D1567432

CHRISTENSEN'S ULTIMATE MOVIE, TV & ROCK 'N' ROLL DIRECTORY

3RD EDITION

CHRISTENSEN'S ULTIMATE MOVIE, TV & ROCK 'N' ROLL DIRECTORY

3RD EDITION

Roger & Karen Christensen

PUBLISHING COMPANY
6065 MISSION GORGE ROAD
SAN DIEGO, CA 92120

Dedication

To our loving parents,
Jo and Chris Christensen
&
Beverley and Douglas Jackson

For all your love, support and prayers,
we graciously dedicate this book
to you, for without your help,
it would have never been possible.

In Loving Memory

Neil P. "Gaba" Carter
1904 - 1985

Everrett L. Christensen
1923 - 1984

Kenneth R. Jackson
1934 - 1986

Very Special Thanks To

Georgia Terry
Sy Sussman
Paul Hunt
Tom Jordan

for all of your

. . . *caring guidance*
. . . *endless patience*
. . . *professional expertise*
. . . *endless encouragement*
. . . *and most of all for your unconditional friendships*

Christensen's Ultimate Movie, TV & Rock 'N' Roll Directory, 3rd Edition

Published by Cardiff-By-The-Sea Publishing Company,
6065 Mission Gorge Road, San Diego, CA 92120

Printed in the United States of America by Arcata Book Group in San Diego, California and Kingsport Press., Kingsport, Tennessee.

ISBN 0-960-80383-1

CONTENTS

Advertiser's Index XIII

Acknowledgements XV

Preface XVII

Celebrity Addresses 1

Sy Sussman Celebrity Photograph Catalog 945

Photographic Credits 1,001

Notes 1,005

ADVERTISER'S INDEX

ADDRESS UPDATES .. 241 .. 249 .. 283 .. 311 .. 353 .. 405 .. 507
.... 539 .. 625 .. 669 .. 713 .. 729 .. 767
.... 845 .. 855 .. 885 .. 917 .. 941
GENE ANDROWSKI AUTOGRAPHS & PHOTOGRAPHS.................... 103
ANTIQUE COMPANY (CELEBRITY PHOTOGRAPHS) 85
AUTOGRAPH ALCOVE .... 115 .. 339
AUTOGRAPH COLLECTORS MAGAZINE .... 59 .. 227 .. 275 .. 679
.... 719 .. 787
AUTOGRAPH DEALERS' DIRECTORY ... 155 .. 205 .. 267 .. 383 .. 461
.... 587 .. 651 .. 757 .. 841
AUTOGRAPH REVIEW 209
NANCY BARR-BRANDON (CELEBRITY PHOTOGRAPHS) 61
ROBERT F. BATCHELDER AUTOGRAPHS 409
R. JAMES BENDER PUBLISHING 595
BOB BENNETT (BOOKS) 307
BOOK CASTLE .... 121 .. 146 .. 207 .. 441 .. 649
.... 835 .. 897 .. 943
BOOK FINDER .... 101 .. 231 .. 359 .. 481 .. 577
.... 737 .. 769 .. 909
LANE BRODY FAN CLUB 141
TOM BURFORD FAN CLUB 157
CELEBRITY AUTOGRAPHS .... 97 .. 109 .. 211 .. 279 .. 369
.... 433 .. 613 .. 833
CINEMATIQUES (AUTOGRAPHS) 53
COLLECTORS CINEMA SHOP 13
DAYS OF OUR LIVES CELEBRITY COOKBOOK 99
BARBARA EDEN FAN CLUB 285
ELMER'S NOSTALGIA (AUTOGRAPHS & MEMORABILIA) 71
BOB EVERHART FAN CLUB 303
FAN CLUB DIRECTORY 105
FANDATA COMPUTER SERVICES .... 271 .. 687
FANDOM DIRECTORY .... 163 .. 753
GOLDEN TREASURES (MEMORABILIA) .... 45 .. 245 .. 445 .. 673
PHYLLIS GOLDMAN (AUTOGRAPHS) 29
MICHAEL GUTIERREZ (AUTOGRAPHS) .... 9 .. 91 .. 429 .. 555
HOLLYWOOD MEMORIES (JAMES & DONNA SUTTON) 21
DALE HORNING (AUTOGRAPHS) 181
JEANNE HOYT AUTOGRAPHS .... 23 .. 475 .. 811
INTERNATIONAL FAN LOCATION SERVICE 321
JAMMIE ANN & THE TEXAS REBELETTES 453
JERRY JAYE (ENTERTAINER) 137
RORY KEHLER (AUTOGRAPHS) 113
DAVID KIRCHNER (SINGER) 493
ANN KRAFTHOFER AUTOGRAPHS 77
L'IMAGERIE (ROCK ART & POSTERS) .... 75 .. 295
CECILIA LEE FAN CLUB 525
REBEL LEE FAN CLUB 527
LEGENDS OF SUN RECORDS (PUBLICATION) 641

LEONARDO'S CINEMA CLASSICS .... 4-5 .. 63 .. 297 .. 393
.... 419 .. 659
LESLIE'S RECORD LAND 489
LEW LIPSET (BASEBALL CARDS & PRICE GUIDES) 351
LONE STAR AUTOGRAPHS 87
GLORIA LORING RECORD ALBUM 127
L. W. D. AUTOGRAPHS .... 119 .. 305
JAMES GRANT MAC ALISTER (SPORTS AUTOGRAPHS) 197
STEVAN D. MALLON AUTOGRAPHS 19
ROSA LEE MARTIN FAN CLUB 573
MILTON T. MOORE, JR. (CELEBRITY PHOTOGRAPHS) 37
MOVIE STARS NEWS (PHOTOGRAPHS) .. 41 .. 125 .. 185 .. 361 .. 711
MOVIE WORLD (MEMORABILIA) ...... 401 .. 599 .. 697 .. 755 .. 935
NATIONAL PASTIME (BASEBALL AUTOGRAPHS) .... 10-11 .. 629
NOSTALGIA RECORDS .... 49 .. 133
JERRY OHLINGER'S MOVIE MATERIAL STORE 69
JAMES "REBEL" O'LEARY INTERNATIONAL FAN CLUB 655
OREGON STATE COIN COMPANY (AUTOGRAPHS) 117
RALPH PATICCHIO AUTOGRAPHS 129
PERSONALITIES PLUS+ (AUTOGRAPHS) .... 39 .. 217 .. 561 .. 747
GENE PITNEY FAN CLUB 689
CORDELIA & TOM PLATT AUTOGRAPHS & HISTORICAL MATERIAL 31
FIVE PLATTERS, INC 691
P. M. ANTIQUES & COLLECTABLES ... 81 .. 89 .. 237 .. 255 .. 459
.... 521 .. 783 .. 915
ROCK-A-BILLY AND COUNTRY LEGENDS (PUBLICATION) 289
ROCK AND ROLL LEGENDS (PUBLICATION) 149
R & R ENTERPRISES (AUTOGRAPHS) .... 27 .. 331 .. 477
ROCK-O-GRAPHS (AUTOGRAPHS) ...... 43 .. 143 .. 397 .. 551 .. 923
SEARLE'S AUTOGRAPHS 67
SUSANNE SEVEREID FAN CLUB 781
STAR SIGNS (AUTOGRAPHS) 153
STARWORLD (MEMORABILIA) 73
STELLAR UNIT (VOCAL GROUP) 823
TERRY SMITH & FRIENDS (FAN CLUB) 807
VINCE SMITH FAN CLUB 809
SPORTS AUTOGRAPHS (MAGAZINE) .... 95 .. 259 .. 501 .. 707
.... 773 .. 851
MRS. STEVENS (AUTOGRAPHS) 83
SUN PHOTO ALBUM (PUBLICATION) 721
SY SUSSMAN CELEBRITY PHOTOGRAPHS .... 51 .. 167 .. 187 .. 243
.... 291 .. 329 .. 373 .. 427 .. 469 .. 545 .. 601
.... 645 .. 723 .. 759 .. 777 .. 803 .. 843 .. 869
.... 905 .. 931 .. 945-999 (THE COMPLETE CATALOG)
GEORGIA TERRY AUTOGRAPHS .... 7 .. 140 .. 189 .. 227 .. 367
.... 435 .. 515 .. 533 .. 605
.... 683 .. 739 .. 887
TOTAL ORGANIZATION (PUBLICATION) 173
MARK VARDAKIS AUTOGRAPHS 159
SETH VOGAL AUTOGRAPHS & PHOTOGRAPHS 32-33
MIKE WEHRMANN AUTOGRAPHS 16-17
SCOTT J. WINSLOW ASSOCIATES (AUTOGRAPHS & STOCKS) 151

ACKNOWLEDGEMENTS

The authors wish to thank the following people and organizations for their help in making this book possible:

A & M RECORDS
ABC/DUNHILL RECORDS
JON ALLAN
BILL ALTHAUS
AMERICAN BALLET SOCIETY
AMERICAN BROADCASTING CO.
RON ANDERSON
GENE ANDROWSKI
RAY ANTHONY
ANTIQUE COMPANY
APPLE RECORDS
ARISTA RECORDS
THOMAS K. ARNOLD
MICHAEL ARSULICH
ASSOCIATED FILM DISTRIBUTION
ASYLUM RECORDS
ATCO RECORDS
ATLANTIC RECORDS
AUTOGRAPH ALCOVE
AUTOGRAPH COLLECTORS MAGAZINE
AUTOGRAPH REVIEW
AVCO EMBASSY PICTURES
RICHARD AVEDON
FABIAN BACHRACH
NANCY BARR-BRANDON
LAURA BARTON
ROBERT F. BATCHELDER
PHIL BATTAGLIA
KENNETH BEALER
BEARSVILLE RECORDS
MARIAN BEHLMAN
R. JAMES BENDER
BOB BENNETT
NEIL BENTON
PETER BERES
BRUNO BERNARD
BIG REEL
H. B. BOAH
BOOK CASTLE
BOOK FINDER
BOSTON GLOBE
NICK BOUGAS
TERRY BOWERS
HARVEY BRANDWEIN
HARRY BRODERSON
LANE BRODY
BROTHER RECORDS
GEORGE BROWN
JAMES BROWN
BRUNO OF HOLLYWOOD
BRUNSWICK RECORDS
RONALD J. CAIN
LORETTA CALFEE
BOB CALTRIDER
CAPITOL RECORDS
JOHN R. CARPENTER
HAZEL "GAMA" CARTER
MICHAEL CARTER
NEIL "GABA" CARTER
BOB CHAMBERS
KATHY CHAPPLE
KEN CHAPPLE
JOE CHARLES
SETH CHASE
CHRIS CHRISTENSEN
DIANA CHRISTENSEN
ERNIE CHRISTENSEN
JO CHRISTENSEN
KIMBY CHRISTENSEN
MARK CHRISTENSEN
MIKE CHRISTENSEN
ROBERT CHRISTENSEN
STEPHEN CHRISTENSEN
CHRYSALIS RECORDS
CINEMA CENTER FILMS
CINEMATIQUES
ALAN CLARK
COLLECTORS CINEMA SHOP
COLUMBIA BROADCASTING SYSTEM
COLUMBIA PICTURES
COLUMBIA RECORDS
CONCORD JAZZ RECORDS
TOM CORCORAN
SANDY COUTSAKIS
KEITH COWANS
BEVERLY CROSS
D. C. COMICS
DAILY VARIETY
DENNIS DANIELS
S. A. DANJAQ
ANTHONY DARIUS
DAVE & JESSIE
GLENN DAVIS
DAY SPRING RECORDS
DE LAURENTIIS CORP.
G. R. DEAN, JR
LARRY W. DENHAM
BILL DOSSEY
JUDI DOSSEY
BOB EATON
BARBARA EDEN
STEVE EDRINGTON
ELEKTRA RECORDS
DAVID ELKOUBY
ELMER'S NOSTALGIA
EMI/AMERICAN RECORDS
EPIC RECORDS
ERIC PORTRAIT ASSOCIATED
BOB EVERHART
JONATHAN EXLEY
WALDEN S. FABRY
FAME PICTURES
FAN CLUB DIRECTORY
FANDATA COMPUTER SERVICES
FANDON DIRECTORY
FANTASY HONEY RECORDS
CARLA FARRELL
J. F. FAWLS
FILMWAYS PICTURES
FIRST NATIONAL PICTURES
JOE FONTANA
HOWARD A. FORTENBERRY
GALAXY RECORDS
JERRY GERARD
GOLDEN TRASURES
PHYLLIS GOLDMAN
LYNN GOLDSMITH, INC.
PAM GRAVES
PHIL GRUNDY
MIKE GUTIERREZ
HAGIWARA/PARKER
HANNA-BARBERA PRODUCTIONS
BILL HARRIS
KENNEDY HARRIS
SCOTT HENSEL
RICK HERRMANN
JANICE HOLBERT
BOBBY HOLLAND
HOLLYWOOD MEMORIES
HOLLYWOOD REPORTER
DALE HORNING
JEANNE HOYT
PAUL HUNT
ARTHUR HYDE
INT'L FAN LOCATION SERVICE
ITALIAN FILM DIRECTORS GUILD
J. F. F. AUTOGRAPHS
BEVERLEY JACKSON
BRUCE JACKSON
CHRISTOPHER JACKSON
DANETTE JACKSON
DAVID JACKSON
DOUGLAS JACKSON
KARLA JACKSON
MITZI JACKSON
JAMMIE ANN
JERRY JAYE
JEREMIAH RECORDS
CAROLE JOHNSON
SARAH JOHNSON
TOM JORDAN
RORY KEHLER
MARCIE KIRK
DAVID KIRSCHNER
PAULA KLAW
ANN KRAFTHOFER
KRAGEN & CO.
JOE KRAUS
JAMES J KRIEGSMANN
L'IMAGERIE
L. W. D. AUTOGRAPHS
BERNIE LANG
HARRY LANGDON PHOTOGRAPHY
NEALE LANIGAN
BERNIE LANSKY
JIM LARSON
LESINI LATU
LAUFER COMPANY
SHORTY LAVENDER
SLICK LAWSON
CAPT. KEN LAZIER
RON LEBETSAMER
BUDDY LEE ATTRACTIONS
CECILIA LEE
REBEL LEE
RACHEL LEISTIKOW
LEONARDO'S CINEMA CLASSICS
ERROLL LESLIE
LIBERTY RECORDS
LEW LIPSET
LONE STAR AUTOGRAPHS
JOE LONG
CARL LOPEZ
GLORIA LORING
LOS ANGELES TIMES
FRANK LUDLOW
BILL LUETGE
ALAN LUNGSTROM
JAMES GRANT MAC ALISTER
MR. & MRS. GEORGE MAC LEOD
STEVAN D. MALLON
MARY ELLEN MARK
DOUG MARKS
ROSA LEEE MARTIN
KEITH MC ALLISTER
DAVID MC GRATH
JIM MC GUIRE
MCA RECORDS
MERCURY RECORDS
MGM PICTURES
MONTEREY PENINSULA ARTISTS
MOONGLOW RECORDS
MILTON T. MOORE, JR
BARBARA MORRISON
WILL MORRIS
BARRY MORSE FAN CLUB
MOVIE STAR NEWS
MOVIE WORLD
EDIE MUNROE
JOE MUNROE
LARRY MUNROE
GORDON MUNRO
JOE NABBEFELD
NASTIONAL PASTIME
NATIONAL BROADCASTING CO.
NEW YORK YANKEES
JOHN NIMESGREN
NOSTALGIA RECORDS
STAN NOVAK
EDDIE O'CAMPO
JAMES " REBEL" O'LEARY
MICHAEL OCHS
JERRY OHLINGER
JIM OLESON
OREGON STATE COIN COMPANY
OSMOND CORPORATION
P. M. ANTIQUES & COLLECTABLES
MARK PALMER
PAMELA T. PALMER
PARAMOUNT PICTURES
BEVERLY PARKER
RALPH PATICCHIO
PERSONALITIES PLUS

JAMIE PETERSON
JIM PETERSON
KELLY PETERSON
KRISTIN PETERSON
PHILADELPHIA INT'L RECORDS
GENE PITNEY
PLANET RECORDS
CORDELIA & TOM PLATT
THE FIVE PLATTERS
ADAM POWELL
DAVID POWERS
JERRY POWERS
JOHN PROVINCE
R & R ENTERPRISES
R. K. O. PICTURES
BARTON RANDALL
RCA RECORDS
JOHN E. REED
HERB RITTS
PAUL ROBERTS
TONY RODRIQUEZ
ROLLING STONES RECORDS
BOB ROPER
ROY'S MEMORY SHOP
SAN DIEGO UNION-TRIBUNE
MIKE SCHAAD
SCOTT SCHUTTE
SEDAKA MUSIC COMPANY
NORMAN SEEFF
SUSANNE SEVEREID
MAURICE SEYMOUR
JIM SHEA
SUSAN SHIELDS
BOB SMITH
PASTOR & MRS. ROYCE SMITH
TERRY SMITH
VINCE SMITH
SUSANNE SMOLKA
SOLAR RECORDS
LEONARD SORGI
HOLLY SPECHT
MIKE SPECHT
SPORTS AUTOGRAPHS
SPOTLITE ENTERPRISES
RANDEE ST. NICHOLAS
PAUL STANLEY
VIVIAN STANLEY
STAR SIGNS
STARWORLD
STELLAR UNIT
MRS. STEVENS
R. STRAUSS
DOUG STRAW
JOANNE SULLIVAN
SY SUSSMAN
DONNA SUTTON
JAMES L. SUTTON
SWAN SONG RECORDS
MARTHA SWOPE
GEORGIA TERRY
SCOTT THOMPSON
TOTAL ORGANIZATION
TRIANGLE PUBLICATIONS
BLANCHE "TRINA" TRINAJSTICK
JIM TWELMEYER
20TH CENTURY - FOX FILMS
20TH CENTURY - FOX RECORDS
UNITED ARTISTS PICTURES
UNITED ARTISTS RECORDS
UNIVERSAL CITY STUDIOS
USA TODAY
TONY VAN
MARK VARDAKIS
VALERIE ROSE VAUGHN
SETH VOGAL
KEVIN WALLACE
WALT DISNEY STUDIOS
WARNER BROTHERS FILMS
WARNER BROTHERS RECORDS
WARNER/REPRISE RECORDS
MIKE WEHRMAN
LEO WEIDENBENNER
WEINSTEIN, WEINSTEIN & BURKE
ROBERT WEISS
DICK WESTMORELAND
JIM WIGGANS
SCOTT WINSLOW
WORD RECORDS
WORLD BOXING ASSOCIATION
DAVE YOUNG

PREFACE

Christensen's Ultimate Movie, TV & Rock 'N' Roll Directory (3rd Edition) is an encyclopedic listing which contains more than 50,000 entries in the form of celebrity addresses, memorabilia listings, and photographic reproductions. It is the most extensive directory of its kind ever published.

The purpose of this directory is to assist the thousands of fans who want to write letters to people in the entertainment industry. We feel the cross-section of celebrities represented is quite extensive and covers a wide range of diversified talent. This directory can be most useful in requesting an autographed picture of your favorite movie star, sending a birthday greeting to your favorite soap opera hero, requesting a copy of a TV script from the actual writer, asking the advice of a prominent director, composer or cartoonist, which technical school they recommend, or probing the mind of the controversial film critic to find out what might be this year's box office "sleeper."

Looking for an old movie poster of your favorite movie? How about a nice 8 x 10 glossy portrait of your favorite star? Where might you find an audio cassette from your old favorite radio serial or a mint copy of the first album the Beatles ever recorded? Do you know who was on the front cover of the very first TV Guide? Would you like to purchase any of this valuable memorabilia for your collection? You'll find this and more in this directory.

Throughout the many years of the entertainment industry, various booklets, magazines and maps to the stars' homes have been published. The purpose of the Celebrity Address section of this directory is to provide a thorough source whereby fans can reach their favorite celebrities by one means only — via the U.S. Postal System. We do not, in publishing this directory, nor in our own collecting practices of celebrities' autographs, advocate or encourage fans to visit any of the celebrities, either at their place of residence or business. Most celebrities are quite good about responding to fan mail. Please be patient in your desire for a reply and always include a self-addressed, stamped envelope of appropriate size and postage to accommodate your request.

We assume no responsibility for addresses in the book which are incorrect due to a celebrity moving from a place of residence and not leaving a forwarding address, the changing of agents, managers and/or public relation firms, the refusal to accept and/or answer mail, non-renewal of a membership in a Guild, Union or Local, death, disease or divorce. Nor do we insinuate that every personality personally answers his or her mail.

This directory, since its inception in 1979, has taken over 40,000 hours of time-consuming, painstaking research and labor. It will be biennially published with address update supplements issued in between editions.

It is not only a vast nostalgic trip into the past but also an extensive look at the present. Truly the entertainment directory that deserves only one title, ***Christensen's Ultimate Movie, TV & Rock 'N' Roll Directory.***

— Roger and Karen Christensen

Susanne Severeid

CELEBRITY ADDRESSES

A FROG FROM WISCONSIN	CONTORTIONIST	HALL, 138 FROG HOLLOW RD	CHURCHVILLE, PA	18966
A-BONES, THE	ROCK & ROLL GROUP	LINTRUPER STR 39	1000 BERLIN 49	WEST GERMANY
A-HA	ROCK & ROLL GROUP	HIGH ST, HEALEY BORDEN	NANTS GU 358 BG	ENGLAND
AABERG, PHILIP	MUSICIAN	POST OFFICE BOX 9388	STANFORD, CA	94305
AADLAND, BEVERLY	ACTRESS	POST OFFICE BOX 1115	CANYON COUNTRY, CA	91350
AAGAARD, KENNETH J	TV EXECUTIVE	NBC TELEVISION NETWORK		
		30 ROCKEFELLER PLAZA	NEW YORK, NY	10112
AAL, ANDREA	ACTRESS	13111 VENTURA BLVD #204	STUDIO CITY, CA	91604
AALDA, MARIANN	ACTRESS	9100 SUNSET BLVD #210	LOS ANGELES, CA	90069
AAMES, ANGELA	ACTRESS-MODEL	6310 SAN VICENTE BLVD #407	LOS ANGELES, CA	90048
AAMES, WILLIE	ACTOR-SINGER	845 VIA DE LA PAZ	PACIFIC PALISADES, CA	90272
AARON, ALLISON	ACTRESS	POST OFFICE BOX 1058	LA MESA, CA	92044
AARON, BETSY	NEWS CORRESPONDENT	ABC NEWS, 7 W 66TH ST	NEW YORK, NY	10023
AARON, CHLOE	TV PRODUCER-EXECUTIVE	PBS-TV, 609 5TH AVE	NEW YORK, NY	10017
AARON, HENRY	BASEBALL	1611 ADAMS DR, SW	ATLANTA, GA	30311
AARON, LEE	SINGER-SONGWRITER	41 BRITAIN ST #200	TORONTO, ONT	CANADA
AARON, MICHAEL	NEWS CORRESPONDENT	1326 NORTHVIEW RD	BALTIMORE, MD	21218
AARON, PAUL	FILM WRITER-DIRECTOR	1604 COURTNEY AVE	LOS ANGELES, CA	90046
AARONSON, JOSHUA	NEWS CORRESPONDENT	5413 EL CAMINO	COLUMBIA, MD	21044
ABAJAN, MARIA	SOPRANO	CAMI, 165 W 57TH ST	NEW YORK, NY	10019
ABARBANEL, SAM	WRITER	1118 FAIRFAX AVEVUE #14	LOS ANGELES, CA	90019
ABATEMARCO, FRANK	TV WRITER	8955 BEVERLY BLVD	LOS ANGELES, CA	90048
ABBADO, CLAUDIO	COMPOSER	220 E MICHIGAN AVE	CHICAGO, IL	60604
ABBAS, YAVAR	WRITER-PRODUCER	FACE FILMS, 16 DEAN RD		
		HOUNSLOW	MIDDLESEX TW3 2EL	ENGLAND
ABBASSI, ELIZABETH	ACTRESS	43 E 60TH ST	NEW YORK, NY	10022
ABBATE-CALDWELL, NANCY	ACTRESS-DANCER	1855 E VISTA WY	VISTA, CA	92083
ABBENE, BERNARD	WRITER	7809 FAUST ST AVE	CANOGA PARK, CA	91304
ABBEY, ALAN DAVID	NEWS CORRESPONDENT	1201 CONNECTICUT AVE, NW	WASHINGTON, DC	20036
ABBOT, BRUCE	ACTOR	15760 VENTURA BLVD #1730	ENCINO, CA	91436
ABBOTT, CHARLES J	NEWS CORRESPONDENT	1210 N TAFT ST #610	ARLINGTON, VA	22201
ABBOTT, DIAHNEE	ACTRESS	560 TIGERTAIL RD	LOS ANGELES, CA	90049
ABBOTT, GEORGE	WRITER-PRODUCER	1270 6TH AVE	NEW YORK, NY	10020
		51 W 52ND ST	NEW YORK, NY	10019
ABBOTT, JANE	ACTRESS	4925 INDIAN WOOD RD #377	CULVER CITY, CA	90230
ABBOTT, JOHN	ACTOR	6424 IVARENE AVE	LOS ANGELES, CA	90068
ABBOTT, NORMAN	WRITER-PRODUCER	625 N CAMDEN DR	BEVERLY HILLS, CA	90210
ABBOTT, PHILIP	ACTOR-DIRECTOR	5400 SHIRLEY AVE	TARZANA, CA	92356
ABBOTT, SHEPARD	SCREENWRITER	555 W 57TH ST #1230	NEW YORK, NY	10019
ABBOTT, WILLIAM L	PHOTOJOURNALIST	9739 GOOD LUCK RD #12	SEABROOK, MD	20706
ABBOTT, WILLIAM R	NEWS CORRESPONDENT	2025 "M" ST, NW	WASHINGTON, DC	20036
ABBOTT-FISH, CHRIS	TV WRITER-PRODUCER	10390 SANTA MONICA BLVD #310	LOS ANGELES, CA	90025
ABBOUD, SAMIA G	NEWS CORRESPONDENT	2109 GREENERY LN #301	WHEATON, MD	20906
ABC	ROCK & ROLL GROUP	9200 SUNSET BLVD #PH-15	LOS ANGELES, CA	90069
ABDO, NICHOLAS	DIRECTOR-PRODUCER	13829 RIVERSIDE DR	SHERMAN OAKS, CA	91423
ABDON, CHARLES	DRUMMER	256 COLERIDGE CT	ANTIOCH, TN	37013
ABDUL-ALI, HASSAN	PHOTOGRAPHER	4201 MASSACHUSETTS AVE, NW	WASHINGTON, DC	20016
ABDUL-JABBAR, KAREEM	ACTOR-BASKETBALL	POST OFFICE BOX 10	INGLEWOOD, CA	90306
ABDULLAH THE BUTCHER	WRESTLER	WORLD CLASS WRESTLING		
		SOUTHWEST SPORTS, INC		
		DALLAS SPORTATORIUM		
		1000 S INDUSTRIAL BLVD	DALLAS, TX	75207
ABEL, ELIE	WRITER	1590 DANA AVE	PALO ALTO, CA	94303
ABEL, RAY	WRITER-PRODUCER	SHORE DR	PORT CHESTER, NY	10573
ABEL, ROBERT J	WRITER-PRODUCER	953 N HIGHLAND AVE	LOS ANGELES, CA	90038
ABEL, RUDOLPH E	TV DIRECTOR	3689 GLENDON AVE #4	LOS ANGELES, CA	90034
ABELEW, ALAN	ACTOR	4078 CAMINO REAL	LOS ANGELES, CA	90065
ABELL, DAVID	CONDUCTOR	1776 BROADWAY #504	NEW YORK, NY	10019
ABELSON, ALAN	EDITOR	BARRON'S, 420 LEXINGTON AVE	NEW YORK, NY	10170
ABERCROMBIE, IAN	ACTOR	POST OFFICE BOX 10906	BEVERLY HILLS, CA	90213
ABERCROMBIE, JOHN	JAZZ QUARTET	KURLAND, 173 BRIGHTON AVE	BOSTON, MA	02134
ABERCROMBIE, THOMAS J	PHOTOGRAPHER	WEST RIVER RD	SHADY SIDE, MD	20867
ABERDEEN, ROBERT	ACTOR	301 W 108TH ST	NEW YORK, NY	10025
ABERG, SIV	ACTRESS-MODEL	SHERMAN, 348 S REXFORD DR	BEVERLY HILLS, CA	90212
ABERLIN, BETTY	ACTRESS	19 W 44TH ST #1500	NEW YORK, NY	10036
ABERNATHY, JAMES L	TV EXECUTIVE	40 CENTRAL PARK W	NEW YORK, NY	10019
ABERNATHY, LOUISA	ACTRESS	7621 HOLLYWOOD BLVD #B	LOS ANGELES, CA	90046
ABERNATHY, RALPH DAVID	EVANGELIST	690 LAVERNE DR, NW	ATLANTA, GA	30318
ABERNATHY, ROBERT	NEWS CORRESPONDENT	NBC-TV, NEWS DEPARTMENT		
		30 ROCKEFELLER PLAZA	NEW YORK, NY	10112
ABEY, DENNIS	WRITER-PRODUCER	AB & C, 36 PERCY ST	LONDON W1	ENGLAND
ABEYTA, PAUL A	WRITER	22260 AVE SAN LUIS	WOODLAND HILLS, CA	91364
ABNEY, WILLIAM	ACTOR	TRANS CREATIVE MGMT		
		300 FULHAM RD	LONDON SW10	ENGLAND
ABRAHAM, DAWN	ACTRESS	8721 SUNSET BLVD #202	LOS ANGELES, CA	90069
ABRAHAM, F MURRAY	ACTOR	888 7TH AVE #1800	NEW YORK, NY	10019

WILLIE AAMES

BROOKE ADAMS

JULIE ADAMS

IRIS ADRIAN

AIR SUPPLY

EDDIE ALBERT

ALAN ALDA

KRISTIAN ALFONSO

NANCY ALLEN

Name	Occupation	Address	City	Zip/Country
ABRAHAM, RALPH E	TV DIRECTOR	588 THE PARKWAY	MAMARONECK, NY	10543
ABRAHAM, SETH	FILM EXECUTIVE	HOME BOX OFFICE		
		1100 AVE OF THE AMERICAS	NEW YORK, NY	10036
ABRAHAMS, ANDREW	REPORTER	TIME & PEOPLE MAGAZINE		
		TIME & LIFE BUILDING		
		ROCKEFELLER CENTER	NEW YORK, NY	10020
ABRAHAMS, DORIS COLE	THEATER PRODUCER	TRANSART PRODUCTIONS		
		1501 BROADWAY	NEW YORK, NY	10036
ABRAHAMS, JIM	FILM WRITER-DIRECTOR	19746 PACIFIC COAST HWY	MALIBU, CA	90265
ABRAHAMS, MORT	WRITER-PRODUCER	3936 ETHEL AVE	NORTH HOLLYWOOD, CA	91604
ABRAM, DONALD L	GUITARIST	SEE - KELLY, JUDD		
ABRAMHOFF, SHARYN	WRITER	2312 PISANI PL	VENICE, CA	90291
ABRAMOWITZ, DAVID	TV WRITER	8955 BEVERLY BLVD	LOS ANGELES, CA	90048
ABRAMOWITZ, JAY B	TV DIRECTOR	346 1/2 N SPAULDING AVE	LOS ANGELES, CA	90036
ABRAMS, EARL B	NEWS CORRESPONDENT	3518 N UTAH ST	ARLINGTON, VA	22207
ABRAMS, GERALD	PRODUCER	COLUMBIA PICTURES TV		
		COLUMBIA PLAZA	BURBANK, CA	91505
ABRAMS, MUHAL RICHARD	PIANIST	POST OFFICE BOX 612		
		TIMES SQUARE STATION	NEW YORK, NY	10108
ABRAMS, PAUL E	GUITARIST	216 VILLAGE GREEN DR	NASHVILLE, TN	37217
ABRAMS & ANDERSON	COMEDY DUO	POST OFFICE BOX 4585	PORTSMOUTH, NH	03801
ABRAMSON, RUDY	NEWS CORRESPONDENT	11806 TREE FERN CT	RESTON, VA	22097
ABRAVANEL, DAVID B	COMPOSER	1251 N CRESCENT HGTS BLVD	LOS ANGELES, CA	90046
ABRAVANEL, MAURICE	MUSIC DIRECTOR	123 W TEMPLE ST S	SALT LAKE CITY, UT	84101
ABRAWSKI, JERZY G	COMPOSER	6648 S ROCKWELL ST #A-494	CHICAGO, IL	60629
ABROMS, EDWARD	FILM EDITOR	ACE, 4416 1/2 FINLEY AVE	LOS ANGELES, CA	90027
ABROMS, EDWARD M	FILM DIRECTOR	1866 MARLOWE ST	THOUSAND OAKS, CA	91360
ABRUZZO, RAY	ACTOR	ICM, 8899 BEVERLY BLVD	LOS ANGELES, CA	90048
ABSALOM, JOHN	TENOR	POST OFFICE BOX 188		
		STATION A	TORONTO, ONT	CANADA
ABSOLUTE GREY	ROCK & ROLL GROUP	POST OFFICE BOX 390		
		OLD CHELSEA STATION	NEW YORK, NY	10113
ABSTON, DEAN	ACTOR	5000 LANKERSHIM BLVD #5	NORTH HOLLYWOOD, CA	91601
ABU-FADIL	NEWS CORRESPONDENT	4103 "W" ST #202	WASHINGTON, DC	20007
AC/DC	ROCK & ROLL GROUP	ATI, 888 7TH AVE, 21ST FLOOR	NEW YORK, NY	10106
ACAMPORA, ROBERT JOHN	NEWS CORRESPONDENT	8423 ALAMEDA CT	ALEXANDRIA, VA	22309
ACCARDO, SALVATORE	VIOLINIST	CAMI, 165 W 57TH ST	NEW YORK, NY	10019
ACCEPT	ROCK & ROLL GROUP	GABY HAUKE MANAGEMENT		
		AM ANGELSDORN 47	D-5024 PULHEIM	WEST GERMANY
ACCIAIOLI, CARMEN T	GUITARIST	GENERAL DELIVERY	RED RIVER, NM	87558
ACCIANI, ROBERT D	ACTOR	1202 CARLTON WY	VENICE, CA	90291
ACE, JOHNNY	WRESTLER	NATIONAL WRESTLING ALLIANCE		
		JIM CROCKETT PROMOTIONS		
		421 BRIARBEND DR	CHARLOTTE, NC	28209
ACE, THE	STUD	SEE - RASMUSSEN, R J "ACE"		
ACEL, ERVIN	CONDUCTOR	POST OFFICE BOX 131	SPRINGFIELD, VA	22150
ACES & EIGHTS	C & W GROUP	GREG, 1686 CATALPA RD	CLEVELAND, OH	44112
ACES UP	ROCK & ROLL GROUP	POST OFFICE BOX 448	RADFORD, VA	24141
ACETI, JOSEPH	TV DIRECTOR	225 CENTRAL PARK W	NEW YORK, NY	10024
ACETO, LOUIS J	NEWS CORRESPONDENT	NBC-TV, NEWS DEPARTMENT		
		4001 NEBRASKA AVE, NW	WASHINGTON, DC	20016
ACHUCARRO, JOAQUIN	PIANIST	GERSHUNOFF, 502 PARK AVE	NEW YORK, NY	10022
ACKELSON, JON D	WRITER-PRODUCER	179 N REXFORD DR	BEVERLY HILLS, CA	90210
ACKER, CINDY	ACTRESS	MARTEL, 7813 SUNSET BLVD	LOS ANGELES, CA	90046
ACKER, SANDY	ACTRESS	MARTEL, 7813 SUNSET BLVD	LOS ANGELES, CA	90046
ACKER, SHARON	ACTRESS	9744 WILSHIRE BLVD #306	BEVERLY HILLS, CA	90212
ACKERMAN, BETTYE	ACTRESS	302 N ALPINE DR	BEVERLY HILLS, CA	90210
ACKERMAN, HAROLD	WRITER	7206 WOODROW WILSON DR	LOS ANGELES, CA	90068
ACKERMAN, HARRY S	TV PRODUCER	4525 LEMP AVE	NORTH HOLLYWOOD, CA	91602
ACKERMAN, LESLIE	ACTRESS	9220 SUNSET BLVD #625	LOS ANGELES, CA	90069
ACKERMAN, STEVE	WRITER	4525 LEMP AVE	NORTH HOLLYWOOD, CA	91602
ACKERMAN, WILLIE	DRUMMER	POST OFFICE BOX 22651	NASHVILLE, TN	37202
ACKLAND, JOSS	ACTOR	ICM, 388-396 OXFORD ST	LONDON W1	ENGLAND
ACKROYD, DAVID	ACTOR	12425 OTSEGO ST	NORTH HOLLYWOOD, CA	91607
ACKROYD, TIMOTHY	ACTOR	43 LANSDOWNE CRESCENT		
		HOLLAND PARK	LONDON W11 2NN	ENGLAND
ACOVONE, JAY	ACTOR	151 S EL CAMINO DR	BEVERLY HILLS, CA	90212
ACQUANETTA	ACTRESS	ROSS, 4415 N ARCADIA LN	PHOENIX, AZ	85018
ACREE, DENNIS	ACTOR	1615 BUTLER AVE #17	LOS ANGELES, CA	90025
ACRIM, KEITH JAY	BODY BUILDER	2801 MEADOW LARK DR	SAN DIEGO, CA	92123
ACS, JANOS	CONDUCTOR	POST OFFICE BOX 131	SPRINGFIELD, VA	22150
ACUFF, ROY	SINGER	POST OFFICE BOX 4623	NASHVILLE, TN	37216
ACUNTO, RICHARD	ACTOR	7473 MULHOLLAND DR	LOS ANGELES, CA	90046
ADAIR, DEBORAH	ACTRESS	9000 SUNSET BLVD #1112	LOS ANGELES, CA	90069
ADAIR, WILLIAM D	AUTO HARPIST	122 LEWISBURG AVE	FRANKLIN, TN	37064
ADAM, MARGIE	SINGER-GUITARIST	POST OFFICE BOX 7217	BERKELEY, CA	94707
ADAM, PETER	DIRECTOR-PRODUCER	24 EARL'S TERR	LONDON W8	ENGLAND
ADAM, SCOTT	FILM DIRECTOR	12714 HORTENSE ST	STUDIO CITY, CA	91604
ADAM, THEO	BASSO-BARITONE	MARIEDL ANDERS ARTISTS MGMT		
		535 EL CAMINO DEL MAR ST	SAN FRANCISCO, CA	94121
ADAMO, RALPH	TV WRITER	8955 BEVERLY BLVD	LOS ANGELES, CA	90048
ADAMO, SAM	ACTOR	1741 N IVAR AVE #221	LOS ANGELES, CA	90028
ADAMO, SHERRY	ACTRESS	8230 BEVERLY BLVD #23	LOS ANGELES, CA	90048

Name	Occupation	Address	City	Zip
ADAMS, ALAN E	NEWS CORRESPONDENT	3030 MACOMB ST, NW	WASHINGTON, DC	20008
ADAMS, ALEXIS	ACTRESS	1643 LINDACREST DR	BEVERLY HILLS, CA	90210
ADAMS, ANGELA	ACTRESS	9744 WILSHIRE BLVD #306	BEVERLY HILLS, CA	90212
ADAMS, ANTHONY W	COMPOSER-CONDUCTOR	5021 STROHM AVE	NORTH HOLLYWOOD, CA	91601
ADAMS, ARTHUR	ACTOR	1256 LONGWOOD AVE	LOS ANGELES, CA	90019
ADAMS, ASHBY	ACTOR	9200 SUNSET BLVD #1210	LOS ANGELES, CA	90069
ADAMS, BEVERLY	ACTRESS-MODEL	SEE - SASSOON, BEVERLY ADAMS		
ADAMS, BROOKE	ACTRESS	8672 LOOKOUT MOUNTAIN DR	LOS ANGELES, CA	90046
ADAMS, BRYAN	SINGER	406-68 WATER ST #406	VANCOUVER, BC R2H 2M2	CANADA
ADAMS, CAROLYN	DANCER	144 W 121ST ST	NEW YORK, NY	10027
ADAMS, CASEY	ACTOR	SEE - SHOWALTER, MAX		
ADAMS, CHRISTOPHER R	ACTOR	1003 N GENESEE AVE	HOLLYWOOD, CA	90046
ADAMS, CINDA	ACTRESS	8730 SUNSET BLVD #400	LOS ANGELES, CA	90069
ADAMS, CINDY	FILM CRITIC	N Y POST, 210 SOUTH ST	NEW YORK, NY	10002
ADAMS, CLAUDIA C	TV WRITER	PLESHETTE, 2700 N BEACHWOOD DR	LOS ANGELES, CA	90068
ADAMS, DAVE	DRUMMER	POST OFFICE BOX 233	ANTIOCH, TN	37013
ADAMS, DAVE	WRITER	12132 E 187TH ST	ARTESIA, CA	90701
ADAMS, DON	ACT-WRI-DIR	8955 BEVERLY BLVD	LOS ANGELES, CA	90048
ADAMS, DONALD H	SAXOPHONIST	ROUTE 6, BOX 371	CLARKSVILLE, TN	37040
ADAMS, DOROTHY	ACTRESS	1316 S BEVERLY GLEN BLVD	LOS ANGELES, CA	90024
ADAMS, EARLE	ACTOR	546 N CITRUS AVE	LOS ANGELES, CA	90036
ADAMS, EDDIE	PHOTOGRAPHER	TIME/TIME & LIFE BLDG		
		ROCKEFELLER CENTER	NEW YORK, NY	10020
ADAMS, EDIE	ACTRESS-SINGER	8040 OKEAN TERR	LOS ANGELES, CA	90046
ADAMS, EDWARD	PHOTOGRAPHER	435 W 57TH ST	NEW YORK, NY	10017
ADAMS, ELWYN	VIOLINIST	KAY, 58 W 58TH ST	NEW YORK, NY	10019
ADAMS, GARRY W	GUITARIST	ROUTE #1	ALLENDALE, IL	62410
ADAMS, GARY LEE	GUITARIST	7545 MARGARET	TAYLOR, MI	48180
ADAMS, GENTLEMAN CHRIS	WRESTLER	WORLD CLASS WRESTLING		
		SOUTHWEST SPORTS, INC		
		DALLAS SPORTATORIUM		
		1000 S INDUSTRIAL BLVD	DALLAS, TX	75207
ADAMS, GEORGE	SAXOPHONIST	POST OFFICE BOX 201	WAGENINGEN	HOLLAND
ADAMS, GEORGE C	GUITARIST	2660 N MOUNT GILEND RD	BLOOMINGTON, IN	47401
ADAMS, HARRY G	ACTOR	11701 TEXAS AVE #106	LOS ANGELES, CA	90025
ADAMS, JACQUELINE	NEWS CORRESPONDENT	CBS NEWS, 2020 "M" ST, NW	WASHINGTON, DC	20036
ADAMS, JAMES H	NEWS CORRESPONDENT	631 3RD ST, NE	WASHINGTON, DC	20002
ADAMS, JAMES M	NEWS CORRESPONDENT	5151 WISCONSIN AVE, NW	WASHINGTON, DC	20016
ADAMS, JASON	ACTOR	ABC-TV, "RYAN'S HOPE"		
		1330 AVE OF THE AMERICAS	NEW YORK, NY	10019
ADAMS, JEAN	ACTRESS	1605 N CAHUENGA BLVD #202	LOS ANGELES, CA	90028
ADAMS, JEANNE	ACTRESS	132 S REEVES DR	BEVERLY HILLS, CA	90212
ADAMS, JENNIFER	ACTRESS	439 S LA CIENEGA BLVD #120	LOS ANGELES, CA	90048
ADAMS, JOEY	ACT-WRI-COMED	160 W 46TH ST	NEW YORK, NY	10036
ADAMS, JOHN C	COMPOSER-CONDUCTOR	S F SYMPHONY ORCHESTRA		
		DAVIES HALL		
		201 VAN NESS AVE	SAN FRANCISCO, CA	94102
ADAMS, JULIE	ACTRESS	7060 HOLLYWOOD BLVD #610	HOLLYWOOD, CA	90028
ADAMS, KAY	SINGER	TAYLOR, 2401 12TH AVE S	NASHVILLE, TN	37204
ADAMS, KELLY WOOD	ACTRESS-WRITER	250 W 57TH ST #2317	NEW YORK, NY	10107
ADAMS, KRISTI M	ACTRESS	8322 BEVERLY BLVD #202	LOS ANGELES, CA	90048
ADAMS, LAUREL	ACTRESS	FELBER, 2126 N CAHUENGA BLVD	LOS ANGELES, CA	90068
ADAMS, LEW V	TV DIRECTOR	17233 WARRINGTON DR	GRANADA HILLS, CA	91344
ADAMS, LILLIAN	ACTRESS	8961 SUNSET BLVD #B	LOS ANGELES, CA	90069
ADAMS, LOIS	ACTRESS	9744 WILSHIRE BLVD #306	BEVERLY HILLS, CA	90212
ADAMS, MARC D	NEWS CORRESPONDENT	3528 EDMUNDS ST, NW	WASHINGTON, DC	20007
ADAMS, MARLA	ACTRESS	247 S BEVERLY DR #102	BEVERLY HILLS, CA	90210
ADAMS, MARY KAY	ACTRESS	CBS-TV, "THE GUIDING LIGHT"		
		51 W 52ND ST	NEW YORK, NY	10019
ADAMS, MASON	ACTOR	2006 STRADELLA RD	LOS ANGELES, CA	90077
ADAMS, MAUD	ACTRESS-MODEL	2299 CENTURY HILL	LOS ANGELES, CA	90067
ADAMS, NATHAN M	NEWS CORRESPONDENT	321 S PITT ST	ALEXANDRA, VA	22314
ADAMS, NELSON B	MUSICIAN	MC KENDREE MANOR		
		4347 LEBANON RD	HERMITAGE, TN	37076
ADAMS, PARK, III	MUSICIAN	8715-B AVE "B"	BROOKLYN, NY	11236
ADAMS, PEPPER	SAXOPHONIST	UPTOWN RECORDS COMPANY		
		276 PEARL ST	KINGSTON, NY	12401
ADAMS, RAY	ACTOR	870 N OCCIDENTAL BLVD #1	LOS ANGELES, CA	90026
ADAMS, RICHARD	TV WRITER	8955 BEVERLY BLVD	LOS ANGELES, CA	90048
ADAMS, RICHARD	AUTHOR	26 CHURCH ST, WHITCHURCH	HANTS	ENGLAND
ADAMS, RICHEY D	NEWS CORRESPONDENT	4001 BRANDYWINE ST, NW	WASHINGTON, DC	20016
ADAMS, ROBERT E	NEWS CORRESPONDENT	2500 WISCONSIN AVE, NW	WASHINGTON, DC	20007
ADAMS, ROGER	TALENT AGENT	10100 SANTA MONICA BLVD #1600	LOS ANGELES, CA	90067
ADAMS, STANLEY	LYRICIST	3 ORCHARD LN	KINGS POINT, NY	11024
ADAMS, STEVEN S	TV WRITER	8955 BEVERLY BLVD	LOS ANGELES, CA	90048
ADAMS, SUSAN	ACTRESS	9229 SUNSET BLVD #306	LOS ANGELES, CA	90069
ADAMS, TIMOTHY J	NEWS CORRESPONDENT	3607 MC KINLEY ST, NW	WASHINGTON, DC	20015
ADAMS, TOM	ACTOR	29 KINGS RD	LONDON SW3	ENGLAND
ADAMS, TONY	ACTOR	LADKIN, 11 ALDWYCH	LONDON WC2	ENGLAND
ADAMS, TONY	FILM PRODUCER	1888 CENTURY PARK E #1616	LOS ANGELES, CA	90067
ADAMS, TRACEY	ACTRESS	13402 WYANDOTTE ST	NORTH HOLLYWOOD, CA	91605
ADAMS-MC QUEEN, NEILE	ACTRESS	2323 BOWMONT DR	BEVERLY HILLS, CA	90210
ADAMSON, AL	FILM DIRECTOR	INDEPENDENT-INTERNATIONAL		
		165 W 46TH ST	NEW YORK, NY	10036
ADAMSON, PETER	ACTOR	WALMERSLEY OLD RD, BURY	LANCS	ENGLAND

AUTOGRAPHED BASEBALL PHOTOS

The following 8 x 10 black and white photos are each individually autographed by the player and show him as he appeared during his career. These are all high quality photos and would be a valuable addition to the collections of both the hobbyist and the investor. They are priced at $5 each; 25 or more different photos $4 each.

Cal Abrams(Bkn)
Ace Adams (NYG)
Bobby Adams(Cub)
Buster Adams(StL)
'Sparky' Adams (Cub)
Ethan Allen(Cub)
George Altman(Cub)
Sandy Amoros(Bkn)
Bob Anderson(Cub)
Sparky Anderson(Phl)
Nate Andrews(BosB)
Ken Aspromonte(Was)
Joe Astroth(A's)
Eldon Auker(StL B)
Earl Averill Jr.(Cub)
Jim Bagby Jr.(Cle)
Floyd Baker(Chi)
Gene Baker(Cub)
Rex Barney(Bkn)
Red Barrett(BosB)
Tony Bartirome(Pit)
Hank Bauer(NYY)
Frank Baumann(Chi)
Johnny Beazley(StL)
Ray Benge(Bkn)
Wally Berger(BosB)
Ray Berres(Bkn)
Huck Betts(BosB)
Bill Bevans(NYY)
Ewell Blackwell(Cin)
Don Blasingame(StL)
Buddy Blattner (NYG)
Jimmy Bloodsworth(Was)
Jim Bolger(Cub)
Milt Bolling(Bos)
Ray Boone(Det)
Steve Boros(Det)
Hank Borowy(NYY)
Ed Bouchee(Phil)
Joe Bowman(Pit)
Bob Boyd (Balt)
Clete Boyer(NYY,KC)
Bobby Bragan(Bkn)
Jackie Brandt(SF)
Harry Brecheen(StL)
Ed Bressoud(NYG)
Ernie Broglio(StL)
Jim Brosnen(Cin)
Mace Brown(Pit)
Tommy Brown(Bkn)
Billy Bruton(Mil)
Jimmy Bucher(Bkn)
Tommy Byrne(NYY)
Sam Calderone(NYG)
Bruce Campbell(Clev)
Andy Carey (NYY)
George Case(Was)
Pete Castiglione(Pit)
Phil Caveretta(Cub)
Bob Cerv(NYY)
Ron Cey(Cub)
Spud Chandler(NYY)
Ben Chapman (NYY)
Sam Chapman(A's)
Allie Clark(Clev)
Harland Clift(StL B)
Dick Cole(Pit)
Ray Coleman(StL)
Joe Collins(NYY)
Jimmy Cooney(NYG)
Pete Coscarat(Bkn)
Harry Craft(Cin)
Roger Craig(Bkn)
Doc Cramer(Det)
Del Crandell(Mil)
Frank Crosetti(NYY)
Al Cuccinello(NYG)
Tony Cuccinello(Bkn)
Guy Cartright(Chi)
Dom Dellessandro(Cub)
*Ray Dandridge(Min M) $8
Harry Danning(NYG)
Jim Davenport(SF)
Jim Delsing(Det)
Murray Dickson(StL)
Chuck Diering(Bal)
Bob Dillinger(StL B)
Joe DeMaestri(NYY)
Gene Desaultes(Bos)
Art Ditmar(NYY)
Jack Dittmer(Mil)
Pete Donahue (Cin)
Dick Donovan(Chi)
Moe Drabowsky(Cub)
Ryne Duren(NYY)
Don Elston(Cub)
Woody English(Cub)
Del Ennis(Phi)
Carl Erskine(LA,Bkn)
Sammy Esposito(Chi)
Chuck Essegian(LA)
Nick Etten(NYY)
Hoot Evers(Det)
Elroy Face(Pit)
Ferris Fain(Chi)
'Boo' Ferriss(Bos)
Elbie Fletcher(Pit)
Dee Fondy(Cub)
Lew Fonseca(Cle)
Art Fowler(Cin)
Herman Franks(Bkn)
Tito Francone(Cle)
Fred Frankhouse(Bkn)
Lonny Frey(Cin)
Carl Furillo(Bkn)
Denny Galehouse(StL B)
Danny Gardella(NYG)
Billy Gardner(Balt)
Ned Garver(A's)
Dick Gernert(Bos)
Al Gionfriddo(Bkn)
Alex Grammas(StL)
Jim Greengrass(StL)
Bob Grim(NYY)
Oscar Grimes(NYY)
Marv Grissom(NYG)
Steve Gromek(Det)
Orval Grove(Chi)
Harry Gumbert(StL)
Dan Gutteridge(StL B)
Bert Haas(Cin)
Warren Hacker(Cub)
Harvey Haddix(StL)
Bob Hale(Balt)
Irv Hall(Ph A's)
Mel Harder (Cle)
Gail Harris(NYG)
Roy Hartsfield(BosB)
Clint Hartung(NYG)
Buddy Hassett(Bkn)
Fred Hatfield(Det)
Joe Hatten(Bkn)
Ray Hayworth(Det)
Bob Hazle(Mil)
Ken Heintzelman(Phi)
Solly Hemus(StL)
Bill Henry(Cin)
Carmen Hill (Pit)
Billy Hitchcock(A's)
Glen Hobbie(Cub)
Billy Hoeft(Det)
Johnny Hopp(StL)
Art Houtteman(Cle)
Willis Hudlin(Cle)
*Carl Hubbell(NYG) $8
Sid Hudson(Was)
Roy Hughes(Cle)
Tex Hughson(Bos)
Billy Hunter(NYY)
*Monte Irvin(NYG) $6
Larry Jansen(NYG)
Randy Jackson(Cub,Bkn)
Hal Jeffcoat(Cub)
Woody Jensen(Pit)
Don Johnson(Cub)
Ernie Johnson(Mil)
Smead Jolly(Chi)
Nippy Jones(StL)
Sheldon Jones(NYG)
Eddie Joost(A's)
Buck Jordan(BosB)
Billy Jurges(NYG)
Willie Kamm(Chi)
Alex Kampouris(Cin)
Ted Kazanski(Phi)
Bob Keegan(Chi)
George Kell(Det)
Bob Kennedy(Chi)
Vern Kennedy(StL B)
Johnny Kerr(Chi)
Clyde King(Bkn)
Johnny Klippstein(Cin)
Ted Kluszewski(Cin)
Don Kolloway(Chi)
Ernie Koy(Bkn)
Johnny Kucks(NYY)
Whitey Kurowski(StL)
Clem Labine(Bkn)
Eddie Lake (Det)
Jim Landis(Chi)
Max Lanier(StL)
Cookie Lavagetto(Bkn)
Vern Law(Pit)
Hal Lee (BosB)
Ken Lehman(Bkn)

Hank Leiber(NYG)
*Bob Lemon(Cle) $6
Jim Lemon(Was)
Don Lenhardt(StL B)
*Buck Leonard(NegL) $10
Buddy Lewis(Was)
Whitey Lockman(NYG)
Johnny Logan(Mil)
Lucky Lohrke(NYG)
Vic Lombardi(Bkn)
Dale Long(Pit)
Ed Lopat(NYY)
Stan Lopata(Phi)
Hector Lopez(NYY)
Turk Lown(Cub)
Jerry Lumpe(NYY)
Don Lund(Det)
Tony Lupien(Bos)
Jerry Lynch(Cinc)
Hank Majeski(Cle)
Les Mallon(BosB)
Frank Malzone(Bos)
Cliff Mapes(NYY)
Marty Marion(StL)
Willard Marshall(NYG)
Stu Martin(StL)
Phil Masi(Bos)
Charlie Maxwell(Det)
Pinky May(Pit)
Bill Mazeroski(Pit)
Mike McCormick(SF)
Barney McCosky(Det)
Lindy McDaniel(StL)
Gil McDougald(NYY)

John McHale(Det)
Don McMahon(Mil)
Roy McMillan(Cin)
Glen McQuillan(StL B)
Cliff Melton(NYG)
Len Merullo(Cub)
George Metkovitch(Bos)
Charlie Metro(Cub)
Russ Meyer(Bkn)
Eddie Miksis(Bkn)
Bob Miller(Phi)
Eddie Miller(Cin)
Stu Miller (NYG)
Bob Milliken(Bkn)
Buster Mills (StL B)
Johnny Mize (StL,NYG)
Vinegar Bend Mizell(StL)
Joe Moore (NYG)
Johnny Moore (Cub)
Randy Moore(Bos)
Bobby Morgan(Bkn)
Walt Moryn(Cub)
Les Moss (StL B)
Don Mossi(Cle)
Don Mueller(NYG)
Ray Mueller(Cin)
Hugh Mulcahy(Phi)
Pat Mullin(Det)
*Stan Musial(StL) $8
George Myatt(Was)
Hal Naragon(Clev)
Ray Narleski(Cle)
Bill Nicholson(Cub)
Butch Nieman(BosB)

Irv Noren(NYY)
Johnny Outlaw(Det)
Marv Owen(Det)
Andy Pafko(Cub)
Milt Pappas(Balt)
Mel Parnell(Bos)
Claude Passeau(Cub)
Hal Peck(A's)
Ray Pepper(StL)
Johnny Pesky(Bos)
Russ Peters(Cle)
Babe Phelps(Bkn)
Dave Philley(Chi)
Billy Pierce(Chi)
Jim Piersall(Bos)
Al Pilarcik(Balt)
Nelson Potter(StL B)
Ken Raffensberger(Cin)
Vic Raschi(NYY)
Jimmy Reese(NYY)
Bill Renna(NYY)
Rip Repulski(StL)
Allie Reynolds(NYY)
Bill Rigney(NYG)
Jim Rivera(Chi)
Eddie Robinson(NYY)
Ed Roebuck(Bkn)
Stan Rojek(Pit)
Al Rosen(Clev)
Goody Rosen(Bkn)
Pete Runnels(Bos)
Bob Rush(Cub)
Jim Russell(Pit)
Marius Russo(NYY)

Connie Ryan(Bos)
Russ Scarritt(Bos)
Hal Schumacher(NYG)
Andy Seminick(Phi)
Joe Sewell(NYY)
Bobby Shantz(NYY)
Rip Sewell(Pit)
Bob Shaw(Chi)
Spec Shea(NYY)
Roy Sievers(Was)
Charlie Silvera(NYY)
Sibi Sisti(BosB)
Enos Slaughter(StL)
Roy Smalley Sr.(Cub)
Al Smith(Chi)
Warren Spahn(BosB)
Daryl Spencer(NYG)
'Tuck' Stainback(NYY)
Jerry Staley(Chi)
George Strickland(Cle)
Joe Stripp(Bkn)
Bobby Sturgeon(Cub)
Pete Suder(A's)
Gus Suhr(Pit)
Clyde Sukeforth(Bkn)
John Sullivan(Was)
Frank Sullivan(Bos)
Frank Thomas(Pit)
Tommy Thomas(Chi)
Bobby Thomson(NYG)
Earl Torgeson(BosB)
Cecil Travis(Was)
Gus Triandos(Bal)
Virgil Trucks(Det)

Bob Turley(NYY)
Jim Turner(NYY)
Elmer Valo(A's)
Mickey Vernon(Was)
Bill Virdon(Pit)
Bill Voiselle(NYG)
Harry Walker(StL)
Jerry Walker(Balt)
Monte Weaver(Wash)
Bob Weiland(StL B)
Phil Weintraub(NYG)
Bill Werber(Bos)
Wally Westlake(StL)
Wes Westrum(NYG)
Whitey Whitehead(NYG)
Bill Wight(Bos)
Jack Wilson(Bos)
Red Wilson(Det)
Mickey Witek(NYG)
Dick Whitman(Bkn)
Pinkey Whitney(Phi)
*Hoyt Wilhelm(NYG,Balt) $6
Deb Williams(A's)
Roger Wolff(Was)
Hal Woodeshick(Was)
Gene Woodling(NYY)
Al Worthington(NYG)
Whit Wyatt(Bkn)
*Early Wynn(Was,Clev) $6
Hank Wyse(Cub)
Al Zarilla(StL B)
Norm Zauchin(Bos)
Don Zimmer(Bkn)
Jim King(Cub)

INDIVIDUALLY SIGNED OFFICIAL AL OR NL BASEBALLS. EACH BALL IS INDIVIDUALLY SIGNED IN THE MANAGER'S SPOT.

Luke Appling	$18.00
Luis Aparicio	18.00
Ernie Banks	18.00
Yogi Berra	18.00
Lou Boudreau	15.00
George Brett	18.00
Steve Carlton	18.00
Rod Carew	18.00
Gary Carter	15.00
Vince Coleman	15.00
Ray Dandridge	15.00
Joe Dimaggio	30.00
Bobby Doerr	15.00
Don Drysdale	15.00
Whitey Ford	15.00
Bob Gibson	15.00
Lefty Gomez	15.00
Rickey Henderson	18.00
Carl Hubbell	18.00
Lou Brock	15.00
Monte Irvin	$15.00
Reggie Jackson	22.00
Fergie Jenkins	15.00
Judy Johnson	18.00
Al Kaline	15.00
George Kell	15.00
Harmon Killebrew	15.00
Ralph Kiner	15.00
Sandy Koufax	20.00
Bob Lemon	15.00
Mickey Mantle	22.00
Juan Marichal	18.00
Eddie Mathews	15.00
Willie Mays	18.00
Johnny Mize	15.00
Stan Musial	15.00
Phil Niekro	15.00
Gaylord Perry	15.00
Pee Wee Reese	15.00
Jim Rice	15.00
Dave Righetti	$15.00
Cal Ripken Jr.	15.00
Robin Roberts	15.00
Brooks Robinson	15.00
Frank Robinson	15.00
Pete Rose	18.00
Nolan Ryan	18.00
Tom Seaver	18.00
Joe Sewell	18.00
Enos Slaughter	15.00
Duke Snider	15.00
Warren Spahn	15.00
D. Strawberry	15.00
Don Sutton	15.00
Hoyt Wilhelm	15.00
Maury Wills	15.00
Billy Williams	15.00
Dave Winfield	15.00
Early Wynn	15.00
C. Yastrzemski	18.00

DISCOUNTS:
Order 6 - 10 different balls: deduct $1.00 from each ball.
Order 11 - 25 different balls: deduct $2.00 from each ball.
Order 26 - 40 balls: deduct $3.00 from each ball.
Order 41 or more different balls: deduct $4.00 from each ball.

POSTAGE: PLEASE ADD $2 PER ORDER FOR POSTAGE AND HANDLING. MAKE ALL CHECKS AND MONEY ORDERS PAYABLE TO: THE NATIONAL PASTIME.
SEND ORDERS TO:
THE NATIONAL PASTIME
93 ISELIN DRIVE, NEW ROCHELLE, NY 10804
(Tel: (914) 576-1755 OR (718) 224-1795)
SEND A S.A.S.E. FOR A COMPLETE LIST OF AVAILABLE PHOTOS AND BASEBALLS.

ADAMSON, ROBERT E L	NEWS CORRESPONDENT	612 4TH PL, SW	WASHINGTON, DC	20024
ADATO, PERRY MILLER	TV DIRECTOR-PRODUCER	3 FRASER RD	WESTPORT, CT	06880
ADC BAND	ROCK & ROLL GROUP	17397 SANTA BARBARA DR	DETROIT, MI	48221
ADCOCK, JOE G	DRUMMER	ROUTE #2	PEQUOT LAKE, MN	56472
ADCOCK, JOHN RICHARD	GUITARIST	1520 NORVEL ST	NASHVILLE, TN	37216
ADCOCK, MARILYN	PIANIST	ROUTE #2	PEQUOT LAKES, MN	56472
ADDAMS, CHARLES	CARTOONIST	N Y MAGAZINE, 25 W 43RD ST	NEW YORK, NY	10036
ADDE, NICHOLAS L	NEWS CORRESPONDENT	3903 SPRUELL DR	KENSINGTON, MD	20895
ADDIS, JOHN	COMPOSER	10100 SANTA MONICA BLVD #1600	LOS ANGELES, CA	90067
ADDISON, ANNE	TV EXECUTIVE	1035 5TH AVE	NEW YORK, NY	10028
ADDISON, DAVID ASHLEY	NEWS CORRESPONDENT	1206 ETON CT, NW	WASHINGTON, DC	20007
ADDISON, JOHN	COMPOSER	3815 W OLIVE AVE #202	BURBANK, CA	91505
ADDISON ALTMAN, NANCY	ACTRESS	APA, 888 7TH AVE, 6TH FLOOR	NEW YORK, NY	10106
ADDRISI BROTHERS, THE	VOCAL DUO	SCOTTI BROS, 2128 PICO BLVD	SANTA MONICA, CA	90405
ADDY, WESLEY	ACTOR	88 CENTRAL PARK W	NEW YORK, NY	10023
ADE, JERRY	TALENT AGENT	200 W 51ST ST #1410	NEW YORK, NY	10019
ADELMAN, BARRY	WRITER-PRODUCER	4745 DEGOVIA AVE	WOODLAND HILLS, CA	91364
ADELMAN, SYBIL	WRITER	10390 SANTA MONICA BLVD #310	LOS ANGELES, CA	90025
ADELSON, GAIL	TV PRODUCER	292 S LA CIENEGA BLVD #205	BEVERLY HILLS, CA	90211
ADELSON, GARY	WRITER	2333 COLDWATER CANYON DR	BEVERLY HILLS, CA	90210
ADELSON, MERV	TV PRODUCER	600 SARBONNE RD	LOS ANGELES, CA	90077
ADERMAN, GARY	NEWS CORRESPONDENT	1900 S EADS ST	ARLINGTON, VA	22202
ADES, DAN	ACTOR	652 N LA JOLLA AVE	LOS ANGELES, CA	90048
ADIAS, BRIAN	WRESTLER	WORLD CLASS WRESTLING		
		SOUTHWEST SPORTS, INC		
		DALLAS SPORTATORIUM		
		1000 S INDUSTRIAL BLVD	DALLAS, TX	75207
ADIDAS, BRIAN	WRESTLER	SEE - ADIAS, BRIAN		
ADJANI, ISABELLE	ACTRESS	33 RUE MARBEUF	PARIS 75008	FRANCE
ADKINS, HAZEL	SINGER-SONGWRITER	POST OFFICE BOX 646		
		COOPER STATION	NEW YORK, NY	10276
ADKISSON, KERRY	WRESTLER	SEE - VON ERICH, KERRY		
ADKISSON, KEVIN	WRESTLER	SEE - VON ERICH, KEVIN		
ADLEMAN, ANDREW W	WRITER	608 STRAND ST #7	SANTA MONICA, CA	90405
ADLER, ABRAHAM	TV DIRECTOR	10 DESSER PL	EDISON, NJ	08817
ADLER, ALAN J	SCREENWRITER	8955 BEVERLY BLVD	LOS ANGELES, CA	90048
ADLER, ALLEN	FILM PRODUCER	ARA ENTS, 195 S BEVERLY DR	BEVERLY HILLS, CA	90210
ADLER, BUDDY	ACTOR	BERZON, 336 E 17TH ST	COSTA MESA, CA	92627
ADLER, EDWARD	TV WRITER	555 W 57TH ST #1230	NEW YORK, NY	10019
ADLER, FELICITY	ACTRESS	20 E 22ND ST #3-D	NEW YORK, NY	10010
ADLER, GARY	ACTOR	CASSELL, 843 N SYCAMORE AVE	LOS ANGELES, CA	90038
ADLER, GERALD L	TV EXECUTIVE	145 N ALMONT DR #115	LOS ANGELES, CA	90048
ADLER, JAMES	PIANIST-COMPOSER	GERSHUNOFF, 502 PARK AVE	NEW YORK, NY	10022
ADLER, JERRY	THEATER DIRECTOR	24 W 69TH ST	NEW YORK, NY	10023
ADLER, JUDY	COLUMNIST	NEWS AMERICA SYNDICATE		
		1703 KAISER AVE	IRVINE, CA	92714
ADLER, KURT	OPERA DIRECTOR	WAR MEMORIAL OPERA HOUSE	SAN FRANCISCO, CA	94102
ADLER, LARRY	ACTOR	26 WYNDHAM ST	LONDON W1	ENGLAND
ADLER, LOU	DIRECTOR-PRODUCER	21756 PACIFIC COAST HWY	MALIBU, CA	90265
ADLER, RICHARD	COMPOSER-LYRICIST	8 E 83RD ST	NEW YORK, NY	10028
ADLER, SAMUEL	CONDUCTOR	54 RAILROAD MILLS RD	PITTSFORD, NY	14534
ADLER, SONIA	NEWS CORRESPONDENT	3301 WOODBINE ST	CHEVY CHASE, MD	20815
ADLER, STELLA	ACTOR-DIRECTOR	130 W 56TH ST	NEW YORK, NY	10019
ADLER, WILLIAM	ACTOR	12901 WARREN AVE	LOS ANGELES, CA	90066
ADLIEBL, BRAD	BARITONE	AFFILIATE ARTISTS, INC		
		37 W 65TH ST, 6TH FLOOR	NEW YORK, NY	10023
ADNOPOZ, DAVID	ACTOR-WRITER	1194 N LOS ROBLES AVE	PASADENA, CA	91104
ADONIS, ADORABLE ADRIAN	WRESTLER	POST OFFICE BOX 3859	STAMFORD, CT	06905
ADORJAN, ANDRAS	FLUTIST	COLBERT, 111 W 57TH ST	NEW YORK, NY	10019
ADOTTA, KIP	COMEDIAN	ICM, 8899 BEVERLY BLVD	LOS ANGELES, CA	90048
ADRENALIN	ROCK & ROLL GROUP	ICM, 40 W 57TH ST	NEW YORK, NY	10019
ADRIAN, DIANE	ACTRESS	1645 S LA CIENEGA BLVD #6	LOS ANGELES, CA	90035
ADRIAN, IRIS	ACTRESS	3341 FLOYD TERR	LOS ANGELES, CA	90068
ADRIAN, LOUIS	CONDUCTOR	4450 MERIDIAN AVE	OXNARD, CA	93030
ADRINE, LYNNE K	NEWS CORRESPONDENT	POST OFFICE BOX 2626	WASHINGTON, DC	20013
ADU, SADE	SINGER	SEE - SADE		
AEBERSOLD-NEIWEEM	PIANO DUO	GREAT LAKES PERFORMING		
		310 E WASHINGTON ST	ANN ARBOR, MI	48104
AEROSMITH	ROCK & ROLL GROUP	COLLINS/BARASSO MGMT		
		215 1ST ST	CAMBRIDGE, MA	02142
AESCHLIMANN, JOHANN	NEWS CORRESPONDENT	1227 33RD ST, NW	WASHINGTON, DC	20007
AFFENS, STEVE C	PHOTOJOURNALIST	3305 LLEWLLYN FIELD RD	OLNEY, MD	20832
AFFLECK, WILLIAM C	TV DIRECTOR	22198 REINHARDT DR	WOODHAVEN, MI	48183
AFI, JIMMY	WRESTLER	SEE - AFI, SIVA		
AFI, SIVI	WRESTLER	POST OFFICE BOX 3859	STAMFORD, CT	06905
AFI, SUPERFLY	WRESTLER	SEE - AFI, SIVA		
AFRIAT, ALAN	TV DIRECTOR-PRODUCER	24 COMBEMARTIN RD	LONDON SW18 5PR	ENGLAND
AFRO-CUBAN BAND	ROCK & ROLL GROUP	LOVE ZAGER PRODUCTIONS		
		1697 BROADWAY	NEW YORK, NY	10019
AFRRIKKA BAMBAATA	SINGER	200 W 51ST ST #1410	NEW YORK, NY	10021
AFSHAR, LILY	GUITARIST	AFFILIATE ARTISTS, INC		
		37 W 65TH ST, 6TH FLOOR	NEW YORK, NY	10023
AGAR, JOHN	ACTOR	639 N HOLLYWOOD WY	BURBANK, CA	91505
AGAZZI, JAMES J	TV WRITER	POST OFFICE BOX 24086	LOS ANGELES, CA	90024
AGELLI, ADAM	ACTOR	8350 SANTA MONICA BLVD #103	LOS ANGELES, CA	90069

Name	Occupation	Address	City	Zip/Country
AGHAYAN, RAY	COSTUME DESIGNER	8636 MELROSE AVE	LOS ANGELES, CA	90069
AGNELLO, JOSEPH	DIRECTOR-PRODUCER	4625 SYLMAR AVE #309	SHERMAN OAKS, CA	91423
AGNEW, BRUCE A	NEWS CORRESPONDENT	3411 TURNER LN	CHEVY CHASE, MD	20815
AGOGLIA, GEORGE S	PUBLISHING EXECUTIVE	THE NATIONAL LAMPOON		
		635 MADISON AVE	NEW YORK, NY	10022
AGRES, THEODORE J	NEWS CORRESPONDENT	5805 84TH AVE	NEW CARROLLTON, MD	20784
AGRESS, JOHN	WRITER	555 W 57TH ST #1230	NEW YORK, NY	10019
AGRIESTI, LOU K	COMPOSER-CONDUCTOR	3518 S TOWNER ST	SANTA ANA, CA	92707
AGRONSKY, MARTIN	TV PRODUCER	1232 31ST ST, NW	WASHINGTON, DC	20007
AGUILA, LEO D	NEWS CORRESPONDENT	1502 S GEORGE MASON DR	ARLINGTON, VA	22204
AGUTTER, JENNY	ACTRESS	8268 MARMONT LN	LOS ANGELES, CA	90069
AHEARN, DAVID M	NEWS CORRESPONDENT	309 S CAROLINA AVE #A, SE	WASHINGTON, DC	20003
AHEARN, DEAN J	NEWS CORRESPONDENT	10114 PHOEBE LN	ADELPHI, MD	20783
AHERN, ALSTON	ACTOR	6430 SUNSET BLVD #1203	LOS ANGELES, CA	90028
AHERN, TIM	NEWS CORRESPONDENT	2139 N OAKLAND ST	ARLINGTON, VA	22207
AHLERS, MICHAEL M	NEWS CORRESPONDENT	14129 FLINT ROCK RD	ROCKVILLE, MD	20853
AHLSTEDT, DOUGLAS	TENOR	61 W 62ND ST #6-F	NEW YORK, NY	10023
AHMANN, SARAH	NEWS CORRESPONDENT	6013 GROSVENOR LN	BETHESDA, MD	20814
AHMANN, TIMOTHY D	NEWS CORRESPONDENT	3714 MORRISON ST, NW	WASHINGTON, DC	20015
AHN, RALPH	ACTOR	14709 CLYMER ST	MISSION HILLS, CA	91345
AHNEMANN, MICHAEL	WRITER	8955 BEVERLY BLVD	LOS ANGELES, CA	90048
AHNSJO, CLAES H	TENOR	CAMI, 165 W 57TH ST	NEW YORK, NY	10019
AHRENS, LYNN	WRITER	555 W 57TH ST #1230	NEW YORK, NY	10019
AIDEKMAN, ALAN	TV WRITER	6371 W 5TH ST	LOS ANGELES, CA	90048
AIDEM, MONTY	TV WRITER	6701 WYNNE AVE	RESEDA, CA	91355
AIDMAN, BETTY LINTON	ACTRESS	525 N PALM DR	BEVERLY HILLS, CA	90210
AIDMAN, CHARLES	ACT-WRI-DIR	525 N PALM DR	BEVERLY HILLS, CA	90210
AIELLO, DANNY	ACTOR	1697 BROADWAY #504	NEW YORK, NY	10019
AIKEN, JONATHAN FRANCIS	NEWS CORRESPONDENT	1825 "K" ST, NW	WASHINGTON, DC	20006
AIKINS, BILL	PIANIST	2835 E VEGAS VALLEY DR	LAS VEGAS, NV	89121
AILES, ROGER	PRODUCER-DIRECTOR	230 CENTRAL PARK S	NEW YORK, NY	10019
AILEY, ALVIN	CHOREOGRAPHER	C C DANCE, 229 E 59TH ST	NEW YORK, NY	10022
AIMARD, PIERRE-LAURENT	PIANIST	119 W 57TH ST #1505	NEW YORK, NY	10019
AIMEE, ANOUK	ACTRESS	10 AVE GEORGE V	PARIS 75008	FRANCE
AINLEY, ANTHONY	ACTOR	2 EMMERDALE DR	LONDON NW9 ODT	ENGLAND
AINLEY, SIMON	ACTOR	6605 HOLLYWOOD BLVD #220	HOLLYWOOD, CA	90028
AINSLEE, MARIAN	WRITER	8955 BEVERLY BLVD	LOS ANGELES, CA	90048
AIR SUPPLY	ROCK & ROLL GROUP	6 BEAUCHAMP PL	LONDON SW3 1NG	ENGLAND
AIRBAND, THE	ROCK & ROLL GROUP	POST OFFICE BOX 222	BLACK HAWK, SD	57718
AIROZO, DAVID JOHN	NEWS CORRESPONDENT	4201 MASSACHUSETTS AVE #3046	WASHINGTON, DC	20016
AIRRACE	ROCK & ROLL GROUP	ATI, 888 7TH AVE, 21ST FLOOR	NEW YORK, NY	10106
AITAY, VICTOR	VIOLINIST	212 OAK KNOLL TERR	HIGHLAND PARK, IL	60035
AITKEN, LEE	WRITER-EDITOR	TIME & PEOPLE MAGAZINE		
		TIME & LIFE BUILDING		
		ROCKEFELLER CENTER	NEW YORK, NY	10020
AJAYE, FRANKLYN	COMEDIAN-ACTOR	ICM, 8899 BEVERLY BLVD	LOS ANGELES, CA	90048
AJMONE-MARSAN, GUIDO	CONDUCTOR	ICM, 40 W 57TH ST	NEW YORK, NY	10019
AKBAR, SCANDOR	WRESTLING MANAGER	WORLD CLASS WRESTLING		
		SOUTHWEST SPORTS, INC		
		DALLAS SPORTATORIUM		
		1000 S INDUSTRIAL BLVD	DALLAS, TX	75207
AKER, JANET A	NEWS CORRESPONDENT	5516 BROAD BEACH RD, NW	WASHINGTON, DC	20015
AKERMAN, JOSEPH L	WRITER	1858 FOX HILLS DR	LOS ANGELES, CA	90025
AKERS, ANDRA	ACTRESS	9022 VISTA GRANDE ST	LOS ANGELES, CA	90069
AKERS, KAREN	ACTRESS	9255 SUNSET BLVD #505	LOS ANGELES, CA	90069
AKERS, KAREN	SINGER	1205 FRANKLIN AVE	GARDEN CITY, NY	11530
AKERS, TIMOTHY WAYNE	MUSIC ARRANGER	112 ACKLEN PARK DR #A-7	NASHVILLE, TN	37203
AKIN, JULIE	ACTRESS	CED, 261 S ROBERTSON BLVD	BEVERLY HILLS, CA	90211
AKINS, CLAUDE	ACTOR	805 S HUDSON AVE	PASADENA, CA	91106
AKINS, JEWEL	SINGER-SONGWRITER	GOOD, 2500 NW 39TH ST	OKLAHOMA CITY, OK	73112
AKIYOSHI, TOSHIKO	COMPOSER-PIANIST	5820 WILSHIRE BLVD #301	LOS ANGELES, CA	90036
AKKAD, MOUSTAPHA	DIRECTOR-PRODUCER	TWICKENHAM, THE BARONS		
		SAINT MARGARETS		
		TWICKENHAM	MIDDLESEX	ENGLAND
AKO	ROCK & ROLL GROUP	AZTEC, 20531 PLUMMER ST	CHATSWORTH, CA	91311
AKS, CATHERINE	SOPRANO	254 W 93RD ST #8	NEW YORK, NY	10025
AKUNE, SHUKO	ACTRESS	9200 SUNSET BLVD #1210	LOS ANGELES, CA	90028
ALABAMA	C & W GROUP	DALE MORRIS MANAGEMENT		
		818 19TH AVE S	NASHVILLE, TN	37203
ALAIMO, MARC	ACTOR	9255 SUNSET BLVD #510	LOS ANGELES, CA	90069
ALAIMO, MICHAEL L	WRITER	8955 BEVERLY BLVD	LOS ANGELES, CA	90048
ALAN, BUDDY	SINGER	1225 N CHESTER AVE	BAKERSFIELD, CA	93308
ALAN, ROBBY	GUITARIST	GENERAL DELIVERY	TACNA, AZ	85352
ALAN, SYLVIA	TV WRITER	8955 BEVERLY BLVD	LOS ANGELES, CA	90048
ALARIMO, JOHN	WRITER	POST OFFICE BOX 1446	STUDIO CITY, CA	91604
ALARM, THE	ROCK & ROLL GROUP	3 E 54TH ST #1400	NEW YORK, NY	10022
ALBA, ROSE	ACTRESS	60 CHANDOS PL	LONDON WC 2	ENGLAND
ALBANESE, LICIA	SOPRANO	800 PARK AVE	NEW YORK, NY	10021
ALBANESE, MICHAEL	TV DIRECTOR	132 HIGH ST	LEONIA, NJ	07605
ALBANO, CAPTAIN LOU	WRESTLER-MANAGER	POST OFFICE BOX 3859	STAMFORD, CT	06905
ALBANO, JOHN F	WRITER	555 W 57TH ST #1230	NEW YORK, NY	10019
ALBANS, SAMUEL	WRITER	1417 VETERAN AVE #201	LOS ANGELES, CA	90024
ALBANY, JOE	PIANIST	STEEPLECHASE RECORDS		
		FLINTERENDEN 4, 4TH	DK-2300 COPENHAGEN	SO DENMARK
ALBARINO, RICHARD	WRITER	8955 BEVERLY BLVD	LOS ANGELES, CA	90048

ALABAMA

Jeff Cook • Randy Owen • Mark Herndon • Teddy Gentry

ASIA

Greg Lake • Steve Howe • Geoff Downes • Carl Palmer

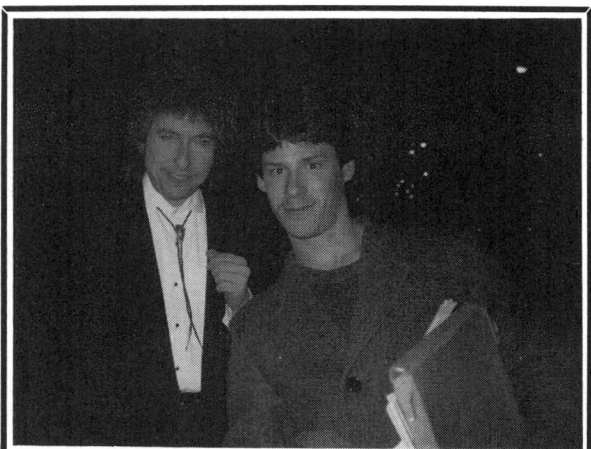

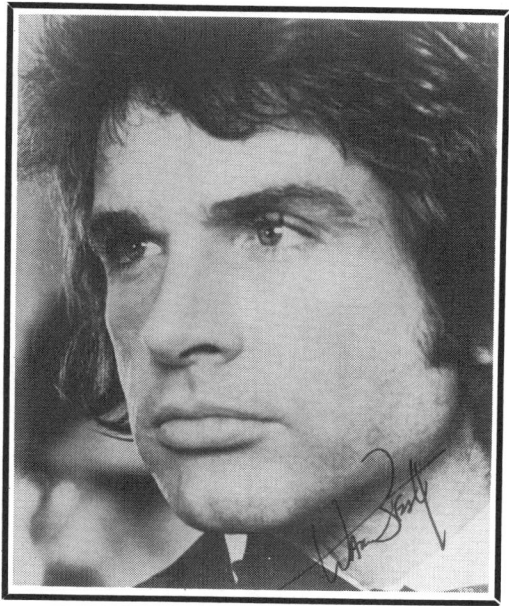

Name	Occupation	Address	City	ZIP
ALBAUGH, EDWIN D, JR	NEWS CORRESPONDENT	6401 CARDINAL LN	COLUMBIA, MD	21044
ALBECK, ANDY	FILM EXECUTIVE	729 7TH AVE	NEW YORK, NY	10019
ALBEE, EDWARD	WRITER-PRODUCER	14 HARRISON ST	NEW YORK, NY	10013
ALBERG, MILDRED F	WRITER-PRODUCER	555 W 57TH ST #1230	NEW YORK, NY	10019
ALBERGHETTI, ANNA MARIA	ACTRESS-SINGER	2337 BENEDICT CANYON RD	BEVERLY HILLS, CA	90210
ALBERICI, LINDA	ACTRESS	3151 W CAHUENGA BLVD #310	LOS ANGELES, CA	90068
ALBERT, ANDREW S	NEWS CORRESPONDENT	2801 QUEBEC ST #348, NW	WASHINGTON, DC	20008
ALBERT, DONNIE RAY	SINGER	CAMI, 165 W 57TH ST	NEW YORK, NY	10019
ALBERT, EDDIE	ACTOR	719 AMALFI DR	PACIFIC PAL, CA	90272
ALBERT, EDWARD	ACTOR	27320 WINDING WY	MALIBU, CA	90265
ALBERT, EDWARD A	GUITARIST	POST OFFICE BOX 45	ELLINGTON, MO	63638
ALBERT, JAN	WRITER	555 W 57TH ST #1230	NEW YORK, NY	10019
ALBERT, JOANN	ACTRESS	FELBER, 2126 N CAHUENGA BLVD	LOS ANGELES, CA	90068
ALBERT, JOEL R	NEWS CORRESPONDENT	NBC-TV, NEWS DEPARTMENT		
		4001 NEBRASKA AVE, NW	WASHINGTON, DC	20016
ALBERT, KENNETH	GUITARIST	300 BAKERTOWN RD #20-H	ANTIOCH, TN	37013
ALBERT, MARV	SPORTSCASTER	NBC-TV, SPORTS DEPARTMENT		
		30 ROCKEFELLER PLAZA	NEW YORK, NY	10112
ALBERT, WIL	ACTOR	151 N SAN VICENTE BLVD #208	BEVERLY HILLS, CA	90211
ALBERT, WILLIAM C	NEWS CORRESPONDENT	5151 WISCONSIN AVE, NW	WASHINGTON, DC	20016
ALBERTI, MERCEDES	ACTRESS	8721 SUNSET BLVD #200	LOS ANGELES, CA	90069
ALBERTS, AL & THE ORIGINALS	VOCAL GROUP	CEE, 193 KONHAUS RD	MECHANICSBURG, PA	17055
ALBERTS, EUNICE	CONTRALTO	254 W 93RD ST #8	NEW YORK, NY	10025
ALBERTSON, DAVID	NEWS CORRESPONDENT	1608 N RANDOLPH ST	ARLINGTON, VA	22207
ALBERTSON, MAURA DHU	ACTRESS	1618 SUNSET PLAZA DR	LOS ANGELES, CA	90069
ALBET, DEBORAH L	NEWS CORRESPONDENT	400 NATIONAL PRESS BLDG		
		529 14TH ST, NW	WASHINGTON, DC	20045
ALBI, DOMINICK	WRITER-PRODUCER	45 W 60TH ST #6-D	NEW YORK, NY	10023
ALBIDREZ, LUIS	WRITER	13419 HARVEST AVE	NORWALK, CA	90650
ALBIN, ANDY	ACTOR	1717 N HIGHLAND AVE #414	LOS ANGELES, CA	90028
ALBIN, DOLORES	ACTRESS	13006 WOODBRIDGE ST	NORTH HOLLYWOOD, CA	91604
ALBO, JOHN	WRITER	8955 BEVERLY BLVD	LOS ANGELES, CA	90048
ALBRECHT, ARDON D	TV WRITER	8955 BEVERLY BLVD	LOS ANGELES, CA	90048
ALBRECHT, GERD	CONDUCTOR	MARIEDL ANDERS ARTISTS MGMT		
		535 EL CAMINO DEL MAR ST	SAN FRANCISCO, CA	94121
ALBRECHT, HOWARD	TV WRITER	3632 BEVERLY RIDGE DR	SHERMAN OAKS, CA	91423
ALBRECHT, JOIE	WRITER	8955 BEVERLY BLVD	LOS ANGELES, CA	90048
ALBRECHT, PATRICIA A	ACTRESS	1803 1/2 N VAN NESS AVE	HOLLYWOOD, CA	90028
ALBRECHT, PEGGY FREES	ACTRESS-WRITER	20701 WELLS DR	WOODLAND HILLS, CA	91364
ALBRECHT, RICHARD	TV WRITER	20500 AETNA ST	WOODLAND HILLS, CA	91367
ALBRECHT, ROBERT	DIRECTOR	3017 N CLIFTON AVE	CHICAGO, IL	60657
ALBRIGHT, ANNE R	WRITER	555 W 57TH ST #1230	NEW YORK, NY	10019
ALBRIGHT, DIANE	NEWS REPORTER	THE NATIONAL ENQUIRER		
		600 SE COAST AVE	LANTANA, FL	33464
ALBRIGHT, LOLA	ACTRESS	9000 SUNSET BLVD #801	LOS ANGELES, CA	90069
ALBRIGHT, MAX	DRUMMER	POST OFFICE BOX 50082	WASHINGTON, DC	20004
ALBRIGHT, RAYMOND	TALENT AGENT	15 HIGH ST #621	HARTFORD, CT	06103
ALBRIGHT, RICHARD D	DRUMMER	ROUTE #6, PEACH HOLLOW RD	FRANKLIN, TN	37064
ALBRIGHT, VICTORIA	ACTRESS	6430 SUNSET BLVD #1203	LOS ANGELES, CA	90028
ALBRO, MICHAEL	TV DIRECTOR	384 N SUMMIT AVE #203	GAITHERSBURG, MD	20877
ALBULET HIGH WIRE DUO	HIGH WIRE DUO	HALL, 138 FROH HOLLOW RD	CHURCHVILLE, PA	18966
ALCADE, LAURA	ACTRESS	1001 N KENTER AVE	LOS ANGELES, CA	90049
ALCAIDE, CHRIS	ACTOR	SF & A, 121 N SAN VICENTE BLVD	BEVERLY HILLS, CA	90211
ALCANTARA, THEO	CONDUCTOR	ICM, 40 W 57TH ST	NEW YORK, NY	10019
ALCH, ALAN	WRITER	125 WASHINGTON AVE #F	SANTA MONICA, CA	90403
ALCIVAR, BOB E	COMPOSER	12713 CHANDLER BLVD	NORTH HOLLYWOOD, CA	91607
ALCORN, JANET	SOPRANO	3003 VAN NESS ST #W-205, NW	WASHINGTON, DC	20008
ALCOTT, ABIGAIL K	NEWS CORRESPONDENT	ABC-TV, NEWS DEPARTMENT		
		1717 DE SALES ST, NW	WASHINGTON, DC	20036
ALCROFT, JAMIE	ACT-WRI-COMED	151 S EL CAMINO DR	BEVERLY HILLS, CA	90212
ALDA, ALAN	ACT-WRI-DIR	MCA/UNIVERSAL STUDIOS, INC		
		100 UNIVERSAL CITY PLAZA #507	UNIVERSAL CITY, CA	91608
ALDA, ANTONY	ACTOR	6433 PEACH AVE	VAN NUYS, CA	91406
ALDA, ELIZABETH	ACTRESS	19432 COLLIER ST	TARZANA, CA	91356
ALDA, RUTANYA	ACTRESS	19 W 44TH ST #1500	NEW YORK, NY	10036
ALDEBERT, LOUIS J	COMPOSER	6215 LONGRIDGE AVE	VAN NUYS, CA	91401
ALDEN, GINGER	MODEL	4152 ROYAL CREST PL	MEMPHIS, TN	38138
ALDEN, JEROME	WRITER	555 W 57TH ST #1230	NEW YORK, NY	10019
ALDEN, KAY	TV WRITER	CBS TELEVISION NETWORK		
		"THE YOUNG & THE RESTLESS"		
		7800 BEVERLY BLVD	LOS ANGELES, CA	90036
ALDEN, NORMAN	ACTOR	345 S CRESCENT DR	BEVERLY HILLS, CA	90212
ALDEN, PRISCILLA K	WRITER	555 W 57TH ST #1230	NEW YORK, NY	10019
ALDERESTS, THE	JAZZ GROUP	POST OFFICE BOX 48041	LOS ANGELES, CA	90048
ALDERETE, ROSEMARY	WRITER-PRODUCER	816 S MONTEBELLO BLVD	MONTEBELLO, CA	90640
ALDERMAN, JANE	CASTING DIRECTOR	679 N MICHIGAN AVE	CHICAGO, IL	60611
ALDINGER, CHARLES SCOTT	NEWS CORRESPONDENT	1300 ARMY-NAVY DR	ARLINGTON, VA	22202
ALDO NOVA	ROCK & ROLL GROUP	PEARLMAN, 228 W 55TH ST	NEW YORK, NY	10019
ALDON, LYNDA	ACTRESS-MODEL	13111 VENTURA BLVD #204	STUDIO CITY, CA	91604
ALDREDGE, DAWN	TV WRITER	8955 BEVERLY BLVD	LOS ANGELES, CA	90048
ALDREDGE, THEONI V	COSTUME DESIGNER	425 LAFAYETTE ST	NEW YORK, NY	10003
ALDRICH, ADELL	TV DIRECTOR	556 S NORTON AVE	LOS ANGELES, CA	90020
ALDRICH, CHARLES W	NEWS CORRESPONDENT	2525 S 2ND ST	ARLINGTON, VA	22204
ALDRICH, JAMES P	WRITER	555 W 57TH ST #1230	NEW YORK, NY	10019
ALDRICH, NANCY L	NEWS CORRESPONDENT	1900 LYTTONSVILLE RD	SILVER SPRING, MD	20910

ALDRICH, RHONDA	ACTRESS	SHERMAN, 348 S REXFORD DR	BEVERLY HILLS, CA	90212
ALDRICH, WILLIAM M	FILM PRODUCER	606 N LARCHMONT BLVD #209	LOS ANGELES, CA	90004
ALDRIDGE, VIRGINIA	ACTRESS-WRITER	976 1/2 PALM AVE	LOS ANGELES, CA	90069
ALDRIDGE NASLUND, KAY	ACTRESS	PENOBSCOT BAY	CAMDEN, ME	04847
ALDRIDGE SISTERS, THE	VOCAL DUO	ICM, 40 W 57TH ST	NEW YORK, NY	10019
ALEANDRI, EMELISE	ACTRESS	229 E 12TH ST	NEW YORK, NY	10011
ALECK, JIMMY	ACTOR	8721 SUNSET BLVD #202	LOS ANGELES, CA	90069
ALEKSANDER, GRANT	ACTOR	CBS TELEVISION NETWORK		
		"THE GUIDING LIGHT"		
		51 W 52ND ST	NEW YORK, NY	10019
ALER, JOHN	TENOR	JCB, 155 W 68TH ST	NEW YORK, NY	10023
ALESIA, FRANK	WRITER-PRODUCER	805 N ELM DR	BEVERLY HILLS, CA	90210
ALETHIA	ROCK & ROLL GROUP	1254 LAMAR CIR #312	MEMPHIS, TN	38114
ALETTER, FRANK	ACTOR	5430 CORBIN AVE	TARZANA, CA	91356
ALETTER, KYLE	ACTRESS	12139 JEANETTE PL	GRANADA HILLS, CA	91344
ALEX, MARILYN	ACTRESS	3330 BARHAM BLVD #103	LOS ANGELES, CA	90068
ALEX, MICHAEL	WRITER	8955 BEVERLY BLVD	LOS ANGELES, CXA	90048
ALEXANDER, ANDREW	TV PRODUCER	10100 SANTA MONICA BLVD #348	LOS ANGELES, CA	90067
ALEXANDER, ANDREW NELSON	NEWS CORRESPONDENT	2925 43RD ST, NW	WASHINGTON, DC	20016
ALEXANDER, ANTHONY	ACTOR	8721 SUNSET BLVD #202	LOS ANGELES, CA	90069
ALEXANDER, AXEL	COMPOSER-CONDUCTOR	BERT BRECHT STR #2	BAD VILBEL 6368	WEST GERMANY
ALEXANDER, CHARLES P	WRITER-EDITOR	TIME/TIME & LIFE BLDG		
		ROCKEFELLER CENTER	NEW YORK, NY	10020
ALEXANDER, DAN	DIRECTOR	DGA, 7950 SUNSET BLVD	LOS ANGELES, CA	90046
ALEXANDER, DAVID	TV DIRECTOR	3907 GOODLAND AVE	NORTH HOLLYWOOD, CA	91604
ALEXANDER, DENISE	ACTRESS	NBC-TV, "ANOTHER WORLD"		
		30 ROCKEFELLER PLAZA	NEW YORK, NY	10112
ALEXANDER, E NICK	WRITER	8955 BEVERLY BLVD	LOS ANGELES, CA	90048
ALEXANDER, FAY	STUNT DRIVER	POST OFFICE BOX 87	WEST LEBANON, NY	12195
ALEXANDER, HAL	TV DIRECTOR	24211 PHILIPRIMM ST	WOODLAND HILLS, CA	91364
ALEXANDER, HOLMES	NEWS CORRESPONDENT	922 25TH ST, NW	WASHINGTON, DC	20037
ALEXANDER, JANE	ACTRESS	RURAL ROUTE #2, GORDON RD	CARMEL, NY	10512
ALEXANDER, JEFF	COMPOSER-CONDUCTOR	921 N SPAULDING AVE #5	LOS ANGELES, CA	90046
ALEXANDER, JESSE	TV EDITOR	17820 HATTON ST	RESEDA, CA	91335
ALEXANDER, JOHN	TENOR	METROPOLITAN OPERA HOUSE		
		LINCOLN CENTER	NEW YORK, NY	10023
ALEXANDER, KAI	ACTRESS	SCHOEMAN, 2600 W VICTORY BLVD	BURBANK, CA	91505
ALEXANDER, KARL	TV WRITER	8955 BEVERLY BLVD	LOS ANGELES, CA	90048
ALEXANDER, KIRK	DIRECTOR	132 E 61ST ST	NEW YORK, NY	10021
ALEXANDER, KRIS	BODYBUILDER	POST OFFICE BOX 1490		
		RADIO CITY STATION	NEW YORK, NY	10101
ALEXANDER, LARRY	TV WRITER	8955 BEVERLY BLVD	LOS ANGELES, CA	90048
ALEXANDER, LAWRENCE	BARITONE	1776 BROADWAY #504	NEW YORK, NY	10019
ALEXANDER, LAWRENCE E	DIRECTOR	ZOE, 663 5TH AVE	NEW YORK, NY	10022
ALEXANDER, LESTER M	WRITER	8955 BEVERLY BLVD	LOS ANGELES, CA	90048
ALEXANDER, LLOYD	WRITER	1005 DREXEL AVE	DREXEL HILL, PA	19026
ALEXANDER, LORI E	COMPOSER	3711 S CANFIELD	LOS ANGELES, CA	90034
ALEXANDER, LOUIS	ACTOR	10000 RIVERSIDE DR #3	TOLUCA LAKE, CA	91602
ALEXANDER, MONTY	PIANIST	POST OFFICE BOX 845	CONCORD, CA	94522
ALEXANDER, MONTY, TRIO	JAZZ TRIO	CAMI, 165 W 57TH ST	NEW YORK, NY	10019
ALEXANDER, NEWELL	ACTOR	11726 SAN VICENTE BLVD #300	LOS ANGELES, CA	90049
ALEXANDER, RICHARD "DICK"	ACTOR	23388 MULHOLLAND DR	WOODLAND HILLS, CA	91364
ALEXANDER, ROBERTA	SOPRANO	CAMI, 165 W 57TH ST	NEW YORK, NY	10019
ALEXANDER, RONALD G	WRITER	8955 BEVERLY BLVD	LOS ANGELES, CA	90048
ALEXANDER, ROSEMARY	REPORTER	TIME & PEOPLE MAGAZINE		
		TIME & LIFE BUILDING		
		ROCKEFELLER CENTER	NEW YORK, NY	10020
ALEXANDER, SAMUEL	DIRECTOR	ZEPLIN, 850 7TH AVE	NEW YORK, NY	10019
ALEXANDER, STEVEN L	PHOTOGRAPHER	8210 ELLINGSON DR	CHEVY CHASE, MD	20815
ALEXANDER, TERENCE	ACTOR	ICM, 388-396 OXFORD ST	LONDON W1	ENGLAND
ALEXANDER, THEA	AUTHORESS	POST OFFICE BOX 26880	TEMPE, AZ	85282
ALEXANDER, THOMAS R	COMPOSER	837 HUNTLEY DR	LOS ANGELES, CA	90069
ALEXANDER, VAN	CONDUCTOR	16373 ROYAL HILLS DR	ENCINO, CA	91436
ALEXANDER, WAYNE	ACTOR	9300 WILSHIRE BLVD #410	BEVERLY HILLS, CA	90212
ALEXANDRA, TIANA	WRITER-PRODUCER	8730 SUNSET BLVD #PH- W	LOS ANGELES, CA	90069
ALEXANDROAIE, CONSTANTIN	NEWS CORRESPONDENT	1201 CONNECTICUT AVE, NW	WASHINGTON, DC	20036
ALEXIS, KIM	MODEL	ELITE MODELS AGENCY		
		150 E 58TH ST	NEW YORK, NY	10022
ALFARO, ALBERTO M	NEWS CORRESPONDENT	2753 W GEORGE MASON RD	FALLS CHURCH, VA	22042
ALFASA, JOE	ACTOR	LEONETTI, 6526 SUNSET BLVD	HOLLYWOOD, CA	90028
ALFIERI, CESARE	CONDUCTOR	253 W 73RD ST #7-M	NEW YORK, NY	10023
ALFONSO, ELISA	WRITER	555 W 57TH ST #1230	NEW YORK, NY	10019
ALFONSO, KRISTIAN	ACTRESS	201 N ROBERTON BLVD #A	BEVERLY HILLS, CA	90211
ALFONSO, OZZIE	DIRECTOR	46 LEWIS PARKWAY	YONKERS, NY	10705
ALFONSO LADY BURKET	TRAPEZE ACT	POST OFFICE BOX 87	WEST LEBANON, NY	12195
ALFORD, BRENDA	SINGER	EAI, 2211 INDUSTRIAL BLVD	SARASOTA, FL	33580
ALFORD, EMERY E	DRUMMER	461 CLAREMOOR DR	BOWLING GREEN, KY	42101
ALFORD, MARY	TALENT AGENT	POST OFFICE BOX 39	BOSTON, MA	02122
ALGER, JOHN	WRITER	555 W 57TH ST #1230	NEW YORK, NY	10019
ALGER, PAT	SINGER	SEE - TRAUM, ARTIE		
ALHANTI, IRIS	ACTRESS	7929 W NORTON AVE	LOS ANGELES, CA	90046
ALI, MOSHIN	NEWS CORRESPONDENT	3001 VEAZEY TERR, NW	WASHINGTON, DC	20008
ALI, MUHAMMAD	BOXER-ACTOR	POST OFFICE BOX 187	BERRIEN SPRINGS, MI	49103
ALI HASSAN ARAB	ACROBATIC TROUPE	HALL, 138 FROG HOLLOW RD	CHURCHVILLE, PA	18966
ALIAS, JOHN	WRITER	555 W 57TH ST #1230	NEW YORK, NY	10019

ALIBERTI, LUCIA	SOPRANO	CAMI, 165 W 57TH ST	NEW YORK, NY	10019
ALICIA, ANA	ACTRESS	9744 WILSHIRE BLVD #206	BEVERLY HILLS, CA	90212
ALICJA	ROCK & ROLL GROUP	POST OFFICE BOX 256577	CHICAGO, IL	60625
ALINDER, DALLAS	ACTOR	1825 TAFT AVE	HOLLYWOOD, CA	90028
ALISON, DOROTHY	ACTRESS-WRITER	7 LYNDHURST TERR	LONDON NW3	ENGLAND
ALIVE!	JAZZ GROUP	ALIVE RECORDS COMPANY		
		1000 NAVARRO BLUFF RD	ALBION, CA	95410
ALKOFF, RENE	WRITER	8955 BEVERLY BLVD	LOS ANGELES, CA	90048
ALKON, SELIG	WRITER	555 W 57TH ST #1230	NEW YORK, NY	10019
ALL NEW JET STAR WARRIOR	AERIAL ACT	HALL, 138 FROG HOLLOW RD	CHURCHVILLE, PA	18966
ALLAN, ELKAN	WRITER-PRODUCER	8 GAINSBOROUGH RD	IPSWICH IP4 2UR	ENGLAND
ALLAN, HUGH	ACTOR	POST OFFICE BOX 18446	MEMPHIS, TN	38118
ALLAN, JED	ACTOR	9300 WILSHIRE BLVD #410	BEVERLY HILLS, CA	90212
ALLAN, TED	SCREENWRITER	ZIMRING, 151 S EL CAMINO DR	BEVERLY HILLS, CA	90212
ALLAND, WILLIAM	WRITER	8955 BEVERLY BLVD	LOS ANGELES, CA	90048
ALLANSON, SUSIE	ACTRESS	LENZ, 1456 E CHARLESTON BLVD	LAS VEGAS, NV	89104
ALLARD, JEANNE	ACTRESS	10 RUE PRADIER	PARIS 75019	FRANCE
ALLARD, JOHN W	NEWS CORRESPONDENT	340 NATIONAL PRESS BLDG	WASHINGTON, DC	20045
		529 14TH ST, NW	WASHINGTON, DC	20045
ALLEE, PAT	WRITER	8955 BEVERLY BLVD	LOS ANGELES, CA	90048
ALLEGHENY EXPRESS	C & W GROUP	PROCESS, 439 WILEY AVE	FRANKLIN, PA	16323
ALLEMANDI, ANTONELLO	CONDUCTOR	1182 MARKET ST #311	SAN FRANCISCO, CA	94102
ALLEN, AL	COMPOSER	MASON, 1299 OCEAN AVE	SANTA MONICA, CA	90401
ALLEN, ALLEN D	COMPOSER-CONDUCTOR	17114 DEVONSHIRE ST	NORTHRIDGE, CA	91325
ALLEN, AMY	ACTRESS	6430 SUNSET BLVD #701	LOS ANGELES, CA	90028
ALLEN, ARIA	WRITER	8955 BEVERLY BLVD	LOS ANGELES, CA	90048
ALLEN, B J	PIANIST-ORGANIST	BASKINS SQ #B-8	GATLINBURG, TN	37738
ALLEN, BETTY	MEZZO-SOPRANO	CAMI, 165 W 57TH ST	NEW YORK, NY	10016
ALLEN, BOB "TEX"	ACTOR	2 SUMMIT CT	OYSTER BAY, LI, NY	11771
ALLEN, BUDDY	TALENT AGENT	65 W 55TH ST #6-C	NEW YORK, NY	10019
ALLEN, BYRON	COMEDIAN	1875 CENTURY PARK E #2200	LOS ANGELES, CA	90067
ALLEN, CHAD	ACTOR	SAVAGE, 6212 BANNER AVE	LOS ANGELES, CA	90038
ALLEN, CHRIS	WRITER	8955 BEVERLY BLVD	LOS ANGELES, CA	90048
ALLEN, CONNIE FACH	SINGER-GUITARIST	810 BELLEVUE RD #231	NASHVILLE, TN	37221
ALLEN, COREY	ACT-WRI-DIR	8642 HOLLYWOOD BLVD	LOS ANGELES, CA	90046
ALLEN, CURTIS L	GUITARIST	435 LYNWOOD BLVD	NASHVILLE, TN	37205
ALLEN, CURTIS LYNN	WRITER	22329 KITTRIDGE ST	CANOGA PARK, CA	91303
ALLEN, DAN FACH	GUITARIST	810 BELLEVUE RD #231	NASHVILLE, TN	37221
ALLEN, DANIEL L	NEWS CORRESPONDENT	7806 APPLEDORE CT	FALLS CHURCH, VA	22043
ALLEN, DAVID R	NEWS CORRESPONDENT	340 NATIONAL PRESS BLDG	WASHINGTON, DC	20045
ALLEN, DAYTON	ACTOR	956 DOBBS FERRY RD	WHITE PLAINS, NY	10607
ALLEN, DEBBIE	ACT-DAN-SING	9255 SUNSET BLVD #1115	LOS ANGELES, CA	90069
ALLEN, DEDE	FILM EDITOR	ACE, 4416 1/2 FINLEY AVE	LOS ANGELES, CA	90027
ALLEN, EUGENE	WRITER	8955 BEVERLY BLVD	LOS ANGELES, CA	90048
ALLEN, GARY	ACTOR	9255 SUNSET BLVD #1105	LOS ANGELES, CA	90069
ALLEN, GENE	DIRECTOR	3452 MANDEVILLE CANYON RD	LOS ANGELES, CA	90049
ALLEN, GLYNN B	GUITARIST	508 ALBANY ST	HERMITAGE, TN	37076
ALLEN, GREGORY	PIANIST	ACE ENTS, 4201 BALCONES DR	AUSTIN, TX	78731
ALLEN, HARRY L	DRUMMER	812 JOSEPH AVE	NASHVILLE, TN	37207
ALLEN, HENRY W	WRITER	4618 LOUISE AVE	ENCINO, CA	91316
ALLEN, IRVING	PRODUCER	6 ROEBUCK HOUSE, PALACE ST	LONDON SW 1	ENGLAND
ALLEN, IRWIN	DIRECTOR-PRODUCER	1050 STRADELLA RD	LOS ANGELES, CA	90024
ALLEN, JAMES E	WRITER	8955 BEVERLY BLVD	LOS ANGELES, CA	90048
ALLEN, JAY PRESSON	FILM WRITER-PRODUCER	TOPHET RD	ROXBURY, CT	06783
ALLEN, JERRY	ART DIRECTOR	TV GUIDE, 100 MATSONFORD RD	RADNOR, PA	19088
ALLEN, JOAN	ACTRESS	SF & A, 121 N SAN VICENTE BLVD	BEVERLY HILLS, CA	90211
ALLEN, JODIE T	NEWS CORRESPONDENT	3100 FOXHALL RD, NW	WASHINGTON, DC	20016
ALLEN, JOE P	GUITARIST	ROUTE #1, NEW HOPE RD	HERMITAGE, TN	37076
ALLEN, JOHN	ACTOR	954-A 16TH ST	SANTA MONICA, CA	90403
ALLEN, JOHN T	PHOTOGRAPHER	5200 SANGAMORE RD	BETHESDA, MD	20816
ALLEN, JONELLE	ACTRES-SINGER	9229 SUNSET BLVD #306	LOS ANGELES, CA	90069
ALLEN, KAREN	ACTRESS	122 E 10TH ST	NEW YORK, NY	10013
ALLEN, KAREN	SPORTS WRITER	POST OFFICE BOX 500	WASHINGTON, DC	20044
ALLEN, KEVIN	SINGER	38 MUSIC SQUARE E #111	NASHVILLE, TN	37203
ALLEN, KEVIN SCOTT	ACTOR	434 N STANLEY AVE	LOS ANGELES, CA	90036
ALLEN, LEE	SINGER	OLDIES, 5218 ALMONT ST	LOS ANGELES, CA	90032
ALLEN, LEWIS	FILM-TV DIRECTOR	2829 MANDEVILLE CANYON RD	LOS ANGELES, CA	90049
ALLEN, LEWIS M	PRODUCER	1500 BROADWAY	NEW YORK, NY	10036
ALLEN, LINDA	SINGER	POST OFFICE BOX 5881	BELLINGHAM, WA	98227
ALLEN, LINDA-LOU	SINGER-ACTRESS	MILLION, 12 PRAED MEWS	LONDON W2 1QY	ENGLAND
ALLEN, LISA J	NEWS CORRESPONDENT	400 N CAPITOL ST, NW	WASHINGTON, DC	20001
ALLEN, MAC KENZIE	ACTOR	9165 SUNSET BLVD #202	LOS ANGELES, CA	90069
ALLEN, MAC KENZIE	ACTRESS	200 W 57TH ST #1303	NEW YORK, NY	10019
ALLEN, MARILYN	ACTRESS	8949 SUNSET BLVD #203	LOS ANGELES, CA	90069
ALLEN, MARLON B	NEWS CORRESPONDENT	2710 10TH ST, NE	WASHINGTON, DC	20018
ALLEN, MARTY	ACTOR-COMEDIAN	WEBB, 7500 DEVISTA DR	LOS ANGELES, CA	90046
ALLEN, MEL	SPORTSCASTER	YANKEE STADIUM	BRONX, NY	10451
ALLEN, MELVIN F	ACTOR	9864 CAYUGA AVE	PACOIMA, CA	91331
ALLEN, NANCY	HARPIST	CAMI, 165 W 57TH ST	NEW YORK, NY	10019
ALLEN, NANCY	ACTRESS	409 N CAMDEN DR #105	BEVERLY HILLS, CA	90210

Name	Occupation	Address	City	Code
ALLEN, PENELOPE	ACTRESS	WRITERS & ARTISTS AGENCY		
		162 W 56TH ST	NEW YORK, NY	10019
ALLEN, PETER	SINGER-COMPOSER	6 W 77TH ST	NEW YORK, NY	10022
ALLEN, PHILLIP RICHARD	ACTOR	POST OFFICE BOX 5617	BEVERLY HILLS, CA	90210
ALLEN, PRISCILLA	ACTRESS	CARPENTER, 1516-W REDWOOD ST	SAN DIEGO, CA	92101
ALLEN, RAE	ACTRESS	ICM, 8899 BEVERLY BLVD	LOS ANGELES, CA	90048
ALLEN, RAE J	DIRECTOR	200 3RD AVE	VENICE, CA	90291
ALLEN, RANCE	SINGER	JACKSON, 2405 BOSTON BLVD	DETROIT, MI	48206
ALLEN, REX, JR	SINGER	POST OFFICE BOX 15245	NASHVILLE, TN	37215
ALLEN, REX, SR	ACTOR-SINGER	13134 HARTSOOK ST	SHERMAN OAKS, CA	91423
ALLEN, RICHIE	BASEBALL	POST OFFICEBOX 204	SELLERSVILLE, PA	18960
ALLEN, ROY	TV DIRECTOR-PRODUCER	CBS-TV, 524 W 57TH ST	NEW YORK, NY	10019
ALLEN, SCOTT ARTHUR	ACTOR	11176 HUSTON ST	NORTH HOLLYWOOD, CA	91601
ALLEN, SIAN BARBARA	ACTRESS-WRITER	1622 SIERRA BONITA AVE	LOS ANGELES, CA	90046
ALLEN, STEVE	ACT-WRI-COMED-COMP	16185 WOODVALE RD	ENCINO, CA	91436
ALLEN, STEVE	TALENT AGENT	65 W 55TH ST #6-C	NEW YORK, NY	10019
ALLEN, STUART	TV DIRECTOR-PRODUCER	EAST MIRAMAR		
		UPPER BONCHURCH		
		VENTNOR	I O WRIGHT PO38 1QB	ENGLAND
ALLEN, TERRY	WRESTLER	SEE - MAGNUM T A		
ALLEN, TODD	ACTOR	ICM, 8899 BEVERLY BLVD	LOS ANGELES, CA	90048
ALLEN, TONY	SINGER	OLDIES, 5218 ALMONT ST	LOS ANGELES, CA	90032
ALLEN, TREE	MODEL	7060 HOLLYWOOD BLVD #1010	LOS ANGELES, CA	90028
ALLEN, VALERIE P	WRITER	8955 BEVERLY BLVD	LOS ANGELES, CA	90048
ALLEN, VICKIE	NEWS CORRESPONDENT	1825 "K" ST, NW	WASHINGTON, DC	20006
ALLEN, WOODY	ACT-COMED-WRI-DIR	ROLLINS/JOFFE MGMT		
		130 W 57TH ST	NEW YORK, NY	10019
ALLEN & ROSSI	COMEDY DUO	DAVID FISHOF PRODUCTIONS		
		1755 BROADWAY	NEW YORK, NY	10019
ALLER, ROBERT	WRITER	8955 BEVERLY BLVD	LOS ANGELES, CA	90048
ALLERS, FRANZ	ORCHESTRA CONDUCTER	CAMI, 165 W 57TH ST	NEW YORK, NY	10019
ALLERS, TONY	GUITARIST	POST OFFICE BOX 521	HENDERSONVILLE, TN	37075
ALLEY, KIRSTIE	ACTRESS	3715 AVENIDA DEL SOL	STUDIO CITY, CA	91604
ALLGOOD, PAUL B, JR	NEWS CORRESPONDENT	2300 PIMMIT DR #613	FALLS CHURCH, VA	22043
ALLIE, REGGIE	GUITARIST	308 CHEROKEE RD	HENDERSONVILLE, TN	37075
ALLIGOOD, DAVID L	GUITARIST	3203-D RALEIGH ST	DALLAS, TX	75219
ALLIN, JEFF	ACTOR	11726 SAN VICENTE BLVD #300	LOS ANGELES, CA	90049
ALLIN, MICHAEL	WRITER	8955 BEVERLY BLVD	LOS ANGELES, CA	90048
ALLIS, SAMUEL G	NEWS CORRESPONDENT	3227 TENNYSON ST, NW	WASHINGTON, DC	20015
ALLIS, TIM	WRITER-EDITOR	PEOPLE/TIME & LIFE BLDG		
		ROCKEFELLER CENTER	NEW YORK, NY	10020
ALLISON, BRIAN LEE	DRUMMER	3510 GOLF ST #2	NASHVILLE, TN	37216
ALLISON, CHARLES GARY	WRITER-PRODUCER	1302 N ALEXANDRIA AVE	LOS ANGELES, CA	90027
ALLISON, CYNTHIA	NEWS CORRESPONDENT	KNBC-TV, 3000 W ALAMEDA AVE	BURBANK, CA	91523
ALLISON, DEBORAH	ACTRESS	ABC-TV NETWORK, "LOVING"		
		1330 AVE OF THE AMERICAS	NEW YORK, NY	10019
ALLISON, JERRY	DRUMMER-SONGWRITER	ROUTE #1, BOX 222	LYLES, TN	37098
ALLISON, JUDITH D	WRITER-PRODUCER	8042 WOODROW WILSON DR	LOS ANGELES, CA	90046
ALLISON, KEITH	SINGER-GUITARIST	381 BURNING TREE DR	NASHVILLE, TN	37076
ALLISON, MAT	ACTRESS	2 BRATENAHL PL	CLEVELAND, OH	44108
ALLISON, MICHAEL	ACTOR	208 S BEVERLY DR #4	BEVERLY HILLS, CA	90212
ALLISON, MOSE	PIANIST-COMPOSER	POST OFFICE BOX 210103	SAN FRANCISCO, CA	94121
ALLISON, PATRICIA	ACTRESS	8350 SANTA MONICA BLVD #103	LOS ANGELES, CA	90069
ALLISON, ROBIN HILLARY	DIRECTOR	2115 KERWOOD AVE	LOS ANGELES, CA	90025
ALLISON, SANDY	CASTING DIRECTOR	SAMUELSONS FILM COMPANBY		
		303 CRICKLEWOOD BROADWAY	LONDON NW2	ENGLAND
ALLISON, SUE	NEWS REPORTER	LIFE/TIME & LIFE BLDG		
		ROCKEFELLER CENTER	NEW YORK, NY	10020
ALLISON, VIRGINIA	WRITER	555 W 57TH ST #1230	NEW YORK, NY	10019
ALLIZON, MARIE B	NEWS CORRESPONDENT	3618 VALLEY DR	ALEXANDRIA, VA	22302
ALLMAN, CHER BONO	ACTRESS-SINGER	SEE - CHER		
ALLMAN, ELVIA	ACTRESS	6380 WILSHIRE BLVD #1600	LOS ANGELES, CA	90048
ALLMAN, GREG	SINGER-MUSICIAN	STRIKE FORCE MGMT		
		130 SOUTH AVE	MARIETTA, GA	30060
ALLMAN, GREG, BAND	ROCK & ROLL GROUP	STRIKE FORCE MGMT		
		130 SOUTH AVE	MARIETTA, GA	30060
ALLMAN, JOHN L	WRITER	8955 BEVERLY BLVD	LOS ANGELES, CA	90048
ALLMAN, LEE	COMPOSER	POST OFFICE BOX 2588	LOS ANGELES, CA	90077
ALLMOND, DOUGLAS	PHOTOGRAPHER	320 FRANKLIN AVE	SILVER SPRING, MD	20901
ALLNUTT, WENDY	ACTRESS	JAMES, 14 HILL ST, RICHMOND	SURREY TW9 ITN	ENGLAND
ALLOTTA, ALBERT	DIRECTOR	185 E 85TH ST	NEW YORK, NY	10028
ALLPORT, CHRISTOPHER	ACTOR	SF & A, 121 N SAN VICENTE BLVD	BEVERLY HILLS, CA	90211
ALLSUP, TOMMY D	GUITARIST	113 MEADOWS	BURLESON, TX	76028
ALLYN, WILLIAM	FILM PRODUCER	12031 VENTURA BLVD #3	STUDIO CITY, CA	91604
ALLYSON, JUNE	ACTRESS	ASHROW, 1651 N FOOTHILL RD	OJAI, CA	93023
ALM, RICHARD G	NEWS CORRESPONDENT	2142 "O" ST, NW	WASHINGTON, DC	20037
ALMEIDA, LAURINDO	GUITARIST-COMPOSER	4104 WITZELL DR	SHERMAN OAKS, CA	91423
ALMENDROS, NESTER	CINEMATOGRAPHER	47 RUE AVE MAIRE	PARIS 3E	FRANCE
ALMODOVAR, ROBERT	ACTOR	6834 CAMROSE DR	HOLLYWOOD, CA	90068
ALMOND, PAUL	WRITER-PRODUCER	1272 REDPATH CRESCENT	MONTREAL, QUE H3G 2K1	CANADA
ALMSTROM, RENEE	MODEL	POST OFFICE BOX 7211	MOUNTAIN VIEW, CA	94043
ALOI, CINDY LYNN	DIRECTOR	DGA, 110 W 57TH ST	NEW YORK, NY	10019
ALON, RAMI	WRITER	1111 GLENVILLE DR	LOS ANGELES, CA	90035
ALONI, AMI	COMPOSER-CONDUCER	4026 BENEDICT CANYON DR	SHERMAN OAKS, CA	91423
ALONSO, MARIA CONCHITA	ACTRESS	8377 GREGORY WY	BEVERLY HILLS, CA	90211

REX ALLEN, SR.

WOODY ALLEN

JUNE ALLYSON

KIRK ALYN

MOREY AMSTERDAM

ADAM ANT

URSULA ANDRESS

RICHARD DEAN ANDERSON

DANA ANDREWS

Name	Occupation	Address	City	ZIP/Country
ALONSO-ZALDIVAR, RICARDO	NEWS CORRESPONDENT	1319 "F" ST #600, NW	WASHINGTON, DC	20004
ALONZO, JOHN A	CINEMATOGRAPHER	310 AVONDALE AVE	LOS ANGELES, CA	90049
ALPER, ALLAN M	COMPOSER-CONDUCTOR	128 N SWALL DR #4	LOS ANGELES, CA	90048
ALPER, LINDA	ACTRESS	16200 QUEMADA RD	ENCINO, CA	91436
ALPERIN, HARVEY J	WRITER	8955 BEVERLY BLVD	LOS ANGELES, CA	90048
ALPERT, ARTHUR M	WRITER	555 W 57TH ST #1230	NEW YORK, NY	10019
ALPERT, BRIAN F	PHOTOGRAPHER	202 E 42ND ST	NEW YORK, NY	10017
ALPERT, DAVID	WRITER-PRODUCER	3900 VENTURA CANYON AVE	SHERMAN OAKS, CA	91423
ALPERT, DAVID R	WRITER	555 W 57TH ST #1230	NEW YORK, NY	10019
ALPERT, HERB	MUS-COMP-EXEC	31930 PACIFIC COAST HWY	MALIBU, CA	90265
ALPERT, HERB & THE TIJUANA BRAS	MUSICAL GROUP	1888 CENTURY PARK E #1400	LOS ANGELES, CA	90067
ALPERT, HOLLIS	WRITER	POST OFFICE BOX 142	SHELTER ISLAND, NY	11964
ALPERT, ROBERT	WRITER	555 W 57TH ST #1230	NEW YORK, NY	10019
ALPINE HARMONAIRES, THE	VOCAL GROUP	POST OFFICE BOX 16	WALNUT CREEK, OH	44687
ALQUIST, JIM	ACTOR	6736 LAUREL CANYON BLVD #306	NORTH HOLLYWOOD, CA	91606
ALSBERG, ARTHUR WILLIAM	WRITER	3816 LONGRIDGE AVE	SHERMAN OAKS, CA	91423
ALSOP, JOSEPH	WRITER	2720 DUMBARTON AVE, NW	WASHINGTON, DC	20007
ALSTON, HOWARD P	TV PRODUCER	10033 VALLEY SPRING LN	NORTH HOLLYWOOD, CA	91602
ALSTON, SHIRLEY	SINGER	KNIGHT, 185 CLINTON AVE	STATEN ISLAND, NY	10301
ALT, CAROL	MODEL	ELITE MODELS, 150 E 58TH ST	NEW YORK, NY	10022
ALTA MODA	ROCK & ROLL GROUP	41 BRITAIN ST #200	TORONTO, ONT	CANADA
ALTAY, DERIN	ACTRESS	330 S SPALDING DR #309	BEVERLY HILLS, CA	90212
ALTEMEYER, PAUL	TV PRODUCER	NBC TELEVISION NETWORK	NEW YORK, NY	10112
ALTENBURGER, CHRISTIAN	VIOLINIST	CAMI, 165 W 57TH ST	NEW YORK, NY	10019
ALTER, ALLEN	WRITER	555 W 57TH ST #1230	NEW YORK, NY	10019
ALTER, ERIC	SCREENWRITER	8955 BEVERLY BLVD	LOS ANGELES, CA	90048
ALTER, PAUL	TV DIRECTOR-PRODUCER	1030 DELLA DR	BEVERLY HILLS, CA	90210
ALTFILISH, LINDA	ACTRESS	846 4TH ST #205	SANTA MONICA, CA	90403
ALTMAN, JEFF	COMEDIAN-ACTOR	151 S EL CAMINO DR	BEVERLY HILLS, CA	90212
ALTMAN, MILT	DIRECTOR	14889 JADESTONE DR	SHERMAN OAKS, CA	91403
ALTMAN, NANCY ALLISON	ACTRESS	SEE - ALLISON ALTMAN, NANCY		
ALTMAN, RICHARD	ACTOR	208 S BEVERLY DR #4	BEVERLY HILLS, CA	90212
ALTMAN, ROBERT	WRITER-PRODUCER	128 CENTRAL PARK S #4-B	NEW YORK, NY	10019
ALTMAN, ROBERTA	WRITER	555 W 57TH ST #1230	NEW YORK, NY	10019
ALTMEYER, PAUL C	WRITER	555 W 57TH ST #1230	NEW YORK, NY	10019
ALTON, BILL	DIRECTOR	238 E 61ST ST	NEW YORK, NY	10021
ALTON, EDWARD H	COMPOSER	5814 1/2 COLFAX AVE	NORTH HOLLYWOOD, CA	91601
ALTSHULER, JOEL	COMPOSER-CONDUCTOR	15420 GAULT ST	VAN NUYS, CA	91406
ALU, AL	ACTOR	7109 1/2 HILLSIDE AVE	HOLLYWOOD, CA	90046
ALU, CHERYL	TV WRITER	7109 1/2 HILLSIDE AVE	HOLLYWOOD, CA	90046
ALVA, LUIGI	TENOR	VIA MOSCOVA 46-3	MILAN	ITALY
ALVAREZ, ABRAHAM	ACTOR	6310 SAN VICENTE BLVD #407	LOS ANGELES, CA	90048
ALVAREZ, CARMEN	ACTRESS	2501 W BURBANK BLVD #304	BURBANK, CA	91505
ALVAREZ, CARMEN	PIANIST	POST OFFICE BOX U	REDDING, CT	06875
ALVERSON, DAVE	ACTOR	1350 N HIGHLAND AVE #24	HOLLYWOOD, CA	90028
ALVES, JOSEPH	DIRECTOR-PRODUCER	4176 ROSARIO RD	WOODLAND HILLS, CA	91364
ALVEY, JAY DAVID	PHOTOGRAPHER	21 BELL BLUFF CT	GAITHERSBURG, MD	20760
ALVEY, MICHAEL	DRUMMER	3317 TOWNE RIDGE DR	ANTIOCH, TN	37013
ALVEY, MURRAY	PHOTOGRAPHER	8815 SUNDALE DR	SILVER SPRING, MD	20910
ALVIN, JOHN	ACTOR	3518 W CAHUENGA BLVD #316	LOS ANGELES, CA	90068
ALVIN, PHIL	SINGER-GUITARIST	VISION MANAGEMENT COMPANY		
		2112 N CAHUENGA BLVD	LOS ANGELES, CA	90068
ALWAYS, BILLY	SINGER-SONGWRITER	MITCHELL, 1320 S LAUDERDALE	MEMPHIS, TN	38106
ALWOOD, DENNIS	ACTOR	4624 CAHUENGA BLVD #303	NORTH HOLLYWOOD, CA	91602
ALWYN, JONATHAN	TV DIRECTOR-PRODUCER	3 SPENCER GARDENS	LONDON SW14 7AH	ENGLAND
ALYN, KIRK	ACTOR	POST OFFICE BOX 200	SUN CITY, CA	92381
ALZADO, LYLE	ACTOR-FOOTBALL	902 N BEDFORD DR	BEVERLY HILLS, CA	90210
AMADON, GREG	PHOTOJOURNALIST	CBS NEWS-AMERICAN EMBASSY		
		P & C, BOX M	00140 HELSINKI	FINLAND
AMADOR, ANDREW	ACTOR	8075 W 3RD ST #303	LOS ANGELES, CA	90048
AMADOR, LUPE	ACTRESS	1607 N EL CENTRO AVE #23	LOS ANGELES, CA	90028
AMANI, KIMYA	WRITER	8955 BEVERLY BLVD	LOS ANGELES, CA	90048
AMARA, LUCINE	SOPRANO	260 W END AVE #7-A	NEW YORK, NY	10023
AMATEAU, RODNEY	FILM WRITER-DIRECTOR	133 1/2 S LINDEN DR	BEVERLY HILLS, CA	90212
AMATO, JOHN	WRITER	4521 COLBATH AVE #305	SHERMAN OAKS, CA	91423
AMATO, JULIE	ACTRESS	356 S SWALL DR	BEVERLY HILLS, CA	90211
AMATO, THOMAS A	CONDUCTOR	1855 SIERA SAGE LN	RENO, NV	89509
AMAZEMENT PARK REVUE	MUSIC GROUP	32500 CONCORD DR #221	MADISON HEIGHTS, MI	48071
AMAZING RHYTHM ACES, THE	C & W GROUP	VARIETY ARTISTS INTL, INC		
		9730 NEMO ST, 3RD FLOOR	LOS ANGELES, CA	90069
AMBANDOS, JAMES	WRITER	555 W 57TH ST #1230	NEW YORK, NY	10019
AMBER, MICHELLE L	NEWS CORRESPONDENT	205 S YOAKUM PARKWAY #503	ALEXANDRIA, VA	22304
AMBROSE, DAVIS E	WRITER	9000 SUNSET BLVD #1200	LOS ANGELES, CA	90069
AMBROSE, NANCY J	NEWS CORRESPONDENT	4201 CATHEDRAL AVE	WASHINGTON, DC	20016
AMBROSE, TISH	ACTRESS	9333 OSO AVE #1	CHATSWORTH, CA	91311
AMBROSON, DONALD A	CONDUCTOR	1303 W 25TH ST	UPLAND, CA	91786
AMECHE, DON	ACTOR	9220 SUNSET BLVD #625	LOS ANGELES, CA	90069
AMELING, ELLY	SOPRANO	SOFFER, 130 W 56TH ST	NEW YORK, NY	10019
AMELON, DEBORAH L	WRITER	616 VETERAN AVE #112	LOS ANGELES, CA	90024
AMER, NICHOLAS	ACTOR	14 GREAT RUSSELL ST	LONDON WC1	ENGLAND
AMERICA	ROCK & ROLL GROUP	8730 SUNSET BLVD #PH-W	LOS ANGELES, CA	90069
AMERICA, CAPTAIN	WRESTLER-ACTOR	SEE - STUDD, BIG JOHN		
AMERICAN DREAM, THE	WRESTLER	SEE - RHODES, DUSTY		
AMERICAN GIRLS, THE	ROCK & ROLL GROUP	FRONTIER BOOKING INTL		
		1776 BROADWAY, 6TH FLOOR	NEW YORK, NY	10019

AMERSON, TAMMY	ACTRESS	ABC-TV, "ONE LIFE TO LIVE"		
		1330 AVE OF THE AMERICAS	NEW YORK, NY	10019
AMES, ANDRES	WRITER	555 W 57TH ST #1230	NEW YORK, NY	10019
AMES, CHRISTOPHER	WRITER	8955 BEVERLY BLVD	LOS ANGELES, CA	90048
AMES, ED	SINGER-ACTOR	1457 CLARIDGE DR	BEVERLY HILLS, CA	90210
AMES, H P	ACTOR	CARPENTER, 1516-W REDWOOD ST	SAN DIEGO, CA	92101
AMES, LEON	ACTOR	23388 MULHOLLAND DR	WOODLAND HILLS, CA	91364
AMES, RACHEL	ACTRESS	8075 W 3RD ST #303	LOS ANGELES, CA	90048
AMES, ROBERT J	NEWS CORRESPONDENT	8862 BLADE GREEN LN	COLUMBIA, MD	21045
AMES, WILMER, JR	NEWS REPORTER	TIME/TIME & LIFE BLDG		
		ROCKEFELLER CENTER	NEW YORK, NY	10020
AMES-REGAN, HARRIETTE	DIRECTOR	POST OFFICE BOX 3680	SANTA MONICA, CA	90403
AMESTOY, MICHAEL F, JR	WRITER	3330 CLUB DR	LOS ANGELES, CA	90064
AMGOTT, MADELINE K	WRITER	555 W 57TH ST #1230	NEW YORK, NY	10019
AMIS, KINGSLEY	NOVELIST	CLOWES, 19 JEFFREY'S PL	LONDON NW1	ENGLAND
AMLEN, SEYMOUR	TV EXECUTIVE	ABC TELEVISION NETWORK		
		1330 AVE OF THE AMERICAS	NEW YORK, NY	10019
AMMERMAN, STUART A	NEWS CORRESPONDENT	2139 WISCONSIN AVE, NW	WASHINGTON, DC	20007
AMOLSCH, ARTHUR L	NEWS CORRESPONDENT	8903 HOOE'S RD	LORTON, VA079	22079
AMONETTE, BILLY J	TRUMPETER	2822 LUMAR LN	NASHVILLE, TN	37214
AMONICK, HOWARD	WRITER	555 W 57TH ST #1230	NEW YORK, NY	10019
AMOROSI, MICHAEL D	COMPOSER	8467 W 4TH ST	LOS ANGELES, CA	90048
AMORY, CLEVELAND	WRITER	140 W 57TH ST	NEW YORK, NY	10019
AMOS, FAMOUS	COOKIE ENTREPRENEUR	SEE - AMOS, WALLY "FAMOUS"		
AMOS, JAMES L	PHOTOGRAPHER	POST OFFICE BOX 118	CENTERVILLE, MD	21617
AMOS, JOHN	ACTOR	15570 OLDEN ST	SYLMAR, CA	91342
AMOS, RICHARD A	TV DIRECTOR	1029 N BEVERLY GLEN BLVD	LOS ANGELES, CA	90077
AMOS, ROBIN S	WRITER	1336 N HARPER AVE	LOS ANGELES, CA	90046
AMOS, WALLY "FAMOUS"	COOKIE ENTREPRENEUR	215 LANIPO DR	KAILUA, HI	96734
AMOUR, DENA	ACTRESS	5330 LANKERSHIM BLVD #210	NORTH HOLLYWOOD, CA	91601
AMOYAL, PIERRE	VIOLINIST	GLOTZ, 141 BD SAINT-MICHEL	PARIS 75005	FRANCE
AMPLE, ANNIE	ACTRESS-DANCER	POST OFFICE BOX 60563	LAS VEGAS, NV	89160
AMRAM, DAVID	COND-COMP-MUS	461 6TH AVE	NEW YORK, NY	10011
AMSLER, CLYDE R	COMPOSER	POST OFFICE BOX 599	ANZA, CA	92306
AMSTERDAM, MOREY	ACTOR-COMEDIAN	1012 N HILLCREST RD	BEVERLY HILLS, CA	90210
AMUZEMENT PARK	ROCK & ROLL GROUP	MIRUS, 2440 LAKESIDE AVE	CLEVELAND, OH	44144
AMY, FRANK	DIRECTOR-PRODUCER	601 E PLANTATION CIR	PLANTATION, FL	33324
AMY, GEORGE	DIRECTOR-EDITOR	14142 COHASSET ST	VAN NUYS, CA	91405
AMY, GILBERT	COMPOSER-ORCH LEADER	10 RUE CARPEAUX	COURBEVOIE 92400	FRANCE
AMYES, JULIAN	TV DIRECTOR	4 PALLISER CT, PALLISER RD	LONDON W14 9ED	ENGLAND
ANA-ALICIA	ACTRESS	SEE - ALICIA, ANA		
ANABLE, THOM	DIRECTOR	2050 N LAS PALMAS AVE	HOLLYWOOD, CA	90068
ANACANI	SINGER	TERRY, 909 PARKVIEW AVE	LODI, CA	95240
ANAGNOST, DINO	CONDUCTOR	59 E 54TH ST #81	NEW YORK, NY	10022
ANASTASI, PATRICK	NEWS CORRESPONDENT	4400 JENIFER ST, NW	WASHINGTON, DC	20015
ANASTASINI FAMILY	ACROBATS	POST OFFICE BOX 87	WEST LEBANON, NY	12195
ANASTI, RUDOLPH T	WRITER	5701 CASE AVE	NORTH HOLLYWOOD, CA	91601
ANCELL, KENNETH	DIRECTOR	923 MICHIGAN AVE	EVANSTON, IL	60202
ANCIER, GARTH RICHARD	TV EXECUTIVE	NBC-TV, 3000 W ALAMEDA AVE	BURBANK, CA	91523
ANDELSON, SHELDON	DIRECTOR	900 STRADELLA RD	LOS ANGELES, CA	90077
ANDEREGG, PETER	WRITER	6615 FRANKLIN AVE #219	LOS ANGELES, CA	90028
ANDERMAN, MAUREEN	ACTRESS	211 S BEVERLY DR #201	BEVERLY HILLS, CA	90212
ANDERS, CHRIS	ACTOR	2700 NEILSON WY #1321	SANTA MONICA, CA	90405
ANDERS, CHRIS	SINGER	PENNY, 30 GUINAN ST	WALTHAM, MA	02154
ANDERS, GEORGE	ACTOR	6331 HOLLYWOOD BLVD #924	LOS ANGELES, CA	90028
ANDERS, JAMIE	ACTOR	1784 N SYCAMORE AVE #108	HOLLYWOOD, CA	90028
ANDERS, KAREN	ACTRESS	15119 SYLVAN ST	VAN NUYS, CA	91411
ANDERS, KRISTOFFER C	ACTOR	1738 CANYON DR #301	LOS ANGELES, CA	90028
ANDERS, LUANA	ACTRESS-WRITER	12734 WOODRIDGE ST	STUDIO CITY, CA	91604
ANDERS, MIKE	NEWS CORRESPONDENT	9356 CHERRY HILL RD	COLLEGE PARK, MD	20740
ANDERS, REA	TV DIRECTOR	12391 RED HILL AVE	SANTA ANA, CA	92705
ANDERS, SUSAN J	ACTRESS	5330 LANKERSHIM BLVD #210	NORTH HOLLYWOOD, CA	91601
ANDERSEN, BRIGETTE	ACTRESS	1450 BELFAST DR	LOS ANGELES, CA	90069
ANDERSEN, ISA	ACTRESS	KOHNER, 9169 SUNSET BLVD	LOS ANGELES, CA	90069
ANDERSEN, KARSTEN	CONDUCTOR	POST OFFICE BOX U	REDDING, CT	06875
ANDERSON, ADRIENNE	SONGWRITER	1560 N LAUREL AVE #109	LOS ANGELES, CA	90046
ANDERSON, ALFRED	BARITONE	POST OFFICE BOX 884	NEW YORK, NY	10023
ANDERSON, ARN	WRESTLER	NATIONAL WRESTLING ALLIANCE		
		JIM CROCKETT PROMOTIONS		
		421 BRIARBEND DR	CHARLOTTE, NC	28209
ANDERSON, ARTHUR	ACTOR	87 PERRY ST	NEW YORK, NY	10014
ANDERSON, BARBARA	ACTRESS	BURNETT, 10140 ANGELO CIR	BEVERLY HILLS, CA	90210
ANDERSON, BILL	GUITARIST	4223 LEBANON RD #201	HERMITAGE, TN	37076
ANDERSON, BILL	SINGER	POST OFFICE BOX 121089	NASHVILLE, TN	37212
ANDERSON, BILLY	WRESTLER	POST OFFICE BOX 3859	STAMFORD, CT	06905
ANDERSON, BRAD	CARTOONIST	422 SANTA MARINA CT	ESCONDIDO, CA	92025
ANDERSON, BRUCE	HIGH WIRE ACT	POST OFFICE BOX 87	WEST LEBANON, NY	12195
ANDERSON, BRUCE	SPORTS WRITER	SPORTS ILLUSTRATED MAGAZINE		
		TIME & LIFE BUILDING		
		ROCKEFELLER CENTER	NEW YORK, NY	10020
ANDERSON, BRYAN J	CINEMATOGRAPHER	921 BUTTERFIELD RD	SAN ANSELMO, CA	94960

Name	Occupation	Address	City	Zip
ANDERSON, BURNETT	NEWS CORRESPONDENT	632 "A" ST, SE	WASHINGTON, DC	20003
ANDERSON, CARL D	NEWS CORRESPONDENT	400 N CAPITOL ST, NW	WASHINGTON, DC	20001
ANDERSON, CHERYL	ACTRESS	15010 VENTURA BLVD #219	SHERMAN OAKS, CA	91403
ANDERSON, CHOPPER	SINGER-GUITARIST	4905 NEVADA AVE	NASHVILLE, TN	37209
ANDERSON, CORBY	NEWS CORRESPONDENT	503 FONTAINE ST	ALEXANDRIA, VA	22302
ANDERSON, DARYL	ACTOR	5923 WILBUR AVE	TARZANA, CA	91356
ANDERSON, DAVID	JOURNALIST	8 INNESS RD	TENAFLY, NJ	07670
ANDERSON, DAVID E	DIRECTOR-PRODUCER	385 ROSEWOOD AVE	WINNETKA, IL	60093
ANDERSON, DEBBIE	SINGER	POST OFFICE BOX 110423	NASHVILLE, TN	37211
ANDERSON, DIANE R	NEWS CORRESPONDENT	11526 HEARTHSTONE CT	RESTON, VA	22091
ANDERSON, DINAH	BODYBUILDER	POST OFFICE BOX 1773	BIG SPRING, TX	79721
ANDERSON, DONALD E	FILM EXECUTIVE	2049 CENTURY PARK E #4170	LOS ANGELES, CA	90067
ANDERSON, DONNA	ACTRESS	3330 BARHAM BLVD #103	LOS ANGELES, CA	90068
ANDERSON, DOUG	ACTOR	7 RUSSELL RD	GARDEN CITY, NY	11530
ANDERSON, DUKEY	CLOWN	2701 COTTAGE WY #14	SACRAMENTO, CA	95825
ANDERSON, DUSTY	ACTRESS	NEGULESCO, 20508 MANDEL ST	CANOGA PARK, CA	91306
ANDERSON, EDDY	DRUMMER	421 CARL MILLER DR	ANTIOCH, TN	37013
ANDERSON, ELIZABETH B	WRITER	840 HAVERFORD AVE	PACIFIC PALISADES, CA	90272
ANDERSON, ERIC	SINGER-COMPOSER	50 W 34TH ST 11-C5	NEW YORK, NY	10001
ANDERSON, ERNEST	ACTOR	8075 W 3RD ST #303	LOS ANGELES, CA	90048
ANDERSON, ERNESTINE	SINGER	POST OFFICE BOX 845	CONCORD, CA	94522
ANDERSON, FLIP	GUITARIST	508 EWING DR	NASHVILLE, TN	37207
ANDERSON, G BERNIE	DRUMMER	112 EASTLAWN DR	GOODLETTSVILLE, TN	37072
ANDERSON, GARRY W	GUITARIST	4821 BLUE SPRINGS DR	NASHVILLE, TN	37211
ANDERSON, GERRY	FILM PRODUCER	AARON BURR PICTURES		
		BRAY STUDIOS, WATER OAKLEY		
		WINDSOR	BERKSHIRE	ENGLAND
ANDERSON, HARRY	ACTOR-COMEDIAN	KRAGEN, 1112 N SHERBOURNE AVE	LOS ANGELES, CA	90069
ANDERSON, HASKELL V, III	ACTOR	8949 SUNSET BLVD #203	LOS ANGELES, CA	90069
ANDERSON, HESPER	WRITER	8955 BEVERLY BLVD	LOS ANGELES, CA	90048
ANDERSON, HOWARD A	CINEMATOGRAPHER	POST OFFICE 2230	HOLLYWOOD, CA	90078
ANDERSON, INGRID	ACTRESS	400 S BEVERLY DR #216	BEVERLY HILLS, CA	90212
ANDERSON, JACK	COLUMNIST	1401 16TH ST, NW	WASHINGTON, DC	20036
ANDERSON, JACK	NEWS CORRESPONDENT	7801 KACHINA LN	BETHESDA, MD	20817
ANDERSON, JOHN	ACTOR	9000 SUNSET BLVD #1112	LOS ANGELES, CA	90069
ANDERSON, JOHN	SINGER-SONGWRITER	1901 18TH AVE S #101	NASHVILLE, TN	37212
ANDERSON, JOHN MAXWELL	COMPOSER-ARRANGER	2158 SUNSET PLAZA DR	LOS ANGELES, CA	90069
ANDERSON, JON	TV CRITIC	THE CHICAGO TRIBUNE		
		TRIBUNE TOWER		
		435 N MICHIGAN AVE	CHICAGO, IL	60611
ANDERSON, JON	TV DIRECTOR	150 S BARRINGTON AVE #1	LOS ANGELES, CA	90049
ANDERSON, JOSEF M	TV WRITER	10100 SANTA MONICA BLVD #1600	LOS ANGELES, CA	90067
ANDERSON, JUDITH	ACTRESS	808 SAN YSIDRO LN	SANTA BARBARA, CA	93102
ANDERSON, KATHLEEN	WRITER	8955 BEVERLY BLVD	LOS ANGELES, CA	90048
ANDERSON, KELLY	MODEL	FORD MODEL AGENCY		
		344 E 59TH ST	NEW YORK, NY	10022
ANDERSON, KEVIN M	SINGER-GUITARIST	111 WHITSETT RD #B-5	NASHVILLE, TN	37211
ANDERSON, LEE TROELL	PHOTOGRAPHER	632 "A" ST, SE	WASHINGTON, DC	20003
		RAINBERRY CT	DELRAY BEACH, FL	33445
ANDERSON, LEONARD E	DIRECTOR	2924 NW 7TH CT #A		
ANDERSON, LEWIS B	COMPOSER	888 8TH AVE #182	NEW YORK, NY	10019
ANDERSON, LEWIS J	GUITARIST	7988 HWY 100	NASHVILLE, TN	37221
ANDERSON, LINDSAY	FILM WRITER-DIRECTOR	9 STIRLING MANSIONS		
		CANFIELD GARDENS	LONDON NW6 3JT	ENGLAND
ANDERSON, LONI	ACTRESS	245 CAROLWOOD DR	LOS ANGELES, CA	90024
ANDERSON, LOUIE	COMEDIAN	10100 SANTA MONICA BLVD #1600	LOS ANGELES, CA	90067
ANDERSON, LURUTH	CONDUCTOR	2723 VIA VERBENA	SAN CLEMENTE, CA	92672
ANDERSON, LYNN	SINGER	POST OFFICE BOX 120428	NASHVILLE, TN	37212
ANDERSON, MACK B	TV DIRECTOR	KABC-TV, 4151 PROSPECT AVE	LOS ANGELES, CA	90027
ANDERSON, MARGO	DIRECTOR	294 MARGUERITA LN	PASADENA, CA	91106
ANDERSON, MARIAN	SINGER	MARIANNA, JOE'S HILL RD	DANBURY, CT	06811
ANDERSON, MARILYN	WRITER	8955 BEVERLY BLVD	LOS ANGELES, CA	90048
ANDERSON, MARY	ACTRESS	1127 NORMAN PL	LOS ANGELES, CA	90049
ANDERSON, MAX W	FILM DIRECTOR	454 SEATON ST #3	LOS ANGELES, CA	90013
ANDERSON, MC KEE	ACTRESS	8075 W 3RD ST #303	LOS ANGELES, CA	90048
ANDERSON, MELISSA SUE	ACTRESS	4160 LAUREL GROVE AVE	STUDIO CITY, CA	91604
ANDERSON, MELODY	ACTRESS	151 S EL CAMINO DR	BEVERLY HILLS, CA	90212
ANDERSON, MICHAEL	FILM DIRECTOR	9255 SUNSET BLVD #910	LOS ANGELES, CA	90069
ANDERSON, MICHAEL	FILM DIRECTOR	FILM RIGHTS LIMITED		
		113 WARDOUR ST	LONDON W1	ENGLAND
ANDERSON, MICHAEL, JR	ACTOR	7466 BEVERLY BLVD #205	LOS ANGELES, CA	90036
ANDERSON, NANCY	ACTRESS	12926 RIVERSIDE DR #C	SHERMAN OAKS, CA	91423
ANDERSON, OLE	WRESTLER	NATIONAL WRESTLING ALLIANCE		
		JIM CROCKETT PROMOTIONS		
		421 BRIARBEND DR	CHARLOTTE, NC	28209
ANDERSON, PAT	ACTRESS	7466 BEVERLY BLVD #205	LOS ANGELES, CA	90036
ANDERSON, PATRICK J	NEWS CORRESPONDENT	5151 WISCONSIN AVE, NW	WASHINGTON, DC	20016
ANDERSON, PAUL BERTRAND	WRITER	1314 N HAYWORTH AVE #301	LOS ANGELES, CA	90046
ANDERSON, R DOUGLAS	DRUMMER	POST OFFICE BOX 147	AUBURN, KY	42206
ANDERSON, RAY	TROMBONIST	ENJA/MUSE RECORDS CO		
		160 W 71ST ST	NEW YORK, NY	10023
ANDERSON, RENEE	ACTRESS	2052 PARAMOUNT DR	LOS ANGELES, CA	90068
ANDERSON, RICHARD	ACTOR	10120 CIELO DR	BEVERLY HILLS, CA	90210
ANDERSON, RICHARD DEAN	ACTOR	8275 W NORTON AVE	LOS ANGELES, CA	90046
ANDERSON, ROBERT	PLAYWRIGHT	ICM, 8899 BEVERLY BLVD	LOS ANGELES, CA	90048

SETH VOGEL

IN PERSON AUTOGRAPHS

Over the last few years through various ways I have been able to obtain autographs of most major recording stars and some movie & T.V. personalities. All of the autographs I sell were obtained in person by myself, not through the mail or purchased from other dealers, so you can be sure of authenticity. Please send a business size S.A.S.E. for complete list, or call for more information.

8 X 10 PHOTOS

COLOR — $4.00 B&W — $2.50

These attractive photos are perfect for getting autographed, collecting and displaying. The number in ( ) indicates how many different color and/or B&W poses are available. I get many new photos from week to week, so please let me know if you are looking for something not listed. Postage and Handling: 1 - 4 Photos — $1.00; 5 - 10 Photos — $1.50; 11 or more — $2.00. Wholesale prices are available — please call or write. Photo key chains are available on many of the celebrities listed. Call or write about your favorites. I also have many baseball photos as well as most other sports.

ABBOTT & COSTELLO - B & W (2)
ALAN ALDA - COLOR (1)
WOODY ALLEN - COLOR (2), B & W (1)
LONI ANDERSON - COLOR (2)
RICHARD DEAN ANDERSON - COLOR (2)
JULIE ANDREWS - COLOR (2), B & W 1
FRED ASTAIRE & GINGER ROGERS - B & W (1)
FRED ASTAIRE & RITA HAYWORTH - B & W (1)
CHRIS ATKINS - COLOR (2)
CATHERINE BACH - COLOR (1)
KEVIN BACON - COLOR (1)
SCOTT BAIO - COLOR (6)
CARROLL BAKER - COLOR (1)
ALEX BALDWIN - COLOR (1)
LUCILLE BALL & DESI ARNAZ, JR - B & W (1)
LUCILLE BALL - COLOR (2), B & W (3)
PETER BARTON - COLOR (3)
MIKHAEL BARYSHNIKOV - COLOR (2)
JASON BATEMAN - COLOR (2)
JUSTINE BATEMAN - COLOR (1)
BATMAN & ROBIN - COLOR (1)
STEVEN BAUER - COLOR (1)
JENNIFER BEALS - COLOR (1)

WARREN BEATTY - B & W (1)
WALLACE BEERY - B & W (1)
JOHN BELUSHI - COLOR (1)
JOHN BELUSHI & DAN ACKROYD - COLOR (1)
INGRID BERGMAN - COLOR (1)
VALERIE BERTINELLI - COLOR (2)
BRIAN BLOOM - COLOR (2)
HUMPHREY BOGART - COLOR (5), B & W (14)
STEVE BOND - COLOR (2)
PAT BOONE - COLOR (1)
CLARA BOW - B & W (2)
BRUCE BOXLEITNER - COLOR (2)
MARLON BRANDO - COLOR (4), B & W (3)
JEFF BRIDGES - COLOR (1)
CRISTIE BRINKLEY - COLOR (2)
MATTHEW BRODERICK - COLOR (3)
JAMES BROLIN - COLOR (1)
CHARLES BRONSON - COLOR (3), B & W (1)
PIERCE BROSNAN - COLOR (4)
RICHARD BURTON - COLOR (1), B & W (1)
JAMES CAGNEY - COLOR (2), B & W (11)
KIRK CAMERON - COLOR (8)
ART CARNEY - B & W (3)

LYNDA CARTER - COLOR (3)
RICHARD CHAMBERLAIN - COLOR (1)
LON CHANEY - B & W (1)
CHARLIE CHAPLIN - B & W (3)
CHER - COLOR (4)
MONTGOMERY CLIFT - COLOR (1)
CLAUDETTE COLBERT - COLOR (1), B & W (2)
JOAN COLLINS - (4)
SEAN CONNERY - COLOR (3)
CHUCK CONNORS - B & W (1)
GARY COOPER - COLOR (1), B & W (3)
JACKIE COOPER - B & W (2)
TERI COPELY - COLOR (1)
COSBY SHOW CAST - COLOR (1)
BING CROSBY & BOB HOPE - B & W (1)
TOM CRUISE - COLOR (10)
JAMIE LEE CURTIS - COLOR (2)
TODD CURTIS - COLOR (1)
TONY CURTIS - COLOR (2)
JOHN CUSAK - COLOR (1)
MICHAEL DAMIEN - COLOR (2)
RODNEY DANGERFIELD - COLOR (1)
TED DANSON - COLOR (3)

TONY DANZA - COLOR (3)
SAMMY DAVIS, JR - B & W (1)
BETTE DAVIS - COLOR (2), B & W (1)
OLIVIA DE HAVILLAND - COLOR (1)
ROBERT DE NIRO - COLOR (2), B & W (2)
DEAD END KIDS - B & W (1)
JAMES DEAN - COLOR (7), B & W (8)
BO DEREK - COLOR (2)
MARLENE DIETRICH - COLOR (1), B & W (2)
MATT DILLON - COLOR (7)
PATRICK DUFFY - COLOR (1)
DYNASTY CAST - COLOR (1)
CLINT EASTWOOD - COLOR (11), B & W (8)
BARBARA EDEN - B & W (1)
EMILO ESTEVEZ - COLOR (3)
ERIK ESTRADA - B & W (1)
LINDA EVANS - COLOR (2)
GREG EVIGAN - COLOR (1)
DOUGLAS FAIRBANKS, JR - COLOR (1), B & W (1)
MORGAN FAIRCHILD - COLOR (6)
FAME CAST - COLOR (1)
SHEA FARRELL - COLOR (1)
W C FIELDS - COLOR (2), B & W (1)

CARRIE FISHER - COLOR (1)
ERROL FLYNN - B & W (8)
HARRISON FORD - COLOR (5), B & W
MICHAEL J FOX - COLOR (13)
CLARK GABLE - COLOR (4), B & W (10)
AVA GARDNER - COLOR (1), B & W (1)
JOHN GARFIELD - B & W (2)
JUDY GARLAND - B & W (6)
JUDY GARLAND & MICKEY ROONEY - COLOR (1)
JAMES GARNER - B & W (1)
LEIF GARRETT - COLOR (1)
MITCH GAYLORD - COLOR (2)
TONY GEARY - COLOR (2)
JASON GEDRICK - COLOR (2)
RICHARD GERE - COLOR (7), B & W (1)
GHOSTBUSTERS CAST - COLOR (1)
MEL GIBSON - COLOR (10)
JACKIE GLEASON - COLOR (3), B & W (4)
JACKIE GLEASON & ART CARNEY - B & W (5)
JACKIE GLEASON & AUDREY MEADOWS - B & W (3)
PAULETTE GODDARD - B & W (1)
GODFATHER CAST - COLOR (1). B & W (3)
GLORIA GRAHAME - B & W (1)
CARY GRANT - COLOR (2), B & W (2)
GROWING PAINS CAST - COLOR (1)
LARRY HAGMAN - COLOR (1)
MARK HAMILL - COLOR (3)
HARRY HAMLIN - COLOR (1)
TOM HANKS - COLOR (1)
JEAN HARLOW - B & W (1)
MARK HARMON - COLOR (1)
GREGORY HARRISON - COLOR (1)
HART TO HART CAST - COLOR (1)
LISA HARTMAN - COLOR (1)
DAVID HASSELHOFF - COLOR (3)
RITA HAYWORTH - COLOR (1)
KATHERINE HEPBURN - COLOR (1), B & W (2)
PEE WEE HERMAN - COLOR (2)
JON ERIK HEXUM - COLOR (5)
HILL STREET BLUES CAST - COLOR (3)
GREGORY HINES - COLOR (1)
ALFRED HITCHCOCK - COLOR (1)
DUSTIN HOFFMAN - B & W (1)
HONEYMOONERS CAST - B & W (2)
BOB HOPE - B & W (1)
LEE HORSLEY - COLOR (3)
C THOMAS HOWELL - COLOR (11)
ROCK HUDSON - COLOR (1)
BILLY HUFSEY - COLOR (3)
TAB HUNTER - B & W (1)
I LOVE LUCY CAST - B & W (1)
JOHN JAMES - COLOR (4)
DON JOHNSON - COLOR (9)
DON JOHNSON & PHILIP MICHAEL THOMAS - COLOR (7)
GRACE JONES - COLOR (1)
BORIS KARLOFF - B & W (1)
BUSTER KEATON - B & W (1)
DIANE KEATON - COLOR (1)
GENE KELLY - COLOR (1), B & W (2)
GRACE KELLY - COLOR (1), B & W (2)
VAL KILMER - COLOR (2)
PAUL KING - COLOR (2)
NASTASSIA KINSKI - COLOR (1)
MICHAEL KNIGHT - COLOR (1)
FREDDY KRIEGER - COLOR (1)
ALAN LADD - COLOR (1), B & W (2)
VERONICA LAKE - COLOR (1), B & W (2)
LORENZO LAMAS - COLOR (2)
BURT LANCASTER - B & W (3)
LAUREL & HARDY - B & W (5)
KELLY LE BROCK - COLOR (1)
HEDY LE MARR - COLOR (1), B & W (2)
BRUCE LEE - COLOR (3), B & W 2)
VIVIAN LEIGH - COLOR (3), B & W (3)
JERRY LEWIS & DEAN MARTIN - B & W (1)
JERRY LEWIS - B & W (1)
LIBERACE - B & W (1) LIBERACE - B & W (1)
HEATHER LOCKLEAR - COLOR (9)
CAROLE LOMBARD - B & W (2)
LONE RANGER & TONTO - B & W (1)
SOPHIA LOREN - COLOR (2)
ROB LOWE - COLOR (12)
BELA LUGOSI - B & W (1)
RALPH MACCHIO - COLOR (7)
LEE MAJORS - COLOR (1)
JAYNE MANSFIELD - COLOR (1)
LEE MARVIN - B & W (1)
GROUCHO MARX - B & W (1)
MARX BROTHERS - B & W (1)
MASH CAST - COLOR (4), B & W (1)
JOHNNY MATHIS- COLOR (1)
ANDREW MC CARTHY - COLOR (2)
FRED MC MURRAY - B & W (1)
AUDREY MEADOWS - B & W (1)
MIAMI VICE CAST - COLOR (1)
ALYSSA MILANO - COLOR (1)
RAY MILLAND - COLOR (1), B & W (2)
BARRY MILLER CAST - B & W (1)
LIZA MINELLI - B & W (1)
ROBERT MITCHUM - COLOR (1)
MARILYN MONROE - COLOR (11), B & W (6)
CLAYTON MOORE - B & W (1)
DEMI MOORE - COLOR (2)
ROGER MOORE - COLOR (5)
MUNSTERS CAST - COLOR (1)
EDDIE MURPHY - COLOR (7), B & W (1)
JUDD NELSON - COLOR (1)
PAUL NEWMAN - COLOR (3), B & W (2)
JACK NICHOLSON - COLOR (1)
STEPHEN NICHOLAS - COLOR (2)
LEONARD NIMOY - COLOR (3)
CHUCK NORRIS - COLOR (3)
KIM NOVAK - COLOR (3), B & W (2)
ODD COUPLE CAST (TV SHOW) - B & W (2)
ODD COUPLE CAST (MOVIE) - B & W (1)
ONE DAY AT A TIME CAST - COLOR (1)
OUR GANG CAST - B & W (7)
OUTSIDERS CAST - COLOR (1)
AL PACINO - COLOR (11), B & W (9)
MICHAEL PARE - COLOR (1), B & W (1)
JAMESON PARKER - COLOR (1)
DOLLY PARTON - COLOR (1)
GREGORY PECK - B & W (2)
BRUCE PENHALL - COLOR (3)
ANTHONY PERKINS - B & W (1)
PAT PETERSON - COLOR (1)
RIVER PHOENIX - COLOR (2)
WILLIAM POWELL - B & W (1)
TYRONE POWERS - COLOR (2), B & W (1)
ELVIS PRESLEY - COLOR (12), B & W (8)
VICTORIA PRINCIPAL - COLOR (2), B & W (1)
ANTHONY QUINN - B & W (1)
ANTHONY QUINN - B & W (1)
GEORGE RAFT - B & W (1)
RONALD REAGON - B & W (2)
PETER RECKELL - B & W (8)
PETER RECKELL & KRISTIAN ALFONSO - COLOR (1)
ROBERT REDFORD - COLOR (5), B & W (5)
GEORGE REEVES - B & W (1)
BURT REYNOLDS - COLOR (2), B & W (2)
ALFONSO RIBIERO - COLOR (1)
DON RICKLES - B & W (1)
MOLLY RINGWALD - COLOR (2)
EDWARD G ROBINSON - B & W (2)
ROY ROGERS - COLOR (3), B & W (2)
TRISTAN ROGERS - COLOR (4)
MICKEY ROURKE - COLOR (1)
JANE RUSSELL - COLOR (2), B & W (2)
EMMA SAMMS - COLOR (1)
SCARECROW & MRS KING CAST - COLOR (1)
GLEN SCARPELLI - COLOR (1)
ROY SCHIEDER - COLOR (1)
JOHN SCHNEIDER - COLOR (3)
RICKY SCHROEDER - COLOR (5)
ARNOLD SCHWARTZENEGGER - COLOR (8)
GEORGE C SCOTT - B & W (1)
TOM SELLECK - COLOR (12), B & W (1)
WILLIAM SHATNER - COLOR (3)
CHARLIE SHEEN - COLOR (3)
CYBIL SHEPHERD - COLOR (1)
ANN SHERIDAN - COLOR (1)
BROOKE SHIELDS - COLRO (4)
GRANT SHOW - COLOR (1)
PHIL SILVERS - B & W (1)
FRANK SINATRA - COLOR (9), B & W (8)
MARC SINGER - COLOR (1)
RED SKELTON - B & W (2)
HELEN SLATER - COLOR (1)
DAVID SOUL - B & W (2)
RICK SPRINGFIELD - COLOR (9)
SYLVESTER STALLONE - COLOR (16)
JOHN STAMOS - COLOR (8)
BARBARA STANWYCK - COLOR (1)
STAR TREK CAST - COLOR (3), B & W (1)
STAR WARS CAST - COLOR (1)
MERYL STREEP - COLOR (2)
BARBRA STRIESAND - COLOR (5), B & W (3)
GLORIA SWANSON - COLOR (2)
PATRICK SWAYZE - COLOR (2)
MR T - COLOR (3)
ELIZABETH TAYLOR - COLOR (3)
ROBERT TAYLOR - COLOR (1), B & W (1)
SHIRLEY TEMPLE - B & W (8)
HEATHER THOMAS - COLOR (6)
PHILLIP MICHAEL THOMAS - COLOR (5)
THREE STOOGES - COLOR (1), B & W (12)
CHERYL TIEGS - COLOR (1)
GENE TIERNEY - COLOR (1)
SPENCER TRACY - B & W (3)
JOHN TRAVOLTA - COLOR (10)
LANA TURNER - COLOR (2), B & W (1)
CICELY TYSON - B & W (1)
ROBERT URICH - COLOR (1)
JAN-MICHAEL VINCENT - COLOR (1)
JACK WAGNER - COLOR (15)
ROBERT WAGNER - COLOR (2)
MALCOM-JAMAL WARNER - COLOR (1)
JOHN WAYNE - COLOR (5), B & W (7)
JOHNNY WEISMULLER - B & W (2)
RAQUEL WELCH - COLOR (2), B & W (1)
MAE WEST - COLOR (1), B & W (3)
WHIZ KIDS CAST - COLOR (1) WHIZ KIDS CAST - COLOR (1)
BILLY DEE WILLIAMS - COLOR (4)
BRUCE WILLIS - COLOR (8)
BRUCE WILLIS & CYBIL SHEPHERD - COLOR (3), B & W (1)
HENRY WINKLER - B & W (1)
WIZARD OF OZ CAST - COLOR (4), B & W (3)
NATALIE WOOD - COLOR (2), B & W (1)
JEFF YAGHER - COLOR (1)
LORETTA YOUNG - COLOR (1)
BILLY ZABKA - COLOR (2)
PIA ZADORA - COLOR (1)

8 x 10 COLOR PHOTOGRAPHS — $4.00 EACH

ABC
AC/DC
AC/DC — Angus Young
Bryan Adams (10)
Aerosmith
A-ha (7)
A-ha — Morten Harkett (2)
Alabama
The Alarm
Adam Ant (4)
Arcadia (2)
Bangles (3)
Beach Boys (2)
Beastie Boys (3)
Beatles (7)
Beatles — Paul McCartney (5)
Beatles — George Harrison (2)
Beatles — Ringo Starr (2)
Beatles — John Lennon and Yoko Ono (2)
Pat Benetar (6)
Chuck Berry — b&w
Bon Jovi (3)
Jon Bon Jovi (14)
David Bowie (8)
Boy George (9)
James Brown
Jackson Browne
Belinda Carlyle (3)
Cars (3)
Johnny Cash
Ray Charles
Cinderella
Eric Clapton (4)
Phil Collins (5)
Crosby, Stills, & Nash
Morris Day
Dead or Alive — Pete Burns
Debarge
El Debarge
Def Leppard (4)
Depeche Mode
Neil Diamond (3)
Dio (2)
Doors (2)
Doors — Jim Morrison
Dream Academy
Duran Duran — 5 members (12)
Duran Duran — 3 members (2)
Duran Duran — John Taylor (8)
Duran Duran — Simon Le Bon (6)
Duran Duran — Nick Rhodes (6)
Duran Duran — Andy Taylor (5)
Duran Duran — Roger Taylor (4)
Bob Dylan (3)
Sheila E
Sheena Easton (2)
Eurythmics (2)
Fabulous T-Birds with Stevie Ray Vaughn
Samantha Fox (6)
Samantha Fox — nude topless (3)
Peter Gabriel
Marvin Gaye
General Public
Genesis — with Gabriel and Hackett (2)
Genesis — current 3 members (6)
Grateful Dead (2)
Grateful Dead — Jerry Garcia
Grateful Dead — Bob Weir
Hall and Oates (3)
Debbie Harry (2)
Corey Hart (2)
Heart (2)
Heart — Anne and Nancy
Jimmy Hendrix (3)
Hooters (5)
Crissie Hynde (3)
Billy Idol (10)
INXS (2)
INXS — Michael Hutchence
Iron Maiden (5)
Julio Iglesias (3)
Janet Jackson (3)
Michael Jackson (16)
Joan Jett (4)
Billy Joel (3)
Billy Joel — with Cristie Brinkley
Elton John (3)
Olivia Newton-John (5)
Don Johnson (9)
Howard Jones (2)
Journey (4)
Journey — Steve Perry
Judas Priest (2)
Judas Priest — Rob Halford
Kiss — current members (2)
Kiss — with Mark St. John
Kiss — with Vinny Vincent
Kiss — Gene Simmons (4)
Kiss — Paul Stanley (3)
Kiss — Vinny Vincent
Kiss — Gene and Paul (3)
Kiss — Paul and Bruce Kulick
Kiss — Gene, Paul & Vinny in concert
Patti Labelle
Cyndi Lauper (5)
Led Zeppelin — Plant, Page & Jones
Led Zeppelin — Robert Plant (6)
Led Zeppelin — Jimmy Page (4)
Led Zeppelin — Plant & Page (2)
Led Zeppelin — group in concert
Julian Lennon (7)
Huey Lewis and The News
Huey Lewis (4)
Loverboy (2)
Madonna (14)
Barry Manilow
John Cougar Mellencamp (5)
Men At Work (2)
Menudo (7)
Metallica (2)
Bette Midler (2)
Monkees (5)
Monkees — with Nesmith
Motley Crue (9)
Motley Crue — Vince Neil (7)
Motley Crue — Tommy Lee (4)
Motley Crue — Nikki Sixx (2)
Motley Crue — Mick Mars (2)
Motley Crue — Vince & Nikki
Mr. Mister (5)
Mr. Mister — Richard Page
Eddie Murphy (4)
New Edition (3)
Stevie Nicks (6)
Billy Ocean
Ozzy Osbourne (8)
The Outfield
Robert Palmer (2)
Gregg Peters
Pet Shop Boys
Tom Petty (2)
Tom Petty and the Heartbreakers
Pointer Sisters
The Police (5)
Power Station
Elvis Presley (12)
Prince (8)
Quiet Riot (3)
Ratt (3)
Randy Rhodes (3)
Lionel Richie (6)
Kenny Rogers
Rolling Stones (5)
Rolling Stones — Mick Jagger (5)
Rolling Stones — Keith Richards (2)
Rolling Stones — Jagger and Richards
Diana Ross (6)
David Lee Roth (9)
Mike Rutherford
Sade (4)
Carlos Santana
Brian Setzer
Simple Minds
Frank Sinatra (6)
Rick Springfield (10)
Bruce Springsteen (8)
Billy Squier (4)
Starship
Steve Stephens
Rod Stewart (6)
Sting (9)
Styx (2)
Stray Cats (5)
Barbra Streisand (5)
Donna Summer
Talking Heads
Tears For Fears (7)
Thompson Twins (2)
Tina Turner (8)
Twisted Sister (4)
Twisted Sister — Dee Snider (2)
U2 (7)
U2 — Bono (5)
Van Halen with Hagar (2)
Van Halen with Roth (2)
Eddie Van Halen (6)
Eddie Van Halen and David Lee Roth
Jack Wagner (8)
John Waite (2)
Dionne Warwick
W.A.S.P.
Wham (6)
Wham — George Michael (6)
Wham — Andrew Rigeley (2)
The Who (2)
The Who — Roger Daltrey (2)
The Who — Pete Townshend (2)
The Who — Daltrey and Townshend
Bruce Willis (5)
Stevie Wonder
Neil Young (3)
Paul Young (3)

SETH VOGEL

2157 Ocean Avenue • Brooklyn, NY 11229
(718) 375-2654

Name	Occupation	Address	City	Zip/Country
ANDERSON, ROBERT M	DIRECTOR	284 MARION AVE	MILL VALLEY, CA	94941
ANDERSON, ROBIN	WRITER	8955 BEVERLY BLVD	LOS ANGELES, CA	90048
ANDERSON, ROLAND	ACTOR	11149 MONTANA AVE	LOS ANGELES, CA	90049
ANDERSON, RON	WINE EXPERT	2801 MEADOW LARK DR	SAN DIEGO, CA	92123
ANDERSON, RUSS	ACTOR	ABC-TV, "ONE LIFE TO LIVE"		
		1330 AVE OF THE AMERICAS	NEW YORK, NY	10019
ANDERSON, RUSSELL	ACTOR	1350 N HIGHLAND AVE #24	HOLLYWOOD, CA	90028
ANDERSON, RUTH M	COMPOSER	2678 N BEACHWOOD DR	LOS ANGELES, CA	90068
ANDERSON, SAM	ACTOR	9200 SUNSET BLVD #1210	LOS ANGELES, CA	90069
ANDERSON, SAM L	WRITER	8955 BEVERLY BLVD	LOS ANGELES, CA	90048
ANDERSON, SHERI L	TV WRITER	CBS-TV, "THE GUIDING LIGHT"		
		51 W 52ND ST	NEW YORK, NY	10019
ANDERSON, SHERYL J	WRITER	8375 FOUNTAIN AVE #308	LOS ANGELES, CA	90069
ANDERSON, SPARKY	BASEBALL	4077 N VERDE VISTA DR	THOUSAND OAKS, CA	91360
ANDERSON, STEVE C	WRITER	555 W 57TH ST #1230	NEW YORK, NY	10019
ANDERSON, STEVEN A	ACTOR	11001 FULLBRIGHT AVE	CHATSWORTH, CA	91311
ANDERSON, SYLVIA	WRITER-PRODUCER	PINEWOOD STUDIOS, IVER HEATH	BUCKS SLO ONH	ENGLAND
ANDERSON, TAYLOR	ACTOR	5330 LANKERSHIM BLVD #210	NORTH HOLLYWOOD, CA	91601
ANDERSON, THOMAS S	WRITER	555 W 57TH ST #1230	NEW YORK, NY	10019
ANDERSON, VALERIE	SINGER	PROCESS, 439 WILEY AVE	FRANKLIN, PA	16323
ANDERSON, WILLIAM C	WRITER	8955 BEVERLY BLVD	LOS ANGELES, CA	90048
ANDERSON, WILLIAM R	GUITARIST-PIANIST	108 S GRAYCROFT AVE	MADISON, TN	37115
ANDERSON-HARDT, JANE	WRITER	555 W 57TH ST #1230	NEW YORK, NY	10019
ANDERSON-LEE, MARY	NEWS CORRESPONDENT	3024 WISCONSIN AVE #B-101, NW	WASHINGTON, DC	20016
ANDERSSON, BIBI	ACTRESS	TYKO VAGEN 28	LIDINGO	SWEDEN
ANDERSSON, NORMAN	BASSO-BARITONE	61 W 62ND ST #6-F	NEW YORK, NY	10023
ANDES, JOHN	ACTOR	NEW, 300 E GLENOAKS BLVD	GLENDALE, CA	91207
ANDON, KURT	ACTOR	1725 CAMINO PALMERO #232	LOS ANGELES, CA	90046
ANDOR, PAUL	ACTOR	123 W 93RD ST	NEW YORK, NY	10025
ANDRADE, DANIEL "HANK THE DRIFT	SINGER	POST OFFICE DRAWER 520	STAFFORD, TX	77477
ANDRADE, ROSARIO	SOPRANO	61 W 62ND ST #6-F	NEW YORK, NY	10023
ANDRE, JILL	ACTRESS	3800 BARHAM BLVD #303	LOS ANGELES, CA	90068
ANDRE, MAURICE	TRUMPETER	CAMI, 165 W 57TH ST	NEW YORK, NY	10019
ANDRE THE GIANT	WRESTLER	POST OFFICE BOX 3859	STAMFORD, CT	06905
ANDREA, GERALD	WRITER	555 W 57TH ST #1230	NEW YORK, NY	10019
ANDREA THE LADY GIANT	WRESTLING VALET	SEE - BABY DOLL		
ANDREAS, MICHAEL	COMPOSER	461 CARROLL CANAL	MARINA DEL REY, CA	90292
ANDREAS, SHELLEY	CASTING DIRECTOR	679 N MICHIGAN AVE	CHICAGO, IL	60611
ANDREEFF, STARR	ACTRESS	9229 SUNSET BLVD #607	LOS ANGELES, CA	90069
ANDREOLA, HOWARD	ACTOR	356 S CAMDEN DR	BEVERLY HILLS, CA	90212
ANDREOLLI, FLORINDO	TENOR	CAMI, 165 W 57TH ST	NEW YORK, NY	10019
ANDREOZZI, GENNARO	TV DIRECTOR	118 E 25TH ST	NEW YORK, NY	10010
ANDRESEN, ROBERT	WRITER	555 W 57TH ST #1230	NEW YORK, NY	10019
ANDRESON, LAILA	SOPRANO	61 W 62ND ST #6-F	NEW YORK, NY	10023
ANDRESS, URSULA	ACTRESS	DANIKOFENWEG 95	3072 OSTERMUNDINGEN	SWITZERLAND
ANDREW & THE UPSTARTS	ROCK & ROLL GROUP	POST OFFICE BOX 3483	NASHVILLE, TN	37219
ANDREWS, A BART	WRITER	1321 N STANLEY AVE	LOS ANGELES, CA	90046
ANDREWS, ANDY	COMEDIAN	POST OFFICE BOX 26131	BIRMINGHAM, AL	35226
ANDREWS, ANN	ACTRESS	675 MADISON AVE	NEW YORK, NY	10021
ANDREWS, ANTHONY	ACTOR	ICM, 388-396 OXFORD ST	LONDON W1	ENGLAND
ANDREWS, BUD	ACTOR	NBC-TV, 30 ROCKEFELLER PLAZA	NEW YORK, NY	10112
ANDREWS, CHARLES E	WRITER	555 W 57TH ST #1230	NEW YORK, NY	10019
ANDREWS, DANA	ACTOR	4238 BEEMAN AVE	STUDIO CITY, CA	91603
ANDREWS, DANA R	WRITER	8955 BEVERLY BLVD	LOS ANGELES, CA	90048
ANDREWS, DONALD JAMES	DRUMMER	3118 MOOREWOOD DR	NASHVILLE, TN	37207
ANDREWS, HARRY	ACTOR	CHURCH FARM OASTS		
		SALEHURST, ROBERTSBRIDGE	SUSSEX	ENGLAND
ANDREWS, JAN P	NEWS CORRESPONDENT	2025 "M" ST, NW	WASHINGTON, DC	20036
ANDREWS, JULIE	SINGER-ACTRESS	1888 CENTURY PARK E #1616	LOS ANGELES, CA	90067
ANDREWS, KATHLEEN W	PUBLISHING EXECUTIVE	UNIVERSAL PRESS SYNDICATE		
		4900 MAIN ST, 9TH FLOOR	KANSAS CITY, MO	62114
ANDREWS, LEE, & THE HEARTS	VOCAL GROUP	MARS, 168 ORCHID DR	PEARL RIVER, NY	10965
ANDREWS, MARK	ACTOR	6640 SUNSET BLVD #203	LOS ANGELES, CA	90028
ANDREWS, MARSHA	SOPRANO	756 7TH AVE #67	NEW YORK, NY	10019
ANDREWS, MAXENE	SINGER-ACTRESS	5119 GAVIOTA AVE	ENCINO, CA	91436
ANDREWS, NANCY LEIGH	ACTRESS	FELBER, 2126 N CAHUENGA BLVD	LOS ANGELES, CA	90068
ANDREWS, NORMAN J	ACTOR	4619 MELROSE AVE	LOS ANGELES, CA	90029
ANDREWS, PATTI	SINGER	POST OFFICE BOX 1793	ENCINO, CA	91316
ANDREWS, PETER	TV DIRECTOR	13-16 CONRAD LN	VIRGINIA BEACH, VA	23454
ANDREWS, PETER A	WRITER	8955 BEVERLY BLVD	LOS ANGELES, CA	90048
ANDREWS, PETER L	FILM PRODUCER	POST OFFICE BOX 1-ET	LONDON W1A 1ET	ENGLAND
ANDREWS, RALPH H	WRITER	8955 BEVERLY BLVD	LOS ANGELES, CA	90048
ANDREWS, ROBERT ALLAN	GUITARIST	196 NEW SHACKLE ISLAND RD	HENDERSONVILLE, TN	37075
ANDREWS, ROBERT M	NEWS CORRESPONDENT	1615 INLET CT	RESTON, VA	22090
ANDREWS, SHEILA	SINGER	TAYLOR, 2401 12TH AVE S	NASHVILLE, TN	37204
ANDREWS, TIGE	ACTOR-WRITER	4914 ENCINO TERR	ENCINO, CA	91316
ANDREWS, TINA	ACTRESS	9255 SUNSET BLVD #1105	LOS ANGELES, CA	90069
ANDREWS, WALTER E, JR	NEWS CORRESPONDENT	1400 S JOYCE ST #A-809	ARLINGTON, VA	22202
ANDRO, NINA	ACTRESS	1021 12TH ST #102	SANTA MONICA, CA	90403
ANDRONICOS, BASIL E	NEWS CORRESPONDENT	200 N MAPLE AVE #103	FALLS CHRUCH, VA	22046
ANDRUS, DAVID H	WRITER	8955 BEVERLY BLVD	LOS ANGELES, CA	90048
ANDRUS, JEFF	WRITER	8955 BEVERLY BLVD	LOS ANGELES, CA	90048
ANDRUS, MARK D	WRITER	8955 BEVERLY BLVD	LOS ANGELES, CA	90048
ANDRUS/BLACKWOOD CO	C & W GROUP	POST OFFICE BOX 17272	MEMPHIS, TN	38187
ANDUJAR, JOAQUIN	BASEBALL	JUAN DEACOSTA #10A SAN PEDRO	DE MARCORIS	DOM REP

JULIE ANDREWS

PAUL ANKA

ANN-MARGRET

SUSAN ANTON

EVE ARDEN

ALAN ARKIN

JAMES ARNESS

EDDY ARNOLD

PEGGY ASHCROFT

Name	Occupation	Address	City
ANELLI, ADRIANA	SOPRANO	CAMI, 165 W 57TH ST	NEW YORK, NY 10019
ANELLO, JOHN, JR	SINGER	POST OFFICE BOX 703	PLACENTIA, CA 92670
ANFINSEN, TOM	ACTOR	924 20TH ST #6	SANTA MONICA, CA 90403
ANGE, DONALD WARD	PIANIST	2215 MARKHAM CT	CHARLOTTE, NC 28205
ANGEL	ACTRESS	7131 OWENSMOUTH AVE #104-B	CANOGA PARK, CA 91303
ANGEL	ROCK & ROLL GROUP	ATI, 888 7TH AVE, 21ST FLOOR	NEW YORK, NY 10019
ANGEL, ADRIENNE	ACTRESS	530 RIVERSIDE DR	NEW YORK, NY 10027
ANGEL, DAVID R	COMPOSER	357 CRANE BLVD	LOS ANGELES, CA 90065
ANGEL, TOMMY	WRESTLER	NATIONAL WRESTLING ALLIANCE	
		JIM CROCKETT PROMOTIONS	
		421 BRIARBEND DR	CHARLOTTE, NC 28209
ANGEL, VANESSA	ACTRESS	853 7TH AVE #9-A	NEW YORK, NY 10019
ANGEL CITY	RHYTHM & BLUES GROUP	10100 SANTA MONICA BLVD #1600	LOS ANGELES, CA 90067
ANGELAKOVA, CHRISTINA	MEZZO-SOPRANO	CAMI, 165 W 57TH ST	NEW YORK, NY 10019
ANGELES, MARK	PHOTOGRAPHER	1303 N ODE ST #225	ARLINGTON, VA 22209
ANGELIN, PATRICIA	ACTRESS	ICM, 8899 BEVERLY BLVD	LOS ANGELES, CA 90048
ANGELIS, KIM	SINGER-VIOLINIST	POST OFFICE BOX 1027	HERMOSA BEACH, CA 90254
ANGELL, DAVID	TV WRITER	8383 WILSHIRE BLVD #923	BEVERLY HILLS, CA 90211
ANGELL, DAVID L	WRITER	4136 BELLINGHAM AVE	STUDIO CITY, CA 91604
ANGELL, ROGER	WRITER	1261 MADISON AVE	NEW YORK, NY 10028
ANGELLO, ROBERT P	GUITARIST	124 1/2 W WALNUT ST	OGLESBY, IL 61348
ANGELO, BONNIE	NEWS CORREPONDENT	TIME/TIME & LIFE BLDG	
		ROCKEFELLER CENTER	NEW YORK, NY 10020
ANGELO, SUSAN	ACTRESS	4731 LAUREL CANYON BLVD #5	NORTH HOLLYWOOD, CA 91607
ANGELS, THE	VOCAL GROUP	MARS, 168 ORCHID DR	PEARL RIVER, NY 10965
ANGELUS, MURIEL	ACTRESS	379 BELDEN HILL RD	WILTON, CT 06897
ANGER, DAROL	VIOLINIST	POST OFFICE BOX 9388	STANFORD, CA 94305
ANGER, KENNETH	DIRECTOR	354 E 91ST ST #9	NEW YORK, NY 10128
ANGERS, AVRIL	ACT-COMED-SING	PETER CHARLESWORTH, LTD	
		68 OLD BROMPTON RD	LONDON SW7 3LQ ENGLAND
ANGIER, JOSEPH	WRITER	555 W 57TH ST #1230	NEW YORK, NY 10019
ANGLADE, CATHERINE	TV PRODUCER	10 RUE VILLEHARDOUIN	PARIS 75003 FRANCE
ANGLE, JAMES LESLIE	NEWS CORRESPONDENT	2323 NEBRASKA AVE, NW	WASHINGTON, DC 20016
ANGLE, MARTHA	NEWS CORRESPONDENT	3550 CHESAPEAKE ST, NW	WASHINGTON, DC 20008
ANGLIM, PHILIP	ACTOR	21650 PACIFIC COAST HWY	MALIBU, CA 90265
ANGLIN, SONNY	SINGER	POST OFFICE BOX 1104	HARVEY, LA 70059
ANGOR, DAROL	VIOLINIST	POST OFFICE BOX 9388	STANFORD, CA 94305
ANGOTTI, JOSEPH	TV EXECUTIVE	NBC TELEVISION NETWORK	
		30 ROCKEFELLER PLAZA	NEW YORK, NY 10112
ANGOTTI, NICK	ACTOR	19816 INGOMAR ST	CANOGA PARK, CA 91306
ANGRES, RICHARD D	WRITER	20 BROOKS AVE #301	VENICE, CA 90291
ANGUS, ALLAN	DIRECTOR	7743 MINSTREL AVE	CANOGA PARK, CA 91304
ANHALT, EDWARD	WRITER-PRODUCER	500 AMALFI DR	PACIFIC PALISADES, CA 90272
ANHOLT, TONY	ACTOR	126 KENNINGTON PARK RD	LONDON SE11 4DJ ENGLAND
ANIEVAS, AGUSTIN	PIANIST	HILLYER, 250 W 57TH ST	NEW YORK, NY 10107
ANIMOTION	ROCK & ROLL GROUP	POST OFFICE BOX 67037	LOS ANGELES, CA 90067
ANISTON, JOHN	ACTOR	KNBC-TV, "DAYS OF OUR LIVES"	
		3000 W ALAMEDA AVE	BURBANK, CA 91523
ANKA, PAUL	SINGER	POST OFFICE BOX 100	CARMEL, CA 93921
ANKLAM, FRED, JR	COLUMNIST	POST OFFICE BOX 500	WASHINGTON, DC 20044
ANKLAM, FREDERICK M, JR	NEWS CORRESPONDENT	3471 S STAFFORD ST	ARLINGTON, VA 22206
ANKRUM, DAVID	ACTOR	657 N LA CIENEGA BLVD	LOS ANGELES, CA 90069
ANN-MARGRET	ACTRESS-SINGER	2707 BENEDICT CANYON RD	BEVERLY HILLS, CA 90210
ANNABELLA	ACTRESS	1 RUE PIERRET	NEUILLY 92200 FRANCE
ANNAKIN, KENNETH	FILM WRITER-DIRECTOR	MORRIS, 147-149 WARDOUR ST	LONDON W1V 3TB ENGLAND
ANNAUD, JEAN-JACQUES	FILM DIRECTOR	ICM, 8899 BEVERLY BLVD	LOS ANGELES, CA 90048
ANNE MARIE	SINGER	LEE STOLLER, 120 HICKORY ST	MADISON, TN 37115
ANNE-MARIE	ACTRESS-MODEL	POST OFFICE BOX 9	STREAMWOOD, IL 60103
ANNENBERG, WALLIS	PUBLISHING EXECUTIVE	1026 RIDGEDALE DR	BEVERLY HILLS, CA 90210
ANNENBERG, WALTER	PUBLISHING EXECUTIVE	POST OFFICE BOX 98	RANCHO MIRAGE, CA 92270
ANNESE, FRANK	ACTOR	3800 BARHAM BLVD #303	LOS ANGELES, CA 90068
ANNETT, PAUL	WRITER-PRODUCER	FRASER, 91 REGENT ST	LONDON W1R 8RV ENGLAND
ANNIS, BARBARA	NEWS CORRESPONDENT	1770 "T" ST, NW	WASHINGTON, DC 20009
ANNIS, FRANCESCA	ACTRESS	2 VICKARAGE CT	LONDON W8 ENGLAND
ANNIS, RICHARD	ACTOR	5418 WILLOW CREST AVE #6	NORTH HOLLYWOOD, CA 91601
ANOTHER MULE	RHYTHM & BLUES GROUP	BETH TAYLOR MGMT	
		2501 TALBOT AVE	LOUISVILLE, KY 40205
ANRIG, GREG, JR	NEWS CORRESPONDENT	2201 VIRGINIA AVE, NW	WASHINGTON, DC 20037
ANSARA, BEVERLY	ACTRESS	8721 SUNSET BLVD #202	LOS ANGELES, CA 90069
ANSARA, EDWARD	ACTOR	8831 SUNSET BLVD #402	LOS ANGELES, CA 90069
ANSARA, MICHAEL	ACTOR	4624 PARK MIRASOL	CALABASAS, CA 91302
ANSEL, JEROME	DIRECTOR	141 5TH AVE	NEW YORK, NY 10010
ANSEN, DAVID	FILM CRITIC	NEWSWEEK, 444 MADISON AVE	NEW YORK, NY 10022
ANSEN, JOHN	TV DIRECTOR	ABC-TV, 4151 PROSPECT AVE	HOLLYWOOD, CA 90027
ANSEN, JOSEPH	WRITER	1950 S BEVERLY GLEN BLVD #302	LOS ANGELES, CA 90025
ANSHUTZ, RICHARD L	CONDUCTOR	1645 SIERRA GARDENS DR #205	ROSEVILLE, CA 95678
ANSON, RUTH	ACTRESS-WRITER	3330 BARHAM BLVD #103	LOS ANGELES, CA 90068
ANSPACH, SUSAN	ACTRESS	473 16TH ST	SANTA MONICA, CA 90402
ANSPAUGH, DAVID	TV DIRECTOR-PRODUCER	7358 W 83RD ST	LOS ANGELES, CA 90045
ANSTEY, EDGAR	FILM PRODUCER	6 HURST CLOSE	LONDON NW 11 ENGLAND
ANT, ADAM	SINGER	POST OFFICE BOX 4QT	LONDON W1A ENGLAND

CELEBRITY PHOTOS

The Immortal
STEVE REEVES

Now available! The classic series of poses photographed by Tony Lanza when Steve won the 1947 "Mr. America" title. 8 x 10 black & white prints from the original negatives are $3.00 each plus postage. Send S.A.S.E. for free catalogue to:

Milton T. Moore, Jr.
P.O. Box 140280
Dallas, Texas 75214-0280

One of the world's largest collections of film personality photographs, with emphasis on rare candids and European material. Send a S.A.S.E. with want-list to:

Milton T. Moore, Jr.
P.O. Box 140280
Dallas, Texas 75214-0280

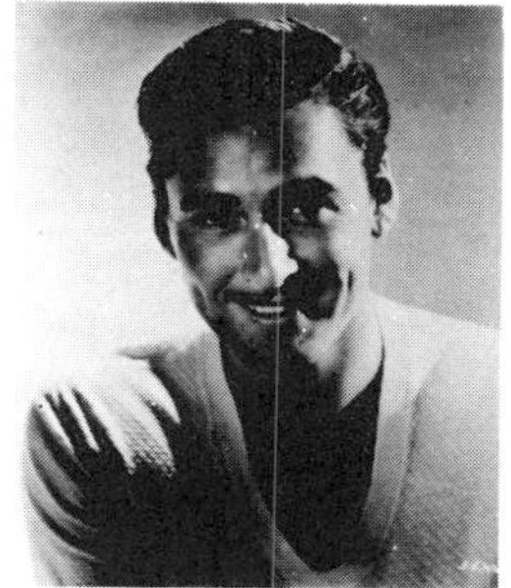

Name	Occupation	Address	City	Zip/Country
ANT LIONS, THE	ROCK & ROLL GROUP	NAKED MANGO MUSIC CO		
		5050 BLUFF PL	EL CAJON, CA	92020
ANTEVIL, JEFFREY H	NEWS CORRESPONDENT	17 W ROSEMONT AVE	ALEXANDRIA, VA	22301
ANTHAN, GEORGE	NEWS CORRESPONDENT	9108 FRIARS RD	BETHESDA, MD	20034
ANTHONY, AL	CONDUCTOR	7823 ALLOTT AVE	PANORAMA CITY, CA	91402
ANTHONY, FRANK	TV DIRECTOR-PRODUCER	ENTERTAINMENT TONIGHT		
		PARAMOUNT TELEVISION		
		5555 MELROSE AVE	LOS ANGELES, CA	90038
ANTHONY, FRANK S	DIRECTOR	DGA, 110 W 57TH ST	NEW YORK, NY	10019
ANTHONY, GERALD	ACTOR	ROUHANA, 1 WORLD TRADE CTR	NEW YORK, NY	10048
ANTHONY, GUY	HYPNOTIST	276 CAMBRIDGE ST #4	BOSTON, MA	02134
ANTHONY, JOSEPH	THEATER DIRECTOR	POST OFFICE BOX 4	WATERVILLE VALLEY, NH	03223
ANTHONY, LEE	ACTOR	9200 SUNSET BLVD #909	LOS ANGELES, CA	90069
ANTHONY, LINDA	GUITARIST	4024 WOODMONT BLVD #B	NASHVILLE, TN	37205
ANTHONY, LYSETTE	ACTRESS	CONWAY, EAGLE HOUSE		
		109 JERMYN ST	LONDON SW1	ENGLAND
ANTHONY, MARK	ACTOR-WRITER	590 N VERMONT AVE	LOS ANGELES, CA	90004
ANTHONY, MARK	DIRECTOR	3808 RIVERSIDE DR	BURBANK, CA	91505
ANTHONY, PETER	COMEDIAN	21243 VENTURA BLVD #243	WOODLAND HILLS, CA	91364
ANTHONY, RAY	ORCHESTRA LEADER	9288 KINGLET DR	LOS ANGELES, CA	90069
ANTHONY, SAL, & VISIONS	VOCAL GROUP	JOYCE, 2028 CHESTNUT ST	PHILADELPHIA, PA	19103
ANTILLA, SUSAN	COLUMNIST	POST OFFICE BOX 500	WASHINGTON, DC	20044
ANTILLE, LISA	ACTRESS	9000 SUNSET BLVD #801	LOS ANGELES, CA	90069
ANTOINE, ANN-MARIE	SOPRANO	225 W 34TH ST #1012	NEW YORK, NY	10001
ANTON, AL	ACTOR	121 N ROBERTSON BLVD #B	BEVERLY HILLS, CA	90211
ANTON, JOHN J	DIRECTOR	635 CLINTON PL	BEVERLY HILLS, CA	90210
ANTON, ROBERT	ACTOR	1350 N HIGHLAND AVE #24	HOLLYWOOD, CA	90028
ANTON, ROBERT	COSTUME DESIGNER	CBS-TV, "THE GUIDING LIGHT"		
		51 W 52ND ST	NEW YORK, NY	10019
ANTON, SUSAN	ACTRESS	14755 VENTURA BLVD #1	SHERMAN OAKS, CA	91403
ANTONACCI, GREG	ACTOR-DIRECTOR	14223 GREENLEAF ST	SHERMAN OAKS, CA	91423
ANTONELLI, LAURA	ACTRESS	VIA ANDREA GIARDINA 8	ROME 00191	ITALY
ANTONEN, MEL	SPORTS WRITER	POST OFFICE BOX 500	WASHINGTON, DC	20044
ANTONIO, JIM	ACTOR	9021 MELROSE AVE #304	LOS ANGELES, CA	90069
ANTONIO, LANE	ACTRESS	530 GAYLORD DR	BURBANK, CA	91505
ANTONIO, LOU	ACT-WRI-DIR	530 GAYLORD DR	BURBANK, CA	91505
ANTONIONI, MICHELANGELO	FILM DIRECTOR	VIA VINCENZO TIBERIO 18	ROME	ITALY
ANTONOFSKY, RUTH	ACTRESS	463 WEST ST	NEW YORK, NY	10014
ANTONOW, JUSTIN	WRITER	1301 BROCKTON AVE #13A	LOS ANGELES, CA	90025
ANTONOWSKY, MARVIN	FILM EXECUTIVE	COLUMBIA PICTURES		
		COLUMBIA PLAZA	BURBANK, CA	91505
ANTOON, A J	DIRECTOR	DGA, 7950 SUNSET BLVD	LOS ANGELES, CA	90046
ANVIL	ROCK & ROLL GROUP	41 BRITAIN ST #200	TORONTO, ONT	CANADA
ANVIL, THE	WRESTLER	SEE - NEIDHART, JIM "THE ANVIL"		
ANZAROOT, JOSHUA	COMPOSER-CONDUCTOR	827 1/2 N CITRUS AVE	LOS ANGELES, CA	90038
AOKI, ROCKY	FOOD ENTREPRENEUR	8685 NW 53RD TERR	MIAMI, FL	33155
APARICIO, LUIS	BASEBALL	CALLE 67 #26-82	MARACAIBO	VENEZUELA
APCA, LEONARD M	NEWS CORRESPONDENT	3524 N DINWIDDIE ST	ARLINGTON, VA	22207
APICK, MARY	ACTRESS	8230 BEVERLY BLVD #23	LOS ANGELES, CA	90048
APLON, BORIS	ACTOR	FARRELL, 10500 MAGNOLIA BLVD	NORTH HOLLYWOOD, CA	91601
APOCALYPSE	ROCK & ROLL GROUP	POST OFFICE BOX 942	RAPID CITY, SD	57709
APOLLONIA	ACTRESS	SEE - KOTERO, APOLLONIA		
APOLLONIA 6	VOCAL GROUP	POST OFFICE BOX 44812	HOPKINS, MN	55343
APPEL, STANLEY	TV PRODUCER	18 BRAMLEY CRESCENT		
		GANTS HILL, ILFORD	ESSEX	ENGLAND
APPEL, WENDY	DIRECTOR	DGA, 7950 SUNSET BLVD	LOS ANGELES, CA	90046
APPELBAUM, LAWRENCE	DIRECTOR	508 N CRESCENT DR	BEVERLY HILLS, CA	90210
APPELL, DON	WRITER	8955 BEVERLY BLVD	LOS ANGELES, CA	90048
APPET, LEAH	WRITER	116 N SWEETZER AVE	LOS ANGELES, CA	90048
APPLE, EDITH S	NEWS CORRESPONDENT	413 "N" ST, SW	WASHINGTON, DC	20024
APPLE, MAX	SCREENWRITER	8955 BEVERLY BLVD	LOS ANGELES, CA	90048
APPLE VIPER	ROCK & ROLL GROUP	41 BRITAIN ST #200	TORONTO, ONT	CANADA
APPLEBAUM, CORY	WRITER	8955 BEVERLY BLVD	LOS ANGELES, CA	90048
APPLEGATE, CHRISTINA	ACTRESS	LYNN, 20411 CHAPTER DR	WOODLAND HILLS, CA	91364
APPLEGATE, PHYLLIS	ACTRESS	208 S BEVERLY DR #8	BEVERLY HILLS, CA	90212
APPLEGATE, ROYCE D	ACTOR	15301 VENTURA BLVD #345	STUDIO CITY, CA	91403
APPLEMAN, HERBERT	WRITER-PRODUCER	2637 GOLFVIEW DR	TROY, MI	48084
APPLEMAN, SID	COMPOSER	1714 MINDA DR	EUGENE, OR	97401
APPLETON, VEDA	ACTRESS	11030 VENTURA BLVD #3	STUDIO CITY, CA	91604
APPLEWHITE, J SCOTT	PHOTOGRAPHER	5130 CONNECTICUT AVE #A, NW	WASHINGTON, DC	20008
APPLING, LUKE	BASEBALL	RURAL ROUTE #7, BRAGG RD	CUMMINGS, GA	30130
APPLING, RON	DIRECTOR	555 W SHAW AVE #15	FRESNO, CA	93704
APREA, JOHN	ACTOR	12750 VENTURA BLVD #102	STUDIO CITY, CA	91604
APRIL WINE	ROCK & ROLL GROUP	FLOOD, 354 YOUVILLE ST	MONTREAL, PQ H2Y 2C3	CANADA
APSTEIN, ELLIOTT	WRITER	6734 ESPLANADE	PLAYA DEL REY, CA	90293
APSTEIN, THEODORE	WRITER	1000 NORMAN PL	LOS ANGELES, CA	90049
APTED, MICHAEL	FILM DIRECTOR	1051 VILLA VIEW DR	PACIFIC PALISADES, CA	90272
APTER, BILL	WRESTLING WRITER	POST OFFICE BOX 48	ROCKVILLE CENTRE, NY	11571
APTER, HAROLD	WRITER	1944 N WHITLEY AVE #310	LOS ANGELES, CA	90068
AR & THE ROCKIN' RICOCHETTES	ROCK & ROLL GROUP	3717 W 50TH ST #L-2	MINNEAPOLIS, MN	55410
ARAGALL, GIACOMO	TENOR	CAMI, 165 W 57TH ST	NEW YORK, NY	10019
ARAGALL, JAIME	SINGER	LOMBARDO, 30 W 60TH ST	NEW YORK, NY	10023
ARAGON, JESSE	ACTOR	400 S BEVERLY DR #216	BEVERLY HILLS, CA	90212
ARAGONES, SERGIO	CARTOONIST	MAD MAGAZINE, INC		
		485 MADISON AVE	NEW YORK, NY	10022

ARAI, KENJI	NEWS CORRESPONDENT	7338 EL DORADO RD	MC LEAN, VA	22102
ARAIZA, FRANCISCO	TENOR	CAMI, 165 W 57TH ST	NEW YORK, NY	10019
ARANA, ANA R	WRITER	555 W 57TH ST #1230	NEW YORK, NY	10019
ARANGO, DOUGLAS	WRITER	POST OFFICE BOX 1768	STUDIO CITY, CA	91604
ARANHA, RAY	WRITER	555 W 57TH ST #1230	NEW YORK, NY	10019
ARATOW, PAUL	WRITER	8955 BEVERLY BLVD	LOS ANGELES, CA	90048
ARBEID, BEN	FILM PRODUCER	ICM, 388-396 OXFORD ST	LONDON W1	ENGLAND
ARBEID, MURRAY	FASHION DESIGNER	87-91 NEW BOND ST	LONDON W1	ENGLAND
ARBESSIER, LOUIS	ACTOR	33 RUE ARTHUR ROZIER	PARIS 75019	FRANCE
ARBOGAST, ROBERT L	WRITER	3092 RODERICK PL	LOS ANGELES, CA	90065
ARBUS, ALLAN	ACTOR	9100 SUNSET BLVD #200	LOS ANGELES, CA	90069
ARBUS, LOREEN J	WRITER	8955 BEVERLY BLVD	LOS ANGELES, CA	90048
ARBUSTO, DOMENIC	DIRECTOR	333 E 49TH ST #LE	NEW YORK, NY	10017
ARC, KATHLEEN	ACTRESS	120 S VICTORY BLVD #104	BURBANK, CA	91502
ARCE, MANUEL	WRITER	555 W 57TH ST #1230	NEW YORK, NY	10019
ARCEDI, TED	WRESTLER	POST OFFICE BOX 3859	STAMFORD, CT	06905
ARCH ANGELS, THE	ROCK & ROLL GROUP	BASTEIN, 644 WARWICK ST	BROOKLYN, NY	11207
ARCHARD, BERNARD	ACTOR	66 CLONCURRY ST	LONDON SW6	ENGLAND
ARCHER, ANNE	ACTRESS	10510 SANDAL LN	LOS ANGELES, CA	90077
ARCHER, BEVERLY	ACTRESS	STONE, 1052 CAROL DR	LOS ANGELES, CA	90069
ARCHER, CHARLES L	GUITARIST	POST OFFICE BOX 4544	NASHVILLE, TN	37216
ARCHER, KATE	WRITER	8955 BEVERLY BLVD	LOS ANGELES, CA	90048
ARCHER, NICHOLAS	TV EXECUTIVE	ABC-TV, 7 W 66TH ST	NEW YORK, NY	10023
ARCHERD, ARMY	COLUMNIST	442 HILGARD AVE	LOS ANGELES, CA	90024
ARCHERD, EVAN P	WRITER	10124 LA TUNA CYN RD	SUN VALLEY, CA	91352
ARCHERD, SELMA	ACTRESS	442 HILGARD AVE	LOS ANGELES, CA	90024
ARCHIBALD, DOTTIE	COMEDIENNE	8955 BEVERLY BLVD	LOS ANGELES, CA	90048
ARCHIBALD, GEORGE H	NEWS CORRESPONDENT	2352 SOFTWIND CT	RESTON, VA	22091
ARDAM, ELZBIETA	SOPRANO	ICM, 40 W 57TH ST	NEW YORK, NY	10019
ARDELL, PHILIP	WRITER	555 W 57TH ST #1230	NEW YORK, NY	10019
ARDEN, EVE	ACTRESS	9066 SAINT IVES DR	LOS ANGELES, CA	90069
ARDEN, TONI	SINGER	34-34 75TH ST	JACKSON HEIGHTS, NY	11372
ARDIES, THOMAS G	WRITER	8955 BEVERLY BLVD	LOS ANGELES, CA	90048
ARDIN, MILAGROS E	NEWS CORRESPONDENT	4400 JENIFER ST, NW	WASHINGTON, DC	20015
ARDOIN, JOHN A	WRITER	555 W 57TH ST #1230	NEW YORK, NY	10019
ARDOLINO, EMILE	TV DIRECTOR	24 5TH AVE #814	NEW YORK, NY	10011
ARDOLINO, PAUL	PRODUCER	1807 TAFT AVE #4	LOS ANGELES, CA	90028
ARENA, MAURIZIO	CONDUCTOR	61 W 62ND ST #6-F	NEW YORK, NY	10023
ARENAL, JULIE	CHOREOGRAPHER	205 E 10TH ST	NEW YORK, NY	10003
ARENO, LOIS	ACTRESS-MODEL	9145 CHARLEVILLE BLVD #305	BEVERLY HILLS, CA	90212
ARESCO, JOEY	ACTOR	409 N CAMDEN DR #203-A	BEVERLY HILLS, CA	90210
ARGENT, DOUGLAS	TV DIRECTOR-PRODUCER	55 KENTON AVE		
		SUNBURY-ON-THAMES	MIDDLESEX	ENGLAND
ARGENTIERI, ALDO	NEWS CORRESPONDENT	3827 ALBEMARLE ST, NW	WASHINGTON, DC	20016
ARGENTO, DOMINICK	COMPOSER	MINNESOTA UNIVERSITY		
		MUSIC DEPARTMENT	MINNEAPOLIS, MN	55455
ARGERICH, MARTHA	PIANIST	CAMI, 165 W 57TH ST	NEW YORK, NY	10019
ARGEROPLOS, GEORGE	PHOTOGRAPHER	311 JAMAICA AVE	MEDFORD, NY	11763
ARGIRO, JAMES	COMPOSER-CONDUCTOR	11042 AQUA VISTA ST #6	NORTH HOLLYWOOD, CA	91602
ARGO, ALLISON	ACTRESS	54 NAVY ST	VENICE, CA	90291
ARGOUD, KARIN	ACTRESS	10100 SANTA MONICA BLVD #1600	LOS ANGELES, CA	90067
ARIAN, MICHAEL	NEWS CORRESPONDENT	1215 N FORT MYER DR #708	ARLINGTON, VA	22209
ARIAS, RON	WRITER	TIME & PEOPLE MAGAZINE		
		TIME & LIFE BUILDING		
		ROCKEFELLER CENTER	NEW YORK, NY	10020
ARIEFF, IRWIN B	NEWS CORRESPONDENT	2761 WOODLEY PL, NW	WASHINGTON, DC	20008
ARIEL TRIO	MUSICAL TRIO	431 S DEARBORN ST #1504	CHICAGO, IL	60605
ARIOSO TRIO	MUSICAL TRIO	61 W 62ND ST #6-F	NEW YORK, NY	10023
ARIS, BEN	ACTOR	BARRY BROWN, 47 W SQ	LONDON SE11	ENGLAND
ARISTO, GIORGIO	TENOR	CAMI, 165 W 57TH ST	NEW YORK, NY	10019
ARIZONA SMOKE REVUE	C & W GROUP	RNJ, 11514 CALVERT ST	NORTH HOLLYWOOD, CA	91606
ARKIN, ADAM	ACTOR-WRITER	50 RIDGE DR	CHAPPAQUE, NY	10514
ARKIN, ALAN	ACTOR-DIRECTOR	50 RIDGE DR	CHAPPAQUE, NY	10514
ARKIN, DAVID	ACTOR	2376 GLENDON AVE	LOS ANGELES, CA	90064
ARKIN, MICHAEL	ACTOR	484 W 43RD ST #24-P	NEW YORK, NY	10036
ARKING, LINDA	WRITER	555 W 57TH ST #1230	NEW YORK, NY	10019
ARKOFF, LOUIS F	EXECUTIVE	1517 N BEVERLY BLVD	BEVERLY HILLS, CA	90210
ARKOFF, SAMUEL Z	FILM PRODUCER	3205 OAKDELL LN	STUDIO CITY, CA	91604
ARKUS, ALBERT	DIRECTOR	2 PADDOCK LN	GREAT NECK, NY	11020
ARKUSH, ALAN	FILM-TV DIRECTOR	151 S EL CAMINO DR	BEVERLY HILLS, CA	90212
ARKUSH, ALLAN PAUL	DIRECTOR	14134 CHANDLER BLVD	VAN NUYS, CA	91401
ARLEDGE, JAMES	GUITARIST-PIANIST	311 DEER PARK CIR	NASHVILLE, TN	37205
ARLEDGE, ROONE	TV DIRECTOR-PRODUCER	ABC TELEVISION NETWORK		
		1330 AVE OF THE AMERICAS	NEW YORK, NY	10019
ARLEN, ALICE A	SCREENWRITER	555 W 57TH ST #1230	NEW YORK, NY	10019
ARLEN, ELIZABETH	ACTRESS	12720 MATTESON AVE #4	LOS ANGELES, CA	90066
ARLEN, GARY H	EDITOR-PUBLISHER	7315 WISCONSIN AVE #600	BETHESDA, MD	20814
ARLEN, GARY H	NEWS CORRESPONDENT	6407 LANDON LN	BETHESDA, MD	20817
ARLEN, MICHAEL	WRITER	NEW YORKER, 23 W 43RD ST	NEW YORK, NY	10036
ARLETT, RICHARD	WRITER	9300 SIERRA MAR DR	LOS ANGELES, CA	90069
ARLETTY	ACTRESS	14 RUE DE RIMUSET	PARIS 75016	FRANCE
ARLT, LEWIS	ACTOR	BARRY, 165 W 46TH ST	NEW YORK, NY	10036
ARMAGNAC, GARY	ACTOR	870 N VINE ST #G	LOS ANGELES, CA	90038
ARMANI, DEBRA	ACTRESS	316 27TH ST	HERMOSA BEACH, CA	90254
ARMANI, GIORGIO	FASHION DESIGNER	GIORGIO'S, 650 5TH AVE	NEW YORK, NY	10019

Name	Occupation	Address	City	ZIP/Country
ARMATRADING, JOAN	SINGER-GUITARIST	RUNNING DOG MANAGEMENT 27 QUEENSDALE PL	LONDON W11	ENGLAND
ARMBRISTER, TREVOR	NEWS CORRESPONDENT	6670 HILLANDALE RD	CHEVY CHASE, MD	20815
		1 DAG HAMMARSKJOLD PLAZA	NEW YORK, NY	10017
ARMBRUSTER, ANN	WRITER-EDITOR	US MAGAZINE COMPANY		
ARMBRUSTER, DEBBIE A	WRITER	555 W 57TH ST #1230	NEW YORK, NY	10019
ARMBRUSTER, RICHARD	ACTOR	1401 N FULLER AVE #6	LOS ANGELES, CA	90046
ARMEN, MARGARET	WRITER	5707 WALLIS LN	WOODLAND HILLS, CA	91367
ARMENDARIZ, PEDRO, JR	ACTOR	9200 SUNSET BLVD #909	LOS ANGELES, CA	90069
ARMENTROUT, LEE	DIRECTOR	801 ERIE ST	OAK PARK, IL	60302
ARMER, ALAN A	DIRECTOR-PRODUCER	266 BRONWOOD AVE	LOS ANGELES, CA	90049
ARMISTEAD, THOMAS	TV DIRECTOR-PRODUCER	10373 ASHTON AVE	LOS ANGELES, CA	90024
ARMITAGE, GEORGE	WRITER-PRODUCER	1113 N BEVERLY GLEN BLVD	LOS ANGELES, CA	90024
ARMOR, JOYCE	TV WRITER	8955 BEVERLY BLVD	LOS ANGELES, CA	90048
ARMOR, KAY	WRITER	6725 SUNSET BLVD #506	LOS ANGELES, CA	90028
ARMOUR-BURNS, THOMAS	BARITONE	260 W END AVE #7-A	NEW YORK, NY	10023
ARMOURY SHOW, THE	ROCK & ROLL GROUP	POST OFFICE BOX 107-A	LONDON N6 5RU	ENGLAND
ARMS, RUSSELL	ACTOR-SINGER	11855 MAGNOLIA BLVD #21	NORTH HOLLYWOOD, CA	91607
ARMSTRONG, ALUN	ACTOR	8 COLEFORD RD, WANDSWORTH	LONDON SW18	ENGLAND
ARMSTRONG, ANDRA H	NEWS CORRESPONDENT	4607 CONNECTICUT AVE #302, NW	WASHINGTON, DC	20008
ARMSTRONG, BESS	ACTRESS	500 S SEPULVEDA BLVD #500	LOS ANGELES, CA	90049
ARMSTRONG, BILL	TV WRITER	8955 BEVERLY BLVD	LOS ANGELES, CA	90048
ARMSTRONG, CURTIS	ACTOR	247 S BEVERLY DR #102	BEVERLY HILLS, CA	90210
ARMSTRONG, ELIZABETH S	NEWS CORRESPONDENT	400 N BRYAN ST	ARLINGTON, VA	22201
ARMSTRONG, GILLIAN	FILM DIRECTOR	MS JUDY FOX SCOTT 151 S EL CAMINO DR	BEVERLY HILLS, CA	90212
ARMSTRONG, HELEN	VIOLINIST	POST OFFICE BOX U	REDDING, CT	06875
ARMSTRONG, HERB	ACTOR	11476 HUSTON ST	NORTH HOLLYWOOD, CA	91601
ARMSTRONG, J GARY	TRUMPETER	1617 LEBANON RD #F-4	NASHVILLE, TN	37210
ARMSTRONG, JACK	ACTOR	ABC-TV, "ALL MY CHILDREN" 1330 AVE OF THE AMERICAS	NEW YORK, NY	10019
ARMSTRONG, JAMES D	CONDUCTOR	7916 4TH ST	DOWNEY, CA	90241
ARMSTRONG, JIM	CARTOONIST	NEWS AMERICA SYNDICATE 1703 KAISER AVE	IRVINE, CA	92714
ARMSTRONG, JOHN	ACTOR	125 W 16TH ST	NEW YORK, NY	10011
ARMSTRONG, JOHN A	NEWS CORRES-PROD	5104 BALTIMORE AVE	BETHESDA, MD	20816
ARMSTRONG, KARAN	SOPRANO	CAMI, 165 W 57TH ST	NEW YORK, NY	10019
ARMSTRONG, MARY	ACTRESS	8721 SUNSET BLVD #202	LOS ANGELES, CA	90069
ARMSTRONG, MARYLEE	TRUMPETER	2113 BROOKVIEW DR	NASHVILLE, TN	37214
ARMSTRONG, MICHAEL	ACT-WRI-DIR	HATTON, 18 JERMYN ST	LONDON SW1	ENGLAND
ARMSTRONG, MOIRA	TV DIRECTOR	10 CEYLON RD	LONDON W14 OPY	ENGLAND
ARMSTRONG, NANCY	SOPRANO	AARON, 25 HUNTINGTON AVE	BOSTON, MA	02116
ARMSTRONG, PETER	PIANIST	POST OFFICE BOX 131	SPRINGFIELD, VA	22150
ARMSTRONG, R G	ACTOR	CONTEMPORARY ARTISTS 132 S LASKY DR	BEVERLY HILLS, CA	90212
ARMSTRONG, REBEKKA	MODEL	MODELS & PROMOTIONS AGENCY 8560 SUNSET BLVD, 10TH FLOOR	LOS ANGELES, CA	90069
ARMSTRONG, RICHARD	NEWS CORRESPONDENT	515 MURDOCK RD	BALTIMORE, MD	21212
ARMSTRONG, RICHARD B	TV DIRECTOR	1910 WINDHAM LN	SILVER SPRING, MD	20902
ARMSTRONG, ROBIN	ACTOR	6716 CLYBOURN AVE #243	NORTH HOLLYWOOD, CA	91606
ARMSTRONG, SHEILA	SOPRANO	CAMI, 165 W 57TH ST	NEW YORK, NY	10019
ARMSTRONG, TOM	CARTOONIST	NEWS AMERICA SYNDICATE 1703 KAISER AVE	IRVINE, CA	92714
ARMSTRONG, TOM C	WRITER	9200 SUNSET BLVD #909	LOS ANGELES, CA	90069
ARMSTRONG, VALORIE	ACTRESS	19 W 44TH ST #1500	NEW YORK, NY	10036
ARMSTRONG, WALTER R	NEWS CORRESPONDENT	1755 S JEFFERSON DAVIS HWY	ARLINGTON, VA	22202
ARMUS, BURTON S	TV WRITER-PRODUCER	2501 CAROB DR	LOS ANGELES, CA	90046
ARNATT, JOHN	ACTOR	3 WARREN COTTAGES WOODLAND WY, KINGSWOOD	SURREY KT20 6NN	ENGLAND
ARNAUD, DANIELE	ACTRESS	LIGHT, 113 N ROBERTSON BLVD	LOS ANGELES, CA	90048
ARNAUD, LEON	COMPOSER-CONDUCTOR	215 BUCK SHOALS RD	HAMPTONVILLE, NC	27020
ARNAZ, DESI, JR	ACTOR	POST OFFICE BOX 2000	OJAI, CA	93023
ARNAZ, LUCI	ACTRESS	271 CENTRAL PARK W	NEW YORK, NY	10024
ARNDT, A PAUL	TV DIRECTOR	236 S RIDGELAND AVE	OAK PARK, IL	60302
ARNER, GWEN	ACTRESS	10100 SANTA MONICA BLVD #1600	LOS ANGELES, CA	90067
ARNESS, JAMES	ACTOR	POST OFFICE BOX 10480	GLENDALE, CA	91209
ARNETT, HAZEL	WRITER	555 W 57TH ST #1230	NEW YORK, NY	10019
ARNETT, JAMES M	FILM DIRECTOR	940 N LA JOLLA AVE	LOS ANGELES, CA	90046
ARNETT, SHERRY	MODEL	MODELS & PROMOTIONS AGENCY 8560 SUNSET BLVD, 10TH FLOOR	LOS ANGELES, CA	90069
ARNETTE, JEANNETTA	ACTRESS	POST OFFICE BOX 5617	BEVERLY HILLS, CA	90210
ARNGRIM, ALISON	ACTRESS	7949 SELMA AVE #15	LOS ANGELES, CA	90046
ARNN, JOHN M	PIANIST-SAXOPHONIST	724 HARPETH PARKWAY W	NASHVILLE, TN	37221
ARNO, ED	CARTOONIST	POST OFFICE BOX 4203	NEW YORK, NY	10017
ARNO, FRANK	ACTOR	5339 NEWCASTLE AVE	ENCINO, CA	91316
ARNOLD, ALAN	SCREENWRITER	20 PEMBRIDGE CRESCENT	LONDON W11	ENGLAND
ARNOLD, BERNARD "BUDDY"	WRITER	8955 BEVERLY BLVD	LOS ANGELES, CA	90048
ARNOLD, CHERYL	SINGER-MODEL	POST OFFICE BOX 189	BOTHELL, WA	98011
ARNOLD, CRAIG W	NEWS CORRESPONDENT	C-SPAN, NEWS DEPARTMENT 400 N CAPITOL ST, NW	WASHINGTON, DC	20001
ARNOLD, DANNY	WRITER-PRODUCER	1293 SUNSET PLAZA DR	LOS ANGELES, CA	90069
ARNOLD, DAVID	BARITONE	POST OFFICE BOX 345	ROOSEVELT, NJ	08555
ARNOLD, EDDY	SINGER	FRANKLIN RD, BOX 97	BRENTWOOD, TN	37027
ARNOLD, GARY	FILM CRITIC	5133 N 1ST ST	ARLINGTON, VA	22203
ARNOLD, H B	DIRECTOR	2720 N MILDRED AVE #3	CHICAGO, IL	60614

Name	Occupation	Address	City	Zip/Country
ARNOLD, HENRI	JUMBLE WRITER	TRIBUNE MEDIA SERVICES 64 E CONCORD ST	ORLANDO, FL	32801
ARNOLD, JACK	DIRECTOR-PRODUCER	4860 NOMAD DR	WOODLAND HILLS, CA	91364
ARNOLD, JAMES	TV DIRECTOR	40 ARAN RD	WESTWOOD, MA	02090
ARNOLD, JENNIFER	WRITER	555 W 57TH ST #1230	NEW YORK, NY	10019
ARNOLD, JERRY	DRUMMER	441 CAPRI DR	NASHVILLE, TN	37209
ARNOLD, JIM	TV WRITER	8955 BEVERLY BLVD	LOS ANGELES, CA	90048
ARNOLD, JOHN	DIRECTOR-PRODUCER	GRAPHIC FILMS COMPANY 2 LOWER JAMES ST	LONDON W1R 3PN	ENGLAND
ARNOLD, JOHN, BAND	C & W GROUP	POST OFFICE BOX 121089	NASHVILLE, TN	37212
ARNOLD, MADISON	ACTOR	9220 SUNSET BLVD #202	LOS ANGELES, CA	90069
ARNOLD, MALCOLM	BARITONE	61 W 62ND ST #6-F	NEW YORK, NY	10023
ARNOLD, MARCELLE	ACTOR	60 BLVD ST GERMAIN	PARIS 75005	FRANCE
ARNOLD, MARK	ACTOR	10100 SANTA MONICA BLVD #1600	LOS ANGELES, CA	90067
ARNOLD, NEWTON DENNIS	WRITER-PRODUCER	16996 STRAWBERRY DR	ENCINO, CA	91436
ARNOLD, NICK	TV WRITER	555 W 57TH ST #1230	NEW YORK, NY	10019
ARNOLD, PETER G	WRITER	555 W 57TH ST #1230	NEW YORK, NY	10019
ARNOLD, PHIL	GUITARIST	206 ACKLEN PARK DR	NASHVILLE, TN	37203
ARNOLD, SUSAN	CASTING DIRECTOR	POST OFFICE BOX 5718	SHERMAN OAKS, CA	91403
ARNOLD, TAFF	COMEDIAN	TERRY, 909 PARKVIEW AVE	LODI, CA	95240
ARNOLD, THOMAS K	MUSIC CRITIC-WRITER	701 "B" ST #501	SAN DIEGO, CA	92101
ARNONE, LEE	ACTRESS	5000 LANKERSHIM BLVD #5	NORTH HOLLYWOOD, CA	91601
ARNONE, VINCENT	TENOR	200 W 70TH ST #7-F	NEW YORK, NY	10023
ARNOSI, MIA	AERIALIST	HALL, 138 FROG HOLLOW RD	CHURCHVILLE, PA	18966
ARNOSI AERIAL CRADLE DUO	AERIAL CRADLE DUO	HALL, 138 FROG HOLLOW RD	CHURCHVILLE, PA	18966
ARNOTT, ROBERT M	TV WRITER	8955 BEVERLY BLVD	LOS ANGELES, CA	90048
ARNOUL, FRANCOISE	ACTRESS	32 RUE MONSIER LE PRINCE	PARIS 75006	FRANCE
ARNST, TERRILL DIANNE	CELLIST	1908 ACKLEN AVE #E	NASHVILLE, TN	37212
ARNSTEIN, LARRY	TV WRITER	2639 1/2 3RD ST	SANTA MONICA, CA	90405
ARNSTEN, STEFAN	ACTOR	1326 DAWNRIDGE DR	BEVERLY HILLS, CA	90210
ARONE, JAMES	ACTOR	1531 COMMONWEALTH AVE	LOS ANGELES, CA	90027
ARONIN, MICHAEL J	ACTOR	3800 BARHAM BLVD #303	LOS ANGELES, CA	90068
ARONOFF, ANITA	SOPRANO	111 W 57TH ST #1209	NEW YORK, NY	10019
ARONOW, HAL	WRITER	555 W 57TH ST #1230	NEW YORK, NY	10019
ARONOWITZ, JOEL	TV DIRECTOR	CBS-TV, 524 W 57TH ST	NEW YORK, NY	10019
ARONSON, BRAD	DIRECTOR	8109 WILLOW GLEN RD	LOS ANGELES, CA	90046
ARONSON, JOSEPH	CARICATURIST	HALL, 138 FROG HOLLOW RD	CHURCHVILLE, PA	18966
ARONSON, JOSHUA	DIRECTOR	260 5TH AVE	NEW YORK, NY	10001
ARONSON, JUDIE	ACTRESS	409 N CAMDEN AVE #105	BEVERLY HILLS, CA	90210
ARONSON, MERRY	WRITER	555 W 57TH ST #1230	NEW YORK, NY	10019
ARONSON, MEYER	WRITER	555 W 57TH ST #1230	NEW YORK, NY	10019
ARPA, PEGGY	ACTRESS	5330 LANKERSHIM BLVD #210	NORTH HOLLYWOOD, CA	91601
ARPINO, GERALD	CHOREOGRAPHER	JOFFREY, 130 W 56TH ST	NEW YORK, NY	10019
ARQUETTE, LEWIS	ACTOR-WRITER	616 N GOWER ST	LOS ANGELES, CA	90004
ARQUETTE, ROSANNA	ACTRESS	13596 CONTOUR DR	SHERMAN OAKS, CA	91423
ARRANGA, IRENE	ACTRESS	909 N SIERRA BONITA AVE #7	LOS ANGELES, CA	90046
ARRANTS, ROD	ACTOR	9229 SUNSET BLVD #306	LOS ANGELES, CA	90069
ARRATA, BILL	ACTOR	THE ATHLETES REGISTRY 2221 S BARRY AVE	LOS ANGELES, CA	90064
ARRAU, CLAUDIO	PIANIST	ICM, 40 W 57TH ST	NEW YORK, NY	10019
ARRENDELL, EDWARD	TALENT AGENT	POST OFFICE BOX 55398	WASHINGTON, DC	20040
ARRIENDA, GERALDINE J	COMPOSER	1719 GIRVIN RD	JACKSONVILLE, FL	32225
ARRIGHI, MEL	WRITER	555 W 57TH ST #1230	NEW YORK, NY	10019
ARRINGTON, BRITT	NEWS CORRESPONDENT	4461 CONNECTICUT AVE, NW	WASHINGTON, DC	20008
ARRINGTON, JAMES A	GUITARIST	POST OFFICE BOX 446	JOELTON, TN	37080
ARRINGTON, PERCY	PHOTOJOURNALIST	7300 RIVER HILL RD	OXON HILL, MD	20021
ARRINGTON, STEVE	SINGER	THE KONGLATHER AGENCY 1775 BROADWAY, 7TH FLOOR	NEW YORK, NY	10019
ARRIOLA, GUS	CARTOONIST	POST OFFICE BOX 3275	CARMEL, CA	93921
ARRIOLA, SERGIO, III	ACTOR	27412 WARRIOR DR	RANCHO PALOS VERDES, C	90274
ARROW, JOEY	GUITARIST	3730 BURRUS ST	NASHVILLE, TN	37216
ARROWS, THE	ROCK & ROLL GROUP	41 BRITAIN ST #200	TORONTO, ONT	CANADA
ARROWSMITH, TRACEY L	NEWS CORRESPONDENT	C-SPAN, NEWS DEPARTMENT 400 N CAPITOL ST, NW	WASHINGTON, DC	20001
ARROYO, MARTINA	SOPRANO	59 E 54TH ST #81	NEW YORK, NY	10022
ARROYO, ROGER	CLOWN	2701 COTTAGE WY #14	SACRAMENTO, CA	95825
ARSLANIAN, OSCAR	PRODUCER-MANAGER	6671 SUNSET BLVD #1502	HOLLYWOOD, CA	90028
ART ENSEMBLE OF CHICAGO	MUSICAL GROUP	5322 S DREXEL BLVD	CHICAGO, IL	60615
ARTHUR, ALICE	COMEDIENNE	PERLE, 4475 VINELAND AVE	STUDIO CITY, CA	91602
ARTHUR, BEATRICE	ACTRESS	2000 OLD RANCH RD	LOS ANGELES, CA	90049
ARTHUR, CAROL	ACTRESS	9744 WILSHIRE BLVD #206	BEVERLY HILLS, CA	90212
ARTHUR, DAVID S	TV WRITER	4330 WINDWARD CIR	DALLAS, TX	75252
ARTHUR, JEAN	ACTRESS	29398 OCEAN VIEW	CARMEL, CA	93921
ARTHUR, JOHN	TV WRITER	8955 BEVERLY BLVD	LOS ANGELES, CA	90048
ARTHUR, KAREN	TV-FILM DIRECTOR	19130 PACIFIC COAST HWY #8	MALIBU, CA	90265
ARTHUR, MAUREEN	ACTRESS	6310 SAN VICENTE BLVD #407	LOS ANGELES, CA	90048
ARTHUR, REBECA	ACTRESS	9229 SUNSET BLVD #306	LOS ANGELES, CA	90069
ARTHUR, ROBERT	TV WRITER	8955 BEVERLY BLVD	LOS ANGELES, CA	90048
ARTHUR, ROBERT	PRODUCER	9330 CHEROKEE LN	BEVERLY HILLS, CA	90210
ARTHUR, ROBERT	PRODUCER	1711 KINGS WY	LOS ANGELES, CA	90069
ARTHUR, SHERWOOD	DIRECTOR	DGA, 110 W 57TH ST	NEW YORK, NY	10019
ARTHUR, TERRY	PHOTOGRAPHER	1225 PROVIDENCE TERR	MC LEAN, VA	22101
ARTHUR, WILLIAM B, JR	NEWS CORRESPONDENT	6702 KIRKLEY AVE	MC LEAN, VA	22101
ARTHURS, RICHARD, JR	NEWS CORRESPONDENT	2906 LANDOVER ST	ALEXANDRIA, VA	22305
ARTISE, BRANDYN	ACTRESS	870 N VINE ST #B	LOS ANGELES, CA	90035

ARTYMIW, LYDIA	PIANIST	POST OFFICE BOX 30	TENAFLY, NJ	07670
ARVIDSON, CHERYL R	NEWS CORRESPONDENT	1370 "E" ST, NE	WASHINGTON, DC	20002
ARVIN, REED	PIANIST	6576 CABOT DR	NASHVILLE, TN	37209
ARWOOD, DONNA	ACTRESS	1496 N KINGS RD	LOS ANGELES, CA	90069
ASCIU, NICULAE	CARTOONIST	POST OFFICE BOX 4203	NEW YORK, NY	10017
ASCOT, LUIS	PIANIST	KAY, 58 W 58TH ST	NEW YORK, NY	10019
ASCOUGH, STANLEY L	WRITER	11983 LAURELWOOD DR #5	STUDIO CITY, CA	91604
ASEFFA, ALEXANDER	ACTOR	6430 SUNSET BLVD #1203	LOS ANGELES, CA	90028
ASH, GLENN	SINGER	7837 MASON AVE	CANOGA PARK, CA	91306
ASH, LESLIE	ACTRESS	4 CT LODGE		
		48 SLOANE SQUARE	LONDON SW1	ENGLAND
ASH, MARY KAY	COSMETIC EXECUTIVE	8787 N STEMMONS FREEWAY	DALLAS, TX	75247
ASH, MONTY	ACTOR	10850 RIVERSIDE DR #505	NORTH HOLLYWOOD, CA	91602
ASH, ROD M	TV WRITER	8955 BEVERLY BLVD	LOS ANGELES, CA	90048
ASHBAKER, HANS GREGORY	TENOR	CAMI, 165 W 57TH ST	NEW YORK, NY	10019
ASHBROOK, DAPHNE LEE	ACTRESS	1827 CANYON DR #6	HOLLYWOOD, CA	90028
ASHBY, HAL	FILM DIRECTOR	23416 MALIBU COLONY DR	MALIBU, CA	90265
ASHBY, JOHN W	WRITER	8955 BEVERLY BLVD	LOS ANGELES, CA	90048
ASHCROFT, DAME PEGGY	ACTRESS	40 FROGNAL LN, HAMPSTEAD	LONDON NW3	ENGLAND
ASHE, ARTHUR	TENNIS	360 E 72ND ST #C-1801	NEW YORK, NY	10021
ASHE, EVE BRENT	ACTRESS	3518 W CAHUENGA BLVD #316	LOS ANGELES, CA	90068
ASHE, JAMES F	PHOTOGRAPHER	6220 BERLEE DR	ALEXANDRIA, VA	22312
ASHE, JENNIFER	ACTRESS	CBS-TV, "AS THE WORLD TURNS"		
		51 W 52ND ST	NEW YORK, NY	10019
ASHE, JERRY	WRITER	8955 BEVERLY BLVD	LOS ANGELES, CA	90048
ASHE, MARTIN	ACTOR	8721 SUNSET BLVD #200	LOS ANGELES, CA	90069
ASHE, MICHAEL	ACTOR	3330 BARHAM BLVD #103	LOS ANGELES, CA	90068
ASHE, TERRY	PHOTOGRAPHER	TIME/TIME & LIFE BLDG		
		ROCKEFELLER CENTER	NEW YORK, NY	10020
ASHER, JANE	ACTRESS	CHATTO & LINNIT, LTD		
		PRINCE OF WALES THEATRE		
		COVENTRY ST	LONDON WC2	ENGLAND
ASHER, MARK	NEWS CORRESPONDENT	2829 CONNECTICUT AVE, NW	WASHINGTON, DC	20008
ASHER, MICHAEL D	CONDUCTOR	10936 1/2 HESBY ST	NORTH HOLLYWOOD, CA	91601
ASHER, MILTON D	CONDUCTOR	1631 LIVONIA AVE	LOS ANGELES, CA	90035
ASHER, PETER	RECORD PROD-AGT	644 N DOHENY DR	LOS ANGELES, CA	90069
ASHER, ROBERT L	NEWS CORRESPONDENT	6443 BARNABY ST, NW	WASHINGTON, DC	20015
ASHER, WILLIAM MILTON	WRITER-PRODUCER	17461 CAMINO YATASTO	PACIFIC PALISADES, CA	90272
ASHERTON DONAT, RENEE	ACTRESS	28 ELSWORTHY RD	LONDON NW3	ENGLAND
ASHFORD, DAVID	ACTOR	53 MOAT DR, HARROW	MIDDLESEX	ENGLAND
ASHFORD, NICHOLAS H	NEWS CORRESPONDENT	3938 MORRISON ST, NW	WASHINGTON, DC	20015
ASHFORD & SIMPSON	VOCAL DUO	RADIO CITY MUSIC HALL PRODS		
		1260 AVE OF THE AMERICAS	NEW YORK, NY	10020
ASHKENASI, SHMUEL	VIOLINIST	MARIEDL ANDERS ARTISTS MGMT		
		535 EL CAMINO DEL MAR ST	SAN FRANCISCO, CA	94121
ASHKENAZY, VLADIMIR	PIANIST	ICM, 40 W 57TH ST	NEW YORK, NY	10019
ASHLAND, CAMILA	ACTRESS	SF & A, 121 N SAN VICENTE BLVD	BEVERLY HILLS, CA	90211
ASHLEY, BECCA C	ACTRESS	9220 SUNSET BLVD #625	LOS ANGELES, CA	90069
ASHLEY, BENJAMIN	TV WRITER	8955 BEVERLY BLVD	LOS ANGELES, CA	90048
ASHLEY, DOUGLAS G	PHOTOGRAPHER	872 DURSLEY DR	BLOOMFIELD HILLS, MI	48013
ASHLEY, EDWARD	ACTOR	1879 BENECIA AVE	LOS ANGELES, CA	90025
ASHLEY, ELIZABETH	ACTRESS	9010 DORRINGTON AVE	LOS ANGELES, CA	90048
ASHLEY, JENNIFER	ACTRESS-MODEL	200 N ROBERTSON BLVD #219	BEVERLY HILLS, CA	90211
ASHLEY, JOHN	ACTOR-PRODUCER	3355 ALANA DR	SHERMAN OAKS, CA	91403
ASHLEY, LEON	SINGER-GUITARIST	POST OFFICE BOX 567	HENDERSONVILLE, TN	37075
ASHLEY, SUSANNE	ACTRESS	6310 SAN VICENTE BLVD #407	LOS ANGELES, CA	90048
ASHLEY, SUZANNE	MODEL	POST OFFICE BOX 7211	MOUNTAIN VIEW, CA	94043
ASHLEY, TED	COMMUNICATIONS EXEC	WARNER COMMUNICATIONS		
		75 ROCKEFELLER PLAZA	NEW YORK, NY	10020
ASHLEY, WILLIAM C	NEWS CORRESPONDENT	1755 S JEFFERSON DAVIS HWY	ARLINGTON, VA	22202
ASHLEY, WILSON S	WRITER	8955 BEVERLY BLVD	LOS ANGELES, CA	90048
ASHMAN, CHUCK	WRITER	111 N LAYTON DR	LOS ANGELES, CA	90049
ASHMAN, PENELOPE W	WRITER	555 W 57TH ST #1230	NEW YORK, NY	10019
ASHMORE, FRANK	ACTOR	6310 SAN VICENTE BLVD #407	LOS ANGELES, CA	90048
ASHTON, BRAD	TV-RADIO WRITER	288 SAINT PAUL'S RD		
		ISLINGTON	LONDON N1 2LR	ENGLAND
ASHTON, DAVID	ACTOR	SIMONS, 9 NEAL ST	LONDON WC2H 9PU	ENGLAND
ASHTON, DUDLEY SHAW	FILM DIRECTOR	3 DORSET HOUSE, THE AVE		
		BRANKSOME, POOLE	DORSET BH13 6HE	ENGLAND
ASHTON, JEROME	NEWS CORRESPONDENT	1800 METZEROTT RD #408	ADELPHI, MD	20783
ASHTON, JOHN DAVID	ACTOR	247 S BEVERLY DR #102	BEVERLY HILLS, CA	90210
ASHTON, LAURA	ACTRESS	KOHNER, 9169 SUNSET BLVD	LOS ANGELES, CA	90069
ASHWORTH, AUDIE	GUITARIST	POST OFFICE BOX 22635	NASHVILLE, TN	37202
ASHWORTH, ERNEST B	GUITARIST	ROUTE #4	LEWISBURG, TN	37091
ASHWORTH, ERNIE	SINGER	POST OFFICE BOX 171132	NASHVILLE, TN	37217
ASHWORTH, KENT P	NEWS CORRESPONDENT	2608 N GEORGE MASON DR	ARLINGTON, VA	22207
ASHWORTH, MIKE	GUITARIST	POST OFFICE BOX 221	LAVERGNE, TN	37086
ASIA	ROCK & ROLL GROUP	SUN ARTISTES, 9 HILLGATE ST	LONDON W8 7SP	ENGLAND
ASIMOV, ISAAC	AUTHOR	10 W 66TH ST #33-A	NEW YORK, NY	10023
ASINOF, ELIOT	WRITER	555 W 57TH ST #1230	NEW YORK, NY	10019
ASKEW, LUKE	ACTOR	247 S BEVERLY DR #102	BEVERLY HILLS, CA	90210
ASKEY, GILBERT A	CONDUCTOR	1309 S REDONDO BLVD	LOS ANGELES, CA	90019
ASKIN, LEON	ACTOR-DIRECTOR	625 N REXFORD DR	BEVERLY HILLS, CA	90210
ASKIN, PETER	WRITER	555 W 57TH ST #1230	NEW YORK, NY	10019
ASKIN, STEVE	NEWS CORRESPONDENT	1481 MONROE ST	WASHINGTON, DC	20010

ASHFORD & SIMPSON

ELIZABETH ASHLEY

JOHN ASTIN

CHET ATKINS

CHRISTOPHER ATKINS

MARY ASTOR

PATTI AUSTIN

GENE AUTRY

HOYT AXTON

ASKINS, MONROE, SR	DIRECTOR	4560 W HEMLOCK AVE		
		MANDALAY BAY	OXNARD, CA	93030
ASKWITH, ROBIN	ACTOR	ICM, 388-396 OXFORD ST	LONDON W1	ENGLAND
ASLAKSEN, DUANE	RECORD PRODUCER	POST OFFICE BOX 22129	SAN FRANCISCO, CA	94122
ASLEEP AT THE WHEEL	ROCK & ROLL GROUP	POST OFFICE BOX 463	AUSTIN, TX	78767
ASMAN, KATHRYN	MEZZO-SOPRANO	MUNRO, 334 W 72ND ST	NEW YORK, NY	10023
ASMAN, ROBERT W	NEWS CORRESPONDENT	NBC-TV, NEWS DEPARTMENT		
		4001 NEBRASKA AVE, NW	WASHINGTON, DC	20016
ASMUSSEN, WILLIAM W	DIRECTOR-PRODUCER	21601 ERWIN DR	WOODLAND HILLS, CA	91367
ASNER, EDWARD	ACTOR	3855 LANKERSHIM BLVD	NORTH HOLLYWOOD, CA	91604
ASPEL, MICHAEL	RADIO PERSONALITY	CAPITOL, EUSTON TOWER	LONDON NW1	ENGLAND
ASPINALL, TIM	WRITER-PRODUCER	62 HARTSWOOD RD	LONDON W11	ENGLAND
ASPINWALL, EVERETT H, JR	WRITER	555 W 57TH ST #1230	NEW YORK, NY	10019
ASQUITH, DON R	WRITER-PRODUCER	446 SHERMAN CANAL	VENICE, CA	90291
ASSA, RENE	ACTOR	3359 ROWENA AVE #2	LOS ANGELES, CA	90027
ASSAD, SERGIO & ODAIR	GUITAR DUO	SHAW CONCERTS, 1995 BROADWAY	NEW YORK, NY	10023
ASSAEL, DAVID	TV WRITER	530 N POINSETTIA PL	LOS ANGELES, CA	90036
ASSANTE, ARMAND	ACTOR	ICM, 8899 BEVERLY BLVD	LOS ANGELES, CA	90048
ASSASSIN #2	WRESTLER	SEE - HERNANDEZ, HERCULES		
ASSELIN, PAUL	DIRECTOR	11668 TERRY HILL PL	LOS ANGELES, CA	90049
ASSEYEV, TAMARA	FILM PRODUCER	1500 CHELTEN WY	SOUTH PASADENA, CA	91030
ASSOCIATION, THE	ROCK & ROLL GROUP	9000 SUNSET BLVD #1200	LOS ANGELES, CA	90069
AST, PAT	ACTRESS	1336 3/4 N JUNE ST	LOS ANGELES, CA	90028
ASTAIRE, JARVIS	FILM PRODUCER	JARAS, 21 CAVENDISH PL	LONDON W1M 9DL	ENGLAND
ASTAR, BEN	ACTOR	1801 N STANLEY AVE	LOS ANGELES, CA	90046
ASTIN, JOHN	ACT-WRI-DIR	1271 STONER AVE #408	LOS ANGELES, CA	90025
ASTIN, MAC KENZIE	ACTOR	266 DENSLOW AVE	LOS ANGELES, CA	90049
ASTIN, PATTY DUKE	ACTRESS	SEE - DUKE, PATTY		
ASTIN, SEAN	ACTOR	266 DENSLOW AVE	LOS ANGELES, CA	90049
ASTOURIAN, JERRY	ACTOR	4302 RAINTREE CIR	CULVER CITY, CA	90230
ASTROW, JO ANNE O	WRITER	8955 BEVERLY BLVD	LOS ANGELES, CA	90048
ATHERTON, DAVID	CONDUCTOR	SHAW CONCERTS, 1995 BROADWAY	NEW YORK, NY	10023
ATHERTON, JAMES	TENOR	CONE, 221 W 57TH ST	NEW YORK, NY	10019
ATHERTON, JAMES E	DRUMMER	8028 STALLION CT	NASHVILLE, TN	37221
ATHERTON, JAMES K W	PHOTOJOURNALIST	2913 STANTON AVE	SILVER SPRING, MD	20910
ATHERTON, WILLIAM	ACTOR	11726 SAN VICENTE BLVD #300	LOS ANGELES, CA	90049
ATKIN, HENRY	ACTOR	CAGNEY & LACEY, 2630 LACY ST	LOS ANGELES, CA	90031
ATKIN, HILLARY C	WRITER	1227 10TH ST #3	SANTA MONICA, CA	90401
ATKINS	ROCK & ROLL GROUP	9454 WILSHIRE BLVD #309	BEVERLY HILLS, CA	90212
ATKINS, CHET	GUITARIST	806 17TH AVE S	NASHVILLE, TN	37203
ATKINS, CHRISTOPHER	ACTOR	3751 SUNSWEPT DR	STUDIO CITY, CA	91604
ATKINS, DAVE	SINGER	9271 S WAYNE RD	ROMULUS, MI	48174
ATKINS, EILEEN	ACTRESS	65 ENNISMORE GARDENS	LONDON SW7	ENGLAND
ATKINS, GEORGE	TV WRITER	8955 BEVERLY BLVD	LOS ANGELES, CA	90048
ATKINS, IRVIN S	TV DIRECTOR	1450 SUNSET PLAZA DR	LOS ANGELES, CA	90069
ATKINS, PAMELA S	NEWS CORRESPONDENT	6058 LEESBURG PIKE	FALLS CHURCH, VA	22041
ATKINS, TOM	ACTOR	211 S BEVERLY DR #201	BEVERLY HILLS, CA	90212
ATKINS, VIRGINIA L	NEWS CORRESPONDENT	10023 GREENROCK RD	SILVER SPRING, MD	20901
ATKINS, WILLIAM L	PHOTOGRAPHER	5305 PORTSMOUTH RD	FAIRFAX, VA	22032
ATKINSON, BEVERLY HOPE	ACTRESS	8350 SANTA MONICA BLVD #206-A	LOS ANGELES, CA	90069
ATKINSON, BUTLER M	WRITER	12659 MOORPARK ST #9	STUDIO CITY, CA	91604
ATKINSON, DON	ACTOR	68 ST MARKS PL	NEW YORK, NY	10003
ATKINSON, KEITH J	WRITER-PRODUCER	DGA, 7950 SUNSET BLVD	LOS ANGELES, CA	90046
ATKINSON, ROWAN	ACTOR-COMEDIAN	NOEL GAY, 24 DENMARK ST	LONDON WC2H 8NJ	ENGLAND
ATLAN, JEAN-LOUIS	PHOTOGRAPHER	1730 16TH ST, NW	WASHINGTON, DC	20009
ATLANTA	VOCAL GROUP	POST OFFICE BOX 550425	ATLANATA, GA	30355
ATLANTA, MR	WRESTLER	SEE - MC DANIEL, CHIEF WAHOO		
ATLANTA RHYTHM SECTION	ROCK & ROLL GROUP	VARIETY ARTISTS INTL, INC		
		9073 NEMO ST, 3RD FLOOR	LOS ANGELES, CA	90069
ATLANTIC STARR	RHYTHM & BLUES GROUP	10100 SANTA MONICA BLVD #1600	LOS ANGELES, CA	90067
ATLANTICS, THE	VOCAL GROUP	F MUNAO, 113 W 70TH ST	NEW YORK, NY	10023
ATLAS, BLACK	WRESTLER	SEE - ATLAS, TONY		
ATLAS, JACOBA	WRITER	124 S SYRACUSE AVE	LOS ANGELES, CA	90036
ATLAS, LARRY	ACTOR	NBC-TV, 30 ROCKEFELLER PLAZA	NEW YORK, NY	10112
ATLAS, S TERRY	NEWS CORRESPONDENT	3123 N 17TH ST	ARLINGTON, VA	22201
ATLAS, TONY	WRESTLER	WORLD CLASS WRESTLING		
		SOUTHWEST SPORTS, INC		
		DALLAS SPORTATORIUM		
		1000 S INDUSTRIAL BLVD	DALLAS, TX	75207
ATOMIX, THE	ROCK & ROLL GROUP	POST OFFICE BOX 1600	HAVERHILL, MA	01831
ATTALLAH, NAIM	FILM-TV PRODUCER	45 POLAND ST	LONDON W1	ENGLAND
ATTANASIO, PAUL	FILM CRITIC	THE WASHINGTON POST		
		1150 15TH ST, NW	WASHINGTON, DC	20071
ATTARD, TONY	WRITER-PRODUCER	41 WOODLAND RISE		
		MUSWELL HILL	LONDON N10 3UN	ENGLAND
ATTAWAY, FRITZ E	FILM EXECUTIVE	PERFORMING ARTISTS		
		1600 "I" ST, NW	WASHINGTON, DC	20036
ATTAWAY, LEROY B	WRITER	555 W 57TH ST #1230	NEW YORK, NY	10019
ATTAWAY, RUTH	ACTRESS	400 W 43RD ST	NEW YORK, NY	10036
ATTAWAY, WILLIAM	TV WRITER	555 W 57TH ST #1230	NEW YORK, NY	10019
ATTEBURY, CLARK M	TV DIRECTOR	19968 LANCASTER	HARPER WOODS, MI	48225
ATTELL, TONI	ACTRESS	6736 LAUREL CANYON BLVD #306	NORTH HOLLYWOOD, CA	91606
ATTENBOROUGH, DAVID	TV PRODUCER	5 PARK RD, RICHMOND	SURREY	ENGLAND
ATTENBOROUGH, DAVID	WRITER-PRODUCER	BBC-TV CENTRE, WOOD LN		
		SHEPHERDS BUSH	LONDON W12	ENGLAND

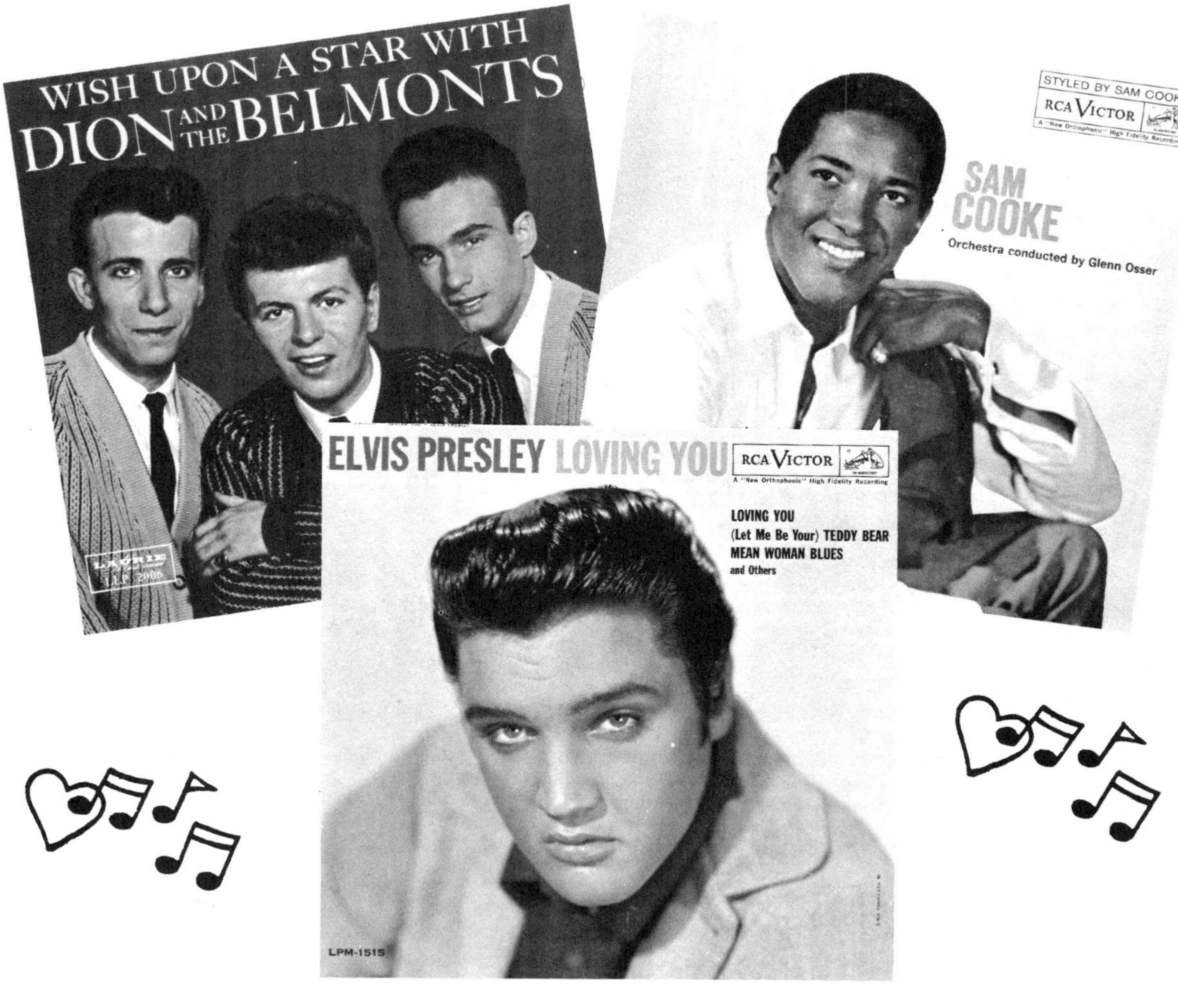

Name	Occupation	Address	City	Zip / Country
ATTENBOROUGH, RICHARD	ACT-WRI-PROD	OLD FARMS, BEAVER LODGE		
		RICHMOND GREEN	SURREY	ENGLAND
ATTERBURY, MALCOLM	ACTOR	605 N CAMDEN DR	BEVERLY HILLS, CA	90210
ATTERBURY, MALCOLM, JR	DIRECTOR	3446 CRANE CT	CLAREMONT, CA	91711
ATTIAS, DANIEL	FILM DIRECTOR	534 23RD ST	SANTA MONICA, CA	90402
ATTILA	ROCK & ROLL GROUP	POST OFFICE BOX 5205	BABYLON, NY	11707
ATWATER, GLADYS	WRITER	8955 BEVERLY BLVD	LOS ANGELES, CA	90048
ATWELL, NORMAN "JO JO"	CLOWN	2701 COTTAGE WY #14	SACRAMENTO, CA	95825
ATWOOD, MARILYN	NEWS CORRESPONDENT	2510 VIRGINIA AVE, NW	WASHINGTON, DC	20037
ATWOOD, TIMOTHY E	GUITARIST	574 BLAKE MOORE	LAVERGNE, TN	37086
ATZMON, MOSHE	CONDUCTOR	ICM, 40 W 57TH ST	NEW YORK, NY	10019
AUBEL, BARBARA	SOPRANO	CAMI, 165 W 57TH ST	NEW YORK, NY	10019
AUBERJONOIS, RENE	ACTOR	448 S ARDEN BLVD	LOS ANGELES, CA	90020
AUBREY, JAMES	ACTOR	67 DURLSTON RD	LONDON E5	ENGLAND
AUBREY, JAMES T	PRODUCER	1426 SEABRIGHT PL	BEVERLY HILLS, CA	90210
AUBREY, LIZABETH	ACTRESS	6310 SAN VICENTE BLVD #407	LOS ANGELES, CA	90048
AUBREY, OLIVER	ACTOR	4789 VINELAND AVE #100	NORTH HOLLYWOOD, CA	91602
AUBREY, SKYE	ACTRESS	ICM, 8899 BEVERLY BLVD	LOS ANGELES, CA	90048
AUBRY, DANIEL L	WRITER	8955 BEVERLY BLVD	LOS ANGELES, CA	90048
AUBRY, DANIELLE	ACTRESS	208 S BEVERLY DR #4	BEVERLY HILLS, CA	90212
AUBRY, RENEE	ACTRESS	357 S REXFORD DR #203	BEVERLY HILLS, CA	90212
AUBRY, TIMOTHY R	PHOTOGRAPHER	3 WASHINGTON CIR, NW	WASHINGTON, DC	20007
AUBUCHON, J REMI	DIRECTOR	DGA, 7950 SUNSET BLVD	LOS ANGELES, CA	90046
AUBUCHON, JACQUES	ACTOR	20978 RIOS ST	WOODLAND HILLS, CA	91364
AUBUCHON, JEAN	ACTRESS	6430 SUNSET BLVD #701	LOS ANGELES, CA	90028
AUBUCHON, JOHN B	NEWS CORRESPONDENT	184 CALHOUN ST	EDGEWATER, MD	21037
AUBURNE, PATRICA	ACTRESS	4789 VINELAND AVE #100	NORTH HOLLYWOOD, CA	91602
AUCHINCLOSS, GORDON	WRITER	555 W 57TH ST #1230	NEW YORK, NY	10019
AUCHINCLOSS, KENNETH	PUBLISH EXECUTIVE	NEWSWEEK, 444 MADISON AVE	NEW YORK, NY	10022
AUCOIN, WILLIAM	DIRECTOR	645 MADISON AVE	NEW YORK, NY	10022
AUDD, RICHARD M	COMPOSER-CONDUCTOR	17400 BURBANK BLVD #206	ENCINO, CA	91316
AUDIARD, MICHEL	WRITER	ARTMEDIA, 10 AVE GEORGE V	PARIS 75008	FRANCE
AUDICK, GEORGE M	NEWS CORRESPONDENT	400 N CAPITOL ST, NW	WASHINGTON, DC	20001
AUDLEY, MAXINE	ACTRESS	EVANS, 52 BEAUCHAMP PL	LONDON SW3	ENGLAND
AUDLEY, NANCY	TV WRITER	854 NOWITA PL	VENICE, CA	90291
AUDRA	VOCAL DUO	TWM, 641 LEXINGTON AVE	NEW YORK, NY	10022
AUER, EDWARD	PIANIST	POST OFFICE BOX 1515	NEW YORK, NY	10023
AUER, MILES BOHM	TALENT AGENT	8162 MANITOBA ST #119	PLAYA DEL REY, CA	90291
AUERBACH, DAVID	TV EXECUTIVE	11811 W OLYMPIC BLVD	LOS ANGELES, CA	90064
AUERBACH, DAVID	TV DIRECTOR	8636 LOOKOUT MOUNTAIN AVE	LOS ANGELES, CA	90046
AUERBACH, GERALD	DIRECTOR	23 MAPLE LN	ESSEX FALLS, NJ	07021
AUERBACH, JANE	TV WRITER-EXECUTIVE	10272 DUNLEER DR	LOS ANGELES, CA	90064
AUERBACH, LARRY	DIRECTOR	32 COUNTRY RD	MAMARONECK, NY	10543
AUERBACH, LARRY	TV DIRECTOR	ABC-TV, "ONE LIFE TO LIVE"		
		1330 AVE OF THE AMERICAS	NEW YORK, NY	10019
AUERBACH, NORBERT	FILM EXECUTIVE	729 7TH AVE	NEW YORK, NY	10019
AUERBACH, RICHARD	DIRECTOR-PRODUCER	105 SHERMAN AVE W	WHITE PLAINS, NY	10607
AUERBACH, STUART C	NEWS CORRESPONDENT	4624 ASBURY PL, NW	WASHINGTON, DC	20016
AUFDERHEIDE, PAT	NEWS CORRESPONDENT	3136 17TH ST, NW	WASHINGTON, DC	20010
AUG, STEPHEN	NEWS CORRESPONDENT	ABC NEWS, 7 W 66TH ST	NEW YORK, NY	10023
AUGER, ARLEEN	SOPRANO	IMG ARTISTS, 22 E 71ST ST	NEW YORK, NY	10021
AUGER, CLAUDINE	ACTRESS	151 S EL CAMINO DR	BEVERLY HILLS, CA	90212
AUGUST	ROCK & ROLL GROUP	CAPURSO, 6 IMPERIAL RD	WORCHESTER, MA	01604
AUGUST, BOB	COLUMNIST	UNIVERSAL PRESS SYNDICATE		
		4900 MAIN ST, 9TH FLOOR	KANSAS CITY, MO	62114
AUGUST, HELEN	WRITER	8955 BEVERLY BLVD	LOS ANGELES, CA	90048
AUGUST, MELISSA	NEWS CORRESPONDENT	9225 COLEVILLE RD	SILVER SPRING, MD	20910
AUGUST, TOM	WRITER	SEE - LEVITT, ALFRED L		
AUGUSTAIN, IRA	ACTOR	9200 SUNSET BLVD #909	LOS ANGELES, CA	90069
AUGUSTINI, MAURO	BASSO-BARITONE	111 W 57TH ST #1209	NEW YORK, NY	10019
AUKOFER, FRANK A	NEWS CORRESPONDENT	4015 THORNTON ST	ANNANDALE, VA	22203
AULETTA, ROBERT	CONDUCTOR	3844 VALLEYBRINK RD	LOS ANGELES, CA	90039
AUMAIER, BEVERLY	CLOWN	2701 COTTAGE WY #14	SACRAMENTO, CA	95825
AUMAIER, DEON	CLOWN	2701 COTTAGE WY #14	SACRAMENTO, CA	95825
AUMONT, JEAN-PIERRE	ACTOR	LORCASTER AGENCE		
		27 RUE DE RICHELIER	PARIS 75001	FRANCE
AURANDT, RICHARD D	COMPOSER-CONDUCTOR	10406 MAGNOLIA BLVD	NORTH HOLLYWOOD, CA	91601
AUREL, JEAN	WRITER	40 RUE LAURISTON	PARIS 75116	FRANCE
AURELIO, RICHARD	COMMUNICATIONS EXEC	WARNER COMMUNICATIONS		
		1211 AVE OF THE AMERICAS	NEW YORK, NY	10036
AURITT, JOAN REISNER	DIRECTOR	175 W 73RD ST	NEW YORK, NY	10023
AUSLEY, JOHN	WRITER	8955 BEVERLY BLVD	LOS ANGELES, CA	90048
AUSSEL, ROBERTO	GUITARIST	GERSHUNOFF, 502 PARK AVE	NEW YORK, NY	10022
AUSTEN, IAN	NEWS CORRESPONDENT	1331 PENNSYLVANIA AVE, NW	WASHINGTON, DC	20004
AUSTIN, ALAN	WRITER	8955 BEVERLY BLVD	LOS ANGELES, CA	90048
AUSTIN, ANDREW	WRITER	555 W 57TH ST #1230	NEW YORK, NY	10019
AUSTIN, DOROTHEA	COMPOSER	FINELL, 155 W 68TH ST	NEW YORK, NY	10023
AUSTIN, JENNIE	SINGER	O & L, 10051 GREENLEAF	SANTA FE SPRINGS, CA	90670
AUSTIN, KAREN	ACTRESS	9220 SUNSET BLVD #625	LOS ANGELES, CA	90069
AUSTIN, KAY	SINGER	FROST/FROST, 3985 W TAFT DR	SPOKANE, WA	99208
AUSTIN, LYN	THEATER PRODUCER	18 E 68TH ST	NEW YORK, NY	10021
AUSTIN, MICHAEL	SCREENWRITER	1888 CENTURY PARK E #1400	LOS ANGELES, CA	90067
AUSTIN, MICHAEL	TENOR	LEW, 204 W 10TH ST	NEW YORK, NY	10014
AUSTIN, PATTI	SINGER	10100 SANTA MONICA BLVD #1600	LOS ANGELES, CA	90067

AUSTIN, RAY	COMPOSER-CONDUCTOR	1545 GLENOVER DR	PASADENA, CA	91105
AUSTIN, RAY	TV DIRECTOR	8855 HOLLYWOOD BLVD	LOS ANGELES, CA	90068
AUSTIN, ROBERT	DRUMMER	820 SUTTON HILL RD	NASHVILLE, TN	37204
AUSTIN, RONALD	WRITER-PRODUCER	1888 CENTURY PARK E #1400	LOS ANGELES, CA	90067
AUSTIN, TERI	ACTRESS	2121 AVE OF THE STARS #410	LOS ANGELES, CA	90067
AUSTRALIA	C & W GROUP	TAYLOR, 2401 12TH AVE S	NASHVILLE, TN	37204
AUTANT-LARA, CLAUDE	DIRECTOR	66 RUE LEPIC	PARIS 75018	FRANCE
AUTH, TONY	CARTOONIST	PHILADELPHIA INQUIRER		
		400 N BROAD ST	PHILADELPHIA, PA	19101
AUTH, WILLIAM COLLINS	PHOTOGRAPHER	1054 KNIGHT LN	HERNDON, VA	22070
AUTOGRAPH	ROCK & ROLL GROUP	17530 VENTURA BLVD #105	ENCINO, CA	91316
AUTRY, DAVID E	NEWS CORRESPONDENT	1830 CALIFORNIA ST, NW	WASHINGTON, DC	20009
AUTRY, GENE	ACT-SING-EXEC	3171 BROOKDALE RD	NORTH HOLLYWOOD, CA	91604
AUTUMN	VOCAL GROUP	POST OFFICE BOX O	EXCELSIOR, MN	55331
AUTUORI, EMILE	ACTOR	4555 SYLMAR AVE #117	SHERMAN OAKS, CA	91423
AVAKIAN, ARAM	DIRECTOR	151 S EL CAMINO DR	BEVERLY HILLS, CA	90212
AVAKIAN, TERRY	ACTOR	11734 WILSHIRE BLVD #C-1516	LOS ANGELES, CA	90025
AVALON, FRANKIE	ACTOR-SINGER	24965 KIT CARSON DR	HIDDEN HILLS, CA	91302
AVANT, CLARENCE	TALENT AGENT	3580 WILSHIRE BLVD #1820	LOS ANGELES, CA	90011
AVAR, JANOS	NEWS CORRESPONDENT	4515 WILLARD AVE	CHEVY CHASE, MD	20815
AVEDIS, HOWARD "HIKMET"	WRITER-DIRECTOR	13521 RAND DR	SHERMAN OAKS, CA	91423
AVEDON, BARBARA HAMMER	WRITER	2317 OAKWOOD AVE	VENICE, CA	90291
AVEDON, RICHARD	PHOTOGRAPHER	407 E 75TH ST	NEW YORK, NY	10021
AVENUE	ROCK & ROLL GROUP	1254 LAMAR AVE #312	MEMPHIS, TN	38114
AVERAGE WHITE BAND, THE	ROCK & ROLL GROUP	3 E 54TH ST #1400	NEW YORK, NY	10022
AVERBACK, HY	FILM-TV DIRECTOR	1525 BLUE JAY WY	LOS ANGELES, CA	90069
AVERY, BRIAN	ACTOR	721 N LA BREA AVE #200	LOS ANGELES, CA	90038
AVERY, JAMES	ACTOR	LIGHT, 113 N ROBERTSON BLVD	LOS ANGELES, CA	90048
AVERY, JEANNE	COLUMNIST	NEWS AMERICA SYNDICATE		
		1703 KAISER AVE	IRVINE, CA	92714
AVERY, MARGARET	ACTRESS	2807 PELHAM PL	LOS ANGELES, CA	90068
AVERY, PATRICIA A	NEWS CORRESPONDENT	2500 "Q" ST, NW	WASHINGTON, DC	20007
AVERY, RICK	STUNTMAN	3518 W CAHUENGA BLVD #300	LOS ANGELES, CA	90068
AVERY, SID	DIRECTOR	3875 BEVERLY RIDGE DR	SHERMAN OAKS, CA	91423
AVERY, VAL	ACTOR	84 GROVE ST #19	NEW YORK, NY	10014
AVIAN, BOB	THEATER PRODUCER	QUAD PRODS, 890 BROADWAY	NEW YORK, NY	10003
AVILA, CHRISTINE	ACTRESS	11726 SAN VICENTE BLVD #300	LOS ANGELES, CA	90049
AVILA, CYNTHIA	ACTRESS	13334 VALLEY VISTA BLVD	VAN NUYS, CA	91423
AVILA, FRANK	ACTOR	8820 SUNSET BLVD #ANB	LOS ANGELES, CA	90069
AVILDSEN, JOHN G	FILM WRITER-DIRECTOR	45 E 89TH ST #37-A	NEW YORK, NY	10028
AVILDSEN, THOMAS K	FILM DIRECTOR	7501 TOPEKA DR	RESEDA, CA	91335
AVILDSEN, TOM	FILM DIRECTOR	9200 SUNSET BLVD #201	LOS ANGELES, CA	90069
AVINS, MIMI	WRITER-EDITOR	US MAGAZINE COMPANY		
		1 DAG HAMMARSKJOLD PLAZA	NEW YORK, NY	10017
AVION	ROCK & ROLL GROUP	POST OFFICE BOX 404	PENT HILLS NSW 2RO	AUSTRALIA
AVNER, PHILIP J	NEWS CORRESPONDENT	1825 "K" ST, NW	WASHINGTON, DC	20006
AVNET, JONATHAN	FILM-TV DIRECTOR	20911 W COLINA DR	TOPANGA CANYON, CA	90290
AVOLA, ALEXANDER A	COMPOSER-CONDUCTOR	10944 MOORPARK ST	NORTH HOLLYWOOD, CA	91602
AVRAMOV, BOGIDAR V	CONDUCTOR	321 N REXFORD DR	BEVERLY HILLS, CA	90210
AVRECH, ROBERT J	WRITER	211 S BEVERLY DR #201	BEVERLY HILLS, CA	90212
AVRIL, FRANCK	OBOIST	AFFILIATE ARTISTS, INC		
		37 W 65TH ST, 6TH FLOOR	NEW YORK, NY	10023
AX	WRESTLER	SEE - DEMOLITION		
AX, EMANUEL	PIANIST	ICM, 40 W 57TH ST	NEW YORK, NY	10019
AXE	ROCK & ROLL GROUP	ATI, 888 7TH AVE, 21ST FLOOR	NEW YORK, NY	10106
AXELMAN, ARTHUR	TALENT AGENT	151 S EL CAMINO DR	BEVERLY HILLS, CA	90212
AXELROD, DAVID	COMPOSER-CONDUCTOR	5856 1/2 WOODMAN AVE	VAN NUYS, CA	91401
AXELROD, DAVID	TV WRITER	555 W 57TH ST #1230	NEW YORK, NY	10019
AXELROD, GEORGE	PLAYWRIGHT	1840 CARLA RIDGE ST	BEVERLY HILLS, CA	90210
AXELROD, JONATHAN	TV EXECUTIVE	8960 SAINT IVES DR	LOS ANGELES, CA	90069
AXELROD, JONATHAN	WRITER	1243 N WETHERLY DR	LOS ANGELES, CA	90069
AXELROD, NINA	ACTRESS	STONE, 1052 CAROL DR	LOS ANGELES, CA	90069
AXELROD, ROBERT	ACTOR	2074 PARAMOUNT DR #305	LOS ANGELES, CA	90068
AXTHELM, PETE	SPORTSCASTER	NBC-TV, SPORTS DEPARTMENT		
		30 ROCKEFELLER PLAZA	NEW YORK, NY	10112
AXTON, HOYT	SINGER-SONGWRITER	POST OFFICE BOX 614	TAHOE CITY, CA	95730
AYALA ACROBATIC TROUPE	ACROBATIC TROUPE	HALL, 138 FROG HOLLOW RD	CHURCHVILLE, PA	18966
AYATOLLAH, SHEIK	WRESTLER	SEE - BLACKWELL, CRUSHER JERRY		
AYBAR, ANDY	ACTOR	1607 N EL CENTRO AVE #23	LOS ANGELES, CA	90028
AYER, HAROLD	ACTOR	4228 CAMELLIA AVE	NORTH HOLLYWOOD, CA	91604
AYER, SIMON	CASTING DIRECTOR	MTM, 4024 RADFORD AVE	STUDIO CITY, CA	91604
AYEROFF, FREDERICK	WRITER	1553 DURANGO AVE	LOS ANGELES, CA	90035
AYERS, CLIFF	SINGER-RECORD PROD	62 MUSIC SQUARE W	NASHVILLE, TN	37203
AYERS, GERALD	SCREENWRITER	151 S EL CAMINO DR	BEVERLY HILLS, CA	90212
AYERS, ROY	VIBRAHARPIST	1860 BROADWAY #1518	NEW YORK, NY	10023
AYERS, VIRGINIA	WRITER	8955 BEVERLY BLVD	LOS ANGELES, CA	90048
AYKROYD, DAN	ACT-WRI-COMED	8955 BEVERLY BLVD	LOS ANGELES, CA	90048
AYKROYD, PETER	WRITER	555 W 57TH ST #1230	NEW YORK, NY	10019
AYLESWORTH, JOHN	WRITER	3217 OVERLAND AVE #7103	LOS ANGELES, CA	90034
AYRES, B DRUMMOND, JR	NEWS CORRESPONDENT	6807 NESBITT PL	MC LEAN, VA	22101
AYRES, DESIREE KERNS	ACTRESS	LIGHT, 113 N ROBERTSON BLVD	LOS ANGELES, CA	90048
AYRES, EUGENE C	WRITER	12618 SARAH ST	STUDIO CITY, CA	91604
AYRES, GERALD	WRITER-PRODUCER	1403 N LAUREL AVE #A	LOS ANGELES, CA	90046
AYRES, LEAH	ACTRESS	8500 WILSHIRE BLVD #506	BEVERLY HILLS, CA	90211
AYRES, LEW	ACTOR	675 WALTHER WY	LOS ANGELES, CA	90049

Name	Occupation	Address	City	Zip / Country
AYRES, MARAY	ACTRESS	SCHOEMAN, 2600 W VICTORY BLVD	BURBANK, CA	91505
AYRES, ROSALIND	ACTRESS	LONDON MANAGEMENT, LTD		
		235-241 REGENT ST	LONDON W1A 2JT	ENGLAND
AZAGURY, JACQUES	FASHION DESIGNER	16 HOLLEN ST	LONDON W1	ENGLAND
AZAROW, MARTIN	ACTOR	15010 VENTURA BLVD #219	SHERMAN OAKS, CA	91403
AZELTON, PHIL	CONDUCTOR	1208 SUNSET AVE	SANTA MONICA, CA	90405
AZENBERG, EMANUEL	THEATER PRODUCER	165 W 46TH ST	NEW YORK, NY	10036
AZENZER, ARTHUR	CONDUCTOR	6447 ELLENVIEW AVE	CANOGA PARK, CA	91307
AZEVEDO, HELEN	TV PRODUCER	ESTRADA, 1875 CENTURY PARK E	LOS ANGELES, CA	90067
AZIMUTH	JAZZ GROUP	ECM RECORDS COMPANY		
		GLEICHMANNSTRABE 10	8000 MUNCHEN 60	GERMANY
AZKOUL, JAD	GUITARIST	AFFILIATE ARTISTS, INC		
		37 W 65TH ST, 6TH FLOOR	NEW YORK, NY	10023
AZLANT, EDWARD	TV WRITER	8955 BEVERLY BLVD	LOS ANGELES, CA	90048
AZNAVOUR, CHARLES	SINGER	4 AVE DE LIEULEE	GALLUIS 78	FRANCE
AZOFF, IRVING	FILM PROD-RECORD EXEC	MCA RECORDS COMPANY		
		70 UNIVERSAL CITY PLAZA	UNIVERSAL CITY, CA	91608
AZTEC CAMERA	ROCK & ROLL GROUP	ICM, 40 W 57TH ST	NEW YORK, NY	10019
AZUMA, ATSUKO	SOPRANO	59 E 54TH ST #81	NEW YORK, NY	10022
AZYMUTH	JAZZ TRIO	POST OFFICE BOX 1040	24000 NITEROI	BRAZIL
AZYMUTH	ROCK & ROLL GROUP	POST OFFICE BOX 7308	CARMEL, CA	93923
AZZARA, CANDICE	ACTRESS	8500 WILSHIRE BLVD #506	BEVERLY HILLS, CA	90211
AZZARI, THOMAS	DIRECTOR	17847 TARZANA ST	ENCINO, CA	91316
AZZARITI, THOMAS	WRITER	555 W 57TH ST #1230	NEW YORK, NY	10019
AZZERI, JOSE	WRESTLER	SEE - IRON SHEIK, THE		
AZZOLI, VAL	RECORD EXECUTIVE	ANTHEM, 189 CARLTON ST	TORONTO, ONT M5A 2K7	CANADA

Name	Occupation	Address	City	Zip / Country
B A D	ROCK & ROLL GROUP	SEE - BIG AUDIO DYNAMITE		
B G K	ROCK & ROLL GROUP	POST OFFICE BOX 70397	AMSTERDAM 1007 KJ	HOLLAND
B PEOPLE	ROCK & ROLL GROUP	POST OFFICE BOX 2428	EL SEGUNDO, CA	90245
B STREET BOMBERS	ROCK & ROLL GROUP	ROCKFEVER, 535 BROADWAY	LAWRENCE, MA	01841
B T EXPRESS	SOUL GROUP	DAVIS, 366 HALSEY ST	BROOKLYN, NY	11216
B T O	ROCK & ROLL GROUP	SEE - BACHMAN-TURNER OVERDRIVE		
B-52'S	ROCK & ROLL GROUP	GARY FURFIST, OVERLAND PRODS		
		1775 BROADWAY, 7TH FLOOR	NEW YORK, NY	10019
BABA, DONALD P	COMPOSER	477 W GAINSBOROUGH RD #106	THOUSAND OAKS, CA	91360
BABAK, RENATA	MEZZO-SOPRANO	GERSHUNOFF, 502 PARK AVE	NEW YORK, NY	10022
BABBIN, JAQUELINE	WRITER-PRODUCER	ABC TELEVISION NETWORK		
		1330 AVE OF THE AMERICAS	NEW YORK, NY	10019
BABBITT, HARRY	CONDUCTOR	7 RUE SAINT CLOUD	NEWPORT BEACH, CA	92660
BABBS, DONNA	SINGER	BROTHERS, 141 DUNBAR AVE	FORDS, NJ	08863
BABCOCK, BARBARA	ACTRESS	211 S BEVERLY DR #201	BEVERLY HILLS, CA	90212
BABCOCK, BRUCE H	COMPOSER	8404 MAMMOTH AVE	PANORAMA CITY, CA	91402
BABCOCK, CHARLES R	NEWS CORRESPONDENT	5220 41ST ST, NW	WASHINGTON, DC	20015
BABCOCK, EDWARD C	COMPOSER-CONDUCTOR	POST OFFICE BOX 44	BRANT LAKE, NY	12815
BABCOCK, JOHN C	TALENT AGENT	518 N LA CIENEGA BLVD	LOS ANGELES, CA	90048
BABCOCK, JOSEPH	GUITARIST	ROUTE #1, PEYTONSVILLE	FRANKLIN, TN	37064
BABCOCK, MARTHA K	REPORTER	TIME & PEOPLE MAGAZINE		
		TIME & LIFE BUILDING		
		ROCKEFELLER CENTER	NEW YORK, NY	10020
BABE, THOMAS	WRITER	555 W 57TH ST #1230	NEW YORK, NY	10019
BABET, PHILIP	WRITER	1037 HYPERION AVE #208	LOS ANGELES, CA	90029
BABILONIA, TAI	ICE SKATER	13889 VALLEY VISTA BLVD	SHERMAN OAKS, CA	91423
BABKA, NANCY	ACTRESS	5000 LANKERSHIM BLVD #5	NORTH HOLLYWOOD, CA	91601
BABSON, THOMAS	ACTOR	9165 SUNSET BLVD #202	LOS ANGELES, CA	90069
BABY DOLL	WRESTLING VALET	NATIONAL WRESTLING ALLIANCE		
		JIM CROCKETT PROMOTIONS		
		421 BRIARBEND DR	CHARLOTTE, NC	28209
BABY PEGGY	ACTRESS	SEE - MONTGOMERY, BABY PEGGY		
BABY SANDY	ACTRESS	SEE - MAGEE, SANDRA LEE		
		HENVILLE		
BABYSITTERS, THE	ROCK & ROLL GROUP	41 BRITAIN ST #200	TORONTO, ONT	CANADA
BACA, LINDA	CASTING DIRECTOR	451 N LA CIENEGA BLVD	LOS ANGELES, CA	90048
BACAL, DAVE	COMPOSER	7850 MORELLA AVE	NORTH HOLLYWOOD, CA	91605
BACAL, HARVEY	COMPOSER	7244 HILLSIDE AVE #309	LOS ANGELES, CA	90046
BACALL, AARON	CARTOONIST	POST OFFICE BOX 4203	NEW YORK, NY	10017
BACALL, LAUREN	ACTRESS	1 W 72ND ST #43	NEW YORK, NY	10023
BACALLA, DONNA LEE	ACTRESS	451 SAN VICENTE BLVD #9	SANTA MONICA, CA	90402
BACCO, DEIDRE M	VIOLINIST	2404 OAKLAND AVE	NASHVILLE, TN	37212
BACCO, SAMUEL DAVID	PERCUSSIONIST	2404 OAKLAND AVE	NASHVILLE, TN	37212
BACH, BARBARA	ACTRESS	TITTENHURST PARK, ASCOT	SURREY	ENGLAND
BACH, BYRON	CELLIST	6239 BRESSLYN RD	NASHVILLE, TN	37205
BACH, CATHERINE	ACTRESS	14000 DAVANA TERR	SHERMAN OAKS, CA	91403
BACH, DANILO	SCREENWRITER	1001 GEORGINA AVE	SANTA MONICA, CA	90402
BACH, DEL-BOURREE	BASS	45 W 60TH ST #4-K	NEW YORK, NY	10023
BACH, MICKEY	COLUMNIST	NEWS AMERICA SYNDICATE		
		1703 KAISER AVE	IRVINE, CA	92714

THE B-52'S
Kate Pierson • Keith Strickland • Cindy Wilson • Fred Schneider • Ricky Wilson

THE BANGLES
Debbie Peterson • Vicki Peterson • Susanna Hoffs • Michael Steele

Name	Occupation	Address	City	Zip
BACH, STEVE	PIANIST	POST OFFICE BOX 1027	HERMOSA BEACH, CA	90254
BACH, STEVEN	FILM WRITER-PRODUCER	746 S ORANGE DR	LOS ANGELES, CA	90036
BACHAND, LORRAINE P	NEWS CORRESPONDENT	1719 PRESTON RD	ALEXANDRIA, VA	22302
BACHARACH, BURT	COMPOSER-PIANIST	658 NIMES RD	LOS ANGELES, CA	90077
BACHARDY, DON	WRITER	145 ADELAIDE DR	SANTA MONICA, CA	90402
BACHELER, DAVID F	NEWS CORRESPONDENT	6505 LIGNUM ST	SPRINGFIELD, VA	22150
BACHELOR, STEPHANIE	ACTRESS	HURLEY MANAGEMENT		
		2231 W CHARLESTON BLVD	LAS VEGAS, NV	89102
BACHMAN, RANDY	SINGER	2029 CENTURY PARK E #450	LOS ANGELES, CA	90067
BACHMAN-TURNER OVERDRIVE	ROCK & ROLL GROUP	S L FELDMAN & ASSOCIATES		
		1534 W 2ND AVE, 3RD FLOOR	VANCOUVER, BC V6J 1H2	CANADA
BACHMANN, LAWRENCE P	WRITER	9224 ALCOTT ST	LOS ANGELES, CA	90035
BACHNER, ANNETTE	DIRECTOR	360 1ST AVE	NEW YORK, NY	10010
BACHRACH, BRADFORD K	PHOTOGRAPHER	50 WINDSOR RD	WELLESLEY HILLS, MA	02181
BACHRACH, CHARLES L	BROADCAST EXECUTIVE	OGILVY, 2 E 48TH ST	NEW YORK, NY	10017
BACHRACH, LOUIS F	PHOTOGRAPHER	41 SOMERSET RD	WEST NEWTON, MA	02165
BACK, ANDREE	SOPRANO	POST OFFICE BOX U	REDDING, CT	06875
BACK BAY BRASS QUINTET	BRASS QUINTET	POST OFFICE BOX 20548	NEW YORK, NY	10025
BACK BEHIND THE BARN BOYS	C & W GROUP	POST OFFICE BOX O	EXCELSIOR, MN	55331
BACKDOORS, THE	ROCK & ROLL GROUP	41 BRITAIN ST #200	TORONTO, ONT	CANADA
BACKE, JOHN D	TV EXECUTIVE	224 CREST RD	RIDGEWOOD, NJ	07450
BACKER, BRIAN	ACTOR	10100 SANTA MONICA BLVD #1600	LOS ANGELES, CA	90067
BACKES, ALICE	ACTRESS	8721 SUNSET BLVD #103	LOS ANGELES, CA	90069
BACKSTREET	C & W GROUP	4615 SOUTHWEST FREEWAY #475	HOUSTON, TX	77027
BACKUS, HENNY	ACTRESS	10914 BELLAGIO RD	LOS ANGELES, CA	90077
BACKUS, JIM	ACTOR	10914 BELLAGIO RD	LOS ANGELES, CA	90077
BACON, DONALD C	NEWS CORRESPONDENT	3809 EAST-WEST HWY	CHEVY CHASE, MD	20815
BACON, KENNETH H	NEWS CORRESPONDENT	1715 HOBAN RD, NW	WASHINGTON, DC	20007
BACON, KEVIN	ACTOR	194 RIVERSIDE DR #7-B	NEW YORK, NY	10023
BACON, MICHAEL	GUITARIST	MIMSA MUSIC, RD #2	PHOENIXVILLE, PA	19460
BACON, RONALD B	DIRECTOR	1402 OLD TOPANGA CANYON RD	TOPANGA, CA	90290
BACOS, CATHERINE A	TV WRITER	8955 BEVERLY BLVD	LOS ANGELES, CA	90048
BACOS, GEORGE	WRITER	1332 N CITRUS AVE #1	LOS ANGELES, CA	90028
BAD	ROCK & ROLL GROUP	SEE - BIG AUDIO DYNAMITE		
BAD COMPANY	ROCK & ROLL GROUP	E S "BUD" PRAGER MANAGEMENT		
		1790 BROADWAY, PENTHOUSE	NEW YORK, NY	10019
BADAMO, VERA G	WRITER	555 W 57TH ST #1230	NEW YORK, NY	10019
BADAT, RANDALL M	WRITER-PRODUCER	2428 CLARK AVE	VENICE, CA	90291
BADD MAXX	ROCK & ROLL GROUP	POST OFFICE BOX 942	RAPID CITY, SD	57709
BADDELEY, HERMIONE	ACTRESS	9000 SUNSET BLVD #807	LOS ANGELES, CA	90069
BADEA, CHRISTIAN	CONDUCTOR	ICM, 40 W 57TH ST	NEW YORK, NY	10019
BADEL, SARAH	ACTRESS	PLUNKET GREEN, 91 REGENT ST	LONDON W1	ENGLAND
BADHAM, JOHN	FILM DIRECTOR	1707 MANDEVILLE LN	LOS ANGELES, CA	90049
BADHWAR, INDY	NEWS CORRESPONDENT	1024 WELSH DR	ROCKVILLE, MD	20852
BADINGS, HENK	COMPOSER	HUGTEN 5, 6026 RG	MAARHEEZE	NETHERLAND
BADIYI, REZA	TV DIRECTOR	8952 DICKS ST	LOS ANGELES, CA	90069
BADLER, JANE	ACTRESS	10000 SANTA MONICA BLVD #305	LOS ANGELES, CA	90067
BADUKA-SKODA, PAULK	PIANIST	5811 S DORCHESTER AVE	CHICAGO, IL	60637
BAER, ART	WRITER-PRODUCER	2225 MALAGA RD	LOS ANGELES, CA	90068
BAER, DONALD	DIRECTOR	520 N ARDEN DR	BEVERLY HILLS, CA	90212
BAER, J A	TV EXECUTIVE	CBS-TV, 51 W 52ND ST	NEW YORK, NY	10019
BAER, JILL	TV WRITER	8955 BEVERLY BLVD	LOS ANGELES, CA	90048
BAER, MAX, JR	ACTOR-DIRECTOR	15541 LE MAY ST	VAN NUYS, CA	91406
BAER, MERIDITH	ACTRESS-WRITER	2720 LA CUESTA DR	LOS ANGELES, CA	90046
BAER, OLAF	BARITONE	MARIEDL ANDERS ARTISTS MGMT		
		535 EL CAMINO DEL MAR ST	SAN FRANCISCO, CA	94121
BAER, PARLEY	ACTOR	4967 BILMOOR AVE	TARZANA, CA	91356
BAER, RANDY CRAIG	WRITER	2604 BERKELEY AVE	LOS ANGELES, CA	90026
BAER, RHODA	PHOTOGRAPHER	1648 BEEKMAN PL #A, NW	WASHINGTON, DC	20009
BAER, RICHARD	TV WRITER	812 N LINDEN DR	BEVERLY HILLS, CA	90210
BAER, ROBERT M	PHOTOGRAPHER	15322 OLD FREDERICK RD	EMMITSBURG, MD	21727
BAERE, GEOFFREY C	SCREENWRITER	8955 BEVERLY BLVD	LOS ANGELES, CA	90048
BAERG, THEODORE	BARITONE	CAMI, 165 W 57TH ST	NEW YORK, NY	10019
BAERWALD, SUSAN	TV DIRECTOR	NBC-TV, 3000 W ALAMEDA AVE	BURBANK, CA	91523
BAERWITZ, JERRY	FILM DIRECTOR	4600 VIA DOLCE #107	MARINA DEL REY, CA	90292
BAEZ, JOAN	SINGER	934 SANTA CRUZ	MENLO PARK, CA	94025
BAEZA, IFA	TV WRITER	ICM, 8899 BEVERLY BLVD	LOS ANGELES, CA	90048
BAFF, REGINA	ACTRESS	853 7TH AVE #9-A	NEW YORK, NY	10019
BAFFICO, JAMES A	DIRECTOR	216 MIDLAND AVE	MONTCLAIR, NJ	07042
BAGDASARIAN, CAROL	ACTRESS	1465 LINDACREST DR	BEVERLY HILLS, CA	90210
BAGDASARIAN, ROSS	ACTOR	1465 LINDACREST DR	BEVERLY HILLS, CA	90210
BAGEN, THOMAS GEORGE	WRITER	2038 HOLLY DR #4	LOS ANGELES, CA	90068
BAGGETT, ROBERT SCOTT	GUITARIST	3308 LEBANON RD #20	HERMITAGE, TN	37076
BAGGETTA, VINCENT	ACTOR	4144 CRISP CYN RD	SHERMAN OAKS, CA	91403
BAGLEY, DON	COMPOSER	8440 CANBY AVE	NORTHRIDGE, CA	91325
BAGLIONI, BRUNA	MEZZO-SOPRANO	61 W 62ND ST #6-F	NEW YORK, NY	10023
BAGNALL, THOMAS J	NEWS CORRESPONDENT	2139 WISCONSIN AVE, NW	WASHINGTON, DC	20007
BAGNATO, BARRY	WRITER	555 W 57TH ST #1230	NEW YORK, NY	10019
BAGNI-DUBOV, GWEN	SCREENWRITER	5700 RHODES AVE	NORTH HOLLYWOOD, CA	91607
BAHLER, JOHN C	COMPOSER	1606 N HIGHLAND AVE	LOS ANGELES, CA	90028
BAHLER, THOMAS L	COMPOSER	217 S CARMELINA ST	LOS ANGELES, CA	90049
BAHRUTH, WILLIAM H	PHOTOGRAPHER	9737 LAKE SHORE DR	GAITHERSBURG, MD	20879
BAIL, CHUCK	FILM DIRECTOR	1421 MORNINGSIDE DR	BURBANK, CA	91506

BARBARA BACH

CATHARINE BACH

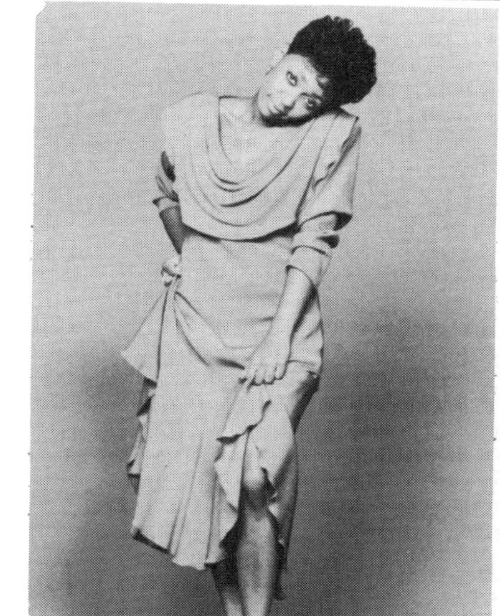
ANITA BAKER

PHILLIP BAILEY

RAZZY BAILEY

PEARL BAILEY

CARROLL BAKER

LUCILLE BALL

ANNE BANCROFT

Name	Occupation	Address	City	Code
BAILES, DON & TONY STARR SHOW	VOCAL GROUP	POST OFFICE BOX 11276	ROCHESTER, NY	14611
BAILEY, ANNE HOWARD	TV WRITER	445 N BEDFORD DR #PH	BEVERLY HILLS, CA	90210
BAILEY, BECKY	NEWS CORRESPONDENT	1755 S JEFFERSON DAVIS HWY	ARLINGTON, VA	22202
BAILEY, BRAD	WRITER	8955 BEVERLY BLVD	LOS ANGELES, CA	90048
BAILEY, CARL	PHOTOGRAPHER	1317 XAVERIA DR	SILVER SPRING, MD	20903
BAILEY, CHARLES W, II	NEWS CORRESPONDENT	2025 "M" ST, NW	WASHINGTON, DC	20036
BAILEY, DAVID	ACTOR	10 E 44TH ST #700	NEW YORK, NY	10017
BAILEY, DENNIS	TENOR	CAMI, 165 W 57TH ST	NEW YORK, NY	10019
BAILEY, DEREK	TV DIRECTOR	ROGER HANCOCK MANAGEMENT		
		8 WATERLOO PL, PALL MALL	LONDON SW1Y 4AW	ENGLAND
BAILEY, DOROTHY	WRITER	8955 BEVERLY BLVD	LOS ANGELES, CA	90048
BAILEY, DOUG	WRITER	8955 BEVERLY BLVD	LOS ANGELES, CA	90048
BAILEY, EDWARD J	WRITER	555 W 57TH ST #1230	NEW YORK, NY	10019
BAILEY, G W	ACTOR	11726 SAN VICENTE BLVD #300	LOS ANGELES, CA	90049
BAILEY, ILOMAY	SINGER	101 W 57TH ST #17-B	NEW YORK, NY	10019
BAILEY, IRENE D	WRITER	555 W 57TH ST #1230	NEW YORK, NY	10019
BAILEY, JEFF D	TRUMPETER	135 FOREST RETREAT	HENDERSONVILLE, TN	37075
BAILEY, JIM	ACTOR	721 N LA BREA AVE #201	LOS ANGELES, CA	90038
BAILEY, JOEL	ACTOR	211 S BEVERLY DR #107	BEVERLY HILLS, CA	90212
BAILEY, JOHN ABRAMS	GUITARIST	6006 BALTIC DR	HERMITAGE, TN	37076
BAILEY, JOSEPH	PHOTOGRAPHER	1226 N CHAMBLISS ST	ALEXANDRIA, VA	22312
BAILEY, JOSEPH	TV WRITER	CHILDREN'S TV WORKSHOP		
		1 LINCOLN PLAZA	NEW YORK, NY	10023
BAILEY, LARRY D	COMPOSER	2223 S 10TH ST	KANSAS CITY, KS	66103
BAILEY, MARVIN LLOYD	DIRECTOR	110 W ILLINOIS ST	CHICAGO, IL	60610
BAILEY, NORMAN	BARITONE	CONE, 221 W 57TH ST	NEW YORK, NY	10019
BAILEY, PATRICK E	WRITER	8955 BEVERLY BLVD	LOS ANGELES, CA	90048
BAILEY, PEARL	SINGER-ACTRESS	POST OFFICE BOX L	LAKE HAVASU CITY, AZ	86403
BAILEY, PHILIP	SINGER-SONGWRITER	1888 CENTURY PARK E #1400	LOS ANGELES, CA	90067
BAILEY, R L	WRITER	8955 BEVERLY BLVD	LOS ANGELES, CA	90048
BAILEY, RAZZY	SINGER	417 SANDERS FERRY RD	HENDERSONVILLE, TN	37075
BAILEY, ROBIN	ACTOR	DGLA, PANTON HOUSE		
		25 HAYMARKET	LONDON SW1	ENGLAND
BAILEY, SHERMAN	ACTOR	5641 MARSHALL DR	HUNTINGTON BEACH, CA	92649
BAILEY, TOM A	ACTOR	12926 RIVERSIDE DR #C	SHERMAN OAKS, CA	91423
BAILEY, WENDELL	TV EXECUTIVE	NATIONAL CABLE TV ASSOCIATION		
		1724 MASSACHUSETTS AVE, SW	WASHINGTON, DC	20036
BAILEY, WILLIAM, III	DRUMMER	2010 LINDEN AVE #1	NASHVILLE, TN	37212
BAIM, HAROLD	WRITER-PRODUCER	54 CHESTER CLOSE S		
		REGENT'S PARK	LONDON NW1 4JG	ENGLAND
BAIN, BARBARA	ACTRESS	10351 SANTA MONICA BLVD #211	LOS ANGELES, CA	90025
BAIN, CONRAD	ACTOR	1230 CHICKORY LN	LOS ANGELES, CA	90049
BAIN, DONALD S	WRITER	555 W 57TH ST #1230	NEW YORK, NY	10019
BAINBRIDGE, JOHN	WRITER	THE NEW YORKER		
		25 W 43RD ST	NEW YORK, NY	10036
BAIO, JIMMY	ACTOR	151 S EL CAMINO DR	BEVERLY HILLS, CA	90212
BAIO, SCOTT	ACTOR	POST OFFICE BOX 5617	BEVERLY HILLS, CA	90210
BAIRD, BIL	PUPPETEER	41 UNION SQ	NEW YORK, NY	10003
BAIRD, JULIANNE	SOPRANO	BYERS-SCHWALBE, 1 5TH AVE	NEW YORK, NY	10003
BAIRD, MIKE L	COMPOSER	2734 MORNINGSIDE ST	PASADENA, CA	91107
BAIRD, ROBERT	SCREENWRITER	8955 BEVERLY BLVD	LOS ANGELES, CA	90048
BAIRD, ROY	FILM PRODUCER	ROYMARK, 112 WARDOUR ST	LONDON W1	ENGLAND
BAIRD, STEPHEN	SINGER	276 CAMBRIDGE ST #4	BOSTON, MA	02134
BAIRD, STEPHEN	STREETSINGER	276 CAMBRIDGE ST #4	BOSTON, MA	02134
BAIRSTOW, SCOTT	ACTOR	322 S SWALL DR	LOS ANGELES, CA	90048
BAISDEN, HARRY L	NEWS CORRESPONDENT	3523 SLADE RUN DR	FALLS CHURCH, VA	22042
BAKALYAN, DICK	ACTOR-WRITER	1070 S BEDFORD ST	LOS ANGELES, CA	90035
BAKER, ALAN	TV PRODUCER	344 S LAS PALMAS AVE	LOS ANGELES, CA	90020
BAKER, ALAN H	DIRECTOR	431 PENN VALLEY RD	NARBERTH, PA	19072
BAKER, ALICE	MEZZO-SOPRANO	CAMI, 165 W 57TH ST	NEW YORK, NY	10019
BAKER, ALLEN	WRITER	8955 BEVERLY BLVD	LOS ANGELES, CA	90048
BAKER, ALONZO	WRITER	208 VERNAL DR	CHOWCHILLA, CA	93610
BAKER, BENNY	ACTOR	5004 CANOGA AVE	WOODLAND HILLS, CA	91364
BAKER, BILL	COMPOSER	16843 LIGGETT AVE	SEPULVEDA, CA	91343
BAKER, BLANCHE	ACTRESS	LIONEL LARNER, 130 W 57TH ST	NEW YORK, NY	10019
BAKER, BRADLEY P	NEWS CORRESPONDENT	236 MASSACHUSETTS AVE, NE	WASHINGTON, DC	20002
BAKER, BUDDY	COMPOSER-CONDUCTOR	3200 W LA ROTONDA #110	PALOS VERDES, CA	90274
BAKER, BUTCH	SINGER-GUITARIST	QUINN, 2948 FRANKLIN RD	NASHVILLE, TN	37204
BAKER, CARROLL	ACTRESS	ICM, 388-396 OXFORD ST	LONDON W1	ENGLAND
BAKER, CHET	TRUMPETER	POST OFFICE BOX 8003	104-20 STOCKHOLM	SWEDEN
BAKER, COLIN	ACTOR	BURNETT, 42 GRAFTON HOUSE		
		2-3 GOLDEN SQ	LONDON W1	ENGLAND
BAKER, CYNTHIA	ACTRESS	200 N ROBERTSON BLVD #308	BEVERLY HILLS, CA	90210
BAKER, DAME JANET	MEZZO-SOPRANO	SHAW CONCERTS, 1995 BROADWAY	NEW YORK, NY	10023
BAKER, DARRELL	ACTOR	19 W 44TH ST #1500	NEW YORK, NY	10036
BAKER, DEBORAH	TV WRITER	555 W 57TH ST #1230	NEW YORK, NY	10019
BAKER, DENNIS J	GUITARIST	14891 BROWNSTONE LN	WESTMINSTER, CA	92683
BAKER, DIANE	ACTRESS-DIRECTOR	8485 MELROSE PL #E	LOS ANGELES, CA	90069
BAKER, DOUGLAS J	DIRECTOR	AMERICAN EMBASSY, ICA	APO, NY	09284
BAKER, DUSTY	BASEBALL	24525 PALERMO DR	CALABASAS, CA	91302
BAKER, ELIZABETH	NEWS CORRESPONDENT	5005 GARFIELD ST, NW	WASHINGTON, DC	20016
BAKER, ELLIOTT	TV WRITER	555 W 57TH ST #1230	NEW YORK, NY	10019
BAKER, FIELDER	TV WRITER	8955 BEVERLY BLVD	LOS ANGELES, CA	90048
BAKER, GALE	ACTRESS	208 S BEVERLY DR #4	BEVERLY HILLS, CA	90212
BAKER, GARY C	GUITARIST	2313 WINFORD AVE	NASHVILLE, TN	37211

Name	Occupation	Address	City
BAKER, GEORGE	ACTOR	ICM, 388-396 OXFORD ST	LONDON W1 ENGLAND
BAKER, GEORGETTE	ACTRESS	8820 SUNSET BLVD #ANB	LOS ANGELES, CA 90069
BAKER, GRAHAM P	FILM DIRECTOR	2706 LA CUESTA DR	LOS ANGELES, CA 90046
BAKER, GREGG	BARITONE	CAMI, 165 W 57TH ST	NEW YORK, NY 10019
BAKER, JACK	TV DIRECTOR	10430 CHEVIOT DR	LOS ANGELES, CA 90064
BAKER, JAMES	WRITER	8955 BEVERLY BLVD	LOS ANGELES, CA 90048
BAKER, JAMES F	TV DIRECTOR	591 VIRGINIA DR	TIBURON, CA 94920
BAKER, JANET ABBOTT	MEZZO-SOPRANO	450 EDGEWARE RD	LONDON W2 ENGLAND
BAKER, JIMMIE	TV DIRECTOR	1637 N BEVERLY DR	BEVERLY HILLS, CA 90210
BAKER, JIMMY G	GUITARIST-DOBROIST	741 BROOK HOLLOW RD	NASHVILLE, TN 37205
BAKER, JOBY	ACTOR	2533 ZORADA DR	LOS ANGELES, CA 90046
BAKER, JOE DON	ACTOR	23339 HATTERAS ST	WOODLAND HILLS, CA 91367
BAKER, JOHN P	DRUMMER	1226 GRANDVIEW DR	NASHVILLE, TN 37215
BAKER, JOSEPH	WRITER	8955 BEVERLY BLVD	LOS ANGELES, CA 90048
BAKER, JULIUS	FLUTIST	GERSHUNOFF, 502 PARK AVE	NEW YORK, NY 10022
BAKER, KAI	ACTRESS	8949 SUNSET BLVD #203	LOS ANGELES, CA 90069
BAKER, KATHRYN L	NEWS CORRESPONDENT	4550 CONNECTICUT AVE, NW	WASHINGTON, DC 20008
BAKER, KENNETH	VIOLINIST	POST OFFICE BOX 51	GOODLETTSVILLE, TN 37072
BAKER, KIMBERLY	ACTRESS	8949 SUNSET BLVD #203	LOS ANGELES, CA 90069
BAKER, KIRSTEN	ACTRESS	568 RIALTO AVE	VENICE, CA 90291
BAKER, KURT	DIRECTOR	DGA, 7950 SUNSET BLVD	LOS ANGELES, CA 90046
BAKER, LAURA	OBOIST	3297 ELM HILL PIKE	NASHVILLE, TN 37214
BAKER, MARGERY CLAIRE	TV PRODUCER	CBS-TV, 524 W 57TH ST	NEW YORK, NY 10019
BAKER, MARINA AUGUSTA	ACTRESS-MODEL	MODELS & PROMOTIONS AGENCY	
		8560 SUNSET BLVD, 10TH FLOOR	LOS ANGELES, CA 90069
BAKER, MARION L	CELLIST	8654 BURTON PARISH CT #204	MANASSAS, VA 22110
BAKER, MICHAEL T	GUITARIST	251 N SHACKLE ISLAND RD	HENDERSONVILLE, TN 37075
BAKER, NORMAN L	NEWS CORRESPONDENT	SUMMERSET	DELAPLANE, VA 22025
BAKER, PENNY	ACTRESS-MODEL	9744 WILSHIRE BLVD #306	BEVERLY HILLS, CA 90212
BAKER, RAY R	GUITARIST-PIANIST	POST OFFICE BOX 162	MADISON, TN 37115
BAKER, RAYMOND	ACTOR	10100 SANTA MONICA BLVD #1600	LOS ANGELES, CA 90067
BAKER, RICHARD	NEWS REPORTER	THE NATIONAL ENQUIRER	
		600 SE COAST AVE	LANTANA, FL 33464
BAKER, RICHARD	WRITER	8955 BEVERLY BLVD	LOS ANGELES, CA 90048
BAKER, ROBERT HART	CONDUCTOR	GERSHUNOFF, 502 PARK AVE	NEW YORK, NY 10022
BAKER, ROBERT S	TV DIRECTOR-PRODUCER	THORN-EMI ELSTREE STUDIOS	
		BOREHAMWOOD	HERTS ENGLAND
BAKER, ROD	TV WRITER	1650 WESTWOOD BLVD #201	LOS ANGELES, CA 90024
BAKER, ROY WARD	FILM DIRECTOR	LEADING ARTISTS, LTD	
		60 SAINT JAMES'S ST	LONDON SW1 ENGLAND
BAKER, RUTH	VIOLINIST	3804 WOODMONT LN	NASHVILLE, TN 37215
BAKER, SALLY	ACTRESS	9056 SANTA MONICA BLVD #201	LOS ANGELES, CA 90069
BAKER, SALLY	TV WRITER	8955 BEVERLY BLVD	LOS ANGELES, CA 90048
BAKER, TOM	ACTOR	LONDON MANAGEMENT, LTD	
		235-241 REGENT ST	LONDON W1A 2JT ENGLAND
BAKER, VIRGINIA	ACTRESS	SEE - PALANCE, VIRGINIA BAKER	
BAKER, WARREN	TV EXECUTIVE	NBC-TV, 3000 W ALAMEDA AVE	BURBANK, CA 91523
BAKER, WARREN A	TV DIRECTOR	16731 BAHAMA ST	SEPULVEDA, CA 91343
BAKER, WILLIAM F	TV EXECUTIVE	GROUP W SATELLITE	
		90 PARK AVE	NEW YORK, NY 10016
BAKER, WILLIAM W	DIRECTOR	3552 SUMMERFIELD DR	SHERMAN OAKS, CA 91423
BAKER, WINTHROP, III	WRITER	555 W 57TH ST #1230	NEW YORK, NY 10019
BAKEWELL, WILLIAM	ACTOR	1745 SELBY AVE #16	LOS ANGELES, CA 90024
BAKEY, ED	ACTOR	3518 W CAHUENGA BLVD #316	LOS ANGELES, CA 90068
BAKKE, ERIC LARS	PHOTOGRAPHER	1054 STEELE ST	DENVER, CO 80206
BAKKEN, VICKI	ACTRESS	8230 BEVERLY BLVD #23	LOS ANGELES, CA 90048
BAKKER, JIM & TAMMY FAYE	TV EVANGELISTS	POSTMASTER/GENERAL DELIVERY	GATLINBURG, TN 37738
BAKSHI, RALPH	ANI-WRI-DIR	GANG, 6400 SUNSET BLVD	LOS ANGELES, CA 90028
BAKST, LAWRENCE	TENOR	AFFILIATE ARTISTS, INC	
		37 W 65TH ST, 6TH FLOOR	NEW YORK, NY 10023
BAL, ADRIAN	RECORD EXECUTIVE	POST OFFICE BOX 369	LA CANADA, CA 91011
BAL, HENRY KAIMU	ACTOR	439 S LA CIENEGA BLVD #117	LOS ANGELES, CA 90048
BALABAN, BOB	ACTOR	390 W END AVE	NEW YORK, NY 10024
BALABAN, ROBERT	WRITER	8955 BEVERLY BLVD	LOS ANGELES, CA 90048
BALASH, MURIEL	TV DIRECTOR	421 W 57TH ST	NEW YORK, NY 10019
BALASKI, BELINDA	ACTRESS	1434 1/2 N CURSON AVE	LOS ANGELES, CA 90046
BALBOA, JOHN	WRESTLER	POST OFFICE BOX 3859	STAMFORD, CT 06905
BALCER, RENE	WRITER	ICM, 8899 BEVERLY BLVD	LOS ANGELES, CA 90048
BALCH, JACK	WRITER	555 W 57TH ST #1230	NEW YORK, NY 10019
BALCOMB, STUART V	COMPOSER-CONDUCTOR	5018 BALBOA BLVD	ENCINO, CA 91436
BALDACCHINO, JOSEPH F, JR	NEWS CORRESPONDENT	12419 STRETTON LN	BOWIE, MD 20715
BALDAUFF, PATRIK	ACTOR	POST OFFICE BOX 69405	LOS ANGELES, CA 90069
BALDAVIN, BARBARA	ACTRESS	228 17TH ST	MANHATTAN BEACH, CA 90266
BALDAVIN, BARBARA	CASTING DIRECTOR	WARNER-HOLLYWOOD STUDIOS	
		1041 N FORMOSA AVE	LOS ANGELES, CA 90046
BALDEN, JAMES E	TV DIRECTOR	1879 E ALTADENA DR	ALTADENA, CA 91001
BALDING, REBECCA	ACTRESS	4300 COQUETTE PL	TARZANA, CA 91356
BALDINI, DONALD L	NEWS CORRESPONDENT	939 26TH ST, NW	WASHINGTON, DC 20036
BALDRY, LONG JOHN	SINGER-MUSICIAN	41 BRITAIN ST #200	TORONTO, ONT CANADA
BALDWIN, ALEC	ACTOR	14755 VENTURA BLVD #1-170	SHERMAN OAKS, CA 91403
BALDWIN, BILL	SINGER	TALENT MASTERS AGENCY	
		1019 17TH AVE S	NASHVILLE, TN 37212
BALDWIN, BONNIE	SINGER	PROCESS, 439 WILEY AVE	FRANKLIN, PA 16323
BALDWIN, ERIC	WRITER	8955 BEVERLY BLVD	LOS ANGELES, CA 90048

Name	Occupation	Address	City	Zip
BALDWIN, GERALD	TV PRODUCER	HANNA, 3400 CAHUENGA BLVD	LOS ANGELES, CA	90068
BALDWIN, JAMES	AUTHOR	ACTION, 17 GROVE ST	NEW YORK, NY	10014
BALDWIN, JANIT	ACTRESS	8508 BRIER DR	LOS ANGELES, CA	90046
BALDWIN, JOE	SINGER	GOOD, 2500 NW 39 ST	OKLAHOMA CITY, OK	73112
BALDWIN, JUDITH	ACTRESS	CBS TELEVISION NETWORK		
		"THE BOLD & THE BEAUTIFUL"		
		7800 BEVERLY BLVD	LOS ANGELES, CA	90036
BALDWIN, JUDY	ACTRESS	3800 BARHAM BLVD #303	LOS ANGELES, CA	90068
BALDWIN, KATY	ACTRESS	113 N SAN VICENTE BLVD #202	BEVERLY HILLS, CA	90211
BALDWIN, MARK	GUITARIST	2929 SELENA DR #K-154	NASHVILLE, TN	37211
BALDWIN, MARK F	NEWS CORRESPONDENT	6122 EDSALL RD #202	ALEXANDRIA, VA	22304
BALDWIN, PETER D	FILM DIRECTOR	575 N BEVERLY BLVD	LOS ANGELES, CA	90077
BALDWIN, PETER I	SCREENWRITER	8955 BEVERLY BLVD	LOS ANGELES, CA	90048
BALDWIN, ROBERT, JR	WRITER	555 W 57TH ST #1230	NEW YORK, NY	10019
BALDWIN, STANLEY	GUITARIST-SAXOPHONIST	626 OAKLEY DR	NASHVILLE, TN	37220
BALE, CHRISTOPHER	NEWS CORRESPONDENT	4317 SELKIRK DR	FAIRFAX, VA	22032
BALE, ELVIN	AERIALIST	HALL, 138 FROG HOLLOW RD	CHURCHVILLE, PA	18966
BALENDA, CARLA	ACTRESS	RUTTER, 15848 WOODVALE RD	ENCINO, CA	91436
BALHATCHET, BOB	ACTOR	6330 WOODMAN AVE	VAN NUYS, CA	91401
BALIK, JOHN	BODYBUILDER	POST OFFICE BOX 777	SANTA MONICA, CA	90406
BALIN, INA	ACTRESS	200 W 57TH ST #1303	NEW YORK, NY	10019
BALIN, MARTY	SINGER-SONGWRITER	GREAT PYRAMID MGMT		
		10 WATERVILLE ST	SAN FRANCISCO, CA	94124
BALIN, RICHARD	ACTOR	4959 DENNY AVE	NORTH HOLLYWOOD, CA	91601
BALIN, ROCHELLE	ACTRESS	4959 DENNY AVE	NORTH HOLLYWOOD, CA	91601
BALINT DUO	MUSICAL DUO	FINELL, 155 W 68TH ST	NEW YORK, NY	10023
BALKAN, DAVID H	TV WRITER-PRODUCER	16815 GRESHAM ST	SEPULVEDA, CA	91343
BALL, ANNE	WRITER	555 W 57TH ST #1230	NEW YORK, NY	10019
BALL, AUDREY	NEWS REPORTER	TIME/TIME & LIFE BLDG		
		ROCKEFELLER CENTER	NEW YORK, NY	10020
BALL, JOHN	DIRECTOR	BAY CREST, HUNTINGTON	LONG ISLAND, NY	11743
BALL, LARRY D	CONDUCTOR	19008 COLBECK ST	CARSON, CA	90746
BALL, LUCILLE	ACTRESS	1000 N ROXBURY DR	BEVERLY HILLS, CA	90210
BALL, MARCIA	SINGER-PIANIST	ATS MANAGEMENT		
		3300 HOLLYWOOD AVE	AUSTIN, TX	78722
BALL, NICHOLAS	ACTOR	KENNINGTON PARK RD		
		WALWORTH	LONDON SE17	ENGLAND
BALL, ROGER D	GUITARIST	POST OFFICE BOX 428	WHITE HOUSE, TN	37188
BALL, SHERWOOD	WRITER-MUSICIAN	473 16TH ST	SANTA MONICA, CA	90402
BALL, SUSAN	SOPRANO	61 W 62ND ST #6-F	NEW YORK, NY	10023
BALL, WILLIAM	DIRECTOR-PRODUCER	450 GEARY ST	SAN FRANCISCO, CA	94102
BALLACE, ELAINE	ACTRESS	4265 COLFAX AVE #10	STUDIO CITY, CA	91604
BALLAM, MICHAEL	TENOR	ICM, 40 W 57TH ST	NEW YORK, NY	10019
BALLANCE, BILL	RADIO PERSONALITY	KFMB RADIO, 7677 ENGINEER RD	SAN DIEGO, CA	92111
BALLANTINE, CARL	ACTOR-COMEDIAN	10850 RIVERSIDE DR #501	NORTH HOLLYWOOD, CA	91602
BALLANTINE, EDDIE	CONDUCTOR	7830 LOWELL AVE	SKOKIE, IL	60076
BALLANTINE, SARA	ACTRESS	FARRELL, 10500 MAGNOLIA BLVD	NORTH HOLLYWOOD, CA	91601
BALLANTINE, TOBY	STILTWALKER	HALL, 138 FROG HOLLOW RD	CHURCHVILLE, PA	18966
BALLARD, CARROLL	FILM DIRECTOR	POST OFFICE BOX 239	CALISTOGA, CA	94515
BALLARD, CHRISTINE	TV WRITER-DIRECTOR	4216 ETHEL AVE	STUDIO CITY, CA	91604
BALLARD, CORNELIUS	TV WRITER	8955 BEVERLY BLVD	LOS ANGELES, CA	90048
BALLARD, DANNY	COMEDIAN	MAGNAN, 1121 NORTHRUP, NW	GRAND RAPIDS, MI	49504
BALLARD, DASHIELL N	WRITER	555 W 57TH ST #1230	NEW YORK, NY	10019
BALLARD, DENNIS P	NEWS CORRESPONDENT	340 NATIONAL PRESS BLDG		
		529 14TH ST, NW	WASHINGTON, DC	20045
BALLARD, HANK & THE MIDNIGHTERS	SOUL GROUP	T MAC NEIL MANAGEMENT		
		11457 HARRISBURG RD	LOS ALAMITOS, CA	90720
BALLARD, JOHN	WRITER	8955 BEVERLY BLVD	LOS ANGELES, CA	90048
BALLARD, KAYE	ACTRESS-SINGER	211 E 70TH ST #20-C	NEW YORK, NY	10021
BALLARD, LUCIEN	CINEMATOGRAPHER	1054 RODEO AVE	PEBBLE BEACH, CA	93953
BALLARD, LUCINDA	COSTUME DESIGNER	180 E END AVE	NEW YORK, NY	10028
BALLARD, RAY	ACTOR	12955 RIVERSIDE DR #303	SHERMAN OAKS, CA	91423
BALLARD, SARAH	SPORTS WRITER	SPORTS ILLISTRATED MAGAZINE		
		TIME & LIFE BUILDING		
		ROCKEFELLER CENTER	NEW YORK, NY	10020
BALLESTEROS, AARON P	COMPOSER	8130 REDLANDS ST #16	MARINA DEL REY, CA	90291
BALLEW, MICHAEL	SINGER	RECORD ONE MANAGEMENT		
		13849 VENTURA BLVD	SHERMAN OAKS, CA	91423
BALLIETT, WHITNEY	WRITER-CRITIC	THE NEW YORKER		
		25 W 43RD ST	NEW YORK, NY	10036
BALLIF, VERA	ACTRESS	3869 DEERVALE DR	SHERMAN OAKS, CA	91403
BALLINGER, JOSHUA J	WRITER	555 W 57TH ST #1230	NEW YORK, NY	10019
BALLUCK, DON	TV WRITER	11566 MORRISON ST	NORTH HOLLYWOOD, CA	91601
BALMAGIA, LARRY	TV WRITER	2315 HILL ST	SANTA MONICA, CA	90405
BALME, JERRY	TV PRODUCER	11516 RIVERSIDE DR #3	NORTH HOLLYWOOD, CA	91602
BALME, JOHN	CONDUCTOR	CONE, 221 W 57TH ST	NEW YORK, NY	10019
BALOFF, PETER I	SCREENWRITER	7041 WOODROW WILSON DR	LOS ANGELES, CA	90068
BALOUGH, BARBARA	ACTRESS	6310 SAN VICENTE BLVD #407	LOS ANGELES, CA	90048
BALSAM, ARTHUR	PIANIST	258 RIVERSIDE DR	NEW YORK, NY	10025
BALSAM, MARTIN	ACTOR	HOTEL OLCOTT, 27 W 72ND ST	NEW YORK, NY	10011
BALSAM, TALIA	ACTRESS	959 N CROFT AVE	LOS ANGELES, CA	90069
BALSLEY, PHILIP	SINGER	ROUTE #1, BOX 33-A	SWOOPE, VA	24479
BALSZ, BARBARA	CASTING DIRECTOR	CALIFORNIA CASTING CO		
		346 1/2 N SYCAMORE AVE	HOLLYWOOD, CA	90036
BALTIN, STEVEN M	WRITER	555 W 57TH ST #1230	NEW YORK, NY	10019

BALTSA, AGNES	MEZZO-SOPRANO	CAMI, 165 W 57TH ST	NEW YORK, NY 10019
BALTZER, ALICE	WRITER	8955 BEVERLY BLVD	LOS ANGELES, CA 90048
BALZ, DANIEL J	NEWS CORRESPONDENT	626 MASSACHUSETTS AVE, NE	WASHINGTON, DC 20002
BALZER, GEORGE M	TV WRITER	6616 LANGDON AVE	VAN NUYS, CA 91406
BAM BAM	WRESTLER	SEE - GORDY, TERRY "BAM BAM"	
BAMBARA, TONI	WRITER	555 W 57TH ST #1230	NEW YORK, NY 10019
BAMBER, GEORGE E	WRITER	3836 ALTURA AVE	LA CRESCENTA, CA 91214
BAMBERGER, ANDREW F	TV DIRECTOR	27 THE HAMLET	PELHAM MANOR, NY 10803
BAMBERGER, GEORGE	BASEBALL	455 N BATH CLUB BLVD	N REDINGTON BEACH, FL 33708
BAMBOO	ROCK & ROLL GROUP	41 BRITAIN ST #200	TORONTO, ONT CANADA
BAMFORD, ROGER	TV DIRECTOR-PRODUCER	2 GORDON RD, CHISWICK	LONDON W4 ENGLAND
BANACH, JOHN	ACTOR	JAYMES, 327 N LAUREL AVE	LOS ANGELES, CA 90048
BANALES, JORGE A	NEWS CORRESPONDENT	7227 JAYHAWK ST	ANNANDALE, VA 22003
BANAS, ARLENE O	ACTRESS	718 N KINGS RD #306	LOS ANGELES, CA 90069
BANAS, CHRISTINE S	TV PRODUCER	CBS-TV, "AS THE WORLD TURNS"	
		51 W 52ND ST	NEW YORK, NY 10019
BANAS, ROBERT	CHOREO-DIR-PROD	5143 GLORIA AVE	ENCINO, CA 91436
BANCROFT, ANNE	ACT-WRI-DIR	915 N FOOTHILL RD	BEVERLY HILLS, CA 90210
BANCROFT, JOHN R	NEWS CORRESPONDENT	108 BONIFANT RD	SILVER SPRING, MD 20904
BAND, ALBERT	PROD-WRI-DIR	1639 BLUE JAY WY	LOS ANGELES, CA 90069
BAND, CHARLES	FILM PRODUCER	EMPIRE ENTERPRISES	
		1551 N LA BREA AVE	LOS ANGELES, CA 90028
BANDANA	C & W GROUP	POST OFFICE BOX 121089	NASHVILLE, TN 37212
BANDKLAYDER, STEVE	WRITER	555 W 57TH ST #1230	NEW YORK, NY 10019
BANDY, CHARLIE	SINGER	POST OFFICE BOX 29262	INDIANPOLIS, IN 46229
BANDY, KARROLL M	ACTOR	2030 HOLLY DR #H	LOS ANGELES, CA 90068
BANDY, LELAND A	NEWS CORRESPONDENT	6817 OLD STAGE RD	ROCKVILLE, MD 20852
BANDY, MOE	SINGER	POST OFFICE BOX 1373	LEWISVILLE, TX 75067
BANDY, WILLIAM LAUREN	GUITARIST	549 E MAIN #C-27	HENDERSONVILLE, TN 37075
BANES, LIONEL	CINEMATOGRAPHER	213 CREIGHTON AVE	
		EAST FINCHLEY	LONDON N2 ENGLAND
BANFIELD, KENNETH "CURLY"	CLOWN	2701 COTTAGE WY #14	SACRAMENTO, CA 95825
BANG, BILLY	VIOLINIST	CELLULOID RECORDS	
		260 W 39TH ST	NEW YORK, NY 10018
BANG BANG	ROCK & ROLL GROUP	VARIETY ARTISTS INTL, INC	
		9073 NEMO ST, 3RD FLOOR	LOS ANGELES, CA 90069
BANGERT, CHARLES A	DIRECTOR-PRODUCER	145 NOD RD	RIDGEFIELD, CT 06877
BANGERTER, MICHAEL	ACTOR	E E SMITH, 10 WYNDHAM PL	LONDON W1 ENGLAND
BANGLES, THE	ROCK & ROLL GROUP	L A P D, 633 N LA BREA AVE	LOS ANGELES, CA 90036
BANISH MISFORTUNE	JAZZ TRIO	IAM, 10572 JASON LN	COLUMBIA, MD 21044
BANK, WILLIAM	NEWS CORRESPONDENT	200 W GEORGE MASON RD	FALLS CHRUCH, VA 22046
BANKER, STEPHEN	NEWS CORRESPONDENT	5078 FULTON ST, NW	WASHINGTON, DC 20016
BANKLER-JUKES, STEPHEN	TV PRODUCER	WOOD, 9 GOLDEN SQ	LONDON W1 ENGLAND
BANKS, BRENTON BOLDEN	VIOLINIST	386 S BURNSIDE AVE #11-C	LOS ANGELES, CA 90036
BANKS, C J	TV WRITER	8955 BEVERLY BLVD	LOS ANGELES, CA 90048
BANKS, C TILLERY	ACTRESS	FELBER, 2126 N CAHUENGA BLVD	LOS ANGELES, CA 90068
BANKS, DAVID	WRITER	8955 BEVERLY BLVD	LOS ANGELES, CA 90048
BANKS, ERNIE	BASEBALL	10660 WILSHIRE BLVD #408	LOS ANGELES, CA 90024
BANKS, HOWARD	NEWS CORRESPONDENT	4312 46TH ST, NW	WASHINGTON, DC 20016
BANKS, JONATHAN	ACTOR	909 EUCLID ST #8	SANTA MONICA, CA 90403
BANKS, LAURA	ACTRESS	FELBER, 2126 N CAHUENGA BLVD	LOS ANGELES, CA 90068
BANKS, MARK	NEWS CORRESPONDENT	1428 MONROE ST	WASHINGTON, DC 20010
BANKSTON, ARNOLD	ACTOR	POST OFFICE BOX 1096	LOS ANGELES, CA 90078
BANKY, VILMA	ACTRESS	316 N ROSSMORE AVE	LOS ANGELES, CA 90004
BANNARD, ROBERT	ACTOR	27 W 96TH ST	NEW YORK, NY 10025
BANNEN, IAN	ACTOR	REDWAY, 16 BERNERS ST	LONDON W1 ENGLAND
BANNER, ALICE B	WRITER	8955 BEVERLY BLVD	LOS ANGELES, CA 90048
BANNER, BOB	DIRECTOR-PRODUCER	9037 ALTO CEDRO DR	BEVERLY HILLS, CA 90210
BANNER, JONATHAN	PUBLISHING	VIEW, 150 E 58TH ST	NEW YORK, NY 10155
BANNICK, LISA A	TV WRITER	9000 SUNSET BLVD #1200	LOS ANGELES, CA 90069
BANNISTER, REGGIE	ACTOR	1006 RIDGEWOOD ST	LONG BEACH, CA 90807
BANNISTER, TERVOR	ACTOR	30 THE AVENUE	
		SAINT MARGARETS	TWICKENHAM ENGLAND
BANNON, JACK	ACTOR	5832 NAGLE AVE	VAN NUYS, CA 91401
BANNON, JIM	ACTOR	616 N HIGHLAND DR	OJAI, CA 93023
BANNON, R C	SINGER	POST OFFICE BOX 23110	NASHVILLE, TN 37202
BANNON, TIMOTHY G	NEWS CORRESPONDENT	8910 BRADFORD RD	SILVER SPRING, MD 20901
BANOW, JOEL	DIRECTOR	19 WELLINGTON TERR	WHITE PLAINS, NY 10607
BANT, GEORGE E	CONDUCTOR	53 OTTER COVE DR	OLD SAYBROOK, CT 06475
BANTA, GLORIA	TV WRITER	1326 BENEDICT CANYON DR	BEVERLY HILLS, CA 90210
BANTA, MILTON C	WRITER	8955 BEVERLY BLVD	LOS ANGELES, CA 90048
BANZET, JOSETTE	ACTRESS	870 N VINE ST #G	LOS ANGELES, CA 90038
BAPTISTE, THOMAS	ACTOR-SINGER	77 MELROSE AVE	LONDON NW2 ENGLAND
BAQUERIZO, ENRIQUE	BARITONE	LEW, 204 W 10TH ST	NEW YORK, NY 10014
BAR, JACQUES	FILM PRODUCER	28 RUE DE FRANQUEVILL	PARIS 75016 FRANCE
BAR-DAVID, MAURICE	TV DIRECTOR	14705 TUSTIN ST	SHERMAN OAKS, CA 91403
BAR-ILLAN, DAVID	PIANIST	CAMI, 165 W 57TH ST	NEW YORK, NY 10019
BAR-YOTAM, REUVEN	WRITER	8955 BEVERLY BLVD	LOS ANGELES, CA 90048
BARAD, THOMAS K	TALENT AGENT	7285 FRANKLIN AVE #E	LOS ANGELES, CA 90046
BARAGONE, TOMMY	ACTOR	2626 KANSAS AVE #1	SANTA MONICA, CA 90404
BARAK, ARI	ACTOR	9021 MELROSE AVE #304	LOS ANGELES, CA 90069
BARANSKI, CHRISTINE	ACTRESS	10100 SANTA MONICA BLVD #1600	LOS ANGELES, CA 90067
BARASCH, NORMAN	WRITER	1438 RISING GLEN RD	LOS ANGELES, CA 90069
BARASH, JEAN E	WRITER	825 AMALFI DR	PACIFIC PALISADES, CA 90272
BARASORDA, ANTONIO	TENOR	CAMI, 165 W 57TH ST	NEW YORK, NY 10019

MOE BANDY

BOBBY BARE

LYNN BARI

BINNIE BARNES

RONA BARRETT

CHUCK BARRIS

GENE BARRY

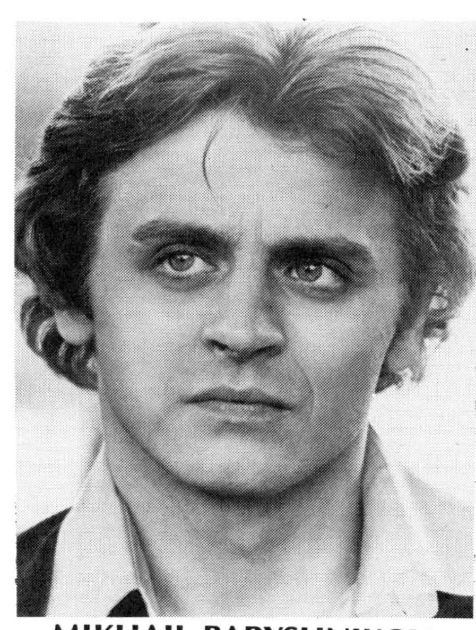
MIKHAIL BARYSHNIKOV

JAMIE LYN BAUER

BARBAGALLO, JAMES	PIANIST	POST OFFICE BOX 20548	NEW YORK, NY	10025
BARBARIAN, THE	WRESTLER	SEE - KONGA THE BARBARIAN		
BARBARIAN, THE	WRESTLER	SEE - NORD THE BARBARIAN		
BARBARIANS, THE	BODYBUILDERS	2210 WILSHIRE BLVD #726	SANTA MONICA, CA	90403
BARBAROSSA, JOSCIK	ACTOR	BRITISH ACTORS EQUITY		
		8 HARLEY ST	LONDON W1	ENGLAND
BARBASH, BOB	SCREENWRITER	8955 BEVERLY BLVD	LOS ANGELES, CA	90048
BARBASH, FRED	NEWS CORRESPONDENT	2799 28TH ST, NW	WASHINGTON, DC	20008
BARBAUX, CHRISTINE	SOPRANO	CAMI, 165 W 57TH ST	NEW YORK, NY	10019
BARBEAU, ADRIENNE	ACTRESS	POST OFFICE BOX 1334	NORTH HOLLYWOOD, CA	91604
BARBEE, CHARLES	CINEMATOGRAPHER	5235 WOODLUKE AVE	WOODLAND HILLS, CA	91367
BARBEE, DIANNE B	SAXOPHONIST	909 BEECH BEND DR	NASHVILLE, TN	37221
BARBEE, ROY	DRUMMER	909 BEECH BEND DR	NASHVILLE, TN	37221
BARBER, BETTY	GUITARIST	303 MARKET ST #5	PORTLAND, OR	37148
BARBER, BILL "RAJUN"	SAXOPHONIST	1225 BOONEHILL RD #Y-1	SUMMERVILLE, SC	29483
BARBER, CYNTHIA J C	NEWS CORRESPONDENT	4001 BRANDYWINE ST, NW	WASHINGTON, DC	20016
BARBER, GLENN	GUITARIST	POST OFFICE BOX 1214	HENDERSONVILLE, TN	37075
BARBER, GLYNIS	ACTRESS	113 WARDOUR ST	LONDON W1V 3TD	ENGLAND
BARBER, JOHNNIE	DRUMMER	402 N 16TH ST	NASHVILLE, TN	37206
BARBER, MORGAN A, JR	TV DIRECTOR	330 W 58TH ST	NEW YORK, NY	10019
BARBER, RANDY	WRESTLER	NATIONAL WRESTLING ALLIANCE		
		JIM CROCKETT PROMOTIONS		
		421 BRIARBEND DR	CHARLOTTE, NC	28209
BARBER, RED	SPORTSCASTER	3013 BROOKMONT DR	TALLAHASSEE, FL	32312
BARBER, ROWLAND	TV WRITER	2216 S BENTLEY AVE #16	LOS ANGELES, CA	90064
BARBERA, NEAL	SCREENWRITER	8955 BEVERLY BLVD	LOS ANGELES, CA	90048
BARBERI, KATIE	ACTRESS	1717 N HIGHLAND AVE #414	LOS ANGELES, CA	90028
BARBI, VINCENT	ACTOR	1230 COLE AVE #103	LOS ANGELES, CA	90038
BARBIER, CHRISTIAN	ACTOR	LES CHAGRANTS	VALENSOLE 04210	FRANCE
BARBIERI, DR MICHAEL	BODYBUILDER	8050 WATSON RD #169	SAINT LOUIS, MO	63119
BARBIERI, ERNEST J	DIRECTOR	1777 1ST AVE	NEW YORK, NY	10028
BARBIERI, GATO	SAXOPHONIST	200 W 51ST ST #1410	NEW YORK, NY	10019
BARBOSA-LIMA, CARLOS	GUITARIST	SHAW CONCERTS, 1995 BROADWAY	NEW YORK, NY	10023
BARBOUR, JOHN	WRITER-COMEDIAN	8955 BEVERLY BLVD	LOS ANGELES, CA	90048
BARBOUR, KEITH	ACTOR-SINGER	9220 SUNSET BLVD #218	LOS ANGELES, CA	90069
BARBOUR, ROSS	SINGER	17233 RAYEN ST	NORTHRIDGE, CA	91325
BARBULEE, MADELEINE	ACTRESS	7 RUE LENTONNETT	PARIS 75009	FRANCE
BARBUTTI, PETE	COMEDIAN	POST OFFICE BOX 3819	LA MESA, CA	92044
BARCELLE, SHEILA	ACTRESS	8075 W 3RD ST #303	LOS ANGELES, CA	90048
BARCLAY, DIANE	SOPRANO	AFFILIATE ARTISTS, INC		
		37 W 65TH ST, 6TH FLOOR	NEW YORK, NY	10023
BARCLAY, JERED	ACTOR	9165 SUNSET BLVD #202	LOS ANGELES, CA	90069
BARCLAY, RUE	SINGER	VISTONE, 6331 SANTA MONICA BLVD	HOLLYWOOD, CA	90038
BARCROFT, JUDITH	ACTRESS	DOLAN, 50-06 63RD ST	WOODSIDE, NJ	11377
BARCUS, KEN	NEWS CORRESPONDENT	2616 COLSTON DR	CHEVY CHASE, MD	20815
BARCUS, STEPHEN J	DIRECTOR	25 DERWEN RD	BALA CYNWYD, PA	19004
BARCZA, PETER	BARITONE	SARDOS, 180 W END AVE	NEW YORK, NY	10023
BARCZAK, ANNA-MARIA	WRITER	555 W 57TH ST #1230	NEW YORK, NY	10019
BARCZAK, M JESSIE	NEWS CORRESPONDENT	11902 SAINT JOHNSBURY CT	RESTON, VA	22091
BARD, RACHEL	ACTRESS	6430 SUNSET BLVD #701	LOS ANGELES, CA	90028
BARDACH, ANN L	WRITER	134 S PALM DR	BEVERLY HILLS, CA	90212
BARDI, ANGELO	ACTOR	COOPDU SPECHT MANAGEMENT		
		27-29 RUE BOURG-TIBOURG	PARIS 75004	FRANCE
BARDO, BOB	TV PRODUCER	ABC-TV, "GENERAL HOSPITAL"		
		1438 N GOWER ST	LOS ANGELES, CA	90028
BARDOT, BRIGITTE	ACTRESS	LA MADRIQUE, AIX-EN-PROVENCE	SAINT TROPEZ 83990	FRANCE
BARDWELL, JEAN	ACTRESS	439 S LA CIENEGA BLVD #117	LOS ANGELES, CA	90048
BARE, BOBBY	SINGER-SONGWRITER	POST OFFICE BOX 121312	NASHVILLE, TN	37212
BAREL, ZVI	NEWS CORRESPONDENT	2810 29TH ST, NW	WASHINGTON, DC	20008
BARENBOIM, DANIEL	CONDUCTOR	HOLT, 122 WIGMORE ST	LONDON W1	ENGLAND
BARFIELD, JUNE T	WRITER	555 W 57TH ST #1230	NEW YORK, NY	10019
BARGAMIAN, ALBERT	PHOTOJOURNALIST	13 DAVID CT	SILVER SPRING, MD	20904
BARGER, BRIAN	NEWS CORRESPONDENT	1539 MONROE ST, NW	WASHINGTON, DC	20010
BARGER, MILLARD I	NEWS CORRESPONDENT	2208 KING PL, NW	WASHINGTON, DC	20007
BARHYDT, FRANK	WRITER	1510 ROLLIN ST	SOUTH PASADENA, CA	91030
BARISH, KEITH	FILM PRODUCER	1800 CENTURY PARK E #1100	LOS ANGELES, CA	90067
BARISH, LEORA	SCREENWRITER	151 S EL CAMINO DR	BEVERLY HILLS, CA	90212
BARKAN, HELEN	TALENT AGENT	AIMEE, 13743 VICTORY BLVD	VAN NUYS, CA	91401
BARKAN, MARK	WRITER	555 W 57TH ST #1230	NEW YORK, NY	10019
BARKAYS, THE	RHYTHM & BLUES GROUP	200 W 51ST ST #1410	NEW YORK, NY	10019
BARKER, BOB	TV HOST	1851 OUTPOST DR	LOS ANGELES, CA	90069
BARKER, LYNN	TV WRITER	8955 BEVERLY BLVD	LOS ANGELES, CA	90048
BARKER, MARGARET	ACTRESS	69 W 9TH ST	NEW YORK, NY	10011
BARKER, RONNIE	ACTOR	BBC-TV CENTRE, WOOD LN		
		SHEPHERDS BUSH	LONDON W12	ENGLAND
BARKER, STEVE	TV WRITER	8955 BEVERLY BLVD	LOS ANGELES, CA	90048
BARKER, SUSAN	ACTRESS	FELBER, 2126 N CAHUENGA BLVD	LOS ANGELES, CA	90068
BARKER, VICKI	NEWS CORRESPONDENT	1400 "I" ST, NW	WASHINGTON, DC	20005
BARKER, WARREN E	COMPOSER-CONDUCTOR	ROUTE #3, BOX 3503	RED BLUFF, CA	96080
BARKETT, R B	DIRECTOR	551 S 35TH ST	SAN DIEGO, CA	92113
BARKIN, ELLEN	ACTRESS	10 E 44TH ST #700	NEW YORK, NY	10017
BARKIN, GEORGE	WRITER	THE NATIONAL LAMPOON		
		635 MADISON AVE	NEW YORK, NY	10022
BARKIN, HASKELL	TV WRITER	14636 MARTHA ST	VAN NUYS, CA	91411

Name	Occupation	Address	City	Zip
BARKIN, MARCIE	ACTRESS	230 S LUCERNE BLVD	LOS ANGELES, CA	90004
BARKLEY, DEANNE	TV PRODUCER	COMWORD, 15301 VENTURA BLVD	SHERMAN OAKS, CA	91403
BARKLEY, DEANNE	WRITER	555 W 57TH ST #1230	NEW YORK, NY	10019
BARKLEY, ROGER J	ACTOR-WRITER	5435 BURNING TREE DR	LA CANADA, CA	91011
BARKLEY, TAMARA	ACTRESS	1036 N CROFT AVE	LOS ANGELES, CA	90069
BARKS, CARL	CARTOONIST	31180 S G KEARNEY	TEMECULA, CA	92390
BARKS, JOSEPH V	NEWS CORRESPONDENT	505 5TH ST, NE	WASHINGTON, DC	20002
BARKWORTH, PETER	ACTOR	47 FLASK WALK	LONDON NW3	ENGLAND
BARLOW, ANNA MARIE	WRITER	555 W 57TH ST #1230	NEW YORK, NY	10019
BARLOW, DAVID E	WRITER-PRODUCER	28 HENRY TREE TERR	TORONTO, ONT M5A 4A1	CANADA
BARLOW, ELIZABETH	WRITER	555 W 57TH ST #1230	NEW YORK, NY	10019
BARLOW, JACK	SINGER	ROUTE #2, BOX 434	BURNS, TN	37029
BARLOW, JENNIFER	ACTRESS	12725 VENTURA BLVD #E	STUDIO CITY, CA	91604
BARLOW, MICHAEL W	WRITER-PRODUCER	415 MONTANA AVE	SANTA MONICA, CA	90403
BARLOW, RANDY	SINGER	5514 KELLY RD	BRENTWOOD, TN	37027
BARLOW, RAY	ACTOR	9025 WILSHIRE BLVD #309	BEVERLY HILLS, CA	90211
BARLOW, RICHARD H	DIRECTOR	411 E 53RD ST	NEW YORK, NY	10022
BARLOW, WILLIAM	DIRECTOR	106 KEITH RD	NEWPORT NEWS, VA	23606
BARMAK, IRA	SCREENWRITER	2711 BOWMONT DR	BEVERLY HILLS, CA	90210
BARMAT, BETSY J	NEWS CORRESPONDENT	2133 WISCONSIN AVE, NW	WASHINGTON, DC	20007
BARNABA, JOSEPH	ACTOR	6919 TOBIAS AVE	VAN NUYS, CA	91405
BARNABA, JOSEPH G	COMPOSER	15474 ALBRIGHT ST	PACIFIC PALISADES, CA	90272
BARNARD, ELAINE	ACTRESS	BERZON, 336 E 17TH ST	COSTA MESA, CA	92627
BARNARD, JERRY	EVANGELIST	POST OFFICE BOX 413	SAN DIEGO, CA	92112
BARNARD, PETER J	NEWS CORRESPONDENT	1080 WISCONSIN AVE, NW	WASHINGTON, DC	20007
BARNARD, RICHARD C	NEWS CORRESPONDENT	1805 N OAKLAND ST	ARLINGTON, VA	22207
BARNARD, TONY	ACTOR	3345 MENTONE AVE #8	LOS ANGELES, CA	90035
BARNAS, RAYMOND E	TV DIRECTOR	1485 WEBSTER LN	DES PLAINES, IL	60018
BARNATHAN, JACQUELINE F	WRITER	555 W 57TH ST #1230	NEW YORK, NY	10019
BARNATHAN, JULIUS	TV EXECUTIVE	ABC-TV, 7 W 66TH ST	NEW YORK, NY	10023
BARNES, BILLY	WRITER	8955 BEVERLY BLVD	LOS ANGELES, CA	90048
BARNES, BINNIE	ACTRESS	838 N DOHENY DR #B	LOS ANGELES, CA	90069
BARNES, CAROL & CINDY	VOCAL DUO	NATA, 84 AMARANTH ST E		
		GRAND VALLEY	ONTARIO LON 1GO	CANADA
BARNES, DALLAS	TV WRITER	8955 BEVERLY BLVD	LOS ANGELES, CA	90048
BARNES, EDWARD	NEWS REPORTER	LIFE/TIME & LIFE BLDG		
		ROCKEFELLER CENTER	NEW YORK, NY	10020
BARNES, FREDERIC W, JR	NEWS CORRESPONDENT	4400 S 1ST ST	ARLINGTON, VA	22204
BARNES, JANET S	NEWS CORRESPONDENT	5205 MASSACHUSETTS AVE, NW	WASHINGTON, DC	20816
BARNES, JIMMY	SINGER-SONGWRITER	41 BRITAIN ST #200	TORONTO, ONT	CANADA
BARNES, JO ANNE	TV WRITER	8955 BEVERLY BLVD	LOS ANGELES, CA	90048
BARNES, JOANNA	ACTRESS-WRITER	400 S BEVERLY DR #216	BEVERLY HILLS, CA	90212
BARNES, JOHN	TV WRITER	8955 BEVERLY BLVD	LOS ANGELES, CA	90048
BARNES, JULIAN	ACTOR	9000 SUNSET BLVD #801	LOS ANGELES, CA	90069
BARNES, KATHLEEN J	WRITER	4702 ETHEL AVE	SHERMAN OAKS, CA	91423
BARNES, MARSHALL	GUITARIST	1229 OLD DICKERSON RD #B-9	GOODLETTSVILLE, TN	37072
BARNES, MAX T	GUITARIST	500 BRINKLEY LN	WHITE HOUSE, TN	37188
BARNES, MICHAEL	ACTOR	LIGHT, 113 N ROBERTSON BLVD	LOS ANGELES, CA	90048
BARNES, PRISCILLA	ACTRESS	432 S HAMEL RD #303	LOS ANGELES, CA	90048
BARNES, RAYFORD	ACTOR	4321 OCEAN DR	MANHATTAN BEACH, CA	90266
BARNES, RON	WRESTLER	SEE - GARVIN, RONNIE		
BARNES, WADE	ACTOR	20 BEEKMAN PL	NEW YORK, NY	10022
BARNET, CHARLIE	CONDUCTOR	1085 MARSHALL WY	PALM SPRINGS, CA	92262
BARNETT, BERT & COLUMBIA	RHYTHM & BLUES GROUP	BLANTON, 2638 TWO NOTCH RD	COLUMBIA, SC	29204
BARNETT, DAVID	PIANIST-COMPOSER	3 LEDGEBROOK CT	WESTON, CT	06883
BARNETT, DAVID L	NEWS CORRESPONDENT	7215 BEECHWOOD RD	ALEXANDRIA, VA	22307
BARNETT, DONALD E	GUITARIST-BANJOIST	1651 MC KOOL AVE	STREAMWOOD, IL	60103
BARNETT, EDWARD A	DIRECTOR	60 E 9TH ST #339	NEW YORK, NY	10003
BARNETT, EILEEN	ACTRESS-SINGER	9255 SUNSET BLVD #603	LOS ANGELES, CA	90069
BARNETT, JACK	WRITER-PRODUCER	508 N CRESCENT DR	BEVERLY HILLS, CA	90210
BARNETT, JAMES C, JR	WRITER	13446 ERWIN ST	VAN NUYS, CA	91401
BARNETT, JERRY	CARTOONIST	POST OFFICE BOX 145	INDIANAPOLIS, IN	46206
BARNETT, JOAN	TV EXECUTIVE	ALAN LANDSBURG PRODUCTIONS		
		11811 W OLYMPIC BLVD	LOS ANGELES, CA	90064
BARNETT, JOHN M	CONDUCTOR	CALLE SAN ALVARO 1882	RIO PIEDRAS, PR	00926
BARNETT, KAREN M	DIRECTOR	3200 N LAKE SHORE DR #1202	CHICAGO, IL	60657
BARNETT, KEN	SCREENWRITER	8955 BEVERLY BLVD	LOS ANGELES, CA	90048
BARNETT, MARK	GUITARIST-BANJOIST	ROUTE #2, ANDERSON LN	HENDERSONVILLE, TN	37075
BARNETT, ROBERT L	TV DIRECTOR	319 ANAPALAU ST	HONOLULU, HI	96825
BARNETT, SANFORD H	WRITER	4217 WHITSETT AVE	STUDIO CITY, CA	91604
BARNETT, STEPHEN	FILM DIRECTOR	5231 SAN FELICIANO DR	WOODLAND HILLS, CA	91364
BARNETTE, IRWIN T	WRITER	3333 W 2ND ST #51-118	LOS ANGELES, CA	90004
BARNGROVER, JAMES V, JR	CONDUCTOR	4422 SANDBURG WY	IRVINE, CA	92664
BARNHARDT, ROBERLEIGH H	COMPOSER	507 E CYPRESS AVE #C	BURBANK, CA	91501
BARNHART, DON LEWIS	ACTOR-DIRECTOR	275 VALLEY DR	HERMOSA BEACH, CA	90254
BARNHILL, JOE BOB	GUITARIST	1303 LIPSCOMB DR	BRENTWOOD, TN	37027
BARNHIZER, DAVID	DIRECTOR	DGA, 110 W 57TH ST	NEW YORK, NY	10019
BARNUM, H B, III	ACTOR	7300 MULHOLLAND DR	LOS ANGELES, CA	90046
BARNWELL, JOHN	WRITER-PRODUCER	POST OFFICE BOX 1337	BIG BEAR LAKE, CA	92315
BARODY, GEORGE	TALENT AGENT	POST OFFICE BOX 252	AUBURN, NY	13021
BARON, ALLEN	WRITER-PRODUCER	407 S SPALDING DR #11	BEVERLY HILLS, CA	90212
BARON, DAVID	ACTOR	BROWN, 47 WEST SQ	LONDON SE11	ENGLAND
BARON, DEBORAH R	TV WRITER	7655 HOLLYWOOD BLVD #1	LOS ANGELES, CA	90046
BARON, HELEN	ACTRESS	7471 MELROSE AVE #11	LOS ANGELES, CA	90046
BARON, JOANNE	ACTRESS	870 N VINE ST #G	LOS ANGELES, CA	90038

BARON, MARY	ACTRESS	348 E OLIVE AVE #K	BURBANK, CA	91502
BARON, MILLE	ACTRESS	1741 N IVAR AVE #221	LOS ANGELES, CA	90028
BARON, SUZANNE	EDITOR	3 RUE PAUL-FEVAR	PARIS 75018	FRANCE
BARON, VALIA	ACTRESS	10845 LINDBROOK DR #3	LOS ANGELES, CA	90024
BARONDESS, BARBARA	ACTRESS	MAC LEAN, 630 PARK AVE	NEW YORK, NY	10021
BARONE, JOAN S	TV WRITER-PRODUCER	3530 EDMUNDS ST, NW	WASHINGTON, DC	20007
BARONE, MARCANTONIO	PIANIST	AFFILIATE ARTISTS, INC		
		37 W 65TH ST, 6TH FLOOR	NEW YORK, NY	10023
BARONE, MICHAEL	NEWS CORRESPONDENT	3530 EDMUNDS ST	WASHINGTON, DC	20007
BAROUH, STAN	PHOTOGRAPHER	6607 WESTMORELAND AVE	TAKOMA PARK, MD	20912
BARR, ADRIENNE E	WRITER	555 W 57TH ST #1230	NEW YORK, NY	10019
BARR, ANTHONY	DIRECTOR-PRODUCER	13516 GAULT ST	VAN NUYS, CA	91405
BARR, BILL	TV WRITER	8955 BEVERLY BLVD	LOS ANGELES, CA	90048
BARR, DONALD J	PUBLISHING EXECUTIVE	SPORTS ILLUSTRATED MAGAZINE		
		TIME & LIFE BUILDING		
		ROCKEFELLER CENTER	NEW YORK, NY	10020
BARR, DOUG	ACTOR	515 S IRVING BLVD	LOS ANGELES, CA	90020
BARR, JESSE "BULLDOG"	WRESTLER	SEE - FUNK, JIMMY JACK		
BARR, JULIA	ACTRESS	ABRAMS ARTISTS & ASSOCIATES		
		420 MADISON AVE, 14TH FLOOR	NEW YORK, NY	10017
BARR, MATTHEW FRANCIS	SCREENWRITER	8955 BEVERLY BLVD	LOS ANGELES, CA	90048
BARR, RICHARD	DIRECTOR-PRODUCER	26 W 8TH ST	NEW YORK, NY	10011
BARR, RICK & AMERICAN BLUES	BLUES GROUP	RAB, 158 S BROADWAY	LAWRENCE, MA	01843
BARR, ROBERT	TV CRITIC	THE ASSOCIATED PRESS		
		50 ROCKEFELLER PLAZA	NEW YORK, NY	10020
BARR, ROBERT A	NEWS CORRESPONDENT	7317 LEESVILLE BLVD	SPRINGFIELD, VA	22151
BARR, ROSEANNE	COMEDIENNE-ACTRESS	SCOTTI BROS, 2128 PICO BLVD	SANTA MONICA, CA	90405
BARR, SHARON	ACTRESS	ICM, 8899 BEVERLY BLVD	LOS ANGELES, CA	90048
BARR, STEVE	CARTOONIST	TRIBUNE MEDIA SERVICES		
		64 E CONCORD ST	ORLANDO, FL	32801
BARR, TONY	TV EXECUTIVE	CBS-TV, 6121 SUNSET BLVD	LOS ANGELES, CA	90028
BARR, WILLIAM H	TV WRITER-PRODUCER	3690 BARHAM BLVD #G-219	LOS ANGELES, CA	90069
BARRA, VANDA	ACTRESS	9300 WILSHIRE BLVD #410	BEVERLY HILLS, CA	90212
BARRACLOUGH, JENNY	FILM DIRECTOR	86 NARROW ST	LONDON E14	ENGLAND
BARRAULT, JEAN-LOUIS	ACTOR	MADELEINE RENAUD AGENCY		
		18 AVE PRES WILSON	PARIS 75116	FRANCE
BARRAULT, MARIE-CHRISTINE	ACTRESS	DE LISBONNE 19	PARIS 75008	FRANCE
BARREAUX, ROSLYN	WRITER	555 W 57TH ST #1230	NEW YORK, NY	10019
BARRERA, JOE O	COMPOSER	5230 CLINTON ST #10	LOS ANGELES, CA	90004
BARREREA, GIULIA	SOPRANO	61 W 62ND ST #6-F	NEW YORK, NY	10023
BARRET, EARL	WRITER-PRODUCER	4239 SHERMAN OAKS AVE	SHERMAN OAKS, CA	91403
BARRET, LESLIE	ACTRESS	203 W 81ST ST	NEW YORK, NY	10024
BARRETT, BETTY	FRENCH HORN	POST OFFICE BOX 12424	NASHVILLE, TN	37212
BARRETT, BUCKY	GUITARIST	POST OFFICE BOX 40891	NASHVILLE, TN	37204
BARRETT, CHRISTOPHER	ACTOR	11227 HORTENSE ST	NORTH HOLLYWOOD, CA	91602
BARRETT, GREG	SINGER-GUITARIST	1900 ROSEWOOD AVE #A-6	NASHVILLE, TN	37212
BARRETT, HELEN A	WRITER	555 W 57TH ST #1230	NEW YORK, NY	10019
BARRETT, JACK E	WRITER	4267 NEOSHO AVE	LOS ANGELES, CA	90066
BARRETT, JAMES LEE	WRITER-PRODUCER	8955 BEVERLY BLVD	LOS ANGELES, CA	90048
BARRETT, JOHN R	TV WRITER	8955 BEVERLY BLVD	LOS ANGELES, CA	90048
BARRETT, JUNE	ACTRESS	6944 FERNHILL DR	MALIBU, CA	90265
BARRETT, LAURENCE I	POLITICAL CORRES	3001 VEAZY TERR, NW	WASHINGTON, DC	20008
BARRETT, LESLIE	ACTOR	203 W 81ST ST	NEW YORK, NY	10024
BARRETT, MARIANNE	ACTRES	8230 BEVERLY BLVD #23	BEVERLY HILLS, CA	90048
BARRETT, MARVIN GALBRAITH	JOURNALIST	35 CLAREMONT AVE	NEW YORK, NY	10027
BARRETT, RON	CARTOONIST	THE NATIONAL LAMPOON		
		635 MADISON AVE	NEW YORK, NY	10022
BARRETT, RONA	TV PERSONALITY	POST OFFICE BOX 1410	BEVERLY HILLS, CA	90213
BARRETT, STAN	DIRECTOR	ROCKING K RANCH	BISHOP, CA	93514
BARRETT, STEPHANIE	SCREENWRITER	8955 BEVERLY BLVD	LOS ANGELES, CA	90048
BARRETT, TIM	ACTOR	JOAN GRAY MANAGEMENT		
		29 SUNBURY CT ISLAND		
		SUNBURY-ON-THAMES	MIDDLESEX	ENGLAND
BARRETT & SMITH	VOCAL DUO	4111 LINCOLN BLVD #211	MARINA DEL REY, CA	90292
BARRETT-BROWNING, JUNE	ACTRESS	400 S BEVERLY DR #216	BEVERLY HILLS, CA	90212
BARRI, STEVE	PRODUCER-SONGWRITER	MOTOWN RECORDS COMPANY		
		6255 SUNSET BLVD	HOLLYWOOD, CA	90028
BARRIE, BARBARA	ACTRESS	465 W END AVE	NEW YORK, NY	10024
BARRIE, BENITA	WRITER	8955 BEVERLY BLVD	LOS ANGELES, CA	90048
BARRIE, MICHAEL P	WRITER	1423 SAN YSIDRO DR	BEVERLY HILLS, CA	90210
BARRIER, ERNESTINE	ACTRESS	PATCO, 10525 STRATHMORE DR	LOS ANGELES, CA	90024
BARRIER, MAURICE	ACTOR	ARTMEDIA, 10 AVE GEORGE	PARIS 75008	FRANCE
BARRINGER, FELICITY	NEWS CORRESPONDENT	2850 28TH ST, NW	WASHINGTON, DC	20008
BARRIS, ALEX P	WRITER	8955 BEVERLY BLVD	LOS ANGELES, CA	90048
BARRIS, CHUCK	TV HOST-PRODUCER	9060 SAINT IVES DR	LOS ANGELES, CA	90069
BARRON, ARTHUR S	WRITER	555 W 57TH ST #1230	NEW YORK, NY	10019
BARRON, BARBARA	ACTRESS	711 E ELMWOOD AVE	BURBANK, CA	91501
BARRON, BRIAN	NEWS CORRESPONDENT	1 GOLDSBORO CT	BETHESDA, MD	20817
BARRON, FRED	WRITER	8428 MELROSE PL	LOS ANGELES, CA	90069
BARRON, JEFFREY	WRITER	8431 BLACKBURN AVE	LOS ANGELES, CA	90048
BARRON, JOHN	ACTOR	GREEN & UNDERWOOD, INC		
		3 THE BROADWAY		
		GUNNERSBURY LN	LONDON W3 8HR	ENGLAND
BARRON, RICHARD H	CONDUCTOR	8208 ROMAINE ST	LOS ANGELES, CA	90046
BARRON, ROBERT V	ACTOR-WRITER	10503 RIVERSIDE DR #7	NORTH HOLLYWOOD, CA	91602

Name	Occupation	Address	City	Code
BARRON, STEVE	ACTOR	LIMELIGHT FILMS		
		36 SOHO SQ	LONDON W1	ENGLAND
BARRON, WILLIAM A, JR	DIRECTOR	1310 HEULU ST #1901	HONOLULU, HI	96822
BARRON, ZELDA	FILM DIRECTOR	LIMELIGHT FILMS		
		36 SOHO SQ	LONDON W1	ENGLAND
BARROSSE, PAUL A	WRITER	555 W 57TH ST #1230	NEW YORK, NY	10019
BARROW, BERNARD	ACTOR	ABC-TV, "RYAN'S HOPE"		
		1330 AVE OF THE AMERICAS	NEW YORK, NY	10019
BARROW, HENRY	SCREENWRITER	8955 BEVERLY BLVD	LOS ANGELES, CA	90048
BARROWS, APRIL	SINGER	POST OFFICE BOX 121201	NASHVILLE, TN	37212
BARROWS, DAN	ACTOR	15037 HAMLIN ST	VAN NUYS, CA	91411
BARROWS, GEORGE	ACTOR	6631 ATOLL AVE	NORTH HOLLYWOOD, CA	91606
BARROWS, MERCER, III	ACTOR	KNBC-TV, "DAYS OF OUR LIVES"		
		3000 W ALAMEDA AVE	BURBANK, CA	91523
BARROWS, ROBERT GUY	ACTOR-WRITER	8955 BEVERLY BLVD	LOS ANGELES, CA	90048
BARROWS, SAMANTHA	ACTRESS	KNBC-TV, "DAYS OF OUR LIVES"		
		3000 W ALAMEDA AVE	BURBANK, CA	91523
BARRS, NORMAN	ACTOR	55 E 78TH ST	NEW YORK, NY	10021
BARRUECO, MANUEL	GUITARIST	CAMI, 165 W 57TH ST	NEW YORK, NY	10019
BARRY, BETTY	ACTRESS	622 N MAPLE DR	BEVERLY HILLS, CA	90210
BARRY, BRUCE STUART	DIRECTOR	2435 YORKTOWN ST	OCEANSIDE, NY	11572
BARRY, CHRISTOPHER	WRITER-PRODUCER	BBC-TV CENTRE, WOOD LN		
		SHEPHERDS BUSH	LONDON W12	ENGLAND
BARRY, CHRISTOPHER C	WRITER-PRODUCER	ALL DIRECTIONS, LTD		
		10 WYNDHAM PL	LONDON W1H 1AS	ENGLAND
BARRY, DAN	CARTOONIST	KING FEATURES SYNDICATE		
		235 E 45TH ST	NEW YORK, NY	10017
BARRY, DAVE	COMEDIAN	21243 VENTURA BLVD #243	WOODLAND HILLS, CA	91364
BARRY, DAVID	SCREENWRITER	8955 BEVERLY BLVD	LOS ANGELES, CA	90048
BARRY, DOLAN J	PHOTOGRAPHER	274 LINCOLN ST	WORCESTER, MA	01605
BARRY, GENE	ACTOR	622 N MAPLE DR	BEVERLY HILLS, CA	90210
BARRY, GUERIN	ACTOR	806 1/2 N MARTEL AVE	LOS ANGELES, CA	90046
BARRY, J J	WRITER	8955 BEVERLY BLVD	LOS ANGELES, CA	90006
BARRY, JEFF	COMPOSER	9100 SUNSET BLVD #200	LOS ANGELES, CA	90069
BARRY, JOHN	COMPOSER	2741 HUTTON DR	BEVERLY HILLS, CA	90210
BARRY, JOHN M	NEWS CORRESPONDENT	1629 COLUMBIA RD, NW	WASHINGTON, DC	20009
BARRY, JULIAN	WRITER	10006 WESTWANDA DR	BEVERLY HILLS, CA	90210
BARRY, JULIE	ACTRESS	12926 RIVERSIDE DR #C	SHERMAN OAKS, CA	91423
BARRY, JUNE	ACTRESS	LONDON MANAGEMENT, LTD		
		235-241 REGENT ST	LONDON W1A 2JT	ENGLAND
BARRY, KENNETH	COMPOSER	950 N ARROWHEAD AVE	SAN BERNARDINO, CA	92410
BARRY, KENNETH D	NEWS CORRESPONDENT	2022 COLUMBIA RD, NW	WASHINGTON, DC	20009
BARRY, LEN	SINGER	JOYCE AGENCY, 435 E 79TH ST	NEW YORK, NY	10021
BARRY, LLOYD F	PIANIST	1019 PATRICIA DR #C-106	NASHVILLE, TN	37217
BARRY, LYNDA J	CARTOONIST	THE READER, 635 STATE ST	SAN DIEGO, CA	92101
BARRY, MATTHEW	ACTOR	POST OFFICE BOX 1684	STUDIO CITY, CA	91604
BARRY, MIRANDA	WRITER	555 W 57TH ST #1230	NEW YORK, NY	10019
BARRY, PATRICIA	ACTRESS	POST OFFICE BOX 49895	LOS ANGELES, CA	90049
BARRY, PATRICK S	TV WRITER	STEPHAN J CANNELL PRODS		
		7083 HOLLYWOOD BLVD	HOLLYWOOD, CA	90028
BARRY, PAUL	ACTOR	505 E LINCOLN AVE	MOUNT VERNON, NY	10552
BARRY, PHILIP, JR	WRITER-PRODUCER	POST OFFICE BOX 49895	LOS ANGELES, CA	90049
BARRY, R Z	WRITER	8955 BEVERLY BLVD	LOS ANGELES, CA	90048
BARRY, SY	CARTOONIST	34 SARATOGA DR	JERICHO, NY	11753
BARRY, THEODORE L, III	WRITER	555 W 57TH ST #1230	NEW YORK, NY	10019
BARRY, WESLEY	ACTOR	GENERAL DELIVERY	WITTER SPRINGS, CA	95493
BARRY O	WRESTLER	POST OFFICE BOX 3859	STAMFORD, CT	06905
BARRYMORE, DREW	ACTRESS	JAID, 3960 LAUREL CANYON BLVD	STUDIO CITY, CA	91604
BARRYMORE, JOHN B, III	ACTOR	8036 JOVENITA CANYON RD	LOS ANGELES, CA	90046
BARSACQ, YVES	ACTOR	20 RUE DU CADET, RENE MOUCHO	PARIS 75014	FRANCE
BARSALONA, FRANK	AGENT	3 E 54TH ST #1400	NEW YORK, NY	10022
BARSELOU, PAUL	ACTOR	6736 LAUREL CANYON BLVD #306	NORTH HOLLYWOOD, CA	91606
BARSEVICH, MICHAEL	TV DIRECTOR	2524 COLUMBIA AVE #2	PITTSSBURGH, PA	15218
BARSHAI, RUDOLF	CONDUCTOR	ICM, 40 W 57TH ST	NEW YORK, NY	10019
BARSOCCHINI, PETER	TV WRITER	11317 VALLEY SPRING LN	NORTH HOLLYWOOD, CA	91602
BARSON, LUCIEN	ACTOR	127 AVE J B CLEMENT	BOULOGNE 92100	FRANCE
BARSTOW, RICHARD	CHOR-DIR-PROD	200 W 54TH ST	NEW YORK, NY	10019
BART, ALVIN	TALENT AGENT	4146 LANKERSHIM BLVD #300	NORTH HOLLYWOOD, CA	91602
BART, BLACK	WRESTLER	SEE - BLACK BART		
BART, CHRIS	ACTRESS	8150 BEVERLY BLVD #303	LOS ANGELES, CA	90048
BART, DUFFY	WRITER	8955 BEVERLY BLVD	LOS ANGELES, CA	90048
BART, LIONEL	LYRICIST-COMPOSER	MAX NAUGHTON LOWE		
		200 FULHAM RD	LONDON SW10	ENGLAND
BART, PETER	FILM PRODUCER	2270 BETTY LN	BEVERLY HILLS, CA	90210
BARTEL, JEAN	ACTRESS	208 S BEVERLY DR #4	BEVERLY HILLS, CA	90212
BARTEL, PAUL	ACTOR-DIRECTOR	DGA, 7950 SUNSET BLVD	HOLLYWOOD, CA	90046
BARTELME, JOE	NEWS DIRECTOR	NBC TELEVISION NETWORK		
		30 ROCKEFELLER PLAZA	NEW YORK, NY	10112
BARTH, CARL	DIRECTOR	DGA, 7950 SUNSET BLVD	LOS ANGELES, CA	90046
BARTH, EDDIE	ACTOR	8075 W 3RD ST #303	LOS ANGELES, CA	90048
BARTH, HENRY	DIRECTOR	143 CUPSAW LAKE DR	RINGWOOD, NJ	07456
BARTH, JEFFREY J	NEWS CORRESPONDENT	3839 BEECHER ST, NW	WASHINGTON, DC	20007
BARTHA, CLARRY	SOPRANO	61 W 62ND ST #6-F	NEW YORK, NY	10023
BARTHOLOME, TRICIA	ACTRESS	8075 W 3RD ST #303	LOS ANGELES, CA	90048

Name	Occupation	Address	City	ZIP
BARTHOLOMEW, LINDA	PIANIST-GUITARIST	705 TARVER ST	MONROE, LA	71201
BARTLE, BARRY	ACTOR	439 S LA CIENEGA BLVD #120	LOS ANGELES, CA	90048
BARTLES, ALFRED H	CELLIST	7000 STUTTGARD 50		
		OBERE WAIBLINGER	STR 158	WEST GERMANY
BARTLETT, BONNIE	ACTRESS	DANIELS, 14242 PIERCE ST	ARLETA, CA	91331
BARTLETT, CHARLES	ACTOR	3800 BARHAM BLVD #303	LOS ANGELES, CA	90068
BARTLETT, CHUCK	GUITARIST	236 MANZANO RD	MADISON, TN	37115
BARTLETT, HALL	WRITER-PRODUCER	861 STONE CANYON RD	LOS ANGELES, CA	90077
BARTLETT, JUANITA	TV PRODUCER	4000 WARNER BLVD	BURBANK, CA	91522
BARTLETT, JUANITA LAULEE	WRITER	15950 VALLEY VISTA BLVD	ENCINO, CA	91436
BARTLETT, MARTINE	ACTRESS-WRITER	1233 N HARPER AVE	LOS ANGELES, CA	90046
BARTLETT, SCOTT	SCREENWRITER	2042 GREEN ST	SAN FRANCISCO, CA	94123
BARTMAN, BILL	ACTOR	10375 WILSHIRE BLVD	LOS ANGELES, CA	90024
BARTMAN, WILLIAM	TV DIRECTOR	4247 KESTER AVE	SHERMAN OAKS, CA	91403
BARTMAN, WILLIAM J	NEWS CORRESPONDENT	1736 QUEENS LN #192	ARLINGTON, VA	22201
BARTO, DOMINIC	ACTOR	8350 SANTA MONICA BLVD #103	LOS ANGELES, CA	90069
BARTO, GORDON	DIRECTOR	320 RIO VISTA PL	SANTA FE, NM	87501
BARTOLD, NORMAN	ACTOR	439 S LA CIENEGA BLVD #120	LOS ANGELES, CA	90048
BARTOLD, VIRGINIA	CONDUCTOR	9285 FLICKER PL	LOS ANGELES, CA	90069
BARTOLETTI, BRUNO	CONDUCTOR	LYRIC OPERA, 20 N WACKER DR	CHICAGO, IL	60606
BARTOLINI, LANDO	TENOR	61 W 62ND ST #6-F	NEW YORK, NY	10023
BARTON, ANTHONY	ACTOR	151 N SAN VICENTE BLVD #208	BEVERLY HILLS, CA	90211
BARTON, DAN	ACTOR	14716 WEDDINGTON ST	VAN NUYS, CA	91411
BARTON, DAVID	GUITARIST	POST OFFICE BOX 24727	NASHVILLE, TN	37202
BARTON, DEREK	ACTOR	930 WESTBOURNE DR #400	LOS ANGELES, CA	90069
BARTON, DIANA	ACTRESS	11350 VENTURA BLVD #206	STUDIO CITY, CA	91604
BARTON, EARL	DIRECTOR	11639 SUNSHINE TERR	STUDIO CITY, CA	91604
BARTON, ERNESTINE	WRITER	212 SAN VICENTE BLVD #H	SANTA MONICA, CA	90402
BARTON, FRANK	PRODUCER	4000 WARNER BLVD	BURBANK, CA	91522
BARTON, FRANKLIN L	WRITER	9226 SIERRA MAR DR	LOS ANGELES, CA	90069
BARTON, GARY	CASTING DIRECTOR	CBS-TV, 6121 SUNSET BLVD	LOS ANGELES, CA	90028
BARTON, JEANNIE DIMTER	ACTRESS	WILLIAMSON, 932 N LA BREA AVE	LOS ANGELES, CA	90038
BARTON, KENT	CARTOONIST	NEWS AMERICA SYNDICATE		
		1703 KAISER AVE	IRVING, CA	92714
BARTON, LARRY	ACTOR	4629 FULTON AVE	SHERMAN OAKS, CA	91423
BARTON, MARY ANN	CASTING DIRECTOR	PARAMOUNT, 5555 MELROSE AVE	LOS ANGELES, CA	90038
BARTON, OLIVIA L	NEWS CORRESPONDENT	17 1/2 6TH ST, SE	WASHINGTON, DC	20003
BARTON, PETER	ACTOR	311 S DOHENY DR #305	LOS ANGELES, CA	90048
BARTON, PETER B	WRITER	555 W 57TH ST #1230	NEW YORK, NY	10019
BARTON, SAMUEL	ACTOR	484 W 43RD ST #28-G	NEW YORK, NY	10036
BARTON, TRUITT C	WRITER	555 W 57TH ST #1230	NEW YORK, NY	10019
BARTOO, MARION	WRITER	3548 CARNATION AVE	LOS ANGELES, CA	90026
BARTOS, MICHAEL	CONDUCTOR	ROSENFIELD, 714 LADD RD	BRONX, NY	10471
BARTRON, HARRY	ACTOR	3532 MENTONE AVE #A	LOS ANGELES, CA	90034
BARTSCH, TED	ACTOR	1828 NE 4TH AVE	MIAMI, FL	33132
BARTUSSEK, WALTER	MIME	360 CENTRAL PARK W #16-G	NEW YORK, NY	10025
BARTY, BILLY	ACTOR	4502 FARMDALE AVE	NORTH HOLLYWOOD, CA	91602
BARTZ, GARY	MUSICIAN	BACKSTAGE MANAGEMENT		
		8919 SUNSET BLVD	LOS ANGELES, CA	90069
BARUCH, ANDRE	RADIO-TV PERSONALITY	9955 DURANT DR #305	BEVERLY HILLS, CA	90212
BARUCH, RALPH M	TV EXECUTIVE	VIACOM INTERNATIONAL, INC		
		1211 AVE OF THE AMERICAS	NEW YORK, NY	10036
BARWOOD, HAL	SCREENWRITER	234 N KENWOOD ST #109	GLENDALE, CA	91206
BARYSHNIKOV, MIKHAIL	BALLET DANCER	35 E 12TH ST #5-D	NEW YORK, NY	10018
BARZMAN, BEN	WRITER	1738 N OGDEN DR	LOS ANGELES, CA	90046
BARZMAN, NORMA	WRITER	1738 N OGDEN DR	LOS ANGELES, CA	90046
BARZYK, FREDERICK F	DIRECTOR	12 BROOK ST	CHELMSFORD, MA	01824
BARZYK, SHARON	NEWS CORRESPONDENT	1725 "K" ST #608, NW	WASHINGTON, DC	20006
BASACKER, CATHY	BODYBUILDER	3836 CAIRNS WY	MODESTO, CA	95356
BASACKER, RICK	BODYBUILDER	3836 CAIRNS WY	MODESTO, CA	95356
BASCH, HARRY	ACTOR-WRITER	920 1/2 S SERRANO AVE	LOS ANGELES, CA	90006
BASCOM, CHERYL	CASTING DIRECTOR	446 N GOLDEN MALL	BURBANK, CA	91502
BASCOM, FRAN	CASTING DIRECTOR	COLUMBIA PICTURES		
		COLUMBIA PLAZA #120	BURBANK, CA	91505
BASCOM, JON P	NEWS CORRESPONDENT	ABC-TV, NEWS DEPARTMENT	WASHINGTON, DC	20036
		1717 DE SALES ST, NW	WASHINGTON, DC	20036
BASEMAN, BO J	SINGER-GUITARIST	506 WANDA DR	NASHVILLE, TN	37210
BASEMAN, DANNY	GUITARIST-DRUMMER	261 SAILFISH CT	ANTIOCH, TN	37013
BASENKO, BEN	ACTOR	240 CENTRAL PARK S	NEW YORK, NY	10019
BASER, MICHAEL S	TV WRITER-PRODUCER	10633 COMMERCE AVE	TUJUNGA, CA	91042
BASEY, JILL	ACTRESS	5656 BELLINGHAM AVE	NORTH HOLLYWOOD, CA	91607
BASH, OTTO EDWARD	DRUMMER	1913 ASHWOOD AVE	NASHVILLE, TN	37212
BASHER	WRESTLER	SEE - MOD SQUAD, THE		
BASHKIROFF, PETER V	WRITER	8955 BEVERLY BLVD	LOS ANGELES, CA	90048
BASICHIS, GORDON ALLEN	WRITER	9255 SUNSET BLVD #411	LOS ANGELES, CA	90069
BASIL, MICKEY	MUSIC ARRANGER	7985 CHARLOTTE PIKE	NASHVILLE, TN	37209
BASIL, TONI	SINGER	9595 WILSHIRE BLVD #505	BEVERLY HILLS, CA	90212
BASILE, NADINE	ACTRESS	15 BLVD LANNES	PARIS 75116	FRANCE
BASINGER, KIM	ACTRESS-MODEL	4833 DON JUAN PL	WOODLAND HILLS, CA	91364
BASINSKI, DAVE	DIRECTOR	920 STRAND	MANHATTAN BEACH, CA	90266
BASKCOMB, JOHN	ACTOR	CAPE HOUSE, CORNWALL		
		SAINT JUST, PENZANCE	CORNWALL	ENGLAND
BASKER, PAMELA	CASTING DIRECTOR	9911 W PICO BLVD		
		4TH FLOOR	LOS ANGELES, CA	90035
BASKERVILLE, CAROL	WRITER	7225 HOLLYWOOD BLVD #223	LOS ANGELES, CA	90046
BASKERVILLE, PRISCILLA	SOPRANO	LEW, 204 W 10TH ST	NEW YORK, NY	10014

Name	Occupation	Address	City	Code
BASKERVILLE, TIMOTHY D	WRITER	7225 HOLLYWOOD BLVD #223	LOS ANGELES, CA	90046
BASKIN, ELYA	ACTOR	151 S EL CAMINO DR	BEVERLY HILLS, CA	90212
BASKIN, JOHN	TV WRITER-PRODUCER	216 N LAYTON DR	LOS ANGELES, CA	90049
BASKIN, ROBERTA	NEWS CORRESPONDENT	4420 CONNECTICUT AVE, NW	WASHINGTON, DC	20008
BASKIN, RONALD	WRITER	555 W 57TH ST #1230	NEW YORK, NY	10019
BASKIN, SUSAN F	TV WRITER	8955 BEVERLY BLVD	LOS ANGELES, CA	90048
BASLER, JAMES R	WRITER	8955 BEVERLY BLVD	LOS ANGELES, CA	90048
BASORE, STU	GUITARIST	916 BEAUMONT DR	MADISON, TN	37115
BASQUIN, PETER	PIANIST	AMERICAN CHAMBER		
		890 W END AVE	NEW YORK, NY	10025
BASS, A	TV WRITER	8955 BEVERLY BLVD	LOS ANGELES, CA	90048
BASS, ALFIE	ACTOR	SIMONS, 9 NEAL ST	LONDON WC2H 9PU	ENGLAND
BASS, BOBBY	DIRECTOR	DGA, 7950 SUNSET BLVD	LOS ANGELES, CA	90046
BASS, BOBBY	STUNTMAN	6024 BUCKINGHAM PKWY	CULVER CITY, CA	90230
BASS, CLARENCE	BODYBUILDER	528 CHAMA ST, NE	ALBUQUERQUE, NM	87108
BASS, EMORY	ACTOR	10000 SANTA MONICA BLVD #305	LOS ANGELES, CA	90067
BASS, GARY E	DIRECTOR	308 E 85TH ST	NEW YORK, NY	10028
BASS, KEVIN	ACTOR	1045 N EDINBURGH AVE #5	LOS ANGELES, CA	90046
BASS, RICHARD	GUITARIST	101 PEAR TREE DR	HENDERSONVILLE, TN	37075
BASS, ROBERT N	NEWS CORRESPONDENT	1012 14TH ST, NW	WASHINGTON, DC	20005
BASS, RONALD	SCREENWRITER	2029 CENTURY PARK E #1330	LOS ANGELES, CA	90067
BASS, SAUL	DIRECTOR-PRODUCER	337 S LAS PALMAS AVE	LOS ANGELES, CA	90020
BASS, VICTORIA	ACTRESS	9220 SUNSET BLVD #625	LOS ANGELES, CA	90069
BASS, WARREN	ACTOR	9200 SUNSET BLVD #1210	LOS ANGELES, CA	90069
BASSET, BRIAN	CARTOONIST	UNIVERSAL PRESS SYNDICATE		
		4900 MAIN ST, 9TH FLOOR	KANSAS CITY, MO	62114
BASSETT, BRUCE W	WRITER	555 W 57TH ST #1230	NEW YORK, NY	10019
BASSETT, LESLIE	COMPOSER	1618 HARBAL DR	ANN ARBOR, MI	48105
BASSETT, RALPH	BASSO-BARITONE	254 W 93RD ST #8	NEW YORK, NY	10025
BASSETT, STEVE	ACTOR	CBS-TV, "AS THE WORLD TURNS"		
		51 W 52ND ST	NEW YORK, NY	10019
BASSETT, WILLIAM H	ACTOR	14664 1/2 VICTORY BLVD	VAN NUYS, CA	91411
BASSEY, BERNARD	WRITER	1128 N VISTA ST #2	LOS ANGELES, CA	90046
BASSEY, JENNIFER	ACTRESS	THE CHELSEA HOTEL		
		222 W 23RD ST	NEW YORK, NY	10014
BASSEY, SHIRLEY	SINGER	10100 SANTA MONICA BLVD #1600	LOS ANGELES, CA	90067
BASSIN, ROBERTA	ACTRESS	120 S VICTORY BLVD #104	BURBANK, CA	91502
BASSING, ROBERT	WRITER	1069 S GENESEE AVE	LOS ANGELES, CA	90019
BASSMAN, GEORGE	COMPOSER-CONDUCTOR	401 S CRESCENT HGTS BLVD	LOS ANGELES, CA	90048
BASSO, BOB	ACTOR	10700 BLUFFSIDE DR #6	STUDIO CITY, CA	91604
BAST, WILLIAM	SCREENWRITER	6691 WHITLEY TERR	LOS ANGELES, CA	90068
BASTA, ANTHONY	TV WRITER	8955 BEVERLY BLVD	LOS ANGELES, CA	90048
BASTABLE, TONY	TV WRITER-DIRECTOR	BURFIELD, 93 CAMBRIDGE ST	LONDON SW1	ENGLAND
BASTEIN, MORGAN	WRESTLER	POST OFFICE BOX 3859	STAMFORD, CT	06905
BASTIA, JEAN	FILM DIRECTOR	56 RUE LA BRUYERE	PARIS 75009	FRANCE
BASTIN, JULES	BASS	1182 MARKET ST #311	SAN FRANCISCO, CA	94102
BASTONE, RON	WRITER	1756 N GARFIELD PL	LOS ANGELES, CA	90028
BAT-ADAM, MICHAL	DIRECTOR	POST OFFICE BOX 229	JERUSALEM	ISRAEL
BATANIDES, ARTHUR	ACTOR	3477 BEVERLY GLEN BLVD	SHERMAN OAKS, CA	91423
BATCHELOR, JOY E	WRITER-PRODUCER	HALAS, 3 KEAN ST	LONDON WC1	ENGLAND
BATE, ANTHONY	ACTOR	PARKER, 55 PARK LN	LONDON W1	ENGLAND
BATE, BRADLEY G	DIRECTOR	5445 N SHERIDAN RD #141	CHICAGO, IL	60640
BATE, HENRY C	DIRECTOR	69 SHORE RD	OLD GREENWICH, CT	06870
BATEMAN, CHARLES	ACTOR	208 S BEVERLY DR #4	BEVERLY HILLS, CA	90212
BATEMAN, EARL C, III	WRITER	555 W 57TH ST #1230	NEW YORK, NY	10019
BATEMAN, JAMES R	WRITER	8955 BEVERLY BLVD	LOS ANGELES, CA	90048
BATEMAN, JASON	ACTOR	ICM, 8899 BEVERLY BLVD	LOS ANGELES, CA	90048
BATEMAN, JUSTINE	ACTRESS	8004 WOODROW WILSON DR	LOS ANGELES, CA	90046
BATEMAN, KENT	TV DIRECTOR	21510 MERCHENA ST	WOODLAND HILLS, CA	91364
BATEMAN, SUZANNE	ACTRESS	8380 MELROSE AVE #207	LOS ANGELES, CA	90069
BATES, ALAN	ACTOR	CHATTO & LINNIT, LTD		
		PRINCE OF WALES THEATRE		
		COVENTRY ST	LONDON W1	ENGLAND
BATES, CARY N	WRITER	555 W 57TH ST #1230	NEW YORK, NY	10019
BATES, JAMES B	COMPOSER	14335 HUSTON ST #210	SHERMAN OAKS, CA	91423
BATES, JEFFREY PETER	WRITER	11157 SARAH ST	NORTH HOLLYWOOD, CA	91602
BATES, JOHN E	WRITER	8955 BEVERLY BLVD	LOS ANGELES, CA	90048
BATES, KATHRINE	ACTRESS	1605 N CAHUENGA BLVD #202	LOS ANGELES, CA	90028
BATES, LEON	PIANIST	POST OFFICE BOX 27539	PHILADELPHIA, PA	19118
BATES, PEG LEG	MUSICIAN		KERHONKSON, NY	12446
BATES, RALPH	ACTOR	SAINT JAMES'S MGMT		
		22 GROOM PL	LONDON SW1X 7BA	ENGLAND
BATES, RHONDA	ACTRESS	THOMAS, 9243 1/2 DOHENY RD	LOS ANGELES, CA	90069
BATES, ROBIN	WRITER	555 W 57TH ST #1230	NEW YORK, NY	10019
BATIUK, TOM	CARTOONIST	NEWS AMERICA SYNDICATE		
		1703 KAISER AVE	IRVINE, CA	92714
BATIZ, ENRIQUE	CONDUCTOR	GERSHUNOFF, 502 PARK AVE	NEW YORK, NY	10022
BATJER, MARGARET	VIOLINIST	ROSENFIELD, 714 LADD RD	BRONX, NY	10471
BATMOBILE	ROCK & ROLL GROUP	KIX 4 U RECORDS		
		BACHSTRAAT 6	2421 TS NIEUWKOOP	HOLLAND
BATTAGLIA, P A	CARPENTER	2801 MEADOW LARK DR	SAN DIEGO, CA	92123
BATTAILE, JANET W	NEWS CORRESPONDENT	3716 JOCELYN ST	WASHINGTON, DC	20015

BATTEN, BART	WRESTLER	WORLD CLASS WRESTLING		
		SOUTHWEST SPORTS, INC		
		DALLAS SPORTATORIUM		
		1000 S INDUSTRIAL BLVD	DALLAS, TX	75207
BATTEN, BRAD	WRESTLER	WORLD CLASS WRESTLING		
		SOUTHWEST SPORTS, INC		
		DALLAS SPORTATORIUM		
		1000 S INDUSTRIAL BLVD	DALLAS, TX	75207
BATTEN, MARK	WRESTLER	SEE - BATTEN, BART		
BATTEN, MARY	WRITER	PURCELL, 964 2ND AVE	NEW YORK, NY	10022
BATTEN, RODNEY SIMS	PHOTOJOURNALIST	1407 JEFFERSON ST	HYATTSVILLE, MD	20782
BATTEN, THOMAS	ACTOR	145 W 71ST ST	NEW YORK, NY	10023
BATTEN, TONY	DIRECTOR	POST OFFICE BOX 339	NEW YORK, NY	10101
BATTIS, EMERY	ACTOR	120 MARVELWOOD DR	NEW HAVEN, CT	06515
BATTISTA, LLOYD	ACTOR	THE WILLIAM MORRIS AGENCY		
		1350 AVE OF THE AMERICAS	NEW YORK, NY	10019
BATTISTA, NED	CONDUCTOR	SOFFER, 130 W 56TH ST	NEW YORK, NY	10019
BATTISTONE, CATHERINE	ACTRESS	5220 BEN AVE	NORTH HOLLYWOOD, CA	91607
BATTLE, DONALD L	NEWS CORRESPONDENT	3501 MADISON ST	HYATTSVILLE, MD	20782
BATTLE, DONALD L	NEWS CORRESPONDENT	3501 MADISON ST	HYATTSVILLE, MD	20782
BATTLE, KATHLEEN	SOPRANO	CAMI, 165 W 57TH ST	NEW YORK, NY	10019
BATTLE, LLOYD A	NEWS CORRESPONDENT	2139 WISCONSIN AVE, NW	WASHINGTON, DC	20007
BATTLECRY	ROCK & ROLL GROUP	POST OFFICE BOX 2896	TORRANCE, CA	90509
BATTOCCHIO, ROY	WRITER	8160 MULHOLLAND TERR	LOS ANGELES, CA	90046
BATTY, PETER	WRITER-PRODUCER	CLAREMONT HOUSE, RENFRE	SURREY KT2 7NT	ENGLAND
BATTYE, MICHAEL	NEWS CORRESPONDENT	1610 19TH ST	WASHINGTON, DC	20009
BATY, ROBERT	WRITER	8955 BEVERLY BLVD	LOS ANGELES, CA	90048
BAUBLITZ, ROBERT K	TV WRITER	927 2ND ST #9	SANTA MONICA, CA	90403
BAUDO, SERGE	CONDUCTOR	SHAW CONCERTS, 1995 BROADWAY	NEW YORK, NY	10023
BAUER, BARBARA H	WRITER	555 W 57TH ST #1230	NEW YORK, NY	10019
BAUER, BELINDA	ACTRESS	10100 SANTA MONICA BLVD #1600	LOS ANGELES, CA	90067
BAUER, BRUCE	ACTOR	10000 SANTA MONICA BLVD #304	LOS ANGELES, CA	90067
BAUER, ELI	CARTOONIST	POST OFFICE BOX 4203	NEW YORK, NY	10017
BAUER, HANS J	WRITER	8955 BEVERLY BLVD	LOS ANGELES, CA	90048
BAUER, JAIME LYN	ACTRESS	15301 VENTURA BLVD #345	SHERMAN OAKS, CA	91403
BAUER, JOHN H	PHOTOGRAPHER	5612 TILIA CT	BURKE, VA	22015
BAUER, ROBERT A	NEWS CORRESPONDENT	3733 MASSACHUSETTS AVE	WASHINGTON, DC	20016
BAUER, STEVEN	ACTOR	8340 DE LONGPRE AVE #F	LOS ANGELES, CA	90069
BAUGH, PHIL R	GUITARIST	621 BEL AIR DR	NASHVILLE, TN	37217
BAUGHMAN, J ROSS	PHOTOJOURNALIST	105 5TH AVE	NEW YORK, NY	10003
BAUGHMAN, TOM	GUITARIST	3502 WOOD BRIDGE DR	NASHVILLE, TN	37217
BAUM, EDWARD	NEWS CORRESPONDENT	1736 WILLARD ST, NW	WASHINGTON, DC	20009
BAUM, RALPH	FILM DIRECTOR	15 RUE SAINT-PIERRE	NEUILLY 92200	FRANCE
BAUM, ROBERT	CABLE EXECUTIVE	CABLE ENTERTAINMENT		
		295 MADISON AVE	NEW YORK, NY	10017
BAUM, THOMAS	SCREENWRITER	9255 SUNSET BLVD #710	LOS ANGELES, CA	90069
BAUMAN, JEROME	CABLE EXECUTIVE	CABLE ENTERTAINMENT		
		295 MADISON AVE	NEW YORK, NY	10017
BAUMAN, JOE "BOWZER"	SINGER-ACTOR-VJ	POST OFFICE BOX 895		
		TIMES SQUARE STATION	NEW YORK, NY	10108
BAUMAN, STEVEN	WRITER	555 W 57TH ST #1230	NEW YORK, NY	10019
BAUMANN	ROCK & ROLL GROUP	2 W 45TH ST #1102	NEW YORK, NY	10036
BAUMANN, HERMANN	FRENCH HORN	59 E 54TH ST #81	NEW YORK, NY	10022
BAUMANN, KATHRINE	ACTRESS-MODEL	8485 MELROSE PL #E	LOS ANGELES, CA	90069
BAUMANN, LUDWIG	BARITONE	CAMI, 165 W 57TH ST	NEW YORK, NY	10019
BAUMEL, SUSAN B	NEWS CORRESPONDENT	5151 WISCONSIN AVE, NW	WASHINGTON, DC	20016
BAUMES, WILFORD L	WRITER	21910 PACIFIC COAST HWY	MALIBU, CA	90265
BAUMGARNER, JAMES D	NEWS CORRESPONDENT	7513 SPRINGLAKE DR #B-2	BETHESA, MD	20817
BAUMGART, GILBERT P	COMPOSER	11471 ALBERS ST	NORTH HOLLYWOOD, CA	91601
BAUMGARTEN, CRAIG	TV PRODUCER-EXECUTIVE	LORIMAR-TELEPICTURES		
		3970 OVERLAND AVE	CULVER CITY, CA	90230
BAUMOHL, BERNARD	NEWS REPORTER	TIME/TIME & LIFE BLDG		
		ROCKEFELLER CENTER	NEW YORK, NY	10020
BAUR, ELIZABETH	ACTRESS	CONTEMPORARY ARTISTS		
		132 S LASKY DR	BEVERLY HILLS, CA	90212
BAUR, FRANK	DIRECTOR	543 TOYOPA DR	PACIFIC PALISADES, CA	90272
BAUSCH, PINA	CHOREOGRAPHER	WUPPETALER BUHNEN		
		BALLETDIREKYION		
		SPINNSTRASSE	5600 WUPPERTAL 2	WEST GERMANY
BAVAN, YOLANDE	ACTRESS	102 PARK PL	BROOKLYN, NY	11217
BAVIER, FRANCIS	ACTRESS	503 W ELK ST	SILER CITY, NC	27344
BAXLEY, BARBARA	ACTRESS	150 W 87TH ST	NEW YORK, NY	10024
BAXLEY, CRAIG R	STUNTMAN-TV DIRECTOR	12065 EDDLESTON DR	NORTHRIDGE, CA	91326
BAXLEY, GARY	DIRECTOR	12258 HESBY ST	NORTH HOLLYWOOD, CA	91607
BAXLEY, PAUL, JR	DIRECTOR	DGA, 7950 SUNSET BLVD	LOS ANGELES, CA	90046
BAXT, GEORGE L	WRITER	8955 BEVERLY BLVD	LOS ANGELES, CA	90048
BAXTER, CLAYTON	TV WRITER	8955 BEVERLY BLVD	LOS ANGELES, CA	90048
BAXTER, ELLEN	TV DIRECTOR	SHAPIRO, TAXON & KOPELL		
		1180 AVE OF THE AMERICAS	NEW YORK, NY	10036
BAXTER, GLENN E	TRUMPETER	POST OFFICE BOX 2468	RENO, NV	79505
BAXTER, KAY	BODYBUILDER	POST OFFICE BOX 746	VENICE, CA	90291
BAXTER, LES	COMPOSER-CONDUCTOR	6430 SUNSET BLVD #1002	HOLLYWOOD, CA	90028

STEVEN BAUER

FRANCIS BAVIER

WARREN BEATTY

HARRY BELAFONTE

BARBARA BEL GEDDES

BELLAMY BROTHERS

RALPH BELLAMY

DIRK BENEDICT

GEORGE BENSON

BAXTER, MEREDITH	ACTRESS	SEE - BIRNEY, MEREDITH BAXTER	
BAXTER, RICHARD	DIRECTOR	RURAL DELIVERY #2, BOX 195A LINVAL	RINGOES, NJ 08551
BAXTER, RICHARD W	WRITER	8955 BEVERLY BLVD	LOS ANGELES, CA 90048
BAXTER, RONNIE	DIRECTOR-PRODUCER	101 MANYGATE LN, SHEPPERTON	MIDDLESEX ENGLAND
BAXTER, STANLEY	ACTOR-COMEDIAN	DAVID WHITE, 31 KINGS RD	LONDON SW3 ENGLAND
BAXTER, THERESE	ACTRESS	6605 HOLLYWOOD BLVD #220	HOLLYWOOD, CA 90028
BAXTER-DONLEY, MARCI	ACTRESS	FELBER, 2126 N CAHUENGA BLVD	LOS ANGELES, CA 90068
BAXTRESSER, JEANNE	FLUTIST	GERSHUNOFF, 502 PARK AVE	NEW YORK, NY 10022
BAY, BEN GHOU	YOGI-FAKIR	2701 COTTAGE WY #14	SACRAMENTO, CA 95825
BAY, FRANCES	ACTRESS	247 S BEVERLY DR #102	BEVERLY HILLS, CA 90210
BAY, HOWARD	SET DESIGNER	159 W 53RD ST	NEW YORK, NY 10019
BAY, SUSAN	ACTRESS-DIRECTOR	11537 HESBY ST	NORTH HOLLYWOOD, CA 91601
BAY, VICTOR	COMPOSER-CONDUCTOR	520 S BURNSIDE AVE #12-E	LOS ANGELES, CA 90036
BAY CITY ROLLERS, THE	ROCK & ROLL GROUP	27 PRESTON GRANGE RD PRESTON PANS E	LOTHIAN SCOTLAND
BAYER, ANN	WRITER-EDITOR	LIFE/TIME & LIFE BLDG ROCKEFELLER CENTER	NEW YORK, NY 10020
BAYER, FRANK	CASTING DIRECTOR	THE MARK TAPER FORUM 135 N GRAND AVE	LOS ANGELES, CA 90012
BAYERS, EDWARD, JR	GUITARIST	606 ERMAC DR	NASHVILLE, TN 37210
BAYES, JOANNE	ACTRESS	205 W 54TH ST	NEW YORK, NY 10019
BAYHA, HOWARD S	DIRECTOR	DGA, 110 W 57TH ST	NEW YORK, NY 10019
BAYLDON, GEOFFREY	ACTOR	8 SHERWOOD CLOSE	LONDON SW13 ENGLAND
BAYLIS, JAMES	DIRECTOR-PRODUCER	9 NORTH LN	CHAPPAQUA, NY 10514
BAYLOR, BARBARA W	WRITER	555 W 57TH ST #1230	NEW YORK, NY 10019
BAYLOR, DON	BASEBALL	250 TRUMAN, BOX 476	CHESSKILL, NJ 07626
BAZADONA, MICHAEL	DIRECTOR	110-07 73RD RD	FOREST HILLS, NY 11375
BAZELON, IRWIN A	COMPOSER-CONDUCTOR	142 E 71ST ST #4-A	NEW YORK, NY 10021
BB & Q BAND	ROCK & ROLL GROUP	233 W 26TH ST #1-W	NEW YORK, NY 10001
BEACH, BENNIE P	TRUMPETER	1670 NORMAL BLVD	BOWLING GREEN, KY 42101
BEACH, BILLIE	ACTRESS	2314 PACIFIC AVE #D	VENICE, CA 90291
BEACH, JAMES	ACTOR	8721 SUNSET BLVD #202	LOS ANGELES, CA 90069
BEACH, JAMES C	WRITER	555 W 57TH ST #1230	NEW YORK, NY 10019
BEACH, JOHN R	NEWS CORRESPONDENT	6441 SILVER RIDGE	ALEXANDRIA, VA 22310
BEACH BOYS, THE	ROCK & ROLL GROUP	17531 SUNSET BLVD #303	PACIFIC PALISADES, CA 90272
BEACHAM, STEPHANIE	ACTRESS	FRASER, 91 REGENT ST	LONDON W1R 8RU ENGLAND
BEADLE, JEREMY	TV PERSONALITY	NOEL GAY, 24 DENMARK ST	LONDON WC2 ENGLAND
BEADLES, LYNN EDGAR	SINGER	POST OFFICE BOX 110423	NASHVILLE, TN 37211
BEAGLE, E HAMPTON	ACTOR	9744 WILSHIRE BLVD #306	BEVERLY HILLS, CA 90212
BEAGLE, PETER	WRITER	311 E RIANDA RD	WATSONVILLE, CA 95076
BEAIRD, JOHN R	SCREENWRITER	8955 BEVERLY BLVD	LOS ANGELES, CA 90048
BEAIRD, LARRY E	GUITARIST	4112 BELMONT BLVD	NASHVILLE, TN 37215
BEAL, EDDIE T	COMPOSER-CONDUCTOR	3866 WILLOW CREST AVE #8	STUDIO CITY, CA 91604
BEAL, JOHN	ACTOR	205 W 54TH ST	NEW YORK, NY 10019
BEAL, JOHN E	FILM DIRECTOR	7242 AVENIDA ALTISIMA	RANCHO PALOS VERDES, C. 90274
BEAL, JOHN EVERETT	MUSICIAN	6520 AMIGO AVE	RESEDA, CA 91335
BEAL, KENN	GUITARIST	POST OFFICE BOX 122	SULLIVAN'S ISLAND, SC 29482
BEAL, TANDY	DANCER	AFFILIATE ARTISTS, INC 37 W 65TH ST, 6TH FLOOR	NEW YORK, NY 10023
BEALE, BETTY	TV COLUMNIST-CORRES	2926 GARFIELD ST, NW	WASHINGTON, DC 20008
BEALE, PETER	FILM PRODUCER	61 EARLS CT RD	LONDON W8 ENGLAND
BEALL, GARY G	PHOTOGRAPHER	14050 TRIDELPHIA MILL RD	DAYTON, MD 21036
BEALL, WILLIAM C	PHOTOGRAPHER	7850 AUDOBON AVE	ALEXANDRIA, VA 22306
BEALMEAR, ROBERT F	WRITER	1796 GRIFFITH PARK BLVD	LOS ANGELES, CA 90026
BEALS, FREDERICK	ACTOR	400 CARROLL AVE	MAMARONECK, NY 10543
BEALS, JENNIFER	ACTRESS-DANCER	100 YORK ST #3-C	NEW HAVEN, CT 06520
BEAN, GERALD	DIRECTOR	840 THAYER AVE	LOS ANGELES, CA 90024
BEAN, HENRY S	SCREENWRITER	348 RENNIE AVE	VENICE, CA 90291
BEAN, ORSON	ACTOR-COMEDIAN	1650 BROADWAY #406	NEW YORK, NY 10019
BEAN, ROBERT B	DIRECTOR	DGA, 110 W 57TH ST	NEW YORK, NY 10019
BEANE, HILARY	ACTRESS	654 N LARCHMONT BLVD	LOS ANGELES, CA 90004
BEANES, DAVID L	DIRECTOR	DGA, 7950 SUNSET BLVD	LOS ANGELES, CA 90046
BEANS, WILFRED W	ACTOR	5631 VENICE BLVD	LOS ANGELES, CA 90019
BEAR, RICHARD T	SINGER	3 E 54TH ST #1400	NEW YORK, NY 10022
BEARD, HENRY	TV WRITER	555 W 57TH ST #1230	NEW YORK, NY 10019
BEARD, SYD	ACTOR	10845 LINDBROOK DR #3	LOS ANGELES, CA 90024
BEARDE, CHRIS D	WRITER-PRODUCER	28106 PACIFIC COAST HWY	MALIBU, CA 90265
BEARDSLEY, ALICE	ACTRESS	ABRAMS ARTISTS & ASSOCIATES 420 MADISON AVE, 14TH FLOOR	NEW YORK, NY 10017
BEARDSLEY, KAREN	SOPRANO	CAMI, 165 W 57TH ST	NEW YORK, NY 10019
BEARDSLEY, T M	NEWS CORRESPONDENT	1641 WISCONSIN AVE #4, NW	WASHINGTON, DC 20007
BEARSE, AMANDA	ACTRESS	1888 CENTURY PARK E #1400	LOS ANGELES, CA 90067
BEASCOECHEA, FRANK P	TV DIRECTOR	24612 MALIBU RD	MALIBU, CA 90265
BEASLEY, ALLYCE	ACTRESS	KOHNER, 9169 SUNSET BLVD	LOS ANGELES, CA 90069
BEASLEY, H CULLY, III	MUSICIAN	1602 LEAF AVE	MURFREESBORO, TN 37130
BEASLEY, LARRY	GUITARIST	ROUTE #6, BOX 38 COUNTRY ESTATES	RUSSELL SPRINGS, KY 42642
BEASOR, TERRENCE	ACTOR	2800 NEILSON WY	SANTA MONICA, CA 90405
BEASTIE BOYS, THE	RAP GROUP	298 ELIZABETH ST	NEW YORK, NY 10012
BEAT, THE	ROCK & ROLL GROUP	POST OFFICE BOX 320	BIRMINGHAM B29 7PR ENGLAND
BEAT TEMPTATION	ROCK & ROLL GROUP	POST OFFICE BOX 570	ROCKVILLE CENTRE, NY 11571
BEATON, ALEX	DIRECTOR-PRODUCER	1625 RANCHO AVE	GLENDALE, CA 91201
BEATON, RON	SPORTS WRITER	POST OFFICE BOX 500	WASHINGTON, DC 20044
BEATTIE, ANN	WRITER	555 W 57TH ST #1230	NEW YORK, NY 10019

Name	Occupation	Address	City	Zip
BEATTIE, BRUCE	CARTOONIST	POST OFFICE BOX 431	DAYTON BEACH, FL	32015
BEATTIE, LAURA	ACTRESS	223 W 70TH ST	NEW YORK, NY	10023
BEATTIE, LYNDA	ACTRESS	6126 SAINT CLAIR AVE	NORTH HOLLYWOOD, CA	91606
BEATTIE, VICTOR B, III	NEWS CORRESPONDENT	4109 HOFFMAN DR	WOODBRIDGE, VA	22193
BEATTS, ANNE	WRITER	555 W 57TH ST #1230	NEW YORK, NY	10019
BEATTY, C ROGER	WRITER-PRODUCER	13336 CHANDLER BLVD	VAN NUYS, CA	91401
BEATTY, EDGAR K	DIRECTOR	3932 E COMMERCE RD	MILFORD, MI	48042
BEATTY, JOHN LEE	SCENIC DESIGNER	107 W 86TH ST	NEW YORK, NY	10024
BEATTY, KERRY DWAYNE	SAXOPHONIST	1004 CALVERT ST	NASHVILLE, TN	37216
BEATTY, NED	ACTOR	2706 N BEACHWOOD DR	LOS ANGELES, CA	90068
BEATTY, WARREN	ACT-WRI-DIR	13671 MULHOLLAND DR	BEVERLY HILLS, CA	90210
BEAU, TOBY	ROCK & ROLL GROUP	AUCOIN, 645 MADISON AVE	NEW YORK, NY	10022
BEAUCARD, EMILE	ACTOR	427 N CANON DR #205	BEVERLY HILLS, CA	90210
BEAUCHAMP, DANIELLE M	NEWS CORRESPONDENT	241 "G" ST, SW	WASHINGTON, DC	20024
BEAUCHAMP, MARY M	WRITER	12012 MOORPARK ST #5	STUDIO CITY, CA	91604
BEAUDINE, CRAIG	TV DIRECTOR	10101 ODESSA AVE	SEPULVEDA, CA	91343
BEAUDINE, SKIP	FILM DIRECTOR	4717 POE AVE	WOODLAND HILLS, CA	91367
BEAUDINE, WILLIAM, JR	DIRECTOR-PRODUCER	5461 BOTHWELL RD	TARZANA, CA	91356
BEAULIEU, TONI	COMPOSER	1549 WESTERN AVE	GLENDALE, CA	91201
BEAUMONT, CHRIS	ACTOR	911 S SPAULDING AVE	LOS ANGELES, CA	90036
BEAUMONT, CHRISTOPHER	TV WRITER	8955 BEVERLY BLVD	LOS ANGELES, CA	90048
BEAUMONT, GABRIELLE	TV DIRECTOR-PRODUCER	3456 ALANA DR	SHERMAN OAKS, CA	91403
BEAUMONT, RALPH	CASTING DIRECTOR	THE AHMANSON THEATER		
		135 N GRAND AVE	LOS ANGELES, CA	90012
BEAUTIFUL BOBBY	WRESTLER	SEE - EATON, BEAUTIFUL BOBBY		
BEAVER, STAN	GUITARIST	3630 WELDON DR	CHATTANOOGA, TN	37412
BEAVER, WALT	ACTOR	10000 RIVERSIDE DR #12-14	TOLUCA LAKE, CA	91602
BEBAN, RICHARD W	TV WRITER	8955 BEVERLY BLVD	LOS ANGELES, CA	90048
BECHE, MIKE R	WRITER	4363 CLYBOURN AVE	NORTH HOLLYWOOD, CA	91602
BECHER, JOHN C	ACTOR	43 GREENWICH AVE	NEW YORK, NY	10014
BECHTEL, ALAN	STUNTMAN	HALL, 138 FROG HOLLOW RD	CHURCHVILLE, PA	18966
BECHTEL, BIG JOHN	GUITARIST	316 S MAIN ST	TELFORD, PA	18969
BECK, BILLY	ACTOR	8350 SANTA MONICA BLVD #206	LOS ANGELES, CA	90069
BECK, BRYAN	ACTOR	ABC-TV, 1438 N GOWER ST	LOS ANGELES, CA	90028
BECK, ELIZABETH	NEWS CORRESPONDENT	2214 CASTLE ROCK SQ	RESTON, VA	22093
BECK, GEORGE	WRITER-PRODUCER	14040 TAHITI WY #512	MARINA DEL REY, CA	90292
BECK, JACK	WRITER	8955 BEVERLY BLVD	LOS ANGELES, CA	90048
BECK, JACK W	CINEMATOGRAPHER	114 E 71ST ST	NEW YORK, NY	10021
BECK, JEFF	SINGER-GUITARIST	ERNEST CHAPMAN MANAGEMENT		
		11 OLD LINCOLN'S INN	LONDON WC2	ENGLAND
BECK, JENNIFER	ACTRESS	12725 VENTURA BLVD #E	STUDIO CITY, CA	91604
BECK, JODY	NEWS CORRESPONDENT	NBC NEWS, NEWS DEPARTMENT		
		4001 NEBRASKA AVE, NW	WASHINGTON, DC	20016
BECK, JOHN	ACTOR	10000 SANTA MONICA BLVD #305	LOS ANGELES, CA	90067
BECK, JOHN F	WRITER	8955 BEVERLY BLVD	LOS ANGELES, CA	90048
BECK, JULIAN	DESIGN-DIR-PROD	800 W END AVE	NEW YORK, NY	10225
BECK, KIMBERLY	ACTRESS-MODEL	SEE - BECK-HILTON, KIMBERLY		
BECK, MARILYN	COLUMNIST-CRITIC	2132 EL ROBLE LN	BEVERLY HILLS, CA	90210
BECK, MARTIN	ACTOR	8831 SUNSET BLVD #402	LOS ANGELES, CA	90069
BECK, MICHAEL	ACTOR	1553 BRENTWOOD AVE	WESTLAKE VILLAGE, CA	91361
BECK, NOELLE	ACTRESS	ABC-TV NETWORK, "LOVING"		
		1330 AVE OF THE AMERICAS	NEW YORK, NY	10019
BECK, SHERMAN	WRITER-DIRECTOR	147 HUNTINGTON BAY RD	HUNTINGTON, NY	11743
BECK-HILTON, KIMBERLY	ACTRESS-MODEL	500 S SEPULVEDA BLVD #510	LOS ANGELES, CA	90049
BECKER, ANTONIE	ACTRESS	8428 MELROSE PL #C	LOS ANGELES, CA	90069
BECKER, ARNOLD	TV EXECUTIVE	CBS-TV, 51 W 52ND ST	NEW YORK, NY	10019
BECKER, BEAR	DRUMMER	1513 N 48TH ST #39-6	OMAHA, NE	68104
BECKER, DEBBIE	SPORTS WRITER	POST OFFICE BOX 500	WASHINGTON, DC	20044
BECKER, H W "FRITZ"	CONDUCTOR	1055 E FLAMINGO RD #219	LAS VEGAS, NV	89109
BECKER, HAROLD	FILM DIRECTOR	7722 SENALDA RD	LOS ANGELES, CA	90068
BECKER, HAZEL	NEWS CORRESPONDENT	3315 MORRISON ST, NW	WASHINGTON, DC	20015
BECKER, RICHARD	MUSIC PUBLISHER	POST OFFICE BOX 144	DEAL, NJ	07723
BECKER, STEPHEN	WRITER	RUSSELL & VOLKENING		
		551 5TH AVE	NEW YORK, NY	10176
BECKER, TERRY	FILM-TV DIRECTOR	8338 SKYLINE DR	HOLLYWOOD, CA	90046
BECKERMAN, ARNOLD	DIRECTOR	153 E 32ND ST	NEW YORK, NY	10016
BECKERMAN, BARRY	WRITER	8955 BEVERLY BLVD	LOS ANGELES, CA	90048
BECKERMAN, SIDNEY	FILM PRODUCER	WARNER-HOLLYWOOD STUDIOS		
		1041 N FORMOSA AVE	LOS ANGELES, CA	90046
BECKETT, ANN M	SCREENWRITER	13532 CONTOUR DR	SHERMAN OAKS, CA	91423
BECKETT, ELTON	ACTOR	ABC-TV, "ALL MY CHILDREN"		
		1330 AVE OF THE AMERICAS	NEW YORK, NY	10019
BECKETT, WHEELER	CONDUCTOR-COMPOSER	23 GILMOUR CIR	CONSTANTIA CAPE	S AFRICA
BECKHAM, ROBERT	MUSIC PUBLISHER	COMBINE, 35 MUSIC SQUARE E	NASHVILLE, TN	37203
BECKLES, ALBERT	BODYBUILDER	POST OFFICE BOX 5005	MISSION HILLS, CA	91345
BECKLEY, BARBRA ANN	ACTRESS	2110 MEADOW VALLEY TERR	LOS ANGELES, CA	90039
BECKLEY, WILLIAM	ACTOR	9165 SUNSET BLVD #202	LOS ANGELES, CA	90069
BECKMAN, HENRY	ACTOR	208 S BEVERLY DR #4	BEVERLY HILLS, CA	90212
BECKMAN, HENRY	WRITER	8955 BEVERLY BLVD	LOS ANGELES, CA	90048
BECKMAN, TOM	CLOWN	2701 COTTAGE WY #14	SACRAMENTO, CA	95825
BECKNER, STEVEN K	NEWS CORRESPONDENT	1608 19TH ST, NW	WASHINGTON, DC	20002
BECKSTROM, LYNN	MEZZO-SOPRANO	LIEBERMAN, 11 RIVERSIDE DR	NEW YORK, NY	10023
BECKWITH, ALAN	ACTOR	3928 CARPENTER AVE #102	STUDIO CITY, CA	91604
BECKWITH, DAVID C	NEWS CORRESPONDENT	5301 BROAD BRANCH RD, NW	WASHINGTON, DC	20015
BECKWITH, DOUGLAS CHARLES	TV WRITER	1025 N KINGS RD	LOS ANGELES, CA	90069

Name	Occupation	Address	City	Zip
BEDARD, BOB	WRESTLER	SEE - GOULET, RENE		
BEDARD, PAUL	NEWS CORRESPONDENT	2315 40TH ST, NW	WASHINGTON, DC	20016
BEDDOE, DON	ACTOR	26801 VIA GRANDE	MISSION VIEJO, CA	92675
BEDELIA, BONNIE	ACTRESS	2082 TOPANGA SKYLINE DR	TOPANGA, CA	90290
BEDELL, SALLY	WRITER	N Y TIMES, 229 W 43RD ST	NEW YORK, NY	10036
BEDFORD, BRIAN	ACTOR	211 S BEVERLY DR #201	BEVERLY HILLS, CA	90212
BEDFORD, EDDIE CLAYTON	GUITARIST	4017 NAVAHO TRAIL	NASHVILLE, TN	37211
BEDFORD, TERRENCE L	DIRECTOR	THE JENNIE COMPANY		
		153 W 79TH ST	NEW YORK, NY	10024
BEDI, KABIR	ACTOR	1222 HILLDALE AVE	LOS ANGELES, CA	90069
BEDNAR, RUDY GERARD	DIRECTOR	DGA, 110 W 57TH ST	NEW YORK, NY	10019
BEDWAY, ART	BODYBUILDER	WEST VIRGINIA NPC DISTRICT		
		BOARD OF TRADING BLDG		
		12TH & CHAPLIN ST	WHEELING, WV	26003
BEE, HARRY	HARMONICIST	5300 POWERLINE RD #202	FORT LAUDERDALE, FL	33309
BEE, MOLLY	ACTRESS-SINGER	POST OFFICE BOX 1310	CANYON COUNTRY, CA	91351
BEE, ROY	GUITARIST	812 TUCKAHOE DR	MADISON, TN	37115
BEE GEES, THE	ROCK & ROLL GROUP	1112 N SHERBOURNE DR	LOS ANGELES, CA	90069
BEEBE, BARBARA	ACTRESS	3630 BARHAM BLVD #2201	LOS ANGELES, CA	90068
BEEBE, PAUL	COLUMNIST	POST OFFICE BOX 500	WASHINGTON, DC	20044
BEECHER, ROBERT	ACTOR	1605 N CAHUENGA BLVD #202	LOS ANGELES, CA	90028
BEECHER, WILLIAM M	NEWS CORRESPONDENT	7911 ROBISON RD	BETHESDA, MD	20084
BEECROFT, DAVID	ACTOR	ABC TELEVISION NETWORK		
		1330 AVE OF THE AMERICAS	NEW YORK, NY	10019
BEEFCAKE, BRUTUS	WRESTLER	POST OFFICE BOX 3859	STAMFORD, CT	06905
BEEGAN, DANIEL H	NEWS CORRESPONDENT	5208 S 10TH PL	ARLINGTON, VA	22204
BEEK, JAMES B	NEWS CORRESPONDENT	2500 WISCONSIN AVE #425, NW	WASHINGTON, DC	20007
BEEKER, JEFF	ACTOR	4321 KLING ST #20	BURBANK, CA	91505
BEEKMAN, RANDALL W	NEWS CORRESPONDENT	5229 S 10TH PL	ARLINGTON, VA	22204
BEELBY, MALCOLM	COMPOSER-CONDUCTOR	117 S VAN NESS AVE	LOS ANGELES, CA	90004
BEELER, MARIAN	ACTRESS	6132 GLEN HOLLY ST	LOS ANGELES, CA	90068
BEEN, PATTI	ACTRESS	4943 LAUREL CANYON RD	NORTH HOLLYWOOD, CA	91607
BEENE, GEOFFREY	FASHION DESIGNER	550 7TH AVE	NEW YORK, NY	10018
BEER, HANS L	CONDUCTOR	7225 HOLLYWOOD BLVD #218	LOS ANGELES, CA	90046
BEER, LUCILLE	MEZZO-SOPRANO	59 E 54TH ST #81	NEW YORK, NY	10022
BEERS, ANDREW C	NEWS CORRESPONDENT	POST OFFICE BOX 3504	ANNAPOLIS, MD	21403
BEERS, BOB	SINGER	POST OFFICE BOX 655	HUDSON, OH	44236
BEERS, CAROLE A	WRITER	4343 CAMELLIA AVE	STUDIO CITY, CA	91604
BEERS, JACK	ACTOR	RICHMOND HILL RD	GREENWICH, CT	06830
BEERY, BARBARA	WRITER	3855 VENTURA CANYON AVE	SHERMAN OAKS, CA	91423
BEERY, BUCKLIND	ACTOR	17823 TARZANA ST	ENCINO, CA	91316
BEERY, NOAH, JR	ACTOR	POST OFFICE BOX 108	KEENE, CA	93531
BEERY, RITA	ACTRESS	27 THORNWOOD ACRES	SCOTTSDALE, AZ	85251
BEERY, WALTER	ACTOR	5330 LANKERSHIM BLVD #210	NORTH HOLLYWOOD, CA	91601
BEES, JULIE	PIANIST	POST OFFICE BOX U	REDDING, CT	06875
BEESMEYER, RICHARD L	TV EXECUTIVE	ABC TELEVISION NETWORK		
		1330 AVE OF THE AMERICAS	NEW YORK, NY	10019
BEESON, JACK	COMPOSER	404 RIVERSIDE DR	NEW YORK, NY	10025
BEESTON, PAUL	CINEMATOGRAPHER	TREE HOUSE, HEUSDEN WY		
		GERRARDS CROSS	BUCKS	ENGLAND
BEESTON, WILLIAM R C	NEWS CORRESPONDENT	1696 32ND ST, NW	WASHINGTON, DC	20007
BEGA, LESLIE	ACTRESS	8322 BEVERLY BLVD #202	LOS ANGELES, CA	90048
BEGEL, CINDY J	WRITER	1253 BARRY AVE #2	LOS ANGELES, CA	90025
BEGELMAN, DAVID	FILM EXECUTIVE	705 N LINDEN DR	BEVERLY HILLS, CA	90210
BEGGS, HAGAN	ACTOR	15010 VENTURA BLVD #219	SHERMAN OAKS, CA	91403
BEGLEITER, RALPH J	NEWS CORRESPONDENT	9820 BETTEKER LN	POTOMAC, MD	20854
BEGLEY, ED, JR	ACTOR	211 S BEVERLY DR #107	BEVERLY HILLS, CA	90212
BEGLEY, JOSEPH	GUITARIST-PIANIST	3730 BURRUS ST	NASHVILLE, TN	37216
BEGLEY, KATHRYN J	WRITER	555 W 57TH ST #1230	NEW YORK, NY	10019
BEGLOV, MICHAEL S	NEWS CORRESPONDENT	5461 SHEFFIELD CT #112	ALEXANDRIA, VA	22311
BEGUN, HOWARD J	COMPOSER	4068 TUJUNGA AVE #C	STUDIO CITY, CA	91604
BEHAR, HENRY	TV WRITER-DIRECTOR	13930 OLD HARBOR LN	MARINA DEL REY, CA	90292
BEHAR, JOSEPH	TV DIRECTOR	22760 FLAMINGO ST	WOODLAND HILLS, CA	91364
BEHAR, PHYLLIS	ACTRESS	ICM, 40 W 57TH ST	NEW YORK, NY	10019
BEHLMER, RUDY	DIRECTOR	3972 TROPICAL DR	STUDIO CITY, CA	91604
BEHM, MARC	SCREENWRITER	8955 BEVERLY BLVD	LOS ANGELES, CA	90048
BEHN, NOEL	WRITER	555 W 57TH ST #1230	NEW YORK, NY	10019
BEHR, IRA S	TV WRITER	8955 BEVERLY BLVD	LOS ANGELES, CA	90048
BEHR, JACK	WRITER	2460 BEVERLY AVE	SANTA MONICA, CA	90405
BEHR, PETER	NEWS CORRESPONDENT	412 N CHERRY ST	FALLS CHURCH, VA	22046
BEHR, WAYNE ALAN	TENOR	SULLIVAN, 390 W END AVE	NEW YORK, NY	10024
BEHREND, JACK	DIRECTOR	918 HINMAN AVE	EVANSTON, IL	60202
BEHRENS, BERNARD	ACTOR	SF & A, 121 N SAN VICENTE BLVD	BEVERLY HILLS, CA	90211
BEHRENS, HILDEGARD	SOPRANO	CAMI, 165 W 57TH ST	NEW YORK, NY	10019
BEHRMAN, KEVIN M	TV DIRECTOR	109 SEWARD AVE	MINEOLA, NY	11501
BEHRSTOCK, ROGER	ACTOR	212 S LINDON DR	BEVERLY HILLS, CA	90212
BEICH, ALBERT C	WRITER	8955 BEVERLY BLVD	LOS ANGELES, CA	90048
BEIGEL, PHILIP	TV DIRECTOR	20 W 64TH ST	NEW YORK, NY	10023
BEILINA, NINA	VIOLINIST	119 W 57TH ST #1505	NEW YORK, NY	10019
BEINER, ROBERT C	DIRECTOR	49 KENMORE ST	STATEN ISLAND, NY	10312
BEISER, H DARR	PHOTOGRAPHER	1718 "P" ST #708, NE	WASHINGTON, DC	20036
BEKER, MARILYN	WRITER	8955 BEVERLY BLVD	LOS ANGELES, CA	90048
BEKKER, PETER O E, JR	WRITER	555 W 57TH ST #1230	NEW YORK, NY	10019
BEL, GARY L	WRITER	555 W 57TH ST #1230	NEW YORK, NY	10019
BEL GEDDES, BARBARA	ACTRESS	15 MILL ST	PUTNAM VALLEY, NY	10579
BEL-FIRES, THE	ROCK & ROLL GROUP	POST OFFICE BOX 784	SIERRA MADRE, CA	91024

THE ANTIQUE CO.
MOVIE STILLS
8X10 GLOSSIES
FABULOUS SELECTION OF OVER
500 HIGH QUALITY PHOTOGRAPHS
ILLUSTRATED CATALOG $1.00
RETAIL AND WHOLESALE
THE ANTIQUE CO.
3186 E. THOUSAND OAKS BLVD.
THOUSAND OAKS, CA 91362
805 - 497-7793

Name	Occupation	Address	City	Zip
BELACK, DORIS	ACTRESS	9220 SUNSET BLVD #202	LOS ANGELES, CA	90069
BELAFONTE, GINA	ACTRESS	ABC-TV, "ALL MY CHILDREN"		
		1330 AVE OF THE AMERICAS	NEW YORK, NY	10019
BELAFONTE, HARRY	ACTOR-SINGER	157 W 57TH ST	NEW YORK, NY	10019
BELAFONTE-HARPER, SHARI	MODEL-ACTRESS	3546 LONGRIDGE AVE	SHERMAN OAKS, CA	91423
BELAIR, MARK	WRITER	555 W 57TH ST #1230	NEW YORK, NY	10019
BELAIR, ROXANE	NEWS CORRESPONDENT	400 N CAPITOL ST, NW	WASHINGTON, DC	20001
BELAMARIC, MIRO	CONDUCTOR	61 W 62ND ST #6-F	NEW YORK, NY	10023
BELANGER, SHARLENE	TV WRITER-DIRECTOR	356 S ELM DR #3	BEVERLY HILLS, CA	90212
BELASCO, LEON	ACTOR	4048 VENTURA CANYON AVE	SHERMAN OAKS, CA	91423
BELCHER, JAMES W	WRITER	6909 OPORTO DR	HOLLYWOOD, CA	90068
BELDIN, SCOTT	ACTOR	LENZ, 1456 E CHARLESTON BLVD	LAS VEGAS, NV	89104
BELFER, HAL B	CHOREO-DIRECTOR	3407 HUXLEY ST #23	LOS ANGELES, CA	90027
BELFONTE, HARRY	SINGER-ACTOR	300 W END AVE	NEW YORK, NY	10023
BELFORD, CHRISTINE	ACTRESS	201 N ROBERTSON BLVD #A	BEVERLY HILLS, CA	90211
BELINFANTE, FRIEDA	CONDUCTOR	490 MYRTLE ST	LAGUNA BCH, CA	92651
BELITA	ACTRESS-BALLERIA	ROSE COTTAGE		
		42 CRABTREE LN	LONDON SW6	ENGLAND
BELKEN, JAMES E	SAXOPHONIST	2641 DOVE MEADOW	GARLAND, TX	75043
BELKIN, BORIS	VIOLINIST	ICM, 40 W 57TH ST	NEW YORK, NY	10019
BELKIN, GARY	WRITER	10787 WILSHIRE BLVD #1201	LOS ANGELES, CA	90024
BELKIN, HARRIET	WRITER	516 N LAUREL AVE	LOS ANGELES, CA	90048
BELKIN, NORMAN	WRITER	516 N LAUREL AVE	LOS ANGELES, CA	90048
BELKIN, PEARL	WRITER	10787 WILSHIRE BLVD #1201	LOS ANGELES, CA	90024
BELL, ALAN	WRITER-PRODUCER	CCA MGMT, 4 CT LODGE		
		48 SLOANE SQ	LONDON SW1W 8AT	ENGLAND
BELL, BRAND	WRITER	28220 AGOURA RD	AGOURA, CA	91301
BELL, CHARLES ROBERT	DIRECTOR	100 E BROADWAY	ROSLYN, NY	11576
BELL, DAVE	DIRECTOR	5700 HILL OAK DR	HOLLYWOOD, CA	90068
BELL, DAVID	TV DIRECTOR-PRODUCER	ROGER HANCOCK MANAGEMENT		
		8 WATERLOO PL, PALL MALL	LONDON SW1Y 4AW	ENGLAND
BELL, DAVID "MR CPR"	BODYBUILDER	2801 MEADOW LARK DR	SAN DIEGO, CA	92123
BELL, DAVID A	COMPOSER-CONDUCTOR	1542 B HARVARD ST	SANTA MONICA, CA	90404
BELL, DIANA A	WRITER	8955 BEVERLY BLVD	LOS ANGELES, CA	90048
BELL, ERIC	TV DIRECTOR	NBC TELEVISION NETWORK		
		30 ROCKEFELLER PLAZA	NEW YORK, NY	10112
BELL, FRANK	PIANIST	POST OFFICE BOX 1421	ATLANTA, GA	30301
BELL, GEORGE D, JR	WRITER	555 W 57TH ST #1230	NEW YORK, NY	10019
BELL, HAL	FILM DIRECTOR	1900 W PARKSIDE AVE	BURBANK, CA	91506
BELL, J D & THE SILVER SPURS	C & W GROUP	ACE PRODUCTIONS		
		3407 GREEN RIDGE DR	NASHVILLE, TN	37214
BELL, JAMES "COOL PAPA"	BASEBALL	3034 DICKSON	SAINT LOUIS, MO	63106
BELL, JANE UPTON	TV DIRECTOR	12225 SAN VICENTE BLVD	LOS ANGELES, CA	90049
BELL, JOHN F, JR	SAXOPHONIST	1831 GREEN HILLS DR	NASHVILLE, TN	37215
BELL, JOHN J	TV DIRECTOR	11-C HERITAGE SOUND	MILFORD, CT	06460
BELL, JOHN T	WRITER	8955 BEVERLY BLVD	LOS ANGELES, CA	90048
BELL, JOSHUA	VIOLINIST	IMG ARTISTS, 22 E 71ST ST	NEW YORK, NY	10021
BELL, KENNETH	SINGER	254 W 93RD ST #8	NEW YORK, NY	10025
BELL, KENNETH E	GUITARIST	ROUTE #4, NEW HWY 96-W	FRANKLIN, TN	37064
BELL, LAURALEE	ACTRESS	CBS TELEVISION NETWORK		
		"THE YOUNG & THE RESTLESS"		
		7800 BEVERLY BLVD	LOS ANGELES, CA	90036
BELL, LEONARD	ACTOR	9744 WILSHIRE BLVD #306	BEVERLY HILLS, CA	90212
BELL, LINDA L	WRITER	8955 BEVERLY BLVD	LOS ANGELES, CA	90048
BELL, MARTIN	NEWS CORRESPONDENT	4600 DUKE ST	ALEXANDRIA, VA	22304
BELL, MARTY	WRITER	555 W 57TH ST #1230	NEW YORK, NY	10019
BELL, MICHAEL	ACTOR	THOMAS, 9243 1/2 DOHENY RD	LOS ANGELES, CA	90069
BELL, MICHAEL	ACTOR	CED, 261 S ROBERTSON BLVD	BEVERLY HILLS, CA	90211
BELL, NEAL	WRITER	555 W 57TH ST #1230	NEW YORK, NY	10019
BELL, RALPH S	WRITER	555 W 57TH ST #1230	NEW YORK, NY	10019
BELL, ROBERT O	NEWS CORRESPONDENT	1333 "H" ST, NW	WASHINGTON, DC	20005
BELL, STEVE	NEWS CORRESPONDENT	ABC-TV, NEWS DEPARTMENT		
		1717 DE SALES ST, NW	WASHINGTON, DC	20036
BELL, TOM	ACTOR	ICM, 388-396 OXFORD ST	LONDON W1	ENGLAND
BELL, TOMMY	SINGER	SCOTT DEAN, 428 HILL ST	RENO, NV	89501
BELL, VANESSA	ACTRESS	ABC-TV, "ALL MY CHILDREN"		
		1330 AVE OF THE AMERICAS	NEW YORK, NY	10019
BELL, WILLIAM J	TV WRITER-PRODUCER	209 E LAKE SHORE DR	CHICAGO, IL	60611
BELLAH, JAMES	WRITER	19030 MIRANDA ST	TARZANA, CA	91356
BELLAK, GEORGE	TV WRITER	555 W 57TH ST #1230	NEW YORK, NY	10019
BELLAMY, ANNE	ACTRESS	6380 WILSHIRE BLVD #1600	LOS ANGELES, CA	90048
BELLAMY, DIANA	ACTRESS	721 N LA BREA AVE #200	LOS ANGELES, CA	90038
BELLAMY, EARL	DIRECTOR-PRODUCER	6111 EL ESCORPION RD	WOODLAND HILLS, CA	91367
BELLAMY, NED	ACTOR	10920 WILSHIRE BLVD #220	LOS ANGELES, CA	90024
BELLAMY, RALPH	ACTOR	8173 MULHOLLAND TERR	LOS ANGELES, CA	90046
BELLAMY BROTHERS, THE	VOCAL DUO	112 21ST AVE S #204	NASHVILLE, TN	37203
BELLAND, BRUCE G	TV WRITER	8955 BEVERLY BLVD	LOS ANGELES, CA	90048
BELLAR, JOHNNIE E	GUITARIST	BOX 145, OLIVER DR	ASHLAND CITY, TN	37015
BELLAR, JOHNNY WAYNE	GUITARIST	POST OFFICE BOX 145	ASHLAND CITY, TN	37015
BELLAVER, HARRY	ACTOR	116 SUMMIT AVE	TAPPAN, NY	10983
BELLER, KATHLEEN	ACTRESS	10351 SANTA MONICA BLVD #211	LOS ANGELES, CA	90025
BELLER, MARY LINN	ACTRESS	29 CARRIAGE HOUSE LN	MAMARONECK, NY	10543
BELLFLOWER, NELLIE	ACTRESS	1302 N SWEETZER AVE #601	LOS ANGELES, CA	90069
BELLI, MELVIN	ATTORNEY	3052 PACIFIC AVE	SAN FRANCISCO, CA	94115
BELLIKOFF, RICHARD	WRITER	8955 BEVERLY BLVD	LOS ANGELES, CA	90048

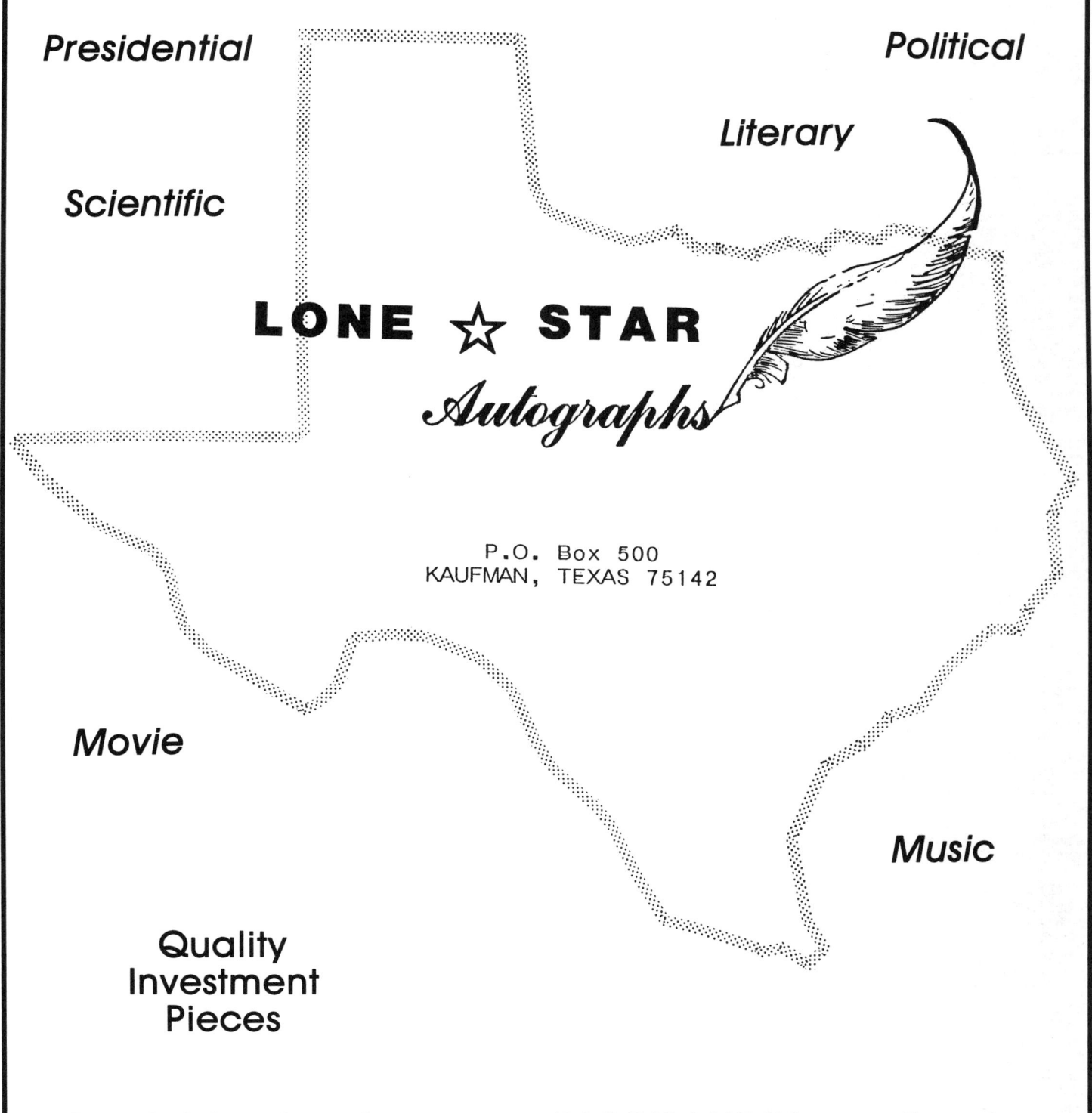

Name	Occupation	Address	City	Zip
BELLIN, LEWIS	COMPOSER	THE BEACON HOTEL		
		75TH & BROADWAY	NEW YORK, NY	10023
BELLIN, THOMAS	ACTOR	721 N LA BREA AVE #200	LOS ANGELES, CA	90038
BELLING, DAVINA	FILM PRODUCER	10 PEMBRIDGE PL	LONDON W2 4XB	ENGLAND
BELLING, SUSAN	SOPRANO	ALLIED, 170 W 74TH ST	NEW YORK, NY	10023
BELLINGHAM, LYNDA	ACTRESS	SARABAND ASSOCIATES AGENCY		
		153 PETHERTON RD, HIGHBURY	LONDON N5	ENGLAND
BELLINI, CAL	ACTOR	15010 VENTURA BLVD #234	SHERMAN OAKS, CA	91403
BELLINI, GABRIELE	CONDUCTOR	61 W 62ND ST #6-F	NEW YORK, NY	10023
BELLISARIO, DONALD P	TV PRODUCER	MCA/UNIVERSAL STUDIOS, INC		
		100 UNIVERSAL CITY PLAZA	UNIVERSAL CITY, CA	91608
BELLO, STEPHEN	SCREENWRITER	2269 LA GRANADA DR	HOLLYWOOD, CA	90068
BELLOMO, SALVATORE	WRESTLER	POST OFFICE BOX 3859	STAMFORD, CT	06905
BELLOW, SAUL	WRITER	1126 E 59TH ST	CHICAGO, IL	60637
BELLOWS, JAMES	TV PRODUCER	ABC TELEVISION NETWORK		
		1330 AVE OF THE AMERICAS	NEW YORK, NY	10019
BELLSON, LOUIE	DRUMMER	POST OFFICE BOX L	LAKE HAVASU, AZ	86403
BELLSON, LOUIE, QUARTET	JAZZ QUARTET	HOFFER, 233 1/2 E 48TH ST	NEW YORK, NY	10017
BELLWOOD, PAMELA	ACTRESS-PHOTOGRAPHER	7444 WOODROW WILSON DR	LOS ANGELES, CA	90046
BELLWOOD, PETER L	SCREENWRITER	8955 BEVERLY BLVD	LOS ANGELES, CA	90048
BELMONT, FRANK L	DIRECTOR	DGA, 110 W 57TH ST	NEW YORK, NY	10019
BELMONTS, THE	VOCAL GROUP	MARS, 168 ORCHID DR	PEARL RIVER, NY	10965
BELOHLAVEK, JIRI	CONDUCTOR	MARIEDL ANDERS ARTISTS MGMT		
		535 EL CAMINO DEL MAR ST	SAN FRANCISCO, CA	94121
BELOIN, EDMUND	WRITER	8955 BEVERLY BLVD	LOS ANGELES, CA	90048
BELOUS, PAUL M	WRITER	8955 BEVERLY BLVD	LOS ANGELES, CA	90048
BELSER, DANA C	GUITARIST	5543 OLD HICKORY BLVD	NASHVILLE, TN	37218
BELSON, JERRY	FILM WRITER-DIRECTOR	8047 WOODROW WILSON DR	LOS ANGELES, CA	90046
BELTON, MARY C	NEWS CORRESPONDENT	1825 "K" ST, NW	WASHINGTON, DC	20006
BELTRAN, ALMA	ACTRESS	8820 SUNSET BLVD #ANB	LOS ANGELES, CA	90069
BELTRAN, ROBERT	ACTOR	1930 CENTURY PARK W #303	LOS ANGELES, CA	90067
BELTZ, WILLIAM A	NEWS CORRESPONDENT	1001 HERBERT SPRINGS RD	ALEXANDRA, VA	22308
BELTZER, YVONNE ROSE	WRITER	1239 N VALLEY ST	BURBANK, CA	91505
BELUSHI, JAMES	ACTOR	1888 CENTURY PARK E #1400	LOS ANGELES, CA	90067
BELVILLE, BONNIE	ACTRESS	8230 BEVERLY BLVD #23	LOS ANGELES, CA	90048
BELZER, RICHARD	COMEDIAN	151 S EL CAMINO DR	BEVERLY HILLS, CA	90212
BEN-DOR, GISELE BUKA	CONDUCTOR	ROSENFIELD, 714 LADD RD	BRONX, NY	10471
BENAC, NANCY	NEWS CORRESPONDENT	4620 S 28TH RD #B	ARLINGTON, VA	22206
BENACHKOVA, GABRIELA	SOPRANO	MARIEDL ANDERS ARTISTS MGMT		
		535 EL CAMINO DEL MAR ST	SAN FRANCISCO, CA	94121
BENAIR, JONATHAN	WRITER	450 N HAYWORTH AVE	LOS ANGELES, CA	90048
BENAKE, JOHN	CLOWN	2701 COTTAGE WY #14	SACRAMENTO, CA	95825
BENARD, FRANK M	ACTOR	6430 SUNSET BLVD #701	LOS ANGELES, CA	90028
BENATAR, PAT	SINGER	NEW STAR, 60 W 70TH ST	NEW YORK, NY	10023
BENCE, JOHN T	WRITER	555 W 57TH ST #1230	NEW YORK, NY	10019
BENCH, JOHNNY	BASEBALL	POST OFFICE BOX 2486	CINCINNATI, OH	45201
BENCHLEY, PETER	AUTHOR	35 BOUDINOT ST	PRINCETON, NJ	08540
BENCIVENGO, RICHARD	DIRECTOR	327 W 89TH ST #5-R	NEW YORK, NY	10024
BENCZIK, TERRY A	WRITER	555 W 57TH ST #1230	NEW YORK, NY	10019
BENDALL, ROBERT	ACTOR	870 N VINE ST #G	LOS ANGELES, CA	90038
BENDEL, JOHN	WRITER	THE NATIONAL LAMPOON		
		635 MADISON AVE	NEW YORK, NY	10022
BENDER, BOB	DIRECTOR	4000 SUNNYSLOPE AVE	SHERMAN OAKS, CA	91423
BENDER, DAVID	TENOR	111 W 57TH ST #1209	NEW YORK, NY	10019
BENDER, EILEEN	ACTRESS	6331 HOLLYWOOD BLVD #924	LOS ANGELES, CA	90028
BENDER, HOWARD	TENOR	CONE, 221 W 57TH ST	NEW YORK, NY	10019
BENDER, JACK L	TV WRITER-DIRECTOR	1424 ORIOLE DR	LOS ANGELES, CA	90069
BENDER, JOAN	WRITER-DIRECTOR	414 E 52ND ST	NEW YORK, NY	10022
BENDER, JOHANNES P	CONDUCTOR	1619 ALAMITAS AVE	MONROVIA, CA	91016
BENDER, JUDITH	NEWS CORRESPONDENT	3003 VAN NESS ST, NW	WASHINGTON, DC	20008
BENDER, KAY	TV WRITER	8955 BEVERLY BLVD	LOS ANGELES, CA	90048
BENDER, LESLIE MICHAEL	TV DIRECTOR	699 EDGEWOOD DR	MILL VALLEY, CA	94941
BENDER, PHILLIP C	TV DIRECTOR	1283 MUSTANG DR	DANVILLE, CA	94526
BENDER, SID	COMPOSER	11326 CHADWELL	LAKEWOOD, CA	90715
BENDEROTH, ALEXANDER	WRITER	555 W 57TH ST #1230	NEW YORK, NY	10019
BENDERSKY, SARAH	PHOTO EDITOR	US MAGAZINE COMPANY		
		1 DAG HAMMARSKJOLD PLAZA	NEW YORK, NY	10017
BENDETSON, BOB S	TV WRITER	6401 W 6TH ST	LOS ANGELES, CA	90048
BENDETSON, HOWARD M	TV WRITER	13331 MOORPARK ST #338	SHERMAN OAKS, CA	91423
BENDETSON, JANE	WRITER	555 W 57TH ST #1230	NEW YORK, NY	10019
BENDETT, KATHY	ACTRESS	2431 BRIARCREST RD	BEVERLY HILLS, CA	90210
BENDICK, ROBERT L	TV DIRECTOR	19 SEA VIEW	GUILFORD, CT	06437
BENDIX, MICHAEL	TV WRITER	8955 BEVERLY BLVD	LOS ANGELES, CA	90048
BENDOKAS, RICK	GUITARIST	1030 17TH AVE S	NASHVILLE, TN	37212
BENEDEK, BARBARA	SCREENWRITER	1888 CENTURY PARK E #1400	LOS ANGELES, CA	90067
BENEDEK, LASLO	DIRECTOR	70 BANK ST	NEW YORK, NY	10014
BENEDEK, THOMAS R	WRITER	10427 WILSHIRE BLVD #22	LOS ANGELES, CA	90024
BENEDEK, TOM	SCREENWRITER	8955 BEVERLY BLVD	LOS ANGELES, CA	90048
BENEDETTO, RICHARD	COLUMNIST	POST OFFICE BOX 500	WASHINGTON, DC	20044
BENEDETTO, ROBERT E	TV WRITER	8955 BEVERLY BLVD	LOS ANGELES, CA	90048
BENEDICT, BILLY	ACTOR	SEE - BENEDICT, WILLIAM		
BENEDICT, DIRK	ACTOR	9000 SUNSET BLVD #1112	LOS ANGELES, CA	90069
BENEDICT, JAY	ACTOR	25 KEMPE RD	LONDON NW6	ENGLAND
BENEDICT, JOAN	ACTRESS	10000 RIVERSIDE DR #3	TOLUCA LAKE, CA	91602
BENEDICT, NICHOLAS	ACTOR	7466 BEVERLY BLVD #205	LOS ANGELES, CA	90036

NAME	OCCUPATION	ADDRESS	CITY	ZIP/COUNTRY
BENEDICT, PAUL	ACTOR	9300 WILSHIRE BLVD #410	BEVERLY HILLS, CA	90212
BENEDICT, ROBERT	ACTOR	11240 MAGNOLIA BLVD #202	NORTH HOLLYWOOD, CA	91601
BENEDICT, WILLIAM	ACTOR	1347 N ORANGE GROVE AVE	LOS ANGELES, CA	90046
BENEDICT, WILLIAM H, SR	PHOTOGRAPHER	2919 STUART DR	FALLS CHURCH, VA	22042
BENEKE, TEX	ORCHESTRA LEADER	HECKER, 2275 FAUST AVE	LONG BEACH, CA	90815
BENEMANN, JAMES BURNS	NEWS CORRESPONDENT	400 N CAPITOL ST, NW	WASHINGTON, DC	20001
BENENSON, ROBERT ALAN	NEWS CORRESPONDENT	1204 S WASHINGTON ST	ALEXANDRIA, VA	22314
BENES, JAMES T	WRITER	555 W 57TH ST #1230	NEW YORK, NY	10019
BENEST, GLEN M	SCREENWRITER	953 11TH ST #1	SANTA MONICA, CA	90403
BENFELL, CAROL R	NEWS CORRESPONDENT	4108 LEE HWY	ARLINGTON, VA	22207
BENFIELD, DEREK	ACTOR	4 BERKELEY RD	LONDON SW13 9L2	ENGLAND
BENGSTON, PAUL	CASTING DIRECTER	12345 VENTURA BLVD #N	STUDIO CITY, CA	91604
BENHAM, BARBARA	ACTRESS	3518 W CAHUENGA BLVD #315	HOLLYWOOD, CA	90068
BENHAM, GEORGE DOUGLAS	GUITARIST	POST OFFICE BOX 17303	NASHVILLE, TN	37217
BENHAM, HELEN	PIANIST	KAY, 58 W 58TH ST	NEW YORK, NY	10019
BENICKES, MILES L	WRITER	3220 PHILO ST	LOS ANGELES, CA	90064
BENJAMIN, ANN	TV DIRECTOR	ABC-TV, 7 W 66TH ST	NEW YORK, NY	10023
BENJAMIN, BURTON	WRITER	555 W 57TH ST #1230	NEW YORK, NY	10019
BENJAMIN, BURTON	TV PRODUCER	CBS-TV, 524 W 57TH ST	NEW YORK, NY	10019
BENJAMIN, CYNTHIA	TV WRITER	555 W 57TH ST #1230	NEW YORK, NY	10019
BENJAMIN, FLOELLA	ACTRESS	TAYLOR, 73 PALACE RD	LONDON SW2 3LB	ENGLAND
BENJAMIN, JAMES E	WRITER	555 W 57TH ST #1230	NEW YORK, NY	10019
BENJAMIN, JEFF	WRITER	8955 BEVERLY BLVD	LOS ANGELES, CA	90048
BENJAMIN, JORDAN	ACTOR	ABC-TV, "GENERAL HOSPITAL"		
		1438 N GOWER ST	LOS ANGELES, CA	90028
BENJAMIN, PAUL	ACTOR	10351 SANTA MONICA BLVD #211	LOS ANGELES, CA	90025
BENJAMIN, RICHARD	ACTOR-DIRECTOR	719 N FOOTHILL RD	BEVERLY HILLS, CA	90210
BENJAMINSON, WENDY ANN	NEWS CORRESPONDENT	1457 CHAPIN ST, NW	WASHINGTON, DC	20009
BENKMAN, HERBERT F	ACTOR	7504 HOLLYWOOD BLVD #3	LOS ANGELES, CA	90046
BENN, HARRY	FILM PRODUCER	7 BELLMOUNT WOOD AVE		
		WATFORD	HERTS WD1 3BN	ENGLAND
BENN, NATHAN	PHOTOGRAPHER	NGS PHOTO DEPARTMENT		
		17TH & "M" STS, NW	WASHINGTON, DC	20036
BENNER, RICHARD	DIRECTOR	228 W 4TH ST #4	NEW YORK, NY	10014
BENNET, SPENCER G	FILM DIRECTOR	6074 SELMA AVE	HOLLYWOOD, CA	90028
BENNETH, JOHN	COLUMNIST	7720 EL CAMINO REAL #2-C	RANCHO LA COSTA, CA	92008
BENNETT, ALAN	ACTOR-WRITER	CHATTO & LINNIT, LTD		
		PRINCE OF WALES THEATRE		
		COVENTRY ST	LONDON W1	ENGLAND
BENNETT, BRUCE	ACTOR	2702 FORESTER RD	LOS ANGELES, CA	90064
BENNETT, CAROL	NEWS CORRESPONDENT	115 SOUTHWOOD AVE	SILVER SPRING, MD	20901
BENNETT, CAROLE	TALENT AGENT	150 S BARRINGTON AVE #1	LOS ANGELES, CA	90049
BENNETT, CHARLES	WRITER-DIRECTOR	1720 COLDWATER CANYON DR	BEVERLY HILLS, CA	90210
BENNETT, CONNIE LEE	WRITER	6439 MOORE DR	LOS ANGELES, CA	90048
BENNETT, DEREK JAMES	TV DIRECTOR-PRODUCER	THE MEWS, RED LODGE		
		BUSTON RD, DISLEY	CHESHIRE	ENGLAND
BENNETT, DIANNE	WRITER	8955 BEVERLY BLVD	LOS ANGELES, CA	90048
BENNETT, FRAN	ACTRESS	2125 W SILVER LAKE DR	LOS ANGELES, CA	90039
BENNETT, HARVE	WRI-DIR-PROD	12907 SUNSET BLVD	LOS ANGELES, CA	90049
BENNETT, HOLLY	ACTRESS	7910 GIRARD AVE	LA JOLLA, CA	92037
BENNETT, HYWEL	ACTOR	REDWAY, 16 BERNERS ST	LONDON W1P 3DD	ENGLAND
BENNETT, JILL	ACTRESS	SHARKEY, 90 REGENT ST	LONDON W1	ENGLAND
BENNETT, JOAN	ACTRESS	67 CHASE RD N	NORTH SCARSDALE, NY	10583
BENNETT, JOAN	MODEL	MODELS & PROMOTIONS AGENCY		
		8560 SUNSET BLVD, 10TH FLOOR	LOS ANGELES, CA	90069
BENNETT, JOHN	ACTOR	SAINT JAMES'S MGMT		
		22 GROOM PL	LONDON SW1	ENGLAND
BENNETT, JOHN L	NEWS CORRESPONDENT	7045 LEEWOOD FOREST DR	SPRINGFIELD, VA	22151
BENNETT, JONATHAN	ACTOR	10850 RIVERSIDE DR #505	NORTH HOLLYWOOD, CA	91602
BENNETT, JULIE	ACTRESS	9200 SUNSET BLVD #909	LOS ANGELES, CA	90069
BENNETT, KELLY	ACTRESS	10351 SANTA MONICA BLVD #211	LOS ANGELES, CA	90025
BENNETT, LINDA	MEZZO-SOPRANO	VKD INTERNATIONAL ARTISTS		
		220 SHEPPARD AVE E		
		WILLOWDALE	TORONTO, ONT M2N 3A9	CANADA
BENNETT, LYNETTE	ACTRESS	165 PARK ROW #10-F	NEW YORK, NY	10038
BENNETT, MACK S	GUITARIST	POST OFFICE BOX 97		
		TURNBULL RD	WHITE BLUFF, TN	37187
BENNETT, MATT	ACTOR	4132 TOLUCA LAKE AVE	BURBANK, CA	91505
BENNETT, MEG	ACTRESS-WRITER	9220 SUNSET BLVD #625	LOS ANGELES, CA	90069
BENNETT, PETER	ACTOR	39 BEDFORD GARDENS	LONDON W8 7EF	ENGLAND
BENNETT, RALPH K	NEWS CORRESPONDENT	7500 OLD CHESTER RD	BETHESDA, MD	20817
BENNETT, RANDY	ACTOR	1912 1/2 HILLCREST RD	LOS ANGELES, CA	90068
BENNETT, RICHARD CHARLES	TV DIRECTOR	17136 INDEX ST	GRANADA HILLS, CA	91344
BENNETT, RICHARD RODNEY	COMPOSER	LONDON MANAGEMENT, LTD		
		235-241 REGENT ST	LONDON W1A 2JT	ENGLAND
BENNETT, ROBERT	NEWS CORRESPONDENT	1601 18TH ST, NW	WASHINGTON, DC	20009
BENNETT, RONALD T	PHOTOGRAPHER	7203 EARLY ST	ANNANDALE, VA	22003
BENNETT, RUTH	TV WRITER	1888 CENTURY PARK E #1107	LOS ANGELES, CA	90067
BENNETT, RUTH A	TV WRITER	8955 BEVERLY BLVD	LOS ANGELES, CA	90048
BENNETT, SEYMOUR	WRITER	6439 MOORE DR	LOS ANGELES, CA	90048
BENNETT, SHARON	COLORATURA	PERLS, 7 W 96TH ST	NEW YORK, NY	10025
BENNETT, SUSAN J	NEWS CORRESPONDENT	7045 LEEWOOD FOREST DR	SPRINGFIELD, VA	22151
BENNETT, TONY	SINGER-ACTOR	101 W 55TH ST	NEW YORK, NY	10019
BENNETT, WALLACE S	SCREENWRITER	8955 BEVERLY BLVD	LOS ANGELES, CA	90048

Name	Occupation	Address	City/State	Zip
BENNETT, WALTER E	PHOTOGRAPHER	654-A 15TH ST S	ARLINGTON, VA	22202
BENNETT, WILLIAM R	WRITER	555 W 57TH ST #1230	NEW YORK, NY	10019
BENNETTS, BRUCE R	ACTOR	4240 PROMENADE WY #130	MARINA DEL REY, CA	90292
BENNEWITZ, JAMES RICK	TV DIRECTOR	3426 N KNOLL DR	LOS ANGELES, CA	90068
BENNINGTON, WILLIAM	TV DIRECTOR	27500 BUENA VISTA ST	HEMET, CA	92343
BENOWITZ, ROY	COMPOSER	464 S BERENDO ST #305	LOS ANGELES, CA	90020
BENSCHEIDT, CARL	TV DIRECTOR	911 S MASSELIN AVE	LOS ANGELES, CA	90036
BENSFIELD, RICHARD E	WRITER-PRODUCER	201 OCEAN AVE #1706-B	SANTA MONICA, CA	90402
BENSINK, JOHN	WRITER	555 W 57TH ST #1230	NEW YORK, NY	10019
BENSLEY, RUSS	TV PRODUCER	CBS-TV, 524 W 57TH ST	NEW YORK, NY	10019
BENSLEY, RUSS	WRITER-PRODUCER	171 HANSON LN	NEW ROCHELLE, NY	10804
BENSO, BEVERLY	MEZZO-SOPRANO	200 W 70TH ST #7-F	NEW YORK, NY	10023
BENSON, ANNETTE	CASTING DIRECTOR	10573 W PICO BLVD #103	LOS ANGELES, CA	90064
BENSON, GEORGE	SINGER-GUITARIST	19 HOLOMAKANI PL	LA HAINA, HI	96761
BENSON, GEORGE	RINGMASTER	HALL, 138 FROG HOLLOW RD	CHURCHVILLE, PA	18966
BENSON, GRAHAM	FILM PRODUCER	MOSTPOINT LIMITED		
		31 LARKHALL RISE		
		CLAPHAM	LONDON SW4 6HU	ENGLAND
BENSON, HARRY C	ACTOR	211 S BEVERLY DR #107	BEVERLY HILLS, CA	90212
BENSON, HUGH	TV PRODUCER	222 N CANON DR	BEVERLY HILLS, CA	90210
BENSON, JAY	TV WRITER-PRODUCER	18628 ROCOSO PL	TARZANA, CA	91356
BENSON, JEFFREY	TALENT AGENT	1900 AVE OF THE STARS #2375	LOS ANGELES, CA	90067
BENSON, MARTIN	ACT-WRI-DIR	THE ROMAN ROAD STUDIO		
		COLONEY ST, SAINT ALBANS	HERTS	ENGLAND
BENSON, MILES	NEWS CORRESPONDENT	7812 SYCAMORE DR	FALLS CHURCH, VA	22042
BENSON, PAMELA S	NEWS CORRESPONDENT	6423 BLUEBILL LN	ALEXANDRIA, VA	22307
BENSON, PAT	ACTRESS	6380 WILSHIRE BLVD #1600	LOS ANGELES, CA	90048
BENSON, REX	ACTOR-WRITER	1607 N EL CENTRO AVE #22	HOLLYWOOD, CA	90028
BENSON, ROBBY	ACTOR-WRITER	4830 BREWSTER DR	TARZANA, CA	91356
BENSON, ROY P	NEWS CORRESPONDENT	9203 NEW HAMPSHIRE AVE	SILVER SPRING, MD	20903
BENSON, SHARON	WRITER	8955 BEVERLY BLVD	LOS ANGELES, CA	90048
BENSON, SHEILA	FILM CRITIC	L A TIMES NEWSPAPER		
		TIMES MIRROR SQUARE	LOS ANGELES, CA	90053
BENSON, STEVE	CARTOONIST	POST OFFICE BOX 1950	PHOENIX, AZ	85001
BENSON, VICKIE SUE	ACTRESS-MODEL	400 S BEVERLY DR #216	BEVERLY HILLS, CA	90212
BENSON, VICTORIA	TV DIRECTOR	189 EXETER WY	HILLSIDE, NJ	07205
BENTINE, MICHAEL	ACTOR-COMEDIAN	LITTLE TYLERS, SANDOWN	SURREY	ENGLAND
BENTLEY, JAMES L	NEWS CORRESPONDENT	1017 COLUMBUS DR	STAFFORD, VA	22554
BENTLEY, JOHN	ACTOR	WEDGWOOD HOUSE, PETWORT	SURREY	ENGLAND
BENTLEY, ROBERT L	WRITER	8955 BEVERLY BLVD	LOS ANGELES, CA	90048
BENTLEY, SAVANNAH	ACTRESS	8225 LOOKOUT MOUNTAIN AVE	LOS ANGELES, CA	90046
BENTON, BARBI	ACTRESS-MODEL	POST OFFICE BOX 7114	PASADENA, CA	91109
BENTON, BYRON	RECORD EXECUTIVE	BAGATELLE RECORDS CO		
		400 SAN JACINTO ST	HOUSTON, TX	77002
BENTON, DANIEL KING	ACTOR-WRITER	7924 WOODMAN AVE #55	VAN NUYS, CA	91402
BENTON, DOUGLAS CARLTON	WRITER-PRODUCER	4924 CALVIN AVE	TARZANA, CA	91356
BENTON, FRAN	WRITER	8955 BEVERLY BLVD	LOS ANGELES, CA	90048
BENTON, JOE	NEWS CORRESPONDENT	ABC NEWS, 7 W 66TH ST	NEW YORK, NY	10023
BENTON, LEE	ACTRESS	1930 CENTURY PARK W #303	LOS ANGELES, CA	90067
BENTON, MONROE	NEWS CORRESPONDENT	1201 CONNECTICUT AVE, NW	WASHINGTON, DC	20036
BENTON, ROBERT A	FILM WRITER-DIRECTOR	ICM, 40 W 57TH ST	NEW YORK, NY	10019
BENTON, SUZANNE	ACTRESS	2360 SUNSET PLAZA DR	LOS ANGELES, CA	90069
BENTS, KEVIN	GUITARIST	3773 NORTHSHORE	EAU CLAIRE, WI	54701
BENTWOOD, L T	TV WRITER	8955 BEVERLY BLVD	LOS ANGELES, CA	90048
BENZ, DONNA KEI	ACTRESS	7466 BEVERLY BLVD #205	LOS ANGELES, CA	90036
BENZ, GARY	DIRECTOR	12345 VENTURA BLVD #H	STUDIO CITY, CA	91604
BERARDINO, JOHN	ACTOR	1719 AMBASSADOR DR	BEVERLY HILLS, CA	90210
BERCOV, BRIAN R	COMPOSER-CONDUCTOR	3884 FRANKLIN AVE	LOS ANGELES, CA	90027
BERCOVICI, ALFRED	WRITER	555 W 57TH ST #1230	NEW YORK, NY	10019
BERCOVICI, ERIC	WRITER-PRODUCER	154 S LAYTON DR	LOS ANGELES, CA	90049
BERCOVICI, JULIAN	WRITER	204 S OAKHURST DR	BEVERLY HILLS, CA	90212
BERCOVICI, KAREN	ACTRESS	154 S LAYTON DR	LOS ANGELES, CA	90049
BERCOVICI, LEONARD	WRITER	969 HILGARD AVE	LOS ANGELES, CA	90024
BERCOVICI, LUCA	ACTOR	445 N BEDFORD DR #PH	BEVERLY HILLS, CA	90210
BERCOVICI, LUCA J	FILM WRITER-DIRECTOR	2226 PENMAR AVE	VENICE, CA	90291
BERCOVITCH, REUBEN	WRITER-PRODUCER	139 S CARMELINA AVE	LOS ANGELES, CA	90049
BERDIS, BERT	TV WRITER	1100 N ALTA LOMA RD #80	LOS ANGELES, CA	90069
BERENBACH, NITA	WRITER	555 W 57TH ST #1230	NEW YORK, NY	10019
BERENGER, TOM	ACTOR	853 7TH AVE #9-A	NEW YORK, NY	10019
BERENHAUS, EDWARD	WRITER	8955 BEVERLY BLVD	LOS ANGELES, CA	90048
BERENSON, CRAIG	ACTOR	1418 N HIGHLAND AVE #102	LOS ANGELES, CA	90028
BERENSON, MARISA	ACTRESS	80 AVE CHARLES DE GAULLE	NEUILLY 92200	FRANCE
BERENSTAIN, STAN	TV WRITER	8955 BEVERLY BLVD	LOS ANGELES, CA	90048
BERENSTEIN, MORT	DIRECTOR	4925 WHITSETT AVE #201	NORTH HOLLYWOOD, CA	91607
BERES, PETER "THE SKIPPER"	BUSINESS AGENT	2801 MEADOW LARK DR	SAN DIEGO, CA	92123
BERESFORD, BRUCE	FILM DIRECTOR	3 MARATHON RD #13		
		DARLING POINT 2027	SYDNEY NSW 2027	AUSTRALIA
BERESWILL, JOSEPH W	PHOTOGRAPHER	2548 COLUMBUS AVE	OCEANSIDE, NY	11572
BEREZOWSKI, MAKAYMILIAN	NEWS CORRESPONDENT	4000 TUNLAW RD	WASHINGTON, DC	20007
BERG, BARRY	WRITER	555 W 57TH ST #1230	NEW YORK, NY	10019
BERG, CARMEN	MODEL	POST OFFICE BOX 7211	MOUNTAIN VIEW, CA	94043
BERG, CURT	COMPOSER	524 N AVON ST	BURBANK, CA	91505
BERG, DANIEL J	DIRECTOR	DGA, 110 W 57TH ST	NEW YORK, NY	10019
BERG, DAVE	ARTIST-WRITER	MAD MAGAZINE, INC		
		485 MADISON AVE	NEW YORK, NY	10022

BARBI BENTON

CANDICE BERGEN

SANDAHL BERGMAN

KEN BERRY

LEONARD BERNSTEIN

VALERIE BERTINELLI

TURHAN BEY

BIG COUNTRY

TONY BILL

Name	Occupation	Address	City, State	Zip
BERG, DAVE	TV WRITER	8955 BEVERLY BLVD	LOS ANGELES, CA	90048
BERG, DICK	TV PRODUCER	151 S EL CAMINO DR	BEVERLY HILLS, CA	90212
BERG, HAMILTON	WRITER	8955 BEVERLY BLVD	LOS ANGELES, CA	90048
BERG, ILENE AMY	TV PRODUCER	ABC CIRCLE FILMS CO		
		4151 PROSPECT AVE	LOS ANGELES, CA	90027
BERG, JAMES B	TV WRITER	8955 BEVERLY BLVD	LOS ANGELES, CA	90048
BERG, JEFF	TALENT AGENT	ICM, 8899 BEVERLY BLVD	LOS ANGELES, CA	90048
BERG, JUDITH	WRITER	8955 BEVERLY BLVD	LOS ANGELES, CA	90048
BERG, KEN	TV WRITER	2102 KELTON AVE	LOS ANGELES, CA	90045
BERG, LEE	WRITER	8955 BEVERLY BLVD	LOS ANGELES, CA	90048
BERG, RICHARD J	WRITER	151 S EL CAMINO DR	BEVERLY HILLS, CA	90212
BERG, SANDRA I	WRITER	8955 BEVERLY BLVD	LOS ANGELES, CA	90048
BERG, STEPHEN	NEWS CORRESPONDENT	4120 WOODBINE ST	CHEVY CHASE, MD	20815
BERG, STUART	DIRECTOR	5820 MAMMOTH AVE	VAN NUYS, CA	91401
BERG & PRINCE MIME CO	VOCAL MIME	POST OFFICE BOX 20548	NEW YORK, NY	10025
BERG,, ALBAN, QUARTET	MUSIC ENSEMBLE	ICM, 40 W 57TH ST	NEW YORK, NY	10019
BERGE, BRENDA	MEZZO-SOPRANO	200 W 70TH ST #7-F	NEW YORK, NY	10023
BERGEL, ERICH	CONDUCTOR	MARIEDL ANDERS ARTISTS MGMT		
		535 EL CAMINO DEL MAR ST	SAN FRANCISCO, CA	94121
BERGEN, CANDICE	ACTRESS	222 CENTRAL PARK S	NEW YORK, NY	10019
BERGEN, FRANCES	ACTRESS	8485 MELROSE PL #E	LOS ANGELES, CA	90069
BERGEN, JERRY	ACTOR	200 W 54TH ST	NEW YORK, NY	10019
BERGEN, POLLY	ACTRESS	3624 MOUNTAIN VIEW AVE	STUDIO CITY, CA	91604
BERGER, ALAN	ACTOR-WRITER	1127 9TH ST #102	SANTA MONICA, CA	90403
BERGER, ANNA	ACTRESS	19 W 44TH ST #1500	NEW YORK, NY	10036
BERGER, DAN	WINE EXPERT	POST OFFICE BOX 569	SANTA ROSA, CA	95402
BERGER, ELIZABETH	ACTRESS	208 S BEVERLY DR #4	BEVERLY HILLS, CA	90212
BERGER, FRED W	FILM EDITOR	1560 KELTON AVE	LOS ANGELES, CA	90024
BERGER, GREGG	ACTOR	7415 LURLINE AVE	CANOGA PARK, CA	91306
BERGER, HARVEY	SCREENWRITER	3621 STEWART AVE	LOS ANGELES, CA	90066
BERGER, HELMUT	ACTOR	PERFALLSTRASSE 8000	MUNICH 80	WEST GERMANY
BERGER, JAMES R	NEWS CORRESPONDENT	20 FRANKLIN AVE	SILVER SPRING, MD	20901
BERGER, JULIUS	CELLIST	IAPR, KINCORA, BEER RD		
		SEATON	DEVON	ENGLAND
BERGER, LOU	TV WRITER	555 W 57TH ST #1230	NEW YORK, NY	10019
BERGER, MARILYN	NEWS CORRESPONDENT	ABC NEWS, 7 W 66TH ST	NEW YORK, NY	10023
BERGER, MEL	ACTOR	8961 SUNSET BLVD #B	LOS ANGELES, CA	90069
BERGER, RICHARD L	FILM EXECUTIVE	637 N WILCOX AVE	LOS ANGELES, CA	90004
BERGER, RICK	TV EXECUTIVE	CBS-TV, 7800 BEVERLY BLVD	LOS ANGELES, CA	90036
BERGER, ROBERT BRYAN	ACTOR	4746 VENTURA CANYON AVE	SHERMAN OAKS, CA	91423
BERGER, SENTA	ACTRESS	ROBT-KOCH-STRASSE 10	GRUNWALD 8022	W GERMANY
BERGER, ZACHARY	ACTOR	6605 HOLLYWOOD BLVD #220	HOLLYWOOD, CA	90028
BERGERE, LEE	ACTOR	2267 CENTURY HILL	LOS ANGELES, CA	90067
BERGERON, ELZA	CASTING DIRECTOR	12031 VENTURA BLVD #1	STUDIO CITY, CA	91601
BERGESON, DOREEN	PRODUCER	STARK PRODS, COLUMBIA PL	BURBANK, CA	91505
BERGGREN, ARTHUR	ACTOR	611 1/2 OCEAN PARK BLVD	SANTA MONICA, CA	90405
BERGGREN, TROY	ACTRESS	11974 MOORPARK ST #6	NORTH HOLLYWOOD, CA	91604
BERGHER, GARY	ACTOR	16814 HART ST	VAN NUYS, CA	91406
BERGHOF, HERBERT	ACTOR	120 BANK ST	NEW YORK, NY	10014
BERGLAND, BOND	SINGER	POST OFFICE BOX 20956		
		THOMPSON STATION	NEW YORK, NY	10009
BERGLUND, ALFRED J	WRITER	555 W 57TH ST #1230	NEW YORK, NY	10019
BERGLUND, PAAVO	CONDUCTOR	ICM, 40 W 57 THE ST	NEW YORK, NY	10019
BERGMAN, ALAN	LYRICIST	714 N MAPLE DR	BEVERLY HILLS, CA	90210
BERGMAN, ANDREW	WRITER-PRODUCER	10100 SANTA MONICA BLVD #1600	LOS ANGELES, CA	90067
BERGMAN, HAROLD	ACTOR	8424 SW 103RD AVE	MIAMI, FL	33173
BERGMAN, KLAS	NEWS CORRESPONDENT	1406 30TH ST, NW	WASHINGTON, DC	20007
BERGMAN, MARILYN	LYRICIST	714 N MAPLE DR	BEVERLY HILLS, CA	90210
BERGMAN, PETER	ACTOR	165 W 46TH ST #409	NEW YORK, NY	10036
BERGMAN, PHILIP S	WRITER	555 W 57TH ST #1230	NEW YORK, NY	10019
BERGMAN, RICHARD	ACTOR	6143 AUCKLAND AVE	NORTH HOLLYWOOD, CA	91606
BERGMAN, SANDAHL	ACTRESS-MODEL	ICM, 8899 BEVERLY BLVD	LOS ANGELES, CA	90048
BERGMAN, TED	TV WRITER	11108 OPHIR DR	LOS ANGELES, CA	90024
BERGMANN, ALAN S	TV DIRECTOR	6330 ALLOTT AVE	VAN NUYS, CA	91401
BERGONZI, CARLO	TENOR	CAMI, 165 W 57TH ST	NEW YORK, NY	10019
BERGQUIST, ELEANOR	SOPRANO	CAMI, 165 W 57TH ST	NEW YORK, NY	10019
BERGREN, ERIC	SCREENWRITER	1015 GAYLEY AVE #201	LOS ANGELES, CA	90024
BERGSTEIN, ELEANOR	SCREENWRITER	555 W 57TH ST #1230	NEW YORK, NY	10019
BERGSTROM, CATHERINE	ACTRESS	1 SPINNAKER ST #1	MARINA DEL REY, CA	90292
BERGSTROM, KARL G	NEWS CORRESPONDENT	6126 BROAD BRANCH RD, NW	WASHINGTON, DC	20015
BERGSTROM, KIRK E	WRITER	8955 BEVERLY BLVD	LOS ANGELES, CA	90048
BERGSTROM, VERN	ACCORDIONIS	640 WESTBORD DR	NASHVILLE, TN	37209
BERINBAUM, MARTIN	TRUMPETER	CAMI, 165 W 57TH ST	NEW YORK, NY	10019
BERINI, BIANCA	MEZZO-SOPRANO	61 W 62ND ST #6-F	NEW YORK, NY	10023
BERIO, LUCIANO	COMPOSER-CONDUCTOR	ICM, 40 W 57TH ST	NEW YORK, NY	10019
BERJER, BARBARA	ACTRESS	NBC-TV, "ANOTHER WORLD"		
		30 ROCKEFELLER PLAZA	NEW YORK, NY	10112
BERK, BARRY	TV DIRECTOR	10555 BLYTHE AVE	LOS ANGELES, CA	90064
BERK, HOWARD	SCREENWRITER	2290 STRADELLA RD	LOS ANGELES, CA	90077
BERK, JAY	NEWS CORRESPONDENT	400 N CAPITOL ST, NW	WASHINGTON, DC	20001
BERK, KATHLEEN E	FLUTIST	1831 GREEN HILLS DR	NASHVILLE, TN	37215
BERK, MICHAEL	TV WRITER	ICM, 8899 BEVERLY BLVD	LOS ANGELES, CA	90048

Name	Occupation	Address	City	Zip
BERKE, ED	ACTOR	LEONETTI, 6526 SUNSET BLVD	HOLLYWOOD, CA	90028
BERKE, LESTER W	WRITER-PRODUCER	9200 SUNSET BLVD #909	LOS ANGELES, CA	90069
BERKE, RONNI	WRITER	555 W 57TH ST #1230	NEW YORK, NY	10019
BERKELEY, CONAN	WRITER	2117 HOLLY DR	LOS ANGELES, CA	90068
BERKMAN, AL	COMPOSER-CONDUCTOR	384 N SAN VICENTE BLVD	LOS ANGELES, CA	90048
BERKMAN, JOHN D	COMPOSER	POST OFFICE BOX 1407	LOS ANGELES, CA	90078
BERKOFF, STEVEN	ACTOR	HAMPER, 193 WARDOUR ST	LONDON W1	ENGLAND
BERKOFSKY, MICHAEL	DIRECTOR	1026 S CARMELINA AVE	LOS ANGELES, CA	90069
BERKOWITZ, BARBARA	TV WRITER	8955 BEVERLY BLVD	LOS ANGELES, CA	90048
BERKOWITZ, BOB	ACTOR	8075 W 3RD ST #303	LOS ANGELES, CA	90048
BERKOWITZ, BOB	NEWS CORRESPONDENT	ABC NEWS, 7 W 66TH ST	NEW YORK, NY	10023
BERKOWSKY, PAUL F	THEATER PRODUCER	1549 BROADWAY	NEW YORK, NY	10036
BERKY, BOB	MIME	SHAFMAN, 723 7TH AVE	NEW YORK, NY	10019
BERLATSKY, DAVID	DIRECTOR	8261 W NORTON AVE #4	LOS ANGELES, CA	90046
BERLE, MILTON	ACTOR-COMEDIAN	711 N ALPINE DR	BEVERLY HILLS, CA	90210
BERLIN	ROCK & ROLL GROUP	10100 SANTA MONICA BLVD #1600	LOS ANGELES, CA	90067
BERLIN, CAROLE	TV WRITER	8955 BEVERLY BLVD	LOS ANGELES, CA	90048
BERLIN, IRVING	COMPOSER	1290 AVE OF THE AMERICAS	NEW YORK, NY	10019
BERLIN, PETER R	TV WRITER	8955 BEVERLY BLVD	LOS ANGELES, CA	90048
BERLIN, RICK & BERLIN	ROCK & ROLL GROUP	25 HUNTINGTON AVE #420	BOSTON, MA	02116
BERLINGER, WARREN	ACTOR	10642 ARNEL PL	CHATSWORTH, CA	91311
BERMAN, CHRIS	SPORTSCASTER	ESPN, ESPN PLAZA	BRISTOL, CT	06010
BERMAN, DAVID Z	DIRECTOR	530 E 72ND ST	NEW YORK, NY	10021
BERMAN, DONALD	NEWS PRODUCER	ENTERTAINMENT TONIGHT		
		PARAMOUNT TELEVISION		
		5555 MELROSE AVE	LOS ANGELES, CA	90038
BERMAN, JESSICA A	NEWS CORRESPONDENT	1111 18TH ST, NW	WASHINGTON, DC	20036
BERMAN, LAZAR	PIANIST	LEISER, DORCHESTER TOWERS		
		155 W 68TH ST	NEW YORK, NY	10023
BERMAN, MARTIN	TV PRODUCER	ICM, 8899 BEVERLY BLVD	LOS ANGELES, CA	90048
BERMAN, MONTY	CINEMATOGRAPHER	THORN EMI ELSTREE STUDIOS		
		BOREHAMWOOD	HERTS	ENGLAND
BERMAN, PANDRO S	FILM PRODUCER	914 N ROXBURY DR	BEVERLY HILLS, CA	90210
BERMAN, PATTI JAN	NEWS CORRESPONDENT	400 N CAPITOL ST, NW	WASHINGTON, DC	20001
BERMAN, PEGGY T	NEWS REPORTER	TIME/TIME & LIFE BLDG		
		ROCKEFELLER CENTER	NEW YORK, NY	10020
BERMAN, RICHARD	TALENT AGENT	6380 WILSHIRE BLVD #910	LOS ANGELES, CA	90048
BERMAN, SHELLEY	COMEDIAN	WEBB, 7500 DEVISTA DR	LOS ANGELES, CA	90048
BERMAN, STEVE	TV EXECUTIVE	CBS-TV, 7800 BEVERLY BLVD	LOS ANGELES, CA	90036
BERMAN, STEVEN	WRITER	555 W 57TH ST #1230	NEW YORK, NY	10019
BERMAN, SUSAN	WRITER	8955 BEVERLY BLVD	LOS ANGELES, CA	90048
BERMAN, TED	FILM WRITER-DIRECTOR	500 S BUENA VISTA ST	BURBANK, CA	91521
BERMANN, HERBERT	WRITER	8955 BEVERLY BLVD	LOS ANGELES, CA	90048
BERMPOHL, CHARLES T	NEWS CORRESPONDENT	1002 "G" ST, SE	WASHINGTON, DC	20003
BERMUDEZ, VIVIAN	BODYBUILDER	POST OFFICE BOX 8837	SAN JUAN, PR	00910
BERNABEI, JOHN	ACTOR	11583 MAGNOLIA BLVD	NORTH HOLLYWOOD, CA	91601
BERNAL, RICHARD	DIRECTOR	520 N MICHIGAN AVE #436	CHICAGO, IL	60611
BERNARD, ANDRE	TRUMPETER	CAMI, 165 W 57TH ST	NEW YORK, NY	10019
BERNARD, ANNABELLE	SOPRANO	1776 BROADWAY #504	NEW YORK, NY	10019
BERNARD, CRYSTAL	ACTRESS	15301 VENTURA BLVD #345	SHERMAN OAKS, CA	91403
BERNARD, DUSTIN	FILM DIRECTOR	726 N ROXBURY DR	BEVERLY HILLS, CA	90210
BERNARD, ED	ACTOR	7461 BEVERLY BLVD #400	LOS ANGELES, CA	90036
BERNARD, FRANCE	ACTOR	9300 WILSHIRE BLVD #410	BEVERLY HILLS, CA	90212
BERNARD, FRANK M	ACTOR	6430 SUNSET BLVD #1203	LOS ANGELES, CA	90028
BERNARD, GUETTA	NEWS CORRESPONDENT	2701 "N" ST, NW	WASHINGTON, DC	20007
BERNARD, HERBERT	DIRECTOR	1956 LUCILLE AVE	LOS ANGELES, CA	90039
BERNARD, IAN	SCREENWRITER	8955 BEVERLY BLVD	LOS ANGELES, CA	90048
BERNARD, JAMES	COMPOSER	LONDON MANAGEMENT, LTD		
		235-241 REGENT ST	LONDON W1A 2JT	ENGLAND
BERNARD, JASON	ACTOR	9220 SUNSET BLVD #625	LOS ANGELES, CA	90069
BERNARD, JAY	ACTOR	1741 N IVAR AVE #221	LOS ANGELES, CA	90028
BERNARD, JOHNNY	SINGER	PTA, 208 ST COACHMAN DR	LAWTON, OK	73501
BERNARD, JOSEPH	ACTOR	8019 1/2 MELROSE AVE #3	LOS ANGELES, CA	90046
BERNARD, JOSEPH	WRITER	8955 BEVERLY BLVD	LOS ANGELES, CA	90048
BERNARD, JUDD	WRITER	8955 BEVERLY BLVD	LOS ANGELES, CA	90048
BERNARD, ROBYN	ACTRESS	1100 N ALTA LOMA RD #707	LOS ANGELES, CA	90069
BERNARD, WADE ALAN	GUITARIST	ROUTE #2, BOX 128	CHRISTIANA, TN	37037
BERNARDI, JACK	ACTOR	1284 N HAVENHURST DR	LOS ANGELES, CA	90046
BERNARDI, MARIO	CONDUCTOR	POST OFFICE BOX 188		
		STATION A	TORONTO, ONT	CANADA
BERNAU, CHRISTOPHER	ACTOR	CBS-TV, "THE GUIDING LIGHT"		
		51 W 52ND ST	NEW YORK, NY	10019
BERNBAUM, PAUL L	WRITER	8955 BEVERLY BLVD	LOS ANGELES, CA	90048
BERNDS, EDWARD L	WRITER	6456 WOODMAN AVE	VAN NUYS, CA	91401
BERNHARD, BARBARA	WRITER	555 W 57TH ST #1230	NEW YORK, NY	10019
BERNHARD, HARVEY	ACTOR	10351 SANTA MONICA BLVD #211	LOS ANGELES, CA	90025
BERNHARD, J P	WRITER	8955 BEVERLY BLVD	LOS ANGELES, CA	90048
BERNHARD, KENTON DAVID	NEWS CORRESPONDENT	9416 GAMBA CT	VIENNA, VA	22180
BERNHARD, SANDRA	COMEDIENNE-ACTRESS	10100 SANTA MONICA BLVD #1600	LOS ANGELES, CA	90067
BERNHARDI, LEE	DIRECTOR	4475 WHITE OAK PL	ENCINO, CA	91316
BERNHARDT, KATHLEEN	WRITER	555 W 57TH ST #1230	NEW YORK, NY	10019
BERNHARDT, KEVIN	ACTOR	ABC-TV ENTERTAINMENT CENTER		
		2040 AVE OF THE STARS	LOS ANGELES, CA	90067
BERNHARDT, MELVIN	DIRECTOR	DURHAM, 123 W 74TH ST	NEW YORK, NY	10023

Name	Occupation	Address	City	Zip
BERNHARDT, ROBERT	CONDUCTOR	1776 BROADWAY #504	NEW YORK, NY	10019
BERNHAUT, MICHAEL	DIRECTOR	112 W 76TH ST	NEW YORK, NY	10023
BERNHEIM, ALAIN	FILM PRODUCER	9209 CORDELL DR	LOS ANGELES, CA	90069
BERNHEIMER, MARTIN	MUSIC-DANCE CRITIC	L A TIMES NEWSPAPER		
		TIMES MIRROR SQUARE	LOS ANGELES, CA	90053
BERNINI, JEFFREY S	SCREENWRITER	15206 LA MAIDA ST	SHERMAN OAKS, CA	91403
BERNOUSSI, FARID	NEWS CORRESPONDENT	1245 4TH ST #504, SW	WASHINGTON, DC	20024
BERNS, FRED	NEWS CORRESPONDENT	148 "G" ST, SW	WASHINGTON, DC	20024
BERNS, GERALD	ACTOR	11350 VENTURA BLVD #206	STUDIO CITY, CA	91604
BERNS, WALLY K	ACTOR	2135 N PASS AVE	BURBANK, CA	91505
BERNSEN, CORBIN	ACTOR	1145 GAYLEY AVE #309	LOS ANGELES, CA	90024
BERNSTEIN, ARMYAN	WRITER-PRODUCER	BARZINI, 9021 MELROSE AVE	LOS ANGELES, CA	90069
BERNSTEIN, BARRY	DIRECTOR	DGA, 7950 SUNSET BLVD	LOS ANGELES, CA	90046
BERNSTEIN, BILL	FILM EXECUTIVE	1875 CENTURY PARK E #300	LOS ANGELES, CA	90067
BERNSTEIN, CAL	TV DIRECTOR	DOVE, 722 N SEWARD ST	LOS ANGELES, CA	90038
BERNSTEIN, CARL	WRITER	2753 ONTARIO RD, NW	WASHINGTON, DC	20009
BERNSTEIN, CHARLES	COMPOSER-CONDUCTOR	POST OFFICE BOX 11413	BEVERLY HILLS, CA	90213
BERNSTEIN, ELLIOT	TV EXECUTIVE	315 E 72ND ST	NEW YORK, NY	10021
BERNSTEIN, ELMER	COMPOSER-CONDUCTOR	1801 AVE OF THE STARS #911	LOS ANGELES, CA	90067
BERNSTEIN, ERIC S	TV WRITER	8955 BEVERLY BLVD	LOS ANGELES, CA	90048
BERNSTEIN, FRED A	WRITER	TIME & PEOPLE MAGAZINE		
		TIME & LIFE BUILDING		
		ROCKEFELLER CENTER	NEW YORK, NY	10020
BERNSTEIN, GEORGE J	TV EXECUTIVE	CBS-TV, 6121 SUNSET BLVD	LOS ANGELES, CA	90028
BERNSTEIN, GIORA	CONDUCTOR	GERSHUNOFF, 502 PARK AVE	NEW YORK, NY	10022
BERNSTEIN, GIORA G	CONDUCTOR	755 7TH ST	BOULDER, CO	80302
BERNSTEIN, IRA	CASTING DIRECTOR	ABC-TV, 4151 PROSPECT AVE	LOS ANGELES, CA	90027
BERNSTEIN, IRA	THEATER PRODUCER	15 E 48TH ST	NEW YORK, NY	10017
BERNSTEIN, JACK B	DIRECTOR-PRODUCER	KLEIN, 4565 SHERMAN OAKS AVE	SHERMAN OAKS, CA	91403
BERNSTEIN, JACLYN	ACTRESS	1450 BELFAST DR	LOS ANGELES, CA	90069
BERNSTEIN, JANE	WRITER	555 W 57TH ST #1230	NEW YORK, NY	10019
BERNSTEIN, JAY	TALENT AGENT	1888 CENTURY PARK E #622	LOS ANGELES, CA	90067
BERNSTEIN, JERRY	TV DIRECTOR	13127 MORRISON ST	SHERMAN OAKS, CA	91423
BERNSTEIN, JOAN E	WRITER	555 W 57TH ST #1230	NEW YORK, NY	10019
BERNSTEIN, JORDAN	DIRECTOR	3716 MALIBU COLONY DR	MALIBU, CA	90265
BERNSTEIN, LEONARD	COMPOSER-CONDUCTOR	205 W 57TH ST	NEW YORK, NY	10019
BERNSTEIN, LINDA	ACTRESS	6470 DEEP DELL PL	LOS ANGELES, CA	90068
BERNSTEIN, NAN	FILM DIRECTOR	MC CARTHY RD	TYRINGHAM, MA	02164
BERNSTEIN, PETER W	NEWS CORRESPONDENT	3126 WOOLEY RD, NW	WASHINGTON, DC	20008
BERNSTEIN, RICK	TALENT AGENT	BRB, 666 N ROBERTSON BLVD	LOS ANGELES, CA	90060
BERNSTEIN, STEWART K	FILM WRITER-DIRECTOR	13044 HARTSOOK ST	SHERMAN OAKS, CA	91423
BERNSTEIN, WALTER	WRITER-DIRECTOR	320 CENTRAL PARK W	NEW YORK, NY	10025
BERNSTORF, CAROL C	BASSOONIST	7327 N PAULINA ST #3	CHICAGO, IL	60626
BERNUTH, CHARLES P	ACTOR	3989 SUNSWEPT DR	STUDIO CITY, CA	91604
BEROFF, MICHEL	PIANIST	CAMI, 165 W 57TH ST	NEW YORK, NY	10019
BEROFF & COLLARD	PIANO DUO	LEISER, DORCHESTER TOWERS		
		155 W 68TH ST	NEW YORK, NY	10023
BERRA, YOGI	BASEBALL	19 HIGHLAND AVE	MONTCLAIR, NJ	07042
BERRE, ANTONIO	NEWS CORRESPONDENT	219-A E WINDSOR AVE	ALEXANDRIA, VA	22301
BERRI, ROBERT	ACTOR	9 RUE DE PAUERETTES	CROISSY 78290	FRANCE
BERRILL, JACK	CARTOONIST	TRIBUNE MEDIA SERVICES		
		64 E CONCORD ST	ORLANDO, FL	32801
BERRY, AL	ACTOR	3360 N TOPANGA CANYON BLVD	TOPANGA, CA	90290
BERRY, CHUCK	SINGER-SONGWRITER	BUCKNER RD	WENTZVILLE, MO	63385
BERRY, CLAYTON	ACTOR	170 W 74TH ST #708	NEW YORK, NY	10023
BERRY, DAVID M	DRUMMER	ROUTE #2, BROWN BRIDGE RD	COVINGTON, GA	30209
BERRY, ERIC	ACTOR	247 S BEVERLY DR #102	BEVERLY HILLS, CA	90212
BERRY, FRED	ACTOR	15010 VENTURA BLVD #234	SHERMAN OAKS, CA	91403
BERRY, JAMES C	WRITER	8955 BEVERLY BLVD	LOS ANGELES, CA	90048
BERRY, JAMES L	NEWS CORRESPONDENT	4461 CONNECTICUT AVE, NW	WASHINGTON, DC	20008
BERRY, JIM	CARTOONIST	NEWSPAPER ENTERTAINMENT		
		200 PARK AVE	NEW YORK, NY	10017
BERRY, JOHN	WRITER-PRODUCER	299 W 12TH ST	NEW YORK, NY	10014
BERRY, JOHN M	NEWS CORRESPONDENT	1207 DUKE ST	ALEXANDRIA, VA	22314
BERRY, JUNE	ACTRESS	15010 VENTURA BLVD #219	SHERMAN OAKS, CA	91403
BERRY, KEN	ACTOR-DANCER	4704 CAHUENGA BLVD	NORTH HOLLYWOOD, CA	91602
BERRY, LEONARD J	WRITER	555 W 57TH ST #1230	NEW YORK, NY	10019
BERRY, MICHAEL P	NEWS CORRESPONDENT	1333 "H" ST, NW	WASHINGTON, DC	20005
BERRY, PAT	WRITER	10 COLUMBUS CIR #1300	NEW YORK, NY	10019
BERRY, PAUL L, JR	NEWS CORRESPONDENT	4461 CONNECTICUT AVE, NW	WASHINGTON, DC	20008
BERRY, WALTER	BARITONE	59 E 54TH ST #81	NEW YORK, NY	10022
BERRYHILL, SHARON	ACTRESS	12375 HERBERT ST	LOS ANGELES, CA	90066
BERRYMAN, MICHAEL	ACTOR	9744 WILSHIRE BLVD #306	BEVERLY HILLS, CA	90212
BERSON, DENIS	TV WRITER	MANN, 1 OLD COMPTON ST	LONDON W1	ENGLAND
BERT, LILIAN	ACTRESS	1 RUE JOSEPH GRANIER	PARIS 75007	FRANCE
BERTELSEN, PEGGY	BODYBUILDER	224 SPOKANE AVE	WHITEFISH, MT	59937
BERTELSEN, TROY	BODYBUILDER	224 SPOAKNE AVE	WHITEFISH, MT	59937
BERTHELSEN, J C	WRITER	11905 KLING ST #18	NORTH HOLLYWOOD, CA	91607
BERTHRONG, DEIRDRE	ACTRESS	12121 HERBERT ST	LOS ANGELES, CA	90066
BERTI, DEHL F	WRITER	555 W 57TH ST #1230	NEW YORK, NY	10019
BERTINELLI, VALERIE	ACTRESS	8500 WILSHIRE BLVD #506	BEVERLY HILLS, CA	90211
BERTINI, GARY	CONDUCTOR	ICM, 40 W 57TH ST	NEW YORK, NY	10019
BERTINI FAMILY, CLARA VALLA	CYCLISTS	HALL, 138 FROG HOLLOW RD	CHURCHVILLE, PA	18966
BERTISH, SUZANNE	ACTRESS	HEATH, PARAMOUNT HOUSE		
		162-170 WARDOUR ST	LONDON W1V 3AT	ENGLAND

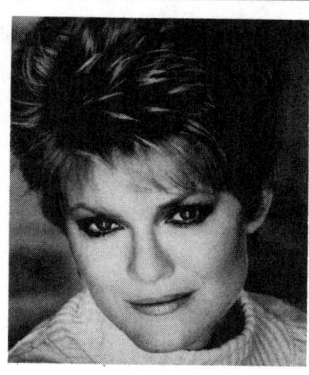

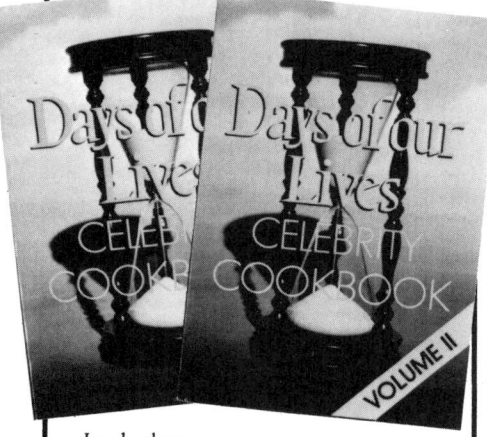

Name	Occupation	Address	City	Zip/Country
BERTLOFF, CLARK & PAULA	TRAPEZE ACT	HALL, 138 FROG HOLLOW RD	CHURCHVILLE, PA	18966
BERTOLUCCI, BERNARDO	FILM DIRECTOR	MINISTER OF TOURISM		
		VIA DELLA FERRATELLA #51	ROME 00184	ITALY
BERTON, PAMELA C	ACTRESS	3335 WOOD TERR #A	LOS ANGELES, CA	90027
BERTON, STUART	ACTOR	4026 MARY ELLEN AVE	STUDIO CITY, CA	91604
BERTRAM, LANIE	TV WRITER	ABC-TV, "ONE LIFE TO LIVE"		
		1330 AVE OF THE AMERICAS	NEW YORK, NY	10019
BERTRAND, COLETTE	ACTRESS	9229 SUNSET BLVD #611	LOS ANGELES, CA	90069
BERUH, JOSEPH	THEATER-FILM PRODUCER	1650 BROADWAY	NEW YORK, NY	10019
BERWALD, LAWRENCE	SINGER-GUITARIST	183 KENNER AVE	NASHVILLE, TN	37205
BERWICK, IRVIN	TV DIRECTOR	16241 DARCIA PL	ENCINO, CA	91436
BERWICK, JAMES	ACTOR	ROSE COTTAGE		
		42 CRABTREE LN	LONDON SW6	ENGLAND
BERWICK, JOHN	ACTOR	11930 MAYFIELD AVE #12	LOS ANGELES, CA	90049
BERWICK, RAY D	WRITER	13009 BLAIRWOOD DR	STUDIO CITY, CA	91604
BESBAS, PETER	ACTOR	1730 N EDGEMONT ST	LOS ANGELES, CA	90027
BESCH, BIBI	ACTRESS	9220 SUNSET BLVD #625	LOS ANGELES, CA	90069
BESEDICK, SUSANNE	WRITER	445 S DETROIT ST #203	LOS ANGELES, CA	90036
BESHER, ALEXANDER	COLUMNIST	CHRONICLE FEATURES		
		870 MARKET ST	SAN FRANCISCO, CA	94102
BESNER, STEVEN	TV DIRECTOR	CBS-TV, 524 W 57TH ST	NEW YORK, NY	10019
BESS, GORDON	CARTOONIST	KING FEATURES SYNDICATE		
		235 E 45TH ST	NEW YORK, NY	10017
BESS, STEPHEN FRANKLIN	DRUMMER	ROUTE #12, TEMPLE RD	FRANKLIN, TN	37064
BESSELL, TED	ACTOR-DIRECTOR	1454 STONE CANYON RD	LOS ANGELES, CA	90077
BESSER, JOE	ACTOR	5103 BILOXI AVE	NORTH HOLLYWOOD, CA	91601
BEST, FRANK M	NEWS CORRESPONDENT	2310 CALIFORNIA ST, NW	WASHINGTON, DC	20008
BEST, HENRY RANDY	GUITARIST	102 MAUREEN DR	HENDERSONVILLE, TN	37075
BEST, JAMES	ACT-WRI-DIR	9744 WILSHIRE BLVD #306	BEVERLY HILLS, CA	90212
BEST, MARTIN	TROUBADOUR	BYERS-SCHWALBE, 1 5TH AVE	NEW YORK, NY	10003
BEST, MICHAEL	TENOR	CAMI, 165 W 57TH ST	NEW YORK, NY	10019
BEST, RICHARD	FILM EDITOR	39 THE GREENWAY, ICKENHAM	MIDDLESEX	ENGLAND
BEST, THE	WRESTLER	SEE - ORTON, COWBOY BOB		
BEST OF FRIENDS	FOLK GROUP	PRODUCERS, 5109 OAKHAVEN LN	TAMPA, FL	33617
BESTENI, BARBARA A	WRITER	555 W 57TH ST #1230	NEW YORK, NY	10019
BESWICK, ELLEN	NEWS CORRESPONDENT	1320 21ST ST, NW	WASHINGTON, DC	20037
BESWICKE, MARTINE	ACTRESS	9220 SUNSET BLVD #625	LOS ANGELES, CA	90069
BETANCOURT, ANNE	ACTRESS	8820 SUNSET BLVD #ANB	LOS ANGELES, CA	90069
BETANCOURT, JEANNE	WRITER	555 W 57TH ST #1230	NEW YORK, NY	10019
BETCHLEY, LEE	ACTRESS	ICM, 8899 BEVERLY BLVD	LOS ANGELES, CA	90048
BETHANCOURT, THOMAS E	TV WRITER	8955 BEVERLY BLVD	LOS ANGELES, CA	90048
BETHEL, TERRY	GUITARIST	POST OFFICE BOX 5	PLEASANTVIEW, TN	37146
BETHENCOURT, FRANCIS	ACTOR	166 W 72ND ST	NEW YORK, NY	10023
BETHUNE, IVY	ACTRESS	3096 LAKE HOLLYWOOD DR	LOS ANGELES, CA	90068
BETHUNE, LLOYD	DIRECTOR-PRODUCER	5550 PATTILAR AVE	WOODLAND HILLS, CA	91367
BETHUNE, ZINA	ACTRESS	3096 LAKE HOLLYWOOD DR	LOS ANGELES, CA	90068
BETTEN, MARY	ACTRESS	12725 VENTURA BLVD #E	STUDIO CITY, CA	91604
BETTGER, LYNE	ACTOR	7060 HOLLYWOOD BLVD #610	LOS ANGELES, CA	90028
BETTI, HENRY	COMPOSER	69 BLVD BINEAU	NEUILLY 92200	FRANCE
BETTIN, SANDRA	ACTRESS	151 S EL CAMINO DR	BEVERLY HILLS, CA	90212
BETTIN, VAL	ACTOR	1234 6TH ST	HERMOSA BEACH, CA	90254
BETTMAN, GILBERT, JR	TV DIRECTOR	10521 SELKIRK LN	LOS ANGELES, CA	90024
BETTS, DICKEY	SINGER	210 25TH AVE N #N-101	NASHVILLE, TN	37203
BETTS, E MITCHELL, III	NEWS CORRESPONDENT	2704 FEDERAL LN	BOWIE, MD	20715
BETTS, HARRY R, JR	COMPOSER	21462 PACIFIC COAST HWY	HUNTINGTON BCH, CA	92648
BETTS, JACK	ACTOR	J MICHAEL BLOOM AGENCY		
		233 PARK AVE S, 10TH FLOOR	NEW YORK, NY	10017
BETTS,, HALL & LEAVELL	ROCK & ROLL GROUP	ICM, 40 W 57TH ST	NEW YORK, NY	10019
BETUEL, JONATHAN	FILM WRITER-DIRECTOR	445 N BEDFORD DR #PH	BEVERLY HILLS, CA	90210
BETZ, PAT	TV EXECUTIVE	NBC-TV, 3000 W ALAMEDA AVE	BURBANK, CA	91523
BETZINA, SANDRA	FASHION CRITIC	CHRONICLE FEATURES		
		870 MARKET ST	SAN FRANCISCO, CA	94102
BETZLER, GERI	ACTRESS	400 S BEVERLY DR #216	BEVERLY HILLS, CA	90212
BEUDERT, MARK	TENOR	LEW, 204 W 10TH ST	NEW YORK, NY	10014
BEUTEL, BILL	TV COMMENTATOR	WABC-TV, 7 LINCOLN SQ	NEW YORK, NY	10023
BEUTEL, JACK	ACTOR	MARINA BAY YACHT CLUB		
		2175 STATE RD #84	FORT LAUDERDALE, FL	33308
BEUTH, EUGENE	DIRECTOR	145 E 27TH ST	NEW YORK, NY	10016
BEVELS, KYLE G	DIRECTOR	131 RIVERSIDE DR	NEW YORK, NY	10024
BEVERIDGE, GEORGE	NEWSPAPERMAN	9302 KINGSLEY AVE	BETHESDA, MD	20014
BEVINS, TIMOTHY B	NEWS CORRESPONDENT	4914 RIDGEWOOD RD	ALEXANDRIA, VA	22312
BEWES, RODNEY	ACTOR	ICM, 388-396 OXFORD ST	LONDON W1	ENGLAND
BEXLEY, DON "BUBBA"	ACTOR	6626 HAYVENHURST AVE #10	VAN NUYS, CA	91406
BEY, TURHAN	ACTOR	PRADIGASSE 47	1190 WEIN X1X	AUSTRIA
BEYER, TROY	ACTRESS	7357 WOODROW WILSON DR	LOS ANGELES, CA	90046
BEYERS, BILL	ACTOR	9255 SUNSET BLVD #510	LOS ANGELES, CA	90069
BEYMER, RICHARD	ACTOR	38701 N 20TH ST #E-213	PALMDALE, CA	93550
BEYNON, RICHARD	TV WRITER-PRODUCER	16 WESTMORELAND RD		
		BARNES	LONDON SW13 9RY	ENGLAND
BEZIAT, RICHARD F	GUITARIST	2804 ACKLEN AVE	NASHVILLE, TN	37212
BEZZERIDES, A I	TV WRITER	19950 COLLIER ST	WOODLAND HILLS, CA	91364
BIALIC, TRUDY	WRITER	555 W 57TH ST #1230	NEW YORK, NY	10019
BIANCHI, EDWARD	FILM DIRECTOR	36 GRAMMERCY PARK E	NEW YORK, NY	10003
BIANCHINI, JOHN	ACTOR	4613 SAN ANDREAS AVE	LOS ANGELES, CA	90065
BIANCO, FRANK F	DIRECTOR	908 W ARMITAGE AVE	CHICAGO, IL	60614

Name	Occupation	Address	City	Zip
BIANCONI, PHILIPPE	PIANIST	GERSHUNOFF, 502 PARK AVE	NEW YORK, NY	10022
BIBAS, FRANK P	TV DIRECTOR-PRODUCER	45 GREENWICH HILLS DR	GREENWICH, CT	06830
BIBER, MEHMET	PHOTOGRAPHER	8910 MORELAND LN	ANNANDALE, VA	22003
BIBLE, FRANCES	MEZZO-SOPRANO	GEWALD, 58 W 58TH ST	NEW YORK, NY	10019
BICAT, TONY	TV WRITER-DIRECTOR	FERRIMANS, CHURCHILL	OXON	ENGLAND
BICK, JERRY	FILM PRODUCER	1520 CAMDEN AVE #105	LOS ANGELES, CA	90025
BICKELL, BETH	ACTOR	9021 MELROSE AVE #304	LOS ANGELES, CA	90069
BICKERTON, SARAH-JANE	ACTRESS	WIMBLEDON, THE BROADWAY		
		WIMBLEDON	LONDON SW19	ENGLAND
BICKFORD, KEVIN	CLOWN	2701 COTTAGE WY #14	SACRAMENTO, CA	95825
BICKFORD, LOVETT	TV DIRECTOR	NEW HOUSE FARM		
		STONEGATE, WADHURST	ESSEX	ENGLAND
BICKLEY, BILL	PRODUCER	1041 N FORMOSA AVE	LOS ANGELES, CA	90046
BICKLEY, WILLIAM S	TV WRITER	8955 BEVERLY BLVD	LOS ANGELES, CA	90048
BICKNELL, GENE	ACTOR	JAYMES, 327 N LAUREL AVE	LOS ANGELES, CA	90048
BIDDICK, GUY M	COMPOSER	18127 ROSCOE BLVD #6	NORTHRIDGE, CA	91324
BIDDLE, WAYNE	NEWS CORRESPONDENT	1000 CONNECTICUT AVE, NW	WASHINGTON, DC	20036
BIDERMAN, ANN	WRITER	10359 1/2 ASHTON AVE	LOS ANGELES, CA	90024
BIDWELL, JOE	RECORD EXECUTIVE	BIRC RECORDS COMPANY		
		601 E BLACKRIDGE DR	TUCSON, AZ	85705
BIEDERMAN, DANIEL A	AUTHOR	8955 BEVERLY BLVD	LOS ANGELES, CA	90048
BIEHL, GENE	SINGER	ROSEWOOD, ROUTE #7, BOX 28	LAKE CITY, FL	32055
BIEHN, MICHAEL	ACTOR	14818 VALERIO ST	VAN NUYS, CA	91405
BIELAK, ROBERT S	TV WRITER	3774 WADE ST	LOS ANGELES, CA	90066
BIELECKI, BOB	DIRECTOR	11574 SUNSHINE TERR	STUDIO CITY, CA	91604
BIEMILER, LAWRENCE	NEWS CORRESPONDENT	1202 S WASHINGTON ST #808-C	ALEXANDRIA, VA	22314
BIEN, WALTER N	WRITER	4640 MONARCA DR	TARZANA, CA	91356
BIENER, THOMAS J	WRITER	7810 AMESTOY AVE	VAN NUYS, CA	91406
BIERBAUER, CHARLES J	NEWS CORRESPONDENT	CNN, 2133 WISCONSIN AVE, NW	WASHINGTON, DC	20007
BIERDZ, THOM	ACTOR	9100 SUNSET BLVD #200	LOS ANGELES, CA	90069
BIERI, RAMON	ACTOR	19963 ARCE ST	NORTHRIDGE, CA	91324
BIERNAT, STANLEY	GUITARIST	106 BALE ST	GALLATIN, TN	37066
BIEWER, BARBARA H	WRITER	27061 CROSSGLADE AVE #7	CANYON COUNTRY, CA	91351
BIG AL & THE HI FI'S	VOCAL GROUP	POST OFFICE BOX 18368	DENVER, CO	80218
BIG BLACK	ROCK & ROLL GROUP	D M RILEY MANAGEMENT		
		3539 N FREMONT ST	CHICAGO, IL	60613
BIG BOYS, THE	ROCK & ROLL GROUP	POST OFFICE BOX 12424	AUSTIN, TX	78711
BIG BUBBA	WRESTLER	SEE - ROGERS, BIG BUBBA		
BIG COUNTRY	ROCK & ROLL GROUP	ATI, 888 7TH AVE, 21ST FLOOR	NEW YORK, NY	10106
BIG DADDY	WRESTLER	SEE - JUNKYARD DOG, THE		
BIG SKY MUDD FLAPP	ROCK & ROLL GROUP	9777 HARWIN ST #101	HOUSTON, TX	77036
BIG SNUKA	WRESTLER	SEE - SNUKA, JIMMY "SUPERFLY"		
BIG STREET	ROCK & ROLL GROUP	3 E 54TH ST #1400	NEW YORK, NY	10022
BIGELOW, BAM BAM	WRESTLER	WORLD CLASS WRESTLING		
		SOUTHWEST SPORTS, INC		
		DALLAS SPORTATORIUM		
		1000 S INDUSTRIAL BLVD	DALLAS, TX	75207
BIGELOW, KATHRYN	SCREENWRITER	ICM, 8899 BEVERLY BLVD	LOS ANGELES, CA	90048
BIGELOW, SCOTT	WRESTLER	SEE - BIGELOW, BAM BAM		
BIGELOW, TARYN L	WRITER	8955 BEVERLY BLVD	LOS ANGELES, CA	90048
BIGGER, JAMES	NEWS CORRESPONDENT	NBC-TV, NEWS DEPARTMENT		
		4001 NEBRASKA AVE, NW	WASHINGTON, DC	20016
BIGGER, WILLIAM A	SAXOPHONIST-FLUTIST	100 W ELM ST	ASHLAND CITY, TN	37015
BIGGINS, CHRISTOPHER	ACTOR	MARTIN, 7 WINDMILL ST	LONDON W1P 1HF	ENGLAND
BIHELLER, ROBERT	WRITER-PRODUCER	2049 CENTURY PARK E #1320	LOS ANGELES, CA	90067
BIKALES, ERIC	COMPOSER	14118 ERWIN ST	VAN NUYS, CA	91401
BIKEL, OFRA	WRITER	555 W 57TH ST #1230	NEW YORK, NY	10019
BIKEL, THEODORE	ACTOR	HONEY MILL RD	GEORGETOWN, CT	06829
BILBREY, RONALD	GUITARIST	ROUTE 4, BOX 88	COOKEVILLE, TN	38501
BILES, ERNEST L, JR	GUITARIST	141 NEESE DR #U-454	NASHVILLE, TN	37211
BILEZIKJIAN, JOHN H	COMPOSER-CONDUCTOR	POST OFFICE BOX 2434	LAGUNA HILLS, CA	92653
BILGER, CAROL	ACTRESS	8075 W 3RD ST #303	LOS ANGELES, CA	90048
BILGER, DAVID	SAXOPHONIST	KAY, 58 W 58TH ST	NEW YORK, NY	10019
BILGER DUO	MUSICAL DUO	KAY, 58 W 58TH ST	NEW YORK, NY	10019
BILIK, JERRY H	COMPOSER-WRITER	4202 MATILIJA AVE	SHERMAN OAKS, CA	91423
BILL, TONY	ACTOR-DIRECTOR	73 MARKET ST	VENICE, CA	90291
BILL JACK	WRESTLER	SEE - HAYNES, BILLY JACK		
BILLINGS, LINDA	NEWS CORRESPONDENT	3416 PORTER ST, NW	WASHINGTON, DC	20016
BILLINGSLEA, BEAU	ACTOR	CED, 261 S ROBERTSON BLVD	BEVERLY HILLS, CA	90211
BILLINGSLEY, ALAN R	COMPOSER	19145 HAYNES ST #2	RESEDA, CA	91335
BILLINGSLEY, BARBARA	ACTRESS	3330 BARHAM BLVD #103	LOS ANGELES, CA	90068
BILLINGSLEY, DICK	ACTOR	3575 W CAHUENGA BLVD #320	LOS ANGELES, CA	90069
BILLINGSLEY, NEIL	ACTOR	BRIAN AGENCY, 250 W 57TH ST	NEW YORK, NY	10107
BILLINGTON, KEVIN	FILM DIRECTOR	A D PETERS & CO, LTD		
		10 BUCKINGHAM ST	LONDON WC2	ENGLAND
BILLINGTON, MICHAEL	ACTOR	BRUNSKILL, 169 QUEEN'S GATE	LONDON SW7 5EH	ENGLAND
BILLINGTON, MICHAEL	ACTOR	1930 CENTURY PARK W #303	LOS ANGELES, CA	90067
BILLINGTON, SHELBY	ACTRESS	10000 SANTA MONICA BLVD #305	LOS ANGELES, CA	90067
BILLINGTON, TOM	WRESTLER	SEE - DYNAMITE KID, THE		
BILLS, JEAN S	CELLIST	1619 E MAIN ST	MURFREESBORO, TN	37130
BILLY & THE BEATERS	ROCK & ROLL GROUP	SCHWARTZ, 1015 N FAIRFAX AVE	LOS ANGELES, CA	90046
BILLY JACK	WRESTLER	SEE - HAYNES, BILLY JACK		
BILLY THE KID	ROCK & ROLL GROUP	8255 SUNSET BLVD #100	LOS ANGELES, CA	90046

Name	Occupation	Address	City	Zip
BILSON, BRUCE	TV DIRECTOR	4444 RADFORD AVE	NORTH HOLLYWOOD, CA	91607
BILSON, DANNY	WRITER	8955 BEVERLY BLVD	LOS ANGELES, CA	90048
BILSON, MALCOLM	PIANIST	BYERS-SCHWALBE, 1 5TH AVE	NEW YORK, NY	10003
BILSON, MALCOLM	PIANIST	MC RAE, 2130 CARLETON ST	BERKELEY, CA	94704
BIMROSE, ARTHUR	CARTOONIST	1320 SW BROADWAY	PORTLAND, OR	97201
BINA, JAN	ACTRESS	2101 N BEACHWOOD DR	HOLLYWOOD, CA	90068
BINDER, DAVID	NEWS CORRESPONDENT	1000 CONNECTICUT AVE, NW	WASHINGTON, DC	20036
BINDER, JOHN	WRITER-PRODUCER	12229 FALKIRK LN	LOS ANGELES, CA	90049
BINDER, RALPH J	PHOTOJOURNALIST	3307-B S WAKEFIELD ST	ARLINGTON, VA	22206
BINDER, STEVE	WRITER-PRODUCER	855 S BUNDY DR	LOS ANGELES, CA	90049
BINDER, STEVE	TALENT AGENT	BRB, 666 N ROBERTSON BLVD	LOS ANGELES, CA	90060
BING, JULIUS	ACTOR	20 W 72ND ST	NEW YORK, NY	10023
BING, LEON	WRITER	8955 BEVERLY BLVD	LOS ANGELES, CA	90048
BING, MACK	DIRECTOR	8000 WOODROW WILSON DR	LOS ANGELES, CA	90046
BING, SIR RUDOLPH	OPERA EXECUTIVE	CAMI, 165 W 57TH ST	NEW YORK, NY	10019
BINGHAM, BARBARA M	ACTRESS	9250 WILSHIRE BLVD #208	BEVERLY HILLS, CA	90212
BINGHAM, EMELYNE	GUITARIST	RURAL ROUTE #78		
		DAHLIA DR	BRENTWOOD, TN	37027
BINGHAM, H MELANIE	SINGER-GUITARIST	5646 AMALIE DR #75	NASHVILLE, TN	37211
BINGHAM, OLEN	GUITARIST	5825 NW 33RD ST	GAINESVILLE, FL	32601
BINGHAM, WALTER	WRITER-EDITOR	SPORTS ILLUSTRATED MAGAZINE		
		TIME & LIFE BUILDING		
		ROCKEFELLER CENTER	NEW YORK, NY	10020
BINI, CARLO	TENOR	CAMI, 165 W 57TH ST	NEW YORK, NY	10019
BINK, BARBARA H	NEWS CORRESPONDENT	1515 N 12TH ST	ARLINGTON, VA	22209
BINKLEY, GEORGE, III	VIOLINIST	1300 GRAYBAR LN	NASHVILLE, TN	37215
BINKLEY, LANE	ACTRESS	165 W 46TH ST #409	NEW YORK, NY	10036
BINKLEY, PAUL CARROLL	GUITARIST	920 DRUMMOND DR	NASHVILLE, TN	37211
BINKLEY, ROBERT	SAXOPHONIST	5181 REGENT DR	NASHVILLE, TN	37220
BINKS, PORTER L	PHOTOGRAPHER	132 12TH ST, NE	WASHINGTON, DC	20002
BINNS, EDWARD	ACTOR	123 S WOODBURN DR	LOS ANGELES, CA	90049
BINSTEIN, MICHAEL	NEWS CORRESPONDENT	12000 OLD GEORGETOWN RD	ROCKVILLE, MD	20852
BINYON, CONRAD	ACTOR	17805 S MARGATE ST	ENCINO, CA	91436
BIONCO, JACKIE-LOU	SINGER	POST OFFICE BOX 63	ORINDA, CA	94563
BIONDI, FRANK J, JR	CABLE EXECUTIVE	HOME BOX OFFICE PICTURES		
		1100 AVE OF THE AMERICAS	NEW YORK, NY	10036
BIONDI, LEE	TV WRITER	8955 BEVERLY BLVD	LOS ANGELES, CA	90048
BIOS, SAM	MUSICIAN	9777 HARWIN ST #101	HOUSTON, TX	77036
BIPED	C & W GROUP	M M M, 3442 NIES ST	FORT WORTH, TX	72010
BIRAUD, MAURICE	ACTOR	J NAIN CHRIK, 31 CHAMPS	PARIS 75008	FRANCE
BIRBROWER, STEWART M	DIRECTOR	DGA, 110 W 57TH ST	NEW YORK, NY	10019
BIRCH, MARY LAINE	DIRECTOR	520 N MICHIGAN AVE #436	CHICAGO, IL	60611
BIRCH, MICHAEL	DIRECTOR	2138 N HUDSON AVE	CHICAGO, IL	60614
BIRCH, MIRIAM E	WRITER	8955 BEVERLY BLVD	LOS ANGELES, CA	90048
BIRCH, PATRICIA	DIRECTOR	SHAPIRO, TAXON & KOPELL		
		1180 AVE OF THE AMERICAS	NEW YORK, NY	10036
BIRCH, PETER H	DIRECTOR	797 NORTH ST	WHITE PLAINS, NY	10605
BIRCH, WILLIAM H	TV DIRECTOR	5653 N WINTHROP AVE	CHICAGO, IL	60660
BIRCHARD, ROBERT S	WRITER	3207 BROOKHILL ST	LA CRESCENTA, CA	91214
BIRD, BILLIE	ACTRESS	9229 SUNSET BLVD #306	LOS ANGELES, CA	90069
BIRD, CHARLES, JR	CONDUCTOR	POST OFFICE BOX 2908	LOS ANGELES, CA	90028
BIRD, JOHN	ACTOR-WRITER	CHATTO & LINNIT, LTD		
		PRINCE OF WALES THEATRE		
		COVENTRY ST	LONDON WC2	ENGLAND
BIRD, KAI	NEWS CORRESPONDENT	1852 COLUMBIA RD, NW	WASHINGTON, DC	20009
BIRD, LAWRENCE	WRITER	8955 BEVERLY BLVD	LOS ANGELES, CA	90048
BIRD, MICHAEL	TV WRITER	FRASER, 91 REGENT ST	LONDON W1R 8RU	ENGLAND
BIRD, NORMAN	ACTOR	LONDON MANAGEMENT, LTD		
		235-241 REGENT ST	LONDON W1A 2JT	ENGLAND
BIRD, STEWART	WRITER	555 W 57TH ST #1230	NEW YORK, NY	10019
BIRDMAN, THE	WRESTLER	SEE - WARE, KOKO B		
BIRDSALL, VIRGINIA	WRITER	555 W 57TH ST #1230	NEW YORK, NY	10019
BIRDSONG, BOB	BODYBUILDER	POST OFFICE BOX 4333	PALM SPRINGS, CA	92263
BIRET, IDIL	PIANIST	LEISER, DORCHESTER TOWERS		
		155 W 68TH ST	NEW YORK, NY	10023
BIRK, JOHN	ACTOR	30000 HASLEY CYN RD #57	SAUGUS, CA	91350
BIRK, RAYE	ACTOR	247 S BEVERLY DR #102	BEVERLY HILLS, CA	90210
BIRKETT, BERNADETTE	ACTRESS	11726 SAN VICENTE BLVD #300	LOS ANGELES, CA	90049
BIRKETT, MICHAEL	TV DIRECTOR-PRODUCER	HOUSE OF LORDS	LONDON SW1	ENGLAND
BIRKIN, JANE	ACTRESS	M ISRAEL, 56 RUE DE PAS	PARIS 75016	FRANCE
BIRKINSHAW, ALAN	WRITER-PRODUCER	ICM, 388-396 OXFORD ST	LONDON W1	ENGLAND
BIRMAN, LEN	ACTOR	10000 SANTA MONICA BLVD #305	LOS ANGELES, CA	90067
BIRMKRANT, SAM	THEATER CRITIC	POST OFFICE BOX 1127	MALIBU, CA	90265
BIRNBAUM, BENJAMIN	WRITER	555 W 57TH ST #1230	NEW YORK, NY	10019
BIRNBAUM, JEFFREY H	NEWS CORRESPONDENT	4805 HARTFORD AVE	SILVER SPRING, MD	20910
BIRNBAUM, JESSE	WRITER-EDITOR	PEOPLE/TIME & LIFE BLDG		
		ROCKEFELLER CENTER	NEW YORK, NY	10020
BIRNBAUM, PHILIP	WRITER	8955 BEVERLY BLVD	LOS ANGELES, CA	90048
BIRNBAUM, ROBERT	WRITER-PRODUCER	4048 STONE CANYON AVE	SHERMAN OAKS, CA	91403
BIRNBAUM, STEPHEN	COLUMNIST	TRIBUNE MEDIA SERVICES		
		64 E CONCORD ST	ORLANDO, FL	32801
BIRNBAUM, STUART	TV WRITER	8955 BEVERLY BLVD	LOS ANGELES, CA	90048
BIRNEY, DAVID	ACTOR	10100 SANTA MONICA BLVD #700	LOS ANGELES, CA	90067
BIRNEY, FRANK	ACTOR	11631 LAURELCREST DR	STUDIO CITY, CA	91604
BIRNEY, MEREDITH BAXTER	ACTRESS	10100 SANTA MONICA BLVD #700	LOS ANGELES, CA	90067

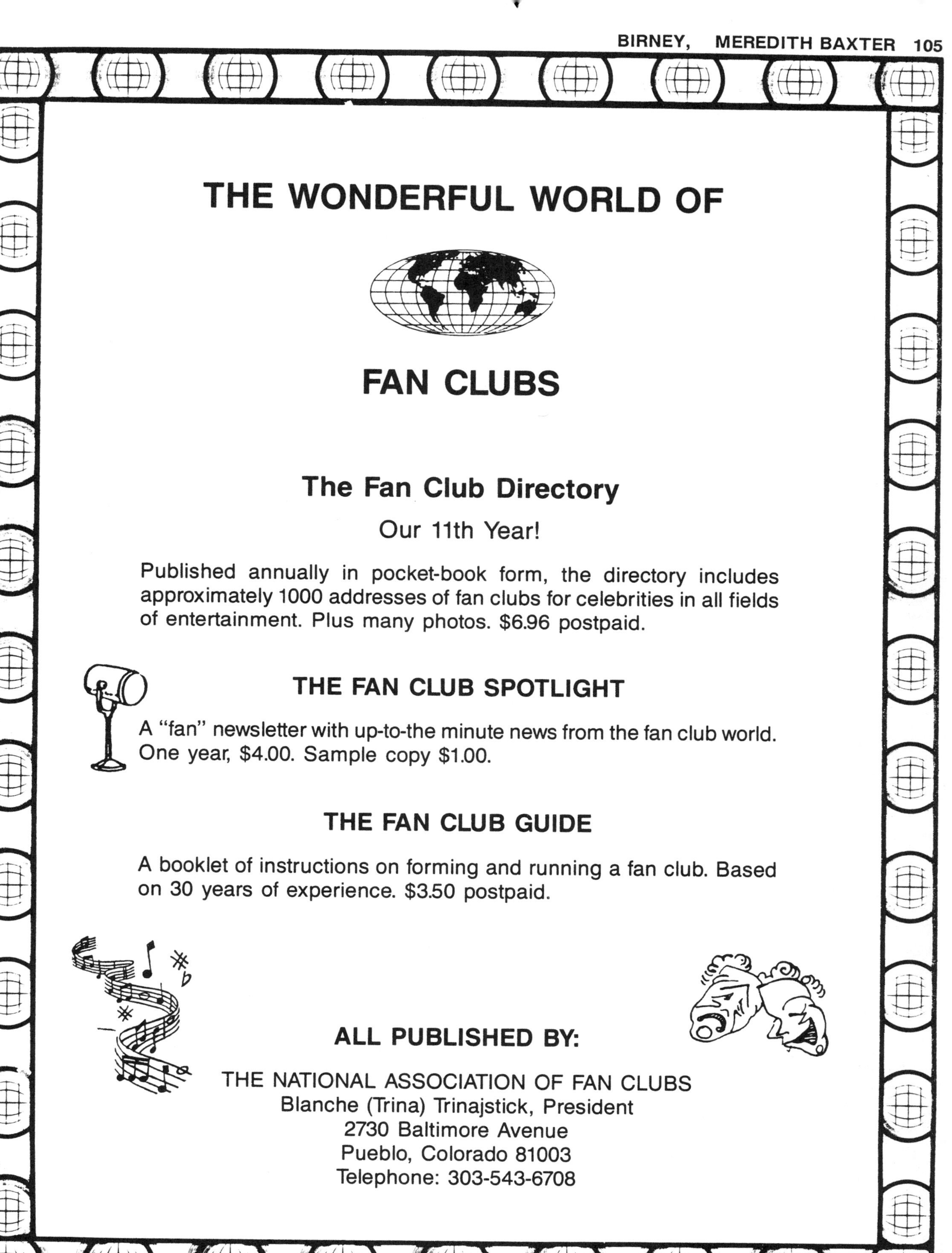

THE WONDERFUL WORLD OF
FAN CLUBS
The Fan Club Directory
Our 11th Year!
Published annually in pocket-book form, the directory includes approximately 1000 addresses of fan clubs for celebrities in all fields of entertainment. Plus many photos. $6.96 postpaid.
THE FAN CLUB SPOTLIGHT
A "fan" newsletter with up-to-the minute news from the fan club world. One year, $4.00. Sample copy $1.00.
THE FAN CLUB GUIDE
A booklet of instructions on forming and running a fan club. Based on 30 years of experience. $3.50 postpaid.
ALL PUBLISHED BY:
THE NATIONAL ASSOCIATION OF FAN CLUBS
Blanche (Trina) Trinajstick, President
2730 Baltimore Avenue
Pueblo, Colorado 81003
Telephone: 303-543-6708

Name	Occupation	Address	City/State	Zip
BIRNEY, REED	ACTOR	9220 SUNSET BLVD #625	LOS ANGELES, CA	90069
BIRNKRANT, DON	CINEMATOGRAPHER	3620 GLENRIDGE DR	SHERMAN OAKS, CA	91423
BIRO, FRANK	ACTOR	10000 RIVERSIDE DR #3	TOLUCA LAKE, CA	91602
BIROC, JOSEPH	CINEMATOGRAPHER	4427 PETIT AVE	ENCINO, CA	91316
BISCARDI, CHESTER	ACTOR	542 AVE OF THE AMERICAS #4-R	NEW YORK, NY	10011
BISCARDI, JESSICA	ACTRESS	POST OFFICE BOX 38596	LOS ANGELES, CA	90038
BISCHEL, DWIGHT W	WRITER-PRODUCER	2108 EWING AVE	EVANSTON, IL	60201
BISCHOF, LARRY	WRITER	8131 LLOYD AVE	NORTH HOLLYWOOD, CA	91605
BISHARA, GHASSAN K	NEWS CORRESPONDENT	9035 BLARNEY STONE DR	SPRINGFIELD, VA	22152
BISHOP, BILL	ACTOR	6605 HOLLYWOOD BLVD #220	HOLLYWOOD, CA	90028
BISHOP, BILLY	CONDUCTOR	17454 TAMP O'SHANTER DR	POWAY, CA	92064
BISHOP, DONALD	ACTOR	11319 SUNSHINE TERR	STUDIO CITY, CA	91604
BISHOP, ELVIN	SINGER-GUITARIST	CRABSHAW CONCERTS		
		338 VILLAGE LN	LOS GATOS, CA	95030
BISHOP, ELVIN, BAND	ROCK & ROLL GROUP	CRABSHAW CONCERTS		
		338 VILLAGE LN	LOS GATOS, CA	95030
BISHOP, FRED	ACTOR	7813 OAKWOOD AVE	LOS ANGELES, CA	90036
BISHOP, GEORGE V	WRITER	14941 HAWK DR	PALMDALE, CA	93550
BISHOP, HAYWARD	DRUMMER	4550 PACKARD DR	NASHVILLE, TN	37211
BISHOP, JANICE	ACTRESS	WRIGHT, 8422 MELROSE PL	LOS ANGELES, CA	90069
BISHOP, JENNIFER	ACTRESS	9870 VIDOR DR	LOS ANGELES, CA	90035
BISHOP, JERRY G	TV HOST	KFMB-TV, 7677 ENGINEER RD	SAN DIEGO, CA	92111
BISHOP, JIM "RIGGIO"	FILM DIRECTOR	POST OFFICE BOX 868	LITCHFIELD, CT	06759
BISHOP, JIMMY & TURNING POINT	ROCK & ROLL GROUP	POST OFFICE BOX 11283	RICHMOND, VA	23230
BISHOP, JOEY	ACTOR-COMEDIAN	534 VIA LIDO NORD	NEWPORT BEACH, CA	92660
BISHOP, JUDITH M	WRITER	555 W 57TH ST #1230	NEW YORK, NY	10019
BISHOP, KELLY	ACTRESS	9255 SUNSET BLVD #1105	LOS ANGELES, CA	90069
BISHOP, LARRY	ACTOR	9744 WILSHIRE BLVD #206	BEVERLY HILLS, CA	90212
BISHOP, LOANNE	ACTRESS	3907 W ALAMEDA AVE #101	BURBANK, CA	91505
BISHOP, MORIN	SPORTS REPORTER	SPORTS ILLUSTRATED MAGAZINE		
		TIME & LIFE BUILDING		
		ROCKEFELLER CENTER	NEW YORK, NY	10020
BISHOP, PATRICK FRANCIS	ACTOR	ABC-TV, "GENERAL HOSPITAL"		
		1438 N GOWER ST	LOS ANGELES, CA	90028
BISHOP, RONALD A	TV WRITER	555 RADCLIFFE AVE	PACIFIC PALISADES, CA	90272
BISHOP, STEPHEN	SINGER-COMPOSER	10100 SANTA MONICA BLVD #1600	LOS ANGELES, CA	90067
BISHOP, THOM	ACTOR	8383 WILSHIRE BLVD #1024	BEVERLY HILLS, CA	90211
BISHOP, WESDON	WRITER	10811 WILKINS AVE	LOS ANGELES, CA	90024
BISHOP-KOVACEVICH, STEPHEN	PIANIST	LEISER, DORCHESTER TOWERS		
		155 W 68TH ST	NEW YORK, NY	10023
BISKUP, BILL	ACTOR	POST OFFICE BOX 10854	GLENDALE, CA	91209
BISMARCK, MYRNA	SOPRANO	111 W 57TH ST #1209	NEW YORK, NY	10019
BISNEY, JOHN F	NEWS CORRESPONDENT	1776 "C" ST, NW	WASHINGTON, DC	20006
BISNO, LESLIE	ACTOR	1449 S HOLT AVE	LOS ANGELES, CA	90035
BISOGLIO, VAL	ACTOR	7466 BEVERLY BLVD #205	LOS ANGELES, CA	90036
BISQUE, MARCIA	ACTRESS	15210 MORRISON ST	SHERMAN OAKS, CA	91403
BISSELL, ROGER E	MUSIC ARRANGER	4415 LONE OAK RD	NASHVILLE, TN	37215
BISSELL, WHIT	ACTOR	10301 CHRYSANTHEMUM LN	LOS ANGELES, CA	90077
BISSET, JACQUELINE	ACTRESS	1815 BENEDICT CANYON DR	BEVERLY HILLS, CA	90210
BISSON, NAPOLEON	BUFFO BARITONE	SARDOS, 180 W END AVE	NEW YORK, NY	10023
BITCH	ROCK & ROLL GROUP	22458 VENTURA BLVD #E	WOODLAND HILLS, CA	91364
BITSCH, CHARLES	FILM DIRECTOR	5 PASS DU CHEMIN-VERT	PARIS 75001	FRANCE
BITTENCOURT, RENATO	NEWS CORRESPONDENT	950 25TH ST #321-N, NW	WASHINGTON, DC	20037
BITTLE, JERRY	CARTOONIST	UNIVERSAL PRESS SYNDICATE		
		4900 MAIN ST, 9TH FLOOR	KANSAS CITY, MO	62114
BIVENS, ERNIE	SINGER	38 MUSIC SQUARE E #216	NASHVILLE, TN	37203
BIVENS, ERNIE, III	SINGER	38 MUSIC SQUARE E #216	NASHVILLE, TN	37203
BIXBY, BILL	ACTOR-DIRECTOR	9100 SUNSET BLVD #200	LOS ANGELES, CA	90069
BJARNASON, KRISTI	CELLIST	333 TAYLOR AVE N #202	SEATTLE, WA	98109
BJERKLIE, DAVID	NEWS REPORTER	TIME/TIME & LIFE BLDG		
		ROCKEFELLER CENTER	NEW YORK, NY	10020
BJERRE, MIRIAM	WRITER	8955 BEVERLY BLVD	LOS ANGELES, CA	90048
BJOERLING, ROLF	TENOR	POST OFFICE BOX 27539	PHILADELPHIA, PA	19118
BJONER, INGRID	SOPRANO	CAMI, 165 W 57TH ST	NEW YORK, NY	10019
BJORKLUND, WILLARD	WRITER	555 W 57TH ST #1230	NEW YORK, NY	10019
BJORLIN, ULF	CONDUCTOR	GERSHUNOFF, 502 PARK AVE	NEW YORK, NY	10022
BJORN, ANNA	MODER-ACTRESS	KOHNER, 9169 SUNSET BLVD	LOS ANGELES, CA	90069
BJURMAN, SUSAN	ACTRESS	786 TORTUOSO WY	LOS ANGELES, CA	90077
BLACK, ALBERT H	WRITER	555 W 57TH ST #1230	NEW YORK, NY	10019
BLACK, ANTHONY	NEWS CORRESPONDENT	1301 PENNSYLVANIA AVE, NW	WASHINGTON, DC	20004
BLACK, BILL, COMBO	MUSIC GROUP	ENTERTAINMENT DIRECTIONS		
		5893 FOX BEND COVE E	MEMPHIS, TN	38115
BLACK, CATHLEEN	PUBLISHING EXECUTIVE	POST OFFICE BOX 500	WASHINGTON, DC	20044
BLACK, CHARLES F	GUITARIST	WALKER, TRUE & CHERRY		
		1710 GRAND AVE	NASHVILLE, TN	37212
BLACK, CILLA	SINGER-ACTRESS	HINDWORTH MANAGEMENT		
		235-241 REGENT ST	LONDON W1A 2JT	ENGLAND
BLACK, DAVID	DIRECTOR-PRODUCER	251 E 51ST ST	NEW YORK, NY	10022
BLACK, DON	LYRICIST	ROGER HANCOCK MANAGEMENT		
		8 WATERLOO PL, PALL MALL	LONDON SW1Y 4AW	ENGLAND
BLACK, GERRY	ACTOR	8721 SUNSET BLVD #202	LOS ANGELES, CA	90069
BLACK. ISOBEL	ACTRESS	LWA TALENT, 66 HAYMARKET	LONDON SW1Y 4RF	ENGLAND
BLACK, JAY & THE AMERICAN	ROCK & ROLL GROUP	BROTHERS, 141 DUNBAR AVE	FORDS, NJ	08863
BLACK, JERRY	ACTOR	PIONEER EQUINE CLINIC		
		11501 PIONEER AVE	OAK DALE, CA	95361

JOEY BISHOP

JACQUELINE BISSET

BILL BIXBY

HONOR BLACKMAN

ROBERT BLAKE

SUSAN BLAKELY

MEL BLANC

ANN BLYTH

DEBBY BOONE

Name	Occupation	Address	City	Zip
BLACK, JOHN	FILM WRITER-PRODUCER	27 BERWICK ST	LONDON W1V 3RF	ENGLAND
BLACK, JOHN D F	WRITER-PRODUCER	845 KENISTON AVE	LOS ANGELES, CA	90005
BLACK, JOHN T	NEWS CORRESPONDENT	11235 OAKLEAF DR	SILVER SPRING, MD	20901
BLACK, KAREN	ACTRESS	9255 SUNSET BLVD #510	LOS ANGELES, CA	90069
BLACK, MARIANNE	ACTRESS	420 N SYCAMORE AVE #1	LOS ANGELES, CA	90036
BLACK, MAXENE	NEWS CORRESPONDENT	WABC-TV, 7 LINCOLN SQ	NEW YORK, NY	10023
BLACK, NOEL	FILM WRITER-DIRECTOR	120 GREENFIELD AVE	LOS ANGELES, CA	90049
BLACK, PATRICIA F	WRITER	8955 BEVERLY BLVD	LOS ANGELES, CA	90048
BLACK, PETER	NEWS REPORTER	THE NATIONAL ENQUIRER		
		600 SE COAST AVE	LANTANA, FL	33464
BLACK, RICHARD	WRITER-PRODUCER	4020 PACHECO DR	SHERMAN OAKS, CA	91403
BLACK, ROBERT	SAXOPHONIST	POST OFFICE BOX 160	HIGHLAND PARK, IL	60035
BLACK, ROBERT	CONDUCTOR	FINELL, 155 W 68TH ST	NEW YORK, NY	10023
BLACK, ROBERT F	NEWS CORRESPONDENT	518 DUKE ST	ALEXANDRIA, VA	22314
BLACK, S NORMAN	NEWS CORRESPONDENT	11307 PALISADES CT	KENSINGTON, MD	20895
BLACK, SENA AYN	ACTRESS	940 HANCOCK AVE #17	LOS ANGELES, CA	90069
BLACK, SHIRLEY TEMPLE	ACTRESS	115 LAKEVIEW DR	WOODSIDE, CA	94062
BLACK, STANLEY	CONDUCTOR-COMPOSER	118 WARDOUR ST	LONDON W1V 4BT	ENGLAND
BLACK, STEPHEN	TV WRITER	8955 BEVERLY BLVD	LOS ANGELES, CA	90048
BLACK, WILLIAM	PIANIST	ROSENFIELD, 714 LADD RD	BRONX, NY	10471
BLACK BART	WRESTLER	WORLD CLASS WRESTLING		
		SOUTHWEST SPORTS, INC		
		DALLAS SPORTATORIUM		
		1000 S INDUSTRIAL BLVD	DALLAS, TX	75207
BLACK CRUSHER	WRESTLER	SEE - MASKED SUPERSTAR, THE		
BLACK DIAMOND STRINGERS, THE	C & W GROUP	POST OFFICE BOX 156	ROSELLE, NJ	07203
BLACK FLAG	ROCK & ROLL GROUP	POST OFFICE BOX 1	LAWNDALE, CA	90260
BLACK IVORY	ROCK & ROLL GROUP	RALPH MERCADO, 1650 BROADWAY	NEW YORK, NY	10019
BLACK MOUNTAIN STRING BAND, THE	C & W GROUP	POST OFFICE BOX 156	ROSELLE, NJ	07203
BLACK OAK ARKANSAS	ROCK & ROLL GROUP	SOUTHERN TALENT AGENCY		
		2925 FALLOWRIDGE CT	SNELLVILLE, GA	30278
BLACK ROSE	ROCK & ROLL GROUP	ATI, 888 7TH AVE, 21ST FLOOR	NEW YORK, NY	10106
BLACK SABBATH	ROCK & ROLL GROUP	8730 SUNSET BLVD #200	LOS ANGELES, CA	90069
BLACK SHEED	ROCK & ROLL GROUP	POST OFFICE BOX 2428	EL SEGUNDO, CA	90245
BLACKBURN, BRYAN	TV PRODUCER	SONNY ZAHL ASSOCIATES, LTD		
		57 GREAT CUMBERLAND PL	LONDON W1	ENGLAND
BLACKBURN, BRYAN	TV WRITER	8955 BEVERLY BLVD	LOS ANGELES, CA	90048
BLACKBURN, CLARICE	TV WRITER	555 W 57TH ST #1230	NEW YORK, NY	10019
BLACKBURN, CLARICE	TV WRITER	ABC-TV, "ALL MY CHILDREN"		
		1330 AVE OF THE AMERICAS	NEW YORK, NY	10019
BLACKBURN, DANIEL M	WRITER	3611 LOWRY RD	LOS ANGELES, CA	90027
BLACKBURN, DOROTHY	ACTRESS	903 PARK AVE	NEW YORK, NY	10021
BLACKBURN, GRETA	ACTRESS	STONE, 1052 CAROL DR	LOS ANGELES, CA	90069
BLACKBURN, JANE	ACTRESS	414 KING'S RD	LONDON SW10	ENGLAND
BLACKBURN, TOM W	WRITER	8955 BEVERLY BLVD	LOS ANGELES, CA	90048
BLACKBYRDS, THE	VOCAL GROUP	527 MADISON AVE #1012	NEW YORK, NY	10022
BLACKFOOT	ROCK & ROLL GROUP	ATI, 888 7TH AVE, 21ST FLOOR	NEW YORK, NY	10106
BLACKFOOT, J	SINGER	POST OFFICE BOX 161240	MEMPHIS, TN	38186
BLACKFOOT, JAY	SINGER	200 W 51ST ST #1410	NEW YORK, NMY	10019
BLACKJACK	ROCK & ROLL GROUP	ARTISTS 1, 35 BRENTWOOD	FARMINGVILLE, NY	11738
BLACKJACKS, THE	ROCK & ROLL GROUP	POST OFFICE BOX 205	BROOKLINE, MA	02146
BLACKMAN, CHARLES	CONDUCTOR	10611 STONE CANYON RD	DALLAS, TX	75230
BLACKMAN, HONOR	ACTRESS	LONDON MANAGEMENT, LTD		
		235-241 REGENT ST	LONDON W1A 2JT	ENGLAND
BLACKMON, BUDDY	GUITARIST	2711 HEMINGWAY DR	NASHVILLE, TN	37215
BLACKMON, DAVID	MANDOLINIST	812 BEECH BEND DR	NASHVILLE, TN	37221
BLACKMORE, STEPHANIE	ACTRESS	7461 BEVERLY BLVD #400	LOS ANGELES, CA	90036
BLACKOFF, EDWARD	ACTOR	11030 VENTURA BLVD #3	STUDIO CITY, CA	91604
BLACKSTONE, HARRY, JR	MAGICIAN	POST OFFICE BOX 3819	LA MESA, CA	92044
BLACKSTONE, JOHN	NEWS CORRESPONDENT	CBS-TV, 68 KNIGHTSBRIDGE	LONDON SW1	ENGLAND
BLACKSTONE, SUSAN	ACTRESS	SAVAGE, 6212 BANNER AVE	LOS ANGELES, CA	90038
BLACKTON, JAY S	COMPOSER-ARRANGER	9209 MONOGRAM AVE	SEPULVEDA, CA	91343
BLACKTON, JENNIE	WRITER	8955 BEVERLY BLVD	LOS ANGELES, CA	90048
BLACKTON TRIMBLE, MARION	ACTRESS	HACIENDA CARE CENTER		
		1899 N RAYMOND AVE	PASADENA, CA	91103
BLACKWELL, ALAN LEE	SINGER	O & L, 10051 GREENLEAF	SANTA FE SPRINGS, CA	90670
BLACKWELL, CRUSHER JERRY	WRESTLER	AMERICAN WRESTLING ASSOC		
		MINNEAPLOIS WRESTLING		
		10001 WAYZATA BLVD	MINNETONKA, MN	55345
BLACKWELL, EARL "MR"	DESIGNER-PUBLISHER	1780 BROADWAY #300	NEW YORK, NY	10019
BLACKWELL, FARMER	WRESTLER	SEE - BLACKWELL, CRUSHER JERRY		
BLACKWELL, HAROLYN	SOPRANO	AFFILIATE ARTISTS, INC		
		37 W 65TH ST, 6TH FLOOR	NEW YORK, NY	10023
BLACKWELL, JEROME A	ACTOR	1823 EL CERRITO PL #F	LOS ANGELES, CA	90068
BLACKWELL, KEN	SCREENWRITER	8955 BEVERLY BLVD	LOS ANGELES, CA	90048
BLACKWELL, LAURA J	WRITER	555 W 57TH ST #1230	NEW YORK, NY	10019
BLACKWELL, MR	DESIGNER-PUBLISHER	SEE - BLACKWELL, EARL "MR"		
BLACKWELL, TOM	GUITARIST	811 CHICKASAW AVE	NASHVILLE, TN	37207
BLACKWOOD, BILLY	SINGER-GUITARIST	102 DILLON DR	HENDERSONVILLE, TN	37075
BLACKWOOD, CHERYL PRUITT	SINGER	POST OFFICE BOX 17272	MEMPHIS, TN	38187
BLACKWOOD, HERMOINE	COMPOSER	2849 ARMACOST AVE	LOS ANGELES, CA	90064
BLACKWOOD, NINA	MUSIC CORRESPONDENT	ENTERTAINMENT TONIGHT		
		5555 MELROSE AVE	LOS ANGELES, CA	90038

BLACKWOOD, R W	SINGER	POST OFFICE BOX 17272	MEMPHIS, TN	38187
BLACKWOOD BROTHERS, THE	C & W GROUP	POST OFFICE BOX 17272	MEMPHIS, TN	38187
BLACKWOOD QUARTET, THE	VOCAL GROUP	POST OFFICE BOX 17272	MEMPHIS, TN	38187
BLACKWOOD SINGERS, THE	GOSPEL GROUP	POST OFFICE BOX 17272	MEMPHIS, TN	38187
BLACQUE, TAUREAN	ACTOR	9255 SUNSET BLVD #1105	LOS ANGELES, CA	90069
BLADE, T & THE FABULOUS ESQUIRE	ROCK & ROLL GROUP	25 HUNTINGTON AVE #420	BOSTON, MA	02116
BLADE RUNNER	WRESTLER	SEE - STING, BLADE RUNNER		
BLADE RUNNER BART	WRESTLER	SEE - DINGO WARRIOR		
BLAGOF, RAY L	COMPOSER	4557 SIMPSON AVE	NORTH HOLLYWOOD, CA	91607
BLAILOCK, STEPHEN	GUITARIST	1905 DICKERSON RD #26	NASHVILLE, TN	37207
BLAINE, MARTIN	ACTOR	21458 RAMBLA VISTA	MALIBU, CA	90265
BLAINE, WILLIAN	PIANIST	POST OFFICE BOX U	REDDING, CT	06875
BLAIR, ALPHA	ACTRESS	8755 BURTON WY	LOS ANGELES, CA	90048
BLAIR, B BRIAN	WRESTLER	POST OFFICE BOX 3859	STAMFORD, CT	06905
BLAIR, BETSY	ACTRESS	11 CHALCOT GARDENS		
		ENGLAND'S LN	LONDON NW3	ENGLAND
BLAIR, DENNIS	TV WRITER	555 W 57TH ST #1230	NEW YORK, NY	10019
BLAIR, HAROLD LEO	GUITARIST	ROUTE #2, BOX 939	MOREHEAD, KY	40351
BLAIR, ISLA	ACTRESS	19 ULLSWATER RD	LONDON SW13	ENGLAND
BLAIR, JAMES	CONDUCTOR	GERSHUNOFF, 502 PARK AVE	NEW YORK, NY	10022
BLAIR, JAMES P	PHOTOGRAPHER	1411 30TH ST, NW	WASHINGTON, DC	20037
BLAIR, JOAN	ACTRESS	2100 N BEACHWOOD DR #211	LOS ANGELES, CA	90068
BLAIR, JON	WRITER-PRODUCER	20 WILLOW BRIDGE RD	LONDON N1 2LA	ENGLAND
BLAIR, JOYCE	ACTRESS	BURNETT, 42 GRAFTON HOUSE		
		2-3 GOLDEN SQ	LONDON W1	ENGLAND
BLAIR, LAWRENCE T	WRITER	8955 BEVERLY BLVD	LOS ANGELES, CA	90048
BLAIR, LES	TV DIRECTOR	63 OAKFIELD RD	LONDON N4 4LD	ENGLAND
BLAIR, LINDA	ACTRESS	1930 CENTURY PARK W #303	LOS ANGELES, CA	90067
BLAIR, LIONEL	TV PERSONALITY-DANCER	68 OLD BROMPTON RD	LONDON SW7	ENGLAND
BLAIR, NICKY	ACTOR	8730 SUNSET BLVD	LOS ANGELES, CA	90069
BLAIR, WENDY	NEWS CORRESPONDENT	2480 16TH ST	WASHINGTON, DC	20009
BLAIR STRING QUARTET, THE	STRING QUARTET	240 W 98TH ST #13-A	NEW YORK, NY	10025
BLAIRE, KENDALL J	WRITER	8955 BEVERLY BLVD	LOS ANGELES, CA	90048
BLAISDELL, BRAD	ACTOR	641 N NAOMI ST	BURBANK, CA	91505
BLAKE, AMANDA	ACTRESS	ICM, 8899 BEVERLY BLVD	LOS ANGELES, CA	90048
BLAKE, BUD	CARTOONIST	POST OFFICE BOX 23	RUMSON, NJ	07760
BLAKE, BUDDY	WRESTLER	POST OFFICE BOX 3859	STAMFORD, CT	06905
BLAKE, CHARLES	ACTOR	8721 SUNSET BLVD #200	LOS ANGELES, CA	90069
BLAKE, ELIZABETH	WRITER	555 W 57TH ST #1230	NEW YORK, NY	10019
BLAKE, ELLEN	CASTING DIRECTOR	AKA CASTING, 6522 HAYES DR	LOS ANGELES, CA	90048
BLAKE, ELTA	ACTRESS	594 GARFIELD AVE	S PASADENA, CA	91030
BLAKE, GAYLE	ACTRESS	5051 WILKINSON AVE	NORTH HOLLYWOOD, CA	91607
BLAKE, GEOFFREY	ACTOR	9220 SUNSET BLVD #625	LOS ANGELES, CA	90069
BLAKE, GERALD	TV DIRECTOR	DAWSON, 31 KINGS RD	LONDON SW3	ENGLAND
BLAKE, HOWARD	COMPOSER	18 KENSINGTON CT PL #6	LONDON W8 5BJ	ENGLAND
BLAKE, JOHN	SINGER	HEARTLAND, 660 DOUGLAS	ALTAMONTE SPRINGS, FL	32714
BLAKE, KATHARINE	ACTRESS-WRITER	LADKIN, 11 ALDWYCH	LONDON WC2	ENGLAND
BLAKE, MERRITT	TALENT AGENT	2121 AVE OF THE STARS #410	LOS ANGELES, CA	90067
BLAKE, MICHAEL FRANCIS	ACTOR	12242 MOORPARK ST	STUDIO CITY, CA	91604
BLAKE, MICHAEL H, JR	NEWS CORRESPONDENT	2201 "L" ST #200, NW	WASHINGTON, DC	20037
BLAKE, NANCY	CELLIST	POST OFFICE BOX 584	TRENTON, GA	30752
BLAKE, NORMAN	SINGER-GUITARIST	POST OFFICE BOX 9188	COLORADO SPRINGS, CO	80932
BLAKE, PATRICIA	WRITER-EDITOR	TIME/TIME & LIFE BLDG		
		ROCKEFELLER CENTER	NEW YORK, NY	10020
BLAKE, PAUL ALAN	DIRECTOR	DGA, 7950 SUNSET BLVD	LOS ANGELES, CA	90046
BLAKE, PETER	ACTOR	FRASER, 91 REGENT ST	LONDON W1	ENGLAND
BLAKE, PHILLIP R	WRITER	8955 BEVERLY BLVD	LOS ANGELES, CA	90048
BLAKE, REBECCA	DIRECTOR	DGA, 110 W 57TH ST	NEW YORK, NY	10019
BLAKE, ROBERT	ACTOR	11604 DILLING ST	NORTH HOLLYWOOD, CA	91604
BLAKE, ROCKWELL	TENOR	CAMI, 165 W 57TH ST	NEW YORK, NY	10019
BLAKE, SONDRA	ACTRESS	7466 BEVERLY BLVD #205	LOS ANGELES, CA	90028
BLAKE, STEPHANIE	ACTRESS	9025 WILSHIRE BLVD #309	BEVERLY HILLS, CA	90211
BLAKE, TIMOTHY	ACTRESS	1643 SUNSET PLAZA DR	LOS ANGELES, CA	90069
BLAKE, WALLY	COMEDIAN	32500 CONCORD DR #211	MADISON NEIGHTS, MI	48071
BLAKE, WHITNEY	ACTRESS	211 S BEVERLY DR #107	BEVERLY HILLS, CA	90212
BLAKELEY, RONEE	SINGER-ACTRESS	400 S BEVERLY DR #216	BEVERLY HILLS, CA	90212
BLAKELY, EDDIE	SINGER-GUITARIST	300 16TH ST	OLD HICKORY, TN	37138
BLAKELY, JAMES	ACTOR	517 N RODEO DR	BEVERLY HILLS, CA	90210
BLAKELY, STEPHEN B	NEWS CORRESPONDENT	1309 N ODE ST #534	ARLINGTON, VA	22209
BLAKELY, SUSAN	ACTRESS	ICM, 8899 BEVERLY BLVD	LOS ANGELES, CA	90048
BLAKEMORE, BILL	TV EXECUTIVE	ABC TELEVISION NETWORK		
		1330 AVE OF THE AMERICAS	NEW YORK, NY	10019
BLAKEMORE, MARSHA D	NEWS CORRESPONDENT	2130 "P" ST #812, NW	WASHINGTON, DC	20037
BLAKEMORE, MICHAEL	FILM DIRECTOR	11-A SAINT MARTIN		
		ALMSHOUSES, BAYHAM ST	LONDON NW1	ENGLAND
BLAKER, CHARLES R	COMPOSER-CONDUCTOR	1142 S SIERRA BONITA AVE #7	LOS ANGELES, CA	90019
BLAKESLEE, CAROL A	NEWS CORRESPONDENT	141 12TH ST, NE	WASHINGTON, DC	20002
BLAKEY, ART & THE JAZZ MESSENGE	JAZZ GROUP	BRIDGE, 106 FORT GREEN PL	BROOKLYN, NY	11217
BLAKLEY, MICHAEL	ACTOR	16607 RUNNYMEDE ST	VAN NUYS, CA	91406
BLAKLEY, RONEE	SINGER-ACTRESS	9701 WILSHIRE BLVD #700	BEVERLY HILLS, CA	90211
BLALOCK, CECELIA	NEWS CORRESPONDENT	9206 VOLLMERHAUSEN RD	JESSUP, MD	20794
BLANC, MEL	ACTOR-VOICE OVERS	266 TOYOPA DR	PACIFIC PALISADES, CA	90272
BLANC, NOEL BARTON	WRITER	702 N RODEO DR	BEVERLY HILLS, CA	90210
BLANC-ROSNER, LARRAINE	ACTRESS	KOHNER, 9169 SUNSET BLVD	LOS ANGELES, CA	90069
BLANCHARD, LARRY H	NEWS CORRESPONDENT	1621 IRVING ST, NW	WASHINGTON, DC	20010

THE BLASTERS

Bill Bateman • Gene Taylor • Dave Alvin • John Bazz • Phil Alvin

BON JOVI

David Rashbaum • Alec John Such • Jon Bon Jovi • Tico Torres • Richie Sambora

BLANCHARD, NINA	TALENT AGENT	8145 MULHOLLAND DR	LOS ANGELES, CA	90046
BLANCHARD, SUSAN	ACTRESS-MODEL	900 CHAPEA RD	PASADENA, CA	91107
BLANCHARD, TULLY	WRESTLER	NATIONAL WRESTLING ALLIANCE		
		JIM CROCKETT PROMOTIONS		
		421 BRIARBEND DR	CHARLOTTE, NC	28209
BLANCHART, DIRK	SINGER	GRAMAVISION RECORDS		
		260 W BROADWAY	NEW YORK, NY	10013
BLANCHET, SHARON B	NEWS CORRESPONDENT	4707 CONNECTICUT AVE, NW	WASHINGTON, DC	20008
BLANCHETTE, FRANCES LYELL	GUITARIST	1008 9TH ST	OLD HICKORY, TN	37138
BLAND, BOBBY "BLUE"	SINGER	108 N AUBURNDALE #1010	MEMPHIS, TN	38104
BLAND, ELIZABETH L	NEWS REPORTER	TIME/TIME & LIFE BLDG		
		ROCKEFELLER CENTER	NEW YORK, NY	10020
BLANE, SALLY	ACTRESS	1114 S ROXBURY DR	LOS ANGELES, CA	90035
BLANEY, H CLAY	THEATER PRODUCER	300 W 55TH ST	NEW YORK, NY	10019
BLANK, LAWRENCE J	CONDUCTOR	200 W 86TH ST #19-M	NEW YORK, NY	10024
BLANK, PETER L	NEWS CORRESPONDENT	4564 AIRLIE WY	ANNANDALE, VA	22003
BLANK, THOMAS JEFFREY	FILM WRITER-DIRECTOR	5707 TOPANGA CANYON BLVD #1	WOODLAND HILLS, CA	91367
BLANKENSHIP, JOHNNY	SINGER	O & L, 10051 GREENLEAF	SANTA FE SPRINGS, CA	90670
BLANKERS, LAURENS ARTHUR	CELLIST	1100 16TH AVE S #1	NASHVILLE, TN	37212
BLANKFIELD, MARK	ACTOR	141 S EL CAMINO DR #205	BEVERLY HILLS, CA	90212
BLANKS, WILLIAM W	WRITER	1737 COLLEGE VIEW PL	LOS ANGELES, CA	90041
BLANTON, ARELL	ACTOR	4191 GREENBUSH AVE	SHERMAN OAKS, CA	91423
BLANTON, JEREMY	DANCER	210 W 19TH ST	NEW YORK, NY	10011
BLASBERG, JOEL	WRITER	8955 BEVERLY BLVD	LOS ANGELES, CA	90048
BLASER, LYNN	SOPRANO	200 W 70TH ST #7-F	NEW YORK, NY	10023
BLASI, ANGELA	SOPRANO	CAMI, 165 W 57TH ST	NEW YORK, NY	10019
BLASOR, DENISE	ACTRESS	LEONETTI, 6526 SUNSET BLVD	HOLLYWOOD, CA	90028
BLASS, BILL	FASHION DESIGNER	550 7TH AVE	NEW YORK, NY	10019
BLASSIE, FREDDIE	WRESTLER-MANAGER	POST OFFICE BOX 3859	STAMFORD, CT	06905
BLASSMAN, FRED	WRESTLER-MANAGER	SEE - BLASSIE, FREDDIE		
BLASTERS, THE	ROCK & ROLL GROUP	VISION MANAGEMENT CO		
		2112 N CAHUENGA BLVD	LOS ANGELES, CA	90068
BLASUCCI, RICHARD	ACTOR-WRITER	10424 BLOOMFIELD ST	NORTH HOLLYWOOD, CA	91602
BLATCH, HELEN	ACTRESS	LONDON ACTORS AGENCY		
		248 KENTISH TOWN RD	LONDON NW5	ENGLAND
BLATCHLEY, JOSEPH	ACTOR	7 FORDWYCH RD	LONDON NW2	ENGLAND
BLATT, DANIEL H	FILM PRODUCER	BLATT/SINGER PRODUCTIONS		
		COLUMBIA PICTURES		
		COLUMBIA PLAZA E	BURBANK, CA	91504
BLATT, DAVID R	TV DIRECTOR	147 E 85TH ST #5-D	NEW YORK, NY	10028
BLATT, LESLIE	WRITER	555 W 57TH ST #1230	NEW YORK, NY	10019
BLATTY, WILLIAM PETER	FILM WRITER-PRODUCER	21 ALDEN RD	GREENWICH, CT	06830
BLATZ, KATHLEEN L	WRITER	1018 EUCLID ST #201	SANTA MONICA, CA	90403
BLAU, PETER E	NEWS CORRESPONDENT	3900 TUNLAW RD #119	WASHINGTON, DC	20007
BLAU, RAPHAEL D	WRITER	555 W 57TH ST #1230	NEW YORK, NY	10019
BLAUSTEIN, BARRY M	FILM-TV WRITER	9000 SUNSET BLVD #1200	LOS ANGELES, CA	90069
BLAUSTEIN, JULIAN	PRODUCER	10126 ANGELO VIEW DR	BEVERLY HILLS, CA	90210
BLAXILL, PETER	ACTOR	321 W 22ND ST	NEW YORK, NY	10011
BLAYLOCK, KENNETH LEE	PHOTOJOURNALIST	2817 N FRANKLIN RD	ARLINGTON, VA	22201
BLAYLOCK, PEGGY AHERN	ACTRESS	24529 DEEP WELL RD	CALABASAS, CA	91302
BLAZER, ARTHUR R	WRITER	555 W 57TH ST #1230	NEW YORK, NY	10019
BLEACH, BARRY M	WRITER	8074 FAREHOLM DR #5	LOS ANGELES, CA	90046
BLECHMAN, COREY	TV WRITER	1015 GAYLEY AVE #301	LOS ANGELES, CA	90024
BLECHMAN, R O	CARTOONIST	POST OFFICE BOX 4203	NEW YORK, NY	10017
BLECKER, RHODA	STORY EDITOR	7024 SYLVIA AVE	RESEDA, CA	91335
BLECKNER, JEFF	DIRECTOR	4815 DUNMAN AVE	WOODLAND HILLS, CA	91364
BLECKNER, PETER NEIL	TV DIRECTOR	17 W 67TH ST #10-A	NEW YORK, NY	10023
BLEDSOE, KATHRYN M	NEWS CORRESPONDENT	12 S VAN DORN ST #V-504	ALEXANDRIA, VA	22304
BLEDSOE, KENNY	DRUMMER	1033 16TH AVE N	NASHVILLE, TN	37208
BLEE, DEBRA	ACTRESS	3907 W ALAMEDA AVE #101	BURBANK, CA	91505
BLEECK, DOUGLAS	DIRECTOR	2120 N BEVERLY GLEN BLVD	LOS ANGELES, CA	90077
BLEECKER, TOM	WRITER	8955 BEVERLY BLVD	LOS ANGELES, CA	90048
BLEES, ROBERT	WRITER-PRODUCER	1373 BECKWITH AVE	LOS ANGELES, CA	90049
BLEETH, YASMINE	ACTRESS	ABC-TV, "RYAN'S HOPE"		
		1330 AVE OF THE AMERICAS	NEW YORK, NY	10019
BLEGEN, JUDITH	SOPRANO	59 E 54TH ST #81	NEW YORK, NY	10022
BLEICH, BILL	TV WRITER	ICM, 8899 BEVERLY BLVD	LOS ANGELES, CA	90048
BLEICHMAN, NORMAN GARY	WRITER	10635 BLYTHE AVE	LOS ANGELES, CA	90064
BLEIER, NANCY	ACTRESS	6430 SUNSET BLVD #1203	LOS ANGELES, CA	90028
BLEIFER, JOHN	ACTOR	832 S MADDELIN AVE	LOS ANGELES, CA	90036
BLEIWEISS, ALLEN	ACTOR	1605 N CAHUENGA BLVD #202	LOS ANGELES, CA	90028
BLEIWEISS, NANCY	ACTRESS	9220 SUNSET BLVD #202	LOS ANGELES, CA	90069
BLENDICK, JAMES	ACTOR	SF & A, 121 N SAN VICENTE BLVD	BEVERLY HILLS, CA	90211
BLESSED, BRIAN	ACTOR	MILLER MANAGEMENT		
		82 BROOM PARK, TEDDINGTON	MIDDLESEX	ENGLAND
BLESSING, BERT	SCREENWRITER	555 W 57TH ST #1230	NEW YORK, NY	10019
BLESSING, JACK	ACTOR	10390 SANTA MONICA BLVD #310	LOS ANGELES, CA	90025
BLESSINGTON, EDWARD	ACTOR	4444 HAZELTINE AVE #130	SHERMAN OAKS, CA	91423
BLEVINS, SCOTTY LEE	GUITARIST	311 OLD SHACKLE ISLAND	HENDERSONVILLE, TN	37075
BLEVINS, TONE	WRITER	8955 BEVERLY BLVD	LOS ANGELES, CA	90048
BLEVINS, WINIFRED E	WRITER	8955 BEVERLY BLVD	LOS ANGELES, CA	90048
BLEY, CARLA	PIANIST-COMPOSER	KURLAND, 173 BRIGHTON AVE	BOSTON, MA	02134
BLEYER, ROBERT	TV DIRECTOR	31 MURRAY HILL DR	SCARSDALE, NY	10583
BLICKER, SEYMOUR	WRITER	8955 BEVERLY BLVD	LOS ANGELES, CA	90048
BLIHOVDE, MARVIN	MUSICIAN	214 OLD HICKORY BLVD #198	NASHVILLE, TN	37221

Name	Occupation	Address	City	Zip
BLINDER, DONNA C	WRITER	10508 CLEARWOOD CT	LOS ANGELES, CA	90077
BLINKO THE CLOWN	CLOWN	2701 COTTAGE WY #14	SACRAMENTO, CA	95825
BLINN, ROGER	ACTOR	264 RUE SAINT-HONORE	PARIS 75001	FRANCE
BLINN, TONY	BODYBUILDER	CAFBB, 53 SUZOR	SAINT HUBERT, QUE J3Y	CANADA
BLINN, WILLIAM FREDERICK	WRITER-PRODUCER	16964 IVADEL PL	ENCINO, CA	91436
BLISS, ALLISON	TV DIRECTOR	2 VISTA VERDE CT	SAN FRANCISCO, CA	94131
BLISS, BILL	ACTOR	9250 WILSHIRE BLVD #208	BEVERLY HILLS, CA	90212
BLISS, BRADLEY	ACTRESS	247 S BEVERLY DR #102	BEVERLY HILLS, CA	90210
BLISS, IMOGENE	ACTRESS	319 W 77TH ST #5	NEW YORK, NY	10024
BLISS, THOMAS A	TV DIRECTOR	1776 KELTON AVE	LOS ANGELES, CA	90024
BLITMAN, NAN	TALENT AGENT	1888 CENTURY PARK E #1400	LOS ANGELES, CA	90067
BLITZER, BARRY	TV WRITER	16315 AKRON ST	PACIFIC PALISADES, CA	90272
BLITZER, WOLF	NEWS CORRESPONDENT	929 FARM HAVEN DR	ROCKVILLE, MD	20852
BLOCH, ANDREW	ACTOR	870 N VINE ST #G	LOS ANGELES, CA	90038
BLOCH, BORIS	PIANIST	1776 BROADWAY #504	NEW YORK, NY	10019
BLOCH, CHARLES B	FILM PRODUCER	5039 BLUEBELL AVE	NORTH HOLLYWOOD, CA	91607
BLOCH, JOHN W	WRITER-PRODUCER	2248 MANDEVILLE CANYON RD	LOS ANGELES, CA	90049
BLOCH, MERWIN A	WRITER	555 W 57TH ST #1230	NEW YORK, NY	10019
BLOCH, ROBERT	WRITER	2111 SUNSET CREST DR	LOS ANGELES, CA	90046
BLOCH, WALTER	TV WRITER	8955 BEVERLY BLVD	LOS ANGELES, CA	90048
BLOCHWITZ, HANS PETER	TENOR	IMG ARTISTS, 22 E 71ST ST	NEW YORK, NY	10021
BLOCK, BETH	WRITER	8955 BEVERLY BLVD	LOS ANGELES, CA	90048
BLOCK, BRUCE A	DIRECTOR	DGA, 7950 SUNSET BLVD	LOS ANGELES, CA	90046
BLOCK, CHAD	ACTOR	2501 W BURBANK BLVD #304	BURBANK, CA	91505
BLOCK, HENRY	TAX EXPERT	NEWS AMERICA SYNDICATE		
		1703 KAISER AVE	IRVINE, CA	92714
BLOCK, HERBERT	CARTOONIST	THE WASHINGTON POST		
		1150 15TH ST, NW	WASHINGTON, DC	20071
BLOCK, JULIAN	TAX EXPERT-COLUMNIST	TRIBUNE MEDIA SERVICES		
		64 E CONCORD ST	ORLANDO, FL	32801
BLOCK, KENAN S	NEWS CORRESPONDENT	1939 17TH ST, NW	WASHINGTON, DC	20009
BLOCK, LARRY	ACTOR	7761 WHITE OAK AVE	RESEDA, CA	91335
BLOCK, MERVIN A	WRITER	140 W END AVE	NEW YORK, NY	10023
BLOCK, RORY	SINGER-GUITARIST	CONCERTED EFFORTS, INC		
		110 MADISON AVE	NEWTONVILLE, MA	02160
BLOCK, RUTH W	WRITER	8955 BEVERLY BLVD	LOS ANGELES, CA	90048
BLOCK, VICTOR I	NEWS CORRESPONDENT	5415 CONNECTICUT AVE #823, NW	WASHINGTON, DC	20015
BLOCK, WILLARD	COMMUNICATIONS EXEC	VIACOM INTERNATIONAL, INC		
		1211 AVE OF THE AMERICAS	NEW YORK, NY	10036
BLOCKER, DIRK	ACTOR	11726 SAN VICENTE BLVD #300	LOS ANGELES, CA	90049
BLOCKER, JUDY	PIANIST	1412 BRECKENRIDGE CT	WHITE CREEK, TN	37189
BLOCKS, THE	SWORD BALANCERS	POST OFFICE BOX 87	WEST LEBANON, NY	12195
BLODGETT, MICHAEL	ACTOR	10485 NATIONAL BLVD #22	LOS ANGELES, CA	90034
BLODGETT, VIRGINIA L	NEWS CORRESPONDENT	472 NATIONAL PRESS BLDG		
		529 14TH ST, NW	WASHINGTON, DC	20045
BLOEBAUM, LANE M	WRITER	6914 N WILLARD AVE	SAN GABRIEL, CA	91775
BLOHM, GARY	WRITER-PRODUCER	7259 BIRDVIEW AVE	MALIBU, CA	90265
BLOM, ANTON	NEWS CORRESPONDENT	8024 FENWAY RD	BETHESDA, MD	20817
BLOMMAERT, JULIEN	BODYBUILDER	ACB GYM, 9 HOPE LN B-8200	BRUGGE	BELGIUM
BLOMQUIST, TOM	WRITER-PRODUCER	4769 ELMER AVE	NORTH HOLLYWOOD, CA	91602
BLONDE BOMBER, THE	WRESTLER	SEE - STEVENS, RAY		
		"THE CRIPPLER"		
BLOOD, RICHARD	WRESTLER	SEE - STEAMBOAT, RICKY		
		"THE DRAGON"		
BLOOD, STEPHEN T	ACTOR	10845 LINDBROOK DR #3	LOS ANGELES, CA	90024
BLOOD ON THE SADDLE	ROCK & ROLL GROUP	CYNX MGMT, 1405 CAMDEN AVE	LOS ANGELES, CA	90024
BLOODLUST	ROCK & ROLL GROUP	POST OFFICE BOX 2428	EL SEGUNDO, CA	90245
BLOODWORTH, LINDA	TV WRITER-PRODUCER	MOZARK PRODUCTIONS CO		
		COLUMBIA TELEVISION		
		COLUMBIA PLAZA E	BURBANK, CA	91505
BLOOM, ANNE	ACTRESS-COMEDIENNE	656 W KNOLL DR #303	LOS ANGELES, CA	90069
BLOOM, ARTHUR	DIRECTOR-PRODUCER	530 W 57TH ST	NEW YORK, NY	10019
BLOOM, BILL ALAN	WRITER	656 W KNOLL DR #303	LOS ANGELES, CA	90069
BLOOM, BRIAN	ACTOR	CBS-TV, "AS THE WORLD TURNS"		
		51 W 52ND ST	NEW YORK, NY	10019
BLOOM, CLAIRE	ACTRESS	15 FAWCETT ST	LONDON SW10	ENGLAND
BLOOM, ERIC L	SCREENWRITER	1221 10TH ST #6	SANTA MONICA, CA	90401
BLOOM, GEORGE ARTHUR	WRITER	426 SMITHWOOD DR	BEVERLY HILLS, CA	90212
BLOOM, GEORGE JAY	TV WRITER	435 GEORGIAN RD	LA CANADA, CA	91011
BLOOM, HAROLD JACK	TV WRITER	9255 DOHENY RD	LOS ANGELES, CA	90069
BLOOM, HERBERT I	NEWS CORRESPONDENT	2205 CALIFORNIA ST, NW	WASHINGTON, DC	20008
BLOOM, JAMES	DIRECTOR-PRODUCER	BLUE IRIS, 850 KEELER AVE	BERKELEY, CA	94707
BLOOM, JEFFREY	WRITER-PRODUCER	10100 SANTA MONICA BLVD #1600	LOS ANGELES, CA	90067
BLOOM, JOHN	ACTOR	8721 SUNSET BLVD #103	LOS ANGELES, CA	90069
BLOOM, JOHN	FILM EDITOR	10100 SANTA MONICA BLVD #1600	LOS ANGELES, CA	90067
BLOOM, LINDSAY	ACTRESS	POST OFFICE BOX 2188	HOLLYWOOD, CA	90078
BLOOM, RICHARD A	PHOTOGRAPHER	2001 WETHERSFIELD CT	RESTON, VA	22091
BLOOM, SANFORD J	DIRECTOR	WLS-TV, 190 N STATE ST	CHICAGO, IL	60601
BLOOM, STEVEN L	SCREENWRITER	8955 BEVERLY BLVD	LOS ANGELES, CA	90048
BLOOM, VERNA	ACTRESS	19 W 44TH ST #1500	NEW YORK, NY	10036
BLOOMBERG, BEVERLY	TV WRITER	8955 BEVERLY BLVD	LOS ANGELES, CA	90048
BLOOMBERG, RON	TV WRITER	5224 DONNA AVE	TARZANA, CA	91356
BLOOMBERG, STUART J	TV EXECUTIVE	3825 SAN RAFAEL AVE	LOS ANGELES, CA	90065
BLOOMFIELD, ARTHUR	MUSIC CRITIC	2229 WEBSTER ST	SAN FRANCISCO, CA	94115
BLOOMFIELD, GEORGE	WRITER-PRODUCER	ADMIRAL RD #50	TORONTO, ONT M5R 2LR	CANADA

Name	Occupation	Address	City/State	Zip/Country
BLOOMGARDEN, JOHN	THEATER PRODUCER	275 CENTRAL PARK W	NEW YORK, NY	10024
BLOOMGARDEN, LEE OSCAR	WRITER	420 S LA FAYETTE PARK PL	LOS ANGELES, CA	90057
BLOOMSTEIN, HENRY H	WRITER	8955 BEVERLY BLVD	LOS ANGELES, CA	90048
BLOOMSTEIN, REX	FILM-TV DIRECTOR	25 WILLOW RD	LONDON NW3	ENGLAND
BLORE, CATHERINE	ACTRESS	10439 VALLEY SPRING LN	NORTH HOLLYWOOD, CA	91602
BLORE, CHUCK	WRITER	3644 BUENA PARK DR	STUDIO CITY, CA	91604
BLOSSER, FRED	NEWS CORRESPONDENT	4216 SIDEBURN RD	FAIRFAX, VA	22030
BLOSSER, JOHN	NEWS REPORTER	THE NATIONAL ENQUIRER		
		600 SE COAST AVE	LANTANA, FL	33464
BLOSSOM, ROBERTS	ACTOR	10100 SANTA MONICA BLVD #1600	LOS ANGELES, CA	90067
BLOTTO	ROCK & ROLL GROUP	POST OFFICE BOX 306	MYSTIC, CT	06355
BLOUNT, JOHN	RECORD EXECUTIVE	BENTE RECORDS COMPANY		
		382 CENTRAL PARK W	NEW YORK, NY	10025
BLOUNT, LISA	ACTRESS	151 S EL CAMINO DR	BEVERLY HILLS, CA	90212
BLOUNT, ROY A, JR	WRITER	8955 BEVERLY BLVD	LOS ANGELES, CA	90048
BLOW, KURTIS	RAPPER-RAPWRITER	201 EASTERN PARKWAY #3-K	BROOKLYN, NY	11238
BLUCHER, JAY J	NEWS CORRESPONDENT	4202 N WASHINGTON BLVD #2	ARLINGTON, VA	22201
BLUE, ANTHONY DIAS	WINE CRITIC	CHRONICLE FEATURES		
		870 MARKET ST	SAN FRANCISCO, CA	94102
BLUE, CARROLL P	WRITER	8955 BEVERLY BLVD	LOS ANGELES, CA	90048
BLUE, DAVID S	NEWS CORRESPONDENT	141 12TH ST #18, NW	WASHINGTON, DC	20002
BLUE, PETER T	PIANIST	249 CENTRAL PARK W #12-A	NEW YORK, NY	10024
BLUE, STEVEN N	TV DIRECTOR	WLS-TV, 190 N STATE ST	CHICAGO, IL	60601
BLUE, VIDA	BASEBALL	POST OFFICE BOX 14438	OAKLAND, CA	94614
BLUE BANDANA COUNTRY BAND	C & W GROUP	CUDE, 519 N HALIFAX AVE	DAYTONA BCH, FL	32018
BLUE IS HEAVEN	ROCK & ROLL GROUP	DESMOND, 23 UPPER SHEPPHERD	DUBLIN 1	IRELAND
BLUE MAX	ROCK & ROLL GROUP	POST OFFICE BOX 448	RADFORD, VA	24141
BLUE OYSTER CULT	ROCK & ROLL GROUP	SANDY PEARLMAN MGMT		
		228 W 55TH ST	NEW YORK, NY	10019
BLUE RIDGE & THE BLUE RIDGE BAN	C & W GROUP	TESSIER, 505 CANTON PASS	MADISON, TN	37115
BLUE SKY BAND	JAZZ GROUP	POST OFFICE BOX 684	DES MOINES, IA	50303
BLUE TRAPEZE	ROCK & ROLL GROUP	POST OFFICE BOX 6863	FULLERTON, CA	92631
BLUEBERRY HELLBELLIES, THE	ROCK & ROLL GROUP	61-71 COLLIER ST	LONDON N1 9BE	ENGLAND
BLUEGRASS CARDINALS, THE	C & W GROUP	POST OFFICE DRAWER 160	HENDERSONVILLE, TN	37075
BLUEGRASS GOSPELETTES, THE	GOSPEL GROUP	ROSEWOOD, ROUTE #7, BOX 28	LAKE CITY, FL	32055
BLUESBUSTERS, THE	ROCK & ROLL GROUP	450 14TH ST #201, NW	ATLANTA, GA	30318
BLUESTEIN, STEVE	ACTOR-WRITER	4931 COLDWATER CANYON AVE	SHERMAN OAKS, CA	91423
BLUESTONE, ED	WRITER	8955 BEVERLY BLVD	LOS ANGELES, CA	90048
BLUESTONE, FRED W	MUSICIAN	6636 JOCELYN HOLLOW RD	NASHVILLE, TN	37205
BLUESTONE, GEORGE	WRITER	8955 BEVERLY BLVD	LOS ANGELES, CA	90048
BLUM, DEBORAH B	TV WRITER	8955 BEVERLY BLVD	LOS ANGELES, CA	90048
BLUM, EDWIN HARVEY	WRITER	801 N RODEO DR	BEVERLY HILLS, CA	90210
BLUM, HARRY N	FILM PRODUCER	494 TUALLITAN RD	LOS ANGELES, CA	90049
BLUM, MARK	ACTOR	151 S EL CAMINO DR	BEVERLY HILLS, CA	90212
BLUM, MICHAEL	TV DIRECTOR	423 MADISON AVE	NEW YORK, NY	10017
BLUM, RALPH	WRITER	8955 BEVERLY BLVD	LOS ANGELES, CA	90048
BLUM, ROBERT P	WRITER	555 W 57TH ST #1230	NEW YORK, NY	10019
BLUM, STANFORD	WRITER-PRODUCER	4222 WOODMAN AVE	SHERMAN OAKS, CA	91423
BLUM, TINA	ACTRESS	6640 SUNSET BLVD #203	LOS ANGELES, CA	90028
BLUMBERG, DAVID E	COMPOSER	3309 LAUREL CANYON BLVD	STUDIO CITY, CA	91604
BLUME, HOWARD	DIRECTOR	1501 BROADWAY #2600	NEW YORK, NY	10036
BLUME, JUDY	WRITER	8955 BEVERLY BLVD	LOS ANGELES, CA	90048
BLUMENTHAL, HOWARD	CONSUMER EXPERT	N Y TIMES SYNDICATION		
		130 5TH AVE	NEW YORK, NY	10011
BLUMFIELD, COLEMAN	PIANIST	SHAW CONCERTS, 1995 BROADWAY	NEW YORK, NY	10023
BLUMGARTEN, JAMES	WRITER	555 W 57TH ST #1230	NEW YORK, NY	10019
BLUMOFE, ROBERT F	FILM PRODUCER	1100 ALTA LOMA RD #1005	LOS ANGELES, CA	90069
BLUNT, BETTY ANDREW	WRITER	3521 WONDER VIEW DR	LOS ANGELES, CA	90068
BLUNT, CHARLOTTE	ACTRESS	9229 SUNSET BLVD #306	LOS ANGELES, CA	90069
BLUSTEIN, PAUL	NEWS CORRESPONDENT	2127 CALIFORNIA ST, NW	WASHINGTON, DC	20008
BLUTO, JOHN	ACTOR	8350 SANTA MONICA BLVD #104	LOS ANGELES, CA	90069
BLY, DENNIS	NEWS CORRESPONDENT	3915 S 16TH ST	ARLINGTON, VA	22204
BLYDON, JOHN	TV EXECUTIVE	RKO-NEDERLANDER PRODS		
		1440 BROADWAY	NEW YORK, NY	10018
BLYE, ALLAN	WRITER-PRODUCER	16014 SKYTOP RD	ENCINO, CA	91316
BLYE, MARGARET	ACTRESS	8495 FOUNTAIN AVE #E-2	LOS ANGELES, CA	90069
BLYSTONE, RICHARD M	NEWS CORRESPONDENT	CNN, 31 FOLEY ST	LONDON W1	ENGLAND
BLYTH, ANN	ACTRESS	6 TOLUCA ESTATES DR	NORTH HOLLYWOOD, CA	91602
BLYTH, HENRY	SCREENWRITER	SOUTHERN DOWN, ROTTINGDEAN	SUSSEX	ENGLAND
BLYTH, JEFF	WRITER	15010 VENTURA BLVD #219	SHERMAN OAKS, CA	91403
BLYTH, MYRNA	WRITER	555 W 57TH ST #1230	NEW YORK, NY	10019
BLYTHE, ERIC	ACTOR	58 JANE ST	NEW YORK, NY	10014
BLYTHE, EUGENE	CASTING DIRECTOR	4024 RADFORD AVE	STUDIO CITY, CA	91604
BLYTHE, JANUS	ACTRESS	3151 W CAHUENGA BLVD #310	LOS ANGELES, CA	90068
BLYTHE, JOHN	ACTOR	19 BELVEDERE CLOSE		
		TEDDINGTON	MIDDLESEX	ENGLAND
BLYTHE, PETER	ACTOR	21 ENNISMORE GARDENS	LONDON SW7	ENGLAND
BLYTHE, ROBYN	ACTRESS	2501 W BURBANK BLVD #304	BURBANK, CA	91505
BOAH, H B	ACTRESS-MODEL	POST OFFICE BOX 1380	SANTEE, CA	92071
BOAM, JEFFREY D	SCREENWRITER	17170 KINZIE ST	NORTHRIDGE, CA	91325
BOAN, JOE	COMPOSER	3518 THE STRAND	HERMOSA BEACH, CA	90254
BOARDMAN, CHRISTOPHER E	COMPOSER	13135 ROSE AVE	LOS ANGELES, CA	90066
BOARDMAN, ELEANOR	ACTRESS	240 SANTA ROSA LN	SANTA BARBARA, CA	93108
BOARDMAN, ERIC	TV WRITER	6120 WINANS DR #11	LOS ANGELES, CA	90068
BOARDMAN, MARK H	NEWS CORRESPONDENT	4500 S FOUR MILE RUN DR	ARLINGTON, VA	22204

Name	Occupation	Address	City	Zip
BOARDMAN, TRUE	ACTOR-WRITER	13900 MARQUESAS WY #C-6	MARINA DEL REY, CA	90292
BOARDMAN, WILLIAM M	TV WRITER	555 W 57TH ST #1230	NEW YORK, NY	10019
BOARDO, LIZ	SINGER	PENNY, 30 GUINAN ST	WALTHAM, MA	02154
BOATMAN, J ROBERT	TV DIRECTOR	1226 WINDING WY	NASHVILLE, TN	37216
BOATMAN, JOHN	NEWS CORRESPONDENT	1263 KALORAMA RD #4-A, NW	WASHINGTON, DC	20009
BOATWRIGHT, GINGER H	MUSICIAN	4601 PACKARD DR #J-174	NASHVILLE, TN	37211
BOAZ, CHARLES "CHUCK"	ACTOR	290 9TH AVE	NEW YORK, NY	10001
BOBECKER, MARK	SINGER	3125 19TH ST #217	BAKERSFIELD, CA	93301
BOBKER, LEE	DIRECTOR	61 SARA LN	NEW ROCHELLE, NY	10804
BOBO, CRAZY "C"	AUTHOR-COACH	SEE - BOSSMAN, T		
BOBO, WILLIE	MUSICIAN	9220 SUNSET BLVD #212	LOS ANGELES, CA	90069
BOBRICK, NEIL	DIRECTOR	152 FINISTERRE #S-152	LINDENWOLD, NJ	08021
BOBRICK, SAM	TV WRITER-DIRECTOR	5300 OAK PARK AVE	ENCINO, CA	91316
BOBROWSKY, IGOR	WRITER	555 W 57TH ST #1230	NEW YORK, NY	10019
BOBS, THE	ROCK & ROLL GROUP	GREAT AMERICAN MUSIC HALL		
		859 O'FARRELL ST	SAN FRANCISCO, CA	94109
BOCCARDO, JOHN	TV WRITER	21569 PASEO SERRA	MALIBU, CA	90265
BOCHCO, STEVEN	WRITER-PRODUCER	694 AMALFI DR	PACIFIC PALISADES, CA	90272
BOCHNER, HART	ACTOR	10032 WESTWANDA DR	BEVERLY HILLS, CA	90210
BOCHNER, LLOYD	ACTOR	42 HALDEMAN RD	SANTA MONICA, CA	90402
BOCK, FRED	COMPOSER-CONDUCTOR	5404 TOPEKA DR	TARZANA, CA	91356
BOCK, JERRY	COMPOSER	ASCAP, 1 LINCOLN PLAZA	NEW YORK, NY	10023
BOCKHOLT, ROBERT, JR	COMPOSER	11625 LA MAIDA ST	NORTH HOLLYWOOD, CA	91601
BOCKMAN, DANIEL H	TV WRITER	8955 BEVERLY BLVD	LOS ANGELES, CA	90048
BOCKNEK, LAWRENCE A	PHOTOGRAPHER	10154 VILLAGE KNOLLS CT	OAKTON, VA	22124
BOCKWINKEL, NICK	WRESTLER	AMERICAN WRESTLING ASSOC		
		MINNEAPLOIS WRESTLING		
		10001 WAYZATA BLVD	MINNETONKA, MN	55345
BODARD, MEG	FILM PRODUCER	19 RUE MONTROSIER	NEUILLY 92200	FRANCE
BODE, KEN	NEWS CORRESPONDENT	NBC-TV, NEWS DEPARTMENT		
		4001 NEBRASKA AVE, NW	WASHINGTON, DC	20016
BODE, RALF D	DIRECTOR	DGA, 110 W 57TH ST	NEW YORK, NY	10019
BODE, WILLIAM T	WRITER	555 W 57TH ST #1230	NEW YORK, NY	10019
BODENHAMER, GREGORY	AUTHOR	1234 W CHAPMAN AVE #203	ORANGE, CA	92668
BODIN, THOMAS C	NEWS CORRESPONDENT	1201 CONNECTICUT AVE, NW	WASHINGTON, DC	20036
BODLANDER, GERALD	NEWS CORRESPONDENT	1825 "K" ST, NW	WASHINGTON, DC	20006
BODMER, MARY T	WRITER	555 W 57TH ST #1230	NEW YORK, NY	10019
BODNAR, JANET	NEWS CORRESPONDENT	1200 RUPPERT RD	SILVER SPRING, MD	20903
BODNAR, JOHN	NEWS CORRESPONDENT	2139 WISCONSIN AVE, NW	WASHINGTON, DC	20007
BODNER, HELENE	ACTRESS	3330 BARHAM BLVD #103	LOS ANGELES, CA	90068
BODOLAI, JOE	TV WRITER	555 W 57TH ST #1230	NEW YORK, NY	10019
BODWELL, PHILIP	TV DIRECTOR-PRODUCER	1900 OLD BRIAR RD	HIGHLAND PK, IL	60601
BODY ELECTRIC	ROCK & ROLL GROUP	41 BRITAIN ST #200	TORONTO, ONT	CANADA
BODZIN, ZELMA	PIANIST	243 W END AVE #907	NEW YORK, NY	10023
BOEHM, ELIZABETH W	TV WRITER	8955 BEVERLY BLVD	LOS ANGELES, CA	90048
BOEHM, HAROLD J	WRITER	8955 BEVERLY BLVD	LOS ANGELES, CA	90048
BOEHM, SYDNEY	SCREENWRITER	9000 CYNTHIA ST #311	LOS ANGELES, CA	90069
BOEKE, JIM	ACTOR	3518 W CAHUENGA BLVD #316	LOS ANGELES, CA	90068
BOELSEN, JIM	ACTOR	10850 RIVERSIDE DR #505	NORTH HOLLYWOOD, CA	91602
BOENZI, NEAL	PHOTOGRAPHER	43 SOLBURY MOUNTAIN RD	NEW HOPE, PA	18938
BOERSMA, JAMES G	COMPOSER-CONDUCTOR	3910 BROWN ST	OCEANSIDE, CA	92054
BOESCH, CHRISTIAN	BARITONE	CAMI, 165 W 57TH ST	NEW YORK, NY	10019
BOETTCHER, KATHY	ACTRESS	LEONETTI, 6526 SUNSET BLVD	HOLLYWOOD, CA	90028
BOETTCHER, WOLFGANG	CELLIST	482 FT WASHINGTON AVE #1-H	NEW YORK, NY	10033
BOETTICHER, BUDD	FILM DIRECTOR	23969 GREEN HAVEN LN	RAMONA, CA	92065
BOFFERY, JEAN	PHOTOGRAPHER	8 AVE DE LA MAYE	VERSAILLES 78000	FRANCE
BOFFEY, PHILIP M	NEWS CORRESPONDENT	5511 MONTGOMERY ST	CHEVY CHASE, MD	20815
BOFILL, ANGELA	SINGER	1385 YORK AVE #6-B	NEW YORK, NY	10021
BOGAERTS, THEO	VIOLINIST	416 LUTI DR	NASHVILLE, TN	37210
BOGAN, SANDRA	ACTRESS	STONE, 1052 CAROL DR	LOS ANGELES, CA	90069
BOGARDE, DIRK	ACTOR	06 CHATEAUNEUF	DE GRASSE	FRANCE
BOGARDUS, JANINE	SOPRANO	45 W 60TH ST #4-K	NEW YORK, NY	10023
BOGART, JOHN PAUL	BASS	61 W 62ND ST #6-F	NEW YORK, NY	10023
BOGART, LINDA SCRUGGS	ACTRESS	11223 LAURIE DR	STUDIO CITY, CA	91604
BOGART, PAUL	TV WRITER-DIRECTOR	1033 CAROL DR #403	LOS ANGELES, CA	90069
BOGART, PETER G	DIRECTOR	202 N LA PEER DR #6	BEVERLY HILLS, CA	90211
BOGAZIANOS, VASILI	ACTOR	165 W 46TH ST #409	NEW YORK, NY	10036
BOGDAN, THOMAS	TENOR	200 W 70TH ST #7-F	NEW YORK, NY	10023
BOGDANOVICH, MARY	ACTRESS	200 S SPAULDING DR #D	BEVERLY HILLS, CA	90212
BOGDANOVICH, PETER	FILM WRITER-DIRECTOR	212 COPA DE ORO RD	LOS ANGELES, CA	90077
BOGEN, JOY	SOPRANO	111 W 57TH ST #1209	NEW YORK, NY	10019
BOGERT, WILLIAM	ACTOR	247 S BEVERLY DR #102	BEVERLY HILLS, CA	90210
BOGGIANO, CARLO-CAPRA A	NEWS CORRESPONDENT	3601 S 2ND ST	ARLINGTON, VA	22204
BOGGS, BILL	TV HOST	WNEW-TV, 205 E 67TH ST	NEW YORK, NY	10021
BOGGS, JEFFREY PARK	DRUMMER	293 YELTON CT	NASHVILLE, TN	37211
BOGGS, RICHARD S	NEWS CORRESPONDENT	5213 WESTBARD AVE	BETHESDA, MD	20816
BOGGS, WADE	BASEBALL	599 MARMORA AVE	TAMPA, FL	33606
BOGLE, STEPHANIE	SOPRANO	VKD INTERNATIONAL ARTISTS		
		220 SHEPPARD AVE E		
		WILLOWDALE	TORONTO, ONT M2N 3A9	CANADA
BOHANNON, HAMILTON	SINGER	PHASE II, 189 N ORATON PKWY	EAST ORANGE, NJ	07017
BOHANNON, JIM	RADIO PERSONALITY	MUTUAL BROADCASTING SYSTEM		
		1755 S J DAVIS HWY	ARLINGTON, VA	22202
BOHANNON, JUDY	ACTRESS	439 S LA CIENEGA BLVD #120	BEVERLY HILLS, CA	90048

Name	Occupation	Address	City	Zip/Country
BOHAY, HEIDI	ACTRESS	9229 SUNSET BLVD #306	LOS ANGELES, CA	90069
BOHEM, ENDRE	SCREENWRITER	1629 N CRESCENT HGTS BLVD	LOS ANGELES, CA	90069
BOHEM, HILDA GORDON	SCREENWRITER	1629 N CRESCENT HGTS BLVD	LOS ANGELES, CA	90069
BOHL, DONALD A	DIRECTOR-PRODUCER	631 INTRACOASTAL DR	FORT LAUDERDALE, FL	33304
BOHL, STAR	WRITER	1818 COLLEGE CIR	LONG BEACH, CA	90815
BOHLIG, BLAIRE	ACTRESS	8721 SUNSET BLVD #203	LOS ANGELES, CA	90069
BOHN, CHRIS	ACTOR	205 NVAC AVE	PELHAM, NY	10803
BOHRER, ALEXANDER	COMPOSER	7810 LAUREL CANYON BLVD #11	NORTH HOLLYWOOD, CA	91605
BOHRER, CORINNE	ACTRESS	10390 SANTA MONICA BLVD #310	LOS ANGELES, CA	90025
BOISROND, MICHEL	FILM DIRECTOR	19 RUE DE LISBONNE	PARIS 75008	FRANCE
BOISSET, YVES	FILM DIRECTOR	248 BLVD RASPAIL	PARIS 75014	FRANCE
BOKAR, HAL	ACTOR	6723 KRAFT AVE	NORTH HOLLYWOOD, CA	91606
BOKHOF, EDWARD F	DIRECTOR	POMO TIERRA RANCH	YORKVILLE, CA	95494
BOKOVA, JANA	FILM-TV DIRECTOR	3 HOLLY VILLAS		
		WELLESLEY AVE	LONDON W6	ENGLAND
BOKY, COLETTE	SOPRANO	61 W 62ND ST #6-F	NEW YORK, NY	10023
BOLAM, JAMES	ACTOR	BURNETT, 42 GRAFTON HOUSE		
		2-3 GOLDEN SQ	LONDON W1	ENGLAND
BOLAND, EDDIE	GUITARIST	601 CALISTA RD	WHITE HOUSE, TN	37188
BOLAND, EUGENE	WRITER	8955 BEVERLY BLVD	LOS ANGELES, CA	90048
BOLAND, NORA	ACTRESS	208 S BEVERLY DR #8	BEVERLY HILLS, CA	90212
BOLCOM & MORRIS	MUSIC DUO	SHAW CONCERTS, 1995 BROADWAY	NEW YORK, NY	10023
BOLD, MARY DOUTHIT	PIANIST	3221 DUVAL ST	AUSTIN, TX	78705
BOLD LIGHTNING	ROCK & ROLL GROUP	POST OFFICE BOX 942	RAPID CITY, SD	57709
BOLDIZAR, JANE	ACTRESS	5312 RADFORD AVE #5	NORTH HOLLYWOOD, CA	91607
BOLDREY, RICHARD	CONDUCTOR	431 DEARBORN ST #1504	CHICAGO, IL	60605
BOLE, CLIFFORD	TV DIRECTOR	2049 CENTURY PARK E #1320	LOS ANGELES, CA	90067
BOLEN, GARY	ACTOR	2031 DRACENA DR #314	LOS ANGELES, CA	90027
BOLES, LANNY	DRUMMER	1728 HILLMONT DR	NASHVILLE, TN	37215
BOLES, WILLIAM	NEWS CORRESPONDENT	210 7TH ST, NW	WASHINGTON, DC	20003
BOLET, ALBERTO	CONDUCTOR	6328 E 5TH ST	LONG BEACH, CA	90803
BOLET, JORGE	PIANIST	CAMI, 165 W 57TH ST	NEW YORK, NY	10019
BOLGER, JOHN	ACTOR	10 E 44TH ST #700	NEW YORK, NY	10017
BOLINS, CHET	SINGER	POST OFFICE BOX 25	KENDALL PARK, NJ	08824
BOLKAN, FLORINDA	ACTRESS	2200 COLDWATER CANYON DR	BEVERLY HILLS, CA	90210
BOLLE, FRANK	CARTOONIST	TRIBUNE MEDIA SERVICES		
		64 E CONCORD ST	ORLANDO, FL	32801
BOLLEN, ROGER	CARTOONIST	36675 EAGLE RD	WILLOUGHBY HILLS, OH	44094
BOLLING, CLAUDE	SINGER	155 W 72ND ST #706	NEW YORK, NY	10023
BOLLING, CLAUDE	PIANIST	KURLAND, 173 BRIGHTON AVE	BOSTON, MA	02134
BOLLING, TIFFANY	ACTRESS	8019 1/2 MELROSE AVE #3	LOS ANGELES, CA	90046
BOLLINGER, JANE	WRITER	555 W 57TH ST #1230	NEW YORK, NY	10019
BOLO	WRESTLER	SEE - MASKED SUPERSTAR, THE		
BOLO, TERRY	ACTRESS	8484 WILSHIRE BLVD #235	BEVERLY HILLS, CA	90211
BOLO MONGOL	WRESTLER	SEE - MASKED SUPERSTAR, THE		
BOLOGNA, JOSEPH	ACT-WRI-DIR	613 ARDEN DR	BEVERLY HILLS, CA	90210
BOLOGNA, PHILIP	TENOR	AFFILIATE ARTISTS, INC		
		37 W 65TH ST, 6TH FLOOR	NEW YORK, NY	10023
BOLOTIN, CRAIG M	WRITER	1888 CENTURY PARK E #1400	LOS ANGELES, CA	90067
BOLSTER, STEPHEN	ACTOR	19 W 44TH ST #1500	NEW YORK, NY	10036
BOLT, BEN	TV DIRECTOR	30 STANHOPE GARDENS	LONDON SW7	ENGLAND
BOLT, JONATHAN	ACTOR	15 E 10TH ST	NEW YORK, NY	10003
BOLT, ROBERT	SCREENWRITER	64 CROCKFORD PARK RD		
		ADDLESTONE, WEYBRIDGE	SURREY	ENGLAND
BOLTE, GISELA	NEWS CORRESPONDENT	6952 KYLEAKIN CT	MC LEAN, VA	22101
BOLTINOFF, HENRY	CARTOONIST	KING FEATURES SYNDICATE		
		235 E 45TH ST	NEW YORK, NY	10017
BOLTON, EMILY	ACTRESS-SINGER	ICM, 388-396 OXFORD ST	LONDON W1	ENGLAND
BOMAN, DRAKE	ACTOR	439 S LA CIENEGA BLVD #11	LOS ANGELES, CA	90048
BOMB, ADAM, BAND	ROCK & ROLL GROUP	65 W 55TH ST #306	NEW YORK, NY	10019
BOMBECK, ERMA	WRITER-TV PERS	NEWS AMERICA SYNDICATE		
		1703 KAISER AVE	IRVINE, CA	92714
BOMSTER, MARK W	NEWS CORRESPONDENT	1803 BILTMORE ST #402, NW	WASHINGTON, DC	20009
BON JOVI	ROCK & ROLL GROUP	MC GHEE ENTERTAINMENT		
		240 CENTRAL PARK S	NEW YORK, NY	10019
BONACUM, LESLIE M	NEWS CORRESPONDENT	1718 CORCORAN ST, NW	WASHINGTON, DC	20009
BONADUCE, CELIA	WRITER	WALLERSTEIN, 9301 SUNSET BLVD	BEVERLY HILLS, CA	90210
BONADUCE, JOSEPH A	WRITER	4236 ENSENEDA DR	WOODLAND HILLS, CA	91364
BONAFEDE, DOM	NEWS CORRESPONDENT	4532 MACOMB ST, NW	WASHINGTON, DC	20016
BONANOME, FRANCO	TENOR	CAMI, 165 W 57TH ST	NEW YORK, NY	10019
BONAR, IVAN	ACTOR	1356 N GARDNER ST	LOS ANGELES, CA	90046
BONART, GARY	ACTOR	1607 N EL CENTRO AVE #23	LOS ANGELES, CA	90028
BONASSI, RAYMOND GENE	TV DIRECTOR	4317 REYES DR	TARZANA, CA	91356
BONATA, VINCE	ACTOR	1741 N IVAR AVE #221	HOLLYWOOD, CA	90028
BONAVERA, ALFREDO	CONDUCTOR	61 W 62ND ST #6-F	NEW YORK, NY	10023
BONAZZI, ELAINE	MEZZO-SOPRANO	LEW, 204 W 10TH ST	NEW YORK, NY	10014
BOND, DAVID	ACTOR	AIMEE, 13743 VICTORY BLVD	VAN NUYS, CA	91401
BOND, DAVID	NEWS CORRESPONDENT	3049 HEATHER LN	FALLS CHURCH, VA	22044
BOND, DEREK	ACTOR	BROOK HOUSE, 7 WOODLAND RD		
		BARNES COMMON	LONDON	ENGLAND
BOND, GARY	ACTOR	19 ELEANOR GROVE	LONDON SW13	ENGLAND
BOND, JULIAN	SCREENWRITER	A D PETERS & CO, LTD		
		10 BUCKINGHAM ST	LONDON WC2N 6BU	ENGLAND

Name	Occupation	Address	City/State	Zip/Country
BOND, LELAND B	COMPOSER	13524 RYE ST #7	SHERMAN OAKS, CA	91423
BOND, LILLIAN	ACTRESS	TESSIER, 9016 WHITE OAK	NORTHRIDGE, CA	91325
BOND, MICHAEL	ACTOR	211 S BEVERLY DR #201	BEVERLY HILLS, CA	90212
BOND, NANCY S	TV WRITER	8955 BEVERLY BLVD	LOS ANGELES, CA	90048
BOND, PHILIP	ACTOR	50 HIGH ST, ABERGWYLLF	WEST GAMORGAN SA13 3YN	ENGLAND
BOND, RALEIGH	ACTOR	POST OFFICE BOX 5617	BEVERLY HILLS, CA	90210
BOND, RUDOLPH "RUDY"	ACTOR	11 E 87TH ST	NEW YORK, NY	10028
BOND, SIMON	CARTOONIST	POST OFFICE BOX 4203	NEW YORK, NY	10017
BOND, STEVE	ACTOR	3608 GRAND CANAL ESPLANADE	MARINA DEL REY, CA	90292
BOND, TIMOTHY	WRITER	555 W 57TH ST #1230	NEW YORK, NY	10019
BOND, TOMMY	ACTOR	KFSN-TV, 177 "G" ST	FRESNO, CA	93706
BONDARCHUK, SERGEI	DIRECTOR	GORKEY ST 9	75 MOSCOW 9	USSR
BONDELLI, PHIL	DIRECTOR	21015 ARMINTA ST	CANOGA PARK, CA	91304
BONDS, GARY "U S"	SINGER	BROTHERS, 141 DUNBAR AVE	FORDS, NJ	08863
BONDY, SUSAN	COLUMNIST-RADIO PERS	NEWS AMERICA SYNDICATE		
		1703 KAISER AVE	IRVINE, CA	92714
BONE, WARREN	GUITARIST	721 BROWNLEE DR	NASHVILLE, TN	37205
BONELESS ONES, THE	ROCK & ROLL GROUP	POST OFFICE BOX 2081	BERKELEY, CA	94702
BONERZ, PETER	ACTOR-DIRECTOR	3637 LOWRY RD	LOS ANGELES, CA	90027
BONET, LISA	ACTRESS	8322 BEVERLY BLVD #202	LOS ANGELES, CA	90048
BONGOS, THE	ROCK & ROLL GROUP	3 E 54TH ST #1400	NEW YORK, NY	10022
BONI, JOHN	WRITER	7932 HILLSIDE AVE	LOS ANGELES, CA	90046
BONIFER, MICHAEL	TV WRITER	8955 BEVERLY BLVD	LOS ANGELES, CA	90048
BONILLA, HENRY	WRITER	555 W 57TH ST #1230	NEW YORK, NY	10019
BONITA	RHYTHM & BLUES GROUP	B D R MANAGEMENT COMPANY		
		2 DALLAS COMM COMPLEX		
		6309 N O'CONNOR ST #122	IRVINE, TX	75060
BONKOWSKI, JERRY	SPORTS WRITER	POST OFFICE BOX 500	WASHINGTON, DC	20044
BONN, RONALD	WRITER	555 W 57TH ST #1230	NEW YORK, NY	10019
BONNELL, JAY	ACTOR	327 E 93RD ST	NEW YORK, NY	10023
BONNELL, TERENCE A	COMPOSER	5985 DOVETAIL DR	AGOURA, CA	91301
BONNEMERE, EDWARD	COMPOSER	FINELL, 155 W 68TH ST	NEW YORK, NY	10023
BONNER, FRANK	ACTOR-DIRECTOR	10351 SANTA MONICA BLVD #211	LOS ANGELES, CA	90025
BONNER, MAJORIE	ACTRESS	344 N OAKHURST DR	BEVERLY HILLS, CA	90210
BONNER, TONY	ACTOR	1930 CENTURY PARK W #303	LOS ANGELES, CA	90067
BONNET, JAMES	TV WRITER	8955 BEVERLY BLVD	LOS ANGELES, CA	90048
BONNEY, BARBARA	SOPRANO	CAMI, 165 W 57TH ST	NEW YORK, NY	10019
BONNEY, ROBERT	WRITER	8955 BEVERLY BLVD	LOS ANGELES, CA	90048
BONO, CHER	SINGER-ACTRESS	SEE - CHER		
BONO, SONNY	ACT-SING-PROD	250 W CAMINO BUENA VISTA PK	PALM SPRINGS, CA	92262
BONO-COELHO, SUSIE	ACTRESS-MODEL	SEE - COELHO, SUSIE		
BONOFF, KARLA	SINGER-COMPOSER	1691 N CRESCENT HGTS BLVD	LOS ANGELES, CA	90069
BONOMO, OCTAVE	CONDUCTOR	5023 DELACROIX RD	ROLLING HILLS EST, CA	90274
BONSIGNORI, UMBERTO	TV DIRECTOR	115 W 86TH ST #4-D	NEW YORK, NY	10024
BONTA, VANNA	ACTRESS	2165 BEACHWOOD TERR	LOS ANGELES, CA	90068
BONVENTRI, PETER V	WRITER	555 W 57TH ST #1230	NEW YORK, NY	10019
BONYNGE, RICHARD	CONDUCTOR	COLBERT, 111 W 57TH ST	NEW YORK, NY	10019
BOODA, LARRY L	NEWS JOURNALIST	3170 N POLLARD ST	ARLINGTON, VA	22207
BOOGIE BOYS, THE	SOUL GROUP	HUSH PRODS, 231 W 58TH ST	NEW YORK, NY	10019
BOOKE, SORRELL	ACT-WRI-DIR	POST OFFICE BOX 1105	STUDIO CITY, CA	91604
BOOKER, BOB	TV WRITER-PRODUCER	ABC-TV, 4151 PROSPECT AVE	LOS ANGELES, CA	90027
BOOKER, SIMEON	NEWS CORRESPONDENT	114 DUDDINGTON PL, SE	WASHINGTON, DC	20003
BOOKER, SIMON	TV PRODUCER	60 GOLDNEY RD	LONDON W9	ENGLAND
BOOKER, SUE	TV DIRECTOR-PRODUCER	2870 N TOWNE AVE #158	POMONA, CA	91767
BOOKHULTZ, BRUCE W	NEWS CORRESPONDENT	19201 JERICHO DR	GAITHERSBURG, MD	20760
BOOKMAN, ROBERT	TV EXECUTIVE	1270 SUNSET PLAZA DR	LOS ANGELES, CA	90069
BOOKWALTER, DEVEREN	ACTOR-DIRECTOR	134 W 4TH ST	NEW YORK, NY	10012
BOOM, TAKA	SINGER	LE CLUB BOOM		
		83 RIVERSIDE DR	NEW YORK, NY	10024
BOOMTOWN RATS, THE	ROCK & ROLL GROUP	O'KELLY, 44 SEYMOUR PL	LONDON W1	ENGLAND
BOONE, ASHLEY	FILM EXECUTIVE	11955 PINNACLE PL	BEVERLY HILLS, CA	90210
BOONE, BRENDON	ACTOR	9601 WILSHIRE BLVD #GL-11	BEVERLY HILLS, CA	90210
BOONE, CHERRY	SINGER	904 N BEVERLY DR	BEVERLY HILLS, CA	90210
BOONE, DAN, JR	MUSIC ARRANGER	ROUTE #3, SNEED RD	FRANKLIN, TN	37064
BOONE, DANIEL K	MUSICIAN	5268 EDMONDSON PIKE #70	NASHVILLE, TN	37211
BOONE, DEBBY	SINGER	15315 MAGNOLIA BLVD #208	SHERMAN OAKS, CA	91403
BOONE, LARRY	SINGER	904 N BEVERLY DR	BEVERLY HILLS, CA	90210
BOONE, LINDY	SINGER	904 N BEVERLY DR	BEVERLY HILLS, CA	90210
BOONE, PAT	SINGER-ACTOR	904 N BEVERLY DR	BEVERLY HILLS, CA	90210
BOONE, RANDY	ACTOR	200 N ROBERTSON BLVD #308	BEVERLY HILLS, CA	90210
BOONE, TIM	SINGER	4810 OLD HICKORY BLVD #C-8	HERMITAGE, TN	37076
BOORMAN, JOHN	FILM DIRECTOR	THE GLEBE, ANNAMOE	COUNTY OF WICKLOW	IRELAND
BOORSTIN, JONATHAN	FILM DIRECTOR	4007 AVE DEL SOL	STUDIO CITY, CA	91604
BOORSTIN, PAUL TERRY	WRITER	9915 WESTWANDA DR	BEVERLY HILS, CA	90210
BOORSTIN, SHARON	WRITER	9915 WESTWANDA DR	BEVERLY HILLS, CA	90210
BOOSLER, ELAYNE	COMEDIENNE	1004 S LA JOLLA AVE	LOS ANGELES, CA	90035
BOOSTROM, DEBORA	MODEL	MODELS & PROMOTIONS AGENCY		
		8560 SUNSET BLVD, 10TH FLOOR	LOS ANGELES, CA	90069
BOOTH, ADRIAN	ACTOR	3922 GLENRIDGE DR	SHERMAN OAKS, CA	91423
BOOTH, ANTHONY	ACTOR	TUDOR SUITE, THE DEAN WATER		
		WILMSLOW RD, WOODFORD	CHESHIRE SK7 1RJ	ENGLAND
BOOTH, CONNIE	ACTRESS	CHATTO & LINNIT, LTD		
		PRINCE OF WALES THEATRE		
		COVENTRY ST	LONDON WC2	ENGLAND
BOOTH, EARL M	TV WRITER	10526 WYTON DR	LOS ANGELES, CA	90024

SHIRLEY BOOTH

ERNEST BORGNINE

DAVID BOWIE

BRUCE BOXLEITNER

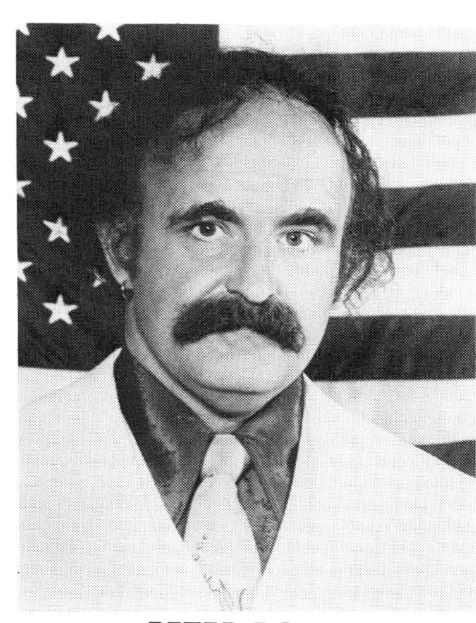

PETER BOYLE

EDDIE BRACKEN

KLAUS MARIA BRANDAUER

MARLON BRANDO

TERESA BREWER

Name	Occupation	Address	City	Zip
BOOTH, GEORGE	CARTOONIST	UNIVERSAL PRESS SYNDICATE		
		4900 MAIN ST, 9TH FLOOR	KANSAS CITY, MO	62114
BOOTH, JAMES	ACTOR	1901 AVE OF THE STARS #840	LOS ANGELES, CA	90067
BOOTH, JAMES	SCREENWRITER	8955 BEVERLY BLVD	LOS ANGELES, CA	90048
BOOTH, JERRY	ACTOR	LIGHT, 113 N ROBERTSON BLVD	LOS ANGELES, CA	90048
BOOTH, LOREE	CASTING DIRECTOR	TLC, 1580 CROSSROADS OF WORLD	LOS ANGELES, CA	90028
BOOTH, MARGARET	FILM EDITOR	ACE, 4416 1/2 FINLEY AVE	LOS ANGELES, CA	90027
BOOTH, PHILIP	BASS	PERLS, 7 W 96TH ST	NEW YORK, NY	10025
BOOTH, SHIRLEY	ACTRESS	POST OFFICE BOX 103	CHATHAM, MA	02633
BOOTH, THOMAS	TENOR	CAMI, 165 W 57 TH ST	NEW YORK, NY	10019
BOOTH, TRUDY	CASTING DIRECTOR	TLC, 1580 CROSSROADS OF WORLD	LOS ANGELES, CA	90028
BOOTHBY, VICTORIA	ACTRESS	HARTIG, 527 MADISON AVE	NEW YORK, NY	10022
BOOTHE, BECKY	PIANIST	747 N DUE WEST AVE	MADISON, TN	37115
BOOTHE, POWERS	ACTOR	4319 MANSON AVE	WOODLAND HILLS, CA	91364
BOOTSY	RHYTHM & BLUES GROUP	414 E WALNUT ST #920	CINCINNATI, OH	45202
BOOZELL, ANNE	NEWS CORRESPONDENT	AMERICAN UNIVERSITY		
		4400 MASSACHUSETTS AVE, NW	WASHINGTON, DC	20016
BOOZER, DIANE T	NEWS CORRESPONDENT	1111 18TH ST, NW	WASHINGTON, DC	20036
BORCHERT, CHARLES	GUITARIST	POST OFFICE BOX 886	MADISON, TN	37115
BORCHERT, DEBRAN	ACTRESS	6430 SUNSET BLVD #701	LOS ANGELES, CA	90028
BORCHERT, RUDOLPH	WRITER	28856 CLIFFSIDE DR	MALIBU, CA	90265
BORCHETTA, SCOTT CLARK	GUITARIST	303 REMBRANDT RD	OLD HICKORY, TN	37138
BORDE, MARK	FILM PRODUCER	1800 N HIGHLAND AVE #600	HOLLYWOOD, CA	90028
BORDE, SEYMOUR	FILM EXECUTIVE	1800 N HIGHLAND AVE #600	HOLLYWOOD, CA	90028
BORDEN, ALICE	ACTRESS	120 S VICTORY BLVD #104	BURBANK, CA	91502
BORDEN, DAVID	COMPOSER-MUSICIAN	ROHR & HOWLETT MGMT		
		425 RIVERSIDE DR	NEW YORK, NY	10025
BORDEN, EUGENE	NEWS CORRESPONDENT	1001 SPRING ST	SILVER SPRING, MD	20910
BORDEN, JASON J	COMPOSER	POST OFFICE BOX 480169	LOS ANGELES, CA	90048
BORDEN, JERRY DON	DRUMMER	309 MILLWOOD DR	NASHVILLE, TN	37217
BORDEN, LARRY	MUSICIAN	4601 PACKARD DR #C-288	NASHVILLE, TN	37211
BORDEN, LYNN	ACTRESS	16808 OAK VIEW DR	ENCINO, CA	91436
BORDEN, STEVE "JUSTICE"	WRESTLER	SEE - STING, BLADE RUNNER		
BORDEN, VIOLA	ACTRESS	SAMUELSON, 32-31 190TH ST	FLUSHING, NY	11358
BORDMAN, PAUL	ACTOR	348 E OLIVE AVE #K	BURBANK, CA	91502
BORDONALI, PETER	GUITARIST	205 CEDAR CREEK PL	NASHVILLE, TN	37205
BORELLI, CARLA	ACTRESS	320 E 57TH ST #12-C	NEW YORK, NY	10107
BORETZ, ALVIN	TV WRITER	1888 CENTURY PARK E #1400	LOS ANGELES, CA	90067
BORETZ, BENJAMIN	COMPOSER	RIVER RD	BARRYTOWN, NY	12504
BORG, BJORN	TENNIS	LIESTORIE AVENUE		
		PRINCESS GRACE	MONTE CARLO	MONACO
BORG, JOHN E	MUSICIAN	318 HARVARD AVE	NASHVILLE, TN	37205
BORG, RICHARD	ACTOR	200 W 57TH ST #1303	NEW YORK, NY	10019
BORGE, VICTOR	PIANIST	FIELDPOINT PARK	GREENWICH, CT	06830
BORGER, GLORIA	NEWS CORRESPONDENT	2813 35TH ST, NW	WASHINGTON, DC	20007
BORGERS, EDWARD W	TV WRITER	8955 BEVERLY BLVD	LOS ANGELES, CA	90048
BORGHI, DOUGLAS S	WRITER	8955 BEVERLY BLVD	LOS ANGELES, CA	90048
BORGIDA, DAVID	NEWS CORRESPONDENT	6507 ELGIN LN	BETHESDA, MD	20817
BORGMAN, JAMES	CARTOONIST	617 VINE ST	CINCINNATI, OH	45201
BORGMAN, KIT	WRITER	555 W 57TH ST #1230	NEW YORK, NY	10019
BORGNINE, ERNEST	ACTOR	3055 LAKE GLEN DR	BEVERLY HILLS, CA	90210
BORGNINE, TOVE	ACTRESS	3055 LAKE GLEN DR	BEVERLY HILLS, CA	90210
BORIS, ROBERT	FILM WRITER-DIRECTOR	8955 BEVERLY BLVD	LOS ANGELES, CA	90048
BORISOFF, NORMAN	TV WRITER	555 W 57TH ST #1230	NEW YORK, NY	10019
BORKOWSKI, MONICA C	NEWS CORRESPONDENT	2701 CONNECTICUT AVE, NW	WASHINGTON, DC	20008
BORLAND, CARROLL	ACTRESS	1643 EDGECLIFFE DR	LOS ANGELES, CA	90026
BORLAND, GLORIA C	NEWS CORRESPONDENT	10243 WINDING CREEK	GERMANTOWN, MD	20874
BORMAN, FRANK	ASTRONAUT	205 W BOULZ RD		
		BUILDING 4, SUITE #4	LAS CRUCES, NM	88005
BORMAN, GARY	TALENT AGENT	POST OFFICE BOX 5880	SHERMAN OAKS, CA	91413
BORMET, GARRY R	TV WRITER	8955 BEVERLY BLVD	LOS ANGELES, CA	90048
BORN, ROSCOE	ACTOR	ABC TELEVISION NETWORK		
		1330 AVE OF THE AMERICAS	NEW YORK, NY	10019
BORNE, HAL	COMPOSER-CONDUCTOR	8787 SHOREHAM DR #104	LOS ANGELES, CA	90069
BORNE, MATT	WRESTLER	WORLD CLASS WRESTLING		
		SOUTHWEST SPORTS, INC		
		DALLAS SPORTATORIUM		
		1000 S INDUSTRIAL BLVD	DALLAS, TX	75207
BORNSTEIN, STEVEN	TV EXECUTIVE	ESPN, ESPN PLAZA	BRISTOL, CT	06010
BOROFF, PHIL	ACTOR	BERZON, 336 E 17TH ST	COSTA MESA, CA	92627
BOROK, EMANUEL	CONCERTMAST	251 HUNTINGTON AVE	BOSTON, MA	02115
BOROWITZ, ANDY S	TV WRITER	289 BELOIT AVE	LOS ANGELES, CA	90049
BOROWITZ, SUSAN	WRITER	289 BELOIT AVE	LOS ANGELES, CA	90049
BORQUEZ, TIMOTHY JON	ACTOR	14234 HOYT ST	ARLETA, CA	91331
BORRELL, NEIL	DIRECTOR	305 RIVERSIDE DR	NEW YORK, NY	10025
BORRELLI, JIM	ACTOR	133 E ALHAMBRA RD	ALHAMBRA, CA	91801
BORSELLA, BILL	ACTOR	3045 ARROWHEAD DR	LOS ANGELES, CA	90068
BORSOS, PHILIP	FILM DIRECTOR	264 SEATON ST	TORONTO, ONT M5A 2T4	CANADA
BORTMAN, MICHAEL E	TV WRITER	4365 CHEVY CHASE DR	LA CANADA, CA	91011
BORTNICK, EVAN	TENOR	MUNRO, 334 W 72ND ST	NEW YORK, NY	10023
BORUT, TOM	ACTOR	15534 AQUA VERDE DR	LOS ANGELES, CA	90077
BORY, JEAN-MARL	ACTOR	AGENCIE F DE GAND		
		38 RUE DE LISBONNE	PARIS 75008	FRANCE
BORZAGE, FRANK E	NEWS CORRESPONDENT	1300 ARLINGTON RIDGE RD	ARLINGTON, VA	22202
BOSACKI, JEFFRY B	CONDUCTOR	7985 SANTA MONICA BLVD #109	LOS ANGELES, CA	90046

Name	Occupation	Address	City	Zip/Country
BOSARGE, BETTY B	NEWS CORRESPONDENT	3031 BORGE ST #311	OAKTON, VA	22124
BOSCHE, WILLIAM R	WRITER	4232 KLUMP AVE	NORTH HOLLYWOOD, CA	91602
BOSCO, PHILIP	ACTOR	10000 SANTA MONICA BLVD #305	LOS ANGELES, CA	90067
BOSHART, ED	NEWS CORRESPONDENT	3004 LEE HWY #D	ARLINGTON, VA	22201
BOSLEY, ROZ	ACTRESS	10850 RIVERSIDE DR #501	NORTH HOLLYWOOD, CA	91602
BOSLEY, TOM	ACTOR	2822 ROYSTON PL	BEVERLY HILLS, CA	90210
BOSMA, JOHN T	NEWS CORRESPONDENT	742 N EDISON ST	ARLINGTON, VA	22305
BOSNER, PAUL	TV DIRECTOR-PRODUCER	3327 MOCKINGBIRD LN	DALLAS, TX	75205
BOSS	ROCK & ROLL GROUP	319 PENSHURST ST	WILLOUGHBY NSW 2068	AUSTRALIA
BOSS, CLAY	STUNTMAN	3518 W CAHUENGA BLVD #300	LOS ANGELES, CA	90068
BOSSMAN, T	AUTHOR-COACH	2801 MEADOW LARK DR	SAN DIEGO, CA	92123
BOSSOM, BARBARA	ACTRESS	BOCHCO, 694 AMALFI DR	PACIFIC PALISADES, CA	90272
BOSTIC, KARL	WRITER	555 W 57TH ST #1230	NEW YORK, NY	10019
BOSTON	ROCK & ROLL GROUP	SR & D MANAGEMENT		
		1560 TRAPELO RD	WALTHAM, MA	02154
BOSTON, BERNIE	PHOTOGRAPHER	7809 LEWINSVILLE RD	MC LEAN, VA	22102
BOSTON, DAVID E	TV WRITER	8955 BEVERLY BLVD	LOS ANGELES, CA	90048
BOSTWICK, BARRY	ACTOR	2770 HUTTON DR	BEVERLY HILLS, CA	90210
BOSTWICK, EUGENIA	ACTRESS	3330 BARHAM BLVD #103	LOS ANGELES, CA	90068
BOSTWICK, HAROLD	ACTOR	8831 SUNSET BLVD #402	LOS ANGELES, CA	90069
BOSTWICK, JACKSON	ACTOR	HUNTER, 132 S LASKY DR	BEVERLY HILLS, CA	90212
BOSUSTOW, NICK	FILM PRODUCER	1156 GALLOWAY ST	PACIFIC PALISADES, CA	90272
BOSUSTOW, STEPHEN	FILM PRODUCER	1649 11TH ST	SANTA MONICA, CA	90404
BOSWELL, CHARLES	ACTOR	3800 BARHAM BLVD #303	LOS ANGELES, CA	90068
BOSWELL, TREVOR, TRAPEZE TROUPE	TRAPEZE TROUPE	HALL, 138 FROG HOLLOW RD	CHURCHVILLE, PA	18966
BOSWELL, VET	SINGER-ACTOR	801 PEMART AVE	PEEKSKILL, NY	10566
BOSWELL, VICTOR R, JR	PHOTOGRAPHER	35-H RIDGE RD, GREENBELT RD	GREENBELT, MD	20770
BOSWORTH, PATRICIA	WRITER	555 W 57TH ST #1230	NEW YORK, NY	10019
BOTCHIN, HILARY	CASTING DIRECTOR	ABC-TV ENTERTAINMENT CENTER		
		2020 AVE OF THE STARS	LOS ANGELES, CA	90067
BOTERO, MONICA	ACTRESS	1605 N CAHUENGA BLVD #202	LOS ANGELES, CA	90028
BOTHAM, NOEL	NEWS REPORTER	THE NATIONAL ENQUIRER		
		600 SE COAST AVE	LANTANA, FL	33464
BOTKIN, PERRY, JR	COMP-ARR-MUS	12999 BLAIRWOOD DR	STUDIO CITY, CA	91604
BOTSFORD, LINDA	NEWS CORRESPONDENT	600 N OVERLOOK DR	ALEXANDRIA, VA	22305
BOTTARO, PAM	ACTRESS	747 N LAFAYETTE PARK PL	LOS ANGELES, CA	90026
BOTTCHER, FRED	NEWS CORRESPONDENT	1699 S JOYCE ST #C-815	ARLINGTON, VA	22202
BOTTINI, IVY	ACTRESS	WILLIAMS-CIMINI AGENCY		
		816 N LA CIENGEGA BLVD	LOS ANGELES, CA	90069
BOTTLES, THE	VOCAL GROUP	9025 WILSHIRE BLVD #303	BEVERLY HILLS, CA	90211
BOTTNER, BARBARA	WRITER	803 N CITRUS AVE	LOS ANGELES, CA	90038
BOTTOMS, JOSEPH	ACTOR	1901 AVE OF THE STARS #840	LOS ANGELES, CA	90067
BOTTOMS, SAMUEL	ACTOR	10648 BLOOMFIELD ST	NORTH HOLLYWOOD, CA	91602
BOTTOMS, TIMOTHY	ACTOR	1790 LAS CANOAS RD	SANTA MONICA, CA	93105
BOTTORFF, DANA	NEWS CORRESPONDENT	1924 1/2 BILTMORE ST, NW	WASHINGTON, DC	20009
BOTTORFF, STEVE S	WRITER	555 W 57TH ST #1230	NEW YORK, NY	10019
BOTWINICK, AMY	ACTRESS	POST OFFICE BOX 4115	MALIBU, CA	90265
BOTZOW, RUFUS	THEATER PRODUCER	35 W 76TH ST	NEW YORK, NY	10023
BOTZUM, JOHN R	NEWS CORRESPONDENT	1101 RIDGE RD	ARLINGTON, VA	22202
BOUBOULIDI, RITA	PIANIST	756 7TH AVE #67	NEW YORK, NY	10019
BOUCHE, CLAUDINE	EDITOR	3 RUE NICOLO	PARIS 75016	FRANCE
BOUCHER, GENE	BARITONE	235 W 76TH ST	NEW YORK, NY	10023
BOUCHER, MICHELE	SOPRANO	CAMI, 165 W 57TH ST	NEW YORK, NY	10019
BOUCHER, SAVANNAH SMITH	ACTRESS	SF & A, 121 N SAN VICENTE BLVD	BEVERLY HILLS, CA	90211
BOUCHET, BARBARA	ACTRESS-MODEL	VIA TAGLIAMENTO 25	ROME	ITALY
BOUDREAU, LOU	BASEBALL	15600 ELLIS AVE	DOLTON, IL	60419
BOUDREAUX, PAUL	NEWS CORRESPONDENT	1404 N 12TH ST #24	ARLINGTON, VA	22209
BOUDROT, MEL	ACTOR	342 W 46TH ST	NEW YORK, NY	10036
BOUGAS, NICK	ARTIST-CARTOONIST	212 N GOLDEN MALL	BURBANK, CA	91502
BOUGHTON, EDWARD F	DIRECTOR-PRODUCER	114 GARDEN DR	ALBERTSON, NY	11507
BOUGHTON, VICTORIA	SPORTS WRITER-EDITOR	SPORTS ILLUSTRATED MAGAZINE		
		TIME & LIFE BUILIDNG		
		ROCKEFELLER CENTER	NEW YORK, NY	10020
BOUGIE, GARIN	ACTOR	6640 SUNSET BLVD #203	LOS ANGELES, CA	90028
BOUILLET, EDWARD E	SAXOPHONIST	278 INDIAN LAKE RD	HENDERSONVILLE, TN	37075
BOULANGER, DANIEL	WRITER	ARTMEDIA, 10 AVE GEORGE V	PARIS 75008	FRANCE
BOULANGER, LEON W	MANDOLINIST	204 TYNE BAY DR	HENDERSONVILLE, TN	37075
BOULAY, PETER C	WRITER	555 W 57TH ST #1230	NEW YORK, NY	10019
BOULAYE, PATTI	SINGER	33 CORK ST	LONDON W1	ENGLAND
BOULDER, DIZZY	WRESTLER	SEE - BEEFCAKE, BRUTUS		
BOULDER, EDDIE	WRESTLER	SEE - BEEFCAKE, BRUTUS		
BOULDER, TERRY "THE HULK"	WRESTLER	SEE - HOGAN, HULK		
BOULEY, FRANK	ACTOR	197 ELM AVE	TEANECK, NJ	07666
BOULEY, RAYMOND	WRITER	555 W 57TH ST #1230	NEW YORK, NY	10019
BOULEYN, KATHRYN	SOPRANO	CAMI, 165 W 57TH ST	NEW YORK, NY	10019
BOULEZ, PIERRE	COMPOSER-CONDUCTOR	POSTFACH 22	BADEN-BADEN	GERMANY
BOULTING, INGRID	ACTRESS	9229 SUNSET BLVD #306	LOS ANGELES, CA	90069
BOULTING, ROY	DIRECTOR-PRODUCER	8-A GLEBE PL	CHELSEA SW3	ENGLAND
BOULTON, MILO	ACTOR	469 N WATERWAY DR	SATELLITE BEACH, FL	32937
BOULWARE, BILL	TV WRITER	8955 BEVERLY BLVD	LOS ANGELES, CA	90048
BOURDON, JACQUES	FILM DIRECTOR	45 AVE DES TERNES	PARIS 75017	FRANCE
BOURDON STREET JASS BAND, THE	JAZZ GROUP	AARON, 25 HUNTINGTON AVE	BOSTON, MA	02116
BOURGHOLTZER, FRANK	NEWS CORRESPONDENT	1133 LINCOLN BLVD	SANTA MONICA, CA	90403
BOURGUIGNON, SERGE	FILM DIRECTOR	18 RUE DE CAL-MALTERRE	PARIS 75016	FRANCE
BOURJAILY, VANCE	NOVELIST	REDBIRD FARM ROUTE #3	IOWA CITY, IA	52240

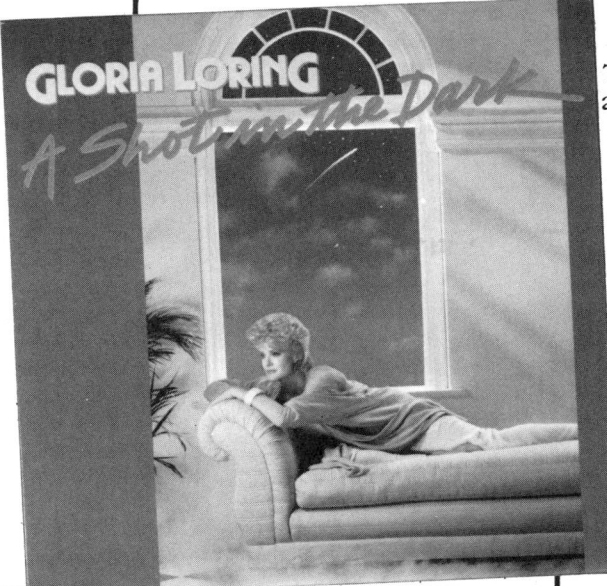

Name	Occupation	Address	City	Zip
BOURKE, RORY M	GUITARIST	212 ROBIN HILL RD	NASHVILLE, TN	37205
BOURNE, ST CLAIR C	WRITER	8955 BEVERLY BLVD	LOS ANGELES, CA	90048
BOURNE, STEVEN	ACTOR	1720 PACIFIC AVE #335	VENICE, CA	90291
BOURSEILLER, ANTOINE	ACTOR	15 RUE DE MIRIMESNI	PARIS 75008	FRANCE
BOUSSON, PATRICE Y	ACTRESS	484 S ROXBURY DR #102	BEVERLY HILLS, CA	90212
BOUTON, BRUCE	GUITARIST-DOBROIST	1402 CEDAR LN	NASHVILLE, TN	37212
BOUTROSS, THOMAS	DIRECTOR-PRODUCER	1952 N BEACHWOOD DR	HOLLYWOOD, CA	90068
BOVA, JOSEPH A	ACTOR	168 E 74TH ST	NEW YORK, NY	10021
BOVINO, PAUL	ACTOR	8820 SUNSET BLVD #ANB	LOS ANGELES, CA	90069
BOW, SIMMY	ACTOR	10000 RIVERSIDE DR #3	TOLUCA LAKE, CA	91602
BOWA, LARRY	BASEBALL	315 MAGNOLIA DR	CLEARWATER, FL	33516
BOWAB, JOHN	TV DIRECTOR	2598 GREENVALLEY RD	LOS ANGELES, CA	90046
BOWAN, SIBYL	ACTRESS	425 W 23RD ST	NEW YORK, NY	10011
BOWDEN, CHARLES	DIRECTOR-PRODUCER	919 3RD AVE	NEW YORK, NY	10022
BOWDEN, DORIS	ACTRESS	1108 TOWER RD	BEVERLY HILLS, CA	90210
BOWDEN, JOHN, JR	PHOTOGRAPHER	2621 SPENCER RD	CHEVY CHASE, MD	20815
BOWE, SHEILA M	TV DIRECTOR-PRODUCER	54 7TH AVE S	NEW YORK, NY	10014
BOWEN, ANNE	WRITER	555 W 57TH ST #1230	NEW YORK, NY	10019
BOWEN, DENNIS	ACTOR	11216 HORTENSE ST	NORTH HOLLYWOOD, CA	91602
BOWEN, EZRA	WRITER-EDITOR	TIME/TIME & LIFE BLDG ROCKEFELLER CENTER	NEW YORK, NY	10020
BOWEN, GARY L	DIRECTOR	74 WILLOW AVE	LARCHMONT, NY	10538
BOWEN, IAN C	NEWS CORRESPONDENT	1600 S JOYCE ST #1106	ARLINGTON, VA	22202
BOWEN, JERRY	NEWS CORRESPONDENT	CBS NEWS, 7800 BEVERLY BLVD	LOS ANGELES, CA	90036
BOWEN, KENNETH L	WRITER	555 W 57TH ST #1230	NEW YORK, NY	10019
BOWEN, LAUREL PAGE	ACTRESS	11216 HORTENSE ST	NORTH HOLLYWOOD, CA	91602
BOWEN, ROGER	ACTOR	9000 SUNSET BLVD #801	LOS ANGELES, CA	90069
BOWEN, TIMOTHY J	NEWS CORRESPONDENT	529 14TH ST, NW	WASHINGTON, DC	20045
BOWEN, VONNA	ACTRESS	8721 SUNSET BLVD #202	LOS ANGELES, CA	90069
BOWENS, CAROLYNE J	WRITER	8955 BEVERLY BLVD	LOS ANGELES, CA	90048
BOWER, ANTOINETTE	ACTRESS	1529 N BEVERLY GLEN BLVD	LOS ANGELES, CA	90024
BOWER, HOLLY	WRITER	555 W 57TH ST #1230	NEW YORK, NY	10019
BOWER, TOM	ACTOR	9220 SUNSET BLVD #625	LOS ANGELES, CA	90069
BOWERS, BILL	SINGER	POST OFFICE BOX 1025	BOERNE, TX	78006
BOWERS, EDWIN W	NEWS CORRESPONDENT	10204 TYBURN TERR	BETHESDA, MD	20814
BOWERS, ERIC L	WRITER	8955 BEVERLY BLVD	LOS ANGELES, CA	90048
BOWERS, GEORGE A	DIRECTOR-PRODUCER	6417 MARYLAND DR	LOS ANGELES, CA	90048
BOWERS, GEORGE A, JR	DIRECTOR	DGA, 7950 SUNSET BLVD	LOS ANGELES, CA	90046
BOWERS, LALLY	ACTRESS	37 ROSSLYN AVE	LONDON SW13	ENGLAND
BOWERS, RICHARD J	NEWS CORRESPONDENT	1827 KALORAMA RD, NW	WASHINGTON, DC	20008
BOWERS, WILLIAM	WRITER-PRODUCER	8955 BEVERLY BLVD	LOS ANGELES, CA	90048
BOWIE, DAVID	SINGER-ACTOR	641 5TH AVE #22-Q	NEW YORK, NY	10022
BOWIE, LESTER	MUSICIAN	ECM, 509 MADISON AVE	NEW YORK, NY	10022
BOWKER, JUDI	ACTRESS	147-149 WARDOUR ST	LONDON W1	ENGLAND
BOWKER, ROBERT E	TV DIRECTOR	11360 SUNSET BLVD	LOS ANGELES, CA	90049
BOWLER, ANTON	TV DIRECTOR-PRODUCER	5 CHEYNE PL	LONDON SW3	ENGLAND
BOWLER, RICHARD	ACTOR	930 2ND AVE	NEW YORK, NY	10022
BOWLES, BILLY	ACTOR	22127 BARBACOA DR	SAUGUS, CA	91350
BOWLES, PAUL	COMPOSER-WRITER	THE WILLIAM MORRIS AGENCY 1350 AVE OF THE AMERICAS	NEW YORK, NY	10019
BOWLES, PETER	ACTOR	LEADING ARTISTS, LTD 60 SAINT JAMES'S ST	LONDON SW1	ENGLAND
BOWLING, DAVE	GUITARIST	POST OFFICE BOX 643	MOUNT JULIET, TN	37122
BOWMAN, BERNADETTE	ACTRESS	CARPENTER, 1516-W REDWOOD ST	SAN DIEGO, CA	92101
BOWMAN, CHUCK	TV DIRECTOR-PRODUCER	5204 LA FOREST DR	LA CANADA, CA	91011
BOWMAN, DAVID	ACTOR	1350 N HIGHLAND AVE #24	HOLLYWOOD, CA	90028
BOWMAN, DAVID	ORGANIST	15 HIGH ST #621	HARTFORD, CT	06103
BOWMAN, DEREK	TALENT AGENT	1 UPPER BROOK ST	LONDON W1	ENGLAND
BOWMAN, EILEEN	ACTRESS	CARPENTER, 1516-W REDWOOD ST	SAN DIEGO, CA	92101
BOWMAN, GAIL	ACTRESS	536 1/2 N ORANGE DR	LOS ANGELES, CA	90036
BOWMAN, GLENN	NEWS CORRESPONDENT	4817 HALE HAVEN	ELLICOTT CITY, MD	21043
BOWMAN, JAMES	TENOR	CAMI, 165 W 57TH ST	NEW YORK, NY	10019
BOWMAN, LISA	ACTRESS	9300 WILSHIRE BLVD #410	BEVERLY HILLS, CA	90212
BOWMAN, PAMELA	ACTRESS	9105 CARMELITA AVE #1	BEVERLY HILLS, CA	90210
BOWMAN, TERESA	ACTRESS	15010 VENTURA BLVD #219	SHERMAN OAKS, CA	91403
BOWMAN, VALERIA	NEWS CORRESPONDENT	9208 SPRINGHILL LN #304	GREENBELT, MD	20770
BOWSER, DANIEL E	WRITER	8955 BEVERLY BLVD	LOS ANGELES, CA	90048
BOWSER, KEN	CARTOONIST	TRIBUNE MEDIA SERVICES 64 E CONCORD ST	ORLANDO, FL	32801
BOWSER, SUSAN R	PHOTOGRAPHER	3702 SHEPHERD ST	CHEVY CHASE, MD	20815
BOX, BETTY	FILM PRODUCER	PINEWOOD STUDIOS, IVER HEATH	BUCKS SLO ONH	ENGLAND
BOX, BILLY	GUITARIST	1431 18TH AVE	E MOLINE, IL	61244
BOX, BRENDA M	NEWS CORRESPONDENT	1000 WILSON BLVD	ROSSLYN, VA	22209
BOX, CHARLES D	MUSIS ARRANGER	119-B MASON AVE	NASHVILLE, TN	37202
BOX, EUEL	COMPOSER-CONDUCTOR	5930 BEEMAN AVE	NORTH HOLLYWOOD, CA	91607
BOX, JOHN	FILM PRODUCER	MORRIS, 147-149 WARDOUR ST	LONDON W1V 3TB	ENGLAND
BOX, THE	ROCK & ROLL GROUP	41 BRITAIN ST #200	TORONTO, ONT	CANADA
BOX, WILLIAM G	WRITER	12543 HARTLAND ST	NORTH HOLLYWOOD, CA	91605
BOXALL, JAMES A, JR	NEWS CORRESPONDENT	4439 PARK RD	ALEXANDRIA, VA	22312
BOXCAR WILLIE	SINGER	26949 CHAGRIN BLVD #203	CLEVELAND, OH	44122
BOXER, SARAH	WRITER-EDITOR	DISCOVER/TIME & LIFE BLDG ROCKEFELLER CENTER	NEW YORK, NY	10020
BOXLEITNER, BRUCE	ACTOR	24500 JOHN COLTER RD	HIDDEN HILLS, CA	91302

Name	Occupation	Address	City	Zip
BOXTOPS, THE	ROCK & ROLL GROUP	2011 FERRY AVE #U-19	CAMDEN, NJ	08104
BOY, NATURE	WRESTLING MASCOT	SEE - NATURE BOY		
BOY, PRETTY	WRESTLER	SEE - SOMERS, DOUG		
		"PRETTY BOY"		
BOY GEORGE	SINGER-COMPOSER	SEE - GEORGE, BOY		
BOYAJIAN, ARAM	WRITER-PRODUCER	50 W 96TH ST	NEW YORK, NY	10025
BOYAR, SULLY	ACTOR	166-40 21ST AVE	WHITESTONE, NY	11357
BOYCE, JOSEPH N	NEWS CORREPONDENT	TIME/TIME & LIFE BLDG		
		ROCKEFELLER CENTER	NEW YORK, NY	10020
BOYD, BONITA	FLUTIST	59 E 54TH ST #81	NEW YORK, NY	10022
BOYD, BRENDAN	COLUMNIST	UNIVERSAL PRESS SYNDICATE		
		4900 MAIN ST, 9TH FLOOR	KANSAS CITY, MO	62114
BOYD, CHARLES	ACTOR	3800 BARHAM BLVD #303	LOS ANGELES, CA	90068
BOYD, DENNIS "OIL CAN"	BASEBALL	1611 20TH ST	MERIDIAN, MS	39301
BOYD, DON	DIRECTOR-PRODUCER	BOYD'S, 9 GREAT NEWPORT ST	LONDON WC2	ENGLAND
BOYD, FORREST J	NEWS CORRESPONDENT	1333 "F" ST, NW	WASHINGTON, DC	20004
BOYD, GEORGE D	TV DIRECTOR	30 PALOMA AVE	VENICE, CA	90291
BOYD, GERALD M	NEWS CORRESPONDENT	1325 15TH ST #603, NW	WASHINGTON, DC	20005
BOYD, GUY	ACTOR	10000 SANTA MONICA BLVD #305	LOS ANGELES, CA	90067
BOYD, HAL H	CONDUCTOR	7234 HWY #9	FELTON, CA	95018
BOYD, JERRY D	NEWS CORRESPONDENT	1940 UPPER LAKE DR	RESTON, VA	22091
BOYD, JIMMY	ACTOR-SINGER	LIGHT, 113 N ROBERTSON BLVD	LOS ANGELES, CA	90048
BOYD, JOHN	NEWS CORRESPONDENT	4405 1ST PL S	ARLINGTON, VA	22204
BOYD, JOHN D	PHOTOGRAPHER	2621 SPENCER RD	CHEVY CHASE, MD	20815
BOYD, LIONA	GUITARIST	7060 HOLLYWOOD BLVD #1212	LOS ANGELES, CA	90028
BOYD, LIONA	GUITARIST	GURTMAN, 162 W 56TH ST	NEW YORK, NY	10019
BOYD, MARLEE	ACTRESS	95 ASPEN WY	ROLLING HILLS, CA	90274
BOYD, ROBERT SKINNER	NEWS CORRESPONDENT	5625 OGDEN ST	BETHESDA, MD	20816
BOYD, TAMYL	ACTRESS-SINGER	1304 S MANSFIELD AVE	LOS ANGELES, CA	90019
BOYER, DAVID S	PHOTOGRAPHER	9406 LOCUST HILL RD	BETHESDA, MD	20014
BOYER, RICHARD ALLEN	GUITARIST	POST OFFICE BOX 800	HENDERSONVILLE, TN	37075
BOYER, ROBERT D	PHOTOJOURNALIST	NBC-TV, NEWS DEPARTMENT	WASHINGTON, DC	20016
		4001 NEBRASKA AVE, NW	WASHINGTON, DC	20016
BOYETT, BOB	TV WRITER-PRODUCER	10124 EMPYREAN WY #201	LOS ANGELES, CA	90067
BOYETT, WILLIAM	ACTOR	LIGHT, 113 N ROBERTSON BLVD	LOS ANGELES, CA	90048
BOYETTE, MIKE	WRESTLER	MID SOUTH SPORTS, INC		
		UNIVERSAL WRESTLING		
		5001 SPRING VALLEY RD	DALLAS, TX	75244
BOYINGTON, GREGORY "PAPPY"	AVAITOR	1730 COLUMBIA DR E	FRESNO, CA	93727
BOYLAN, JOHN	SINGER	2015 NICHOLS CANYON RD	LOS ANGELES, CA	90046
BOYLAN, MARY	ACTRESS	400 W 58TH ST	NEW YORK, NY	10019
BOYLE, BARBARA	FILM EXECUTIVE	11600 SAN VICENTE ST	LOS ANGELES, CA	90049
BOYLE, BESS T	WRITER	8955 BEVERLY BLVD	LOS ANGELES, CA	90048
BOYLE, DONALD	WRITER-PRODUCER	3351 OAKDELL RD	STUDIO CITY, CA	91604
BOYLE, GARY	ACTOR	8730 SUNSET BLVD #400	LOS ANGELES, CA	90069
BOYLE, INEZ RODEN	CELLIST	4809 MERRILL LN	NASHVILLE, TN	37211
BOYLE, J DAVID, II	VIOLINIST	4809 MERRILL LN	NASHVILLE, TN	37211
BOYLE, JAMES F	WRITER	1832 W SILVER LAKE DR	LOS ANGELES, CA	90026
BOYLE, JOHN A	WRITER	8955 BEVERLY BLVD	LOS ANGELES, CA	90048
BOYLE, PETER	ACTOR	ROBBINS & STIELMAN		
		1700 BROADWAY	NEW YORK, NY	10019
BOYLE, ROBERT F	ART DIRECTOR	6904 LOS TILOS RD	LOS ANGELES, CA	90068
BOYLE, WILLIAM J	WRITER	555 W 57TH ST #1230	NEW YORK, NY	10019
BOYNTON, PETER	ACTOR	CBS TELEVISION NETWORK		
		"AS THE WORLD TURNS"		
		51 W 52ND ST	NEW YORK, NY	10019
BOYRIVEN, PATRICK	TV DIRECTOR	15622 ROYAL OAK RD	ENCINO, CA	91436
BOYS, THE	ROCK & ROLL GROUP	10020 PIONEER BLVD #B-104	SANTE FE SPRINGS, CA	90670
BOYS BRIGADE, THE	ROCK & ROLL GROUP	ATI, 888 7TH AVE, 21ST FLOOR	NEW YORK, NY	10106
BOYUM, MAURIE	ACTOR	5430 ROUND MEADOW RD	CALABASAS, CA	91302
BOYUM, STEPHEN M	DIRECTOR	5661 BUSCH DR	MALIBU, CA	90265
BOZICH, JOE	BODYBUILDER	POST OFFICE BOX 11883	FRESNO, CA	93775
BOZICK, PETER A	PHOTOGRAPHER	10420 THREE DOCTORS RD	DUNKIRK, MD	20754
BOZMAN, LARRY	WRITER	555 W 57TH ST #1230	NEW YORK, NY	10019
BOZZUFI, MARCEL	ACTOR	ARTMEDIA, 10 AVE GEORGE V	PARIS 75008	FRANCE
BRAASKMA, ROY	ACTOR	MARY CROSBY, 2130 4TH AVE	SAN DIEGO, CA	92101
BRABAZON, JAMES	WRITER-PRODUCER	36 KINGSWOOD RD, CHISWICK	LONDON W4 5ET	ENGLAND
BRABEAU, SUSAN	ACTRESS	1627 N PASS AVE	BURBANK, CA	91505
BRABLEC, RADEK A	NEWS CORRESPONDENT	2025 "M" ST, NW	WASHINGTON, DC	20036
BRABOURNE, LORD	FILM PRODUCER	G W FILMS COMPANY		
		41 MONTPELIER WALK	LONDON SW7	ENGLAND
BRACALI, GIAMPAOLO	CONDUCTOR	61 W 62ND ST #6-F	NEW YORK, NY	10023
BRACCI, TEDA	ACTRESS	7721 HOLLYWOOD BLVD #2	LOS ANGELES, CA	90046
BRACE, CLEMENT	ACTOR	1617 TOWER GROVE DR	BEVERLY HILLS, CA	90210
BRACH, BIRDIE	ACTRESS	5330 LANKERSHIM BLVD #210	NORTH HOLLYWOOD, CA	91601
BRACH, GERALD	SCREENWRITER	THE WRITERS GUILD		
		430 EDGEWARE RD	LONDON W2 1EH	ENGLAND
BRACHT, ROLAND	SINGER	CAMI, 165 W 57TH ST	NEW YORK, NY	10019
BRACK, REGINALD K, JR	PUBLISHING EXECUTIVE	LIFE/TIME & LIFE BLDG		
		ROCKEFELLER CENTER	NEW YORK, NY	10020
BRACK, WILLIAM DENNIS	PHOTOGRAPHER	3609 WOODHILL PL	FAIRFAX, VA	22030
BRACKEEN, JOANNE, TRIO	JAZZ TRIO	KEANE, 49 E 96TH ST	NEW YORK, NY	10028
BRACKEN, DOROTHY	ACTRESS	8075 W 3RD ST #303	LOS ANGELES, CA	90048
BRACKEN, EDDIE	ACTOR	69 DOUGLAS RD	GLEN RIDGE, NJ	07028
BRACKEN, PEG	ACTRESS	66 KAHANA PL	LAHAINA, HI	96761

Name	Occupation	Address	City	Zip
BRACKMAN, JACOB	SCREENWRITER	555 W 57TH ST #1230	NEW YORK, NY	10019
BRADBURY, JANET LANE	ACTRESS	651 ORCHARD DR	BURBANK, CA	91506
BRADBURY, RAY	AUTHOR	10265 CHEVIOT DR	LOS ANGELES, CA	90064
BRADDOCK, ROBERT	ACTOR	NEW, 300 E GLENOAKS BLVD	GLENDALE, CA	91207
BRADEE, RICHARD	NEWS CORRESPONDENT	6209 BARDU AVE	SPRINGFIELD, VA	22152
BRADEN, BERNARD	ACT-WRI-PROD	ADANAC, 2 OVINGTON SQ	LONDON SW3	ENGLAND
BRADEN, ELISABETH	SOPRANO	LEW, 204 W 10TH ST	NEW YORK, NY	10014
BRADEN, NANCY R	WRITER	555 W 57TH ST #1230	NEW YORK, NY	10019
BRADEN, THOMAS W	TV HOST	CNN, 1050 TECHWOOD DR, NW	ATLANTA, GA	30318
BRADFORD, ART	ACTOR	4421 KLING ST #4	BURBANK, CA	91505
BRADFORD, GREG	ACTOR	3752 REDWOOD AVE	LOS ANGELES, CA	90066
BRADFORD, HANK	TV WRITER	8955 BEVERLY BLVD	LOS ANGELES, CA	90048
BRADFORD, HAZEL M	NEWS CORRESPONDENT	2153 CALIFORNIA ST #604, NW	WASHINGTON, DC	20008
BRADFORD, JANE	WRITER	8955 BEVERLY BLVD	LOS ANGELES, CA	90048
BRADFORD, JOHN M	TV WRITER	8955 BEVERLY BLVD	LOS ANGELES, CA	90048
BRADFORD, LAURIE	NEWS CORRESPONDENT	1004 PALMER RD	FORT WASHINGTON, MD	20744
BRADFORD, RICHARD	ACTOR	SF & A, 121 N SAN VICENTE BLVD	BEVERLY HILLS, CA	90211
BRADFORD, RICHARD R	WRITER	8955 BEVERLY BLVD	LOS ANGELES, CA	90048
BRADFORD, ROBERT	FILM EXECUTIVE	350 5TH AVE	NEW YORK, NY	10118
BRADFORD, RONALD E	NEWS EDITOR	1450 SPRUCE TREE DR	DIAMOND BAR, CA	91765
BRADFORD, STEVE	PIANIST	6421 ORION AVE	VAN NUYS, CA	91406
BRADFORD, TERRY	ACTOR	32 BUXTON RD, STRATFORD	LONDON E15 1QU	ENGLAND
BRADLEE, BENJAMIN	JOURNALIST	1712 21ST ST, NW	WASHINGTON, DC	20009
BRADLEY, BOB	WRESTLER	POST OFFICE BOX 3859	STAMFORD, CT	06905
BRADLEY, DAI	ACTOR	LARRY DALZELL ASSOCIATES		
		126 KENNINGTON PARK RD	LONDON SE11	ENGLAND
BRADLEY, DAN	STUNTMAN	3518 W CAHUENGA BLVD #300	LOS ANGELES, CA	90068
BRADLEY, DAN	WRITER	8955 BEVERLY BLVD	LOS ANGELES, CA	90048
BRADLEY, DAVID	DIRECTOR	1781 N CRESCENT HGTS BLVD	HOLLYWOOD, CA	90069
BRADLEY, DEE DEE	CASTING DIRECTOR	6565 SUNSET BLVD, 4TH FLOOR	LOS ANGELES, CA	90028
BRADLEY, ED	NEWSCASTER	10 COLUMBUS CIR #1270	NEW YORK, NY	10019
BRADLEY, GWENDOLYN	SOPRANO	CAMI, 165 W 57TH ST	NEW YORK, NY	10019
BRADLEY, HAROLD RAY	GUITARIST-BANJOIST	303 BAYSHORE DR	HENDERSONVILLE, TN	37075
BRADLEY, JAMES	FILM DIRECTOR	1860 VERDUGO KNOLLS DR	GLENDALE, CA	91208
BRADLEY, JAMES L, JR	NEWS CORRESPONDENT	122 "C" ST, NW	WASHINGTON, DC	20001
BRADLEY, JAN	ACTRESS	9200 SUNSET BLVD #909	LOS ANGELES, CA	90069
BRADLEY, JERRY	GUITARIST	30 MUSIC SQUARE W	NASHVILLE, TN	37203
BRADLEY, JILL	SINGER	POST OFFICE BOX 111510	NASHVILLE, TN	37211
BRADLEY, KATHLEEN J	ACTRESS	4476 VICTORIA PARK DR	LOS ANGELES, CA	90019
BRADLEY, KITTY B	WRITER	8955 BEVERLY BLVD	LOS ANGELES, CA	90048
BRADLEY, MICHAEL	WRITER	555 W 57TH ST #1230	NEW YORK, NY	10019
BRADLEY, OWEN	PIANIST	1609 HAWKINS ST	NASHVILLE, TN	37203
BRADLEY, PAT "RICK"	WRITER	8955 BEVERLY BLVD	LOS ANGELES, CA	90048
BRADLEY, STEPHEN	ACTOR	10850 RIVERSIDE DR #501	NORTH HOLLYWOOD, CA	91602
BRADLEY, STEWART	ACTOR	8721 SUNSET BLVD #103	LOS ANGELES, CA	90069
BRADLEY, WILBERT	ACTOR	1509 N CRESCENT HGTS BLVD #7	LOS ANGELES, CA	90069
BRADSHAW, BOOKER	WRITER	1520 PRINCETON ST #1	SANTA MONICA, CA	90404
BRADSHAW, CHARLES	BODYBUILDER	POST OFFICE BOX 566155	OCEANSIDE, CA	92056
BRADSHAW, TERRY	ACTOR-FOOTBALL	POST OFFICE BOX 1607	SHREVEPORT, LA	71165
BRADSHAW, THOMAS	TENOR	111 W 57TH ST #1209	NEW YORK, NY	10019
BRADSHAW, THORNTON F	ENTERTAINMENT EXEC	RCA, 30 ROCKEFELLER PLAZA	NEW YORK, NY	10112
BRADSHAW & BUENO	PIANO DUO	POST OFFICE BOX U	REDDING, CT	06875
BRADY, BEN	WRITER	8955 BEVERLY BLVD	LOS ANGELES, CA	90048
BRADY, JERRY	DIRECTOR	POST OFFICE BOX 9026	MARINA DEL REY, CA	90292
BRADY, JOHN	WRITER	8955 BEVERLY BLVD	LOS ANGELES, CA	90048
BRADY, KATHLEEN	NEWS REPORTER	TIME/TIME & LIFE BLDG		
		ROCKEFELLER CENTER	NEW YORK, NY	10020
BRADY, KATHLEEN A	NEWS CORRESPONDENT	5110 38TH ST, NW	WASHINGTON, DC	20016
BRADY, MARY ELLEN	NEWS CORRESPONDENT	18617 CALYPSO PL	GAITHERSBURG, MD	20879
BRADY, PATRICK	ACTOR	3050 W 7TH ST #200	LOS ANGELES, CA	90005
BRADY, PAUL	SINGER	DAMAGE MGMT, 192 WALTON	LONDON SW3	ENGLAND
BRADY, RAY	NEWS CORRESPONDENT	CBS NEWS, 524 W 57TH ST	NEW YORK, NY	10019
BRADY, RUTH	ACTRESS	ROAD, 11180 VALLEY SPRING PL	NORTH HOLLYWOOD, CA	91602
BRAEDEN, ERIC	ACTOR	13723 ROMANY DR	PACIFIC PALISADES, CA	90272
BRAENDEL, GREGORY	ACTOR	6126 GLEN ALDER ST	LOS ANGELES, CA	90068
BRAFA, TONY	ACTOR	12121 LA MAIDA ST #17	NORTH HOLLYWOOD, CA	91607
BRAFF, DAVID	TV WRITER	2818 HIGHLAND AVE	SANTA MONICA, CA	90405
BRAFFORD, ELIZABETH	WRITER	555 W 57TH ST #1230	NEW YORK, NY	10019
BRAGDON, PETER	NEWS CORRESPONDENT	2912 18TH ST, NW	WASHINGTON, DC	20009
BRAGG, CHARLES	WRITER	8955 BEVERLY BLVD	LOS ANGELES, CA	90048
BRAGG, GEORGIA	ACTRESS	2019 PONTIUS AVE	LOS ANGELES, CA	90025
BRAGG, MELVYN	TV WRITER	12 HAMPSTEAD HILL GARDE	LONDON NW3	ENGLAND
BRAHA, HERB	ACTOR	1433 N ORANGE GROVE AVE	LOS ANGELES, CA	90046
BRAHM, JOHN	FILM DIRECTOR	19419 PACIFIC COAST HWY	MALIBU, CA	90265
BRAINARD, WENDY	ACTRESS	3800 BARHAM BLVD #303	LOS ANGELES, CA	90068
BRAITHWAITE, KEN	NEWS CORRESPONDENT	1702 SUMMIT PL #405, NW	WASHINGTON, DC	20009
BRAKE, PATRICIA	ACTRESS	44 PERRYN RD	LONDON W3 7NA	ENGLAND
BRALVER, BOB	STUNTMAN	3518 W CAHUENGA BLVD #300	LOS ANGELES, CA	90068
BRALVER, CHARLENE	TV WRITER	17589 CAMINO YATASTO	PACIFIC PALISADES, CA	90272
BRALVER, ROBERT	TV WRITER-DIRECTOR	17589 CAMINO YATASTO	PACIFIC PALISADES, CA	90272
BRAME, WILLIAM	FILM DIRECTOR	1111 HEATHERSIDE RD	PASADENA, CA	91105
BRAMLEY, WILLIAM	ACTOR	19101 ARCHWOOD ST	RESEDA, CA	91335
BRAMS, DICK	PRODUCER	MCA/UNIVERSAL STUDIOS, INC		
		100 UNIVERSAL CITY PLAZA	UNIVERSAL CITY, CA	91608
BRANCATO, ROBIN F	WRITER	555 W 57TH ST #1230	NEW YORK, NY	10019

Name	Occupation	Address	City	ZIP
BRANCH, WILLIAM	PLAYWRIGHT	53 CORTLANDT AVE	NEW ROCHELLE, NY	10801
BRANCHAUD, GARY	GUITARIST	410 SUNSET DR	MOUNT JULIET, TN	37122
BRANCHE, GLENWOOD	WRITER	555 W 57TH ST #1230	NEW YORK, NY	10019
BRAND, ANTHONY	TV DIRECTOR	3253 BENDA ST	LOS ANGELES, CA	90068
BRAND, DAVID	WRITER-EDITOR	TIME/TIME & LIFE BLDG		
		ROCKEFELLER CENTER	NEW YORK, NY	10020
BRAND, JOSHUA	TV WRITER	11400 CHENAULT ST	LOS ANGELES, CA	90049
BRAND, LARRY	TV WRITER	8955 BEVERLY BLVD	LOS ANGELES, CA	90048
BRAND, OSCAR	SINGER	360 CENTRAL PARK W #16-G	NEW YORK, NY	10025
BRAND, ROBERT N	WRITER	8383 WILSHIRE BLVD #923	BEVERLY HILLS, CA	90211
BRAND, SYBIL	ACTRESS	703 N REXFORD DR	BEVERLY HILLS, CA	90210
BRANDA, RICHARD	ACTOR	8945 MC LENNAN LN	SEPULVEDA, CA	91343
BRANDAUER, KLAUS MARIA	ACTRESS	BARTENSTEINGASSE 8/9	A-1010 VIENNA	AUSTRIA
BRANDEIS, RUTH	ACTRESS	47 8TH AVE #4	NEW YORK, NY	10014
BRANDEL, MARC	TV WRITER	8955 BEVERLY BLVD	LOS ANGELES, CA	90048
BRANDES, DAVID	WRITER	8428 MELROSE PL #C	LOS ANGELES, CA	90069
BRANDES, RALPH H	DIRECTOR	DGA, 110 W 57TH ST	NEW YORK, NY	10019
BRANDIN, MARC	ACTOR	1725 CAMINO PALMERO ST	LOS ANGELES, CA	90046
BRANDIS, ROLF W	WRITER-PRODUCER	1022 SHERIDAN RD	EVANSTON, IL	60202
BRANDMAN, MICHAEL	TV WRITER	2062 N VINE ST	HOLLYWOOD, CA	90068
BRANDNER, GARY	SCREENWRITER	8955 BEVERLY BLVD	LOS ANGELES, CA	90048
BRANDO, MARLON	ACTOR-DIRECTOR	12900 MULHOLLAND DR	BEVERLY HILLS, CA	90210
BRANDON, BRUMSIC, JR	CARTOONIST	210 RUSHMORE ST	WESTBURY, NY	11590
BRANDON, GEORGE F	NEWS CORRESPONDENT	11719 GALT AVE	WHEATON, MD	20902
BRANDON, HENRY	ACTOR	1033 N SPALDING AVE	LOS ANGELES, CA	90046
BRANDON, HENRY	CONDUCTOR	300 N STATE ST	CHICAGO, IL	60610
BRANDON, JOHN	ACTOR	8350 SANTA MONICA BLVD #103	LOS ANGELES, CA	90069
BRANDON, MICHAEL	ACTOR	453 S BARRINGTON AVE	LOS ANGELES, CA	90049
BRANDON, MILTON	CLOWN	2701 COTTAGE WY #14	SACRAMENTO, CA	95825
BRANDON, PRISCILLA THAYER	NEWS CORRESPONDENT	11719 GALT AVE	WHEATON, MD	20902
BRANDON BULL, THE	WRESTLER	SEE - ORNDORFF, PAUL		
		"MR WONDERFUL"		
BRANDS, X	ACTOR	17171 ROSCOE BLVD #104	NORTHRIDGE, CA	91325
BRANDSTEIN, EVE	TV PRODUCER	EMBASSY TV, 1438 N GOWER ST	LOS ANGELES, CA	90028
BRANDSTETTER, JOHN	BARITONE	AFFILIATE ARTISTS, INC		
		37 W 65TH ST, 6TH FLOOR	NEW YORK, NY	10023
BRANDT, ANDREW	WRITER	555 W 57TH ST #1230	NEW YORK, NY	10019
BRANDT, CARL	COMPOSER	11758 BLIX ST	NORTH HOLLYWOOD, CA	91607
BRANDT, DONNA M	NEWS CORRESPONDENT	NBC-TV, NEWS DEPARTMENT		
		4001 NEBRASKA AVE, NW	WASHINGTON, DC	20016
BRANDT, EDWARD A	COMPOSER	POST OFFICE BOX 3232	NORTH HOLLYWOOD, CA	91609
BRANDT, ELLEN	ACTRESS	8900 BURTON WY #204	BEVERLY HILLS, CA	90211
BRANDT, FRANK M	DIRECTOR	DGA, 7950 SUNSET BLVD	LOS ANGELES, CA	90046
BRANDT, GEOFF	LITERARY AGENT	9000 SUNSET BLVD #1200	LOS ANGELES, CA	90069
BRANDT, HANK	ACTOR	CONTEMPORARY ARTISTS		
		132 S LASKY DR	BEVERLY HILLS, CA	90212
BRANDT, JANET	ACTRESS	1625 SUMMITRIDGE DR	BEVERLY HILLS, CA	90210
BRANDT, MIA D	WRITER	555 W 57TH ST #1230	NEW YORK, NY	10019
BRANDT, MICHAEL	ACT-WRI-DIR	WEALD HOUSE, PLUCKLEY	KENT	ENGLAND
BRANDT, SHELLEY	SINGER	NBA, 2605 NORTHRIDGE DR	GARLAND, TX	75043
BRANDT, THOMAS D	NEWS CORRESPONDENT	3212 WOODLAND AVE	ALEXANDRIA, VA	22304
BRANDT, VICTOR	ACTOR	859 CAMINO COLIBRI	CALABASAS, CA	91302
BRANDT, YANNA KROYT	WRITER-PRODUCER	1349 LEXINGTON AVE	NEW YORK, NY	10028
BRANDZEL, ROBERT	CONDUCTOR	15760 MORRISON ST	ENCINO, CA	91436
BRANEGAN, JAY	NEWS CORRESPONDENT	2129 FLORIDA AVE, NW	WASHINGTON, DC	20008
BRANIGAN, LAURA	SINGER-SONGWRITER	GRAND, 128 N LA PEER DR	BEVERLY HILLS, CA	90211
BRANNAN, SPADY	GUITARIST	2708 W LINDEN AVE	NASHVILLE, TN	37212
BRANNEN, RALPH	ACTOR	1038 1/2 S ORANGE DR	LOS ANGELES, CA	90019
BRANNING, PENELOPE	ACTRESS	1071 S ORANGE GROVE AVE	LOS ANGELES, CA	90019
BRANNON, DEL	SINGER	POST OFFICE BOX 171132	NASHVILLE, TN	37217
BRANNON, KIPPI	SINGER	BINKLEY, 1322 SPRINGFIELD	VILLAGEVILLE, TN	37072
BRANNON, PAUL	GUITARIST	6025 CORTEZ CT	HERMITAGE, TN	37076
BRANNON, THOMAS	GUITARIST	4400 BELMONT PARK TERR	NASHVILLE, TN	37215
BRANSCOME, JAMES	NEWS CORRESPONDENT	5901 MOUNT EAGLE	ALEXANDRIA, VA	22303
BRANSON, ALLEGRA	WRITER	555 W 57TH ST #1230	NEW YORK, NY	10019
BRANTLEY, STEPHEN L	GUITARIST	4332 KENILWOOD DR	NASHVILLE, TN	37204
BRAO, LYNNE F	WRITER	8955 BEVERLY BLVD	LOS ANGELES, CA	90048
BRASCIA, DOMINICK	ACTOR	12725 VENTURA BLVD #E	STUDIO CITY, CA	91604
BRASCIA, JOHN F	SCREENWRITER	8955 BEVERLY BLVD	LOS ANGELES, CA	90048
BRASERO, EL	WRESTLER	CAPITOL INTERNATIONAL		
		11844 MARKET ST	NORTH LIMA, OH	44452
BRASH, PETER	WRITER	555 W 57TH ST #1230	NEW YORK, NY	10019
BRASHAR, JAIE	WRITER	8703 KATHERINE AVE	VAN NUYS, CA	91402
BRASON, JOHN	TV WRITER	GRAHAM'S FIELD	GORING ON THAMES	ENGLAND
BRASS CONSTRUCTION	SOUL GROUP	850 7TH AVE #1102	NEW YORK, NY	10019
BRASSELLE, BEN	TRUMPETER	1705 TAMMANY DR	NASHVILLE, TN	37206
BRASSOUR, CLAUDE	ACTOR	ARTMEDIA, 10 AVE GEORGE	PARIS 75008	FRANCE
BRASWELL, DAVID	DRUMMER	138 KAREN DR	MOUNT JULIET, TN	37122
BRASWELL, JERRY	GUITARIST	527 HICKORY VIEW DR	NASHVILLE, TN	37211
BRASWELL BROTHERS, THE	C & W GROUP	VB, 5520 14TH ST W	BRADENTON, FL	33507
BRATCHER, JOE	ACTOR	131 S ORANGE DR	LOS ANGELES, CA	90036

Name	Occupation	Address	City	Zip
BRATH, ELOMBE	WRITER	555 W 57TH ST #1230	NEW YORK, NY	10019
BRATMAN, STEVEN E	WRITER	555 W 57TH ST #1230	NEW YORK, NY	10019
BRAUCHLI, BERNARD	HARPSICHORD	POST OFFICE BOX 131	SPRINGFIELD, VA	22150
BRAUDE, LAURIE	ACTOR	24 PARK AVE	VENICE, CA	90291
BRAUDY, SUSAN	WRITER-EDITOR	US MAGAZINE COMPANY		
		1 DAG HAMMARSKJOLD PLAZA	NEW YORK, NY	10017
BRAUN, CLIFFORD H	DIRECTOR	1846 MISSION HILL LN	NORTHBROOK, IL	60062
BRAUN, DAVID	RECORD EXECUTIVE	716 N ELM DR	BEVERLY HILLS, CA	90210
BRAUN, JOSEF	COMPOSER	500 N MAIN ST	SPRINGDALE, AR	72764
BRAUN, JUDITH	WRITER	555 W 57TH ST #1230	NEW YORK, NY	10019
BRAUN, VICTOR	BARITONE	CAMI, 165 W 57TH ST	NEW YORK, NY	10019
BRAUN, ZEV	FILM PRODUCER	97 FREMONT PL	LOS ANGELES, CA	90005
BRAUNER, ASHER	ACTOR	10000 SANTA MONICA BLVD #305	LOS ANGELES, CA	90067
BRAUNSTEIN, GENE H	TV WRITER	8955 BEVERLY BLVD	LOS ANGELES, CA	90048
BRAUNSTEIN, GEORGE G	PRODUCER	1001 N KENTER AVE	LOS ANGELES, CA	90049
BRAUNSTEIN, LAURA	SCREENWRITER	1001 N KENTER AVE	LOS ANGELES, CA	90049
BRAUS, MORTIMER	WRITER	410 S HAUSER BLVD	LOS ANGELES, CA	90036
BRAVER, RITA	NEWS CORRESPONDENT	CBS NEWS, 2020 "M" ST, NW	WASHINGTON, DC	20036
BRAVERMAN, BART	ACTOR	823 S PLYMOUTH BLVD #10	LOS ANGELES, CA	90005
BRAVERMAN, CHUCK	TV DIRECTOR-PRODUCER	1237 7TH ST	SANTA MONICA, CA	90401
BRAVERMAN, DAVID	WRITER	8955 BEVERLY BLVD	LOS ANGELES, CA	90048
BRAVERMAN, MARVIN	TV WRITER	8955 BEVERLY BLVD	LOS ANGELES, CA	90048
BRAVERMAN, MICHAEL	TV PRODUCER	MCA/UNIVERSAL STUDIOS, INC		
		100 UNIVERSAL CITY PLAZA	UNIVERSAL CITY, CA	91608
BRAVERMAN, MICHAEL B	TV WRITER-DIRECTOR	3636 DELLVALE PL	ENCINO, CA	91436
BRAVERMAN, ROBERT	DIRECTOR	69 MARION AVE	MERRICK, NY	11556
BRAVO, DINO	WRESTLER	POST OFFICE BOX 3859	STAMFORD, CT	06905
BRAWLEY, PEGGY	REPORTER	TIME & PEOPLE MAGAZINE		
		TIME & LIFE BUILDING		
		ROCKEFELLER CENTER	NEW YORK, NY	10020
BRAWNER, DONALD	PHOTOGRAPHER	4313 3RD ST, NW	WASHINGTON, DC	20011
BRAWNER, WAYNE	DRUMMER	154 CHIPPENDALE DR	HENDERSONVILLE, TN	37075
BRAXTON, ANTHONY	MUSICIAN-COMPOSER	2490 CHANNING WY #406	BERKELEY, CA	94704
BRAXTON, MARY D	NEWS CORRESPONDENT	4461 CONNECTICUT AVE, NW	WASHINGTON, DC	20008
BRAXTON, STEPHANIE	ACTRESS-WRITER	500 S SEPULVEDA BLVD #510	LOS ANGELES, CA	90049
BRAYFIELD, DOUGLAS	COMPOSER-LYRICIST	3815 W OLIVE AVE #202	BURBANK, CA	91505
BRAYNE, WILLIAM	TV DIRECTOR	31 HOLLAND PARK	LONDON W11	ENGLAND
BRAYTON, MARIAN	TV PRODUCER	CBS-TV, 6121 SUNSET BLVD	LOS ANGELES, CA	90028
BRAZAITIS, THOMAS J	NEWS CORRESPONDENT	2302 COLSTON DR	SILVER SPRING, MD	20910
BRAZDA, JEROME F	NEWS CORRESPONDENT	3767 KELLER AVE	ALEXANDRIA, VA	22302
BRAZIL, BO BO	WRESTLER	CAPITOL INTERNATIONAL		
		11844 MARKET ST	NORTH LIMA, OH	44452
BRAZIL, SCOTT	TV PRODUCER	MTM, 4024 RADFORD AVE	STUDIO CITY, CA	91604
BRAZZI, ROSANNO	ACTOR	VIA G B MARTINI 13	ROME	ITALY
BREAGY, JAMES C	NEWS CORRESPONDENT	2924 N 2ND ST	ARLINGTON, VA	22201
BREAKS, THE	ROCK & ROLL GROUP	ICM, 40 W 57TH ST	NEW YORK, NY	10019
BREAM, JULIAN	GUITARIST	SHAW CONCERTS, 1995 BROADWAY	NEW YORK, NY	10023
BREAST, WINIFRED	AUTO HARPIST	2410 VALLEY BROOK RD	NASHVILLE, TN	37215
BREATHED, BERKE	CARTOONIST	THE WASHINGTON POST		
		WRITERS GROUP		
		1150 15TH ST, NW	WASHINGTON, DC	20071
BREAUX, MARC	DIRECTOR	6090 HAROLD WY	HOLLYWOOD, CA	90028
BRECHER, IRVING	WRITER-PRODUCER	10590 WILSHIRE BLVD #1001	LOS ANGELES, CA	90024
BRECHER, JIM	TV WRITER-PRODUCER	LORIMAR-TELEPICTURES		
		3970 OVERLAND AVE	CULVER CITY, CA	90230
BRECHNER, DANIEL	NEWS CORRESPONDENT	1755 S JEFFERSON DAVIS HWY	ARLINGTON, VA	22202
BRECK, PETER	ACTOR	9744 WILSHIRE BLVD #306	BEVERLY HILLS, CA	90212
BRECKMAN, ANDREW	TV WRITER	555 W 57TH ST #1230	NEW YORK, NY	10019
BRECKNER, DENNIS	ACTOR	6736 LAUREL CANYON BLVD #306	NORTH HOLLYWOOD, CA	91606
BREDEMAN, DANIEL	WRITER	555 W 57TH ST #1230	NEW YORK, NY	10019
BREDEMEIER, JUDI	NEWS CORRESPONDENT	6111 MOONPATTERNS TRAIL	FAIRFAX STATION, VA	22039
BREDEMEIER, KENNETH H	NEWS CORRESPONDENT	6111 MOONPATTERNS TRAIL	FAIRFAX STATION, VA	22039
BREDHOFF, SUSAN	ACTRESS	1310 E ORANGE GROVE BLVD	PADADENA, CA	91104
BREDOUW, JEROME	WRITER	3394 CHARLESTON WY	LOS ANGELES, CA	90068
BREDWELL, MERLE E	TV DIRECTOR	4 RANCH RD	UPPER SADDLE RIVER, NJ	07458
BREE, BARLEY	MUSICIAN	170 CAMERON DR	HOLLAND, PA	18966
BREECE, NANCY	SOPRANO	45 W 60TH ST #4-K	NEW YORK, NY	10023
BREECH, KATHRYN	ACTRESS	ABRAMS ARTISTS & ASSOCIATES		
		420 MADISON AVE, 14TH FLOOR	NEW YORK, NY	10017
BREEDEN, GENE	GUITARIST	139 ROBERTA DR	HENDERSONVILLE, TN	37075
BREEN, DANNY	ACTOR-COMEDIAN	POST OFFICE BOX 2350	HOLLYWOOD, CA	90078
BREEN, NELSON E	WRITER	555 W 57TH ST #1230	NEW YORK, NY	10019
BREEN, PAULETTE	ACTRESS	8721 SUNSET BLVD #103	LOS ANGELES, CA	90069
BREESE, ELEANOR B	WRITER	8955 BEVERLY BLVD	LOS ANGELES, CA	90048
BREESE, PENELOPE	PHOTOGRAPHER	616 "D" ST, NE	WASHINGTON, DC	20002
BREEZE, CRYSTAL	ACTRESS	C-V, 1029 N HARPER AVE	LOS ANGELES, CA	90046
BREGER, MARTIN L	SAXOPHONIST	1913 OAKHAMPTON PL	BRENTWOOD, TN	37027
BREGMAN, BUDDY	DIRECTOR-PRODUCER	4155 WITZEL DR	SHERMAN OAKS, CA	91423
BREGMAN, ELI JOSEPH	WRITER	11338 JOFFRE ST	LOS ANGELES, CA	90049
BREGMAN, MARTIN	FILM PRODUCER	MCA/UNIVERSAL STUDIOS, INC		
		100 UNIVERSAL CITY PLAZA	UNIVERSAL CITY, CA	91608
BREGMAN, ROBERT M	WRITER	8955 BEVERLY BLVD	LOS ANGELES, CA	90048
BREGMAN, SUZANNE	ACTRESS	4155 WITZEL DR	SHERMAN OAKS, CA	91423
BREGMAN, SUZANNE L	WRITER	8955 BEVERLY BLVD	LOS ANGELES, CA	90048

BREGMAN, TRACEY E	ACTRESS	1723 SAN YSIDRO DR	BEVERLY HILLS, CA	90210
BREGONZI, ALEC	ACTOR	36 KNOLL RD, WANDSWORTH	LONDON SW18 2DF	ENGLAND
BREHM, GREGORY A	WRITER	8955 BEVERLY BLVD	LOS ANGELES, CA	90048
BREIMER, STEPHEN	SCREENWRITER	5030 1/2 LEMON GROVE AVE	LOS ANGELES, CA	90029
BREINER, CARY M	WRITER	555 W 57TH ST #1230	NEW YORK, NY	10019
BREINER, JERRY	GUITARIST	POST OFFICE BOX 341	OJAI, CA	93023
BRELAND, DON	GUITARIST	329 ROCKLAND RD	HENDERSONVILLE, TN	37075
BREMER, LESLEE	MODEL	POST OFFICE BOX 7211	MOUNTAIN VIEW, CA	94043
BREMER, WILLIAM R	TV WRITER	8955 BEVERLY BLVD	LOS ANGELES, CA	90048
BREMERS, BEVERLY	SINGER	WILLIAMSON, 932 N LA BREA AVE	LOS ANGELES, CA	90038
BREMNER, BRIAN	NEWS CORRESPONDENT	3934 MILITARY RD, NW	WASHINGTON, DC	20015
BREMSETH, LLOYD	ACTOR	1217 GREENACRE AVE	LOS ANGELES, CA	90046
BREN, GENE	CONDUCTOR	14726 KILLION ST	VAN NUYS, CA	91401
BRENAN, GERALD	WRITER	ALHAURIN EL GRANDE	MALAGA	SPAIN
BRENDEL, ALFRED	PIANIST	COLBERT, 111 W 57TH ST	NEW YORK, NY	10019
BRENDEL, WOLFGANG	BARITONE	CAMI, 165 W 57TH ST	NEW YORK, NY	10019
BRENDER, MARK E	NEWS CORRESPONDENT	4419 N 7TH ST	ARLINGTON, VA	22203
BRENLIN, GEORGE	ACTOR	7565 MULHOLLAND DR	LOS ANGELES, CA	90046
BRENNA, SUSAN	NEWS CORRESPONDENT	3002 RODMAN ST #303, NW	WASHINGTON, DC	20008
BRENNA, TONY	NEWS REPORTER	THE NATIONAL ENQUIRER		
		600 SE COAST AVE	LANTANA, FL	33464
BRENNAN, ALLISON	ACTRESS	243 W 4TH ST	NEW YORK, NY	10014
BRENNAN, EILEEN	ACTRESS	4256 BECK AVE	NORTH HOLLYWOOD, CA	91604
BRENNAN, MELISSA	ACTRESS	KNBC-TV, "DAYS OF OUR LIVES"		
		3000 W ALAMEDA AVE	BURBANK, CA	91523
BRENNAN, MISSY	ACTRESS	SEE - BRENNAN, MELISSA		
BRENNAN, ROBERT E	TV WRITER	8955 BEVERLY BLVD	LOS ANGELES, CA	90048
BRENNAN, TERI	ACTRESS	230 E 32ND ST	NEW YORK, NY	10016
BRENNAN, WALTER A, JR	DIRECTOR-PRODUCER	17829 TULSA ST	GRANADA HILLS, CA	91344
BRENNAN, WILLIAM C	DIRECTOR	33 NEWBURY ST	BOSTON, MA	02116
BRENNEIS, GERD	TENOR	111 W 57TH ST #1209	NEW YORK, NY	10019
BRENNER, ALBERT	ART DIRECTOR	10100 SANTA MONICA BLVD #1600	LOS ANGELES, CA	90067
BRENNER, ALFRED	WRITER	708 GREENTREE RD	PACIFIC PALAISADES, CA	90272
BRENNER, DAVID	COMEDIAN	THE WILLIAM MORRIS AGENCY		
		1350 AVE OF THE AMERICAS	NEW YORK, NY	10019
BRENNER, DORI	ACTRESS	649 N HUNTLEY DR	LOS ANGELES, CA	90069
BRENNER, EVE	ACTRESS	STAR, 17502 PARTHENIA ST	NORTHRIDGE, CA	91325
BRENNER, HARVEY B	TV WRITER	8955 BEVERLY BLVD	LOS ANGELES, CA	90048
BRENNER, LEONARD	ART DIRECTOR	MAD MAGAZINE, INC		
		485 MADISON AVE	NEW YORK, NY	10022
BRENNER, RAY	WRITER	6517 MATILIJA AVE	VAN NUYS, CA	91401
BRENNERT, ALAN	TV WRITER	14010 CAPTAINS ROW DR #343	MARINA DEL REY, CA	90292
BRENT, EVE	ACTRESS	SEE - ASHE, EVE BRENT		
BRENTWOOD, MICHAEL	TV WRITER	555 W 57TH ST #1230	NEW YORK, NY	10019
BRESCINO, ADOLPHO	WRESTLER	SEE - BRAVO, DINO		
BRESEE, BOBBIE	ACTRESS-MODEL	POST OFFICE BOX 1222	HOLLYWOOD, CA	90028
BRESH, TOM	SINGER	3907 W ALAMEDA AVE #101	BURBANK, CA	91505
BRESLER, FENTON	TV WRITER	9 WOODWARD SQ	LONDON W14 8DP	ENGLAND
BRESLER, SANDY	TALENT AGENT	15760 VENTURA BLVD #1730	ENCINO, CA	91436
BRESLOW, LOU	WRITER	825 GRETNA GREEN WY #O	LOS ANGELES, CA	90049
BRESLOW, MARC	DIRECTOR	9454 WILSHIRE BLVD #405	BEVERLY HILLS, CA	90212
BRESNAN, WILLIAM	CABLE EXECUTIVE	GROUP W CABLE, 888 7TH AVE	NEW YORK, NY	10106
BRESNIKOFF, BORIS	WRESTLER	SEE - VOLKOFF, NIKOLAI		
BRESSLAW, BERNARD	ACTOR	THE NORMAN PAYNE AGENCY		
		28 QUEENS RD, WEYBRIDGE	SURREY KT13 9UT	ENGLAND
BRESSLER, CHARLES	TENOR	KAPLAN, 115 COLLEGE ST	BURLINGTON, VT	05401
BRESSLER, JACOV	CASTING DIRECTOR	5330 LANKERSHIM BLVD #205	NORTH HOLLYWOOD, CA	91601
BRESSON, ROBERT	FILM DIRECTOR	49 QUAI DE BOURBON	PARIS 75004	FRANCE
BREST, MARTIN	FILM WRITER-DIRECTOR	207 N SWALL DR	BEVERLY HILLS, CA	90211
BRESTOFF, RICHARD	ACTOR	4621 COUNCIL ST #3	LOS ANGELES, CA	90004
BRETNOR, REGINALD	WRITER	FARQUHARSON, 250 W 57TH ST	NEW YORK, NY	10107
BRETONNIERRE, JEAN	ACTOR	21 RUE DES FOURGERES	PARIS 75020	FRANCE
BRETT, GEORGE	BASEBALL	POST OFFICE BOX 1969	KANSAS CITY, MO	64141
BRETT, JEREMY	ACTOR	8322 BEVERLY BLVD #202	LOS ANGELES, CA	90048
BREVIG, PER	MUSICIAN	JUILLIARD SCHOOL OF MUSIC		
		LINCOLN CENTER	NEW YORK, NY	10023
BREWARY, FRANCIS	PHOTOGRAPHER	4119 BAFFIN BAY LN	ROCKVILLE, MD	20853
BREWED	ROCK & ROLL GROUP	BIRD, 4905 S ATLANTIC AVE	DAYTONA BEACH, FL	32019
BREWER, BOB	NEWS CORRESPONDENT	206 11TH ST, SE	WASHINGTON, DC	20003
BREWER, EUGENE	GUITARIST	ROUTE #3, BOX 94	CHARLOTTE, TN	37036
BREWER, GEOF	STUNTMAN	3518 W CAHUENGA BLVD #300	LOS ANGELES, CA	90068
BREWER, JAMES	ACTOR	AIMEE, 13743 VICTORY BLVD	VAN NUYS, CA	91401
BREWER, JAMESON	SCREENWRITER	8955 BEVERLY BLVD	LOS ANGELES, CA	90048
BREWER, NORM	NEWS CORRESPONDENT	8509 BRADMOOR DR	BETHESDA, MD	20817
BREWER, TERESA	SINGER	394 PINEBROOK BLVD	NEW ROCHELLE, NY	10803
BREWER, TIMOTHY	GUITARIST	ROUTE #1, BOX 324	GREENBRIER, TN	37073
BREWER, WILLIAM C, JR	NEWS CORRESPONDENT	2438 20TH ST, NW	WASHINGTON, DC	20009
BREWINGTON, PETER	SPORTS WRITER	POST OFFICE BOX 500	WASHINGTON, DC	20044
BREWSTER, CAROL	ACTRESS	8721 W SUNSET BLVD #203	LOS ANGELES, CA	90069
BREWSTER, D K	SINGER	PAU, RUSTIC ACRES	JASPER, IN	47546
BREWSTER, DIANE	ACTRESS	9255 SUNSET BLVD #610	LOS ANGELES, CA	90069
BREWSTER, STEVE	DRUMMER	314 CRESTWOOD DR	TULLAHOMA, TN	37338

Name	Occupation	Address	City	Zip/Country
BREWSTER, TODD	WRITER-REPORTER	LIFE/TIME & LIFE BLDG		
		ROCKEFELLER CENTER	NEW YORK, NY	10020
BREWTON, MAIA	ACTRESS	KELMAN, 7813 SUNSET BLVD	LOS ANGELES, CA	90046
BREY, CARTER	CELLIST	ICM, 40 W 57TH ST	NEW YORK, NY	10019
BREZ, ETHEL M	TV WRITER	ABC-TV, "ONE LIFE TO LIVE"		
		1330 AVE OF THE AMERICAS	NEW YORK, NY	10019
BREZ, MELVIN E	TV WRITER	ABC-TV, "ONE LIFE TO LIVE"		
		1330 AVE OF THE AMERICAS	NEW YORK, NY	10019
BREZANY, EUGENE, III	ACTOR	6339 IVARENE AVE	HOLLYWOOD, CA	90068
BREZNER, BRETT	FILM EDITOR	3239 DERONDA DR	HOLLYWOOD, CA	90068
BREZNER, LARRY	FILM-TV PRODUCER	3239 DERONDA DR	HOLLYWOOD, CA	90068
BRIALY, JEAN-CLAUDE	ACTOR	3 PL DES VOSGES	PARIS 75004	FRANCE
BRIAN, DAVID	ACTOR	3922 GLENRIDGE DR	SHERMAN OAKS, CA	91423
BRIANT, MICHAEL E	FILM-TV DIRECTOR	LONDON MANAGEMENT, LTD		
		235-241 REGENT ST	LONDON W1A 2JT	ENGLAND
BRIANT, SHANE	ACTOR	THE RICHARD STONE AGENCY		
		18 YORK BUILDINGS, ADELPHI	LONDON WC2	ENGLAND
BRIARHOPPERS, THE	BLUEGRASS GROUP	POST OFFICE BOX 25371	CHARLOTTE, NC	28212
BRICE, JOHN	DIRECTOR	2929 LAS ALTURAS ST	LOS ANGELES, CA	90068
BRICK	SOUL GROUP	11355 W OLYMPIC BLVD #555	LOS ANGELES, CA	90064
BRICK, EDDIE	SINGER	POST OFFICE BOX C	RIVER EDGE, NJ	07661
BRICKELL, BETH	WRITER-DIRECTOR	DGA, 7950 SUNSET BLVD	LOS ANGELES, CA	90046
BRICKELL, CLAUDE	ACTOR	7250 FRANKLIN AVE #911	LOS ANGELES, CA	90046
BRICKEN, JULES	DIRECTOR	POST OFFICE BOX 3641	INCLINE VILLAGE, NV	89450
BRICKER, REBECCA	WRITER-EDITOR	PEOPLE/TIME & LIFE BLDG		
		ROCKEFELLER CENTER	NEW YORK, NY	10020
BRICKHOUSE, JACK	RADIO ANNOUNCER	2501 W BRADLEY PL	CHICAGO, IL	60618
BRICKMAN, MARSHALL	FILM WRITER-DIRECTOR	BERNSTEIN & FREEDMAN CO		
		228 W 55TH ST, 2ND FLOOR	NEW YORK, NY	10019
BRICKMAN, MORRIE	CARTOONIST	KING FEATURES SYNDICATE		
		235 E 45TH ST	NEW YORK, NY	10017
BRICKMAN, PAUL M	FILM WRITER-DIRECTOR	10100 SANTA MONICA BLVD #1600	LOS ANGELES, CA	90067
BRICUSSE, LESLIE	COMPOSER-LYRICIST	1106 SAN YSIDRO DR	BEVERLY HILLS, CA	90210
BRIDGES, ALAN J S	TV DIRECTOR	THE OLD MANOR FARM		
		CHRUCH ST		
		SUNBURY-ON-THAMES	MIDDLESEX TWIG GRG	ENGLAND
BRIDGES, ALICIA	SINGER	SECOND WAVE RECORDS		
		4400 MARKET ST	OAKLAND, CA	94608
BRIDGES, BEAU	ACTOR-DIRECTOR	EBM, 132 S RODEO DR	BEVERLY HILLS, CA	90212
BRIDGES, BETTY	ACTRESS	KOHNER, 9169 SUNSET BLVD	LOS ANGELES, CA	90069
BRIDGES, JACK	ACTOR	8949 SUNSET BLVD #203	LOS ANGELES, CA	90069
BRIDGES, JAMES	FILM WRITER-DIRECTOR	449 SKYEWIAY RD	LOS ANGELES, CA	90049
BRIDGES, JAMES, JR	ACTOR	20253 ELKWOOD ST	CANOGA PARK, CA	91306
BRIDGES, JEFF	ACTOR	436 ADELAIDE	SANTA MONICA, CA	90402
BRIDGES, JERRY	GUITARIST	1225 HABER DR	BRENTWOOD, TN	37027
BRIDGES, JIM	GUITARIST	2904 WESTERN HILLS DR	NASHVILLE, TN	37214
BRIDGES, LLOYD	ACTOR	225 LORING AVE	LOS ANGELES, CA	90024
BRIDGES, STANLEY	COMPOSER	10233 OVERLAND TRAIL	CHERRY VALLEY, CA	92223
BRIDGES, TODD	ACTOR	17260 RAVEN ST	NORTHRIDGE, CA	91306
BRIDGEWATER, DEE DEE	SINGER-ACTRESS	POST OFFICE BOX 5617	BEVERLY HILLS, CA	90210
BRIDGHAM, KENNETH R	PHOTOJOURNALIST	5804 BROADMORE ST	ALEXANDRIA, VA	22310
BRIDGMAN, ANNE C	NEWS CORRESPONDENT	1727 MASSACHUSETTS AVE #715	WASHINGTON, DC	20036
BRIERS, RICHARD	ACTOR	ICM, 388-396 OXFORD ST	LONDON W1	ENGLAND
BRIGADE, THE	ROCK & ROLL TRIO	POST OFFICE BOX 67-A-64	LOS ANGELES, CA	90067
BRIGANTI, ALBERT J	WRITER	555 W 57TH ST #1230	NEW YORK, NY	10019
BRIGGLE, STOCKTON F	TV DIRECTOR-PRODUCER	6217 GLEN AIRY DR	LOS ANGELES, CA	90068
BRIGGS, DAVID	HARPSICHORDIST	GELFAND-MACNOW MGMT		
		5 MUSIC CIRCLE N	NASHVILLE, TN	37203
BRIGGS, JOE BOB	COLUMNIST	UNIVERSAL PRESS SYNDICATE		
		4900 MAIN ST, 9TH FLOOR	KANSAS CITY, MO	62114
BRIGGS, JOHNNY	ACTOR	99 WILTON ST, SOUTHBRIDGE	WEST MIDLANDS	ENGLAND
BRIGGS, RICHARD A	WRITER	8955 BEVERLY BLVD	LOS ANGELES, CA	90048
BRIGGS, ROBERT	BASS	119 W 57TH ST #1015	NEW YORK, NY	10019
BRIGGS, SHAWN TIMOTHY	NEWS CORRESPONDENT	2939 NEWARK ST, NW	WASHINGTON, DC	20008
BRIGGS, SUSAN	NEWS CORRESPONDENT	215 WALES ALLEY	ALEXANDRIA, VA	22314
BRIGHAM, RED	SINGER	WCME, 2 HAWKES AVE	OSSINING, NY	10562
BRIGHT, JOHN	WRITER	8955 BEVERLY BLVD	LOS ANGELES, CA	90048
BRIGHT, JOHN R	GUITARIST	2209 ABBOTT MARTIN RD	NASHVILLE, TN	37215
BRIGHT, KEVIN S	WRITER	8955 BEVERLY BLVD	LOS ANGELES, CA	90048
BRIGHT, PETER	TV DIRECTOR	1901 LEMOYNE ST	LOS ANGELES, CA	90026
BRIGHT, RICHARD S	ACTOR	36 E 57TH ST	NEW YORK, NY	10022
BRIGHT, ROBERT A	CONDUCTOR	500 N BUNDY DR	LOS ANGELES, CA	90049
BRIGHT, RONNELL L	COMPOSER-CONDUCTOR	211 W 56TH ST #31-E	NEW YORK, NY	10019
BRIGHTMAN, HOMER H	WRITER	8955 BEVERLY BLVD	LOS ANGELES, CA	90048
BRIGHTMAN, SAMUEL C	NEWS CORRESPONDENT	6308 CRATHIE LN	BETHESDA, MD	20016
BRIGHTON ROCK	ROCK & ROLL GROUP	41 BRITAIN ST #200	TORONTO, ONT	CANADA
BRIGLIA, RICHARD E	TV DIRECTOR-PRODUCER	587 1ST AVE #2-R	NEW YORK, NY	10016
BRIGNARDELLO, MIKE	GUITARIST	399 TANGLEWOOD CT	NASHVILLE, TN	37211
BRILES, CHARLES	ACTOR	18312 SCHOOLCRAFT ST	RESEDA, CA	91335
BRILEY, DONNA	ACTRESS	9744 WILSHIRE BLVD #306	BEVERLY HILLS, CA	90212
BRILEY, JOHN	TV WRITER	TREVONE, 24 HIGHLAND RD	BUCKINGSHIRE	ENGLAND
BRILEY, JOHN RICHARD	SCREENWRITER	ICM, 40 W 57TH ST	NEW YORK, NY	10019
BRILEY, MARTIN	SINGER-SONGWRITER	POST OFFICE BOX 7451	NEW YORK, NY	10022
BRILL, CHARLIE	ACTOR	6310 SAN VICENTE BLVD #407	LOS ANGELES, CA	90048

Name	Occupation	Address	City	ZIP
BRILL, MARTY	ACTOR-WRITER	19375 ROSITA ST	TARZANA, CA	91356
BRILLSTEIN, BERNIE	TALENT AGENT	912 N CRESCENT DR	BEVERLY HILLS, CA	90210
BRILLSTEIN, LEIGH	TALENT AGENT	912 N CRESCENT DR	BEVERLY HILLS, CA	90210
BRIM, MARGARET L	WRITER	555 W 57TH ST #1230	NEW YORK, NY	10019
BRIMHALL, CYNTHIA	MODEL	MODELS & PROMOTIONS AGENCY		
		8560 SUNSET BLVD, 10TH FLOOR	LOS ANGELES, CA	90069
BRIMLEY, WILFRED	ACTOR	1888 CENTURY PARK E #1400	LOS ANGELES, CA	90067
BRIN, SUSANNAH	ACTRESS	3508 MOORE ST	LOS ANGELES, CA	90066
BRINCKERHOFF, BURT	TV DIRECTOR	151 S EL CAMINO DR	BEVERLY HILLS, CA	90212
BRINCKERHOFF, PETER A	DIRECTOR	393 W END AVE	NEW YORK, NY	10024
BRINE, MARK	GUITARIST	1113 FORREST AVE #C	NASHVILLE, TN	37206
BRINEGAR, PAUL	ACTOR	17322 HALSEY ST	GRANADA HILLS, CA	91344
BRINGELSON, MARK	ACTOR	1538 N DETROIT ST #6	LOS ANGELES, CA	90046
BRINKLEY, CHRISTIE	MODEL-ACTRESS	344 E 59TH ST	NEW YORK, NY	10022
BRINKLEY, DAVID	TV HOST	ABC-TV, NEWS DEPARTMENT		
		1717 DE SALES ST, NW	WASHINGTON, DC	20036
BRINKLEY, DONALD	WRITER-PRODUCER	22626 PACIFIC COAST HWY	MALIBU, CA	90265
BRINKLEY, JOEL	NEWS CORRESPONDENT	2224 39TH PL, NW	WASHINGTON, DC	20007
BRINKLEY, JOHN	NEWS CORRESPONDENT	8008 WELLINGTON RD	ALEXANDRIA, VA	22308
BRION, KEITH	CONDUCTOR	SHAW CONCERTS, 1995 BROADWAY	NEW YORK, NY	10023
BRISBIN, DAVID	ACTOR	ABC-TV, "ALL MY CHILDREN"		
		1330 AVE OF THE AMERICAS	NEW YORK, NY	10019
BRISCOE, JIMMY	ACTOR	10000 RIVERSIDE DR #3	TOLUCA LAKE, CA	91602
BRISCOE, ROBERT	ACTOR	10000 RIVERSIDE DR #3	TOLUCA LAKE, CA	91602
BRISEBOIS, DANIELLE	ACTRESS	20044-42 CHASE ST	CANOGA PARK, CA	91306
BRISK, BARRY	CONDUCTOR	5450 FENWOOD AVE	WOODLAND HILLS, CA	91364
BRISKER, GORDON I	COMPOSER	7 CONCORD SQ #2	BOSTON, MA	02118
BRISKER, GORDON, QUINTET	JAZZ QUINTET	POST OFFICE BOX 48081	LOS ANGELES, CA	90048
BRISKER, MITCHELL	FILM DIRECTOR	3675 FREDONIA DR	LOS ANGELES, CA	90068
BRISKEY, JACKLYNN BURROD	CASTING DIRECTOR	3970 OVERLAND AVE #700	CULVER CITY, CA	90230
BRISKIN, MORT	WRITER-PRODUCER	146 N ALMONT DR #4	LOS ANGELES, CA	90048
BRISLIN, RAY D	PHOTOGRAPHER	3717 N NELSON ST	ARLINGTON, VA	22207
BRISLIN, RAYMOND D	NEWS CORRESPONDENT	3132 "M" ST, NW	WASHINGTON, DC	20007
BRISTOW, BOYD	SINGER	220 CAPITOL VIEW DR #B	NASHVILLE, TN	37207
BRISTOW, MELISSA STAR	NEWS CORRESPONDENT	1401 S BARTON ST #224	ARLINGTON, VA	22204
BRITAIN, RADIE	COMPOSER	1945 N CURSON ST	LOS ANGELES, CA	90046
BRITISH BULLDOGS, THE	WRESTLING DUO	POST OFFICE BOX 3859	STAMFORD, CT	06905
BRITO, ALBERT E	TV DIRECTOR	312 N WILLAND ST	SAN FRANCISCO, CA	94118
BRITO, TERESITA	NEWS CORRESPONDENT	444 N CAPITOL ST, NW	WASHINGTON, DC	20001
BRITT, ANDREW	TV WRITER	8955 BEVERLY BLVD	LOS ANGELES, CA	90048
BRITT, ANGELA	NEWS CORRESPONDENT	407 NAILEY RD	LANDOVER, MD	20785
BRITT, DEPP	GUITARIST	420 WALTON LN #F-28	MADISON, TN	37115
BRITT, KELLY	ACTRESS	3575 W CAHUENGA BLVD #320	LOS ANGELES, CA	90068
BRITT, MAY	ACTRESS	11726 SAN VICENTE BLVD #300	LOS ANGELES, CA	90049
BRITT, MELENDY	ACTRESS	551 S PARISH PL	BURBANK, CA	91506
BRITTANY, LINDA LOVE	ACTRESS	3518 W CAHUENGA BLVD #315	LOS ANGELES, CA	90068
BRITTANY, MORGAN	ACTRESS-MODEL	18060 BORIS DR	ENCINO, CA	91316
BRITTO, DARBY	DIRECTOR	DGA, 110 W 57TH ST	NEW YORK, NY	10019
BRITTON, DAVID	TENOR	COLBERT, 111 W 57TH ST	NEW YORK, NY	10019
BRITTON, MICHAEL L	WRITER	8955 BEVERLY BLVD	LOS ANGELES, CA	90048
BRITTON, TONY	ACTOR	ICM, 388-396 OXFORD ST	LONDON W1	ENGLAND
BRITTON, TRACY L	WRITER	1418 N HIGHLAND AVE #102	LOS ANGELES, CA	90028
BRITTON BROTHERS, THE	VOCAL GROUP	KNODLE, 7609 GLEASON RD	EDINA, MN	55435
BRIVIC, BOB	ACTOR	305 W 13TH ST	NEW YORK, NY	10014
BRIZENDINE, PAUL	COMPOSER	4821 SALEM WY	CARMICHAEL, CA	95608
BROAD, WILLIAM	SINGER-SONGWRITER	SEE - IDOL, BILLY		
BROADAX, ALBERT P	WRITER	555 W 57TH ST #1230	NEW YORK, NY	10019
BROADBENT, ALAN L	CONDUCTOR	5609 RADFORD AVE	NORTH HOLLYWOOD, CA	91607
BROADHURST, KENT	ACTOR	10 E 44TH ST #700	NEW YORK, NY	10017
BROADIE, RICHARD G	COMPOSER	POST OFFICE BOX 615	PALM SPRINGS, CA	92263
BROCCO, PETER	ACTOR	8721 SUNSET BLVD #103	LOS ANGELES, CA	90069
BROCCOLI, ALBERT R "CUBBY"	FILM PRODUCER	809 HILLCREST RD	BEVERLY HILLS, CA	90210
BROCINER, MICHEL	NEWS CORRESPONDENT	4500 SALEM LN, NW	WASHINGTON, DC	20036
BROCK, CHRIS	FILM DIRECTOR	THE HIDE, 30 RUSCOMBE GARDENS		
		DATCHET	BERKS	ENGLAND
BROCK, J S	GUITARIST	ROUTE #2, GOOSECREEK BY-PA	FRANKLIN, TN	37064
BROCK, JIMMY	GUITARIST	317 SENTINEL DR	NASHVILLE, TN	37209
BROCK, LOU	BASEBALL	12595 DURBIN DR	SAINT LOUIS, MO	63141
BROCK, NANCY	ACTRESS	609 N DOHENY DR #B	BEVERLY HILLS, CA	90210
BROCK, STANLEY	ACTOR	12725 VENTURA BLVD #E	STUDIO CITY, CA	91604
BROCK, TRICIA	WRITER-PRODUCER	1046 MADISON AVE	NEW YORK, NY	10021
BROCKHURST, ROBERT	PHOTOGRAPHER	2214 TULIP DR	FALLS CHURCH, VA	22046
BROCKMAN, MICHAEL S	TV EXECUTIVE	CBS-TV, 6121 SUNSET BLVD	LOS ANGELES, CA	90028
BROCKWAY, MERRILL	WRITER-PRODUCER	276 RIVERSIDE DR	NEW YORK, NY	10025
BRODER, DAVID S	NEWS CORRESPONDENT	4024 N 27TH ST	ARLINGTON, VA	22207
BRODER, DICK	FILM-TV PRODUCER	PLAYBOY, 9046 SUNSET BLVD	LOS ANGELES, CA	90069
BRODERICK, ALFRED E	TV DIRECTOR	271 ADELPHI ST	BROOKLYN, NY	11205
BRODERICK, LORRAINE	TV WRITER	ABC-TV, "ALL MY CHILDREN"		
		1330 AVE OF THE AMERICAS	NEW YORK, NY	10019
BRODERICK, MARY	NEWS CORRESPONDENT	4461 CONNECTICUT AVE, NW	WASHINGTON, DC	20008
BRODERICK, MATTHEW	ACTOR	27 WASHINGTON SQ N	NEW YORK, NY	10011
BRODERSON, FRED C	DIRECTOR	520 N MICHIGAN AVE #436	CHICAGO, IL	60611
BRODHEAD, JAMES E	ACTOR	3642 LONGVIEW VALLEY	SHERMAN OAKS, CA	91423
BRODIE, DON	ACTOR	4410 AVOCADO ST #3	LOS ANGELES, CA	90027
BRODIE, JOHN	FOOTBALL-ANNOUNCER	260 SURRY PL	LOS ALTOS, CA	94022

JEFF BRIDGES

CHRISTIE BRINKLEY

MORGAN BRITTANY

MATTHEW BRODERICK

STEVE BRODIE

DR. JOYCE BROTHERS

RAND BROOKS

MEL BROOKS

PIERCE BROSNAN

BRODIE, KEVIN	ACTOR	3240 SUMACRIDGE DR	MALIBU, CA	90265
BRODIE, KEVIN	DIRECTOR	32752 PACIFIC COAST HWY	MALIBU, CA	90265
BRODIE, STEVE	ACTOR	6742 SUNNYBRAE AVE	CANOGA PARK, CA	91306
BRODINE, DOROTHY	WRITER	555 W 57TH ST #1230	NEW YORK, NY	10019
BRODKIN, HERBERT	TV PRODUCER	TITUS PRODS, 211 E 51ST ST	NEW YORK, NY	10022
BRODKMEYER, BOB, QUARTET	JAZZ QUARTET	POST OFFICE BOX 845	CONCORD, CA	94522
BRODNEY, KENNETH	WRITER	555 W 57TH ST #1230	NEW YORK, NY	10019
BRODNEY, OSCAR	WRITER-PRODUCER	450 S MAPLE DR #305	BEVERLY HILLS, CA	90212
BRODNICK, MARILYNN	ACTRESS	366 N SPAULDING AVE #14	LOS ANGELES, CA	90036
BRODSKY, ARTHUR R	NEWS CORRESPONDENT	3907 PALMIRA LN	WHEATON, MD	20906
BRODY, BRUISER	WRESTLER	WORLD CLASS WRESTLING		
		SOUTHWEST SPORTS, INC		
		DALLAS SPORTATORIUM		
		1000 S INDUSTRIAL BLVD	DALLAS, TX	75207
BRODY, FRANK	WRESTLER	SEE - BRODY, BRUISER		
BRODY, KING KONG	WRESTLER	SEE - BRODY, BRUISER		
BRODY, LANE	SINGER	POST OFFICE BOX 24775	NASHVILLE, TN	37202
BRODY, LARRY	TV WRITER	8955 BEVERLY BLVD	LOS ANGELES, CA	90048
BRODY, MEREDITH	WRITER	8955 BEVERLY BLVD	LOS ANGELES, CA	90048
BRODY, RONNIE	ACTOR	9 BEAUFIELD CLOSE, SELSEY	SUSSEX	ENGLAND
BRODY, SCOTT	TV WRITER	8955 BEVERLY BLVD	LOS ANGELES, CA	90048
BROFFMAN, CRAIG A	NEWS CORRESPONDENT	2133 WISCONSIN AVE, NW	WASHINGTON, DC	20007
BROGAN, JIMMY	COMEDIAN	ICM, 8899 BEVERLY BLVD	LOS ANGELES, CA	90048
BROGAN, PAMELA	NEWS CORRESPONDENT	5637 RAPID ROW CT	BURKE, VA	22015
BROGDON, BENJAMIN F, III	GUITARIST	3820 SYFEROUTE LN	NASHVILLE, TN	37211
BROGLIATTI, BARBARA	DIRECTOR	15034 MARBLE DR	SHERMAN OAKS, CA	91403
BROHN, BILL D	CONDUCTOR	250 W 85TH ST	NEW YORK, NY	10024
BROKAW, JOANNE	TV EXECUTIVE	CBS-TV, 51 W 52ND ST	NEW YORK, NY	10019
BROKAW, NORMAN	TALENT AGENT	530 VICK ST	BEVERLY HILLS, CA	90210
BROKE, RICHARD	FILM PRODUCER	HEATH, PARAMOUNT HOUSE		
		162-170 WARDOUR ST	LONDON W1V 3AT	ENGLAND
BROKOW, TOM	BROADCAST JOURNALIST	941 PARK AVE #14-C	NEW YORK, NY	10025
BROKS, CHARLES	CARTOONIST	1612 CRESTHILL RD	BIRMINGHAM, AL	35213
BROLIN, JAMES	ACTOR	8721 SAINT IVES DR	LOS ANGELES, CA	90069
BROLIN, JOSH	ACTOR	895 BUENA VISTA AVE	SANTA BARBARA, CA	93108
BROMBERG, CONRAD	TV WRITER-PRODUCER	555 W 57TH ST #1230	NEW YORK, NY	10019
BROMBERG, DAVID	SINGER-GUITARIST	POST OFFICE BOX 9109	SAN RAFAEL, CA	94912
BROMBERG, DEBORAH A	WRITER	555 W 57TH ST #1230	NEW YORK, NY	10019
BROMFIELD, JOHN	ACTOR	1750 WHITTIER AVE	COSTA MESA, CA	92627
BROMFIELD, LOIS	COMEDIAN	151 S EL CAMINO DR	BEVERLY HILLS, CA	90212
BROMFIELD, REX	DIRECTOR	1237 HOWE ST	VANCOUVER, BC	CANADA
BROMFIELD, VALRI	COMEDIENNE-WRITER	11726 SAN VICENTE BLVD #300	LOS ANGELES, CA	90049
BROMHEAD, MICHAEL	FILM EXECUTIVE	THORN-EMI SCREEN ENTS		
		9489 DAYTON WY	BEVERLY HILLS, CA	90210

Name	Occupation	Address	City	Zip/Country
BROMLEY DAVENPORT, HARRY	TV WRITER-DIRECTOR	11 WESTCHESTER HOUSE		
		SEYMOUR ST	LONDON W2 2JG	ENGLAND
BROMLY, ALAN	TV DIRECTOR-PRODUCER	SMITH, 10 WYNDHAM PL	LONDON W1H 14S	ENGLAND
BRONDER, WILLIAM	ACTOR	7621 GENTRY AVE	NORTH HOLLYWOOD, CA	91605
BRONFELD, STEWART	WRITER	555 W 57TH ST #1230	NEW YORK, NY	10019
BRONFMAN, YEFIM	PIANIST	ICM, 40 W 57TH ST	NEW YORK, NY	10019
BRONNER, FRITZ	ACTOR	FIELDS, 165 W 46TH ST	NEW YORK, NY	10036
BRONNER BROTHERS, THE	SOUL DUO	POST OFFICE BOX 115269	ATLANTA, GA	30310
BRONSKI BEAT	ROCK & ROLL GROUP	134 WIGMORE ST	LONDON W1	ENGLAND
BRONSON, CHARLES	ACTOR	121 UDINE WY	LOS ANGELES, CA	90077
BRONSON, DAN	WRITER	8955 BEVERLY BLVD	LOS ANGELES, CA	90048
BRONSON, HAROLD	RECORD EXECUTIVE	RHINO RECORDS COMPANY		
		1720 WESTWOOD BLVD	LOS ANGELES, CA	90024
BRONSON, KIM	ACTRESS	15010 VENTURA BLVD #219	SHERMAN OAKS, CA	91403
BRONSON, LILLIAN	ACTRESS	TREASURE ISLAND TRAILOR PARK		
		PLAZA #5	LAGUNA BEACH, CA	92651
BRONSON, MICHAEL	OPERA DIRECTOR	METROPOLITAN OPERA		
		520 W 27TH ST	NEW YORK, NY	10001
BRONSON, PANDORA	ACTRESS	102 W 75TH ST	NEW YORK, NY	10023
BRONX ARTS ENSEMBLE	CHAMBER ORCHESTRA	POST OFFICE BOX 20548	NEW YORK, NY	10025
BRONZ	ROCK & ROLL GROUP	BRON MGMT, 100 CHALK FAR	LONDON NW1 8EH	ENGLAND
BROOD, THE	ROCK & ROLL GROUP	POST OFFICE BOX 34871	LOS ANGELES, CA	90034
BROOK, FAITH	ACTRESS	CONWAY, EAGLE HOUSE		
		109 JERMYN ST	LONDON SW1	ENGLAND
BROOK, LYNDON	ACTOR-WRITER	87 FINLEY ST	LONDON SW6	ENGLAND
BROOK, PETER	DIRECTOR-PRODUCER	CICT, 9 RUE DU CIRQUE	PARIS 8	FRANCE
BROOKE, ELIZABETH	NEWS CORRESPONDENT	9517 ROCKPORT RD	VIENNA, VA	22180
BROOKE, HILLARY	ACTRESS	KLUNE, 40 VIA CASTITAS	BONSALL, CA	92003
BROOKE, O KERN, JR	GUITARIST	1204 THOMPSON AVE	SEVERN, MD	21144
BROOKE, PETER R	WRITER	8955 BEVERLY BLVD	LOS ANGELES, CA	90048
BROOKE, SANDY	ACTRESS	5000 LANKERSHIM BLVD #5	NORTH HOLLYWOOD, CA	91601
BROOKE, WALTER	ACTOR	4313 BEN AVE	NORTH HOLLYWOOD, CA	91604
BROOKE-TAYLOR, TIM	ACTOR-WRITER	ROUND COPSE, ALLEYNS LN	BERKS SL6 9AE	ENGLAND
BROOKER, GARY	SINGER-COMPOSER	STRONGMAN MANAGEMENT		
		BANDA HOUSE		
		CAMBRIDGE GROVE	LONDON W6 8LE	ENGLAND
BROOKER, JOAN	TV WRITER	8955 BEVERLY BLVD	LOS ANGELES, CA	90048
BROOKES, DIANA	ACTRESS	427 N CANON DR #205	BEVERLY HILLS, CA	90210
BROOKES, JACQUELINE	ACTRESS	10100 SANTA MONICA BLVD #1600	LOS ANGELES, CA	90067
BROOKES, WARREN	ECONOMIST-COLUMNIST	THE DETROIT NEWS		
		615 LAFAYETTE BLVD	DETROIT, MI	48231
BROOKING, KEVIN	CLOWN	2701 COTTAGE WY #14	SACRAMENTO, CA	95825
BROOKINS, GARY	CARTOONIST	POST OFFICE BOX C-32333	RICHMOND, VA	23293
BROOKLYN BRIDGE, THE	ROCK & ROLL GROUP	BROTHERS, 141 DUNBAR AVE	FORDS, NJ	08863
BROOKLYN DREAMS	VOCAL GROUP	MUNRO, 1224 N VINE ST	LOS ANGELES, CA	90038
BROOKMAN, MICHAEL S	TV EXECUTIVE	CBS-TV, 7800 BEVERLY BLVD	LOS ANGELES, CA	90036
BROOKS, ALAN	WRITER	555 W 57TH ST #1230	NEW YORK, NY	10019
BROOKS, ALAN D	DIRECTOR	DGA, 110 W 57TH ST	NEW YORK, NY	10019
BROOKS, ALBERT	ACT-WRI-DIR	1880 CENTURY PARK E #900	LOS ANGELES, CA	90067
BROOKS, C R	WRITER	8955 BEVERLY BLVD	LOS ANGELES, CA	90048
BROOKS, CHRISTOPHER W	DRUMMER	28 WESTOVERHILL RD	TORONTO, ONT M6C 3L5	CANADA
BROOKS, CINDY	MODEL	MODELS & PROMOTIONS AGENCY		
		8560 SUNSET BLVD, 10TH FLOOR	LOS ANGELES, CA	90069
BROOKS, CLYDE	DRUMMER	208 BASKIN DR	NASHVILLE, TN	37205
BROOKS, D J	WRITER	8955 BEVERLY BLVD	LOS ANGELES, CA	90048
BROOKS, DAVID	ACTOR	400 W 43RD ST #40-E	NEW YORK, NY	10036
BROOKS, DAVID	FILM CRITIC	THE WASHINGTON TIMES		
		3600 NEW YORK AVE, NE	WASHINGTON, DC	20002
BROOKS, DEAN	ACTOR	17601 HAYNES ST	VAN NUYS, CA	91406
BROOKS, DONALD	COSTUME DESIGNER	LOCAL 22, 218 W 40TH ST	LOS ANGELES, CA	90018
BROOKS, DONNIE	COMEDIAN	2701 COTTAGE WY #14	SACRAMENTO, CA	95825
BROOKS, DUDLEY M	PHOTOGRAPHER	8750 GEORGIA AVE	SILVER SPRING, MD	20910
BROOKS, DWIGHT	FILM DIRECTOR	POST OFFICE BOX 102	GRASS VALLEY, CA	95945
BROOKS, ERIN & DON SHIPLEY	VOCAL DUO	POST OFFICE BOX 42466	TUCSON, AZ	85733
BROOKS, FOSTER	COMEDIAN	18116 CHADRON CIR	ENCINO, CA	91316
BROOKS, GEORGE W	TV DIRECTOR	20224 SHERMAN WY #41	CANOGA PARK, CA	91306
BROOKS, HAZEL	ACTRESS	ROSS, 754 TORTUOSA WY	LOS ANGELES, CA	90024
BROOKS, HINDI	WRITER	6430 SUNSET BLVD #1203	LOS ANGELES, CA	90028
BROOKS, JAMES	CONDUCTOR	GERSHUNOFF, 502 PARK AVE	NEW YORK, NY	10022
BROOKS, JAMES L	TV WRITER-PRODUCER	31708 BROAD BEACH RD	MALIBU, CA	90265
BROOKS, JANET N	PIANIST	1504 VILLA PL	NASHVILLE, TN	37212
BROOKS, JOEL	ACTOR	SF & A, 121 N SAN VICENTE BLVD	BEVERLY HILLS, CA	90211
BROOKS, JOSEPH	WRITER-PRODUCER	41-A E 74TH ST	NEW YORK, NY	10021
BROOKS, KAREN	SINGER	POST OFFICE BOX 1983	PEARLAND, TX	77588
BROOKS, KATIE	SINGER	CEE, 193 KONHAUS RD	MECHANICSBURG, PA	17055
BROOKS, KILLER	WRESTLER	WORLD CLASS WRESTLING		
		SOUTHWEST SPORTS, INC		
		DALLAS SPORTATORIUM		
		1000 S INDUSTRIAL BLVD	DALLAS, TX	75207
BROOKS, LONNIE	MUSICIAN	POST OFFICE BOX 60234	CHICAGO, IL	60660
BROOKS, MARILYN	FASHION DESIGNER	263 ADELAIDE ST W	TORONTO, ONT M5H 1Y1	CANADA
BROOKS, MARTIN E	ACTOR	LIGHT, 113 N ROBERTSON BLVD	LOS ANGELES, CA	90048
BROOKS, MEL	ACT-WRI-DIR	10201 W PICO BLVD	LOS ANGELES, CA	90035
BROOKS, NORMAN A	WRITER	555 W 57TH ST #1230	NEW YORK, NY	10019
BROOKS, NORMAN G	TV PRODUCER	11600 WASHINGTON PL #20	LOS ANGELES, CA	90066

Name	Occupation	Address	City	Zip/Country
BROOKS, TERI FOSTER	ACTRESS	18116 CHADRON CIR	ENCINO, CA	91316
BROOKS, THOMAS O	PIANIST	1421 MOHAWK TRAIL	MADISON, TN	37115
BROOKS, TIM	WRESTLER	SEE - BROOKS, KILLER		
BROOKS, TITA	WRITER	5211 VELOZ AVE	TARZANA, CA	91356
BROOKS BROTHERS BAND, THE	VOCAL GROUP	POST OFFICE BOX 111510	NASHVILLE, TN	37211
BROOKSBANK, LES	ANIMATION DIRECTOR	WOOD HOUSE, 500 LEEDS RD	BRADFORD BD3 9RU	ENGLAND
BROOKSHIER, TOM	SPORTSCASTER	CBS SPORTS, 51 W 52ND ST	NEW YORK, NY	10019
BROOM, BOBBY	SINGER	1697 BROADWAY #600	NEW YORK, NY	10019
BROOME, PAUL	DRUMMER	3208 KNOBDALE RD	NASHVILLE, TN	37214
BROOMFIELD, CRUSHER	WRESTLER	SEE - ONE MAN GANG		
BROOMFIELD, NICHOLAS	TV DIRECTOR	22 HYLDA CT		
		SAINT ALBANS RD	LONDON NW5	ENGLAND
BROPHY, KEVIN M	ACTOR	15010 HAMLIN ST	VAN NUYS, CA	91411
BROSE, RICHARD	ACTOR	10850 RIVERSIDE DR #505	NORTH HOLLYWOOD, CA	91602
BROSNAN, JAMES W "WOODY"	NEWS CORRESPONDENT	209 HODGES LN	TAKOMA PARK, MD	20912
BROSNAN, JOHN	WRITER	555 W 57TH ST #1230	NEW YORK, NY	10019
BROSNAN, PIERCE	ACTOR-MODEL	2101 CASTILIAN DR	LOS ANGELES, CA	90068
BROSSET, CLAUDE	ACTOR	GEORGES LAMBERT AGENCE		
		13 BIS AVE DE		
		LA MOTTE PIQUET	PARIS 75007	FRANCE
BROSTEN, HARVE	WRI-DIR-PROD	35 W 92ND ST	NEW YORK, NY	10025
BROTHERS, DR JOYCE	PSYCHOLOGIST	1530 PALISADES AVE	FORT LEE, NJ	07024
BROTHERS FOUR, THE	VOCAL DUO	POST OFFICE BOX 220219	CHARLOTTE, NC	28222
BROTHERS JOHNSON, THE	SOUL DUO	7250 BEVERLY BLVD #200	LOS ANGELES, CA	90036
BROTMAN, JOYCE	TV WRITER-PRODUCER	2338 1/2 S BEVERLY GLEN BLVD	LOS ANGELES, CA	90064
BROTT, BORIS	CONDUCTOR	SHAW CONCERTS, 1995 BROADWAY	NEW YORK, NY	10023
BROUDY, SAUL, BAND	FOLK GROUP	105 S 22ND ST	PHILADELPHIA, PA	19103
BROUGH, CANDI	ACTRESS-MODEL	JAYMES, 327 N LAUREL AVE	LOS ANGELES, CA	90048
BROUGH, CHRISTOPHER J	WRITER	ICM, 8899 BEVERLY BLVD	LOS ANGELES, CA	90048
BROUGH, RANDI	ACTRESS-MODEL	JAYMES, 327 N LAUREL AVE	LOS ANGELES, CA	90048
BROUGH, WALTER	WRITER-PRODUCER	8955 BEVERLY BLVD	LOS ANGELES, CA	90048
BROUGHTON, BRUCE	COMPOSER	3815 W OLIVE AVE #201	BURBANK, CA	91505
BROUGHTON, DIANE E	TV WRITER	8955 BEVERLY BLVD	LOS ANGELES, CA	90048
BROUGHTON, MICHAEL D	WRITER	8955 BEVERLY BLVD	LOS ANGELES, CA	90048
BROUN, CHARLES W, JR	TV DIRECTOR-PRODUCER	2238 HILLVIEW DR	SARASOTA, FL	33579
BROUSSARD, SAM	GUITARIST	5646 AMALIE DR #D-71	NASHVILLE, TN	37211
BROWER, BROCK	WRITER	555 W 57TH ST #1230	NEW YORK, NY	10019
BROWER, MONTGOMERY	WRITER-EDITOR	PEOPLE/TIME & LIFE BLDG		
		ROCKEFELLER CENTER	NEW YORK, NY	10020
BROWER, STUART	TV EXECUTIVE	995 BRENTAL RD	PASADENA, CA	91105
BROWN, ALBERT B	TV DIRECTOR	745 CRANE BLVD	LOS ANGELES, CA	90065
BROWN, ANGELA	ACTRESS	ESSANAY, 75 HAMMERSMITH RD	LONDON W14 8UZ	ENGLAND
BROWN, ARVIN	DIRECTOR	222 SARGENT DR	NEW HAVEN, CT	06511
BROWN, B KEITH	PIANIST	1022 16TH AVE S	NASHVILLE, TN	37212
BROWN, BARRY A	DIRECTOR	DGA, 7950 SUNSET BLVD	LOS ANGELES, CA	90046
BROWN, BARRY K	DIRECTOR-PRODUCER	BRILLIG PRODUCTIONS		
		300 CENTRAL PARK W	NEW YORK, NY	10024
BROWN, BARRY M	THEATER PRODUCER	250 W 52ND ST	NEW YORK, NY	10019
BROWN, BEVERLY	ACTRESS	9255 SUNSET BLVD #603	LOS ANGELES, CA	90069
BROWN, BLAIR	ACTRESS	JORDAN, 3704 CARBON CYN RD	MALIBU, CA	90265
BROWN, BOB	SPORTS WRITER-EDITOR	SPORTS ILLUSTRATED MAGAZINE		
		TIME & LIFE BUILDING		
		ROCKEFELLER CENTER	NEW YORK, NY	10020
BROWN, BOBBIE	SINGER	POST OFFICE BOX B	CARLISLE, IA	50047
BROWN, BRUCE R	SINGER-GUITARIST	180 WALLACE RD #S-13	NASHVILLE, TN	37211
BROWN, BRYAN	ACTOR	10100 SANTA MONICA BLVD #1600	LOS ANGELES, CA	90067
BROWN, CAMERON C	NEWS CORRESPONDENT	2133 WISCONSIN AVE, NW	WASHINGTON, DC	20007
BROWN, CANDY ANN	ACTRESS	1349 S CURSON AVE	LOS ANGELES, CA	90019
BROWN, CARY	WRITER-PRODUCER	12952 WOODBRIDGE ST	STUDIO CITY, CA	91604
BROWN, CHARLIE & THE COASTERS	VOCAL GROUP	JOYCE, 2028 CHESTNUT ST	PHILADELPHIA, PA	19103
BROWN, CHARLOTTE	WRITER-PRODUCER	801 THAYER AVE	LOS ANGELES, CA	90024
BROWN, CHRISTOPHER J	ACTOR	1560 N LAUREL AVE #206	LOS ANGELES, CA	90046
BROWN, CLARENCE	ACTOR	10850 RIVERSIDE DR #505	NORTH HOLLYWOOD, CA	91602
BROWN, CLARENCE "GATESMOUTH"	SINGER-GUITARIST	POST OFFICE BOX 958	BOGALUSA, LA	70427
BROWN, CRAIG E	COMPOSER	11708 S FELTON	HAWTHORNE, CA	90250
BROWN, D W	ACTOR	KOHNER, 9169 SUNSET BLVD	LOS ANGELES, CA	90069
BROWN, DANIEL	NEWS CORRESPONDENT	2139 WYOMING AVE #32, NW	WASHINGTON, DC	20008
BROWN, DAVID	FILM PRODUCER	1 W 81ST ST	NEW YORK, NY	10024
BROWN, DAVID "G B"	TV WRITER	8955 BEVERLY BLVD	LOS ANGELES, CA	90048
BROWN, DENNIS	SINGER	THE MUSIC COMPANY		
		14097 NW 19TH AVE	OPA LOCKA, FL	33054
BROWN, DENNY	WRESTLER	NATIONAL WRESTLING ALLIANCE		
		JIM CROCKETT PROMOTIONS		
		421 BRIARBEND DR	CHARLOTTE, NC	28209
BROWN, DONALD C, JR	NEWS CORRESPONDENT	3246 DUCK POND CT	HERNDON, VA	22071
BROWN, DWIGHT	NEWS CORRESPONDENT	NBC-TV, NEWS DEPARTMENT		
		4001 NEBRASKA AVE, NW	WASHINGTON, DC	20016
BROWN, EARL	COMPOSER-CONDUCTOR	ICI, 799 BROADWAY	NEW YORK, NY	10003
BROWN, EDGAR W, JR	NEWS CORRESPONDENT	NBC-TV, NEWS DEPARTMENT		
		4001 NEBRASKA AVE, NW	WASHINGTON, DC	20016
BROWN, EDMUND G "JERRY"	POLITICIAN	8942 WONDERLAND PARK	LOS ANGELES, CA	90046
BROWN, EDWARD R	CINEMATOGRAPHER	POST OFFICE BOX 2230	HOLLYWOOD, CA	90078
BROWN, ELAINE M	WRITER	555 W 57TH ST #1230	NEW YORK, NY	10019
BROWN, ELLA MAE	ACTRESS	3330 BARHAM BLVD #103	LOS ANGELES, CA	90068

CANDI BROUGH

RANDI BROUGH

JACKSON BROWNE

DAVE BRUBECK

ANITA BRYANT

LINDSAY BUCKINGHAM

JIMMY BUFFETT

BROOKE BUNDY

GEORGE BURNS

Name	Occupation	Address	City	Zip
BROWN, ELLEN	DIRECTOR	DGA, 7950 SUNSET BLVD	LOS ANGELES, CA	90046
BROWN, ERIC	ACTOR	ICM, 8899 BEVERLY BLVD	LOS ANGELES, CA	90048
BROWN, ERIC F	WRITER	8955 BEVERLY BLVD	LOS ANGELES, CA	90048
BROWN, ERNIE	ACTOR	6380 WILSHIRE BLVD #1600	LOS ANGELES, CA	90048
BROWN, FAITH	SINGER-ACTRESS	MILLION DOLLAR MUSIC CO		
		12 PRAED MEWS	LONDON W2 1QY	ENGLAND
BROWN, FRANK HYLO, JR	VIOLINIST	115 N BELMONT AVE	SPRINGFIELD, OH	45503
BROWN, G MAC	DIRECTOR-PRODUCER	425 E 63RD ST #8-EW	NEW YORK, NY	10021
BROWN, GAIL	ACTRESS	ICM, 40 W 57TH ST	NEW YORK, NY	10019
BROWN, GARY M	TV DIRECTOR	880 W 1ST ST #407	LOS ANGELES, CA	90012
BROWN, GAYE	ACTRESS	94 TANTALLOWN RD	LONDON SW12	ENGLAND
BROWN, GEORG STANFORD	ACTOR-DIRECTOR	1 SPINNAKER ST #13	VENICE, CA	90291
BROWN, GEORGE	FILM PRODUCER	REDWAY, 16 BERNERS ST	LONDON W1	ENGLAND
BROWN, GWENDOLYN	ACTRESS	1585 CROSSROADS OF WORLD	HOLLYWOOD, CA	90028
BROWN, H ARTHUR	CONDUCTOR-VIOLINIST	5961 CHULA VISTA WY	LOS ANGELES, CA	90068
BROWN, HARRY P	SCREENWRITER	8955 BEVERLY BLVD	LOS ANGELES, CA	90048
BROWN, HELEN	ACTRESS	8721 SUNSET BLVD #200	LOS ANGELES, CA	90069
BROWN, HELEN GURLEY	AUTHORESS-EDITOR	1 W 81ST ST	NEW YORK, NY	10024
BROWN, HENRY METRIC	PHOTOJOURNALIST	ABC-TV, PHOTO DEPARTMENT		
		1717 DE SALES ST, NW	WASHINGTON, DC	20036
BROWN, HILARY	NEWS CORRESPONDENT	ABC NEWS, 7 W 66TH ST	NEW YORK, NY	10023
BROWN, HIMAN	DIRECTOR	221 W 26TH ST	NEW YORK, NY	10001
BROWN, JACK	ACTOR	9220 SUNSET BLVD #218	LOS ANGELES, CA	90069
BROWN, JAKI	CASTING DIRECTOR	869 N SAN VICENTE BLVD	LOS ANGELES, CA	90048
BROWN, JAMES	CRITIC	L A TIMES NEWSPAPER		
		TIMES MIRROR SQUARE	LOS ANGELES, CA	90053
BROWN, JAMES	SINGER-SONGWRITER	BROTHERS, 141 DUNBAR AVE	FORDS, NJ	08863
BROWN, JAMES H	DIRECTOR-PRODUCER	13900 NW PASSAGE #310	MARINA DEL REY, CA	90292

Name	Occupation	Address	City	Zip
BROWN, JAMES L	ACTOR	20543 TIARA ST	WOODLAND HILLS, CA	91367
BROWN, JANET	ACTRESS	BERNARD LEE, MOORCROFT LODGE		
		FARLEIGH COMMON, WARLINGHAM	SURREY CR3 9PE	ENGLAND
BROWN, JANIS	NEWS CORRESPONDENT	17735 SHIRLEY DR	ASHTON, MD	20861
BROWN, JANNA	ACTRESS	208 S BEVERLY DR #8	BEVERLY HILLS, CA	90212
BROWN, JEFFERIE L	NEWS CORRESPONDENT	400 N CAPITOL ST, NW	WASHINGTON, DC	20001
BROWN, JEFFREY D	FILM DIRECTOR	445 N BEDFORD DR #PH	BEVERLY HILLS, CA	90210
BROWN, JIM	ACTOR-FOOTBALL	1851 SUNSET PLAZA DR	LOS ANGELES, CA	90069
BROWN, JIM ED	SINGER	7000 CLOVERLAND DR	BRENTWOOD, TN	37027
BROWN, JIM R	GUITARIST	311 OLD SHACKLE ISLAND	HENDERSONVILLE, TN	37075
BROWN, JOCELYN	SINGER	200 W 51ST ST #1410	NEW YORK, NY	10019
BROWN, JOHN	BODYBUILDER	POST OFFICE BOX 6696	FULLERTON, CA	92634
BROWN, JOHN E, JR	WRITER	555 W 57TH ST #1230	NEW YORK, NY	10019
BROWN, JOHNNY	PERFORMER	2732 WOODHAVEN DR	LOS ANGELES, CA	90068
BROWN, JUDITH L	NEWS CORRESPONDENT	5532 ASCOT CT	ALEXANDRIA, VA	22311
BROWN, JUDY	ACTRESS	MARX, 11130 HUSTON ST	NORTH HOLLYWOOD, CA	91601
BROWN, JULIE	ACTRESS	ICM, 8899 BEVERLY BLVD	LOS ANGELES, CA	90048
BROWN, JULIUS B	NEWS CORRESPONDENT	611 49TH ST, NE	WASHINGTON, DC	20019
BROWN, KARL	WRITER	8955 BEVERLY BLVD	LOS ANGELES, CA	90048
BROWN, KATHLEEN A	NEWS CORRESPONDENT	122 "C" ST, NW	WASHINGTON, DC	20001
BROWN, KIM	SINGER	1888 CENTURY PARK E #1400	LOS ANGELES, CA	90067
BROWN, LAWRENCE P	CONDUCTOR-PIANIST	222 MOCKINGBIRD TRAIL	PALM BEACH, FL	33480
BROWN, LAWRENCE W	NEWS CORRESPONDENT	1825 "K" ST, NW	WASHINGTON, DC	20006
BROWN, LES	ORCHESTRA LEADER	POST OFFICE BOX 3996	WESTLAKE VILLAGE, CA	91361
BROWN, LES	TV CRITIC	131 N CHATSWORTH	LARCHMONT, NY	10538
BROWN, LES R, SR	CONDUCTOR	POST OFFICE BOX 3996	WESTLAKE VILLAGE, CA	91359
BROWN, LEW	ACTOR	NBC-TV, 3000 W ALAMEDA AVE	BURBANK, CA	91523
BROWN, LEW G	ACTOR	8121 GONZAGA AVE	LOS ANGELES, CA	90045
BROWN, LISA	ACTRESS	CBS-TV, "AS THE WORLD TURNS"		
		51 W 52ND ST	NEW YORK, NY	10019
BROWN, LLOYD ELKIN	GUITARIST-BANJOIST	302 CANE RIDGE RD #1503	ANTIOCH, TN	37013
BROWN, LOUIS	WRITER	555 W 57TH ST #1230	NEW YORK, NY	10019
BROWN, LOUIS T	GUITARIST	KELLY RD	BRENTWOOD, TN	37027
BROWN, LUTHER, JR	NEWS CORRESPONDENT	NBC-TV, NEWS DEPARTMENT		
		4001 NEBRASKA AVE, NW	NEW YORK, NY	10022
BROWN, M K	CARTOONIST	THE NATIONAL LAMPOON		
		635 MADISON AVE	NEW YORK, NY	10022
BROWN, MARCIA	AUTHOR	SCRIBNER'S, 597 5TH AVE	NEW YORK, NY	10017
BROWN, MARTHA	WRITER	555 W 57TH ST #1230	NEW YORK, NY	10019
BROWN, MAXINE	SINGER	POST OFFICE BOX 82	GREAT NECK, NY	11021
BROWN, MEG	ACTRESS	6640 SUNSET BLVD #203	LOS ANGELES, CA	90028
BROWN, MENDE	TV DIRECTOR	39 OLOLA AVE	VAUCLUSE NSW 2030	AUSTRALIA
BROWN, MICHAEL HUNT	NEWS CORRESPONDENT	5901 LITTLE FALLS RD	ARLINGTON, VA	22207
BROWN, MICHAEL LALOR	WRITER	23740 WEBB RD	CHATSWORTH, CA	91311
BROWN, MICHAEL M	DIRECTOR	10 KENT CT	CLARENDON HILLS, IL	60514
BROWN, MICHAEL M	NEWS CORRESPONDENT	629 S WALTER DR #453-A	ARLINGTON, VA	22204
BROWN, MIKE	DIRECTOR	POST OFFICE BOX 47	BEDFORD MK40 3HD	ENGLAND
BROWN, NELSON C	NEWS CORRESPONDENT	330 INDEPENDENCE AVE, SW	WASHINGTON, DC	20547
BROWN, OLIVIA	ACTRESS	LIGHT, 113 N ROBERTSON BLVD	LOS ANGELES, CA	90048
BROWN, OLLIE	SINGER-PERCUSSIONIST	POLYDOR RECORDS, 810 7TH AVE	NEW YORK, NY	10019
BROWN, PAMELA	ACTRESS	9165 SUNSET BLVD #202	LOS ANGELES, CA	90069
BROWN, PETER	ACTOR	3408 THE STRAND	MANHATTAN BEACH, CA	90266
BROWN, PETER A	NEWS CORRESPONDENT	429 7TH ST, SE	WASHINGTON, DC	20003
BROWN, PETER J	DIRECTOR	706 SKYLINE TRAIL	TOPANGA CANYON, CA	90290
BROWN, PHYLLIS GEORGE	TV PERSONALITY	SEE - GEORGE BROWN, PHYLLIS		
BROWN, RALPH B	NEWS CORRESPONDENT	323 13TH ST, NE	WASHINGTON, DC	20002
BROWN, RAY, ALL-STARS	JAZZ GROUP	POST OFFICE BOX 845	CONCORD, CA	94522
BROWN, REB	ACTOR	9000 SUNSET BLVD #1112	LOS ANGELES, CA	90069
BROWN, RITA MAE	AUTHOR-TV WRITER	JULIAN BACH, 747 3RD AVE	NEW YORK, NY	10017
BROWN, ROGER AARON	ACTOR	400 S BEVERLY DR #216	BEVERLY HILLS, CA	90212
BROWN, ROGER COTTON	DIRECTOR	1055 COTTONWOOD PASS RD	GYPSUM, CO	81637
BROWN, ROSS	CASTING DIRECTOR	7319 BEVERLY BLVD #10	LOS ANGELES, CA	90036
BROWN, RUTH	SINGER	POST OFFICE BOX 19114	LAS VEGAS, NV	89119
BROWN, SHARON	SINGER	PROFILE RECORDS CO		
		250 W 57TH ST	NEW YORK, NY	10107
BROWN, SHIRLEY L	ACTRESS	50 SHORE BLVD	BROOKLYN, NY	11235
BROWN, SLADE	THEATER PRODUCER	1175 YORK AVE	NEW YORK, NY	10021
BROWN, STAN	GUITARIST-BANJOIST	2943 HILLHURST DR #49	NASHVILLE, TN	37207
BROWN, STEPHEN R	PHOTOGRAPHER	1882 COLUMBIA RD, NW	WASHINGTON, DC	20009
BROWN, STEVE	WRITER-PRODUCER	1650 WESTWOOD BLVD #201	LOS ANGELES, CA	90024
BROWN, SUSAN	ACTRESS	9000 SUNSET BLVD #1200	LOS ANGELES, CA	90069
BROWN, T GRAHAM	SINGER	STARBOUND, 128 VOLUNTEER DR	HENDERSONVILLE, TN	37075
BROWN, TERRY M	RECORD EXECUTIVE	AIRWAVE, 6381 HOLLYWOOD BLVD	HOLLYWOOD, CA	90028
BROWN, THOMAS M	NEWS CORRESPONDENT	6908 VARNUM ST	LANDOVER HILLS, MD	20784
BROWN, THOMAS TERRELL	GUITARIST	ROUTE #1	LIZELLA, GA	31052
BROWN, TIM	ACTOR	CBS-TV, 7800 BEVERLY BLVD	LOS ANGELES, CA	90036
BROWN, TIMOTHY	ACTOR	3151 W CAHUENGA BLVD #310	LOS ANGELES, CA	90068
BROWN, TONY	PIANIST	803 KENDALL DR	NASHVILLE, TN	37209
BROWN, VANESSA	ACTRESS	14340 MULHOLLAND DR	LOS ANGELES, CA	90024
BROWN, VICKI LYNNE	NEWS CORRESPONDENT	302 "G" ST, SE	WASHINGTON, DC	20003
BROWN, VICTORIA D	WRITER	555 W 57TH ST #1230	NEW YORK, NY	10019
BROWN, VIRGE	SINGER	PROCESS, 439 WILEY AVE	FRANKLIN, PA	16323
BROWN, VIVIAN	ACTRESS	1418 N HIGHLAND AVE #102	LOS ANGELES, CA	90028
BROWN, WALTER P	ACTOR	103 RALPH ST	BELLEVILLE, NJ	07109
BROWN, WILLIAM	PRODUCER	WORLDWIDE, 2520 W OLIVE AVE	BURBANK, CA	91505

Name	Occupation	Address	City	Zip
BROWN, WILLIAM	TENOR	SHAW CONCERTS, 1995 BROADWAY	NEW YORK, NY	10023
BROWN, WILLIAM F	WRITER	555 W 57TH ST #1230	NEW YORK, NY	10019
BROWN, WILLIAM JIM	DIRECTOR	93 CENTRAL AVE	AMITYVILLE, NY	11701
BROWN, WILLIAM S	WRITER	555 W 57TH ST #1230	NEW YORK, NY	10019
BROWN, WILLIE	DRUMMER	4346 HAIGHT AVE	CINCINNATI, OH	45223
BROWN, WINIFRED FAIX	SOPRANO	61 W 62ND ST #6-F	NEW YORK, NY	10023
BROWN, WOODY	ACTOR	151 S EL CAMINO DR	BEVERLY HILLS, CA	90212
BROWNE, ANGELA	ACTRESS	ESSANAY LIMITED		
		SAINT MARTIN THEATRE		
		WEST ST	LONDON WC2	ENGLAND
BROWNE, ARTHUR, JR	WRITER	12021 VALLEYHEART DR #303	STUDIO CITY, CA	91604
BROWNE, AUTUMN	ACTRESS	8721 SUNSET BLVD #200	LOS ANGELES, CA	90069
BROWNE, CORAL	ACTRESS	PRICE, 9255 SWALLOW DR	LOS ANGELES, CA	90049
BROWNE, DANIEL GREGORY	WRITER	8955 BEVERLY BLVD	LOS ANGELES, CA	90048
BROWNE, DEL	ACTRESS	92 JAY ST	KATONAH, NY	10536
BROWNE, DIK	CARTOONIST	COMLY AVE	PORT CHESTER, NY	10573
BROWNE, HOWARD C	WRITER	8955 BEVERLY BLVD	LOS ANGELES, CA	90048
BROWNE, JACKSON	SINGER-COMPOSER	1888 CENTURY PARK E #1400	LOS ANGELES, CA	90067
BROWNE, JESSICA	ACTRESS	1509 N CRESCENT HGTS BLVD #7	LOS ANGELES, CA	90069
BROWNE, KALE	ACTOR	NBC-TV, "ANOTHER WORLD"		
		30 ROCKEFELLER PLAZA	NEW YORK, NY	10112
BROWNE, KATHY	ACTRESS	9903 KIP DR	BEVERLY HILLS, CA	90210
BROWNE, KENDALL CARLY	ACTRESS	240 N CRESCENT DR #300	BEVERLY HILLS, CA	90210
BROWNE, L VIRGINIA	TV WRITER	CBS-TV, 51 W 52ND ST	NEW YORK, NY	10019
BROWNE, MALCOM	JOURNALIST	36 E 36TH ST	NEW YORK, NY	10016
BROWNE, MARJORIE STAPP	ACTRESS	6430 SUNSET BLVD #1203	LOS ANGELES, CA	90028
BROWNE, ROBERT ALAN	ACTOR	6430 SUNSET BLVD #1203	LOS ANGELES, CA	90028
BROWNE, ROSCOE LEE	ACT-WRI-DIR	3531 WONDER VIEW DR	LOS ANGELES, CA	90068
BROWNE, TOM	SINGER	B & B BOOKING, 3477 BROADWAY	NEW YORK, NY	10031
BROWNELL, BARBARA	ACTRESS	5101 LEDGE AVE	NORTH HOLLYWOOD, CA	91601
BROWNELL, JOHN	NEWS CORRESPONDENT	1740 "T" ST, NW	WASHINGTON, DC	20009
BROWNER, SKIP	GUITARIST	110 DIDDLE DR	HENDERSONVILLE, TN	37075
BROWNING, BOB	GUITARIST	427 GREEN HARBOR CT	OLD HICKORY, TN	37138
BROWNING, DAVID W	WRITER	8955 BEVERLY BLVD	LOS ANGELES, CA	90048
BROWNING, EARL S, JR	NEWS CORRESPONDENT	9916 BROADVIEW DR	FAIRFAX, VA	22030
BROWNING, JOHN	PIANIST	CAMI, 165 W 57TH ST	NEW YORK, NY	10019
BROWNING, JOHN S	CONDUCTOR	2621 N COMMONWEATH AVE	LOS ANGELES, CA	90027
BROWNING, KIRK	DIRECTOR	80 CENTRAL PARK W	NEW YORK, NY	10023
BROWNING, PHILIP L	WRITER	8955 BEVERLY BLVD	LOS ANGELES, CA	90048
BROWNING, RICOU R	WRITER-PRODUCER	5221 SW 196TH LN	FORT LAUDERDALE, FL	33332
BROWNING, ROD	ACTOR-WRITER	3642 ALTA MESA DR	STUDIO CITY, CA	91604
BROWNLEE, CHERI	TV DIRECTOR	ENTERTAINMENT TONIGHT		
		PARAMOUNT TELEVISION		
		5555 MELROSE AVE	LOS ANGELES, CA	90038
BROWNLEE, DONALD E	NEWS CORRESPONDENT	5611 5TH ST N	ARLINGTON, VA	22205
BROWNLEE, SHANNON	WRITER-EDITOR	DISCOVER/TIME & LIFE BLDG		
		ROCKEFELLER CENTER	NEW YORK, NY	10020
BROWNRIDGE, KENT	PUBLISHING EXECUTIVE	US MAGAZINE COMPANY		
		1 DAG HAMMARSKJOLD PLAZA	NEW YORK, NY	10017
BROWNSTEIN, RONALD	NEWS CORRESPONDENT	2617 WOODLEY PL, NW	WASHINGTON, DC	20008
BROXTON	MUSIC GROUP	DBA, 4630 DEEPDALE DR	CORPUS CHRISTI, TX	78413
BROYLES, DICK	GUITARIST	POST OFFICE BOX 27072	JACKSONVILLE, FL	32205
BROYLES, ROBERT	ACTOR	2311 SCOTT AVE	LOS ANGELES, CA	90026
BROYLES, WILLIAM, JR	WRITER	POST OFFICE BOX 1569	AUSTIN, TX	78767
BROZOWSKI, ANTHONY J	NEWS CORRESPONDENT	4507 HANOVER CT	DALE CITY, VA	
BRUBACH, HOLLY B	WRITER	555 W 57TH ST #1230	NEW YORK, NY	10019
BRUBECK, DAVE	PIANIST	221 MILLSTONE RD	WILTON, CT	06897
BRUBECK-LA VERNE TRIO	JAZZ TRIO	1527 MANORVILLE RD	WEST SAUGERTIES, NY	12477
BRUCE, ASHLEY	TV DIRECTOR-PRODUCER	156 HIGH ST, BILDESTON	SUFFOLK	ENGLAND
BRUCE, BRIDGET	ACTRESS	8285 SUNSET BLVD #12	LOS ANGELES, CA	90046
BRUCE, CAROL	ACTRESS	1361 N LAUREL AVE	LOS ANGELES, CA	90046
BRUCE, ED	SINGER	1022 16TH AVE S	NASHVILLE, TN	37212
BRUCE, EVE	ACTRESS	11030 VENTURA BLVD #3	STUDIO CITY, CA	91604
BRUCE, HERBERT	MUSICIAN	306 BEACON HILL DR	MOUNT JULIET, TN	37122
BRUCE, JOHN	TV DIRECTOR	SPOKEMEN, 1 CRAVEN HILL	LONDON W2	ENGLAND
BRUCE, KITTY	SINGER	ANDREW FRANCES, 31 HARRISON ST	NEW YORK, NY	10019
BRUCE, MURRAY	DIRECTOR	463 WEST ST	NEW YORK, NY	10014
BRUCE, ROBERT	WRITER	555 W 57TH ST #1230	NEW YORK, NY	10019
BRUCE, SHERRY	SOPRANO	254 W 93RD ST #8	NEW YORK, NY	10025
BRUCK, BELLA	ACTRESS	13952 BORA BORA WY #314	MARINA DEL REY, CA	90292
BRUCK, CHARLES	ACTOR	8484 WILSHIRE BLVD #235	BEVERLY HILLS, CA	90211
BRUCK, KARL	ACTOR	404 S BENTON WY	LOS ANGELES, CA	90057
BRUCKHEIM, DR ALLAN H	COLUMNIST	TRIBUNE MEDIA SERVICES		
		64 E CONCORD ST	ORLANDO, FL	32801
BRUCKHEIMER, JERRY	FILM PRODUCER	PARAMOUNT PICTURES CORP		
		5555 MELROSE AVE	LOS ANGELES, CA	90038
BRUCKNER, D J R	FILM CRITIC	N Y TIMES, 229 W 43RD ST	NEW YORK, NY	10036
BRUDER, PATRICIA	ACTRESS	CBS-TV, "AS THE WORLD TURNS"		
		51 W 52ND ST	NEW YORK, NY	10019
BRUEGGEN, FRANS	FLUTIST-CONDUCTOR	LEE MC RAE, 2130 CARLETON ST	BERKELEY, CA	94704
BRUESTLE, BEAUMONT	ACTOR	2149 PANORAMA TERR	LOS ANGELES, CA	90039
BRUHL, HEIDI	ACTRESS	OBERER SEEWEG 13-B	D-8130 STARNBERG	WEST GERMANY
BRUHNS, WIBKE	NEWS CORRESPONDENT	2810 29TH ST, NW	WASHINGTON, DC	20008
BRUISER BRODY	WRESTLER	SEE - BRODY, BRUISER		
BRULE, CLAUDE	ACTOR	36-Q VAINATIONAL	PUTREAUX 92800	FRANCE

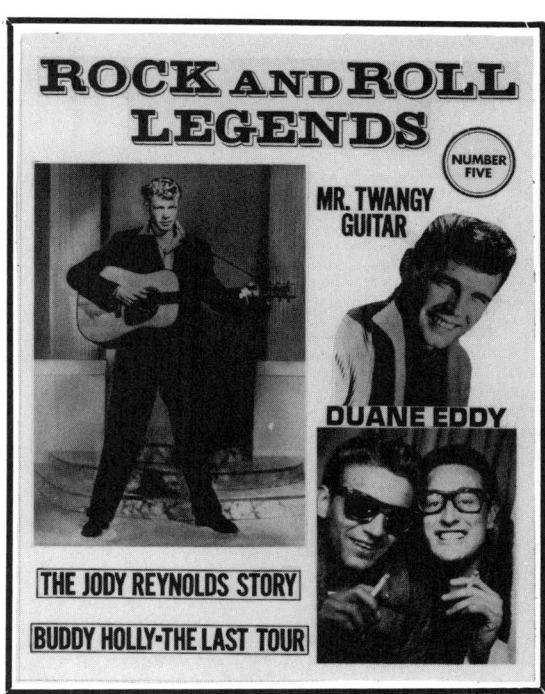

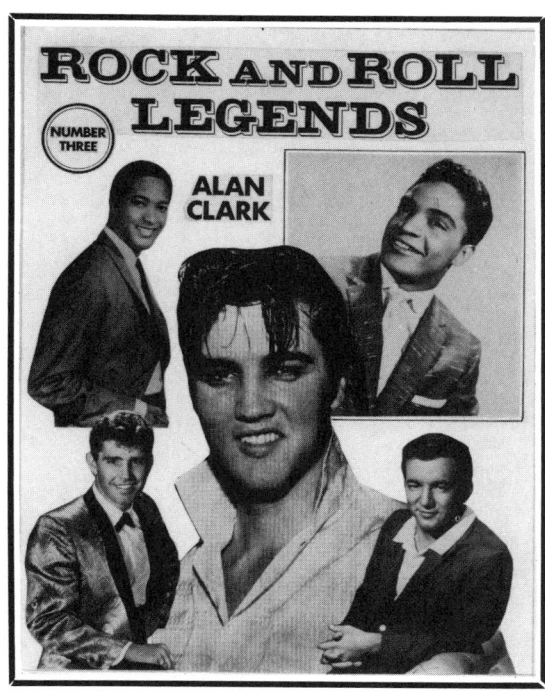

Name	Occupation	Address	City	Zip/Country
BRULL, PAMELA	ACTRESS	9255 SUNSET BLVD #1105	LOS ANGELES, CA	90069
BRUM, ALLAN	WRITER	8955 BEVERLY BLVD	LOS ANGELES, CA	90048
BRUMMER, ALEX	NEWS CORRESPONDENT	4801 BENDING LN, NW	WASHINGTON, DC	20007
BRUNDIN, BO	ACTOR	211 S BEVERLY DR #107	BEVERLY HILLS, CA	90212
BRUNEL, LUIS	FILM DIRECTOR	72 AVE DES CHAMPS ELYSE	PARIS 75008	FRANCE
BRUNELLE, TOM	ACTOR	7146 LA PRESA DR	LOS ANGELES, CA	90068
BRUNER, ANNE	ACTRESS	9165 SUNSET BLVD #202	LOS ANGELES, CA	90069
BRUNER, JAMES	SCREENWRITER	8383 WILSHIRE BLVD #923	BEVERLY HILLS, CA	90211
BRUNER, RICHARD W	WRITER	555 W 57TH ST #1230	NEW YORK, NY	10019
BRUNET, GENEVIEVE	ACTRESS	115 RE DE LA POMPE	PARIS 75116	FRANCE
BRUNETTI, ARENTINA	ACTRESS	2011 HOLLY HILL TERR	HOLLYWOOD, CA	90068
BRUNI, PETER	ACTOR	1613 N VISTA ST	LOS ANGELES, CA	90046
BRUNN, LOTTIE	JUGGLER	POST OFFICE BOX 87	WEST LEBANON, NY	12195
BRUNNER, DON	ACTOR	6430 SUNSET BLVD #1203	LOS ANGELES, CA	90028
BRUNNER, RICHARD	TENOR	61 W 62ND ST #6-F	NEW YORK, NY	10023
BRUNNER, ROBERT DWIGHT	TV WRITER-PRODUCER	17161 GRESHAM ST	NORTHRIDGE, CA	91325
BRUNNER, ROBERT F	COMPOSER-CONDUCTOR	169 N BOWLING GREEN WY	LOS ANGELES, CA	90049
BRUNO, CATHERINE	ACTRESS	200 W 57TH ST #1303	NEW YORK, NY	10019
BRUNO, DONNA	MEZZO-SOPRANO	CONE, 221 W 57TH ST	NEW YORK, NY	10019
BRUNO, MAURO	COMPOSER-CONDUCTOR	16934 MOONCREST DR	ENCINO, CA	91316
BRUNS, GEORGE	COMPOSER	POST OFFICE BOX 57	SANDY, OR	97055
BRUNS, MONA	ACTRESS	THOMAS, 4140 WARNER BLVD #210	BURBANK, CA	91522
BRUNS, PHILIP	ACTOR	1901 AVE OF THE STARS #840	LOS ANGELES, CA	90067
BRUNS, RICHARD	NEWS REPORTER	TIME/TIME & LIFE BLDG		
		ROCKEFELLER CENTER	NEW YORK, NY	10020
BRUNS, SCOTT	NEWS CORRESPONDENT	NBC-TV, NEWS DEPARTMENT		
		4001 NEBRASKA AVE, NW	WASHINGTON, DC	20016
BRUNSSEN, KAREN	MEZZO-SOPRANO	59 E 54TH ST #81	NEW YORK, NY	10022
BRUNSWICK, J P	WRITER	555 W 57TH ST #1230	NEW YORK, NY	10019
BRUNTON, GREG	CINEMATOGRAPHER	7715 SUNSET BLVD #150	LOS ANGELES, CA	90046
BRUNZELL, JUMPING JIM	WRESTLER	POST OFFICE BOX 3859	STAMFORD, CT	06905
BRUSCANTINI, SESTO	BARITONE	61 W 62ND ST #6-F	NEW YORK, NY	10023
BRUSH, ROBERT L, JR	TV WRITER	555 W 57TH ST #1230	NEW YORK, NY	10019
BRUSKOFF, JACK	ACTOR	4166 TUJUNGA AVE	STUDIO CITY, CA	91604
BRUSON, RENATO	BARITONE	CAMI, 165 W 57TH ST	NEW YORK, NY	10019
BRUSTADT, MARILYN	SOPRANO	45 W 60TH ST #4-K	NEW YORK, NY	10023
BRUSTIN, MICHELE	TV EXECUTIVE	NBC-TV, 3000 W ALAMEDA AVE	BURBANK, CA	91523
BRUTON, ERIC	WRITER	WHITE HOUSE, WIDMER END	BUCKS	ENGLAND
BRUTON, MARY WQ	WRITER	555 W 57TH ST #1230	NEW YORK, NY	10019
BRUTUS BEEFCAKE	WRESTLER	SEE - BEEFCAKE, BRUTUS		
BRUYERE, CHRISTIAN G	WRITER	8955 BEVERLY BLVD	LOS ANGELES, CA	90048
BRY, ELLEN	ACTRESS	9220 SUNSET BLVD #625	LOS ANGELES, CA	90069
BRYAN, BILL	WRITER	8955 BEVERLY BLVD	LOS ANGELES, CA	90048
BRYAN, DORA	ACTRESS	11 MARINE PARADE, BRIGHTON	SUSSEX	ENGLAND
BRYAN, JAMES E	FIDDLER	POST OFFICE BOX 111	MENTONE, AL	35984
BRYAN, LAWRENCE	ACTOR	ABC-TV, "GENERAL HOSPITAL"		
		1438 N GOWER ST	LOS ANGELES, CA	90028
BRYAN, ROBERT L, JR	NEWS CORRESPONDENT	5713 MARBEL ARCH WY	ALEXANDRIA, VA	22310
BRYAN, SHIRLEY	ACTRESS	HARBOR VILLAGE #28-D	BRANFORD, CT	06405
BRYAN, TIC	GUITARIST	POST OFFICE BOX 857	LEBANON, TN	37087
BRYANT, ANITA	SINGER	66 PACES WEST CT	ATLANTA, GA	30327
BRYANT, CHRIS	WRITER	8955 BEVERLY BLVD	LOS ANGELES, CA	90048
BRYANT, DAVID PAUL	PIANIST	ARDAVAN, 1606 N ARGYLE AVE	LOS ANGELES, CA	90028
BRYANT, JOHN	ACTOR	1585 CROSSROADS OF WORLD #107	HOLLYWOOD, CA	90028
BRYANT, JOSHUA	ACTOR	9744 WILSHIRE BLVD #206	BEVERLY HILLS, CA	90212
BRYANT, LEE	ACTRESS	9300 WILSHIRE BLVD #410	BEVERLY HILLS, CA	90212
BRYANT, MEG	NEWS CORRESPONDENT	4652-B S 28TH ST	ARLINGTON, VA	22206
BRYANT, MICHAEL	ACTOR	38 KILLYON RD	LONDON SW8	ENGLAND
BRYANT, PAMELA JEAN	ACTRESS-MODEL	8721 SUNSET BLVD #200	LOS ANGELES, CA	90069
BRYANT, WALTER E	COMPOSER-CONDUCTOR	1511 NE VIVION RD #12	GLADSTONE, MO	64118
BRYANT, WEB	ILLUSTRATOR	POST OFFICE BOX 500	WASHINGTON, DC	20044
BRYANT, WILLIAM	ACTOR	3518 W CAHUENGA BLVD #316	LOS ANGELES, CA	90068
BRYANT, WILLIAM J	ACTOR	1607 N EL CENTRO AVE #22	HOLLYWOOD, CA	90028
BRYAR, CLAUDIA	ACTRESS	4721 LAUREL CANYON BLVD #211	NORTH HOLLYWOOD, CA	91607
BRYAR, PAUL	ACTOR	9034 SUNSET BLVD #200	LOS ANGELES, CA	90069
BRYCE, JAMES	SCREENWRITER	555 W 57TH ST #1230	NEW YORK, NY	10019
BRYCE, SCOTT	ACTOR	CBS-TV, "AS THE WORLD TURNS"		
		51 W 52ND ST	NEW YORK, NY	10019
BRYDEN, BILL	FILM WRITER-DIRECTOR	FRASER, 91 REGENT ST	LONDON W1R 8RU	ENGLAND
BRYDEN, JANE	SOPRANO	254 W 93RD ST #8	NEW YORK, NY	10025
BRYER, MAXIMILLIAN	DIRECTOR	15363 MULHOLLAND DR	LOS ANGELES, CA	90077
BRYGGMAN, LARRY	ACTOR	CBS-TV, "AS THE WORLD TURNS"		
		51 W 52ND ST	NEW YORK, NY	10019
BRYN-JULSON, PHYLLIS	SOPRANO	COLBERT, 111 W 57TH ST	NEW YORK, NY	10019
BRYNE, BARBARA	ACTRESS	11726 SAN VICENTE BLVD #300	LOS ANGELES, CA	90049
BRYSAC, SHAREEN M	WRITER-PRODUCER	50 W 96TH ST	NEW YORK, NY	10025
BRYSON, A C	WRITER	8955 BEVERLY BLVD	LOS ANGELES, CA	90048
BRYSON, GAIL	ACTRESS	10000 RIVERSIDE DR #3	TOLUCA LAKE, CA	91602
BRYSON, PEABO	SINGER-SONGWRITER	1290 S OMNI INTERNATIONAL	ATLANTA, GA	30303
BRYSON, ROBERT P	SINGER-SONGWRITER	SEE - BRYSON, PEABO		
BRYTTAN, ADRIAN	CONDUCTOR	45 W 60TH ST #4-K	NEW YORK, NY	10023
BUBALO, RUDOLPH	COMPOSER	333 TAYLOR AVE N #202	SEATTLE, WA	98109
BUBEK, ALBERT	BODYBUILDER	POST OFFICE BOX 800-323	8000 MUNICH 80	WEST GERMANY
BUCCHINO, JOHN J	COMPOSER	527 N LAUREL AVE	LOS ANGELES, CA	90048

Name	Occupation	Address	City/State	ZIP
BUCCI, MARC	COMPOSER	5625 BECK AVE	NORTH HOLLYWOOD, CA	91601
BUCCOLA, DONALD	DIRECTOR	DGA, 7950 SUNSET BLVD	LOS ANGELES, CA	90046
BUCHAN, BETSY S	NEWS CORRESPONDENT	3374 WOODBURN RD	ANNANDALE, VA	22003
BUCHANAN, BUCK	VIOLINIST	2000 W WESTLEY RD, NW	ATLANTA, GA	90327
BUCHANAN, IAN	ACTOR	ABC-TV, "GENERAL HOSPITAL"		
		1438 N GOWER ST	LOS ANGELES, CA	90028
BUCHANAN, JAMES D	MUSIC ARRANGER	POST OFFICE BOX 1726	MORGANTON, NC	28655
BUCHANAN, JAMES D	WRITER-PRODUCER	21222 LOPEZ ST	WOODLAND HILLS, CA	91364
BUCHANAN, JENNIFER	ACTRESS	9165 SUNSET BLVD #202	LOS ANGELES, CA	90069
BUCHANAN, JOAN	SCREENWRITER	8955 BEVERLY BLVD	LOS ANGELES, CA	90048
BUCHANAN, LARRY	FILM WRITER-DIRECTOR	5440 LINDLEY AVE #205	ENCINO, CA	91316
BUCHANAN, MICHAEL C	NEWS CORRESPONDENT	4001 BRANDYWINE ST, NW	WASHINGTON, DC	20016
BUCHANAN, MORRIS	ACTOR	842 N FAIR OAKS AVE	PASADENA, CA	91103
BUCHANAN, PATRICK JOSEPH	TV HOST	1017 SAVILE LN N	MC LEAN, WA	22101
BUCHANAN, ROY	SINGER-GUITARIST	SLATUS, 332 W 22ND ST	NEW YORK, NY	10011
BUCHANAN, SONNY	FIDDLER	POST OFFICE BOX 182	NEW JOHNSONVILLE, TN	37134
BUCHBINDER, RUDOLF	PIANIST	CAMI, 165 W 57TH ST	NEW YORK, NY	10019
BUCHHOLZ, HORST	ACTOR	POSTMASTER/GENERAL DELIVERY	6068 LENZER HEIBE	SWITZERLAND
BUCHMAN, HAROLD	WRITER	8955 BEVERLY BLVD	LOS ANGELES, CA	90048
BUCHWALD, ART	COLUMNIST	1750 PENNSYLVANIA AVE, NW	WASHINGTON, DC	20006
BUCK, CRAIG	TV WRITER	151 S EL CAMINO DR	BEVERLY HILLS, CA	90212
BUCK, DAVID	ACTOR	PERFORMING ARTS, 1 HIND ST	LONDON W1	ENGLAND
BUCK, GEORGE	ACTOR	853 7TH AVE #9-A	NEW YORK, NY	10019
BUCK, JACK	SPORTSCASTER	CBS SPORTS, 51 W 52ND ST	NEW YORK, NY	10019
BUCK, MARY	CASTING DIRECTOR	4051 RADFORD AVE #B	STUDIO CITY, CA	91604
BUCK, RONALD L	SCREENWRITER	21606 PACIFIC COAST HWY	MALIBU, CA	90265
BUCK, SONNY BUD	SAXOPHONIST	511 CHESTERFIELD AVE #2-G	NASHVILLE, TN	37212
BUCK, STEVE	GUITARIST	102 LAKE TERRACE DR	HENDERSONVILLE, TN	37075
BUCK'S STOVE & RANGE COMPANY	BLUEGRASS GROUP	POST OFFICE BOX 1487	MILWAUKEE, WI	53201
BUCK-N-WING BAND, THE	C & W GROUP	PAU, RUSTIC ACRES	JASPER, IN	47546
BUCKAROOS, THE	C & W GROUP	OMAC, 237 W YOSEMITE AVE	MANTECA, CA	95336
BUCKEYE	ROCK & ROLL GROUP	9229 SUNSET BLVD #625	LOS ANGELES, CA	90069
BUCKEYE STRINGS, THE	C & W GROUP	POST OFFICE BOX 655	HUDSON, OH	44236
BUCKHANTZ, ALLAN	DIRECTOR	215 S MAPLE DR	BEVERLY HILLS, CA	90212
BUCKHOLTZ, TOM	DIRECTOR	3224 N RIVER RD	PT ALLEN, LA	70767
BUCKINGHAM, LINDSEY	SINGER-SONGWRITER	MICHAEL BROKOW MANAGEMENT		
		3389 CAMINO DE LA CUMBRE	SHERMAN OAKS, CA	91423
BUCKINGHAM, STEVE	GUITARIST	POST OFFICE BOX 998	LEBANON, TN	37087
BUCKINGHAMS, THE	ROCK & ROLL GROUP	DAVID FISHOFF PRODS		
		1775 BROADWAY	NEW YORK, NY	10019
BUCKLEY, BETTY	ACTRESS	10100 SANTA MONICA BLVD #1600	LOS ANGELES, CA	90067
BUCKLEY, CATHERINE	WRITER	555 W 57TH ST #1230	NEW YORK, NY	10019
BUCKLEY, CATHERINE L	NEWS CORRESPONDENT	8215 CEDAR ST	SILVER SPRING, MD	20910
BUCKLEY, EMERSON	CONDUCTOR	1776 BROADWAY #504	NEW YORK, NY	10019
BUCKLEY, J TAYLOR	NEWS EDITOR	POST OFFICE BOX 500	WASHINGTON, DC	20044
BUCKLEY, JAMES	DIRECTOR	1042 18TH AVE	HONOLULU, HI	96816
BUCKLEY, KATHLEEN M	NEWS CORRESPONDENT	3237 S 6TH ST	ARLINGTON, VA	22204
BUCKLEY, KEITH	ACTOR	18 NETHERTON RD	TWICKENHAM	ENGLAND
BUCKLEY, LINDA M	NEWS CORRESPONDENT	3029 HEATHCOTE RD	WALDORF, MD	20601
BUCKLEY, RICHARD	CONDUCTOR	1776 BROADWAY #504	NEW YORK, NY	10019
BUCKLEY, RICHARD	WRITER	555 W 57TH ST #1230	NEW YORK, NY	10019
BUCKLEY, RICHARD L	NEWS CORRESPONDENT	8215 CEDAR ST	SILVER SPRING, MD	20910
BUCKLEY, WILLIAM F, JR	AUTHOR-EDITOR	778 PARK AVE	NEW YORK, NY	10016
BUCKLEY, WILLIAM G	DIRECTOR	2 HALF MILE COMMON	WESTPORT, CT	06880
BUCKLEY, WILLIAM T	WRITER	555 W 57TH ST #1230	NEW YORK, NY	10019
BUCKMAN, TARA	ACTRESS	11715 LA MAIDA ST	NORTH HOLLYWOOD, CA	91607
BUCKMAN, TARA	ACTRESS	9744 WILSHIRE BLVD #306	BEVERLY HILLS, CA	90212
BUCKNER, BETTY	ACTRESS	6000 MONTEREY RD #B	LOS ANGELES, CA	90042
BUCKNER, BILL	BASEBALL	3 MC DONALD CIR	ANDOVER, MA	01810
BUCKNER, BRAD	TV WRITER-PRODUCER	2017 N TAFT AVE	LOS ANGELES, CA	90068
BUCKNER, JUDITH F	WRITER	1216 WASHINGTON BLVD	VENICE, CA	90291
BUCKWALTER, JOHN	ACTOR	117 W 57TH ST	NEW YORK, NY	10019
BUCKWHEAT ZYDECO	CAJUN BAND	CONCERTED EFFORTS		
		110 MADISON AVE	NEWTONVILLE, MA	02160
BUDAHN, PHILIP J	NEWS CORRESPONDENT	4327 RAVENSWORTH RD #119	ANNANDALE, VA	22003
BUDAI, LIVIA	MEZZO-SOPRANO	111 W 57TH ST #1209	NEW YORK, NY	10019
BUDAI, THOMAS P	PHOTOJOURNALIST	1711 N 17TH ST	ARLINGTON, VA	22209
BUDAY, DON	WRITER	3620 LANKERSHIM BLVD	LOS ANGELES, CA	90068
BUDD, ANDRIA	WRITER	555 W 57TH ST #1230	NEW YORK, NY	10019
BUDD, JOE	ACTOR	6533 HOLLYWOOD BLVD #201	HOLLYWOOD, CA	90028
BUDD, JULIE	ACTRESS	6430 SUNSET BLVD #1203	LOS ANGELES, CA	90028
BUDD, ROY	COMPOSER	91 RUE DU FAUBOURG		
		SAINT-HUNORE	PARIS 75008	FRANCE
BUDD, TERENCE	ACTOR	29 RYLETTE RD	LONDON W12	ENGLAND
BUDDY, AVERY	SCREENWRITER	8955 BEVERLY BLVD	LOS ANGELES, CA	90048
BUDGE, KATIE	ACTRESS	6430 SUNSET BLVD #701	LOS ANGELES, CA	90028
BUDIANSKY, STEPHEN	NEWS CORRESPONDENT	ROUTE #4	FREDERICK, MD	21701
BUDIN, ELBERT	DIRECTOR	15 HEATHCOTE RD	SCARSDALE, NY	10583
BUDIN, JEFFREY	COMPOSER-CONDUCTOR	3324 BEETHOVEN ST	LOS ANGELES, CA	90066
BUDRYS, ALGIRDAS J	WRITER	8955 BEVERLY BLVD	LOS ANGELES, CA	90048
BUECHNER, DAVID	PIANIST	SOFFER, 130 W 56TH ST	NEW YORK, NY	10019
BUEHLER, JUNE KNIGHT	ACTRESS	SEE - KNIGHT, JUNE		
BUELL, JAMES M	WRITER	555 W 57TH ST #1230	NEW YORK, NY	10019
BUELL, JOANNA JACOBS	GUITARIST	3246 NIAGARA DR	NASHVILLE, TN	37214
BUERKLE, MARILYN L	NEWS CORRESPONDENT	400 N CAPITOL ST, NW	WASHINGTON, DC	20001

Name	Occupation	Address	City	Code
BUFANO, VINCENT	ACTOR	4543 COLDWATER CANYON AVE	STUDIO CITY, CA	91604
BUFFETT, JIMMY	SINGER-SONGWRITER	FRONT LINE MANAGEMENT		
		80 UNIVERSAL CITY PLAZA	UNIVERSAL CITY, CA	91608
BUFFIN, CAROL	WRESTLING CORRES	THE WORLD WRESTLING		
		FEDERATION MAGAZINE		
		TITAN SPORTS PUBS		
		1055 SUMMER ST	STAMFORD, CT	06905
BUFFONE, MICHELE	ACTRESS	371 N GARDNER ST	LOS ANGELES, CA	90036
BUFMAN, ZEV	THEATER PRODUCER	1466 BROADWAY	NEW YORK, NY	10036
BUGDEN, SUE	ACTRESS	6545 SIMPSON AVE #19	NORTH HOLLYWOOD, CA	91606
BUGGLES, THE	ROCK & ROLL GROUP	ISLAND RECORDS COMPANY		
		22 SAINT PETERS SQ	LONDON W69 NW	ENGLAND
BUGIN, HARRY	ACTOR	88-08 32ND AVE	JACKSON HEIGHTS, NY	11369
BUGLIOSI, VINCENT	ATTORNEY-AUTHOR	9300 WILSHIRE BLVD #470	BEVERLY HILLS, CA	90210
BUHAI, JEFF	SCREENWRITER	454 S IRVING BLVD	LOS ANGELES, CA	90020
BUHLER, MICHAELA	NEWS CORRESPONDENT	142 N CAROLINA AVE, SE	WASHINGTON, DC	20003
BUHRMAN, DOROTHY	ACTRESS	12800 MOORPARK ST #15	STUDIO CITY, CA	91604
BUJOLD, GENEVIEVE	ACTRESS	1849 SAWTELLE BLVD #500	LOS ANGELES, CA	90025
BUKA, DONALD	ACTOR	317 W 89TH ST	NEW YORK, NY	10024
BUKSBAUM, DAVID	TV DIRECTOR	CBS-TV, 524 W 57TH ST	NEW YORK, NY	10019
BUKTENICA, RAY	ACTOR	11873 ROCHESTER AVE	LOS ANGELES, CA	90025
BULASKY, DAVID	ACTOR	250 W 57TH ST #2317	NEW YORK, NY	10107
BULIFANT, JOYCE	ACTRESS	6310 SAN VICENTE BLVD #407	LOS ANGELES, CA	90048
BULL, DAVID J G	NEWS CORRESPONDENT	2413 ECCLESTON ST	SILVER SPRING, MD	20902
BULL, DEBBY	WRITER-EDITOR	US MAGAZINE COMPANY		
		1 DAG HAMMARSKJOLD PLAZA	NEW YORK, NY	10017
BULL, RICHARD	ACTOR	151 N SAN VICENTE BLVD #208	BEVERLY HILLS, CA	90211
BULL, SHELDON	WRITER	16258 DORILEE LN	ENCINO, CA	91436
BULLARD, CECE	ACTRESS	11240 MAGNOLIA BLVD #202	NORTH HOLLYWOOD, CA	91601
BULLARD, GENE	TENOR	GEWALD, 58 W 58TH ST	NEW YORK, NY	10019
BULLARD, JOHN SPENCE	PHOTOJOURNALIST	6611 BIRCHLEIGH WY	ALEXANDRIA, VA	22310
BULLARD, NIGEL	ACTOR	3840 POTOMAC AVE #15	LOS ANGELES, CA	90008
BULLDOG	WRESTLER	SEE - KENT, BULLDOG DON		
BULLEY, TONY	TV DIRECTOR	NINA BLATT, THE COACH HOUSE		
		1-A LARPENT AVE	LONDON SW15	ENGLAND
BULLING, ERICH	CONDUCTOR	15220 LA MAIDA ST	SHERMAN OAKS, CA	91403
BULLINGTON, DEWEL	VIOLINIST	ROUTE #3, WILLOW LAKE DR	PORTLAND, TN	37148
BULLINGTON, PERRY	ACTOR	849 MARCO PL	VENICE, CA	90291
BULLION, LARRY CURTIS	PIANIST	220 CHAPEL AVE	NASHVILLE, TN	37206
BULLOCK, EARL	ACTOR	427 N CANON DR #205	BEVERLY HILLS, CA	90210
BULLOCK, HARVEY	TV WRITER	8955 BEVERLY BLVD	LOS ANGELES, CA	90048
BULLOCK, JM JACKSON	ACTOR	6210 TEMPLE HILL DR	LOS ANGELES, CA	90069
BULLUCK, VICANGELO	SCREENWRITER	8955 BEVERLY BLVD	LOS ANGELES, CA	90048
BULLY, RALPH	WRESTLING REFEREE	WORLD CLASS WRESTLING		
		SOUTHWEST SPORTS, INC		
		DALLAS SPORTATORIUM		
		1000 S INDUSTRIAL BLVD	DALLAS, TX	75207
BULVA, JOSEF	PIANIST	CAMI, 165 W 57TH ST	NEW YORK, NY	10019
BUMATAI, DANIELLE	SINGER	ICM, 8899 BEVERLY BLVD	LOS ANGELES, CA	90048
BUMBRY, GRACE	SOPRANO	119 W 57TH ST #1015	NEW YORK, NY	10019
BUMESS, TAD	COLUMNIST	NEWS AMERICA SYNDICATE		
		1703 KAISER AVE	IRVINE, CA	92714
BUMSTEAD, J P	ACTOR	10405 FOOTHILL BLVD	LAKE VIEW, CA	91342
BUMSTED, BRADLEY E	NEWS CORRESPONDENT	2911 ROGERS DR	FALLS CHURCH, VA	22043
BUNCH, CHRISTOPHER R	WRITER	432 27TH ST	MANHATTAN BEACH, CA	90266
BUNCH, JACK D	WRITER	8955 BEVERLY BLVD	LOS ANGELES, CA	90048
BUNCH, MARIANNE	ACTRESS	8485 MELROSE PL #E	LOS ANGELES, CA	90069
BUNCH, VELTON RAY	CONDUCTOR	10640 JOHANNA AVE	SUNLAND, CA	91040
BUNDOCK, SUSAN	NEWS CORRESPONDENT	400 N CAPITOL ST, NW	WASHINGTON, DC	20001
BUNDY, BROOKE	ACTRESS	833 N MARTEL AVE	LOS ANGELES, CA	90046
BUNDY, CHARLES E	GUITARIST	POST OFFICE BOX 121483	NASHVILLE, TN	37212
BUNDY, CHRIS	WRESTLER	SEE - BUNDY, KING KONG		
BUNDY, KING KONG	WRESTLER	POST OFFICE BOX 3859	STAMFORD, CT	06905
BUNEL, JEAN-LUIS	ACTOR	14 RUE DES ARTISTES	PARIS 92800	FRANCE
BUNGERT, DOUGLAS	ACTOR	10920 ROSE AVE #2	LOS ANGELES, CA	90034
BUNIM, MARY-ELLIS	TV PRODUCER	402 E 76TH ST	NEW YORK, NY	10021
BUNIS, MIKE	PIANIST	2713 BELMONT BLVD	NASHVILLE, TN	37212
BUNKER, EDWARD	WRITER	555 W 57TH ST #1230	NEW YORK, NY	10019
BUNKER, LARRY	COMPOSER	2244 LIVE OAK DR E	LOS ANGELES, CA	90068
BUNKS, CAREY	CLOWN	2701 COTTAGE WY #14	SACRAMENTO, CA	95825
BUNNAGE, AVIS	ACTRESS	NEMS, 31 KINGS RD	LONDON SW3	ENGLAND
BUNNELL, JANE	MEZZO-SOPRANO	HILLYER, 250 W 57TH ST	NEW YORK, NY	10107
BUNNELL, ROBERT A	NEWS CORRESPONDENT	4226 COLUMBIA PIKE #21	ARLINGTON, VA	22204
BUNNING, JIM	BASEBALL	30 WINSTON HILL RD	FORT THOMAS, KY	41075
BUNNYDROMS, THE	ROCK & ROLL GROUP	1704 N 5TH ST	PHILADELPHIA, PA	19122
BUNTING, FINDLAY	WRITER	1015 GAYLEY AVE #301	LOS ANGELES, CA	90024
BUNTZ, GINA	DANCER	AFFILIATE ARTISTS, INC		
		37 W 65TH ST, 6TH FLOOR	NEW YORK, NY	10023
BUNUEL, JOYCE	WRITER	555 W 57TH ST #1230	NEW YORK, NY	10019
BUNUEL, LUIS	DIRECTOR	GREENWICH FILM PRODUCTIONS		
		72 AVE DES CHAMPS-ELYSEES	PARIS 75008	FRANCE
BUNUEL, RAFAEL A	WRITER	8955 BEVERLY BLVD	LOS ANGELES, CA	90048
BUNZOW, JOHN	SINGER	2112 W LINDEN AVE	NASHVILLE, TN	37212
BUOY UP	ROCK & ROLL GROUP	41 BRITAIN ST #200	TORONTO, ONT	CANADA
BURANSKAS, KAREN	CELLIST	KAY, 58 W 58TH ST	NEW YORK, NY	10019

Name	Occupation	Address	City	Zip
BURBANK, JOE	PHOTOGRAPHER	5023 WISSIOMING RD	BETHESDA, MD	20085
BURCH, CURTIS E, JR	GUITARIST	POST OFFICE BOX 189	SMITH GROVE, KY	42171
BURCH, JACKIE	CASTING DIRECTOR	MCA/UNIVERSAL STUDIOS, INC		
		100 UNIVERSAL CITY PLAZA	UNIVERSAL CITY, CA	91608
BURCH, JANE	ACTRESS	1451 1/2 N MANSFIELD AVE	LOS ANGELES, CA	90028
BURCH, RICHARD O	GUITARIST-BANJOIST	ROUTE #8	GLASGOW, KY	42141
BURCH, SHELLY	ACTRESS	ABC-TV, "ONE LIFE TO LIVE"		
		1330 AVE OF THE AMERICAS	NEW YORK, NY	10019
BURCH, SHERRY WILLIS	ACTRESS	341 1/2 N STANLEY AVE	LOS ANGELES, CA	90036
BURCH, VERNON	SINGER-GUITARIST	6430 SUNSET BLVD #1516	LOS ANGELES, CA	90028
BURCH, WILLIAM JAMES	COMPOSER	777 MARION AVE	PALO ALTO, CA	94301
BURCHER, CHARLES	FIDDLER	2401 OAKLAND AVE	NASHVILLE, TN	37212
BURCHETT, PHIL & LARRY	VOCAL DUO	POST OFFICE BOX 211	EAST PRAIRIE, MO	63845
BURCHETTE, ROBERT	PHOTOGRAPHER	ROUTE #1, 1733 DREVAR TRAIL	ANNAPOLIS, MD	21401
BURCHFIELD, STEPHANIE	ACTRESS	2275 VASANTA WY	HOLLYWOOD, CA	90068
BURCHINAL, FREDERICK	BARITONE	CAMI, 165 W 57TH ST	NEW YORK, NY	10019
BURDEAU, GEORGE	TV DIRECTOR	12330 OSBORNE #34	HANSEN HILLS, CA	91331
BURDETTE, AGNES	GUITARIST	610 N GRAYCROFT AVE	MADISON, TN	37115
BURDETTE, AVERY L	PIANIST	119 37TH AVE N	NASHVILLE, TN	37209
BURDETTE, LOU	BASEBALL	2837 GULF OF MEXICO DR	LONGBOAT KEY, FL	33548
BURDITT, GEORGE	TV WRITER-PRODUCER	1009 E WALNUT AVE	BURBANK, CA	91501
BURDITT, JOYCE	TV WRITER	1009 E WALNUT AVE	BURBANK, CA	91501
BUREAU, KAREN	SOPRANO	COLBERT, 111 W 57TH ST	NEW YORK, NY	10019
BUREY, JOSEPH M	NEWS CORRESPONDENT	3221 CONNECTICUT AVE #405, NW	WASHINGTON, DC	20008
BURFORD, TOM	ACTOR	20 SUNNYSIDE AVE #241	MILL VALLEY, CA	94941
BURGDORF, BARBARA	ACTRESS	11516 MOORPARK ST #6	NORTH HOLLYWOOD, CA	91602
BURGE, DAVID	PIANIST	149 IRVING RD	ROCHESTER, NY	14618
BURGE, GREGG	SINGER	ICM, 8899 BEVERLY BLVD	LOS ANGELES, CA	90048
BURGER, NEAL R	WRITER	4308 ALCOVE AVE	STUDIO CITY, CA	91604
BURGER, ROBERT I	NEWS REPORTER	TIME/TIME & LIFE BLDG		
		ROCKEFELLER CENTER	NEW YORK, NY	10020
BURGESS, ANTHONY	ACTOR	44 RUE GRIMALDI	MONTE CARLO	MONACO
BURGESS, CHET	BROADCAST JOURNALIST	125 ELYSIAN WY, NW	ATLANTA, GA	30327
BURGESS, COLE	SAXOPHONIST	3611 MEADOWBROOK AVE	NASHVILLE, TN	37205
BURGESS, DAVE	GUITARIST	815 18TH AVE S	NASHVILLE, TN	37203
BURGESS, DICK	COMEDIAN	CEE, 193 KONHAUS RD	MECHANICSBURG, PA	17055
BURGESS, GRANVILLE W	TV WRITER	555 W 57TH ST #1230	NEW YORK, NY	10019
BURGESS, MARY	SOPRANO	CAMI, 165 W 57TH ST	NEW YORK, NY	10019
BURGESS, THOMAS F	NEWS CORRESPONDENT	6344 SHAUNDALE DR	SPRINGFIELD, VA	22152
BURGESS, VIVIENNE	ACTRESS	ACTORUM, 21 TOWER ST	LONDON WC 2	ENGLAND
BURGESS, WILMA	SINGER	POST OFFICE DRAWER #1	MADISON, TN	37203
BURGGRAF, PAUL S	DIRECTOR	220 E 54TH ST #6-C	NEW YORK, NY	10022
BURGHEIM, RICHARD A	PUBLISHING EXECUTIVE	TELEVISION-CABLE WEEK		
		1271 AVE OF THE AMERICAS	NEW YORK, NY	10020
BURGON, GEOFFREY	COMPOSER	FIRST COMPOSERS COMPANY		
		14 NEW BURLINGTON ST	LONDON W1X 2LR	ENGLAND
BURGOS, ROBERT	ACTOR	753 1/2 N CITRUS AVE	LOS ANGELES, CA	90038
BURGUNDY THREE, THE	MUSIC TRIO	260 W END AVE #7-A	NEW YORK, NY	10023
BURKE, ALFRED	ACTOR	32 HELLERDON AVE	LONDON SW13	ENGLAND
BURKE, ANDREW	WRITER	14144 VENTURA BLVD #200	SHERMAN OAKS, CA	91423
BURKE, CHUCKY	DRUMMER	715 HART AVE	NASHVILLE, TN	37206
BURKE, DAVE	COMPOSER	8211 BOBBYBOYAR AVE	CANOGA PARK, CA	91304
BURKE, DAVID	TV PRODUCER	NBC TEVELISION NETWORK		
		30 ROCKEFELLER PLAZA	NEW YORK, NY	10112
BURKE, DAVID L	ACTOR	12206 HILLSLOPE ST	STUDIO CITY, CA	91604
BURKE, DAVID W	TV EXECUTIVE	ABC-TV, 7 W 66TH ST	NEW YORK, NY	10023
BURKE, DELTA	ACTRESS	POST OFFICE BOX 1276	NORTH HOLLYWOOD, CA	91604
BURKE, DENISE W	TV EXECUTIVE	ABC TELEVISION NETWORK		
		1330 AVE OF THE AMERICAS	NEW YORK, NY	10019
BURKE, FLORA	ACTRESS	8721 SUNSET BLVD #200	LOS ANGELES, CA	90069
BURKE, FRENCHIE	SINGER	POST OFFICE BOX 225	NACOGDOCHES, TX	75963
BURKE, JAMES	TV WRITER-PRODUCER	CLOWES, 22 PRINCE ALBERT RD	LONDON NW1 7ST	ENGLAND
BURKE, JOHNNY	SINGER	PT & M MANAGEMENT		
		2464 BRASILIA CIR	MISS, ONT L5N 2G1	CANADA
BURKE, JOSEPH	ACTOR	1717 N HIGHLAND AVE #414	LOS ANGELES, CA	90028
BURKE, KELLY	NEWS CORRESPONDENT	WRC-TV, NEWS DEPARTMENT		
		4001 NEBRASKA AVE, NW	WASHINGTON, DC	20016
BURKE, MARTYN	DIRECTOR	ICM, 8899 BEVERLY BLVD	LOS ANGELES, CA	90048
BURKE, MARYBETH	NEWS CORRESPONDENT	3504 "T" ST, NW	WASHINGTON, DC	20007
BURKE, PATRICK SULLIVAN	ACTOR	14155 MAGNOLIA BLVD #120	SHERMAN OAKS, CA	91423
BURKE, PAUL	ACTOR	6310 SAN VICENTE BLVD #407	LOS ANGELES, CA	90048
BURKE, SOLOMON	SINGER	JE MGMT, 200 W 57TH ST	NEW YORK, NY	10019
BURKE, SUSAN	ACTRESS	1418 N HIGHLAND AVE #102	LOS ANGELES, CA	90028
BURKELY, DENNIS	ACTOR	1930 CENTURY PARK W #303	LOS ANGELES, CA	90067
BURKETT, FREIDA	SAXOPHONIST	2460 CROCKER SPRINGS RD	GOODLETTSVILLE, TN	37072
BURKETT, JERRY	ACCORDIONIST	2460 CROCKER SPRINGS RD	GOODLETTSVILLE, TN	37072
BURKH, DENNIS	COMPOSER-CONDUCTOR	POST OFFICE BOX U	REDDING, CT	06875
BURKHARDT, RICHARD	NEWS CORRESPONDENT	653 E CAPITOL ST #1, NW	WASHINGTON, DC	20003
BURKHARDT, ROBERT	NEWS CORRESPONDENT	POST OFFICE BOX W	SHEPHERDSTOWN, WV	25443
BURKHART, JEFF C	SCREENWRITER	8955 BEVERLY BLVD	LOS ANGELES, CA	90048
BURKLEY, DENNIS	ACTOR	5145 COSTELLO AVE	SHERMAN OAKS, CA	91423
BURKLEY, H LLOYD	DIRECTOR	121 BARTRAM RD	MARLTON, NJ	08053

Name	Occupation	Address	City	Zip
BURKLY, KATHLEEN	DRUMMER	1131 BROADWAY #1	SOMERVILLE, MA	02144
BURKONS, HOWARD	ACTOR	4012 COLDWATER CANYON AVE	STUDIO CITY, CA	91604
BURKOW, STEVE	TV WRITER	ABC-TV, "ALL MY CHILDREN"		
		1330 AVE OF THE AMERICAS	NEW YORK, NY	10019
BURLAGE, JOHN D	NEWS CORRESPONDENT	7917 BUBBLING BROOK CIR	SPRINGFIELD, VA	22153
BURLBAUGH, GEORGE L	NEWS CORRESPONDENT	1012 BAYBERRY DR	ARNOLD, MD	21012
BURLEY, MARK	PRODUCER	MCA/UNIVERSAL STUDIOS, INC		
		100 UNIVERSAL CITY PLAZA	UNIVERSAL CITY, CA	91608
BURLEY, MARK ALAN	DIRECTOR	11250 LAURIE DR	STUDIO CITY, CA	91604
BURMAS, RONALD M	NEWS CORRESPONDENT	1201 CONNECTICUT AVE, NW	WASHINGTON, DC	20036
BURMEISTER, DOUGLAS	ACTOR	124 W 71ST ST	NEW YORK, NY	10023
BURMESTER, BRUCE	TV DIRECTOR	19618 WEEBURN LN	TARZANA, CA	91356
BURN, JONATHAN	ACTOR	69 CHIPPENHAM RD #2	LONDON W9	ENGLAND
BURNARD, SANDY	ACTRESS	721 N LA BREA AVE #200	LOS ANGELES, CA	90028
BURNETT, BOBBY	COMEDIAN	CEE, 193 KONHAUS RD	MECHANICSBURG, PA	17055
BURNETT, CAROL	ACTRESS	10601 WILSHIRE BLVD #501	LOS ANGELES, CA	90024
BURNETT, DAVID	PHOTOGRAPHER	328 W 19TH ST	NEW YORK, NY	10011
BURNETT, JIM	CARTOONIST	KING FEATURES SYNDICATE		
		235 E 45TH ST	NEW YORK, NY	10017
BURNETT, JOHN	WRITER	555 W 57TH ST #1230	NEW YORK, NY	10019
BURNETT, MURRAY	WRITER	555 W 57TH ST #1230	NEW YORK, NY	10019
BURNETT, NANCY	ACTRESS	8721 SUNSET BLVD #103	LOS ANGELES, CA	90069
BURNETT, RAYMOND CHRIS	NEWS CORRESPONDENT	18341 ALLSPICE DR	GERMANTOWN, MD	20874
BURNETT, T-BONE	SINGER	6255 SUNSET BLVD #1214	HOLLYWOOD, CA	90028
BURNETTE, BILLY	SINGER-GUITARIST	10100 SANTA MONICA BLVD #1600	LOS ANGELES, CA	90067
BURNETTE, GARY	BANJOIST	POST OFFICE BOX 120113	NASHVILLE, TN	37212
BURNETTE, ROCKY	SINGER	1900 AVE OF THE STARS #2530	LOS ANGELES, CA	90067
BURNETTE, SONNY	GUITARIST	108 CRESTMONT DR	HENDERSONVILLE, TN	37075
BURNEY, STEVE	ACTOR	29 W 84TH ST #1-B	NEW YORK, NY	10024
BURNHAM, DAVID	NEWS CORRESPONDENT	524 6TH ST, SE	WASHINGTON, DC	20003
BURNHAM, EDWARD	TV WRITER	1240 YALE ST	SANTA MONICA, CA	90404
BURNHAM, STEPHEN C	SCREENWRITER	729 1/2 N FORMOSA AVE	LOS ANGELES, CA	90046
BURNIER, JEANNINE	TV WRITER	8955 BEVERLY BLVD	LOS ANGELES, CA	90048
BURNING BRIDGES, THE	ROCK & ROLL GROUP	POST OFFICE BOX 81973	SAN DIEGO, CA	92138
BURNING SENSATIONS	SOUL GROUP	4570 ENCINO AVE	ENCINO, CA	91316
BURNING SPEAR	RHYTHM & BLUES GROUP	FAST LANE PRODUCTIONS		
		4590 MAC ARTHUR BLVD, NW	WASHINGTON, DC	20007
BURNS, ALAN	FILM DIRECTOR	34 W COLUMBIA ST	HEMPSTEAD, NY	11550
BURNS, ALLAN P	WRITER-PRODUCER	1660 MANDEVILLE CANYON BLVD	LOS ANGELES, CA	90049
BURNS, BONNIE	DIRECTOR-PRODUCER	10523 MARS LN	LOS ANGELES, CA	90077
BURNS, BRENDAN	ACTOR	12749 HART ST	NORTH HOLLYWOOD, CA	91605
BURNS, CATHERINE	ACTRESS	211 S BEVERLY DR #201	BEVERLY HILLS, CA	90212
BURNS, CHRISTOPHER W	NEWS CORRESPONDENT	1825 "K" ST, NW	WASHINGTON, DC	20006
BURNS, DAVID A	GUITARIST	ROUTE #1, SNAIL SHELL CAVE	ROCKVALE, TN	37153
BURNS, DAVID S	PHOTOGRAPHER	2665 HOMECREST AVE	BROOKLYN, NY	11235
BURNS, DIANE J	PIANIST	2824 WINDEMERE DR	NASHVILLE, TN	37214
BURNS, EILEEN	ACTRESS	400 W 43RD ST	NEW YORK, NY	10036
BURNS, ERIC	NEWS-TV CORRES	NBC-TV, NEWS DEPARTMENT		
		30 ROCKEFELLER PLAZA	NEW YORK, NY	10112
BURNS, FRANCIS	SCREENWRITER	8955 BEVERLY BLVD	LOS ANGELES, CA	90048
BURNS, FRANK	DIRECTOR	DGA, 110 W 57TH ST	NEW YORK, NY	10019
BURNS, GARY	TV WRITER	8955 BEVERLY BLVD	LOS ANGELES, CA	90048
BURNS, GEORGE	ACTOR-COMEDIAN	720 N MAPLE DR	BEVERLY HILLS, CA	90210
BURNS, JACK	ACTOR-COMEDIAN	8075 W 3RD ST #303	LOS ANGELES, CA	90048
BURNS, JETHRO	MUSICIAN	POST OFFICE BOX 1487	MILWAUKEE, WI	53201
BURNS, JOE A	WRITER-PRODUCER	1155 N BRAND BLVD #802	GLENDALE, CA	91202
BURNS, JOHN F	ACTOR-WRITER	8955 BEVERLY BLVD	LOS ANGELES, CA	90048
BURNS, JOHN F	PRODUCER	30010 ANDROMEDA LN	MALIBU, CA	90265
BURNS, JUDY A	WRITER	9200 SUNSET BLVD #531	LOS ANGELES, CA	90069
BURNS, KATHRYN SUE	ACTRESS	1741 N IVAR AVE #221	LOS ANGELES, CA	90028
BURNS, KEITH	WRITER-DIRECTOR	6026 MESA AVE	LOS ANGELES, CA	90042
BURNS, MARILYN	ACTRESS	MARX, 11130 HUSTON ST	NORTH HOLLYWOOD, CA	91601
BURNS, MARK	ACTOR	44 TEMPERLEY RD	LONDON SW12	ENGLAND
BURNS, PATRICE	ACTRESS	5330 LANKERSHIM BLVD #210	NORTH HOLLYWOOD, CA	91601
BURNS, RALPH J	COMPOSER-CONDUCTOR	7416 WOODROW WILSON DR	LOS ANGELES, CA	90046
BURNS, ROBERT D	NEWS CORRESPONDENT	1755 S JEFFERSON DAVIS HWY	ARLINGTON, VA	22202
BURNS, ROBERT LEWIS	MUSIC ARRANGER	5001 MC LENDON DR	ANTIOCH, TN	37013
BURNS, ROJO	GUITARIST	POST OFFICE BOX 21331	NASHVILLE, TN	37221
BURNS, RON	WRITER	8955 BEVERLY BLVD	LOS ANGELES, CA	90048
BURNS, STAN	TV WRITER	8955 BEVERLY BLVD	LOS ANGELES, CA	90048
BURNS, STEPHEN	TRUMPETER	AFFILIATE ARTISTS, INC		
		37 W 65TH ST, 6TH FLOOR	NEW YORK, NY	10023
BURNS, TIMOTHY	TV WRITER	2077 N BEVERLY GLEN BLVD	LOS ANGELES, CA	90077
BURNS, VERONICA	REPORTER	TIME & PEOPLE MAGAZINE		
		TIME & LIFE BUILDING		
		ROCKEFELLER CENTER	NEW YORK, NY	10020
BURNS, VICKIE	WRITER	555 W 57TH ST #1230	NEW YORK, NY	10019
BURNS, WARREN O	COMPOSER	11714 TERRABELLA ST	LAKE VIEW TERRACE, CA	91342
BURNS, WILFRED	COMPOSER-CONDUCTOR	RONDO LIME GROVE		
		WEST CLANDON	SURREY	ENGLAND
BURNS-BISOGNO, LOUISA	TV WRITER	555 W 57TH ST #1230	NEW YORK, NY	10019
BURNSIDE, DENNIS J	PIANIST	26 LORI LN	MOUNT JULIET, TN	37122
BURR, BRIAN	MUSICIAN	2523 STINSON RD	NASHVILLE, TN	37214
BURR, COURTNEY	THEATER PRODUCER	5 TUDOR CITY PL	NEW YORK, NY	10017
BURR, DICK	ACTOR	9220 SUNSET BLVD #218	LOS ANGELES, CA	90069

Name	Occupation	Address	City	Zip/Country
BURR, FRITZI	ACTRESS	1752 PREUSS RD	LOS ANGELES, CA	90035
BURR, LONNIE	ACTOR-WRITER	3518 W CAHUENGA BLVD #316	LOS ANGELES, CA	90068
BURR, OSCAR	SINGER	POST OFFICE BOX 25371	CHARLOTTE, NC	28212
BURR, RAYMOND	ACTOR-DIRECTOR	POST OFFICE BOX 678	GEYSERVILLE, CA	95441
BURR, ROBERT	ACTOR	19 W 44TH ST #1500	NEW YORK, NY	10036
BURR, WALTER S	DIRECTOR	11632 VENTURA BLVD #203	STUDIO CITY, CA	91604
BURRELL, GINA EHRLICH	ACTRESS	8927 HOLLY PL	LOS ANGELES, CA	90046
BURRELL, JAN	ACTRESS	8721 SUNSET BLVD #200	LOS ANGELES, CA	90069
BURRELL, KENNY, TRIO	JAZZ TRIO	KEANE, 49 E 96TH ST	NEW YORK, NY	10128
BURRELL, MARYEDITH	ACTRESS-WRITER	435 N SWEETZER AVE	LOS ANGELES, CA	90048
BURRELL, PETER JOHN	WRITER-PRODUCER	8927 HOLLY PL	LOS ANGELES, CA	90046
BURRELLE, ELIZABETH	ACTRESS	500 S SEPULVEDA BLVD #510	LOS ANGELES, CA	90049
BURRILL, TIMOTHY	FILM PRODUCER	51 LANSDOWNE RD	LONDON W11 2LG	ENGLAND
BURRINGTON, DAVID	NEWS CORRESPONDENT	NBC-TV, NEWS DEPARTMENT		
		30 ROCKEFELLER PLAZA	NEW YORK, NY	10112
BURROUGHS, HENRY	PHOTOGRAPHER	SHADY OAKS MANOR		
		ROUTE #1, BOX 65	WEST RIVER, MD	20881
BURROWES, NORMA	SOPRANO	CAMI, 165 W 57TH ST	NEW YORK, NY	10019
BURROWS, BARBARA BAKER	PHOTO EDITOR	LIFE/TIME & LIFE BLDG		
		ROCKEFELLER CENTER	NEW YORK, NY	10020
BURROWS, CANDICE	MEZZO-SOPRANO	POST OFFICE BOX 884	NEW YORK, NY	10023
BURROWS, JAMES	WRITER-PRODUCER	6974 LOS TILOS RD	LOS ANGELES, CA	90068
BURROWS, THOMAS	DIRECTOR	5637 OCEAN BLVD	LA CANADA, CA	91011
BURROWS, VICTORIA	CASTING DIRECTOR	1600 N HIGHLAND AVE #7	LOS ANGELES, CA	90028
BURRS, LESLIE	FLUTIST	AFFILIATE ARTISTS, INC		
		37 W 65TH ST, 6TH FLOOR	NEW YORK, NY	10023
BURRUD, BILL	FILM PRODUCER	17045 S PACIFIC ST	SUNSET BEACH, CA	90742
BURSKEY, ALLAN	COMEDIAN	ICM, 8899 BEVERLY BLVD	LOS ANGELES, CA	90048
BURSTEIN, FRED	ACTOR-DIRECTOR	5122 QUAKERTOWN AVE	WOODLAND HILLS, CA	91364
BURSTEIN, MARC	DIRECTOR	1111 ARLINGTON BLVD	ARLINGTON, VA	22209
BURSTYN, ELLEN	ACTRESS	POST OFFICE BOX 217	PALISADES, NY	10964
BURT, ANDREW	ACTOR	GREEN & UNDERWOOD, LTD		
		3 THE PARADE		
		GUNNERSBURY LN	LONDON W3 8HR	ENGLAND
BURT, CHRIS	DIRECTOR-PRODUCER	58 DEVONSHIRE RD	LONDON W4	ENGLAND
BURT, MICHAEL	BASSO-BARITONE	CAMI, 165 W 57TH ST	NEW YORK, NY	10019
BURTNICK, GLEN	SINGER-COMPOSER	E S "BUD" PRAGER MANAGEMENT		
		1790 BROADWAY, PENTHOUSE	NEW YORK, NY	10019
BURTON, AL	WRI-PROD-COMP-EXEC	2300 COLDWATER CANYON DR	BEVERLY HILLS, CA	90210
BURTON, AMY	SOPRANO	CONE, 221 W 57TH ST	NEW YORK, NY	10019
BURTON, BAMBI	TV WRITER	8955 BEVERLY BLVD	LOS ANGELES, CA	90048
BURTON, BYRD	BANJOIST	500 PARAGON MILLS RD #N-17	NASHVILLE, TN	37211
BURTON, DONALD	ACTOR	BRYAN DREW, LTD		
		MEZZANINE QUADRANT HOUSE		
		80-82 REGENT ST	LONDON W1	ENGLAND
BURTON, EDDIE	GUITARIST	143 LAKESHORE DR	OLD HICKORY, TN	37138
BURTON, GARY, QUARTET	JAZZ QUARTET	KURLAND, 173 BRIGHTON AVE	BOSTON, MA	02134
BURTON, HAL	STUNTMAN	3518 W CAHUENGA BLVD #300	LOS ANGELES, CA	90068
BURTON, HUMPHREY M	DIRECTOR	123 OAKWOOD CT	LONDON W14 8LA	ENGLAND
BURTON, JAY	SCREENWRITER	8955 BEVERLY BLVD	LOS ANGELES, CA	90048
BURTON, JIM	AUTHOR-BASEBALL	121 CEDAR LN	TEANECK, NJ	07666
BURTON, JULIAN	ACTOR	2700 N CAHUENGA BLVD #430	LOS ANGELES, CA	90068
BURTON, KATE	ACTRESS	9004 ASHCROFT AVE	LOS ANGELES, CA	90048
BURTON, LANCE	MAGICIAN	10350 SANTA MONICA BLVD #210	LOS ANGELES, CA	90025
BURTON, LAURIE	ACTRESS	1418 N HIGHLAND AVE #102	LOS ANGELES, CA	90028
BURTON, LEVAR	ACTOR	13417 INWOOD DR	SHERMAN OAKS, CA	91423
BURTON, NORMAN	ACTOR	3641 MEADVILLE DR	SHERMAN OAKS, CA	91403
BURTON, PHILIP, JR	WRITER-PRODUCER	CBS-TV, 524 W 57TH ST	NEW YORK, NY	10019
BURTON, ROBERT	ACTOR	BRET ADAMS, 448 W 44TH ST	NEW YORK, NY	10036
BURTON, SANDRA	NEWS CORREPONDENT	TIME/TIME & LIFE BLDG		
		ROCKEFELLER CENTER	NEW YORK, NY	10020
BURTON, SHELLY	SCREENWRITER	8955 BEVERLY BLVD	LOS ANGELES, CA	90048
BURTON, TONY	ACTOR	8350 SANTA MONICA BLVD #103	LOS ANGELES, CA	90069
BURTON, WARREN	ACTOR	SCHUMER-OUBRE, 1697 BROADWAY	NEW YORK, NY	10019
BURTON, WENDELL	ACTOR	7722 GENTRY AVE	NORTH HOLLYWOOD, CA	91605
BUSBY, DARYL	TV WRITER	8955 BEVERLY BLVD	LOS ANGELES, CA	90048
BUSCAGLIA, DR LEO	COLUMNIST-AUTHOR	N Y TIMES SYNDICATION		
		130 5TH AVE	NEW YORK, NY	10011
BUSCH, NIVEN	WRITER	2625 BAKER ST	SAN FRANCISCO, CA	94123
BUSCHING, MARIANNA	MEZZO-SOPRANO	254 W 93RD ST #8	NEW YORK, NY	10025
BUSEY, GARY	ACTOR-SINGER	6053 PASEO CANYON DR	MALIBU, CA	90265
BUSFIELD, TIM	ACTOR	9744 WILSHIRE BLVD #206	BEVERLY HILLS, CA	90212
BUSH, BECKY	ACTRESS	10390 SANTA MONICA BLVD #310	LOS ANGELES, CA	90025
BUSH, BILLY GREEN	ACTOR	12725 VENTURA BLVD #E	STUDIO CITY, CA	91604
BUSH, DICK	CINEMATOGRAPHER	1 HILLSIDE COTTAGE		
		TOWER HILL, STAWELL		
		BRIDGWATER	SOMERSET	ENGLAND
BUSH, GENE	DOBROIST	ROUTE #1, BOX 165	KINGSTON SPRINGS, TN	37082
BUSH, GRAND	ACTOR	1917 W JEFFERSON BLVD	LOS ANGELES, CA	90018
BUSH, JAMES	ACTOR	3270 LAUREL CANYON BLVD	STUDIO CITY, CA	91604
BUSH, LARRY	NEWS CORRESPONDENT	410 11TH ST #13, NE	WASHINGTON, DC	20002
BUSH, NORMAN	ACTOR	311 E 23RD ST	NEW YORK, NY	10011

RAYMOND BURR

PAT BUTTRAM

LEVAR BURTON

EDD BYRNES

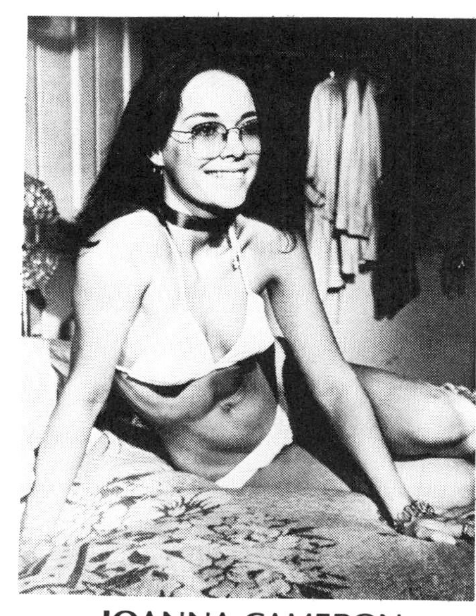
JOANNA CAMERON

KIRK CAMERON

JOSEPH CAMPANELLA

GLEN CAMPBELL

WILLIAM CAMPBELL

Name	Occupation	Address	City	Zip
BUSH, OWEN	ACTOR	8350 SANTA MONICA BLVD #206-A	LOS ANGELES, CA	90069
BUSH, PHYLLIS KIRK	ACTRESS	SEE - KIRK, PHYLLIS		
BUSH, REBECCAH	ACTRESS	10390 SANTA MONICA BLVD #310	LOS ANGELES, CA	90025
BUSH, SAM	MANDOLINIST	111 OLD HICKORY BLVD #E-1	NASHVILLE, TN	37221
BUSH, STAN	SINGER	ICM, 40 W 57TH ST	NEW YORK, NY	10019
BUSH, TED J	NEWS CORRESPONDENT	8449 TOLLHOUSE RD	ANNANDALE, VA	22003
BUSH, WARREN V	WRITER	8955 BEVERLY BLVD	LOS ANGELES, CA	90048
BUSH, WILLIAM	ACTOR	400 W 43RD ST #31-T	NEW YORK, NY	10036
BUSHELMAN, JOHN	FILM DIRECTOR	11972 SUNSHINE TERRACE DR	STUDIO CITY, CA	91604
BUSHNELL, LEWIS W	DIRECTOR	DGA, 110 W 57TH ST	NEW YORK, NY	10019
BUSHNELL, WILLIAM	WRITER-DIRECTOR	2751 PELHAM PL	LOS ANGELES, CA	90068
BUSIA, AKOSUA	ACTRESS	12725 VENTURA BLVD #E	STUDIO CITY, CA	91604
BUSINO, ORLANDO	CARTOONIST	12 SHADOW HILL RD	RIDGEFIELD, CT	06877
BUSOWSKI, PETER A	NEWS CORRESPONDENT	109 4TH ST, NE	WASHINGTON, DC	20002
BUSSARD, STEVEN W	WRITER	10606 KINNARD AVE	LOS ANGELES, CA	90024
BUSSE, BARRY	TENOR	CAMI, 165 W 57TH ST	NEW YORK, NY	10019
BUSTANY, DON	RADIO WRITER-PRODUCER	3456 BEN LOMOND PL	LOS ANGELES, CA	90027
BUSTANY, JUDITH	TV WRITER	3456 BEN LOMOND PL	LOS ANGELES, CA	90027
BUSTERUD, JAMES	BARITONE	CAMI, 165 W 57TH ST	NEW YORK, NY	10019
BUSTOS, OCTAVIO	GUITARIST	KAY, 58 W 58TH ST	NEW YORK, NY	10019
BUTCHER, PAUL A	TRUMPETER	105 ROSEBANK AVE	NASHVILLE, TN	37206
BUTCHER, ROBERT E	NEWS CORRESPONDENT	2025 "M" ST, NW	WASHINGTON, DC	20036
BUTCHER, STEPHEN	TV DIRECTOR	20 GRAFTON RD, ACTON	LONDON W3 6PB	ENGLAND
BUTCHER, TED	TV PRODUCER	ABC-TV, 4151 PROSPECT AVE	LOS ANGELES, CA	90027
BUTCHER AXIS, JON	SINGER-GUITARIST	ATI, 888 7TH AVE, 21ST FLOOR	NEW YORK, NY	10106
BUTCHOCK, STEVE	NEWS CORRESPONDENT	POST OFFICE BOX 1062	MANASSAS, VA	22110
BUTERA, M LEE	NEWS CORRESPONDENT	4006 VIRGINIA ST	CHEVY CHASE, MD	20815
BUTKIS, DICK	ACTOR-FOOTBALL	151 S EL CAMINO DR	BEVERLY HILLS, CA	90212
BUTLER, AARON C	WRITER	8955 BEVERLY BLVD	LOS ANGELES, CA	90048
BUTLER, ALBERT WAYNE	SAXOPHONIST	3230 DOVERSIDE DR	NASHVILLE, TN	37207
BUTLER, ARTIE	COMPOSER-CONDUCER	4146 LANKERSHIM BLVD #300	NORTH HOLLYWOOD, CA	91602
BUTLER, BILL	CINEMATOGRAPHER	POST OFFICE 2230	HOLLYWOOD, CA	90078
BUTLER, CARL	SINGER-GUITARIST	ROUTE #5, BOX 250	FRANKLIN, TN	37064
BUTLER, CHER	MODEL	MODELS & PROMOTIONS AGENCY		
		8560 SUNSET BLVD, 10TH FLOOR	LOS ANGELES, CA	90069
BUTLER, DAWS	ACTOR-VOICE OVERS	244 S OAKHURST DR	BEVERLY HILLS, CA	90212
BUTLER, DEAN	ACTOR	8075 W 3RD ST #303	LOS ANGELES, CA	90048
BUTLER, ERIC	GUITARIST	14 FAIRWAY DR	NASHVILLE, TN	37214
BUTLER, FERRIS	TV WRITER	555 W 57TH ST #1230	NEW YORK, NY	10019
BUTLER, HOLLY	ACTRESS	1585 CROSSROADS OF WORLD #107	HOLLYWOOD, CA	90028
BUTLER, JAMES	BASS	61 W 62ND ST #6-F	NEW YORK, NY	10023
BUTLER, JEAN ROUVEROL	WRITER	2103 WASHINGTON AVE	SANTA MONICA, CA	90403
BUTLER, JERRY	SINGER-SONGWRITER	PHILADELPHIA INTERNATIONAL		
		RECORDS COMPANY		
		63 E ADAMS ST	CHICAGO, IL	60603
BUTLER, KATE	MEZZO-SOPRANO	CAMI, 165 W 57TH ST	NEW YORK, NY	10019
BUTLER, KENT	ACTOR	518 N FAIRVIEW ST	BURBANK, CA	91505
BUTLER, LARRY	PIANIST	POST OFFICE BOX 121318	NASHVILLE, TN	37212
BUTLER, MICHAEL CHRISTOPHER	CINEMATOGRAPHER	14023 VALLEY VISTA BLVD	SHERMAN OAKS, CA	91423
BUTLER, MICHAEL P	SCREENWRITER	1650 WESTWOOD BLVD #201	LOS ANGELES, CA	90024
BUTLER, RICHARD E, JR	TV DIRECTOR	19447 ROSITA ST	TARZANA, CA	91356
BUTLER, ROBERT	TV DIRECTOR	650 CLUB VIEW DR	LOS ANGELES, CA	90024
BUTLER, ROBERT M	NEWS CORRESPONDENT	500 23RD ST #1101, NW	WASHINGTON, DC	20037
BUTLER, SHEA E	TV WRITER	8955 BEVERLY BLVD	LOS ANGELES, CA	90048
BUTLER, WILMER CABLE	DIRECTOR	DGA, 7950 SUNSET BLVD	LOS ANGELES, CA	90046
BUTRICK, MERRITT	ACTOR	211 S BEVERLY DR #201	BEVERLY HILLS, CA	90212
BUTRUM, HILLOUS	GUITARIST	2816 BARCLAY DR	NASHVILLE, TN	37206
BUTT, RAY	TV DIRECTOR	CHALFONT SAINT GILES		
		22 KINGS RD	BUCKS	ENGLAND
BUTT, YONDANI	CONDUCTOR	KAY, 58 W 58TH ST	NEW YORK, NY	10019
BUTTELMANN, KENT	BODYBUILDER	POST OFFICE BOX 11883	FRESNO, CA	93775
BUTTERS, BRIAN	NEWS CORRESPONDENT	11106 JOLLY WY	KENSINGTON, MD	20895
BUTTERWORTH, SHANE	ACTRESS	POST OFFICE BOX 5617	BEVERLY HILLS, CA	90210
BUTTERY, JOHN	FILM-TV PRODUCER	DINGLE RD, MIDDLETON	MANCHESTER	ENGLAND
BUTTON, CHARLES D	COMPOSER	331 N CALIFORNIA ST	BURBANK, CA	91505
BUTTON, DICK	TV PRODUCER	888 7TH ST	NEW YORK, NY	10106
BUTTONS, RED	ACTOR	778 TORTUOSO WY	LOS ANGELES, CA	90077
BUTTRAM, TERRY WAYNE	DRUMMER	104 EVERGREEN CIR	HENDERSONVILLE, TN	37075
BUTTREY, KENNETH	DRUMMER	POST OFFICE BOX 302	HENDERSONVILLE, TN	37075
BUTTREY, ORVILLE	DRUMMER	121 BOSTRING DR	HENDERSONVILLE, TN	37075
BUTTS, DOROTHY	ACTRESS	151 N SAN VICENTE BLVD #208	BEVERLY HILLS, CA	90211
BUTTS, R DALE	COMPOSER-CONDUCTOR	10470 KINNARD AVE	LOS ANGELES, CA	90024
BUXBAUM, JAMES M	WRITER	8955 BEVERLY BLVD	LOS ANGELES, CA	90048
BUXTON, FRANK	WRITER-PRODUCER	273 S WESTGATE AVE	LOS ANGELES, CA	90049
BUXTON, SIMON	TV PRODUCER	149 TOTTENHAM CT RD	LONDON W1	ENGLAND
BUYSE, EMILE J	FILM EXECUTIVE	1320 CARLA LN	BEVERLY HILLS, CA	90210
BUZAN, ALLEN	GUITARIST	ROUTE #5	LEWISBURG, TN	37091
BUZBY, ZANE	ACTRESS-WRITER	2117 HOLLY DR	LOS ANGELES, CA	90068
BUZENBERG, WILLIAM E	NEWS CORRESPONDENT	11675 STOCKBRIDGE LN	RESTON, VA	22090
BUZZI, RUTH	ACTRESS	9000 SUNSET BLVD #1105	LOS ANGELES, CA	90069
BUZZTONES, THE	ROCK & ROLL GROUP	POST OFFICE BOX 8125	ANN ARBOR, MI	48107
BYBEE, ARIEL	MEZZO-SOPRANO	LEW, 204 W 10TH ST	NEW YORK, NY	10014
BYBEE, KLAIR	ACTOR	8250 LANKERSHIM BLVD #6-MAPLE	NORTH HOLLYWOOD, CA	91605
BYER, LAWRENCE N	WRITER	555 W 57TH ST #1230	NEW YORK, NY	10019
BYERLEY, SCOTCH	ACTOR	8350 SANTA MONICA BLVD #103	LOS ANGELES, CA	90069

Name	Occupation	Address	City	Zip
BYERS, BRENDA	SINGER	32500 CONCORD DR #221	MADISON HEIGHTS, MI	48071
BYERS, BRENDA & THE NEIGHBORS	MUSICAL GROUP	32500 CONCORD DR #221	MADISON HGTS, MI	48071
BYERS, PAUL H	NEWS CORRESPONDENT	CBS NEWS, 2020 "M" ST, NW	WASHINGTON, DC	20036
BYERS, WILLIAM	COMPOSER-CONDUCTOR	28822 BONIFACE DR	MALIBU, CA	90265
BYGRAVES, MAX	ACTOR	JENNIFER MAFFINI MGMT		
		66 ROEBUCK HOUSE		
		PALACE ST	LONDON SW1	ENGLAND
BYLSMA, ANNER	CELLIST	LEE MC RAE MANAGEMENT		
		2130 CARLETON ST	BERKELEY, CA	94704
BYNER, JOHN	COMEDIAN-WRITER	5863 RAMIREZ CANYON RD	MALIBU, CA	90265
BYNES, EDD	ACTOR	STONE, 1052 CAROL DR	LOS ANGELES, CA	90069
BYRD, ANDY	GUITARIST	2300 SHARONDALE DR	NASHVILLE, TN	37212
BYRD, ANNE GEE	ACTRESS	11156 KLING ST	NORTH HOLLYWOOD, CA	91602
BYRD, BILL	GUITARIST	218 FAIRFAX AVE	NASHVILLE, TN	37212
BYRD, BILLY	FIDDLER	19306 WALTZ RD	NEW BOSTON, MI	48164
BYRD, CARL	ACTOR	1111 HACIENDA PL #B	LOS ANGELES, CA	90069
BYRD, CHARLIE, TRIO	JAZZ TRIO	POST OFFICE BOX 1515	NEW YORK, NY	10023
BYRD, DARVIN B	GUITARIST	POST OFFICE BOX 732	HENDERSONVILLE, TN	37075
BYRD, DAVID	PIANIST	961 CARLIN ST	GOODLETTSVILLE, TN	37072
BYRD, DAVID	ACTOR	870 N VINE ST #G	LOS ANGELES, CA	90038
BYRD, DONALD & 125TH ST BAND	JAZZ GROUP	10100 SANTA MONICA BLVD #1600	LOS ANGELES, CA	90067
BYRD, EDDY MACK	GUITARIST	14736 S DORCHESTER	DOLTON, IL	60419
BYRD, JERRY	GUITARIST	POST OFFICE BOX 15026	HONOLULU, HI	96815
BYRD, JOHN	FILM WRITER-DIRECTOR	61 ARTHUR RD, WIMBLEDON	LONDON SW19	ENGLAND
BYRD, JOSEPH	GUITARIST	POST OFFICE BOX 732	HENDERSONVILLE, TN	37075
BYRD, JOSEPH	COMPOSER	13206 DEWEY ST	LOS ANGELES, CA	90066
BYRD, LARRICE	GUITARIST	3829 HYDES FERRY PIKE	NASHVILLE, TN	37218
BYRD, LEE	NEWS CORRESPONDENT	4431 S 34TH ST	ARLINGTON, VA	22206
BYRD, LEVON	ACTOR	2301 CARMONA AVE #111	LOS ANGELES, CA	90016
BYRD, P P	WRITER	555 W 57TH ST #1230	NEW YORK, NY	10019
BYRD, RANDY	DOBROIST	POST OFFICE BOX 732	HENDERSONVILLE, TN	37075
BYRD, SAMUEL	BARITONE	CONE, 221 W 57TH ST	NEW YORK, NY	10019
BYRD, TOM	ACTOR	9744 WILSHIRE BLVD #206	BEVERLY HILLS, CA	90212
BYRD, WILLIAM H, JR	NEWS CORRESPONDENT	510 21ST ST #114, NW	WASHINGTON, DC	20006
BYRD, WYNTER C S	NEWS CORRESPONDENT	2139 WISCONSIN AVE, NW	WASHINGTON, DC	20007
BYRD-NETHERY, MIRIAM	ACTRESS	9744 WILSHIRE BLVD #206	BEVERLY HILLS, CA	90212
BYRDE, EDYE	ACTRESS	647 E 227TH ST	BRONX, NY	10466
BYRDS, THE	ROCK & ROLL GROUP	SCOTT DEAN, 428 HILL ST	RENO, NV	89501
BYRGE, DUANE	FILM CRITIC	6715 SUNSET BLVD	LOS ANGELES, CA	90028
BYRGE, DUANE P	TV WRITER	8955 BEVERLY BLVD	LOS ANGELES, CA	90048
BYRNE, ERICA	TV WRITER	8955 BEVERLY BLVD	LOS ANGELES, CA	90048
BYRNE, JOHNNY	TV WRITER	LINDA SEIFERT ASSOCIATES		
		8-A BRUNSWICK GARDENS	LONDON W8 4AJ	ENGLAND
BYRNE, JOSEPH P	TV WRITER-PRODUCER	3210 OAKDELL LN	STUDIO CITY, CA	91604
BYRNE, MARTHA	ACTRESS	CBS-TV, "AS THE WORLD TURNS"		
		51 W 52ND ST	NEW YORK, NY	10019
BYRNE, MARY	TV EXECUTIVE	30 W 60TH ST	NEW YORK, NY	10023
BYRNE, MICHAEL	ACTOR	CONWAY, EAGLE HOUSE		
		109 JERMYN ST	LONDON SW1	ENGLAND
BYRNE, MYLES	TV DIRECTOR	CINESCENE CINEMA		
		64 NORTH ST	BRIGHTON	ENGLAND
BYRNE, ROBERT	CHESS COLUMNIST	N Y TIMES, 229 W 43RD ST	NEW YORK, NY	10036
BYRNE, ROBERT F	NEWS CORRESPONDENT	1726 INDEPENDENCE AVE, SE	WASHINGTON, DC	20003
BYRNES, BURKE	ACTOR	12725 VENTURA BLVD #E	STUDIO CITY, CA	91604
BYRNES, DENNIS L	NEWS CORRESPONDENT	2025 "M" ST, NW	WASHINGTON, DC	20036
BYRNES, EDD	ACTOR	STONE, 1052 CAROL DR	LOS ANGELES, CA	90069
BYRNES, JAMES	TV WRITER	4820 MULHOLLAND DR	LOS ANGELES, CA	90046
BYRNES, MAUREEN	ACTRESS	837 VENICE BLVD	VENICE, CA	90291
BYRNES, ROSEMARY	NEWS REPORTER	TIME/TIME & LIFE BLDG		
		ROCKEFELLER CENTER	NEW YORK, NY	10020
BYRNIE, DON	NEWS CORRESPONDENT	3003 VAN NESS ST, NW	WASHINGTON, DC	20008
BYRNS, ALLAN	ACTOR	11936 BURBANK BLVD #10	NORTH HOLLYWOOD, CA	91607
BYROM, LARRY	GUITARIST	ROUTE #4	FRANKLIN, TN	37064
BYRON, ANTOINETTE	ACTRESS	ABC-TV, "ALL MY CHILDREN"		
		1330 AVE OF THE AMERICAS	NEW YORK, NY	10019
BYRON, DIANE	WRITER	8955 BEVERLY BLVD	LOS ANGELES, CA	90048
BYRON, JEANE	ACTRESS	FELBER, 2126 N CAHUENGA BLVD	LOS ANGELES, CA	90068
BYRON, JEFFREY	ACTOR	247 S BEVERLY DR #102	BEVERLY HILLS, CA	90210
BYRON, KATHLEEN	ACTRESS	POST OFFICE BOX 130, HOVE	EAST SUSSEX BN3 6QU	ENGLAND
BYRON, MICHAEL	ACTOR	807 S CURSON AVE	LOS ANGELES, CA	90036
BYRUM, JOHN	FILM WRITER-DIRECTOR	7435 WOODROW WILSON DR	LOS ANGELES, CA	90046
BYWATERS, THOMAS S	WRITER-PRODUCER	ABC TELEVISION NETWORK		
		1330 AVE OF THE AMERICAS	NEW YORK, NY	10019

Name	Occupation	Address	City	Zip
CAAN, JAMES	ACTOR-DIRECTOR	1435 STONE CANYON RD	LOS ANGELES, CA	90077
CABALLE, MONTSERRAT	SOPRANO	CAMI, 165 W 57TH ST	NEW YORK, NY	10019
CABE, BRIG	PHOTOGRAPHER	5504 KEMPTON DR	SPRINGFIELD, VA	22151

Name	Occupation	Address	City	Zip
CABE, GARY LEE	GUITARIST	408 BRINKLEY LN	WHITE HOUSE, TN	37188
CABOT, CEIL	ACTRESS	10850 RIVERSIDE DR #501	NORTH HOLLYWOOD, CA	91602
CABRERA-RAMIREZ, PABLO A	TV DIRECTOR	210 W 89TH ST #10-A	NEW YORK, NY	10024
CACAS, MAX A	NEWS CORRESPONDENT	1406 COLONY RD	OXON HILL, MD	20745
CACAVAS, JOHN	COMPOSER-CONDUCTOR	524 N BEVERLY DR	BEVERLY HILLS, CA	90210
CACAVIO, TERRY	TV WRITER	ABC-TV, "ALL MY CHILDREN"		
		1330 AVE OF THE AMERICAS	NEW YORK, NY	10019
CACCAVALLO, CATHERINE	SOPRANO	431 S DEARBORN ST #1504	CHICAGO, IL	60605
CADELL, AVA	ACTRESS-MODEL	435 S LA CIENEGA BLVD #20	LOS ANGELES, CA	90048
CADELL, SIMON	ACTOR	MAC NAUGHTON LOWE		
		200 FULHAM RD	LONDON SW10	ENGLAND
CADEN, FRANK	TV DIRECTOR	80-02 192ND ST	JAMAICA ESTATES, NY	11423
CADENE, M J	WRITER	8955 BEVERLY BLVD	LOS ANGELES, CA	90048
CADMAN, JOSHUA	ACTOR	3800 BARHAM BLVD #303	LOS ANGELES, CA	90068
CADOGAN, ALICE	ACTRESS	11726 SAN VICENTE BLVD #300	LOS ANGELES, CA	90049
CADORET, JEAN-PAUL	NEWS CORRESPONDENT	6018 N 20TH ST	ARLINGTON, VA	22205
CADORETTE, MARY	ACTRESS	ICM, 8899 BEVERLY BLVD	LOS ANGELES, CA	90048
CADY, CARLY M	TV WRITER	233 S LA FAYETTE PARK PL	LOS ANGELES, CA	90057
CADY, FRANK	ACTOR	9021 MELROSE AVE #304	LOS ANGELES, CA	90069
CADY, JAMES	DIRECTOR	40 25TH AVE	VEVICE, CA	90291
CAEN, HERB	COLUMNIST	SAN FRANCISCO CHRONICLE		
		901 MISSION ST	SAN FRANCISCO, CA	94119
CAESAR, HARRY	ACTOR	1112 W 41ST PL	LOS ANGELES, CA	90037
CAESAR, IRVING	LYRICIST-COMPOSER	HOTEL PARK SHERATION		
		870 7TH AVE	NEW YORK, NY	10019
CAESAR, SHIRLEY	SINGER	10100 SANTA MONICA BLVD #1600	LOS ANGELES, CA	90067
CAESAR, SID	ACTOR-COMEDIAN	1910 LOMA VISTA DR	BEVERLY HILLS, CA	90210
CAESAR, TIFFANI	ACTRESS	CBS-TV, "AS THE WORLD TURNS"		
		51 W 52ND ST	NEW YORK, NY	10019
CAFARELLA, ANTONIO E	COMPOSER	1450 FAIR OAKS BLVD	PASADENA, CA	91103
CAFFARO, CHERI	ACTRESS-WRITER	650 N BRONSON AVE #H-102	HOLLYWOOD, CA	90004
CAFFERTY, JOHN & THE BEAVER BAN	ROCK & ROLL GROUP	ARNOLD FREEDMAN MANAGEMENT		
		1200 PROVIDENCE HWY	SHARON, MA	02067
CAFFEY, MICHAEL	DIRECTOR	2049 CENTURY PARK E #1320	LOS ANGELES, CA	90067
CAGAN, RICHARD	WRITER	555 W 57TH ST #1230	NEW YORK, NY	10019
CAGE, JOHN	COMPOSER	101 W 18TH ST	NEW YORK, NY	10011
CAGE, NICOLAS	ACTOR	151 S EL CAMINO DR	BEVERLY HILLS, CA	90212
CAGGIANO, JOHN JOSEPH	DIRECTOR	DGA, 7950 SUNSET BLVD	LOS ANGELES, CA	90046
CAGLE, CHARLES	ACTOR	344 W 72ND ST	NEW YORK, NY	10023
CAGNEY, BILL	ACTOR-PRODUCER	2800 BAYSHORE DR	NEWPORT BEACH, CA	92663
CAGNEY, TIM	TV WRITER	9911 W PICO BLVD #1490	LOS ANGELES, CA	90035
CAGNEY, WILLIAM J	ACTOR	2800 BAYSHORE DR	NEWPORT BEACH, CA	92663
CAHALAN, TERENCE	WRITER	1122 HACIENDA PL	LOS ANGELES, CA	90069
CAHAN, GEORGE	DIRECTOR	4433 LAKESIDE DR	BURBANK, CA	91505
CAHAN, VICKY	NEWS CORRESPONDENT	2726 ORDWAY ST	WASHINGTON, DC	20008
CAHILL, BARRY	ACTOR	12711 HACIENDA DR	NORTH HOLLYWOOD, CA	91604
CAHILL, GERALD M	WRITER	7426 WISH AVE	VAN NUYS, CA	91406
CAHILL, JAMES	ACTOR	400 W 43RD ST #11-G	NEW YORK, NY	10036
CAHILL, JEROME S	NEWS CORRESPONDENT	11672 MEDITERRANEAN CT	RESTON, VA	22090
CAHILL, TERESA	SOPRANO	1776 BROADWAY #504	NEW YORK, NY	10019
CAHLING, ANDREAS	BODYBUILDER	POST OFFICE BOX 929	VENICE, CA	90291
CAHN, CATHY	ACTRESS	6852 CAMROSE DR	LOS ANGELES, CA	90068
CAHN, DANN	TV DIRECTOR	856 LEONARD RD	LOS ANGELES, CA	90049
CAHN, SAMMY	LYRICIST-COMPOSER	704 N CANON DR	BEVERLY HILLS, CA	90210
CAIDEN, MARTIN	WRITER	8955 BEVERLY BLVD	LOS ANGELES, CA	90048
CAILLOU, ALAN	ACTOR-TV WRITER	9165 SUNSET BLVD #202	LOS ANGELES, CA	90069
CAIN, BRUCE	BARITONE	431 S DEARBORN ST #1504	CHICAGO, IL	60605
CAIN, CHRISTOPHER	FILM DIRECTOR	5901 CLOVER HGTS	MALIBU, CA	90265
CAIN, JACKIE	SINGER	ROSENFIELD, 714 LADD RD	BRONX, NY	10471
CAIN, JACKIE & ROY KRAL	JAZZ DUO	HARTSTEIN, 8822 EVANVIEW DR	LOS ANGELES, CA	90069
CAIN, JOY DUCKETT	SPORTS REPORTER	SPORTS ILLUSTRATED MAGAZINE		
		TIME & LIFE BUILDING		
		ROCKEFELLER CENTER	NEW YORK, NY	10020
CAIN, LISA	ACTRESS	WRIGHT, 136 E 57TH ST	NEW YORK, NY	10022
CAIN, MADELYN	ACTRESS	9255 SUNSET BLVD #603	LOS ANGELES, CA	90069
CAIN, RANDY K	SAXOPHONIST	4903 TANGLEWOOD DR	NASHVILLE, TN	37216
CAIN, STEPHEN	PHOTOGRAPHER	1436 OAK ST	WASHINGTON, DC	20010
CAIN, TANE	SINGER-GUITARIST	3 E 54TH ST #1400	NEW YORK, NY	10022
CAIN, THOMAS G	MUSICIAN	4404 SYUMARTRA DR	NASHVILLE, TN	37218
CAIN, WILLIAM	ACTOR	484 W 43RD ST	NEW YORK, NY	10036
CAINE, HOWARD	ACTOR	6131 COLDWATER CANYON BLVD	NORTH HOLLYWOOD, CA	91606
CAINE, MARTI	COMEDIENNE	JOHNIE PELLER, STONE GROVE		
		OFF TREE, ROOT WALK		
		BROOMHILL	SHEFFIELD S10 2SW	ENGLAND
CAINE, MICHAEL	ACTOR	1309 DAVIES DR	BEVERLY HILLS, CA	90210
CAINE, RICHARD	ACTOR	15010 VENTURA BLVD #219	SHERMAN OAKS, CA	91403
CAIRE, CLAY S	DRUMMER	2612 WOODLAWN DR	NASHVILLE, TN	37212
CAIRNEY, JOHN	ACTOR	197 ONSLOW DR	GLASGLOW G31 2QE	ENGLAND
CAITLIN, ELISE	ACTRESS	327 N ORLANDO AVE	LOS ANGELES, CA	90048
CAJATI, MARIO L	COMPOSER-CONDUCTOR	7735 FLORENCE AVE	DOWNEY, CA	90240
CAKMIS, BILL	ACTOR	POST OFFICE BOX 480361	LOS ANGELES, CA	90048
CALA, JOSEPH MICHAEL	ACTOR	3890 CARPENTER AVE	STUDIO CITY, CA	91604

Name	Occupation	Address	City	Zip
CALABRESE, PETER ROBERT	TV EXECUTIVE	ICM, 8899 BEVERLY BLVD	LOS ANGELES, CA	90048
CALABRESE, ZARO	WRITER	555 W 57TH ST #1230	NEW YORK, NY	10019
CALABRO, KARIN	COLORATURA	PERLS, 7 W 96TH ST	NEW YORK, NY	10025
CALAHAN, WALTER P	PHOTOGRAPHER	4656 S 34TH ST #B-2	ARLINGTON, VA	22206
CALAMITY JANE & THE COWPUNKS	C & W GROUP	9000 SUNSET BLVD #1200	LOS ANGELES, CA	90069
CALAWAY, BELLE	ACTRESS	8322 BEVERLY BLVD #202	LOS ANGELES, CA	90048
CALDE, MARK A	WRITER	7405 OGELSBY AVE	LOS ANGELES, CA	90045
CALDER, GILCHRIST	TV DIRECTOR	34 KEW GREEN, RICHMOND	SURREY	ENGLAND
CALDER, IAIN	EDITOR-PUBLISHER	THE NATIONAL ENQUIRER		
		600 SE COAST AVE	LANTANA, FL	33464
CALDERON, JAVIER	GUITARIST	POST OFFICE BOX 9532	MADISON, WI	53715
CALDERON, JULIA	ACTRESS	6430 SUNSET BLVD #1203	LOS ANGELES, CA	90028
CALDERON, SERGIO	ACTOR	LIGHT, 113 N ROBERTSON BLVD	LOS ANGELES, CA	90048
CALDERWOOD, ROBERT M	COMPOSER-CONDUCTOR	12208 LOUISE AVE	GRANADA HILLS, CA	91344
CALDWELL, BOBBY	SINGER-GUITARIST	ASSOCIATED BOOKING CORP		
		1995 BROADWAY, 5TH FLOOR	NEW YORK, NY	10023
CALDWELL, CAROL	TV WRITER	555 W 57TH ST #1230	NEW YORK, NY	10019
CALDWELL, CECELIA H	WRITER	8955 BEVERLY BLVD	LOS ANGELES, CA	90048
CALDWELL, DAVID	TV DIRECTOR	26934 HALIFAX PL	HAYWARD, CA	94542
CALDWELL, DAVID E	TV DIRECTOR	POST OFFICE BOX 585	CHESTER, CA	96020
CALDWELL, JOHN	CARTOONIST	THE NATIONAL LAMPOON		
		635 MADISON AVE	NEW YORK, NY	10022
CALDWELL, JOHNNY	CONDUCTOR	POST OFFICE BOX 60885	OKLAHOMA CITY, OK	73146
CALDWELL, JOSEPH	WRITER	555 W 57TH ST #1230	NEW YORK, NY	10019
CALDWELL, ROBERT L	SAXOPHONIST	5400 BURGESS AVE #4	NASHVILLE, TN	37209
CALDWELL, STEPHEN P	TV DIRECTOR-PRODUCER	2285 BEACHWOOD DR	LOS ANGELES, CA	90068
CALDWELL, TAYLOR	AUTHORESS	IVANHOE LN	GREENWICH, CT	06830
CALE, J J	SINGER-GUITARIST	POST OFFICE BOX 210103	SAN FRANCISCO, CA	94121
CALE, JOHN W	SINGER	POST OFFICE BOX 22635	NASHVILLE, TN	37202
CALEB, J R	TV WRITER	555 W 57TH ST #1230	NEW YORK, NY	10019
CALFA, DON	ACTOR	1520 N HAYWORTH AVE #10	LOS ANGELES, CA	90046
CALHOUN, DARRELL	NEWS CORRESPONDENT	1755 S JEFFERSON DAVIS HWY	ARLINGTON, VA	22202
CALHOUN, JACK	GUITARIST	416 BROAD ST	NASHVILLE, TN	37203
CALHOUN, JERRY	GUITARIST	416 BROAD ST	NASHVILLE, TN	37203
CALHOUN, ROBERT	TV PRODUCER	CBS-TV, "AS THE WORLD TURNS"		
		51 W 52ND ST	NEW YORK, NY	10019
CALHOUN, ROBERT P	DIRECTOR	1501 BROADWAY #2600	NEW YORK, NY	10036
CALHOUN, RORY	ACTOR	11532 CHIQUITA ST	STUDIO CITY, CA	91604
CALI, JOSEPH	ACTOR	1707 CLEARVIEW DR	BEVERLY HILLS, CA	90210
CALIANDRO, THOMAS V	NEWS CORRESPONDENT	230 N JACKSON ST	ARLINGTON, VA	22201
CALIFANO, ARTHUR	DIRECTOR	DGA, 110 W 57TH ST	NEW YORK, NY	10019
CALIFANO, GARY L	DIRECTOR	COOPER, 28 W 25TH ST	NEW YORK, NY	10010
CALIFORNIA DOLL	WRESTLER	GORGEOUS GIRLS OF WRESTLING		
		RIVIERA HOTEL & CASINO		
		DAVID B MC LANE PRODS		
		2901 S LAS VEGAS BLVD	LAS VEGAS, NV	89109
CALIO, JIM	WRITER-EDITOR	PEOPLE/TIME & LIFE BLDG		
		ROCKEFELLER CENTER	NEW YORK, NY	10020
CALIS, RAPHAEL J	NEWS CORRESPONDENT	6308 HERKOS CT	BETHESDA, MD	20817
CALKINS, JOHNNY	ACTOR	5719 COLUMBUS AVE	VAN NUYS, CA	91411
CALL, ANTHONY	ACTOR	ABC-TV, "ONE LIFE TO LIVE"		
		1330 AVE OF THE AMERICAS	NEW YORK, NY	10019
CALL, BRANDON	ACTOR	KELMAN, 7813 SUNSET BLVD	LOS ANGELES, CA	90046
CALL, EDWARD	ACTOR	15010 VENTURA BLVD #219	SHERMAN OAKS, CA	91403
CALL, THE	ROCK & ROLL GROUP	HEATON, 6858 LOS ALTOS PL	HOLLYWOOD, CA	90068
CALLAGHAN, MICHAEL J, JR	WRITER	555 W 57TH ST #1230	NEW YORK, NY	10019
CALLAHAN, ANNE M	NEWS CORRESPONDENT	5021 SEMINARY RD	ALEXANDRIA, VA	22311
CALLAHAN, E J	ACTOR	3330 BARHAM BLVD #103	LOS ANGELES, CA	90068
CALLAHAN, GEORGE E	WRITER	10437 ALMAYO AVE	LOS ANGELES, CA	90064
CALLAHAN, GREG	ACTOR	470 N SAN VICENTE BLVD #102	LOS ANGELES, CA	90048
CALLAHAN, JAMES	ACTOR	12725 VENTURA BLVD #E	STUDIO CITY, CA	91604
CALLAHAN, JOHN	ACTOR	POST OFFICE BOX 5617	BEVERLY HILLS, CA	90210
CALLAHAN, KRISTINA	ACTRESS	3800 BARHAM BLVD #303	LOS ANGELES, CA	90068
CALLAHAN, LEE	ACTRESS	360 CENTRAL PARK W	NEW YORK, NY	10025
CALLAHAN, MARY PATRICIA	NEWS CORRESPONDENT	7002 EXETER RD	BETHESEDA, MD	20814
CALLAHAN, SHEILIA	NEWS CORRESPONDENT	1307 CONDUCTOR WY	SILVER SPRING, MD	20904
CALLAHAN, TOM	WRITER-EDITOR	TIME/TIME & LIFE BLDG		
		ROCKEFELLER CENTER	NEW YORK, NY	10020
CALLAN, CECILE	ACTRESS	9744 WILSHIRE BLVD #206	BEVERLY HILLS, CA	90212
CALLAN, CHRIS	ACTRESS	WEBB, 7500 DEVISTA DR	LOS ANGELES, CA	90046
CALLAN, K	ACTRESS	4957 MATILIJA AVE	SHERMAN OAKS, CA	91423
CALLAN, MICHAEL	ACTOR	6310 SAN VICENTE BLVD #407	LOS ANGELES, CA	90048
CALLANDER, BRUCE	NEWS CORRESPONDENT	9948 MURNAME ST	VIENNA, VA	22180
CALLAS, CHARLIE	COMEDIAN-ACTOR	9000 SUNSET BLVD #502	LOS ANGELES, CA	90069
CALLAWAY, NANCY LYNN	TV DIRECTOR	18 BRAYTON ST	ENGLEWOOD, NJ	07631
CALLAWAY, THOMAS	ACTOR	10000 SANTA MONICA BLVD #305	LOS ANGELES, CA	90067
CALLEI-TREBEK, ELAINE	WRITER	2661 CARMAR DR	LOS ANGELES, CA	90046
CALLEN, CECILE	ACTRESS	9744 WILSHIRE BLVD #206	BEVERLY HILLS, CA	90212
CALLENDER, COLIN	TV PRODUCER	CALLENDER, 39 LONG ACRE	LONDON WC2 9JZ	ENGLAND
CALLENDER, GEORGE S	COMPOSER	8120 CANBY AVE #4	RESEDA, CA	91335
CALLEO, RICCARDO	TENOR	59 E 54TH ST #81	NEW YORK, NY	10022
CALLIE, MICHAEL A	WRITER	8955 BEVERLY BLVD	LOS ANGELES, CA	90048
CALLIHAN, CLAIR C	DIRECTOR	422 CENTRAL AVE	WILMETTE, IL	60091
CALLINAN, DICK	ACTOR	7720 SW 51ST AVE	MIAMI, FL	33143
CALLINAN, TOM	MUSICIAN	276 CAMBRIDGE ST #4	BOSTON, MA	02134

Name	Occupation	Address	City	Zip/Country
CALLOW, SIMON	ACTOR	60 FINBOROUGH RD	LONDON SW10	ENGLAND
CALLOWAY, CAB	SINGER-COMPOSER	1040 KNOLLWOOD RD	WHITE PLAINS, NY	10603
CALLOWAY, KIRK	ACTOR	13619 S BERENDO AVE	GARDENA, CA	90247
CALLUM, MYLES	WRITER-EDITOR	TV GUIDE, 100 MATSONFORD RD	RADNOR, PA	19088
CALMES, JACKIE	NEWS CORRESPONDENT	713 19TH ST, SE	WASHINGTON, DC	20003
CALVE, JEAN-FRANCOIS	ACTOR	1 RUE DE NAVARRE	PARIS 75010	FRANCE
CALVERT, HENRY	ACTOR	19 COMMERCE ST	NEW YORK, NY	10014
CALVERT, LUCILE	ACTRESS	1 CHRISTOPHER ST	NEW YORK, NY	10014
CALVET, CORINNE	ACTRESS	1431 OCEAN AVE #109	SANTA MONICA, CA	90401
CALVIN, JOHN	ACTOR	1794 WASHINGTON WY	VENICE, CA	90291
CAMACHO, JULIO C	NEWS CORRESPONDENT	6631 WAKEFIELD DR	ALEXANDRIA, VA	22307
CAMANIA, MADHU	NEWS CORRESPONDENT	NBC-TV, NEWS DEPARTMENT		
		4001 NEBRASKA AVE, NW	WASHINGTON, DC	20016
CAMARATA, SALVADOR	COMPOSER-CONDUCTOR	12141 IREDELL ST	STUDIO CITY, CA	91604
CAMBERN, DONN	TV DIRECTOR	11611 AMANDA DR	STUDIO CITY, CA	91604
CAMBOU, DON	WRITER	618 BOCCACCIO WY	VENICE, CA	90291
CAMBRELING, SYLVAIN	CONDUCTOR	ICM, 40 W 57TH ST	NEW YORK, NY	10019
CAMDEN, GLORIA	ACTRESS	9300 WILSHIRE BLVD #410	BEVERLY HILLS, CA	90212
CAMEO	SOUL GROUP	1422 W PEACHTREE ST #816, NW	ATLANTA, GA	30309
CAMERON, BEN	ACTOR	1605 N CAHUENGA BLVD #202	LOS ANGELES, CA	90028
CAMERON, CHRISTOPHER	BASSO-BARITONE	VKD INTERNATIONAL ARTISTS		
		220 SHEPPARD AVE E		
		WILLOWDALE	TORONTO, ONT M2N 3A9	CANADA
CAMERON, CHRISTOPHER	TENOR	61 W 62ND ST #6-F	NEW YORK, NY	10023
CAMERON, CISSE	ACTRESS	POST OFFICE BOX 2012	MALIBU, CA	90265
CAMERON, DAVE	ACTOR	5720 DONNA AVE	TARZANA, CA	91356
CAMERON, DAVID E	ACTOR	FELBER, 2126 N CAHUENGA BLVD	LOS ANGELES, CA	90068
CAMERON, DAVID O	ACTOR	2146 1/2 N BEACHWOOD DR	LOS ANGELES, CA	90068
CAMERON, DEAN	ACTOR	1717 N HIGHLAND AVE #414	LOS ANGELES, CA	90028
CAMERON, DOUG	SINGER	41 BRITAIN ST #200	TORONTO, ONT	CANADA
CAMERON, FAYE	ACTRESS	8484 WILSHIRE BLVD #235	BEVERLY HILLS, CA	90211
CAMERON, GAIL BRYANT	ACTRESS	5319 VICTORIA AVE	LOS ANGELES, CA	90043
CAMERON, GARY A	PHOTOGRAPHER	6532 79TH PL	CABIN JOHN, MD	20818
CAMERON, JANE	ACTRESS	NBC-TV, "ANOTHER WORLD"		
		30 ROCKEFELLER PLAZA	NEW YORK, NY	10112
CAMERON, JOANNA	ACTRESS-DIRECTOR	POST OFFICE BOX 8569	UNIVERSAL CITY, CA	91608
CAMERON, JOHN	COMPOSER-CONDUCTOR	ROGER HANCOCK MANAGEMENT		
		8 WATERLOO, PALL MALL	LONDON W1	ENGLAND
CAMERON, JOHN ALLAN	SINGER	4881 YONGE ST #412	TORONTO, ONT M2N 5X3	CANADA
CAMERON, JULIA	TV WRITER	8955 BEVERLY BLVD	LOS ANGELES, CA	90048
CAMERON, KIRK	ACTOR	8369 SAUSALITO AVE	CANOGA PARK, CA	91304
CAMERON, RAY	WRITER-PRODUCER	5 HOLLYCROFT AVE	LONDON NW3	ENGLAND
CAMERON, SUE	TALENT AGENT	445 N BEDORD DR #PH	BEVERLY HILLS, CA	90210
CAMFIELD, DOUGLAS	FILM-TV DIRECTOR	LONDON MANAGEMENT, LTD		
		235-241 REGENT ST	LONDON W1A 2JT	ENGLAND
CAMIEL, ERIC S	DIRECTOR	210 MIDDLE RIVER RD	DANBURY, CT	06810
CAMMANN, FREDERIC G	TV DIRECTOR	15 E 91ST ST	NEW YORK, NY	10028
CAMMELL, DONALD	WRITER-PRODUCER	151 S EL CAMINO DR	BEVERLY HILLS, CA	90212
CAMP, COLLEEN	ACTRESS	12359 EMELITA ST	NORTH HOLLYWOOD, CA	91607
CAMP, HAMILTON	ACTOR	10100 SANTA MONICA BLVD #1600	LOS ANGELES, CA	90067
CAMP, HELEN PAGE	ACTRESS	9300 WILSHIRE BLVD #410	BEVERLY HILLS, CA	90212
CAMP, JOSEPH M	FILM DIRECTOR	DGA, 110 W 57TH ST	NEW YORK, NY	10019
CAMP, JOSEPH S, JR	WRITER-PRODUCER	10300 N CENTRAL EXPRESSWAY	DALLAS, TX	75231
CAMP, KAYE WILSON	MUSICIAN	1207 MC ALPINE AVE	NASHVILLE, TN	37216
CAMP, MARK E	MUSIC ARRANGER	1100 GRANVILLE RD #705	FRANKLIN, TN	37064
CAMP, RICHARD B	TV WRITER	555 W 57TH ST #1230	NEW YORK, NY	10019
CAMP, THOMAS J	WRITER	8955 BEVERLY BLVD	LOS ANGELES, CA	90048
CAMPAGNA, DAVID	ACTOR	8450 DE LONGPRE AVE #16	LOS ANGELES, CA	90069
CAMPANELLA, FRANK	ACTOR	151 S EL CAMINO DR	BEVERLY HILLS, CA	90212
CAMPANELLA, JOSEPH	ACTOR	4647 ARCOLA AVE	NORTH HOLLYWOOD, CA	91602
CAMPANELLA, ROY, JR	WRITER-PRODUCER	8383 WILSHIRE BLVD #923	BEVERLY HILLS, CA	90211
CAMPANELLA, ROY, SR	BASEBALL	6213 CAPISTRANO AVE	WOODLAND HILLS, CA	91367
CAMPBELL, ARCH	THEATER CRITIC	WRC-TV, NEWS DEPARTMENT		
		4001 NEBRASKA AVE, NW	WASHINGTON, DC	20016
CAMPBELL, ARCHIE	COMEDIAN-ACTOR	POST OFFICE BOX 189	BRENTWOOD, TN	37027
CAMPBELL, BARBARA	NEWS CORRESPONDENT	1400 "I" ST, NW	WASHINGTON, DC	20005
CAMPBELL, BRUCE	ACTOR	THE CHELSEA HOTEL		
		222 W 23RD ST	NEW YORK, NY	10011
CAMPBELL, BRUCE R	WRITER	555 W 57TH ST #1230	NEW YORK, NY	10019
CAMPBELL, BRUCE V	COMPOSER	8322 TOPEKA DR	NORTHRIDGE, CA	91324
CAMPBELL, CANDACE	NEWS CORRESPONDENT	2950 VAN NESS ST, NW	WASHINGTON, DC	20008
CAMPBELL, CARLOS	ACTOR	837 10TH ST #7	SANTA MONICA, CA	90403
CAMPBELL, CAROL	TV WRITER	JEOPARDY, 1541 N VINE ST	HOLLYWOOD, CA	90028
CAMPBELL, CAROLYN E	SINGER	629 AMERICAN RD	NASHVILLE, TN	37209
CAMPBELL, CHARLES A	GUITARIST	913 20TH AVE S #23	NASHVILLE, TN	37212
CAMPBELL, CHERYL	ACTRESS	HOPE & LYNNE, 5 MILNER PL	LONDON N1 1TN	ENGLAND
CAMPBELL, COLIN	ACTOR	3521 GRIFFITH PARK BLVD	LOS ANGELES, CA	90027
CAMPBELL, DEBBIE	SINGER	HALSEY, 3225 S NORWOOD AVE	TULSA, OK	74135
CAMPBELL, DON	NEWS CORRESPONDENT	5800 QUANTRELL AVE	ALEXANDRIA, VA	22312
CAMPBELL, ELIZABETH A	WRITER	8955 BEVERLY BLVD	LOS ANGELES, CA	90048
CAMPBELL, GLEN	SING-ACT-COMP	1900 AVE OF THE STARS #2530	LOS ANGELES, CA	90067
CAMPBELL, JAMES	CLARINETIST	5720 MOSHOLU AVE #300	RIVERDALE, NY	10471
CAMPBELL, JANE	ACTRESS	120 S VICTORY BLVD #104	BURBANK, CA	91502
CAMPBELL, JOAN	MEZZO-SOPRANO	HILLYER, 250 W 57TH ST	NEW YORK, NY	10107
CAMPBELL, JOHN	SINGER-GUITARIST	POST OFFICE BOX 2520	NACOGDOCHES, TX	75963

CAMEO

THE COMMODORES

Ronald La Pread • Thomas McClary • Walter "Clyde" Orange • Milan Williams • William King

CAMPBELL, JUDY	SINGER-ACTRESS	21 OLD CHURCH ST, CHELS	LONDON SW3	ENGLAND
CAMPBELL, JULIA	ACTRESS	KNBC-TV, "SANTA BARBARA"		
		3000 W ALAMEDA AVE	BURBANK, CA	91523
CAMPBELL, JULIE	SPORTS WRITER-EDITOR	SPORTS ILLUSTRATED MAGAZINE		
		TIME & LIFE BUILDING		
		ROCKEFELLER CENTER	NEW YORK, NY	10020
CAMPBELL, KENNETH L	DIRECTOR-PRODUCER	3704 BARHAM BLVD #E-208	LOS ANGELES, CA	90068
CAMPBELL, KENNETH M	NEWS CORRESPONDENT	9429 FOREST HAVEN DR	ALEXANDRIA, VA	22309
CAMPBELL, LOUISE	ACTRESS-SINGER	46 ROWAYTON AVE	ROWAYTON, CT	06853
CAMPBELL, MAE E	ACTRESS	8230 BEVERLY BLVD #23	LOS ANGELES, CA	90048
CAMPBELL, MICHAEL	WRITER	8955 BEVERLY BLVD	LOS ANGELES, CA	90048
CAMPBELL, MIKE	GUITARIST	9017-B OLD SMYRNA RD	BRENTWOOD, TN	37027
CAMPBELL, NICHOLAS	ACTOR	10390 SANTA MONICA BLVD #310	LOS ANGELES, CA	90025
CAMPBELL, NORMAN	FILM DIRECTOR	20 GEORGE HENRY BLVD		
		WILLOWDALE	TORONTO, ONT M2J 1E2	CANADA
CAMPBELL, PATRICK	ACTOR	8721 SUNSET BLVD #200	LOS ANGELES, CA	90069
CAMPBELL, R W	WRITER	8955 BEVERLY BLVD	LOS ANGELES, CA	90048
CAMPBELL, ROBERT F	WRITER	555 W 57TH ST #1230	NEW YORK, NY	10019
CAMPBELL, TOM G	GUITARIST	104 COLE DR	HENDERSONVILLE, TN	37075
CAMPBELL, WILLIAM	PHOTOGRAPHER	TIME/TIME & LIFE BLDG		
		ROCKEFELLER CENTER	NEW YORK, NY	10020
CAMPBELL, WILLIAM J	ACTOR	21502 VELICATA ST	WOODLAND HILLS, CA	91364
CAMPERO, ANA MARIA	NEWS CORRESPONDENT	4450 S PARK AVE #410, NE	WASHINGTON, DC	20815
CAMPHUIS, RICHARD	ACTOR	4424 WOODMAN AVE #204	SHERMAN OAKS, CA	91423
CAMPION, CLIFFORD	WRITER	1473 3/4 HAVENHURST DR	LOS ANGELES, CA	90046
CAMPO, FRANK P	COMPOSER	12336 MILBANK ST	STUDIO CITY, CA	91604
CAMPORI, ANGELO	CONDUCTOR	61 W 62ND ST #6-F	NEW YORK, NY	10023
CAMPOS, CYNTHIA	TALENT AGENT	1901 AVE OF THE STARS #840	LOS ANGELES, CA	90067
CAMPOS, VICTOR	ACTOR	8350 SANTA MONICA BLVD #23	LOS ANGELES, CA	90069
CAMPUS, MICHAEL	FILM DIRECTOR	2121 KRESS ST	LOS ANGELES, CA	90046
CAMPUS, PAMELA	CASTING DIRECTOR	8833 SUNSET BLVD #305	LOS ANGELES, CA	90069
CAN-AM CONNECTION, THE	WRESTLING TAG TEAM	POST OFFICE BOX 3859	STAMFORD, CT	06905
CANAAN, CHRISTOPHER	TV WRITER	8955 BEVERLY BLVD	LOS ANGELES, CA	90048
CANADAY, EDWARD LYNN	GUITARIST	111 SCOTCH ST	HENDERSONVILLE, TN	37075
CANADIAN BUMBLE BEE, THE	WRESTLER	SEE - BLACKWELL, CRUSHER JERRY		
CANADIAN ROAD WARRIOR, THE	WRESTLER	CAPITOL INTERNATIONAL		
		11844 MARKET ST	NORTH LIMA, OH	44452
CANADY, ALVA	GUITARIST	POST OFFICE BOX 363	LAKE WACCAMAW, NC	28450
CANAN, MARTHA	NEWS CORRESPONDENT	1933 18TH ST #104, NW	WASHINGTON, DC	20009
CANARY, DAVID	ACTOR	903 S MANSFIELD AVE	LOS ANGELES, CA	90036
CANAVAN, MICHAEL	ACTOR	9255 SUNSET BLVD #603	LOS ANGELES, CA	90069
CANBY, VINCENT	FILM CRITIC	215 W 88TH ST	NEW YORK, NY	10024
CANCELLARE, CHARLES	PHOTOGRAPHER	2828 CONNECTICUT AVE #411, NW	WASHINGTON, DC	20008
CANCELLARE, FRANK	PHOTOGRAPHER	109 S UTAH ST	ARLINGTON, VA	22204
CANCILLA, ELAINE	ACTRESS	232 W 23RD ST	NEW YORK, NY	10011
CANDELA	ROCK & ROLL GROUP	PROGRESS RECORDS COMPANY		
		5500 AVION PARK DR	HIGHLAND HEIGHTS, OH	44143
CANDELARIA, JOHN	BASEBALL	POST OFFICE BOX 2000		
		MAIN OFFICE STATION	ANAHEIM, CA	92803
CANDIOTTY, MARK	TALENT AGENT	120 S VICTORY BLVD #104	BURBANK, CA	91502
CANDOLI, PETER	ACTOR-TRUMPETER	12451 MULHOLLAND DR	BEVERLY HILLS, CA	90210
CANDY, JOHN	ACT-WRI-COMED	12328 MONTANA AVE	LOS ANGELES, CA	90049
CANE, PETER	WRITER	555 W 57TH ST #1230	NEW YORK, NY	10019
CANE, RIC	ACTOR	11687 WEDDINGTON ST	NORTH HOLLYWOOD, CA	91601
CANESTRELLIS, THE	TRAMPOLINE TROUPE	HALL, 138 FROG HOLLOW RD	CHURCHVILLE, PA	18966
CANETTI, ELIAS	WRITER	FARRAR, 19 UNION SQ W	NEW YORK, NY	10003
CANFIELD, MARGARET	ACTRESS	FARRELL, 10500 MAGNOLIA BLVD	NORTH HOLLYWOOD, CA	91601
CANFIELD, MARSHA	NEWS CORRESPONDENT	102 KING HENRY CT	ALEXANDRIA, VA	22134
CANFIELD, MARY GRACE	ACTRESS	10850 RIVERSIDE DR #501	NORTH HOLLYWOOD, CA	91602
CANFIELD, WILLIAM	CARTOONIST	143 WAYSIDE RD	TINTO FALLS, NJ	07724
CANGIALOSI, ANTHONY R	WRITER	8955 BEVERLY BLVD	LOS ANGELES, CA	90048
CANIDA, DAVE	GUITARIST	MOSLEY TRAILER PARK #17	FRANKLIN, TN	37064
CANIFF, MILTON	CARTOONIST	KING FEATURES SYNDICATE		
		235 E 45TH ST	NEW YORK, NY	10017
CANINO, BRUNO	PIANIST	MARIEDL ANDERS ARTISTS MGMT		
		535 EL CAMINO DEL MAR ST	SAN FRANCISCO, CA	94121
CANKO, ROBERT ELIOT	ACTOR	KNBC-TV, "DAYS OF OUR LIVES"		
		3000 W ALAMEDA AVE	BURBANK, CA	91523
CANNELL, STEPHEN J	TV WRITER-PRODUCER	875 LA LOMA RD	PASADENA, CA	91105
CANNING, JAMES	ACTOR	POST OFFICE BOX 5617	BEVERLY HILLS, CA	90210
CANNON, ACE	SINGER	POST OFFICE BOX 121089	NASHVILLE, TN	37212
CANNON, BUDDY	GUITARIST	ROUTE #2, BOX 403	KINGSTON SPRINGS, TN	37082
CANNON, CARL M	NEWS CORRESPONDENT	ROUTE #2, BOX 363	THE PLAINS, VA	22171
CANNON, CHRIS	WRESTLER	SEE - BUNDY, KING KONG		
CANNON, DORAN WILLIAM	SCREENWRITER	2671 LA CUESTA DR	LOS ANGELES, CA	90046
CANNON, DYAN	ACTRESS-WRITER	98 MALIBU COLONY DR	MALIBU, CA	90265
CANNON, FREDDY	SINGER-SONGWRITER	18641 CASSANDRA ST	TARZANA, CA	91356
CANNON, HAROLD	ACTOR	BERZON, 336 E 17TH ST	COSTA MESA, CA	92627
CANNON, HARRY	ACTOR	15048 GREENLEAF ST	SHERMAN OAKS, CA	91403
CANNON, J D	ACTOR	9300 WILSHIRE BLVD #410	BEVERLY HILLS, CA	90212
CANNON, JIMMI	SINGER	MC CATER, ROUTE #16, BOX 3	MOBILE, AL	36609
CANNON, JOHN	ACTOR	110-45 QUEENS BLVD	FOREST HILLS, CA	11375
CANNON, KATHERINE	ACTRESS	15301 VENTURA BLVD #345	SHERMAN OAKS, CA	91403
CANNON, LOU	NEWS CORRESPONDENT	WASHINGTON POST NEWSPAPER		
		1150 15TH ST, NW	WASHINGTON, DC	20071

DYAN CANNON

CANTINFLAS

IRENE CARA

CLAUDIA CARDINALE

HARRY CAREY, JR.

ART CARNEY

ALLAN CARR

JOHN CARRADINE

MADELEINE CARROLL

Name	Occupation	Address	City	Zip/Country
CANNON, REUBEN	CASTING DIRECTOR	7083 HOLLYWOOD BLVD #306	LOS ANGELES, CA	90028
CANNON, RICHARD A	WRITER	555 W 57TH ST #1230	NEW YORK, NY	10019
CANNON, TOM	WRITER	8955 BEVERLY BLVD	LOS ANGELES, CA	90048
CANNON, TOMMY & BOBBY BALL	COMEDY DUO	IAR, 235-241 REGENT ST	LONDON W1A 2JT	ENGLAND
CANNONS, THE	C & W GROUP	MANDRELL, 713 W MAIN ST	HENDERSONVILLE, TN	37075
CANO, CRAIG	NEWS CORRESPONDENT	8800 MANCHESTER RD #8	SILVER SPRING, MD	20901
CANO, TERRY J	COMPOSER	18434 COLLINS ST #8	TARZANA, CA	91356
CANON, PETER	ACTOR	1128 N VISTA ST #4	LOS ANGELES, CA	90046
CANOVA, DIANA	ACTRESS	10100 SANTA MONICA BLVD #1600	LOS ANGELES, CA	90067
CANSINO, RICHARD	ACTOR	1975 N BEACHWOOD DR #307	HOLLYWOOD, CA	90068
CANTARELLI, GIUSEPPE	CONDUCTOR	1005 N SWEETZER #24	LOS ANGELES, CA	90069
CANTER, M KATHLEEN	NEWS CORRESPONDENT	4836 69TH PL	HYATTSVILLE, MD	20784
CANTER, STANLEY S	SCREENWRITER	8955 BEVERLY BLVD	LOS ANGELES, CA	90048
CANTER, TIM	GUITARIST	POST OFFICE BOX 91	RED BOILING SPRINGS, T.	37150
CANTER, WALTER	WRITER	555 W 57TH ST #1230	NEW YORK, NY	10019
CANTILENA	MUSICAL DUO	MANNING MUSIC MGMT		
		935 NW 19TH AVE	PORTLAND, OR	97207
CANTILENA WIND QUINTENT	WIND QUINTET	FROTHINGHAM, 40 GROVE ST	WESSESLEY, MA	02181
CANTINFLAS	COMEDIAN-ACTOR	AVENUE INSURSENTES SUR 377	MEXICO D F	MEXICO
CANTON, NEIL	FILM PRODUCER	MCA/UNIVERSAL STUDIOS, INC		
		100 UNIVERSAL CITY PLAZA		
		BUILDING #47	UNIVERSAL CITY, CA	91608
CANTONE, VIC	CARTOONIST	DAILY, 220 E 42ND ST	NEW YORK, NY	10017
CANTOR, ARTHUR	THEATER PRODUCER	234 W 44TH ST	NEW YORK, NY	10036
CANTOR, BENJAMIN	WRITER	555 W 57TH ST #1230	NEW YORK, NY	10019
CANTOR, MARILYN	ACTRESS	211 CENTRAL PARK W	NEW YORK, NY	10024
CANTRELL, BYRON	COMPOSER-CONDUCTOR	6831 BOTHWELL RD	RESEDA, CA	91335
CANTRELL, LANA	SINGER	300 E 71ST ST	NEW YORK, NY	10021
CANTRELL, WILLIAM	GUITARIST	1254 MC GAVOCK PIKE	NASHVILLE, TN	37216
CANTU, DOLORES	ACTRESS	9300 WILSHIRE BLVD #410	BEVERLY HILLS, CA	90212
CANUTT, TAP	DIRECTOR	15856 BEAVER RUN RD	CANYON COUNTRY, CA	91351
CANYON	C & W GROUP	POST OFFICE BOX 1373	LEWISVILLE, TX	75067
CANYON, CHRIS	WRESTLER	SEE - BUNDY, KING KONG		
CANYON, CRIPPLER	WRESTLER	SEE - BUNDY, KING KONG		
CANZANO, FRANK	ACTOR	15 CHARLES ST	NEW YORK, NY	10014
CAPACCIO, ANTHONY W	NEWS CORRESPONDENT	105 6TH ST, NE	WASHINGTON, DC	20002
CAPALBO, CARMEN	DIRECTOR-PRODUCER	CARPENTER, 254 W 73RD ST	NEW YORK, NY	10023
CAPARROS, ERNESTO	DIRECTOR	DGA, 110 W 57TH ST	NEW YORK, NY	10019
CAPECCHI, RENATO	BARITONE	CAMI, 165 W 57TH ST	NEW YORK, NY	10019
CAPEN, CRIS	ACTOR	6210 WINANS DR	LOS ANGELES, CA	90068
CAPERS, VIRGINIA	ACTRESS	390 S HAUSER BLVD	LOS ANGELES, CA	90036
CAPETANOS, LEON	SCREENWRITER	8431 FOUNTAIN AVE #C	LOS ANGELES, CA	90069
CAPICE, PHILIP	TV PRODUCER	1359 MILLER DR	LOS ANGELES, CA	90069
CAPIZZI, BILL	ACTOR	6147 COLFAX AVE	NORTH HOLLYWOOD, CA	91606
CAPKA, CAROL	ACTRESS	18120 KINZIE ST	NORTHRIDGE, CA	91325
CAPLAIN, ROBERT	WRITER	1033 HILGARD AVE #409	LOS ANGELES, CA	90024
CAPLAN, JANE	NEWS CORRESPONDENT	4201 CATHEDRAL AVE, NW	WASHINGTON, DC	20016
CAPLAN, TWINK	ACTRESS	6430 SUNSET BLVD #1203	LOS ANGELES, CA	90028
CAPLIN, GUY	TV DIRECTOR-PRODUCER	YORKSHIRE TV CENTRE	LEEDS LS3 1JS	ENGLAND
CAPOLON, CARL	TV DIRECTOR	ABC TELEVISION NETWORK		
		1330 AVE OF THE AMERICAS	NEW YORK, NY	10019
CAPONE, GLORIA	SOPRANO	CAMI, 165 W 57TH ST	NEW YORK, NY	10019
CAPORALE, ESTHER	WRITER	145 S ELM DR	BEVERLY HILLS, CA	90212
CAPOZZOLA, CARMEN	COMPOSER	411 36TH ST	UNION CITY, NJ	07087
CAPPLEMAN, CHARLES	TV EXECUTIVE	CBS-TV, 51 W 52ND ST	NEW YORK, NY	10019
CAPPONE, NORBERTO	PIANIST	MANNING MUSIC MGMT		
		935 NW 19TH AVE	PORTLAND, OR	97209
CAPPS, DENNIS D	WRITER	8955 BEVERLY BLVD	LOS ANGELES, CA	90048
CAPPS, JAMES	DOBROIST	138 KAREN DR	MOUNT JULIET, TN	37122
CAPRA, FRANK, JR	FILM PRODUCER	2427 BANYAN DR	LOS ANGELES, CA	90049
CAPRA, FRANK, SR	FILM WRITER-DIRECTOR	POST OFFICE BOX 98	LA QUINTA, CA	92253
CAPRA, PRISCILLA	NEWS CORRESPONDENT	1101 ARLINGTON RIDGE RD	ARLINGTON, VA	22202
CAPRA, TOM	DIRECTOR-PRODUCER	116 W 78TH ST	NEW YORK, NY	10024
CAPRI, AHNA	ACTRESS	8227 FOUNTAIN AVE #2	LOS ANGELES, CA	90046
CAPRON, BRIAN	ACTOR	PLANT & FROGGATT, LTD		
		JULIAN HOUSE		
		4 WINDMILL ST	LONDON W1	ENGLAND
CAPSHAW, KATE	ACTRESS	1888 CENTURY PARK E #1400	LOS ANGELES, CA	90067
CAPTAIN & TENNILLE, THE	MUSIC DUO	POST OFFICE BOX 262	GLENBROOK, NV	89413
CAPTAIN AMERICA	WRESTLER-ACTOR	SEE - STUDD, BIG JOHN		
CAPTAIN CIRCUS	CANNONBALL ACT	HALL, 138 FROG HOLLOW RD	CHURCHVILLE, PA	18966
CAPTAIN REDNECK	WRESTLER	SEE - MURDOCH, DICK		
CAPTOR, ROXANNE	ACTRESS	5330 LANKERSHIM BLVD #210	NORTH HOLLYWOOD, CA	91601
CAPUCINE	ACTRESS	CHEMIN DE PRIMCIOSE 6	LAUSANNE 1007	SWITZERLAND
CAPUTO, PHILIP	AUTHOR	HOLT, 383 MADISON AVE	NEW YORK, NY	10017
CARA, IRENE	ACTRESS-SINGER	POST OFFICE BOX 135	MASSAPEQUE PARK, NY	11762
CARABATSOS, JAMES	SCREENWRITER	8955 BEVERLY BLVD	LOS ANGELES, CA	90048
CARABATSOS, STEVEN	SCREENWRITER	POST OFFICE BOX 753	MALIBU, CA	90265
CARAS, ROGER	NEWS CORRESPONDENT	ABC-TV, NEWS DEPARTMENT		
		1330 AVE OF THE AMERICAS	NEW YORK, NY	10019
CARBO, HENRY	ACTOR	5137 WEST BLVD	LOS ANGELES, CA	90043
CARBONE, CARL A	DIRECTOR-PRODUCER	225 E 36TH ST	NEW YORK, NMY	10016

CARBY, FANNY	ACTRESS	3 THURLOW RD, GARDEN FLOOR	LONDON NW3	ENGLAND
CARD, JUNE	SOPRANO	CAMI, 165 W 57TH ST	NEW YORK, NY	10019
CARD, LAMAR	DIRECTOR-PRODUCER	7318 WOODROW WILSON DR	LOS ANGELES, CA	90046
CARD, WILLIAM	MUSICIAN	206 GRAYCROFT DR	MADISON, TN	37115
CARDAN, CHRISTINA	ACTRESS	FARRELL, 10500 MAGNOLIA BLVD	NORTH HOLLYWOOD, CA	91601
CARDARAS, MARY	WRITER	555 W 57TH ST #1230	NEW YORK, NY	10019
CARDEA, FRANK, JR	TV WRITER-PRODUCER	1960 LAUGHLIN PARK DR	LOS ANGELES, CA	90027
CARDELL, PATRICIA	ACTRESS	7469 MELROSE AVE #30	LOS ANGELES, CA	90046
CARDENAS, HERNAN	FILM DIRECTOR	201 CRANDON BLVD #1102	KEY BISCAYNE, FL	33149
CARDENES, ANDRES	VIOLINIST	AIA, 60 E 42ND ST	NEW YORK, NY	10165
CARDER, ELIZABETH	ACTRESS	9601 WILSHIRE BLVD #GL-11	BEVERLY HILLS, CA	90210
CARDIFF, JACK	FILM DIRECTOR	LEPINE-SMITH, 10 WYNDHAM PL	LONDON W1	ENGLAND
CARDIN, PIERRE	FASHION DESIGNER	59 RUE DU FAULBOURG		
		SAINT-HONORE	PARIS 75008	FRANCE
CARDINAL, CYNDI	ACTRESS	401 1/2 HOWLAND CANAL	VENICE, CA	90291
CARDINALE, CLAUDIA	ACTRESS	VIDES PIAZZA, PITAGORA	ROME	ITALY
CARDIS, DEE	MUSICIAN	119 HILLCREST RD	GOODLETTSVILLE, TN	37072
CARDIS, VICTOR	DRUMMER	119 HILLCREST RD	NASHVILLE, TN	37072
CARDONA, ANNETTE	ACTRESS	KOHNER, 9169 SUNSET BLVD	LOS ANGELES, CA	90069
CARDONA, ROBERT	WRITER-PRODUCER	1901 AVE OF THE STARS #840	LOS ANGELES, CA	90067
CARDOS, JOHN "BUD"	ACTOR-DIRECTOR	19116 ENADIA WY	RESEDA, CA	91335
CARELLI, RICHARD	NEWS CORRESPONDENT	6 HOLLY DR	GAITHERSBURG, MD	20877
CAREW, ALYCE S	PRODUCER	1420 N BEACHWOOD DR #7	LOS ANGELES, CA	90028
CAREW, COLIN A, JR	WRITER	3127 NICHOLS CANYON RD	LOS ANGELES, CA	90046
CAREW, PETER	ACTOR	151 N SAN VICENTE BLVD #208	BEVERLY HILLS, CA	90211
CAREW, ROD	BASEBALL	5144 E CRESCENT DR	ANAHEIM, CA	92807
CAREW, TOPPER	WRITER-PRODUCER	1420 N BEACHWOOD DR	LOS ANGELES, CA	90028
CAREY, GEORGE E	ACTOR	10701 RIVERSIDE DR #13	TOLUCA LAKE, CA	91602
CAREY, HARRY, JR	ACTOR	1801 SANTA MONICA RD	CARPINTERIA, CA	93013
CAREY, JACK	SPORTS WRITER	POST OFFICE BOX 500	WASHINGTON, DC	20044
CAREY, JOSEPH C	NEWS CORRESPONDENT	2800 ONTARIO RD #305, NW	WASHINGTON, DC	20009
CAREY, KATHI	ACTRESS	13111 VENTURA BLVD #204	STUDIO CITY, CA	91604
CAREY, MAC DONALD	ACTOR	1543 BENEDICT CANYON DR	BEVERLY HILLS, CA	90210
CAREY, MICHELE	ACTRESS	9636 YOAKUM DR	BEVERLY HILLS, CA	90210
CAREY, OLIVE FULLER	ACTRESS	1801 SANTA MONICA RD	CARPINTERIA, CA	93013
CAREY, PHILIP	ACTOR	427 N CANON DR #205	BEVERLY HILLS, CA	90210
CAREY, RON	ACTOR	8500 WILSHIRE BLVD #506	BEVERLY HILLS, CA	90211
CAREY, TIMOTHY AGOGLIA	ACTOR	POST OFFICE BOX 8589	UNIVERSAL CITY, CA	91608
CAREY-JONES, SELENA	ACTRESS	32 ACACIA RD	LONDON NW8	ENGLAND
CARGILL, HENSON	SINGER	CENTER, 408 W PARK AVE	OKLAHOMA CITY, OK	73102
CARGILL, MARK K	COMPOSER	1937 W 94TH ST	LOS ANGELES, CA	90047
CARGILL, PATRICK	ACTOR	LONDON MANAGEMENT, LTD		
		235-241 REGENT ST	LONDON W1A 2JT	ENGLAND
CARHART, EILEEN	TV DIRECTOR	11101 1/4 CAMARILLO ST	NORTH HOLLYWOOD, CA	91602
CARIAGA, DANIEL	MUSIC CRITIC	L A TIMES NEWSPAPER		
		TIMES MIRROR SQUARE	LOS ANGELES, CA	90053
CARIAGA, MARVELLEE	MEZZO-SOPRANO	CONE, 221 W 57TH ST	NEW YORK, NY	10019
CARIBBEAN KNIGHTS, THE	C & W GROUP	CUDE, 519 N HALIFAX AVE	DAYTON BEACH, FL	32018
CARIDI, CARMINE	ACTOR	9200 SUNSET BLVD #909	LOS ANGELES, CA	90069
CARILLO	ROCK & ROLL GROUP	3 E 54TH ST #1400	NEW YORK, NY	10022
CARINO, MERLE	PIANIST	1030 N C ST	LAKE WORTH, FL	33460
CARIOU, LEN	ACTOR	211 S BEVERLY DR #201	BEVERLY HILLS, CA	90212
CARISLE, CHRIS	WRITER	555 W 57TH ST #1230	NEW YOEK, NY	10019
CARISTI, VINCENT	ACTOR	732 N HARPER AVE	LOS ANGELES, CA	90046
CARIZZMA, JIMMY	SINGER	JOYCE, 2028 CHESTNUT ST	PHILADELPHIA, PA	19103
CARLE, CYNTHIA	ACTRESS	9744 WILSHIRE BLVD #206	BEVERLY HILLS, CA	90212
CARLE, FRANKIE	PIANIST-COMPOSER	29500 HEATHER CLIFF RD	MALIBU, CA	90265
CARLEN, CATHERINE	ACTRESS	247 S BEVERLY DR #102	BEVERLY HILLS, CA	90210
CARLILE, DAVID	ACTOR	8721 SUNSET BLVD #200	LOS ANGELES, CA	90069
CARLILE, TOM	SINGER	TALENT MASTER AGENCY		
		1019 17TH AVE S	NASHVILLE, TN	37212
CARLIN, DANIEL A	CONDUCTOR	6635 SHELTONDALE AVE	CANOGA PARK, CA	91307
CARLIN, GEORGE	COMEDIAN	HAMZA, 901 BRINGHAM AVE	LOS ANGELES, CA	90049
CARLIN, GLORIA	ACTRESS	9220 SUNSET BLVD #625	LOS ANGELES, CA	90069
CARLIN, JACQUELINE	ACTRESS-MODRL	7684 WOODROW WILSON DR	LOS ANGELES, CA	90046
CARLIN, LYNN	ACTRESS	24504 WINGFIELD RD	CALABASAS, CA	91302
CARLINER, MARK	FILM PRODUCER	11700 LAUREL WOOD DR	STUDIO CITY, CA	91604
CARLINER, MARK P	SCREENWRITER	555 W 57TH ST #1230	NEW YORK, NY	10019
CARLINO, LEWIS JOHN	WRITER-DIRECTOR	991 OAKMONT DR	LOS ANGELES, CA	90049
CARLISLE, BELINDA	SINGER-SONGWRITER	10100 SANTA MONICA BLVD #1600	LOS ANGELES, CA	90067
CARLISLE, BILL	SINGER	ROUTE #3, BOX 444	GOODLETTSVILLE, TN	37072
CARLISLE, JODI	ACTRESS	ICM, 8899 BEVERLY BLVD	LOS ANGELES, CA	90048
CARLISLE, KATE	NEWS CORRESPONDENT	441 1/2 2ND ST, SE	WASHINGTON, DC	20003
CARLISLE, KEVIN B	TV DIRECTOR	2022 N SYCAMORE AVE	HOLLYWOOD, CA	90068
CARLISLE, KITTY	ACTRESS	32 E 64TH ST	NEW YORK, NY	10021
CARLISLE, MICHAEL	SINGER	ROUTE #2, BOX 3343, GREER RD	GOODLETTSVILLE, TN	37072
CARLISLE, ROBERT W	DIRECTOR	45422 INDIAN WELLS LN	INDIAN WELLS, CA	92260
CARLISLE, STEVE	SINGER	28001 CHARGRIN BLVD #205	CLEVELAND, OH	44122
CARLISLE, WILLIAM T, JR	GUITARIST	1853 UNION HILL RD	GOODLETTSVILLE, TN	37072
CARLON, FRAN	ACTRESS	451 W END AVE	NEW YORK, NY	10024
CARLSON, ALVER	NEWS CORRESPONDENT	9637 PERCUSSION WY	VIENNA, VA	22180
CARLSON, CHRISTOPHER F	PHOTOJOURNALIST	8409 STONEGATE DR	ANNANDALE, VA	22003
CARLSON, CLAUDINE	MEZZO-SOPRANO	ICM, 40 W 57TH ST	NEW YORK, NY	10019
CARLSON, CRAIG	TV WRITER	ABC-TV, "ONE LIFE TO LIVE"		
		1330 AVE OF THE AMERICAS	NEW YORK, NY	10019

Name	Occupation	Address	City	Zip
CARLSON, CURT	ACTOR	10850 RIVERSIDE DR #505	NORTH HOLLYWOOD, CA	91602
CARLSON, DONALD L	DIRECTOR-PRODUCER	1937 NORTH DR	GLENVIEW, IL	60025
CARLSON, EUGENE	NEWS CORRESPONDENT	6617 31ST ST, NW	WASHINGTON, DC	20015
CARLSON, GAIL RAE	ACTRESS	9441 WILSHIRE BLVD #620-D	BEVERLY HILLS, CA	90210
CARLSON, HERBERT P	NEWS CORRESPONDENT	2215 DAIRY FARM RD	GAMBRILLS, MD	21054
CARLSON, JIM	TV WRITER	8955 BEVERLY BLVD	LOS ANGELES, CA	90048
CARLSON, KAREN	ACTRESS	3700 VENTURA CANYON AVE	SHERMAN OAKS, CA	91423
CARLSON, LAURA	ACTRESS	9220 SUNSET BLVD #202	LOS ANGELES, CA	90069
CARLSON, LENUS	BARITONE	CAMI, 165 W 57TH ST	NEW YORK, NY	10019
CARLSON, LINDA	ACTRESS	9220 SUNSET BLVD #625	LOS ANGELES, CA	90069
CARLSON, ROBERT A	DIRECTOR	1323 HOLMBY AVE	LOS ANGELES, CA	90024
CARLSON, SANDY	ACTRESS	9777 WILSHIRE BLVD #707	BEVERLY HILLS, CA	90212
CARLSON, STEVE	ACT-WRI-DIR	9441 WILSHIRE BLVD #620-D	BEVERLY HILLS, CA	90210
CARLTON, CARL	SINGER	DAVID RUBINSON MGMT		
		827 FOLSOM ST	SAN FRANCISCO, CA	94107
CARLTON, HOPE MARIE	ACTRESS-MODEL	9744 WILSHIRE BLVD #306	BEVERLY HILLS, CA	90212
CARLTON, LARRY	GUITARIST	3208 W CAHUENGA BLVD #42	LOS ANGELES, CA	90068
CARLTON, STEVE	BASEBALL	16240 HOLTS LAKE DR	CHESTERFIELD, MO	63017
CARLTON, TIMOTHY	ACTOR	SARABAND ASSOCIATES AGENCY		
		153 PETHERTON RD, HIGHBURY	LONDON N5	ENGLAND
CARLYLE, AILEEN	ACTRESS	2267 EL CONTENTO DR	LOS ANGELES, CA	90068
CARLYLE, JOHN	ACTOR	9220 SUNSET BLVD #218	LOS ANGELES, CA	90069
CARLYLE, RICHARD	ACTOR	11240 MAGNOLIA BLVD #202	NORTH HOLLYWOOD, CA	91601
CARMEN, ERIC	SINGER-SONGWRITER	BARUCK, 1046 CAROL DR	LOS ANGELES, CA	90069
CARMEN, JULIE	ACTRESS	9220 SUNSET BLVD #625	LOS ANGELES, CA	90069
CARMEN, ROBERT D	WRITER	8955 BEVERLY BLVD	LOS ANGELES, CA	90048
CARMICHAEL, DAN	NEWS CORRESPONDENT	5703 LAWSON HILL CT	ALEXANDRIA, VA	22310
CARMICHAEL, IAN	ACTOR-PRODUCER	LONDON MANAGEMENT, LTD		
		235-241 REGENT ST	LONDON W1A 2JT	ENGLAND
CARMICHAEL, ROBERT J	TV DIRECTOR	3419 LOS PINOS DR	SANTA BARBARA, CA	93105
CARN, JEAN	SINGER	HUSH PRODS, 231 W 58TH ST	NEW YORK, NY	10019
CARNE, JEAN	SINGER	POST OFFICE BOX 27641	PHILADELPHIA, PA	27641
CARNE, JUDY	ACTRESS	CARNE LODGE, CHAPEL BRAMPTON	NORTHAMPTONSHIRE	ENGLAND
CARNEGIE, ROBERT	ACTOR	9300 WILSHIRE BLVD #410	BEVERLY HILLS, CA	90212
CARNER, CHARLES	WRITER	555 W 57TH ST #1230	NEW YORK, NY	10019
CARNER, CHARLES R	SCREENWRITER	8417 HAROLD WY	LOS ANGELES, CA	90069
CARNES, KIM	SINGER-SONGWRITER	1112 N SHERBOURNE DR	LOS ANGELES, CA	90069
CARNEVALE, MARY LOUISE	NEWS CORRESPONDENT	1900 S EADS ST	ARLINGTON, VA	22202
CARNEY, ART	ACTOR	RURAL ROUTE #20, BOX 911	WESTBROOK, CT	06498
CARNEY, DONALD M	DIRECTOR-PRODUCER	60 CENTRAL AVE	PELHAM, NY	10803
CARNEY, FRED	ACTOR	1429 N HAVENHURST DR	LOS ANGELES, CA	90046
CARNEY, KAY	ACTRESS	396 BLEECKER ST	NEW YORK, NY	10014
CARNEY, LARRY	NEWS CORRESPONDENT	5565 COLUMBIA PIKE #514	ARLINGTON, VA	22204
CARNEY, THOMAS R	WRITER	555 W 57TH ST #1230	NEW YORK, NY	10019
CARNEY, WILL	ACTOR	427 N CANON DR #205	BEVERLY HILLS, CA	90210
CAROL, LINDA	ACTRESS	8019 1/2 MELROSE AVE #3	LOS ANGELES, CA	90046
CAROLEI, JOSEPH A	TV DIRECTOR	45 W 67TH ST #11-C	NEW YORK, NY	10023
CAROLINA JAM BROTHERS, THE	ROCK & ROLL GROUP	POST OFFICE BOX 448	RADFORD, VA	24141
CAROLL, STANESS	ACTRESS	8721 SUNSET BLVD #202	LOS ANGELES, CA	90069
CARON, GLENN G	TV WRITER-PRODUCER	5474 JED SMITH RD	HIDDEN HILLS, CA	91302
CARON, LESLIE	ACTRESS	6 RUE DE BELLECHASSE		
		7TH DISTRICT	PARIS 75007	FRANCE
CARON, SANDRA	ACTRESS	7471 MELROSE AVE #11	LOS ANGELES, CA	90046
CAROTHERS, A J	SCREENWRITER	217 S BURLINGAME AVE	LOS ANGELES, CA	90049
CARPEL, ANDY	DIRECTOR	8618 DISCOVERY BLVD	WALKERSVILLE, IN	21793
CARPENTER, BETTY WIDBY	PIANIST	POST OFFICE BOX 4545	NASHVILLE, TN	37216
CARPENTER, BOBBY	MUSICIAN	ROUTE #3, CHESTNUT ST	BOWLING GREEN, KY	42101
CARPENTER, CARLETON	ACTOR	CHARDAVOYNE RD	WARWICK, NY	10990
CARPENTER, EDWARD	WRITER	555 W 57TH ST #1230	NEW YORK, NY	10019
CARPENTER, HOWARD R	VIOLINIST	1730 CHESTNUT ST	BOWLING GREEN, KY	42101
CARPENTER, JAMES	ACTOR	AFFILIATE ARTISTS, INC		
		37 W 65TH ST, 6TH FLOOR	NEW YORK, NY	10023
CARPENTER, JOHN	ACTOR	HEAVEN-ON-EARTH STABLES	LAKE VIEW TERRACE, CA	91342
CARPENTER, JOHN	FILM WRITER-DIRECTOR	DGA, 7950 SUNSET BLVD	LOS ANGELES, CA	90046
CARPENTER, JOHN R	AUTHOR-WRITER	2801 MEADOW LARK DR	SAN DIEGO, CA	92123
CARPENTER, RICHARD	PIANIST-COMPOSER	8341 LUBEC AVE	DOWNEY, CA	90241
CARPENTER, RICHARD E	SINGER	512 LEEANNE DR	NASHVILLE, TN	37211
CARPENTER, SCOTT (LT CMDR)	ASTRONAUT	1183 STRADELLA RD	LOS ANGELES, CA	90077
CARPENTER, TED	EDITOR-PUBLISHER	2917 COVINGTON RD	SILVER SPRINGS, MD	20910
CARPENTER, TERESA	WRITER	555 W 57TH ST #1230	NEW YORK, NY	10019
CARPER, DON	CONDUCTOR	28303 HAZELRIDGE DR	PALOS VERDES ESTATES,	90274
CARPER, ELSIE	NEWS CORRESPONDENT	4421 WINDOM PL, NW	WASHINGTON, DC	20016
CARPER, JEAN	AUTHOR	1018 W PEACHTREE ST, NW	ATLANTA, GA	30309
CARR, ALLAN	FILM WRITER-PRODUCER	1220 BENEDICT CANYON DR	BEVERLY HILLS, CA	90210
CARR, BETTY ANN	ACTRESS	8949 SUNSET BLVD #203	LOS ANGELES, CA	90069
CARR, CAMILLA	ACTRESS	427 N CANON DR #205	BEVERLY HILLS, CA	90210
CARR, COLIN	CELLIST	1776 BROADWAY #504	NEW YORK, NY	10019
CARR, DARLEEN	ACTRESS	8721 SUNSET BLVD #202	LOS ANGELES, CA	90069
CARR, DAVE "BOAT"	GUITARIST	200 NESBITT LN #21	MADISON, TN	37115
CARR, DIDI	ACTRESS	9105 CARMELITA AVE #1	BEVERLY HILLS, CA	90210
CARR, GORDON	TV PRODUCER-JOURN	BBC TV NEWS, TV CENTRE		
		WOOD LN	LONDON W12	ENGLAND
CARR, JANE	ACTRESS	PLANT & FROGGATT, LTD		
		JULIAN HOUSE		
		4 WINDMILL ST	LONDON W1	ENGLAND

CARR, JOHN	FILM WRITER-DIRECTOR	PAN-AMERICAN PICTURES	
		9033 WILSHIRE BLVD	BEVERLY HILLS, CA 90211
CARR, JUNE	SINGER	3620 CENTRAL AVE	NASHVILLE, TN 37205
CARR, LAURIE	ACTRESS-MODEL	MODELS & PROMOTIONS AGENCY	
		8560 SUNSET BLVD, 10TH FLOOR	LOS ANGELES, CA 90069
CARR, LUCIEN	NEWS CORRESPONDENT	1844 ONTARIO PL, NW	WASHINGTON, DC 20009
CARR, MARTIN	WRITER-PRODUCER	305 W 86TH ST	NEW YORK, NY 10024
CARR, PATRICIA	ACTRESS	8831 SUNSET BLVD #402	LOS ANGELES, CA 90069
CARR, PATRICIA E	NEWS CORRESPONDENT	9410 GAMBA CT	VIENNA, VA 22180
CARR, PAUL	ACTOR-WRITER	3800 BARHAM BLVD #303	LOS ANGELES, CA 90068
CARR, RICHARD GRANT	TV WRITER	8955 BEVERLY BLVD	LOS ANGELES, CA 90048
CARR, TEDDY S	GUITARIST	204 DONOHO AVE	LAFAYETTE, TN 37083
CARR, THOMAS	FILM DIRECTOR	1365 WEYMOUTH LN	VENTURA, CA 93003
CARR, VICKIE	SINGER	2289 BETTY LN	BEVERLY HILLS, CA 90210
CARR, WENDY D	NEWS CORRESPONDENT	203 W WINDSOR AVE	ALEXANDRIA, VA 22301
CARR-BOSLEY, PATRICIA	ACTRESS	2822 ROYSTON PL	BEVERLY HILLS, CA 90210
CARRACK, PAUL	SINGER	ATI, 888 7TH AVE, 21ST FLOOR	NEW YORK, NY 10106
CARRADINE, CAROLYN	ACTRESS	2350 SUNSET PLAZA DR	LOS ANGELES, CA 90069
CARRADINE, DAVID	ACTOR	7101 WOODROW WILSON DR	LOS ANGELES, CA 90046
CARRADINE, JOHN	ACTOR	WEBB, 7500 DEVISTA DR	LOS ANGELES, CA 90046
CARRADINE, KEITH	ACTOR-SINGER	151 S EL CAMINO DR	BEVERLY HILLS, CA 90212
CARRADINE, ROBERT	ACTOR	7453 MULHOLLAND DR	LOS ANGELES, CA 90046
CARRAHER, JACK E	COMPOSER	2416 BRYCE CT	LAWRENCE, KS 66044
CARRAWAY, STEVE	NEWS CORRESPONDENT	NBC-TV, NEWS DEPARTMENT	
		4001 NEBRASKA AVE, NW	WASHINGTON, DC 20016
CARRELL, MARTHA	TALENT AGENT	6605 HOLLYWOOD BLVD #220	HOLLYWOOD, CA 90028
CARREN, DAVID BENNETT	TV WRITER	2458 GLYNDON AVE	VENICE, CA 90291
CARRENO, JOSE	NEWS CORRESPONDENT	2500 "Q" ST #641, NW	WASHINGTON, DC 20007
CARREOW, JACK	TV WRITER	519 S CAMINO REAL	REDONDO BEACH, CA 90277
CARRERA, BARBARA	ACTRESS-MODEL	15430 MILLDALE DR	LOS ANGELES, CA 90077
CARRERA, GINA	ACTRESS	9333 OSO AVE #1	CHATSWORTH, CA 91311
CARRERAS, JOSE	TENOR	COPERA CABALLE	
		VIA AUGUSTA 59	BARCELONA SPAIN
CARRERAS, SIR JAMES	FILM EXECUTIVE	QUEEN ANNE COTTAGE	
		FRIDAY ST, HENLEY-ON-THAMES	OXFORDSHIRE ENGLAND
CARRERE, LEON	TV DIRECTOR	220 W CHANNEL RD	SANTA MONICA, CA 90402
CARRERE, TIA	ACTRESS	7060 HOLLYWOOD BLVD #1010	LOS ANGELES, CA 90028
CARREY, JIM	ACTOR-COMEDIAN	ICM, 8899 BEVERLY BLVD	LOS ANGELES, CA 90048
CARRICART, ROBERT	ACTOR	205 AVE "G"	REDONDO BEACH, CA 90277
CARRICO, MARK	SINGER	LUTZ, 5625 "O" STREET BLDG	LINCOLN, NE 68510
CARRIER, ALBERT	ACTOR	7640 MULHOLLAND DR	LOS ANGELES, CA 90046
CARRIER, JUDY	FIDDLER-BANJOIST	POST OFFICE BOX 721	GOODLETTSVILLE, TN 37072
CARRIER, MATHIEW	ACTOR	79 BLVD SAINT-MICHEL	PARIS 75009 FRANCE
CARRIERE, GLORY-ANNE	SINGER	4680 ELK LAKE DR #304	VICTORIA, BC V8Z 5M1 CANADA
CARRIGAN, JERRY	DRUMMER	119 HOLLY FOREST	NASHVILLE, TN 37221
CARRILLIO, PEDRO	HIGH WIRE ACT	POST OFFICE BOX 87	WEST LEBANON, NY 12195
CARRINGTON, CAROL	ACTRESS	8721 SUNSET BLVD #2092	LOS ANGELES, CA 90069
CARRINGTON, LAURA	ACTRESS	ABC-TV, "ONE LIFE TO LIVE"	
		1330 AVE OF THE AMERICAS	NEW YORK, NY 10019
CARRINGTON, PATRICIA	WRITER	555 W 57TH ST #1230	NEW YORK, NY 10019
CARRINGTON, ROBERT	SCREENWRITER	10811 WILKINS AVE	LOS ANGELES, CA 90024
CARRINGTON, TIMOTHY T	NEWS CORRESPONDENT	6637 BARNABY ST, NW	WASHINGTON, DC 20015
CARRINGTON, WENDY	WRITER	8955 BEVERLY BLVD	LOS ANGELES, CA 90048
CARROLI, SILVANO	BARITONE	61 W 62ND ST #6-F	NEW YORK, NY 10023
CARROLL, BEESON	ACTOR	1930 CENTURY PARK W #303	LOS ANGELES, CA 90067
CARROLL, BELINDA	ACTRESS	BURNETT, 42 GRAFTON HOUSE	
		2-3 GOLDEN SQ	LONDON W1 ENGLAND
CARROLL, BOB, JR	TV PRODUCER	RWG, 8428 MELROSE PL	LOS ANGELES, CA 90069
CARROLL, BRUCE	WRITER	555 W 57TH ST #1230	NEW YORK, NY 10019
CARROLL, CORINNE	ACTRESS	10000 RIVERSIDE DR #3	TOLUCA LAKE, CA 91602
CARROLL, DAVID	TV WRITER	8955 BEVERLY BLVD	LOS ANGELES, CA 90048
CARROLL, DIAHANN	ACTRESS-SINGER	9108 ALANDA PL	BEVERLY HILLS, CA 90210
CARROLL, EDDIE	ACTOR	7461 SUNSET BLVD #400	LOS ANGELES, CA 90036
CARROLL, FRANCINE	WRITER	8955 BEVERLY BLVD	LOS ANGELES, CA 90048
CARROLL, GORDON	FILM PRODUCER	9080 SHOREHAM DR #C	LOS ANGELES, CA 90067
CARROLL, J LARRY	SCREENWRITER	8955 BEVERLY BLVD	LOS ANGELES, CA 90048
CARROLL, JAMES F	ACTOR	JARRETT, 220 E 63RD ST	NEW YORK, NY 10021
CARROLL, JAMES R	NEWS CORRESPONDENT	1119 BEVERLY DR	ALEXANDRIA, VA 22302
CARROLL, JANET	ACTRESS	409 N CAMDEN DR #203-A	BEVERLY HILLS, CA 90210
CARROLL, JANICE	ACTRESS	13923 DAVENTRY ST	PACOIMA, CA 91331
CARROLL, JOE	GUITARIST	110 HARRIS CT #C-4	GOODLETTSVILLE, TN 37216
CARROLL, KATHLEEN	FILM CRITIC	220 E 42ND ST	NEW YORK, NY 10017
CARROLL, LARRY	BROADCAST JOURNALIST	8019 1/2 MELROSE AVE #3	LOS ANGELES, CA 90046
CARROLL, LESTER	CARTOONIST	21100 BEACHWOOD DR	ROCKY RIVER, OH 44116
CARROLL, LISA HART	ACTRESS	ICM, 8899 BEVERLY BLVD	LOS ANGELES, CA 90048
CARROLL, MADELEINE	ACTRESS	EL MADRONAL, NEAR RONDA	COSTA DEL SOL SPAIN
CARROLL, MARTHA	TALENT AGENT	6605 HOLLYWOOD BLVD #220	HOLLYWOOD, CA 90028
CARROLL, PAT	ACTRESS	POST OFFICE BOX 252	HIGH FALLS, NY 12440
CARROLL, PAUL	GUITARIST	1316 KENWOOD DR	NASHVILLE, TN 37216
CARROLL, RAY	MUSIC ARRANGER	ROUTE #8, JEFF DAVIS DR	FRANKLIN, TN 37064
CARROLL, ROBERT G, JR	WRITER-PRODUCER	8141 CORNETT DR	LOS ANGELES, CA 90046
CARROLL, ROGER G	GUITARIST	2313 OAKHURST	SPRINGFIELD, TN 37172
CARROLL, RONNIE	SINGER	LYNCH, 57 DUKE ST	LONDON W1 ENGLAND
CARROLL, SIDNEY	TV WRITER	555 W 57TH ST #1230	NEW YORK, NY 10019

JOHNNY CARSON

SUNSET CARSON

CARTER FAMILY

JOHNNY CASH

DAVID CASSIDY

CAROL CHANNING

STOCKARD CHANNING

TOM CHAPIN

RAY CHARLES

Name	Occupation	Address	City	ZIP
CARROLL, STACY	ACTRESS	SHERMAN, 348 S REXFORD DR	BEVERLY HILLS, CA	90212
CARROLL, SUSETTE	ACTRESS	9200 SUNSET BLVD #909	LOS ANGELES, CA	90069
CARROLL, TOD	TV WRITER	555 W 57TH ST #1230	NEW YORK, NY	10019
CARROLL, VICTORIA	ACTRESS	9744 WILSHIRE BLVD #306	BEVERLY HILLS, CA	90212
CARROLL, VINCENT	NEWS CORRESPONDENT	1728 CORCORAN ST #C, NW	WASHINGTON, DC	20009
CARROLL, VINNETTE	ACT-WRI-DIR	227 W 17TH ST	NEW YORK, NY	10011
CARRUTHERS, JULIE	ACTRESS	10000 RIVERSIDE DR #3	TOLUCA LAKE, CA	91602
CARRUTHERS, WILLIAM H	DIRECTOR-PRODUCER	506 S BRONSON AVE	LOS ANGELES, CA	90020
CARRY, JULIUS	ACTOR	427 N CANON DR #205	BEVERLY HILLS, CA	90210
CARRY, JULIUS J, III	ACTOR	427 N CANON DR #205	BEVERLY HILLS, CA	90210
CARS, THE	ROCK & ROLL GROUP	LOOKOUT, 9120 SUNSET BLVD	LOS ANGELES, CA	90069
CARSEL, HARRIET	ACTRESS	24520 WELBY WY	WESTHILLS, CA	91307
CARSEY, JOHN J	WRITER	8955 BEVERLY BLVD	LOS ANGELES, CA	90048
CARSEY, MARCY	TV PRODUCER	1438 N GOWER ST #376	LOS ANGELES, CA	90028
CARSON, DARWYN	ACTRESS	5726 CAMELLIA AVE #205	NORTH HOLLYWOOD, CA	91601
CARSON, JEANNIE	ACTRESS	250 W 57TH ST #2317	NEW YORK, NY	10107
CARSON, JOHN	ACTOR	JAMESON, 7 W EATON PLACE MEWS	LONDON SW1	ENGLAND
CARSON, JOHN DAVID	ACTOR	8322 BEVERLY BLVD #202	LOS ANGELES, CA	90048
CARSON, JOHNNY	TV HOST-COMEDIAN	NBC-TV, 3000 W ALAMEDA AVE	BURBANK, CA	91523
CARSON, L M "KIT"	SCREENWRITER	THE WILLIAM MORRIS AGENCY		
		1350 AVE OF THE AMERICAS	NEW YORK, NY	10019
CARSON, MICHAEL A	NEWS CORRESPONDENT	6130 FRANCONIA STATION LN	ALEXANDRIA, VA	22310
CARSON, RUBIN	WRITER	8955 BEVERLY BLVD	LOS ANGELES, CA	90048
CARSON, STEPHEN DALE	PIANIST	2300 ELLIOTT AVE	NASHVILLE, TN	37204
CARSON, SUNSET	ACTOR	11159 DINO CIR #42	GARDEN GROVE, CA	90264
CARTENSEN, MARGIT	ACTRESS	JACKSON, 59 KNIGHTSBRIDGE	LONDON SW1X 7RA	ENGLAND
CARTER, ALFRED W	WRITER	8955 BEVERLY BLVD	LOS ANGELES, CA	90048
CARTER, BETTY	SINGER	KURLAND, 173 BRIGHTON AVE	BOSTON, MA	02134
CARTER, BEVERLY	TV WRITER	8955 BEVERLY BLVD	LOS ANGELES, CA	90048
CARTER, BILL	SINGER	FREE LOW, 1209 BAYLOR ST	AUSTIN, TX	78703
CARTER, BOB	SAXOPHONIST	706 WESTWOOD DR	TULLAHOMA, TN	37388
CARTER, C CARROLL	NEWS CORRESPONDENT	5016 LOWELL ST, NW	WASHINGTON, DC	20016
CARTER, CHERYL	ACTRESS	12403 MAGNOLIA BLVD	NORTH HOLLYWOOD, CA	91607
CARTER, CHRIS	WRESTLER	CAPITOL INTERNATIONAL		
		11844 MARKET ST	NORTH LIMA, OH	44452
CARTER, CRAIG C	NEWS CORRESPONDENT	100 SCHUYLER RD #102	BETHESDA, MD	20901
CARTER, CYNTHIA A	NEWS CORRESPONDENT	1039 N MC KINLEY RD	ARLINGTON, VA	22205
CARTER, DIXIE	ACTRESS	SEE - CARTER HOLBROOK, DIXIE		
CARTER, FINN	ACTOR	CBS-TV, "AS THE WORLD TURNS"		
		51 W 52ND ST	NEW YORK, NY	10019
CARTER, FRED "THE FLASH"	GUITARIST	810 DICKERSON RD	GOODLETTSVILLE, TN	37072
CARTER, HELEN	ACCORDIONIST	ROUTE #2, BOX 21-A	DICKSON, TN	37055
CARTER, HODDING	NEWS CORRESPONDENT	FRANK GOODMAN, 1776 BROADWAY	NEW YORK, NY	10019
CARTER, J PAT	PHOTOGRAPHER	7420 PARK HGTS AVE	BALTIMORE, MD	21208
CARTER, JACK	COMEDIAN-ACTOR	1023 CHEVY CHASE DR	BEVERLY HILLS, CA	90210
CARTER, JIMMY	PRESIDENT-AUTHOR	MARANATHA BAPTIST CHURCH		
		SUNDAY SCHOOL OFFICE	PLAINS, GA	31780
CARTER, JIMMY R	FIDDLER	683 HUNTINGTON PARKWAY	NASHVILLE, TN	37211
CARTER, JODY	ACTRESS	13111 VENTURA BLVD #102	STUDIO CITY, CA	91604
CARTER, JOHN	ACTOR	4721 LAUREL CANYON BLVD #211	NORTH HOLLYWOOD, CA	91607
CARTER, JOHN R	NEWS CORRESPONDENT	1617 N ABINGDON ST	ARLINGTON, VA	22207
CARTER, JOHN S	NEWS CORRESPONDENT	715 "D" ST, NE	WASHINGTON, DC	20002
CARTER, JUDY	ACTRESS	239 PACIFIC ST #K	SANTA MONICA, CA	90405
CARTER, LAURA	WRITER	8955 BEVERLY BLVD	LOS ANGELES, CA	90048
CARTER, LES	TV WRITER	8955 BEVERLY BLVD	LOS ANGELES, CA	90048
CARTER, LYNDA	ACTRESS-SINGER	POST OFFICE BOX 5973	SHERMAN OAKS, CA	91413
CARTER, MAURICE	ART DIRECTOR	LEE END, HURLEY	BERKS	ENGLAND
CARTER, MEL	SINGER-ACTOR	6380 WILSHIRE BLVD #1600	LOS ANGELES, CA	90048
CARTER, MITCH	ACTOR	870 N VINE ST #G	LOS ANGELES, CA	90038
CARTER, NANCY	ACTRESS	13111 VENTURA BLVD #102	STUDIO CITY, CA	91604
CARTER, NELL	ACTRESS-SINGER	10100 SANTA MONICA BLVD #1600	LOS ANGELES, CA	90067
CARTER, PAT	GUITARIST	GELFAND-BRESLAUER MGMT		
		7 MUSIC CIRCLE N	NASHVILLE, TN	37203
CARTER, RALPH	ACTOR	104-60 WUEENS BLVD #1-D	FOREST HILLS, NY	11375
CARTER, RANDY	DIRECTOR	6287 VINE WY	HOLLYWOOD, CA	90068
CARTER, ROSALYN	FIRST LADY-AUTHORESS	MARANATHA BAPTIST CHURCH		
		SUNDAY SCHOOL OFFICE	PLAINS, GA	31780
CARTER, SUSAN	WRITER	8955 BEVERLY BLVD	LOS ANGELES, CA	90048
CARTER, SUSAN ELIZABETH	NEWS CORRESPONDENT	1908 FLORIDA AVE #314, NW	WASHINGTON, DC	20009
CARTER, SUZY	ACTRESS	113 N SAN VICENTE BLVD #202	BEVERLY HILLS, CA	90211
CARTER, TERRY	ACTOR	447 9TH ST	SANTA MONICA, CA	90402
CARTER, THOMAS	ACTOR-DIRECTOR	ICM, 8899 BEVERLY BLVD	LOS ANGELES, CA	90048
CARTER, THOMAS G, JR	WRITER	8955 BEVERLY BLVD	LOS ANGELES, CA	90048
CARTER, VIRGINIA	TV WRITER	8955 BEVERLY BLVD	LOS ANGELES, CA	90048
CARTER, VIRGINIA L	TV EXECUTIVE	TAT COMMUNICATIONS		
		1901 AVE OF THE STARS	LOS ANGELES, CA	90067
CARTER, W HODDING, III	NEWS CORRESPONDENT	211 S SAINT ASAPH ST	ALEXANDRIA, VA	22314
CARTER, WALTER C, JR	DOBROIST	2609 W LINDEN AVE	NASHVILLE, TN	37212
CARTER FAMILY, THE	VOCAL GROUP	POST OFFICE BOX 508	HENDERSONVILLE, TN	37075
CARTER HOLBROOK, DIXIE	ACTRESS	10100 SANTA MONICA BLVD #1600	LOS ANGELES, CA	90067
CARTER-COX, ANN	SOPRANO	POST OFFICE BOX 20548	NEW YORK, NY	10025
CARTERET, ANNA	ACTRESS	55 WINTERBROOK RD	HERNE HILL SE24	ENGLAND
CARTHEL, THIN MAN	DRUMMER	POST OFFICE BOX 8013	NASHVILLE, TN	37207

THE CARS

Ben Orr • David Robinson • Ric Ocasek • Elliot Easton • Greg Hawkes

FOR MY GOOD FRIEND KEITH MC ALLISTER, "LET THE GOOD TIMES ROLL."

Name	Occupation	Address	City/State	Zip
CARTIER, ASHLEY	WRESTLER	GORGEOUS LADIES OF WRESTLING		
		RIVIERA HOTEL & CASINO		
		DAVID B MC LANE PRODS		
		2901 S LAS VEGAS BLVD	LAS VEGAS, NV	89109
CARTLAND, BARBARA	NOVELIST	CAMFIELD PL, HATFIELD	HERTFORDSHIRE	ENGLAND
CARTLIDLE, WILLIAM	FILM PRODUCER	THE OLD MILL, LANGSTONE	HANTS PO9 1RY	ENGLAND
CARTNER, WILLIAM	WRITER-PRODUCER	LAPWING MEADOW, ROCKCLIFF	CUMBS	ENGLAND
CARTUNES, THE	ROCK & ROLL GROUP	POST OFFICE BOX 448	RADFORD, VA	24141
CARTWRIGHT, ANGELA	ACTRESS	10143 RIVERSIDE DR	NORTH HOLLYWOOD, CA	91602
CARTWRIGHT, JORCA	ACTRESS	10250 SUNSET BLVD	LOS ANGELES, CA	90024
CARTWRIGHT, JUSTIN	WRITER-PRODUCER	58-A COLEBROOKE ROW	LONDON N1	ENGLAND
CARTWRIGHT, LYNN	ACTRESS	10000 RIVERSIDE DR #3	TOLUCA LAKE, CA	91602
CARTWRIGHT, VERONICA	ACTRESS	2128 BEACHWOOD TERR	LOS ANGELES, CA	90068
CARUSO, ANTHONY	ACTOR	1706 MANDEVILLE LN	LOS ANGELES, CA	90049
CARUSO, CAROL A	WRITER	8955 BEVERLY BLVD	LOS ANGELES, CA	90048
CARUSO, DEE K	WRITER	8955 BEVERLY BLVD	LOS ANGELES, CA	90048
CARUSO, DONALD K	WRITER	11916 SATAIR TERR	LOS ANGELES, CA	90049
CARUSO, JOSEPH G, JR	WRITER	555 W 57TH ST #1230	NEW YORK, NY	10019
CARUSO, KRISTIN	ACTRESS	1803 N WILTON PL #104	HOLLYWOOD, CA	90028
CARUSO, RICHARD	ACTOR	915 POPPY ST	LOS ANGELES, CA	90042
CARUSO, SAM	WRITER	8955 BEVERLY BLVD	LOS ANGELES, CA	90048
CARVELL, JANET	GUITARIST	224 LUCILLE ST	NASHVILLE, TN	37207
CARVELL, LONE STAR	GUITARIST	POST OFFICE BOX 8224	NASHVILLE, TN	37207
CARVER, JOHN DAVID	GUITARIST	POST OFFICE BOX 681	LEBANON, TN	37087
CARVER, JOHNNY	SINGER-SONGWRITER	WILLIAMS-CIMINI AGENCY		
		816 N LA CIENEGA BLVD	LOS ANGELES, CA	90069
CARVER, MARY	ACTRESS	9300 WILSHIRE BLVD #410	BEVERLY HILLS, CA	90212
CARVER, RANDALL	ACTOR	12032 1/2 GUERIN ST	STUDIO CITY, CA	91604
CARVER, RAYMOND	WRITER	555 W 57TH ST #1230	NEW YORK, NY	10019
CARVER, RON L	COMPOSER-CONDUCTOR	1637 N VINE ST #713	LOS ANGELES, CA	90028
CARVER, STEVE	FILM DIRECTOR	1010 PACIFIC AVE	VENICE, CA	90291
CARVEY, DANA	COMEDIENNE	ICM, 8899 BEVERLY BLVD	LOS ANGELES, CA	90048
CARY, CHRISTOPHER	ACTOR	9744 WILSHIRE BLVD #306	BEVERLY HILLS, CA	90212
CARY, LOU	SINGER	ICM, 8899 BEVERLY BLVD	LOS ANGELES, CA	90048
CASADESUS, GABY	PIANIST	GERSHUNOFF, 502 PARK AVE	NEW YORK, NY	10022
CASADOS, ELOY PHIL	ACTOR	840 N AVE #63	LOS ANGELES, CA	90042
CASADY, CORT	TV WRITER	1543 SUNSET PLAZA DR	LOS ANGELES, CA	90069
CASAGRANDE, ALAN H	COMPOSER	9169 ALCOTT ST #7	LOS ANGELES, CA	90035
CASALAINA, VINCENT	DIRECTOR	DGA, 110 W 57TH ST	NEW YORK, NY	10019
CASALE, GERALD V	WRITER	8955 BEVERLY BLVD	LOS ANGELES, CA	90048
CASAMENTO, VICTOR	PHOTOGRAPHER	11337 FAIRFAX DR	GREAT FALLS, VA	22006
CASAZZA, JANICE	TV WRITER	132 1/2 N MAPLE ST	BURBANK, CA	91505
CASBY, MARIA	WRITER	555 W 57TH ST #1230	NEW YORK, NY	10019
CASCINO, JERILYN M	WRITER	555 W 57TH ST #1230	NEW YORK, NY	10019
CASE, ALLEN	ACTOR	15010 VENTURA BLVD #219	SHERMAN OAKS, CA	91403
CASE, EUGENE L	WRITER-PRODUCER	445 PARK AVE	NEW YORK, NY	10022
CASE, HAROLD	CINEMATOGRAPHER	34 CUNNINGHAM PARK, HARROW	MIDDLESEX HA1 4QL	ENGLAND
CASE, NELSON, JR	WRITER	555 W 57TH ST #1230	NEW YORK, NY	10019
CASE, TOM	ACTOR	1717 N HIGHLAND AVE #614	LOS ANGEELS, CA	90028
CASEI, NEDDA	MEZZO-SOPRANO	15 W 72ND ST	NEW YORK, NY	10023
CASELLA, DONNA	SOPRANO	111 W 57TH ST #1209	NEW YORK, NY	10019
CASELLA, MARTIN	WRITER	8955 BEVERLY BLVD	LOS ANGELES, CA	90048
CASELLA, PAMELA	SOPRANO	CAMI, 165 W 57TH ST	NEW YORK, NY	10019
CASELLI, LAMAR	DIRECTOR	6019 BUFFALO AVE #B	VAN NUYS, CA	91401
CASEY, BERNIE	ACTOR-FOOTBALL	3022 FALL AVE	LOS ANGELES, CA	90019
CASEY, CAROLE	ACTRESS	11030 VENTURA BLVD #3	STUDIO CITY, CA	91604
CASEY, COLLEEN	ACTRESS-SINGER	721 N LA BREA AVE #200	LOS ANGELES, CA	90038
CASEY, HARRY "K C"	SINGER-ACTOR	7764 NW 71ST ST	MIAMI, FL	33166
CASEY, JEANE	ACTRESS	8721 SUNSET BLVD #200	LOS ANGELES, CA	90069
CASEY, JOHN	COMMUNICATION EXEC	THE UNITED SATELLITE		
		COMMUNICATIONS COMPANY		
		1345 AVE OF THE AMERICAS	NEW YORK, NY	10105
CASEY, JULIE	ACTRESS	3761 LAS FLORES CANYON RD	MALIBU, CA	90265
CASEY, LAWRENCE	ACTOR	4139 VANETTA PL	STUDIO CITY, CA	91604
CASEY, PATRICK C	NEWS CORRESPONDENT	4461 CONNECTICUT AVE, NW	WASHINGTON, DC	20008
CASEY, PAUL A	TV WRITER	9100 SUNSET BLVD #340	LOS ANGELES, CA	90069
CASEY, PETER	TV WRITER-PRODUCER	1650 WESTWOOD BLVD #201	LOS ANGELES, CA	90024
CASEY, SCOTT	WRESTLER	WORLD CLASS WRESTLING		
		SOUTHWEST SPORTS, INC		
		DALLAS SPORTATORIUM		
		1000 S INDUSTRIAL BLVD	DALLAS, TX	75207
CASEY, SCOTT	WRESTLER	POST OFFICE BOX 3859	STAMFORD, CT	06905
CASEY, WARREN	COMPOSER-LYRICIST	ICM, 40 W 57TH ST	NEW YORK, NY	10019
CASH, ANTHONY	DIRECTOR-PRODUCER	7 LILLYVILLE RD	LONDON SW6	ENGLAND
CASH, JACK	WRITER	1333 N STANLEY AVE #A-17	LOS ANGELES, CA	90046
CASH, JIM	WRITER	8955 BEVERLY BLVD	LOS ANGELES, CA	90048
CASH, JIM S	ACTOR	3924 LAUREL CANYON BLVD #4	STUDIO CITY, CA	91604
CASH, JOHN CARTER	SINGER	711 SUMMERFIELD DR	HENDERSONVILLE, TN	37075
CASH, JOHNNY	SINGER-SONGWRITER	711 SUMMERFIELD DR	HENDERSONVILLE, TN	37075
CASH, JUNE CARTER	SINGER-GUITARIST	711 SUMMERFIELD DR	HENDERSONVILLE, TN	37075
CASH, ROSALIND	ACTRESS	247 S BEVERLY DR #102	BEVERLY HILLS, CA	90210
CASH, ROSANNE	SINGER-SONGWRITER	SIDE ONE MANAGEMENT AGENCY		
		1775 BROADWAY, 7TH FLOOR	NEW YORK, NY	10019
CASH, TOMMY	SINGER-SONGWRITER	50 MUSIC SQUARE E #806	NASHVILLE, TN	37203

WHERE ARE THEY NOW?

Even though this book contains thousands of celebrities' addresses, the whereabouts of many screen veterans is virtually unknown. Early film buffs with addresses or other related information on these artists, please write: DALE HORNING, P. O. BOX 35-467, 7 OAKS STATION, DETROIT, MI 48235-0467. Please Note — This is but a partial list. Thank you.

ADULT ACTORS

Katharine Alexander
Rosemary Ames
Lona Andre
Poupee Androit
Armida
Monica Bannister
Jess Barker
Mona Barrie
Phyllis Barrington
Michael Bartlett
Finis Barton
Stephen Bekassy
Dean Benton
Barbara Bestar
Lydia Bilbrook
Irene Biller
Francelia Billington
Pamela Blake
Beatrice Blinn
Karin Booth
Kenny Bowers
Lorraine Bridges
Esther Brodelet
Everett Brown
Stanley Brown
Frankie Burke
Wyn Cahoon
Jewell Carmen
Virginia Carroll
Janice Chambers
Ruth Channing
Hally (Hal E.) Chester
Lita Chevret
Ann Christy
Judy Clark
Dorinda Clifton
Bill Cody, Jr.
Anita Colby
Inez Cooper
Tito Coral
Marcelle Corday
Ann Corio
Mady Correll
Bob Curwood
Patricia Dane
Vondell Dare
Dorothy Dayton
Irene Delroy
Anthony Dexter
Florence Dudley
Yvette Dugay
Dorothy Dwan
Richard Emory
Wera Engels
Ann Evers
June Filmer
Madeline Forbes
Ann Forrest
Sylvia Froos
Dale Fuller
Mary Fuller
Gwen Gaze
Florence George
Charles Gerrard
Helen Gilbert
Grace Goodall
Edna May Harris
Hazel Hayes
Jean Heather
Louise Henry
Harriet Hoctor
Pee Wee Holmes
Ula Holt
Kenneth Howell
John B. Hubbard
Gladys Hulette
Henry Hunter
Ada Ince
Betty Jaynes
Joyzelle Joyner
Donald Keith
Barbara Kent
Dorothea Kent
Carlotta King
Ivan Kirov
Scott Kolk
Marina Koshetz
Anna Kostant
Molly Lamont
Charles Lang
Keith Larsen
Louise Latimer
Priscilla Lawson
Donrue Leighton
Dorothy Libaire
Morton Lowry
Beverly Loyd
Lya Lys
Sari Maritza
Mitzi Mayfair
Charlotte Merriam
Lynn Merrick
Emile Meyer
Conchita Montenegro
Toshia Mori
Ann Morriss
Lucille Norman
Richard Norris
Zelma O'Neal
Dorothy Page
Dorothy Patrick
Edward Pawley
Joan Perry
Lucien Prival
Frances Ramsden
Rebel Randall
Allene Ray
Jeff Richards
Mayna Roberti
Lee Roberts
Ann Robinson
Tutta Rolf
Charles Ruppert
Anne Sargent
Loretta Sayers
Marina Schubert
Toni Seven
Maria Shelton
Marla Shelton
Jack Sherrill
Diane Sinclair
Eve Southern
Mark Stevens
June Storey
Gertrude Sutton
Gloria Talbott
Colin Tapley
Viva Tattersall
Brad Taylor
Ethelind Terry
Ruth Terry
Rosemary Theby
Fay Tincher
Ruth Tobey
Vivian Tobin
Aabel Trunnelle
Luis Trenker
Adland Varno
Virginia Verrill
Margaret Vyner
Dale Walsh
Amelita Ward
Lee and Lyn Wilde
Chili Williams
Howard Wilson
Edward Woods
Gloria Youngblood

CHILD ACTORS

Tad Alexander
Baby Leroy
Johnny Calkins
Francis W. Carpenter
Ann Carter
Fay Chaldecott
Janet Chapman
Joyce Coad
Cora Sue Collins
Billy Cook
Bobbie Cox
Douglas Croft
David Durand
Gordon Gebert
Patsy (Diana) Hale
Jackie Horner
Mary Ann Jackson
Marilyn Knowlden
Mickey Kuhn
Connie Marshall
Peggy McIntire
Sharon McManus
Sharyn Moffett
Jackie Moran
Bobbie Nelson
Richard Nichols
Larry Nunn
Buster Phelps
Jane Preston
Donald Profitt
Mickey Rentschler
Eric Roberts
Matty Roubert
Dorothy Ann Seese
Ronald Sinclair
Mary Thomas
Ann E. Todd
Richard Tyler
Linda Ware
Janis Wilson
Edna May Wonacott
Sarita Wooten
Charlene Wyatt

Name	Occupation	Address	City	Zip
CASHDAN, LINDA	NEWS CORRESPONDENT	2502 CUTTBOURNE PL, NW	WASHINGTON, DC	20009
CASHDOLLAR, GARY	ACTOR	6605 HOLLYWOOD BLVD #220	HOLLYWOOD, CA	90028
CASHMAN, WILLIAM	RECORD EXECUTIVE	POST OFFICE BOX 31475	TUCSON, AZ	85751
CASIANO, MARCOS	DRUMMER	2615 VALLEYBROOK DR	HUNTSVILLE, AL	35811
CASNER, MARY CAROL	SINGER	816 HIGHLAND PARK CT	NASHVILLE, TN	37205
CASNER, NORM	GUITARIST	816 HIGHLAND PARK CT	NASHVILLE, TN	37205
CASNOFF, PHIL	ACTOR	POST OFFICE BOX 5617	BEVERLY HILLS, CA	90210
CASO, LAURENCE A	TV EXECUTIVE	CBS-TV, 51 W 52ND ST	NEW YORK, NY	10019
CASO, PATRICIA	TV PRODUCER	WABC-TV, 7 LINCOLN SQ	NEW YORK, NY	10023
CASOLLA, GIOVANNA	SOPRANO	61 W 62ND ST #6-F	NEW YORK, NY	10023
CASON, BARBARA	ACTRESS	9220 SUNSET BLVD #202	LOS ANGELES, CA	90069
CASON, BUZZ	GUITARIST	2804 AZALEA PL	NASHVILLE, TN	37204
CASORLA, RICK	ACTOR	1028 CAROL DR	LOS ANGELES, CA	90069
CASPARY, DENNIS	ACTOR	8465 SAMRA DR	CANOGA PARK, CA	91304
CASPER, ROBERT	ACTOR	427 N CANON DR #205	BEVERLY HILLS, CA	90210
CASS, DAVID S	DIRECTOR	15021 LARKSPUR ST	SYLMAR, CA	91342
CASS, PEGGY	ACTRESS	200 E 62ND ST	NEW YORK, NY	10021
CASS, RONNIE	WRITER-COMPOSER	27A ELSWORTHY RD	LONDON NW3 3BT	ENGLAND
CASSARO, ALAN	GUITARIST	3552 NORMANDY RD	SHAKER HEIGHTS, OH	44120
CASSAT, GEORGANNE	HARPIST	AFFILIATE ARTISTS, INC		
		37 W 65TH ST, 6TH FLOOR	NEW YORK, NY	10023
CASSAVETES, JOHN	ACT-WRI-DIR	7917 WOODROW WILSON DR	LOS ANGELES, CA	90046
CASSAVETES, NICK	ACTOR	151 S EL CAMINO DR	BEVERLY HILLS, CA	90212
CASSEDY, KATHLEEN G	NEWS CORRESPONDENT	3340 GUNSTON RD	ALEXANDRIA, VA	22302
CASSEL, JEAN-PIERRE	ACTOR	ICM, 388-396 OXFORD ST	LONDON W1	ENGLAND
CASSEL, SEYMOUR	ACTOR	1427 N KINGS RD	LOS ANGELES, CA	90069
CASSELLS, ANDREW M	PHOTOJOURNALIST	2125 DOCKET LN	VIENNA, VA	22180
CASSIDAY, BRUCE	WRITER	555 W 57TH ST #1230	NEW YORK, NY	10019
CASSIDY, ALAN	WRITER	8955 BEVERLY BLVD	LOS ANGELES, CA	90048
CASSIDY, ALICE	CASTING DIRECTOR	10201 W PICO BLVD #4	LOS ANGELES, CA	90035
CASSIDY, ANN PENNINGTON	MODEL	1801 AVE OF THE STARS #911	LOS ANGELES, CA	90067
CASSIDY, BRUCE	COMPOSER	7319 RUBIO AVE	VAN NUYS, CA	91406
CASSIDY, DAVID	ACTER-SINGER	151 S EL CAMINO DR	BEVERLY HILLS, CA	90212
CASSIDY, JEAN C	WRITER	8955 BEVERLY BLVD	LOS ANGELES, CA	90048
CASSIDY, JOANNA	ACTRESS	10351 SANTA MONICA BLVD #211	LOS ANGELES, CA	90025
CASSIDY, MARTIN	ACTOR	9220 SUNSET BLVD #202	LOS ANGELES, CA	90069
CASSIDY, RYAN	ACTOR	701 N OAKHURST DR	BEVERLY HILLS, CA	90210
CASSIDY, SHAUN	ACTOR-SINGER	1801 AVE OF THE STARS #911	LOS ANGELES, CA	90067
CASSIDY, WILLIAM	DIRECTOR	DGA, 7950 SUNSET BLVD	LOS ANGELES, CA	90046
CASSIERE, GLORY ANN	SINGER	4680 ELK LAKE DR #304	VICTORIA, BC V8Z 5M1	CANADA
CASSILLY, RICHARD	TENOR	59 E 54TH ST #81	NEW YORK, NY	10022
CASSINI, OLEG	FASHION DESIGNER	257 PARK AVE #F-3	NEW YORK, NY	10010
CASSITY, JAMES J	FILM WRITER-PRODUCER	10858 DANUBE AVE	GRANADA HILLS, CA	91344
CASSITY, RIC	GUITARIST	5309 TOWNES CT	NASHVILLE, TN	37211
CASSMORE, JUDITH	ACTRESS	721 N LA BREA AVE #200	LOS ANGELES, CA	90038
CASSOLAS, CONSTANTINE	TENOR	POST OFFICE BOX 884	NEW YORK, NY	10023
CASSON, PHILIP	TV DIRECTOR	21E BALCOMBE ST	LONDON NW1	ENGLAND
CASSTEVENS, JOHN MARK	BANJOIST	3415 HOPKINS LN	NASHVILLE, TN	37215
CASSUTO, ALVARO	CONDUCTOR	SHAW CONCERTS, 1995 BROADWAY	NEW YORK, NY	10023
CASSUTT, MICHAEL	WRITER-TV EXEC	5523 RANCHITO AVE	VAN NUYS, CA	91401
CAST, EDWARD	ACT-WRI-DIR	SAINT JAMES'S MGMT		
		22 GROOM PL	LONDON SW1X 7BA	ENGLAND
CAST, TRICIA	ACTRESS	3800 BARHAM BLVD #303	LOS ANGELES, CA	90068
CASTAGNETTA, GRACE	PIANIST	383 UNION AVE	WOODBRIDGE, NJ	07075
CASTANEDA, LORNA	SOPRANO	756 7TH AVE #67	NEW YORK, NY	10019
CASTEL, COLLETTE	ACTRESS	36 BIS, QUAI LOUIS BLER	PARIS 75016	FRANCE
CASTEL, NICO	TENOR	170 W END AVE	NEW YORK, NY	10023
CASTELAR, LOUIS	WRITER	555 W 57TH ST #1230	NEW YORK, NY	10019
CASTELLANO, FREDDIE	ACTOR	15 PALOMA AVE #102	VENICE, CA	90291
CASTELLANO, RICHARD	ACTOR	592 PENN AVE	TEANECK, NJ	07666
CASTELLANOS, PABLO	CONDUCTOR	FINELL, 155 W 68TH ST	NEW YORK, NY	10023
CASTELLI, LOUIS P	TV DIRECTOR-PRODUCER	HEARST/ABC-TV		
		555 5TH AVE	NEW YORK, NY	10017
CASTELLINO, WILLIAM J	ACTOR	732 N HARPER AVE	LOS ANGELES, CA	90046
CASTENS, ED	PHOTOGRAPHER	POST OFFICE BOX 1382	SPRINGFIELD, VA	22151
CASTILLO, CANDY	ACTOR	4216 ARICA AVE	ROSEMEAD, CA	91770
CASTILLO, GERALD	ACTOR	6858 DE LONGPRE AVE #3	HOLLYWOOD, CA	90028
CASTLE, CHARLES	TV WRITER-DIRECTOR	EWHURST GREEN, ROBERTSBRIDGE	SUSSEX	ENGLAND
CASTLE, JOHN	ACTOR	LARRY DALZELL ASSOCIATES		
		126 KENNINGTON PARK RD	LONDON SE11 4DJ	ENGLAND
CASTLE, JOYCE	MEZZO-SOPRANO	CAMI, 165 W 57TH ST	NEW YORK, NY	10019
CASTLE, NICK	FILM WRITER-DIRECTOR	8458 RIDPATH DR	LOS ANGELES, CA	90046
CASTLE, ROY	ACTOR	LONDON MANAGEMENT, LTD		
		235-241 REGENT ST	LONDON W1A 2JT	ENGLAND
CASTLE FAMILY, THE	MUSICAL GROUP	CEE, 193 KONHAUS RD	MECHANICSBURG, PA	17055
CASTLEMAN, BOOMER	BANJOIST	POST OFFICE BOX 120723	NASHVILLE, TN	37212
CASTLEMAN, CHARLES	VIOLINIST	GURTMAN, 162 W 56TH ST	NEW YORK, NY	10019
CASTLEMAN, MIKE	GUITARIST	298 PORT DR	MADISON, TN	37115
CASTNER, EDWARD	NEWS CORRESPONDENT	1705 DE SALES ST, NW	WASHINGTON, DC	20036
CASTNER, EDWARD R	PHOTOGRAPHER	6009 GROSVENOR LN	BETHESDA, MD	20814
CASTNER, MICHAEL	NEWS CORRESPONDENT	400 NATIONAL PRESS BLDG		
		529 14TH ST, NW	WASHINGTON, DC	20045
CASTOR, JIMMY	SINGER	ITZLER, 110 E 59TH ST	NEW YORK, NY	10022
CASTREJON DUO	AERIAL SPACE WHEELERS	HALL, 138 FROG HOLLOW RD	CHURCHVILLE, PA	18966
CASTRO, DAVID I	TV WRITER	8955 BEVERLY BLVD	LOS ANGELES, CA	90048

Name	Occupation	Address	City	Zip
CASTRO, JANICE	WRITER-EDITOR	TIME/TIME & LIFE BLDG		
		ROCKEFELLER CENTER	NEW YORK, NY	10020
CASTRO, JOE	COMPOSER-CONDUCTOR	2812 COLANTHE AVE	LAS VEGAS, NV	89102
CASTRO, LUIZ DE MOURA	PIANIST	GERSHUNOFF, 502 PARK AVE	NEW YORK, NY	10022
CASTRO, SHIP, BAND	RHYTHM & BLUES GROUP	POST OFFICE BOX 210103	SAN FRANCISCO, CA	94121
CASTRO-ALBERTY, MARGARITA	SOPRANO	CAMI, 165 W 57TH ST	NEW YORK, NY	10019
CASTRONOVO, VAL	NEWS REPORTER	TIME/TIME & LIFE BLDG		
		ROCKEFELLER CENTER	NEW YORK, NY	10020
CASWELL, BILL	GUITARIST	POST OFFICE BOX 121272	NASHVILLE, TN	37212
CASWELL, OZZIE	COMPOSER-CONDUCTOR	240 ACARI DR	LOS ANGELES, CA	90049
CATALA, MURIEL	ACTRESS	JACQUES ITAH AGENCE		
		15 RUE CHATEAUBRIAND	PARIS 75016	FRANCE
CATALANO, NICHOLAS	WRITER	555 W 57TH ST #1230	NEW YORK, NY	10019
CATCHING, J P "BILL"	DIRECTOR	POST OFFICE BOX 1008	STUDIO CITY, CA	91604
CATCHINGS, JOHN	CELLIST	4242 SPRING ST #31	LA MESA, CA	92041
CATE, BENJAMIN W	NEWS CORRESPONDENT	TIME/TIME & LIFE BLDG		
		ROCKEFELLER CENTER	NEW YORK, NY	10020
CATE BROTHERS, THE	VOCAL DUO	LOOKOUT, 9120 SUNSET BLVD	LOS ANGELES, CA	90069
CATER, JOHN	ACTOR	LONDON MANAGEMENT, LTD		
		235-241 REGENT ST	LONDON W1A 2JT	ENGLAND
CATES, GEORGE	CONDUCTOR	1221 OCEAN AVE #1107	SANTA MONICA, CA	90401
CATES, GILBERT	FILM DIRECTOR	936 HILTS AVE	LOS ANGELES, CA	90024
CATES, JOSEPH	WRITER-PRODUCER	119 W 57TH ST #915	NEW YORK, NY	10019
CATES, LISA	SINGER	2121 BLAIR BLVD	NASHVILLE, TN	37212
CATES, MADELYN	ACTRESS	3800 BARHAM BLVD #303	LOS ANGELES, CA	90068
CATES, MADLYN	ACTRESS	155 BANK ST	NEW YORK, NY	10014
CATES, MARCY LYNN	MANDOLINIST	ROUTE #5, BOX 320	LEBANON, TN	37087
CATES, MARJORIE ANN	MANDOLINIST	1538 CAMPBELL RD	GOODLETTSVILLE, TN	37072
CATES, PHOEBE	ACTRESS	1888 CENTURY PARK E #1400	LOS ANGELES, CA	90067
CATES, RON	TV DIRECTOR	2835 OAKPOINT DR	LOS ANGELES, CA	90068
CATES, THE	ROCK & ROLL GROUP	OVATION, 1249 WAUKEGAN RD	GLENVIEW, IL	60025
CATHCART, DICK	COMPOSER	6414 LUBAO AVE	WOODLAND HILLS, CA	91364
CATHCART, JACK W	COMPOSER	2635 WYANDOTTE ST #1	LAS VEGAS, NV	89102
CATHCART, KATHRYN	CONDUCTOR	61 W 62ND ST #6-F	NEW YORK, NY	10023
CATHERINE, ESCOUDE & LOCKWOOD	JAZZ TRIO	KURLAND, 173 BRIGHTON AVE	BOSTON, MA	02134
CATILLAC	ROCK & ROLL GROUP	3717 W 50TH ST #L-2	MINNEAPOLIS, MN	55410
CATINGUB, MATTHEW M	COMPOSER-CONDUCTOR	7120 BELLAIRE AVE	NORTH HOLLYWOOD, CA	91605
CATLETT, MARY JO	ACTRESS	4375 FARMDALE AVE	NORTH HOLLYWOOD, CA	91604
CATLIN, MICHAEL	ACTOR	3495 LA SOMBRA DR	LOS ANGELES, CA	90068
CATLIN, VICTORIA	ACTRESS	208 S BEVERLY DR #8	BEVERLY HILLS, CA	90212
CATLING, BOYD	WRITER-PRODUCER	84 ST DIONIS RD	LONDON SW6	ENGLAND
CATLING, DARREL	WRITER-PRODUCER	TRAVELLERS REST, CHURCH ST	HERTS	ENGLAND
CATO, CONNIE	SINGER	TESSIER, 505 CANTON PASS	MADISON, TN	37115
CATS CAN FLY	ROCK & ROLL GROUP	41 BRITAIN ST #200	TORONTO, ONT	CANADA
CATT, RICHARD	ACTOR	1327 STANFORD ST #5	SANTA MONICA, CA	90404
CATTANO, JANET	ACTRESS	615 ASHTABULA ST #2	PASADENA, CA	91104
CATTRALL, KIM	ACTRESS	151 S EL CAMINO DR	BEVERLY HILLS, CA	90212
CAU, JEAN	ACTOR	13 RUE DE SEINE	PARIS 75006	FRANCE
CAUDELL, LANE	ACTOR	9105 CARMELITA AVE #1	BEVERLY HILLS, CA	90210
CAUDLE, SHEILA	NEWS CORRESPONDENT	3520 N 14TH ST	ARLINGTON, VA	22201
CAUGHLIN, JAMES	TV WRITER	8955 BEVERLY BLVD	LOS ANGELES, CA	90048
CAULEY, HARRY	WRITER	8955 BEVERLY BLVD	LOS ANGELES, CA	90048
CAULFIELD, MAXWELL	ACTOR	4036 FOOTHILL RD	CARPINTERIA, CA	93013
CAUSEY, MIKE	NEWS CORRESPONDENT	7709 TOMLINSON AVE	CABIN JOHN, MD	20818
CAUTHERN, KENNETH	WRITER	13949 WEDDINGTON ST	VAN NUYS, CA	91401
CAUTIOUS DREAMS	ROCK & ROLL GROUP	100 BULIAM LN	AUSTIN, TX	78746
CAVALERI, RAY	TALENT AGENT	6605 HOLLYWOOD BLVD #220	HOLLYWOOD, CA	90028
CAVALIER, CARRIE E	ACTRESS	3200 WYOMING AVE	BURBANK, CA	91505
CAVALIER, JOE	DIRECTOR	4185 ARCH DR	STUDIO CITY, CA	91604
CAVALIERE, FELIX	SINGER-PIANIST	65 W 55TH ST #306	NEW YORK, NY	10019
CAVALLO, ROBERT	FILM PRODUCER	11340 W OLYMPIC BLVD #357	LOS ANGELES, CA	90064
CAVANAGH, JOSEPH J	NEWS CORRESPONDENT	2503 DE WITT AVE	ALEXANDRIA, VA	22301
CAVANAUGH, JAMES J	CONDUCTOR	1631 SEAL WY	SEAL BEACH, CA	90740
CAVANAUGH, MICHAEL	ACTOR	SF & A, 121 N SAN VICENTE BLVD	BEVERLY HILLS, CA	90211
CAVANAUGH, NICK	ACTOR	120 S VICTORY BLVD #104	BURBANK, CA	91502
CAVAS, CHRISTOPHER P	TV DIRECTOR	5350 MAC ARTHUR BLVD, NW	WASHINGTON, DC	20016
CAVAZZINI, JAMES J	TV EXECUTIVE	ESPN, 355 LEXINGTON AVE	NEW YORK, NY	10017
CAVE, NICK & THE BAD SEEDS	ROCK & ROLL GROUP	POST OFFICE BOX 570	ROCKVILLE CENTRE, NY	11571
CAVE, RAY	PUBLISHING EXECUTIVE	TIME/TIME & LIFE BLDG		
		ROCKEFELLER CENTER	NEW YORK, NY	10020
CAVENDER, KENNETH	TV WRITER	555 W 57TH ST #1230	NEW YORK, NY	10019
CAVENDISH, ROBERT	ACTOR	4 BOLINGBROKE RD	LONDON W14	ENGLAND
CAVESTANI, FRANK J	TV WRITER	7120 PACIFIC VIEW DR	LOS ANGELES, CA	90068
CAVETT, DICK	TV HOST-COMEDIAN	109 E 79TH ST #2C	NEW YORK, NY	10019
CAVETT, MORGAN A	COMPOSER	7923 1/2 NORTON AVE	LOS ANGELES, CA	90046
CAVOLINA, LAWRENCE A	TV DIRECTOR	214-31 38TH AVE	NEW YORK, NY	11361
CAVONIS, PAUL	ACTOR	602 N CAMDEN DR	BEVERLY HILLS, CA	90210
CAWLEY, EVONNE GOOLAGONG	TENNIS	80 DUNTROON AVE	ROSEVILLE NSW	AUSTRALIA
CAWLFIELD, CONSTANCE	ACTRESS	17009 JEANINE PL	GRANADA HILLS, CA	91344
CAWSTON, RICHARD	TV DIRECTOR-PRODUCER	25 LOWER ADDISON GARDENS	LONDON W14 8BG	ENGLAND
CAWTHORNE, DAVID M	NEWS CORRESPONDENT	6323 RIVERDALE RD	RIVERDALE, MD	20737
CAYLOR, FLORENCE B	CONDUCTOR	191 ORANGE DR	SAN LUIS OBISPO, CA	93401
CAYLOR, JAMIE	FILM EDITOR	ACE, 4416 1/2 FINLEY AVE	LOS ANGELES, CA	90027
CAZALAS, ROBERT P	NEWS CORRESPONDENT	11482 BINGHAM TERR	RESTON, VA	22091
CAZARES, MICHAEL A	WRITER	8955 BEVERLY BLVD	LOS ANGELES, CA	90048

Name	Occupation	Address	City	Zip
CAZDEN, JOANNA	SINGER-GUITARIST	POST OFFICE BOX 36-M-37	LOS ANGELES, CA	90036
CAZENOVE, CHRISTOPHER	ACTOR	CHATTO & LINNIT, LTD		
		PRINCE OF WALES THEATRE		
		COVENTRY ST	LONDON WC2	ENGLAND
CEASE, WESLEY J	CONDUCTOR	POST OFFICE BOX 2043	GLENDALE, CA	91209
CECALA, GUY D	NEWS CORRESPONDENT	7204 CHESTNUT ST	CHEVY CHASE, MD	20015
CECCALDI, DANIEL	ACTOR	81 RUE DE LONGCHAMP	NEUILLY 92200	FRANCE
CECCATO, ALDO	CONDUCTOR	ICM, 40 W 57TH ST	NEW YORK, NY	10019
CECCHELE, GIANFRANCO	TENOR	CAMI, 165 W 57TH ST	NEW YORK, NY	10019
CECERE, TONY	STUNTMAN	3518 W CAHUENGA BLVD #300	LOS ANGELES, CA	90068
CECHVALA, ALPHONSE A	COMPOSER	1346 VALE VIEW AVE	GLENDORA, CA	91740
CECIL, JANE	ACTRESS	1697 BROADWAY	NEW YORK, NY	10019
CECIL, JONATHAN	ACTOR	FEAST, 43-A PRINCESS RD	LONDON NW1	ENGLAND
CECIL, VANDER	WRITER	8955 BEVERLY BLVD	LOS ANGELES, CA	90048
CECILIA-MENDEZ, ZEIDA E	FILM DIRECTOR	2150 CENTER AVE #3-A	FORT LEE, NJ	07024
CEDAR, JON	ACTOR	2717 LAUREL CANYON BLVD	LOS ANGELES, CA	90046
CEDAR, LARRY	ACTOR	5741 VESPER AVE	VAN NUYS, CA	91411
CEDAR, LOREN	ACTRESS	CED, 261 S ROBERTSON BLVD	BEVERLY HILLS, CA	90211
CEDAR, LORRIE	ACTRESS	2717 LAUREL CANYON BLVD	LOS ANGELES, CA	90046
CEDAR, MICHAEL	ACTOR	5119 NAGLE AVE	SHERMAN OAKS, CA	91423
CEDAR CREEK	C & W GROUP	POST OFFICE BOX 1763	HENDERSONVILLE, TN	37075
CEDENO, CESAR	BASEBALL	77 CARPENTER RIDGE	BLUE ASH, OH	45241
CEE, GARY W	WRITER	555 W 57TH ST #1230	NEW YORK, NY	10019
CEE, ROBBIE	SINGER	1680 N VINE ST #214	HOLLYWOOD, CA	90028
CELARDO, JOHN	COMICS EDITOR	KING FEATURES SYNDICATE		
		235 E 45TH ST	NEW YORK, NY	10017
CELEBRE, JOHN A	NEWS CORRESPONDENT	12320 KEMMERTON LN	BOWIE, MD	20715
CELENTINO, LUCIANO	WRITER-PRODUCER	ANGLO-FORTUNATO FILMS		
		118 PICCADILLY		
		PARK LN #14	LONDON W1	ENGLAND
CELESTE, SUZANNE	ACTRESS	5330 LANKERSHIM BLVD #210	NORTH HOLLYWOOD, CA	91601
CELLAN-JONES, JAMES G	TV DIRECTOR	19 CUMBERLAND RD, KEW	SURREY	ENGLAND
CELLINO, MARIA ELENA	WRITER	2206 LAS LUNAS ST	PASADENA, CA	91107
CELTIC FROST	ROCK & ROLL GROUP	SECOND DIVISION MGMT		
		5 CROSBY ST	NEW YORK, NY	10013
CENEDELLA, ROBERT	WRITER	555 W 57TH ST #1230	NEW YORK, NY	10019
CENTRONS, THE	AERIAL MOTORCYCLISTS	HALL, 138 FROG HOLLOW RD	CHURCHVILLE, PA	18966
CEO, JOSEPH	VIOLIST	ROSENFIELD, 714 LADD RD	BRONX, NY	10471
CERDA, EVON	ACTRESS	8820 SUNSET BLVD #ANB	LOS ANGELES, CA	90069
CERES, VELA	ACTRESS	311 CAMPBELL ST	WOODBRIDGE, NJ	07095
CERF, CHRISTOPHER	WRITER	555 W 57TH ST #1230	NEW YORK, NY	10019
CERLETTY, MARIE M	NEWS CORRESPONDENT	1705 DE SALES ST, NW	WASHINGTON, DC	20036
CERNAN, EUGENE	ASTRONAUT	900 TOWN & COUNTRY LN	HOUSTON, TX	77024
CERNY, FLORIAN	BARITONE	61 W 62ND ST #6-F	NEW YORK, NY	10023
CERNY, PAVEL	DIRECTOR	11927 MAGNOLIA BLVD #18	NORTH HOLLYWOOD, CA	91607
CERRELLA, GINNY	WRITER	1416 N HAVENHURST DR #1	LOS ANGELES, CA	90046
CERTO, AL	NEWS CORRESPONDENT	400 N CAPITOL ST, NW	WASHINGTON, DC	20001
CERTO, ALBERT J, JR	NEWS CORRESPONDENT	2139 WISCONSIN AVE, NW	WASHINGTON, DC	20007
CERVAMI, ANTHONY	TV EXECUTIVE	NBC TELEVISION NETWORK	NEW YORK, NY	10112
		30 ROCKEFELLER PLAZA	NEW YORK, NY	10112
CERVANTES, GARY	ACTOR	2240 MARDEL AVE	WHITTIER, CA	90601
CERVI, BRUCE	ACTOR-WRITER	12042 GERALD AVE	GRANADA HILLS, CA	91344
CESLIK, CAROLYN	TV EXECUTIVE	CBS-TV, 51 W 52ND ST	NEW YORK, NY	10019
CESSNA, HAL	NEWS CORRESPONDENT	400 N CAPITOL ST, NW	WASHINGTON, DC	20001
CESSNA, ROBERT	WRITER	555 W 57TH ST #1230	NEW YORK, NY	10019
CEY, RON	BASEBALL	22714 CREOLE RD	WOODLAND HILLS, CA	91364
CHAAPEL, EARL	FILM-TV PRODUCER	DARBO, 9142 CALAHENA BLVD	LOS ANGELES, CA	90016
CHAD, SHELDON	WRITER	8955 BEVERLY BLVD	LOS ANGELES, CA	90048
CHAD & JEREMY	VOCAL DUO	9000 SUNSET BLVD #1200	LOS ANGELES, CA	90069
CHADBON, TOM	ACTOR	2 WOODSIDE COTTAGE		
		MIDDLE OLD PARK, FARNHAM	SURREY GU9 OAP	ENGLAND
CHADDERTON, JUNE RANDOLPH	WRITER	654 1/2 KELTON AVE	LOS ANGELES, CA	90024
CHADWICK, ALEXANDER B	NEWS CORRESPONDENT	2025 "M" ST, NW	WASHINGTON, DC	20036
CHADWICK, JOHN	NEWS CORRESPONDENT	5304 FALMOUTH RD	BETHESDA, MD	20816
CHAFFEE, C DAVID	NEWS CORRESPONDENT	18720 GINGER CT	GERMANTOWN, MD	20874
CHAFFEE, SUZY	TV PERSONALITY	5106 WOODWIND LN	ANAHEIM, CA	92807
CHAFFEY, DON	TV DIRECTOR	7020 LA PRESA DR	LOS ANGELES, CA	90068
CHAFFIN, KATHY	ACTRESS	200 N ROBERTSON BLVD #219	BEVERLY HILLS, CA	90211
CHAILLY, RICCARDO	CONDUCTOR	ICM, 40 W 57TH ST	NEW YORK, NY	10019
CHAIN, BARBARA	WRITER	835 S HUDSON AVE	LOS ANGELES, CA	90005
CHAIN, MICHAEL	WRITER-COMPOSER	835 S HUDSON AVE	LOS ANGELES, CA	90005
CHAIN LINK FENCE	ROCK & ROLL GROUP	25 HUNTINGTON AVE #420	BOSTON, MA	02116
CHAINSAW	WRESTLER	GORGEOUS GIRLS OF WRESTLING		
		RIVIERA HOTEL & CASINO		
		DAVID B MC LANE PRODS		
		2901 S LAS VEGAS BLVD	LAS VEGAS, NV	89109
CHAIS, PAMELA HERBERT	WRITER	611 N OAKHURST DR	BEVERLY HILLS, CA	90210
CHAKIRAS, GEORGE	ACTOR	1010 N PALM AVE	LOS ANGELES, CA	90069
CHAKRAPANI, RAGHAVENDRA	NEWS CORRESPONDENT	4701 WILLARD AVE #1531	CHEVY CHASE, MD	20015
CHALK CIRCLE	ROCK & ROLL GROUP	CHRIS PEGG, 163 CRESCENT RD	TORONTO, ONT M4W 1V1	CANADA
CHALKER, CURLY	DOROIST	3401 WRIGHT AVE	N LAS VEGAS, NV	89110
CHALKER, MARGARET	SOPRANO	CAMI, 165 W 57TH ST	NEW YORK, NY	10019
CHALLEY, TINA	ACTRESS	8961 SUNSET BLVD #B	LOS ANGELES, CA	90069
CHALLIS, CHRISTOPHER	CINEMATOGRAPHER	THE SUN HOUSE, EAST ASHLING		
		CHICHESTER	SUSSEX	ENGLAND

Name	Occupation	Address	City/State	Zip/Country
CHALLIS, DRUMMOND	DIRECTOR-PRODUCER	GALACTIC, 9 1/2 CHARLOT MEWS	LONDON W1	ENGLAND
CHALMERS, CHARLIE	SAXOPHONIST	810 BELLVUE RD #280	NASHVILLE, TN	37221
CHALOM, MARC	TV EXECUTIVE	HEARST/ABC-TV		
		555 5TH AVE	NEW YORK, NY	10019
CHALOW, THEA	TV WRITER	555 W 57TH ST #1230	NEW YORK, NY	10019
CHALVET, JACQUES	COMPOSER	221 AVE DE FABRON	NICE 06200	FRANCE
CHAMBERLAIN, JEFF	ACTOR	4220 ALLOTT AVE	SHERMAN OAKS, CA	91423
CHAMBERLAIN, JEROME P	TV DIRECTOR	10 LAKE DR W	WAYNE, NJ	07470
CHAMBERLAIN, JOHN	COMMENTATOR	KING FEATURES SYNDICATE		
		235 E 45TH ST	NEW YORK, NY	10017
CHAMBERLAIN, LACHELLE	ACTRESS	4220 ALLOTT AVE	SHERMAN OAKS, CA	91423
CHAMBERLAIN, RICHARD	ACTOR-PRODUCER	2771 HUTTON DR	BEVERLY HILLS, CA	90210
CHAMBERLAIN, STUART H, JR	WRITER	555 W 57TH ST #1230	NEW YORK, NY	10019
CHAMBERLAIN, WILT	BASKETBALL	15216 ANTELO PL	LOS ANGELES, CA	90077
CHAMBERLAYNE, PYE	NEWS CORRESPONDENT	1114 PRINCE ST	ALEXANDRIA, VA	22314
CHAMBERLIN, CRAN	WRITER	8955 BEVERLY BLVD	LOS ANGELES, CA	90048
CHAMBERLIN, HAP	TV DIRECTOR	3467 PRIMERA DR	HOLLYWOOD, CA	90068
CHAMBERLIN, LEE	ACTOR	ABC-TV, "ALL MY CHILDREN"		
		1330 AVE OF THE AMERICAS	NEW YORK, NY	10019
CHAMBERS, ANDREA	WRITER-EDITOR	PEOPLE/TIME & LIFE BLDG		
		ROCKEFELLER CENTER	NEW YORK, NY	10020
CHAMBERS, CATHY	SINGER	PEEVER, 2464 BRASILIA CIR	MISSISSAUGA, ONTARIO	CANADA
CHAMBERS, DAN	ACTOR	6640 SUNSET BLVD #203	LOS ANGELES, CA	90028
CHAMBERS, DAVID L	TV WRITER	151 S EL CAMINO DR	BEVERLY HILLS, CA	90212
CHAMBERS, DEAN	CLOWN	2701 COTTAGE WY #14	SACRAMENTO, CA	95825
CHAMBERS, DIANE	ACTRESS	757 S ORANGE GROVE BLVD #1	PASADENA, CA	91105
CHAMBERS, ERNEST	TV WRITER-PRODUCER	1438 N GOWER ST	LOS ANGELES, CA	90028
CHAMBERS, EVERETT	WRITER-PRODUCER	1277 SUNSET PLAZA DR	LOS ANGELES, CA	90069
CHAMBERS, GARRY	FILM-TV WRITER	APRIL YOUNG, 31 KINGS RD	LONDON SW3	ENGLAND
CHAMBERS, GERALD	GUITARIST	POST OFFICE BOX 150871	NASHVILLE, TN	37215
CHAMBERS, JEFF	MUSICIAN	3257 NEW TOWNE RD	ANTIOCH, TN	37013
CHAMBERS, JEFFREY R	TV DIRECTOR	4726 1/2 FORMAN LN	NORTH HOLLYWOOD, CA	91602
CHAMBERS, KATHLYN	TV PRODUCER	CBS-TV, "THE GUIDING LIGHT"		
		51 W 52ND ST	NEW YORK, NY	10019
CHAMBERS, MARILYN	ACTRESS	4528 W CHARLESTON BLVD	LAS VEGAS, NV	89102
CHAMBERS, RICHARD O	DIRECTOR	1310 S WESTHOLME AVE	LOS ANGELES, CA	90024
CHAMBERS, ROBERT	GUITARIST	4237 LITTLE MARROWBONE	JOELTON, TN	37080
CHAMBERS, TERRY	FILM EDITOR	7230 WISH AVE	VAN NUYS, CA	91406
CHAMBERS BROTHERS, THE	SOUL GROUP	WILLARD ALEXANDER, INC		
		660 MADISON AVE	NEW YORK, NY	10021
CHAMBLISS, CHIP	DRUMMER	505 IDLEWILD AVE	MADISON, TN	37115
CHAMBLISS, CHRIS	BASEBALL	54 IVY CHASE ST	ATLANTA, GA	30342
CHAMBLISS, RALPH ED	DRUMMER	3112 CEDARCROFT DR	ANTIOCH, TN	37013
CHAMBLISS, WILLIAM DAVID	SAXOPHONIST	2210 SHARONDALE DR	NASHVILLE, TN	37215
CHAMMAS, ALAIN	WRITER	8955 BEVERLY BLVD	LOS ANGELES, CA	90048
CHAMMETTE, FRANCOIS	ACTOR	13 RUE DE TRETAIGNE	PARIS 75018	FRANCE
CHAMPAGNE	VOCAL GROUP	GROUP, 801 N WESTMOUNT ST	LOS ANGELES, CA	90069
CHAMPAGNE, CHRISTOPHER	NEWS CORRESPONDENT	1201 CONNECTICUT AVE, NW	WASHINGTON, DC	20036
CHAMPION	ROCK & ROLL GROUP	DIXON-PROPAS MGMT		
		180 BLOOR ST W	TORONTO, ONT	CANADA
CHAMPION, DAVID	CONDUCTOR	229 15TH ST	MANHATTAN BEACH, CA	90266
CHAMPION, FERN	CASTING DIRECTOR	9911 W PICO BLVD, 4TH FLOOR	LOS ANGELES, CA	90035
CHAMPION, JOHN	WRITER-PRODUCER	16157 MORRISON ST	ENCINO, CA	91436
CHAMPION, MARGE	DANCER-ACTRESS	SAGAL, 31 STONEY BROOK	GREAT BARRINGTON, MA	01230
CHAMPION, TODD	WRESTLER	NATIONAL WRESTLING ALLIANCE		
		JIM CROCKETT PROMOTIONS		
		421 BRIARBEND DR	CHARLOTTE, NC	28209
CHAMPLIN, BILL	SINGER	BARUCK, 1046 CAROL DR	LOS ANGELES, CA	90069
CHAMPLIN, CHARLES	FILM CRITIC	2169 LINDA FLORA DR	LOS ANGELES, CA	90077
CHAMPS, THE	ROCK & ROLL GROUP	OLDIES, 5218 ALMONT ST	LOS ANGELES, CA	90032
CHAN, DAVID	PHOTOGRAPHER	MODELS & PROMOTIONS AGENCY		
		8560 SUNSET BLVD, 10TH FLOOR	LOS ANGELES, CA	90069
CHAN, ERNIE	ARTIST	4131 VALE AVE	OAKLAND, CA	94619
CHANCE, BARRY	GUITARIST	106 MORNINGVIEW CT	MADISON, TN	37115
CHANCE, EMILY	ACTRESS	3800 BARHAM BLVD #303	LOS ANGELES, CA	90068
CHANCE, LARRY & THE EARLS	VOCAL GROUP	MARS, 168 ORCHID DR	PEARL RIVER, NY	10965
CHANCE, LIGHTNIN'	GUITARIST	106 MORNINGVIEW CT	MADISON, TN	37115
CHANCE BROTHERS, THE	C & W GROUP	KEITH CASE COMPANY		
		1016 16TH AVE S	NASHVILLE, TN	37212
CHANCELLOR, ANDREA	NEWS CORRESPONDENT	3045 S ABINGDON ST	ARLINGTON, VA	22202
CHANCELLOR, JOHN	BROADCAST JOURNALIST	NBC-TV, NEWS DEPARTMENT		
		30 ROCKEFELLER PLAZA	NEW YORK, NY	10112
CHANCELLOR, MARY	TV WRITER	8955 BEVERLY BLVD	LOS ANGELES, CA	90048
CHANCEY, HARRY, JR	TV WRITER	555 W 57TH ST #1230	NEW YORK, NY	10019
CHANCEY, RON	GUITARIST	MCA RECORDS COMPANY		
		27 MUSIC SQUARE W	NASHVILLE, TN	37203
CHANDA, NAYAN R	NEWS CORRESPONDENT	8708 MELWOOD RD	BETHESDA, MD	20817
CHANDLEE, HARRY C	WRITER	8955 BEVERLY BLVD	LOS ANGELES, CA	90048
CHANDLEE, RICHARD CREEL	WRITER	610 N ROSE ST	BURBANK, CA	91505
CHANDLER, ALBERT "HAPPY"	BASEBALL EXECUTIVE	191 ELM ST	VERSAILLES, KY	40383
CHANDLER, CHICK	ACTOR	510 ANITA ST	LAGUNA BEACH, CA	92651
CHANDLER, ESTEE	ACTRESS	9200 SUNSET BLVD #931	LOS ANGELES, CA	90069
CHANDLER, GENE	SINGER	ASSOCIATED BOOKING CORP		
		1955 BROADWAY, 5TH FLOOR	NEW YORK, NY	10023
CHANDLER, JAMES	ACTOR	11240 MAGNOLIA BLVD #202	NORTH HOLLYWOOD, CA	91601

Name	Occupation	Address	City	Zip
CHANDLER, JEFFREY ALAN	ACTOR	9229 SUNSET BLVD #306	LOS ANGELES, CA	90069
CHANDLER, JOHN DAVID	ACTOR	421 N PASS AVE #5	BURBANK, CA	91505
CHANDLER, JOY	ACTRESS	1607 N EL CENTRO AVE #22	HOLLYWOOD, CA	90028
CHANDLER, JUNE	ACTRESS	LEONETTI, 6526 SUNSET BLVD	HOLLYWOOD, CA	90028
CHANDLER, MICHAEL	WRITER	8955 BEVERLY BLVD	LOS ANGELES, CA	90048
CHANDLER, ROBERT	TV EXECUTIVE	CBS-TV, 530 W 57TH ST	NEW YORK, NY	10019
CHANDLER, RUTH	NEWS CORRESPONDENT	4607 CONNECTICUT AVE, NW	WASHINGTON, DC	20008
CHANEL, PATRICE	ACTRESS	19216 ANDMARK AVE	CARSON, CA	90746
CHANEY, HAROLD LEE	SCREENWRITER	13201 ROSCOE BLVD	SUN VALLEY, CA	91352
CHANG, CATHY	BODYBUILDER	PHYSIQUE WORLD, INC		
		735 SHERIDAN ST #9	HONOLULU, HI	96814
CHANG, DONALD	BODYBUILDER	PHYSIQUE WORLD, INC		
		735 SHERIDAN ST #9	HONOLULU, HI	96814
CHANG, TISA	ACTRESS	305 RIVERSIDE DR	NEW YORK, NY	10025
CHANGE	RHYTHM & BLUES GROUP	200 W 51ST ST #1410	NEW YORK, NY	10019
CHANGING BODIES, THE	ROCK & ROLL GROUP	POST OFFICE BOX 8125	ANN ARBOR, MI	48107
CHANIN, JOHN G	DIRECTOR	15 CHRISTY LN	SPARTA, NJ	07871
CHANIN, STACEY	WRITER	555 W 57TH ST #1230	NEW YORK, NY	10019
CHANKIN, SIDNEY	ACTOR	9025 WILSHIRE BLVD #309	BEVERLY HILLS, CA	90211
CHANNEL, BRUCE	GUITARIST	504 WILLIAMSBURG RD	MOUNT JULIET, TN	37122
CHANNING, CAROL	ACTRESS	9301 FLICKER WY	LOS ANGELES, CA	90069
CHANNING, STOCKARD	ACTRESS	10880 WILSHIRE BLVD #2110	LOS ANGELES, CA	90024
CHANTELS, THE	VOCAL GROUP	TRUMBALL PRODUCTIONS		
		60 SEAMAN AVE	BROOKLYN, NY	11222
CHANTLER, DAVID T	WRITER	14001 PALAWAN WY #PH-18	MARINA DEL REY, CA	90292
CHANTLER-DICK, PEGGY	WRITER	8955 BEVERLY BLVD	LOS ANGELES, CA	90048
CHANTREY, MARVIN	VIOLINIST	1109 CHATEAU LN	NASHVILLE, TN	37215
CHAO, ROSALIND	ACTRESS	8322 BEVERLY BLVD #202	LOS ANGELES, CA	90048
CHAPEL, LOYITA	ACTRESS	9300 WILSHIRE BLVD #410	BEVERLY HILLS, CA	90212
CHAPIN, DOUG	FILM PRODUCER	415 N CRESCENT DR	BEVERLY HILLS, CA	90210
CHAPIN, LAUREN	ACTRESS	POST OFFICE BOX 922	KILLEEN, TX	76541
CHAPIN, SCHUYLER	OPERA EXECUTIVE	POST OFFICE BOX 20548	NEW YORK, NY	10025
CHAPIN, TOM	SINGER	KRAGEN, 8 CADMAN PLAZA	BROOKLYN, NY	11201
CHAPLAIN, HILARY	FIREEATER-JUGGLER	276 CAMBRIDGE ST #4	BOSTON, MA	02134
CHAPLIN, GERALDINE	ACTRESS	MARIA DE MOLINA 12	MADRID 6	SPAIN
CHAPLIN, LITA GREY	ACTRESS	8440 FOUNTAIN AVE #302	HOLLYWOOD, CA	90069
CHAPMAN, ALAN	COMPOSER	4853 STRATFORD RD	LOS ANGELES, CA	90042
CHAPMAN, DANIEL	NEWS CORRESPONDENT	3507 IDAHO AVE, NW	WASHINGTON, DC	20016
CHAPMAN, DAVID ELEY	FILM DIRECTOR	650 W END AVE	NEW YORK, NY	10025
CHAPMAN, GRAHAM	ACTOR-WRITER	2 PARK SQ W	LONDON NW1	ENGLAND
CHAPMAN, JOSEPH	ACTOR	151 N SAN VICENTE BLVD #208	BEVERLY HILLS, CA	90211
CHAPMAN, JUDITH	ACTRESS	9255 SUNSET BLVD #1105	LOS ANGELES, CA	90069
CHAPMAN, LEE	FILM DIRECTOR	2359 STANLEY HILLS DR	LOS ANGELES, CA	90046
CHAPMAN, LEIGH	SCREENWRITER	8955 BEVERLY BLVD	LOS ANGELES, CA	90048
CHAPMAN, LONNY	ACTOR	3973 GOODLAND AVE	STUDIO CITY, CA	91604
CHAPMAN, MARK	FILM DIRECTOR	ASPECT, 36 PERCY ST	LONDON W1	ENGLAND
CHAPMAN, MARSHALL	GUITARIST	1906 SOUTH ST #704	NASHVILLE, TN	37212
CHAPMAN, MICHAEL	TV WRITER-PRODUCER	MAX NAUGHTON LOWE		
		200 FULHAM RD	LONDON SW10	ENGLAND
CHAPMAN, MICHAEL C	FILM DIRECTOR	DGA, 7950 SUNSET BLVD	LOS ANGELES, CA	90046
CHAPMAN, MIKE	SINGER	FEVER, 50-A E 167TH ST	BRONX, NY	10452
CHAPMAN, PAUL STEPHEN	GUITARIST	2026 ROSECLIFF RD	NASHVILLE, TN	37206
CHAPMAN, PRISCILLA	SCREENWRITER	8955 BEVERLY BLVD	LOS ANGELES, CA	90048
CHAPMAN, R STANLEY	NEWS CORRESPONDENT	5330 N 37TH ST	ARLINGTON, VA	22207
CHAPMAN, RICHARD	TV PRODUCER	MCA/UNIVERSAL STUDIOS, INC		
		100 UNIVERSAL CITY PLAZA	UNIVERSAL CITY, CA	91608
CHAPMAN, RICHARD E	TV WRITER	8955 BEVERLY BLVD	LOS ANGELES, CA	90048
CHAPMAN, ROBIN	NEWS CORRESPONDENT	4461 CONNECTICUT AVE, NW	WASHINGTON, DC	20008
CHAPMAN, STEPHEN	COMMENTATOR	THE CHICAGO TRIBUNE		
		TRIBUNE TOWER		
		435 N MICHIGAN AVE	CHICAGO, IL	60611
CHAPMAN, STEVEN RICHARD	GUITARIST	308 HUNTERS RUN LN	MOUNT JULIET, TN	37122
CHAPMAN, THOMAS C	SCREENWRITER	8955 BEVERLY BLVD	LOS ANGELES, CA	90048
CHAPPELEAR, CHARLES	GUITARIST	108 HAZELWOOD DR	HENDERSONVILLE, TN	37075
CHAPPELL, JOHN	ACTOR	9744 WILSHIRE BLVD #206	BEVERLY HILLS, CA	90212
CHAPUIS, ISABELLE	FLUTIST	KAY, 58 W 58TH ST	NEW YORK, NY	10019
CHARADES, THE	VOCAL GROUP	5300 POWERLINE RD #202	FORT LAUDERDALE, FL	33309
CHARAMELLA, JACK	GUITARIST	2803 BRANSFORD AVE	NASHVILLE, TN	37204
CHARBONNEAU, NAN	CASTING DIRECTOR	166 E SUPERIOR ST #412	CHICAGO, IL	60611
CHARDY, ALFONSO	NEWS CORRESPONDENT	1200 N NASH ST #1117	ARLINGTON, VA	22209
CHARISSE, CYD	ACTRESS-DANCER	2328 CENTURY HILL	LOS ANGELES, CA	90067
CHARLES, CAROLINE	FASHION DESIGNER	9 BEAUCHAMP PL	LONDON SW3	ENGLAND
CHARLES, ERNEST A	WRITER	8955 BEVERLY BLVD	LOS ANGELES, CA	90048
CHARLES, GLEN	WRITER-PRODUCER	1716 WESTRIDGE RD	LOS ANGELES, CA	90049
CHARLES, GLORIA	ACTRESS	3800 BARHAM BLVD #303	LOS ANGELES, CA	90068
CHARLES, HARRIET	WRITER	1064 N CATALINA AVE	PASADENA, CA	91104
CHARLES, KEITH	ACTOR	9200 SUNSET BLVD #1210	LOS ANGELES, CA	90069
CHARLES, KEITH	WRITER	555 W 57TH ST #1230	NEW YORK, NY	10019
CHARLES, LARRY	TV WRITER	8955 BEVERLY BLVD	LOS ANGELES, CA	90048
CHARLES, LESLIE D	WRITER	9917 LANCER CT	BEVERLY HILLS, CA	90210

LIGHTS! CAMERA! ACTION!
GEORGIA TERRY AUTOGRAPHS
We work actively from your WANT lists.
840 N.E. COCHRAN AVENUE
GRESHAM, OREGON 97030
FREE CATALOG
REASONABLE PRICES
Specializing in the ENTERTAINMENT field.
FAST, FRIENDLY SERVICE
Member U.A.C.C.
Collector since 1952
Dealer since 1978
LIGHTS! CAMERA! ACTION!
(503) 667-0950
LIGHTS! CAMERA! ACTION!

Name	Occupation	Address	City	Zip
CHARLES, LESLIE SEBASTIAN	SINGER-COMPOSER	SEE - OCEAN, BILLY		
CHARLES, MARIA	ACTRESS	BROWN, 47 WEST SQ	LONDON SE11	ENGLAND
CHARLES, MARTHA	ACTRESS	HAZEL MC MILLAN		
		126 N DOHENY DR	BEVERLY HILLS, CA	90211
CHARLES, MICHAEL	NEWS CORRESPONDENT	4206 WASHINGTON BLVD	ARLINGTON, VA	22201
CHARLES, MONA	ACTRESS	9777 WILSHIRE BLVD #707	BEVERLY HILLS, CA	90212
CHARLES, NICK	SPORTSCASTER	CNN, 1050 TECHWOOD DR, NW	ATLANTA, GA	30318
CHARLES, RAY	SINGER-PIANIST	2107 W WASHINGTON BLVD #2	LOS ANGELES, CA	90018
CHARLES, SUZETTE	MISS AMERICA	151 S EL CAMINO DR	BEVERLY HILLS, CA	90212
CHARLES, ZACHARY	ACTOR	FARRELL, 10500 MAGNOLIA BLVD	NORTH HOLLYWOOD, CA	91601
CHARLESON, IAN	ACTOR	CONWAY, EAGLE HOUSE		
		109 JERMYN ST	LONDON SW1	ENGLAND
CHARLESON, LESLIE	ACTRESS	ABC-TV, "GENERAL HOSPITAL"		
		1438 N GOWER ST	LOS ANGELES, CA	90028
CHARLSON, CARL	DIRECTOR	DGA, 110 W 57TH ST	NEW YORK, NY	10019
CHARLSTON, ELSA	SOPRANO	MUGDAN, 84 PROSPECT AVE	DOUGLASTON, NY	11363
CHARLSTON, RONDI	SOPRANO	SULLIVAN, 390 W END AVE	NEW YORK, NY	10024
CHARM, NIKKI	ACTRESS	16005 SHERMAN WY #204	VAN NUYS, CA	91406
CHARMOLI, TONY	DIRECTOR-CHOREO	1271 SUNSET PLAZA DR	LOS ANGELES, CA	90069
CHARNAY, LYNNE	ACTRESS	75 CENTRAL PARK W	NEW YORK, NY	10023
CHARNEY, JORDAN	ACTOR	9229 SUNSET BLVD #306	LOS ANGELES, CA	90069
CHARNIN, MARTIN	WRITER-PRODUCER	BEAM ONE LTD, 850 7TH AVE	NEW YORK, NY	10019
CHARNOTA, ANTHONY	ACTOR	7250 FRANKLIN AVE #506	LOS ANGELES, CA	90046
CHARNOW, STEVEN	WRITER	143 OCEAN PARK BLVD	SANTA MONICA, CA	90405
CHARNY, SUZANNE	ACTRESS	11240 MAGNOLIA BLVD #202	NORTH HOLLYWOOD, CA	91601
CHARO	SINGER	1801 LEXINGTON RD	BEVERLY HILLS, CA	90210
CHARONE, IRWIN	ACTOR	8721 SUNSET BLVD #103	LOS ANGELES, CA	90069
CHARRELL, LISSA	WRITER	8955 BEVERLY BLVD	LOS ANGELES, CA	90048
CHARREN, PEGGY	TV EXECUTIVE	ACT, 46 AUSTIN ST	NEWTONVILLE, MA	02160
CHARTERIS, LESLIE	WRITER	LEVETT, 8 SOUTHAMPTON ROW	LONDON WC1	ENGLAND
CHARTOFF, MELANIE	ACTRESS	1333 N STANLEY AVE #14	LOS ANGELES, CA	90046
CHARTOFF, ROBERT	FILM PRODUCER	10125 W WASHINGTON BLVD	CULVER CITY, CA	90230
CHARTOK, LEA	WRITER	8955 BEVERLY BLVD	LOS ANGELES, CA	90048
CHARYN, JEROME	WRITER	555 W 57TH ST #1230	NEW YORK, NY	10019
CHAS	COMEDIAN	MAGNAN, 1121 NORTHRUP DR, NW	GRAND RAPIDS, MI	48504
CHASE	ROCK & ROLL GROUP	516 SE MORRISON ST #420	PORTLAND, OR	97214
CHASE, BARRIE	ACTRESS-DANCER	3750 BEVERLY RIDGE DR	SHERMAN OAKS, CA	91423
CHASE, BARRY OLIVER	TV EXECUTIVE	PBS, 475 L'ENFANT PLAZA	WASHINGTON, DC	20024
CHASE, BRODIE	WRESTLER	NATIONAL WRESTLING ALLIANCE		
		JIM CROCKETT PROMOTIONS		
		421 BRIARBEND DR	CHARLOTTE, NC	28209
CHASE, CAROL	SINGER	6255 SUNSET BLVD #1019	LOS ANGELES, CA	90028
CHASE, CHEVY	ACTOR-WRITER	8436 W 3RD ST #650	LOS ANGELES, CA	90048
CHASE, CHRIS	TV HOST	151 S EL CAMINO DR	BEVERLY HILLS, CA	90212
CHASE, DAVID	TV WRITER-PRODUCER	1888 CENTURY PARK E #1400	LOS ANGELES, CA	90067
CHASE, DAVID H	PHOTOJOURNALIST	5902 RIDGEVIEW DR	ALEXANDRIA, VA	22310
CHASE, DAVID HENRY	WRITER	13215 RIVIERA RANCH RD	LOS ANGELES, CA	90049
CHASE, FRANK	TV WRITER	213 OCEAN AVE	SANTA MONICA, CA	90403
CHASE, GARY J	COMPOSER	7920 MC LAREN AVE	CANOGA PARK, CA	91304
CHASE, LAUREN	ACTRESS	9744 WILSHIRE BLVD #206	BEVERLY HILLS, CA	90212
CHASE, LEONARD	TV PRODUCER	5 REGENT SQ	LONDON WC1	ENGLAND
CHASE, LORRAINE	ACTRESS	PETER CHARLESWORTH, LTD		
		68 OLD BROMPTON RD	LONDON SW7 3LQ	ENGLAND
CHASE, MARTIN M	NEWS CORRESPONDENT	4902 DORSET AVE, NW	WASHINGTON, DC	20815
CHASE, RAMONA	WRITER	213 OCEAN AVE	SANTA MONICA, CA	90402
CHASE, REBECCA	NEWS CORRESPONDENT	ABC NEWS, 7 W 66TH ST	NEW YORK, NY	10023
CHASE, STEPHAN	ACTOR	19 SHEEN GATE GARDENS	LONDON SW14	ENGLAND
CHASE, STEPHANIE	VIOLINIST	59 E 54TH ST #81	NEW YORK, NY	10022
CHASE, SYLVIA	NEWS CORRESPONDENT	ABC NEWS - "20/20"		
		1330 AVE OF THE AMERICAS	NEW YORK, NY	10019
CHASE, WILLIAM L	NEWS CORRESPONDENT	4902 NEWPORT AVE	BETHESDA, MD	20815
CHASE & PARK	TRAMPOLINE ACT	HALL, 138 FROG HOLLOW RD	CHURCHVILLE, PA	18966
CHASE FORWARD	C & W GROUP	POST OFFICE BOX 6025	NEWPORT NEWS, VA	23606
CHASEN, HEATHER	ACTRESS	RJPM, 59 KNIGHTSBRIDGE	LONDON SW1X 7RA	ENGLAND
CHASER BAND, THE	ROCK & ROLL GROUP	POST OFFICE BOX 830	ALBANY, NY	12201
CHASIN, HELEN	WRITER	555 W 57TH ST #1230	NEW YORK, NY	10019
CHASIN, PHYLLIS	ACTRESS	2640 1/2 23RD ST	SANTA MONICA, CA	90405
CHASIN, ROBERT	TV EXECUTIVE	COLUMBIA PICTURES TV		
		COLUMBIA PLAZA	BURBANK, CA	91505
CHASIN' THE BLUES	RHYTHM & BLUES GROUP	276 CAMBRIDGE ST #4	BOSTON, MA	02134
CHASMAN, DAVID	WRITER	1505 CARLA RIDGE DR	BEVERLY HILLS, CA	90210
CHASON, MYRA	ACTRESS	435 S LA CIENEGA BLVD #20	LOS ANGELES, CA	90048
CHAST, ROZ	CARTOONIST	POST OFFICE BOX 4203	NEW YORK, NY	10017
CHASTAIN, DAVE, BAND	ROCK & ROLL GROUP	VARIETY ARTISTS INTL, INC		
		9073 NEMO ST, 3RD FLOOR	LOS ANGELES, CA	90069
CHASTAIN, DON	ACTOR	4229 VIA ALONDRA	PALOS VERDES, CA	90274
CHASTAIN, JANE	ACTRESS	3219 CYN LAKE DR	HOLLYWOOD, CA	90068
CHATER, GEOFFREY	ACTOR	LEADING PLAYERS MGMT		
		31 KING'S RD	LONDON SW3	ENGLAND
CHATFIELD, LESLIE	TV DIRECTOR-PRODUCER	GREEN & UNDERWOOD, LTD		
		THE BROADWAY		
		GUNNERSBURY LN	LONDON W3 8HR	ENGLAND
CHATFIELD, ROCCINA M	TV WRITER	6639 SUNNYSLOPE AVE	VAN NUYS, CA	91401
CHATFIELD-TAYLOR, CONSTANCE	NEWS CORRESPONDENT	13 W LINDEN ST	ALEXANDRIA, VA	22301
CHATINOVER, MARVIN A	ACTOR	22 AVALON RD	GREAT NECK, NY	11021

CHARO

CHER

ERIC CLAPTON

ALAN CLARK

DICK CLARK

ROY CLARK

MIKE CLIFFORD

DEBRA CLINGER

THE COASTERS

Name	Occupation	Address	City	Zip
CHATMAN, DELLE	ACTRESS	5607 LA MIRADA AVE #402	LOS ANGELES, CA	90038
CHAULS, ROBERT N	COMPOSER-CONDUCTOR	3451 VALLEY MEADOW RD	SHERMAN OAKS, CA	91403
CHAUSSON, CARLOS	BASSO-BARITONE	AFFILIATE ARTISTS, INC		
		37 W 65TH ST, 6TH FLOOR	NEW YORK, NY	10023
CHAUVIN, LILYAN	ACT-WRI-DIR	3841 EUREKA DR	STUDIO CITY, CA	91604
CHAVEZ, ABRAHAM, JR	CONDUCTOR	GERSHUNOFF, 502 PARK AVE	NEW YORK, NY	10022
CHAVEZ, JOHN A	TV EXECUTIVE	ABC-TV, 2040 AVE OF THE STARS	LOS ANGELES, CA	90067
CHAYKIN, DANIEL	DIRECTOR	DGA, 110 W 57TH ST	NEW YORK, NY	10019
CHAYKIN, MAURY	ACTOR	11726 SAN VICENTE BLVD #300	LOS ANGELES, CA	90049
CHEAP TRICK	ROCK & ROLL GROUP	KEN ADAMANY & ASSOCIATES		
		315 W GORHAM ST	MADISON, WI	53703
CHEATHAM, BILL	GUITARIST	4107 ESTES RD	NASHVILLE, TN	37215
CHEATHAM, JAMES R	COMPOSER	7836 CAMINO RAPOSA	SAN DIEGO, CA	92122
CHEATHAM, JEAN E	COMPOSER	7836 CAMINO RAPOSA	SAN DIEGO, CA	92122
CHEATHAM, MARIE	ACTRESS	KOHNER, 9169 SUNSET BLVD	LOS ANGELES, CA	90069
CHECCO, AL	ACTOR	4029 COLDWATER CANYON AVE	STUDIO CITY, CA	91604
CHECKER, CHUBBY	SINGER-SONGWRITER	1650 BROADWAY #1011	NEW YORK, NY	10019
CHECKMATES, THE	VOCAL GROUP	ASSOCIATED BOOKING CORP		
		1995 BROADWAY, 5TH FLOOR	NEW YORK, NY	10023
CHEEK, DOUGLAS W	WRITER-PRODUCER	DGA, 110 W 57TH ST	NEW YORK, NY	10019
CHEEK, JOHN	SINGER	59 E 54TH ST #81	NEW YORK, NY	10022
CHEEK, MOLLY	ACTRESS	15301 VENTURA BLVD #345	SHERMAN OAKS, CA	91403
CHEELY, GEORGE	NEWS CORRESPONDENT	NBC-TV, NEWS DEPARTMENT		
		4001 NEBRASKA AVE, NW	WASHINGTON, DC	20016
CHEER, MAX	ROCK & ROLL GROUP	SEE - MAX CHEER		
CHEERLEADERS, THE	WRESTLING TAG TEAM	GORGEOUS GIRLS OF WRESTLING		
		RIVIERA HOTEL & CASINO		
		DAVID B MC LANE PRODS		
		2901 S LAS VEGAS BLVD	LAS VEGAS, NV	89109
CHEERS, DUANE MICHAEL	NEWS CORRESPONDENT	920 WESTMINISTER ST, NW	WASHINGTON, DC	20001
CHEEVER, RUSSELL A	COMPOSER	25 MARGARITA	CAMARILLO, CA	93010
CHEFFEY, MARY	ACTRESS	KENNEDY, 2768 WOODWARDIA AVE	LOS ANGELES, CA	90024
CHEHAK, TOM	TV WRITER-PRODUCER	5442 ALLOTT AVE	VAN NUYS, CA	91401
CHEIKEN, SUSAN A	NEWS CORRESPONDENT	4201 MASSACHUSETTS AVE, NW	WASHINGTON, DC	20016
CHELF, WILLIAM DUNBAR	MUSIC ARRANGER	903 RUSSELL ST	NASHVILLE, TN	32206
CHELL, GRETCHEN	NEWS CORRESPONDENT	2715 S INGE ST	ARLINGTON, VA	22202
CHELSEA	ROCK & ROLL GROUP	BROTHERS, 141 DUNBAR AVE	FORDS, NJ	08863
CHELSI, LARRO	ACTOR	17 PARK AVE	NEW YORK, NY	10016
CHELSI, LAWRENCE	ACTOR	151 N SAN VICENTE BLVD #208	BEVERLY HILLS, CA	90211
CHELSOM, PETER	ACTOR	SHARKEY, 90 REGENT ST	LONDON W1	ENGLAND
CHEN, ALLAN	NEWS REPORTER	DISCOVER/TIME & LIFE BLDG		
		ROCKEFELLER CENTER	NEW YORK, NY	10020
CHEN, LELAND	VIOLINIST	ANGLO-SWISS ARTISTS MGMT		
		16 MUSWELL HILL RD, HIGHGATE	LONDON N6 5UG	ENGLAND
CHEN, TAI-CHANG	PIANIST	POST OFFICE BOX 20548	NEW YORK, NY	10025
CHEN, TINA	ACTRESS	ICM, 8899 BEVERLY BLVD	LOS ANGELES, CA	90048
CHENAULT, CYNTHIA	WRITER	201 W 22ND ST #H-23	SAN PEDRO, CA	90731
CHENAULT, ROBERT	TV DIRECTOR	201 W 22ND ST #H-23	SAN PEDRO, CA	90731
CHENEVEY, PAUL	CONDUCTOR	260 W END AVE #7-A	NEW YORK, NY	10023
CHENEY, TOM	CARTOONIST	THE NATIONAL LAMPOON		
		635 MADISON AVE	NEW YORK, NY	10022
CHENG, LYDIA	BODYBUILDER	POST OFFICE BOX 1490		
		RADIO CITY STATION	NEW YORK, NY	10101
CHENG, MARIA	DANCER	AFFILIATE ARTISTS, INC		
		37 W 65TH ST, 6TH FLOOR	NEW YORK, NY	10023
CHENG, STEPHEN	ACTOR-WRITER	395 RIVERSIDE DR	NEW YORK, NY	10025
CHENG-ZONG, YIN	PIANIST	SHAW CONCERTS, 1995 BROADWAY	NEW YORK, NY	10023
CHENIER, CLIFTON	MUSICIAN	9777 HARWIN ST #101	HOUSTON, TX	77036
CHENNAULT, ANNA	AUTHOR	2510 VIRGINIA AVE #1404, NW	WASHINGTON, DC	20005
CHENOWETH, KARIN	NEWS CORRESPONDENT	2008 LUZERNE AVE	CHEVY CHASE, MD	20910
CHENOWITH, ELLEN	CASTING DIRECTOR	1888 CENTURY PARK E #1888	LOS ANGELES, CA	90067
CHEQUERED PAST	ROCK & ROLL GROUP	ATI, 888 7TH AVE, 21ST FLOOR	NEW YORK, NY	10106
CHER	SINGER-ACTRESS	2727 BENEDICT CANYON DR	BEVERLY HILLS, CA	90210
CHERBACK, CYNTHIA	WRITER	11912 RIVERDALE DR #3	NORTH HOLLYWOOD, CA	91607
CHERE, LIU	SOPRANO	KAY, 58 W 58TH ST	NEW YORK, NY	10019
CHERELLE	SINGER	200 W 51ST ST #1410	NEW YORK, NY	10019
CHERESKIN, LOWELL	WRITER	555 W 57TH ST #1230	NEW YORK, NY	10019
CHERKASSKY, SHURA	PIANIST	SHAW CONCERTS, 1995 BROADWAY	NEW YORK, NY	10023
CHERMAK, CY	WRITER-PRODUCER	20224 DELITA DR	WOODLAND HILLS, CA	91364
CHERNAK, JERALD	DIRECTOR	12 ASHWOOD PL	PARSIPPANY, NJ	07054
CHERNER, REID	SPORTS WRITER	POST OFFICE BOX 500	WASHINGTON, DC	20044
CHERNOFF, JOEL	NEWS CORRESPONDENT	6414 WINGATE ST	ALEXANDRIA, VA	22312
CHERNUS, SONIA	WRITER	11520 DONA EVITA DR	STUDIO CITY, CA	91604
CHERONES, THOMAS H, JR	WRITER-PRODUCER	3177 LINDO ST	HOLLYWOOD, CA	90068
CHERRELL, GWEN	ACTRESS-WRITER	CADELL & RAYMAN, LTD		
		2 SOUTHWOOD LN	LONDON N6 5EE	ENGLAND
CHERRILL, DAVID	TV DIRECTOR	52 WOODLAND RISE		
		STUDHAM, NEAR DUNSTABLE	BEDFORDSHIRE	ENGLAND
CHERRIX, ROBERT P, JR	PHOTOJOURNALIST	1705 "P" ST #54, NW	WASHINGTON, DC	20036
CHERRY, BYRON	ACTOR	9744 WILSHIRE BLVD #306	BEVERLY HILLS, CA	90212
CHERRY, CARLA	ACTRESS	CUZZINS, 250 W 57TH ST	NEW YORK, NY	10019
CHERRY, CAROLE S	TV WRITER	8955 BEVERLY BLVD	LOS ANGELES, CA	90048
CHERRY, STANLEY	WRITER-PRODUCER	11222 VENTURA BLVD	STUDIO CITY, CA	91604

Name	Occupation	Address	City	Zip
CHERRY, TOM	MUSIC ARRANGER	2908 DONNA HILL DR	NASHVILLE, TN	37214
CHERRY BOMBZ, THE	ROCK & ROLL GROUP	41 BRITAIN ST #200	TORONTO, ONT	CANADA
CHERTOK, JACK	FILM PRODUCER	515 OCEAN AVE N #305	SANTA MONICA, CA	90402
CHERWIN, PETER	CABLE EXECUTIVE	SHOWTIME, 1633 BROADWAY	NEW YORK, NY	10019
CHESHE, STEVEN T	COMPOSER	1123 OCEAN PARK BLVD #C	SANTA MONICA, CA	90405
CHESHIRE, HERBERT W	NEWS CORRESPONDENT	2475 VIRGINIA AVE #818, NW	WASHINGTON, DC	20037
CHESIS, LINDA	FLUTIST	157 W 57TH ST #1100	NEW YORK, NY	10019
CHESIS/CUTLER DUO	MUSICAL DUO	157 W 57TH ST #1100	NEW YORK, NY	10019
CHESLER, MARC D	WRITER	8955 BEVERLY BLVD	LOS ANGELES, CA	90048
CHESLEY, HOWARD M	TV WRITER	1908 MONTANA AVE	SANTA MONICA, CA	90403
CHESNEY, DIANA	ACTRESS	8721 SUNSET BLVD #103	LOS ANGELES, CA	90069
CHESNEY, RONALD	WRITER-PRODUCER	1 GROSVENOR GARDENS	LONDON NW11 OHH	ENGLAND
CHESNUTT, JUDY	ACTRESS	JARRETT, 220 E 63RD ST	NEW YORK, NY	10021
CHESSER, LARRY G	NEWS CORRESPONDENT	9771 LAKEPOINT DR	BURKE, VA	22015
CHESSLER, ABDREA	WRITER	555 W 57TH ST #1230	NEW YORK, NY	10019
CHESSOR, JOHN B	GUITARIST	1417 MC GAVOCK PIKE	NASHVILLE, TN	37216
CHESSYRE, ROBERT C	NEWS CORRESPONDENT	4944 LOWELL ST, NW	WASHINGTON, DC	20016
CHESTER, COLBY	ACTOR	1245 N ORCHARD DR	BURBANK, CA	91506
CHESTER, DAVID T	NEWS CORRESPONDENT	1755 JEFFERSON DAVIS HWY	ARLINGTON, VA	22202
CHESTER, GIRAUD	TV EXECUTIVE	GOODSON-TODMAN COMPANY		
		375 PARK AVE	NEW YORK, NY	10022
CHESTER, LYNN	ACTRESS	9220 SUNSET BLVD #202	LOS ANGELES, CA	90069
CHESTER STRING QUARTET	STRING QUARTET	POST OFFICE BOX 30	TENAFLY, NJ	07670
CHESTERFIELD KINGS, THE	ROCK & ROLL GROUP	MIRRORS RECORDS CO		
		645 TITUS AVE	ROCHESTER, NY	14617
CHESTNUT, ROBERT	ACTOR	247 S BEVERLY DR #102	BEVERLY HILLS, CA	90210
CHETWYND, LIONEL	SCREENWRITER	2401 S HACIENDA BLVD #311	HACIENDA HGTS, CA	91745
CHEUNG, GEORGE KEE	ACTOR	9229 SUNSET BLVD #306	LOS ANGELES, CA	90069
CHEVALIER, DOUGLAS	PHOTOGRAPHER	5301 WILSON LN	BETHESDA, MD	20014
CHEVILLAT, BRUCE	TV DIRECTOR	1626 CERRO GORDO ST	LOS ANGELES, CA	90026
CHEVRON, DOLORES	TALENT AGENT	4051 RADFORD AVE #A	STUDIO CITY, CA	91604
CHEW, RICHARD F	WRITER	8955 BEVERLY BLVD	LOS ANGELES, CA	90048
CHEW, SAM, JR	ACTOR	9165 SUNSET BLVD #202	LOS ANGELES, CA	90069
CHEYNE, HANK	ACTOR	NBC-TV, "ANOTHER WORLD"		
		30 ROCKEFELLER PLAZA	NEW YORK, NY	10112
CHI-LITES, THE	SOUL GROUP	250 W 57TH ST #330	NEW YORK, NY	10107
CHIANG, OSCAR	NEWS REPORTER	TIME/TIME & LIFE BLDG		
		ROCKEFELLER CENTER	NEW YORK, NY	10020
CHIARA, MARIA	SOPRANO	CAMI, 165 W 57TH ST	NEW YORK, NY	10019
CHIAVOLA, KATHY	GUITARIST	1408 MC KENNIE AVE	NASHVILLE, TN	37206
CHIBBARO, LOUIS M	NEWS CORRESPONDENT	516 "A" ST, NE	WASHINGTON, DC	20002
CHIC	SOUL GROUP	250 W 57TH ST #330	NEW YORK, NY	10107
CHICAGO	ROCK & ROLL GROUP	FRONT LINE MANAGEMENT		
		80 UNIVERSAL CITY PLAZA	UNIVERSAL CITY, CA	91608
CHICAGO, FREDDIE	TV WRITER	8955 BEVERLY BLVD	LOS ANGELES, CA	90048
CHICAGO CITY LIMITS	COMEDY DUO	EAGLES, 305 E 24TH ST	NEW YORK, NY	10010
CHICAGO KNOCKERS	MUD WRESTLERS	POST OFFICE BOX 2038	GLENVIEW, IL	60025
CHICH, BOB	TALENT AGENT	348 E 9TH ST #10	NEW YORK, NY	10003
CHICOS, CATHERINE N	WRITER	555 W 57TH ST #1230	NEW YORK, NY	10019
CHIECO, FORTUNATO F	WRITER	555 W 57TH ST #1230	NEW YORK, NY	10019
CHIEN, ALEC	PIANIST	AFFILIATE ARTISTS, INC		
		37 W 65TH ST, 6TH FLOOR	NEW YORK, NY	10023
CHIFFONS, THE	VOCAL GROUP	KNIGHT, 185 CLINTON AVE	STATEN ISLAND, NY	10301
CHIGER, HENRY	WRITER	555 W 57TH ST #1230	NEW YORK, NY	10019
CHIHARA, PAUL	COMPOSER-CONDUCTOR	3815 W OLIVE AVE #202	BURBANK, CA	91505
CHILD, ELIZABETH	NEWS CORRESPONDENT	2800 ONTARIO RD, NW	WASHINGTON, DC	20009
CHILD, JEREMY	ACTOR	26 MADRID RD	LONDON SW13	ENGLAND
CHILD, JULIA	TV PERSONALITY	WGBH-TV, 125 WESTERN AVE	BOSTON, MA	02134
CHILD, MARILYN	ACTRESS	3151 W CAHUENGA BLVD #310	LOS ANGELES, CA	90068
CHILDERS, BUDDY	COMPOSER	616 N RUSH ST #1611	CHICAGO, IL	60611
CHILDRESS, ALICE	PLAYWRIGHT	555 W 57TH ST #1230	NEW YORK, NY	10019
CHILDS, RALPH	GUITARIST	323 LAUDERDALE RD	NASHVILLE, TN	37205
CHILDS, SUZANNE	ACTRESS	21910 PACIFIC COAST HWY	MALIBU, CA	90265
CHILDS, TED	TV DIRECTOR-PRODUCER	FRASER, 91 REGENT ST	LONDON W1	ENGLAND
CHILDS, TOMMI LYNN	PHOTOGRAPHER	1430 "S" ST, NW	WASHINGTON, DC	20009
CHILES, LINDEN	ACTOR	2521 TOPANGA SKYLINE	TOPANGA, CA	90290
CHILES, LOIS	ACTRESS	644 SAN LORENZO ST	SANTA MONICA, CA	90402
CHILEWICH, MARTIN D	WRITER	555 W 57TH ST #1230	NEW YORK, NY	10019
CHILL, THE	ROCK & ROLL GROUP	VARIETY ARTISTS INTL, INC		
		9073 NEMO ST, 3RD FLOOR	LOS ANGELES, CA	90069
CHILLIWACK	ROCK & ROLL GROUP	41 BRITAIN ST #200	TORONTO, ONT	CANADA
CHILTON, JOHN	ACTOR	2211 OCEAN AVE	SANTA MONICA, CA	90405
CHILVERS, COLIN A	DIRECTOR	DGA, 110 W 57TH ST	NEW YORK, NY	10019
CHIMES FAMILY, THE	HARMONICA VIRTUOSOS	2701 COTTAGE WY #14	SACRAMENTO, CA	95825
CHIN, ANNIE	WRITER	8955 BEVERLY BLVD	LOS ANGELES, CA	90048
CHIN, CLINT	ACTOR	91 GROVE ST	PASSIAC, NJ	07055
CHIN, GLEN	ACTOR	3430 3/4 DREW ST	LOS ANGELES, CA	90065
CHINICH, MICHAEL	CASTING DIRECTOR	MCA/UNIVERSAL STUDIOS, INC		
		100 UNIVERSAL CITY PLAZA	UNIVERSAL CITY, CA	91608
CHINIQUY, RONALD	WRITER	12021 VALLEY HEART DR #1	STUDIO CITY, CA	91604
CHINN, JOHN	WRITER	555 W 57TH ST #1230	NEW YORK, NY	10019
CHINN, PHILIP	WRITER	555 W 57TH ST #1230	NEW YORK, NY	10019
CHION-KENNEY, LINDA	NEWS CORRESPONDENT	5560 ASCOT CT #122	ALEXANDRIA, VA	22311
CHIPELLO, PAUL W	COMPOSER-CONDUCTOR	6313 PEACH AVE	VAN NUYS, CA	91401
CHIPMAN, PETER	SINGER	4680 ELK LAKE DR #304	VICTORIA, BC V8Z 5M1	CANADA

CHIRKINIAN, FRANK	TV DIRECTOR-PRODUCER	CBS-TV, 51 W 52ND ST	NEW YORK, NY	10019
CHISHOLM, DAVID J	TV WRITER	8955 BEVERLY BLVD	LOS ANGELES, CA	90048
CHISHOLM, JOHN	CINEMATOGRAPHER	7715 SUNSET BLVD #150	LOS ANGELES, CA	90046
CHISZAR, DAN	NEWS CORRESPONDENT	1844 ONTARIO PL, NW	WASHINGTON, DC	20009
CHITRE, DILIP V	NEWS CORRESPONDENT	8310 LEGATION RD	NEW CARROLLTON, MD	20784
CHMURA, GABRIEL	CONDUCTOR	SHAW CONCERTS, 1995 BROADWAY	NEW YORK, NY	10023
CHO, NAM-DO	NEWS CORRESPONDENT	6014 FOREST HOLLOW LN	SPRINGFIELD, VA	22152
CHO, RAYMOND	CONDUCTOR	3123 W 8TH ST #208	LOS ANGELES, CA	90005
CHO, YOUNG-AE	SOPRANO	1182 MARKET ST #311	SAN FRANCISCO, CA	94102
CHOATE, DON WAYNE	GUITARIST	ROUTE #2, OLD CHARLOTTE PIKE	NASHVILLE, TN	37209
CHOCOLATE MILK	SOUL GROUP	POST OFFICE BOX 19004	NEW ORLEANS, LA	70179
CHODER, JILL	ACTRESS	EISEN, 154 E 61ST ST	NEW YORK, NY	10021
CHODERKER, GEORGE	TV DIRECTOR	10282 KINCARDINE AVE	LOS ANGELES, CA	90064
CHODOROV, JEROME	WRITER	131 S MAPLE DR #304	BEVERLY HILLS, CA	90212
CHODOROV, STEPHEN	WRITER-PRODUCER	CAMERA 3 PRODUCTIONS 555 W 57TH ST	NEW YORK, NY	10019
CHODOS, DANIEL	ACTOR	2242 CLIFFORD ST	LOS ANGELES, CA	90026
CHODOS, GABRIEL	PIANIST	AARON, 25 HUNTINGTON AVE	BOSTON, MA	02116
CHOLAKIAN, KEVORK	WRITER	555 W 57TH ST #1230	NEW YORK, NY	10019
CHOLAKIS, JOHN E	DIRECTOR	240 CENTRAL PARK S	NEW YORK, NY	10019
CHOLET, BLANCHE	ACTRESS	43 W 93RD ST	NEW YORK, NY	10025
CHOMAN, THOMAS	NEWS CORRESPONDENT	2020 N CALVERT ST	ARLINGTON, VA	22201
CHOMSKY, DAVID	TV WRITER	1942 PELHAM AVE #16	LOS ANGELES, CA	90025
CHOMSKY, MARVIN	DIRECTOR	4707 OCEAN FRONT WALK	VENICE, CA	90291
CHOMYN, JOSEPH K	TV DIRECTOR	6 ARMHERST PL	UPPER MONTCLAIR, NJ	07043
CHONG, MICHAEL	ACTOR	3151 W CAHUENGA BLVD #310	LOS ANGELES, CA	90068
CHONG, RAE DAWN	ACTRESS	10100 SANTA MONICA BLVD #1600	LOS ANGELES, CA	90067
CHONG, THOMAS	ACT-WRI-DIR	11661 SAN VICENTE BLVD #1010	LOS ANGELES, CA	90049
CHOOKASIAN, LILI	CONTRALTO	59 E 54TH ST #81	NEW YORK, NY	10022
CHOOLUCK, LEON	DIRECTOR-PRODUCER	6531 RANCHITO AVE	VAN NUYS, CA	91401
CHORОROS, WILLIAM	DIRECTOR	DGA, 110 W 57TH ST	NEW YORK, NY	10019
CHOU, SHEAU-HEI	NEWS CORRESPONDENT	784 AZALEA DR	ROCKVILLE, MD	20850
CHOW, RAYMOND	FILM EXECUTIVE	GOLDEN HARVEST GROUP 8 HAMMER HILL RD	KOWLOON	HONG KONG
CHOY, EUGENE	ACTOR	4731 LAUREL CANYON BLVD #5	NORTH HOLLYWOOD, CA	91607
CHOYKE, WILLIAM J	NEWS CORRESPONDENT	3132 BIRCH ST, NW	WASHINGTON, DC	20015
CHRAMOFF, NORMAN	ACTOR	650 WESTMOUNT DR	LOS ANGELES, CA	90069
CHRAPEK, DONNA	WRITER	555 W 57TH ST #1230	NEW YORK, NY	10019
CHRIS, MARILYN	ACTRESS	ABC-TV, "ONE LIFE TO LIVE" 1330 AVE OF THE AMERICAS	NEW YORK, NY	10019
CHRISAFIS, CHRIS	FILM PRODUCER	PINEWOOD STUDIOS, IVER HEATH	BUCKINGHAMSHIRE	ENGLAND
CHRISMAN, JOSEPH GENE	DRUMMER	223 PEYTONSVILLE RD	FRANKLIN, TN	37064
CHRISMAN, WOODY PAUL	BANJOIST	308 N WILSON BLVD	NASHVILLE, TN	37205
CHRISSENS, LES	AERIAL CRADLE DUO	HALL, 138 FROG HOLLOW RD	CHURCHVILLE, PA	18966
CHRISSENS, THE	AERIAL CRADLE DUO	SEE - CHRISSENS, LES		
CHRISTENSEN, BEVERLY	ACTRESS	4789 VINELAND AVE #100	NORTH HOLLYWOOD, CA	91602
CHRISTENSEN, BRUCE L	TV EXECUTIVE	NATIONAL ASSOC OF PUBLIC TV 955 L'ENFANT PLAZA, SW	WASHINGTON, DC	20024
CHRISTENSEN, CHRIS	CONDUCTOR	POST OFFICE BOX U	REDDING, CT	06875
CHRISTENSEN, JEAN	NEWS CORRESPONDENT	1728 NEW HAMPSHIRE AVE, NW	WASHINGTON, DC	20009
CHRISTENSEN, KENNETH	PIANIST	120 HICKORY ST	MADISON, TN	37115
CHRISTENSEN, ROY	CELLIST	1807 TYNE BLVD	NASHVILLE, TN	37215
CHRISTENSEN, VIRGINIA	VIOLINIST	1807 TYNE BLVD	NASHVILLE, TN	37215
CHRISTI, PANOS	ACTOR	3330 BARHAM BLVD #103	LOS ANGELES, CA	90068
CHRISTIAN, CHRIS	MUSICIAN	2020 SUNNYSIDE DR	BRENTWOOD, TN	37027
CHRISTIAN, CLAUDIA	ACTRESS	9200 SUNSET BLVD #931	LOS ANGELES, CA	90069
CHRISTIAN, H R	SCREENWRITER	1888 CENTURY PARK E #1400	LOS ANGELES, CA	90067
CHRISTIAN, LEIGH	ACTRESS-MODEL	8322 BEVERLY BLVD #202	LOS ANGELES, CA	90048
CHRISTIAN, MARK	GUITARIST	4164 EASTVIEW DR	NASHVILLE, TN	37211
CHRISTIAN, MARK	BODYBUILDER	GOLD'S GYM, 360 HAMPTON DR	VENICE, CA	90291
CHRISTIAN, MEG	SINGER-GUITARIST	OLIVIA RECORDS CO 4400 MARKET ST	OAKLAND, CA	94608
CHRISTIAN, RICHARD S	DIRECTOR	POST OFFICE BOX 3085	PRINCETON, NJ	08540
CHRISTIAN, ROGER	FILM DIRECTOR	24 BLOEMFONTEIN AVE	LONDON W12	ENGLAND
CHRISTIAN, S M BOBBY	COMPOSER	531 N EAST AVE	OAK PARK, IL	60302
CHRISTIAN & CHRISTIAN	C & W GROUP	LUTZ, 5625 "O" STREET BLDG	LINCOLN, NE	68510
CHRISTIANI, MARA	TRAPEZIST	HALL, 138 FROG HOLLOW RD	CHURCHVILLE, PA	18966
CHRISTIANSEN, CHERYL	ACTRESS	9753 GREGORY WY	BEVERLY HILLS, CA	90212
CHRISTIANSON, PEGGY	TV EXECUTIVE	500 S BUENA VISTA ST	BURBANK, CA	91521
CHRISTIE, JULIE	ACTRESS	23 LINDEN GARDENS	LONDON W2	ENGLAND
CHRISTIE, LOU	SINGER	YOUNG, 1645 E 50TH ST #10-H	CHICAGO, IL	60615
CHRISTIE, SHANNON	ACTRESS	5330 LANKERSHIM BLVD #210	NORTH HOLLYWOOD, CA	91601
CHRISTIN, JUDITH	MEZZO-SOPRANO	CAMI, 165 W 57TH ST	NEW YORK, NY	10019
CHRISTINE, VIRGINIA	ACTRESS	12348 ROCHEDALE LN	LOS ANGELES, CA	90049
CHRISTMAN, GLADYS	WRITER	8955 BEVERLY BLVD	LOS ANGELES, CA	90048
CHRISTMAN, RICK	TENOR	LIEBERMAN, 11 RIVERSIDE DR	NEW YORK, NY	10023
CHRISTMAN, SHARON	SOPRANO	61 W 62ND ST #6-F	NEW YORK, NY	10023
CHRISTMAS	ROCK & ROLL GROUP	BIG TIME RECORDS COMPANY 6777 HOLLYWOOD BLVD	HOLLYWOOD, CA	90028
CHRISTMAS, ERIC	ACTOR	211 S BEVERLY DR #107	BEVERLY HILLS, CA	90212
CHRISTOPHER, A L	TV WRITER	8955 BEVERLY BLVD	LOS ANGELES, CA	90048
CHRISTOPHER, AL	NEWS CORRESPONDENT	7858 SNEAD LN	FALLS CHURCH, VA	22043
CHRISTOPHER, ALTA	ACTRESS	5193 CANOGA AVE	WOODLAND HILLS, CA	91364
CHRISTOPHER, DENNIS	ACTOR	151 S EL CAMINO DR	BEVERLY HILLS, CA	90212
CHRISTOPHER, EUNICE	ACTRESS	3800 BARHAM BLVD #303	LOS ANGELES, CA	90068

Name	Occupation	Address	City	ZIP
CHRISTOPHER, FAITH	ACTRESS	3330 BARHAM BLVD #103	LOS ANGELES, CA	90068
CHRISTOPHER, GUY	ACTOR	1418 N HIGHLAND AVE #102	LOS ANGELES, CA	90028
CHRISTOPHER, JOHNNY	GUITARIST	POST OFFICE BOX 120485	NASHVILLE, TN	37212
CHRISTOPHER, JORDAN	ACTOR	300 CENTRAL PARK E	NEW YORK, NY	10024
CHRISTOPHER, KEVIN	TV HOST	TBS, 1050 TECHWOOD DR, NW	ATLANTA, GA	30318
CHRISTOPHER, MARC	ACTOR	14027 GARBER ST	ARLETA, CA	91331
CHRISTOPHER, P	SINGER	JOYCE, 2028 CHESTNUT ST	PHILADELPHIA, PA	19103
CHRISTOPHER, ROBERT J	ACTOR	4789 VINELAND AVE #100	NORTH HOLLYWOOD, CA	91602
CHRISTOPHER, SYBIL BURTON	ACTRESS	300 CENTRAL PARK W	NEW YORK, NY	10024
CHRISTOPHER, THOM	ACTOR	1930 CENTURY PARK W #303	LOS ANGELES, CA	90067
CHRISTOPHER, WILLIAM	ACTOR	574 BELLEFONTAINE ST	PASADENA, CA	91105
CHRISTOPOULOS, GEORGE	ACTOR	418 REES ST #B	PLAYA DEL REY, CA	90291
CHRISTOS, MARIANNA	SOPRANO	CAMI, 165 W 57TH ST	NEW YORK, NY	10019
CHRISTY, JEFFREY B	NEWS CORRESPONDENT	1126 S CAROLINA AVE, SE	WASHINGTON, DC	20003
CHROMCHAK, RUDY	ACTOR	1330 N HARPER AVE #106	LOS ANGELES, CA	90046
CHRONIS, BELLA	ACTRESS	845 S MANSFIELD AVE	LOS ANGELES, CA	90036
CHRONOPOULOS, GENE	ACTOR	1551 MIDVALE AVE	LOS ANGELES, CA	90024
CHRUCH, GEORGE J	WRITER-EDITOR	TIME/TIME & LIFE BLDG		
CHRYSTAL, CHRIS	NEWS CORRESPONDENT	2939 VAN NESS ST #216, NW	WASHINGTON, DC	20008
CHRZAN, NAT	NEWS EDITOR	THE NATIONAL ENQUIRER		
		600 SE COAST AVE	LANTANA, FL	33464
CHU, DANIEL	WRITER-EDITOR	PEOPLE/TIME & LIFE BLDG		
		ROCKEFELLER CENTER	NEW YORK, NY	10020
CHUA-EOAN, HOWARD G	NEWS REPORTER	TIME/TIME & LIFE BLDG		
		ROCKEFELLER CENTER	NEW YORK, NY	10020
CHUDLER, CRAIG	NEWS CORRESPONDENT	1825 "T" ST, NW	WASHINGTON, DC	20009
CHUDNOW, BYRON	TV DIRECTOR-PRODUCER	918 S WESTGATE AVE #4	LOS ANGELES, CA	90049
CHUDNOW, RICHARD G	ACTOR-WRITER	8955 BEVERLY BLVD	LOS ANGELES, CA	90048
CHULAY, JOHN	TV DIRECTOR	317 MARKHAM PL	PASADENA, CA	91105
CHUNG, CONNIE	NEWS CORRESPONDENT	NBC-TV, NEWS DEPARTMENT		
		30 ROCKEFELLER PLAZA	NEW YORK, NY	10112
CHUNG, KYUNG WHA	VIOLINIST	CAMI, 165 W 57TH ST	NEW YORK, NY	10019
CHUNG, MYUNG-WHUM	CONDUCTOR	ICM, 40 W 57TH ST	NEW YORK, NY	10019
CHUNG, MYUNG-WHUN	CONDUCTOR	180 W END AVE #21	NEW YORK, NY	10023
CHURCH, JIMMY	GUITARIST	1803 15TH AVE S	NASHVILLE, TN	37212
CHURCH, SUZANNE	ACTRESS	LM AGY, 213-A EDGWARE RD	LONDON W2	ENGLAND
CHURCHILL, DONALD	ACTOR-WRITER	41 FITZROY RD	LONDON NW1	ENGLAND
CHURCHILL, STEVE	FLUTIST	311 SETH PL	ROCKVILLE, MO	20850
CHURNIN, NANCY	TV WRITER	8955 BEVERLY BLVD	LOS ANGELES, CA	90048
CIANI, PAUL	WRITER-PRODUCER	DARRYL BROWN MGMT		
		WIMBLEDON THEATRE	LONDON SW19	ENGLAND
CIANNELLA, GIULIANO	TENOR	CAMI, 165 W 57TH ST	NEW YORK, NY	10019
CIAPPESSONI, PAUL	TV DIRECTOR	THE BARN, MANOR HOUSE CT		
		SHEPPERTON	MIDDLESEX	ENGLAND
CIBBER, COLLEY	TV WRITER	8955 BEVERLY BLVD	LOS ANGELES, CA	90048
CIBELLA, ROSS M	DIRECTOR	1711 BEACON ST	WABAN, MA	02168
CIBELLI, RENATO	ACTOR	245 W 25TH ST	NEW YORK, NY	10001
CICCOLINI, ALDO	PIANIST	IMG ARTISTS, 22 E 71ST ST	NEW YORK, NY	10021
CICHOWSKI, JOHN W	WRITER	555 W 57TH ST #1230	NEW YORK, NY	10019
CIESINSKI, KATHERINE	MEZZO-SOPRANO	CAMI, 165 W 57TH ST	NEW YORK, NY	10019
CIESINSKI, KRISTINE	SOPRANO	CAMI, 165 W 57TH ST	NEW YORK, NY	10019
CILETTI, MILES	WRITER	12237 LA MAIDA ST	NORTH HOLLYWOOD, CA	91607
CIMINO, LEONARDO	ACTOR	10100 SANTA MONICA BLVD #1600	LOS ANGELES, CA	90067
CIMINO, MICHAEL	WRITER-PRODUCER	9015 ALTA CEDRO DR	BEVERLY HILLS, CA	90210
CIMONS, MARLENE F	NEWS CORRESPONDENT	4813 WESTWAY DR	BETHESDA, MD	20816
CINADER, ROBERT A	WRITER-PRODUCER	9046 SUNSET BLVD #202	LOS ANGELES, CA	90069
CINARDO, NICK	ACTOR	18625 CLARK ST #101	TARZANA, CA	91356
CINCOTTA, CARMINE	WRITER	555 W 57TH ST #1230	NEW YORK, NY	10019
CINDERELLA	ROCK & ROLL GROUP	POST OFFICE BOX 642	PAOLI, PA	19301
CINTRON, SHARON	ACTRESS	211 S BEVERLY DR #107	BEVERLY HILLS, CA	90212
CIOFFI, CHARLES	ACTOR	GLOVER AVE	NORWALK, CT	06850
CIOFFI, LOU	NEWS CORRESPONDENT	ABC NEWS, 7 W 66TH ST	NEW YORK, NY	10023
CIOLLI, RITA F	NEWS CORRESPONDENT	1725 NEW HAMPSHIRE AVE, NW	WASHINGTON, DC	20009
CIOMPI QUARTET	STRING QUARTET	POST OFFICE BOX 20548	NEW YORK, NY	10025
CIOROMILA, MARIANA	MEZZO-SOPRANO	CAMI, 165 W 57TH ST	NEW YORK, NY	10019
CIPES, ARIANNE ULMER	FILM EXECUTIVE	3651 STONE CANYON RD	LOS ANGELES, CA	90077
CIPRIANO, EILEEN	ACTRESS	5330 LANKERSHIM BLVD #210	NORTH HOLLYWOOD, CA	91601
CIRACE, ROBERT H	PHOTOGRAPHER	POST OFFICE BOX 3510	ARLINGTON, VA	22203
CIRCUS, CAPTAIN	CANNONBALL ACT	SEE - CAPTAIN CIRCUS		
CIRILLINO, JOHNNY	CLOWN	2701 COTTAGE WY #14	SACRAMENTO, CA	95825
CIRILLO, ANTHONY F	DIRECTOR	37 E 28TH ST	NEW YORK, NY	10016
CIRILLO, LAWRENCE	TV DIRECTOR	1 HARTLAND AVE	HUNTINGTON STATION, NY	11746
CIRIMELE, ALBERT	ACTOR	1044 N SWEETZER AVE	LOS ANGELES, CA	90069
CIRKER, IRA	TV DIRECTOR	235 E 22ND ST	NEW YORK, NY	10010
CIRRONE, PHILIP	WRITER	555 W 57TH ST #1230	NEW YORK, NY	10019
CISEWSKI, LARRY	KNIFETHROWER	POST OFFICE BOX 3819	LA MESA, CA	92044
CITRANO, THOMAS D	TV WRITER	ABC-TV, "GENERAL HOSPITAL"		
		1438 N GOWER ST	LOS ANGELES, CA	90028
CITRON, HERMAN	TALENT AGENT	9255 SUNSET BLVD #910	LOS ANGELES, CA	90069
CITRON, RICHARD D	DIRECTOR-PRODUCER	365 W END AVE	NEW YORK, NY	10024
CITY ON EDGE	ROCK & ROLL GROUP	2256 PEPPERMINT LN	LEMON GROVE, CA	92045
CITYFOLKS COUNTRY BAND	C & W GROUP	CUDE, 519 N HALIFAX AVE	DAYTONA BEACH, FL	32018
CIUPKA, RICHARD	DIRECTOR	71 CORNWALL ST	QUEBEC	CANADA
CIURCA, CLEOPATRA	MEZZO-SOPRANO	CAMI, 165 W 57TH ST	NEW YORK, NY	10019
CIVITA, DIANA	ACTRESS	PARRIOTT, 5159 AMESTOY AVE	ENCINO, CA	91316

Name	Occupation	Address	City	Zip
CIVITELLO, LINDA ANN	WRITER	3741 JASMINE AVE #5	LOS ANGELES, CA	90034
CLAIR, BERNICE	ACTRESS	46 EUCALYPTUS KNOLL	MILL VALLEY, CA	94941
CLAIR, DICK	ACTOR	9744 WILSHIRE BLVD #206	BEVERLY HILLS, CA	90212
CLAIR, ETHLYNE	ACTRESS	FROST, 20174 VILLAGE #2	CAMARILLO, CA	93010
CLAIR, RICHARD	TV WRITER	8955 BEVERLY BLVD	LOS ANGELES, CA	90048
CLAIRE, ADELE	ACTRESS	ATA, 2437 E WASHINGTON BLVD	PASADENA, CA	91104
CLAIRE, JAN	ACTRESS	5330 LANKERSHIM BLVD #210	NORTH HOLLYWOOD, CA	91601
CLAIRMONT, ELVA	WRITER	555 W 57TH ST #1230	NEW YORK, NY	10019
CLAMAN, BARBARA	CASTING DIRECTOR	6565 SUNSET BLVD #412	LOS ANGELES, CA	90028
CLAMAN, JUNE	ACTRESS	4721 LAUREL CANYON BLVD #211	NORTH HOLLYWOOD, CA	91607
CLANCY, MARTIN J	TV DIRECTOR-PRODUCER	ABC-TV, 7 W 66TH ST	NEW YORK, NY	10023
CLANCY, TOM	ACTOR	4123 PATRICK HENRY PL	AQUARA, CA	91301
CLANCY BROTHERS, THE	FOLK GROUP	ROTHSCHILD, 330 E 48TH ST	NEW YORK, NY	10017
CLANTON, DARRELL	SINGER	TAYLOR, 2401 12TH AVE S	NASHVILLE, TN	37204
CLANTON, RONNY H	GUITARIST	109 LINDY MURFF CT	ANTIOCH, TN	37013
CLAPHAM, JODI	WRITER	8955 BEVERLY BLVD	LOS ANGELES, CA	90048
CLAPP, NICHOLAS R	WRITER-PRODUCER	2515 LAUREL PASS AVE	LOS ANGELES, CA	90046
CLAPTON, ERIC	SINGER-GUITARIST	67 BROOK ST	LONDON W1	ENGLAND
CLARDY, LARRY	ACTOR	1203 S LA CIENEGA BLVD #D	LOS ANGELES, CA	90035
CLAREY, CYNTHIA	MEZZO-SOPRANO	119 W 57TH ST #1505	NEW YORK, NY	10019
CLARIDGE, CHRISTIE	ACTRESS	20541 NORTHRIDGE RD	CHATSWORTH, CA	91311
CLARIDGE, WESTBROOK	WRITER	2210 6TH ST	SANTA MONICA, CA	90405
CLARITY, JAMES	NEWS CORRESPONDENT	2130 "P" ST, NW	WASHINGTON, DC	20037
CLARK, AL	FILM PRODUCER	VIRGIN FILMS, 328 KENSAL RD	LONDON W10	ENGLAND
CLARK, ALAN	SINGER-SONGWRITER	POST OFFICE BOX 1062	WEST COVINA, CA	91793
CLARK, ALEXANDER	ACTOR	175 W 79TH ST	NEW YORK, NY	10024
CLARK, ANNA	MODEL	MODELS & PROMOTIONS AGENCY		
		8560 SUNSET BLVD, 10TH FLOOR	LOS ANGELES, CA	90069
CLARK, BARRY F	TV WRITER	8955 BEVERLY BLVD	LOS ANGELES, CA	90048
CLARK, BOB	FILM WRITER-DIRECTOR	9200 SUNSET BLVD #808	LOS ANGELES, CA	90069
CLARK, BOB	NEWS CORRESPONDENT	ABC NEWS, 7 W 66TH ST	NEW YORK, NY	10023
CLARK, BRIAN	SCREENWRITER	8955 BEVERLY BLVD	LOS ANGELES, CA	90048
CLARK, BROOKS	SPORTS WRITER	SPORTS ILLUSTRATED MAGAZINE		
		TIME & LIFE BUILDING		
		ROCKEFELLER CENTER	NEW YORK, NY	10020
CLARK, BRUCE "B D"	SCREENWRITER	KANT, 233 WILSHIRE BLVD	SANTA MONICA, CA	90401
CLARK, BYRON	ACTOR	745 N ALFRED ST #PH	LOS ANGELES, CA	90069
CLARK, CANDY	ACTRESS	10390 SANTA MONICA BLVD #310	LOS ANGELES, CA	90025
CLARK, CHARLES S	NEWS CORRESPONDENT	800 DEVON PL	ALEXANDRIA, VA	22314
CLARK, CHRISTIE	ACTRESS	KNBC-TV, "DAYS OF OUR LIVES"		
		3000 W ALAMEDA AVE	BURBANK, CA	91523
CLARK, CYD	ACTRESS	11922 KLING ST #106	NORTH HOLLYWOOD, CA	91607
CLARK, DANE	ACTOR-DIRECTOR	1680 OLD OAK RD	LOS ANGELES, CA	90049
CLARK, DAVID	DIRECTOR-PRODUCER	CLARABI PRODUCTIONS CO		
		4 HILLCREST GARDENS		
		HINCHLEY, WOOD, ESHER	SURREY KT10 OBS	ENGLAND
CLARK, DAVID C, JR	WRITER	555 W 57TH ST #1230	NEW YORK, NY	10019
CLARK, DAVID W	WRITER	555 W 57TH ST #1230	NEW YORK, NY	10019
CLARK, DENNIS L	WRITER	8955 BEVERLY BLVD	LOS ANGELES, CA	90048
CLARK, DEREK	TV DIRECTOR-PRODUCER	CLARABI PRODUCTIONS CO		
		4 HILLCREST GARDENS		
		HINCHLEY, WOOD, ESHER	SURREY KT10 OBS	ENGLAND
CLARK, DICK	TV HOST-PRODUCER	3003 W OLIVE AVE	BURBANK, CA	91505
CLARK, DICK	SINGER	UTI, 1907 DIVISION ST	NASHVILLE, TN	37202
CLARK, DON A	WRITER	8955 BEVERLY BLVD	LOS ANGELES, CA	90048
CLARK, DORAN	ACTRESS	211 S BEVERLY DR #201	BEVERLY HILLS, CA	90212
CLARK, EDWARD W	PHOTOGRAPHER	4570 MAC ARTHUR BLVD	BETHESDA, MD	20816
CLARK, ELIZABETH	TV WRITER	8955 BEVERLY BLVD	LOS ANGELES, CA	90048
CLARK, EVERT B	NEWS CORRESPONDENT	9605 PINKNEY CT	POTOMAC, MD	20850
CLARK, GLORYETTE	FILM EDITOR	3611 WILLOW CREST AVE	STUDIO CITY, CA	91604
CLARK, GORDON	ACTOR	10000 RIVERSIDE DR #3	TOLUCA LAKE, CA	91602
CLARK, GRAHAM	TENOR	COLBERT, 111 W 57TH ST	NEW YORK, NY	10019
CLARK, GUY	SINGER	ROUTE #4, CROSSWINDS	MOUNT JULIET, TN	37122
CLARK, JAMES	TENOR	POST OFFICE BOX 884	NEW YORK, NY	10023
CLARK, JAMES A	FILM DIRECTOR	34 KENSINGTON SQ	LONDON W8	ENGLAND
CLARK, JAMES B	DIRECTOR	10051-5 VALLEY CIRCLE BLVD	CHATSWORTH, CA	91311
CLARK, JANET	ACTRESS	6430 SUNSET BLVD #1203	LOS ANGELES, CA	90028
CLARK, JOEL	TV WRITER	8955 BEVERLY BLVD	LOS ANGELES, CA	90048
CLARK, JOHN	TV DIRECTOR	POST OFFICE BOX 1207	TOPANGA CANYON, CA	90290
CLARK, JOHN S, III	WRITER	555 W 57TH ST #1230	NEW YORK, NY	10019
CLARK, KAREN	TV WRITER	8955 BEVERLY BLVD	LOS ANGELES, CA	90048
CLARK, KEN	NEWS REPORTOR	THE CHICAGO TRIBUNE		
		TRIBUNE TOWER		
		435 N MICHIGAN AVE	CHICAGO, IL	60611
CLARK, L KAREEMA	NEWS CORRESPONDENT	5232 N CAPITOL ST	WASHINGTON, DC	20011
CLARK, LARRY	COMEDIAN	1022 N PALM AVE #2	LOS ANGELES, CA	90069
CLARK, LISA S	NEWS CORRESPONDENT	400 N CAPITOL ST, NW	WASHINGTON, DC	20001
CLARK, LYNN	ACTRESS	KNBC-TV, "SANTA BARBARA"		
		3000 W ALAMEDA AVE	BURBANK, CA	91523
CLARK, MARILYN	ACTRESS	135 CENTRAL PARK W	NEW YORK, NY	10023
CLARK, MATT	ACTOR	KOHNER, 9169 SUNSET BLVD	LOS ANGELES, CA	90069
CLARK, MICHAEL	GUITARIST	ROUTE #2, FOREST HARBOR DR	HENDERSONVILLE, TN	37075
CLARK, MICHAEL J	CABLE EXECUTIVE	SHOWTIME ENTERTAINMENT		
		10900 WILSHIRE BLVD	LOS ANGELES, CA	90024
CLARK, NORA GOLDSTEIN	NEWS CORRESPONDENT	6724 2ND ST, NW	WASHINGTON, DC	20012

CLARK, OLIVER	ACTOR	9200 SUNSET BLVD #1210	LOS ANGELES, CA	90069
CLARK, OLIVER	TV WRITER	8955 BEVERLY BLVD	LOS ANGELES, CA	90048
CLARK, PETULA	SINGER-ACTRESS	POST OFFICE BOX 498	QUAKERTOWN, PA	18951
CLARK, R A "RAC"	TV PRODUCER	3003 W OLIVE AVE	BURBANK, CA	91505
CLARK, RICHARD J	BARITONE	61 W 62ND ST #6-F	NEW YORK, NY	10023
CLARK, ROBERT	ORGANIST	15 HIGH ST #621	HARTFORD, CT	06103
CLARK, ROBERT	WRITER-DIRECTOR	DGA, 110 W 57TH ST	NEW YORK, NY	10019
CLARK, ROBERT C	COMPOSER	POST OFFICE BOX 4121	MALIBU, CA	90265
CLARK, ROBIN S	DIRECTOR	CPB, 1901 AVE OF THE STARS	LOS ANGELES, CA	90067
CLARK, RONALD	WRITER	151 S EL CAMINO DR	BEVERLY HILLS, CA	90212
CLARK, ROSS	ACTOR	336 HERMITAGE LN	AZUSA, CA	91702
CLARK, ROY	SINGER-GUITARIST	1800 FORREST BLVD	TULSA, OK	74114
CLARK, ROYDON E	DIRECTOR	9483 WHEATLAND AVE	SUNLAND, CA	91040
CLARK, STEPHEN R	NEWS CORRESPONDENT	236 MASSACHUSETTS AVE, NE	WASHINGTON, DC	20002
CLARK, SUSAN	ACTRESS	7943 WOODROW WILSON DR	LOS ANGELES, CA	90046
CLARK, T ELLSWORTH	ACTOR	10850 RIVERSIDE DR #505	NORTH HOLLYWOOD, CA	91602
CLARK, TEX	GUITARIST	POST OFFICE BOX 365	GULF BREEZE, FL	32561
CLARK, THEODORE E	NEWS CORRESPONDENT	1615 "Q" ST, NW	WASHINGTON, DC	20009
CLARK, TIMOTHY	BARITONE	GREAT LAKES PERFORMING		
		310 E WASHINGTON ST	ANN ARBOR, MI	48104
CLARK, TIMOTHY B	NEWS CORRESPONDENT	5532 GREYSTONE ST	CHEVY CHASE, MD	20815
CLARK, TRAVIS	CASTING DIRECTOR	POST OFFICE BOX 69-1495	LOS ANGELES, CA	90069
CLARK, WAYNE	FASHION DESIGNER	49 SPADINA AVE, 5TH FLOOR	TORONTO, ONT M5V 2J1	CANADA
CLARK, WILLIAM	TV WRITER	8955 BEVERLY BLVD	LOS ANGELES, CA	90048
CLARK, WILLIAM G	ACTOR	4908 FRAN PL #203	ALEXANDRIA, VA	22312
CLARK SISTERS, THE	GOSPEL TRIO	10100 SANTA MONICA BLVD #1600	LOS ANGELES, CA	90067
CLARK-PENDARVIS, CHINA	WRITER	555 W 57TH ST #1230	NEW YORK, NY	10019
CLARKE, ALAN	TV DIRECTOR	123 HARLEY ST	LONDON W1	ENGLAND
CLARKE, ANGELA	ACTRESS	7557 MULHOLLAND DR	LOS ANGELES, CA	90046
CLARKE, ARTHUR C	AUTHOR	4715 GREGORY'S RD	COLOMBO 7	CEYLON
CLARKE, BOB	CARTOONIST	MAD MAGAZINE, INC		
		485 MADISON AVE	NEW YORK, NY	10022
CLARKE, BRIAN D	DIRECTOR	DGA, 110 W 57TH ST	NEW YORK, NY	10019
CLARKE, BRIAN PATRICK	ACTOR	5 TOLUCA ESTATES DR	NORTH HOLLYWOOD, CA	91602
CLARKE, CAMERON	ACTOR	1585 CROSSROADS OF WORLD #107	LOS ANGELES, CA	90028
CLARKE, COLEMAN I	NEWS CORRESPONDENT	1333 "H" ST, NW	WASHINGTON, DC	20005
CLARKE, DAVID	ACTOR	225 CENTRAL PARK W	NEW YORK, NY	10024
CLARKE, GERALD	WRITER-EDITOR	TIME/TIME & LIFE BLDG		
		ROCKEFELLER CENTER	NEW YORK, NY	10020
CLARKE, JAMES D	NEWS CORRESPONDENT	4461 CONNECTICUT AVE, NW	WASHINGTON, DC	20008
CLARKE, JOHN	ACTOR	KNBC-TV, "DAYS OF OUR LIVES"		
		3000 W ALAMEDA AVE	BURBANK, CA	91523
CLARKE, JORDAN	ACTOR	CBS-TV, "THE GUIDING LIGHT"		
		51 W 52ND ST	NEW YORK, NY	10019
CLARKE, KARIN	SOPRANO	JCB, 155 W 68TH ST	NEW YORK, NY	10023
CLARKE, KATHARINE	WRITER	19 W 44TH ST #1500	NEW YORK, NY	10036
CLARKE, LARRY	WRESTLER	NATIONAL WRESTLING ALLIANCE		
		JIM CROCKETT PROMOTIONS		
		421 BRIARBEND DR	CHARLOTTE, NC	28209
CLARKE, LOGAN	ACTOR	1350 N HIGHLAND AVE #24	HOLLYWOOD, CA	90028
CLARKE, MAE	ACTRESS	23388 MULHOLLAND DR	WOODLAND HILLS, CA	91364
CLARKE, MALCOLM	TV DIRECTOR	314 E 41ST ST #805	NEW YORK, NY	10017
CLARKE, MARGARET	WRITER	555 W 57TH ST #1230	NEW YORK, NY	10019
CLARKE, RICHARD	ACTOR	40 STUYVESANT ST	NEW YORK, NY	10003
CLARKE, RICHARD W	ACTOR	350 E 57TH ST	NEW YORK, NY	10022
CLARKE, ROBERT	ACTOR	4841 GENTRY AVE	NORTH HOLLYWOOD, CA	91607
CLARKE, ROY	WRITER	LEMON, 24 POTTERY LN	LONDON W11	ENGLAND
CLARKE, STANLEY	GUITARIST-COMPOSER	POST OFFICE BOX 25863	LOS ANGELES, CA	90025
CLARKE, TRISHA	ACTRESS	DOWER HOUSE, CALEHILL PARK		
		LITTLE CHART, ASHFORD	KENT	ENGLAND
CLARKSON, CHANNING	CASTING DIRECTOR	LONG, 8615 SHERWOOD DR	LOS ANGELES, CA	90069
CLARKSON, CHANNING	ACTOR	POST OFFICE BOX 441	PACIFIC PALISADES, CA	90272
CLARKSON, LANA	ACTRESS	3151 W CAHUENGA BLVD #310	LOS ANGELES, CA	90068
CLARKSON, MARIANNE	TV WRITER	8955 BEVERLY BLVD	LOS ANGELES, CA	90048
CLARKSON, STEPHEN	WRITER-PRODUCER	PECKHAMS, NORTH LN		
		WEST HOATHLY		
		EAST GRINSTEAD	SUSSEX	ENGLAND
CLARKSON, WILLIAM C	TV DIRECTOR	1449 W GEORGE ST	CHICAGO, IL	60614
CLARY, ROBERT	ACTOR	10001 SUNDIAL LN	BEVERLY HILLS, CA	90210
CLARY, TIMOTHY A	PHOTOGRAPHER	707 "A" ST, NE	WASHINGTON, DC	20002
CLASH, THE	ROCK & ROLL GROUP	268 CAMDEN RD	LONDON NW1	ENGLAND
CLASSICS IV	ROCK & ROLL GROUP	1650 BROADWAY #611	NEW YORK, NY	10019
CLATWORTHY, DAVID	BARITONE	59 E 54TH ST #81	NEW YORK, NY	10022
CLAUDIER, ANNETTE	ACTRESS	208 S BEVERLY DR #4	BEVERLY HILLS, CA	90212
CLAUDIO, ANDREA	ACTRESS	3644 BARCELONA ST	LAS VEGAS, NV	89121
CLAUDIO, JEAN	ACTOR	9255 SUNSET BLVD #505	LOS ANGELES, CA	90069
CLAUSEN, ALF H	COMPOSER-CONDUCTOR	3853 ROYAL WOODS DR	SHERMAN OAKS, CA	91403
CLAUSEN, ALIS	ACTRESS	1208 E AVE "R" #2	PALMDALE, CA	93550
CLAUSER, SUZANNE	WRITER	ICM, 8899 BEVERLY BLVD	LOS ANGELES, CA	90048
CLAUSI, JOHN	BANJOIST	517 ALEXANDER DR	FRANKLIN, TN	37064
CLAUSSEN, MARC J	DIRECTOR	520 N MICHIGAN AVE #436	CHICAGO, IL	60611
CLAVEL, ROBERT	COMPOSER	2024 RUE EMILE-DUBOIS	PARIS 75014	FRANCE
CLAVELL, JAMES	WRITER-PRODUCER	2006 THAYER AVE	LOS ANGELES, CA	90025
CLAVER, BOB	DIRECTOR-PRODUCER	22244 PACIFIC COAST HWY	MALIBU, CA	90265
CLAWSON, TIM	SCREENWRITER	8955 BEVERLY BLVD	LOS ANGELES, CA	90048

Name	Occupation	Address	City	Code
CLAXTON, NICHOLAS	DIRECTOR-PRODUCER	FRASER, 91 REGENT ST	LONDON W1	ENGLAND
CLAXTON, WILLIAM F	TV DIRECTOR-PRODUCER	1065 NAPOLI DR	PACIFIC PALISADES, CA	90272
CLAXTON, WILLIAM J	DIRECTOR	1368 ANGELO DR	BEVERLY HILLS, CA	90210
CLAY, BRUCE	WRESTLER	SEE - REED, BUTCH "THE NATURAL"		
CLAY, JAMIE	GUITARIST	815 HAMBLEN RD	MADISON, TN	37115
CLAY, JUANIN	ACTRESS	200 W 57TH ST #1303	NEW YORK, NY	10019
CLAY, MARCELLO R	ACTOR	4845 CLELAND AVE	LOS ANGELES, CA	90065
CLAY, NICHOLAS	ACTOR	WHITE, 31 KINGS RD	LONDON SW3	ENGLAND
CLAYBORNE, ROY	SINGER	POST OFFICE BOX 740368	HOUSTON, TX	77274
CLAYBURGH, JILL	ACTRESS	10318 VIRETTA LN	LOS ANGELES, CA	90024
CLAYTON, EDGAR	DOBROIST	ROUTE #6, BOX 45	HAMILTON, AL	35570
CLAYTON, JACK	FILM DIRECTOR	THE HERON'S FLIGHT		
		HIGHFIELD PARK, MARLOW	BUCKS	ENGLAND
CLAYTON, KENNY	COMPOSER-CONDUCTOR	BRUNSKILL, 169 QUEENSGATE #8	LONDON SW 7	ENGLAND
CLAYTON, LEE TRUELOVE	GUITARIST	35 MUSIC SQUARE E	NASHVILLE, TN	37203
CLAYTON, MILES	ACTOR	918 MALTMAN AVE	LOS ANGELES, CA	90026
CLAYTON, THE	LARIATS & WHIPS	HALL, 138 FROG HOLLOW RD	CHURCHVILLE, PA	18966
CLAYTON, WILLIAM E	NEWS CORRESPONDENT	3402 HALCYON DR	ALEXANDRIA, VA	22305
CLAYTON, WILLIAM F	ACTOR	CASSELL, 843 N SYCAMORE AVE	LOS ANGELES, CA	90038
CLAYWORTH, JUNE	ACTRESS	1641 VETERAN AVE	LOS ANGELES, CA	90024
CLEAMANN, WILLIAM J	NEWS CORRESPONDENT	4913 STICKLEY RD	ROCKVILLE, MD	20852
CLEARLIGHT	ROCK & ROLL GROUP	41 BRITAIN ST #200	TORONTO, ONT	CANADA
CLEARY, DANIEL J	MUSIC ARRANGER	810 BELLEVUE RD #100	NASHVILLE, TN	37221
CLEARY, EILEEN S	NEWS CORRESPONDENT	400 N CAPITOL ST, NW	WASHINGTON, DC	20001
CLEAVES, ROBERT	ACTOR	5432 LA MIRADA AVE	LOS ANGELES, CA	90029
CLEESE, JOHN	ACTOR-WRITER	ROGER HANCOCK MANAGEMENT		
		8 WATERLOO PL, PALL MALL	LONDON SW1Y 4AW	ENGLAND
CLEFTONES, THE	VOCAL GROUP	MARS, 168 ORCHID DR	PEARL RIVER, NY	10965
CLEGG, TERENCE	FILM PRODUCER	51 HOLLAND ST	LONDON W8 8JB	ENGLAND
CLEIN, HAROLD	WRITER	8836 LOOKOUT MOUNTAIN AVE	LOS ANGELES, CA	90046
CLEM-ALLEN, CHERYL	MODEL	POST OFFICE BOX 2338	BEVERLY HILLS, CA	90213
CLEMENCIC, RENE	CONDUCTOR	1182 MARKET ST #311	SAN FRANCISCO, CA	94102
CLEMENS, BRIAN H	TV WRITER-PRODUCER	REDWAY, 16 BERNERS ST	LONDON W1	ENGLAND
CLEMENS, ROGER	BASEBALL	10131 BEEKMAN PLACE DR	HOUSTON, TX	77043
CLEMENT, JACK	GUITARIST	POST OFFICE BOX 120477	NASHVILLE, TN	37212
CLEMENT, JOSEPH E	WRITER	555 W 57TH ST #1230	NEW YORK, NY	10019
CLEMENT, RENE	FILM DIRECTOR	91 AVE HENRI-MARTIN	PARIS 75016	FRANCE
CLEMENT, RICHARD	WRITER-PRODUCER	37 CLAREVILLE ST	LONDON SW1	ENGLAND
CLEMENTE, JOHN R	DIRECTOR	1955 MONON ST	LOS ANGELES, CA	90027
CLEMENTE, MICHAEL A	WRITER	555 W 57TH ST #1230	NEW YORK, NY	10019
CLEMENTS, BOOTS	SINGER	POST OFFICE BOX 8875	UNIVERSAL CITY, CA	91608
CLEMENTS, CAL	PRODUCER	MCA/UNIVERSAL STUDIOS, INC		
		100 UNIVERSAL CITY PLAZA	UNIVERSAL CITY, CA	91608
CLEMENTS, CALVIN J, SR	TV WRITER	18796 PASADERO DR	TARZANA, CA	91356
CLEMENTS, CALVIN, JR	TV WRITER	23050 CASS AVE	WOODLAND HILLS, CA	91364
CLEMENTS, JACK C	WRITER	8955 BEVERLY BLVD	LOS ANGELES, CA	90048
CLEMENTS, RANDY	ACTOR	250 W 57TH ST #2317	NEW YORK, NY	10107
CLEMENTS, RICHARD	COMPOSER-CONDUCTOR	5000 CALATRANA DR	WOODLAND HILLS, CA	91364
CLEMENTS, SIR JOHN	ACTOR	7 ROYAL CRESCENT, BRIGHTON	SUSSEX	ENGLAND
CLEMENTS, STEVE	TV WRITER	8955 BEVERLY BLVD	LOS ANGELES, CA	90048
CLEMENTS, VASSAR	FIDDLER-COMPOSER	POST OFFICE BOX 397	MOUNT JULIET, TN	37122
CLEMENTS, ZEKE	MANDOLINIST	POST OFFICE BOX 22035	NASHVILLE, TN	37202
CLEMMONS, LARRY	WRITER	8955 BEVERLY BLVD	LOS ANGELES, CA	90048
CLEMMONS HERITAGE GOSPEL SINGER	GOSPEL GROUP	CLEMMONS, 1203 E ETHEL ST	DOUGLAS, GA	31333
CLEMONS, CLARENCE	SINGER-SAXOPHONIST	SANFORD-NEIMAN MGMT		
		701 IVY ST	PITTSBURGH, PA	15232
CLEMONS, CLARENCE & THE RED	ROCK & ROLL GROUP	ICM, 40 W 57TH ST	NEW YORK, NY	10019
CLEMONS, JOHN	WRITER	8955 BEVERLY BLVD	LOS ANGELES, CA	90048
CLEMONS, REBECCA	ACTRESS	10920 WILSHIRE BLVD #220	LOS ANGELES, CA	90024
CLENNON, DAVID	ACTOR	1476 S SHERBOURNE DR	LOS ANGELES, CA	90035
CLEPPER, PATRICK M	WRITER	GLASS, 28 BERKELEY SQ	LONDON W1X 6HD	ENGLAND
CLEVELAND, ODESSA	ACTRESS	6058 FAIR AVE	NORTH HOLLYWOOD, CA	91606
CLEVELAND, PATIENCE	ACTRESS	21321 PROVIDENCIA ST	WOODLAND HILLS, CA	91364
CLEVELAND QUARTET	MUSIC ENSEMBLE	ICM, 40 W 57TH ST	NEW YORK, NY	10019
CLIBURN, VAN	PIANIST	455 WILDER PL	SHREVEPORT, LA	71104
CLIFF, JIMMY	SINGER	10100 SANTA MONICA BLVD #1600	LOS ANGELES, CA	90067
CLIFFHANGERS, THE	C & W GROUP	2791 COTTAGE WY #14	SACRAMENTO, CA	95825
CLIFFORD, GARRY	NEWS CORRESPONDENT	146 GRAFTON ST	CHEVY CHASE, MD	20815
CLIFFORD, GRAEME	DIRECTOR	21750 CASTLEWOOD DR	MALIBU, CA	90265
CLIFFORD, JACQUI & FURY	MUSICAL GROUP	AZTEC, 20531 PLUMMER ST	CHATSWORTH, CA	91311
CLIFFORD, LINDA	SINGER	BORZOI MUSIC ARTISTS		
		222 DUNCAN ST	SAN FRANCISCO, CA	94131
CLIFFORD, MIKE	SINGER	3518 W CAHUENGA BLVD #209	LOS ANGELES, CA	90068
CLIFFORD, ROBERT J	COMPOSER	14114 GLADESIDE DR	LA MIRADA, CA	90638
CLIFT, ELEANOR	NEWS CORRESPONDENT	5455 30TH ST, NW	WASHINGTON, DC	20015
CLIFT, RALPH M	ACTOR	5111 DENNY AVE #6	NORTH HOLLYWOOD, CA	91601
CLIFT, W BROOKS	DIRECTOR	5455 30TH ST, NW	WASHINGTON, DC	20015
CLIFTON, GEORGE	ACTOR	9469 BEACHY AVE	ARLETA, CA	91331
CLIFTON, PATTI	ACTRESS	7060 HOLLYWOOD BLVD #610	LOS ANGELES, CA	90028
CLIFTONES, THE	VOCAL GROUP	MARS, 168 ORCHID DR	PEARL RIVER, NY	10965
CLIMAX BLUES BAND	ROCK & ROLL GROUP	3 E 54TH ST #1400	NEW YORK, NY	10022
CLINE, HAROLD "DICK"	TV DIRECTOR	NBC TELEVISION NETWORK		
		30 ROCKEFELLER PLAZA	NEW YORK, NY	10112
CLINE, RICHARD	CARTOONIST	POST OFFICE BOX 4203	NEW YORK, NY	10017

Name	Occupation	Address	City	Zip
CLINE, TAMMY	SINGER	2701 COTTAGE WY #14	SACRAMENTO, CA	95825
CLINE, THORNTON	PIANIST	1010 10TH AVE S	NASHVILLE, TN	37212
CLINGER, DEBRA	ACTRESS	4415 AUCKLAND AVE	HOLLYWOOD, CA	91602
CLINTO, EDWARD	SCREENWRITER	555 W 57TH ST #1230	NEW YORK, NY	10019
CLINTON, GEORGE	SINGER	EGMITT INC, ARCHIE IVY		
		2418 W THOREAU ST	INGLEWOOD, CA	90303
CLISE, JOHN MICHAEL	GUITARIST	513 E MAIN ST	WAVERLY, TN	37185
CLIVE, JOHN	ACTOR-WRITER	11 QUEEN'S CRESCENT, RICHMOND	SURREY	ENGLAND
CLOEREC, RENE	COMPOSER	7 RUE DU PRES-V-PAUCHET	VAUCRESSON 92420	FRANCE
CLOHERTY, JOHN J, JR	NEWS CORRESPONDENT	NBC-TV, NEWS DEPARTMENT		
		4001 NEBRASKA AVE, NW	WASHINGTON, DC	20016
CLOKE, JOHN	ACTOR	HUDSON HOUSE, BOX 7082	ARDSLEY-ON-HUDSON, NY	10503
CLONES, THE	ROCK & ROLL GROUP	HUMAN, 6219 MILLBROOK RD	BRENTWOOD, TN	37027
CLOONEY, ROSEMARY	SINGER	1019 N ROXBURY DR	BEVERLY HILLS, CA	90210
CLOOSE, ROBERT	DIRECTOR	454 HOT SPRING RD	SANTA BARBARA, CA	93108
CLORE, LEON	FILM PRODUCER	FILM CONTRACTS, LTD		
		2 LOWER JAMES ST	LONDON W1R 3PN	ENGLAND
CLOSE, DEL	ACTOR	1509 N CRESCENT HGTS BLVD #7	LOS ANGELES, CA	90069
CLOSE, GLENN	ACTRESS	969 5TH AVE	NEW YORK, NY	10021
CLOSE, SHIRLEY	MEZZO-SOPRANO	MUNRO, 334 W 72ND ST	NEW YORK, NY	10023
CLOTH, SHERWIN	WRITER	555 W 57TH ST #1230	NEW YORK, NY	10019
CLOTHIER, BARRY	BODYBUILDER	1456 GUERRERO ST	SAN FRANCISCO, CA	94110
CLOTWORTHY, ROBERT	ACTOR	122 S HARPER AVE	LOS ANGELES, CA	90048
CLOUD, HAMILTON S, II	TV EXECUTIVE	NBC-TV, 3000 W ALAMEDA AVE	BURBANK, CA	91523
CLOUGH, APRIL	ACTRESS	LIGHT, 113 N ROBERTSON BLVD	LOS ANGELES, CA	90048
CLOUGH, BRENDA W	NEWS CORRESPONDENT	9872 SWEET MINT DR	VIENNA, VA	22180
CLOUGH, JOHN SCOTT	ACTOR	KOHNER, 9169 SUNSET BLVD	LOS ANGELES, CA	90069
CLOUSE, ROBERT	FILM WRITER-DIRECTOR	32356 W MULHOLLAND WY	MALIBU, CA	90265
CLOVER, DAVID	ACTOR	8961 SUNSET BLVD #B	LOS ANGELES, CA	90069
CLOVERS, THE	VOCAL GROUP	POST OFFICE BOX 262	CARTERET, NJ	07008
CLOWARD, CONSTANCE	SOPRANO	61 W 62ND ST #6-F	NEW YORK, NY	10023
CLOWER, JERRY	COMEDIAN	POST OFFICE BOX 121089	NASHVILLE, TN	37212
CLUB FOOT ORCHESTRA	ROCK & ROLL GROUP	2440 16TH ST #213	SAN FRANCISCO, CA	94103
CLUESS, CHRISTOPHER J	WRITER	1112 MAPLE ST	SANTA MONICA, CA	90405
CLURMAN, HAROLD	FILM CRITIC	205 W 57TH ST	NEW YORK, NY	10019
CLUTTERBUCK, GRAHAM	FILM PRODUCER	FILMFAIR, JACOBS WELL MEWS	LONDON W1	ENGLND
CLYDE, JEREMY	ACT-SING-COMP	9744 WILSHIRE BLVD #206	BEVERLY HILLS, CA	90212
COANE, JAMES B	DIRECTOR	240 CENTRAL PARK S	NEW YORK, NY	10019
COASTERS, THE	VOCAL GROUP	BROTHERS, 141 DUNBAR AVE	FORDS, NJ	08863
COATES, ANNE	FILM PRODUCER	64 CHELSEA PARK GARDENS	LONDON SW3	ENGLAND
COATES, CAROLYN	ACTRESS	211 S BEVERLY DR #201	BEVERLY HILLS, CA	90212
COATES, JUDITH A	NEWS CORRESPONDENT	1825 "K" ST, NW	WASHINGTON, DC	20006
COATES, KEVIN PAUL	WRITER	8955 BEVERLY BLVD	LOS ANGELES, CA	90048
COATES, MATTHEW H	NEWS CORRESPONDENT	AMERICAN UNIVERSITY		
		4400 MASSACUSETTS AVE, NW	WASHINGTON, DC	20016
COATES, ODIA	SINGER	1061 E FLAMINGO RD #7	LAS VEGAS, NV	89119
COATES, PHYLLIS	ACTRESS	POST OFFICE BOX 3664	CARMEL, CA	93921
COATES-WEST, CAROLE	TV EXECUTIVE	NBC-TV, 3000 W ALAMEDA AVE	BURBANK, CA	91523
COBB, ARNETT	MUSICIAN	9777 HARWIN ST #101	HOUSTON, TX	77036
COBB, CATLIN	DANCER	AFFILIATE ARTISTS, INC		
		37 W 65TH ST, 6TH FLOOR	NEW YORK, NY	10023
COBB, CECIL RAY	GUITARIST	8218 LUREE LN	HERMITAGE, TN	37076
COBB, CHERYL	SOPRANO	POST OFFICE BOX 345	ROOSEVELT, NJ	08555
COBB, JO DIANE	PHOTOGRAPHER	1913 37TH ST, NW	WASHINGTON, DC	20007
COBB, JULIE	ACTRESS	10437 SARAH ST	NORTH HOLLYWOOD, CA	91602
COBB, RANDALL "TEX"	ACTOR-BOXER	2121 AVE OF THE STARS #410	LOS ANGELES, CA	90067
COBB, RON	GUITARIST	6901 STONE CREEK RD	NASHVILLE, TN	37221
COBB, STANLEY	NEWS CORRESPONDENT	8590 MAIN AVE	PASADENA, MD	21122
COBB, TOMMY	GUITARIST	226 BONNABROOK DR	HERMITAGE, TN	37076
COBB, TYRONE	WRITER	8955 BEVERLY BLVD	LOS ANGELES, CA	90048
COBB, VINCENT	ACTOR	1935 LIVONIA AVE	LOS ANGELES, CA	90034
COBEN, SHERRY	TV WRITER	555 W 57TH ST #1230	NEW YORK, NY	10019
COBHAM, BILLY	DRUMMER	POST OFFICE BOX 514	MARIETTA, GA	30061
COBIN, THOMAS P	WRITER	555 W 57TH ST #1230	NEW YORK, NY	10019
COBLENZ, WALTER	FILM-TV PRODUCER	440 S MC CADDEN PL	LOS ANGELES, CA	90020
COBLER, JAN	ACTRESS	8075 W 3RD ST #303	LOS ANGELES, CA	90038
COBURN, DON	BANJOIST	400 SYCAMORE #B-4	FRANKLIN, TN	37064
COBURN, JAMES	ACTOR-DIRECTOR	3930 HOLLYLINE AVE	SHERMAN OAKS, CA	91413
COBURN, PAMELA	SOPRANO	CAMI, 165 W 57TH ST	NEW YORK, NY	10019
COBURN, WILLIAM J	CONDUCTOR	3855 BROADVIEW DR	LOS ANGELES, CA	90068
COCA, IMOGENE	ACTRESS	200 E 66TH ST	NEW YORK, NY	10021
COCCHINI, GEORGE	GUITARIST	600 WHISPERING HILLS DR	NASHVILLE, TN	37211
COCCIA, ANDREA	NEWS CORRESPONDENT	2020 "F" ST #906, NW	WASHINGTON, DC	20006
COCHARIO, DANNY	ACTOR	11751 HORTENSE ST	NORTH HOLLYWOOD, CA	91607
COCHRAN, CHUCK	PIANIST	1011 MANLEY LN	BRENTWOOD, TN	37027
COCHRAN, GARLAND	SONGWRITER	ROUTE #2, BOX 448		
		LATTAMER LN	HENERSONVILLE, TN	37505
COCHRAN, HANK	SINGER-SONGWRITER	POST OFFICE BOX 120537	NASHVILLE, TN	37212
COCHRAN, JOHN	NEWS CORRESPONDENT	NBC-TV, NEWS DEPARTMENT		
		30 ROCKEFELLER PLAZA	NEW YORK, NY	10112
COCHRAN, JOSEPH	WRITER	555 W 57TH ST #1230	NEW YORK, NY	10019
COCHRAN, RONNIE	GUITARIST	104 GREENLAWN DR	HENDERSONVILLE, TN	37075
COCHRAN, TODD T	COMPOSER	5731 TOPANGA CANYON BLVD	WOODLAND HILLS, CA	92367
COCHRAN, WAYNE & THE C C RIDERS	ROCK & ROLL GROUP	13719 VENTURA BLVD #H	SHERMAN OAKS, CA	91423
COCHRAN, WILLIAM	TENOR	59 E 54TH ST #81	NEW YORK, NY	10022

IMOGENE COCA

DAVID ALLAN COE

NATALIE COLE

GARY COLEMAN

PERRY COMO

JOAN COLLINS

PHIL COLLINS

JOHN CONLEE

EARL THOMAS CONLEY

NAME	OCCUPATION	ADDRESS	CITY	ZIP/COUNTRY
COCKBURN, BRUCE	SINGER-SONGWRITER	98 QUEEN ST E #201	TORONTO, ONT M5C 1S6	CANADA
COCKBURN, LESLIE C	WRITER-PRODUCER	DGA, 110 W 57TH ST	NEW YORK, NY	10019
COCKER, JOE	SINGER	435 E 79TH ST	NEW YORK, NY	10021
COCKRELL, FRANK	ACTOR	13408 CHANDLER BLVD	VAN NUYS, CA	91401
COCKS, JAY	MUSIC CRITIC-WRITER	TIME/TIME & LIFE BLDG		
		ROCKEFELLER CENTER	NEW YORK, NY	10020
COCO THE CLOWN	CLOWN	HALL, 138 FROG HOLLOW RD	CHURCHVILLE, PA	18966
CODDINGTON, LYNN	NEWS CORRESPONDENT	3307 PORTER ST, NW	WASHINGTON, DC	20008
CODY, BUCK	SINGER	38 MUSIC SQUARE E #216	NASHVILLE, TN	37203
CODY, COMMANDER, BAND	ROCK & ROLL GROUP	VARIETY ARTISTS INTL, INC		
		9073 NEMO ST, 3RD FLOOR	LOS ANGELES, CA	90069
CODY, IRON EYES	ACTOR	2013 GRIFFITH PARK BLVD	LOS ANGELES, CA	90039
CODY, SEBASTIAN	FILM DIRECTOR	18 PHILLIMORE PL	LONDON W8	ENGLAND
COE, BOYER	BODYBUILDER	POST OFFICE BOX 5877	HUNTINGTON BEACH, CA	92646
COE, DAVID ALLAN	SINGER-SONGWRITER	ROUTE #3, BOX 549	DICKSON, TN	37055
COE, GEORGE	ACTOR	POST OFFICE BOX 5617	BEVERLY HILLS, CA	90210
COE, LIZ	TV WRITER	1511 SUNSET PLAZA DR	LOS ANGELES, CA	90069
COE, MICHELLE	WRITER	555 W 57TH ST #1230	NEW YORK, NY	10019
COELHO, SUSIE	ACTRESS-MODEL	2814 HUTTON DR	BEVERLY HILLS, CA	90210
COEN, FRANKLIN	WRITER	318 N MAPLE DR #402	BEVERLY HILLS, CA	90210
COEN, GUIDO	FILM PRODUCER	KENSINGTON PARK GARDENS		
		4 THE LODGE	LONDON W11	ENGLAND
COFEY, BRIAN	TV WRITER	8955 BEVERLY BLVD	LOS ANGELES, CA	90048
COFFEY, ALDON L	NEWS CORRESPONDENT	5326 LA ROCHELLE CT	ALEXANDRIA, VA	22310
COFFEY, DENNIS	MUSICIAN	19631 W 8 MILE RD	DETROIT, MI	48219
COFFEY, EDWARD HOPE, III	WRITER	9442 SIERRA MAR PL	LOS ANGELES, CA	90069
COFFEY, JOHN L	TV DIRECTOR	54 HAVERFORD RD	HICKSVILLE, NY	11801
COFFEY, JOSEPH F	DIRECTOR	112 E 17TH ST	NEW YORK, NY	10003
COFFEY, NANCY	NEWS CORRESPONDENT	3521 39TH ST, NW	WASHINGTON, DC	20016
COFFEY, RAYMOND R	NEWS CORRESPONDENT	6305 HARDY DR	MC LEAN, VA	22101
COFFIELD, PETER	ACTOR	333 E 13TH ST	NEW YORK, NY	10003
COFFIN, DICK	COMEDIAN	276 CAMBRIDGE ST #4	BOSTON, MA	02134
COFFIN, DICK	IMPRESSIONIST	276 CAMBRIDGE ST #4	BOSTON, MA	02134
COFFIN, JAMES B	NEWS CORRESPONDENT	1220 N MEADE ST #1	ARLINGTON, VA	22209
COFFIN, STANTON	ACTOR	1217 1/8 N FAIRFAX AVE	LOS ANGELES, CA	90046
COFFIN, TRIS	ACTOR	2314 PIER AVE	SANTA MONICA, CA	90405
COFFMAN, MARY B	NEWS CORRESPONDENT	122 "C" ST, NW	WASHINGTON, DC	20001
COFFMAN, RAMON	COLUMNIST	NEWS AMERICA SYNDICATE		
		1703 KAISER AVE	IRVINE, CA	92714
COGAN, DAVID	THEATER PRODUCER	350 5TH AVE	NEW YORK, NY	10001
COGAN, RHODIE	ACTRESS	3800 BARHAM BLVD #303	LOS ANGELES, CA	90068
COGGIN, W ROY	DIRECTOR	64 W 21ST ST	NEW YORK, NY	10010
COGGINS, KRISTINA	ACTRESS	3800 BARHAM BLVD #303	LOS ANGELES, CA	90068
COGHLAN, FRANK	ACTOR	4789 VINELAND AVE #100	NORTH HOLLYWOOD, CA	91602
COGHLAN, FRANK, JR	ACTOR	12522 ARGYLE AVE	LOS ALAMITOS, CA	90720
COGHLAN, LIBBEY	ACTRESS	470 N SAN VICENTE BLVD #1	LOS ANGELES, CA	90048
COGLIANO, PHILIP A	COMPOSER	36 WOODLAND RD	JAMAICA PLAIN, MA	02130
COHAN, JEFFREY	FLUTIST	POST OFFICE BOX U	REDDING, CT	06875
COHAN, MARTIN	WRITER-PRODUCER	5693 SPREADING OAK DR	LOS ANGELES, CA	90068
COHEN, ALEXANDER H	THEATER-TV PRODUCER	THE SHUBERT THEATER		
		225 W 44TH ST	NEW YORK, NY	10036
COHEN, ANNETTE	DIRECTOR	77 ROXBOROUGH DR	TORONTO, ONT M4W 1X2	CANADA
COHEN, BARBARA S	TV EXEC-NEWS CORRES	2617 WOODLEY PL, NW	WASHINGTON, DC	20008
COHEN, BARNEY	WRITER	555 W 57TH ST #1230	NEW YORK, NY	10019
COHEN, BERNARD I	TV PRODUCER	ABC-TV, 7 W 66TH ST	NEW YORK, NY	10023
COHEN, CHARLES Z	SCREENWRITER	8955 BEVERLY BLVD	LOS ANGELES, CA	90048
COHEN, DANIEL A	NEWS CORRESPONDENT	5151 WISCONSIN AVE, NW	WASHINGTON, DC	20016
COHEN, DENIS	COMPOSER-CONDUCTOR	IAPR, KINCORA, BEER RD		
		SEATON	DEVON	ENGLAND
COHEN, ELLIS A	TV WRITER-PRODUCER	920 N KINGS RD #226	LOS ANGELES, CA	90069
COHEN, ERIC	TV WRITER	8955 BEVERLY BLVD	LOS ANGELES, CA	90048
COHEN, FRANKLIN	CLARINETIST	SHAW CONCERTS, 1995 BROADWAY	NEW YORK, NY	10023
COHEN, FRED	CABLE EXECUTIVE	HOME BOX OFFICE PICTURES		
		1100 AVE OF THE AMERICAS	NEW YORK, NY	10036
COHEN, FRED H	TV DIRECTOR	8509 PATTON RD	WYNDMOOR, PA	19118
COHEN, GARY	WRITER	555 W 57TH ST #1230	NEW YORK, NY	10019
COHEN, GERRY	DIRECTOR	250 W 85TH ST	NEW YORK, NY	10024
COHEN, GERRY	TV DIRECTOR	3825 SHANNON RD	LOS ANGELES, CA	90027
COHEN, HAROLD D	CINEMATOGRAPHER	847 COMMONWEALTH AVE	VENICE, CA	90291
COHEN, HARVEY R	COMPOSER	14066-7 VAN NUYS BLVD	ARLETA, CA	91331
COHEN, HERMAN	WRITER-PRODUCER	7 HESTER RD	LONDON SW1	ENGLAND
COHEN, HILDY PARKS	WRITER-PRODUCER	DGA, 110 W 57TH ST	NEW YORK, NY	10019
COHEN, JACOB	COMEDIAN-ACTOR	SEE - DANGERFIELD, RODNEY		
COHEN, JANE E	TV EXECUTIVE	NAB, 1771 "N" ST, NW	WASHINGTON, DC	20036
COHEN, JOSEPH	DIRECTOR-CHOREO	484 W 43RD ST	NEW YORK, NY	10036
COHEN, JOSEPH M	ENTERTAINMENT EXEC	MADISON SQ GARDEN NETWORK		
		2 PENNSYLVANIA PLAZA	NEW YORK, NY	10119
COHEN, LARRY	WRITER-PRODUCER	2111 COLDWATER CANYON DR	BEVERLY HILLS, CA	90210
COHEN, LAWRENCE D	SCREENWRITER	151 S EL CAMINO DR	BEVERLY HILLS, CA	90212
COHEN, LAWRENCE J	TV WRITER	8955 BEVERLY BLVD	LOS ANGELES, CA	90048
COHEN, LEONARD	SINGER-SONGWRITER	ATI, 888 7TH AVE, 21ST FLOOR	NEW YORK, NY	10019
COHEN, LORI B	OBOIST	12025 WASHINGTON ST #42	ALEXANDRIA, VA	22314
COHEN, M CHARLES	WRITER	8955 BEVERLY BLVD	LOS ANGELES, CA	90048
COHEN, MARK H	TV EXECUTIVE	ABC-TV, 1330 AVE OF AMERICAS	NEW YORK, NY	10019
COHEN, MARTY	COMEDIAN	10351 SANTA MONICA BLVD #211	LOS ANGELES, CA	90025

Name	Occupation	Address	City/State	Zip
COHEN, MITCHELL WAYNE	TV WRITER	8383 WILSHIRE BLVD #923	BEVERLY HILLS, CA	90211
COHEN, NAT	FILM DIRECTOR	30 GOLDEN SQ	LONDON W1A 4QX	ENGLAND
COHEN, PAUL	DIRECTOR	15 HIGHLAND RD	WESTPORT, CT	06880
COHEN, RICHARD	NEWS CORRESPONDENT	2617 WOODLEY PL, NW	WASHINGTON, DC	20008
COHEN, RICHARD E	NEWS CORRESPONDENT	2352 N VERNON ST	ARLINGTON, VA	22207
COHEN, RICHARD M	DIRECTOR	585 W END AVE #12-G	NEW YORK, NY	10024
COHEN, ROB	WRITER-PRODUCER	1383 MILLER PL	LOS ANGELES, CA	90069
COHEN, ROB	FILM PRODUCER	1800 CENTURY PARK E #1100	LOS ANGELES, CA	90067
COHEN, ROBERT	CELLIST	SHAW CONCERTS, 1995 BROADWAY	NEW YORK, NY	10023
COHEN, ROBERT CARL	SCREENWRITER	401 S CAMDEN DR #7	BEVERLY HILLS, CA	90212
COHEN, ROBERT L	NEWS CORRESPONDENT	403 11TH ST, SE	WASHINGTON, DC	20003
COHEN, RONALD E	NEWS CORRESPONDENT	8105 WHITES FORD WY	POTOMAC, MD	20854
COHEN, RONALD M	WRITER	2446 N COMMONWEALTH AVE	LOS ANGELES, CA	90027
COHEN, SCOOTER	ACTOR	1717 N HIGHLAND AVE #414	HOLLYWOOD, CA	90028
COHEN, SHARLEEN COOPER	WRITER	1888 CENTURY PARK E #1400	LOS ANGELES, CA	90067
COHEN, STEPHAN L	WRITER	555 W 57TH ST #1230	NEW YORK, NY	10019
COHEN, STEVEN	WRESTLER	SEE - SIMPSON, STEVE		
COHEN, THOMAS A	DIRECTOR-PRODUCER	FREELAND-COPPER, WHITE & COOPER		
		100 CALIFORNIA ST	SAN FRANCISCO, CA	94111
COHEN, WILLIAM	THEATER PRODUCER	THEATRE NOW, 1515 BROADWAY	NEW YORK, NY	10036
COHEN-ROSS, JUDITH L	WRITER	29606 MEADOWMIST WY	AGOURA HILLS, CA	91301
COHL, CLAUDIA	EDITOR-COLUMNIST	FAMILY COMPUTING CO		
		730 BROADWAY	NEW YORK, NY	10003
COHN, ALAN M	WRITER	555 W 57TH ST #1230	NEW YORK, NY	10019
COHN, BRUCE	SCREENWRITER	ICM, 8899 BEVERLY BLVD	LOS ANGELES, CA	90048
COHN, D'VERA	NEWS CORRESPONDENT	5827 MOUNT VERNON DR	ALEXANDRIA, VA	22303
COHN, DAVID	ACTOR	10524 MONOGRAM AVE	GRANADA HILLS, CA	91344
COHN, DAVID	CASTING DIRECTOR	12023 1/2 VENTURA BLVD	STUDIO CITY, CA	91604
COHN, JEFF	TV WRITER	8955 BEVERLY BLVD	LOS ANGELES, CA	90048
COHN, LEON M	NEWS CORRESPONDENT	5448 33RD ST, NW	WASHINGTON, DC	20015
COHN, MARY W	NEWS CORRESPONDENT	5448 33RD ST, NW	WASHINGTON, DC	20015
COHN, SAM	TALENT AGENT	ICM, 40 W 57TH ST	NEW YORK, NY	10019
COHN, VICTOR E	NEWS CORRESPONDENT	6303 CONTENTION CT	BETHESDA, MD	20817
COHODAS, NADINE	NEWS CORRESPONDENT	2122 CALIFORNIA ST #257, NW	WASHINGTON, DC	20008
COHOON, CHRIS S	WRITER	1823 12TH ST #3	SANTA MONICA, CA	90404
COIT, MARGARET	WRITER	386 PARK AVE	RUTHERFORD, NJ	07070
COKER, KATHERINE E	TV WRITER	978 WELLESLEY AVE	LOS ANGELES, CA	90049
COKER, PAUL	CARTOONIST	MAD MAGAZINE, INC		
		485 MADISON AVE	NEW YORK, NY	10022
COKER, PAUL	PIANIST	ANGLO-SWISS ARTISTS MGMT		
		16 MUSWELL HILL RD, HIGHGATE	LONDON N6 5UG	ENGLAND
COKLISS, HARLEY	TV DIRECTOR	25 MILMAN RD	LONDON NW6	ENGLAND
COL LUCKY	RINGMASTER	SEE - LARABEE, COL LUCKY		
COLACIOPPO, TULLIO	CONDUCTOR	POST OFFICE BOX 884	NEW YORK, NY	10023
COLARUSSO, CHARLES A	WRITER	2225 MALAGA RD	LOS ANGELES, CA	90048
COLBERT, CLAUDETTE	ACTRESS	BELLERIVE SAINT PETER	BARBADOS	WEST INDIES
COLBERT, EARL	ACTOR	8051 WILLOW GLEN RD	LOS ANGELES, CA	90046
COLBERT, IVY	ACTRESS	2239 GREENFIELD AVE	LOS ANGELES, CA	90064
COLBERT, ROBERT	ACTOR	151 OCEAN PARK BLVD	SANTA MONICA, CA	90405
COLBERT, THOMAS J	WRITER	8955 BEVERLY BLVD	LOS ANGELES, CA	90048
COLBERT, VERDELL & OFFSPRIN	GOSPEL GROUP	POST OFFICE BOX 2095	PHILADELPHIA, PA	19103
COLBURN, DON	NEWS CORRESPONDENT	5332 29TH ST, NW	WASHINGTON, DC	20015
COLBURN, HOLLY	ACTRESS	8730 SUNSET BLVD #400	LOS ANGELES, CA	90069
COLBURNE, MAURICE	ACTOR	44 AINGER RD	LONDON NW3	ENGLAND
COLBY, ALFRED W	NEWS CORRESPONDENT	5304 ATLEE PL	SPRINGFIELD, VA	22151
COLBY, PHIL	ACTOR	1401 VALLEY VIEW RD #21	GLENDALE, CA	91202
COLBY, RONALD	ACTOR	15010 VENTURA BLVD #219	SHERMAN OAKS, CA	91403
COLBY, RONALD B	WRITER	8955 BEVERLY BLVD	LOS ANGELES, CA	90048
COLCORD, RAY, III	WRITER-MUSICIAN	5453 AGNES AVE	NORTH HOLLYWOOD, CA	91607
COLDER, BEN	SINGER	TESSIER, 505 CANTON PASS	MADISON, TN	37115
COLE, ALEX	COMEDIAN	POST OFFICE BOX 9532	MADISON, WI	53715
COLE, ALLAN	TV WRITER	8955 BEVERLY BLVD	LOS ANGELES, CA	90048
COLE, BENJAMIN R	NEWS CORRESPONDENT	4101 N RANDOLPH ST	ARLINGTON, VA	22207
COLE, BRYAN E	NEWS CORRESPONDENT	2139 WISCONSIN AVE, NW	WASHINGTON, DC	20007
COLE, CHARLES	WRITER	555 W 57TH ST #1230	NEW YORK, NY	10019
COLE, CLAY	WRITER	555 W 57TH ST #1230	NEW YORK, NY	10019
COLE, DALLAS	ACTRESS	3907 W ALAMEDA AVE #101	BURBANK, CA	91505
COLE, DANNY LEE	WRITER	14144 VENTURA BLVD #200	SHERMAN OAKS, CA	91423
COLE, DENNIS	ACTOR	CONTEMPORARY ARTISTS		
		132 S LASKY DR	BEVERLY HILLS, CA	90212
COLE, EVAN	ACTOR	6843 WILLIS AVE	VAN NUYS, CA	91405
COLE, GEORGE	ACTOR	"DONNELLY", NEWNHAM HILL		
		BOTTOM, NETTLEFORD	OXFORDSHIRE	ENGLAND
COLE, LARRY	WRITER	8955 BEVERLY BLVD	LOS ANGELES, CA	90048
COLE, MICHAEL	ACTOR	9000 SUNSET BLVD #801	LOS ANGELES, CA	90069
COLE, NATALIE	SINGER	11780 MOORPARK ST #C	STUDIO CITY, CA	91604
COLE, OLIVIA	ACTRESS	200 W 57TH ST #1303	NEW YORK, NY	10019
COLE, RAY	ACTOR	1350 N HIGHLAND AVE #24	HOLLYWOOD, CA	90028
COLE, ROBERT L	NEWS CORRESPONDENT	330 INDEPENDENCE AVE, SW	WASHINGTON, DC	20547
COLE, ROYAL	WRITER	16754 E AVE "X" #33	LLANO, CA	93544
COLE, SAMI JO	SINGER	MORRIS, 2325 CRESTMOOR DR	NASHVILLE, TN	37215
COLE, SIDNEY	TV DIRECTOR-PRODUCER	40 WARWICK RD	LONDON W5	ENGLAND
COLE, STEVEN	TENOR	CAMI, 165 W 57TH ST	NEW YORK, NY	10019
COLE, TINA	ACTRESS	FELBER, 2126 N CAHUENGA BLVD	LOS ANGELES, CA	90068
COLE, TRILLY	FIDDLER	313 1/2 CHURCH ST	NASHVILLE, TN	37201

Name	Occupation	Address	City	Zip/Country
COLE, VINSON	TENOR	CAMI, 165 W 57TH ST	NEW YORK, NY	10019
COLE, WILLIAM G	NEWS CORRESPONDENT	4461 CONNECTICUT AVE, NW	WASHINGTON, DC	20008
COLE-ADAMS, PETER	NEWS CORRESPONDENT	3308 CATHEDRAL AVE	WASHINGTON, DC	20008
COLEMAN, ALBERT	VIOLINIST	POST OFFICE BOX 723172	ATLANTA, GA	30339
COLEMAN, ALLEN J	WRITER	555 W 57TH ST #1230	NEW YORK, NY	10019
COLEMAN, CHARLOTTE	ACTRESS	40 WARWICK RD	LONDON W5	ENGLAND
COLEMAN, CY	PIANIST-COMPOSER	161 W 54TH ST	NEW YORK, NY	10023
COLEMAN, DABNEY	ACTOR	401 SURFVIEW AVE	PACIFIC PALISADES, CA	90272
COLEMAN, DEL	WRITER	8955 BEVERLY BLVD	LOS ANGELES, CA	90048
COLEMAN, DEREK	ACTOR	15010 VENTURA BLVD #234	SHERMAN OAKS, CA	91403
COLEMAN, DON	ACTOR	POST OFFICE BOX 567	WILLITS, CA	95490
COLEMAN, FRANCIS	TV PRODUCER	45 ONSLOW GARDENS	LONDON N10	ENGLAND
COLEMAN, GARY	ACTOR	9229 SUNSET BLVD #611	LOS ANGELES, CA	90069
COLEMAN, HENRY	TV PRODUCER	AARON SPELLING PRODS		
		4000 WARNER BLVD	BURBANK, CA	91522
COLEMAN, HERBERT	FILM DIRECTOR	687 SAN MORITZ DR		
		FOREST LAKES	BAYFIELD, CO	81122
COLEMAN, HERBERT J	NEWS CORRESPONDENT	300 WALKER RD	GREAT FALLS, VA	22066
COLEMAN, JACK	ACTOR	9220 SUNSET BLVD #625	LOS ANGELES, CA	90069
COLEMAN, JANET	WRITER	8955 BEVERLY BLVD	LOS ANGELES, CA	90048
COLEMAN, JANET	NEWS CORRESPONDENT	1221 EDGEVALE RD	SILVER SPRING, MD	20910
COLEMAN, JOHN	TV EXECUTIVE	2840 MOUNT WILKINSON PARKWAY	ATLANTA, GA	30339
COLEMAN, JOHN W	DIRECTOR	4524 RHODELLA AVE	CLAREMONT, CA	91711
COLEMAN, LINDSEY	SOPRANO	POST OFFICE BOX 884	NEW YORK, NY	10023
COLEMAN, LISA	ACTRESS	45 ONSLOW GARDENS	LONDON N10	ENGLAND
COLEMAN, MICHAEL	GUITARIST	7548 ROLLING RIVER PARKWAY	NASHVILLE, TN	37221
COLEMAN, MILTON R	NEWS CORRESPONDENT	3174 WESTOVER DR, SE	WASHINGTON, DC	20020
COLEMAN, NANCY	ACTRESS	THE MANHATTAN PLAZA		
		484 W 43RD ST	NEW YORK, NY	10036
COLEMAN, ORNETTE	MUSICIAN	POST OFFICE BOX 106	NEW YORK, NY	10013
COLEMAN, RAHN	ACTOR	9220 SUNSET BLVD #202	LOS ANGELES, CA	90069
COLEMAN & STUART	COMEDY DUO	10845 LINDBROOK DR #3	LOS ANGELES, CA	90024
COLENBACK, JOHN	ACTOR	8560 RIDPATH DR	LOS ANGELES, CA	90046
COLES, CHARLES "HONI"	ACTOR	19 W 44TH ST #1500	NEW YORK, NY	10036
COLETTI, APUL	VIOLIST	JCB, 155 W 68TH ST	NEW YORK, NY	10023
COLETTI & CHASTAIN	VIOLIST-VIOLINIST	JCB, 155 W 68TH ST	NEW YORK, NY	10023
COLEY, JOHN FORF	SINGER-SONGWRITER	10100 SANTA MONICA BLVD #1600	LOS ANGELES, CA	90067
COLEY, THOMAS	ACTOR	145 W 79TH ST	NEW YORK, NY	10024
COLFORD, STEVEN W	NEWS CORRESPONDENT	4233 S 35TH ST	ARLINGTON, VA	22206
COLGAN, MICHAEL J	DIRECTOR	DGA, 7950 SUNSET BLVD	LOS ANGELES, CA	90046
COLHOUN, JACK	NEWS CORRESPONDENT	1434 "C" ST, SE	WASHINGTON, DC	20003
COLHOUR, DONALD	TV EXECUTIVE	ABC-TV ENTERTAINMENT CENTER		
		2040 AVE OF THE STARS	LOS ANGELES, CA	90067
COLICK, LEWIS A	WRITER	416 N VISTA ST	LOS ANGELES, CA	90036
COLICOS, JOHN	ACTOR	1757 RIVERSIDE DR	GLENDALE, CA	91201
COLIN, MARGARET	ACTRESS	10 E 44TH ST #700	NEW YORK, NY	10017
COLITTI, RIK	ACTOR	215 SEBONAC RD	SOUTHAMPTON, NY	11968
COLLA, RICHARD	DIRECTOR	2533 GREENVALLEY RD	LOS ANGELES, CA	90046
COLLAMORE, JEROME	ACTOR	147-05 SANFORD AVE	FLUSHING, NY	11355
COLLARD, JEAN-PHILIPPE	PIANIST	LEISER, DORCHESTER TOWERS		
		155 W 68TH ST	NEW YORK, NY	10023
COLLEARY, ROBERT J	TV WRITER	10537 VALLEY SPRING LN	NORTH HOLLYWOOD, CA	91602
COLLEARY, ROBERT M	TV WRITER	10537 VALLEY SPRING LN	NORTH HOLLYWOOD, CA	91602
COLLECTOR, ROBERT O	WRITER	8955 BEVERLY BLVD	LOS ANGELES, CA	90048
COLLENTINE, BARBARA	ACTRESS	151 N SAN VICENTE BLVD #208	BEVERLY HILLS, CA	90211
COLLERAN, WILLIAM	WRITER-PRODUCER	1535 N LAS PALMAS AVE #32	LOS ANGELES, CA	90028
COLLEY, DON PEDRO	ACTOR	4721 LAUREL CANYON BLVD #211	NORTH HOLLYWOOD, CA	91607
COLLEY, KENNETH	ACTOR	64-A NOTTING HILL GATE	LONDON W11	ENGLAND
COLLEY, PETER M	PLAYWRIGHT	250 W 57TH ST	NEW YORK, NY	10107
COLLIE, MARK	GUITARIST	1201 BELL RD	ANTIOCH, TN	37013
COLLIER, ADELINE	TV WRITER-PRODUCER	47 BERWICK ST	LONDON W1V 3RA	ENGLAND
COLLIER, ANNIE	WRITER-EDITOR	US MAGAZINE COMPANY		
		1 DAG HAMMARSKJOLD PLAZA	NEW YORK, NY	10017
COLLIER, BARBARA	SOPRANO	200 W 70TH ST #7-F	NEW YORK, NY	10023
COLLIER, CHERYL	WRITER	555 W 57TH ST #1230	NEW YORK, NY	10019
COLLIER, EARL W	COMPOSER	7745 ETON AVE	CANOGA PARK, CA	91304
COLLIER, ERICH	TV WRITER	8955 BEVERLY BLVD	LOS ANGELES, CA	90048
COLLIER, JAMES	WRITER-PRODUCER	11345 BRILL DR	STUDIO CITY, CA	91604
COLLIER, JENSEN	ACTRESS	POST OFFICE BOX 69405	LOS ANGELES, CA	90069
COLLIER, MARIAN	ACTRESS	427 N CANON DR #205	BEVERLY HILLS, CA	90210
COLLIER, PAUL G	DRUMMER	4301 SOMERDALE LN	CHARLOTTE, NC	28205
COLLIGAN, JOE	ACTOR	LIGHT, 113 N ROBERTSON BLVD	LOS ANGELES, CA	90048
COLLIN, DOROTHY	NEWS CORRESPONDENT	238 9TH ST, SE	WASHINGTON, DC	20003
COLLIN, MARGARET H	COMPOSER	6250 TELEGRAPH RD #109	VENTURA, CA	93003
COLLIN, REGINALD	DIRECTOR-PRODUCER	BAFTA, 195 PICCADILY	LONDON W1V 9LG	ENGLAND
COLLIN, RICHARD	WRITER-PRODUCER	17 PONSONBY PL	LONDON SW1P 4PS	ENGLAND
COLLINGS, DAVID	ACTOR	26 CLERMONT TERR		
		PRESTON PARK, BRIGHTON	SUSSEX	ENGLAND
COLLINS, ALANA	ACTRESS	391 N CAROLWOOD DR	LOS ANGELES, CA	90077
COLLINS, ANNE	WRITER	8955 BEVERLY BLVD	LOS ANGELES, CA	90048
COLLINS, BETH	ACTRESS	10 E 44TH ST #700	NEW YORK, NY	10017
COLLINS, BOB L	DRUMMER	2720 WINSLOW ST	IRVING, TX	75065
COLLINS, BRENT	ACTOR	NBC-TV, "ANOTHER WORLD"		
		30 ROCKEFELLER PLAZA	NEW YORK, NY	10112
COLLINS, BRIAN	ACTOR	208 S BEVERLY DR #4	BEVERLY HILLS, CA	90212
COLLINS, BRIAN	NEWS CORRESPONDENT	4124 EDMUNDS ST #303, NW	WASHINGTON, DC	20007

Name	Occupation	Address	City	Zip
COLLINS, BRUCE D	CABLE EXECUTIVE	400 N CAPITOL ST #155, NW	WASHINGTON, DC	20001
COLLINS, BURTON	ACTOR	1803 CARNEGIE LN	REDONDO BEACH, CA	90278
COLLINS, C T	ACTOR	7616 HOLLYWOOD BL#304	LOS ANGELES, CA	90046
COLLINS, CAREENA	ACTRESS	WESTERN, 15745 STAGG ST	VAN NUYS, CA	91411
COLLINS, CARRIE	TV PRODUCER	400 N CAPITOL ST #155, NW	WASHINGTON, DC	20001
COLLINS, CHARLIE	GUITARIST	2501 SANDY DR	NASHVILLE, TN	37216
COLLINS, CHRISTINA	NEWS CORRESPONDENT	437 15TH ST, NE	WASHINGTON, DC	20002
COLLINS, DOUG	ACTOR	2230 S BEVERLY GLEN BLVD #208	LOS ANGELES, CA	90064
COLLINS, DOUG	BODYGUARD	EVENT MANAGEMENT CO		
		3662 KATELLA AVE	LOS ALAMITOS, CA	90720
COLLINS, ERNIE	ACTOR	14144 DICKENS ST	SHERMAN OAKS, CA	91423
COLLINS, ERNIE L	MUSIC ARRANGER	1515 DENISE CT	ANTIOCH, TN	37013
COLLINS, GARY	ACTOR-TV HOST	2751 HUTTON DR	BEVERLY HILLS, CA	90210
COLLINS, GREG	WRITER	8955 BEVERLY BLVD	LOS ANGELES, CA	90048
COLLINS, GUNTHER	WRITER-PRODUCER	21917 GRANT AVE	TORRANCE, CA	90503
COLLINS, GWEN	GUITARIST	POST OFFICE BOX 1947	LAKE CITY, FL	32055
COLLINS, IAN DAVID	TV DIRECTOR	304 W 88TH ST #3-C	NEW YORK, NY	10024
COLLINS, JACK	ACTOR	CED, 261 S ROBERTSON BLVD	BEVERLY HILLS, CA	90211
COLLINS, JACKIE	AUTHORESS	BLOCK, 7911 3/8 W NORTON AVE	HOLLYWOOD, CA	90046
COLLINS, JAY	MUSIC ARRANGER	POST OFFICE BOX 815	BRENTWOOD, TN	37027
COLLINS, JERRY	GUITARIST	POST OFFICE BOX 1947	LAKE CITY, FL	32055
COLLINS, JOAN	ACTRESS-PRODUCER	1196 CABRILLO DR	BEVERLY HILLS, CA	90210
COLLINS, JOHN	NEWS CORRESPONDENT	5820 JAMESTOWN RD	HYATTSVILLE, MD	20782
COLLINS, JOHN B	TV WRITER	8955 BEVERLY BLVD	LOS ANGELES, CA	90048
COLLINS, JOHNNIE, III	ACTOR	MALIBU LAKE MOUNTATIN CLUB		
		29033 WESTLAKE VISTA DR	AGOURA, CA	92301
COLLINS, JUDY	SINGER-SONGWRITER	POST OFFICE BOX 1296	NEW YORK, NY	10025
COLLINS, KAREN A	NEWS CORRESPONDENT	4420 CONNECTICUT AVE, NW	WASHINGTON, DC	20008
COLLINS, KATE	ACTRESS	ABC-TV, "ALL MY CHILDREN"		
		1330 AVE OF THE AMERICAS	NEW YORK, NY	10019
COLLINS, KEVIN	WRESTLER	POST OFFICE BOX 3859	STAMFORD, CT	06905
COLLINS, LESLIE W	DIRECTOR	BBDO, 385 MADISON AVE	NEW YORK, NY	10017
COLLINS, LEWIS	ACTOR	MOPES FARMHOUSE, DENHAM LN		
		CHALFON SAINT PETER	BUCKS SL9 04H	ENGLAND
COLLINS, MAX	CARTOONIST	TRIBUNE MEDIA SERVICES		
		64 E CONCORD ST	ORLANDO, FL	32801
COLLINS, MICHAEL	WRITER	555 W 57TH ST #1230	NEW YORK, NY	10019
COLLINS, MICHAEL C	ACTOR	1974 HILLCREST RD	LOS ANGELES, CA	90068
COLLINS, MONICA	TV CRITIC	POST OFFICE BOX 500	WASHINGTON, DC	20044
COLLINS, PAT	HYPNOTIST	524 W 57TH ST	NEW YORK, NY	10019
COLLINS, PATRICK	ACTOR	9200 SUNSET BLVD #1210	LOS ANGELES, CA	90069
COLLINS, PATRICK J	NEWS CORRESPONDENT	4461 CONNECTICUT AVE, NW	WASHINGTON, DC	20008
COLLINS, PETER	NEWS CORRESPONDENT	ABC-TV, 7 W 66TH ST	NEW YORK, NY	10019
COLLINS, PHIL	SINGER-DRUMMER	SHALFORD	SURREY	ENGLAND
COLLINS, RICHARD J	WRITER	200 ACARI DR	LOS ANGELES, CA	90049
COLLINS, RICK	ACTOR	POST OFFICE BOX 981	LEE'S SUMMIT, MO	64063
COLLINS, RISE	ACTOR	AFFILIATE ARTISTS, INC		
		37 W 65TH ST, 6TH FLOOR	NEW YORK, NY	10023
COLLINS, ROBERT	CINEMATOGRAPHER	7715 SUNSET BLVD #150	LOS ANGELES, CA	90046
COLLINS, ROBERT	TV WRITER	8955 BEVERLY BLVD	LOS ANGELES, CA	90048
COLLINS, ROBERT L	DIRECTOR	1888 CENTURY PARK E #1400	LOS ANGELES, CA	90067
COLLINS, ROBERTA	ACTRESS	8721 SUNSET BLVD #202	LOS ANGELES, CA	90069
COLLINS, SAMUEL LEE	GUITARIST	2660 MOUNT GILEAD	BLOOMINGTON, TN	47401
COLLINS, STEPHEN	ACTOR	1416 N HAVENHURST DR #3-B	LOS ANGELES, CA	90046
COLLINS, SUGAR FOOT	GUITARIST	THE GREEN TREE INN		
		14173 GREEN TREE BLVD	VICTORVILLE, CA	92392
COLLINS, W O, JR	VIOLINIST	4400 BELMONT PARK TERR	NASHVILLE, TN	37215
COLLINS, WILLIAM BOOTSY	SINGER	MORRIS, 2325 CRESTMOOR RD	NASHVILLE, TN	37215
COLLINS, WILLIAM D	GUITARIST	4809 NEBRASKA AVE	NASHVILLE, TN	37209
COLLINS SISTERS, THE	VOCAL DUO	TESSIER, 505 CANTON PASS	MADISON, TN	37115
COLLIS, ALAN	WRITER	8955 BEVERLY BLVD	LOS ANGELES, CA	90048
COLLIS, ARTHUR B	WRITER	555 W 57TH ST #1230	NEW YORK, NY	10019
COLLISON, DANIEL J	NEWS CORRESPONDENT	2205 N PICKETT ST	ALEXANDRIA, VA	22304
COLLOFF, ROGER	TV EXECUTIVE	CBS-TV, 524 W 57TH ST	NEW YORK, NY	10019
COLLOGAN, DAVID L	NEWS CORRESPONDENT	2820 HATHAWAY TERR	SILVER SPRING, MD	20906
COLLOM, STEVE	GUITARIST	541 BREWER DR	NASHVILLE, TN	37211
COLLOPY, CONNIE	VIOLINIST	4029 WESTLAWN DR #B-2	NASHVILLE, TN	37209
COLLURA, FRANCO	CONDUCTOR	GERSHUNOFF, 502 PARK AVE	NEW YORK, NY	10022
COLMAN, BOOTH	ACTOR	8024 W NORTON AVE	LOS ANGELES, CA	90046
COLMAN, HENRY	TV WRITER-PRODUCER	423 LINNIE CANAL	VENICE, CA	90291
COLMAN, JOEL	DIRECTOR	755 BROOKTREE RD	PACIFIC PALISADES, CA	90272
COLMERAUER, DANIEL M	TV WRITER	3518 W CAHUENGA BLVD #318	LOS ANGELES, CA	90068
COLMES, WALTER	FILM DIRECTOR	5425 SW 77TH CT #1080	MIAMI, FL	33155
COLMUS, GERALDINE	GUITARIST	424 GRAPEVINE AVE	MADISON, TN	37115
COLODNER, JOEL	ACTOR	9000 SUNSET BLVD #200	LOS ANGELES, CA	90069
COLODNY, LESTER	DIRECTOR	DORCHER, 15 E 48TH ST	NEW YORK, NY	10017
COLODZIN, ROBERT S	DIRECTOR	7 WAKE ROBIN LN	STAMFORD, CT	06903
COLOMBIER, MICHEL	MUSICIAN	POST OFFICE BOX 779	MILL VALLEY, CA	94942
COLOMBU, FRANCO	BODYBUILDER	2389 WESTWOOD BLVD	LOS ANGELES, CA	90025
COLOMBY, HARRY	TV WRITER-PRODUCER	4139 WOODCLIFF RD	SHERMAN OAKS, CA	91403
COLOMBY, SCOTT	ACTOR	1425 QUEENS RD	LOS ANGELES, CA	90069
COLON, ALEX	ACTOR	POST OFFICE BOX 1221	STUDIO CITY, CA	91604
COLOR ME GONE	ROCK & ROLL GROUP	POST OFFICE BOX 5841	KANSAS CITY, MO	64111
COLOR TV	ROCK & ROLL GROUP	9881 EDGAR PL	LA MESA, CA	92041

200,000 Books
Back Issue Magazines
100,000 Paperback Books
Comics (New & Old)
Newspapers 1890 to date
Sheet Music
Records
Historic WWI and WWII Posters

Name	Occupation	Address	City/State	Zip
COLORADO, HORTENSIA	ACTRESS	247 S BEVERLY DR #102	BEVERLY HILLS, CA	90210
COLORADO QUARTET, THE	STRING QUARTET	5720 MOSHOLU AVE #300	RIVERDALE, NY	10471
COLPITTS, CISSY	ACTRESS	SEE - CAMERON, CISSE		
COLSON, CHARLES	AUTHOR	POST OFFICE BOX 40562	WASHINGTON, DC	20016
COLSON-DODGE, JANICE	WRITER	8955 BEVERLY BLVD	LOS ANGELES, CA	90048
COLT, GEORGE HOWE	WRITER-EDITOR	LIFE/TIME & LIFE BLDG		
		ROCKEFELLER CENTER	NEW YORK, NY	10020
COLT, MARSHALL	ACTOR	923 OCEAN AVE #5	SANTA MONICA, CA	90403
COLTER, JESSI	SINGER	1117 17TH AVE S	NASHVILLE, TN	37203
COLTON, BARBARA	ACTRESS	117 W 13TH ST	NEW YORK, NY	10011
COLTON, CHEVI	ACTRESS	300 CENTRAL PARK W	NEW YORK, NY	10024
COLTON, JACQUE LYNN	ACTRESS	4116 W VERDUGO AVE	BURBANK, CA	91505
COLTON, WILLIAM J	PHOTOGRAPHER	6600 BLVD E #16-N	WEST NEW YORK, NJ	07093
COLTRANE, CHI	SINGER	5955 TUXEDO TERR	LOS ANGELES, CA	90068
COLUMBU, FRANCO	ACTOR-BODYBUILDER	POST OFFICE BOX 1250	SANTA MONICA, CA	90406
COLUMBUS, CHRIS	SCREENWRITER	8955 BEVERLY BLVD	LOS ANGELES, CA	90048
COLVIG, VANCE	ACTOR	4789 VINELAND AVE #100	NORTH HOLLYWOOD, CA	91602
COLVIN, JACK L	ACTOR-DIRECTOR	3404 LARISSA DR	LOS ANGELES, CA	90026
COLVIN, LEON M, JR	WRITER	555 W 57TH ST #1230	NEW YORK, NY	10019
COLVIN, MARIE C	NEWS CORRESPONDENT	1844 ONTARIO PL, NW	WASHINGTON, DC	20009
COMBA, FRED W	COMPOSER	54 CRAGMONT AVE	SAN FRANCISCO, CA	94116
COMBE, TIMOTHY	TV DIRECTOR	ELLISON COMBE MANAGEMENT		
		17 RICHMOND HILL, RICHMOND	SURREY TW10 6RE	ENGLAND
COMBEMALE, JEAN-LOUP R	NEWS CORRESPONDENT	POST OFFICE BOX 309	GAINESVILLE, VA	22065
COMBEST, GAYLEN A	WRITER	555 W 57TH ST #1230	NEW YORK, NY	10019
COMBEST, PHILIP M	TV WRITER	8955 BEVERLY BLVD	LOS ANGELES, CA	90048
COMBOPIANO, CLAIRE	LYRIC SPINTO	431 S DEARBORN ST #1504	CHICAGO, IL	60605
COMBS, DEBBIE	ACTRESS	9300 WILSHIRE BLVD #410	BEVERLY HILLS, CA	90212
COMBS, FREDERICK	ACTOR	1152 N HOOVER ST	LOS ANGELES, CA	90029
COMBS, RON	GUITARIST	704 BERRY RD #C-3	NASHVILLE, TN	37204
COMDEN, BETTY	WRITER	117 E 95TH ST	NEW YORK, NY	10028
COMELY, RICHARD	CARTOONIST	POST OFFICE BOX 345		
		STATION A	TORONTO, ONT M5W 1C2	CANADA
COMER, ANJANETTE	ACTRESS	15010 VENTURA BLVD #219	SHERMAN OAKS, CA	91403
COMER, TOM	GUITARIST	1701 BLAIR BLVD #D	NASHVILLE, TN	37212
COMERFORD, CLINTON P	WRITER	528 E FOOTHILL BLVD	GLENDORA, CA	91740
COMET, CATHERINE	CONDUCTOR	SHAW CONCERTS, 1995 BROADWAY	NEW YORK, NY	10023
COMFORT, JOHN	FILM PRODUCER	32 ABBOTS HOUSE		
		SAINT MARY ABBOTS TERRACE	LONDON W14	ENGLAND
COMFORT, ROBERT	TV WRITER	8955 BEVERLY BLVD	LOS ANGELES, CA	90048
COMI, PAUL	ACTOR	1665 OAK KNOLL AVE	SAN MARINO, CA	91108
COMICI, ELIZABETH L	TV WRITER	15415 MILLDALE DR	LOS ANGELES, CA	90077
COMICI, LUCIANO	TV WRITER	15415 MILLDALE DR	LOS ANGELES, CA	90077
COMINOS, NICHOLAS	WRITER-PRODUCER	THE CAMBRIDGE TOWER		
		1801 LAVACA ST	AUSTIN, TX	78701
COMISKEY, ROBERT J	DIRECTOR	DGA, 110 W 57TH ST	NEW YORK, NY	10019
COMISSIONA, SERGIU	CONDUCTOR	ICM, 40 W 57TH ST	NEW YORK, NY	10019
COMISSIONG, LYDIA NICOLE	ACTRESS	3800 BARHAM BLVD #303	LOS ANGELES, CA	90068
COMMANDER CODY BAND	ROCK & ROLL GROUP	SEE - CODY, COMMANDER, BAND		
COMMIRE, ANNE	PLAYWRIGHT	81-R OSWEGATCHIE RD	WATERFORD, CT	06385
COMMODORES, THE	SOUL GROUP	3151 W CAHUENGA BLVD #235	LOS ANGELES, CA	90068
COMMONS, DAVID	WRITER-PRODUCER	1835 CAMINO PALMERO ST	LOS ANGELES, CA	90046
COMO, PERRY	SINGER	305 NORTHERN BLVD #3-A	GREAT NECK, NY	11021
COMORA, BETTY	SINGER	POST OFFICE BOX C	RIVER EDGE, NJ	07661
COMPANY	GOSPEL GROUP	POST OFFICE BOX 10298	COLORADO SPRINGS, CO	80932
COMPTON, ANN	NEWS CORRESPONDENT	ABC-TV, NEWS DEPARTMENT		
		1717 DE SALES ST, NW	WASHINGTON, DC	20036
COMPTON, BURL	SINGER	GROUP, 1957 KILBURN DR	ATLANTA, GA	30324
COMPTON, FORREST	ACTOR	TAL REP, 20 E 53RD ST	NEW YORK, NY	10022
COMPTON, JAMES M	NEWS CORRESPONDENT	NBC-TV, NEWS DEPARTMENT		
		30 ROCKEFELLER PLAZA	NEW YORK, NY	10112
COMPTON, JOYCE	ACTRESS	4125 DANANA RD	SHERMAN OAKS, CA	91403
COMPTON, JULEEN	SCREENWRITER	8955 BEVERLY BLVD	LOS ANGELES, CA	90048
COMPTON, RICHARD	WRITER-PRODUCER	9000 SUNSET BLVD #1200	LOS ANGELES, CA	90069
COMPTONS, THE	C & W GROUP	ACE PRODUCTIONS		
		3407 GREEN RIDGE DR	NASHVILLE, TN	37214
COMSTOCK, FRANK G	COMPOSER-CONDUCTOR	3966 ALADDIN DR	HUNTINGTON HARBOUR, CA	92649
CON SPIRITO	WOODWIND QUINTET	FINELL, 155 W 68TH ST	NEW YORK, NY	10023
CONATY, JOHN L	NEWS CORRESPONDENT	4461 CONNECTICUT AVE, NW	WASHINGTON, DC	20008
CONAWAY, JEFF	ACTOR	10390 WILSHIRE BLVD #714	LOS ANGELES, CA	90024
CONBOY, JOHN J	TV DIRECTOR-PRODUCER	CBS-TV, 7800 BEVERLY BLVD	LOS ANGELES, CA	90036
CONCANNON, LEON	TALENT AGENT	OLD SOUTH HEAD RD #17/79	BONDI JUNCTION NSW	AUSTRALIA
CONCEICAO, JACK	WRITER	555 W 57TH ST #1230	NEW YORK, NY	10019
CONCERT A TRE	MUSICAL TRIO	CPS, 34 66TH PL	LONG BEACH, CA	90803
CONCONI, CHARLES N	NEWS CORRESPONDENT	2929 28TH ST, NW	WASHINGTON, DC	20008
CONDE, RITA	ACTRESS	1607 N EL CENTRO AVE #22	HOLLYWOOD, CA	90028
CONDO, ADAM J	NEWS CORRESPONDENT	5911 BROADVIEW DR	ALEXANDRIA, VA	22310
CONDON, GEORGE E, JR	NEWS CORRESPONDENT	403 MANSFIELD RD	SILVER SPRING, MD	20910
CONDON, MAGGIE MC GRAW	DIRECTOR	20 5TH AVE	NEW YORK, NY	10011
CONDON, WILLIAM	SCREENWRITER	8955 BEVERLY BLVD	LOS ANGELES, CA	90048
CONDOS, DIMO	ACTOR	75 BANK ST	NEW YORK, NY	10014
CONDREY, LOVERBOY DENNIS	WRESTLER	NATIONAL WRESTLING ALLIANCE		
		JIM CROCKETT PROMOTIONS		
		421 BRIARBEND DR	CHARLOTTE, NC	28209

Name	Occupation	Address	City	Zip
CONDRIN, JOANNE	SOPRANO	111 W 57TH ST #1209	NEW YORK, NY	10019
CONE, TOM	CARTOONIST	TRIBUNE MEDIA SERVICES		
		64 E CONCORD ST	ORLANDO, FL	32801
CONEY, CHARLES LEE	NEWS CORRESPONDENT	4990 SENTINEL DR #102	BETHESDA, MD	20816
CONEY HATCH	ROCK & ROLL GROUP	41 BRITAIN ST #200	TORONTO, ONT	CANADA
CONFORTE, RUTH	CASTING DIRECTOR	POST OFFICE BOX 5718	SHERMAN OAKS, CA	91403
CONFORTI, GINO	ACTOR	9220 SUNSET BLVD #202	LOS ANGELES, CA	90069
CONFORTI, JOE	DIRECTOR	49 PARK AVE	NEW YORK, NY	10011
CONFUNKSHUN	RHYTHM & BLUES GROUP	200 W 51ST ST #1410	NEW YORK, NY	10019
CONGDON, JAMES	ACTOR	340 RIVERSIDE DR	NEW YORK, NY	10025
CONGER, DEAN	PHOTOGRAPHER	6604 MELODY LN	BETHESDA, MD	20034
CONGER, ERIC	ACTOR	484 W 43RD ST #37-F	NEW YORK, NY	10036
CONIFF, RAY	COMPOSER	2154 HERCULES DR	LOS ANGELES, CA	90046
CONKLIN, BILL	ACTOR	439 S LA CIENEGA BLVD #120	LOS ANGELES, CA	90048
CONKLIN, PATRICIA	ACTRESS	10850 RIVERSIDE DR #505	NORTH HOLLYWOOD, CA	91602
CONKLIN, PAUL	PHOTOGRAPHER	3900 TUNLAW RD, NW	WASHINGTON, DC	20007
CONKLIN, PEGGY	ACTRESS	THOMPSON, 142 E 71ST ST	NEW YORK, NY	10021
CONKLIN, RODERICK B	WRITER	8955 BEVERLY BLVD	LOS ANGELES, CA	90048
CONKLING, J D	WRITER	8955 BEVERLY BLVD	LOS ANGELES, CA	90048
CONKWRIGHT, LYNN	BODYBUILDER	POST OFFICE BOX 4235	VIRGINIA BEACH, CA	23454
CONLAN, CAMMIE KING	ACTRESS	SEE - KING CONLAN, CAMMIE		
CONLAN, JAMES S	WRITER	555 W 57TH ST #1230	NEW YORK, NY	10019
CONLAN, JOHN	BASEBALL	7810 E MARIPOSA DR	SCOTTSDALE, AZ	85251
CONLAN, MICHAEL F	NEWS CORRESPONDENT	113 5TH ST, NE	WASHINGTON, DC	20002
CONLEE, JOHN	SINGER-SONGWRITER	340-B TRINITY LN W	NASHVILLE, TN	37207
CONLEY, CORINNE	ACTRESS	9021 MELROSE AVE #304	LOS ANGELES, CA	90069
CONLEY, DARLENE	ACTRESS	ABC-TV, "GENERAL HOSPITAL"		
		1438 N GOWER ST	LOS ANGELES, CA	90028
CONLEY, DAVID L	DRUMMER	1022-B WESTCHESTER DR	MADISON, TN	37115
CONLEY, DAVID M	DIRECTOR	DGA, 110 W 57TH ST	NEW YORK, NY	10019
CONLEY, DAWN	ACTRESS	9777 WILSHIRE BLVD #707	BEVERLY HILLS, CA	90212
CONLEY, EARL THOMAS	SINGER-SONGWRITER	2809 GLENOAKS DR	NASHVILLE, TN	37214
CONLEY, JOE	ACTOR	10332 CHRISTINE PL	CHATSWORTH, CA	91311
CONLEY, JOHN L	NEWS CORRESPONDENT	874 CHESTNUT TREE DR	ANNAPOLIS, MD	21401
CONLEY, MICHAEL C	WRITER	8955 BEVERLY BLVD	LOS ANGELES, CA	90048
CONLIN, NOEL	ACTOR	4317 CROWNFIELD CT	WESTLAKE VILLAGE, CA	91361
CONLIN, NOREEN P	TV PRODUCER	13577 VALLEYHEART DR N	SHERMAN OAKS, CA	91423
CONLON, JAMES	CONDUCTOR	CAMI, 165 W 57TH ST	NEW YORK, NY	10019
CONN, DIDI	ACTRESS	14820 VALLEY VISTA BLVD	SHERMAN OAKS, CA	91403
CONN, FRANK	ACTOR	5330 LANKERSHIM BLVD #210	NORTH HOLLYWOOD, CA	91601
CONN, KELLY ANN	ACTRESS	9229 SUNSET BLVD #306	LOS ANGELES, CA	90069
CONN, TONY	COMPOSER	5503 BECK AVE #B	NORTH HOLLYWOOD, CA	91601
CONN, WILLIAM A, JR	SAXOPHONIST	100 ANDERSON RD	HENDERSONVILLE, TN	37075
CONNAL, SCOTTY	TV EXCUTIVE	ESPN, ESPN PLAZA	BRISTOL, CT	06010
CONNELL, ALAN R	WRITER	555 W 57TH ST #1230	NEW YORK, NY	10019
CONNELL, CHRISTOPHER	NEWS CORRESPONDENT	2021 "K" ST, NW	WASHINGTON, DC	20006
CONNELL, DAVID D	TV WRITER-EXECUTIVE	CHILDREN'S TV WORSHOP		
		1 LINCOLN PLAZA	NEW YORK, NY	10023
CONNELL, JOLYCON C N	NEWS CORRESPONDENT	3148 "O" ST, NW	WASHINGTON, DC	20008
CONNELL, KATHLEEN	ACTRESS	ANDERSON, 5923 WILBUR AVE	TARZANA, CA	91356
CONNELL, RICK	DRUMMER	3741 HILLBROOK DR	NASHVILLE, TN	37211
CONNELLS, THE	ROCK & ROLL GROUP	BLACK PARK RECORDS		
		1614 PARK DR	RALEIGH, NC	27605
CONNELLY, CHRIS	ACTOR	10016 TOLUCA LAKE AVE	TOLUCA LAKE, CA	91602
CONNELLY, JOAN	NEWS CORRESPONDENT	2315 HUIDEKOPER PL, NW	WASHINGTON, DC	20007
CONNELLY, LARRY E	COMPOSER	824 N LINCOLN ST	BURBANK, CA	91506
CONNER, DENNIS	YACHTSMAN	401 W "A" ST #615	SAN DIEGO, CA	92101
CONNER, KATHLEEN	CASTING DIRECTOR	POST OFFICE BOX 5718	SHERMAN OAKS, CA	91403
CONNER, ZOE	ACTRESS	8721 SUNSET BLVD #200	LOS ANGELES, CA	90069
CONNERS, DENNIS	PROUDCER	RIVER RUN PRODUCTIONS		
		1040 N LAS PALMAS AVE	LOS ANGELES, CA	90038
CONNERY, JASON	ACTOR	22 BISHOPS RD	LONDON SW6 7AB	ENGLAND
CONNERY, SEAN	ACTOR	FUENTE DEL RODEO		
		CASA MALIBU, NUEVA		
		ANDALUSIA	MALAGA	SPAIN
CONNIE	SINGER	PURPLE MOON PRODS		
		271 E 17TH ST	HIALEAH, FL	33010
CONNIFF, JUNE	ACTRESS	5330 LANKERSHIM BLVD #210	NORTH HOLLYWOOD, CA	91601
CONNOCK, JIM	FILM EDITOR	28 SUSSEX MANSIONS		
		OLD BROMPTON RD	LONDON SW7	ENGLAND
CONNOLLY, BILLY	ACTOR	GOLDSMITH, 360 OXFORD ST	LONDON W1	ENGLAND
CONNOLLY, CAMILLE C	NEWS CORRESPONDENT	1333 "H" ST, NW	WASHINGTON, DC	20005
CONNOLLY, JAMES G	DIRECTOR	DGA, 110 W 57TH ST	NEW YORK, NY	10019
CONNOLLY, JOSEPH M	NEWS CORRESPONDENT	4646 40TH ST, NW	WASHINGTON, DC	20016
CONNOLLY, NORMA	ACTRESS	9000 SUNSET BLVD #1200	LOS ANGELES, CA	90069
CONNOLLY, RAY	WRITER	8955 BEVERLY BLVD	LOS ANGELES, CA	90048
CONNOR, CHRISTINE	WRITER	555 W 57TH ST #1230	NEW YORK, NY	10019
CONNOR, JAMES T	NEWS CORRESPONDENT	NBC-TV, NEWS DEPARTMENT		
		4001 NEBRASKA AVE, NW	WASHINGTON, DC	20016
CONNOR, JOHN	NEWS CORRESPONDENT	4910 N 13TH ST	ARLINGTON, VA	22205
CONNOR, KEVIN G	WRITER-PRODUCER	MERRILL, 4260 ARCOLA AVE	TOLUCA LAKE, CA	91602
CONNOR, MICHAEL	ACTOR	1416 N HAVENHURST DR	LOS ANGELES, CA	90046
CONNOR, MICHAEL	NEWS CORRESPONDENT	ABC NEWS, 7 W 66TH ST	NEW YORK, NY	10023
CONNOR, PATRICK	ACTOR	109 SAINT ALBANS RD		
		SANDRIDGE, SAINT ALBANS	HERTS AL4 9LH	ENGLAND

Name	Occupation	Address	City	Zip
CONNOR, WHITFIELD	ACTOR	5 LADDER HILL RD S	WESTON, CT	06883
CONNORS, CAROL	SONGWRITER	333 N PALM DR #206	BEVERLY HILLS, CA	90210
CONNORS, CHUCK	ACTOR-BASEBALL	8306 WILSHIRE BLVD #252	BEVERLY HILLS, CA	90211
CONNORS, EDWARD M	NEWS CORRESPONDENT	623 MARYLAND AVE, NE	WASHINGTON, DC	20002
CONNORS, KATHRYN	ACTRESS	CUZZINS, 250 W 57TH ST	NEW YORK, NY	10107
CONNORS, MIKE	ACTOR	4810 LOUISE AVE	ENCINO, CA	91316
CONNORS, SUSAN	ACTRESS	1757 N KINGSLEY DR #211	HOLLYWOOD, CA	90027
CONNORS, THOMAS J	NEWS CORRESPONDENT	3044 HOLMES RUN RD	FALLS CHURCH, VA	22042
CONNORS, THOMAS J, III	DIRECTOR	DGA, 7950 SUNSET BLVD	LOS ANGELES, CA	90046
CONOVER, MARGARET LYNN	NEWS CORRESPONDENT	30 E MASONIC VIEW AVE	ALEXANDRIA, VA	22301
CONRAD, BARBARA	MEZZO-SOPRANO	59 E 54TH ST #81	NEW YORK, NY	10022
CONRAD, CHRISTIAN	ACTOR	21316 PACIFIC COAST HWY	MALIBU, CA	90265
CONRAD, CHRISTINE	WRITER	8955 BEVERLY BLVD	LOS ANGELES, CA	90048
CONRAD, CONSTANCE	ACTRESS	KEY, 45 BURLINGTON AVE	LEONARDO, NJ	07737
CONRAD, DEREK	WRITER-PRODUCER	3 KINGLY ST	LONDON W1R 5LR	ENGLAND
CONRAD, FRED R	PHOTOGRAPHER	78 WINDSOR PL	GLEN RIDGE, NJ	07028
CONRAD, JACK H	WRITER	8955 BEVERLY BLVD	LOS ANGELES, CA	90048
CONRAD, JON J	DIRECTOR	9224 MARMORA	MORTON GROVE, IL	66053
CONRAD, NANCY	ACTRESS	11666 GOSHEN AVE #305	LOS ANGELES, CA	90049
CONRAD, PAUL	CARTOONIST	28649 CRESTRIDGE RD	PALOS VERDES, CA	90274
CONRAD, RICHARD	TENOR	POST OFFICE BOX 20548	NEW YORK, NY	10025
CONRAD, ROBERT	ACTOR-WRITER	21316 PACIFIC COAST HWY	MALIBU, CA	9265
CONRAD, SHANE	ACTOR	21316 PACIFIC COAST HWY	MALIBU, CA	90265
CONRAD, SID	ACTOR	18954 STRATHERN ST	RESEDA, CA	91335
CONRAD, SIMA	ACTRESS	31377 PACIFIC COAST HWY	MALIBU, CA	90265
CONRAD, WILLIAM	ACTOR-RADIO PERS	POST OFFICE BOX 1633	BEVERLY HILLS, CA	90213
CONRAN, JASPER	FASHION DESIGNER	49-50 GREAT MARLBOROUGH ST	LONDON W1	ENGLAND
CONROY, BURT	ACTOR	11240 MAGNOLIA BLVD #202	NORTH HOLLYWOOD, CA	91601
CONROY, DAVID	FILM WRITER-PRODUCER	16 WOODLANDS RD	LONDON SW13	ENGLAND
CONROY, FRANCES F	WRITER	555 W 57TH ST #1230	NEW YORK, NY	10019
CONROY, JARLATH	ACTOR	ROBERT KASS, 156 5TH AVE	NEW YORK, NY	10010
CONROY, KEVIN	ACTOR	211 S BEVERLY DR #201	BEVERLY HILLS, CA	90212
CONS, CARL	WRITER-PRODUCER	6622 LINDLEY AVE	RESDEDA, CA	91335
CONSIDINE, DENNIS J	TV EXECUTIVE	11541 LAUREL CREST DR	STUDIO CITY, CA	91604
CONSIDINE, JOHN	ACTOR-WRITER	1624 N GARDNER ST	LOS ANGELES, CA	90046
CONSIDINE, TIM	ACT-WRI-DIR	10328 VIRETTA LN	LOS ANGELES, CA	90077
CONSOLO, SAL	ACTOR	8721 SUNSET BLVD #200	LOS ANGELES, CA	90069
CONSTABLE, ANNE	NEWS CORRESPONDENT	6223 UTAH AVE, NW	WASHINGTON, DC	20015
CONSTANTIN, GAVRAS	WRITER-PRODUCER	244 RUE SAINT JACQUES	PARIS	FRANCE
CONSTANTINE, MICHAEL	ACTOR	1476 S SHERNANDOAH ST #301	LOS ANGELES, CA	90035
CONTA, IOSIF	CONDUCTOR	POST OFFICE BOX 131	SPRINGFIELD, VA	22150
CONTARDO, JOHN	ACTOR	1418 N HIGHLAND AVE #102	LOS ANGELES, CA	90028
CONTE, CHRISTOPHER	NEWS CORRESPONDENT	615 PERSHING DR	SILVER SPRING, MD	20910
CONTE, JOHN	ACTOR	75600 BERYL DR	INDIAN WELLS, CA	92260
CONTE, JOSEPH A	DIRECTOR	860 NORTH ST	GREENWICH, CT	06830
CONTI, BILL	COMPOSER-ARRANGER	117 FREMONT PL W	LOS ANGELES, CA	90005
CONTI, ROBERT J	COMPOSER	518 N JUANITA AVE	REDONDO BEACH, CA	90277
CONTI, ROBERT W	WRITER	8955 BEVERLY BLVD	LOS ANGELES, CA	90048
CONTI, TOM	ACTOR	CHATTO & LINNIT, LTD		
		PRINCE OF WALES THEATRE		
		COVENTRY ST	LONDON WC2	ENGLAND
CONTI-GUGLIA, RICHARD & JOHN	PIANO DUO	SHAW CONCERTS, 1995 BROADWAY	NEW YORK, NY	10023
CONTRERAS, LUIS	ACTOR	4731 LAUREL CANYON BLVD #5	NORTH HOLLYWOOD, CA	91607
CONTRERAS, ROBERTO	ACTOR	10000 RIVERSIDE DR #3	TOLUCA LAKE, CA	91602
CONTROLLERS, THE	VOCAL GROUP	400-A 56TH ST	FAIRFIELD, AL	35064
CONTRUCCI, LANCE	WRITER	THE NATIONAL LAMPOON		
		635 MADISON AVE	NEW YORK, NY	10022
CONVERSE, DAVE	TRUMPETER	6046 BETHANY BLVD	NASHVILLE, TN	37221
CONVERSE, FRANK	ACTOR	BOX 101, BELDEN ISLAND	STONY CREEK, CT	06405
CONVERSE, MELISSA	ACTRESS	368 GRENOLA ST	PACIFIC PALISADES, CA	90272
CONVERSE, PEGGY	ACTRESS	2525 BRIARCREST RD	BEVERLY HILLS, CA	90210
CONVERSE, TONY	PRODUCER	PEREGRINE, 9229 SUNSET BLVD	LOS ANGELES, CA	90069
CONVICT	ROCK & ROLL GROUP	POST OFFICE BOX 212	ISSINGTON, ONT M9A 4X2	CANADA
CONVY, ANNE	SCREENWRITER	560 TOYOPA DR	PACIFIC PALISADES, CA	90272
CONVY, BERT	ACTOR	560 TOYOPA DR	PACIFIC PALISADES, CA	90272
CONVY, JENNIFER	ACTRESS	560 TOYOPA DR	PACIFIC PALISADES, CA	90272
CONWAY, BERT	ACTOR	5401 SEPULVEDA BLVD #49	VAN NUYS, CA	91411
CONWAY, BLAKE	ACTOR	439 S LA CIENEGA BLVD #117	LOS ANGELES, CA	90048
CONWAY, CHRISTINE R	NEWS CORRESPONDENT	2025 "M" ST, NW	WASHINGTON, DC	20036
CONWAY, CHRISTOPHER	NEWS CORRESPONDENT	NBC-TV, NEWS DEPARTMENT		
		4001 NEBRASKA AVE, NW	WASHINGTON, DC	20016
CONWAY, ELAINE	TV EXECUTIVE	NBC TELEVISION NETWORK		
		30 ROCKEFELLER PLAZA	NEW YORK, NY	10112
CONWAY, GARY	ACTOR	2035 MANDEVILLE CANYON RD	LOS ANGELES, CA	90049
CONWAY, GERARD F	WRITER	8955 BEVERLY BLVD	LOS ANGELES, CA	90048
CONWAY, JAMES L	WRITER-PRODUCER	4300 COQUETTE PL	TARZANA, CA	91356
CONWAY, KARLA	MODEL	SEE - CONWAY-SACHI, KARLA		
CONWAY, KEVIN	ACTOR	10390 SANTA MONICA BLVD #310	LOS ANGELES, CA	90025
CONWAY, MAUREEN C	WRITER	555 W 57TH ST #1230	NEW YORK, NY	10019
CONWAY, RICHARD S	WRITER	8955 BEVERLY BLVD	LOS ANGELES, CA	90048
CONWAY, TIM	ACTOR-DIRECTOR	10905 OHIO AVE #305	LOS ANGELES, CA	90024
CONWAY, WILLIAM M	NEWS CORRESPONDENT	8918 PEORIA CT	SPRINGFIELD, VA	22153
CONWAY BROTHERS, THE	SOUL GROUP	POST OFFICE BOX 2206	SHREVEPORT, LA	71166
CONWELL, CAROLYN	ACTRESS	1350 N HIGHLAND AVE	LOS ANGELES, CA	90028
CONWELL, JOHN	CASTING DIRECTOR	2542 BENEDICT CANYON DR	BEVERLY HILLS, CA	90210

CHUCK CONNERS

SEAN CONNERY

ELISHA COOK

JACKIE COOPER

LYDIA CORNELL

HOWARD COSELL

ELVIS COSTELLO

JACQUES COUSTEAU

JEANNE CRAIN

CONWELL, TOMMY & YOUNG RUMBLERS	ROCK & ROLL GROUP	CORNERSTONE MANAGEMENT		
		23 E LANCASTER AVE	ARDMORE, PA	19003
CONY, EDWARD	JOURNALIST	7 GULL'S COVE	MANHASSET, NY	11030
COODER, RY	GUITARIST-SONGWRITER	326 ENTRADA DR	SANTA MONICA, CA	90402
COOK, ANCEL	ACTRESS	25844 LUCILLE AVE	LOMITA, CA	90717
COOK, ANTHONY P	WRITER	8955 BEVERLY BLVD	LOS ANGELES, CA	90048
COOK, BARBARA	NEWS CORRESPONDENT	4319 DAHILL PL	ALEXANDRIA, VA	22312
COOK, CARLA	MEZZO-SOPRANO	CAMI, 165 W 57TH ST	NEW YORK, NY	10019
COOK, CAROLE	ACTRESS	8829 ASHCROFT AVE	LOS ANGELES, CA	90022
COOK, CHRISTOPHER	TV DIRECTOR-PRODUCER	23-A WARWICK AVE	LONDON W9 2PS	ENGLAND
COOK, DAVID	ACTOR-WRITER	LEADING PLAYERS MGMT		
		31 KING'S ROAD	LONDON SW3	ENGLAND
COOK, DAVID T	NEWS CORRESPONDENT	1025 S 20TH ST	ARLINGTON, VA	22202
COOK, DEBORAH	SOPRANO	61 W 62ND ST #6-F	NEW YORK, NY	10023
COOK, DENNIS	PHOTOGRAPHER	4319 DAHILL PL	ALEXANDRIA, VA	22312
COOK, DORIA	ACTRESS	9246 SIERRA MAR DR	LOS ANGELES, CA	90069
COOK, ED	DRUMMER	116 CHERYL DR	HENDERSONVILLE, TN	37075
COOK, ELISHA, JR	ACTOR	POST OFFICE BOX 335	BISHOP, CA	93514
COOK, FIELDER	TV DIRECTOR-PRODUCER	10585 BRADBURY RD	LOS ANGELES, CA	90064
COOK, FRANK T	NEWS CORRESPONDENT	3524 S 7TH ST	ARLINGTON, VA	22204
COOK, FRED	ACTOR	7 E 14TH ST	NEW YORK, NY	10003
COOK, FREDRIC	ACTOR	3208 W CAHUENGA BLVD	LOS ANGELES, CA	90068
COOK, GEORGE H, III	PHOTOGRAPHER	7850 AMERICANA CIR	GLEN BURNIE, MD	21061
COOK, JOSEPH	TV WRITER	555 W 57TH ST #1230	NEW YORK, NY	10019
COOK, JULIE	ACTRESS	3151 W CAHUENGA BLVD #310	LOS ANGELES, CA	90068
COOK, NATHAN	ACTOR	2121 AVE OF THE STARS #410	LOS ANGELES, CA	90067
COOK, NEILSON	ACTOR	6605 HOLLYWOOD BLVD #220	HOLLYWOOD, CA	90028
COOK, NORMAN W	DIRECTOR	17130 BURBANK BLVD #204	ENCINO, CA	91316
COOK, PATRICK M	DIRECTOR	139 BELL AVE	HASBROUCK HEIGHTS, NJ	07604
COOK, PAUL R	DRUMMER	2131 ELM HILL PIKE #U-3	NASHVILLE, TN	37210
COOK, PETER	ACTOR-COMEDIAN	24 PERRRINE WALK	LONDON NW3	ENGLAND
COOK, REBECCA	SOPRANO	1182 MARKET ST #311	SAN FRANCISCO, CA	94102
COOK, RHODES	NEWS CORRESPONDENT	3804 HUMMER RD	ANNANDALE, VA	22003
COOK, ROBIN	SCREENWRITER	555 W 57TH ST #1230	NEW YORK, NY	10019
COOK, RODERICK	ACTOR	1650 BROADWAY #302	NEW YORK, NY	10019
COOK, RODERICK	THEATER PRODUCER	425 E 51ST ST	NEW YORK, NY	10022
COOK, ROGER	PIANIST	4006 ESTES RD	NASHVILLE, TN	37215
COOK, RON	ACTOR	FEAST, 43-A PRINCESS RD	LONDON NW1	ENGLAND
COOK, SAMONA	SINGER	PERLE, 4475 VINELAND AVE	STUDIO CITY, CA	91602
COOK, STANTON	PUBLISHING EXECUTIVE	THE CHICAGO TRIBUNE		
		TRIBUNE TOWER		
		435 N MICHIGAN AVE	CHICAGO, IL	60611
COOK, TERRY	BASSO-BARITONE	59 E 54TH ST #81	NEW YORK, NY	10022
COOK, THOMAS S	SCREENWRITER	5950 FOOTHILL DR	LOS ANGELES, CA	90068
COOK, TOM	TV PRODUCER	MCA/UNIVERSAL STUDIOS, INC		
		100 UNIVERSAL CITY PLAZA	UNIVERSAL CITY, CA	91608
COOK, TOMMY	ACTOR	4572 VIA MARINA #307	MARINA DEL REY, CA	90292
COOK, WHITFIELD	WRITER	8955 BEVERLY BLVD	LOS ANGELES, CA	90048
COOK, WILLIAM J	NEWS CORRESPONDENT	3501 FARM HILL DR	FALLS CHURCH, VA	22044
COOKE, ALAN	TV DIRECTOR	7670 WOODROW WILSON DR	LOS ANGELES, CA	90046
COOKE, ALAN	WRITER-PRODUCER	2 CARDIGAN RD, RICHMOND	SURREY	ENGLAND
COOKE, BRIAN	TV WRITER	FRASER, 91 REGENT ST	LONDON W1	ENGLAND
COOKE, GREG	WRITER	555 W 57TH ST #1230	NEW YORK, NY	10019
COOKE, JENNIFER	ACTRESS	151 S EL CAMINO DR	BEVERLY HILLS, CA	90212
COOKE, JOHN	CABLE EXECUTIVE	2951 E 28TH ST #2000	SANTA MONICA, CA	90405
COOKE, JOHN BYRNE	NOVELIST	POST OFFICE BOX 68	TETON VILLAGE, WY	83025
COOKE, SUSAN	PRODUCER	101 OCEAN AVE #D-8	SANTA MONICA, CA	90402
COOKSEY, DANNY	ACTOR	11350 VENTURA BLVD #206	STUDIO CITY, CA	91604
COOKSEY, DANNY	SINGER	WOOD, 2901 EPPERLY DR	DEL CITY, OK	73115
COOKSEY, DARRYL	ACTOR	3575 W CAHUENGA BLVD #320	LOS ANGELES, CA	90068
COOKSON, GARY	ACTOR	54 W 70TH ST	NEW YORK, NY	10023
COOKSON, GEORGINA	ACTRESS	APARTADO 62, SANTA EULA	IBIZA	SPAIN
COOKSON, PETER	ACTOR	156 E 62ND ST	NEW YORK, NY	10021
COOLEY, RICK	ACTOR	9777 WILSHIRE BLVD #707	BEVERLY HILLS, CA	90212
COOLEY, VICTOR	NEWS CORRESPONDENT	13511 COLLINWOOD TERR	SILVER SPRING, MD	20904
COOLIDGE, MARTHA	FILM DIRECTOR	1305 PARK AVE	BEVERLY HILLS, CA	90210
COOLIDGE, RITA	SINGER-ACTRESS	9454 WILSHIRE BLVD #206	BEVERLY HILLS, CA	90212
COOMBS, LINDA J	WRITER	555 W 57TH ST #1230	NEW YORK, NY	10019
COOMBS, PAT	ACTRESS	5 WENDELA CT		
		HARROW-ON-THE-HILL	MIDDLESEX	ENGLAND
COOMES, AVERY	GUITARIST	5003 MARCHANT DR	NASHVILLE, TN	37211
COONEY, GERRY	BOXER	22501 LINDEN BLVD	CAMBRIA HEIGHTS, NY	11411
COONEY, JOAN GANZ	TV EXECUTIVE	CHILDREN'S TV WORKSHOP		
		1 LINCOLN PLAZA	NEW YORK, NY	10023
COONEY, ROBERT B	NEWS CORRESPONDENT	2621 COLSTON DR	CHEVY CHASE, MD	20815
COOPER, ADRIAN	FILM PRODUCER	SAINT CATHERINE'S DRAMA ST	GUILFORD	ENGLAND
COOPER, ALICE	ROCK & ROLL GROUP	ALIVE ENTERTAINMENT		
		8271 SUNSET BLVD	LOS ANGELES, CA	90046
COOPER, ALICE	SINGER-SONGWRITER	4135 E KEIM ST	PARADISE VALLEY, AZ	85253
COOPER, ANN	NEWS CORRESPONDENT	1753 SWANN ST, NW	WASHINGTON, DC	20007
COOPER, BEN	ACTOR	9777 WILSHIRE BLVD #707	BEVERLY HILLS, CA	90212
COOPER, BOB	COMPOSER	3548 STONEWOOD DR	SHERMAN OAKS, CA	91403
COOPER, CATHERINE M	NEWS CORRESPONDENT	2512 1/2 EAST PL, NW	WASHINGTON, DC	20007

COOPER, CHAS	ACTOR	120 S VICTORY BLVD #104	BURBANK, CA	91502
COOPER, DAN	WRITER-PRODUCER	1060 PARK AVE	NEW YORK, NY	10128
COOPER, DENNIS	TV WRITER	8955 BEVERLY BLVD	LOS ANGELES, CA	90048
COOPER, EDWIN	ACTOR	RURAL FARM DELIVERY #5		
		PARMALEE HILL RD	NEWTON, CT	06470
COOPER, ERIC	WRESTLER	POST OFFICE BOX 3859	STAMFORD, CT	06905
COOPER, GARY L	DIRECTOR	DGA, 7950 SUNSET BLVD	LOS ANGELES, CA	90046
COOPER, GEORGE A	ACTOR	FRASER, 91 REGENT ST	LONDON W1	ENGLAND
COOPER, GUY	TV DIRECTOR	600 E OLIVE AVE	BURBANK, CA	91501
COOPER, HAL	WRITER-PRODUCER	2651 HUTTON DR	BEVERLY HILLS, CA	90210
COOPER, HENRY	TV PERSONALITY	36 BRAMPTON GROVE	LONDON NW4	ENGLAND
COOPER, J C	ACTRESS	SHERMAN, 348 S REXFORD DR	BEVERLY HILLS, CA	90212
COOPER, JACKIE	ACTOR-DIRECTOR	9621 ROYALTON DR	BEVERLY HILLS, CA	90210
COOPER, JAY L	COMPOSER	9465 WILSHIRE BLVD #800	BEVERLY HILLS, CA	90212
COOPER, JEANNE	ACTRESS	2472 COLDWATER CANYON DR	BEVERLY HILLS, CA	90210
COOPER, JOHN	DIRECTOR-PRODUCER	18 PELHAM CRESCENT		
		THE PARK	NOTTINGHAM NG1 6GN	ENGLAND
COOPER, JOHN GARY	DIRECTOR	520 N MICHIGAN AVE #436	CHICAGO, IL	60611
COOPER, JOHN KAYE	TV DIRECTOR-PRODUCER	ROGER HANCOCK MANAGEMENT		
		8 WATERLOO PL, PALL MALL	LONDON SW1Y 4AW	ENGLAND
COOPER, JOSHUA D	NEWS CORRESPONDENT	CBS NEWS, 2020 "M" ST, NW	WASHINGTON, DC	20036
COOPER, KAREN	TV EXECUTIVE	CBS-TV, 6121 SUNSET BLVD	LOS ANGELES, CA	90028
COOPER, LAWRENCE	BARITONE	CAMI, 165 W 57TH ST	NEW YORK, NY	10019
COOPER, LISA	MODEL	AMBROSE, 1466 BROADWAY	NEW YORK, NY	10036
COOPER, MAGGIE	ACTRESS	445 N BEDFORD DR #PH	BEVERLY HILLS, CA	90210
COOPER, MARGO	WRITER	8955 BEVERLY BLVD	LOS ANGELES, CA	90048
COOPER, MARY H	NEWS CORRESPONDENT	7104 OAK RIDGE RD	FALLS CHURCH, VA	22042
COOPER, NATALIE	SCREENWRITER	8955 BEVERLY BLVD	LOS ANGELES, CA	90048
COOPER, PAUL	RECORD EXECUTIVE	ATLANTIC RECORDS COMPANY		
		9229 SUNSET BLVD	LOS ANGELES, CA	90069
COOPER, PAUL	WRITER	14144 VENTURA BLVD #200	SHERMAN OAKS, CA	91423
COOPER, PETER H	DIRECTOR	28 W 25TH ST	NEW YORK, NY	10010
COOPER, RAY	MUSICIAN-FILM PROD	HAND MADE FILMS CO		
		26 CADOGAN SQ	LONDON SW1X OJP	ENGLAND
COOPER, RICHARD T	NEWS CORRESPONDENT	210 S LEE ST	ALEXANDRIA, VA	22314
COOPER, ROBERT	FILM PRODUCER	11500 W OLYMPIC BLVD #300	LOS ANGELES, CA	90064
COOPER, ROBERT	FILM PRODUCER	78 SCOLLARD ST	TORONTO, ONT M5R 1GA	CANADA
COOPER, ROY	ACTOR	202 SOUNDVIEW AVE #29	STAMFORD, CT	06902
COOPER, STUART	TV DIRECTOR	8428 MELROSE PL #C	LOS ANGELES, CA	90068
COOPER, SUSAN	WRITER	ICM, 40 W 57TH ST	NEW YORK, NY	10019
COOPER, TAMAR	ACTRESS	2265 N BEVERLY GLEN PL	LOS ANGELES, CA	90077
COOPER, WILMA LEE	SINGER-GUITARIST	606 DAVIS DR	BRENTWOOD, TN	37027
COOPER, WILMA LEE & CLINCH	BLUEGRASS GROUP	POST OFFICE BOX 809	GOODLETTSVILLE, TN	37072
COOPER, ZACKIE C	COMPOSER	1634 N WESTERLY TERR	LOS ANGELES, CA	90026
COOPERMAN, ALVIN	TV PRODUCER	146 CENTRAL PARK W	NEW YORK, NY	10023
COOPERMAN, JACK	FILM DIRECTOR	POST OFFICE BOX 5118	BEVERLY HILLS, CA	90210
COOPERSMITH, JEROME	WRITER	555 W 57TH ST #1230	NEW YORK, NY	10019
COOPERSTEIN, EDWIN	TV DIRECTOR	7745 N TATUM BLVD	PARADISE VALLEY, AZ	85253
COOPLE, TY	ACTOR	429 W 45TH ST #4-FW	NEW YORK, NY	10036
COPAGE, ERIC V	NEWS REPORTER	LIFE/TIME & LIFE BLDG		
		ROCKEFELLER CENTER	NEW YORK, NY	10020
COPAGE, JOHN	ACTOR	455 S ALMONT DR	BEVERLY HILLS, CA	90211
COPAGE, MARC	ACTOR	455 S ALMONT DR	BEVERLY HILLS, CA	90211
COPELAND, ALAN	CONDUCTOR	POST OFFICE BOX 393	AGOURA, CA	91301
COPELAND, JOHN	ACTRESS	88 CENTRAL PARK W	NEW YORK, NY	10023
COPELAND, KENNETH	EVANGELIST	POST OFFICE BOX 2908	FORT WORTH, TX	76113
COPELAND, MARTIN W	SCREENWRITER	10351 SANTA MONICA BLVD #211	LOS ANGELES, CA	90025
COPELAND, MAURICE	ACTOR	47 ROCKWOOD DR	LARCHMONT, NY	10538
COPELAND, STEWART	DRUMMER-SONGWRITER	FIRSTIR MANAGEMENT, LTD		
		194 KENSINGTON PARK RD	LONDON W11	ENGLAND
COPELAND, WILLIAM	WRITER	8955 BEVERLY BLVD	LOS ANGELES, CA	90048
COPERNICUS	ROCK & ROLL GROUP	POST OFFICE BOX 150	BROOKLYN, NY	11217
COPLAND, AARON	COMPOSER	1538 "L" WASHINGTON ST	PEEKSKILL, NY	10566
COPLEY, PAUL	ACTOR	FEAST, 43-A PRINCESS RD	LONDON NW1	ENGLAND
COPLEY, TERI	ACTRESS	3654 POTOSI AVE	STUDIO CITY, CA	91604
COPLEY-MAYER, TERI	ACTRESS-MODEL	SEE - COPLEY, TERI		
COPNDAX, KATE D	WRITER	555 W 57TH ST #1230	NEW YORK, NY	10019
COPPERFIELD, DAVID	MAGICIAN	9107 WILSHIRE BLVD #500	BEVERLY HILLS, CA	90210
COPPOLA, CARMINE	COMPOSER-CONDUCTOR	19813 GILMORE ST	WOODLAND HILLS, CA	91367
COPPOLA, FRANCIS FORD	WRITER-PRODUCER	916 KEARNY ST	SAN FRANCISCO, CA	94133
COPPOLA, FRANK	ACTOR	573 N WINDSOR BLVD	LOS ANGELES, CA	90004
COPPOLA, LOUIS A	TV WRITER	555 W 57TH ST #1230	NEW YORK, NY	10019
COPPOLA, MICHELE	NEWS CORRESPONDENT	3010 WISCONSIN AVE #E-11, NW	WASHINGTON, DC	20016
COPPOLA, VINCENT V	WRITER	8955 BEVERLY BLVD	LOS ANGELES, CA	90048
COQUILLON, JOHN	CIMENATOGRAPHER	CCA MGMT, 4 CT LODGE		
		48 SLOANE SQ	LONDON SW1W 8AT	ENGLAND
CORBEIL, CLAUDE	BASSO-BARITONE	CAMI, 165 W 57TH ST	NEW YORK, NY	10019
CORBELLI, ALESSANDRO	BARITONE	CAMI, 165 W 57TH ST	NEW YORK, NY	10019
CORBETH, ALAN S	NEWS CORRESPONDENT	2025 "M" ST, NW	WASHINGTON, DC	20036
CORBETT, CHRISTOPHER	TALENT AGENT	15 HIGH ST #621	HARTFORD, CT	06103
CORBETT, GRETCHEN	ACTRESS	2600 RINCONIA DR	LOS ANGELES, CA	90068
CORBETT, MATTHEW	ACTOR	VINCENT SHAW, 20 JAY MEWS	LONDON SW7 2EP	ENGLAND
CORBETT, MICHAEL	ACTOR	11726 SAN VICENTE BLVD #300	LOS ANGELES, CA	90049
CORBETT, RONNIE	COMEDIAN	SONNY ZALE ASSOCIATES		
		57 GREAT CUMBERLAND PL	LONDON W1H 7LJ	ENGLAND

Name	Occupation	Address	City	Zip
CORBETT, TY	DRUMMER	POST OFFICE BOX 179	ANTIOCH, TN	37013
CORBIN, ALBERT	ACTOR	714 GREENWICH ST	NEW YORK, NY	10014
CORBIN, BARRY	ACTOR	11726 SAN VICENTE BLVD #300	LOS ANGELES, CA	90049
CORBIN/HANNER BAND	C & W GROUP	HALSEY, 3225 S NORWOOD AVE	TULSA, OK	74135
CORBY, ELLEN	ACTRESS	THE WESTWOOD HORIZONS		
		947 TIVERTON AVE	LOS ANGELES, CA	90024
CORCORAN, BRIAN	ACTOR	2502 1/2 CHANDLER BLVD	BURBANK, CA	91505
CORCORAN, HUGH V	WRITER	8955 BEVERLY BLVD	LOS ANGELES, CA	90048
CORCORAN, KERRY	ACTOR	350 S MADISON AVE #126	PASADENA, CA	91101
CORCORAN, NOREEN	ACTRESS	18016 COLLINS ST	ENCINO, CA	91316
CORD, ALEX	ACTOR	7387 WOODROW WILSON DR	LOS ANGELES, CA	90046
CORD, ERIK	DIRECTOR	8350 SANTA MONICA BLVD #206	LOS ANGELES, CA	90069
CORDAY, BARBARA	TV WRITER-PRODUCER	615 S ROSSMORE AVE	LOS ANGELES, CA	90005
CORDAY, KEN	TV PRODUCER	10343 VALLEY SPRING LN	TOLUCA LAKE, CA	91602
CORDAY, MRS TED	TV PRODUCER	4000 WARNER BLVD #8-139	BURBANK, CA	91522
CORDDRY, CHARLES W	NEWS CORRESPONDENT	4304 GLENRIDGE ST	KENSINGTON, MD	20895
CORDELL, CATHERINE	SOPRANO	260 W END AVE #7-A	NEW YORK, NY	10023
CORDELL, CATHLEEN	ACTOR	1850 N WHITLEY AVE #419	LOS ANGELES, CA	90028
CORDELL, MELINDA	ACTRESS	FARRELL, 10500 MAGNOLIA BLVD	NORTH HOLLYWOOD, CA	91601
CORDEN, HENRY	ACTOR	3697 GOODLAND AVE	STUDIO CITY, CA	91604
CORDERO, MARIA-ELENA	ACTRESS	17240 REVELLO DR	PACIFIC PALISADES, CA	90272
CORDES, KATHRYN	ACTRESS	195 W 10TH ST #2-B	NEW YORK, NY	10014
CORDIC, REGIS J	ACTOR	8410 ALLENWOOD RD	LOS ANGELES, CA	90046
CORDOVA, CAESAR	ACTOR	4789 VINELAND AVE #100	NORTH HOLLYWOOD, CA	91602
CORDOVA, MARGARITA	ACTRESS	10000 RIVERSIDE DR #3	TOLUCA LAKE, CA	91602
CORDOVA, PAMELA	ACTRESS	723 N BEDFORD DR	BEVERLY HILLS, CA	90210
CORDRAY, RONALD E	NEWS CORRESPONDENT	6813 VALLEY BROOK DR	FALLS CHURCH, VA	22042
CORDTZ, HOWARD	NEWS CORRESPONDENT	ABC NEWS, 7 W 66TH ST	NEW YORK, NY	10023
CORDUNER, ALLAN	ACTOR	51 EL PARK GARDENS #M	LONDON SW10	ENGLAND
CORDY, ANNIE	ACTRESS	LA ROSERAIE	BIEVRES 91570	FRANCE
CORE, NATALIE	ACTRESS	8322 BEVERLY BLVD #202	LOS ANGELES, CA	90048
COREA, CHICK	MUSICIAN	33 ABBOTT AVE	EVERETT, MA	02149
COREA, NICHOLAS JOHN	WRITER-PRODUCER	14101 DICKENS ST #6	SHERMAN OAKS, CA	91423
CORELLI, FRANCO	TENOR	CAMI, 165 W 57TH ST	NEW YORK, NY	10019
CORENFLOS, J T	GUITARIST	335 FOREST PARK RD #36	MADISON, TN	37115
COREY, JEFF	ACTOR-DIRECTOR	29445 BLUEWATER RD	MALIBU, CA	90265
COREY, PROF IRWIN	COMEDIAN	58 NASSAU	GREAT NECK, NY	11022
CORGIAT, GARRY	ACTOR	8400 DE LONGPRE AVE #315	LOS ANGELES, CA	90069
CORGILE, WILLIAM C	NEWS CORRESPONDENT	4707 6TH PL, NE	WASHINGTON, DC	20017
CORINIS, DIMITRI	WRITER-PRODUCER	19 WESTBOURNE TERR #D	LONDON W2 6QT	ENGLAND
CORIO, ANN	BURLESQUE	CARUSO, 1706 MANDEVILLE LN	LOS ANGELES, CA	90049
CORK, ALLEN T	NEWS CORRESPONDENT	5151 WISCONSIN AVE, NW	WASHINGTON, DC	20016
CORKE, FREDERICK	WRITER	555 W 57TH ST #1230	NEW YORK, NY	10019
CORLETTE, BARBARA	ACTRESS	1585 CROSSROADS OF WORLD	HOLLYWOOD, CA	90028
CORLEY, AL	SINGER	ALEX GROB MANAGEMENT		
		THEATERSTRASSE 10	8024 ZURICH	SWITZERLAND
CORLEY, PAT	ACTOR	STONE, 1052 CAROL DR	LOS ANGELES, CA	90069
CORLEY, WILLIAM A	WRITER	555 W 57TH ST #1230	NEW YORK, NY	10019
CORLISS, RICHARD	FILM CRITIC-WRITER	TIME/TIME & LIFE BLDG		
		ROCKEFELLER CENTER	NEW YORK, NY	10020
CORMAN, AVERY	WRITER	555 W 57TH ST #1230	NEW YORK, NY	10019
CORMAN, CIS	CASTING DIRECTOR	1 GULF & WESTERN PLAZA	NEW YORK, NY	10023
CORMAN, EUGENE H	FILM PRODUCER	615 N ALTA DR	BEVERLY HILLS, CA	90210
CORMAN, JULIE	FILM PRODUCER	TRINITY PRODUCTIONS CO		
		11600 SAN VICENTE BLVD	LOS ANGELES, CA	90049
CORMAN, ROGER	WRITER-PRODUCER	NEW HORIZON PICTURES CO		
		11600 SAN VICENTE BLVD	LOS ANGELES, CA	90049
CORN, LAURA	ACTRESS	8019 1/2 MELROSE AVE #3	LOS ANGELES, CA	90046
CORNACHIO, DONNA	WRITER	555 W 57TH ST #1230	NEW YORK, NY	10019
CORNEAL, JOHN STEPHEN	DRUMMER	POST OFFICE BOX 127	AUBURNDALE, FL	33823
CORNELIUS, DON	TV PRODUCER	12685 MULHOLLAND DR	BEVERLY HILLS, CA	90210
CORNELIUS, HELEN	SINGER	WORLD CLASS TALENT AGY		
		1522 DEMONBREUN ST	NASHVILLE, TN	37203
CORNELIUS, RON	GUITARIST	7899 RIVER RD	NASHVILLE, TN	37209
CORNELIUS BROTHERS & SISTER ROS	VOCAL GROUP	CAROLINA ATTRACTIONS		
		203 CULVER AVE	CHARLESTON, SC	29407
CORNELL, DENNIS	CASTING DIRECTOR	EMBASSY TV, 1438 N GOWER ST	LOS ANGELES, CA	90028
CORNELL, DON	SINGER	POST OFFICE BOX C	RIVER EDGE, NJ	07661
CORNELL, LYDIA	ACTRESS-MODEL	2048 ROSCOMARE RD	LOS ANGELES, CA	90077
CORNET, ROBERT J	TV EXECUTIVE	NBC TELEVISION NETWORK		
		30 ROCKEFELLER PLAZA	NEW YORK, NY	10112
CORNETT, STANLEY	TENOR	IMG ARTISTS, 22 E 71ST ST	NEW YORK, NY	10021
CORNETTE, JIM	WRESTLING MANAGER	NATIONAL WRESTLING ALLIANCE		
		JIM CROCKETT PROMOTIONS		
		421 BRIARBEND DR	CHARLOTTE, NC	28209
CORNFIELD, BETTY	TV WRITER	555 W 57TH ST #1230	NEW YORK, NY	10019
CORNFIELD, EDITH	PIANIST	ROSENFIELD, 714 LADD RD	BRONX, NY	10471
CORNISH, DOUG	DIRECTOR	11266 DORLAND ST	WHITTIER, CA	90606
CORNISH, EDWARD	COLUMNIST	7720 EL CAMINO REAL #2-C	RANCHO LA COSTA, CA	92008
CORNTHWAITE, ROBERT	ACTOR	11656 JACARANDA AVE	HESPERIA, CA	92345
CORNWELL, JUDY	ACTRESS	LADKIN, 11 GARRICK ST	LONDON WC2	ENGLAND
CORPORA, THOMAS	TV EXECUTIVE	POST OFFICE BOX 467	ATLANTA, GA	30301
CORPORON, JOHN R	TV EXECUTIVE	INN, 11 WPIX PLAZA	NEW YORK, NY	10017

Name	Occupation	Address	City	Zip
CORRADO, GUS	ACTOR	1626 S WOOSTER ST	LOS ANGELES, CA	90035
CORRALES, PILITA	SINGER	POST OFFICE BOX 63	ORINDA, CA	94563
CORRELL, CHARLES	CINEMATOGRAPHER	3872 LAS FLORES CANYON RD #1	MALIBU, CA	90265
CORRELL, RICHARD	TV WRITER	8955 BEVERLY BLVD	LOS ANGELES, CA	90048
CORRI, NICK	ACTOR	151 S EL CAMINO DR	BEVERLY HILLS, CA	90212
CORRIGAN, C RICHARD	NEWS CORRESPONDENT	3335 TENNYSON ST, NW	WASHINGTON, DC	20015
CORRIGAN, DOUGLAS	ACTOR	2828 N FLOWER ST	SANTA ANA, CA	92706
CORRIGAN, JIM	PIANIST	114 LAKEWOOD CIR	SMYRNA, TN	37167
CORRINGTON, JOHN W	TV WRITER	8955 BEVERLY BLVD	LOS ANGELES, CA	90048
CORRINGTON, JOYCE H	TV WRITER	8955 BEVERLY BLVD	LOS ANGELES, CA	90048
CORROSION OF CONFORMITY	ROCK & ROLL GROUP	POST OFFICE BOX 5091	RALEIGH, NC	27607
CORRY, EARLE	CONDUCTOR	130 W PITKIN AVE	PUEBLO, CO	81004
CORRY, WILLIAM R	WRITER	8955 BEVERLY BLVD	LOS ANGELES, CA	90048
CORSARO, FRANK	OPERA DIRECTOR	33 RIVERSIDE DR	NEW YORK, NY	10023
CORSAUT, ANITA	ACTRESS	10850 RIVERSIDE DR #501	NORTH HOLLYWOOD, CA	91602
CORSENTINO, FRANK	ACTOR	5352 APPIAN WY	LONG BEACH, CA	90803
CORSO-PLITT, KAREN	ACTRESS	5631 SUNNYSLOPE AVE	VAN NUYS, CA	91401
CORT, BILL	ACTOR	9255 SUNSET BLVD #603	LOS ANGELES, CA	90069
CORT, BUD	ACTOR	2749 LYRIC AVE	LOS ANGELES, CA	90027
CORTES, ROBERT	PRODUCER	MCA/UNIVERSAL STUDIOS, INC		
		100 UNIVERSAL CITY PLAZA	UNIVERSAL CTIY, CA	91608
CORTESE, JOE	ACTOR	10100 SANTA MONICA BLVD #1600	LOS ANGELES, CA	90067
CORTEZ, MIGUEL	TENOR	59 E 54TH ST #81	NEW YORK, NY	10022
CORTEZ, STANLEY	CINEMATOGRAPHER	1512 SUNSET PLAZA DR	LOS ANGELES, CA	90069
CORTINAS, PEDRO	VIOLINIST	POST OFFICE BOX 131	SPRINGFIELD, VA	22150
CORTLAND, NICHOLAS	ACTOR	250 W 57TH ST #2317	NEW YORK, NY	10107
CORUJO, ROBERT	WRITER	555 W 57TH ST #1230	NEW YORK, NY	10019
CORVO, DAVID	WRITER	3870 RAMBLA ORIENTA	MALIBU, CA	90265
CORWIN, HANK	DOBROIST	ROUTE #2, BOX 210-U30		
		ANGLIN RD	FAIRVIEW, TN	37062
CORWIN, M J	TV EXECUTIVE	NBC-TV, 3000 W ALAMEDA AVE	BURBANK, CA	91523
CORWIN, MARK ROBERT	TV DIRECTOR	5748 HILLVIEW PARK AVE	VAN NUYS, CA	91401
CORWIN, NORMAN	WRITER-PRODUCER	1840 FAIRBURN AVE #302	LOS ANGELES, CA	90025
CORWIN, RAYMOND A	DIRECTOR	370 RIVERSIDE DR	NEW YORK, NY	10025
CORWIN, SHERRILL	ACTOR	838 N DOHENRY DR #PH-C	LOS ANGELES, CA	90069
CORYELL, LARRY	MUSICIAN	5 WATCHILL RD	WESTPORT, CT	06880
CORZINE, MICHAEL	ORGANIST	15 HIGH ST #621	HARTFORD, CT	06103
COSAND, LARRY	ACTOR	1214 N CLARK ST #9	LOS ANGELES, CA	90069
COSBY, BILL	ACTOR-COMEDIAN	BARDWELL FERRY RD, BOX 808	GREENFIELD, MA	01301
COSCARELLI, DONALD	FILM DIRECTOR	4132 FULTON AVE	SHERMAN OAKS, CA	91423
COSEL, WILLIAM N	DIRECTOR	335 HURON AVE	CAMBRIDGE, MA	02138
COSELL, HOWARD	SPORTSCASTER	150 E 69TH ST	NEW YORK, NY	10021
COSGROVE, JOHN	DIRECTOR	BELL, 3211 W CAHUENGA BLVD	LOS ANGELES, CA	90068
COSMATOS, GEORGE P	FILM DIRECTOR	151 S EL CAMINO DR	BEVERLY HILLS, CA	90212
COSNER, BOBBY	WRITER	555 W 57TH ST #1230	NEW YORK, NY	10019
COSPITO, FRED	WRITER	555 W 57TH ST #1230	NEW YORK, NY	10019
COSSA, DOMINIC	BARITONE	COLBERT, 111 W 57TH ST	NEW YORK, NY	10019
COSSETT, PIERRE	PRODUCER	8899 BEVERLY BLVD #900	LOS ANGELES, CA	90048
COSSINS, JAMES	ACTOR	LEADING ARTISTS, LTD		
		60 SAINT JAMES'S ST	LONDON SW1	ENGLAND
COSSON, PIERRE	FILM DIRECTOR	RUE DU PRESSOIR	EPISRHUS 95810	FRANCE
COSSOTTO, FIORENZA	MEZZO-SOPRANO	CAMI, 165 W 57TH ST	NEW YORK, NY	10019
COSSU, SCOTT	PIANIST	POST OFFICE BOX 9388	STANFORD, CA	94305
COST, THOMAS M	WRITER	5800 SHIRLEY AVE	TARZANA, CA	91356
COSTA, COSIE	ACTOR	2816 N FREDERICK ST	BURBANK, CA	91504
COSTA, JOSEPH	PHOTOGRAPHER	25301 OUTLOOK DR	CARMEL, CA	93923
COSTA, MARY	SOPRANO	1182 MARKET ST #311	SAN FRANCISCO, CA	94102
COSTA, SEQUEIRA	PIANIST	GERSHUNOFF, 502 PARK AVE	NEW YORK, NY	10022
COSTA-GAVRAS, HENRI "CONSTANTIN	FILM WRITER-DIRECTOR	244 RUE SAINT JACQUES	PARIS 75005	FRANCE
COSTA-GREENSPON, MURIEL	MEZZO-SOPRANO	GERSHUNOFF, 502 PARK AVE	NEW YORK, NY	10022
COSTA-REIS, EDGARDO	NEWS CORRESPONDENT	6507 WILMETT RD	BETHESDA, MD	20817
COSTAPERARIA, BARBARA M	WRITER	12308 EMELITA ST	NORTH HOLLYWOOD, CA	91607
COSTAS, BOB	SPORTSCASTER	NBC-TV, SPORTS DEPARTMENT		
		30 ROCKEFELLER PLAZA	NEW YORK, NY	10112
COSTE, PHILLIPPE	NEWS CORRESPONDENT	4515 VERPLANCKE PL, NW	WASHINGTON, DC	20016
COSTELLO, ANTHONY	ACTOR	211 S BEVERLY DR #201	BEVERLY HILLS, CA	90212
COSTELLO, BRIAN	WRESTLER	AMERICAN WRESTLING ASSOC		
		MINNEAPLOIS WRESTLING		
		10001 WAYZATA BLVD	MINNETONKA, MN	55345
COSTELLO, ELVIS & THE ATTRACTIO	ROCK & ROLL GROUP	GLOBAL RIVIIERA, WESTERN HOUSE		
		9028 GREAT GUEST RD	MIDDLESEX TW8 9EW	ENGLAND
COSTELLO, J D	WRESTLING MANAGER	NATIONAL WRESTLING ALLIANCE		
		JIM CROCKETT PROMOTIONS		
		421 BRIARBEND DR	CHARLOTTE, NC	28209
COSTELLO, JOHN	WRITER	555 W 57TH ST #1230	NEW YORK, NY	10019
COSTELLO, MARICLAIRE	ACTRESS	SF & A, 121 N SAN VICENTE BLVD	BEVERLY HILLS, CA	90211
COSTELLO, MARJORIE	PUBLISHING EXECUTIVE	VIDEOGRAPHY MAGAZINE		
		475 PARK AVE	NEW YORK, NY	10016
COSTELLO, MARK	ACTOR	8230 BEVERLY BLVD #23	LOS ANGELES, CA	90048
COSTELLO, ROBERT E	DIRECTOR	NARWAL, 161 W 57TH ST	NEW YORK, NY	10019
COSTELLO, WARD	ACTOR	247 S BEVERLY DR #102	BEVERLY HILLS, CA	90210
COSTER, CANDACE	ACTRESS	345 N PALM DR #8	BEVERLY HILLS, CA	90210
COSTER, NICOLAS	ACTOR	1624 N GARDNER ST	LOS ANGELES, CA	90046
COSTI, AL R	COMPOSER	9838 WHEATLAND	SUNLAND, CA	91040
COSTICK, LOUISE R	NEWS CORRESPONDENT	3420 ANNANDALE RD	FALLS CHURCH, VA	22042

Name	Occupation	Address	City	Zip/Country
COSTIGAN, JAMES	SCREENWRITER	8955 BEVERLY BLVD	LOS ANGELES, CA	90048
COSTIKYAN, ANDREW M	DIRECTOR	567 HAPP RD	NORTHFIELD, IL	60093
COSTIKYAN, FRANCES H	WRITER	8955 BEVERLY BLVD	LOS ANGELES, CA	90048
COSTON, SUZANNE	TV PRODUCER	ICM, 8899 BEVERLY BLVD	LOS ANGELES, CA	90048
COTHRAN, MICHAEL H	PIANIST	2503 SUNSET PL	NASHVILLE, TN	37212
COTHRAN, WILLIAM	ACTOR-WRITER	3850 WAWONA ST	LOS ANGELES, CA	90065
COTLER, ALAN B	SCREENWRITER	8955 BEVERLY BLVD	LOS ANGELES, CA	90048
COTLER, GORDON	TV WRITER	555 W 57TH ST #1230	NEW YORK, NY	10019
COTRUBAS, ILEANA	SOPRANO	ICM, 40 W 57TH ST	NEW YORK, NY	10019
COTSWORTH, STAATS	ACTOR	360 E 55TH ST	NEW YORK, NY	10022
COTT, GERRY	SINGER	41 BRITAIN ST #200	TORONTO, ONT	CANADA
COTT, RIDLEY	FILM DIRECTOR	6-10 LEXINGTON ST	LONDON W1	ENGLAND
COTTEN, JOSEPH	ACTOR	1993 MESA DR	PALM SPRINGS, CA	92264
COTTEN, RICHARD MANSEL	GUITARIST	1815 21ST AVE S	NASHVILLE, TN	37212
COTTLE, GRAHAM D	FILM PRODUCER	SENTA PRODUCTIONS		
		CHANCERY HOUSE		
		CHANCERY LN	LONDON WC2	ENGLAND
COTTLE, GRAHAM DAVID	DIRECTOR	8261 MARMONT LN	LOS ANGELES, CA	90069
COTTOM, EVERETT M	NEWS CORRESPONDENT	2800 ONTARIO RD, NW	WASHINGTON, DC	20009
COTTON, GENE	SINGER-GUITARIST	ROUTE #3, SWEENEY HOLLOW RD	FRANKLIN, TN	37064
COTTON, JACK	GUITARIST	5141 LANA RENEE CT	HERMITAGE, TN	37076
COTTON, JAMES, BAND	JAZZ GROUP	KENNERLY, 11541 S HALE AVE	CHICAGO, IL	60643
COTTON, OLIVER	ACTOR	GREEN & UNDERWOOD, LTD		
		3 THE BROADWAY		
		GUNNERSBURY LN	LONDON W3 8HR	ENGLAND
COTTON, PAUL	SINGER-SONGWRITER	4804 KELVIN AVE	WOODLAND HILLS, CA	91364
COTTON-ATES, CAROLINA	SINGER	POST OFFICE BOX 730	BAKERSFIELD, CA	93302
COTTONWOOD	MUSICAL GROUP	LUTZ, 5625 "O" STREET BLDG	LINCOLN, NE	68510
COTTS, GERALD VOSS	DIRECTOR	627 W END AVE	NEW YORK, NY	10024
COUCH, CHARLES EDWARD	DIRECTOR	DGA, 7950 SUNSET BLVD	LOS ANGELES, CA	90046
COUCH, CHESTER	DRUMMER	4101 UTAH AVE	NASHVILLE, TN	37209
COUDOUX, SYLVAIN	NEWS CORRESPONDENT	4651 SEMINARY RD	ALEXANDRIA, VA	22304
COUFFER, JACK	WRITER-PRODUCER	ICM, 8899 BEVERLY BLVD	LOS ANGELES, CA	90048
COUGAR, JOHN	SINGER-SONGWRITER	SEE - MELLENCAMP, JOHN COUGAR		
COUGAR JAY	WRESTLER	NATIONAL WRESTLING ALLIANCE		
		JIM CROCKETT PROMOTIONS		
		421 BRIARBEND DR	CHARLOTTE, NC	28209
COUGHLAN, GREGORY S	NEWS CORRESPONDENT	5212 GRINNELL ST	FAIRFAX, VA	22032
COUGHLIN, ELLEN K	NEWS CORRESPONDENT	213 13TH ST, SE	WASHINGTON, DC	20003
COULIER, DAVID	ACTOR	11726 SAN VICENTE BLVD #300	LOS ANGELES, CA	90049
COULOURIS, GEORGE	ACTOR	CHESTNUT COTTAGE		
		VALE OF HEATH, HAMPSTEAD	LONDON NW3	ENGLAND
COULSON, COTTON	PHOTOGRAPHER	745 10TH ST, SE	WASHINGTON, DC	20003
COULSON, PETER	DIRECTOR-PRODUCER	15 EYOT GARDENS	LONDON W6 9TN	ENGLAND
COULTER, ELIZABETH	ACTRESS	9165 SUNSET BLVD #202	LOS ANGELES, CA	90069
COUNTRY GAZETTE, THE	VOCAL GROUP	FOLKLORE, 1671 APPIAN WY	SANTA MONICA, CA	90401
COUNTRY GENTLEMEN, THE	VOCAL GROUP	ROUTE #2, BOX 640	WARRENTON, VA	22186
COUNTRY GOLD EXPRESS	C & W GROUP	POST OFFICE BOX 4234	PANORAMA CITY, CA	91412
COUNTRY LIBERATION, THE	VOCAL GROUP	POST OFFICE BOX 3153	GLENDALE, CA	91201
COUNTRY PARSON	GOSPEL GROUP	POST OFFICE BOX AB	EUSTIS, FL	32727
COUNTRY SPIRIT BAND	C & W GROUP	CUDE, 519 N HALIFAX AVE	DAYTONA BEACH, FL	37212
COUNTRYMAN, JOHN R	SINGER-SONGWRITER	SEE - RUSSELL, JOHNNY		
COUNTRYMAN, SCOTT	STUD-TRACK & FIELD	2801 MEADOW LARK DR	SAN DIEGO, CA	92123
COUNTS, RICHARD	WRESTLING WRITER	POST OFFICE BOX 48	ROCKVILLE CENTRE, NY	11571
COUPLAND, DIANA	ACTRESS	BD, 81 SHAFTESBURY AVE	LONDON W1	ENGLAND
COUPPEE, ED	ACTOR	12168 OXNARD ST	NORTH HOLLYWOOD, CA	91606
COURAGE, ALEXANDER	COMPOSER-CONDUCTOR	23344 PALOMA BLANCA	MALIBU, CA	90265
COURAGE, CAROLYN	ACTRESS	BRYAN DREW, LTD		
		MEZZANINE QUADRANT HOUSE		
		80-82 REGENT ST	LONDON W1	ENGLAND
COURBASH, YMA	TV WRITER	8955 BEVERLY BLVD	LOS ANGELES, CA	90048
COURCEL, NICOLE	ACTRESS	G BEAUME, 3 QUAI MALAQUAIS	PARIS 75006	FRANCE
COURCOL, CHRISTINE	NEWS CORRESPONDENT	6004 34TH PL, NW	WASHINGTON, DC	20015
COURLEY, JIM	CLOWN	2701 COTTAGE WY #14	SACRAMENTO, CA	95825
COURT, GERALDINE	ACTRESS	19 W 44TH ST #1500	NEW YORK, NY	10036
COURT, HAZEL	ACTRESS	1111 SAN VICENTE BLVD	SANTA MONICA, CA	90402
COURTENAY, MARGARET	ACTRESS	16 BROOKFIELD RD	LONDON W4	ENGLAND
COURTENAY, TOM	ACTOR	ICM, 388-396 OXFORD ST	LONDON W1	ENGLAND
COURTLAND, JEROME	DIRECTOR	2224 THE TERRACE	LOS ANGELES, CA	90049
COURTLAND, JOHN C	DIRECTOR	4909 BELLAIRE AVE	NORTH HOLLYWOOD, CA	91607
COURTLEIGH, BOB	ACTOR	3321 LANDA ST	LOS ANGELES, CA	90039
COURTNEY, ALEX	ACTOR	3351 OAK GLEN DR	LOS ANGELES, CA	90068
COURTNEY, JAMES	SINGER	CAMI, 165 W 57TH ST	NEW YORK, NY	10019
COURTNEY, NICHOLAS	ACTOR	118 CRAWFORD ST	LONDON W1H 1AF	ENGLAND
COUSIN LUKE	WRESTLER	POST OFFICE BOX 3859	STAMFORD, CT	06905
COUSINS, CHRISTOPHER	ACTOR	NBC-TV, "ANOTHER WORLD"		
		30 ROCKEFELLER PLAZA	NEW YORK, NY	10112
COUSTEAU, JACQUES	OCEANOGRAPHER	777 3RD AVE	NEW YORK, NY	10017
COUSY, BOB	BASKETBALL	459 SALISBURY ST	WORCESTER, MA	01609
COUTARD, RAOUL	FILM DIRECTOR	138 BLVD MURAT	PARIS 75016	FRANCE
COUTURIE, ANNE SPIESS	WRITER	8955 BEVERLY BLVD	LOS ANGELES, CA	90048
COUTURIE, BILL D	WRITER	8955 BEVERLY BLVD	LOS ANGELES, CA	90048
COVAN, DE FORREST	DANCER	5545 CARLSON WY #301	LOS ANGELES, CA	90028
COVAULT, CRAIG	NEWS CORRESPONDENT	1933 BATON DR	VIENNA, VA	22180
COVELLI, JOHN	PIANIST	POST OFFICE BOX U	REDDING, CT	06875

Name	Occupation	Address	City	Zip
COVER, FRANKLIN	ACTOR	11726 SAN VICENTE BLVD #300	LOS ANGELES, CA	90049
COVERT, DAVE	SINGER	POST OFFICE BOX 171132	NASHVILLE, TN	37217
COVERT, DONALD	CONDUCTOR	KAY, 58 W 58TH ST	NEW YORK, NY	10019
COVERT, JAMES	ACTOR	9230 OLYMPIC BLVD #203	BEVERLY HILLS, CA	90212
COVIELLO, ROBERTO	BARITONE	61 W 62ND ST #6-F	NEW YORK, NY	10023
COVINGTON, BOB	WRITER	555 W 57TH ST #1230	NEW YORK, NY	10019
COVINGTON, HILBURN	DIRECTOR	2816 NICHOLS CANYON RD	LOS ANGELES, CA	90046
COVY, ROSANNE	ACTRESS	3800 BARHAM BLVD #303	LOS ANGELES, CA	90068
COWAN, CLAUDIA	ACTRESS	3907 W ALAMEDA AVE #101	BURBANK, CA	91505
COWAN, CLAYTON L	COMPOSER	15749 MERCED AVE	CHINO, CA	91710
COWAN, EDWARD	NEWS CORRESPONDENT	3924 HARRISON ST, NW	WASHINGTON, DC	20015
COWAN, MICHAEL A	TV DIRECTOR	3756 EFFINGHAM PL	LOS ANGELES, CA	90027
COWAN, RICHARD	BASSO-BARITONE	MUNRO, 334 W 72ND ST	NEW YORK, NY	10023
COWAN, RICHARD	NEWS CORRESPONDENT	2727 29TH ST, NW	WASHINGTON, DC	20008
COWAN, SIGMUND	BARITONE	HILLYER, 250 W 57TH ST	NEW YORK, NY	10107
COWAN, WAYNE	WRESTLER	SEE - MANTEL, DUTCH		
COWAN, WILL	FILM DIRECTOR	9140 BROOKSHIRE AVE	DOWNEY, CA	90240
COWARD, LOUISE P	NEWS CORRESPONDENT	3411 LOWELL ST, NW	WASHINGTON, DC	20016
COWBOY BOB	WRESTLER	SEE - ORTON, COWBOY BOB		
COWBOY JAZZ	C & W GROUP	LST, 2138 FLAG MARSH RD	MOUNT AIRY, MD	21771
COWDEN, JACK	WRITER	8955 BEVERLY BLVD	LOS ANGELES, CA	90048
COWELL, STANLEY	PIANIST	KURLAND, 173 BRIGHTON AVE	BOSTON, MA	02134
COWEN, DONNA	ACTRESS	340 S OCEAN BLVD	PALM BEACH, FL	33480
COWEN, EUGENE S	TV EXECUTIVE	ABC-TV, NEWS DEPARTMENT		
		1717 DE SALES ST, NW	WASHINGTON, DC	20036
COWEN, FRANK	COMPOSER	POST OFFICE BOX 395	ROSAMOND, CA	93560
COWEN, ROBERT M, JR	NEWS CORRESPONDENT	9113 WILLOW POND LN	POTOMAC, MD	20854
COWEN, RON	TV WRITER	620 VIA DE LA PAZ	PACIFIC PALISADES, CA	90272
COWGILL, LINDA J	TV WRITER	8955 BEVERLY BLVD	LOS ANGELES, CA	90048
COWL, DARRYL	ACTOR	3 RUE EDOUARD NORTIER	NEUILLY 92200	FRANCE
COWLES, MATHEW	ACTOR	50 DELANCY ST	NEW YORK, NY	10002
COWLES, MATTHEW	ACTOR	ABC-TV NETWORK, "LOVING"		
		1330 AVE OF THE AMERICAS	NEW YORK, NY	10019
COWLES, SYMON B	TV EXECUTIVE	ABC TELEVISION NETWORK		
		1330 AVE OF THE AMERICAS	NEW YORK, NY	10019
COWLEY, GILBERT H, JR	WRITER	555 W 57TH ST #1230	NEW YORK, NY	10019
COWLEY, WILLIAM	ACTOR	5850 CANOGA AVE #110	WOODLAND HILLS, CA	91367
COWLEY, WILLIAM M, III	WRITER	2544 HUTTON DR	BEVERLY HILLS, CA	90210
COX, AINSLEE	CONDUCTOR	157 W 57TH ST #1100	NEW YORK, NY	10019
COX, ASHLEY	ACTRESS-MODEL	328 W COLORADO AVE	GLENDORA, CA	91740
COX, BOWMAN	NEWS CORRESPONDENT	2418 59TH PL	CHEVERLY, MD	20785
COX, BRIAN	ACTOR	LARRY DALZELL ASSOCIATES		
		126 KENNINGTON PARK RD	LONDON SE11 4DJ	ENGLAND
COX, CHRISTINA	ACTRESS	3151 W CAHUENGA BLVD #310	LOS ANGELES, CA	90068
COX, COURTNEY	ACTRESS	FRONTIER BOOKING INTL		
		8600 MELROSE AVE	LOS ANGELES, CA	90069
COX, CRAWFORD	ACTOR	8640 HILLROSE ST #E-12	SUNLAND, CA	91040
COX, DAVID M	WRITER	8955 BEVERLY BLVD	LOS ANGELES, CA	90048
COX, EUGENE ALLEN	BANJOIST	2333 PENNINGTON BEACH RD	NASHVILLE, TN	37210
COX, GARY D	WRITER	8955 BEVERLY BLVD	LOS ANGELES, CA	90048
COX, GARY DON	ACTOR	10000 SANTA MONICA BLVD #305	LOS ANGELES, CA	90067
COX, JAMES	COLUMNIST	POST OFFICE BOX 500	WASHINGTON, DC	20044
COX, JAMES RUSSELL	TV DIRECTOR	1872 W TEDMAR AVE	ANAHEIM, CA	92804
COX, JOSHUA	ACTOR	ABC-TV, "ONE LIFE TO LIVE"		
		1330 AVE OF THE AMERICAS	NEW YORK, NY	10019
COX, KENNETH	BASS	HILLYER, 250 W 57TH ST	NEW YORK, NY	10107
COX, KENNETH STEWART	TRUMPETER	4301 APPLEWOOD	MATTESON, IL	60443
COX, MARY	SCREENWRITER	8955 BEVERLY BLVD	LOS ANGELES, CA	90048
COX, MICHAEL GRAHAM	ACTOR	32 CLIFTON GARDENS	LONDON W9	ENGLAND
COX, MICHAEL STEPHEN	TV DIRECTOR-PRODUCER	GRANADA TV CENTRE	MANCHESTER M60 9EA	ENGLAND
COX, MONTY	STUNTMAN	3518 W CAHUENGA BLVD #300	LOS ANGELES, CA	90068
COX, NELL	WRITER-PRODUCER	1629 GEORGINA AVE	SANTA MONICA, CA	90403
COX, PAUL E	NEWS CORRESPONDENT	2021 N ROOSEVELT ST	ARLINGTON, VA	22205
COX, RICHARD	ACTOR	2121 AVE OF THE STARS #410	LOS ANGELES, CA	90067
COX, RICHARD	TV-CABLE EXECUTIVE	CBS-TV, 51 W 52ND ST	NEW YORK, NY	10019
COX, RICHARD M	DIRECTOR	933 TOWLSTON RD	MC LEAN, VA	22102
COX, ROGER	DRUMMER	510 HERITAGE DR #B-1	MADISON, TN	37115
COX, RONNY	ACTOR-FILM PRODUCER	ICM, 8899 BEVERLY BLVD	LOS ANGELES, CA	90048
COX, STEVE	WRESTLER	UNIVERSAL WRESTLING FEDERATION		
		MID SOUTH SPORTS, INC		
		5001 SPRING VALLEY RD	DALLAS, TX	75244
COX, TONY	CABLE EXECUTIVE	HOME BOX OFFICE PICTURES		
		1100 AVE OF THE AMERICAS	NEW YORK, NY	10036
COX, WESLEY J	WRITER	KOHNER, 9169 SUNSET BLVD	LOS ANGELES, CA	90069
COX, WILLIAM	GUITARIST	516 BOB WHITE CT	NASHVILLE, TN	37218
COX, WILLIAM R	WRITER	3974 BEVERLY GLEN BLVD	SHERMAN OAKS, CA	91423
COYLE, HARRY J	TV DIRECTOR	70 ALPINE DR	WAYNE, NJ	07470
COYLE, MARCIA A	NEWS CORRESPONDENT	119 LAFAYETTE AVE	ANNAPOLIS, MD	21401
COYLE, PAUL ROBERT	TV WRITER	9911 W PICO BLVD #1490	LOS ANGELES, CA	90035
COYLE, SUSAN	ACTRESS	1042 E WALNUT AVE	BURBANK, CA	91501
COYOTE, PETER	ACTOR	SF & A, 121 N SAN VICENTE BLVD	BEVERLY HILLS, CA	90211
COZART, RANDY	DRUMMER	1011-B BROADMOOR DR	NASHVILLE, TN	37216
COZART, TOMMY	DRUMMER	1238 ADAMS ST	FRANKLIN, TN	37064
COZENS, VIVIENNE	TV DIRECTOR	29 COURTNELL ST	LONDON W2	ENGLAND
COZYRIS, GEORGE A	WRITER	8955 BEVERLY BLVD	LOS ANGELES, CA	90048

Name	Occupation	Address	City	Zip
COZZA, MICHAEL A	NEWS CORRESPONDENT	400 N CAPITOL ST, NW	WASHINGTON, DC	20001
COZZENS, MIMI	ACTRESS	STONE, 1052 CAROL DR	LOS ANGELES, CA	90069
COZZI, MIKE	TV DIRECTOR	8508 CASABA AVE	CANOGA PARK, CA	91306
CRABB, ALAN	TENOR	1776 BROADWAY #504	NEW YORK, NY	10019
CRABB, LAWRENCE	WRITER-PRODUCER	1 HILL CLOSE	LONDON NW2 6RE	ENGLAND
CRABBE, CUFFY	ACTOR	11216 N 74TH ST	SCOTTSDALE, AZ	85260
CRABBY, TABBY	GUITARIST	1030 16TH AVE S	NASHVILLE, TN	37212
CRABE, JAMES	CINEMATOGRAPHER	222 NICHOLS CANYON RD	LOS ANGELES, CA	90046
CRABTREE, MICHAEL	ACTOR	9200 SUNSET BLVD #1210	LOS ANGELES, CA	90069
CRADDOCK, BILLY "CRASH"	SINGER-SONGWRITER	POST OFFICE BOX 121089	NASHVILLE, TN	37212
CRADDOCK, RON	TV DIRECTOR-PRODUCER	WOODSTONE, KIDMORE END		
		READING	BERKS	ENGLAND
CRAFT, CARL C	NEWS CORRESPONDENT	5274 LONSDALE DR	SPRINGFIELD, VA	22151
CRAFT, GARLAND	PIANIST	POST OFFICE BOX 1763	HENDERSONVILLE, TN	37075
CRAFT, PAUL CHARLES	BANJOIST	669 S BELVEDERE BLVD	MEMPHIS, TN	38104
CRAFT, ROBERT J	WRITER	23279 WELBY WY	CANOGA PARK, CA	91307
CRAFTS, EDWARD	BARITONE	CAMI, 165 W 57TH ST	NEW YORK, NY	10019
CRAFTS, RITA	ACTRESS	2541 6TH ST	SANTA MONICA, CA	90405
CRAGG, STEPHEN	TV DIRECTOR	12415 VALLEYHEART DR	STUDIO CITY, CA	91604
CRAGG, STEVEN	PRODUCER	MCA/UNIVERSAL STUDIOS, INC		
		100 UNIVERSAL CITY PLAZA	UNIVERSAL CITY, CA	91608
CRAGGS, JULIAN	DIRECTOR	1419 DAUPHINE ST	NEW ORLEANS, LA	70116
CRAIG, CARL	ACTOR	3281 N FAIR OAKS AVE	ALTADENA, CA	91001
CRAIG, CATHERINE	ACTRESS	PRESTON, 1035 FAIRWAY DR	MONTECITO, CA	93108
CRAIG, DAVID	COLUMNIST	POST OFFICE BOX 500	WASHINGTON, DC	20044
CRAIG, DAVID COBB	NEWS REPORTER	LIFE/TIME & LIFE BLDG		
		ROCKEFELLER CENTER	NEW YORK, NY	10020
CRAIG, DEAN K	TV EXECUTIVE	NBC-TV, 3000 W ALAMEDA AVE	BURBANK, CA	91523
CRAIG, HELEN	ACTRESS	BEAL, 205 W 54TH ST	NEW YORK, NY	10019
CRAIG, JIM	NEWS CORRESPONDENT	6008 JEWELL CT	ALEXANDRIA, VA	22312
CRAIG, JOHN	ACTOR	9200 SUNSET BLVD #909	LOS ANGELES, CA	90069
CRAIG, LOMAN EARL	GUITARIST	3939 APACHE TRAIL #V-4	ANTIOCH, TN	37013
CRAIG, MICHAEL	ACTOR	ICM, 388-396 OXFORD ST	LONDON W1	ENGLAND
CRAIG, PATRICIA	SOPRANO	61 W 62ND ST #6-F	NEW YORK, NY	10023
CRAIG, ROGER	BASEBALL	2453 CANORA AVE	ALPINE, CA	92331
CRAIG, W SCOTT	DIRECTOR-PRODUCER	1924 A N MOHAWK ST #11	CHICAGO, IL	60614
CRAIG, WENDY	ACTRESS	HATTON, 18 JERMYN ST	LONDON SW1	ENGLAND
CRAIG, YVONNE	ACTRESS	1221 OCEAN AVE #202	SANTA MONICA, CA	90401
CRAIG COUNTRY BOYS, THE	C & W GROUP	BMP, 732 BRANDON AVE, SW	ROANOKE, VA	24015
CRAIG-RAYMOND, PETER	WRITER-PRODUCER	28 LORDSHIP LN	LONDON SE22	ENGLAND
CRAIN, BILLY	DRUMMER	2227 SCHOOL RD	LAND O LAKES, FL	33539
CRAIN, JEANNE	ACTRESS	354 HILGARD AVE	LOS ANGELES, CA	90024
CRAIN, JOHN THOMAS	GUITARIST	ROUTE #4, BLAZER LN	FRANKLIN, TN	37064
CRAIN, SCOTT	NEWS CORRESPONDENT	400 N CAPITOL ST, NW	WASHINGTON, DC	20001
CRAIN, WILLIAM	FILM DIRECTOR	POST OFFICE BOX 744	BEVERLY HILLS, CA	90213
CRAIS, ROBERT	WRITER	12829 LANDALE ST	STUDIO CITY, CA	91604
CRAM, ROBERT	FLUTIST	200 W 70TH ST #7-F	NEW YORK, NY	10023
CRAMER, DOUGLAS A	TV WRITER-PRODUCER	738 SARBONNE RD	LOS ANGELES, CA	90077
CRAMER, FLOYD	PIANIST	SUTTON, 119 W 57TH ST	NEW YORK, NY	10019
CRAMER, GRANT	ACTOR	6310 SAN VICENTE BLVD #407	LOS ANGELES, CA	90048
CRAMER, ROSS G	DIRECTOR	DGA, 110 W 57TH ST	NEW YORK, NY	10019
CRAMPTON, BARBARA	ACTRESS	427 N CANON DR #205	BEVERLY HILLS, CA	90212
CRAN, WILLIAM	WRITER	555 W 57TH ST #1230	NEW YORK, NY	10019
CRANDALL, CECIL A	COMPOSER	1441 MERRIMAN DR	GLENDALE, CA	91202
CRANDALL, CHERYL LOUISE	ACTRESS	6515 SUNSET BLVD #401	LOS ANGELES, CA	90028
CRANDALL, JENNIFER	PHOTO EDITOR	US MAGAZINE COMPANY		
		1 DAG HAMMARSKJOLD PLAZA	NEW YORK, NY	10017
CRANE, ALBERT H, III	TV EXECUTIVE	CBS-TV, 51 W 52ND ST	NEW YORK, NY	10019
CRANE, BRANDON	ACTOR	1717 N HIGHLAND AVE #414	LOS ANGELES, CA	90028
CRANE, DAVID H	COMPOSER	3725 S TOPANGA BLVD	MALIBU, CA	90265
CRANE, HARRY	WRITER	9014 ALTO CEDRO DR	BEVERLY HILLS, CA	90210
CRANE, KENNETH	FILM DIRECTOR	6627 LINDENHURST AVE	LOS ANGELES, CA	90048
CRANE, LES	TV-RADIO HOST	424 S REXFORD DR	BEVERLY HILLS, CA	90212
CRANE, PETER MAURICE	DIRECTOR-PRODUCER	333 W 86TH ST	NEW YORK, NY	10024
CRANEY, TRUDY	SOPRANO	756 7TH AVE #67	NEW YORK, NY	10019
CRANFILL, DAVID V	DIRECTOR	520 N MICHIGAN AVE #436	CHICAGO, IL	60611
CRANFORD, JOHN R	NEWS CORRESPONDENT	1701 LOGMILL LN	GAITHERSBURG, MD	20879
CRANSHAW, PATRICK	ACTOR	8165 KATHERINE AVE	PANORAMA CITY, CA	91402
CRANSTON, BRYAN	ACTOR	POST OFFICE BOX 69405	LOS ANGELES, CA	90069
CRANSTON, MARY KATE	NEWS CORRESPONDENT	2700 "Q" ST, NW	WASHINGTON, DC	20007
CRASH, JIMMY	SINGER	CRAIG DAVID, 20 PLAZA PL	LIVINGSTON, NJ	07039
CRASH 'N FLASH	TRAMPOLINISTS	HALL, 138 FROG HOLLOW RD	CHURCHVILLE, PA	18966
CRASH CREW	SOUL GROUP	SUGARHILL RECORDS		
		96 WEST ST	ENGLEWOOD, NJ	07631
CRATTY, BILL	DANCER	AFFILIATE ARTISTS, INC		
		37 W 65TH ST, 6TH FLOOR	NEW YORK, NY	10023
CRATTY, CAROL A	NEWS CORRESPONDENT	2133 WISCONSIN AVE, NW	WASHINGTON, DC	20007
CRAVEN, CAROL	TV DIRECTOR	137 E 66TH ST	NEW YORK, NY	10021
CRAVEN, GARTH	DIRECTOR	21751 AZURELEE DR	MALIBU, CA	90265
CRAVEN, GEMMA	ACTRESS	RICHARDS, 42 HAZLEBURY RD	LONDON SW6	ENGLAND
CRAVEN, PEGGY	ACTRESS	LLOYD, 1813 OLD RANCH RD	LOS ANGELES, CA	90049
CRAVEN, RICHARD	DIRECTOR	137 E 66TH ST	NEW YORK, NY	10021
CRAVEN, RICHARD	FILM PRODUCER	39 ANTRIM MANSIONS	LONDON NW3 4XV	ENGLAND
CRAVEN, THOMAS	DIRECTOR	83 HEWLETT AVE	POINT LOOKOUT, NY	11569
CRAVEN, THOMAS, JR	PHOTOJOURNALIST	6529 KERNS RD	FALLS CHURCH, VA	22044

CRAVEN, WESLEY	WRITER-PRODUCER	2015 NAVY ST	SANTA MONICA, CA	90405
CRAVER, MARTHA L	NEWS CORRESPONDENT	4550 CONNECTICUT AVE #706, NW	WASHINGTON, DC	20008
CRAVIOTTE, DARLENE	SCREENWRITER	LEVIEN, 1202 N POINSETTIA DR	LOS ANGELES, CA	90046
CRAWFISH BAND	C & W GROUP	POST OFFICE BOX 5412	BUENA PARK, CA	90620
CRAWFORD, ANTHONY	MANDOLINIST	2701 NODYNE CIR	NASHVILLE, TN	37214
CRAWFORD, C C	WRITER	555 W 57TH ST #1230	NEW YORK, NY	10019
CRAWFORD, CALVIN	GUITARIST	135 HILLS DALE DR	HENDERSONVILLE, TN	37075
CRAWFORD, CASEY	NEWS CORRESPONDENT	2122 LEROY PL, NW	WASHINGTON, DC	20008
CRAWFORD, CHERYL	THEATER PRODUCER	400 E 52ND ST	NEW YORK, NY	10022
CRAWFORD, CHRISTINA	AUTHORESS	KOONTZ, 4630 MIRADOR PL	TARZANA, CA	91356
CRAWFORD, FRANK B, JR	DIRECTOR-PRODUCER	7838 SHOSONE AVE	NORTHRIDGE, CA	91325
CRAWFORD, HARDIN	GUITARIST	732 MADISON BLVD	MADISON, TN	37115
CRAWFORD, HARRIET B	COMPOSER	5505 TOPEKA DR	TARZANA, CA	91356
CRAWFORD, JAMES	NEWS CORRESPONDENT	101 N CAROLINA AVE, SE	WASHINGTON, DC	20003
CRAWFORD, JOANNA	TV WRITER	151 S EL CAMINO DR	BEVERLY HILLS, CA	90212
CRAWFORD, JOHN	ACTOR	3800 BARHAM BLVD #303	LOS ANGELES, CA	90068
CRAWFORD, JOHN	STUNTMAN	POST OFFICE BOX 1770	STUDIO CITY, CA	91604
CRAWFORD, JOSEPH A	ACTOR	8800 KITTYHAWK AVE	LOS ANGELES, CA	90045
CRAWFORD, LEE	ACTRESS	3800 BARHAM BLVD #303	LOS ANGELES, CA	90068
CRAWFORD, MARK H	NEWS CORRESPONDENT	4617 COLUMBIA RD	ANNANDALE, VA	22003
CRAWFORD, MERRITT A, JR	NEWS CORRESPONDENT	1825 "K" ST, NW	WASHINGTON, DC	20006
CRAWFORD, MICHAEL	ACTOR	CHATTO & LINNIT, LTD		
		PRINCE OF WALES THEATRE		
		COVENTRY ST	LONDON WC2	ENGLAND
CRAWFORD, MICHAEL	CARTOONIST	POST OFFICE BOX 4203	NEW YORK, NY	10017
CRAWFORD, NANCY V	WRITER	8955 BEVERLY BLVD	LOS ANGELES, CA	90048
CRAWFORD, OLIVER	TV WRITER	8955 BEVERLY BLVD	LOS ANGELES, CA	90048
CRAWFORD, PENELOPE	PIANIST	GREAT LAKES PERFORMING		
		310 E WASHINGTON ST	ANN ARBOR, MI	48104
CRAWFORD, RANDY	SINGER	FRITZ/TURNER MANAGEMENT		
		648 N ROBERTSON BLVD	LOS ANGELES, CA	90069
CRAWFORD, ROBERT	FILM PRODUCER	PAN-ARTS PRODUCTIONS		
		4000 WARNER BLVD	BURBANK, CA	91522
CRAWFORD, STEPHEN J	WRITER	8955 BEVERLY BLVD	LOS ANGELES, CA	90048
CRAWFORD, WALTER C	NEWS CORRESPONDENT	4461 CONNECTICUT AVE, NW	WASHINGTON, DC	20008
CRAWFORD, WAYNE	ACTOR	KOHNER, 9169 SUNSET BLVD	LOS ANGELES, CA	90069
CRAWFORD, WAYNE	FILM PRODUCER	9220 SUNSET BLVD #212	LOS ANGELES, CA	90069
CRAWFORD, WAYNE	SCREENWRITER	8955 BEVERLY BLVD	LOS ANGELES, CA	90048
CRAWL AWAY MACHINE	ROCK & ROLL GROUP	1230 GRANT AVE #531	SAN FRANCISCO, CA	94133
CRAY, ROBERT, BAND	RHYTHM & BLUES GROUP	POST OFFICE BOX 210103	SAN FRANCISCO, CA	94121
CRAYS, DURRELL ROYCE	WRITER-PRODUCER	11650 MAYFIELD AVE #1	LOS ANGELES, CA	90049
CREACH, EVERETT	STUNT DIRECTOR	9355 NOBLE AVE	SEPULVEDA, CA	91343
CREACH, PAPA JOHN	SINGER-GUITARIST	SYLVAKIAN MUSIC COMPANY		
		1122 S LA JOLLA AVE	LOS ANGELES, CA	90035
CREAMER, RAYMOND W	PHOTOGRAPHER	9919 PINEHURST AVE	FAIRFAX, VA	22030
CREAR, JOHNNY	ACTOR	8831 SUNSET BLVD #PH-A	LOS ANGELES, CA	90069
CREASON, SAMMY	DRUMMER	601 BOYD MILL AVE #B-4	FRANKLIN, TN	37064
CREASY, WILLIAM N, JR	DIRECTOR	8 OAK BEND	BRONXVILLE, NY	10708
CRECHALES, ANTHONY	WRITER	12031 HOFFMAN ST #6	STUDIO CITY, CA	91604
CREDLE, GARY	TV PRODUCER	WARNER BROTHERS TV		
		4000 WARNER BLVD	BURBANK, CA	91522
CREECH, KATHRYN H	TV EXECUTIVE	HEARST/ABC-TV		
		555 5TH AVE	NEW YORK, NY	10017
CREECH, PHILIP	TENOR	CAMI, 165 W 57TH ST	NEW YORK, NY	10019
CREEDY, KATHRYN B	NEWS CORRESPONDENT	822 S ARLINGTON HILL DR #204	ARLINGTON, VA	22204
CREEPS, THE	ROCK & ROLL GROUP	POST OFFICE BOX 2175-53102	LIDKOPING	SWEDEN
CREGEEN, PETER	TV DIRECTOR-PRODUCER	38 STRAWBERRY HILL RD		
		TWICKENHAM	MIDDLESEX	ENGLAND
CREMEDAS, A E	NEWS CORRES-WRITER	ABC-TV, NEWS DEPARTMENT		
		1717 DE SALES ST, NW	WASHINGTON, DC	20036
CRENNA, RICHARD	ACTOR-DIRECTOR	3951 VALLEY MEADOW RD	ENCINO, CA	91436
CRENSHAW, ALBERT B	NEWS CORRESPONDENT	321 E CAPITOL ST, NW	WASHINGTON, DC	20003
CRENSHAW, ELIZABETH A	NEWS CORRESPONDENT	NBC-TV, NEWS DEPARTMENT		
		4001 NEBRASKA AVE, NW	WASHINGTON, DC	20016
CRENSHAW, GEORGE	CARTOONIST	NEWS AMERICA SYNDICATE		
		1703 KAISER AVE	IRVINE, CA	92714
CRENSHAW, MARSHALL	SINGER-SONGWRITER	200 W 57TH ST #1403	NEW YORK, NY	10019
CRENSHAW, RANDEL L	COMPOSER	913 1/2 S OLIVE AVE	ALHAMBRA, CA	91803
CRESCENDOS, THE	VOCAL GROUP	OLDIES, 5218 ALMONT ST	LOS ANGELES, CA	90032
CRESPIN, REGINE	SOPRANO	119 W 57TH ST #1505	NEW YORK, NY	10019
CRESPO, GLENN A	WRITER	555 W 57TH ST #1230	NEW YORK, NY	10019
CRESSON, JAMES	THEATER PRODUCER	4001 AVENIDA DEL SOL	STUDIO CITY, CA	91604
CRETONES, THE	VOCAL GROUP	EPSTEIN, 644 N DOHENY DR	LOS ANGELES, CA	90069
CREW, LARRY CLINTON	GUITARIST	1145 FERNBANK AVE	MADISON, TN	37115
CREW CUTS, THE	VOCAL GROUP	BROWN, 29 CEDAR ST	CRESKILL, NJ	07626
CREWS, ART	WRESTLER	UNIVERSAL WRESTLING FEDERATION		
		MID SOUTH SPORTS, INC		
		116 W BRECKINRIDGE	BIXBY, OK	74008
CRIBBINS, BERNARD	ACTOR	59 FRITH ST	LONDON W1	ENGLAND
CRICHTON, CHARLES	FILM DIRECTOR	MAX NAUGHTON LOWE		
		200 FULHAM RD	LONDON SW10 9PN	ENGLAND
CRICHTON, JUDY F	WRITER-PRODUCER	DGA, 110 W 57TH ST	NEW YORK, NY	10019
CRICHTON, MICHAEL	FILM WRITER-DIRECTOR	1750 14TH ST #C	SANTA MONICA, CA	90404
CRICHTON, ROBIN	TV DIRECTOR-PRODUCER	EDINBURGH FILM PRODUCTIONS		
		9 MILE BURN, BY PENICUIK	MIDLOTHIAN EH26 9LT	SCOTLAND

JOHNNY CRAWFORD

RICHARD CRENNA

HUME CRONYN

CATHY LEE CROSBY

TOM CRUISE

THE CRUSADERS

BOB CUMMINGS

JAMIE LEE CURTIS

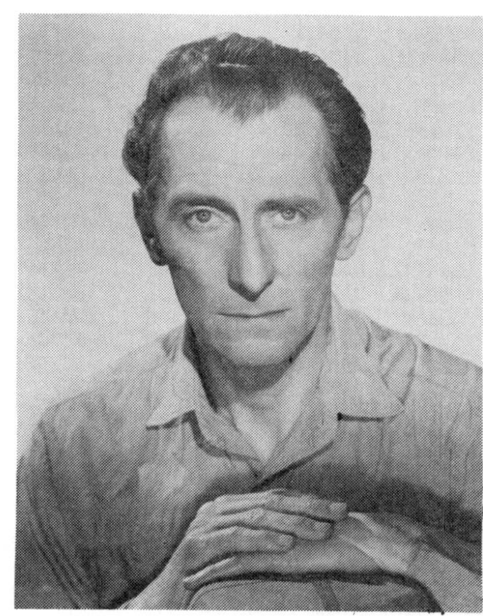

PETER CUSHING

Name	Occupation	Address	City
CRICK, ED	ACTOR	3518 W CAHUENGA BLVD #316	LOS ANGELES, CA 90068
CRICKETS, THE	ROCK & ROLL GROUP	HOFFMAN TALENT, INC	
		15500 WAYZATA BLVD	
		1011 12 OAKS CENTER	WAYZATA, MN 55391
CRIDER, BOB	SINGER	851-D OLD HICKORY BLVD	JACKSON, TN 38301
CRIGGER, HARRY	ACTOR	5709 SILVA ST	LAKEWOOD, CA 90713
CRIGGER, TRIGGER	PIANIST	115 QUEEN ANN DR	MADISON, TN 37115
CRILE, GEORGE, III	TV WRITER-PRODUCER	CBS-TV, 524 W 57TH ST	NEW YORK, NY 10019
CRIM, SARAH K	NEWS CORRESPONDENT	3419 MEDINA AVE	BOWIE, MD 20715
CRINKLEY, RICHMOND	THEATER PRODUCER	59 W 71ST ST	NEW YORK, NY 10023
CRIPPLER, THE	WRESTLER	SEE - BUNDY, KING KONG	
CRIPPLER, THE	WRESTLER	SEE - STEVENS, RAY	
		"THE CRIPPLER"	
CRIPPS, ERIK	DIRECTOR	POST OFFICE BOX 321	QUEEN ANNE, MD 21657
CRIQUI, DON	SPORTSCASTER	NBC-TV, SPORTS DEPARTMENT	
		30 ROCKEFELLER PLAZA	NEW YORK, NY 10112
CRISAFULLI, V JAMES	COMPOSER	245 N MANHATTAN PL	LOS ANGELES, CA 90004
CRISCI, EUGENE W	WRITER	1339 WESLEYAN AVE	WALNUT, CA 91789
CRISP, QUENTIN	ACTOR	7 AVE MANSIONS	
		FINCHLEY RD	LONDON NW3 ENGLAND
CRISP, TRACEY	ACTRESS	40 CENTRAL PARK S	NEW YORK, NY 10023
CRISPELL, EDDIE	ACTRESS	536 N LA CIENEGA BLVD #A	LOS ANGELES, CA 90048
CRISS, PETER	DRUMMER-SINGER	AUCOIN, 645 MADISON AVE	NEW YORK, NY 10022
CRIST, JUDITH	FILM CRITIC	180 RIVERSIDE DR	NEW YORK, NY 10024
CRIST, RICHARD	SINGER	59 E 54TH ST #81	NEW YORK, NY 10022
CRISTAL, LINDA	ACTRESS	9129 HAZEN DR	BEVERLY HILLS, CA 90210
CRISTIANI	UNICYCLISTS	HALL, 138 FROG HOLLOW RD	CHURCHVILLE, PA 18966
CRISTOFER, MICHAEL	ACTOR	151 S EL CAMINO DR	BEVERLY HILLS, CA 90212
CRISTOFER, MICHAEL	SCREENWRITER	8955 BEVERLY BLVD	LOS ANGELES, CA 90048
CRISWELL, KAREN	ACTRESS	LEONETTI, 6526 SUNSET BLVD	HOLLYWOOD, CA 90028
CRITCHFIELD, DONALD D	NEWS CORRESPONDENT	NBC-TV, NEWS DEPARTMENT	
		4001 NEBRASKA AVE, NW	WASHINGTON, DC 20016
CRITCHFIELD, JAMES F	WRITER-PRODUCER	22 THORNTON AVE	VENICE, CA 90291
CRITTENDEN, DIANNE	CASTING DIRECTOR	POST OFFICE BOX 1305	WOODLAND HILLS, CA 91364
CRITTENDEN, JORDAN	WRITER	8955 BEVERLY BLVD	LOS ANGELES, CA 90048
CROCK, STANLEY	NEWS CORRESPONDENT	5007 NEBRASKA AVE, NW	WASHINGTON, DC 20008
CROCKER, CARTER	TV WRITER	8955 BEVERLY BLVD	LOS ANGELES, CA 90048
CROCKER, JAMES S	WRITER	15746 MORRISON ST	ENCINO, CA 91436
CROCKER, ROBERT R	CONDUCTOR	POST OFFICE BOX 5192	HACIENDA HEIGHTS, CA 91745
CROCKETT, BILLY	MUSIC ARRANER	6576 CABOT DR	NASHVILLE, TN 37209
CROCKETT, DAVID	WRESTLING ANNOUNCER	NATIONAL WRESTLING ALLIANCE	
		JIM CROCKETT PROMOTIONS	
		421 BRIARBEND DR	CHARLOTTE, NC 28209
CROCKETT, GIBSON	CARTOONIST	4713 GREAT OAK RD	ROCKVILLE, MD 20853
CROCKETT, KARLENE	ACTRESS	4408 CAHUENGA BLVD	NORTH HOLLYWOOD, CA 91602
CROCKETT, UNCLE STEVE & THE LOG	C & W GROUP	WARREN, 116 PRINCETON RD	LINDEN, NJ 07036
CROCKFORD, PAUL	TALENT AGENT	OUTLAW MGMT, 145 OXFORD ST	LONDON W1 ENGLAND
CROES, CARY	WRITER	555 W 57TH ST #1230	NEW YORK, NY 10019
CROFOOT, TERRY	TV DIRECTOR	KABC-TV, 4151 PROSPECT AVE	LOS ANGELES, CA 90027
CROFT, ALYSON	ACTRESS	1450 BELFAST DR	LOS ANGELES, CA 90069
CROFT, RICHARD	TENOR	CAMI, 165 W 57TH ST	NEW YORK, NY 10019
CROFT, SANDY	SINGER	BIRDSONG, 2714 WESTWOOD DR	NASHVILLE, TN 37204
CROFWELL, JAMES	ACTOR	4237 LONGRIDGE AVE	STUDIO CITY, CA 91604
CROMLEY, ALLAN W	NEWS CORRESPONDENT	3320 STONEYBRAE DR	FALLS CHURCH, VA 22044
CROMLEY, RAY	NEWS CORRESPONDENT	1912 MARTHA'S RD	ALEXANDRIA, VA 22307
CROMMIE, KAREN T	WRITER-PRODUCER	DGA, 7950 SUNSET BLVD	LOS ANGELES, CA 90046
CROMPTON, CHARLES L	WRITER	8955 BEVERLY BLVD	LOS ANGELES, CA 90048
CROMWELL, GLORIA	ACTRESS	9229 SUNSET BLVD #306	LOS ANGELES, CA 90069
CROMWELL, JAMES	ACTOR	POST OFFICE BOX 5617	BEVERLY HILLS, CA 90210
CRON, CLAUDIA	ACTRESS	200 W 57TH ST #1303	NEW YORK, NY 10019
CRONAN, MICHAEL	CARTOONIST	POST OFFICE BOX	SAN DIEGO, CA 92112
CRONENBERG, DAVID	FILM WRITER-DIRECTOR	184 COTTINGHAM ST	TORONTO, ONT M4V 7C7 CANADA
CRONENWETH, JORDAN	CINEMATOGRAPHER	2276 S BEVERLY GLEN BLVD	LOS ANGELES, CA 90064
CRONIN, MARY	NEWS CORRESPONDENT	TIME/TIME & LIFE BLDG	
		ROCKEFELLER CENTER	NEW YORK, NY 10020
CRONIN, PATRICK	ACTOR	131 S ARDEN BLVD	LOS ANGELES, CA 90004
CRONIN, SEAN	NEWS CORRESPONDENT	2500 "Q" ST, NW	WASHINGTON, DC 20007
CRONKITE, KATHY	ACTRESS-AUTHORESS	DMI, 250 W 57TH ST	NEW YORK, NY 10107
CRONKITE, WALTER	BROADCAST JOURNALIST	519 E 84TH ST	NEW YORK, NY 10028
CRONLEY, JAY W	WRITER	8955 BEVERLY BLVD	LOS ANGELES, CA 90048
CRONYN, HUME	ACTOR	165 W 46TH ST #409	NEW YORK, NY 10036
CRONYN, TANDY	ACTRESS	151 S EL CAMINO DR	BEVERLY HILLS, CA 90212
CROOK, CLIVE	NEWS CORRESPONDENT	1331 PENNSYLVANIA AVE, NW	WASHINGTON, DC 20004
CROOK, EDDY	MUSIC ARRANGER	107 CHIPPENDALE DR	HENDERSONVILLE, TN 37075
CROOK, HERMAN MARSHALL	MUSICIAN	1618 RUSSELL ST	NASHVILLE, TN 37206
CROOK, JACK	GUITARIST	1458 E CEDAR LN	MADISON, TN 37115
CROOKHAM, WADE	ACTOR	7100 HILLSIDE AVE #502	HOLLYWOOD, CA 90046
CROOKS, LEON D, JR	DRUMMER	300 KATE ST #L-8	MADISON, TN 37115
CROOM, CARL ERSKINE	ACTOR	813 W 103RD ST	LOS ANGELES, CA 90044
CROPPER, ANNA	ACTRESS	FEAST, 43-A PRINCESS RD	LONDON NW1 ENGLAND
CROSBIE, ANNETTE	ACTRESS	23 WILTON CRESCENT, WIMBLEDON	LONDON SW19 ENGLAND
CROSBY, BOB	MUSICIAN	939 COAST BLVD	LA JOLLA, CA 92037
CROSBY, CATHY LEE	ACTRESS-MODEL	10488 EASTBORNE AVE #308	LOS ANGELES, CA 90024
CROSBY, DAVID	SINGER-SONGWRITER	BILL SIDDONS & ASSOCIATES	
		1588 CROSSROADS OF WORLD	HOLLYWOOD, CA 90028

CROSBY, DENISE	ACTOR	9200 SUNSET BLVD #1210	LOS ANGELES, CA 90069
CROSBY, GARY	SINGER	1856 LOMA VISTA DR	BEVERLY HILLS, CA 90210
CROSBY, GEORGE	PRODUCER	MCA/UNIVERSAL STUDIOS, INC	
		100 UNIVERSAL CITY PLAZA	UNIVERSAL CITY, CA 91608
CROSBY, JOAN	ACTRESS-WRITER	5036 STROHM AVE	NORTH HOLLYWOOD, CA 91601
CROSBY, JOHN	CASTING DIRECTOR	ABC-TV ENTERTAINMENT CENTER	
		2040 AVE OF THE STARS	LOS ANGELES, CA 90067
CROSBY, KATHRYN	ACTRESS	101 ROBBIN DR	HILLSBOROUGH, CA 94010
CROSBY, MARY	ACTRESS	2875 S BARRYMORE DR	MALIBU, CA 90265
CROSBY, NORM	COMEDIAN-ACTOR	1400 LONDONDERRY PL	LOS ANGELES, CA 90069
CROSBY, PEGGY JOYCE	ACTRESS	13329 MAGNOLIA BLVD	SHERMAN OAKS, CA 91423
CROSBY, PHILIP	ACTOR	21801 PROVIDENCIA ST	WOODLAND HILLS, CA 91364
CROSBY, THOMAS A	NEWS CORRESPONDENT	330 INDEPENDENCE AVE, SW	WASHINGTON, DC 20547
CROSBY, STILLS & NASH	ROCK & ROLL GROUP	BILL SIDDONS & ASSOCIATES	
		1588 CROSSROADS OF WORLD	HOLLYWOOD, CA 90028
CROSLAND, ALAN	FILM DIRECTOR	16905 SCENTIC PL	PACIFIC PALISADES, CA 90272
CROSLAND, CHERYL	ACTRESS	518 N FAIRVIEW ST	BURBANK, CA 91505
CROSLAND, STEVEN JAY	WRITER	1426 1/2 PORTIA ST	LOS ANGELES, CA 90026
CROSON, STEVE	GUITARIST	3502 WOODBRIDGE DR	NASHVILLE, TN 37217
CROSS, ALISON	SCREENWRITER	1148 SIERRA ALTA WY	LOS ANGELES, CA 90069
CROSS, BEN	ACTOR	29 BURLINGTON GARDENS	LONDON W4 ENGLAND
CROSS, BILL	ACTOR	ICM, 8899 BEVERLY BLVD	LOS ANGELES, CA 90048
CROSS, CHRISTOPHER	SINGER-SONGWRITER	114 W 7TH ST #717	AUSTIN, TX 78701
CROSS, JAMES R	DIRECTOR-PRODUCER	WISTERIA PATH	SANDS POINT, NY 11050
		1330 AVE OF THE AMERICAS	NEW YORK, NY 10019
CROSS, MIKE	SINGER	POST OFFICE BOX 1556	GAINESVILLE, FL 32602
CROSS, MURPHY	ACTRESS	11726 SAN VICENTE BLVD #300	LOS ANGELES, CA 90049
CROSS, RICHARD	SINGER	59 E 54TH ST #81	NEW YORK, NY 10022
CROSS, STEVEN P	WRITER	8955 BEVERLY BLVD	LOS ANGELES, CA 90048
CROSSFIELD, HENRY H	TV WRITER	555 W 57TH ST #1230	NEW YORK, NY 10019
CROSSMAN, DAVID	DIRECTOR	58 WICKHAM RD, BECKENHAM	KENT ENGLAND
CROSSMAN, GREGORY	WRITER	8955 BEVERLY BLVD	LOS ANGELES, CA 90048
CROSSON, ROBERT	ACTOR	11240 MAGNOLIA BLVD #202	NORTH HOLLYWOOD, CA 91601
CROSSWIND	C & W GROUP	SCA, 46 E HERBERT AVE	SALT LAKE CITY, UT 84111
CROTTY, DANIEL	ACTOR	708 BAY ST #B	SANTA MONICA, CA 90405
CROUCH, ANDRAE	SINGER-SONGWRITER	34213 COAST HIGHWAY #H	DANA POINT, CA 92629
CROUCH, BRYON	TV DIRECTOR	11450 BOLAS ST	LOS ANGELES, CA 90049
CROUCH, COLLEEN ZENK	ACTRESS	SEE - ZENK, COLLEEN	
CROUCH, PAUL	GUITARIST	300 KATE ST #E-3	MADISON, TN 37115
CROUCH, TIM	FIDDLER	ROUTE #1	CAVE CITY, AR 72521
CROUSE, LINDSAY	ACTRESS	ICM, 8899 BEVERLY BLVD	LOS ANGELES, CA 90048
CROUSE, TIMOTHY	WRITER	8955 BEVERLY BLVD	LOS ANGELES, CA 90048
CROW, ALVIN	SINGER	ATS MGMT, 3300 HOLLYWOOD AVE	AUSTIN, TX 78722
CROW, ASHLEY	ACTRESS	CBS-TV, "AS THE WORLD TURNS"	
		51 W 52ND ST	NEW YORK, NY 10019
CROW, BRYAN	DRUMMER	POST OFFICE 707	CLARKSVILLE, TN 37040
CROW, PATRICK	NEWS CORRESPONDENT	4205 LINDEN ST	FAIRFAX, VA 22030
CROW, ROBERT	ACTOR	BERZON, 336 E 17TH ST	COSTA MESA, CA 92627
CROWDER, JOHN	ACTOR	7727 ORION AVE	VAN NUYS, CA 91406
CROWE, ADELL	NEWS CORRESPONDENT	4350 ALTON PL, NW	WASHINGTON, DC 20016
CROWE, CAMERON	FILM WRITER-PRODUCER	151 S EL CAMINO DR	BEVERLY HILLS, CA 90212
CROWE, CHRISTOPHER	WRITER-PRODUCER	11922 IREDELL ST	STUDIO CITY, CA 91604
CROWE, FRANK	TV WRITER	8955 BEVERLY BLVD	LOS ANGELES, CA 90048
CROWE, GORDON	THEATER PRODUCER	30 E 40TH ST	NEW YORK, NY 10016
CROWE, J D & THE NEW SOUTH	BLUEGRASS GROUP	POST OFFICE BOX 1210	HAMILTON, OH 45012
CROWE, SUSAN	SINGER	DELICATE ARTIST MANAGEMENT	
		1379 LA MARCHANT ST, HALIFAX	NOVA SCOTIA B3J 3K6 CANADA
CROWELL, RODNEY	SINGER-SONGWRITER	NEW STAR ENTERPRISES	
		60 W 70TH ST	NEW YORK, NY 10023
CROWELL, ROSANNE CASH	SINGER	SEE - CASH, ROSANNE	
CROWL, JOHN A	NEWS CORRESPONDENT	1819 CORCORAN ST, NW	WASHINGTON, DC 20037
CROWLEY, CANDY A	NEWS CORRESPONDENT	1825 "K" ST, NW	WASHINGTON, DC 20006
CROWLEY, CARL FERMAN	DRUMMER	3604 RICHLAND AVE	NASHVILLE, TN 37205
CROWLEY, DEBRA	ACTRESS	8721 SUNSET BLVD #200	LOS ANGELES, CA 90069
CROWLEY, ED	ACTOR	142 W END AVE	NEW YORK, NY 10023
CROWLEY, GREG U	NEWS CORRESPONDENT	2811 CATHEDRAL AVE, NW	WASHINGTON, DC 20008
CROWLEY, MART	WRITER	8955 BEVERLY BLVD	LOS ANGELES, CA 90048
CROWLEY, MARY E	NEWS CORRESPONDENT	625 RAY DR	SILVER SPRING, MD 20910
CROWLEY, MORRISON E	NEWS CORRESPONDENT	1000 WILSON BLVD	ROSSLYN, VA 22209
CROWLEY, PATRICIA	ACTRESS	551 PERUGIA WY	LOS ANGELES, CA 90077
CROWLEY, THERESA	NEWS CORRESPONDENT	5-J LAUREL HILL RD	GREENBELT, MD 20770
CROWN HEIGHTS AFFAIR	JAZZ GROUP	250 W 57TH ST #1315	NEW YORK, NY 10107
CROWNE, JAMES D	NEWS CORRESPONDENT	2802 BUXMONT LN	BOWIE, MD 20715
CROWNE, TONYA	ACTRESS	KELMAN, 7813 SUNSET BLVD	LOS ANGELES, CA 90046
CROWNER, STUART W	WRITER-PRODUCER	4821 WESTPARK DR	NORTH HOLLYWOOD, CA 91601
CROWTHER, JOHN	SCREENWRITER	13900 PANAY WY #DN-15	MARINA DEL REY, CA 90292
CROWTHER, LESLIE	ACTOR-COMEDIAN	LONDON MANAGEMENT, LTD	
		235-241 REGENT ST	LONDON W1A 2JT ENGLAND
CROXTON, DEE	ACTRESS	9200 SUNSET BLVD #909	LOS ANGELES, CA 90069
CROY, GEORGE E, JR	COMPOSER	20449 ACRE ST	CANOGA PARK, CA 91306
CROYDON, JOAN	ACTRESS	2 BEEKMAN PL	NEW YORK, NY 10022
CRUICKSHANK, ANDREW	ACTOR	33 CARLISLE MANSIONS	
		CARLISLE PL	LONDON SW1 ENGLAND
CRUICKSHANK, PAULA L	NEWS CORRESPONDENT	2601 S WATER REED DR #C	ARLINGTON, VA 22206
CRUICKSHANKS, REID	ACTOR	4201 VIA MARINA	MARINA DEL REY, CA 90292

Name	Occupation	Address	City	Code
CRUISE, TOM	ACTOR	14775 VENTURA BLVD #1-710	SHERMAN OAKS, CA	91403
CRUM, JAMES	TV DIRECTOR	5075 WESTSLOPE LN	LA CANADA, CA	91011
CRUM, JOHN E	NEWS CORRESPONDENT	2139 WISCONSIN AVE, NW	WASHINGTON, DC	20007
CRUM, MARTIN	GUITARIST	404 OLD HICKORY PL	MADISON, TN	37115
CRUMB, CYNTHIA REED	VIOLINIST	3015 POSTON AVE #2	NASHVILLE, TN	37203
CRUMB, GEORGE	COMPOSER	240 KIRK LN	MEDIA, PA	19063
CRUMP, DONALD J	PHOTOGRAPHER	5222 LIGHT ST	SPRINGFIELD, VA	22151
CRUMP, OWEN	WRITER-PRODUCER	9015 ELEVADO AVE	LOS ANGELES, CA	90069
CRUSADERS, THE	JAZZ GROUP	8467 BEVERLY BLVD #100	LOS ANGELES, CA	90048
CRUSE	GOSPEL GROUP	ROUTE # 3, BOX 116	FLINT, TX	75762
CRUSETURNER, WAYNE	WRITER	5345 SEPULVEDA BLVD #242	VAN NUYS, CA	91411
CRUSHER, BILLY	WRESTLER	SEE - MASKED SUPERSTAR, THE		
CRUSHER, BLACK	WRESTLER	SEE - MASKED SUPERSTAR, THE		
CRUSHER, THE	WRESTLER	SEE - BLACKWELL, CRUSHER JERRY		
CRUSHER DARSO	WRESTLER	SEE - KHRUSHCHEV, KHRUSHER		
CRUTCHER, BRETT R	DIRECTOR	DGA, 7950 SUNSET BLVD	LOS ANGELES, CA	90046
CRUTCHER, GARY	WRITER	8955 BEVERLY BLVD	LOS ANGELES, CA	90048
CRUTCHFIELD, JERRY D	PERCUSSIONIST	1106 17TH AVE S	NASHVILLE, TN	37212
CRUTCHLEY, ANTHONY	TV WRITER	103 N END AVE		
		FITZ JAMES AVE	LONDON W14	ENGLAND
CRUTCHLEY, ROSALIE	ACTRESS	LONDON MANAGEMENT, LTD		
		235-241 REGENT ST	LONDON W1A 2JT	ENGLAND
CRUTHIRDS, JOANN	VIOLINIST	401 MC DONALD DR	NASHVILLE, TN	37217
CRUTSINGER, MARTIN S	NEWS CORRESPONDENT	2007 N INGLEWOOD ST	ARLINGTON, VA	22205
CRUZ, BRANDON	ACTOR	7466 BEVERLY BLVD #205	LOS ANGELES, CA	90036
CRUZ, GREGORY NORMAN	ACTOR	1119 S ORME AVE	LOS ANGELES, CA	90023
CRUZ, JOSE	BASEBALL	B-15 JARDINES LAFAYETTE	ARROYO, PR	00615
CRUZ-ROMO, GILDA	SOPRANO	CAMI, 165 W 57TH ST	NEW YORK, NY	10019
CRUZADOS, THE	ROCK & ROLL GROUP	POST OFFICE BOX 2426	HOLLYWOOD, CA	90078
CRYER, BARRY	ACTOR-WRITER	BRIAN CODD MANAGEMENT		
		8 WATERLOO, PALL MALL	LONDON SW1Y 4AW	ENGLAND
CRYER, GRETCHEN	WRITER	555 W 57TH ST #1230	NEW YORK, NY	10019
CRYERS, THE	ROCK & ROLL GROUP	375 PARK AVE #2004	NEW YORK, NY	10004
CRYPTIC SLAUGHTER	ROCK & ROLL GROUP	2210 WILSHIRE BLVD #161	SANTA MONICA, CA	90403
CRYSTAL	C & W GROUP	LUTZ, 5625 "O" STREET BLDG	LINCOLN, NE	68510
CRYSTAL, BILLY	ACTOR-COMEDIAN	ROLLINS, 801 WESTMOUNT DR	LOS ANGELES, CA	90069
CRYSTAL, LESTER M	TV EXECUTIVE	WNET-TV/13, 356 W 58TH ST	NEW YORK, NY	10019
CRYSTAL, RICHARD	ACTOR-WRITER	737 N MC CADDEN PL	LOS ANGELES, CA	90038
CRYSTAL, ROSS L	NEWS CORRESPONDENT	5225 POOKS HILL RD	BETHESDA, MD	20814
CRYSTALS, THE	VOCAL GROUP	MARS, 168 ORCHID DR	PEARL RIVER, NY	10965
CSAKY, MICK	TV DIRECTOR-PRODUCER	11 GRAPE ST	LONDON WC2	ENGLAND
CSENCSITS, CANDY	BODYBUILDER	RURAL DELIVERY #1, BOX 746	LENHARTSVILLE, PA	19534
CSIKI, ANTHONY	TV DIRECTOR	6926 PACIFIC VIEW DR	LOS ANGELES, CA	90068
CSONGOS, FRANK T	NEWS CORRESPONDENT	1900 S EADS ST	ARLINGTON, VA	22202
CUA, RICK	SINGER	POST OFFICE BOX 723591	ATLANTA, GA	30339
CUBERLI, LELLA	SOPRANO	CAMI, 165 W 57TH ST	NEW YORK, NY	10019
CUCCI, FRANK	WRITER	555 W 57TH ST #1230	NEW YORK, NY	10019
CUCUMBERS, THE	ROCK & ROLL GROUP	LOCK BOX 7295	NEW YORK, NY	10116
CUDDEBACK, ALEC RICHARD	WRITER	10757 HORTENSE ST #407	NORTH HOLLYWOOD, CA	91602
CUESTA, ANGEL M	DIRECTOR	5 RANDOLPH DR	DIX HILLS, NY	11746
CUEVA, IVONNE	WRITER	555 W 57TH ST #1230	NEW YORK, NY	10019
CUEVAS, LOUIS	WRITER	555 W 57TH ST #1230	NEW YORK, NY	10019
CUEVAS, NELSON D	ACTOR	7674 OAKDALE AVE	CANOGA PARK, CA	91306
CUGAT, CHARRO	SINGER	1801 LEXINGTON RD	BEVERLY HILLS, CA	90212
CUGAT, XAVIER	BANDLEADER	RITZ HOTEL	BARCELONA	SPAIN
CUKA, FRANCES	ACTRESS	MILLER, 82 BROOM PARK		
		TEDDINGTON	MIDDLESEX TW11 9NY	ENGLAND
CULBERTSON, DIANE	WRITER-EDITOR	POST OFFICE BOX 500	WASHINGTON, DC	20044
CULBERTSON, FRED W	WRITER	10975 PEORIA ST	SUN VALLEY, CA	91352
CULBERTSON, KEVIN A	NEWS CORRESPONDENT	529 14TH ST, NW	WASHINGTON, DC	20045
CULEA, MELINDA	ACTRESS	2627 OUTPOST DR	LOS ANGELES, CA	90068
CULHANE, DAVID	NEWS CORRESPONDENT	CBS NEWS, 524 W 57TH ST	NEW YORK, NY	10019
CULHANE, JOHN	TV WRITER	555 W 57TH ST #1230	NEW YORK, NY	10019
CULHANE, SHAMUS	DIRECTOR	325 W END AVE	NEW YORK, NY	10023
CULLBERG, BIRGIT	CHOREOGRAPHER	SVENSKA RIKSTEATERN		
		RASUNDAVAGEN 150	S-171 30 SOLNA	SWEDEN
CULLEN, ALMA	TV WRITER	LEMON, 24 POTTERY LN	LONDON W11	ENGLAND
CULLEN, BRETT	ACTOR	POST OFFICE BOX 5617	BEVERLY HILLS, CA	90210
CULLEN, IAN	ACTOR-WRITER	RICHARD STONE, 2 CONNOP WY		
		FRIMLEY, CAMBERLEY	SURREY GU16 5PX	ENGLAND
CULLEN, JAMES J	WRITER	555 W 57TH ST #1230	NEW YORK, NY	10019
CULLEN, PATRICIA	COMPOSER	6404 WILSHIRE BLVD #800	LOS ANGELES, CA	90048
CULLEN, PATRICK J	WRITER	555 W 57TH ST #1230	NEW YORK, NY	10019
CULLEN, PATRICK J	NEWS CORRESPONDENT	412 11TH ST, SE	WASHINGTON, DC	20003
CULLEN, WILLIAM KIRBY	ACTOR	9300 WILSHIRE BLVD #410	BEVERLY HILLS, CA	90212
CULLERS, RANDY LEE	DRUMMER	717 ALLEN PASS	MADISON, TN	37115
CULLIN, GEORGE	NEWS CORRESPONDENT	NBC NEWS, 4001 NEBRASKA AVE, NW	WASHINGTON, DC	20016
CULLINGHAM, G MARK	TV DIRECTOR	POST OFFICE BOX 694	CENTER MORICHES, NY	11934
CULLINGHAM, MARK	TV DIRECTOR	34 STOCKWELL PARK RD	LONDON SW9	ENGLAND
CULLITON, CAROLYN	TV WRITER	ICM, 40 W 57TH ST	NEW YORK, NY	10019
CULLITON, RICHARD	TV WRITER	ICM, 40 W 57TH ST	NEW YORK, NY	10019
CULLLEN, EDWARD F	DIRECTOR	250 W 57TH ST	NEW YORK, NY	10019
CULLUM, JOHN	ACTER-SINGER	ICM, 40 W 57TH ST	NEW YORK, NY	10019
CULLUM, LEO	CARTOONIST	POST OFFICE BOX 4203	NEW YORK, NY	10017

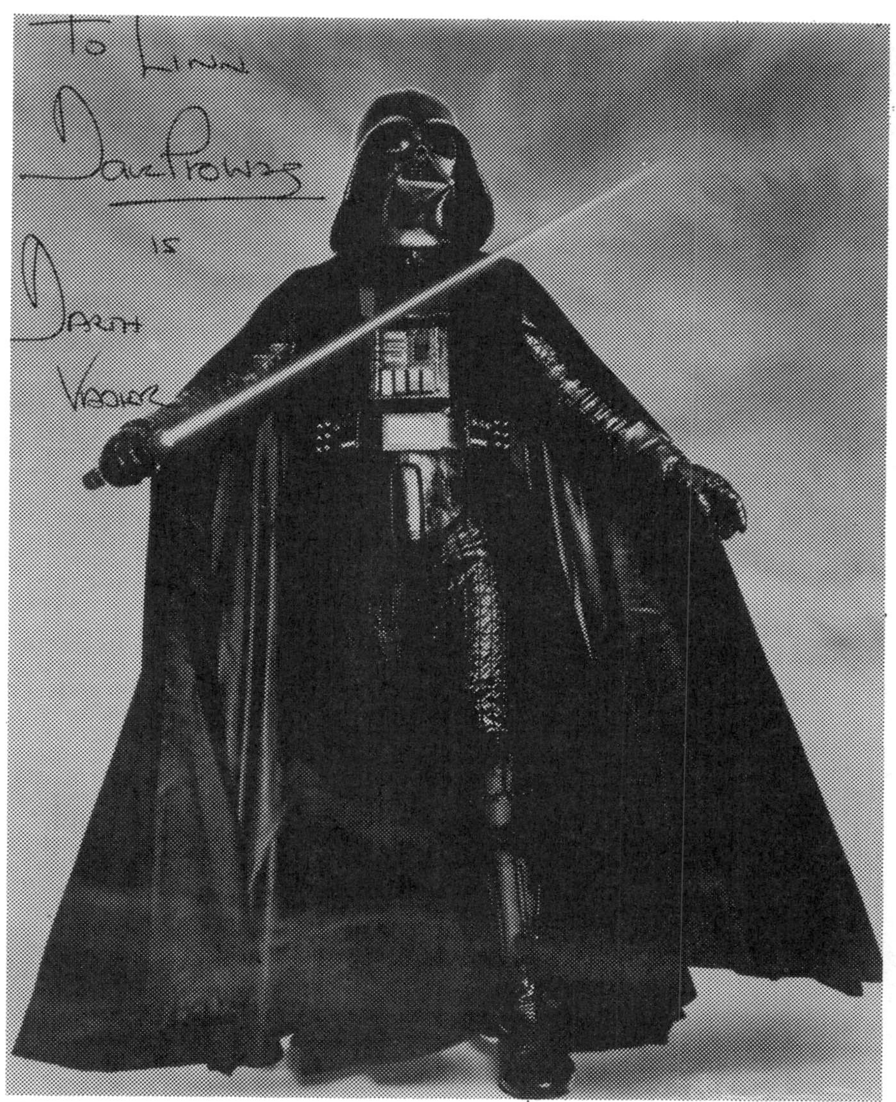

Name	Occupation	Address	City/State	Zip
CULP, JASON	ACTOR	9332 READCREST DR	BEVERLY HILLS, CA	90210
CULP, JOE BILL	SINGER	ROUTE #9, BOX 340	BENTON, KY	42025
CULP, JOSEPH	ACTOR	9332 READCREST DR	BEVERLY HILLS, CA	90210
CULP, JOSH	ACTOR	9332 READCREST DR	BEVERLY HILLS, CA	90210
CULP, RACHEL	ACTRESS	9332 READCREST DR	BEVERLY HILLS, CA	90210
CULP, ROBERT	ACT-WRI-DIR	9332 READCREST DR	BEVERLY HILLS, CA	90210
CULTURE CLUB	ROCK & ROLL GROUP	34-A GREEN LN, NORTHWOOD	MIDDLESEX	ENGLAND
CULVER, CARMEN	TV WRITER	9046 SUNSET BLVD #202	LOS ANGELES, CA	90069
CULVER, CAROL	ACTRESS	3575 W CAHUENGA BLVD #243	LOS ANGELES, CA	90068
CULVER, CASSE & BELLE STARR BAN	C & W GROUP	RMP, 200 WESTMORELAND AVE	WHITE PLAINS, NY	10606
CULVER, FELIX	TV WRITER	8955 BEVERLY BLVD	LOS ANGELES, CA	90048
CULVER, JAMES H	NEWS CORRESPONDENT	365 "O" ST, SW	WASHINGTON, DC	20025
CULVER, MICHAEL	ACTOR	5 CLANCARTY RD	LONDON SW6	ENGLAND
CUMBERLAND, DAVID	BASSO-BARITONE	CONE, 221 W 57TH ST	NEW YORK, NY	10019
CUMMING, RICHARD J	WRITER	555 W 57TH ST #1230	NEW YORK, NY	10019
CUMMINGS, BLONDELL	DANCER	AFFILIATE ARTISTS, INC		
		37 W 65TH ST, 6TH FLOOR	NEW YORK, NY	10023
CUMMINGS, BOB	ACTOR	516 HAVERKAMP DR	GLENDALE, CA	91206
CUMMINGS, BRAD	VENTRILOQUIST	8350 SANTA MONICA BLVD #102	LOS ANGELES, CA	90069
CUMMINGS, BRIAN	ACTOR	25020 AVE BALITA	VALENCIA, CA	91355
CUMMINGS, BRUCE	NEWS CORRESPONDENT	NBC-TV, NEWS DEPARTMENT		
		4001 NEBRASKA AVE, NW	WASHINGTON, DC	20016
CUMMINGS, CONSTANCE	ACTRESS	66 OLD CHURCH ST	LONDON SW3	ENGLAND
CUMMINGS, DREW	DIRECTOR	1528 NORTHVIEW DR	WESTLAKE VGE, CA	91362
CUMMINGS, GANTIETT	RECORD EXECUTIVE	POST OFFICE BOX 8263	HALEDON, NJ	07508
CUMMINGS, IRVING, JR	WRITER	11516 MOORPARK ST #9	NORTH HOLLYWOOD, CA	91602
CUMMINGS, KEN	ACTOR	3330 BARHAM BLVD #103	LOS ANGELES, CA	90068
CUMMINGS, MARILYN A	TV DIRECTOR	34 ANNAPOLIS RD	MILTON, MA	02186
CUMMINGS, MICHAEL	ACTOR	10351 SANTA MONICA BLVD #211	LOS ANGELES, CA	90025
CUMMINGS, PARKE	WRITER	178 COMPO RD S	WESTPORT, CT	06880
CUMMINGS, PETER THWEATT	GUITARIST	469 W 57TH ST #4-E	NEW YORK, NY	10019
CUMMINGS, QUINN	ACTRESS	1501 N KINGS RD	LOS ANGELES, CA	90069
CUMMINGS, ROBERT	ACTOR	SEE - CUMMINGS, BOB		
CUMMINGS, TAM	NEWS CORRESPONDENT	2600-B ARLINGTON BLVD	ARLINGTON, VA	22204
CUMMINS, BRIAN KENNAWAY	WRITER-PRODUCER	2372 CANYON DR	LOS ANGELES, CA	90068
CUMMINS, CLYDE FOLEY	GUITARIST	1310 TARRYWOOD LN	NASHVILLE, TN	37217
CUMMINS, ELI	ACTOR	4731 LAUREL CANYON BLVD #5	NORTH HOLLYWOOD, CA	91607
CUMMINS, JIM	PHOTOGRAPHER	75 PROSPECT ST	EAST ORANGE, NJ	07018
CUNEFF, RAY	TV WRITER	8955 BEVERLY BLVD	LOS ANGELES, CA	90048
CUNHA, RICHARD E	DIRECTOR	DGA, 7950 SUNSET BLVD	LOS ANGELES, CA	90046
CUNIBERTI, BETTY	NEWS CORRESPONDENT	3102 "N" ST, NW	WASHINGTON, DC	20007
CUNIFF, LOIS F	WRITER	555 W 57TH ST #1230	NEW YORK, NY	10019
CUNIFF, ROBERT	WRITER	555 W 57TH ST #1230	NEW YORK, NY	10019
CUNLIFFE, DAVID	TV DIRECTOR-PRODUCER	JOY JAMESON, LTD		
		7 W EATON PLACE MEWS	LONDON SW1	ENGLAND
CUNNEFF, THOMAS	FILM CRITIC-REPORTER	TIME & PEOPLE MAGAZINE		
		TIME & LIFE BUILDING		
		ROCKEFELLER CENTER	NEW YORK, NY	10020
CUNNIFF, HERBERT J	DIRECTOR	NBC-TV, 3000 W ALAMEDA AVE	BURBANK, CA	91523
CUNNINGHAM, BARRY	NEWS CORRESPONDENT	1728 NEW HAMPSHIRE AVE, NW	WASHINGTON, DC	20009
CUNNINGHAM, CORNELIUS	TV DIRECTOR	23 MITCHELL RD	PORT WASHINGTON, NY	11050
CUNNINGHAM, DEBRA	ACTRESS	2160 S BEVERLY GLEN BLVD	LOS ANGELES, CA	90025
CUNNINGHAM, GEORGE	TRUMPETER	2813 BELMONT BLVD	NASHVILLE, TN	37212
CUNNINGHAM, HEALY	ACTRESS	445 N BEDFORD DR #PH	BEVERLY HILLS, CA	90210
CUNNINGHAM, JAMES	SAXOPHONIST	ALPHA, 685 W END AVE	NEW YORK, NY	10025
CUNNINGHAM, JOHN	ACTOR	9229 SUNSET BLVD #306	LOS ANGELES, CA	90069
CUNNINGHAM, MARYBETH	WRITER	555 W 57TH ST #1230	NEW YORK, NY	10019
CUNNINGHAM, SEAN S	DIRECTOR-PRODUCER	155 LONG LOTS RD	WESTPORT, CT	06880
CUNNINGHAM, TIM	ACTOR	8831 SUNSET BLVD #402	LOS ANGELES, CA	90069
CUNNINGHAM, TODD H	NEWS CORRESPONDENT	5733 LEVERETT CT #370	ALEXANDRIA, VA	22311
CUNNINGHAM, WALT	MUSIC ARRANGER	5292 EDMONDSON PL #1314	NASHVILLE, TN	37211
CUNNINGHAM, WENDELL	SINGER	POST OFFICE BOX 25371	CHARLOTTE, NC	28212
CUNNINGHAM-CHANG	MUSICAL DUO	ALPHA, 685 W END AVE	NEW YORK, NY	10025
CUONG, PHAM GIA	PHOTOGRAPHER	2209 S BUCHANAN ST	ARLINGTON, VA	22206
CUPIDO, ALBERTO	TENOR	CAMI, 165 W 57TH ST	NEW YORK, NY	10019
CUPP, DANA E, JR	GUITARIST	POST OFFICE BOX 4172	CENTER LINE, MI	48015
CURB, MIKE	RECORD PRODUCER	1820 CARLA RIDGE	BEVERLY HILLS, CA	90210
CURETON, DAVID L	NEWS CORRESPONDENT	1755 S JEFFERSON DAVIS HWY	ARLINGTON, VA	22202
CURI, ALEX	ACTOR	2028 STEWART ST #B	SANTA MONICA, CA	90404
CURIEL, DEBORAH L	NEWS CORRESPONDENT	400 N CAPITOL ST, NW	WASHINGTON, DC	20001
CURLE, CHRIS	BROADCAST JOURNALIST	CNN, 1050 TECHWOOD DR, NW	ATLANTA, GA	30318
CURLEE, NANCY	TV WRITER	CBS-TV, "THE GUIDING LIGHT"		
		51 W 52ND ST	NEW YORK, NY	10019
CURLESS, DICK	SINGER	PENNY, 30 GUINAN ST	WALTHAM, MA	02154
CURLEY, CARLO	ORGANIST	CAMI, 165 W 57TH ST	NEW YORK, NY	10019
CURLEY, GEORGE	ACTOR	415 W 50TH ST	NEW YORK, NY	10019
CURLEY, JOHN J	PUBLISHING EXECUTIVE	POST OFFICE BOX 500	WASHINGTON, DC	20044
CURLEY, THOMAS	PUBLISHING EXECUTIVE	POST OFFICE BOX 500	WASHINGTON, DC	20044
CURLIN, JAMES W	NEWS CORRESPONDENT	2928 28TH ST, NW	WASHINGTON, DC	20007
CURLY THE CLOWN	CLOWN	POST OFFICE BOX 87	WEST LEBANON, NY	12195
CURNEW, TIM	WRITER	8955 BEVERLY BLVD	LOS ANGELES, CA	90048
CURRAM, ROLAND	ACTOR	14 BLENKARNE RD	LONDON SW11	ENGLAND
CURRAN, ED	NEWS CORRESPONDENT	9411 RUSSELL RD	SILVER SPRING, MD	20910
CURRAN, ELIZABETH	FILM PRODUCER	ELSINORE FILMS, LTD		
		39 MIDDLE MEAD, HOOK	HANTS	ENGLAND

Name	Occupation	Address	City	Zip/Country
CURRAN, KEVIN	TV WRITER	THE WILLIAM MORRIS AGENCY		
		1350 AVE OF THE AMERICAS	NEW YORK, NY	10019
CURRAN, LARRY	ACTOR	8721 SUNSET BLVD #200	LOS ANGELES, CA	90069
CURRAN, LAURA H	NEWS CORRESPONDENT	5151 WISCONSIN AVE, NW	WASHINGTON, DC	20016
CURRAN, LEIGH	TV WRITER	555 W 57TH ST #1230	NEW YORK, NY	10019
CURRAN, MAUREEN	NEWS CORRESPONDENT	2323 40TH PL #303, NW	WASHINGTON, DC	20007
CURRAN, MICK	WRITER	8955 BEVERLY BLVD	LOS ANGELES, CA	90048
CURRAN, PATRICK J	NEWS CORRESPONDENT	400 N CAPITOL ST, NW	WASHINGTON, DC	20001
CURRAN, PETER	FILM WRITER-DIRECTOR	ELSINORE FILMS, LTD		
		39 MIDDLE MEAD, HOOK	HANTS	ENGLAND
CURRENCE, CINDY K	NEWS CORRESPONDENT	1000 22ND ST #6, NW	WASHINGTON, DC	20037
CURRERI, LEE	ACTOR-TV WRITER	19 HORIZON AVE	VENICE, CA	90291
CURRIE, DANIEL	ACTOR	BENSON, 518 TOLUCA PARK DR	BURBANK, CA	91505
CURRIE, LOUISE	ACTRESS	GOOD, 1317 DELRESTO DR	BEVERLY HILLS, CA	90210
CURRIE, MICHAEL	ACTOR	11726 SAN VICENTE BLVD #300	LOS ANGELES, CA	90049
CURRIE, SONDRA	ACTRESS	LEVI, 3951 LONGRIDGE AVE	SHERMAN OAKS, CA	91423
CURRIE, CHERIE & MARIE	ROCK & ROLL GROUP	151 S EL CAMINO DR	BEVERLY HILLS, CA	90212
CURRIER, LAUREN	SCREENWRITER	8955 BEVERLY BLVD	LOS ANGELES, CA	90048
CURRIER, TERRENCE P	ACTOR	1602 N MC KINLEY RD	ARLINGTON, VA	22205
CURRLIN, LEE	TV EXECUTIVE	NBC-TV, 30 ROCKEFELLER PLAZA	NEW YORK, NY	10112
CURRY, ANNE E	ACTRESS	8920 WILSHIRBLVD #303	LOS ANGELES, CA	90069
CURRY, DAVID	WRITER-MUSICIAN	10514 WIPPLE ST	NORTH HOLLYWOOD, CA	91602
CURRY, DIANE	MEZZO-SOPRANO	CAMI, 165 W 57TH ST	NEW YORK, NY	10019
CURRY, FLYING FRED	WRESTLER	CAPITOL INTERNATIONAL		
		11844 MARKET ST	NORTH LIMA, OH	44452
CURRY, GEORGE E	NEWS CORRESPONDENT	1622-C BELMONT ST, NW	WASHINGTON, DC	20009
CURRY, JACK	TV CRITIC	POST OFFICE BOX 500	WASHINGTON, DC	20044
CURRY, JULIAN	ACTOR	M M MARTIN, 7 WINDMILL ST	LONDON W1	ENGLAND
CURRY, TIM	ACTOR	CAMERON-HAYWOOD & COMPANY		
		3 LORD NAPIER PL	LONDON W6	ENGLAND
CURRY, TOM	NEWS REPORTER	TIME/TIME & LIFE BLDG		
CURTAN, DEBORAH A	CASTING DIRECTOR	NBC-TV, 3000 W ALAMEDA AVE	BURBANK, CA	91523
CURTEIS, IAN	WRITER-PRODUCER	MILL HOUSE, CIRENCESTER		
		COLIN SAINT ALDWYNS	GLOS	ENGLAND
CURTIN, JANE	ACTRESS	11726 SAN VICENTE BLVD #300	LOS ANGELES, CA	90049
CURTIN, JIM "E"	SINGER	JOYCE, 2028 CHESTNUT ST	PHILADELPHIA, PA	19103
CURTIN, ROBERT	ACTOR	1418 N HIGHLAND AVE #102	LOS ANGELES, CA	90028
CURTIN, TOMMY	JUGGLER	HALL, 138 FROG HOLLOW RD	CHURCHVILLE, PA	18966
CURTIN, VALERIE	ACTRESS-WRITER	15622 MEADOWGATE RD	ENCINO, CA	91316
CURTIS, ALAN	ACT-WRI-DIR	36 ERNEST GARDENS	LONDON W4	ENGLAND
CURTIS, CRAIG	ACTOR	9230 OLYMPIC BLVD #203	BEVERLY HILLS, CA	90212
CURTIS, DAL	CARTOONIST	NEWS AMERICA SYNDICATE		
		1703 KAISER AVE	IRVINE, CA	92714
CURTIS, DAN	DIRECTOR-PRODUCER	5451 MARATHON ST	HOLLYWOOD, CA	90038
CURTIS, JAMIE LEE	ACTRESS	1416 N HAVENHURST DR #6-C	LOS ANGELES, CA	90046
CURTIS, JOHN	MUSIC ARRANGER	1973 SUNNYSIDE DR	BRENTWOOD, TN	37027
CURTIS, KEENE	ACTOR	6363 IVARENE AVE	HOLLYWOOD, CA	90068
CURTIS, KEN	ACTOR	9441 WILSHIRE BLVD #620-D	BEVERLY HILLS, CA	90210
CURTIS, LIANE	ACTRESS	KOHNER, 9169 SUNSET BLVD	LOS ANGELES, CA	90069
CURTIS, MARQUEETA L	WRITER	555 W 57TH ST #1230	NEW YORK, NY	10019
CURTIS, MEL	WRITER	8955 BEVERLY BLVD	LOS ANGELES, CA	90048
CURTIS, PHYLLIS	SINGER	80 HIGH ST	NEW HAVEN, CT	06511
CURTIS, RICHARD	GUITARIST	851 ALLISON DR	COLUMBUS, OH	43207
CURTIS, ROBERT A	WRITER	8955 BEVERLY BLVD	LOS ANGELES, CA	90048
CURTIS, ROBERT L	DIRECTOR	6143 PASEO CANYON DR	MALIBU, CA	90265
CURTIS, ROBIN	ACTRESS	870 N VINE ST #B	LOS ANGELES, CA	90038
CURTIS, SCOTT	ACTOR	NBC-TV, 3000 W ALAMEDA AVE	BURBANK, CA	91523
CURTIS, SONNY	SINGER-SONGWRITER	ROUTE #2, BOX 61	DICKSON, TN	37055
CURTIS, SYNKA A	DIRECTOR	520 N MICHIGAN AVE #436	CHICAGO, IL	60611
CURTIS, TODD	ACTOR	2046 14TH ST #10	SANTA MONICA, CA	90405
CURTIS, TONY	ACTOR	10351 SANTA MONICA BLVD #211	LOS ANGELES, CA	90025
CURTIS, TONY	ART DIRECTOR	1 SURREY HOUSE		
		PORTSMOUTH RD, CAMBERLEY	SURREY	ENGLAND
CURTIS, WADE	GUITARIST	POST OFFICE BOX 4740	NASHVILLE, TN	37216
CURTISS, MARK	WRITER	8955 BEVERLY BLVD	LOS ANGELES, CA	90048
CURTIZ, GABRIEL	ACTOR	3625 LAUREL CANYON BLVD	NORTH HOLLYWOOD, CA	91604
CURTOLA, BOBBY	SINGER	576 WOLF WILLOW RD	EDMONTON, ALB T5T 1E5	CANADA
CURY, IVAN	TV DIRECTOR	2620 11TH ST #13	SANTA MONICA, CA	90405
CUSACK, BELINDA	TV DIRECTOR	202 E 35TH ST	NEW YORK, NY	10016
CUSACK, CYRIL	ACTOR	30 LOWER HATCH ST	DUBLIN 2	IRELAND
CUSACK, JOHN	ACTOR	1509 N CRESCENT HGTS BLVD #7	LOS ANGELES, CA	90069
CUSACK, MARGARET	SOPRANO	1776 BROADWAY #504	NEW YORK, NY	10019
CUSACK, SINEAD	ACTRESS	HUTTON, 200 FULHAM RD	LONDON SW10	ENGLAND
CUSHING, PETER	ACTOR	SEASALTER, WHITSTABLE	KENT	ENGLAND
CUSHMAN, CHARLIE	MANDOLINIST	1800 WALLACE RD, NOB HILL	NASHVILLE, TN	37211
CUSIMANO, HENRY	ACTOR	8721 SUNSET BLVD #203	LOS ANGELES, CA	90069
CUSOLITO, ROBERT L	WRITER	555 W 57TH ST #1230	NEW YORK, NY	10019
CUSTANCE, MICHAEL	TV DIRECTOR	50 CHURCH RD, RICHMOND	SURREY	ENGLAND
CUTCHLOW, GAIL	ACTRESS	1693 E CALAVERAS ST	ALTADENA, CA	91001
CUTCLIFFE, JOHN	TALENT AGENT	AVENT, 3805 W MAGNOLIA BLVD	BURBANK, CA	91505
CUTELL, LOU	ACTOR	1923 N CRESCENT HGTS BLVD	LOS ANGELES, CA	90069
CUTHBERT, NEIL	TV WRITER	555 W 57TH ST #1230	NEW YORK, NY	10019
CUTHBERTSON, ALLAN	ACTOR	15 BERRYLANDS, SURBITON	SURREY	ENGLAND
CUTHBERTSON, IAIN	ACTOR-DIRECTOR	FRENCH'S, 26 BINNEY ST	LONDON W1	ENGLAND

Name	Occupation	Address	City, State	ZIP
CUTHRIELL, ROBERT E	NEWS CORRESPONDENT	4740 CONNECTICUT AVE #1002, NW	WASHINGTON, DC	20008
CUTLER, B J	NEWS CORRESPONDENT	2735 "P" ST, NW	WASHINGTON, DC	20007
CUTLER, BARRY	ACTOR	310 S KENMORE AVE #1	LOS ANGELES, CA	90020
CUTLER, BRIAN	ACTOR	5505 CLYBOURN AVE	NORTH HOLLYWOOD, CA	91601
CUTLER, DEVORAH	WRITER	BUSKIN, 2029 CENTURY PARK E	LOS ANGELES, CA	90067
CUTLER, JERRY	WRITER-PRODUCER	8955 BEVERLY BLVD	LOS ANGELES, CA	90048
CUTLER, LESLIE B	ACTOR-DIRECTOR	344 W 72ND ST	NEW YORK, NY	10023
CUTLER, NELIDA GONZALEZ	NEWS REPORTER	TIME/TIME & LIFE BLDG		
		ROCKEFELLER CENTER	NEW YORK, NY	10020
CUTLER, RON "ROLAND"	WRITER	554 S SAN VICENTE BLVD #3	LOS ANGELES, CA	90048
CUTLER, SARA	HARPIST	157 W 57TH ST #1100	NEW YORK, NY	10017
CUTLER, STAN	WRITER	10100 SANTA MONICA BLVD #1600	LOS ANGELES, CA	90067
CUTLER, WENDY	ACTRESS	STONE, 1052 CAROL DR	LOS ANGELES, CA	90069
CUTNER, NAOMI V	NEWS REPORTER	LIFE/TIME & LIFE BLDG		
		ROCKEFELLER CENTER	NEW YORK, NY	10020
CUYUERS, LUC	NEWS CORRESPONDENT	201 N JACKSON ST	ARLINGTON, VA	22201
CYBULSKI, JERZY K	TV WRITER	8955 BEVERLY BLVD	LOS ANGELES, CA	90048
CYCLONAIS	RING MASTER	POST OFFICE BOX 87	WEST LEBANON, NY	12195
CYCLONIANS, THE	UNICYCLISTS	HALL, 138 FROG HOLLOW RD	CHURCHVILLE, PA	18966
CYMONE, ANDRE	SINGER	ICM, 40 W 57TH ST	NEW YORK, NY	10019
CYNKO, CYNTHIA	ACTRESS	4740 VANTAGE AVE #2	NORTH HOLLYWOOD, CA	91607
CYPHER, JON	ACTOR	4458 MATILIJA AVE	SHERMAN OAKS, CA	91423
CYPHERS, CHARLES	ACTOR	10949 FRUITLAND DR #17	STUDIO CITY, CA	91604
CYTRON, SAMUEL D	COMPOSER	1620 N STANLEY AVE	LOS ANGELES, CA	90046
CYTRON, SHIRLEY	ACTRESS	6605 HOLLYWOOD BLVD #200	HOLLYWOOD, CA	90028
CZECH, GREG	TV DIRECTOR	ENTERTAINMENT TONIGHT		
		PARAMOUNT TELEVISION		
		5555 MELROSE AVE	LOS ANGELES, CA	90038
CZIFFRA, GEORGES	PIANIST	LEISER, DORCHESTER TOWERS		
		115 W 68TH ST	NEW YORK, NY	10023
CZIFRA-TOUBOUL	MUCICAL DUO	POST OFFICE BOX 131	SPRINGFIELD, VA	22150
CZYS, KENNETH E	DIRECTOR	424 STAPLES AVE	SAN FRANCISCO, CA	94112

Name	Occupation	Address	City/State	Zip/Country
D R I	ROCK & ROLL GROUP	POST OFFICE BOX 2428	EL SEGUNDO, CA	90245
D TRAIN	RHYTHM & BLUES GROUP	PRELUDE RECORDS COMPANY		
		342 WESTMINISTER AVE	ELIZABETH, NJ	07208
D'ABO, OLIVIA	ACTRESS	10100 SANTA MONICA BLVD #1600	LOS ANGELES, CA	90067
D'ACQUISTO, RICHARD	DRUMMER	1805 ELECTRIC AVE	NASHVILLE, TN	37206
D'ADDIO, DANIEL	TRUMPETER	GREAT LAKES PERFORMING		
		310 E WASHINGTON ST	ANN ARBOR, MI	48104
D'AGOSTA, JOE	CASTING DIRECTOR	10900 WILSHIRE BLVD		
		4TH FLOOR	LOS ANGELES, CA	90024
D'AMBOISE, JACQUES	CHOREOGRAPHER	NATIONAL DANCE INSTITUTE		
		244 W 71ST ST	NEW YORK, NY	10023
D'AMBROSE, CAMILLE	WRITER	8955 BEVERLY BLVD	LOS ANGELES, CA	90048
D'AMICO, FIAMMA IZZO	SOPRANO	CAMI, 165 W 57TH ST	NEW YORK, NY	10019
D'ANGELO, BEVERLY	ACTRESS	8730 SUNSET BLVD #PH-W	LOS ANGELES, CA	90069
D'ANGELO, BILL	PRODUCER	GROUP W, 3801 BARHAM BLVD	LOS ANGELES, CA	90068
D'ANGELO, WILLIAM P	WRITER-PRODUCER	1107 N BAYFRONT	BALBOA ISLAND, CA	92662
D'ANJOLELL, RICHARD M	DIRECTOR	140 SYCAMORE MILLS RD	MEDIA, PA	19063
D'ANNA, SALVATORE L	NEWS CORRESPONDENT	2030 "M" ST, NW	WASHINGTON, DC	20036
D'ANNIBALE, THOMAS J	NEWS CORRESPONDENT	ABC-TV, NEWS DEPARTMENT		
		1717 DE SALES ST, NW	WASHINGTON, DC	20036
D'ANNIBALE, THOMAS JOSEPH	PHOTOGRAPHER	10919 FOX SPARROW CT	FAIRFAX, VA	22032
D'ANTONI, PHILIP	WRITER-PRODUCER	8 E 63RD ST	NEW YORK, NY	10021
D'ANTONIO, CARMEN	ACTRESS	SCHOEMAN, 2600 W VICTORY BLVD	BURBANK, CA	91505
D'ANTONIO, DENNIS	NEWS REPORTER	THE NATIONAL ENQUIRER		
		600 SE COAST AVE	LANTANA, FL	33464
D'ARBANVILLE, PATTI	ACTRESS	814 10TH ST	SANTA MONICA, CA	90403
D'ARCHAMBEAU, PIERRE	VIOLINIST	IAPR, KINCORA		
		BEER RD, SEATON	DEVON	ENGLAND
D'ARIANO, RAY	WRITER	555 W 57TH ST #1230	NEW YORK, NY	10019
D'ARNAL, DAVID	ACTOR	350 N GENESEE AVE #2	LOS ANGELES, CA	90036
D'ASCOLI, BERNARD	PIANIST	SHAW CONCERTS, 1995 BROADWAY	NEW YORK, NY	10023
D'AURIA, CAROL	WRITER	555 W 57TH ST #1230	NEW YORK, NY	10019
D'AURIA, TOM	FASHION DESIGNER	561 RICHMOND ST, 2ND FLOOR	TORONTO, ONT M5V 1V7	CANADA
D'AVRAY, WILLIAM	TV WRITER	8955 BEVERLY BLVD	LOS ANGELES, CA	90048
D'ETES, PAULA	WRITER	8955 BEVERLY BLVD	LOS ANGELES, CA	90048
D'INCECCO, JOAN	CASTING DIRECTOR	ABC-TV, 101 W 67TH ST	NEW YORK, NY	10023
D'JOHNS, JACK	SINGER	A & S, 3039 BROCKPORT RD	SPENCERPORT, NY	14559
D'USSEAU, LORING	DIRECTOR-PRODUCER	8420 KIRKWOOD DR	HOLLYWOOD, CA	90046
DA CAMERA	MUSICAL GROUP	5720 MOSHOLU AVE #300	RIVERDALE, NY	10471
DA COSTA, MORTON	ACTOR-DIRECTOR	20 DORETHY RD	WEST REDDING, CT	06896
DA PRON, LOUIS	ACTOR-DANCER	5743 LAKE LINDERO DR	AGOURA, CA	91301
DA SILVA, MARIO	BODYBUILDER	POST OFFICE BOX 36643	LOS ANGELES, CA	90036
DAAS, THE	ROCK & ROLL GROUP	POST OFFICE BOX 11283	RICHMOND, VA	23230
DAB, BARBARA	ACTRESS	5429 NEWCASTLE AVE #318	ENCINO, CA	91316
DABBS, HENRY	DIRECTOR-PRODUCER	24 WHITTIER DR	ENGLISHTOWN, NJ	07726
DABNEY, AUGUSTA	ACTRESS	NORTH MOUNTAIN DR	DOBBS FERRY, NY	10522
DABNEY, JOHN A	WRITER-PRODUCER	1721 N DILLON ST	LOS ANGELES, CA	90026
DACQMINE, JACQUES	ACTOR	49 RUE DE VERSAILLES		
		DE MESNIL	SAINT-DENNIS 78320	FRANCE
DACRI, STEVE	ACTOR	8899 BEVERLY BLVD #402	LOS ANGELES, CA	90048
DACYS, MILDA	ACTRESS	943 7TH ST #2	SANTA MONICA, CA	90403
DADAP, MICHAEL A	GUITARIST	ALPHA, 685 W END AVE	NEW YORK, NY	10025
DADAP-MA	MUSICAL DUO	ALPHA, 685 W END AVE	NEW YORK, NY	10025
DADARIO, JEAN L	TV DIRECTOR	1661 WILLIAMBRIDGE RD	BRONX, NY	10461
DADISMAN, E KING	COMPOSER	4384 LEMP AVE	STUDIO CITY, CA	91604
DAFOE, WILLEM	ACTOR	SF & A, 121 N SAN VICENTE BLVD	BEVERLY HILLS, CA	90211
DAGGETT, LUCY	ACTRESS	348 E OLIVE AVE #K	BURBANK, CA	91502
DAHEIM, JOHN J	DIRECTOR	937 S PACIFIC ST	OCEANSIDE, CA	92054
DAHL, ARLENE	ACTRESS	150 E 72ND ST	NEW YORK, NY	10021
DAHL, ROALD	WRITER	GIPSY HOUSE, GREAT MISSEENDEN	BUCKINGHAMPSHIRE	ENGLAND
DAILEY, DIANE P	TV WRITER	8955 BEVERLY BLVD	LOS ANGELES, CA	90048
DAILEY, ROBERT	DIRECTOR	CBS-TV, 51 W 52ND ST	NEW YORK, NY	10019
DAILY, BILL	ACTOR	5245 E COLDWATER CANYON AVE	VAN NUYS, CA	91401
DAILY, WILLIAM E	DIRECTOR	DGA, 7950 SUNSET BLVD	LOS ANGELES, CA	90046
DAKAR, LAINI	ACTRESS	4789 VINELAND AVE #100	NORTH HOLLYWOOD, CA	91602
DAKIL, VICTORIA	ACTRESS	9777 WILSHIRE BLVD #707	BEVERLY HILLS, CA	90212
DAKOTA	ROCK & ROLL GROUP	STEVENSON, 115 E MAIN ST	NEWARK, NJ	19711
DAKSS, BRIAN	WRITER	555 W 57TH ST #1230	NEW YORK, NY	10019
DALBEY, DIANE	WRITER	4700 NATICK AVE #311	SHERMAN OAKS, CA	91403
DALBY, LYNN	ACTRESS	MAHONEY MANAGEMENT		
		30 CHALFONT CT, BAKER ST	LONDON NW1	ENGLAND
DALE, AL	NEWS CORRESPONDENT	ABC NEWS, 7 W 66TH ST	NEW YORK, NY	10023
DALE, BRUCE A	PHOTOGRAPHER	1546 N IVANHOE ST	ARLINGTON, VA	22205
DALE, CLAMMA	SOPRANO	CAMI, 165 W 57TH ST	NEW YORK, NY	10019
DALE, DANIEL	ACTOR	NBC-TV, "ANOTHER WORLD"		
		30 ROCKEFELLER PLAZA	NEW YORK, NY	10112

BEVERLY D'ANGELO

ARLENE DAHL

TYNE DALY

RODNEY DANGERFIELD

BLYTHE DANNER

CESARE DANOVA

BETTE DAVIS

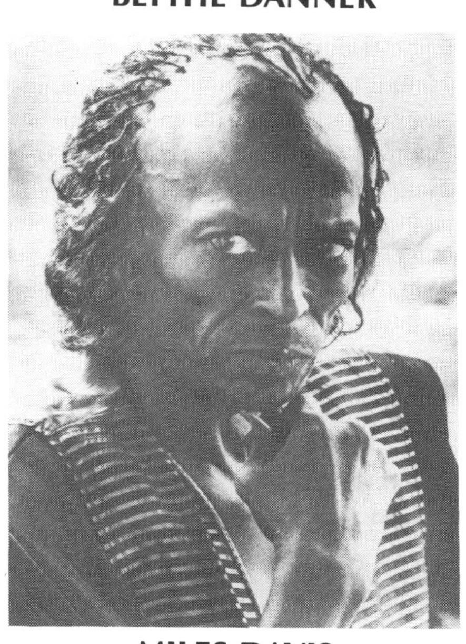
MILES DAVIS

SAMMY DAVIS

Name	Occupation	Address	City	Zip/Country
DALE, DICK	SINGER-GUITARIST	TERRY, 909 PARKVIEW AVE	LODI, CA	95240
DALE, DUCHESS	ACTRESS	11653 ACAMA ST	STUDIO CITY, CA	91604
DALE, GROVER	DIRECTOR	ICM, 40 W 57TH ST	NEW YORK, NY	10019
DALE, JIM	ACTOR	26 PEMBRIDGE VILLAS	LONDON W11	ENGLAND
DALE, JOHN R "JACK"	COMPOSER-CONDUCTOR	6836 ALDEA AVE	VAN NUYS, CA	91406
DALE, KENNY	SINGER	POST OFFICE BOX 23470	NASHVILLE, TN	37202
DALE, LAURENCE	TENOR	CAMI, 165 W 57TH ST	NEW YORK, NY	10019
DALE, REGINALD	NEWS CORRESPONDENT	3600 "T" ST, NW	WASHINGTON, DC	20007
DALE, RONNIE	GUITARIST	2822 COLONIAL CIR	NASHVILLE, TN	37214
DALE, TED	WRITER	8955 BEVERLY BLVD	LOS ANGELES, CA	90048
DALECKI, KENNETH B	NEWS CORRESPONDENT	9121 WALDEN RD	SILVER SPRING, MD	20901
DALES, MARY J	NEWS CORRESPONDENT	12509 CASTLELEIGH PL	SILVER SPRING, MD	20904
DALESANDRO, JAMES	ACTOR	12926 RIVERSIDE DR #C	STUDIO CITY, CA	91423
DALEY, HARRY	WRITER	555 W 57TH ST #1230	NEW YORK, NY	10019
DALEY, JAN B	ACTRESS	9777 WILSHIRE BLVD #707	BEVERLY HILLS, CA	90212
DALEY, KATHRYN	ACTRESS	9100 SUNSET BLVD #200	LOS ANGELES, CA	90069
DALEY, ROBERT A	FILM PRODUCER	POST OFFICE BOX 8509	UNIVERSAL CITY, CA	91608
DALEY, SHARON	WRITER	8955 BEVERLY BLVD	LOS ANGELES, CA	90048
DALEY, WILLIAM A	WRITER	19317 STARE ST	NORTHRIDGE, CA	91324
DALI, SALVADOR	ARTIST	POINT LLIGAT	CADAQUES	SPAIN
DALLAS BRASS ENSEMBLE	MUSIC ENSEMBLE	FEGAN, 6638 MAPLE AVE	DALLAS, TX	75235
DALLENBACH, WALTER	WRITER	2682 WOODSTOCK RD	LOS ANGELES, CA	90046
DALLER, RICHARD DAVID	TRUMPETER	9 JUDICIAL ST	PITTSBURGH, PA	15211
DALLESANDRO, JOE	ACTOR	7285 FRANKLIN AVE #E	LOS ANGELES, CA	90046
DALLIN, LEON	COMPOSER	POST OFFICE BOX 2400	SEAL BEACH, CA	90740
DALLIS, DR NICHOLAS P	CARTOON WRITER	7315 E MC LELLAN BLVD	SCOTTSDALE, AZ	85253
DALRYMPLE, JEAN	THEATER PRODUCER	150 W 55TH ST	NEW YORK, NY	10019
DALTON, ABBY	ACTRESS	15301 VENTURA BLVD #345	SHERMAN OAKS, CA	91403
DALTON, AUDREY	ACTRESS	SIMENZ, 15227 DEL GADO DR	SHERMAN OAKS, CA	91403
DALTON, DARREL	WRESTLER	NATIONAL WRESTLING ALLIANCE		
		JIM CROCKETT PROMOTIONS		
		421 BRIARBEND DR	CHARLOTTE, NC	28209
DALTON, DEBORAH	ACTRESS	9100 SUNSET BLVD #200	LOS ANGELES, CA	90069
DALTON, LACY J	SINGER-SINGER	TEN TEN MANAGEMENT		
		1010 16TH AVE S	NASHVILLE, TN	37212
DALTON, TIMOTHY	ACTOR	3 FRISTON ST	LONDON SW6	ENGLAND
DALTON, WALTER	ACTOR-WRITER	4011 STONE CANYON AVE	SHERMAN OAKS, CA	91403
DALTON, WILLIAM PATRICK	NEWS CORRESPONDENT	4201 OGLETHORPE ST #203	HYATTSVILLE, MD	20781
DALTRY, LAURA	WRITER	POST OFFICE BOX 9506	MARINA DEL REY, CA	90265
DALTRY, ROGER	SINGER-ACTOR	5 MILNER PL	LONDON N1	ENGLAND
DALVA, ROBERT	WRITER-PRODUCER	THE ZOETROPE STUDIOS		
		1040 N LAS PALMAS AVE	HOLLYWOOD, CA	90038
DALVAN, ROBERT	ACTOR	58 RUE MICHEL-ANGE	PARIS 75017	FRANCE
DALY, FRANK	ACTOR	400 W 43RD ST #10-P	NEW YORK, NY	10036
DALY, JOHN	FILM PRODUCER	HEMDALE, 1118 N WETHERLY DR	LOS ANGELES, CA	90069
DALY, JOHN	NEWS CORRESPONDENT	732 S ALFRED ST	ALEXANDRIA, VA	22314
DALY, JOHN CHARLES	RADIO-TV PERSONALITY	1070 PARK AVE	NEW YORK, NY	10028
DALY, JONATHAN	ACTOR	9220 SUNSET BLVD #202	LOS ANGELES, CA	90069
DALY, MAUREEN P	WRITER	9200 SUNSET BLVD #601	LOS ANGELES, CA	90069
DALY, RAD	ACTOR	4258 BEVERLY GLEN BLVD	SHERMAN OAKS, CA	91423
DALY, ROBERT	FILM-TV EXECUTIVE	444 LORING AVE	LOS ANGELES, CA	90024
DALY, SMILEY, JR	CLOWN	2701 COTTAGE WY #14	SACRAMENTO, CA	95825
DALY, TIMOTHY	ACTOR	151 S EL CAMINO DR	BEVERLY HILLS, CA	90212
DALY, TYNE	ACTRESS	1 SPINNAKER ST #13	VENICE, CA	90292
DALY, WILLIAM J	NEWS CORRESPONDENT	3387 STUYVANESANT PL, NW	WASHINGTON, DC	20015
DALZELL, JEFFREY	SINGER-GUITARIST	POST OFFICE BOX 158332	NASHVILLE, TN	37215
DAMANTE-SHAW, SUSAN	ACTRESS	12725 VENTURA BLVD #E	STUDIO CITY, CA	91604
DAMATO, JOE	ACTOR	8285 SUNSET BLVD #12	LOS ANGELES, CA	90046
DAMES, ROBERT L	WRITER-PRODUCER	5329 TOPEKA DR	TARZANA, CA	91356
DAMIAN, MICHAEL	ACTOR	24337 MULHOLLAND HWY	CALABASAS, CA	91302
DAMIANI, LEO G	CONDUCTOR	1909 MANNING ST	BURBANK, CA	91505
DAMIEN THORNE	ROCK & ROLL GROUP	JACKAL'S PACK MGMT		
		2533 S 58TH CT	CICERO, IL	60650
DAMMANN, APRIL A	WRITER	7065 HILLSIDE AVE	HOLLYWOOD, CA	90068
DAMMETT, BLACKIE	ACTOR	1004 N LA JOLLA AVE	LOS ANGELES, CA	90046
DAMON, GABRIEL	ACTOR	8961 SUNSET BLVD #B	LOS ANGELES, CA	90069
DAMON, MARK	ACTOR	16990 STRAWBERRY DR	ENCINO, CA	91316
DAMON, STUART	ACTOR	367 N VAN NESS AVE	LOS ANGELES, CA	90004
DAMONE, VIC	SINGER	9108 ALANDA PL	BEVERLY HILLS, CA	90210
DAMSEL, CHARLES	BARITONE	CONE, 221 W 57TH ST	NEW YORK, NY	10019
DAMSKI, MELVIN	WRITER-PRODUCER	10533 DUNLEER DR	LOS ANGELES, CA	90064
DANA, BARBARA	ACTRESS-WRITER	ARKIN, 50 RIDGE DR	CHAPPAQUE, NY	10514
DANA, BILL	ACTOR-COMEDIAN	1008 9TH ST #A	SANTA MONICA, CA	90403
DANA, JUSTIN	ACTOR	13111 VENTURA BLVD #102	STUDIO CITY, CA	91604
DANA, MORDO	ACTOR	FELBER, 2126 N CAHUENGA BLVD	LOS ANGELES, CA	90068
DANA, VIOLA	ACTRESS	23388 MULHOLLAND DR	WOODLAND HILLS, CA	91364
DANAE, KARA	PIANIST	POST OFFICE BOX 131	SPRINGFIELD, VA	22150
DANAHER, KAREN	TV DIRECTOR-PRODUCER	NBC-TV, 3000 W ALAMEDA AVE	BURBANK, CA	91523
DANAHY, MICHAEL	ACTOR	2235 1/2 N CAHUENGA BLVD	HOLLYWOOD, CA	90068
DANARE, MALCOLM	ACTOR	CONTEMPORARY ARTISTS		
		132 S LASKY DR	BEVERLY HILLS, CA	90212
DANBY, NICHOLAS	ORGANIST	15 HIGH ST #621	HARTFORD, CT	06103

Name	Occupation	Address	City/Country
DANCE, CHARLES	ACTOR	DAWSON, 31 KINGS RD	LONDON SW3 ENGLAND
DANCH, WILLIAM	WRITER	8955 BEVERLY BLVD	LOS ANGELES, CA 90048
DANCY, JOHN	NEWS CORRESPONDENT	NBC-TV, NEWS DEPARTMENT	
		4001 NEBRASKA AVE, NW	WASHINGTON, DC 20016
DANDO, SUZANNE	ACTRESS	LIMELIGHT, WALLHURST ST	W SUSSEX ENGLAND
DANDREA, RONALD	FILM EXECUTIVE	8 HAMMER HILL RD	KOWLOON HONG KONG
DANDRIDGE, DON	ACTOR	1527 S OGDEN DR	LOS ANGELES, CA 90019
DANDRIDGE, FRANK	TV WRITER	WGA, 8955 SUNSET BLVD	LOS ANGELES, CA 90048
DANDRIDGE, RUBY	ACTRESS	BALDWIN HILLS CARE CENTER	
		3737 DON FELIPE DR	LOS ANGELES, CA 90008
DANE, ANN	ACTRESS	10100 SANTA MONICA BLVD #1600	LOS ANGELES, CA 90067
DANE, HOLLY	ACTOR	13906 FIJI WY #344	MARINA DEL REY, CA 90292
DANE, LAWRENCE	ACTOR	8019 1/2 MELROSE AVE #3	LOS ANGELES, CA 90046
DANEMAN, PAUL	ACTOR-WRITER	CHATTO & LINNIT, LTD	
		PRINCE OF WALES THEATRE	
		COVENTRY ST	LONDON WC2 ENGLAND
DANESE, SHERA	ACTRESS	151 S EL CAMINO DR	BEVERLY HILLS, CA 90212
DANGERFIELD, MAX	TV WRITER	8955 BEVERLY BLVD	LOS ANGELES, CA 90048
DANGERFIELD, RODNEY	COMEDIAN-ACTOR	520 E 77TH ST	NEW YORK, NY 10021
DANIAS, STARR	ACTRESS-DANCER	30 W 63RD ST #30-K	NEW YORK, NY 10023
DANIEL	C & W GROUP	STOLLER, 120 HICKORY ST	MADISON, TN 37115
DANIEL	SINGER	POST OFFICE BOX 25083	NASHVILLE, TN 37202
DANIEL, ANN	TV EXECUTIVE	ABC-TV, 4151 PROSPECT AVE	LOS ANGELES, CA 90027
DANIEL, BEAU	ACTOR	11240 MAGNOLIA BLVD #202	NORTH HOLLYWOOD, CA 91601
DANIEL, CYRUS	MUSICIAN	2416 ABBOTT MARTIN RD	NASHVILLE, TN 37215
DANIEL, ELIOT H	CONDUCTOR	FAIR PLAY RD	SOMERSET, CA 95684
DANIEL, GERALD	COMPOSER-CONDUCTOR	1850 CARFAX	LONG BEACH, CA 90815
DANIEL, JAY	TV DIRECTOR	5933 ROD AVE	WOODLAND HILLS, CA 91367
DANIEL, JAY	ACTOR	11726 SAN VICENTE BLVD #300	LOS ANGELES, CA 90049
DANIEL, JAY	TV PRODUCER	ABC-TV, 9911 W PICO BLVD	LOS ANGELES, CA 90035
DANIEL, JENNIFER	ACTRESS	FILM RIGHTS, LTD	
		113 WARDOUR ST	LONDON ENGLAND
DANIEL, MARGARET TRUMAN	AUTHORESS	830 PARK AVE	NEW YORK, NY 10028
DANIEL, NANCY	NEWS CORRESPONDENT	2602 TUNLAW RD, NW	WASHINGTON, DC 20036
DANIEL, ROD	FILM DIRECTOR	19414 OLIVOS DR	TARZANA, CA 91356
DANIEL, ROGER	GUITARIST	721 OLD DUE WEST AVE	MADISON, TN 37115
DANIEL, SAM	MUSICIAN	POST OFFICE BOX 623	LEXINGTON, MS 39095
DANIEL, TAMARA	ACTRESS	149 W 13TH ST	NEW YORK, NY 10011
DANIEL'S, MR JACK, ORIGINAL	C & W GROUP	POST OFFICE BOX 418	BRENTWOOD, TN 37027
DANIELEWSKI, TAD	DIRECTOR	9300 WILSHIRE BLVD #410	BEVERLY HILLS, CA 90212
DANIELLE	ACTRESS	17029 DEVONSHIRE ST #155	NORTHRIDGE, CA 91325
DANIELLE, SUZANNE	ACTRESS	91 REGENT ST	LONDON W1 ENGLAND
DANIELS, BARBARA	SOPRANO	CAMI, 165 W 57TH ST	NEW YORK, NY 10019
DANIELS, BARBARA	NEWS CORRESPONDENT	400 N CAPITOL ST, NW	WASHINGTON, DC 20001
DANIELS, BILL	CABLE EXECUTIVE	DANIELS & ASSOCIATES	
		5720 EL CAMINO REAL	CARLSBAD, CA 92008
DANIELS, BILL	COLUMNIST	VARIETY, 1400 N CAHUENGA BLVD	HOLLYWOOD, CA 90028
DANIELS, BILLY	SINGER	2200 BEECH KNOLL RD	LOS ANGELES, CA 90046
DANIELS, BOBBY	DRUMMER	7383 BRIDLE DR	NASHVILLE, TN 37221
DANIELS, CHARLIE, BAND	C & W GROUP	210 25TH AVE N #N-101	NASHVILLE, TN 37203
DANIELS, DARI	TV WRITER	8955 BEVERLY BLVD	LOS ANGELES, CA 90048
DANIELS, DAVID MASON	ACTOR	113 N SAN VICENTE BLVD #202	BEVERLY HILLS, CA 90211
DANIELS, GARY HUGH	ACTOR	420 N ONTARIO ST	BURBANK, CA 91505
DANIELS, JACK B	DIRECTOR	349 N OAKHURST DR	BEVERLY HILLS, CA 90210
DANIELS, JUDITH	EDITOR-PUBLISHER	LIFE/TIME & LIFE BLDG	
		ROCKEFELLER CENTER	NEW YORK, NY 10020
DANIELS, MARC	TV DIRECTOR	12534 OTSEGO ST	NORTH HOLLYWOOD, CA 91607
DANIELS, PAUL	MAGICIAN	140 BECKETT RD, DONCASTER	SOUTH YORKSHIRE ENGLAND
DANIELS, PHIL	ACTOR	HOPE & LYNE, 5 MILNER PL	LONDON N1 ENGLAND
DANIELS, ROBERT M	ART DIRECTOR	DISCOVER/TIME & LIFE BLDG	
		ROCKEFELLER CENTER	NEW YORK, NY 10020
DANIELS, RUDY	ACTOR	5330 LANKERSHIM BLVD #210	NORTH HOLLYWOOD, CA 91601
DANIELS, STANLEY E	WRITER-PRODUCER	4754 ALONZO AVE	ENCINO, CA 91316
DANIELS, TIM	SINGER-GUITARIST	119 HICKORY HGTS DR	HENDERSONVILLE, TN 37075
DANIELS, WILLIAM	ACTOR	14242 PIERCE ST	ARLETA, CA 91331
DANIELSON, ROCKY	CINEMATOGRAPHER	7715 SUNSET BLVD #150	LOS ANGELES, CA 90046
DANILOFF, NICHOLAS	NEWS CORRESPONDENT	U S NEWS & WORLD REPORT	
		2400 "N" ST, NW	WASHINGTON, DC 20037
DANILOFF, RUTH	NEWS CORRESPONDENT	DISCOVER/TIME & LIFE BLDG	
		ROCKEFELLER CENTER	NEW YORK, NY 10020
DANILOVA, ALEXANDRA	BALLERINA	100 W 57TH ST	NEW YORK, NY 10019
DANK, HARRY N	WRITER	555 W 57TH ST #1230	NEW YORK, NY 10019
DANKWORTH, JOHN	MUSICIAN-COMPOSER	THE OLD RECTORY, WAVENDON	MILTON KEYNES MK17 8LT ENGLAND
DANN, MIKE	TV EXECUTIVE	ABC TELEVISION NETWORK	
		1330 AVE OF THE AMERICAS	NEW YORK, NY 10019

DANN, SAMUEL H	WRITER	555 W 57TH ST #1230	NEW YORK, NY 10019
DANN, VICTORIA	WRITER	8955 BEVERLY BLVD	LOS ANGELES, CA 90048
DANNE, TERRY D	CONDUCTOR	10681 VALLEYHEART DR	STUDIO CITY, CA 91604
DANNEMILLER, CHRISTI	SINGER	GOOD, 2500 NW 39TH ST	OKLAHOMA CITY, OK 73112
DANNER, BLYTHE	ACTRESS	304 21ST ST	SANTA MONICA, CA 90402
DANNER, DAVID WILLIAM	NEWS CORRESPONDENT	3896 PORTER ST, NW	WASHINGTON, DC 20016
DANNHAUSER, WILLIAM	TV EXECUTIVE	NBC TELEVISION NETWORK	
		30 ROCKEFELLER PLAZA	NEW YORK, NY 10112
DANNING, SYBIL	ACTRESS-MODEL	8578 WALNUT DR	LOS ANGELES, CA 90004
DANNIS, RAY	ACTOR	965 LAKE ST	VENICE, CA 90291
DANNON, ROBERT	ACTOR	3330 BARHAM BLVD #103	LOS ANGELES, CA 90068
DANNY & THE JUNIORS	VOCAL GROUP	MARS, 168 ORCHID DR	PEARL RIVER, NY 10965
DANO, LINDA	ACTRESS	113 N SAN VICENTE BLVD #202	BEVERLY HILLS, CA 90211
DANO, RICHARD	ACTOR	7060 HOLLYWOOD BLVD #610	LOS ANGELES, CA 90028
DANO, ROYAL	ACTOR	517 20TH ST	SANTA MONICA, CA 90402
DANOVA, CESARE	ACTOR	8721 SUNSET BLVD #209	LOS ANGELES, CA 90069
DANSBURY, PATRICIA A	NEWS CORRESPONDENT	1722 19TH ST #501, NW	WASHINGTON, DC 20009
DANSBY, WILLIAM	BASSO-BARITONE	LEW, 204 W 10TH ST	NEW YORK, NY 10014
DANSEREAU, ED	PIANIST	1625 MEDIA DR	BOWLING GREEN, KY 42101
DANSKA, DOLORES F	DIRECTOR-PRODUCER	711 AMSTERDAM AVE	NEW YORK, NY 10025
DANSKA, HERBERT	WRITER-PRODUCER	9601 WILSHIRE BLVD #642	BEVERLY HILLS, CA 90210
DANSON, TED	ACTOR	10780 SANTA MONICA BLVD #280	LOS ANGELES, CA 90025
DANTE, JOE	FILM DIRECTOR	2321 HOLLY DR	HOLLYWOOD, CA 90068
DANTE, MICHAEL	ACTOR	9200 SUNSET BLVD #909	LOS ANGELES, CA 90069
DANTE, NICHOLAS	PLAYWRIGHT	250 W 75TH ST	NEW YORK, NY 10023
DANTINE, NIKI	ACTRESS	707 N PALM DR	BEVERLY HILLS, CA 90210
DANTON, RAY	ACTOR-DIRECTOR	DGA, 7950 SUNSET BLVD	LOS ANGELES, CA 90046
DANTZSCHER, BARRY C	WRITER	13414 OXNARD ST	VAN NUYS, CA 91401
DANUS, BONNIE BENOV	WRITER	400 N OAKHURST DR #101	BEVERLY HILLS, CA 90210
DANUS, RICHARD CHRISTIAN	WRITER	432 N PALM DR	BEVERLY HILLS, CA 90210
DANUTA, THE SPIDER GODDESS	AERIALIST	HALL, 138 FROG HOLLOW RD	CHURCHVILLE, PA 18966
DANZA, JOHN	DIRECTOR	140 GLENWOOD AVE	LEONIA, NJ 07605
DANZA, TONY	ACTOR	7300 WOODROW WILSON DR	LOS ANGELES, CA 90046
DANZIG, MICHAEL H	WRITER	1920 HILLCREST RD #9	LOS ANGELES, CA 90068
DANZIGER, DENNIS JAY	TV WRITER	10549 NORTHVALE RD	LOS ANGELES, CA 90064
DANZIGER, MAIA	ACTRESS	J MICHAEL BLOOM AGENCY	
		233 PARK AVE S, 10TH FLOOR	NEW YORK, NY 10017
DANZY, ROSCOE, JR	COMPOSER	13120 VICTORY BLVD #11	VAN NUYS, CA 91401
DAPAR, JOSEPHINE N	COMPOSER	6910 DAY ST	TUJUNGA, CA 91042
DAPRATO, WILLIAM J	ACTOR	220 E 27TH ST	NEW YORK, NY 10016
DARA, ENZO	SINGER	CAMI, 165 W 57TH ST	NEW YORK, NY 10019
DARBO, PATRIKA	ACTRESS	346 N AVON ST	BURBANK, CA 91505
DARBY, KIM	ACTRESS	11726 SAN VICENTE BLVD #300	LOS ANGELES, CA 90049
DARC, MIREILLE	ACTRESS	ADEL PRO, 4 RUE CHAMBIGES	PARIS 75008 FRANCE
DARCEY, RICHARD G	PHOTOGRAPHER	1314 CONSTITUTION AVE, NE	WASHINGTON, DC 20002
DARCEY-BARTLETT, SUSAN W	NEWS CORRESPONDENT	3133 CONNECTICUT AVE #916, NW	WASHINGTON, DC 20008
DARCY, GEORGINE	ACTRESS	7044 LOS TILOS RD	HOLLYWOOD, CA 90068
DARCY, ROBERT	ACTOR	3151 W CAHUENGA BLVD #310	LOS ANGELES, CA 90068
DARDEN, SEVERN	ACTOR	3220 LAUREL CANYON BLVD	STUDIO CITY, CA 91604
DARE, BARBARA	ACTRESS	ESSEX, 8841 WILBUR BLVD	NORTHRIDGE, CA 91324
DARENSBERT, JOE	MUSICIAN	22233 AVE SAN LUIS	WOODLAND HILLS, CA 91364
DARGET, CHANTAL	ACTRESS	15 RUE DE MIROMESNIL	PARIS 75008 FRANCE
DARIAN, ANITA	SOPRANO	GEWALD, 58 W 58TH ST	NEW YORK, NY 10019
DARIO & ARNAUD	JUGGLERS	276 CAMBRIDGE ST #4	BOSTON, MA 02134
DARION, JOE	LYRICIST	PINNACLE RD	LYME, NH 03768
DARION, SIDNEY	TV EXECUTIVE-WRITER	276 RIVERSIDE DR	NEW YORK, NY 10025
DARK, GREGORY	FILM DIRECTOR	158-A SOUTHFIELD RD	CHISWICK W4 1AN ENGLAND
DARK, JOHN	FILM PRODUCER	PINEWOOD STUDIOS, IVER HEATH	BUCKS SLO ONH ENGLAND
DARK, JOHNNY	COMEDIAN	1100 N ALTA LOMA RD #707	LOS ANGELES, CA 90069
DARK AGE	ROCK & ROLL GROUP	5455 SARD ST	ALTA LOMA, CA 91701
DARK JOURNEY	WERSTLING VALET	UNIVERSAL WRESTLING FEDERATION	
		MID SOUTH SPORTS, INC	
		116 W BRECKINRIDGE	BIXBY, OK 74008
DARKROOM	ROCK & ROLL GROUP	41 BRITAIN ST #200	TORONTO, ONT CANADA
DARLEY, CHRIS	DIRECTOR	4092 DEERVALE DR	SHERMAN OAKS, CA 91403
DARLEY, DICK	TV DIRECTOR	3383 TARECO DR	HOLLYWOOD, CA 90068
DARLING, BRUCE E	TV WRITER	8955 BEVERLY BLVD	LOS ANGELES, CA 90048
DARLING, JOAN	WRITER-DIRECTOR	DGA, 7950 SUNSET BLVD	LOS ANGELES, CA 90046
DARLING & CALE	ROCK & ROLL GROUP	POST OFFICE BOX 448	RADFORD, VA 24141
DARLOW, MICHAEL	WRITER-PRODUCER	PIP, 74 NEWMAN ST	LONDON W1 ENGLAND
DARNALL, JOHN	GUITARIST	4407 ALCOTT DR	NASHVILLE, TN 37215
DARNELL, CYTHIA	TV WRITER	9100 SUNSET BLVD #340	LOS ANGELES, CA 90069
DARNELL, JIMMY	MUSICIAN	1505 GOLF ST	NASHVILLE, TN 37216
DARNELL, JOHN H	NEWS CORRESPONDENT	400 N CAPITOL ST, NW	WASHINGTON, DC 20001
DARNELL, ROBERT	ACTOR	9220 SUNSET BLVD #202	LOS ANGELES, CA 90069
DARNEY, TONI	ACTRESS	7 W 16TH ST	NEW YORK, NY 10011
DARRELL, DAVID	ACTOR	7309 FRANKLIN AVE #102	LOS ANGELES, CA 90046
DARRELL, JIM	WRESTLER	SEE - ZHUKOV, BORIS	
DARRELL, JUDITH	WRITER	555 W 57TH ST #1230	NEW YORK, NY 10019
DARRELL, MICHAEL	ACTOR	3050 W 7TH ST #200	LOS ANGELES, CA 90005
DARREN, JAMES	ACTOR-SINGER	POST OFFICE BOX 1088	BEVERLY HILLS, CA 90213
DARRENKAMP, JOHN	BARITONE	HILLYER, 250 W 57TH ST	NEW YORK, NY 10107
DARRID, WILLIAM	WRITER	4035 MADELIA AVE	SHERMAN OAKS, CA 91403
DARRIEUX, DANIELLE	ACTRESS	3 QUAI MALAIVAIS	PARIS 75006 FRANCE

Name	Occupation	Address	City	Zip
DARRO, KELLY	ACTRESS	10850 RIVERSIDE DR #505	NORTH HOLLYWOOD, CA	91602
DARROW, HENRY	ACTOR	15010 VENTURA BLVD #234	SHERMAN OAKS, CA	91403
DARROW, WHITNEY, JR	CARTOONIST	331 NEWTOWN TURNPIKE	WILTON, CT	06897
DARSO, CHRUSHER	WRESTLER	SEE - KHRUSHCHEV, KHRUSHER		
DARSO, MAN MOUNTAIN	WRESTLER	SEE - KHRUSHCHEV, KHRUSHER		
DARSOW, BARRY	WRESTLER	SEE - KHRUSHCHEV, KHRUSHER		
DARST, GUY B, JR	NEWS CORRESPONDENT	1338 4TH ST, SW	WASHINGTON, DC	20024
DART, JUSTIN	ACTOR	8480 BEVERLY BLVD	LOS ANGELES, CA	90048
DART, ROBERT E	NEWS CORRESPONDENT	331 LEWIS ST	VIENNA, VA	22180
DART, STEPHEN M	WRITER	3555 BEVERLY GLEN BLVD	SHERMAN OAKS, CA	91423
DARVAS, TEDDY	FILM EDITOR	1 ROTHWELL ST	LONDON NW1 8YH	ENGLAND
DASHEV, DAVID	WRITER	8955 BEVERLY BLVD	LOS ANGELES, CA	90048
DASSIN, JULES	ACTOR-DIRECTOR	25 ANAGNOSTOPOULON ST	ATHENS	GREECE
DATZ, DAVID	ACTOR	1066 CONCHA ST	ALTADENA, CA	91001
DAUBER, PHILIP	WRITER-PRODUCER	1454 CEDAR ST	BERKELEY, CA	94702
DAUENHAUER, TOMM	WRITER	8955 BEVERLY BLVD	LOS ANGELES, CA	90048
DAUER, PATRICIA A	WRITER	555 W 57TH ST #1230	NEW YORK, NY	10019
DAUFMAN, DAVE	COLUMNIST	VARIETY, 1400 N CAHUENGA BLVD	HOLLYWOOD, CA	90028
DAUGHERTY, GREGORY S	MUSICIAN	7207 OLD SHEPHERDSVILLE	LOUISVILLE, KY	40219
DAUGHERTY, HERSCHEL	TV DIRECTOR	925 SANTE FE DR	ENCINITAS, CA	92024
DAUGHERTY, ROBERT A	PHOTOGRAPHER	6425 ICHABOD PL	FALLS CHURCH, VA	22042
DAUGHERTY, TERRY	ACTRESS	8640 W 3RD ST #2	LOS ANGELES, CA	90048
DAUGHERTY, TOMMY	PIANIST	333 RAIN DROP LN	HENDERSONVILLE, TN	37075
DAUGHTON, JAMES	ACTOR	415 N SYCAMORE AVE #102	LOS ANGELES, CA	90036
DAVALOS, DICK	ACTOR-DIRECTOR	1958 VESTAL AVE	LOS ANGELES, CA	90026
DAVALOS, ELYSSA	ACTRESS	1958 VESTAL AVE	LOS ANGELES, CA	90026
DAVE & SUGAR	C & W GROUP	POST OFFICE BOX 121089	NASHVILLE, TN	37212
DAVELUY, RAYMOND	ORGANIST	15 HIGH ST #621	HARTFORD, CT	06103
DAVENALL, ANTHONY	TV DIRECTOR	37 RANDOLPH CRESCENT	LONDON W9	ENGLAND
DAVENPORT, ALICE	WRITER	555 W 57TH ST #1230	NEW YORK, NY	10019
DAVENPORT, CLAIRE	ACTRESS	27 ROYAL CRESCENT	LONDON W11	ENGLAND
DAVENPORT, DONALD J, JR	WRITER	8955 BEVERLY BLVD	LOS ANGELES, CA	90048
DAVENPORT, EDWARD OLIN	MUSIC CRITIC	THE DAKOTA, 1 W 72ND ST	NEW YORK, NY	10023
DAVENPORT, GEORGE LEWIS	CABLE EXECUTIVE	COX CABLE COMMUNICATIONS		
		219 PERIMETER CENTER PKWY	ATLANTA, GA	30346
DAVENPORT, HORACE N, JR	MUSICIAN	5208 ALPHA, BOX 76707	LEWISVILLE, TX	75056
DAVENPORT, MARY	ACTRESS	215 E 68TH ST	NEW YORK, NY	10021
DAVENPORT, MATT LEE	SINGER-GUITARIST	111 BEECHWOOD CT	HENDERSONVILLE, TN	37075
DAVENPORT, NIGEL	ACTOR	STONE, 1052 CAROL DR	LOS ANGELES, CA	90069
DAVENPORT, RALPH W	TV WRITER	8955 BEVERLY BLVD	LOS ANGELES, CA	90048
DAVENPORT, WILLIAM D	WRITER	8955 BEVERLY BLVD	LOS ANGELES, CA	90048
DAVI, CLIFTON	ACTOR-CLERGYMAN	9145 SUNSET BLVD #228	LOS ANGELES, CA	90069
DAVI, ROBERT	ACTOR	POST OFFICE BOX 5617	BEVERLY HILLS, CA	90210
DAVIAU, ALLEN	CINEMATOGRAPHER	2249 BRONSON HILL DR	LOS ANGELES, CA	90069
DAVICH, MARTIN A	COMPOSER	3480 BARHAM BLVD #215	LOS ANGELES, CA	90068
DAVICH, MARTY	ACTOR	KNBC-TV, "DAYS OF OUR LIVES"		
		3000 W ALAMEDA AVE	BURBANK, CA	91523
DAVICH, MATTHEW STEPHEN	SAXOPHONIST	1145 FERNBANK AVE	MADISON, TN	37115
DAVID, ALTOVISE	ACTRESS-MODEL	1151 SUMMIT DR	BEVERLY HILLS, CA	90210
DAVID, ANDREA	WRITER	555 W 57TH ST #1230	NEW YORK, NY	10019
DAVID, ANDREW	CONDUCTOR	SHAW CONCERTS, 1995 BROADWAY	NEW YORK, NY	10023
DAVID, ART	ACTOR	POST OFFICE BOX 11	BLOOMBURG, TX	75556
DAVID, B J	DIRECTOR	POST OFFICE BOX 2175	TOLUCA LAKE, CA	91602
DAVID, BOB	FLUTIST	3000 HILLSBORO RD #87	NASHVILLE, TN	37215
DAVID, BOWEN	CONDUCTOR	379 GRANT PARK PL, SE	ATLANTA, GA	30315
DAVID, BUB	STUNTMAN	3518 W CAHUENGA BLVD #300	LOS ANGELES, CA	90068
DAVID, CAROLE R	ACTRESS	7060 HOLLYWOOD BLVD #610	LOS ANGELES, CA	90028
DAVID, CLIVE	RECORD EXECUTIVE	88 CENTRAL PARK W	NEW YORK, NY	10019
DAVID, COSTO I, JR	MUSIC ARRANGER	452 MOSS TRAIL #K-2	GOODLETTSVILLE, TN	37072
DAVID, CYNTHIA	ACTRESS	928 1/2 S SERRANO AVE	LOS ANGELES, CA	90006
DAVID, DAVID H	COMPOSER-CONDUCTOR	POST OFFICE BOX 24-B30	LOS ANGELES, CA	90024
DAVID, GOLDA F	WRITER	8955 BEVERLY BLVD	LOS ANGELES, CA	90048
DAVID, HAL	LYRICIST	24 W 55TH ST	NEW YORK, NY	10019
DAVID, HUGH	ACT-WRI-DIR	WILDACRE, 10 PARSONAGE	BERKS SL4 5EN	ENGLAND
DAVID, HUMPHREY	ACTOR	16 ARLINGTOPN TERR	EDGEWATER, NJ	07020
DAVID, JEFFREY L	TV WRITER	8955 BEVERLY BLVD	LOS ANGELES, CA	90048
DAVID, JERRY	WRITER-PRODUCER	1250 LA COLLINA DR	BEVERLY HILLS, CA	90210
DAVID, JOANNA	ACTRESS	25 MAIDA AVE	LONDON W2	ENGLAND
DAVID, KATE	ACTRESS	11-C SUNDERLAND TERR	LONDON W2 5PA	ENGLAND
DAVID, LARRY G	TV WRITER	8955 BEVERLY BLVD	LOS ANGELES, CA	90048
DAVID, MACK	COMPOSER	1575 TOLEDO CIR	PALM SPRINGS, CA	92262
DAVID, MADELINE B	TV WRITER	555 W 57TH ST #1230	NEW YORK, NY	10019
DAVID, MARJORIE S	WRITER	445 N BEDFORD DR #PH	BEVERLY HILLS, CA	90210
DAVID, MICHAEL ROBERT	WRITER	10442 GLORIA AVE	GRANADA HILLS, CA	91344
DAVID, MOLLY	ACTRESS	10000 RIVERSIDE DR #12-14	TOLUCA LAKE, CA	91602
DAVID, NICOLE	TALENT AGENT	10100 SANTA MONICA BLVD #1600	LOS ANGELES, CA	90067
DAVID, NOUR RUNA	PHOTOGRAPHER	4015 N 27TH RD	ARLINGTON, VA	22207
DAVID, PIERRE	FILM PRODUCER	1888 CENTURY PARK E #622	LOS ANGELES, CA	90067
DAVID, RICHARD J	WRITER	8955 BEVERLY BLVD	LOS ANGELES, CA	90048
DAVID, RICK DAKOTA	GUITARIST	1326 WINTHORNE DR	NASHVILLE, TN	37217
DAVID, RONALD L	PHOTOGRAPHER	4015 N 27TH RD	ARLINGTON, VA	22207
DAVID, SAUL	WRITER	13216 CUMPSTON ST	VAN NUYS, CA	91401
DAVID, WILLIAM J	WRITER	8955 BEVERLY BLVD	LOS ANGELES, CA	90048
DAVID & DAVID	ROCK & ROLL GROUP	M F C MANAGEMENT COMPANY		
		1428 S SHERBOURNE DR	LOS ANGELES, CA	90035

Name	Occupation	Address	City	Code
DAVID & THE GIANTS	GOSPEL GROUP	POST OFFICE BOX 723591	ATLANTA, GA	30339
DAVIDOFF, JUDITH	CELLIST	61 W 62ND ST #6-F	NEW YORK, NY	10023
DAVIDOFF, LOLITA	ACTRESS	8383 WILSHIRE BLVD #1024	BEVERLY HILLS, CA	90211
DAVIDOVICH, BELLA	PIANIST	LEISER, DORCHESTER TOWERS		
		155 W 68TH ST	NEW YORK, NY	10023
DAVIDOVICI, ROBERT	VIOLINIST	SHAW CONCERTS, 1995 BROADWAY	NEW YORK, NY	10023
DAVIDS, HOLLACE G	WRITER	1880 CENTURY PARK E #618	LOS ANGELES, CA	90067
DAVIDS, PAUL	SCREENWRITER	435 HOLLAND AVE	LOS ANGELES, CA	90042
DAVIDSON, ARLENE	SCREENWRITER	8955 BEVERLY BLVD	LOS ANGELES, CA	90048
DAVIDSON, BILL	WRITER	8955 BEVERLY BLVD	LOS ANGELES, CA	90048
DAVIDSON, BOAZ	DIRECTOR	CANNON, 9911 W PICO BLVD	LOS ANGELES, CA	90035
DAVIDSON, DARYL D	GUITARIST	POST OFFICE BOX 705	BRANSON, MO	65616
DAVIDSON, DIANA	MEZZO-SOPRANO	45 W 60TH ST #4-K	NEW YORK, NY	10023
DAVIDSON, DOUG	ACTOR	3641 E CHEVY CHASE DR	GLENDALE, CA	91206
DAVIDSON, EILEEN	ACTRESS	6363 WILSHIRE BLVD #600	LOS ANGELES, CA	90048
DAVIDSON, EMIL G	WRITER	12125 HOLLYGLEN PL	STUDIO CITY, CA	91604
DAVIDSON, GERALD	WRITER	8955 BEVERLY BLVD	LOS ANGELES, CA	90048
DAVIDSON, GORDON	DIRECTOR	165 MABERY RD	SANTA MONICA, CA	90402
DAVIDSON, HARLEY	WRESTLER	SEE - HILBILLY JIM		
DAVIDSON, JIM	COMEDIAN	IAR, 235-241 REGENT ST	LONDON W1A 2JT	ENGLAND
DAVIDSON, JOE	NEWS CORRESPONDENT	2906 25TH ST, NE	WASHINGTON, DC	20018
DAVIDSON, JOHN	SINGER-ACTOR	20944 PACIFIC COAST HWY	MALIBU, CA	90265
DAVIDSON, JOY	MEZZO-SOPRANO	5751 SW 74TH AVE	MIAMI, FL	33143
DAVIDSON, LEWIS WINSTON	WRITER	8955 BEVERLY BLVD	LOS ANGELES, CA	90048
DAVIDSON, MARK	WRITER	8955 BEVERLY BLVD	LOS ANGELES, CA	90048
DAVIDSON, MARK L	WRITER	555 W 57TH ST #1230	NEW YORK, NY	10019
DAVIDSON, MARTIN	FILM WRITER-DIRECTOR	1505 VIEWSITE TERR	LOS ANGELES, CA	90069
DAVIDSON, RALPH P	PUBLISHING EXECUTIVE	TIME & LIFE MAGAZINES		
		TIME & LIFE BUILDING		
		ROCKEFELLER CENTER	NEW YORK, NY	10020
DAVIDSON, ROD	ACTOR	10359 MONTE MAR DR	LOS ANGELES, CA	90064
DAVIDSON, SARA J	WRITER	8955 BEVERLY BLVD	LOS ANGELES, CA	90048
DAVIDSON, WILLIAM J	WRITER	1666 THAYER AVE #202	LOS ANGELES, CA	90024
DAVIDSON, ZEKE	ACTOR	POST OFFICE BOX 347	ANNA, IL	62906
DAVIES, ARTHUR	TENOR	61 W 62ND ST #6-F	NEW YORK, NY	10023
DAVIES, BRIAN	ACTOR	6355 N LEMON AVE	SAN GABRIEL, CA	91775
DAVIES, CAROL	WRITER	8955 BEVERLY BLVD	LOS ANGELES, CA	90048
DAVIES, DANIEL	ACTOR	4558 CAMELLIA AVE	NORTH HOLLYWOOD, CA	91602
DAVIES, GAIL	SINGER-SONGWRITER	246 CHEROKEE RD	NASHVILLE, TN	37205
DAVIES, GARETH	TV PRODUCER	MTM, 4024 RADFORD AVE	STUDIO CITY, CA	91604
DAVIES, GEOFFREY	ACTOR	CROUCH, 59 FRITH ST	LONDON W1V 5TA	ENGLAND
DAVIES, HEATHER	DIRECTOR-PRODUCER	CHESS VALLEY FILMS, LTD		
		FILM HOUSE, LITTEL CHALFONT	BUCKS	ENGLAND
DAVIES, JACK	SCREENWRITER	8955 BEVERLY BLVD	LOS ANGELES, CA	90048
DAVIES, JAN	ACTRESS	76 MICHELDEVER RD	LEE SE12 8LU	ENGLAND
DAVIES, JANICE	ACTRESS	4558 CAMELLIA AVE	NORTH HOLLYWOOD, CA	91602
DAVIES, JOHN	BASSO-BARITONE	MUNRO, 334 W 72ND ST	NEW YORK, NY	10023
DAVIES, JOHN	TV DIRECTOR-PRODUCER	MARSTON HILL FARM		
		THORPE MANDEVILLE		
		NEAR BANBURY	OXON	ENGLAND
DAVIES, JOHN HOWARD	FILM DIRECTOR	LONDON MANAGEMENT, LTD		
		235-241 REGENT ST	LONDON W1A 2JT	ENGLAND
DAVIES, JOHN RHYS	ACTOR	CCA MGMT, 4 CT LODGE		
		48 SLOANE SQ	LONDON SW1	ENGLAND
DAVIES, KEN	STAMP DESIGNER	POST OFFICE BOX 902	MADISON, CT	06443
DAVIES, LANE	ACTOR	247 BEVERLY DR #102	BEVERLY HILLS, CA	90210
DAVIES, PAUL	FILM EDITOR	SCAR COTTAGE, DORSTONE	HEREFORDSHIRE	ENGLAND
DAVIES, PETER	ACTOR	ABC-TV NETWORK, "LOVING"		
		1330 AVE OF THE AMERICAS	NEW YORK, NY	10019
DAVIES, RICHARD	ACTOR	1605 N CAHUENGA BLVD #202	LOS ANGELES, CA	90028
DAVIES, RICHARD B	TV DIRECTOR	6939 MAMMOTH AVE	LOS ANGELES, CA	90026
DAVIES, STEPHEN	ACTOR	9255 SUNSET BLVD #610	LOS ANGELES, CA	90069
DAVIES, STEPHEN A	NEWS CORRESPONDENT	13173 AUTUMN HILL LN	HERNDON, VA	22071
DAVIES, WILLIAM C	CONDUCTOR	5548 ELMER AVE	NORTH HOLLYWOOD, CA	91601
DAVIES, WINDSOR	ACTOR	19 W EATON PLACE MEWS		
		EATON SQ	LONDON SW1	ENGLAND
DAVILA, RAUL	ACTOR	ABC-TV, "ONE LIFE TO LIVE"		
		1330 AVE OF THE AMERICAS	NEW YORK, NY	10019
DAVINE, ROBERT	ACCORDIONIST	425 RIVERSIDE DR #5-G	NEW YORK, NY	10025
DAVIS, ALLAN	DIRECTOR	ICM, 388-396 OXFORD ST	LONDON W1	ENGLAND
DAVIS, ANDREW	FILM DIRECTOR	10351 SANTA MONICA BLVD #211	LOS ANGELES, CA	90025
DAVIS, ANGELA	AUTHOR-LECTURER	SAN FRANCISCO STATE UNIV		
		ETHNIC STUDIES DEPT		
		1600 HOLLOWAY AVE	SAN FRANCISCO, CA	94132
DAVIS, ANTHONY	COMPOSER-PIANIST	AIA, 60 E 42ND ST	NEW YORK, NY	10165
DAVIS, B J	MANDOLINIST	3008 FALMOUTH DR	LOUISVILLE, KY	40205
DAVIS, BARBARA	NEWS CORRESPONDENT	2729 ORDWAY ST #4, NW	WASHINGTON, DC	20008
DAVIS, BEN	ACTOR	6565 SUNSET BLVD #525-A	HOLLYWOOD, CA	90068
DAVIS, BETH R	NEWS CORRESPONDENT	4046 ULINE AVE	ALEXANDRIA, VA	22304
DAVIS, BETTE	ACTRESS	555 5TH AVE #1900	NEW YORK, NY	10017
DAVIS, BILL	DIRECTOR	DGA, 7950 SUNSET BLVD	LOS ANGELES, CA	90046
DAVIS, BILL C	WRITER	555 W 57TH ST #1230	NEW YORK, NY	10019
DAVIS, BILLY NEWTON	SINGER	41 BRITAIN ST #200	TORONTO, ONT	CANADA
DAVIS, BRAD	ACTOR	4302 TEESDALE AVE	STUDIO CITY, CA	91604
DAVIS, BRENT	ACTOR	8350 SANTA MONICA BLVD #102	LOS ANGELES, CA	90069

Name	Occupation	Address	City	Zip
DAVIS, BYRON M	CONDUCTOR	1236 CEDAREDGE CT	LOS ANGELES, CA	90041
DAVIS, CARL	COMPOSER	EATON MUSIC, 8 W EATON PL	LONDON SW1X 8LS	ENGLAND
DAVIS, CAROL LEE	PERCUSSIONIST	106 KAREN CT	BRENTWOOD, TN	37027
DAVIS, CHALMERS	PIANIST	ROUTE #2, BOX 22	KILLEN, AL	35645
DAVIS, CHARLES	ACTOR	1350 N HIGHLAND AVE #24	HOLLYWOOD, CA	90028
DAVIS, CHIP	RECORD PROD-EXEC	GRAMAVISION RECORDS		
		260 W BROADWAY	NEW YORK, NY	10013
DAVIS, CLIFTON	ACTOR-CLERGYMAN	THE LOMA LINDA UNIVERSITY		
		SEVENTH-DAY ADVENTIST		
		CHURCH OF LOMA LINDA		
		24701 UNIVERSITY AVE	LOMA LINDA, CA	92354
DAVIS, CRITT	ACTOR	9235 1/2 DOHENY RD	LOS ANGELES, CA	90069
DAVIS, D'MITCH	ACTOR	8721 SUNSET BLVD #200	LOS ANGELES, CA	90069
DAVIS, DANIEL	ACTOR	9220 SUNSET BLVD #625	LOS ANGELES, CA	90069
DAVIS, DANNY	GUITARIST	ROUTE #3, BOX 224	WAYNESBORO, TN	38485
DAVIS, DANNY	TRUMPETER	POST OFFICE BOX 1546	NASHVILLE, TN	37202
DAVIS, DANNY	WRESTLING REFEREE	POST OFFICE BOX 3859	STAMFORD, CT	06905
DAVIS, DAVID	TV PRODUCER	ICM, 8899 BEVERLY BLVD	LOS ANGELES, CA	90048
DAVIS, DAVID	WRITER-PRODUCER	DGA, 7950 SUNSET BLVD	LOS ANGELES, CA	90046
DAVIS, DEBORAH	TV WRITER	8955 BEVERLY BLVD	LOS ANGELES, CA	90048
DAVIS, DESMOND	FILM DIRECTOR	REDWAY, 16 BERNERS ST	LONDON W1P 3DD	ENGLAND
DAVIS, DIANA P	WRITER	555 W 57TH ST #1230	NEW YORK, NY	10019
DAVIS, DON	COMPOSER-CONDUCTOR	19221 SHERMAN WY #28	RESEDA, CA	91335
DAVIS, DON G	DIRECTOR	POST OFFICE BOX861	NEW YORK, NY	10030
DAVIS, DONALD I	DIRECTOR	4854 ENCINO AVE	ENCINO, CA	91316
DAVIS, ED	THEATER PRODUCER	THEATRE NOW, 1515 BROADWAY	NEW YORK, NY	10036
DAVIS, EDITH	SOPRANO	MUNRO, 334 W 72ND ST	NEW YORK, NY	10023
DAVIS, ELIAS S	TV WRITER	3311 LEDGEWOOD DR	LOS ANGELES, CA	90068
DAVIS, ELLEN	WRITER	555 W 57TH ST #1230	NEW YORK, NY	10019
DAVIS, ELLEN S	WRITER	10 COLUMBUS CIR #1300	NEW YORK, NY	10019
DAVIS, ELLSWORTH J	PHOTOGRAPHER	4831 MEADE ST, NE	WASHINGTON, DC	20019
DAVIS, EMILY	ACTRESS	LEONETTI, 6526 SUNSET BLVD	HOLLYWOOD, CA	90028
DAVIS, ERIK	ACTOR	2820 3RD ST #3	SANTA MONICA, CA	90405
DAVIS, GEENA	ACTRESS	211 S BEVERLY DR #201	BEVERLY HILLS, CA	90212
DAVIS, GEORGE BUD	DIRECTOR	DGA, 7950 SUNSET BLVD	LOS ANGELES, CA	90046
DAVIS, GERRY	WRITER-EDITOR	65 MIDDLE LN, HORNSEY	LONDON N8 8PE	ENGLAND
DAVIS, GLEN	DRUMMER	106 KAREN CT	BRENTWOOD, TN	37027
DAVIS, GLENN	ACTOR	4428 AGNES AVE	NORTH HOLLYWOOD, CA	91607
DAVIS, GLENN	BASEBALL	POST OFFICE BOX 14025	SAVANNAH, GA	31416
DAVIS, GUY	ACTOR	ABC-TV, "ONE LIFE TO LIVE"		
		1330 AVE OF THE AMERICAS	NEW YORK, NY	10019
DAVIS, GWEN	TV WRITER	8955 BEVERLY BLVD	LOS ANGELES, CA	90048
DAVIS, H FREDERICK	CONDUCTOR	5738 SIMPSON AVE	NORTH HOLLYWOOD, CA	91607
DAVIS, HAL	DIRECTOR	441 E 20TH ST	NEW YORK, NY	10010
DAVIS, IVAN	TV WRITER	8955 BEVERLY BLVD	LOS ANGELES, CA	90048
DAVIS, IVAN	PIANST	GERSHUNOFF, 502 PARK AVE	NEW YORK, NY	10022
DAVIS, IVAN	TV WRITER	8955 BEVERLY BLVD	LOS ANGELES, CA	90048
DAVIS, IVOR	COLUMNIST	N Y TIMES SYNDICATION		
		130 5TH AVE	NEW YORK, NY	10011
DAVIS, J RODNEY	DIRECTOR	DGA, 7950 SUNSET BLVD	LOS ANGELES, CA	90046
DAVIS, JACK	CARTOONIST	MAD MAGAZINE, INC		
		485 MADISON AVE	NEW YORK, NY	10022
DAVIS, JAMES H	SINGER-COMPOSER	POST OFFICE BOX 15826	BATON ROUGE, LA	70895
DAVIS, JIM	CARTOONIST	UNITED FEATURE SYNDICATE		
		200 PARK AVE	NEW YORK, NY	10166
DAVIS, JIM	WRITER	10960 WILSHIRE BLVD #924	LOS ANGELES, CA	90024
DAVIS, JOEL	WRITER	DAVIES, 3518 W CAHUENGA BLVD	LOS ANGELES, CA	90068
DAVIS, JOHN	TV DIRECTOR-PRODUCER	MARSTON HILL FARM, THOR	OXON	ENGLAND
DAVIS, JOHN	TV DIRECTOR-PRODUCER	20 BROCKLEY AVE, STANMORE	MIDDLESEX	ENGLAND
DAVIS, JOHN E	COMPOSER	5105 VARNA AVE	SHERMAN OAKS, CA	91423
DAVIS, JOHN WALTER	ACTOR	1418 N HIGHLAND AVE #102	LOS ANGELES, CA	90028
DAVIS, JOSEPH A	NEWS CORRESPONDENT	1202 HEMLOCK ST, NW	WASHINGTON, DC	20012
DAVIS, JOYCE	ACTRESS	11726 SAN VICENTE BLVD #300	LOS ANGELES, CA	90049
DAVIS, JUDY	ACTRESS	151 S EL CAMINO DR	BEVERLY HILLS, CA	90212
DAVIS, JULIE ANN	TV WRITER	JEOPARDY, 1541 N VINE ST	HOLLYWOOD, CA	90028
DAVIS, KAREN L	WRITER	WILLIAM M CAUTHERN		
		13949 WEDDINGTON ST	VAN NUYS, CA	91401
DAVIS, KATHERINE E	NEWS CORRESPONDENT	1751 LANIER PL, NW	WASHINGTON, DC	20009
DAVIS, KENNETH L	GUITARIST	824 E KIBBY ST	LIMA, OH	45804
DAVIS, LANCE E	WRITER	8955 BEVERLY BLVD	LOS ANGELES, CA	90048
DAVIS, LARRY M	DIRECTOR	714 N SWEETZER AVE #5	LOS ANGELES, CA	90069
DAVIS, LEILA	NEWS CORRESPONDENT	9 W LINDEN ST	ALEXANDRIA, VA	22309
DAVIS, LENDA	ACTRESS	9601 WILSHIRE BLVD #GL-11	BEVERLY HILLS, CA	90210
DAVIS, LOUIS W	NEWS CORRESPONDENT	3321 ROCKY MOUNT RD	FAIRFAX, VA	22031
DAVIS, LOWELL	ARTIST	FLATLANDER GALL		
		107 E 3RD ST	CARTHAGE, MO	64836
DAVIS, LUTHER	WRITER-PRODUCER	PICTURES, 18 W 55TH ST	NEW YORK, NY	10019
DAVIS, LUTHER	WRITER	2049 CENTURY PARK E #1320	LOS ANGELES, CA	90067
DAVIS, LYNNE	ORGANIST	15 HIGH ST #621	HARTFORD, CT	06103
DAVIS, MAC	SINGER-ACTOR	759 NIMES RD	LOS ANGELES, CA	90024
DAVIS, MADELYN MARTIN	TV WRITER	142 N BRIGHTON ST	BURBANK, CA	91506
DAVIS, MANNY	SAXOPHONIST	3287 W 17TH ST	CLEVELAND, OH	44109
DAVIS, MARILYN MC COO	SINGER-ACTRESS	SEE - MC COO, MARILYN		
DAVIS, MARTY	ACTOR	1605 N CAHUENGA BLVD #202	LOS ANGELES, CA	90028
DAVIS, MARVIN	FILM EXECUTIVE	1120 SCHUYLER RD	BEVERLY HILLS, CA	90210

DAVIS, MARY	NEWS CORRESPONDENT	9707 FAIRWAY AVE	SILVER SPRING, MD	20901
DAVIS, MAURICE EMMETT	WRITER	8955 BEVERLY BLVD	LOS ANGELES, CA	90048
DAVIS, MICHAEL	ACTOR	151 S EL CAMINO DR	BEVERLY HILLS, CA	90212
DAVIS, MICHAEL	VIOLINIST	GREAT LAKES PERFORMING		
		310 E WASHINGTON ST	ANN ARBOR, MI	48104
DAVIS, MICHAEL A	TV WRITER	555 W 57TH ST #1230	NEW YORK, NY	10019
DAVIS, MICHAEL LEE	GUITARIST	4915 SALEM DR	NASHVILLE, TN	37211
DAVIS, MIKE	SPORTS WRITER	POST OFFICE BOX 500	WASHINGTON, DC	20044
DAVIS, MILES	TRUMPETER	315 W 70TH ST	NEW YORK, NY	10023
DAVIS, MIMI	ACTRESS	OSCARS & ABRAMS MGMT		
		59 BERKELEY ST	TORONTO, ONT M5A 2W5	CANADA
DAVIS, MORGAN	SINGER	41 BRITAIN ST #200	TORONTO, ONT	CANADA
DAVIS, NANCY	ACTRESS	SEE - REAGAN, NANCY		
DAVIS, NOLAN	WRITER	8955 BEVERLY BLVD	LOS ANGELES, CA	90048
DAVIS, OSCEOLA	SOPRANO	61 W 62ND ST #6-F	NEW YORK, NY	10023
DAVIS, OSSIE	ACT-WRI-DIR	44 CORTLAND AVE	NEW ROCHELLE, NY	10801
DAVIS, PAT L	MANDOLINIST	3020 S ROENA ST	INDIANAPOLIS, IN	46241
DAVIS, PATRICK "GRAMPY"	ACTOR	8831 SUNSET BLVD #402	LOS ANGELES, CA	90069
DAVIS, PAUL	SINGER-SONGWRITER	POST OFFICE BOX 7308	CARMEL, CA	93921
DAVIS, PAUL E	TV DIRECTOR	7439 OSTROM AVE	VAN NUYS, CA	91406

DAVIS, PESHA PAUL	DIRECTOR	8242 HILLSIDE AVE	LOS ANGELES, CA	90069
DAVIS, PETER	TV WRITER-PRODUCER	320 CENTRAL PARK W	NEW YORK, NY	10025
DAVIS, PETER	FILM-TV PRODUCER	1438 N GOWER ST #401	LOS ANGELES, CA	90028
DAVIS, PETER MAXWELL	COMPOSER	JUDY ARNOLD MANAGEMENT		
		SOUTH HOGARTH RD #3	LONDON SW5	ENGLAND
DAVIS, PHIL	WRITER	8955 BEVERLY BLVD	LOS ANGELES, CA	90048
DAVIS, PHILLIS	SINGER	POST OFFICE BOX 171132	NASHVILLE, TN	37217
DAVIS, PHYLLIS	ACTRESS	8721 SUNSET BLVD #200	LOS ANGELES, CA	90069
DAVIS, RHETT	SINGER-GUITARIST	261 DELVIN DR	ANTIOCH, TN	37013
DAVIS, RICK	MIME	AFFILIATE ARTISTS, INC		
		37 W 65TH ST, 6TH FLOOR	NEW YORK, NY	10023
DAVIS, ROBERT	WRITER	555 W 57TH ST #1230	NEW YORK, NY	10019
DAVIS, ROBERT L, JR	DIRECTOR	DGA, 110 W 57TH ST	NEW YORK, NY	10019
DAVIS, ROBERT P	SCREENWRITER	555 W 57TH ST #1230	NEW YORK, NY	10019
DAVIS, ROGER	ACTOR	6380 WILSHIRE BLVD #910	LOS ANGELES, CA	90048
DAVIS, RON	ACTOR	8721 SUNSET BLVD #203	LOS ANGELES, CA	90069
DAVIS, RUBY DEE	ACTRESS-WRITER	44 CORTLAND AVE	NEW ROCHELLE, NY	10801
DAVIS, RUSTY	GUITARIST	ROUTE #3, BOX 224	WAYNESBORO, TN	38485
DAVIS, SAMMY, JR	ACTOR-SINGER-DANCER	1151 SUMMIT DR	BEVERLY HILLS, CA	90210
DAVIS, SAMMY, SR	ENTERTAINER	1435 HARRIDGE DR	BEVERLY HILLS, CA	90210
DAVIS, SID	TV EXECUTIVE	NBC-TV, NEWS DEPARTMENT		
		4001 NEBRASKA AVE, NW	WASHINGTON, DC	20016
DAVIS, SIDNEY	WRITER	555 W 57TH ST #1230	NEW YORK, NY	10019
DAVIS, SIDNEY A	NEWS CORRESPONDENT	7103 ARRAN PL	BETHESDA, MD	20817
DAVIS, SKEETER	SINGER	508 SEWARD RD	BRENTWOOD, TN	37027
DAVIS, SPENCER, GROUP	ROCK & ROLL GROUP	12457 VENTURA BLVD #103	STUDIO CITY, CA	91604
DAVIS, SPIG	MUSICIAN	205 W DIVISION ST	MOUNT JULIET, TN	37122
DAVIS, STANLEY	MUSIC EDITOR	4378 CAHUENGA BLVD	NORTH HOLLYWOOD, CA	91602
DAVIS, STEVE	BODYBUILDER	23115 LYONS AVE	NEWHALL, CA	91321
DAVIS, STORM	BASEBALL	POST OFFICE BOX 14025	SAVANNAH, GA	31416
DAVIS, SUSAN	ACTRESS	9255 SUNSET BLVD #603	LOS ANGELES, CA	90069
DAVIS, THOMAS J	TV WRITER	555 W 57TH ST #1230	NEW YORK, NY	10019
DAVIS, TODD	ACTOR	9441 WILSHIRE BLVD #620-D	BEVERLY HILLS, CA	90210
DAVIS, TYRONE	SINGER-SONGWRITER	ASSOCIATED BOOKING CORP		
		1995 BROADWAY, 5TH FLOOR	NEW YORK, NY	10023
DAVIS, WALTER H	WRITER	ICM, 8899 BEVERLY BLVD	LOS ANGELES, CA	90048
DAVIS, WALTER HALSEY	TV PRODUCER	ICM, 8899 BEVERLY BLVD	LOS ANGELES, CA	90048
DAVIS, WILLARD S, JR	WRITER	8955 BEVERLY BLVD	LOS ANGELES, CA	90048
DAVIS-GOFF, ANNABEL C	WRITER	8955 BEVERLY BLVD	LOS ANGELES, CA	90048
DAVISON, BRUCE	ACTOR	2415 GREENVALLEY RD	LOS ANGELES, CA	90046
DAVISON, BRUCE	MUSICIAN	4301 KLING ST #24	BURBANK, CA	91505
DAVISON, JON	FILM PRODUCER	POST OFFICE BOX 5617	BEVERLY HILLS, CA	90210
DAVISON, PETER	ACTOR	30 CHALFONT CT, BAKER ST	LONDON NW1 5RS	ENGLAND
DAVISON, PETER S	COMPOSER	1924 EUCLID ST	SANTA MONICA, CA	90404
DAVITT, MARK	ACTOR	8831 SUNSET BLVD #402	LOS ANGELES, CA	90069
DAVY, ERNEST C	WRITER	555 W 57TH ST #1230	NEW YORK, NY	10019
DAVYDOV, ANATOLY E	WRITER	8955 BEVERLY BLVD	LOS ANGELES, CA	90048
DAW, RICHARD W	NEWS CORRESPONDENT	1907 S FALLSMEAD WY	POTOMAC, MD	20854
DAW, TERENCE	TV DIRECTOR	35 COMPTON RD #D		
		WINCHMORE HILL	LONDON N21	ENGLAND
DAWBER, PAM	ACTRESS	PONY PRODS, COLUMBIA PLAZA	BURBANK, CA	91505
DAWIDOFF, T NICHOLAS	SPORTS REPORTER	SPORTS ILLUSTRATED MAGAZINE		
		TIME & LIFE BUILDING		
		ROCKEFELLER CENTER	NEW YORK, NY	10020
DAWKINS, JOHNNY	TV WRITER	8955 BEVERLY BLVD	LOS ANGELES, CA	90048
DAWN, HAZEL	ACTRESS	15 STUYVESANT OVAL	NEW YORK, NY	10009
DAWN, VIOLA	ACTRESS	23388 MULHOLLAND DR	WOODLAND HILLS, CA	91364
DAWSON, ANDRE	BASEBALL	6295 SW 58TH PL	MIAMI, FL	33143
DAWSON, CLIFF	SINGER	BROADWALK ENTERPRISES		
		200 W 58TH ST	NEW YORK, NY	10019
DAWSON, DEBORAH ZOE	TV WRITER-PRODUCER	B L S & ASSOCIATES		
		800 S ROBERTSON BLVD	LOS ANGELES, CA	90035
DAWSON, FRANK R, III	WRITER	8955 BEVERLY BLVD	LOS ANGELES, CA	90048
DAWSON, GORDON T	WRITER-PRODUCER	10100 SANTA MONICA BLVD #1600	LOS ANGELES, CA	90067
DAWSON, JANE	TV DIRECTOR	515 N SPAULDING AVE	LOS ANGELES, CA	90036
DAWSON, JAY THOMAS	MUSIC ARRANGER	4421 BRUSH HILL RD	NASHVILLE, TN	37216
DAWSON, JOHN S	DIRECTOR	1505 SAN FELIPE DR	BOULDER CITY, NV	89005
DAWSON, LEN	SPORTSCASTER	NBC-TV, SPORTS DEPARTMENT		
		30 ROCKEFELLER PLAZA	NEW YORK, NY	10112
DAWSON, LESLIE	ACTOR-COMEDIAN	GARTH HOUSE, ISLAY RD	LYTHAM	ENGLAND
DAWSON, MIMI WEYFORTH	COMMUNICATION EXEC	FCC, 1919 "M" ST, NW	WASHINGTON, DC	20554
DAWSON, RICHARD	ACTOR	1117 ANGELO DR	BEVERLY HILLS, CA	90210
DAWSON, ZEKE	MUSIC ARRANGER	ROUTE #2, BOX 95	DICKSON, TN	37055
DAY, ARLAN	SINGER	PASHA MUSIC, 5615 MELROE AVE	HOLLYWOOD, CA	90038
DAY, BARRY	DRUMMER	107 ROSEBANK AVE	NASHVILLE, TN	37206
DAY, BILL	CARTOONIST	THE DETROIT FREE PRESS		
		321 W LAFAYETTE BLVD	DETROIT, MI	48231
DAY, CHON	CARTOONIST	22 CROSS ST	WESTERLY, RI	02891
DAY, CLAYTON	ACTOR	POST OFFICE BOX 5617	BEVERLY HILLS, CA	90210
DAY, CLIFF	DIRECTOR-PRODUCER	CJD PRODS, 12 MOOR ST	LONDON W1	ENGLAND
DAY, CORA LEE	ACTRESS	1823 S COCHRAN AVE	LOS ANGELES, CA	90019
DAY, DENNIS	SINGER	2401 MANDEVILLE CANYON RD	LOS ANGELES, CA	90049
DAY, DORIS	ACTRESS	POST OFFICE BOX 223163	CARMEL, CA	93922
DAY, DORIS (WESTERNS)	ACTRESS	RENNA, 16222 MONTEREY LN #279	HUNTINGTON HARBOR, CA	92649
DAY, EVERETT A	WRITER	555 W 57TH ST #1230	NEW YORK, NY	10019

Name	Occupation	Address	City	ZIP
DAY, GERRY	TV WRITER	1546 N FAIRFAX AVE	LOS ANGELES, CA	90046
DAY, JAMES	TV EXECUTIVE	1 LINCOLN PLAZA #300	NEW YORK, NY	10023
DAY, JEFF	NEWS CORRESPONDENT	2929 CONNECTICUT AVE #207, NW	WASHINGTON, DC	20008
DAY, JERRY	ACTOR	5735 VINELAND AVE	NORTH HOLLYWOOD, CA	91601
DAY, JIMMY	GUITARIST	POST OFFICE BOX 381	BUDA, TX	78610
DAY, JOHN S	NEWS CORRESPONDENT	1220 MARYLAND AVE, NE	WASHINGTON, DC	20002
DAY, JONATHAN	WRITER	555 W 57TH ST #1230	NEW YORK, NY	10019
DAY, LARAINE	ACTRESS	GRILIKHES, 2256 SELBY AVE	LOS ANGELES, CA	90046
DAY, LINDA GAIL	TV DIRECTOR	3335 COY DR	SHERMAN OAKS, 91423	
DAY, LYNDA	ACTRESS	SEE - GEORGE, LYNDA DAY		
DAY, MEREDITH	SINGER	AMIE RECORDS COMPANY		
		567 EMERALD DR	VISTA, CA	92083
DAY, OTIS & THE KNIGHTS	SOUL GROUP	AMERICAN ENTERPRISES		
		239 W OLIVE AVE	BURBANK, CA	91502
DAY, PHYLLIS	ACCORDIONIST	4574 ARTELIA DR	ANTIOCH, TN	37013
DAY, ROBERT	CARTOONIST	ROUTE #1	GRAVETTE, AR	72736
DAY, RUDY	TV WRITER	8955 BEVERLY BLVD	LOS ANGELES, CA	90048
DAY, SONNY	GUITARIST	107 ROSEBANK AVE	NASHVILLE, TN	37206
DAYAN, DAVID	ACTOR	11726 SAN VICENTE BLVD #300	LOS ANGELES, CA	90049
DAYTON	ROCK & ROLL GROUP	SANDRIDGE, 1940 VICTORIA AVE	DAYTON, OH	45406
DAYTON, DAN	DIRECTOR	1449 LAUREL WY	BEVERLY HILLS, CA	90210
DAYTON, DANNY	ACTOR	9300 WILSHIRE BLVD #410	BEVERLY HILLS, CA	90212
DAYTON, HOWARD	ACTOR	11237 BRADDOCK DR	CULVER CITY, CA	90230
DAYTON, JUNE	ACTRESS	6310 SAN VICENTE BLVD #407	LOS ANGELES, CA	90048
DAYTON, LYMAN	DIRECTOR-PRODUCER	1021 VALLEY VIEW DR	ST GEORGE, UT	84770
DAZZ BAND, THE	RHYTHM & BLUES GROUP	LEFT BANK MANAGEMENT		
		2519 CARMEN CREST DR	LOS ANGELES, CA	90068
DE ALMEIDA, ANTONIO J	CONDUCTOR	13210 SAINT-REMY-DE PROVEN	MAS DE ROMANIN	FRANCE
DE ANDA, PETER	ACTOR	929 N LARRABEE ST #10	LOS ANGELES, CA	90069
DE ANGELO, DOLRORES	ACTRESS	8640 W 3RD ST #2	LOS ANGELES, CA	90048
DE AZEVEDO, ALEXIS K	COMPOSER-CONDUCER	POST OFFICE BOX 2228	NORTH HOLLYWOOD, CA	91602
DE BAER, JEAN	ACTRESS	9200 SUNSET BLVD #1210	LOS ANGELES, CA	90069
DE BANZIE, LOIS	ACTRESS	116 PINEHURST AVE	NEW YORK, NY	10033
DE BARGE	SOUL GROUP	6255 SUNSET BLVD #624	HOLLYWOOD, CA	90028
DE BARGE, CHICO	SINGER-WRITER	POST OFFICE BOX 491423	LOS ANGELES, CA	90049
DE BARGE, EL	SINGER	6255 SUNSET BLVD #624	LOS ANGELES, CA	90028
DE BARI, IRENE	ACTRESS	2425 MEADOW VALLEY TERR	LOS ANGELES, CA	90039
DE BAUN, RICHARD F	WRITER	8955 BEVERLY BLVD	LOS ANGELES, CA	90048
DE BEER, BARON	ACTOR	ATA, 2437 E WASHINGTON BLVD	PASADENA, CA	91104
DE BEER, GENE	ACTOR	5086 MARMOL DR	WOODLAND HILLS, CA	91364
DE BEERS, COLONEL	WRESTLER	AMERICAN WRESTLING ASSOC		
		MINNEAPLOIS WRESTLING		
		10001 WAYZATA BLVD	MINNETONKA, MN	55345
DE BELL, KRISTINE	ACTRESS	3800 BARHAM BLVD #303	LOS ANGELES, CA	90068
DE BELLIS, JOHN	TV WRITER	555 W 57TH ST #1230	NEW YORK, NY	10019
DE BENEDICTIS, RICHARD	COMPOSER	1430 GEORGINA AVE	SANTA MONICA, CA	90402
DE BENNING, BURR	ACTOR	4235 KINGFISHER RD	CALABASAS, CA	91302
DE BLASIO, EDWARD P	TV WRITER-PRODUCER	SPELLING, 1041 N FORMOSA AVE	LOS ANGELES, CA	90046
DE BOER, LEE	CABLE EXECUTIVE	THE CINEMAX CORPORATION		
		1271 AVE OF THE AMERICAS	NEW YORK, NY	10020
DE BOISE, ALLEN N	WRITER	8955 BEVERLY BLVD	LOS ANGELES, CA	90048
DE BONO, JERRY	WRITER	4653 W 1ST ST	LOS ANGELES, CA	90004
DE BORBA, DOROTHY	ACTRESS	1810 MONTECITO CIR	LIVERMORE, CA	94550
DE BOST, MICHEL	FLUTIST	MARIEDL ANDERS ARTISTS MGMT		
		535 EL CAMINO DEL MAR ST	SAN FRANCISCO, CA	94121
DE BRITO, DENNIS	WRITER	555 W 57TH ST #1230	NEW YORK, NY	10019
DE BROUX, LEE	ACTOR	8646 CASABA AVE	CANOGA PARK, CA	91306
DE BRUIN, SANDRA M	ACTRESS-WRITER	8955 BEVERLY BLVD	LOS ANGELES, CA	90048
DE BURGH, CHRIS	SINGER-GUITARIST	THE MISMANAGEMENT AGENCY		
		3805 W MAGNOLIA BLVD	BURBANK, CA	91505
DE BURGOS, RAFAEL FRUHBECK	CONDUCTOR	SHAW CONCERTS, 1995 BROADWAY	NEW YORK, NY	10023
DE CAMP, ROSEMARY	ACTRESS	317 CAMINO DE LOS COLIN	REDONDO BEACH, CA	90277
DE CAPRIO, AL	DIRECTOR	203 E CHESTER ST	VALLEY STREAM, NY	11580
DE CARL, NANCY	ACTRESS	4615 WINNETKA AVE	WOODLAND HILLS, CA	91364
DE CARLO, RITA	MEZZO-SOPRANO	SARDOS, 180 W END AVE	NEW YORK, NY	10023
DE CARLO, YVONNE	ACTRESS	1665 N BRONSON AVE #914	LOS ANGELES, CA	90028
DE CHIARO, GIOVANNI	GUITARIST	15 HIGH ST #621	HARTFORD, CT	06103
DE CICCO, PAT	ACTOR	50 SUTTON PL S	NEW YORK, NY	10022
DE CLAMECY, DREE	WRITER	28312 RIDGEFALLS CT	RANCHO PALOS VERDES, CA	90274
DE CLUE, DENNIS	WRITER	555 W 57TH ST #1230	NEW YORK, NY	10019
DE COIT, DICK	ACTOR	652 VERNON AVE #4	VENICE, CA	90291
DE CORDOVA, FREDERICK	FILM-TV DIRECTOR	1875 CARLA RIDGE	BEVERLY HILLS, CA	90210
DE CORDOVA, VINCENT	BARITONE	POST OFFICE BOX 884	NEW YORK, NY	10023
DE COSTA, DARRELL PHILLIP	DIRECTOR	DGA, 7950 SUNSET BLVD	LOS ANGELES, CA	90046
DE CROOS, JEAN	CELLIST	POST OFFICE BOX U	REDDING, CT	06875
DE CROOS & DECHENNE	MUSICAL DUO	POST OFFICE BOX U	REDDING, CT	06875
DE CUIR, GABRIELLE	ACTRESS	208 ADELAIDE DR	SANTA MONICA, CA	90402
DE FARIA, WALT	WRITER-PRODUCER	1515 LINDACREST DR	BEVERLY HILLS, CA	90210
DE FARRA, LOUIS	ACTOR	1621 W 221ST ST	TORRANCE, CA	90501
DE FAZIO, SAM	ACTOR	7632 HOLLYWOOD BLVD #4	LOS ANGELES, CA	90046
DE FELITTA, FRANK	WRITER-PRODUCER	3008 PAULCREST DR	LOS ANGELES, CA	90046
DE FERRO, GREG	BODYBUILDER	POST OFFICE BOX 8427	CHERRY HILL, NJ	08002
DE FILIPPI, AMEDEO	COMPOSER-CONDUCTOR	4101 WILKINSON AVE	STUDIO CITY, CA	91604
DE FORD, FRANK	TV WRITER	555 W 57TH ST #1230	NEW YORK, NY	10019
DE FORE, DON	ACTOR	2496 MANDEVILLE CANYON RD	LOS ANGELES, CA	90049

Name	Occupation	Address	City	Zip/Country
DE FOREST, JUNE	VIOLINIST	ACC, 890 W END AVE	NEW YORK, NY	10025
DE FRANCO, B F	COMPOSER	POST OFFICE BOX 252	SUNNYSIDE, FL	32461
DE FRANCO, BUDDY, QUARTET	JAZZ QUARTET	WILLARD ALEXANDER, INC		
		660 MADISON AVE	NEW YORK, NY	10021
DE FRANK, ROBERT	ACTOR	241 W 15TH ST	NEW YORK, NY	10011
DE FRANK, THOMAS	NEWS CORRESPONDENT	608 S CAROLINA AVE, SE	WASHINGTON, DC	20003
DE FREHN, RAYMOND C	NEWS CORRESPONDENT	2139 WISCONSIN AVE, NW	WASHINGTON, DC	20007
DE FUNES, LOUIS	ACTOR	CHATEAU DE CLERMONT	44 CLERMONT	FRANCE
DE GAETANI, JAN	MEZZO-SOPRANO	HURLBURT, 140 W 79TH ST	NEW YORK, NY	10024
DE GALLO, URSULA NADASDY	NEWS REPORTER	TIME/TIME & LIFE BLDG		
		ROCKEFELLER CENTER	NEW YORK, NY	10020
DE GASTYNE, MICHELE	NEWS CORRESPONDENT	2701 ARLINGTON DR #204	ALEXANDRIA, VA	22306
DE GEORGE, CRAIG	WRESTLING CORRES	POST OFFICE BOX 3859	STAMFORD, CT	06905
DE GEORGE, JOHNNY, JR	DRUMMER	739 HARPETH BEND DR	NASHVILLE, TN	37221
DE GRASSI, ALEX	GUITARIST	POST OFFICE BOX 604	CONIFER, CO	80433
DE GRAY, CLIFFORD E	NEWS CORRESPONDENT	5465 N MORGAN ST	ALEXANDRIA, VA	22312
DE GROOT, TED E	DIRECTOR	708 FORESTDALE RD	ROYAL OAK, MI	48067
DE GROOTE, STEVEN	PIANIST	ICM, 40 W 57TH ST	NEW YORK, NY	10019
DE GUERE, PHILIP	TV WRITER-PRODUCER	5315 YARMOUTH AVE #111	ENCINO, CA	91316
DE GUZMAN, MICHAEL	WRITER	1557 N ORANGE GROVE AVE	LOS ANGELES, CA	90046
DE HAVEN, CARTER, III	DIRECTOR-PRODUCER	5170 W 2ND ST	LOS ANGELES, CA	90004
DE HAVEN, GLORIA	ACTRESS	ABC-TV, "RYAN'S HOPE"		
		1330 AVE OF THE AMERICAS	NEW YORK, NY	10019
DE HAVEN, PENNY	SINGER	POST OFFICE BOX 83	BRENTWOOD, TN	37027
DE HAVEN, RICHARD	ACTOR	8380 MELROSE AVE #207	LOS ANGELES, CA	90069
DE HAVILLAND, OLIVIA	ACTRESS	3 RUE BENOUVILLE	PARIS 75116	FRANCE
DE HETRE, KATHERINE	ACTRESS	12750 VENTURA BLVD #102	STUDIO CITY, CA	91604
DE JARNATT, STEVE	WRITER-PRODUCER	8955 BEVERLY BLVD	LOS ANGELES, CA	90048
DE JESUS, CARLOS	TV DIRECTOR	55 W 11TH ST	NEW YORK, NY	10011
DE JOHNETTE, JACK	MUSICIAN	SILVER HOLLOW RD	WILLOW, NY	11201
DE JONGH, JAMES	WRITER	555 W 57TH ST #1230	NEW YORK, NY	10019
DE KOKER, RICHARD	WRITER	8955 BEVERLY BLVD	LOS ANGELES, CA	90048
DE KONINCK, MARC	NEWS CORRESPONDENT	5603 SURREY ST	CHEVY CHASE, MD	20815
DE KORTE, PAUL D	CONDUCTOR	HANNA-BARBERA PRODUCTIONS		
		3400 W CAHUENGA BLVD	LOS ANGELES, CA	90068
DE KOVA, FRANK	ACTOR	7471 MELROSE AVE #11	LOS ANGELES, CA	90046
DE KOVEN, LENORE	TV DIRECTOR	229 E 79TH ST	NEW YORK, NY	10021
DE KOVEN, ROGER	ACTOR	360 W CENTRAL PARK W	NEW YORK, NY	10025
DE LA CHAMBERS, ANNE M	WRITER	555 W 57TH ST #1230	NEW YORK, NY	10019
DE LA CROIX, RAVEN	ACTRESS-MODEL	MARX, 11130 HUSTON ST	NORTH HOLLYWOOD, CA	91601
DE LA FUENTE, ALFRED	ACTOR	1362 OCEAN AVE	BROOKLYN, NY	11230
DE LA PENA, GILBERT	ACTOR	15632 LE MARSH ST	SEPULVEDA, CA	91343
DE LA RENTA, OSCAR	FASHION DESIGNER	550 7TH AVE	NEW YORK, NY	10018
DE LA ROSA, EVELYN	SOPRANO	1182 MARKET ST #311	SAN FRANCISCO, CA	94102
DE LA TOUR, FRANCES	ACTRESS	2 SOUTHWOOD LN, HIGHGATE	LONDON N6	ENGLAND
DE LAIN, MARGUERITE	ACTRESS	8350 SANTA MONICA BLVD #103	LOS ANGELES, CA	90069
DE LAMA, GEORGE	NEWS CORRESPONDENT	1615 "Q" ST, NW	WASHINGTON, DC	20009
DE LANCIE, JOHN	ACTOR	1808 HANSCOM DR	SOUTH PASADENA, CA	91030
DE LAND, BILL	ACTOR	AIMEE, 13743 VICTORY BLVD	VAN NUYS, CA	91401
DE LANDRI, CARLA	WRITER	555 W 57TH ST #1230	NEW YORK, NY	10019
DE LANEY, ETHEL & HER BUCKEYE S	C & W GROUP	POST OFFICE BOX 655	HUDSON, OH	44236
DE LANEY, GLORIA	ACTRESS	9200 SUNSET BLVD #909	LOS ANGELES, CA	90069
DE LANEY, KIM	ACTRESS	J MICHAEL BLOOM AGENCY		
		233 PARK AVE S, 10TH FLOOR	NEW YORK, NY	10017
DE LANEY, STEVE	NEWS CORRESPONDENT	NBC-TV, NEWS DEPARTMENT		
		4001 NEBRASKA AVE, NW	WASHINGTON, DC	20016
DE LANO, LEE	ACTOR	13615 VALERIO ST #B	VAN NUYS, CA	91405
DE LANO, MICHAEL	ACTOR	13671 DRONFIELD AVE	SYLMAR, CA	91342
DE LANY, DANA	ACTRESS	165 W 46TH ST #710	NEW YORK, NY	10036
DE LANY, PAT	ACTRESS	10000 RIVERSIDE DR #3	TOLUCA LAKE, CA	91602
DE LARROCHA, ALICIA	PIANIST	CAMI, 165 W 57TH ST	NEW YORK, NY	10019
DE LAURENTIIS, DINO	FILM PRODUCER	VIA DELLA VASCA NAVALE 58	ROME	ITALY
DE LAURENTIIS, RAFFAELLA	PRODUCER	724 S VICTORY BLVD		
		2ND FLOOR	BURBANK, CA	91502
DE LAURENTIS, ROBERT	SCREENWRITER	8955 BEVERLY BLVD	LOS ANGELES, CA	90048
DE LAWDER FAMILY, THE	GOSPEL GROUP	POST OFFICE BOX 2145	MORGANTOWN, WV	26507
DE LAY, DOROTHY	VIOLINIST	349 N BROADWAY	UPPER NYACK, NY	10960
DE LEEUW, LISA	ACTRESS-WRITER	CABALLERO, 7920 ALABAMA AVE	CANOGA PARK, CA	91304
DE LIA, ANTHONY J	TV WRITER	8955 BEVERLY BLVD	LOS ANGELES, CA	90048
DE LIAGRE, ALFRED, JR	DIRECTOR-PRODUCER	245 W 52ND ST	NEW YORK, NY	10019
DE LINE, DONALD	CASTING DIRECTOR	2040 AVE OF THE STARS	LOS ANGELES, CA	90067
DE LISLE, THOMAS J	WRITER	8955 BEVERLY BLVD	LOS ANGELES, CA	90048
DE LON, NATHALIE	ACTRESS	GEORGES BEAUME AGENCE		
		3 QUAI MALAQUAIS	PARIS 75006	FRANCE
DE LONG, LESLIE ANN	NEWS CORRESPONDENT	3332 SPRING LN	FALLS CHURCH, VA	20041
DE LONGIS, ANTHONY	ACTOR	1262 1/2 N KINGSLEY DR	LOS ANGELES, CA	90029
DE LORME, DANIEL	ACTOR	16 RUE DE MARIGNAN	PARIS 75008	FRANCE
DE LORT, GUY JEAN	PHOTOGRAPHER	25 S FLOYD ST	ALEXANDRIA, VA	22304
DE LOS, MICHAEL	BASSO-BARITONE	MMM, 935 NW 19TH AVE	PORTLAND, OR	97209
DE LOS ANGELES, VICTORIA	SOPRANO	119 W 57TH ST #1505	NEW YORK, NY	10019
DE LOUISE, RICHARD	NEWS CORRESPONDENT	6501 STONEHAM RD	BETHESDA, MD	20817
DE LUCA, RUDY	WRITER-PRODUCER	DGA, 7950 SUNSET BLVD	LOS ANGELES, CA	90046
DE LUCA, THOMAS G	BANJOIST	1712 LINDEN AVE #2	NASHVILLE, TN	37212
DE LUCIA, PACO	GUITARIST	KURLAND, 173 BRIGHTON AVE	BOSTON, MA	02134
DE LUCIA, VITO	PHOTOGRAPHER	56 SAINT ANDREWS LN	GLEN COVE, NY	11542

GLORIA DE HAVEN

OLIVIA DE HAVILLAND

DINO DE LAURENTIIS

DOM DE LUISE

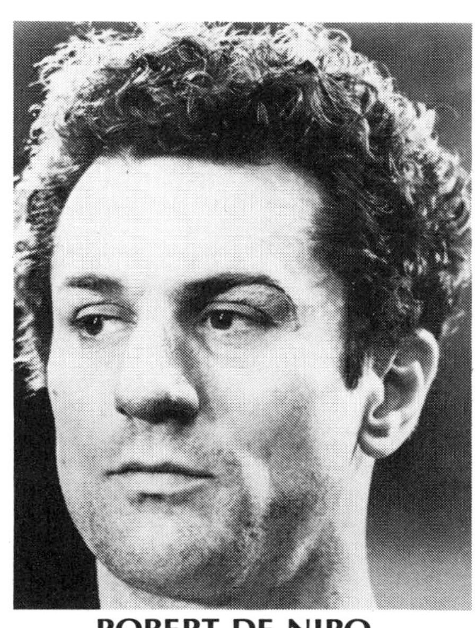
ROBERT DE NIRO

JOYCE DE WITT

DENNIS DE YOUNG

EDDIE DEAN

FRANCIS DEE

Name	Occupation	Address	City	Zip
DE LUGACH, ALBERT	REPORTER	4313 PRICE ST	LOS ANGELES, CA	90027
DE LUGG, MILTON	ACCORDIONIST-ARRANGER	2740 CLARAY AVE	LOS ANGELES, CA	90024
DE LUISE, DOM	ACTOR-DIRECTOR	1186 CORISCA DR	PACIFIC PALISADES, CA	90272
DE LUISE, PETER	ACTOR	151 S EL CAMINO DR	BEVERLY HILLS, CA	90212
DE LUN, LI	CONDUCTOR	SHAW CONCERTS, 1995 BROADWAY	NEW YORK, NY	10023
DE LUNA, MIKE	STUNTMAN	3518 W CAHUENGA BLVD #300	LOS ANGELES, CA	90068
DE MAIO, RICHARD R	DIRECTOR	2451 WEBB AVE	NEW YORK, NY	10468
DE MANN, ROBERT	ACTOR	894 1/2 W KNOLL DR	LOS ANGELES, CA	90069
DE MARCH, KENT	ACTRESS	9744 WILSHIRE BLVD #306	BEVERLY HILLS, CA	90212
DE MARCO, JOHN G	WRITER	8955 BEVERLY BLVD	LOS ANGELES, CA	90048
DE MARCO, NICHOLAS	DIRECTOR	560 SUMMIT AVE	ORADELL, NJ	07649
DE MARSEILLE, FREDERIC	TENOR	45 W 60TH ST #4-K	NEW YORK, NY	10023
DE MARTINI, TOM	WRITER	8955 BEVERLY BLVD	LOS ANGELES, CA	90048
DE MASO, LAURI K	NEWS CORRESPONDENT	3710 CALVERT ST, NW	WASHINGTON, DC	20007
DE MAVE, JACK	ACTOR	4329 COLFAX AVE	STUDIO CITY, CA	91604
DE MAY, JANET	ACTRESS	113 N SAN VICENTE BLVD #202	BEVERLY HILLS, CA	90211
DE MAY, SALLY	ACTRESS	325 W 45TH ST	NEW YORK, NY	10036
DE MEO, PAUL J	WRITER	721 N LA JOLLA AVE	LOS ANGELES, CA	90046
DE MEY, BERRY	BODYBUILDER	POST OFFICE BOX 11883	FRESNO, CA	93775
DE MICHELE, RAYNER "REMO"	CONDUCTOR	1637 N VINE ST #414	LOS ANGELES, CA	90028
DE MILLA, WAYNE	BODYBUILDER	POST OFFICE BOX 1490		
		RADIO CITY STATION	NEW YORK, NY	10101
DE MILLE, AGNES	CHOREOGRAPHER	THE SOCIETY OF STAGE		
		DIRECTORS & CHOREOGRAPHERS		
		1501 BROADWAY	NEW YORK, NY	10036
DE MILLE, KATHERINE	ACTRESS	645 OCAMPO DR	PACIFIC PALISADES, CA	90272
DE MORAES, RON	TV DIRECTOR	17250 SUNSET BLVD #303	PACIFIC PALISADES, CA	90272
DE MORNAY, REBECCA	ACTRESS	1888 CENTURY PARK E #1400	LOS ANGELES, CA	90067
DE MOTT, JOHN S	WRITER-EDITOR	TIME/TIME & LIFE BLDG		
		ROCKEFELLER CENTER	NEW YORK, NY	10020
DE MUNN, JEFFREY	ACTOR	LANTZ, 888 7TH AVE, 25TH FLOOR	NEW YORK, NY	10106
DE MURCIE, DENISE	WRITER	555 W 57TH ST #1230	NEW YORK, NY	10019
DE NEUT, RICHARD	WRITER	8476 FOUNTAIN AVE	LOS ANGELES, CA	90069
DE NIRO, PATRICIA	TALENT AGENT	9777 WILSHIRE BLVD #707	BEVERLY HILLS, CA	90212
DE NIRO, ROBERT	ACTOR	1501 BROADWAY #2600	NEW YORK, NY	10036
DE NOIA, NICK	TV DIRECTOR	4319 LAUREL GROVE AVE	STUDIO CITY, CA	91604
DE ORE, BILL	CARTOONIST	POST OFFICE BOX 225537	DALLAS, TX	75265
DE PAIVA, JAMES	ACTOR	ABC-TV, "ONE LIFE TO LIVE"		
		1330 AVE OF THE AMERICAS	NEW YORK, NY	10019
DE PALMA, BRIAN	WRITER-PRODUCER	DGA, 110 W 57TH ST	NEW YORK, NY	10019
DE PAOLA, ALESSIO	DIRECTOR	4017 N 45TH PL	PHOENIX, AZ	85018
DE PAOLIS, RON	WRITER	555 W 57TH ST #1230	NEW YORK, NY	10019
DE PAOLO, THERESA	ACTRESS	15010 VENTURA BLVD #219	SHERMAN OAKS, CA	91403
DE PASQUALE, JOSEPH	VIOLIST	GERSHUNOFF, 502 PARK AVE	NEW YORK, NY	10022
DE PASS, STEVE	SINGER	EAGLES, 305 E 24TH ST	NEW YORK, NY	10010
DE PASSE, SUZANNE	TV WRITER	1100 N ALTA LOMA RD #805	LOS ANGELES, CA	90069
DE PAUL, GENE	COMPOSER	9607 CALVIN AVE	NORTHRIDGE, CA	91324
DE PAUL, JUDITH	TV PRODUCER	GROSVENOR HOUSE HOTEL		
		PARK LN	LONDON	ENGLAND
DE PEW, JOSEPH	DIRECTOR	15316 SKY HIGH DR	ESCONDIDO, CA	92025
DE PEYER, GERVASE	CLARINETIST	GERSHUNOFF, 502 PARK AVE	NEW YORK, NY	10022
DE POMPA, BARBARA	NEWS CORRESPONDENT	4264 CHARLEY ST	OLNEY, MD	20832
DE PRIEST, HERMAN W	PIANIST	4646 NOLENSVILLE RD #D-14	NASHVILLE, TN	37211
DE PRIEST, JAMES	CONDUCTOR	142 W END AVE #3	NEW YORK, NY	10023
DE PRIEST, MARGARET	TV WRITER	8955 BEVERLY BLVD	LOS ANGELES, CA	90048
DE QUINZIO, MARILYN	WRITER	555 W 57TH ST #1230	NEW YORK, NY	10019
DE RENZI, VICTOR	CONDUCTOR	LEW, 204 W 10TH ST	NEW YORK, NY	10014
DE RITA, CURLY JOE	ACTOR	10611 MOORPARK AVE	NORTH HOLLYWOOD, CA	91601
DE ROSE, CHRISTOPHER	ACTOR	9040 HARRAIT ST #4	LOS ANGELES, CA	90069
DE ROTHSCHILD, NICHOLAS	TV PRODUCER	STUDIO FILM LABS		
		68 WARDOUR ST	LONDON W1	ENGLAND
DE ROY, RICHARD	WRITER	334 S CYN VIEW DR	LOS ANGELES, CA	90049
DE RUGERIIS, JOSEPH	CONDUCTOR	61 W 62ND ST #6-F	NEW YORK, NY	10023
DE SAILLY, JEAN	ACTOR	53 QUAI DES GRANDS AUGUSTINS	PARIS 75006	FRANCE
DE SALES, FRANCIS A	ACTOR	5729 MAMMOTH AVE	VAN NUYS, CA	91401
DE SALVO, ANNE	ACTRESS	10100 SANTA MONICA BLVD #1600	LOS ANGELES, CA	90067
DE SANTIS, PATRICK	ACTOR	6310 SAN VICENTE BLVD #407	LOS ANGELES, CA	90048
DE SHANNON, JACKIE	SINGER-SONGWRITER	STONE, 1052 N CAROL DR	LOS ANGELES, CA	90069
DE SHAZO, ANNE V	WRITER	555 W 57TH ST #1230	NEW YORK, NY	10019
DE SHIELDS, ANDRE	ACTOR	256 W 21ST ST	NEW YORK, NY	10011
DE SILVA, RANJIT	NEWS CORRESPONDENT	12060 GREYWING SQ	RESTON, VA	22091
DE SIMONE-FEINSTEI, ANNA	WRITER	555 W 57TH ST #1230	NEW YORK, NY	10019
DE SOUZA, STEVEN E	SCREENWRITER	16476 REFUGIO RD	ENCINO, CA	91436
DE TITTA, ARTHUR	PHOTOGRAPHER	74 VIA MINORCA	CATHEDRAL CITY, CA	92234
DE TOTH, ANDRE	WRITER-PRODUCER	3690 BARHAM BLVD #6-307	LOS ANGELES, CA	90068
DE VALLY, RAYMOND	TV DIRECTOR	600 E CAMBRIDGE DR	BURBANK, CA	91504
DE VANY, EDWARD H	WRITER-PRODUCER	312 W WEATHERSPOON	SANFORD, NC	27330
DE VARGAS, VAL	ACTOR	427 N CANON DR #205	BEVERLY HILLS, CA	90210
DE VARONA, DONNA	SPORTS ANALYST	NBC-TV, SPORTS DEPARTMENT		
		30 ROCKEFELLER PLAZA	NEW YORK, NY	10112
DE VASQUEZ, DEVIN	ACTRESS-MODEL	MODELS & PROMOTIONS AGENCY		
		8560 SUNSET BLVD, 10TH FLOOR	LOS ANGELES, CA	90069
DE VAUGHN, ALTEOUISE	SOPRANO	SULLIVAN, 390 W END AVE	NEW YORK, NY	10024
DE VEAUX, RONALD	NEWS CORRESPONDENT	529 14TH ST, NW	WASHINGTON, DC	20045
DE VENISH, ROSS	FILM DIRECTOR	SPOKESMAN, 1 CRAVEN HILL	LONDON W2 3EP	ENGLAND

DE VERE COLE, TRISTAN	TV DIRECTOR-PRODUCER	ODSTOCK MANOR, SALIBURY	WILTS SP5 4JA	ENGLAND
DE VILLE, MICHEL	FILM DIRECTOR	32 RUE REINHARDT	BOULOGNE 92100	FRANCE
DE VILLE, MINK	ROCK & ROLL GROUP	SEE - MINK DEVILLE		
DE VINEY, JOHN H	DIRECTOR	DGA, 110 W 57TH ST	NEW YORK, NY	10019
DE VINNEY, ROBERT L	WRITER	8955 BEVERLY BLVD	LOS ANGELES, CA	90048
DE VITO, DANNY	ACTOR-DIRECTOR	1746 COURTNEY AVE	LOS ANGELES, CA	90046
DE VITO, HANK	GUITARIST	ROUTE #5	FRANKLIN, TN	37064
DE VITO, KARLA	ACTRESS	POST OFFICE BOX 1305	WOODLAND HILLS, CA	91364
DE VITT, TIMOTHY R	DIRECTOR	18 STUYVESANT OVAL	NEW YORK, NY	10009
DE VORE, CHRISTOPHER	SCREENWRITER	8955 BEVERLY BLVD	LOS ANGELES, CA	90048
DE VORZON, BARRY	COMPOSER-MUSICIAN	1323 E VALLEY RD	SANTA BARBARA, CA	93108
DE VOTO, JOSEPH	DIRECTOR	333 E 69TH ST	NEW YORK, NY	10021
DE VRIES, DAVIS G	DIRECTOR	100 RIVERSIDE DR	NEW YORK, NY	10024
DE VRIES, HAN	OBOIST	SOFFER, 130 W 56TH ST	NEW YORK, NY	10019
DE VRIES, LLOYD A	WRITER	555 W 57TH ST #1230	NEW YORK, NY	10019
DE WAART, EDO	CONDUCTOR	107 WAR MEMORIAL VETS BLDG	SAN FRANCISCO, CA	94102
DE WAAY, LARRY	FILM PRODUCER	PINEWOOD STUDIOS, IVER HEATH	BUCKS	ENGLAND
DE WAYNE FAMILY, BEN	JUGGLERS	HALL, 138 FROG HOLLOW RD	CHURCHVILLE, PA	18966
DE WINDT, SHEILA	ACTRESS	15301 VENTURA BLVD #345	SHERMAN OAKS, CA	91403
DE WINTER, JO	ACTRESS	9220 SUNSET BLVD #202	LOS ANGELES, CA	90069
DE WIT, JACQUELINE	ACTRESS	436 S ALANDELE AVEVUE		
		PARK LA BREA	LOS ANGELES, CA	90036
DE WIT, LEW	SONGWRITER	312 BALDWIN DR	STAUNTON, VA	24401
DE WITT, FAY	ACTRESS	2012 LA BREA TERR	LOS ANGELES, CA	90046
DE WITT, JAMES H	WRITER	8955 BEVERLY BLVD	LOS ANGELES, CA	90048
DE WITT, JOYCE	ACTRESS	201 OCEAN AVE #1406-P	SANTA MONICA, CA	90402
DE WITT, MIRIAM	WRITER	8955 BEVERLY BLVD	LOS ANGELES, CA	90048
DE WITT, ROGER	COMPOSER	3347 PASEO-HALCON	SAN CLEMENTE, CA	92672
DE WITT, TERRY	PHOTOJOURNALIST	4116 MOUNT OLNEY RD	OLNEY, MD	20832
DE WOLF, KAREN	WRITER	8955 BEVERLY BLVD	LOS ANGELES, CA	90048
DE YOUNG, CLIFF	ACTOR	ICM, 8899 BEVERLY BLVD	LOS ANGELES, CA	90048
DE YOUNG, DENNIS	SINGER-SONGWRITER	GOLD STARSHIP MANAGEMENT		
		3575 W CAHUENGA BLVD	LOS ANGELES, CA	90068
DE YOUNG, GYPSI	ACTRESS	1930 CENTURY PARK W #303	LOS ANGELES, CA	90067
DE ZAYAS, RODRIGO	GUITARIST	KAY, 58 W 58TH ST	NEW YORK, NY	10019
DE-FILM	ROCK & ROLL GROUP	100 HAMILTON PLAZA #520	PATTERSON, NJ	07505
DEA, JANE	SINGER	POST OFFICE BOX 25371	CHARLOTTE, NC	28212
DEACON, ERIC	ACTOR	LOUIS HAMMOND MGMT		
		45 GOLDEN HOUSE		
		29 GREAT PULTENEY ST	LONDON W1	ENGLAND
DEAD MILKMEN, THE	ROCK & ROLL GROUP	POST OFFICE BOX 42684	PHILADELPHIA, PA	19101
DEADLINE	ROCK & ROLL GROUP	CELLUOID RECORDS CO		
		155 W 29TH ST	NEW YORK, NY	10001
DEADLY EARNEST	ROCK & ROLL GROUP	GREG, 1686 CATALPA RD	CLEVELAND, OH	44112
DEADLY NIGHTSHADE	C & W GROUP	RMP, 200 WESTMORELAND AVE	WHITE PLAINS, NY	10606
DEADRICK, GAIL R	CONDUCTOR	POST OFFICE BOX 69281	LOS ANGELES, CA	90069
DEADRICK, VINCENT PAUL, JR	ACTOR	18012 RAYMER ST	NORTHRIDGE, CA	91325
DEAL, BILL & THE RHONDELLS	ROCK & ROLL GROUP	1604 W HILLTOP SQ #308	VIRGINIA BEACH, VA	23451
DEAL, MEL	GUITARIST	ROUTE #1, BOX 327	THOMPSON STATION, TN	37179
DEAL, THE	ROCK & ROLL GROUP	3 E 54TH ST #1400	NEW YORK, NY	10022
DEAN, BARTON	WRITER	1117 EUCLID ST #7	SANTA MONICA, CA	90403
DEAN, BUBBA	DRUMMER	1019 PATRICIA DR #E-205	NASHVILLE, TN	37217
DEAN, DEBRA	SOPRANO	45 W 60TH ST #4-K	NEW YORK, NY	10023
DEAN, ED	WRESTLER	POST OFFICE BOX 3859	STAMFORD, CT	06905
DEAN, EDDIE	ACTOR-SINGER	32161 SAILVIEW LN	WESTLAKE VILLAGE, CA	91360
DEAN, FELICITY	ACTRESS	151 S EL CAMINO DR	BEVERLY HILLS, CA	90212
DEAN, FLOY	ACTRESS	6640 SUNSET BLVD #203	LOS ANGELES, CA	90028
DEAN, G R, JR	FILM CRITIC	SAN DIEGO'S CHOICE MAGAZINE		
		1939 GRAND AVE	SAN DIEGO, CA	92109
DEAN, GREG	CLOWN	2701 COTTAGE WY #14	SACRAMENTO, CA	95825
DEAN, ISABEL	ACTRESS	FEAST, 43-A PRINCESS RD	LONDON NW1	ENGLAND
DEAN, JIMMY	SINGER	JIMMY DEAN MEAT COMPANY, INC		
		1341 W MOCKINGBIRD LN #1100-E	DALLAS, TX	75247
DEAN, JOHN	AUTHOR	9496 REMBERT LN	BEVERLY HILLS, CA	90210
DEAN, MARGIA	ACTRESS	ALVAREZ, BUCKEYE BUIDLING		
		8500 WILSHIRE BLVD	BEVERLY HILLS, CA	90211
DEAN, MORTON	NEWS CORRESPONDENT	CBS NEWS, 524 W 57TH ST	NEW YORK, NY	10019
DEAN, PRISCILLA	ACTRESS	411 BROAD AVE	LEONIA, NJ	07605
DEAN, ROBERT G, JR	DRUMMER	POST OFFICE BOX 110546	NASHVILLE, TN	37211
DEAN, RON	ACTOR	1509 N CRESCENT HGTS BLVD #7	LOS ANGELES, CA	90069
DEAN, TIM	GUITARIST	5675 AMALIE DR	NASHVILLE, TN	37211
DEAN, TOM	GUITARIST	5675 AMALIE DR	NASHVILLE, TN	37211
DEANE, ELIZABETH K	WRITER-PRODUCER	555 W 57TH ST #1230	NEW YORK, NY	10019
DEANE, WILLIAM T	WRITER	555 W 57TH ST #1230	NEW YORK, NY	10019
DEAR, JULIE	NEWS CORRESPONDENT	2400 "N" ST, NW	WASHINGTON, DC	20037
DEAR, WILLIAM	FILM DIRECTOR	HISK, 10950 VENTURA BLVD	STUDIO CITY, CA	91604
DEARDEN, JAMES	FILM WRITER-DIRECTOR	7 CHESILTON RD	LONDON SW6 5AA	ENGLAND
DEARDEN, ROBIN	ACTRESS	10390 SANTA MONICA BLVD #310	LOS ANGELES, CA	90025
DEARIE, BLOSSOM	SINGER	DAFFODIL RECORDS COMPANY		
		POST OFFICE BOX 21	EAST DURHAM, NY	12423
DEARING, DAN	SAXOPHONIST	5001 MC LENDON DR	ANTIOCH, TN	37013
DEARMORE, TERRY DEE	SINGER-GUITARIST	133 RICE RD	HENDERSONVILLE, TN	37075
DEARTH, BILL	ACTOR	5330 LANKERSHIM BLVD #210	NORTH HOLLYWOOD, CA	91601
DEAS, JUSTIN	ACTOR	KNBC-TV, "SANTA BARBARA"		
		3000 W ALAMEDA AVE	BURBANK, CA	91523

G. R. DEAN, JR.

"America's Leading Film Critic"

DEASON, PAUL	WRITER-PRODUCER	10550 OHIO AVE	LOS ANGELES, CA	90024
DEATH, DR	WRESTLER	SEE - WILLIAMS, STEVE		
		"DR DEATH"		
DEATON, SUSAN MARIE	NEWS CORRESPONDENT	1846 INGLESIDE TERR, NW	WASHINGTON, DC	20010
DEATON, VERNON	WRESTLER	NATIONAL WRESTLING ALLIANCE		
		JIM CROCKETT PROMOTIONS		
		421 BRIARBEND DR	CHARLOTTE, NC	28209
DEATS, PAULA H	TV WRITER	8955 BEVERLY BLVD	LOS ANGELES, CA	90048
DEATS, RICK	ACTOR	8721 SUNSET BLVD #202	LOS ANGELES, CA	90069
DEAVEN, JOHN	ACTOR	5217 3/4 VIRGINIA AVE	LOS ANGELES, CA	90029
DEBARTOLO, DICK	WRITER	MAD MAGAZINE, INC		
		485 MADISON AVE	NEW YORK, NY	10022
DEBBIE SUE	SINGER	PROCESS, 439 WILEY AVE	FRANKLIN, PA	16323
DEBHAM, BETTY	WRITER-COLUMNIST	UNIVERSAL PRESS SYNDICATE		
		4900 MAIN ST, 9TH FLOOR	KANSAS CITY, MO	62114
DEBIN, DAVID	TV WRITER	5613 VALLEY OAK DR	LOS ANGELES, CA	90068
DEBIN, JOHN	PRODUCER	1119 MC CADDEN PL	LOS ANGELES, CA	90038
DEBNEY, JOHN C	COMPOSER	2722 N BRIGHTON ST	BURBANK, CA	91504
DEBUTANTE, DEBBIE	WRESTLER	SEE - CHEERLEADERS, THE		
DECEIVOR	ROCK & ROLL GROUP	POST OFFICE BOX 256577	CHICAGO, IL	60625
DECHTER, BRADLEY G	COMPOSER	641 27TH ST	MANHATTAN BEACH, CA	90266
DECHTER, TED	COMPOSER	22921 CALIFA ST	WOODLAND HILLS, CA	91367
DECKER, JOHN D	WRITER	555 W 57TH ST #1230	NEW YORK, NY	10019
DECKER, LIONEL	ACTOR	1418 N HIGHLAND AVE #102	LOS ANGELES, CA	90028
DECKER, PAUL	CASTING DIRECTOR	NBC TELEVISION NETWORK		
		3000 W ALAMEDA AVE #308	BURBANK, CA	91523
DECRY	ROCK & ROLL GROUP	POST OFFICE BOX 242	POMONA, CA	91769
DECTER, EDWARD	WRITER	8955 BEVERLY BLVD	LOS ANGELES, CA	90048
DED RINGER	ROCK & ROLL GROUP	VARIETY ARTISTS INTL, INC		
		9073 NEMO ST, 3RD FLOOR	LOS ANGELES, CA	90069
DEDINI, ELDON	CARTOONIST	POST OFFICE BOX 1630	MONTEREY, CA	93940
DEE, DAVID	DIRECTOR	14 E 52ND ST	NEW YORK, NY	10022
DEE, FRANCES	ACTRESS	RURAL ROUTE #1	CAMARILLO, CA	93010
DEE, JIMMY	DRUMMER	ROUTE #12, SUNNYSIDE DR	MURFREESBORO, TN	37130
DEE, JOEY & THE STAR-LIGHTERS	VOCAL GROUP	BROTHERS, 141 DUNBAR AVE	FORDS, NJ	08863
DEE, JOHNNY & THE ROCKET 88'S	C & W GROUP	NATIONAL BOOKING AGENCY		
		2605 NORTHRIDGE DR	GARLAND, TX	75043
DEE, RUBY	ACTRESS	44 CORTLAND AVE	NEW ROCHELLE, NY	10801
DEE, SANDRA	ACTRESS	LIGHT, 113 N ROBERTSON BLVD	LOS ANGELES, CA	90048
DEE, TANYA	SINGER	POST OFFICE BOX 171132	NASHVILLE, TN	37217
DEEB, GARY	TV CRITIC-COLUMNIST	NEWS AMERICA SYNDICATE		
		1703 KAISER AVE	IRVINE, CA	92714
DEEGAN, MARY JANE	ACTRESS	5055 WILLOW CREST AVE	NORTH HOLLYWOOD, CA	91601
DEEL, SANDRA	ACTRESS	1717 N STANLEY AVE	LOS ANGELES, CA	90046
DEELE, THE	RHYTHM & BLUES GROUP	200 W 51ST ST #1410	NEW YORK, NY	10019
DEELEY, MICHAEL	FILM PRODUCER	CONSOLIDATED FILMS & TV		
		8 CORNWALL TERRACE	LONDON NW1	ENGLAND
DEELY, DONNA	NEWS CORRESPONDENT	3400 OLD DIMINION DR	ARLINGTON, VA	22207
DEEMS, MICKEY	ACTOR-DIRECTOR	13114 WEDDINGTON ST	VAN NUYS, CA	91401
DEEP PURPLE	ROCK & ROLL GROUP	THAMES TALENT AGENCY		
		45 E PUTNAM AVE	GREENWICH, CT	06830
DEES, GERALD BRUCE	GUITARIST	4912 MILLERWOOD DR	NASHVILLE, TN	37211
DEES, JULIE	COMEDIENNE	8730 SUNSET BLVD #PH-W	LOS ANGELES, CA	90069
DEES, RICK	RADIO-TV PERSONALITY	19580 WELLS DR	TARZANA, CA	91356
DEEZEN, EDDIE	ACTOR	400 S BEVERLY DR #216	BEVERLY HILLS, CA	90212
DEF LEPPARD	ROCK & ROLL GROUP	80 WARWICK GARDENS	LONDON W14 8PR	ENGLAND
DEFFENBAUGH, JO ELLA	ACTRESS	6310 W 5TH ST	LOS ANGELES, CA	90048
DEFIANCE	ROCK & ROLL GROUP	CEE, 193 KONHAUS RD	MECHANICSBURG, PA	17055
DEFORD, FRANK	SPORTS WRITER-EDITOR	SPORTS ILLUSTRATED MAGAZINE		
		TIME & LIFE BUILDING		
		ROCKEFELLER CENTER	NEW YORK, NY	10020
DEFREITAS, SCOTT	ACTOR	CBS-TV, "AS THE WORLD TURNS"		
		51 W 52ND ST	NEW YORK, NY	10019
DEFTERIOS, JOHN K	NEWS CORRESPONDENT	236 MASSACHUSETTS AVE, NE	WASHINGTON, DC	20036
DEGATINA, JOHN	COMPOSER	570 N ROSSMORE AVE	LOS ANGELES, CA	90004
DEGHY, GUY	ACTOR-WRITER	41 FILMER RD	LONDON SW6 7JJ	ENGLAND
DEGLER, STANLEY E	NEWS CORRESPONDENT	2723 N OAKLAND ST	ARLINGTON, VA	22207
DEHNER, JOHN	ACTOR	9255 SUNSET BLVD #610	LOS ANGELES, CA	90069
DEHRAN, BERNARD	ACTOR	82 AVE DE VILLIERS	PARIS 75017	FRANCE
DEIBEL, MARY	NEWS CORRESPONDENT	3038 CHESTNUT ST, NW	WASHINGTON, DC	20015
DEICHMAN, DAVID C	CONDUCTOR	14834 WYANDOTTE ST	VAN NUYS, CA	91405
DEICHMAN, JOHN CHARLES	CONDUCTOR	1640 SUNNYSIDE TERR	SAN PEDRO, CA	90732
DEIGHTON, LEN	WRITER	FAIRYMOUNT, BLACKROCK		
		DUNDALK	COUNTY LOUTH	IRELAND
DEIGNAN, MARTINA	ACTRESS	9200 SUNSET BLVD #1210	LOS ANGELES, CA	90069
DEIS, JEAN	TENOR	243 W END AVE #907	NEW YORK, NY	10023
DEKKER, FRED	WRITER	8955 BEVERLY BLVD	LOS ANGELES, CA	90048
DEKLE, BILL	MUSIC ARRANGER	1605 16TH AVE S #8	NASHVILLE, TN	37212
DEKNATEL, JANE	CABLE EXECUTIVE	2049 CENTURY PARK E #4170	LOS ANGELES, CA	90067
DEKTOR, LESLIE MICHAEL	FILM-TV DIRECTOR	3923 GOODLAND AVE	STUDIO CITY, CA	91604
DEL AMITRI	ROCK & ROLL GROUP	POST OFFICE BOX 615	LONDON SE 1YS	ENGLAND
DEL BARRIO, GEORGE G	COMPOSER-CONDUCTOR	5826 CANTALOUPE AVE	VAN NUYS, CA	91401
DEL CAMPOS, DYAN	ACTRESS	5330 LANKERSHIM BLVD #210	NORTH HOLLYWOOD, CA	91601
DEL CARLO, JOHN	BASSO-BARITONE	CAMI, 165 W 57TH ST	NEW YORK, NY	10019

SANDRA DEE

CATHERINE DENEUVE

BOB DENVER

JOHN DENVER

BO DEREK

JOHN DEREK

SUSAN DEY

DON DIAMONT

ANGIE DICKINSON

DEL CASTILLO, LLOYD G	COMPOSER	2008 PREUSS RD	LOS ANGELES, CA	90034
DEL CASTILLO MORANTE, MARK	ACTOR	4120 MONROE ST	LOS ANGELES, CA	90029
DEL FOSS, RAOUL	ACTOR	3 RUE DE VERDUN	VIARMES 95270	FRANCE
DEL GIUDICE, VINCENT	NEWS CORRESPONDENT	503 N ROOSEVELT BLVD	FALLS CHURCH, VA	22044
DEL GRANDE, LOUIS	ACTOR-WRITER	32 N SHERBOURNE ST	TORONTO, ONT M4W 2T3	CANADA
DEL LA RENTA, OSCAR	FASHION DESIGNER	BROOK HILL FARM		
		SKIFF MOUNTAIN RD	KENT, CT	06757
DEL LORDS, THE	ROCK & ROLL GROUP	188 1ST AVE #6	NEW YORK, NY	10009
DEL MAINE, BARRY	PRODUCER	9 LANCASTER DR, HAMPSTEAD	LONDON NW3	ENGLAND
DEL MONTE, RICHARD	ACTOR	8350 SANTA MONICA BLVD #103	LOS ANGELES, CA	90069
DEL PIERO, FABRIZIO	NEWS CORRESPONDENT	4919 MASSACHUSETTS AVE, NW	WASHINGTON, DC	20016
DEL POZO, PAUL C	TV DIRECTOR	WNJU-TV, 1020 BROAD ST	NEWARK, NJ	07102
DEL RAY, SANDRA	SINGER	ROSEWOOD, ROUTE #7, BOX 285	LAKE CITY, FL	32055
DEL RE, CARLA	SOPRANO	CAMI, 165 W 57TH ST	NEW YORK, NY	10019
DEL REY, PILAR	ACTRESS	8820 SUNSET BLVD #ANB	LOS ANGELES, CA	90069
DEL RIO, VANESSA	ACTRESS	163 JORALEMON ST #1544	BROOKLYN, NY	11201
DEL TREDICI, DAVID	COMPOSER-PIANIST	463 WEST ST #G-121	NEW YORK, NY	10014
DEL-RAYS, THE	ROCK & ROLL GROUP	POST OFFICE BOX 262	CARTERET, NJ	07008
DEL-VIKINGS, THE	VOCAL GROUP	5300 POWERLINE RD #202	FORT LAUDERDALE, FL	33309
DELAMARTER, RADHA	ACTRESS	9165 SUNSET BLVD #202	LOS ANGELES, CA	90069
DELANEY, JAMES ROBERT	TV DIRECTOR	292 SPOOK ROCK RD	SUFFERN, NY	10901
DELAPLANE, FRANK H	NEWS CORRESPONDENT	1200 N NASH ST	ARLINGTON, VA	22209
DELAPLANE, STAN	COLUMNIST	CHRONICLE FEATURES		
		870 MARKET ST	SAN FRANCISCO, CA	94102
DELASSANDRO, NICHOLAS	NEWS CORRESPONDENT	1755 S JEFFERSON DAVIS HWY	ARLINGTON, VA	22202
DELAY, JEROME	PHOTOGRAPHER	POST OFFICE BOX 20875	ALEXANDRIA, VA	22320
DELEHANTY, ANNE	ACTRESS	ABC-TV, "ALL MY CHILDREN"		
		1330 AVE OF THE AMERICAS	NEW YORK, NY	10019
DELEON, AL	PIANIST	POST OFFICE BOX 1293	HENDERSONVILLE, TN	37075
DELERUE, GEORGES	COMPOSER	54 RUE DE TOCQUEVILLE	PARIS 75017	FRANCE
DELFINO, FRANK	ACTOR	1441 PASO REAL AVE #270	ROWLAND HEIGHTS, CA	91748
DELFONICS, THE	VOCAL GROUP	2011 FERRY AVE #U-19	CAMDEN, NJ	08104
DELFONT, LORD	FILM EXECUTIVE	17 GOLDEN SQ	LONDON W1R 3AG	ENGLAND
DELGADO, KIM	ACTOR	GEFFEN, 17 W 71ST ST	NEW YORK, NY	10023
DELIRIOUS PINK	ROCK & ROLL GROUP	POST OFFICE BOX 4429	AUSTIN, TX	78765
DELL, CHARLIE	ACTOR	3800 BARHAM BLVD #303	LOS ANGELES, CA	90068
DELL, GEORGIA	ACTRESS	8721 SUNSET BLVD #202	LOS ANGELES, CA	90069
DELL, MYRNA	ACTRESS	12958 VALLEYHEART DR	STUDIO CITY, CA	91604
DELL, SANDY	ACTRESS	9601 WILSHIRE BLVD #GL-11	BEVERLY HILLS, CA	90210
DELLA MALVA, JOSEPH	ACTOR	151 S EL CAMINO DR	BEVERLY HILLS, CA	90212
DELLA PIETRA, CARLINA F	TV WRITER	555 W 57TH ST #1230	NEW YORK, NY	10019
DELLA PORTA, AGOSTINO	NEWS CORRESPONDENT	2737 DEVONSHIRE PL, NW	WASHINGTON, DC	20008
DELLA SORTE, JOSEPH	ACTOR	1422 1/2 N SIERRA BONITA AVE	LOS ANGELES, CA	90046
DELLAR, MELVIN D	FILM DIRECTOR	125 TURQUOISE AVE	BALBOA ISLAND, CA	92662
DELLIGAN, WILLIAM F	WRITER	555 W 57TH ST #1230	NEW YORK, NY	10019
DELLINGER, ROBERT	TV WRITER-PRODUCER	21 WESTMINSTER AVE #201	VENICE, CA	90291
DELLO JOIO, NORMAN	COMPOSER	POST OFFICE BOX 154	EAST HAMPTON, NY	11937
DELLS, DOROTHY	ACTRESS	1026 TIVERTON AVE #207	LOS ANGELES, CA	90024
DELLS, THE	VOCAL GROUP	JOYCE AGENCY, 435 E 79TH ST	NEW YORK, NY	10021
DELO, KEN	SINGER	TERRY, 909 PARKVIEW AVE	LODI, CA	95240
DELON, ALAIN	ACTOR	ADEL PRO, 4 RUE DE CHAMBIGES	PARIS 75008	FRANCE
DELOY, GEORGE	ACTOR	KNBC-TV, "DAYS OF OUR LIVES"		
		3000 W ALAMEDA AVE	BURBANK, CA	91523
DELPHIN & ROMAIN	PIANO DUO	240 W 98TH ST #13-A	NEW YORK, NY	10025
DELSON, JAMES	WRITER	555 W 57TH ST #1230	NEW YORK, NY	10019
DEMAK, RICHARD	SPORTS REPORTER	SPORTS ILLUSTRATED MAGAZINE		
		TIME & LIFE BUILDING		
		ROCKEFELLER CENTER	NEW YORK, NY	10020
DEMBECKI, STAN	ACTOR	220 MARKET ST #7	VENICE, CA	90291
DEMBERG, LISA	TV WRITER	345 S COCHRAN AVE #7	LOS ANGELES, CA	90036
DEMBO, ROBERT J	WRITER	555 W 57TH ST #1230	NEW YORK, NY	10019
DEMETRACOPOULOS, ELIAS P	NEWS CORRESPONDENT	1280 21ST ST, NW	WASHINGTON, DC	20036
DEMIAN, MARCUS	WRITER	1850 N WHITLEY AVE	HOLLYWOOD, CA	90028
DEMING, WANG	NEWS CORRESPONDENT	4816 BUTTERWORTH PL, NW	WASHINGTON, DC	20016
DEMKOVICH, LINDA E	NEWS CORRESPONDENT	3602 S WAKEFIELD ST	ARLINGTON, VA	22206
DEMME, EVELYN PURCELL	DIRECTOR-PRODUCER	9000 SUNSET BLVD #1115	LOS ANGELES, CA	90069
DEMME, JONATHAN	FILM WRITER-DIRECTOR	9000 SUNSET BLVD #1115	LOS ANGELES, CA	90069
DEMOLITION (AXE & SMASH)	WRESTLING TAG TEAM	POST OFFICE BOX 3859	STAMFORD, CT	06905
DEMOREST, STEPHAN	TV WRITER	CBS-TV, "THE GUIDING LIGHT"		
		51 W 52ND ST	NEW YORK, NY	10019
DEMPSEY, JAMES C	GUITARIST	COLE'S MOBILE PARK #42	HENDERSON, KY	42420
DEMPSEY, JAMES TIMOTHY	GUITARIST	COLE'S MOBILE PARK #42	HENDERSON, KY	42420
DEMPSEY, JEROME	ACTOR	19 W 44TH ST #1500	NEW YORK, NY	10036
DEMPSTER, CAROL	ACTRESS	5815 LA JOLLA MESA DR	LA JOLLA, CA	92037
DEMPSTER, NIGEL	WRITER	10 BUCKINGHAM ST	LONDON WC2	ENGLAND
DEMUS, JORG	PIANIST	SOFFER, 130 W 56TH ST	NEW YORK, NY	10019
DEMY, JACQUES	DIRECTOR	86 RUE DAGUERRE	PARIS 75014	FRANCE
DENBAUM, DREW	WRITER	151 S EL CAMINO DR	BEVERLY HILLS, CA	90212
DENBY, DAVID	FILM CRITIC	N Y MAGAZINE, 755 2ND AVE	NEW YORK, NY	10017
DENCH, JUDI	ACTRESS	LEADING ARTISTS, LTD		
		60 SAINT JAMES'S ST	LONDON SW1	ENGLAND
DENEM, SUE	WRITER	8955 BEVERLY BLVD	LOS ANGELES, CA	90048
DENERSTEIN, ROBERT	FILM CRITIC	POST OFFICE BOX 719	DENVER, CO	80204
DENEUVE, CATHERINE	ACTRESS	ARTMEDIA, 10 AVE GEORGE V	PARIS 75008	FRANCE
DENG, YUN	MEZZO-SOPRANO	CAMI, 165 W 57TH ST	NEW YORK, NY	10019

Name	Occupation	Address	City	Zip
DENGEL, RONI	TV WRITER	555 W 57TH ST #1230	NEW YORK, NY	10019
DENHAM, MAURICE	ACTOR	44 BRUNSWICK GARDENS #2	LONDON W8	ENGLAND
DENHART, THOMAS E	DIRECTOR	OGILVY, 2 E 48TH ST	NEW YORK, NY	10017
DENHOLTZ, ELAINE G	WRITER	555 W 57TH ST #1230	NEW YORK, NY	10019
DENIS, BURKE	ACTOR	6331 HOLLYWOOD BLVD #924	LOS ANGELES, CA	90028
DENIS, PAUL	WRITER	555 W 57TH ST #1230	NEW YORK, NY	10019
DENISON, MICHAEL	ACTOR	2 CUMBERLAND PL	LONDON NW1	ENGLAND
DENISON, ROBERT G	ACTOR	7449 ALDEA AVE	VAN NUYS, CA	91406
DENKER, HENRY	PLAYWRIGHT	241 CENTRAL PARK W	NEW YORK, NY	10024
DENLINGER, J KENNETH	NEWS CORRESPONDENT	4513 MINUTEMAN DR	ROCKVILLE, MD	20853
DENMAN, JOHN	CLARINETIST	KAY, 58 W 58TH ST	NEW YORK, NY	10019
DENMAN DUO	MUSICAL DUO	KAY, 58 W 58TH ST	NEW YORK, NY	10019
DENN, MARIE	ACTRESS	22831 NADINE CIR #B	TORRANCE, CA	90505
DENNARD, ROGER	ACTOR	3800 BARHAM BLVD #303	LOS ANGELES, CA	90068
DENNEHY, AL	FILM DIRECTOR	POST OFFICE BOX 5165	SHERMAN OAKS, CA	91403
DENNEHY, BRIAN	ACTOR	SF & A, 121 N SAN VICENTE BLVD	BEVERLY HILLS, CA	90211
DENNEN, BARRY	ACTOR	870 N VINE ST #G	LOS ANGELES, CA	90038
DENNETT, JIM	DIRECTOR	20575 CHENEY DR	TOPANGA CANYON, CA	90290
DENNEY, AL B, JR	CINEMATOGRAPHER	8635 YOLANDA AVE #3	NORTHRIDGE, CA	91324
DENNEY, CHARLES	ACTOR	1 W 67TH ST	NEW YORK, NY	10023
DENNEY, KATHLEEN	ACTRESS	121 N ROBERTSON BLVD #B	BEVERLY HILLS, CA	90211
DENNEY, NORA	ACTRESS	15010 VENTURA BLVD #219	SHERMAN OAKS, CA	91403
DENNIS, ALFRED	ACTOR	312 N LOUISE ST #212	GLENDALE, CA	91206
DENNIS, ALLAN	DIRECTOR	461 PARK AVE S	NEW YORK, NY	10016
DENNIS, CHARLES	TV WRITER	8955 BEVERLY BLVD	LOS ANGELES, CA	90048
DENNIS, DIANA	BODYBUILDER	POST OFFICE BOX 3671	NEWPORT BEACH, CA	92663
DENNIS, GILL	WRITER	8955 BEVERLY BLVD	LOS ANGELES, CA	90048
DENNIS, GINGER	SINGER	POST OFFICE BOX 171132	NASHVILLE, TN	37217
DENNIS, GUY	GUITARIST-BANJOIST	2127-B BLAIR BLVD	NASHVILLE, TN	37212
DENNIS, JOHN	ACTOR	8721 SUNSET BLVD #103	LOS ANGELES, CA	90069
DENNIS, PETE	DRUMMER	7216 OLD BURKETT RD	ANTIOCH, TN	37013
DENNIS, QUITMAN	MUSICIAN	4001 ANDERSON RD #105	NASHVILLE, TN	37217
DENNIS, ROBERT C	WRITER	8082 MULHOLLAND DR	HOLLYWOOD, CA	90046
DENNIS, SANDY	ACTRESS	93 N SYLVAN RD	WESTPORT, CT	06880
DENNIS, SHARON	DRUMMER	219 PEBBLE BROOK	NASHVILLE, TN	37221
DENNISON, RACHEL PARTON	ACTRESS	9255 SUNSET BLVD #1115	LOS ANGELES, CA	90069
DENNISON, RICHARD	PIANIST	ROUTE #5, WILSON PIKE	FRANKLIN, TN	37064
DENNISON, SALLY	CASTING DIRECTOR	POST OFFICE BOX 5718	SHERMAN OAKS, CA	91403
DENNISTON, LESLIE	ACTRESS	10 E 44TH ST #700	NEW YORK, NY	10017
DENNISTON, LYLE W	NEWS CORRESPONDENT	1325 18TH ST #308, NW	WASHINGTON, DC	20036
DENNY, J WILLIAM	MUSIC PUBLISHER	800 CALDWELL LN	NASHVILLE, TN	37204
DENNY, LINDA	AUTO HARPIST	POST OFFICE BOX 1267	HENDERSONVILLE, TN	37075
DENNY, MARTIN	COMPOSER	4080 BLACK POINT RD	HONOLULU, HI	96816
DENNY & LEE	ILLUSIONIST	HALL, 138 FROG HOLLOW RD	CHURCHVILLE, PA	18966
DENOFF, SAMUEL	TV WRITER-PRODUCER	428 N CARMELINA AVE	LOS ANGELES, CA	90049
DENOS, JOHN	ACTOR	CBS TELEVISION NETWORK		
		"THE YOUNG & THE RESTLESS"		
		7800 BEVERLY BLVD	LOS ANGELES, CA	90036
DENSFORD, LYNN E	NEWS CORRESPONDENT	1721 BEULAH RD	VIENNA, VA	22180
DENSHAM, PEN	FILM WRITER-DIRECTOR	7235 SYCAMORE TRAIL	HOLLYWOOD, CA	90068
DENSMORE, JOHN	MUSICIAN	11737 CRESCENDA ST	LOS ANGELES, CA	90046
DENSMORE, STEVEN C	NEWS CORRESPONDENT	8574 HAYSHED LN	COLUMBIA, MD	21045
DENSON, FRANK W	COMPOSER	846 WILADONDA DR	LA CANADA, CA	91011
DENSON, JOHN LANE	TRUMPETER	511 JONES ST #B-4	OLD HICKORY, TN	37138
DENTON, CHRISTA	ACTRESS	SAVAGE, 6212 BANNER AVE	LOS ANGELES, CA	90038
DENTON, ELLEN	WRITER	555 W 57TH ST #1230	NEW YORK, NY	10019
DENTON, JACK	ACTOR	8256 CANTERBURY AVE	SUN VALLEY, CA	91352
DENTON, KATHY	ACTRESS	1339 FEDERAL AVE #3	LOS ANGELES, CA	90025
DENTON, LEN	WRESTLER	SEE - GRAPPLER, THE		
DENVER, BILL	SINGER	PROCESS, 439 WILEY AVE	FRANKLIN, PA	16323
DENVER, BOB	ACTOR	POST OFFICE BOX 426	PACIFIC PALISADES, CA	90272
DENVER, JOHN	SINGER-SONGWRITER	POST OFFICE BOX 1587	ASPEN, CO	81612
DENZIEN, RICK	SINGER	POST OFFICE BOX 314	AMBER, PA	19002
DEODATO	MUSIC GROUP	SONNENBERG, 83 RIVERSIDE DR	NEW YORK, NY	10024
DEODATO, EUMIR	COMPOSER	565 5TH AVE #600	NEW YORK, NY	10017
DEPECHE MODE	ROCK & ROLL GROUP	200 W 57TH ST #1403	NEW YORK, NY	10019
DEPEW, ART	CONDUCTOR	11530 HUSTON ST	NORTH HOLLYWOOD, CA	91601
DEPUTY DAWG BAND	C & W GROUP	POST OFFICE BOX O	EXCELSIOR, MN	55331
DER MARDEROSIAN, ALAN DICKRAN	COMPOSER	12547 CHANDLER BLVD #4	NORTH HOLLYWOOD, CA	91607
DEREK, BO	ACTRESS-MODEL	3625 ROBLAR	SANTA YNEZ, CA	93460
DEREK, JOHN	ACT-WRI-DIR	3625 ROBLAR	SANTA YNEZ, CA	93460
DEREK, SEAN CATHERINE	WRITER-ACTRESS	8955 BEVERLY BLVD	LOS ANGELES, CA	90048
DERFNER, DORI	WRITER	1223 AMALFI DR	PACIFIC PALISADES, CA	90272
DERLOSHON, GERALD B	SCREENWRITER	8955 BEVERLY BLVD	LOS ANGELES, CA	90048
DERMAN, WILLIAM	WRITER	8955 BEVERLY BLVD	LOS ANGELES, CA	90048
DERN, BRUCE	ACTOR	23430 MALIBU COLONY DR	MALIBU, CA	90265
DERN, LAURA	ACTRESS	9243 1/2 DOHENY RD	LOS ANGELES, CA	90069
DERNESCH, HELGA	MEZZO-SOPRANO	CAMI, 165 W 57TH ST	NEW YORK, NY	10019
DERR, RICHARD	ACTOR	151 S EL CAMINO DR	BEVERLY HILLS, CA	90212
DERRICK, VERNON	FIDDLER	ROUTE #3, BOX 438	ARAB, AL	35016
DERRICKS, CLEAVANT	ACTOR	SF & A, 121 N SAN VICENTE BLVD	BEVERLY HILLS, CA	90211
DERRINGER	ROCK & ROLL GROUP	LUTZ, 5625 "O" STREET BLDG	LINCOLN, NE	68510
DERRIS, STEVE J	TV DIRECTOR	325 E 64TH ST	NEW YORK, NY	10036
DERROUGH, NEIL E	TV EXECUTIVE	CBS-TV, 51 W 52ND ST	NEW YORK, NY	10019
DERRY, CHARLES	TV DIRECTOR	8660 MERKEL RD	DEXTER, MI	48130

DEPECHE MODE

DIRE STRAITS

John Illsley • David Knopfler • Mark Knopfler • Pick Withers

Name	Occupation	Address	City	Zip/Country
DERVAL, LAMYA	ACTRESS	208 S BEVERLY DR #4	BEVERLY HILLS, CA	90212
DERVARICS, CHARLES J	NEWS CORRESPONDENT	1201 S SCOTT ST	ARLINGTON, VA	22204
DES BARRES, MICHAEL	SINGER	POST OFFICE BOX 4160	HOLLYWOOD, CA	90078
DES BARRES, PAMELA	ACTRESS	943 N VISTA ST	LOS ANGELES, CA	90046
DESATOFF, PAUL	TV DIRECTOR	2944 MARIQUITA ST	LONG BEACH, CA	90803
DESBY, FRANK H	COMPOSER-CONDUCTOR	6234 SCENIC AVE	LOS ANGELES, CA	90068
DESCALZI, GUILLERMO	NEWS CORRESPONDENT	217 12TH ST, SE	WASHINGTON, DC	20003
DESCENDENTS, THE	ROCK & ROLL GROUP	POST OFFICE BOX 1224	LOMITA, CA	90717
DESCHANEL, CALEB	CINEMATOGRAPHER	844 CHAUTAUQUA BLVD	PACIFIC PALISADES, CA	90272
DESCHANEL, MARY JO	ACTRESS	844 CHAUTAUQUA BLVD	PACIFIC PALISADES, CA	90272
DESCRIERES, GEORGES	ACTOR	15 PL DU MARCHE	ST MONORE 75001	FRANCE
DESDERI, CLAUDIO	BARITONE	CAMI, 165 W 57TH ST	NEW YORK, NY	10019
DESERT ROSE	C & W GROUP	POST OFFICE BOX 8305	HARWIN, TX	77036
DESFOR, MAX	PHOTOGRAPHER	8811 COLESVILLE RD	SILVER SPRING, MD	20910
DESIDERIO, ROBERT	ACTOR	3410 WRIGHTVIEW DR	STUDIO CITY, CA	91604
DESMARETS, SOPHIE	ACTRESS	GEORGES BEAUME AGENCE		
		3 QUAI MALAQUAIS	PARIS 75006	FRANCE
DESMOND, DICK	SCREENWRITER	8955 BEVERLY BLVD	LOS ANGELES, CA	90048
DESMOND, EDWARD W	WRITER-EDITOR	TIME/TIME & LIFE BLDG		
		ROCKEFELLER CENTER	NEW YORK, NY	10020
DESMOND, JOHN J	DIRECTOR	165 E 66TH ST	NEW YORK, NY	10021
DESMOND CHILD	ROCK & ROLL GROUP	1780 BROADWAY #1208	NEW YORK, NY	10019
DESMONI-HORNE, MADDY	TV EXECUTIVE	CBS-TV, 7800 BEVERLY BLVD	LOS ANGELES, CA	90036
DESPRES, LORAINE	WRITER	6403 SEASTAR DR	MALIBU, CA	90265
DESRUISSEAUX, PAUL	NEWS CORRESPONDENT	5917 WILMETT RD	BETHESDA, MD	20817
DESSI, DANIELA	SOPRANO	CAMI, 165 W 57TH ST	NEW YORK, NY	10019
DESTINATION	SOUL GROUP	JOYCE AGENCY, 435 E 79TH ST	NEW YORK, NY	10021
DESTINE, JEAN-LEON	CHOREOGRAPHER-DANCER	676 RIVERSIDE DR	NEW YORK, NY	10031
DESTROYER, SUPER	WRESTLER	SEE - SPOILER, THE		
DESTRUCTION	ROCK & ROLL GROUP	POST OFFICE BOX 2428	EL SEGUNDO, CA	90245
DESZERAY	ROCK & ROLL GROUP	VARIETY ARTISTS INTL, INC		
		9073 NEMO ST, 3RD FLOOR	LOS ANGELES, CA	90069
DETAMORE, OSCAR	BANJOIST	300 S PLANT #1-A	BOERNE, TX	78006
DETENTE	ROCK & ROLL GROUP	POST OFFICE BOX 2428	EL SEGUNDO, CA	90245
DETERS, THOMAS C, MD	BODYBUILDER	POST OFFICE BOX 64301	CHICAHO, IL	60664
DETIEGE, DAVE	WRITER	8955 BEVERLY BLVD	LOS ANGELES, CA	90048
DEUBEL, ROBERT	DIRECTOR-PRODUCER	THE WILLIAM MORRIS AGENCY		
		1350 AVE OF THE AMERICAS	NEW YORK, NY	10019
DEUCE	MUSICAL DUO	484 W 43RD ST #34-H	NEW YORK, NY	10036
DEUTEKOM, CRISTINA	SOPRANO	CAMI, 165 W 57TH ST	NEW YORK, NY	10019
DEUTSCH, DAVID	FILM PRODUCER	WATERGATE FILMS, LTD		
		10 BUCKINGHAM ST	LONDON WC 2N 6BU	ENGLAND
DEUTSCH, DAVID GEORGE	SCREENWRITER	2311 CHEREMOYA AVE	LOS ANGELES, CA	90068
DEUTSCH, DAVID S	TV DIRECTOR	1243 "C" ST, SE	WASHINGTON, DC	20003
DEUTSCH, HELEN	SCREENWRITER	1185 PARK AVE	NEW YORK, NY	10128
DEUTSCH, RICHARD H	NEWS CORRESPONDENT	1940 BILTMORE ST, NW	WASHINGTON, DC	20009
DEUTSCH, RUTH	TV WRITER	JEOPARDY, 1541 N VINE ST	HOLLYWOOD, CA	90028
DEUTSCH, STEVEN	FILM PRODUCER	150 S EL CAMINO DR #205	BEVERLY HILLS, CA	90212
DEVADAS, REJAN	PHOTOGRAPHER	214 HARDY PL	ROCKVILLE, MD	20852
DEVANE, WILLIAM	ACTOR	15027 VALLEY VISTA BLVD	SHERMAN OAKS, CA	91403
DEVASTATION, INC	WRESTLING TAG TEAM	UNIVERSAL WRESTLING FEDERATION		
		MID SOUTH SPORTS, INC		
		5001 SPRING VALLEY RD	DALLAS, TX	75244
DEVER, TOM	ACTOR	5953 1/4 CARLTON WY	LOS ANGELES, CA	90028
DEVERAUX, SUZI & THE NASHVILLE	C & W GROUP	154 CHIPPENDALE DR	HENDERSONVILLE, TN	37075
DEVEREAUX, DAVID EARL	TV DIRECTOR	2870 DERBY RD	BIRMINGHAM, MI	48008
DEVEREUX, ROBERT	FILM PRODUCER	VIRGIN FILMS, 328 KENSAL RD	LONDON W10	ENGLAND
DEVERY, LOUISE	ACTRESS	25 82ND ST	SEA ISLE CITY, NJ	08243
DEVIA, MARIELLA	SOPRANO	61 W 62ND ST #6-F	NEW YORK, NY	10023
DEVILLE, MINK	ROCK & ROLL GROUP	SEE - MINK DEVILLE		
DEVINE	ACTOR-ACTRESS	MILSTEAD, 40 E 58TH ST	NEW YORK, NY	10022
DEVINE, JERRY	WRITER	8955 BEVERLY BLVD	LOS ANGELES, CA	90048
DEVINE, JOHN	NEWS CORRESPONDENT	1324 4TH ST, SW	WASHINGTON, DC	20024
DEVINE, L F	WRITER	555 W 57TH ST #1230	NEW YORK, NY	10019
DEVLET, TED	DIRECTOR	SPS, 310 E 46TH ST	NEW YORK, NY	10017
DEVLIN, C TAD	WRITER	8955 BEVERLY BLVD	LOS ANGELES, CA	90048
DEVLIN, DESMOND	WRITER	MAD MAGAZINE, INC		
		485 MADISON AVE	NEW YORK, NY	10022
DEVLIN, DON	WRITER	8577 BRIER DR	LOS ANGELES, CA	90046
DEVLIN, MICHAEL	BASSO-BARITONE	CAMI, 165 W 57TH ST	NEW YORK, NY	10019
DEVO	ROCK & ROLL GROUP	LOOKOUT, 9120 SUNSET BLVD	LOS ANGELES, CA	90069
DEVOLL, RAY	TENOR	KAY, 58 W 58TH ST	NEW YORK, NY	10019
DEVON, LAURA	ACTRESS	1201 TOWER GROVE DR	BEVERLY HILLS, CA	90210
DEVON, RICHARD	ACTOR	5727 CANOGA AVE	WOODLAND HILLS, CA	91367
DEVON, TONY	ACTOR	BAGS ZIMMERMAN PRODS		
		101 W 57TH ST	NEW YORK, NY	10019
DEVONNES, THE	VOCAL GROUP	DEANGELIS, 79 KINGSLAND AVE	BROOKLYN, NY	11211
DEVORE, GARY M	SCREENWRITER	1403 MARINETTE RD	PACIFIC PALISADES, CA	90272
DEVORE, KIM	WRITER	8955 BEVERLY BLVD	LOS ANGELES, CA	90048
DEVOYON, PASCAL	PIANIST	LEISER, DORCHESTER TOWERS		
		155 W 68TH ST	NEW YORK, NY	10023
DEVROY, ANN	NEWS CORRESPONDENT	830 11TH ST, NE	WASHINGTON, DC	20002
DEW, CEDRIC D	WRITER	555 W 57TH ST #1230	NEW YORK, NY	10019
DEWAR, HELEN	NEWS CORRESPONDENT	1 POTOMAC CT	ALEXANDRIA, VA	22314
DEWBERRY, DEAN & PENNY	JAZZ DUO	POST OFFICE BOX 302	KEYSTONE HEIGHTS, FL	32656

DEWESE, LARRY	GUITARIST	5101 LINBAR DR #J-114	NASHVILLE, TN	37211
DEWEY, CLEON	PIANIST	3996 LAWING DR	NASHVILLE, TN	37207
DEWEY, DAVID D	TV DIRECTOR	CBS-TV, 524 W 57TH ST	NEW YORK, NY	10019
DEWEY, RAY	COMPOSER-CONDUCTOR	3641 CROWNRIDGE DR	SHERMAN OAKS, CA	91403
DEWEY-CARTER, JOHN	ACTOR	9220 SUNSET BLVD #202	LOS ANGELES, CA	90069
DEWHURST, COLLEEN	ACTRESS	FLOOD FARM, BOUTONVILLE	SOUTH SALEM, NY	10590
DEXTER, DOROTHY	ACTRESS	8230 BEVERLY BLVD #23	LOS ANGELES, CA	90048
DEXTER, MAURY	TV DIRECTOR	1384 CAMINO MAGENTA	THOUSAND OAKS, CA	91360
DEXTER, RON	COMPOSER	930 N WETHERLY DR	LOS ANGELES, CA	90069
DEXTER, RON P	DIRECTOR	8675 EDWIN DR	LOS ANGELES, CA	90046
DEY, JANET	ACTRESS	3330 BARHAM BLVD #103	LOS ANGELES, CA	90068
DEY, SUSAN	ACTRESS	151 S EL CAMINO DR	BEVERLY HILLS, CA	90212
DEYELL, PETER R J	TV DIRECTOR	10742 CAMARILLO ST	TOLUCA LAKE, CA	91602
DEZI-RAE	RHYTHM & BLUES GROUP	LCS, 1627 16TH AVE S	NASHVILLE, TN	37212
DFX-2	ROCK & ROLL GROUP	11744 DARLINGTON AVE #20	LOS ANGELES, CA	90049
DI BELLA, BENITO	BARITONE	61 W 62ND ST #6-F	NEW YORK, NY	10023
DI BELLA, VINCENT W	GUITARIST	510 N 17TH #B	NASHVILLE, TN	37206
DI BENEDETTO, GARY DEE	GUITARIST	1909 W OGLETHORPE AVE	ALBANY, GA	31707
DI BENEDETTO, WILLIAM R	NEWS CORRESPONDENT	15213 CRESCENT ST	WOODBRIDGE, VA	22193
DI BIASE, TED	WRESTLER	UNIVERSAL WRESTLING FEDERATION		
		MID SOUTH SPORTS, INC		
		5001 SPRING VALLEY RD	DALLAS, TX	75244
DI BIASI, CYNTHIA	NEWS CORRESPONDENT	2304 ASHBORO DR	CHEVY CHASE, MD	20815
DI BONA, VINCENT J	DIRECTOR-PRODUCER	1912 THAYER AVE	LOS ANGELES, CA	90025
DI BONAVENTURA, ANTHONY	PIANIST	SHAW CONCERTS, 1995 BROADWAY	NEW YORK, NY	10023
DI CENZO, GEORGE	ACTOR	500 25TH ST	SANTA MONICA, CA	90402
DI CESARE, EZIO	TENOR	61 W 62ND ST #6-F	NEW YORK, NY	10023
DI CICCO, BOBBY	ACTOR	11726 SAN VICENTE BLVD #300	LOS ANGELES, CA	90049
DI FALCO, TONY	ACTOR	1418 N HIGHLAND AVE #102	LOS ANGELES, CA	90028
DI FRANCO, LORETTA	SOPRANO	61 W 62ND ST #6-F	NEW YORK, NY	10023
DI GIUSEPPE, ENRICO	TENOR	CAMI, 165 W 57TH ST	NEW YORK, NY	10019
DI GREGORIO, TAZ	PIANIST	109 BIG HORN CT	OLD HICKORY, TN	37138
DI LELLO, RICHARD	SCREENWRITER	1420 BEL AIR RD	LOS ANGELES, CA	90077
DI LEO, MARIO	CINEMATOGRAPHER	7617 KESTER AVE	VAN NUYS, CA	91405
DI LEVA, ANTHONY J	ACTOR	160 W 73RD ST	NEW YORK, NY	10023
DI LORENZO, EDWARD D	WRITER	8955 BEVERLY BLVD	LOS ANGELES, CA	90048
DI MAGGIO, JOE	BASEBALL	2150 BEACH ST	SAN FRANCISCO, CA	94123
DI MAGGIO, MADELINE	TV WRITER	8955 BEVERLY BLVD	LOS ANGELES, CA	90048
DI MAGGIO, MARY	TV WRITER	8955 BEVERLY BLVD	LOS ANGELES, CA	90048
DI MARCO, SALVATORE C	PHOTOGRAPHER	1002 COBBS ST	DREXEL HILL, PA	19026
DI MARCO, TONY	WRITER	9300 WILSHIRE BLVD #410	BEVERLY HILLS, CA	90212
DI MASSA, ERNANI V, JR	TV WRITER-PRODUCER	23237 KESWICK ST	CANOGA PARK, CA	91304
DI MEOLA, AL	GUITARIST	KURLAND, 173 BRIGHTON AVE	BOSTON, MA	02134
DI MILO, TONY	ACTOR	10000 RIVERSIDE DR #3	TOLUCA LAKE, CA	91602
DI MISCIO, ANTHONY	COMPOSER	1045 N BUENA VISTA ST	BURBANK, CA	91505
DI MITRI, RICHARD	TV WRITER	8955 BEVERLY BLVD	LOS ANGELES, CA	90048
DI MOMENICO, DINO	TENOR	CAMI, 165 W 57TH ST	NEW YORK, NY	10019
DI MONA, JOSEPH	WRITER	555 W 57TH ST #1230	NEW YORK, NY	10019
DI MORA, SHANE	BODYBUILDER	POST OFFICE BOX 11883	FRESNO, CA	93775
DI MUCCI, DION	SINGER	19301 VENTURA BLVD #205	TARZANA, CA	91356
DI NALLO, GREGORY S	WRITER	958 24TH ST	SANTA MONICA, CA	90403
DI PAOLO, TONIO	TENOR	CONE, 221 W 57TH ST	NEW YORK, NY	10019
DI PASQUALE, JAMES	COMPOSER-LYRICIST	3815 W OLIVE AVE #202	BURBANK, CA	91505
DI PASQUALE, JAMES A	COMPOSER	4058 WOODMAN AVE	SHERMAN OAKS, CA	91423
DI PEGO, GERALD	WRITER-PRODUCER	610 MARGUERITA AVE	SANTA MONICA, CA	90402
DI PIERO, BOB	GUITARIST	1111 DRAUGHON AVE	NASHVILLE, TN	37204
DI PIETRO, ROBERT B	WRITER	8955 BEVERLY BLVD	LOS ANGELES, CA	90048
DI PRETA, TONY	CARTOONIST	NEWS AMERICA SYNDICATE		
		1703 KAISER AVE	IRVINE, CA	92714
DI RE, FLO	ACTRESS	1092 LOMA DR	HERMOSA BEACH, CA	90254
DI REDA, JOE	ACTOR	ABC-TV, "GENERAL HOSPITAL"		
		1438 N GOWER ST	LOS ANGELES, CA	90028
DI ROMA, RON	SINGER	JOYCE, 2028 CHESTNUT ST	PHILADELPHIA, PA	19103
DI SHELL, WALTER D, MD	TV WRITER	4610 AZALIA DR	TARZANA, CA	91356
DI STEFANO, DANIEL M	TV WRITER	9431 BIANCA AVE	NORTHRIDGE, CA	91325
DI TILLIO, LAWRENCE GABRIEL	WRITER	1441 1/2 S HOLT AVE	LOS ANGELES, CA	90035
DI TONTO, DOUGLAS P	WRITER	8955 BEVERLY BLVD	LOS ANGELES, CA	90048
DI TOSTI, BEN	COMPOSER-CONDUCTOR	1645 CAMINO DE VILLAS	BURBANK, CA	91501
DI ZENZO, CHARLES	TV WRITER	420 VIA ALMAR	PALOS VERDES, CA	90274
DI ZENZO, PATRICIA	TV WRITER	420 VIA ALMAR	PALOS VERDES, CA	90274
DIAL, DICK	DIRECTOR	3220 COLONY VIEW CIR	MALIBU, CA	90265
DIAL, WILLIAM	PRODUCER	MCA/UNIVERSAL STUDIOS, INC		
		100 UNIVERSAL CITY PLAZA	UNIVERSAL CITY, CA	91608
DIAL, WILLIAM ALLEN	ACTOR-WRITER	4171 WITZEL DR	SHERMAN OAKS, CA	91423
DIALSINGH, CAROLANN	NEWS CORRESPONDENT	244 60TH ST #303, NE	WASHINGTON, DC	20019
DIAMOND, ARNOLD	ACTOR	32 BELSIZE CT, WEDDERBU	LONDON NW3 5QJ	ENGLAND
DIAMOND, BARRY	COMEDIAN	9000 SUNSET BLVD #1112	LOS ANGELES, CA	90069
DIAMOND, BOBBY	ACTOR	5309 COMERCIO WY	WOODLAND HILLS, CA	91367
DIAMOND, DAVID	COMPOSER	249 EDGERTON ST	ROCHESTER, NY	14607
DIAMOND, DON	ACTOR	10000 RIVERSIDE DR #3	TOLUCA LAKE, CA	91602
DIAMOND, I A L	SCREENWRITER	313 EL CAMINO DR	BEVERLY HILLS, CA	90212
DIAMOND, ISIDORE	SCREENWRITER	SEE - DIAMOND, I A L		
DIAMOND, JAMIE	WRITER	8955 BEVERLY BLVD	LOS ANGELES, CA	90048
DIAMOND, JEFFREY L	TV PRODUCER	ABC-TV, 7 W 66TH ST	NEW YORK, NY	10023
DIAMOND, JILL	WRITER	555 W 57TH ST #1230	NEW YORK, NY	10019

DIAMOND, JOEL, EXPERIENCE	SOUL GROUP	SILVER BLUE MANAGEMENT		
		220 CENTRAL PARK S	NEW YORK, NY	10019
DIAMOND, MATTHEW	CHOREOGRAPHER	29 W 21ST ST, 4TH FLOOR	NEW YORK, NY	10010
DIAMOND, NEIL	SINGER-SONGWRITER	161 S MAPLETON DR	LOS ANGELES, CA	90024
DIAMOND, PAUL	TV WRITER	8955 BEVERLY BLVD	LOS ANGELES, CA	90048
DIAMOND, PHYLLIS	NEWS CORRESPONDENT	1231 25TH ST, NW	WASHINGTON, DC	20037
DIAMOND, ROBERT G	FILM DIRECTOR	DGA, 7950 SUNSET BLVD	LOS ANGELES, CA	90046
DIAMOND, ROBERT R	TV DIRECTOR	680 W END AVE	NEW YORK, NY	10025
DIAMOND, VERNON K	TV DIRECTOR	5 DUXBURY RD	GREAT NECK, NY	11023
DIAMOND LIL	C & W GROUP	GROUP, 1957 KILBURN DR	ATLANTA, GA	30324
		23509 BALTAR ST	CANOGA PARK, CA	91304
DIAMONDS, THE	ROCK & ROLL GROUP	POST OFFICE BOX 448	RADFORD, VA	24141
DIAMONDS, THE	VOCAL GROUP	FIRST CHAIR MANAGEMENT		
		23509 BALTER ST	CANOGA PARK, CA	91304
DIAMONSTEIN, BARBARALEE	WRITER	555 W 57TH ST #1230	NEW YORK, NY	10019
DIAMONT, DON	ACTOR	CBS TELEVISION NETWORK		
		"THE YOUNG & THE RESTLESS"		
		7800 BEVERLY BLVD	LOS ANGELES, CA	90036
DIAMONT, KATHI	TV HOST	KFMB-TV, 7677 ENGINEER RD	SAN DIEGO, CA	92111
DIANA, HRH PRINCESS	PRINCESS	KENSINGTON PALACE	LONDON W8	ENGLAND
DIAZ, BETTE	WRITER	555 W 57TH ST #1230	NEW YORK, NY	10019
DIAZ, EDITH	ACTRESS	POST OFFICE BOX 8775	NORTH HOLLYWOOD, CA	91608
DIAZ, GREGORY T	NEWS CORRESPONDENT	7246 JILLSPRING CT	SPRINGFIELD, VA	22152
DIAZ, JAIME	SPORTS WRITER-EDITOR	SPORTS ILLUSTRATED MAGAZINE		
		TIME & LIFE BUILDING		
		ROCKEFELLER CENTER	NEW YORK, NY	10020
DIAZ, JUSTINO	SINGER	140 W END AVE	NEW YORK, NY	10023
DIAZ, MILKA	CONTRALTO	260 W END AVE #7-A	NEW YORK, NY	10023
DIAZ, RUDY	ACTOR	10000 RIVERSIDE DR #3	TOLUCA LAKE, CA	91602
DIBIE, GEORGE	TV DIRECTOR	14537 HESBY ST	SHERMAN OAKS, CA	91403
DICHTER, MISHA	PIANIST	ICM, 40 W 57TH ST	NEW YORK, NY	10019
DICHTER, MISHA & CIPA	PIANO DUO	ICM, 40 W 57TH ST	NEW YORK, NY	10019
DICK, DAVID	NEWS CORRESPONDENT	CBS NEWS, 524 W 57TH ST	NEW YORK, NY	10019
DICK, DOUGLAS	ACTOR	604 GRETNA GREEN WY	LOS ANGELES, CA	90049
DICK, JAMES	PIANIST	59 E 54TH ST #81	NEW YORK, NY	10022
DICK, JAMES F	WRITER	555 W 57TH ST #1230	NEW YORK, NY	10019
DICK, PEGGY CHANTLER	WRITER	604 GRETNA GREEN WY	LOS ANGELES, CA	90049
DICK & DEE DEE	VOCAL DUO	MONARCH, 9227 NICHOLS ST	BELLFLOWER, CA	90706
DICKENS, LITTLE JIMMY	SINGER	510 W CONCORD	BRENTWOOD, TN	37027
DICKENSON, JAMES R	NEWS CORRESPONDENT	4101 GLENROSE ST	KENSINGTON, MD	20895
DICKEROW, GLENN	VIOLINIST	GERSHUNOFF, 502 PARK AVE	NEW YORK, NY	10022
DICKERSON, CHRIS	BODYBUILDER	GOLD'S GYM, 360 HAMPTON DR	VENICE, CA	90291
DICKERSON, DANNY ROSS	PIANIST	POST OFFICE BOX 120913	NASHVILLE, TN	37212
DICKERSON, GEORGE	ACTOR	8350 SANTA MONICA BLVD #103	LOS ANGELES, CA	90069
DICKERSON, NANCY	NEWS CORRESPONDENT	1063 THOMAS JEFFERSON ST, NW	WASHINGTON, DC	20007
DICKERSON, NEAL A	WRITER	555 W 57TH ST #1230	NEW YORK, NY	10019
DICKEY, BILL	BASEBALL	114 E 5TH ST	LITTLE ROCK, AR	72203
DICKEY, GLENN	COLUMNIST-WRITER	120 FLORENCE AVE	OAKLAND, CA	94618
DICKEY, JAMES	POET-NOVELIST	4620 LELIAS CT		
		LAKE KATHERINE	COLUMBIA, SC	29206
DICKEY, LUCINDA	ACTRESS	10351 SANTA MONICA BLVD #211	LOS ANGELES, CA	90025
DICKIEBIRDS, THE	ROCK & ROLL GROUP	POST OFFICE BOX 6025	NEWPORT NEWS, VA	23606
DICKIES, THE	ROCK & ROLL GROUP	POST OFFICE BOX 651	LA MIRADA, CA	90637
DICKINSON, ANGIE	ACTRESS	9580 LIME ORCHARD RD	BEVERLY HILLS, CA	90210
DICKINSON, BOB	CINEMATOGRAPHER	7715 SUNSET BLVD #150	LOS ANGELES, CA	90046
DICKINSON, CHRISTINE	ACTRESS	9744 WILSHIRE BLVD #206	BEVERLY HILLS, CA	90212
DICKINSON, JAMES G	NEWS CORRESPONDENT	ROUTE #3	HEDGESVILLE, WV	25427
DICKINSON, PAMELA	GUITARIST	4574 ARTELIA DR	ANTIOCH, TN	37013
DICKINSON, REBECCA L	NEWS CORRESPONDENT	1529 S GEORGE MASON DR	ARLINGTON, VA	22204
DICKINSON, WILLIAM G	DRUMMER	280 TANGLEWOOD CT	NASHVILLE, TN	37211
DICKMAN, CAROL A	DIRECTOR	1552 NE QUAYSIDE TERR	MIAMI, FL	33138
DICKMAN, IRVING R	WRITER	555 W 57TH ST #1230	NEW YORK, NY	10019
DICKSON, BARBARA	ACTRESS-SINGER	RICHMOND BUILDINGS, DEAN ST	LONDON W1	ENGLAND
DICKSON, BRENDA	ACTRESS	10100 EMPYREAN WY #302	LOS ANGELES, CA	90067
DICKSON, DAVID A	COMPOSER	382 E DEL MAR BLVD #3	PASADENA, CA	91101
DICKSON, DORA	SINGER	POST OFFICE BOX 82	GREENBRIER, TN	37073
DICKSON, STEPHEN	BARITONE	CAMI, 165 W 57TH ST	NEW YORK, NY	10019
DICKSON, WALLACE G	NEWS CORRESPONDENT	1743 "P" ST, NW	WASHINGTON, DC	20036
DIDATO, SALVATORE V	PUZZLE-GAME WRITER	NEWS AMERICA SYNDICATE		
		1703 KAISER AVE	IRVINE, CA	92714
DIDDLEY, BO	SINGER-GUITARIST	OTELSBERG, 5530 KEOKUK AVE	WOODLAND HILLS, CA	92364
DIDION, JOAN	SCREENWRITER	8955 BEVERLY BLVD	LOS ANGELES, CA	90048
DIE KREUZEN	ROCK & ROLL GROUP	POST OFFICE BOX 92181	MILWAUKEE, WI	53202
DIEDERICH, SUSAN	WRITER	555 W 57TH ST #1230	NEW YORK, NY	10019
DIEDERICH, WILLIAM P	WRITER	555 W 57TH ST #1230	NEW YORK, NY	10019
DIEHENN, ART	DIRECTOR	5817 PACKARD ST	LOS ANGELES, CA	90019
DIEHL, DIGBY R	FILM CRITIC-WRITER	788 S LAKE AVE	PASADENA, CA	91106
DIEHL, JOHN	ACTOR	3800 BARHAM BLVD #303	LOS ANGELES, CA	90068
DIEKHAUS, GRACE	TV WRITER-PRODUCER	CBS-TV, 524 W 57TH ST	NEW YORK, NY	10019
DIEKMEYER, HANS	NEWS CORRESPONDENT	3132 "M" ST, NW	WASHINGTON, DC	20007
DIEMECKE, ENRIQUE	CONDUCTOR	AFFILIATE ARTISTS, INC		
		37 W 65TH ST, 6TH FLOOR	NEW YORK, NY	10023
DIEMER, THOMAS K	NEWS CORRESPONDENT	930 NATIONAL PRESS BLDG		
		529 14TH ST, NW	WASHINGTON, DC	20045
DIERKOP, CHARLES	ACTOR	7845 TUJUNGA AVE	NORTH HOLLYWOOD, CA	91605

Name	Occupation	Address	City	Zip
DIERKS, DONALD	MUSIC CRITIC	POST OFFICE BOX 191	SAN DIEGO, CA	92112
DIES, BARBARA A	WRITER	8955 BEVERLY BLVD	LOS ANGELES, CA	90048
DIESEL	ROCK & ROLL GROUP	LIBERT, 13457 RAND DR	SHERMAN OAKS, CA	91423
DIETHER, ANTON	SCREENWRITER	POST OFFICE BOX 1982	LOS ANGELES, CA	90028
DIETRICH, CINDI	ACTRESS	FLICK EAST-WEST TALENTS		
		9045 NEMO ST	LOS ANGELES, CA	90069
DIETRICH, DENA	ACTRESS	4006 MADELIA AVE	SHERMAN OAKS, CA	91403
DIETRICH, JAMES	CONDUCTOR	11547 HESBY ST	NORTH HOLLYWOOD, CA	91601
DIETRICH, MARLENE	ACTRESS	12 AVE MONTAIGNE	PARIS 8E	FRANCE
DIETRICH, RAY H	DIRECTOR	10125 DE SOTO AVE #40	CHATSWORTH, CA	91311
DIETRICH, RICHARD A	TV DIRECTOR	1088 WASHINGTON CIR	NORTHVILLE, MI	48167
DIETRICK, GARTH	DIRECTOR	65 HOBBY DR	RIDGEFIELD, CT	06877
DIETSCH, JAMES	BARITONE	61 W 62ND ST #6-F	NEW YORK, NY	10023
DIETZ, EILEEN	ACTRESS	2036 VISTA DEL MAR AVE	LOS ANGELES, CA	90068
DIETZ, HOWARD	LYRICIST-WRITER	180 E END AVE	NEW YORK, NY	10028
DIETZ, LAWRENCE S	TV WRITER	8955 BEVERLY BLVD	LOS ANGELES, CA	90048
DIEZ, MANNY	WRITER	8955 BEVERLY BLVD	LOS ANGELES, CA	90048
DIFFERENCE, THE	ROCK & ROLL GROUP	VARIETY ARTISTS INTL, INC		
		9073 NEMO ST, 3RD FLOOR	LOS ANGELES, CA	90069
DIFFRING, ANTON	ACTOR	MORRIS, 147-149 WARDOUR ST	LONDON W1V 3TB	ENGLAND
DIGBY, DENNIS	GUITARIST	8167 HARDING RD	NASHVILLE, TN	37221
DIGGINS, PETER	BALLET EXECUTIVE	133 W 71ST ST	NEW YORK, NY	10023
DIGGS, DAVID H	COMPOSER	POST OFFICE BOX 1834	STUDIO CITY, CA	91604
DIGGS, GWENDOLYN C	NEWS CORRESPONDENT	11552 LOCKWOOD DR #D-1	SILVER SPRING, MD	20904
DIGGS, JOHN	ACTOR	3518 W CAHUENGA BLVD #316	LOS ANGELES, CA	90068
DIGIAIMO, LOUIS	CASTING DIRECTOR	POST OFFICE BOX 5296	NEW YORK, NY	10150
DILBERT, BERNARD	TV WRITER	LAKE, 1103 GLENDON AVE	LOS ANGELES, CA	90024
DILBERTO, GIOIA	WRITER-EDITOR	PEOPLE/TIME & LIFE BLDG		
		ROCKEFELLER CENTER	NEW YORK, NY	10020
DILG, LARRY	ACTOR	2439 IVANHOE DR	LOS ANGELES, CA	90039
DILL, JAMES SCOBEY, JR	SAXOPHONIST	3813 BRIARCLIFF CT	NASHVILLE, TN	37211
DILLARD, ALBERT N, JR	PUBLISHING EXECUTIVE	SAN DIEGO'S CHOICE MAGAZINE		
		1939 GRAND AVE	SAN DIEGO, CA	92109
DILLARD, ANNIE	AUTHOR	GREGORY, 2 TUDOR PL	NEW YORK, NY	10017
DILLARD, SUZANNE	ACTRESS	8230 BEVERLY BLVD #23	LOS ANGELES, CA	90048
DILLARDS, THE	BLUEGRASS GROUP	KEITH CASE COMPANY		
		1016 16TH AVE S	NASHVILLE, TN	37212
DILLE, KARREN	ACTRESS	6457 MAMMOTH AVE	VAN NUYS, CA	91401
DILLE, ROBERT N	WRITER	1400 KELTON AVE #203	LOS ANGELES, CA	90024
DILLER, BARRY	FILM EXECUTIVE	1940 COLDWATER CANYON DR	BEVERLY HILLS, CA	90210
DILLER, JOHN C	CABLE EXECUTIVE	THE ENTERTAINMENT CHANNEL		
		1133 AVE OF THE AMERICAS	NEW YORK, NY	10036
DILLER, JULIE	ACTRESS	163 S ROCKINGHAM AVE	LOS ANGELES, CA	90049
DILLER, PHYLLIS	ACTRESS-COMEDIENNE	163 S ROCKINGHAM AVE	LOS ANGELES, CA	90049
DILLIN, JOHN	NEWS CORRESPONDENT	5525 N 15TH ST	ARLINGTON, VA	22205
DILLINDER, ERMA	COMPOSER	5864 HARCO ST	LONG BEACH, CA	90808
DILLINGER	C & W GROUP	TAYLOR, 2401 12TH AVE S	NASHVILLE, TN	37204
DILLINGHAM, CRAIG	SINGER	10880 WILSHIRE BLVD #912	LOS ANGELES, CA	90024
DILLMAN, BRADFORD	ACTOR	770 HOT SPRINGS RD	SANTA BARBARA, CA	93103
DILLMAN, DAISY	SINGER	POST OFFICE BOX O	EXCELSIOR, MN	55331
DILLMAN BAND, THE	ROCK & ROLL GROUP	POST OFFICE BOX O	MINNEAPOLIS, MN	55331
DILLON, BRENDAN THOMAS	ACTOR	4721 LAUREL CANYON BLVD #211	NORTH HOLLYWOOD, CA	91607
DILLON, DANIEL P	TV DIRECTOR	717-C COLE ST	SAINT LOUIS, MO	63101
DILLON, DAVID D	ACTOR	612 BRANCH AVE	LITTLE RIVER, NJ	07739
DILLON, DEAN	SINGER	MC COLLUM, 21 ELM PL	PRINCETON, IL	61356
DILLON, JAMES	FILM DIRECTOR	9579 OLYMPIC BLVD	BEVERLY HILLS, CA	90212
DILLON, JAMES J	WRESTLING MANAGER	NATIONAL WRESTLING ALLIANCE		
		JIM CROCKETT PROMOTIONS		
		421 BRIARBEND DR	CHARLOTTE, NC	28209
DILLON, JOHN JOSEPH	TV DIRECTOR	241 PENNSYLVANIA AVE	CRESTWOOD, NY	10707
DILLON, KEVIN	ACTOR	49 W 9TH ST	NEW YORK, NY	10010
DILLON, LAURIE	WRITER	8955 BEVERLY BLVD	LOS ANGELES, CA	90048
DILLON, MARK	DIRECTOR	13441 SYLVAN ST	VAN NUYS, CA	91401
DILLON, MATT	ACTOR	49 W 9TH ST	NEW YORK, NY	10010
DILLON, MELINDA	ACTRESS	225 W 34TH ST #1012	NEW YORK, NY	10122
DILLON, MIA	ACTRESS	151 S EL CAMINO DR	BEVERLY HILLS, CA	90212
DILLON, RICHARD	WRITER	8955 BEVERLY BLVD	LOS ANGELES, CA	90048
DILLON, RICHARD A	WRITER	8955 BEVERLY BLVD	LOS ANGELES, CA	90048
DILLON, RITA	TV PRODUCER	1438 N GOWER ST	LOS ANGELES, CA	90028
DILLON, ROBERT	SCREENWRITER	8955 BEVERLY BLVD	LOS ANGELES, CA	90048
DILLON, SUSAN J	NEWS CORRESPONDENT	3520 "T" ST, NW	WASHINGTON, DC	20007
DILLON, TIMOTHY P	PHOTOGRAPHER	1120 PARK ST, NE	WASHINGTON, DC	20002
DILLS, GEOFFREY E	NEWS CORRESPONDENT	2924 FAULKNER PL	KENSINGTON, MD	20895
DILNIK, GEORGE S	TV WRITER	8955 BEVERLY BLVD	LOS ANGELES, CA	90048
DILNIK, JOHN F	TV WRITER	8955 BEVERLY BLVD	LOS ANGELES, CA	90048
DILTZ, HENRY	PHOTOGRAPHER-SINGER	8777 LOOKOUT MOUNTAIN AVE	LOS ANGELES, CA	90046
DIMANT, ABEL	NEWS CORRESPONDENT	6730 N 26TH ST	ARLINGTON, VA	22213
DIMBLEBY, JONATHAN	AUTHOR	ROSEMAN, 8 POLAND ST	LONDON W1	ENGLAND
DIMEO, DIANE	CASTING DIRECTOR	8272 SUNSET BLVD	LOS ANGELES, CA	90046
DIMOCK, GIOIA L	PHOTOGRAPHER	6833 RADCLIFFE DR	ALEXANDRIA, VA	22307
DIMOND, DIANE	NEWS CORRESPONDENT	1776 "C" ST, NW	WASHINGTON, DC	20006
DIMSDALE, HOWARD	WRITER	2662 CARMAR DR	LOS ANGELES, CA	90046
DIMSDALE, JOHN H	NEWS CORRESPONDENT	499 S CAPITOL ST, SW	WASHINGTON, DC	20003
DIMTER, JEANNIE	ACTRESS	5000 LANKERSHIM BLVD #5	NORTH HOLLYWOOD, CA	91601
DINEHART, ALAN	WRITER	5040 TUJUNGA AVE #16	NORTH HOLLYWOOD, CA	91601

MARLENE DIETRICH

ALBERT N. DILLARD, JR.

BRADFORD DILLMAN

MATT DILLON

DION DI MUCCI

DONNA DIXON

TROY DONAHUE

TONY DOW

SANDY DUNCAN

DINEHART, JENNIFER WOOMER	NEWS CORRESPONDENT	3481 MILDRED DR	FALLS CHURCH, VA 22042
DINGLE, KAY	ACTRESS	8265 SUNSET BLVD #202	LOS ANGELES, CA 90069
DINGO WARRIOR	WRESTLER	WORLD CLASS WRESTLING	
		SOUTHWEST SPORTS, INC	
		DALLAS SPORTATORIUM	
		1000 S INDUSTRIAL BLVD	DALLAS, TX 75207
DINMAN, DICK	ACTOR	5255 BELLINGHAM AVE #215	NORTH HOLLYWOOD, CA 91607
DINMAN, DICK	CASTING DIRECTOR	1350 N HIGHLAND AVE #6	LOS ANGELES, CA 90028
DINNING, ACE	SINGER-GUITARIST	ROUTE #1, BOX 1	SUNRISE BCH, MO 65079
DINOME, JERRY	ACTOR	8500 WILSHIRE BLVD #506	BEVERLY HILLS, CA 90211
DINOTA, PAT	ACTRESS	1951 1/2 N ARGYLE AVE	HOLLYWOOD, CA 90068
DIO	ROCK & ROLL GROUP	18653 VENTURA BLVD #307	TARZANA, CA 91356
DIO, RONNIE JAMES	SINGER-SONGWRITER	5315 LAUREL CANYON BLVD #101	NORTH HOLLYWOOD, CA 91601
DIOGUARDI, PAUL C	COMPOSER-CONDUCTOR	11517 CUMPSTON ST #1	NORTH HOLLYWOOD, CA 91601
DION	SINGER-SONGWRITER	SEE - DI MUCCI, DION	
DION, COLLEEN	ACTRESS	ABC-TV NETWORK, "LOVING"	
		1330 AVE OF THE AMERICAS	NEW YORK, NY 10019
DIOS, KELLY	TV DIRECTOR	1234 WESTGATE AVE #2	LOS ANGELES, CA 90025
DIRE STRAITS, THE	ROCK & ROLL GROUP	DAMAGE MANAGEMENT, LTD	
		10 SOUTHWICK MEWS	LONDON W2 ENGLAND
DIRICKSON, BARBARA	ACTRESS	247 S BEVERLY DR #102	BEVERLY HILLS, CA 90210
DIRKSON, DOUGLAS	ACTOR	740 W 24TH ST #10	SAN PEDRO, CA 90731
DIRT, PHIL & THE DOZERS	ROCK & ROLL GROUP	COVER, 1425 N STAR RD	COLUMBUS, OH 43212
DIRTY WHITE BOY #1	WRESTLER	SEE - GRAPPLER, THE	
DISHY, BOB	ACTOR-WRITER	20 E 9TH ST	NEW YORK, NY 10003
DISKIN, JOY MATTHEWS	ACTRESS	4225 GLEN ALBYN DR	LOS ANGELES, CA 90065
DISKIN, PHIL	ACTOR	4225 GLEN ALBYN DR	LOS ANGELES, CA 90065
DISNEY, ROY E	WRITER-PRODUCER	4300 ARCOLA AVE	NORTH HOLLYWOOD, CA 91602
DISNEY, ROY P	ANIMATOR	11650 SUNSHINE TERR	STUDIO CITY, CA 91604
DISSELKAMP, HENRY B	NEWS CORRESPONDENT	2139 WISCONSIN AVE, NW	WASHINGTON, DC 20007
DISTAL, SACHA	SINGER	3 QUAI MALAQUAIS	PARIS 75006 FRANCE
DITTRICH, JOHN H	DRUMMER	141 NEESE DR #J-49	NASHVILLE, TN 37211
DIVE-O-LEAN	TRAMPOLINE ACT	HALL, 138 FROG HOLLOW RD	CHURCHVILLE, PA 18966
DIVINE	ACTOR-ACTRESS	HARRIS GLENN MILSTEAD	
		40 E 58TH ST	NEW YORK, NY 10022
DIVINE	ROCK & ROLL GROUP	B JAY MGMT, 2025 BROADWAY	NEW YORK, NY 10023
DIVINE, HOWARD	DRUMMER	630 W SWAN ST	SPRINGFIELD, MO 65807
DIVINYLS	ROCK & ROLL GROUP	ACROSS THE PACIFIC MANAGEMENT	
		THE WATERTOWER, UNIT #104	
		ROSEHILL ST	SYDNEY NSW 2016 AUSTRALIA
DIVISEK, BARBARA	CASTING DIRECTOR	2741 WOODHAVERN DR	LOS ANGELES, CA 90068
DIVISEK, KAREN	CASTING DIRECTOR	2741 WOODHAVEN DR	LOS ANGELES, CA 90068
DIXIE DOUGHBOYS, THE	C & W GROUP	380 LEXINGTON AVE #1119	NEW YORK, NY 10017
DIXIE DREGS, THE	ROCK & ROLL GROUP	5775 PEACHTREE DUNWOODY	ATLANTA, GA 30342
DIXIE HOTSHOTS, THE	C & W GROUP	LUTZ, 5625 "O" STREET BLDG	LINCOLN, NE 68510
DIXIE HUMMINGBIRDS, THE	VOCAL GROUP	LIEGNER, 1860 BROADWAY	NEW YORK, NY 10023
DIXIELAND RHYTHM KINGS, THE	DIXIELAND BAND	POST OFFICE BOX 20548	NEW YORK, NY 10025
DIXIT, NORMA	ACTRESS	24 WHITTON MANOR RD, ISLEWORTH	MIDDLESEX TW7 7NL ENGLAND
DIXON, ALICIA	ACTRESS	4185 ARCH DR #316	STUDIO CITY, CA 91604
DIXON, BEVERLY	ACTRESS	4919 COLDWATER CANYON AVE #6	SHERMAN OAKS, CA 91423
DIXON, BUZZ	WRITER	8955 BEVERLY BLVD	LOS ANGELES, CA 90048
DIXON, CHRISTOPHER P	FILM DIRECTOR	116 E 63RD ST	NEW YORK, NY 10021
DIXON, DAVID A	WRITER	8955 BEVERLY BLVD	LOS ANGELES, CA 90048
DIXON, DIANNE	WRITER	8955 BEVERLY BLVD	LOS ANGELES, CA 90048
DIXON, DON	SINGER-SONGWRITER	POST OFFICE BOX 237	CARRBORO, NC 27510
DIXON, DONNA	ACTRESS	EDRICK, 8955 NORMA PL	LOS ANGELES, CA 90069
DIXON, GLENN	ACTOR	3330 BARHAM BLVD #103	LOS ANGELES, CA 90068
DIXON, IVAN	ACTOR-DIRECTOR	3432 N MARGENGO AVE	ALTADENA, CA 91001
DIXON, JAMES	WRITER	8955 BEVERLY BLVD	LOS ANGELES, CA 90048
DIXON, JEANNE	PSYCHIC	1225 CONECTICUT AVE #411, NW	WASHINGTON, DC 20036
DIXON, JESSY	SINGER	2008 S YALE ST #F	SANTA ANA, CA 92704
DIXON, JOHN ROBERT	ACTOR	3800 BARHAM BLVD #303	LOS ANGELES, CA 90068
DIXON, MASON	C & W GROUP	SEE - MASON DIXON	
DIXON, PENNY C	WRITER-PRODUCER	555 W 57TH ST #1230	NEW YORK, NY 10019
DIXON, PETER	ACTOR	1350 EDGECLIFFE DR #10	LOS ANGELES, CA 90026
DIXON, PETER LEE	TV WRITER	31875 SEA LEVEL DR	MALIBU, CA 90265
DIXON, ROBERT	GUITARIST	300 BOOTH CALLOWAY #244	HURST, TX 76053
DIXON, SARAH H	WRITER-PRODUCER	31875 SEA LEVEL DR	MALIBU, CA 90265
DIXON, WILLIE & THE CHICAGO BLU	BLUES GROUP	CAMERON, 822 HILLGROVE AVE	WESTERN SPRINGS, IL 60558
DIXON HOUSE BAND	JAZZ BAND	POST OFFICE BOX 66558	SEATTLE, WA 98166
DIXONS, THE	GOSPEL GROUP	POST OFFICE BOX 614	HAZLEHURST, MS 39083
DIZON, JESSE	ACTOR-WRITER	807 CENTINELA AVE	SANTA MONICA, CA 90403
DJOKIC, MICHELLE	CELLIST	AFFILIATE ARTISTS, INC	
		37 W 65TH ST, 6TH FLOOR	NEW YORK, NY 10023
DJUPEDAL, BIRGIT	SOPRANO	PERLS, 7 W 96TH ST	NEW YORK, NY 10025
DMYTRYK, EDWARD	DIRECTOR	8729 LOOKOUT MOUNTAIN AVE	LOS ANGELES, CA 90046
DMYTRYK, MICHAEL J	DIRECTOR	DGA, 7950 SUNSET BLVD	LOS ANGELES, CA 90046
DO QUI, ROBERT	ACTOR	1529 S ELLSMERE AVE	LOS ANGELES, CA 90019
DO QUI, SHEA	ACTRESS	1717 N HIGHLAND AVE #414	LOS ANGELES, CA 90028
DOAN, MICHAEL F	NEWS CORRESPONDENT	3316 N 21ST AVE	ARLINGTON, VA 22207
DOANE, SAMANTHA	ACTRESS	20550 STAGG ST	CANOGA PARK, CA 91306
DOBAL, MICHAEL J	NEWS CORRESPONDENT	2139 WISCONSIN AVE, NW	WASHINGTON, DC 20007
DOBBINS, BILL	WRITER-BODYBUILDER	2012 VETERAN AVE	LOS ANGELES, CA 90025
DOBBINS, GARY LAWRENCE	GUITARIST	4841 LYNN DR	NASHVILLE, TN 37211
DOBBS, CHARLOTTE M	TV WRITER	1818 FAIRBURN AVE #303	LOS ANGELES, CA 90025

Name	Occupation	Address	City	Zip/Country
DOBBS, GREG	NEWS CORRESPONDENT	ABC NEWS, 8 CARBURTON ST	LONDON W1	ENGLAND
DOBBS, MATTIWILDA	SOPRANO	POST OFFICE BOX 27539	PHILADELPHIA, PA	19118
DOBBS, WILLIAM ARTHUR	TV DIRECTOR	4927 ESKRIDGE TERR, NW	WASHINGTON, DC	20016
DOBENI, PATSY	PIANIST	1801 BEECHWOOD AVE	NASHVILLE, TN	37212
DOBIE, ALAN	ACTOR	PONTUS, MOLASH	KENT CT4 8HW	ENGLAND
DOBISH, GAIL	SOPRANO	CAMI, 165 W 57TH ST	NEW YORK, NY	10019
DOBKIN, KATHERINE L	WRITER	555 W 57TH ST #1230	NEW YORK, NY	10019
DOBKIN, LAWRENCE	ACT-WRI-DIR	1787 OLD RANCH RD	LOS ANGELES, CA	90049
DOBKOWITZ, ROGER	TV PRODUCER	CBS TELEVISION NETWORK		
		"THE PRICE IS RIGHT"		
		7800 BEVERLY BLVD	LOS ANGELES, CA	90036
DOBRIN, DUILIO	CONDUCTOR	IAM, 10572 JASON LN	COLUMBIA, MD	21044
DOBROFSKY, NEAL H	WRITER	839 19TH ST	SANTA MONICA, CA	90403
DOBROW, JOELLE	TV DIRECTOR-PRODUCER	1615 REDCLIFF AVE	LOS ANGELES, CA	90026
DOBSON, BRIDGET	TV WRITER-PRODUCER	221 E CONSTANCE AVE	SANTA BARBARA, CA	93105
DOBSON, JAMES	ACTOR	8464 COLE CREST DR	LOS ANGELES, CA	90046
DOBSON, JEROME	TV WRITER-PRODUCER	221 E CONSTANCE AVE	SANTA BARBARA, CA	93105
DOBSON, JIMMY	WRITER-AUTHOR	3601 HAYVENHURST AVE	ENCINO, CA	91436
DOBSON, KEVIN	ACTOR	11930 KREDELL ST	STUDIO CITY, CA	91604
DOBTCHEFF, VERNON	ACTOR	MC REDDIE, 91 REGENT ST	LONDON W1	ENGLAND
DOBYNS, LLOYD	BROADCAST JOURNALIST	300 CENTRAL PARK W	NEW YORK, NY	10024
DOCHERTY, JAMES J	SCREENWRITER	8955 BEVERLY BLVD	LOS ANGELES, CA	90048
DOCHERTY, RICH	DIRECTOR	40 W 86TH ST #2-D	NEW YORK, NY	10024
DOCHTERMANN, RUDOLPH	WRITER-PRODUCER	12801 MARTHA ST	NORTH HOLLYWOOD, CA	91607
DOCHTERMANN, WOLFRAM J	DIRECTOR	46 SANTO DOMINGO DR	RANCHO MIRAGE, CA	92270
DOCKERY, JOHN	GUITARIST	111 OLD HICKORY BLVD #207	NASHVILLE, TN	37221
DOCKEY, RUDY	CLOWN	2701 COTTAGE WY #14	SACRAMENTO, CA	95825
DOCKSTADER, DONNA	CASTING DIRECTOR	MCA/UNIVERSAL STUDIOS, INC		
		100 UNIVERSAL CITY PLAZA	UNIVERSAL CITY, CA	91608
DOCTOR & THE MEDICS	ROCK & ROLL GROUP	53 GREEK ST	LONDON W1	ENGLAND
DOCTOROW, E L	SCREENWRITER	8955 BEVERLY BLVD	LOS ANGELES, CA	90048
DOCTORS, THE	ROCK & ROLL GROUP	VARIETY ARTISTS INTL, INC		
		9073 NEMO ST, 3RD FLOOR	LOS ANGELES, CA	90069
DODA, CAROL	DANCER	THE CONDOR CLUB		
		300 COLUMBUS AVE	SAN FRANCISCO, CA	94133
DODD, BARBARA	ACTRESS	8322 BEVERLY BLVD #202	LOS ANGELES, CA	90048
DODD, ED	CARTOONIST	POST OFFICE BOX 760	GAINESVILLE, GA	30503
DODD, KEN	COMEDIAN-SINGER	76 THOMAS LN, KNOTTY ASH	LIVERPOOL	ENGLAND
DODDS, ROBERT	ACTOR	123 N MAPLE ST #D	BURBANK, CA	91505
DODGE, CHARLES S	NEWS CORRESPONDENT	9214 THREE OAKS DR	SILVER SPRING, MD	20901
DODGE, RICHARD	DIRECTOR	2254 N GOWER ST	LOS ANGELES, CA	90068
DODGE, SUE ELLEN	SINGER	6750 W 75TH ST, MARKADE 75		
		BUILDING #2-A	OVERLAND PARK, KS	66204
DODSON, DENNIS	BODYGUARD	2801 MEADOW LARK DR	SAN DIEGO, CA	92123
DODSON, JACK	ACTOR	3800 BARHAM BLVD #303	LOS ANGELES, CA	90068
DODSON, JAMES	GUITARIST	3111 LAUREL FOREST DR	NASHVILLE, TN	37214
DODSON, RICHARD E	NEWS CORRESPONDENT	NBC-TV, NEWS DEPARTMENT		
		4001 NEBRASKA AVE, NW	WASHINGTON, DC	20016
DODY, SANFORD	WRITER	555 W 57TH ST #1230	NEW YORK, NY	10019
DOE, CHARLES	NEWS CORRESPONDENT	1901 WYCOMING AVE #57, NW	WASHINGTON, DC	20009
DOE, KELLY	CARTOONIST	POST OFFICE 5533	SAN JOSE, CA	95190
DOEBELE, CONSTANCE J	NEWS CORRESPONDENT	400 N CAPITOL ST, NW	WASHINGTON, DC	20001
DOEL, FRANCES M	WRITER	11611 CHENAULT ST #219	LOS ANGELES, CA	90049
DOERNER, WILLIAM R	WRITER-EDITOR	TIME/TIME & LIFE BLDG		
		ROCKEFELLER CENTER	NEW YORK, NY	10020
DOERR, BOBBY	BASEBALL	33705 ILLAMO AGNESS RD	AGNESS, OR	97406
DOESE, HELENA	SOPRANO	COLBERT, 111 W 57TH ST	NEW YORK, NY	10019
DOGGETT, ENID A	NEWS CORRESPONDENT	1825 "K" ST, NW	WASHINGTON, DC	20006
DOGGETT'S, BILL, HONKY TONK COM	ROCK & ROLL GROUP	OLDIES, 5218 ALMONT ST	LOS ANGELES, CA	90032
DOGGY STYLE	ROCK & ROLL GROUP	DXSX, 634 PINEHURST AVE	PLACENTIA, CA	92670
DOHENY, LAWRENCE	TV DIRECTOR	38 COLGATE DR	PLAINVIEW, NY	11803
DOHERTY, CARROLL	NEWS CORRESPONDENT	3220 CONNECTICUT AVE, NW	WASHINGTON, DC	20009
DOHERTY, MARIANNE	ACTRESS	8350 SANTA MONICA BLVD #103	LOS ANGELES, CA	90069
DOHERTY, PETE	WRESTLER	POST OFFICE BOX 3859	STAMFORD, CT	06905
DOHERTY, ROBERT P	NEWS CORRESPONDENT	817 W 38TH ST	BALTIMORE, MD	21211
DOHERTY, SAHM	PHOTOGRAPHER	TIME/TIME & LIFE BLDG		
		ROCKEFELLER CENTER	NEW YORK, NY	10020
DOIG, DONALD	TENOR	431 S DEARBORN ST #1504	CHICAGO, IL	60605
DOKKEN	ROCK & ROLL GROUP	Q TIME, 80 WARWICK GARDENS	LONDON W14 8PR	ENGLAND
DOKOFF, BARRY M	CINEMATOGRAPHER	31770 BROAD BEACH RD	MALIBU, CA	90265
DOKOVSKA, PAVLINA	PIANIST	POST OFFICE BOX 20548	NEW YORK, NY	10025
DOKTOR, PAUL	MUSICIAN	215 W 88TH ST	NEW YORK, NY	10024
DOLAN, ANTHONY	JOURNALIST	1600 PENNSYLVANIA AVE, NW	WASHINGTON, DC	20500
DOLAN, DON	ACTOR	14228 EMELITA ST	VAN NUYS, CA	91401
DOLAN, JACK	NEWS CORRESPONDENT	1701 MASSACHUSETTS AVE, NW	WASHINGTON, DC	20036
DOLAN, JAMES M, JR	NEWS CORRESPONDENT	156 "F" ST, SE	WASHINGTON, DC	20003
DOLAN, JULIE	ACTRESS	8721 SUNSET BLVD #103	LOS ANGELES, CA	90069
DOLAN, MARY ANNE	COLUMNIST	UNIVERSAL PRESS SYNDICATE		
		4900 MAIN ST, 9TH FLOOR	KANSAS CITY, MO	62114
DOLAN, PATRICK FRANCIS	NEWS CORRESPONDENT	6266 MELODY LN	DALLAS, TX	75231
DOLAN, TRENT	ACTOR	1408 RISING GLEN RD	LOS ANGELES, CA	90069
DOLBY, THOMAS	SINGER-SONGWRITER	20 MANCHESTER SQ	LONDON W1	ENGLAND
DOLEMAN, GUY	ACTOR	9165 SUNSET BLVD #202	LOS ANGELES, CA	90069
DOLENZ, MICKEY	ACT-MUS-PROD	SEIFERT, 8-A BRUNSWICK GARDENS	LONDON W8	ENGLAND

Name	Occupation	Address	City	Code
DOLEYS, MARY LYNNE	FRENCH HORNIST	180 WALLACE RD #E-10	NASHVILLE, TN	37211
DOLIN, ELLIOTT D	GUITARIST	POST OFFICE BOX 150307	NASHVILLE, TN	37215
DOLIN, GERALD	COMPOSER	5961 CHULA VISTA WY #5	LOS ANGELES, CA	90068
DOLL, BABY	WRESTLING VALET	SEE - BABY DOLL		
DOLL, CHRISTOPHER	TV PRODUCER	WHITE BRIARS, SLINFOLD, HORSHAM	SUSSEX RH13 7RP	ENGLAND
DOLLAGHAN, PATRICK	ACTOR	7528 1/8 LEXINGTON AVE	LOS ANGELES, CA	90046
DOLLAR, JOHN	GUITARIST	42-D MUSIC SQUARE W	NASHVILLE, TN	37203
DOLLINGER, STEPHEN	DIRECTOR	4734 BALBOA AVE	ENCINO, CA	91316
DOLLISON, SONJA D	NEWS CORRESPONDENT	NBC-TV, NEWS DEPARTMENT		
		4001 NEBRASKA AVE, NW	WASHINGTON, DC	20016
DOLLY SISTERS, THE	AERIAL TRIO	HALL, 138 FROG HOLLOW RD	CHURCHVILLE, PA	18966
DOLMAN, ROBERT H	TV WRITER	4716 INDIANOLA WY	LA CANADA, CA	91011
DOLMETSCH, CARL	VIOLINIST	JESSES, HASLEMERE	SURREY GU27	ENGLAND
DOLNY, JOSEPH J	COMPOSER	5116 CAROLI LN	LA CANADA, CA	91011
DOLPHIN, JOSEPH	ACTOR	698 W END AVE	NEW YORK, NY	10025
DOLTER, GERALD	BARITONE	CAMI, 165 W 57TH ST	NEW YORK, NY	10019
DOMBASLE, ARIELLE	ACTRESS	KOHNER, 9169 SUNSET BLVD	LOS ANGELES, CA	90069
DOMBROSKI, JOE	PHOTOGRAPHER	62 S HOWELL AVE	FARMINGVILLE, NY	11738
DOMBROWSKI, CATHY H	NEWS CORRESPONDENT	14120 HUCKLEBERRY LN	SILVER SPRING, MD	20906
DOMENICO, TONDO	CONDUCTOR	POST OFFICE BOX 131	SPRINGFIELD, VA	22150
DOMINELLO, LAWRENCE A	COMPOSER	1219 N COLUMBUS AVE #C	GLENDALE, CA	91202
DOMINGO, PLACIDO	TENOR	3 TROY CT, KENSINGTON HIGH	LONDON W8	ENGLAND
DOMINGUEZ, ALBERT	PIANIST	CPS, 34 66TH PL	LONG BEACH, CA	90803
DOMINGUEZ, RUBEN	TENOR	61 W 62ND ST #6-F	NEW YORK, NY	10023
DOMINO, FATS	SINGER-PIANIST	5525 MARAIS ST	NEW ORLEANS, LA	70117
DOMOKOS, CHARLES A	WRITER	21205 LESSEN ST #4	CHATSWORTH, CA	91311
DON, CARL	ACTOR	333 W 57TH ST	NEW YORK, NY	10019
DON & DEWEY	VOCAL DUO	OLDIES, 5218 ALMONT ST	LOS ANGELES, CA	90032
DONAHOE, TERRY	ACTRESS	ABC-TV, "ONE LIFE TO LIVE"		
		1330 AVE OF THE AMERICAS	NEW YORK, NY	10019
DONAHOE, WALTER J, JR	NEWS CORRESPONDENT	NBC-TV, NEWS DEPARTMENT		
		4001 NEBRASKA AVE, NW	WASHINGTON, DC	20016
DONAHUE, BARBARA L S	DIRECTOR	370 ROUND HILL RD	GREENWICH, CT	06830
DONAHUE, CHRISTINE	SOPRANO	LEW, 204 W 10TH ST	NEW YORK, NY	10014
DONAHUE, ELINOR	ACTRESS	4525 LEMP AVE	NORTH HOLLYWOOD, CA	91602
DONAHUE, JAMES	ACTOR	BALDWIN, 501 5TH AVE	NEW YORK, NY	10017
DONAHUE, MARILOU	SOPRANO	KAY, 58 W 58TH ST	NEW YORK, NY	10019
DONAHUE, MARY ANN	WRITER	555 W 57TH ST #1230	NEW YORK, NY	10019
DONAHUE, PHIL	TV HOST-AUTHOR	300 CENTRAL PARK W	NEW YORK, NY	10024
DONAHUE, TROY	ACTOR	9255 SUNSET BLVD #510	LOS ANGELES, CA	90069
DONALD, FLOYD L	NEWS CORRESPONDENT	4461 CONNECTICUT AVE, NW	WASHINGTON, DC	20006
DONALD, JONATHAN	WRITER	555 W 57TH ST #1230	NEW YORK, NY	10019
DONALD, JULIANA	ACTRESS	10100 SANTA MONICA BLVD #1600	LOS ANGELES, CA	90067
DONALD, WILLIAM D	NEWS CORRESPONDENT	5426 ALTA VISTA RD	BETHESDA, MD	20910
DONALDSON, FREDERICK	TENOR	61 W 62ND ST #6-F	NEW YORK, NY	10023
DONALDSON, HERBERT	COMPOSER	14409 VALLEY VISTA BLVD	SHERMAN OAKS, CA	91403
DONALDSON, JAMES V	NEWS CORRESPONDENT	5878 WOOD FLOWER CT	BURKE, VA	22015
DONALDSON, SAM	JOURNALIST	11404 FAIRFAX DR	GREAT FALLS, VA	22066
DONALLY, ANDREW	FILM PRODUCER	36 WELLINGTON CT		
		WELLINGTON RD		
		SAINT JOHN'S RD	LONDON NW8	ENGLAND
DONALSON, ELYSE	ACTRESS	5330 LANKERSHIM BLVD #210	NORTH HOLLYWOOD, CA	91601
DONAT, PETER	ACTOR	POST OFFICE BOX 5617	BEVERLY HILLS, CA	90210
DONAT, ZDZISLAWA	SOPRANO	CAMI, 165 W 57TH ST	NEW YORK, NY	10019
DONATI, WILLIAM	COMPOSER	11550 KLING ST	NORTH HOLLYWOOD, CA	91602
DONATI, WILLIAM R	DIRECTOR	106 MAC DOUGAL ST #15	NEW YORK, NY	10012
DONATO, JUDITH A	WRITER	555 W 57TH ST #1230	NEW YORK, NY	10019
DONDERO, PAUL	MUSICIAN	POST OFFICE BOX 9388	STANFORD, CA	94305
DONEN, STANLEY	FILM DIRECTOR	9626 OAK PASS RD	BEVERLY HILLS, CA	90210
DONFELD	COSTUME DESIGNER	2900 HUTTON DR	BEVERLY HILLS, CA	90210
DONHAM, DAVID	ACTOR	8831 SUNSET BLVD #402	LOS ANGELES, CA	90069
DONIAN, BRIAN	TV CRITIC	POST OFFICE BOX 500	WASHINGTON, DC	20044
DONIGER, JACOB L	NEWS CORRESPONDENT	1825 "K" ST, NW	WASHINGTON, DC	20006
DONIGER, WALTER	WRITER-PRODUCER	555 HUNTLEY DR	LOS ANGELES, CA	90048
DONLAN, THOMAS G	NEWS CORRESPONDENT	6516 JAY MILLER DR	FALLS CHURCH, VA	22041
DONLAN, YOLANDE	ACTRESS-WRITER	11 MELLINA PL	LONDON NW8	ENGLAND
DONLEY, JOHN	NEWS CORRESPONDENT	NBC-TV, NEWS DEPARTMENT		
		4001 NEBRASKA AVE, NW	WASHINGTON, DC	20016
DONLEY, JOHN	TV WRITER	127 S LARCHMONT BLVD	LOS ANGELES, CA	90004
DONLEY, ROBERT M	WRITER	8955 BEVERLY BLVD	LOS ANGELES, CA	90048
DONNE, GEOFFREY	ACTOR	9165 SUNSET BLVD #202	LOS ANGELES, CA	90069
DONNELL, GORDON	WRITER	8955 BEVERLY BLVD	LOS ANGELES, CA	90048
DONNELL, JEFF	ACTRESS	1326 N HAYWORTH AVE #15	LOS ANGELES, CA	90046
DONNELL, KATHY	SCREENWRITER	1340 SANBORN AVE	LOS ANGELES, CA	90027
DONNELLEY, ALEX	ACTRESS	9744 WILSHIRE BLVD #206	BEVERLY HILLS, CA	90212
DONNELLY, DEIRDRE	WRITER	8955 BEVERLY BLVD	LOS ANGELES, CA	90048
DONNELLY, DENNIS M	DIRECTOR	9777 WILSHIRE BLVD #600	BEVERLY HILLS, CA	90212
DONNELLY, HARRISON H	NEWS CORRESPONDENT	415 LINCOLN AVE	TAKOMA PARK, MD	20912
DONNELLY, KEVIN P	DIRECTOR	4834 SALEM VILLAGE PL	CULVER CITY, CA	90230
DONNELLY, LIZA	CARTOONIST	POST OFFICE BOX 4203	NEW YORK, NY	10017
DONNELLY, PHILIP	GUITARIST	324 BLACKMAN RD	NASHVILLE, TN	37211
DONNELLY, SALLY B	NEWS REPORTER	TIME/TIME & LIFE BLDG		
		ROCKEFELLER CENTER	NEW YORK, NY	10020
DONNELLY, SHARON	NEWS CORRESPONDENT	1301 PENNSYLVANIA AVE, NW	WASHINGTON, DC	20004
DONNELLY, THOMAS	NEWS CORRESPONDENT	4442 GREENWICH PARKWAY, NW	WASHINGTON, DC	20007

of THE AUTOGRAPH DEALERS' DIRECTORY*

3rd Edition

for information write:

Georgia Terry
840 N.E. Cochran Ave.
Gresham, Oregon 97030
(503) 667-0950

Name	Occupation	Address	City	Zip/Country
DONNELLY, THOMAS M	SCREENWRITER	8955 BEVERLY BLVD	LOS ANGELES, CA	90048
DONNELLY, TIM	ACTOR	4092 FARMDALE AVE	STUDIO CITY, CA	91604
DONNER, CHICK	GUITARIST	999 VALLEY BLVD	ELYRIA, OH	44035
DONNER, CLIVE	FILM DIRECTOR	1466 N KINGS RD	LOS ANGELES, CA	90069
DONNER, JILL SHERMAN	TV WRITER	1888 CENTURY PARK E #1107	LOS ANGELES, CA	90067
DONNER, JORN	DIRECTOR	POHJOISRANTA 12	00170 HELSINKI 17	FINLAND
DONNER, RICHARD	FILM DIRECTOR	1444 FOREST KNOLL DR	LOS ANGELES, CA	90069
DONNER, ROBERT	ACTOR	4031 HAYVENHURST AVE	ENCINO, CA	91436
DONNO, EDDY	DIRECTOR	5051 BILOXI AVE	NORTH HOLLYWOOD, CA	91601
DONOFF, MARTIN S	TV WRITER	555 W 57TH ST #1230	NEW YORK, NY	10019
DONOGHUE, CAROLE J	NEWS CORRESPONDENT	7249 PARKWOOD CT #303	FALLS CHURCH, VA	22042
DONOGHUE, MARY AGNES	WRITER	427 ALTA AVE	SANTA MONICA, CA	90402
DONOGHUE, WILLIAM	COLUMNIST	TRIBUNE MEDIA SERVICES		
		64 E CONCORD ST	ORLANDO, FL	32801
DONOHOE, PETER	PIANIST	5720 MOSHOLU AVE #300	RIVERDALE, NY	10471
DONOHUE, CHRISTINE W	NEWS CORRESPONDENT	13906 CRISTO CT	CENTERVILLE, VA	22020
DONOHUE, DR PAUL	COLUMNIST	NEWS AMERICA SYNDICATE		
		1703 KAISER AVE	IRVINE, CA	92714
DONOHUE, ROBERT P	TV DIRECTOR	WJZ-TV, TELEVISION HILL	BALTIMORE, MD	21211
DONOSKY, LEAH	NEWS CORRESPONDENT	2117 1/2 "O" ST, NW	WASHINGTON, DC	20037
DONOVAN	SINGER-SONGWRITER	POST OFFICE BOX 472	LONDON SW7 2QB	ENGLAND
DONOVAN, ARLENE	FILM PRODUCER	ICM, 40 W 57TH ST	NEW YORK, NY	10019
DONOVAN, ERIN	ACTRESS	15055 MC KENDREE AVE	PACIFIC PALISADES, CA	90272
DONOVAN, KING	ACTOR-DIRECTOR	200 E 66TH ST	NEW YORK, NY	10021
DONOVAN, LISA	ACTRESS	13111 VENTURA BLVD #204	STUDIO CITY, CA	91604
DONOVAN, LISA ANN	SINGER-COMPOSER	927 18TH ST #E	SANTA MONICA, CA	90403
DONOVAN, LISA L	ACTRESS	10707 CAMARILLO ST #308	NORTH HOLLYWOOD, CA	91602
DONOVAN, MARK V	WRITER-EDITOR	PEOPLE/TIME & LIFE BLDG		
		ROCKEFELLER CENTER	NEW YORK, NY	10020
DONOVAN, MARTHA I	NEWS CORRESPONDENT	1755 S JEFFERSON DAVIS HWY	ARLINGTON, VA	22202
DONOVAN, MARTIN	WRITER	10871 VICENZA WY	LOS ANGELES, CA	90077
DONOVAN, TATE	ACTOR	CONTEMPORARY ARTISTS		
		132 S LASKY DR	BEVERLY HILLS, CA	90212
DONOVAN, TIMOTHY G	NEWS CORRESPONDENT	9804 NATICK RD	BURKE, VA	22015
DONOVAN, TOM	DIRECTOR-PRODUCER	650 PARK AVE	NEW YORK, NY	10021
DONOVAN, TOM	WRITER	8955 BEVERLY BLVD	LOS ANGELES, CA	90048
DONOVAN, WARDE	ACTOR	10850 RIVERSIDE DR #505	NORTH HOLLYWOOD, CA	91602
DONSKOI, MARK	DIRECTOR	UNION OF CINEMATOGRAPHISTS		
		USSR, 14 VASSILIEVSKAYA UL	MOSCOW	USSR
DONVAN, JOHN	NEWS CORRESPONDENT	ABC NEWS, 8 CARBURTON ST	LONDON W1	ENGLAND
DOOCY, STEPHEN J	NEWS CORRESPONDENT	NBC-TV, NEWS DEPARTMENT		
		4001 NEBRASKA AVE, NW	WASHINGTON, DC	20016
DOOHAN, ANITA	WRITER	8955 BEVERLY BLVD	LOS ANGELES, CA	90048
DOOHAN, JAMES	ACTOR	POST OFFICE BOX 1100	BURBANK, CA	91507
DOOLAN, TRISH	ACTRESS	419 WINDSOR PL	OCEANSIDE, NY	11572
DOOLEY, J ROSCOE	GUITARIST	336 CANE RIDGE RD #209	ANTIOCH, TN	37013
DOOLEY, JEFFREY	COUNTERTENO	LIEBERMAN, 11 RIVERSIDE DR	NEW YORK, NY	10023
DOOLEY, MELANIE	NEWS CORRESPONDENT	1231 25TH ST, NW	WASHINGTON, DC	20520
DOOLEY, PAUL	SCREENWRITER	555 W 57TH ST #1230	NEW YORK, NY	10019
DOOLEY, PAUL	SINGER-SONGWRITER	MORGAN COMMUNICATIONS		
		301 W 53RD ST	NEW YORK, NY	10019
DOOLEY, RAE	ACTRESS	HARRIS AVE, RD #1	LINCOLN, RI	02865
DOOLEY, RAY	ACTOR	AFFILIATE ARTISTS, INC		
		37 W 65TH ST, 6TH FLOOR	NEW YORK, NY	10023
DOOLEY, WILLIAM	BARITONE	CAMI, 165 W 57TH ST	NEW YORK, NY	10019
DOOLITTLE, ROBERT	ACTOR	1021 N EDINBURGH AVE #2	LOS ANGELES, CA	90046
DOONICAN, VAL	SINGER	B LEE, 1 GODSTONE RD		
DOPPELT, JACK C	WRITER	555 W 57TH ST #1230	NEW YORK, NY	10019
DOPPELT, MARGERY	WRITER	2325 HOLLYRIDGE DR	LOS ANGELES, CA	90068
DOR, KARIN	ACTRESS	TSINTAUERSTRASSE 80	D-8000 MUNICH 82	WEST GERMANY
DORAN, ANN	ACTRESS	1610 N ORANGE GROVE AVE	LOS ANGELES, CA	90046
DORAN, JOHN	TV WRITER-PRODUCER	GRAMPIAN TELEVISION PLC		
		QUEEN'S CROSS	ABERDEEN	SCOTLAND
DORAN, MATT H	COMPOSER	11432 CHENAULT ST	LOS ANGELES, CA	90049
DORAN, PHILLIP G	TV WRITER	311 OCEAN AVE #302	SANTA MONICA, CA	90402
DORAN, TAKAYO	ACTRESS	10590 WILSHIRE BLVD #1601	LOS ANGELES, CA	90024
DORATI, ANTAL	CONDUCTOR	CAMI, 165 W 57TH ST	NEW YORK, NY	10019
DORDI, PATRIZIA	SOPRANO	CAMI, 165 W 57TH ST	NEW YORK, NY	10019
DORE, MARGARET J	NEWS CORRESPONDENT	4461 CONNECTICUT AVE, NW	WASHINGTON, DC	20008
DORE, ROBERT E	NEWS CORRESPONDENT	11200 LOCKWOOD DR	SILVER SPRING, MD	20901
DOREMUS, JENNIFER	NEWS CORRESPONDENT	1455 "Q" ST, NW	WASHINGTON, DC	20009
DORES, JURGEN	ACTOR	ABC-TV, "GENERAL HOSPITAL"		
		1438 N GOWER ST	LOS ANGELES, CA	90028
DORFF, MATTHEW	WRITER	8955 BEVERLY BLVD	LOS ANGELES, CA	90048
DORFMAN, ANDREA	NEWS REPORTER	TIME/TIME & LIFE BLDG		
		ROCKEFELLER CENTER	NEW YORK, NY	10020
DORFMAN, DAN	COLUMNIST	NEWS AMERICA SYNDICATE		
		1703 KAISER AVE	IRVINE, CA	92714
DORFMAN, SID	TV WRITER	8955 BEVERLY BLVD	LOS ANGELES, CA	90048
DORFMAN, STANLEY	DIRECTOR-PRODUCER	2556 DEARBORN DR	LOS ANGELES, CA	90068
DORFMAN, STEVEN	TV WRITER	JEOPARDY, 1541 N VINE ST	HOLLYWOOD, CA	90028
DORFSMAN, LOUIS	BROADCAST EXECUTIVE	80 STATION RD	GREAT NECK, NY	11023
DORI, MI	VIOLINIST	ICM, 40 W 57TH ST	NEW YORK, NY	10019
DORIN, PHOEBE	ACTRESS-WRITER	8857 WONDERLAND AVE	LOS ANGELES, CA	90046
DORIO, RICK	WRITER	8955 BEVERLY BLVD	LOS ANGELES, CA	90048

Name	Occupation	Address	City/State	Zip
DORKIN, MICHAEL	ACTOR	530 PARK AVE	NEW YORK, NY	10021
DORLAND, GILBERT N	WRITER	8955 BEVERLY BLVD	LOS ANGELES, CA	90048
DORMAN, MARY	NEWS CORRESPONDENT	NBC-TV, NEWS DEPARTMENT		
		4001 NEBRASKA AVE, NW	WASHINGTON, DC	20016
DORMAN, RANDY	GUITARIST	4621 WOODSIDE DR	OLD HICKORY, TN	37138
DORN, DOLORES	ACTRESS	9200 SUNSET BLVD #909	LOS ANGELES, CA	90069
DORN, MICHAEL	ACTOR	9300 WILSHIRE BLVD #410	BEVERLY HILLS, CA	90212
DORN, RUDI	TV DIRECTOR	31 ASHGROVE PL	DON MILLS, ONT	CANADA
DORNAN, DON	TV DIRECTOR	15459 DICKENS ST	SHERMAN OAKS, CA	91403
DORNE, PHYLLIS	ACTRESS	6290 SUNSET BLVD #326	LOS ANGELES, CA	90028
DORNEMANN, JOAN	CONDUCTOR	FINELL, 155 W 68TH ST	NEW YORK, NY	10023
DORNEY, DICK	MUSICIAN	817 MARLIN PASS	MADISON, TN	37115
DORNING, STACY	ACTRESS	CCA MGMT, 4 CT LODGE		
		48 SLOANE SQ	LONDON SW1	ENGLAND
DORNISCH, WILLIAM PAUL	FILM EDITOR	150 S BARRINGTON AVE #1	LOS ANGELES, CA	90049
DOROCHER, ROCKY STONE	GUITARIST	4500 SPENCER HWY	PASADENA, CA	77504
DOROUGH, LORI	MODEL	POST OFFICE BOX 7211	MOUNTAIN VIEW, CA	94043
DOROUGH, ROBERT L	COMPOSER	RURAL DELIVERY #1, BOX 1514	MT BETHEL, PA	18343
DORR, DAVID	ACTOR	LESTER, 110 W 40TH ST	NEW YORK, NY	10018
DORRIS, DAVID T	MUSIC ARRANGER	5028 REGENT DR	NASHVILLE, TN	37220
DORROUGH, HENRY EDGAR, JR	GUITARIST	3813 BEDFORD AVE	NASHVILLE, TN	37215
DORSEY, JENNIFER	NEWS CORRESPONDENT	3829 WARREN ST, NW	WASHINGTON, DC	20016
DORSEY, JOE	ACTOR	9255 SUNSET BLVD #1105	LOS ANGELES, CA	90069
DORSEY, JOHN	DIRECTOR-PRODUCER	11912 RIVERSIDE DR #11	NORTH HOLLYWOOD, CA	91607
DORSEY, REGINALD T	ACTOR	3800 BARHAM BLVD #303	LOS ANGELES, CA	90068
DORSEY, TOMMY GLENN	PIANIST	146 GRASSLAND DR	GALLATIN, TN	37066
DORSO, RICHARD J	WRITER	1100 N ALTA LOMA RD	LOS ANGELES, CA	90069
DORST, SALLY	NEWS REPORTER	DISCOVER/TIME & LIFE BLDG		
		ROCKEFELLER CENTER	NEW YORK, NY	10020
DORTORT, DAVID	WRITER-PRODUCER	133 UDINE WY	LOS ANGELES, CA	90077
DORWARD, KENNETH L	TV WRITER	8955 BEVERLY BLVD	LOS ANGELES, CA	90048
DOSS, TERI LYNN	MODEL	POST OFFICE BOX 7211	MOUNTAIN VIEW, CA	94043
DOSTER, BUCKY	GUITARIST	2313 E HILL DR	MADISON, TN	37115
DOSTER, MICHAEL THOMAS	GUITARIST	1005 ESTES RD	NASHVILLE, TN	37215
DOTRICE, KAREN	ACTRESS	ICM, 388-396 OXFORD ST	LONDON W1	ENGLAND
DOTRICE, MICHELE	ACTRESS	CCA MGMT, 4 CT LODGE		
		48 SLOANE SQ	LONDON SW1	ENGLAND
DOTRICE, ROY	ACTOR	HUTTON, 200 FULHAM RD	LONDON SW10	ENGLAND
DOTSON, BOB	NEWS CORRESPONDENT	NBC-TV, NEWS DEPARTMENT		
		30 ROCKEFELLER PLAZA	NEW YORK, NY	10112
DOTTEN, BOB	MUSICIAN	POST OFFICE BOX 456	LA VERGNE, TN	37086
DOTTIE MAE	C & W GROUP	SWALIK, 448 SCHOOL ST	WOODBRIDGE, NJ	07095
DOUBET, STEVE	ACTOR	1629 CALIFORNIA AVE	SANTA MONICA, CA	90403
DOUBLE DARE	ROCK & ROLL GROUP	41 BRITAIN ST #200	TORONTO, ONT	CANADA
DOUBLE IMAGE	JAZZ GROUP	509 MADISON AVE #512	NEW YORK, NY	10022
DOUBLEDAY, FRANK	ACTOR	5061 ELMWOOD AVE	LOS ANGELES, CA	90004
DOUBRAVA, DAVE	NEWS CORRESPONDENT	609 MASSACHUSETTS AVE, NE	WASHINGTON, DC	20002
DOUCETTE, J DUKE	ACTOR	POST OFFICE BOX 657	MONTAUK, NY	11954
DOUCETTE, JEFF	ACTOR	1315 N SIERRA BONITA AVE	LOS ANGELES, CA	90046
DOUCETTE, JOHN	ACTOR	POST OFFICE BOX 252	CABAZON, CA	92230
DOUCHETTE, MICHAEL	GUITARIST	POST OFFICE BOX 1183	HENDERSONVILLE, TN	37075
DOUDT, E M	DIRECTOR	DGA, 110 W 57TH ST	NEW YORK, NY	10019
DOUG & THE SLUGS	ROCK & ROLL GROUP	41 BRITAIN ST #200	TORONTO, ONT	CANADA
DOUGAN, MICHAEL	CRITIC	110 5TH ST	SAN FRANCISCO, CA	94103
DOUGHERTY, DOUG	TV DIRECTOR	4219 W OLIVE AVE #327	BURBANK, CA	91505
DOUGHERTY, JEANNE	ACTRESS	3239 BENNETT DR	LOS ANGELES, CA	90068
DOUGHERTY, LEE	SOPRANO	POST OFFICE BOX U	REDDING, CT	06875
DOUGHERTY, MARGOT	NEWS REPORTER	LIFE/TIME & LIFE BLDG		
		ROCKEFELLER CENTER	NEW YORK, NY	10020
DOUGHERTY, MARION	CASTING DIRECTOR	TBS, 4000 WARNER BLVD	BURBANK, CA	91522
DOUGHERTY, PAUL G	NEWS CORRESPONDENT	400 N CAPITOL ST, NW	WASHINGTON, DC	20001
DOUGHERTY, STEVEN	WRITER-EDITOR	TIME & PEOPLE MAGAZINE		
		TIME & LIFE BUILDING		
		ROCKEFELLER CENTER	NEW YORK, NY	10020
DOUGLAS, ANDREW B	NEWS CORRESPONDENT	7016 EXFAIR RD	BETHESDA, MD	20817
DOUGLAS, ANGELA	ACTRESS	ICM, 388-396 OXFORD ST	LONDON W1	ENGLAND
DOUGLAS, CHARLIE	SINGER	TAYLOR, 2401 12TH AVE S	NASHVILLE, TN	37204
DOUGLAS, DAMON	ACTOR	10000 RIVERSIDE DR #3	TOLUCA LAKE, CA	91602
DOUGLAS, DIANA	ACTRESS	305 MADISON AVE #4419	NEW YORK, NY	10165
DOUGLAS, DONNA	ACTRESS-SINGER	POST OFFICE BOX 49455	LOS ANGELES, CA	90049
DOUGLAS, ERIC	ACTOR	7060 HOLLYWOOD BLVD #610	LOS ANGELES, CA	90028
DOUGLAS, GORDON	FILM DIRECTOR	6600 W 6TH ST	LOS ANGELES, CA	90048
DOUGLAS, JACK	ACTOR	18-20 YORK BLDGS, ADELPHI	LONDON WC2N 6JY	ENGLAND
DOUGLAS, JACK	ACTOR-COMEDIAN	PETER PRICHARD, LTD		
		118 BEAUFORT ST, CHELSEA	LONDON SW3 6BU	ENGLAND
DOUGLAS, JACK	WRITER	555 W 57TH ST #1230	NEW YORK, NY	10019
DOUGLAS, JERRY	ACTOR	11753 MAYFIELD AVE	LOS ANGELES, CA	90049
DOUGLAS, JERRY	DOBROIST	502 WESLEY AVE	NASHVILLE, TN	37207
DOUGLAS, JOSEPHINE	TV DIRECTOR-PRODUCER	WHITE BRIARS, SLINFOLD		
		NEAR HORSHAM	SUSSEX	ENGLAND
DOUGLAS, KIRK	ACTOR-DIRECTOR	805 N REXFORD DR	BEVERLY HILLS, CA	90210
DOUGLAS, MAC GREGOR	WRITER	8955 BEVERLY BLVD	LOS ANGELES, CA	90048
DOUGLAS, MICHAEL	ACTOR-PRODUCER	POST OFFICE BOX 49054	LOS ANGELES, CA	90049
DOUGLAS, MIKE	TV HOST-SINGER	565 PERUGIA WY	LOS ANGELES, CA	90077
DOUGLAS, PAMELA	TV WRITER	1650 WESTWOOD BLVD #201	LOS ANGELES, CA	90024

Name	Occupation	Address	City	Code
DOUGLAS, PAULETTE	TV DIRECTOR	112 W 76TH ST #1-R	NEW YORK, NY	10023
DOUGLAS, PETER	PRODUCER	MCA/UNIVERSAL STUDIOS, INC		
		100 UNIVERSAL CITY PLAZA	UNIVERSAL CITY, CA	91608
DOUGLAS, PETER V	WRITER	8955 BEVERLY BLVD	LOS ANGELES, CA	90048
DOUGLAS, ROBERT	ACTOR-DIRECTOR	SEA BLUFF, 1810 PARLIAMENT RD	LEUCADIA, CA	92024
DOUGLAS, SARAH	ACTRESS	MAX NAUGHTON LOWE		
		200 FULHAM RD	LONDON SW10 9PN	ENGLAND
DOUGLAS, SHEILA D	NEWS CORRESPONDENT	4461 CONNECTICUT AVE, NW	WASHINGTON, DC	20008
DOUGLAS, WARREN	TV WRITER	8955 BEVERLY BLVD	LOS ANGELES, CA	90048
DOUGLAS, WAYNE, JR	TALENT AGENT	2600 NONCONNAH BLVD #390	MEMPHIS, TN	38132
DOUGLASS, DAVID R	NEWS CORRESPONDENT	1362 ELM GROVE CIR	SILVER SPRING, MD	20904
DOUGLASS, ROBYN	ACTRESS	10 CANTERBURY CT	WILMETTE, IL	60091
DOUGNAC, FRANCE	ACTRESS	BABETTE POUGE, 6 SQUARE		
		VILLARET DE JOYEUSE	PARIS 75017	FRANCE
DOUMANIAN, JEAN	TV WRITER	555 W 57TH ST #1230	NEW YORK, NY	10019
DOURIF, BRAD	ACTRESS	2342 BENEDICT CANYON DR	BEVERLY HILLS, CA	90210
DOUTHETTE, DANI	ACTRESS	6736 LAUREL CANYON BLVD #306	NORTH HOLLYWOOD, CA	91606
DOUTHIT, RANDALL	TV PRODUCER	2133 WISCONSIN AVE, NW	WASHINGTON, DC	20007
DOVE, BILLIE	ACTRESS	THUNDERBIRD COUNTRY CLUB		
		70612 HWY 111	RANCHO MIRAGE, CA	92270
DOVE, RONNIE	SINGER-SONGWRITER	107 DORAL DR	FRANKLIN, TN	37064
DOVE, SANDRA F	NEWS CORRESPONDENT	9206 HAMILTON DR	FAIRFAX, VA	22031
DOVE, ULYSSES	DANCER-CHOREOGRAPHER	272 W 84TH ST	NEW YORK, NY	10024
DOVELLS, THE	VOCAL GROUP	BROTHERS, 141 DUNBAR AVE	FORDS, NJ	08863
DOW, DAVID	NEWS CORRESPONDENT	CBS-TV, NEWS DEPARTMENT		
		7800 BEVERLY BLVD	LOS ANGELES, CA	90036
DOW, HAROLD	NEWS CORRESPONDENT	CBS NEWS, 524 W 57TH ST	NEW YORK, NY	10019
DOW, JUDITH	SINGER	GERSHUNOFF, 502 PARK AVE	NEW YORK, NY	10022
DOW, PEGGY	ACTRESS	HELMERICH, 2121 S YORKSTOWN AVE	TULSA, OK	74114
DOW, TONY	ACTOR	18 VENICE BLVD #C	VENICE, CA	90291
DOWD, M'EL	ACTRESS	155 SOUTHSIDE AVE	HASTING-ON-HUDSON, NY	10706
DOWD, NANCY	SCREENWRITER	6310 HEATHER DR	LOS ANGELES, CA	90068
DOWDELL, ROBERT	ACTOR	427 N CANON DR #205	BEVERLY HILLS, CA	90210
DOWELL, JAMES	GUITARIST	ROUTE #2, BUFFALO RD	NASHVILLE, TN	37209
DOWELL, WILLIAM	NEWS CORRESPONDENT	DISCOVER/TIME & LIFE BLDG		
		ROCKEFELLER CENTER	NEW YORK, NY	10020
DOWIE, FREDA	ACTRESS	ELLISON-COMBE ASSOCIATES		
		17 RICHMOND HILL, RICHMOND	SURREY	ENGLAND
DOWLING, CHET	TV WRITER-PRODUCER	8955 BEVERLY BLVD	LOS ANGELES, CA	90048
DOWLING, CLAUDIA GLENN	WRITER-EDITOR	LIFE/TIME & LIFE BLDG		
		ROCKEFELLER CENTER	NEW YORK, NY	10020
DOWLING, DORIS	ACTRESS	9026 ELEVADO AVE	LOS ANGELES, CA	90069
DOWLING, PATRICK	ACTOR-DIRECTOR	11 ROYAL RD, TEDDINGTON	MIDDLESEX	ENGLAND
DOWLING, RICHARD W	WRITER	555 W 57TH ST #1230	NEW YORK, NY	10019
DOWN, ANGELA	ACTRESS	STONE, 18 YORK BUILDINGS	LONDON WC2	ENGLAND
DOWN, LESLEY-ANNE	ACTRESS	124 UDINE WY	LOS ANGELES, CA	90077
DOWN, LINDA A	WRITER	555 W 57TH ST #1230	NEW YORK, NY	10019
DOWN, RENA	WRITER-PRODUCER	834 LINCOLN BLVD #5	SANTA MONICA, CA	90403
DOWN AVENUE	ROCK & ROLL GROUP	25 HUNTINGTON AVE #420	BOSTON, MA	02116
DOWNCHILD BLUES BAND	BLUES BAND	41 BRITAIN ST #200	TORONTO, ONT	CANADA
DOWNE, EDWARD R, JR	THEATER PRODUCER	824 5TH AVE	NEW YORK, NY	10021
DOWNES, BARRY E	TV WRITER	555 W 57TH ST #1230	NEW YORK, NY	10019
DOWNES, BOB	NEWS CORRESPONDENT	5736 N 6TH ST	ARLINGTON, VA	22205
DOWNEY, JAMES M	TV WRITER	555 W 57TH ST #1230	NEW YORK, NY	10019
DOWNEY, ROBERT	ACTOR	1888 CENTURY PARK E #1400	LOS ANGELES, CA	90067
DOWNEY, ROBERT	DIRECTOR	8497 CRESCENT DR	HOLLYWOOD, CA	90046
DOWNIE, LEONARD	NEWS CORRESPONDENT	2737 DEVONSHIRE PL, NW	WASHINGTON, DC	20008
DOWNING, BIG AL	SINGER	2800 NEILSON WAY #412	SANTA MONICA, CA	90405
DOWNING, DAVID	ACTOR	23938 HAMLIN ST	CANOGA PARK, CA	91307
DOWNING, LAWRENCE A	PHOTOGRAPHER	3821 TAFT AVE	ALEXANDRIA, VA	22304
DOWNING, STEPHEN M	WRITER	9022 SUNSET BLVD #531	LOS ANGELES, CA	90069
DOWNS, HUGH	TV HOST-JOURNALIST	POST OFFICE BOX 1132	CAREFREE, AZ	85331
DOWNS, JOHNNY	ACTOR-DANCER	1114 ORANGE ST	CORONADO, CA	92118
DOWNS, M A	ACTOR	10701 RIVERSIDE DR #13	TOLUCA LAKE, CA	91602
DOWNS, N W	WRITER	555 W 57TH ST #1230	NEW YORK, NY	10019
DOWNS, RICHARD W	GUITARIST	321 PIONEER LN	NASHVILLE, TN	37206
DOWNTIME	ROCK & ROLL GROUP	25 HUNTINGTON AVE #420	BOSTON, MA	02116
DOYEN, JACQUELINE	ACTRESS	3 RUE DE REGARD	PARIS 75006	FRANCE
DOYLE, ANDREW C	DIRECTOR	4261 HAMPSHIRE GREEN CT	LAS VEGAS, NV	89110
DOYLE, BRIAN JAMES	NEWS CORRESPONDENT	1920 BRISBANE ST	SILVER SPRING, MD	20902
DOYLE, CHRISTOPHER	STUNTMAN	5318 W CAHUENGA BLVD #300	LOS ANGELES, CA	90068
DOYLE, DAVID	ACTOR-DIRECTOR	4731 NOELINE AVE	ENCINO, CA	91436
DOYLE, EDDIE	SINGER	PROCESS, 439 WILEY AVE	FRANKLIN, PA	16323
DOYLE, ENOS LYNN	ACTOR	1933 N BEACHWOOD DR #20	LOS ANGELES, CA	90068
DOYLE, HELEN SEN	NEWS REPORTER	TIME/TIME & LIFE BLDG		
		ROCKEFELLER CENTER	NEW YORK, NY	10020
DOYLE, JAMES H	NEWS CORRESPONDENT	5121 BALTAN RD	BETHESDA, MD	20816
DOYLE, JAMES S	NEWS CORRESPONDENT	6401 TONE DR	BETHESDA, MD	20817
DOYLE, KATHLEEN H	NEWS CORRESPONDENT	340 NATIONAL PRESS BLDG		
		529 14TH ST, NW	WASHINGTON, DC	20045
DOYLE, MARTIN	ACTOR	9220 SUNSET BLVD #202	LOS ANGELES, CA	90069
DOYLE, RON	ACTOR	11137 ARCHWOOD ST	NORTH HOLLYWOOD, CA	91606
DOYLE-MURRAY, BRIAN	ACTOR-TV WRITER	555 W 57TH ST #1230	NEW YORK, NY	10019
DOZER, DAVID	WRITER	8955 BEVERLY BLVD	LOS ANGELES, CA	90048
DOZIER, AARON	ACTOR	9220 SUNSET BLVD #202	LOS ANGELES, CA	90069

DOZIER, LAMONT	SINGER	4175 STANSBURY AVE	SHERMAN OAKS, CA	91423
DOZIER, ROBERT J	TV WRITER	8955 BEVERLY BLVD	LOS ANGELES, CA	90048
DR COOL & HIS NEW BREED BLUES B	BLUES GROUP	POST OFFICE BOX 11321		
		FLAGLER STATION	MIAMI, FL	33101
DR CORN'S ELECTRIC GRASS BAND	BLUEGRASS GROUP	DOWNING, 3038 E BURNSIDE ST	PORTLAND, OR	97214
DR DEATH	WRESTLER	SEE - WILLIAMS, STEVE		
		"DR DEATH"		
DR DEMENTO	RADIO PERSONALITY	POST OFFICE BOX 884	CULVER CITY, CA	90230
DR FEELGOOD	ROCK & ROLL GROUP	3 E 54TH ST #1400	NEW YORK, NY	10022
DR HOOK	ROCK & ROLL GROUP	POST OFFICE BOX 121017	NASHVILLE, TN	37212
DR JOHN	SINGER-SONGWRITER	927 N CALLOLLSON AVE	NEW ORLEANS, LA	70119
DR K & THE SHANTAYS	MUSICAL GROUP	POST OFFICE BOX 222	BLACK HAWK, SD	57718
DR KNOW	ROCK & ROLL GROUP	POST OFFICE BOX 7263	OAKLAND, CA	93031
DR SEUSS	AUTHOR	SEE - GEISEL, TED		
DRABINSKY, GARTH	FILM PRODUCER	CINEPLEX CORPORATION		
		214 KING STREET W	TORONTO, ONT M5H 1K4	CANADA
DRAFFEN, BILL	SINGER-GUITARIST	POST OFFICE BOX 120981	NASHVILLE, TN	37212
DRAGAS, M L	WRITER	555 W 57TH ST #1230	NEW YORK, NY	10019
DRAGO, BILLY	ACTOR	3800 BARHAM BLVD #303	LOS ANGELES, CA	90068
DRAGON, THE	WRESTLER	SEE - STEAMBOAT, RICKY		
		"THE DRAGON"		
DRAGON, TONI	SINGER	SEE - CAPTAIN & TENNILLE, THE		
DRAGONI, CARLA	ACTRESS	939 CANDLEWOOD LAKE RD	NEW MILFORD, CT	06776
DRAGONI, MARIA	SOPRANO	CAMI, 165 W 57TH ST	NEW YORK, NY	10019

Name	Occupation	Address	City	ZIP
DRAGOTI, STAN	WRITER-PRODUCER	755 STRADELLA RD	LOS ANGELES, CA	90077
DRAI, VICTOR	FILM PRODUCER	1201 DELRESTO DR	BEVERLY HILLS, CA	90210
DRAIN, MARGARET A	WRITER	555 W 57TH ST #1230	NEW YORK, NY	10019
DRAKE, ADRIAN	ACTOR	8721 SUNSET BLVD #202	LOS ANGELES, CA	90069
DRAKE, ALAN	COMEDIAN	21243 VENTURA BLVD #243	WOODLAND HILLS, CA	91364
DRAKE, ALLAN	ACTOR	5456 BOTHWELL RD	TARZANA, CA	91356
DRAKE, ARNOLD A	WRITER	555 W 57TH ST #1230	NEW YORK, NY	10019
DRAKE, BETSY	ACTRESS	6 CHEYNE GARDENS #3	LONDON SW3	ENGLAND
DRAKE, BRUCE	NEWS CORRESPONDENT	2900 CONNECTICUT AVE, NW	WASHINGTON, DC	20008
DRAKE, BUD	CARTOONIST	KING FEATURES SYNDICATE		
		235 E 45TH ST	NEW YORK, NY	10017
DRAKE, CHARLIE	ACT-WRI-COMED	IAR, 235-241 REGENT ST	LONDON W1A 2JT	ENGLAND
DRAKE, COLIN	ACTOR	1741 N IVAR AVE #221	LOS ANGELES, CA	90028
DRAKE, DONA	ACTRESS	425 N OAKHURST DR #213	BEVERLY HILLS, CA	90210
DRAKE, ELLIOTT R	WRITER-PRODUCER	67 HILTON AVE	GARDEN CITY, NJ	11530
DRAKE, ERVIN	WRITER	555 W 57TH ST #1230	NEW YORK, NY	10019
DRAKE, FRANCES	ACTRESS	1511 SUMMITRIDGE DR	BEVERLY HILLS, CA	90210
DRAKE, GABRIELLE	ACTRESS	FRASER, 91 REGENT ST	LONDON W1	ENGLAND
DRAKE, JIM	TV DIRECTOR	5145 CALVIN AVE	TARZANA, CA	91356
DRAKE, LAURA	ACTRESS	SCHOEMAN, 2600 W VICTORY BLVD	BURBANK, CA	91505
DRAKE, MADELEINE	ACTRESS	11240 MAGNOLIA AVE #202	NORTH HOLLYWOOD, CA	91601
DRAKE, MICHELE	ACTRES-MODEL	FARRELL, 10500 MAGNOLIA BLVD	NORTH HOLLYWOOD, CA	91601
DRAKE, PAUL	ACTOR	211 S BEVERLY DR #201	BEVERLY HILLS, CA	90212
DRAKE, PAULINA	PIANIST	MMM, 935 NW 19TH AVE	PORTLAND, OR	97209
DRAKE, PETE	DOBROIST	809 18TH AVE S	NASHVILLE, TN	37203
DRAKE, PHIL	MUSICIAN	4917 MILLERWOOD DR	NASHVILLE, TN	37211
DRAKE, RONALD	ACTOR	ABC-TV, "ALL MY CHILDREN"		
		1330 AVE OF THE AMERICAS	NEW YORK, NY	10019
DRAKE, ROSS	WRITER-EDITOR	PEOPLE/TIME & LIFE BLDG		
		ROCKEFELLER CENTER	NEW YORK, NY	10020
DRAKE, STAN	CARTOONIST	KING FEATURES SYNDICATE		
		235 E 45TH ST	NEW YORK, NY	10017
DRAKE, STANLEY	CARTOONIST	46 POST RD E	WESTPORT, CT	06880
DRAKE, SYLVIE	THEATER CRITIC	701 "B" ST #501	SAN DIEGO, CA	92101
DRAKE, THOMAS Y	SCREENWRITER	8955 BEVERLY BLVD	LOS ANGELES, CA	90048
DRAKE, WILLIAM	BARITONE	45 W 60TH ST #4-K	NEW YORK, NY	10023
DRAPER, FREDA	SINGER	POST OFFICE BOX 656	INDEPENDENCE, MO	64052
DRAPER, HARRY	VIOLINIST	3322 FAIRMONT DR #2	NASHVILLE, TN	37203
DRAPER, NATALIE	ACTRESS	GOFF, 86 MALIBU COLONY DR	MALIBU, CA	90265
DRAPER, PETER	TV-FILM WRITER	1 SUMMER LN, BRIXHAM	DEVON	ENGLAND
DRAPER, POLLY	ACTRESS	211 S BEVERLY DR #201	BEVERLY HILLS, CA	90212
DRAPER, ROBERTA H	NEWS CORRESPONDENT	NBC-TV, NEWS DEPARTMENT		
		4001 NEBRASKA AVE, NW	WASHINGTON, DC	20016
DRAPKIN, ARNOLD H	PHOTO EDITOR	TIME/TIME & LIFE BLDG		
		ROCKEFELLER CENTER	NEW YORK, NY	10020
DRASNIN, IRV	WRITER-PRODUCER	180 E 79TH ST #10-D	NEW YORK, NY	10021
DRASNIN, ROBERT J	COMPOSER-CONDUCTOR	17115 NANETTE ST	GRANADA HILLS, CA	91344
DRATH, VIOLA HERMS	NEWS CORRESPONDENT	3206 "Q" ST, NW	WASHINGTON, DC	20007
DRAY, DIANE F	WRITER	555 W 57TH ST #1230	NEW YORK, NY	10019
DRAYER, DAVE	SINGER	PROCESS, 439 WILEY AVE	FRANKLIN, PA	16323
DRAYNE, MARY	WRITER	555 W 57TH ST #1230	NEW YORK, NY	10019
DRAYTON, LESLIE C	COMPOSER	3441 S DUNSMUIR AVE	LOS ANGELES, CA	90016
DREAM EXPRESS	SOUL GROUP	PDQ, 1474 N KINGS RD	LOS ANGELES, CA	90069
DREAM TEAM, THE	WRESTLING TAG TEAM	SEE - NEW DREAM TEAM, THE		
DREESEN, TOM	COMEDIAN	5155 COSTELLO AVE	SHERMAN OAKS, CA	91423
DREIDAME, DANA	ACTRESS	4141 ELENDA ST #3	CULVER CITY, CA	90230
DREIFUSS, ARTHUR	WRITER-PRODUCER	3950 LOS FELIZ BLVD #210	LOS ANGELES, CA	90027
DREITH, DENNIS J	COMPOSER	4820 1/2 CLEON AVE	NORTH HOLLYWOOD, CA	91601
DRENNAN, NOEL	ACTOR-SINGER	81 DOWNTON AVE	LONDON SW2	ENGLAND
DRENNAN, PATTI	WRITER	8955 BEVERLY BLVD	LOS ANGELES, CA	90048
DRESCHER, FRAN	ACTRESS	7708 WOODROW WILSON DR	LOS ANGELES, CA	90046
DRESDEN, JOHN	ACTOR	950 N KINGS RD #137	LOS ANGELES, CA	90069
DRESNER, HAL	SCREENWRITER	1569 BENEDICT CANYON DR	BEVERLY HILLS, CA	90210
DRESS, SAMUEL	DIRECTOR	4606 ATOLL AVE	SHERMAN OAKS, CA	91423
DRESSEN, TOM	COMEDIAN	5155 COSTELLO AVE	SHERMAN OAKS, CA	91423
DRESSER, LEE	SINGER	17530 VENTURA BLVD #108	ENCINO, CA	91316
DRESSER, NORINE S	WRITER	3093 SAINT GEORGE ST	LOS ANGELES, CA	90027
DRESSLER, LIEUX	ACTRESS	15760 VENTURA BLVD #1730	ENCINO, CA	91436
DREW, CHRISTOPHER	SCREENWRITER	38 CARROLL HOUSE		
		CRAVEN TERRACE	LONDON W2	ENGLAND
DREW, ELIZABETH	NEWS CORRESPONDENT	3112 WOODLEY RD	WASHINGTON, DC	20008
DREW, ELLEN	ACTRESS	POST OFFICE BOX 344	PALM DESERT, CA	92260
DREW, RICK	WRITER	8955 BEVERLY BLVD	LOS ANGELES, CA	90048
DREW, ROBERT J	ACTOR	6 SUNSET LN	PORT WASHINGTON, NY	11050
DREW, ROLAND	ACTOR	1117 6TH ST #A-12	SANTA MONICA, CA	90403
DREW, ROY	FILM PRODUCER	2 ORCHARD RISE, SHIRLEY	CROYDON CRO 7QY	ENGLAND
DREXELL, OLIVER P, JR	TV WRITER	555 W 57TH ST #1230	NEW YORK, NY	10019
DREXLER, ROSALYN	PLAYWRIGHT	ROSENSTONE, 3 E 48TH ST	NEW YORK, NY	10017
DREYFUS, KAREN	VIOLIST	POST OFFICE BOX 131	SPRINGFIELD, VA	22150
DREYFUSS, IRA J	NEWS CORRESPONDENT	1825 "K" ST, NW	WASHINGTON, DC	20006
DREYFUSS, LORIN	SCREENWRITER	8955 BEVERLY BLVD	LOS ANGELES, CA	90048
DREYFUSS, RANDOLPH	ACTOR	D EISEN, 154 E 61ST ST	NEW YORK, NY	10021
DREYFUSS, RICHARD	ACTOR	2809 NICHOLS CANYON RD	LOS ANGELES, CA	90046
DRIBBEN, ELIZABETH L	WRITER	555 W 57TH ST #1230	NEW YORK, NY	10019
DRIER, MOOSIE	ACTOR	8485 MELROSE PL #E	LOS ANGELES, CA	90069

ELLEN DREW

JAMES DRURY

IRENE DUNNE

ROBERT DUVALL

BOB DYLAN

SHEENA EASTON

CLINT EASTWOOD

DUANE EDDY

BARBARA EDEN

Name	Occupation	Address	City	Zip
DRIFTERS, THE	VOCAL GROUP	J BIRD BOOKING AGENCY		
		4905 S ATLANTIC AVE	DAYTON BEACH, FL	32019
DRIFTWOOD, JIMMY	SINGER	FEGAN, 6638 MAPLE AVE	DALLAS, TX	75235
DRIGGERS, DON	WRESTLER	POST OFFICE BOX 3859	STAMFORD, CT	06905
DRIGGERS, JIM	ACTOR	1605 N CAHUENGA BLVD #202	LOS ANGELES, CA	90028
DRIGGS, DENNIS L	COMPOSER	1351 N ORANGE DR #207	LOS ANGELES, CA	90028
DRIMMER, JOHN	SCREENWRITER	555 W 57TH ST #1230	NEW YORK, NY	10019
DRINKALL, ROGER	CELLIST	KAY, 58 W 58TH ST	NEW YORK, NY	10019
DRINKARD, JAMES P	NEWS CORRESPONDENT	6814 DARBY LN	SPRINGFIELD, VA	22150
DRINKWATER, TERRY	NEWS CORRESPONDENT	941 HILTS AVE	LOS ANGELES, CA	90024
DRISCHELL, RALPH	ACTOR	LIGHT, 113 N ROBERTSON BLVD	LOS ANGELES, CA	90048
DRISCOLL, LAWRASON	ACTOR	837 VENICE BLVD	VENICE, CA	90291
DRISEBOIS, DANIELLE	ACTRESS	9200 SUNSET BLVD #620	LOS ANGELES, CA	90069
DRISKILL, WILLIAM	SCREENWRITER	8955 BEVERLY BLVD	LOS ANGELES, CA	90048
DRIVALA, JENNY	SOPRANO	CAMI, 165 W 57TH ST	NEW YORK, NY	10019
DRIVAS, ROBERT	ACTOR-DIRECTOR	376 BLEECKER ST	NEW YORK, NY	10014
DRIVER, DONALD	DIRECTOR	DGA, 110 W 57TH ST	NEW YORK, NY	10019
DRIVER, JOHN S	TV WRITER-DIRECTOR	ASKENASE, 6217 GLEN AIR DR	LOS ANGELES, CA	90068
DROMGOOLE, PATRICK	TV DIRECTOR-PRODUCER	HTV CENTRE, BATH RD	BRISTOL BS4 2HG	ENGLAND
DROP IN THE GRAY	ROCK & ROLL GROUP	VARIETY ARTISTS INTL, INC		
		9073 NEMO ST, 3RD FLOOR	LOS ANGELES, CA	90069
DROSNIN, DEBORAH	NEWS CORRESPONDENT	2800 ONTARIO RD, NW	WASHINGTON, DC	20009
DROSSMAN, ALLAN H	WRITER	555 W 57TH ST #1230	NEW YORK, NY	10019
DROTT, JOAN	ACTRESS	24 SUMMIT PL	NEWBURY PORT, MA	01950
DRU, JOANNE	ACTRESS	1455 CARLA RIDGE	BEVERLY HILLS, CA	90210
DRUCE, JEFFRY	ACTOR	4117 MICHAEL AVE	LOS ANGELES, CA	90066
DRUCE, OLGA	ACTRESS	152 E 94TH ST	NEW YORK, NY	10028
DRUCK, MARK	WRITER	555 W 57TH ST #1230	NEW YORK, NY	10019
DRUCKER, BRUCE	TV DIRECTOR	WCVB-TV, 5 TV PL	NEEDHAM, MA	02192
DRUCKER, DORIS	CARTOONIST	POST OFFICE BOX 4203	NEW YORK, NY	10017
DRUCKER, GARY	WRITER	8955 BEVERLY BLVD	LOS ANGELES, CA	90048
DRUCKER, JEROLD P	WRITER	5560 RANTHOM AVE	WOODLAND HILLS, CA	91367
DRUCKER, MORT	CARTOONIST	MAD MAGAZINE, INC		
		485 MADISON AVE	NEW YORK, NY	10022
DRUCKMAN, JACOB	CONDUCTOR	SOFFER, 130 W 56TH ST	NEW YORK, NY	10019
DRUIAN, RAFAEL	VIOLINIST	JCB, 155 W 68TH ST	NEW YORK, NY	10023
DRULEY, TOM	SINGER-GUITARIST	POST OFFICE BOX 73	GOODLETTSVILLE, TN	37072
DRUMMOND, ALICE	ACTRESS	242 E 26TH ST	NEW YORK, NY	10010
DRUMMOND, TIM	GUITARIST	POST OFFICE BOX 5091	SHERMAN OAKS, CA	91403
DRUMMUND & HICKS	JAZZ DUO	BRIDGE, 106 FORT GREENE PL	BROOKLYN, NY	11217
DRUMMY, SAM	CINEMATOGRAPHER	7715 SUNSET BLVD #150	LOS ANGELES, CA	90046
DRURY, DRUMMOND	DIRECTOR	DGA, 110 W 57TH ST	NEW YORK, NY	10019
DRURY, JAMES	ACTOR	WEBB, 7500 DEVISTA DR	LOS ANGELES, CA	90046
DRURY, STEPHEN	PIANIST	AFFILIATE ARTISTS, INC		
		37 W 65TH ST, 6TH FLOOR	NEW YORK, NY	10023
DRUSKY, ROY	SINGER-SONGWRITER	ROUTE #4, BOX 79-A		
		BUCKLODGE RD	PORTLAND, TN	37148
DRUYAN, ANN	TV WRITER	8955 BEVERLY BLVD	LOS ANGELES, CA	90048
DRUZHININ, ALEXANDER N	NEWS CORRESPONDENT	1401 BLAIR MILL RD	SILVER SPRING, MD	20910
DRYDEN, MACK	ACTOR	151 S EL CAMINO DR	BEVERLY HILLS, CA	90212
DRYDEN, MACK L	WRITER	203 DIMMICK AVE	VENICE, CA	90291
DRYER, DAVID CARL	DIRECTOR	16140 MOORPARK ST	ENCINO, CA	91346
DRYER, FRED	ACTOR-FOOTBALL	151 S EL CAMINO DR	BEVERLY HILLS, CA	90212
DRYER, ROBERT	ACTOR	3151 W CAHUENGA BLVD #310	LOS ANGELES, CA	90068
DRYHURST, CHRISTOPHER	FILM DIRECTOR	2 BYRON VILLAS, VALE OF HEATH		
		HAMPSTEAD	LONDON NW3	ENGLAND
DRYHURST, EDWARD	FILM WRITER-PRODUCER	9 NORTHWOOD HALL, HORNSEY LN	LONDON N6 5PE	ENGLAND
DRYHURST, MICHAEL	FILM PRODUCER	21 BROADLANDS AVE	SHEP-ON-THAMES	ENGLAND
DRYSDALE, DON	SPORTSCASTER	78 COLGATE	RANCHO MIRAGE, CA	92270
DRYSDALE, PHILIP E	WRITER	555 W 57TH ST #1230	NEW YORK, NY	10019
DU BAIN, DONNA	ACTRESS	1231 FLANDERS RD	LA CANADA, CA	91011
DU BARRY, DENISE	ACTRESS	3083 1/2 RAMBLA PACIFICA	MALIBU, CA	90265
DU BOIS, GARY	NEWS CORRESPONDENT	7455 BOUNDARY AVE	MANASSAS, VA	22111
DU BOIS, JA'NET	ACTRESS	6310 SAN VICENTE BLVD #407	LOS ANGELES, CA	90048
DU BOIS, MARK	TENOR	VKD INTERNATIONAL ARTISTS		
		220 SHEPPARD AVE E		
		WILLOWDALE	TORONTO, ONT M2N 3A9	CANADA
DU BOIS, MARTA	ACTRESS	9220 SUNSET BLVD #625	LOS ANGELES, CA	90069
DU BOIS, RICHARD	ACTOR	LIONEL LARNER, 130 W 57TH ST	NEW YORK, NY	10019
DU BOIS, ROGER	HIGHPOLE ACT	POST OFFICE BOX 87	WEST LEBANON, NY	12195
DU BOST, PAULETTE	ACTRESS	23 RUE DE BELVEDERE	BOULOGNE 92100	FRANCE
DU BROCK, NEAL	THEATER PRODUCER	STUDIO ARENA, 681 MAIN ST	BUFFALO, NY	14203
DU PONT, HELEN	WRITER	8955 BEVERLY BLVD	LOS ANGELES, CA	90048
DU PONT, PENNY	CASTING DIRECTOR	COLUMBIA PICTURES TV		
		COLUMBIA PLAZA	BURBANK, CA	91505
DU PRE, JACQUELINE	VIOLONCELLIST	HOLT, 134 WIGMORE ST	LONDON W1	ENGLAND
DU PREE, DAVID	SPORTS WRITER	POST OFFICE BOX 500	WASHINGTON, DC	20044
DU PUY, MELISSA	MUSICIAN	108 THOMPSON LN #A-10	NASHVILLE, TN	37211
DU VAL, DOUGLAS	ACTOR	5850 CANOGA AVE #110	WOODLAND HILLS, CA	91367
DUANE, FRANK	WRITER	8955 BEVERLY BLVD	LOS ANGELES, CA	90048
DUBBINS, DON	ACTOR	17020 SUNSET BLVD #9	PACIFIC PALISADES, CA	90272
DUBELMAN, RICHARD S	WRITER-PRODUCER	1 LAURIE DR	ENGLEWOOD CLIFFS, NJ	07632
DUBERSTEIN, BARBARA F	WRITER	555 W 57TH ST #1230	NEW YORK, NY	10019
DUBILL, ROBERT A	NEWS EDITOR	POST OFFICE BOX 500	WASHINGTON, DC	20044
DUBIN, CHARLES S	TV DIRECTOR	651 LORNA LN	LOS ANGELES, CA	90049

Name	Occupation	Address	City	ZIP/Country
DUBIN, LAURENCE L	DIRECTOR	POST OFFICE BOX 78	LIVINGSTON, NY	12541
DUBIN, MORTON DONALD	DIRECTOR	63 W 83RD ST	NEW YORK, NY	10024
DUBNO, DANIEL N	WRITER	555 W 57TH ST #1230	NEW YORK, NY	10019
DUBOIS, DOODLES	TV WRITER	8955 BEVERLY BLVD	LOS ANGELES, CA	90048
DUBOV, ADAM	TV WRITER	5700 RHODES AVE	NORTH HOLLYWOOD, CA	91607
DUBS, THE	VOCAL GROUP	OLDIES, 5218 ALMONT ST	LOS ANGELES, CA	90032
DUBSKY, HARRY	EQUILIBRIST	HALL, 138 FROG HOLLOW RD	CHURCHVILLE, PA	18966
DUBY, JACQUES	ACTOR	4 RUE ST-ROCH	PARIS 75001	FRANCE
DUCAT, SUZANNE B	NEWS CORRESPONDENT	POST OFFICE BOX 2626	WASHINGTON, DC	20013
DUCE, SHARON	ACTRESS	75 KENSINGTON GARDENS S	LONDON W2	ENGLAND
DUCHABLE, FRANCOIS-RENE	PIANIST	LEISER, DORCHESTER TOWERS		
		155 W 68TH ST	NEW YORK, NY	10023
DUCHEMIN, ANDRE-GILLES	FLUTIST	POST OFFICE BOX U	REDDING, CT	06875
DUCHIN, PETER	PIANIST	305 MADISON AVE #956	NEW YORK, NY	10165
DUCHOW, PETE	PRODUCER	4000 WARNER BLVD #76	BURBANK, CA	91522
DUCHOWNY, ROGER	DIRECTOR	7352 BIRDVIEW AVE	MALIBU, CA	90265
DUCK, MARILYN	NEWS CORRESPONDENT	310 E CAPITOL ST #F, NE	WASHINGTON, DC	20003
DUCKHAM, GRAEME	TV-FILM DIRECTOR	7 CORRIB HEIGHTS		
		30 CRESCENT RD	LONDON N8	ENGLAND
DUCKWORTH, DORTHA	ACTRESS	200 W 54TH ST	NEW YORK, NY	10019
DUCKY, PRINCESS	TV WRITER	8955 BEVERLY BLVD	LOS ANGELES, CA	90048
DUCLON, DAVID W	TV WRITER-PRODUCER	NBC-TV, 3000 W ALAMEDA AVE	BURBANK, CA	91523
DUCLOUX, WALTER	CONDUCTOR	2 WILDWIND POINT	AUSTIN, TX	78746
DUCOMMUN, RICK	COMEDIAN	9000 SUNSET BLVD #1200	LOS ANGELES, CA	90069
DUDGEON-RANSDELL, COLLEEN	WRITER	555 W 57TH ST #1230	NEW YORK, NY	10019
DUDIKOFF, MICHAEL	ACTOR	21322 MILDRED AVE	TORRANCE, CA	90503
DUDLEY, CAROL	CASTING DIRECTOR	REUBEN CANNON & ASSOCIATES		
		2020 AVE OF THE STARS		
		4TH FLOOR	LOS ANGELES, CA	90067
DUDLEY, DAVE	SINGER-SONGWRITER	ACE PRODUCTIONS		
		3407 GREEN RIDGE DR	NASHVILLE, TN	37214
DUDLEY, JONATHAN	CONDUCTOR	121 WAVERLY PL	NEW YORK, NY	10011
DUDLEY, ROBERT S	NEWS CORRESPONDENT	1931 RHODE ISLAND	MC LEAN, VA	22101
DUDLEY, TERENCE	WRITER-PRODUCER	GLASS, 28 BERKELEY SQ	LONDON W1X 6HD	ENGLAND
DUELL, D WILLIAM	ACTOR	4 PARK AVE	NEW YORK, NY	10016
DUERR, ROBERT KENNETH	CONDUCTOR	80 N EUCLID AVE #401	PASADENA, CA	91101
DUESING, DALE	BARITONE	CAMI, 165 W 57TH ST	NEW YORK, NY	10019
DUFALLO, RICHARD	CONDUCTOR	1776 BROADWAY #504	NEW YORK, NY	10019
DUFF, HOWARD	ACTOR	NBC-TV, 30 ROCKEFELLER PLAZA	NEW YORK, NY	10112
DUFF, NORWICH	ACTOR	SIMMONS, 9 NEAL ST	LONDON WC2H 9PU	ENGLAND
DUFF, PATRICIA	ACTRESS	151 S EL CAMINO DR	BEVERLY HILLS, CA	90212
DUFFEK, PATTY	MODEL	MODELS & PROMOTIONS AGENCY		
		8560 SUNSET BLVD, 10TH FLOOR	LOS ANGELES, CA	90069
DUFFELL, PETER	TV WRITER-DIRECTOR	HEATH, PARAMOUNT HOUSE		
		162-170 WARDOUR ST	LONDON W1V 3AT	ENGLAND
DUFFY, AL	TV WRITER	8955 BEVERLY BLVD	LOS ANGELES, CA	90048
DUFFY, DAVID	NEWS REPORTER	THE NATIONAL ENQUIRER		
		600 SE COAST AVE	LANTANA, FL	33464
DUFFY, HELEN	ACTRESS	5330 LANKERSHIM BLVD #210	NORTH HOLLYWOOD, CA	91601
DUFFY, JAMES E	TV EXECUTIVE	ABC TELEVISION NETWORK		
		1330 AVE OF THE AMERICAS	NEW YORK, NY	10019
DUFFY, JAMES STUART	ACTOR	4345 OCEAN VIEW DR	MALIBU, CA	90265
DUFFY, JULIA	ACTRESS-DIRECTOR	870 N VINE ST #213	LOS ANGELES, CA	90038
DUFFY, MARTHA	WRITER-EDITOR	TIME/TIME & LIFE BLDG		
		ROCKEFELLER CENTER	NEW YORK, NY	10020
DUFFY, PATRICK	ACTOR-DIRECTOR	5010 PALOMAR DR	TARZANA, CA	91356
DUFFY, WILLIAM	ACTOR	12926 RIVERSIDE DR #C	SHERMAN OAKS, CA	91423
DUFOUR, VAL	ACTOR	40 W 22ND ST	NEW YORK, NY	10010
DUGAN, DENNIS	ACTOR	1331 N HAYWORTH AVE	LOS ANGELES, CA	90046
DUGAN, JAMES	ACTOR	9777 WILSHIRE BLVD #707	BEVERLY HILLS, CA	90212
DUGAN, JOHN T	TV WRITER	8955 BEVERLY BLVD	LOS ANGELES, CA	90048
DUGAN, JUDITH	NEWS CORRESPONDENT	3824 VAN NESS ST, NW	WASHINGTON, DC	20016
DUGAN, MARY	COMPOSER	2560 "D" HWY #273	ANDERSON, CA	96007
DUGAN, MICHAEL	FILM DIRECTOR	3822 E 1ST ST	LONG BEACH, CA	90803
DUGAN, SUSAN	ACTRESS	9025 WILSHIRE BLVD #309	BEVERLY HILLS, CA	90211
DUGGAN, ANDREW	ACTOR	711 S BEVERLY GLEN BLVD	LOS ANGELES, CA	90024
DUGGAN, DEBRA	ACTRESS	247 S BEVERLY DR #102	BEVERLY HILLS, CA	90210
DUGGAN, HACKSAW JIM	WRESTLER	POST OFFICE BOX 3859	STAMFORD, CT	06905
DUGGAN, RICHARD	ACTOR	711 S BEVERLY GLEN BLVD	LOS ANGELES, CA	90024
DUGGAN, TOMMY	ACTOR	808 HOWARD HOUSE, DOLPHIN SQ	LONDON SW1	ENGLAND
DUGGIN, FREDDY	GUITARIST	1009 FRANKLIN RD	MURFREESBORO, TN	37130
DUGOSH, DARRYL	SINGER	3198 ROYAL LN #204	DALLAS, TX	75229
DUGOW, IRIS	CABLE EXECUTIVE	2049 CENTURY PARK E #4170	LOS ANGELES, CA	90067
DUGUAY, RON	ACTOR	150 E 58TH ST #2610	NEW YORK, NY	10021
DUHON, BESSYL	VIOLINIST	ROUTE #2, BOX 125	CHRISTIANA, TN	37037
DUKANE, SY	ACTOR	610 N ORLANDO AVE #204	LOS ANGELES, CA	90048
DUKAS, JAMES G	ACTOR	39 W 67TH ST	NEW YORK, NY	10023
DUKE, BILL	ACTOR	10351 SANTA MONICA BLVD #211	LOS ANGELES, CA	90025
DUKE, BILL	TV DIRECTOR	2200 BROADVIEW TERR	LOS ANGELES, CA	90068
DUKE, DARYL	FILM DIRECTOR	1153 LILLOOET RD	NORTH VANCOUVER, BC	CANADA
DUKE, DAVID A	COMPOSER	831 TEAKWOOD RD	LOS ANGELES, CA	90049
DUKE, FREDDE	ACTRESS	2240 S BENTLEY AVE	LOS ANGELES, CA	90064
DUKE, GEORGE	MUSICIAN-PRODUCER	6430 SUNSET BLVD #1500	HOLLYWOOD, CA	90028
DUKE, JOHN ROBERT	MUSICIAN	1935 ROBINSON RD	MURFREESBORO, TN	37130
DUKE, MATHILDE	VIOLINIST	2116 HARDING PL	NASHVILLE, TN	37215

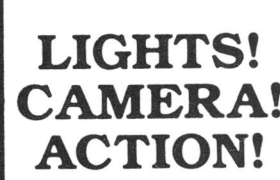

Name	Occupation	Address	City	Zip
DUKE, PATTY	ACTRESS	266 DENSLOW AVE	LOS ANGELES, CA	90049
DUKE, PAUL W	NEWS CORRESPONDENT	4257 FORDHAM RD, NW	WASHINGTON, DC	20816
DUKE, ROBIN	TV WRITER	555 W 57TH ST #1230	NEW YORK, NY	10019
DUKE & THE DRIPS	VOCAL GROUP	POST OFFICE BOX 222	BLACK HAWK, SD	57718
DUKE OF PADUCAH	BANJOIST	625 FARRELL PARKWAY	NASHVILLE, TN	37220
DUKEHART, THOMAS V, JR	PHOTOJOURNALIST	3810 JENIFER ST, NW	WASHINGTON, DC	20015
DUKERT, BETTY C	NEWS CORRESPONDENT	NBC-TV, NEWS DEPARTMENT		
		4001 NEBRASKA AVE, NW	WASHINGTON, DC	20016
DUKES, DAVID	ACTOR	ICM, 8899 BEVERLY BLVD	LOS ANGELES, CA	90048
DUKES, THE	ROCK & ROLL GROUP	ALEX SCOTT, 11 CHARTFIELD SQ	LONDON SW15	ENGLAND
DUKES, THOMAS M	RECORD EXECUTIVE	ARIANA, 808 S PANTANO RD	TUCSON, AZ	85710
DUKESMEN, THE	JAZZ GROUP	HOFFER, 233 1/2 E 48TH ST	NEW YORK, NY	10017
DUKORE, LAWRENCE	SCREENWRITER	RLR ASSOC, LTD, 7 W 51ST ST	NEW YORK, NY	10019
DULANEY, SHARON E	DIRECTOR	DGA, 110 W 57TH ST	NEW YORK, NY	10019
DULIN, DAN	ACTOR	38 W 31ST ST #403	NEW YORK, NY	10001
DULLAGHAN, JAMES R	TV EXECUTIVE	ESPN, ESPN PLAZA	BRISTOL, CT	06010
DULLEA, KEIR	ACTOR	6 DOGWOOD LN	WESTPORT, CT	06880
DULO, JANE	ACTRESS	904 HILLDALE AVE #2	LOS ANGELES, CA	90069
DUMAS, ANDRE	ACTOR	19 AVE DE CHATEAU	MAUDON 92190	FRANCE
DUMAS, DUKE	GUITARIST	149 MAPLE DR	HENDERSONVILLE, TN	37075
DUMAS, JERRY	CARTOONIST	KING FEATURES SYNDICATE		
		235 E 45TH ST	NEW YORK, NY	10017
DUMAS, JOHN	FILM DIRECTOR	2601 MARLU DR	LOS ANGELES, CA	90046
DUMAS, JOHN J	FILM EDITOR	ACE, 4416 1/2 FINLEY AVE	LOS ANGELES, CA	90027
DUMAS, ROGER	ACTOR	GEORGES LAMBERT AGENCE		
		13 BIS AVE LA MOTTE PIQUET	PARIS 75007	FRANCE
DUMAURIER, DAME DAPHNE	PLAYWRIGHT	KILMARTH, PAR	CORNWALL	ENGLAND
DUMM, JOHN RICKLEY	TV WRITER-PRODUCER	2056 BEL AIRE DR	GLENDALE, CA	91201
DUMONT, PAUL	ACTOR	14 E 52ND ST	NEW YORK, NY	10022
DUMPTRUCK	ROCK & ROLL GROUP	POST OFFICE BOX 551	BROOKLINE, MA	02146
DUNAGIN, RALPH	ARTIST	NEWS AMERICA SYNDICATE		
		1703 KAISER AVE	IRVINE, CA	92714
DUNARD, DAVID	ACTOR	1630 N EDGEMONT ST #E-9	LOS ANGELES, CA	90027
DUNAS, RONALD S	WRITER	10643 SOMMA WY	LOS ANGELES, CA	90077
DUNAVAN, PATRICK	DIRECTOR-PRODUCER	2315 KENILWORTH AVE	LOS ANGELES, CA	90039
DUNAWAY, DON CARLOS	SCREENWRITER	445 N BEDFORD DR #PH	BEVERLY HILLS, CA	90210
DUNBAR, DIXIE	DANCER-ACTRESS	KING, 5905 N BAY RD	MIAMI BEACH, FL	33140
DUNBAR, MARY-ELLEN	ACTRESS	10351 SANTA MONICA BLVD #211	LOS ANGELES, CA	90025
DUNBAR, MIKE	MUSICIAN	304 GREENWAY AVE	NASHVILLE, TN	37205
DUNCAN, ANGUS	ACTOR	6736 LAUREL CANYON BLVD #306	NORTH HOLLYWOOD, CA	91606
DUNCAN, CRAIG	GUITARIST	105 BOSTRING DR	HENDERSONVILLE, TN	37075
DUNCAN, DEXTER	PIANIST	2502 ESSEX PL #B	NASHVILLE, TN	37212
DUNCAN, ELISHA	NEWS CORRESPONDENT	12219 DALEWOOD DR	WHEATON, MD	20902
DUNCAN, HERB	ACTOR	SUNNYRIDGE RD	HARRISON, NY	10528
DUNCAN, JOHNNY	SINGER	ROUTE #2, BOX 356	STEPHENVILLE, TX	76401
DUNCAN, JUDITH A	TV DIRECTOR	554 FOREST HILL RD	LAKE FOREST, IL	60045
DUNCAN, LANNY	ACTOR	336 N ISABEL ST	GLENDALE, CA	91206
DUNCAN, MARY	ACTRESS	SANFORD, 321 TANGIER AVE	PALM BEACH, FL	33480
DUNCAN, MEREDITH	ACTRESS	4257 CLYBOURN AVE	NORTH HOLLYWOOD, CA	91602
DUNCAN, MICHAEL	WRITER	555 W 57TH ST #1230	NEW YORK, NY	10019
DUNCAN, PATRICK	SCREENWRITER	8955 BEVERLY BLVD	LOS ANGELES, CA	90048
DUNCAN, PETER	ACTOR	WALLHAM GROVE	LONDON SW6	ENGLAND
DUNCAN, PHILIP	NEWS CORRESPONDENT	3100 JOHN MARSHALL DR	ARLINGTON, VA	22207
DUNCAN, RICHARD L	WRITER-EDITOR	TIME & DISCOVER MAGAZINES		
		TIME & LIFE BUILDING		
		ROCKEFELLER CENTER	NEW YORK, NY	10020
DUNCAN, ROBERT	WRITER	555 W 57TH ST #1230	NEW YORK, NY	10019
DUNCAN, ROBERT B	WRITER-PRODUCER	4360 TROOST AVE	STUDIO CITY, CA	91604
DUNCAN, SANDY	ACTRESS	8743 ASHCROFT AVE	LOS ANGELES, CA	90048
DUNCAN, TERRY WAYNE	GUITARIST	79 BUFFALO TRAIL	MOUNT JULIET, TN	37122
DUNCAN, TODD	PHOTOGRAPHER	92 MANOR RD	HUNTINGTON, NY	11743
DUNCAN, VIVIAN	ACTRESS	1985 N WINERY AVE #103	FRESNO, CA	93703
DUNCAN, WAYNE	ACTOR	8701 DELGANY AVE #215	PLAYA DEL REY, CA	90291
DUNCKEL, JOE	COMEDIAN	9777 HARWIN ST #101	HOUSTON, TX	77036
DUNDAS, JENNIE	ACTRESS	9200 SUNSET BLVD #1210	LOS ANGELES, CA	90069
DUNDAS, ZITA	ACTRESS-WRITER	84 SUTHERLAND AVE	LONDON W9 2QS	ENGLAND
DUNDEE, SUPERSTAR BILL	WRESTLER	NATIONAL WRESTLING ALLIANCE		
		JIM CROCKETT PROMOTIONS		
		421 BRIARBEND DR	CHARLOTTE, NC	28209
DUNGAN, FRANK	TV WRITER-PRODUCER	151 S EL CAMINO DR	BEVERLY HILLS, CA	90212
DUNHAM, DON A	SINGER-GUITARIST	123 STIRTON RD	NASHVILLE, TN	37210
DUNHAM, JAMES	VIOLIST	CCS, 4478 PURDUE AVE	CULVER CITY, CA	90230
DUNHAM, JOANNA	ACTRESS	19 CROFTDOWN RD, CHISWICK	LONDON W4	ENGLAND
DUNHAM, RICHARD S	NEWS CORRESPONDENT	928 S 20TH ST	ARLINGTON, VA	22202
DUNHAM, WILL	NEWS CORRESPONDENT	2121 "H" ST, NW	WASHINGTON, DC	20037
DUNING, GEORGE W	COMPOSER	13455 VENTURA BLVD #207	SHERMAN OAKS, CA	91423
DUNKEL, PAUL	CONDUCTOR	GURTMAN, 162 W 56TH ST	NEW YORK, NY	10019
DUNLAP, AL	ACTOR	8721 SUNSET BLVD #200	LOS ANGELES, CA	90069
DUNLAP, CARLA	BODYBUILDER	THE DIAMOND GYM		
		732 IRVINGTON AVE	MAPLEWOOD, NJ	07040
DUNLAP, HENRY GENE	PIANIST	ROUTE #3, BOX 261-A	ASHLAND CITY, TN	37015
DUNLAP, MARGOT R	NEWS CORRESPONDENT	NBC-TV, NEWS DEPARTMENT		
		4001 NEBRASKA AVE, NW	WASHINGTON, DC	20016
DUNLAP, PAMELA	ACTRESS	12725 VENTURA BLVD #E	STUDIO CITY, CA	91604

DUNLAP, RICHARD D	TV DIRECTOR	484 W 43RD ST #38-E	NEW YORK, NY 10036
DUNLAP, ROBERT	ACTOR	8721 SUNSET BLVD #200	LOS ANGELES, CA 90069
DUNLOP, LESLEY	ACTRESS	2 GERALDINE RD, CHISWICK	LONDON W4 ENGLAND
DUNLOP, MICHAEL	TV PRODUCER	A D PETERS & CO, LTD	
		10 BUCKINGHAM ST	LONDON WC2N 6BU ENGLAND
DUNLOP, PATRICK M	TV WRITER	8955 BEVERLY BLVD	LOS ANGELES, CA 90048
DUNMEYER, EARL E	NEWS CORRESPONDENT	1227 LONG CORNER RD	MOUNT AIRY, MD 21771
DUNMIRE, JOHN P	PHOTOJOURNALIST	105 HOPELAND LN	STERLING, VA 22170
DUNN, ALDEN B	COMPOSER-CONDUCTOR	1918 COLLEGE VISTA AVE	WALNUT, CA 91789
DUNN, BILL	GUITARIST	180 WALLACE RD #F-16	NASHVILLE, TN 37211
DUNN, BOB	CARTOONIST	KING FEATURES SYNDICATE	
		235 E 45TH ST	NEW YORK, NY 10017
DUNN, CAL	DIRECTOR	ROUTE #3, BOX 86-L	
		SUNLIT HILLS	SANTE FE, NM 87501
DUNN, CHRIS WATERS	GUITARIST	5628 KENDALL DR	NASHVILLE, TN 37209
DUNN, CLIVE	ACTOR-COMEDIAN	31 NASSAU RD	LONDON SW13 ENGLAND
DUNN, DANNY	GUITARIST	26 DUPREE DR	MC KINNEY, TX 75069
DUNN, MICHAEL	NEWS CORRESPONDENT	1755 S JEFFERSON DAVIS HWY	ARLINGTON, VA 22202
DUNN, MIGNON	MEZZO-SOPRANO	CAMI, 165 W 57TH ST	NEW YORK, NY 10019
DUNN, RICHARD	CONDUCTOR	27 SKYLINE CIR	SANTA BARBARA, CA 93109
DUNN, ROBERT J	WRITER	8955 BEVERLY BLVD	LOS ANGELES, CA 90048
DUNN, RON	DIRECTOR	13324 DENVER CIR N	STERLING HEIGHTS, MI 48077
DUNN, SUSAN	SOPRANO	HILLYER, 250 W 57TH ST	NEW YORK, NY 10107
DUNN, THOMAS	CONDUCTOR	157 W 57TH ST #1100	NEW YORK, NY 10019
DUNN, TRISHA	ACTRESS	8721 SUNSET BLVD #103	LOS ANGELES, CA 90069
DUNN, WILLIAM	COLUMNIST	POST OFFICE BOX 500	WASHINGTON, DC 20044
DUNNAGAN, MICHAEL	ACTOR	685 W GRANDVIEW AVE	SIERRA MADRE, CA 91024
DUNNAM, STEPHANIE	ACTRESS	9744 WILSHIRE BLVD #206	BEVERLY HILLS, CA 90212
DUNNE, GRIFFIN	ACTOR-PRODUCER	10100 SANTA MONICA BLVD #1600	LOS ANGELES, CA 90067
DUNNE, IRENE	ACTRESS	461 N FARING RD	LOS ANGELES, CA 90024
DUNNE, JAMES PATRICK	COMPOSER	3030 DURAND DR	LOS ANGELES, CA 90068
DUNNE, JOHN GREGORY	NOVELIST	ICM, 40 W 57TH ST	NEW YORK, NY 10019
DUNNE, MURPHY	WRITER	8955 BEVERLY BLVD	LOS ANGELES, CA 90048
DUNNE, MURPHY	ACTOR	1850 1/2 N VISTA ST	LOS ANGELES, CA 90046
DUNNE, NANCY	NEWS CORRESPONDENT	5407 FALLRIVER ROW CT	COLUMBIA, MD 21044
DUNNE, PETER	TV PRODUCER	LORIMAR-TELEPICTURES	
		3970 OVERLAND AVE	CULVER CITY, CA 90230
DUNNE, PHILIP	WRITER-PRODUCER	24708 PACIFIC COAST HWY	MALIBU, CA 90265
DUNNE, TERRY	TALENT AGENT	125 E 15TH ST	NEW YORK, NY 10003
DUNNELL, RAN	DIRECTOR	5800 KELVIN AVE	WOODLAND HILLS, CA 91367
DUNNING, BRUCE	NEWS CORRESPONDENT	CBS NEWS, 524 W 57TH ST	NEW YORK, NY 10019
DUNNOCK, MILDRED	ACTRESS	URMY, RFD POST OFFICE BOX 525	VINEYARD HAVEN, MA 02568
DUNPHY, JERRY	BROADCAST JOURNALIST	KABC-TV, 4151 PROSPECT AVE	LOS ANGELES, CA 90027
DUNROE, MARY ANN	ACTRESS	439 S LA CIENEGA BLVD #117	LOS ANGELES, CA 90048
DUNSHEATH, LISA	ACTRESS	SF & A, 121 N SAN VICENTE BLVD	BEVERLY HILLS, CA 90211
DUNSMORE, BARRIE	NEWS CORRESPONDENT	ABC-TV, NEWS DEPARTMENT	
		1717 DE SALES ST, NW	WASHINGTON, DC 20036
DUNSMUIR, THOMAS D	WRITER	567 RADCLIFFE AVE	PACIFIC PALISADES, CA 90272
DUNSTAN, TOM	ACTOR	3533 KEYSTONE AVE #2	LOS ANGELES, CA 90034
DUO ELMARS	ACROBATS	HALL, 138 FROG HOLLOW RD	CHURCHVILLE, PA 18966
DUPOIS, STARLETTA	ACTRESS	8350 SANTA MONICA BLVD #103	LOS ANGELES, CA 90069
DUPONT, STEPHEN	SINGER	CAMI, 165 W 57TH ST	NEW YORK, NY 10019
DUPOUY, JEAN	TENOR	1182 MARKET ST #311	SAN FRANCISCO, CA 94102
DUPREE, ROBBIE	SINGER	4121 WILSHIRE BLVD #215	LOS ANGELES, CA 90010
DUPREES, THE	VOCAL GROUP	JOHN SALVATO ENTS	
		111 W 6TH ST	BAYONNE, NJ 07002
DUPUY, CHARLOTTE H	NEWS CORRESPONDENT	340 NATIONAL PRESS BLDG	
		529 14TH ST, NW	WASHINGTON, DC 20045
DURACK, ALEXIS	ACTRESS	1741 N IVAR AVE #221	LOS ANGELES, CA 90028
DURAL, JEFFREY P	COMPOSER	149 E 120TH ST	LOS ANGELES, CA 90061
DURALIA, DARLENE	ACTRESS	3935 VINELAND AVE #6	NORTH HOLLYWOOD, CA 91604
DURAN, ROBERTO	BOXER	BOX 157, ARENA COLON	PANAMA CITY PANAMA
DURAN DURAN	ROCK & ROLL GROUP	273 BROAD ST	BIRMINGHAM B12 DS ENGLAND
DURAND, AL	RECORD EXECUTIVE	ALFIE RECORDS COMPANY	
		7769 MELROSE AVE	LOS ANGELES, CA 90046
DURAND, ENRIQUE	NEWS CORRESPONDENT	7739 BURNT TREE DR	MANASSAS, VA 22111
DURAND, JOSEPH W	DIRECTOR	729 CLEARVIEW AVE	WOODBURY HEIGHTS, NJ 08097
DURAND, RUDY	WRITER-PRODUCER	KOALA, 361 N CANON DR	BEVERLY HILLS, CA 90210
DURANG, CHRISTOPHER	WRITER	555 W 57TH ST #1230	NEW YORK, NY 10019
DURANT, CELESTE	WRITER	8955 BEVERLY BLVD	LOS ANGELES, CA 90048
DURANT, JOHN	WRITER	350 10TH AVE S	NAPLES, FL 33940
DURBANO, ART	WRITER-EDITOR	TV GUIDE, 100 MATSONFORD RD	RADNOR, PA 19088
DURBIN, FRAN	NEWS CORRESPONDENT	3869 FAIRFAX SQ	FAIRFAX, VA 22031
DURBRIDGE, FRANCIS	WRITER	4 FAIRACRES, ROEHAMPTON	LONDON SW15 5LX ENGLAND
DURDEN, CHARLES	WRITER	555 W 57TH ST #1230	NEW YORK, NY 10019
DURHAM, BRIAN J	NEWS CORRESPONDENT	2139 WISCONSIN AVE, NW	WASHINGTON, DC 20007
DURHAM, BUDDY	GUITARIST	POST OFFICE BOX 60462	NASHVILLE, TN 37206
DURHAM, CARROLL E	GUITARIST	ROUTE #1, BOX 388	WAYNESBORO, VA 22980
DURHAM, CHRIS	ACTOR	ABC-TV, "RYAN'S HOPE"	
		1330 AVE OF THE AMERICAS	NEW YORK, NY 10019
DURHAM, DEBORAH	NEWS CORRESPONDENT	444 N CAPITOL ST, NW	WASHINGTON, DC 20001
DURHAM, EARL	PRODUCER	FRASER, 11811 W OLYMPIC BLVD	LOS ANGELES, CA 90064
DURHAM, EARL L	TV WRITER	8955 BEVERLY BLVD	LOS ANGELES, CA 90048
DURHAM, LAWRENCE	MANDOLINIST	ROUTE #1, BOX 122	CENTERVILLE, TN 37033
DURHAM BROTHERS, THE	C & W GROUP	742-B LINDEN GREEN DR	HERMITAGE, TN 37076

Name	Occupation	Address	City	Zip/Country
DURICKA, JOHN	PHOTOGRAPHER	4508 NEPTUNE DR	ALEXANDRIA, VA	22309
DURKEE, CUTLER	WRITER-EDITOR	PEOPLE/TIME & LIFE BLDG		
		ROCKEFELLER CENTER	NEW YORK, NY	10020
DURKEE, LINDA	NEWS CORRESPONDENT	672 HILLANDALE RD	CHEVY CHASE, MD	20815
DURKIN, TOM	WRITER	8955 BEVERLY BLVD	LOS ANGELES, CA	90048
DURNING, CHARLES	ACTOR	10590 WILSHIRE BLVD #506	LOS ANGELES, CA	90024
DUROCHER, LEO	BASEBALL	1400 E PALM CANYON DR #210	PALM SPRINGS, CA	92262
DURON, DAVID	WRITER	8955 BEVERLY BLVD	LOS ANGELES, CA	90048
DURON, GILBERT V, III	WRITER	8955 BEVERLY BLVD	LOS ANGELES, CA	90048
DURR, BARBARA	NEWS CORRESPONDENT	3600 "T" ST, NW	WASHINGTON, DC	20007
DURRELL, DON	ACTOR	ABC-TV, "ALL MY CHILDREN"		
		1330 AVE OF THE AMERICAS	NEW YORK, NY	10019
DURRELL, MICHAEL	ACTOR	POST OFFICE BOX 5617	BEVERLY HILLS, CA	90210
DURRETT, RICHARD	MUSICIAN	POST OFFICE BOX 24801	NASHVILLE, TN	37202
DURSLAG, MELVIN	COLUMNIST	523 DALEHURST AVE	LOS ANGELES, CA	90024
DURSO, MICHAEL	WRITER	555 W 57TH ST #1230	NEW YORK, NY	10019
DURSTON, DAVID E	WRITER	8955 BEVERLY BLVD	LOS ANGELES, CA	90048
DURY, IAN & THE BLOCKHEADS	ROCK & ROLL GROUP	ICM, 40 W 57TH ST	NEW YORK, NY	10019
DUSAY, DEBRA	ACTRESS	9255 SUNSET BLVD #603	LOS ANGELES, CA	90069
DUSAY, MARJ	ACTRESS	1930 CENTURY PARK W #303	LOS ANGELES, CA	90067
DUSENBERRY, ANN	ACTRESS	9000 SUNSET BLVD #1200	LOS ANGELES, CA	90069
DUSENBERRY, PHILIP B	SCREENWRITER	555 W 57TH ST #1230	NEW YORK, NY	10019
DUSKIN, KENNETH	DIRECTOR	RURAL DELIVERY #5, BOX 256		
		PRIMROSE ST	KATONAH, NY	10536
DUSKIN, MARVIN	WRITER	555 W 57TH ST #1230	NEW YORK, NY	10019
DUSSAULT, NANCY	ACTRESS	8500 WILSHIRE BLVD #506	BEVERLY HILLS, CA	90211
DUSSAUT, THERESE	PIANIST	POST OFFICE BOX 884	NEW YORK, NY	10023
DUSTON, DIANE A	NEWS CORRESPONDENT	2719 36TH PL, NW	WASHINGTON, DC	20007
DUTCH, DEBORAH	ACTRESS	801 S WOOSTER ST #2	LOS ANGELES, CA	90035
DUTCH, RAYMOND	WRITER	555 W 57TH ST #1230	NEW YORK, NY	10019
DUTEIL, JEFFREY	TV WRITER	9122 AMBOY AVE	SUN VALLEY, CA	91352
DUTOIT, CHARLES	CONDUCTOR	ICM, 40 W 57TH ST	NEW YORK, NY	10019
DUTTINE, JOHN	ACTOR	BROWNE, 13 SAINT MARTIN RD	LONDON SW9	ENGLAND
DUTTON, CHARLES S	ACTOR	151 S EL CAMINO DR	BEVERLY HILLS, CA	90212
DUTTON, JOHN C	DIRECTOR	1289 N CRESCENT HGTS BLVD #A	LOS ANGELES, CA	90046
DUTTON, NAN	CASTING DIRECTOR	9911 W PICO BLVD #1580	LOS ANGELES, CA	90035
DUVALL, JAMES E	NEWS CORRESPONDENT	2828 WISCONSIN AVE, NW	WASHINGTON, DC	20007
DUVALL, LAWRENCE C	NEWS CORRESPONDENT	5151 WISCONSIN AVE, NW	WASHINGTON, DC	20016
DUVALL, ROBERT	ACTOR	257 W 86TH ST	NEW YORK, NY	10024
DUVALL, SHELLEY	ACTRESS	13280 VALLEY VISTA BLVD	SHERMAN OAKS, CA	91423
DUX, PIERRE	ACTOR	ARTMEDIA, 10 AVE GEORGE	PARIS 75008	FRANCE
DUYKERS, JOHN	TENOR	1182 MARKET ST #311	SAN FRANCISCO, CA	94102
DVONCH, RUSSELL	TV WRITER	8955 BEVERLY BLVD	LOS ANGELES, CA	90048
DVORAK, WAYNE	ACTOR	1308 N HAVENHURST DR #5	LOS ANGELES, CA	90046
DVORE, SANDY	ARTIST	9255 SUNSET BLVD #713	LOS ANGELES, CA	90069
DVORE, SANDY	TV DIRECTOR	840 N LARRABEE ST	LOS ANGELES, CA	90069
DWAINE, RONNIE	GUITARIST	POST OFFICE BOX 121614	NASHVILLE, TN	37212
DWAN, ROBERT	DIRECTOR	229 AMALFI DR	SANTA MONICA, CA	90402
DWARES, THE	ROCK & ROLL GROUP	POST OFFICE BOX 7112	BURBANK, CA	91510
DWIER, JENNY REBECCA	ACTRESS	FIELDS, 250 W 57TH ST	NEW YORK, NY	10107
DWIGGINS, DAVID	PRODUCER	RIVER RUN PRDICTIONS		
		1040 N LAS PALMAS AVE	LOS ANGELES, CA	90038
DWIGGINS, SUE	WRITER	8955 BEVERLY BLVD	LOS ANGELES, CA	90048
DWORECK, STUART	VIDEO EDITOR	ENTERTAINMENT TONIGHT		
		PARAMOUNT TELEVISION		
		5555 MELROSE AVE	LOS ANGELES, CA	90038
DWORET, LAURENCE	WRITER	6726 MILNER RD	LOS ANGELES, CA	90068
DWORETZKY, TOM	NEWS REPORTER	DISCOVER/TIME & LIFE BLDG		
		ROCKEFELLER CENTER	NEW YORK, NY	10020
DWORSKI, DAVID	WRITER	31840 SEAFIELD DR	MALIBU, CA	90265
DWORSKI, SUSAN B	WRITER	31840 SEAFIELD DR	MALIBU, CA	90265
DWORSKY, RICHARD	MUSICIAN	POST OFFICE BOX 9388	STANFORD, CA	94305
DWYER, FRANK	ACTOR	243 W 4TH ST #5	NEW YORK, NY	10014
DWYER, LESLIE	ACTOR	PIPPINS, LITTLE PADDOCK	SUSSEX	ENGLAND
		RINGMER, LEWES	SUSSEX	ENGLAND
DWYER, PAULA E	NEWS CORRESPONDENT	2518 SWIFT RUN ST	VIENNA, VA	22180
DWYER, THOMAS	WRITER	555 W 57TH ST #1230	NEW YORK, NY	10019
DWYER-DOBBIN, MARY ALICE	TV PRODUCER	HEARST/ABC-TV		
		555 5TH AVE	NEW YORK, NY	10017
DYBAS, JAMES	ACTOR	14350 ADDISON ST #220	SHERMAN OAKS, CA	91423
DYER, CHARLES CORNELIUS	DIRECTOR	DGA, 110 W 57TH ST	NEW YORK, NY	10019
DYER, EDDY C	ACTOR	1418 N HIGHLAND AVE #102	LOS ANGELES, CA	90028
DYER, JAMES E, JR	NEWS CORRESPONDENT	4461 CONNECTICUT AVE, NW	WASHINGTON, DC	20008
DYER, WILLIAM DAVID	PIANIST	2512 OAKLAND AVE	NASHVILLE, TN	37212
DYKEMA, SCOTT A	NEWS CORRESPONDENT	626 NORTH IVY ST	ARLINGTON, VA	22201
DYKEWICZ, PAUL G	NEWS CORRESPONDENT	13113 TAMARACK RD	SILVER SPRING, MD	20904
DYKINGA, JACK	PHOTOJOURNALIST	POST OFFICE BOX 26807	TUCSON, AZ	85726
DYKMAN, JOAN DAY	ACTRESS	10000 RIVERSIDE DR #12-14	TOLUCA LAKE, CA	91602
DYKSTRA, JOHN C	DIRECTOR	6842 VALJEAN AVE	VAN NUYS, CA	91406
DYLAN, BOB	SINGER-SONGWRITER	7156 BIRDVIEW AVE	MALIBU, CA	90265
DYMALLY, AMENTHA V	ACTRESS	2366 W 23RD ST	LOS ANGELES, CA	90018
DYNAMITE KID, THE	WRESTLER	SEE - BRITISH BULLDOGS, THE		
DYNARSKI, GENE	ACTOR	435 S LA CIENEGA BLVD #108	LOS ANGELES, CA	90048
DYNATONES, THE	ROCK & ROLL GROUP	ROUNDER RECORDS, 1 CAMP ST	CAMBRIDGE, MA	02140
DYNE, MICHAEL	WRITER	555 W 57TH ST #1230	NEW YORK, NY	10019

EARTH, WIND & FIRE

ECHO & THE BUNNYMEN

Les Pattinson • Pete De Freitas • Ian McCulloch • Will Sergeant

DYRECTOR, JOYCE	WRITER	756 1/2 N CROFT AVE	LOS ANGELES, CA	90069
DYRECTOR, STANLEY	ACTOR-WRITER	756 1/2 N CROFT AVE	LOS ANGELES, CA	90069
DYRENFORTH, DR H O	ACTOR	3489 ASHWOOD AVE	LOS ANGELES, CA	90066
DYSART, RICHARD A	ACTOR	654 COPELAND CT	SANTA MONICA, CA	90405
DYSERT, ALAN	ACTOR	304 W 88TH ST	NEW YORK, NY	10024
DYSON, ANNE	ACTRESS	16 WILMINGTON HOUSE		
		18 HIGHBURY CRESCENT	LONDON N5	ENGLAND
DYSON, BOBBY	GUITARIST	3378 EZELL RD	NASHVILLE, TN	37211
DYSON, NOEL	ACTRESS	18 PETHERTON RD, GARDEN FLAT	LONDON N5	ENGLAND
DYSON, RONNIE	SINGER	65 W 55TH ST #6-C	NEW YORK, NY	10019
DZUNDZA, GEORGE	ACTOR	211 S BEVERLY BLVD #201	BEVERLY HILLS, CA	90212

E

E, SHEILA	SINGER-MUSICIAN	11355 W OLYMPIC BLVD #555	LOS ANGELES, CA	90064
E L O	ROCK & ROLL GROUP	SEE - ELECTRIC LIGHT ORCHESTRA		
EADES, RONALD LEE	SAXOPHONIST	POST OFFICE BOX 2861	MUSCLE SHOALS, AL	35660
EADIE, BILL	WRESTLER	SEE - MASKED SUPERSTAR, THE		
EADY, DAVID	TV WRITER-DIRECTOR	59-A ALBERT DR	LONDON SW19 6LD	ENGLAND
EAGAN, SHERMAN G	TV DIRECTOR	23 HOLLOW TREE RIDGE	DARIEN, CT	06820
EAGLE, BOBBY BOLD	WRESTLER	AMERICAN WRESTLING ASSOC		
		MINNEAPLOIS WRESTLING		
		10001 WAYZATA BLVD	MINNETONKA, MN	55345
EAGLE, JACK	ACTOR	63 CONTINENTAL AVE	FOREST HILLS, NY	11375
EAGLE, JACQUELINE	NEWS CORRESPONDENT	2020 "F" ST, NW	WASHINGTON, DC	20006
EAGLE, JEFF	ACTOR	13111 VENTURA BLVD #204	STUDIO CITY, CA	91604
EAGLE, MARY	PRODUCER	MCA/UNIVERSAL STUDIOS, INC		
		100 UNIVERSAL CITY PLAZA	UNIVERSAL CITY, CA	91608
EAGLE, STARSHIP	WRESTLER	SEE - SPIVEY, DANIEL		
		.... "GOLDEN BOY"		
EAGLESON, LEONARD	TENOR	59 E 54TH ST #81	NEW YORK, NY	10022
EAKINS, HENRY E	NEWS CORRESPONDENT	3231 YUMA ST, NW	WASHINGTON, DC	20008
EAMES, JOHN	ACTOR	9220 SUNSET BLVD #202	LOS ANGELES, CA	90069
EANES, JIM	SINGER	MCS, 301 SHAKESPEARE AVE	MADISON, TN	37115
EARING, ROBERT E	WRITER	555 W 57TH ST #1230	NEW YORK, NY	10019
EARL, DONALD	GUITARIST	554 SAVELY DR	HENDERSONVILLE, TN	37075
EARL, ELIZABETH	ACTRESS	5226 BECKFORD AVE	TARZANA, CA	91356
EARL, MAUREEN	WRITER	8955 BEVERLY BLVD	LOS ANGELES, CA	90048
EARLE, ANITRA	TV WRITER	8955 BEVERLY BLVD	LOS ANGELES, CA	90048
EARLE, STEVE	SINGER-SONGWRITER	SIDE ONE MANAGEMENT		
		1775 BROADWAY, 7TH FLOOR	NEW YORK, NY	10019
EARLEY, CANDICE	ACTRESS	14 W 44TH ST #1500	NEW YORK, NY	10036
EARLL, ROBERT	WRITER	9022 SUNSET BLVD #531	LOS ANGELES, CA	90069
EARNHARDT, DAVID C	DIRECTOR	DGA, 110 W 57TH ST	NEW YORK, NY	10019
EARONS, THE	RHYTHM & BLUES GROUP	200 W 51ST ST #1410	NEW YORK, NY	10019
EARTH, WIND & FIRE	SOUL GROUP	11355 W OLYMPIC BLVD #555	LOS ANGELES, CA	90064
EARTH QUAKE	ROCK & ROLL GROUP	POST OFFICE BOX 589	BERKELEY, CA	94701
EARWOOD, MUNDO	MUSICIAN	3012 N MAIN ST	HOUSTON, TX	77009
EASLEY, DOUGLAS	ACTOR	200 W 16TH ST	NEW YORK, NY	10011
EASLEY, JAMES LAVELL	SINGER	POST OFFICE BOX 30166	MEMPHIS, TN	38130
EAST, JEFF	ACTOR	2516 HARGROVE DR	LOS ANGELES, CA	90068
EAST, JOHN M	ACTOR-WRITER	22 GIBSON'S HILL	LONDON SW16 3JP	ENGLAND
EAST & WEST COAST DOO-WOP	VOCAL GROUP	OLDIES, 5218 ALMONT ST	LOS ANGELES, CA	90032
EASTBURN, JOSEPH	ACTOR	85 CHRISTOPHER ST #6-B	NEW YORK, NY	10014
EASTERBROOK, GREGG	NEWS CORRESPONDENT	520 CONSTITUTION AVE, NE	WASHINGTON, DC	20002
EASTERBROOK, LESLIE	ACTRESS	ABC-TV, "RYAN'S HOPE"		
		1330 AVE OF THE AMERICAS	NEW YORK, NY	10019
EASTHAM, RICHARD	ACTOR	1529 ORIOLE LN	LOS ANGELES, CA	90069
EASTIN, STEPHEN	ACTOR	15010 VENTURA BLVD #219	SHERMAN OAKS, CA	91403
EASTMAN, ALAN	WRITER	555 W 57TH ST #1230	NEW YORK, NY	10019
EASTMAN, CHARLES	WRITER-PRODUCER	113 27TH ST #B	MANHATTAN BEACH, CA	90266
EASTMAN, LYNN	ACTRESS	8721 SUNSET BLVD #200	LOS ANGELES, CA	90069
EASTMAN, PETER A	ACTOR	112 GREENE ST	NEW YORK, NY	10012
EASTMAN, SPENCER	WRITER	8955 BEVERLY BLVD	LOS ANGELES, CA	90048
EASTON, BRUCE J	WRITER	8955 BEVERLY BLVD	LOS ANGELES, CA	90048
EASTON, ELLIOT	SINGER-SONGWRITER	LOOKOUT, 9120 SUNSET BLVD	LOS ANGELES, CA	90069
EASTON, ERIC B	NEWS CORRESPONDENT	9805 BRISTOL AVE	SILVER SPRINGS, MD	20901
EASTON, JACK	COMPOSER-CONDUCTOR	295 CENTRAL PARK W	NEW YORK, NY	10024
EASTON, ROBERT	ACTOR	1000 S PASADENA AVE	PASADENA, CA	91105
EASTON, SHAWN	ACTOR	151 S EL CAMINO DR	BEVERLY HILLS, CA	90212
EASTON, SHEENA	SINGER-SONGWRITER	WASSERMAN, 5954 WILKINSON AVE	NORTH HOLLYWOOD, CA	91607
EASTWOOD, ALISON	ACTRESS	MALPASO PRODUCTIONS		
		1900 AVE OF THE STARS	LOS ANGELES, CA	90067
EASTWOOD, CLINT	ACTOR-DIRECTOR	MALPASO PRODUCTIONS		
		1900 AVE OF THE STARS	LOS ANGELES, CA	90067
EASTWOOD, KYLE	ACTOR	MALPASO PRODUCTIONS		
		1900 AVE OF THE STARS	LOS ANGELES, CA	90067
EATON, ANTHONY	VIDEO PRODUCER	10100 SANTA MONICA BLVD #1600	LOS ANGELES, CA	90067

EATON, BEAUTIFUL BOBBY	WRESTLER	NATIONAL WRESTLING ALLIANCE	....
	....	JIM CROCKETT PROMOTIONS	....
	....	421 BRIARBEND DR	CHARLOTTE, NC 28209
EATON, BOB	TV EXECUTIVE	NBC-TV, 3000 W ALAMEDA AVE	BURBANK, CA 91523
EATON, DIAN	ACTRESS	12320 CHANDLER BLVD #12	NORTH HOLLYWOOD, CA 91607
EATON, DONALD P H	TV WRITER	8955 BEVERLY BLVD	LOS ANGELES, CA 90048
EATON, REBECCA	WRITER	555 W 57TH ST #1230	NEW YORK, NY 10019
EATON, SHIRLEY	ACTRESS	2 BUCKS AVE, OXHEY	HERTS .... ENGLAND
EATON, WILLIAM	NEWS REPORTOR	1875 "I" ST, NW	WASHINGTON, DC 20006
EAVES, JAMES E	PHOTOGRAPHER	12497 LOLLY POST LN	WOODBRIDGE, VA 22192
EBB, FRED	LYRICIST	146 CENTRAL PARK W #14-D	NEW YORK, NY 10023
EBBECKE, MICHAEL	BARITONE	CAMI, 165 W 57TH ST	NEW YORK, NY 10019

Name	Occupation	Address	City	Zip
EBER, JOSE	HAIR STYLIST	1230 N HORN AVE #530	LOS ANGELES, CA	90069
EBERHARDT, RICHARD	POET	5 WEBSTER TERR	HANOVER, NH	03755
EBERLE, ROBERT C	DIRECTOR	DGA, 110 W 57TH ST	NEW YORK, NY	10019
EBERSOLE, CHRISTINE	ACTRESS	THE WILLIAM MORRIS AGENCY		
		1350 AVE OF THE AMERICAS	NEW YORK, NY	10019
EBERT, ALAN M	WRITER	555 W 57TH ST #1230	NEW YORK, NY	10019
EBERT, ROGER	FILM CRITIC	509 W DICKENS AVE	CHICAGO, IL	60614
EBERTS, JOHN "JAKE"	FILM PRODUCER	3 AUDLEY SQ	LONDON W1	ENGLAND
EBIN, DAVID J	WRITER	555 W 57TH ST #1230	NEW YORK, NY	10019
EBONEE, WEBB	SINGER	POST OFFICE BOX 161076	MEMPHIS, TN	38116
EBONY	WRESTLER	GORGEOUS GIRLS OF WRESTLING		
		RIVIERA HOTEL & CASINO		
		DAVID B MC LANE PRODS		
		2901 S LAS VEGAS BLVD	LAS VEGAS, NV	89109
EBRAHIM, GRETCHEN	TV WRITER	630 BIENVENEDA AVE	PACIFIC PALISADES, CA	90272
EBSEN, BONNIE	ACTRESS	POST OFFICE BOX 356	AGOURA, CA	91301
EBSEN, BUDDY	ACTOR	POST OFFICE BOX 356	AGOURA, CA	91301
EBY, DEBORAH	NEWS CORRESPONDENT	10010 COLUMBINE	GREAT FALLS, VA	22066
EBY, GEORGE	ENTERTAINMENT EXEC	11679 DONA ALICIA PL	STUDIO CITY, CA	91604
EBY, JOHN	ACTOR	733 N SEWARD ST	LOS ANGELES, CA	90038
EBZERY, JOAN	NEWS CORRESPONDENT	5342 E 41ST ST	NEW YORK, NY	10017
ECCLES, AIMEE	ACTRESS	15010 VENTURA BLVD #219	SHERMAN OAKS, CA	91403
ECHAVE, JOHN	PHOTOGRAPHER	6623 WESTERN AVE, NW	WASHINGTON, DC	20015
ECHEVERRIA, DIEGO	TV WRITER	555 W 57TH ST #1230	NEW YORK, NY	10019
ECHOLLAS, JEM	ACTOR	3330 BARHAM BLVD #103	LOS ANGELES, CA	90068
ECKE, WALTER	WRITER	555 W 57TH ST #1230	NEW YORK, NY	10019
ECKELS, NANCY D	WRITER	5100 RIVERTON AVE #4	NORTH HOLLYWOOD, CA	91601
ECKERSLEY, DENNIS	BASEBALL	263 MORSE RD	SUDBURY, MA	01776
ECKERT, BARTON M	NEWS CORRESPONDENT	400 NATIONAL PRESS BLDG		
		529 14TH ST, NW	WASHINGTON, DC	20045
ECKHAUS, RICHARD B	TV WRITER	8955 BEVERLY BLVD	LOS ANGELES, CA	90048
ECKHERT, JULIE	NEWS CORRESPONDENT	WABC-TV, 7 LINCOLN SQ	NEW YORK, NY	10023
ECKHOFF, HERBERT	SINGER	59 E 54TH ST #81	NEW YORK, NY	10022
ECKHOUSE, JAMES	ACTOR	11726 SAN VICENTE BLVD #300	LOS ANGELES, CA	90049
ECKSTEIN, GEORGE	WRITER-PRODUCER	1900 AVE OF THE STARS #2375	LOS ANGELES, CA	90067
ECKSTINE, BILLY	SINGER	1118 15TH ST #4	SANTA MONICA, CA	90403
ECONOMOU, ROSE-MARIE	WRITER	555 W 57TH ST #1230	NEW YORK, NY	10019
ECSTEIN, JOHN	CLOWN	2701 COTTAGE WY #14	SACRAMENTO, CA	95825
EDDIE, JOHN	SINGER	130 W 57TH ST #2-A	NEW YORK, NY	10019
EDDINGS, CYNTHIA	WRITER	555 W 57TH ST #1230	NEW YORK, NY	10019
EDDINGTON, PAUL	ACTOR	ICM, 388-396 OXFORD ST	LONDON W1	ENGLAND
EDDINS, JAMES DONALD	TV DIRECTOR	420 BROOKSHIRE DR	COLUMBIA, SC	29210
EDDO, NANCY	WRITER	5516 CORTEEN PL #15	NORTH HOLLYWOOD, CA	91607
EDDY, DUANE	SINGER-GUITARIST	POST OFFICE BOX 10771	ZEPHYR COVE, NV	89448
EDDY, HELEN JEROME	ACTRESS	90 EPISCOPALIAN HOME		
		1428 S MARENGO AVE	ALHAMBRA, CA	91803
EDDY, TIMOTHY	CELLIST	200 W 70TH ST #7-F	NEW YORK, NY	10023
EDELBERG, ALICIA	VIOLINIST	LIEBERMAN, 11 RIVERSIDE DR	NEW YORK, NY	10023
EDELBERG, LOU	ACTOR	3800 BARHAM BLVD #303	LOS ANGELES, CA	90068
EDELHART, YVETTE	ACTRESS	ABRAMS ARTISTS & ASSOCIATES		
		420 MADISON AVE, 14TH FLOOR	NEW YORK, NY	10017
EDELMAN, HERB	ACTOR	147 N OLD TOPANGA CANYON RD	TOPANGA, CA	90290
EDELMAN, JONATHAN	SCREENWRITER	2419 BEVERLY AVE #1	SANTA MONICA, CA	90405
EDELMAN, JULIUS	DIRECTOR	21-15 34TH AVE	LONG ISLAND, CA	11106
EDELMAN, SERGEI	PIANIST	SHAW CONCERTS, 1995 BROADWAY	NEW YORK, NY	10023
EDELMAN, SUSIE	CASTING DIRECTOR	4051 RADFORD AVE, BUILDING #5	STUDIO CITY, CA	91604
EDELSTEIN, RICK	WRITER-PRODUCER	747 GAYLEY AVE	LOS ANGELES, CA	90024
EDEN	ROCK & ROLL GROUP	POST OFFICE BOX 6681	HERMOSA BEACH, CA	92615
EDEN, BARBARA	ACTRESS-PRODUCER	1332 N ULSTER ST	ALLENTOWN, PA	18103
EDEN, RICHARD	ACTOR	KNBC-TV, "SANTA BARBARA"		
		3000 W ALAMEDA AVE	BURBANK, CA	91523
EDEN & TAMIR	PIANO DUO	KAY, 58 W 58TH ST	NEW YORK, NY	10019
EDENTON, POLLY R	SINGER	2556 BAKER STATION RD	GOODLETTSVILLE, TN	37072
EDENTON, RAY	GUITARIST	ROUTE #3	GOODLETTSVILLE, TN	37072
EDGAR, ROBERTA	WRITER	703 N FOOTHILL RD	BEVERLY HILLS, CA	90210
EDGAR, WILLIAM ALFRED	WRITER	703 N FOOTHILL RD	BEVERLY HILLS, CA	90210
EDGCOMB, JAMES	ACTOR	15010 VENTURA BLVD #219	SHERMAN OAKS, CA	91403
EDGERTON, JUSTIN	TV WRITER	8955 BEVERLY BLVD	LOS ANGELES, CA	90048
EDGLEY, LESLIE	WRITER	8955 BEVERLY BLVD	LOS ANGELES, CA	90048
EDINGER, CHRISTIANE	VIOLINIST	59 E 54TH ST #81	NEW YORK, NY	10022
EDISON, THOMAS E	WRITER	8955 BEVERLY BLVD	LOS ANGELES, CA	90048
EDLER, LEW	ACTOR	6430 SUNSET BLVD #1203	LOS ANGELES, CA	90028
EDLIN, LAURA	WRITER	555 W 57TH ST #1230	NEW YORK, NY	10019
EDLUND, RICHARD	CINEMATOGRAPHER	POST OFFICE BOX 2230	HOLLYWOOD, CA	90078
EDMISTON, WALTER	ACTOR	15010 VENTURA BLVD #219	SHERMAN OAKS, CA	91403
EDMONDS, BERNARD M	WRITER	555 W 57TH ST #1230	NEW YORK, NY	10019
EDMONDS, LOUIS	ACTOR	250 W 57TH ST #2317	NEW YORK, NY	10107
EDMONDS, ROBERT J	DIRECTOR	1132 W LUNT AVE #9-D	CHICAGO, IL	60626
EDMONDS, RONALD A	PHOTOGRAPHER	5500 EASTON DR	SPRINGFIELD, VA	22151
EDMONDSON, DONNA	MODEL	MODELS & PROMOTIONS AGENCY		
		8560 SUNSET BLVD, 10TH FLOOR	LOS ANGELES, CA	90069
EDMONDSON, RODNEY M	DRUMMER	595 HICKS RD #13-K	NASHVILLE, TN	37221
EDMONSTON, MARY-KATE	ACTRESS	438 N SWEETZER AVE	LOS ANGELES, CA	90048
EDMUNDS, DAVE	SINGER-GUITARIST	POLAR UNION MANAGEMENT		
		119-121 FRESTON RD	LONDON W11 4DB	ENGLAND

Name	Occupation	Address	City	ZIP
EDMUNDS, DAVID E	SAXOPHONIST	413 BRAMBLEWOOD DR	NASHVILLE, TN	37211
EDMUNDS, LAVINA W	NEWS CORRESPONDENT	700 CATHEDRAL ST #4-F	BALTIMORE, MD	21201
EDMUNDS, MALCOLM W	DIRECTOR	1712 W GRIFFIN PL	CHICAGO, IL	60643
EDMUNDS, MARIANNA	WRITER	555 W 57TH ST #1230	NEW YORK, NY	10019
EDSALL, THOMAS B	NEWS CORRESPONDENT	511 4TH AVE, SE	WASHINGTON, DC	20003
EDSEY, CHRISTINE	ACTRESS	1032 HYPERION AVE	LOS ANGELES, CA	90029
EDSON, ERIC	WRITER	BLOOM, 800 S ROBERTSON BLVD	LOS ANGELES, CA	90035
EDSON, HILARY	ACTRESS	9000 SUNSET BLVD #1200	LOS ANGELES, CA	90069
EDWARD, JIMMY	ACTOR	PETER CHARLESWORTH, LTD		
		68 OLD BROMPTON RD	LONDON SW7 3LQ	ENGLAND
EDWARD, KIM H	PHOTOGRAPHER	5067 DRY WELL CT	COLUMBIA, MD	21045
EDWARDO	PERCH POLE DUO	HALL, 138 FROG HOLLOW RD	CHURCHVILLE, PA	18966
EDWARDS, ANNE M	WRITER	555 W 57TH ST #1230	NEW YORK, NY	10019
EDWARDS, ANTHONY	ACTOR	211 S BEVERLY DR #201	BEVERLY HILLS, CA	90212
EDWARDS, BARBARA	ACTRESS-MODEL	MODELS & PROMOTIONS AGENCY		
		8560 SUNSET BLVD, 10TH FLOOR	LOS ANGELES, CA	90069
EDWARDS, BLAKE	WRITER-PRODUCER	1888 CENTURY PARK E #1616	LOS ANGELES, CA	90067
EDWARDS, BURT	ACTOR	208 S BEVERLY DR #4	BEVERLY HILLS, CA	90212
EDWARDS, DOUGLAS	BROADCAST JOURNALIST	CBS NEWS, 51 W 52ND ST	NEW YORK, NY	10019
EDWARDS, E PAUL	TV WRITER	8955 BEVERLY BLVD	LOS ANGELES, CA	90048
EDWARDS, EDWARD	ACTOR	726 IDAHO AVE #105	SANTA MONICA, CA	90403
EDWARDS, ELLA RAINO	ACTRESS	9255 SUNSET BLVD #610	LOS ANGELES, CA	90069
EDWARDS, FRED L	DRUMMER	ROUTE #4, BOX 51	PORTLAND, TN	37148
EDWARDS, GAIL	ACTRESS	POST OFFICE BOX 5617	BEVERLY HILLS, CA	90212
EDWARDS, GARY	DRUMMER	POST OFFICE BOX 391	ANTIOCH, TN	37013
EDWARDS, GEOFF	TV HOST	2172 CENTURY HILL	LOS ANGELES, CA	90067
EDWARDS, GEOFF	FILM EDITOR	1034 N LA JOLLA AVE	LOS ANGELES, CA	90046
EDWARDS, GEOFFREY B	SCREENWRITER	8955 BEVERLY BLVD	LOS ANGELES, CA	90048
EDWARDS, GEORGE	DOBROIST	111 CREEKWOOD LN	HENDERSONVILLE, TN	37075
EDWARDS, GEORGE	PRODUCER	650 N BRONSON AVE	LOS ANGELES, CA	90004
EDWARDS, GEORGE L	SCREENWRITER	8955 BEVERLY BLVD	LOS ANGELES, CA	90048
EDWARDS, GLYNN	ACTOR	GREEN & UNDERWOOD, LTD		
		3 THE BROADWAY		
		GUNNERSBURY LN	LONDON W3 8HR	ENGLAND
EDWARDS, HANLEY E	COMPOSER	2131 3RD AVE	LOS ANGELES, CA	90018
EDWARDS, HENRY	WRITER	555 W 57TH ST #1230	NEW YORK, NY	10019
EDWARDS, J L	WRITER	555 W 57TH ST #1230	NEW YORK, NY	10019
EDWARDS, JAMES RAY	GUITARIST	POST OFFICE BOX 40209	NASHVILLE, TN	37204
EDWARDS, JASON	ACTOR	1418 N HIGHLAND AVE #102	LOS ANGELES, CA	90028
EDWARDS, JENNIFER BLAKE	ACTRESS	1888 CENTURY PARK E #1616	LOS ANGELES, CA	90067
EDWARDS, JOAN	NEWS CORRESPONDENT	2950 VAN NESS ST, NW	WASHINGTON, DC	20008
EDWARDS, JOHN H	ACTOR	3129 HIGHLAND VIEW DR	BURBANK, CA	91504
EDWARDS, JONATHAN	SINGER-SONGWRITER	KEITH CASE COMPANY		
		1016 16TH AVE S	NASHVILLE, TN	37212
EDWARDS, JOSEPH L	GUITARIST	9006 FORREST LAWN DR		
		ROUTE #5	BRENTWOOD, TN	37027
EDWARDS, MARK	SINGER-DRUMMER	POST OFFICE BOX 15812	NORTH HOLLYWOOD, CA	91615
EDWARDS, MAX	MUSICIAN	VARIETY ARTISTS INTL, INC		
		9073 NEMO ST, 3RD FLOOR	LOS ANGELES, CA	90069
EDWARDS, PADDI	ACTRESS	9229 SUNSET BLVD #306	LOS ANGELES, CA	90069
EDWARDS, PAUL F	TV WRITER-DIRECTOR	16812 CHARMEL LN	PACIFIC PALISADES, CA	90272
EDWARDS, RALPH	TV HOST-PRODUCER	1717 N HIGHLAND AVE, 10TH FLOOR	LOS ANGELES, CA	90028
EDWARDS, RANDALL	ACTRESS	247 S BEVERLY DR #102	BEVERLY HILLS, CA	90212
EDWARDS, RICHARD	BANJOIST	POST OFFICE BOX 120672	NASHVILLE, TN	37212
EDWARDS, ROBERT A	NEWS CORRESPONDENT	2025 "M" ST, NW	WASHINGTON, DC	20036
EDWARDS, RONA	ACTRESS	151 N SAN VICENTE BLVD #208	BEVERLY HILLS, CA	90211
EDWARDS, RONNIE CLAIRE	ACTRESS	STONE, 1052 CAROL DR	LOS ANGELES, CA	90069
EDWARDS, ROY	SINGER	POST OFFICE BOX 98	FOREST HILLS, CA	11375
EDWARDS, RYAN	BARITONE	61 W 62ND ST #6-F	NEW YORK, NY	10023
EDWARDS, SI	DRUMMER	114 BOSTRING DR	HENDERSONVILLE, TN	37075
EDWARDS, STACY	ACTRESS	KNBC-TV, "SANTA BARBARA"		
		3000 W ALAMEDA AVE	BURBANK, CA	91523
EDWARDS, STEPHANIE	ACTRESS	8075 W 3RD ST #303	LOS ANGELES, CA	90048
EDWARDS, STEVE	TV HOST	KABC-TV, 4151 PROSPECT AVE	LOS ANGELES, CA	90027
EDWARDS, STEWART W	NEWS CORRESPONDENT	1755 S JEFFERSON DAVIS HWY	ARLINGTON, VA	22202
EDWARDS, THOMAS JACKSON	PIANIST	ROUTE #2, BOX 204	ASHLAND CITY, TN	37015
EDWARDS, VINCENT	ACT-WRI-DIR	4267 MARINA CITY DR #60	MARINA DEL REY, CA	90292
EDWING, DON	WRITER	MAD MAGAZINE, INC		
		485 MADISON AVE	NEW YORK, NY	10022
EELLS, GEORGE	NOVELIST	514 N RODEO DR	BEVERLY HILLS, CA	90210
EFFIGIES, THE	ROCK & ROLL GROUP	POST OFFICE BOX 42684	PHILADELPHIA, PA	19101
EFFRON, DAVID	CONDUCTOR	59 E 54TH ST #81	NEW YORK, NY	10022
EFFRON, ERIC	NEWS CORRESPONDENT	643 1/2 "E" ST, NE	WASHINGTON, DC	20002
EFRAIN, CONRAD	WRESTLER	SEE - JONES, S D		
EFRON, MARSHALL H	WRITER	555 W 57TH ST #1230	NEW YORK, NY	10019
EGAN, LANCE	WRITER	8955 BEVERLY BLVD	LOS ANGELES, CA	90048
EGAN, MARK	TV WRITER	8955 BEVERLY BLVD	LOS ANGELES, CA	90048
EGAN, PETER	ACTOR	FRASER, 91 REGENT ST	LONDON W1	ENGLAND
EGAN, RICHARD	ACTOR	11907 CHAPARAL ST	LOS ANGELES, CA	90049
EGAN, RICHMOND J	NEWS CORRESPONDENT	4408 8TH ST, NE	WASHINGTON, DC	20017
EGAN, SAM	TV PRODUCER	LARSON, 10201 W PICO BLVD	LOS ANGELES, CA	90035
EGAN, SAM	TV WRITER-DIRECTOR	521 12TH ST	SANTA MONICA, CA	90402

DAVE EDMUNDS

JULIE EDGE

PENNY EDWARDS

VINCE EDWARDS

BRITT EKLAND

JACK ELAM

SAM ELLIOTT

WILLIAM GRAY ESPY

EMILO ESTEVEZ

EGAN, TRACY	NEWS CORRESPONDENT	WABC-TV, 7 LINCOLN SQ	NEW YORK, NY	10023
EGE, JULIE	ACTRESS-MODEL	56 SUFFOLK RD	LONDON SW13	ENGLAND
EGE, KONRAD	NEWS CORRESPONDENT	3435 BROWN ST #22, NW	WASHINGTON, DC	20010
EGER, JEFFREY	WRITER	555 W 57TH ST #1230	NEW YORK, NY	10019
EGER, JOSEPH	CONDUCTOR	40 W 67TH ST	NEW YORK, NY	10023
EGERTON, CAL	WRITER	8955 BEVERLY BLVD	LOS ANGELES, CA	90048
EGGAR, SAMANTHA	ACTRESS	STONE, 1052 CAROL DR	LOS ANGELES, CA	90069
EGGART, HARRY R	DIRECTOR	41 SPICER RD	WESTPORT, CT	06880
EGGBEER, WILLIAM T	NEWS CORRESPONDENT	5911 WOODLAND	TAKOMA PARK, MD	20912
EGGERS, BOB	GUITARIST	229 DANYA CREST DR	NASHVILLE, TN	37214
EGGERS, KEVIN	TV WRITER	555 W 57TH ST #1230	NEW YORK, NY	10019
EGGERS, ROBERT	DIRECTOR	3386 FRYMAN PL	STUDIO CITY, CA	91604
EGGERT, NICOLE	ACTRESS	12725 VENTURA BLVD #E	STUDIO CITY, CA	91604
EGGERTON, JOHN S	NEWS CORRESPONDENT	7455 LITLE RIVER TURNPIKE	ANNANDALE, VA	22003
EGLEE, CHARLES	SCREENWRITER	1023 17TH ST #C	SANTA MONICA, CA	90403
EGNATZ, GARY A	COMPOSER	6076 FRANKLIN AVE	LOS ANGELES, CA	90028
EGOROV, YOURI	PIANIST	SHAW CONCERTS, 1995 BROADWAY	NEW YORK, NY	10023
EHLERS, BETH	ACTRESS	9229 SUNSET BLVD #306	LOS ANGELES, CA	90069
EHRENBERG, HALAYNE	WRITER	555 W 57TH ST #1230	NEW YORK, NY	10019
EHRENHALT, ALAN	NEWS CORRESPONDENT	1411 N HIGHLAND ST	ARLINGTON, VA	22201
EHRIN, JOHN	ACTOR	8831 SUNSET BLVD #402	LOS ANGELES, CA	90069
EHRLICH, AARON	DIRECTOR	414 E 52ND ST	NEW YORK, NY	10022
EHRLICH, JANICE	ACTRESS	13111 VENTURA BLVD #204	STUDIO CITY, CA	91604
EHRLICH, JAYNE	WRITER	8955 BEVERLY BLVD	LOS ANGELES, CA	90048
EHRLICH, JESSE	ACTOR	439 S LA CIENEGA BLVD #117	LOS ANGELES, CA	90048
EHRLICH, KEN	WRITER-PRODUCER	17200 OAK VIEW DR	ENCINO, CA	91316
EHRLICH, MAX	WRITER	10459 WILSHIRE BLVD	LOS ANGELES, CA	90024
EHRLICH, SOL	DIRECTOR	49 W 53RD ST	NEW YORK, NY	10019
EHRLICH, STU	TALENT AGENT	9701 WILSHIRE BLVD #800	BEVERLY HILLS, CA	90212
EHRLICHMAN, JOHN	AUTHOR	POST OFFICE BOX 5559	SANTE FE, NM	87502
EHRLING, SIXTEN	CONDUCTOR	ICM, 40 W 57TH ST	NEW YORK, NY	10019
EHRMANN, PAUL	TV WRITER	8955 BEVERLY BLVD	LOS ANGELES, CA	90048
EICH, JOSEPH F	CONDUCTOR	1301 N GENESEE AVE	LOS ANGELES, CA	90046
EICHELBURGER, ROBERT	SAXOPHONIST	ROUTE #2, COUNTRYLINE RD	FAIRVIEW, TN	37062
EICHER, SHELBY JOSEPH	MANDOLINIST	4616 E 68TH ST	TULSA, OK	74136
EICHERN, CHERI	ACTRESS-SINGER	747 S DUNSMUIR AVE	LOS ANGELES, CA	90036
EICHHORN, LISA	ACTRESS	581 FLANDERS RD	WOODBURY, CT	06798
EICHLER, UDI	DIRECTOR-PRODUCER	16 CUMBERLAND RD, KEW	SURREY	ENGLAND
EICHSTEADT, GARY	PIANIST	500 PARAGON MILLS #J-3	NASHVILLE, TN	37211
EIDSON, CARL, JR	OBOIST	POST OFFICE BOX 182		
		RIDGEWOOD STATION	GOODLETTSVILLE, TN	37072
EIDSVOOG, JOHN C	CONDUCTOR	12305 HARTSOOK ST	NORTH HOLLYWOOD, CA	91607
EIFFERT, LEO J, JR	SINGER	POST OFFICE BOX 5412	BUENA VISTA, CA	90620
EIKENBERRY, JILL	ACTRESS	211 S BEVERLY DR #201	BEVERLY HILLS, CA	90212
EILAND, KENNETH S	ACTOR	5756 CRANER AVE	NORTH HOLLYWOOD, CA	91601
EILBACHER, CYNTHIA	ACTRESS	2860 PACIFIC VIEW TERR	LOS ANGELES, CA	90068
EILBACHER, LISA	ACTRESS	10100 SANTA MONICA BLVD #1600	LOS ANGELES, CA	90067
EILBER, JANET	ACTRESS	ICM, 40 W 57TH ST	NEW YORK, NY	10019
EILER, JIM W	WRITER	8955 BEVERLY BLVD	LOS ANGELES, CA	90048
EINBERG, FRANNE	WRITER	10524 BLYTHE AVE	LOS ANGELES, CA	90064
EINFRANK, BOB	ACTOR	5020 TUJUNGA AVE #211	NORTH HOLLYWOOD, CA	91601
EINHORN, LAWRENCE	TV DIRECTOR	5001 OAKDALE AVE	WOODLAND HILLS, CA	91364
EINHORN, MARVIN D	TV DIRECTOR	150 W 79TH ST #6-A	NEW YORK, NY	10024
EINSTEIN, BOB	ACTOR-WRITER	8955 BEVERLY BLVD	LOS ANGELES, CA	90048
EINSTEIN, CHARLES	WRITER	8955 BEVERLY BLVD	LOS ANGELES, CA	90048
EINSTEIN, PAUL	NEWS CORRESPONDENT	POST OFFICE BOX 362	SYKESVILLE, MD	21784
EIRABIE, GHANI	NEWS CORRESPONDENT	5535 COLUMBIA PIKE	ARLINGTON, VA	22204
EISELE, ROBERT	SCREENWRITER	9255 SUNSET BLVD #505	LOS ANGELES, CA	90069
EISEN, GAIL L	WRITER	555 W 57TH ST #1230	NEW YORK, NY	10019
EISEN, JACK E	NEWS CORRESPONDENT	1730 ARLINGTON BLVD	ARLINGTON, VA	22209
EISENBACH, ROBERT	LITERARY AGENCY	760 N LA CIENEGA BLVD	LOS ANGELES, CA	90069
EISENBARTH, RONALD RAY	PHOTOJOURNALIST	625 CENTER ST #201	HERNDON, VA	22070
EISENBERG, HARRY	TV WRITER	JEOPARDY, 1541 N VINE ST	HOLLYWOOD, CA	90028
EISENBERG, IRA	WRITER-PRODUCER	30 BERRY ST	SAN FRANCISCO, CA	94107
EISENBERG, LESLIE J	WRITER	555 W 57TH ST #1230	NEW YORK, NY	10019
EISENBERG, MAX	WRITER	6356 MARYLAND DR	LOS ANGELES, CA	90048
EISENBERG, NAT B	DIRECTOR-PRODUCER	202 E 35TH ST	NEW YORK, NY	10016
EISENMAN, ROBIN G	ACTRESS	5065 GOODLAND AVE	NORTH HOLLYWOOD, CA	91607
EISENMANN, GUSTAVE W	DIRECTOR	375 HIGHLAND AVE	SAN FRANCISCO, CA	94110
EISENMANN, IKE	ACTOR	5306 NORWICH AVE	VAN NUYS, CA	91411
EISENSON, ARTHUR M	TV WRITER	12737 INDIANAPOLIS ST	LOS ANGELES, CA	90035
EISENSTADT, STEVEN	NEWS CORRESPONDENT	1333 "F" ST, NW	WASHINGTON, DC	20004
EISENSTAEDT, ALFRED	PHOTOGRAPHER	TIME/TIME & LIFE BLDG		
		ROCKEFELLER CENTER	NEW YORK, NY	10020
EISENSTOCK, ALAN	TV WRITER	533 N MC CADDEN PL	LOS ANGELES, CA	90004
EISERER, LEONARD A	NEWS CORRESPONDENT	9101 SLIGO CREEK PARKWAY	SILVER SPRING, MD	20901
EISGRAU, MIKE	WRITER	555 W 57TH ST #1230	NEW YORK, NY	10019
EISINGER, LARRY	COLUMNIST	TRIBUNE MEDIA SERVICES		
		64 E CONCORD ST	ORLANDO, FL	32801
EISLER, DAVID	TENOR	SARDOS, 180 W END AVE	NEW YORK, NY	10023
EISLER, PAUL A	SAXOPHONIST	141 NEESE DR #J-22	NASHVILLE, TN	37211
EISLEY, ANTHONY	ACTOR	9441 WILSHIRE BLVD #620-D	BEVERLY HILLS, CA	90210
EISMAN, HY	CARTOONIST	KING FEATURES SYNDICATE		
		235 E 45TH ST	NEW YORK, NY	10017
EISMANN, BERNARD N	TV WRITER	555 W 57TH ST #1230	NEW YORK, NY	10019

Name	Occupation	Address	City	Zip
EISNER, ARTHUR	ACTOR	13336 EBELL ST	VAN NUYS, CA	91402
EISNER, DAVID	ACTOR	260 RIVERSIDE DR #10-G	NEW YORK, NY	10025
EISNER, JANE B	WRITER	283 BEL AIR RD	LOS ANGELES, CA	90077
EITEN, EMILY B	WRITER	555 W 57TH ST #1230	NEW YORK, NY	10019
EITEN, GARY	ACTOR	JARRETT, 220 E 63RD ST	NEW YORK, NY	10021
EITNER, DON	ACTOR-DIRECTOR	10915 HESBY ST	NORTH HOLLYWOOD, CA	91601
EIZONAS, TOM	SINGER-GUITARIST	2737 PENNINGTON BEND RD	NASHVILLE, TN	37214
EKINS, DONNA	ACTRESS	1841 COURTNEY AVE	HOLLYWOOD, CA	90046
EKLAND, BRITT	ACTRESS	1744 N DOHENY DR	LOS ANGELES, CA	90069
EKSTRAND, BRADFORD L	ACTOR	1750 1/2 LUCRETIA AVE	LOS ANGELES, CA	90026
EL BRASERO	WRESTLER	SEE - BRASERO, EL		
EL CHICANO	ROCK & ROLL GROUP	AZTEC, 20531 PLUMMER ST	CHATSWORTH, CA	91311
EL LOBO	WRESTLER	NATIONAL WRESTLING ALLIANCE		
		JIM CROCKETT PROMOTIONS		
		421 BRIARBEND DR	CHARLOTTE, NC	28209
EL MASQUERES	WRESTLING TAG TEAM	CAPITOL INTERNATIONAL		
		11844 MARKET ST	NORTH LIMA, OH	44452
EL SEBAI, NADIA H	WRITER	555 W 57TH ST #1230	NEW YORK, NY	10019
EL-KAISSE, SHEIK ADNAN	WRESTLING MANAGER	AMERICAN WRESTLING ASSOC		
		MINNEAPLOIS WRESTLING		
		10001 WAYZATA BLVD	MINNETONKA, MN	55345
ELAM, JACK	ACTOR	POST OFFICE BOX 5718	SANTA BARBARA, CA	93108
ELANJIAN, GEORGE, JR	TV DIRECTOR	8312 MAPLE DR	LOS ANGELES, CA	90046
ELBLING, HAROLD PETER	TV WRITER	8955 BEVERLY BLVD	LOS ANGELES, CA	90048
ELBO, RICARDO G	NEWS CORRESPONDENT	2310 HOMESTEAD DR	SILVER SPRING, MD	20902
ELCAR, DANA	ACTOR-DIRECTOR	22920 HATTERAS ST	WOODLAND HILLS, CA	91367
ELCAR, NORA	ACTRESS	22920 HATTERAS ST	WOODLAND HILLS, CA	91367
ELDER, ANN W	TV WRITER	1811 COURTNEY AVE	LOS ANGELES, CA	90046
ELDER, JUDITH	ACTRESS	320 S CAMAC ST	PHILADELPHIA, CA	19107
ELDER, JUDYANN	ACTRESS	9220 SUNSET BLVD #202	LOS ANGELES, CA	90069
ELDER, LONNE, III	SCREENWRITER	7615 GLADE AVE #110	CANOGA PARK, CA	91304
ELDER, MARK	CONDUCTOR	ICM, 40 W 57TH ST	NEW YORK, NY	10019
ELDER, PAUL R	ACTOR	5330 LANKERSHIM BLVD #210	NORTH HOLLYWOOD, CA	91601
ELDER, ROBERT	NEWS CORRESPONDENT	3101 38TH ST, NW	WASHINGTON, DC	20016
ELDER, WILLIAM E	WRITER	8955 BEVERLY BLVD	LOS ANGELES, CA	90048
ELDREDGE, GORDON S	WRITER	8955 BEVERLY BLVD	LOS ANGELES, CA	90048
ELDREDGE, GRADY	GUITARIST	203 SEALEY DR #1-107	MADISON, TN	37115
ELDREDGE, NICK	ACTOR	870 N VINE ST #G	LOS ANGELES, CA	90038
ELDREDGE, TERRY WAYNE	GUITARIST	203 SEALEY DR #1-107	MADISON, TN	37115
ELECTRIC LIGHT ORCHESTRA	ROCK & ROLL GROUP	113-117 WARDOUR ST	LONDON W1	ENGLAND
ELECTRIC PEACE	ROCK & ROLL GROUP	POST OFFICE BOX 2428	EL SEGUNDO, CA	90245
ELEGANTS, THE	VOCAL GROUP	KNIGHT, 185 CLINTON AVE	STATEN ISLAND, NY	10301
ELENA, SUESIE	ACTRESS	9200 SUNSET BLVD #909	LOS ANGELES, CA	90069
ELES, SANDOR	ACTOR	BRIAN WHEELER MANAGEMENT		
		19 STRAND ON THE GREEN	LONDON W4	ENGLAND
ELEVATORS, THE	ROCK & ROLL GROUP	CHICKLES, 15 MANSFIELD ST	BOSTON, MA	02134
ELFAND, MARTIN	FILM PRODUCER	9486 LLOYDCREST DR	BEVERLY HILLS, CA	90210
ELFERMAN, GEORGE	BODYBUILDER	953 E SAHARA AVE #11-A	LAS VEGAS, NV	89104
ELFIN, MEL	NEWS CORRESPONDENT	4515 30TH ST, NW	WASHINGTON, DC	20008
ELFMAN, BLOSSOM	TV WRITER	476 GREENCRAIG RD	LOS ANGELES, CA	90049
ELFORD, JENNIE	WRITER	10536 MOORPARK ST	NORTH HOLLYWOOD, CA	91602
ELG, TAINA	ACTRESS	HARTIG, 527 MADISON AVE	NEW YORK, NY	10022
ELGAR, AVRIL	ACTRESS	FRENCH'S, 26 BINNEY ST	LONDON W1	ENGLAND
ELGART, LARRY	ORCHESTRA LEADER	55 E 74TH ST	NEW YORK, NY	10021
ELIAS, ALIX	ACTRESS	8285 SUNSET BLVD #12	LOS ANGELES, CA	90046
ELIAS, CAROLINE	WRITER	8955 BEVERLY BLVD	LOS ANGELES, CA	90048
ELIAS, CHERYL N	WRITER	555 W 57TH ST #1230	NEW YORK, NY	10019
ELIAS, HECTOR	ACTOR	828 N MANSFIELD AVE	LOS ANGELES, CA	90038
ELIAS, JEANNIE	ACTRESS	8380 MELROSE AVE #207	LOS ANGELES, CA	90069
ELIAS, LOUIS	TV WRITER	8955 BEVERLY BLVD	LOS ANGELES, CA	90048
ELIAS, MICHAEL	SCREENWRITER	10036 REEVESBURY DR	BEVERLY HILLS, CA	90210
ELIAS, ROBERT	WRITER	8955 BEVERLY BLVD	LOS ANGELES, CA	90048
ELIAS, ROSALIND	MEZZO-SOPRANO	CAMI, 165 W 57TH ST	NEW YORK, NY	10019
ELIASON, JOHN	TV WRITER	10960 WILSHIRE BLVD #922	LOS ANGELES, CA	90024
ELIASON, JOYCE	SCREENWRITER	8955 BEVERLY BLVD	LOS ANGELES, CA	90048
ELIC, JOSIP	ACTOR	POST OFFICE BOX 793	NEW YORK, NY	10022
ELIKANN, LARRY	TV-FILM DIRECTOR	100 S DOHENY DR	LOS ANGELES, CA	90048
ELIKANN, PETER T	NEWS CORRESPONDENT	NBC NEWS, 4001 NEBRASKA AVE, NW	WASHINGTON, DC	20016
ELINSON, JACK	TV WRITER-PRODUCER	3313 BUTLER AVE	LOS ANGELES, CA	90066
ELIOPOULOS, PHOEBE	NEWS CORRESPONDENT	4900 BATTERY LN #406	BETHESDA, MD	20814
ELIOT, MARC	WRITER	8955 BEVERLY BLVD	LOS ANGELES, CA	90048
ELIOT, TAMARA	ACTRESS	545 MESA LILA RD	GLENDALE, CA	91208
ELISCO, BLASE	TV WRITER	8955 BEVERLY BLVD	LOS ANGELES, CA	90048
ELIZABETH, MISS	WRESTLING VALET	SEE - MISS ELIZABETH		
ELIZONDO, HECTOR	ACTOR	262 W 107TH ST #8-A	NEW YORK, NY	10025
ELIZONDO-BRAUCH DUO	MUSICAL DUO	POST OFFICE BOX 131	SPRINGFIELD, VA	22150
ELKES, TERRENCE A	CABLE EXECUTIVE	VIACOM INTERNATIONAL, INC		
		1211 AVE OF THE AMERICAS	NEW YORK, NY	10036
ELKIN, STANLEY	WRITER	8955 BEVERLY BLVD	LOS ANGELES, CA	90048
ELKINS, HILLARD	PRODUCER	1966 OUTPOST CIR	LOS ANGELES, CA	90068
ELKINS, SAUL	WRITER	1230 EDRIS DR	LOS ANGELES, CA	90035
ELLEMENT, JOHN A	NEWS CORRESPONDENT	654 "F" ST, NE	WASHINGTON, DC	20002
ELLENSTEIN, DAVID	ACTOR	5525 COSTELLO AVE	VAN NUYS, CA	91401
ELLENSTEIN, ROBERT	ACTOR-DIRECTOR	5215 SEPULVEDA BLVD #23-F	CULVER CITY, CA	90230
ELLENWOOD, GARY	NEWS CORRESPONDENT	400 N CAPITOL ST, NW	WASHINGTON, DC	20001

ELLERBE, HARRY	ACTOR	1896 WYCLIFF RD, NW	ATLANTA, GA	30309
ELLERBEE, LINDA	BROADCAST JOURNALIST	ABC NEWS, 7 W 66TH ST	NEW YORK, NY	10023
ELLERING, PRECIOUS PAUL	WRESTLER	NATIONAL WRESTLING ALLIANCE		
		JIM CROCKETT PROMOTIONS		
		421 BRIARBEND DR	CHARLOTTE, NC	28209
ELLERS, PENNY	CASTING DIRECTOR	2049 CENTURY PARK E #4100	LOS ANGELES, CA	90067
ELLGAARD, PETER	NEWS CORRESPONDENT	3926 GEORGETOWN CT, NW	WASHINGTON, DC	20007
ELLINGTON, MERCER	MUSICIAN	DOCTOR JAZZ RECORDS COMPANY		
		1414 AVE OF THE AMERICAS	NEW YORK, NY	10019
ELLIOT, BIFF	ACTOR	1350 N HIGHLAND AVE #24	HOLLYWOOD, CA	90028
ELLIOT, DAVID	DIRECTOR	200 W 90TH ST	NEW YORK, NY	10024
ELLIOT, JANE	ACTRESS	10100 SANTA MONICA BLVD #1600	LOS ANGELES, CA	90067
ELLIOT, MARIAN	TV WRITER	8955 BEVERLY BLVD	LOS ANGELES, CA	90048
ELLIOT, MICHAEL	DIRECTOR	15 W 72ND ST	NEW YORK, NY	10023
ELLIOT, NEIL	ACTOR	807 HYPERION AVE #1	LOS ANGELES, CA	90029
ELLIOT, PETER V	TV WRITER	8955 BEVERLY BLVD	LOS ANGELES, CA	90048
ELLIOT, ROBERT	DIRECTOR	DGA, 110 W 57TH ST	NEW YORK, NY	10019
ELLIOT, STEPHEN	TV DIRECTOR	239 E 79TH ST	NEW YORK, NY	10021
ELLIOT, STEPHEN B	DIRECTOR	120 W 97TH ST	NEW YORK, NY	10025
ELLIOT, SUSAN	TV WRITER	8955 BEVERLY BLVD	LOS ANGELES, CA	90048
ELLIOTT, AL	GUITARIST	POST OFFICE BOX 10	BIG STONE GAP, VA	24219
ELLIOTT, BARRY	DIRECTOR	932 N LA BREA AVE	HOLLYWOOD, CA	90038
ELLIOTT, BOB	COMEDIAN	420 LEXINGTON AVE	NEW YORK, NY	10021
ELLIOTT, CHRIS	TV WRITER	ICM, 8899 BEVERLY BLVD	LOS ANGELES, CA	90048
ELLIOTT, DALE	ACTOR	8831 SUNSET BLVD #402	LOS ANGELES, CA	90069
ELLIOTT, DAVID	ACTOR	11726 SAN VICENTE BLVD #300	LOS ANGELES, CA	90049
ELLIOTT, DAVID	FILM CRITIC	POST OFFICE BOX 191	SAN DIEGO, CA	92112
ELLIOTT, DAVID G	FRENCH HORNIST	171 HEDGEWOOD CT	LEXINGTON, KY	40509
ELLIOTT, DEAN	COMPOSER-CONDUCTOR	22410 MARTHA ST	WOODLAND HILLS, CA	91364
ELLIOTT, DENHOLM	ACTOR	75 ALBERT ST		
		REGENTS PARK	LONDON NW1	ENGLAND
ELLIOTT, FRANCIS E	VIOLINIST	760 WELCH AVE #1	COOKEVILLE, TN	38501
ELLIOTT, GLENN	SINGER	POST OFFICE BOX 29543	ATLANTA, GA	30359
ELLIOTT, JACK	ACTOR	10100 SANTA MONICA BLVD #1600	LOS ANGELES, CA	90067
ELLIOTT, JACK	CONDUCTOR	9312 SANTA MONICA BLVD	BEVERLY HILLS, CA	90210
ELLIOTT, LANG	THEATER PRODUCER	POST OFFICE BOX 7419	THOUSAND OAKS, CA	91359
ELLIOTT, LEONARD	ACTOR	400 E 50TH ST	NEW YORK, NY	10022
ELLIOTT, MIKE	GUITARIST	2131 ELM HILL PIKE #A-2	NASHVILLE, TN	37210
ELLIOTT, PATRICIA	ACTRESS	151 S EL CAMINO DR	BEVERLY HILLS, CA	90212
ELLIOTT, PAUL	TENOR	1182 MARKET ST #31	SAN FRANCISCO, CA	94102
ELLIOTT, PAUL	TV WRITER	8955 BEVERLY BLVD	LOS ANGELES, CA	90048
ELLIOTT, PAUL C	SCREENWRITER	14144 VENTURA BLVD #200	SHERMAN OAKS, CA	91423
ELLIOTT, PEGGY	WRITER	8955 BEVERLY BLVD	LOS ANGELES, CA	90048
ELLIOTT, PETER	FILM EDITOR	3 VIRGINIA CLOSE		
		BLACKSMITH'S LN, LALEHAM	MIDDLESEX	ENGLAND
ELLIOTT, RAMBLIN' JACK	SINGER-SONGWRITER	DAY PRODS, 300 W 55TH ST	NEW YORK, NY	10019
ELLIOTT, ROBERT B	TV WRITER	555 W 57TH ST #1230	NEW YORK, NY	10019
ELLIOTT, RON	GUITARIST	3991 DICKERSON RD	NASHVILLE, TN	37207
ELLIOTT, ROSS	ACTOR	5702 GRAVES AVE	ENCINO, CA	91316
ELLIOTT, SAM	ACTOR	33050 PACIFIC COAST HWY	MALIBU, CA	90265
ELLIOTT, STEPHEN	ACTOR	3948 WOODFIELD DR	SHERMAN OAKS, CA	91403
ELLIOTTE, JOHN	WRITER	8955 BEVERLY BLVD	LOS ANGELES, CA	90048
ELLIS, ANTHONY	ACTOR	8350 SANTA MONICA BLVD #103	LOS ANGELES, CA	90069
ELLIS, ARTHUR	FILM WRITER-DIRECTOR	16 GRANVILLE MANSIONS		
		SHEPHERDS BUSH GREEN	LONDON W12	ENGLAND
ELLIS, BRENT	BARITONE	CAMI, 165 W 57TH ST	NEW YORK, NY	10019
ELLIS, BRIAN T	WRITER	555 W 57TH ST #1230	NEW YORK, NY	10019
ELLIS, CAROLINE	ACTRESS	AIDA FOSTER, 33 ABBEY LODGE		
		PARK RD	LONDON NW8 7RJ	ENGLAND
ELLIS, DAVID	NEWS REPORTER	TIME/TIME & LIFE BLDG		
		ROCKEFELLER CENTER	NEW YORK, NY	10020
ELLIS, DAVID RICHARD	DIRECTOR	6587 TAMARIND ST	AGOURA, CA	91301
ELLIS, DONALD E	DIRECTOR	404 NOBLE CREEK DR, NW	ATLANTA, GA	30327
ELLIS, GENE	WRITER	555 W 57TH ST #1230	NEW YORK, NY	10019
ELLIS, GRETCHEN S	WRITER	8955 BEVERLY BLVD	LOS ANGELES, CA	90048
ELLIS, HAROLD E	COMPOSER-CONDUCTOR	1861 WHITLEY AVE	LOS ANGELES, CA	90028
ELLIS, HERB, TRIO	GUITARIST	LAMBROS, 582 SPA CREEK LANDING	ANNAPOLIS, MD	21403
ELLIS, JEFFREY	SCREENWRITER	8955 BEVERLY BLVD	LOS ANGELES, CA	90048
ELLIS, JIM	MUSICIAN	ROUTE #1, BOX 104	KINGSTON SPRINGS, TN	37082
ELLIS, KENNETH R	WRITER-PRODUCER	3200 BURDECK DR	OAKLAND, CA	94602
ELLIS, MERLE	COLUMNIST	CHRONICLE FEATURES		
		870 MARKET ST	SAN FRANCISCO, CA	94102
ELLIS, OSIAN	HARPIST	CAMI, 165 W 57TH ST	NEW YORK, NY	10019
ELLIS, PATRICIA	NEWS CORRESPONDENT	2122 CALIFORNIA ST, NW	WASHINGTON, DC	20008
ELLIS, PEGGY A	WRITER	555 W 57TH ST #1230	NEW YORK, NY	10019
ELLIS, PERRY	FASHION DESIGNER	575 7TH AVE	NEW YORK, NY	10018
ELLIS, RALPH	WRITER	555 W 57TH ST #1230	NEW YORK, NY	10019
ELLIS, RAMEY	ACTRESS	1239 WASHINGTON BLVD	VENICE, CA	90291
ELLIS, RAYMOND S	CONDUCTOR	12821 MOORPARK ST #8	STUDIO CITY, CA	91604
ELLIS, REX	GUITARIST	ROUTE #2, BOX 359	BETHPAGE, TN	37022
ELLIS, RICHARD	PHOTOGRAPHER	1508 "Q" ST, NW	WASHINGTON, DC	20009
ELLIS, RICHARD W	DIRECTOR	DGA, 110 W 57TH ST	NEW YORK, NY	10019
ELLIS, ROBERT D	WRITER	8955 BEVERLY BLVD	LOS ANGELES, CA	90048
ELLIS, ROGER	ACTOR	POST OFFICE BOX 543	ENCINO, CA	91426
ELLIS, SIDNEY	WRITER	238 ENTRADA DR	SANTA MONICA, CA	90402

ELLIS, THERESA	MANDOLINIST	POST OFFICE BOX 121141	NASHVILLE, TN	37212
ELLIS, TOTTIE	COLUMNIST	POST OFFICE BOX 500	WASHINGTON, DC	20044
ELLISON, BARRY	BARITONE	MUNRO, 334 W 72ND ST	NEW YORK, NY	10023
ELLISON, BOB	TV WRITER	8955 BEVERLY BLVD	LOS ANGELES, CA	90048
ELLISON, HARLAN	AUTHOR-WRITER	3484 COY DR	SHERMAN OAKS, CA	91423
ELLISON, JAMES	ACTOR	1143 HIGH RD	MONTECITO, CA	93108
ELLISON, JAMES S	TV DIRECTOR	424 W END AVE	NEW YORK, NY	10024
ELLISON, L R	WRITER	555 W 57TH ST #1230	NEW YORK, NY	10019
ELLISON, ROBERT J	WRITER	11474 BELLAGIO RD	LOS ANGELES, CA	90049
ELLISOR, CONNI	VIOLINIST	6436 FLEETWOOD DR	NASHVILLE, TN	37209
ELLITHORPE, BUDDY	PIANIST	182 ARCHWOOD PL	MADISON, TN	37115
ELLMAN, DONALD M, JR	PUBLISHING EXECUTIVE	TIME/TIME & LIFE BLDG		
		ROCKEFELLER CENTER	NEW YORK, NY	10020
ELLNER, EDDIE	WRESTLING WRITER	POST OFFICE BOX 48	ROCKVILLE CENTRE, NY	11571
ELLS, GEORGE	WRITER	8955 BEVERLY BLVD	LOS ANGELES, CA	90048
ELLS, MARLAINE	FLUTIST	801 CANTON PASS	MADISON, TN	37115
ELLS, WARREN	SINGER-GUITARIST	801 CANTON PASS	MADISON, TN	37115
ELLSBERG, DANIEL	AUTHOR	90 NORWOOD AVE	KENSINGTON, CA	94707
ELLSWORTH, WARREN	TENOR	CAMI, 165 W 57TH ST	NEW YORK, NY	10019
ELMAN, EUGENE	ACTOR	540 N ORLANDO AVE #6	LOS ANGELES, CA	90048
ELMAN, IRVING	WRITER-PRODUCER	430 PUERTO DEL MAR	PACIFIC PALISADES, CA	90272
ELMAN, JUDITH S	WRITER	555 W 57TH ST #1230	NEW YORK, NY	10019
ELMAN, LOUIS	TV DIRECTOR	LEAH INTERNATIONAL ANVIL		
		DENHAM STUDIOS, DENHAM	MIDDLESEX	ENGLAND
ELMAN, MILDRED M	WRITER	430 PUERTO DEL MAR	PACIFIC PALISADES, CA	90272
ELMER, SANDRA	DRUMMER	3502 WOOD BRIDGE DR	NASHVILLE, TN	37217
ELMER-DE WITT, PHILIP	WRITER-EDITOR	TIME/TIME & LIFE BLDG		
		ROCKEFELLER CENTER	NEW YORK, NY	10020
ELMES, FRED	ACTOR	438 NORWICH DR	HOLLYWOOD, CA	90048
ELMORE, STEVE	ACTOR	1650 BROADWAY #302	NEW YORK, NY	10019
ELPHICK, MICHAEL	ACTOR	37 DENNINGTON PARK RD	LONDON NW6	ENGLAND
ELROD, JACK	CARTOONIST	NEWS AMERICA SYNDICATE		
		1703 KAISER AVE	IRVINE, CA	92714
ELSASSER, GLEN R	NEWS CORRESPONDENT	319 "C" ST, NE	WASHINGTON, DC	20002
ELSE, JON	WRITER	8955 BEVERLY BLVD	LOS ANGELES, CA	90048
ELSENBACH, JOHN	CINEMATOGRAPHER	POST OFFICE BOX 2230	HOLLYWOOD, CA	90078
ELSING, EVELYN	CELLIST	3003 VAN NESS ST #W-205, NW	WASHINGTON, DC	20008
ELSON, DONALD	ACTOR	2456 HIDALGO AVE	LOS ANGELES, CA	90039
ELSON, JOHN	WRITER-EDITOR	TIME/TIME & LIFE BLDG		
		ROCKEFELLER CENTER	NEW YORK, NY	10020
ELSTAD, LINDA BARRIC	TV WRITER	788 BROOKTREE RD	PACIFIC PALISADES, CA	90272
ELSWIT, JEROME	NEWS CORRESPONDENT	2810 OAKTON MANOR CT	OAKTON, VA	22124
ELTERMAN, JUDI	TV DIRECTOR	4265 MARINA CITY DR	MARINA DEL REY, CA	90292
ELTON, WILLIAM	COMPOSER-CONDUCTOR	431 N CITRUS AVE	LOS ANGELES, CA	90036
ELVINGTON, D GLENN	NEWS CORRESPONDENT	6008 HARDWICK PL	WASHINGTON, DC	20002
ELVIRA	ACTRESS	SEE - PETERSON, CASSANDRA		
ELVIRA, PABLO	BASSO-BARITONE	111 W 57TH ST #1209	NEW YORK, NY	10019
ELVIS BROTHERS, THE	ROCK & ROLL TRIO	KEN ADAMANY & ASSOCIATES		
		BOSS OF THE WORLD INDUSTRIES		
		315 W GORMAN ST	MADISON, WI	53703
ELWARD, JAMES	WRITER	555 W 57TH ST #1230	NEW YORK, NY	10019
ELWES, CARY	ACTOR	WINKAST FILMS, PINEWOOD STUDIOS		
		IVER HEATH	BUCKS	ENGLAND
ELWES, CASSIAN	FILM PRODUCER	10202 W WASHINGTON BLVD		
		LION BUILDING, ROOM #207	CULVER CITY, CA	90230
ELY, JOE	SINGER-SONGWRITER	POST OFFICE BOX 160668	AUSTIN, TX	78716
ELY, RON	ACTOR	1617 CASALE RD	PACIFIC PALISADES, CA	90272
ELYSE, TARYN	ACTRESS	6605 HOLLYWOOD BLVD #220	HOLLYWOOD, CA	90028
EMANUEL	FASHION DESIGNER	26-A BROOK ST	LONDON W1	ENGLAND
EMBER, LOIS	NEWS CORRESPONDENT	8314 CARRLEIGH PARKWAY	SPRINGFIELD, VA	22152
EMBER, MAX	WRITER	2331 OUTPOST DR	LOS ANGELES, CA	90068
EMBERG, KELLY	MODEL	ELITE MODELS, 150 E 58TH ST	NEW YORK, NY	10022
EMBLEN, CLOVIS	ACTRESS	19816 GRAND VIEW DR #A	TOPANGA CANYON, CA	90290
EMBREE, MARC	BASSO-BARITONE	LEW, 204 W 10TH ST	NEW YORK, NY	10014
EMBREY, GEORGE A	NEWS CORRESPONDENT	6820 DEAN DR	MC LEAN, VA	22101
EMELIANOFF, ANDRE	CELLIST	243 W END AVE #907	NEW YORK, NY	10023
EMERSON, BONNIE	ACTRESS	ABC-TV, "GENERAL HOSPITAL"		
		1438 N GOWER ST	LOS ANGELES, CA	90028
EMERSON, DOUGLAS	ACTOR	KELMAN, 7813 SUNSET BLVD	LOS ANGELES, CA	90046
EMERSON, GALE	ACTRESS	8949 SUNSET BLVD #203	LOS ANGELES, CA	90069
EMERSON, JOANNA	TV WRITER	8955 BEVERLY BLVD	LOS ANGELES, CA	90048
EMERSON, KARRIE	ACTRESS-MODEL	8350 SANTA MONICA BLVD #206	LOS ANGELES, CA	90069
EMERSON, LAKE & POWELL	ROCK & ROLL TRIO	ALEX GROB, THEATERSTRASSE	POSTFACH 8024	SWITZERLAND
EMERSON STRING QUARTET	STRING QUARTET	KAPLAN, 115 COLLEGE ST	BURLINGTON, VT	05401
EMERY, JAMES	ACTOR	9255 SUNSET BLVD #603	LOS ANGELES, CA	90069
EMERY, MATT	ACTOR	439 S LA CIENEGA BLVD #120	LOS ANGELES, CA	90048
EMES, IAN	FILM DIRECTOR	134 ROYAL COLLEGE ST	LONDON NW1	ENGLAND
EMHARDT, ROBERT	ACTOR	9220 SUNSET BLVD #202	LOS ANGELES, CA	90069
EMIL, MICHAEL	ACTOR	409 N CAMDEN DR #105	BEVERLY HILLS, CA	90210
EMMERICH, JOZIE	NEWS CORRESPONDENT	ABC-TV, NEWS DEPARTMENT		
		1330 AVE OF THE AMERICAS	NEW YORK, NY	10019
EMMERICH, KLAUS	NEWS CORRESPONDENT	1206 ETON CT, NW	WASHINGTON, DC	20007
EMMETT, RAY	GUITARIST	POST OFFICE BOX 631	HENDERSONVILLE, TN	37075
EMMETT, ROBERT	WRITER	555 W 57TH ST #1230	NEW YORK, NY	10019
EMMICH, CLIFF	ACTOR	5312 BELLINGHAM AVE #2	NORTH HOLLYWOOD, CA	91607

Name	Occupation	Address	City	Zip
EMMONS, BLAKE	ACTOR	12725 VENTURA BLVD #E	STUDIO CITY, CA	91604
EMMONS, BLAKE, & PHOENIX	C & W GROUP	4680 ELK LAKE DR #304	VICTORIA, BC V8Z 5M1	CANADA
EMMONS, BOBBY	PIANIST	ROUTE #2, JOHNSON CHAPEL RD	BRENTWOOD, TN	37027
EMMONS, BUDDY GENE	GUITARIST	4852 CONCORD DR	HERMITAGE, TN	37076
EMMONS, CYNTHIA	ACTRESS	5330 LANKERSHIM BLVD #210	NORTH HOLLYWOOD, CA	91601
EMMONS, KAREN	NEWS REPORTER	LIFE/TIME & LIFE BLDG		
		ROCKEFELLER CENTER	NEW YORK, NY	10020
EMMONS, LARRY	GUITARIST	64 BUFFALO TRAIL	MOUNT JULIET, TN	37122
EMORY, ALAN S	NEWS CORRESPONDENT	6302 CROSSWOODS CIR	FALLS CHURCH, VA	22044
EMOTIONS, THE	SOUL GROUP	MARS, 168 ORCHID DR	PEARL RIVER, NY	10965
EMPIRE	ROCK & ROLL GROUP	JOYCE, 2028 CHESTNUT ST	PHILADELPHIA, PA	19103
EMPSON, WILLIAM	PIANIST	6700 RODNEY CT	NASHVILLE, TN	37205
ENACHESCU, ELEONORA	SOPRANO	KAY, 58 W 58TH ST	NEW YORK, NY	10019
ENBERG, DICK	SPORTSCASTER	NBC-TV, SPORTS DEPARTMENT		
		30 ROCKEFELLER PLAZA	NEW YORK, NY	10112
ENCHANTMENT	VOCAL GROUP	POST OFFICE BOX 82	GREAT NECK, NY	11021
ENCINAS, ALVARO	NEWS CORRESPONDENT	444 N CAPITOL ST, NW	WASHINGTON, DC	20001
ENDARA, JOSE R	WRITER	555 W 57TH ST #1230	NEW YORK, NY	10019
ENDE, MICHAEL	AUTHOR	U K THIENEMANNS, VERLAG	STUTTGRAT 7000-1	W GERMANY
ENDERS, HOWARD	WRITER-PRODUCER	19 FOREST PARK AVE	LARCHMONT, NY	10538
ENDERS, ROBERT	WRITER-PRODUCER	1110 BENEDICT CANYON DR	BEVERLY HILLS, CA	90210
ENDERSBY, CLIVE	WRITER	9301 WILSHIRE BLVD #800	BEVERLY HILLS, CA	90212
ENDES, JOE	ACTOR	1352 N LAS PALMAS AVE #1	HOLLYWOOD, CA	90028
ENDICOTT, BETTY W	NEWS CORRESPONDENT	5151 WISCONSIN AVE, NW	WASHINGTON, DC	20016
ENDLER, ESTELLE	FILM PRODUCER	3920 SUNNY OAK RD	SHERMAN OAKS, CA	91403
ENDLER, MICHAEL	FILM WRITER-PRODUCER	3920 SUNNY OAK RD	SHERMAN OAKS, CA	91403
ENDLESS SUMMER	ROCK & ROLL GROUP	41 BRITAIN ST #200	TORONTO, ONT	CANADA
ENDO, AKIRA	CONDUCTOR	8853 MOUNTAIN RIDGE CIR	AUSTIN, TX	78759
ENDSLEY, MELVIN	GUITARIST	ROUTE #3, BOX 155	HEBER SPRINGS, AR	72543
ENEMY WITHIN, THE	ROCK & ROLL GROUP	THE WHITE HOUSE, THE STREET		
		NORTH LOPHAM, DISS	NORFOLK IP2Z 2LU	ENGLAND
ENESCO STRING QUARTET	STRING QUARTET	KAPLAN, 115 COLLEGE ST	BURLINGTON, VT	05401
ENEVOLDSEN, ROBERT M	COMPOSER	20621 AETNA ST	WOODLAND HILLS, CA	91367
ENEY, WOODY	ACTOR	211 S BEVERLY BLVD #201	BEVERLY HILLS, CA	90212
ENG, JONATHAN	NEWS CORRESPONDENT	1738 "R" ST, NW	WASHINGTON, DC	20009
ENG, RICHARD	ACTOR	433 W 24TH ST #1-E	NEW YORK, NY	10011
ENG, STEVE	SINGER-SONGWRITER	POST OFFICE BOX 110423	NASHVILLE, TN	37211
ENGBERG, ERIC	NEWS CORRESPONDENT	CBS NEWS, 2020 "M" ST, NW	WASHINGTON, DC	20036
ENGEL, CHARLES	TV PRODUCER	MCA/UNIVERSAL STUDIOS, INC		
		100 UNIVERSAL CITY PLAZA	UNIVERSAL CITY, CA	91608
ENGEL, GEORGIA	ACTRESS	350 W 57TH ST #10-E	NEW YORK, NY	10019
ENGEL, KATHLEEN	WRITER	555 W 57TH ST #1230	NEW YORK, NY	10019
ENGEL, MARGARET	NEWS CORRESPONDENT	5319 YORKTOWN RD	BETHESDA, MD	20816
ENGEL, MARY	ACTRESS	8900 BOULEVARD EAST	NORTH BERGEN, NJ	07047
ENGEL, RUTH C	ACTRESS	3330 BARHAM BLVD #103	LOS ANGELES, CA	90068
ENGEL, SUSAN	ACTRESS	FEAST, 43-A PRINCESS RD	LONDON NW1	ENGLAND
ENGELBACH, DAVID	SCREENWRITER	12 24TH AVE #9	VENICE, CA	90291
ENGELBERG, FRED	WRITER	8955 BEVERLY BLVD	LOS ANGELES, CA	90048
ENGELBERG, MICHAEL	WRITER	8955 BEVERLY BLVD	LOS ANGELES, CA	90048
ENGELGAU, DONNA	NEWS CORRESPONDENT	2146 FLORIDA AVE, NW	WASHINGTON, DC	20008
ENGELHARDT, DEAN	DIRECTOR	404 N DANEHURST AVE	COVINA, CA	91724
ENGELHARDT, THOMAS	CARTOONIST	900 N 12TH BLVD	SAINT LOUIS, MO	63101
ENGELMAN, GUS	WRITER	555 W 57TH ST #1230	NEW YORK, NY	10019
ENGELMAN, ROBERT	NEWS CORRESPONDENT	5406 CONNECTICUT AVE #707, NW	WASHINGTON, DC	20015
ENGELSON, GEORGE J	ACTOR	11640 HAMLIN ST	NORTH HOLLYWOOD, CA	91606
ENGER, PAUL	WRITER	555 W57TH ST #1230	NEW YORK, NY	10019
ENGERER, BRIGITTE	PIANIST	ICM, 40 W 57TH ST	NEW YORK, NY	10019
ENGLAND, HAL	ACTOR	11030 VENTURA BLVD #3	STUDIO CITY, CA	91604
ENGLAND, JOHN	ACTOR	9250 WILSHIRE BLVD #208	BEVERLY HILLS, CA	90212
ENGLAND DAN	SINGER-SONGWRITER	SEE - SEALS, DAN		
ENGLANDER, DAVID	WRITER	555 W 57TH ST #1230	NEW YORK, NY	10019
ENGLANDER, MELBA	ACTRESS	6736 LAUREL CANYON BLVD #306	NORTH HOLLYWOOD, CA	91606
ENGLANDER, ROGER	DIRECTOR-PRODUCER	15 SAINT LUKES PL	NEW YORK, NY	10014
ENGLEHART	CARTOONIST	THE HARTFORD COURANT		
		285 BROAD ST	HARTFORD, CT	06115
ENGLER, LORI-NAN	ACTRESS	200 W 57TH ST #1303	NEW YORK, NY	10019
ENGLERT, KURT	NEWS CORRESPONDENT	3225 GRACE ST, NW	WASHINGTON, DC	20007
ENGLES, JUDITH	TV WRITER	555 W 57TH ST #1230	NEW YORK, NY	10019
ENGLISH, ARTHUR	ACTOR	FREEMAN, 4 CROMWELL GROVE		
		HAMMERSMITH	LONDON W6 7RG	ENGLAND
ENGLISH, BRAD	ACTOR	11494 DELLMONT DR	TUJUNGA, CA	91042
ENGLISH, CAMERON	ACTOR	6404 WILSHIRE BLVD #800	LOS ANGELES, CA	90048
ENGLISH, CAREY W	NEWS CORRESPONDENT	9221 FOREST HAVEN DR	ALEXANDRIA, VA	22309
ENGLISH, DIANE	TV WRITER	8955 BEVERLY BLVD	LOS ANGELES, CA	90048
ENGLISH, JAMES MICHAEL	NEWS CORRESPONDENT	3629 OLD MILFORD MILL RD	BALTIMORE, MD	21207
ENGLISH, JIM	CABLE EXECUTIVE	SHOWTIME ENTERTAINMENT		
		1633 BROADWAY	NEW YORK, NY	10019
ENGLISH, JIMMY	GUITARIST	1011-C PIERCE RD	MADISON, TN	37115
ENGLISH, JOE	DRUMMER	ROUTE #1, BOX 40-A	ARRINGTON, TN	37014
ENGLISH, JOE, BAND	GOSPEL GROUP	365 GREAT CIRCLE DR	NASHVILLE, TN	37228
ENGLISH, PHILIP	ACTOR	9021 MELROSE AVE #304	LOS ANGELES, CA	90069
ENGLISH, PRISCILLA	SCREENWRITER	9941 YOUNG DR #A	BEVERLY HILLS, CA	90212
ENGLISH, VICTORIA	WRITER	555 W 57TH ST #1230	NEW YORK, NY	10019
ENGLISH DOGS, THE	ROCK & ROLL GROUP	IMPORT RECORDS COMPANY		
		149-03 GUY R BREWER BLVD	JAMAICA, NY	11434

ENGLUND, GEORGE H	DIRECTOR-PRODUCER	765 BROOKTREE RD	PACIFIC PALISADES, CA	90272
ENGLUND, GEORGE H	MUSICIAN	2041 MANDEVILLE CANYON RD	LOS ANGELES, CA	90049
ENGLUND, ROBERT	ACTOR	7060 HOLLYWOOD BLVD #610	LOS ANGELES, CA	90028
ENGMAN, NANCY	ACTRESS	6640 SUNSET BLVD #203	LOS ANGELES, CA	90028
ENIVEL, BO	ACTOR	549 HAWLEY AVE	BRIDGEPORT, CT	06606
ENNIS, CARMENE	SINGER	289 S BARRINGTON AVE #101	LOS ANGELES, CA	90049
ENO, BRIAN	SINGER-PRODUCER	OPAL, 330 HARROW RD	LONDON W9 2HP	ENGLAND
ENO, ROGER	SINGER-MUSICIAN	OPAL, 330 HARROW RD	LONDON W9 2HP	ENGLAND
ENOCH, RUSSELL	ACTOR	FEAST, 43-A PRINCESS RD	LONDON NW1	ENGLAND
ENRICH, EDWARD	ACTOR	20884 TIARA ST	WOODLAND HILLS, CA	91367
ENRICO, ROBERT	FILM DIRECTOR	ARTMEDIA, 10 AVE GEORGE V	PARIS 75008	FRANCE
ENRIGHT, DAN	TV PRODUCER	1888 CENTURY PARK E #1100	LOS ANGELES, CA	90067
ENRIGHT, DON	SCREENWRITER	1253 AMALFI DR	PACIFIC PALISADES, CA	90272
ENRIGHT, ERICA	WRITER	1253 AMALFI DR	PACIFIC PALISADES, CA	90272
ENRIQUEZ, RENE	ACTOR	4664 LAUREL GROVE AVENUYE	VAN NUYS, CA	91604
ENSEMBLE CHANTERELLE	MUSIC TRIO	POST OFFICE BOX 20548	NEW YORK, NY	10025
ENSIGN, MICHAEL	ACTOR	LIGHT, 113 N ROBERTSON BLVD	LOS ANGELES, CA	90048
ENSLEY, ANNETTE	ACTRESS	1865 3/4 S SYCAMORE AVE	LOS ANGELES, CA	90019
ENTELIS, AMY R	TV PRODUCER	ABC-TV, 7 W 66TH ST	NEW YORK, NY	10023
ENTNER, WARREN	MUSICIAN-TAL AGT	1021 S STEARNS DR	LOS ANGELES, CA	90035
ENTON-FRIEDKIN, GREGORY	ACTOR-WRITER	1811 VETERAN AVE	LOS ANGELES, CA	90025
ENTREMONT, PHILIPPE	PIANIST	ICM, 40 W 57TH ST	NEW YORK, NY	10019
EOFF, TERRI	ACTRESS	NBC TELEVISION NETWORK		
		30 ROCKEFELLER PLAZA	NEW YORK, NY	10112
EPHRON, AMY	FILM EXECUTIVE	8439 KIRKWOOD DR	LOS ANGELES, CA	90046
EPHRON, DELIA	WRITER	1464 GLENVILLE DR	LOS ANGELES, CA	90035
EPHRON, HENRY	SCREENWRITER	8439 KIRKWOOD DR	LOS ANGELES, CA	90046
EPHRON, NORA	SCREENWRITER	2211 BROADWAY	NEW YORK, NY	10024
EPPER, ANDREW	STUNTMAN	3518 W CAHUENGA BLVD #300	LOS ANGELES, CA	90068
EPPER, JEANNIE	STUNTWOMAN	3518 W CAHUENGA BLVD #206	LOS ANGELES, CA	90068
EPPLER, KYLE T	NEWS CORRESPONDENT	6837 HEATHERWAY CT	ALEXANDRIA, VA	22310
EPPS, JACK, JR	SCREENWRITER	425 SKEWIAY RD	LOS ANGELES, CA	90049
EPSTEIN, AARON B	NEWS CORRESPONDENT	7017 AMY LN	BETHESDA, MD	20034
EPSTEIN, ALLEN	TV PRODUCER	10100 SANTA MONICA BLVD #1600	LOS ANGELES, CA	90067
EPSTEIN, ANDREW	TV WRITER	8955 BEVERLY BLVD	LOS ANGELES, CA	90048
EPSTEIN, BOB E	WRITER	555 W 57TH ST #1230	NEW YORK, NY	10019
EPSTEIN, DANIEL	PIANIST	POST OFFICE BOX U	REDDING, CT	06875
EPSTEIN, DASHA	THEATER PRODUCER	720 PARK AVE	NEW YORK, NY	10021
EPSTEIN, DAVID	CONDUCTOR	59 E 54TH ST #81	NEW YORK, NY	10022
EPSTEIN, DAVID	TV WRITER	555 W 57TH ST #1230	NEW YORK, NY	10019
EPSTEIN, DAVID SCHAFFER	DIRECTOR	315 CENTRAL PARK W	NEW YORK, NY	10025
EPSTEIN, DONALD K	WRITER	555 W 57TH ST #1230	NEW YORK, NY	10019
EPSTEIN, JACOB	TV WRITER	ICM, 8899 BEVERLY BLVD	LOS ANGELES, CA	90048
EPSTEIN, JANET B	FLUTIST	1912 19TH AVE S	NASHVILLE, TN	37212
EPSTEIN, JEROME	WRITER	8955 BEVERLY BLVD	LOS ANGELES, CA	90048
EPSTEIN, JON	STUNTMAN	3518 W CAHUENGA BLVD #300	LOS ANGELES, CA	90068
EPSTEIN, JON	TV WRITER-PRODUCER	1988 COLDWATER CANYON DR	BEVERLY HILLS, CA	90210
EPSTEIN, JULIUS J	SCREENWRITER	10556 FONTENELLE WY	LOS ANGELES, CA	90077
EPSTEIN, STANLEY	DIRECTOR	310 W 72ND ST	NEW YORK, NY	10023
ERB, EARL M	GUITARIST	ROUTE #5, BOX 320	LEBANON, TN	37087
ERB, HELMUT	TRUMPETER	IAPR, KINCORA, BEER RD		
		SEATON	DEVON	ENGLAND
ERBE, BONNIE G	NEWS CORRESPONDENT	1400 "I" ST, NW	WASHINGTON, DC	20005
ERCH, NIELS	WRITER	732 1/2 N DETROIT ST	LOS ANGELES, CA	90046
ERDELYI, MIKLOS	CONDUCTOR	111 W 57TH ST #1209	NEW YORK, NY	10019
ERDMAN, RICHARD	ACTOR-DIRECTOR	23160 OSTRONIC DR	WOODLAND HILLS, CA	91367
ERGAS, JOSEPH	WRITER	555 W 57TH ST #1230	NEW YORK, NY	10019
ERHART, THOMAS, JR	ACTOR	862 W NEWPORT AVE	CHICAGO, IL	60657
ERIC, MARTIN	ACTOR	6290 SUNSET BLVD #326	LOS ANGELES, CA	90028
ERICKSON, DIANE	ACTRESS	445 BEDFORD DR #PH	BEVERLY HILLS, CA	90210
ERICKSON, KAAREN	SOPRANO	59 E 54TH ST #81	NEW YORK, NY	10022
ERICKSON, MERCEDES	NEWS CORRESPONDENT	7007 EXETER RD	BETHESDA, MD	20814
ERICKSON, ROKY	SINGER-WRITER	POST OFFICE BOX 22129	SAN FRANCISCO, CA	94122
ERICKSON, SKIP	NEWS CORRESPONDENT	400 N CAPITOL ST, NW	WASHINGTON, DC	20001
ERICKSON, TRICIA	AGENT-MODEL	ERICKSON MODELING AGENCY		
		1483 CHAIN BRIDGE RD	MC LEAN, VA	22101
ERICSON, ANITA	MEZZO-SOPRANO	45 W 60TH ST #4-K	NEW YORK, NY	10023
ERICSON, DEVON	ACTRESS	12725 VENTURA BLVD #E	STUDIO CITY, CA	91604
ERICSON, HELEN	NEWS CORRESPONDENT	614 E CAPITOL ST, NE	WASHINGTON, DC	20003
ERICSON, JOHN	ACTOR	15010 VENTURA BLVD #219	SHERMAN OAKS, CA	91403
ERICSON, KAREN	ACTRESS	12659 MOORPARK ST #12	STUDIO CITY, CA	91604
ERICSON, MILLY	ACTRESS	3575 W CAHUENGA BLVD #320	LOS ANGELES, CA	90068
ERICSON, NICOLE	ACTRESS	3575 W CAHUENGA BLVD #320	LOS ANGELES, CA	90068
ERIKSON, STEEN	ACTOR	FELBER, 2126 N CAHUENGA BLVD	LOS ANGELES, CA	90068
ERISMAN, ZOE	PIANIST	KAY, 58 W 58TH ST	NEW YORK, NY	10019
ERKMAN, JOE	GUITARIST	6001 OLD HICKORY BLVD #24	HERMITAGE, TN	37076
ERLANGER, DAVID MICHAEL	COMPOSER	6200 CANTERBURY DR #205	CULVER CITY, CA	90230
ERLENBORN, DANIEL R	NEWS CORRESPONDENT	CBS NEWS, 2020 "M" ST, NW	WASHINGTON, DC	20036
ERLENBORN, RAY	ACTOR	8344 MELROSE AVE #29	LOS ANGELES, CA	90069
ERLICH, HARVEY	ACTOR	8961 SUNSET BLVD #B	LOS ANGELES, CA	90069
ERLICH, KEN	PRODUCER	17200 OAKVIEW DR	ENCINO, CA	91316
ERLICHMAN, MARTY	PRODUCER	MIKO, 1040 N LAS PALMAS AVE	LOS ANGELES, CA	90038
ERLICHT, LEWIS H	TV EXECUTIVE	ABC-TV ENTERTAINMENT CENTER		
		2040 AVE OF THE STARS	LOS ANGELES, CA	90067
ERMAN, JOHN	TV-FILM DIRECTOR	978 CASIANO RD	LOS ANGELES, CA	90049

ERNEST, ROGER CRAIG	WRITER	266 WISCONSIN AVE	LONG BEACH, CA	90803
ERSHLER, MARGARET	WRITER	555 W 57TH ST #1230	NEW YORK, NY	10019
ERSKINE, CHRIS M	TV DIRECTOR	330 W RUSSELL	BARRINGTON, IL	60610
ERTEGUN, AHMET	RECORD EXECUTIVE	75 ROCKEFELLER PLAZA	NEW YORK, NY	10019
ERTH	ROCK & ROLL GROUP	POST OFFICE BOX 332	BONITA, CA	92002
ERTMANN, JOHN F	DIRECTOR	DGA, 110 W 57TH ST	NEW YORK, NY	10019
ERVIN, JUDITH	TV WRITER	8955 BEVERLY BLVD	LOS ANGELES, CA	90048
ERVIN, WENDY	ACTRESS	8721 SUNSET BLVD #200	LOS ANGELES, CA	90069
ERVING, JULIUS	BASKETBALL-ACTOR	POST OFFICE BOX 25040		
		SOUTHPARK STATION	PHILADELPHIA, PA	19147
ERWIN, BILL	ACTOR	12324 MOORPARK ST	STUDIO CITY, CA	91604
ERWIN, DAVID	GUITARIST	35 SAN GABRIEL CT	OLD HICKORY, TN	37138
ERYOMINA, LARISSA	ACTRESS	KOHNER, 9169 SUNSET BLVD	LOS ANGELES, CA	90069
ESCH, DAVID	ACTOR	14214 COHASSET ST	VAN NUYS, CA	91405
ESCHELBACHER, DAVID	TV PRODUCER	ABC-TV, 38 W 66TH ST	NEW YORK, NY	10023
ESCHENBACH, CHRISTOPH	PIANIST	CAMI, 165 W 57TH ST	NEW YORK, NY	10019
ESCOSA & RADO	MUSICAL DUO	CAMI, 165 W 57TH ST	NEW YORK, NY	10019
ESCOVEDO, PETE	MUSICIAN	GIRLS WORLD, 1926 33RD AVE	OAKLAND, CA	94601
ESCOVEDO, SHEILA	SINGER-MUSICIAN	SEE - E, SHEILA		
ESCUDERO, MARIO	GUITARIST	HILLYER, 250 W 57TH ST	NEW YORK, NY	10107
ESFANDIARY, H AUSTIN	NEWS CORRESPONDENT	4401 SEDGWICK ST, NW	WASHINGTON, DC	20016
ESFORMES, NATE	ACTOR-WRITER	7266 FRANKLIN AVE #16	LOS ANGELES, CA	90046
ESHAM, FAITH	SOPRANO	CAMI, 165 W 57TH ST	NEW YORK, NY	10019
ESHBACH, LLOYD ARTHUR	WRITER	220 S RAILROAD ST	MEYERSTOWN, PA	17067
ESKEL, BEVERLY	SINGER	RAB, 158 S BROADWAY	LAWRENCE, MA	01843
ESKEY, KENNETH	NEWS CORRESPONDENT	5102 BALTIMORE AVE	BETHESDA, MD	20816
ESKIN, VIRGINIA	PIANIST	CAMI, 165 W 57TH ST	NEW YORK, NY	10019
ESKOW, JOHN	WRITER	555 W 57TH ST #1230	NEW YORK, NY	10019
ESKRIDGE, REGINALD	RECORD EXECUTIVE	1508 HARLEM ST #1508	MEMPHIS, TN	38114
ESLIN, JAMES	ACTOR	7406 ENFIELD AVE	RESEDA, CA	91335
ESMOND, CARL	ACTOR	576 TIGERTAIL RD	LOS ANGELES, CA	90049
ESPARZA, MONTESUMA	WRITER-PRODUCER	2036 LEMOYNE ST	LOS ANGELES, CA	90026
ESPINOZA, MAURO	NEWS CORRESPONDENT	11507 FEBRUARY CIR #304	SILVER SPRING, MD	20904
ESPO, DAVID M	NEWS CORRESPONDENT	1229 SOUTHVIEW RD	BALTIMORE, MD	21218
ESPOSITO, JOSEPH	DRUMMER	416 N OAKHURST DR #105	BEVERLY HILLS, CA	90210
ESPOSITO, SALVATORE	DIRECTOR	520 N MICHIGAN AVE #436	CHICAGO, IL	60611
ESPY, WILLIAM GRAY	ACTOR	853 7TH AVE #9-A	NEW YORK, NY	10019
ESSEX, DAVID	SINGER-ACTOR	109 EASTBOURNE MEWS	LONDON W2	ENGLAND
ESSEX, HARRY J	WRITER-PRODUCER	9303 READCREST DR	BEVERLY HILLS, CA	90210
ESSLINGER, MARK ERIC	TV WRITER	8955 BEVERLY BLVD	LOS ANGELES, CA	90048
ESSOE, GABE	WRITER	8955 BEVERLY BLVD	LOS ANGELES, CA	90048
ESSRIG, MICHAEL	ACTOR	11716 WOODLEY AVE	GRANADA HILLS, CA	91344
ESSWOOD, PAUL	TENOR	119 W 57TH ST #1505	NEW YORK, NY	10019
ESTABROOK, CHRISTINE	ACTRESS	10100 SANTA MONICA BLVD #1600	LOS ANGELES, CA	90067
ESTERMAN, LAURA	ACTRESS	11726 SAN VICENTE BLVD #300	LOS ANGELES, CA	90049
ESTES, BARRY H	ACTOR	8270 W NORTON AVE #8	HOLLYWOOD, CA	90046
ESTES, ROB	ACTOR	KNBC-TV, "DAYS OF OUR LIVES"		
		3000 W ALAMEDA AVE	BURBANK, CA	91523
ESTES, SIMON	BASSO-BARITONE	CAMI, 165 W 57TH ST	NEW YORK, NY	10019
ESTEVEZ, EMILIO	ACTOR-WRITER	SHEEN, 6916 DUME DR	MALIBU, CA	90265
ESTEVEZ, RAMON	ACTOR	SHEEN, 6916 DUME DR	MALIBU, CA	90265
ESTILL, CYNTHIA	BASSOONIST	1625 STOKES LN	NASHVILLE, TN	37215
ESTILL, JERRY R	NEWS CORRESPONDENT	4401 LEE HWY	ARLINGTON, VA	22207
ESTILL, MARGARET C	VIOLINIST	910 WOODMONT BLVD #M-7	NASHVILLE, TN	37204
ESTILL, ROBERT E	NEWS CORRESPONDENT	6407 HANOVER AVE	SPRINGFIELD, VA	22150
ESTIN, KENNETH A	TV WRITER	8955 BEVERLY BLVD	LOS ANGELES, CA	90048
ESTLEMAN, LOREN	WRITER	PUECHNER, 2625 N 36TH ST	MILWAUKEE, WI	53210
ESTRADA, ERIK	ACTOR	11350 VENTURA BLVD	STUDIO CITY, CA	91604
ESTRADA, LEE	SINGER	POST OFFICE BOX 263	HASBROUCK HEIGHTS, NJ	07604
ESTRADA, PETER J	NEWS CORRESPONDENT	4461 CONNECTICUT AVE, NW	WASHINGTON, DC	20008
ESTRIN, JONATHAN	ACTOR-WRITER	2919 GRAND CANAL	VENICE, CA	90291
ESTRIN, PATRICIA	ACTRESS	9229 SUNSET BLVD #306	LOS ANGELES, CA	90069
ESTROM, JACK	ACTOR	1310 N JUNE ST	LOS ANGELES, CA	90028
ESTRUELAS, JUAN B	NEWS CORRESPONDENT	4850 CONNECTICUT AVE #1216, NW	WASHINGTON, DC	20008
ESTVAN, VALERIE	ACTRESS	10850 RIVERSIDE DR #505	NORTH HOLLYWOOD, CA	91602
ESZEKI, TIBOR J, JR	NEWS CORRESPONDENT	9149 SEPTEMBER LN	SILVER SPRING, MD	20901
ESZTERHAS, JOSEPH A	SCREENWRITER	8955 BEVERLY BLVD	LOS ANGELES, CA	90048
ETCHEN, GRACE	ACTRESS	6430 SUNSET BLVD #701	LOS ANGELES, CA	90028
ETCHISON, DENNIS W	WRITER	2041 N BEVERLY GLEN BLVD	LOS ANGELES, CA	90077
ETERNITY	GOSPEL GROUP	6750 W 75TH ST, MARKADE 75		
		BUILDING #2-A	OVERLAND PARK, KS	66204
ETHRIDGE, ROBYN	ACTOR	CARPENTER, 1516-W REDWOOD ST	SAN DIEGO, CA	92101
ETO, TOSHIYA	VIOLINIST	1776 BROADWAY #504	NEW YORK, NY	10019
ETTENSON, HERB	CROSSWORD WRITER	TRIBUNE MEDIA SERVICES		
		64 E CONCORD ST	ORLANDO, FL	32801
ETTINGER, RICHARD B	TV DIRECTOR	3238 BEECHWOOD BLVD	PITTSBURGH, PA	15217
ETTLINGER, DON	WRITER	555 W 57TH ST #1230	NEW YORK, NY	10019
ETTLINGER, JOHN	DIRECTOR-PRODUCER	520 HAYNES AVE	BEVERLY HILLS, CA	90210
ETTORE, JOHN J	NEWS CORRESPONDENT	2814 38TH ST, NW	WASHINGTON, DC	20007
EUBANKS, BOB	TV HOST	POST OFFICE BOX 269	AGOURA, CA	91301
EUBANKS, JACK	GUITARIST	110 LA PLAZA DR	HENDERSONVILLE, TN	37075
EUBANKS, KEVIN	GUITARIST	HOFFER, 233 E 48TH ST	NEW YORK, NY	10017
EUBANKS, RACHEL	COMPOSER	4928 CRENSHAW BLVD	LOS ANGELES, CA	90043
EUGENE & MICHAEL	SKYCYCLE ACT	HALL, 138 FROG HOLLOW RD	CHURCHVILLE, PA	18966
EUNSON, DALE	WRITER	2707 6TH ST	SANTA MONICA, CA	90405

EVERLY BROTHERS
Phil • Don

EXILE

Name	Occupation	Address	City	Zip / Country
EURE, WESLEY	ACTOR	POST OFFICE BOX 69405	LOS ANGELES, CA	90069
EUROGLIDERS, THE	ROCK & ROLL GROUP	POST OFFICE BOX 979		
		BONDI JUNCTION	SYDNEY 2022	AUSTRALIA
EURYTHMICS, THE	ROCK & ROCK DUO	POST OFFICE BOX 245	LONDON N8	ENGLAND
EUSTIS, RICHARD	SCREENWRITER	8955 BEVERLY BLVD	LOS ANGELES, CA	90048
EVANGELAUF, JEAN	NEWS CORRESPONDENT	2122 MASSACHUSETTS AVE, NW	WASHINGTON, DC	20008
EVANIER, MARK	TV WRITER	6282 DREXEL AVE	LOS ANGELES, CA	90048
EVANS, ALISON	ACTRESS	4225 ETHEL AVE #20	STUDIO CITY, CA	91604
EVANS, ANDREA	ACTRESS	10351 SANTA MONICA BLVD #211	LOS ANGELES, CA	90025
EVANS, ANNE	SOPRANO	CONE, 221 W 57TH ST	NEW YORK, NY	10019
EVANS, ART J	ACTOR-DIRECTOR	3800 BARHAM BLVD #303	LOS ANGELES, CA	90068
EVANS, BARBARA	TV WRITER	8955 BEVERLY BLVD	LOS ANGELES, CA	90048
EVANS, BARRY	ACTOR	HARRY MALONE, LTD		
		89 RIVERVIEW GARDENS	LONDON SW13	ENGLAND
EVANS, BRUCE A	WRITER-PRODUCER	8218 HOLLYWOOD BLVD	LOS ANGELES, CA	90069
EVANS, BUCK	GUITARIST	ROUTE #2, BOX 252	NUNNELLY, TN	37137
EVANS, CHEMIN	CASTING DIRECTOR	4024 RADFORD AVE	STUDIO CITY, CA	91604
EVANS, CRISPIN	TV DIRECTOR-PRODUCER	ARLINGTON, 1 CHARLOTTE	LONDON W1	ENGLAND
EVANS, DALE	ACTRESS	ROGERS, 15650 SENECA RD	VICTORVILLE, CA	92392
EVANS, DARRELL	BASEBALL	354 PROVENCAL RD	DETROIT, MI	48236
EVANS, DIRK	WRITER	8955 BEVERLY BLVD	LOS ANGELES, CA	90048
EVANS, DWIGHT	BASEBALL	3 JORDAN RD	LYNNFIELD, MA	01940
EVANS, EDWARD R	DIRECTOR	403 BRECKENRIDGE DR #2	HUNTSVILLE, AL	35802
EVANS, EVANS	ACTRESS	101 MALIBU COLONY RD	MALIBU, CA	90265
EVANS, GAYNELLE J	NEWS CORRESPONDENT	3104 16TH ST, NW	WASHINGTON, DC	20010
EVANS, GENE	ACTOR	1583 CHURCH ST	VENTURA, CA	93001
EVANS, GEOFFREY	TV DIRECTOR-PRODUCER	GREENAGE PRODUCTIONS, LTD		
		47 LAMBS CONDUIT ST	LONDON WC1	ENGLAND
EVANS, GEORGE	CARTOONIST	KING FEATURES SYNDICATE		
		235 E 45TH ST	NEW YORK, NY	10017
EVANS, GERAINT	SINGER	SEE - EVANS, SIR GERAINT		
EVANS, GREG	CARTOONIST	NEWS AMERICA SYNDICATE		
		1703 KAISER AVE	IRVINE, CA	92714
EVANS, HAROLD	NEWS CORRESPONDENT	2501 "M" ST #705, NW	WASHINGTON, DC	20037
EVANS, JACQUI	ACTRESS	3151 W CAHUENGA BLVD #310	LOS ANGELES, CA	90068
EVANS, JANICE	NEWS CORRESPONDENT	CBS NEWS, 2020 "M" ST, NW	WASHINGTON, DC	20036
EVANS, JERRY	TV DIRECTOR	1 SUNSET DR	SUMMIT, NJ	07901
EVANS, JOE	CASTING DIRECTOR	POST OFFICE BOX 10704	GLENDALE, CA	91209
EVANS, JOSEPH	TENOR	POST OFFICE BOX 1515	NEW YORK, NY	10023
EVANS, LEO B	WRITER	8955 BEVERLY BLVD	LOS ANGELES, CA	90048
EVANS, LESLEY	ACTRESS	4150 RIVERSIDE DR #204	BURBANK, CA	91505
EVANS, LINDA	ACTRESS	9115 HAZEN DR	BEVERLY HILLS, CA	90210
EVANS, LLOYD RANNEY	ART DIRECTOR	CBS-TV, "AS THE WORLD TURNS"		
		51 W 52ND ST	NEW YORK, NY	10019
EVANS, MARK	PIANIST	3636 16TH ST #B-564, NW	WASHINGTON, DC	20010
EVANS, MARTIN A	DIRECTOR	4235 KESTER AVE	SHERMAN OAKS, CA	91403
EVANS, MARTY	DIRECTOR	DGA, 7950 SUNSET BLVD	LOS ANGELES, CA	90046
EVANS, MARY BETH	ACTRESS	151 N SAN VICENTE BLVD #208	BEVERLY HILLS, CA	90211
EVANS, MAX	WRITER	8955 BEVERLY BLVD	LOS ANGELES, CA	90048
EVANS, MELISSA	SOPRANO	MARIEDL ANDERS ARTISTS MGMT		
		535 EL CAMINO DEL MAR ST	SAN FRANCISCO, CA	94121
EVANS, MICHAEL	ACTOR-WRITER	12530 COLLINS ST	NORTH HOLLYWOOD, CA	91605
EVANS, MICHAEL	PHOTOGRAPHER	TIME/TIME & LIFE BLDG		
		ROCKEFELLER CENTER	NEW YORK, NY	10020
EVANS, MIKE	EVANGELIST-AUTHOR	POST OFFICE 709	BEDFORD, TX	76021
EVANS, PETER	ACTOR	ICM, 8899 BEVERLY BLVD	LOS ANGELES, CA	90048
EVANS, RICHARD	TV WRITER-PRODUCER	27 HOVE PARK VILLAS, HOVE	SUSSEY	ENGLAND
EVANS, RICHARD	ACTOR	211 S BEVERLY DR #107	BEVERLY HILLS, CA	90212
EVANS, ROBERT	PRODUCER-ACTOR	1052 WOODLAWN DR	BEVERLY HILLS, CA	90210
EVANS, ROSS	ACTOR	1605 N CAHUENGA BLVD #202	LOS ANGELES, CA	90028
EVANS, ROSS S, JR	NEWS CORRESPONDENT	310 SKYHILL RD	ALEXANDRIA, VA	22314
EVANS, ROWLAND	COLUMNIST	NEWS AMERICA SYNDICATE		
		1703 KAISER AVE	IRVINE, CA	92714
EVANS, SALLY	WRITER	8955 BEVERLY BLVD	LOS ANGELES, CA	90048
EVANS, SANDRA	NEWS CORRESPONDENT	1300 ARMY-NAVY DR #812	ARLINGTON, VA	22202
EVANS, SIR GERAINT	SINGER	17 HIGHCLIFFE		
		32 ALBEMARLE ST, BECKENHAM	KENT	ENGLAND
EVANS, STEVEN LEE	COMPOSER	2377 MALCOM AVE	LOS ANGELES, CA	90064
EVANS, TENNIEL	ACTOR	CANDLEMAS, JORDANS	BUCKS	ENGLAND
EVANS, TERRENCE	ACTOR	15010 VENTURA BLVD #219	SHERMAN OAKS, CA	91403
EVANS, TROY	ACTOR	1350 N HIGHLAND AVE #24	HOLLYWOOD, CA	90028
EVANS-MASSEY, ANDREA	ACTRESS	10351 SANTA MONICA BLVD #211	LOS ANGELES, CA	90025
EVE, TREVOR	ACTOR	MORRIS, 147-149 WARDOUR ST	LONDON W1V 3TB	ENGLAND
EVELYN	SINGER	CICR, 9271 S WAYNE RD	ROMULUS, MI	48174
EVENCE, FRANCIS	NEWS CORRESPONDENT	4655 S 36TH ST	ARLINGTON, VA	22205
EVENSON, KIMBERLY	ACTRESS-MODEL	9000 SUNSET BLVD #1112	LOS ANGELES, CA	90069
EVERETT, CHAD	ACTOR	19901 NORTHRIDGE RD	CHATSWORTH, CA	91311
EVERETT, DEAN	NEWS CORRESPONDENT	1755 JEFFERSON DAVIS HWY	ARLINGTON, VA	22202
EVERETT, ELAINE	ACTRESS	1421 N AVE 47	LOS ANGELES, CA	90042
EVERETT, KENNY	TV-RADIO PERSONALITY	45 QUEENSGATE MEWS	LONDON SW7	ENGLAND
EVERETT, PERCIVAL L	WRITER	555 W 57TH ST #1230	NEW YORK, NY	10019
EVERETT, RUPERT	ACTOR	HEATH, PARAMOUNT HOUSE		
		162-170 WARDOUR ST	LONDON W1V 3AT	ENGLAND
EVERETT, SHELBY GRANT	ACTRESS	19901 NORTHRIDGE RD	CHATSWORTH, CA	91311
EVERETT, TOM	SINGER-ACTOR	9255 SUNSET BLVD #510	LOS ANGELES, CA	90069

THE EURYTHMICS

LINDA EVANS

CHAD EVERETT

GREG EVIGAN

DOUGLAS FAIRBANKS, JR.

MORGAN FAIRCHILD

JINX FALKENBURG

JAMES FARENTINO

ANTONIO FARGAS

Name	Occupation	Address	City	Zip
EVERETTE, LEON	SINGER-GUITARIST	POST OFFICE BOX 13009-A	ORLANDO, FL	32809
EVERHARD, NANCY	ACTRESS	151 S EL CAMINO DR	BEVERLY HILLS, CA	90212
EVERHART, BOB	SINGER-SONGWRITER	106 NAVAJO	COUNCIL BLUFFS, IA	51501
EVERHART, GALEN	ACTRESS	6430 SUNSET BLVD #1203	LOS ANGELES, CA	90028
EVERHART, REX	ACTOR	42 N COMPO RD	WESTPORT, CT	06880
EVERING, JAMES V	TV WRITER	2438 N BEACHWOOD DR	LOS ANGELES, CA	90068
EVERITT, RICHARD	TV PRODUCER	LAUREL MOUNT, RICHMOND RD		
		BOWDEN	CHESHIRE	ENGLAND
EVERLY, DON	SINGER-SONGWRITER	10100 SANTA MONICA BLVD #1600	LOS ANGELES, CA	90067
EVERLY, PHIL	SINGER-SONGWRITER	10414 CAMARILLO ST	NORTH HOLLYWOOD, CA	91602
EVERLY, TRISH	ACTRESS	2175 CENTURY WOODS WY	LOS ANGELES, CA	90067
EVERLY BROTHERS, THE	VOCAL DUO	10100 SANTA MONICA BLVD #1600	LOS ANGELES, CA	90067
EVERS, JASON	ACTOR	232 N CRESCENT DR #101	BEVERLY HILLS, CA	90210
EVERSON, CORY	BODYBUILDER	7324 RESEDA BLVD #208	RESEDA, CA	91335
EVERSON, JEFF	BODYBUILDER	7324 RESEDA BLVD #208	RESEDA, CA	91335
EVERT-LLOYD, CHRIS	TENNIS	1628 NE 7TH PL	FORT LAUDERDALE, FL	37204
EVERTS, KELLIE	AUTHOR-PREACHER	LEITNER & ASSOCIATES		
		1415 ELBRIDGE PAYNE RD	CHESTERFIELD, MO	63017
EVERYMAN'S NIGHTMARE	WRESTLER	SEE - STING		
EVERYTHING BUT GIRL	ROCK & ROCK DUO	200 W 57TH ST #1403	NEW YORK, NY	10019
EVIGAN, GREG	ACTOR-SINGER	6030 GRACIOSA DR	LOS ANGELES, CA	90068
EVITTS, DAVID	BARITONE	POST OFFICE BOX 1515	NEW YORK, NY	10023
EVRY, MARTA	NEWS CORRESPONDENT	2139 WISCONSIN AVE, NW	WASHINGTON, DC	20007
EVSTATIEVA, STEFKA	SOPRANO	CAMI, 165 W 57TH ST	NEW YORK, NY	10019
EWALD, WILLIAM F	WRITER-EDITOR	TIME/TIME & LIFE BLDG		
		ROCKEFELLER CENTER	NEW YORK, NY	10020
EWALT, JOSEPH H	NEWS CORRESPONDENT	1776 "C" ST, NW	WASHINGTON, DC	20006
EWELL, CODAY	CASTING DIRECTOR	20TH CENTURY-FOX PICTURES		
		10201 W PICO BLVD		
		BUNGALOW #1	LOS ANGELES, CA	90035
EWEN, ALAN	GUITARIST	106 SHERBROOK LN	HENDERSONVILLE, TN	37075
EWEN, GREGORY	DRUMMER	231 NEW SHACKLE ISLAND	HENDERSONVILLE, TN	37075
EWEN, LINDA	ACTRESS	262 1/2 S SPALDING DR #6	BEVERLY HILLS, CA	90212
EWERS, MIKE	CARTOONIST	POST OFFICE BOX 4203	NEW YORK, NY	10017
EWING, DIANA	WRITER	407 SAN VICENTE BLVD	SANTA MONICA, CA	90402
EWING, GORDON	ACTOR	3502 ST ELIZABETH RD	GLENDALE, CA	91206
EWING, JOHN CHRISTY	ACTOR	368 GRENOLA ST	PACIFIC PALISADES, CA	90272
EWING, LAURENCE LEE	NEWS CORRESPONDENT	4541 CASABLANCA CT	ANNANDALE, VA	22003
EWING, ROGER	ACTOR	7733 HAMPTON AVE #4	LOS ANGELES, CA	90046
EWING, WILLIAM R	WRITER	8955 BEVERLY BLVD	LOS ANGELES, CA	90048
EXCITER	ROCK & ROLL GROUP	POST OFFICE BOX 6010	SHERMAN OAKS, CA	91413
EXECUTIONER, THE	WRESTLER	CAPITOL INTERNATIONAL		
		11844 MARKET ST	NORTH LIMA, OH	44452
EXECUTIONER #2	WRESTLER-ACTOR	SEE - STUDD, BIG JOHN		
EXILE	C & W GROUP	8730 SUNSET BLVD #PH-W	LOS ANGELES, CA	90069
EXPLODING WHITE MICE	ROCK & ROLL GROUP	POST OFFICE BOX 136		
		RUNDLE MALL	ADELAIDE 5000	S AUSTRALIA
EXPRESSWAY	C & W GROUP	4615 SW FREEWAY #475	HOUSTON, TX	77027
EXTON, CLIVE	TV WRITER	A D PETERS & CO, LTD		
		10 BUCKINGHAM ST	LONDON WC2	ENGLAND
EXUDE	ROCK & ROLL GROUP	GREENWALD, 20445 GRAMERCY PL	TORRANCE, CA	90501
EXXPLORER	ROCK & ROLL GROUP	POST OFFICE BOX 2428	EL SEGUNDO, CA	90245
EYE EYE	ROCK & ROLL GROUP	41 BRITAIN ST #200	TORONTO, ONT	CANADA
EYE TO EYE	ROCK & ROLL GROUP	ICM, 40 W 57TH ST	NEW YORK, NY	10019
EYEN, TOM	LYRICIST	ICM, 40 W 57TH ST	NEW YORK, NY	10019
EYER, RICHARD	ACTOR	ROCKING "K" RANCH	BISHOP, CA	93514
EYRE, DAVID M, JR	SCREENWRITER	555 W 57TH ST #1230	NEW YORK, NY	10019
EYSTER, JENIFER N	WRITER	555 W 57TH ST #1230	NEW YORK, NY	10019
EZRA, MARK	SCREENWRITER	22 ROYAL CRESCENT	LONDON W11	ENGLAND

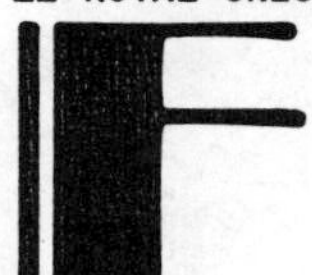

Name	Occupation	Address	City	Zip
F M	ROCK & ROLL GROUP	2067 BROADWAY #B	NEW YORK, NY	10023
F U'S, THE	ROCK & ROLL GROUP	BOB FURAPPLES, 45 LYDON WY	DORCHESTER, MA	02124
FABARES, SHELLEY	ACTRESS	POST OFFICE BOX 6010-85	SHERMAN OAKS, CA	91413
FABBRI, DAVID	BASSO-BARITONE	111 W 57TH ST #1209	NEW YORK, NY	10019
FABER, GEORGE D	AUTHOR-EXECUTIVE	VIACOM COMMUNICATIONS		
		10900 WILSHIRE BLVD	LOS ANGELES, CA	90024
FABER, MORT	CONDUCTOR	1123 GARFIELD AVE	MARINA DEL REY, CA	90292
FABER, ROBERT	WRITER-PRODUCER	1524 STRADELLA RD	LOS ANGELES, CA	90077
FABIAN, AVA	ACTRESS-MODEL	MODELS & PROMOTIONS AGENCY		
		8560 SUNSET BLVD, 10TH FLOOR	LOS ANGELES, CA	90069
FABIAN, THECLA R	NEWS CORRESPONDENT	309 MARYLAND AVE #7, NE	WASHINGTON, DC	20002
FABIANI, JOEL	ACTOR	9220 SUNSET BLVD #202	LOS ANGELES, CA	90069
FABINYI, JEREMY	TALENT AGENT	OLD SOUTH HEAD RD #17/79	BONDI JUNCTION NSW	AUSTRALIA
FABRAY, NANETTE	ACTRESS	14360 SUNSET BLVD	PACIFIC PALISADES, CA	90272
FABRIQUE, TINA	SINGER	360 CENTRAL PARK W #16-G	NEW YORK, NY	10025
FABULOUS THUNDERBIRDS, THE	ROCK & ROLL GROUP	POST OFFICE BOX 17006	AUSTIN, TX	78760
FACE TO FACE	ROCK & ROLL GROUP	HART & HINKLE MANAGEMENT		
		17 CADMAN PLAZA W	BROOKLYN, NY	11201
FACE TO FACE	ROCK & ROLL GROUP	25 HUNTINGTON AVE #420	BOSTON, MA	02116

BOB EVERHART

106 Navajo
Council Bluffs
Iowa, 51501

Don't Miss Bob Everhart's Greatest Festival!

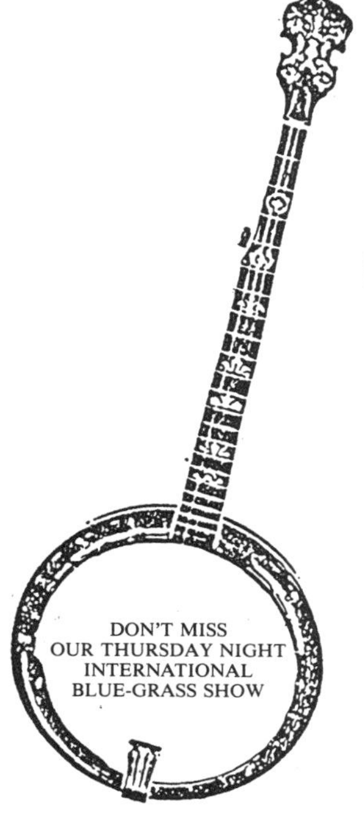

DON'T MISS
OUR THURSDAY NIGHT
INTERNATIONAL
BLUE-GRASS SHOW

12th Old-Time Country Music Festival

SEPT. 3-7, 1987

Pottawattamie County Fairgrounds

AVOCA IOWA

$20,000 Prizes

CHAMPIONSHIPS
National Accordian
International Country Singer
International Bluegrass Band
National Gandy Dancer
National Harmonica
International Comedy Group
National Rag-Time Piano
World's Spoon & Bone
Iowa State Checkers
National Country Instrument
Jimmy Rodgers Yodeling
Great Plains Story Telling
Iowa State Cribbage
Pioneer Arts & Crafts
National Whistlers
Hank Williams Songwriters
Hatchet Throwing
International Performers

CHAMPIONSHIPS
Iowa State Banjo
Iowa State Mandolin
Mid-America Fiddle
Fur-Trader Tipi Village
Iowa State Square Dance
Biggest Grasshopper Contest
Woody Guthrie Folksinger
Mid-West Flat-Top Guitar
Mid-West Dobro Guitar
Mid-West Dulcimer
Mid-America Junior
National Autoharp
Great Plains Clog Dance
Mid-West Horse Shoe
International Toad Hop
Scavenger Hunt
Roy Acuff YoYo Champion
Legends Of Our Time

ALL ACTS & CONTESTS SUBJECT TO CHANGE
NO DRUGS OR ALCOHOL ALLOWED

Bob Everhart, Director
106 Navajo
Council Bluffs, Iowa 51501

Name	Occupation	Address	City	Zip
FACEDANCER	ROCK & ROLL GROUP	5225 POOKS HILL RD #162	SOUTH BETHESDA, MD	20014
FACH, CHARLES	SAXOPHONIST	5516 S STANFORD DR	NASHVILLE, TN	37215
FACINELLI, ROBERTA E	WRITER	555 W 57TH ST #1230	NEW YORK, NY	10019
FACKELMANN, KATHY A	NEWS CORRESPONDENT	3701 CONNECTICUT AVE #915, NW	WASHINGTON, DC	20008
FACTOR, ALAN JAY	FILM DIRECTOR	404 N ROXBURY DR #800	BEVERLY HILLS, CA	90210
FADE TO BLACK	ROCK & ROLL GROUP	1230 GRANT AVE #531	SAN FRANCISCO, CA	94133
FADER, SUNNY	WRITER	8955 BEVERLY BLVD	LOS ANGELES, CA	90048
FADIMAN, ANNE	WRITER-EDITOR	LIFE/TIME & LIFE BLDG		
		ROCKEFELLER CENTER	NEW YORK, NY	10020
FADIMAN, CLIFTON	TV PERSONALITY	3222 CAMPANIL DR	SANTA BARBARA, CA	93109
FAER, STANLEY M	TV DIRECTOR	301 E 62ND ST	NEW YORK, NY	10021
FAGA, GARY	ACTOR	31637 SEA LEVEL DR	MALIBU, CA	90265
FAGAN, ANDREW H	DIRECTOR	358 N VAN NESS AVE	LOS ANGELES, CA	90004
FAGAN, JIM	ACTOR	TUSH, 119 W 57TH ST	NEW YORK, NY	10019
FAGAN, KEVIN	CARTOONIST	UNITED FEATURE SYNDICATE		
		200 PARK AVE	NEW YORK, NY	10017
FAGEN, ARTHUR	CONDUCTOR	61 W 62ND ST #6-F	NEW YORK, NY	10023
FAGEN, DONALD	SINGER-SONGWRITER	24109 MALIBU RD	MALIBU, CA	90265
FAGEN, LESLEY D	WRITER	555 W 57TH ST #1230	NEW YORK, NY	10019
FAGER, JOHN	WRITER	555 W 57TH ST #1230	NEW YORK, NY	10019
FAHEY, JEFF	ACTOR	9000 SUNSET BLVD #1200	LOS ANGELES, CA	90069
FAHEY, JOHN	GUITARIST	4230 SW VIEWPOINT TERR #12	PORTLAND, OR	97201
FAICHNEY, JAMES B	WRITER-PRODUCER	LAKESIDE DR	MONSON, MA	01057
FAIN, JACQUELYN	NEWS CORRESPONDENT	2133 WISCONSIN AVE, NW	WASHINGTON, DC	20007
FAIN, JAMES E	NEWS CORRESPONDENT	2276 CATHEDRAL AVE, NW	WASHINGTON, DC	20008
FAIN, JOHNNY	ACTOR	25154 MALIBU RD #1	MALIBU, CA	90265
FAIN, SAMMY	COMPOSER	1640 SAN YSIDRO DR	BEVERLY HILLS, CA	90210
FAIR, LA LANYA	ACTRESS	4421 KLING ST #17	BURBANK, CA	91505
FAIRBAIRN, BRUCE	ACTOR	2121 AVE OF THE STARS #410	LOS ANGELES, CA	90067
FAIRBANKS, DOUGLAS, JR	ACTOR	448 N LAKE WY	PALM BEACH, FL	33480
FAIRBANKS, JERRY	DIRECTOR-PRODUCER	826 N COLE AVE	HOLLYWOOD, CA	90038
FAIRCHILD, BARBARA	SINGER	HALLMARK DIRECTION CO		
		15 MUSIC SQUARE W	NASHVILLE, TN	37203
FAIRCHILD, BOBBY	WHIPS & KNIFE TOSSER	HALL, 138 FROG HOLLOW RD	CHURCHVILLE, PA	18966
FAIRCHILD, MARGARET	ACTRESS	6310 SAN VICENTE BLVD #407	LOS ANGELES, CA	90048
FAIRCHILD, MORGAN	ACTRESS	POST OFFICE BOX 8170	UNIVERSAL CITY, CA	91608
FAIRCHILD, TOMMY	GUITARIST	4125 STARWOOD DR	MEMPHIS, TN	38115
FAIRCHILD, WILLIAM	TV WRITER-DIRECTOR	DOUGLAS RAE MANAGEMENT		
		28 CHARING CROSS RD	LONDON WC2	ENGLAND
FAIRCLOTH, JAMES	GUITARIST	314 SPRING ST	EUREKA SPRINGS, AR	72632
FAIRFAX, FERDINAND	FILM WRITER-DIRECTOR	HEATH, PARAMOUNT HOUSE		
		162-170 WARDOUR ST	LONDON W1V 3AT	ENGLAND
FAIRFAX, SARAH	ACTRESS	120 S VICTORY BLVD #104	BURBANK, CA	91502
FAIRFIELD, ROBIN	FILM PRODUCER	116 BACTON TOWER		
		KISMORE CIRCUS	LONDON NW5 4PX	ENGLAND
FAIRHURST, LYN	FILM-TV WRITER	124 DOLLIS HILL LN	LONDON NW2	ENGLAND
FAIRLEY, RON	SPORTSCASTER	23140 PARK SORRENTO	CALABASAS, CA	91302
FAIRMAN, MICHAEL	ACT-WRI-DIR	6615 FRANKLIN AVE #119	HOLLYWOOD, CA	90028
FAIRPORT CONVENTION	ROCK & ROLL GROUP	POST OFFICE BOX 37, BANBURY	OXON	ENGLAND
FAISON, MATTHEW	ACTOR	13701 KAGEL CANYON RD	SYLMAR, CA	91342
FAISON, SANDY	ACTRESS	211 S BEVERLY DR #201	BEVERLY HILLS, CA	90212
FAITH, ADAM	SINGER-ACTOR	CROCKHAM HILL, EDENBRIDGE	KENT	ENGLAND
FAITH NO MORE	ROCK & ROLL GROUP	POST OFFICE BOX 988	SAN FRANCISCO, CA	94101
FAITHFULL, MARIANNE	SINGER-SONGWRITER	YEW TREE COTTAGE, ALDRIDGE	BERKS	ENGLAND
FAJARDO, PHILLIP	DRUMMER	ROUTE #9, LOT 29, COOKS CORNER	MURFREESBORO, TN	37130
FALANA, LOLA	SINGER-ACTRESS	3121 S MARYLAND PARKWAY #216	LAS VEGAS, NV	89109
FALCK, EDWARD	NEWS CORRESPONDENT	3001 VEAZEY TERR, NW	WASHINGTON, DC	20008
FALCO	SINGER-SONGWRITER	GIG RECORDS, KAERNTRIERING #17	VIENNA 1919	AUSTRIA
FALCO, MICHAEL ANTHONY	ACTOR	MINE HILL RD	CORNWALL, NY	12518
FALCON, BILLY	SINGER	POST OFFICE BOX 602	WOODCLIFF LAKE, NJ	07675
FALCON, ELLEN	TV DIRECTOR	4809 ARCOLA AVE	TOLUCA LAKE, CA	91601
FALCON, ERROL A	DIRECTOR	7955 SW 146TH CT	MIAMI, FL	33143
FALCON, RUTH	SOPRANO	CAMI, 165 W 57TH ST	NEW YORK, NY	10019
FALCONER, THEODORE E	WRITER	6139 BLUEBELL AVE	NORTH HOLLYWOOD, CA	91606
FALK, HARRY	DIRECTOR	1289 SUNSET PLAZA DR	LOS ANGELES, CA	90069
FALK, LAURA NELSON	SCREENWRITER	21070 PACIFIC COAST HWY	MALIBU, CA	90265

Name	Occupation	Address	City	Zip
FALK, LEE	CARTOONIST	KING FEATURES SYNDICATE		
		235 E 45TH ST	NEW YORK, NY	10017
FALK, PETER	ACTOR-DIRECTOR	1004 N ROXBURY DR	BEVERLY HILLS, CA	90210
FALK, TOM	WRITER	21070 PACIFIC COAST HWY	MALIBU, CA	90265
FALKENBERG, KORT	ACTOR	20831 BURBANK BLVD	WOODLAND HILLS, CA	91367
FALKENBERG, PAUL V	DIRECTOR	15 W 67TH ST	NEW YORK, NY	10023
FALKENBURG, JINX	ACTRESS	10 SHELTER ROCK RD	MANHASSET, LI, NY	11030
FALKERSON, LINDA J	NEWS CORRESPONDENT	100 W UNIVERSITY PARKWAY, NW	WASHINGTON, DC	21210
FALKNOR, RICHARD W C	NEWS CORRESPONDENT	SCIENTIST'S CLIFFS	REPUBLIC, MD	20676
FALLETTA, JOANN	CONDUCTOR	SOFFER, 130 W 56TH ST	NEW YORK, NY	10019
FALLICK, MORTON	DIRECTOR	23885 KILLION ST	WOODLAND HILLS, CA	91367
FALLON, DAVID	WRITER	555 W 57TH ST #1230	NEW YORK, NY	10019
FALLON, JOEL R	WRITER	426 S GRIFFITH PARK DR	BURBANK, CA	91506
FALLON, KATHRYN JACKSON	NEWS REPORTER	TIME/TIME & LIFE BLDG		
		ROCKEFELLER CENTER	NEW YORK, NY	10020
FALOTICO, CREIGHTON	ACTOR	5431 JED SMITH RD	CALABASAS, CA	91302
FALSE PROPHETS, THE	ROCK & ROLL GROUP	POST OFFICE BOX 11458	SAN FRANCISCO, CA	94101
FALSEY, JOHN	TV PRODUCER	10100 SANTA MONICA BLVD #1600	LOS ANGELES, CA	90067
FALSEY, JOHN, JR	TV WRITER	8955 BEVERLY BLVD	LOS ANGELES, CA	90048
FALVELLO, NINA J	NEWS CORRESPONDENT	4461 CONNECTICUT AVE, NW	WASHINGTON, DC	20008
FALWELL, REV JERRY	EVANGELIST	THOMAS ROAD BAPTIST CHURCH		
		701 THOMAS RD	LYNCHBURG, VA	24502
FAMIGLIETTI, LEONARD G	NEWS CORRESPONDENT	4550 CONECTICUT AVE #615, NW	WASHINGTON, DC	20008
FAMILY BROWN, THE	C & W GROUP	71 BIRCHVIEW RD	NEPEAN, ONT K2G 3G3	CANADA
FAMOUS AMOS	COOKIE ENTREPRENEUR	SEE - AMOS, WALLY "FAMOUS"		
FANARO, BARRY P	TV WRITER	13914 BORA BORA WY #318	MARINA DEL REY, CA	90292
FANCHER, HAMPTON	SCREENWRITER	262 N OLD TOPANGA CANYON RD	TOPANGA, CA	90290
FANDANGO	ROCK & ROLL GROUP	NEWMARK, 793 BINGHAM RD	RIDGEWOOD, NJ	07540
FANN, AL	ACTOR	19649 CITRONIA ST	NORTHRIDGE, CA	91324
FANNING, BOB	GUITARIST	ROUTE #2, SHARBOT LAKE	ONTARIO	CANADA
FANNING, DAVID E	WRITER	8955 BEVERLY BLVD	LOS ANGELES, CA	90048
FANNING, JOHN	BARITONE	VKD INTERNATIONAL ARTISTS		
		220 SHEPPARD AVE N		
		WILLOWDALE	TORONTO, ONT M2N 3A9	CANADA
FANNING, ODOM	NEWS CORRESPONDENT	9206 BULLS RUN PARKWAY	BETHESDA, MD	20817
FANT, LESA	ACTRESS	19602 LANARK ST	RESEDA, CA	91335
FANT, LOU	ACTOR	19602 LANARK ST	RESEDA, CA	91335
FANT, WILLIAM H S	NEWS CORRESPONDENT	2302 41ST ST, NW	WASHINGTON, DC	20007
FANTASTIC VIOLINAIRES, THE	VIOLIN ENSEMBLE	4803 BISSONETTE #146	BEL AIRE, TX	77401
FANTASTICS, THE	WRESTLING TAG TEAM	UNIVERSAL WRESTLING FEDERATION		
		MID SOUTH SPORTS, INC		
		5001 SPRING VALLEY RD	DALLAS, TX	75244
FANTO, CLARENCE A	WRITER	555 W 57TH ST #1230	NEW YORK, NY	10019
FANTUS, KARIN D	WRITER	555 W 57TH ST #1230	NEW YORK, NY	10019
FARACY, STEPHANIE	ACTRESS	10390 SANTA MONICA BLVD #310	LOS ANGELES, CA	90025
FARAGO, ERNESTO	VIOLINIST	POST OFFICE BOX 131	SPRINGFIELD, VA	22150
FARAGO, GABRIEL	GUITARIST	112 SAIN AVE	HENDERSONVILLE, TN	37075
FARAGO, JOE	ACTOR	835 HOPKINS WY #313	REDONDO BEACH, CA	90277
FARAGO, MARCEL	CELLIST	POST OFFICE BOX 131	SPRINGFIELD, VA	22150
FARAGO DUO	MUSICAL DUO	POST OFFICE BOX 131	SPRINGFIELD, VA	22150
FARALLA, WILLIAM	DIRECTOR	448 MARVIEW DR	SOLANA BEACH, CA	92075
FARBER, J J	WRITER	8955 BEVERLY BLVD	LOS ANGELES, CA	90048
FARBER, STEPHEN	WRITER	10611 WILKINS AVE #6	LOS ANGELES, CA	90024
FARBERMAN, HAROLD	CONDUCTOR	1776 BROADWAY #504	NEW YORK, NY	10019
FARBERMAN, RACHELLE	CASTING DIRECTOR	20TH CENTURY FOX PICTURES		
		10201 W PICO BLVD, TRAILER #71	LOS ANGELES, CA	90035
FARBMAN, PAUL	ACTOR	2832 EXPOSITION BLVD	SANTA MONICA, CA	90404
FARENHEIT	ROCK & ROLL GROUP	25 HUNTINGTON AVE #420	BOSTON, MA	02116
FARENTINO, JAMES	ACTOR	1340 LONDONDERRY PL	LOS ANGELES, CA	90069
FARGAS, ANTONIO	ACTOR	ABC-TV, "ALL MY CHILDREN"		
		1330 AVE OF THE AMERICAS	NEW YORK, NY	10019
FARGNOLI, STEVEN	TALENT AGENT	11355 W OLYMPIC BLVD #555	LOS ANGELES, CA	90064
FARGO, DONNA	SINGER	POST OFFICE BOX 15385	NASHVILLE, TN	37215
FARGO, JOHNNY	WRESTLER	SEE - VALENTINE, GREG		
		"THE HAMMER"		
FARGO, LOUIS J	DIRECTOR	2419 OCEAN FRONT WALK #3	VENICE, CA	90291
FARINA, DENNIS	ACTOR	1509 N CRESCENT HGTS BLVD #7	LOS ANGELES, CA	90069
FARINA, FRANCO	TENOR	CAMI, 165 W 57TH ST	NEW YORK, NY	10019
FARINA, MICHAEL F	TV DIRECTOR	235 W 70TH ST	NEW YORK, NY	10023
FARINA, MIMI	SINGER	WOLFGANG ARTISTS, 201 11TH ST	SAN FRANCISCO, CA	94103
FARINA, SANTO	SINGER	POST OFFICE BOX 1064	SETAUKET, NY	11733
FARINELLI, PATTI	MODEL	MODELS & PROMOTIONS AGENCY		
		8560 SUNSET BLVD, 10TH FLOOR	LOS ANGELES, CA	90069
FARINI, JOE	WRESTLER	SEE - SAVOLDI, JUMPING JOE		
FARKAS, B RAY	NEWS CORRESPONDENT	NBC NEWS, 4001 NEBRASKA AVE, NW	WASHINGTON, DC	20016
FARKAS, MARK D	NEWS CORRESPONDENT	400 N CAPITOL ST, NW	WASHINGTON, DC	20001
FARLEIGH, LYNN	ACTRESS	CONWAY, EAGLE HOUSE		
		109 JERMYN ST	LONDON SW1	ENGLAND
FARLEY, CAROLE	SOPRANO	111 W 57TH ST #1209	NEW YORK, NY	10019
FARLEY, EDWARD	TRUMPETER	3427 BENHAM AVE	NASHVILLE, TN	37215
FARLEY, MORGAN	ACTOR	CONVENT SAINT BIRGITTE		
		VIKINGSBORG	DARIEN, CT	06820
FARLEY, SUSAN	PHOTOGRAPHER	100 W MASON AVE	ALEXANDRIA, VA	22301

Name	Occupation	Address	City	Zip
FARMER, ART, QUARTET	JAZZ QUARTET	KEANE, 49 E 96TH ST	NEW YORK, NY	10128
FARMER, BUDDY	ACTOR	LEONETTI, 6526 SUNSET BLVD	HOLLYWOOD, CA	90028
FARMER, DON	BROADCAST JOURNALIST	MARTIN KRALL, 1800 "M" ST, NW	WASHINGTON, DC	20036
FARMER, FRANK	ACTOR	8961 SUNSET BLVD #B	LOS ANGELES, CA	90069
FARMER, GARY	MUSICIAN	POST OFFICE BOX 22375	NASHVILLE, TN	37202
FARMER, GENE	TV WRITER	555 W 57TH ST #1230	NEW YORK, NY	10019
FARMER, JAMES	GUITARIST	197 TANKSLEY AVE	NASHVILLE, TN	37211
FARMER, JERRILYN S	TV WRITER	8955 BEVERLY BLVD	LOS ANGELES, CA	90048
FARMER, JOHN A	ACTOR-WRITER	5542 SUNNYSLOPE AVE	VAN NUYS, CA	91401
FARMER, KIPLYN R	CABLE EXECUTIVE	8252 S HARVARD AVE	TULSA, OK	74136
FARMER, REGINALD H	WRITER	POST OFFICE BOX 1040	STUDIO CITY, CA	91604
FARMER'S DAUGHTER, THE	WRESTLER	SEE - SALLY THE FARMER'S DAUGHTER		
FARNEY, DENNIS D	NEWS CORRESPONDENT	222 S ALFRED ST	ALEXANDRIA, VA	22314
FARNON, SHANNON	ACTRESS	12743 MILBANK ST	STUDIO CITY, CA	91604
FARNSWORTH, CLYDE H	NEWS CORRESPONDENT	5353 COLUMBIA PIKE	ARLINGTON, VA	22204
FARNSWORTH, RICHARD	ACTOR	3800 BARHAM BLVD #303	LOS ANGELES, CA	90068
FARNSWORTH, ROBERT	PIANIST	1521 GRAYBAR AVE	MADISON, TN	37215
FARNSWORTH, STEPHEN J	NEWS CORRESPONDENT	58 WALNUT AVE	TAKOMA PARK, MD	20912
FARNUM, DOUGLASS P	NEWS CORRESPONDENT	NBC-TV, NEWS DEPARTMENT 4001 NEBRASKA AVE, NW	WASHINGTON, DC	20016
FARPOUR, SHOLEH	ACTRESS	KOHNER, 9169 SUNSET BLVD	LOS ANGELES, CA	90069
FARQUHAR, RALPH	TV WRITER	1300 1/2 N SYCAMORE AVE	LOS ANGELES, CA	90028
FARR, BERNARD E	CONDUCTOR	300 N RAMPART ST #158	ORANGE, CA	92667
FARR, FELICIA	ACTRESS	141 S EL CAMINO DR #201	BEVERLY HILLS, CA	90212
FARR, GIDEON	TV WRITER	8955 BEVERLY BLVD	LOS ANGELES, CA	90048
FARR, GORDON	WRITER-PRODUCER	8161 LAUREL VIEW DR	LOS ANGELES, CA	90069
FARR, JAMIE	ACTOR-DIRECTOR	POST OFFICE BOX 8519	CALABASAS, CA	91302
FARR, KIMBERLY	ACTRESS	1509 N CRESCENT HGTS BLVD #7	LOS ANGELES, CA	90069
FARR, TONY	GUITARIST	701 GRAYCROFT AVE	MADISON, TN	37115
FARRANT, TREVOR A	SCREENWRITER	8955 BEVERLY BLVD	LOS ANGELES, CA	90048
FARRAR, BILL	MUSICIAN	612 BATON ROUGE CT	HERMITAGE, TN	37076
FARRAR, FREDERIC DOUGLAS	DIRECTOR	DGA, 110 W 57TH ST	NEW YORK, NY	10019
FARREL, BRIONI	ACTRESS	208 S BEVERLY DR #8	BEVERLY HILLS, CA	90212
FARRELL, BRIAN	ACTOR	18432 LINNET ST	TARZANA, CA	91356
FARRELL, CHARLES (AMERICAN)	ACTOR	630 TACHEVAH DR	PALM SPRINGS, CA	92262
FARRELL, CHARLES (ENGLISH)	ACTOR	GREEN ROOM CLUB, 9 ADAMS ST	LONDON WC2	ENGLAND
FARRELL, CHARLES S	NEWS CORRESPONDENT	1450 HARVARD ST #B, NW	WASHINGTON, DC	20009
FARRELL, COLIN	ACTOR	17 FOUNDRY ST, BRIGHTON	SUSSEX	ENGLAND
FARRELL, DANIEL B	PHOTOGRAPHER	291 MERRIFIELD AVE	OCEANSIDE, NY	11572
FARRELL, GAIL	ACTRESS	16022 MEADOWCREST RD	SHERMAN OAKS, CA	91403
FARRELL, GINGER	ACTRESS	FELBER, 2126 N CAHUENGA BLVD	LOS ANGELES, CA	90068
FARRELL, JUDY	ACTRESS	9220 SUNSET BLVD #202	LOS ANGELES, CA	90069
FARRELL, JUDY L	TV WRITER	8955 BEVERLY BLVD	LOS ANGELES, CA	90048
FARRELL, KEVIN	NEWS CORRESPONDENT	1726 "U" ST, NW	WASHINGTON, DC	20009
FARRELL, MARTY	TV WRITER	14144 VENTURA BLVD #200	SHERMAN OAKS, CA	91423
FARRELL, MARY	ACTRESS	11726 SAN VICENTE BLVD #300	LOS ANGELES, CA	90049
FARRELL, MIKE	ACT-WRI-DIR	POST OFFICE BOX 5961-306	SHERMAN OAKS, CA	91413
FARRELL, PETER	TV DIRECTOR	8 GROVE LODGE, CROSS DEEP TWICKENHAM	MIDDLESEX	ENGLAND
FARRELL, ROBERT E	NEWS CORRESPONDENT	2400 VIRGINIA AVE #C-823	WASHINGTON, DC	20037
FARRELL, SHAWNA	SOPRANO	POST OFFICE BOX 188 STATION A	TORONTO, ONT	CANADA
FARRELL, SHEA	ACTOR	9220 SUNSET BLVD #625	LOS ANGELES, CA	90069
FARRELL, TERRENCE	GUITARIST	KAY, 58 W 58TH ST	NEW YORK, NY	10019
FARRELL, TERRY	ACTRESS	9200 SUNSET BLVD #1210	LOS ANGELES, CA	90069
FARRELL, TOMMY	ACTOR	5225 RIVERTON AVE	NORTH HOLLYWOOD, CA	91601
FARRELL, TOMMY F	WRITER	8955 BEVERLY BLVD	LOS ANGELES, CA	90048
FARRELL, WILLIAM E	NEWS CORRESPONDENT	2130 "P" ST, NW	WASHINGTON, DC	20037
FARRELL, WILLIAM PATRICK	DIRECTOR	518 E 80TH ST #2-P	NEW YORK, NY	10021
FARRER, JOHN	CONDUCTOR	CPS, 34 66TH PL	LONG BEACH, CA	90803
FARRIES, CHRISTOPHER	ACTOR	CAREY, 126 KENNINGTON PARK RD	LONDON SE11 4DJ	ENGLAND
FARRINGTON, HUGH	ACTRESS	439 S LA CIENEGA BLVD #117	LOS ANGELES, CA	90048
FARRIS, FREDERICK J	NEWS CORRESPONDENT	2830 RITTENHOUSE ST, NW	WASHINGTON, DC	20015
FARRIS, HOLLIE	TRUMPETER	525 SKYVIEW DR	NASHVILLE, TN	37206
FARRIS, JANET	PIANIST	295 LAKESIDE DR	ASHLAND CITY, TN	37015
FARRIS, JOHN	WRITER	8955 BEVERLY BLVD	LOS ANGELES, CA	90048
FARRIS, JOSEPH	CARTOONIST	POST OFFICE BOX 4203	NEW YORK, NY	10017
FARRIS, JUDITH	CONTRALTO	SULLIVAN, 390 W END AVE	NEW YORK, NY	10024
FARRIS, MARY LEE	SOPRANO	61 W 62ND ST #6-F	NEW YORK, NY	10023
FARROW, DAVID M	FILM DIRECTOR	1915 CERRO GORDO ST	LOS ANGELES, CA	90039
FARROW, LAWRENCE G	COMPOSER-CONDUCTOR	373 N WESTERN AVE #18	LOS ANGELES, CA	90004
FARROW, MIA	ACTRESS	136 CENTRAL PARK W	NEW YORK, NY	10023
FARROW, STAN	ACTOR	8831 SUNSET BLVD #402	LOS ANGELES, CA	90069
FASBENDER, ROBERT	WRITER	555 W 57TH ST #1230	NEW YORK, NY	10019
FASCIANO, DEBRA J	WRITER	5914 W 85TH PL	LOS ANGELES, CA	90045
FASHION	ROCK & ROLL GROUP	ATI, 888 7TH AVE, 21ST FLOOR	NEW YORK, NY	10106
FASSBAENDER, BRIGITTE	MEZZO-SOPRANO	CAMI, 165 W 57TH ST	NEW YORK, NY	10019
FAST, HOWARD	WRITER	HOUGHTON MIFFIN, 2 PARK ST	BOSTON, MA	02107
FAST, JONATHAN D	WRITER	555 W 57TH ST #1230	NEW YORK, NY	10019

DONNA FARGO

SHEA FARRELL

FARRAH FAWCETT

ALICE FAYE

FREDDY FENDER

NORMAN FELL

JOSE FERRER

MEL FERRER

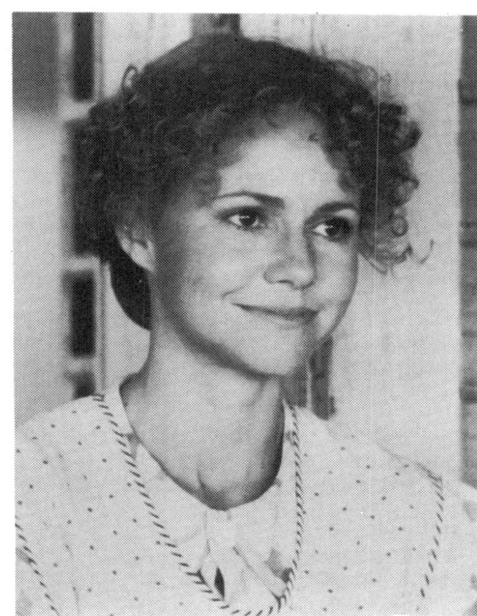
SALLY FIELD

Name	Occupation	Address	City	Zip/Country
FASTWAY	ROCK & ROLL GROUP	PART ROCK MANAGEMENT		
		4 MOUNTAGU ROW, BAKER ROW	LONDON W1H 1AB	ENGLAND
FAT AMMON'S BAND	ROCK & ROLL GROUP	210 81ST ST #4	VIRGINIA BEACH, VA	23451
FAT BOYS, THE	RAP GROUP	SUTRA RECORDS, TINE PAN APPLE		
		1790 BROADWAY	NEW YORK, NY	10009
FAT CITY BAND, THE	ROCK & ROLL GROUP	25 HUNTINGTON AVE #420	BOSTON, MA	02116
FATBACK	ROCK & ROLL GROUP	POST OFFICE BOX 151	SAINT ALBANS, NY	11412
FATES WARNING	ROCK & ROLL GROUP	POST OFFICE BOX 2428	EL SEGUNDO, CA	90245
FATOVICH, PETER A	TV DIRECTOR	156 HOLLYWOOD AVE	TUCKAHOE, NY	10707
FATTIBENE, JAMES F	NEWS CORRESPONDENT	8805 WINTHROP DR	ALEXANDRIA, VA	22308
FATZINGER, CRAIG R	PHOTOJOURNALIST	8308 EAST RIDGE AVE #F	TAKOMA PARK, MD	20912
FAUER, JONATHAN	TV DIRECTOR	500 E 83RD ST	NEW YORK, NY	10028
FAULCONER, CATHERINE	TV WRITER	555 W 57TH ST #1230	NEW YORK, NY	10019
FAULDS, ANDREW	ACTOR	14 ALBEMARLE ST	LONDON W1	ENGLAND
FAULKNER, CAROLINE	ACTRESS	161 E 89TH ST	NEW YORK, NY	10028
FAULKNER, JAMES	ACTOR	HATTON, 18 JERMYN ST	LONDON SW1	ENGLAND
FAULKNER, JULIA	SOPRANO	CAMI, 165 W 57TH ST	NEW YORK, NY	10019
FAULKNER, LELAND	MIME	AFFILIATE ARTISTS, INC,		
		37 W 65TH ST, 6TH FLOOR	NEW YORK, NY	10023
FAULKNER, NANCY	WRITER	8955 BEVERLY BLVD	LOS ANGELES, CA	90048
FAULKNER, NORBERT	WRITER	8955 BEVERLY BLVD	LOS ANGELES, CA	90048
FAULKNER, STEPHANIE	ACTRESS	2010 S SPAULDING AVE	LOS ANGELES, CA	90016
FAULKNER, TIM	ACTOR	6 CLAREVILLE ST	LONDON SW7	ENGLAND
FAULKNER, TRADER	ACTOR	21 LEXHAM GARDENS #15	LONDON W8 5JJ	ENGLAND
FAURE, MICHEL	NEWS CORRESPONDENT	4824 LINNEAN AVE, NW	WASHINGTON, DC	20008
FAUST, JOE	ACTOR	9777 WILSHIRE BLVD #707	BEVERLY HILLS, CA	90212
FAUSTINO, DAVID	ACTOR	8075 W 3RD ST #303	LOS ANGELES, CA	90048
FAVREAUX, LOU	ACTOR	438 N SWEETZER AVE	LOS ANGELES, CA	90048
FAW, BOB	NEWS CORRESPONDENT	CBS NEWS, 2 REHOV, CARLEBACH	TEL AVIV	ISRAEL
FAWCETT, ALLEN	ACTOR-TV HOST	9200 SUNSET BLVD #414	LOS ANGELES, CA	90069
FAWCETT, FARRAH	ACTRESS-MODEL	3130 ANTELO RD	LOS ANGELES, CA	90024
FAY, DEIDRE	TV WRITER-PRODUCER	EMBASSY TV, 1438 N GOWER ST	LOS ANGELES, CA	90028
FAY, DOROTHY	ACTRESS	RITTER, 14151 VALLEY VISTA BL	SHERMAN OAKS, CA	91423
FAY, EDDY	ACTOR	330 E 49TH ST	NEW YORK, NY	10017
FAY, THERESA VILLANI	CELLIST	POST OFFICE BOX 131	SPRINGFIELD, VA	22150
FAYE, ALICE	ACTRESS-SINGER	49400 JOHN F KENNEDY TRAIL	PALM DESERT, CA	92260
FAYMAN, WILLIAM	FILM PRODUCER	FGH FILM CONSORTIUM		
		74 BRIDPORT ST, ALBERT PARK	VICTORIA 3206	AUSTRALIA
FAYNA, LOWELL	GUITARIST	POST OFFICE BOX 653	GOODLETTSVILLE, TN	37072
FAZAH, ADIB	BARITONE	61 W 62ND ST #6-F	NEW YORK, NY	10023
FEAR	ROCK & ROLL GROUP	POST OFFICE BOX 2428	EL SEGUNDO, CA	90245
FEARN, KATHLEEN A	WRITER	8955 BEVERLY BLVD	LOS ANGELES, CA	90048
FEARN, SHEILA	ACTRESS	BROWNE, 13 ST MARTINS RD	LONDON SW9	ENGLAND
FEASEL, DARLENE	ACTRESS	5812 WHITSETT AVE	NORTH HOLLYWOOD, CA	91607
FEATHER, JACQUELINE M	TV WRITER	8955 BEVERLY BLVD	LOS ANGELES, CA	90048
FEATHER, LEONARD	AUTHOR-JAZZ CRITIC	13833 RIVERSIDE DR	SHERMAN OAKS, CA	91423
FEATHERS, CHARLIE	SINGER	POST OFFICE BOX 242	HORSESHOE BEND, AR	72512
FEAVER, DOUGLAS B	NEWS CORRESPONDENT	205 SUMMERS DR	ALEXANDRIA, VA	22301
FEAZELL, JIM	SCREENWRITER	8955 BEVERLY BLVD	LOS ANGELES, CA	90048
FEBLES, MICHAEL	PERCUSSIONIST	583 MOSS LANDING DR	ANTIOCH, TN	37013
FED'S, THE	ROCK & ROLL GROUP	9777 HARWIN ST #101	HOUSTON, TX	77036
FEDDERSON, DON	TV PRODUCER	16071 ROYAL OAK	ENCINO, CA	91436
FEDER, BART S	WRITER	555 W 57TH ST #1230	NEW YORK, NY	10019
FEDER, DAVID L	FILM WRITER-PRODUCER	5800 OWENSMOUTH AVE #32	WOODLAND HILLS, CA	91367
FEDER, DON	COLUMNIST	BOSTON HERALD, 1 HERALD SQ	BOSTON, MA	02106
FEDER, ROBERT	TV-RADIO REPORTER	THE CHICAGO SUN-TIMES		
		401 N WABASH AVE	CHICAGO, IL	60611
FEDER, RUTH	WRITER	8955 BEVERLY BLVD	LOS ANGELES, CA	90048
FEDERBUSH, ARNOLD	WRITER	840 S SERRANO AVE #305	LOS ANGELES, CA	90005
FEE, MELINDA O	ACTRESS	9255 SUNSET BLVD #603	LOS ANGELES, CA	90069
FEEL, THE	ROCK & ROLL GROUP	THE GROUP, INC, 1957 KILBURN DR	ATLANTA, GA	30324
FEELABEELIA	ROCK & ROLL GROUP	QWEST RECORDS COMPANY		
		7250 BEVERLY BLVD	LOS ANGELES, CA	90036
FEELEY, TERENCE	PLAYWRIGHT	55 DRAYTON GARDENS		
		SOUTH KENSINGTON	LONDON SW10	ENGLAND
FEELIES, THE	ROCK & ROLL GROUP	BALLFIELD PRODS, 9 BERNARD AVE	HALEDIN, NJ	07508
FEENER, PAMELA	ACTRESS	1758 N ORANGE DR #17	HOLLYWOOD, CA	90028
FEERO, ROBERT	ACTOR	CONTEMPORARY ARTISTS		
		132 S LASKY DR	BEVERLY HILLS, CA	90212
FEES, JARRE-BETH	ACTRESS	6406 FRANKLIN AVE #5	LOS ANGELES, CA	90028
FEFERMAN, LINDA	WRITER	555 W 57TH ST #1230	NEW YORK, NY	10019
FEGHALI, JOSE	PIANIST	IMG ARTISTS, 22 E 71ST ST	NEW YORK, NY	10021
FEGLEY, RICHARD	PHOTOGRAPHER	MODELS & PROMOTIONS AGENCY		
		8560 SUNSET BLVD, 10TH FLOOR	LOS ANGELES, CA	90069
FEHR, KAJA	FILM EDITOR	POST OFFICE BOX 5617	BEVERLY HILLS, CA	90210
FEHR, RUDI	EXECUTIVE PRODUCER	3410 LA SOMBRA DR	LOS ANGELES, CA	90068
FEHR, STEPHEN C	NEWS CORRESPONDENT	11556 FEBRUARY CIR	SILVER SPRING, MD	20904
FEHRLE, PHILIP D	WRITER	691 COUNTRY CLUB DR	BURBANK, CA	91501
FEIBLEMAN, PETER	SCREENWRITER	263 LOMA AVE	LONG BEACH, CA	90803
FEIERMAN, JACK W	CONDUCTOR	13120 HARTSOOK ST	SHERMAN OAKS, CA	91423
FEIFER, GEORGE	WRITER	555 W 57TH ST #1230	NEW YORK, NY	10019
FEIFFER, JUDITH R	WRITER	555 W 57TH ST #1230	NEW YORK, NY	10019
FEIFFER, JULES	WRITER	325 W END AVE	NEW YORK, NY	10023
FEIGELSON, J D	WRITER-PRODUCER	8955 BEVERLY BLVD	LOS ANGELES, CA	90048
FEIGENBAUM, JOEL J	TV WRITER-DIRECTOR	1888 CENTURY PARK E #1107	LOS ANGELES, CA	90067

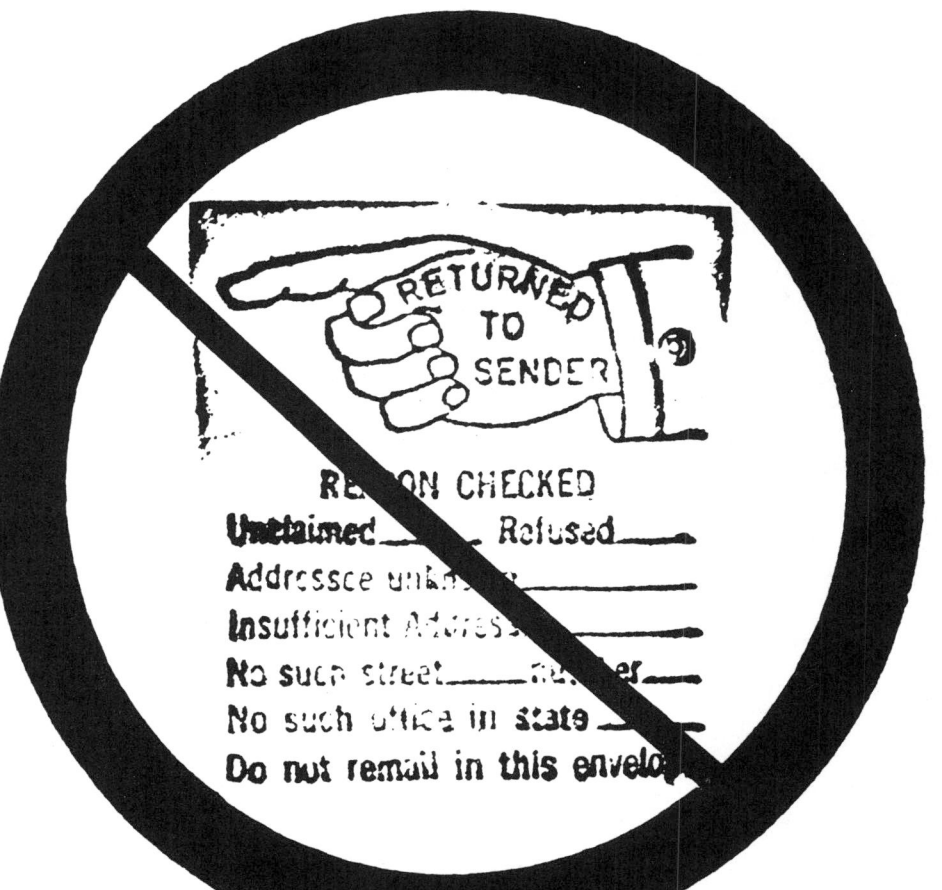

Name	Occupation	Address	City/State	Zip
FEIL, GERALD	DIRECTOR	1160 CYPRESS AVE	HERMOSA BEACH, CA	90254
FEIL, HILA	WRITER	555 W 57TH ST #1230	NEW YORK, NY	10019
FEIL, KENNETH	PHOTOGRAPHER	1000 WATER ST, SW	WASHINGTON, DC	20024
FEIN, BENA A	NEWS CORRESPONDENT	1915 KALORAMA RD, NW	WASHINGTON, DC	20009
FEIN, DAVID	CONDUCTOR	FINELL, 155 W 68TH ST	NEW YORK, NY	10023
FEIN, IRVING	TV EXECUTIVE	1100 N ALTA LOMA RD	LOS ANGELES, CA	90069
FEIN, JUDITH	WRITER	8955 BEVERLY BLVD	LOS ANGELES, CA	90048
FEINBERG, DAVID	WRITER	555 W 57TH ST #1230	NEW YORK, NY	10019
FEINBERG, JANE	CASTING DIRECTOR	20TH CENTURY FOX FILMS		
		10201 W PICO BLVD	LOS ANGELES, CA	90035
FEINBERG, LAWRENCE W	NEWS CORRESPONDENT	3520 LEGATION ST, NW	WASHINGTON, DC	20015
FEINBERG, ROBERT E	TV WRITER	555 W 57TH ST #1230	NEW YORK, NY	10019
FEINBERG, RONALD	ACTOR	220 S REEVES DR	BEVERLY HILLS, CA	90212
FEINBERG, STEPHEN N	WRITER	8955 BEVERLY BLVD	LOS ANGELES, CA	90048
FEINGOLD, VIRGINIA	ACTRESS	612 WESTBOURNE DR #8	LOS ANGELES, CA	90069
FEININGER, ANDREAS	PHOTOGRAPHER	18 ELIZABETH LN	NEW MILFORD, CT	06776
FEINMAN, BARBARA	NEWS CORRESPONDENT	622 MARYLAND AVE, NE	WASHINGTON, DC	20002
FEINSILBER, MYRON "MIKE"	NEWS CORRESPONDENT	5154 34TH ST, NW	WASHINGTON, DC	20008
FEINSTEIN, ALAN	ACTOR	1230 N SWEETZER AVE	LOS ANGELES, CA	90069
FEINTHEL, ROGER	NEWS CORRESPONDENT	5509 NORTHFIELD RD	BETHESDA, MD	20817
FEIRSTEIN, BRUCE J	AUTHOR-WRITER	DELL BOOKS COMPANY		
		1 DAG HAMMARSKJOLD PLAZA	NEW YORK, NY	10017
FEIRSTEIN, FREDERICK	WRITER	555 W 57TH ST #1230	NEW YORK, NY	10019
FEITSHANS, BUZZ	FILM PRODUCER	MGM/UA PRODUCTIONS		
		10202 WASHINGTON BLVD	CULVER CITY, CA	90230
FEJER, TIBOR	COMPOSER-CONDUCTOR	8440 DE LONGPRE AVE	LOS ANGELES, CA	90069
FEKE, STEPHEN JAMES	WRITER	11719 EL CERRO LN	STUDIO CITY, CA	91604
FEKETE, CHARLES	PHOTOJOURNALIST	154 E COLONIL HWY	HAMILTON, VA	22068
FELCYN, CHRISTOPHER M	TV DIRECTOR	4316 W 13 MILE RD #B-12	ROYAL OAK, MI	48072
FELD, FRITZ	ACTOR	12348 ROCHEDALE LN	LOS ANGELES, CA	90049
FELD, JOEL D	TV DIRECTOR	200 E 90TH ST #19-E	NEW YORK, NY	10023
FELD, PHILIP	DIRECTOR	1001 91ST ST	BAY HARBOR ISLAND, FL	33154
FELD, STEVEN	WRITER	8955 BEVERLY BLVD	LOS ANGELES, CA	90048
FELDBERG, STEPHEN	WRITER	555 W 57TH ST #1230	NEW YORK, NY	10019
FELDER, CLARENCE	ACTOR	10100 SANTA MONICA BLVD #1600	LOS ANGELES, CA	90067
FELDER, DON	SINGER-SONGWRITER	10880 WILSHIRE BLVD #2110	LOS ANGELES, CA	90024
FELDER, LOU	ACTOR	15010 VENTURA BLVD #219	SHERMAN OAKS, CA	91403
FELDER, WILTON	MUSICIAN	4485 MYRTLE AVE	LONG BEACH, CA	90807
FELDINGER, FRANK A	WRITER	7960 SELMA AVE #303	LOS ANGELES, CA	90046
FELDMAN, BRUCE	WRITER	8955 BEVERLY BLVD	LOS ANGELES, CA	90048
FELDMAN, CAROLE	NEWS CORRESPONDENT	3110 WISCONSIN AVE, NW	WASHINGTON, DC	20016
FELDMAN, CHARLES STUART	DIRECTOR	DGA, 110 W 57TH ST	NEW YORK, NY	10019
FELDMAN, CHESTER	DIRECTOR	304 CASTLE DR	ENGLEWOOD, NJ	07632
FELDMAN, DANIEL M	TV DIRECTOR	451 BROOME ST #5-E	NEW YORK, NY	10013
FELDMAN, DENNIS	SCREENWRITER	8955 BEVERLY BLVD	LOS ANGELES, CA	90048
FELDMAN, EDWARD H	WRITER-PRODUCER	2003 EL CERRITO PL	LOS ANGELES, CA	90068
FELDMAN, EDWARD S	ACTOR	POST OFFICE BOX 5617	BEVERLY HILLS, CA	90210
FELDMAN, EDWARD S	FILM PRODUCER	FELDMAN/MEEKER COMPANY		
		PARAMOUNT PICTURES CORP		
		5555 MELROSE AVE	LOS ANGELES, CA	90038
FELDMAN, GENE	WRITER	555 W 57TH ST #1230	NEW YORK, NY	10019
FELDMAN, JACK L	DIRECTOR-PRODUCER	FORDHAM, 6430 SUNSET BLVD	HOLLYWOOD, CA	90028
FELDMAN, JOAN M	NEWS CORRESPONDENT	4312 46TH ST, NW	WASHINGTON, DC	20016
FELDMAN, LESTER	DIRECTOR	DGA, 110 W 57TH ST	NEW YORK, NY	10019
FELDMAN, MARIE	VIOLINIST	POST OFFICE BOX 24731	NASHVILLE, TN	37202
FELDMAN, MAXINE	SINGER	POST OFFICE BOX 114	BOSTON, MA	02117
FELDMAN, RANDOLPH ROBERT	SCREENWRITER	6946 CAMROSE DR	LOS ANGELES, CA	90068
FELDMAN, RANDY PAUL	PHOTOJOURNALIST	10507 WEYMOUTH ST #3	BETHESDA, MD	20814
FELDMAN, RUTHE	TV WRITER	8955 BEVERLY BLVD	LOS ANGELES, CA	90048
FELDMAN, SAM	WRITER	8955 BEVERLY BLVD	LOS ANGELES, CA	90048
FELDMAN, SCOTT H	NEWS CORRESPONDENT	400 N CAPITOL ST, NW	WASHINGTON, DC	20001
FELDMAN, WILLIAM H	NEWS CORRESPONDENT	301 VEAZY TERR, NW	WASHINGTON, DC	20008
FELDON, BARBARA	ACTRESS-MODEL	1888 CENTURY PARK E #1400	LOS ANGELES, CA	90067
FELDON, SUSAN	ACTRESS	6380 WILSHIRE BLVD #1600	LOS ANGELES, CA	90048
FELDSHUH, TOVAH	ACTRESS	110 RIVERSIDE DR #16-F	NEW YORK, NY	10024
FELICE, JACK	TV DIRECTOR	75 CLIFFORD AVE	PELHAM, NY	10803
FELICIANO, JOSE	SINGER-GUITARIST	8961 SUNSET BLVD #2-B	LOS ANGELES, CA	90069
FELIX, JOE	CONDUCTOR	2117 POWER ST	HERMOSA BEACH, CA	90254
FELIX, MARIA	ACTRESS	MELCHOR OCAMPO 309-403	MEXICO 7 DF	MEXICO
FELIX, MARTA	MEZZO-SOPRANO	LIEBERMAN, 11 RIVERSIDE DR	NEW YORK, NY	10023
FELIX, OTTO	ACTOR	2147 N BEVERLY GLEN BLVD	LOS ANGELES, CA	90077
FELIX & JARVIS	SOUL GROUP	TANN/FAGENSON MGMT		
		14750 PURITAN ST	DETROIT, MI	48227
FELL, HERMAN	TV DIRECTOR	434 ROSCOE ST	CHICAGO, IL	60657
FELL, IAN	TV DIRECTOR-PRODUCER	YTV, KIRKSTALL RD	LEEDS LS3 1JS	ENGLAND
FELL, NORMAN	ACTOR	445 N BEDFORD DR #PH	BEVERLY HILLS, CA	90210
FELLER, BOB	BASEBALL	POST OFFICE BOX 157	GATES MILLS, OH	44040
FELLER, DICK	SINGER	POST OFFICE BOX 121264	NASHVILLE, TN	37212
FELLER, RICHARD D	GUITARIST	POST OFFICE BOX 23613	NASHVILLE, TN	37202
FELLER, SIDNEY H	CONDUCTOR	4216 VILLAGE 4		
		LEISURE VILLAGE	CAMARILLO, CA	93010
FELLINI, FEDERICO	WRITER-PRODUCER	141A VIA MARGUTTA 110	ROME	ITALY
FELLOWS, EDITH	ACTRESS	2016 1/2 VISTA DEL MAR	LOS ANGELES, CA	90068
FELONY	ROCK & ROLL GROUP	POST OFFICE BOX 33664	LOS ANGELES, CA	90033
FELSHER, MURRAY	NEWS CORRESPONDENT	POST OFFICE BOX 20	GERMANTOWN, MD	20874

FELTHAM, KERRY	DIRECTOR-PRODUCER	650 LAS LOMAS	PACIFIC PALISADES, CA 90272
FELTNER, ERIN	SINGER	LCS ENTS, 1627 16TH AVE S	NASHVILLE, TN 37212
FELTON, JOHN	NEWS CORRESPONDENT	5602 OAKMONT AVE	BETHESDA, MD 20817
FELTON, NORMAN	TV WRITER-PRODUCER	22146 PACIFIC COAST HWY	MALIBU, CA 90265
FELTS, JUDY	PIANIST	2628 WESTERN HILLS DR	NASHVILLE, TN 37214
FELTS, NARVEL	SINGER	TAYLOR, 2401 12TH AVE S	NASHVILLE, TN 37204
FELZER, SHARON J	NEWS CORRESPONDENT	400 N CAPITOL ST, NW	WASHINGTON, DC 20001
FEMIA, JOHN	SINGER	1650 BROADWAY #714	NEW YORK, NY 10019
FEMINO, JAMES	SINGER-GUITARIST	MUSIC SERVICES OF AMERICA	
		252 MENNONITE RD	COLLEGEVILLE, PA 19426
FENADY, ANDREW J	FILM WRITER-PRODUCER	126 N ROSSMERE AVE	LOS ANGELES, CA 90004
FENADY, GEORG	TV DIRECTOR	602 N CHEROKEE AVE	LOS ANGELES, CA 90004
FENDEL, DAN L	TV WRITER	1951 SELBY AVE #5	LOS ANGELES, CA 90025
FENDER, FREDDY	SINGER-SONGWRITER	POST OFFICE BOX 4003	BEVERLY HILLS, CA 90213
FENDRICK, DAVID	ACTOR	360 CENTRAL PARK W #16-G	NEW YORK, NY 10025
FENEMORE, HILDA	ACTRESS	MAHONEY, 30 CHALFONT CT	LONDON NW1 ENGLAND
FENICHEL, JAY	ACTOR	4076 ALBRIGHT AVE	LOS ANGELES, CA 90066
FENMORE, TANYA	ACTRESS	3018 HUTTON PL	BEVERLY HILLS, CA 90210
FENN, SHERILYN	ACTRESS	1901 AVE OF THE STARS #840	LOS ANGELES, CA 90067
FENNELL, FREDERICK	CONDUCTOR	111 W 57TH ST #1203	NEW YORK, NY 10019
FENNELLY, PARKER	ACTOR	597 CROTON AVE	PEEKSKILL, NY 10566
FENNEMAN, CLIFFORD	TV DIRECTOR	13007 DEBBY ST	VAN NUYS, CA 91401
FENNEMAN, GEORGE	TV HOST	13214 MOORPARK ST #206	SHERMAN OAKS, CA 91423
FENSKE, MARK	ACTOR	4150 ARCH DR #2	STUDIO CITY, CA 91604
FENTON, MIKE	CASTING DIRECTOR	20TH CENTURY FOX FILMS	
		10201 W PICO BLVD	LOS ANGELES, CA 90035
FENTON, NORMAN	TV DIRECTOR	WAVENDON, MANOR PARK, ILKLEY	YORKSHIRE ENGLAND
FENTON, ROBERT L	PRODUCER	MCA/UNIVERSAL STUDIOS, INC	
		100 UNIVERSAL CITY PLAZA	UNIVERSAL CITY, CA 91608
FENTON, THOMAS T	NEWS CORRESPONDENT	CBS NEWS, 524 W 57TH ST	NEW YORK, NY 10019
FENWICK, PEG	WRITER	8955 BEVERLY BLVD	LOS ANGELES, CA 90048
FERA, DARLA M	NEWS CORRESPONDENT	5112 CONNECTICUT AVE #210, NW	WASHINGTON, DC 20008
FERA, GREG	TV DIRECTOR	7019 WOODSTONE PL	CANOGA PARK, CA 91307
FERBER, BRUCE	TV WRITER	13526 MORRISON ST	SHERMAN OAKS, CA 91423
FERBER, MEL	DIRECTOR-PRODUCER	5141 ENCINO AVE	ENCINO, CA 91316
FERBER, STEVE	NEWS CORRESPONDENT	3060 SOUTHERN ELM CT	FAIRFAX, VA 22031
FERDEN, BRUCE	CONDUCTOR	COLBERT, 111 W 57TH ST	NEW YORK, NY 10019
FERDIN, PAMELYN	ACTRESS	2030 CUMMINGS DR	LOS ANGELES, CA 90027
FERGUS, PATRICIA M	NEWS CORRESPONDENT	1825 "K" ST, NW	WASHINGTON, DC 20006
FERGUSON, ALLYN	ACTOR	8601 WILSHIRE BLVD #1000	BEVERLY HILLS, CA 90211
FERGUSON, ALLYN	CONDUCTOR	12941 MOORPARK ST #4	STUDIO CITY, CA 91604
FERGUSON, BIANCA	ACTRESS	254 S HORBART BLVD	LOS ANGELES, CA 90004
FERGUSON, BOBBIE	ACTRESS	LIGHT, 113 N ROBERTSON BLVD	LOS ANGELES, CA 90048
FERGUSON, BRADLEY	WRITER	555 W 57TH ST #1230	NEW YORK, NY 10019
FERGUSON, DONALD N	WRITER	8955 BEVERLY BLVD	LOS ANGELES, CA 90048
FERGUSON, ERNEST	MANDOLINIST	ROUTE #2	ADAMS, TN 37010
FERGUSON, FRANCES	ACTRESS	1919 N ARGYLE AVE #711	HOLLYWOOD, CA 90068
FERGUSON, GRAEME	FILM DIRECTOR	417 CARLTON ST	TORONTO, ONT M5A 2M3 CANADA
FERGUSON, J DON	ACTOR	1 CHANTILLY CT	SAVANNAH, GA 31406
FERGUSON, JAY	SINGER	POST OFFICE BOX U	TARZANA, CA 91356
FERGUSON, JIM	SINGER-GUITARIST	2406 BELMONT BLVD	NASHVILLE, TN 37212
FERGUSON, JOHN	WRITER	8955 BEVERLY BLVD	LOS ANGELES, CA 90048
FERGUSON, JOHN M	WRITER	555 W 57TH ST #1230	NEW YORK, NY 10019
FERGUSON, JOHNNY	SINGER-SONGWRITER	POST OFFICE BOX 24970	NASHVILLE, TN 37202
FERGUSON, JULIA	PHOTOGRAPHER	2805 ST PAUL ST	BALTIMORE, MD 21218
FERGUSON, KATHERINE R	NEWS CORRESPONDENT	3236 MC KINLEY ST, NW	WASHINGTON, DC 20015
FERGUSON, KATHLEEN	WRITER	8955 BEVERLY BLVD	LOS ANGELES, CA 90048
FERGUSON, LARRY	SCREENWRITER	8955 BEVERLY BLVD	LOS ANGELES, CA 90048
FERGUSON, LYNNDA	ACTRESS	9165 SUNSET BLVD #202	LOS ANGELES, CA 90069
FERGUSON, MAYNARD	TRUMPETER	POST OFFICE BOX 716	OJAI, CA 93023
FERGUSON, MICHAEL	TV DIRECTOR-PRODUCER	LARRY DALZELL ASSOCIATES	
		126 KENNINGTON PARK RD	LONDON SE11 4DT ENGLAND
FERGUSON, TONI	VIOLINIST	2406 BELMONT BLVD	NASHVILLE, TN 37212
FERGUSON, WALTER	MUSICIAN	135 BRINKHAVEN #74	MADISON, TN 37115
FERN, THERESA M	WRITER	555 W 57TH ST #1230	NEW YORK, NY 10019
FERNANDES, MIGUEL	ACTOR	12750 VENTURA BLVD #102	STUDIO CITY, CA 91604
FERNANDEZ, EDUARDO	GUITARIST	SHAW CONCERTS, 1995 BROADWAY	NEW YORK, NY 10023
FERNANDEZ, MANNY	WRESTLER	NATIONAL WRESTLING ALLIANCE	
		JIM CROCKETT PROMOTIONS	
		421 BRIARBEND DR	CHARLOTTE, NC 28209
FERNANDEZ, WILHELMENIA	SOPRANO	MUNRO, 334 W 72ND ST	NEW YORK, NY 10023
FERNBACH, ALEXANDER	DIRECTOR	DGA, 110 W 57TH ST	NEW YORK, NY 10019
FERRAIOLO, ANGELA	WRITER	555 W 57TH ST #1230	NEW YORK, NY 10019
FERRANDINI, DEAN	STUNTMAN	3518 W CAHUENGA BLVD #300	LOS ANGELES, CA 90068
FERRANDINI, DEAN R	DIRECTOR	POST OFFICE BOX 6201	BEVERLY HILLS, CA 90212
FERRANO, DOLORES MARIE	DIRECTOR	727 WESTBOURNE DR #307	LOS ANGELES, CA 90069
FERRANTE & TEICHER	PIANO DUO	POST OFFICE BOX 8248	VAN NUYS, CA 91409
FERRARA, PETER S	WRITER	8955 BEVERLY BLVD	LOS ANGELES, CA 90048
FERRARA, SUSAN E	WRITER	555 W 57TH ST #1230	NEW YORK, NY 10019
FERRARE, ASHLEY	ACTRESS	8380 MELROSE AVE #310	LOS ANGELES, CA 90069
FERRARE, CRISTINA	ACTRESS-MODEL-TV HOST	152 GRANVILLE AVE	LOS ANGELES, CA 90049
FERRARI, TINA	WRESTLER	GORGEOUS GIRLS OF WRESTLING	
		RIVIERA HOTEL & CASINO	
		DAVID B MC LANE PRODS	
		2901 S LAS VEGAS BLVD	LAS VEGAS, NV 89109

Name	Occupation	Address	City	Zip
FERRARINI, ALIDA	SOPRANO	CAMI, 165 W 57TH ST	NEW YORK, NY	10019
FERRARO, GERALDINE	POLITICIAN	22 DEEPDENE RD	FOREST HILLS, CA	11375
FERRARO, RALPH A	COMPOSER	467 W RUSTIC RD	SANTA MONICA, CA	90402
FERRARO, ROBERT	WRITER	555 W 57TH ST #1230	NEW YORK, NY	10019
FERRARO, THOMAS M	NEWS CORRESPONDENT	3777 GUNSTON RD	ALEXANDRIA, VA	22302
FERRARO, TONY G	CONDUCTOR	2122 GRIFFITH PARK BLVD	LOS ANGELES, CA	90039
FERRATTI, REBECCA	MODEL	MODELS & PROMOTIONS AGENCY		
		8560 SUNSET BLVD, 10TH FLOOR	LOS ANGELES, CA	90069
FERRE, JEAN	WRESTLER	SEE - ANDRE THE GIANT		
FERREIRA, WILLIAM	PIANIST	5101 LINBAR DR #G-105	NASHVILLE, TN	37211
FERRELL, CONCHATA	ACTRESS	1347 N SEWARD ST	HOLLYWOOD, CA	90028
FERRELL, KRISTI	ACTRESS	9220 SUNSET BLVD #202	LOS ANGELES, CA	90069
FERRELL, RICK	BASEBALL	2199 GOLFVIEW DR	TROY, MI	48084
FERRENTINO, HENRY	ACTOR	405 BROAD ST	BLOOMFIELD, NJ	07003
FERREOL, ANDREA	ACTRESS	11726 SAN VICENTE BLVD #300	LOS ANGELES, CA	90049
FERRER, JOSE	ACTOR-DIRECTOR	POST OFFICE BOX 616	MIAMI, FL	33133
		ROCKEFELLER CENTER	NEW YORK, NY	10020
FERRER, JOSE M, III	WRITER-EDITOR	TIME/TIME & LIFE BLDG		
FERRER, LUPITA	ACTRESS	861 STONE CANYON RD	LOS ANGELES, CA	90077
FERRER, MARIA	ACTRESS	1019 N ROXBURY DR	BEVERLY HILLS, CA	90210
FERRER, MEL	ACTOR	2220 AVE OF THE STARS #2006	LOS ANGELES, CA	90067
FERRER, MIGUEL	ACTOR	1019 N ROXBURY DR	BEVERLY HILLS, CA	90210
FERRER, RAFAEL	ACTOR	1019 N ROXBURY DR	BEVERLY HILLS, CA	90210
FERRERO, MARTIN	ACTOR	1607 N EL CENTRO AVE #23	LOS ANGELES, CA	90028
FERRI, ROBERT J, JR	NEWS CORRESPONDENT	1211 33RD ST, NW	WASHINGTON, DC	20007
FERRIER, GARRY T	TV WRITER	8955 BEVERLY BLVD	LOS ANGELES, CA	90048
FERRIER, MARINA	ACTRESS	6736 LAUREL CANYON BLVD #306	NORTH HOLLYWOOD, CA	91606
FERRIGNO, LOU	ACTOR-BODY BUILDIER	621 17TH ST	SANTA MONICA, CA	90402
FERRIN, RALPH W	DIRECTOR	22410 HATTERAS ST	WOODLAND HILLS, CA	91367
FERRIN, RICHARD R	CONDUCTOR	220 S MICHIGAN AVE	CHICAGO, IL	60604
FERRIS, CRAIG T	NEWS CORRESPONDENT	3937 MILITARY RD, NW	WASHINGTON, DC	20015
FERRIS, DAVID A	WRITER	8955 BEVERLY BLVD	LOS ANGELES, CA	90048
FERRIS, IRENA	ACTRESS	445 N BEDFORD DR #PH	BEVERLY HILLS, CA	90210
FERRIS, JOHN	SCREENWRITER	9200 SUNSET BLVD #531	LOS ANGELES, CA	90069
FERRIS, MARTHA	ACTRESS	9255 SUNSET BLVD #510	LOS ANGELES, CA	90069
FERRIS, ROBERT N	RADIO WRITER	222 5TH AVE	VENICE, CA	90291
FERRO, JEFFREY	TV WRITER	8955 BEVERLY BLVD	LOS ANGELES, CA	90048
FERRO, MATHILDE	WRITER	8955 BEVERLY BLVD	LOS ANGELES, CA	90048
FERRONE, DAN	ACTOR	22605 MULHOLLAND DR	WOODLAND HILLS, CA	92364
FERRUGIA, JOHN A	NEWS CORRESPONDENT	CBS NEWS, 2020 "M" ST, NW	WASHINGTON, DC	20036
FERRY, BRYAN	SINGER-SONGWRITER	E G MANAGEMENT, LTD		
		63-A KINGS RD	LONDON SW3 4NT	ENGLAND
FERTIG, STEVEN	CASTING DIRECTOR	4043 RADFORD AVE	STUDIO CITY, CA	91604
FERTIK, BILL	CINEMATOGRAPHER	251 W 89TH ST	NEW YORK, NY	10024
FERULLO, JOSEPH M	WRITER	555 W 57TH ST #1230	NEW YORK, NY	10019
FESSLER, PAMELA	NEWS CORRESPONDENT	6118 SWANSEA ST	BETHESDA, MD	20817
FESTINGER, FRED	ACTOR	17830 SHERMAN WY #280	RESEDA, CA	91335
FESTIVAL	MUSICAL GROUP	1300 DIVISION ST #103	NASHVILLE, TN	37203
FETNER, MARK	TV DIRECTOR	50 BULAIRE RD	EAST ROCKWAY, NY	11518
FETTA, FRANK P	CONDUCTOR	5843 EUCALYPTUS LN	LOS ANGELES, CA	90042
FETTERMAN, PETER	FILM PRODUCER	MIDAS PRODS, 9 GRAPE ST	LONDON WC2H 8DR	ENGLAND
FETTY, DARRELL	ACTOR	4262 CAHUENGA BLVD	NORTH HOLLYWOOD, CA	91602
FEUER, CY	THEATER DIR-PROD	502 PARK AVE	NEW YORK, NY	10022
FEUER, DEBRA	ACTRESS	1901 AVE OF THE STARS #840	LOS ANGELES, CA	90067
FEUER, RUSTY	ACTRESS	LENZ, 1456 E CHARLESTON BLVD	LAS VEGAS, NV	89104
FEUERHERD, JOSEPH	NEWS CORRESPONDENT	653 E CAPITOL ST, NW	WASHINGTON, DC	20003
FEUERSTEIN, EDIE	WRITER	555 W 57TH ST #1230	NEW YORK, NY	10019
FEUILLERE, EDWIGE	ACTOR	19 RUE EUGENE MANUEL	PARIS 75016	FRANCE
FEVER, MIKE	WRESTLER	POST OFFICE BOX 3859	STAMFORD, CT	06905
FEVES, RICHARD H	CONDUCTOR	3432 WONDERVIEW DR	LOS ANGELES, CA	90068
FEY, JIM	SINGER-GUITARIST	3615 ROBIN RD	NASHVILLE, TN	37204
FIALKA, JOHN J	NEWS CORRESPONDENT	1959 ROCKINGHAM ST	MC LEAN, VA	22101
FIALKOWSKA, JANINA	PIANIST	ICM, 40 W 57TH ST	NEW YORK, NY	10019
FICALORA, ANTHONY	DIRECTOR	28 E 29TH ST	NEW YORK, NY	10016
FICARA, JOHN F	PHOTOGRAPHER	1101 MARYLAND AVE, NE	WASHINGTON, DC	20002
FICARRA, JOHN	EDITOR-WRITER	MAD MAGAZINE, INC		
		485 MADISON AVE	NEW YORK, NY	10022
FICATIER, CAROL	MODEL	MODELS & PROMOTIONS AGENCY		
		8560 SUNSET BLVD, 10TH FLOOR	LOS ANGELES, CA	90069
FICHENBERG, ROBERT G	NEWS CORRESPONDENT	107 CAMERON MEWS	ALEXANDRIA, VA	22314
FICKETT, MARY	ACTRESS	ABC-TV, "ALL MY CHILDREN"		
		1330 AVE OF THE AMERICAS	NEW YORK, NY	10019
FICTION GROOVE	ROCK & ROLL GROUP	POST OFFICE BOX 325	READING RG1 7AN	ENGLAND
FIDANQUE, DEL	ACTOR	ALBANY POST RD	GARRISON, NY	10524
FIDLER, JIMMY	ACTOR	POST OFFICE BOX 4027	WESTLAKE VILLAGE, CA	91359
FIEDEL, BRAD	SINGER-COMPOSER	11726 LAURELWOOD DR	STUDIO CITY, CA	91604
FIEDLER, E ROBERT	TV DIRECTOR	13959 LA MAIDA ST	SHERMAN OAKS, CA	91423
FIEDLER, JAMES D, JR	PHOTOGRAPHER	14910 FOREST LANDING CIR	ROCKVILLE, MD	20850
FIEDLER, JOHN	ACTOR	18770 EDLEEN DR	TARZANA, CA	91356
FIEDLER, PETER	DIRECTOR-PRODUCER	173 HERRICK RD	BOXFORD, MA	01921
FIELD, ANDREW R	NEWS CORRESPONDENT	4461 CONNECTICUT AVE, NW	WASHINGTON, DC	20008
FIELD, BILLY	TV WRITER	8955 BEVERLY BLVD	LOS ANGELES, CA	90048
FIELD, CAROLE H	ACTRESS	11030 AQUA VISTA ST	NORTH HOLLYWOOD, CA	91602
FIELD, CHELSEA	ACTRESS	445 N BEDFORD DR #PH	BEVERLY HILLS, CA	90210
FIELD, DAVID	NEWS CORRESPONDENT	1722 19TH ST #305, NW	WASHINGTON, DC	20009

KIM FIELDS

ALBERT FINNEY

FANNIE FLAGG

MICK FLEETWOOD

RHONDA FLEMING

JOHN FOGERTY

PETER FONDA

ERNIE FORD

GLENN FORD

FIELD, ELLIOT	ACTOR	8344 MELROSE AVE #29	LOS ANGELES, CA	90069
FIELD, FERN	WRITER-PRODUCER	13935 TAHITI WY #147	MARINA DEL REY, CA	90292
FIELD, FREDERICK "TED"	FILM PRODUCER	10900 WILSHIRE BLVD #1400	LOS ANGELES, CA	90024
FIELD, GUSTAVE	WRITER	8955 BEVERLY BLVD	LOS ANGELES, CA	90048
FIELD, HOWARD O	WRITER	1516 1/2 SUNSET PLAZA DR	LOS ANGELES, CA	90069
FIELD, LEONARD S	TV-THEATER PRODUCER	1697 BROADWAY	NEW YORK, NY	10019
FIELD, LYNN	TV EXECUTIVE	CBS-TV, 7800 BEVERLY BLVD	LOS ANGELES, CA	90036
FIELD, PAUL L	WRITER-PRODUCER	119 WHITE PLAINS RD	BRONXVILLE, NY	10708
FIELD, ROY	FILM DIRECTOR	REDROFF COTTAGE, TEMPLEWOOD LN		
		FARNHAM COMMON	BUCKS SL2 3HA	ENGLAND
FIELD, SALLY	ACTRESS	10880 WILSHIRE BLVD #2110	LOS ANGELES, CA	90024
FIELD, SIDNEY	WRITER	2440 S BARRINGTON AVE #1	LOS ANGELES, CA	90064
FIELD, SYLVIA	ACTRESS	3263 VIA ALTIMIRA	FALLBROOK, CA	92028
FIELD, THEODORE S, JR	WRITER	555 W 57TH ST #1230	NEW YORK, NY	10019
FIELDER, PAT P	TV WRITER	10040 REEVESBURY DR	BEVERLY HILLS, CA	90210
FIELDER, RICHARD	TV WRITER-PRODUCER	1900 AVE OF THE STARS #2375	LOS ANGELES, CA	90067
FIELDER/ALLISON DUO	MUSICAL DUO	FROTHINGHAM, 40 GROVE ST	WESSESLEY, MA	02181
FIELDING, BYRON	NEWS CORRESPONDENT	1789 LANIER PL, NW	WASHINGTON, DC	20009
FIELDING, DOROTHY	ACTRESS	9100 SUNSET BLVD #200	LOS ANGELES, CA	90069
FIELDING, JANET	ACTRESS	IAR, 235-241 REGENT ST	LONDON W1A 2JT	ENGLAND
FIELDS, BRANDON	SAXOPHONIST	NOVA RECORDS, 1061 BROXTON AVE	LOS ANGELES, CA	90024
FIELDS, CAROLE	TALENT AGENT	9255 SUNSET BLVD #603	LOS ANGELES, CA	90069
FIELDS, CHARLIE	GUITARIST	44 MUSIC SQUARE E	NASHVILLE, TN	37203
FIELDS, CHERYL M	NEWS CORRESPONDENT	3001 VEAZEY TERR #1626, NW	WASHINGTON, DC	20008
FIELDS, CHIP	ACTRESS	6430 SUNSET BLVD #1203	LOS ANGELES, CA	90028
FIELDS, DEBBIE	COOKIE ENTREPRENEUR	POST OFFICE BOX 680370	PARK CITY, UT	84068
FIELDS, DON	SINGER	LUTZ, 5625 "O" STREET BLDG	LINCOLN, NE	68510
FIELDS, EDITH	ACTRESS	POST OFFICE BOX 5617	BEVERLY HILLS, CA	90210
FIELDS, FREDDIE	FILM PRODUCER	MGM, 10202 W WASHINGTON BLVD	CULVER CITY, CA	90230
FIELDS, GREG F	TV WRITER	8955 BEVERLY BLVD	LOS ANGELES, CA	90048
FIELDS, HOWARD	NEWS CORRESPONDENT	716 S WAYNE ST	ARLINGTON, VA	22204
FIELDS, JAMES H	PIANIST	1420 LONDONDALE PARKWAY #9	NEWARK, OH	43055
FIELDS, JEFF	WRITER	555 W 57TH ST #1230	NEW YORK, NY	10019
FIELDS, JOYCE	PIANIST	260 W END AVE #7-A	NEW YORK, NY	10023
FIELDS, KATHRYN	SOPRANO	254 W 93RD ST #8	NEW YORK, NY	10025
FIELDS, KIM RHOCHELLE	ACTRESS	ATA, 2437 E WASHINGTON BLVD	PASADENA, CA	91104
FIELDS, LILIAN	ACTRESS	8831 SUNSET BLVD #402	LOS ANGELES, CA	90069
FIELDS, LYNDSEY	ACTRESS	435 S LA CIENEGA BLVD #108	LOS ANGELES, CA	90048
FIELDS, MONROE	SINGER-GUITARIST	5048 WHITES CREEK PIKE	WHITES CREEK, TN	37189
FIELDS, MRS	COOKIE ENTREPRENEUR	SEE - FIELDS, DEBBIE		
FIELDS, PETER ALLEN	TV WRITER	8955 BEVERLY BLVD	LOS ANGELES, CA	90048
FIELDS, RICHARD "DIMPLES"	SINGER	200 W 51ST ST #1410	NEW YORK, NY	10019
FIELDS, TARA	ACTRESS	9052 LLOYD PL	LOS ANGELES, CA	90069
FIELDS, TERRY LEE	DRUMMER	231-B STADIUM DR	HENDERSONVILLE, TN	37075
FIELDS, THOMAS G	DIRECTOR	POST OFFICE BOX 14371	ORLANDO, FL	32857
FIELDSTONES, THE	RHYTHM & BLUES GROUP	1254 LAMAR DR #312	MEMPHIS, TN	38114
FIELMAN, SHELDON	PHOTOJOURNALIST	4513 PRESTWOOD DR	OLNEY, MD	20832
FIER, DEBBIE	PIANIST	POST OFFICE BOX 63	WENDELL, MA	01379
FIERRO, PAUL	ACTOR	8618 APPIAN WY	LOS ANGELES, CA	90046
FIFE, RANDY	DIRECTOR	311 PARK BROOK DR	DALLAS, TX	75218
FIFITA, KING	WRESTLER	SEE - TONGA, KING		
FIFTH AVENUE BAND	C & W GROUP	LUTZ, 5625 "O" STREET BLDG	LINCOLN, NE	68510
FIFTH DIMENSION, THE	VOCAL GROUP	MARC GORDON, 1022 N PALM AVE	LOS ANGELES, CA	90069
50'S SUN SESSION ROCK-A-BILLY	ROCK & ROLL GROUP	OLDIES, 5218 ALMONT ST	LOS ANGELES, CA	90032
54'40	ROCK & ROLL GROUP	41 BRITAIN ST #200	TORONTO, ONT	CANADA
FIGUEROA, EFRAIN	ACTOR	LEONETTI, 6526 SUNSET BLVD	HOLLYWOOD, CA	90028
FIGUEROA, JOHN L	TV WRITER	8955 BEVERLY BLVD	LOS ANGELES, CA	90048
FIGUEROA, RUBEN	ACTOR	826 COLUMBUS AVE	NEW YORK, NY	10026
FIGURES ON A BEACH	ROCK & ROLL GROUP	CEREMONY, 1431 WASHINGTON BLVD	DETROIT, MI	48226
FIGUS, LISA	ACTRESS	9165 SUNSET BLVD #202	LOS ANGELES, CA	90069
FILERMAN, MICHAEL	TV WRITER-PRODUCER	7533 WOODROW WILSON DR	LOS ANGELES, CA	90046
FILICE, ERNEST C	COMPOSER	5500-1-E PASEO DEL LAGO	LAGUNA HILLS, CA	92653
FILIPOVIC, IGOR	TENOR	61 W 62ND ST #6-F	NEW YORK, NY	10023
FILKIN, DAVID	TV PRODUCER	29 BLOOMFIELD RD		
		KINGSTON UPON THAMES	SURREY	ENGLAND
FILM AT ELEVEN	ROCK & ROLL GROUP	VARIETY ARTISTS INTL, INC		
		9073 NEMO ST, 3RD FLOOR	LOS ANGELES, CA	90069
FILPI, CARMEN	ACTOR	6569 DE LONGPRE AVE	LOS ANGELES, CA	90028
FILTEAU, JEROME F	NEWS CORRESPONDENT	8013 NICKY CT	LAUREL, MD	20707
FIMPLE, DENNIS	ACTOR	3518 W CAHUENGA BLVD #316	LOS ANGELES, CA	90068
FIMRITE, RON	SPORTS WRITER-EDITOR	SPORTS ILLUSTRATED MAGAZINE		
		TIME & LIFE BUILDING		
		ROCKEFELLER CENTER	NEW YORK, NY	10020
FINAMORE, CHARLES A	NEWS CORRESPONDENT	6713 DOANE AVE	SPRINGFIELD, VA	22152
FINCH, BRIAN	TV WRITER	A D PETERS, LTD		
		10 BUCKINGHAM ST	LONDON WC2	ENGLAND
FINCH, JON	ACTOR	NEASRADER, 135 NEW KINGS RD	LONDON SW6 4SL	ENGLAND
FINCH, MARTINA	ACTRESS	9000 SUNSET BLVD #1200	LOS ANGELES, CA	90069
FINCH, SAMANTHA	ACTRESS	ANN WRIGHT, 136 E 57TH ST	NEW YORK, NY	10022
FINCHER, JACK	WRITER	8955 BEVERLY BLVD	LOS ANGELES, CA	90048
FINCKEL, DAVID	CELLIST	KAPLAN, 115 COLLEGE ST	BURLINGTON, VT	05401
FINDLATER, JOHN	ACTOR	1047 S GENESEE AVE	LOS ANGELES, CA	90019
FINDLEY, MARY	VIOLINIST	IAM, 10572 JASON LN	COLUMBIA, MD	21044
FINE, BILLY	FILM PRODUCER	9229 SUNSET BLVD #320	LOS ANGELES, CA	90069
FINE, DELIA	TV PRODUCER	WABC-TV, 7 LINCOLN SQ	NEW YORK, NY	10023

FINE, HOLLY	PHOTOGRAPHER	2300 CHAIN BRIDGE RD, NW	WASHINGTON, DC	20016
FINE, LEON	WRITER	555 W 57TH ST #1230	NEW YORK, NY	10019
FINE, MORTON N	SCREENWRITER	595 E CHANNEL RD	SANTA MONICA, CA	90402
FINE, NATE	PHOTOGRAPHER	9214 KINGSBURY DR	SILVER SPRING, MD	20910
FINE, PAUL	PHOTOGRAPHER	2300 CHAIN BRIDGE RD, NW	WASHINGTON, DC	20016
FINE, PAUL R	DIRECTOR	2300 CHAIN BRIDGE RD, NW	WASHINGTON, DC	20016
FINE, SYLVIA	TV WRITER	8955 BEVERLY BLVD	LOS ANGELES, CA	90048
FINE ARTS BRASS QUINTET	BRASS QUINTET	CCS, 4478 PURDUE AVE	CULVER CITY, CA	90230
FINE YOUNG CANNIBALS, THE	ROCK & ROLL GROUP	AGM MGMT, 1312 N LA BREA AVE	HOLLYWOOD, CA	90028
FINEGAN, JAMES J, JR	NEWS CORRESPONDENT	3048 S BUCHANAN ST	ARLINGTON, VA	22206
FINEHOUT, ROBERT	CABLE EXECUTIVE	MODERN TALKING PICTURE SERVICES		
		45 ROCKEFELLER PLAZA	NEW YORK, NY	10020
FINELL, ALYCE	TV WRITER-PRODUCER	301 E 79TH ST	NEW YORK, NY	10021
FINEMAN, HOWARD	NEWS CORRESPONDENT	4105 HARRISON ST, NW	WASHINGTON, DC	20015
FINEMAN, JOSEPH	WRITER	9351 W OLYMPIC BLVD	BEVERLY HILLS, CA	90212
FINESTRA, CARMEN	WRITER	404 S COCHRAN AVE	LOS ANGELES, CA	90036
FINFER, JUNE K	WRITER	555 W 57TH ST #1230	NEW YORK, NY	10019
FINGERETT, SALLY	SINGER	29 COMMONWEALTH AVE #705	BOSTON, MA	02116
FINGERS, ROLAND	BASEBALL	1268 HIDDEN MOUNTAIN DR	EL CAJON, CA	92020
FINIZZA, EILEEN	ACTRESS	130 S CARSON RD	BEVERLY HILLS, CA	90211
FINK, MANFRED	TENOR	CAMI, 165 W 57TH ST	NEW YORK, NY	10019
FINK, MARK	TV WRITER	13040 WOODBRIDGE ST	STUDIO CITY, CA	91604
FINK, SUE	SINGER-GUITARIST	2801-B OCEAN PARK BLVD #66	SANTA MONICA, CA	90405
FINKEL, FYVUSH	ACTOR	155 E 50TH ST	NEW YORK, NY	10022
FINKEL, GEORGE	TV DIRECTOR-PRODUCER	110 BRENTWOOD DR	MOUNT LAUREL, NJ	08054
FINKEL, HOWARD	RING ANNOUCER	POST OFFICE BOX 3859	STAMFORD, CT	06905
FINKEL, ROBERT	WRITER-PRODUCER	12560 THE VISTA	LOS ANGELES, CVA	90049
FINKEL, SHELLEY	TALENT AGENT	310 MADISON AVE #804	NEW YORK, NY	10017
FINKELMAN, JEFFREY K	WRITER	555 W 57TH ST #1230	NEW YORK, NY	10019
FINKELSTEIN, JULIAN S	TV DIRECTOR	54 BLISS AVE	TENAFLY, NJ	07670
FINKELSTEIN, STEVEN	WRITER	8955 BEVERLY BLVD	LOS ANGELES, CA	90048
FINKLE, DAVID R	WRITER	555 W 57TH ST #1230	NEW YORK, NY	10019
FINKLEMAN, KENNETH C	WRITER-PRODUCER	151 S EL CAMINO DR	BEVERLY HILLS, CA	90212
FINKO, DAVID	COMPOSER	482 FORT WASHINGTON AVE #1-H	NEW YORK, NY	10033
FINLAND, BRUCE F	NEWS CORRESPONDENT	400 N CAPITOL ST, NW	WASHINGTON, DC	20001
FINLAY, FRANK	ACTOR	AL PARKER LTD, 50 MOUNT ST		
		PARK LN	LONDON W1	ENGLAND
FINLAYSON, ALEX	ACTOR	8075 W 3RD ST #303	LOS ANGELES, CA	90048
FINLAYSON, ROBERT ALLAN	NEWS CORRESPONDENT	7636 E ARBORY CT	LAUREL, MD	20707
FINLEY, CHARLES N	WRITER	555 W 57TH ST #1230	NEW YORK, NY	10019
FINLEY, GREG	ACTOR	3518 W CAHUENGA BLVD #316	LOS ANGELES, CA	90068
FINLEY, KENNETH Q	WRITER-PRODUCER	908 E HARVARD RD	BURBANK, CA	91501
FINLEY, RONALD T	DIRECTOR	260 W 72ND ST	NEW YORK, NY	10023
FINLEY, W FRANKLYN	SCREENWRITER	555 W 57TH ST #1230	NEW YORK, NY	10019
FINLEY, WILLIAM	ACTOR	POST OFFICE BOX 5617	BEVERLY HILLS, CA	90210
FINLEY, WILLIAM	SCREENWRITER	151 S EL CAMINO DR	BEVERLY HILLS, CA	90212
FINN, HERBERT	TV WRITER	4058 CAMELLIA AVE	STUDIO CITY, CA	91604
FINN, MALLY	CASTING DIRECTOR	9911 W PICO BLVD #1580	LOS ANGELES, CA	90035
FINN, ROBYN	ACTRESS	TERRIT TALENT, 432 PARK AVE	NEW YORK, NY	10022
FINNEGAN, J P	ACTOR	9639 VIA RIMINI	BURBANK, CA	91504
FINNEGAN, JACK	ACTOR	435 E 85TH ST	NEW YORK, NY	10028
FINNEGAN, JOHN	ACTOR	7471 MELROSE AVE #11	LOS ANGELES, CA	90046
FINNEGAN, PATRICIA	TV PRODUCER	4225 COLDWATER CANYON DR	STUDIO CITY, CA	91604
FINNEGAN, WILLIAM P	FILM WRITER-PRODUCER	4225 COLDWATER CANYON DR	STUDIO CITY, CA	91604
FINNEGAN, WILLIAM R	FILM WRITER-PRODUCER	3074 FRANKLIN CANYON DR	BEVERLY HILLS, CA	90210
FINNERMAN, GERALD	CINEMATOGRAPHER	3211 OAKDELL LN	STUDIO CITY, CA	91604
FINNEY, ALBERT	ACTOR	39 SEYMOUR WALK	LONDON SW10	ENGLAND
FINNEY, EILEEN	ACTRESS	8485 MELROSE PL #E	LOS ANGELES, CA	90069
FINNEY, JOHN W	NEWS CORRESPONDENT	5275 WATSON ST, NW	WASHINGTON, DC	20016
FINNEY, SARA V	TV WRITER	1233 1/2 S CITRUS AVE	LOS ANGELES, CA	90019
FINNIGAN, MICHAEL	PHOTOGRAPHER	806 MARYLAND AVE, NE	WASHINGTON, DC	20002
FINNIGAN, THOMAS	TV WRITER	8955 BEVERLY BLVD	LOS ANGELES, CA	90048
FINNIGAN, VINCENT A	PHOTOGRAPHER	806 MARYLAND AVE, NW	WASHINGTON, DC	20002
FINNILAE, BIRGIT	CONTRALTO	COLBERT, 111 W 57TH ST	NEW YORK, NY	10019
FINUCANE, TOM	ACTOR	11175 HUSTON ST #29	NORTH HOLLYWOOD, CA	91601
FIONA	SINGER	10100 SANTA MONICA BLVD #1600	LOS ANGELES, CA	90067
FIONDELLA, JAY	WRITER	1657 OCEAN AVE #3	SANTA MONICA, CA	90401
FIORAMONTI, GLORY	STUNTWOMEN	3518 W CAHUENGA BLVD #206	LOS ANGELES, CA	90068
FIORE, ALBERT A	DIRECTOR	128 MALLORY AVE	JERSEY CITY, NJ	07304
FIORE, BILL	ACTOR	10 E 44TH ST #700	NEW YORK, NY	10017
FIORE, FRANK V	CONDUCTOR	243 E WILBUR RD #320	THOUSAND OAKS, CA	91360
FIORE, ROBERT	WRITER-PRODUCER	141 GARDEN CITY AVE	POINT LOOKOUT, NY	11569
FIORENTINO, JACQUES	PRODUCER	933 N CROFT AVE	LOS ANGELES, CA	90069
FIORENTINO, LINDA	ACTRESS	1888 CENTURY PARK E #1400	LOS ANGELES, CA	90067
FIORILLO, ELISA	ACTRESS	3575 W CAHUENGA BLVD #320	LOS ANGELES, CA	90068
FIORITO, JOHN	ACTOR	2501 W BURBANK BLVD #304	BURBANK, CA	91505
FIORITO, JOHN	BASSO-BARITONE	61 W 62ND ST #6-F	NEW YORK, NY	10023
FIRBANK, ANN	ACTRESS	HEATH, PARAMOUNT HOUSE		
		162-170 WARDOUR ST	LONDON W1V 3AT	ENGLAND
FIRE, RICHARD	ACTOR	1509 N CRESCENT HGTS BLVD	LOS ANGELES, CA	90069
FIRE WATER BAND	C & W GROUP	RAU, RUSTIC ACRES	JASPER, IN	47546
FIREBALLS, THE	ROCK & ROLL GROUP	OLDIES, 5218 ALMONT ST	LOS ANGELES, CA	90032
FIREFALL	ROCK & ROLL GROUP	FANTASMA PRODUCTIONS		
		2000 S DIXIE HWY	WEST PALM BEACH, FL	33401
FIREHOUSE	C & W GROUP	POST OFFICE BOX O	EXCELSIOR, MN	55331

Name	Occupation	Address	City/State	Zip
FIREMAN, KENNETH HOWARD	NEWS CORRESPONDENT	2901 CONNECTICUT AVE #510, NW	WASHINGTON, DC	20008
FIREMAN, MARVIN	DIRECTOR	DGA, 110 W 57TH ST	NEW YORK, NY	10019
FIRESTONE, ADRIA	MEZZO-SOPRANO	HILLYER, 250 W 57TH ST	NEW YORK, NY	10107
FIRESTONE, EDDIE	ACTOR	14319 GREENLEAF ST	SHERMAN OAKS, CA	91423
FIRESTONE, RICHARD D	NEWS CORRESPONDENT	6559 SWEET FERN	COLUMBIA, MD	21045
FIRKUSNY, RUDOLF	PIANIST	59 E 54TH ST #81	NEW YORK, NY	10022
FIRM, THE	ROCK & ROLL GROUP	ATLANTIC RECORDS		
		75 ROCKEFELLER PLAZA	NEW YORK, NY	10019
FIRMANI, LILLIAN	NEWS CORRESPONDENT	11807 RIVERSHORE DR	DUNKIRK, MD	20754
FIRST CHOICE	VOCAL GROUP	JOYCE AGENCY, 435 E 79TH ST	NEW YORK, NY	10021
FIRST LIGHT	ROCK & ROLL GROUP	POST OFFICE BOX 8125	ANN ARBOR, MI	48107
FIRTH, COLIN	ACTOR	22 W END TERRACE, WINCHESTER	HANTS	ENGLAND
FIRTH, PETER	ACTOR	PLANT & FROGGATT, LTD		
		THE JULIAN HOUSE		
		4 WINDMILL ST	LONDON W1	ENGLAND
FISCHER, ANNIE	PIANIST	LEISER, DORCHESTER TOWERS		
		155 W 68TH ST	NEW YORK, NY	10023
FISCHER, BRENT S C	COMPOSER	3832 LAUREL CANYON BLVD	STUDIO CITY, CA	91604
FISCHER, BRUCE M	ACTOR	6000 COCOS DR #4	LOS ANGELES, CA	90068
FISCHER, CARL	TV DIRECTOR	121 E 83RD ST	NEW YORK, NY	10028
FISCHER, CLARE	COMPOSER-CONDUCTOR	3832 LAUREL CANYON BLVD	STUDIO CITY, CA	91604
FISCHER, EDWARD	WRITER	555 W 57TH ST #1230	NEW YORK, NY	10019
FISCHER, GEOFFREY	WRITER-PRODUCER	1900 AVE OF THE STARS #2375	LOS ANGELES, CA	90067
FISCHER, IDA	TALENT AGENT	6565 SUNSET BLVD #525-A	HOLLYWOOD, CA	90028
FISCHER, IVAN	CONDUCTOR	ICM, 40 W 57TH ST	NEW YORK, NY	10019
FISCHER, JANICE	TV WRITER	8955 BEVERLY BLVD	LOS ANGELES, CA	90048
FISCHER, PAUL	WRITER	555 W 57TH ST #1230	NEW YORK, NY	10019
FISCHER, PETER S	TV WRITER-PRODUCER	MCA/UNIVERSAL STUDIOS, INC		
		100 UNIVERSAL CITY PLAZA	UNIVERSAL CITY, CA	91608
FISCHER, RONALD	DRUMMER	247 TOWNES DR	NASHVILLE, TN	37211
FISCHER, STEPHEN C	TV WRITER	8955 BEVERLY BLVD	LOS ANGELES, CA	90048
FISCHER, STEWART R	COMPOSER-CONDUCTOR	19112 FRIENDLY VALLEY PARKWAY	NEWHALL, CA	91321
FISCHER, WILLIAM P	TV PRODUCER	1977 N DRACENA DR	LOS ANGELES, CA	90027
FISCHER-DIESKAU, DIETRICH	BARITONE	COLBERT, 111 W 57TH ST	NEW YORK, NY	10019
FISCHMANN, RUEL	TV WRITER	4637 MAYTIME LN	CULVER CITY, CA	90230
FISCHOFF, GEORGE	COMPOSER-PIANIST	MM GROUP, 48 W 38TH ST	NEW YORK, NY	10018
FISCHOFF, STUART P	WRITER	5911 CYN HGTS LN	LOS ANGELES, CA	90068
FISHBEIN, GERSHON W	NEWS CORRESPONDENT	408 NEALE CT	SILVER SPRING, MD	20901
FISHBIEN, BARNET	SCREENWRITER	8955 BEVERLY BLVD	LOS ANGELES, CA	90048
FISHER, ALBERT C	DIRECTOR-PRODUCER	333 W 86TH ST #PH-2006	NEW YORK, NY	10024
FISHER, AMEEL J	TV WRITER	6 STUYVESANT OVAL	NEW YORK, NY	10009
FISHER, ANDREW, IV	WRITER	555 W 57TH ST #1230	NEW YORK, NY	10019
FISHER, ARTHUR	WRITER-PRODUCER	DGA, 7950 SUNSET BLVD	LOS ANGELES, CA	90046
FISHER, CARRIE	ACTRESS	9555 OAK PASS RD	BEVERLY HILLS, CA	90210
FISHER, CINDY	ACTRESS	3641 E CHEVY CHASE DR	GLENDALE, CA	91206
FISHER, CRAIG	FILM-TV EXECUTIVE	233 E 52ND ST	NEW YORK, NY	10022
FISHER, CRAIG B	WRITER	555 W 57TH ST #1230	NEW YORK, NY	10019
FISHER, DAVID	SCREENWRITER	8955 BEVERLY BLVD	LOS ANGELES, CA	90048
FISHER, DEBRA	WRITER	555 W 57TH ST #1230	NEW YORK, NY	10019
FISHER, ED	CARTOONIST	POST OFFICE BOX 4203	NEW YORK, NY	10017
FISHER, EDDIE	SINGER-ACTOR	CHARLES RAPP ENTS		
		1650 BROADWAY	NEW YORK, NY	10019
FISHER, GAIL	ACTRESS	WEBB, 7500 DEVISTA DR	LOS ANGELES, CA	90046
FISHER, GAIL L	WRITER	8955 BEVERLY BLVD	LOS ANGELES, CA	90048
FISHER, HELEN A	WRITER	555 W 57TH ST #1230	NEW YORK, NY	10019
FISHER, JOELY	ACTRESS	STEVENS, 243 DELFERN DR	LOS ANGELES, CA	90077
FISHER, JON	DIRECTOR	DGA, 110 W 57TH ST	NEW YORK, NY	10019
FISHER, JULES	THEATER PRODUCER	126 5TH AVE	NEW YORK, NY	10011
FISHER, LOLA	ACTRESS	1768 S SHERBOURNE DR	LOS ANGELES, CA	90035
FISHER, M F K	WRITER	13935 SONOMA HWY	GLEN ELLEN, CA	95442
FISHER, MARTIN	PRODUCER	3855 LANKERSHIM BLVD #122	NORTH HOLLYWOOD, CA	91604
FISHER, MARY JANE	NEWS CORRESPONDENT	3140 HIGHLAND PL, NW	WASHINGTON, DC	20008
FISHER, MAXINE	ACTRESS	CASSELL, 843 N SYCAMORE ST	LOS ANGELES, CA	90038
FISHER, MICHAEL R	TV WRITER-PRODUCER	8955 BEVERLY BLVD	LOS ANGELES, CA	90048
FISHER, PAUL A	NEWS CORRESPONDENT	12410 KENSINGTON LN	BOWIE, MD	20715
FISHER, RICHARD A	TV WRITER	8955 BEVERLY BLVD	LOS ANGELES, CA	90048
FISHER, RICHARD C	NEWS CORRESPONDENT	236 MASSACHUSETTS AVE, NE	WASHINGTON, DC	20002
FISHER, ROBERT H	TV WRITER	8955 BEVERLY BLVD	LOS ANGELES, CA	90048
FISHER, ROBERT J	DIRECTOR	4930 COLDWATER CANYON AVE #220	SHERMAN OAKS, CA	91423
FISHER, ROBERT S	ACTOR	1426 N HOOVER ST #4	LOS ANGELES, CA	90027
FISHER, RUSS	COMEDIAN	32500 CONCORD DR #221	MADISON HEIGHTS, MI	48071
FISHER, SANFORD H	TV EXECUTIVE	CORPORATION FOR ENTERTAINMENT		
		AND LEARNING		
		515 MADISON AVE	NEW YORK, NY	10022
FISHER, STEPHANIE	MODEL	POST OFFICE BOX 7211	MOUNTAIN VIEW, CA	94043
FISHER, STEVEN J	TV WRITER	8955 BEVERLY BLVD	LOS ANGELES, CA	90048
FISHER, TERRY	TV PRODUCER	ORION TV, 2630 LACY ST	LOS ANGELES, CA	90031
FISHER, TERRY LOUISE	TV WRITER-PRODUCER	8439 SUNSET BLVD #102	LOS ANGELES, CA	90069
FISHKO, ROBERT S	THEATER PRODUCER	1501 BROADWAY	NEW YORK, NY	10036
FISHMAN, ALLEN	COLUMNIST	TRIBUNE MEDIA SERVICES		
		64 E CONCORD ST	ORLANDO, FL	32801
FISHMAN, JANET	DIRECTOR-PRODUCER	333 E 79TH ST	NEW YORK, NY	10021
FISHMAN, JANICE I	WRITER	8955 BEVERLY BLVD	LOS ANGELES, CA	90048
FISHMAN, JEFF	ACTOR	8322 BEVERLY BLVD #202	LOS ANGELES, CA	90048
FISHMAN, ROBERT A	TV DIRECTOR	101 GROVE POINT RD	WESTPORT, CT	06880

Name	Occupation	Address	City	Zip/Country
FISICHELLA, SALVATORE	TENOR	CAMI, 165 W 57TH ST	NEW YORK, NY	10019
FISK, CARLTON	BASEBALL	16612 CATAWBA RD	LOCKPORT, IL	60441
FISK, ELIOT	GUITARIST	ICM, 40 W 57TH ST	NEW YORK, NY	10019
FISK, JACK	FILM DIRECTOR	BEAU VAL FARM, BOX #7	COBHAM, VA	22929
FISK, VICKI	SINGER	GERSHUNOFF, 502 PARK AVE	NEW YORK, NY	10022
FISKIN, JEFFREY A	SCREENWRITER	6107 TEMPLE HILL DR	LOS ANGELES, CA	90068
FISSORE, ENRICO	BASSO-BARITONE	61 W 62ND ST #6-F	NEW YORK, NY	10023
FISZ, BENJAMIN	FILM PRODUCER	51 S AUDLEY ST	LONDON W1	ENGLAND
FITCH, BERNARD	TENOR	61 W 62ND ST #6-F	NEW YORK, NY	10023
FITSGERALD, NEIL	ACTOR	32 GRAMERCY PARK S	NEW YORK, NY	10003
FITTS, KENNETH L	TV PRODUCER	CBS-TV, "AS THE WORLD TURNS"		
		51 W 52ND ST	NEW YORK, NY	10019
FITTS, RICK	ACTOR	2054 1/2 RODNEY DR	LOS ANGELES, CA	90027
FITZ, ALEXANDER	ACTOR	26 1/2 18TH AVE	VENICE, CA	90291
FITZ, REGINALD	NEWS REPORTER	THE NATIONAL ENQUIRER		
		600 SE COAST AVE	LANTANA, FL	33464
FITZALAN, MARSHA	ACTRESS	HEATH, PARAMOUNT HOUSE		
		162-170 WARDOUR ST	LONDON W1V 3AT	ENGLAND
FITZER, JOHN L	COMPOSER	3156 KALLIN AVE	LONG BEACH, CA	90808
FITZGERALD, ANNE	CARTOONIST	KING FEATURES SYNDICATE		
		235 E 45TH ST	NEW YORK, NY	10017
FITZGERALD, ANNE P	NEWS CORRESPONDENT	151 DUDDINGTON PL, SE	WASHINGTON, DC	20003
FITZGERALD, BENEDICT R	WRITER	555 W 57TH ST #1230	NEW YORK, NY	10019
FITZGERALD, CHER QUINN	ACTRESS	8721 SUNSET BLVD #200	LOS ANGELES, CA	90069
FITZGERALD, DAN L	DIRECTOR	1410 1/2 HAVENHURST DR	HOLLYWOOD, CA	90046
FITZGERALD, ELLA	SINGER	908 WHITTIER DR	BEVERLY HILLS, CA	90210
FITZGERALD, EUGENIA M	NEWS CORRESPONDENT	4461 CONNECTICUT AVE, NW	WASHINGTON, DC	20008
FITZGERALD, FERN	ACTRESS	MC CARTHY, 4958 WOODMAN AVE		
		SUITE #108	SHERMAN OAKS, CA	91423
FITZGERALD, GERALDINE	ACTRESS	50 E 79TH ST	NEW YORK, NY	10019
FITZGERALD, JACK	ACTOR	8721 SUNSET BLVD #203	LOS ANGELES, CA	90069
FITZGERALD, JACK	WRITER	8955 BEVERLY BLVD	LOS ANGELES, CA	90048
FITZGERALD, JOHN F	NEWS CORRESPONDENT	151 DUDDINGTON PL, SE	WASHINGTON, DC	20003
FITZGERALD, KATHLEEN	DIRECTOR	DGA, 110 W 57TH ST	NEW YORK, NY	10019
FITZGERALD, KATHLEEN	ACTRESS	427 N CANON DR #205	BEVERLY HILLS, CA	90210
FITZGERALD, MICHAEL	PRODUCER	MCA/UNIVERSAL STUDIOS, INC		
		100 UNIVERSAL CITY PLAZA	UNIVERSAL CITY, CA	91608
FITZGERALD, NEIL	ACTOR	32 GRAMERCY PARK S	NEW YORK, NY	10003
FITZGERALD, RAYMOND A	DIRECTOR	546 E 87TH ST	NEW YORK, NY	10028
FITZGERALD, ROB	ACTOR	6430 SUNSET BLVD #1203	LOS ANGELES, CA	90028
FITZGERALD, SARA	NEWS CORRESPONDENT	3900 VACATION LN	ARLINGTON, VA	22207
FITZGERALD, VALERIE	ACTRESS	9000 SUNSET BLVD #1112	LOS ANGELES, CA	90069
FITZGERALD, WAYNE R	DIRECTOR	1878 LAUREL CANYON BLVD	LOS ANGELES, CA	90046
FITZHUGH, PATRICK	GUITARIST	400 LYNWOOD BLVD	NASHVILLE, TN	37205
FITZPATRICK, AILEEN	ACTRESS	1999 N SYCAMORE AVE #1	LOS ANGELES, CA	90068
FITZPATRICK, BRIAN	ACTOR	ABC-TV, "ALL MY CHILDREN"		
		1330 AVE OF THE AMERICAS	NEW YORK, NY	10019
FITZPATRICK, JAMES F	NEWS CORRESPONDENT	7203 46TH ST	CHEVY CHASE, MD	20815
FITZPATRICK, L S F	NEWS CORRESPONDENT	9411 LEE HWY #308	FAIRFAX, VA	22031
FITZPATRICK, RAYMOND	ACTOR	40 1/2 27TH PL	VENICE, CA	90291
FITZPATRICK, WILLIAM	VIOLINIST	4205 MURPHY RD	NASHVILLE, TN	37209
FITZSIMMONS, ROBERT T	ACTOR	76 RIVERSIDE DR	NEW YORK, NY	10024
FITZSIMMONS, TOM	ACTOR	247 S BEVERLY DR #102	BEVERLY HILLS, CA	90210
FITZSTEPHENS, JOHN J	DIRECTOR	235 W 76TH ST	NEW YORK, NY	10023
FITZWATER, MICHAEL S	DIRECTOR	DGA, 110 W 57TH ST	NEW YORK, NY	10019
FIVE DISCS, THE	VOCAL GROUP	POST OFFICE BOX 262	CARTERET, NJ	07008
FIVE PLATTERS, THE	VOCAL GROUP	SEE - PLATTERS, THE		
FIVE PM	MUSICAL GROUP	DBA MGMT, 4630 DEEPDALE DR	CORPUS CHRISTI, TX	78413
FIVE SATINS, THE	VOCAL GROUP	BROTHERS, 141 DUNBAR AVE	FORDS, NJ	08863
FIVE STAR	VOCAL GROUP	POST OFFICE BOX 29, ROMFORD	ESSEX RM7 OST	ENGLAND
FIVESON, ROBERT S	WRITER	2365 TEVOIT ST	LOS ANGELES, CA	90039
FIX, JANET L	NEWS CORRESPONDENT	2329 40TH PL, NW	WASHINGTON, DC	20007
FIXEL, ARTHUR	MUSIC ARRANGER	2929 SELENA DR #J-127	NASHVILLE, TN	37211
FIXX, THE	ROCK & ROLL GROUP	POST OFFICE BOX 4XN	LONDON W1A 4XN	ENGLAND
FIZDALE, JONATHAN	WRITER	14230 MULHOLLAND DR	LOS ANGELES, CA	90077
FIZEL, DOUGLAS	NEWS CORRESPONDENT	984 NATIONAL PRESS BLDG		
		529 14TH ST, NW	WASHINGTON, DC	20045
FJELL, JUDY	SINGER-GUITARIST	POST OFFICE BOX 56	CORVALLIS, OR	97339
FLACK, BARBARA	WRITER	555 W 57TH ST #1230	NEW YORK, NY	10019
FLACK, ROBERTA	SINGER-SONGWRITER	THE DAKOTA, 1 W 72ND ST	NEW YORK, NY	10023
FLACK, TIM	CASTING DIRECTOR	1438 N GOWER ST #432	LOS ANGELES, CA	90028
FLACKE, RAYMOND JAMES	GUITARIST	2601 HILLSBORO RD #M-1	NASHVILLE, TN	37212
FLAG	ROCK & ROLL GROUP	SCOTTI BROS, 2128 PICO BLVD	SANTA MONICA, CA	90405
FLAGELLO, EZIO	SINGER	1776 BROADWAY #504	NEW YORK, NY	10019
FLAGG, DON	FILM DIRECTOR	11847 RIVERSIDE DR	NORTH HOLLYWOOD, CA	91607
FLAGG, FANNIE	ACTRESS	1520 WILLINA LN	MONTECITO, CA	93108
FLAHERTY, EDWARD	DIRECTOR	9594 NEWFAME CIR	FOUNTAIN VALLEY, CA	92708
FLAHERTY, JOE	ACTOR-WRITER-PRODUCER	SCTV, 110 LOMBARD ST	TORONTO, ONT M5C 1M3	CANADA
FLAHERTY, JOHN D	WRITER	8955 BEVERLY BLVD	LOS ANGELES, CA	90048
FLAHERTY, JOSEPH P	TV WRITER	8955 BEVERLY BLVD	LOS ANGELES, CA	90048
FLAHERTY, MICHAEL JAMES	NEWS CORRESPONDENT	1739 19TH ST, NW	WASHINGTON, DC	20009
FLAHERTY, PAUL M	WRITER	8955 BEVERLY BLVD	LOS ANGELES, CA	90048
FLAHERTY, THOMAS E	COMPOSER	5151 EL RIO AVE	LOS ANGELES, CA	90041
FLAHERTY, VINCENT X	ACTOR	11240 MAGNOLIA BLVD #202	NORTH HOLLYWOOD, CA	91601

Name	Occupation	Address	City	ZIP
FLAIR, RIC	WRESTLER	NATIONAL WRESTLING ALLIANCE		
		JIM CROCKETT PROMOTIONS		
		421 BRIARBEND DR	CHARLOTTE, NC	28209
FLAMBEAU, PERE ANTOINE	COMEDIAN	333 SAINT CHARLES AVE #500	NEW ORLEANS, LA	70130
FLAMIN GROOVIES, THE	ROCK & ROLL GROUP	SIRE RECORDS COMPANY		
		75 ROCKEFELLER PLAZA	NEW YORK, NY	10019
FLAMIN' OH'S, THE	ROCK & ROLL GROUP	VARIETY ARTISTS INTL, INC		
		9073 NEMO ST, 3RD FLOOR	LOS ANGELES, CA	90069
FLAMING LIPS, THE	ROCK & ROLL GROUP	POST OFFICE BOX 2428	EL SEGUNDO, CA	90245
FLAMINGOS, THE	VOCAL GROUP	25 HIGH ST	SOUTHBOROUGH, MA	01772
FLAMMING, PETER	GUITARIST	5003 NEVADA AVE	NASHVILLE, TN	37209
FLANAGAN, FIONNULA	ACTRESS	9220 SUNSET BLVD #625	LOS ANGELES, CA	90069
FLANAGAN, JUDITH	ACTRESS	9220 SUNSET BLVD #625	LOS ANGELES, CA	90069
FLANDERS, ED	ACTOR	32918 CALLE DE BURITTA	MALIBU, CA	90265
FLANIGAN, JAMES C	NEWS CORRESPONDENT	907 6TH ST, SW #401	WASHINGTON, DC	20024
FLANIGAN, LAUREN	SOPRANO	253 W 73RD ST #7-M	NEW YORK, NY	10023
FLANNERY, SUSAN	ACTRESS	146 N ALMONT DR #8	LOS ANGELES, CA	90048
FLANNERY, THOMAS	CARTOONIST	518 ORKNEY RD	BALTIMORE, MD	21212
FLANTER, JILL	ACTRESS	4789 VINELAND AVE #100	NORTH HOLLYWOOD, CA	91602
FLANZ, NEIL	GUITARIST	622 BOSCOBEL ST	NASHVILLE, TN	37206
FLASH & THE PAN	ROCK & ROLL GROUP	LEBER, 65 W 55TH ST	NEW YORK, NY	10019
FLASH CADILLAC	ROCK & ROLL GROUP	POST OFFICE BOX 6588	SAN ANTONIO, TX	78209
FLASHCATS, THE	VOCAL GROUP	TENTH HOUR, 4806 LIBERTY AVE	PITTSBURGH, PA	15224
FLATLEY, WILLIAM	ACTOR	10845 LINDBROOK DR #3	LOS ANGELES, CA	90024
FLATT, ERNEST	DIRECTOR-CHOREORAPHER	POST OFFICE BOX 40	VALLEY CENTER, CA	92082
FLAUM, MARSHALL	WRITER-PRODUCER	301 S RODEO DR	BEVERLY HILLS, CA	90212
FLAX, PHYLLIS	ACTRESS	8831 SUNSET BLVD #402	LOS ANGELES, CA	90069
FLECK, BELA	BANJOIST	4328 LINDAWOOD DR	NASHVILLE, TN	37215
FLECK, MICHAEL	ACTOR	1617 POINT VIEW ST	LOS ANGELES, CA	90035
FLECK, WILLIAM	BASS	MUNRO, 334 W 72ND ST	NEW YORK, NY	10023
FLEDER, ROB	SPORTS WRITER-EDITOR	SPORTS ILLUSTRATED MAGAZINE		
		TIME & LIFE BUILDING		
		ROCKEFELLER CENTER	NEW YORK, NY	10020
FLEEKS, ERIC	ACTOR	5000 LANKERSHIM BLVD #5	NORTH HOLLYWOOD, CA	91601
FLEER, ALICIA	ACTRESS	5035 CATALON AVE	WOODLAND HILLS, CA	91364
FLEER, HARRY	ACTOR	5035 CATALON AVE	WOODLAND HILLS, CA	91364
FLEETWOOD, ANSLEY	PIANIST	4206 LONE OAK RD	NASHVILLE, TN	37215
FLEETWOOD, MICK	DRUMMER-SONGWRITER	11435 BELLAGIO RD	LOS ANGELES, CA	90049
FLEETWOODS, THE	VOCAL GROUP	POST OFFICE BOX 262	CARTERET, NJ	07008
FLEICHER, ANDREA	NEWS CORRESPONDENT	2800 WOODLEY RD, NW	WASHINGTON, DC	20008
FLEISCHER, CHARLES	ACTOR	8212 W NORTON AVE	LOS ANGELES, CA	90046
FLEISCHER, JULIE	TV WRITER	8955 BEVERLY BLVD	LOS ANGELES, CA	90048
FLEISCHER, RICHARD	FILM DIRECTOR	169 S ROCKINGHAM AVE	LOS ANGELES, CA	90049
FLEISCHMAN, ALBERT S	TV WRITER	305 10TH ST	SANTA MONICA, CA	90402
FLEISCHMAN, PAUL	WRITER	8955 BEVERLY BLVD	LOS ANGELES, CA	90048
FLEISCHMAN, ROBERT	SINGER	3 E 54TH ST #1400	NEW YORK, NY	10022
FLEISCHMAN, STEPHEN	TV PRODUCER	ABC TELEVISION NETWORK		
		1330 AVE OF THE AMERICAS	NEW YORK, NY	10019
FLEISCHMAN, STEPHEN E	WRITER-PRODUCER	33 W 93RD ST	NEW YORK, NY	10025
FLEISCHNER, MORTON J	WRITER	555 W 57TH ST #1230	NEW YORK, NY	10019
FLEISHER, CAROL L	WRITER	8955 BEVERLY BLVD	LOS ANGELES, CA	90048
FLEISHER, LEON	PIANIST-CONDUCTOR	CAMI, 165 W 57TH ST	NEW YORK, NY	10019
FLEMING, B B	SINGER	POST OFFICE BOX 11321		
		FLAGLER STATION	MIAMI, FL	33101
FLEMING, JAMES F	WRITER	555 W 57TH ST #1230	NEW YORK, NY	10019
FLEMING, PAMELA S	TV EXEC-NEWS CORRES	22005 FOXLAIR RD	GAITHERSBURG, MD	20879
FLEMING, PEGGY	SKATER	POST OFFICE BOX 173	LOS GATOS, CA	95031
FLEMING, PENELOPE	WRITER	8955 BEVERLY BLVD	LOS ANGELES, CA	90048
FLEMING, RHONDA	ACTRESS	9255 DOHENY RD #1602	LOS ANGELES, CA	90069
FLEMING, ROBERT	WRITER-PRODUCER	5 SOUTH VILLAS, CAMDEN	LONDON NW1	ENGLAND
FLEMING, ROBERT	RECORD EXECUTIVE	POST OFFICE BOX 169	HOLLYWOOD, CA	90028
FLEMING, STEWART R	NEWS CORRESPONDENT	2237 48TH ST, NW	WASHINGTON, DC	20007
FLEMING, THOMAS	WRITER	315 E 72ND ST	NEW YORK, NY	10021
FLEMING, VAN	WRITER	8955 BEVERLY BLVD	LOS ANGELES, CA	90048
FLEMYNG, GORDON	TV DIRECTOR	1 ALBERT RD, WILMSLOW	CHESHIRE	ENGLAND
FLEMYNG, ROBERT	ACTOR	4 NETHERBOURNE RD	LONDON SW4	ENGLAND
FLENNIKEN, SHARY	CARTOONIST-WRITER	THE NATIONAL LAMPOON		
		635 MADISON AVE	NEW YORK, NY	10022
FLESER, APRIL	ACTRESS	24235 BURBANK BLVD	WOODLAND HILLS, CA	91367
FLESHER, GERALD	WRITER	8955 BEVERLY BLVD	LOS ANGELES, CA	90048
FLETCHER, AARON	ACTOR	CED, 261 S ROBERTSON BLVD	BEVERLY HILLS, CA	90211
FLETCHER, BILL	ACTOR	15301 VENTURA BLVD #345	SHERMAN OAKS, CA	91403
FLETCHER, BRAMWELL	ACTOR	ROUTE #1	MARLBOROUGH, NH	03455
FLETCHER, DIANE	ACTRESS	11726 SAN VICENTE BLVD #300	LOS ANGELES, CA	90049
FLETCHER, JACK	ACTOR	569 N ROSSMORE AVE #609	LOS ANGELES, CA	90004
FLETCHER, JACK	PHOTOGRAPHER	ROUTE #2, BOX 213	HURLOCK, MD	21643
FLETCHER, LESTER C	ACTOR	9028 LLOYD PL	LOS ANGELES, CA	90069
FLETCHER, LOUISE	ACTRESS	1520 CAMDEN AVE #105	LOS ANGELES, CA	90025
FLETCHER, MARTIN	TV PROD-CORRES	NBC NEWS, 73 AVE DES CHAMPS	PARIS	FRANCE
FLETCHER, STEVE	ACTOR	ABC-TV, "ONE LIFE TO LIVE"		
		1330 AVE OF THE AMERICAS	NEW YORK, NY	10019
FLICK, BOB	TV WRITER	ENTERTAINMENT TONIGHT		
		PARAMOUNT TELEVISION		
		5555 MELROSE AVE	LOS ANGELES, CA	90038
FLICK, VICTOR H	COMPOSER-CONDUCTOR	1385 N GILBERT ST #145	FULLERTON, CA	92633

FLICKER, JULIE E	WRITER	555 W 57TH ST #1230	NEW YORK, NY	10019
FLICKER, TED	DIRECTOR	DGA, 7950 SUNSET BLVD	HOLLYWOOD, CA	90046
FLICKER, THEODORE	TV WRITER-PRODUCER	1801 AVE OF THE STARS	LOS ANGELES, CA	90067
FLICKINGER, CHARLES E	ACTOR	435 W WILSON AVE	GLENDALE, CA	91203
FLIES, THE	ROCK & ROLL GROUP	POST OFFICE BOX 570	ROCKVILLE CENTRE, NY	11571
FLIGHT	DISCO GROUP	LIVELY LADY, 3778 DUNHILL RD	WATAGH, NY	11793
FLINT, PERRY	NEWS CORRESPONDENT	4224 1/2 RIVER RD, NW	WASHINGTON, DC	20016
FLINT, ROGER	DIRECTOR	1015 N ORLANDO AVE	LOS ANGELES, CA	90069
FLIP CITY	ACROBATIC TROUPE	HALL, 138 FROG HOLLOW RD	CHURCHVILLE, PA	18966
FLIPPER	ROCK & ROLL GROUP	SUBTERRANEAN RECORDS		
		577 VALENCIA ST	SAN FRANCISCO, CA	94110
FLIPPIN, LUCY LEE	ACTRESS	1753 CANFIELD AVE	LOS ANGELES, CA	90035
FLIRTS, THE	ROCK & ROLL GROUP	1776 BROADWAY #1801	NEW YORK, NY	10019
FLO & EDDIE	VOCAL DUO	COHEN MGMT, 5831 SUNSET BLVD	LOS ANGELES, CA	90028
FLOCK, JEFF	TV WRITER-PRODUCER	CHICAGO MERCHANDISE MART #409	CHICAGO, IL	60634
FLOCK OF SEAGULLS	ROCK & ROLL GROUP	POST OFFICE BOX 145, HARROW	MIDDLESEX HA2 ORT	ENGLAND
FLOIED, DAVID	GUITARIST	ROUTE #4, BOX 38	CENTERVILLE, TN	37033
FLOOD, ANN	ACTRESS	19 W 44TH ST #1500	NEW YORK, NY	10036
FLOOD, GAY	SPORTS WRITER-EDITOR	SPORTS ILLUSTRATED MAGAZINE		
		TIME & LIFE BUILDING		
		ROCKEFELLER CENTER	NEW YORK, NY	10020
FLOR, CLAUS PETER	CONDUCTOR	MARIEDL ANDERS ARTISTS MGMT		
		535 EL CAMINO DEL MAR ST	SAN FRANCISCO, CA	94121
FLOREA, JOHN	DIRECTOR-PRODUCER	11730 MOORPARK ST #B	STUDIO CITY, CA	91604
FLOREN, MYRON	COMPOSER	26 GEORGEFF RD	RANCHO PALOS VERDES, C.	90274
FLORENCE, JOSEPH	ACTOR	112 S AVE 66 #2	LOS ANGELES, CA	90042
FLORES DUO, THE	CRADEL ACT	HALL, 138 FROG HOLLOW RD	CHURCHVILLE, PA	18966
FLOREZ, MARILYN	MEZZO-SOPRANO	111 W 57TH ST #1209	NEW YORK, NY	10019
FLORIMONTE, LOUIS	WRITER	25376 N AVE CAPPELA	VALENCIA, CA	91355
FLORIO, ANDY	COMPOSER	1634 WESTERLY TERR	LOS ANGELES, CA	90026
FLORIO, ROBERT	FILM EDITOR	ACE, 4416 1/2 FINLEY AVE	LOS ANGELES, CA	90027
FLORSHEIM, HENRY	WRITER	555 W 57TH ST #1230	NEW YORK, NY	10019
FLORY, MED	ACTOR	6044 ENSIGN AVE	NORTH HOLLYWOOD, CA	91606
FLOTSAM AND JETSAM	ROCK & ROLL GROUP	SHOCKIN MANAGEMENT, BOX 6	RUSHCUTTERS BAY NSW	AUSTRALIA
FLOWER, GEORGE "BUCK"	ACTOR	11812 PENDLETON ST	SUN VALLEY, CA	91352
FLOWER, ROBIN	SINGER-GUITARIST	POST OFFICE BOX 3505	BERKELEY, CA	94703
FLOWERS, DANIEL	GUITARIST	ROUTE #1, WILSON PIKE	ARRINGTON, TN	37017
FLOWERS, JERRY	GUITARIST	4919 DARLINGTON DR	NASHVILLE, TN	37211
FLOWERS, WAYLAND	VENTRILOQUIST	7929 HOLLYWOOD BLVD	LOS ANGELES, CA	90046
FLOYD, ALPHA	SOPRANO	POST OFFICE BOX 27539	PHILADELPHIA, PA	19118
FLOYD, CLARENCE, III	ACTOR	12725 VENTURA BLVD #E	STUDIO CITY, CA	91604
FLOYD, EDDIE	SINGER	2272 DEADRICK AVE	MEMPHIS, TN	38114
FLOYD, TOMMY	GUITARIST	4987 EDMONDSON PIKE	NASHVILLE, TN	37211
FLOYD, WILLIAM	WRITER	8955 BEVERLY BLVD	LOS ANGELES, CA	90048
FLUELLEN, JOEL	ACTOR	1253 S WILTON PL	LOS ANGELES, CA	90019
FLUTIE, DOUG	FOOTBALL	21 SPRING VALLEY RD	NATICK, MA	01760
FLUTY, STEVE	NEWS CORRESPONDENT	8538 FREYMAN DR #211	CHEVY CHASE, MD	20815
FLY, RICHARD H	NEWS CORRESPONDENT	128 TENNESSEE AVE, NE	WASHINGTON, DC	20002
FLYING CABALLEROS TRAPEZE TROUP	TEETERBOARDERS	HALL, 138 FROG HOLLOW RD	CHURCHVILLE, PA	18966
FLYING CACERES TRAPEZE TROUPE	TRAPEZE TROUPE	HALL, 138 FROG HOLLOW RD	CHURCHVILLE, PA	18966
FLYING CORTEZ, THE	TRAPEZE TROUPE	HALL, 138 FROG HOLLOW RD	CHURCHVILLE, PA	18966
FLYING ESPANAS, THE	TRAPEZE ACT	HALL, 138 FROG HOLLOW RD	CHURCHVILLE, PA	18966
FLYING LA RAYS, THE	TRAPEZE ACT	POST OFFICE BOX 87	WEST LEBANON, NY	12195
FLYING LANES, THE	FLYING TRAPEZE ACT	POST OFFICE BOX 87	WEST LEBANON, NY	12195
FLYING PAGES, THE	TRAPEZE ACT	SEE - PAGES, THE FLYING		
FLYING TORRALBAS, THE	AERIAL ACT	HALL, 138 FROG HOLLOW RD	CHURCHVILLE, PA	18966
FLYNN, CHARLES	GUITARIST	306 N DIVISION ST	MOUNT VERNON, OH	43050
FLYNN, DONALD R	TV WRITER	555 W 57TH ST #1230	NEW YORK, NY	10019
FLYNN, FRANCIS P	DIRECTOR	13701 RIVERSIDE DR	SHERMAN OAKS, CA	91423
FLYNN, GERTRUDE	ACTRESS	9009 WONDERLAND AVE	LOS ANGELES, CA	90046
FLYNN, JAMES	ACTOR	POST OFFICE BOX 1115	CANYON CITY, CA	91351
FLYNN, JOHN E	WRITER-DIRECTOR	574 LATIMER RD	SANTA MONICA, CA	90402
FLYNN, MICHAEL	NEWS CORRESPONDENT	12343 QUAIL WOODS DR	GERMANTOWN, MD	20874
FLYNN, MIRIAM	ACTRESS	10000 SANTA MONICA BLVD #305	LOS ANGELES, CA	90067
FLYNN, PATRICK	CONDUCTOR	61 W 62ND ST #6-F	NEW YORK, NY	10023
FLYNN, THOMAS F	WRITER	555 W 57TH ST #1230	NEW YORK, NY	10019
FLYNT, ALTHEA	PUBLISHER	9211 ROBIN DR	LOS ANGELES, CA	90046
FLYNT, LARRY	PUBLISHER	9211 ROBIN DR	LOS ANGELES, CA	90069
FM	ROCK & ROLL GROUP	41 BRITAIN ST #200	TORONTO, ONT	CANADA
FOCA-RODI, GEORGE	PIANIST-COMPOSER	POST OFFICE BOX 20072		
		GREELEY SQUARE STATION	NEW YORK, NY	10001
FOCH, NINA	ACTRESS	POST OFFICE BOX 1884	BEVERLY HILLS, CA	90213
FODOR, EUGENE	VIOLINIST	22314 N TURKEY CREEK RD	MORRISON, CO	80465
FOERSTER, TREY	PUBLISHING EXECUTIVE	GOLDMINE, 700 E STATE ST	IOLA, WI	54990
FOGARTY, BRENDA J	ACTRESS	10831 HUSTON ST	NORTH HOLLYWOOD, CA	91601
FOGARTY, JACK PATRICK	ACTOR	294 HIGHWOOD ST	TEANECK, NJ	07666
FOGARTY, JACK V	TV WRITER	12432 SANFORD ST	LOS ANGELES, CA	90066
FOGARTY, JOHN R	NEWS CORRESPONDENT	5002 JAMESTOWN RD	BETHESDA, MD	20816
FOGARTY, JOSEPH R	COMMUNICATIONS EXEC	FCC, 1919 "M" ST, NW	WASHINGTON, DC	20554
FOGEL, IRA G	TV DIRECTOR	15 W 72ND ST	NEW YORK, NY	10023
FOGEL, JERRY P	ACTOR	826 W 59TH TERR	KANSAS CITY, MO	64113
FOGELBERG, DAN	SINGER-SONGWRITER	9044 MELROSE AVE #306	LOS ANGELES, CA	90069
FOGELSON, ANDREW	FILM PRODUCER	4000 WARNER BLVD, PROD 2-1201	BURBANK, CA	91505
FOGERTY, JOHN	SINGER-SONGWRITER	POST OFFICE BOX 9245	BERKELEY, CA	94709
FOGHAT	ROCK & ROLL GROUP	1783 MASSACHUSETTS AVE #2	CAMBRIDGE, MA	02140

Name	Occupation	Address	City	Zip/Country
FOGLE, ELLEN L	TV WRITER	555 W 57TH ST #1230	NEW YORK, NY	10019
FOGLE, HAROLD	GUITARIST	300 LIBERTY CIR #B-26	MADISON, TN	37115
FOLB, JAY	TV WRITER	1652 COMSTOCK AVE	LOS ANGELES, CA	90024
FOLDI, ANDREW	SINGER	59 E 54TH ST #81	NEW YORK, NY	10022
FOLEY, IRENE	WRITER	555 W 57TH ST #1230	NEW YORK, NY	10019
FOLEY, JAMES	WRITER-PRODUCER	1888 CENTURY PARK E #1400	LOS ANGELES, CA	90067
FOLEY, MARY JO	NEWS CORRESPONDENT	18 4TH ST #1, NE	WASHINGTON, DC	20002
FOLEY, THERESA M	NEWS CORRESPONDENT	208 10TH ST, SE	WASHINGTON, DC	20003
FOLEY, THOMAS J	NEWS CORRESPONDENT	5013 34TH RD N	ARLINGTON, VA	22207
FOLGER, EDWARD	WRITER-PRODUCER	POST OFFICE BOX 124	FROBISHER BAY NWT XOA	CANADA
FOLGER, FRANKLIN	CARTOONIST	NEWS AMERICA SYNDICATE		
		1703 KAISER AVE	IRVINE, CA	92714
FOLK, ROBERT E	COMPOSER-CONDUCTOR	10708 STRADELLA CT	LOS ANGELES, CA	90077
FOLKERS, RICHARD A	PHOTOGRAPHER	10612 WOODSDALE DR	SILVER SPRING, MD	20901
FOLLETT, JAMES	TV WRITER	SCHEHALLIEN, WOODSIDE RD		
		CHIDDINGFOLD	SURREY	ENGLAND
FOLSEY, GEORGE	FILM PRODUCER	MCA/UNIVERSAL STUDIOS, INC		
		100 UNIVERSAL CITY PLAZA	UNIVERSAL CITY, CA	91608
FOLSEY, GEORGE, JR	ACTOR-DIRECTOR	350 N CLIFFWOOD AVE	LOS ANGELES, CA	90049
FOLSOM, AL	WRITER-PRODUCER	13856 BORA BORA WY #11	MARINA DEL REY, CA	90292
FOLSOM, ALLAN R	TV WRITER	22545 CARBON MESA RD	MALIBU, CA	90265
FONAROW, JERRY	WRITER	8955 BEVERLY BLVD	LOS ANGELES, CA	90048
FONDA, JANE	ACTRESS-WRITER	POST OFFICE BOX 491355	LOS ANGELES, CA	90049
FONDA, PETER	ACT-WRI-DIR	INDIAN HILL RANCH	LIVINGSTON, MT	59047
FONER, NAOMI	TV WRITER	226 S NORTON AVE	LOS ANGELES, CA	90004
FONG, BENSON	ACTOR	7236 OUTPOST COVE	LOS ANGELES, CA	90068
FONG, JON	ACTOR	435 S LA CIENEGA BLVD #108	LOS ANGELES, CA	90048
FONG, KAM	ACTRESS	3907 W ALAMEDA AVE #101	BURBANK, CA	91523
FONG, LISA	ACTRESS	6310 SAN VICENTE BLVD #407	LOS ANGELES, CA	90048
FONG-TORRES, BEN S	WRITER	8955 BEVERLY BLVD	LOS ANGELES, CA	90048
FONTAINE, ALISHA	ACTRESS	439 S LA CIENEGA BLVD #120	LOS ANGELES, CA	90048
FONTAINE, CHAR	ACTRESS	22442 MAYCOTTE RD	WOODLAND HILLS, CA	91364
FONTAINE, JOAN	ACTRESS	POST OFFICE BOX 222600	CARMEL, CA	93922
FONTAINE, MOLLY	ACTRESS	12725 VENTURA BLVD #E	STUDIO CITY, CA	91604
FONTANA, CARL R	WRITER	8955 BEVERLY BLVD	LOS ANGELES, CA	90048
FONTANA, D J	DRUMMER	493 BRENT LAWN DR	NASHVILLE, TN	37220
FONTANA, DOROTHY C	WRITER	11862 MOORPARK ST #D	STUDIO CITY, CA	91604
FONTANA, GABRIELE	SOPRANO	MARIEDL ANDERS ARTISTS MGMT		
		535 EL CAMINO DEL MAR ST	SAN FRANCISCO, CA	94121
FONTANA, RICHARD	TV WRITER	8955 BEVERLY BLVD	LOS ANGELES, CA	90048
FONTANA, TOM	TV WRITER	555 W 57TH ST #1230	NEW YORK, NY	10019
FONTANA, TOM	TV WRITER-PRODUCER	CBS-TV, 4024 RADFORD AVE	STUDIO CITY, CA	91604
FONTANA, WAYNE & THE MINDBENDER	ROCK & ROLL GROUP	BRIAN CANNON MANAGEMENT		
		BOX 81, RUYTON, OLDHAM	MANCHESTER OL2 5DG	ENGLAND
FONTANE, CHAR	ACTRESS	870 N VINE ST #G	LOS ANGELES, CA	90038
FONTES, MONTSERRAT	WRITER	8955 BEVERLY BLVD	LOS ANGELES, CA	90048
FONTEYN, MARGOT	BALLERINA	ESTA FETA, EL SORADO 6-1140	PANAMA CITY 6	PANAMA
FONTINELL, FRANCIS J	WRITER	555 W 57TH ST #1230	NEW YORK, NY	10019
FONVIELLE, LLOYD	SCREENWRITER	8955 BEVERLY BLVD	LOS ANGELES, CA	90048
FOOKES, GARY P	PHOTOGRAPHER	12800 LACY DR	SILVER SPRING, MD	20904
FOOLS, THE	ROCK & ROLL GROUP	CASTLE MUSIC INTL		
		923 5TH AVE	NEW YORK, NY	10021
FOOT, MOIRA	ACTRESS	FOSTER, 33 ABBEY LODGE		
		PARK RD	LONDON NW8 7RJ	ENGLAND
FOOT LOOSE	RHYTHM & BLUES GROUP	108 SHARON DR	WEST MONROE, LA	71291
FOOTE, DOROTHY COOPER	SCREENWRITER	8955 BEVERLY BLVD	LOS ANGELES, CA	90048
FOOTE, HORTON	SCREENWRITER	LUCY KROLL, 390 W END AVE	NEW YORK, NY	10024
FORAKER, LOIS	ACTRESS	KOHNER, 9169 SUNSET BLVD	LOS ANGELES, CA	90069
FORAY, JUNE	ACTRESS	22745 ERWIN ST	WOODLAND HILLS, CA	91367
FORBERT, STEVE	SINGER	611 BROADWAY #822	NEW YORK, NY	10012
FORBES, BRENDA	ACTRESS	SHEPERD, BOX 607		
		SNEED'S LANDING	PALISADES, NY	10964
FORBES, BRYAN	WRITER-DIRECTOR	7 PINES, WENTWORTH	SURREY	ENGLAND
FORBES, CHRIS	ACTRESS	12060 LAUREL TERR DR	STUDIO CITY, CA	91604
FORBES, DAVID	PRODUCER	11908 VENTURA BLVD #200	STUDIO CITY, CA	91604
FORBES, DON	TV DIRECTOR	1347 MILLER DR	LOS ANGELES, CA	90069
FORBES, GORDON	SPORTS WRITER	POST OFFICE BOX 500	WASHINGTON, DC	20044
FORCE, MIKE	WRESTLER	NATIONAL WRESTLING ALLIANCE		
		JIM CROCKETT PROMOTIONS		
		421 BRIARBEND DR	CHARLOTTE, NC	28209
FORCE, THE	ROCK & ROLL GROUP	POST OFFICE BOX 272	LONDON N20 0B4	ENGLAND
FORCE M D'S	RAP GROUP	HUSH PRODS, 231 W 58TH ST	NEW YORK, NY	10019
FORCUCCI, MICHAEL S	NEWS CORRESPONDENT	527 N ARMISTEAD ST	ALEXANDRIA, VA	22312
FORD, "TENNESEE" ERNIE	SINGER	255 MATHACHE DR	PORTOLA VALLEY, CA	94025
FORD, BETTE	ACTRESS	9220 SUNSET BLVD #625	LOS ANGELES, CA	90069
FORD, BETTY	FIRST LADY-AUTHOR	POST OFFICE BOX 927	RANCHO MIRAGE, CA	92270
FORD, CONSTANCE	ACTRESS	244 E 53RD ST	NEW YORK, NY	10022
FORD, DEREK JOHN	FILM WRITER-DIRECTOR	BEELINE FILMS, BEELEIGH	ESSEX	ENGLAND
FORD, DOROTHY	ACTRESS	BANE, 13906 FIJI WY #344	MARINA DEL REY, CA	90292
FORD, EILEEN	TALENT AGENT	344 E 59TH ST	NEW YORK, NY	10022
FORD, FRANKIE	SINGER-SONGWRITER	POST OFFICE BOX 1830	NEW ORLEANS, LA	70053
FORD, GERALD R	PRESIDENT-AUTHOR	POST OFFICE BOX 927	RANCHO MIRAGE, CA	92270
FORD, GLENN	ACTOR	911 OXFORD WY	BEVERLY HILLS, CA	90210

Name	Occupation	Address	City	Zip
FORD, HARRISON	ACTOR	POST OFFICE BOX 5617	BEVERLY HILLS, CA	90210
FORD, JANE E	NEWS CORRESPONDENT	3009 TYSON LN	BOWIE, MD	20715
FORD, JEAN H	TV WRITER	8955 BEVERLY BLVD	LOS ANGELES, CA	90048
FORD, JESSE H	WRITER	8955 BEVERLY BLVD	LOS ANGELES, CA	90048
FORD, LITA	SINGER	8383 WILSHIRE BLVD #546	BEVERLY HILLS, CA	90211
FORD, LOUIS	DIRECTOR	2111 JEFFERSON DAVIS HW	ARLINGTON, VA	22202
FORD, MELISSA MATHISON	SCREENWRITER	SEE - MATHESON, MELISSA FORD		
FORD, MICHAEL	NEWS CORRESPONDENT	218 5TH ST, NE	WASHINGTON, DC	20002
FORD, MICK	ACTOR	47 GLENGARRY RD, DULWICH	LONDON SE22 8QA	ENGLAND
FORD, NANCY	TV WRITER	555 W 57TH ST #1230	NEW YORK, NY	10019
FORD, OLGA M	WRITER	555 W 57TH ST #1230	NEW YORK, NY	10019
FORD, PENNYE	SINGER	TOTAL EXPERIENCE RECORDS CO		
		1800 N ARGYLE AVE, 3RD FLOOR	HOLLYWOOD, CA	90028
FORD, PETER SHANN	BROADCAST JOURNALIST	GELLER MGMT, 250 W 57TH ST	NEW YORK, NY	10019
FORD, RANDALL	SAXOPHONIST	1419 CLIFTON LN	NASHVILLE, TN	37215
FORD, REBAKKAH S	WRITER	1949 BUCKINGHAM RD	LOS ANGELES, CA	90016
FORD, RICHARD	WRITER	555 W 57TH ST #1230	NEW YORK, NY	10019
FORD, RITA D	NEWS CORRESPONDENT	8750 GEORGIA AVE #1507-B	SILVER SPRING, MD	20910
FORD, ROBERT C	WRITER-PRODUCER	281 LAMBERT RD	NEW CANAAN, CT	06840
FORD, RUTH	ACTRESS	THE DAKOTA, 1 W 72ND ST	NEW YORK, NY	10023
FORD, SALLY	PIANIST	308 WHITE OAK	HARTSVILLE, TN	37074
FORD, SAM	NEWS CORRESPONDENT	CBS NEWS, 2020 "M" ST, NW	WASHINGTON, DC	20036
FORD, SEAN J	NEWS CORRESPONDENT	5851 QUANTRELL AVE #402	ALEXANDRIA, VA	22312
FORD, STEPHEN	ACTOR	ROUTE #1, BOX 90	SAN LUIS OBISPO, CA	93401
FORD, STEVEN	MUSICIAN	1708 MARTIN ST	NASHVILLE, TN	37210
FORD, TERENCE	ACTOR	9255 SUNSET BLVD #510	LOS ANGELES, CA	90069
FORD, THOMAS I	WRITER-PRODUCER	PARK DR S	RYE, NY	10580
FORD, TONY A	TV WRITER	8955 BEVERLY BLVD	LOS ANGELES, CA	90048
FORD, WHITEY	BASEBALL	38 SCHOOLHOUSE LN	LAKE SUCCESS, NY	11020
FORD, WILLIAM	TALENT AGENT	119 W 57TH ST #901	NEW YORK, NY	10019
FORDE, EUGENE	DIRECTOR-ACTOR	155 E ALTA GREEN	PORT HUENEME, CA	93041
FORECAST	JAZZ GROUP	POST OFFICE BOX 1556	GAINESVILLE, FL	32602
FOREIGNER	ROCK & ROLL GROUP	E S "BUD" PRAGER MANAGEMENT		
		1790 BROADWAY, PENTHOUSE	NEW YORK, NY	10019
FOREMAN, DEBRA	ACTRESS	1888 CENTURY PARK E #1400	LOS ANGELES, CA	90067
FOREMAN, GEORGE	BOXER	6 W RIVERCREST DR	HOUSTON, TX	77042
FOREMAN, JOHN	FILM PRODUCER	TVI, 517 W 35TH ST	NEW YORK, NY	10001
FOREMAN, STEPHEN H	WRITER-PRODUCER	405 E 54TH ST #9-D	NEW YORK, NY	10022
FORESTER, DAVID	CONDUCTOR	11593 KLING ST	NORTH HOLLYWOOD, CA	91602
FORESTER SISTERS, THE	C & W GROUP	128 VOLUNTEER DR	HENDERSONVILLE, TN	37075
FORGIONE, BOB N	DIRECTOR	12 W 37TH ST	NEW YORK, NY	10018
FORGUSON, RICKY	GUITARIST	600 WHISPERING HILLS DR	NASHVILLE, TN	37211
FORKUM, WILLIAM	DRUMMER	2921 WINGATE AVE	NASHVILLE, TN	37211
FORMA, WARREN	WRITER	555 W 57TH ST #1230	NEW YORK, NY	10019
FORMAN, JOHN	FILM PRODUCER	ICM, 40 W 57TH ST	NEW YORK, NY	10019
FORMAN, MILOS	FILM DIRECTOR	555 MADISON AVE #2700	NEW YORK, NY	10020
FORMAN, ROBERT	WRITER	555 W 57TH ST #1230	NEW YORK, NY	10019
FORMAN, SIR DENIS	TV EXECUTIVE	GRANADA TV, 36 GOLDEN SQ	LONDON W1	ENGLAND
FORMAN, STEPHEN L	WRITER	555 W 57TH ST #1230	NEW YORK, NY	10019
FORMAN, TOM	CARTOONIST	5755 RAINBOW HILL	AGOURA, CA	91301
FORMICA, SALVATORE EDWARD	DIRECTOR	12704 MONTCLAIR DR	SILVER SPRING, MD	20904
FORMICOLA, FIL	ACTOR	6000 COCOS DR	LOS ANGELES, CA	90068
FORMULA 5	SOUL GROUP	JALEM PRODS, 4512 W 30TH ST	LOS ANGELES, CA	90016
FORNASARY FAMILY, THE	ACROBATS	POST OFFICE BOX 87	WEST LEBANON, NY	12195
FORNES, MARIA	PLAYWRIGHT	1 SHERIDAN SQ	NEW YORK, NY	10014
FORNESS, LAWRENCE	GUITARIST	POST OFFICE BOX 120974	NASHVILLE, TN	37212
FORNEY, PHILLIP	SINGER-GUITARIST	113 WESTLAWN DR	GOODLETTSVILLE, TN	37072
FORONJY, RICHARD	ACTOR	137 N SWEETZER AVE	LOS ANGELES, CA	90048
FORRELL, GENE	CONDUCTOR	3003 VAN NESS ST #W-205, NW	WASHINGTON, DC	20008
FORREST, ARTHUR	DIRECTOR-PRODUCER	10366 HOLMAN AVE	LOS ANGELES, CA	90024
FORREST, CLEMENT	SINGER	BOUVIER RECORDS, 144 S 1ST ST	BURBANK, CA	91502
FORREST, FREDERIC	ACTOR	13111 VENTURA BLVD #204	STUDIO CITY, CA	91604
FORREST, HELEN	SINGER	POST OFFICE BOX 1	TOLUCA LAKE, CA	91602
FORREST, LEW	ACTOR	BERZON, 336 E 17TH ST	COSTA MESA, CA	92627
FORREST, PHIL	MUSIC ARRANGER	2207 CABIN HILL RD	NASHVILLE, TN	37214
FORREST, STEVE	ACTOR	10620 WILKINS AVE #3	LOS ANGELES, CA	90024
FORRESTAL, ELIZABETH K	WRITER	555 W 57TH ST #1230	NEW YORK, NY	10019
FORRESTER, BOB	MUSICIAN	925 TODD PREIS DR #Z-40	NASHVILLE, TN	37221
FORRESTER, HOLGIE	ACTRESS	SCHOEMAN, 2600 W VICTORY BLVD	BURBANK, CA	91505
FORRESTER, HOWDY	VIOLINIST	925 TODD PREIS DR #Z-40	NASHVILLE, TN	37221
FORRESTER, JOE	GUITARIST	4341 THOMAS DR #D-19	PANAMA CITY BEACH, FL	32407
FORRESTER, LARRY	TV WRITER-PRODUCER	MEANWYLE BAKAT		
		4715 VANALDEN AVE	TARZANA, CA	91356
FORRESTER, MAUREEN	CONTRALTO	SHAW CONCERTS, 1995 BROADWAY	NEW YORK, NY	10023
FORRESTER, RHETT	SINGER	POST OFFICE BOX 252	AUBURN, NY	13021
FORRESTER, STEPHEN	NEWS CORRESPONDENT	121 2ND ST, SE	WASHINGTON, DC	20002
FORRESTER, WILENE	ACCORDIONIST	925 TODD PREIS DR #Z-40	NASHVILLE, TN	37221
FORSBERG, ROLF	WRITER-PRODUCER	380 TOYON RD	SIERRA MADRE, CA	91024
FORSLUND, CONSTANCE	ACTRESS	ICM, 8899 BEVERLY BLVD	LOS ANGELES, CA	90048
FORST, JUDITH	MEZZO-SOPRANO	CAMI, 165 W 57TH ST	NEW YORK, NY	10019
FORST-LARSEN, LISSER	BODYBUILDER	KANINGARDSVEJ 53	2830 VIRUM	DENMARK
FORSTADT, REBECCA	ACTRESS	9601 WILSHIRE BLVD #GL-11	BEVERLY HILLS, CA	90210

HARRISON FORD

FABIAN FORTE

BOB FOSSE

MICHAEL J. FOX

PETER FRAMPTON

ARLENE FRANCIS

CONNIE FRANCIS

GENIE FRANCIS

JAMES FRANCISCUS

Name	Occupation	Address	City	Zip/Country
FORSTATER, MARK	FILM PRODUCER	42-A DEVONSHIRE CLOSE		
		PORTLAND PL	LONDON W1 N1LL	ENGLAND
FORSTER, ROBERT	ACTOR	108 MAC DOUGALL ST #2-D	NEW YORK, NY	10012
FORSTMAN, PAUL	GUITARIST	3618 CENTRAL AVE	NASHVILLE, TN	37205
FORSYTH, BILL	FILM DIRECTOR	LAKE FILM PRODS, 20 WINTON DR	GLASGOW G-12	SCOTLAND
FORSYTH, BRIGIT	ACTRESS	CONWAY, EAGLE HOUSE		
		109 JERMYN ST	LONDON W1	ENGLAND
FORSYTH, BRUCE	TV PERSONALITY	STRALDARRAN, WENTWORTH DR		
		VIRGINIA WATER	SURREY	ENGLAND
FORSYTH, ROSEMARY	ACTRESS	1591 BENEDICT CANYON DR	BEVERLY HILLS, CA	90210
FORSYTHE, CHARLES	THEATER PRODUCER	1841 BROADWAY	NEW YORK, NY	10023
FORSYTHE, ERIC	ACTOR	152 SHAWNEE RD	ARDMORE, PA	19003
FORSYTHE, FREDERICK	WRITER	17 CONWAY ST	LONDON W1P SHL	ENGLAND
FORSYTHE, HENDERSON	ACTOR	204 ELM ST	TENAFLY, NJ	07670
FORSYTHE, JOHN	ACTOR	14215 SUNSET BLVD	PACIFIC PALISADES, CA	90272
FORTE, CHET	TV DIRECTOR	3 GLENWOOD DR	SADDLE RIVER, NJ	07458
FORTE, FABIAN	ACTOR-SINGER	11806 MOORPARK ST #H	STUDIO CITY, CA	91604
FORTE, WILLIAM	DRUMMER	6535 PREMIER DR #H-1	NASHVILLE, TN	37209
FORTNER, ROBERT	MUSICIAN	1060 PENINSULA	GALLATIN, TN	37066
FORTNEY, LINDA	TV WRITER	8955 BEVERLY BLVD	LOS ANGELES, CA	90048
FORTSON, EDWIN B, JR	WRITER	400 S JUNE ST	LOS ANGELES, CA	90020
FORTUNATE SONS, THE	ROCK & ROLL GROUP	9 RIDGEMONT RD, SAINT ALBANS	HERTSHIRE	ENGLAND
FORTUNATO, CHRIS	WRITER	8955 BEVERLY BLVD	LOS ANGELES, CA	90048
FORTUNATO, D'ANNA	MEZZO-SOPRANO	59 E 54TH ST #81	NEW YORK, NY	10022
FORTUNE, GEORGE	BASSO-BARITONE	111 W 57TH ST #1209	NEW YORK, NY	10019
FORTUNE, MICKEY	GUITARIST	6017 PLANTATION DR	HERMITAGE, TN	37076
45 GRAVE	ROCK & ROLL GROUP	1626 N WILCOX #358	HOLLYWOOD, CA	90028
FORWARD, ROBERT H, SR	WRITER-PRODUCER	550 S BARRINGTON AVE	LOS ANGELES, CA	90049
FORWARD, WILLIAM	ACTOR	550 S BARRINGTON AVE	LOS ANGELES, CA	90049
FOSHKO, ALLAN	DIRECTOR	STUDIO, 305 W 52ND ST	NEW YORK, NY	10019
FOSHKO, ROBERT	WRITER	3710 HAYVENHURST AVE	ENCINO, CA	91316
FOSS, LUKAS	CONDUCTOR	59 E 54TH ST #81	NEW YORK, NY	10022
FOSSELIUS, ERNIE	WRITER	8955 BEVERLY BLVD	LOS ANGELES, CA	90048
FOSSET, APRIL	SWAPOLE ACT	POST OFFICE BOX 87	WEST LEBANON, NY	12195
FOSSET FAMILY, THE	SWAYPOLE ACT	POST OFFICE BOX 87	WEST LEBANON, NY	12195
FOSTER, ALAN D	SCREENWRITER	8955 BEVERLY BLVD	LOS ANGELES, CA	90048
FOSTER, AMI	ACTRESS	3575 W CAHUENGA BLVD #320	LOS ANGELES, CA	90068
FOSTER, BARRY	ACTOR	AL PARKER, 55 PARK LN	LONDON W1	ENGLAND
FOSTER, BENNETT	TV WRITER	8955 BEVERLY BLVD	LOS ANGELES, CA	90048
FOSTER, BILL R	TV DIRECTOR	12325 MOORPARK ST	STUDIO CITY, CA	91604
FOSTER, C MICHAEL	GUITARIST	ROUTE #5, CHEROKEE RD	GALLATIN, TN	37066
FOSTER, CASSANDRA	ACTRESS	11574 IOWA AVE #105	LOS ANGELES, CA	90025
FOSTER, CHRISTINE	TV EXECUTIVE	GROUP W PRODUCTIONS CO		
		70 UNIVERSAL CITY PLAZA	UNIVERSAL CITY, CA	91608
FOSTER, DAN, JR	SINGER-GUITARIST	ROUTE #1, BOX 104	SUMMERTOWN, TN	38483
FOSTER, DAVID	FILM PRODUCER	719 N PALM DR	BEVERLY HILLS, CA	90210
FOSTER, DAVID	TV DIRECTOR-PRODUCER	KINGS COTTAGE, THE SQUARE		
		COSTOCK, NEAR LOUGHBOROUGH	LEICESTERSHIRE LE12 6X	ENGLAND
FOSTER, DAVID W	COMP-ARR-PROD-PIANO	10351 WHIPPLE ST	NORTH HOLLYWOOD, CA	91602
FOSTER, FLOYD L, JR	ACTOR	1830 S SAINT ANDREWS PL #8	LOS ANGELES, CA	90019
FOSTER, FRANCES	ACTRESS	146 E 49TH ST	NEW YORK, NY	10019
FOSTER, GEORGE	BASEBALL	POST OFFICE BOX 11098	GREENWICH, CT	06830
FOSTER, IRENE	PIANIST	4016 IVY DR	NASHVILLE, TN	37216
FOSTER, JAMES E	NEWS CORRESPONDENT	8110 DAYTON ST	LORTON, VA	22079
FOSTER, JEAN RENEE	ACTRESS	431 N SYCAMORE AVE #103	LOS ANGELES, CA	90036
FOSTER, JIM	SINGER	41 BRITAIN ST #200	TORONTO, ONT	CANADA
FOSTER, JODIE	ACTRESS	3700 WILSHIRE BLVD #900	LOS ANGELES, CA	90010
FOSTER, JOHNNY	GUITARIST	4977 EDMONDSON PIKE	NASHVILLE, TN	37211
FOSTER, KAREN P	NEWS CORRESPONDENT	2030 "M" ST, NW	WASHINGTON, DC	20036
FOSTER, KIMBERLY	ACTRESS	1717 N HIGHLAND AVE #90	LOS ANGELES, CA	90028
FOSTER, LAWRENCE	CONDUCTOR	ICM, 40 W 57TH ST	NEW YORK, NY	10019
FOSTER, LAWRENCE D	NEWS CORRESPONDENT	1656 PRESTON RD	ALEXANDRIA, VA	22302
FOSTER, LLOYD DAVID	SINGER	POST OFFICE BOX 1373	LEWISVILLE, TX	75067
FOSTER, MEG	ACTRESS	211 S BEVERLY DR #201	BEVERLY HILLS, CA	90212
FOSTER, NORAH	ACTRESS	4301 KLING ST #25	BURBANK, CA	91505
FOSTER, ORVILLE	COMPOSER	334 E OCEAN BLVD #305	LONG BEACH, CA	90802
FOSTER, RICHARD	NEWS CORRESPONDENT	5315 42ND ST, NW	WASHINGTON, DC	20015
FOSTER, RICHARD S	NEWS CORRESPONDENT	400 N CAPITOL ST, NW	WASHINGTON, DC	20001
FOSTER, ROBERT O	TV WRITER-DIRECTOR	8955 BEVERLY BLVD	LOS ANGELES, CA	90048
FOSTER, ROBERT W	WRITER-PRODUCER	1005 N CROFT AVE #6	LOS ANGELES, CA	90069
FOSTER, RON	ACTOR	8833 SUNSET BLVD #308	LOS ANGELES, CA	90069
FOSTER, SUSAN	ACTRESS	4721 LAUREL CANYON BLVD #211	NORTH HOLLYWOOD, CA	91607
FOSTER, THOMAS E	NEWS CORRESPONDENT	8 VALLEY LAKE PL	COCKEYSVILLE, MD	21030
FOTI, JACQUES	ACTOR	7461 BEVERLY BLVD #400	LOS ANGELES, CA	90036
FOTOMAKER	ROCK & ROLL GROUP	S L HOOD, 719 GREENWICH ST	NEW YORK, NY	10014
FOTRE, VINCENT G	WRITER	1227 ROBERTO LN	LOS ANGELES, CA	90077
FOTT, SOLIE	VIOLINIST	117 TALTON DR	CLARKSVILLE, TN	37040
FOTY, THOMAS C	NEWS CORRESPONDENT	2001 N ADAMS ST	ARLINGTON, VA	22201
FOUHY, EDWARD	TV EXECUTIVE	ABC-TV, NEWS DEPARTMENT		
		1717 DE SALES ST, NW	WASHINGTON, DC	20036
FOULK, ROBERT	ACTOR	9 WILLIAMSBURG LN	ROLLING HILLS, CA	90274
FOUNTAIN, PETE	CLARINETIST	AS WAS, 2 POLDRAS ST	NEW ORLEANS, LA	70140
FOUNTAINHEAD, THE	ROCK & ROLL GROUP	CHINA RECORDS COMPANY		
		27 QUEENSDALE PL	LONDON W11 4SQ	ENGLAND
FOUR ACES, THE	VOCAL GROUP	12 MARSHAL ST #8-Q	IRVINGTON, NJ	07111
FOUR FRESHMAN, THE	VOCAL GROUP	601 S RANCHO DR #C-18	LAS VEGAS, NV	89106

FOREIGNER

Dennis Elliott • Rick Wills • Lou Gramm • Mick Jones

THE FOUR TOPS

Obie Benson • Duke Fakir • Levi Stubbs • Lawrence Payton

Name	Occupation	Address	City/State	Zip
FOUR GUYS, THE	VOCAL GROUP	AUDIOGRAPH, 20 MUSIC SQUARE	NASHVILLE, TN	37203
FOUR HORSEMEN, THE	WRESTLING QUARTET	SEE - ANDERSON, ARN		
		SEE - BLANCHARD, TULLY		
		SEE - FLAIR, RIC		
		SEE - LUGER, LEX		
FOUR LADS, THE	VOCAL GROUP	32500 CONCORD DR #221	MADISON HEIGHTS, MI	48071
FOUR SEASONS, THE	ROCK & ROLL GROUP	MARS, 168 ORCHID DR	PEARL RIVER, NY	10965
FOUR TOPS, THE	VOCAL GROUP	200 W 51ST ST #1410	NEW YORK, NY	10019
FOURNIER, EUGENE A	TV WRITER	8955 BEVERLY BLVD	LOS ANGELES, CA	90048
FOURNIER, RIFT	WRITER-PRODUCER	10535 WILSHIRE BLVD #610	LOS ANGELES, CA	90024
FOUSER, DONALD B	DIRECTOR-PRODUCER	19 N MAIN ST	IPSWICH, MA	01938
FOUTS, KENNETH A, JR	TV DIRECTOR	DGA, 110 W 57TH ST	NEW YORK, NY	10019
FOUTZ, ANTHONY	WRITER	8955 BEVERLY BLVD	LOS ANGELES, CA	90048
FOWLDS, DEREK	ACTOR	BURNETT, 42 GRAFTON HOUSE		
		2-3 GOLDEN SQ	LONDON W1	ENGLAND
FOWLER, CHRISTINA	ACTRESS	10118 ALDEA AVE	NORTHRIDGE, CA	91325
FOWLER, DON	GUITAIST	ROUTE #1, BOX 159-A	PEGRAM, TN	37143
FOWLER, E T "BUBBA"	GUITARIST	POST OFFICE BOX 150	KRUM, TX	76249
FOWLER, GENE, JR	FILM DIRECTOR	7261 OUTPOST COVE DR	HOLLYWOOD, CA	90068
FOWLER, HARRY	ACTOR	ESSANAY, SAINT MARTIN'S		
		THEATRE, WEST ST	LONDON WC2	ENGLAND
FOWLER, JAMES EMMET	ACTOR	10118 ALDEA AVE	NORTHRIDGE, CA	91325
FOWLER, JOHN	CABLE EXECUTIVE	WARNER AMEX CABLE COMM		
		75 ROCKEFELLER PLAZA	NEW YORK, NY	10019
FOWLER, JOHN	TENOR	CAMI, 165 W 57TH ST	NEW YORK, NY	10019
FOWLER, MARJORIE	TV WRITER	9200 SUNSET BLVD #531	LOS ANGELES, CA	90069
FOWLER, MARK S	COMMUNICATIONS EXEC	FCC, 1919 "M" ST, NW	WASHINGTON, DC	20554
FOWLER, ROBERT	FILM DIRECTOR	ICM, 8899 BEVERLY BLVD	LOS ANGELES, CA	90048
FOWLER, RODNEY	WRITER	555 W 57TH ST #1230	NEW YORK, NY	10019
FOWLES, GLENYS	SOPRANO	HILLYER, 250 W 57TH ST	NEW YORK, NY	10107
FOWLES, JOHN	NOVELIST	ASA, 52 FLORAL ST	LONDON WC2	ENGLAND
FOWLEY, DOUGLAS V	ACTOR	969 HILGARD AVE	LOS ANGELES, CA	90024
FOX, ALAN	WRESTLER	NATIONAL WRESTLING ALLIANCE		
		JIM CROCKETT PROMOTIONS		
		421 BRIARBEND DR	CHARLOTTE, NC	28209
FOX, ANNE-MARIE	MODEL	MODELS & PROMOTIONS AGENCY		
		8560 SUNSET BLVD, 10TH FLOOR	LOS ANGELES, CA	90069
FOX, ARNIM "CURLY"	GUITARIST	POST OFFICE BOX 157	GRAYSVILLE, TN	37338
FOX, BARBARA	SOPRANO	1776 BROADWAY #504	NEW YORK, NY	10019
FOX, BERNARD	ACTOR	6736 LAUREL CANYON BLVD #306	NORTH HOLLYWOOD, CA	91606
FOX, BERTIL	BODYBUILDER	POST OFFICE BOX 531	CANOGA PARK, CA	91305
FOX, CHARLES	COMPOSER-CONDUCTOR	16231 MEADOW RIDGE WY	ENCINO, CA	91316
FOX, DAVID	TV DIRECTOR	46 W 65TH ST	NEW YORK, NY	10023
FOX, DOLLY	ACTRESS	211 S BEVERLY DR #201	BEVERLY HILLS, CA	90212
FOX, DONALD R	PHOTOGRAPHER	19512 BODMER AVE	POOLESVILLE, MD	20837
FOX, EDWARD	ACTOR	25 MAIDA AVE	LONDON W2	ENGLAND
FOX, FRED, S, JR	TV WRITER	4217 EMPRESS AVE	ENCINO, CA	91436
FOX, JACK D	WRITER	8955 BEVERLY BLVD	LOS ANGELES, CA	90048
FOX, JAMES	ACTOR	3 SPENCER PARK RD	LONDON SW18	ENGLAND
FOX, JERRY L	GUITARIST	2408-B DALEBROOK CT	NASHVILLE, TN	37206
FOX, JOHN G	DIRECTOR-PRODUCER	215 W 91ST ST	NEW YORK, NY	10023
FOX, JOHN G	WRITER	555 W 57TH ST #1230	NEW YORK, NY	10019
FOX, JONATHAN CHARLES	ACTOR	120 S VICTORY BLVD #104	BURBANK, CA	91502
FOX, JUDY E	NEWS CORRESPONDENT	10951 DEBORAH DR	POTOMAC, MD	20854
FOX, JUDY SCOTT	TALENT AGENT	151 S EL CAMINO DR	BEVERLY HILLS, CA	90212
FOX, KENT	SINGER	POST OFFICE BOX 2271	PALM SPRINGS, CA	92263
FOX, LYNN G, JR	PIANIST	ROUTE #6	FRANKLIN, TN	37064
FOX, M BERNARD	WRITER-PRODUCER	DGA, 7950 SUNSET BLVD	LOS ANGELES, CA	90046
FOX, MAGGIE	WRITER	555 W 57TH ST #1230	NEW YORK, NY	10019
FOX, MARILYN ELAINE	ACTRESS	141 1/2 OCEAN PARK BLVD	SANTA MONICA, CA	90405
FOX, MAXINE	THEATER PRODUCER	1501 BROADWAY	NEW YORK, NY	10036
FOX, MICHAEL	ACTOR	8485 MELROSE PL #E	LOS ANGELES, CA	90069
FOX, MICHAEL	TV DIRECTOR	6425 NAGLE AVE	VAN NUYS, CA	91401
FOX, MICHAEL J	ACTOR-DIRECTOR	9255 SUNSET BLVD #710	LOS ANGELES, CA	90069
FOX, MICHAEL S	WRITER	10356 ASHTON AVE	LOS ANGELES, CA	90024
FOX, NORM C	TV WRITER	8955 BEVERLY BLVD	LOS ANGELES, CA	90048
FOX, PETER	ACTOR	228 23RD ST	MANHATTAN BEACH, CA	90266
FOX, RANDY BRENT	DRUMMER	ROUTE #6	FRANKLIN, TN	37064
FOX, ROY	DRUMMER	ROUTE #6	FRANKLIN, TN	37064
FOX, SAMANTHA	SINGER-MODEL	RCA RECORDS COMPANY		
		1133 AVE OF THE AMERICAS	NEW YORK, NY	10036
FOX, SONNY	TV PRODUCER	1447 N KINGS RD	LOS ANGELES, CA	90069
FOX, STEVE	NEWS CORRESPONDENT	ABC NEWS, 7 W 66TH ST	NEW YORK, NY	10023
FOX, TERRY	WRITER	8955 BEVERLY BLVD	LOS ANGELES, CA	90048
FOX, THELMA GRACE	PIANIST	9253 1/2 HILL HAVEN DR	HOPKINSVILLE, KY	42240
FOX, THEODORE	WRITER	8955 BEVERLY BLVD	LOS ANGELES, CA	90048
FOX, WALTER	SCREENWRITER	8955 BEVERLY BLVD	LOS ANGELES, CA	90048
FOX, WILLIAM	WRITER	555 W 57TH ST #1230	NEW YORK, NY	10019
FOX, WILLIAM	DIRECTOR	15 EDWARD RD, BROMLEY	KENT	ENGLAND
FOX BROTHERS, THE	GOSPEL GROUP	FRONTIER, 422 W HIGH AVE	NEW PHILADELPHIA, OH	44663
FOX-HOOVER, NANCY	SOPRANO	POST OFFICE BOX 27539	PHILADELPHIA, PA	19118
FOXWELL, IVAN	FILM PRODUCER	CLEMENT HOUSE, 99 ALDWYCH	LONDON WC2 B4JY	ENGLAND
FOXWORTH, ROBERT	ACTOR	1230 BENEDICT CANYON DR	BEVERLY HILLS, CA	90210
FOXX	VOCAL TRIO	MALACO RECORDS COMPANY		
		3023 W NORTHSIDE DR	JACKSON, MS	39213

Name	Occupation	Address	City	Zip
FOXX, ELIZABETH	ACTRESS	3907 W ALAMDEA AVE #101	BURBANK, CA	91505
FOXX, REDD	ACTOR-COMEDIAN	933 N LA BREA AVE	LOS ANGELES, CA	90038
FOXY	SOUL-DISCO GROUP	4100 W FLAGLER ST #B-2	MIAMI, FL	33134
FOY, LOUIS	NEWS CORRESPONDENT	1612 "K" ST #400, NW	WASHINGTON, DC	20006
FOY, NANCY	CASTING DIRECTOR	POST OFFICE BOX 5718	SHERMAN OAKS, CA	91403
FOY, NANCY	ACTRESS	3424 TROY DR	LOS ANGELES, CA	90068
FRABOTTA, DON	ACTOR	5036 RIVERTON AVE #2	NORTH HOLLYWOOD, CA	91601
FRABOTTA, JUDITH	NEWS CORRESPONDENT	839 LINDEN CIR	TAKOMA PARK, MD	20912
FRACHON, ALAIN	NEWS CORRESPONDENT	2711 ORDWAY ST, NW	WASHINGTON, DC	20008
FRACHTENBERG, EMANUEL	WRITER	555 W 57TH ST #1230	NEW YORK, NY	10019
FRADON, DANA	CARTOONIST	POST OFFICE BOX 4203	NEW YORK, NY	10017
FRADON, RAMONA	CARTOONIST	TRIBUNE MEDIA SERVICES		
		64 E CONCORD ST	ORLANDO, FL	32801
FRAENKEL, WOLFGANG	COMPOSER-CONDUCTOR	143 S LAPEER DR	LOS ANGELES, CA	90048
FRAGER, MALCOLM	PIANIST	CAMI, 165 W 57TH ST	NEW YORK, NY	10019
FRAGOYANNIS, PETER	NEWS CORRESPONDENT	400 N CAPITOL ST, NW	WASHINGTON, DC	20001
FRAILEY, FREDERICK W	NEWS CORRESPONDENT	821 S LEE ST	ALEXANDRIA, VA	22014
FRAKER, WILLIAM A	CINEMATOGRAPHER	POST OFFICE BOX 2230	HOLLYWOOD, CA	90078
FRAKES, JONATHAN	ACTOR	211 S BEVERLY DR #201	BEVERLY HILLS, CA	90212
FRALEY, JOSEPH REX	SCREENWRITER	8955 BEVERLY BLVD	LOS ANGELES, CA	90048
FRAM, ALAN	NEWS CORRESPONDENT	2939 VAN NESS ST #938, NW	WASHINGTON, DC	20008
FRAME, JOHN A	NEWS CORRESPONDENT	5617 JOHNSON AVE	BETHESDA, MD	20817
FRAME, PAMELA	CELLIST	AFFILIATE ARTISTS, INC		
		37 W 65TH ST, 6TH FLOOR	NEW YORK, NY	10023
FRAME, PETER W	CABLE EXECUTIVE	HOME BOX OFFICE PICTURES		
		1100 AVE OF THE AMERICAS	NEW YORK, NY	10036
FRAMPTON, BETSY K	PHOTOGRAPHER	3411 36TH ST, NW	WASHINGTON, DC	20016
FRAMPTON, MARC	KEYBOARDIST	POST OFFICE BOX 12403		
		NORTH SIDE STATION	ATLANTA, GA	30355
FRAMPTON, PETER	SINGER-GUITARIST	HIT & RUN MUSIC, LTD		
		81-83 WALTON ST	LONDON SW3 2HR	ENGLAND
FRANCARRO & ESTRALITA	AERIAL CRADEL ACT	HALL, 138 FROG HOLLOW RD	CHURCHVILLE, PA	18966
FRANCAVILLO, ROBERT L	MUSIC ARRANGER	6700 CABOT DR #O-14	NASHVILLE, TN	37209
FRANCE, BOYD	NEWS CORRESPONDENT	10304 SUMMIT AVE	KENSINGTON, MD	20795
FRANCE, MILIAN B	WRITER	8955 BEVERLY BLVD	LOS ANGELES, CA	90048
FRANCES, HELENE	ACTRESS-PRODUCER	8721 SUNSET BLVD #102	LOS ANGELES, CA	90069
FRANCESCA, ALBA	ACTRESS	4455 LOS FELIZ BLVD #802	LOS ANGELES, CA	90027
FRANCESCH, HOMERO	PIANIST	HILLYER, 250 W 57TH ST	NEW YORK, NY	10107
FRANCHINI, BRUCE	TV DIRECTOR	4600 VIA MARINA #107	MARINA DEL REY, CA	90292
FRANCHOT, RICHARD	DIRECTOR	1146 HACIENDA PL	LOS ANGELES, CA	90069
FRANCINE, ANNE	ACTRESS	75 CHARLES ST	NEW YORK, NY	10014
FRANCIOSA, TONY	ACTOR	567 TIGERTAIL RD	LOS ANGELES, CA	90049
FRANCIS, AL	CINEMATOGRAPHER	POST OFFICE BOX 2230	HOLLYWOOD, CA	90078
FRANCIS, ANNE	ACTRESS	POST OFFICE BOX 5417	SANTA BARBARA, CA	93103
FRANCIS, ARLENE	ACTRESS	RITZ TOWERS, 59TH & PARK AVE	NEW YORK, NY	10021
FRANCIS, BARBARA	WRITER	8955 BEVERLY BLVD	LOS ANGELES, CA	90048
FRANCIS, BEV	BODYBUILDER	POST OFFICE BOX 250	GLEN OAKS, NY	11004
FRANCIS, CONNIE	SINGER-ACTRESS	1975 HOWARD AVE	POTTSVILLE, PA	17901
FRANCIS, DEREK	ACTOR	9 VINEYARD HILL RD	LONDON SW19	ENGLAND
FRANCIS, FREDDIE	TV DIRECTOR	58 WHEATLANDS, HESTON VILLAGE	MIDDLESEX	ENGLAND
FRANCIS, FREDERICK N	NEWS CORRESPONDENT	NBC NEWS, 4001 NEBRASKA AVE, NW	WASHINGTON, DC	20016
FRANCIS, GENIE	ACTRESS	15237 MAGNOLIA BLVD #C	SHERMAN OAKS, CA	91403
FRANCIS, GILBERT D, JR	WRITER	555 W 57TH ST #1230	NEW YORK, NY	10019
FRANCIS, JAN	ACTRESS	LEADING ARTISTS, LTD		
		60 SAINT JAMES'S ST	LONDON SW1	ENGLAND
FRANCIS, JOHN	ACTOR	9255 SUNSET BLVD #505	LOS ANGELES, CA	90069
FRANCIS, KEVIN	FILM PRODUCER	TYBURN, PINEWOOD STUDIOS		
		IVER HEATH	BUCKS	ENGLAND
FRANCIS, LINDA	CASTING DIRECTOR	POST OFFICE BOX 5718	SHERMAN OAKS, CA	91403
FRANCIS, MISSY	ACTRESS	8075 W 3RD ST #303	LOS ANGELES, CA	90048
FRANCIS, POLLY	WRITER	8955 BEVERLY BLVD	LOS ANGELES, CA	90048
FRANCIS, RAYMOND	ACTOR	FRASER, 91 REGENT ST	LONDON W1R 8RU	ENGLAND
FRANCIS, TIFFANY ANN	ACTRESS	KELMAN, 7813 SUNSET BLVD	LOS ANGELES, CA	90046
FRANCIS, WILLIAM V, JR	DIRECTOR	POST OFFICE BOX 1352	NEW YORK, NY	10185
FRANCISCUS, JAMES	ACTOR	12549 ADDISON ST	NORTH HOLLYWOOD, CA	91607
FRANCK, EDWARD A	DIRECTOR-PRODUCER	136 SICKELTOWN RD	WEST NYACK, NY	10994
FRANCO, ABEL	ACTOR	8230 BEVERLY BLVD #23	LOS ANGELES, CA	90048
FRANCO, DICK	JUGGLER	HALL, 138 FROG HOLLOW RD	CHURCHVILLE, PA	18966
FRANCO, JUDITH A	NEWS CORRESPONDENT	2025 "M" ST, NW	WASHINGTON, DC	20036
FRANCONI DUO, THE	TRAPEZE ACT	HALL, 138 FROG HOLLOW RD	CHURCHVILLE, PA	18966
FRANDSEN, JON C	NEWS CORRESPONDENT	1875 NEWTON ST, NW	WASHINGTON, DC	20010
FRANGIONE, NANCY	ACTRESS	ABRAMS ARTISTS & ASSOCIATES		
		420 MADISON AVE, 14TH FLOOR	NEW YORK, NY	10017
FRANK, ALAN G	DIRECTOR	127 W 79TH ST	NEW YORK, NY	10024
FRANK, ALLAN DODDS	NEWS CORRESPONDENT	1906 S LYNN ST	ARLINGTON, VA	22202
FRANK, ALLAN L	NEWS CORRESPONDENT	8811 COLESVILLE RD #925	SILVER SPRING, MD	20910
FRANK, ASTRID	ACTOR-DIRECTOR	CCA MGMT, 4 CT LODGE		
		48 SLOANE SQ	LONDON SW1W 8AT	ENGLAND
FRANK, BEN	ACTOR	8037 HEMET PL	LOS ANGELES, CA	90046
FRANK, BOB	ACTOR	AIMEE, 13743 VICTORY BLVD	VAN NUYS, CA	91401
FRANK, CHARLES	ACTOR	900 CHAPEA RD	PASADENA, CA	91107
FRANK, CHRISTINA	ACTRESS	9777 WILSHIRE BLVD #707	BEVERLY HILLS, CA	90212
FRANK, CLAUDE	PIANIST	CAMI, 165 W 57TH ST	NEW YORK, NY	10019
FRANK, DAVID M	CONDUCTOR	2971 BRIAR KNOLL DR	LOS ANGELES, CA	90046
FRANK, DEBRA	TV WRITER	9300 WILSHIRE BLVD #410	BEVERLY HILLS, CA	90212

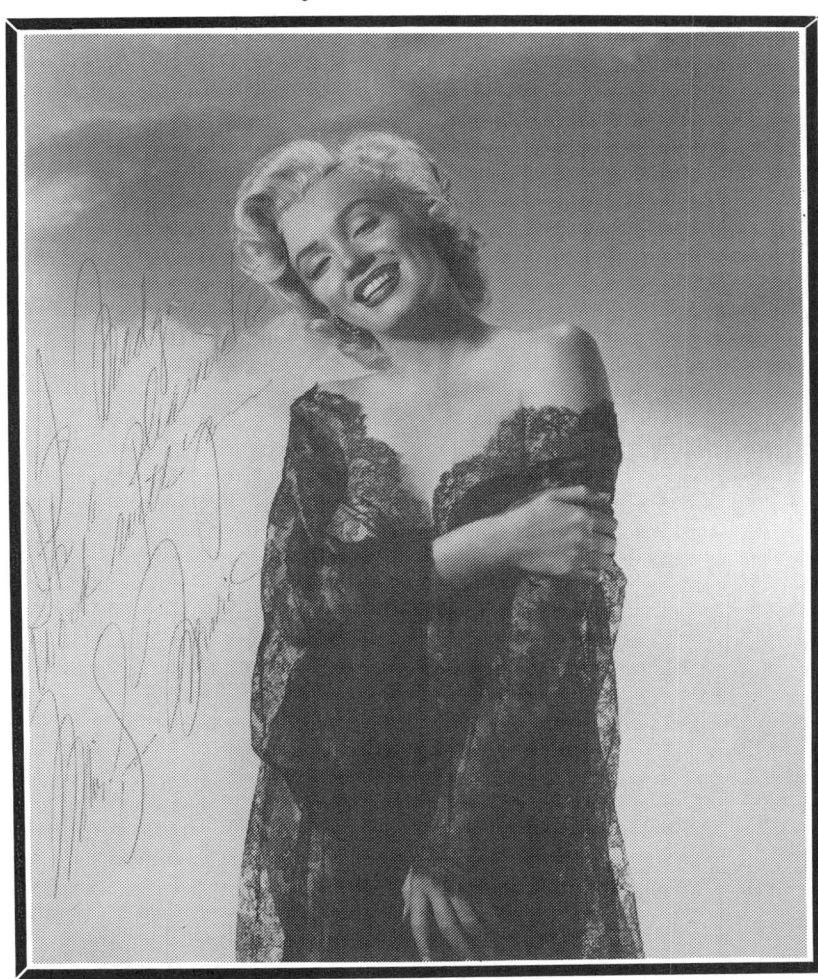

FRANK, GAIL E	DIRECTOR-PRODUCER	360 E 55TH ST	NEW YORK, NY	10022
FRANK, GARY	ACTOR	323 S ANITA AVE	LOS ANGELES, CA	90049
FRANK, HARRIET, JR	SCREENWRITER	8955 BEVERLY BLVD	LOS ANGELES, CA	90048
FRANK, JACQUELINE	NEWS CORRESPONDENT	2907 S DINWIDDIE ST	ARLINGTON, VA	22206
FRANK, JOANNA	ACTRESS	1124 N LARRABEE ST	LOS ANGELES, CA	90069
FRANK, JOSEPH	TENOR	CAMI, 165 W 57TH ST	NEW YORK, NY	10019
FRANK, LAWRENCE	PHOTOGRAPHER	784 COLUMBUS AVE	NEW YORK, NY	10025
FRANK, MELVIN	FILM WRITER-DIRECTOR	3859 MANDEVILLE CANYON RD	LOS ANGELES, CA	90049
FRANK, MILO	WRITER-PRODUCER	1125 ANTELO DR	BEVERLY HILLS, CA	90210
FRANK, MORRY H	WRITER	8955 BEVERLY BLVD	LOS ANGELES, CA	90048
FRANK, PHIL	CARTOONIST	NEWS AMERICA SYNDICATE		
		1703 KAISER AVE	IRVINE, CA	92714
FRANK, REUBEN	TV EXECUTIVE	NBC TELEVISION NETWORK		
		30 ROCKEFELLER PLAZA	NEW YORK, NY	10112
FRANK, RICHARD S	NEWS CORRESPONDENT	5111 WESSLING LN	BETHESDA, MD	20814
FRANK, SANFORD J	WRITER	555 W 57TH ST #1230	NEW YORK, NY	10019
FRANK, SELIG	TV DIRECTOR	10331 RIVERSIDE DR #103	NORTH HOLLYWOOD, CA	91602
FRANK, SHERMAN	CONDUCTOR	47 MARGARET CT	TOMS RIVER, NJ	08753
FRANK, TONY	ACTOR	9744 WILSHIRE BLVD #206	BEVERLY HILLS, CA	90212
FRANK, WILLIAM H	NEWS CORRESPONDENT	1810 SANFORD RD	SILVER SPRING, MD	20902
FRANKAU, JOHN	TV DIRECTOR-PRODUCER	ROGER HANCOCK, 8 WATERLOO PL	LONDON SW1Y 4AW	ENGLAND
FRANKE, KEITH	WRESTLER	SEE - ADONIS, ADORABLE ADRIAN		
FRANKEL, ART	ACTOR	8721 SUNSET BLVD #202	LOS ANGELES, CA	90069
FRANKEL, CYRIL	ACTOR	KRUGER, 22 MORLEY HOUSE		
		314 REGENT ST	LONDON W1	ENGLAND
FRANKEL, DORIS	WRITER	555 W 57TH ST #1230	NEW YORK, NY	10019
FRANKEL, ERNEST	WRITER-PRODUCER	19501 ROSITA ST	TARZANA, CA	91536
FRANKEL, JOHN	WRESTLER	SEE - TATUM, JOHN "HOLLYWOOD"		
FRANKEL, MAX	COLUMNIST	N Y TIMES, 229 W 43RD ST	NEW YORK, NY	10036
FRANKEN, AL	COMEDIAN-WRITER	10000 SANTA MONICA BLVD #305	LOS ANGELES, CA	90067
FRANKEN, OWEN	PHOTOGRAPHER	61 W 8TH ST	NEW YORK, NY	10011
FRANKEN, ROBERT E	NEWS CORRESPONDENT	324 4TH ST, SE	WASHINGTON, DC	20036
FRANKEN, STEVE	ACTOR	3704 WHITESPEAK DR	SHERMAN OAKS, CA	91403
FRANKENHEIMER, JOHN	DIRECTOR-PRODUCER	101 MALIBU COLONY DR	MALIBU, CA	90265
FRANKES, GEORGEOUS KEITH	WRESTLER	SEE - ADONIS, ADORABLE ADRIAN		
FRANKES, KEITH	WRESTLER	SEE - ADONIS, ADORABLE ADRIAN		
FRANKFATHER, WILLIAM	ACTOR	1246 VICTORIA AVE	LOS ANGELES, CA	90019
FRANKHAM, DAVID	ACTOR	9165 SUNSET BLVD #202	LOS ANGELES, CA	90069
FRANKHAUSER, MERRELL	SINGER-GUITARIST	POST OFFICE BOX 1504	ARROYO GRANDE, CA	93420
FRANKHAUSER, MERRELL & THE MAUI	ROCK & ROLL GROUP	348 COLLEGE ST #301	BURLINGTON, VT	05401
FRANKIE	WRESTLING BIRD	POST OFFICE BOX 3859	STAMFORD, CT	06905
FRANKIE GOES TO HOLLYWOOD	ROCK & ROLL GROUP	POST OFFICE BOX 160	LIVERPOOL L6G 8BT	ENGLAND
FRANKLIN, ARETHA	SINGER-SONGWRITER	1364 COUNTRY CLUB DR	WEST BLOOMFIELD, MI	48013
FRANKLIN, BENJAMIN A	NEWS CORRESPONDENT	11404 ROKEBY AVE	GARRETT PARK, MD	20896
FRANKLIN, BONNIE	ACTRESS	POOLHOUSE PRODUCTIONS		
		4113 1/2 RADFORD AVE	STUDIO CITY, CA	91604
FRANKLIN, CARL	ACTOR	4402 VICTORIA PARK DR	LOS ANGELES, CA	90019
FRANKLIN, CECIL	SINGER	16919 STANSBURY ST	DETROIT, MI	48235
FRANKLIN, DANIEL JAY	FILM-TV WRITER	8955 BEVERLY BLVD	LOS ANGELES, CA	90048
FRANKLIN, DIANE	ACTRESS	JARRETT, 220 E 63RD ST	NEW YORK, NY	10021
FRANKLIN, DON	ACTOR	1509 N CRESCENT HGTS BLVD #7	LOS ANGELES, CA	90069
FRANKLIN, ELLEN	TV EXECUTIVE	ABC-TV ENTERTAINMENT CENTER		
		2040 AVE OF THE STARS	LOS ANGELES, CA	90067
FRANKLIN, GARY	FILM CRITIC	KABC-TV, 4151 PROSPECT AVE	LOS ANGELES, CA	90027
FRANKLIN, GEORGE	TV WRITER	8955 BEVERLY BLVD	LOS ANGELES, CA	90048
FRANKLIN, GRETCHEN	ACTRESS	BURNETT, 42 GRAFTON HOUSE		
		2-3 GOLDEN SQ	LONDON W1	ENGLAND
FRANKLIN, HARRY S	FILM WRITER-DIRECTOR	10118 EMPYREAN WY #304	LOS ANGELES, CA	90067
FRANKLIN, HOWARD W	WRITER	8955 BEVERLY BLVD	LOS ANGELES, CA	90048
FRANKLIN, JEFF	SCREENWRITER	8955 BEVERLY BLVD	LOS ANGELES, CA	90048
FRANKLIN, JIM	TV DIRECTOR	BBC-TV CENTRE, WOOD LN		
		SHEPHERS BUSH	LONDON W12	ENGLAND
FRANKLIN, JOE	TV HOST	WOR-TV, 1440 BROADWAY	NEW YORK, NY	10019
FRANKLIN, LAWRENCE	CONDUCTOR	28500 BRADLEY RD #183	SUN CITY, CA	92381
FRANKLIN, LOUISE	ACTRESS	2425 7TH AVE	LOS ANGELES, CA	90018
FRANKLIN, NANCY	ACTRESS	165 W 46TH ST #409	NEW YORK, NY	10036
FRANKLIN, NANCY	TV WRITER	555 W 57TH ST #1230	NEW YORK, NY	10019
FRANKLIN, PAMELA	ACTRESS	1280 SUNSET PLAZA DR	LOS ANGELES, CA	90069
FRANKLIN, PAUL	GUITARIST	712 MAY DR	MADISON, TN	37115
FRANKLIN, RICHARD B	FILM DIRECTOR	11726 SAN VICENTE BLVD #300	LOS ANGELES, CA	90049
FRANKLIN, RODNEY	SINGER	151 S EL CAMINO DR	BEVERLY HILLS, CA	90212
FRANKLIN, WENDELL JAMES	DIRECTOR	432 S CURSON AVE #9-G	LOS ANGELES, CA	90036
FRANKLYN, SABINA	ACTRESS	LEADING ARTISTS, LTD		
		60 SAINT JAMES'S ST	LONDON SW1	ENGLAND
FRANKLYN, WILLIAM	ACTOR-DIRECTOR	29 CHARLWOOD RD	LONDON SW15 1QA	ENGLAND
FRANKLYN-ROBBINS, JOHN	ACTOR	CONWAY, EAGLE HOUSE		
		109 JERMYN ST	LONDON SW1	ENGLAND
FRANKOVICH, MIKE	FILM PRODUCER	838 N DOHENY DR #B	LOS ANGELES, CA	90069
FRANKOVICH, PETER	TV EXECUTIVE	CBS-TV, 6121 SUNSET BLVD	LOS ANGELES, CA	90028
FRANKS, CHARLES V	PHOTOGRAPHER	508 SHERWOOD CIR	CONNELLSVILLE, PA	15425
FRANKS, IAN	CINEMATOGRAPHER	THE DOWER HOUSE		
		SERGE HILL LN, BEDMOND	HERTS	ENGLAND
FRANKS, JACK P	WRITER	555 W 57TH ST #1230	NEW YORK, NY	10019
FRANKS, JEROLD	CASTING DIRECTOR	8480 BEVERLY BLVD #165	LOS ANGELES, CA	90048
FRANKS, JERRY	CASTING DIRECTOR	10202 W WASHINGTON BLVD #M-105	CULVER CITY, CA	90230

ARETHA FRANKLIN

JANIE FRICKE

ROBERT FULLER

ANNETTE FUNICELLO

ZSA ZSA GABOR

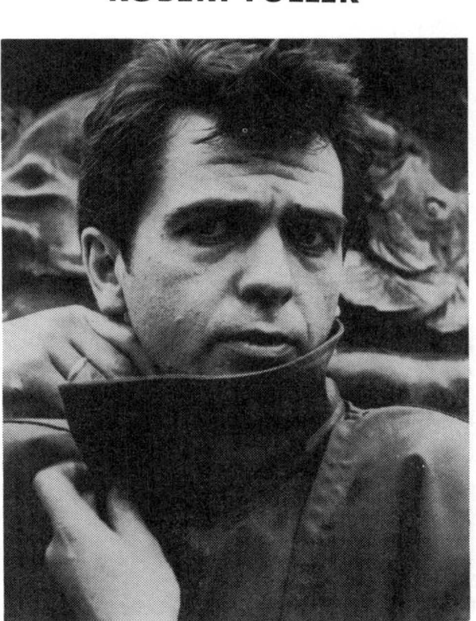
PETER GABRIEL

GALLAGHER

DON GALLOWAY

GRETA GARBO

FRANKS, MICHAEL	SINGER-GUITARIST	151 S EL CAMINO DR	BEVERLY HILLS, CA	90212
FRANN, MARY	ACTRESS	2790 HUTTON DR	BEVERLY HILLS, CA	90210
FRANSECKY, ROGER	CABLE EXECUTIVE	HOME BOX OFFICE PICTURES		
		1100 AVE OF THE AMERICAS	NEW YORK, NY	10036
FRANTZ, FRANK C	NEWS CORRESPONDENT	3604 DEVILWOOD CT	FAIRFAX, VA	22030
FRANTZ, JUSTUS	PIANIST	CAMI, 165 W 57TH ST	NEW YORK, NY	10019
FRANZ, ARTHUR	ACTOR	32960 PACIFIC COAST HWY	MALIBU, CA	90265
FRANZ, CAROLINE J	TV WRITER	CBS-TV, "AS THE WORLD TURNS"		
		51 W 52ND ST	NEW YORK, NY	10019
FRANZ, DENNIS	ACTOR	9255 SUNSET BLVD #1105	LOS ANGELES, CA	90069
FRANZ, KATHERINE SHELDON	TV WRITER	8955 BEVERLY BLVD	LOS ANGELES, CA	90048
FRANZ, ROBERT	DIRECTOR	45 W 45TH ST	NEW YORK, NY	10036
FRANZETTA, KENNETH	MUSICIAN	3912 CAMBRIDGE AVE	NASHVILLE, TN	37205
FRANZONI, DAVID H	WRITER	2 SEA COLONY DR	SANTA MONICA, CA	90405
FRANZUSOFF, VICTOR	NEWS CORRESPONDENT	10402 CLINTON AVE	SILVER SPRING, MD	20902
FRASCINO, ED	CARTOONIST	POST OFFICE BOX 4203	NEW YORK, NY	10017
FRASER, BILL	ACTOR	CROUCH, 59 FRITH ST	LONDON W1	ENGLAND
FRASER, BOB	ACTOR-WRITER	8955 BEVERLY BLVD	LOS ANGELES, CA	90048
FRASER, BOB	TV PRODUCER	1438 N GOWER ST, 4TH FLOOR	LOS ANGELES, CA	90028
FRASER, FORREST L	DIRECTOR	DGA, 7950 SUNSET BLVD	LOS ANGELES, CA	90046
FRASER, HARRIET	CASTING DIRECTOR	3518 W CAHUENGA BLVD #206	HOLLYWOOD, CA	90068
FRASER, IAN	COMPOSER-CONDUCTOR	2386 SUNSET HGTS DR	LOS ANGELES, CA	90046
FRASER, JILL	COMPOSER	15209 VALERIO ST	VAN NUYS, CA	91405
FRASER, JOHN	ACTOR	FRASER, 91 REGENT ST	LONDON W1	ENGLAND
FRASER, LIZ	ACTRESS	BURNETT, 42 GRAFTON HOUSE		
		2-3 GOLDEN SQ	LONDON W1	ENGLAND
FRASER, PATRICIA	ACTRESS	289 SAINT ALBANS AVE	SOUTH PASADENA, CA	91030
FRASER, PHYLLIS	ACTRESS	R F WAGNER, 425 PARK AVE	NEW YORK, NY	10022
FRASER, PRUDENCE	TV WRITER	8955 BEVERLY BLVD	LOS ANGELES, CA	90048
FRASER, RONALD	ACTOR	LONDON MANAGEMENT, LTD		
		235-241 REGENT ST	LONDON W1A 2JT	ENGLAND
FRASER, SHELAGH	ACTRESS	12 CAROLINE TERR		
		SLOANE SQ	LONDON SW1	ENGLAND
FRASER, TOM	DIRECTOR	79 CHARLES ST	NEW YORK, NY	10014
FRASER, WILFRED R, JR	PHOTOJOURNALIST	20159 HOB HILL WY	GAITHERSBURG, MD	20879
FRASURE, KENNETH	GUITARIST	2161 BYRUM AVE	NASHVILLE, TN	37203
FRATTI, MARIO	WRITER	555 W 57TH ST #1230	NEW YORK, NY	10019
FRAVIER, AL	SINGER	PROCESS, 439 WILEY AVE	FRANKLIN, PA	16323
FRAWLEY, JAMES	FILM DIRECTOR	MAYA, 9229 SUNSET BLVD	LOS ANGELES, CA	90069
FRAZE, BARBARA J	NEWS CORRESPONDENT	16576 ROYAL CT	WOODBRIDGE, VA	22191
FRAZER, DAN	ACTOR	9220 SUNSET BLVD #202	LOS ANGELES, CA	90069
FRAZER, LIZ	ACTRESS	29 KINGS RD	LONDON SW3	ENGLAND
FRAZER-JONES, PETER	TV PRODUCER	THAMES TELEVISION, TEDDINGTON	MIDDLESEX TW11 9NT	ENGLAND
FRAZIER, BRUCE H	CONDUCTOR	2927 N MYERS ST	BURBANK, CA	91504
FRAZIER, DALLAS	SINGER-SONGWRITER	ROUTE 5, BOX 133, LH PIKE	GALLATIN, TN	37066
FRAZIER, DANNY MACK	SINGER-GUITARIST	570 MC MURRAY DR #D-24	NASHVILLE, TN	37211
FRAZIER, HARRY	ACTOR	5152 LA VISTA CT	LOS ANGELES, CA	90004
FRAZIER, JIMMY B	FILM EDITOR	842 E CAMBRIDGE DR	BURBANK, CA	91504
FRAZIER, JODY	SAXOPHONIST	6529 MERCOMATIC CT	NASHVILLE, TN	37209
FRAZIER, JOE	BOXER-SINGER	2917 N BROAD ST	PHILADELPHIA, PA	19132
FRAZIER, KERMIT G	WRITER	555 W 57TH ST #1230	NEW YORK, NY	10019
FRAZIER, L D	SINGER	2528-A W JEROME AVE	CHICAGO, IL	60645
FRAZIER, PATRICIA	CELLIST	POST OFFICE BOX 772	MADISON, TN	37115
FRAZIER, SHEILA A	ACTRESS	3800 BARHAM BLVD #303	LOS ANGELES, CA	90068
FRAZIER, STEPHEN	NEWS CORRESPONDENT	NBC JAPAN, NTV, YOBANCH	TOKYO 102	JAPAN
FRAZIER, YVONNE	SOPRANO	POST OFFICE BOX 884	NEW YORK, NY	10023
FRAZOR, TERENCE	CONDUCTOR	GERSHUNOFF, 502 PARK AVE	NEW YORK, NY	10022
FREAM, TERESA KAY	PIANIST	416 WANDA DR	NASHVILLE, TN	37214
FREBERG, STAN	ACTOR-DIRECTOR	DGA, 7950 SUNSET BLVD	LOS ANGELES, CA	90046
FREDELL, ERIC A	NEWS CORRESPONDENT	1737-B "Q" ST, NW	WASHINGTON, DC	20009
FREDERICK, JOHN C	WRITER	8955 BEVERLY BLVD	LOS ANGELES, CA	90048
FREDERICK, ROBERT A	WRITER	8955 BEVERLY BLVD	LOS ANGELES, CA	90048
FREDERICKS, FRED	CARTOONIST	BRIDGE RD, BOX 475	EASTHAM, MA	02642
FREDERICKS, KEITH	SINGER	45 TUDOR CITY PL #911	NEW YORK, NY	10016
FREDERICKS, SCOTT	ACTOR	HOWES & PRIOR, LTD		
		66 BERKELEY HOUSE, HAY HILL	LONDON W1X 7LH	ENGLAND
FREDIANI, PAUL	ACTOR	251 S LAMER ST	BURBANK, CA	91506
FREDMAN, ROCHELLE	WRITER	8955 BEVERLY BLVD	LOS ANGELES, CA	90048
FREDRICK, KYLE	GUITARIST	2123 FAIRFAX AVE #12	NASHVILLE, TN	37212
FREDRICK, PAUL	WRESTLER-MANAGER	SEE - JONES, PAUL		
FREDRICKS, DIANA	ACTRESS	427 N CANON DR #205	BEVERLY HILLS, CA	90210
FREDRICKS, RICHARD	BARITONE	EV ASSOC, 145 E 52ND ST	NEW YORK, NY	10022
FREDRIK, BURRY	THEATER PRODUCER	165 W 46TH ST	NEW YORK, NY	10036
FREDRIK, KAREN	ACTRESS	1418 N HIGHLAND AVE #102	LOS ANGELES, CA	90028
FREDRIKSSON, STIG GUNNAR	NEWS CORRESPONDENT	1233 NATIONAL PRESS BLDG		
		529 14TH ST, NW	WASHINGTON, DC	20045
FREDRIX, PAUL MORGAN	ACTOR	802 HILLDALE AVE #7	LOS ANGELES, CA	90069
FREE AGENT	ROCK & ROLL GROUP	VARIETY ARTISTS INTL, INC		
		9073 NEMO ST, 3RD FLOOR	LOS ANGELES, CA	90069
FREE FLIGHT	JAZZ GROUP	GURTMAN, 162 W 56TH ST	NEW YORK, NY	10019
FREE NOT LUNCH BAND!	FOLK GROUP	POST OFFICE BOX 9532	MADISON, WI	53715
FREEBAIRN-SMITH, IAN	COMPOSER	4362 LEMP AVE	STUDIO CITY, CA	91604
FREEBIRD, THE	WRESTLER	SEE - HAYES, MICHAEL "P S"		
FREED, BERT	ACTOR	418 N BOWLING GREEN WY	LOS ANGELES, CA	90049
FREED, DONALD	WRITER	8955 BEVERLY BLVD	LOS ANGELES, CA	90048

Name	Occupation	Address	City	Zip
FREED, HERB	WRITER-DIRECTOR	120 N ORANGE DR	LOS ANGELES, CA	90036
FREED, LEONARD	PHOTOGRAPHER	463 WEST ST	NEW YORK, NY	10014
FREEDMAN, GENE	ACTOR	4731 LAUREL CANYON BLVD #5	NORTH HOLLYWOOD, CA	91607
FREEDMAN, JAMES L	WRITER	8955 BEVERLY BLVD	LOS ANGELES, CA	90048
FREEDMAN, JERROLD	DIRECTOR	9220 SUNSET BLVD #206	LOS ANGELES, CA	90069
FREEDMAN, LEWIS	TV DIRECTOR-PRODUCER	THE CORPORATION FOR		
		PUBLIC BROADCASTING		
		1111 16TH ST, NW	WASHINGTON, DC	20036
FREEDMAN, MIKE	TV DIRECTOR	5 N WAGON RD	BELL CANYON, CA	91307
FREEDMAN, ROB	DIRECTOR	DGA, 110 W 57TH ST	NEW YORK, NY	10019
FREEDMAN, ROBERT	WRITER	1650 BROADWAY #501	NEW YORK, NY	10019
FREEDMAN, STEVEN ALLAN	DIRECTOR	DGA, 7950 SUNSET BLVD	LOS ANGELES, CA	90046
FREEDMAN, WINIFRED	ACTRESS	9229 SUNSET BLVD #306	LOS ANGELES, CA	90069
FREEK, BALDUR	NEWS CORRESPONDENT	3005 CLEVELAND AVE, NW	WASHINGTON, DC	20008
FREEMAN, AL, JR	ACTOR-DIRECTOR	10 W 66TH ST #14-K	NEW YORK, NY	10023
FREEMAN, ALLAN K	NEWS CORRESPONDENT	1755 S JEFFERSON DAVIS HWY	ARLINGTON, VA	22202
FREEMAN, ALLYN I	TV WRITER	1239 N SWEETZER AVE	LOS ANGELES, CA	90069
FREEMAN, ARNY	ACTOR	70 GROVE ST	NEW YORK, NY	10014
FREEMAN, BEA	ACTRESS	120 W 3RD ST	NEW YORK, NY	10012
FREEMAN, BOBBY	SINGER	OLDIES, 5218 ALMONT ST	LOS ANGELES, CA	90032
FREEMAN, BUD	TV WRITER	8955 BEVERLY BLVD	LOS ANGELES, CA	90048
FREEMAN, CARRIE	ACTRESS	15900 SUNSET BLVD #2	PACIFIC PALISADES, CA	90272
FREEMAN, CARROLL	TENOR	59 E 54TH ST #81	NEW YORK, NY	10022
FREEMAN, CELIA	WRITER	50 S HILL PARK	LONDON NW3	ENGLAND
FREEMAN, DAMITA JO	ACTRESS	9012 7TH AVE	INGLEWOOD, CA	90305
FREEMAN, DAVID	SCREENWRITER	8955 BEVERLY BLVD	LOS ANGELES, CA	90048
FREEMAN, DAVID	TV WRITER	117 CHEVENING RD	LONDON NW6	ENGLAND
FREEMAN, DEVERY	SCREENWRITER	9481 CHEROKEE LN	BEVERLY HILLS, CA	90210
FREEMAN, DICK	COMEDIAN	MAGNAN, 1121 NORTHRUP DR, NW	GRAND RAPIDS, MI	49504
FREEMAN, DON	COLUMNIST	POST OFFICE BOX 191	SAN DIEGO, CA	92112
FREEMAN, ED	CONDUCTOR-ARRANGER	8439 RIDPATH DR	LOS ANGELES, CA	90046
FREEMAN, EMILY P	WRITER	555 W 57TH ST #1230	NEW YORK, NY	10019
FREEMAN, EVERETT	WRITER	8955 BEVERLY BLVD	LOS ANGELES, CA	90048
FREEMAN, FRED	TV WRITER	602 25TH ST	SANTA MONICA, CA	90402
FREEMAN, IRVING M	WRITER	555 W 57TH ST #1230	NEW YORK, NY	10019
FREEMAN, JOAN	FILM WRITER-DIRECTOR	8350 SANTA MONICA BLVD #103	LOS ANGELES, CA	90069
FREEMAN, JOHN NORMAN	WRITER	8955 BEVERLY BLVD	LOS ANGELES, CA	90048
FREEMAN, JUDITH A	WRITER	8955 BEVERLY BLVD	LOS ANGELES, CA	90048
FREEMAN, JUDITH L	NEWS CORRESPONDENT	2100 CONNECTICUT AVE #409, NW	WASHINGTON, DC	20008
FREEMAN, KATHLEEN	ACTRESS	6247 ORION AVE	VAN NUYS, CA	91411
FREEMAN, KAY	ACTRESS	12725 VENTURA BLVD #E	STUDIO CITY, CA	91604
FREEMAN, LISA M	ACTRESS	1440 23RD ST #314	SANTA MONICA, CA	90404
FREEMAN, LISA S	WRITER	555 W 57TH ST #1230	NEW YORK, NY	10019
FREEMAN, MARION C	TV WRITER	11906 GOSHEN AVE #1	LOS ANGELES, CA	90049
FREEMAN, MICHAEL	WRITER	8955 BEVERLY BLVD	LOS ANGELES, CA	90048
FREEMAN, MICKEY	ACTOR	433 W 34TH ST	NEW YORK, NY	10120
FREEMAN, MONA	ACTOR	608 N ALPINE DR	BEVERLY HILLS, CA	90210
FREEMAN, MORGAN	ACTOR	10100 SANTA MONICA BLVD #1600	LOS ANGELES, CA	90067
FREEMAN, PAUL	ACTOR	211 S BEVERLY DR #201	BEVERLY HILLS, CA	90212
FREEMAN, PAUL	ACTOR	MC REDDIE, 91 REGENT ST	LONDON W1	ENGLAND
FREEMAN, PAUL	CONDUCTOR	POST OFFICE BOX 27539	PHILADELPHIA, PA	19118
FREEMAN, PAUL	WRITER	8955 BEVERLY BLVD	LOS ANGELES, CA	90048
FREEMAN, PAUL	TV DIRECTOR	330 E 49TH ST	NEW YORK, NY	10017
FREEMAN, ROLAND L	PHOTOGRAPHER	117 INGRAHAM ST, NW	WASHINGTON, DC	20011
FREEMAN, SANDY	ACTRESS	LIGHT, 113 N ROBERTSON BLVD	LOS ANGELES, CA	90048
FREEMAN, SETH	WRITER-PRODUCER	1465 CAPRI DR	PACIFIC PALISADES, CA	90272
FREES, PAUL	DIRECTOR	DGA, 110 W 57TH ST	NEW YORK, NY	10019
FREEZE, JAMES GORDON	MUSICIAN	811 FAIR AVE	LAWRENCEBURG, TN	38464
FREEZER, HARLENE J	WRITER	555 W 57TH ST #1230	NEW YORK, NY	10019
FREHM, WALTER	CARTOONIST	KING FEATURES SYNDICATE		
		235 E 45TH ST	NEW YORK, NY	10017
FREI, SALLY	ACTRESS	3544 JASMINE AVE #9	LOS ANGELES, CA	90034
FREIBERGER, FRED	TV WRITER	10390 WILSHIRE BLVD	LOS ANGELES, CA	90024
FREIBERGER, VENCESLAVA	SOPRANO	111 W 57TH ST #1209	NEW YORK, NY	10019
FREIBUS, FLORIDA	ACTRESS	227 ANAPAMER ST	SANTA BARBARA, CA	93101
FREIDMAN, SEYMOUR	TV EXECUTIVE	COLUMBIA PICTURES TV		
		COLUMBIA PLAZA	BURBANK, CA	91505
FREILICH, JEFFREY	TV WRITER	10594 HOLMAN AVE	LOS ANGELES, CA	90024
FREIMAN, RICHARD D	TV WRITER	8955 BEVERLY BLVD	LOS ANGELES, CA	90048
FREIRE, NELSON	PIANIST	CAMI, 165 W 57TH ST	NEW YORK, NY	10019
FREITAG, DOROTHEA	COMPOSER	2 LINCOLN SQ	NEW YORK, NY	10023
FREIVOGEL, MARGARET W	NEWS CORRESPONDENT	5905 ROOSEVELT ST	BETHESDA, MD	20817
FREIVOGEL, WILLIAM	NEWS CORRESPONDENT	5905 ROOSEVELT ST	BETHESDA, MD	20817
FREIWALD, ERIC W	WRITER	8955 BEVERLY BLVD	LOS ANGELES, CA	90048
FREIZER, LOUIS A	WRITER	555 W 57TH ST #1230	NEW YORK, NY	10019
FRELENG, FRIZ	DIRECTOR-PRODUCER	1058 S ALFRED ST	LOS ANGELES, CA	90035
FREMIN, JOURDAN	ACTOR	POST OFFICE BOX 5617	BEVERLY HILLS, CA	90210
FRENCH, ALLISON	WRITER	555 W 57TH ST #1230	NEW YORK, NY	10019
FRENCH, ARTHUR T	ACTOR	233 E 80TH ST	NEW YORK, NY	10021
FRENCH, BRANDY	WRITER	8955 BEVERLY BLVD	LOS ANGELES, CA	90048
FRENCH, BRUCE	ACTOR	SF & A, 121 N SAN VICENTE BLVD	BEVERLY HILLS, CA	90211
FRENCH, DAVID T	NEWS CORRESPONDENT	1911 DALMATION DR	MC LEAN, VA	22101
FRENCH, LEIGH	ACTRESS	STONE, 1052 CAROL DR	LOS ANGELES, CA	90069
FRENCH, SUSAN	ACTRESS	40 HALDEMAN RD	SANTA MONICA, CA	90402

Name	Occupation	Address	City	Zip
FRENCH, SUSAN S	MUSICIAN	11934 RIVERSIDE DR #110	NORTH HOLLYWOOD, CA	91607
FRENCH, VALERIE	ACTRESS	309 W 57TH ST	NEW YORK, NY	10019
FRENCH, VALERIE	WRESTLING VALET	SEE - SUNSHINE		
FRENCH, VICTOR	ACTOR-DIRECTOR	4514 FARMDALE AVE	NORTH HOLLYWOOD, CA	91602
FRENCH GIANT, THE	WRESTLER	SEE - ANDRE THE GIANT		
FRENI, MIRELLA	SOPRANO	119 W 57TH ST #1505	NEW YORK, NY	10019
FRENI, ROSEMARIE	MEZZO-SOPRANO	HILLYER, 250 W 57TH ST	NEW YORK, NY	10107
FRENKE, EUGENE	FILM WRITER-DIRECTOR	2022 COLDWATER CANYON DR	BEVERLY HILLS, CA	90210
FRENZER, BILL	ACTOR	11240 MAGNOLIA BLVD #202	NORTH HOLLYWOOD, CA	91601
FRESCO, DAVID	ACTOR	4121 VIA MARINA #313	MARINA DEL REY, CA	90292
FRESCO, JOHN	COMPOSER	4567 WHITE OAK PL	ENCINO, CA	91316
FRESCO, ROBERT	WRITER	555 W 57TH ST #1230	NEW YORK, NY	10019
FRESH	ROCK & ROLL GROUP	DMR, WILSON BUILDING #316	SYRACUSE, NY	13202
FRESH, DOUG E & THE GET FRESH C	RAPPERS	GTI, 1700 BROADWAY, 10TH FLOOR	NEW YORK, NY	10019
FRESH AIRE	MUSICIAL GROUP	GRAMAVISION RECORDS		
		577 VALENCIA ST	SAN FRANCISCO, CA	94110
FRESSON, BERNARD	ACTOR	GEORGES BEAUME AGENCE		
		3 QUAI MALAQUAIS	PARIS 75006	FRANCE
FREUDBERG, FRANK	COLUMNIST	POST OFFICE BOX 500	WASHINGTON, DC	20044
FREUDBERG, JUDITH	WRITER	555 W 57TH ST #1230	NEW YORK, NY	10019
FREUDENBERGER, DANIEL N	TV WRITER-DIRECTOR	10486 LORENZO PL	LOS ANGELES, CA	90064
FREUND, PHILLIP	WRITER	555 W 57TH ST #1230	NEW YORK, NY	10019
FREUNDLICH, PETER	WRITER	555 W 57TH ST #1230	NEW YORK, NY	10019
FREY, GLENN	SINGER-SONGWRITER	10100 SANTA MONICA BLVD #1600	LOS ANGELES, CA	90067
FREY, LEONARD	ACTOR	180 WAVERLY PL	NEW YORK, NY	10014
FREY, RUDI	PHOTOGRAPHER	TIME/TIME & LIFE BLDG		
		ROCKEFELLER CENTER	NEW YORK, NY	10020
FREYTAG, ARNY	PHOTOGRAPHER	22735 MAC FARLANE DR	WOODLAND HILLS, CA	91364
FRIBERG, CARL L	CONDUCTOR	3334 BONNIE HILL DR	LOS ANGELES, CA	90068
FRICHTWIG	ROCK & ROLL GROUP	SUBTERRANEAN RECORDS		
		577 VALENCIA ST	SAN FRANCISCO, CA	94110
FRICKE, JANIE	SINGER	POST OFFICE BOX 798	LANCASTER, TX	75146
FRICKE, JOHN	BROADCAST JOURNALIST	CNN, 1050 TECHWOOD DR, NW	ATLANTA, GA	30318
FRIDAY, FRANCESCA	WRITER	8955 BEVERLY BLVD	LOS ANGELES, CA	90048
FRIDAY, JON	RINGMASTER	HALL, 138 FROG HOLLOW RD	CHURCHVILLE, PA	18966
FRIDAY, NANCY	AUTHORESS	ICM, 40 W 57TH ST	NEW YORK, NY	10019
FRIDELL, SQUIRE	ACTOR	9200 SUNSET BLVD #1210	LOS ANGELES, CA	90069
FRIDRICH, GEORGE J	PHOTOJOURNALIST	11812 GREGERSCROFT RD	POTOMAC, MD	20854
FRIEBUS, FLORIDA	ACTRESS	5550 WILSHIRE BLVD #306	LOS ANGELES, CA	90069
FRIED, GERALD	COMPOSER-CONDUCTOR	1801 AVE OF THE STARS #911	LOS ANGELES, CA	90067
FRIED, LEONARD	NEWS CORRESPONDENT	1662 WAINWRIGHT DR	RESTON, VA	22090
FRIED, MIRIAM	VIOLINIST	SHAW CONCERTS, 1995 BROADWAY	NEW YORK, NY	10023
FRIED, PAUL	FLUTIST	ROSENFIELD, 714 LADD RD	BRONX, NY	10471
FRIED & BISS	VIOLIN DUO	SHAW CONCERTS, 1995 BROADWAY	NEW YORK, NY	10023
FRIEDAN, BETTY	AUTHORESS	1 LINCOLN PLAZA	NEW YORK, NY	10023
FRIEDBERG, RICK	WRITER-PRODUCER	439 S PALM DR	BEVERLY HILLS, CA	90212
FRIEDE, STEPHANIE	SOPRANO	LEW, 204 W 10TH ST	NEW YORK, NY	10014
FRIEDEN, TERRY R	NEWS CORRESPONDENT	2133 WISCONSIN AVE, NW	WASHINGTON, DC	20007
FRIEDENBERG, RICHARD	WRITER-PRODUCER	5847 KEOKUK AVE	WOODLAND HILLS, CA	91367
FRIEDENBERG, WALTER	NEWS CORRESPONDENT	10030 COLVIN RUN RD	GREAT FALLS, VA	22066
FRIEDER, SOL	ACTOR	POST OFFICE BOX 235	NEW YORK, NY	10003
FRIEDGEN, JULIE	TV WRITER	8955 BEVERLY BLVD	LOS ANGELES, CA	90048
FRIEDKIN, WILLIAM	FILM WRITER-DIRECTOR	124 UDINE WY	LOS ANGELES, CA	90024
FRIEDL, ROBERT J	WRITER	10022 MELVIN AVE	NORTHRIDGE, CA	91324
FRIEDLANDER, HOWARD	TV WRITER	8955 BEVERLY BLVD	LOS ANGELES, CA	90048
FRIEDLANDER, LEONARD	TV PRODUCER	KNBC-TV, "SANTA BARBARA"		
		3000 W ALAMEDA AVE	BURBANK, CA	91523
FRIEDMAN, AL	WRITER	8955 BEVERLY BLVD	LOS ANGELES, CA	90048
FRIEDMAN, ALAN FOSTER	TV WRITER	8955 BEVERLY BLVD	LOS ANGELES, CA	90048
FRIEDMAN, BARBARA	TV DIRECTOR	35 E 75TH ST	NEW YORK, NY	10021
FRIEDMAN, BONNIE	TV DIRECTOR	4327 LOWER HONOAPIILANI	LAHAINA, HI	96761
FRIEDMAN, BRUCE JAY	SCREENWRITER	8955 BEVERLY BLVD	LOS ANGELES, CA	90048
FRIEDMAN, BUDD	TV-COMEDY PRODUCER	THE IMPROV, 8162 MELROSE AVE	LOS ANGELES, CA	90046
FRIEDMAN, DAVID	ACTOR	6430 SUNSET BLVD #1203	HOLLYWOOD, CA	90028
FRIEDMAN, DAVID	NEWS CORRESPONDENT	1401 BLAIR MILL RD #1719	SILVER SPRING, MD	20910
FRIEDMAN, DAVID JERROLD	AUTHOR	8939 CANBY AVE	NORTHRIDGE, CA	91325
FRIEDMAN, DICK	WRITER-EDITOR	TV GUIDE, 100 MATSONFORD RD	RADNOR, PA	19088
FRIEDMAN, DREW	CARTOONIST	THE NATIONAL LAMPOON		
		635 MADISON AVE	NEW YORK, NY	10022
FRIEDMAN, ERICK	VIOLINIST	IAM, 111 W 57TH ST	NEW YORK, NY	10019
FRIEDMAN, GABRIEL	VIOLINIST	POST OFFICE BOX 131	SPRINGFIELD, VA	22150
FRIEDMAN, HAROLD	DIRECTOR	420 LEXINGTON AVE #2716	NEW YORK, NY	10017
FRIEDMAN, IRA	PUBLISHING EXECUTIVE	10 COLUMBUS CIR #1300	NEW YORK, NY	10019
FRIEDMAN, JACK	WRITER-EDITOR	TIME & PEOPLE MAGAZINE		
		TIME & LIFE BUILDING		
		ROCKEFELLER CENTER	NEW YORK, NY	10020
FRIEDMAN, JOHN S	NEWS CORRESPONDENT	2939 VAN NESS ST, NW	WASHINGTON, DC	20008
FRIEDMAN, JOSH ALAN	WRITER	THE NATIONAL LAMPOON		
FRIEDMAN, JUDITH S	DIRECTOR	421 CUSTER AVE	EVANSTON, IL	60202
FRIEDMAN, KENNETH	SCREENWRITER	555 W 57TH ST #1230	NEW YORK, NY	10019
FRIEDMAN, KENNETH A	WRITER	8955 BEVERLY BLVD	LOS ANGELES, CA	90048
FRIEDMAN, KIM H	DIRECTOR	DGA, 7950 SUNSET BLVD	LOS ANGELES, CA	90046
FRIEDMAN, KIM PAUL	DIRECTOR-PRODUCER	13030 MOORPARK ST	STUDIO CITY, CA	91604
FRIEDMAN, KINKY	SINGER	MANGO PRODS, 511 COZZENS LN	NORTH BRUNSWICK, NJ	08902

Name	Occupation	Address	City	ZIP
FRIEDMAN, PAUL L	ACTOR	6380 WILSHIRE BLVD #1600	LOS ANGELES, CA	90048
FRIEDMAN, PAUL L	TV WRITER	ICM, 8899 BEVERLY BLVD	LOS ANGELES, CA	90048
FRIEDMAN, PHILIP	WRITER	8955 BEVERLY BLVD	LOS ANGELES, CA	90048
FRIEDMAN, ROBERT	WRITER	555 W 57TH ST #1230	NEW YORK, NY	10019
FRIEDMAN, ROBERT A	WRITER	8955 BEVERLY BLVD	LOS ANGELES, CA	90048
FRIEDMAN, RONALD	TV WRITER	1280 COLDWATER CANYON DR	BEVERLY HILLS, CA	90210
FRIEDMAN, SAMUEL	CONDUCTOR	POST OFFICE BOX 131	SPRINGFIELD, VA	22150
FRIEDMAN, SARA ANN	TV WRITER	555 W 57TH ST #1230	NEW YORK, NY	10019
FRIEDMAN, SAUL	NEWS CORRESPONDENT	4237 KINGS RD	EDGEWATER, MD	20137
FRIEDMAN, SEYMOUR MARK	FILM DIRECTOR	1960 COLDWATER CANYON DR	BEVERLY HILLS, CA	90210
FRIEDMAN, SONYA	TV HOST	USA CABLE NETWORK		
		208 HARRISTOWN RD	GLEN ROCK, NJ	07452
FRIEDMAN, STANLEY A	COMPOSER	187 S MARENGO AVE #6	PASADENA, CA	91101
FRIEDMAN, STANLEY D	WRITER-PRODUCER	555 W 57TH ST #1230	NEW YORK, NY	10019
FRIEDMAN, STEPHANIE	MEZZO-SOPRANO	1182 MARKET ST #311	SAN FRANCISCO, CA	94102
FRIEDMAN, STEPHEN	FILM PRODUCER	1901 AVE OF THE STARS #540	LOS ANGELES, CA	90067
FRIEDMAN, STEVE	TV PRODUCER	NBC-TV, 30 ROCKEFELLER PLAZA	NEW YORK, NY	10112
FRIEDMAN, STEVEN A	WRITER	8955 BEVERLY BLVD	LOS ANGELES, CA	90048
FRIEDMAN, THOMAS	WRITER	555 W 57TH ST #1230	NEW YORK, NY	10019
FRIEDMAN, VIKTOR	PIANIST	POST OFFICE BOX U	REDDING, CT	06875
FRIEDMANN, ANTHONY	FILM WRITER-DIRECTOR	PANTHEON, 38 MT PLEASANT	LONDON WC1X OAP	ENGLAND
FRIEDMANN, GERARD	TENOR	111 W 57TH ST #1209	NEW YORK, NY	10019
FRIEDRICH, EMILY	NEWS CORRESPONDENT	3003 VAN NESS ST, NW	WASHINGTON, DC	20008
FRIEDRICH, LIESEL C	WRITER	555 W 57TH ST #1230	NEW YORK, NY	10019
FRIEDRICH, OTTO	WRITER-EDITOR	TIME/TIME & LIFE BLDG		
		ROCKEFELLER CENTER	NEW YORK, NY	10020
FRIEDRICHS, HANS-JOACHIM	NEWS CORRESPONDENT	1077 31ST ST, NW	WASHINGTON, DC	20007
FRIEND, DAVID M	WRITER-EDITOR	LIFE/TIME & LIFE BLDG		
		ROCKEFELLER CENTER	NEW YORK, NY	10020
FRIEND, MARTYN	TV DIRECTOR	16 ALBANY MANSIONS		
		ALBERT BRIDGE RD	LONDON SW11	ENGLAND
FRIEND, ROBERT	FILM DIRECTOR	932 N LARRABEE ST #307	LOS ANGELES, CA	90069
FRIENDLY, ANDY	TV WRITER	1472 RISING GLEN RD	LOS ANGELES, CA	90069
FRIENDLY, ED	TV PRODUCER	1110 BEL AIR PL	LOS ANGELES, CA	90077
FRIENDLY, FRED W	COMMUNICATIONS EXEC	NAB, 1771 "N" ST, NW	WASHINGTON, DC	20036
FRIENDSHIP	JAZZ GROUP	1901 AVE OF THE STARS #1240	LOS ANGELES, CA	90067
FRIES, BUTCH E	NEWS CORRESPONDENT	230 N EDISON ST	ARLINGTON, VA	22203
FRIES, CHARLES	TV PRODUCER-EXECUTIVE	971 ALPINE DR	BEVERLY HILLS, CA	90210
FRIES, SANDY	TV WRITER	14144 VENTURA BLVD #200	SHERMAN OAKS, CA	91423
FRIESEN, DAVID & JOHN STOWE	VOCAL DUO	2490 CHANNING WY #406	BERKELEY, CA	94704
FRIESEN, EUGENE	CELLIST	POST OFFICE BOX 9388	STANFORD, CA	94305
FRIMEL, RUDE V	COMPOSER	MCA/UNIVERSAL STUDIOS, INC		
		100 UNIVERSAL CITY PLAZA	UNIVERSAL CITY, CA	91608
FRIPP, ROBERT	GUIATRIST	ROUTE #1, BOX 279	CHARLESTON, WV	25414
FRIPP, ROBERT & THE LEAGUE OF C	ROCK & ROLL GROUP	JEM RECORDS COMPANY		
		3619 KENNEDY RD	SOUTH PLAINFIELD, NJ	07080
FRISBIE, ALEXANDER L, JR	DIRECTOR	POST OFFICE BOX 574	BROOKLINE, MA	02146
FRISCHMANN, ROBERT S	WRITER	555 W 57TH ST #1230	NEW YORK, NY	10019
FRISHBERG, DAVE	MUSICIAN	HARTSTEIN, 8822 EVANVIEW DR	LOS ANGELES, CA	90069
FRISHMAN, DANIEL	ACTOR	10000 RIVERSIDE DR #3	TOLUCA LAKE, CA	91602
FRISTOE, ALLEN J	TV DIRECTOR	441 W END AVE	NEW YORK, NY	10024
FRITSCH, GUNTHER	TV DIRECTOR	265 MARGUERITA LN	PASADENA, CA	91106
FRITTS, DONALD RAY	MUSICIAN	POST OFFICE BOX 158094	NASHVILLE, TN	37215
FRITTS, VAUGHN	BARITONE	POST OFFICE BOX 884	NEW YORK, NY	10023
FRITZ, RICHARD E	COMPOSER-CONDUCTOR	7709 HOSFORD AVE	LOS ANGELES, CA	90045
FRITZ, SARA	NEWS CORRESPONDENT	232 8TH ST, SE	WASHINGTON, DC	20003
FRITZHAND, JAMES	TV WRITER	1645 WOODS DR	LOS ANGELES, CA	90069
FRITZINGER, GRACE	ACTRESS	244 MUIRFIELD RD	LOS ANGELES, CA	90004
FRIZZELL, DAVID & SHELLY WEST	VOCAL DUO	1302 DIVISION ST #102	NASHVILLE, TN	37203
FRIZZELL, JIMMY CLAY	GUITARIST	5280 EDMONDSON PIKE #11	NASHVILLE, TN	37211
FROBE, GERT	ACTOR	MANAGEMENT JOVANOVIC, PERFALL	8000 MUCHEN 80	WEST GERMANY
FROEBER, RICHARD R	COMPOSER	POST OFFICE BOX 2166	LOS ANGELES, CA	90028
FROEHLICH, BILL	TV WRITER	8955 BEVERLY BLVD	LOS ANGELES, CA	90048
FROEHLICH, GUSTAV	ACTOR	CASA AL MURO	CH-6614 BRISSAGO	
			TESSIN	SWITERLAND
FROHMAN, CLAYTON	SCREENWRITER	8955 BEVERLY BLVD	LOS ANGELES, CA	90048
FROHMAN, LORNE	WRITER	14144 VENTURA BLVD #200	SHERMAN OAKS, CA	91423
FROHMAN, MELVYN	SCREENWRITER	2051 PELHAM AVE	LOS ANGELES, CA	90025
FROLOV, DIANE	TV WRITER	3148 WAVERLY DR	LOS ANGELES, CA	90027
FROME, MILTON	ACTOR	12802 HORTENSE ST	NORTH HOLLYWOOD, CA	91604
FROMM, JOSEPH	NEWS CORRESPONDENT	1344 PINE TREE RD	MC LEAN, VA	22101
FROMMER, BEN	ACTOR	8322 BEVERLY BLVD #202	LOS ANGELES, CA	90048
FROMMERT, PETER J	TV DIRECTOR	9235 SILVERSIDE DR	SOUTH LYON, MI	48178
FROMSON, CAROLYN	ACTRESS	1230 HORN AVE #100	LOS ANGELES, CA	90069
FRONS, BRIAN	TV EXECUTIVE	NBC-TV, 3000 W ALAMEDA AVE	BURBANK, CA	91523
FRONTIERE, DOMINIC	COMPOSER-CONDUCTOR	10410 BELLAGIO RD	LOS ANGELES, CA	90024
FROST, BOBBY JEAN	MUSIC ARRANGER	2137 JUNE DR	NASHVILLE, TN	37214
FROST, CYNTHIA	ACTRESS	1605 N CAHUENGA BLVD #202	LOS ANGELES, CA	90028
FROST, DAVID	TV HOST	46 EGERTON CRESCENT	LONDON SW3	ENGLAND
FROST, DONNA L	SINGER	210-B TILLMAN LN	NASHVILLE, TN	37206

Name	Occupation	Address	City	Zip
FROST, JEAN	CASTING DIRECTOR	MCA / UNIVERSAL STUDIOS		
		100 UNIVERSAL CITY PLAZA	UNIVERSAL CITY, CA	91608
FROST, JEAN SARAH	ACTRESS	2341 SCARFF ST	LOS ANGELES, CA	90007
FROST, KATHERINE A	WRITER	555 W 57TH ST #1230	NEW YORK, NY	10019
FROST, LINDSAY	ACTRESS	CBS-TV, "AS THE WORLD TURNS"		
		51 W 52ND ST	NEW YORK, NY	10019
FROST, MARK	TV WRITER	8955 BEVERLY BLVD	LOS ANGELES, CA	90048
FROST, RALPH L	FILM WRITER-DIRECTOR	7813 HILLSIDE AVE	LOS ANGELES, CA	90046
FROST, RAY SANFORD	DRUMMER	508 N MAPLE ST #A	MURFREESBORO, TN	37130
FROSTIG, RICHARD M	WRITER	555 W 57TH ST #1230	NEW YORK, NY	10019
FROUG, WILLIAM	WRITER-PRODUCER	3419 WOODCLIFF RD	SHERMAN OAKS, CA	91403
FRUCHTMAN, MILTON	TV DIRECTOR-PRODUCER	180 MADISON AVE #1407	NEW YORK, NY	10016
FRUET, WILLIAM	DIRECTOR	51 OLIVE ST	TORONTO, ONT M6G 1T7	CANADA
FRUSONI, MAURIZIO	TENOR	CAMI, 165 W 57TH ST	NEW YORK, NY	10019
FRY, BILL	JUGGLER	HALL, 138 FROG HOLLOW RD	CHURCHVILLE, PA	18966
FRY, DEBBIE	SINGER	LUTZ, 5625 "O" STREET BLDG	LINCOLN, NE	68510
FRY, ED	ACTOR	NBC-TV, "ANOTHER WORLD"		
		30 ROCKEFELLER PLAZA	NEW YORK, NY	10112
FRY, GARY D	COMPOSER-CONDUCTOR	3950 LYONS ST	EVANSTON, IL	60203
FRY, MICHAEL	CARTOONIST	THE WASHINGTON POST		
		WRITERS GROUP		
		1150 15TH ST, NW	WASHINGTON, DC	20071
FRYE, ROBERT E	DIRECTOR	6006 GRACIOSA DR	LOS ANGELES, CA	90068
FRYE, ROBERT E	TV PRODUCER	ABC-TV, 7 W 66TH ST	NEW YORK, NY	10023
FRYE, SEAN	ACTOR	1930 CENTURY PARK W #30	LOS ANGELES, CA	90067
FRYE, STUART	DIRECTOR	1404 S BAY FRONT	BALBOA ISLAND, CA	92662
FRYER, ROBERT	THEATER PRODUCER	PRODUCERS CIRCLE COMPANY		
		1350 AVE OF THE AMERICAS	NEW YORK, NY	10019
FRYERS, EDWIN D	WRITER	555 W 57TH ST #1230	NEW YORK, NY	10019
FRYMAN, NICHOLAS C	COMPOSER	310 N VAN NESS AVE #6	LOS ANGELES, CA	90004
FU, NORMAN C	NEWS CORRESPONDENT	9013 PADDOCK LN	POTOMAC, MD	20854
FUCCI, WILLIAM J	DIRECTOR	12 W 37TH ST	NEW YORK, NY	10018
FUCHS, C EMIL	COMPOSER	455 N CRESCENT HGTS BLVD	LOS ANGELES, CA	90048
FUCHS, DANIEL	WRITER	8955 BEVERLY BLVD	LOS ANGELES, CA	90048
FUCHS, DICK	ACTOR	1412 N GORDON ST	HOLLYWOOD, CA	90028
FUCHS, JOSEPH	VIOLINIST	GURTMAN, 162 W 56TH ST	NEW YORK, NY	10019
FUCHS, LEO	ACTOR	609 N KILKEA DR	LOS ANGELES, CA	90048
FUCHS, LILLIAN	VIOLIST	KAY, 58 W 58TH ST	NEW YORK, NY	10019
FUCHS, LILLIAN & STRING TRIO	STRING TRIO	KAY, 58 W 58TH ST	NEW YORK, NY	10019
FUCHS, MICHAEL J	CABLE EXECUTIVE	HBO, 1100 AVE OF THE AMERICAS	NEW YORK, NY	10036
FUCHS, THOMAS	WRITER	1427 N HAYWORTH AVE #D	LOS ANGELES, CA	90046
FUDGE, ALAN	ACTOR	355 S REXFORD DR	BEVERLY HILLS, CA	90212
FUENTES, ERNIE	ACTOR	16636 RUNNYMEDE ST	VAN NUYS, CA	91406
FUENTES, LUIS	COMPOSER	98 RUE LEPIC	PARIS 75018	FRANCE
FUENTES, PAUL	WRITER-PRODUCER	12345 CALIFA ST	NORTH HOLLYWOOD, CA	91607
FUERBRINGER, JONATHAN	NEWS CORRESPONDENT	1424 LONGFELLOW ST, NW	WASHINGTON, DC	20011
FUEST, ROBERT	TV WRITER-DIRECTOR	NEMS, 31 KINGS RD	LONDON SW3	ENGLAND
FUJI, MR	WRESTLER-MANAGER	POST OFFICE BOX 3859	STAMFORD, CT	06905
FUJIMORI, WARREN	ACTOR	10800 WESCOTT AVE	SUNLAND, CA	91040
FUJIOKA, JOHN	ACTOR	8831 SUNSET BLVD #402	LOS ANGELES, CA	90069
FUJIWARA, HAMAO	VIOLINIST	KAPLAN, 115 COLLEGE ST	BURLINGTON, VT	05401
FUJIWARA, HARRY	WRESTLER-MANAGER	SEE - FUJI, MR		
FUJIWARA, MARI	CELLIST	SHAW CONCERTS, 1995 BROADWAY	NEW YORK, NY	10023
FULD, BRIAN	ACTOR	6 GEORGEFF RD	ROLLING HILLS, CA	90274
FULKERSON, GREGORY	VIOLINIST	500 5TH AVE #2050	NEW YORK, NY	10110
FULL, JIM	TV WRITER	8955 BEVERLY BLVD	LOS ANGELES, CA	90048
FULL, JOHN	PHOTOGRAPHER	701 DELAWARE AVE, SW	WASHINGTON, DC	20024
FULL HOUSE	ROCK & ROLL GROUP	POST OFFICE BOX 263	HASBROUCK HEIGHTS, NJ	07604
FULL MOON	ROCK & ROLL GROUP	PAT RAINS, 9034 SUNSET BLVD	LOS ANGELES, CA	90069
FULL TIME MEN	ROCK & ROLL GROUP	POST OFFICE BOX 112	HOBOKEN, NJ	07030
FULLAM, LARRY NEIL	GUITARIST	1252 SHAWNEE RD	MADISON, TN	37115
FULLENWIDER, FRAN	ACTRESS	JAMES, 110 WESTBOURNE GROVE	LONDON W11	ENGLAND
FULLER, CHARLES	SCREENWRITER	THE WILLIAM MORRIS AGENCY		
		1350 AVE OF THE AMERICAS	NEW YORK, NY	10019
FULLER, CHRISTA	ACTRESS	7628 WOODROW WILSON DR	LOS ANGELES, CA	90046
FULLER, DIANE	WRITER	555 W 57TH ST #1230	NEW YORK, NY	10019
FULLER, ERWIN	ACTOR	122 S SYCAMORE AVE	LOS ANGELES, CA	90036
FULLER, FRED P, JR	NEWS CORRESPONDENT	1020 N QUINCY ST	ARLINGTON, VA	22201
FULLER, GALE	MEZZO-SOPRAANO	POST OFFICE BOX 20548	NEW YORK, NY	10025
FULLER, JERRY	SINGER-SONGWRITER	WILLIAMS-CIMINI AGENCY		
		816 N LA CIENEGA BLVD	LOS ANGELES, CA	90069
FULLER, JOHN G	WRITER	555 W 57TH ST #1230	NEW YORK, NY	10019
FULLER, JOHNNY	BODYBUILDER	3002 E 20TH ST	TUCSON, AZ	85716
FULLER, LANCE	ACTOR	8831 SUNSET BLVD #402	LOS ANGELES, CA	90069
FULLER, LESLIE	COMPOSER-LYRICIST	151 S EL CAMINO DR	BEVERLY HILLS, CA	90212
FULLER, LORENZO	ACTOR	155 W 68TH ST	NEW YORK, NY	10023
FULLER, MICHAEL	WRITER	2565 1/2 GLEN GREEN ST	LOS ANGELES, CA	90068
FULLER, PARMER	COMPOSER-CONDUCTOR	911 MALCOLM AVE	LOS ANGELES, CA	90024
FULLER, PEGGY	WRITER	8955 BEVERLY BLVD	LOS ANGELES, CA	90048
FULLER, PENNY	ACTRESS	12428 HESBY ST	NORTH HOLLYWOOD, CA	91607
FULLER, ROBERT	ACTOR	6640 SUNSET BLVD #203	LOS ANGELES, CA	90028
FULLER, SAMUEL	FILM WRITER-PRODUCER	7628 WOODROW WILSON DR	LOS ANGELES, CA	90046
FULLERTON, JOHN HENRY	TRUMPETER	405 S MARIA	HEBBRONVILLE, TX	78361
FULLERTON, RICHARD S	ACTOR	431 N SPAULDING AVE	LOS ANGELES, CA	90036

Name	Occupation	Address	City	Zip
FULLERTON, SANDI	TV DIRECTOR	8264 GOULD AVE	LOS ANGELES, CA	90046
FULMORE, CHUCK, TRIO	GOSPEL GROUP	4031 FORNI RD	PLACERVILLE, CA	95667
FULTON, BOBBY	WRESTLER	UNIVERSAL WRESTLING FEDERATION		
		MID SOUTH SPORTS, INC		
		116 W BRECKINRIDGE	BIXBY, OK	74008
FULTON, DEWAYNE	HARPIST	CAMI, 165 W 57TH ST	NEW YORK, NY	10019
FULTON, EDWARD	MUSICIAN	720 E NASHBORO BLVD	NASHVILLE, TN	37214
FULTON, EILEEN	ACTRESS	CBS-TV, "AS THE WORLD TURNS"		
		51 W 52ND ST	NEW YORK, NY	10019
FULTON, LAURAN	SOPRANO	253 W 73RD ST #7-M	NEW YORK, NY	10023
FULTON, WENDY	ACTRESS	KOHNER, 9169 SUNSET BLVD	LOS ANGELES, CA	90069
FULTS, RICHARD J	ACTOR	4763 NOBLE AVE	SHERMAN OAKS, CA	91403
FUNABASHI, YOICHI	NEWS CORRESPONDENT	5019 SANGAMORE RD	BETHESDA, MD	20816
FUNAI, HELEN	ACTRESS	1930 CENTURY PARK W #30	LOS ANGELES, CA	90067
FUNICELLO, ANNETTE	ACTRESS	16202 SANDY LN	ENCINO, CA	91436
FUNK, DANIEL	TV DIRECTOR	636 E HARVARD RD #D	BURBANK, CA	91501
FUNK, JIMMY JACK	WRESTLER	POST OFFICE BOX 3859	STAMFORD, CT	06905
FUNK, ROBERT F	NEWS CORRESPONDENT	7019 SHERIDONNA LN	ALEXANDRIA, VA	22310
FUNK BROTHERS, THE	WRESTLING TAG TEAM	POST OFFICE BOX 3859	STAMFORD, CT	06905
FUNKADELICS, THE	SOUL GROUP	FAR OUT, 7417 SUNSET BLVD	HOLLYWOOD, CA	90046
FUNNY BOYS, THE	COMEDY DUO	EAI, 2211 INDUSTRIAL BLVD	SARASOTA, FL	33580
FUNT, ALLEN	TV HOST-DIRECTOR	DGA, 110 W 57TH ST	NEW YORK, NY	10019
FUNT, DAVID W	DIRECTOR	SUNTREE, 220 E 23RD ST	NEW YORK, NY	10010
FURE, TRET	SINGER-GUITARIST	OLIVIA RECORDS, 4400 MARKET ST	OAKLAND, CA	94608
FUREY, JOHN	ACTOR	1829 1/2 WESTHOLME AVE	LOS ANGELES, CA	90025
FUREY, THOMAS J	WRITER	555 W 57TH ST #1230	NEW YORK, NY	10019
FURGURSON, CASSIE T	NEWS CORRES-REPORTER	4805 SEDGWICK ST, NW	WASHINGTON, DC	20016
FURGURSON, ERNEST B	NEWS CORRESPONDENT	4805 SEDGWICK ST, NW	WASHINGTON, DC	20016
FURIA, JOHN, JR	TV WRITER	17147 OAK VIEW DR	ENCINO, CA	91316
FURIE, SIDNEY J	WRITER-PRODUCER	1191 ANGELO DR	BEVERLY HILLS, CA	90210
FURINO, FRANK V	WRITER-PRODUCER	3900 GLENRIDGE DR	SHERMAN OAKS, CA	91423
FURLAN, ALAN	ACTOR	665 ELM GROVE RD	ELM GROVE, WI	53122
FURLANETTO, FERRUCCIO	SINGER	CAMI, 165 W 57TH ST	NEW YORK, NY	10019
FURLAUD, MAXIME	WRITER	555 W 57TH ST #1230	NEW YORK, NY	10019
FURLONG, JOHN	ACTOR	5250 WOODMAN AVE	VAN NUYS, CA	91401
FURLOW, ROBERT S	NEWS CORRESPONDENT	1028 N LIVINGSTON ST	ARLINGTON, VA	22205
FURMAN, MARY ANN	ACTRESS	505 AVONDALE AVE #A	LOS ANGELES, CA	90049
FURMSTON, DAVID J	COMPOSER-CONDUCTOR	804 N LINDEN DR	BEVERLY HILLS, CA	90210
FURNELL, BILL	ACTOR	1134 9TH ST #H	SANTA MONICA, CA	90403
FURST, STEPHEN	ACTOR	15010 VENTURA BLVD #219	SHERMAN OAKS, CA	91403
FURTH, DANIEL	MUSICIAN	3656 MAYFLOWER PL	NASHVILLE, TN	37204
FURTH, GEORGE	ACTOR-WRITER	307 W 4TH ST	NEW YORK, NY	10014
FURTH, JANE	NEWS REPORTER	LIFE/TIME & LIFE BLDG		
		ROCKEFELLER CENTER	NEW YORK, NY	10020
FURTH, MARY	CELLIST	3656 MAYFLOWER PL	NASHVILLE, TN	37204
FURY, RON	WRESTLER	SEE - MASKED SUPERSTAR, THE		
FUSARI, LOUIS	DIRECTOR	10084 ROSCOE BLVD	SUN VALLEY, CA	91352
FUSCHI, OLEGNA	PIANIST	GURTMAN, 162 W 56TH ST	NEW YORK, NY	10019
FUSCO, PAUL	PHOTOGRAPHER	7 MELODY LN	MILL VALLEY, CA	94941
FUSELIER, OLIVER	ACTOR	323 VETERAN AVE	LOS ANGELES, CA	90024
FUSHAN, NANCY H	NEWS CORRESPONDENT	2025 "M" ST, NW	WASHINGTON, DC	20036
FUTRELL, MICHELE	DIRECTOR	999 N DOHENY DR #509	LOS ANGELES, CA	90069
FUTROWSKY, DAVID	NEWS CORRESPONDENT	5151 WISCONSIN AVE, NW	WASHINGTON, DC	20016
FUVOULO, JOHN	WRESTLER	SEE - KONGA THE BARBARIAN		
FUZZ TONES, THE	ROCK & ROLL GROUP	POST OFFICE BOX 2520	NACOGDOCHES, TX	75963
FX	ROCK & ROLL GROUP	IDEAL MGMT, 138 NELSON RD		
		SOUTH MELBOURNE	VICTORIA 3205	AUSTRALIA
FYANES, JOANN M	NEWS CORRESPONDENT	NBC-TV, NEWS DEPARTMENT		
		4001 NEBRASKA AVE, NW	WASHINGTON, DC	20016
FYFE, PETER	HARPSICHORD	900 BROADWAY	NASHVILLE, TN	37203
FYSON, CAROLYN	ACTRESS	15605 WOODFIELD PL	SHERMAN OAKS, CA	91403

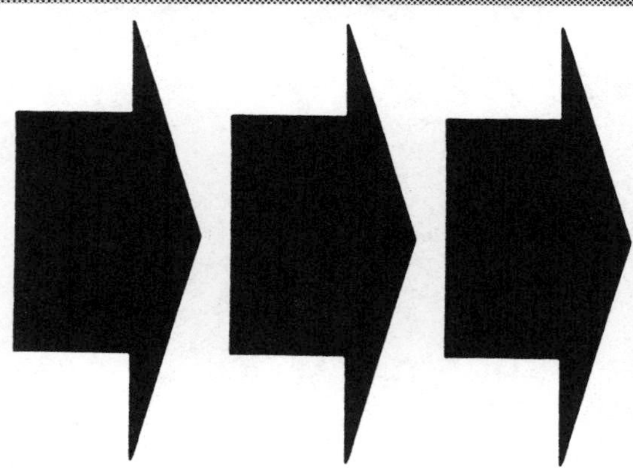

GALLOWAY, JOSEPH L	NEWS CORRESPONDENT	12600 GARMAN DR	NOKESVILLE, VA	22123
GALLOWAY, LINDA	ACTRESS	13001 BLAIRWOOD DR	NORTH HOLLYWOOD, CA	91604
GALLOWAY, MICHAEL	ACTOR	DULCINA EISEN MANAGEMENT		
		154 E 61ST ST	NEW YORK, NY	10021
GALLOWAY, PAMELA	ACTRESS	6310 SAN VICENTE BLVD #407	LOS ANGELES, CA	90048
GALLU, SAMUEL	WRITER	555 W 57TH ST #1230	NEW YORK, NY	10019
GALLUB, MARTHA	ACTRESS	9255 SUNSET BLVD #510	LOS ANGELES, CA	90069
GALLUN, RAYMOND Z	WRITER	110-20 71ST AVE	FOREST HILLS, CA	11375
GALMEYER, FRANK N	NEWS CORRESPONDENT	1755 S JEFFERSON DAVIS HWY	ARLINGTON, VA	22202
GALORENZO, EDWARD A	WRITER	555 W 57TH ST #1230	LOS ANGELES, CA	10019
GALOVIC, MARTI M	WRITER	555 W 57TH ST #1230	NEW YORK, NY	10019
GALTON, RAY	RADIO-TV WRITER	LE BARS, 18 QUEEN ANNE	LONDON W1	ENGLAND
GALVANY, MARISA	SOPRANO	61 W 62ND ST #6-F	NEW YORK, NY	10023
GALVIN, RAY	ACTOR	5529 HAZELBROOK AVE	LAKEWOOD, CA	90712
GALWAY, JAMES	FLUTIST	ICM, 40 W 57TH ST	NEW YORK, NY	10019
GAM, RITA	ACTRESS	10351 SANTA MONICA BLVD #211	LOS ANGELES, CA	90025
GAMAREKIAN, BARBARA S	NEWS CORRESPONDENT	3133 "O" ST, NW	WASHINGTON, DC	20007
GAMBARELLI, MARIA	ACTRESS	50 CENTRAL PARK W	NEW YORK, NY	10023
GAMBERONI, KATHRYN	SOPRANO	CAMI, 165 W 57TH ST	NEW YORK, NY	10019
GAMBLE, DUNCAN	ACTOR	1080 NOWITA PL	VENICE, CA	90291
GAMBLE, ED	CARTOONIST	POST OFFICE BOX 1949-F	JACKSONVILLE, FL	32231
GAMBLE, JOHN	TV EXECUTIVE	1245 N CRESCENT HGTS BLVD	LOS ANGELES, CA	90046
GAMBLE, KENNETH	RECORD PRODUCER	309 S BROAD ST	PHILADELPHIA, PA	19107
GAMBLE, OSCAR	BASEBALL	108 TENSAW RD	MONTGOMERY, AL	36117
GAMBLE, TRACY C	WRITER	555 W 57TH ST #1230	NEW YORK, NY	10019
GAMBLE, WILLIAM K	NEWS CORRESPONDENT	NBC NEWS, 4001 NEBRASKA AVE, NW	WASHINGTON, DC	20016
GAMBLER	ROCK & ROLL GROUP	496 W ANN ARBOR TRIAL #204	PLYMOUTH, MI	48170
GAMBRELL, JEANNE	ACTRESS	8721 SUNSET BLVD #203	LOS ANGELES, CA	90069
GAME THEORY	ROCK & ROLL GROUP	POST OFFICE BOX 2428	EL SEGUNDO, CA	90245
GAMMELL, ROBIN	ACTOR	2121 AVE OF THE STARS #410	LOS ANGELES, CA	90067
GAMMILL, TOM W	TV WRITER	555 W 57TH ST #1230	NEW YORK, NY	10019
GAMMON, CLIVE	SPORTS WRITER-EDITOR	SPORTS ILLUSTRATED MAGAZINE		
		TIME & LIFE BUILDING		
		ROCKEFELLER CENTER	NEW YORK, NY	10020
GAMMON, JAMES	ACTOR	641 N POINSETTA PL	LOS ANGELES, CA	90036
GAMMON, MICHAEL R	WRITER	8955 BEVERLY BLVD	LOS ANGELES, CA	90048
GAMMONS, PETER	SPORTS WRITER-EDITOR	SPORTS ILLUSTRATED MAGAZINE		
		TIME & LIFE BUILDING		
		ROCKEFELLER CENTER	NEW YORK, NY	10020
GAMPEL, CHRIS	ACTOR	400 W 43RD ST	NEW YORK, NY	10036
GAMSON, CHERYL	ACTRESS	6116 ALCOVE AVE	NORTH HOLLYWOOD, CA	91605
GANAHL, NANCY	NEWS CORRESPONDENT	2428 19TH ST #4, NW	WASHINGTON, DC	20009
GANCIE, VINCENT M	NEWS CORRESPONDENT	5151 WISCONSIN AVE, NW	WASHINGTON, DC	20016
GANDOL, ANITA	BODYBUILDER	LIFTERS FITNESS CENTER		
		47 S TELEGRAPH RD	PONTIAC, MI	48052
GANG GREEN	ROCK & ROLL GROUP	15 BARROWS ST	ALLSTON, MA	02314
GANGEL, GIG	MODEL	MODELS & PROMOTIONS AGENCY		
		8560 SUNSET BLVD, 10TH FLOOR	LOS ANGELES, CA	90069
GANGEL, JAMIE S	NEWS CORRESPONDENT	NBC-TV, NEWS DEPARTMENT	WASHINGTON, DC	20016
		4001 NEBRASKA AVE, NW	WASHINGTON, DC	20016
GANIS, GLENDA	WRITER	8745 WONDERLAND AVE	LOS ANGELES, CA	90046
GANLEY, MICHAEL J	NEWS CORRESPONDENT	1414 22ND ST, NW	WASHINGTON, DC	20037
GANN, ERNEST	AUTHOR	RED MILL FARM	SAN JUAN ISLAND, WA	98250
GANNON, HANK	PIANIST	4667 27TH AVE N	SAINT PETERSBURG, FL	33713
GANNON, JAMES	WRITER	555 W 57TH ST #1230	NEW YORK, NY	10019
GANNON, JOSEPH M	TV WRITER	STONE, 1052 CAROL DR	LOS ANGELES, CA	90069
GANNON, MARY R	WRITER	555 W 57TH ST #1230	NEW YORK, NY	10019
GANSBERG, ALAN	WRITER	8955 BEVERLY BLVD	LOS ANGELES, CA	90048
GANT, MARYA	ACTRESS	6331 HOLLYWOOD BLVD #924	LOS ANGELES, CA	90028
GANTMAN, JOSEPH	WRITER	8955 BEVERLY BLVD	LOS ANGELES, CA	90048
GANZ, ARMIN	WRITER	555 W 57TH ST #1230	NEW YORK, NY	10019
GANZ, BRIAN	PIANIST	3003 VAN NESS ST #W-205, NW	WASHINGTON, DC	20008
GANZ, JEFFREY JAY	DIRECTOR-PRODUCER	2136 NICHOLS CANYON RD	LOS ANGELES, CA	90046
GANZ, LOWELL	TV WRITER-DIRECTOR	3950 LONGRIDGE AVE	SHERMAN OAKS, CA	91423
GANZ, TONY	FILM PRODUCER	500 S BUENA VISTA ST		
		ANIMATION BUILDING #164	BURBANK, CA	91521
GANZEL, MARK	ACTOR	1145 S FORMOSA AVE #3	LOS ANGELES, CA	90046
GANZEL, TERESA	ACTRESS	6431 LA PUNTA DR	LOS ANGELES, CA	90068
GANZER, ALVIN	FILM-TV DIRECTOR	31673 W FOXFIELD DR	WESTLAKE VILLAGE, CA	91367
GAP BAND	RHYTHM & BLUES GROUP	200 W 51ST ST #1410	NEW YORK, NY	10019
GARAGIOLA, JOE	RADIO-TV PERSONALITY	6221 E HUNTRESS DR	PARADISE VALLEY, AZ	85253
GARAMONE, JAMES A	NEWS CORRESPONDENT	4420 SCARBOROUGH SQ	ALEXANDRA, VA	22309
GARAS, KAZ	ACTOR-DIRECTOR	31276 BAILARD RD	MALIBU, CA	90265
GARAVAGLIA, ROBERT C	WRITER	555 W 57TH ST #1230	NEW YORK, NY	10019
GARAY, VAL C	RECORD PRODUCER	13200 CHELTENHAM DR	SHERMAN OAKS, CA	91413
GARBAREK, JAN	SAXOPHONIST	KURLAND, 173 BRIGHTON AVE	BOSTON, MA	02134
GARBAREK, JIM	MUSICIAN	KURLAND, 173 BRIGHTON AVE	BOSTON, MA	02134
GARBER, DAVID M	WRITER-PRODUCER	13469 GALEWOOD ST	SHERMAN OAKS, CA	91423
GARBER, HARRIET M	NEWS CORRES-WRITER	4409 RANDALE CT	OLNEY, MD	20832
GARBER, TERRI	ACTRESS	8500 WILSHIRE BLVD #506	BEVERLY HILLS, CA	90211
GARBO, GRETA	ACTRESS	450 E 52ND ST	NEW YORK, NY	10022
GARCHER, DENNIS	CABLE EXECUTIVE	HOME BOX OFFICE PICTURES		
		1100 AVE OF THE AMERICAS	NEW YORK, NY	10036
GARCIA, ALBERTO	BARITONE	45 W 60TH ST #4-K	NEW YORK, NY	10023
GARCIA, ANDY	ACTOR	211 S BEVERLY DR #201	BEVERLY HILLS, CA	90212

Name	Occupation	Address	City	Zip
GARCIA, C ROBERTO	NEWS CORRESPONDENT	6416 BROOKSIDE DR	CHEVY CHASE, MD	20815
GARCIA, DAVID	WRITER	8955 BEVERLY BLVD	LOS ANGELES, CA	90048
GARCIA, GERMIN, JR	SINGER	POST OFFICE BOX 17472	NASHVILLE, TN	37217
GARCIA, GUY D	WRITER-EDITOR	TIME/TIME & LIFE BLDG		
		ROCKEFELLER CENTER	NEW YORK, NY	10020
GARCIA, JOHN CARLOS	COMPOSER	POST OFFICE BOX 733	POMONA, CA	91766
GARCIA, RICHARD D	NEWS CORRESPONDENT	13465 HIGGS CT	HERNDON, VA	22071
GARCIA, RUSSELL	COMPOSER-CONDUCTOR	6836 WOODMAN AVE #7	VAN NUYS, CA	91405
GARCIA, STELLA	ACTRESS	5850 CANOGA AVE #110	WOODLAND HILLS, CA	91367
GARCIA-ASENSIO, ENRIQUE	CONDUCTOR	1776 BROADWAY #504	NEW YORK, NY	10019
GARD-WORNSON, CHERYL	WRITER	1421 N LAUREL AVE #5	LOS ANGELES, CA	90046
GARDE, BETTY	ACTRESS	3928 CARPENTER AVE #202	STUDIO CITY, CA	91604
GARDELLA, KAY	TV CRITIC	NEW YORK DAILY NEWS		
		220 E 42ND ST	NEW YORK, NY	10017
GARDEN, CLAUDE	HARMONICA	FROTHINGHAM, 40 GROVE ST	WESSESLEY, MA	02181
GARDEN, GRAEME	ACTOR-WRITER	16 FARM AVE	LONDON NW2	ENGLAND
GARDEN, IRA	DIRECTOR	FORDHAM, 6430 SUNSET BLVD	HOLLYWOOD, CA	90028
GARDENIA, VINCENT	ACTOR	888 7TH AVE #2500	NEW YORK, NY	10106
GARDETT, ROBERT	ACTOR	LIGHT, 113 N ROBERTSON BLVD	LOS ANGELES, CA	90048
GARDNER, ANN	ACTRESS	201 W 86TH ST #PH W-17	NEW YORK, NY	10024
GARDNER, ARTHUR	PRODUCER	9570 WILSHIRE BLVD #400	BEVERLY HILLS, CA	90212
GARDNER, ARTHUR H	SCREENWRITER	300 N SWALL DR	BEVERLY HILLS, CA	90211
GARDNER, AVA	ACTRESS	34 ENNISMORE GARDENS	LONDON SW7	ENGLAND
GARDNER, DARREL W	CONDUCTOR	1158 LEEWARD WY	ANAHEIM, CA	92801
GARDNER, GAIL	SPORTSCASTER	ESPN, ESPN PLAZA	BRISTOL, CT	06010
GARDNER, GERALD	SCREENWRITER	466 S CAMDEN DR	BEVERLY HILLS, CA	90212
GARDNER, HERBERT	WRITER	555 W 57TH ST #1230	NEW YORK, NY	10019
GARDNER, HY	TV-RADIO PERSONALITY	5601 N BAYSHORE DR	MIAMI, FL	33137
GARDNER, JAKE	BARITONE	119 W 57TH ST #1505	NEW YORK, NY	10019
GARDNER, JEAN	FILM PRODUCER	1445 N BEVERLY GLEN BLVD	LOS ANGELES, CA	90077
GARDNER, JOAN	ACTRESS	8075 W 3RD ST #303	LOS ANGELES, CA	90048
GARDNER, JOHN	GUITARIST	2732 MC KIEGE DR	NASHVILLE, TN	37214
GARDNER, KAY	FLUTIST	POST OFFICE BOX 3124	DURHAM, NC	27705
GARDNER, KAY	FLUTIST-DULCIMER	POST OFFICE BOX 33	STONINGTON, ME	04681
GARDNER, LEONARD C	WRITER	8955 BEVERLY BLVD	LOS ANGELES, CA	90048
GARDNER, MARILYN	COLUMNIST	NEWS AMERICA SYNDICATE		
		1703 KAISER AVE	IRVINE, CA	92714
GARDNER, RANDY	SKATER	4640 GLENCOVE AVE #6	MARINA DEL REY, CA	90292
GARDNER, STEVE & MARIA	GOSPEL DUO	6750 W 75TH ST, MARKADE 75		
		BUILDING #2-A	OVERLAND PARK, KS	66204
GARDNER, WINNIE	ACTRESS	9200 SUNSET BLVD #931	LOS ANGELES, CA	90069
GARDONYI, FRANK	DIRECTOR	2585 DEARBORN DR	HOLLYWOOD, CA	90028
GAREA, TONY	WRESTLER	POST OFFICE BOX 3859	STAMFORD, CT	06905
GARELIK, GLENN	WRITOR-EDITOR	DISCOVER/TIME & LIFE BLDG		
		ROCKEFELLER CENTER	NEW YORK, NY	10020
GAREN, LEO	TV WRITER	2417 WILSON AVE	VENICE, CA	90291
GAREN, SCOTT	TV DIRECTOR-PRODUCER	617 9TH ST	SANTA MONICA, CA	90402
GARFEIN, JACK	DIRECTOR-PRODUCER	ACTORS & DIRECTORS LAB		
		412 W 42ND ST	NEW YORK, NY	10036
GARFIELD, ALLEN	ACTOR	13019 MONTANA AVE	LOS ANGELES, CA	90049
GARFIELD, BRIAN	SCREENWRITER	10390 SANTA MONICA BLVD #310	LOS ANGELES, CA	90025
GARFIELD, SUSAN	WRITER	555 W 57TH ST #1230	NEW YORK, NY	10019
GARFINKLE, LOUIS A	SCREENWRITER	14127 MARGATE ST	VAN NUYS, CA	91401
GARFUNKEL, ART	SING-ACT-COMP	24 MARKHAM PL	STATEN ISLAND, NY	10314
GARGAN, LESLIE H	TV WRITER	6816 WOODROW WILSON DR	LOS ANGELES, CA	90068
GARGARO, WILLIAM, JR	WRITER	6226 SCENIC AVE	LOS ANGELES, CA	90068
GARGIULO, MICHAEL R	TV DIRECTOR-PRODUCER	301 E 21ST ST	NEW YORK, NY	10010
GARIBALDI, MARCO	WRITER-DIRECTOR	PRESLEY, 1167 SUMMIT DR	BEVERLY HILLS, CA	90210
GARIGLIETTI, RANDY	BANJOIST	566 UPSHAW DR	NASHVILLE, TN	37214
GARIN, MICHAEL	PUBLISHING EXECUTIVE	US MAGAZINE COMPANY		
		1 DAG HAMMARSKJOLD PLAZA	NEW YORK, NY	10017
GARLAND, BEVERLY	ACTRESS	8014 BRIAR SUMMIT DR	LOS ANGELES, CA	90046
GARLAND, GEOFF	ACTOR	340 W 11TH ST	NEW YORK, NY	10014
GARLAND, HANK	GUITARIST	ROUTE #1, BOX 370, TWIN BROOKS	INMAN, SC	29347
GARLAND, ROBERT	SCREENWRITER	8955 BEVERLY BLVD	LOS ANGELES, CA	90048
GARLAND, SUSAN B	NEWS CORRESPONDENT	4004 BEECHER ST, NW	WASHINGTON, DC	20007
GARLAND, TRISH	ACTRESS	12223 CALIFA ST	NORTH HOLLYWOOD, CA	91607
GARLAND, WILLIAM	NEWS CORRESPONDENT	6194 GREENWOOD DR #1	FALLS CHURCH, VA	22044
GARLICK, LINDA	WRITER	555 W 57TH ST #1230	NEW YORK, NY	10019
GARMAN, STEPHANIE	TV WRITER	14144 VENTURA BLVD #200	SHERMAN OAKS, CA	91423
GARMENT, SUZANNE	NEWS CORRESPONDENT	4125 52ND ST, NW	WASHINGTON, DC	20016
GARNER, ANTHONY CRAIG	DRUMMER	617 HIDDEN HILL DR	HERMITAGE, TN	37076
GARNER, BRADLEY	FLUTIST	POST OFFICE BOX 20548	NEW YORK, NY	10025
GARNER, CHARLES	GUITARIST	ROUTE #2	NUNNELLY, TN	37137
GARNER, DIANE K	NEWS CORRESPONDENT	9101 ASPEN PARK CT	LORTON, VA	22079
GARNER, FRANCOISE	SOPRANO	CAMI, 165 W 57TH ST	NEW YORK, NY	10019
GARNER, GIGI	SINGER	33 OAKMONT DR	LOS ANGELES, CA	90049
GARNER, JACK	ACTOR	11820 CHANDER BLVD #5	NORTH HOLLYWOOD, CA	91607
GARNER, JAMES	ACTOR-DIRECTOR	33 OAKMONT DR	LOS ANGELES, CA	90049
GARNER, KATINA	ACTRESS	11827 ARMINTA ST	NORTH HOLLYWOOD, CA	91605
GARNER, LEE	GUITARIST	ROUTE #3	SMYRNA, TN	37167
GARNER, MARTIN	ACTOR	870 N VINE ST #G	LOS ANGELES, CA	90038
GARNER, PAUL "MOUSIE"	ACTOR	7220 HOLLYWOOD BLVD #230	LOS ANGELES, CA	90046
GARNER, RAY	DIRECTOR	POSTMASTER/GENERAL DELIVERY	IDYLLWILD, CA	92349
GARNER, ROBERT L	COMPOSER	10 LAWSON PL #6	YELLOW SPRINGS, OH	45387

AVA GARDNER

DAVID GATES

JOHN GAVIN

CRYSTAL GAYLE

TONY GEARY

BOB GELDOF

BOY GEORGE

PHYLLIS GEORGE

ANDY GIBB

GARNER, SALLY A	WRITER	8955 BEVERLY BLVD	LOS ANGELES, CA	90048
GARNER, SHAY	ACTRESS	120 S VICTORY BLVD #104	BURBANK, CA	91502
GARNES, LEE	CINEMATOGRAPHER	POST OFFICE 2230	HOLLYWOOD, CA	90078
GARNETT, GALE	ACTRESS	9200 SUNSET BLVD #1210	LOS ANGELES, CA	90069
GARNETT, RICHARD	COMPOSER	2429 N BEACHWOOD DR #2	LOS ANGELES, CA	90068
GARNETT, TONY	PRODUCER	3903 W OLIVE AVE #343	BURBANK, CA	91522
GARNETT, TONY	SCREENWRITER	8955 BEVERLY BLVD	LOS ANGELES, CA	90048
GARNITZ, BERNARD	COMPOSER	538 PIER ST #6-A	SANTA MONICA, CA	90405
GAROFALO, JOSEPH	TENOR	LIEBERMAN, 11 RIVERSIDE DR	NEW YORK, NY	10023
GAROFALO, JOSEPH A	SCREENWRITER	8955 BEVERLY BLVD	LOS ANGELES, CA	90048
GAROFALO, TONY	WRITER	16205 MORRISON ST	ENCINO, CA	91436
GARR, MICHAEL L	WRITER-PRODUCER	2008 1/2 VISTA DEL MAR ST	LOS ANGELES, CA	90068
GARR, TERI	ACTRESS	1462 RISING GLEN RD	LOS ANGELES, CA	90069
GARRARD, DON	BASS	VKD INTERNATIONAL ARTISTS		
		220 SHEPPARD AVE E		
		WILLOWDALE	TORONTO, ONT M2N 3A9	CANADA
GARRATY, TIMOTHY C	NEWS CORRESPONDENT	529 14TH ST	WASHINGTON, DC	20045
GARRELS, ANNE	NEWS CORRESPONDENT	ABC-TV, NEWS DEPARTMENT		
		1717 DE SALES ST, NW	WASHINGTON, DC	20036
GARRETSON, ROBERT M	NEWS CORRESPONDENT	7254 DONNELL PL	FORESTVILLE, MD	20747
GARRETT, BOB	WRITER	8955 BEVERLY BLVD	LOS ANGELES, CA	90048
GARRETT, BRAD	COMEDIAN	9243 1/2 DOHENY RD	LOS ANGELES, CA	90069
GARRETT, DAVID	TV WRITER	555 W 57TH ST #1230	NEW YORK, NY	10019
GARRETT, ELIZA	ACTRESS	3800 BARHAM BLVD #303	LOS ANGELES, CA	90068
GARRETT, ERIC	BASSO-BARITONE	61 W 62ND ST #6-F	NEW YORK, NY	10023
GARRETT, GARY	WRITER	8955 BEVERLY BLVD	LOS ANGELES, CA	90048
GARRETT, GEORGE P	WRITER	555 W 57TH ST #1230	NEW YORK, NY	10019
GARRETT, HANK	ACTOR	LIGHT, 113 N ROBERTSON BLVD	LOS ANGELES, CA	90048
GARRETT, JAMES	ACTOR	KOHNER, 9169 SUNSET BLVD	LOS ANGELES, CA	90069
GARRETT, LEIF	ACTOR-SINGER	7473 MULHOLLAND DR	LOS ANGELES, CA	90046
GARRETT, LILA	WRITER-PRODUCER	1356 LAUREL WY	BEVERLY HILLS, CA	90210
GARRETT, MAUREEN	ACTRESS	888 7TH AVE #201	NEW YORK, NY	10019
GARRETT, ROGER	TV WRITER	8955 BEVERLY BLVD	LOS ANGELES, CA	90048
GARRETT, SNUFF	TALENT AGENT	6255 SUNSET BLVD #1019	LOS ANGELES, CA	90028
GARRETT, VALERY	WRITER	8955 BEVERLY BLVD	LOS ANGELES, CA	90048
GARRETT, WILBUR E	PHOTOGRAPHER	209 SENSCA RD	GREAT FALLS, VA	22066
GARRICK, BARBARA	ACTRESS	ABC-TV, "ONE LIFE TO LIVE"		
		1330 AVE OF THE AMERICAS	NEW YORK, NY	10019
GARRICK, EDWARD	FILM DIRECTOR	1827 JEWETT DR	LOS ANGELES, CA	90046
GARRICK, STEVEN A	COMPOSER	23739 SANDALWOOD ST	CANOGA PARK, CA	91307
GARRISH, PAUL	DRUMMER	505 CLEMATIS DR	NASHVILLE, TN	37205
GARRISH, SONNY	GUITARIST-DOBROIST	113 CALDWELL DR	HENDERSONVILLE, TN	37075
GARRISON, DAVID E	ACTOR	9220 SUNSET BLVD #625	LOS ANGELES, CA	90069
GARRISON, GREG	DIRECTOR	3400 W ALAMEDA AVE	BURBANK, CA	91523
GARRISON, JON	TENOR	59 E 54TH ST #81	NEW YORK, NY	10022
GARRISON, LARRY	PRODUCER	4432 AGNES AVE	NORTH HOLLYWOOD, CA	91607
GARRISON, LLOYD	WRITER-EDITOR	TIME/TIME & LIFE BLDG		
		ROCKEFELLER CENTER	NEW YORK, NY	10020
GARRISON & VAN DYKE BAND	ROCK & ROLL GROUP	200 W 57TH ST #206	NEW YORK, NY	10019
GARRONI, WILLIAM	DIRECTOR	11 ALLISON DR	ENGLEWOOD CLIFFS, NJ	07632
GARSON, GREER	ACTRESS	3525 TURTLE CREEK RD	DALLAS, TX	75219
GARSON, HENRY	WRITER	411 N PALM DR #3	BEVERLY HILLS, CA	90210
GARSON, JOHN	ACTOR	415 E 71ST ST	NEW YORK, NY	10021
GARSON, MORT	CONDUCTOR	11824-H MOORPARK ST	STUDIO CITY, CA	91604
GARSTANG, JAMES	PIANIST	3253 NIAGARA DR	NASHVILLE, TN	37214
GARTIN, SANDY RUSSEL	TV EXECUTIVE	151 W 86TH ST	NEW YORK, NY	10024
GARTZMAN, MELINDA	CASTING DIRECTOR	3970 OVERLAND AVE #700	CULVER CITY, CA	90230
GARVER, KATHY	ACTRESS	8721 SUNSET BLVD #200	LOS ANGELES, CA	90069
GARVER, LLOYD	TV WRITER-PRODUCER	10474 ILONA AVE	LOS ANGELES, CA	90064
GARVER, RAY	GUITARIST	ROUTE #1	FRANKLIN, TN	37064
GARVEY, CHARLOTTE	NEWS CORRESPONDENT	2201 "L" ST, NW	WASHINGTON, DC	20037
GARVEY, CYNTHIA	TV HOST	944 PARK AVE #14-A	NEW YORK, NY	10028
GARVEY, STEVE	BASEBALL	9449 FRIARS RD	SAN DIEGO, CA	92121
GARVIN, CLINTON	MUSIC ARRANGER	916 MESA ST	MORRO BAY, CA	93442
GARVIN, GLENN	NEWS CORRESPONDENT	1418 "F" ST, NE	WASHINGTON, DC	20002
GARVIN, GORGEOUS JIMMY	WRESTLER	NATIONAL WRESTLING ALLIANCE		
		JIM CROCKETT PROMOTIONS		
		421 BRIARBEND DR	CHARLOTTE, NC	28209
GARVIN, KAREN E	WRITER	8955 BEVERLY BLVD	LOS ANGELES, CA	90048
GARVIN, KARL	TRUMPETER	4012 BRUSH HILL RD	NASHVILLE, TN	37216
GARVIN, RONNIE	WRESTLER	NATIONAL WRESTLING ALLIANCE		
		JIM CROCKETT PROMOTIONS		
		421 BRIARBEND DR	CHARLOTTE, NC	28209
GARWOOD, JOHN	ACTOR	8628 FONTANA ST	DOWNEY, CA	90241
GARY, A PETER	COMPOSER-CONDUCTOR	1328 S BUNDY DR #9	LOS ANGELES, CA	90025
GARY, CAROL D	TV WRITER	8955 BEVERLY BLVD	LOS ANGELES, CA	90048
GARY, GARNEY	NEWS CORRESPONDENT	400 N CAPITOL ST, NW	WASHINGTON, DC	20001
GARY, HAROLD	ACTOR	2109 BROADWAY	NEW YORK, NY	10023
GARY, JOHN	SINGER	32500 CONCORD DR #221	MADISON HEIGHTS, MI	48071
GARY, LINDA	ACTRESS	208 S BEVERLY DR #4	BEVERLY HILLS, CA	90212
GARY, LORRAINE	ACTRESS	1158 TOWER RD	BEVERLY HILLS, CA	90210
GARY, SAM	TV DIRECTOR	8770 CRESCENT DR	LOS ANGELES, CA	90046
GARY O	SINGER-COMPOSER	761 JANE ST #15	TORONTO, ONT M6N 4B4	CANADA
GARZA, JANISS	ACTRESS	1750 CAMINO PALMERO #52	LOS ANGELES, CA	90046
GASBARRO, MARK F	COMPOSER	17540 HIAWATHA ST	GRANADA HILLS, CA	91344

GASCO, ERNESTO	ACTOR	55-41 96TH ST	ELMHURST, NY 11368
GASCOINE, JILL	ACTRESS	MARTIN, 7 WINDMILL ST	LONDON W1P 1HF ENGLAND
GASDIA, CECILIA	SOPRANO	119 W 57TH ST #1505	NEW YORK, NY 10019
GASPARD-HUIT, PIERRE	FILM DIRECTOR	25 BIS RUE JASMIN	PARIS 75016 FRANCE
GASPARI, RICHARD	BODYBUILDER	POST OFFICE BOX 29	MILLTOWN, NJ 08850
GASPER, JAMES M	RECORD EXECUTIVE	ARIANA, 808 S PANTANO RD	TUCSON, AZ 85710
GASS, MARC J	DIRECTOR	8501 BRIER DR	HOLLYWOOD, CA 90046
GASS, MICHAEL	WRITER	555 W 57TH ST #1230	NEW YORK, NY 10019
GASSEN, MARIE LOUISE	ACTRESS	8230 BEVERLY BLVD #23	LOS ANGELES, CA 90048
GASSMAN, VITTORIO	ACTOR	GUISEPPE PROSA	
		VIA SAN DOMINICO	2 BIS ROME ITALY
GASSMANN, JENNIE	ACTRESS	1450 BELFAST DR	LOS ANGELES, CA 90069
GAST, HAROLD	TV WRITER-PRODUCER	281 LORING AVE	LOS ANGELES, CA 90024
GASTON, ED	TRUMPETER	920 DRUMMOND DR	NASHVILLE, TN 37211
GASTON, LAVESTIA	SINGER	4696 COLUMBINE CT	MEMPHIS, TN 38118
GATELEY, ROBERT	GUITARIST	407 NAWAKUA TRAIL	NASHVILLE, TN 37215
GATELY, GEORGE	CARTOONIST	MC NAUGHT SYNDICATE	
		60 E 42ND ST	NEW YORK, NY 10036
GATELY, JAMES E	NEWS CORRESPONDENT	400 N CAPITOL ST, NW	WASHINGTON, DC 20001
GATES, DAVID	SINGER-SONGWRITER	24344 ROLLING VIEW RD	HIDDEN HILLS, CA 91302
GATES, JAMES S	TV DIRECTOR	24952 KIT CARSON RD	HIDDEN HILLS, CA 91302
GATES, LARRY	ACTOR	1901 AVE OF THE STARS #840	LOS ANGELES, CA 90067
GATES, NANCY	ACTRESS	HAYES, 200 CONWAY AVE	LOS ANGELES, CA 90024
GATES, RICHARD	ACTOR	2055 N LAS PALMAS AVE	LOS ANGELES, CA 90068
GATES, TUDOR	WRITER-PRODUCER	DRUMBEAT, 17-A MERCER ST	LONDON WC2H 9QJ ENGLAND
GATEWOOD, JOHNNY	SINGER	ROUTE #2, BOX 73	INMAN, KS 67546
GATI, ISTVAN	BASSO-BARITONE	111 W 57TH ST #1209	NEW YORK, NY 10019
GATI, LASZLO	CONDUCTOR	482 FORT WASHINGTON AVE #1-H	NEW YORK, NY 10033
GATLIN, JERRY JOE	DIRECTOR	DGA, 7950 SUNSET BLVD	LOS ANGELES, CA 90046
GATLIN, LARRY	SINGER-SONGWRITER	2 MARYLAND FARMS #322	BRENTWOOD, TN 37027
GATLIN, LARRY & THE GATLIN BROT	C & W GROUP	2 MARYLAND FARMS #322	BRENTWOOD, TN 37027
GATLIN, RUDY	SINGER-SONGWRITER	2 MARYLAND FARMS #322	BRENTWOOD, TN 37027
GATLIN, STEVE	SINGER-SONGWRITER	2 MARYLAND FARMS #322	BRENTWOOD, TN 37027
GATORWOLF, STEVE	WRESTLER	POST OFFICE BOX 3859	STAMFORD, CT 06905
GATTI, JENNIFER	ACTRESS	CBS-TV, "THE GUIDING LIGHT"	
		51 W 52ND ST	NEW YORK, NY 10019
GATTO, PETER	ACTOR	RAGLYN, 60 E 42ND ST	NEW YORK, NY 10165
GATTY, MARY ANN	NEWS CORRESPONDENT	5332 TEN OAKS RD	CLARKSVILLE, MD 21029
GATTY, ROBERT C	NEWS CORRESPONDENT	5332 TEN OAKS RD	CLARKSVILLE, MD 21029
GATWOOD, JODY	VIOLINIST	3003 VAN NESS ST #W-205, NW	WASHINGTON, DC 20008
GAUBERT, JAMES	BODYBUILDER	POST OFFICE BOX 2343	LAFAYETTE, LA 70502
GAUDUCHON, NICOLE	FILM EDITOR	11 AVE GEORGES-BIZET	LE VESINET 78110 FRANCE
GAUGHRAN, KEN	WRITER	555 W 57TH ST #1230	NEW YORK, NY 10019
GAUL, PATRICIA	ACTRESS	13205 CHELTENHAM DR	SHERMAN OAKS, CA 91423
GAULT, BRIGITTE	ACTRESS	8230 BEVERLY BLVD #23	LOS ANGELES, CA 90048
GAULT, JENNY	ACTRESS	333 E 49TH ST	NEW YORK, NY 10017
GAUNT, JOHN J M	NEWS CORRESPONDENT	2005 N UPLAND ST	ARLINGTON, VA 22207
GAUTHIER, ARTHUR R	NEWS CORRESPONDENT	ABC-TV, NEWS DEPARTMENT	
		1717 DE SALES ST, NW	WASHINGTON, DC 20036
GAUTHIER, JACK	ACTOR	19 RUE JEAN-LECLAIRE	PARIS 75017 FRANCE
GAUTIER, DICK	ACTOR-WRITER	12747 ADDISON ST	NORTH HOLLYWOOD, CA 91607
GAUVIN, PAUL	GUITARIST	2002 ASHWOOD AVE	NASHVILLE, TN 37212
GAVA, CASSANDRA	ACTRESS	151 S EL CAMINO DR	BEVERLY HILLS, CA 90212
GAVALA, YULA	WRITER-PRODUCER	651 LORNA LN	LOS ANGELES, CA 90049
GAVELL, ANN B	NEWS CORRESPONDENT	7308 BROXBURN CT	BETHESDA, MD 20817
GAVIATI, RONALD M	DIRECTOR	5800 SUNSET BLVD	HOLLYWOOD, CA 90028
GAVIN, BARRIE	DIRECTOR-PRODUCER	SADLER'S COTTAGE, HIGH ST	
		CHALFORD	GLOS GL6 8DJ ENGLAND
GAVIN, DELANE "MIKE"	TV DIRECTOR	4660 WILLIS AVE	SHERMAN OAKS, CA 91403
GAVIN, JAMES WILLIAM	DIRECTOR	DGA, 7950 SUNSET BLVD	LOS ANGELES, CA 90046
GAVIN, JOHN	ACTOR	2145 CENTURY HILL	LOS ANGELES, CA 90067
GAVRAS-COSTA	FILM DIRECTOR	SA AU CAPITAL DE 300.00	
		244 RUE SAINT-JACQUES	PARIS 75005 FRANCE
GAVRILOV, ANDREI	PIANIST	ICM, 40 W 57TH ST	NEW YORK, NY 10019
GAWRYCH, RONEE L	WRITER	555 W 57TH ST #1230	NEW YORK, NY 10019
GAY, BARBARA ANN	PIANIST	158 EVERGREEN CIR	HENDERSONVILLE, TN 37075
GAY, JOHN	TV WRITER	1636 SAN ONOFRE DR	PACIFIC PALISADES, CA 90272
GAY, LANCE C	NEWS CORRESPONDENT	1730 ARLINGTON BLVD #103	ARLINGTON, VA 22209
GAY, MICHAEL	ACTOR	JARRETT, 220 E 63RD ST	NEW YORK, NY 10021
GAYBIS, ANNIE	ACTRESS-SINGER	999 N DOHENY DR #1005	LOS ANGELES, CA 90069
GAYDEN, MAC	GUITARIST	3506 FRANKLIN RD	NASHVILLE, TN 37204
GAYDOES, STEVEN M	WRITER	ICM, 8899 BEVERLY BLVD	LOS ANGELES, CA 90048
GAYE, NORA	ACTRESS	9601 WILSHIRE BLVD #GL-11	BEVERLY HILLS, CA 90210
GAYER, CATHERINE	SOPRANO	KAY, 58 W 58TH ST	NEW YORK, NY 10019
GAYER, JOSEPHA	MEZZO-SOPRANO	1776 BROADWAY #504	NEW YORK, NY 10019
GAYLE, CRYSTAL	SINGER	51 MUSIC SQUARE E	NASHVILLE, TN 37203
GAYLE, JACKIE	COMEDIAN	13109 CHANDLER BLVD	VAN NUYS, CA 91401
GAYLE, MONICA	ACTRESS	725 S BARRINGTON AVE #204	LOS ANGELES, CA 90049
GAYLE, NANCY	TV WRITER	8955 BEVERLY BLVD	LOS ANGELES, CA 90048
GAYLE, ROZELLE	ACTOR	1766 S STEARNS DR	LOS ANGELES, CA 90035
GAYLEN-TRENN, AMELIA	TV WRITER	555 W 57TH ST #1230	NEW YORK, NY 10019
GAYLIN, GEORGE	PHOTOGRAPHER	1101 BAHAMA BEND #F-2	COCONUT CREEK, FL 33066
GAYLOR, MARY L	WRITER	555 W 57TH ST #1230	NEW YORK, NY 10019
GAYLORD, JEFF	WRESTLER	UNIVERSAL WRESTLING FEDERATION	
		MID SOUTH SPORTS, INC	
		5001 SPRING VALLEY RD	DALLAS, TX 75244

GAYLORD, MITCH	ACTOR	8485 MELROSE AVE #E	LOS ANGELES, CA	90069
GAYLORD & HOLIDAY	COMEDY DUO	32500 CONCORD DR #221	MADISON HEIGHTS, MI	48071
GAYMAN, LOWELL	NEWS CORRESPONDENT	7311 WILLOW AVE	TAKOMA PARK, MD	20912
GAYNES, GEORGE	ACTOR-DIRECTOR	4234 BABCOCK AVE	STUDIO CITY, CA	91604
GAYNES, LLOYD	TV DIRECTOR	6918 OPORTO DR	HOLLYWOOD, CA	90068
GAYNOR, GLORIA	SINGER	MALCOLM FELD AGENCY		
		15 ATHERTON PL		
		LONGFORD AVE, SOUTHALL	MIDDLESEX UB1 3QT	ENGLAND
GAYNOR, GRACE	ACTRESS	9850 YOAKUM DR	BEVERLY HILLS, CA	90210
GAYNOR, JOCK	ACTOR	9850 YOAKUM DR	BEVERLY HILLS, CA	90210
GAYNOR, JOHN	WRITER	8955 BEVERLY BLVD	LOS ANGELES, CA	90048
GAYNOR, MITZI	ACTRESS-DANCER	610 N ARDEN DR	BEVERLY HILLS, CA	90210
GAYTON, JOE	SCREENWRITER	8955 BEVERLY BLVD	LOS ANGELES, CA	90048
GAZELL, PHIL	PERCUSSIONIST	ROUTE #5, BOX 303	LEBANON, TN	37087
GAZELLA, KIM M	NEWS CORRESPONDENT	1740 "S" ST, NW	WASHINGTON, DC	20009
GAZNICK, TONY	ACTOR	843 TIPTON TERR	LOS ANGELES, CA	90042
GAZZANIGA, DON	ACTOR-DIRECTOR	14758 MORRISON ST	SHERMAN OAKS, CA	91403
GAZZARA, BEN	ACTOR-DIRECTOR	1501 BROADWAY #2600	NEW YORK, NY	10036
GAZZO, MICHAEL	SCREENWRITER	ICM, 8899 BEVERLY BLVD	LOS ANGELES, CA	90048
GAZZO, MICHAEL V	ACTOR	9000 SUNSET BLVD #1112	LOS ANGELES, CA	90069
GEARY, ANTHONY	ACTOR	7010 PACIFIC VIEW DR	LOS ANGELES, CA	90068
GEARY, RICK	CARTOONIST	THE NATIONAL LAMPOON		
		635 MADISON AVE	NEW YORK, NY	10022
GEBHARDT, WILLIAM A	NEWS CORRESPONDENT	NBC-TV, NEWS DEPARTMENT		
		4001 NEBRASKA AVE, NW	WASHINGTON, DC	20016
GEBOY, GARY J	NEWS CORRESPONDENT	5151 WISCONSIN AVE, NW	WASHINGTON, DC	20016
GEDDA, GEORGE	NEWS CORRESPONDENT	8360 GREENSBORO DR #102	MC LEAN, VA	22102
GEDDA, NICOLAI	TENOR	SHAW CONCERTS, 1995 BROADWAY	NEW YORK, NY	10023
GEDDES, BETH R	TV WRITER	12039 WEDDINGTON ST	NORTH HOLLYWOOD, CA	91607
GEDDES, BRUCE	FILM DIRECTOR	4988 VINCENT AVE	LOS ANGELES, CA	90041
GEDDES, RALPH	MUSICIAN	522 GLENPARK DR	NASHVILLE, TN	37217
GEDEON, CONROY A	ACTOR	12725 VENTURA BLVD #E	STUDIO CITY, CA	91604
GEDRICK, JASON	ACTOR	10100 SANTA MONICA BLVD #1600	LOS ANGELES, CA	90067
GEE, CHRISTOPHER LYNDON	CONDUCTOR	111 W 57TH ST #1203	NEW YORK, NY	10019
GEE, DONALD	ACTOR	HOPE & LYNE, 5 MILNER PL	LONDON N1	ENGLAND
GEE, MASTER	WRESTLER	SEE - WELLES, GEORGE		
GEE, PRUNELLA	ACTRESS	CROUCH, 59 FRITH ST	LONDON W1	ENGLAND
GEEHAN, JAMES	NEWS CORRESPONDENT	2503 "I" ST, NW	WASHINGTON, DC	20037
GEER, AUSSIE C	WRITER	555 W 57TH ST #1230	NEW YORK, NY	10019
GEER, ELLEN	ACTRESS	21418 W ENTRADA RD	TOPANGA, CA	90290
GEER, HAL	WRITER-PRODUCER	WARNER BROTHERS, INC		
		4000 WARNER BLVD	BURBANK, CA	91522
GEER, HAROLD	DIRECTOR-PRODUCER	776 BENNETT ST	SIMI VALLEY, CA	93065
GEER, STEPHEN	NEWS CORRESPONDENT	ABC NEWS, 7 W 66TH ST	NEW YORK, NY	10023
GEER, THAD	ACTOR	1419 N TOPANGA CANYON BLVD	TOPANGA, CA	90290
GEESLIN, CAMPBELL	WRITER-EDITOR	LIFE/TIME & LIFE BLDG		
		ROCKEFELLER CENTER	NEW YORK, NY	10020
GEESLIN, NED	WRITER-EDITOR	PEOPLE/TIME & LIFE BLDG		
		ROCKEFELLER CENTER	NEW YORK, NY	10020
GEESON, JUDY	ACTRESS	STONE, 1052 CAROL DR	LOS ANGELES, CA	90069
GEFFEN, DAVID	RECORD-FILM EXECUTIVE	1225 ANGELO RD	BEVERLY HILLS, CA	90210
GEFFNER, DEBORAH	ACTRESS	9744 WILSHIRE BLVD #306	BEVERLY HILLS, CA	90212
GEFSKY, HAL	TALENT AGENT	8650 PINE TREE PL	LOS ANGELES, CA	90069
GEHMAN, MARTHA	ACTRESS	151 S EL CAMINO DR	BEVERLY HILLS, CA	90212
GEHRIG, BETTY	PIANIST	3810 PICTURE RIDGE	NASHVILLE, TN	37216
GEHRING, TED	ACTOR	9744 WILSHIRE BLVD #306	BEVERLY HILLS, CA	90212
GEHRINGER, CHARLIE	BASEBALL	32301 LAHSER RD	BIRMINGHAM, MI	48010
GEIGER, GEORGE	TV WRITER	151 S EL CAMINO DR	BEVERLY HILLS, CA	90212
GEIGER, GEORGE	PRODUCER	4000 WARNER BLVD	BURBANK, CA	91522
GEIGER, MIRIAM	WRITER	7676 HOLLYWOOD BLVD #7	LOS ANGELES, CA	90046
GEILS BAND, J	ROCK & ROLL GROUP	KRAGEN, 8 CADMAN PLAZA	BROOKLYN, NY	11201
GEISEL, JEROME M	NEWS CORRESPONDENT	3438 S WAKEFIELD ST	ARLINGTON, VA	22206
GEISEL, TED	AUTHOR	7301 ENCELIA DR	SAN DIEGO, CA	92037
GEISINGER, ELLIOTT PAUL	DIRECTOR	THE FILM COMPANY		
		1600 BROADWAY	NEW YORK, NY	10019
GEISS, TONY	TV WRITER	CHILDREN'S TV WORKSHOP		
		1 LINCOLN PLAZA	NEW YORK, NY	10023
GELB, CLIFF	WRITER	555 W 57TH ST #1230	NEW YORK, NY	10019
GELB, JODY	ACTRESS	9229 SUNSET BLVD #306	LOS ANGELES, CA	90069
GELB, LESLIE H	NEWS CORRESPONDENT	2405 ELBA CT	ALEXANDRIA, VA	22306
GELB, MICHAEL	NEWS CORRESPONDENT	2226 N KENSINGTON ST	ARLINGTON, VA	22205
GELB, SONDRA	MEZZO-SOPRANO	PERLS, 7 W 96TH ST	NEW YORK, NY	10025
GELBAND, MYRA	SPORTS WRITER-EDITOR	SPORTS ILLUSTRATED MAGAZINE		
		TIME & LIFE BUILDING		
		ROCKEFELLER CENTER	NEW YORK, NY	10020
GELBART, LARRY	WRITER-PRODUCER	807 N ALPINE DR	BEVERLY HILLS, CA	90210
GELBER, BRUNO LEONARDO	PIANIST	COLBERT, 111 W 57TH ST	NEW YORK, NY	10019
GELBER, JACK	WRITER	555 W 57TH ST #1230	NEW YORK, NY	10019
GELBMANN, LARRY	ACTOR	5235 VIRGINIA AVE	LOS ANGELES, CA	90029
GELD, KARYL	WRITER	14455 DUNBAR PL	SHERMAN OAKS, CA	91423
GELDOF, BOB	SINGER-HUMANITARIAN	DAVINGTON PRIORY	LONDON	ENGLAND
GELFOND, BERYL	DIRECTOR	3217 FRYMAN RD	STUDIO CITY, CA	91604
GELGUR, DONNA	WRITER	8955 BEVERLY BLVD	LOS ANGELES, CA	90048
GELIN, DANIEL	FILM DIRECTOR	92 BLVD MURAT	PARIS 75016	FRANCE

GELIN, XAVIER	ACTOR	16 RUE DE MARIGNAN	PARIS 75008	FRANCE
GELINE, ROBERT J	TV EXECUTIVE	NBC-TV, 30 ROCKEFELLER PLAZA	NEW YORK, NY	10112
GELLER, HERBERT	COMPOSER	JULIUS VOSSELERSTRASSE	2000 HAMBURG 54 566-78	GERMANY
GELLER, MATT	TV WRITER	10982 ROEBLIND AVE #438	LOS ANGELES, CA	90024
GELLER, NANCY	TV PRODUCER	10100 SANTA MONICA BLVD #1600	LOS ANGELES, CA	90067
GELLER, NORM	CONDUCTOR	3538 TWAIN AVE	LAS VEGAS, NV	89121
GELLER, ROBERT	TV PRODUCER-EXECUTIVE	LEARNING IN FOCUS		
		310 MADISON AVE	NEW YORK, NY	10017
GELLER, ROBERT	WRITER	555 W 57TH ST #1230	NEW YORK, NY	10019
GELLER, STEPHEN	WRITER	8955 BEVERLY BLVD	LOS ANGELES, CA	90048
GELLER, URI	PSYCHIC	POST OFFICE BOX 5175	NEW YORK, NY	10150
GELLERMAN, BRUCE E	NEWS CORRESPONDENT	2025 "M" ST, NW	WASHINGTON, DC	20036
GELLMAN, ALEXANDER	ACTOR	3 E MOUNT AIRY RD	CROTON-ON-HUDSON, NY	10520
GELLMAN, MICHAEL	ACTOR-WRITER	8955 BEVERLY BLVD	LOS ANGELES, CA	90048
GELMAN, ALAN DAVID	ACTOR	1418 N HIGHLAND AVE #102	LOS ANGELES, CA	90028
GELMAN, LARRY	ACTOR	5121 GREENBUSH AVE	SHERMAN OAKS, CA	91423
GELMAN, LAURIE	TV WRITER	12232 HUSTON ST	NORTH HOLLYWOOD, CA	91607
GELMAN, MILTON S	WRITER-PRODUCER	13905 MILBANK ST	SHERMAN OAKS, CA	91423
GELMAN, MORRIE	COLUMNIST	VARIETY, 1400 N CAHUENGA BLVD	HOLLYWOOD, CA	90028
GELMIS, JOSEPH	FILM CRITIC	1500 BROADWAY #2201	NEW YORK, NY	10036
GELOTTE, BOB	DRUMMER	775 MYHR DR	NASHVILLE, TN	37221
GELSEY, ERWIN S	WRITER	9160 BEVERLY BLVD #302	BEVERLY HILLS, CA	90210
GELTNER, SHARON	NEWS CORRESPONDENT	5763 EXETER CT #260	ALEXANDRIA, VA	22311
GEMPERLEIN, JOYCE A	NEWS CORRESPONDENT	3860 RODMAN ST, NW	WASHINGTON, DC	20016
GENDEL, MARK	GUITARIST	100 VALLEY GREEN CT	ANTIOCH, TN	37013
GENDELMAN, JEFF	ACTOR	ABC-TV NETWORK, "LOVING"		
		1330 AVE OF THE AMERICAS	NEW YORK, NY	10019
GENE, LONNIE	SINGER	JIMKA, 600 NEVAN RD	VIRGINIA BEACH, VA	23451
GENELIN, ALAN MICHAEL	WRITER	13169 CHELTENHAM DR	SHERMAN OAKS, CA	91423
GENERAL BAND	C & W GROUP	JOHNNY VINE, ROUTE #1	SULPHUR SPRINGS, TX	75482
GENERAL CAINE	ROCK & ROLL GROUP	151 S EL CAMINO DR	BEVERLY HILLS, CA	90212
GENERATION X	ROCK & ROLL GROUP	JOSEPH, 184 GLOUCESTER	LONDON NW1	ENGLAND
GENESIS	ROCK & ROLL TRIO	HIT & RUN MUSIC, LTD		
		81-83 WALTON ST	LONDON SW3 2HR	ENGLAND
GENGE, PAUL	ACTOR	5607 LA MIRADA AVE #406	LOS ANGELES, CA	90038
GENISE, LIVIA	ACTRESS	7050 FLORAMORGAN TRAIL	TUJUNGA, CA	91042
GENNARELLI, CHARLES A	DIRECTOR	7 PHILLIPS LN	RYE, NY	10580
GENOVESE, MIKE	ACTOR	1509 N CRESCENT HGTS BLVD #7	LOS ANGELES, CA	90069
GENSON, DON	WRITER	144 S MC CARTHY DR	BEVERLY HILLS, CA	90212
GENT, GEORGE D "PETER"	SCREENWRITER	8955 BEVERLY BLVD	LOS ANGELES, CA	90048
GENTEEL, LINDA	PIANIST	7060 HOLLYWOOD BLVD #1212	HOLLYWOOD, CA	90028
GENTLEMAN	WRESTLER	SEE - ADAMS, CHRIS "GENTLEMAN"		
GENTNER, RICK	WRESTLER	AMERICAN WRESTLING ASSOC		
		MINNEAPLOIS WRESTLING		
		10001 WAYZATA BLVD	MINNETONKA, MN	55345
GENTRY, BOBBIE	SINGER-SONGWRITER	19801 WELLS DR	WOODLAND HILLS, CA	91364
GENTRY, RENEE	ACTRESS	6430 SUNSET BLVD #701	HOLLYWOOD, CA	90028
GENTRY, ROBERT	ACTOR	ABC-TV, "ALL MY CHILDREN"		
		1330 AVE OF THE AMERICAS	NEW YORK, NY	10019
GENUS, KARL	TV DIRECTOR	1049 ALPINE VILLA DR	ALTADENA, CA	91001
GENZMER, HARALD	CONDUCTOR	IAPR, KINCORA, BEER RD, SEATON	DEVON	ENGLAND
GEOFFREYS, STEPHEN	ACTOR	9200 SUNSET BLVD #1210	LOS ANGELES, CA	90069
GEOGHAN, JIM	TV WRITER	804 MANSFIELD AVE	LOS ANGELES, CA	90038
GEORGE, BARBARA	ACTRESS-WRITER	1437 N HAVENHURST DR	LOS ANGELES, CA	90046
GEORGE, BOY	SINGER-COMPOSER	34-A GREEN LN, NORTHWOOD	MIDDLESEX	ENGLAND
GEORGE, DOROETHA	NEWS CORRESPONDENT	5305 TUSCARAWAS RD	BETHESDA, MD	20816
GEORGE, EARL	ACTOR	4445 POST RD	RIVERDALE, NY	10471
GEORGE, GEORGE L	DIRECTOR-PRODUCER	685 W END AVE	NEW YORK, NY	10025
GEORGE, GEORGE W	THEATER PRODUCER	60 W 55TH ST	NEW YORK, NY	10019
GEORGE, GEORGE W	WRITER	8955 BEVERLY BLVD	LOS ANGELES, CA	90048
GEORGE, GORGEOUS	WRESTLER	GRANT, BLESSED HOPE CHURCH		
		BLESSED HOPE RD	YORK, SC	29745
GEORGE, HOWARD	ACTOR-WRITER	1746 N ORANGE DR #1002	LOS ANGELES, CA	90028
GEORGE, JENNIFER	ACTRESS	3575 W CAHUENGA BLVD #320	LOS ANGELES, CA	90068
GEORGE, JEROME	NEWS REPORTER	THE NATIONAL ENQUIRER		
		600 SE COAST AVE	LANTANA, FL	33464
GEORGE, JOE	ACTOR	6736 LAUREL CANYON BLVD #306	NORTH HOLLYWOOD, CA	91606
GEORGE, JON A	SCREENWRITER	8955 BEVERLY BLVD	LOS ANGELES, CA	90048
GEORGE, LYNDA DAY	ACTRESS	1501 S SIMMONS AVE	LOS ANGELES, CA	90022
GEORGE, PHYLLIS	TV PERSONALITY	SEE - GEORGE BROWN, PHYLLIS		
GEORGE, ROBERT	TV WRITER	8955 BEVERLY BLVD	LOS ANGELES, CA	90048
GEORGE, SUSAN	ACTRESS	838 N DOHENY DR #1201	LOS ANGELES, CA	90069
GEORGE, TANYA L	ACTRESS	KELMAN, 7813 SUNSET BLVD	LOS ANGELES, CA	90046
GEORGE, WALLY	TV HOST	POST OFFICE BOX 787	LOS ANGELES, CA	90028
GEORGE BROWN, PHYLLIS	TV PERSONALITY	CAVE HILL LN, BOX 4308	LEXINGTON, KY	40511
GEORGEOUS GEORGE	WRESTLER	SEE - GEORGE, GORGEOUS		
GEORGES, HARVEY	PHOTOGRAPHER	6603 TUCKER AVE	MC LEAN, VA	22101
GEORGES, LIZ	ACTRESS	6736 LAUREL CANYON BLVD #306	NORTH HOLLYWOOD, CA	91606
GEORGEVICH, DEJAN	DIRECTOR	42 CROTON AVE	HASTINGS-ON-HUDSON, NY	10706
GEORGIADE, NICHOLAS	ACTOR	3429 COUNTRY CLUB DR	LOS ANGELES, CA	90019
GERACE, LOIS	ACTRESS	6767 IRONDALE AVE	CANOGA PARK, CA	91306
GERADO, ANDREW	ACTOR	ROSS, 60 E 42ND ST	NEW YORK, NY	10165
GERAGHTY, ANNE F	NEWS CORRESPONDENT	1214 OLDE TOWNE RD	ALEXANDRIA, VA	22304
GERAGHTY, JANE	TALENT AGENT	3 E 54TH ST #1400	NEW YORK, NY	10022
GERAGHTY, MAURY	TV WRITER-DIRECTOR	1557 S RIVERSIDE DR	PALM SPRINGS, CA	92262

Name	Occupation	Address	City	Zip
GERARD, ANNE	SCREENWRITER	8955 BEVERLY BLVD	LOS ANGELES, CA	90048
GERARD, DAVID	CLOWN	2701 COTTAGE WY #14	SACRAMENTO, CA	95825
GERARD, GIL	ACTOR	10000 SANTA MONICA BLVD #305	LOS ANGELES, CA	90067
GERARD, J S	KARATE EXPERT	2801 MEADOW LARK DR	SAN DIEGO, CA	92123
GERARD, MARGARET	ACTRESS	MANN, 1 OLD COMPTON ST	LONDON W1	ENGLAND
GERARD, MERWIN	TV WRITER	857 BURNSIDE AVE	LOS ANGELES, CA	90036
GERATY, FRANK	CINEMATOGRAPHER	7715 SUNSET BLVD #150	LOS ANGELES, CA	90046
GERBER, BILL	TALENT AGENT	LOOKOUT, 9120 SUNSET BLVD	LOS ANGELES, CA	90069
GERBER, DAISY	FILM DIRECTOR	9617 OAK PASS RD	BEVERLY HILLS, CA	90210
GERBER, DAVID	TV PRODUCER	10800 CHALON RD	LOS ANGELES, CA	90077
GERBER, EDWARD W	CONDUCTOR	12406 CHERRY	KANSAS CITY, MO	64145
GERBER, ELLA	ACTRESS	329 E 58TH ST	NEW YORK, NY	10022
GERBER, JAY	ACTOR	16732 MC CORMICK ST	ENCINO, CA	91436
GERBER, STEVE	WRITER	8955 BEVERLY BLVD	LOS ANGELES, CA	90048
GERBERG, MORT	CARTOONIST	POST OFFICE BOX 4203	NEW YORK, NY	10017
GERDAU, RICHARD	TV WRITER-DIRECTOR	9200 SUNSET BLVD #808	LOS ANGELES, CA	90069
GERE, RICHARD	ACTOR	26 E 10TH ST #PH	NEW YORK, NY	10003
GERECHT, ASH	NEWS CORRESPONDENT	1109 RUPPERT RD	SILVER SPRING, MD	20903
GEREN, TOM	CINEMATOGRAPHER	7715 SUNSET BLVD #150	LOS ANGELES, CA	90046
GERHARD, DEBORAH	PHOTOGRAPHER	1255 N HAMPSHIRE AVE #320, NW	WASHINGTON, DC	20036
GERHART, KENNETH C	WRITER	555 W 57TH ST #1230	NEW YORK, NY	10019
GERICKE, THOMAS J	WRITER	2322 LYRIC AVE	LOS ANGELES, CA	90027
GERINGAS, DAVID	CELLIST	MARIEDL ANDERS ARTISTS MGMT		
		535 EL CAMINO DEL MAR ST	SAN FRANCISCO, CA	94121
GERKEN, ELLEN	ACTRESS	646 S BARRINGTON AVE #213	LOS ANGELES, CA	90049
GERLACH, EUGENE	PHOTOJOURNALIST	9301 CHANUTE DR	BETHESDA, MD	20814
GERLACH, GEORGE R	PHOTOJOURNALIST	4720 HARDESTY RD	HUNTINGTOWN, MD	20639
GERLE, ROBERT	CONDUCTOR	3003 VAN NESS ST, NW	WASHINGTON, DC	20008
GERMINO, MARK & THE FOLK 'N' RO	FOLK-ROCK GROUP	34 MUSIC SQUARE E	NASHVILLE, TN	37203
GERMOND, JACK W	NEWS CORRESPONDENT	6613 VIRGINIA VIEW CT	BETHESDA, MD	20816
GERO, FRANK	THEATER PRODUCER	1140 BROADWAY	NEW YORK, NY	10001
GERO, MARK	THEATER PRODUCER	214 E 89TH ST	NEW YORK, NY	10028
GERONIMI, CLYDE	ANIMATOR-DIRECTOR	1069 BUCKINGHAM LN	NEWPORT BEACH, CA	92660
GERRARD, JEFF	CASTING DIRECTOR	CARSON, 10643 RIVERSIDE DR	NORTH HOLLYWOOD, CA	91602
GERRISH, FLO	ACTRESS	11240 MAGNOLIA BLVD #202	NORTH HOLLYWOOD, CA	91601
GERRITY, DANIEL	ACTOR	1752 N SERRANO AVE #604	LOS ANGELES, CA	90027
GERROLD, DAVID	WRITER	8955 BEVERLY BLVD	LOS ANGELES, CA	90048
GERRY, TONI	ACTRESS	3151 W CAHUENGA BLVD #310	LOS ANGELES, CA	90068
GERRY & THE PACEMAKERS	ROCK & ROLL GROUP	28-A MANOR ROW	BRADFORD BDL 3QU	ENGLAND
GERSHE, LEONARD	TV WRITER	9400 EDEN DR	BEVERLY HILLS, CA	90210
GERSHFIELD, JONATHAN	FILM WRITER-DIRECTOR	16 DENBIGH RD, GARDEN FLAT	LONDON W11	ENGLAND
GERSHMAN, BEN	WRITER	451 SAN VICENTE BLVD #1	SANTA MONICA, CA	90402
GERSHUNY, THEODORE	WRITER	555 W 57TH ST #1230	NEW YORK, NY	10019
GERSMEHL, MARK S	PIANIST	111 OLD HICKORY BLVD #354	NASHVILLE, TN	37221
GERSON, PHILIP	ACTOR-WRITER	1310 N VISTA ST	LOS ANGELES, CA	90046
GERSTEIN, DANNY	ACTOR	49 W 88TH ST #3	NEW YORK, NY	10024
GERSTEL, STEVEN	NEWS CORRESPONDENT	1635 COLONIAL TERR	ARLINGTON, VA	22209
GERSTEN, BERNARD	THEATER PRODUCER	QUAD PRODS, 890 BROADWAY	NEW YORK, NY	10003
GERSTEN, GERRY	CARTOONIST	MAD MAGAZINE, INC		
		485 MADISON AVE	NEW YORK, NY	10022
GERSTENZANG, JAMES	NEWS CORRESPONDENT	7427 12TH ST, NW	WASHINGTON, DC	20012
GERTH, JEFF	NEWS CORRESPONDENT	4201 CATHEDRAL AVE #808-W, NW	WASHINGTON, DC	20016
GERTLER, DEBRA J	PHOTOGRAPHER	1101 S WASHINGTON ST #92-C	ALEXANDRIA, VA	22314
GERTZ, IRVING	COMPOSER-CONDUCTOR	351 VETERAN AVE	LOS ANGELES, CA	90024
GERTZ, JAMI	ACTRESS	POST OFFICE BOX 5617	BEVERLY HILLS, CA	90210
GERTZ, STEPHEN J	WRITER	8955 BEVERLY BLVD	LOS ANGELES, CA	90048
GERULAITAS, VITAS	TENNIS	1 ERIEVIEW PLAZA	CLEVELAND, OH	44114
GESCHWIND, JOE	ACTOR	226 GRUBER CT	WEST HEMPSTEAD, NY	11552
GESNER, CLARK	WRITER	555 W 57TH ST #1230	NEW YORK, NY	10019
GESSENDORF, MECHTHILD	SOPRANO	CAMI, 165 W 57TH ST	NEW YORK, NY	10019
GESSLER, JOAN E	WRITER	13416 RAMONA PARKWAY	BALDWIN PARK, NY	91706
GESSNER, HAL	TV DIRECTOR-PRODUCER	30 W 15TH ST	NEW YORK, NY	10011
GEST, KATHRYN W	NEWS CORRESPONDENT	6221 WESTERN AVE, NW	WASHINGTON, DC	20015
GEST, TED	NEWS CORRESPONDENT	6221 WESTERN AVE, NW	WASHINGTON, DC	20015
GET SMART	ROCK & ROLL TRIO	POST OFFICE BOX 3800		
		MERCHANDISE MART	CHICAGO, IL	60654
GETCHELL, FRANKLIN	TV WRITER	555 W 57TH ST #1230	NEW YORK, NY	10019
GETCHELL, ROBERT L	SCREENWRITER	8730 HOLLYWOOD HILLS RD	LOS ANGELES, CA	90046
GETHERS, ERIC	TV WRITER	2759 WOODSHIRE DR	LOS ANGELES, CA	90068
GETHERS, PETER	WRITER	555 W 57TH ST #1230	NEW YORK, NY	10019
GETHERS, STEVEN	TV WRITER-DIRECTOR	9100 HAZEN DR	BEVERLY HILLS, CA	90210
GETLIN, SCOTT	ACTOR	183 N MARTEL AVE #260	LOS ANGELES, CA	90036
GETSI, JOSEPH M	MUSICIAN	324 E FAIRVIEW RD	OAK RIDGE, TN	37830
GETSI, MARK	GUITARIST	49 INTRA CITY TRAILER PARK	BOWLING GREEN, KY	42101
GETTENGER, BRAD	ACTOR	101 W 69TH ST #3-B	NEW YORK, NY	10023
GETTINGER, STEPHEN	NEWS CORRESPONDENT	1741 "T" ST #104, NW	WASHINGTON, DC	20009
GETTLER, RACHEL	MEZZO-SOPRANO	HILLYER, 250 W 57TH ST	NEW YORK, NY	10107
GETTLER, RACHEL	SINGER	2109 BROADWAY #10-10	NEW YORK, NY	10023
GETTLIN, ROBERT H	NEWS CORRESPONDENT	2144 CALIFORNIA ST #905, NW	WASHINGTON, DC	20008
GETTY, ESTELLE	ACTRESS	68-85 218TH ST	BAYSIDE, NY	11364
GETTY, GORDON	COMPOSER	1199 PARK AVE #1-E	NEW YORK, NY	10028
GETTY, GORDON P	PHILANTHROPIST	THE JOHN PAUL GETTY MUSEUM		
		17985 PACIFIC COAST HWY	MALIBU, CA	90265
GETZ, DON	FILM EXECUTIVE	PLAYPONT, 47 DEAN ST	LONDON W1V 5HL	ENGLAND
GETZ, JOHN	ACTOR	POST OFFICE BOX 5617	BEVERLY HILLS, CA	90210

Name	Occupation	Address	City	Zip
GETZ, ROBERT	TV PRODUCER	CBS-TV, 524 W 57TH ST	NEW YORK, NY	10019
GETZ, STAN	SAXOPHONIST	SHADOWBROOK	IRVINGTON, NY	10533
GEWIRTZ, HOWARD	TV WRITER	12301 ROCHEDALE LN	LOS ANGELES, CA	90049
GEYER, GEORGIE ANNE	JOURNALIST	UPS, TIME & LIFE BUILDING		
		1271 AVE OF THE AMERICAS #3717	NEW YORK, NY	10020
GEYER, STEPHEN G	COMPOSER	118 PACIFIC ST	SANTA MONICA, CA	90405
GHAZARIAN, SONA	SOPRANO	CAMI, 165 W 57TH ST	NEW YORK, NY	10019
GHAZLO, ANTHONY	ACTOR	6736 LAUREL CANYON BLVD #306	NORTH HOLLYWOOD, CA	91606
GHEHREAB, DEHAB	NEWS CORRESPONDENT	1615 S 28TH ST #1	ARLINGTON, VA	22206
GHERTNER, CAROLE	ACTRESS	11429 YOLANDA AVE	NORTHRIDGE, CA	91326
GHIAUROV, NICOLAI	BASSO-BARITONE	CAMI, 165 W 57TH ST	NEW YORK, NY	10019
GHIGLIA, OSCAR	GUITARIST	COLBERT, 111 W 57TH ST	NEW YORK, NY	10019
GHIUSELEV, NICOLA	SINGER	CAMI, 165 W 57TH ST	NEW YORK, NY	10019
GHOSTLEY, ALICE	ACTRESS	3800 REKLAW DR	NORTH HOLLYWOOD, CA	91604
GIACHETTI, RICHIE	ACTOR-BOXING TRAINER	ROUND 15, 10400 LORRAINE AVE	CLEVELAND, OH	44136
GIACOMINI, GIUSEPPE	TENOR	61 W 62ND ST #6-F	NEW YORK, NY	10023
GIACOMO, CAROL A	NEWS CORRESPONDENT	1209 LINDEN PL, NE	WASHINGTON, DC	20002
GIAIOTTI, BONALDO	BASS	61 W 62ND ST #6-F	NEW YORK, NY	10023
GIAMBALVO, LOUIS	ACTOR	10100 SANTA MONICA BLVD #1600	LOS ANGELES, CA	90067
GIANGIULIO, RICHARD	TRUMPETER	POST OFFICE BOX 160	HIGHLAND PARK, IL	60035
GIANNINI, CHERYL	ACTRESS	AFFILIATE ARTISTS, INC		
		37 W 65TH ST, 6TH FLOOR	NEW YORK, NY	10023
GIANOTTI, PETER	NEWS CORRESPONDENT	1725 NEW HAMPSHIRE AVE #501, NW	WASHINGTON, DC	20009
GIANT, THE	WRESTLER	SEE - ANDRE THE GIANT		
GIANT MACHINE	WRESTLER	SEE - ANDRE THE GIANT		
GIANT SAND	ROCK & ROLL TRIO	2509 N CAMPBELL AVE #202	TUSCON, AZ	85719
GIAQUINTO, JOSEPH E	TV EXECUTIVE	ABC-TV, 1330 AVE OF AMERICAS	NEW YORK, NY	10019
GIARDINA, GARY	BASSO-BARITONE	LIEBERMAN, 11 RIVERSIDE DR	NEW YORK, NY	10023
GIARDINO, MARK	ACTOR	4545 TALOFA AVE	NORTH HOLLYWOOD, CA	91602
GIARNIERO, RICHARD P	WRITER	555 W 57TH ST #1230	NEW YORK, NY	10019
GIATTI, IAN	ACTOR	3575 W CAHUENGA BLVD #320	LOS ANGELES, CA	90068
GIBB, ANDY	SINGER-SONGWRITER	POST OFFICE BOX 8179	MIAMI BEACH, FL	33139
GIBB, BARRY	SINGER-SONGWRITER	KRAGEN, 1112 N SHERBOURNE DR	LOS ANGELES, CA	90069
GIBB, CYNTHIA	ACTRESS	19 W 44TH ST #1500	NEW YORK, NY	10036
GIBB, MAURICE	SINGER-SONGWRITER	KRAGEN, 1112 N SHERBOURNE DR	LOS ANGELES, CA	90069
GIBB, ROBIN	SINGER-SONGWRITER	KRAGEN, 1112 N SHERBOURNE DR	LOS ANGELES, CA	90069
GIBB, STEPHEN M	MUSIC ARRANGER	2120 CHESTMOOR DR #41	NASHVILLE, TN	37215
GIBB, TOM	CARTOONIST	HERITAGE FEATURES SYNDICATE		
		214 MASSACHUSETTS AVE, NE	WASHINGTON, DC	20002
GIBBON, MICHAEL	TV DIRECTOR	7 ALTON RD	LONDON SW15	ENGLAND
GIBBON, SAMUEL YOUNG, JR	DIRECTOR	CHILDREN'S TV WORKSHOP		
		1 LINCOLN PLAZA	NEW YORK, NY	10023
GIBBONS, BEVERLY	PIANIST	POST OFFICE BOX 20548	NEW YORK, NY	10025
GIBBONS, DON L	NEWS CORRESPONDENT	6236 18TH RD	ARLINGTON, VA	22205
GIBBONS, DONNA	ACTRESS	11726 SAN VICENTE BLVD #300	LOS ANGELES, CA	90049
GIBBONS, GENE	NEWS CORRESPONDENT	907 DE WOLFE DR	ALEXANDRIA, VA	22308
GIBBONS, JOHN	HARPSICHORDIST	AARON, 25 HUNTINGTON AVE	BOSTON, MA	02116
GIBBONS, LEEZA	NEWS CORRESPONDENT	ENTERTAINMENT TONIGHT		
		PARAMOUNT TELEVISION		
		5555 MELROSE AVE	LOS ANGELES, CA	90038
GIBBONS, STEVE, BAND	ROCK & ROLL GROUP	3 E 54TH ST #1400	NEW YORK, NY	10022
GIBBONS, THOMAS B	NEWS CORRESPONDENT	4431 S 36TH ST #B-2	ARLINGTON, VA	22206
GIBBS, ADRIAN	ACTOR	43 BAALBEC RD, HIGHBURY	LONDON N5	ENGLAND
GIBBS, ALAN R	DIRECTOR	3518 W CAHUENGA BLVD #300	LOS ANGELES, CA	90068
GIBBS, BILL & HIS COUNTRY HAMS	C & W GROUP	POST OFFICE BOX 11321		
		FLAGLER STATION	MIAMI, FL	33101
GIBBS, EMILIE	NEWS CORRESPONDENT	5431 SHEFFIELD CT	ALEXANDRIA, VA	22311
GIBBS, GEORGIA	SINGER	GERVASI, 765 5TH AVE	NEW YORK, NY	10021
GIBBS, MARLA	ACTRESS	1607 N EL CENTRO AVE #2	LOS ANGELES, CA	90028
GIBBS, MICHAEL	CONDUCTOR	KURLAND, 173 BRIGHTON AVE	BOSTON, MA	02134
GIBBS, NANCY R	NEWS REPORTER	TIME/TIME & LIFE BLDG		
		ROCKEFELLER CENTER	NEW YORK, NY	10020
GIBBS, NORMAN ALEXANDER	ACTOR	3907 W ALAMEDA AVE #101	BURBANK, CA	91505
GIBBS, RICHARD K	COMPOSER	7921 AURA AVE	RESEDA, CA	91335
GIBBS, SCOTT	DIRECTOR	DGA, 7950 SUNSET BLVD	LOS ANGELES, CA	90046
GIBBS, TERRI	SINGER-SONGWRITER	414 GIBBS CIR	GROVETOWN, GA	30813
GIBBS, TERRY	WRESTLER	POST OFFICE BOX 3859	STAMFORD, CT	06905
GIBLIN, JOHN J	ACTOR	1056 1/4 N OXFORD AVE	LOS ANGELES, CA	90029
GIBNEY, SHERIDAN	WRITER	8955 BEVERLY BLVD	LOS ANGELES, CA	90048
GIBSON, ALAN	TV DIRECTOR-PRODUCER	55 PORTLAND RD	LONDON W11	ENGLAND
GIBSON, ALEXANDER	CONDUCTOR	SEE - GIBSON, SIR ALEXANDER		
GIBSON, BOB	SINGER	PRODUCERS, 5109 OAK HAVEN LN	TAMPA, FL	33617
GIBSON, BOB	BASEBALL	215 BELLEVIEW BLVD S	BELLEVIEW, NE	68005
GIBSON, BRIAN	CINEMATOGRAPHER	3 FITZROY SQ	LONDON W1P 5AN	ENGLAND
GIBSON, BRIAN J	FILM DIRECTOR	65 GREENHILL, HAMPSTEAD	LONDON NW3	ENGLAND
GIBSON, CAL	ACTOR	7300 LANKERSHIM BLVD #135	NORTH HOLLYWOOD, CA	91605
GIBSON, CHANNING	TV WRITER	8955 BEVERLY BLVD	LOS ANGELES, CA	90048
GIBSON, CHARLES D	NEWS CORRESPONDENT	3511 RITTENHOUSE ST, NW	WASHINGTON, DC	20015
GIBSON, CURT	GUITARIST	808 BROADMOOR DR	NASHVILLE, TN	37216
GIBSON, DON	SINGER-GUITARIST	38 MUSIC SQUARE E #300	NASHVILLE, TN	37203
GIBSON, FRANK L, JR	NEWS CORRESPONDENT	12614 BILLINGTON RD	SILVER SPRING, MD	20904
GIBSON, GERRY	ACTOR	3800 BARHAM BLVD #303	LOS ANGELES, CA	90068
GIBSON, HARRIETT	FILM PRODUCER	843 21ST ST #1	SANTA MONICA, CA	90403
GIBSON, HENRY	ACTOR	24840 PACIFIC COAST HWY	MALIBU, CA	90265
GIBSON, HENRY R	WRITER	555 W 57TH ST #1230	NEW YORK, NY	10019

GIBSON, JACK	RADIO PERSONALITY	BILLYE LOVE, JACK THE RAPPER		
		2637 BARKWATER DR	ORLANDO, FL	32809
GIBSON, JEAN LEWIS	COMPOSER	4108 TUJUNGA AVE	STUDIO CITY, CA	91604
GIBSON, JOE F	GUITARIST	2432 INGA AVE	NASHVILLE, TN	37206
GIBSON, JOHN R	NEWS CORRESPONDENT	4105 40TH ST N	ARLINGTON, VA	22207
GIBSON, JONATHAN D	WRITER	8955 BEVERLY BLVD	LOS ANGELES, CA	90048
GIBSON, KENT	DIRECTOR	1508 N CRESCENT HGTS BLVD	HOLLYWOOD, CA	90046
GIBSON, KIRK	BASEBALL	1082 OAK POINTE DR	PONTIAC, MI	48054
GIBSON, LOIS	WRITER	8955 BEVERLY BLVD	LOS ANGELES, CA	90048
GIBSON, MEL	ACTOR-WRITER	SHANAHAN MANAGEMNET		
		129 BOURKE ST	WOOLLOOMOOLOO NSW 2011	AUSTRALIA
GIBSON, MELANIE	ACTRESS	10 BUSHWOOD, LEYTONSTON	LONDON E11	ENGLAND
GIBSON, MICHAEL	CONDUCTOR	POST OFFICE BOX 131	SPRINGFIELD, VA	22150
GIBSON, PIERS	FILM PRODUCER	CINDERELLA PRODUCTIONS		
		5 D'ARBLAY ST	LONDON W1	ENGLAND
GIBSON, RICK	GUITARIST	ROUTE #4, 206 LAKESIDE DR	ASHLAND CITY, TN	37015
GIBSON, ROBERT	WRESTLER	NATIONAL WRESTLING ALLIANCE		
		JIM CROCKETT PROMOTIONS		
		421 BRIARBEND DR	CHARLOTTE, NC	28209
GIBSON, ROBERTA J	WRITER	8955 BEVERLY BLVD	LOS ANGELES, CA	90048
GIBSON, RUSS	ACTOR	BURLEWS #5, HWY 71	BRIELLE, NJ	08730
GIBSON, SANDY	WRITER	8955 BEVERLY BLVD	LOS ANGELES, CA	90048
GIBSON, SIR ALEXANDER	CONDUCTOR	ICM, 40 W 57TH ST	NEW YORK, NY	10019
GIBSON, STEVEN A	GUITARIST	POST OFFICE BOX 150451	NASHVILLE, TN	37215
GIBSON, STEVEN D	GUITARIST	808 BROADMOOR DR	NASHVILLE, TN	37216
GIBSON, WALTER P, JR	SAXOPHONIST	818 TANNAHILL DR	HUNTSVILLE, AL	35802
GIBSON, WILLIAM E	NEWS CORRESPONDENT	816 "E" ST, SE	WASHINGTON, DC	20003
GIBSON, WILLIAM J	TV DIRECTOR	4121 REDWOOD AVE	LOS ANGELES, CA	90066
GIBSON BROTHERS, THE	VOCAL GROUP	ISLAND RECORDS COMPANY		
		7720 SUNSET BLVD	LOS ANGELES, CA	90046
GIBSONS, THE	GOSPEL GROUP	POST OFFICE BOX 124	KIRBYVILLE, TX	75956
GIDCOMB, JOHNNY	GUITARIST	210 PLEASANT DR	COLUMBIA, TN	38401
GIDDENS, JAMES	DIRECTOR	DGA, 7950 SUNSET BLVD	LOS ANGELES, CA	90046
GIDDING, NELSON	WRITER	234 VANCE ST	PACIFIC PALISADES, CA	90272
GIDEON, BOND	ACTRESS	427 N CANON DR #205	BEVERLY HILLS, CA	90210
GIDEON, RAYMOND	SCREENWRITER	3524 MULTIVIEW DR	LOS ANGELES, CA	90068
GIDLEY, PAMELA	ACTRESS	ICM, 8899 BEVERLY BLVD	LOS ANGELES, CA	90048
GIELGUD, JOHN	ACTOR	SEE - GIELGUD, SIR JOHN		
GIELGUD, SIR JOHN	ACTOR	SOUTH PAVILLION		
		WOTTEN-UNDERWOOD, AYLESBURY	BUCKS	ENGLAND
GIERASCH, STEFAN	ACTOR	211 S BEVERLY DR #201	BEVERLY HILLS, CA	90212
GIERE, GLENN	TV DIRECTOR	208 W SHORE TRAIL	SPARTA, NJ	07871
GIESE, WILLIAM	NEWS CORRESPONDENT	7001 FLORIDA ST	CHEVY CHASE, FL	20815
GIESLER, RODNEY	WRITER-PRODUCER	5 PARK CHASE, GUILDFORD	SURREY GU1 1ES	ENGLAND
GIFFEN, RALPH R	DIRECTOR	633 HERITAGE VILLAGE #B	SOUTHBURY, CT	06488
GIFFORD, COURTNEY	NEWS CORRESPONDENT	5504 ANDREWS CHAPEL CT	FAIRFAX, VA	22032
GIFFORD, FRANK	NEWS CORRESPONDENT	1755 S JEFFERSON DAVIS HWY	ARLINGTON, VA	22202
GIFFORD, FRANK	SPORTSCASTER-FOOTBALL	355 TACONIC RD	GREENWICH, CT	06830
GIFFORD, GLORIA	ACTRESS	CONTEMPORARY ARTISTS		
		132 S LASKY DR	BEVERLY HILLS, CA	90212
GIFFORD, HAZEN	ACTOR	5 PETER COOPER RD	NEW YORK, NY	10010
GIFFORD, LEWIS L B	DIRECTOR	548 E 87TH ST	NEW YORK, NY	10016
GIFFORD, THOMAS	SCREENWRITER	8955 BEVERLY BLVD	LOS ANGELES, CA	90048
GIFFORD, WENDY	ACTRESS	CONWAY, EAGLE HOUSE		
		109 JERMYN ST	LONDON SW1	ENGLAND
GIFTOS, ELAINE	ACTRESS	3907 W ALAMEDA AVE #101	BURBANK, CA	91505
GIGER, ANTHONY	ACTOR	4361 ROSEWOOD AVE	LOS ANGELES, CA	90004
GIGLI, ORMOND	DIRECTOR	327 E 58TH ST	NEW YORK, NY	10022
GIL, JEAN-LOUIS	ORGANIST	15 HIGH ST #621	HARTFORD, CT	06103
GIL, JOANE	WRITER	8955 BEVERLY BLVD	LOS ANGELES, CA	90048
GILAD, YEHUDA	CONDUCTOR	953 N LAUREL AVE	LOS ANGELES, CA	90046
GILBEAUX, EUGENE A	COMPOSER	1020 GIRARD ST	SAN FRANCISCO, CA	94134
GILBERT, ADAM HILL	TV WRITER-PRODUCER	1590 SUNSET PLAZA DR	LOS ANGELES, CA	90069
GILBERT, ALAN	WRITER	8955 BEVERLY BLVD	LOS ANGELES, CA	90048
GILBERT, AMBER	ACTRESS	KNBC-TV, "DAYS OF OUR LIVES"		
		3000 W ALAMEDA AVE	BURBANK, CA	91523
GILBERT, BRUCE	FILM PRODUCER	AMERICAN FILMWORKS CO		
		4000 WARNER BLVD	BURBANK, CA	91522
GILBERT, CHARLES	ACTOR	400 W 43RD ST #42-N	NEW YORK, NY	10036
GILBERT, CRAIG P	WRITER	555 W 57TH ST #1230	NEW YORK, NY	10019
GILBERT, DAVE	WRITER	8955 BEVERLY BLVD	LOS ANGELES, CA	90048
GILBERT, DAVID G	WRITER	8955 BEVERLY BLVD	LOS ANGELES, CA	90048
GILBERT, EDDIE "HOT STUFF"	WRESTLER	UNIVERSAL WRESTLING FEDERATION		
		MID SOUTH SPORTS, INC		
		5001 SPRING VALLEY RD	DALLAS, TX	75244
GILBERT, EDMUND	ACTOR	6310 SAN VICENTE BLVD #407	LOS ANGELES, CA	90048
GILBERT, GARY	GUITARIST	PRESTON RD, BOX 456	ANTIOCH, TN	37013
GILBERT, GARY	TV WRITER	555 W 57TH ST #1230	NEW YORK, NY	10019
GILBERT, GULSHIN	ACTRESS	8831 SUNSET BLVD #402	LOS ANGELES, CA	90069
GILBERT, HERSCHEL BURKE	COMPOSER-CONDUCTOR	2451 NICHOLS CANYON PL	LOS ANGELES, CA	90046
GILBERT, IRENE	ACTRESS	10000 RIVERSIDE DR #3	TOLUCA LAKE, CA	91602
GILBERT, JAMES	DIRECTOR-PRODUCER	29 SYDNEY RD, RICHMOND	SURREY	ENGLAND
GILBERT, JIMMIE	CONDUCTOR	1771 KENNETH WY	PASADENA, CA	91103
GILBERT, JULIE G	WRITER	555 W 57TH ST #1230	NEW YORK, NY	10019
GILBERT, KENNETH	ACTOR	POST OFFICE BOX 130, HOVE	EAST SUSSEX BN3 6QU	ENGLAND

MEL GIBSON

MICKEY GILLEY

BABE GILLIAM

PAUL MICHAEL GLASER

SHARON GLESS

BOBBY GOLDSBORO

EYDIE GORME

GALE GORDON

GEORGE GOBEL

GILBERT, KENNETH C	DIRECTOR	KENANN, 6111 W 75TH ST	LOS ANGELES, CA	90045
GILBERT, KEVIN TIMOTHY	PHOTOGRAPHER	1168 JEFFREY DR	CROFTON, MD	21114
GILBERT, LEWIS	WRITER-PRODUCER	BAKER ROOKE, CLEMENT HOUSE		
		99 ALDWYCH	LONDON WC2 BJY	ENGLAND
GILBERT, MELISSA	ACTRESS	9255 SUNSET BLVD #1115	LOS ANGELES, CA	90069
GILBERT, MICKEY	DIRECTOR	DGA, 7950 SUNSET BLVD	LOS ANGELES, CA	90046
GILBERT, MIKE	NEWS CORRESPONDENT	708 LIVE OAK DR	MC LEAN, VA	22101
GILBERT, PAUL	TV PRODUCER	"DANCE FEVER," 1541 N VINE ST	HOLLYWOOD, CA	90028
GILBERT, PHILIP	ACTOR	LITTLE END, GREAT MISSENDEN	BUCKS	ENGLAND
GILBERT, RON	TV PRODUCER	MCA/UNIVERSAL STUDIOS, INC		
		100 UNIVERSAL CITY PLAZA #507	UNIVERSAL CITY, CA	91608
GILBERT, RUTH	ACTRESS	1070 PARK AVE	NEW YORK, NY	10028
GILBERT, STANLEY E	CINEMATOGRAPHER	DGA, 7950 SUNSET BLVD	LOS ANGELES, CA	90046
GILBERT, STANLEY J	NEWS CORRESPONDENT	6118 LYNLEY TERR	ALEXANDRIA, VA	22310
GILBERT, STEVE J	WRITER	8955 BEVERLY BLVD	LOS ANGELES, CA	90048
GILBERT, TIM	STUNTMAN	3518 W CAHUENGA BLVD #300	LOS ANGELES, CA	90069
GILBRIDE, JOE "THE HUMAN TORCH"	HUMAN TORCH	POST OFFICE BOX 8872		
		UNIVERSAL CITY STATION	UNIVERSAL CITY, CA	91608
GILBRIDGE, JOE	STUNTMAN	3518 W CAHUENGA BLVD #300	LOS ANGELES, CA	90068
GILDER, NICK	SINGER-COMPOSER	6354 VAN NUYS BLVD #150	VAN NUYS, CA	91401
GILDER, ROSAMOND	DRAMA CRITIC	24 GRAMERCY PARK	NEW YORK, NY	10003
GILDNER, BARBARA	ACTRESS	1217 S WESTGATE AVE #H	LOS ANGELES, CA	90025
GILER, DAVID	WRITER-PRODUCER	7874 WOODROW WILSON DR	LOS ANGELES, CA	90046
GILER, LYNNE D	WRITER	609 SAINT CLOUD RD	LOS ANGELES, CA	90077
GILES, JOHNNY	COMPOSER-CONDUCTOR	POST OFFICE BOX 244	APTOS, CA	95003
GILES, LEONARD A	MUSIC ARRANGER	488 LEMONT DR #1-182	NASHVILLE, TN	37216
GILFILLAN, SUE ANN	ACTRESS	247 S BEVERLY DR #102	BEVERLY HILLS, CA	90210
GILFORD, GWYNNE	ACTOR-WRITER	15010 VENTURA BLVD #219	SHERMAN OAKS, CA	91403
GILFORD, JACK	ACTOR	ICM, 40 W 57TH ST	NEW YORK, NY	10019
GILFRY, RODNEY	BARITONE	59 E 54TH ST #81	NEW YORK, NY	10022
GILKA, ROBERT E	PHOTOGRAPHER	4664 N 25TH ST	ARLINGTON, VA	22207
GILKINSON, JEFF	GUITARIST	POST OFFICE BOX 23255	NASHVILLE, TN	37202
GILL, ANDREW	STUNTMAN	3518 W CAHUENGA BLVD #300	LOS ANGELES, CA	90068
GILL, DEREK	WRITER	700 ESPLANADE ST #34	REDONDO BEACH, CA	90277
GILL, ELIZABETH	TV WRITER	959 GALLOWAY ST	PACIFIC PALISADES, CA	90272
GILL, JACK	STUNTMAN	18060 BORIS DR	ENCINO, CA	91316
GILL, JOHNNY	SINGER-PIANIST	330 W 58TH ST #4-H	NEW YORK, NY	10019
GILL, KATHLEEN D	NEWS CORRESPONDENT	5415 N 36TH RD	ARLINGTON, VA	22207
GILL, KENT	GUITARIST	712 ROBINSON PL	SHREVEPORT, LA	71104
GILL, MICHAEL	TV DIRECTOR	GILL, 16 NEWMAN PASS	LONDON W1	ENGLAND
GILL, VINCE	SINGER-SONGWRITER	7250 BEVERLY BLVD #200	LOS ANGELES, CA	90036
GILL, WILL, JR	ACTOR	8721 SUNSET BLVD #103	LOS ANGELES, CA	90069
GILLACH, JOSEPH P	WRITER	555 W 57TH ST #1230	NEW YORK, NY	10019
GILLARD, STUART	WRITER-PRODUCER	9744 WILSHIRE BLVD #206	BEVERLY HILLS, CA	90212
GILLEN, LINDA	ACTRESS	POST OFFICE BOX 5617	BEVERLY HILLS, CA	90210
GILLERAN, TOM	ACTOR	574 GREENCRAIG RD	LOS ANGELES, CA	90049
GILLES, DONALD B	TV WRITER	555 W 57TH ST #1230	NEW YORK, NY	10019
GILLES, GENEVIEVE	ACTRESS	THE DAKOTA, 1 W 72ND ST	NEW YORK, NY	10023
GILLES, NICHOLAS	TV EXECUTIVE	1111 PARK AVE	NEW YORK, NY	10028
GILLESBERG, CAROL	WRITER	555 W 57TH ST #1230	NEW YORK, NY	10019
GILLESPIE, ANGELA JO	NEWS CORRESPONDENT	9321 HUMPHRIES DR	BURKE, VA	22015
GILLESPIE, ANN	ACTRESS	J MICHAEL BLOOM AGENCY		
		233 PARK AVE S, 10TH FLOOR	NEW YORK, NY	10017
GILLESPIE, DIZZY	TRUMPETER	477 N WOODLANDS ST	ENGLEWOOD, NJ	07631
GILLESPIE, HENRY	CABLE EXECUTIVE	TBS, 1050 TECHWOOD DR, NW	ATLANTA, GA	30318
GILLESPIE, JEAN	ACTRESS	135 S CANON DR	BEVERLY HILLS, CA	90212
GILLESPIE, PHILLIP E	PHOTOGRAPHER	4451 ELAN CT	ANNANDALE, VA	22003
GILLESPIE, ROBERT	ACTOR-DIRECTOR	10 IRVING RD	LONDON W14 OJS	ENGLAND
GILLETT, JOHN	FILM CRITIC	BRITISH FILM INSTITUTE		
		127 CHARING CROSS RD	LONDON WC2	ENGLAND
GILLETTE, ANITA	ACTRESS	SF & A, 121 N SAN VICENTE BLVD	BEVERLY HILLS, CA	90211
GILLETTE, DAVID	NEWS CORRESPONDENT	5112 CLINTON RD	ALEXANDRIA, VA	22312
GILLETTE, RUTH	ACTRESS	12737 MOORPARK ST	STUDIO CITY, CA	91604
GILLETTE, STEVE	SINGER-SONGWRITER	SEGAL, 1116 N CORY AVE	LOS ANGELES, CA	90069
GILLEY, MICKEY	SINGER-SONGWRITER	9255 SUNSET BLVD #706	LOS ANGELES, CA	90069
GILLEY, ROBERT B	NEWS CORRESPONDENT	2139 WISCONSIN AVE, NW	WASHINGTON, DC	20007
GILLIAM, BABE	ACTRESS	9025 WILSHIRE BLVD #309	BEVERLY HILLS, CA	90211
GILLIAM, BURTON	ACTOR	825 N BEACHWOOD DR	BURBANK, CA	91506
GILLIAM, TERRY	ANI-DIR-ACT	14 NEAL'S YARD	LONDON WC1	ENGLAND
GILLIAM, TERRY	FILM DIRECTOR	METHUEN, 2330 MIDLAND AVE	AGIN, ONT M1S 1P7	CANADA
GILLIAM, TERRY V	WRITER-PRODUCER	51 S HILL PARK	LONDON NW3	ENGLAND
GILLIAT, LESLIE	FILM PRODUCER	13 SHERIDAN PL		
		ROXBOROUGH PARK		
		HARROW-ON-THE-HILL	MIDDLESEX	ENGLAND
GILLIGAN, JOHN P	TV WRITER	3120 SCOTLAND ST #A	LOS ANGELES, CA	90039
GILLIGAN, SONJA C	WRITER	555 W 57TH ST #1230	NEW YORK, NY	10019
GILLILAND, DEBORAH	TV WRITER	14144 VENTURA BLVD #200	SHERMAN OAKS, CA	91423
GILLILAND, RICHARD	ACTOR	9145 SUNSET BLVD #228	LOS ANGELES, CA	90069
GILLIN, HUGH	ACTOR	15010 VENTURA BLVD #219	SHERMAN OAKS, CA	91403
GILLION, CARL	SINGER	BUTTS, 1002 KIRBY DR	NASHVILLE, TN	37217
GILLION, CARL	MANDOLINIST	1002 KIRBY DR	NASHVILLE, TN	37217
GILLIS, JACKSON C	TV WRITER	4980 VANALDEN AVE	TARZANA, CA	91356
GILLIS, JOHN	CINEMATOGRAPHER	7715 SUNSET BLVD #150	LOS ANGELES, CA	90046
GILLIS, MARY	ACTRESS	1975 N BEACHWOOD DR #31	LOS ANGELES, CA	90068

Name	Occupation	Address	City	Code
GILLIS, VERNA	TALENT AGENT	SOUNDSCAPE, 500 W 52ND ST	NEW YORK, NY	10019
GILLON, DAVE	GUITARIST	2002 SWEETBRIAR AVE	NASHVILLE, TN	37212
GILLOT, NICK	TV PRODUCER	169 QUEENSGATE #8	LONDON SW7	ENGLAND
GILLOTTE, WENDY J	WRITER	555 W 57TH ST #1230	NEW YORK, NY	10019
GILLSON, CAROL A	TV WRITER-PRODUCER	4519 GLORIA AVE	ENCINO, CA	91436
GILLUM, VERN	DIRECTOR	8640 PINETREE PL	HOLLYWOOD, CA	90069
GILMAN, EDWARD M	PHOTOGRAPHER	3231 ADAMS CT	FAIRFAX, VA	22030
GILMAN, KENNETH	ACTOR	3516 MULTIVIEW DR	LOS ANGELES, CA	90068
GILMAN, KENNETH DAVID	ACTOR	10000 SANTA MONICA BLVD #305	LOS ANGELES, CA	90067
GILMAN, LOIS	NEWS REPORTER	TIME/TIME & LIFE BLDG		
		ROCKEFELLER CENTER	NEW YORK, NY	10020
GILMARTIN, PATRICIA A	NEWS CORRESPONDENT	4911 S 31ST ST	ARLINGTON, VA	22206
GILMER, ROB	PRODUCER	4000 WARNER BLVD	BURBANK, CA	91522
GILMER, ROBERT W	TV WRITER	13308 CHELTENHAM DR	SHERMAN OAKS, CA	91423
GILMORE, BO-DEAN	SINGER-GUITARIST	500 SADDLE DR	NASHVILLE, TN	37221
GILMORE, DANIEL F	NEWS CORRESPONDENT	3701 S GEORGE MASON #1304-N	FALLS CHURCH, VA	22041
GILMORE, DENIS	ACTOR	AIDE FOSTE, 33 ABBEY LODGE		
		PARK RD	LONDON NW8 7RJ	ENGLAND
GILMORE, GAIL	MEZZO-SOPRANO	CAMI, 165 W 57TH ST	NEW YORK, NY	10019
GILMORE, JOAN C	WRITER	555 W 57TH ST #1230	NEW YORK, NY	10019
GILMORE, JOHN	TENOR	59 E 54TH ST #81	NEW YORK, NY	10022
GILMORE, PETER	ACTOR	MORRIS, 147-149 WARDOUR ST	LONDON W1V 3TB	ENGLAND
GILMORE, ROBERT B	TV DIRECTOR	5573 MASON AVE	WOODLAND HILLS, CA	91367
GILMORE, RUTH M	WRITER	555 W 57TH ST #1230	NEW YORK, NY	10019
GILMORE, WALTER L, JR	TV DIRECTOR	345 S SPARKS ST	BURBANK, CA	91506
GILMOUR, BILL	TV DIRECTOR	12 LANSDOWNE RD, SALE	CHESHIRE	ENGLAND
GILMOUR, SANDY	NEWS CORRESPONDENT	NBC NEWS, QUIAN MEN HOTEL #8	PEKING	CHINA
GILPIN, JEAN	ACTRESS	13111 VENTURA BLVD #204	STUDIO CITY, CA	91604
GILROY, DAN	COLUMNIST	VARIETY, 1400 N CAHUENGA BLVD	HOLLYWOOD, CA	90028
GILROY, FRANK D	WRITER-PRODUCER	DGA, 7950 SUNSET BLVD	LOS ANGELES, CA	90046
GILSTON, SAMUEL M	NEWS CORRESPONDENT	5308 CRESTEDGE LN	ROCKVILLE, MD	20853
GILVEZAN, DAN	ACTOR	9220 SUNSET BLVD #202	LOS ANGELES, CA	90069
GIMBEL, NORMAN	LYRICIST-SONGWRITER	1172 CENTINELA AVE #3	SANTA MONICA, CA	90403
GIMBEL, PETER	DIRECTOR-PRODUCER	10 E 63RD ST	NEW YORK, NY	10021
GIMBEL, ROGER	PRODUCER	PEREGRINE, 1428 S SHERBOURNE DR	LOS ANGELES, CA	90069
GIMBLE, JOHNNY	MUSICIAN	1204 CLUB CIR	SALADO, TX	76571
GIMENEZ, RAUL	TENOR	61 W 62ND ST #6-F	NEW YORK, NY	10023
GIMLIN, HOYT	NEWS CORRESPONDENT	2626 N QUANTICO ST	ARLINGTON, VA	22207
GIMPEL, SANDRA	DIRECTOR	11944 OTSEGO ST	NORTH HOLLYWOOD, CA	91607
GINDES, MARK	SCREENWRITER	1584 PALISADES DR	PACIFIC PALISADES, CA	90272
GINDOFF, BRYAN	SCREENWRITER	2820 DELL AVE	VENICE, CA	90291
GINESTA, FRANCISCO	NEWS CORRESPONDENT	444 N CAPITOL ST, NW	WASHINGTON, DC	20001
GING, JACK	ACTOR	25234 MALIBU RD	MALIBU, CA	90265
GINGOLD, DAN	DIRECTOR	3540 BEVERLY RIDGE DR	SHERMAN OAKS, CA	91403
GINNA, ROBERT E, JR	WRITER	555 W 57TH ST #1230	NEW YORK, NY	10019
GINNANE, ANTONY I	FILM PRODUCER	74 BRIDPORT ST		
		ALBERT PARK	VICTORIA 3206	AUSTRALIA
GINNES, ABRAM	TV WRITER	9713 SANTA MONICA BLVD	BEVERLY HILLS, CA	90210
GINNES, JUDITH BINDER	WRITER	326 S BENTLEY AVE	LOS ANGELES, CA	90049
GINOVSKY, JOHN S	NEWS CORRESPONDENT	120 E CHURCHILL ST	BALTIMORE, MD	21230
GINSBACH, PAM	NEWS CORRESPONDENT	1007 E TAYLOR RUN PARKWAY	ALEXANDRIA, VA	22302
GINSBERG, ALLEN	POET	CITY LIGHTS, 261 COLUMBIA AVE	SAN FRANCISCO, CA	94133
GINSBERG, JUDAH B	NEWS CORRESPONDENT	6423 BLUEBILL LN	ALEXANDRIA, VA	22307
GINSBURG, BENSON	PHOTOJOURNALIST	1346 29TH ST, NW	WASHINGTON, DC	20007
GINSBURG, ROBIN	ACTRESS	1307 15TH ST #1	SANTA MONICA, CA	90404
GINTY, ROBERT	ACTOR	4023 GOODLAND PL	STUDIO CITY, CA	91604
GIOFFRE, MARISA	TV WRITER	555 W 57TH ST #1230	NEW YORK, NY	10019
GIOFRIDDO, MARK	PIANIST	CAPURSO, 6 IMPERIAL RD	WORCESTER, MA	01604
GIOLITO, RICK	ACTOR	CBS-TV, "AS THE WORLD TURNS"		
		51 W 52ND ST	NEW YORK, NY	10019
GIORDANO, JOHN	CONDUCTOR	1776 BROADWAY #504	NEW YORK, NY	10019
GIORDANO, TONY	DIRECTOR	40 W 74TH ST	NEW YORK, NY	10023
GIORGIO, ANTHONY	ACTOR	9441 WILSHIRE BLVD #620-D	BEVERLY HILLS, CA	90210
GIOSA, SUE	ACTRESS	9220 SUNSET BLVD #202	LOS ANGELES, CA	90069
GIOVANNINETTI, REYNALD	CONDUCTOR	COLBERT, 111 W 57TH ST	NEW YORK, NY	10019
GIOVANNINI, CAESAR	COMPOSER	POST OFFICE BOX 1503	SEDONA, AZ	86336
GIOVI, MARLENE	ACTRESS	9900 DURANT DR #C	BEVERLY HILLS, CA	90212
GIPS, ROBERT E	DIRECTOR-PRODUCER	2040 CUMMINGS DR	LOS ANGELES, CA	90027
GIPSON, MELINDA	NEWS CORRESPONDENT	2850 S COLUMBUS ST	ARLINGTON, VA	22206
GIR, FRANCOIS	FILM DIRECTOR	95810 GRISY-LES-PLATRES	PARIS	FRANCE
GIRALDI, ROBERT N	DIRECTOR	DGA, 110 W 57TH ST	NEW YORK, NY	10019
GIRARD, BERNARD	DIRECTOR	DGA, 7950 SUNSET BLVD	HOLLYWOOD, CA	90046
GIRARD, ELISA	SINGER	ACE, 3407 GREEN RIDGE DR	NASHVILLE, TN	37204
GIRARD, JACQUES	PHOTOGRAPHER	3060 OLIVER ST, NW	WASHINGTON, DC	20015
GIRARD, KENNETH S	WRITER	8955 BEVERLY BLVD	LOS ANGELES, CA	90048
GIRARD, LOUIS	ACTOR	POST OFFICE BOX 476	BRANCHVILLE, NJ	07826
GIRARD, STEPHEN	TV EXECUTIVE	COLUMBIA PICTURES TV		
		COLUMBIA PLAZA	BURBANK, CA	91505
GIRARD, WENDY	ACTRESS	1173 N ARDMORE AVE #3	LOS ANGELES, CA	90029
GIRARDOT, ANNIE	ACTRESS	J NAINCHRIC, 31 CHAMPS-ELYSEES	PARIS 75008	FRANCE
GIRLS NEXT DOOR, THE	C & W GROUP	MTM RECORDS, 21 MUSIC SQUARE E	NASHVILLE, TN	37203
GIRLS NIGHT OUT	ROCK & ROLL GROUP	25 HUNTINGTON AVE #420	BOSTON, MA	02116
GIRLSCHOOL	ROCK & ROLL GROUP	BARRY ARMY, 98 PUDDLETON CRES		
		CANFORD HEATH, POOLE	DORSET	ENGLAND
GIRNEY, SHEILA	ACTRESS	NESFIELD, 34 DEAN ST	LONDON W1	ENGLAND

Name	Occupation	Address	City/State	Zip
GIRODAY, FRANCOIS	ACTOR	ABC-TV, "RYAN'S HOPE"		
		1330 AVE OF THE AMERICAS	NEW YORK, NY	10019
GIRON, ARTHUR	WRITER	555 W 57TH ST #1230	NEW YORK, NY	10019
GIRONDA, VINCE	BODYBUILDER	VINCE'S GYM, 11262 VENTURA BL	STUDIO CITY, CA	91604
GIROTTI, ALESSIO	WRITER	8955 BEVERLY BLVD	LOS ANGELES, CA	90048
GIROUX, JACKIE	ACTRESS	8721 SUNSET BLVD #202	LOS ANGELES, CA	90069
GISERMAN, LOU	NEWS CORRESPONDENT	1400 "I" ST, NW	WASHINGTON, DC	20005
GISH, LILLIAN	ACTRESS	430 E 57TH ST	NEW YORK, NY	10022
GISH, SHEILA	ACTRESS	CONWAY, EAGLE HOUSE		
		109 JERMYN ST	LONDON SW1	ENGLAND
GISMONTI, EGBERTO	GUITARIST	KURLAND, 173 BRIGHTON AVE	BOSTON, MA	02134
GISONDI, TONI ANN	ACTRESS	1450 BELFAST DR	LOS ANGELES, CA	90069
GISSEN, JAY	WRITER-EDITOR	US MAGAZINE COMPANY		
		1 DAG HAMMARSKJOLD PLAZA	NEW YORK, NY	10017
GIST, ROBERT	DIRECTOR	4675 WILLIS AVE	SHERMAN OAKS, CA	91403
GIST, ROD	ACTOR-WRITER	1111 S RIDGELEY DR	LOS ANGELES, CA	90019
GITLITZ, DAVID P	NEWS CORRESPONDENT	8692 MISSION RD	JESSUP, MD	20794
GITOMER, MICHAEL	ACTOR	239 N ORCHARD DR	BURBANK, CA	91506
GITTELMAN, DEIDRE	DIRECTOR	DGA, 110 W 57TH ST	NEW YORK, NY	10019
GITTELMAN, PHIL	WRITER-PRODUCER	135 E 36TH ST	NEW YORK, NY	10016
GITTELMAN, PHILLIP B	AGENT	1221 N KINGS RD #PH-405	LOS ANGELES, CA	90069
GITTINS, ROBERT C	DIRECTOR	DGA, 7950 SUNSET BLVD	LOS ANGELES, CA	90046
GITTLEMAN, NEAL	CONDUCTOR	AFFILIATE ARTISTS, INC		
		37 W 65TH ST, 6TH FLOOR	NEW YORK, NY	10023
GITTLIN, JOYCE	ACTRESS-WRITER	6234 W 6TH ST	LOS ANGELES, CA	90048
GIUFFRE, JAMES P	COMPOSER	STONE MILL, BOX 302	WEST STOCKBRIDGE, MA	01266
GIUFFRIA	ROCK & ROLL GROUP	WINTERLAND, 890 TENNESSEE ST	SAN FRANCISCO, CA	94107
GIULINI, CARLO MARIA	CONDUCTOR	LOS ANGELES PHILHARMONIC		
		135 N GRAND AVE	LOS ANGELES, CA	90012
GIUNTA, JOSEPH	CONDUCTOR	1776 BROADWAY #504	NEW YORK, NY	10019
GIUSTO, THOMAS M	NEWS CORRESPONDENT	ABC-TV, NEWS DEPARTMENT		
		1717 DE SALES ST, NW	WASHINGTON, DC	20036
GJELTEN, TOM	NEWS CORRESPONDENT	1312 22ND ST, NW	WASHINGTON, DC	20037
GLADIATORS, THE	ROCK & ROLL GROUP	CONCERTED, 312 SALEM ST	MEDFORD, MA	02155
GLADIATORS, THE	WRESTLING TAG TEAM	NATIONAL WRESTLING ALLIANCE		
		JIM CROCKETT PROMOTIONS		
		421 BRIARBEND DR	CHARLOTTE, NC	28209
GLADSTON, JENNIFER	WRITER	1221 OCEAN AVE #401	SANTA MONICA, CA	90401
GLADSTONE, BERNARD	COLUMNIST	N Y TIMES, 229 W 43RD ST	NEW YORK, NY	10036
GLADSTONE, DANA	ACTOR	1336 N ALTA VISTA BLVD	LOS ANGELES, CA	90046
GLADSTONE, FRANCIS J	WRITER	555 W 57TH ST #1230	NEW YORK, NY	10019
GLADWELL, DAVID	FILM DIRECTOR	8 CALDERVALE RD	LONDON SW4	ENGLAND
GLADWISH, HUGH	FILM DIRECTOR	GLADWISH & BLAIR, LTD		
		STONEYDEEP #11		
		TWICKENHAM RD, TEDDINGTON	MIDDLESEX TW11 8BL	ENGLAND
GLAIHENGAUZ, JULIUS	CONDUCTOR	482 FORT WASHINGTON AVE #1-H	NEW YORK, NY	10033
GLAISTER, GERARD	TV PRODUCER	32 ABBOTSMEDE CLOSE		
		STRAWBERRY HILL, TWICKENHAM	MIDDLESEX	ENGLAND
GLANDBARD, MAX	DIRECTOR	195 MOHAWK DR	RIVER EDGE, NJ	07661
GLANTZ, STEPHEN	TV WRITER	8955 BEVERLY BLVD	LOS ANGELES, CA	90048
GLASCO, GORDON G	WRITER	8955 BEVERLY BLVD	LOS ANGELES, CA	90048
GLASELL, DON LEON	WRITER-PRODUCER	331 KEDZIE ST	EVANSTON, IL	60202
GLASER, CHUCK	SINGER-GUITARIST	916 19TH AVE S	NASHVILLE, TN	37212
GLASER, JAN	CASTING DIRECTOR	8480 BEVERLY BLVD #165	LOS ANGELES, CA	90048
GLASER, JIM	SINGER	TAYLOR, 2401 12TH AVE S	NASHVILLE, TN	37204
GLASER, JOSEPH R	COMPOSER	639 HILL ST #C	SANTA MONICA, CA	90405
GLASER, MARJORIE	NEWS CORRESPONDENT	1509 "R" ST, NW	WASHINGTON, DC	20009
GLASER, PAUL MICHAEL	ACTOR-DIRECTOR	317 GEORGINA AVE	SANTA MONICA, CA	90402
GLASER, ROBERT L	CABLE EXECUTIVE	VIACOM INTERNATIONAL, INC		
		1211 AVE OF THE AMERICAS	NEW YORK, NY	10036
		9 MUSIC SQUARE W	NASHVILLE, TN	37203
GLASER, TOMPALL & HIS OUTLAWS	C & W GROUP	PORTER & ROUSSELL MGMT		
GLASER, VERA	NEWS CORRESPONDENT	5000 CATHEDRAL AVE, NW	WASHINGTON, DC	20016
GLASGOW, DALE	ILLUSTRATOR	POST OFFICE BOX 500	WASHINGTON, DC	20044
GLASGOW, ROBERT	ORGANIST	15 HIGH ST #621	HARTFORD, CT	06103
GLASS, ANDREW J	NEWS CORRESPONDENT	2901 BRANDYWINE ST, NW	WASHINGTON, DC	20008
GLASS, CHARLES	BODYBUILDER	742 E 88TH PL	LOS ANGELES, CA	90002
GLASS, CHARLES	NEWS CORRESPONDENT	ABC-TV, NEWS DEPARTMENT		
		POST OFFICE BOX 1135168		
		GEFINOR CENTER 1602, BLOCK B	BEIRUT	LEBANON
GLASS, ED	GUITARIST	4701 LEBANON PIKE	HERMITAGE, TN	37076
GLASS, JERALYN	ACTRESS	1733 PASEO DEL MAR	PALOS VERDES, CA	90274
GLASS, JOANNA M	WRITER	555 W 57TH ST #1230	NEW YORK, NY	10019
GLASS, PAMELA	NEWS CORRESPONDENT	5500 FRIENDSHIP BLVD #2226-N	CHEVY CHASE, MD	20815
GLASS, PHILIP	COMPOSER	853 BROADWAY #2120	NEW YORK, NY	10003
GLASS, ROBERT P	NEWS CORRESPONDENT	7910 FAIRFAX RD	ALEXANDRIA, VA	22308
GLASS, RON	ACTOR	2485 WILD OAK DR	LOS ANGELES, CA	90068
GLASS, SALLY R	WRITER	555 W 57TH ST #1230	NEW YORK, NY	10019
GLASS, SANFORD	SCREENWRITER	8955 BEVERLY BLVD	LOS ANGELES, CA	90048
GLASS, SEAMON	ACTOR	814 6TH ST #4	SANTA MONICA, CA	90403
GLASS, STEPHEN	TALENT AGENT	761 JANE ST #15	TORONTO, ONT M6N 4B4	CANADA
GLASS, SYDNEY A	TV WRITER	2004 MILAN AVE	SOUTH PASADENA, CA	91030
GLASS HAMMER	C & W GROUP	TALENT MASTER AGENCY		
		1019 17TH AVE S	NASHVILLE, TN	37212

Name	Occupation	Address	City	Zip/Country
GLASS PYRAMID	ROCK & ROLL GROUP	GOOD, 2500 NW 39TH ST	OKLAHOMA CITY, OK	73112
GLASS TIGER	ROCK & ROLL GROUP	238 DAVENPORT RD #126	TORONTO, ONT M5R 1J6	CANADA
GLASSER, ALBERT	COMPOSER-CONDUCTOR	11812 BELLAGIO RD	LOS ANGELES, CA	90049
GLASSER, BARRY H	WRITER	1417 PEARL ST #6	SANTA MONICA, CA	90405
GLASSER, BERNARD	DIRECTOR	POST OFFICE BOX 67635	LOS ANGELES, CA	90067
GLASSER, DAVID B	NEWS CORRESPONDENT	2025 "M" ST, NW	WASHINGTON, DC	20036
GLASSER, KERRY S	DIRECTOR	400 E 54TH ST	NEW YORK, NY	10022
GLASSER, LEONARD	DIRECTOR-PRODUCER	8109 GLADE AVE	CANOGA PARK, CA	91304
GLASSMAN, ALLAN	TENOR	AFFILIATE ARTISTS, INC		
		37 W 65TH ST, 6TH FLOOR	NEW YORK, NY	10023
GLASSMAN, PAULETTE M	WRITER-PRODUCER	DGA, 110 W 57TH ST	NEW YORK, NY	10019
GLASSMAN, SETH S	DIRECTOR	484 W 43RD ST #19-B	NEW YORK, NY	10036
GLASSMEYER, STEVEN	MUSICIAN	POST OFFICE BOX 140551	NASHVILLE, TN	37214
GLATTES, WOLFGANG	FILM DIRECTOR	3801 RHODES AVE	NORTH HOLLYWOOD, CA	91604
GLATZER, RICHARD M	WRITER	555 W 57TH ST #1230	NEW YORK, NY	10019
GLAUBER, STEPHEN A	WRITER	555 W 57TH ST #1230	NEW YORK, NY	10019
GLAUBERG, JOE	TV WRITER	12570 ROSY CIR	LOS ANGELES, CA	90066
GLAZE, GARY	TENOR	JCB, 155 W 68TH ST	NEW YORK, NY	10023
GLAZER, BARRY	TV DIRECTOR-PRODUCER	1227 SUNSET PLAZA DR	LOS ANGELES, CA	90069
GLAZER, DAVID	CLARINETIST	25 CENTRAL PARK W	NEW YORK, NY	10023
GLAZER, MITCHELL	WRITER	555 W 57TH ST #1230	NEW YORK, NY	10019
GLAZER, VICTOR B	COMPOSER-CONDUCTOR	1304 WOODLOW CT	WESTLAKE VILLAGE, CA	91361
GLAZIER, MARY	ACTRESS	10850 RIVERSIDE DR #505	NORTH HOLLYWOOD, CA	91602
GLEAMING SPIRES, THE	ROCK & ROLL GROUP	POST OFFICE BOX 1421	HOLLYWOOD, CA	90028
GLEASON, JOANNA	ACTRESS	9000 SUNSET BLVD #1200	LOS ANGELES, CA	90069
GLEASON, MICHAEL	TV WRITER-PRODUCER	MTM, 4024 RADFORD AVE	STUDIO CITY, CA	91604
GLEASON, PAUL	ACTOR	9220 SUNSET BLVD #625	LOS ANGELES, CA	90069
GLECKMAN, HOWARD	NEWS CORRESPONDENT	2710 MACOMB ST, NW	WASHINGTON, DC	20008
GLEESON, REDMOND	ACTOR	9000 SUNSET BLVD #1112	LOS ANGELES, CA	90069
GLEN, JOHN	FILM DIRECTOR	9-A BARKSTON GARDENS	LONDON SW5	ENGLAND
GLEN, MAXWELL	COLUMNIST	NEWS AMERICA SYNDICATE		
		1703 KAISER AVE	IRVINE, CA	92714
GLEN, ROBERT M	NEWS CORRESPONDENT	1537 FOXHALL RD, NW	WASHINGTON, DC	20007
GLENISTER, JOHN	TV DIRECTOR	MURPHY-BROWN MGMT		
		162 REGENT ST	LONDON W1R 5TA	ENGLAND
GLENN, BILL	TV DIRECTOR	CBS TELEVISION NETWORK		
		"THE BOLD & THE BEAUTIFUL"		
		7800 BEVERLY BLVD	LOS ANGELES, CA	90036
GLENN, CARRICK	ACTRESS	TRAVIS, 250 W 57TH ST	NEW YORK, NY	10107
GLENN, CHARLES	TV EXECUTIVE	2247 STRADELLA RD	LOS ANGELES, CA	90077
GLENN, CHRISTOPHER	BROADCAST JOURNALIST	CBS-TV, 51 W 52ND ST	NEW YORK, NY	10019
GLENN, DENNIS	DIRECTOR	520 N MICHIGAN AVE #436	CHICAGO, IL	60611
GLENN, KAREN J	NEWS CORRESPONDENT	1120 VERMONT AVE, NW	WASHINGTON, DC	20005
GLENN, SCOTT	ACTOR	POST OFFICE BOX 1902	SANTA FE, NM	87504
GLENN, WILLIAM E	DIRECTOR	DGA, 7950 SUNSET BLVD	LOS ANGELES, CA	90046
GLENNDENING, ED	ARTIST	8285 SUNSET BLVD #3	LOS ANGELES, CA	90046
GLENNON, JEAN	SOPRANO	45 W 60TH ST #4-K	NEW YORK, NY	10023
GLENNON, MICHAEL	NEWS CORRESPONDENT	3127-A "N" ST, NW	WASHINGTON, DC	20007
GLENNON, THOMAS J	WRITER	555 W 57TH ST #1230	NEW YORK, NY	10019
GLENVILLE, PETER	DIRECTOR	DGA, 110 W 57TH ST	NEW YORK, NY	10019
GLESEN, ERICA	BODYBUILDER	PAUL GRAHAM MANAGEMENT		
		288 THE GRAND PARADE	RAMSGATE BEACH	AUSTRALIA
GLESS, SHARON	ACTRESS	4709 TEESDALE AVE	STUDIO CITY, CA	91604
GLEYSTEEN, SANDY	NEWS CORRESPONDENT	NBC-TV, NEWS DEPARTMENT		
		4001 NEBRASKA AVE, NW	WASHINGTON, DC	20016
GLICK, MARIAN	WRITER	555 W 57TH ST #1230	NEW YORK, NY	10019
GLICKENHAUS, JAMES W	WRITER-PRODUCER	1619 BROADWAY #303	NEW YORK, NY	10019
GLICKMAN, JOEL	WRITER-PRODUCER	DGA, 7950 SUNSET BLVD	HOLLYWOOD, CA	90046
GLICKMAN, SUSAN	CASTING DIRECTOR	ABC-TV ENTERTAINMENT CENTER		
		2040 AVE OF THE STARS	LOS ANGELES, CA	90067
GLICKMAN, SYLVIA	PIANIST	POST OFFICE BOX U	REDDING, CT	06875
GLIEBERMAN, CARY H	WRITER	8955 BEVERLY BLVD	LOS ANGELES, CA	90048
GLINES, JOHN	WRITER	555 W 57TH ST #1230	NEW YORK, NY	10019
GLINN, BURTON	PHOTOGRAPHER	41 CENTRAL PARK W	NEW YORK, NY	10023
GLINWOOD, TERRY	FILM DIRECTOR	120 PALL MALL	LONDON SW1	ENGLAND
GLIONA, MICHAEL A	DIRECTOR	DGA, 7950 SUNSET BLVD	LOS ANGELES, CA	90046
GLOBE OF DEATH	MOTORCYCLIST	HALL, 138 FROG HOLLOW RD	CHURCHVILLE, PA	18966
GLOBUS, YORAM	PRODUCER-EXECUTIVE	CANNON FILM GROUP		
		640 S SAN VICENTE BLVD	LOS ANGELES, CA	90048
GLORIONS, THE	CRADLE-PERCH DUO	HALL, 138 FROG HOLLOW RD	CHURCHVILLE, PA	18966
GLOSSER, DANIEL	CONDUCTOR	750 S SPAULDING AVE #31	LOS ANGELES, CA	90036
GLOSSOP, PETER	BARITONE	61 W 62ND ST #6-F	NEW YORK, NY	10023
GLOUNER, RICHARD C	CINEMATOGRAPHER	POST OFFICE BOX 2230	HOLLYWOOD, CA	90078
GLOVER, BRIAN	ACTOR	DEWOLFE, 1 ROBERT ST	LONDON WC2N 6BH	ENGLAND
GLOVER, BRUCE	ACTOR	11449 WOODBINE ST	LOS ANGELES, CA	90066
GLOVER, BRUCE E	CONDUCTOR	POST OFFICE BOX 10413	MARINA DEL REY, CA	90295
GLOVER, CRISPIN	ACTOR	11449 WOODBINE ST	LOS ANGELES, CA	90066
GLOVER, DANNY	ACTOR	829 SHRADER ST	SAN FRANCISCO, CA	94117
GLOVER, FRED	ACTOR	BERZON, 336 E 17TH ST	COSTA MESA, CA	92627
GLOVER, JIM	SINGER	GREG, 1686 CATALPA RD	CLEVELAND, OH	44112
GLOVER, JULIAN	ACTOR	CONWAY, EAGLE HOUSE		
		109 JERMYN ST	LONDON SW1	ENGLAND
GLOVER, KENT	WRESTLER	NATIONAL WRESTLING ALLIANCE		
		JIM CROCKETT PROMOTIONS		
		421 BRIARBEND DR	CHARLOTTE, NC	28209

Name	Occupation	Address	City	Zip
GLOVER, WILLIAM	ACTOR	247 S BEVERLY DR #102	BEVERLY HILLS, CA	90210
GLOVER, WILLIAM	THEATER CRITIC	4 E 88TH ST	NEW YORK, NY	10028
GLOW, BRIAN	PRESTIDIGITATOR	59 E 54TH ST #81	NEW YORK, NY	10022
GLUCK, MARVIN A	TV WRITER	19988 OBSERVATION DR	TOPANGA CANYON, CA	90290
GLUCK, STEPHEN HENRY	DIRECTOR	DGA, 110 W 57TH ST	NEW YORK, NY	10019
GLUCKSMAN, MARGE	CASTING DIRECTOR	7800 BEVERLY BLVD	LOS ANGELES, CA	90036
GLUCKSMAN, MARGIE	TV EXECUTIVE	CBS-TV, 6121 SUNSET BLVD	LOS ANGELES, CA	90028
GLUECKMAN, ALAN J	SCREENWRITER	8955 BEVERLY BLVD	LOS ANGELES, CA	90048
GLUM, GARY L, MD	BODYBUILDER	5250 W CENTURY BLVD #614	LOS ANGELES, CA	90045
GLUSKIN, MICHAEL	ACTOR	619 N HOLLISTON AVE #4	PASADENA, CA	91106
GLUT, DONALD F	WRITER	2805 N KEYSTONE ST	BURBANK, CA	91504
GLYNN, J MICHAEL	NEWS REPORTER	THE NATIONAL ENQUIRER		
		600 SE COAST AVE	LANTANA, FL	33464
GLYNN, JEANNE DAVIS	TV WRITER	555 W 57TH ST #1230	NEW YORK, NY	10019
GLYNN, MICHAEL	TV PRODUCER	32 BEDFORD ROW	LONDON WC1R 4HE	ENGLAND
GLYNN, VICTOR	FILM PRODUCER	21 LONDON PL	OXFORD	ENGLAND
GLYNNE, DEREK	TV EXECUTIVE	17 WILTON PL	LONDON SW1	ENGLAND
GMITER, BERNARD	PHOTOJOURNALIST	11904 DEVILWOOD DR	POTOMAC, MD	20854
GNAM, ADRIAN	CONDUCTOR	POST OFFICE BOX 27539	PHILADELPHIA, PA	19118
GNEISER, ROBERT H	NEWS CORRESPONDENT	8103 LILLY STONE DR	BETHESDA, MD	20817
GOAD, LARRY	GUITARIST	211 DIANNE DR	MADISON, TN	37115
GOBBLE, DEBORAH E	WRITER	555 W 57TH ST #1230	NEW YORK, NY	10019
GOBEL, GEORGE	ACTOR	4201 CLEAR VALLEY DR	ENCINO, CA	91316
GOBETTI, MARIA	ACTRESS	12833 LANDALE ST	NORTH HOLLYWOOD, CA	91604
GODARD, JEAN-LUC	FILM DIRECTOR	SONIMAGE, 99 RUE DU ROULE	NEUILLY 92200	FRANCE
GODBEY, GARY	GUITARIST	704 BERRY RD #D-3	NASHVILLE, TN	37204
GODDARD, GARY	SCREENWRITER	8955 BEVERLY BLVD	LOS ANGELES, CA	90048
GODDARD, JIM	TV DIRECTOR	7 CHISWICK QUAY	LONDON W4 3UR	ENGLAND
GODDARD, JOHN	ACTOR	5125 FULTON AVE	SHERMAN OAKS, CA	91423
GODDARD, KEITH	CINEMATOGRAPHER	EASTFIELD COTTAGES		
		TIDEBROOK, WADHURST	EAST SUSSEX TN5 6PF	ENGLAND
GODDARD, LIZA	ACTRESS	BURNETT, 42 GRAFTON HOUSE		
		2-3 GOLDEN SQ	LONDON W1	ENGLAND
GODDARD, MARK	ACTOR	7466 BEVERLY BLVD #205	LOS ANGELES, CA	90036
GODDARD, PAULETTE	ACTRESS	RITZ TOWERS, 465 PARK AVE	NEW YORK, NY	10022
GODDARD, RAYMOND J	PHOTOJOURNALIST	3900 IVYDALE DR	ANNANDALE, VA	22003
GODDARD, SCOTT	SINGER	2250 N ONTARIO ST	BURBANK, CA	91504
GODDARD, VIC	SINGER	UPSIDE RECORDS COMPANY		
		225 LAFAYETTE ST	NEW YORK, NY	10012
GODEERE, WILLIAM B	NEWS CORRESPONDENT	NBC NEWS, 4001 NEBRASKA AVE, NW	WASHINGTON, DC	20016
GODFREY, ALAN S	TV WRITER	8955 BEVERLY BLVD	LOS ANGELES, CA	90048
GODFREY, DEREK	ACTOR	33 ALMA SQ	LONDON NW8	ENGLAND
GODFREY, LONNIE	DRUMMER	302 NOKES DR	HENDERSONVILLE, TN	37075
GODFREY, MARK R	PHOTOGRAPHER	3526 N 3RD ST	ARLINGTON, VA	22201
GODFREY, NEIL G	NEWS CORRESPONDENT	101 "G" ST #A-619, SW	WASHINGTON, DC	20024
GODLER, JACK	WRITER	555 W 57TH ST #1230	NEW YORK, NY	10019
GODUNOV, ALEXANDER	DANCER	1815 BENEDICT CANYON DR	BEVERLY HILLS, CA	90210
GODWIN, FRANK	WRITER-PRODUCER	11 TOWNSEND HOUSE, DEAN ST	LONDON W1	ENGLAND
GODWIN, STEPHEN J	ACTOR	9200 SUNSET BLVD #1210	LOS ANGELES, CA	90069
GODZ, THE	ROCK & ROLL GROUP	FRIEDHEIM, 659 1/2 3RD ST	COLUMBUS, OH	43206
GOEBEL, JOCHEN	NEWS CORRESPONDENT	4525 DOREST AVE	CHEVY CHASE, MD	20815
GOELLER, DAVID	NEWS CORRESPONDENT	676 4TH ST, NE	WASHINGTON, DC	20002
GOETZ, CANDACE	SOPRANO	61 W 62ND ST #6-F	NEW YORK, NY	10023
GOETZ, PETER MICHAEL	ACTOR	9200 SUNSET BLVD #1210	LOS ANGELES, CA	90069
GOETZ, THEODORE	DIRECTOR	13457 CHANDLER BLVD	VAN NUYS, CA	91401
GOETZ, WERNER	TENOR	111 W 57TH ST #1209	NEW YORK, NY	10019
GOETZMAN, GARY	ACTOR	11558 RIVERSIDE DR	NORTH HOLLYWOOD, CA	91602
GOFER BROKE SWING BAND	C & W GROUP	GREG, 1686 CATALPA RD	CLEVELAND, OH	44112
GOFF, IVAN CLAYTON	TV WRITER-PRODUCER	86 MALIBU COLONY DR	MALIBU, CA	90265
GOFFNEY, BRENDA	NEWS CORRESPONDENT	2101 NEW HAMPSHIRE AVE, NW	WASHINGTON, DC	20009
GOFORTH, STEVEN	GUITARIST	54 MOBIL VILLAGE	HENDERSONVILLE, TN	37075
GOGGIN, WILLIAM T	NEWS CORRESPONDENT	1201 CONNECTICUT AVE, NW	WASHINGTON, DC	20036
GOIN, JON	SINGER-GUITARIST	344 WIMPOLE DR	NASHVILLE, TN	37211
GOING, RON	MUSICIAN	3530 CLAREMORE AVE	LONG BEACH, CA	90808
GOINS, JESSE	ACTOR	247 S BEVERLY DR #102	BEVERLY HILLS, CA	90210
GOKEY, WILLIAM	BANJOIST	1213 STATE ST	OGDENSBURG, NY	13669
GOLAN, GILA	ACTRESS	M B ROSEHAUS, 767 5TH AVE	NEW YORK, NY	10022
GOLAN, MENAHEM	PRODUCER-EXECUTIVE	CANNON FILM GROUP		
		640 S SAN VICENTE BLVD	LOS ANGELES, CA	90048
GOLAND, ALAN	TV DIRECTOR-PRODUCER	1024 STEARNS DR	LOS ANGELES, CA	90035
GOLANI, RIVKA	VIOLIST	5720 MOSHOLU AVE #300	RIVERDALE, NY	10471
GOLD, ANDREW	SINGER-SONGWRITER	2565 ZORADA DR	LOS ANGELES, CA	90046
GOLD, AVRAM D	WRITER	146 N ARNAZ DR #D	BEVERLY HILLS, CA	90211
GOLD, BARRY	TV WRITER	8955 BEVERLY BLVD	LOS ANGELES, CA	90048
GOLD, DAVID	WRESTLER	POST OFFICE BOX 3859	STAMFORD, CT	06905
GOLD, DONALD L	TV WRITER	8955 BEVERLY BLVD	LOS ANGELES, CA	90048
GOLD, DONNA F	WRITER	8955 BEVERLY BLVD	LOS ANGELES, CA	90048
GOLD, ERNEST	COMPOSER	269 N BELLINO DR	PACIFIC PALISADES, CA	90272
GOLD, HEIDI	ACTRESS	11726 SAN VICENTE BLVD #300	LOS ANGELES, CA	90049
GOLD, JACK	FILM-TV DIRECTOR	A D PETERS & CO, LTD		
		10 BUCKINGHAM ST	LONDON WC2	ENGLAND
GOLD, JEFF	TV DIRECTOR-PRODUCER	300 E 51ST ST	NEW YORK, NY	10022
GOLD, LESLIE J	NEWS CORRESPONDENT	2301 CATHEDRAL AVE #403, NW	WASHINGTON, DC	20008
GOLD, LLOYD	TV WRITER	ABC-TV, "ONE LIFE TO LIVE"		
		1330 AVE OF THE AMERICAS	NEW YORK, NY	10019

PAULETE GODDARD

WHOOPI GOLDBERG

FRANK GORSHIN

ELLIOTT GOULD

FARLEY GRANGER

STEWART GRANGER

EDDY GRANT

BONITA GRANVILLE

PETER GRAVES

Name	Occupation	Address	City	ZIP
GOLD, MISSY	ACTRESS	KELMAN, 7813 SUNSET BLVD	LOS ANGELES, CA	90046
GOLD, PAUL H	DIRECTOR	401 E 74TH ST	NEW YORK, NY	10021
GOLD, RUSSELL	ACTOR	89 MAC DOUGAL ST	NEW YORK, NY	10012
GOLD, STEVEN	CASTING DIRECTOR	THE RALEIGH STUDIOS		
		650 N BRONSON AVE	LOS ANGELES, CA	90004
GOLD, SYLVIANE	WRITER	555 W 57TH ST #1230	NEW YORK, NY	10019
GOLD, TRACEY	ACTRESS	12725 VENTURA BLVD #E	STUDIO CITY, CA	91604
GOLD RUSH	C & W GROUP	POST OFFICE BOX 1909	MILL VALLEY, CA	94942
GOLDBERG, ALAN B	WRITER	555 W 57TH ST #1230	NEW YORK, NY	10019
GOLDBERG, ANDY S	TV WRITER	8955 BEVERLY BLVD	LOS ANGELES, CA	90048
GOLDBERG, BERNARD	NEWS CORRESPONDENT	CBS TV, NEWS DEPARTMENT		
		1800 CENTURY BLVD, NE	ATLANTA, GA	30345
GOLDBERG, BETTY	TV WRITER-DIRECTOR	1042 CORNING ST	LOS ANGELES, CA	90035
GOLDBERG, DIEGO	PHOTOGRAPHER	75 E END AVE	NEW YORK, NY	10028
GOLDBERG, DONALD F	NEWS CORRESPONDENT	8754 PRESTON PL	CHEVY CHASE, MD	20815
GOLDBERG, GARY D	TV WRITER-PRODUCER	PARAMOUNT, 5451 MARATHON ST	HOLLYWOOD, CA	90038
GOLDBERG, GARY DAVID	WRITER-PRODUCER	139 S ANITA AVE	LOS ANGELES, CA	90049
GOLDBERG, HOWARD S	WRITER	1358 N ALTA VISTA BLVD	LOS ANGELES, CA	90046
GOLDBERG, JEANNE	DIETITIAN-COLUMNIST	THE WASHINGTON POST		
		WRITERS GROUP		
		1150 15TH ST, NW	WASHINGTON, DC	20071
GOLDBERG, JEROLD M	WRITER	8955 BEVERLY BLVD	LOS ANGELES, CA	90048
GOLDBERG, JOANN	DIRECTOR	DGA, 7950 SUNSET BLVD	LOS ANGELES, CA	90046
GOLDBERG, JOANN	TV WRITER	555 W 57TH ST #1230	NEW YORK, NY	10019
GOLDBERG, JOEL	WRITER	555 W 57TH ST #1230	NEW YORK, NY	10019
GOLDBERG, LEONARD	TV-FILM PRODUCER	235 LADERA DR	BEVERLY HILLS, CA	90210
GOLDBERG, MARSHALL	TV WRITER	8955 BEVERLY BLVD	LOS ANGELES, CA	90048
GOLDBERG, MEL	TV WRITER	8955 BEVERLY BLVD	LOS ANGELES, CA	90048
GOLDBERG, RALPH E	TV EXECUTIVE	CBS-TV, 524 W 57TH ST	NEW YORK, NY	10019
GOLDBERG, REINER	TENOR	CAMI, 165 W 57TH ST	NEW YORK, NY	10019
GOLDBERG, RICKI A	WRITER	555 W 57TH ST #1230	NEW YORK, NY	10019
GOLDBERG, SHARON	ACTRESS	2269 N BEACHWOOD DR #203	LOS ANGELES, CA	90068
GOLDBERG, SHARON	CHOREOGRAPHER	2106 MOUNT OLYMPUS DR	LOS ANGELES, CA	90046
GOLDBERG, STEVE	NEWS CORRESPONDENT	3129 SLEEPY HOLLOW RD	FALLS CHURCH, VA	22042
GOLDBERG, SUSAN S	TV WRITER	9300 WILSHIRE BLVD #410	BEVERLY HILLS, CA	90212
GOLDBERG, WHOOPI	COMEDIENNE-ACTRESS	2212 MC KINLEY AVE	BERKELEY, CA	94703
GOLDBLATT, STEPHEN	DIRECTOR	DGA, 7950 SUNSET BLVD	LOS ANGELES, CA	90046
GOLDBLUM, JEFF	ACTOR	13205 CHELTENHAM DR	SHERMAN OAKS, CA	91423
GOLDCHAIN, MAURICE H	NEWS CORRESPONDENT	9208 CROCKETT PL	UPPER MARLBORO, MD	20772
GOLDEMBERG, ROSE LEIMAN	TV WRITER-PRODUCER	10100 SANTA MONICA BLVD #1600	LOS ANGELES, CA	90067
GOLDEN, ALEX	ACTOR-DIRECTOR	8286 PRESSON PL	LOS ANGELES, CA	90069
GOLDEN, ALEXANDER R	CONDUCTOR	8286 PRESSON PL	LOS ANGELES, CA	90069
GOLDEN, DIZZY	WRESTLER	SEE - BEEFCAKE, BRUTUS		
GOLDEN, EMILY	MEZZO-SOPRANO	CAMI, 165 W 57TH ST	NEW YORK, NY	10019
GOLDEN, FREDERIC	WRITER-EDITOR	DISCOVER/TIME & LIFE BLDG		
		ROCKEFELLER CENTER	NEW YORK, NY	10020
GOLDEN, GENE	MUSICIAN	200 BONNA OAKS DR	HERMITAGE, TN	37076
GOLDEN, HERB	TV WRITER-PRODUCER	4108 SAUGUS AVE	SHERMAN OAKS, CA	91403
GOLDEN, JAMES R	NEWS CORRESPONDENT	4850 CONNECTICUT AVE, NW	WASHINGTON, DC	20008
GOLDEN, JEROME B	TV EXECUTIVE	ABC TELEVISION NETWORK		
		1330 AVE OF THE AMERICAS	NEW YORK, NY	10019
GOLDEN, JOHN F	WRITER	8955 BEVERLY BLVD	LOS ANGELES, CA	90048
GOLDEN, LARRY	ACTOR	ABC-TV, "ALL MY CHILDREN"		
		1330 AVE OF THE AMERICAS	NEW YORK, NY	10019
GOLDEN, LAURA	SONGWRITER	11554 1/2 HUSTON ST	NORTH HOLLYWOOD, CA	91601
GOLDEN, MURRAY	TV DIRECTOR	15739 MULHOLLAND PL	LOS ANGELES, CA	90049
GOLDEN, OLIVE FULLER	ACTRESS	SEE - CAREY, OLIVE FULLER		
GOLDEN, RICHARD A	NEWS CORRESPONDENT	7405 CARMINE ST	ANNANDALE, VA	22003
GOLDEN, RUTH	SOPRANO	AFFILIATE ARTISTS, INC		
		37 W 65TH ST, 6TH FLOOR	NEW YORK, NY	10023
GOLDEN, STERLING	WRESTLER	SEE - HOGAN, HULK		
GOLDEN, TIMOTHY	NEWS CORRESPONDENT	609 2ND ST, NE	WASHINGTON, DC	20002
GOLDEN, WILLIAM LEE	SINGER-SONGWRITER	329 ROCKLAND RD	HENDERSONVILLE, TN	37075
GOLDEN EARRING	ROCK & ROLL GROUP	65 W 55TH ST #306	NEW YORK, NY	10019
GOLDEN HORDE, THE	ROCK & ROLL GROUP	MEDIA BURN RECORDS		
		36 HANWAY ST	LONDON W1	ENGLAND
GOLDEN SISTERS, THE	ACROBATIC DUO	HALL, 138 FROG HOLLOW RD	CHURCHVILLE, PA	18966
GOLDEN-GOTTLIEB, PHYLLIS	TV EXECUTIVE	500 S BUENA VISTA ST	BURBANK, CA	91521
GOLDENBERG, BILLY	COMPOSER	10037 VALLEY SPRING LN	NORTH HOLLYWOOD, CA	91602
GOLDENBERG, DEVIN M	WRITER	8955 BEVERLY BLVD	LOS ANGELES, CA	90048
GOLDENBERG, GENE S	NEWS CORRESPONDENT	5100 WYCOMING RD	BETHESDA, MD	20816
GOLDENBERG, HARVEY J	ACTOR	1807 N CHEROKEE AVE	LOS ANGELES, CA	90028
GOLDENSON, LEONARD H	TV EXECUTIVE	ABC TELEVISION NETWORK		
		1330 AVE OF THE AMERICAS	NEW YORK, NY	10019
GOLDFARB, PETER	DIRECTOR	781 5TH AVE	NEW YORK, NY	10021
GOLDFEIN, ALAN	TV WRITER	8955 BEVERLY BLVD	LOS ANGELES, CA	90048
GOLDFEIN, MICHAEL D	NEWS CORRESPONDENT	7211 LAKE COVE DR	ALEXANDRIA, VA	22310
GOLDHOR, DAVID	DIRECTOR	EAGLE EYE FILM COMPANY		
		4019 TUJUNGA AVE	STUDIO CITY, CA	91604
GOLDIN, MARILYN	WRITER	534 WESTMOUNT DR	LOS ANGELES, CA	90048
GOLDIN, MARION	TV PRODUCER	ABC-TV, 7 W 66TH ST	NEW YORK, NY	10023
GOLDING, LOUISE DIANA	ACTRESS	367 N SIERRA BONITA AVE	LOS ANGELES, CA	90036
GOLDING, PAUL	TV WRITER	5007 STONEY CREEK RD #433	CULVER CITY, CA	90230

GOLDMAN, BO	SCREENWRITER	8955 BEVERLY BLVD	LOS ANGELES, CA	90048
GOLDMAN, BYRON	THEATER PRODUCER	1270 AVE OF THE AMERICAS	NEW YORK, NY	10020
GOLDMAN, CAROLE	ACTRESS	8383 WILSHIRE BLVD #1024	BEVERLY HILLS, CA	90211
GOLDMAN, DANNY	CASTING DIRECTOR	1625 N STANLEY AVE	LOS ANGELES, CA	90046
GOLDMAN, DONALD	DIRECTOR	9759 SOPHIA AVE	SEPULVEDA, CA	91343
GOLDMAN, EDMUND	FILM PRODUCER	MANSON INTL PICTURES		
		9145 SUNSET BLVD	LOS ANGELES, CA	90069
GOLDMAN, ERWIN	WRITER	2800 NEILSON WY #902	SANTA MONICA, CA	90405
GOLDMAN, GINA	WRITER	8250 FOUNTAIN AVE #C	LOS ANGELES, CA	90046
GOLDMAN, GREGORY	WRITER-PRODUCER	2016 OCEAN DR	MANHATTAN BEACH, CA	90266
GOLDMAN, HAROLD I	TV WRITER	2341 DONELLA CIR	LOS ANGELES, CA	90077
GOLDMAN, JACK	COMPOSER	11317 HERBERT ST	LOS ANGELES, CA	90066
GOLDMAN, JAMES	PLAYWRIGHT	ICM, 40 W 57TH ST	NEW YORK, NY	10019
GOLDMAN, JEFF S	NEWS CORRESPONDENT	POST OFFICE BOX 2626	WASHINGTON, DC	20013
GOLDMAN, LAWRENCE LOUIS	WRITER	13470 MARGATE ST	VAN NUYS, CA	91401
GOLDMAN, LESLIE	DIRECTOR	330 W 55TH ST	NEW YORK, NY	10019
GOLDMAN, LORRY	ACTOR	1310 N SWEETZER AVE #205	LOS ANGELES, CA	90069
GOLDMAN, MARCY	ACTRESS	116 N GALE DR #22	BEVERLY HILLS, CA	90211
GOLDMAN, MARGARET A	TV WRITER	9633 BEVERLYWOOD ST	LOS ANGELES, CA	90034
GOLDMAN, MARTIN	FILM DIRECTOR	POST OFFICE BOX 370	WILSON, WY	83014
GOLDMAN, MAURICE	COMPOSER-CONDUCTOR	23001 BIGLER ST	WOODLAND HILLS, CA	91364
GOLDMAN, MICHAEL	FILM EXEC-PROD	11355 OLYMPIC BLVD #500	LOS ANGELES, CA	90064
GOLDMAN, PEGGY	TV WRITER	SEE - GOLDMAN, MARGARET A		
GOLDMAN, RICHARD A	TV WRITER	8955 BEVERLY BLVD	LOS ANGELES, CA	90048
GOLDMAN, ROBERT P	WRITER	555 W 57TH ST #1230	NEW YORK, NY	10019
GOLDMAN, ROY	ACTOR	1713 BRYN MAWN AVE	SANTA MONICA, CA	90405
GOLDMAN, RUDI	PRODUCER	400 S BEVERLY DR #214	BEVERLY HILLS, CA	90212
GOLDMAN, SHEPARD	WRITER	COHN, GLICKSTEIN & LURIE		
		1370 AVE OF THE AMERICAS	NEW YORK, NY	10019
GOLDMAN, SHERWIN	THEATER PRODUCER	1501 BROADWAY	NEW YORK, NY	10036
GOLDMAN, WENDY	ACTRESS	211 S BEVERLY DR #201	BEVERLY HILLS, CA	90212
GOLDMAN, WENDY ANN	ACTRESS	3518 W CAHUENGA BLVD #318	LOS ANGELES, CA	90068
GOLDMAN, WILLIAM	SCREENWRITER	740 PARK AVE	NEW YORK, NY	10021
GOLDMAN, WILLIAM	TV DIRECTOR	4 INDIANCREEK RD	MATAWAN, NJ	07747
GOLDONI, LELIA	ACTRESS	15459 WYANDOTTE ST	VAN NUYS, CA	91406
GOLDRUP, RAY	TV WRITER	8955 BEVERLY BLVD	LOS ANGELES, CA	90048
GOLDSBORO, BOBBY	SINGER-SONGWRITER	POST OFFICE BOX 6706		
		GREEN HILLS STATION	NASHVILLE, TN	37215
GOLDSCHMIDT, JOHN	TV DIRECTOR	46 CASCADE AVE	LONDON N10 3PU	ENGLAND
GOLDSCHMIDT, STEVEN	NEWS CORRESPONDENT	5111 S 8TH RD #403	ARLINGTON, VA	22204
GOLDSMITH, BRUCE LEIGH	WRITER-PRODUCER	9722 OAK PASS RD	BEVERLY HILLS, CA	90210
GOLDSMITH, DAVID	WRITER	8955 BEVERLY BLVD	LOS ANGELES, CA	90048
GOLDSMITH, GLORIA	WRITER	8440 DE LONGPRE AVE #10	LOS ANGELES, CA	90069
GOLDSMITH, JERRY	COMPOSER-CONDUCTOR	2049 CENTURY PARK E #37	LOS ANGELES, CA	90067
GOLDSMITH, JOEL	COMPOSER	10100 SANTA MONICA BLVD #1600	LOS ANGELES, CA	90067
GOLDSMITH, JONATHAN	ACTOR	POST OFFICE BOX 9464	MARINA DEL REY, CA	90292
GOLDSMITH, LYNN	DIRECTOR	15 E 61ST ST	NEW YORK, NY	10021
GOLDSMITH, MALISSA	ACTRESS	POST OFFICE BOX 75	DEMAREST, NJ	07627
GOLDSMITH, MARTIN M	TV WRITER	13643 OAK CANYON AVE	SHERMAN OAKS, CA	91423
GOLDSMITH, MERWIN	ACTOR	66 W 88TH ST	NEW YORK, NY	10024
GOLDSMITH, RAYMOND	TV PRODUCER	47 GRAHAM TERR	LONDON SW1W 8HN	ENGLAND
GOLDSMITH, TOMMY	GUITARIST	ROUTE #1, CORCORD RD	BRENTWOOD, TN	37027
GOLDSMITH & HURLONG	MUSICAL DUO	LIEBERMAN, 11 RIVERSIDE DR	NEW YORK, NY	10023
GOLDSON, BENNY	COMPOSER	1140 BROADWAY #1006	NEW YORK, NY	10001
GOLDSTEIN, ABE	CLOWN	2701 COTTAGE WY #14	SACRAMENTO, CA	95825
GOLDSTEIN, ALLEN	TV WRITER	8955 BEVERLY BLVD	LOS ANGELES, CA	90048
GOLDSTEIN, ANDREA	TV WRITER	8955 BEVERLY BLVD	LOS ANGELES, CA	90048
GOLDSTEIN, CHARLES A	TV EXECUTIVE	19463 HATTON ST	RESEDA, CA	91335
GOLDSTEIN, ELLEN J	WRITER	555 W 57TH ST #1230	NEW YORK, NY	10019
GOLDSTEIN, JEFFREY	DIRECTOR	DGA, 7950 SUNSET BLVD	LOS ANGELES, CA	90046
GOLDSTEIN, LEE	TV WRITER	14058 DAVANA TERR	SHERMAN OAKS, CA	91423
GOLDSTEIN, MARTIN M	TV WRITER	ICM, 8899 BEVERLY BLVD	LOS ANGELES, CA	90048
GOLDSTEIN, MAX	WRITER	555 W 57TH ST #1230	NEW YORK, NY	10019
GOLDSTEIN, MITCHELL M	DIRECTOR	604 JAEGER CT	SICKLERVILLE, NJ	05801
GOLDSTEIN, NEIL	WRITER	555 W 57TH ST #1230	NEW YORK, NY	10019
GOLDSTEIN, NORMAN	DIRECTOR	DGA, 110 W 57TH ST	NEW YORK, NY	10019
GOLDSTEIN, PATRICK	FILM CRITIC	L A TIMES NEWSPAPER		
		TIME MIRROR SQUARE	LOS ANGELES, CA	90053
GOLDSTEIN, REBECCA	ACTRESS-WRITER	6121 1/2 GLEN TOWER ST	LOS ANGELES, CA	90068
GOLDSTEIN, ROBIN S	NEWS CORRESPONDENT	3220 CONNECTICUT AVE, NW	WASHINGTON, DC	20008
GOLDSTEIN, RONALD H	COMPOSER-CONDUCTOR	9740 DONNA AVE	NORTHRIDGE, CA	91324
GOLDSTEIN, SHELLY	TV WRITER	8955 BEVERLY BLVD	LOS ANGELES, CA	90048
GOLDSTEIN, WILLIAM	COMPOSER-CONDUCTOR	8521 ALLENWOOD RD	LOS ANGELES, CA	90046
GOLDSTEIN, WILLIAM I	WRITER	9255 SUNSET BLVD #1122	LOS ANGELES, CA	90069
GOLDSTONE, DEENA	TV WRITER	5672 TYRON RD	LOS ANGELES, CA	90068
GOLDSTONE, DUKE	DIRECTOR	351 N PALM DR #120	BEVERLY HILLS, CA	90210
GOLDSTONE, JAMES	FILM WRITER-DIRECTOR	344 CONWAY AVE	LOS ANGELES, CA	90024
GOLDSTONE, JOHN	FILM PRODUCER	SIEFERT, 8-A BRUNSWICK GARDENS	LONDON W8 4AJ	ENGLAND
GOLDSTONE, PATRICIA E	WRITER	8955 BEVERLY BLVD	LOS ANGELES, CA	90048
GOLDSTONE, RAYMOND E	TV WRITER	14128 EMELITA ST	VAN NUYS, CA	91401
GOLDSTONE, RICHARD G	DIRECTOR	ICM, 8899 BEVERLY BLVD	LOS ANGELES, CA	90048
GOLDTHWAIT, BOB	ACTOR-COMEDIAN	ICM, 8899 BEVERLY BLVD	LOS ANGELES, CA	90048
GOLDWASSER, LAWRENCE L	DIRECTOR	686 QUAKER ST	CHAPPAQUA, NY	10514
GOLDWATER, BARRY	U S SENATOR	6250 HOGAHN	PARADISE VALLEY, AZ	85253
GOLDWYN, SAMUEL, JR	DIRECTOR-PRODUCER	1200 LAUREL LN	BEVERLY HILLS, CA	90210

Name	Occupation	Address	City	Zip
GOLITZEN, ALEXANDER	ART DIRECTOR	14880 VALLEY VISTA BLVD	VAN NUYS, CA	91403
GOLLADAY, SAMUEL MARK	GUITARIST	POST OFFICE BOX 373	HERMITAGE, TN	37076
GOLLANCE, RICHARD	TV WRITER	2686 WOODSTOCK RD	LOS ANGELES, CA	90046
GOLLARD, JEROME T	WRITER	8955 BEVERLY BLVD	LOS ANGELES, CA	90048
GOLONKA, ARLENE	ACTRESS	153 S REEVES DR	BEVERLY HILLS, CA	90212
GOLOVIN, ALEXIS	PIANIST	GERSHUNOFF, 502 PARK AVE	NEW YORK, NY	10022
GOLPHIN, VINCENT F	NEWS CORRESPONDENT	7403 TAYLOR ST	HYATTSVILLE, MD	20784
GOLS, MARCAL	CONDUCTOR	POST OFFICE BOX 131	SPRINGFIELD, VA	22150
GOLTRA, KATHERINE	NEWS CORRESPONDENT	1755 S JEFFERSON DAVIS HWY	ARLINGTON, VA	22202
GOLTZ, GENE	NEWS CORRESPONDENT	10205 PIERCE DR	SILVER SPRING, MD	20901
GOMAVITZ, LEWIS	DIRECTOR	10831 SYLVIA AVE	NORTHRIDGE, CA	91326
GOMBERG, RALPH	OBOIST	GERSHUNOFF, 502 PARK AVE	NEW YORK, NY	10022
GOMBERG, SY L	SCREENWRITER	13233 RIVIERA RANCH RD	LOS ANGELES, CA	90049
GOMES, GEORGE	DIRECTOR	217 E 49TH ST	NEW YORK, NY	10017
GOMEZ, ALLEN M	TV DIRECTOR	2071 SYDNEY DR	NORTH MERRICK, NY	11566
GOMEZ, DANIEL M	DIRECTOR-PRODUCER	217 BETTYHILL AVE	DUARTE, CA	91010
GOMEZ, EDWARD M	NEWS REPORTER	TIME/TIME & LIFE BLDG		
		ROCKEFELLER CENTER	NEW YORK, NY	10020
GOMEZ, JENNIFER	SPORTS REPORTER	SPORTS ILLUSTRATED MAGAZINE		
		TIME & LIFE BUILDING		
		ROCKEFELLER CENTER	NEW YORK, NY	10020
GOMEZ, LEFTY	BASEBALL	26 SAN BENITO WY	NOVATO, CA	94947
GOMEZ, LEROY	SINGER	BACK STAGE, 8919 SUNSET BLVD	LOS ANGELES, CA	90069
GOMEZ, MIKE	ACTOR	8230 BEVERLY BLVD #23	LOS ANGELES, CA	90048
GOMEZ, PANCHITO	ACTOR	POST OFFICE BOX 7016	BURBANK, CA	91510
GOMM, IAN	SINGER-GUITARIST	CHARLY RECORDS COMPANY		
		156-166 ILDERTON RD	LONDON SE15 1NT	ENGLAND
GOMMERMAN, STEVE	WRITER	8955 BEVERLY BLVD	LOS ANGELES, CA	90048
GOMPERTZ, ROLF	WRITER	6516 BEN AVE	NORTH HOLLYWOOD, CA	91606
GONCALVES, MANUEL	ROLA-BOLIST	HALL, 138 FROG HOLLOW RD	CHURCHVILLE, PA	18966
GONDEK, JULIANA	SOPRANO	AFFILIATE ARTISTS, INC		
		37 W 65TH ST, 6TH FLOOR	NEW YORK, NY	10023
GONE	ROCK & ROLL GROUP	POST OFFICE BOX 1	LAWNDALE, CA	90260
GONE FISHIN'	ROCK & ROLL GROUP	POST OFFICE BOX 2428	EL SEGUNDO, CA	90245
GONSHAK, IRWIN	WRITER	555 W 57TH ST #1230	NEW YORK, NY	10019
GONYEA, DALE	SINGER	7916 1/8 W NORTON AVE	LOS ANGELES, CA	90046
GONZALES, CARLOS	PHOTOGRAPHER	3813 LEGATION ST, NW	WASHINGTON, DC	20015
GONZALES, MARY M	TV DIRECTOR	519 N ELECTRIC AVE #7	ALHAMBRA, CA	91801
GONZALES, PAUL	BOXER	129 PASEO LOS ALISIS	LOS ANGELES, CA	90033
GONZALEZ	ROCK & ROLL GROUP	200 W 51ST ST #1410	NEW YORK, NY	10019
GONZALEZ, ANN MARIA	SOPRANO	61 W 62ND ST #6-F	NEW YORK, NY	10023
GONZALEZ, CARLOS A	NEWS CORRESPONDENT	5151 WISCONSIN AVE, NW	WASHINGTON, DC	20012
GONZALEZ, DALMACIO	TENOR	CAMI, 165 W 57TH ST	NEW YORK, NY	10019
GONZALEZ, ERNESTO	ACTOR	195 PRINCE ST	NEW YORK, NY	10012
GONZALEZ, GLORIA	TV WRITER	555 W 57TH ST #1230	NEW YORK, NY	10019
GONZALEZ, JOHN MICHAEL	DIRECTOR	DGA, 110 W 57TH ST	NEW YORK, NY	10019
GONZALEZ, PEDRO	WRESTLER	POST OFFICE BOX 3859	STAMFORD, CT	06905
GONZALEZ, RENE	WRITER	555 W 57TH ST #1230	NEW YORK, NY	10019
GONZALEZ, RUBEN	VIOLINIST	500 5TH AVE #2050	NEW YORK, NY	10110
GONZALEZ-GONZALEZ, PEDRO	ACTOR	4154 CHARLES AVE	CULVER CITY, CA	90230
GOOD, ART	RADIO PERSONALITY	KIFM RADIO 98, 5125 CONVOY ST	SAN DIEGO, CA	92111
GOOD, BOB	HAND BALANCER	BTC ENTERPRISES		
		600 HAYMONT DR	EASTON, PA	18042
GOOD, DENNIS	TROMBONIST	5325 BARRELL SPRINGS HOLLOW	FRANKLIN, TN	37064
GOOD, LARRY & THE GOODTIMES SHO	C & W GROUP	627 COUNTRY VIEW ESTATE	COLUMBUS, NE	68601
GOOD, MICHAEL	PHOTOGRAPHER	5 BLUE SILO CT	GAITHERSBURG, MD	20878
GOOD BROTHERS, THE	C & W GROUP	41 BRITAIN ST #200	TORONTO, ONT	CANADA
GOOD COMPANY	MUSICAL GROUP	GOOD, 2500 NW 39TH ST	OKLAHOMA CITY, OK	73112
GOOD OL' PERSONS, THE	BLUEGRASS GROUP	POST OFFICE BOX O	EL CERRITO, CA	94530
GOOD RATS, THE	ROCK & ROLL GROUP	ICM, 40 W 57TH ST	NEW YORK, NY	10019
GOODALL, GRAYSON "HUT 1-2-3"	DRILL INSTRUCTOR	2801 MEADOW LARK DR	SAN DIEGO, CA	92123
GOODE, FRITZ	DIRECTOR	6249 RODGERTON DR	HOLLYWOOD, CA	90068
GOODE, MARK I	DIRECTOR	1640 35TH ST, NW	WASHINGTON, DC	20007
GOODE, MORTON	WRITER	555 W 57TH ST #1230	NEW YORK, NY	10019
GOODE, RICHARD	PIANIST	BYERS-SCHWALBE, 1 5TH AVE	NEW YORK, NY	10003
GOODELL, GREGORY	WRITER-PRODUCER	1228 N FLORES ST	LOS ANGELES, CA	90069
GOODELL, HAROLD	ACTOR	1633 VISTA DEL MAR ST #201	LOS ANGELES, CA	90028
GOODEN, DWIGHT	BASEBALL	3101 E ELM ST	TAMPA, FL	33610
GOODEN, ROBERT	ACTOR	11240 MAGNOLIA BLVD #202	NORTH HOLLYWOOD, CA	91601
GOODEN, ROBERT	ACTOR-WRITER	3407 WARNER BLVD #B	BURBANK, CA	91505
GOODENOUGH-BARTON, GAY	ACTRESS	13827 E FOSTER AVE	BALDWIN PARK, CA	91706
GOODEVE, GRANT	ACTOR	9200 SUNSET BLVD #931	LOS ANGELES, CA	90069
GOODFELLOW, ALEXANDER S	NEWS CORRESPONDENT	NBC NEWS, 4001 NEBRASKA AVE, NW	WASHINGTON, DC	20016
GOODFORD, JACK	DIRECTOR	295 CARLTON ST	TORONTO, ONT M5A 2L6	CANADA
GOODFRIEND, LYNDA	ACTRESS	LIGHT, 113 N ROBERTSON BLVD	LOS ANGELES, CA	90048
GOODHART, JOANNE W	TV DIRECTOR	EUE SCREEN GEMS		
		222 E 44TH ST	NEW YORK, NY	10017
GOODHART, WILLIAM M	SCREENWRITER	555 W 57TH ST #1230	NEW YORK, NY	10019
GOODISH, FRANK	WRESTLER	SEE - BORDY, BRUISER		
GOODISH, FRANK "THE HAMMER"	WRESTLER	SEE - BRODY, BRUISER		
GOODMAN, ALAN	NEWS CORRESPONDENT	24-C AUBURN CT	ALEXANDRIA, VA	22305
GOODMAN, ALBERT M	TV WRITER	8955 BEVERLY BLVD	LOS ANGELES, CA	90048
GOODMAN, DAVID Z	TV WRITER	8955 BEVERLY BLVD	LOS ANGELES, CA	90048
GOODMAN, DODY	ACTRESS	1 IRONSIDES ST #12	MARINA DEL REY, CA	90292
GOODMAN, DON	WRITER	8955 BEVERLY BLVD	LOS ANGELES, CA	90048

Name	Occupation	Address	City/State	Zip
GOODMAN, ELLEN	COLUMNIST	THE BOSTON GLOBE		
		135 MORRISSEY RD	BOSTON, MA	02107
GOODMAN, EVELYN	WRITER	1123 N FULLER AVE #302	LOS ANGELES, CA	90046
GOODMAN, GEORGE J	WRITER	8955 BEVERLY BLVD	LOS ANGELES, CA	90048
GOODMAN, HAL	TV WRITER	8955 BEVERLY BLVD	LOS ANGELES, CA	90048
GOODMAN, HANNAH G	WRITER	555 W 57TH ST #1230	NEW YORK, NY	10019
GOODMAN, HARRY	PHOTOGRAPHER	3217 PAULINE DR	CHEVY CHASE, MD	20815
GOODMAN, JEFFREY S	PHOTOJOURNALIST	4225 SLEAFORD RD	BETHESDA, MD	20014
GOODMAN, JOHN	ACTOR	POST OFFICE BOX 5617	BEVERLY HILLS, CA	90210
GOODMAN, JON W	WRITER	19252 LUDLOW ST	NORTHRIDGE, CA	91326
GOODMAN, JOSEPH L	ACTOR	8075 W 3RD ST #303	LOS ANGELES, CA	90048
GOODMAN, LAWRENCE	WRITER	555 W 57TH ST #1230	NEW YORK, NY	10019
GOODMAN, LEE	DIRECTOR	3105 GULF OF MEXICO DR	LONGBOAT KEY, FL	33548
GOODMAN, LESLIE A	WRITER	555 W 57TH ST #1230	NEW YORK, NY	10019
GOODMAN, MARK	VIDEO JOCKEY	POST OFFICE BOX 1370	NEW YORK, NY	10101
GOODMAN, MAURICE	WRITER-PRODUCER	11179 BERTRAND AVE	GRANADA HILLS, CA	91344
GOODMAN, MILES	COMPOSER	11812 SAN VICENTE BLVD #200	LOS ANGELES, CA	90049
GOODMAN, PETER J	WRITER	555 W 57TH ST #1230	NEW YORK, NY	10019
GOODMAN, PHILIP S	WRITER	555 W 57TH ST #1230	NEW YORK, NY	10019
GOODMAN, ROBERT E	TV DIRECTOR	DGA, 110 W 57TH ST	NEW YORK, NY	10019
GOODMAN, ROGER	HARPSICHORDIST	AFFILIATE ARTISTS, INC		
		37 W 65TH ST, 6TH FLOOR	NEW YORK, NY	10023
GOODMAN, RONALD L	WRITER	555 W 57TH ST #1230	NEW YORK, NY	10019
GOODMAN, STUART	DIRECTOR	170 W 73RD ST	NEW YORK, NY	10023
GOODMAN, W H	PIANIST	POST OFFICE BOX 13	MADISONVILLE, KY	42431
GOODMAN, WALTER	WRITER	N Y TIMES, 229 W 43RD ST	NEW YORK, NY	10036
GOODMAN, WILLARD	WRITER-PRODUCER	6200 VISTA DEL MAR	PLAYA DEL REY, CA	90291
GOODNIGHT, GARY	SINGER	KENNEDY, 2125 8TH AVE S	NASHVILLE, TN	37204
GOODNOFF, SOL	DIRECTOR	ROUTE #8-A	PLAINFIELD, MA	01070
GOODPASTER, EDWIN W	NEWS CORRESPONDENT	5309 WANETA RD	BETHESDA, MD	20816
GOODRICH, DANIEL D	PHOTOGRAPHER	105 MARINERS WY	COPIAGUE, NY	11726
GOODRICH, DEBORAH	ACTRESS	9220 SUNSET BLVD #625	LOS ANGELES, CA	90069
GOODRICH, ROBERT E	DIRECTOR	DGA, 110 W 57TH ST	NEW YORK, NY	10019
GOODRICH, THEODOCIA	ACTRESS	13111 VENTURA BLVD #102	STUDIO CITY, CA	91604
GOODROW, GARRY	ACTOR	7466 BEVERLY BLVD #205	LOS ANGELES, CA	90036
GOODROW, MICHAEL	ACTOR	49 BREEZE AVE #1	VENICE, CA	90291
GOODRUM, CHARLES P	TV DIRECTOR	1702 SAN MIGUEL DR	SAINT CHARLES, MO	63301
GOODRUM, CHARLES R	PIANIST	31 WOODY LN	WESTPORT, CT	06880
GOODSON, ANN	MEZZO-SOPRANO	61 W 62ND ST #6-F	NEW YORK, NY	10023
GOODSON, JONATHAN M	DIRECTOR	DGA, 7950 SUNSET BLVD	LOS ANGELES, CA	90046
GOODSON, JOSEPH	TV DIRECTOR	858 RIDGE RD	LAKE ARROWHEAD, CA	92352
GOODSON, JOSEPH A	TV WRITER	8955 BEVERLY BLVD	LOS ANGELES, CA	90048
GOODSON, MARK	TV PRODUCER	375 PARK AVE	NEW YORK, NY	10152
GOODSPEED, PETER F	NEWS CORRESPONDENT	1316 NEW HAMPSHIRE AVE #505, NW	WASHINGTON, DC	20036
GOODSTONE, TONY	ACTOR	10000 RIVERSIDE DR #3	TOLUCA LAKE, CA	91602
GOODWIN, CHIP, BAND	MUSICAL GROUP	LUTZ, 5625 "O" STREET BLDG	LINCOLN, NE	68510
GOODWIN, DERRICK	TV DIRECTOR	MACK HOUSE COTTAGE		
		NETHER LYPIATT	GLOS	ENGLAND
GOODWIN, DOUG	COMPOSER	24758 HERMOSILLA CT	CALABASAS, CA	91302
GOODWIN, GERALD	COMEDIAN	1007 BUCKINGHAM RD	GARNER, NC	27529
GOODWIN, HAROLD	ACTOR	21 ALBERT RD, TWICKENHAM	MIDDLESEX	ENGLAND
GOODWIN, JAMES	ACTOR	CBS-TV, "THE GUIDING LIGHT"		
		51 W 52ND ST	NEW YORK, NY	10019
GOODWIN, JOHN M, III	ACTOR	706 N BUSHNELL AVE	ALHAMBRA, CA	91801
GOODWIN, JOSEPH	GUITARIST	POST OFFICE BOX 3421	ALBANY, GA	31706
GOODWIN, MICHAEL	ACTOR	9200 SUNSET BLVD #414	LOS ANGELES, CA	90069
GOODWIN, PAUL	TRUMPETER	ROUTE #1	HERMITAGE, TN	37076
GOODWIN, RICHARD	FILM PRODUCER	GRICE'S, 119 ROTHERHITH ST	LONDON SE16 4NF	ENGLAND
GOODWIN, ROBERT S	WRITER	8955 BEVERLY BLVD	LOS ANGELES, CA	90048
GOODWIN, ROBERT WILLIAM	TV WRITER-PRODUCER	33267 W DECKER SCHOOL RD	MALIBU, CA	90265
GOODWIN, RONALD ALFRED	COMPOSER-CONDUCTOR	BLACK NEST COTTAGE		
		HOCKFORD LN, BRIMPTON COMMON	READING RG7 4RP	ENGLAND
GOODWIN, RUTH	SINGER	POST OFFICE BOX 171132	NASHVILLE, TN	37217
GOODWIN, WILLIAM	GUITARIST	1303 N GALLATIN RD, DRAWER H	MADISON, TN	37115
GOOLAGONG, EVONNE	TENNIS	SEE - CAWLEY, EVONNE GOOLAGONG		
GOORNEY, HOWARD	ACTOR	PLANT & FROGGATT, LTD		
		JULIAN HOUSE		
		4 WINDMILL ST	LONDON W1	ENGLAND
GOORWITZ, ALLEN	ACTOR	13019 MONTANA AVE	LOS ANGELES, CA	90049
GOOSE CREEK SYMPHONY	BLUEGRASS GROUP	CAPITOL RECORDS COMPANY		
		PUBLIC RELATIONS DEPT		
		1750 N VINE ST	LOS ANGELES, CA	90028
GOOTSAN, GEORGE A	DIRECTOR	529 N MICHIGAN AVE	CHICAGO, IL	60611
GORANCHEVA, KRISTINA	SOPRANO	111 W 57TH ST #1209	NEW YORK, NY	10019
GORDAN, DAN	ACTOR	10351 SANTA MONICA BLVD #211	LOS ANGELES, CA	90025
GORDEAN, WILLIAM DRAKE	DIRECTOR	19517 BOWER DR	TOPANGA, CA	90290
GORDON, AARON SONNY	TV WRITER	3752 TRACY ST	LOS ANGELES, CA	90027
GORDON, ALIXE	CASTING DIRECTOR	POST OFFICE BOX 5718	SHERMAN OAKS, CA	91403
GORDON, ALVIN LAWRENCE	TV WRITER	789 WESTHOLME AVE	LOS ANGELES, CA	90024
GORDON, ANTHONY	ACTOR	ABC-TV, "GENERAL HOSPITAL"		
		1438 N GOWER ST	LOS ANGELES, CA	90028
GORDON, ARLENE	WRITER	8955 BEVERLY BLVD	LOS ANGELES, CA	90048
GORDON, BARRY	ACTOR	LEONETTI, 6526 SUNSET BLVD	HOLLYWOOD, CA	90028
GORDON, BERNARD	SCREENWRITER	1383 LONDONDERRY PL	LOS ANGELES, CA	90069
GORDON, BERT	WRITER-PRODUCER	9640 ARBY DR	BEVERLY HILLS, CA	90210

Name	Occupation	Address	City	Zip
GORDON, BRUCE	ACTOR	ROUTE #4, BOX 247	SANTA FE, NM	87501
GORDON, BRYAN	ACTOR-WRITER	854 19TH ST	SANTA MONICA, CA	90403
GORDON, CHARLES A	TV WRITER	10518 CHEVIOT DR	LOS ANGELES, CA	90064
GORDON, CHARLIE M	WRITER	8955 BEVERLY BLVD	LOS ANGELES, CA	90048
GORDON, CLARKE	ACTOR	13429 CANTARA ST	VAN NUYS, CA	91402
GORDON, CLAUDE	CONDUCTOR	19522 LEADWELL ST	RESEDA, CA	91335
GORDON, CLEO	ACTRESS	5330 LANKERSHIM BLVD #210	NORTH HOLLYWOOD, CA	91601
GORDON, DAN	SCREENWRITER	8955 BEVERLY BLVD	LOS ANGELES, CA	90048
GORDON, DANIEL	ACTOR	32-40 91ST ST	JACKSON HEIGHTS, NY	11369
GORDON, DANIEL H	ACTOR	205 E 63RD ST	NEW YORK, NY	10021
GORDON, DAVID	TENOR	59 E 54TH ST #81	NEW YORK, NY	10022
GORDON, DAVID	WRITER	8955 BEVERLY BLVD	LOS ANGELES, CA	90048
GORDON, DENISE A	WRITER-PRODUCER	31 MERCER ST #3-C	NEW YORK, NY	10013
GORDON, DEXTER	SAXOPHONIST	MS MGMT, 130 E 31ST ST	NEW YORK, NY	10016
GORDON, DON	ACTOR	2095 LINDA FLORA DR	LOS ANGELES, CA	90077
GORDON, DOUGLAS	ACTOR	100 LA SALLE ST	NEW YORK, NY	10027
GORDON, EDITH W	CONDUCTOR	5458 BEAUMONT	LA JOLLA, CA	92037
GORDON, EDWIN	SCREENWRITER	554 S SAN VICENTE BLVD #3	LOS ANGELES, CA	90048
GORDON, EVERETT H	CONDUCTOR	8819 EVANVIEW DR	LOS ANGELES, CA	90069
GORDON, FLORENCE LA RUE	SINGER	SEE - LA RUE, FLORENCE		
GORDON, GALE	ACTOR	POST OFFICE BOX 126	BORREGO SPRINGS, CA	92004
GORDON, GEOFFREY	ACTOR	4181 KLING ST #4	BURBANK, CA	91505
GORDON, GERALD	ACTOR	6310 SAN VICENTE BLVD #407	LOS ANGELES, CA	90048
GORDON, GREG	NEWS CORRESPONDENT	338 8TH ST, NE	WASHINGTON, DC	20002
GORDON, HANNAH	ACTRESS	WHITE, 31 KINGS RD	LONDON SW3	ENGLAND
GORDON, HAROLD	WRITER	25253 MALIBU RD	MALIBU, CA	90265
GORDON, JAMES K	NEWS CORRESPONDENT	2503 SPENCER RD	SILVER SPRING, MD	20910
GORDON, JANE	PUBLISHING	VIEW MAGAZINE, 150 E 58TH ST	NEW YORK, NY	10155
GORDON, JILL	TV WRITER	8955 BEVERLY BLVD	LOS ANGELES, CA	90048
GORDON, JUDITH ANN	THEATER PRODUCER	7 E 84TH ST	NEW YORK, NY	10028
GORDON, LAWRENCE	FILM PRODUCER	10201 W PICO BLVD	LOS ANGELES, CA	90035
GORDON, LAWRENCE	WRITER	8955 BEVERLY BLVD	LOS ANGELES, CA	90048
GORDON, LAWRENCE D, SR	COMPOSER	4257 SHADYGLADE AVE	STUDIO CITY, CA	91604
GORDON, LEAH SHANKS	WRITER-EDITOR	TIME/TIME & LIFE BLDG		
		ROCKEFELLER CENTER	NEW YORK, NY	10020
GORDON, LEO V	ACTOR-WRITER	9977 WORNOM AVE	SUNLAND, CA	91040
GORDON, MARC	TALENT AGENT	1244 OZETA TERR	LOS ANGELES, CA	90069
GORDON, MARGIE	TV WRITER	8955 BEVERLY BLVD	LOS ANGELES, CA	90048
GORDON, MARIANNE	ACTRESS	KRAGEN, 1112 N SHERBORUNE DR	LOS ANGELES, CA	90069
GORDON, MARK	ACTOR	10 E 44TH ST #700	NEW YORK, NY	10017
GORDON, MARK	TV DIRECTOR	323 W 83RD ST	NEW YORK, NY	10024
GORDON, MICHAEL	FILM DIRECTOR	DGA, 7950 SUNSET BLVD	LOS ANGELES, CA	90046
GORDON, MICHAEL R	NEWS CORRESPONDENT	4431 FESSENDEN ST, NW	WASHINGTON, DC	20016
GORDON, NEIL BRUCE	DIRECTOR	1321 WELLESLEY AVE	LOS ANGELES, CA	90025
GORDON, PATRICIA A	NEWS CORRESPONDENT	1415 RHODE ISLAND AVE, NW	WASHINGTON, DC	20005
GORDON, REGINA L	TV DIRECTOR	13342 CROCKER ST	LOS ANGELES, CA	90061
GORDON, RICHARD	FILM PRODUCER	119 W 57TH ST #319	NEW YORK, NY	10019
GORDON, RICHARD	WRITER	1 CRAVEN HILL	LONDON W2 3EP	ENGLAND
GORDON, ROBERT	SINGER	3 E 54TH ST #1400	NEW YORK, NY	10022
GORDON, ROBERT	DIRECTOR	DGA, 7950 SUNSET BLVD	LOS ANGELES, CA	90046
GORDON, SHIRLEY	WRITER	8955 BEVERLY BLVD	LOS ANGELES, CA	90048
GORDON, STEVE	WRITER-PRODUCER	151 S EL CAMINO DR	BEVERLY HILLS, CA	90212
GORDON, STEVEN & NADYA	PIANO DUO	CAMI, 165 W 57TH ST	NEW YORK, NY	10019
GORDON, STEVEN A	CONDUCTOR	11821 MAGNOLIA BLVD #5	NORTH HOLLYWOOD, CA	91607
GORDON, WILLIAM D	TV WRITER-PRODUCER	3208 STONER AVE	LOS ANGELES, CA	90066
GORDONE, CHARLES	PLAYWRIGHT	BOBBS-MERRILL COMPANY		
		4300 W 62ND ST	INDIANPOLIS, IN	46206
GORDY, ALISON	ACTRESS	13111 VENTURA BLVD #102	STUDIO CITY, CA	91604
GORDY, BERRY	RECORD EXECUTIVE	878 STRADELLA RD	LOS ANGELES, CA	90077
GORDY, DENISE	ACTRESS	151 S EL CAMINO DR	BEVERLY HILLS, CA	90212
GORDY, FULLER	RECORD EXECUTIVE	2378 ACHILLES DR	LOS ANGELES, CA	90046
GORDY, TERRY "BAM BAM"	WRESTLER	UNIVERSAL WRESTLING FEDERATION		
		MID SOUTH SPORTS, INC		
		5001 SPRING VALLEY RD	DALLAS, TX	75244
GORE, ALBERT	GUITARIST	116 SAVELY CT	HENDERSONVILLE, TN	37075
GORE, CHARLES	GUITARIST	2505 BLAIR BLVD	NASHVILLE, TN	37212
GORE, CHRISTOPHER	TV WRITER	555 W 57TH ST #1230	NEW YORK, NY	10019
GORE, DENNIS M	COMPOSER-CONDUCTOR	355 NW 189TH ST	SEATTLE, WA	98177
GORE, JOHN	GUITARIST	ROUTE #6, BOX 235-A		
		OLD HARRISTOWN RD	ASHLAND CITY, TN	37015
GORE, LESLEY	SINGER-ACTRESS	141 VERNON AVE	PATERSON, NJ	07503
GORE, MICHAEL	COMPOSER	310 W END AVE #12-C	NEW YORK, NY	10023
GORE, STEVEN R "NICK"	TV WRITER	8955 BEVERLY BLVD	LOS ANGELES, CA	90048
GOREN, CHARLES	BRIDGE EXPERT-WRITER	TRIBUNE MEDIA SERVICES		
		64 E CONCORD ST	ORLANDO, FL	32801
GOREN, ROWBY	WRITER	14144 VENTURA BLVD #200	SHERMAN OAKS, CA	91423
GORES, JOSEPH N	TV WRITER	9200 SUNSET BLVD #531	LOS ANGELES, CA	90069
GOREY, HAYS	NEWS CORRESPONDENT	4606 TOURNAY RD	BETHESDA, MD	20816
GORFAIN, LOUIS H	TV WRITER	APA, 888 7TH AVE, 21ST FLOOR	NEW YORK, NY	10106
GORGANO, CHARLES	ACTOR	8820 SUNSET BLVD #ANB	LOS ANGELES, CA	90069
GORHAM, PAMELA	ACTRESS	3575 W CAHUENGA BLVD #243	LOS ANGELES, CA	90068
GORI, KATHLEEN	SCREENWRITER	1127 9TH ST #102	SANTA MONICA, CA	90403
GORIN, NORMAN	WRITER	555 W 57TH ST #1230	NEW YORK, NY	10019
GORING. MARIUS	ACTOR	FILM RIGHTS, LTD, HAMMER HOUSE		
		113 WARDOUR ST	LONDON W1V 4EH	ENGLAND

GORLIN, RENA	NEWS CORRESPONDENT	3516 "W" PL #202	WASHINGTON, DC	20007
GORMAN, BOB	ACTOR	1240 N GARDNER ST	LOS ANGELES, CA	90046
GORMAN, CAROLYN W	NEWS CORRESPONDENT	6250 15TH PL	ARLINGTON, VA	22205
GORMAN, CHRISTINE	NEWS REPORTER	TIME/TIME & LIFE BLDG		
		ROCKEFELLER CENTER	NEW YORK, NY	10020
GORMAN, CLIFF	ACTOR	333 W 57TH ST	NEW YORK, NY	10019
GORMAN, MARI	ACTRESS	117 1/2 N SYCAMORE AVE	LOS ANGELES, CA	90036
GORMAN, STEVEN J	NEWS CORRESPONDENT	516 "A" ST #101, NE	WASHINGTON, DC	20002
GORMAN-JACOBS, JUDY	SINGER	ICEBERG RECORDS COMPANY		
		207 E BUFFALO ST	MILWAUKEE, WI	53202
GORME, EYDIE	SINGER	820 GREENWAY DR	BEVERLY HILLS, CA	90210
GORMLEY, ROBERT	ACTOR	543 N SYCAMORE AVE #11	LOS ANGELES, CA	90036
GORNEL, RANDY	ACTOR	1525 MONTANA AVE #A	SANTA MONICA, CA	90403
GORODETSKY, EDDIE	WRITER	8955 BEVERLY BLVD	LOS ANGELES, CA	90048
GORODETZKY, CARL	VIOLINIST	3526 RICHLAND AVE	NASHVILLE, TN	37205
GORODETZKY, CAROL	VIOLINIST	3526 RICHLAND AVE	NASHVILLE, TN	37205
GOROG, LASZLO	SCREENWRITER	5124 WILKINSON AVE	NORTH HOLLYWOOD, CA	91607
GOROKHOVSKY, ZINOVY	COMPOSER	1005 N STANLEY AVE #206	LOS ANGELES, CA	90046
GOROW, RONALD F	COMPOSER	POST OFFICE BOX 1131	LOS ANGELES, CA	90078
GORRELL, BOB	CARTOONIST	POST OFFICE BOX C-32333	RICHMOND, VA	23293
GORRIE, JOHN	TV DIRECTOR	41 CAMPDEN ST	LONDON W8	ENGLAND
GORRIN, MICHAEL	ACTOR	160 W 77TH ST	NEW YORK, NY	10024
GORRY, WILLIAM J	PHOTOGRAPHER	6581 LITTLE FALLS RD	ARLINGTON, VA	22213
GORSHIN, FRANK	ACTOR-COMEDIAN	POST OFFICE BOX 48559	LOS ANGELES, CA	90048
GORSKY, EDWARD	NEWS CORRESPONDENT	NBC-TV, NEWS DEPARTMENT		
		4001 NEBRASKA AVE, NW	WASHINGTON, DC	20016
GORTON, CLARENCE "DUTCH"	VIOLINIST	753 BRESSLYN RD	NASHVILLE, TN	37205
GOSA, JAMES	ACTOR	5727 OSO AVE	WOODLAND HILLS, CA	91367
GOSDIN, VERN	SINGER-SONGWRITER	818 18TH AVE S #300	NASHVILLE, TN	37203
GOSE, DULCINDA	WRITER	9039 PHYLLIS AVE	LOS ANGELES, CA	90069
GOSEY, CHARLES D	TV DIRECTOR	1804 SNOW MEADOW LN #T-2	BALTIMORE, MD	21209
GOSHKO, JOHN M	NEWS CORRESPONDENT	9810 SUMMIT AVE	KENSINGTON, MD	20895
GOSPEL LADS, THE	GOSPEL GROUP	6750 W 75TH ST, MARKADE 75		
		BUILDING #2-A	OVERLAND PARK, KS	66212
GOSS, DAVID	ACTOR	7471 MELROSE AVE #11	HOLLYWOOD, CA	90046
GOSS, JAMES W	WRITER	8955 BEVERLY BLVD	LOS ANGELES, CA	90048
GOSSAGE, GOOSE	BASEBALL	10565 VIACHA WY	SAN DIEGO, CA	92124
GOSSETT, JIMMY	DRUMMER	3808 CREEKSIDE DR	NASHVILLE, TN	37211
GOSSETT, LOUIS, JR	ACTOR-DIRECTOR	5916 BONSALL DR	MALIBU, CA	90265
GOTCHER, RICHARD	NEWS CORRESPONDENT	3349 S 5TH ST	ARLINGTON, VA	22204
GOTELL, WALTER	ACTOR	1930 CENTURY PARK W #30	LOS ANGELES, CA	90067
GOTTESFELD, DOV	ACTOR-WRITER	8955 BEVERLY BLVD	LOS ANGELES, CA	90048
GOTTFRIED, MARTIN	DRAMA CRITIC	17 96TH ST E	NEW YORK, NY	10020
GOTTLIEB, ALEX	WRITER-PRODUCER	921 10TH ST #110	SANTA MONICA, CA	90403
GOTTLIEB, BERNARD V	CONDUCTOR	1237 CRESTBROOK PL	ANAHEIM, CA	92805
GOTTLIEB, CARL	WRITER-DIRECTOR	8328 FOUNTAIN AVE #C	LOS ANGELES, CA	90069
GOTTLIEB, DAVID N	DIRECTOR	POST OFFICE BOX 924	TOPANGA CANYON, CA	90290
GOTTLIEB, JEROME	TV EXECUTIVE	MGM-UA TELEVISION		
		10202 W WASHINGTON BLVD	CULVER CITY, CA	90230
GOTTLIEB, LARRY	TV WRITER-PRODUCER	2133 REDLOCK CT	LOS ANGELES, CA	90039
GOTTLIEB, LISA	WRITER	8955 BEVERLY BLVD	LOS ANGELES, CA	90048
GOTTLIEB, MICHAEL	DIRECTOR	2436 WASHINGTON AVE	SANTA MONICA, CA	90403
GOTTLIEB, MORTON	THEATER PRODUCER	165 W 46TH ST	NEW YORK, NY	10036
GOTTLIEB, PAUL	WRITER	555 W 57TH ST #1230	NEW YORK, NY	10019
GOTTLIEB, RICHARD M	TV DIRECTOR	1717 N HIGHLAND AVE #1000	LOS ANGELES, CA	90028
GOTTLIEB, ROBERT M	NEWS CORRESPONDENT	1725 17TH ST #115, NW	WASHINGTON, DC	20009
GOTTLIEB, TARYN	WRITER	555 W 57TH ST #1230	NEW YORK, NY	10019
GOTTRON, MARTHA V	NEWS CORRESPONDENT	5602 OAKMONT AVE	BETHESDA, MD	20817
GOTTSCHALK, ROBERT	DIRECTOR	18618 OXNARD ST	TARZANA, CA	91356
GOUGH, ERIN	ACTRESS	SCHOEMAN, 2600 W VICTORY BLVD	BURBANK, CA	91505
GOULD, BERNI	WRITER	126 MABERY RD	SANTA MONICA, CA	90402
GOULD, CHERYL	TV PRODUCER	NBC TELEVISION NETWORK		
		30 ROCKEFELLER PLAZA	NEW YORK, NY	10112
GOULD, CLIFF	TV WRITER	8955 BEVERLY BLVD	LOS ANGELES, CA	90048
GOULD, DANNY	COMPOSER-CONDUCTOR	12315 RYE ST	STUDIO CITY, CA	91604
GOULD, DIANA	TV PRODUCER	AARON SPELLING PRODUCTIONS		
		1041 N FORMOSA AVE	LOS ANGELES, CA	90046
GOULD, DIANA	TV WRITER	267 MABERRY RD	SANTA MONICA, CA	90402
GOULD, DOROTHY	ACTRESS	CORWIN, 838 N DOHENY DR	LOS ANGELES, CA	90069
GOULD, ELEANOR CODY	ACTRESS	360 W 22ND ST	NEW YORK, NY	10011
GOULD, ELLIOTT	ACTOR	12169 GREENROCK LN	LOS ANGELES, CA	90049
GOULD, HAROLD	ACTOR	912 EL MEDIO AVE	PACIFIC PALISADES, CA	90272
GOULD, HEYWOOD	SCREENWRITER	555 W 57TH ST #1230	NEW YORK, NY	10019
GOULD, JANE	TV WRITER	8955 BEVERLY BLVD	LOS ANGELES, CA	90048
GOULD, JON	FILM PRODUCER	PARAMOUNT PICTURES CORP		
		5555 MELROSE AVE	LOS ANGELES, CA	90038
GOULD, LEE A	NEWS CORRESPONDENT	2950 VAN NESS ST #429, NW	WASHINGTON, DC	20008
GOULD, MARK	TRUMPETER	SOFFER, 130 W 56TH ST	NEW YORK, NY	10019
GOULD, MARTY	CONDUCTOR	THE SARTINI PLAZA		
		900 BRUSH ST #418	LAS VEGAS, NV	89107
GOULD, MORTON	COMPOSER-CONDUCTOR	327 MELBOURNE RD	GREAT NECK, NY	11021
GOULD, SANDRA	ACTRESS	6736 LAUREL CANYON BLVD #306	NORTH HOLLYWOOD, CA	91606
GOULD, SID	ACTOR	351 S PECK DR	BEVERLY HILLS, CA	90212

GOULD, SUSAN	WRITER	555 W 57TH ST #1230	NEW YORK, NY	10019
GOULD, VAL	ACTOR	8484 WILSHIRE BLVD #235	BEVERLY HILLS, CA	90211
GOULDING, RAY	ACT-WRI-COMED	420 LEXINGTON AVE	NEW YORK, NY	10017
GOULET, CHRISTOPHER	ACTOR	ICM, 8899 BEVERLY BLVD	LOS ANGELES, CA	90048
GOULET, NICOLETTE	ACTRESS	MICHAEL HARTIG, 114 E 28TH ST	NEW YORK, NY	10016
GOULET, RENE	WRESTLER	POST OFFICE BOX 3859	STAMFORD, CT	06905
GOULET, ROBERT	SINGER	3110 MONTE ROSA AVE	LAS VEGAS, NV	89120
GOULET, SGT JACQUES	WRESTLER	SEE - GOULET, RENE		
GOULLIERE, RENE	WRESTLER	SEE - GOULET, RENE		
GOURDINE, LITTLE ANTHONY	SINGER	23610 KENTWORTHY AVE	HARBOR CITY, CA	90710
GOURLEY, JAMIE D	ACTRESS	5000 LANKERSHIM BLVD #5	NORTH HOLLYWOOD, CA	91601
GOURVITZ, PAUL H	WRITER	555 W 57TH ST #1230	NEW YORK, NY	10019
GOUTMAN, CHRISTOPHER PAUL	TV DIRECTOR	10 W 66TH ST	NEW YORK, NY	10023
GOVE	C & W GROUP	POST OFFICE BOX 1556	GAINESVILLE, FL	32602
GOVER, DOUGLAS J	TV DIRECTOR	7803 VIA FOGGIA	BURBANK, CA	91504
GOWAN	ROCK & ROLL GROUP	41 BRITAIN ST #200	TORONTO, ONT	CANADA
GOWAN, BILL	CLOWN	2701 COTTAGE WY #14	SACRAMENTO, CA	95825
GOWANS, DAVID J	BASSOONIST	1702 OLIVE	MURRAY, KY	42071
GOWDY, CURT	SPORTCASTER-TV HOST	33 FRANKLIN ST	LAWRENCE, MA	01840
GOWEN, JERRY	GUITARIST	2131 ELM HILL PIKE #F-1	NASHVILLE, TN	37210
GOWER, RANDY	GUITARIST	ROUTE #1	FRANKLIN, TN	37064
GOWERS, BRUCE	DIRECTOR	2153 KRESS ST	LOS ANGELES, CA	90046
GOWERS, WARREN	GUITARIST	ROUTE #3	FRANKLIN, TN	37064
GOYAL, RAGHBIR	NEWS CORRESPONDENT	9426 PACKARD WY	BURKE, VA	22015
GOYETTE, DESIREE	COMPOSER-ACTRESS	POST OFFICE BOX 10622	BEVERLY HILLS, CA	90213
GOZ, HARRY	ACTOR	SCHAPIRO, 122 E 42ND ST	NEW YORK, NY	10168
GRABER, KATHY	ACTRESS	15010 VENTURA BLVD #219	SHERMAN OAKS, CA	91403
GRABOWSKI, GENE	NEWS CORRESPONDENT	9111 LINDALE DR	BETHESDA, MD	20817
GRACE, ARTHUR	PHOTOGRAPHER	1928 35TH PL, NW	WASHINGTON, DC	20007
GRACE, BUD	CARTOONIST	POST OFFICE BOX 4203	NEW YORK, NY	10017
GRACE, FRANCES K	WRITER	555 W 57TH ST #1230	NEW YORK, NY	10019
GRACE, FREDI & RHINSTONE	C & W GROUP	SOUTH/OMNI INTERNATIONAL #1290	ATLANTA, GA	30303
GRACE, JASON R	DIRECTOR	CLARK HILL RD	OLD LYME, CT	06371
GRACE, MICHAEL L	WRITER	4520 RUSSELL AVE	LOS ANGELES, CA	90027
GRACE, NIKOLAS	ACTOR	SARABAND ASSOCIATES AGENCY		
		153 PETHERTON RD, HIGHBURY	LONDON N5	ENGLAND
GRAD, PETER	TV EXECUTIVE	POST OFFICE BOX 900	BEVERLY HILLS, CA	90213
GRADE, LORD LEW	FILM EXECUTIVE	EMBASSY, 3 AUDLEY SQ	LONDON W1Y 5DR	ENGLAND
GRADE, MICHAEL	TV EXECUTIVE	BBC-TV CENTRE, WOOD LN		
		SHEPHERDS BUSH	LONDON W12	ENGLAND
GRADINGER, EDWARD BARRY	FILM EXECUTIVE	POST OFFICE BOX 900	BEVERLY HILLS, CA	90213
GRADISON, ROBIN	NEWS CORRES-WRITER	ABC-TV, NEWS DEPARTMENT	WASHINGTON, DC	20036
		1717 DE SALES ST, NW	WASHINGTON, DC	20036
GRADUS, BEN	TV WRITER-DIRECTOR	161 GREENWAY S	FOREST HILLS GARDENS,	11375
GRADY, DON	ACTOR	3575 W CAHUENGA BLVD #320	LOS ANGELES, CA	90068
GRADY, ERNEST "SANDY"	NEWS CORRESPONDENT	1400 JOYCE ST #A-906	ARLINGTON, VA	22202
GRADY, JAMES	WRITER	555 W 57TH ST #1230	NEW YORK, NY	10019
GRADY, MARY	TALENT AGENT	3575 W CAHUENGA BLVD #320	LOS ANGELES, CA	90068
GRAF, DAVID	ACTOR	151 N SAN VICENTE BLVD #208	BEVERLY HILLS, CA	90211
GRAF, ELLY	TV DIRECTOR	457 W 57TH ST	NEW YORK, NY	10019
GRAF, ENRIQUE	PIANIST	POST OFFICE BOX 22456	BALTIMORE, MD	21203
GRAF, WILLIAM N	FILM PRODUCER	1100 N ALTA LOMA RD #603	LOS ANGELES, CA	90069
GRAFA, JULIE	SINGER	GOOD, 2500 NW 39TH ST	OKLAHOMA CITY, OK	73112
GRAFAS, VAN ANGELO, II	BODYBUILDER	BODY-BUILDER ENTS		
		40 PROSPECT ST	SUMMIT, NJ	07901
GRAFF, ILENE	ACTRESS	10100 SANTA MONICA BLVD #1600	LOS ANGELES, CA	90067
GRAFF, J WILLIAM	NEWS CORRESPONDENT	12847 TEWKSBURY DR	HERNDON, VA	22071
GRAFF, ROBERT D	DIRECTOR	116 E 68TH ST	NEW YORK, NY	10021
GRAFF, THOMAS DUNCAN	DIRECTOR	50 W 96TH ST #1-A	NEW YORK, NY	10025
GRAFFIUS, JOHN H	DIRECTOR	515 UNIVERSITY PL	GROSSE POINTE CITY, MI	48230
GRAFFMAN, GARY	PIANIST	POST OFFICE BOX 30	TENAFLY, NJ	07670
GRAFTON, JIMMY	TV WRITER	10 LESLEY CT		
		23 STRUTTON GROUND	LONDON SW1	ENGLAND
GRAFTON, SUE	TV WRITER-PRODUCER	1015 GAYLEY AVE #301	LOS ANGELES, CA	90024
GRAGLIA, RICHARD E	WRITER	8955 BEVERLY BLVD	LOS ANGELES, CA	90048
GRAHAM, ALEX	CARTOONIST	NEWS AMERICA SYNDICATE		
		1703 KAISER AVE	IRVINE, CA	92714
GRAHAM, BILL	ROCK PROMOTER	POST OFFICE BOX 1994	SAN FRANCISCO, CA	94101
GRAHAM, BILLY	EVANGELIST	SEE - GRAHAM, REV BILLY		
GRAHAM, BILLY "SUPERSTAR"	WRESTLER	POST OFFICE BOX 3859	STAMFORD, CT	06905
GRAHAM, BOB	FILM DIRECTOR	1926 HILLCREST RD	LOS ANGELES, CA	90068
GRAHAM, BRUCE	WRITER	GOLDSTEIN, 99 PARK AVE	NEW YORK, NY	10016
GRAHAM, CAROLE	BODYBUILDER	288 THE GRAND PARADE	RAMSGATE BEACH	AUSTRALIA
GRAHAM, DAVID	CASTING DIRECTOR	POST OFFICE BOX 69277	LOS ANGELES, CA	90069
GRAHAM, DAVID M	NEWS CORRESPONDENT	1308 S WALTER REED DR	ARLINGTON, VA	22204
GRAHAM, DONALD G	TV DIRECTOR	32625 CLAIRVIEW RD	FARMINGTON HILLS, MI	48018
GRAHAM, DOUGLAS	TV WRITER	8955 BEVERLY BLVD	LOS ANGELES, CA	90048
GRAHAM, DR JERRY	WRESTLER	CAPITOL INTERNATIONAL		
		11844 MARKET ST	NORTH LIMA, OH	44452
GRAHAM, EDDIE	GUITARIST	9561 RYLIE CREST	DALLAS, TX	75217
GRAHAM, ELIZABETH	SOPRANO	SULLIVAN, 390 W END AVE	NEW YORK, NY	10024
GRAHAM, EVARTS A	NEWS CORRESPONDENT	540 "N" ST, SW	WASHINGTON, DC	20024
GRAHAM, FRED	LAW-NEWS CORRES	2149 CALIFORNIA ST, NW	WASHINGTON, DC	20008
GRAHAM, GARY	ACTOR	183 N MARTEL AVE #260	LOS ANGELES, CA	90036
GRAHAM, GERRIT	ACTOR-WRITER	6201 GLEN OAK ST	LOS ANGELES, CA	90068

GRAHAM, HERB K	ACTOR	8484 WILSHIRE BLVD #235	BEVERLY HILLS, CA	90211
GRAHAM, IRVIN	ACTOR-WRITER	360 E 55TH ST	NEW YORK, NY	10022
GRAHAM, JANICE L	SCREENWRITER	8955 BEVERLY BLVD	LOS ANGELES, CA	90048
GRAHAM, JOHN MICHAEL	ACTOR	14955 OTSEGO ST	SHERMAN OAKS, CA	91403
GRAHAM, KATHARINE	PUBLISH EXECUTIVE	NEWSWEEK, 444 MADISON AVE	NEW YORK, NY	10022
GRAHAM, KENNETH F	ACTOR	1746 N ORANGE DR #803	LOS ANGELES, CA	90028
GRAHAM, LARRY	PIANIST	425 RIVERSIDE DR #5-G	NEW YORK, NY	10025
GRAHAM, LARRY	SINGER-GUITARIST	MISTER I MOUSE, LTD		
		920 DICKSON ST	MARINA DEL REY, CA	90292
GRAHAM, LYLA	ACTRESS	151 N SAN VICENTE BLVD #208	BEVERLY HILLS, CA	90211
GRAHAM, MARTHA	DANCER	316 E 63RD ST	NEW YORK, NY	10021
GRAHAM, NANCY L	WRITER	8955 BEVERLY BLVD	LOS ANGELES, CA	90048
GRAHAM, PAUL	BODYBUILDER	288 THE GRAND PARADE	RAMSGATE BEACH	AUSTRALIA
GRAHAM, PAUL C	WRITER	555 W 57TH ST #1230	NEW YORK, NY	10019
GRAHAM, RANALD	WRITER	8955 BEVERLY BLVD	LOS ANGELES, CA	90048
GRAHAM, REV BILLY	EVANGELIST	1300 HARMON PL	MINNEAPOLIS, MN	55403
GRAHAM, RONALD	PIANIST	KAY, 58 W 58TH ST	NEW YORK, NY	10019
GRAHAM, RONALD M	TV WRITER	8955 BEVERLY BLVD	LOS ANGELES, CA	90048
GRAHAM, SHARON	MEZZO-SOPRANO	61 W 62ND ST #6-F	NEW YORK, NY	10023
GRAHAM, TAMMY	MUSICIAN	POST OFFICE BOX 592	HENDERSONVILLE, TN	37075
GRAHAM, VIRGINIA	TV HOST	LIGHT, 113 N ROBERTSON BLVD	LOS ANGELES, CA	90048
GRAHAM, WILLIAM A	DIRECTOR	21510 CALLE DEL BARCO	MALIBU, CA	90265
GRAHAME, GERALD	TENOR	CAMI, 165 W 57TH ST	NEW YORK, NY	10019
GRAHN, NANCY	ACTRESS	9220 SUNSET BLVD #202	LOS ANGELES, CA	90069
GRAIMAN, JACK	COMEDIAN	6380 WILSHIRE BLVD #1600	LOS ANGELES, CA	90048
GRAIS, MICHAEL	SCREENWRITER	683 HAMPDEN PL	PACIFIC PALISADES, CA	90272
GRALNICK, JEFF	TV PRODUCER	ABC-TV, 7 W 66TH ST	NEW YORK, NY	10023
GRAMALIA, ROSE	WRITER	6057 BECK AVE	NORTH HOLLYWOOD, CA	91606
GRAMBS, JEFFREY W	WRITER	555 W 57TH ST #1230	NEW YORK, NY	10019
GRAMM, LOU	SINGER-SONGWRITER	E S "BUD" PRAGER MANAGEMENT		
		1790 BROADWAY, PENTHOUSE	NEW YORK, NY	10019
GRAMMER, BILLY	SINGER-GUITARIST	ROUTE #1	NOLENSVILLE, TN	37135
GRAN SCENA	CLASSICAL GROUP	SHAFMAN INTERNATIONAL		
		723 7TH AVE	NEW YORK, NY	10019
GRANAT, DIANE	NEWS CORRESPONDENT	2422 39TH PL, NW	WASHINGTON, DC	20007
GRAND JUNCTION	C & W GROUP	LUTZ, 5625 "O" STREET BLDG	LINCOLN, NE	68510
GRAND MASTER FLASH	RAPPER-RAPWRITER	200 W 51ST ST #1410	NEW YORK, NY	10019
GRAND MASTER MELLE-MEL	RAPPER-RAPWRITER	200 W 51ST ST #1410	NEW YORK, NY	10019
GRANDE, JUDY	NEWS CORRESPONDENT	1401 N OAK ST	ARLINGTON, VA	22209
GRANDON, RONALD E	NEWS CORRESPONDENT	1730 S MONROE ST	ARLINGTON, VA	22204
GRANDY, FRED	ACTOR-CONGRESSMAN	4511 COUNTRY CLUB BLVD	SIOUX CITY, IA	51104
GRANDY, JAN GOUGH	TV WRITER	33 19TH AVE	VENICE, CA	90291
GRANER, GERTRUDE	ACTRESS	7072 HAWTHORN AVE	LOS ANGELES, CA	90028
GRANET, BERT	WRITER	350 ENTRADA DR	SANTA MONICA, CA	90402
GRANET, IRMA	ACTRESS	4448 TYRONE AVE	SHERMAN OAKS, CA	91423
GRANGENOIS, MIRIELLE	NEWS CORRESPONDENT	1246 LINDEN PL, NE	WASHINGTON, DC	20002
GRANGER, DEREK	TV PRODUCER	82 PALACE GARDENS	LONDON W8	ENGLAND
GRANGER, DOROTHY	ACTRESS	HILDER, 11903 W PICO BLVD	LOS ANGELES, CA	90064
GRANGER, FARLEY	ACTOR	18 W 72ND ST #25-D	NEW YORK, NY	10023
GRANGER, KAY	SINGER	1300 DIVISION ST #103	NASHVILLE, TN	37203
GRANGER, PAPPY	CLOWN	2701 COTTAGE WY #14	SACRAMENTO, CA	95825
GRANGER, PERCY	TV WRITER	165 W 46TH ST #409	NEW YORK, NY	10036
GRANGER, SHANTON	ACTOR	450 E 84TH ST	NEW YORK, NY	10028
GRANGER, STEWART	ACTOR	8485 MELROSE PL #E	LOS ANGELES, CA	90069
GRANICK, MELVIN	WRITER	555 W 57TH ST #1230	NEW YORK, NY	10019
GRANITO, LIVIA	DIRECTOR	DGA, 7950 SUNSET BLVD	LOS ANGELES, CA	90046
GRANO, JOHN R	NEWS CORRESPONDENT	10013 CORNWALL RD	FAIRFAX, VA	22030
GRANOT, ODED	NEWS CORRESPONDENT	318 LORRAINE DR	ROCKVILLE, MD	20852
GRANT, AMY	SINGER-SONGWRITER	POST OFFICE BOX 50701	NASHVILLE, TN	37205
GRANT, ARMAND	TV WRITER-PRODUCER	2270 BOWMONT DR	BEVERLY HILLS, CA	90210
GRANT, B DONALD	TV EXECUTIVE	CBS-TV, 7800 BEVERLY BLVD	LOS ANGELES, CA	90036
GRANT, BARRA	ACTRESS-WRITER	151 S EL CAMINO DR	BEVERLY HILLS, CA	90212
GRANT, BERNICE	WRITER	555 W 57TH ST #1230	NEW YORK, NY	10019
GRANT, BILL	BODYBUILDER	MARGOT, LES GRAND PARADE	1261 BOGIS-BOSSEY	SWITZERLAND
GRANT, BOB	MUSICIAN	15413 DOTY ST	LAWNDALE, CA	90260
GRANT, DR TONI	RADIO PERSONALITY	1289 SUNSET PLAZA DR	LOS ANGELES, CA	90069
GRANT, EDDY	SINGER-WRITER	POST OFFICE BOX 212	LONDON	ENGLAND
GRANT, FAYE	ACTRESS	ICM, 8899 BEVERLY BLVD	LOS ANGELES, CA	90048
GRANT, GEORGE	WRESTLER	SEE - GEORGE, GORGEOUS		
GRANT, GEORGE C	ACTOR	15010 VENTURA BLVD #219	SHERMAN OAKS, CA	91403
GRANT, GIL	TV WRITER	8955 BEVERLY BLVD	LOS ANGELES, CA	90048
GRANT, GOGI	SINGER	1709 AMBASSADOR AVE	BEVERLY HILLS, CA	90210
GRANT, GORDON W	ACTOR	3414 1/2 S SEPULVEDA BLVD	LOS ANGELES, CA	90034
GRANT, HANK	WRITER	6715 SUNSET BLVD	HOLLYWOOD, CA	90028
GRANT, JERRY	COMPOSER	6040 VANTAGE AVE	NORTH HOLLYWOOD, CA	91606
GRANT, JOE	GUITARIST	249 LAKE TERR DR	HENDERSONVILLE, TN	37075
GRANT, JOHNNY	TV HOST	KTLA-TV, 5800 SUNSET BLVD	HOLLYWOOD, CA	90028
GRANT, KATIE	ACTRESS	1650 BROADWAY #302	NEW YORK, NY	10019
GRANT, LEE	ACTRESS-DIRECTOR	151 S EL CAMINO DR	BEVERLY HILLS, CA	90212
GRANT, LEE H	TV WRITER	962 1ST ST #D	HERMOSA BEACH, CA	90006
GRANT, LEE J	WRITER	5417 ENCINO AVE	ENCINO, CA	91316
GRANT, LORRAINE	ACTRESS	10850 RIVERSIDE DR #410	NORTH HOLLYWOOD, CA	91609
GRANT, MARK ALLEN	ACTOR	12713 CASWELL AVE #1	LOS ANGELES, CA	90066
GRANT, MARSHALL	GUITARIST-TAL AGT	POST OFFICE BOX 492	HERNANDO, MS	38632
GRANT, MERRILL	TV WRITER-PRODUCER	6 CAYUGA RD	SCARSDALE, NY	10583

Name	Occupation	Address	City, State	Zip
GRANT, MITCHELL E	WRITER	555 W 57TH ST #1230	NEW YORK, NY	10019
GRANT, NEVA	NEWS CORRESPONDENT	1748 SWANN ST, NW	WASHINGTON, DC	20009
GRANT, PERRY	TV WRITER-PRODUCER	727 OCAMPO DR	PACIFIC PALISADES, CA	90272
GRANT, RON	RECORDING ENGINEER	3815 W OLIVE AVE #202	BURBANK, CA	91505
GRANT, ROSLYN	NEWS CORRESPONDENT	2725 POPLAR ST, NW	WASHINGTON, DC	20007
GRANT, SAM	GUITARIST	700 PATRICIA DR #A-3	NASHVILLE, TN	37217
GRANT, SARINA C	ACTRESS	11927 MAGNOLIA BLVD #13	NORTH HOLLYWOOD, CA	91607
GRANT, SHELBY	ACTRESS	SEE - EVERETT, SHELBY GRANT		
GRANT, TOM	SINGER	323 MELVIN JONES RD	NASHVILLE, TN	37217
GRANT, TOM	SINGER-GUITARIST	234 CUMBERLAND CIR	NASHVILLE, TN	37214
GRANT & WINN	PIANO DUO	GREAT LAKES PERFORMING		
		310 E WASHINGTON ST	ANN ARBOR, MI	48104
GRANTHAM, CLINTON	GUITARIST	2712 W LINDEN AVE	NASHVILLE, TN	37212
GRANTHAM, GEORGE	DRUMMER	729 ALBAR DR	NASHVILLE, TN	37221
GRANTS, MAURICE A	CONDUCTOR	11319 ALETHEA DR	SUNLAND, CA	91040
GRANVILLE, BONITA	ACTRESS-PRODUCER	WRATHER, 172 DELFERN DR	LOS ANGELES, CA	90077
GRANZ, NORMAN	RECORD PRODUCER	1110 DOLORITA AVE	GLENDALE, CA	91208
GRAPE, MOBY	ROCK & ROLL GROUP	SEE - MOBY GRAPE		
GRAPES, CHERIE	SINGER	1111 MC CHESNEY AVE	NASHVILLE, TN	37221
GRAPES, JOHN	GUITARIST	1111 MC CHESNEY AVE	NASHVILLE, TN	37216
GRAPPLER, THE	WRESTLER	WORLD CLASS WRESTLING		
		SOUTHWEST SPORTS, INC		
		DALLAS SPORTATORIUM		
		1000 S INDUSTRIAL BLVD	DALLAS, TX	75207
GRAPPLER #1	WRESTLER	SEE - GRAPPLER, THE		
GRAPPLER #2	WRESTLER	WORLD CLASS WRESTLING		
		SOUTHWEST SPORTS, INC		
		DALLAS SPORTATORIUM		
		1000 S INDUSTRIAL BLVD	DALLAS, TX	75207
GRASS ROOTS, THE	ROCK & ROLL GROUP	10880 WILSHIRE BLVD #912	LOS ANGELES, CA	90024
GRASSANO, WILLIAM J	NEWS CORRESPONDENT	1919 CALVERT ST, NW	WASHINGTON, DC	20007
GRASSELLI, DIANA	SINGER	3 E 54TH ST #1400	NEW YORK, NY	10022
GRASSHOFF, ALEX	WRITER-PRODUCER	7845 TORREYSON DR	LOS ANGELES, CA	90046
GRASSIE, JOHN E	DIRECTOR	1120 DENNIS CT	SILVER SPRING, MD	20901
GRASSLE, KAREN	ACTRESS	POST OFFICE BOX 493	PACIFIC PALISADES, CA	90272
GRASSO, JUNE R	WRITER	555 W 57TH ST #1230	NEW YORK, NY	10019
GRASSO, NEIL J	PHOTOGRAPHER	1000 ARNON CHAPEL RD	GREAT FALLS, VA	22066
GRATEFUL DEAD	ROCK & ROLL GROUP	POST OFFICE BOX 1566		
		MAIN OFFICE STATION	MONTCLAIR, NJ	07043
GRATOVICH/GOLMON DUO	MUSICAL DUO	FROTHINGHAM, 40 GROVE ST	WESSESLEY, MA	02181
GRATTON, BILL	ACTOR	8350 SANTA MONICA BLVD #103	LOS ANGELES, CA	90069
GRATTON, RICHARD	BARITONE	JCB, 155 W 68TH ST	NEW YORK, NY	10023
GRAU, SHIRLEY ANN	WRITER	BRANDT & BRANDT, 1501 BROADWAY	NEW YORK, NY	10036
GRAUL, EWALD	COMPOSER-CONDUCTOR	528 S RAMPAROUTE BLVD #2	LOS ANGELES, CA	90057
GRAUMAN, WALTER	TV DIRECTOR-PRODUCER	244 BABCOCK AVE	LOS ANGELES, CA	90049
GRAUSE, DONNA	MODEL	POST OFFICE BOX 7211	MOUNTAIN VIEW, CA	94043
GRAVAGE, BOB	ACTOR	8250 LANKERSHIM BLVD PARK #14	NORTH HOLLYWOOD, CA	91605
GRAVATTE, MARIANNE	ACTRESS-MODEL	MODELS & PROMOTIONS AGENCY		
		8560 SUNSET BLVD, 10TH FLOOR	LOS ANGELES, CA	90069
GRAVER, FRED	TV WRITER	THE WILLIAM MORRIS AGENCY		
		1350 AVE OF THE AMERICAS	NEW YORK, NY	10019
GRAVES, AMANDA LEE	ACTRESS	660 E CHANNEL RD	SANTA MONICA, CA	90402
GRAVES, ERNEST	ACTOR	323 W 83RD ST	NEW YORK, NY	10024
GRAVES, JASON	ACTOR	8484 WILSHIRE BLVD #235	BEVERLY HILLS, CA	90211
GRAVES, JOEL RYAN	ACTOR	1717 N HIGHLAND AVE #41	HOLLYWOOD, CA	90028
GRAVES, JOSH, JR	GUITARIST	182 LAKESIDE PARK DR	HENDERSONVILLE, TN	37075
GRAVES, JOSH, SR	GUITARIST	810 CHADWELL DR	MADISON, TN	37115
GRAVES, LINDSAY	NEWS CORRESPONDENT	2411 MENOKIN DR	ALEXANDRIA, VA	22302
GRAVES, NELSON M	NEWS CORRESPONDENT	156 13TH ST, SE	WASHINGTON, DC	20003
GRAVES, PETER	ACTOR	ICM, 388-396 OXFORD ST	LONDON W1	ENGLAND
GRAVES, PETER	ACTOR-DIRECTOR	660 E CHANNEL RD	SANTA MONICA, CA	90402
GRAVES, PETER & ATLANTIAN	JAZZ BAND	2501 S OCEAN DR	HOLLYWOOD, FL	33019
GRAVLIN, VIRGINIA	ACTRESS	425 RIVERSIDE DR	NEW YORK, NY	10025
GRAY, ANTHONY	ACTOR	3050 W 7TH ST #200	LOS ANGELES, CA	90005
GRAY, BARTON	COMPOSER	5129 ALTA DR	LAS VEGAS, NV	89107
GRAY, BEATRICE	ACTRESS	6430 SUNSET BLVD #1203	LOS ANGELES, CA	90028
GRAY, BILLY	ACTOR	19612 GRAND VIEW DR	TOPANGA CANYON, CA	90290
GRAY, BRUCE	ACTOR	9165 SUNSET BLVD #202	LOS ANGELES, CA	90069
GRAY, CALEB	WRITER	555 W 57TH ST #1230	NEW YORK, NY	10019
GRAY, CHARLES	ACTOR	LONDON MANAGEMENT, LTD		
		235-241 REGENT ST	LONDON W1A 2JT	ENGLAND
GRAY, COLEEN	ACTRESS	1432 N KENWOOD ST	BURBANK, CA	91505
GRAY, CYNTHIA	ACTRESS	9000 SUNSET BLVD #1200	LOS ANGELES, CA	90069
GRAY, DAVID	ACTOR	GRAHAM MGMT, 25 BROOKDALE RD		
		BRAMHALL HALL	CHESHIRE	ENGLAND
GRAY, DOBIE	SINGER-SONGWRITER	210 25TH AVE N #N-101	NASHVILLE, TN	37203
GRAY, DUANE D	WRITER	555 W 57TH ST #1230	NEW YORK, NY	10019
GRAY, ELIZABETH A	WRITER	8955 BEVERLY BLVD	LOS ANGELES, CA	90048
GRAY, ERIN	ACTRESS	500 S SEPULVEDA BLVD #510	LOS ANGELES, CA	90049
GRAY, ESTHER E	ACTRESS	10 E 44TH ST #700	NEW YORK, NY	10017
GRAY, GARY	WRITER	8955 BEVERLY BLVD	LOS ANGELES, CA	90048
GRAY, GEORGE	WRESTLER	SEE - ONE MAN GANG		
GRAY, J T	GUITARIST	1148 VULTEE BLVD #2	NASHVILLE, TN	37217
GRAY, JAN	SINGER	TAYLOR, 2401 12TH AVE S	NASHVILLE, TN	37204
GRAY, JEROME	ACTOR	10351 SANTA MONICA BLVD #211	LOS ANGELES, CA	90025

GRAY, LINDA	ACTRESS-DIRECTOR	151 S EL CAMINO DR	BEVERLY HILLS, CA	90212
GRAY, LINDA ESTHER	SOPRANO	CAMI, 165 W 57TH ST	NEW YORK, NY	10019
GRAY, MARK	SINGER	151 S EL CAMINO DR	BEVERLY HILLS, CA	90212
GRAY, MARK	SINGER	POST OFFICE BOX 19489	AUSTIN, TX	78760
GRAY, MIKE	WRITER-PRODUCER	20373 EVERDING LN	TOPANGA CANYON, CA	90290
GRAY, NICK	TV DIRECTOR-PRODUCER	76 BROADGATE LN, HORSFORTH	LEEDS	ENGLAND
GRAY, NORM	DIRECTOR	11138 AQUA VISTA ST #25	STUDIO CITY, CA	91602
GRAY, PAUL	WRITER-EDITOR	TIME/TIME & LIFE BLDG		
		ROCKEFELLER CENTER	NEW YORK, NY	10020
GRAY, ROBERT	ACTOR	211 S BEVERLY DR #201	BEVERLY HILLS, CA	90212
GRAY, RUDY	SCREENWRITER	KLAUSNER, 71 PARK AVE	NEW YORK, NY	10016
GRAY, SIMON	PLAYWRIGHT	DAISH, 83 EASTBOURNE MEWS	LONDON W2 6LQ	ENGLAND
GRAY, SPALDING	WRITER-ACTOR	PROGRAM DEVELOPMENT		
		136 E 65TH ST	NEW YORK, NY	10021
GRAY, STANLEY LEROY	WRITER	401 W WELLS ST	SAN GABRIEL, CA	91776
GRAY, THOMAS	FILM EXECUTIVE	GOLDEN HARVEST PICTURES		
		9884 SANTA MONICA BLVD	BEVERLY HILLS, CA	90212
GRAY, VELEKKA	ACTRESS	10000 RIVERSIDE DR #3	TOLUCA LAKE, CA	91602
GRAY, WAYNE	GUITARIST	104 DIANNE DR, SW	FAIRVIEW, TN	37062
GRAY, WILLIAM	SCREENWRITER	POST OFFICE BOX 5617	BEVERLY HILLS, CA	90210
GRAYCO, HELEN	SINGER	GATSBY, 11500 SAN VICENTE BLVD	LOS ANGELES, CA	90049
GRAYDON, JAY J	COMPOSER	POST OFFICE BOX 1507	STUDIO CITY, CA	91604
GRAYSON, KATHRYN	ACTRESS-SINGER	2009 LA MESA DR	SANTA MONICA, CA	90402
GRAYSON, LARRY	TV PERSONALITY	THE GARLANDS, HINCKLEY RD	WARWICKS	ENGLAND
GRAYSON, ROBERT	TENOR	HILLYER, 250 W 57TH ST	NEW YORK, NY	10107
GRAZER, BRIAN	FILM PRODUCER	20434 ROCA CHICA DR	MALIBU, CA	90265
GRAZIANO, ROCKY	BOXER	300 E 57TH ST	NEW YORK, NY	10022
GRAZIER, JOHN F	MUSIC ARRANGER	4121 ABERDEEN RD	NASHVILLE, TN	37205
GRDNIC, JOY	COMEDIENNE	16565 SAN FERNANDO MISSION BLVD	GRANADA HILLS, CA	91344
GREAT HOSSEIN ARAB, THE	WRESTLER	SEE - IRON SHEIK, THE		
GREAT PRETENDERS, THE	VOCAL GROUP	COVER, 1425 N STAR RD	COLUMBUS, OH	43212
GREAT SNUKA	WRESTLER	SEE - SNUKA, JIMMY "SUPERFLY"		
GREAT WHITE	ROCK & ROLL GROUP	3 E 54TH ST #1400	NEW YORK, NY	10022
GREAT WOJO, THE	WRESTLER	CAPITOL INTERNATIONAL		
		11844 MARKET ST	NORTH LIMA, OH	44452
GREATER NEW YORK YOUTH WIND ENS	WIND ENSEMBLE	756 7TH AVE #67	NEW YORK, NY	10019
GREAVES, WILLIAM	WRITER-PRODUCER	230 W 55TH ST #26-D	NEW YORK, NY	10019
GRECO, BUDDY	SINGER	9200 SUNSET BLVD #621	LOS ANGELES, CA	90069
GRECO, CLAUDIA	WRITER	555 W 57TH ST #1230	NEW YORK, NY	10019
GRECO, JOSE	CHOREOGRAPHER	224 W 49TH ST	NEW YORK, NY	10019
GRECO, KATHY	TV PRODUCER	CBS-TV, "THE PRICE IS RIGHT"		
		7800 BEVERLY BLVD	LOS ANGELES, CA	90036
GRECO, KRISTINE	ACTRESS	14225 RIVERSIDE DR	SHERMAN OAKS, CA	91423
GRECO, TONY	SINGER	8271 MELROSE AVE #106	LOS ANGELES, CA	90046
GREEDY, ALLAN	DIRECTOR	28647 VISCO CT	SAUGUS, CA	91350
GREEK, JANET C	WRITER	25136 MALIBU RD	MALIBU, CA	90265
GREEK, JIMMY THE	ODDSMAKER	SEE - SNYDER, JIMMY "THE GREEK"		
GREEN, ADAM D	WRITER	555 W 57TH ST #1230	NEW YORK, NY	10019
GREEN, ADOLPH	ACTOR-WRITER	211 CENTRAL PARK W #19-E	NEW YORK, NY	10024
GREEN, AL	SINGER-PREACHER	POST OFFICE 456	MEMPHIS, TN	38053
GREEN, ALAN	NEWS CORRESPONDENT	2627 39TH ST, NW	WASHINGTON, DC	20007
GREEN, ALAN R	DIRECTOR	32049 WATERSIDE LN	WESTLAKE VILLAGE, CA	91361
GREEN, ALLAN	DIRECTOR	110 PASCACK RD	PEARL RIVER, NY	10965
GREEN, ALLEN J	TV DIRECTOR	1601 3RD AVE	NEW YORK, NY	10128
GREEN, AMANDA J	WRITER	8955 BEVERLY BLVD	LOS ANGELES, CA	90048
GREEN, AMY B	NEWS CORRESPONDENT	1545 18TH ST, NW	WASHINGTON, DC	20036
GREEN, BARRY	DOUBLE BASS	FROTHINGHAM, 40 GROVE ST	WESSESLEY, MA	02181
GREEN, BARRY	GUITARIST	600 ROTHWOOD AVE #A-12	MADISON, TN	37115
GREEN, BILL	SINGER	4047 NACO-PERRIN BLVD #110	SAN ANTONIO, TX	78217
GREEN, BONITA C	TV WRITER	8955 BEVERLY BLVD	LOS ANGELES, CA	90048
GREEN, BRUCE SETH	TV DIRECTOR	1729 BRYN MAWR AVE	SANTA MONICA, CA	90405
GREEN, CAROL A	WRITER	8955 BEVERLY BLVD	LOS ANGELES, CA	90048
GREEN, CAROL L	FILM DIRECTOR	11575 MOORPARK AVE #207	STUDIO CITY, CA	91602
GREEN, CHARLES A	NEWS CORRESPONDENT	7221 16TH AVE	TAKOMA PARK, MD	20012
GREEN, CHIC	DIRECTOR	POST OFFICE BOX 1527	EAST HAMPTON, NY	11937
GREEN, CHRISTOPHER WARREN	VIOLINIST	ANGLO-SWISS ARTISTS MGMT		
		16 MUSWELL HILL RD, HIGHGATE	LONDON N6 5UG	ENGLAND
GREEN, CLIFFORD J	WRITER	8955 BEVERLY BLVD	LOS ANGELES, CA	90048
GREEN, CONNIE	WRITER	555 W 57TH ST #1230	NEW YORK, NY	10019
GREEN, DAVID	FILM DIRECTOR	HEATH, PARAMOUNT HOUSE		
		162-170 WARDOUR ST	LONDON W1V 3AT	ENGLAND
GREEN, DOROTHY	ACTRESS	12725 VENTURA BLVD #E	STUDIO CITY, CA	91604
GREEN, DOROTHY E	PIANIST	604 OAKLAND DR	MADISON, TN	37115
GREEN, DOUGLAS B	GUITARIST	334 HARVARD AVE	NASHVILLE, TN	37205
GREEN, DOUGLAS E	DIRECTOR-PRODUCER	MCA/UNIVERSAL STUDIOS, INC		
		100 UNIVERSAL CITYT PLAZA	UNIVERSAL CITY, CA	91608
GREEN, ELLEN R	WRITER	8955 BEVERLY BLVD	LOS ANGELES, CA	90048
GREEN, ELVIRA	MEZZO-SOPRANO	253 W 73RD ST #7-M	NEW YORK, NY	10023
GREEN, FELICIA A	WRITER	555 W 57TH ST #1230	NEW YORK, NY	10019
GREEN, FRANCIS	CONDUCTOR	1970 N NEW HAMPSHIRE AVE	LOS ANGELES, CA	90027
GREEN, GARARD	ACTOR	7 WOOD LN CLOSE, IVER HEATH	BUCKS SLO OLH	ENGLAND
GREEN, GERALD	TV WRITER	THE WILLIAM MORRIS AGENCY		
		1350 AVE OF THE AMERICAS	NEW YORK, NY	10019
GREEN, GUY	WRITER-PRODUCER	REDWAY, 16 BERNERS ST	LONDON W1P 3DD	ENGLAND
GREEN, GUY M	DIRECTOR	POST OFFICE BOX 5617	BEVERLY HILLS, CA	90210

KATHRYN GRAYSON

KERRI GREEN

PAM GRIER

MERV GRIFFIN

ANDY GRIFFITH

ARLO GUTHRIE

FRED GWYNNE

SHELLEY HACK

GENE HACKMAN

Name	Occupation	Address	City
GREEN, HARRY P	ACTOR	3330 BARHAM BLVD #103	LOS ANGELES, CA 90068
GREEN, HILTON	FILM PRODUCER	MCA/UNIVERSAL STUDIOS, INC	
		100 UNIVERSAL CITY PLAZA	UNIVERSAL CITY, CA 91608
GREEN, I BERNARD	DIRECTOR	24 STAFFIRE DR	SCHAUMBURG, IL 60194
GREEN, IVAN	TALENT AGENT	9911 W PICO BLVD #1490	LOS ANGELES, CA 90035
GREEN, JACK	SINGER	41 BRITAIN ST #200	TORONTO, ONT CANADA
GREEN, JAMES	ACTOR	60 POPES GROVE, TWICKENHAM	MIDDLESEX ENGLAND
GREEN, JAY	UNICYCLIST	SPOTFIELD, 84 ELM ST PRODUCTIONS	WESTFIELD, NJ 07090
GREEN, JERRY	JUGGLER	POST OFFICE BOX 87	WEST LEBANON, NY 12195
GREEN, JIM	TV PRODUCER	10100 SANTA MONICA BLVD #1600	LOS ANGELES, CA 90067
GREEN, JOHN L	SAXOPHONIST	825 YOUNGS LN	NASHVILLE, TN 37207
GREEN, JOHNNY	COMPOSER-CONDUCTOR	903 N BEDFORD DR	BEVERLY HILLS, CA 90210
GREEN, JONATHAN	TENOR	MUNRO, 334 W 72ND ST	NEW YORK, NY 10023
GREEN, KATHERINE D	TV WRITER	13616 VALLEY VISTA BLVD	SHERMAN OAKS, CA 91423
GREEN, KELLYE	CASTING DIRECTOR	9903 SANTA MONICA BLVD #102	BEVERLY HILLS, CA 90212
GREEN, LAURA DIRKSEN	MUSICIAN	SPRINGER, 1001 ROLANDVUE RD	BALTIMORE, MD 21204
GREEN, LEIGHTON	ACTRESS	6640 SUNSET BLVD #203	HOLLYWOOD, CA 90028
GREEN, LES	FILM EDITOR	ACE, 4416 1/2 FINLEY AVE	LOS ANGELES, CA 90027
GREEN, LESLIE L	DIRECTOR	DGA, 7950 SUNSET BLVD	LOS ANGELES, CA 90046
GREEN, LLOYD LAMAR	GUITARIST	604 OAKLAND DR	MADISON, TN 37115
GREEN, LONI	SINGER	ATTRACTIONS TALENT AGENCY	
		6525 N FRANCISCO AVE	CHICAGO, IL 60645
GREEN, MARC E	WRITER	10341 KESWICK AVE	LOS ANGELES, CA 90064
GREEN, MARTIN	WRITER-PRODUCER	DGA, 7950 SUNSET BLVD	LOS ANGELES, CA 90046
GREEN, MAURY	TV WRITER	8955 BEVERLY BLVD	LOS ANGELES, CA 90048
GREEN, MERRILL JOHNS	TV WRITER	8955 BEVERLY BLVD	LOS ANGELES, CA 90048
GREEN, MICHAEL	FILM PROD-EXEC	NATIONAL HOUSE, 60 WARD	LONDON W1 ENGLAND
GREEN, MICHAEL	NEWS CORRESPONDENT	105 "E" ST, SE	WASHINGTON, DC 20003
GREEN, MICHAEL C	FILM PRODUCER	4020 TOWHEE DR	CALABASAS, CA 91302
GREEN, MICHELLE	WRITER-EDITOR	TIME & PEOPLE MAGAZINE	
		TIME & LIFE BUILDING	
		ROCKEFELLER CENTER	NEW YORK, NY 10020
GREEN, MORT	WRITER-PRODUCER	320 S ELM DR #1	BEVERLY HILLS, CA 90212
GREEN, NANCY	CELLIST	ROSENFIELD, 714 LADD RD	BRONX, NY 10471
GREEN, NANCY	NEWS CORRESPONDENT	1977 BILTMORE ST, NW	WASHINGTON, DC 20009
GREEN, NANCY	SOPRANO	CAMI, 165 W 57TH ST	NEW YORK, NY 10019
GREEN, PATRICIA M	WRITER	451 RIVERSIDE DR	BURBANK, CA 91506
GREEN, PAULA	DIRECTOR	145 W 86TH ST	NEW YORK, NY 10024
GREEN, RAY	TV PRODUCER	METROMEDIA, 5746 SUNSET BLVD	LOS ANGELES, CA 90028
GREEN, RICKI	NEWS CORRESPONDENT	2947 MACOMB ST, NW	WASHINGTON, DC 20008
GREEN, ROBERT D	NEWS CORRESPONDENT	1425 S EADS ST #602	ARLINGTON, VA 22202
GREEN, ROBERT L, JR	GUITARIST	300 BAKERTOWN RD #5-E	ANTIOCH, TN 37013
GREEN, ROBERT M	DIRECTOR	DGA, 7950 SUNSET BLVD	LOS ANGELES, CA 90046
GREEN, ROBIN DOUGLAS	GUITARIST	604 OAKLAND DR	MADISON, TN 37115
GREEN, RUBIN C	WRITER	8955 BEVERLY BLVD	LOS ANGELES, CA 90048
GREEN, SIDNEY C	TV WRITER	8955 BEVERLY BLVD	LOS ANGELES, CA 90048
GREEN, SOSKITA H	WRITER	555 W 57TH ST #1230	NEW YORK, NY 10019
GREEN, SYLVIA	COMPOSER	153 S MAPLE DR	BEVERLY HILLS, CA 90212
GREEN, TAMARA L	WRITER	8955 BEVERLY BLVD	LOS ANGELES, CA 90048
GREEN, TERRY	TV DIRECTOR	EUSTON, 365 EUSTON RD	LONDON NW1 ENGLAND
GREEN, TOM	TV CRITIC	POST OFFICE BOX 500	WASHINGTON, DC 20044
GREEN, VERNON & THE MEDAL MEDAL	ROCK & ROLL GROUP	OLDIES, 5218 ALMONT ST	LOS ANGELES, CA 90032
GREEN, WALON C	WRITER-PRODUCER	3089 SEAHORSE AVE	VENTURA, CA 93001
GREEN, WALT	WRITER	8955 BEVERLY BLVD	LOS ANGELES, CA 90048
GREEN, WAYLOR	TV WRITER-PRODUCER	8955 BEVERLY BLVD	LOS ANGELES, CA 90048
GREEN, WILLIAM	WRITER	555 W 57TH ST #1230	NEW YORK, NY 10019
GREEN ON RED	ROCK & ROLL GROUP	POST OFFICE BOX 2896	TORRANCE, CA 90509
GREEN RIVER	ROCK & ROLL GROUP	41 BRITAIN ST #200	TORONTO, ONT CANADA
GREENAWALD, SHERI	SOPRANO	CAMI, 165 W 57TH ST	NEW YORK, NY 10019
GREENAWAY, NORMA	NEWS CORRESPONDENT	3500 39TH ST #F-672, NW	WASHINGTON, DC 20016
GREENBAUM, EVERETT	TV WRITER	4507 NOELINE AVE	ENCINO, CA 91436
GREENBAUM, SAM	TV WRITER	8955 BEVERLY BLVD	LOS ANGELES, CA 90048
GREENBERG, BOB	TV WRITER	151 S EL CAMINO DR	BEVERLY HILLS, CA 90212
GREENBERG, BURTON L	DIRECTOR	28 E 10TH ST	NEW YORK, NY 10003
GREENBERG, CHUCK	LYRICONIST	POST OFFICE BOX 9388	STANFORD, CA 94305
GREENBERG, DANIEL S	NEWS CORRESPONDENT	3736 KANAWHA ST, NW	WASHINGTON, DC 20015
GREENBERG, EDWARD	DIRECTOR	DGA, 7950 SUNSET BLVD	LOS ANGELES, CA 90046
GREENBERG, HENRY F	SCREENWRITER	8955 BEVERLY BLVD	LOS ANGELES, CA 90048
GREENBERG, JEFF	ACTOR	1280 N LAUREL AVE #18	LOS ANGELES, CA 90046
GREENBERG, JERRY	TV WRITER	8955 BEVERLY BLVD	LOS ANGELES, CA 90048
GREENBERG, JOAN D	WRITER	8955 BEVERLY BLVD	LOS ANGELES, CA 90048
GREENBERG, KENNY	GUITARIST	POST OFFICE BOX 90943	NASHVILLE, TN 37209
GREENBERG, NIKKI FINKE	NEWS CORRESPONDENT	2737 DEVONSHIRE PL #104, NW	WASHINGTON, DC 20008
GREENBERG, NORMAN	FRENCH HORN	POST OFFICE BOX 255	OSHTEMO, MI 49077
GREENBERG, PAUL W	TV WRITER-DIRECTOR	DGA, 110 W 57TH ST	NEW YORK, NY 10019
GREENBERG, PETER S	WRITER	8955 BEVERLY BLVD	LOS ANGELES, CA 90048
GREENBERG, RICHARD A	DIRECTOR	240 MADISON AVE	NEW YORK, NY 10016
GREENBERG, ROBERT S	NEWS CORRESPONDENT	3903 JENIFER ST, NW	WASHINGTON, DC 20015
GREENBERG, RODNEY	DIRECTOR	61 BRANDS HILL AVE	
		HIGH WYCOMBE	BUCKS HP13 5PY ENGLAND
GREENBERG, SHARI R	WRITER	555 W 57TH ST #1230	NEW YORK, NY 10019
GREENBERG, SONDRA E	MODEL	MODELS & PROMOTIONS AGENCY	
		8560 SUNSET BLVD, 10TH FLOOR	LOS ANGELES, CA 90069
GREENBERG, STANLEY R	TV WRITER	8955 BEVERLY BLVD	LOS ANGELES, CA 90048
GREENBERG, STEVEN	TV WRITER	8955 BEVERLY BLVD	LOS ANGELES, CA 90048

Name	Occupation	Address	City	Zip
GREENBERG, SYLVIA	SOPRANO	CAMI, 165 W 57TH ST	NEW YORK, NY	10019
GREENBLATT, LARRY S	WRITER	555 W 57TH ST #1230	NEW YORK, NY	10019
GREENBURG, DAN	WRITER	9000 SUNSET BLVD #1200	LOS ANGELES, CA	90069
GREENBURG, EARL	TV PRODUCER	COLUMBIA PICTURES		
		COLUMBIA PLAZA		
		PRODUCERS BUILDING	BURBANK, CA	91505
GREENBURG, EARL D	TV DIRECTOR	1807 NICHOLS CANYON RD	LOS ANGELES, CA	90046
GREENE, A C	WRITER	8955 BEVERLY BLVD	LOS ANGELES, CA	90048
GREENE, ARTHUR	PIANIST	AARON, 25 HUNTINGTON AVE	BOSTON, MA	02116
GREENE, ARTHUR M	COMPOSER-CONDUCTOR	529 W 42ND ST	NEW YORK, NY	10036
GREENE, BARNEY	COMPOSER	12619 HORTENSE ST	STUDIO CITY, CA	91604
GREENE, BOB	COLUMNIST	THE CHICAGO TRIBUNE		
		TRIBUNE TOWER		
		435 N MICHIGAN AVE	CHICAGO, IL	60611
GREENE, BOB	NEWS CORRESPONDENT	ABC NEWS, 7 W 66TH ST	NEW YORK, NY	10023
GREENE, BRIAN	ACTOR	7471 MELROSE AVE #11	LOS ANGELES, CA	90046
GREENE, BUDDY	OBOIST	9401 ROBERTS DR #10-B	ATLANTA, GA	30354
GREENE, CLARENCE	GUITARIST	1511 DICKERSON RD #B-17	NASHVILLE, TN	37207
GREENE, CLARENCE	SCREENWRITER	8955 BEVERLY BLVD	LOS ANGELES, CA	90048
GREENE, DANIEL	ACTOR	1507 S SHERBOURNE DR #3	LOS ANGELES, CA	90035
GREENE, DAVID	WRITER-PRODUCER	4225 COLDWATER CANYON AVE	STUDIO CITY, CA	91604
GREENE, DIANE	NEWS CORRESPONDENT	400 N CAPITOL ST, NW	WASHINGTON, DC	20001
GREENE, EDWARD	COMPOSER	11033 FRUITLAND DR #6	STUDIO CITY, CA	91604
GREENE, ELLEN	ACTRESS-SINGER	151 S EL CAMINO DR	BEVERLY HILLS, CA	90212
GREENE, GRAHAM	AUTHOR	PALAIS DES FLEURS		
		AVENUE PASTEUR	ANTIBES 06600	FRANCE
GREENE, HAROLD	WRITER	8955 BEVERLY BLVD	LOS ANGELES, CA	90048
GREENE, HAROLD R	LIT-TAL AGENT	760 N LA CIENEGA BLVD	LOS ANGELES, CA	90069
GREENE, HERBERT S	TV DIRECTOR	4176 ARCH DR	STUDIO CITY, CA	91604
GREENE, J W, JR	WRITER	555 W 57TH ST #1230	NEW YORK, NY	10019
GREENE, JACK	SINGER	POST OFFICE BOX 4966	LITTLE ROCK, AR	72214
GREENE, JACKIE	PHOTOGRAPHER	1334 LEEGATE RD, NW	WASHINGTON, DC	20012
GREENE, JAMES	ACTOR	60 POPES GROVE, TWICKENHAM	MIDDLESEX	ENGLAND
GREENE, JANICE L	NEWS CORRESPONDENT	5439 HAWTHORNE PL, NW	WASHINGTON, DC	20016
GREENE, JAVOTTE SUTTON	ACTRESS	225 HAMILTON AVE	NEW ROCHELLE, NY	10801
GREENE, JEFF	TALENT AGENT	PURPLE MOON PRODUCTIONS		
		271 E 17TH ST	HIALEAH, FL	33010
GREENE, JERI-ANN	ACTRESS	1710 MONTE CIELO DR	BEVERLY HILLS, CA	90210
GREENE, JOHN L	WRITER	8955 BEVERLY BLVD	LOS ANGELES, CA	90048
GREENE, JOSHUA	CONDUCTOR	61 W 62ND ST #6-F	NEW YORK, NY	10023
GREENE, JOYCE E	ACTRESS	6605 HOLLYWOOD BLVD #220	HOLLYWOOD, CA	90028
GREENE, KELLIE	COMPOSER	12301 VIEWCREST RD	STUDIO CITY, CA	91604
GREENE, KIRA	NEWS CORRESPONDENT	2115 N SYCAMORE ST	ARLINGTON, VA	22205
GREENE, LARRY	COMPOSER-CONDUCTOR	1151 SUNSET HILLS RD	LOS ANGELES, CA	90069
GREENE, LYN	ACTRESS	9220 SUNSET BLVD #202	LOS ANGELES, CA	90069
GREENE, MARGARET M	WRITER	555 W 57TH ST #1230	NEW YORK, NY	10019
GREENE, MATT	ACTOR	360 S ELM DR	BEVERLY HILLS, CA	90212
GREENE, MICHAEL	ACTOR	9025 WILSHIRE BLVD #309	BEVERLY HILLS, CA	90211
GREENE, MICHELE	ACTRESS	KOHNER, 9169 SUNSET BLVD	LOS ANGELES, CA	90069
GREENE, MILTON	CONDUCTOR	2149 HERCULES DR	LOS ANGELES, CA	90046
GREENE, MILTON H	DIRECTOR	244 LAKE MERCED HILLS ST	SAN FRANCISCO, CA	94132
GREENE, MORT	TV WRITER	8955 BEVERLY BLVD	LOS ANGELES, CA	90048
GREENE, NOEL	TV DIRECTOR-PRODUCER	36-A GRAFTON SQ	LONDON SW4 ODB	ENGLAND
GREENE, OTIS GARY	ACTOR	990 PALM AVE #A-12	LOS ANGELES, CA	90069
GREENE, ROBIN	NEWS CORRESPONDENT	1400 "I" ST, NW	WASHINGTON, DC	20005
GREENE, SHECKY	COMEDIAN	1245 RANCHO DR	LAS VEGAS, NV	89101
GREENE, SHEPPARD M	TV WRITER	555 W 57TH ST #1230	NEW YORK, NY	10019
GREENE, SPARKY	DIRECTOR	DGA, 7950 SUNSET BLVD	LOS ANGELES, CA	90046
GREENE, STEVE	SCREENWRITER	555 W 57TH ST #1230	NEW YORK, NY	10019
GREENE, TOM	WRITER-PRODUCER	2049 CENTURY PARK E #13	LOS ANGELES, CA	90067
GREENE, WALTER W	COMPOSER-CONDUCTOR	15175 KINAI RD	APPLE VALLEY, CA	92307
GREENFELD, JOSH	SCREENWRITER	14637 BESTER BLVD	PACIFIC PALISADES, CA	90272
GREENFIELD, BARRY	WRITER	632 PACIFIC ST #2	SANTA MONICA, CA	90405
GREENFIELD, BARRY S	DIRECTOR	7 ROBINS TERR	HIGHLAND LAKES, NJ	07422
GREENFIELD, GRETCHEN	CONTRALTO	59 E 54TH ST #81	NEW YORK, NY	10022
GREENFIELD, H JEFF	TV WRITER	555 W 57TH ST #1230	NEW YORK, NY	10019
GREENFIELD, JEFF	WRITER-COLUMNIST	UNIVERSAL PRESS SYNDICATE		
		4900 MAIN ST, 9TH FLOOR	KANSAS CITY, MO	62114
GREENFIELD, LEO	FILM EXECUTIVE	1811 RISING GLEN RD	LOS ANGELES, CA	90069
GREENFIELD, MEG	NEWS CORRESPONDENT	3318 "R" ST, NW	WASHINGTON, DC	20007
GREENFIELD, MIKE	TALENT AGENT	9000 SUNSET BLVD #1112	LOS ANGELES, CA	90069
GREENFIELD, ROBERT B	WRITER	8955 BEVERLY BLVD	LOS ANGELES, CA	90048
GREENHILL, MITCH	SINGER	FOLKLORE, 1671 APPIAN WY	SANTA MONICA, CA	90401
GREENHOUSE, LINDA	NEWS CORRESPONDENT	5410 SPANGLER AVE	BETHESDA, MD	20816
GREENHOUSE, MARTHA	ACTRESS	1230 PARK AVE	NEW YORK, NY	10028
GREENHUNT, ROBERT	FILM PRODUCER	ROLLINS / JOFFE, 130 W 57TH ST	NEW YORK, NY	10019
GREENLAND, SETH	TV WRITER	8955 BEVERLY BLVD	LOS ANGELES, CA	90048
GREENLAW, REBECCA A	DIRECTOR	4225 ETHEL AVE #27	STUDIO CITY, CA	91604
GREENLEE, DAVID	ACTOR	120 S VICTORY BLVD #104	BURBANK, CA	91502
GREENLUND, ALYS	COMPOSER	659 GRETNA GREEN WY	LOS ANGELES, CA	90049
GREENS, ELISA JOY	VIOLINIST	3200 OVERLOOK DR #B	NASHVILLE, TN	37212
GREENSPAN, BUD	WRITER-PRODUCER	CAPPY, 33 E 68TH ST	NEW YORK, NY	10021
GREENSPAN, MARK	NEWS CORRESPONDENT	1013 MASSACHUSETTS AVE, NE	WASHINGTON, DC	20002

GREENWALD, JOHN	WRITER-EDITOR	TIME/TIME & LIFE BLDG		
		ROCKEFELLER CENTER	NEW YORK, NY	10020
GREENWALD, MICHAEL	WRITER	8955 BEVERLY BLVD	LOS ANGELES, CA	90048
GREENWALD, NANCY	TV WRITER	3633 MOUNTAIN VIEW AVE	LOS ANGELES, CA	90066
GREENWALD, ROBERT	TV DIRECTOR	53 27TH AVE	VENICE, CA	90291
GREENWALD, ROBERT	TV PRODUCER	10202 W WASHINGTON BLVD	CULVER CITY, CA	90230
GREENWALT, DAVID	SCREENWRITER	417 SYCAMORE RD	SANTA MONICA, CA	90402
GREENWAY, GREG	SINGER	ENTERTAINMENT CONCEPTS		
		29 COMMONWEALTH AVE	BOSTON, MA	02116
GREENWOOD, BILL	NEWS CORRESPONDENT	ABC-TV, NEWS DEPARTMENT		
		1717 DE SALES ST, NW	WASHINGTON, DC	20036
GREENWOOD, JOAN	ACTRESS	27 SLAIDBURN ST	CHELSEA SW10	ENGLAND
GREENWOOD, LAURA D	SCREENWRITER	8955 BEVERLY BLVD	LOS ANGELES, CA	90048
GREENWOOD, LEE	SINGER-SONGWRITER	1111 16TH AVE S #200	NASHVILLE, TN	37212
GREENWOOD, LORNA	VIOLINIST	907 N 16TH ST	NASHVILLE, TN	37206
GREENWOOD, MARC	DRUMMER	2706 JOYA DR	NASHVILLE, TN	37214
GREENWOOD, MICHAEL	ACTOR	14 KINGSTON HOUSE EAST		
		PRINCES GATE	LONDON SW7 1LJ	ENGLAND
GREER, BILL	TV WRITER	8955 BEVERLY BLVD	LOS ANGELES, CA	90048
GREER, BRODIE	ACTOR	2035 FAIRBURN AVE	LOS ANGELES, CA	90025
GREER, DABBS	ACTOR	POST OFFICE BOX 322	PASADENA, CA	91102
GREER, DARRELL	ACTOR	180 S AVE 53	LOS ANGELES, CA	90042
GREER, GEORGE	WRITER	8468 HATILLO AVE	CANOGA PARK, CA	91306
GREER, GORDON	TENOR	61 W 62ND ST #6-F	NEW YORK, NY	10023
GREER, JANE	ACTRESS	10390 SANTA MONICA BLVD #310	LOS ANGELES, CA	90025
GREER, JANE "BETTY"	ACTRESS	LASKER, 966 MORAGA DR	LOS ANGELES, CA	90049
GREER, KATHLEEN	WRITER-PRODUCER	4422 BEN AVE	NORTH HOLLYWOOD, CA	91607
GREER, RICHARD	DIRECTOR	RURAL DELIVERY #1, CENTER RD	SCIPIO CENTER, NY	13147
GREER, ROBIN	ACTRESS	3907 W ALAMEDA AVE #101	BURBANK, CA	91505
GREFE, WILLIAM	DIRECTOR-PRODUCER	14390 MUSTANG TRAIL	FORT LAUDERDALE, FL	33330
GREG, JULIE	WRITER	555 W 57TH ST #1230	NEW YORK, NY	10019
GREGG, COLIN	TV DIRECTOR-PRODUCER	116 FALCONBERG CT	LONDON W1	ENGLAND
GREGG, DIANA L	NEWS CORRESPONDENT	3840 PORTER ST #B-380, NW	WASHINGTON, DC	20016
GREGG, JULIE	ACTRESS	8019 1/2 MELROSE AVE #3	LOS ANGELES, CA	90046
GREGG, PAUL	GUITARIST	830 GLASTONBURY RD #510	NASHVILLE, TN	37217
GREGG, SHARON	ACTRESS	1607 N EL CENTRO AVE #22	HOLLYWOOD, CA	90028
GREGG, WALTER P	DIRECTOR	227 E 31ST ST	NEW YORK, NY	10016
GREGGORY, DAVID	WRITER	1737 VIEWMONT DR	LOS ANGELES, CA	90069
GREGOR, ADAM	ACTOR	1350 N HIGHLAND AVE #24	HOLLYWOOD, CA	90028
GREGORIO, ROSE	ACTRESS	247 S BEVERLY DR #102	BEVERLY HILLS, CA	90212
GREGORY, ANDRE	ACTOR	10100 SANTA MONICA BLVD #1600	LOS ANGELES, CA	90067
GREGORY, ARTHUR U	TV PRODUCER	11548 ACAMA ST	NORTH HOLLYWOOD, CA	91604
GREGORY, BETTINA	NEWS CORRESPONDENT	ABC-TV, NEWS DEPARTMENT		
		1717 DE SALES ST, NW	WASHINGTON, DC	20036
GREGORY, CONSTANTINE	ACTOR	172 CLONMORE ST	LONDON SW10	ENGLAND
GREGORY, DON	THEATER PRODUCER	9200 SUNSET BLVD	LOS ANGELES, CA	90069
GREGORY, ENA	ACTRESS	32131 COAST HWY	SOUTH LAGUNA, CA	92677
GREGORY, HUBERT	GUITARIST	1011 STOCKELL ST	NASHVILLE, TN	37207
GREGORY, JACK	ACTOR	3330 BARHAM BLVD #103	LOS ANGELES, CA	90068
GREGORY, JACK	SAXOPHONIST	145 DERBY LN, ROUTE #7	FRANKLIN, TN	37064
GREGORY, JAMES	ACTOR	23 OAKMONT DR	LOS ANGELES, CA	90049
GREGORY, JOHN	FILM PRODUCER	50 GREAT RUSSELL ST	LONDON WC1	ENGLAND
GREGORY, KEITH	GUITARIST	1010 GRACELAWN DR	BRENTWOOD, TN	37027
GREGORY, MARY	ACTRESS	1350 N HIGHLAND AVE #24	HOLLYWOOD, CA	90028
GREGORY, MELVIN	GUITARIST	130 LORRAINE DR	GALLATIN, TN	37066
GREGORY, MICHAEL	MUSICIAN	KURLAND, 173 BRIGHTON AVE	BOSTON, MA	02134
GREGORY, MICHAEL	ACTOR	15010 VENTURA BLVD #219	SHERMAN OAKS, CA	91403
GREGORY, MOLLIE	SCREENWRITER	3278 WILSHIRE BLVD #401	LOS ANGELES, CA	90010
GREGORY, NATALIE	ACTRESS	12725 VENTURA BLVD #E	STUDIO CITY, CA	91604
GREGORY, PAUL	FILM PRODUCER	POST OFFICE BOX 38	PALM SPRINGS, CA	92262
GREGORY, RUTH	ACTRESS	400 W 43RD ST #32-A	NEW YORK, NY	10036
GREGORY, SHAREE	ACTRESS	12725 VENTURA BLVD #E	STUDIO CITY, CA	91604
GREGORY, SUSAN	SOPRANO	POST OFFICE BOX U	REDDING, CT	06875
GREGORY, TERRY	SINGER	AL GALLICO, 120 E 56TH ST	NEW YORK, NY	10022
GREGORY, WILLIAM H	NEWS CORRESPONDENT	227 FALCON RIDGE RD	GREAT FALLS, VA	22066
GREGSON, RICHARD J	TV WRITER	8955 BEVERLY BLVD	LOS ANGELES, CA	90048
GREIDER, WILLIAM H	NEWS CORRESPONDENT	5931 UTAH AVE, NW	WASHINGTON, DC	20015
GREIF, STEPHEN	ACTOR	BURNETT, 42 GRAFTON HOUSE		
		2-3 GOLDEN SQ	LONDON W1	ENGLAND
GREIFER, LEWIS	WRITER	8955 BEVERLY BLVD	LOS ANGELES, CA	90048
GREINER, JUSTINE	MODEL	MODELS & PROMOTIONS AGENCY		
		8560 SUNSET BLVD, 10TH FLOOR	LOS ANGELES, CA	90069
GREISER, BOB	PHOTOGRAPHER	1427 31ST ST	SAN DIEGO, CA	92102
GREISMAN, ALAN	FILM PRODUCER	10880 WILSHIRE BLVD #2110	LOS ANGELES, CA	90024
GREISMAN, GORDON JAMES	SCREENWRITER	1845 CALGARY LN	LOS ANGELES, CA	90024
GRELLET, GILBERT	NEWS CORRESPONDENT	5005 PATH TERR	BETHESDA, MD	20816
GRENIER, CYNTHIA	WRITER	8955 BEVERLY BLVD	LOS ANGELES, CA	90048
GRENIER, JACQUES	NEWS CORRESPONDENT	ABC NEWS, POST OFFICE BOX 4516	JOHNANNESBURG 2000	SOUTH AFRICA
GRESH, THEODORE M	CONDUCTOR	8118 TILDEN AVE	PANORAMA CITY, CA	91402
GRESOCK, FRANCIS	NEWS CORRESPONDENT	8 W SRPING ST	ALEXANDRIA, VA	22301
GRETH, ROMA	WRITER	555 W 57TH ST #1230	NEW YORK, NY	10019
GRETZKY, WAYNE	HOCKEY	7424 118TH AVE	EDMONTON, ALB T5B 4M9	CANADA
GREVE, FRANK J	NEWS CORRESPONDENT	6209 30TH ST, NW	WASHINGTON, DC	20015
GREY, BARRY M	WRITER	8955 BEVERLY BLVD	LOS ANGELES, CA	90048
GREY, JOEL	ACTOR-SINGER	NINA FIREMAN, 266 W 73RD ST	NEW YORK, NY	10023

Name	Occupation	Address	City	Zip
GREY, LARRY	ACTOR	35 W 90TH ST	NEW YORK, NY	10024
GREY, VIRGINIA	ACTRESS	15101 MAGNOLIA BLVD #5-H	SHERMAN OAKS, CA	91403
GREY, ZANE	SINGER	POST OFFICE BOX O	EXCELSIOR, MN	55331
GREYHOSKY, BABS	TV WRITER-PRODUCER	9046 SUNSET BLVD #202	LOS ANGELES, CA	90069
GREYN, CLINTON	ACTOR	14 GARWAY RD	LONDON W2	ENGLAND
GREYSON, KAREN	ACTRESS	12433 MOORPARK ST #213	STUDIO CITY, CA	91604
GREYTAK, EUGENE	ACTOR	4789 VINELAND AVE #100	NORTH HOLLYWOOD, CA	91602
GREYWITT, MICHAEL P	WRITER	8955 BEVERLY BLVD	LOS ANGELES, CA	90048
GRIBBIN, TOM & THE SALTWATER BA	C & W GROUP	POST OFFICE BOX 8945	MADEIRA BEACH, FL	33738
GRICE, GARRY	TENOR	111 W 57TH ST #1209	NEW YORK, NY	10019
GRIECO, RICHARD	ACTOR	ABC-TV, "ONE LIFE TO LIVE"		
GRIEF, STEPHEN	ACTOR	LONDON MANAGEMENT, LTD		
		235-241 REGENT ST	LONDON W1A 2JT	ENGLAND
GRIEGO, SANDRA	ACTRESS	3151 W CAHUENGA BLVD #310	LOS ANGELES, CA	90068
GRIEM, HELMUT	ACTOR	AGENTUR LENTZ, HOLBERNSTRASSE 4	8000 MUNICH 80	W GERMANY
GRIER, PAM	ACTRESS	9220 SUNSET BLVD #625	LOS ANGELES, CA	90069
GRIER, PETER	NEWS CORRESPONDENT	3140 WISCONSIN AVE #516, NW	WASHINGTON, DC	20016
GRIER, ROD	ACTOR	6546 SEPULVEDA BLVD #207	VAN NUYS, CA	91411
GRIER, ROSEY	ACTOR	11656 MONTANA AVE #301	LOS ANGELES, CA	90049
GRIES, JONATHAN	ACTOR	827 4TH ST #306	SANTA MONICA, CA	90403
GRIEVE, ANDREW	FILM DIRECTOR	2 DARTMOUTH PARK AVE	LONDON NW5	ENGLAND
GRIEVE, MARVIN	WRITER	555 W 57TH ST #1230	NEW YORK, NY	10019
GRIEVES, DUG	GUITARIST	158 VULCO DR	HENDERSONVILLE, TN	37075
GRIFASI, JOE	ACTOR	APA, 888 7TH AVE, 21ST FLOOR	NEW YORK, NY	10106
GRIFF, RAY	SINGER-GUITARIST	POST OFFICE BOX 23245	NASHVILLE, TN	37202
GRIFF BAND	ROCK & ROLL TRIO	9777 HARWIN ST #101	HOUSTON, TX	77036
GRIFFEL, KAY	SOPRANO	SELLHEIM, TAUNUSSTR 10	5303 BORHEIM 3	WEST GERMANY
GRIFFEN, STUART	TALENT AGENT	1888 CENTURY PARK E #1400	LOS ANGELES, CA	90067
GRIFFETH, SIMONE	ACTRESS-MODEL	7702 FIRENZE AVE	LOS ANGELES, CA	90046
GRIFFIN, CHRISTOPHER	TV DIRECTOR-PRODUCER	THE OLD POST HOUSE, WILMCOTE	STRATFORD-UPON-AVON	ENGLAND
GRIFFIN, EILEEN	NEWS CORRESPONDENT	2480 16TH ST, NW	WASHINGTON, DC	20009
GRIFFIN, HENRY L	PHOTOGRAPHER	3214 GUMWOOD DR	UNIVERSITY HILL, MD	20783
GRIFFIN, JACK	ACTOR	9777 WILSHIRE BLVD #707	BEVERLY HILLS, CA	90212
GRIFFIN, JOHNNY	SAXOPHONIST	MS MGMT, 150 E 35TH ST	NEW YORK, NY	10016
GRIFFIN, JOHNNY, QUARTET	JAZZ QUARTET	HOFFER, 233 1/2 E 48TH ST	NEW YORK, NY	10017
GRIFFIN, KEN	TV PRODUCER	WILLOW COTTAGE, SELSEY RD		
		SIDLESHAM	WEST SUSSEX PO 7LR	ENGLAND
GRIFFIN, MERV	SINGER-HOST-PRODUCER	1541 N VINE ST	LOS ANGELES, CA	90028
GRIFFIN, NANCY L	NEWS REPORTER	LIFE/TIME & LIFE BLDG		
		ROCKEFELLER CENTER	NEW YORK, NY	10020
GRIFFIN, RODMAN	NEWS REPORTER	TIME/TIME & LIFE BLDG		
		ROCKEFELLER CENTER	NEW YORK, NY	10020
GRIFFIN, SEAN D	NEWS CORRESPONDENT	1320 N FORT MEYER DR	ARLINGTON, VA	22209
GRIFFIN, SUNNY	ACTRESS	ICM, 8899 BEVERLY BLVD	LOS ANGELES, CA	90048
GRIFFIS, WILLIAM	ACTOR	9021 MELROSE AVE #304	LOS ANGELES, CA	90069
GRIFFITH, ANDY	ACTOR	4445 CARTWRIGHT AVE #11	NORTH HOLLYWOOD, CA	91602
GRIFFITH, BENNY	SINGER	5137 AURIESVILLE	HAZELWOOD, MO	63042
GRIFFITH, BILL	CARTOONIST	KING FEATURES SYNDICATE		
		235 E 45TH ST	NEW YORK, NY	10017
GRIFFITH, BILL	WRITER	8955 BEVERLY BLVD	LOS ANGELES, CA	90048
GRIFFITH, CHARLES B	WRITER-PRODUCER	1650 WESTWOOD BLVD #201	LOS ANGELES, CA	90024
GRIFFITH, JAMES	ACTOR	9777 WILSHIRE BLVD #707	BEVERLY HILLS, CA	90212
GRIFFITH, JAMES A	GUITARIST	1312 SHADY LAWN DR	CLARKSVILLE, TN	37040
GRIFFITH, KENNETH	ACTOR-PRODUCER	ICM, 388-396 OXFORD ST	LONDON W1	ENGLAND
GRIFFITH, KRISTIN	ACTRESS	211 S BEVERLY DR #201	BEVERLY HILLS, CA	90212
GRIFFITH, MELANIE	ACTRESS	8340 DE LONGPRE AVE #F	LOS ANGELES, CA	90069
GRIFFITH, NANCI	SINGER-SONGWRITER	POST OFFICE BOX 121684	NASHVILLE, TN	37212
GRIFFITH, SANDI	SINGER	LUTZ, 1626 VINE ST	LOS ANGELES, CA	90028
GRIFFITH, THOMAS IAN	ACTOR	NBC-TV, "ANOTHER WORLD"		
		30 ROCKEFELLER PLAZA	NEW YORK, NY	10112
GRIFFITHS, DAVID	NEWS CORRESPONDENT	22022 DICKERSON RD	DICKERSON, MD	20842
GRIFFITHS, DEREK	ACTOR-COMEDIAN	AZA, 652 FINCHLEY RD	LONDON NW11	ENGLAND
GRIFFITHS, LEON	TV WRITER	A D PETERS, LTD		
		10 BUCKINGHAM ST	LONDON WC2	ENGLAND
GRIFFITHS, MARK L	FILM WRITER-DIRECTOR	10945 AYRES AVE	LOS ANGELES, CA	90064
GRIFFITHS, RICHARD	ACTOR	LEADING ARTISTS, LTD		
		60 SAINT JAMES'S ST	LONDON SW1	ENGLAND
GRIGOR, NANCY	ACTRESS	3907 W ALAMEDA AVE #101	BURBANK, CA	91505
GRIGSBY, DEAN L	COMPOSER	ROUTE #1, BOX 363-A-9	FOREST GROVE, OR	97116
GRILES, EDD	ENTERTAINMENT EXEC	HORIZON ENTERTAINMENT		
		919 3RD AVE	NEW YORK, NY	10022
GRILIKHES, MICHEL M	WRITER	463 S ELM DR	BEVERLY HILLS, CA	90212
GRILLO, DENNIS	COMPOSER	245 E 62ND ST	NEW YORK, NY	10021
GRILLO, JANET L	WRITER	555 W 57TH ST #1230	NEW YORK, NY	10019
GRILLO, JOANN	MEZZO-SOPRANO	1550 75TH ST	BROOKLYN, NY	10018
GRILLO, JOHN	ACTOR	HOWES & PRIOR, LTD		
		66 BERKELEY HOUSE, HAY HILL	LONDON W1X 7LH	ENGLAND
GRILLO, MICHAEL FRANCIS	FILM DIRECTOR	3474 LAURELVALE DR	STUDIO CITY, CA	91604
GRIM REAPER	ROCK & ROLL GROUP	111 BROADWAY #611	NEW YORK, NY	10010
GRIMALDI, GIAN ROSS	DIRECTOR	7516 WOODROW WILSON DR	LOS ANGELES, CA	90046
GRIMALDI, GINO	TV PRODUCER	MCA/UNIVERSAL STUDIOS, INC		
		100 UNIVERSAL CITY PLAZA	UNIVERSAL CITY, CA	91608
GRIMALDI, HUGO	DIRECTOR	220 SAN VICENTE BLVD #507	SANTA MONICA, CA	90402
GRIMES, GARY	ACTOR	112 S HELBERTA AVE	REDONDO BEACH, CA	90277
GRIMES, J WILLIAM	CABLE EXECUTIVE	ESPN, ESPN PLAZA	BRISTOL, CT	06010

Name	Occupation	Address	City, State	Zip
GRIMES, STEPHEN	ART DIRECTOR	KOHNER, 9169 SUNSET BLVD	LOS ANGELES, CA	90069
GRIMES, TAMMY	ACTRESS-SINGER	6 E 74TH ST	NEW YORK, NY	10021
GRIMINELLI, ANDREA	FLUTIST	119 W 57TH ST #1505	NEW YORK, NY	10019
GRIMM, MARIA	ACTRESS	300 N SWALL DR #215	BEVERLY HILLS, CA	90211
GRIMM, MICKEY	PIANIST	4732 VOLUNTEER DR	ANTIOCH, TN	37013
GRIMSBY, ROGER	BROADCAST JOURNALIST	WABC-TV, 7 LINCOLN SQ	NEW YORK, NY	10023
GRIMSLEY, GREER	BARITONE	AFFILIATE ARTISTS, INC		
		37 W 65TH ST, 6TH FLOOR	NEW YORK, NY	10023
GRIND, THE	ROCK & ROLL GROUP	POST OFFICE BOX 4087	MISSOULA, MT	59806
GRINER, NORMAN	DIRECTOR	DGA, 110 W 57TH ST	NEW YORK, NY	10019
GRINKER, CHARLES	WRITER-DIRECTOR	THE CORPORATION FOR		
		ENTERTAINMENT & LEARNING		
		515 MADISON AVE	NEW YORK, NY	10022
GRINNAGE, JACK	ACTOR	1234 N HAYWORTH AVE #10	LOS ANGELES, CA	90046
GRINSTEAD, LINDA M	ACTRESS	505 S LAKE ST	BURBANK, CA	91502
GRIPPO, JOELYN A	WRITER	10915 1/2 WELLWORTH AVE	LOS ANGELES, CA	90024
GRISHAM, DOYLE	GUITARIST	210 FOREST PARK RD	MADISON, TN	37115
GRISHAW, JAMES	GUITARIST	3571 GAILYNN DR	CINCINNATI, OH	45211
GRISHMAN, ALAN	VIOLINIST	POST OFFICE BOX U	REDDING, CT	06875
GRISHMAN & HA CHIU	MUSICAL DUO	POST OFFICE BOX U	REDDING, CT	06875
GRISMAN, DAVID, QUARTET	JAZZ QUARTET	KURLAND, 173 BRIGHTON AVE	BOSTON, MA	02134
GRISMER, RAY	COMPOSER	6520 RIVERGROVE DR	DOWNEY, CA	90240
GRIST, RERI	SOPRANO	CAMI, 165 W 57TH ST	NEW YORK, NY	10019
GRISWOLD, GRIZZY	DRUMMER	995 BRILEY PARKWAY	NASHVILLE, TN	37217
GRIZZARD, GEORGE	ACTOR	400 E 54TH ST	NEW YORK, NY	10022
GRIZZARD, JOE	GUITARIST	306 E TIMMONS ST	NASHVILLE, TN	37211
GRIZZARD, LEWIS	AUTHOR-COLUMNIST	POST OFFICE BOX 4689	ATLANTA, GA	30302
GRIZZLY	WRESTLER	SEE - SMITH, JAKE "GRIZZLY"		
GROBY, FRANK	ACTOR	3967 PAIGE ST	LOS ANGELES, CA	90031
GRODE, GEOFFREY THOMAS	WRITER	451 N GENESEE AVE	LOS ANGELES, CA	90036
GRODIN, CHARLES	ACTOR-WRITER	445 N BEDFORD DR #PH	BEVERLY HILLS, CA	90210
GROENENDAAL, CRIS	TENOR	LEW, 204 W 10TH ST	NEW YORK, NY	10014
GROENING, MATT	CARTOONIST	313 28TH ST	VENICE, CA	90291
GROER, RICHARD C	NEWS CORRESPONDENT	2730 WISCONSIN AVE, NW	WASHINGTON, DC	20007
GROFE, FERDE	WRITER	8955 BEVERLY BLVD	LOS ANGELES, CA	90048
GROGAN, DAVID W	NEWS CORRESPONDENT	2013 COLUMBIA RD, NW	WASHINGTON, DC	20008
GROGAN, STEVE	FOOTBALL	17 LAUREL RD	SHARON, MA	02067
GROH, DAVID	ACTOR	3800 BARHAM BLVD #303	LOS ANGELES, CA	90068
GROHS, CAROL	MUSICIAN	3631 SARATOGA AVE	NASHVILLE, TN	37205
GROLLMAN, ELAINE	ACTRESS	64-29 231ST ST	BAYSIDE, NY	11364
GRONENTHAL, MAX	SINGER	POST OFFICE BOX 4217	NORTH HOLLYWOOD, CA	91607
GRONER, BRIAN	VIOLINIST	416 WANDA DR	NASHVILLE, TN	37214
GRONNING, PIA	ACTRESS	8285 SUNSET BLVD #12	LOS ANGELES, CA	90046
GRONROOS, WALTON	BARITONE	CAMI, 165 W 57TH ST	NEW YORK, NY	10019
GROODY, WILLIAM N	NEWS CORRESPONDENT	1755 S JEFFERSON DAVIS HWY	ARLINGTON, DC	22202
GROOM, SAM	ACTOR	9229 SUNSET BLVD #306	LOS ANGELES, CA	90069
GROOME, MALCOLM	ACTOR	ABC-TV, "RYAN'S HOPE"		
		1330 AVE OF THE AMERICAS	NEW YORK, NY	10019
GROPP, GERALD	GUITARIST	4160 EASTVIEW DR	NASHVILLE, TN	37211
GROSBARD, ULA	FILM DIRECTOR	29 W 10TH ST	NEW YORK, NY	10011
GROSJEAN, JAMES	VIOLINIST	4068 KINGS LN	NASHVILLE, TN	37218
GROSKOPF, AUBREY	FILM EXECUTIVE	12636 BEATRICE ST	LOS ANGELES, CA	90066
GROSLAND, CRAIG	DRUMMER	1201 CEDAR LN	NASHVILLE, TN	37212
GROSS, ALAN P	WRITER	555 W 57TH ST #1230	NEW YORK, NY	10019
GROSS, ARVE	ACTOR	LIGHT, 113 N ROBERTSON BLVD	LOS ANGELES, CA	90048
GROSS, DAVID	ACTOR	1418 N HIGHLAND AVE #10	LOS ANGELES, CA	90028
GROSS, DAVID JOSEPH	PHOTOJOURNALIST	2907 N UNDERWOOD ST	ARLINGTON, VA	22213
GROSS, DAVID P	CONDUCTOR	13490 MAHOGANY DR	RENO, NV	89511
GROSS, HERBERT	TV EXECUTIVE	CBS-TV, 6121 SUNSET BLVD	LOS ANGELES, CA	90028
GROSS, JACK, JR	TV WRITER	132 S PALM DR	BEVERLY HILLS, CA	90212
GROSS, JOEL	WRITER	555 W 57TH ST #1230	NEW YORK, NY	10019
GROSS, KEN	WRITER-EDITOR	TIME & PEOPLE MAGAZINE		
		TIME & LIFE BUILDING		
		ROCKEFELLER CENTER	NEW YORK, NY	10020
GROSS, KENNETH H	LITERARY AGENT	8428 MELROSE PL #C	LOS ANGELES, CA	90069
GROSS, LARRY	SCREENWRITER	8955 BEVERLY BLVD	LOS ANGELES, CA	90048
GROSS, LEONARD	WRITER	8955 BEVERLY BLVD	LOS ANGELES, CA	90048
GROSS, LLOYD J	DIRECTOR	33 ORCHARD HILL RD	NEWTOWN, CT	06470
GROSS, MARCY	WRITER	8955 BEVERLY BLVD	LOS ANGELES, CA	90048
GROSS, MARGE	ACTRESS-WRITER	1930 CENTURY PARK W #30	LOS ANGELES, CA	90067
GROSS, MAUREEN O	WRITER	555 W 57TH ST #1230	NEW YORK, NY	10019
GROSS, MICHAEL	ACTOR	1801 CENTURY PARK E #1400	LOS ANGELES, CA	90067
GROSS, MICHAEL	VIDEO EDITOR	ENTERTAINMENT TONIGHT		
		PARAMOUNT TELEVISION		
		5555 MELROSE AVE	LOS ANGELES, CA	90038
GROSS, PETER A	VIDEO EXECUTIVE	TIME/LIFE VIDEO, INC		
		1271 AVE OF THE AMERICAS	NEW YORK, NY	10020
GROSS, RICHARD C	NEWS CORRESPONDENT	2730 WISCONSIN AVE, NW	WASHINGTON, DC	20007
GROSS, ROBERT P	DIRECTOR	149 BLEEKER ST	NEW YORK, NY	10012
GROSS, SAM	CARTOONIST	POST OFFICE BOX 4203	NEW YORK, NY	10017
GROSS, SHELLY	THEATER PRODUCER	MUSIC FAIR ENTERPRISES		
		555 CITY LINE AVE	BALA CYNWOOD, PA	19004
GROSSAN, MARK STEVEN	WRITER-PRODUCER	508 N CANON DR	BEVERLY HILLS, CA	90210
GROSSBACH, ROBERT	SCREENWRITER	LEIBOWITZ, 858 STEWART	GARDEN CITY, NY	11530
GROSSBERG, JACK	DIRECTOR-PRODUCER	10 PONY CIR	ROSLYN HEIGHTS, NY	11577

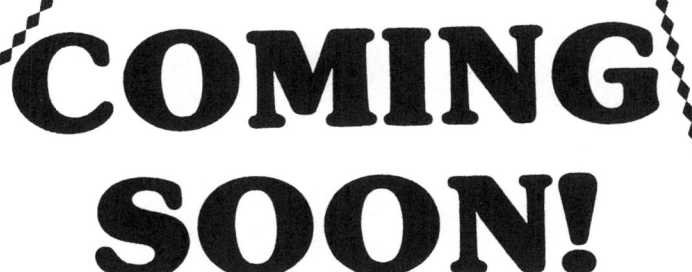

Name	Occupation	Address	City	Zip
GROSSELFINGER, BURT	ACTOR	84 BOURNDALE RD S	MANHASSET, NY	11030
GROSSER, ARTHUR E	WRITER	555 W 57TH ST #1230	NEW YORK, NY	10019
GROSSFELD, SIDNEY H	DIRECTOR	6152 KENWATER AVE	WOODLAND HILLS, CA	91364
GROSSLIGHT, PETER	TALENT AGENT	10100 SANTA MONICA BLVD #1600	LOS ANGELES, CA	90067
GROSSMAN, ARNOLD	WRITER	8955 BEVERLY BLVD	LOS ANGELES, CA	90048
GROSSMAN, BUDD	TV WRITER	8955 BEVERLY BLVD	LOS ANGELES, CA	90048
GROSSMAN, DAVID	DIRECTOR	11009 OHIO AVE	LOS ANGELES, CA	90025
GROSSMAN, DAVIS S	NEWS CORRESPONDENT	20233 SHIPLEY TERR	GERMANTOWN, MD	20874
GROSSMAN, DIXIE BROWN	WRITER	6948 LENA AVE	CANOGA PARK, CA	91307
GROSSMAN, DOUGLAS A	SCREENWRITER	8955 BEVERLY BLVD	LOS ANGELES, CA	90048
GROSSMAN, GARY H	TV PRODUCER	9000 SUNSET BLVD #1200	LOS ANGELES, CA	90069
GROSSMAN, HENRY	TENOR	LIEBERMAN, 11 RIVERSIDE DR	NEW YORK, NY	10023
GROSSMAN, KENNETH L	FILM EXECUTIVE	10728 WELLWORTH AVE	LOS ANGELES, CA	90024
GROSSMAN, LAWRENCE K	TV EXECUTIVE	PBS, 475 L'ENFANT PLAZA, NW	WASHINGTON, DC	20024
GROSSMAN, LYNN	TV WRITER	8955 BEVERLY BLVD	LOS ANGELES, CA	90048
GROSSMAN, SANFORD	TV DIRECTOR	CBS-TV, 51 W 52ND ST	NEW YORK, NY	10019
GROSSMAN, STEFAN	SINGER-GUITARIST	FOLKLORE, 1671 APPIAN WY	SANTA MONICA, CA	90401
GROSSMAN, TERRY	TV WRITER	8955 BEVERLY BLVD	LOS ANGELES, CA	90048
GROSSMANN, SUZANNE	WRITER	555 W 57TH ST #1230	NEW YORK, NY	10019
GROSSO, SONNY	TV WRITER	555 W 57TH ST #1230	NEW YORK, NY	10019
GROSVENOR, GILBERT	PHOTOGRAPHER	1259 CREST LN	MC LEAN, VA	22101
GROSZ, GREGORY MICHAEL	WRITER-PRODUCER	1219 ORANGE GROVE AVE	GLENDALE, CA	91205
GROTH, ROBIN	NEWS CORRESPONDENT	ABC-TV ENTERTAINMENT CENTER		
		2040 AVE OF THE STARS	LOS ANGELES, CA	90067
GROUBERT, MARK	WRITER	THE NATIONAL LAMPOON		
		635 MADISON AVE	NEW YORK, NY	10022
GROUND, ROBERT	WRI-DIR-PROD	4412 N 53RD LN #3	PHOENIX, AZ	85031
GROUND ZERO	ROCK & ROLL GROUP	41 BRITAIN ST #200	TORONTO, ONT	CANADA
GROUP, MITCHELL	ACTOR-WRITER	7935 BLACKBURN AVE	LOS ANGELES, CA	90048
GROUT, AL	JUGGLER	BTC ENTERPRISES		
		600 HAYMONT DR	EASTON, PA	18042
GROUT, JAMES	ACTOR	CROUCH, 59 FRITH ST	LONDON W1	ENGLAND
GROVE, GEORGE W, JR	MUSIC ARRANGER	POST OFFICE BOX 241	BLOWING ROCK, NC	28605
GROVER, EDWARD	ACTOR-WRITER	17 SYCAMORE LN	ROLLING HILLS, CA	90274
GROVER, LINDA	TV WRITER	8955 BEVERLY BLVD	LOS ANGELES, CA	90048
GROVER, RONALD G	NEWS CORRESPONDENT	7007 FLORIDA ST	CHEVY CHASE, MD	20815
GROVER, STANLEY	ACTOR	208 S BEVERLY DR #4	BEVERLY HILLS, CA	90212
GROVES, CAROLYN	ACTRESS	SOGLIO, 423 MADISON AVE	NEW YORK, NY	10017
GROVES, CHARLES	CONDUCTOR	SEE - GROVE, SIR CHARLES		
GROVES, HERMAN	TV WRITER	4657 ARRIBA DR	TARZANA, CA	91356
GROVES, JOHN PATRICK	TV WRITER	2912 PACIFIC AVE	MANHATTAN BEACH, CA	90266
GROVES, SIR CHARLES	CONDUCTOR	1776 BROADWAY #504	NEW YORK, NY	10019
GROW, RON	TV PRODUCER	WARNER BROTHERS TV		
		4000 WARNER BLVD	BURBANK, CA	91522
GRUBBS, GARY	ACTOR	9744 WILSHIRE BLVD #206	BEVERLY HILLS, CA	90212
GRUBEROVA, EDITA	SOPRANO	CAMI, 165 W 57TH ST	NEW YORK, NY	10019
GRUBERT, CARL	CARTOONIST	918 WOODLAWN ST	DES PLAINES, IL	60016
GRUEN, GABBY	ACTOR	936 21ST ST #F	SANTA MONICA, CA	90403
GRUENBERG, AXEL A	DIRECTOR	621 SAN VICENTE BLVD	SANTA MONICA, CA	90402
GRUENBERG, MARK	NEWS CORRESPONDENT	4000 CATHEDRAL AVE, NW	WASHINGTON, DC	20016
GRUENEBERG, BILL	ACTOR	8721 SUNSET BLVD #200	LOS ANGELES, CA	90069
GRUENER, ALLAN	ACTOR	1080 S 10TH AVE	ARCADIA, CA	91006
GRUESOMES, THE	ROCK & ROLL GROUP	POST OFFICE BOX 182		
		STATION F	MONTREAL, QUE H3J 2L1	CANADA
GRUIFF, SAM	NEWS CORRESPONDENT	5425 CONNECTICUT AVE, NW	WASHINGTON, DC	20015
GRUMBLES, WILLIAM H	CABLE EXECUTIVE	HOME BOX OFFICE PICTURES		
		1100 AVE OF THE AMERICAS	NEW YORK, NY	10036
GRUMIAUX, ARTHUR	VIOLINIST	59 E 54TH ST #81	NEW YORK, NY	10022
GRUMMAN, FRANCIS	DIRECTOR	1200 OLIVE DR	LOS ANGELES, CA	90069
GRUNDHEBER, FRANZ	BARITONE	CAMI, 165 W 57TH ST	NEW YORK, NY	10019
GRUNDY, REG	TV PRODUCER	THE GRUNDY ORGANISATION		
		GRUNDY HOUSE, 448 PACIFIC HWY		
		ARTARMON	SYDNEY	AUSTRALIA
GRUNER, ANTHONY	FILM-TV EXECUTIVE	TALBOT-TV, 21 POLAND ST	LONDON W1	ENGLAND
GRUNFELD, GABRIEL	ACTOR-WRITER	750 S SPAULDING AVE #20	LOS ANGELES, CA	90036
GRUNWALD, HENRY ANATOLE	EDITOR-PUBLISHER	TIME & LIFE MAGAZINES		
		TIME & LIFE BUILDING		
		ROCKEFELLER CENTER	NEW YORK, NY	10020
GRUSIN, DAVE	COMPOSER	4011 HOPEVALE DR	SHERMAN OAKS, CA	91405
GRUSIN, LARRY M	WRITER	8380 WARING AVE #102	LOS ANGELES, CA	90069
GRUWELL, SHELLEY	BODYBUILDER	POST OFFICE BOX 1329	CLOVIS, CA	93612
GRYMES, STEPHEN B	TV DIRECTOR	561 BABBLING BROOK LN	VALLEY COTTAGE, NY	10989
GRYMKOWSKI, PETE	BODYBUILDER	GOLD'S GYM, 360 HAMPTON DR	VENICE, CA	90291
GUADAGNO, ANTON	CONDUCTOR	111 W 57TH ST #1209	NEW YORK, NY	10019
GUADALCANAL DIARY	ROCK & ROLL GROUP	POST OFFICE BOX 1584	MARIETTA, GA	30061
GUARD, CHRISTOPHER	ACTOR	2 GERALDINE RD	LONDON W4	ENGLAND
GUARD, DAVE	SINGER-SONGWRITER	601 S RANCHO DR #C-18	LAS VEGAS, NV	89106
GUARD, SALLY	SPORTS REPORTER	SPORTS ILLUSTRATED MAGAZINE		
		TIME & LIFE BUILDING		
		ROCKEFELLER CENTER	NEW YORK, NY	10020
GUARDINO, CHARLES	ACTOR	7300 FRANKLIN AVE #649	LOS ANGELES, CA	90046
GUARDINO, HARRY	ACTOR	9738 ARBY DR	BEVERLY HILLS, CA	90210
GUARDINO, JEROME	ACTOR	6565 SUNSET BLVD #525-A	HOLLYWOOD, CA	90068
GUARE, JOHN	SCREENWRITER	555 W 57TH ST #1230	NEW YORK, NY	10019
GUARIGLIA, MARIA	SOPRANO	SARDOS, 180 W END AVE	NEW YORK, NY	10023

Name	Occupation	Address	City/State	Zip
GUARINO, CHRISTOPHER J	NEWS CORRESPONDENT	2133 WISCONSIN AVE, NW	WASHINGTON, DC	20007
GUARINO, ROBERT	TENOR	CAMI, 165 W 57TH ST	NEW YORK, NY	10019
GUARNERI STRING QUARTET	STRING QUARTER	POST OFFICE BOX 30	TENAFLY, NJ	07670
GUAY, REGINA A	NEWS CORRESPONDENT	9607 CARRIAGE RD	KENSINGTON, MD	20985
GUAY, TOM	NEWS CORRESPONDENT	9115 WALDEN RD	SILVER SPRING, MD	20901
GUBER, LEE	THEATER PRODUCER	32 E 57TH ST	NEW YORK, NY	10022
GUBER, PETER	FILM PRODUCER	GUBER-PETERS PRODUCTIONS		
		4000 WARNER BLVD	BURBANK, CA	91522
GUBRUD, IRENE	SOPRANO	ICM, 40 W 57TH ST	NEW YORK, NY	10019
GUCCIONE, BOB	PUBLISHER	PENTHOUSE, 1965 BROADWAY	NEW YORK, NY	10023
GUDEGAST, HANS	ACTOR	SEE - BRAEDEN, ERIC		
GUDENKAUF, ANNE E	NEWS CORRESPONDENT	2025 "M" ST, NW	WASHINGTON, DC	20036
GUDGEON, SUSAN	MEZZO-SOPRANO	POST OFFICE BOX 188, STATION A	TORONTO, ONT	CANADA
GUEDEL, JOHN	WRITER-PRODUCER	8455 FOUNTAIN AVE #408	LOS ANGELES, CA	90069
GUEFEN, ANTHONY	COMPOSER-CONDUCTOR	1042 VISTA ST #3	LOS ANGELES, CA	90046
GUELL, LUISA MARIA	MUSICIAN	9777 HARWIN ST #101	HOUSTON, TX	77036
GUENETTE, ROBERT	WRITER-PRODUCER	2130 TRENTLY LN	BEVERLY HILLS, CA	90210
GUERCIO, JAMES WILLIAM	DIRECTOR-PRODUCER	CARIBOU RANCH	NEDERLAND, CO	80466
GUERDAT, ANDREW DAVID	TV WRITER	8955 BEVERLY BLVD	LOS ANGELES, CA	90048
GUERIN, ANN	REPORTER	TIME & PEOPLE MAGAZINE		
		TIME & LIFE BUILDING		
		ROCKEFELLER CENTER	NEW YORK, NY	10020
GUERRA, CASTULO	ACTOR	211 S BEVERLY DR #201	BEVERLY HILLS, CA	90212
GUERRERA, INEZ	WRITER	555 W 57TH ST #1230	NEW YORK, NY	10019
GUERRERAS	HIGH WIRE ACT	POST OFFICE BOX 87	WEST LEBANON, NY	12195
GUERRERO, CHAVO	WRESTLER	UNIVERSAL WRESTLING FEDERATION		
		MID SOUTH SPORTS, INC		
		5001 SPRING VALLEY RD	DALLAS, TX	75244
GUERRERO, DANIEL H	COMPOSER	747 S KINGSLEY DR #7	LOS ANGELES, CA	90005
GUERRERO, EVELYN	ACTRESS	10000 RIVERSIDE DR #3	TOLUCA LAKE, CA	91602
GUERRERO, HECTOR "PISTOLAS"	WRESTLER	NATIONAL WRESTLING ALLIANCE		
		JIM CROCKETT PROMOTIONS		
		421 BRIARBEND DR	CHARLOTTE, NC	28209
GUERRERO, PEDRO	BASEBALL	535 S PLYMOUTH BLVD	LOS ANGELES, CA	90020
GUERRI, RUTH	MODEL	MODELS & PROMOTIONS AGENCY		
		8560 SUNSET BLVD, 10TH FLOOR	LOS ANGELES, CA	90069
GUEST, CHRISTOPHER	ACTOR-WRITER	518 N SYCAMORE AVE	LOS ANGELES, CA	90036
GUEST, ELLISA HADEN	SCREENWRITER	555 W 57TH ST #1230	NEW YORK, NY	10019
GUEST, JEAN	CASTING DIRECTOR	CBS-TV, 7800 BEVERLY BLVD	LOS ANGELES, CA	90036
GUEST, LANCE	ACTOR	962 S GRANVILLE AVE #5	LOS ANGELES, CA	90049
GUEST, REVEL	DIRECTOR-PRODUCER	9 HOLLAND PARK	LONDON W11	ENGLAND
GUEST, VAL	WRITER-PRODUCER	9 CAVENDISH SQ	LONDON W1	ENGLAND
GUETTA, BERNARD	NEWS CORRESPONDENT	2701 "N" ST, NW	WASHINGTON, DC	20007
GUETTEL, HENRY	THEATER PRODUCER	115 CENTRAL PARK W	NEW YORK, NY	10023
GUFFEY, ROGER	PIANIST	CANDLELIGHT APARTMENTS #13	GALLATIN, TN	37066
GUIDA, THOMAS WILLIAM	DIRECTOR	1681 BLOOMFIELD PL #539	BLOOMFIELD HILLS, MI	48013
GUIDRY, VERNON A, JR	NEWS CORRESPONDENT	10211 KINDLY CT	GAITHERSBURG, MD	20879
GUILAROFF, SYDNEY	HAIRDRESSER	POST OFFICE BOX 253	BEVERLY HILLS, CA	90213
GUILBAUD, HERVE	NEWS CORRESPONDENT	9315 W PARK DR	BETHESDA, MD	20814
GUILBAULT, ARTHUR	GUITARIST	4833 LEESA ANN LN	HERMITAGE, TN	37076
GUILBERT, ANN	ACTRESS	870 N VINE ST #G	LOS ANGELES, CA	90038
GUILBERT, ANN MORGAN	ACTRESS	550 ERSKINE DR	PACIFIC PALISADES, CA	90272
GUILD, S ROLLINS	DIRECTOR	POST OFFICE BOX 551	WOODSTOCK, NY	12498
GUILFORD, CAROL	WRITER	8955 BEVERLY BLVD	LOS ANGELES, CA	90048
GUILFOYLE, PAUL	ACTOR	129 E 29TH ST	NEW YORK, NY	10016
GUILLAUME, ROBERT	ACTOR	4925 PALO DR	TARZANA, CA	91356
GUILLERMIN, JOHN	FILM DIRECTOR	309 S ROCKINGHAM AVE	LOS ANGELES, CA	90049
GUILLORY, BENNET	ACTOR	15010 VENTURA BLVD #219	SHERMAN OAKS, CA	91403
GUIMARAES, LEILA	SOPRANO	45 W 60TH ST #4-K	NEW YORK, NY	10023
GUINAN, ROBERT	ACTOR	1356 E 58TH ST	BROOKLYN, NY	11234
GUINN	SOUL GROUP	POST OFFICE BOX 11981	PHILADELPHIA, PA	19145
GUINN, LESLIE	SINGER	59 E 54TH ST #81	NEW YORK, NY	10022
GUINNESS, SIR ALEC	ACTOR-DIRECTOR	KETTLEBROOK MEADOWS		
		STEEP MARSH, PETERSFORD	HAMPSHIRE	ENGLAND
GUISE, GREGORY W	NEWS CORRESPONDENT	4001 BRANDYWINE ST	WASHINGTON, DC	20016
GUISEWITE, CATHY	CARTOONIST	NEWS AMERICA SYNDICATE		
		1703 KAISER AVE	IRVINE, CA	92714
GUIZAR, TITO	ACTOR-GUITARIST	THE SIERRA MADRE		
		640 LOMAS DE CHAPRILETEPEO	MEXICO CITY 10	
			DF 09999	MEXICO
GUIZON, FRENCHIA	ACTOR	4025 PALMYRA RD #31	LOS ANGELES, CA	90008
GULAGER, CLU	ACTOR	POST OFFICE BOX 852	WOODLAND HILLS, CA	91364
GULDEMIR, UFUK	NEWS CORRESPONDENT	925 25TH ST, NW	WASHINGTON, DC	20037
GULINO, DENIS G	NEWS CORRESPONDENT	4316 ADRIENNE DR	ALEXANDRIA, VA	22309
GULLEY, JOHN KEN	GUITARIST	12 CHAUCER CIR	BARRIE, ONT L4N 4T7	CANADA
GULLI, FRANCO	VIOLINIST	CAMI, 165 W 57TH ST	NEW YORK, NY	10019
GULLIVER, DOROTHY	ACTRESS	PROCTOR, 247 S ORANGE DR	LOS ANGELES, CA	90036
GULLSTRAND, DONNA	SOPRANO	200 W 70TH ST #7-F	NEW YORK, NY	10023
GULYAS, DENES	TENOR	61 W 62ND ST #6-F	NEW YORK, NY	10023
GUMBEL, BRYANT	BROADCASTER	30 ROCKEFELLER PLAZA #1508	NEW YORK, NY	10112
GUMBEL, GREG	SPORTSCASTER	ESPN, ESPN PLAZA	BRISTOL, CT	06010
GUMP, DAVID	NEWS CORRESPONDENT	719 BARTON ST	ARLINGTON, VA	22209
GUN CLUB, THE	ROCK & ROLL GROUP	61 SILVERLEIGH RD		
		THORNTON HEATH	SURREY CR4 602	ENGLAND

GUNDEN, TAMI	SINGER	POST OFFICE BOX 723591	ATLANTA, GA	30339
GUNDERSEN, KARI	NEWS CORRESPONDENT	5112 CONNECTICUT AVE, NW	WASHINGTON, DC	20008
GUNN, GEORGE WILLIAM	NEWS CORRESPONDENT	8910 LYNNHURST DR	FAIRFAX, VA	22031
GUNN, HARTFORD N, JR	CABLE EXECUTIVE	1301 PENNSYLVANIA AVE, N	WASHINGTON, DC	20004
GUNN, JAMES H, JR	GUITARIST	1238 KENMORE PL	NASHVILLE, TN	37216
GUNN, JOSEPH A	TV WRITER	8955 BEVERLY BLVD	LOS ANGELES, CA	90048
GUNN, MOSES	ACTOR	9220 SUNSET BLVD #202	LOS ANGELES, CA	90069
GUNN, NICHOLAS	ACTOR	247 S BEVERLY DR #102	BEVERLY HILLS, CA	90210
GUNN, UTE W	NEWS CORRESPONDENT	2139 WISCONSIN AVE, NW	WASHINGTON, DC	20007
GUNN, WILLIAM	WRITER	555 W 57TH ST #1230	NEW YORK, NY	10019
GUNNELS, MERRIE RAE	ECONOMIST	2801 MEADOW LARK DR	SAN DIEGO, CA	92123
GUNNER, RODERICK	FILM-TV EXECUTIVE	D D A, 57 BEAK ST	LONDON W1	ENGLAND
GUNNING, CHRISTOPHER	COMPOSER	THE OLD RECTORY, MILL LN		
		MONKS RISBOROUGH	BUCKS HP17 9LG	ENGLAND
GUNTER, CORNELL & THE COASTERS	VOCAL GROUP	POST OFFICE BOX 552	CUPERTINO, CA	95014
GUNTER, PATRICIA LEE	BASSOONIST	3004 BRIGHTWOOD AVE	NASHVILLE, TN	37212
GUNTHER, C RONALD	DIRECTOR	7631 ORIOLE DR	NILES, IL	60648
GUNTS, BRENT O, JR	DIRECTOR	DGA, 110 W 57TH ST	NEW YORK, NY	10019
GUNTZELMAN, DANIEL J	TV WRITER-DIRECTOR	15069 RAYNETA DR	SHERMAN OAKS, CA	91403
GUNZENHAUSER, STEPHEN	CONDUCTOR	GERSHUNOFF, 502 PARK AVE	NEW YORK, NY	10022
GUPTA, SNEH	ACTRESS	T C M, 300 FULHAM RD	LONDON SW10	ENGLAND
GURBST, MIMI	WRITER	555 W 57TH ST #1230	NEW YORK, NY	10019
GURDINE, JAMES G	WRITER	12726 VANOWEN ST	NORTH HOLLYWOOD, CA	91605
GUREN, PETER	CARTOONIST	NEWS AMERICA SYNDICATE		
		1703 KAISER AVE	IRVINE, CA	92714
GURIN, PHILIP	WRITER	555 W 57TH ST #1230	NEW YORK, NY	10019
GURMAN, RICHARD	TV WRITER	6440 COLGATE AVE	LOS ANGELES, CA	90048
GURNEE, HAL	TV DIRECTOR	DUNBAR RD	SHARON, CT	06069
GURNER, GARY S	TV WRITER	853 16TH ST #6	SANTA MONICA, CA	90403
GURNEY, A R, JR	PLAYWRIGHT	120 W 70TH ST	NEW YORK, NY	10023
GURNEY, ROBERT J, JR	WRITER	555 W 57TH ST #1230	NEW YORK, NY	10019
GUROK, NOAH D	WRITER	555 W 57TH ST #1230	NEW YORK, NY	10019
GURRIN, GEOFFREY	DIRECTOR	THE OLD STUDIO, AMBERLEY	WEST SUSSEX	ENGLAND
GURSKY, GREGG	NEWS CORRESPONDENT	400 N CAPITOL ST, NW	WASHINGTON, DC	20001
GURWITT, ROBERT	NEWS CORRESPONDENT	2706 N KEY BLVD	ARLINGTON, VA	22201
GUSEV, VLADIMIR	NEWS CORRESPONDENT	1401 BLAIR MILL RD	SILVER SPRING, MD	20910
GUSS, JACK R	TV WRITER	10500 MARS LN	LOS ANGELES, CA	90077
GUSS, LOUIS	ACTOR	6310 SAN VICENTE BLVD #407	LOS ANGELES, CA	90048
GUSSOW, MEL	CRITIC	N Y TIMES, 229 W 43RD ST	NEW YORK, NY	10036
GUSTAFON & CO	ILLUSIONISTS	HALL, 138 FROG HOLLOW RD	CHURCHVILLE, PA	18966
GUSTAFSON, CHARLES G	CONDUCTOR	1750 NORFOLK AVE #3	SAINT PAUL, MN	55116
GUSTAFSON, NANCY	SOPRANO	CAMI, 165 W 57TH ST	NEW YORK, NY	10019
GUSTAOTOS, JOSEPH	WRITER	555 W 57TH ST #1230	NEW YORK, NY	10019
GUTCHEON, BETH R	SCREENWRITER	555 W 57TH ST #1230	NEW YORK, NY	10019
GUTENBERG, ARLAN P	WRITER	8955 BEVERLY BLVD	LOS ANGELES, CA	90048
GUTERMAN, SHERYL L	TV WRITER	1335 9TH ST #4	SANTA MONICA, CA	90401
GUTFIELD, ROSE	NEWS CORRESPONDENT	1823 BILTMORE ST, NW	WASHINGTON, DC	20009
GUTHMAN, LESTER	WRITER	555 W 57TH ST #1230	NEW YORK, NY	10019
GUTHRIE, ANDY	NEWS CORRESPONDENT	6826 DEER SPRING CT	FALLS CHURCH, VA	22043
GUTHRIE, ARLO	SINGER-SONGWRITER	THE FARM	WASHINGTON, MA	01223
GUTHRIE, DAVID	TV WRITER	8955 BEVERLY BLVD	LOS ANGELES, CA	90048
GUTHRIE, JANET	ACTRESS	343 E 30TH ST #312-N	NEW YORK, NY	10016
GUTHRIE, LYNN H	DIRECTOR	23238 CANZONET ST	WOODLAND HILLS, CA	91367
GUTHRIE, RICHARD	ACTOR	3271 1/2 ROWENA AVE	LOS ANGELES, CA	90027
GUTIERREZ, GERALD	TV DIRECTOR	ROBERTS, 157 W 57TH ST	NEW YORK, NY	10019
GUTIERREZ, HORACIO	PIANIST	CAMI, 165 W 57TH ST	NEW YORK, NY	10019
GUTIERREZ, VICENTE	SCREENWRITER	8955 BEVERLY BLVD	LOS ANGELES, CA	90048
GUTIERREZ, VINCE R	TV WRITER	9100 SUNSET BLVD #340	LOS ANGELES, CA	90069
GUTIS	FLYING ACTS	POST OFFICE BOX 87	WEST LEBANON, NY	12195
GUTKNECHT, CAROL	SOPRANO	CAMI, 165 W 57TH ST	NEW YORK, NY	10019
GUTMAN, AMY J	NEWS CORRESPONDENT	CBS NEWS, 2020 "M" ST, NW	WASHINGTON, DC	20036
GUTMAN, NATASHA	CELLIST	MARIEDL ANDERS ARTISTS MGMT		
		535 EL CAMINO DEL MAR ST	SAN FRANCISCO, CA	94121
GUTMAN, ROY	NEWS CORRESPONDENT	2201 LEELAND DR	FALLS CHURCH, VA	22043
GUTMAN, SCOTT R	WRITER	555 W 57TH ST #1230	NEW YORK, NY	10019
GUTMANN, HANNA	NEWS CORRESPONDENT	9209 THREE OAKS DR	SILVER SPRING, MD	20901
GUTOWSKI, ROBERT M	TV EXECUTIVE	ESPN, ESPN PLAZA	BRISTOL, CT	06010
GUTTENBERG, STEVE	ACTOR	3818 SHERVIEW DR	SHERMAN OAKS, CA	91413
GUTTER, ROBERT	CONDUCTOR	SOFFER, 130 W 56TH ST	NEW YORK, NY	10019
GUTTERIDGE, LUCY	ACTRESS	9255 SUNSET BLVD #505	LOS ANGELES, CA	90069
GUTTFREUND, ANDRE RUBEN	DIRECTOR	DGA, 7950 SUNSET BLVD	LOS ANGELES, CA	90046
GUTTMAN, RICHARD A	WRITER	8955 BEVERLY BLVD	LOS ANGELES, CA	90048
GUTTMAN, ROBERT J	NEWS CORRESPONDENT	209 "C" ST, NE	WASHINGTON, DC	20002
GUTWILLIG, ROBERT ALAN	WRITER	2237 NICHOLS CANYON RD	LOS ANGELES, CA	90046
GUY & RALNA	VOCAL DUO	9200 SUNSET BLVD #808	LOS ANGELES, CA	90069
GUYER, JOYCE	SOPRANO	61 W 62ND ST #6-F	NEW YORK, NY	10023
GUYLAS, ELLEN M	TV WRITER	7432 CERVANTES PL	LOS ANGELES, CA	90046
GUYLER, DERYCK	ACTOR	180 NORBURY CRESCENT, NORBURY	LONDON SW16	ENGLAND
GUZA, ROBERT O	WRITER	2423 RONDA VISTA DR	LOS ANGELES, CA	90027
GUZA, ROBERT, JR	TV WRITER	ABC-TV, "GENERAL HOSPITAL"		
		1438 N GOWER ST	LOS ANGELES, CA	90028
GUZMAN, ARMANDO	NEWS CORRESPONDENT	3902 CHERRYWOOD LN	ANNANDALE, VA	22003
		POST OFFICE BOX 87	WEST LEBANON, NY	12195
GUZZO, DANIEL J	WRITER	555 W 57TH ST #1230	NEW YORK, NY	10019
GWERTZMAN, BERNARD M	NEWS CORRESPONDENT	4416 "Q" ST, NW	WASHINGTON, DC	20007

Name	Occupation	Address	City	Zip
GWILLIM, JACK	ACTOR	STONE, 1052 CAROL DR	LOS ANGELES, CA	90069
GWILYM, MIKE	ACTOR	PLANT & FROGGATT, LTD		
		JULIAN HOUSE		
		4 WINDMILL ST	LONDON W1	ENGLAND
GWOZDZ, LAWRENCE	SAXOPHONIST	POST OFFICE BOX 131	SPRINGFIELD, VA	22150
GWYNNE, FRED	ACTOR	888 7TH AVE #1602	NEW YORK, NY	10019
GYLLENHAAL, STEPHEN	WRITER-PRODUCER	226 S NORTON AVE	LOS ANGELES, CA	90004
GYORY, ANNE	WRITER	555 W 57TH ST #1230	NEW YORK, NY	10019
GYPSY	MUSICAL GROUP	MARSH, 1704 W LAKE ST	MINNEAPOLIS, MN	55408
GYPSY CHILD	ROCK & ROLL GROUP	POST OFFICE BOX 1467	NEW SMYRNA BEACH, FL	32070
GYSIN, FRANCIS	TV PRODUCER	NCB FILMS, DUNELM, ARKLEY	HERTS	ENGLAND
GYTRI, LOWELL	ACTOR	1734 N TAFT AVE #11	LOS ANGELES, CA	90028

Name	Occupation	Address	City	Zip
HA, A	ROCK & ROLL GROUP	SEE - A HA		
HAAGENSEN, ROBERT RISBERG	DIRECTOR	2427 WASHINGTON AVE	OCEANSIDE, NY	11572
HAAKE, JAMES "GYPSY"	ACTOR	SF & A, 121 N SAN VICENTE BLVD	BEVERLY HILLS, CA	90211
HAAS, CHARLES	SCREENWRITER	151 S EL CAMINO DR	BEVERLY HILLS, CA	90212
HAAS, CHARLES F	DIRECTOR	12626 HORTENSE ST	STUDIO CITY, CA	91604
HAAS, CLIFFORD B	NEWS CORRESPONDENT	4250 GARRISON ST, NW	WASHINGTON, DC	20016
HAAS, DOLLY	ACTRESS	HIRSCHFIELD, 122 E 95TH ST	NEW YORK, NY	10028
HAAS, ED	TV WRITER	8955 BEVERLY BLVD	LOS ANGELES, CA	90048
HAAS, EMILY T	WRITER	8955 BEVERLY BLVD	LOS ANGELES, CA	90048
HAAS, HAROLD	FILM EXECUTIVE	303 S ALMONT DR	LOS ANGELES, CA	90048
HAAS, KENNETH R, II	WRITER	555 W 57TH ST #1230	NEW YORK, NY	10019
HAAS, LUKAS	ACTOR	12725 VENTURA BLVD #E	STUDIO CITY, CA	91604
HAAS, STEVEN	TENOR	61 W 62ND ST #6-F	NEW YORK, NY	10023
HAASE, HEATHER	ACTRESS	1717 N HIGHLAND AVE #41	LOS ANGELES, CA	90028
HAASE, ROD	ACTOR	9040 HARRATT ST #5	LOS ANGELES, CA	90069
HABER, BERNARD	DIRECTOR	71 BEVERLY RD	GREAT NECK, NY	11021
HABER, CORY	NEWS CORRESPONDENT	NBC-TV, NEWS DEPARTMENT		
		4001 NEBRASKA AVE, NW	WASHINGTON, DC	20016
HABER, JOYCE	WRITER-COLUMNIST	1005 N REXFORD DR	LOS ANGELES, CA	90210
HABER, LES	TV PRODUCER	350 E 52ND ST #6-D	NEW YORK, NY	10022
HABER, LOUIS M	WRITER	555 W 57TH ST #1230	NEW YORK, NY	10019
HABEREK, JUDY	NEWS CORRESPONDENT	6803 ALLEGHENY AVE	TAKOMA PARK, MD	20912
HABERMAN, DONALD G	TV WRITER	5538 CASE AVE	NORTH HOLLYWOOD, CA	91601
HABIB, GEORGE	TV PRODUCER	NBC-TV, 3000 W ALAMEDA AVE	BURBANK, CA	91523
HABIB, GEORGE J	DIRECTOR	5165 CALATRAMA DR	WOODLAND HILLS, CA	91364
HACK, RICHARD	ACTOR	131 N WETHERLY DR #304	LOS ANGELES, CA	90048
HACK, RICHARD	CRITIC	6715 SUNSET BLVD	HOLLYWOOD, CA	90028
HACK, SHELLEY	ACTRESS-MODEL	2530 CAROB DR	LOS ANGELES, CA	90046
HACKEL, DAN	BROADCAST JOURNALIST	CNN, 1050 TECHWOOD DR, NW	ATLANTA, GA	30318
HACKEL, DAVID M	TV WRITER	4221 COLFAX AVE #1	STUDIO CITY, CA	91604
HACKENSACK HAMMER, THE	WRESTLER	SEE - WOLFE, BUDDY		
HACKER, JOSEPH	ACTOR	211 S BEVERLY DR #107	BEVERLY HILLS, CA	90212
HACKER, PATRICIA	TALENT AGENT	445 N BEDFORD DR #PH	BEVERLY HILLS, CA	90210
HACKER, RANDI	WRITER	8955 BEVERLY BLVD	LOS ANGELES, CA	90048
HACKES, PETER QUINN	NEWS CORRESPONDENT	NBC-TV, NEWS DEPARTMENT		
		4001 NEBRASKA AVE, NW	WASHINGTON, DC	20016
HACKETT, ALBERT	TV WRITER	8955 BEVERLY BLVD	LOS ANGELES, CA	90048
HACKETT, BUDDY	COMEDIAN-ACTOR	800 N WHITTIER DR	BEVERLY HILLS, CA	90210
HACKETT, F ARTHUR	DIRECTOR	20808 E GLEN HAVEN	NORTHVILLE, MI	48167
HACKETT, GEORGE A	CONDUCTOR	3651 CRESTMONT AVE	LOS ANGELES, CA	90026
HACKETT, PAT	WRITER	555 W 57TH ST #1230	NEW YORK, NY	10019
HACKETT, ROBERT J	WRITER	1888 CENTURY PARK E #1400	LOS ANGELES, CA	90067
HACKETT, SANDY	ACTRESS	800 N WHITTIER DR	BEVERLY HILLS, CA	90210
HACKETT, STEVE	SINGER-SONGWRITER	200 W 57TH ST #1403	NEW YORK, NY	10019
HACKFORD, TAYLOR	WRITER-PRODUCER	6620 CAHUENGA TERR	LOS ANGELES, CA	90068
HACKIN, DENNIS E	SCREENWRITER	555 W 57TH ST #1230	NEW YORK, NY	10019
HACKMAN, GENE	ACTOR	1888 CENTURY PARK E #1400	LOS ANGELES, CA	90067
HACKNEY, ALAN	TV WRITER	MANN, 1 OLD COMPTON ST	LONDON W1	ENGLAND
HACKSAW JIM	WRESTLER	SEE - DUGGAN, HACKSAW JIM		
HACSI, LOUIS	ACTOR	10850 RIVERSIDE DR #410	NORTH HOLLYWOOD, CA	91609
HADDOCK, JULIE ANNE	ACTRESS	6430 SUNSET BLVD #1203	LOS ANGELES, CA	90028
HADDOCK, MARCUS	TENOR	59 E 54TH ST #81	NEW YORK, NY	10022
HADDOCK, RON	DIRECTOR-PRODUCER	CHESS VALLEY FILMS, LTD		
		FILM HOUSE, LITTLE CHALFONT	BUCKS	ENGLAND
HADDON, JUDITH	SOPRANO	CAMI, 165 W 57TH ST	NEW YORK, NY	10019
HADDON, LARRY	ACTOR	208 S BEVERLY DR #4	BEVERLY HILLS, CA	90212
HADDOW, JEFFREY	TV WRITER	555 W 57TH ST #1230	NEW YORK, NY	10019
HADLEY, BRETT	ACTOR	1930 CENTURY PARK W #30	LOS ANGELES, CA	90067
HADLEY, JERRY	TENOR	LEW, 204 W 10TH ST	NEW YORK, NY	10014
HADLEY, RICHARD D	NEWS CORRESPONDENT	1300 N MEADE ST #22	ARLINGTON, VA	22209
HADLOCK, CHANNING M	WRITER-PRODUCER	60 GRAMERCY PARK N	NEW YORK, NY	10010
HADLOW, MICHAEL	ACTOR	6736 LAUREL CANYON BLVD #306	NORTH HOLLYWOOD, CA	91606
HAEBERLE, HORATIUS	SCREENWRITER	8955 BEVERLY BLVD	LOS ANGELES, CA	90048
HAEDERLE, THOMAS M	NEWS CORRESPONDENT	148 "G" ST, SW	WASHINGTON, DC	20024

Name	Occupation	Address	City/State	Zip
HAEFLIGER, ERNST	TENOR	COLBERT, 111 W 57TH ST	NEW YORK, NY	10019
HAENEN, ANNE	MEZZO-SOPRANO	59 E 54TH ST #81	NEW YORK, NY	10022
HAFFNER, CRAIG ALLEN	TV WRITER	4200 TEESDALE AVE	STUDIO CITY, CA	91604
HAGAN, CHET	TV WRITER	555 W 57TH ST #1230	NEW YORK, NY	10019
HAGAN, MOLLY	ACTRESS	8383 WILSHIRE BLVD #1024	BEVERLY HILLS, CA	90211
HAGAN, RICHARD M	NEWS CORRESPONDENT	419 E HOWELL AVE	ALEXANDRIA, VA	22301
HAGAR, SAMMY	SINGER-GUITARIST	9229 SUNSET BLVD #625	LOS ANGELES, CA	90069
HAGARD, J HARVEY	WRITER	5275 SEPULVEDA AVE	SAN BERNARDINO, CA	92404
HAGEGARD, HAKAN	BARITONE	59 E 54TH ST #81	NEW YORK, NY	10022
HAGEN, BEA	ACTRESS	120 S VICTORY BLVD #104	BURBANK, CA	91502
HAGEN, BETTY-JEAN	VIOLINIST	POST OFFICE BOX 188		
		STATION A	TORONTO, ONT	CANADA
HAGEN, E DEANE	COMPOSER	7900 SALE AVE	CANOGA PARK, CA	91304
HAGEN, EARLE	COMPOSER	23845 PARK BELMONTE	CALABASAS, CA	91302
HAGEN, KEVIN	ACTOR	8350 SANTA MONICA BLVD #103	LOS ANGELES, CA	90069
HAGEN, NINA	SINGER	FRONTIER BOOKING INTL		
		8600 MELROSE AVE	LOS ANGELES, CA	90069
HAGEN, ROSS	ACTOR	4721 LAUREL CANYON BLVD #211	NORTH HOLLYWOOD, CA	91607
HAGEN, STEPHANIE	ACTRESS	9255 SUNSET BLVD #603	LOS ANGELES, CA	90069
HAGEN, UTA	ACTRESS	KROLL, 390 W END AVE	NEW YORK, NY	10024
HAGER, GEORGE	NEWS CORRESPONDENT	703 "A" ST, NE	WASHINGTON, DC	20002
HAGER, JIM	SINGER-ACTOR	2057 LAUREL CANYON BLVD	LOS ANGELES, CA	90046
HAGER, JOAN BELL	SINGER	429 DAVIDSON RD	NASHVILLE, TN	37205
HAGER, JON	SINGER-ACTOR	8661 HOLLYWOOD BLVD	LOS ANGELES, CA	90069
HAGER, LEOPOLD	CONDUCTOR	59 E 54TH ST #81	NEW YORK, NY	10022
HAGER, MARY	NEWS CORRESPONDENT	1607 8TH PL	MC LEAN, VA	22101
HAGER, PHILIP	NEWS CORRESPONDENT	1607 8TH PL	MC LEAN, VA	22101
HAGER, ROBERT	NEWS CORRESPONDENT	NBC-TV, NEWS DEPARTMENT		
		4001 NEBRASKA AVE, NW	WASHINGTON, DC	20016
HAGERMAN, PAUL S	WRITER	555 W 57TH ST #1230	NEW YORK, NY	10019
HAGERS, THE	C & W DUO	POST OFFICE BOX 121153	NASHVILLE, TN	37212
HAGERTY, JULIE	ACTRESS	ICM, 8899 BEVERLY BLVD	NEW YORK, NY	90048
HAGGANDER, MARI-ANNE	SOPRANO	119 W 57TH ST #1505	NEW YORK, NY	10019
HAGGARD, MARTY	SINGER-SONGWRITER	17530 VENTURA BLVD #108	ENCINO, CA	91316
HAGGARD, MERLE	SINGER	6988 RAMLIN LN	BELLA VISTA, CA	96008
HAGGARD, NATHAN R	TV DIRECTOR	22255 NEEDLES ST	CHATSWORTH, CA	91311
HAGGARD, PAUL, JR	TV WRITER	8955 BEVERLY BLVD	LOS ANGELES, CA	90048
HAGGARD, PIERS	TV DIRECTOR	DOUGLAS RAE MANAGEMENT		
		28 CHARING CROSS RD	LONDON WC2	ENGLAND
HAGGARD, STEVE	SINGER	4 PARK AVE #7-N	NEW YORK, NY	10016
HAGGERTY, DAN	ACTOR	427 N CANON DR #205	BEVERLY HILLS, CA	90210
HAGGERTY, DON	ACTOR	7722 GREENBUSH AVE	VAN NUYS, CA	91402
HAGGERTY, H B	ACTOR	9744 WILSHIRE BLVD #306	BEVERLY HILLS, CA	90212
HAGGERTY, PATRICK B	NEWS CORRESPONDENT	9509 CLEMENT RD	SILVER SPRING, MD	20910
HAGGERTY, TIM	CARTOONIST	POST OFFICE BOX 4203	NEW YORK, NY	10017
HAGGIS, BLAKE	TV WRITER	555 W 57TH ST #1230	NEW YORK, NY	10019
HAGGIS, PAUL	TV WRITER	12804 HATTERAS ST	NORTH HOLLYWOOD, CA	91607
HAGIN, JOHN F	NEWS CORRESPONDENT	1080 WISCONSIN AVE, NW	WASHINGTON, DC	20007
HAGINS, MONTROSE	ACTRESS	1607 N EL CENTRO AVE #22	HOLLYWOOD, CA	90028
HAGLER, MARVELOUS MARVIN	BOXER	MARVELOUS ENTERPRISES		
		24 WARD ST	BROCKTON, MA	02401
HAGLUND, CECILIA	ACTRESS	204 W 14TH ST #5-A	NEW YORK, NY	10011
HAGLUND, KEITH ALAN	NEWS CORRESPONDENT	4900 VAN MASDAG CT	ANNANDALE, VA	22003
HAGMAN, HEIDI	ACTRESS	23730 MALIBU COLONY DR	MALIBU, CA	90265
HAGMAN, LARRY	ACTOR-DIRECTOR	23730 MALIBU COLONY DR	MALIBU, CA	90265
HAGMANN, STUART	FILM DIRECTOR	150 S WOODBURN DR	LOS ANGELES, CA	90049
HAGON, GARRICK	ACTOR	21 HILLIER RD	LONDON SW11	ENGLAND
HAGSTROM, BARBARA B	TV WRITER	CBS-TV, "AS THE WORLD TURNS"		
		51 W 52ND ST	NEW YORK, NY	10019
HAGSTROM, JERRY	NEWS CORRESPONDENT	2127 CALIFORNIA ST #104, NW	WASHINGTON, DC	20036
HAGUE, ALBERT	ACTOR-COMPOSER	4265 MARINA CITY DR #909	MARINA DEL REY, CA	90292
HAHN, ARCHIE	ACTOR	6380 WILSHIRE BLVD #910	LOS ANGELES, CA	90048
HAHN, DAVID W	DIRECTOR	33 RIVERSIDE DR	NEW YORK, NY	10023
HAHN, DIETER H	TV DIRECTOR	201 E 15TH ST #6-G	NEW YORK, NY	10003
HAHN, MARIAN	PIANIST	AARON, 25 HUNTINGTON AVE	BOSTON, MA	02116
HAHN, PAUL	ACTOR	3316 ROWENA AVE #3	LOS ANGELES, CA	90027
HAHN, PHIL H	TV WRITER	11845 KLING ST	NORTH HOLLYWOOD, CA	91607
HAHN, SUSAN L	NEWS CORRESPONDENT	4600 DUKE ST #1200	ALEXANDRIA, VA	22304
HAID, CHARLES	ACTOR-PRODUCER	4376 FORMAN AVE	NORTH HOLLYWOOD, CA	91602
HAID, DAVID	ACTOR	11726 SAN VICENTE BLVD #300	LOS ANGELES, CA	90049
HAIGH, KENNETH	ACTOR	REDWAY, 16 BERNERS ST	LONDON W1P 3DD	ENGLAND
HAIGHT, GORDON	ACTOR	1022 GALLOWAY ST	PACIFIC PALISADES, CA	90272
HAIGHT, LENNIE	VIOLINIST	POST OFFICE BOX 120163	NASHVILLE, TN	37212
HAILEY, ARTHUR	WRITER	POST OFFICE BOX N-7776, LYFOND	NASSAU	BAHAMAS
HAILEY, ELIZABETH F	WRITER	11747 CANTON PL	STUDIO CITY, CA	91604
HAILEY, OLIVER	SCREENWRITER	11747 CANTON PL	STUDIO CITY, CA	91604
HAIM, COREY	ACTOR	LIGHT, 113 N ROBERTSON BLVD	LOS ANGELES, CA	90048
HAIMOVITZ, JULES	CABLE EXECUTIVE	VIACOM INTERNATIONAL, INC		
		1211 AVE OF THE AMERICAS	NEW YORK, NY	10036
HAIMOVITZ, MATT	CELLIST	ICM, 40 W 57TH ST	NEW YORK, NY	10019
HAINES, CALVIN	DRUMMER	2120 BELMONT BLVD #C-3	NASHVILLE, TN	37212
HAINES, CHARLES T	MUSIC ARRANGER	ROUTE #3, BOX 369, MIRES RD	MOUNT JULIET, TN	37122
HAINES, CONNIE	SINGER	POPST OFFICE BOX 1	TOLUCA LAKE, CA	91602
HAINES, F L "ROY"	COMPOSER-CONDUCTOR	7726 JAMIESON AVE	RESEDA, CA	91335
HAINES, LARRY	ACTOR	HIDDEN MEADOW RD	WESTON, CT	06883

MERLE HAGGARD

DAN HAGGERTY

CONNIE HAINES

MONTE HALE

JACKIE EARLE HALEY

HUNTZ HALL

DOROTHY HAMILL

TOM HANKS

TY HARDIN

Name	Occupation	Address	City	Zip
HAINES, RANDA	TV DIRECTOR	1429 AVON PARK TERR	LOS ANGELES, CA	90026
HAINES, ROB	GUITARIST	612 TEMPLEWOOD DR	NASHVILLE, TN	37214
HAINES, WILLIAM W	WRITER	8955 BEVERLY BLVD	LOS ANGELES, CA	90048
HAINES-STILES, GEOFFREY	TV DIRECTOR	776 S MADISION AVE	PASADENA, CA	91106
HAINING, MARK	ACTOR	2491 N GOWER ST	LOS ANGELES, CA	90068
HAIRCUT ONE HUNDRED	ROCK & ROLL GROUP	T B A INTERNATIONAL		
		24 HANOVER SQ	LONDON W1	ENGLAND
HAIRSTON, CURTIS	SINGER	130 W 57TH ST #8-B	NEW YORK, NY	10019
HAIRSTON, HAROLD "HAPPY"	ACTOR-BASKETBALL	13222 ADMIRAL AVE #G	MARINA DEL REY, CA	90292
HAIRSTON, JESTER	ACTOR	5047 VALLEY RIDGE AVE	LOS ANGELES, CA	90043
HAIRSTON, ROBERT L	NEWS CORRESPONDENT	9209 CONSTANTINE DR	FORT WASHINGTON, MD	20744
HAJACOS, ROBERT	FIDDLER	231 IRIS DR	HENDERSONVILLE, TN	37075
HAJAK, RON	ACTOR	208 S BEVERLY DR #4	BEVERLY HILLS, CA	90212
HAJE, KHRYSTYNE	ACTRESS	9000 SUNSET BLVD #801	LOS ANGELES, CA	90069
HAKE, ARDELL B	COMPOSER	5306 LA FOREST DR	LA CANADA, CA	91011
HAKEL, PETER J	PHOTOJOUNRLAIST	6041 CHESHIRE DR	BETHESDA, MD	20814
HAKOBIAN, ALEX	SCREENWRITER	4528 VISTA DEL MONTE #6	SHERMAN OAKS, CA	91403
HAKOSHIMA, YASS	MIME	POST OFFICE BOX 884	NEW YORK, NY	10023
HAKU	WRESTLER	POST OFFICE BOX 3859	STAMFORD, CT	06905
HAKU, ISLANDER	WRESTLER	SEE - TONGA, KING		
HALAS, JOHN	FILM PRODUCER	EDUCATIONAL FILM CENTRE		
		3-7 KEAN ST	LONDON WC2	ENGLAND
HALASZ, GEORGE	WRITER	332 BONHILL RD	LOS ANGELES, CA	90049
HALASZ, LASZLO	CONDUCTOR	3 LEEDS DR	PORT WASHINGTON, NY	11050
HALBROOK, CELESTE	PIANIST	4403 SUNNYBROOK DR	NASHVILLE, TN	37205
HALDEMAN, H R	AUTHOR-POLITICAN	443 N MC CADDEN PL	LOS ANGELES, CA	90004
HALDEMAN, JOE W	WRITER	555 W 57TH ST #1230	NEW YORK, NY	10019
HALDEMAN, TIM	ACTOR	4257 LINCOLN AVE	CULVER CITY, CA	90230
HALE, ALAN	ACTOR	1418 N ORANGE GROVE AVE	LOS ANGELES, CA	90046
HALE, BARBARA	ACTRESS	14155 MAGNOLIA BLVD #4	SHERMAN OAKS, CA	91403
HALE, BERNADETTE	ACTRESS	1327 N VISTA ST	LOS ANGELES, CA	90046
HALE, BILLY	TV DIRECTOR	151 S EL CAMINO DR	BEVERLY HILLS, CA	90212
HALE, CHERYL	SINGER	POST OFFICE BOX 282	HARTSELLE, AL	35640
HALE, DIANA	ACTRESS	1327 N VISTA ST	LOS ANGELES, CA	90046
HALE, ELLEN	NEWS CORRESPONDENT	2800 ONTARIO RD, NW	WASHINGTON, DC	20009
HALE, FRANK G	WRITER	8955 BEVERLY BLVD	LOS ANGELES, CA	90048
HALE, GEORGINA	ACTRESS	74-A SAINT JOHNS		
		WOOD HIGH ST	LONDON NW8	ENGLAND
HALE, HELEN	ACTRESS	166 W 75TH ST	NEW YORK, NY	10023
HALE, JEAN	ACTRESS	401 SURFVIEW AVE	PACIFIC PALISADES, CA	90272
HALE, MONTE	ACTOR	POST OFFICE BOX 1960	SANTA MONICA, CA	90406
HALE, ROBERT	BASSO-BARITONE	1776 BROADWAY #504	NEW YORK, NY	10019
HALE, RON	ACTOR	ABC-TV, "RYAN'S HOPE"		
		1330 AVE OF THE AMERICAS	NEW YORK, NY	10019
HALE, SCOTT	ACTOR-WRITER	8955 BEVERLY BLVD	LOS ANGELES, CA	90048
HALE, WILLIAM B	TV DIRECTOR	9601 WILSHIRE BLVD #642	BEVERLY HILLS, CA	90210
HALEY, ALEX	AUTHOR	POST OFFICE BOX 3338	BEVERLY HILLS, CA	90213
HALEY, HAROLD D	WRITER	555 W 57TH ST #1230	NEW YORK, NY	10019
HALEY, JACK, JR	WRITER-PRODUCER	1443 DEVLIN DR	LOS ANGELES, CA	90069
HALEY, JACKIE EARLE	ACTOR	22716 LEADWELL ST	CANOGA PARK, CA	91307
HALEY, WILLIAM	MUSICIAN	111 ACKLEN PARK DR #A-2	NASHVILLE, TN	37203
HALEY'S, BILL, COMETS	ROCK & ROLL GROUP	2011 FERRY AVE #U-19	CAMDEN, NJ	08104
HALFORD, BRUCE B	DIRECTOR	2549 N CATALINA ST	LOS ANGELES, CA	90027
HALFVARSON, ERIC	BASSO-BARITONE	MUNRO, 334 W 72ND ST	NEW YORK, NY	10023
HALICKI, H B	FILM PRODUCER	18511 S MARIPOSA AVE	GARDENA, CA	90248
HALL, ADRIAN	DIRECTOR	176 PLEASANT ST	PROVIDENCE, RI	02906
HALL, ADRIAN	WRITER	555 W 57TH ST #1230	NEW YORK, NY	10019
HALL, ALBERT	ACTOR	11726 SAN VICENTE BLVD #300	LOS ANGELES, CA	90049
HALL, ANTHONY MICHAEL	ACTOR	9200 SUNSET BLVD #1210	LOS ANGELES, CA	90069
HALL, BARBARA E	TV WRITER	8955 BEVERLY BLVD	LOS ANGELES, CA	90048
HALL, BRUCE	ACTOR	CRESCENT DR	HOPEWELL JUNCTION, NY	12533
HALL, BRUCE	NEWS CORRESPONDENT	CBS NEWS, 524 W 57TH ST	NEW YORK, NY	10019
HALL, CARLA RIGGS	SINGER-SONGWRITER	SEE - RIGGS-HALL, CARLA		
HALL, CHERYL	ACTRESS	DEWOLFE, 1 ROBERT ST	LONDON WC2N 6BH	ENGLAND
HALL, CONRAD L	DIRECTOR	1310 N SWEETZER AVE #60	LOS ANGELES, CA	90069
HALL, DARYL	SINGER-SONGWRITER	130 W 57TH ST #2-A	NEW YORK, NY	10019
HALL, DAVID	TV EXECUTIVE	THE NASHVILLE NETWORK		
		2806 OPRYLAND DR	NASHVILLE, TN	37214
HALL, DEAN	CINEMATOGRAPHER	7715 SUNSET BLVD #1150	LOS ANGELES, CA	90046
HALL, DEIDRE	ACTRESS	13201 BLOOMFIELD ST	SHERMAN OAKS, CA	91423
HALL, DELORES	ENTERTAINER	APA, 120 W 57TH ST	NEW YORK, NY	10019
HALL, DONALD L	TV WRITER	8955 BEVERLY BLVD	LOS ANGELES, CA	90048
HALL, FAWN	SECRETARY-MODEL	ERICKSON MODELING AGENCY		
		1483 CHAIN BRIDGE RD	MC LEAN, VA	22101
HALL, GARY L	DIRECTOR	2203 MICHELTORENA ST	LOS ANGELES, CA	90039
HALL, HARRIET	ACTRESS	9255 SUNSET BLVD #603	LOS ANGELES, CA	90069
HALL, HARRY GUY	COMPOSER	968 1/2 W KENSINGTON RD	LOS ANGELES, CA	90026
HALL, HARRY S	WRITER	8955 BEVERLY BLVD	LOS ANGELES, CA	90048
HALL, HUNTZ	ACTOR	12512 CHANDLER BLVD #307	NORTH HOLLYWOOD, CA	91607
HALL, J D	ACTOR	3800 BARHAM BLVD #303	LOS ANGELES, CA	90068
HALL, JAMES	ACTOR	7060 HOLLYWOOD BLVD #610	LOS ANGELES, CA	90028
HALL, JAMES	GUITARIST-SONGWRITER	49 W 12TH ST	NEW YORK, NY	10011
HALL, JAMES ANDREW	TV WRITER	49 RICHMOND PARK AVE		
		BOURNEMOUTH	DORSET	ENGLAND
HALL, JAMES LEWES	MUSIC ARRANGER	8106 WIKLE RD	BRENTWOOD, TN	37027

HALL, JAMES M	TV WRITER	8955 BEVERLY BLVD	LOS ANGELES, CA 90048
HALL, JANICE	SOPRANO	CAMI, 165 W 57TH ST	NEW YORK, NY 10019
HALL, JERRY	MODEL	81 WIMPLE ST	LONDON W1 ENGLAND
HALL, JIM	GUITARIST	KURLAND, 173 BRIGHTON AVE	BOSTON, MA 02134
HALL, JIMMY	SAXOPHONIST	3632 MAYFLOWER PL	NASHVILLE, TN 37204
HALL, JIMMY	SINGER	8106 WILKE RD	BRENTWOOD, TN 37027
HALL, JOHN	TV WRITER	8955 BEVERLY BLVD	LOS ANGELES, CA 90048
HALL, JOHN	NEWS CORRESPONDENT	7125 CAROL LN	FALLS CHURCH, VA 22041
HALL, JOHN BARRACIOUG	DIRECTOR	DGA, 110 W 57TH ST	NEW YORK, NY 10019
HALL, JOHNNY	SINGER	6750 W 75TH ST, MARKADE 75	
		BUILDING #2-A	OVERLAND PARK, KS 66204
HALL, JOSEPH L	DIRECTOR-PRODUCER	80 THUNDER RD	HOLBROOK, NY 11741
HALL, KAREN	TV WRITER	BRODER, 9046 SUNSET BLVD	LOS ANGELES, CA 90056
HALL, LANI	SINGER-SONGWRITER	SEE - HALL ALPERT, LANI	
HALL, LEONARD E	PIANIST	1913 ELECTRIC AVE	NASHVILLE, TN 37206
HALL, LOIS	ACTRESS	8961 SUNSET BLVD #B	LOS ANGELES, CA 90069
HALL, MARTIN	TV WRITER-PRODUCER	MASTERSCREEN ENTERTAINMENT	
		LORRIMER HOUSE, 47 DEAN ST	LONDON W1 ENGLAND
HALL, MATTHEW	WRITER	555 W 57TH ST #1230	NEW YORK, NY 10019
HALL, MONTY	TV HOST	519 N ARDEN DR	BEVERLY HILLS, CA 90210
HALL, NORMAN	TV DIRECTOR	11 AMHERST RD	GREAT NECK, NY 11021
HALL, PARNELL	SCREENWRITER	555 W 57TH ST #1230	NEW YORK, NY 10019
HALL, PETER	FILM DIRECTOR	WALL HOUSE, MONGEWELL PARK	
		WALLINGFORD	BERKS ENGLAND
HALL, PHILIP BAKER	ACTOR	5160 1/2 CLINTON ST	LOS ANGELES, CA 90004
HALL, RANDY	SINGER	1888 CENTURY PARK E #1400	LOS ANGELES, CA 90067
HALL, RICH T	ACT-COMED-WRI	POST OFFICE BOX 2350	HOLLYWOOD, CA 90078
HALL, RICHARD D	WRITER	555 W 57TH ST #1230	NEW YORK, NY 10019
HALL, ROBERT E	TV DIRECTOR	3591 WINCROSS DR	MEMPHIS, TN 38119
HALL, RUTH	ACTRESS	422 ALANDALE AVE	LOS ANGELES, CA 90036
HALL, SAM	TV WRITER	555 W 57TH ST #1230	NEW YORK, NY 10019
HALL, SANDS	ACTOR	3739 MULTIVIEW DR	LOS ANGELES, CA 90068
HALL, SCOTT	WRESTLER	AMERICAN WRESTLING ASSOC	
		MINNEAPLOIS WRESTLING	
		10001 WAYZATA BLVD	MINNETONKA, MN 55345
HALL, SHASHAWNEE	ACTOR	3800 BARHAM BLVD #303	LOS ANGELES, CA 90068
HALL, STEVEN	PIANIST	POST OFFICE BOX 450727	ATLANTA, GA 30345
HALL, SUSAN	FILM PRODUCER	200 W 58TH ST	NEW YORK, NY 10019
HALL, TERRY	TV PERSONAL	93 GRANGE RD, SOLIHULL	WEST MIDLANDS B91 1B2 ENGLAND
HALL, THOMAS M	VIOLINIST	2800 LAKE SHORE DR #320	CHICAGO, IL 60657
HALL, TOM T	SINGER-SONGWRITER	1512 HAWKINS ST	NASHVILLE, TN 37203
HALL, VICTOR O	CONDUCTOR	13921 BESSEMER ST #20	VAN NUYS, CA 91401
HALL, W S	MUSICIAN	8106 WIKLE RD	BRENTWOOD, TN 37027
HALL, WILLIE	GUITARIST	306 VILLAGE GREEN DR	NASHVILLE, TN 37217
HALL, WILLIS	PLAYWRIGHT	LONDON MANAGEMENT, LTD	
		235-241 REGENT ST	LONDON W1A 2JT ENGLAND
HALL & OATES	ROCK & ROCK DUO	130 W 57TH ST #2-A	NEW YORK, NY 10019
HALL ALPERT, LANI	SINGER-SONGWRITER	31930 PACIFIC COAST HWY	MALIBU, CA 90265
HALLAHAN, CHARLES	ACTOR	10100 SANTA MONICA BLVD #1600	LOS ANGELES, CA 90067
HALLAM, JOHN	ACTOR	51 LANSDOWNE GARDENS	LONDON SW8 ENGLAND
HALLANAN, D BLAKE	NEWS REPORTER	TIME/TIME & LIFE BLDG	
		ROCKEFELLER CENTER	NEW YORK, NY 10020
HALLAREN, JANE	ACTRESS	11726 SAN VICENTE BLVD #300	LOS ANGELES, CA 90049
HALLER, DANIEL	TV DIRECTOR	5364 JED SMITH RD	HIDDEN HILLS, CA 91302
HALLER, SCOTT	FILM CRITIC-WRITER	PEOPLE/TIME & LIFE BLDG	
		ROCKEFELLER CENTER	NEW YORK, NY 10020
HALLEY, GUSTAVO	SINGER	45 W 60TH ST #4-K	NEW YORK, NY 10023
HALLICK, TOM	ACTOR	13900 TAHITI WY	MARINA DEL REY, CA 90292
HALLIDAY, AL & THE HURRICANES	ROCK & ROLL GROUP	25 HUNTINGTON AVE #420	BOSTON, MA 02116
HALLIGAN, PEG	CASTING DIRECTOR	REUBEN CANNON & ASSOCIATES	
		7083 HOLLYWOOD BLVD	LOS ANGELES, CA 90028
HALLIGAN, RICHARD B	COMPOSER	2509 ROSCOMARE RD	LOS ANGELES, CA 90024
HALLIWELL, LESLIE	AUTHOR	GRANADA, 36 GOLDEN SQ	LONDON W1 ENGLAND
HALLORAN, RICHARD	NEWS CORRESPONDENT	2939 VAN NESS ST, NW	WASHINGTON, DC 20008
HALLOW, RALPH Z	NEWS CORRESPONDENT	4600 CONNECTICUT AVE #924, NW	WASHINGTON, DC 20008
HALLS, CLIVE	TV DIRECTOR	6 CEDAR RD, BARNES	LONDON SW13 ENGLAND
HALLSTROM, HOLLY	MODEL	8901 WONDERLAND AVE	LOS ANGELES, CA 90046
HALLYDAY, JOHNNY	SINGER	16 AVE DU PDT WILSON	PARIS 75116 FRANCE
HALMI, ROBERT, JR	TV PRODUCER	ICM, 889 BEVERLY BLVD	LOS ANGELES, CA 90048
HALMOS, E E, JR	NEWS CORRESPONDENT	POST OFFICE BOX 132	POLLESVILLE, MD 20837
HALMOS, ROZSIKA	ACTRESS	6380 WILSHIRE BLVD #1600	LOS ANGELES, CA 90048
HALONEN, DOUGLAS J	NEWS CORRESPONDENT	2000 N CALVERT ST #2	ARLINGTON, VA 22201
HALPER, ROBERT M	TV DIRECTOR	250 W 94TH ST	NEW YORK, NY 10025
HALPERIN, MICHAEL H	TV WRITER	3610 STONE CANYON AVE	SHERMAN OAKS, CA 91403
HALPERN, ANN	ACTRESS	8961 SUNSET BLVD #B	LOS ANGELES, CA 90069
HALPERN, DR HOWARD	COLUMNIST	N Y TIMES SYNDICATION	
		130 5TH AVE	NEW YORK, NY 10011
HALPERN, MEREDITH A	NEWS CORRESPONDENT	400 NATIONAL PRESS BLDG	
		529 14TH ST, NW	WASHINGTON, DC 20045
HALSEY, BRETT	ACTOR	141 N GRAND AVE	PASADENA, CA 91103
HALSEY, JAMES	TALENT AGENT	3225 S NORWOOD AVE	TULSA, OK 74135
HALSEY, SHERMAN	TALENT AGENT	POST OFFICE BOX 4003	BEVERLY HILLS, CA 90213
HALSTEAD, DIRCK	PHOTOGRAPHER	3332 "P" ST, NW	WASHINGTON, DC 20007
HALSTED, DANA	ACTRESS	3151 W CAHUENGA BLVD #310	LOS ANGELES, CA 90068
HALTON, PETER	ACTOR	560 GLENWOOD RD #205	GLENDALE, CA 91202

HALTON, TONY	DIRECTOR	JENNIE, 127 W 79TH ST	NEW YORK, NY	10024
HALVORSON, GARY A	TV DIRECTOR	136 LAWRENCE ST	BROOKLYN, NY	11201
HAM, LARRY	COLUMNIST	TRIBUNE MEDIA SERVICES		
		64 E CONCORD ST	ORLANDO, FL	32801
HAM, ROD	GUITARIST	6001 OLD HICKORY BLVD #29	HERMITAGE, TN	37076
HAMAGUCHI, TED TETSUO	ACTOR	5152 MARATHON ST	LOS ANGELES, CA	90038
HAMALAINEN, ALOYSIA CATHERINE	NEWS CORRESPONDENT	7911 FENTON ST	SILVER SPRING, MD	20910
HAMARI, JULIA	MEZZO-SOPRANO	61 W 62ND ST #6-F	NEW YORK, NY	10023
HAMATY, EMILE	ACTOR	1914 N ALEXANDRIA AVE	LOS ANGELES, CA	90027
HAMBLEN, STUART	SINGER	POST OFFICE BOX 8085	UNIVERSAL CITY, CA	91608
HAMBLEN, SUZY	SINGER	POST OFFICE BOX 8085	UNIVERSAL CITY, CA	91608
HAMBLETON, T EDWARD	THEATER PRODUCER	1640 BROADWAY	NEW YORK, NY	10019
HAMBRICK, MICHAEL K	NEWS CORRESPONDENT	NBC NEWS, 4001 NEBRASKA AVE, NW	WASHINGTON, DC	20016
HAMBURG, HARRY	DIRECTOR	DGA, 7950 SUNSET BLVD	LOS ANGELES, CA	90046
HAMBURG, HARRY	PHOTOGRAPHER	1012 YARDLEY RD	YARDLEY, PA	19067
HAMBURGER STEW	GUITARIST	SEE - HAMMOND, HAMBURGER STEW		
HAMEL, ALAN	TV PERSONALITY	10342 MISSISSIPPI AVE	LOS ANGELES, CA	90025
HAMEL, VERONICA	ACTRESS	129 N WOODBURN DR	LOS ANGELES, CA	90049
HAMELINE, GERARD	DIRECTOR	DGA, 110 W 57TH ST	NEW YORK, NY	10019
HAMER, JOSEPH	ACTOR	10 E 44TH ST #700	NEW YORK, NY	10017
HAMER, RUSTY	ACTOR	GENERAL DELIVERY	DE RIDDER, LA	70634
HAMERMAN, MILT	CASTING DIRECTOR	MCA/UNIVERSAL STUDIOS, INC		
		100 UNIVERSAL CITY PLAZA	UNIVERSAL CITY, CA	91608
HAMERSKI, THOMAS L	NEWS CORRESPONDENT	8065 ROUND MOON CIR	JESSUP, MD	20794
HAMILL, DOROTHY	SKATER	2569 BENEDICT CANYON DR	BEVERLY HILLS, CA	90210
HAMILL, MARK	ACTOR	POST OFFICE BOX 55	MALIBU, CA	90265
HAMILL, PETE	WRITER	555 W 57TH ST #1230	NEW YORK, NY	10019
HAMILTON, ANDREW M	GUITARIST	308 PANAMINT DR	ANTIOCH, TN	37013
HAMILTON, BERNIE	ACTOR	1272 WEST BLVD	LOS ANGELES, CA	90019
HAMILTON, CHICO, QUINTET	JAZZ QUINTET	ARTHUR SHAFMAN INTL		
		723 7TH AVE	NEW YORK, NY	10019
HAMILTON, COLIN	ACTOR	3518 W CAHUENGA BLVD #316	LOS ANGELES, CA	90068
HAMILTON, DAN	ACTOR	500 S SEPULVEDA BLVD #510	LOS ANGELES, CA	90049
HAMILTON, DAVID	BARITONE	LEW, 204 W 10TH ST	NEW YORK, NY	10014
HAMILTON, DAVID	TV-RADIO PERSONALITY	MPC ARTISTS, 113 WARDOUR ST	LONDON W1	ENGLAND
HAMILTON, DAVID C	NEWS CORRESPONDENT	5251 RIDGE CT	FAIRFAX, VA	22032
HAMILTON, DEAN	ACTOR	1100 N ALTA LOMA RD #707	LOS ANGELES, CA	90069
HAMILTON, E THOMAS	GUITARIST	4008 COLORADO AVE	NASHVILLE, TN	37209
HAMILTON, GAY	ACTRESS	26 OAK GROVE	LONDON NW2 3LP	ENGLAND
HAMILTON, GEORGE	ACTOR	4770 KESTER AVE	SHERMAN OAKS, CA	91403
HAMILTON, GEORGE, IV	SINGER	POST OFFICE BOX 727	MATTHEWS, NC	28105
HAMILTON, GUY	FILM DIRECTOR	LONDON MANAGEMENT, LTD		
		235-241 REGENT ST	LONDON W1A 2JT	ENGLAND
HAMILTON, IAIN	COMPOSER	40 PARK AVE	NEW YORK, NY	10016
HAMILTON, JAMES	SCREENWRITER	8955 BEVERLY BLVD	LOS ANGELES, CA	90048
HAMILTON, JOE	TV DIRECTOR-PRODUCER	991 N ALPINE DR	BEVERLY HILLS, CA	90210
HAMILTON, JOHN F	PIANIST	1020 CLEARVIEW DR	MOUNT JULIET, TN	37122
HAMILTON, KIM	ACTRESS	7466 BEVERLY BLVD #205	LOS ANGELES, CA	90036
HAMILTON, LAURA	VIOLINIST	POST OFFICE BOX 20548	NEW YORK, NY	10025
HAMILTON, LEIGH	ACTRESS	11726 SAN VICENTE BLVD #300	LOS ANGELES, CA	90049
HAMILTON, LINDA	ACTRESS	10100 SANTA MONICA BLVD #1600	LOS ANGELES, CA	90067
HAMILTON, LYNN	ACTRESS	4721 LAUREL CANYON BLVD #211	NORTH HOLLYWOOD, CA	91607
HAMILTON, MARTHA M	NEWS CORRESPONDENT	3615 ALBEMARLE ST, NW	WASHINGTON, DC	20008
HAMILTON, MICHAEL S	DIRECTOR	637-D WESTBOURNE DR	LOS ANGELES, CA	90069
HAMILTON, RANDY	ACTOR	LIGHT, 113 N ROBERTSON BLVD	LOS ANGELES, CA	90048
HAMILTON, RICHARD W	ACTOR	10100 SANTA MONICA BLVD #1600	LOS ANGELES, CA	90067
HAMILTON, RICHARD, JR	COMPOSER	412 S MC CADDEN PL	LOS ANGELES, CA	90020
HAMILTON, ROBERT	TV WRITER	8955 BEVERLY BLVD	LOS ANGELES, CA	90048
HAMILTON, ROBERT K	PHOTOGRAPHER	10914 MAIDEN DR	BOWIE, MD	20715
HAMILTON, ROBERTA A	FLUTIST	308 PANAMINT DR	NASHVILLE, TN	37211
HAMILTON, TAMMAS J	PHOTOGRAPHER	1611 45TH ST, NW	WASHINGTON, DC	20007
HAMILTON, TOM	SINGER	10 THE LEDGES RD	NEWTON, MA	02158
HAMILTON, WARREN W, JR	WRITER	8955 BEVERLY BLVD	LOS ANGELES, CA	90048
HAMILTON, WILLIAM	CARTOONIST	400 W 43RD ST	NEW YORK, NY	10036
HAMLET, BRENDA	WRITER	555 W 57TH ST #1230	NEW YORK, NY	10019
HAMLETT, JACKSON	DRUMMER	357 WALES DR	NASHVILLE, TN	37211
HAMLIN, HARRY	ACTOR	8185 GOULD AVE	LOS ANGELES, CA	90046
HAMLIN, JOHN	TV EXECUTIVE	ABC-TV, 4151 PROSPECT AVE	LOS ANGELES, CA	90027
HAMLISCH, MARVIN	COMPOSER-PIANIST	22024 PACIFIC COAST HWY	MALIBU, CA	90265
HAMLYN, MICHAEL	TV PRODUCER	MIDNIGHT FILMS COMPANY		
		1-2 SLINGSBY PL, LONG ACRE	LONDON EC2	ENGLAND
HAMM, CHARLIE	GUITARIST	309 WINDEMERE DR	STAUNTON, VA	24401
HAMM, LISA M	NEWS CORRESPONDENT	4614 38TH ST, NW	WASHINGTON, DC	20016
HAMM, RICK	DRUMMER	1719 ALLISON PL	NASHVILLE, TN	37203
HAMM, SAM	SCREENWRITER	EISENBACH-GREENE, INC		
		760 N LA CIENEGA BLVD	LOS ANGELES, CA	90069
HAMMAN, SKEETER	SINGER	CUDE, 519 N HALIFAX AVE	DAYTONA BEACH, FL	32018
HAMMER, ALVIN	ACTOR	8514 LOOKOUT MOUNTAIN AVE	LOS ANGELES, CA	90046
HAMMER, BEN	ACTOR	6310 SAN VICENTE BLVD #407	LOS ANGELES, CA	90048
HAMMER, CHARLES J	WRITER	555 W 57TH ST #1230	NEW YORK, NY	10019
HAMMER, DENNIS	TV PRODUCER	AARON SPELLING PRODUCTIONS		
		1041 N FORMOSA AVE	LOS ANGELES, CA	90046
HAMMER, HACKENSACK	WRESTLER	SEE - WOLFE, BUDDY		
HAMMER, JAN	SINGER-SONGWRITER	2 W 45TH ST #1102	NEW YORK, NY	10036
HAMMER, JAY	ACTOR	247 S BEVERLY DR #102	BEVERLY HILLS, CA	90210

Name	Occupation	Address	City	Zip
HAMMER, MICHAEL J	NEWS CORRESPONDENT	2950 VAN NESS ST, NW	WASHINGTON, DC	20008
HAMMER, PAMELA L	TV WRITER	555 W 57TH ST #1230	NEW YORK, NY	10019
HAMMER, RICHARD	WRITER	555 W 57TH ST #1230	NEW YORK, NY	10019
HAMMERSTEIN, JANE-HOWARD	WRITER	9255 SUNSET BLVD #505	LOS ANGELES, CA	90069
HAMMETT, MIKE	ACTOR	10982 ROEBLING AVE #308	LOS ANGELES, CA	90024
HAMMIL, JOEL	WRITER	2743 ELLISON DR	BEVERLY HILLS, CA	90210
HAMMILL, PETER	SINGER-GUITARIST	POST OFFICE BOX 2428	EL SEGUNDO, CA	90245
HAMMOND, ALBERT	SINGER-SONGWRITER	9200 SUNSET BLVD #1215	LOS ANGELES, CA	90069
HAMMOND, BILLY	ACTOR	471-C RIVERSIDE DR	BURBANK, CA	91505
HAMMOND, BRAD	WRITER	8955 BEVERLY BLVD	LOS ANGELES, CA	90048
HAMMOND, BRUCE	CARTOONIST	UNIVERSAL PRESS SYNDICATE		
		4900 MAIN ST, 9TH FLOOR	KANSAS CITY, MO	62114
HAMMOND, CHUCK	GUITARIST	699 W 239TH ST #2-C	RIVERDALE, NY	10463
HAMMOND, DIANA	TV WRITER	8955 BEVERLY BLVD	LOS ANGELES, CA	90048
HAMMOND, H J	WRITER	8955 BEVERLY BLVD	LOS ANGELES, CA	90048
HAMMOND, HAMBURGER STEW	GUITARIST	2547 MURFREESBORO RD	NASHVILLE, TN	37217
HAMMOND, JOHN	SINGER-GUITARIST	POST OFFICE BOX 210103	SAN FRANCISCO, CA	94121
HAMMOND, JON M	DIRECTOR	DGA, 110 W 57TH ST	NEW YORK, NY	10019
HAMMOND, JULIET	ACTRESS	MARGARET RAMSAY, LTD		
		14-A GOODWINS CT		
		SAINT MARTINS LN	LONDON WC2N 4LL	ENGLAND
HAMMOND, MARGO	ACTRESS	DMI, 250 W 57TH ST	NEW YORK, NY	10107
HAMMOND, MARK	ACTOR	1253 N HAVENHURST DR #204	LOS ANGELES, CA	90046
HAMMOND, MARK F	DRUMMER	2423 KIMBERLY DR	NASHVILLE, TN	37214
HAMMOND, NICHOLAS	ACTOR	16413 AKRON ST	PACIFIC PALISADES, CA	90272
HAMMOND, PETER	TV PRODUCER	ENTERTAINMENT TONIGHT		
		PARAMOUNT TELEVISION		
		5555 MELROSE AVE	LOS ANGELES, CA	90038
HAMMOND, PETER	WRITER-PRODUCER	CHATTO & LINNIT, LTD		
		PRINCE OF WALES THEATRE		
		COVENTRY ST	LONDON WC2	ENGLAND
HAMMOND, PETER R	TV WRITER	8955 BEVERLY BLVD	LOS ANGELES, CA	90048
HAMMOND, VERNON	TALENT AGENT	POST OFFICE BOX 55398	WASHINGTON, DC	20040
HAMMONS, PAUL A	WRITER-PRODUCER	45 W 60TH ST #23-F	NEW YORK, NY	10023
HAMMONS, THOMAS	BASSO-BARITONE	POST OFFICE BOX 884	NEW YORK, NY	10023
HAMNER, EARL	TV WRITER-PRODUCER	11575 AMANDA DR	STUDIO CITY, CA	91604
HAMNER, J GARY	TV WRITER	167 1/2 S SYCAMORE AVE	LOS ANGELES, CA	90036
HAMNER, LINDA ELIN	TV WRITER	167 1/2 S SYCAMORE AVE	LOS ANGELES, CA	90036
HAMNER, ROBERT	WRITER-PRODUCER	268 S LASKY DR #304	BEVERLY HILLS, CA	90212
HAMNER, SARA	WRITER	555 W 57TH ST #1230	NEW YORK, NY	10019
HAMNER, SCOTT M	TV WRITER	CONTEMPORARY ARTISTS		
		132 S LASKY DR	BEVERLY HILLS, CA	90212
HAMNETT, KATHARINE	FASHION DESIGNER	83 SHEPPERTON RD	LONDON N1	ENGLAND
HAMPLE, STUART E	WRITER	555 W 57TH ST #1230	NEW YORK, NY	10019
HAMPSHIRE, SUSAN	ACTRESS	BILLING RD	LONDON SW10	ENGLAND
HAMPSON, THOMAS	BARITONE	CAMI, 165 W 57TH ST	NEW YORK, NY	10019
HAMPTON, BONNIE	CELLIST	1182 MARKET ST #311	SAN FRANCISCO, CA	94102
HAMPTON, CHRISTOPHER	SCREENWRITER	MARGARET RAMSAY, LTD		
		14-A GOODWINS CT		
		SAINT MARTINS LN	LONDON WC2N 4LL	ENGLAND
HAMPTON, DEBORRA	ACTRESS	LEONETTI, 6526 SUNSET BLVD	HOLLYWOOD, CA	90028
HAMPTON, GEORGE	WRITER	8955 BEVERLY BLVD	LOS ANGELES, CA	90048
HAMPTON, HENRY	VIOLINIST	917 HUROUTE DR	NASHVILLE, TN	37214
HAMPTON, JAMES	ACTOR-WRITER	8955 BEVERLY BLVD	LOS ANGELES, CA	90048
HAMPTON, LIONEL	MUSICIAN	20 W 64TH ST #28-K	NEW YORK, NY	10023
HAMPTON, ORVILLE	SCREENWRITER	1033 6TH ST #302	SANTA MONICA, CA	90403
HAMPTON, PAUL	ACTOR	9000 SUNSET BLVD #801	LOS ANGELES, CA	90069
HAMPTON, ROGER	ACTOR	321 CAMERON PL #5	GLENDALE, CA	91207
HAMPTON, TERRY WAYNE	SINGER-GUITARIST	POST OFFICE BOX 101	GREENBRIER, TN	37073
HAMPTON, TIM	FILM PRODUCER	HATTON HOUSE, HATTON HILL		
		WINDLESHAM	SURREY	ENGLAND
HAMRICK, DONALD	TENOR	253 W 73RD ST #7-M	NEW YORK, NY	10023
HAN, MAGGIE	ACTRESS	9200 SUNSET BLVD #1210	LOS ANGELES, CA	90069
HANALIS, BLANCHE	SCREENWRITER	14144 VENTURA BLVD #200	SHERMAN OAKS, CA	91423
HANANI, YEHUDA	CELLIST	AIA, 60 E 42ND ST	NEW YORK, NY	10165
HANCHETTE, JOHN M	NEWS CORRESPONDENT	2658 CARROLLTON RD	ANNAPOLIS, MD	21403
HANCOCK, BUTCH	SINGER	ATS MGMT, 3300 HOLLYWOOD AVE	AUSTIN, TX	78722
HANCOCK, DAVID	GUITARIST	127 ARMAND DR	SAVALAND, AL	36571
HANCOCK, HERBIE	PIANIST-COMPOSER	1250 N DOHENY DR	LOS ANGELES, CA	90069
HANCOCK, JOHN D	FILM WRITER-DIRECTOR	21531 DEERPATH LN	MALIBU, CA	90265
HANCOCK, PRENTIS	ACTOR	7 ELM PARK GARDENS #23		
		CHELSEA	LONDON SW10	ENGLAND
HAND, CHIP	WRITER	8955 BEVERLY BLVD	LOS ANGELES, CA	90048
HANDEL, LEO A	DIRECTOR	8730 SUNSET BLVD	LOS ANGELES, CA	90069
HANDELMAN, DAVID	FILM EXECUTIVE	600 BONHILL RD	LOS ANGELES, CA	90049
HANDELMAN, STANLEY MYRON	ACT-WRI-COMED	5922 WOODMAN AVE #10	VAN NUYS, CA	91401
HANDELSMAN, J B	CARTOONIST	POST OFFICE BOX 4203	NEW YORK, NY	10017
HANDEY, JACK W	TV WRITER	8314 MARMONT LN	LOS ANGELES, CA	90069
HANDL, IRENE	ACTRESS	31 VISCOUNT CT		
		1 PEMBRIDGE VILLAS	LONDON W2 4XA	ENGLAND
HANDLER, DAVID L	DIRECTOR	15 W 84TH ST	NEW YORK, NY	10024
HANDLER, DAVID R	WRITER	555 W 57TH ST #1230	NEW YORK, NY	10019
HANDLER, MARC R	WRITER	8955 BEVERLY BLVD	LOS ANGELES, CA	90048
HANDLEY, ALAN	DIRECTOR	DGA, 7950 SUNSET BLVD	LOS ANGELES, CA	90046
HANDLEY, DREW R	DIRECTOR	6732 AMBER CT	ALTA LOMA, CA	91701

HANDY, JAMES	ACTOR	110 W 40TH ST #2401	NEW YORK, NY 10018
HANDY, JOHN	SINGER	2490 CHANNING WY #406	BERKELEY, CA 94704
HANEY, ANNE	ACTRESS	10390 SANTA MONICA BLVD #310	LOS ANGELES, CA 90025
HANEY, LEE	BODYBUILDER	POST OFFICE BOX 491263	ATLANTA, GA 30349
HANEY, LYNN	SINGER	RUSTRON, 200 WESTMORELAND AVE	WHITE PLAINS, NY 10606
HANEY, MICHAEL	ACTOR	AFFILIATE ARTISTS, INC	
		37 W 65TH ST, 6TH FLOOR	NEW YORK, NY 10023
HANEY, SONJA	ACTRESS	10915 HESBY ST	NORTH HOLLYWOOD, CA 91601
HANGEN, BRUCE	CONDUCTOR	SHAW CONCERTS, 1995 BROADWAY	NEW YORK, NY 10023
HANGMAN, THE	WRESTLER	SEE - BLACK BART	
HANIAN, SHARON	ACTRESS	8484 WILSHIRE BLVD #235	BEVERLY HILLS, CA 90211
HANKAL, BOB	TV DIRECTOR	420 CENTRAL PARK W #5-K	NEW YORK, NY 10025
HANKIN, LARRY	ACTOR	1046 N SPAULDING AVE #8	LOS ANGELES, CA 90046
HANKIN, SAMUEL F	NEWS CORRESPONDENT	11700 OLD COLUMBIA PIKE #416	SILVER SPRING, MD 20904
HANKINS, RICHARD C	ART DIRECTOR	CBS-TV, "THE GUIDING LIGHT"	
		51 W 52ND ST	NEW YORK, NY 10019
HANKINS, ROBERT E	DIRECTOR	DGA, 7950 SUNSET BLVD	LOS ANGELES, CA 90046
HANKINSON, STEPHANIE	ACTRESS	14358 MAGNOLIA BLVD #130	SHERMAN OAKS, CA 91423
HANKOFF, PETER	WRITER	1316 1/2 N FORMOSA AVE	LOS ANGELES, CA 90046
HANKS, MICHAEL	CASTING DIRECTOR	11047 WESTWOOD BLVD	CULVER CITY, CA 90230
HANKS, PAUL	SINGER	MORGAN, 21 FLEETWOOD	JACKSON, OH 45640
HANKS, STEVE	ACTOR	9220 SUNSET BLVD #620	LOS ANGELES, CA 90069
HANKS, TOM	ACTOR	120 E 56TH ST #600	NEW YORK, NY 10022
HANLEY, BARBARA	CASTING DIRECTOR	1040 N LAS PALMAS AVE	HOLLYWOOD, CA 90038
HANLEY, BRIDGET	ACTRESS	16671 OAK VIEW DR	ENCINO, CA 91436
HANLEY, GEARY, BAND	C & W GROUP	17530 VENTURA BLVD #108	ENCINO, CA 91316
HANLEY, JENNY	ACTRESS	JOHN MAHONY, 30 CHALFONT CT	
		BAKER ST	LONDON NW1 ENGLAND
HANLEY, ROBERT	ACTOR	POST OFFICE BOX 6611	BURBANK, CA 91510
HANLEY, THOMAS F, JR	WRITER	10317 MISSISSIPPI AVE	LOS ANGELES, CA 90025
HANLEY, WILLIAM	TV WRITER	555 W 57TH ST #1230	NEW YORK, NY 10019
HANMER, DON	ACTOR	7414 W 85TH ST	LOS ANGELES, CA 90045
HANNA, MARK	WRITER	8955 BEVERLY BLVD	LOS ANGELES, CA 90048
HANNA, SAM A	NEWS CORRESPONDENT	610 MELROSE ST	ALEXANDRIA, VA 22302
HANNAFORD, JIM	MUSICIAN	549-B MAPLEWOOD LN	NASHVILLE, TN 37216
HANNAH, CINDY	ACTRESS	ABC-TV, "ALL MY CHILDREN"	
		1330 AVE OF THE AMERICAS	NEW YORK, NY 10019
HANNAH, DARRYL	ACTRESS	151 S EL CAMINO DR	BEVERLY HILLS, CA 90212
HANNAH, JAMES G	NEWS CORRESPONDENT	1023 N EDGEWOOD ST	ARLINGTON, VA 22201
HANNAH, PAGE	ACTRESS	9000 SUNSET BLVD #1200	LOS ANGELES, CA 90069
HANNAN, THOMAS	BASSO-BUFFO	PERLS, 7 W 96TH ST	NEW YORK, NY 10025
HANNAWAY, DORIAN R	TV WRITER	1276 N HAYWORTH AVE	LOS ANGELES, CA 90046
HANNEN, NORMAN	NEWS CORRESPONDENT	14700 STURDEVANT RD	SILVER SPRING, MD 20904
HANNIBAL, JULIA	ACTRESS	9744 WILSHIRE BLVD #306	BEVERLY HILLS, CA 90212
HANNIBAL, LYDIA	ACTRESS	ABC-TV, "RYAN'S HOPE"	
		1330 AVE OF THE AMERICAS	NEW YORK, NY 10019
HANNIFIN, JERRY	NEWS CORRESPONDENT	1001 WILSON BLVD	ARLINGTON, VA 22209
HANNIFIN, SUE BUTLER	NEWS CORRESPONDENT	1001 WILSON BLVD #608	ARLINGTON, VA 22209
HANNON, THOMAS F, JR	NEWS CORRESPONDENT	2611 DUMBARTON ST, NW	WASHINGTON, DC 20008
HANNUM, TOMMY	GUITARIST	1719 ALLSION PL	NASHVILLE, TN 37203
HANOI ROCKS	ROCK & ROLL GROUP	13 PARSON ST #5	LONDON NW4 ENGLAND
HANSARD, SARA	NEWS CORRESPONDENT	6705 WESTMORELAND AVE	TAKOMA PARK, MD 20912
HANSARD, WILLIAM W	DIRECTOR	2 HAVEN ST	BOSTON, MA 02118
HANSEN, AL	ACTOR	1418 N HIGHLAND AVE #102	LOS ANGELES, CA 90028
HANSEN, DANNA	ACTRESS	1418 N HIGHLAND AVE #102	LOS ANGELES, CA 90028
HANSEN, EDWARD A	ANIMATOR	500 S BUENA VISTA ST	BURBANK, CA 91521
HANSEN, J OMAR	ACTOR	1741 N IVAR AVE #221	LOS ANGELES, CA 90028
HANSEN, J WOODS	NEWS CORRESPONDENT	805 ALBANY AVE	ALEXANDRIA, VA 22302
HANSEN, JOHN R	WRITER	8955 BEVERLY BLVD	LOS ANGELES, CA 90048
HANSEN, LE ROY	NEWS CORRESPONDENT	5 VICTORY CT	POTOMAC, MD 20854
HANSEN, NINA	ACTRESS	350 W 24TH ST	NEW YORK, NY 10011
HANSEN, PETER	ACTOR	208 S BEVERLY DR #8	BEVERLY HILLS, CA 90212
HANSEN, RANDY	SINGER	ADAM'S, 827 FOLSOM ST	SAN FRANCISCO, CA 94107
HANSEN, RUTH	TALENT AGENT	12725 VENTURA BLVD #E	STUDIO CITY, CA 91604
HANSEN, SONNY	TV DIRECTOR	POST OFFICE BOX 78	AUGUSTA, NJ 07822
HANSEN, STANLEY ROBERT	TV WRITER	6430 SUNSET BLVD #1203	HOLLYWOOD, CA 90028
HANSON, BARRY	TV DIRECTOR-PRODUCER	HANSTOLL, 7 AMOR RD	LONDON W6 ENGLAND
HANSON, CONNIE	SINGER	POST OFFICE BOX 4340	HOUSTON, TX 77210
HANSON, CURTIS LEE	WRITER-PRODUCER	21 EASTWIND ST	VENICE, CA 90291
HANSON, DANNY	CLOWN	2701 COTTAGE WY #14	SACRAMENTO, CA 95825
HANSON, DAVID J	NEWS CORRESPONDENT	10438 COLLINGHAM DR	FAIRFAX, VA 22032
HANSON, ERIC ALLEN	BARITONE	45 W 60TH ST #4-K	NEW YORK, NY 10023
HANSON, GENE	TV WRITER	8955 BEVERLY BLVD	LOS ANGELES, CA 90048
HANSON, GORDON	ACTOR	8831 SUNSET BLVD #402	LOS ANGELES, CA 90069
HANSON, HOWARD	COMPOSER-CONDUCTOR	326 OAKDALE DR	ROCHESTER, NY 14618
HANSON, JAMES	DIRECTOR	SEE - HANSON, SIR JAMES	
HANSON, KRISTINE	MODEL-NEWS REPORTER	KCRA-TV, 310 10TH ST	SACRAMENTO, CA 95814
HANSON, MARCY	ACTRESS-MODEL	MODELS & PROMOTIONS AGENCY	
		8560 SUNSET BLVD, 10TH FLOOR	LOS ANGELES, CA 90069
HANSON, PRESTON	ACTOR	9328 CAYUGA AVE	SUN VALLEY, CA 91352
HANSON, RICK	SINGER	ROUTE #1, BOX 327	NASHVILLE, TN 47448
HANSON, SIR JAMES	DIRECTOR	180 BROMPTON RD	LONDON SW3 1HF ENGLAND
HANSON, TERRY	TV PRODUCER	4606 EBERLINE CT	STONE MOUNTAIN, GA 30083
HANSSEN, DEIRDRE	WRITER	853 N LARRABEE ST	LOS ANGELES, CA 90069
HANTMAN, CAROL E	WRITER	555 W 57TH ST #1230	NEW YORK, NY 10019

Name	Occupation	Address	City	Zip
HANWRIGHT, JOSEPH C	FILM DIRECTOR	430 WOOD RIVER DR	KETCHUM, ID	83340
HAPPENINGS, THE	VOCAL GROUP	POST OFFICE BOX 262	CARTERET, NJ	07008
HAPPER, TOM	ACTOR	1333 N STANLEY AVE #23	LOS ANGELES, CA	90046
HAPPYFEET	ROCK & ROLL GROUP	POST OFFICE BOX 448	RADFORD, VA	24141
HARA, YASUSHI	NEWS CORRESPONDENT	8719 EWING DR	BETHESDA, MD	20817
HARADA, ERNEST	ACTOR	13952 MOORPARK ST #1	SHERMAN OAKS, CA	91423
HARB, CHARLENE	PIANIST	608 N BROADWAY	KNOXVILLE, TN	37917
HARBACH, BARBARA	ORGANIST	GREAT LAKES PERFORMING		
		310 E WASHINGTON ST	ANN ARBOR, MI	48104
HARBACH, BILL	TV DIRECTOR-PRODUCER	876 PARK AVE #7-N	NEW YORK, NY	10021
HARBACH, OTTO	LYRICIST	876 PARK AVE #7-N	NEW YORK, NY	10021
HARBACH, WILLIAM O	DIRECTOR	876 PARK AVE #7-N	NEW YORK, NY	10021
HARBARTH, TED	ACTOR	6006 LA PRADA ST	LOS ANGELES, CA	90042
HARBER, PAUL	TV WRITER	8955 BEVERLY BLVD	LOS ANGELES, CA	90048
HARBERT, TED	TV EXECUTIVE	ABC-TV ENTERTAINMENT CENTER		
		2040 AVE OF THE STARS	LOS ANGELES, CA	90067
HARBINGERS, THE	GOSPEL GROUP	POST OFFICE BOX 124	KIRBYVILLE, TX	75956
HARBISON, GEORGIA	NEWS REPORTER	TIME/TIME & LIFE BLDG		
		ROCKEFELLER CENTER	NEW YORK, NY	10020
HARBORD, GORDON	THEATER PRODUCER	17 RIDGMOUNT GARDENS	LONDON WC1E 7AR	ENGLAND
HARBRECHT, DOUGLAS	NEWS CORRESPONDENT	10600 WISE OWL WY	GREAT FALLS, VA	22066
HARBURG, EDGAR	LYRICIST	262 CENTRAL PARK W	NEW YORK, NY	10024
HARCOURT, JACK	COMPOSER	120 CARLTON AVE #48	LOS GATOS, CA	95030
HARCOURT, THOMAS	ACTOR	6605 HOLLYWOOD BLVD #220	HOLLYWOOD, CA	90028
HARDAWAY, R E	SINGER	4900 NEBRASKA AVE	NASHVILLE, TN	37209
HARDCASTLE, LOY	DRUMMER	816 LEWISBURG AVE	FRANKLIN, TN	37064
HARDCASTLE, PAUL	SINGER-COMPOSER	19 MANAGEMENT, LTD		
		9 DISRAELI RD	LONDON SW	ENGLAND
HARDEN, ERNEST, JR	ACTOR	11726 SAN VICENTE BLVD #300	LOS ANGELES, CA	90049
HARDEN, HOWARD, JR	TV DIRECTOR	1710 MONTEREY DR	SAN BRUNO, CA	94066
HARDER, JAMES	ACTOR	531 E 72ND ST	NEW YORK, NY	10021
HARDER, WILLIAM E	DIRECTOR	6616 N PONCHARTRAIN BLVD	CHICAGO, IL	60646
HARDESTY, RODNEY	TENOR	SOFFER, 130 W 56TH ST	NEW YORK, NY	10019
HARDIN, FRANCES A	NEWS CORRESPONDENT	2133 WISCONSIN AVE, NW	WASHINGTON, DC	20007
HARDIN, GUS	SINGER	HALSEY, 1111 16TH AVE S	NASHVILLE, TN	37212
HARDIN, JERRY	ACTOR	13422 OXNARD ST	VAN NUYS, CA	91401
HARDIN, MELORA	ACTRESS	11726 SAN VICENTE BLVD #300	LOS ANGELES, CA	90049
HARDIN, PETER	NEWS CORRESPONDENT	3900 TUNLAW RD, NW	WASHINGTON, DC	20007
HARDIN, TY	ACTOR	427 N CANON DR #205	BEVERLY HILLS, CA	90210
HARDING, TERRY	TV DIRECTOR-PRODUCER	WOODFIELD HOUSE, TEMPLE CLOUD	AVON	ENGLAND
HARDMAN, HOLLY	ACTRESS	8721 SUNSET BLVD #202	LOS ANGELES, CA	90069
HARDMAN, RIC	SCREENWRITER	8733 SUNSET BLVD #102	LOS ANGELES, CA	90069
HARDMAN ENELL, KATHLEEN	WRITER	8955 BEVERLY BLVD	LOS ANGELES, CA	90048
HARDT, ELOISE	ACTRESS	8831 SUNSET BLVD #402	LOS ANGELES, CA	90069
HARDWICK, MARY	TV DIRECTOR	13745 1/2 MULHOLLAND DR	BEVERLY HILLS, CA	90210
HARDWICK, PAUL	ACTOR	267 GOLDHURST TERR	LONDON NW6 3EP	ENGLAND
HARDY, CHIP	GUITARIST	4305 IDAHO AVE	NASHVILLE, TN	37209
HARDY, DONA	ACTRESS	8961 SUNSET BLVD #B	LOS ANGELES, CA	90069
HARDY, JOE	TV PRODUCER	ABC TELEVISION NETWORK		
		1330 AVE OF THE AMERICAS	NEW YORK, NY	10019
HARDY, JOHN	FILM PRODUCER	27 ALTON RD, RICHMOND	SURREY	ENGLAND
HARDY, JOSEPH	ACTOR	129 W 147TH ST	NEW YORK, NY	10039
HARDY, JOSEPH	TV DIRECTOR	1888 CENTURY PARK E #1400	LOS ANGELES, CA	90069
HARDY, LUCILLE	ACTRESS	PRICE, 4055 TUJUNGA BLVD	NORTH HOLLYWOOD, CA	91602
HARDY, ROBERT	ACTOR	CHATTO & LINNIT, LTD		
		PRINCE OF WALES THEATRE		
		COVENTRY ST	LONDON LWC2	ENGLAND
HARDY, SARAH	ACTRESS	9009 WONDERLAND AVE	LOS ANGELES, CA	90046
HARDY, SCOTT	TALENT AGENT	9777 WILSHIRE BLVD #707	BEVERLY HILLS, CA	90212
HARDY, WILLIAM	ACTOR	ICM, 8899 BEVERLY BLVD	LOS ANGELES, CA	90048
HARE, DAVID	WRITER-PRODUCER	95 LINDEN GARDENS	LONDON W2	ENGLAND
HARE, WILL	ACTOR	15010 VENTURA BLVD #234	SHERMAN OAKS, CA	91403
HARENS, THOMAS J	TALENT AGENT	POST OFFICE BOX 9556	MINNEAPOLIS, MN	55440
HAREWOOD, DORIAN	ACTRESS	1203 GREENACRE AVE	LOS ANGELES, CA	90046
HARFORD, BETTY	ACTRESS	9165 SUNSET BLVD #202	LOS ANGELES, CA	90069
HARFORD, JOHN C	WRITER	8955 BEVERLY BLVD	LOS ANGELES, CA	90048
HARGITAY, MARISKA	ACTRESS	2370 SUNSET PLAZA DR	LOS ANGELES, CA	90069
HARGITAY, MICKEY	ACTOR	2370 SUNSET PLAZA DR	LOS ANGELES, CA	90069
HARGREAVES, ALLAN	TV PRODUCER	DAVIE, 37 HILL ST	LONDON W1	ENGLAND
HARGREAVES, JOHN LAWRENCE	FILM EXECUTIVE	FIDDLERS GREEN, WOOD LN	BUCKS	ENGLAND
HARGREAVES, ROBERT	ACTOR-SINGER	13 GUNTERSTONE RD	LONDON W14 9BP	ENGLAND
HARGROVE, BRIAN	ACTOR	ABRAMS ARTISTS & ASSOCIATES		
		420 MADISON AVE, 14TH FLOOR	NEW YORK, NY	10017
HARGROVE, DEAN	TV WRITER-PRODUCER	705 CALLE MIRAMAR	REDONDO BEACH, CA	90277
HARGROVE, LINDA	SINGER-SONGWRITER	809 18TH AVE S	NASHVILLE, TN	37203
HARGROVE, MARION	TV WRITER	130 ADELAIDE DR	SANTA MONICA, CA	90402
HARGROVE, MAURICE DEAN	WRITER	474 HALVERN DR	LOS ANGELES, CA	90049
HARGROVE, MICHAEL LEE	PIANIST	POST OFFICE BOX 1307	NEW SMYRNA BEACH, FL	32069
HARGROVE, PARNENEH	WRITER	1014 MANNING AVE	LOS ANGELES, CA	90024
HARGROVE, PHIL	WRITER	8955 BEVERLY BLVD	LOS ANGELES, CA	90048
HARIMOTO, DALE	ACTRESS	LIGHT, 113 N ROBERTSON BLVD	LOS ANGELES, CA	90048
HARING, KEITH	ARTIST	TONY SHAFRAZI GALLERY		
		163 MERCER ST	NEW YORK, NY	10012
HARKER, STEPHENIE J	ACTRESS	1139 N VISTA ST	LOS ANGELES, CA	90046
HARKER, WILEY	ACTOR	STONE, 1052 CAROL DR	LOS ANGELES, CA	90069

Name	Occupation	Address	City	ZIP
HARKINS, JOHN	ACTOR	SF & A, 121 N SAN VICENTE BLVD	BEVERLY HILLS, CA	90211
HARKINS, JOHN L	TV DIRECTOR	190 N STATE ST	CHICAGO, IL	60601
HARKNESS, PETER A	NEWS CORRESPONDENT	5407 MACOMB ST, NW	WASHINGTON, DC	20016
HARKREADER, FIDDLIN SID	FIDDLER	525 SHELBY AVE #801	NASHVILLE, TN	37206
HARLAN, SUSAN	CARTOONIST	POST OFFICE BOX 500	WASHINGTON, DC	20044
HARLEQUIN	ROCK & ROLL GROUP	41 BRITAIN ST #200	TORONTO, ONT	CANADA
HARLIB, MATTHEW E	DIRECTOR	ADFILM, 300 E 40TH ST	NEW YORK, NY	10016
HARLING, NOELLE	ACTRESS	3575 W CAHUENGA BLVD #320	LOS ANGELES, CA	90068
HARLOW, BILL LEE	ACTOR	1607 N EL CENTRO AVE #2	LOS ANGELES, CA	90028
HARLOW, GAIL	WRITER-EDITOR	TV GUIDE, 100 MATSONFORD RD	RADNOR, PA	19088
HARMAN, BARRY	SCREENWRITER	ICM, 8899 BEVERLY BLVD	LOS ANGELES, CA	90048
HARMAN, BUDDY	DRUMMER	POST OFFICE BOX 120302	NASHVILLE, TN	37212
HARMAN, RICKY	WRITER	555 W 57TH ST #1230	NEW YORK, NY	10019
HARMAN, STAN	DRUMMER	3812 LOOKOUT DR	NASHVILLE, TN	37209
HARMETZ, ALJEAN	TV WRITER	2065 KERWOOD AVE	LOS ANGELES, CA	90025
HARMON, BRUCE	TV WRITER	555 W 57TH ST #1230	NEW YORK, NY	10019
HARMON, BRUCE	TV WRITER-NEWS CORRES	1523 N STAFFORD ST	ARLINGTON, VA	22207
HARMON, DEBORAH	ACTRESS	10351 SANTA MONICA BLVD #211	LOS ANGELES, CA	90025
HARMON, JAMES E, JR	NEWS CORRESPONDENT	1755 S JEFFERSON DAVIS HWY	ARLINGTON, VA	22202
HARMON, JEFF B	WRITER-PRODUCER	8955 BEVERLY BLVD	LOS ANGELES, CA	90048
HARMON, JENNIFER	ACTRESS	211 S BEVERLY DR #201	BEVERLY HILLS, CA	90212
HARMON, KELLY	ACTRESS	211 S BEVERLY DR #201	BEVERLY HILLS, CA	90212
HARMON, LARRY "BOZO"	FILM EXEC-CONDUCTOR	650 N BRONSON AVE	HOLLYWOOD, CA	90004
HARMON, MANNY	CONDUCTOR	8350 SANTA MONICA BLVD	LOS ANGELES, CA	90069
HARMON, MARK	ACTOR	9000 SUNSET BLVD #1200	LOS ANGELES, CA	90069
HARMON, ROBERT G, JR	WRITER	8955 BEVERLY BLVD	LOS ANGELES, CA	90048
HARMON, SANDRA	TV WRITER	675 CAMELOT WY #21	LOS ANGELES, CA	90002
HARMON, TOM	SPORTSCASTER	320 N GUNSTON DR	LOS ANGELES, CA	90049
HARMONICA RASCALS, THE	MUSICAL GROUP	CEE, 193 KONHAUS RD	MECHANICSBURG, PA	17055
HARMONY SISTERS, THE	VIOLIN TRIO	FLYING FISH RECORDS CO		
		1304 W SCHUBERT AVE	CHICAGO, IL	60614
HARMS, CARL	ACTOR	230 W END AVE	NEW YORK, NY	10023
HARMS, RACHEL	DANCER	AFFILIATE ARTISTS, INC		
		37 W 65TH ST, 6TH FLOOR	NEW YORK, NY	10023
HARNACK, JOHN	TV DIRECTOR-PRODUCER	1049 21ST ST #4	SANTA MONICA, CA	90403
HARNAGEL, JIM	ACTOR	1595 KENSINGTON RD	SAN MARINO, CA	91108
HARNAGEL, JOHN	ACTOR	1595 KENSINGTON RD	SAN MARINO, CA	91108
HARNED, ALFRED M	COMPOSER	3480 2ND AVE	LOS ANGELES, CA	90018
HARNED, VICTORIA	ACTRESS	11240 MAGNOLIA BLVD #202	NORTH HOLLYWOOD, CA	91601
HARNELL, JOE	COMPOSER	4146 WESLIN AVE	SHERMAN OAKS, CA	91423
HARNESS, WILLIAM	TENOR	CAMI, 165 W 57TH ST	NEW YORK, NY	10019
HARNEY, GREGORY G	DIRECTOR	POST OFFICE BOX 34	LINCOLN, MA	01773
HARNEY, SUSAN	ACTRESS	12750 VENTURA BLVD #102	STUDIO CITY, CA	91604
HARNONCOURT, NIKOLAUS	CONDUCTOR	MARIEDL ANDERS ARTISTS MGMT		
		535 EL CAMINO DEL MAR ST	SAN FRANCISCO, CA	94121
HARNOY, OFRA	CELLIST	GERSHUNOFF, 502 PARK AVE	NEW YORK, NY	10022
HAROLD, MARY-CATHERINE	TV PRODUCER	LORIMAR-TELEPICTURES		
		"KNOTS LANDING"		
		3970 OVERLAND AVE	CULVER CITY, CA	90230
HAROUT, MAGDA	ACTRESS	13452 VOSE ST	VAN NUYS, CA	91405
HARPAZ, UDI EHUD	COMPOSER-CONDUCTOR	5541 LAUREL CANYON BLVD #11	NORTH HOLLYWOOD, CA	91607
HARPER, ACEY C	PHOTOGRAPHER	1021 ARLINGTON BLVD	ARLINGTON, VA	22209
HARPER, ALAN	WRITER	555 W 57TH ST #1230	NEW YORK, NY	10019
HARPER, CANDIDA E	TV DIRECTOR	POST OFFICE BOX 268	WOODY CREEK, CO	81656
HARPER, CHRIS	NEWS CORRESPONDENT	ABC NEWS, 7 W 66TH ST	NEW YORK, NY	10023
HARPER, DAVID W	ACTOR	9777 WILSHIRE BLVD #707	BEVERLY HILLS, CA	90212
HARPER, DIANNE	ACTRESS	7915 VAN NOORD AVE	NORTH HOLLYWOOD, CA	91605
HARPER, GERALD	ACTOR	LARRY DALZELL ASSOCIATES		
		126 KENNINGTON PARK RD	LONDON SE11 4DJ	ENGLAND
HARPER, HENRY	SCREENWRITER	8955 BEVERLY BLVD	LOS ANGELES, CA	90048
HARPER, JESSICA	ACTRESS	151 S EL CAMINO DR	BEVERLY HILLS, CA	90212
HARPER, JOHNNY	GUITARIST	306 VILLAGE GREEN DR	NASHVILLE, TN	37217

MARK HARMON

JULIE HARRIS

PHIL HARRIS

GEORGE HARRISON

GREG HARRISON

REX HARRISON

DEBBIE HARRY

HARRY HARRYHAUSEN

COREY HART

Name	Occupation	Address	City	Zip
HARPER, KEN	THEATER PRODUCER	165 W 46TH ST	NEW YORK, NY	10036
HARPER, MARIA	ACTRESS	CLIFFORD, 109 NEW BOND	LONDON W1	ENGLAND
HARPER, NEILL S	TV DIRECTOR	4458 CARPENTER ST	STUDIO CITY, CA	91604
HARPER, PAUL	ACTOR	427 N CANON DR #205	BEVERLY HILLS, CA	90210
HARPER, RICK	GUITARIST	228 DOWNEYMEADE DR	NASHVILLE, TN	37214
HARPER, ROBERT J, JR	NEWS CORRESPONDENT	NBC-TV, NEWS DEPARTMENT		
		4001 NEBRASKA AVE, NW	WASHINGTON, DC	20016
HARPER, RON	ACTOR	10 E 44TH ST #700	NEW YORK, NY	10017
HARPER, ROSALINDE	NEWS CORRESPONDENT	816 EASLEY ST	SILVER SPRING, MD	20910
HARPER, SAMANTHA	ACTRESS	9300 WILSHIRE BLVD #410	BEVERLY HILLS, CA	90212
HARPER, SCOTT E	COMPOSER	717 1/2 HAYWORTH AVE	LOS ANGELES, CA	90046
HARPER, TESS	ACTRESS	ICM, 8899 BEVERLY BLVD	LOS ANGELES, CA	90048
HARPER, VALERIE	ACTRESS	445 N BEDFORD DR #PH	BEVERLY HILLS, CA	90210
HARPTONES, THE	VOCAL GROUP	55 W 119TH ST	NEW YORK, NY	10026
HARRAR, LINDA	WRITER	555 W 57TH ST #1230	NEW YORK, NY	10019
HARRELL, BILL & THE VIRGINIANS	BLUEGRASS GROUP	380 LEXINGTON AVE #1119	NEW YORK, NY	10017
HARRELL, JACK L	WRITER	8955 BEVERLY BLVD	LOS ANGELES, CA	90048
HARRELL, LYNN	CELLIST	CAMI, 165 W 57TH ST	NEW YORK, NY	10019
HARRER-BUTLER, MARTHA	ACTRESS	4239 SHADYGLADE AVE #4	STUDIO CITY, CA	91604
HARRES, HOLLIE	ACTRESS	5030 TUJUNGA AVE	NORTH HOLLYWOOD, CA	91601
HARRESCHOU, MICHAEL	SCREENWRITER	8033 LOYOLA BLVD	LOS ANGELES, CA	90045
HARRIES, DAVYD	ACTOR	PLANTATION COLLEGE		
		MIDDLE WINTERSLOW		
		NEAR SALISBURY	WILTS	ENGLAND
HARRIES, KATHRYN	SOPRANO	CAMI, 165 W 57TH ST	NEW YORK, NY	10019
HARRIMAN, FAWNE	ACTRESS	200 N ROBERTSON BLVD #219	BEVERLY HILLS, CA	90211
HARRINGTON, ALAN S	WRITER	8955 BEVERLY BLVD	LOS ANGELES, CA	90048
HARRINGTON, CURTIS	DIRECTOR	9000 SUNSET BLVD #1200	LOS ANGELES, CA	90069
HARRINGTON, DANIEL M	WRITER	555 W 57TH ST #1230	NEW YORK, NY	10019
HARRINGTON, DAVID	CLOWN	2701 COTTAGE WY #14	SACRAMENTO, CA	95825
HARRINGTON, LAURA	ACTRESS	10100 SANTA MONICA BLVD #1600	LOS ANGELES, CA	90067
HARRINGTON, LESLIE	TENOR	45 W 60TH ST #4-K	NEW YORK, NY	10023
HARRINGTON, LISA H	NEWS CORRESPONDENT	4501 CONNECTICUT AVE #419, NW	WASHINGTON, DC	20008
HARRINGTON, MARK H, III	WRITER	555 W 57TH ST #1230	NEW YORK, NY	10019
HARRINGTON, PAT, JR	ACTOR-WRITER	2259 LINDA FLORA DR	LOS ANGELES, CA	90077
HARRINGTON, TIM	NEWS CORRESPONDENT	2219 HALL PL, NW	WASHINGTON, DC	20007
HARRIS, ALBERT	COMPOSER-CONDUCTOR	5622 ALLOTT AVE	VAN NUYS, CA	91401
HARRIS, ALFRED	TV WRITER	SWANSON, 8523 SUNSET BLVD	LOS ANGELES, CA	90069
HARRIS, ALLEN W	MUSICIAN	2509 ALVINWOOD DR	NASHVILLE, TN	37214
HARRIS, ANITA	SINGER-ACTRESS	LONDON MANAGEMENT, LTD		
		235-241 REGENT ST	LONDON W1A 2JT	ENGLAND
HARRIS, ANTHONY	NEWS CORRESPONDENT	9310 EDMONDSTON RD #201	GREENBELT, MD	20770
HARRIS, ARNIE	PRODUCER	26011 REDBLUFF ST	CALABASAS, CA	91302
HARRIS, BADNEWS	WRESTLER	SEE - KIMALA		
HARRIS, BARBARA	ACTRESS	31 W 11TH ST	NEW YORK, NY	10010
HARRIS, BRENDA	SOPRANO	HILLYER, 250 W 57TH ST	NEW YORK, NY	10107
HARRIS, BROOKE	WRITER	1501 PEARL ST #3	SANTA MONICA, CA	90405
HARRIS, BURTT	FILM PRODUCER	LUMET/ALLEN, 156 W 56TH ST	NEW YORK, NY	10019
HARRIS, CASSANDRA	ACTRESS	BROSNAN, 8817 PINTO PL	LOS ANGELES, CA	90069
HARRIS, CHARLES	TV DIRECTOR	17 LANGLAND GARDENS	LONDON NW3 6WE	ENGLAND
HARRIS, CHRIS	GUITARIST	POST OFFICE BOX 120753	NASHVILLE, TN	37212
HARRIS, CRAIG W	COMPOSER-CONDUCTOR	POST OFFICE BOX 36-A-45	LOS ANGELES, CA	90036
HARRIS, CYNTHIA	ACTRESS	211 S BEVERLY DR #201	BEVERLY HILLS, CA	90212
HARRIS, DALE	WRITER	555 W 57TH ST #1230	NEW YORK, NY	10019
HARRIS, DAVID	ACTOR	157 W 57TH ST #604	NEW YORK, NY	10019
HARRIS, DAVID D	ACTOR	8285 SUNSET BLVD #12	LOS ANGELES, CA	90046
HARRIS, DAVID V	WRITER	8955 BEVERLY BLVD	LOS ANGELES, CA	90048
HARRIS, DENNY	FILM DIRECTOR	12152 OLYMPIC BLVD	LOS ANGELES, CA	90064
HARRIS, ED	ACTOR	7250 FRANKLIN AVE #105	LOS ANGELES, CA	90046
HARRIS, EDDIE	SAXOPHONIST	BRIDGE, 106 FORT GREENE PL	BROOKLYN, NY	11217
HARRIS, EMMYLOU	SINGER-SONGWRITER	POST OFFICE BOX 4471	NORTH HOLLYWOOD, CA	91607
HARRIS, ERIC	WRESTLER	SEE - BLACK BART		
HARRIS, FABIA	NEWS CORRESPONDENT	9827 OLD GEORGETOWN RD	BETHESDA, MD	20814
HARRIS, HARRIET H	ACTRESS	9229 SUNSET BLVD #306	LOS ANGELES, CA	90069
HARRIS, HARRIETT	ACTRESS	15010 VENTURA BLVD #219	SHERMAN OAKS, CA	91403
HARRIS, HARRY	TV DIRECTOR	10999 RIVERSIDE DR	NORTH HOLLYWOOD, CA	91602
HARRIS, HENRY	ACTOR	8721 SUNSET BLVD #200	LOS ANGELES, CA	90069
HARRIS, HILDA	MEZZO-SOPRANO	IMG ARTISTS, 22 E 71ST ST	NEW YORK, NY	10021
HARRIS, IKE	GUITARIST	309 CROSS TIMBERS DR	NASHVILLE, TN	37221
HARRIS, JAMES B	DIRECTOR	RINGER, 248 1/2 S LASKY DR	BEVERLY HILLS, CA	90212
HARRIS, JAMIE	ACTOR	5000 LANKERSHIM BLVD #5	NORTH HOLLYWOOD, CA	91601
HARRIS, JAY	CARTOONIST	KING FEATURES SYNDICATE		
		235 E 45TH ST	NEW YORK, NY	10017
HARRIS, JAY T	NEWS CORRESPONDENT	5422 MIDSHIP CT	BURKE, VA	22015
HARRIS, JEFF	TV WRITER-DIRECTOR	8428 MELROSE PL #C	LOS ANGELES, CA	90069
HARRIS, JEFFREY D	COMPOSER	3955 COLDWATER CANYON AVE	STUDIO CITY, CA	91604
HARRIS, JILL	ACTRESS	9300 WILSHIRE BLVD #410	BEVERLY HILLS, CA	90212
HARRIS, JIM	WRESTLER	SEE - KIMALA		
HARRIS, JIMMY JAM	SONGWRITER-PRODUCER	FLYTE TYME PRODUCTIONS		
		4330 NICOLLET AVE	MINNEAPOLIS, MN	55409
HARRIS, JOHN S L	COMPOSER-CONDUCTOR	5428 PARADISE VALLEY RD	CALABASAS, CA	91302
HARRIS, JONATHAN	ACTOR	16830 MARMADUKE PL	ENCINO, CA	91436
HARRIS, JOSEPH	THEATER PRODUCER	15 E 48TH ST	NEW YORK, NY	10017
HARRIS, JOSHUA	ACTOR	12725 VENTURA BLVD #E	STUDIO CITY, CA	91604
HARRIS, JULIE	ACTRESS	11345 BRILL DR	STUDIO CITY, CA	91604

HARRIS, JULIE	FASHION DESIGNER	13 PHILLIMORE GARDENS	LONDON W8	ENGLAND
HARRIS, JULIUS	ACTOR	1947 7TH AVE	NEW YORK, NY	10026
HARRIS, KAREN	PRODUCER	MCA/UNIVERSAL STUDIOS, INC		
		100 UNIVERSAL CITY PLAZA	UNIVERSAL CITY, CA	91608
HARRIS, KAREN	TV WRITER	8955 BEVERLY BLVD	LOS ANGELES, CA	90048
HARRIS, KEN	WRITER	8955 BEVERLY BLVD	LOS ANGELES, CA	90048
HARRIS, KIM & REGGIE	FOLK-ROCK DUO	360 CENTRAL PARK W #16-G	NEW YORK, NY	10025
HARRIS, LANA J	PHOTOGRAPHER	1350 BEVERLY RD #703	MC LEAN, VA	22101
HARRIS, LEE	ACTOR	9744 WILSHIRE BLVD #306	BEVERLY HILLS, CA	90212
HARRIS, LOU	COMMENTATOR	TRIBUNE MEDIA SERVICES		
		64 E CONCORD ST	ORLANDO, FL	32801
HARRIS, LOUIS	DIRECTOR	1914 FAIRBURN AVE	LOS ANGELES, CA	90025
HARRIS, LOWELL	ACTOR	9165 SUNSET BLVD #202	LOS ANGELES, CA	90069
HARRIS, LYLE V	NEWS CORRESPONDENT	7100 CHESTNUT ST, NW	WASHINGTON, DC	20012
HARRIS, LYNNE I	NEWS CORRESPONDENT	1121 24TH ST, NW	WASHINGTON, DC	20037
HARRIS, MARILYN	RECORD EXECUTIVE	ANTHEM, 189 CARLTON ST	TORONTO, ONT M5A 2K7	CANADA
HARRIS, MARK J	SCREENWRITER	1043 POINT VIEW ST	LOS ANGELES, CA	90035
HARRIS, MATTHEW	COMPOSER	FINELL, 155 W 68TH ST	NEW YORK, NY	10023
HARRIS, MICHAEL P	NEWS REPORTER	TIME/TIME & LIFE BLDG		
		ROCKEFELLER CENTER	NEW YORK, NY	10020
HARRIS, MICHELLE	NEWS CORRESPONDENT	2038 COLUMBIA PIKE #10	ARLINGTON, VA	22204
HARRIS, OTIS	PIANIST	930 SWINGING BRIDGE RD	OLD HICKORY, TN	37138
HARRIS, PAUL	NEWS CORRESPONDENT	3 W OAK ST	ALEXANDRIA, VA	22301
HARRIS, PAUL V, JR	MUSICIAN	731 BOWFIELD CT	ANTIOCH, TN	37013
HARRIS, PETER	ACTOR	115 W 71ST ST	NEW YORK, NY	10023
HARRIS, PHIL	ACTOR	2155 MAYVIEW DR	LOS ANGELES, CA	90027
HARRIS, PHIL	ORCHESTRA LEADER	49400 J F KENNEDY TRAIL	PALM DESERT, CA	92260
HARRIS, R G	CARTOONIST	THE NATIONAL LAMPOON		
		635 MADISON AVE	NEW YORK, NY	10022
HARRIS, RALPH	NEWS CORRESPONDENT	6312 ALCOTT RD	BETHESDA, MD	20817
HARRIS, RICHARD	ACTOR	POST OFFICE BOX N-1812	NASSAU	BAHAMAS
HARRIS, RICHARD	TV WRITER	HATTON, 18 JERMYN ST	LONDON SW1Y 6HN	ENGLAND
HARRIS, RICHARD S	WRITER	8955 BEVERLY BLVD	LOS ANGELES, CA	90048
HARRIS, RICK "HANGMAN"	WRESTLER	SEE - BLACK BART		
HARRIS, RICKY	WRESTLER	SEE - BLACK BART		
HARRIS, ROBERT A	WRITER	555 W 57TH ST #1230	NEW YORK, NY	10019
HARRIS, ROBERT D	WRITER	8955 BEVERLY BLVD	LOS ANGELES, CA	90048
HARRIS, ROGER	ACTOR	8721 SUNSET BLVD #203	LOS ANGELES, CA	90069
HARRIS, RONALD M	NEWS CORRESPONDENT	8630 WEEMS RD	MANASSAS, VA	22110
HARRIS, ROSEMARY	ACTRESS	55 E 72ND ST	NEW YORK, NY	10021
HARRIS, ROSEMARY ANN	ACTRESS	ICM, 8899 BEVERLY BLVD	LOS ANGELES, CA	90048
HARRIS, ROY MELVIN	GUITARIST	324 LYNN DR	NASHVILLE, TN	37211
HARRIS, SAM	SINGER	256 S ROBERTSON BLVD #3215	BEVERLY HILLS, CA	90211
HARRIS, SID	SCREENWRITER	5146 COLDWATER CANYON AVE	SHERMAN OAKS, CA	91403
HARRIS, SIDNEY	CARTOONIST	POST OFFICE BOX 4203	NEW YORK, NY	10017
HARRIS, SIMONE S	WRITER	555 W 57TH ST #1230	NEW YORK, NY	10019
HARRIS, STAN	DIRECTOR	9200 SUNSET BLVD #428	LOS ANGELES, CA	90069
HARRIS, SUGARBEAR	WRESTLER	SEE - KIMALA		
HARRIS, SUSAN	TV PRODUCER	WITT/THOMAS PPRODUCTIONS		
		1438 N GOWER ST, 4TH FLOOR	LOS ANGELES, CA	90028
HARRIS, SUSAN	TV WRITER	8955 BEVERLY BLVD	LOS ANGELES, CA	90048
HARRIS, SYDNEY J	AUTHOR-COLUMNIST	NEWS AMERICA SYNDICATE		
		1703 KAISER AVE	IRVINE, CA	92714
HARRIS, TED	GUITARIST	POST OFFICE BOX 824	NASHVILLE, TN	37202
HARRIS, THOMAS A	WRITER	555 W 57TH ST #1230	NEW YORK, NY	10019
HARRIS, TIMOTHY H	SCREENWRITER	8955 BEVERLY BLVD	LOS ANGELES, CA	90048
HARRIS, TRACY	ACTOR	6227 MORSE AVE #202	NORTH HOLLYWOOD, CA	91606
HARRIS, VIOLA	ACTRESS	CED, 261 S ROBERTSON BLVD	BEVERLY HILLS, CA	90211
HARRIS, WILLIAM H	ART DIRECTOR	151 S EL CAMINO DR	BEVERLY HILLS, CA	90212
HARRIS, WILSON	SINGER	25 HUNTINGTON AVE #420	BOSTON, MA	02116
HARRISON, CATHRYN	ACTRESS	151 S EL CAMINO DR	BEVERLY HILLS, CA	90212
HARRISON, CLAY	DIRECTOR	6229 AGNES AVE	NORTH HOLLYWOOD, CA	91606
HARRISON, CYNTHIA	ACTRESS	13111 VENTURA BLVD #204	STUDIO CITY, CA	91604
HARRISON, DIXIE	SINGER	POST OFFICE BOX 171132	NASHVILLE, TN	37217
HARRISON, FRED	NEWS CORRESPONDENT	703 S PITT ST	ALEXANDRIA, VA	22314
HARRISON, GEORGE	SINGER-SONGWRITER	FRIAR PARK RD	HENLEY-ON-THAMES	ENGLAND
HARRISON, GREGORY	ACTOR	15509 BRIARWOOD DR	SHERMAN OAKS, CA	91403
HARRISON, HAL	SCREENWRITER	8955 BEVERLY BLVD	LOS ANGELES, CA	90048
HARRISON, JAMIE	WRITER-EDITOR	US MAGAZINE COMPANY		
		1 DAG HAMMARSKJOLD PLAZA	NEW YORK, NY	10017
HARRISON, JEANNE	DIRECTOR	200 E 50TH ST	NEW YORK, NY	10016
HARRISON, JENILEE	ACTRESS-MODEL	3800 BARHAM BLVD #303	LOS ANGELES, CA	90068
HARRISON, JIM T	WRITER	8955 BEVERLY BLVD	LOS ANGELES, CA	90048
HARRISON, JOEL	ACTOR	8961 SUNSET BLVD #B	LOS ANGELES, CA	90069
HARRISON, JOHN WAYNE	GUITARIST	ROUTE #2, ZIEGLER FORT RD	GALLATIN, TN	37066
HARRISON, JOSEPH L, JR	NEWS CORRESPONDENT	124 SMITHWOOD AVE	BALTIMORE, MD	20228
HARRISON, KATHLEEN	ACTRESS	30 COTTENHAM PARK RD	LONDON SW20 OSA	ENGLAND
HARRISON, KEN	COMPOSER	6671 SUNSET BLVD #1574	HOLLYWOOD, CA	90028
HARRISON, KENNETH R	COMPOSER	6420 WILSHIRE BLVD #425	LOS ANGELES, CA	90048
HARRISON, LINDA	ACTRESS	16718 BOLLINGER DR	PACIFIC PALISADES, CA	90272
HARRISON, LINDSAY	SCREENWRITER	8955 BEVERLY BLVD	LOS ANGELES, CA	90048
HARRISON, MARK	ACTOR	12725 VENTURA BLVD #E	STUDIO CITY, CA	91604
HARRISON, MICHAEL	MUSICIAN	POST OFFICE BOX 9388	STANFORD, CA	94305
HARRISON, MIKE	TV DIRECTOR-PRODUCER	74 WINDERMERE RD, EALING	LONDON W5 4TD	ENGLAND
HARRISON, PAT	WRITER	8955 BEVERLY BLVD	LOS ANGELES, CA	90048

JOHN HART

MARIETTE HARTLEY

RICHARD HATCH

GOLDIE HAWN

JILL HAYWORTH

HELEN HAYES

MARILU HENNER

PAUL HENREID

BUCK HENRY

Name	Occupation	Address	City	Zip/Country
HARRISON, PAUL H	GUITARIST	ROUTE #5, WAGGONER RD	FRANKLIN, TN	37064
HARRISON, REX	ACTOR	RITZ HOTEL, PICCADILLY	WEST END W1V 9DG	ENGLAND
HARRISON, ROBIN	PIANIST	200 W 70TH ST #7-F	NEW YORK, NY	10023
HARRISON, RONALD G	DIRECTOR	1201 QUEEN VICTORIA AVE	MISSISSA, ONT L5H 3H2	CANADA
HARRISON, ROY E	DIRECTOR	DGA, 7950 SUNSET BLVD	LOS ANGELES, CA	90046
HARRISON, SALLY	ACTRESS	76 TALGARTH MANSIONS		
		TALGARTH RD	LONDON W14	ENGLAND
HARRISON, TONY	TV DIRECTOR-PRODUCER	GREYSTROKE, CAVENDISH RD		
		BOWDEN, ALTRINCHAM	CHESHIRE	ENGLAND
HARRISON, WES	COMEDIAN	32500 CONCORD DR #221	MADISON HEIGHTS, MI	48071
HARRISON, WILLIAM N	SCREENWRITER	8955 BEVERLY BLVD	LOS ANGELES, CA	90048
HARRISS, WILLIAM L	DRUMMER	POST OFFICE BOX 9698	RIVIERA BEACH, FL	33404
HARRISTON, KEITH	NEWS CORRESPONDENT	6101 16TH ST #528, NW	WASHINGTON, DC	20011
HARRITY, CHARLES W	PHOTOGRAPHER	3311 ARDLEY CT	FALLS CHURCH, VA	22041
HARROLD, JACK	TENOR	CONE, 221 W 57TH ST	NEW YORK, NY	10019
HARROLD, KATHRYN	ACTRESS	POST OFFICE BOX 5617	BEVERLY HILLS, CA	90210
HARRON, DON	TV HOST	POST OFFICE BOX 4700	VANCOUVER, BC V6B 4A3	CANADA
HARRON, DONALD H	WRITER	555 W 57TH ST #1230	NEW YORK, NY	10019
HARROW, LISA	ACTRESS	MAX NAUGHTON LOWE		
		200 FULHAM RD	LONDON SW10	ENGLAND
HARROWER, ELIZABETH	TV WRITER	8955 BEVERLY BLVD	LOS ANGELES, CA	90048
HARRY, DEBORAH "BLONDIE"	SINGER	1775 BROADWAY #700	NEW YORK, NY	10019
HARRY, JACKEE	ACTRESS	KOHNER, 9169 SUNSET BLVD	LOS ANGELES, CA	90069
HARRYHAUSEN, HARRY	ACTOR	2 ILLCHESTER PL	LONDON W14	ENGLAND
HARSCH, JONATHAN	NEWS CORRESPONDENT	1001 THORNWOOD RD	KENSINGTON, MD	20895
HART, AVERY	PLAYWRIGHT	MANTELL, 675 HUDSON ST	NEW YORK, NY	10014
HART, BEVERLY	ACTRESS	8485 MELROSE PL #E	LOS ANGELES, CA	90069
HART, BRET "HIT MAN"	WRESTLER	POST OFFICE BOX 3859	STAMFORD, CT	06905
HART, BRUCE	TV DIRECTOR	200 W 86TH ST	NEW YORK, NY	10024
HART, BRUCE	TV WRITER	ICM, 40 W 57TH ST	NEW YORK, NY	10019
HART, CAROLE	TV WRITER	ICM, 40 W 57TH ST	NEW YORK, NY	10019
HART, CECILIA	ACTRESS	9220 SUNSET BLVD #202	LOS ANGELES, CA	90069
HART, CHARLES J	WRITER	555 W 57TH ST #1230	NEW YORK, NY	10019
HART, CHRISTINA	ACTRESS	DOUBLEDAY, 5061 ELMWOOD AVE	LOS ANGELES, CA	90004
HART, CHRISTOPHER	FILM WRITER-DIRECTOR	10351 SANTA MONICA BLVD #211	LOS ANGELES, CA	90025
HART, COLONEL JIMMY	WRESTLING MANAGER	POST OFFICE BOX 3859	STAMFORD, CT	06905
HART, COREY	SINGER-SONGWRITER	6265 COTE DE LIESSE #200	ST LAURANT, QUE H4T 1C	CANADA
HART, DOLORES	ACTRESS	REGINA LAUDIS CONVENT	BETHLEHEM, CT	06751
HART, DON	TV WRITER	8955 BEVERLY BLVD	LOS ANGELES, CA	90048
HART, DON ERWIN	MUSIC ARRANGER	117 VALLEY WY DR	ANTIOCH, TN	37013
HART, FREDDIE	SINGER	TESSIER, 505 CANTON PASS	MADISON, TN	37115
HART, GARY	POLITICIAN	1748 HIGH ST	DENVER, CO	80201
HART, GARY	WRESTLING MANAGER	WORLD CLASS WRESTLING		
		SOUTHWEST SPORTS, INC		
		DALLAS SPORTATORIUM		
		1000 S INDUSTRIAL BLVD	DALLAS, TX	75207
HART, HARVEY	DIRECTOR	5 SULTAN ST	TORONTO, ONT M5S IL6	CANADA
HART, JAMES L "COLE"	CONDUCTOR	13841 COHASSET ST	VAN NUYS, CA	91405
HART, JEFFREY	COMMENTATOR	KING FEATURES SYNDICATE		
		235 E 45TH ST	NEW YORK, NY	10017
HART, JERRY "CAJUN"	SINGER	POST OFFICE BOX 532	MALIBU, CA	90265
HART, JIM V	WRITER	8955 BEVERLY BLVD	LOS ANGELES, CA	90069
HART, JIMMY	WRESTLING MANAGER	SEE - HART, COLONEL JIMMY		
HART, JOHN	ACTOR	5650 RANCHITO AVE	VAN NUYS, CA	91401
HART, JOHN	NEWS CORRESPONDENT	ICM, 40 W 57TH ST	NEW YORK, NY	10019
HART, JOHNNY	CARTOONIST	NEWS AMERICA SYNDICATE		
		1703 KAISER AVE	IRVINE, CA	92714
HART, KATHY SUE	MUSICIAN	117 VALLEY WY DR	ANTIOCH, TN	37013
HART, LINDA	ACTRESS	9229 SUNSET BLVD #306	LOS ANGELES, CA	90069
HART, LOUISA G	NEWS CORRESPONDENT	5008 WORTHINGTON DR	BETHESDA, MD	20816
HART, MARY	TV HOST	ENTERTAINMENT TONIGHT		
		PARAMOUNT TELEVISION		
		5555 MELROSE AVE	LOS ANGELES, CA	90038
HART, MICHELE	ACTRESS	1332 N CURSON AVE	LOS ANGELES, CA	90046
HART, RALPH	WRITER	1614 S BEVERLY GLEN BLVD	LOS ANGELES, CA	90024
HART, STANLEY	TV WRITER	8955 BEVERLY BLVD	LOS ANGELES, CA	90048
HART, WARREN	DIRECTOR	4345 SAMOSET RD	ROYAL OAK, MI	48072
HART FOUNDATION, THE	WRESTLING TAG TEAM	POST OFFICE BOX 3859	STAMFORD, CT	06905
HART PIANO QUARTET	PIANO QUART	POST OFFICE BOX 188		
		STATION A	TORONTO, ONT	CANADA
HARTER, JOHN R, II	NEWS CORRESPONDENT	4904 BELT RD, NW	WASHINGTON, DC	20016
HARTFIELD, PAUL	TENOR	CAMI, 165 W 57TH ST	NEW YORK, NY	10019
HARTFORD, JOHN	SINGER-SONGWRITER	POST OFFICE BOX 40989	NASHVILLE, TN	37204
HARTFORD, KENNETH	WRITER	8955 BEVERLY BLVD	LOS ANGELES, CA	90048
HARTGE, JOHN	NEWS CORRESPONDENT	1755 S JEFFERSON DAVIS HWY	ARLINGTON, VA	22202
HARTH, SIDNEY	VIOLINIST	SOFFER, 130 W 56TH ST	NEW YORK, NY	10019
HARTIG, HERBERT	TV WRITER	555 W 57TH ST #1230	NEW YORK, NY	10019
HARTIGAN, KEVIN	WRITER-PRODUCER	8955 BEVERLY BLVD	LOS ANGELES, CA	90048
HARTING, DONALD M	WRITER	555 W 57TH ST #1230	NEW YORK, NY	10019
HARTLEY, CYNTHIA	ACTRESS	1930 CENTURY PARK W #30	LOS ANGELES, CA	90067
HARTLEY, MARIETTE	ACTRESS	10100 SANTA MONICA BLVD #2460	LOS ANGELES, CA	90067
HARTLEY, NINA	ACTRESS	1442-A WALNUT ST #242	BERKELEY, CA	94709
HARTLEY, TED	ACTOR	9744 WILSHIRE BLVD #306	BEVERLY HILLS, CA	90212
HARTLIEP, NIKKI LI	SOPRANO	CAMI, 165 W 57TH ST	NEW YORK, NY	10019
HARTMAN, CARL	NEWS CORRESPONDENT	1066 THOMAS JEFFERSON ST, NW	WASHINGTON, DC	20007

Name	Occupation	Address	City	Zip
HARTMAN, DAN	SINGER-SONGWRITER	3 E 54TH ST #1400	NEW YORK, NY	10022
HARTMAN, DAVID	ACTOR-TV HOST	222 CEDAR LN	TEANECK, NJ	07666
HARTMAN, JAN A	TV WRITER	555 W 57TH ST #1230	NEW YORK, NY	10019
HARTMAN, JEANNE	ACTRESS	FELBER, 2126 N CAHUENGA BLVD	LOS ANGELES, CA	90068
HARTMAN, LISA	ACT-SING-MOD	1760 N COURTNEY AVE	LOS ANGELES, CA	90046
HARTMAN, PHIL	SCREENWRITER	8955 BEVERLY BLVD	LOS ANGELES, CA	90048
HARTMAN, SHIRLEY O	WRITER	8955 BEVERLY BLVD	LOS ANGELES, CA	90048
HARTMAN, SUSAN	WRITER	555 W 57TH ST #1230	NEW YORK, NY	10019
HARTMAN, TED	WRITER	8955 BEVERLY BLVD	LOS ANGELES, CA	90048
HARTMAN, WALTER M	MANDOLINIST	312 CAPITOL TOWERS	NASHVILLE, TN	37219
HARTMANN, EDMUND L	TV WRITER-PRODUCER	1223 S ROXBURY DR #104	LOS ANGELES, CA	90035
HARTMANN, ERICH	PHOTOGRAPHER	117 W 78TH ST	NEW YORK, NY	10024
HARTOG, MICHAEL	DIRECTOR	DGA, 7950 SUNSET BLVD	LOS ANGELES, CA	90046
HARTOS, NICO	FILM DIRECTOR	16 WICHITA AVE	ROCKWAY, NJ	07866
HARTSON, MERRILL JARD	NEWS CORRESPONDENT	7427 COLTON LN	MANASSAS, VA	22110
HARTUNG, RAYMOND C	WRITER	338 N CITRUS AVE	LOS ANGELES, CA	90036
HARTWELL, JOHN	WRITER	8955 BEVERLY BLVD	LOS ANGELES, CA	90048
HARTY, RUSSELL	TV PRODUCER	N GAY, 24 DENMARK ST	LONDON WC2	ENGLAND
HARTZ, JIM	TV HOST	PBS, 475 L'ENFANT PLAZA	WASHINGTON, DC	20024
HARU, SUMI	ACTRESS	8235 SANTA MONICA BLVD #202	LOS ANGELES, CA	90046
HARVEY, ALAN E	NEWS CORRESPONDENT	NBC-TV, NEWS DEPARTMENT		
		4001 NEBRASKA AVE, NW	WASHINGTON, DC	20016
HARVEY, ALAN EDWARD	PHOTOGRAPHER	5228 RUSSETT RD	ROCKVILLE, MD	20853
HARVEY, ALEX	GUITARIST	RENTHAL-KAUFMAN MGMT		
		1900 AVE OF THE STARS	LOS ANGELES, CA	90067
HARVEY, ANTHONY	FILM DIRECTOR	MORRIS, 147-149 WARDOUR ST	LONDON W1V 3TB	ENGLAND
HARVEY, BOB	WRITER	8955 BEVERLY BLVD	LOS ANGELES, CA	90048
HARVEY, DAVID A	PHOTOGRAPHER	7205 PINETREE RD	RICHMOND, VA	23229
HARVEY, FRANCIS	DIRECTOR	MS PRODS, 54 MARSHALL ST	LONDON W1	ENGLAND
HARVEY, JAMES D	PHOTOGRAPHER	5020 ALTA VISTA RD	BETHESDA, MD	20814
HARVEY, JERRY F	WRITER	8955 BEVERLY BLVD	LOS ANGELES, CA	90048
HARVEY, KAY	ACTRESS	10850 RIVERSIDE DR #410	NORTH HOLLYWOOD, CA	91609
HARVEY, KEN	GUITARIST	2519 BLAIR BLVD	NASHVILLE, TN	37212
HARVEY, MICHAEL	THEATER PRODUCER	1501 BROADWAY	NEW YORK, NY	10036
HARVEY, PAUL	NEWS ANALYST	1034 PARK AVE	RIVER FOREST, IL	60305
HARVEY, RAYMOND	CONDUCTOR	1776 BROADWAY #504	NEW YORK, NY	10019
HARVEY, STEVE	SPORTS WRITER	UNIVERSAL PRESS SYNDICATE		
		4900 MAIN ST, 9TH FLOOR	KANSAS CITY, MO	62114
HARVEY, SUSAN SEAMANS	COMPOSER	6258 ATOLL AVE	VAN NUYS, CA	91401
HARVIN, LAURENCE	VIOLINIST	ROUTE #2, MEADOW LN	MURFREESBORO, TN	37130
HARVIN, MARIANNA	VIOLINIST	ROUTE #2, MEADOW LN	MURFREESBORO, TN	37130
HARVIN, TEMOTHI	ACTOR	961 EASTERN PARKWAY	BROOKLYN, NY	11213
HARWOOD, GWEN	ACTRESS	19758 WELLS DR	WOODLAND HILLS, CA	91364
HARWOOD, JAMES	ACTOR	3 WEEHAWKEN ST	NEW YORK, NY	10014
HARWOOD, JOHN	NEWS CORRESPONDENT	1747 CHURCH ST #2, NW	WASHINGTON, DC	20036
HARWOOD, MARGARET C	NEWS CORRESPONDENT	1322 DE WITT AVE	ALEXANDRIA, VA	22301
HARWOOD, RICHARD	TV DIRECTOR	16737 KNOLLWOOD DR	GRANADA HILLS, CA	91344
HARWOOD, RONALD	TV WRITER	DAISH, 83 EASTBOURNE MEWS	LONDON W2 6LQ	ENGLAND
HARZ, CLAUDE J	WRITER	8955 BEVERLY BLVD	LOS ANGELES, CA	90048
HASBURGH, PATRICK BURKE	WRITER-PRODUCER	3884 SHERWOOD PL	SHERMAN OAKS, CA	91423
HASELDEN, KATHRYN	ACTRESS	LEONETTI, 6526 SUNSET BLVD	HOLLYWOOD, CA	90028
HASELEY, DONNA	NEWS CORRESPONDENT	5811 READING AVE #282	ALEXANDRIA, VA	22311
HASIN, NINA L	NEWS CORRESPONDENT	3002 RODMAN ST, NW	WASHINGTON, DC	20008
HASKELL, DAVID	ACTOR	9220 SUNSET BLVD #202	LOS ANGELES, CA	90069
HASKELL, JIMMIE	COMPOSER-CONDUCTOR	11800 LAUGHTON WY	NORTHRIDGE, CA	91326
HASKELL, MOLLY	FILM CRITIC	VOGUE MAGAZINE, INC		
		350 MADISON AVE	NEW YORK, NY	10017
HASKELL, PETER	ACTOR	19924 ACRE ST	NORTHRIDGE, CA	91324
HASKINS, DENNIS	ACTOR	9777 WILSHIRE BLVD #707	BEVERLY HILLS, CA	90212
HASLEY, DAVID D	WRITER	8955 BEVERLY BLVD	LOS ANGELES, CA	90048
HASLEY, WILLIAM	ACTRESS-WRITER	1523 N MARTEL AVE	HOLLYWOOD, CA	90046
HASLOP & SANDERS	MUSICAL DUO	CCS, 4478 PURDUE AVE	CULVER CITY, CA	90230
HASS, SABINE	SOPRANO	CAMI, 165 W 57TH ST	NEW YORK, NY	10019
HASSELHOFF, DAVID	ACTOR	4310 SUTTON PL	SHERMAN OAKS, CA	91413
HASSETT, MARILYN	ACTRESS	10000 SANTA MONICA BLVD #305	LOS ANGELES, CA	90067
HASSETT, RAYMOND C	WRITER	555 W 57TH ST #1230	NEW YORK, NY	10019
HASSETT, WALTER D, JR	NEWS CORRESPONDENT	1755 S JEFFERSON DAVIS HWY	ARLINGTON, VA	22202
HASSING, JOYCE MAC KENZIE	ACTRESS	6430 SUNSET BLVD #1203	LOS ANGELES, CA	90028
HASSINGER, SARA L	DIRECTOR	4008 BUCKINGHAM AVE	DETROIT, MI	48224
HASSLER, PATTI	WRITER	555 W 57TH ST #1230	NEW YORK, NY	10019
HASSO, SIGNE	ACTRESS	215 W 90TH ST #7-F	NEW YORK, NY	10024
HASSON, CAROL L	WRITER	555 W 57TH ST #1230	NEW YORK, NY	10019
HASSON, JUDITH	NEWS CORRESPONDENT	403 11TH ST, SE	WASHINGTON, DC	20003
HASSON, RAYMOND	WRITER	555 W 57TH ST #1230	NEW YORK, NY	10019
HASTEY, STAN	NEWS CORRESPONDENT	6047 CLERKENWELL CT	BURKE, VA	20015
HASTINGS, BOB	ACTOR	8075 W 3RD ST #303	LOS ANGELES, CA	90048
HASTINGS, DON	ACTOR	CBS-TV, "AS THE WORLD TURNS"		
		51 W 52ND ST	NEW YORK, NY	10019
HASTINGS, HARRY ROBERT	TV PRODUCER	CURRIEHILL COTTAGE		
		LEO RD, WIMBLEDON	LONDON SW19	ENGLAND
HASTINGS, ROSS	COMPOSER	4 WOODLAWN TERR	CEDAR GROVE, NJ	07009
HATCH, CHRISTOPHER	PHOTOGRAPHER	53 COOLRIDGE RD	MILFORD, CT	06460
HATCH, RICHARD	ACTOR	11726 SAN VICENTE BLVD #300	LOS ANGELES, CA	90049
HATCHER, CHARLES CHANDLER	DIRECTOR	200 LAUREL AVE	CHICAGO, IL	60611
HATCHER, SHIRLEY J	ACTRESS	1407 LINDEN BLVD	BROOKLYN, NY	11212

HATCHET, MOLLY	ROCK & ROLL GROUP	SEE - MOLLY HATCHET	
HATFIELD, BOBBY	SINGER	RILLERA, 9841 HOT SPRINGS DR	HUNTINGTON BEACH, CA 92646
HATFIELD, CAROL A	TV WRITER	8955 BEVERLY BLVD	LOS ANGELES, CA 90048
HATFIELD, DR FRED	BODYBUILDER	POST OFFICE BOX 222	CANOGA PARK, CA 91305
HATFIELD, HURD	ACTOR	BALLINTERRY HOUSE, RATHCORMAC	CO CORK IRELAND
HATHAWAY, BRUCE W	NEWS CORRESPONDENT	1001 26TH ST #404, NW	WASHINGTON, DC 20037
HATOS, STEFAN	TV WRITER	1555 ALEXIS PL	BEVERLY HILLS, CA 90210
HATTMAN, STEPHEN	TV WRITER-PRODUCER	11660 PICTURESQUE DR	STUDIO CITY, CA 91604
HATTON, MAURICE	FILM PRODUCER	MITHRAS, 3 CAMBRIDGE GATE	
		REGENT'S PARK	LONDON NW1 ENGLAND
HATU KID	WRESTLER	POST OFFICE BOX 3859	STAMFORD, CT 06905
HAUBEN, LAURENCE A	WRITER	8955 BEVERLY BLVD	LOS ANGELES, CA 90048
HAUCK, CHARLES R	TV WRITER	4412 ELENDA ST	CULVER CITY, CA 90230
HAUER, RUTGER	ACTOR	151 S EL CAMINO DR	BEVERLY HILLS, CA 90212
HAUFRECT, ALAN	ACTOR-WRITER	3525 COLDWATER CANYON AVE	STUDIO CITY, CA 91604
HAUGHN, JEANNE	SOPRANO	POST OFFICE BOX 884	NEW YORK, NY 10023
HAUGHT, ROBERT L	NEWS CORRESPONDENT	527 S FAIRFAX ST	ALEXANDRIA, VA 22314
HAUGLAND, AAGE	SINGER	CAMI, 165 W 57TH ST	NEW YORK, NY 10019
HAUN, CHRISTOPHER	TV WRITER	8955 BEVERLY BLVD	LOS ANGELES, CA 90048
HAUPT, CHARLES	VIOLINIST	ACC, 890 W END AVE	NEW YORK, NY 10025
HAUPT, DONNA E	NEWS REPORTER	LIFE/TIME & LIFE BLDG	
		ROCKEFELLER CENTER	NEW YORK, NY 10020
HAUPTMAN, WILLIAM T	TV WRITER	555 W 57TH ST #1230	NEW YORK, NY 10019
HAUSER, FAY	ACTRESS	LAM, 6834 HOLLYWOOD BLVD	LOS ANGELES, CA 90028
HAUSER, HAL	WRITER	8955 BEVERLY BLVD	LOS ANGELES, CA 90048
HAUSER, NANCY LOCKE	ACTRESS	8640 W 3RD ST #2	LOS ANGELES, CA 90048
HAUSER, RANDY	DRUMMER	140 ROBIN HOOD CIR	HENDERSONVILLE, TN 37075
HAUSER, RICK	WRITER-PRODUCER	6906 PACIFIC VIEW DR	LOS ANGELES, CA 90068
HAUSER, WINGS	ACTOR	2234 VISTA DEL MAR AVE	LOS ANGELES, CA 90068
HAUSNER, EDWARD	PHOTOGRAPHER	20-11 RADBURN RD	FAIR LAWN, NJ 07410
HAUSNER, JERRY	ACTOR	9255 SUNSET BLVD #1105	LOS ANGELES, CA 90069
HAUSRATH, JAN E	WRITER	8955 BEVERLY BLVD	LOS ANGELES, CA 90048
HAUSRATH, LISE	NEWS CORRESPONDENT	1403 N NASH ST #2	ARLINGTON, VA 22209
HAUSSERMAN, MISCHA	ACTOR	KOHNER, 9169 SUNSET BLVD	LOS ANGELES, CA 90069
HAUTZIG, WALTER	PIANIST	111 W 57TH ST #1209	NEW YORK, NY 10019
HAVEMANN, JOEL	NEWS CORRESPONDENT	3809 WOODBINE ST	CHEVY CHASE, MD 20815
HAVEN, SUE PERKINS	TV WRITER	555 W 57TH ST #1230	NEW YORK, NY 10019
HAVENS, JAMES C	DIRECTOR	DGA, 7950 SUNSET BLVD	LOS ANGELES, CA 90046
HAVENS, RICHIE	SINGER-GUITARIST	10 E 44TH ST #700	NEW YORK, NY 10017
HAVER, JUNE	ACTRESS	MAC MURRAY, 485 HALVERN DR	LOS ANGELES, CA 90049
HAVERS, NIGEL	ACTOR	LEADING ARTISTS, LTD	
		60 SAINT JAMES'S ST	LONDON SW1 ENGLAND
HAVEY, MARKOS & HIS MEXIC	C & W GROUP	POST OFFICE BOX 707	BELMONT, CA 94002
HAVINGA, NICHOLAS, JR	TV DIRECTOR	1250 CORNING ST	LOS ANGELES, CA 90035
HAVNER, CARL	COMPUTER ANALYIST	2801 MEADOW LARK DR	SAN DIEGO, CA 92123
HAVOC	ROCK & ROLL GROUP	1085 VALLEY DR	SUNNYVALE, CA 94087
HAVOC, JUNE	ACTRESS	CANNON CROSSING	WILTON, CT 06879
HAWES, MICHAEL A	WRITER	8955 BEVERLY BLVD	LOS ANGELES, CA 90048
HAWES, TONY	WRITER-COMEDIAN	5329 TAMPA AVE	TARZANA, CA 91356
HAWK, DAVE	BODYBUILDER	POST OFFICE BOX 97007	PITTSBIRGH, PA 15229
HAWK, J W	WRESTLER	CAPITOL INTERNATIONAL	
		11844 MARKET ST	NORTH LIMA, OH 44452
HAWK, JAMES A	NEWS CORRESPONDENT	3101 CRAFFORD DR	FORT WASHINGTON, MD 20744
HAWK, JOHNNY	GUITARIST	ROUTE #3	HARTSVILLE, TN 37074
HAWKE, CHARLIE	ACTOR	3907 W ALAMEDA AVE #101	BURBANK, CA 91505
HAWKESWORTH, JOHN	TV WRITER-PRODUCER	24 COTTERSMORE GARDENS	LONDON W8 ENGLAND
HAWKINS	C & W GROUP	1909 THOMAS AVE #E	PORTSMOUTH, OH 45662
HAWKINS, BOYCE	PIANIST	1011 MURFREESBORO RD #E	FRANKLIN, TN 37064
HAWKINS, CAROL	ACTRESS	7 LAMBOLE RD #17	LONDON NW3 ENGLAND
HAWKINS, CRAWFORD W, JR	DIRECTOR	14021 MARQUESAS WY #10	MARINA DEL REY, CA 90292
HAWKINS, EDWIN, SINGER	GOSPEL GROUP	1971 HOOVER AVE	OAKLAND, CA 94602
HAWKINS, JAY	SINGER-SONGWRITER	SEE - HAWKINS, SCREAMIN' JAY	
HAWKINS, MARTHA	GUITARIST	ROUTE #1, BOX 99	MC EWEN, TN 37101
HAWKINS, ODIE	TV WRITER	8955 BEVERLY BLVD	LOS ANGELES, CA 90048
HAWKINS, PETER	ACTOR	7 HARROWBY CT, HARROWBY ST	LONDON W1H 5FA ENGLAND
HAWKINS, RICHARD R	TV WRITER	4238 RIVERTON AVE	NORTH HOLLYWOOD, CA 91602
HAWKINS, RICK	TV PRODUCER	NBC-TV, 3000 W ALAMEDA AVE	BURBANK, CA 91523
HAWKINS, RUSS	GUITARIST	ROUTE #1, BOX 99	MC EWEN, TN 37101
HAWKINS, SCREAMIN' JAY	SINGER-SONGWRITER	GLITTER MANAGEMENT AGENCY	
		1833 N ORANGE GROVE AVE	LOS ANGELES, CA 90046
HAWKINS, SLIM	GUITARIST	ROUTE #1, BOX 99	MC EWEN, TN 37101
HAWKINS, TOMMY	SPORTSCASTER	2445 BANYON DR	LOS ANGELES, CA 90036
HAWKINS, WALTER & THE HAWKINS	GOSPEL GROUP	10100 SANTA MONICA BLVD #1600	LOS ANGELES, CA 90067
HAWKINS, WARD	WRITER	22770 BRANDYWINE DR	WOODLAND HILLS, CA 91364
HAWKINS-MILLER, SUSAN J	WRITER	6716 CLYBOURN AVE #247	NORTH HOLLYWOOD, CA 91606
HAWLEY, ALEXANDRA	FLUTIST	POST OFFICE BOX U	REDDING, CT 06875
HAWLEY, LOWELL S	WRITER	8955 BEVERLY BLVD	LOS ANGELES, CA 90048
HAWLEY & JANSEN	MUSICAL DUO	POST OFFICE BOX U	REDDING, CT 06875
HAWN, GOLDIE	ACTRESS	1849 SAWTELLE BLVD #500	LOS ANGELES, CA 90025
HAWN, JACK L	WRITER	8955 BEVERLY BLVD	LOS ANGELES, CA 90048
HAWORTH, BARRY J	DIRECTOR	12720 BURBANK BLVD #229	NORTH HOLLYWOOD, CA 91607
HAWORTH, EDWARD S	WRITER-PRODUCER	1500 STONE CANYON RD	LOS ANGELES, CA 90077
HAWORTH, JILL	ACTRESS	ACTORS GROUP, 157 W 57TH ST	NEW YORK, NY 10019
HAWORTH, SPEEDY	MUSICIAN	POST OFFICE BOX 606	FAIRVIEW, TN 37062
HAWTHORNE, JAMES	GUITARIST	MC EVOY, 8040 HARDING AVE	SKOKIE, IL 60076

Name	Occupation	Address	City
HAWTHORNE, NIGEL	ACTOR	5 STUD COTTAGES, BURNT FARM RD	
		CREWES HILL, ENFIELD	MIDDLESEX ENGLAND
HAWTHORNE, OLIVER	TV WRITER	8955 BEVERLY BLVD	LOS ANGELES, CA 90048
HAWTHORNE, TIMOTHY R	WRITER-PRODUCER	13183-A GWYNETH DR	TUSTIN, CA 92680
HAXALL, E LEE	SCREENWRITER	1940 6TH ST #B	SANTA MONICA, CA 90405
HAY, COLIN JAMES	SINGER-SONGWRITER	575 MADISON AVE #600	NEW YORK, NY 10022
HAY, JAMES	WRITER	8955 BEVERLY BLVD	LOS ANGELES, CA 90048
HAYASHI, KENICHIRO	NEWS CORRESPONDENT	6014 KINGSFORD RD	BETHESDA, MD 20817
HAYDEN, DENNIS	ACTOR	1605 N CAHUENGA BLVD #202	LOS ANGELES, CA 90028
HAYDEN, JEFFREY	TV DIRECTOR	10590 WILSHIRE BLVD #408	LOS ANGELES, CA 90024
HAYDEN, LINDA	ACTRESS	5 KINGS CT, HAMMERSMITH	LONDON W6 ENGLAND
HAYDEN, MELISSA	ACTRESS	12725 VENTURA BLVD #E	STUDIO CITY, CA 91604
HAYDEN, RON	ACTOR	8721 SUNSET BLVD #202	LOS ANGELES, CA 90069
HAYDEN, SCOTT	ACTOR	200 N ROBERTSON BLVD #308	BEVERLY HILLS, CA 90210
HAYDEN, TERI	ACTRESS	8949 SUNSET BLVD #203	LOS ANGELES, CA 90069
HAYDEN, TOM	POLITICIAN	POST OFFICE BOX 491355	LOS ANGELES, CA 90049
HAYDON, ETHEL L	WRITER	14277 SUNSET BLVD	PACIFIC PALISADES, CA 90272
HAYDON, TOM	WRITER-PRODUCER	POST OFFICE BOX 1608	NORTH SYDNEY NSW 2060 AUSTRALIA
HAYEK, JULIE	ACTRESS-MODEL	5645 BURNING TREE DR	LA CANADA, CA 91011
HAYERS, SIDNEY	TV DIRECTOR-PRODUCER	10451 WYTON DR	LOS ANGELES, CA 90024
HAYES, AFRIKA	SOPRANO	FROTHINGHAM, 40 GROVE ST	WESSESLEY, MA 02181
HAYES, BERNADETTE	ACTRESS	7112 1/2 LA TIJERA BLVD	LOS ANGELES, CA 90045
HAYES, BILL	ACTOR	4528 BECK AVE	NORTH HOLLYWOOD, CA 91602
HAYES, BILLIE	ACTRESS	8022 SELMA AVE	LOS ANGELES, CA 90046
HAYES, BLAIR K	TV DIRECTOR	51 CLINTON AVE	RIDGEWOOD, NJ 07450
HAYES, BRIAN CAMERON	WRITER	18540 PLUMMER ST #221	NORTHRIDGE, CA 91324
HAYES, BRUCE	ACTOR	7942 NAGLE AVE	NORTH HOLLYWOOD, CA 91605
HAYES, FRANKLIN	WRESTLER	SEE - TATUM, JOHN "HOLLYWOOD"	
HAYES, GLORIA	ACTRESS	KOHNER, 9169 SUNSET BLVD	LOS ANGELES, CA 90069
HAYES, HELEN	ACTRESS	235 N BROADWAY	NYACK, NY 10960
HAYES, ISAAC	SINGER-SONGWRITER	HUSH PRODS, 231 W 58TH ST	NEW YORK, NY 10010
HAYES, JACK J	COMPOSER	8111 ZITOLA TERR	MARINA DEL REY, CA 90292
HAYES, JAMES B	PUBLISHING EXECUTIVE	DISCOVER/TIME & LIFE BLDG	
		ROCKEFELLER CENTER	NEW YORK, NY 10020
HAYES, JAMES MICHAEL	ACTOR	13111 VENTURA BLVD #102	STUDIO CITY, CA 91604
HAYES, JAMES W	TV WRITER	8955 BEVERLY BLVD	LOS ANGELES, CA 90048
HAYES, JEFFREY M	TV WRITER	8955 BEVERLY BLVD	LOS ANGELES, CA 90048
HAYES, JOHN MICHAEL	SCREENWRITER	503 N ALPINE DR	BEVERLY HILLS, CA 90210
HAYES, JONATHAN	TV EXECUTIVE	POST OFFICE BOX 10210	STAMFORD, CT 06904
HAYES, JOSEPH A	WRITER	8955 BEVERLY BLVD	LOS ANGELES, CA 90048
HAYES, JUDE T	WRITER	555 W 57TH ST #1230	NEW YORK, NY 10019
HAYES, LINDA	ACTRESS	CROSBY, 670 BUSCH GARDE	PASADENA, CA 91105
HAYES, LONNY	GUITARIST-BANJOIST	POST OFFICE BOX 1091	LAUERGNE, TN 37086
HAYES, MELVYN	ACTOR	LITTLE BARFIELDS	
		38 GLOVERS RD, REIGATE	SURREY RH2 7LA ENGLAND
HAYES, MICHAEL	FILM WRITER-DIRECTOR	GREENE, 91 REGENT ST	LONDON W1 ENGLAND
HAYES, MICHAEL "FREEBIRD"	WRESTLER	SEE - HAYES, MICHAEL "P S"	
HAYES, MICHAEL "P S"	WRESTLER	UNIVERSAL WRESTLING FEDERATION	
		MID SOUTH SPORTS, INC	
		5001 SPRING VALLEY RD	DALLAS, TX 75244
HAYES, OTIS R, JR	COMPOSER	1731 W 84TH ST	LOS ANGELES, CA 90047
HAYES, PATRICIA	ACTRESS	20 WEST HILL RD	LONDON SW18 ENGLAND
HAYES, PATTY	CASTING DIRECTOR	932 N LA BREA AVE	LOS ANGELES, CA 90038
HAYES, PETER LIND	ACTOR-COMEDIAN	3538 PUEBLO WY	LAS VEGAS, NV 89109
HAYES, RAPHAEL	WRITER	8955 BEVERLY BLVD	LOS ANGELES, CA 90048
HAYES, ROBERT D	GUITARIST	ROUTE #4	CAMDEN, TN 38320
HAYES, RON	ACTOR	10920 WILSHIRE BLVD #220	LOS ANGELES, CA 90024
HAYES, STEVE	TV WRITER	14144 VENTURA BLVD #200	SHERMAN OAKS, CA 91423
HAYES, SUSAN SEAFORTH	ACTRESS	4528 BECK AVE	NORTH HOLLYWOOD, CA 91602
HAYES, TIMOTHY	TV DIRECTOR	322 E 39TH ST	NEW YORK, NY 10016
HAYES, WILLIAM	ACTOR	3151 W CAHUENGA BLVD #310	LOS ANGELES, CA 90068
HAYESON, JIMMY	ACTOR	2289 5TH AVE #12-C	NEW YORK, NY 10037
HAYGOOD, JIM	CLOWN	2701 COTTAGE WY #14	SACRAMENTO, CA 95825
HAYLEY, HAROLD	PHOTOJOURNALIST	1205 LORENE CT	PASADENA, MD 21122
HAYMAN, CYD	ACTRESS	GARDNER, 219-A KINGS RD	LONDON SW3 5EJ ENGLAND
HAYMAN, DAVID T	ACTOR	9165 SUNSET BLVD #202	LOS ANGELES, CA 90069
HAYMAN, RICHARD	COMPOSER-CONDUCTOR	1020 PARK AVE	NEW YORK, NY 10028
HAYMER, JOHNNY	ACTOR	11321 CANTON DR	STUDIO CITY, CA 91604
HAYMER, SUSAN	TV WRITER-DIRECTOR	2883 NICHOLS CANYON RD	LOS ANGELES, CA 90046
HAYMES, DICK, JR	SINGER-ACTOR	180 CENTRAL PARK S	NEW YORK, NY 10019
HAYMON, CYNTHIA	SOPRANO	CAMI, 165 W 57TH ST	NEW YORK, NY 10019
HAYNES, BILLY H	GUITARIST	115 BOXWOOD DR	FRANKLIN, TN 37064
HAYNES, BILLY JACK	WRESTLER	POST OFFICE BOX 3859	STAMFORD, CT 06905
HAYNES, BILLY JACK	WRESTLER	POST OFFICE BOX 3859	STAMFORD, CT 06905
HAYNES, EUGENE, JR	PIANIST-COMPOSER	710 LAFAYETTE ST	JEFFERSON CITY, MO 65101
HAYNES, JOHN	WRITER	8955 BEVERLY BLVD	LOS ANGELES, CA 90048
HAYNES, LINDA	ACTRESS	6363 WILSHIRE BLVD #600	LOS ANGELES, CA 90048
HAYNES, MARSHA	ACTRESS	8350 SANTA MONICA BLVD #103	LOS ANGELES, CA 90069
HAYNES, MICHAEL	ACTOR	11325 RIVERSIDE DR	NORTH HOLLYWOOD, CA 91602
HAYNES, MIKE	TRUMPETER	ROUTE #4, BOX 309-A	TULLAHOMA, TN 37388
HAYNES, ROBERTA	WRITER	8955 BEVERLY BLVD	LOS ANGELES, CA 90048
HAYNES, TIGER	ACTOR	313 W 14TH ST	NEW YORK, NY 10014
HAYNES, WALTER	GUITARIST	ROUTE #1, BOX 92	BURNS, TN 37029
HAYNES, WILLIAM, JR	WRESTLER	SEE - HAYNES, BILLY JACK	
HAYNIE, CINDIE	ACTRESS	6331 HOLLYWOOD BLVD #924	LOS ANGELES, CA 90028

Name	Occupation	Address	City	Zip/Country
HAYNIE, JIM	ACTOR	211 S BEVERLY DR #201	BEVERLY HILLS, CA	90212
HAYS, BILL	TV DIRECTOR	1 CHALLONERER CRESCENT	LONDON W14	ENGLAND
HAYS, CHANTEL	SINGER	POST OFFICE BOX 171132	NASHVILLE, TN	37217
HAYS, DAVID	THEATER PRODUCER	305 GREAT NECK RD	WATERFORD, CT	06385
HAYS, KATHRYN	ACTRESS	BRET ADAMS, 448 W 44TH ST	NEW YORK, NY	10036
HAYS, LEE	WRITER-PRODUCER	113 WAVERLY PL	NEW YORK, NY	10011
HAYS, LOYAL	WRITER	8955 BEVERLY BLVD	LOS ANGELES, CA	90048
HAYS, ROBERT	ACTOR	2607 NICHOLS CANYON RD	LOS ANGELES, CA	90046
HAYS, WILL H, JR	SCREENWRITER	208 UNION FEDERAL BUILDING	CRAWFORDSVILLE, IN	47933
HAYSBERT, DENNIS	ACTOR	3624 CYN CREST RD	ALTADENA, CA	91001
HAYSI EANTAYZEE	ROCK & ROLL GROUP	POST OFFICE BOX 4DR	LONDON W1A 4DR	ENGLAND
HAYT, ANDY	SPORTS PHOTOGRAPHER	SPORTS ILLUSTRATED MAGAZINE		
		TIME & LIFE BUILDING		
		ROCKEFELLER CENTER	NEW YORK, NY	10020
HAYWARD, ANN STEWART	WRITER-PRODUCER	3838 S GIBRALTER AVE	LOS ANGELES, CA	90008
HAYWARD, CHRISTOPHER	TV WRITER-PRODUCER	12546 THE VISTA	LOS ANGELES, CA	90049
HAYWARD, CHUCK	DIRECTOR	9030 WHEATLAND AVE	SUN VALLEY, CA	91352
HAYWARD, DAVID	ACTOR	SF & A, 121 N SAN VICENTE BLVD	BEVERLY HILLS, CA	90211
HAYWARD, DAVID W	MUSICIAN	2813 S TOPANGA CANYON BLVD	MALIBU, CA	90265
HAYWARD, JUSTIN	SINGER-SONGWRITER	TOWERBELL RECORDS COMPANY		
		1 IVERSON RD	LONDON NW6 2QT	ENGLAND
HAYWARD, MICHAEL	DIRECTOR	3308 TICA DR	LOS ANGELES, CA	90027
HAYWARD, WILLIAM L	WRITER	8855 SAINT IVES DR	LOS ANGELES, CA	90069
HAYWIRE	ROCK & ROLL GROUP	41 BRITAIN ST #200	TORONTO, ONT	CANADA
HAYWOOD, LORNA	SOPRANO	59 E 54TH ST #81	NEW YORK, NY	10022
HAYWORTH, JEAN OWENS	ACTRESS	4645 ETHEL AVE	VAN NUYS, CA	91423
HAZARD, JOYCE	ACTRESS	1509 N CRESCENT HGTS BLVD	LOS ANGELES, CA	90069
HAZARD, RICHARD	COMPOSER	657 PERUGIA WY	LOS ANGELES, CA	90077
HAZARD, ROBERT	SINGER	ICM, 40 W 57TH ST	NEW YORK, NY	10019
HAZELWOOD, DEL	PIANIST	1505 RIVERWOOD DR	NASHVILLE, TN	37216
HAZELWOOD, ERROL M	WRITER	555 W 57TH ST #1230	NEW YORK, NY	10019
HEABERLIN, LARRY	SINGER	POST OFFICE BOX 405-A	EDON, MO	65026
HEAD, CHARLES	GUITARIST	611 FREDA VILLA	MADISON, TN	37115
HEAD, MARSHALL	DIRECTOR	1763 CULVER LN	GLENVIEW, IL	60025
HEAD, ROY	SINGER-SONGWRITER	HUGH DANCY, 3095 HWY 301 N	LAKE CORNORANT, MS	38641
HEAD, TEENAGE	ROCK & ROLL GROUP	SEE - TEENAGE HEAD		
HEAD EAST	ROCK & ROLL GROUP	10350 SANTA MONICA BLVD #210	LOS ANGELES, CA	90025
HEADHUNTERS, THE	WRESTLING TAG TEAM	GORGEOUS GIRLS OF WRESTLING		
		RIVIERA HOTEL & CASINO		
		DAVID B MC LANE PRODS		
		2901 S LAS VEGAS BLVD	LAS VEGAS, NV	89109
HEADLINE, WILLIAM	CABLE EXECUTIVE	1050 TECHWOOD DR, NW	ATLANTA, GA	30318
HEADLINE, WILLIAM W	NEWS CORRESPONDENT	2133 WISCONSIN AVE, NW	WASHINGTON, DC	20007
HEADPINS, THE	ROCK & ROLL GROUP	3 E 54TH ST #1400	NEW YORK, NY	10022
HEADPINS, THE	ROCK & ROLL GROUP	41 BRITAIN ST #200	TORONTO, ONT	CANADA
HEADS, BARRIE	TV EXECUTIVE	GRANADA INTERNATIONAL		
		36 GOLDEN SQ	LONDON W1	ENGLAND
HEADY, ROBERT K	COLUMNIST	TRIBUNE MEDIA SERVICES		
		64 E CONCORD ST	ORLANDO, FL	32801
HEAFNER, CAROLYN	SOPRANO	1199 PARK AVE #1-E	NEW YORK, NY	10028
HEAGY, WILL	NEWS CORRESPONDENT	1333 "H" ST, NW	WASHINGTON, DC	20005
HEALD, ANTHONY	ACTOR	AFFILIATE ARTISTS, INC		
		37 W 65TH ST, 6TH FLOOR	NEW YORK, NY	10023
HEALEY, DIANE	TV EXECUTIVE	NBC TELEVISION NETWORK		
		30 ROCKEFELLER PLAZA	NEW YORK, NY	10112
HEALEY, JAMES R	COLUMNIST	POST OFFICE BOX 500	WASHINGTON, DC	20044
HEALEY, MARY	ACTRESS	FRASER, 91 REGENT ST	LONDON W1	ENGLAND
HEALEY, MIKE	TV WRITER-DIRECTOR	25 KNUTSFORD RD, WILMSLOW	CHESHIRE	ENGLAND
HEALEY, MYRON D	ACTOR-WRITER	1461 2ND ST	SISNA, CA	93065
HEALIS, SUSAN	ACTRESS	12007 BURGESS AVE	WHITTIER, CA	90604
HEALY, DAVID	ACTOR	SF & A, 121 N SAN VICENTE BLVD	BEVERLY HILLS, CA	90211
HEALY, MARY	SINGER-ACTRESS	3538 PUEBLO WY	LAS VEGAS, NV	89109
HEALY, REV TIMOTHY S	EDUCATOR-AUTHOR	GEORGETOWN UNIVERSITY		
		DEPARTMENT OF ENGLISH		
		37TH & "O" STS, NW	WASHINGTON, DC	20008
HEALY, ROBERT	NEWS CORRESPONDENT	3711 FESSENDEN ST, NW	WASHINGTON, DC	20016
HEALY, ROBERT LEO	NEWS CORRESPONDENT	2201 "L" ST #414, NW	WASHINGTON, DC	20037
HEAP, JIMMY, JR	DRUMMER	714 NEW DUE WEST AVE #K	MADISON, TN	37115
HEARD, ANN	ACTRESS	KOHNER, 9169 SUNSET BLVD	LOS ANGELES, CA	90069
HEARD, CONNIE	VIOLINIST	867 CURTISWOOD LN	NASHVILLE, TN	37204
HEARD, JOHN	ACTOR	853 7TH AVE #9-A	NEW YORK, NY	10019
HEARN, ANN	ACTRESS	KOHNER, 9169 SUNSET BLVD	LOS ANGELES, CA	90069
HEARN, DAN	SAXOPHONIST	891 ROBERTS RD	COOKVILLE, TN	38501
HEARN, GEORGE	ACTOR	211 S BEVERLY DR #201	BEVERLY HILLS, CA	90212
HEARSHEN, IRA P	COMPOSER-CONDUCTOR	8723 1/2 CEDROS AVE	PANORAMA CITY, CA	91402
HEARST, KEVIN	ACTOR	9715 HENSAL RD	BEVERLY HILLS, CA	90210
HEARST, STEPHEN	TV WRITER-DIRECTOR	78 ELM PARK, STANMORE	MIDDLESEX	ENGLAND
HEARST SHAW, PATRICIA	AUTHORESS	110 5TH ST	SAN FRANCISCO, CA	94103
HEART	ROCK & ROLL GROUP	6300 S CENTER BLVD #200	SEATTLE, WA	98188
HEART OF GOLD, THE	ROCK & ROLL GROUP	POST OFFICE BOX 92	BROOKLYN, NY	11229
HEART THROBS, THE	ROCK & ROLL GROUP	CEE, 193 KONHAUS RD	MECHANICSBURG, PA	17055
HEARTBREAK U S A	ROCK & ROLL GROUP	PREPPY PRODS, 66 W 77TH ST	NEW YORK, NY	10024
HEARTFIXERS, THE	BLUES BAND	450 14TH ST #201, NW	ATLANTA, GA	30318
HEASLEY, MARLA	ACTRESS	1172 CENTINELA AVE #4	SANTA MONICA, CA	90403
HEASTON, TRACY MATTHEW	COMPOSER-CONDUCTOR	POST OFFICE BOX 3316	ONTARIO, CA	91761

Name	Occupation	Address	City	Zip
HEATERS, THE	ROCK & ROLL GROUP	K P PRODS, 132 N DOHENY DR	LOS ANGELES, CA	90048
HEATH, ERIC	ACTOR	9250 WILSHIRE BLVD #208	BEVERLY HILLS, CA	90212
HEATH, JAMES	SAXOPHONIST	112-19 34TH AVE	CORONA, NY	11368
HEATH, JIMMY, QUARTET	JAZZ QUARTET	KURLAND, 173 BRIGHTON AVE	BOSTON, MA	02134
HEATH, LEONARD LAWRENCE	TV WRITER	151 TIGERTAIL RD	LOS ANGELES, CA	90049
HEATH, PETER GRAEME	DIRECTOR	DGA, 110 W 57TH ST	NEW YORK, NY	10019
HEATH, ROBERT	WRITER-PRODUCER	POST OFFICE BOX 5373	NORTH HOLLYWOOD, CA	91616
HEATH BROTHERS, THE	JAZZ GROUP	KURLAND, 173 BRIGHTON AVE	BOSTON, MA	02134
HEATHERTON, JOEY	ACT-SING-DAN	950 3RD AVE #2300	NEW YORK, NY	10022
HEATTER, MERRILL	TV WRITER-PRODUCER	1011 N ROXBURY DR	BEVERLY HILLS, CA	90210
HEATWAVE	SOUL GROUP	POST OFFICE BOX U	TARZANA, CA	91356
HEATWOLE, LUTHER E	MUSIC ARRANGER	2000 TYNE BLVD	NASHVILLE, TN	37215
HEAVEN	JAZZ GROUP	9777 HARWIN ST #101	HOUSTON, TX	77036
HEAVEN	ROCK & ROLL GROUP	ATI, 888 7TH AVE, 21ST FLOOR	NEW YORK, NY	10106
HEAVEN, SIMON	DIRECTOR-PRODUCER	COMPASS, SPITALFIELDS		
		WORKSPACE, 9 HENTAGE ST	LONDON E1 5LJ	ENGLAND
HEAVEN & EARTH	MUSICAL GROUP	POST OFFICE BOX 802096	CHICAGO, IL	60680
HEAVEN 17	ROCK & ROLL GROUP	HEAVENLY MANAGEMENT		
		36 NOTTING HILL GATE	LONDON W11 3HX	ENGLAND
HEAVY METAL SISTERS, THE	WRESTLING TAG TEAM	GORGEOUS LADIES OF WRESTLING		
		RIVIERA HOTEL & CASINO		
		DAVID B MC LANE PRODS		
		2901 S LAS VEGAS BLVD	LAS VEGAS, NV	89109
HEBERLEIN, JULIE	ACTRESS	427 N CANON DR #205	BEVERLY HILLS, CA	90210
HEBERT, GLENN	SINGER	312 W LEE ETTA	GALLATIN, TN	37066
HEBERT, H JOSEF	NEWS CORRESPONDENT	18706 CONSIDINE DR	BROOKEVILLE, MD	20833
HEBERT, PAUL	COMPOSER	13860 MAGNOLIA BLVD	SHERMAN OAKS, CA	91423
HEBERT, RICH	ACTOR	315 W 14TH ST #1-B	NEW YORK, NY	10014
HECHT, ALBERT D	TV DIRECTOR-PRODUCER	24 HUTTON AVE	WEST ORANGE, NJ	07052
HECHT, BARRY A	NEWS CORRESPONDENT	2139 WISCONSIN AVE, NW	WASHINGTON, DC	20007
HECHT, CYNTHIA A	NEWS CORRESPONDENT	1825 "K" ST, NW	WASHINGTON, DC	20006
HECHT, DANIEL	GUIATRIST	POST OFFICE BOX 9388	STANFORD, CA	94305
HECHT, GINA	ACTRESS	1302 N SWEETZER AVE #402	LOS ANGELES, CA	90069
HECHT, HENRY	SPORTS WRITER-EDITOR	SPORTS ILLUSTRATED MAGAZINE		
		TIME & LIFE BUILDING		
		ROCKEFELLER CENTER	NEW YORK, NY	10020
HECHT, JOEL S	TV WRITER	8955 BEVERLY BLVD	LOS ANGELES, CA	90048
HECHT, KEN	TV PRODUCER	EMBASSY-TV, 1438 N GOWER ST	LOS ANGELES, CA	90028
HECHT, KEN	TV WRITER	8955 BEVERLY BLVD	LOS ANGELES, CA	90048
HECHT, PAUL	ACTOR	SCHUMER-OUBRE, 1697 BROADWAY	NEW YORK, NY	10019
HECHT, SYLVIA	TV WRITER	8955 BEVERLY BLVD	LOS ANGELES, CA	90048
HECKART, EILEEN	ACTRESS	135 COMSTOCK HILL RD	NEW CANAAN, CT	06840
HECKER, JULIE M	NEWS CORRESPONDENT	ABC-TV, NEWS DEPARTMENT		
		1717 DE SALES ST, NW	WASHINGTON, DC	20036
HECKER, ROBERT L	TV WRITER	14697 DEERVALE PL	SHERMAN OAKS, CA	91403
HECKERLING, AMY	FILM WRITER-DIRECTOR	ISRAEL, 1282 DEVON AVE	LOS ANGELES, CA	90024
HECKMAN, DONALD J	WRITER	210 N PASS AVE #206	BURBANK, CA	91505
HECKMAN, HUGH M	WRITER	555 W 57TH ST #1230	NEW YORK, NY	10019
HEDAYA, DAN	ACTOR	2101 N BEACHWOOD DR	HOLLYWOOD, CA	90068
HEDGES, MICHAEL	GUITARIST	POST OFFICE BOX 9388	STANFORD, CA	94305
HEDGES, ROGER A	NEWS CORRESPONDENT	2333 OLD TRAIL DR	RESTON, VA	22091
HEDISON, DAVID	ACTOR	445 N BEDFORD DR #PH	BEVERLY HILLS, CA	90210
HEDLEY, JACK	ACTOR	MORRIS, 147-149 WARDOUR ST	LONDON W1V 3TB	ENGLAND
HEDLEY, THOMAS JOHN	SCREENWRITER	NANAS, 9454 WILSHIRE BLVD	BEVERLY HILLS, CA	90212
HEDLUND, CORY L	NEWS CORRESPONDENT	ABC NEWS, 1717 DE SALES ST, NW	WASHINGTON, DC	20036
HEDLUND, RONALD	BASSO-BARITONE	CONE, 221 W 57TH ST	NEW YORK, NY	10019
HEDREN, TIPPI	ACTRESS	6867 SOLEDAD CYN	ACTION, CA	93510
HEELEY, DAVID E	TV DIRECTOR	31 W 31ST ST	NEW YORK, NY	10001
HEENAN, BOBBY "THE BRAIN"	WRESTLING MANAGER	POST OFFICE BOX 3859	STAMFORD, CT	06905
HEENAN, RAYMOND	WRESTLING MANAGER	SEE - HEENAN, BOBBY "THE BRAIN"		
HEERY, SEAN M	NEWS CORRESPONDENT	400 N CAPITOL ST, NW	WASHINGTON, DC	20001
HEFFER, RICHARD ELLIOTT	ACTOR	QDA, 31 KINGS RD	LONDON SW3	ENGLAND
HEFFERNAN, GREGORY	WRITER	5210 CALLE DE ARBOLES	TORRANCE, CA	90505
HEFFLEY, ROY	NEWS CORRESPONDENT	ABC-TV, NEWS DEPARTMENT		
		1717 DE SALES ST, NW	WASHINGTON, DC	20036
HEFFLEY, WAYNE	ACTOR	245 N GRAMERCY PL	LOS ANGELES, CA	90004
HEFFNER, KYLE T	ACTOR	CONTEMPORARY ARTISTS		
		132 S LASKY DR	BEVERLY HILLS, CA	90212
HEFFRON, RICHARD	FILM DIRECTOR	31712 BROAD BEACH RD	MALIBU, CA	90265
HEFLIN, FRANCES	ACTRESS	10 E 44TH ST #700	NEW YORK, NY	10017
HEFLIN, MARTA	ACTRESS	SHUKAT, 340 W 55TH ST	NEW YORK, NY	10019
HEFLIN, NORA	ACTRESS	246 STRAND ST	SANTA MONICA, CA	90405
HEFNER, CHRISTIE	PUBLISHING EXECUTIVE	10236 CHARING CROSS RD	LOS ANGELES, CA	90024
HEFNER, HUGH	PUBLISHING EXECUTIVE	10236 CHARING CROSS RD	LOS ANGELES, CA	90024
HEFTER, SAM	WRITER	341 N ALTA VISTA BLVD	LOS ANGELES, CA	90036
HEFTI, NEAL	COMPOSER	9454 WILSHIRE BLVD #405	BEVERLY HILLS, CA	90212
HEGIERSKI, KATHLEEN	MEZZO-SOPRANO	CAMI, 165 W 57TH ST	NEW YORK, NY	10019
HEGIRA, ANNE	ACTRESS	20 COMMERCE ST	NEW YORK, NY	10014
HEGSTRAND, MICHAEL	WRESTLER	SEE - ROAD WARRIOR HAWK		
HEGYES, ROBERT	ACTOR-DIRECTOR	12117 1/2 HOFFMAN ST	STUDIO CITY, CA	91604
HEHORN, LANNY	ACTOR	5848 ROLLING RD	WOODLAND HILLS, CA	91367
HEIBERGER, JOSEPH	PHOTOGRAPHER	10016 PORTLAND RD	SILVER SPRING, MD	20901
HEIDEN-DRYER, JANICE	ACTRESS	16140 MOORPARK ST	ENCINO, CA	91436
HEIDER, LAWRENCE	CINEMATOGRAPHER	7715 SUNSET BLVD #150	LOS ANGELES, CA	90046
HEIFETZ, DANIEL	VIOLINIST	SHAW CONCERTS, 1995 BROADWAY	NEW YORK, NY	10023

Name	Occupation	Address	City	ZIP
HEIFETZ, JASCHA	VIOLINIST	1520 GILCREST DR	BEVERLY HILLS, CA	90210
HEIGH, HELENE	ACTRESS	1836 1/2 N EDGEMONT ST	HOLLYWOOD, CA	90027
HEIGHLEY, BRUCE	ACTOR	18646 COLLINS ST #3	TARZANA, CA	91356
HEIK, JENS H	NEWS CORRESPONDENT	1077 31ST ST, NW	WASHINGTON, DC	20007
HEIKES, DARRYL L	PHOTOGRAPHER	1220 FOLKSTONE DR	HERNDON, VA	22070
HEIKIN, NANCY	ACTRESS	91 CHRISTOPHER ST	NEW YORK, NY	10014
HEILBRON, LORNA	ACTRESS	169 QUEEN'S GATE #8	LONDON SW7 5EH	ENGLAND
HEILBUT, FRANCIS	PIANIST-CONDUCTOR	GRIGGS, 685 W END AVE	NEW YORK, NY	10025
HEILEMANN, CAROLINE M	NEWS CORRESPONDENT	4318 CUB RUN RD	CHANTILLY, VA	22021
HEILEMANN, DONALD L	PHOTOGRAPHER	4318 CUB RUN RD	CHANTILLY, VA	22021
HEILIG, MORTON L	WRITER-PRODUCER	855 GALLOWAY ST	PACIFIC PALISADES, CA	90272
HEILVEIL, ELAYNE	ACTRESS	6310 SAN VICENTE BLVD #407	LOS ANGELES, CA	90048
HEIM, HENRY J	DRUMMER	7439 HWY 705 #238	NASHVILLE, TN	37221
HEIM, PAULA M	ACTRESS	15870 SILVER STAR LN	CANYON CITY, CA	91351
HEIMANN, RICHARD G	DIRECTOR	3 E 63RD ST	NEW YORK, NY	10021
HEIMEL, CYNTHIA J	WRITER	555 W 57TH ST #1230	NEW YORK, NY	10019
HEIMER, GREGORY W	DIRECTOR	10510 SEABURY LN	LOS ANGELES, CA	90077
HEIMSATH, PETER	PHOTOGRAPHER	SOUTH ARLINGTON MILL DR #2500-D	ARLINGTON, VA	22206
HEINDORF, MICHAEL	COMPOSER	2111 N CAHUENGA BLVD #9	LOS ANGELES, CA	90068
HEINEMAN, LAURIE	ACTRESS	165 W 46TH ST #409	NEW YORK, NY	10036
HEINEMANN, ARTHUR	TV WRITER	3606 MANDEVILLE CANYON RD	LOS ANGELES, CA	90049
HEINEN, KENNETH R	PHOTOGRAPHER	4001 LORCUM LN	ARLINGTON, VA	22207
HEINERS, JEFFREY A	NEWS CORRESPONDENT	400 N CAPITOL ST, NW	WASHINGTON, DC	20001
HEININGER, JAN	WRITER	8955 BEVERLY BLVD	LOS ANGELES, CA	90048
HEINLEIN, ROBERT A	WRITER	6000 BONNY DUNE RD	SANTA CRUZ, CA	95060
HEINLY, DAVID R	NEWS CORRESPONDENT	5910 GRAYSON ST	SPRINGFIELD, VA	22150
HEINSOHN, ELISA	ACTRESS	MGM/UA-TV, 10202 W WASHINGTON BL	CULVER CITY, CA	90230
HEINZ, CHARLES D	TV DIRECTOR	21 BRYAN DR	MONTVALE, NJ	07645
HEINZ, JUDY	ACTRESS	525 S ARDMORE AVE #310	LOS ANGELES, CA	90020
HEINZE, CATHERINE	NEWS CORRESPONDENT	4831 36TH ST #206, NW	WASHINGTON, DC	20008
HEISLER, HAROLD J	DIRECTOR	2044 HOLMBY AVE	LOS ANGELES, CA	90025
HEITZER, HARRY	TV EXECUTIVE	CBS-TV, 7800 BEVERLY BLVD	LOS ANGELES, CA	90036
HEJBAL, FRANK	COMPOSER	POST OFFICE BOX 61-1521	NORTH MIAMI, FL	33161
HEKTOEN, JEANNETTE	TV EXECUTIVE	NBC-TV, 30 ROCKEFELLER PLAZA	NEW YORK, NY	10112
HELBERG, HARRIET	CASTING DIRECTOR	7471 MELROSE AVE #12	LOS ANGELES, CA	90046
HELBERG, SANDY	ACTOR-WRITER	8412 CARLTON WY	LOS ANGELES, CA	90069
HELBURN, WILLIAM D	DIRECTOR	161 E 35TH ST	NEW YORK, NY	10016
HELD, CARL	ACTOR	1817 HILLCREST RD #51	HOLLYWOOD, CA	90068
HELDE, ANNETTE	ACTRESS	AFFILIATE ARTISTS, INC		
		37 W 65TH ST, 6TH FLOOR	NEW YORK, NY	10023
HELDFOND, SUSAN	ACTRESS	358 S HIGHLAND AVE	LOS ANGELES, CA	90036
HELFER, ELLEN BRITT	ACTRESS	18541 DEARBORN ST #17	NORTHRIDGE, CA	91324
HELFER, RALPH D	WRITER-PRODUCER	15840 CEDARFORT DR	SAUGUS, CA	91350
HELFFER, CLAUDE	PIANIST	1182 MARKET ST #311	SAN FRANCISCO, CA	94102
HELFGOTT, DANIEL	WRITER-PRODUCER	12151 LA MAIDA ST	NORTH HOLLYWOOD, CA	91607
HELIN, JACQUELYN	PIANIST	111 W 57TH ST #1203	NEW YORK, NY	10019
HELIOS CREED	ROCK & ROLL GROUP	SUBTERRANEAN RECORDS		
		577 VALENCIA ST	SAN FRANCISCO, CA	94110
HELIX	ROCK & ROLL GROUP	POST OFFICE BOX 577	WATERLOO, ONT N2J 4B8	CANADA
HELLAND, ERIC	ACTOR	7503 WILLOW GLEN RD	LOS ANGELES, CA	90046
HELLBERG, LARS	NEWS CORRESPONDENT	7011 HAMEL HILL CT	MC LEAN, VA	22101
HELLENDALL, INES	ACTRESS	30609 RUE DE LA PIERRE	RANCHO PALOS VERDES, C.	90274
HELLENTHAL, ALBERT W	WRITER-PRODUCER	1256 EL SUR WY	SACRAMENTO, CA	95825
HELLER, BARBARA	TV WRITER	1541 N VINE ST	HOLLYWOOD, CA	90028
HELLER, FRANKLIN M	TV DIRECTOR	1364 ROCKRIMMON RD	STAMFORD, CT	06903
HELLER, JACK	ACTOR	LIGHT, 113 N ROBERTSON BLVD	LOS ANGELES, CA	90048
HELLER, JACK	PIANIST	SEE - HELLER, LITTLE JACK		
HELLER, JAY	WRITER	555 W 57TH ST #1230	NEW YORK, NY	10019
HELLER, JOEL	TV DIRECTOR-PRODUCER	CBS-TV, 524 W 57TH ST	NEW YORK, NY	10019
HELLER, JOEL H	WRITER	555 W 57TH ST #1230	NEW YORK, NY	10019
HELLER, JOSEPH	WRITER	SIMON & SCHUSTER, 630 5TH AVE	NEW YORK, NY	10020
HELLER, KEN	COMPOSER-CONDUCTOR	8993 WONDERLAND AVE	LOS ANGELES, CA	90046
HELLER, LEON	SCREENWRITER	8955 BEVERLY BLVD	LOS ANGELES, CA	90048
HELLER, LITTLE JACK	PIANIST	1850 S CAMINO REAL #7	PALM SPRINGS, CA	92262
HELLER, PAUL	DIRECTOR-PRODUCER	1666 N BEVERLY DR	BEVERLY HILLS, CA	90210
HELLER, RANDEE	ACTRESS	9744 WILSHIRE BLVD #206	BEVERLY HILLS, CA	90212
HELLER, ROB	TALENT AGENT	ICM, 8899 BEVERLY BLVD	LOS ANGELES, CA	90048
HELLER, SCOTT	NEWS CORRESPONDENT	2020 "F" ST #724, NW	WASHINGTON, DC	20006
HELLER-BAKER, JILL	ACTRESS	6605 HOLLYWOOD BLVD #220	HOLLYWOOD, CA	90028
HELLERMAN, FRED	SINGER	83 GOODHILL RD	WESTON, CT	06880
HELLHAMMER	ROCK & ROLL GROUP	POST OFFICE BOX 2896	TORRANCE, CA	90509
HELLING, JAMES A	NEWS CORRESPONDENT	2139 WISCONSIN AVE, NW	WASHINGTON, DC	20007
HELLINGER, WILLIAM	WRITER	8955 BEVERLY BLVD	LOS ANGELES, CA	90048
HELLMAN, JEROME R	DIRECTOR-PRODUCER	68 MALIBU COLONY DR	MALIBU, CA	90265
HELLMAN, MARCEL	FILM PRODUCER	1 ACACIA RD	LONDON NW8 6AD	ENGLAND
HELLMAN, MONTE	WRITER-PRODUCER	8588 APPIAN WY	LOS ANGELES, CA	90046
HELLMAN, PETER	ACTOR	KOHNER, 9169 SUNSET BLVD	LOS ANGELES, CA	90069
HELLOWEEN	ROCK & ROLL GROUP	IRD, 149-03 GUY R BREWER BLVD	JAMAICA, NY	11434
HELLSTROM, GUNNAR	TV DIRECTOR	10816 3/4 LINDBROOK DR	LOS ANGELES, CA	90024
HELLWIG, JIM	WRESTLER	SEE - DINGO WARRIOR		
HELM, ALAN	ACTOR	38 CHEVERTON RD	LONDON N19	ENGLAND
HELM, ANNE	ACTRESS	21857 KOONTZ WY	TOPANGA CANYON, CA	90290
HELM, FRANCES	ACTRESS	55 CENTRAL PARK W	NEW YORK, NY	10023
HELM, LEVON & CATE BROTHERS	ROCK & ROLL GROUP	MAGNA ARTISTS, 595 MADISON AVE	NEW YORK, NY	10022
HELM, PETER J	ACTOR	5424 COLFAX AVE	NORTH HOLLYWOOD, CA	91601

Name	Occupation	Address	City	Zip
HELM, TIFFANY	ACTRESS	8322 BEVERLY BLVD #202	LOS ANGELES, CA	90048
HELMAN, GEOFFREY	TV PRODUCER	9-D LOGAN PL, KENSINGTON	LONDON W8 6QN	ENGLAND
HELMERSON, FRANS	CELLIST	CAMI, 165 W 57TH ST	NEW YORK, NY	10019
HELMICK, PAUL A	DIRECTOR	10333 ODESSA AVE	GRANADA HILLS, CA	91344
HELMOND, KATHERINE	ACTRESS-DIRECTOR	151 S EL CAMINO DR	BEVERLY HILLS, CA	90212
HELMS, BOBBY	SINGER	POST OFFICE BOX 4357	MARIETTA, GA	30065
HELMS, DON	GUITARIST	200 NEPTUNE DR	HENDERSONVILLE, TN	37075
HELMS FAMILY, THE	FOLK GROUP	POST OFFICE BOX 25371	CHARLOTTE, NC	28212
HELOISE	CONSUMER ADVISER	KING FEATURES SYNDICATE		
		235 E 45TH ST	NEW YORK, NY	10017
HELOU, RAJA	WRITER	555 W 57TH ST #1230	NEW YORK, NY	10019
HELPER, MARJORIE GAY	WRITER	540 ALTA AVE	SANTA MONICA, CA	90402
HELRICH, GEOFFREY	ACTOR	2326 1/2 PENMAR AVE	VENICE, CA	90291
HELSTAR	ROCK & ROLL GROUP	POST OFFICE BOX 9217	HOUSTON, TX	77261
HELTON, MELANIE	SOPRANO	AFFILIATE ARTISTS, INC		
		37 W 65TH ST, 6TH FLOOR	NEW YORK, NY	10023
HEMBREE, MARK	GUITARIST	527 SKYVIEW DR	NASHVILLE, TN	37206
HEMBREE, STEVE	GUITARIST	194 TIMBER LAKE DR	HENDERSONVILLE, TN	37075
HEMBY, TOM	GUITARIST	4904 SHERMAN OAKS	NASHVILLE, TN	37211
HEMINGWAY, MARGAUX	ACTRESS-MODEL	POST OFFICE BOX 387	SUN VALLEY, ID	83353
HEMINGWAY, MARIEL	ACTRESS	2020 COLDWATER CANYON DR	BEVERLY HILLS, CA	90210
HEMINGWAY, POLLY	ACTRESS	MARMONT, 302 REGENT ST	LONDON W1	ENGLAND
HEMINGWAY, SANDRA JEAN	NEWS CORRESPONDENT	4701 KENMORE AVE #1211	ALEXANDRIA, VA	22304
HEMINWAY, JOHN H, JR	WRITER	555 W 57TH ST #1230	NEW YORK, NY	10019
HEMION, DWIGHT	TV DIRECTOR-PRODUCER	522 PALISADES BEACH RD	SANTA MONICA, CA	90402
HEMION, MAC	DIRECTOR	POST OFFICE BOX 703	MANTOLOKING, NJ	08738
HEMMIG, ROBERT H	PHOTOGRAPHER	3915 WOODLEY DR	ALEXANDRIA, VA	22309
HEMMINGS, DAVID	ACTOR-DIRECTOR	STONE, 1052 CAROL DR	LOS ANGELES, CA	90069
HEMPEL, ANOUSKA	ACTRESS	THE BLAKES HOTEL		
		3 ROLAND GARDENS	LONDON SW7	ENGLAND
HEMPHILL, SHIRLEY	ACTRESS	539 TRONA AVE	WEST COVINA, CA	91790
HEMPKER, ROBERT	DOBROIST	251 NEW SHACKLE ISLAND	HENDERSONVILLE, TN	37075
HEMPSTONE, SMITH	NEWS CORRESPONDENT	7611 FAIRFAX RD	BETHESDA, MD	20814
HEMSLEY, SHERMAN	ACTOR-COMEDIAN	1907 JEWETT DR	LOS ANGELES, CA	90046
HENCH, RICHARD ALAN	ACTOR-MODEL	1800 EL CENTRO PL #6	HOLLYWOOD, CA	90046
HENCK, FRED W	NEWS CORRESPONDENT	2407 N QUEBEC ST	ARLINGTON, VA	22207
HENCKE, PAUL G	NEWS CORRESPONDENT	6315 NAVAL AVE	LANHAM, MD	20706
HENDEL, KAREN	CASTING DIRECTOR	2049 CENTURY PARK E #4100	LOS ANGELES, CA	90067
HENDEL, LIORA	PIANIST	157 W 57TH ST #1100	NEW YORK, NY	10019
HENDEL, THOMAS	WRITER	8955 BEVERLY BLVD	LOS ANGELES, CA	90048
HENDERER, RHODES	NEWS CORRESPONDENT	2356 N VERMONT ST	ARLINGTON, VA	22207
HENDERSON, ALBERT	ACTOR	247 S BEVERLY DR #102	BEVERLY HILLS, CA	90210
HENDERSON, ALEXANDRA	NEWS CORRESPONDENT	1012 14TH ST, NW	WASHINGTON, DC	20005
HENDERSON, ANNETTE C	WRITER	555 W 57TH ST #1230	NEW YORK, NY	10019
HENDERSON, BILL	ACTOR	10100 SANTA MONICA BLVD #1600	LOS ANGELES, CA	90067
HENDERSON, BRICE	SINGER-GUITARIST	417-A SARVER AVE	MADISON, TN	37115
HENDERSON, CATHRYN	CASTING DIRECTOR	1040 N LAS PALMAS AVE	HOLLYWOOD, CA	90038
HENDERSON, DON	ACTOR	38 ALBANY RD		
		STRATFORD-UPON-AVON	WARWICKS	ENGLAND
HENDERSON, DON	DIRECTOR	1079 E OLIVE AVE	BURBANK, CA	91501
HENDERSON, DUNCAN	FILM DIRECTOR	518 1/2 VETERAN AVE	LOS ANGELES, CA	90024
HENDERSON, FLORENCE	SINGER-ACTRESS	1492 CARLA RIDGE	BEVERLY HILLS, CA	90210
HENDERSON, GARY A	NEWS CORRES-WRITER	9107 KINGSBURY DR	SILVER SPRING, MD	20910
HENDERSON, JAMES J, JR	DIRECTOR	15-1 GRANADA CRESCENT	WHITE PLAINS, NY	10603
HENDERSON, JIM	COLUMNIST	POST OFFICE BOX 500	WASHINGTON, DC	20044
HENDERSON, LUTHER L, III	COMPOSER-CONDUCTOR	POST OFFICE BOX 3602	CULVER CITY, CA	90230
HENDERSON, MAGGIE	TALENT AGENT	247 S BEVERLY DR #102	BEVERLY HILLS, CA	90210
HENDERSON, MAYE	ACTRESS	6515 SUNSET BLVD #300-A	LOS ANGELES, CA	90028
HENDERSON, MICHAEL	SINGER	4856 LAUREL CANYON BLVD	NORTH HOLLYWOOD, CA	91607
HENDERSON, NANCY	NEWS CORRESPONDENT	2724 ORDWAY ST, NW	WASHINGTON, DC	20008
HENDERSON, PAUL	NEWS CORRESPONDENT	1755 S JEFFERSON DAVIS HWY	ARLINGTON, VA	22202
HENDERSON, RICKEY	BASEBALL	10561 ENGLEWOOD DR	OAKLAND, CA	94621
HENDERSON, ROBERT	CONDUCTOR	SHAW CONCERTS, 1995 BROADWAY	NEW YORK, NY	10023
HENDERSON, SKITCH	COMPOSER-CONDUCTOR	HUNT HILL FARM, UPLAND RD		
		RURAL FARM DELIVERY #3	NEW MILFORD, CT	06776
HENDERSON, STEPHEN	ACTOR	AFFILIATE ARTISTS, INC		
		37 W 65TH ST, 6TH FLOOR	NEW YORK, NY	10023
HENDL, WALTER	CONDUCTOR	SHAW CONCERTS, 1995 BROADWAY	NEW YORK, NY	10023
HENDLER, JANIS	TV WRITER	8955 BEVERLY BLVD	LOS ANGELES, CA	90048
HENDLER, LAURI	ACTRESS	9925 1/2 DURANT DR	BEVERLY HILLS, CA	90212
HENDRA, ANTHONY C	WRITER	555 W 57TH ST #1230	NEW YORK, NY	10019
HENDRICK, THOMAS	PIANIST	ROUTE #15, BOX 35, LOVERS LN	BOWLING GREEN, KY	42101
HENDRICKS, BARBARA	SOPRANO	CAMI, 165 W 57TH ST	NEW YORK, NY	10019
HENDRICKS, EVAN D	NEWS CORRESPONDENT	2354 CHAMPLAIN ST, NW	WASHINGTON, DC	20009
HENDRICKS, JON	SINGER	WILLARD ALEXANDER, INC		
		660 MADISON AVE	NEW YORK, NY	10021
HENDRICKS, LAURIE	ACTRESS	6629 COLGATE AVE	LOS ANGELES, CA	90048
HENDRICKS, SKITCH	CASTING DIRECTOR	1438 N GOWER ST	LOS ANGELES, CA	90028
HENDRICKSON, MARK	NEWS CORRESPONDENT	2711 ORDWAY ST #300, NW	WASHINGTON, DC	20008
HENDRIE, CHRIS	ACTOR	4150 RIVERSIDE DR #204	BURBANK, CA	91505
HENDRIX, TONY	DRUMMER	2751 CLINTON CIR	HOPKINSVILLE, KY	42240
HENDRIX SINGERS, JAMES	VOCAL GROUP	POST OFFICE BOX 90639	NASHVILLE, TN	37209
HENDRIXSON, LARRY	DRUMMER	422 SPRINGVIEW DR	NASHVILLE, TN	37214
HENDRY, CHARLES	SAXOPHONIST	4001 ANDERSON RD #147	NASHVILLE, TN	37217
HENDRY, LEE J	ACTRESS	641 GREENBROOK RD	NORTH PLAINFIELD, NJ	07063

Name	Occupation	Address	City	Zip
HENDRYX, SHIRL	SCREENWRITER	12310 DOROTHY ST	LOS ANGELES, CA	90049
HENERSON, JAMES S	TV WRITER-PRODUCER	15300 KINGSWOOD LN	SHERMAN OAKS, CA	91403
HENINBURG, GUSTAV	TV HOST	WNBC-TV, 30 ROCKEFELLER PL	NEW YORK, NY	10112
HENISSART, MARTHA	WRITER	555 W 57TH ST #1230	NEW YORK, NY	10019
HENKEL, OLGA	WRITER	555 W 57TH ST #1230	NEW YORK, NY	10019
HENKIN, HILARY	SCREENWRITER	8955 BEVERLY BLVD	LOS ANGELES, CA	90048
HENKIN, HOWARD	WRITER-PRODUCER	150 E 77TH ST	NEW YORK, NY	10021
HENLEY, ARTHUR	AUTHOR-EDITOR	73-37 AUSTIN ST	FOREST HILLS, NY	11375
HENLEY, BETH	WRITER-ACTRESS	THE WILLIAM MORRIS AGENCY		
		1350 AVE OF THE AMERICAS	NEW YORK, NY	10019
HENLEY, DAVID C	NEWS CORRESPONDENT	3821 LEGATION ST, NW	WASHINGTON, DC	20015
HENLEY, DON	SINGER-SONGWRITER	10880 WILSHIRE BLVD #2110	LOS ANGELES, CA	90024
HENLEY, TREVOR	ACTOR	15501 MOORPARK ST #10	ENCINO, CA	91436
HENLEY, WES	TRUMPETER	1603 JONES BLVD	MURFREESBORO, TN	37130
HENMAN, PAUL J	DIRECTOR	DGA, 7950 SUNSET BLVD	LOS ANGELES, CA	90046
HENN, RICHARD A	COMPOSER-CONDUCTOR	28908 GRAYFOX ST	MALIBU, CA	90265
HENNER, MARILU	ACTRESS	100 S DOHENY DR #1004	LOS ANGELES, CA	90048
HENNESSEY-SMITH, DONNA L	TV DIRECTOR	11 MEADOWBROOK RD	DOVER, MA	02030
HENNESSY, JOHN	FILM PRODUCER	540 TAMARAC RD	PASADENA, CA	91105
HENNIG, CURT	WRESTLER	AMERICAN WRESTLING ASSOC		
		MINNEAPLOIS WRESTLING		
		10001 WAYZATA BLVD	MINNETONKA, MN	55345
HENNIG, JUTTA	NEWS CORRESPONDENT	9216 WATSON RD	SILVER SPING, MD	20910
HENNING, DOUG	MAGICIAN	POST OFFICE BOX 49043	LOS ANGELES, CA	90049
HENNING, LINDA KAYE	ACTRESS	4231 WARNER BLVD	BURBANK, CA	91505
HENNING, PAUL	TV WRITER-PRODUCER	4250 NAVAJO ST	NORTH HOLLYWOOD, CA	91602
HENNINGS, SAM	ACTOR	1100 N ALTA LOMA RD #707	LOS ANGELES, CA	90069
HENOCH, MICHAEL	OBOIST	POST OFFICE BOX 160	HIGHLAND PARK, IL	60035
HENREHAN, JOHN F	NEWS CORRESPONDENT	400 N CAPITOL ST, NW	WASHINGTON, DC	20001
HENRICKSON, BENJAMIN	ACTOR	CBS-TV, "AS THE WORLD TURNS"		
		51 W 52ND ST	NEW YORK, NY	10019
HENRIED, PAUL	ACTOR	18068 BLUE SAIL DR	PACIFIC PALISADES, CA	90272
HENRIKSEN, LANCE	ACTOR	9220 SUNSET BLVD #625	LOS ANGELES, CA	90069
HENRIQUEZ, RON	ACTOR	POST OFFICE BOX 38027	HOLLYWOOD, CA	90038
HENRY, BOB	TV DIRECTOR	11940 SAN VICENTE BLVD	LOS ANGELES, CA	90049
HENRY, BOB	WRITER	8955 BEVERLY BLVD	LOS ANGELES, CA	90048
HENRY, BUCK	WRITER-PRODUCER	760 N LA CIENEGA BLVD	LOS ANGELES, CA	90069
HENRY, CANDICE	ACTRESS	8961 SUNSET BLVD #B	LOS ANGELES, CA	90069
HENRY, CAROL ANN	ACTRESS	CASSELL, 843 N SYCAMORE AVE	LOS ANGELES, CA	90038
HENRY, CLARENCE "FROGMAN"	SINGER-GUITARIST	BOB ASTER, 23 HOLLY DR	LA PLACE, LA	70068
HENRY, DARRYL	WRITER	8955 BEVERLY BLVD	LOS ANGELES, CA	90048
HENRY, DAVID LEE	SCREENWRITER	8955 BEVERLY BLVD	LOS ANGELES, CA	90048
HENRY, DEANNE	ACTRESS	9744 WILSHIRE BLVD #206	BEVERLY HILLS, CA	90212
HENRY, DEBI	SINGER	NBA, 2605 NORTHRIDGE DR	GARLAND, TX	75043
HENRY, ED	NEWS CORRESPONDENT	13306 RIPPLING BROOK DR	SILVER SPRING, MD	20906
HENRY, GIG	TV WRITER	8955 BEVERLY BLVD	LOS ANGELES, CA	90048
HENRY, GLORIA	ACTRESS	15010 VENTURA BLVD #219	SHERMAN OAKS, CA	91403
HENRY, GREGG	ACTOR	8956 APPIAN WY	LOS ANGELES, CA	90046
HENRY, HOYET	GUITARIST	311 LUTIE ST	NASHVILLE, TN	37210
HENRY, JAMES F	TV WRITER	8955 BEVERLY BLVD	LOS ANGELES, CA	90048
HENRY, LENNY	COMEDIAN	LUFF, 294 EARLS CT RD	LONDON SW5 9BB	ENGLAND
HENRY, LOUISE	WRITER	555 W 57TH ST #1230	NEW YORK, NY	10019
HENRY, MIKE	ACTOR-FOOTBALL	9255 SUNSET BLVD #610	LOS ANGELES, CA	90069
HENRY, MIKE	PRODUCER	10803 BLIX ST	NORTH HOLLYWOOD, CA	91602
HENRY, ROGER	DRUMMER	218 WILEY ST	MADISON, TN	37115
HENRY, TROY	DRUMMER	535 MAPLEWOOD LN	NASHVILLE, TN	37216
HENRY, WILLIAM A, III	WRITER-EDITOR	TIME/TIME & LIFE BLDG		
		ROCKEFELLER CENTER	NEW YORK, NY	10020
HENSCHEL, JANE	CONTRALTO	59 E 54TH ST #81	NEW YORK, NY	10022
HENSCHEL, TOM	ACTOR	9601 WILSHIRE BLVD #GL-11	BEVERLY HILLS, CA	90210
HENSEL, HOWARD	TENOR	CONE, 221 W 57TH ST	NEW YORK, NY	10019
HENSEY, TERRY	TV WRITER	8955 BEVERLY BLVD	LOS ANGELES, CA	90048
HENSHAW, JAKE	NEWS CORRESPONDENT	7407 BLACKFORD ST	SPRINGFIELD, VA	22151
HENSHAW, JERE	FILM EXECUTIVE	9541 CHEROKEE LN	BEVERLY HILLS, CA	90210
HENSLER, PAUL G	SCREENWRITER	11901 SUNSET BLVD #211	LOS ANGELES, CA	90049
HENSLEY, DAN	GUITARIST	POST OFFICE BOX 110767	NASHVILLE, TN	37222
HENSLEY, HAROLD	SINGER	POST OFFICE BOX 4234	PANORAMA CITY, CA	91412
HENSLEY, J MIYOKO	TV WRITER	BLOOM, 800 S ROBERTSON BLVD	LOS ANGELES, CA	90035
HENSLEY, JON	ACTOR	CBS-TV, "AS THE WORLD TURNS"		
		51 W 52ND ST	NEW YORK, NY	10019
HENSLEY, STEVE	TV WRITER	BLOOM, 800 S ROBERTSON BLVD	LOS ANGELES, CA	90035
HENSLEY, TERI	SINGER	MC FADDEN ARTISTS CORP		
		818 18TH AVE S	NASHVILLE, TN	37203
HENSLEY, THOMAS R	COMPOSER-CONDUCTOR	ARCHANGEL, 8715 W 3RD ST	LOS ANGELES, CA	90048
HENSLEY, TOMMY R	GUITARIST	2611 ESSEX PL	NASHVILLE, TN	37212
HENSON, JIM	PUPPETER	117 E 69TH ST	NEW YORK, NY	10021
HENSON, NICKY	ACTOR	THE RICHARD STONE AGENCY		
		18-20 YORK BLDGS, ADELPHI	LONDON WC2N 6JY	ENGLAND
HENSON, RHYS C	CONDUCTOR	POST OFFICE BOX 3948	LOS ANGELES, CA	90078
HENSTELL, BRUCE	WRITER	2617 3RD ST	SANTA MONICA, CA	90405
HENTELOFF, ALEX	ACTOR	6400 W 5TH ST	LOS ANGELES, CA	90048
HENTOFF, NATHAN	WRITER-JOURNALIST	25 5TH AVE	NEW YORK, NY	10003
HENTOFF & HOYER	AERIAL CRADLE DUO	HALL, 138 FROG HOLLOW RD	CHURCHVILLE, PA	18966
HENVILLE, SANDRA LEE	ACTRESS	SEE - MAGEE, SANDRA LEE HENVILLE		
HENZ, STEVEN N	WRITER	555 W 57TH ST #1230	NEW YORK, NY	10019

PAMELA HENSLEY

AUDREY HEPBURN

KATHARINE HEPBURN

PEE WEE HERMAN

BARBARA HERSHEY

CHARLETON HESTON

ARTHUR HILL

JOHN HILLERMAN

JUDD HIRSCH

HENZE, HANS WERNER	COMPOSER-CONDUCTOR	ICM, 40 W 57TH ST	NEW YORK, NY	10019
HENZEL, RICHARD	ACTOR	POST OFFICE BOX 160	HIGHLAND PARK, IL	60035
HEPBURN, AUDREY	ACTRESS	CHALET RICE BISSENSTRASSE	GSTAAD	SWITZERLAND
HEPBURN, DEE	ACTRESS	50 CECIL ST, HILLMEAD	GLASGOW	SCOTLAND
HEPBURN, DEIRDRE	ACTRESS	8322 BEVERLY BLVD #202	LOS ANGELES, CA	90048
HEPBURN, KATHARINE	ACTRESS	244 E 49TH ST	NEW YORK, NY	10017
HEPCAT, HARRY & THE BOOGIE	ROCK & ROLL GROUP	MUSKRAT, 44 N CENTRAL AVE	ELMSFORD, NY	10523
HEPPLE, JEANNE	ACTRESS	211 S BEVERLY DR #201	BEVERLY HILLS, CA	90212
HEPTON, BERNARD	DIRECTOR-ACTOR	BRYAN DREW, LTD		
		MEZZANINE QUADRANT HOUSE		
		80-82 REGENT ST	LONDON W1	ENGLAND
HERAL, WILLIAM	DIRECTOR	KGO-TV, 277 GOLDEN GATE AVE	SAN FRANCISCO, CA	94102
HERALD, JOHN, BAND	C & W GROUP	380 LEXINGTON AVE #1119	NEW YORK, NY	10017
HERALD, VERNON	NEWS CORRESPONDENT	400 N CAPITOL ST, NW	WASHINGTON, DC	20001
HERB, ALICE H	WRITER-PRODUCER	DGA, 110 W 57TH ST	NEW YORK, NY	10019
HERB'S HEARD	ROCK & ROLL GROUP	25 HUNTINGTON AVE #420	BOSTON, MA	02116
HERBERT, CLIFFORD W	PHOTOJOURNALIST	9737 MOUNT PISGAH RD	SILVER SPRING, MD	20903
HERBERT, DON "MR WIZARD"	TV PERSONALITY	POST OFFICE BOX 83	CANOGA PARK, CA	91305
HERBERT, EDWARD E	WRITER	555 W 57TH ST #1230	NEW YORK, NY	10019
HERBERT, HENRY	TV DIRECTOR	FRASER, 91 REGENT ST	LONDON W1R 8RU	ENGLAND
HERBERT, PERCY	ACTOR	14 LEAMORE ST	LONDON W6	ENGLAND
HERBERT, PITT	ACTOR	15484 JONFIN ST	MISSION HILLS, CA	91345
HERBERT, TIM	ACTOR	1361 N LAUREL AVE #15	LOS ANGELES, CA	90046
HERBIG, GUNTHER	CONDUCTOR	ICM, 40 W 57TH ST	NEW YORK, NY	10019
HERCULES	WRESTLER	SEE - HERNANDEZ, HERCULES		
HERD, RICHARD	ACTOR	POST OFFICE BOX 5617	BEVERLY HILLS, CA	90210
HEREFORD, KATHRYN	ACTRESS-PRODUCER	914 N ROXBURY DR	BEVERLY HILLS, CA	90210
HERFEL, CHRISTIAN R, JR	DIRECTOR	TRINITY PASS	POUND RIDGE, NY	10576
HERFORD, HENRY	BARITONE	IMG ARTISTS, 22 E 71ST ST	NEW YORK, NY	10021
HERIGSTAD, GORDON	ACTOR	3411 WARNER BLVD #B	BURBANK, CA	91505
HERINCX, RAIMUND	BARITONE	SARDOS, 180 W END AVE	NEW YORK, NY	10023
HERITAGE SINGERS, THE	GOSPEL GROUP	POST OFFICE BOX 1358	PLACERVILLE, CA	95667
HERLAN, RICHARD	TV WRITER	2319 14TH ST #13	SANTA MONICA, CA	90405
HERLIE, EILEEN	ACTRESS	ABC-TV, "ALL MY CHILDREN"		
		1330 AVE OF THE AMERICAS	NEW YORK, NY	10019
HERLIHY, JAMES	PLAYWRIGHT	J GARON, 415 CENTRAL PARK W	NEW YORK, NY	10025
HERLING, JOHN	NEWS CORRESPONDENT	6504 E HALBERT RD	BETHESDA, MD	20034
HERMAN, ANDREA	NEWS CORRESPONDENT	2126 CONNECTICUT AVE #21, NW	WASHINGTON, DC	20008
HERMAN, BILLY	BASEBALL	3111 E GARDEN #33	PALM BEACH GARDENS, FL	33410
HERMAN, BRUCE	ACTOR	1018 9TH ST #10	SANTA MONICA, CA	90403
HERMAN, DAVID CHARLES	PHOTOGRAPHER	4850 CONNECTICUT AVE, NW	WASHINGTON, DC	20008
HERMAN, FRANK G	DIRECTOR	43 W 93RD ST	NEW YORK, NY	10025
HERMAN, GARY B	TV DIRECTOR-PRODUCER	ENTERTAINMENT TONIGHT		
		PARAMOUNT TELEVISION		
		5555 MELROSE AVE	LOS ANGELES, CA	90038
HERMAN, GEORGE E	NEWS CORRESPONDENT	3115 "O" ST, NW	WASHINGTON, DC	20007
HERMAN, GERALD	WRITER-PRODUCER	STARSHOLMA	280 72 KILLEBERG	SWEDEN
HERMAN, HARRY	ACTOR	8220 W NORTON AVE #16	LOS ANGELES, CA	90046
HERMAN, HARVEY	TV DIRECTOR	19 E 88TH ST	NEW YORK, NY	10028
HERMAN, HOWARD B	COMPOSER	6527 RIVERTON AVE	NORTH HOLLYWOOD, CA	91606
HERMAN, JERRY	COMPOSER-LYRICIST	55 CENTRAL PARK W	NEW YORK, NY	10023
HERMAN, KENNETH R, JR	TV DIRECTOR	5050 HOOKTREE RD	LA CANADA, CA	91011
HERMAN, LAWRENCE L	PHOTOJOURNALIST	7 CINZANO CENTER	GAITHERSBURG, MD	20878
HERMAN, MAXINE	TV WRITER	999 N DOHENY DR #403	LOS ANGELES, CA	90069
HERMAN, NADINE	SINGER	POST OFFICE BOX 256577	CHICAGO, IL	60625
HERMAN, NATHAN S	TV WRITER	555 W 57TH ST #1230	NEW YORK, NY	10019
HERMAN, NORMAN	WRITER-PRODUCER	3350 FRYMAN RD	STUDIO CITY, CA	91604
HERMAN, PEE WEE	COMEDIAN-ACTOR	POST OFFICE BOX 48243	LOS ANGELES, CA	90048
HERMAN, RANDY	ACTOR	2628 WASHINGTON AVE	SANTA MONICA, CA	90403
HERMAN, T NORMAN	WRITER-PRODUCER	3350 FRYMAN RD	STUDIO CITY, CA	91604
HERMAN, THELMA	TV WRITER	8955 BEVERLY BLVD	LOS ANGELES, CA	90048
HERMAN, WOODY	BAND LEADER	8620 HOLLYWOOD BLVD	LOS ANGELES, CA	90069
HERMAN HERMITS	ROCK & ROLL GROUP	POST OFFICE BOX 81		
		BUYTON, OLDHAM	MANCHESTER OL2 5DG	ENGLAND
HERMAN ZE GERMAN	DRUMMER	RANDY NAVERT MANAGEMENT		
		3465 ENCINAL CANYON RD	MALIBU, CA	90265
HERMANN, RICHARD	NEWS CORRESPONDENT	5831 N 19TH ST	ARLINGTON, VA	22205
HERMANN, ROLAND	BARITONE	61 W 62ND ST #6-F	NEW YORK, NY	10023
HERMANNS, CARL B	CONDUCTOR	5120 NOBLE AVE	SHERMAN OAKS, CA	91403
HERMISTON, NANCY	SOPRANO	SOFFER, 130 W 56TH ST	NEW YORK, NY	10019
HERN, ART	ACTOR	2449 OAK ST	SANTA MONICA, CA	90405
HERN, BERNIE	ACTOR	11726 SAN VICENTE BLVD #300	LOS ANGELES, CA	90049
HERNANDEZ	TEETERBOARDIST	HALL, 138 FROG HOLLOW RD	CHURCHVILLE, PA	18966
HERNANDEZ, CARLOS E	NEWS CORRESPONDENT	444 N CAPITOL ST, NW	WASHINGTON, DC	20001
HERNANDEZ, HERCULES	WRESTLER	POST OFFICE BOX 3859	STAMFORD, CT	06905
HERNANDEZ, KEITH	BASEBALL	1300 CHRISTMAS VALLEY	CHESTERFIELD, MO	63017
HERNANDEZ, MARCO	ACTOR	5000 LANKERSHIM BLVD #5	NORTH HOLLYWOOD, CA	91601
HERNANDEZ, RAY	WRESTLER	SEE - HERNANDEZ, HERCULES		
HERNANDEZ, WILLIE	BASEBALL	BO ESPINA CALLE C BOX 125	AGUADA, PR	00602
HERNDON, CRAIG G	PHOTOJOURNALIST	4122 ARKANSAS AVE, NW	WASHINGTON, DC	20011
HERNDON, VENABLE	SCREENWRITER	8955 BEVERLY BLVD	LOS ANGELES, CA	90048
HERNDON, WALTER SCOTT	WRITER-PRODUCER	1080 ARMADA DR	PASADENA, CA	91103
HEROLD, PATRICIA	TV DIRECTOR-PRODUCER	589 7TH ST	BROOKLYN, NY	11215
HEROUX, CLAUDE	FILM PRODUCER	3515 RUE BEAUSEJOUR	MONTREAL, QUE H4K 1W5	CANADA
HERR, MICHAEL	SCREENWRITER	555 W 57TH ST #1230	NEW YORK, NY	10019

Name	Occupation	Address	City	Zip
HERRARA, JOSEPH PAUL	ACTOR	7005 LANEWOOD AVE #219	LOS ANGELES, CA	90028
HERRERA, ANTHONY	ACTOR	WRITERS & ARTISTS AGENCY		
		162 W 56TH ST	NEW YORK, NY	10019
HERRERA, SUZANNE M	TV WRITER	15010 VENTURA BLVD #219	SHERMAN OAKS, CA	91403
HERRICK, F HERRICK	DIRECTOR	3633 MACK RD	SAGINAW, MI	48601
HERRIDGE, FRANCES	DANCE CRITIC	305 W 28TH ST	NEW YORK, NY	10001
HERRIN, ANGELIA LOUISE	NEWS CORRESPONDENT	10011 MOSBY RD	FAIRFAX, VA	22032
HERRIN, KYMBERLY	ACTRESS-MODEL	POST OFFICE BOX 22402	SANTA BARBARA, CA	93121
HERRING, LYNN	ACTRESS	ABC-TV, "GENERAL HOSPITAL"		
		1438 N GOWER ST	LOS ANGELES, CA	90028
HERRING, PEMBROKE	FILM EDITOR	22625 GILMORE ST	CANOGA PARK, CA	91307
HERRING-NORTHROP, LYNN	ACTRESS	21919 W CANON DR	TOPANGA CANYON, CA	90290
HERRIOTT, HEIDI	AERIAL ACT	POST OFFICE BOX 87	WEST LEBANON, NY	12195
HERRIOTT, JOHN	CIRCUS RINGMASTER	HALL, 138 FROG HOLLOW RD	CHURCHVILLE, PA	18966
HERRIOTT, PAUL	DIRECTOR	425 E 58TH ST #5-B	NEW YORK, NY	10022
HERRMAN, SABINA	NEWS CORRESPONDENT	3201 ELLICOTT ST, NW	WASHINGTON, DC	20008
HERRMANN, EDWARD	ACTOR	ICM, 8899 BEVERLY BLVD	LOS ANGELES, CA	90048
HERRON, J BARRY	DIRECTOR	324 W CAMINO REAL	ARCADIA, CA	91006
HERRON, PAUL M	NEWS CORRESPONDENT	4016 CLEVELAND ST	KENSINGTON, MD	20895
HERROZO, TINA	ACTRESS	SEE - RAINES, CHRISTINA		
HERSCH, HANK	SPORTS WRITER	SPORTS ILLUSTRATED MAGAZINE		
		TIME & LIFE BUILDING		
		ROCKEFELLER CENTER	NEW YORK, NY	10020
HERSCHENSOHN, BRUCE	WRITER-PRODUCER	ABC-TV, 4151 PROSPECT AVE	HOLLYWOOD, CA	90027
HERSEY, JOHN	WRITER	420 HUMPHREY ST	NEW HAVEN, CT	06511
HERSH, ROBERT D	TV DIRECTOR	RURAL ROUTE #2, BOX 351-B	SOUTH SALEM, NY	10590
HERSH, RONALD S	TV DIRECTOR	70 W 38TH ST	NEW YORK, NY	10018
HERSH, STUART A	WRITER-PRODUCER	41-34 243RD ST	DOUGLASTOWN, NY	11363
HERSHENOV, MILTON	WRITER	16505 VANOWEN ST #110	VAN NUYS, CA	91406
HERSHEWE, S K	WRITER	761 N GOWER ST	LOS ANGELES, CA	90038
HERSHEY, BARBARA	ACTRESS	55 W 90TH ST #1	NEW YORK, NY	10023
HERSHEY, ROBERT D	NEWS CORRESPONDENT	3508 DUNDEE DR	CHEVY CHASE, MD	20815
HERSHEY, WILLIAM LAUDER	NEWS CORRESPONDENT	7902 HATTERAS LN	SPRINGFIELD, VA	22151
HERSKOVITZ, MARSHALL S	WRITER-PRODUCER	905 CENTINELA AVE	SANTA MONICA, CA	90403
HERSKOWITZ, MICKEY	SPORTS WRITER	UNIVERSAL PRESS SYNDICATE		
		4900 MAIN ST, 9TH FLOOR	KANSAS CITY, MO	62114
HERST, JERRY P	COMPOSER	5735 CLOVER DR	OAKLAND, CA	94618
HERSTON, KELSO	GUITARIST	1202 16TH AVE S	NASHVILLE, TN	37212
HERTELENDY, HANNA	ACTRESS	939 1/2 N SIERRA BONITA AVE	LOS ANGELES, CA	90046
HERTFORD, BRIGHTON	ACTRESS	ABC-TV, "GENERAL HOSPITAL"		
		1438 N GOWER ST	LOS ANGELES, CA	90028
HERTLING, JAMES D	NEWS CORRESPONDENT	4230 FESSENDEN ST, NW	WASHINGTON, DC	20016
HERTZ, WILLIAM F	ENTERTAINMENT EXEC	5345 TOPEKA DR	TARZANA, CA	91356
HERTZBERG, MICHAEL	FILM WRITER-PRODUCER	DGA, 7950 SUNSET BLVD	LOS ANGELES, CA	90046
HERTZBERG, ROBERT M	WRITER	555 W 57TH ST #1230	NEW YORK, NY	10019
HERTZBERG, SIDNEY	WRITER	555 W 57TH ST #1230	NEW YORK, NY	10019
HERTZOG, LARRY	TV PRODUCER	STEPHEN J CANNELL PRODS		
		7083 HOLLYWOOD BLVD	LOS ANGELES, CA	90028
HERTZOG, LAWRENCE	TV WRITER	8955 BEVERLY BLVD	LOS ANGELES, CA	90048
HERVEY, IRENE	ACTRESS	10741 MOORPARK ST	NORTH HOLLYWOOD, CA	91602
HERVEY, JASON	ACTOR	8949 SUNSET BLVD #203	LOS ANGELES, CA	90069
HERVEY, RICHARD	ACTOR	8831 SUNSET BLVD #402	LOS ANGELES, CA	90069
HERVEY, WINIFRED	TV WRITER	1900 AVE OF THE STARS #2375	LOS ANGELES, CA	90067
HERZBERG, JACK	DIRECTOR-PRODUCER	4314 KLING ST	BURBANK, CA	91505
HERZBERG, ROBERT A	NEWS CORRESPONDENT	8144 MURRAY HILL DR	FORT WASHINGTON, MD	20744
HERZFELD, JOHN	WRITER-PRODUCER	12820 MILBANK ST	STUDIO CITY, CA	91604
HERZOG, WHITEY	BASEBALL	3613 S FOREST	INDEPENDENCE, MO	64052
HESCHKE, RICHARD	ORGANIST	15 HIGH ST #621	HARTFORD, CT	06103
HESCHONG, NAOMI	WRITER	5132 AMESTOY AVE	ENCINO, CA	91316
HESS, BENNIE	SINGER-GUITARIST	14119 CHRISMAN RD	HOUSTON, TX	77039
HESS, BENTON	CONDUCTOR	MUNRO, 334 W 72ND ST	NEW YORK, NY	10023
HESS, DAVID A	WRITER	1505 BROOKINGS TRAIL	TOPANGA, CA	90290
HESS, DAVID W	NEWS CORRESPONDENT	5411 EASTON DR	SPRINGFIELD, VA	22151
HESS, GLENN H	NEWS CORRESPONDENT	1400 S JOYCE ST #C	ARLINGTON, VA	22202
HESS, JAKE	GUITARIST	510 MEADOW LARK LN	BRENTWOOD, TN	37027
HESS, JAMES	ACTOR	3151 W CAHUENGA BLVD #310	LOS ANGELES, CA	90068
HESS, JOHN D	WRITER	555 W 57TH ST #1230	NEW YORK, NY	10019
HESS, JUDITH	ACTRESS	948 E CAMBRIDGE DR	BURBANK, CA	91504
HESS, MILO	WRITER	555 W 57TH ST #1230	NEW YORK, NY	10019
HESS, NICKIE	ACTRESS	CARPENTER, 1516-W REDWOOD ST	SAN DIEGO, CA	92101
HESS, RONNIE L	WRITER	555 W 57TH ST #1230	NEW YORK, NY	10019
HESS, SUSAN	ACTRESS	J MICHAEL BLOOM AGENCY		
		233 PARK AVE S, 10TH FLOOR	NEW YORK, NY	10017
HESS, TROY	SINGER	14119 CHRISMAN RD	HOUSTON, TX	77039
HESSE, LOUIS	FILM EDITOR	23388 MULHOLLAND DR	WOODLAND HILLS, CA	91364
HESSEMAN, HOWARD	ACTOR-WRITER	7146 LA PESA DR	HOLLYWOOD, CA	90068
HESSLER, GORDON	DIRECTOR	8910 HOLLY PL	LOS ANGELES, CA	90046
HESTER, HOOT	GUITARIST	ROUTE #3, BOX 203	DICKSON, TN	37055
HESTON, CHARLTON	ACTOR-DIRECTOR	2859 COLDWATER CANYON DR	BEVERLY HILLS, CA	90210
HESTON, FRASER	FILM WRITER-PRODUCER	2859 COLDWATER CANYON DR	BEVERLY HILLS, CA	90210
HESTON, JEFF	ACTOR	10 E 44TH ST #700	NEW YORK, NY	10017
HESTON, JOSEPH WERNER	DIRECTOR	DGA, 110 W 57TH ST	NEW YORK, NY	10019
HETU, PIERRE	CONDUCTOR	61 W 62ND ST #6-F	NEW YORK, NY	10023
HETZEL, GERHART	VIOLINIST	MARIEDL ANDERS ARTISTS MGMT		
		535 EL CAMINO DEL MAR ST	SAN FRANCISCO, CA	94121

Name	Occupation	Address	City	Zip
HEU, STEPHEN	ACTOR	4350 TROOST AVE #1	STUDIO CITY, CA	91604
HEUER, ROBERT	FRENCH HORNIST	2115 ASHWOOD AVE	NASHVILLE, TN	37212
HEWES, HENRY	DRAMA CRITIC	1326 MADISON AVE	NEW YORK, NY	10028
HEWETT, JENNI	NEWS CORRESPONDENT	632 E CAPITOL ST #5, NW	WASHINGTON, DC	20003
HEWGLEY, TOM	MUSICIAN	8312 CORTLAND DR	KNOXVILLE, TN	37919
HEWITSON, MICHAEL	ACTOR	8255 BEVERLY BLVD	LOS ANGELES, CA	90048
HEWITT, CHARLES	ACTOR	5647 CARTWRIGHT AVE #47	NORTH HOLLYWOOD, CA	91601
HEWITT, DON	WRITER-PRODUCER	220 CENTRAL PARK S	NEW YORK, NY	10019
HEWITT, FRANKIE	THEATER PRODUCER	FORD'S THEATRE		
		511 10TH ST, NW	WASHINGTON, DC	20005
HEWITT, HEATHER	ACTRESS	6324 TAHOE DR	LOS ANGELES, CA	90068
HEWITT, JACK	PIANIST	430 WINSTON RD, SW	MARIETTA, GA	30060
HEWITT, STEVEN W	TV EXECUTIVE	CBS-TV, 6121 SUNSET BLVD	LOS ANGELES, CA	90028
HEWITT, TED	GUITARIST	4183 APACHE TRAIL	ANTIOCH, TN	37013
HEWLETT, ARTHUR	ACTOR	10 HEATH DR	LONDON NW3	ENGLAND
HEWLETT, DONALD	ACTOR	THE MILL HOUSE, ARGOS HILL		
		ROTHERFIELD	EAST SUSSEX	ENGLAND
HEXTER, HOLLY	NEWS CORRESPONDENT	506 INDEPENDENCE AVE, SE	WASHINGTON, DC	20003
HEY, DALE	WRESTLER	SEE - ROBERTS, BUDDY "JACK"		
HEYCOCK, DAVID	TV PRODUCER	146 MERTON RD #2, WANDSWORTH	LONDON SW18	ENGLAND
HEYDORN, NANCY S	DIRECTOR	15443 HUSTON ST	SHERMAN OAKS, CA	91403
HEYER, JULIA	SOPRANO	45 W 60TH ST #4-K	NEW YORK, NY	10023
HEYES, DOUG, JR	TV WRITER	1900 AVE OF THE STARS #2535	LOS ANGELES, CA	90067
HEYES, DOUGLAS H	WRITER-PRODUCER	1227 COLDWATER CANYON DR	BEVERLY HILLS, CA	90210
HEYMAN, BARTON	ACTOR	151 2ND AVE #1-B	NEW YORK, NY	10003
HEYMAN, JOHN B	FILM PRODUCER	1271 AVE OF THE AMERICAS #730	NEW YORK, NY	10020
HEYMAN, MILLARD	CONDUCTOR	314 CLAYTON ST	WAUKEGAN, IL	60085
HEYMAN, RICHARD X	SINGER-GUITARIST	51 1ST ST #1	NEW YORK, NY	10003
HEYMANN, LEONARD	NEWS CORRESPONDENT	1710 LAMONT ST, NW	WASHINGTOPN, DC	20010
HEYWARD, ANDREW J	WRITER	555 W 57TH ST #1230	NEW YORK, NY	10019
HEYWARD, LOUIS	WRITER-PRODUCER	6819 SEPULVEDA BLVD	VAN NUYS, CA	91405
HEYWARD, LOUIS M	TV WRITER	10717 WILSHIRE BLVD #1003	LOS ANGELES, CA	90024
HEYWOOD, ANNE	ACTRESS	9966 LIEBE DR	BEVERLY HILLS, CA	90210
HEYWORTH, JAMES O	PUBLISHING EXECUTIVE	DISCOVER/TIME & LIFE BLDG		
		ROCKEFELLER CENTER	NEW YORK, NY	10020
HEYWORTH, JIM	CABLE EXECUTIVE	HBO, 1100 AVE OF THE AMERICAS	NEW YORK, NY	10036
HEYWORTH, MALCOLM B	FILM PRODUCER	CHATSWORTH FILMS		
		97-99 DEAN ST	LONDON W1	ENGLAND
HIATT, FRED	NEWS CORRESPONDENT	3624 VAN NESS ST	WASHINGTON, DC	20008
HIATT, KEVIN L	COMPOSER	1218 LODI PL #216	LOS ANGELES, CA	90038
HIATT, MELISSA	WRESTLING VALET	SEE - HYATT, MISSY		
HIATT, MICHAEL	DIRECTOR	DGA, 7950 SUNSET BLVD	LOS ANGELES, CA	90046
HIATT, RUTH	ACTRESS	FRENCH, 2166 CANYON DR	LOS ANGELES, CA	90068
HIBBERD, KEVIN	DIRECTOR-PRODUCER	23 GOSFIELD ST	LONDON S1P 7HB	ENGLAND
HIBLER, CHRISTOPHER A	DIRECTOR	1927 MELWOOD DR	GLENDALE, CA	91207
HICE, VALERIE C	WRITER	8045 LLOYD AVE	NORTH HOLLYWOOD, CA	91605
HICKER, MARILYN FAITH	ACTRESS	3330 BARHAM BLVD #103	LOS ANGELES, CA	90068
HICKERSON, BUDDY	CARTOONIST	THE NATIONAL LAMPOON		
		635 MADISON AVE	NEW YORK, NY	10022
HICKEY, JANICE	WRITER	8955 BEVERLY BLVD	LOS ANGELES, CA	90048
HICKEY, JIM	NEWS CORRESPONDENT	ABC-TV, 7 W 66TH ST	NEW YORK, NY	10019
HICKEY, NEIL	WRITER	TV GUIDE, 25 5TH AVE	NEW YORK, NY	10003
HICKLAND, CATHERINE	ACTRESS	HASSELHOFF, 4310 SUTTON PL	SHERMAN OAKS, CA	91413
HICKMAN, DARRYL	ACT-WRI-PROD	10100 SANTA MONICA BLVD #1600	LOS ANGELES, CA	90067
HICKMAN, DAVID	TRUMPETER	POST OFFICE BOX 27539	PHILADELPHIA, PA	19118
HICKMAN, DWAYNE	ACTOR	812 16TH ST #1	SANTA MONICA, CA	90403
HICKMAN, GAIL MORGAN	TV WRITER	8955 BEVERLY BLVD	LOS ANGELES, CA	90048
HICKMAN, HUDSON ROBERT	TV WRITER	8955 BEVERLY BLVD	LOS ANGELES, CA	90048
HICKMAN, LARRY & RED HOT RIDERS	C & W GROUP	JOYCE, 2028 CHESTNUT ST	PHILADELPHIA, PA	19103
HICKMAN, WILLIAM W	FILM DIRECTOR	82-317 LANCASTER WY	INDIO, CA	92201
HICKOX, BRYAN	WRITER	11726 SAN VICENTE BLVD #300	LOS ANGELES, CA	90049
HICKOX, DOUGLAS	TV DIRECTOR	DOUGLAS RAE MANAGEMENT		
		28 CHARING CROSS RD	LONDON WC2 HOBD	ENGLAND
HICKOX, HARRY	ACTOR	8819 LOOKOUT MOUNTAIN AVE	LOS ANGELES, CA	90046
HICKOX, S BRYAN	TV EXECUTIVE	WARNER BROTHERS, INC		
		4000 WARNER BLVD		
		PRODUCER'S BLDG #4, ROOM 16	BURBANK, CA	91522
HICKS, BRENDA	WRITER	555 W 57TH ST #1230	NEW YORK, NY	10019
HICKS, CATHERINE	ACTRESS	9973 DURANT DR #2	BEVERLY HILLS, CA	90212
HICKS, CHUCK	ACTOR	POST OFFICE BOX 24-A-56	LOS ANGELES, CA	90024
HICKS, DAN	SINGER-SONGWRITER	SAVOY MUSIC, 1111 KEARNET ST	SAN FRANCISCO, CA	94133
HICKS, DAVID LEE	GUITARIST	206 SEALY DR #D-38	MADISON, TN	37115
HICKS, HILLY	ACTOR	708 SANTA BARBARA DR #F	CLAREMONT, CA	91711
HICKS, JACK	BANJOIST	ROUTE #4, BOX 33-B	WESTMORELAND, TN	37186
HICKS, JOANN	ACTRESS	13239 ADDISON ST	SHERMAN OAKS, CA	91423
HICKS, JOHN	SINGER	PENNY, 30 GUINAN ST	WALTHAM, MA	02154
HICKS, JOHN P	COMPOSER	3834 TRACY ST	LOS ANGELES, CA	90027
HICKS, LIANE	ACTRESS	3100 S MANCHESTER ST #810	FALLS CHRUCH, VA	22044
HICKS, MARY	PIANIST	3503 HOOD TRAIL	NASHVILLE, TN	37204
HICKS, MARY M	WRITER	555 W 57TH ST #1230	NEW YORK, NY	10019
HICKS, NEIL D	SCREENWRITER	8955 BEVERLY BLVD	LOS ANGELES, CA	90048
HICKS, ROGER	MUSICIAN	206 SEALEY DR	MADISON, TN	37115
HICKS, RUSSELL	GUITARIST	ROUTE #1, BOX 253-A	PEGRAM, TN	37143

HIDAKA, YOSHIKI	NEWS CORRESPONDENT	444 N CAPITOL ST, NW	WASHINGTON, DC	20001
HIDER, ED	TV WRITER	8955 BEVERLY BLVD	LOS ANGELES, CA	90048
HIEGEL, NANCY J	WRITER	555 W 57TH ST #1230	NEW YORK, NY	10019
HIERONYMUS, RICHARD E	COMPOSER	1161 N HIGHLAND AVE	LOS ANGELES, CA	90038
HIESTAND, EDWARD A	WRITER	555 W 57TH ST #1230	NEW YORK, NY	10019
HIGBIE, BARBARA	PIANIST	POST OFFICE BOX 9388	STANFORD, CA	94305
HIGGINS, ALEXANDER G	NEWS CORRESPONDENT	464 VISTA CT	WALDORF, MD	20601
HIGGINS, BERTIE	SINGER-SONGWRITER	5775 PEACHTREE DUNWOODY	ATLANTA, GA	30342
HIGGINS, COLIN	WRITER-PRODUCER	2844 HUTTON DR	BEVERLY HILLS, CA	90210
HIGGINS, GEORGE V	WRITER	8955 BEVERLY BLVD	LOS ANGELES, CA	90048
HIGGINS, JACK	WRITER	"SEPTEMBERTIDE"		
		MONT DE LA ROCQUE		
		SAINT AUBIN	JERSEY	CHANNEL ISLS
HIGGINS, JAMES	ACTOR	8285 SUNSET BLVD #12	LOS ANGELES, CA	90046
HIGGINS, JOE	ACTOR	10823 CAMARILLO ST	NORTH HOLLYWOOD, CA	91602
HIGGINS, JOEL	ACTOR	10100 SANTA MONICA BLVD #1600	LOS ANGELES, CA	90067
HIGGINS, JOETTE	ACTRESS	ABC-TV, "ALL MY CHILDREN"		
		1330 AVE OF THE AMERICAS	NEW YORK, NY	10019
HIGGINS, JOHN C	WRITER	10371 MISSISSIPPI AVE	LOS ANGELES, CA	90025
HIGGINS, JOHN K	NEWS CORRESPONDENT	6232 32ND PL, NW	WASHINGTON, DC	20015
HIGGINS, MICHAEL	ACTOR	2121 AVE OF THE STARS #410	LOS ANGELES, CA	90067
HIGGINS, THOM BEAU	DIRECTOR	DGA, 110 W 57TH ST	NEW YORK, NY	10019
HIGGS, LARRY Y	TV DIRECTOR-PRODUCER	4660 CERRILLOS DR	WOODLAND HILLS, CA	91364
HIGH, GOLDIE	HIGH WIRE ACT	SEE - KING ARTHUR &		
		.... GOLDIE HIGH		
HIGH, MARK	ACTOR	10920 WILSHIRE BLVD #220	LOS ANGELES, CA	90024
HIGH FASHION	MUSIC GROUP	233 W 26TH ST #1-W	NEW YORK, NY	10001
HIGH INERGY	ROCK & ROLL GROUP	GWEN FULLER, MOTOWN RECORDS		
		6255 SUNSET BLVD	LOS ANGELES, CA	90028
HIGHER GROUND	GOSPEL GROUP	6750 W 75TH ST, MARKADE 75		
		BUILDING #2-A	OVERLAND PARK, KS	66204
HIGHER GROUND BLUEGRASS BAND	BLUEGRASS G	POST OFFICE BOX 942	RAPID CITY, SD	57709
HIGHLAND, FRANKIE R	WRITER	8955 BEVERLY BLVD	LOS ANGELES, CA	90048
HIGHWAY CHILE	ROCK & ROLL GROUP	MELKLAAN 35-A	VELSON NOORD	NETHERLANDS
HIGUCHI, KATHRYN J	WRITER	555 W 57TH ST #1230	NEW YORK, NY	10019
HIKEN, GERALD	ACTOR	2133 1/2 HOLLY DR #A	LOS ANGELES, CA	90068
HILARY, JENNIFER	ACTRESS	LONDON MANAGEMENT, LTD		
		235-241 REGENT ST	LONDON W1A 2JT	ENGLAND
HILBURN, ROBERT	MUSIC CRITIC	L A TIMES NEWSPAPER		
		TIMES MIRROR SQUARE	LOS ANGELES, CA	90053
HILDEBRAND, DAVID & GINGER	FOLK DUO	SPRINGER, 1001 ROLANDVUE RD	BALTIMORE, MD	21204
HILDEBRAND, ROBERT	DRUMMER	411 S 5TH ST	NASHVILLE, TN	37206
HILDEGARDE	SINGER	230 E 48TH ST	NEW YORK, NY	10017
HILDNER, VICTORIA	NEWS CORRESPONDENT	4461 CONNECTICUT AVE, NW	WASHINGTON, DC	20008
HILDRETH, JAMES M	NEWS CORRESPONDENT	5038 PORTSMOUTH RD	FAIRFAX, VA	22032
HILKA, TRISHA	ACTRESS	217 S LINCOLN ST	BURBANK, CA	91506
HILL, ANDREW	TV EXECUTIVE	COLUMBIA PICTURES TV		
		COLUMBIA PLAZA	BURBANK, CA	91505
HILL, ANTHONY	FILM EXECUTIVE	97 OXFORD RD, UXBRIDGE	MIDDLESEX	ENGLAND
HILL, ANTHONY C	WRITER	555 W 57TH ST #1230	NEW YORK, NY	10019
HILL, ARTHUR	ACTOR	1515 CLUB VIEW DR	LOS ANGELES, CA	90024
HILL, BARRY	TV WRITER	4 HURSTHEAD RD, CHEADLE HULME	CHESHIRE SK8 7JR	ENGLAND
HILL, BENJAMIN T, JR	TV DIRECTOR	6842 RANCHITO AVE	VAN NUYS, CA	91405
HILL, BENNY	ACTOR-COMEDIAN	2 QUEENSGATE #7	LONDON SW7	ENGLAND
HILL, BOB	ACTOR	5723 LA MIRADA AVE #1	LOS ANGELES, CA	90038
HILL, DANA	ACTRESS	10351 SANTA MONICA BLVD #211	LOS ANGELES, CA	90025
HILL, DANIELLE	WRITER	555 W 57TH ST #1230	NEW YORK, NY	10019
HILL, DEAN	ACTOR	1509 N CRESCENT HGTS BLVD #7	LOS ANGELES, CA	90069
HILL, DEBRA	FILM PRODUCER	PARAMOUNT PICTURES CORP		
		5555 MELROSE AVE	LOS ANGELES, CA	90038
HILL, DEBRA G	SCREENWRITER	8955 BEVERLY BLVD	LOS ANGELES, CA	90048
HILL, DONALD H	CONDUCTOR	4257 S NORTON AVE	LOS ANGELES, CA	90008
HILL, EDDIE	GUITARIST	2011 RICHARD JONES RD #K-6	NASHVILLE, TN	37214
HILL, ELAINE WELTON	ACTRESS	208 S BEVERLY DR #4	BEVERLY HILLS, CA	90212
HILL, FRANKIE	ACTRESS	1509 N CRESCENT HGTS BLVD #7	LOS ANGELES, CA	90069
HILL, GEORGE ROY	FILM WRITER-DIRECTOR	70 MADISON AVE	NEW YORK, NY	10016
HILL, GREG	TV DIRECTOR	631 BAY ST #6	SANTA MONICA, CA	90405
HILL, HEATHER H	TV DIRECTOR	83 KELLOGG ST	BROOKFIELD, CT	06804
HILL, JACK	SCREENWRITER	8955 BEVERLY BLVD	LOS ANGELES, CA	90048
HILL, JACK	TV DIRECTOR	22014 DE LA OSA ST	WOODLAND HILLS, CA	91364
HILL, JACKSON	WRITER	13235 VALLEYHEART DR	SHERMAN OAKS, CA	91423
HILL, JAMES	TV DIRECTOR	1 ABDALE RD	LONDON W12	ENGLAND
HILL, JIM	TV WRITER-PRODUCER	GOODWIN, 19 LONDON ST	LONDON W2	ENGLAND
HILL, JOHN	SCREENWRITER	9046 SUNSET BLVD #202	LOS ANGELES, CA	90069
HILL, JOHN D	MUSIC ARRANGER	2885 LYNCREST DR	NASHVILLE, TN	37214
HILL, JON	ACTOR	2832 AVENEL ST #7	LOS ANGELES, CA	90039
HILL, KEN	ACTOR	8350 SANTA MONICA BLVD #206-A	LOS ANGELES, CA	90069
HILL, KIMBERLY	TV WRITER	8955 BEVERLY BLVD	LOS ANGELES, CA	90048
HILL, LANGDON	COLUMNIST	UNIVERSAL PRESS SYNDICATE		
		4900 MAIN ST, 9TH FLOOR	KANSAS CITY, MO	62114
HILL, LARRY	DRUMMER	231 NEW SHACKLE ISLAND	HENDERSONVILLE, TN	37075
HILL, LEONARD	TV PRODUCER	MCA/UNIVERSAL STUDIOS, INC		
		100 UNIVERSAL CITY PLAZA	UNIVERSAL CITY, CA	91608
HILL, LEONARD F	TV EXECUTIVE	2519 PERDIDO LN	LOS ANGELES, CA	90077
HILL, LESLIE B	WRITER-PRODUCER	715 PIER AVE	SANTA MONICA, CA	90405

HILL, LYNNE REGGIARDO	WRITER-PRODUCER	1748 FRANKLIN ST	SANTA MONICA, CA 90404
HILL, MARIANA	ACTRESS	KOHNER, 9169 SUNSET BLVD	LOS ANGELES, CA 90069
HILL, MAURICE	ACTOR	208 S BEVERLY DR #4	BEVERLY HILLS, CA 90212
HILL, MAURICE J	ACTOR-WRITER	8573 APPIAN WY	LOS ANGELES, CA 90046
HILL, MICHAEL	TV WRITER	8955 BEVERLY BLVD	LOS ANGELES, CA 90048
HILL, PAMELA	TV DIRECTOR-PRODUCER	169 E 80TH ST	NEW YORK, NY 10021
HILL, PATRICIA S	NEWS CORRESPONDENT	407 17TH ST, SE	WASHINGTON, DC 20003
HILL, PAULA	ACTRESS	1738 CANYON DR #202	LOS ANGELES, CA 90028
HILL, PHIL	GUITARIST	702 COUNTRY SIDE DR	MC KEES ROCK, PA 15136
HILL, R LANCE	WRITER	9000 SUNSET BLVD #1200	LOS ANGELES, CA 90069
HILL, RICHARD	ACTOR	1930 CENTURY PARK W #30	LOS ANGELES, CA 90067
HILL, RICHARD LEE	GUITARIST	ROUTE #4, BOX 4082	BOERNE, TX 78006
HILL, RICK	ACTOR	10100 SANTA MONICA BLVD #1600	LOS ANGELES, CA 90067
HILL, RILEY	ACTOR	POST OFFICE BOX 5251	TUCSON, AZ 85703
HILL, ROBERT J	WRITER	8955 BEVERLY BLVD	LOS ANGELES, CA 90048
HILL, ROD	TRUMPETER	4824 BARCLAY SQ DR	ANTIOCH, TN 37013
HILL, SETH	TV WRITER-DIRECTOR	17130 PALISADES CIR	PACIFIC PALISADES, CA 90272
HILL, STEPHEN	SINGER-GUITARIST	2909 TWIN LAWN DR	NASHVILLE, TN 37214
HILL, STEVEN	ACTOR	10100 SANTA MONICA BLVD #1600	LOS ANGELES, CA 90067
HILL, TERENCE	ACTOR	POST OFFICE BOX 818	STOCKBRIDGE, MA 01262
HILL, THOMAS	ACTOR	KOHNER, 9169 SUNSET BLVD	LOS ANGELES, CA 90069
HILL, VINCE	SINGER	235 REGENT ST	LONDON W1A 2JT ENGLAND
HILL, WALTER	WRITER-PRODUCER	31368 BROAD BEACH RD	MALIBU, CA 90265
HILL, WAYNE	TRUMPETER	2311 ELLIOTT AVE #J-7	NASHVILLE, TN 37204
HILL, WELDON	TV WRITER	8955 BEVERLY BLVD	LOS ANGELES, CA 90048
HILL, WENDY	SOPRANO	FINELL, 155 W 68TH ST	NEW YORK, NY 10023
HILL, WILLIAM B	WRITER	555 W 57TH ST #1230	NEW YORK, NY 10019
HILL, WILLIAM H	COMPOSER-CONDUCTOR	1125 S 5TH AVE	ARCADIA, CA 91006
HILL CITY	C & W GROUP	102 E EXCHANGE AVE #300	FORT WORTH, TX 76106
HILLAIRE, MARCEL	ACTOR	637 1/2 BURNSIDE AVE	LOS ANGELES, CA 90036
HILLARD, TIMOTHY E	NEWS CORRESPONDENT	236 MASSACHUSETTS AVE, NE	WASHINGTON, DC 20002
HILLARY, SIR EDMUND	MOUNTAINEER	228-A REMUERA RD	AUCKLAND SE2 NEW ZEALAND
HILLBILLY JIM	WRESTLER	POST OFFICE BOX 3859	STAMFORD, CT 06905
HILLEL	ACTOR	3575 W CAHUENGA BLVD #320	LOS ANGELES, CA 90068
HILLER, ARTHUR	FILM DIRECTOR	1218 BENEDICT CANYON DR	BEVERLY HILLS, CA 90210
HILLER, DAME WENDY	ACTRESS	SPINDLES, STRATTON RD BEACONSFIELD	BUCKS ENGLAND
HILLER, WALLY	TALENT AGENT	9220 SUNSET BLVD #202	LOS ANGELES, CA 90069
HILLERMAN, JOHN	ACTOR	469 ENA RD, 38TH FLOOR	HONOLULU, HI 96815
HILLEY, KENNETH	GUITARIST	623 TEMPLEWOOD CT	NASHVILLE, TN 37214
HILLGREN, SONJA	NEWS CORRESPONDENT	2800 29TH PL, NW	WASHINGTON, DC 20008
HILLHOUSE, WENDY	MEZZO-SOPRANO	61 W 62ND ST #6-F	NEW YORK, NY 10023
HILLIAN, VANESSA B	PHOTOGRAPHER	5327 AMES ST, NE	WASHINGTON, DC 20019
HILLIARD, ROBERT J	TV WRITER	8955 BEVERLY BLVD	LOS ANGELES, CA 90048
HILLIER, BILL	TV PRODUCER	15303 VENTURA BLVD, 11TH FLOOR	SHERMAN OAKS, CA 91403
HILLIER, DAVID G	DIRECTOR-PRODUCER	6 AVE RD, BRENTFORD	MIDDLESEX TW8 9MS ENGLAND
HILLINGER, CHARLES	WRITER	8955 BEVERLY BLVD	LOS ANGELES, CA 90048
HILLIS, MARGARET	CONDUCTOR	SHAW CONCERTS, 1995 BROADWAY	NEW YORK, NY 10023
HILLKIRK, JOHN	COLUMNIST	POST OFFICE BOX 500	WASHINGTON, DC 20044
HILLMAN, CHRIS	SINGER-MUSICIAN	1377 HANOVER LN	VENTURA, CA 93003
HILLMAN, LORI A	WRITER	555 W 57TH ST #1230	NEW YORK, NY 10019
HILLMAN, LORRAINE P	WRITER	8955 BEVERLY BLVD	LOS ANGELES, CA 90048
HILLMAN, PAUL H	WRITER	555 W 57TH ST #1230	NEW YORK, NY 10019
HILLMAN, RONALD E	COMPOSER	POST OFFICE BOX 5452	BEVERLY HILLS, CA 90210
HILLMAN, WILLIAM B	WRITER-PRODUCER	18251 FRIAR ST	RESEDA, CA 91335
HILLS, ANNE	SINGER	5109 OAK HAVEN LN	TAMPA, FL 33617
HILLS, ANNE	SINGER-GUITARIST	HOGEYE MUSIC, 1920 CENTRAL ST	EVANSTON, IL 60201
HILLS, DICK	TV WRITER	9 ADDINGTON RD, WEST WICKHAM	KENT ENGLAND
HILLS, R WARREN	TV DIRECTOR	3800 HOOPER AVE	BALTIMORE, MD 21211
HILLYER, RAPHAEL	VIOLIST	HILLYER, 250 W 57TH ST	NEW YORK, NY 10107
HILMER, DAVID	CINEMATOGRAPHER	7715 SUNSET BLVD #150	LOS ANGELES, CA 90046
HILMER, DAVID	TV DIRECTOR	12011 ADDISON ST	NORTH HOLLYWOOD, CA 91607
HILTON, GREGG	NEWS CORRESPONDENT	51 "D" ST, NW	WASHINGTON, DC 20003
HILTON, KIMBERLY BECK	ACTRESS	500 S SEPULVEDA BLVD #510	LOS ANGELES, CA 90049
HILTZ, PHYLLIS	VIOLINIST	404 GREENWAY AVE	NASHVILLE, TN 37205
HIMELFARB, JOEL	NEWS CORRESPONDENT	125 "C" ST, SE	WASHINGTON, DC 20003
HIMELFARB, MARVIN	WRITER	6380 WILSHIRE BLVD #910	LOS ANGELES, CA 90048
HIMES, CAROL	TV PRODUCER	PARAMOUNT TELEVISION 5555 MELROSE AVE	LOS ANGELES, CA 90038
HIMES, DAVID	ACTOR	17950 BURBANK BLVD #6	ENCINO, CA 91316
HIMES, ERIC L	DIRECTOR	342 W 71ST ST	NEW YORK, NY 10023
HIMES, SHARON	CASTING DIRECTOR	CBS-TV, 4000 WARNER BLVD	BURBANK, CA 91522
HIMES, TIMOTHY	ACTOR	14417 COHASSET ST	VAN NUYS, CA 91405
HIMMEL, LARRY	TV-RADIO PERSONALITY	KFMB-TV, 7677 ENGINEER RD	SAN DIEGO, CA 92111
HIMMELMAN, PETER	SINGER-SONGWRITER	POST OFFICE BOX 95	RIDGEWOOD, NJ 07541
HIMMELSTEIN, DAVID J	WRITER	555 W 57TH ST #1230	NEW YORK, NY 10019
HINCKLE, DOUG	PHOTOGRAPHER	1000 PERRY ST, NE	WASHINGTON, DC 20014
HINCKLEY, ALFRED	ACTOR	THE MANHATTAN PLAZA 400 W 43RD ST	NEW YORK, NY 10036
HINCKLEY, DAVID	FILM CRITIC	THE N Y DAILY NEWS 220 E 42ND ST	NEW YORK, NY 10017
HINCKS, C J	ACTRESS	7223 WILLOUGHBY AVE #101	LOS ANGELES, CA 90046
HINDE, MADELINE	ACTRESS	MILLER, 82 BROOM PARK TEDDINGTON	MIDDLESEX ENGLAND
HINDEN, STANLEY J	NEWS CORRESPONDENT	10 KIRKWALL CT	POTOMAC, MD 20854

Name	Occupation	Address	City	Zip
HINDERAS, NATALIE	PIANIST	POST OFFICE BOX 27539	PHILADELPHIA, PA	19118
HINDLE, ART	ACTOR	3005 MAIN ST	SANTA MONICA, CA	90405
HINDMAN, EARL	ACTOR	HARTIG, 527 MADISON AVE	NEW YORK, NY	10022
HINDS, BILL	CARTOONIST	UNIVERSAL PRESS SYNDICATE		
		4900 MAIN ST, 9TH FLOOR	KANSAS CITY, MO	62114
HINDS, ESTHER	SOPRANO	SHAW CONCERTS, 1995 BROADWAY	NEW YORK, NY	10023
HINDS, HUGH B	NEWS CORRESPONDENT	824 CHESTNUT TRAIL DR	ANNAPOLIS, MD	21401
HINDY, JOSEPH	ACTOR	2017 1/2 ROSILLA PL	LOS ANGELES, CA	90046
HINDY, PATRICIA	ACTRESS	2017 1/2 ROSILLA PL	LOS ANGELES, CA	90046
HINER, LOUIS C	NEWS CORRESPONDENT	3426 FARM HILL DR	FALLS CHURCH, VA	22044
HINES, BARRY	TV WRITER	LEMON, 24 POTTERY LN	LONDON W11	ENGLAND
HINES, CONNIE	ACTRESS	818 N DOHENY DR #905	LOS ANGELES, CA	90069
HINES, CRAIG	NEWS CORRESPONDENT	707 7TH ST, NW	WASHINGTON, DC	20003
HINES, FRAZER	ACTOR	25 DENMARK ST	LONDON WC2H 8NJ	ENGLAND
HINES, GRAINGER	ACTOR	10557 TROON AVE	LOS ANGELES, CA	90064
HINES, GREGORY	ACTOR	125 BREEZE AVE	VENICE, CA	90291
HINES, JEROME	BASSO	SHAW CONCERTS, 1995 BROADWAY	NEW YORK, NY	10023
HINES, MIMI	ACTRESS	229 OLD POST RD	CAPE CODE, MA	02632
HINES, RONALD	ACTOR	LEADING ARTISTS, LTD		
		60 SAINT JAMES'S ST	LONDON SW1	ENGLAND
HINES, WILLIAM	NEWS CORRESPONDENT	ROUTE #1, BOX 48	LOVETTSVILLE, VA	22080
HINGLE, PAT	ACTOR	11247 KLING ST	NORTH HOLLYWOOD, CA	91602
HINKLER, DIANNE	ACTRESS	6310 SAN VICENTE BLVD #407	LOS ANGELES, CA	90048
HINKLEY, DEL	ACTOR	2513 2ND ST #6	SANTA MONICA, CA	90405
HINMAN, NANCY	ACTRESS	721 N LA BREA AVE #200	LOS ANGELES, CA	90038
HINNANT, CHARLES	BASSOONIST	1420 CUMBER LN	COOKEVILLE, TN	38501
HINSON, DANNY	GUITARIST	313 BURNING TREE APARTMENTS	HERMITAGE, TN	37076
HINSON, JAMES H "JAY"	COMPOSER-CONDUCTOR	421 S LAFAYETTE PARK PL	LOS ANGELES, CA	90057
HINTON, DARBY	ACTOR	1234 BEL AIR RD	LOS ANGELES, CA	90077
HINTON, JAMES DAVID	ACTOR	2808 OAK POINT DR	LOS ANGELES, CA	90068
HINTON, S E	SCREENWRITER	8955 BEVERLY BLVD	LOS ANGELES, CA	90048
HINTON, SAM	SINGER-GUITARIST	9420 LA JOLLA SHORES DR	LA JOLLA, CA	92037
HINZ, VOLKER	PHOTOGRAPHER	POST OFFICE BOX 11696	WASHINGTON, DC	20008
HIONA, SAM	ACTOR	427 N CANON DR #205	BEVERLY HILLS, CA	90210
HIPP, RICHARD FRANCIS	ACTOR	605 N RODEO DR	BEVERLY HILLS, CA	90210
HIPPARD, ROBERT	WRITER	2049 LINNINGTON AVE	LOS ANGELES, CA	90025
HIRAX	ROCK & ROLL GROUP	POST OFFICE BOX 2428	EL SEGUNDO, CA	90245
HIRD, BOB	TV DIRECTOR-PRODUCER	LONDON MANAGEMENT, LTD		
		235-241 REGENT ST	LONDON W1A 2JT	ENGLAND
HIRD, THORA	ACTRESS	OLD LOFT, 21 LEINSTER MEWS		
		LANCASTER GATE	LONDON W2 3EY	ENGLAND
HIRE, LOIS	WRITER	17161 OAK VIEW DR	ENCINO, CA	91316
HIRO	DIRECTOR	50 CENTRAL PARK W	NEW YORK, NY	10023
HIROSHIGE, KIMIKO	ACTRESS	2841 S NORTON AVE	LOS ANGELES, CA	90018
HIROSHIMA	JAZZ GROUP	10100 SANTA MONICA BLVD #1600	LOS ANGELES, CA	90067
HIRSCH, CHARLES S	WRITER	209 E 23RD ST	NEW YORK, NY	10010
HIRSCH, ELROY "CRAZY LEGS"	ACTOR	50 OAK CREEK TRAIL	MADISON, WI	53717
HIRSCH, GLENN	COMEDIAN	ICM, 8899 BEVERLY BLVD	LOS ANGELES, CA	90048
HIRSCH, JAMES GORDON	TV WRITER	1075 CASIANO RD	LOS ANGELES, CA	90049
HIRSCH, JANIS	TV WRITER	8955 BEVERLY BLVD	LOS ANGELES, CA	90048
HIRSCH, JUDD	ACTOR	15760 VENTURA BLVD #1730	ENCINO, CA	91436
HIRSCH, LYNDA	TV CRITIC-COLUMNIST	NEWS AMERICA SYNDICATE		
		1703 KAISER AVE	IRVINE, CA	92714
HIRSCH, STEVE J	NEWS CORRESPONDENT	111 "P" ST, SW	WASHINGTON, DC	20024
HIRSCH, TIBOR	TV DIRECTOR	32 W 53RD ST	NEW YORK, NY	10019
HIRSCHFELD, BURTON	WRITER	555 W 57TH ST #1230	NEW YORK, NY	10019
HIRSCHFELD, GERALD	CINEMATOGRAPHER	904 HIGH VIEW DR	ARROYO GRANDE, CA	93420
HIRSCHFELD, JIM	TV DIRECTOR-PRODUCER	285 CENTRAL PARK W #2-S	NEW YORK, NY	10024
HIRSCHFELD, MARC	CASTING DIRECTOR	EMBASSY-TV, 1438 N GOWER ST	LOS ANGELES, CA	90028
HIRSCHFELD, ROBERT	ACTOR	870 N VINE ST #G	LOS ANGELES, CA	90038
HIRSCHFIELD, AL	CARICATURIST	122 E 95TH ST	NEW YORK, NY	10028
HIRSCHFIELD, ALAN J	FILM EXECUTIVE	10201 PICO BLVD	LOS ANGELES, CA	90064
HIRSCHFIELD, LEONARD	DIRECTOR-PRODUCER	9 E 40TH ST	NEW YORK, NY	10016
HIRSCHHORN, LINDA	SINGER-PRODUCER	POST OFFICE BOX 3929	BERKELEY, CA	94703
HIRSCHL, GARY I	NEWS CORRESPONDENT	2020 "F" ST #207, NW	WASHINGTON, DC	20006
HIRSCHMAN, RAYMOND	TV WRITER	555 W 57TH ST #1230	NEW YORK, NY	10019
HIRSEN, STEVEN	TV DIRECTOR	6174 GLEN OAK WALK	LOS ANGELES, CA	90068
HIRSH, STEPHEN L	NEWS CORRES-WRITER	6665 HILLANDALE RD	CHEVY CHASE, MD	20815
HIRSHAN, LEN	TALENT AGENT	151 S EL CAMINO DR	BEVERLY HILLS, CA	90212
HIRSHENSON, JANET	CASTING DIRECTOR	7319 BEVERLY BLVD #6	LOS ANGELES, CA	90036
HIRSHORN, ROSS	TV WRITER	8955 BEVERLY BLVD	LOS ANGELES, CA	90048
HIRSON, ALICE	ACTRESS	3948 WOODFIELD DR	SHERMAN OAKS, CA	91403
HIRSON, ROGER O	TV WRITER	555 W 57TH ST #1230	NEW YORK, NY	10019
HIRST, DON	NEWS CORRESPONDENT	2027 POWHATAN RD	HYATTSVILLE, MD	20782
HIRST, GRAYSON	TENOR	215 W 75TH ST	NEW YORK, NY	10023
HIRT, AL	TRUMPETER	POST OFFICE BOX 1574	LUTZ, FL	33549
HIRT, CHARLES C	CONDUCTOR	1318 CORDOVA AVE	GLENDALE, CA	91207
HIT MAN, THE	WRESTLER	SEE - HART, BRET "HIT MAN"		
HITCHCOCK, JANE S	WRITER	555 W 57TH ST #1230	NEW YORK, NY	10019
HITCHCOCK, LAURA	THEATER CRITIC	6715 SUNSET BLVD	HOLLYWOOD, CA	90028
HITCHCOCK, WILLIAM G	CONDUCTOR	3640 BERRY DR	STUDIO CITY, CA	91604
HITCHCOCK, WILLIAM M	WRITER	555 W 57TH ST #1230	NEW YORK, NY	10019
HITCHENS, CHRISTOPHER	NEWS CORRESPONDENT	447 15TH ST, NE	WASHINGTON, DC	20002
HITCHENS, THEREA	NEWS CORRESPONDENT	1521 CHURCH ST #1	WASHINGTON, DC	20008
HITE, KATHLEEN	TV WRITER	8955 BEVERLY BLVD	LOS ANGELES, CA	90048

AL HIRT

DUSTIN HOFFMAN

ROBERT HOOKS

BOB HOPE

LENA HORNE

JOHN HOUSEMAN

THELMA HOUSTON

JAN HOWARD

C. THOMAS HOWELL

Name	Occupation	Address	City/State	Zip
HITE, WARREN	WRITER-PRODUCER	731 N ROSE ST	BURBANK, CA	91505
HITER, WAYNE	GUITARIST	13701 OLD HICKORY BLVD	ANTIOCH, TN	37013
HITMAN, THE	WRESTLER	SEE - HART, BRET "HIT MAN"		
HITTLEMAN, CARL K	WRITER-PRODUCER	8365 W 1ST ST	LOS ANGELES, CA	90048
HITZ	ROCK & ROLL GROUP	3717 W 50TH ST #L-2	MINNEAPOLIS, MN	55410
HITZEMAN, SHIRLEY	SINGER	PROCESS, 439 WILEY AVE	FRANKLIN, PA	16323
HITZIG, RUPPERT	WRITER-PRODUCER	34 GRAMMERCY PARK E	NEW YORK, NY	10003
HIVELY, PETE	NEWS CORRESPONDENT	NBC-TV, NEWS DEPARTMENT	WASHINGTON, DC	20016
HIXON, KEN	WRITER	POST OFFICE BOX 5617	BEVERLY HILLS, CA	90210
HJORTSBERG, WILLIAM	TV WRITER	8955 BEVERLY BLVD	LOS ANGELES, CA	90048
HLINKA, WERNER	DIRECTOR	200 WINSTON, TWR #1815	CLIFFSIDE PARK, NJ	07010
HLLANDER, CARLTON H	WRITER	8955 BEVERLY BLVD	LOS ANGELES, CA	90048
HNATYSCHAK, JOHN	BODYBUILDER	POST OFFICE BOX 4045	BAYTONE, NJ	07002
HO, DON	SINGER-SONGWRITER	2005 KALIA AVE	HONOLULU, HI	96815
HO, WAI CHING	ACTRESS	ABC-TV, "ONE LIFE TO LIVE"		
		1330 AVE OF THE AMERICAS	NEW YORK, NY	10019
HOADE, MARTIN	WRITER-PRODUCER	370 1ST AVE	NEW YORK, NY	10010
HOAG, JUDITH	ACTRESS	ABC-TV NETWORK, "LOVING"		
		1330 AVE OF THE AMERICAS	NEW YORK, NY	10019
HOAG, MITZI	ACTRESS	3800 BARHAM BLVD #303	LOS ANGELES, CA	90068
HOAGLAND, CHARLES A	NEWS CORRESPONDENT	NBC-TV, NEWS DEPARTMENT		
		4001 NEBRASKA AVE, NW	WASHINGTON, DC	20016
HOAGLAND, EDWARD	WRITER	WESTBETH, 463 WEST ST	NEW YORK, NY	10014
HOAK, BILL	GUITARIST	118 QUINN CIR	NASHVILLE, TN	37210
HOAN, PHAM BOI	PHOTOJOURNALIST	7921 FREEHOLLOW DR	FALLS CHURCH, VA	22042
HOARE, KEN	TV WRITER	38 CHEVERTON RD	LONDON N19 3AZ	ENGLAND
HOARE, TONY	PLAYWRIGHT	WGGB, 430 EDGWARE RD	LONDON W2 1EH	ENGLAND
HOART, HELEN	NEWS CORRESPONDENT	1814 KILBOURNE PL, NW	WASHINGTON, DC	20010
HOBACK, JAMES	TENOR	119 W 57TH ST #1505	NEW YORK, NY	10019
HOBAN, GORDON	ACTOR-WRITER	1722 REDCLIFF ST	LOS ANGELES, CA	90026
HOBAN, ROBERT	WRITER	1722 REDCLIFF ST	LOS ANGELES, CA	90026
HOBARD, RICK	THEATER PRODUCER	234 W 44TH ST	NEW YORK, NY	10036
HOBART, DEBORAH	ACTRESS	AMBROSE, 1466 BROADWAY	NEW YORK, NY	10036
HOBART, FENTON, JR	SCREENWRITER	8955 BEVERLY BLVD	LOS ANGELES, CA	90048
HOBART, ROSE	ACTRESS	23388 MULHOLLAND DR	WOODLAND HILLS, CA	91364
HOBBS, BECKY	SINGER	TAYLOR, 2401 12TH AVE S	NASHVILLE, TN	37204
HOBBS, LYNDALL GEORGINA	DIRECTOR	DGA, 7950 SUNSET BLVD	LOS ANGELES, CA	90046
HOBBS, MARY GAIL	ACTRESS	14340 ROBLAR PL	SHERMAN OAKS, CA	91423
HOBBS, PETER	ACTOR	1827 21ST ST	SANTA MONICA, CA	90404
HOBBY, PATRICK, JR	TV WRITER	8955 BEVERLY BLVD	LOS ANGELES, CA	90048
HOBEL, JOE	TV PRODUCER	ABC-TV, "ONE LIFE TO LIVE"		
		1330 AVE OF THE AMERICAS	NEW YORK, NY	10019
HOBERMAN, ARTHUR	CONDUCTOR	13625 BASSETT ST	VAN NUYS, CA	91405
HOBIN, BILL	DIRECTOR-PRODUCER	DGA, 110 W 57TH ST	NEW YORK, NY	10019
HOBIN, FREDERICA L	WRITER	126 N SWALL DR	BEVERLY HILLS, CA	90211
HOBLITT, GREGORY	TV WRITER	328 S WESTGATE AVE	LOS ANGELES, CA	90049
HOBSON, CHARLES	WRITER	555 W 57TH ST #1230	NEW YORK, NY	10019
HOBSON, IAN	PIANIST	AIA, 60 E 42ND ST	NEW YORK, NY	10165
HOBSON, JAMES	DIRECTOR-PRODUCER	984 BEL AIR RD	LOS ANGELES, CA	90077
HOBSON, RICHARD	WRITER	555 W 57TH ST #1230	NEW YORK, NY	10019
HOCH, BEVERLY	SOPRANO	59 E 54TH ST #81	NEW YORK, NY	10022
HOCHBERG, LEONARD	WRITER	555 W 57TH ST #1230	NEW YORK, NY	10019
HOCHBERG, VICTORIA	FILM WRITER-DIRECTOR	6825 ALTA LOMA TERR	HOLLYWOOD, CA	90068
HOCHMAN, EARL	WRITER	9950 TOPANGA CANYON BLVD #12	CHATSWORTH, CA	91311
HOCK, ALLISON	TV WRITER	CONTEMPORARY ARTISTS		
		132 S LASKY DR	BEVERLY HILLS, CA	90212
HOCKENSMITH, NED	DRUMMER	2204 18TH AVE S	NASHVILLE, TN	37212
HOCKER, STEPHEN A	NEWS CORRESPONDENT	2139 WISCONSIN AVE, NW	WASHINGTON, DC	20007
HOCKETT, DON	COMPOSER-CONDUCTOR	1504 VIA MONTEMAR	PALOS VERDES, CA	90274
HOCKHEIMER, ELLEN	WRITER	555 W 57TH ST #1230	NEW YORK, NY	10019
HOCKNEY, LYNNE	ACTRESS	9165 SUNSET BLVD #202	LOS ANGELES, CA	90069
HODEK, ANTONIN	ACTOR	3330 BARHAM BLVD #103	LOS ANGELES, CA	90068
HODER, MARK J	COMPOSER	POST OFFICE BOX 71082	LOS ANGELES, CA	90071
HODGE, JIMMY	GUITARIST	ROUTE #1, BOX 201	STEPHENSON, VA	22656
HODGE, LATHAN	WRITER	555 W 57TH ST #1230	NEW YORK, NY	10019
HODGE, MAX EUGENE	TV WRITER	4034 VENTURA CANYON AVE	SHERMAN OAKS, CA	91423
HODGE, PATRICIA	ACTRESS	ICM, 388-396 OXFORD ST	LONDON W1	ENGLAND
HODGE, ROBERT W	WRITER	555 W 57TH ST #1230	NEW YORK, NY	10019
HODGES, ADRIAN	FILM EXECUTIVE	THORN EMI HOUSE		
		UPPER SAINT MARTINS LN	LONDON WC2	ENGLAND
HODGES, ANN	ACTRESS	721 N LA BREA AVE #200	LOS ANGELES, CA	90038
HODGES, GEORGE ROBERT	TV WRITER	1236 N LARRABEE ST	LOS ANGELES, CA	90069
HODGES, JOY	ACTRESS	RD #4, VAN RENSSELAER RD	KATONAH, NY	10536
HODGES, KEN	CINEMATOGRAPHER	21 SOUTH DR, FERRING		
		WORTHING	SUSSEX	ENGLAND
HODGES, MICHAEL	FILM DIRECTOR	70 ELGIN CRESCENT	LONDON	ENGLAND
HODGES, PATRICIA	ACTRESS	NBC-TV, "ANOTHER WORLD"		
		30 ROCKEFELLER PLAZA	NEW YORK, NY	10112
HODGES, SARA PUCKETT	PIANIST	2116 W SHANDON DR	FLORENCE, SC	29501
HODGINS, DICK	CARTOONIST	KING FEATURES SYNDICATE		
		235 E 45TH ST	NEW YORK, NY	10017
HODGKINSON, RANDALL	PIANIST	1776 BROADWAY #504	NEW YORK, NY	10019
HODGSON, ALFREDA	MEZZO-SOPRANO	ICM, 40 W 57TH ST	NEW YORK, NY	10019
HODGSON, DAVID	TV DIRECTOR	306 EUSTON RD	LONDON NW1 3BB	ENGLAND
HODOSH, MARK B	WRITER	11936 GORHAM AVE #105	LOS ANGELES, CA	90049

Name	Occupation	Address	City	ZIP
HODSHIRE, ALLEN Z	DIRECTOR	1333 N SWEETZER AVE #3-A	LOS ANGELES, CA	90069
HOEFFNER, KAROL A	WRITER	8955 BEVERLY BLVD	LOS ANGELES, CA	90048
HOEGSTROM, JON M	DIRECTOR-PRODUCER	POST OFFICE BOX 1410	TAMPA, FL	33601
HOELSCHER, ULF	VIOLINIST	COLBERT, 111 W 57TH ST	NEW YORK, NY	10019
HOELTZ, EDWARD R	COMPOSER	1340 N PARKSIDE AVE	CHICAGO, IL	60651
HOELZER, STANLEY	DRUMMER	6200 BROOKVILLE RD #107	INDIANAPOLIS, IN	46219
HOEPFINGER, LARRY	TROMBONIST	944 SUNSET DR	COOKEVILLE, TN	38501
HOEST, BILL	CARTOONIST	PARADE, 750 3RD AVE	NEW YORK, NY	10017
HOESTEN, RAYMOND J	DIRECTOR	72 ELMSTREE LN	JERICHO, LI, NY	11753
HOEY, MICHAEL A	WRITER-PRODUCER	12364 EMELITA ST	NORTH HOLLYWOOD, CA	91607
HOFF, ROBIN	ACTRESS	15010 VENTURA BLVD #219	SHERMAN OAKS, CA	91403
HOFF, STEPHANIE	ACTRESS	1352 HILL ST	SANTA MONICA, CA	90405
HOFF, SYD	CARTOONIST	POST OFFICE BOX 2463	MIAMI BEACH, FL	33140
HOFFBERG, SY	CINEMATOGRAPHER	POST OFFICE 2230	HOLLYWOOD, CA	90078
HOFFE, ARTHUR	WRITER	1235 N KINGS RD #408	LOS ANGELES, CA	90069
HOFFENBERG, KARL A	WRITER-PRODUCER	234 S BUCKHOUT ST	IRVINGTON, NY	10533
HOFFITT, JOHN CRAIG	DIRECTOR-PRODUCER	13233 STONERIDGE PL	SHERMAN OAKS, CA	91423
HOFFLANDER, SUSAN	MEZZO-SOPRANO	431 S DEARBORN ST #1504	CHICAGO, IL	60605
HOFFMAN, ALICE	SCREENWRITER	555 W 57TH ST #1230	NEW YORK, NY	10019
HOFFMAN, BASIL	ACTOR	13344 OXNARD ST	VAN NUYS, CA	91401
HOFFMAN, BERNARD	DIRECTOR	895 GREEN PL	WOODMERE, NY	11598
HOFFMAN, BOBBY	CASTING DIRECTOR	1438 N GOWER ST	LOS ANGELES, CA	90028
HOFFMAN, DAVID E	TV WRITER	8955 BEVERLY BLVD	LOS ANGELES, CA	90048
HOFFMAN, DAVID H	NEWS CORRESPONDENT	4608 S CHELSEA LN	BETHESDA, MD	20814
HOFFMAN, DEBORAH	HARPIST	3003 VAN NESS ST #W-205, NW	WASHINGTON, DC	20008
HOFFMAN, DONALD B, JR	NEWS CORRESPONDENT	8113 15TH AVE #203	LANGLEY PARK, MD	20783
HOFFMAN, DUKE	SAXOPHONIST	866 BRESSLYN RD	NASHVILLE, TN	37205
HOFFMAN, DUSTIN	ACTOR	PUNCH PRODS, 711 5TH AVE	NEW YORK, NY	10022
HOFFMAN, ELIZABETH	ACTRESS	3330 BARHAM BLVD #103	LOS ANGELES, CA	90068
HOFFMAN, GARY	CELLIST	JCB, 155 W 68TH ST	NEW YORK, NY	10023
HOFFMAN, GARY M	DIRECTOR	4650 FORMAN AVE	TOLUCA LAKE, CA	91602
HOFFMAN, HERMAN	WRITER-PRODUCER	DGA, 7950 SUNSET BLVD	HOLLYWOOD, CA	90046
HOFFMAN, JACK	COMPOSER	6515 SUNSET BLVD #305	LOS ANGELES, CA	90028
HOFFMAN, JAY K	WRITER	555 W 57TH ST #1230	NEW YORK, NY	10019
HOFFMAN, JOSEPH	ACTOR	1607 N EL CENTRO AVE #23	LOS ANGELES, CA	90028
HOFFMAN, JOSEPH	ART DIRECTOR	832 N SWEETZER AVE	LOS ANGELES, CA	90069
HOFFMAN, JOSEPH	WRITER-PRODUCER	1318 WARNER AVE	LOS ANGELES, CA	90024
HOFFMAN, KURT C	NEWS CORRESPONDENT	5816 DANBURY RD	SPRINGFIELD, VA	22150
HOFFMAN, LORI	WRITER	555 W 57TH ST #1230	NEW YORK, NY	10019
HOFFMAN, MILT	DIRECTOR	4231 CANOGA AVE	WOODLAND HILLS, CA	91364
HOFFMAN, PAUL	PIANIST	MUGDAN, 84 PROSPECT AVE	DOUGLASTON, NY	11363
HOFFMAN, PETER	NEWS CORRESPONDENT	5901 BRYN MAWR RD	COLLEGE PARK, MD	20740
HOFFMAN, RICHARD R	GUITARIST	314 LELLYET AVE	NASHVILLE, TN	37209
HOFFMAN, ROBERT J	WRITER	8955 BEVERLY BLVD	LOS ANGELES, CA	90048
HOFFMAN, SASQUATCH	SAXOPHONIST	721 NEW DUE WEST #B-203	MADISON, TN	37115
HOFFMAN, SHERRELL	TV DIRECTOR	243 E 71ST ST	NEW YORK, NY	10021
HOFFMAN, SHIRLEE	NEWS CORRESPONDENT	1320 CORCORAN ST, NW	WASHINGTON, DC	20009
HOFFMAN, STEVEN	DESIGN DIRECTOR	SPORTS ILLUSTRATED MAGAZINE		
		TIME & LIFE BUILDING		
		ROCKEFELLER CENTER	NEW YORK, NY	10020
HOFFMAN, TOBY	VIOLIST	JCB, 155 W 68TH ST	NEW YORK, NY	10023
HOFFMAN, WILLIAM	PLAYWRIGHT	199 PRINCE ST	NEW YORK, NY	10012
HOFFMANN, BETTYE K	TV EXECUTIVE	NBC TELEVISION NETWORK		
		30 ROCKEFELLER PLAZA	NEW YORK, NY	10112
HOFFNER, DAVE	BANJOIST	816 KENDALL DR	NASHVILLE, TN	37209
HOFFS, TAMAR SIMON	WRITER-PRODUCER	307 AVONDALE AVE	LOS ANGELES, CA	90049
HOFLER, ROBERT	WRITER-EDITOR	LIFE/TIME & LIFE BLDG		
		ROCKEFELLER CENTER	NEW YORK, NY	10020
HOFMAN, MARC A	WRITER	8955 BEVERLY BLVD	LOS ANGELES, CA	90048
HOFMANN, PETER	TENOR	CAMI, 165 W 57TH ST	NEW YORK, NY	10019
HOFMEISTER, ELIZABETH WALPOLE	NEWS CORRESPONDENT	6759 BRIGADOON DR	BETHESDA, MD	20817
HOFSISS, JACK	DIRECTOR	DGA, 110 W 57TH ST	NEW YORK, NY	10019
HOGAN, BEN	GOLFER	1917 CANTERBURY DR	FORT WORTH, TX	76107
HOGAN, BILL	NEWS CORRESPONDENT	4418 S 36TH ST	ARLINGTON, VA	22206
HOGAN, DIZZY	WRESTLER	SEE - BEEFCAKE, BRUTUS		
HOGAN, EDDIE	WRESTLER	SEE - BEEFCAKE, BRUTUS		
HOGAN, GERALD	CABLE EXECUTIVE	1050 TECHWOOD DR, NW	ATLANTA, GA	30318
HOGAN, HULK	WRESTLER	POST OFFICE BOX 3859	STAMFORD, CT	06905
HOGAN, JACK	ACTOR	4721 LAUREL CANYON BLVD #211	NORTH HOLLYWOOD, CA	91607
HOGAN, JERRY	TALENT AGENT	247 S BEVERLY DR #102	BEVERLY HILLS, CA	90210
HOGAN, JOHN F	WRITER	8955 BEVERLY BLVD	LOS ANGELES, CA	90048
HOGAN, PAUL	ACTOR	TCN 9 ARTARMON RD	WILLOUGHBY NSW 2068	AUSTRALIA
HOGAN, ROBERT	ACTOR	10390 SANTA MONICA BLVD #310	LOS ANGELES, CA	90025
HOGAN, ROGER E	COMPOSER	13150 PHILLIPPI	SYLMAR, CA	91342
HOGAN, WILLIAM H	WRITER-PRODUCER	1311 MORNINGSIDE DR	BURBANK, CA	91506
HOGARD, BRUCE R	ACTOR	7140 DE LONGPRE AVE #1	LOS ANGELES, CA	90046
HOGESTYN, DRAKE	ACTOR	KNBC-TV, "DAYS OF OUR LIVES"		
		3000 W ALAMEDA AVE	BURBANK, CA	91523
HOGG, IAN	ACTOR	OXGANGS HOUSE, NETTLETON TOP	LINCOLN LN7 6S7	ENGLAND
HOGGAN, MICHAEL B	FILM EDITOR	ACE, 4416 1/2 FINLEY AVE	LOS ANGELES, CA	90027
HOGLAND, CHARLES A	PHOTOGRAPHER	9606 PAGE AVE	BETHESDA, MD	20814
HOGLUND, RUDOLPH	ART DIRECTOR	TIME/TIME & LIFE BLDG		
		ROCKEFELLER CENTER	NEW YORK, NY	10020
HOGUE, ALEXANDER	PAINTER	4052 E 23RD ST	TULSA, OK	74114
HOGUE, JAMES H	NEWS CORRESPONDENT	725 S ROYAL ST	ALEXANDRIA, VA	22314

HOHENRIEDER, MARGARITA	PIANIST	IAPR, KINCORA, BEER RD		
		SEATON	DEVON	ENGLAND
HOILAND, HAROLD	PHOTOJOURNALIST	18800 ALPENGLOW LN	BROOKEVILLE, MD	20729
HOISECK, RONALD F	ACTOR	120 S VICTORY BLVD #104	BURBANK, CA	91502
HOIT, MICHAEL	ACTOR-PRODUCER	2166 RIDGEMONT DR	LOS ANGELES, CA	90046
HOKANSON, MARY ALAN	ACTRESS	3800 BARHAM BLVD #303	LOS ANGELES, CA	90068
HOLBROOK, BILL	CARTOONIST	KING FEATURES SYNDICATE		
		235 E 45TH ST	NEW YORK, NY	10017
HOLBROOK, DIXIE CARTER	ACTRESS	10100 SANTA MONICA BLVD #1600	LOS ANGELES, CA	90067
HOLBROOK, HAL	ACTOR	10000 SANTA MONICA BLVD #305	LOS ANGELES, CA	90067
HOLCH, ARTHUR	WRITER-PRODUCER	49 SUMNER RD	GREENWICH, CT	06830
HOLCHAK, VICTOR	ACTOR	9441 WILSHIRE BLVD #620-D	BEVERLY HILLS, CA	90212
HOLCOMB, CHUCK	GUITARIST	ROUTE #2	MANCHESTER, TN	37355
HOLCOMB, ROD	TV DIRECTOR	1337 BOSTON ST	ALTADENA, CA	91001
HOLCOMBE, WENDY	SINGER	POST OFFICE BOX 607	ALABASTER, AL	35007
HOLDEN, DAVID A	DIRECTOR	POST OFFICE BOX 392	LOS ALAMOS, CA	93440
HOLDEN, GLORIA	ACTRESS	722 W HIGHLAND AVE	REDLANDS, CA	92373
HOLDEN, HENRY	ACTOR	8949 SUNSET BLVD #203	LOS ANGELES, CA	90069
HOLDEN, JAN	WRITER	8955 BEVERLY BLVD	LOS ANGELES, CA	90048
HOLDEN, LAWRENCE	WRITER	4954 HAZELTINE AVE #4	SHERMAN OAKS, CA	91423
HOLDEN, REBECCA	ACTRESS-SINGER	870 N VINE ST #B	LOS ANGELES, CA	90038
HOLDEN, STEPHEN	MUSIC CRITIC	N Y TIMES, 229 W 43RD ST	NEW YORK, NY	10036
HOLDER, CHRIS	ACTOR	247 S BEVERLY DR #102	BEVERLY HILLS, CA	90210
HOLDER, LAURENCE	WRITER	555 W 57TH ST #1230	NEW YORK, NY	10019
HOLDER, RAY	COND-ARR-CHOREO	WEYBREAD HOUSE, WEYBREAD	SUFFOLK	ENGLAND
HOLDERFIELD, ALFRED	GUITARIST	291 TAMPA DR	NASHVILLE, TN	37211
HOLDERNESS, BEAR & THE HOT BEAR	C & W GROUP	HOT BEAR, 420 W PLATTE AVE	COLORADO SPRINGS, CO	80905
HOLDERNESS, SUE	ACTRESS	37 WINDMILL HILL, RUISLIP	MIDDLESEX HA4 8PY	ENGLAND
HOLDRIDGE, LEE E	COMPOSER-CONDUCTOR	1060 SHADOW HILL WY	BEVERLY HILLS, CA	90210
HOLDSWORTH, ALLAN	SINGER-GUITARIST	17609 VENTURA BLVD #212	ENCINO, CA	91316
HOLE, JONATHAN	ACTOR	5024 BALBOA BLVD	ENCINO, CA	91316
HOLE, WILLIAM J, JR	DIRECTOR	23654 CALVERT ST	WOODLAND HILLS, CA	91367
HOLECEK, BARBARA G	WRITER	555 W 57TH ST #1230	NEW YORK, NY	10019
HOLEMAN, ESTELLA L	WRITER	1200 CRENSHAW BLVD	LOS ANGELES, CA	90019
HOLENDER, ADAM	DIRECTOR	136 E 64TH ST	NEW YORK, NY	10021
HOLICKER, HEIDI	ACTRESS	15101 MAGNOLIA BLVD #F-15	SHERMAN OAKS, CA	91403
HOLIDAY, DOC & THE SOUL SURVIVO	ROCK & ROLL GROUP	J BIRD, 4905 S ATLANTIC AVE	DAYTONA BEACH, FL	32019
HOLIDAY, HOPE	ACTRESS	8538 EASTWOOD RD	LOS ANGELES, CA	90046
HOLIDAY, MARVIN "DOC"	SINGER	PROCESS, 439 WILEY AVE	FRANKLIN, PA	16323
HOLIMAN, BOB	SINGER	AM CREAT ENT, 536 E ST	LAS VEGAS, NV	89104
HOLISTER, BOYD	ACTOR	9220 SUNSET BLVD #218	LOS ANGELES, CA	90069
HOLL, ROBERT	BASSO-BARITONE	1182 MARKET ST #311	SAN FRANCISCO, CA	94102
HOLLAND	ROCK & ROLL GROUP	3 E 54TH ST #1400	NEW YORK, NY	10022
HOLLAND, AMY	SINGER	9044 MELROSE AVE #306	LOS ANGELES, CA	90069
HOLLAND, ANEECE M	NEWS CORRESPONDENT	400 N CAPITOL ST, NW	WASHINGTON, DC	20001
HOLLAND, ANTHONY	ACTOR	11726 SAN VICENTE BLVD #300	LOS ANGELES, CA	90049
HOLLAND, BETTY LOU	ACTRESS	162 W 56TH ST	NEW YORK, NY	10019
HOLLAND, BILL	NEWS CORRESPONDENT	4704 40TH ST	HYATTSVILLE, MD	20781
HOLLAND, ERIK	ACTOR	5648 COLUMBUS AVE	VAN NUYS, CA	91411
HOLLAND, GEOFFREY	WRITER	5036 COLDWATER CANYON AVE	SHERMAN OAKS, CA	91423
HOLLAND, GERARD F	WRITER	555 W 57TH ST #1230	NEW YORK, NY	10019
HOLLAND, GLADYS	ACTRESS	15010 VENTURA BLVD #234	SHERMAN OAKS, CA	91403
HOLLAND, JEFFREY	ACTOR	GRIFFITHS, 185 OXFORD ST	LONDON W1R 1TA	ENGLAND
HOLLAND, JERRY	ACTOR	5058 FOUNTAIN AVE	LOS ANGELES, CA	90029
HOLLAND, JOHN	ACTOR	6062 CARLOS AVE	LOS ANGELES, CA	90028
HOLLAND, JOHN F	NEWS CORRESPONDENT	NBC-TV, NEWS DEPARTMENT		
		4001 NEBRASKA AVE, NW	WASHINGTON, DC	20016
HOLLAND, PENNY	ACTRESS	5058 FOUNTAIN AVE	LOS ANGELES, CA	90029
HOLLAND, RANDY	ACTOR-WRITER	9300 WILSHIRE BLVD #410	BEVERLY HILLS, CA	90212
HOLLAND, ROBERT K	NEWS CORRESPONDENT	2515 "K" ST, NW	WASHINGTON, DC	20037
HOLLAND, STEPHEN	WRITER	8955 BEVERLY BLVD	LOS ANGELES, CA	90048
HOLLAND, TOM	WRITER-PRODUCER	10351 SANTA MONICA BLVD #211	LOS ANGELES, CA	90025
HOLLAND, TOMMY	GUITARIST	2714 MURFREESBORO RD #7	ANTIOCH, TN	37013
HOLLANDER, JACK	ACTOR	439 E 71ST ST	NEW YORK, NY	10021
HOLLANDER, LORIN	PIANIST	ICM, 40 W 57TH ST	NEW YORK, NY	10019
HOLLANDER, MELODIE	WRITER	8955 BEVERLY BLVD	LOS ANGELES, CA	90048
HOLLANDER, ROY	WRITER	555 W 57TH ST #1230	NEW YORK, NY	10019
HOLLANDER, XAVIERA	AUTHORESS	PENTHOUSE MAG, 1965 BROADWAY	NEW YORK, NY	10023
HOLLE, MATTHIAS	SINGER	CAMI, 165 W 57TH ST	NEW YORK, NY	10019
HOLLE, MERITA	ACTRESS	10856 1/2 CAMARILLO ST	NORTH HOLLYWOOD, CA	91602
HOLLEB, ALAN	FILM WRITER-DIRECTOR	1653 MALCOLM AVE	LOS ANGELES, CA	90024
HOLLEN, REBECCA	ACTRESS	J MICHAEL BLOOM AGENCY		
		233 PARK AVE S, 10TH FLOOR	NEW YORK, NY	10017
HOLLENBAUGH, GAYLE	FILM PRODUCER	ASTA PRODS, 126 S ORLANDO AVE	LOS ANGELES, CA	90048
HOLLENBECK, PAUL, JR	NEWS CORRESPONDENT	400 N CAPITOL ST, NW	WASHINGTON, DC	20001
HOLLENHORST, JOHN T	NEWS CORRESPONDENT	400 N CAPITOL ST, NW	WASHINGTON, DC	20001
HOLLEQUE, ELIZABETH	SOPRANO	ICM, 40 W 57TH ST	NEW YORK, NY	10019
HOLLERITH, CHARLES, JR	THEATER PRODUCER	18 W 55TH ST	NEW YORK, NY	10019
HOLLEY, BERNARD	ACTOR	3-61 SANDYCOMBE RD, RICHMOND	SURREY TW9 3PR	ENGLAND
HOLLEY, LEE	CARTOONIST	KING FEATURES SYNDICATE		
		235 E 45TH ST	NEW YORK, NY	10017
HOLLIDAY, FRED	ACTOR-TV HOST	4610 FORMAN AVE	NORTH HOLLYWOOD, CA	91602
HOLLIDAY, JENNIFER	SINGER-ACTRESS	9000 SUNSET BLVD #1200	LOS ANGELES, CA	90069
HOLLIDAY, KENE	ACTOR	2051 GARTH AVE	LOS ANGELES, CA	90034
HOLLIDAY, LANNY	WRESTLER	SEE - POFFO, LEAPING LANNY		

Name	Occupation	Address	City	ZIP
HOLLIDAY, POLLY	ACTRESS	LANTZ, 888 7TH AVE, 25TH FLOOR	NEW YORK, NY	10106
HOLLIDAY, ROMAN	ROCK & ROLL GROUP	SEE - ROMAN HOLLIDAY		
HOLLIGER, HEINZ	OBOIST	COLBERT, 111 W 57TH ST	NEW YORK, NY	10019
HOLLIMAN, EARL	ACTOR	POST OFFICE BOX 1969	STUDIO CITY, CA	91604
HOLLIMAN, JOHN, JR	NEWS CORRESPONDENT	2133 WISCONSIN AVE, NW	WASHINGTON, DC	20007
HOLLINGER, MICHAEL	GUITARIST	161 JACKSONIAN DR	HERMITAGE, TN	37076
HOLLINGSWORTH, JIMMIE EARL	DIRECTOR	KAMINSKY, 521 MADISON AVE	NEW YORK, NY	10022
HOLLINGSWORTH, SAMUEL	GUITARIST	4403 CENTRE AVE #C-6	PITTSBURGH, PA	15213
HOLLIS, GARY	ACTOR	9165 SUNSET BLVD #202	LOS ANGELES, CA	90069
HOLLIS, JERRY V	NEWS CORRESPONDENT	2139 WISCONSIN AVE, NW	WASHINGTON, DC	20007
HOLLIS, LOUIS J	PHOTOGRAPHER	7423 CAROL LN	FALLS CHURCH, VA	22042
HOLLISTER, ANNE	NEWS REPORTER	LIFE/TIME & LIFE BLDG		
		ROCKEFELLER CENTER	NEW YORK, NY	10020
HOLLISTER, BOYD	ACTOR	348 E OLIVE AVE #K	BURBANK, CA	91502
HOLLOWAY, DAVID	BARITONE	CAMI, 165 W 57TH ST	NEW YORK, NY	10019
HOLLOWAY, JEAN	ACTRESS-WRITER	215 S KENMORE AVE #3	LOS ANGELES, CA	90004
HOLLOWAY, JULIAN	ACTOR-PRODUCER	BOYACK, 9 CORK ST	LONDON W1	ENGLAND
HOLLOWAY, LINDA	MUSICIAN	1906 BERNARD AVE	NASHVILLE, TN	37212
HOLLOWAY, MARTIN	WRITER	8955 BEVERLY BLVD	LOS ANGELES, CA	90048
HOLLOWAY, SIMEON	ACTOR	6515 SUNSET BLVD #300-A	LOS ANGELES, CA	90028
HOLLOWAY, STERLING	ACTOR	137 N SYCAMORE AVE	LOS ANGELES, CA	90036
HOLLOWELL, PAUL	PIANIST	1503 STRATFORD AVE	NASHVILLE, TN	37216
HOLLWEG, WERNER	TENOR	MARIEDL ANDERS ARTISTS MGMT		
		535 EL CAMINO DEL MAR ST	SAN FRANCISCO, CA	94121
HOLLY, DOYLE	SINGER-GUITARIST	POST OFFICE BOX 148	HENDERSONVILLE, TN	37075
HOLLY, LAUREN	ACTRESS	ABC-TV, "ALL MY CHILDREN"		
		1330 AVE OF THE AMERICAS	NEW YORK, NY	10019
HOLLY, RUTH E	WRITER	555 W 57TH ST #1230	NEW YORK, NY	10019
HOLLYMAN, THOMAS B	DIRECTOR	300 E 40TH ST	NEW YORK, NY	10016
HOLLYWOOD	WRESTLER	GORGEOUS GIRLS OF WRESTLING		
		RIVIERA HOTEL & CASINO		
		DAVID B MC LANE PRODS		
		2901 S LAS VEGAS BLVD	LAS VEGAS, NV	89109
HOLLYWOOD SAXONS, THE	VOCAL GROUP	POST OFFICE BOX 01473	LOS ANGELES, CA	90001
HOLLYWOODS, THE	ROCK & ROLL GROUP	41 BRITAIN ST #200	TORONTO, ONT	CANADA
HOLM, CELESTE	ACTRESS	88 CENTRAL PARK W	NEW YORK, NY	10023
HOLM, IAN	ACTOR	LEADING ARTISTS, LTD		
		60 SAINT JAMES'S ST	LONDON SW1	ENGLAND
HOLM, JOHNNY	SINGER	3717 W 50TH ST #L-2	MINNEAPOLIS, MN	55437
HOLMAN, REX	ACTOR	8721 SUNSET BLVD #103	LOS ANGELES, CA	90069
HOLMAN, W L	COMPOSER	2236 SAN MARCO DR	LOS ANGELES, CA	90068
HOLMBERG-BROOKS, HOLLY	TV WRITER	8955 BEVERLY BLVD	LOS ANGELES, CA	90048
HOLMES, BRENDA JONES	ACTRESS-PRODUCER	11122 LANDALE ST	NORTH HOLLYWOOD, CA	91602
HOLMES, CLINT	ACTOR	151 S EL CAMINO DR	BEVERLY HILLS, CA	90212
HOLMES, CLINT	SINGER	11122 LANDALE ST	NORTH HOLLYWOOD, CA	91602
HOLMES, GROOVE	ORGANIST	JOYCE AGENCY, 435 E 79TH ST	NEW YORK, NY	10021
HOLMES, JAMES R	DIRECTOR-PRODUCER	1033 S DELPHIA ST	PARK RIDGE, IL	60068
HOLMES, JENNIFER	ACTRESS	5329 SUNNYSLOPE AVE	VAN NUYS, CA	91401
HOLMES, JOHN PHILIP, III	NEWS CORRESPONDENT	6940 HANOVER PARKWAY #300	GREENBELT, MD	20770
HOLMES, KENDALL J	NEWS CORRESPONDENT	608 MC NEILL ST	SILVER SPRING, MD	20910
HOLMES, LARRY	BOXER	413 NORTHAMPTON ST	EASTON, PA	18042
HOLMES, MILTON	WRITER	8955 BEVERLY BLVD	LOS ANGELES, CA	90048
HOLMES, RICHARD G	ACTOR	178 E 80TH ST	NEW YORK, NY	10021
HOLMES, ROBERT, JR	MUSIC ARRANGER	2509 BUCHANAN ST	NASHVILLE, TN	37208
HOLMES, RUPERT	SINGER-SONGWRITER	SPOLITE ENTERPRISES, LTD		
		221 W 57TH ST, 9TH FLOOR	NEW YORK, NY	10019
HOLMES, THEODORE E	WRITER	555 W 57TH ST #1230	NEW YORK, NY	10019
HOLMIN, SHARON	ACTRESS	3866 MENTONE AVE	LOS ANGELES, CA	90034
HOLMLUND, DAVID P	WRITER	555 W 57TH ST #1230	NEW YORK, NY	10019
HOLOWCHAK, EUGENE	TV DIRECTOR	8701 METROPOLITAN	WARREN, MI	48093
HOLSLAG, WILLIAM S	WRITER	8955 BEVERLY BLVD	LOS ANGELES, CA	90048
HOLSTRA, JUDITH	CASTING DIRECTOR	8265 SUNSET BLVD #207	LOS ANGELES, CA	90046
HOLT, ARVA	ACTRESS	15010 VENTURA BLVD #219	SHERMAN OAKS, CA	91403
HOLT, BEN	BARITONE	59 E 54TH ST #81	NEW YORK, NY	10022
HOLT, BETTY	PIANIST	ROUTE #1, BOX 422-X	GOODLETTSVILLE, TN	37072
HOLT, CHARLENE	ACTRESS	SEE - HOLT-HIARA, CHARLENE		
HOLT, DENIS	FILM PRODUCER	161 RIDGE LANGLEY, SANDERSTEAD	SURREY	ENGLAND
HOLT, DENNIS	DRUMMER	POST OFFICE BOX 110212	NASHVILLE, TN	37211
HOLT, FRITZ	THEATER PRODUCER	250 W 52ND ST	NEW YORK, NY	10019
HOLT, JENNIFER	ACTRESS	MRS BROOKE MARSH CADWALLADER		
		APARTADO POSTAL 170, CUERNAVACA	MORELES 62000	MEXICO
HOLT, LYNN	ACTRESS	5330 LANKERSHIM BLVD #210	NORTH HOLLYWOOD, CA	91601
HOLT, ROBERT I	TV WRITER	2900 VIA LA SELVA	PALOS VERDES, CA	90274
HOLT, STEPHEN P	NEWS CORRESPONDENT	1444 RHODE ISLAND AVE, NW	WASHINGTON, DC	20036
HOLT, WAYNE	BASSOONIST	5609 KNOB RD	NASHVILLE, TN	37209
HOLT-HIARA, CHARLENE	ACTRESS	9000 SUNSET BLVD #1112	LOS ANGELES, CA	90069
HOLTHOUSE, RICHARD	FILM DIRECTOR	140 FAIRBRIDGE RD	LONDON N19	ENGLAND
HOLTON, MARK	ACTOR	6380 WILSHIRE BLVD #1600	LOS ANGELES, CA	90048
HOLTUM, PAUL	ACTOR	4629 CLARISSA AVE	LOS ANGELES, CA	90027
HOLTZMAN, BOBBI	ACTRESS	BENSON, 518 TOLUCA PARK DR	BURBANK, CA	91505
HOLTZMAN, HENRY	DIRECTOR	33 RIVERSIDE DR	NEW YORK, NY	10023
HOLZBERG, ROGER S	WRITER	4071 PERLITA AVE #C	LOS ANGELES, CA	90039
HOLZER, HANS	SCREENWRITER	555 W 57TH ST #1230	NEW YORK, NY	10019
HOLZMAN, WILLIAM S	WRITER	555 W 57TH ST #1230	NEW YORK, NY	10019
HOMAN, RICHARD L	NEWS CORRESPONDENT	6217 WINNEBAGO RD	BETHESDA, MD	20816

HOMBRES, TRES	ROCK & ROLL GROUP	SEE - TRES HOMBRES		
HOME, BENJAMIN	TV WRITER	8955 BEVERLY BLVD	LOS ANGELES, CA	90048
HOME AND GARDEN	ROCK & ROLL GROUP	AFTER HOURS RECORDS		
		300 PROSPECT AVE	CLEVELAND, OH	44115
HOMEIER, SKIPPY	261 ACTOR	261 S ROBERTSON BLVD	BEVERLY HILLS, CA	90211
HOMER, RAYMOND	DIRECTOR-PRODUCER	165 W 66TH ST	NEW YORK, NY	10023
HOMES, HERBERT	DIRECTOR	21 FORSTER PARKWAY	MOUNT VERNON, NY	10552
HOMSEY, BONNIE ODA	ACTRESS	11240 MAGNOLIA BLVD #202	NORTH HOLLYWOOD, CA	91601
HON, JEAN MARIE	ACTRESS	9255 SUNSET BLVD #1105	LOS ANGELES, CA	90069
HONAKER, KARL SCOTT	ACTOR	1939 N ARGYLE AVE #36	LOS ANGELES, CA	90068
HONE, FRED	ACTOR	15125 SATICOY ST #126	VAN NUYS, CA	91405
HONEYCOMBE, GORDON	WRITER	DAVIE LTD, 37 HILL ST	LONDON W1	ENGLAND
HONEYMAN, JEFFREY	WRITER	555 W 57TH ST #1230	NEW YORK, NY	10019
HONEYMOON SUITE	ROCK & ROLL GROUP	41 BRITAIN ST #103	TORONTO, ONT M5A 1R7	CANADA
HONG, HEI-KYUNG	SOPRANO	CAMI, 165 W 57TH ST	NEW YORK, NY	10019
HONG, JAMES	ACTOR	8235 SANTA MONICA BLVD #202	LOS ANGELES, CA	90046
HONIG, HOWARD	ACTOR	14418 BENEFIT ST	SHERMAN OAKS, CA	91423
HONIGBERG, ALLEN E	WRITER	555 W 57TH ST #1230	NEW YORK, NY	10019
HONIGBERG, CAROL	PIANIST	POST OFFICE BOX 160	HIGHLAND PARK, IL	60035
HONIGBERG, GAIL R	COMEDY WRITER	2220 AVE OF THE STARS #1906	LOS ANGELES, CA	90067
HONKAMP, HELEN	ACTRESS	336 W 89TH ST #3	NEW YORK, NY	10024
HONKY TONK HEROES	C & W GROUP	POST OFFICE BOX O	EXCELSIOR, MN	55331
HONKY TONK MAN, THE	WRESTLER	POST OFFICE BOX 3859	STAMFORD, CT	06905
HONTHANER, RONALD W	WRITER	12353 SARAH ST	STUDIO CITY, CA	91604
HOOD, CHUCK L	DIRECTOR	1015 E PROVIDENCIA AVE	BURBANK, CA	91501
HOOD, DON	ACTOR	400 S BEVERLY DR #216	BEVERLY HILLS, CA	90212
HOOD, DON	ACTOR	9200 SUNSET BLVD #1210	LOS ANGELES, CA	90069
HOOD, MORAG	ACTRESS	54-A FOUNTAYNE RD	LONDON N16	ENGLAND
HOOD, ROBIN LEE	PHOTOGRAPHER	STATE CAPITOL BUILDING	NASHVILLE, TN	37219
HOOD, THE	WRESTLER	SEE - MANTELL, JOHNNY		
HOODOO GURUS	ROCK & ROLL GROUP	HARBOUR AGENCY PTY, LTD		
		63 WILLIAM ST, 3RD FLOOR	SYDNEY NSW 2000	AUSTRALIA
HOOK, JANET	NEWS CORRESPONDENT	2009 WYOMING AVE, NW	WASHINGTON, DC	20009
HOOKER	ROCK & ROLL GROUP	POST OFFICE BOX 448	RADFORD, VA	24141
HOOKER, BUDDY JOE	FILM DIRECTOR	3518 W CAHUENGA BLVD #100	LOS ANGELES, CA	90068
HOOKER, GARY	GUITARIST	1412 17TH AVE S	NASHVILLE, TN	37212
HOOKER, JAMES	PIANIST	ROUTE #2, LEWISBURG PIKE	FRANKLIN, TN	37064
HOOKER, JOHN LEE	SINGER-GUITARIST	POST OFFICE BOX 210103	SAN FRANCISCO, CA	94121
HOOKS, CALLY	ACTRESS	2510 LYRIC AVE	LOS ANGELES, CA	90027
HOOKS, DAVID	ACTOR	2212 N CAHUENGA BLVD #206	HOLLYWOOD, CA	90068
HOOKS, ED	ACTOR	2510 LYRIC AVE	LOS ANGELES, CA	90027
HOOKS, JAN	ACTRESS	9300 WILSHIRE BLVD #410	BEVERLY HILLS, CA	90212
HOOKS, KEVIN	ACTOR-DIRECTOR	1809 N NAOMI ST	BURBANK, CA	91505
HOOKS, ROBERT	ACTOR	1873 SUNSET PLAZA DR	LOS ANGELES, CA	90069
HOOKS, WILLIAM G	CABLE EXECUTIVE	HOME BOX OFFICE PICTURES		
		1100 AVE OF THE AMERICAS	NEW YORK, NY	10036
HOOL, LANCE	ACTOR	13747 ROMANY DR	PACIFIC PALISADES, CA	90272
HOOPER, BAYARD	WRITER-EDITOR	DISCOVER/TIME & LIFE BLDG		
		ROCKEFELLER CENTER	NEW YORK, NY	10020
HOOPER, BUDDY	RECORD EXECUTIVE	POST OFFICE BOX 84	HERMITAGE, TN	37076
HOOPER, LESTER J, III	COMPOSER	4432 SEVENOAKS CT	WESTLAKE VILLAGE, CA	91361
HOOPER, MARY ANN	WRITER	8955 BEVERLY BLVD	LOS ANGELES, CA	90048
HOOPER, PETER	ACTOR	ICM, 8899 BEVERLY BLVD	LOS ANGELES, CA	90048
HOOPER, ROBERT F	NEWS CORRESPONDENT	2021 BROOKS DR	FORESTVILLE, MD	20747
HOOPER, SUSAN MARY	NEWS CORRESPONDENT	2929 CONNECTICUT AVE #404, NW	WASHINGTON, DC	20008
HOOPER, TOBE	FILM DIRECTOR	820 TOYOPA DR	PACIFIC PALISADES, CA	90272
HOOPES, CORA R	NEWS CORRESPONDENT	6433 WISCAWSET RD	BETHESDA, MD	20816
HOOPES, TERENCE J	NEWS CORRESPONDENT	2121 COLUMBIA PIKE	ARLINGTON, VA	22204
HOOSE, MONICA	NEWS CORRESPONDENT	POST OFFICE BOX 2626	WASHINGTON, DC	20013
HOOTEN, LONZO	GUITARIST	ROUTE #1, BOX 235	CROSS PLAINS, TN	37049
HOOTERS, THE	ROCK & ROLL GROUP	CORNERSTONE MANAGEMENT		
		23 E LANCASTER AVE	ARDMORE, PA	19003
HOOTKINS, WILLIAM	ACTOR	188 CROMWELL RD	LONDON SW5	ENGLAND
HOOVER, CHARLES A	CONDUCTOR	12757 VENICE BLVD #3	LOS ANGELES, CA	90066
HOOVER, JOSEPH	ACTOR	4158 SHADYGLADE AVE	STUDIO CITY, CA	91604
HOOVER, KERWIN	NEWS EDITOR	1504 S MARENGO AVE	PASADENA, CA	91106
HOOVER, PHIL	ACTOR	8721 SUNSET BLVD #202	LOS ANGELES, CA	90069
HOOVER, ROBERT	NOVELIST	G BORCHARDT, 136 E 57TH ST	NEW YORK, NY	10022
HOOVER, TONI L	PHOTOJOURNALIST	11437 CHERRY HILL RD	BELTSVILLE, MD	20705
HOPE, BOB	ACTOR-COMEDIAN	10346 MOORPARK ST	NORTH HOLLYWOOD, CA	91602
HOPE, LESLIE	ACTRESS	10100 SANTA MONICA BLVD #1600	LOS ANGELES, CA	90067
HOPE, LINDA	ACTRESS	10400 MOORPARK ST	NORTH HOLLYWOOD, CA	91602
HOPE, PAUL B	NEWS CORRESPONDENT	6917 CABIN JOHN RD	SPRINGFIELD, VA	22150
HOPKINS, ANNE	NEWS REPORTER	TIME/TIME & LIFE BLDG		
		ROCKEFELLER CENTER	NEW YORK, NY	10020
HOPKINS, ANTHONY	ACTOR	7 HIGH PARK RD, KEW	SURREY TW9 3BL	ENGLAND
HOPKINS, BIG MIKE	SINGER	POST OFFICE BOX 448	RADFORD, VA	24141
HOPKINS, BO	ACTOR	6620 ETHEL AVE	NORTH HOLLYWOOD, CA	91606
HOPKINS, BOBB	ACTOR	3800 BARHAM BLVD #303	LOS ANGELES, CA	90068
HOPKINS, JANE	ACTRESS	9021 MELROSE AVE #304	LOS ANGELES, CA	90069
HOPKINS, JOHN	SCREENWRITER	24 MALMAINS WY, BECKENHAM	KENT	ENGLAND
HOPKINS, JOHN R	SCREENWRITER	151 S EL CAMINO DR	BEVERLY HILLS, CA	90212
HOPKINS, LINDA	SINGER	2055 N IVAR ST #PH	LOS ANGELES, CA	90068
HOPKINS, NICKY	MUSICIAN	19912 ARCHWOOD ST	CANOGA PARK, CA	91306
HOPKINS, ROBERT S	WRITER	8733 SUNSET BLVD #102	LOS ANGELES, CA	90069

HOPKINS, SHIRLEY KNIGHT	ACTRESS	24 MAILMANS WY, BECKENHAM	KENT	ENGLAND
HOPKINS, TELMA	ACTRESS-SINGER	445 N BEFORD DR #PH	BEVERLY HILLS, CA	90210
HOPKINS, WILLIAM CARLISLE	TV WRITER	8955 BEVERLY BLVD	LOS ANGELES, CA	90048
HOPKINSON, PETER	ACTOR-DIRECTOR	GLASS, 28 BERKELEY SQ	LONDON W1X 6HD	ENGLAND
HOPMAN, GERALD	WRITER	2764 WOODWARDIA DR	LOS ANGELES, CA	90077
HOPPE, ARTHUR	POLITICAL SATIRIST	CHRONICLE FEATURES		
		870 MARKET ST	SAN FRANCISCO, CA	94102
HOPPER, DENNIS	ACTOR-DIRECTOR	POST OFFICE BOX 1889		
		LOS GALLOS	TAOS, NM	87571
HOPPER, HAROLD H	DIRECTOR	815 AVENIDA SALVADOR	SAN CLEMENTE, CA	92672
HOPPER, JERRY	FILM DIRECTOR	815 AVENIDA SALVADOR	SAN CLEMENTE, CA	92672
HOPPER, ROBERT D	NEWS CORRESPONDENT	1280 21ST ST, NW	WASHINGTON, DC	20036
HOPPERS, LONNIE	BANJOIST	POST OFFICE BOX 265	REEDS SPRING, MO	65737
HOPPS, KEVIN CROSBY	WRITER	25840 TURQUESA DR	VALENCIA, CA	91355
HOPSON, AL	ACTOR	439 S LA CIENEGA BLVD #120	LOS ANGELES, CA	90048
HORAN, BARBARA	ACTRESS	500 S SEPULVEDA BLVD #510	LOS ANGELES, CA	90049
HORAN, DON	DIRECTOR	248 CROWN RD	BOONTON, NJ	07005
HORAN, JAMES	ACTOR	7469 MELROSE AVE #30	LOS ANGELES, CA	90046
HORAN, MICHAEL	NEWS CORRESPONDENT	5151 WISCONSIN AVE, NW	WASHINGTON, DC	20012
HORETEL, BRUCE G	PHOTOGRAPHER	825 DUKE ST	ALEXANDRIA, VA	22314
HORGAN, PATRICK	ACTOR	201 E 89TH ST	NEW YORK, NY	10028
HORGAN, SUSAN BEDSON	TV WRITER-PRODUCER	CBS-TV, "AS THE WORLD TURNS"		
		51 W 52ND ST	NEW YORK, NY	10019
HORGER, EMORY	DIRECTOR	10721 ADDISON ST	NORTH HOLLYWOOD, CA	91601
HORICKE, FRED	PIANIST	GERSHUNOFF, 502 PARK AVE	NEW YORK, NY	10022
HORIGOME, YUZUKO	VIOLINIST	CAMI, 165 W 57TH ST	NEW YORK, NY	10019
HORKY, JAMES E	TV DIRECTOR	212 N VALLEY ST #14	BURBANK, CA	91505
HORL, RAY	WRITER	8955 BEVERLY BLVD	LOS ANGELES, CA	90048
HORN, ALAN	TV PRODUCER	1901 AVE OF THE STARS	LOS ANGELES, CA	90067
HORN, LEW	ACTOR	421 S LAFAYETTE PARK BLVD	LOS ANGELES, CA	90057
HORN, PAUL	MUSICIAN	4680 ELK LAKE DR #304	VICTORIA, BC	CANADA
HORN, ROBIN F	COMPOSER	2219 BEN LOMOND DR	LOS ANGELES, CA	90027
HORN, STEVE	DIRECTOR	DGA, 7950 SUNSET BLVD	LOS ANGELES, CA	90046
HORN, VOLKER	TENOR	CAMI, 165 W 57TH ST	NEW YORK, NY	10019
HORNADAY, JEFF	ACTOR	14465 DICKENS ST	SHERMAN OAKS, CA	91423
HORNBURGER, DARYL	GUITARIST	ROUTE #1	MC EWEN, TN	37101
HORNBY, FREDERICK H	WRITER	555 W 57TH ST #1230	NEW YORK, NY	10019
HORNE, CHARLES	PHOTOGRAPHER	ROUTE 1, BOX 499	MARATHON, FL	33050
HORNE, ERROL	ACTOR	11905 KLING ST #19	NORTH HOLLYWOOD, CA	91607
HORNE, LENA	SINGER	1090 VERMONT AVE #929, NW	WASHINGTON, DC	20005
HORNE, MARILYN	MEZZO-SOPRANO	CAMI, 165 W 57TH ST	NEW YORK, NY	10019
HORNE, SUZI	ACTRESS	3800 BARHAM BLVD #303	LOS ANGELES, CA	90068
HORNE, VICTORIA	ACTRESS	OAKIE, 18650 DEVONSHIRE ST	NORTHRIDGE, CA	91324
HORNER, CHUCK	TV WRITER	555 W 57TH ST #1230	NEW YORK, NY	10019
HORNER, HARRY	FILM DIRECTOR	728 BROOKTREE RD	PACIFIC PALISADES, CA	90272
HORNER, JACK	ACTOR	3518 W CAHUENGA BLVD #315	LOS ANGELES, CA	90068
HORNER, JAMES	COMPOSER	728 BROOKTREE RD	PACIFIC PALISADES, CA	90272
HORNER, RICHARD	THEATER PRODUCER	65 W 55TH ST	NEW YORK, NY	10019
HORNER, TIM	WRESTLER	NATIONAL WRESTLING ALLIANCE		
		JIM CROCKETT PROMOTIONS		
		421 BRIARBEND DR	CHARLOTTE, NC	28209
HORNER, VIVIAN	CABLE EXECUTIVE	WARNER CABLE COMMUNICATIONS		
		75 ROCKEFELLER PLAZA	NEW YORK, NY	10019
HORNICK, JOY G	TV WRITER	555 W 57TH ST #1230	NEW YORK, NY	10019
HORNIK, GOTTFRIED	BARITONE	MARIEDL ANDERS ARTISTS MGMT		
		535 EL CAMINO DEL MAR ST	SAN FRANCISCO, CA	94121
HORNISHER, CHRISTINA	WRITER	3998 SUNSWEPT DR	STUDIO CITY, CA	91604
HORNSBY, BRUCE & THE RANGE	ROCK & ROLL GROUP	TIM NEECE MANAGEMENT		
		10513 CUSHDON AVE	LOS ANGELES, CA	90064
HOROVITZ, ISRAEL	PLAYWRIGHT	SAFIER, 667 MADISON AVE	NEW YORK, NY	10021
HOROVITZ, LOUIS J	TV DIRECTOR	8944 CRESCENT DR	LOS ANGELES, CA	90046
HOROWICZ, MICHAEL A	WRITER	555 W 57TH ST #1230	NEW YORK, NY	10019
HOROWITZ, ANDREW M	WRITER	8955 BEVERLY BLVD	LOS ANGELES, CA	90048
HOROWITZ, ANTHONY	COMPOSER	13843 OXNARD ST #38	VAN NUYS, CA	91401
HOROWITZ, DAVID	TV HOST	9012 BEVERLY BLVD	LOS ANGELES, CA	90048
HOROWITZ, EDWARD D	CABLE EXECUTIVE	HOME BOX OFFICE PICTURES		
		1100 AVE OF THE AMERICAS	NEW YORK, NY	10036
HOROWITZ, JANICE M	NEWS REPORTER	TIME/TIME & LIFE BLDG		
		ROCKEFELLER CENTER	NEW YORK, NY	10020
HOROWITZ, RICHARD	TIMPANIST	THE METROPOLITAN OPERA		
		LINCOLN CENTER	NEW YORK, NY	10023
HOROWITZ, SARI	NEWS CORRESPONDENT	2700 CONNECTICUT AVE #702-A, NW	WASHINGTON, DC	20008
HOROWITZ, VLADIMER	PIANIST	SHAW CONCERTS, 1995 BROADWAY	NEW YORK, NY	10023
HORROCK, NICHOLAS M	NEWS CORRESPONDENT	719 S LEE ST	ALEXANDRIA, VA	22314
HORSBRUGH, OLIVER	FILM DIRECTOR	126 HAMPTON RD, TWICKEHAM	MIDDLESEX	ENGLAND
HORSEY, DAVID	CARTOONIST	TRIBUNE MEDIA SERVICES		
		64 E CONCORD ST	ORLANDO, FL	32801
HORSFALL, BERNARD	ACTOR	34 CHATSWORTH WY	LONDON SE27	ENGLAND
HORSH, JANET R	NEWS CORRESPONDENT	NATIONAL PRESS BUILDING		
		529 14TH ST, NW	WASHINGTON, DC	20045
HORSLEY, LEE	ACTOR	1941 CUMMINGS DR	LOS ANGELES, CA	90027
HORST FAMILY SINGERS, THE	GOSPEL GROUP	705 GASCHE	WOOSTER, OH	44691
HORSTMAN, JUDITH	NEWS CORRESPONDENT	2136 "R" ST, NW	WASHINGTON, DC	20008
HORSTMEYER, ROY	GUITARIST	ROUTE #4, BOX 443-J	LEBANON, TN	37087
HORSZOWSKI, MIECZYSLAW	PIANIST	COLBERT, 111 W 57TH ST	NEW YORK, NY	10019

HORTON, BOBBY LEE	NEWS CORRESPONDENT	1735 NEW HAMPSHIRE AVE #404, NW	WASHINGTON, DC	20009
HORTON, ELLEN P	NEWS CORRESPONDENT	3601 N 17TH ST	ARLINGTON, VA	22207
HORTON, JOHN J	DIRECTOR	17 SURREYHILL PL	HUNTINGTON, NY	11743
HORTON, LOUISE	ACTRESS	259 E 78TH ST	NEW YORK, NY	10021
HORTON, PETER	ACTOR	151 S EL CAMINO DR	BEVERLY HILLS, CA	90212
HORTON, RICHARD P	GUITARIST-SAXOPHONIST	1905 YORKSTONE CIR	COLLEGE PARK, GA	30349
HORTON, ROBERT	ACTOR	5317 ANDASOL AVE	ENCINO, CA	91316
HORTON, WILLIE	BASEBALL	19312 STEEL ST	DETROIT, MI	48235
HORVAT, ALEX	WRITER	8955 BEVERLY BLVD	LOS ANGELES, CA	90048
HORVATH, GYULA	CONDUCTOR	POST OFFICE BOX 131	SPRINGFIELD, VA	22150
HORVATH, IMRE	WRITER	555 W 57TH ST #1230	NEW YORK, NY	10019
HORVATH, JOHN	DIRECTOR	145 E 52ND ST	NEW YORK, NY	10022
HORVITZ, LOUIS J	TV DIRECTOR	8944 CRESCENT DR	LOS ANGELES, CA	90046
HORWICH, FRANCES	ACTRESS-TV HOST	WMAQ TEELEVISION STATION		
		MERCHANDISE MART PLAZA	CHICAGO, IL	60654
HORWITT, ARNOLD	WRITER	555 W 57TH ST #1230	NEW YORK, NY	10019
HORWITZ, MICHAEL F	DIRECTOR	DGA, 7950 SUNSET BLVD	LOS ANGELES, CA	90046
HORWITZ, MURRAY L	WRITER	555 W 57TH ST #1230	NEW YORK, NY	10019
HOSBEIN, JAMES	ACTOR	ABRAMS ARTISTS & ASSOCIATES		
		420 MADISON AVE, 14TH FLOOR	NEW YORK, NY	10017
HOSEA, BOBBY	ACTOR	8484 WILSHIRE BLVD #235	BEVERLY HILLS, CA	90211
HOSEFROS, PAUL	PHOTOGRAPHER	907 6TH ST, SW	WASHINGTON, DC	20024
HOSENBALL, MARK	NEWS CORRESPONDENT	7249 PARKWOOD CT #303	FALLS CHURCH, VA	22042
HOSIE, STANLEY	WRITER	555 W 57TH ST #1230	NEW YORK, NY	10019
HOSKINS, BOB	ACTOR	HOPE & LYNE, 5 MILNER PL	LONDON N1	ENGLAND
HOSKINS, BOB	ACTOR	9200 SUNSET BLVD #1210	LOS ANGELES, CA	90069
HOSPODAR, JUNE C	WRITER	17239 ARCHWOOD ST	VAN NUYS, CA	91406
HOSSEIN, IRON SHEIK	WRESTLER	SEE - IRON SHEIK, THE		
HOSSEIN, ROBERT	ACTOR	17 RUE DE LA TREMOILLE	PARIS 75008	FRANCE
HOSTLER, KAREN A	NEWS CORRESPONDENT	12 CONSTITUTION AVE, NW	WASHINGTON, DC	21401
HOT ICE	RHYTHM & BLUES GROUP	POST OFFICE BOX 2095	PHILADELPHIA, PA	19103
HOT RIZE	BLUEGRASS GROUP	KEITH CASE COMPANY		
		1016 16TH AVE S	NASHVILLE, TN	37212
HOT ROD, THE	WRESTLER	SEE - PIPER, ROWDY RODDY		
HOT SHOT	ROCK & ROLL GROUP	BROTHERS, 141 DUNBAR AVE	FORD, NJ	08863
HOT STUFF	WRESTLER	SEE - GILBERT, EDDIE		
		"HOT STUFF"		
HOTALING, EDWARD	NEWS CORRESPONDENT	3506 LEGATION ST, NW	WASHINGTON, DC	20015
HOTCHKIS, JOAN	ACTRESS	201 OCEAN AVE #509-P	SANTA MONICA, CA	90402
HOTCHNER, A E	WRITER	555 W 57TH ST #1230	NEW YORK, NY	10019
HOTCHNER, TRACY	ACTRESS-WRITER	8955 BEVERLY BLVD	LOS ANGELES, CA	90048
HOTEL	ROCK & ROLL GROUP	POST OFFICE BOX 24570	NASHVILLE, TN	37202
HOTROD, CHEVY KEVY & THE FLASHB	ROCK & ROLL GROUP	3717 W 50TH ST #L-2	MINNEAPOLIS, MN	55410
HOTTELET, RICHARD C	NEWS CORRESPONDENT	CBS NEWS, 524 W 57TH ST	NEW YORK, NY	10019
HOTTON, DONALD	ACTOR	9021 MELROSE AVE #304	LOS ANGELES, CA	90069
HOTY, DEE	ACTRESS	9229 SUNSET BLVD #306	LOS ANGELES, CA	90069
HOTZ, WILLIAM G	PHOTOGRAPHER	619 ROCKAWAY BEACH AVE	BALTIMORE, MD	21221
HOUCK, JOY N, JR	SCREENWRITER	8955 BEVERLY BLVD	LOS ANGELES, CA	90048
HOUGH, JOHN	FILM DIRECTOR	REDWAY, 16 BERNERS ST	LONDON W1	ENGLAND
HOUGH, RICHARD W	WRITER	555 W 57TH ST #1230	NEW YORK, NY	10019
HOUGH, STANLEY	TV DIRECTOR	CBS-TV, 4024 N RADFORD AVE	STUDIO CITY, CA	91604
HOUGH, STEPHEN	PIANIST	CAMI, 165 W 57TH ST	NEW YORK, NY	10019
HOUGHTON, A E, JR	WRITER	8544 WALNUT DR	LOS ANGELES, CA	90046
HOUGHTON, DON	TV WRITER-PRODUCER	UNNA & DURBRIDGE, LTD		
		24-32 POTTERY LN		
		HOLLAND PARK	LONDON W11	ENGLAND
HOUGHTON, JAMES	ACTOR-WRITER	8544 WALNUT DR	LOS ANGELES, CA	90046
HOUGHTON, JOHN	NEWS CORRESPONDENT	114 N JACKSON ST	ARLINGTON, VA	22201
HOUGHTON, KATHLEEN	ACTRESS	134 STEELE RD	WEST HARTFORD, CT	06119
HOUGHTON, MONA	TV WRITER	8544 WALNUT DR	LOS ANGELES, CA	90046
HOUGHTON, WANDA	WRITER	1591 SUNSET PLAZA DR	LOS ANGELES, CA	90069
HOULDEY, MICHAEL	DIRECTOR-PRODUCER	14 LOWTHER RD, BARNES	LONDON SW13 9ND	ENGLAND
HOUNDS, THE	ROCK & ROLL GROUP	505 N LAKE SHORE DR #65	CHICAGO, IL	60611
HOUSE, ANDERSON G	SCREENWRITER	1922 WESTHOLME AVE	LOS ANGELES, CA	90025
HOUSE, BUDDY	MUSIC ARRANGER	1000 MC MAHON DR	NASHVILLE, TN	37216
HOUSE, DALE	ACTOR	ABC-TV, "GENERAL HOSPITAL"		
		1438 N GOWER ST	LOS ANGELES, CA	90028
HOUSE, DANA	ACTRESS-MODEL	439 S LA CIENEGA BLVD #120	LOS ANGELES, CA	90048
HOUSE, JAMES	SINGER	ICM, 40 W 57TH ST	NEW YORK, NY	10019
HOUSE, RON	ACTOR	KOHNER, 9169 SUNSET BLVD	LOS ANGELES, CA	90069
HOUSE, RONALD E	WRITER	8955 BEVERLY BLVD	LOS ANGELES, CA	90048
HOUSEHOLD, GEOFFREY	ACTOR	CHURCH HEADLAND, WHITECHUR		
		AYLESBURY	BUCKS	ENGLAND
HOUSEMAN, JOHN	ACTOR-DIRECTOR	12315 GORHAM AVE	LOS ANGELES, CA	90049
HOUSER, JERRY	ACTOR	3236 BENDA ST	LOS ANGELES, CA	90068
HOUSEROCKERS, THE	ROCK & ROLL GROUP	AWOL ENTERTAINMENT		
		157 W 57TH ST	NEW YORK, NY	10019
HOUSTON, ALEX	VENTRILIQUIST	POST OFFICE BOX 82	GREENBRIER, TN	37073
HOUSTON, CHRISTINE	WRITER	8955 BEVERLY BLVD	LOS ANGELES, CA	90048
HOUSTON, CISSY	SINGER	POST OFFICE BOX 82	GREAT NECK, NY	11021
HOUSTON, DAVID	SINGER-GUITARIST	TFE, 324 JOHNSON BUILDING	SHREVEPORT, LA	71101
HOUSTON, DONALD	ACTOR	20 CARROLL HOUSE		
		GLOUCESTER TERR	LONDON W2	ENGLAND
HOUSTON, FITZHUGH	ACTOR	614 S WALNUT ST #4	INGLEWOOD, CA	90301

Name	Occupation	Address	City/State	Zip
HOUSTON, GLYN	ACTOR	5 KINGSWOOD CLOSE, WEYBRIDGE	SURREY	ENGLAND
HOUSTON, JACQUES	CONDUCTOR	3003 VAN NESS ST #W-205, NW	WASHINGTON, DC	20008
HOUSTON, JAMES D	WRITER	8955 BEVERLY BLVD	LOS ANGELES, CA	90048
HOUSTON, JAMES W	TV WRITER	9255 SUNSET BLVD #1122	LOS ANGELES, CA	90069
HOUSTON, JEANNE W	TV WRITER	9255 SUNSET BLVD #1122	LOS ANGELES, CA	90069
HOUSTON, MICHAEL SAMUEL	WRESTLER	SEE - HOUSTON, SAM		
HOUSTON, MIGHTY JOE	SINGER	OLDIES, 5218 ALMONT ST	LOS ANGELES, CA	90032
HOUSTON, PAUL	NEWS CORRESPONDENT	3019 S COLUMBUS ST	ARLINGTON, VA	22206
HOUSTON, ROBERT	SCREENWRITER	8955 BEVERLY BLVD	LOS ANGELES, CA	90048
HOUSTON, SAM	WRESTLER	POST OFFICE BOX 3859	STAMFORD, CT	06905
HOUSTON, THELMA	SINGER	4296 MOUNT VERNON DR	LOS ANGELES, CA	90008
HOUSTON, WHITNEY	SINGER	230 W 55TH #31-B	NEW YORK, NY	10019
HOUTRIDES, JAMES	WRITER	555 W 57TH ST #1230	NEW YORK, NY	10019
HOVANNISIAN, JOHN	ACTOR	11606 TERRY HILL PL	LOS ANGELES, CA	90049
HOVEN, LOUISE	ACTRESS	1211 N POINSETTIA DR #F	LOS ANGELES, CA	90046
HOVENKAMP, JOHN	TALENT AGENT	POST OFFICE BOX 20043		
		COLUMBUS CIR STATION	NEW YORK, NY	10023
HOVERTON, RENEE	MODEL	POST OFFICE BOX 7211	MOUNTAIN VIEW, CA	94043
HOVEY, TAMARA	WRITER	8955 BEVERLY BLVD	LOS ANGELES, CA	90048
HOVHANESS, ALAN	COMPOSER	17259 138TH AVE, SE	RENTON, WA	98055
HOVLAND, JULIE	ACTRESS	30 UNIVERSAL CITY PLAZA #251	UNIVERSAL CITY, CA	91608
HOW, JANE	ACTRESS	51 BRODERICK RD	LONDON SW17	ENGLAND
HOWAR, BARBARA	TV CORRES-COLUMNIST	ENTERTAINMENT TONIGHT		
		PARAMOUNT TELEVISION		
		5555 MELROSE AVE	LOS ANGELES, CA	90038
HOWARD, ALAN	ACTOR	1714 N IVAR AVE #1116	HOLLYWOOD, CA	90028
HOWARD, ALAN ROBERT	WRITER	2370 NICHOLS CANYON RD	LOS ANGELES, CA	90046
HOWARD, ALAN S	ACTOR	4512 ATOLL AVE	SHERMAN OAKS, CA	91423
HOWARD, ALFRED L	WRITER	555 W 57TH ST #1230	NEW YORK, NY	10019
HOWARD, ANDREA	ACTRESS	25708 CLINE RD	CALABASAS, CA	91302
HOWARD, ANN	MEZZO-SOPRANO	61 W 62ND ST #6-F	NEW YORK, NY	10023
HOWARD, ANTHONY	DIRECTOR-PRODUCER	DROVE COTTAGE, NEWBRIDGE		
		NEAR CADNAM	HANTS	ENGLAND
HOWARD, BARBARA	ACTRESS	329 N WETHERLY DR #205	BEVERLY HILLS, CA	90211
HOWARD, BRUCE	TV WRITER	8955 BEVERLY BLVD	LOS ANGELES, CA	90048
HOWARD, CHUBBY	GUITARIST	375 MAYER CT	FRANKLIN, OH	45005
HOWARD, CHUCK	TV EXECUTIVE	ABC TELEVISION NETWORK		
		1330 AVE OF THE AMERICAS	NE YORK, NY	10019
HOWARD, CLARK	AUTHOR	8955 BEVERLY BLVD	LOS ANGELES, CA	90048
HOWARD, CLARK	TV WRITER	JACKINSON, 156 5TH AVE	NEW YORK, NY	10010
HOWARD, CLINT	ACTOR	4286 CLYBOURNE AVE	BURBANK, CA	91505
HOWARD, CY	WRITER-PRODUCER	10230 SUNSET BLVD	LOS ANGELES, CA	90024
HOWARD, D D	ACTRESS	8400 DE LONGPRE AVE #306	LOS ANGELES, CA	90069
HOWARD, DAN	BODYBUILDER	HOWARD'S GYM, 17435 NEWHOPE	FOUNTAIN VALLEY, CA	92708
HOWARD, DENNIS	ACTOR	11726 SAN VICENTE BLVD #300	LOS ANGELES, CA	90049
HOWARD, DORAN T	NEWS CORRESPONDENT	4809 RANDOLPH DR	ANNANDALE, VA	22003
HOWARD, FRANK	BASEBALL	560 SAINT MARYS BLVD	GREEN BAY, WI	54301
HOWARD, GORDON	ACTOR	CARPENTER, 1516-W REDWOOD ST	SAN DIEGO, CA	92101
HOWARD, GREG	CARTOONIST	NEWS AMERICA SYNDICATE		
		1703 KAISER AVE	IRVINE, CA	92714
HOWARD, HARLIN	GUITARIST-SONGWRITER	1625 OTTER CREEK RD	NASHVILLE, TN	37215
HOWARD, HARRY	FILM DIRECTOR	DGA, 7950 SUNSET BLVD	LOS ANGELES, CA	90046
HOWARD, JAN	SINGER	TESSIER, 505 CANTON PASS	MADISON, TN	37115
HOWARD, JASON	ACTOR	60 SAINT MARKS PL	NEW YORK, NY	10003
HOWARD, JERRY	DIRECTOR	DGA, 7950 SUNSET BLVD	LOS ANGELES, CA	90046
HOWARD, JOHN D	GUITARIST	247 COLLIER AVE	NASHVILLE, TN	37211
HOWARD, JOSHUA J	WRITER	555 W 57TH ST #1230	NEW YORK, NY	10019
HOWARD, JOYCE B	WRITER	8955 BEVERLY BLVD	LOS ANGELES, CA	90048
HOWARD, KARIN	FILM DIRECTOR	3541 LANDA ST	LOS ANGELES, CA	90039
HOWARD, KEN	ACTOR	59 E 54TH ST	NEW YORK, NY	10022
HOWARD, LESLIE	PIANIST	ROSENFIELD, 714 LADD RD	BRONX, NY	10471
HOWARD, LINDA	DIRECTOR	18306 DELANO	RESEDA, CA	91335
HOWARD, LISA	ACTRESS	ABC-TV, "ALL MY CHILDREN"		
		1330 AVE OF THE AMERICAS	NEW YORK, NY	10019
HOWARD, LUCY	NEWS CORRESPONDENT	919 22ND ST, NW	WASHINGTON, DC	20037
HOWARD, MARJORIE	ACTRESS	THE WHITBY, 325 W 45TH ST	NEW YORK, NY	10036
HOWARD, MATTHEW	TV WRITER	8955 BEVERLY BLVD	LOS ANGELES, CA	90048
HOWARD, NANCY K	DIRECTOR	POST OFFICE BOX 323	ALPINE, NJ	07620
HOWARD, PAUL	GUITARIST	ROUTE #5, BOX 500	SHREVEPORT, LA	71107
HOWARD, RANCE	ACTOR-WRITER	4286 CLYBOURN AVE	BURBANK, CA	91505
HOWARD, RICHARD	PHOTOGRAPHER	144 HOLWORTHY ST	CAMBRIDGE, MA	02138
HOWARD, ROBERT	TV WRITER	8955 BEVERLY BLVD	LOS ANGELES, CA	90048
HOWARD, RON	ACTOR-DIRECTOR	POST OFFICE BOX 900	BEVERLY HILLS, CA	90213
HOWARD, SANDY	FILM PRODUCER	9255 SUNSET BLVD #1122	LOS ANGELES, CA	90069
HOWARD, SANDY	FILM DIRECTOR	8755 SHOREHAM DR #403	LOS ANGELES, CA	90060
HOWARD, STEPHEN G	DIRECTOR	DGA, 110 W 57TH ST	NEW YORK, NY	10019
HOWARD, SUSAN	ACTRESS	CHRANE, 5071 CALVIN AVE	TARZANA, CA	91356
HOWARD, TERRY	WRITER	555 W 57TH ST #1230	NEW YORK, NY	10019
HOWARD, TERRY H	SINGER	2408 DALEBROOK CT #A	NASHVILLE, TN	37206
HOWARD, THOMAS K	DIRECTOR	3552 CARRIAGE HILL CIR	RANDALLSTOWN, MD	21133
HOWARD, TREVOR	ACTOR	ROWLEY GREEN HOUSE, ARKLEY	HERTS	ENGLAND
HOWARD, TRUSTIN	WRITER	8955 BEVERLY BLVD	LOS ANGELES, CA	90048
HOWARD, VINCE	ACTOR	6515 SUNSET BLVD #300-A	LOS ANGELES, CA	90028
HOWARD, VOLNEY, III	PRODUCER	DON-EL PRODUCTIONS		
		5746 SUNSET BLVD	LOS ANGELES, CA	90028

HOWARD, WARREN E	NEWS CORRESPONDENT	503 2ND ST, NE	WASHINGTON, DC	20002
HOWARD, WILLIAM E	NEWS CORRESPONDENT	1413 28TH ST, NW	WASHINGTON, DC	20007
HOWARD & TIM'S PAID VACATION	ROCK & ROLL GROUP	POST OFFICE BOX 390		
		OLD CHELSEA STATION	NEW YORK, NY	10113
HOWARTH, ALAN	MUSICIAN	2400 E GLENOAKS BLVD	GLENDALE, CA	91206
HOWAT, CLARK	ACTOR	9165 SUNSET BLVD #202	LOS ANGELES, CA	90069
HOWE, HARVEY	WRITER	8955 BEVERLY BLVD	LOS ANGELES, CA	90048
HOWE, MARTHA JANE	CONTRALTO	CONE, 221 W 57TH ST	NEW YORK, NY	10019
HOWE, MICHAEL	ACTOR-SINGER-DANCER	TARLO, 7 FLORAL ST	LONDON WC2	ENGLAND
HOWELL, BILL	DIRECTOR	DGA, 7950 SUNSET BLVD	LOS ANGELES, CA	90046
HOWELL, CHARLENE	ACTRESS	6430 SUNSET BLVD #1203	LOS ANGELES, CA	90028
HOWELL, DAVID L	NEWS CORRESPONDENT	2441 ONTARIO RD, NW	WASHINGTON, DC	20009
HOWELL, GWYNNE	SINGER	COLBERT, 111 W 57TH ST	NEW YORK, NY	10019
HOWELL, HOKE	ACTOR-WRITER	330 S LAMER ST	BURBANK, CA	91506
HOWELL, J KURT	PIANIST	POST OFFICE BOX 120561	NASHVILLE, TN	37212
HOWELL, JEAN	ACTRESS	11240 MAGNOLIA BLVD #202	NORTH HOLLYWOOD, CA	91601
HOWELL, KATHY	WRITER	555 W 57TH ST #1230	NEW YORK, NY	10019
HOWELL, KENNETH E	COMPOSER	1545 COLUMBIA DR	GLENDALE, CA	91205
HOWELL, MARCELA	WRITER	8955 BEVERLY BLVD	LOS ANGELES, CA	90048
HOWELL, MARGARET	ACTRESS	6404 WILSHIRE BLVD #800	LOS ANGELES, CA	90048
HOWELL, MARGARET	FASHION DESIGNER	111 OLD DOVER RD	LONDON SE1	ENGLAND
HOWELL, ROGER	BARITONE	CAMI, 165 W 57TH ST	NEW YORK, NY	10019
HOWELL, T J	JUGGLER-UNICYCLIST	HALL, 138 FROG HOLLOW RD	CHURCHVILLE, PA	18966
HOWER, NELSON L	WRITER	555 W 57TH ST #1230	NEW YORK, NY	10019
HOWERD, FRANKIE	COMEDIAN	306-16 EUSTON RD	LONDON NW13	ENGLAND
HOWERTON, CANDACE	ACTRESS	745 1/2 N GENESEE AVE	LOS ANGELES, CA	90046
HOWERTON, CHARLES	ACTOR	13132 CREWE ST	NORTH HOLLYWOOD, CA	91605
HOWES, HANS	ACTOR	10000 RIVERSIDE DR #3	TOLUCA LAKE, CA	91602
HOWES, SALLY ANN	ACTRESS	19 W 44TH ST #1500	NEW YORK, NY	10036
HOWITT, KAREN	WRITER	555 W 57TH ST #1230	NEW YORK, NY	10019
HOWLAND, BETH	ACTRESS	255 AMALFI DR	SANTA MONICA, CA	90402
HOWLETT, PHILIP G	PUBLISHING EXECUTIVE	DISCOVER/TIME & LIFE BLDG		
		ROCKEFELLER CENTER	NEW YORK, NY	10020
HOWSER, HUELL	TV HOST	450 N ROSSMORE AVE	LOS ANGELES, CA	90004
HOXIE, AL	WRITER	916 N ROXBURY DR	BEVERLY HILLS, CA	90210
HOY, ANNE Q	NEWS CORRESPONDENT	227 S PAYNE ST	ALEXANDER, VA	22314
HOY, BOB	ACTOR	4067 FARMDALE AVE	STUDIO CITY, CA	91604
HOY, ELIZABETH	ACTRESS	KELMAN, 7813 SUNSET BLVD	LOS ANGELES, CA	90046
HOY, FRANK	PHOTOGRAPHER	1322 LIBRA DR	TEMPE, AR	85203
HOY, LINDA	ACTRESS	12725 VENTURA BLVD #E	STUDIO CITY, CA	91604
HOY, THOMAS L	PHOTOGRAPHER	5602 GLOSTER RD, NW	WASHINGTON, DC	20016
HOYER, DONN F	DIRECTOR	25728 WHISPERING TREES	VALENCIA, CA	91355
HOYLE, GEOFF	MIME	AFFILIATE ARTISTS, INC		
		37 W 65TH ST, 6TH FLOOR	NEW YORK, NY	10023
HOYLE, RUSS	WRITER-EDITOR	TIME/TIME & LIFE BLDG		
		ROCKEFELLER CENTER	NEW YORK, NY	10020
HOYOS, RODOLFO	ACTOR	KOHNER, 9169 SUNSET BLVD	LOS ANGELES, CA	90069
HOYT, H AUSTIN	WRITER-PRODUCER	555 W 57TH ST #1230	NEW YORK, NY	10019
HOYT, JOHN	ACTOR	BILLY WOOD, 5730 LANKERSHIM BL	NORTH HOLLYWOOD, CA	91601
HRBEK, KENT	BASEBALL	9109 4TH AVE S	BLOOMINGTON, MN	55420
HRICKO, ANDREA M	WRITER	2506 21ST ST	SANTA MONICA, CA	90405
HSIEH, CHAURKUEN E	NEWS CORRESPONDENT	4540 CONWELL DR	ANNANDALE, VA	22003
HSU, BENEDICT S	NEWS CORRESPONDENT	8600 AQUEDUCT RD	POTOMAC, MD	20854
HSU, FEI-PING	PIANIST	BYERS-SCHWALBE, 1 5TH AVE	NEW YORK, NY	10003
HSU, VICTOR	DIRECTOR	DGA, 7950 SUNSET BLVD	LOS ANGELES, CA	90046
HUBBARD, BRUCE	BARITONE	CAMI, 165 W 57TH ST	NEW YORK, NY	10019
HUBBARD, BRUCE	SINGER	320 E 42ND ST	NEW YORK, NY	10017
HUBBARD, DAVID	ACTOR	8075 W 3RD ST #305	LOS ANGELES, CA	90048
HUBBARD, ELIZABETH	ACTRESS	22 RIVERSIDE DR	NEW YORK, NY	10023
HUBBARD, FREDDIE	TRUMPETER	17609 VENTURA BLVD #212	ENCINO, CA	91316
HUBBARD, JAMES DALE	PHOTOGRAPHER	8104 CHESTER ST	TAKOMA PARK, MD	20912
HUBBARD, JERRY REED	SINGER-ACTOR	SEE - REED, JERRY		
HUBBARD, KIM	REPORTER	TIME & PEOPLE MAGAZINE		
		TIME & LIFE BUILDING		
		ROCKEFELLER CENTER	NEW YORK, NY	10020
HUBBARD, RAY WYLIE	SINGER	ATS MGMT, 3300 HOLLYWOOD AVE	AUSTIN, TX	78722
HUBBELL, CARL	BASEBALL	130 N LESEUER #1		
		SUNCREST APARTMENT #8	MESA, AZ	83205
HUBCAPS, THE	ROCK & ROLL GROUP	POST OFFICE BOX 1388	DOVER, DE	19903
HUBERT, DICK	TV PRODUCER	GATEWAY PRODS, 304 E 45TH ST	NEW YORK, NY	10017
HUBERT, RICHARD F	WRITER	555 W 57TH ST #1230	NEW YORK, NY	10019
HUBERT, RUSS	ACTOR	161 18TH ST	UNION CITY, NJ	07087
HUBERTO, GREAT	AERIAL ACT	POST OFFICE BOX 87	WEST LEBANON, NY	12195
HUBLER, TIMOTHY	PIANIST	2507 OAKLAND AVE #B	NASHVILLE, TN	37212
HUBLEY, GRANT	ACTOR	9220 SUNSET BLVD #625	LOS ANGELES, CA	90069
HUBLEY, SEASON	ACTRESS	8500 WILSHIRE BLVD #506	BEVERLY HILLS, CA	90211
HUCK, BILLY	ACTOR	2160 S BEVERLY GLEN BLVD	LOS ANGELES, CA	90025
HUCKABEE, COOPER	ACTOR	1800 EL CERRITO PL #45	HOLLYWOOD, CA	90068
HUCKELBERRY, JIM	GUITARIST	290 SPARTAN DR	NASHVILLE, TN	37211
HUCKSTEP, LORILYN	ACTRESS	8961 SUNSET BLVD #B	LOS ANGELES, CA	90069
HUDD, ROY	ACTOR	AZA, 652 FINCHLEY RD	LONDON NW11 7NT	ENGLAND
HUDDLE, ELIZABETH	ACTRESS	247 S BEVERLY DR #102	BEVERLY HILLS, CA	90210
HUDDLESTON, DAVID	ACTOR	THE MANHATTAN TOWERS		
		484 W 43RD ST #27-A	NEW YORK, NY	10036

FREDDIE HUBBARD

MARSHA HUNT

KIM HUNTER

TAB HUNTER

BETTY HUTTON

LAUREN HUTTON

PHYLLIS HYMAN

BILLY IDOL

JULIO IGLESIAS

Name	Occupation	Address	City	Zip
HUDDLESTON, GARY	BODYBUILDER	WEST HWY 54, BOX 207	CAMDENTON, MO	65020
HUDDLESTON, GENE	SINGER	PROCESS, 439 WILEY AVE	FRANKLIN, PA	16323
HUDDLESTON, MICHAEL	ACTOR	10390 SANTA MONICA BLVD #310	LOS ANGELES, CA	90025
HUDGINS, CHRISTINE	NEWS CORRESPONDENT	5559 FIRST STATESMAN LN	ALEXANDRIA, VA	23312
HUDINI	ESCAPE ARTIST	POST OFFICE BOX 87	WEST LEBANON, NY	12195
HUDIS, NORMAN I	TV WRITER	10100 SANTA MONICA BLVD #1600	LOS ANGELES, CA	90067
HUDNUT, BILL	ACTOR	179 N SYCAMORE AVE	LOS ANGELES, CA	90036
HUDOCK, JOHN	STORY EDITOR	3639 ROYAL MEADOW RD	SHERMAN OAKS, CA	91403
HUDSON, BETTY	TV EXECUTIVE	NBC TELEVISION NETWORK		
		30 ROCKEFELLER PLAZA	NEW YORK, NY	10112
HUDSON, BILL	SINGER-ACTOR	2808 WESTBROOK AVE	LOS ANGELES, CA	90046
HUDSON, ERNIE	ACTOR	15301 VENTURA BLVD #345	SHERMAN OAKS, CA	91403
HUDSON, FRED	WRITER	555 W 57TH ST #1230	NEW YORK, NY	10019
HUDSON, GARY	TV WRITER	8955 BEVERLY BLVD	LOS ANGELES, CA	90048
HUDSON, HUGH	FILM DIRECTOR	11 QUEEN'S GATE PLACE MEWS	LONDON SW7	ENGLAND
HUDSON, JIM	ACTOR	4731 LAUREL CANYON BLVD #5	NORTH HOLLYWOOD, CA	91607
HUDSON, LAUREN	WRITER	555 W 57TH ST #1230	NEW YORK, NY	10019
HUDSON, TONI	ACTRESS	151 S EL CAMINO DR	BEVERLY HILLS, CA	90212
HUDSON, WILLIAM R	DIRECTOR	30 W 26TH ST	NEW YORK, NY	10010
HUDSON BROTHERS, THE	VOCAL TRIO	10100 SANTA MONICA BLVD #1600	LOS ANGELES, CA	90067
HUDZ, ANTHONY	TV WRITER	6323 WILBUR AVE	RESEDA, CA	91335
HUERTA, ARMANDO M	TV DIRECTOR	4552 COLLEGE VIEW AVE	LOS ANGELES, CA	90041
HUERTA, STEVEN	TV DIRECTOR	25692 LUPITA DR	VALENCIA, CA	90028
HUES CORPORATION, THE	VOCAL TRIO	POST OFFICE BOX 5295	SANTA MONICA, CA	90405
HUFF, BRENT	ACTOR	LIGHT, 113 N ROBERTSON BLVD	LOS ANGELES, CA	90048
HUFF, CLARA	ACTOR-PRODUCER	7501 ASMAN AVE	CANOGA PARK, CA	91307
HUFF, DANN	GUITARIST	865 BELLEVUE RD		
		KNOLLWOOD #K-19	NASHVILLE, TN	37221
HUFF, DAVID	DRUMMER	180 WALLACE RD #U-14	NASHVILLE, TN	37211
HUFF, DONNA	PIANIST	ROUTE #4, OLD HARDING RD	FRANKLIN, TN	37064
HUFF, JOHN N	TV WRITER	11611 MONTANA AVE #6	LOS ANGELES, CA	90049
HUFF, LEON	SONGWRITER-PRODUCER	309 S BROAD ST	PHILADELPHIA, PA	19107
HUFF, RONALD	MUSIC ARRANGER	ROUTE #4, OLD HARDING RD	FRANKLIN, TN	37064
HUFF, VICKI	CASTING DIRECTOR	9911 W PICO BLVD #1580	LOS ANGELES, CA	90035
HUFFAKER, CLAIR	WRITER	8050 SELMA AVE	LOS ANGELES, CA	90046
HUFFMAN, DIANA L	NEWS CORRESPONDENT	7100 MILLWOOD RD	BETHESDA, MD	20817
HUFFMAN, DOUGLAS	DRUMMER	1238 S BRANDT DR	INDIANAPOLIS, IN	46241
HUFFMAN, E BRADFORD	NEWS CORRESPONDENT	5151 WISCONSIN AVE, NW	WASHINGTON, DC	20012
HUFFMAN, J MARK	NEWS CORRESPONDENT	1825 "K" ST, NW	WASHINGTON, DC	20006
HUFFMAN, LARRY D	GUITARIST	819 KENDALL DR	NASHVILLE, TN	37209
HUFFMAN, PHYLLIS	CASTING DIRECTOR	TBS, 4000 WARNER BLVD	BURBANK, CA	91522
HUFFMAN, ROSANNA	ACTRESS	215 S CLIFFWOOD AVE	LOS ANGELES, CA	90049
HUFFMASTER, RAYMOND	GUITARIST	ROUTE #1, BOX 178	LAUDERDALE, MS	39335
HUFFORD, ROGER E	COMPOSER	1058 ELRADO ST	NAPLES, FL	33940
HUFFSTODT, KAREN	SOPRANO	CAMI, 165 W 57TH ST	NEW YORK, NY	10019
HUFSEY, BILLY	ACTOR	19141 GAYLE PL	TARZANA, CA	91356
HUGGER, JONATHON	ACTOR	1722 ASHMORE PL	LOS ANGELES, CA	90026
HUGGETT, MONICA	VIOLINIST	BYERS-SCHWALBE, 1 5TH AVE	NEW YORK, NY	10003
HUGGIE BOY'S ON-STAGE 1950'S	ROCK & ROLL GROUP	OLDIES, 5218 ALMONT ST	LOS ANGELES, CA	90032
HUGGINS, BRENDA	ACTRESS	8721 SUNSET BLVD #202	LOS ANGELES, CA	90069
HUGGINS, ROY	WRITER-PRODUCER	1928 MANDEVILLE CANYON RD	LOS ANGELES, CA	90049
HUGH, JOHN	ACTOR	7852 GLADE AVE	CANOGA PARK, CA	91304
HUGH-KELLY, DANIEL	ACTOR	POST OFFICE BOX 5617	BEVERLY HILLS, CA	90210
HUGHES, ALEXANDRA	MEZZO-SOPRANO	CAMI, 165 W 57TH ST	NEW YORK, NY	10019
HUGHES, ANN C	NEWS CORRESPONDENT	ABC-TV, NEWS DEPARTMENT		
		1717 DE SALES ST, NW	WASHINGTON, DC	20036
HUGHES, BARNARD	ACTOR	250 W 94TH ST	NEW YORK, NY	10025
HUGHES, BRENDAN	ACTOR	1801 CENTURY PARK E #1415	LOS ANGELES, CA	90067
HUGHES, DEL	DIRECTOR	30 NORMAN AVE	AMITYVILLE, NY	11701
HUGHES, DEWEY WILFRED	DIRECTOR	5325 MAC ARTHUR BLVD, NW	WASHINGTON, DC	20016
HUGHES, DICKSON	ACTOR	208 S BEVERLY DR #4	BEVERLY HILLS, CA	90212
HUGHES, ELINOR	DRAMA CRITIC	24 ACADEMY LN	BELLPORT, NY	11713
HUGHES, ERIC	SCREENWRITER	8955 BEVERLY BLVD	LOS ANGELES, CA	90048
HUGHES, ERNEST	COMPOSER	131 DE LA RONDO	OCEANSIDE, CA	92056
HUGHES, FAYE FOSTER	NEWS CORRESPONDENT	200 RHODE ISLAND AVE #319, NE	WASHINGTON, DC	20002
HUGHES, FINOLA	ACTRESS	ABC-TV, "GENERAL HOSPITAL"		
		1438 N GOWER ST	LOS ANGELES, CA	90025
HUGHES, GARETH	TV PRODUCER	17108 BURBANK BLVD	ENCINO, CA	91316
HUGHES, GENE V	GUITARIST	3634 ESTES RD	NASHVILLE, TN	37215
HUGHES, GEOFFREY	ACTOR	LILFORD PARK, LILFORD		
		NEAR OUNDLE	NORTHANTS	ENGLAND
HUGHES, GEORGE W	PHOTOGRAPHER	ABC-TV, NEWS DEPARTMENT		
		1717 DE SALES ST, NW	WASHINGTON, DC	20036
HUGHES, GERALD W	DIRECTOR	POST OFFICE BOX 9223	PITTSBURGH, PA	15224
HUGHES, HEIDI	NEWS CORRESPONDENT	NBC-TV, NEWS DEPARTMENT		
		4001 NEBRASKA AVE, NW	WASHINGTON, DC	20016
HUGHES, HOLLIE	SINGER	3784 REALTY	ADDISON, TX	70551
HUGHES, HUNTER	ACTOR	9777 WILSHIRE BLVD #707	BEVERLY HILLS, CA	90212
HUGHES, JANICE	NEWS CORRESPONDENT	3850 TUNLAW RD, NW	WASHINGTON, DC	20007
HUGHES, JOEL	ACTOR	8484 WILSHIRE BLVD #235	BEVERLY HILLS, CA	90211
HUGHES, JOEL	SINGER	POST OFFICE BOX 500	ROBINSON CREEK, KY	41650
HUGHES, JOHN W	WRITER-PRODUCER	MCA/UNIVERSAL STUDIOS, INC		
		100 UNIVERSAL CITY PLAZA	UNIVERSAL CITY, CA	91608
HUGHES, JUDITH	MEZZO-SOPRANO	260 W END AVE #7-A	NEW YORK, NY	10023
HUGHES, JULIE	CASTING DIRECTOR	311 W 43RD ST	NEW YORK, NY	10036

HUGHES, KATHLEEN	ACTRESS	8818 RISING GLEN PL	LOS ANGELES, CA 90069
HUGHES, KEN	FILM WRITER-DIRECTOR	950 N KINGS RD #364	HOLLYWOOD, CA 90069
HUGHES, MARK STEPHEN	SINGER-GUITARIST	234 E MORTON AVE	NASHVILLE, TN 37211
HUGHES, MARVIN H	MUSIC ARRANGER	2513 LINCOYA CT	NASHVILLE, TN 37214
HUGHES, MICHAEL HILARY	ACTOR	208 S BEVERLY DR #4	BEVERLY HILLS, CA 90212
HUGHES, MISSY	ACTRESS	NBC-TV, "ANOTHER WORLD"	
		30 ROCKEFELLER PLAZA	NEW YORK, NY 10112
HUGHES, NERYS	ACTRESS	THE RICHARD STONE AGENCY	
		18-20 YORK BLDGS, ADELPHI	LONDON WC2N 6JY ENGLAND
HUGHES, PETER	ACTOR	BROWNE, 13 SAINT MARTINS RD	LONDON SW9 ENGLAND
HUGHES, PRINCE A	ACTOR	12189 CLARETTA ST	LAKE VIEW, CA 91342
HUGHES, RICHARD K	DIRECTOR	DGA, 7950 SUNSET BLVD	LOS ANGELES, CA 90046
HUGHES, ROBERT	WRITER-EDITOR	TIME/TIME & LIFE BLDG	
		ROCKEFELLER CENTER	NEW YORK, NY 10020
HUGHES, ROBERT E	FILM DIRECTOR	210 E 36TH ST #12-A	NEW YORK, NY 10016
HUGHES, ROBERT E	COMPOSER-CONDUCTOR	10344 OSO AVE	CHATSWORTH, CA 91311
HUGHES, RONNY	GUITARIST	123 RIDGEWOOD LN	BRENTWOOD, TN 37027
HUGHES, SALLY	ACTRESS	121 N ROBERTSON BLVD #B	BEVERLY HILLS, CA 90211
HUGHES, TERRY	THEATER DIRECTOR	THE WILLIAM MORRIS AGENCY	
		1350 AVE OF THE AMERICAS	NEW YORK, NY 10019
HUGHES, WENDY	ACTRESS	151 S EL CAMINO DR	BEVERLY HILLS, CA 90212
HUGHEY, GENE	GUITARIST	POST OFFICE BOX 1035	HENDERSONVILLE, TN 37075
HUGHEY, JOHN	DOBROIST	410 INDIAN LAKE RD	HENDERSONVILLE, TN 37075
HUGUELY, JAY	WRITER	BRODER, 9046 SUNSET BLVD	LOS ANGELES, CA 90069
HUIE, JOHN	WRITER	555 W 57TH ST #1230	NEW YORK, NY 10019
HUIE, KAREN	ACTRESS	8350 SANTA MONICA BLVD #103	LOS ANGELES, CA 90069
HUIE, WILLIAM B	SCREENWRITER	N BROWN, 407 N MAPLE DR	BEVERLY HILLS, CA 90210
HULCE, THOMAS	ACTOR	SF & A, 121 N SAN VICENTE BLVD	BEVERLY HILLS, CA 90211
HULETTE, DONALD	WRITER	8955 BEVERLY BLVD	LOS ANGELES, CA 90048
HULK, THE	WRESTLER	SEE - HOGAN, HULK	
HULKSTER, THE	WRESTLER	SEE - HOGAN, HULK	
HULL, DIANNE	ACTRESS	7266 FRANKLIN AVE #6	LOS ANGELES, CA 90046
HULL, JENNIFER	NEWS CORRESPONDENT	TIME/TIME & LIFE BLDG	
		ROCKEFELLER CENTER	NEW YORK, NY 10020
HULLETT, BILL	GUITARIST	94 EVELYN AVE	NASHVILLE, TN 37210
HULLETT, DEBORAH	GUITARIST	94 EVELYN AVE	NASHVILLE, TN 37210
HULME, ROBERT D	DIRECTOR	PENTANGLE, 801 WESTMOUNT DR	LOS ANGELES, CA 90069
HULS, EDWARD	BARITONE	PERLS, 7 W 96TH ST	NEW YORK, NY 10025
HUMAN LEAGUE, THE	ROCK & ROLL GROUP	TUNENOISE, 3-A COATES PL	EDINBURGH SCOTLAND
HUMAN TORCH, THE	HUMAN TORCH	SEE - GILBRIDE, JOE	
		"THE HUMAN TORCH"	
HUMBARD, REV REX	EVANGELIST	CATHEDRAL OF TOMORROW	
		2700 STATE RD	CUYAHOGA FALLS, OH 44421
HUMBLE, GWEN	ACTRESS	999 N DOHENY DR #PH-12	LOS ANGELES, CA 90069
HUMBLE, WILLIAM	GUITARIST	2011 GALBRAITH DR	NASHVILLE, TN 37215
HUMBLE PIE	ROCK & ROLL GROUP	65 W 55TH ST #306	NEW YORK, NY 10019
HUME, ALEXANDER	NEWS CORRESPONDENT	5409 BLACKSTONE RD	BETHSEDA, MD 20016
HUME, BRIT	NEWS CORRESPONDENT	5409 BLACKSTONE RD	BETHESDA, MD 20816
HUME, DAVID F	NEWS CORRESPONDENT	1217 MORNINGSIDE LN	ALEXANDRIA, VA 22308
HUME, EDWARD	TV WRITER	10100 SANTA MONICA BLVD #1600	LOS ANGELES, CA 90067
HUME, ELLEN	NEWS CORRESPONDENT	2601 WOODLEY PL, NW	WASHINGTON, DC 20008
HUME, KENNERLY DAVID	PHOTOGRAPHER	3332 "P" ST, NW	WASHINGTON, DC 20007
HUME, MARGARET	NEWS CORRESPONDENT	1333 "H" ST, NW	WASHINGTON, DC 20005
HUME, PAUL	MUSIC EDITOR	3625 TILDEN ST, NW	WASHINGTON, DC 20008
HUMECKE, TONY D	COMPOSER-CONDUCTOR	1721 N KINGSLEY DR	LOS ANGELES, CA 90027
HUMER, AUGUST	ORGANIST	15 HIGH ST #621	HARTFORD, CT 06103
HUMES, MARY-MARGARET	ACTRESS-MODEL	9220 SUNSET BLVD #625	LOS ANGELES, CA 90069
HUMI, PETER JOHN	PROD-CORRES	CNN, VIA DEI ROBILANT I	ROME 00194 ITALY
HUMM, MICHAEL ALAN	WRITER	4244 VIA MARINA #466	MARINA DEL REY, CA 90291
HUMMEL, HOMER R	CONDUCTOR	3526 HOLBORO DR	LOS ANGELES, CA 90027
HUMMEL, JIM	CARTOONIST	POST OFFICE BOX 5533	SAN JOSE, CA 95190
HUMMERT, ANNE	WRITER	555 W 57TH ST #1230	NEW YORK, NY 10019
HUMO, TERRY	NEWS CORRESPONDENT	6170 GREENWOOD DR #202	FALLS CHURCH, VA 22044
HUMPERDINCK, ENGELBERT	SINGER	10100 SUNSET BLVD	LOS ANGELES, CA 90024
HUMPHREY, CAVADA	ACTRESS	KILTY, POST OFFICE BOX 1074	WESTON, CT 06880
HUMPHREY, RON	DRUMMER	305 COUNTRY CT	ANTIOCH, TN 37013
HUMPHREY, STEVEN F	TV WRITER-PRODUCER	8955 BEVERLY BLVD	LOS ANGELES, CA 90048
HUMPHREYS, DAVID	DRUMMER	POST OFFICE BOX 121433	NASHVILLE, TN 37212
HUMPHREYS, JOEL D	WRITER	8955 BEVERLY BLVD	LOS ANGELES, CA 90048
HUMPHREYS, KERRY	MUSICIAN	5200 STANFORD DR	NASHVILLE, TN 37215
HUMPHREYS, MARTHA D	WRITER	8955 BEVERLY BLVD	LOS ANGELES, CA 90048
HUMPHREYS, STEVE	NEWS CORRESPONDENT	1720 LINDEN AVE	BALTIMORE, MD 21217
HUMPHRIES, DAVE	TV DIRECTOR	SEIFERT, 8-A BRUNSWICK	LONDON W8 ENGLAND
HUMPHRIES, MITCH	MUSIC ARRANGER	ROUTE #8, BOX 202-A	COLUMBIA, TN 38401
HUNDLEY, CRAIG	ACTOR	14244 VALLEY VISTA BLVD	SHERMAN OAKS, CA 91423
HUNDLEY, CRAIG L	CONDUCTOR	POST OFFICE BOX 6327	BEVERLY HILLS, CA 90212
HUNGATE, WILLIAM DAVID	MUSIC ARRANGER	ROUTE #5, BOX 99-A	GOODLETTSVILLE, TN 37072
HUNGERFORD, MICHAEL	ACTOR	1605 N CAHUENGA BLVD #202	LOS ANGELES, CA 90028
HUNGRY FOR WHAT	ROCK & ROLL GROUP	POST OFFICE BOX 67-A-64	LOS ANGELES, CA 90067
HUNKINS, LEE	WRITER	555 W 57TH ST #1230	NEW YORK, NY 10019
HUNLEY, CON	SINGER	POST OFFICE BOX 121321	NASHVILLE, TN 37212
HUNLEY, JERRY "COOTIE"	DRUMMER	3746 E RIDGE DR	NASHVILLE, TN 37211
HUNLEY, LEANN	ACTRESS-MODEL	1888 N CRESCENT HEIGHTS BLVD	LOS ANGELES, CA 90069
HUNLEY, WILLIAM	MUSICIAN	701 W MAIN ST	WAVERLY, TN 37185

Name	Occupation	Address	City/State	Zip/Country
HUNNICUTT, ED	SINGER-GUITARIST	MERIT MUSIC CORPORATION		
		815 18TH AVE S	NASHVILLE, TN	37203
HUNNICUTT, GAYLE	ACTRESS	174 REGENTS PARK RD	LONDON NW1	ENGLAND
HUNT, ALBERT R	NEWS CORRESPONDENT	3501 36TH ST, NW	WASHINGTON, DC	20016
HUNT, ALLAN	ACTOR	12413 SARAH ST	STUDIO CITY, CA	91604
HUNT, ALLEN	ACTOR	CED, 261 S ROBERTSON BLVD	BEVERLY HILLS, CA	90211
HUNT, BOB	SCREENWRITER	8955 BEVERLY BLVD	LOS ANGELES, CA	90048
HUNT, CHARLES, JR	SAXOPHONIST	503 N DIVISION	CARTERVILLE, IL	62918
HUNT, E HOWARD	AUTHOR	1245 N 85TH ST	MIAMI, FL	33138
HUNT, FINLEY C, JR	WRITER-PRODUCER	154-A "G" ST, SW	WASHINGTON, DC	20024
HUNT, GARETH	ACTOR	ICM, 388-396 OXFORD ST	LONDON W1	ENGLAND
HUNT, HELEN	ACTRESS	9220 SUNSET BLVD #625	LOS ANGELES, CA	90069
HUNT, KAREN	SOPRANO	CAMI, 165 W 57TH ST	NEW YORK, NY	10019
HUNT, LARRY E	GUITARIST	POST OFFICE BOX 646	LEBANON, TN	37087
HUNT, LAURENCE R	NEWS CORRESPONDENT	2613 DAVISFORD RD	WOODBRIDGE, VA	22192
HUNT, LEIGH R	WRITER	8955 BEVERLY BLVD	LOS ANGELES, CA	90048
HUNT, LESLIE	ACTRESS	SEE - HUNTLEY, LESLIE		
HUNT, LILLIAN	VIOLINIST	1500 CLAIRMONT PL	NASHVILLE, TN	37215
HUNT, LINDA	ACTRESS	457 W 57TH ST	NEW YORK, NY	10019
HUNT, MARSHA	ACTRESS	13131 MAGNOLIA BLVD	VAN NUYS, CA	91403
HUNT, PAUL	AUTHOR-PUBLISHER	POST OFFICE BOX 10907	BURBANK, CA	91510
HUNT, PAUL	PUBLISHER-AUTHOR	POST OFFICE BOX 10907	BURBANK, CA	91510
HUNT, PETER H	WRITER-PRODUCER	1888 CENTURY PARK E #1400	LOS ANGELES, CA	90067
HUNT, PETER R	FILM DIRECTOR	2229 ROSCOMARE RD	LOS ANGELES, CA	90077
HUNT, RUTH	ACTRESS	10100 SANTA MONICA BLVD #1600	LOS ANGELES, CA	90067
HUNT, SUSAN A	WRITER	8955 BEVERLY BLVD	LOS ANGELES, CA	90048
HUNT, TERENCE	NEWS CORRESPONDENT	1907 STRATTON RD	SILVER SPRING, MD	20910
HUNTER, ALAN	VIDEO JOCK	POST OFFICE BOX 1370	NEW YORK, NY	10101
HUNTER, BLAKE	WRITER-PRODUCER	2327 ALTO OAK DR	LOS ANGELES, CA	90068
HUNTER, DIANA	ACTRESS	9777 WILSHIRE BLVD #707	BEVERLY HILLS, CA	90212
HUNTER, EVAN	NOVELIST	179 PERRY AVE	NORWALK, CT	06850
HUNTER, FRANK T	COMPOSER-CONDUCTOR	EAGLE RD ROAD #2, BOX 6	NEWTOWN, PA	18940
HUNTER, FREDERIC	TV WRITER	1900 AVE OF THE STARS #2535	LOS ANGELES, CA	90067
HUNTER, GEORGE ALLEN	GUITARIST	POST OFFICE BOX 88	NORTH VERNON, IN	47265
HUNTER, GRAHAM	CARTOONIST	42 CLONAVOR RD, SILVER	WEST ORANGE, NJ	07052
HUNTER, HOLLY	ACTRESS	KOHNER, 9169 SUNSET BLVD	LOS ANGELES, CA	90069
HUNTER, IAN	SINGER	ATI, 888 7TH AVE, 21ST FLOOR	NEW YORK, NY	10106
HUNTER, IAN MC LELLAN	WRITER	555 W 57TH ST #1230	NEW YORK, NY	10019
HUNTER, JAMES "CATFISH"	BASEBALL	RURAL ROUTE #1, BOX 895	HERTSFORD, NC	27944
HUNTER, JAMES D	DIRECTOR	75 CRESCI BLVD	HAZLET, NJ	07730
HUNTER, JERRY DWIGHT	HARPSICHORDIST	1310 SCHOOL ST	COLUMBIA, TN	38401
HUNTER, JOHN R "JAC"	CONDUCTOR	700 S LAKE AVE #317	PASADENA, CA	91106
HUNTER, KAKI	ACTRESS	POST OFFICE BOX 5617	BEVERLY HILLS, CA	90210
HUNTER, KIM	ACTRESS	42 COMMERCE ST	NEW YORK, NY	10014
HUNTER, LAURA	SAXOPHONIST	AFFILIATE ARTISTS, INC		
		37 W 65TH ST, 6TH FLOOR	NEW YORK, NY	10023
HUNTER, LEW	TV WRITER	554 S SAN VICENTE BLVD #3	LOS ANGELES, CA	90048
HUNTER, MARJORIE	NEWS CORRESPONDENT	3517 "R" ST, NW	WASHINGTON, DC	20007
HUNTER, MARSHA	SOPRANO	POST OFFICE BOX 884	NEW YORK, NY	10023
HUNTER, PAUL	TV WRITER	14144 VENTURA BLVD #200	SHERMAN OAKS, CA	91423
HUNTER, PHYLLIS	SOPRANO	LEW, 204 W 10TH ST	NEW YORK, NY	10014
HUNTER, ROBERT	SINGER	POST OFFICE BOX 92	BROOKLYN, NY	11229
HUNTER, ROBERT RUSSELL	ACTOR	1830 GRACE AVE #3	HOLLYWOOD, CA	90028
HUNTER, ROSS	FILM PRODUCER	370 TROUSDALE PL	BEVERLY HILLS, CA	90210
HUNTER, RUTH	WRITER-EDITOR	US MAGAZINE COMPANY		
		1 DAG HAMMARSKJOLD PLAZA	NEW YORK, NY	10017
HUNTER, TAB	ACTOR	POST OFFICE BOX 11167	BEVERLY HILLS, CA	90213
HUNTER, THOMAS	WRITER	21023 HAPPY TRAILS	TOPANGA, CA	90290
HUNTER, TIM	WRITER-PRODUCER	1888 CENTURY PARK E #1400	LOS ANGELES, CA	90067
HUNTER, WILLIAM	WRITER	8955 BEVERLY BLVD	LOS ANGELES, CA	90048
HUNTER-KILMER, MELISSA A	NEWS CORRESPONDENT	8124 PRESCOTT DR #103	VIENNA, VA	22180
HUNTERS & COLLECTORS	ROCK & ROLL GROUP	POST OFFICE BOX 216		
		ALBERT PARK	VICTORIA 3206	AUSTRALIA
HUNTINGTON, DR ANN	COLUMNIST	TRIBUNE MEDIA SERVICES		
		64 E CONCORD ST	ORLANDO, FL	32801
HUNTINGTON, LOUISA	ACTRESS	361 CLAREMONT AVE	MONTCLAIR, NJ	07042
HUNTLEY, ERNEST	ACTOR	8949 SUNSET BLVD #203	LOS ANGELES, CA	90069
HUNTLEY, JOHN	AUTHOR	22 ISLINGTON GREEN	LONDON N1 8DU	ENGLAND
HUNTLEY, LESLIE	ACTRESS	3151 W CAHUENGA BLVD #310	LOS ANGELES, CA	90068
HUNTLEY, RAYMOND	ACTOR	LEADING ARTISTS, LTD		
		60 SAINT JAMES'S ST	LONDON SW1	ENGLAND
HUNTLEY, ROBERT S	NEWS CORRESPONDENT	2500 N POLLARD ST	ARLINGTON, VA	22207
HUNTSINGER, DAVID	PIANIST	1703 ANTIOCH PIKE	ANTIOCH, TN	37013
HUPPERT, ISABELLE	ACTRESS	ARTMEDIA, 10 AVE GEORGE V	PARIS 75008	FRANCE
HURD, BARRY	WRITER	555 W 57TH ST #1230	NEW YORK, NY	10019
HURD, DAVID	ORGANIST	15 HIGH ST #621	HARTFORD, CT	06103
HURD, GEORGE S	TV DIRECTOR	616 N RUSH ST	CHICAGO, IL	60611
HURD, MARC F	TV DIRECTOR	11520 YOLANDA AVE	NORTHRIDGE, CA	91326
HURKOS, PETER	ACTOR-PSYCHIC	12214 VIEWCREST RD	STUDIO CITY, CA	91604
HURLBURT, JAMES R	COMPOSER	11669 VALERIO ST #241	NORTH HOLLYWOOD, CA	91605
HURLBURT, SID	WRITER-EDITOR	POST OFFICE BOX 500	WASHINGTON, DC	20044
HURLBUT, GLADYS	ACTRESS	116 BYRDCLIFFE RD	WOODSTOCK, NY	12498
HURLEY, FOSTER	WRITER	8955 BEVERLY BLVD	LOS ANGELES, CA	90048
HURLEY, GLEN	COMEDIAN	POST OFFICE BOX 99	AMBOY, IL	61310
HURLEY, JACK	NEWS CORRESPONDENT	400 N CAPITOL ST, NW	WASHINGTON, DC	20001

200,000 Books
Back Issue Magazines
100,000 Paperback Books
Comics (New & Old)
Newspapers 1890 to date
Sheet Music
Records
Historic WWI and WWII Posters

Book Castle
200 N. Golden Mall
Burbank, CA 91502
(818) 845-1563

Name	Occupation	Address	City	Zip
HURLEY, JOSEPH	WRITER	555 W 57TH ST #1230	NEW YORK, NY	10019
HURLEY, MAURICE	TV WRITER	8955 BEVERLY BLVD	LOS ANGELES, CA	90048
HURLL, MICHAEL	TV PRODUCER	BBC-TV CENTRE, WOOD LN		
		SHEPHERS BUSH	LONDON W12	ENGLAND
HURRELL, GEORGE	PHOTOGRAPHER	6702 SAINT CLAIR AVE	NORTH HOLLYWOOD, CA	91606
HURRICANE	ROCK & ROLL GROUP	GREENWALD, 20445 GRAMERCY PL	TORRANCE, CA	90501
HURSEY, CAMI	CASTING DIRECTOR	3970 OVERLAND AVE #700	CULVER CITY, CA	90232
HURSEY, SHERRY	ACTRESS	4822 HOLLOW CORNER RD #276	CULVER CITY, CA	90230
HURST, ALBERTA	COMPOSER	POST OFFICE BOX 6189	LOS OSOS, CA	93402
HURST, DAVID	ACTOR	10100 SANTA MONICA BLVD #1600	LOS ANGELES, CA	90067
HURST, GORDON "HOWDY"	ACTOR	12027 ALBERS ST #C	NORTH HOLLYWOOD, CA	91607
HURST, JACK	MUSIC CRITIC	TRIBUNE MEDIA SERVICES		
		64 E CONCORD ST	ORLANDO, FL	32801
HURST, RICK	ACTOR	151 S EL CAMINO DR	BEVERLY HILLS, CA	90212
HURST, WILLIAM R	NEWS CORRESPONDENT	5423 SHEFFIELD CT #110	ALEXANDRIA, VA	22311
HURT, CINDY	SINGER	CBC, 2135 STERLING RD	DEERFIELD, IL	60015
HURT, JOHN	ACTOR	23 BACK LN	LONDON NW2	ENGLAND
HURT, MARY BETH	ACTRESS	74 5TH AVE	NEW YORK, NY	10010
HURT, WILLIAM	ACTOR	10100 SANTA MONICA BLVD #1600	LOS ANGELES, CA	90067
HURTE, LEROY E	CONDUCTOR	7826 CRENSHAW BLVD	LOS ANGELES, CA	90043
HURTES, HETTIE LYNN	ACTRESS	8607 HOLLYWOOD BLVD	LOS ANGELES, CA	90069
HURWITZ, DAVID	TV WRITER	151 S EL CAMINO DR	BEVERLY HILLS, CA	90212
HURWITZ, HARRY	WRITER-PRODUCER	2049 CENTURY PARK E #1320	LOS ANGELES, CA	90067
HURWITZ, LEO	TV DIRECTOR	617 W END AVE	NEW YORK, NY	10024
HURWITZ, MARK	WRITER	10100 SANTA MONICA BLVD #1600	LOS ANGELES, CA	90067
HURWITZ, RICHARD D	COMPOSER	2168 ALCCYONA DR	LOS ANGELES, CA	90068
HURWITZ, VICTOR	TV DIRECTOR-PRODUCER	27505 BERKSHIRE DR	SOUTHFIELD, MI	48076
HURWOOD, BERNHARDT J	WRITER	555 W 57TH ST #1230	NEW YORK, NY	10019
HUSH, Q T	SOUL GROUP	SEE - Q T HUSH		
HUSH, SUSI	TV PRODUCER	LIMEHOUSE, 43 WHITFIELD ST	LONDON W1	ENGLAND
HUSHMAN, KATHERINE	MODEL	MODELS & PROMOTIONS AGENCY		
		8560 SUNSET BLVD, 10TH FLOOR	LOS ANGELES, CA	90069
HUSKEY, ROY	GUITARIST	1403 ARDEE AVE	NASHVILLE, TN	37216
HUSKEY, RUTH R	GUITARIST	1403 ARDEE AVE	NASHVILLE, TN	37216
HUSKY, FERLIN	SINGER-SONGWRITER	38 MUSIC SQUARE E #116	NASHVILLE, TN	37203
HUSKY, RICK	ACT-WRI-PROD	13565 LUCCA DR	PACIFIC PALISADES, CA	90272
HUSMANN, RON	ACTOR	11550 DILLING ST	STUDIO CITY, CA	91604
HUSON, KATHERINE A	WRITER	555 W 57TH ST #1230	NEW YORK, NY	10019
HUSON, PAUL	WRITER	6691 WHITLEY TERR	LOS ANGELES, CA	90068
HUSS, MICHAEL	DIRECTOR	12 W 96TH ST	NEW YORK, NY	10025
HUSSEIN, WARIS	FILM DIRECTOR	2 THISTLE GROVE	LONDON SW10	ENGLAND
HUSSEY, OLIVIA	ACTRESS	CONTEMPORARY ARTISTS, LTD		
		132 S LASKY DR	BEVERLY HILLS, CA	90212
HUSSEY, RUTH	ACTRESS	3361 DON PABLO DR	CARLSBAD, CA	92008
HUSTON, ANGELICA	ACTRESS	9255 SUNSET BLVD #510	LOS ANGELES, CA	90069
HUSTON, CRAIG W	FILM DIRECTOR	256 S ROBERTSON BLVD	BEVERLY HILLS, CA	90211
HUSTON, JIMMY	SCREENWRITER	8955 BEVERLY BLVD	LOS ANGELES, CA	90048
HUSTON, JOHN	ACT-WRI-DIR	APTDO POSTAL 273, LIBRO	JALISCO 22361	MEXICO
HUSTON, LOU	WRITER	8955 BEVERLY BLVD	LOS ANGELES, CA	90048
HUSTON, PATRICIA	ACTRESS	8380 MELROSE AVE #207	LOS ANGELES, CA	90069
HUSZAR, JOHN L	DIRECTOR-PRODUCER	420 E 55TH ST	NEW YORK, NY	10022
HUTCHENS, MICHAEL	GUITARIST	2804 27TH AVE S	NASHVILLE, TN	37212
HUTCHENS, RONALD	PIANIST	371 WALLACE RD #110	NASHVILLE, TN	37211
HUTCHERSON, BOBBY	VIBRAPHONIST	2490 CHANNING WY #406	BERKELEY, CA	94704
HUTCHERSON, RAY	WRITER	8955 BEVERLY BLVD	LOS ANGELES, CA	90048
HUTCHESON, RON	NEWS CORRESPONDENT	713 10TH ST, SE	WASHINGTON, DC	20003
HUTCHINGS, PHILIP J	DIRECTOR	520 N MICHIGAN AVE #436	CHICAGO, IL	60611
HUTCHINS, J W	SINGER	ROUTE #8, 425 OREBANK RD	KINGSPORT, TN	37664
HUTCHINS, JIM	MUSICIAN	POST OFFICE BOX 25371	CHARLOTTE, NC	28212
HUTCHINS, PAUL H, JR	PHOTOGRAPHER	1607 DOGWOOD RD	TOWSON, MD	21204
HUTCHINS, WILL	ACTOR	3461 WAVERLY DR	LOS ANGELES, CA	90027
HUTCHINS, WILL	CLOWN	2701 COTTAGE WY #14	SACRAMENTO, CA	95825
HUTCHINSON, JOSEPHINE	ACTRESS	360 E 55TH ST	NEW YORK, NY	10022
HUTCHINSON, KAREN	PIANIST	POST OFFICE BOX 300063	DENVER, CO	80203
HUTCHISON, BARBARA BAILEY	SINGER	POST OFFICE BOX 1556	GAINESVILLE, FL	32602
HUTCHISON, FIONA	ACTRESS	ABC-TV, "ONE LIFE TO LIVE"		
		1330 AVE OF THE AMERICAS	NEW YORK, NY	10019
HUTCHISON, ROBERT B	WRITER	8955 BEVERLY BLVD	LOS ANGELES, CA	90048
HUTMAN, JON	ACTOR	1051 N KENTER AVE	LOS ANGELES, CA	90049
HUTSON, LEE	TV WRITER	8955 BEVERLY BLVD	LOS ANGELES, CA	90048
HUTSON, SANDY M	WRITER	8955 BEVERLY BLVD	LOS ANGELES, CA	90048
HUTTENLOCH, RALPH L	PHOTOJOURNALIST	7610 MIDDAY LN	ALEXANDRIA, VA	22306
HUTTENLOCH, WILLIAM R	PHOTOGRAPHER	8229 GREY EAGLE DR	UPPER MARLBORO, MD	20870
HUTTER, CHRISTINA MARIA	ACTRESS	6380 WILSHIRE BLVD #1600	LOS ANGELES, CA	90048
HUTTER, MARK	ACTOR	10000 SANTA MONICA BLVD #305	LOS ANGELES, CA	90067
HUTTO, MAX A	FILM DIRECTOR	560 CERRO ST	ENCINITAS, CA	92024
HUTTON, BETTY	ACTRESS	SALVE REGINA NEWPORT COLLEGE		
		OCHRE POINT AVE	NEWPORT, RI	02840
HUTTON, BRIAN G	FILM DIRECTOR	8848 LOOKOUT MOUNTAIN AVE	LOS ANGELES, CA	90046
HUTTON, DANNY	SINGER-SONGWRITER	2437 HORSESHOE CYN RD	LOS ANGELES, CA	90046
HUTTON, GUNILLA	ACTRESS-SINGER	6310 SAN VICENTE BLVD #407	LOS ANGELES, CA	90048
HUTTON, LAUREN	ACTRESS-MODEL	124 WAVERLY PL	NEW YORK, NY	10011
HUTTON, RICHARD E	WRITER	555 W 57TH ST #1230	NEW YORK, NY	10019
HUTTON, THOMAS J	COMPOSER	3461 OAK GLEN DR	LOS ANGELES, CA	90068

Name	Occupation	Address	City	Zip
HUTTON, TIMOTHY	ACTOR	52 W 82ND ST	NEW YORK, NY	10020
HUXLEY, CRAIG	COMPOSER	11240 MAGNOLIA BLVD #202	NORTH HOLLYWOOD, CA	91601
HUXTABLE, VICKY	ACTRESS	8666 W OLYMPIC BLVD	LOS ANGELES, CA	90035
HUYBREGTS, PIERRE	PIANIST	GEWALD, 58 W 58TH ST	NEW YORK, NY	10019
HUYCK, GLORIA KATZ	FILM WRITER-DIRECTOR	39 OAKMONT DR	LOS ANGELES, CA	90049
HUYCK, WILLARD M, JR	FILM WRITER-DIRECTOR	39 OAKMONT DR	LOS ANGELES, CA	90049
HWANG, DEBORAH	WRITER-PRODUCER	1402 N HAVENHURST DR	LOS ANGELES, CA	90046
HWONG, LUCIA	COMPOSER	H ORENSTEIN, 157 W 57TH ST	NEW YORK, NY	10019
HYAMS, ALAN	COMPOSER-CONDUCTOR	23425 CANDLEWOOD WY	CANOGA PARK, CA	91304
HYAMS, JOSEPH I, JR	WRITER	540 N BEVERLY GLEN BLVD	LOS ANGELES, CA	90077
HYAMS, NESSA	FILM DIRECTOR	1015 GAYLEY AVE #301	LOS ANGELES, CA	90024
HYAMS, PETER	WRITER-PRODUCER	932 HILTS AVE	LOS ANGELES, CA	90024
HYATT, DONALD B	TV DIRECTOR	109 LINDEN AVE	BRANDFORD, CT	06405
HYATT, GEORGE W	NEWS CORRESPONDENT	13318 SCHWENGER PL	HERNDON, VA	22070
HYATT, MISSY	WRESTLING VALET	POST OFFICE BOIX 3859	STAMFORD, CT	06905
HYATT, ROBERT J	WRITER-PRODUCER	6725 SUNSET BLVD #506	HOLLYWOOD, CA	90028
HYATT, WALTER H	PIANIST	4417 MARATHON BLVD	AUSTIN, TX	78756
HYDE, JACQUELYN	ACTRESS	15010 VENTURA BLVD #234	SHERMAN OAKS, CA	91403
HYDE, JAMES P	DRUMMER	300 TAMPA DR	NASHVILLE, TN	37211
HYDE, JOHN	FILM PRODUCER	PSO, 10100 SANTA MONICA BLVD	LOS ANGELES, CA	90067
HYDE, JOHN C	NEWS CORRESPONDENT	1114 MERWOOD DR	TAKOMA PARK, MD	20912
HYDE-WHITE, ALEX	ACTOR	17406 COVELLO ST	VAN NUYS, CA	91316
HYDE-WHITE, WILFRID	ACTOR	23388 MULHOLLAND DR	WOODLAND HILLS, CA	91364
HYLANDS, SCOTT	ACTOR	9229 SUNSET BLVD #306	LOS ANGELES, CA	90069
HYLEN, STEVE LENNART	DIRECTOR	DGA, 7950 SUNSET BLVD	LOS ANGELES, CA	90046
HYLER, JOY	ACTRESS	1001 HAMMOND ST #9	LOS ANGELES, CA	90069
HYLTON, RUSSELL	DOBROIST	3601 MEADOWBROOK AVE	NASHVILLE, TN	37205
HYMAN, BONITA	MEZZO-SOPRANO	45 W 60TH ST #4-K	NEW YORK, NY	10023
HYMAN, CHARLES H	ACTOR	8230 BEVERLY BLVD #23	LOS ANGELES, CA	90048
HYMAN, DICK	PIANIST	GERSHUNOFF, 502 PARK AVE	NEW YORK, NY	10022
HYMAN, EARLE	ACTOR	THE MANHATTAN TOWERS		
		484 W 43RD ST #33-E	NEW YORK, NY	10036
HYMAN, KEITH	PIANIST	413 NORMANDY CIR	NASHVILLE, TN	37209
HYMAN, KENNETH	FILM EXECUTIVE	SHERWOOD HOUSE, TILEHOUSE LN		
		DENHAM	BUCKS	ENGLAND
HYMOFF, ED	WRITER	555 W 57TH ST #1230	NEW YORK, NY	10019
HYND, NOEL	WRITER	555 W 57TH ST #1230	NEW YORK, NY	10019
HYNES, ELIZABETH	SOPRANO	CAMI, 165 W 57TH ST	NEW YORK, NY	10019
HYNES, KEVIN	WRITER	8955 BEVERLY BLVD	LOS ANGELES, CA	90048
HYNNINEN, JORMA	BARITONE	CAMI, 165 W 57TH ST	NEW YORK, NY	10019
HYSER, JOYCE	ACTRESS	151 S EL CAMINO DR	BEVERLY HILLS, CA	90212
HYSLOP, AL	TV EXECUTIVE	CHILDREN'S TV WORKSHOP		
		1 LINCOLN PLAZA	NEW YORK, NY	10023

Name	Occupation	Address	City	Zip
I-TAL	ROCK & ROLL GROUP	POST OFFICE BOX 8125	ANN ARBOR, MI	48107
IACANGELO, PETER	ACTOR	247 S BEVERLY DR #102	BEVERLY HILLS, CA	90210
IACOCCA, LEE	AUTO EXEC-AUTHOR	571 EDGEMERE CT	BLOOMFIELD HILLS, MI	48013
IACOME, JEREMY KANE	WRITER	POST OFFICE BOX 5617	BEVERLY HILLS, CA	90210
		ROCKEFELLER CENTER	NEW YORK, NY	10020
IACONO, JOHN	SPORTS PHOTOGRAPHER	SPORTS ILLUSTRATED MAGAZINE		
		TIME & LIFE BUILDING		
IANNUCCI, SALVATORE J	TV EXECUTIVE	1901 AVE OF THE STARS #666	LOS ANGELES, CA	90067
IBARRAS, THE FLYING	AERIAL ACT	HALL, 138 FROG HOLLOW RD	CHURCHVILLE, PA	18966
IBBETSON, ARTHUR	CINEMATOGRAPHER	TANGLEWOOD, CHALFONT LN		
		CHORLEY WOOD	HERTS	ENGLAND
ICHASO, LEON	WRITER	555 W 57TH ST #1230	NEW YORK, NY	10019
ICHIHARA, TARO	TENOR	CAMI, 165 W 57TH ST	NEW YORK, NY	10019
ICHNIOWSKI, THOMAS	NEWS CORRESPONDENT	10005 THORNWOOD RD	KENSINGTON, MD	20895
ICKO, MARSHA	FILM DIRECTOR	FILM TREE, 8554 MELROSE AVE	LOS ANGELES, CA	90069
ICON	ROCK & ROLL GROUP	MORTICELLI, 3300 MONROE AVE	ROCHESTER, NY	14618
ICTUS	JAZZ BAND	FROTHINGHAM, 40 GROVE ST	WESSESLEY, MA	02181
IDELS, ROBERT B	DIRECTOR-PRODUCER	4301 SUNNYSLOPE AVE	SHERMAN OAKS, CA	91423
IDELSON, WILLIAM	WRITER-PRODUCER	710 BROOKTREE RD	PACIFIC PALISADES, CA	90272
IDEN, MINDI	ACTRESS	3800 BARHAM BLVD #303	LOS ANGELES, CA	90068
IDLE, ERIC	ACTOR-DIRECTOR	20 FITZROY SQ	LONDON W1P 6BB	ENGLAND
IDLE EYES	ROCK & ROLL GROUP	41 BRITAIN ST #200	TORONTO, ONT	CANADA
IDLE TEARS	ROCK & ROLL GROUP	MCA RECORDS COMPANY		
		70 UNIVERSAL CITY PLAZA	UNIVERSAL CITY, CA	91608
IDOL, BILLY	SINGER-SONGWRITER	645 MADISON AVE #35-A	NEW YORK, NY	10022
IEMOLA, EUGENE	FILM DIRECTOR	1870 W 10TH ST	BROOKLYN, NY	11223
IGER, K S	WRITER	555 W 57TH ST #1230	NEW YORK, NY	10019
IGER, ROBERT	TV DIRECTOR	ABC TELEVISION NETWORK		
		1330 AVE OF THE AMERICAS	NEW YORK, NY	10019
IGLAVER, BRUCE	MUSICIAN	POST OFFICE BOX 60234	CHICAGO, IL	60660
IGLEHART, L T, JR	TV WRITER	555 W 57TH ST #1230	NEW YORK, NY	10019
IGLEHEART, WALKER	GUITARIST	4224 1/2 MC CONNELL BLVD	LOS ANGELES, CA	90066
IGLESIAS, JULIO	SINGER	4500 BISCAYNE BLVD #333	MIAMI, FL	10004

Name	Occupation	Address	City	Zip
IGLESIAS, LEE	DIRECTOR	471 AVE OF THE AMERICAS	NEW YORK, NY	10011
IGNATIEV, IGOR V	NEWS CORRESPONDENT	5653 DERBY CT #223	ALEXANDRIA, VA	22311
IGNATIUS, DAVID R	NEWS CORRESPONDENT	2310 "L" ST, NW	WASHINGTON, DC	20037
IKE, REVERAND	EVANGELIST	4140 BROADWAY	NEW YORK, NY	10004
ILAND, TOBY	ACTOR	101 S SWEETZER AVE #103	LOS ANGELES, CA	90048
ILEY, BARBARA	ACTRESS	211 S BEVERLY DR #201	BEVERLY HILLS, CA	90212
ILLES, ROBERT	TV WRITER-PRODUCER	3735 SCADLOCK LN	SHERMAN OAKS, CA	91403
ILLMAN, ARNOLD, MD	BODYBUILDER	4180 SUNRISE HWY	MASSAPEQUA, NY	11758
ILOTT, PAMELA	TV EXECUTIVE	CBS-TV, 524 W 57TH ST	NEW YORK, NY	10019
ILOTT, PAMELA	WRITER	555 W 57TH ST #1230	NEW YORK, NY	10019
ILOTT, TERRY	TV WRITER	6 GREAT CHAPEL ST	LONDON W1	ENGLAND
ILSON, BERNARD	WRITER	555 W 57TH ST #1230	NEW YORK, NY	10019
ILSON, SAUL	TV WRITER-PRODUCER	4522 LOUISE AVE	ENCINO, CA	91316
IMAGES IN VOGUE	ROCK & ROLL GROUP	41 BRITAIN ST #200	TORONTO, ONT	CANADA
IMAGINATION	ROCK & ROLL GROUP	1 LINCOLN RD BUILDING #204	MIAMI BEACH, FL	33139
IMAI, NOBUKO	VIOLIST	CAMI, 165 W 57TH ST	NEW YORK, NY	10019
IMBODEN, OTIS	PHOTOGRAPHER	NGS, 17TH & "M" ST, NW	WASHINGTON, DC	20036
IMHOFF, GARY	ACTOR	1430 N MARTEL AVE #401	HOLLYWOOD, CA	90046
IMI, TONY	CINEMATOGRAPHER	48 CHESTNUT AVE, ESHER	SURREY	ENGLAND
IMMEDIATO, MICKEY	ACTOR	4731 LAUREL CANYON BLVD #5	NORTH HOLLYWOOD, CA	91607
IMMEL, JERROLD	COMPOSER-CONDUCTOR	13532 CONTOUR DR	SHERMAN OAKS, CA	91423
IMMEN, NORBERT G	NEWS CORRESPONDENT	3003 VAN NESS ST, NW	WASHINGTON, DC	20008
IMMERMAN, WILLIAM J	FILM EXECUTIVE	16524 PARK LN CIR	LOS ANGELES, CA	90049
IMPALA'S, THE	ROCK & ROLL GROUP	MARS, 168 ORCHID DR	PEARL RIVER, NY	10965
IMPASTATO, DAVID	DIRECTOR	325 S GRAND AVE	PASADENA, CA	91105
IMPERIALS, THE	VOCAL GROUP	POST OFFICE BOX 17272	MEMPHIS, TN	38187
IMPRESSIONS, THE	VOCAL GROUP	50 MUSIC SQUARE W #804	NASHVILLE, TN	37203
IMPULSE	ROCK & ROLL GROUP	POST OFFICE BOX 448	RADFORD, VA	24141
IMUS, DONALD	RADIO PERSONALITY	555 W 57TH ST #1230	NEW YORK, NY	10019
IN PURSUIT	ROCK & ROLL TRIO	POST OFFICE BOX 121347	NASHVILLE, TN	37212
INBAL, ELIAHU	CONDUCTOR	SHAW CONCERTS, 1995 BROADWAY	NEW YORK, NY	10023
INCH, KEVIN	TV DIRECTOR-PRODUCER	1559 PALISADES DR	PACIFIC PALISADES, CA	90272
INCREDIBLE HULK, THE	WRESTLER	SEE - HOGAN, HULK		
INCROCCI, AGENORE	WRITER	8955 BEVERLY BLVD	LOS ANGELES, CA	90048
INDELLI, JOSEPH D	TV EXECUTIVE	COLUMBIA PICTURES TV		
		COLUMBIA PLAZA	BURBANK, CA	91505
INDERFURTH, RICK	NEWS CORRESPONDENT	ABC-TV, NEWS DEPARTMENT		
		1717 DE SALES ST, NW	WASHINGTON, DC	20036
INDICTOR, LLOYD	CONDUCTOR	936 TUFTS AVE	BURBANK, CA	91504
INDIG, MARK	DIRECTOR	140 W 87TH ST #B	NEW YORK, NY	10024
INFUSINO, DIVINA	MUSIC CRITIC	POST OFFICE BOX 191	SAN DIEGO, CA	92112
INGALLS, DON	TV WRITER-PRODUCER	2049 CENTURY PARK E #1320	LOS ANGELES, CA	90067
INGALLS, JOYCE	ACTRESS	151 S EL CAMINO DR	BEVERLY HILLS, CA	90212
INGBER, MANDY	ACTRESS	9300 WILSHIRE BLVD #410	BEVERLY HILLS, CA	90212
INGELS, MARTY	ACTOR	701 N OAKHURST DR	BEVERLY HILLS, CA	90210
INGELS-CLARK, JEAN	ACTRESS	11514 VENTURA BLVD #A-170	STUDIO CITY, CA	91604
INGERSOLL, BRUCE	NEWS CORRESPONDENT	5467 NEVADA AVE, NW	WASHINGTON, DC	20015
INGERSOLL, JAMES	ACTOR	12509 MILBANK ST	STUDIO CITY, CA	91604
INGERSOLL, MARY	ACTRESS	8721 SUNSET BLVD #200	LOS ANGELES, CA	90069
INGLE, JAMES BARRY	GUITARIST	374 BLACKMAN RD	NASHVILLE, TN	37211
INGLE, JOHN	ACTOR	9200 SUNSET BLVD #909	LOS ANGELES, CA	90069
INGLE, WILLIAM	TENOR	61 W 62ND ST #6-F	NEW YORK, NY	10023
INGLES, EDWARD H	WRITER	555 W 57TH ST #1230	NEW YORK, NY	10019
INGMAN, NICK	COMPOSER-ARRANGER	37-A ALBERT SQ	LONDON SW8	ENGLAND
INGRAFFIA, JOSEPH	DIRECTOR	13411 CONTOUR DR	SHERMAN OAKS, CA	91423
INGRAM, JAMES	SINGER	867 MUIRFIELD RD	LOS ANGELES, CA	90005
INGRAM, JAY	ACTOR	6736 LAUREL CANYON BLVD #306	NORTH HOLLYWOOD, CA	91606
INGRAM, KENNETH	BANJOIST	601 S 12TH ST	NASHVILLE, TN	37206
INGRAMS, JONATHAN	FILM WRITER-DIRECTOR	STANMORE LODGE, HERONSGATE	HERTS WD3 5DN	ENGLAND
INK SPOTS, THE	VOCAL GROUP	1385 YORK AVE #15-H	NEW YORK, NY	10021
INMAN, JIM	TV WRITER	5878 GRACIOSA DR	LOS ANGELES, CA	90068
INMAN, JOHN	ACTOR	W & J THEATRICAL ENTS		
		51-A OAKWOOD RD	LONDON NW11 6RJ	ENGLAND
INMAN, ROGER	TV DIRECTOR	30729 LAKEFRONT DR	AGOURA, CA	91301
INNERST, CAROL	NEWS CORRESPONDENT	18 LAMP POST CT	POTOMAC, MD	20854
INNES, GEORGE	ACTOR	CONWAY, EAGLE HOUSE		
		109 JERMYN ST	LONDON SW1	ENGLAND
INNIS, DAVID	SINGER-GUITARIST	4201 KIRKLAND AVE	NASHVILLE, TN	37215
INNOCENT, HAROLD	ACTOR	ANGEL, 10 GREEK ST	LONDON W1	ENGLAND
INNOCENT MISCHIEF	ROCK & ROLL GROUP	POST OFFICE BOX 942	RAPID CITY, SD	57709
INNOCENTI, FRANK	SAXOPHONIST	3902 PLANTATION DR	HERMITAGE, TN	37076
INNOVATION	RHYTHM & BLUES GROUP	KINGSLAND, 108 SHARON DR	WEST MONROE, LA	71291
INPALER	ROCK & ROLL GROUP	1131 E HAWTHORNE AVE	SAINT PAUL, MN	55106
INSANA, TINA	TV WRITER	8955 BEVERLY BLVD	LOS ANGELES, CA	90048
INSERRA, DONNA	NEWS CORRESPONDENT	5021 45TH ST, NW	WASHINGTON, DC	20016
INTELLIGENT MONSTER, THE	WRESTLER	SEE - BRODY, BRUISER		
INTERCHANGE	MUSICAL GROUP	CENTRAL, 7027 TWIN HILL	DALLAS, TX	75231
INVADER, THE	WRESTLER	SEE - MURDOCH, DICK		
INVISIBLE MAN'S BAND, THE	ROCK & ROLL GROUP	ISLAND RECORDS COMPANY		
		444 MADISON AVE	NEW YORK, NY	10022
INVISIBLECHAINS	ROCK & ROLL GROUP	POST OFFICE BOX 21	SAN PEDRO, CA	90733
INWOOD, STEVE	ACTOR	POST OFFICE BOX 5617	BEVERLY HILLS, CA	90210
INXS	ROCK & ROLL GROUP	8 HAYNES ST #1	NEUTRAL BAY NSW 2089	AUSTRALIA
IONESCO, EUGENE	PLAYWRIGHT	EDITIONS GALLIMARD		
		5 RUE SEBASTIAN-BOTTIN	PARIS 75007	FRANCE

Name	Occupation	Address	City	Zip/Country
IPALE, AHARON	ACTOR	HAMPER, 193 WARDOUR ST	LONDON W1	ENGLAND
IREK & CHUMBLEY	PIANO DUO	157 W 57TH ST #1100	NEW YORK, NY	10019
IRELAND, JILL	ACTRESS	BRONSON, 121 UDINE WY	LOS ANGELES, CA	90077
IRELAND, JOHN	ACTOR	2910 SYCAMORE CYN RD	SANTA BARBARA, CA	93108
IRIS, DONNIE	SINGER	ATI, 888 7TH AVE, 21ST FLOOR	NEW YORK, NY	10106
IRISH ROVERS, THE	VOCAL GROUP	FRONT ROW, 547 HOMER ST	VANCOUVER, BC	CANADA
IRON BUTTERFLY	ROCK & ROLL GROUP	POST OFFICE BOX 1658	FONTANA, CA	92335
IRON MAIDEN	ROCK & ROLL GROUP	RON SMALLWOOD, 22 DANBURY ST	LONDON	ENGLAND
IRON SHEIK, THE	WRESTLER	POST OFFICE BOX 3859	STAMFORD, CT	06905
IRONS, JEREMY	ACTOR	HUTTON, 200 FULHAM RD	LONDON SW10	ENGLAND
IRONSIDE, MICHAEL	ACTOR	10100 SANTA MONICA BLVD #1600	LOS ANGELES, CA	90067
IRVIN, JARRELL L	CONDUCTOR	3823 18TH ST #1	SAN FRANCISCO, CA	94114
IRVIN, JOHN	DIRECTOR	6 LOWER COMMON S	LONDON SW15	ENGLAND
IRVIN, MONTE	BASEBALL	104 SYRACUSE CIR	HOMOSASSA, FL	32646
IRVING, AMY	ACTRESS	10100 SANTA MONICA BLVD #1600	LOS ANGELES, CA	90067
IRVING, RICHARD	DIRECTOR-PRODUCER	492 S SPALDING DR	BEVERLY HILLS, CA	90212
IRVING, ROBERT	CONDUCTOR-PIANIST	160 W END AVE	NEW YORK, NY	10023
IRWIN, AL	WRITER	555 W 57TH ST #1230	NEW YORK, NY	10019
IRWIN, BEN	WRITER	8955 BEVERLY BLVD	LOS ANGELES, CA	90048
IRWIN, DONALD	NEWS CORRESPONDENT	3904 BLACKTHORN ST	CHEVY CHASE, MD	20815
IRWIN, DR BILL	WRESTLER	SEE - IRWIN, WILD BILL		
IRWIN, JAMES B	ASTRONAUT	POST OFFICE BOX 1387	COLORADO SPRINGS, CO	80901
IRWIN, WILD BILL	WRESTLER	UNIVERSAL WRESTLING FEDERATION		
		MID SOUTH SPORTS, INC		
		5001 SPRING VALLEY RD	DALLAS, TX	75244
IRWIN, WYNN	ACTOR	131 N HAMILTON DR #204	BEVERLY HILLS, CA	90211
ISAAC, BILL	BODYBUILDER	THE BIG ISLAND GYM		
		74-5605 ALAPA ST	KAILUA KONA, HI	96740
ISAAC, JEANETTE	NEWS REPORTER	TIME/TIME & LIFE BLDG		
		ROCKEFELLER CENTER	NEW YORK, NY	10020
ISAACS, ANTONY	TV DIRECTOR-PRODUCER	KENSINGTON HOUSE, RICHMOND WY	LONDON W14 OAX	ENGLAND
ISAACS, CAROL	TV EXECUTIVE	CBS-TV, 7800 BEVERLY BLVD	LOS ANGELES, CA	90036
ISAACS, CHARLES	TV WRITER	344 DALEHURST AVE	LOS ANGELES, CA	90024
ISAACS, DAVID	TV WRITER-PRODUCER	9046 SUNSET BLVD #202	LOS ANGELES, CA	90069
ISAACS, JEREMY	TV PRODUCER	60 CHARLOTTE ST	LONDON W1	ENGLAND
ISAACS, NAOMI	TV PRODUCER	17 CANNON PL	LONDON NW3	ENGLAND
ISAACS, PHIL	FILM EXECUTIVE	1742 S BENTLEY AVE	LOS ANGELES, CA	90025
ISAACS, STANLEY	WRITER	15301 VENTURA BLVD #345	SHERMAN OAKS, CA	91403
ISAACS, SUSAN	SCREENWRITER	555 W 57TH ST #1230	NEW YORK, NY	10019
ISAACSON, JASON F	NEWS CORRESPONDENT	506 INDEPENDENCE AVE, SE	WASHINGTON, DC	20003
ISAACSON, KIM	ACTRESS	CASSELL, 843 N SYCAMORE AVE	LOS ANGELES, CA	90038
ISAACSON, MICHAEL N	COMPOSER-CONDUCTOR	4841 ALONZO AVE	ENCINO, CA	91316
ISAACSON, WALTER	WRITER-EDITOR	TIME/TIME & LIFE BLDG		
		ROCKEFELLER CENTER	NEW YORK, NY	10020
ISACKSEN, PETER	ACTOR	LIGHT, 113 N ROBERTSON BLVD	LOS ANGELES, CA	90048
ISACSSON, PAUL	TV EXECUTIVE	CBS-TV, 51 W 52ND ST	NEW YORK, NY	10019
ISBELL, JAMES	DRUMMER	100 MOUNTAINWOOD DR	HENDERSONVILLE, TN	37075
ISBIN, SHARON	GUITARIST	CAMI, 165 W 57TH ST	NEW YORK, NY	10019
ISCOVE, ROBERT	DIRECTOR-CHOREO	8496 HOLLYWOOD BLVD	LOS ANGELES, CA	90069
ISELER, ELMER	CONDUCTOR	MARIEDL ANDERS ARTISTS MGMT		
		535 EL CAMINO DEL MAR ST	SAN FRANCISCO, CA	94121
ISELIN, JOHN JAY	TV EXECUTIVE	356 W 58TH ST	NEW YORK, NY	10019
ISENBERG, GERALD I	TV DIRECTOR-PRODUCER	2208 STRADELLA RD	LOS ANGELES, CA	90077
ISENBERG, ROBERT	ACTOR	4731 LAUREL CANYON BLVD #5	NORTH HOLLYWOOD, CA	91607
ISENBERG, ROBERT	TV WRITER	8955 BEVERLY BLVD	LOS ANGELES, CA	90048
ISERI, HIROFUMI	NEWS CORRESPONDENT	5507 BRITE DR	BETHESDA, MD	20817
ISHAM, CHRISTOPHER	WRITER	555 W 57TH ST #1230	NEW YORK, NY	10019
ISHAQ, SALIM	NEWS CORRESPONDENT	8328 N BROOK LN	BETHESDA, MD	20814
ISHIBASHI, HERBERT, MD	BODYBUILDER	29 SHIPMAN ST #104	HILO, HI	96720
ISHIDA, JAMES	ACTOR	871 N VAIL AVE	MONTEBELLO, CA	90640
ISHIKAWA, HIRONOBU	NEWS CORRESPONDENT	6150 FARVER RD	MC LEAN, VA	22101
ISHIMOTO, DALE	ACTOR	8721 SUNSET BLVD #200	LOS ANGELES, CA	90069
ISIKOFF, MICHAEL	NEWS CORRESPONDENT	2745 29TH ST, NW	WASHINGTON, DC	20008
ISLANDER HAKU	WRESTLER	SEE - TONGA, KING		
ISLANDERS, THE (HAKA & TAMA)	WRESTLING TAG TEAM	POST OFFICE BOX 3859	STAMFORD, CT	06905
ISLEY-JASPER-ISLEY	VOCAL TRIO	ICM, 40 W 57TH ST	NEW YORK, NY	10019
ISRAEL, CHARLES E	WRITER	5922 PENFIELD AVE	WOODLAND HILLS, CA	91367
ISRAEL, DAVID	TV WRITER	8955 BEVERLY BLVD	LOS ANGELES, CA	90048
ISRAEL, NEIL C	WRITER-PRODUCER	8511 BRIER DR	LOS ANGELES, CA	90046
ISREALSON, PETER	DIRECTOR	115 E 87TH ST	NEW YORK, NY	10028
ISTOMIN, EUGENE	PIANIST	225 W 71ST ST	NEW YORK, NY	10023
ITALIAN STALLION, THE	WRESTLER	NATIONAL WRESTLING ALLIANCE		
		JIM CROCKETT PROMOTIONS		
		421 BRIARBEND DR	CHARLOTTE, NC	28209
ITALS, THE	ROCK & ROLL GROUP	CONCERTED, 312 SALEM ST	MEDFORD, MA	02155
ITKIN, PAUL HENRY	ACTOR	948 1/2 N MARTEL LN	LOS ANGELES, CA	90046
ITO, DEE	WRITER	555 W 57TH ST #1230	NEW YORK, NY	10019
ITO, ROBERT	ACTOR	9200 SUNSET BLVD #909	LOS ANGELES, CA	90069
ITO, TADASHI	NEWS CORRESPONDENT	9401 HOLBROOK LN	POTOMAC, MD	20854
ITZKOWITZ, HOWARD	ACTOR-WRITER	1017 10TH ST #14	SANTA MONICA, CA	90403
IVAR, STAN	ACTOR	3800 BARHAM BLVD #303	LOS ANGELES, CA	90068
IVES, BURL	ACTOR-SINGER	1880 VALLEY RD	MONTECITO, CA	93108
IVES, KENNETH	TV DIRECTOR	16 QUEEN'S GARDENS	LONDON W2	ENGLAND

AMY IRVING

BURL IVES

ANNE JACKSON

KATE JACKSON

LAWRENCE H. JACOBS

RICHARD JAECKEL

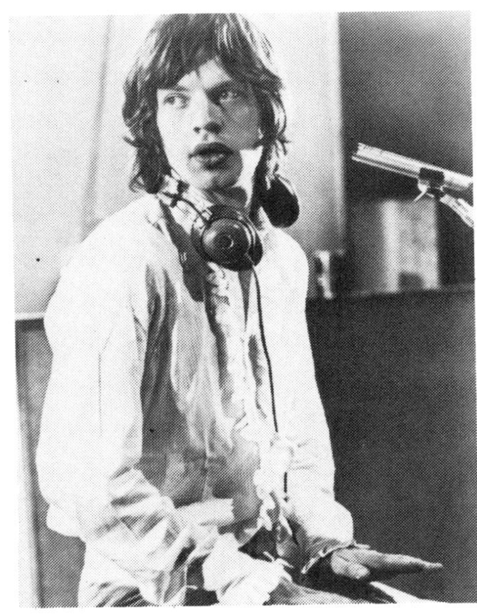
MICK JAGGER

AHMAD JAMAL

RICK JAMES

Name	Occupation	Address	City	Zip
IVEY, DANA	ACTRESS	211 S BEVERLY DR #201	BEVERLY HILLS, CA	90212
IVEY, JUDITH	ACTRESS	10100 SANTA MONICA BLVD #1600	LOS ANGELES, CA	90067
IVINGS, STEVE	COMEDIAN	4680 ELK LAKE DR #304	VICTORIA, BC	CANADA
IVINS, STEVEN D	NEWS CORRESPONDENT	3737 N NELSON ST	ARLINGTON, VA	22207
IVORY, JAMES	FILM DIRECTOR	400 E 52ND ST	NEW YORK, NY	10022
IVORY, JULIE & SNAPSHOT	ROCK & ROLL GROUP	COVER, 1425 N STAR RD	COLUMBUS, OH	43212
IVORY, KAREN K	WRITER	555 W 57TH ST #1230	NEW YORK, NY	10019
IWAKI, HIROYUKI	CONDUCTOR	SHAW CONCERTS, 1995 BROADWAY	NEW YORK, NY	10023
IWAMASTU, MAKO	ACTOR	SEE - MAKO		
IWASAKI, SETSUKO	PIANIST	CAMI, 165 W 57TH ST	NEW YORK, NY	10019
IZAY, VICTOR	ACTOR	216 N PARISH PL	BURBANK, CA	91506
IZUI, RICHARD	PHOTOGRAPHER	MODELS & PROMOTIONS AGENCY		
		8560 SUNSET BLVD, 10TH FLOOR	LOS ANGELES, CA	90069
IZZARD, BRYAN	TV DIRECTOR-PRODUCER	ROGER HANCOCK MANAGEMENT		
		8 WATERLOO PL, PALL MALL	LONDON SW1Y 4AW	ENGLAND

Name	Occupation	Address	City	Zip
J T & THE T-BIRDS	ROCK & ROLL GROUP	LCS, 1627 16TH AVE S	NASHVILLE, TN	37212
J Y D	WRESTLER	SEE - JUNKYARD DOG, THE		
JABLONSKI, DONNA M	NEWS CORRESPONDENT	1120 VERMONT AVE, NW	WASHINGTON, DC	20005
JACK, BILL	WRESTLER	SEE - HAYNES, BILLY JACK		
JACK, MAX	SCREENWRITER	8955 BEVERLY BLVD	LOS ANGELES, CA	90048
JACK, OUT BACK	WRESTLER	SEE - OUT BACK JACK		
JACK, WOLFMAN	RADIO-TV PERSONALITY	6310 SAN VICENTE BLVD #407	LOS ANGELES, CA	90048
JACKER, CORINNE	WRITER	555 W 57TH ST #1230	NEW YORK, NY	10019
JACKLIN, JUDITH	WRITER	555 W 57TH ST #1230	NEW YORK, NY	10019
JACKMAN, FRANCIS P	NEWS CORRESPONDENT	311 MC DONOUGH RD	ANNAPOLIS, MD	21401
JACKMAN, FRED H	TV DIRECTOR	16730 OCTAVIA PL	ENCINO, CA	91436
JACKMAN, LAWRENCE E	TV DIRECTOR	312 W 23RD ST #3-H	NEW YORK, NY	10011
JACKMAN, MICHELE MATIS	TV DIRECTOR	736 N SYCAMORE AVE	LOS ANGELES, CA	90038
JACKMAN, TOM	ACTOR	625 N SYCAMORE AVE #117	LOS ANGELES, CA	90036
JACKS, ROBERT L	FILM WRITER-PRODUCER	18810 TOPANGA BEACH DR	MALIBU, CA	90265
JACKSON, ANNE	ACTRESS	90 RIVERSIDE DR	NEW YORK, NY	10024
JACKSON, BARRY	ACTOR	KEEPERS COTTAGE, WOOD LN		
		BUTLEIGH, GLASTONBURY	SOMERSET	ENGLAND
JACKSON, BETTY	FASHION DESIGNER	33-B TOTTENHAM ST	LONDON W1	ENGLAND
JACKSON, BEVERLY A	TV DIRECTOR	5425 SPRING ST	PHILADELPHIA, PA	19139
JACKSON, BILLY	WRESTLER	SEE - HAYNES, BILLY JACK		
JACKSON, BRAD	ACTOR	1830 N CHEROKEE AVE #507	HOLLYWOOD, CA	90028
JACKSON, BROOKS	NEWS CORRESPONDENT	2812 ADAMS MILL RD, NW	WASHINGTON, DC	20009
JACKSON, CHRISTOPHER	ACTOR	1511 GRAMERCY PL	LOS ANGELES, CA	90019
JACKSON, DAVID S	WRITER	ROBERTS CO, 427 N CANON DR	BEVERLY HILLS, CA	90210
JACKSON, DION	ACTOR	2736 W VIEW ST	LOS ANGELES, CA	90016
JACKSON, EDGAR E, JR	WRITER	555 W 57TH ST #1230	NEW YORK, NY	10019
JACKSON, ELMA V	ACTRESS	4526 DON MIGUEL DR	LOS ANGELES, CA	90008
JACKSON, FELIX	WRITER-PRODUCER	4149 MURIETTA AVE	SHERMAN OAKS, CA	91423
JACKSON, FREDDIE	SINGER-SONGWRITER	HUSH PRODS, 231 W 58TH ST	NEW YORK, NY	10019
JACKSON, GERALD	NEWS CORRESPONDENT	NBC-TV, NEWS DEPARTMENT		
		4001 NEBRASKA AVE, NW	WASHINGTON, DC	20016
JACKSON, GLENDA	ACTRESS	51 HARVEY RD, BLACK	LONDON SE3	ENGLAND
JACKSON, GORDON	ACTOR	9 CHISWICK TERR	BRIGHTON	ENGLAND
JACKSON, GREG	NEWS CORRESPONDENT	ABC NEWS, 7 W 66TH ST	NEW YORK, NY	10023
JACKSON, HAROLD	NEWS CORRESPONDENT	4812 DE RUSSEY PARKWAY	CHEVY CHASE, MD	20815
JACKSON, ISIAH	CONDUCTOR	59 E 54TH ST #81	NEW YORK, NY	10022
JACKSON, J J	VIDEO JOCK	POST OFFICE BOX 1370	NEW YORK, NY	10101
JACKSON, JACK	GUITARIST	2870 SUGARTREE RD	NASHVILLE, TN	37215
JACKSON, JAMES W	DIRECTOR-PRODUCER	223 E 61ST ST	NEW YORK, NY	10021
JACKSON, JAMIE SMITH	ACTRESS	941 FERNWOOD DR	TOPANGA, CA	90290
JACKSON, JANET	ACTRESS-SINGER	4641 HAYVENHURST AVE	ENCINO, CA	91436
JACKSON, JERMAINE	SINGER-COMPOSER	21 OAKMONT DR	LOS ANGELES, CA	90049
JACKSON, JERRY L	WRITER	8955 BEVERLY BLVD	LOS ANGELES, CA	90048
JACKSON, JESSE L	EVANGELIST	SEE - JACKSON, REV JESSE L		
JACKSON, JOE	SINGER-SONGWRITER	BASEMENT MUSIC, 6 PEMBRIDGE RD		
		TRINITY HOUSE, 2ND FLOOR	LONDON W11	ENGLAND
JACKSON, JOE L	GUITARIST	ROUTE #1, BOX 473	HELENA, AL	35080
JACKSON, JOHN M	ACTOR	247 S BEVERLY DR #102	BEVERLY HILLS, CA	90210
JACKSON, JOHN S	GUITARIST	6113 CHICKERING CT	NASHVILLE, TN	37215
JACKSON, JOHN W	GUITARIST	2501 LINCOYA DR #B	NASHVILLE, TN	37214
JACKSON, JUMP & HIS BLUES BAND	BLUES GROUP	R & B, 8959 S OGLESBY AVE	CHICAGO, IL	60617
JACKSON, KARLA	ACTRESS-MODEL	6250 EL CAJON BLVD #103-820	SAN DIEGO, CA	92115
JACKSON, KATE	ACTRESS	2620 BENEDICT CANYON DR	BEVERLY HILLS, CA	90210
JACKSON, KEITH	SPORTSCASTER	ABC SPORTS, 1330 AVE OF AMERICAS	NEW YORK, NY	10019
JACKSON, KENNETH, GROUP	JAZZ GROUP	POST OFFICE BOX 12752	MEMPHIS, TN	38182
JACKSON, LATOYA	SINGER	4641 HAVENHURST AVE	ENCINO, CA	91436
JACKSON, LEO	GUITARIST	ROUTE #1, BOX 263	GOODLETTSVILLE, TN	37072
JACKSON, LEONARD	ACTOR	60 E 42ND ST	NEW YORK, NY	10165
JACKSON, LEONARD	ACTOR	4 PARK AVE	NEW YORK, NY	10016
JACKSON, LEWIS	WRITER	555 W 57TH ST #1230	NEW YORK, NY	10019

Name	Occupation	Address	City	Zip
JACKSON, LLOYD SKIP	GUITARIST	122 CEDAR CREST DR	HENDERSONVILLE, TN	37075
JACKSON, LOYOTA	SINGER	4641 HAYVENHURST AVE	ENCINO, CA	91436
JACKSON, MAGGIE	ACTRESS	300 W 49TH ST	NEW YORK, NY	10019
JACKSON, MARY	ACTRESS	11726 SAN VICENTE BLVD #300	LOS ANGELES, CA	90049
JACKSON, MICHAEL	RADIO PERSONALITY	KABC TALK RADIO 79 AM		
		3321 S LA CIENEGA BLVD	LOS ANGELES, CA	90016
JACKSON, MICHAEL	SINGER-SONGWRITER	4641 HAYVENHURST AVE	ENCINO, CA	91436
JACKSON, MICHAEL GREGORY	SINGER	ARISTA RECORDS, 6 W 57TH ST	NEW YORK, NY	10019
JACKSON, MIKE	WRESTLER	NATIONAL WRESTLING ALLIANCE		
		JIM CROCKETT PROMOTIONS		
		421 BRIARBEND DR	CHARLOTTE, NC	28209
JACKSON, MILLIE	SINGER	KEISHVAL ENTS, 1650 BROADWAY	NEW YORK, NY	10019
JACKSON, MYKE	MUSICIAN	POST OFFICE BOX 110201	NASHVILLE, TN	37211
JACKSON, PATRICK E	GUITARIST	206 KERR AVE	MURFREESBORO, TN	37130
JACKSON, PAUL M, JR	ACTOR	POST OFFICE BOX 90044	GARDENA, CA	90249
JACKSON, PHILIP	ACTOR	PLANT & FROGGATT, LTD		
		JULIAN HOUSE		
		4 WINDMILL ST	LONDON W1	ENGLAND
JACKSON, REBBIE	SINGER	240 LOMBARD ST	THOUSAND OAKS, CA	91360
JACKSON, REGGIE	BASEBALL-SPORTSCASTER	22 YANKEE HILL	OAKLAND, CA	94616
JACKSON, REV JESSE L	EVANGELIST	930 E 50TH ST	CHICAGO, IL	60615
JACKSON, RICHARD	BARITONE	MARIEDL ANDERS ARTISTS MGMT		
		535 EL CAMINO DEL MAR ST	SAN FRANCISCO, CA	94121
JACKSON, RICHARD	THEATER PRODUCER	59 KNIGHTSBRIDGE	LONDON SW1X 7RA	ENGLAND
JACKSON, ROBERT	NEWS CORRESPONDENT	9900 GEORGIA AVE	SILVER SPRING, MD	20902
JACKSON, ROGER	SPORTS WRITER	SPORTS ILLUSTRATED MAGAZINE		
		TIME & LIFE BUILDING		
		ROCKEFELLER CENTER	NEW YORK, NY	10020
JACKSON, SAMMY	ACTOR-RADIO PERS	SEE - JACKSON, SAMMY M		
JACKSON, SAMMY M	ACTOR-RADIO PERS	KMPC RADIO, 5858 SUNSET BLVD	HOLLYWOOD, CA	90028
JACKSON, SHERRY	ACTRESS	4933 ENCINO AVE	ENCINO, CA	91316
JACKSON, SHOT	GUITARIST	3030 HOBSON PIKE	ANTIOCH, TN	37013
JACKSON, STONEWALL, JR	SINGER-SONGWRITER	6007 CLOVERLAND DR	BRENTWOOD, TN	37027
JACKSON, STONEWALL, SR	SINGER-SONGWRITER	6007 CLOVERLAND DR	BRENTWOOD, TN	37027
JACKSON, STONEY	ACTOR	3151 W CAHUENGA BLVD #310	LOS ANGELES, CA	90068
JACKSON, TITO	SINGER	16725 ADDISON ST	ENCINO, CA	91436
JACKSON, TRAVIS	BASEBALL	101 S OLIVE ST	WALDO, AR	71770
JACKSON, VICTORIA	ACTRESS	151 S EL CAMINO DR	BEVERLY HILLS, CA	90212
JACKSON, WADE	GUITARIST	620 TULIP CIR	GALLATIN, TN	37066
JACKSON, WANDA	SINGER	POST OFFICE BOX 7007	OKLAHOMA CITY, OK	73153
JACKSON, WILFRED P	CONDUCTOR	POST OFFICE BOX 73234	LOS ANGELES, CA	90003
JACKSON SOUTHERNAIRES, THE	GOSPEL GROUP	POST OFFICE BOX 9287	JACKSON, MS	39206
JACKSONS, THE	VOCAL GROUP	4641 HAVENHURST AVE	ENCINO, CA	91436
JACO, CHARLES D	NEWS CORRESPONDENT	3407 VALEWOOD DR	OAKTON, VA	22124
JACOB, NORMAN	WRITER	1412 BUTLER AVE #16	LOS ANGELES, CA	90025
JACOBI, DEREK	ACTOR	ICM, 388-396 OXFORD ST	LONDON W1	ENGLAND
JACOBI, LOU	ACTOR	240 CENTRAL PARK S	NEW YORK, NY	10019
JACOBIUS, JERRY	TV WRITER	8955 BEVERLY BLVD	LOS ANGELES, CA	90048
JACOBS, AVIVA	TV DIRECTOR	4202 RAINTREE CIR	CULVER CITY, CA	90230
JACOBS, BARRY A	TV WRITER	8955 BEVERLY BLVD	LOS ANGELES, CA	90048
JACOBS, BERNARD	THEATER PRODUCER	225 W 44TH ST	NEW YORK, NY	10036
JACOBS, CARL	ACTOR	326 E 69TH ST	NEW YORK, NY	10021
JACOBS, CHUCK	GUITARIST	410 SUNSET DR	MOUNT JULIET, TN	37122
JACOBS, DANIEL B	WRITER	555 W 57TH ST #1230	NEW YORK, NY	10019
JACOBS, DAVID	ACTOR-TV HOST	LEWIS-JOELLE, LTD		
		108 FROBISHER HOUSE		
		DOLPHIN SQ	LONDON SW1	ENGLAND
JACOBS, DAVID	TV DIRECTOR-PRODUCER	LORIMAR-TELEPICTURES		
		3970 OVERLAND AVE	CULVER CITY, CA	90230
JACOBS, DAVID MICHAEL	TV WRITER	PLESHETTE, 2700 N BEACHWOOD DR	HOLLYWOOD, CA	90028
JACOBS, DEBBIE	SINGER	1680 N VINE ST #214	HOLLYWOOD, CA	90028
JACOBS, DOLLY	AERIALIST	POST OFFICE BOX 87	WEST LEBANON, NY	12195
JACOBS, EMMA	ACTRESS	CONWAY, EAGLE HOUSE		
		109 JERMYN ST	LONDON SW1	ENGLAND
JACOBS, FRANK	WRITER	555 W 57TH ST #1230	NEW YORK, NY	10019
JACOBS, FRANK	WRITER	MAD MAGAZINE, INC		
		485 MADISON AVE	NEW YORK, NY	10022
JACOBS, GARY	TV WRITER	211 S FULLER AVE #8	LOS ANGELES, CA	90036
JACOBS, HARVEY	WRITER	555 W 57TH ST #1230	NEW YORK, NY	10019
JACOBS, JACK	TV WRITER	8955 BEVERLY BLVD	LOS ANGELES, CA	90048
JACOBS, JAMES F	DIRECTOR-PRODUCER	18625 CASSANDRA ST	TARZANA, CA	91356
JACOBS, JESSE	ACTOR	6515 SUNSET BLVD #300-A	LOS ANGELES, CA	90028
JACOBS, JIM	PLAYWRIGHT	ICM, 40 W 57TH ST	NEW YORK, NY	10019
JACOBS, JOHN	TV DIRECTOR-PRODUCER	78 CHAPEL FIELDS		
		CHARTERHOUSE RD, GODALMING	SURREY	ENGLAND
JACOBS, LAWRENCE-HILTON	ACTOR-SINGER	2110 MOUNT OLYMPUS DR	LOS ANGELES, CA	90046
JACOBS, LEONARD S	DIRECTOR	3 BLUE FERN LN	RANDOLPH, NJ	07869
JACOBS, MARC N	ACTOR	4211 GLENALBYN DR #A	LOS ANGELES, CA	90065
JACOBS, MARILYN	TV DIRECTOR	250 E 39TH ST	NEW YORK, NY	10016
JACOBS, MARTHA	CELLIST	BOX 390-H, LAKEWOOD DR	FAIRVIEW, TN	37062
JACOBS, MARTIN P	COMPOSER	6207 LUBAO AVE	WOODLAND HILLS, CA	91364
JACOBS, MICHAEL	PRODUCER	MCA/UNIVERSAL STUDIOS, INC		
		100 UNIVERSAL CITY PLAZA #507	UNIVERSAL CITY, CA	91608
JACOBS, MICHAEL	TV WRITER	555 W 57TH ST #1230	NEW YORK, NY	10019
JACOBS, RACHEL	ACTRESS	3575 W CAHUENGA BLVD #320	LOS ANGELES, CA	90068

Name	Occupation	Address	City	Zip
JACOBS, RICK	CASTING DIRECTOR	CBS-TV, 7800 BEVERLY BLVD	LOS ANGELES, CA	90036
JACOBS, RICK	TV EXECUTIVE	CBS-TV, 6121 SUNSET BLVD	LOS ANGELES, CA	90028
JACOBS, ROBERT S	WRITER	8955 BEVERLY BLVD	LOS ANGELES, CA	90048
JACOBS, RONALD N	DIRECTOR-PRODUCER	11920 LAUREL HILLS RD	STUDIO CITY, CA	91604
JACOBS, RONALD S	DIRECTOR	JAGUAR PRODUCTIONS, INC		
		285 E 34TH ST	NEW YORK, NY	10010
JACOBS, S RAY	BASSO-BARITONE	CONE, 221 W 57TH ST	NEW YORK, NY	10019
JACOBS, SEAMAN B	TV WRITER	1702 CLEAR VIEW DR	BEVERLY HILLS, CA	90210
JACOBS, WILL	WRITER	THE NATIONAL LAMPOON		
		635 MADISON AVE	NEW YORK, NY	10022
JACOBSEN, EDMUND	VIOLINIST	THE METROPOLITAN OPERA		
		LINCOLN CENTER	NEW YORK, NY	10023
JACOBSEN, RANI	NEWS PRODUCER	ENTERTAINMENT TONIGHT		
		PARAMOUNT TELEVISION		
		5555 MELROSE AVE	LOS ANGELES, CA	90038
JACOBSEN, SALLY A	NEWS CORRESPONDENT	1735 PARK RD, NW	WASHINGTON, DC	20006
JACOBSON, ANDREW	NEWS CORRESPONDENT	1224 BANK ST, NW	WASHINGTON, DC	20007
JACOBSON, ARTHUR	FILM DIRECTOR	6050 CANTERBURY DR, FOX HILLS	CULVER CITY, CA	90230
JACOBSON, DANNY	TV WRITER	8955 BEVERLY BLVD	LOS ANGELES, CA	90048
JACOBSON, DAVID	DIRECTOR	149 DUDLEY RD	WILTON, CT	06897
JACOBSON, DAVID	CARTOONIST	POST OFFICE BOX 4203	NEW YORK, NY	10017
JACOBSON, GELA	ACTRESS	445 N BEDFORD DR #PH	BEVERLY HILLS, CA	90210
JACOBSON, HARVEY	MUSICIAN	POST OFFICE BOX 122	WALTHAM, MA	02154
JACOBSON, JEFFREY I	PHOTOGRAPHER	42 WESTERVELT AVE	STATEN ISLAND, NY	10301
JACOBSON, JILL	ACTRESS	KOHNER, 9169 SUNSET BLVD	LOS ANGELES, CA	90069
JACOBSON, JOHN A	TV DIRECTOR	3352 LOS OLIVOS LN	LA CRESCENTA, CA	91214
JACOBSON, LAURIE	ACTRESS	1905 1/2 N VAN NESS AVE	HOLLYWOOD, CA	90068
JACOBSON, ROBERT L	NEWS CORRESPONDENT	5316 WAPAKONETA RD	BETHESDA, MD	20816
JACOBSON, RUTH	SOPRANO	CONE, 221 W 57TH ST	NEW YORK, NY	10019
JACOBSON, STANLEY	TV WRITER-DIRECTOR	73 CRISWELL CRESCENT	WILLOW, ONT M2N 6G2	CANADA
JACOBSON, WILLIAM	WRITER	8955 BEVERLY BLVD	LOS ANGELES, CA	90048
JACOBSON, WILLIAM JAN	COMPOSER	POST OFFICE BOX 1504	OJAI, CA	93023
JACOBY, BILLY	ACTOR	KELMAN, 7813 SUNSET BLVD	LOS ANGELES, CA	90046
JACOBY, COLEMAN	TV WRITER	555 W 57TH ST #1230	NEW YORK, NY	10019
JACOBY, EDMOND M	NEWS CORRESPONDENT	3209 PLANTATION PARKWAY	FAIRFAX, VA	22030
JACOBY, FRANK D	DIRECTOR	8 W BRANCH RD	WESTPORT, CT	06880
JACOBY, GARY	TENOR	GREAT LAKES PERFORMING		
		310 E WASHINGTON ST	ANN ARBOR, MI	48104
JACOBY, GARY	WRITER	555 W 57TH ST #1230	NEW YORK, NY	10019
JACOBY, INGRID	PIANIST	ANGLO-SWISS ARTISTS MGMT		
		16 MUSWELL HILL RD, HIGHGATE	LONDON N6 5UG	ENGLAND
JACOBY, JOSEPH	TV WRITER	2049 CENTURY PARK E #13	LOS ANGELES, CA	90067
JACOBY, LAURA	ACTRESS	KELMAN, 7813 SUNSET BLVD	LOS ANGELES, CA	90046
JACOBY, SCOTT	ACTOR	12725 VENTURA BLVD #E	STUDIO CITY, CA	91604
JACQUET, JEAN	MUSICIAN	112-44 179TH ST	SAINT ALBANS, NY	11412
JAECK, SCOTT	ACTOR	11726 SAN VICENTE BLVD #300	LOS ANGELES, CA	90049
JAECKEL, RICHARD	ACTOR	POST OFFICE BOX 1818	SANTA MONICA, CA	90406
JAEGER, FREDERICK	ACTOR	6 ORLEANS RD, TWICKENHAM	MIDDLESEX	ENGLAND
JAFFE, ALFRED J	PUBLISHER	TV / RADIO AGE MAGAZINE		
		1270 AVE OF THE AMERICAS	NEW YORK, NY	10020
JAFFE, ANDREW M	NEWS CORRESPONDENT	1701 PENNSYLVANIA AVE #510	WASHINGTON, DC	20006
JAFFE, ANITA L	WRITER	555 W 57TH ST #1230	NEW YORK, NY	10019
JAFFE, CLAUDIO	CELLIST	POST OFFICE BOX 27539	PHILADELPHIA, PA	19118
JAFFE, DIANA	ACTRESS	3324 DURAND DR	HOLLYWOOD, CA	90068
JAFFE, GARY M	NEWS CORRESPONDENT	330 INDEPENDENCE AVE, SW	WASHINGTON, DC	20547
JAFFE, HARRY	NEWS CORRESPONDENT	1612 19TH ST, NW	WASHINGTON, DC	20009
JAFFE, HENRY	TV DIRECTOR	SUNSET GOWER, 1438 N GOWER ST	HOLLYWOOD, CA	90028
JAFFE, HENRY	PRODUCER	1420 N BEACHWOOD DR	LOS ANGELES, CA	90028
JAFFE, HERB	FILM PRODUCER	LAIRD, 9336 W WASHINGTON BLVD	CULVER CITY, CA	90230
JAFFE, JAMES	WRITER	8955 BEVERLY BLVD	LOS ANGELES, CA	90048
JAFFE, JEWEL	WRITER	8955 BEVERLY BLVD	LOS ANGELES, CA	90048
JAFFE, LEO	FILM EXECUTIVE	425 E 58TH ST	NEW YORK, NY	10022
JAFFE, MONTE	BASS	61 W 62ND ST #6-F	NEW YORK, NY	10023
JAFFE, ROBERT J	SCREENWRITER	8955 BEVERLY BLVD	LOS ANGELES, CA	90048
JAFFE, SETH	ACTOR	9200 SUNSET BLVD #1210	LOS ANGELES, CA	90069
JAFFE, STANLEY R	DIRECTOR-PRODUCER	JAFFE/LANSING, 660 MADISON AVE	NEW YORK, NY	10021
JAFFE, STEVE	DIRECTOR-PRODUCER	7302 MULHOLLAND DR	LOS ANGELES, CA	90046
JAFFE, STEVEN CHARLES	WRI-DIR-PROD	1037 16TH ST #6	SANTA MONICA, CA	90403
JAFFE, TALIESIN	ACTOR	1450 BELFAST DR	LOS ANGELES, CA	90069
JAFFEE, AL	CARTOONIST	MAD MAGAZINE, INC		
		485 MADISON AVE	NEW YORK, NY	10022
JAFFEY, HERBERT	WRITER	555 W 57TH ST #1230	NEW YORK, NY	10019
JAFFREY, SAEED	ACTOR	136 HICKS AVE, GREENFORD	MIDDLESEX	ENGLAND
JAGERSKOG, BENGT G	NEWS CORRESPONDENT	1905 MASON HILL DR	ALEXANDRIA, VA	22307
JAGGER, BIANCA	ACTRESS-MODEL	300 CENTRAL PARK W	NEW YORK, NY	10019
JAGGER, CHRIS	SINGER	13719 VENTURA BLVD #H	SHERMAN OAKS, CA	91423
JAGGER, DEAN	ACTOR	326 ADELAIDE DR	SANTA MONICA, CA	90406
JAGGER, MICK	SINGER-ACTOR-WRITER	2 MUNRO TERR	LONDON SW10	ENGLAND
JAGGERS, BOBBY	WRESTLER	NATIONAL WRESTLING ALLIANCE		
		JIM CROCKETT PROMOTIONS		
		421 BRIARBEND DR	CHARLOTTE, NC	28209
JAGLOM, HENRY D	WRITER-PRODUCER	8235 MONTEEL RD	LOS ANGELES, CA	90069
JAGLOM, MICHAEL	FILM DIRECTOR	8235 MONTEEL RD	LOS ANGELES, CA	90069
JAHAN, MARINE	ACTRESS	9220 SUNSET BLVD #625	LOS ANGELES, CA	90069
JAHN, NORMA JEAN	SINGER	10850 RIVERSIDE DR	NORTH HOLLYWOOD, CA	91602

JAHNS, KAREN MARIE	WRITER	43442 N 20TH ST W	LANCASTER, CA	93534
JAICKS, AGAR	TV DIRECTOR	KGO-TV, 277 GOLDEN GATE AVE	SAN FRANCISCO, CA	94102
JAID, ILDIKO	ACTRESS	3960 LAUREL CANYON BLVD	STUDIO CITY, CA	91604
JAK	SINGER	POST OFFICE BOX 691565	LOS ANGELES, CA	90069
JAKLIN, INGE	ACTRESS	1605 N CAHUENGA BLVD #202	LOS ANGELES, CA	90028
JAKOBY, DON	SCREENWRITER	8955 BEVERLY BLVD	LOS ANGELES, CA	90048
JALOMA, RAMIRO	TV DIRECTOR	POST OFFICE BOX 6679	GLENDALE, CA	91205
JAM, JIMMY	SONGWRITER-PRODUCER	SEE - HARRIS, JIMMY JAM		
JAM, THE	SOUL GROUP	POST OFFICE BOX 2105	DAYTON, OH	45401
JAMAALADEEN TACUMA	JAZZ GROUP	1560 BROADWAY #507	NEW YORK, NY	10036
JAMAICAN KID, THE	WRESTLER	CAPITOL INTERNATIONAL		
		11844 MARKET ST	NORTH LIMA, OH	44452
JAMES, ANTHONY	ACTOR	8721 SUNSET BLVD #202	LOS ANGELES, CA	90069
JAMES, BEAU	WRESTLER	SEE - GARVIN, GORGEOUS JIMMY		
JAMES, BILLY	GUITARIST	ROUTE #2, BOX 10	CROZET, VA	22932
JAMES, BOB	PIANIST	IMG ARTISTS, 22 E 71ST ST	NEW YORK, NY	10021
JAMES, BRION	ACTOR	3800 BARHAM BLVD #303	LOS ANGELES, CA	90068
JAMES, CHARITY	ACTRESS	205 S ARNAZ DR #4	BEVERLY HILLS, CA	90211
JAMES, CLARITY "CAROLYNE"	MEZZO-SOPRANO	CAMI, 165 W 57TH ST	NEW YORK, NY	10019
JAMES, CLIFTON	ACTOR	95 BUTTONWOOD DR	DIX HILLS, LI, NY	11726
JAMES, DAVID	CINEMATOGRAPHER	FIR TREE HOUSE, THE BROW		
		CHALFONT SAINT GILES	BUCKS	ENGLAND
JAMES, DON	COMPOSER	2106 MOUNT OLYMPUS DR	LOS ANGELES, CA	90046
JAMES, EDWARD	WRITER	8955 BEVERLY BLVD	LOS ANGELES, CA	90048
JAMES, EDWIN H	NEWS CORRESPONDENT	ROUTE #2	CALIFORNIA, MD	20619
JAMES, ELIZABETH L	WRITER	8955 BEVERLY BLVD	LOS ANGELES, CA	90048
JAMES, ERVAN	GUITARIST	925 ACKLEN AVE	NASHVILLE, TN	37203
JAMES, ETTA	SINGER	165 O'FARRELL ST #208	SAN FRANCISCO, CA	94102
JAMES, FRANCES W, JR	WRITER	555 W 57TH ST #1230	NEW YORK, NY	10019
JAMES, FRANCESCA	TV DIRECTOR	DGA, 110 W 57TH ST	NEW YORK, NY	10019
JAMES, FREDERICK	SCREENWRITER	8955 BEVERLY BLVD	LOS ANGELES, CA	90048
JAMES, GABRIELLE A	WRITER-PRODUCER	20654 BASSETT ST	CANOGA PARK, CA	91306
JAMES, GEORGE	SINGER	POST OFFICE BOX 5563	ROCKFORD, IL	61125
JAMES, GODFREY	ACTOR	THE SHACK, WESTERN RD		
		PEVENSEY BAY	EAST SUSSEX	ENGLAND
JAMES, ISAIAH, JR	DIRECTOR	215 E 24TH ST	NEW YORK, NY	10010
JAMES, J C	SINGER	SEE - WARNER, CHERYL K		
JAMES, JESSICA	SINGER	POST OFFICE BOX 110423	NASHVILLE, TN	37211
JAMES, JIMMY	GUITARIST	ROUTE #1, SLATERS CREEK RD	GOODLETTSVILLE, TN	37072
JAMES, JOHN	ACTOR	7310 MULHOLLAND DR	LOS ANGELES, CA	90046
JAMES, JOHN ELVIS	SINGER	38 MUSIC SQUARE E #216	NASHVILLE, TN	37203
JAMES, JONI	SINGER	1027 N ROXBURY DR	BEVERLY HILLS, CA	90210
JAMES, JOSHUA	ACTOR	11030 VENTURA BLVD #1-A	STUDIO CITY, CA	91604
JAMES, KEN	ACTOR	4731 LAUREL CANYON BLVD #5	NORTH HOLLYWOOD, CA	91607
JAMES, KING	SINGER	POST OFFICE BOX 11321		
		FLAGLER STATION	MIAMI, FL	33101
JAMES, KING	WRESTLER	SEE - VALIANT, JIMMY		
JAMES, LARRY	SINGER	WOOD, 2901 EPPERLY DR	DEL CITY, OK	73115
JAMES, LAURA	ACTRESS	5330 LANKERSHIM BLVD #210	NORTH HOLLYWOOD, CA	91601
JAMES, LEONE	ACTRESS	8666 HOLLYWOOD BLVD	LOS ANGELES, CA	90069
JAMES, LISA	ACTRESS	8956 APPIAN WY	LOS ANGELES, CA	90046
JAMES, LUTHER	TV WRITER-DIRECTOR	556 W AVE 46	LOS ANGELES, CA	90065
JAMES, PAUL	SINGER	41 BRITAIN ST #200	TORONTO, ONT	CANADA
JAMES, REGINA	SINGER	POST OFFICE BOX 11321		
		FLAGLER STATION	MIAMI, FL	33101
JAMES, RICHARD B	DIRECTOR	23870 MADISON ST	TORRANCE, CA	90505
JAMES, RICK	SINGER-SONGWRITER	MARY JANE PRODUCTIONS		
		104 CHAPIN PARKWAY	BUFFALO, NY	14209
JAMES, ROBERT	ACTOR	THE COTTAGE ON THE GREE	WHATFIELD, IPS IP7 6QS	ENGLAND
JAMES, SIDNEY	COMPOSER	3726 BRILLIANT DR	LOS ANGELES, CA	90065
JAMES, SONNY	SINGER-SONGWRITER	MC FADDEN & ASSOCIATES		
		818 18TH AVE S	NASHVILLE, TN	37203
JAMES, STEVE W	ACTOR	ICM, 8899 BEVERLY BLVD	LOS ANGELES, CA	90048
JAMES, TERRY T	COMPOSER-CONDUCTOR	1317 N SWEETZER AVE #8	LOS ANGELES, CA	90069
JAMES, TOMMY & THE SHONDELLS	ROCK & ROLL GROUP	STEPHAN FRANK MANAGEMENT		
		458 W 55TH ST	NEW YORK, NY	10019
JAMES, WILLIAM L	WRITER	8955 BEVERLY BLVD	LOS ANGELES, CA	90048
JAMES, WOODROW C	COMPOSER-CONDUCTOR	6501 KESTER AVE #4	VAN NUYS, CA	91411
JAMES-REESE, CYNDI	ACTRESS	1706 S CRESCENT HGTS BLVD	LOS ANGELES, CA	90035
JAMESON, ADAIR	ACTRESS	1461 2ND ST	SISNA, CA	93065
JAMESON, CONRAD	WRITER	555 W 57TH ST #1230	NEW YORK, NY	10019
JAMESON, JERRY	FILM WRITER-DIRECTOR	10436 KLING ST	NORTH HOLLYWOOD, CA	91602
JAMESON, JOY	TALENT AGENT	7 W EATON PLACE MEWS	LONDON SW1	ENGLAND
JAMESON, LOUISE	ACTRESS	CONWAY, EAGLE HOUSE		
		109 JERMYN ST	LONDON SW1	ENGLAND
JAMESON, PAULINE	ACTRESS	7 WARRINGTON GARDENS	LONDON W9	ENGLAND
JAMESON, REX	ACTOR-COMEDIAN	NEWLEY, 71 MORING RD	LONDON SW17	ENGLAND
JAMIESON, BOB	NEWS CORRESPONDENT	NBC-TV, NEWS DEPARTMENT		
		30 ROCKEFELLER PLAZA	NEW YORK, NY	10112
JAMIESON, EDWARD L	WRITER-EDITOR	TIME/TIME & LIFE BLDG		
		ROCKEFELLER CENTER	NEW YORK, NY	10020
JAMIESON & PAYKIN	CHAMBER DUO	260 W END AVE #7-A	NEW YORK, NY	10023
JAMIN, MILT	ACTOR	10930 1/2 CAMARILLO ST	NORTH HOLLYWOOD, CA	91602
JAMISON, MARSHALL	TV DIRECTOR	POST OFFICE BOX 83111	LINCOLN, NB	68501

Name	Occupation	Address	City	Zip/Country
JAMISON, MILO F, JR	COMPOSER	1231 TENNYSON ST	MANHATTAN BEACH, CA	90266
JAMMIE ANN	SINGER	POST OFFICE BOX 3525	YORK, PA	17402
JAMPEL, BARBARA	TV WRITER	830 N FORD ST	BURBANK, CA	91505
JAMPOL, CLAIRE	WRITER	5002 RAINBOWS END	CULVER CITY, CA	90230
JAMROG, JOSEPH	ACTOR	EISEN, 346 E 50TH ST	NEW YORK, NY	10022
JAN & DEAN	VOCAL DUO	WILLIAM L BERRY / W J B		
		6040 SUNSET BLVD	LOS ANGELES, CA	90028
JANA JAE	SINGER	4815 S HARVARD AVE #250	TULSA, OK	74135
JANAVER, RICHARD	WRITER	3920 WESLIN AVE	SHERMAN OAKS, CA	91423
JANCSO, MIKLOS	DIRECTOR	ROZSA FERENC-UTCA 71 #H	BUDAPEST VI	HUNGARY
JANES, ROBERT	TV WRITER	662 ELKINS RD	LOS ANGELES, CA	90049
JANET, STAN	NEWS CORRESPONDENT	19705 BODMER AVE	POOLESVILLE, MD	20837
JANEWAY, ELIOT	ECONOMIST	15 E 80TH ST	NEW YORK, NY	10021
JANI, ROBERT	THEATER PRODUCER	1260 AVE OF THE AMERICAS	NEW YORK, NY	10020
JANIS, BYRON	PIANIST	ICM, 40 W 57TH ST	NEW YORK, NY	10019
JANIS, CONRAD	ACTOR	300 N SWALL DR #251	BEVERLY HILLS, CA	90211
JANIS, NORMA	ACTRESS	16808 MARILLA ST	SEPULVEDA, CA	91343
JANIS, RYAN	ACTOR	ABC-TV, "ONE LIFE TO LIVE"		
		1330 AVE OF THE AMERICAS	NEW YORK, NY	10019
JANISS, VIVI	ACTRESS	LARCH, 4506 VARNA AVE	SHERMAN OAKS, CA	91423
JANJIGIAN, JANET	NEWS CORRESPONDENT	NBC-TV, NEWS DEPARTMENT		
		4001 NEBRASKA AVE, NW	WASHINGTON, DC	20016
JANKEL, CHAZ	SINGER	ANDREW HEATH, 5 POLAND ST	LONDON W1	ENGLAND
JANKEY, LES	ACTOR	6380 WILSHIRE BLVD #1600	LOS ANGELES, CA	90048
JANKOWSKI, GENE F	TV EXECUTIVE	CBS-TV, 51 W 52ND ST	NEW YORK, NY	10019
JANN, GERALD	ACTOR	842 S CITRUS AVE	LOS ANGELES, CA	90036
JANNETTY, MARTY	WRESTLER	SEE - MIDNIGHT ROCKERS, THE		
JANNEY, WILLIAM	ACTOR	9924 MARCUS AVE	TUJUNGA, CA	91042
JANNI, JOSEPH	FILM PRODUCER	31 BURTON CT	LONDON SW3	ENGLAND
JANO, NEAL	ACTOR	3575 W CAHUENGA BLVD #243	LOS ANGELES, CA	90068
JANOFF, CRAIG ALAN	TV DIRECTOR	46 CHESTNUT HILL, NORTH HILLS	ROSLYN, NY	11576
JANOS, CYNTHIA	ACTRESS	9255 SUNSET BLVD #510	LOS ANGELES, CA	90069
JANOS, JAMES	WRESTLER-ANNOUNCER	SEE - VENTURA, JESSE "THE BODY"		
JANOVER, MICHAEL	SCREENWRITER	950 HARTZELL ST	PACIFIC PALISADES, CA	90272
JANSON, ANDREJS	CONDUCTOR	POST OFFICE BOX 131	SPRINGFIELD, VA	22150
JANSON, KENNETH	DRUMMER	265 LAKESIDE PARK	HENDERSONVILLE, TN	37075
JANSON, LEN	TV WRITER	8955 BEVERLY BLVD	LOS ANGELES, CA	90048
JANUARY, LOIS	ACTRESS	20938 DE MINA ST	WOODLAND HILLS, CA	91364
JANUS	MUSICAL TRIO	431 S DEARBORN ST #1504	CHICAGO, IL	60605
JANZ, PAUL	SINGER	41 BRITAIN ST #200	TORONTO, ONT	CANADA
JAPP, DAVID	TV DIRECTOR-PRODUCER	FIRST COMPOSERS COMPANY		
		14 NEW BURLINGTON ST	LONDON W1X 2LR	ENGLAND
JAQUE, CHRISTIAN	FILM DIRECTOR	42 BIS RUE DE PARIS	BOULOGNE 92100	FRANCE
JARCHOW, BRUCE	ACTOR	9229 SUNSET BLVD #306	LOS ANGELES, CA	90069
JARDINE, DON	WRESTLER	SEE - SPOILER, THE		
JARED, JEFFREY	GUITARIST	106 GRAVES ST	PORTLAND, TN	37148
JARESS, JILL	ACTRESS-WRITER	7935 BLACKBURN AVE	LOS ANGELES, CA	90048
JARKEY, HARRY	COMEDIAN	32500 CONCORD DR #221	MADISON HEIGHTS, MI	48071
JARMAN, CLAUDE, JR	ACTOR	SHAKLEE, 444 MARKET ST	SAN FRANCISCO, CA	94111
JARMAN, DEREK	DIRECTOR-DESIGNER	ELLIS, BFI, 81 DEAN ST	LONDON W1	ENGLAND
JARMAN, JOSEPH	MUSICIAN	611 BROADWAY #214	NEW YORK, NY	10012
JARMES, JON J	ACTOR	1224 E MENDOCINO ST	ALTADENA, CA	91001
JAROFF, LEON	SCIENCE EDITOR	TIME/TIME & LIFE BLDG		
		ROCKEFELLER CENTER	NEW YORK, NY	10020
JAROS, JOE JAN	RECORD EXECUTIVE	AMERICATONE RECORDS CO		
		1817 LOCH LOMAND WY	LAS VEGAS, NV	89102
JAROSLOVSKY, RICH	NEWS CORRESPONDENT	7401 SUMMIT AVE	CHEVY CHASE, MD	20815
JAROSLOW, RUTH	ACTRESS	67 W 68TH ST	NEW YORK, NY	10023
JARRE, MAURICE	COMPOSER	1201 TOWER GROVE DR	BEVERLY HILLS, CA	90210
JARREAU, AL	SINGER	16530 VENTURA BLVD #202	ENCINO, CA	91436
JARRELL, BARBARA	ACTRESS	3316 ALABAMA ST	LA CRESCENTA, CA	91214
JARRELL, KENT	NEWS CORRESPONDENT	1648-B BEEKMAN PL, NW	WASHINGTON, DC	20009
JARRELL, STEVE	SAXOPHONIST	ROUTE #4, BOX 196	ASHLAND CITY, TN	37015
JARRET, GABE	ACTOR	6640 SUNSET BLVD #203	LOS ANGELES, CA	90028
JARRETT, CHRISTOPHER	ACTOR	9255 SUNSET BLVD #603	LOS ANGELES, CA	90069
JARRETT, JERRY	ACTOR	135 W 96TH ST	NEW YORK, NY	10025
JARRETT, RENNE	ACTRESS	3800 BARHAM BLVD #303	LOS ANGELES, CA	90068
JARRICO, PAUL	TV WRITER-PRODUCER	2017 CALIFORNIA AVE	SANTA MONICA, CA	90403
JARRICO, SYLVIA	TV WRITER	8955 BEVERLY BLVD	LOS ANGELES, CA	90048
JARRILL, TOM	BROADCAST JOURNALIST	10 COLUMBUS CIR #1270	NEW YORK, NY	10019
JARROTT, CHARLES	DIRECTOR-ACTOR	THOMPSON, 7 HIGH PARK RD		
		KEW, RICHMOND	SURREY	ENGLAND
JARROTT, CHARLES B	DIRECTOR	6420 WILSHIRE BLVD #1900	LOS ANGELES, CA	90048
JARVIS, ALAN STEELE	NEWS CORRESPONDENT	12868 GRAYPINE PL	HERNDON, VA	22070
JARVIS, GRAHAM	ACTOR	15351 VIA DE LAS OLAS #531	PACIFIC PALISADES, CA	90272
JARVIS, JEFF	WRITER-EDITOR	PEOPLE/TIME & LIFE BLDG		
		ROCKEFELLER CENTER	NEW YORK, NY	10020
JARVIS, JOHN	PIANIST	3101 HADDON RD	LOUISVILLE, KY	40222
JARVIS, LUCILLE H	WRITER	555 W 57TH ST #1230	NEW YORK, NY	10019
JARVIS, LUCY	TV EXEC-PROD	171 W 57TH ST	NEW YORK, NY	10019
JARVIS, MARTIN	ACTOR	YEW TREE COTTAGE		
		SUDBROOK LN, PETERSHAM	SURREY	ENGLAND
JARVIS, MARY LYNCH	PIANIST	POST OFFICE BOX 150725	NASHVILLE, TN	37215
JARVIS, RON	ACTOR	1515 S MARENGO AVE	ALHAMBRA, CA	91803

Country Crazy with

JAMMIE ANN & THE TEXAS REBELETTES

SHOW

Grace Jammie Lee Rose

1987	**FEMALE ENTERTAINER OF THE YEAR** Presented by Melvin Bittner Sr., President Country Musicians
1986	***UNITED WAY Community Spirit & U.S. JAYCEES Appreciation Award***
1985 '86, '87	***Salute to Ernest Tubb • Midnight Jamboree • Fan Fair*** *Nashville Tennessee Country Musicians*
1984	***Blue Rooster: Texas Rebels: Band Award*** ***Ohio State Fair Appreciation Award:*** *Ohio Country Music*
1983	***INTERNATIONAL HORIZON AWARD:*** *O'LEARY BROS. Jim Ed Hamilton*
1982	***C.M.E. FEMALE VOCALIST: JAMMIE ANN***
1981	***M.A.F.C. ENTERTAINER: JAMMIE ANN***
1980	***FEMALE VOCALIST***
1979	***K.C.Z.T. O'LEARY BROS.***
1978	***BAND: TEXAS REBELETTES***

Personal Management: Barbara Hope Agent: J.E. Christiner
Jammie Ann or O'Leary Bros. International Fan Club P.O. BOX 3525 York, PA 17402

Name	Occupation	Address	City	Zip/Country
JARVIS, SCOTT	ACTOR	210 W 16TH ST #4-F	NEW YORK, NY	10011
JASON, DAVID	ACTOR	THE RICHARD STONE AGENCY		
		18-20 YORK BLDGS, ADELPHI	LONDON WC2N 6JY	ENGLAND
JASON, GEORGE A	TV DIRECTOR	346 CALVERT RD	MERION STATION, PA	19066
JASON, HARVEY	WRITER	1280 SUNSET PLAZA DR	LOS ANGELES, CA	90069
JASON, MELINDA	TALENT AGENT	1900 AVE OF THE STARS #2375	LOS ANGELES, CA	90067
JASON, MITCHELL	ACTOR	43 W 93RD ST	NEW YORK, NY	10025
JASON, NEVILLE	ACTOR	40 INVERNESS ST	LONDON NW1 7HB	ENGLAND
JASON, PETER	ACTOR	211 S BEVERLY DR #201	BEVERLY HILLS, CA	90212
JASON, RICK	ACTOR	14822 HARTSOOK ST	SHERMAN OAKS, CA	91403
JASON & THE SCORCHERS	ROCK & ROLL GROUP	2535 FRANKLIN RD #206	NASHVILLE, TN	37204
JASON DRAKE, SYBIL	ACTRESS	POST OFFICE BOX 573	LOS ANGELES, CA	90078
JASTROW, TERRY	DIRECTOR-PRODUCER	10510 SANDAL LN	LOS ANGELES, CA	90077
JAVA	JAZZ GROUP	312 NEWCASTLE WY	MADISON, WI	53704
JAVOR, DEBORAH	ACTRESS	9100 SUNSET BLVD #200	LOS ANGELES, CA	90069
JAWITZ, JUDITH B	WRITER	555 W 57TH ST #1230	NEW YORK, NY	10019
JAY, ANTONY RUPERT	FILM WRITER-PRODUCER	33 MOUNT AVE	LONDON W5	ENGLAND
JAY, COUGAR	WRESTLER	SEE - COUGAR JAY		
JAY, EUGENE STEPHEN	COMPOSER	2616 HOLLYRIDGE DR	LOS ANGELES, CA	90068
JAY, JODIE	SINGER	MBA, 8914 GEORGIAN DR	AUSTIN, TX	78753
JAY, VALERIE	SINGER	45 TUDOR CITY PL #911	NEW YORK, NY	10017
JAY & THE AMERICAS	ROCK & ROLL GROUP	POST OFFICE BOX 262	CARTERET, NJ	07008
JAYANT	ACTOR	15 E 11TH ST #9-C	NEW YORK, NY	10003
JAYE, EDDIE	COMEDIAN	CAPITOL, 11844 MARKET ST	NORTH LIMA, OH	44452
JAYMES, CATHERINE	TALENT AGENT	327 N LAUREL AVE	LOS ANGELES, CA	90048
JAYNES, GREGORY	WRITER-EDITOR	TIME/TIME & LIFE BLDG		
		ROCKEFELLER CENTER	NEW YORK, NY	10020
JAYSON, ROBERT K	TV WRITER	8955 BEVERLY BLVD	LOS ANGELES, CA	90048
JAYSTON, MICHAEL	ACTOR	LEADING ARTISTS, LTD		
		60 SAINT JAMES'S ST	LONDON SW1	ENGLAND
JEADOVIN, BOB	WRESTLER	SEE - JAGGERS, BOBBY		
JEAN, AL	WRITER	151 S EL CAMINO DR	BEVERLY HILLS, CA	90212
JEAN, GLORIA	ACTRESS	6625 VARIEL AVE	CANOGA PARK, CA	91303
JEAN, NORMA	SINGER	SEE - JAHN, NORMA JEAN		
JEAN-BERNARD, MARC	GUITARIST	200 W 70TH ST #7-F	NEW YORK, NY	10023
JEANMAIRE, ZIZI	ACTRESS	22 RUE DE LA PAIX	PARIS 75002	FRANCE
JEANS, CHRISTOPHER	DIRECTOR	40 BEDFORD ST	NEW YORK, NY	10014
JEANS, LUKE	FILM-TV DIRECTOR	109 DOLLIS PARK	LONDON N3	ENGLAND
JEAVONS, COLIN	ACTOR	LONDON MANAGEMENT, LTD		
		235-241 REGENT ST	LONDON W1A 2JT	ENGLAND
JEDICKA, DAN	COLUMNIST	NEWS AMERICA SYNDICATE		
		1703 KAISER AVE	IRVINE, CA	92714
JEFFERIES, PETER	TV DIRECTOR	58 1ST AVE, MORTLAKE	LONDON SW14	ENGLAND
JEFFERS, BECKY	GUITARIST	1336 OLD HICKORY BLVD	NASHVILLE, TN	37207
JEFFERS, RUSSELL	GUITARIST	1336 OLD HICKORY BLVD	NASHVILLE, TN	37207
JEFFERSON, EDDIE & RICHIE COLE	JAZZ DUO	2490 CHANNING WY #406	BERKELEY, CA	94704
JEFFERSON, GERI	WRITER	555 W 57TH ST #1230	NEW YORK, NY	10019
JEFFERSON, ROLAND S	WRITER	8955 BEVERLY BLVD	LOS ANGELES, CA	90048
JEFFERSON STARSHIP, THE	ROCK & ROLL GROUP	SEE - STARSHIP, THE		
JEFFERY, WILLIAM	COMPOSER	5143 VILLAGE GREEN ST	LOS ANGELES, CA	90016
JEFFES, PETER	TENOR	1182 MARKET ST #311	SAN FRANCISCO, CA	94102
JEFFORY, DAWN	ACTRESS	352 N STANLEY AVE	LOS ANGELES, CA	90036
JEFFREY, J KIMMEL	NEWS CORRESPONDENT	2317 HUIDEKOPER PL, NW	WASHINGTON, DC	20007
JEFFREY, JEFFREY D	WRITER	8955 BEVERLY BLVD	LOS ANGELES, CA	90048
JEFFREY, PETER	ACTOR	12 WINCHESTER PL	LONDON N6	ENGLAND
JEFFREY, TOM M	TV DIRECTOR-PRODUCER	SAMSON, 119 PYRMONT ST	PYRMONT NSW 2009	AUSTRALIA
JEFFREYS, ANNE	ACTRESS	STERLING, 121 S BENTLEY AVE	LOS ANGELES, CA	90049
JEFFREYS, GARLAND	SINGER	ICM, 40 W 57TH ST	NEW YORK, NY	10019
JEFFREYS, RONALD	MUSIC ARRANGER	121 APOLLO CT W	ANTIOCH, TN	37013
JEFFRIE, WILLIAM	PERCUSSIONIST	1407 CEDAR LN	NASHVILLE, TN	37212
JEFFRIES, GEORGIA	SCREENWRITER	20750 DUMONT ST	WOODLAND HILLS, CA	91364
JEFFRIES, HERB	SINGER	POST OFFICE BOX C	RIVER EDGE, NJ	07661
JEFFRIES, LIONEL	ACTOR-DIRECTOR	ICM, 388-396 OXFORD ST	LONDON W1	ENGLAND
JEFFRIES, NANCY	RECORD EXECUTIVE	A & M RECORDS COMPANY		
		595 MADISON AVE	NEW YORK, NY	10022
JEFFRIES, PETER	NEWS CORRESPONDENT	NBC-TV, NEWS DEPARTMENT		
		4001 NEBRASKA AVE, NW	WASHINGTON, DC	20016
JEKEL, AUGUST A	DIRECTOR	4222 TROOST AVE #26	STUDIO CITY, CA	91604
JEKOT, DR WALTER	BODYBUILDER	8635 W 3RD ST	LOS ANGELES, CA	90048
JELLICK, HERB	TV EXECUTIVE	ABC-TV, 4151 PROSPECT AVE	LOS ANGELES, CA	90027
JEMISON, TERRY L	NEWS CORRESPONDENT	2804 BOSWELL AVE	ALEXANDRIA, VA	22306
JENIOUS, CRYSTAL	ACTRESS	2441 EXPOSITION PL #1	LOS ANGELES, CA	90018
JENKIN, LEN	TV WRITER	555 W 57TH ST #1230	NEW YORK, NY	10019
JENKINS, ANDREW	DIRECTOR	DGA, 110 W 57TH ST	NEW YORK, NY	10019
JENKINS, BARRY	FILM EXECUTIVE	CANNON FILMS, 167 WARDOUR ST	LONDON W1	ENGLAND
JENKINS, BOB & THE DAM BAND	C & W GROUP	4047 NACO-PERRIN BLVD #110	SAN ANTONIO, TX	78217
JENKINS, BOBBY	GUITARIST	POST OFFICE BOX 488	MOUNT JULIET, TN	37122
JENKINS, CAROL MAYO	ACTRESS	9220 SUNSET BLVD #202	LOS ANGELES, CA	90069
JENKINS, DAL	TV WRITER	8955 BEVERLY BLVD	LOS ANGELES, CA	90048
JENKINS, DAN	WRITER	555 W 57TH ST #1230	NEW YORK, NY	10019
JENKINS, DAVID	CELLIST	6700 CABOT DR #J-20	NASHVILLE, TN	37209
JENKINS, DEL	MUSICAN-SONGWRITER	3119 SANTA CARLOTTA ST	LA CRESCENTA, CA	91214
JENKINS, GEORGE	ART DIRECTOR	740 KINGMAN AVE	SANTA MONICA, CA	90402
JENKINS, GORDON A	NEWS CORRESPONDENT	1530 16TH ST, NW	WASHINGTON, DC	20036
JENKINS, HOWARD P	TV DIRECTOR	17097 MAGNOLIA PARKWAY	SOUTHFIELD, MI	48075

AL JARREAU

KAREN JENSEN

ANN JILLIAN

ELTON JOHN

GLYNIS JOHNS

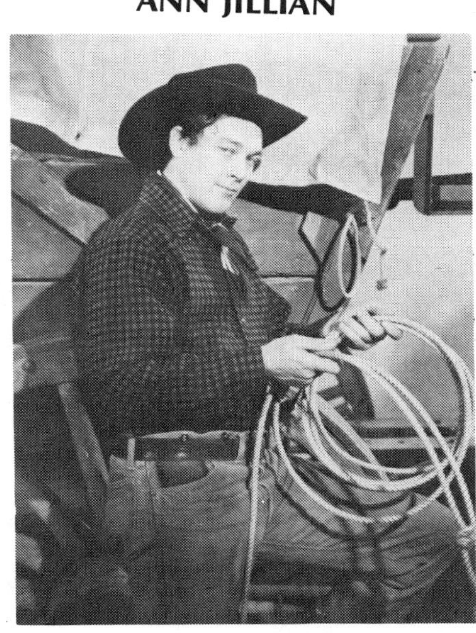
BEN JOHNSON

DON JOHNSON

VAN JOHNSON

LYNN-HOLLY JOHNSON

Name	Occupation	Address	City
JENKINS, JACKIE "BUTCH"	ACTOR	ROUTE #6, BOX 5416	FAIRVIEW, NC 28730
JENKINS, JANE	CASTING DIRECTOR	7319 BEVERLY BLVD #6	LOS ANGELES, CA 90036
JENKINS, JOHN	NEWS CORRESPONDENT	3944 LIVINGSTON ST, NW	WASHINGTON, DC 20015
JENKINS, JOHN W R	DIRECTOR	20 SUTTON PL S	NEW YORK, NY 10022
JENKINS, LARRY "FLASH"	ACTOR	3855 LANKERSHIM BLVD #818	NORTH HOLLYWOOD, CA 91604
JENKINS, LE ROY	VIOLINIST	611 BROADWAY #214	NEW YORK, NY 10012
JENKINS, RICHARD	ACTOR	853 7TH AVE #9-A	NEW YORK, NY 10019
JENKINS, ROGER	TV-FILM DIRECTOR	MAX NAUGHTON LOWE	
		200 FULHAM RD	LONDON SW10 9PN ENGLAND
JENKINS, SANDRA G	WRITER	555 W 57TH ST #1230	NEW YORK, NY 10019
JENKINS, SCOTT	ACTOR	KNBC-TV, "SANTA BARBARA"	
		3000 W ALAMEDA AVE	BURBANK, CA 91523
JENKINS, SUSAN ANN	DIRECTOR-PRODUCER	5250 STROHM AVE	NORTH HOLLYWOOD, CA 91601
JENKINS, T CLIFFORD	CONDUCTOR	8811 CANOGA AVE #302	CANOGA PARK, CA 91304
JENKINS, TERYN	ACTRESS	29500 HEATHERCLIFF RD #155	MALIBU, CA 90265
JENKINS, TIMOTHY	TENOR	COLBERT, 111 W 57TH ST	NEW YORK, NY 10019
JENKINS, WILLIAM L	NEWS CORRESPONDENT	17005 GEORGE WASHINGTON DR	ROCKVILLE, MD 20853
JENKINSON, BRIAN	TV DIRECTOR-PRODUCER	32 HEATON RD	NEWCASTLE-UPON-TYNE ENGLAND
JENKS, SUSAN	NEWS CORRESPONDENT	4820 EARLSTON DR	BETHESDA, MD 20816
JENNER, BARRY	ACTOR	1650 BROADWAY #302	NEW YORK, NY 10019
JENNER, BRUCE	ACTOR-ATHLETE	POST OFFICE BOX 665	MALIBU, CA 90265
JENNER, LINDA THOMPSON	ACTRESS	POST OFFICE BOX 665	MALIBU, CA 90265
JENNERJAHN, MARY LOU	TV EXECUTIVE	CBS-TV, 51 W 52ND ST	NEW YORK, NY 10019
JENNETT, JAMES B	TV DIRECTOR	106 MAGNOLIA DR	DOBBS FERRY, NY 10522
JENNEY, LUCINDA	ACTRESS	200 W 57TH ST #304	NEW YORK, NY 10019
JENNINGS, BRENT	ACTOR	SF & A, 121 N SAN VICENTE BLVD	BEVERLY HILLS, CA 90211
JENNINGS, CHUCK	GUITARIST	14303 SEMINOLE	BALCH SPRINGS, TX 75180
JENNINGS, ELIZABETH	WRITER	8955 BEVERLY BLVD	LOS ANGELES, CA 90048
JENNINGS, GREG	GUITARIST	142 MC GAVOCK PIKE	NASHVILLE, TN 37214
JENNINGS, JOHN ELVIS	SINGER	38 MUSIC SQUARE E	NASHVILLE, TN 37203
JENNINGS, JUNERO	ACTOR	14234 LEMAY ST	VAN NUYS, CA 91405
JENNINGS, LISA NOELLE	NEWS CORRESPONDENT	4127 45TH ST, NW	WASHINGTON, DC 20016
JENNINGS, MARYANNE	ACTRESS	14234 LEMAY ST	VAN NUYS, CA 91405
JENNINGS, PETER	NEWS CORRESPONDENT	1330 AVE OF THE AMERICAS	NEW YORK, NY 10019
JENNINGS, SANDRA	WRITER	555 W 57TH ST #1230	NEW YORK, NY 10019
JENNINGS, STAN	PHOTOGRAPHER	1087 NATIONAL PRESS BLDG	
		529 14TH ST, NW	WASHINGTON, DC 20045
JENNINGS, TOMMY	SINGER-SONGWRITER	ROUTE #3, BOX 396	MOUNT JULIET, TN 37122
JENNINGS, WAYLON	SINGER-SONGWRITER	POST OFFICE BOX 121556	NASHVILLE, TN 37212
JENNINGS, WILLIAM	FILM PRODUCER	POST OFFICE BOX D	TRINIDAD, CA 95570
JENNINGS, WILLIAM D	WRITER	8955 BEVERLY BLVD	LOS ANGELES, CA 90048
JENRETTE, RITA	ACTRESS-MODEL	250 W 57TH ST #2530	NEW YORK, NY 10107
JENS, SALOME	ACTRESS	1716 REDESDALE AVE	LOS ANGELES, CA 90026
JENSEN, BRUCE F	WRITER	555 W 57TH ST #1230	NEW YORK, NY 10019
JENSEN, DICK	SINGER	6399 WILSHIRE BLVD #506	LOS ANGELES, CA 90048
JENSEN, GORDON	SINGER	6750 W 75TH ST, MARKADE 75	
		BUILDING #2-A	OVERLAND PARK, KS 66212
JENSEN, JERRY	ACTOR	TYIAMA, 10648 BALBOA AVE	GRANADA HILLS, CA 91344
JENSEN, KRISTEN	ACTRESS	8322 BEVERLY BLVD #202	LOS ANGELES, CA 90048
JENSEN, LARRY	TV WRITER	8955 BEVERLY BLVD	LOS ANGELES, CA 90048
JENSEN, MAREN	ACTRESS	10880 WILSHIRE BLVD #2110	LOS ANGELES, CA 90069
JENSEN, MARJORIE M	NEWS CORRESPONDENT	3825 DAVIS PL #203, NW	WASHINGTON, DC 20007
JENSEN, MIKE	NEWS CORRESPONDENT	NBC-TV, NEWS DEPARTMENT	
		30 ROCKEFELLER PLAZA	NEW YORK, NY 10112
JENSEN, MONIKA R	WRITER	555 W 57TH ST #1230	NEW YORK, NY 10019
JENSEN, RANDEE LYNNE	ACTRESS	3113 RIVERSIDE DR	BURBANK, CA 91505
JENSEN, SHELLEY	TV DIRECTOR-EDITOR	150 S BARRINGTON AVE #1	LOS ANGELES, CA 90049
JENSEN, SHELLY	TV DIRECTOR	1426 THOMPSON AVE	GLENDALE, CA 91201
JENSEN, STERLING B	ACTOR	311 E 9TH ST	NEW YORK, NY 10003
JENSEN, STUART	CASTING DIRECTOR	PARAMOUNT PICTURES CORP	
		5555 MELROSE AVE	LOS ANGELES, CA 90038
JENSON, DYLANA	VIOLINIST	SHAW CONCERTS, 1995 BROADWAY	NEW YORK, NY 10023
JENSON, GEORGE F	WRITER	8955 BEVERLY BLVD	LOS ANGELES, CA 90048
JENTRY, LARRY	GUITARIST	POST OFFICE BOX 18415	AUSTIN, TX 78760
JERBIC, MARIJAN	CELLIST	GEWALD, 58 W 58TH ST	NEW YORK, NY 10019
JERGENSON, DALE R	COMPOSER	15035 WYANDOTTE ST	VAN NUYS, CA 91406
JERNIGAN, CLARENCE F	COMPOSER	920 KINGS RD #214	LOS ANGELES, CA 90069
JERNIGAN, DOUGLAS	DOBROIST	117 CRANOR DR	WHITE HOUSE, TN 37188
JEROME, ALBERT	TV EXECUTIVE	NBC TELEVISION NETWORK	
		30 ROCKEFELLER PLAZA	NEW YORK, NY 10112
JERSEY, WILLIAM C	DIRECTOR	5915 HOLLIS ST	EMERYVILLE, CA 94608
JERUSALEM, SIEGFRIED	TENOR	MARIEDL ANDERS ARTISTS MGMT	
		535 EL CAMINO DEL MAR ST	SAN FRANCISCO, CA 94121
JESKIN, MICHAEL A	WRITER	POST OFFICE BOX 67531	LOS ANGELES, CA 90067
JESSE, ANITA	ACTRESS	6736 LAUREL CANYON BLVD #306	NORTH HOLLYWOOD, CA 91606
JESSEL, IAN	TV-FILM EXECUTIVE	CBS FILMS, 4024 RADFORD AVE	STUDIO CITY, CA 91604
JESSEL, JANIS ELEANOR	WRITER	8225 HOLLYWOOD BLVD	LOS ANGELES, CA 90069
JESSEL, RAYMOND	TV WRITER	8225 HOLLYWOOD BLVD	LOS ANGELES, CA 90069
JESSELL, HARRY A, JR	NEWS CORRESPONDENT	4311 12TH ST, NE	WASHINGTON, DC 20017
JESSOP, LELAND K	WRITER	753 W 31ST ST	SAN PEDRO, CA 90731
JESSOP, PETER	CINEMATOGRAPHER	16 DARTMOUTH PARK AVE	LONDON NW5 1JN ENGLAND
JESSYE, EVA	SINGER	102 E MADISON ST	PITTSBURG, KS 66762
JESTERS OF DESTINY	ROCK & ROLL GROUP	POST OFFICE BOX 2428	EL SEGUNDO, CA 90245
JET BLACK BERRIES	ROCK & ROLL GROUP	POST OFFICE BOX 2428	EL SEGUNDO, CA 90245
JETER, FELICIA	NEWS CORRESPONDENT	CBS NEWS, 524 W 57TH ST	NEW YORK, NY 10019

JETER, JAMES	ACTOR	788 ALAMEDA ST	ALTADENA, CA 91001
JETHRO TULL	ROCK & ROLL GROUP	WOOLLEY, MAISON ROUGE	
		2 WANSDOWN PL, FULHAM	LONDON SW6 ENGLAND
JETS, THE	RHYTHM & BLUES GROUP	POST OFFICE BOX 437	EXCELSIOR, MN 55331
JETT, JOAN & THE BLACKHEARTS	ROCK & ROLL GROUP	250 W 57TH ST #603	NEW YORK, NY 10107
JEWELL, KATHERINE L	WRITER	555 W 57TH ST #1230	NEW YORK, NY 10019
JEWISON, NORMAN	DIRECTOR-PRODUCER	23752 MALIBU RD	MALIBU, CA 90265
JEZEK, KEN	ACTOR	12725 VENTURA BLVD #E	STUDIO CITY, CA 91604
JEZIORO, JACK	BANJOIST	3316 FALL CREEK DR	NASHVILLE, TN 37214
JHABVALA, RUTH P	WRITER	555 W 57TH ST #1230	NEW YORK, NY 10019
JILLIAN, ANN	ACTRESS-SINGER	MURCIA, 4141 WOODCLIFF RD	SHERMAN OAKS, CA 91403
JILLSON, JOYCE	ASTROLOGER-COLUMNIST	TRIBUNE MEDIA SERVICES	
		64 E CONCORD ST	ORLANDO, FL 32801
JIM, HILLBILLY	WRESTLER	SEE - HILLBILLY JIM	
JIM & JESSE & THE VIRGINIA BOYS	C & W GROUP	POST OFFICE BOX 27	GALLATIN, TN 37066
JIMENO, RAMON A	NEWS CORRESPONDENT	1615 "Q" ST, NW	WASHINGTON, DC 20009
JIMERSON, WENDELL	GUITARIST	1703 BAROUTE WY	MURFREESBORO, TN 37130
JIMIRRO, JAMES P	FILM-TV EXECUTIVE	500 S BUENA VISTA ST	BURBANK, CA 91521
JIMMY, BOBBY & THE CRITTERS	RAP GROUP	6354 VAN NUYS BLVD #174	VAN NUYS, CA 91401
JIMMY JAM	SONGWRITER-PRODUCER	SEE - HARRIS, JIMMY JAM	
JINAKI	ACTRESS	8230 BEVERLY BLVD #23	LOS ANGELES, CA 90048
JINKS, EILEEN R	NEWS CORRESPONDENT	4079 35TH ST N	ARLINGTON, VA 22207
JINNETTE, BETTY	ACTRESS	8235 SANTA MONICA BLVD #315	LOS ANGELES, CA 90046
JINX	ROCK & ROLL GROUP	SEE - WILD BLUE	
JIRAS, ROBERT E	WRITER	555 W 57TH ST #1230	NEW YORK, NY 10019
JIRGENSONS, AIJA	SOPRANO	GREAT LAKES PERFORMING	
		535 EL CAMINO DEL MAR ST	SAN FRANCISCO, CA 94121
JIVE FIVE, THE	VOCAL GROUP	POST OFFICE BOX 499	QUEENS, NY 11365
JLYNE	SINGER	PTA, 208 ST COACHMAN DR	LAWTON, OK 73501
JOACHIM, THOMAS W	WRITER	718 1/2 W 40TH ST	SAN PEDRO, CA 90731
JOBELMANN, HERMAN F	CONDUCTOR	POST OFFICE BOX 8185	PORTLAND, OR 97207
JOBES, HEATH	ACTOR	2348 FELLOWSHIP PARKWAY	LOS ANGELES, CA 90039
JOBIN, ANTONIO CARLOS	GUITARIST-SONGWRITER	HOFFER, 233 1/2 E 48TH ST	NEW YORK, NY 10017
JOBIN, PETER	WRITER	555 W 57TH ST #1230	NEW YORK, NY 10019
JOBLIN, MONIA B	CABLE EXECUTIVE	U S A NETWORK	
		208 HARRISTOWN RD	GLEN ROCK, NJ 07452
JOBOXERS, THE	ROCK & ROLL GROUP	BOXERCARE, IAN MULLARD	
		21 WIGMORE ST	LONDON W1 ENGLAND
JOCELYN, VERN T	NEWS CORRESPONDENT	113 S LEE ST	ALEXANDRIA, VA 22314
JOCHIMSEN, GARY	ACTOR	8921 SUNSET BLVD #B	LOS ANGELES, CA 90069
JODELSOHN, ANITA	ACTRESS	15010 VENTURA BLVD #219	SHERMAN OAKS, CA 91403
JOEL, BILLY	SINGER-SONGWRITER	375 N BROADWAY	JERICHO, NY 11753
JOELSON, BEN	TV WRITER	908 N BEVERLY DR	BEVERLY HILLS, CA 90210
JOFFE, CHARLES H	FILM PRODUCER	860 BIRCHWOOD DR	LOS ANGELES, CA 90024
JOFFE, EDWARD	DIRECTOR-PRODUCER	6 OLDFIELD MEWS, HIGHGATE	LONDON N6 5XA ENGLAND
JOFFE, ROLAND	FILM DIRECTOR	DAISH, 83 EASTBOURNE MEWS	LONDON W2 6LQ ENGLAND
JOFFREY, ROBERT	CHOREOGRAPHER	434 6TH AVE	NEW YORK, NY 10009
JOHANN, ZITA	ACTRESS	SICKLETOWN RD	WEST NYACK, NY 10994
JOHANNES, VICTOR L	FILM DIRECTOR	415 E 85TH ST	NEW YORK, NY 10028
JOHANNESEN, GRANT	PIANIST	59 E 54TH ST #81	NEW YORK, NY 10022
JOHANNSSON, KRISTIAN	TENOR	61 W 62ND ST #6-F	NEW YORK, NY 10023
JOHANNSSON, MATS	NEWS CORRESPONDENT	3414 VOLTA PL, NW	WASHINGTON, DC 20007
JOHANSEN, DAVID	SINGER	3 E 54TH ST #1400	NEW YORK, NY 10022
JOHANSEN, JASON	WRITER	8955 BEVERLY BLVD	LOS ANGELES, CA 90048
JOHANSSON, INGEMAR	BOXER	SVEN EKSTROM	
		RAKEGATON 9 S-41320	GOTEBORG SWEDEN
JOHARI, AZIZI	ACTRESS-MODEL	7060 HOLLYWOOD BLVD #610	HOLLYWOOD, CA 90028
JOHMANN, CAROL A	NEWS REPORTER	TIME/TIME & LIFE BLDG	
		ROCKEFELLER CENTER	NEW YORK, NY 10020
JOHN, DR	SINGER-SONGWRITER	SEE - DR JOHN	
JOHN, ELTON	SINGER-SONGWRITER	40 S AUDLEY ST, MAYFAIR	LONDON W1Y 5DH ENGLAND
JOHN, MASTER	ACROBATIC ACT	SEE - MASTER JOHN	
JOHN, MICHAEL	SINGER	DTP, 5060 RANCHWOOD DR	COCOA, FL 32926
JOHN, ROBERT	SINGER	6430 SUNSET BLVD #1516	LOS ANGELES, CA 90028
JOHN, TONGA	WRESTLER	SEE - KONGA THE BARBARIAN	
JOHNATHON, MICHAEL	SINGER	360 CENTRAL PARK W #16-G	NEW YORK, NY 10025
JOHNNY & THE DISTRACTIONS	ROCK & ROLL GROUP	3 E 54TH ST #1400	NEW YORK, NY 10022
JOHNNY & THE HURRICANES	ROCK & ROLL GROUP	OLDIES, 5218 ALMONT ST	LOS ANGELES, CA 90032
JOHNNY & THE KNUCKLEHEADS	ROCK & ROLL GROUP	POST OFFICE BOX 52241	TULSA, OK 74152
JOHNNY K-9	WRESTLER	POST OFFICE BOX 3859	STAMFORD, CT 06905
JOHNNY V	WRESTLING MANAGER	SEE - V, JOHNNY	
JOHNS, BONNIE	ACTRESS	8831 SUNSET BLVD #402	LOS ANGELES, CA 90069
JOHNS, GLYNIS	ACTRESS	CONTEMPORARY ARTISTS	
		132 S LASKY DR	BEVERLY HILLS, CA 90212
JOHNS, JOHN F	GUITARIST	299 GARRY DR	NASHVILLE, TN 37211
JOHNS, JONNIE	TV WRITER	8955 BEVERLY BLVD	LOS ANGELES, CA 90048
JOHNS, JOSEPH E	NEWS CORRESPONDENT	NBC-TV, NEWS DEPARTMENT	
		4001 NEBRASKA AVE, NW	WASHINGTON, DC 20016
JOHNS, MERVYN	ACTOR	RICHARDS, 42 HAZLEBURY RD	LONDON SW6 ENGLAND
JOHNS, VICTORIA	TV WRITER-PRODUCER	BLOOM, 800 S ROBERTSON BLVD	LOS ANGELES, CA 90035
JOHNS, WILLIAM	TENOR	CAMI, 165 W 57TH ST	NEW YORK, NY 10019
JOHNSON, A DUDLEY, JR	TV WRITER	8955 BEVERLY BLVD	LOS ANGELES, CA 90048
JOHNSON, ALAN S	FILM DIRECTOR	J LENNY, 9701 WILSHIRE BLVD	BEVERLY HILLS, CA 90212
JOHNSON, ALEXANDRA	ACTRESS	SF & A, 121 N SAN VICENTE BLVD	BEVERLY HILLS, CA 90211
JOHNSON, ANNE-MARIE	ACTRESS	5967 W 3RD ST #205	LOS ANGELES, CA 90036

JOHNSON, ANTHONY ROLFE	TENOR	ICM, 40 W 57TH ST	NEW YORK, NY	10019
JOHNSON, ARCH	ACTOR	STARKMAN, 1501 BROADWAY	NEW YORK, NY	10036
JOHNSON, ARTE	ACTOR-COMEDIAN	2725 BOTTLEBRUSH DR	LOS ANGELES, CA	90026
JOHNSON, BARBARA	CASTING DIRECTOR	8300 SANTA MONICA BLVD #203	LOS ANGELES, CA	90069
JOHNSON, BARRY	PIANIST	11726 LEMAY ST #14	NORTH HOLLYWOOD, CA	91606
JOHNSON, BEN	ACTOR	31509 GERMAINE LN	WESTLAKE VILLAGE, CA	91361
JOHNSON, BERTA A	PIANIST	9457 LAS VEGAS BLVD S #16	LAS VEGAS, NV	89123
JOHNSON, BETSEY	FASHION DESIGNER	209 W 38TH ST	NEW YORK, NY	10018
JOHNSON, BILL D	GUITARIST	2175 JUNE DR	NASHVILLE, TN	37214
JOHNSON, BOB	ILLUSTRATOR	1346 4TH ST	SAN RAFAEL, CA	94901
JOHNSON, BONNIE	WRITER-EDITOR	PEOPLE/TIME & LIFE BLDG		
		ROCKEFELLER CENTER	NEW YORK, NY	10020
JOHNSON, BRUCE	CABLE EXECUTIVE	HEARST ABC-TV, 555 5TH AVE	NEW YORK, NY	10019
JOHNSON, BRUCE	TV WRITER	8955 BEVERLY BLVD	LOS ANGELES, CA	90048
JOHNSON, BRUCE	PRODUCER	5555 MELROSE AVE	LOS ANGELES, CA	90038
JOHNSON, BRUCE	PRODUCER	PARAMOUNT PICTURES CORP		
		1221 AVE OF THE AMERICAS	NEW YORK, NY	10036
JOHNSON, CARL E	GUITARIST	1050 PLEASANT HILL RD #F-68	NASHVILLE, TN	37214
JOHNSON, CARL J	ACTOR	335 S COCHRAN AVE #104	LOS ANGELES, CA	90036
JOHNSON, CARL J	DRUMMER	976 E 55TH ST	LOS ANGELES, CA	90011
JOHNSON, CAROL BASS	SINGER	131 FRANCES ST	GALLATIN, TN	37066
JOHNSON, CECIL L	GUITARIST	30908 SOAPMINE RD	BARSTOW, CA	92311
JOHNSON, CHARLES	PRODUCER	MCA/UNIVERSAL STUDIOS, INC		
		100 UNIVERSAL CITY PLAZA	UNIVERSAL CITY, CA	91608
JOHNSON, CHARLES	TV WRITER	8955 BEVERLY BLVD	LOS ANGELES, CA	90048
JOHNSON, CHARLES DE WITT	PERCUSSIONIST	1948 PORTER RD	NASHVILLE, TN	37206
JOHNSON, CHARLES E	DRUMER	811 W REDFIELD RD	TEMPE, AZ	85283
JOHNSON, CHARLES FLOYD	TV WRITER-PRODUCER	1900 AVE OF THE STARS #2535	LOS ANGELES, CA	90067
JOHNSON, CHARLES R	TV WRITER	8955 BEVERLY BLVD	LOS ANGELES, CA	90048
JOHNSON, CHRISTINA L	NEWS CORRESPONDENT	NBC-TV, NEWS DEPARTMENT		
		4001 NEBRASKA AVE, NW	WASHINGTON, DC	20016
JOHNSON, CLAUDE	ACTOR	AIMEE, 13743 VICTORY BLVD	VAN NUYS, CA	91401
JOHNSON, CLIFTON	PHOTOJOURNALIST	3605 CLAIRTON DR	MITCHELLVILLE, MD	20716
JOHNSON, CORKY	NEWS CORRESPONDENT	549 11TH ST, SE	WASHINGTON, DC	20003
JOHNSON, COSLOUGH	TV WRITER	ICM, 8899 BEVERLY BLVD	LOS ANGELES, CA	90048
JOHNSON, CYNTHIA	PHOTOGRAPHER	316 10TH ST, NE	WASHINGTON, DC	20002
JOHNSON, DALE	ACTOR	151 N SAN VICENTE BLVD #208	BEVERLY HILLS, CA	90211
JOHNSON, DANNY R	GUITARIST	POST OFFICE BOX 1151	DUNN, NC	28334
JOHNSON, DAVEY	BASEBALL	4245 BEAR GULLEY RD	WINTER PARK, FL	32789
JOHNSON, DAVID	TV EXECUTIVE	ABC TELEVISION NETWORK		
		1330 AVE OF THE AMERICAS	NEW YORK, NY	10019
JOHNSON, DAVID L	GUITARIST	POST OFFICE BOX 4494	ASPEN, CO	81612
JOHNSON, DEBI NICOLLE	MODEL	MODELS & PROMOTIONS AGENCY		
		8560 SUNSET BLVD, 10TH FLOOR	LOS ANGELES, CA	90069
JOHNSON, DEBORAH	TV PRODUCER	NBC TELEVISION NETWORK		
		30 ROCKEFELLER PLAZA	NEW YORK, NY	10112
JOHNSON, DEBORAH LIV	SINGER-GUITARIST	POST OFFICE BOX 8516	SAN DIEGO, CA	92101
JOHNSON, DENIS	PRODUCER	9 FOUNTAINE RD	LONDON SW2 3TS	ENGLAND
JOHNSON, DIANE L	SCREENWRITER	8955 BEVERLY BLVD	LOS ANGELES, CA	90048
JOHNSON, DIRK	PIANIST	228 SAUNDERS FERRY RD #J-134	HENDERSONVILLE, TN	37075
JOHNSON, DON	ACTOR-SINGER	2895 BISCAYNE BLVD #395	MIAMI, FL	33137
JOHNSON, DON L	TRUMPETER	11554 TARRON AVE	LOS ANGELES, CA	90047
JOHNSON, DONA L	NEWS CORRESPONDENT	12709 WEISS ST	ROCKVILLE, MD	20853
JOHNSON, DOTTS	ACTOR	420 W 130TH ST #64	NEW YORK, NY	10027
JOHNSON, DOUG	NEWS CORRESPONDENT	WABC-TV, 7 LINCOLN SQ	NEW YORK, NY	10023
JOHNSON, DUNCAN	TRUMPETER	301 CHESTER AVE S	BAKERSFIELD, CA	93304
JOHNSON, EARVIN "MAJIC"	BASKETBALL	POST OFFICE BOX 10	INGELWOOD, CA	90306
JOHNSON, ELAINE D	ACTRESS	13950 NW PASSAGE #210	MARINA DEL REY, CA	90292
JOHNSON, ERNEST J	TV DIRECTOR	POST OFFICE BOX 35602	LOS ANGELES, CA	90035
JOHNSON, EVAN	VIOLINIST	POST OFFICE BOX 131	SPRINGFIELD, VA	22150
JOHNSON, F MICHAEL	WRITER	8955 BEVERLY BLVD	LOS ANGELES, CA	90048
JOHNSON, FATS	COMEDIAN	2701 COTTAGE WY #14	SACRAMENTO, CA	95825
JOHNSON, FERD	CARTOONIST	TRIBUNE MEDIA SERVICES		
		64 E CONCORD ST	ORLANDO, FL	32801
JOHNSON, FRANK	CARTOONIST	KING FEATURES SYNDICATE		
		235 E 45TH ST	NEW YORK, NY	10017
JOHNSON, FRED	WRITER	555 W 57TH ST #1230	NEW YORK, NY	10019
JOHNSON, FREDERICK GERALD	ACTOR	5020 EAGLE VIEW TERR	LOS ANGELES, CA	90041
JOHNSON, GARY D	TV WRITER	8955 BEVERLY BLVD	LOS ANGELES, CA	90048
JOHNSON, GARY M	FLUEGEL HORNIST	6010 LEMON AVE	LONG BEACH, CA	90805
JOHNSON, GEOFFREY	CASTING DIRECTOR	JOHNSON/LIFF, 1501 BROADWAY	NEW YORK, NY	10036
JOHNSON, GEORGANN	ACTRESS	9229 SUNSET BLVD #306	LOS ANGELES, CA	90069
JOHNSON, GEORGE CLAYTON	SCREENWRITER	8955 BEVERLY BLVD	LOS ANGELES, CA	90048
JOHNSON, GERALDINE	ACTRESS	8831 SUNSET BLVD #402	LOS ANGELES, CA	90069
JOHNSON, GLENN L	WRITER	8955 BEVERLY BLVD	LOS ANGELES, CA	90048
JOHNSON, GRAY R	FILM DIRECTOR	POST OFFICE BOX 1447	BURBANK, CA	91507
JOHNSON, GREGORY D	NEWS CORRESPONDENT	1825 "K" ST, NW	WASHINGTON, DC	20006
JOHNSON, HAL	SAXOPHONIST	4130 FOOTHILL RD	SANTA BARBARA, CA	90003
JOHNSON, HAROLD V	TRUMPETER-COMPOSER	305 N OAKHURST DR	BEVERLY HILLS, CA	90210
JOHNSON, HARRIET C	COLUMNIST	POST OFFICE BOX 500	WASHINGTON, DC	20044
JOHNSON, HARRIETT	MUSIC CRITIC	164 W 54TH ST	NEW YORK, NY	10019
JOHNSON, HARRY	CLOWN	2701 COTTAGE WY #14	SACRAMENTO, CA	95825
JOHNSON, HARRY B	FLUTIST	418 COVENTRY DR	NASHVILLE, TN	37211
JOHNSON, HAYNES	NEWS CORRESPONDENT	3201 BROAD BRANCH TERR, NW	WASHINGTON, DC	20008
JOHNSON, HELEN	ACTRESS	SEE - WOOD, JUDITH		

Name	Occupation	Address	City	Zip
JOHNSON, HELEN	WRITER	555 W 57TH ST #1230	NEW YORK, NY	10019
JOHNSON, HENRY W	TV WRITER	8955 BEVERLY BLVD	LOS ANGELES, CA	90048
JOHNSON, HILDRED C	TRUMPETER	3953 6TH AVE	LOS ANGELES, CA	90008
JOHNSON, HORACE C	ALTO HORNIST	1031 W 85TH ST	LOS ANGELES, CA	90044
JOHNSON, HOWARD	SINGER	180 W END AVE #1-E	NEW YORK, NY	10023
JOHNSON, HOWARD L	WRITER	12752 MULHOLLAND DR	BEVERLY HILLS, CA	90210
JOHNSON, J J	TROMBONIST-COMPOSER	4001 MURIETTA AVE	SHERMAN OAKS, CA	91423
JOHNSON, JAMES	HELDEN BARITONE	SARDOS, 180 W END AVE	NEW YORK, NY	10023
JOHNSON, JAMES A, JR	SINGER-SONGWRITER	SEE - JAMES, RICK		
JOHNSON, JAMES D	TV DIRECTOR	4840 MAMMOTH AVE	SHERMAN OAKS, CA	91423
JOHNSON, JAMES F	GUITARIST	7115 S MAIN ST	LOS ANGELES, CA	90003
JOHNSON, JAMES HAROLD	MUSICIAN	601 VALLEY AVE #109	BIRMINGHAM, AL	35209
JOHNSON, JAMES MARVIN	GUITARIST	604 LAMAR DR	NASHVILLE, TN	37205
JOHNSON, JAMES-BURR	TV WRITER	8955 BEVERLY BLVD	LOS ANGELES, CA	90048
JOHNSON, JANET	ACTRESS	SEE - JULIEN, JANET		
JOHNSON, JAY	VENTRILOQUIST	9000 SUNSET BLVD #1200	LOS ANGELES, CA	90069
JOHNSON, JAY W	PIANIST	BEAR MOUNTAIN VILLAGE		
		RURAL ROUTE #2	HARRISON, ME	04040
JOHNSON, JEROME L	WRITER	8955 BEVERLY BLVD	LOS ANGELES, CA	90048
JOHNSON, JESSE	SINGER-SONGWRITER	AMERICAN ARTISTS, INC		
		312 WASHINGTON AVE N	MINNEAPOLIS, MN	55401
JOHNSON, JILL	ACTRESS	43 MATHESON RD	LONDON W14	ENGLAND
JOHNSON, JILL A	WRITER	555 W 57TH ST #1230	NEW YORK, NY	10019
JOHNSON, JIMMY	GUITARIST	131 COLEMONT DR	ANTIOCH, TN	37013
JOHNSON, JOE	ACTOR	357 S REXFORD DR #203	BEVERLY HILLS, CA	90212
JOHNSON, JOE	SINGER	STAR, 1311 CANDLELIGHT AVE	DALLAS, TX	75216
JOHNSON, JOHN	NEWS CORRESPONDENT	WABC-TV, 7 LINCOLN SQ	NEW YORK, NY	10023
JOHNSON, JOHN	NEWS CORRESPONDENT	203 "C" ST, NE	WASHINGTON, DC	20002
JOHNSON, JOHN E, JR	TV DIRECTOR	10 W 66TH ST #15-E	NEW YORK, NY	10023
JOHNSON, JOHN H	PUBLISHING EXECUTIVE	JET MAGAZINE, INC		
		820 S MICHIGAN AVE	CHICAHO, IL	60605
JOHNSON, JOHN T	TUBIST	10530 LERIDA PL	CHATSWORTH, CA	91311
JOHNSON, JOHN W	PIANIST	150 S PLYMOUTH BLVD	LOS ANGELES, CA	90004
JOHNSON, JOHNNY S, JR	GUITARIST	220 LISA LN	NASHVILLE, TN	37210
JOHNSON, JOSEPH A	TROMBONIST	6425 RUTHLEE AVE	SAN GABRIEL, CA	91775
JOHNSON, KATHERINE	SOPRANO	756 7TH AVE #67	NEW YORK, NY	10019
JOHNSON, KATHIE LEE	SINGER-TV HOST	GIFFORD, 355 TACONIC RD	GREENWICH, CT	06830
JOHNSON, KATHLEEN	CASTING DIRECTOR	8480 BEVERLY BLVD #148	LOS ANGELES, CA	90048
JOHNSON, KATHLEEN K	WRITER	8955 BEVERLY BLVD	LOS ANGELES, CA	90048
JOHNSON, KATHRYN	NEWS CORRESPONDENT	825 NEW HAMPSHIRE AVE #709, NW	WASHINGTON, DC	20037
JOHNSON, KEN	ACTOR	FELBER, 2126 W CAHUENGA BLVD	LOS ANGELES, CA	90068
JOHNSON, KENNETH C	WRITER-PRODUCER	4319 HAYVENHURST AVE	ENCINO, CA	91436
JOHNSON, KENNETH E	NEWS CORRESPONDENT	4408 WESTBROOK LN	KENSINGTON, MD	20895
JOHNSON, KIRBY D	FRENCH HORNIST	6914 WOODROW WILSON DR	LOS ANGELES, CA	90068
JOHNSON, KRISTINA	REPORTER	TIME & PEOPLE MAGAZINE		
		TIME & LIFE BUILDING		
		ROCKEFELLER CENTER	NEW YORK, NY	10020
JOHNSON, LAMONT	DIRECTOR-PRODUCER	601 PASEO MIRAMAR	PACIFIC PALISADES, CA	90272
JOHNSON, LARRY	SPORTS WRITER	UNIVERSAL PRESS SYNDICATE		
		4900 MAIN ST, 9TH FLOOR	KANSAS CITY, MO	62114
JOHNSON, LARRY H	SCREENWRITER	10960 WILSHIRE BLVD #922	LOS ANGELES, CA	90024
JOHNSON, LAURA	ACTRESS	15760 VENTURA BLVD #1730	ENCINO, CA	91436
JOHNSON, LAURIE	COMPOSER	PRIORY HOUSE, CLAMP HILL		
		STANMORE	MIDDLESEX	ENGLAND
JOHNSON, LEROY	NEWS CORRESPONDENT	NBC-TV, NEWS DEPARTMENT		
		4001 NEBRASKA AVE, NW	WASHINGTON, DC	20016
JOHNSON, LEZLIE BROOKS	FILM DIRECTOR	1290 OAKWOOD DR	TOPANGA CANYON, CA	90290
JOHNSON, LOIS	SINGER	POST OFFICE BOX 50	GOODLETSVILLE, TN	37072
JOHNSON, LOIS W	CONDUCTOR	5015 KESTER AVE #5	SHERMAN OAKS, CA	91423
JOHNSON, LUCY ANTEK	TV EXECUTIVE	NBC TELEVISION NETWORK		
		30 ROCKEFELLER PLAZA	NEW YORK, NY	10112
JOHNSON, LUTHER "GUITAR JR"	GUITARIST	CONCERTED, 312 SALEM ST	MEDFORD, MA	02155
JOHNSON, LYNN-HOLLY	ACTRESS	151 S EL CAMINO DR	BEVERLY HILLS, CA	90212
JOHNSON, MAL	NEWS CORRESPONDENT	400 N CAPITOL ST, NW	WASHINGTON, DC	20001
JOHNSON, MARCUS F	GUITARIST	721 DUE WEST #E-301	MADISON, TN	37115
JOHNSON, MARGUERITE	WRITER-EDITOR	TIME/TIME & LIFE BLDG		
JOHNSON, MARK	FILM PRODUCER	1888 CENTURY PARK E #1400	LOS ANGELES, CA	90067
JOHNSON, MARK	GUITARIST	660 HARDING PL	NASHVILLE, TN	37211
JOHNSON, MARK C	WRITER	8955 BEVERLY BLVD	LOS ANGELES, CA	90048
JOHNSON, MARK M	DIRECTOR-PRODUCER	1290 OAKWOOD DR	TOPANGA CANYON, CA	90290
JOHNSON, MARTIN	GUITARIST	ROUTE #1, BOX 222	WESTMORELAND, TN	37186
JOHNSON, MARY JANE	SINGER	1710 S POLK ST	AMARILLO, TX	79102
JOHNSON, MARY LEA	THEATER PRODUCER	PRODUCERS CIRCLE COMPANY		
		1350 AVE OF THE AMERICAS	NEW YORK, NY	10019
JOHNSON, MARY R	WRITER	555 W 57TH ST #1230	NEW YORK, NY	10019
JOHNSON, MAURICE	PHOTOGRAPHER	3804 RAYMOND ST	CHEVY CHASE, MD	20015
JOHNSON, MEL	CASTING DIRECTOR	MCA/UNIVERSAL STUDIOS, INC		
		100 UNIVERSAL CITY PLAZA	UNIVERSAL CITY, CA	91608
JOHNSON, MELINDA	NEWS CORRESPONDENT	1755 S JEFFERSON DAVIS HWY	ARLINGTON, VA	22202
JOHNSON, MICHAEL	SINGER-GUITARIST	POST OFFICE BOX 40661	NASHVILLE, TN	37204
JOHNSON, MICHELE	TV WRITER	1541 N VINE ST	HOLLYWOOD, CA	90028
JOHNSON, MICHELLE	ACTRESS	400 S BEVERLY DR #216	BEVERLY HILLS, CA	90212
JOHNSON, MIKE	GUITARIST	809 W OLD HICKORY BLVD	MADISON, TN	37115
JOHNSON, MONICA MC GOWAN	SCREENWRITER	8955 BEVERLY BLVD	LOS ANGELES, CA	90048
JOHNSON, NANCY	SOPRANO	CAMI, 165 W 57TH ST	NEW YORK, NY	10019

Name	Occupation	Address	City	Zip/Country
JOHNSON, NICHOLAS R	PIANIST	86 LAS LOMAS RD	DUARTE, CA	91010
JOHNSON, NOEL	ACTOR	218 SAINT MARGARET'S RD		
		SAINT MARGARET'S-ON-THE-THAMES		
		TWICKENHAM	MIDDLESEX	ENGLAND
JOHNSON, NORMAN E	VIOLINIST	1525 POINT VIEW ST	LOS ANGELES, CA	90035
JOHNSON, PAGE	ACTOR	49 GROVE ST	NEW YORK, NY	10014
JOHNSON, PAMELA	AUTO HARPIST	ROUTE #4, BOX 38-A	LEXINGTON, TN	38351
JOHNSON, PAT E	SCREENWRITER	8955 BEVERLY BLVD	LOS ANGELES, CA	90048
JOHNSON, PETER	COLUMNIST	POST OFFICE BOX 500	WASHINGTON, DC	20044
JOHNSON, PETER C	SINGER	225 W 57TH ST #301	NEW YORK, NY	10019
JOHNSON, PHILIP D	PIANIST	2078 SUNNYSIDE DR	BRENTWOOD, TN	37027
JOHNSON, R TOWNLEY	MUSIC ARRANGER	ROUTE #7, HILLAKE DR	LEBANON, TN	37087
JOHNSON, R VERLE	DIRECTOR	4918 SCHUYLER DR	ANNANDALE, VA	22003
JOHNSON, RAFER	ACTOR	9255 SUNSET BLVD #610	LOS ANGELES, CA	90069
JOHNSON, RANDI E	WRITER	8955 BEVERLY BLVD	LOS ANGELES, CA	90048
JOHNSON, RICHARD	ACTOR	ICM, 388-396 OXFORD ST	LONDON W1	ENGLAND
JOHNSON, RICHMOND F	ACTOR	WILLIAMSON, 932 N LA BREA AVE	LOS ANGELES, CA	90038
JOHNSON, ROBERT L	TV EXECUTIVE	BLACK ENTERTAINMENT TV		
		1050 31ST ST, NW	WASHINGTON, DC	20007
JOHNSON, ROBIN	ACTRESS	211 S BEVERLY DR #107	BEVERLY HILLS, CA	90212
JOHNSON, ROGER, JR	DIRECTOR	4240 TEESDALE AVE	STUDIO CITY, CA	91604
JOHNSON, ROLANDA S	NEWS CORRESPONDENT	1077 31ST ST, NW	WASHINGTON, DC	20007
JOHNSON, ROME	GUITARIST	19854 LABRADOR ST	CHATSWORTH, CA	91311
JOHNSON, ROME	SINGER	POST OFFICE 4234	PANORAMA CITY, CA	91412
JOHNSON, ROY, JR	MUSICIAN	3912 ARLINGTON SQ DR #5	HOUSTON, TX	77034
JOHNSON, RUSSELL	ACTOR	2501 W BURBANK BLVD #304	BURBANK, CA	91505
JOHNSON, RYERSON	WRITER	8955 BEVERLY BLVD	LOS ANGELES, CA	90048
JOHNSON, SANDER	ACTOR	10000 RIVERSIDE DR #3	TOLUCA LAKE, CA	91602
JOHNSON, SANDY	NEWS CORRESPONDENT	1841 CORCORAN ST, NW	WASHINGTON, DC	20009
JOHNSON, SARAH	VIOLINIST	AFFILIATE ARTISTS, INC		
		37 W 65TH ST, 6TH FLOOR	NEW YORK, NY	10023
JOHNSON, SCOTT	GUITARIST	NEW MUSIC SERVICE CO		
		500 BROADWAY	NEW YORK, NY	10012
JOHNSON, SCOTT	SCREENWRITER	8955 BEVERLY BLVD	LOS ANGELES, CA	90048
JOHNSON, SHARON	DIRECTOR	4201 VIA MARINA #162	MARINA DEL REY, CA	90292
JOHNSON, SHARON S	NEWS CORRESPONDENT	1316 NEW HAMPSHIRE AVE #101, NW	WASHINGTON, DC	20036
JOHNSON, SHELLY	ACTRESS-MODEL	7060 HOLLYWOOD BLVD #1010	LOS ANGELES, CA	90028
JOHNSON, STANLEY R	DIRECTOR	1922 LAKE ALDEN DR	APOPKA, FL	32703
JOHNSON, STEPHEN	WRITER	8955 BEVERLY BLVD	LOS ANGELES, CA	90048
JOHNSON, STERLING	TV DIRECTOR	1315 S OAKLAND AVE	PASADENA, CA	91106
JOHNSON, STEVE	NEWS CORRESPONDENT	986 FARM HAVEN DR	ROCKVILLE, MD	20852
JOHNSON, STEVE C	DRUMMER	126 WALTON FERRY #B-4	HENDERSONVILLE, TN	37075
JOHNSON, STEVEN R	TROMBONIST	1254 SPAZIER AVE	GLENDALE, CA	91201
JOHNSON, SUNE	FRENCH HORNIST	1446 MILDINE DR	GLENDALE, CA	91208
JOHNSON, THADDEUS L	MUSICIAN	3209 BRAY DR	NASHVILLE, TN	37218
JOHNSON, THOMAS	NEWS CORRESPONDENT	NBC-TV, NEWS DEPARTMENT		
		4001 NEBRASKA AVE, NW	WASHINGTON, DC	20016
JOHNSON, THOMAS H	MUSICIAN	ROUTE #1, BOX 61	LYLES, TN	37098
JOHNSON, TINA	ACTRESS	ICM, 40 W 57TH ST	NEW YORK, NY	10019
JOHNSON, TOM	CARTOONIST	TRIBUNE MEDIA SERVICES		
		64 E CONCORD ST	ORLANDO, FL	32801
JOHNSON, TRAVIS	WRITER-PRODUCER	POST OFFICE BOX 2093	DENTON, TX	76201
JOHNSON, TROY	SINGER	6433 TOPANGA CANYON BLVD #154	CANOGA PARK, CA	91303
JOHNSON, VAN	ACTOR	THE WILLIAM MORRIS AGENCY		
		1350 AVE OF THE AMERICAS	NEW YORK, NY	10019
JOHNSON, VICTORIA	MODEL	8075 W 3RD ST #303	LOS ANGELES, CA	90048
JOHNSON, W D	WRITER	8955 BEVERLY BLVD	LOS ANGELES, CA	90048
JOHNSON, WALTER E, JR	SAXOPHONIST	9966 ROSCOE BLVD	SUN VALLEY, CA	91352
JOHNSON, WALTER I	TRUMPETER	400 S SPARKS ST	BURBANK, CA	91506
JOHNSON, WAYMER L	DIRECTOR	1101 3RD ST #816, SW	WASHINGTON, DC	20024
JOHNSON, WAYNE A	GUITARIST	9901 ROSCOE BLVD	SUN VALLEY, CA	91352
JOHNSON, WILLIAM	PHOTOGRAPHER	4913 STICKLEY RD	ROCKVILLE, MD	20853
JOHNSON, WILLIAM "JUDY"	BASEBALL	3701 KIAMENSI	MARSHALLTOWN, DE	19808
JOHNSON, WILLIAM K	GUITARIST	ROUTE #4	MOUNT JULIET, TN	37122
JOHNSON, WILLIAM OSCAR	SPORTS WRITER-EDITOR	SPORTS ILLUSTRATED MAGAZINE		
		TIME & LIFE BUILDING		
		ROCKEFELLER CENTER	NEW YORK, NY	10020
JOHNSON, WYATT	ACTOR	CARPENTER, 1516-W REDWOOD ST	SAN DIEGO, CA	92101
JOHNSON MOUNTAIN BOYS, THE	C & W GROUP	10235 LEWIS DR	DAMASCUS, MD	20872
JOHNSON-ALDRETE, LORI	DIRECTOR	3015 CATALINA DR	DAVIS, CA	95616
JOHNSON-HAMILTON, JOYCE	CONDUCTOR	KAY, 58 W 58TH ST	NEW YORK, NY	10019
JOHNSON-ROBINSON, MARNI	FRENCH HORN	5124 AUCKLAND AVE	NORTH HOLLYWOOD, CA	91601
		322 MURIEL ST, NE	ALBUQUERQUE, NM	87123
JOHNSONS, THE	ROCK & ROLL GROUP	POST OFFICE BOX 53588	PHILADELPHIA, PA	19105
JOHNSSON, HILLARY	SOPRANO	JCB, 155 W 68TH ST	NEW YORK, NY	10023
JOHNSTON, BOBBY	GUITARIST	1010 18TH AVE S	NASHVILLE, TN	37212
JOHNSTON, DAVID	NEWS CORRESPONDENT	4439 ELLICOTT ST, NW	WASHINGTON, DC	20016
JOHNSTON, ERIC	ACTOR	3575 W CAHUENGA BLVD #320	LOS ANGELES, CA	90068
JOHNSTON, FRANK B	PHOTOGRAPHER	THE LORCOM TOWERS		
		4300 OLD DOMINION DR	ARLINGTON, VA	22207
JOHNSTON, FREDERICK E, JR	DIRECTOR	POST OFFICE BOX 4060	PRINCETON, NJ	08540
JOHNSTON, HOWARD B, SR	MUSICIAN	524 E MARTHONNA RD	MADISON, TN	37115
JOHNSTON, J J	ACTOR	9255 SUNSET BLVD #510	LOS ANGELES, CA	90069
JOHNSTON, JAMES E	DRUMMER	POST OFFICE BOX 24346	NASHVILLE, TN	37202
JOHNSTON, JAMES R	DIRECTOR	140 E 39TH ST	NEW YORK, NY	10016

Name	Occupation	Address	City	Zip
JOHNSTON, JAMES W	NEWS CORRESPONDENT	1755 S JEFFERSON DAVIS HWY	ARLINGTON, VA	22202
JOHNSTON, JANE A	ACTRESS	247 S BEVERLY DR #102	BEVERLY HILLS, CA	90212
JOHNSTON, JERRY RAY	PIANIST	936-B RIVERSIDE DR	NASHVILLE, TN	37206
JOHNSTON, JOHN DENNIS	ACTOR	9744 WILSHIRE BLVD #206	BEVERLY HILLS, CA	90212
JOHNSTON, JOHN R	ACTOR	ABC-TV NETWORK, "LOVING" 1330 AVE OF THE AMERICAS	NEW YORK, NY	10019
JOHNSTON, JULANNE	ACTRESS	RUST, 29 FISHER RD	GROSSE POINTE, MI	48230
JOHNSTON, KENNETH E	FIDDLER	111 WHITSETT AVE #B-7	NASHVILLE, TN	37210
JOHNSTON, LYNN	CARTOONIST	UNIVERSAL PRESS SYNDICATE 4900 MAIN ST, 9TH FLOOR	KANSAS CITY, MO	62114
JOHNSTON, OSWALD	NEWS CORRESPONDENT	4800 QUEBEC ST, NW	WASHINGTON, DC	20016
JOHNSTON, RICHARD O	COMPOSER	7900 SALE AVE	CANOGA PARK, CA	91304
JOHNSTON, RICK	WRITER	555 W 57TH ST #1230	NEW YORK, NY	10019
JOHNSTON, T J	ACTOR	10946 S GROVEDALE DR	WHITTIER, CA	90603
JOHNSTON, TOM, BAND	ROCK & ROLL GROUP	POST OFFICE BOX 878	SONOMA, CA	95476
JOHNSTON, TRACE	SCREENWRITER	8955 BEVERLY BLVD	LOS ANGELES, CA	90048
JOHNSTON, WILLIAM D H	NEWS CORRESPONDENT	1301 20TH ST #405, NW	WASHINGTON, DC	20036
JOHNSTONE, DAVEY	SINGER	9595 WILSHIRE BLVD #505	BEVERLY HILLS, CA	90212
JOHNSTONE, IAIN	DIRECTOR-PRODUCER	16 TOURNAY RD	LONDON SW6	ENGLAND
JOI, MARILYN	ACTRESS	205 S BEVERLY DR #210	BEVERLY HILLS, CA	90212
JOINT HIERS, THE	GOSPEL GROUP	POST OFFICE DRAWER 20146	SAINT PETERSBURG, FL	33742
JOLAS, BETSY	COMPOSER	YALE SCHOOL OF MUSIC 96 WALL ST	NEW HAVEN, CT	06511
JOLGUERA, JOSE G	TV DIRECTOR	12297 SW 204 TERR	MIAMI, FL	33177
JOLL, BARRIE A	DIRECTOR	58 FRITH ST	LONDON W1	ENGLAND
JOLL, PHILLIP	BARITONE	CAMI, 165 W 57TH ST	NEW YORK, NY	10019
JOLLEY, DAVID	FRENCH HORNIST	CAMI, 165 W 57TH ST	NEW YORK, NY	10019
JOLLEY, NORMAN	WRITER	11189 AQUA VISTA ST	NORTH HOLLYWOOD, CA	91602
JOLLEY, STAN	ART DIRECTOR	2965 ST GREGORY RD	GLENDALE, CA	91206
JOLLY, JOE	ACTOR	2614 CLOVERFIELD BLVD	SANTA MONICA, CA	90405
JON & THE NIGHTRIDERS	ROCK & ROLL GROUP	OLDIES, 5218 ALMONT ST	LOS ANGELES, CA	90032
JONAH, DOLLY	ACTRESS	45 E 66TH ST	NEW YORK, NY	10021
JONAS, NORMAN N	NEWS CORRESPONDENT	9032 WEANT DR	GREAT FALLS, VA	22066
JONAS, SHIRLEY	WRITER	555 W 57TH ST #1230	NEW YORK, NY	10019
JONAS, SUSAN	PHOTO EDITOR	DISCOVER/TIME & LIFE BLDG ROCKEFELLER CENTER	NEW YORK, NY	10020
JONAS, THEODORE	TV WRITER	8955 BEVERLY BLVD	LOS ANGELES, CA	90048
JONASON, DAVID A	WRITER	555 W 57TH ST #1230	NEW YORK, NY	10019
JONASON, LOUISA	SOPRANO	CAMI, 165 W 57TH ST	NEW YORK, NY	10019
JONES, A BERNEY	DIRECTOR	142 W END AVE #12-L	NEW YORK, NY	10023
JONES, AARON M	NEWS CORRESPONDENT	1755 S JEFFERSON DAVIS HWY	ARLINGTON, VA	22202
JONES, AL	STUNTMAN	3518 W CAHUENGA BLVD #300	LOS ANGELES, CA	90068
JONES, ALAN	ACTOR	4040 VINELAND AVE #225	STUDIO CITY, CA	91604
JONES, ALBERT H	NEWS CORRESPONDENT	3109 HAWTHORNE ST, NW	WASHINGTON, DC	20008
JONES, ALLAN	ACTOR-SINGER	10 W 66TH ST	NEW YORK, NY	10023
JONES, AMY	WRITER	8955 BEVERLY BLVD	LOS ANGELES, CA	90048
JONES, ANTHONY	WRITER	555 W 57TH ST #1230	NEW YORK, NY	10019
JONES, ANTHONY R	COMPOSER-CONDUCTOR	1016 S CRESCENT HGTS BLVD	LOS ANGELES, CA	90035
JONES, ARTHUR	NEWS CORRESPONDENT	5208 AMPTHILL DR	ALEXANDRIA, VA	22312
JONES, AYVONNE	SINGER-GUITARIST	201 E HOYT	LONG VIEW, TX	75601
JONES, BAIRD	CONDUCTOR	509 35TH ST SW	OKLAHOMA CITY, OK	73109
JONES, BEN	SINGER	5 BLVD, SE	ATLANTA, GA	30312
JONES, BETTY	SOPRANO	LIEBERMAN, 11 RIVERSIDE DR	NEW YORK, NY	10023
JONES, BILL	FILM CRITIC	POST OFFICE BOX 1950	PHOENIX, AZ	85001
JONES, BOBBY & NEW LIFE	GOSPEL GROUP	6750 W 75TH ST, MARKADE 75 BUILDING #2-A	OVERLAND PARK, KS	66204
JONES, CARO	CASTING DIRECTOR	5858 HOLLYWOOD BLVD #403	LOS ANGELES, CA	90046
JONES, CAROL	ACTRESS	6736 LAUREL CANYON BLVD #306	NORTH HOLLYWOOD, CA	91606
JONES, CHARLENE	ACTRESS	415 N CRESCENT DR #320	BEVERLY HILLS, CA	90210
JONES, CHARLES O	TV DIRECTOR	17800 WHITE'S FERRY RD	POOLESVILLE, MD	20837
JONES, CHARLIE	SPORTSCASTER	NBC SPORTS, 3000 W ALAMEDA AVE	BURBANK, CA	91523
JONES, CHARLOTTE	ACTRESS	205 W 57TH ST	NEW YORK, NY	10019
JONES, CHARLOTTE SCHIFF	CABLE EXECUTIVE	SCHIFF-JONES, 1775 BROADWAY	NEW YORK, NY	10019
JONES, CHRISTINE	ACTRESS	FELBER, 2126 N CAHUENGA BLVD	LOS ANGELES, CA	90068
JONES, CHRISTOPHER	ACTOR	4057 SAPPHIRE DR	ENCINO, CA	91436
JONES, CLAIRE	ACTRESS	7256 ROSEWOOD AVE	LOS ANGELES, CA	90036
JONES, CLARK R	TV DIRECTOR	337 W 70TH ST	NEW YORK, NY	10023
JONES, CLAUDE EARL	ACTOR	151 N SAN VICENTE BLVD #208	BEVERLY HILLS, CA	90211
JONES, CRANSTON	WRITER-EDITOR	PEOPLE/TIME & LIFE BLDG ROCKEFELLER CENTER	NEW YORK, NY	10020
JONES, DANNY	MUSICIAN	ROUTE #2, BOX 21-A	DICKSON, TX	37055
JONES, DAVE	FILM DIRECTOR	POST OFFICE BOX 55025	SHERMAN OAKS, CA	91403
JONES, DAVEY	SINGER-ACTOR	21 ELMS RD	LONDON	ENGLAND
JONES, DAVID	FILM EXECUTIVE	VARIETY CLUB, 25 DORSET HOUSE GLOUCESTER PL	LONDON NW1 5AD	ENGLAND
JONES, DAVID	FILM DIRECTOR	9201 WILSHIRE BLVD #202	BEVERLY HILLS, CA	90210
JONES, DAVID LAWRENCE	GUITARIST	ROUTE #2, BOX 21-A	DICKSON, TN	37055
JONES, DEAN	ACTOR	CONTEMPORARY ARTISTS 132 S LASKY DR	BEVERLY HILLS, CA	90212
JONES, DEBORAH	SCREENWRITER	8955 BEVERLY BLVD	LOS ANGELES, CA	90048
JONES, DELLA	MEZZO-SOPRANO	IMG ARTISTS, 22 E 71ST ST	NEW YORK, NY	10021
JONES, DELORES	SOPRANO	SPRINGER, 1001 ROLANDVU RD	BALTIMORE, MD	21204
JONES, DOROTHY M	NEWS CORRESPONDENT	4400 JENIFER ST, NW	WASHINGTON, DC	20015
JONES, EDWARD	TV WRITER-PRODUCER	37 E SHORE DR	BABYLON, NY	11702
JONES, EDWARD M	WRITER	555 W 57TH ST #1230	NEW YORK, NY	10019

JONES, ELVIN	DRUMMER	KEIKO JONES MANAGEMENT		
		415 CENTRAL PARK W	NEW YORK, NY	10025
JONES, ELWYN	TV WRITER	BLAENEINON, PONT SHAN		
		LLANDYSSUL	DYFED	ENGLAND
JONES, ERIC P	DIRECTOR	3521 DAHLIA AVE	LOS ANGELES, CA	90026
JONES, EUGENE	DIRECTOR-PRODUCER	190 E 72ND ST	NEW YORK, NY	10021
JONES, EUGENE S	FILM WRITER-DIRECTOR	461 BELLAGIO TERR	LOS ANGELES, CA	90049
JONES, FREDDIE	ACTOR	IAR, 235-241 REGENT ST	LONDON W1A 2JT	ENGLAND
JONES, FREDDIE	ACTOR	STONE, 1052 CAROL DR	LOS ANGELES, CA	90069
JONES, GARY	ACTOR	19 W 44TH ST #1500	NEW YORK, NY	10036
JONES, GAYNOR	SOPRANO	POST OFFICE BOX 188		
		STATION A	TORONTO, ONT	CANADA
JONES, GEMMA	ACTOR	LARRY DALZELL ASSOCIATES		
		126 KENNINGTON PARK RD	LONDON SE11 4DJ	ENGLAND
JONES, GENE	WRITER	555 W 57TH ST #1230	NEW YORK, NY	10019
JONES, GEORGE	SINGER-COMPOSER	38 MUSIC SQUARE E #300	NASHVILLE, TN	37203
JONES, GERARD	WRITER	THE NATIONAL LAMPOON		
		635 MADISON AVE	NEW YORK, NY	10022
JONES, GERRE L	NEWS CORRESPONDENT	2123 TUNLAW RD, NW	WASHINGTON, DC	20007
JONES, GLENN	SINGER	LOUISE C WEST MANAGEMENT		
		1775 BROADWAY, 7TH FLOOR	NEW YORK, NY	10019
JONES, GRACE	MODEL-ACTRESS	POST OFFICE BOX 82	GREAT NECK, NY	11021
JONES, GRANDPA	SINGER-GUITARIST	POST OFFICE BOX 57	MOUNTAIN VIEW, AR	72560
JONES, GWENDOLYN	MEZZO-SOPRANO	45 W 60TH ST #4-K	NEW YORK, NY	10023
JONES, GWYNETH	SOPRANO	CAMI, 165 W 57TH ST	NEW YORK, NY	10019
JONES, GWYNETH A	WRITER	555 W 57TH ST #1230	NEW YORK, NY	10019
JONES, HARLAN E	MANDOLINIST	110 SHIHMEN CT	ANTIOCH, TN	37013
JONES, HAROLD	FLUTIST	POST OFFICE BOX 27539	PHILADELPHIA, PA	19118
JONES, HAROLD EUGENE	PIANIST	3684 TAMPA DR	NASHVILLE, TN	37211
JONES, HENRY	ACTOR	12221 TWEED LN	LOS ANGELES, CA	90049
JONES, HOWARD	SINGER-SONGWRITER	POST OFFICE BOX 185		
		HIGH WYCOM	BUCKS HP11 2E2	ENGLAND
JONES, IVY	ACTRESS	8075 W 3RD ST #303	LOS ANGELES, CA	90048
JONES, JACK	SINGER-ACTOR	8075 W 3RD ST #303	LOS ANGELES, CA	90048
JONES, JACQUE	TV WRITER	8955 BEVERLY BLVD	LOS ANGELES, CA	90048
JONES, JAMES CELLAN	TV DIRECTOR	19 CUMBERLAND RD, KEW	SURREY	ENGLAND
JONES, JAMES EARL	ACTOR	9255 SUNSET BLVD #1105	LOS ANGELES, CA	90069
JONES, JAN S	GUITARIST	118 BROOKSIDE DR	HENDERSONVILLE, TN	37075
JONES, JANET	ACTRESS	SEE - JONES, JANET MARIE		
JONES, JANET MARIE	ACTRESS	15301 VENTURA BLVD #345	SHERMAN OAKS, CA	91403
JONES, JEFF	WRITER	555 W 57TH ST #1230	NEW YORK, NY	10019
JONES, JEFFREY	ACTOR	9200 SUNSET BLVD #1210	LOS ANGELES, CA	90069
JONES, JEFFREY M	COMPOSER	6456 BLUCHER ST	VAN NUYS, CA	91406
JONES, JEFFREY M	DIRECTOR	520 N MICHIGAN AVE #436	CHICAGO, IL	60611
JONES, JENNIFER	ACTRESS	POST OFFICE BOX 2248	BEVERLY HILLS, CA	90213
JONES, JENNIFER	MEZZO-SOPRANO	CAMI, 165 W 57TH ST	NEW YORK, NY	10019
JONES, JO	MUSICIAN	401 E 64TH ST #4-A	NEW YORK, NY	10021
JONES, JOCELYN	ACTRESS	15010 VENTURA BLVD #219	SHERMAN OAKS, CA	91403
JONES, JOE	CONDUCTOR	10556 ARNWOOD RD	LAKE VIEW TERRACE, CA	91342
JONES, JOE	MUSICIAN	POST OFFICE BOX 275	MOUNT LAUREL, NJ	08054
JONES, JOHN CHRISTOPHER	ACTOR	AFFILIATE ARTISTS, INC		
		37 W 65TH ST, 6TH FLOOR	NEW YORK, NY	10023
JONES, JOHN J	WRITER	555 W 57TH ST #1230	NEW YORK, NY	10019
JONES, JONI L	WRITER	555 W 57TH ST #1230	NEW YORK, NY	10019
JONES, JORGE	GUITARIST	300 LIBERTY CIR #F-1	MADISON, TN	37115
JONES, KEN	ACTOR	23 LAURIER RD	LONDON NW5	ENGLAND
JONES, KEN	CONDUCTOR-ARRANGER	APPLEGARTH, CUCKOO HILL	MIDDLESEX	ENGLAND
JONES, KEN "K O"	ACTOR	869 LEONARD DR	WESTBURY, NY	11590
JONES, KENLEY	NEWS CORRESPONDENT	NBC-TV, NEWS DEPARTMENT		
		30 ROCKEFELLER PLAZA	NEW YORK, NY	10112
JONES, KENNETH V	COMPOSER-CONDUCTOR	HICKWELLS, CHAILEY, NEAR LEWES	SUSSEX	ENGLAND
JONES, KENNETH W	GUITARIST	14 HILL ST	ANNAPOLIS, MD	21401
JONES, KEVIN CARTER	GUITARIST	ROUTE #2, BOX 38, WEEMS RD	DICKSON, TN	37055
JONES, KIT	WRITER	555 W 57TH ST #1230	NEW YORK, NY	10019
JONES, L DEAN, JR	FILM DIRECTOR	440 PANORAMIC HWY	MILL VALLEY, CA	94941
JONES, L Q	ACTOR-DIRECTOR	9000 SUNSET BLVD #1112	LOS ANGELES, CA	90069
JONES, LAURIS L	CONDUCTOR	POST OFFICE BOX 1126	SPRING VALLEY, CA	92077
JONES, LELAND S	WRITER-PRODUCER	124 HARRINGTON AVE	WESTWOOD, CA	07675
JONES, LINDSAY V	ACTRESS	5734 ELMER AVE	NORTH HOLLYWOOD, CA	91601
JONES, MALINDA	VIOLINIST	21 W ROYAL OAKS TOWER		
		4505 HARDING RD	NASHVILLE, TN	37205
JONES, MALLORY	ACTRESS	9000 SUNSET BLVD #1200	LOS ANGELES, CA	90069
JONES, MARCIA MAE	ACTRESS	4541 HAZELTINE AVE #4	SHERMAN OAKS, CA	91423
JONES, MARILYN	ACTRESS	445 N BEDFORD DR #PH	BEVERLY HILLS, CA	90210
JONES, MARK	TV WRITER	8955 BEVERLY BLVD	LOS ANGELES, CA	90048
JONES, MARK ALLEN	GUITARIST	POST OFFICE BOX 57	MOUNTAIN VIEW, AR	72560
JONES, MELVIN L	NEWS CORRESPONDENT	11903 BROADMOOR CT	UPPER MARLBORO, MD	20772
JONES, MICHAEL R	TV DIRECTOR	POST OFFICE BOX 49348	LOS ANGELES, CA	90049
JONES, MICKEY	ACTOR	15010 VENTURA BLVD #219	SHERMAN OAKS, CA	91403
JONES, MIKE W	GUITARIST	208 MORRIS ST	HENDERSONVILLE, TN	37075
JONES, MORRIS	NEWS CORRESPONDENT	5151 WISCONSIN AVE, NW	WASHINGTON, DC	20016
JONES, NANCY	TV PRODUCER	1541 N VINE ST	HOLLYWOOD, CA	90028
JONES, NATALIE	FILM PRODUCER	190 E 72ND ST	NEW YORK, NY	10021
JONES, NEIL R	WRITER	1028 FAY ST	FULTON, NY	13069
JONES, NICKIE	ACTRESS	8961 SUNSET BLVD #B	LOS ANGELES, CA	90069

GRACE JONES

HOWARD JONES

JAMES EARL JONES

RICKIE LEE JONES

SHIRLEY JONES

TOM JONES

RICHARD JORDAN

LOUIS JOURDAN

RAUL JULIA

Name	Occupation	Address	City/State	Zip/Country
JONES, NORMAN	ACTOR	BOYACK, 9 CORK ST	LONDON W1	ENGLAND
JONES, OTIS	TV WRITER	8955 BEVERLY BLVD	LOS ANGELES, CA	90048
JONES, PARNELLI	AUTO RACER	20550 EARL ST	TORRANCE, CA	90503
JONES, PATRICIA	PRODUCER	MGM, 10202 W WASHINGTON BLVD	CULVER CITY, CA	90230
JONES, PATRICIA	TV WRITER	8955 BEVERLY BLVD	LOS ANGELES, CA	90048
JONES, PAUL	WRESTLER-MANAGER	NATIONAL WRESTLING ALLIANCE		
		JIM CROCKETT PROMOTIONS		
		421 BRIARBEND DR	CHARLOTTE, NC	28209
JONES, PEGGY	ACTRESS	9601 WILSHIRE BLVD #GL-11	BEVERLY HILLS, CA	90210
JONES, PETER	ACTOR-WRITER	32 ACACIA RD	LONDON NW8 6AS	ENGLAND
JONES, PETER	WRITER	555 W 57TH ST #1230	NEW YORK, NY	10019
JONES, PHIL	NEWS CORRESPONDENT	CBS NEWS, 2020 "M" ST, NW	WASHINGTON, DC	20036
JONES, PHILIP H	NEWS CORRESPONDENT	5105 WESTPORT RD	CHEVY CHASE, MD	20815
JONES, PHILIP H, II	TROMBONIST	504 BARCLAY SQUARE CT	ANTIOCH, TN	37013
JONES, QUINCY	COMP-ARR-PROD	10880 WILSHIRE BLVD #2110	LOS ANGELES, CA	90024
JONES, RAMONA	MANDOLINIST	POST OFFICE BOX 57	MOUNTAIN VIEW, AR	72560
JONES, RANDY	CARTOONIST	THE NATIONAL LAMPOON		
		635 MADISON AVE	NEW YORK, NY	10022
JONES, RANDY	GUITARIST	3684 TAMPA DR	NASHVILLE, TN	37211
JONES, REESA KAY	SINGER	OPERATION MUSIC ENTERPRISES		
		233 W WOODLAND AVE	OTTUMWA, IA	52501
JONES, RICHARD C	WRITER	8955 BEVERLY BLVD	LOS ANGELES, CA	90048
JONES, RICK V	COMPOSER	1016 S CRESCENT HGTS BLVD	LOS ANGELES, CA	90035
JONES, RICKIE LEE	SINGER-SONGWRITER	10100 SANTA MONICA BLVD #1600	LOS ANGELES, CA	90067
JONES, RICKY LEE	WRESTLER	NATIONAL WRESTLING ALLIANCE		
		JIM CROCKETT PROMOTIONS		
		421 BRIARBEND DR	CHARLOTTE, NC	28209
JONES, ROBERT C	TV WRITER	8955 BEVERLY BLVD	LOS ANGELES, CA	90048
JONES, ROBERT EARL	ACTOR	THE MANHATTAN PLAZA		
		400 W 43RD ST	NEW YORK, NY	10036
JONES, ROBERT M	DIRECTOR	18617 W SOLEDAD CANYON	CANYON CITY, CA	91351
JONES, ROCHELLE A	WRITER	555 W 57TH ST #1230	NEW YORK, NY	10019
JONES, RONALD	TV DIRECTOR-PRODUCER	21 HOLLAND PARK AVE	LONDON W11	ENGLAND
JONES, RONALD N	COMPOSER	11840 RIVERSIDE DR	NORTH HOLLYWOOD, CA	91607
JONES, ROOSEVELT	WRESTLER	SEE - JONES, S D		
JONES, S D	WRESTLER	POST OFFICE BOX 3859	STAMFORD, CT	06905
JONES, SABRA	ACTRESS	2160 OLIVE AVE	LONG BEACH, CA	90806
JONES, SAM J	ACTOR	1717 N HIGHLAND AVE #90	LOS ANGELES, CA	90028
JONES, SAMUEL	CONDUCTOR	2235 SOUTHGATE BLVD	HOUSTON, TX	77030
JONES, SHERRY L	WRITER	555 W 57TH ST #1230	NEW YORK, NY	10019
JONES, SHERYLE R	WRITER	555 W 57TH ST #1230	NEW YORK, NY	10019
JONES, SHIRLEY	ACTRESS	701 N OAKHURST DR	BEVERLY HILLS, CA	90210
JONES, SHIRLEY	SINGER	CAPITOL RECORDS COMPANY		
		1750 N VINE ST	HOLLYWOOD, CA	90028
JONES, SPECIAL DELIVERY	WRESTLER	SEE - JONES, S D		
JONES, TAMARA	MODEL	FORD MODEL AGENCY		
		344 E 59TH ST	NEW YORK, NY	10022
JONES, TAMMIE	WRESTLER	GORGEOUS GIRLS OF WRESTLING		
		RIVIERA HOTEL & CASINO		
		DAVID B MC LANE PRODS		
		2901 S LAS VEGAS BLVD	LAS VEGAS, NV	89109
JONES, TERRY	ACT-WRI-DIR	PYTHON PRODS, 6 CAMBRIDGE GATE	LONDON NW1 4JR	ENGLAND
JONES, TERRY RUSSELL	GUITARIST	371 BURNING TREE DR	HERMITAGE, TN	37076
JONES, TIM	COMEDIAN	ICM, 8899 BEVERLY BLVD	LOS ANGELES, CA	90048
JONES, TOM	DRUMMER	107 MOSS CT	HENDERSONVILLE, TN	37075
JONES, TOM	SINGER	363 COPA DE ORA RD	LOS ANGELES, CA	90077
JONES, TOMMY	GUITARIST	1201 WARNER CT	BRENTWOOD, TN	37027
JONES, TOMMY LEE	ACTOR	ICM, 8899 BEVERLY BLVD	LOS ANGELES, CA	90048
JONES, TRENT	TV WRITER	CBS-TV, "THE GUIDING LIGHT"		
		51 W 52ND ST	NEW YORK, NY	10019
JONES, TREVOR	COMPOSER	9 OWL'S GREEN, DENTON	SUFFOLK	ENGLAND
JONES, WALTER L	WRITER-PRODUCER	DGA, 110 W 57TH ST	NEW YORK, NY	10019
JONES, WELTON	THEATER CRITIC	POST OFFICE BOX 191	SAN DIEGO, CA	92112
JONES GIRLS, THE	VOCAL GROUP	POST OFFICE BOX 6010-761	SHERMAN OAKS, CA	91413
JONESES, THE	ROCK & ROLL GROUP	DR DREAM RECORDS COMPANY		
		833 W COLLINS AVE	ORANGE, CA	92667
JONESS, DONALD R	WRITER	8955 BEVERLY BLVD	LOS ANGELES, CA	90048
JONIK, JOHN	CARTOONIST	POST OFFICE BOX 4203	NEW YORK, NY	10017
JONKE, GARY JOHN	TV WRITER	2624 MANNING AVE	LOS ANGELES, CA	90064
JONSON, KEVIN JOE	DIRECTOR	3201 LANDOVER ST #1621	ALEXANDRIA, VA	22305
JONZUN, MICHAEL	SINGER-GUITARIST	BOSTON INTL MUSIC CO		
		545 BOSTON ST	BOSTON, MA	02116
JORDAN, ALAN	ACTOR	2501 W BURBANK BLVD #304	BURBANK, CA	91505
JORDAN, ARCHIE P	MUSIC ARRANGER	ROUTE #7, SPENCER CREEK RD	FRANKLIN, TN	37064
JORDAN, BOBBI	ACTRESS	1508 S MANSFIELD AVE	LOS ANGELES, CA	90019
JORDAN, CECIL	ACTOR	200 N ROBERTSON BLVD #308	BEVERLY HILLS, CA	90210
JORDAN, DELIA	TV WRITER	8955 BEVERLY BLVD	LOS ANGELES, CA	90048
JORDAN, DIANE	SINGER	152 SHAWNEE RD	MADISON, TN	37115
JORDAN, DULCIE	ACTRESS	6380 WILSHIRE BLVD #1600	LOS ANGELES, CA	90048
JORDAN, GLENN	FILM DIRECTOR	9401 WILSHIRE BLVD #700	BEVERLY HILLS, CA	90212
JORDAN, GLENN A	COMPOSER	11334 CALIFA ST	NORTH HOLLYWOOD, CA	91601
JORDAN, HOWARD	ACTOR	8235 SANTA MONICA BLVD #202	LOS ANGELES, CA	90046
JORDAN, JAMES CARROLL	ACTOR	8333 LOOKOUT MOUNTAIN AVE	LOS ANGELES, CA	90046
JORDAN, JAMES J	DIRECTOR	COAST, 1001 N POINSETTIA PL	HOLLYWOOD, CA	90046
JORDAN, JAY	DRUMMER	POST OFFICE BOX 901	GOODLETTSVILLE, TN	37072

THE JONES GIRLS

THE JUDDS
Wynonna • Naomi

Name	Occupation	Address	City	Zip
JORDAN, JIM	RADIO PERSONALITY	1310 TOWER GROVE DR	BEVERLY HILLS, CA	90210
JORDAN, JOEY	CHAINSAW JUGGLER	POST OFFICE BOX 60122		
		TERMINAL ANNEX	LOS ANGELES, CA	90060
JORDAN, JON	BODYBUILDER	1651 MARMONT AVE	LOS ANGELES, CA	90069
JORDAN, JUDITH	ACTRESS	5639 SATSUMA AVE	NORTH HOLLYWOOD, CA	91601
JORDAN, LARRY K	DIRECTOR-PRODUCER	65 MAIN ST	FRAMINGHAM, MA	01701
JORDAN, MICHAEL J	DIRECTOR	164 W 79TH ST	NEW YORK, NY	10024
JORDAN, MIKE	PIANIST	4895 HWY 20 SE	COVINGTON, GA	30209
JORDAN, MURRAY B	TV DIRECTOR	1605 1/2 S WOOSTER ST	LOS ANGELES, CA	90035
JORDAN, PAUL	ORGANIST	LIEBERMAN, 11 RIVERSIDE DR	NEW YORK, NY	10023
JORDAN, PETER	PHOTOGRAPHER	TIME/TIME & LIFE BLDG		
		ROCKEFELLER CENTER	NEW YORK, NY	10020
JORDAN, RICHARD	ACTOR	3704 CARBON CYN	MALIBU, CA	90265
JORDAN, ROBERT	WRITER	SCHNEE, 11602 COLLETT AVE	GRANADA HILLS, CA	91344
JORDAN, S MARC	ACTOR	KNBC-TV, "DAYS OF OUR LIVES"		
		3000 W ALAMEDA AVE	BURBANK, CA	91523
JORDAN, STANLEY	GUITARIST	C MARTIN, 242 W 30TH ST	NEW YORK, NY	10001
JORDAN, VICTOR HOWARD	GUITARIST	305 JOSAM DR	NASHVILLE, TN	37211
JORDAN, WILL	COMEDIAN	435 W 57TH ST #10-F	NEW YORK, NY	10019
JORDAN, WILLIAM	ACTOR	7466 BEVERLY BLVD #205	LOS ANGELES, CA	90036
JORDEN, JAN	ACTRESS	151 N SAN VICENTE BLVD #208	BEVERLY HILLS, CA	90211
JORGENSEN, DALE R	GUITARIST	2600 S LAKEPORT ST	SIOUX CITY, IA	51106
JORGENSEN, REBEKAH L	DIRECTOR	KARLIN, 1025 CHAUTAUQUA BLVD	PACIFIC PALISADES, CA	90272
JORGENSON, CHRISTINE	AUTHORESS	31752 GRAND CANYON DR	LAGUNA NIGUEL, CA	92677
JORY, TERRILL	CONDUCTOR	111 W 57TH ST #1203	NEW YORK, NY	10019
JOSEFSBERG, MILTON	WRITER-PRODUCER	4256 VALLEY MEADOW RD	ENCINO, CA	91436
JOSELOFF, MICHAEL H	WRITER	555 W 57TH ST #1230	NEW YORK, NY	10019
JOSEPH, ADRIAN H	TV WRITER-PRODUCER	201 LA VEREDA RD	PASADENA, CA	91105
JOSEPH, ALLEN	ACTOR	2134 N VINE ST	LOS ANGELES, CA	90068
JOSEPH, BRYAN K	TV WRITER	2615 CANYON DR	LOS ANGELES, CA	90068
JOSEPH, FRANK S	NEWS CORRESPONDENT	5617 WARWICK PL	CHEVY CHASE, MD	20814
JOSEPH, FREDERICK	ACTOR	6500 YUCCA ST #354	LOS ANGELES, CA	90028
JOSEPH, JACKIE	ACTRESS-WRITER	111 N VALLEY ST	BURBANK, CA	91505
JOSEPH, JAMES	COLUMNIST	UNIVERSAL PRESS SYNDICATE		
		4900 MAIN ST, 9TH FLOOR	KANSAS CITY, MO	62114
JOSEPH, JAMES HERZ	WRITER	11685 GORHAM AVE #6	LOS ANGELES, CA	90049
JOSEPH, KATHY S	TV WRITER	11108 OPHIR DR	LOS ANGELES, CA	90024
JOSEPH, KIM	ACTRESS	1350 N HIGHLAND AVE #24	HOLLYWOOD, CA	90028
JOSEPH, LINDA	GUITARIST	859 BRADFORD AVE	NASHVILLE, TN	37204
JOSEPH, NEAL	MUSIC ARRANGER	3301 TIMBER TRAIL	ANTIOCH, TN	37013
JOSEPH, PAUL	ACTOR	3294 RAMBLA PACIFICIO	MALIBU, CA	90265
JOSEPH, REYNOLDS, JR	WRITER	555 W 57TH ST #1230	NEW YORK, NY	10019
JOSEPH, ROBERT L	TV WRITER	1888 CENTURY PARK E #1400	LOS ANGELES, CA	90067
JOSEPH, RONALD	ACTOR	409 N CAMDEN DR #105	BEVERLY HILLS, CA	90210
JOSEPH, SAMUEL W	WRITER	8955 BEVERLY BLVD	LOS ANGELES, CA	90048
JOSEPH, STANLEY	WRITER-PRODUCER	1 BIRCH LEA, CRAWLEY	SUSSEX RH10 2AR	ENGLAND
JOSEPH, WILFRED	COMPOSER	LONDON MANAGEMENT, LTD		
		235-241 REGENT ST	LONDON W1A 2JT	ENGLAND
JOSEPHS, JENNIFER	ACTRESS	KELMAN, 7813 SUNSET BLVD	LOS ANGELES, CA	90046
JOSEPHSON, JEFFREY	ACTOR	5000 LANKERSHIM BLVD #5	NORTH HOLLYWOOD, CA	91601
JOSEPHSON, ROBERT B	WRITER	8955 BEVERLY BLVD	LOS ANGELES, CA	90048
JOSHUA, LARRY	ACTOR	165 W 46TH ST #710	NEW YORK, NY	10036
JOSHUA, MICHAEL	TV WRITER	555 W 57TH ST #1230	NEW YORK, NY	10019
JOULIN, JEAN-PIERRE	NEWS CORRESPONDENT	3251 PROSPECT ST, NW	WASHINGTON, DC	20007
JOURDAN, LOUIS	ACTOR	1139 MAYBROOK DR	BEVERLY HILLS, CA	90210
JOURNEY	ROCK & ROLL GROUP	POST OFFICE BOX 5952	SAN FRANCISCO, CA	94101
JOURNEY, DARK	WRESTLING VALET	SEE - DARK JOURNEY		
JOWERS, WALTER	GUITARIST	114 BOWLING AVE	NASHVILLE, TN	37205
JOY, CHRISTOPHER	ACTOR-PRODUCER	1034 S OGDEN DR #6	LOS ANGELES, CA	90019
JOY, RON	TV DIRECTOR	333 N PALM DR	BEVERLY HILLS, CA	90210
JOYCE, ADRIEN	SCREENWRITER	SEE - EASTMAN, CAROL		
JOYCE, BOB	HYPNOTIST	276 CAMBRIDGE ST #4	BOSTON, MA	02134
JOYCE, CHRISTOPHER	NEWS CORRESPONDENT	2755 ORDWAY ST #513, NW	WASHINGTON, DC	20009
JOYCE, ED	TV EXECUTIVE	CBS-TV, 524 W 57TH ST	NEW YORK, NY	10019
JOYCE, ELAINE	ACTRESS	724 N ROXBURY DR	BEVERLY HILLS, CA	90210
JOYCE, KRISTIN	WRITER	555 W 57TH ST #1230	NEW YORK, NY	10019
JOYCE, MIKE	SINGER	POST OFFICE BOX 120492	NASHVILLE, TN	37212
JOYCE, PADDY	ACTOR	ANGEL, 10 GREEK ST	LONDON W1V 5LA	ENGLAND
JOYCE, PATRICIA	SCREENWRITER	8955 BEVERLY BLVD	LOS ANGELES, CA	90048
JOYCE, STEPHEN	ACTOR	4150 RIVERSIDE DR #204	BURBANK, CA	91505
JOYCE, WENDELL	ACTOR	8961 SUNSET BLVD #B	LOS ANGELES, CA	90069
JOYCE, WILLIAM	ACTOR	4628 ENCINO AVE	ENCINO, CA	91316
JOYEUX, ODETTE	WRITER	1 RUE SEGUIER	PARIS 75006	FRANCE
JOYNER, DOUGLAS C	NEWS CORRESPONDENT	53 "D" ST, SE	WASHINGTON, DC	20003
JOYNER, JOSEPH	GUITARIST	6691 RIDGE RD	TOBACCOVILLE, NC	27050
JOYNER, MICHELLE	ACTRESS	19 W 44TH ST #1500	NEW YORK, NY	10036
JOYNT, CAROL R	NEWS CORRESPONDENT	CBS NEWS, 2020 "M" ST, NW	WASHINGTON, DC	20036
JOZEFIAK, ROBERT	GUITARIST	106 COLE DR	HENDERSONVILLE, TN	37075
JOZEFSON, JACK	TALENT AGENT	6736 LAUREL CANYON BLVD #306	NORTH HOLLYWOOD, CA	91606
JR CADILLAC	VOCAL GROUP	FAR WEST, 110 BOYLSTON AVE E	SEATTLE, WA	98102
JUABE, ISRAEL	ACTOR	8350 SANTA MONICA BLVD #103	LOS ANGELES, CA	90069
JUAN, DON & THE LARKS	VOCAL GROUP	OLDIES, 5218 ALMONT ST	LOS ANGELES, CA	90032
JUAREZ, BENJAMIN	CONDUCTOR	61 W 62ND ST #6-F	NEW YORK, NY	10023
JUBILEE	C & W GROUP	SCAHILL, 32 BIRCH CRESCENT	ROCHESTER, NY	14607
JUDAS PRIEST	ROCK & ROLL GROUP	3 E 54TH ST #1400	NEW YORK, NY	10022

Name	Occupation	Address	City	Zip/Country
JUDD, EDWARD	ACTOR	25 COTTENHAM PARK RD		
		WIMBLEDON	LONDON SW20	ENGLAND
JUDD, JAMES	CONDUCTOR	ANGLO-SWISS ARTISTS MGMT		
		16 MUSWEL HILL RD, HIGHGATE	LONDON N6 5UG	ENGLAND
JUDDS, THE	VOCAL DUO	POST OFFICE BOX 17087	NASHVILLE, TN	37217
JUDIS, JOHN	NEWS CORRESPONDENT	11201 VALLEY VIEW AVE	KENSINGTON, MD	20895
JUDKINS, GARY	DRUMMER	101 GLENROSE CIR	NASHVILLE, TNM	37210
JUDKINS, RICK	DRUMMER	805 LYNN DR	GOODLETTSVILLE, TN	37072
JUDY, E B "PETE"	ENTREPRENEUR	2801 MEADOW LARK DR	SAN DIEGO, CA	92123
JUDY'S TINY HEAD	ROCK & ROLL GROUP	25 HUNTINGTON AVE #420	BOSTON, MA	02116
JUGGERNAUT	ROCK & ROLL GROUP	POST OFFICE BOX 2428	EL SEGUNDO, CA	90245
JUHL, JERRY R	SCREENWRITER	1113 W JAY ST	TORRANCE, CA	90502
JUHL, SUSAN E	WRITER	555 W 57TH ST #1230	NEW YORK, NY	10019
JUHLIN, DONALD N	NEWS CORRESPONDENT	CBS NEWS, 2020 "M" ST, NW	WASHINGTON, DC	20036
JUHREN, ROBERT M	TV WRITER	555 W 57TH ST #1230	NEW YORK, NY	10019
JUKEBOX ROMANCE	ROCK & ROLL GROUP	POST OFFICE BOX 634	LAWRENCE, KS	66044
JULIA, RAUL	ACTOR	449 E 84TH ST #4-A	NEW YORK, NY	10028
JULIAN, ARTHUR	TV WRITER	443 BELLAGIO TERR	LOS ANGELES, CA	90049
JULIAN, CHUCK	ACTOR	23 TENTERDEN GARDENS	LONDON NW4 1TG	ENGLAND
JULIAN, JANET	ACTRESS	15301 VENTURA BLVD #345	SHERMAN OAKS, CA	91403
JULIAN, MAX	ACT-WRI-PROD	5107 COLDWATER CANYON AVE	SHERMAN OAKS, CA	91423
JULIAN, SALLY	ACTRESS	LEONETTI, 6526 SUNSET BLVD	HOLLYWOOD, CA	90028
JULIANO, LENNY	ACTOR	10000 RIVERSIDE DR #3	TOLUCA LAKE, CA	91602
JULIEN, JAY	TALENT AGENT	1501 BROADWAY #2600	NEW YORK, NY	10036
JULIEN, SYDNEY D	TV WRITER	8955 BEVERLY BLVD	LOS ANGELES, CA	90048
JULIUS, MAXINE	FILM EDITOR	93 WARDOUR ST	LONDON W1	ENGLAND
JULUKA	RHYTHM & BLUES GROUP	10100 SANTA MONICA BLVD #1600	LOS ANGELES, CA	90067
JUMP, GORDON	ACTOR-DIRECTOR	1631 HILLCREST AVE	GLENDALE, CA	91202
JUNG, CALVIN	ACTOR	9744 WILSHIRE BLVD #306	BEVERLY HILLS, CA	90212
JUNG, NATHAN	ACTOR	8235 SANTA MONICA BLVD #202	LOS ANGELES, CA	90046
JUNGERT, ANDREA	ACTRESS	6736 LAUREL CANYON BLVD #306	NORTH HOLLYWOOD, CA	91606
JUNGLE WOMAN	WRESTLER	GORGEOUS LADIES OF WRESTLING		
		RIVIERA HOTEL & CASINO		
		DAVID B MC LANE PRODS		
		2901 S LAS VEGAS BLVD	LAS VEGAS, NV	89109
JUNGMEYER, JACK, JR	WRITER	16190 ROYAL OAK DR	ENCINO, CA	91436
JUNIE LOU	SINGER	PROCESS, 439 WILEY AVE	FRANKLIN, PA	16323
JUNIOR	SINGER	GTI, 1700 BROADWAY, 10TH FLOOR	NEW YORK, NY	10019
JUNKIN, JOHN	ACTOR-WRITER	THE RICHARD STONE AGENCY		
		18-20 YORK BLDGS, ADELPHI	LONDON WC2N 6JY	ENGLAND
JUNKYARD DOG, THE	WRESTLER	POST OFFICE BOX 3859	STAMFORD, CT	06905
JUPITER, JOEY	ACTRESS	11231 OTSEGO ST #101	NORTH HOLLYWOOD, CA	91601
JUPP, NANCY	WRITER	555 W 57TH ST #1230	NEW YORK, NY	10019
JURAN, NATHAN	WRITER-PRODUCER	623 VIA HORQUILLA	PALOS VERDES, CA	90274
JURASIK, PETER	ACTOR	969 1/2 MANZANITA ST	LOS ANGELES, CA	90029
JURDEM, MELVIN	ACTOR	360 TENAFLY RD	ENGLEWOOD, NJ	07631
JURENAS, ASTRA R	NEWS CORRESPONDENT	3924 BENTON ST, NW	WASHINGTON, DC	20007
JUREY, PHILOMENA	NEWS CORRESPONDENT	3211 ROWLAND PL, NW	WASHINGTON, DC	20008
JURGENS, DEANA	ACTRESS	870 N VINE ST #G	LOS ANGELES, CA	90038
JURGENSEN, KAREN	NEWS EDITOR	POST OFFICE BOX 500	WASHINGTON, DC	20044
JURGENSEN, W KEITH	CINEMATOGRAPHER	11232 DONA LOLA DR	STUDIO CITY, CA	91604
JURGENSON, ALBERT	FILM EDITOR	178 QUAI, LOUIS BLERIOT	PARIS 75016	FRANCE
JURIST, ED	TV WRITER	2720 BOTTLEBRUSH DR	LOS ANGELES, CA	90077
JUROW, MARTIN	FILM PRODUCER	3505 RANKIN ST	DALLAS, TX	75205
JURZYKOWSKI, CHRISTINE	FILM PRODUCER	CINETUDES FILM PRODS		
		295 W 4TH ST	NEW YORK, NY	10014
JUST-ICE	SOUL GROUP	FRESH RECORDS, 1974 BROADWAY	NEW YORK, NY	10023
JUSTICE, BASIL A	NEWS CORRESPONDENT	5151 WISCONSIN AVE, NW	WASHINGTON, DC	20016
JUSTICE, CHARLIE	VIOLINIST	833 CHURCHILL DR	FREDERICKSBURG, VA	22401
JUSTICE, EDGAR	ACTOR	1972 1/2 COMMONWEALTH AVE	LOS ANGELES, CA	90027
JUSTICE, JOSEPH DANIEL, III	GUITARIST	1139 TUCKAHOE DR	NASHVILLE, TN	37207
JUSTICE, PAUL	VIOLINIST	ROUTE #1	FORT PAYNE, AL	35967
JUSTICE, SPIRE	GUITARIST	4304 IROQUOIS AVE	NASHVILLE, TN	37205
JUSTIN, JOHN	ACTOR	18 CANFIELD GARDENS	LONDON NW6 3JY	ENGLAND
JUSTIZ, JAKE	TV WRITER	8955 BEVERLY BLVD	LOS ANGELES, CA	90048
JUSTMAN, PAUL	WRITER	555 W 57TH ST #1230	NEW YORK, NY	10019
JUSTUS, WILLIAM	BARITONE	HILLYER, 250 W 57TH ST	NEW YORK, NY	10107
JUTT, STEPHANIE	FLUTIST	AFFILIATE ARTISTS, INC		
		37 W 57TH ST, 6TH FLOOR	NEW YORK, NY	10023
JUTTNER, SHELLY	ACTRESS	2224 THE TERR	LOS ANGELES, CA	90049
JYD	WRESTLER	SEE - JUNKYARD DOG, THE		

Name	Occupation	Address	City	Zip/Country
K B C BAND	ROCK & ROLL GROUP	ARISTA RECORDS, 6 W 57TH ST	NEW YORK, NY	10019
K C & THE SUNSHINE BAND	ROCK & ROLL GROUP	7764 NW 71ST ST	MIAMI, FL	33166
K T P	ROCK & ROLL GROUP	SEE - KISSING THE PINK		

JUNIOR

STEVE KANALY

WILLIAM KATT

DIANE KEATON

HOWARD KEEL

RUBY KEELER

DAVID KEITH

THE KENDALLS

GEORGE KENNEDY

Name	Occupation	Address	City	ZIP
K-9, JOHNNY	WRESTLER	SEE - JOHNNY K-9		
KAAT, JIM	BASEBALL	POST OFFICE BOX 86	GLEN MILLS, PA	19342
KABAIVANSKA, RAINA	SOPRANO	61 W 62ND ST #6-F	NEW YORK, NY	10023
KABASAWA, KATSUHIKO	NEWS CORRESPONDENT	2005 WELLFLEET CT	FALLS CHURCH, VA	22043
KACIN, JAY	DIRECTOR	POST OFFICE BOX 55042	VALENCIA, CA	91355
KACSO, DIANA	PIANIST	ROSENFIELD, 714 LADD RD	BRONX, NY	10471
KACZENDER, GEORGE	DIRECTOR	1550 DR PENFIELD DRIVE	MONTREAL, QUE H3E 1C2	CANADA
KACZMAREK, JANE	ACTRESS	SF & A, 121 N SAN VICENTE BLVD	BEVERLY HILLS, CA	90211
KADAU, CHARLIE	WRITER	MAD MAGAZINE, INC		
		485 MADISON AVE	NEW YORK, NY	10022
KADISON, ELLIS	DIRECTOR	31754 FOXFIELD DR	WESTLAKE VILLAGE, CA	91361
KADLEC, DANIEL	COLUMNIST	POST OFFICE BOX 500	WASHINGTON, DC	20044
KADUSHIN, CAROL	NEWS CORRESPONDENT	122 "C" ST, NW	WASHINGTON, DC	20001
KAEL, PAULINE	FILM CRITIC-AUTHORESS	2 BERKSHIRE HEIGHTS RD	GREAT BARRINGTON, MA	01230
KAFKA, JOSEPH F	NEWS CORRESPONDENT	1825 "K" ST, NW	WASHINGTON, DC	20006
KAFKA, SHERRY	WRITER	555 W 57TH ST #1230	NEW YORK, NY	10019
KAFUN, PAUL A	COMPOSER	8141 AGNES AVE	NORTH HOLLYWOOD, CA	91605
KAGAN, CAREN D	NEWS CORRESPONDENT	1012 14TH ST, NW	WASHINGTON, DC	20005
KAGAN, JEREMY PAUL	WRITER-PRODUCER	2024 N CURSON AVE	LOS ANGELES, CA	90046
KAGAN, MARILYN	ACTRES	909 1/2 S SHERBOURNE DR	LOS ANGELES, CA	90035
KAGAN, MICHAEL H	TV WRITER-DIRECTOR	21626 CEZANNE PL	WOODLAND HILLS, CA	91364
KAGEN, DAVID	ACTOR	9220 SUNSET BLVD #202	LOS ANGELES, CA	90069
KAHAN, JUDITH	ACTRESS	SF & A, 121 N SAN VICENTE BLVD	BEVERLY HILLS, CA	90211
KAHAN, JUDY	TV WRITER	8955 BEVERLY BLVD	LOS ANGELES, CA	90048
KAHAN, STEPHEN	ACTOR	12750 VENTURA BLVD #102	STUDIO CITY, CA	91604
KAHANE, JEFFREY	PIANIST	IMG ARTISTS, 22 E 71ST ST	NEW YORK, NY	10021
KAHANE, ROBERT	TALENT AGENT	10100 SANTA MONICA BLVD #1600	LOS ANGELES, CA	90067
KAHLER, KATHRYN S	NEWS CORRESPONDENT	3100 CONNECTICUT AVE #203, NW	WASHINGTON, DC	20008
KAHLER, LIA	MEZZO-SOPRANO	61 W 62ND ST #6-F	NEW YORK, NY	10023
KAHLERT, JIM	TV WRITER	12121 SHETLAND LN	LOS ANGELES, CA	90069
KAHLON, BEN	ACTOR	1217 11TH ST	MANHATTAN BEACH, CA	90266
KAHN, AL	ACTOR	3518 W CAHUENGA BLVD #315	LOS ANGELES, CA	90068
KAHN, BERNARD M	SCREENWRITER	838 N ORLANDO AVE	LOS ANGELES, CA	90069
KAHN, DAVE	COMPOSER	4629 FULTON AVE #313	SHERMAN OAKS, CA	91423
KAHN, DONALD	CONDUCTOR	G KAHN, 6223 SELMA AVE	LOS ANGELES, CA	90028
KAHN, ED	WRITER	8955 BEVERLY BLVD	LOS ANGELES, CA	90048
KAHN, EDGAR C	DIRECTOR	J W THOMPSON, 466 LEXINGTON AVE	NEW YORK, NY	10028
KAHN, EPHRAIM	NEWS CORRESPONDENT	3610 MACOMB ST, NW	WASHINGTON, DC	20016
KAHN, HARVEY L	ACTOR	4150 ARCH DR #27	STUDIO CITY, CA	91604
KAHN, HELEN	NEWS CORRESPONDENT	3810 MACOMB ST, NW	WASHINGTON, DC	20016
KAHN, IRVING	COMMUNICATIONS EXEC	375 PARK AVE #3701	NEW YORK, NY	10152
KAHN, MADELINE	ACTRESS	975 PARK AVE #9-A	NEW YORK, NY	10028
KAHN, MICHAEL	FILM EDITOR	ACE, 4416 1/2 FINLEY AVE	LOS ANGELES, CA	90027
KAHN, MICHAEL	STAGE DIRECTOR	1 W 72ND ST	NEW YORK, NY	10023
KAHN, MILTON P	WRITER	4219 SAUGUS AVE	VAN NUYS, CA	91403
KAHN, NATHAN	GUITARIST	765 MC MURRAY DR #B-3	NASHVILLE, TN	37211
KAHN, RICHARD	FILM EXECUTIVE	1080 WALLACE RIDGE	BEVERLY HILLS, CA	90210
KAHN, STEPHEN	WRITER	1260 N HAYWORTH AVE #11	LOS ANGELES, CA	90046
KAHN, TERRY C	WRITER	8955 BEVERLY BLVD	LOS ANGELES, CA	90048
KAHN, TOBY	REPORTER	TIME & PEOPLE MAGAZINE		
		TIME & LIFE BUILDING		
		ROCKEFELLER CENTER	NEW YORK, NY	10020
KAHN, TONY	WRITER	555 W 57TH ST #1230	NEW YORK, NY	10019
KAID, JAMERSON	GUITARIST	ROUTE #2, BOX 145	THOMPSON STATION, TN	37179
KAIKKO, PETER E	TV WRITER	19957 RAMBLING RD	COVINA, CA	91724
KAILEY, LIIS	ACTRESS	870 N VINE ST #G	LOS ANGELES, CA	90038
KAIN, DAN	TV HOST	PLAYBOY, 8560 SUNSET BLVD	LOS ANGELES, CA	90069
KAISER, HENRY	ACTOR	1814 IDAHO AVE	SANTA MONICA, CA	90403
KAISER, RICHARD	WRITER	8955 BEVERLY BLVD	LOS ANGELES, CA	90048
KAISER, ROBERT G	NEWS CORRESPONDENT	1711 "S" ST, NW	WASHINGTON, DC	20009
KAISY, ADNON	WRESTLING MANAGER	SEE - EL-KAISSE, SHEIK ADNAN		
KALAJIAN, JERRY	TALENT AGENT	1901 AVE OF THE STARS #840	LOS ANGELES, CA	90067
KALALI, NORMA	FASHION DESIGNER	11 W 56TH ST	NEW YORK, NY	10019
KALASH, CARL	CONDUCTOR	3378 SENECA DR	LAS VEGAS, NV	89109
KALB, BERNARD	NEWS CORRESPONDENT	NBC-TV, NEWS DEPARTMENT		
		4001 NEBRASKA AVE, NW	WASHINGTON, DC	20016
KALB, MARVIN	NEWS CORRESPONDENT	NBC-TV, NEWS DEPARTMENT		
		4001 NEBRASKA AVE, NW	WASHINGTON, DC	20016
KALBER, FLOYD	BROADCAST JOURNALIST	NBC NEWS, 30 ROCKEFELLER PLAZA	NEW YORK, NY	10112
KALCHEIM, LEE H	TV WRITER	55 W 57TH ST #1230	NEW YORK, NY	10019
KALDOR, ERIC	WRITER	8955 BEVERLY BLVD	LOS ANGELES, CA	90048
KALDWELL, ANDREA	ACTRESS	113 N SAN VICENTE BLVD #202	BEVERLY HILLS, CA	90211
KALDWELL, KANDAL	ACTRESS	8285 SUNSET BLVD #12	LOS ANGELES, CA	90046
KALE, PAULA M	NEWS CORRESPONDENT	2133 WISCONSIN AVE, NW	WASHINGTON, DC	20007
KALEM, TONI	ACTRESS	9744 WILSHIRE BLVD #206	BEVERLY HILLS, CA	90212
KALEMBER, PATRICIA	ACTRESS	POST OFFICE BOX 5617	BEVERLY HILLS, CA	90210
KALER, DORIS J	WRITER	1857 FOX HILLS DR	LOS ANGELES, CA	90025
KALFUS, JORDAN	DIRECTOR	2456 ASTRAL DR	LOS ANGELES, CA	90046
KALICHSTEIN, JOSEPH	PIANIST	SHAW CONCERTS, 1995 BROADWAY	NEW YORK, NY	10023
KALIKA	WRITER	2151 S AMARIPOSA AVE	LOS ANGELES, CA	90004
KALINE, AL	BASEBALL	945 TIMBERLAKE DR	BLOOMFIELD HILLS, MI	48013
KALINOSKY, JOHN P	WRITER	8955 BEVERLY BLVD	LOS ANGELES, CA	90048
KALISH, AUSTIN	TV WRITER	5339 LINDLEY AVE #103	TARZANA, CA	91356
KALISH, BRUCE E	TV WRITER-PRODUCER	5339 LINDLEY AVE #103	TARZANA, CA	91356

Name	Occupation	Address	City	ZIP
KALISH, GILBERT	PIANIST	HURLBURT, 140 W 79TH ST	NEW YORK, NY	10024
KALISH, IRMA	TV WRITER	3831 BOWSPRIT CIR	WESTLAKE VILLAGE, CA	91361
KALLIANIOTES, HELENA	ACTRESS-WRITER-DANCER	12850 MULHOLLAND DR	BEVERLY HILLS, CA	90210
KALLIR, LILIAN	PIANIST	CAMI, 165 W 57TH ST	NEW YORK, NY	10019
KALLIS, DANNY	TV WRITER	742 RADCLIFFE AVE	PACIFIC PALISADES, CA	90272
KALLIS, STANLEY	WRITER-PRODUCER	12345 DEERBROOK LN	LOS ANGELES, CA	90049
KALLSEN, RICHARD	WRITER	555 W 57TH ST #1230	NEW YORK, NY	10019
KALMAN, DEBI	ACTRESS	ABRAMS ARTISTS & ASSOCIATES 420 MADISON AVE, 14TH FLOOR	NEW YORK, NY	10017
KALMANOFF, MARTIN	COMPOSER	392 CENTRAL PARK W	NEW YORK, NY	10025
KALMAR, MAGDA	SOPRANO	1182 MARKET ST #311	SAN FRANCISCO, CA	94102
KALOMIRAKIS, THEODORE	ART DIRECTOR	DISCOVER/TIME & LIFE BLDG ROCKEFELLER CENTER	NEW YORK, NY	10020
KALOYEROPOULOS, PAUL G	WRITER	8955 BEVERLY BLVD	LOS ANGELES, CA	90048
KALSER, KONSTANTIN	DIRECTOR-PRODUCER	MARATHON PRODUCTIONS 211 E 51ST ST	NEW YORK, NY	10020
KALTER, SUZY	TV WRITER	283 W RADCLIFFE DR	CLAREMONT, CA	91711
KALUDOV, KALUDI	TENOR	CAMI, 165 W 57TH ST	NEW YORK, NY	10019
KAMAJIAN, AL T	WRITER	555 W 57TH ST #1230	NEW YORK, NY	10019
KAMALA	WRESTLER	SEE - KIMALA		
KAMB, SUSAN	SPORTS WRITER-EDITOR	SPORTS ILLUSTRATED MAGAZINE TIME & LIFE BUILDING ROCKEFELLER CENTER	NEW YORK, NY	10020
KAMBER, STAN	ACTOR	13111 VENTURA BLVD #204	STUDIO CITY, CA	91604
KAMEKONA, DANNY	ACTOR	6605 HOLLYWOOD BLVD #220	HOLLYWOOD, CA	90028
KAMEL, P J	SINGER	STAR, 1311 CANDLELIGHT	DALLAS, TX	75216
KAMEL, STANLEY	ACTOR	2414 DETOUR DR	LOS ANGELES, CA	90068
KAMEN, JEFF	NEWS CORRESPONDENT	400 NATIONAL PRESS BLDG 529 14TH ST, NW	WASHINGTON, DC	20045
KAMEN, ROBERT MARK	SCREENWRITER	8955 BEVERLY BLVD	LOS ANGELES, CA	90048
KAMENIR, DAVID L	COMPOSER	1224 CASIANO RD	LOS ANGELES, CA	90049
KAMER, HANS RUDOLPH	NEWS CORRESPONDENT	1601 30TH ST, NW	WASHINGTON, DC	20007
KAMINS, SUSAN	ACTRESS	117 E 53RD ST	LONG BEACH, CA	90805
KAMINSKY, PETER	WRITER	555 W 57TH ST #1230	NEW YORK, NY	10019
KAMM, LARRY	TV DIRECTOR	420 E 51ST ST #7-F	NEW YORK, NY	10022
KAMMERER, PATRICIA L	WRITER	555 W 57TH ST #1230	NEW YORK, NY	10019
KAMMERMAN, ROY	TV WRITER	9875 RIMMELE DR	BEVERLY HILLS, CA	90210
KAMP, LOUIS	SCREENWRITER	207 S HIGHLAND AVE	LOS ANGELES, CA	90036
KAMPMANN, JUDITH K	WRITER-PRODUCER	812 JACON WY	PACIFIC PALISADES, CA	90272
KAMPMANN, STEVEN W	ACTOR-WRITER	812 JACON WY	PACIFIC PALISADES, CA	90272
KANALY, STEVE	ACTOR	3611 LONGRIDGE AVE	SHERMAN OAKS, CA	91423
KANANACK, ARTHUR	TV EXECUTIVE	ITC ENTERTAINMENT 12711 VENTURA BLVD	STUDIO CITY, CA	91604
KANARECK, MAURICE	TV WRITER-DIRECTOR	3 MEADWAY CT, MEADWAY	LONDON NW11	ENGLAND
KANDEL, ABEN	WRITER	8955 BEVERLY BLVD	LOS ANGELES, CA	90048
KANDEL, STEPHEN	TV WRITER	214 S BEDFORD DR	BEVERLY HILLS, CA	90212
KANDER, JOHN H, II	WRITER	12203 OCTAGON ST	LOS ANGELES, CA	90049
KANE, ANTHONY	ACTOR	70 E 77TH ST	NEW YORK, NY	10021
KANE, ARNOLD	TV WRITER-PRODUCER	8381 HOLLYWOOD BLVD	LOS ANGELES, CA	90069
KANE, ART	DIRECTOR	36 GRAMERCY PARK E	NEW YORK, NY	10003
KANE, ARTIE M	CONDUCTOR	10900 WILSHIRE BLVD #900	LOS ANGELES, CA	90024
KANE, BOB	CARTOONIST	420 E 55TH ST	NEW YORK, NY	10022
KANE, BRUCE	TV WRITER	9300 WILSHIRE BLVD #410	BEVERLY HILLS, CA	90212
KANE, BYRON	DIRECTOR	2231 BENEDICT CANYON DR	BEVERLY HILLS, CA	90210
KANE, CAROL	ACTRESS	250 W 57TH ST #2105	NEW YORK, NY	10019
KANE, HENRY	WRITER	555 W 57TH ST #1230	NEW YORK, NY	10019
KANE, IRVING M	MUSIC ARRANGER	2001 BLAIR BLVD #B	NASHVILLE, TN	37212
KANE, JAYSON	ACTOR	9200 SUNSET BLVD #909	LOS ANGELES, CA	90069
KANE, JOHN	CLOWN	2701 COTTAGE WY #14	SACRAMENTO, CA	95825
KANE, JOSH	TV EXECUTIVE	CBS-TV, 51 W 52ND ST	NEW YORK, NY	10020
KANE, KIERAN	SINGER	POST OFFICE BOX 121089	NASHVILLE, TN	37212
KANE, KRISTI	WRITER	8955 BEVERLY BLVD	LOS ANGELES, CA	90048
KANE, LOUISE	ACTRESS	8721 SUNSET BLVD #200	LOS ANGELES, CA	90069
KANE, MADLEEN	SINGER	1330 SCHUYLER RD	BEVERLY HILLS, CA	90210
KANE, MARY	ACTRESS	ABC-TV, "ALL MY CHILDREN" 1330 AVE OF THE AMERICAS	NEW YORK, NY	10019
KANE, MICHAEL	SCREENWRITER	8955 BEVERLY BLVD	LOS ANGELES, CA	90048
KANE, MICHAEL J	TV DIRECTOR	4565 HAZELTINE AVE #6	SHERMAN OAKS, CA	91423
KANE, PATRICIA F	WRITER	8955 BEVERLY BLVD	LOS ANGELES, CA	90048
KANE, PETER	TV EXECUTIVE	CBS-TV, 7800 BEVERLY BLVD	LOS ANGELES, CA	90036
KANE, RICHARD	MUSICIAN	143 KENNER AVE	NASHVILLE, TN	37205
KANE, ROBERT G	SCREENWRITER	1427 GREENFIELD AVE	LOS ANGELES, CA	90025
KANE, ROBERT M	WRITER	8955 BEVERLY BLVD	LOS ANGELES, CA	90048
KANE, RUBEN	WRESTLER	SEE - GIBSON, ROBERT		
KANE, SCOTT H	DIRECTOR	1621 WILMOT LN	DEERFIELD, IL	60015
KANE, SHARON	BASSOONIST	2502 WESTWOOD AVE	NASHVILLE, TN	37212
KANE, VIVIAN W	WRITER	8955 BEVERLY BLVD	LOS ANGELES, CA	90048
KANEKO, ATSUO	NEWS CORRESPONDENT	6109 DURBIN RD	BETHESDA, MD	20817
KANEW, JEFFREY	FILM DIRECTOR	51 W 83RD ST	NEW YORK, NY	10024
KANFER, STEFAN	WRITER-EDITOR	TIME/TIME & LIFE BLDG ROCKEFELLER CENTER	NEW YORK, NY	10020
KANG, DONG-SUK	VIOLINIST	IMG ARTISTS, 22 E 71ST ST	NEW YORK, NY	10021
KANIN, FAY	WRITER	653 OCEAN FRONT WALK	SANTA MONICA, CA	90402
KANIN, GARSON	WRITER-PRODUCER	200 W 57TH ST #1203	NEW YORK, NY	10019
KANIN, MICHAEL	WRITER	653 OCEAN FRONT WALK	SANTA MONICA, CA	90402

Name	Occupation	Address	City	Zip
KANN, MAYO	RADIO PERSONALITY	116 HERMAN ST	WINTHROP, MA	02152
KANN, STAN	ACTOR	594 N ROSSMORE AVE #4	LOS ANGELES, CA	90004
KANNER, JUDITH	WRITER	8955 BEVERLY BLVD	LOS ANGELES, CA	90048
KANON, JOSEPH	COMPOSER-CONDUCTOR	4236 COLFAX AVE	STUDIO CITY, CA	91604
KANSAS	ROCK & ROLL GROUP	POST OFFICE BOX 7308	CARMEL, CA	93923
KANSAS JAYHAWKS, THE	WRESTLING TAG TEAM	NATIONAL WRESTLING ALLIANCE		
		JIM CROCKETT PROMOTIONS		
		421 BRIARBEND DR	CHARLOTTE, NC	28209
KANT, HAROLD S	WRITER	8955 BEVERLY BLVD	LOS ANGELES, CA	90048
KANTER, DONNA	WRITER-PRODUCER	ICM, 8899 BEVERLY BLVD	LOS ANGELES, CA	90048
KANTER, DORIS	WRITER	15941 WOODVALE RD	ENCINO, CA	91316
KANTER, HAL	WRITER-PRODUCER	15941 WOODVALE RD	ENCINO, CA	91316
KANTER, JAY	FILM EXECUTIVE	726 N ROXBURY DR	BEVERLY HILLS, CA	90210
KANTER, JEFF	WRITER	POST OFFICE BOX 49218	LOS ANGELES, CA	90049
KANTNER-BALIN-CASADY BAND	ROCK & ROLL GROUP	POST OFFICE BOX 15-584	SAN FRANCISCO, CA	94115
KANTOR, ABBE	ACTRESS	6303 ATOLL AVE	VAN NUYS, CA	91401
KANTOR, ALICE K	WRITER	555 W 57TH ST #1230	NEW YORK, NY	10019
KANTOR, IGO	COMPOSER	11501 DUQUE DR	STUDIO CITY, CA	91604
KANTOR, RONALD	DIRECTOR-PRODUCER	524 N CAHUENGA BLVD	LOS ANGELES, CA	90004
KANTOR, SETH	NEWS CORRESPONDENT	5115 WESSLING LN	BETHESDA, MD	20814
KANTOROW, JEAN-JAQUES	VIOLINIST	SHAW CONCERTS, 1995 BROADWAY	NEW YORK, NY	10023
KANWISCHER, ALFRED & HEIDI	PIANO DUO	KAY, 58 W 58TH ST	NEW YORK, NY	10019
KANZLER, SHEILA	NEWS CORRESPONDENT	14809 RESERVE RD	ACCOKEEK, MD	20607
KAPLAN, ALAN I	DIRECTOR	DGA, 110 W 57TH ST	NEW YORK, NY	10019
KAPLAN, DAVID	TV DIRECTOR	1228 HAZEL AVE	PLAINFIELD, NJ	07060
KAPLAN, E JACK	TV WRITER	8955 BEVERLY BLVD	LOS ANGELES, CA	90048
KAPLAN, EDWIN FRANCIS	TV WRITER	1223 SUNSET PLAZA DR #A	LOS ANGELES, CA	90069
KAPLAN, ELLIOT	COMPOSER	4520 SALTILLO ST	WOODLAND HILLS, CA	91364
KAPLAN, FRED	NEWS CORRESPONDENT	1915 KALORAMA RD #204, NW	WASHINGTON, DC	20009
KAPLAN, GABRIEL	COMEDIAN-ACTOR	9551 HIDDEN VALLEY RD	BEVERLY HILLS, CA	90210
KAPLAN, HENRY	DIRECTOR	DGA, 110 W 57TH ST	NEW YORK, NY	10019
KAPLAN, JANE	TV WRITER	ENTERTAINMENT TONIGHT		
		PARAMOUNT TELEVISION		
		5555 MELROSE AVE	LOS ANGELES, CA	90038
KAPLAN, JANICE E	WRITER	555 W 57TH ST #1230	NEW YORK, NY	10019
KAPLAN, JANICE L	NEWS CORRESPONDENT	1317 "F" ST #320, NW	WASHINGTON, DC	20004
KAPLAN, JONATHAN H	DIRECTOR	CHARLEVILLE PRODUCTIONS		
		715 N LA JOLLA AVE	LOS ANGELES, CA	90046
KAPLAN, JONATHAN S	WRITER-PRODUCER	8275 KIRKWOOD DR	LOS ANGELES, CA	90046
KAPLAN, JOSHUA R	WRITER	8955 BEVERLY BLVD	LOS ANGELES, CA	90048
KAPLAN, MADY	ACTRESS	POST OFFICE BOX 5617	BEVERLY HILLS, CA	90210
KAPLAN, MARC	WRITER	1438 10TH ST #5	SANTA MONICA, CA	90401
KAPLAN, MARK	VIOLINIST	1776 BROADWAY #504	NEW YORK, NY	10019
KAPLAN, MARVIN	ACTOR	6310 SAN VICENTE BLVD #407	LOS ANGELES, CA	90048
KAPLAN, MICHAEL	WRITER	8955 BEVERLY BLVD	LOS ANGELES, CA	90048
KAPLAN, NANCY	DIRECTOR	1393 BLUE SPRUCE LN	WANTAGH, NY	11793
KAPLAN, NATE	WRITER	8955 BEVERLY BLVD	LOS ANGELES, CA	90048
KAPLAN, PATTI	DIRECTOR	DGA, 110 W 57TH ST	NEW YORK, NY	10019
KAPLAN, RICHARD	WRITER-PRODUCER	555 W 57TH ST #1230	NEW YORK, NY	10019
KAPLAN, RICK	TV PRODUCER	ABC-TV, 7 W 66TH ST	NEW YORK, NY	10023
KAPLAN, ROBERT D	NEWS CORRESPONDENT	53 "D" ST, SE	WASHINGTON, DC	20003
KAPLAN, ROBERT O	FILM PRODUCER	1112 N SHERBOURNE DR	LOS ANGELES, CA	90069
KAPLAN, ROSALIND	WRITER	555 W 57TH ST #1230	NEW YORK, NY	10019
KAPLAN, SHELDON L	DIRECTOR	29818 KATHERINE ST	MAGNOLIA, TX	77355
KAPLAN, WILLIAM	FILM DIRECTOR	233 LOS PINOS DR	PALM SPRINGS, CA	92264
KAPLEN, LAWRENCE J	WRITER-NEWS CORRES	ABC-TV, NEWS DEPARTMENT		
		1717 DE SALES ST, NW	WASHINGTON, DC	20036
KAPLOW, HERBERT E	NEWS CORRESPONDENT	ABC-TV, NEWS DEPARTMENT		
		1717 DE SALES ST, NW	WASHINGTON, DC	20036
KAPP, JOE	ACTOR-FOOTBALL	2318 PROSSER AVE	LOS ANGELES, CA	90064
KAPP, RICHARD	CONDUCTOR	1776 BROADWAY #504	NEW YORK, NY	10019
KAPP, TIM	JUGGLER	HALL, 138 FROG HOLLOW RD	CHURCHVILLE, PA	18966
KAPRISKY, VALERIE	ACTRESS	BRU, 33 CHAMPS ELYSEES	PARIS 75008	FRANCE
KAPROFF, DANA	CONDUCTOR	1120 EL MEDIO AVE	PACIFIC PALISADES, CA	90272
KAPS, CAROLA	NEWS CORRESPONDENT	982 NATIONAL PRESS BLDG		
		529 14TH ST, NW	WASHINGTON, DC	20045
KAPTUR, RUNE	TALENT AGENT	3151 W CAHUENGA BLVD #310	LOS ANGELES, CA	90068
KARABATSOS, RON	ACTOR	9229 SUNSET BLVD #306	LOS ANGELES, CA	90069
KARABELL, SHELLIE B	WRITER	555 W 57TH ST #1230	NEW YORK, NY	10019
KARAGIANIS, DAVID S	COMPOSER	435 1/2 N SIERRA BONITA AVE	LOS ANGELES, CA	90036
KARAJAN, HERBERT VON	CONDUCTOR	FESTSPIELHAUS	SALZBURG	AUSTRIA
KARAM, EDWARD M	COMPOSER-CONDUCTOR	6175 PASEO CANYON DR	MALIBU, CA	90265
KARAM, SAMIR F	NEWS CORRESPONDENT	1515 JEFFERSON DAVIS HWY	ARLINGTON, VA	22202
KARAN, DONNA	FASHION DESIGNER	550 7TH AVE	NEW YORK, NY	10018
KARANT, MORT	WRITER	8955 BEVERLY BLVD	LOS ANGELES, CA	90048
KARATH, KYM	ACTRESS	638 S SYCAMORE AVE	LOS ANGELES, CA	90036
KARCYKOWSKI, RYSZARD	TENOR	61 W 62ND ST #6-F	NEW YORK, NY	10023
KARDISCH, VAN	WRITER	555 W 57TH ST #1230	NEW YORK, NY	10019
KAREL, RUSS	FILM WRITER-PRODUCER	ROSEMAN, 8 POLAND ST	LONDON W1	ENGLAND
KARELLA, CLARENCE O	CONDUCTOR	POST OFFICE BOX 1132	PALM SPRINGS, CA	92263
KAREN, ANNA	ACTRESS	AIMEE, 13743 VICTORY BLVD	VAN NUYS, CA	91401
KAREN, JAMES	ACTOR	4455 LOS FELIZ BLVD #807	LOS ANGELES, CA	90027
KAREY, GERALD	NEWS CORRESPONDENT	9704 BRUNET AVE	SILVER SPRING, MD	20901
KARIN, RITA	ACTRESS	484 W 43RD ST #11-D	NEW YORK, NY	10036

KARL, STUART	VIDEO EXECUTIVE	KARL-LORIMAR HOME VIDEO	
		17942 COWAN	IRVINE, CA 92714
KARLAN, RICHARD	ACTOR	11235 DILLING ST	NORTH HOLLYWOOD, CA 91602
KARLATOS, OLGA	ACTRESS	E LASHER, 211 W 56TH ST	NEW YORK, NY 10019
KARLEN, BETTY	ACTRESS	439 S LA CIENEGA BLVD #120	LOS ANGELES, CA 90048
KARLEN, JOHN	ACTOR	POST OFFICE BOX 5617	BEVERLY HILLS, CA 90210
KARLIN, FRED	COMPOSER-CONDUCTOR	10736 ASHTON AVE	LOS ANGELES, CA 90024
KARLIN, MIRIAM	ACTRESS	ICM, 388-396 OXFORD ST	LONDON W1 ENGLAND
KARLSON, PHIL	FILM DIRECTOR	3094 PATRICIA AVE	LOS ANGELES, CA 90064
KARLTON & CO	MAGICIAN	HALL, 138 FROG HOLLOW RD	CHURCHVILLE, PA 18966
KARMAN, MAL	WRITER	8955 BEVERLY BLVD	LOS ANGELES, CA 90048
KARMAZYN, DENNIS	CELLIST	CAMI, 165 W 57TH ST	NEW YORK, NY 10019
KARMIN, MONROE W	NEWS CORRESPONDENT	7011 BEECHWOOD DR	CHEVY CHASE, MD 20815
KARNAD, BHARAT	NEWS CORRESPONDENT	2511 WOODLEY RD, NW	WASHINGTON, DC 20008
KARNES, REBECCA	NEWS CORRESPONDENT	205 GUNDRY DR	FALLS CHRUCH, VA 22046
KAROFF, JEFF	PRODUCER	KEVIN BILES, 358 HAMPTON DR	VENICE, CA 90291
KAROS, STEPHANIE	ACTRESS	230 S ROXBURY DR	BEVERLY HILLS, CA 90212
KAROUSATOS, NICHOLAS	BARITONE	AFFILIATE ARTISTS, INC	
		37 W 65TH ST, 6TH FLOOR	NEW YORK, NY 10023
KARP, CATHY	ACTRESS	654 S CLOVERDALE AVE #201	LOS ANGELES, CA 90036
KARP, DAVID	TV WRITER	1116 CORSICA DR	PACIFIC PALISADES, CA 90272
KARP, JEAN	ACTRESS	6139 GLEN TOWER ST	LOS ANGELES, CA 90068
KARPEN, EARL	ACTOR	11030 VENTURA BLVD #3	STUDIO CITY, CA 91604
KARPF, ELINOR	WRITER	24504 W MULHOLLAND HWY	CALABASAS, CA 91302
KARPF, STEPHEN L	WRITER	24504 W MULHOLLAND HWY	CALABASAS, CA 91302
KARR, ALBERT R	NEWS CORRESPONDENT	7608 WHITTIER BLVD	BETHESDA, MD 20817
KARR, AMY ALLEN	ACTRESS	1012 KENISTON AVE	LOS ANGELES, CA 90019
KARR, DANA	GUITARIST	5726 STONEYWAY TRAIL	NASHVILLE, TN 37209
KARR, GARY	DOUBLE BASS	ANGLO-SWISS ARTISTS MGMT	
		16 MUSWELL HILL RD, HIGHGATE	LONDON N6 5UG ENGLAND
KARR, HARRIET	WRITER	8955 BEVERLY BLVD	LOS ANGELES, CA 90048
KARR, JENNIFER	ACTRESS	STONE, 1052 CAROL DR	LOS ANGELES, CA 90069
KARR, PATTI	ACTRESS	247 S BEVERLY DR #102	BEVERLY HILLS, CA 90210
KARR, PHILIP	TALENT AGENT	1012 KENISTON AVE	LOS ANGELES, CA 90019
KARRAS, ALEX	ACTOR	7943 WOODROW WILSON DR	LOS ANGELES, CA 90046
KARRIN, BONNIE	TV PRODUCER	ALAN LANDSBURG PRODUCTIONS	
		11811 W OLYMPIC BLVD	LOS ANGELES, CA 90064
KARS, MICHAEL	WRITER	8955 BEVERLY BLVD	LOS ANGELES, CA 90048
KARSH, YOUSUF	PHOTOGRAPHER	BOX 1931, PRESCOTT HWY	OTTAWA, ONT CANADA
KARSON, ERIC	WRITER-PRODUCER	15027 SHERMAN WY #C	VAN NUYS, CA 91405
KARSON, LEE	TV WRITER	7706 W NORTON AVE #6	LOS ANGELES, CA 90046
KARSON, ROSALIND	WRITER	555 W 57TH ST #1230	NEW YORK, NY 10019
KARTALIAN, BUCK	ACTOR	14757 VALERIO ST	VAN NUYS, CA 91405
KARTIGANER, ESTHER	WRITER	555 W 57TH ST #1230	NEW YORK, NY 10019
KARTOZIAN, THOMAS GEORGE	TV WRITER	8953 KEITH AVE	LOS ANGELES, CA 90069
KARTUN, ALLAN	DIRECTOR	12501 VALLEY SPRING LN	STUDIO CITY, CA 91604
KARVELAS, ROBERT	ACTOR	855 LEVERING AVE #401	LOS ANGELES, CA 90024
KASANDER, PAUL	TV DIRECTOR	100 RIVERSIDE DR	NEW YORK, NY 10024
KASARJIAN, ARTHUR	ACTOR	1168 N NORMANDIE AVE	LOS ANGELES, CA 90029
KASDAN, LAWRENCE	FILM WRITER-PRODUCER	DGA, 7950 SUNSET BLVD	LOS ANGELES, CA 90046
KASDAN, MARK	WRITER	8955 BEVERLY BLVD	LOS ANGELES, CA 90048
KASDORF, LENORE	ACTRESS	10351 SANTA MONICA BLVD #211	LOS ANGELES, CA 90025
KASE, SUSAN	ACTRESS	400 S BEVERLY DR #216	BEVERLY HILLS, CA 90212
KASELL, CARL R	NEWS CORRESPONDENT	5316 TRUMAN AVE	ALEXANDRIA, VA 22304
KASEM, CASEY	RADIO PERS-TV HOST	362 COPA DE ORO RD	LOS ANGELES, CA 90077
KASEM, JEAN	ACTRESS	362 COPA DE ORA RD	LOS ANGELES, CA 90077
KASHA, AL	COMPOSER	337 S EL CAMINO DR	BEVERLY HILLS, CA 90212
KASHA, LAWRENCE	TV WRITER-PRODUCER	2229 GLOAMING WY	BEVERLY HILLS, CA 90210
KASHIF	SINGER	200 W 51ST ST #1410	NEW YORK, NY 10019
KASHIWAHARA, KEN	NEWS CORRESPONDENT	ABC NEWS, 277 GOLDEN GATE AVE	SAN FRANCISCO, CA 94102
KASHKASHIAN, KIM	VIOLIST-VIOLINIST	808 W END AVE #1204	NEW YORK, NY 10025
KASICA, MARYANNE E	TV WRITER	554 S SAN VICENTE BLVD #3	LOS ANGELES, CA 90048
KASOFF, LAWRENCE	TV DIRECTOR	68-36 108TH ST	FOREST HILLS, NY 11375
KASPER, EDWIN T	DIRECTOR	301 W 53RD ST #10-A	NEW YORK, NY 10019
KASPER, GARY F	ACTOR	4731 LAUREL CANYON BLVD #5-A	NORTH HOLLYWOOD, CA 91607
KASPRZYK, JACEK	CONDUCTOR	SHAW CONCERTS, 1995 BROADWAY	NEW YORK, NY 10023
KASS, JEROME A	SCREENWRITER	141 S EL CAMINO DR #110	BEVERLY HILLS, CA 90212
KASS, MARCIA B	NEWS CORRESPONDENT	3701 CONNECTICUT AVE #406, NW	WASHINGTON, DC 20008
KASS, SUSAN	ACTRESS	10000 RIVERSIDE DR #12-14	TOLUCA LAKE, CA 91602
KASSEL, VIRGINIA W	WRITER	555 W 57TH ST #1230	NEW YORK, NY 10019
KASSIR, JOHN	COMEDIAN	EAI, 2211 INDUSTRIAL BLVD	SARASOTA, FL 33580
KASSUL, ART	ACTOR	10901 BLIX ST #1	NORTH HOLLYWOOD, CA 91602
KASTELNIK, CONNIE M	WRITER	555 W 57TH ST #1230	NEW YORK, NY 10019
KASTNER, ELLIOTT	FILM PRODUCER	WINKAST, PINEWOOD STUDIOS	
		IVER HEATH	BUCKS ENGLAND
KASTNER, PETER BERNARD	ACTOR-WRITER	29 PARK AVE	VENICE, CA 90291
KASTOR, ELIZABETH M	NEWS CORRESPONDENT	2500 WISCONSIN AVE, NW	WASHINGTON, DC 20007
KASZA, KATALIN	SOPRANO	1182 MARKET ST #311	SAN FRANCISCO, CA 94102
KATAHN, DICK	VIOLINIST	4607 BELMONT PARK TERR	NASHVILLE, TN 37215
KATAHN, ENID	PIANIST	4607 BELMONT PARK TERR	NASHVILLE, TN 37215
KATAHN, TERRI	FLUTIST	4607 BELMONT PARK TERR	NASHVILLE, TN 37215
KATARINA, ANNA	ACTRESS	1717 N HIGHLAND AVE #41	LOS ANGELES, CA 90028

Name	Occupation	Address	City/State	ZIP
KATCHER, ARAM	ACTOR	9777 WILSHIRE BLVD #707	BEVERLY HILLS, CA	90212
KATER, DAN	CABLE EXECUTIVE	MODERN SATELLITE NETWORK		
		45 ROCKEFELLER PLAZA	NEW YORK, NY	10111
KATES, ANNE	COLUMNIST	POST OFFICE BOX 500	WASHINGTON, DC	20044
KATES, ARTHUR L	CONDUCTOR	41055 VILLAGE 41	CAMARILLO, CA	93010
KATES, BERNARD	ACTOR	BARRY, 165 W 46TH ST	NEW YORK, NY	10036
KATH, CAMELIA	ACTRESS	9040 HARRATT ST #5	LOS ANGELES, CA	90069
KATIMS, DAVID	ACTOR	3500 KELTON AVE #8	LOS ANGELES, CA	90034
KATIMS, MILTON	CONDUCTOR	GERSHUNOFF, 502 PARK AVE	NEW YORK, NY	10022
KATIN, PETER	PIANIST	243 W END AVE #907	NEW YORK, NY	10023
KATKOV, NORMAN	TV WRITER	166 N CYN VIEW DR	LOS ANGELES, CA	90049
KATLEMAN, HARRIS	WRITER-PRODUCER	1250 SHADOW HILL WY	BEVERLY HILLS, CA	90210
KATON-WALDON, ROSEANNE	ACTRESS-MODEL	407 OCEAN FRONT WALK #5	VENICE, CA	90291
KATRINA & THE WAVES	ROCK & ROLL GROUP	28 ADDISON CLOSE		
		FELTWELL RR, THETFORD	NORFOLK 1P2 64DJ	ENGLAND
KATSANOS, STEPHEN	NEWS CORRESPONDENT	3844 HOLLY DR	EDGEWATER, MD	21037
KATSELAS, MILTON	FILM DIRECTOR	2559 N CATALINA AVE	LOS ANGELES, CA	90027
KATSUKI, KIYOHIDE	NEWS CORRESPONDENT	11017 GAINSBOROUGH RD	POTOMAC, MD	20854
KATT, WILLIAM	ACTOR	445 N BEDFORD DR #PH	BEVERLY HILLS, CA	90210
KATTEN, STEVEN	TV DIRECTOR	6201 MULHOLLAND HWY	LOS ANGELES, CA	90068
KATZ, ALLAN	TV WRITER-PRODUCER	1510 FOREST KNOLL DR	LOS ANGELES, CA	90069
KATZ, AMY D	WRITER	555 W 57TH ST #1230	NEW YORK, NY	10019
KATZ, ARTHUR JOEL	WRITER-PRODUCER	703 N PALM DR	BEVERLY HILLS, CA	90210
KATZ, BARRY	NEWS CORRESPONDENT	400 N CAPITOL ST, NW	WASHINGTON, DC	20001
KATZ, BERNARD	CONDUCTOR	2788 34TH AVE	SAN FRANCISCO, CA	94116
KATZ, CRAIG C	NEWS CORRESPONDENT	1755 S JEFFERSON DAVIS HWY	ARLINGTON, VA	22202
KATZ, DONALD R	WRITER	8955 BEVERLY BLVD	LOS ANGELES, CA	90048
KATZ, EDWARD E	DIRECTOR	234 MEADOWBROOK AVE	NORTHBROOK, IL	60062
KATZ, EPHRAIM	WRITER	555 W 57TH ST #1230	NEW YORK, NY	10019
KATZ, GLORIA	FILM WRITER-PRODUCER	39 OAKMONT DR	LOS ANGELES, CA	90049
KATZ, HUBERT B	NEWS CORRESPONDENT	12613 CRAFT LN	BOWIE, MD	20715
KATZ, JOEL	CABLE EXECUTIVE	PLAYBOY, 8560 SUNSET BLVD	LOS ANGELES, CA	90069
KATZ, LEN	NEWS REPORTER	THE NATIONAL ENQUIRER		
		600 SE COAST AVE	LANTANA, FL	33464
KATZ, MARTIN I	PHOTOGRAPHER	POST OFFICE BOX 141	BROOKLANDVILLE, MD	21022
KATZ, MAX J	DIRECTOR	315 E 65TH ST	NEW YORK, NY	10021
KATZ, MIKE	BODYBUILDER	THE WORLD GYM EAST		
		295 TREADWELL ST	HAMDEN, CT	06514
KATZ, NORMAN B	FILM EXECUTIVE	1123 VISTA GRANDE DR	PACIFIC PALISADES, CA	90272
KATZ, PETER J	WRITER	555 W 57TH ST #1230	NEW YORK, NY	10019
KATZ, RICHARD J	TV EXECUTIVE	CBS-TV, 6121 SUNSET BLVD	LOS ANGELES, CA	90028
KATZ, ROBERT I	TV DIRECTOR	3700 S SEPULVEDA BLVD #248	LOS ANGELES, CA	90034
KATZ, SHELLEY	TV WRITER	2186 BROADVIEW TERR	LOS ANGELES, CA	90068
KATZ, SHELLY	PHOTOGRAPHER	TIME/TIME & LIFE BLDG		
		ROCKEFELLER CENTER	NEW YORK, NY	10020
KATZ, STEPHEN	SCREENWRITER	8955 BEVERLY BLVD	LOS ANGELES, CA	90048
KATZ, STEVEN J	NEWS CORRESPONDENT	1825 "K" ST, NW	WASHINGTON, DC	20006
KATZ, SUSAN E	NEWS CORRESPONDENT	1755 S JEFFERSON DAVIS HWY	ARLINGTON, VA	22202
KATZ, WILLIAM	WRITER	FISCHER, 1 E 57TH ST	NEW YORK, NY	10022
KATZER, STAN	ACTOR	565 ESPLANADE ST	REDONDO BEACH, CA	90277
KATZIN, LEE	FILM DIRECTOR	13425 JAVA DR	BEVERLY HILLS, CA	90210
KATZKA, GABRIEL	FILM-TV PRODUCER	151 S EL CAMINO DR	BEVERLY HILLS, CA	90212
KATZMAN, BRUCE	ACTOR	441 N OGDEN DR	LOS ANGELES, CA	90036
KATZMAN, DREW	ACTOR	11564 ADDISON ST	NORTH HOLLYWOOD, CA	91601
KATZMAN, LEONARD	WRITER-PRODUCER	16117 ROYAL OAK RD	ENCINO, CA	91436
KATZMAN, SHERYL LYNN	ACTRESS	16117 ROYAL OAK RD	ENCINO, CA	91436
KATZOFF, MARVIN	ACTOR	1569 N EDGEMONT ST	LOS ANGELES, CA	90027
KAUFER, JERRY	TV EXECUTIVE	VIACOM INTERNATIONAL, INC		
		1211 AVE OF THE AMERICAS	NEW YORK, NY	10036
KAUFER, JONATHAN	WRITER-PRODUCER	8358 RIDPATH DR	LOS ANGELES, CA	90046
KAUFFMAN, KRISTINE	ACTRESS	1136 N LARRABEE ST #204	LOS ANGELES, CA	90069
KAUFFMAN, KURK	WRESTLER	POST OFFICE BOX 3859	STAMFORD, CT	06905
KAUFMAN, ALLAN	WRITER	555 W 57TH ST #1230	NEW YORK, NY	10019
KAUFMAN, ARVIN	TV EXECUTIVE	11970 MONTANA AVE	LOS ANGELES, CA	90049
KAUFMAN, BARRY N	TV WRITER	555 W 57TH ST #1230	NEW YORK, NY	10019
KAUFMAN, BRIAN	TV WRITER	555 W 57TH ST #1230	NEW YORK, NY	10019
KAUFMAN, CANDACE	ACTRESS	SCHOEMAN, 2600 W VICTORY BLVD	BURBANK, CA	91505
KAUFMAN, CHARLES	SCREENWRITER	8955 BEVERLY BLVD	LOS ANGELES, CA	90048
KAUFMAN, DAVID	ACTOR	KELMAN, 7813 SUNSET BLVD	LOS ANGELES, CA	90046
KAUFMAN, HAROLD	DIRECTOR	1324 BENEDICT CANYON DR	BEVERLY HILLS, CA	90210
KAUFMAN, JACK	WRITER-PRODUCER	3835 FAIRWAY AVE	STUDIO CITY, CA	91604
KAUFMAN, KENNETH A	NEWS CORRESPONDENT	10612 GAINSBOROUGH RD	POTOMAC, MD	20854
KAUFMAN, LEONARD B	WRITER-PRODUCER	9026 ELEVADO AVE	LOS ANGELES, CA	90069
KAUFMAN, LLOYD, JR	DIRECTOR-PRODUCER	TROMA INC, 733 9TH AVE	NEW YORK, NY	10019
KAUFMAN, MILLARD	WRITER-PRODUCER	3574 MULTIVIEW DR	LOS ANGELES, CA	90068
KAUFMAN, OLA	ACTRESS	14846 SUTTON ST	SHERMAN OAKS, CA	91403
KAUFMAN, PEARL	PIANIST	GEWALD, 58 W 58TH ST	NEW YORK, NY	10019
KAUFMAN, PHILIP	WRITER-PRODUCER	ICM, 8899 BEVERLY BLVD	LOS ANGELES, CA	90048
KAUFMAN, RICHARD	CONDUCTOR	4237 BEEMAN AVE	STUDIO CITY, CA	91604
KAUFMAN, ROBERT	WRITER-PRODUCER	555 W 57TH ST #1230	NEW YORK, NY	10019
KAUFMAN, RODGER D	SINGER-GUITARIST	ROUTE #3, BOX 109	APOLLO, PA	15613
KAUFMAN, ROSE L	SCREENWRITER	8955 BEVERLY BLVD	LOS ANGELES, CA	90048
KAUFMAN, SETH	ACTOR	11350 VENTURA BLVD #206	STUDIO CITY, CA	91604
KAUFMAN, SID	TV EXECUTIVE	CBS-TV, 51 W 52ND ST	NEW YORK, NY	10019
KAUFMAN, WENDY R	NEWS CORRESPONDENT	2025 "M" ST, NW	WASHINGTON, DC	20036

Name	Occupation	Address	City	ZIP
KAUFMANN, JEROME S	DIRECTOR	225 E 46TH ST	NEW YORK, NY	10017
KAUKONEN, JORMA	SINGER-GUITARIST	BOWMAN, 2400 FULTON ST	SAN FRANCISCO, CA	94118
KAUL, DONALD	COMMENTATOR	TRIBUNE MEDIA SERVICES		
		64 E CONCORD ST	ORLANDO, FL	32801
KAUPE, ALAN	FILM EXECUTIVE	11 PRINCEDALE RD	LONDON W11	ENGLAND
KAVA, CAROLINE	ACTRESS	11726 SAN VICENTE BLVD #300	LOS ANGELES, CA	90049
KAVAFIAN, ANI	VIOLINIST	1776 BROADWAY #504	NEW YORK, NY	10019
KAVAFIAN, IDA	VIOLINIST	POST OFFICE BOX 30	TENAFLY, NJ	07670
KAVANAGH, MICHAEL	ACTOR	1741 N IVAR AVE #221	LOS ANGELES, CA	90028
KAVANAU, TED	CABLE EXECUTIVE	1 SOUTH PRADO	ATLANTA, GA	30309
KAVANAUGH, LEIGH	ACTRESS	9165 SUNSET BLVD #202	LOS ANGELES, CA	90069
KAVESH, LAURA	COLUMNIST	TRIBUNE MEDIA SERVICES		
		64 E CONCORD ST	ORLANDO, FL	32801
KAVNER, STEVEN	ACTOR	430 S CLOVERDALE AVE #22	LOS ANGELES, CA	90036
KAVRAKOS, DIMITRI	BASS	61 W 62ND ST #6-F	NEW YORK, NY	10023
KAVUR, FUAD	FILM PRODUCER	USTINOV, 14 LOWNDES SQ	LONDON SW1	ENGLAND
KAWADRI, ANWAR	FILM DIRECTOR	194 CROMWELL RD	LONDON SW5	ENGLAND
KAWAK, EDWARD	BODYBUILDER	AN DER SCHMIEDE LA		
		D-5024 PULHEIM	SINNERSDORF	WEST GERMANY
KAWAMURA, MIDORI	WRITER	8955 BEVERLY BLVD	LOS ANGELES, CA	90048
KAWASAKI, KIKUO	DIRECTOR	DGA, 7950 SUNSET BLVD	LOS ANGELES, CA	90046
KAWELL, JO ANN	NEWS CORRESPONDENT	2731 ONTARIO RD, NW	WASHINGTON, DC	20009
KAY, ALLEN STEVEN	DIRECTOR	DGA, 110 W 57TH ST	NEW YORK, NY	10019
KAY, BERNARD	ACTOR	MARTIN, 7 WINDMILL ST	LONDON W1P 1HF	ENGLAND
KAY, CHARLES	ACTOR	18 EPPLE RD	LONDON SW6	ENGLAND
KAY, DIANNE	ACTRESS	1559 PALISADES DR	PACIFIC PALISADES, CA	90272
KAY, H B	TV WRITER	8955 BEVERLY BLVD	LOS ANGELES, CA	90048
KAY, JOHN & STEPPENWOLF	ROCK & ROLL GROUP	9454 WILSHIRE BLVD #206	BEVERLY HILLS, CA	90212
KAY, MARY	COSMETIC EXECUTIVE	SEE - ASH, MARY KAY		
KAY, MONTE	TALENT AGENT	7655 CURSON TERR	LOS ANGELES, CA	90046
KAY, PAMELA G	ACTRESS	NBC TELEVISION NETWORK		
KAY, ROBERT, JR	WRITER	8955 BEVERLY BLVD	LOS ANGELES, CA	90048
KAY-GEES	VOCAL GROUP	200 W 57TH ST #1101	NEW YORK, NY	10019
KAYAK	MUSICAL GROUP	NELSON, 1701 QUEENS RD	LOS ANGELES, CA	90069
KAYAN, CYNTHIA	TV PRODUCER	ENTERTAINMENT TONIGHT		
		PARAMOUNT TELEVISION		
		5555 MELROSE AVE	LOS ANGELES, CA	90038
KAYDEN, TONY	TV WRITER	2243 CHEREMOYA AVE	HOLLYWOOD, CA	90068
KAYDEN, WILLIAM	TV WRITER-PRODUCER	999 N DOHENY DR	LOS ANGELES, CA	90069
KAYE, CAREN	ACTRESS	151 S EL CAMINO DR	BEVERLY HILLS, CA	90212
KAYE, CELIA	ACTRESS	MILIUS, 888 LINDA FLORA DR	LOS ANGELES, CA	90049
KAYE, CHARLES E	WRITER	555 W 57TH ST #1230	NEW YORK, NY	10019
KAYE, DIANNA	ACTRESS	8235 SANTA MONICA BLVD #202	LOS ANGELES, CA	90046
KAYE, DUANE R	WRITER	8955 BEVERLY BLVD	LOS ANGELES, CA	90048
KAYE, ELIZABETH	WRITER-EDITOR	US MAGAZINE COMPANY		
		1 DAG HAMMARSKJOLD PLAZA	NEW YORK, NY	10017
KAYE, EVELYN PATRICIA	AUTHOR-JOURNALIST	223 TENEFLY RD	ENGLEWOOD, NJ	07631
KAYE, JOHN	SCREENWRITER	8955 BEVERLY BLVD	LOS ANGELES, CA	90048
KAYE, JONATHAN BARNETT	GUITARIST	2140 KNOLL CREST	ARLINGTON, TX	76014
KAYE, JUDY	ACTRESS	870 N VINE ST #G	LOS ANGELES, CA	90038
KAYE, LILA	ACTRESS	PLANT & FROGGATT, LTD		
		JULIAN HOUSE		
		4 WINDMILL ST	LONDON W1	ENGLAND
KAYE, MATTHEW D	NEWS CORRESPONDENT	POST OPFFICE BOX 510	LEONARDTOWN, MD	20650
KAYE, MELVENA	SINGER	P FITZ, 1421 N LINCOLN ST	BURBANK, CA	91506
KAYE, SANDRA	SINGER	POST OFFICE BOX 344	NOLENSVILLE, TN	37135
KAYE, SYLVIA F	WRITER	8955 BEVERLY BLVD	LOS ANGELES, CA	90048
KAYLOR, ROBERT	FILM DIRECTOR	121 S HARPER AVE	LOS ANGELES, CA	90048
KAYZER, BEAU	ACTOR	2160 CENTURY PARK E #1930	LOS ANGELES, CA	90067
KAZ, NEAL	ACTOR	419 E TUJUNGA AVE	BURBANK, CA	91501
KAZAN, CHRIS	SCREENWRITER	LASKY, 551 5TH AVE	NEW YORK, NY	10176
KAZAN, ELIA	DIRECTOR-PRODUCER	432 W 44TH ST	NEW YORK, NY	10036
KAZAN, LAINIE	SINGER-ACTRESS	9903 SANTA MONICA BLVD #283	BEVERLY HILLS, CA	90212
KAZAN, NICHOLAS	SCREENWRITER	3014 3RD ST	SANTA MONICA, CA	90405
KAZANJIAN, HOWARD G	FILM PRODUCER	2759 DORESTA RD	SAN MARINO, CA	91108
KAZANN, ZITTO	ACTOR	6310 SAN VICENTE BLVD #407	LOS ANGELES, CA	90048
KAZARAS, PETER	TENOR	CAMI, 165 W 57TH ST	NEW YORK, NY	10019
KAZIN, ALFRED	WRITER	CITY UNIVERSITY OF NEW YORK		
		ENGLISH DEPARTMENT		
		33 W 42ND ST	NEW YORK, NY	10036
KAZOOPHONY	CLASSICAL GROUP	ARTHUR SHAFMAN INTL		
		723 7TH AVE	NEW YORK, NY	10019
KAZURINSKY, TIMOTHY J	TV WRITER	555 W 57TH ST #1230	NEW YORK, NY	10019
KEACH, JAMES	ACTOR	154 S PALM DR #F	BEVERLY HILLS, CA	90212
KEACH, STACY, JR	ACTOR-DIRECTOR	27425 WINDING WY	MALIBU, CA	90265
KEACH, STACY, SR	ACTOR	3969 LONGRIDGE AVE	SHERMAN OAKS, CA	91423
KEAGGY, PHIL	SINGER	4701 COLLEGE BLVD #106	LEAWOOD, KS	66211
KEALOHA, JIMMY	WRESTLER	SEE - SNUKA, JIMMY "SUPERFLY"		
KEALOHA, LANIE	WRESTLER	SEE - SNUKA, JIMMY "SUPERFLY"		
KEAN, ALAN	FILM EXECUTIVE	9 GREAT NEWPORT ST	LONDON WC1	ENGLAND
KEAN, BETTY	ACTRESS	1850 N WHITLEY AVE #414	HOLLYWOOD, CA	90028
KEAN, E ARTHUR	WRITER-PRODUCER	24235 VALLEY ST	NEWHALL, CA	91321
KEAN, EDWARD S	NEWS CORRESPONDENT	18342 TIMKO LN	GERMANTOWN, MD	20874
KEAN, GERALD A	WRITER	555 W 57TH ST #1230	NEW YORK, NY	10019
KEAN, JANE	ACTRESS	4332 BEN AVE	STUDIO CITY, CA	91604

Name	Occupation	Address	City	Zip
KEAN, NORMAN	THEATER PRODUCER	280 RIVERSIDE DR	NEW YORK, NY	10026
KEAN, SHERRY	SINGER	41 BRITAIN ST #200	TORONTO, ONT	CANADA
KEANE, BIL	CARTOONIST	5815 E JOSHUA TREE LN	PARADISE VALLEY, AZ	85253
KEANE, BOB M	TV WRITER	1510 SCREENLAND DR	BURBANK, CA	91505
KEANE, CHRISTOPHER L	SCREENWRITER	8955 BEVERLY BLVD	LOS ANGELES, CA	90048
KEANE, DIANE	ACTRESS	BURNETT, 42 GRAFTON HOUSE		
		2-3 GOLDEN SQ	LONDON W1	ENGLAND
KEANE, JAMES	ACTOR	10206 CAMARILLO PL #6	NORTH HOLLYWOOD, CA	91602
KEANE, KERRIE	ACTRESS	1888 CENTURY PARK E #1400	LOS ANGELES, CA	90067
KEARNEY, KARON	ACTRESS	8484 WILSHIRE BLVD #235	BEVERLY HILLS, CA	90211
KEARNEY, PHILIP	WRITER	8955 BEVERLY BLVD	LOS ANGELES, CA	90048
KEARNEY, RAMSEY	GUITARIST	602 INVERNESS AVE	NASHVILLE, TN	37204
KEARNS, BURT F	WRITER	555 W 57TH ST #1230	NEW YORK, NY	10019
KEARNS, CHARLES	ACTOR	415 AVONDALE AVE	LOS ANGELES, CA	90049
KEARNS, JOHN P	GUITARIST	142 MC GAVOCK PIKE	NASHVILLE, TN	37214
KEARNS, ROBERT M	NEWS CORRESPONDENT	7610 HELENA DR	FALLS CHURCH, VA	22043
KEARSE, GEORGE W	NEWS CORRESPONDENT	1333 "H" ST, NW	WASHINGTON, DC	20005
KEATHLEY, GEORGE	DIRECTOR	DGA, 7950 SUNSET BLVD	LOS ANGELES, CA	90046
KEATHLEY, STUART	GUITARIST	4002 ELKINS AVE	NASHVILLE, TN	37209
KEATING, CHARLES	ACTOR	10 E 44TH ST #700	NEW YORK, NY	10017
KEATING, DORIS M	WRITER	8955 BEVERLY BLVD	LOS ANGELES, CA	90048
KEATING, MARY	WRITER	555 W 57TH ST #1230	NEW YORK, NY	10019
KEATON, DIANE	ACTRESS-DIRECTOR	ROTHBERG, 145 CENTRAL PARK W	NEW YORK, NY	10023
KEATON, MICHAEL	ACTOR	1888 CENTURY PARK E #1400	LOS ANGELES, CA	90067
KEATS, ROBERT A	TV WRITER	1326 CENTINELA AVE #2	LOS ANGELES, CA	90025
KEBBE, TOM	CASTING DIRECTOR	4705 FARMDALE AVE	NORTH HOLLYWOOD, CA	91602
KEDROVA, LILA	ACTRESS	ARTMEDIA, 10 AVE GEORGE V	PARIS 75008	FRANCE
KEE, BOB B	COMPOSER	6824 CHIMINEAS AVE	RESEDA, CA	91335
KEE, PAUL	MUSIC ARRANGER	3838 PRIEST LAKE DR	NASHVILLE, TN	37217
KEE, ROBERT	TV DIRECTOR	81 KEW GREEN, RICHMOND	SURREY	ENGLAND
KEEFE, MIKE	CARTOONIST	POST OFFICE BOX 1709	DENVER, CO	80201
KEEFER, DON	ACTOR	4146 ALLOTT AVE	VAN NUYS, CA	91403
KEEFER, JANET H	NEWS CORRESPONDENT	2133 WISCONSIN AVE, NW	WASHINGTON, DC	20007
KEEGAN, BARBARA	ACTRESS	15010 VENTURA BLVD #219	SHERMAN OAKS, CA	91403
KEEHNE, VIRGINIA	ACTRESS	6640 SUNSET BLVD #203	LOS ANGELES, CA	90028
KEEL	ROCK & ROLL GROUP	14755 VENTURA BLVD #1-170	SHERMAN OAKS, CA	91423
KEEL, CHARLENE	TV WRITER	8955 BEVERLY BLVD	LOS ANGELES, CA	90048
KEEL, HOWARD	ACTOR-SINGER	15353 LONGBOW DR	SHERMAN OAKS, CA	91403
KEELE, BETH	WRITER	1042 N CRESCENT HGTS BLVD	LOS ANGELES, CA	90046
KEELER, RUBY	ACTRESS	1221 W COAST HWY #220	NEWPORT BEACH, CA	92661
KEELEY, MARIANNE	WRITER	555 W 57TH ST #1230	NEW YORK, NY	10019
KEELS, BUNKY	PIANIST	524 ROOSEVELT AVE	MADISON, TN	37115
KEELS, MIKE	MUSICIAN	524 ROOSEVELT AVE	MADISON, TN	37115
KEEN, LISA MELINDA	NEWS CORRESPONDENT	913 S 22ND ST	ARLINGTON, VA	22202
KEEN, NOAH	ACTOR	9165 SUNSET BLVD #202	LOS ANGELES, CA	90069
KEEN, STANLEY N	CONDUCTOR	6553 39TH ST, NE	SEATTLE, WA	98115
KEENA, PARIS	NEWS CORRESPONDENT	340 NATIONAL PRESS BLDG		
		529 14TH ST, NW	WASHINGTON, DC	20045
KEENE, MELISSA	ACTRESS	SCHOEMAN, 2600 W VICTORY BLVD	BURBANK, CA	91505
KEENE, TOMMY	SINGER-GUITARIST	GEFFEN RECORDS COMPANY		
		9130 SUNSET BLVD	LOS ANGELES, CA	90069
KEENE, WILLIAM	ACTOR	10839 MORRISON ST #16	NORTH HOLLYWOOD, CA	91601
KEENER, GLENN	GUITARIST	ROUTE #1	PATTONVILLE, TX	75468
KEENER, JOYCE	WRITER	8955 BEVERLY BLVD	LOS ANGELES, CA	90048
KEENER, WAYNE	ACTOR	484 W 43RD ST	NEW YORK, NY	10036
KEENY, KAREN	PHOTOGRAPHER	1906 "R" ST #5, NW	WASHINGTON, DC	20009
KEEP, MICHAEL	ACTOR	9255 SUNSET BLVD #610	LOS ANGELES, CA	90069
KEEP, STEPHEN	ACTOR	9255 SUNSET BLVD #1105	LOS ANGELES, CA	90069
KEEPER, GARY	TV EXECUTIVE	PARAMOUNT TELEVISION		
		5555 MELROSE AVE	LOS ANGELES, CA	90038
KEESEY, LORI	NEWS CORRESPONDENT	15933 YUKON LN	DERWOOD, MD	20855
KEESHAN, BOB	TV HOST	555 W 57TH ST	NEW YORK, NY	10019
KEETEN, KATHY	PUBLISHING EXECUTIVE	OMNI MAGAZINE, 1965 BROADWAY	NEW YORK, NY	10023
KEEVUK, LIBBY	ACTRESS	8831 SUNSET BLVD #402	LOS ANGELES, CA	90069
KEFAUVER, F SCOTT	MUSICIAN	1138 WINDING WY RD	NASHVILLE, TN	37216
KEGL-BOGNAR, DESI	WRITER	555 W 57TH ST #1230	NEW YORK, NY	10019
KEHOE, JACK	ACTOR	11726 SAN VICENTE BLVD #300	LOS ANGELES, CA	90049
KEIDEL, A DALE	DIRECTOR	382 CENTRAL PARK W	NEW YORK, NY	10025
KEIFER, LIZ	ACTRESS	13273 VENTURA BLVD #211	STUDIO CITY, CA	91604
KEIL, DREW	ACTOR	175 W 87TH ST #26-H	NEW YORK, NY	10024
KEIL, FELICITAS	PIANIST	POST OFFICE BOX U	REDDING, CT	06875
KEILL, IAN	TV PRODUCER	4 BOYN HILL CLOSE, MAIDENHEAD	BERKSHIRE SL6 4JD	ENGLAND
KEIM, BETTY LOU	ACTRESS	BERLINGER, 10642 ARNEL PL	CHATSWORTH, CA	91311
KEIN, SYBIL	SINGER	2528-A W JEROME AVE	CHICAGO, IL	60645
KEIR, ANDREW	ACTOR	ICM, 388-396 OXFORD ST	LONDON W1	ENGLAND
KEISER, HENRY B	NEWS CORRESPONDENT	7200 ARMAT DR	BETHESDA, MD	20817
KEISTER, JOHN SHANE	PIANIST	ROUTE #1, ARNO RD	FRANKLIN, TN	37064
KEITEL, HARVEY	ACTOR	ICM, 40 W 57TH ST	NEW YORK, NY	10019
KEITH, ANITA	ACTRESS	8721 SUNSET BLVD #200	LOS ANGELES, CA	90069
KEITH, DAVID	ACTOR	151 S EL CAMINO DR	BEVERLY HILLS, CA	90212
KEITH, DAVID	CONDUCTOR	10238 WHITEGATE AVE	SUNLAND, CA	91040
KEITH, GERREN F	TV DIRECTOR	3332 BLAIR DR	LOS ANGELES, CA	90068
KEITH, J VASHONE	NEWS CORRESPONDENT	1650 HARVARD ST, NW	WASHINGTON, DC	20009
KEITH, JEFFREY ALLEN	TV WRITER	225 N ROSE ST #404	BURBANK, CA	91505

Name	Occupation	Address	City
KEITH, LAWRENCE	ACTOR	SCHUMER-OUBRE, 1697 BROADWAY	NEW YORK, NY 10019
KEITH, PAUL	ACTOR	546 N SIERRA BONITA AVE	LOS ANGELES, CA 90036
KEITH, PENELOPE	ACTRESS	HOWE, 66 BERKELEY HOUSE	
		HAY HILL	LONDON W1 ENGLAND
KEITH, SHEILA	ACTRESS	LEADING PLAYERS, 31 KINGS RD	LONDON SW3 ENGLAND
KEITH, SUSAN	ACTRESS	ABC-TV NETWORK, "LOVING"	
		1330 AVE OF THE AMERICAS	NEW YORK, NY 10019
KEITH, WARREN	PIANIST	415 TUSCULUM RD #C-2	NASHVILLE, TN 37211
KEITHH, BRIAN	ACTOR	8150 BEVERLY BLVD #303	LOS ANGELES, CA 90048
KELADA, ASAAD	TV DIRECTOR	4139 MAMMOTH AVE	SHERMAN OAKS, CA 91423
KELBAUGH, RICHARD	TV WRITER	8955 BEVERLY BLVD	LOS ANGELES, CA 90048
KELBEL, BRUCE A	NEWS CORRESPONDENT	13248 TRIADELPHIA RD	ELLICOTT CITY, MD 21043
KELDERMAN, JAKE	NEWS CORRESPONDENT	8800 MAYWOOD AVE	SILVER SPRING, MD 20910
KELEN, PETER	TENOR	61 W 62ND ST #6-F	NEW YORK, NY 10023
KELINGOS, JOHN A	VIOLINIST	VANDERBILT UNIVERSITY	
KELINGOS, JOHN A	VIOLINIST	BOX 6196, STATION B	NASHVILLE, TN 37235
KELL, GEORGE	BASEBALL	POST OFFICE BOX 158	SWIFTON, AR 72471
KELLAHIN, JAMES	WRITER-PRODUCER	19869 GREENBRIAR DR	TARZANA, CA 91356
KELLARD, GRACE	ACTRESS	1156 MONUMENT ST	PACIFIC PALISADES, CA 90272
KELLARD, PHILLIP	TV WRITER	1156 MONUMENT ST	PACIFIC PALISADES, CA 90272
KELLARD, RICHARD J	TV WRITER	12634 KLING ST	STUDIO CITY, CA 91604
KELLAWAY, ROGER W	COMPOSER	HABER, 16255 VENTURA BLVD	ENCINO, CA 91436
KELLEHER, KRISTINE	NEWS CORRESPONDENT	1705 DE SALES ST, NW	WASHINGTON, DC 20036
KELLEHER, TIMOTHY H	NEWS CORRESPONDENT	340 NATIONAL PRESS BLDG	
		529 14TH ST, NW	WASHINGTON, DC 20045
KELLEMS, HAPPY	PANTOMIMIST	2701 COTTAGE WY #14	SACRAMENTO, CA 95825
KELLER, CASEY	TV WRITER	1900 AVE OF THE STARS #1530	LOS ANGELES, CA 90067
KELLER, DAVID W	WRITER	2515 LA MESA WY	SANTA MONICA, CA 90402
KELLER, DONALD	DIRECTOR	117 WALWORTH AVE	SCARSDALE, NY 10583
KELLER, EYTAN	TV WRITER-PRODUCER	9307 KIRKSIDE RD	LOS ANGELES, CA 90035
KELLER, JUDITH	WRITER	555 W 57TH ST #1230	NEW YORK, NY 10019
KELLER, MARTHE	ACTRESS	LAMONSTRASSE 9	8 MUNICH 80 WEST GERMANY
KELLER, MAX	FILM PRODUCER	INTER PLANETARY PICTURES	
		14225 VENTURA BLVD	SHERMAN OAKS, CA 91423
KELLER, MAY	ACTRESS	8721 SUNSET BLVD #200	LOS ANGELES, CA 90069
KELLER, MICHELINE	FILM PRODUCER	INTER PLANETARY PICTURES	
		14225 VENTURA BLVD	SHERMAN OAKS, CA 91423
KELLER, RONALD E	TRUMPETER	500 DES MOINES DR	HERMITAGE, TN 37076
KELLER, SHELDON	WRITER-PRODUCER	2501 ASTRAL DR	LOS ANGELES, CA 90046
KELLER, THOMAS B	TV EXECUTIVE	PBS, 475 L'ENFANT PLAZA, SW	WASHINGTON, DC 20024
KELLER, WILLIAM G	NEWS CORRESPONDENT	1753 SWANN ST, NW	WASHINGTON, DC 20009
KELLERMAN, SALLY	ACTRESS	7944 WOODROW WILSON DR	LOS ANGELES, CA 90046
KELLERMANN, BARBARA	ACTRESS	ICM, 388-396 OXFORD ST	LONDON W1 ENGLAND
KELLERMANN, SUSAN	ACTRESS	SF & A, 121 N SAN VICENTE BLVD	BEVERLY HILLS, CA 90211
KELLETT, BOB	WRITER-PRODUCER	GANNET FILMS COMPANY	
		EMI ELSTREE STUDIOS	
		BOREHAMWOOD	HERTS ENGLAND
KELLEY, ALBERT	DIRECTOR	3767 ALOMAR DR	SHERMAN OAKS, CA 91403
KELLEY, CHRIS	NEWS CORRESPONDENT	CBS NEWS, 524 W 57TH ST	NEW YORK, NY 10019
KELLEY, DEFOREST	ACTOR	15463 GREENLEAF ST	VAN NUYS, CA 91403
KELLEY, ELLIOT JOE	GUITARIST	3145 LONG BLVD #A	NASHVILLE, TN 37203
KELLEY, KITTY	AUTHORESS	BANTOM BOOKS, 666 5TH AVE	NEW YORK, NY 10103
KELLEY, PATRICK	PRODUCER	PAN-ARTS, 4000 WARNER BLVD	BURBANK, CA 91522
KELLEY, ROBERT W	PHOTOGRAPHER	POST OFFICE BOX 13	EDMONDS, CA 98020
KELLEY, STEVE	CARTOONIST	POST OFFICE BOX 191	SAN DIEGO, CA 92112
KELLEY, TIMOTHY J	WRITER	8955 BEVERLY BLVD	LOS ANGELES, CA 90048
KELLEY, WALTER	WRITER-PRODUCER	6459 SYCAMORE MEADOWS DR	MALIBU, CA 90265
KELLEY, WAYNE	SCREENWRITER	1626 1/2 N VISTA ST	LOS ANGELES, CA 90046
KELLEY, WILLIAM	TV WRITER	501 S FULLLER AVE	LOS ANGELES, CA 90036
KELLEY, WILLIAM	TV EXECUTIVE	NBC TELEVISION NETWORK	
		30 ROCKEFELLER PLAZA	NEW YORK, NY 10112
KELLISON, CATHERINE	WRITER	555 W 57TH ST #1230	NEW YORK, NY 10019
KELLJAN, BOB	WRITER-PRODUCER	9151 WARBLER PL	LOS ANGELES, CA 90069
KELLMAN, BARNET	TV DIRECTOR	718 BROADWAY	NEW YORK, NY 10003
KELLOG, MARJORIE	SCREENWRITER	555 W 57TH ST #1230	NEW YORK, NY 10019
KELLOGG, JOHN G	ACTOR	9200 SUNSET BLVD #1210	LOS ANGELES, CA 90069
KELLOGG, LYNN	ACTRESS-SINGER	10583 SCENARIO LN	LOS ANGELES, CA 90077
KELLUM, ALLAN CARTER	NEWS CORRESPONDENT	1300 S CLEVELAND ST	ARLINGTON, VA 22204
KELLUM, MURRY	SINGER	POST OFFICE BOX 208	GOODLETTSVILLE, TN 37072
KELLY, ALFRED ORR	NEWS CORRESPONDENT	3225 OLIVER ST, NW	WASHINGTON, DC 20015
KELLY, APRIL	TV WRITER	8955 BEVERLY BLVD	LOS ANGELES, CA 90048
KELLY, BARBARA	ACTRESS-WRITER	STUDIO, 5 KIDDERPORE AVE	LONDON NW3 7SX ENGLAND
KELLY, BRIAN	ACTOR	23709 MALIBU COLONY	MALIBU, CA 90265
KELLY, BRUCE	BARITONE	VKD INTERNATIONAL ARTISTS	
		220 SHEPPARD AVE E	
		WILLOWDALE	TORONTO, ONT M2N 3A9 CANADA
KELLY, CALVIN REGINALD	TV WRITER	5830 W GREEN VALLEY CIR #210	CULVER CITY, CA 90230
KELLY, CASEY	WRITER	555 W 57TH ST #1230	NEW YORK, NY 10019
KELLY, CHRIS	TV WRITER	4 CLAIRE RD	CAMBRIDGE CB3 9HN ENGLAND

Name	Occupation	Address	City	Zip/Country
KELLY, DAREN	ACTOR	10000 SANTA MONICA BLVD #305	LOS ANGELES, CA	90067
KELLY, DAVID	ACTOR	IAR, 235-241 REGENT ST	LONDON W1A 2JT	ENGLAND
KELLY, DAVID PATRICK	ACTOR	KOHNER, 9169 SUNSET BLVD	LOS ANGELES, CA	90069
KELLY, DOROTHY	CASTING DIRECTOR	CHELSA VIDEO, 6534 SUNSET BLVD	LOS ANGELES, CA	90028
KELLY, ELLIOT H	CONDUCTOR	691 S IROLO ST #409	LOS ANGELES, CA	90005
KELLY, GENE	ACT-DAN-DIR	DGA, 7950 SUNSET BLVD	LOS ANGELES, CA	90046
KELLY, GREGORY	SPORTS REPORTER	SPORTS ILLUSTRATED MAGAZINE		
		TIME & LIFE BUILDING		
		ROCKEFELLER CENTER	NEW YORK, NY	10020
KELLY, JACK	ACTOR	9255 SUNSET BLVD #1105	LOS ANGELES, CA	90069
KELLY, JAMES	WRITER-EDITOR	TIME/TIME & LIFE BLDG		
		ROCKEFELLER CENTER	NEW YORK, NY	10020
KELLY, JAMES F	ACTOR	10390 SANTA MONICA BLVD #310	LOS ANGELES, CA	90025
KELLY, JAMES PATRICK, III	DIRECTOR	410 W 60TH TERR	KANSAS CITY, MO	64113
KELLY, JERRI	SINGER	CARRERE UK, 22 QUEEN ST	LONDON	ENGLAND
KELLY, JERRI H	GUITARIST	POST OFFICE BOX 24457	NASHVILLE, TN	37202
KELLY, JERRY, BAND	ROCK & ROLL GROUP	SEE - DAKOTA		
KELLY, JIM	SPORTSCASTER	CBS SPORTS, 51 W 52ND ST	NEW YORK, NY	10019
KELLY, JIM	ACTOR	9744 WILSHIRE BLVD #306	BEVERLY HILLS, CA	90212
KELLY, JOAN M	WRITER	555 W 57TH ST #1230	NEW YORK, NY	10019
KELLY, JOHN	ACTOR	8961 SUNSET BLVD #B	LOS ANGELES, CA	90069
KELLY, JOHN G	DIRECTOR-PRODUCER	CBS-TV, 524 W 57TH ST	NEW YORK, NY	10019
KELLY, JOHN S	TALENT AGENT	15760 VENTURA BLVD #1730	ENCINO, CA	91436
KELLY, JOSE	SINGER	VISTONE, 6331 SANTA MONICA BLVD	HOLLYWOOD, CA	90038
KELLY, JUDD	GUITARIST	120 KINGSTON PL #50	BLOOMINGTON, IN	47401
KELLY, KAREN	ACTRESS	15010 VENTURA BLVD #234	SHERMAN OAKS, CA	91403
KELLY, KATHY	WRITER	8955 BEVERLY BLVD	LOS ANGELES, CA	90048
KELLY, KATIE	FILM CRITIC	WABC-TV, 7 LINCOLN SQ	NEW YORK, NY	10023
KELLY, KEVIN "MR MAGNIFICENT"	WRESTLER	AMERICAN WRESTLING ASSOC		
		MINNEAPLOIS WRESTLING		
		10001 WAYZATA BLVD	MINNETONKA, MN	55345
KELLY, KEVIN B	TV DIRECTOR	13 PIERPONT PL	STATEN ISLAND, NY	10314
KELLY, LOREN J	NEWS CORRESPONDENT	2028 16TH ST, NW	WASHINGTON, DC	20009
KELLY, MARGO	ACTRESS	9040 HARRATT ST #5	LOS ANGELES, CA	90069
KELLY, MARGUERITE	COLUMNIST	TRIBUNE MEDIA SERVICES		
		64 E CONCORD ST	ORLANDO, FL	32801
KELLY, MARY P	WRITER	8955 BEVERLY BLVD	LOS ANGELES, CA	90048
KELLY, MATTHEW	ACTOR	REGAN, 11 BELSIZE PARK	LONDON NW3 4ES	ENGLAND
KELLY, MATTHEW	TV PERSONALITY	REAGAN, 78 NEW BOND ST	LONDON W1	ENGLAND
KELLY, MICHAEL	CONDUCTOR	POST OFFICE BOX 131	SPRINGFIELD, VA	22150
KELLY, MICHAEL C	TV DIRECTOR	80 HIGHVIEW AVE	PARK RIDGE, NJ	07656
KELLY, MIKE	WRESTLER	POST OFFICE BOX 3859	STAMFORD, CT	06905
KELLY, PATRICK D	DIRECTOR	PIER 62, W 23RD STATION		
		12TH AVE	NEW YORK, NY	10011
KELLY, PAULA	ACTRESS-DANCER	ICM, 8890 BEVERLY BLVD	LOS ANGELES, CA	90048
KELLY, RICHARD M	GUITARIST	POST OFFICE BOX 745	GALLATIN, TN	37066
KELLY, ROZ	ACTRESS	445 N BEDFORD DR #PH	BEVERLY HILLS, CA	90210
KELLY, SANDRA	COLUMNIST	UNIVERSAL PRESS SYNDICATE		
		4900 MAIN ST, 9TH FLOOR	KANSAS CITY, MO	62114
KELLY, SEAN C	TV WRITER	55 W 57TH ST #1230	NEW YORK, NY	10019
KELLY, THOMAS F	DIRECTOR	360 S BURNSIDE AVE #5-K	LOS ANGELES, CA	90036
KELLY, TOM "SHOTGUN"	TV-RADIO PERSONALITY	POST OFFICE BOX 11985	SAN DIEGO, CA	92111
KELLY, VIRGINIA W	NEWS CORRESPONDENT	3930 CONNECTICUT AVE, NW	WASHINGTON, DC	20008
KELLY, WAYNE	WRITER	8955 BEVERLY BLVD	LOS ANGELES, CA	90048
KELLY, WAYNE P	NEWS CORRESPONDENT	511 ROBINSON CT	ALEXANDRIA, VA	22302
KELLY, WILLIAM J	NEWS CORRESPONDENT	320 N GEORGE MASON DR #4	ARLINGTON, VA	22203
KELLY'S HEROES	MUSICAL GROUP	KTA, 108 SHARON DR	WEST MONROE, LA	71291
KELM, LINDA	SOPRANO	ICM, 40 W 57TH ST	NEW YORK, NY	10019
KELMAN, ALFRED R	TV DIRECTOR	124 E 65TH ST	NEW YORK, NY	10021
KELSEY, CAROL	CASTING DIRECTOR	937 N COLE AVE	LOS ANGELES, CA	90028
KELSEY, DALE	NEWS CORRESPONDENT	4706 SPRUCE AVE	FAIRFAX, VA	22030
KELSEY, LINDA	ACTRESS	30600 SICOMORO DR	MALIBU, CA	90265
KELSEY, LYNNE	TV WRITER	8955 BEVERLY BLVD	LOS ANGELES, CA	90048
KELSH, PETER	COMPOSER	FINELL, 155 W 68TH ST	NEW YORK, NY	10023
KELTON, KEVIN	TV WRITER	11726 SAN VICENTE BLVD #300	LOS ANGELES, CA	90049
KEMBLE, MARK	ACTOR	1605 N CAHUENGA BLVD #202	LOS ANGELES, CA	90028
KEMENY, JOHN	FILM PRODUCER	POST OFFICE BOX 900	BEVERLY HILLS, CA	90213
KEMLER, KATHERINE	FLAUTIST	IAPR, KINCORA, BEER RD		
		SEATON	DEVON	ENGLAND
KEMMER, EDWARD	ACTOR	200 W 57TH ST #1303	NEW YORK, NY	10019
KEMMERLING, WARREN	ACTOR	10819 SHOSHONE AVE	GRANADA HILLS, CA	91344
KEMP, BARRY	TV EXEC-PROD	10100 SANTA MONICA BLVD #348	LOS ANGELES, CA	90067
KEMP, BARRY MICHAEL	TV WRITER	17780 RIDGEWAY RD	GRANADA HILLS, CA	91344
KEMP, DONNA TURNER	DIRECTOR	14052 VALLEYHEART DR #4	SHERMAN OAKS, CA	91423
KEMP, JEREMY	ACTOR	LEADING ARTISTS, LTD		
		60 SAINT JAMES'S ST	LONDON SW1	ENGLAND
KEMP, SALLY	ACTRESS	NBC-TV, 3000 W ALAMEDA AVE	BURBANK, CA	91523
KEMP, WAYNE	SINGER	POST OFFICE BOX 390	PONTOTOC, MS	38863
KEMP-WELCH, JOAN	TV DIRECTOR-PRODUCER	11 CHILWORTH MEWS	LONDON W2	ENGLAND
KEMPEL, ARTHUR B	COMPOSER	2255 N CAHUENGA BLVD #30	LOS ANGELES, CA	90068
KEMPER, DAVID M	WRITER	8955 BEVERLY BLVD	LOS ANGELES, CA	90048
KEMPF, DEBORAH L	PHOTOJOURNALIST	3514 34TH ST, NW	WASHINGTON, DC	20008
KEMPLEY, RITA	FILM CRITIC	THE WASHINGTON POST		
		1150 15TH ST, NW	WASHINGTON, DC	20071
KEMPLEY, WALTER	TV WRITER	8955 BEVERLY BLVD	LOS ANGELES, CA	90048

Name	Occupation	Address	City	Zip/Country
KEMPSTER, NORMAN	NEWS CORRESPONDENT	9503 MIDWOOD RD	SILVER SPRING, MD	20910
KENCKE, JOHN	GUITARIST	137 SHIVEL DR	HENDERSONVILLE, TN	37075
KENDAL, FELICITY	ACTRESS	CHATTO & LINNIT, LTD		
		PRINCE OF WALES THEATRE		
		COVENTRY ST	LONDON WC2	ENGLAND
KENDALL, BEN	COMPOSER	POST OFFICE BOX 1098	PALMA DE MALLORCA	SPAIN
KENDALL, DONALD M	NEWS CORRESPONDENT	1617 COLESBERG ST	SILVER SPRING, MD	20904
KENDALL, GARY	BASSO-BARITONE	1776 BROADWAY #504	NEW YORK, NY	10019
KENDALL, JO	ACTRESS	PLANT & FROGGATT, LTD		
		JULIAN HOUSE		
		4 WINDMILL ST	LONDON WC2	ENGLAND
KENDALL, PETER L	NEWS CORRESPONDENT	CBS NEWS, 2020 "M" ST, NW	WASHINGTON, DC	20036
KENDALL, SARAH	ACTRESS	8484 WILSHIRE BLVD #235	BEVERLY HILLS, CA	90211
KENDALL, SUZY	ACTRESS	DENTHAM HOUSE #44, THE MOUNT	HAMPSTEAD NW3	ENGLAND
KENDALLS, THE	C & W GROUP	WORLD CLASS TALENT AGENCY		
		1522 DEMONBREUN ST	NASHVILLE, TN	37203
KENDRICK, CHARLES	GUITARIST	POST OFFICE BOX 446	SHELAY, NC	28150
KENDRICK, HENRY	ACTOR	5626 E LINDEN ST	TUCSON, AZ	85712
KENDRICKS, EDDIE	SINGER	200 W 57TH ST #907	NEW YORK, NY	10019
KENDY, ARTHUR	NEWS CORRESPONDENT	925 25TH ST, NW	WASHINGTON, DC	20037
KENIN, DAVID	CABLE EXECUTIVE	USA CABLE NETWORK		
		208 HARRISTOWN RD	GLEN ROCK, NJ	07452
KENION, JERRY MANN	WRITER	202 COUNTRY PARK RD	GREENSBORO, NC	27408
KENIS, STEVE	TALENT AGENT	MORRIS, 147-149 WARDOUR ST	LONDON W1V 3TB	ENGLAND
KENNARD, ARTHUR	TALENT AGENT	12220 HUSTON ST	NORTH HOLLYWOOD, CA	91606
KENNARD, DAVID	DIRECTOR-PRODUCER	POST OFFICE BOX 81	PALOS VERDES, CA	90274
KENNEALLY, PHILIP	ACTOR	400 S BURNSIDE AVE #4-B	LOS ANGELES, CA	90036
KENNEDY, ADAM	SCREENWRITER	555 W 57TH ST #1230	NEW YORK, NY	10019
KENNEDY, ADRIENNE LITA	PLAYWRIGHT	172 W 79TH ST	NEW YORK, NY	10021
KENNEDY, ARTHUR	ACTOR	2768 WOODWARDIA DR	LOS ANGELES, CA	90024
KENNEDY, BILL	ACTOR	2100 S OCEAN BLVD #103-S	PALM BEACH, FL	33480
KENNEDY, BURT	FILM WRITER-DIRECTOR	13138 MAGNOLIA BLVD	SHERMAN OAKS, CA	91423
KENNEDY, CAROLINE	CELEBRITY	20 W 20TH ST	NEW YORK, NY	10011
KENNEDY, GENE	SINGER	2125 8TH AVE S	NASHVILLE, TN	37204
KENNEDY, GEORGE	ACTOR	15620 LIVE OAKS SPRINGS CANYON	CANYON COUNTRY, CA	91351
KENNEDY, GORDON S	GUITARIST	6010 MURRAY LN	BRENTWOOD, TN	37027
KENNEDY, HAROLD	NEWS CORRESPONDENT	14901 POPLAR HILL RD	ACOCKEEK, MD	20607
KENNEDY, JACQUELINE	FIRST LADY-AUTHOR	647 5TH AVE	NEW YORK, NY	10028
KENNEDY, JAMES	ACTOR	8230 BEVERLY BLVD #23	LOS ANGELES, CA	90048
KENNEDY, JAMES W	WRITER	8955 BEVERLY BLVD	LOS ANGELES, CA	90048
KENNEDY, JAY R	WRITER	555 W 57TH ST #1230	NEW YORK, NY	10019
KENNEDY, JAYNE	ACTRESS-MODEL	POST OFFICE BOX 491355	LOS ANGELES, CA	90049
KENNEDY, JERRY G	GUITARIST-DOBROIST	6010 MURRAY LN	BRENTWOOD, TN	37027
KENNEDY, JOHN MILTON	ACTOR	6430 SUNSET BLVD #1203	LOS ANGELES, CA	90028
KENNEDY, JOYCE LAIN	COLUMNIST	7720 EL CAMINO REAL #2-C	RANCHO LA COSTA, CA	92008
KENNEDY, KATHLEEN	FILM PRODUCER	MCA/UNIVERSAL STUDIOS, INC		
		100 UNIVERSAL CITY PLAZA	UNIVERSAL CITY, CA	91608
KENNEDY, KEN	DIRECTOR	1302 E BECKER LN	PHOENIX, AZ	85020
KENNEDY, LEON ISAAC	ACTOR-PRODUCER	5565 BONNEVILLE RD	HIDDEN HILLS, CA	91302
KENNEDY, MALLORY	CASTING DIRECTOR	6815 WILLOUGHBY AVE	LOS ANGELES, CA	90038
KENNEDY, MARTIN T	WRITER	A D PETERS & CO, LTD		
		10 BUCKINGHAM ST	LONDON WC2	ENGLAND
KENNEDY, MARY ANN	MUSICIAN	6418 TEMPLE RD	FRANKLIN, TN	37064
KENNEDY, MIMI	ACTRESS	10100 SANTA MONICA BLVD #1600	LOS ANGELES, CA	90067
KENNEDY, NIGEL	VIOLINIST	CAMI, 165 W 57TH ST	NEW YORK, NY	10019
KENNEDY, RAY	SINGER	11340 W OLYMPIC BLVD #357	LOS ANGELES, CA	90064
KENNEDY, RICHARD T	WRITER	555 W 57TH ST #1230	NEW YORK, NY	10019
KENNEDY, RIGG	ACTOR	470 S SAN VICENTE BLVD #204-D	LOS ANGELES, CA	90048
KENNEDY, ROYAL	NEWS CORRESPONDENT	ABC NEWS, 2040 AVE OF THE STARS	LOS ANGELES, CA	90067
KENNEDY, WILLIAM	SCREENWRITER	555 W 57TH ST #1230	NEW YORK, NY	10019
KENNEDY-MARTIN, IAN	WRITER-EDITOR	ROGERS, 29 GOODGE ST	LONDON W1	ENGLAND
KENNEDY-MARTIN, TROY	SCREENWRITER	A D PETERS & CO, LTD		
		10 BUCKINGHAM ST	LONDON WC2	ENGLAND
KENNER, BILL	GUITARIST	1213 DAVIDSON RD	NASHVILLE, TN	37205
KENNERLY, DAVID HUME	PHOTOGRAPHER	3332 "P" ST, NW	WASHINGTON, DC	20007
KENNERLY, DIANE	ACTRESS	9165 SUNSET BLVD #202	LOS ANGELES, CA	90069
KENNERSON, BENNY	PIANIST	125 ROBERTA DR	HENDERSONVILLE, TN	37075
KENNEY, BILL	CASTING DIRECTOR	733 N SEWARD ST	LOS ANGELES, CA	90038
KENNEY, H WESLEY	TV WRITER-PRODUCER	12996 GALEWOOD ST	STUDIO CITY, CA	91604
KENNEY, H WESLEY	TV PRODUCER	CBS-TV, 7800 BEVERLY BLVD	LOS ANGELES, CA	90036
KENNEY, LONA B	TV WRITER	555 W 57TH ST #1230	NEW YORK, NY	10019
KENNEY, SEAN	ACTOR	9441 WILSHIRE BLVD #620-D	BEVERLY HILLS, CA	90210
KENNON, RALPH	DRUMMER	POST OFFICE BOX 1495	HENDERSONVILLE, TN	37075
KENNY, DOUGLAS J	DIRECTOR	152 W 20TH ST	NEW YORK, NY	10011
KENNY, EDWARD J	DIRECTOR	152 W SHORE DR	MARBLEHEAD, MA	01945
KENNY, JOSEPH E	FILM DIRECTOR	7250 SAN LUIS AVE	CARLSBAD, CA	92008
KENNY, YVONNE	SOPRANO	CAMI, 165 W 57TH ST	NEW YORK, NY	10019
KENNY G	SAXOPHONIST	FRITZ/TURNER MANAGEMENT		
		648 N ROBERTSON BLVD	LOS ANGELES, CA	90048
KENRICK, TONY	SCREENWRITER	8955 BEVERLY BLVD	LOS ANGELES, CA	90048
KENSEN, KAREN	ACTRESS	4501 VISTA DEL MONTE AVE #8	SHERMAN OAKS, CA	91403
KENT, ALLEGRA	DANCER	NEW YORK CITY BALLET		
		LINCOLN CENTER PLAZA	NEW YORK, NY	10023
KENT, ART	TV EXECUTIVE	NBC TELEVISION NETWORK		
		30 ROCKEFELLER PLAZA	NEW YORK, NY	10112

JAYNE KENNEDY

DEBORAH KERR

EVELYN KEYES

PERSIS KHAMBATTA

CHAKA KHAN

EVELYN KING

PERRY KING

NASTASSIA KINSKI

PHYLLIS KIRK

Name	Occupation	Address	City / Zip
KENT, BULLDOG DON	WRESTLER	CAPITOL INTERNATIONAL	
		11844 MARKET ST	NORTH LIMA, OH 44452
KENT, CHRISTINA	NEWS CORRESPONDENT	2508 EAST PL, NW	WASHINGTON, DC 20007
KENT, DIAN	WRITER	8955 BEVERLY BLVD	LOS ANGELES, CA 90048
KENT, ENID	ACTRESS	9300 WILSHIRE BLVD #410	BEVERLY HILLS, CA 90212
KENT, GEORGE	CONDUCTOR	7125 FULTON AVE #24	NORTH HOLLYWOOD, CA 91605
KENT, JANICE	ACTRESS	3800 BARHAM BLVD #303	LOS ANGELES, CA 90068
KENT, JEAN	ACTRESS	LONDON MANAGEMENT, LTD	
		235-241 REGENT ST	LONDON W1A 2JT ENGLAND
KENT, JIM	GUITARIST	1300 DIVISION ST #106	NASHVILLE, TN 37203
KENT, JOAN-CAROL	ACTRESS	200 N ROBERTSON BLVD #308	BEVERLY HILLS, CA 90210
KENT, LILA	ACTRESS	9255 SUNSET BLVD #603	LOS ANGELES, CA 90069
KENT, MICHAEL	CONDUCTOR	POST OFFICE BOX 1150	MOUNT SHASTA, CA 96067
KENT, PAUL	ACTOR	37219 N 52ND ST #E	PALMDALE, CA 93550
KENT, STEVEN	TV PRODUCER	KNBC-TV, "SANTA BARBARA"	
		3000 W ALAMEDA AVE	BURBANK, CA 91523
KENT, WALTER	COMPOSER	4611 STARK AVE	WOODLAND HILLS, CA 91364
KENTERA, GEORGE R	NEWS CORRESPONDENT	7808 ACCOTINK PL	ALEXANDRIA, VA 22308
KENTISH, DOUGLAS	FILM PRODUCER	ILLUSTRA, 13 BATEMAN ST	LONDON W1 ENGLAND
KENWITH, HERBERT	DIRECTOR-PRODUCER	1527 SUNSET PLAZA DR	LOS ANGELES, CA 90069
KENWORTHY, THOMAS	NEWS CORRESPONDENT	416 N CHAPELGATE LN	BALTIMORE, MD 21229
KENYON, CURTIS	FILM EXECUTIVE	16145 MORRISON ST	ENCINO, CA 91436
KENYON, MARION	SCREENWRITER	8721 SUNSET BLVD #202	LOS ANGELES, CA 90069
KENYON, SANDY	ACTOR-DIRECTOR	13530 MORRISON ST	SHERMAN OAKS, CA 91423
KENYON, SANDY	NEWS CORRESPONDENT	CNN, 6290 SUNSET BLVD	LOS ANGELES, CA 90028
KEOUGH, LAUREEN	ACTRESS	5330 LANKERSHIM BLVD #210	NORTH HOLLYWOOD, CA 91601
KEPLER, JOHN	ACTOR	808 RADCLIFFE AVE	PACIFIC PALISADES, CA 90272
KEPLER, SHELL	ACTRESS	9441 WILSHIRE BLVD #620-D	BEVERLY HILLS, CA 90212
KERAMIDAS, GEORGE	TV EXECUTIVE	284 VOORHIS AVE	RIVER EDGE, NJ 07661
KERBAWY, HAFORD	DIRECTOR	1025 YORKSHIRE	GROSSE POINT PARK, MI 48230
KERBY, WILLIAM C	SCREENWRITER	9200 SUNSET BLVD #PH-25	LOS ANGELES, CA 90069
KERCHEVAL, KEN	ACTOR	570 N ROSSMARE AVE	LOS ANGELES, CA 90004
KERK, SOREN	ACTRESS	5330 LANKERSHIM BLVD #210	NORTH HOLLYWOOD, CA 91601
KERMISCH, AMOS A	NEWS CORRESPONDENT	2900 N DINWIDDIE ST	ARLINGTON, VA 22207
KERMOYAN, MICHAEL	ACTOR	817 W END AVE	NEW YORK, NY 10025
KERN, BILL	TV DIRECTOR-PRODUCER	9255 SUNSET BLVD #706	LOS ANGELES, CA 90069
KERN, ROBERT J, JR	FILM EDITOR	ACE, 4416 1/2 FINLEY AVE	LOS ANGELES, CA 90027
KERN, RONNI	SCREENWRITER	7339 PACIFIC VIEW DR	LOS ANGELES, CA 90068
KERNDOLE, WALLY	WRESTLER	SEE - KERNODLE, ROCKY	
KERNER, JORDAN R	WRITER	8955 BEVERLY BLVD	LOS ANGELES, CA 90048
KERNER, MICHAEL	TV DIRECTOR	CBS-TV, "AS THE WORLD TURNS"	
		51 W 52ND ST	NEW YORK, NY 10019
KERNOCHAN, SARAH M	WRITER	8955 BEVERLY BLVD	LOS ANGELES, CA 90048
KERNODLE, DON	WRESTLER	NATIONAL WRESTLING ALLIANCE	
		JIM CROCKETT PROMOTIONS	
		421 BRIARBEND DR	CHARLOTTE, NC 28209
KERNODLE, ROCKY	WRESTLER	NATIONAL WRESTLING ALLIANCE	
		JIM CROCKETT PROMOTIONS	
		421 BRIARBEND DR	CHARLOTTE, NC 28209
KERNS, JOANNA	ACTRESS	3529 BEVERLY GLEN DR	SHERMAN OAKS, CA 91423
KERNS, SANDRA	ACTRESS	3800 BARHAM BLVD #303	LOS ANGELES, CA 90068
KERR, ALAN	DRUMMER	550 HARDING PL #102-E	NASHVILLE, TN 37211
KERR, DEBORAH	ACTRESS	WYHERGUT, 7250 KLOSTERS	GRISONS SWITZERLAND
KERR, ELIZABETH	ACTRESS	410 N ROSSMORE AVE	LOS ANGELES, CA 90004
KERR, GLAISTER	FILM EXECUTIVE	1875 CENTURY PARK E #300	LOS ANGELES, CA 90067
KERR, JAY	ACTOR	1901 AVE OF THE STARS #840	LOS ANGELES, CA 90067
KERR, JEAN	PLAYWRIGHT	1 BEACH AVE	LARCHMONT, NY 10538
KERR, JUDY	ACTRESS	6827 PACIFIC VIEW DR	LOS ANGELES, CA 98068
KERR, KAREN	ACTRESS	LENZ, 1456 E CHARLESTON BLVD	LAS VEGAS, NV 89104
KERR, WILLIAM B	ACTOR	16183 ROYAL OAK RD	ENCINO, CA 91436
KERRIDGE, LINDA	ACTRESS-MODEL	FLICK EAST-WEST TALENTS	
		9045 MEMO ST	LOS ANGELES, CA 90069
KERRIGAN, TERRY	CASTING DIRECTOR	4120 W ALAMEDA AVE N #9113	BURBANK, CA 91505
KERRY, ANN	ACTRESS	8075 W 3RD ST #303	LOS ANGELES, CA 90048
KERRY, ANNE	ACTRESS	2121 AVE OF THE STARS #410	LOS ANGELES, CA 90067
KERRY, ERICA	TV WRITER	8955 BEVERLY BLVD	LOS ANGELES, CA 90048
KERSH, KATHY	ACTRESS	13925 MORRISON ST	SHERMAN OAKS, CA 91423
KERSHAW, DOUG	FIDDLER	6537 KESSLER AVE	WOODLAND HILLS, CA 91364
KERSHAW, GLENN	WRITER	555 W 57TH ST #1230	NEW YORK, NY 10019
KERSHAW, H V	WRITER-PRODUCER	ABERGELE	NORTH WALES ENGLAND
KERSHAW, RICHARD	TV-RADIO PERSONALITY	82 PRINCE OF WALES MANSIONS	
		PRINCE OF WALES DR	LONDON SW11 ENGLAND
KERSHAW, STEWART	CONDUCTOR	3003 VAN NESS ST #W-205, NW	WASHINGTON, DC 20008
KERSHAW, WHITNEY	ACTRESS	8730 SUNSET BLVD #400	LOS ANGELES, CA 90069
KERSHNER, IRVIN	FILM DIRECTOR	ROUTE #7, BOX 232	KENT, CT 06757
KERSTEN, PETER	BANJOIST	1412 TOMAHAWK LN	OLATHE, KS 66062
KERVEN, CLAUDE MICHEL	TV DIRECTOR	14 WASHINGTON PL	NEW YORK, NY 10003
KERWIN, BRIAN	ACTOR	10402 1/2 WHEATLAND AVE	SUNLAND, CA 91040
KERWIN, DENNIS	ACTOR	8350 SANTA MONICA BLVD #103	LOS ANGELES, CA 90069
KERWIN, HARRY E	WRITER	8955 BEVERLY BLVD	LOS ANGELES, CA 90048
KERWIN, JOHN J, JR	TV DIRECTOR	3014 NESTALL RD	LAGUNA BEACH, CA 92651
KESEND, ELLEN	SCREENWRITER	2107 1/2 N HIGHLAND AVE #A	LOS ANGELES, CA 90068
KESEY, KEN	WRITER	ROUTE #8, BOX 477	PLEASANT HILL, OR 97401
KESHEN, AMY	DIRECTOR	2425 NE 194TH ST	MIAMI, FL 33180

KESLER, HENRY	DIRECTOR	459 LORING AVE	LOS ANGELES, CA	90024
KESLING, DIANE	MEZZO-SOPRANO	61 W 62ND ST #6-F	NEW YORK, NY	10023
KESSEL, BARNEY	COMPOSER	1125 BEDFORD DR	OKLAHOMA CITY, OK	73116
KESSLER, ANDREA	ACTRESS	151 S EL CAMINO DR	BEVERLY HILLS, CA	90212
KESSLER, BRUCE	DIRECTOR	4444 VIA MARINA	MARINA DEL REY, CA	90292
KESSLER, ELAINE M	NEWS CORRESPONDENT	5051 CLIFFHAVEN DR	ANNANDALE, VA	22003
KESSLER, FRANCINE	ACTRESS	9220 SUNSET BLVD #303	LOS ANGELES, CA	90069
KESSLER, JEROME A	CONDUCTOR	1717 N HIGHLAND AVE #305	LOS ANGELES, CA	90028
KESSLER, LEE	ACTRESS	8920 WILSHIRE BLVD #520	BEVERLY HILLS, CA	90211
KESSLER, LYLE	ACTOR-WRITER	15010 VENTURA BLVD #219	SHERMAN OAKS, CA	91403
KESSLER, MARCH H	WRITER	8955 BEVERLY BLVD	LOS ANGELES, CA	90048
KESSLER, QUIN	ACTRESS	8322 BEVERLY BLVD #202	LOS ANGELES, CA	90048
KESSLER, RALPH	COMPOSER-CONDUCTOR	14400 ADDISON ST	SHERMAN OAKS, CA	91403
KESSLER, TODD E	WRITER-PRODUCER	DGA, 110 W 57TH ST	NEW YORK, NY	10019
KESSLER, ZALE	ACTOR	1953 HILLCREST RD	LOS ANGELES, CA	90068
KESSNER, DANIEL	COMPOSER	FINELL, 155 W 68TH ST	NEW YORK, NY	10023
KESTELMAN, SARA	ACTRESS	113 FORTRESS RD	LONDON NW5	ENGLAND
KESTEN, BRAD	ACTOR	12725 VENTURA BLVD #E	STUDIO CITY, CA	91604
KESTER, MORGAN	ACTRESS	813 VENEZIA AVE	VENICE, CA	90291
KESTNBAUM, ALBERT S	DIRECTOR	2 E LYON FARM	GREENWICH, CT	06830
KETCHAM, HANK	CARTOONIST	POST OFFICE BOX 800	PEBBLE BEACH, CA	93953
KETCHAM, JERRY	DIRECTOR	24348 HIGHLANDER RD	CANOGA PARK, CA	91307
KETCHUM, DAVID	WRITER-PRODUCER	DGA, 7950 SUNSET BLVD	LOS ANGELES, CA	90046
KETCHUM, JANET	FLUTIST	POST OFFICE BOX 27539	PHILADELPHIA, PA	19118
KETER, SHANIT	ACTRESS	427 N CANON DR #205	BEVERLY HILLS, CA	90210
KETEYIAN, ARMEN	SPORTS WRITER	SPORTS ILLUSTRATED MAGAZINE		
		TIME & LIFE BUILDING		
		ROCKEFELLER CENTER	NEW YORK, NY	10020
KEY, JANET	ACTRESS	BROWNE, 13 SAINT MARTINS RD	LONDON SW9	ENGLAND
KEY, TED	CARTOONIST	1694 GLENHARDIE RD	WAYNE, PA	19087
KEYES, CHIP	TV WRITER	ICM, 8899 BEVERLY BLVD	LOS ANGELES, CA	90048
KEYES, DANIEL F	ACTOR	43 W 93RD ST	NEW YORK, NY	10025
KEYES, DOUG	TV WRITER	ICM, 8899 BEVERLY BLVD	LOS ANGELES, CA	90048
KEYES, EVELYN	ACTRESS	1155 N LA CIENEGA BLVD #909	LOS ANGELES, CA	90069
KEYES, PAUL W	TV WRITER-PRODUCER	10543 VALLEY SPRING LN	NORTH HOLLYWOOD, CA	91602
KEYES, PAUL WILLIAM	TV WRITER-PRODUCER	135 SCREENLAND DR	BURBANK, CA	91505
KEYLOUN, MARK	ACTOR	9255 SUNSET BLVD #505	LOS ANGELES, CA	90069
KEYS, GARY	DIRECTOR	228 E 89TH ST	NEW YORK, NY	10028
KEYS, JOE	SINGER	PROCESS, 439 WILEY AVE	FRANKLIN, PA	16323
KEYS, VINCENT R, JR	TV DIRECTOR-PRODUCER	10132 ROVEOUT LN	COLUMBIA, MD	21046
KEYS, WILLIAM	TV WRITER	14144 VENTURA BLVD #200	SHERMAN OAKS, CA	91423
KEZA, T MICHAEL	PHOTOGRAPHER	1855 CALVERT ST, NW	WASHINGTON, DC	20009
KHADDURI, SHIRIN	NEWS CORRESPONDENT	5704 CROMWELL DR	BETHESDA, MD	20816
KHAMBATTA, PERSIS	ACTRESS-MODEL	STONE, 1052 CAROL DR	LOS ANGELES, CA	90069
KHAN, CHAKA	SINGER	POST OFFICE BOX 3125	BEVERLY HILLS, CA	90212
KHANER, JEFFREY	FLUTIST	GERSHUNOFF, 502 PARK AVE	NEW YORK, NY	10022
KHMARA, ED	SCREENWRITER	1945 OVERHILL RD	AGOURA, CA	91301
KHRUSHCHEV, KHRUSHER	WRESTLER	NATIONAL WRESTLING ALLIANCE		
		JIM CROCKETT PROMOTIONS		
		421 BRIARBEND DR	CHARLOTTE, NC	28209
KIAMOS, ELENI NICHOLAS	ACTRESS	25 MINETTA LN	NEW YORK, NY	10012
KIANI, ALI	WRITER	ICM, 8899 BEVERLY BLVD	LOS ANGELES, CA	90048
KIAT, LIAK TENG	NEWS CORRESPONDENT	2401 CALVERT ST #710, NW	WASHINGTON, DC	20008
KIBBE, MICHAEL G	COMPOSER	11311 TIARA ST	NORTH HOLLYWOOD, CA	91601
KIBBE, TOM	ACTOR	31209 PACIFIC COAST HWY	MALIBU, CA	90265
KIBBEE, GORDON	COMPOSER	3815 VALLEY MEADOW RD	ENCINO, CA	91316
KIBBEE, LOIS	ACTRESS-TV WRITER	9220 SUNSET BLVD #202	LOS ANGELES, CA	90069
KIBBIE, DANIEL C	WRITER	5069 ALDEA AVE	ENCINO, CA	91316
KIBRICK, LEONARD	ACTOR	5454 ZELZAH AVE #208	ENCINO, CA	91316
KIBRICK, SIDNEY	ACTOR	711 N OAKHURST DR	BEVERLY HILLS, CA	90210
KICK AXE	ROCK & ROLL GROUP	41 BRITAIN ST #200	TORONTO, ONT	CANADA
KID, HATU	WRESTLER	SEE - HATU KID		
KID CREOLE & THE COCONUTS	ROCK & ROLL GROUP	130 W 57TH ST #2-A	NEW YORK,]NY	10019
KIDD, DAVID H	WRITER	8955 BEVERLY BLVD	LOS ANGELES, CA	90048
KIDD, JONATHAN	ACTOR	7045 HAWTHORN AVE	HOLLYWOOD, CA	90028
KIDD, MICHAEL	ACT-DAN-CHOREO	151 S EL CAMINO DR	BEVERLY HILLS, CA	90212
KIDD, SUSAN M	NEWS CORRESPONDENT	NBC-TV, NEWS DEPARTMENT		
		4001 NEBRASKA AVE, NW	WASHINGTON, DC	20016
KIDDER, MARGOT	ACTRESS	23215 MARIPOSA DE ORO	MALIBU, CA	90265
KIDNEY, STEPHEN C	NEWS CORRESPONDENT	9511 KENTSTONE DR	BETHESDA, MD	20817
KIDS AT WORK	ROCK & ROLL GROUP	POST OFFICE BOX 82	GREAT NECK, NY	11022
KIDS WANNA ROCK	ROCK & ROLL GROUP	41 BRITAIN ST #200	TORONTO, ONT	CANADA
KIDWELL, DON	GUITARIST	18026 SAHARA RD	HAYWARD, CA	94541
KIDZ, THE	ROCK & ROLL GROUP	CAPURO, 6 IMPERIAL RD	WORCESTER, MA	01604
KIEFFER, GARY	PHOTOGRAPHER	4399 ENSBROOK LN	DALE CITY, VA	22193
KIEL, SUE	ACTRESS	SHERMAN, 348 S REXFORD DR	BEVERLY HILLS, CA	90212
KIELY, KATY	NEWS CORRESPONDENT	1735 "U" ST, NW	WASHINGTON, DC	20009
KIERLAND, JOSEPH S	WRITER	2621 CRESTON DR	LOS ANGELES, CA	90068
KIERMAN, KATHY	WRITER	8955 BEVERLY BLVD	LOS ANGELES, CA	90048
KIERNAN, MICHAEL	NEWS CORRESPONDENT	NBC-TV, NEWS DEPARTMENT		
		4001 NEBRASKA AVE, NW	WASHINGTON, DC	20016
KIESER, ELLWOOD E	WRITER	10750 OHIO AVE	LOS ANGELES, CA	90024
KIESER, PHILLIP J	NEWS CORRESPONDENT	14211 ESSEX DR	WOODBRIDGE, VA	22191
KIESLER, KENNETH	CONDUCTOR	POST OFFICE BOX 1515	NEW YORK, NY	10023

KIFF, KALEENA	ACTRESS	6640 SUNSET BLVD #203	LOS ANGELES, CA	90028
KIGER, ROBERT	TV DIRECTOR	8928 ELLIS AVE	LOS ANGELES, CA	90034
KIKER, DOUGLAS	NEWS CORRESPONDENT	NBC-TV, NEWS DEPARTMENT		
		4001 NEBRASKA AVE, NW	WASHINGTON, DC	20016
KILBORN, PETER T	NEWS CORRESPONDENT	113 GRAFTON ST	CHEVY CHASE, MD	20815
KILBURN, TERRY	ACTOR-TEACHER	MEADOWBROOK THEATRE		
		OAKLAND UNIVERSITY		
		WALTON BLVD & SQUIRREL RD	ROCHESTER, MI	48063
KILEY, RICHARD	ACTOR	14323 COLLINS AVE	VAN NUYS, CA	91401
KILEY, TIMOTHY	TV DIRECTOR	1645 SUNSET PLAZA DR	LOS ANGELES, CA	90069
KILGORE, MERLE	SINGER-SONGWRITER	POST OFFICE BOX 120789	NASHVILLE, TN	37203
KILGRUE, KATHLEEN	ACTRESS	63 TEMPLE ST	MATTAPAN, MA	02126
KILIAN, MICHAEL	WRITER-EDITOR	DISCOVER/TIME & LIFE BLDG		
		ROCKEFELLER CENTER	NEW YORK, NY	10020
KILIAN, MICHAEL D	NEWS CORRESPONDENT	1003 HEATHER HILL CT	MC LEAN, VA	22101
KILIANSKI, LILIAN	MEZZO-SOPRANO	POST OFFICE BOX 188		
		STATION A	TORONTO, ONT	CANADA
KILLDOZER	ROCK & ROLL GROUP	ROADKILL MUSIC COMPANY		
		933 WILLIAMSON ST	MADISON, WI	53703
KILLEBREW, GWENDOLYN	MEZZO-SOPRANO	CAMI, 165 W 57TH ST	NEW YORK, NY	10019
KILLEBREW, HARMON	BASEBALL	POST OFFICE BOX 626	ONTARIO, OR	97914
KILLEEN, MARTIN	WRITER	555 W 57TH ST #1230	NEW YORK, NY	10019
KILLELEA, MICHAEL J	PHOTOGRAPHER	127 ABBOTT DR	HUNTINGTON, NY	11743
KILLEN, BUDDY	GUIATRIST	POST OFFICE BOX 1273	NASHVILLE, TN	37203
KILLEN, PATRICK J	NEWS CORRESPONDENT	2761 GREENWAY BLVD	FALLS CHURCH, VA	22042
KILLEN, TOM	GUITARIST	906 KENDALL DR	POPLAR BLUFF, MO	63901
KILLER BEES, THE	WRESTLING TAG TEAM	POST OFFICE BOX 3859	STAMFORD, CT	06905
KILLIAN, PHIL	ACTOR	632 W KNOLL DR	LOS ANGELES, CA	90069
KILLINGSWORTH, CARL S	WRITER	555 W 57TH ST #1230	NEW YORK, NY	10019
KILLMOND, FRANK	ACTOR	5087 SAN FELICIANO DR	WOODLAND HILLS, CA	91364
KILPACK, DEBRA	ACTRESS	211 S BEVERLY DR #107	BEVERLY HILLS, CA	90212
KILPATRICK, ERIC	ACTOR	POST OFFICE BOX 5617	BEVERLY HILLS, CA	90210
KILPATRICK, JAMES C	NEWS CORRESPONDENT	2117 PAUL SPRING RD	ALEXANDRIA, VA	22307
KILPATRICK, JAMES J	COLUMNIST-JOURNALIST	WHITE WALNUT HILL	WOODVILLE, VA	22749
KILPATRICK, LINCOLN	ACTOR	12834 MC LENNAN AVE	GRANADA HILLS, CA	91344
KILTY, JEROME	ACTOR	POST OFFICE BOX 1074	WESTON, CT	06883
KIM, EUGENE	NEWS CORRESPONDENT	1825 "K" ST, NW	WASHINGTON, DC	20006
KIM, EVAN C	ACTOR-WRITER	3218 PECK AVE	SAN PEDRO, CA	90731
KIM, JUNE	ACTRESS	8235 SANTA MONICA BLVD #202	LOS ANGELES, CA	90025
KIM, JUNG AE	SOPRANO	CAMI, 165 W 57TH ST	NEW YORK, NY	10019
KIM, KIM O	ACTRESS	8831 SUNSET BLVD #402	LOS ANGELES, CA	90069
KIM, PAUL W	DIRECTOR	215 PARK ROW #19-A	NEW YORK, NY	10038
KIM, SHINJA	MEZZO-SOPRANO	CAMI, 165 W 57TH ST	NEW YORK, NY	10019
KIM, YOUNG MI	SOPRANO	59 E 54TH ST #81	NEW YORK, NY	10022
KIM, YOUNG UCK	VIOLINIST	CAMI, 165 W 57TH ST	NEW YORK, NY	10019
KIMALA	WRESTLER	POST OFFICE BOX 3859	STAMFORD, CT	06905
KIMBALL	SINGER	CAPURSO, 6 IMPERIAL RD	WORCESTER, MA	01604
KIMBALL, BILLY C	COMEDY WRITER	8955 BEVERLY BLVD	LOS ANGELES, CA	90048
KIMBALL, BRUCE	ACTOR	435 S LA CIENEGA BLVD #108	LOS ANGELES, CA	90048
KIMBALL, JAMES	WRITER	8955 BEVERLY BLVD	LOS ANGELES, CA	90048
KIMBALL, PETER WILDER	TV DIRECTOR	2008 CLIFTON AVE, 1ST FLOOR	CHICAGO, IL	60614
KIMBALL, WARD	ANIMATION DIRECTOR	8910 ARDENDALE AVE	SAN GABRIEL, CA	91775
KIMBERLY, NANCY	ACTRESS	6605 HOLLYWOOD BLVD #220	HOLLYWOOD, CA	90028
KIMBLE, JOHN	TALENT AGENT	10100 SANTA MONICA BLVD #1600	LOS ANGELES, CA	90067
KIMBLE, ROBERT I	FILM EDITOR	ACE, 4416 1/2 FINLEY AVE	LOS ANGELES, CA	90027
KIMBRO, ART	ACTOR	9000 SUNSET BLVD #801	LOS ANGELES, CA	90069
KIMBROUGH, JERRY	SINGER-GUITARIST	2141 BELCOURT AVE #3	NASHVILLE, TN	37212
KIMBROUGH, STEVEN	BARITONE	SULLIVAN, 390 W END AVE	NEW YORK, NY	10024
KIMMEL, BRUCE	WRITER-DIRECTOR	12230 OTSEGO ST	NORTH HOLLYWOOD, CA	91607
KIMMEL, DANA	ACTRESS	3575 W CAHUENGA BLVD #320	LOS ANGELES, CA	90068
KIMMEL, HENRY HOWARD	DIRECTOR	17215 PALISADES CIR	PACIFIC PALISADES, CA	90272
KIMMEL, JEFFREY J	NEWS CORRESPONDENT	2317 HUIDENKOPER PL, NW	WASHINGTON, DC	20007
KIMMEL, JOEL	ACTOR-WRITER	638 N KILKEA DR	LOS ANGELES, CA	90048
KIMMONS, KENNETH	ACTOR	8352 FOUNTAIN AVE #D-1	LOS ANGELES, CA	90069
KINARD, KAREN ANN	NEWS CORRESPONDENT	5130 CONNECTICUT AVE #A, NW	WASHINGTON, DC	20008
KINBERG, JUD	WRITER-PRODUCER	10538 WYTON DR	LOS ANGELES, CA	90024
KINCAID, ARON	ACTOR	13111 VENTURA BLVD #204	STUDIO CITY, CA	91604
KINCAID, CLIFF	NEWS CORRESPONDENT	9 MEADOW LN	WALDORF, MD	20601
KINCAID, J D	SINGER	OME, 233 W WOODLAND AVE	OTTUMWA, IA	52501
KINCAID, JASON	ACTOR	8485 MELROSE PL #E	LOS ANGELES, CA	90069
KINCAID, WAYNE	GUITARIST	115 TIMBERLANE DR, SW	FAIRVIEW, TN	37062
KINCSES, VERONIKA	SOPRANO	61 W 62ND ST #6-F	NEW YORK, NY	10023
KIND, DIANE	ACTRESS	8871 BURTON WY #303	LOS ANGELES, CA	90048
KIND, JOHN	TV WRITER	8955 BEVERLY BLVD	LOS ANGELES, CA	90048
KIND, ROSLYN	ACTRESS	8871 BURTON WY #303	LOS ANGELES, CA	90048
KINDIG, LEONARD	DRUMMER	506 HARDING PL	NASHVILLE, TN	37211
KINDLE, ANDY J	DIRECTOR	6321 NEWTOWN CIR #B-1	TAMPA, FL	33615
KINDLE, TOM	ACTOR	8029 W NORTON AVE #1	LOS ANGELES, CA	90046
KINDLEY, JEFFREY	TV WRITER	555 W 57TH ST #1230	NEW YORK, NY	10019
KING, ALAN	COMEDIAN-ACTOR	665 5TH AVE	NEW YORK, NY	10022
KING, ALANA	ACTRESS	8831 SUNSET BLVD #402	LOS ANGELES, CA	90069
KING, ALBERT	SINGER-GUITARIST	ASSOCIATED BOOKING CORP		
		1995 BROADWAY, 5TH FLOOR	NEW YORK, NY	10023

Name	Occupation	Address	City	Zip
KING, ANDREA	ACTRESS	222 S SPALDING DR	BEVERLY HILLS, CA	90212
KING, B B	SINGER-GUITARIST	POST OFFICE BOX 16707	MEMPHIS, TN	38131
KING, BEN E	SINGER-SONGWRITER	KNIGHT, 185 CLINTON AVE	STATEN ISLAND, NY	10301
KING, BILLIE JEAN	TENNIS	2029 CENTURY PARK E #1200	LOS ANGELES, CA	90067
KING, BRETT	ACTOR	CORAL SANDS HOTEL	HARBOR ISLAND	BAHAMAS
KING, BRUCE E	DIRECTOR	403 W 54TH ST	NEW YORK, NY	10019
KING, CAROLE	SINGER-SONGWRITER	ROBINSON BAR RANCH	STANLEY, ID	83278
KING, CAROLYN B	TV WRITER	8955 BEVERLY BLVD	LOS ANGELES, CA	90048
KING, CHERYL	COMEDIENNE	POST OFFICE BOX 1556	GAINESVILLE, TN	32602
KING, CLAIRE	PIANIST	111 OLD HICKORY BLVD #312	NASHVILLE, TN	37211
KING, CLAUDE	SINGER	HOT, 306 W CHURCH ST	HORSESHOE BEND, AR	72512
KING, COLLEEN R	WRITER	555 W 57TH ST #1230	NEW YORK, NY	10019
KING, CORINE	SINGER	PROCESS, 439 WILEY AVE	FRANKLIN, PA	16323
KING, DAMU	ACTOR	POST OFFICE BOX 48410	LOS ANGELES, CA	90048
KING, DENNIS	COMPOSER	34 NEW END SQ	LONDON NW3 1LS	ENGLAND
KING, DON	SINGER	POST OFFICE BOX 121089	NASHVILLE, TN	37212
KING, DONALD	TV DIRECTOR	143 W 80TH ST	NEW YORK, NY	10024
KING, DONALD A	GUITARIST	5109 HILSON RD	NASHVILLE, TN	37211
KING, DONALD EMERSON	TV WRITER	8955 BEVERLY BLVD	LOS ANGELES, CA	90048
KING, DURNFORD	DIRECTOR-PRODUCER	1423 EUCLID ST	SANTA MONICA, CA	90404
KING, ED	MUSICIAN	POST OFFICE BOX 510	WOODBINE, NJ	08270
KING, EMERY	NEWS CORRESPONDENT	NBC-TV, NEWS DEPARTMENT		
		4001 NEBRASKA AVE, NW	WASHINGTON, DC	20016
KING, EVELYN "CHAMPAGNE"	SINGER	119 W 57TH ST #901	NEW YORK, NY	10019
KING, FREEMAN	ACTOR	10926 BLUFFSIDE DR #15	STUDIO CITY, CA	91604
KING, GREGORY WESTON	SCREENWRITER	8955 BEVERLY BLVD	LOS ANGELES, CA	90048
KING, JACKIE	SINGER	BRAD SIMON ORGANIZATION		
		445 E 80TH ST	NEW YORK, NY	10021
KING, JAMES	SINGER	POST OFFICE BOX 11321		
		FLAGLER STATION	MIAMI, FL	33101
KING, JAMES	TENOR	CAMI, 165 W 57TH ST	NEW YORK, NY	10019
KING, JAMES C, JR	COMPOSER	23047 SCHOOLCRAFT ST	CANOGA PARK, CA	91307
KING, JEFF	SCREENWRITER	555 W 57TH ST #1230	NEW YORK, NY	10019
KING, JERRY	TV EXECUTIVE	ABC TELEVISION NETWORK		
		1330 AVE OF THE AMERICAS	NEW YORK, NY	10019
KING, JOE	CABLE EXECUTIVE	2049 CENTURY PARK E #4170	LOS ANGELES, CA	90067
KING, JOHN	TV DIRECTOR	CHURCH BARTON, HIGH LITTLETON	AVON BS18 5HQ	ENGLAND
KING, JOHN "DUSTY"	ACTOR	POST OFFICE BOX 487	RANCHO SANTA FE, CA	92067
KING, JULIANA	NEWS CORRESPONDENT	3029 SYLVAN DR	FALLS CHURCH, VA	22042
KING, KEVIN	ACTOR	17083 PALISADES CIR	PACIFIC PALISADES, CA	90272
KING, KIP	ACTOR	4428 STERN AVE	SHERMAN OAKS, CA	91403
KING, LARRY	RADIO PERSONALITY	1101 30TH ST, NW	WASHINGTON, DC	20007
KING, LARRY L	SCREENWRITER	555 W 57TH ST #1230	NEW YORK, NY	10019
KING, LESLIE E	WRITER	8955 BEVERLY BLVD	LOS ANGELES, CA	90048
KING, LOUIS	CONDUCTOR	3790 HAZELWOOD AVE #4	LAS VEGAS, NV	89109
KING, LYNWOOD B	TV DIRECTOR	12 BEEKMAN PL	NEW YORK, NY	10022
KING, MABEL	ACTRESS	7100 TEESDALE AVE	NORTH HOLLYWOOD, CA	91605
KING, MACK P, JR	GUITARIST	808 E 145TH AVE	TAMPA, FL	33612
KING, MARSHALL A	TV WRITER	8955 BEVERLY BLVD	LOS ANGELES, CA	90048
KING, MARY E	WRITER	555 W 57TH ST #1230	NEW YORK, NY	10019
KING, MEEGAN	ACTOR	5050 WOODMAN AVE #20	SHERMAN OAKS, CA	91423
KING, MORGANA	SINGER	9744 WILSHIRE BLVD #306	BEVERLY HILLS, CA	90212
KING, NANCY	NEWS CORRESPONDENT	1511 FOREST LN	MC LEAN, VA	22101
KING, PAUL	TALENT AGENT	OUTLAW MGMT, 145 OXFORD ST	LONDON W1	ENGLAND
KING, PAUL D	WRITER	8955 BEVERLY BLVD	LOS ANGELES, CA	90048
KING, PEE WEE	MUSICIAN	240 W JEFFERSON ST	LOUISVILLE, KY	40202
KING, PEE WEE, REDD STEWART & C	C & W GROUP	TESSIER, 505 CANTON PASS	MADISON, TN	37115
KING, PERRY	ACTOR	1888 CENTURY PARK E #1400	LOS ANGELES, CA	90067
KING, PETER	FILM EXECUTIVE	6 GREAT CHAPEL ST	LONDON W1V 4BR	ENGLAND
KING, PETER	WRESTLING WRITER	POST OFFICE BOX 48	ROCKVILLE CENTRE, NY	11571
KING, RAMSAY	CASTING DIRECTOR	POST OFFICE BOX 5718	SHERMAN OAKS, CA	91403
KING, RICHARD ALAN	TV DIRECTOR	PINE MOUNTAIN CLUB		
		2157 BRENTWOOD PL	FRAZIER PARK, CA	93225
KING, RICHARD I	MUSICIAN	332 TAMWORTH DR	NASHVILLE, TN	37214
KING, ROY	ACTOR	80-35 246TH ST	BELLEROSE, L I, NY	11426
KING, SETH	NEWS CORRESPONDENT	7600 EDENWOOD CT	BETHESDA, MD	20817
KING, STEPHEN	NOVELIST	POST OFFICE BOX 1186	BANGOR, ME	04401
KING, STEVEN M	COMPOSER	2861 PIEDMONT AVE	LA CRESCENTA, CA	91214
KING, SUSAN	NEWS CORRESPONDENT	NBC-TV, NEWS DEPARTMENT		
		4001 NEBRASKA AVE, NW	WASHINGTON, DC	20016
KING, THOMAS J	TV DIRECTOR	180 W END AVE #5-M	NEW YORK, NY	10023
KING, TIM	TV DIRECTOR	3 PARSONS GREEN LN	LONDON SW6	ENGLAND
KING, TOM	TV WRITER	853 7TH AVE #9-A	NEW YORK, NY	10019
KING, TOMMY	ACTOR	80-35 246TH ST	BELLEROSE, L I, NY	11426
KING, TONY	ACTOR	1333 N SWEETZER AVE	LOS ANGELES, CA	90046
KING, VIKI	TV WRITER	8955 BEVERLY BLVD	LOS ANGELES, CA	90048
KING, WAYNE D	SAXOPHONIST	ROUTE #6, BOX 487	RINGGOLD, GA	30736
KING, ZALMAN	ACTOR-WRITER	1393 ROSE AVE	VENICE, CA	90291
KING, ZEKE	GUITARIST	ROUTE #1, BOX 255	OAK GROVE, KY	42262
KING ARTHUR	HIGH WIRE ACT	HALL, 138 FROG HOLLOW RD	CHURCHVILLE, PA	18966
KING ARTHUR & GOLDIE HIGH	HIGH WIRE DUO	HALL, 138 FROG HOLLOW RD	CHURCHVILLE, PA	18966
KING CONLON, CAMMIE	ACTRESS	10643 SUNSET BLVD	LOS ANGELES, CA	90024
KING CRIMSON	ROCK & ROLL GROUP	E G MGMT, 161 W 54TH ST	NEW YORK, NY	10019

Name	Occupation	Address	City	Zip/Country
KING JAMES	WRESTLER	SEE - VALIANT, JIMMY		
KING KONG	WRESTLER	SEE - BUNDY, KING KONG		
KING KONG TONGA	WRESTLER	SEE - TONGA, KING		
KING NEPTUNE & THE SEA SERPENTS	ROCK & ROLL GROUP	OLDIES, 5218 ALMONT ST	LOS ANGELES, CA	90032
KING'S ENGLISH	ROCK & ROLL GROUP	AMERICAN FAMOUS TALENT		
		504 W ARLINGTON PL	CHICAGO, IL	60614
KING-SORENSEN, CAROLE	SINGER-SONGWRITER	15760 VENTURA BLVD #1730	ENCINO, CA	91436
KING-WADE, DIXIE	ACTRESS	8949 SUNSET BLVD #203	LOS ANGELES, CA	90069
KINGHAM, BERNARD	FILM-TV PRODUCER	ACC HOUSE, GREAT CUMBERLAND PL	LONDON W1A 1AG	ENGLAND
KINGHORN, DAVID J	TV WRITER	151 S EL CAMINO DR	BEVERLY HILLS, CA	90212
KINGI, HENRY	ACTOR-STUNTMAN	3580 AVE DEL SOL	STUDIO CITY, CA	91604
KINGMAN, DAVE	BASEBALL	818 W BUSSE AVE	MOUNT PROSPECT, IL	60056
KINGS, THE	ROCK & ROLL GROUP	41 BRITAIN ST #200	TORONTO, ONT	CANADA
KINGSBRIDGE, JOHN	TV WRITER	8955 BEVERLY BLVD	LOS ANGELES, CA	90048
KINGSBURY-SMITH, JOSEPH	NEWS CORRESPONDENT	ROUTE #665	WATERFORD, VA	22190
KINGSLEY, BEN	ACTOR	NEW PENWORTH HOUSE		
		STRATFORD UPON AVON	WARWICKSHIRE OV3 7QX	ENGLAND
KINGSLEY, DANITZA	ACTRESS-MODEL	1901 AVE OF THE STARS #840	LOS ANGELES, CA	90067
KINGSLEY, DOROTHY	WRITER	8955 BEVERLY BLVD	LOS ANGELES, CA	90048
KINGSLEY, EMILY P	WRITER	555 W 57TH ST #1230	NEW YORK, NY	10019
KINGSLEY, NATHAN	NEWS CORRESPONDENT	4217 LELAND ST	CHEVY CHASE, MD	20815
KINGSLEY, SIDNEY	PLAYWRIGHT	DRAMA GUILD, 234 W 44TH ST	NEW YORK, NY	10036
KINGSLEY-SMITH, TERRENCE	WRITER	1290 1/2 DEVON AVE	LOS ANGELES, CA	90024
KINGSMEN, THE	ROCK & ROLL GROUP	STERLING TALENT ENTERPRISES		
		11369 SW LAKEWOOD CT	TIGARD, OR	97223
KINGSON, JAMES G	WRITER	8955 BEVERLY BLVD	LOS ANGELES, CA	90048
KINGSON, ROME C	WRITER	3414 S SEPULVEDA BLVD #7	LOS ANGELES, CA	90034
KINGSTON, JAMES G	WRITER	POST OFFICE BOX 203	ROCKY POINT, NY	11778
KINGSTON, WILLIAM	FILM EXECUTIVE	HONISTER GARDENS, STANMORE	MIDDLESEX	ENGLAND
KINGSTON TRIO, THE	VOCAL TRIO	601 S RANCHO DR #C-18	LAS VEGAS, NV	89106
KINGWILL, JAY	THEATER PRODUCER	226 W 47TH ST	NEW YORK, NY	10036
KINISKI, NICK	WRESTLER	POST OFFICE BOX 3859	STAMFORD, CT	06905
KINISON, SCREAMING SAMMY	COMEDIAN-ACTOR	21241 VENTURA BLVD #251	WOODLAND HILLS, CA	91364
KINKEAD, MAEVE	ACTRESS	ICM, 40 W 57TH ST	NEW YORK, NY	10019
KINKS, THE	ROCK & ROLL GROUP	LARRY PAGE, 29 RUSTON MEWS	LONDON W11 1RB	ENGLAND
KINLEY, DAVID D	CABLE EXECUTIVE	POST OFFICE BOX 13	PLEASANTON, CA	94566
KINMONTH, MARGY	FILM DIRECTOR	FOXTROT, 45 ELGIN CRESCENT	LONDON W11	ENGLAND
KINNAMAN, MELANIE	ACTRESS	9255 SUNSET BLVD #510	LOS ANGELES, CA	90069
KINNEAL, KEN	TALENT AGENT	POST OFFICE BOX 66558	SEATTLE, WA	98166
KINNEAR, ROY	ACTOR	THE RICHARD STONE AGENCY		
		18-20 YORK BLDGS, ADELPHI	LONDON WC2N 6JY	ENGLAND
KINNELL, GALWAY	POET	432 HUDSON ST	NEW YORK, NY	10014
KINNEY, BARBARA G	PHOTOGRAPHER	326-A COMMERCE ST	ALEXANDRIA, VA	22314
KINNEY, DORIS G	NEWS REPORTER	LIFE/TIME & LIFE BLDG		
		ROCKEFELLER CENTER	NEW YORK, NY	10020
KINNEY, MICHAEL	ACTOR	8949 SUNSET BLVD #203	LOS ANGELES, CA	90069
KINNOCH, RONALD G	WRITER	8955 BEVERLY BLVD	LOS ANGELES, CA	90048
KINO, LLOYD	ACTOR	3036 MALABAR ST	LOS ANGELES, CA	90063
KINON, RICHARD	DIRECTOR	360 S CRESCENT DR	BEVERLY HILLS, CA	90212
KINOY, DANIEL P	WRITER	555 W 57TH ST #1230	NEW YORK, NY	10019
KINOY, ERNEST	TV WRITER	66 LEWIS PARKWAY	YONKERS, NY	10705
KINSEY, LANCE	ACTOR	7471 MELROSE AVE #11	LOS ANGELES, CA	90046
KINSEY, MIKE	ACTOR	HIGHVIEW CT, HARROW WEALD	MIDDLESEX	ENGLAND
KINSEY, TONY	COMPOSER-ARRANGER	CCA MGMT, 4 CT LODGE		
		48 SLOANE SQ	LONDON SW1W 8AT	ENGLAND
KINSKEY, LEONID	ACTOR	11652 HUSTON ST	NORTH HOLLYWOOD, CA	91601
KINSKI, KLAUS	ACTOR	ARTMEDIA, 10 AVE GEORGE V	PARIS 75008	FRANCE
KINSKI, NASTASSJA	ACTRESS-MODEL	GEORGES BEAUME AGENCE		
		3 QUAI MALAQUAIS	PARIS 75006	FRANCE
KINSLEY, MICHAEL E	NEWS CORRESPONDENT	1511 22ND ST, NW	WASHINGTON, DC	20037
KINSOLVING, LESTER	NEWS CORRESPONDENT	1517 BEULAH RD	VIENNA, VA	22180
KINSOLVING, WILLIAM	WRITER	ICM, 8899 BEVERLY BLVD	LOS ANGELES, CA	90048
KINZEL, CAROLE	TALENT AGENT	ICM, 8899 BEVERLY BLVD	LOS ANGELES, CA	90048
KIPLING, BOGDAN	NEWS CORRESPONDENT	2803 "Q" ST, NW	WASHINGTON, DC	20007
KIPLINGER, AUSTIN H	NEWS CORRESPONDENT	16801 RIVER RD	POOLESVILLE, MD	20837
KIPNESS, JOSEPH	THEATER PRODUCER	KIPPYS PRODS, 144 W 52ND ST	NEW YORK, NY	10019
KIPNIS, IGOR	HARPSICHORDIST	AIA, 60 E 42ND ST	NEW YORK, NY	10165
KIPP, RAY	NEWS CORRESPONDENT	2700 WILLOW DR	VIENNA, VA	22180
KIPPYCASH, JOHN	DIRECTOR	DGA, 110 W 57TH ST	NEW YORK, NY	10019
KIRBY, ALEX	TV DIRECTOR	ANCHORAGE, WOODLANDS RD		
		PORTISHEAD	BRISTOL	ENGLAND
KIRBY, BRUCE	ACTOR	629 N ORLANDO AVE #3	LOS ANGELES, CA	90048
KIRBY, BRUNO	ACTOR	SF & A, 121 N SAN VICENTE BLVD	BEVERLY HILLS, CA	90211
KIRBY, DAVE	GUITARIST	ROUTE #8, BOX 69	LEBANON, TN	37083
KIRBY, DURWARD	SCREENWRITER	3714 1/2 BERRY DR	STUDIO CITY, CA	91604
KIRBY, GEORGE	COMEDIAN	4173 SOMERSET DR #3	LOS ANGELES, CA	90008
KIRBY, JACK	GUITARIST	2131 ELM HILL PIKE #B-31	NASHVILLE, TN	37210
KIRBY, JAMES H, JR	PIANIST	4017 NAVAHO TRAIL	NASHVILLE, TN	37211
KIRBY, JOHN	ACTOR	4317 AVOCADO ST	LOS ANGELES, CA	90027
KIRBY, JOHN	SINGER	102 E EXCHANGE AVE #300	FORT WORTH, TX	76106
KIRBY, JOHN W	NEWS CORRESPONDENT	CBS NEWS, 2020 "M" ST, NW	WASHINGTON, DC	20036
KIRBY, K E S	NEWS CORRESPONDENT	2402 20TH ST, NW	WASHINGTON, DC	20009
KIRBY, KEN	GUITARIST	457 JANETTE AVE	GOODLETTSVILLE, TN	37072
KIRBY, RANDALL	WRITER	8955 BEVERLY BLVD	LOS ANGELES, CA	90048
KIRBY, RON L	SINGER-PIANIST	500 N 17TH ST	NASHVILLE, TN	37206

Name	Occupation	Address	City	Zip
KIRBY, WADE	GUITARIST	321 WALTON LN #K-142	MADISON, TN	37115
KIRCH, CASANOVA JACK	GUITARIST	POST OFFICE BOX 111	STANLEY, ID	83278
KIRCHER, VALERIE	WRITER-PRODUCER	1556 RIDGEWAY DR	GLENDALE, CA	91202
KIRCHHOFF, HERBERT	NEWS CORRESPONDENT	3003 DUNBAR ST	ALEXANDRIA, VA	22306
KIRCHMAIER, CORINE	VIOLINIST	7625 E CAMELBACK RD #441-B	SCOTTSDALE, AZ	85251
KIRCHMAR, ANITA J	NEWS CORRESPONDENT	ABC-TV, NEWS DEPARTMENT		
		1717 DE SALES ST, NW	WASHINGTON, DC	20036
KIRCHNER, CORPORAL	WRESTLER	POST OFFICE BOX 3859	STAMFORD, CT	06905
KIRCHNER, DAVID	SINGER-SONGWRITER	106 BUTLEIGH CT	GOODLETTSVILLE, TN	37072
KIRCHNER, FRANK	TRUMPETER	3831 VALLEY RIDGE DR	NASHVILLE, TN	37211
KIRCHNER, JANE	FLUTIST	3831 VALLEY RIDGE DR	NASHVILLE, TN	37211
KIRCHNER, MIKE	WRESTLER	SEE - KIRCHNER, CORPORAL		
KIRGO, DIANA	TV WRITER	14504 GREENLEAF ST	SHERMAN OAKS, CA	91403
KIRGO, GEORGE	TV WRITER	178 N CARMELINA AVE	LOS ANGELES, CA	90049
KIRGO, JULIE	TV WRITER-PRODUCER	KAUFMAN, 14540 GREENLEAF ST	SHERMAN OAKS, CA	91403
KIRK, ALLAN	BASSO-BARITONE	260 W END AVE #7-A	NEW YORK, NY	10023
KIRK, BEN	MUSIC ARRANGER	3028 VISTA VALLEY CT	NASHVILLE, TN	37218
KIRK, BONNIE	SOPRANO	253 W 73RD ST #7-M	NEW YORK, NY	10023
KIRK, JAY	COMEDIAN	CEE, 193 KONHAUS RD	MECHANICSBURG, PA	17055
KIRK, LISA	SINGER-ACTRESS	340 W 57TH ST	NEW YORK, NY	10019
KIRK, REBA V	COMPOSER	10059 GLEN GROVE CT	ELK GROVE, CA	95624
KIRKBY, EMMA	SOPRANO	BYERS-SCHWALBE, 1 5TH AVE	NEW YORK, NY	10003
KIRKCONNELL, CLARE	ACTRESS	7473 MULHOLLAND DR	LOS ANGELES, CA	90046
KIRKES, SHIRLEY	ACTRESS	11620 TEXAS AVE	LOS ANGELES, CA	90025
KIRKHAM, DOUGLAS	DRUMMER	632 ROCHELLE DR	NASHVILLE, TN	37220
KIRKLAND, BILLY	SINGER	KRAGEN, 1112 N SHERBOURNE DR	LOS ANGELES, CA	90069
KIRKLAND, DENNIS	TV DIRECTOR-PRODUCER	181 UXBRIDGED RD #5		
		HAMPTON HILL	MIDDLESEX	ENGLAND
KIRKLAND, GLENDA	SOPRANO	GREAT LAKES PERFORMING ARISTS		
		310 E WASHINGTON ST	ANN ARBOR, MI	48104
KIRKLAND, LARRY	GUITARIST	POST OFFICE BOX 396	WAYNESBORO, TN	38485
KIRKLAND, PAT	CASTING DIRECTOR	MCA/UNIVERSAL STUDIOS, INC		
		100 UNIVERSAL CITY PLAZA	UNIVERSAL CITY, CA	91608
KIRKLAND, RAY	GUITARIST	452 MOSS TRAIL DR #D-13	GOODLETTSVILLE, TN	37072
KIRKLAND, SALLY	ACTRESS	1930 OCEAN AVE #11	SANTA MONICA, CA	90405
KIRKMAN, DONALD C	NEWS CORRESPONDENT	8416 BRIAR CREEK DR	ANNANDALE, VA	22003
KIRKMAN, TERRY R	WRITER	1089 S GENESEE AVE	LOS ANGELES, CA	90019
KIRKPATRICK, CURLY	SPORTS WRITER-EDITOR	SPORTS ILLUSTRATED MAGAZINE		
		TIME & LIFE BUILDING		
		ROCKEFELLER CENTER	NEW YORK, NY	10020
KIRKPATRICK, DAVID	SCREENWRITER	8955 BEVERLY BLVD	LOS ANGELES, CA	90048
KIRKWOOD, ALEXANDER	ACTOR	5850 CANOGA AVE #110	WOODLAND HILLS, CA	91367
KIRKWOOD, GENE	FILM PRODUCER	1221 STONE CANYON RD	LOS ANGELES, CA	90077
KIRKWOOD, JAMES	ACTOR	19 W 44TH ST #1500	NEW YORK, NY	10036
KIRKWOOD, JAMES	PLAYWRIGHT	58 OYSTER SHORES RD	EAST HAMPTON, NY	11937
KIRKWOOD, JAMES	WRITER	484 W 43RD ST #45-R	NEW YORK, NY	10036
KIRSCHBAUM, BRUCE	TV WRITER	1617 N ORANGE GROVE AVE	LOS ANGELES, CA	90046
KIRSCHBAUM, EDWARD JOHN	PHOTOGRAPHER	102 N WOLFE ST	BALTIMORE, MD	21231
KIRSCHEN, ALAN	ACTOR	3410 PAUL AVE	BRONX, NY	10468
KIRSCHENBAUM, SUSAN	TV WRITER	ABC-TV, "ALL MY CHILDREN"		
		1330 AVE OF THE AMERICAS	NEW YORK, NY	10019
KIRSCHNER, CORPORAL	WRESTLER	POST OFFICE BOX 3859	STAMFORD, CT	06905
KIRSCHTEN, J DICKEN	NEWS CORRESPONDENT	3602 S WAKEFIELD ST	ARLINGTON, VA	22206
KIRSH, JILL	ACTRESS	6100 SHADYGLADE AVE	NORTH HOLLYWOOD, CA	91606
KIRSHBAUM, RALPH	CELLIST	COLBERT, 111 W 57TH ST	NEW YORK, NY	10019
KIRSHENBAUM, JERRY	WRITER-EDITOR	SPORTS ILLUSTRATED MAGAZINE		
		TIME & LIFE BUILDING		
		ROCKEFELLER CENTER	NEW YORK, NY	10020
KIRSTEN, DOROTHY	SOPRANO	A D ALZHEIMER'S CENTER		
		70 E LAKE ST	CHICAGO, IL	60601
KIRSTEN, KRISTINA	ACTRESS	8949 SUNSET BLVD #203	LOS ANGELES, CA	90069
KIRSTIN, KRISTINA	ACTRESS	6533 HOLLYWOOD BLVD #201	HOLLYWOOD, CA	90028
KIRTLAND, LOUISE	ACTRESS	ANSONIA, 73RD ST & BROADWAY		
		SUITE #1714	NEW YORK, NY	10023
KISCH, TONY	WRITER	THE NATIONAL LAMPOON		
		635 MADISON AVE	NEW YORK, NY	10022
KISELSTEIN, SHELLY L	WRITER	232 S LASKY DR	BEVERLY HILLS, CA	90212
KISER, TERRY	ACTOR-COMEDIAN	10390 SANTA MONICA BLVD #310	LOS ANGELES, CA	90025
KISER, VIRGINIA	ACTRESS	9300 WILSHIRE BLVD #410	BEVERLY HILLS, CA	90212
KISH, JIMMY	SINGER-GUITARIST	200 DEDHAM DR	NASHVILLE, TN	37214
KISH, JOE	RECORD EXECUTIVE	1508 HARLEM ST #206	MEMPHIS, TN	38174
KISHI, RUSSELL	WRITER	8955 BEVERLY BLVD	LOS ANGELES, CA	90048
KISHON, EPHRAIM	FILM DIRECTOR	POST OFFICE BOX 229	JERUSALEM	ISRAEL
KISS	ROCK & ROLL GROUP	POST OFFICE BOX 840	WESTBURY, NY	11590
KISSAL, BRUCE M	NEWS CORRESPONDENT	7610 MIDDAY LN	ALEXANDRIA, VA	22306
KISSIN, AMANDA	WRITER	555 W 57TH ST #1230	NEW YORK, NY	10019
KISSING THE PINK	ROCK & ROLL GROUP	MAGNET/POLYGRAM RECORDS		
		810 7TH AVE	NEW YORK, NY	10019
KISSINGER, DR HENRY	AUTHOR	435 E 52ND ST	NEW YORK, NY	10022
KIST, THOMAS	MUSICIAN	POST OFFICE BOX 22952	NASHVILLE, TN	37202
KITAEN, TAWNY	ACTRESS	445 N BEDFORD DR #PH	BEVERLY HILLS, CA	90210
KITAIENKO, DIMITRI	CONDUCTOR	MARIEDL ANDERS ARTISTS MGMT		
		535 EL CAMINO DEL MAR ST	SAN FRANCISCO, CA	94121
KITAJ, LEM	WRITER	8955 BEVERLY BLVD	LOS ANGELES, CA	90048

Truly one of the most entertaining acts in country music today

DAVID

Dynamic! Classic Country... Concert Entertainer!

On the one side is the "real" country music, the ballads of the common man. On the other side is the newer country-pop; standing in between is David Kirchner, a 22-year-old nationally acclaimed singer/songwriter.

"Country music is God's music, there's a song out there everyone can relate to. At least half of the people coming to our shows have heard only the newer country pop, they haven't heard the old-fashioned country, I try to give them a taste of both."

Kirchner has performed across the country at fairs, theatres, opries, malls, and some of the nation's largest festivals including Jamboree USA, Jimmie Rodgers', and Hank Williams' since he was 13 years old. He has also performed on some of the top country music television shows including Ralph Emory, Nashville Music Country, and R.F.D. Country, all originating out of Nashville.

He has coordinated country festivals for some of Chicagoland's largest malls; become a quite well known, and respected pageant entertainer; produced opry shows throughout the Chicagoland area; and performed on the renowned Ernest Tubb Midnight Jamboree in Nashville. Also performing at Fan Fair, & DJ Convention.

David has earned the honors of being called "Another Hank Williams", "Junior Edition of Roy Clark", and "Teenage Fox" from the CM of Colorado. His many awards include: Golden Guitar Awards for 1976 and '78 from the CMF of Colorado; "Best Teenage Vocalist-Chicago land"; "Best Male Vocalist" and "Entertainer of the Year" from the CMS of Kentucky for 82 and was inducted into the Colorado Country Music Hall of Fame, youngest member to date).

His single "Cheatin' Side of Life" was on the Cashbox National Charts, and received excellent reviews from DJ's across the country.

His new single, "Fancy Lady" also hit Cbx. Ntl. & Feature Pick Charts.

David appeals to an all age audience, draws huge crowds wherever he performs, receiving standing ovations one after another. His two octave range, facial expressions and emotions, combined with sensational showmanship, captivate his audiences, securing a very real, warm place in their hearts.

BOOKING

Kirchner Enterprises
106 Butleigh Court
Goodlettsville, Tn. 37072
615-859-3286

Destined to be one of our great Country Music Stars, and once you hear him you will agree.

Name	Occupation	Address	City
KITAJIMA, OSAMU	MUSICIAN	9000 SUNSET BLVD #611	LOS ANGELES, CA 90069
KITCHEN, MICHAEL	ACTOR	94-A CECILE PARK	LONDON N8 ENGLAND
KITE, LESA	TV WRITER	8955 BEVERLY BLVD	LOS ANGELES, CA 90048
KITEI, MICHAEL	TV DIRECTOR	5526 GALBRAITH RD	CINCINNATI, OH 45236
KITEMAN III	AERIAL ACT	HALL, 138 FROG HOLLOW RD	CHURCHVILLE, PA 18966
KITMAN, MARVIN	TV CRITIC	NEWSDAY, 1500 BROADWAY	NEW YORK, NY 10036
KITT, EARTHA	SINGER-ACTOR	ICM, 8899 BEVERLY BLVD	LOS ANGELES, CA 90048
KITTLE, ROBERT A	NEWS CORRESPONDENT	714 BERRY ST	FALLS CHURCH, VA 22042
KITTLESON, JOHN R	FILM DIRECTOR	2401 JOLLY DR	BURBANK, CA 91504
KITTLESON, SUSIE	CASTING DIRECTOR	1302 N SWEETZER ST	LOS ANGELES, CA 90069
KITTRELL, LISA	ACTRESS	49 MORTON ST #4-B	NEW YORK, NY 10014
KITTS, ROBERT JOHN	WRITER-PRODUCER	29 BELSIZE PARK GARDENS	LONDON NW3 ENGLAND
KIVLIN, TERENCE	NEWS CORRESPONDENT	1750 PENNSYLVANIA AVE, NW	WASHINGTON, DC 20006
KIZER, JAMES S	NEWS CORRESPONDENT	47 RYE CT	GAITHERSBURG, MD 20878
KIZZIER, GARY M	WRITER	8955 BEVERLY BLVD	LOS ANGELES, CA 90048
KJAR, JOAN	ACTRESS	15729 ROSE ST	VAN NUYS, CA 91406
KJAR, TYLER	TALENT AGENT	8961 SUNSET BLVD #B	LOS ANGELES, CA 90069
KJELLAN, ALF	ACTOR-DIRECTOR	12630 MULHOLLAND DR	BEVERLY HILLS, CA 90210
KLADSTRUP, DON	NEWS CORRESPONDENT	CBS NEWS, 524 W 57TH ST	NEW YORK, NY 10019
KLAGES, BILL	CINEMATOGRAPHER	7715 SUNSET BLVD #150	LOS ANGELES, CA 90046
KLANE, BOB	WRITER-PRODUCER	2357 KIMBRIDGE RD	BEVERLY HILLS, CA 90210
KLAPIS, RALPH	BARITONE	GREAT LAKES PERFORMING	
		310 E WASHINGTON ST	ANN ARBOR, MI 48104
KLASE, IRVING E	CONDUCTOR	248 S PALM DR	BEVERLY HILLS, CA 90212
KLASS, PHILIP J	NEWS CORRESPONDENT	404 "N" ST, SW	WASHINGTON, DC 20024
KLASSABIAN, GLORIA	NEWS CORRESPONDENT	7401 EASTMORELAND RD #803	ANNANDALE, VA 22003
KLATMAN, CAROL	TV WRITER	2351 OCEAN AVE	VENICE, CA 90291
KLATMAN, CHRISTOPHER J	COMPOSER	2351 OCEAN AVE	MARINA DEL REY, CA 90292
KLATZKIN, LEON	COMPOSER-CONDUCTOR	2276 S BEVERLY GLEN BLVD #307	LOS ANGELES, CA 90064
KLAUBER, GERTAN	ACTOR	21 YALE CT, HONEYBOURNE RD	LONDON NW6 ENGLAND
KLAVAN, ROSS	WRITER	555 W 57TH ST #1230	NEW YORK, NY 10019
KLAVUN, WALTER J	ACTOR	32 GRAMERCY PARK S	NEW YORK, NY 10003
KLAWITTER, JOHN	FILM DIRECTOR	4917 MEDINA DR	WOODLAND HILLS, CA 91364
KLAY, ANDOR C	NEWS CORRESPONDENT	3402 GARFIELD ST, NW	WASHINGTON, DC 20007
KLAYTEN, MELVERNE	ACTRESS	10850 RIVERSIDE DR #505	NORTH HOLLYWOOD, CA 91602
KLEBAU, JAMES D	PHOTOJOURNALIST	5806 MAIDEN LN	BETHESDA, MD 20817
KLEBER, DAVID	PHOTOJOURNALIST	950 FARM HAVEN DR	ROCKVILLE, MD 20852
KLEE, BERNHARD	CONDUCTOR	COLBERT, 111 W 57TH ST	NEW YORK, NY 10019
KLEFFMAN, ERVIN H	CONDUCTOR	1100 S GARFIELD AVE	ALHAMBRA, CA 91801
KLEILER, FRANK M	NEWS CORRESPONDENT	9100 WARREN ST	SILVER SPRING, MD 20910
KLEIN, ANNE	FASHION DESIGNER	205 W 39TH ST	NEW YORK, NY 10018
KLEIN, ARTHUR W	TV DIRECTOR	ABC-TV, 39 W 66TH ST	NEW YORK, NY 10023
KLEIN, BARUCH	COMPOSER	484 INVERNESS DR	PACIFICA, CA 94044
KLEIN, BILL	TV EXECUTIVE	CBS-TV, 6121 SUNSET BLVD	LOS ANGELES, CA 90028
KLEIN, CALVIN	FASHION DESIGNER	205 W 39TH ST	NEW YORK, NY 10018
KLEIN, CARRIE	ACTRESS	13111 VENTURA BLVD #204	STUDIO CITY, CA 91604
KLEIN, DANIEL M	WRITER	555 W 57TH ST #1230	NEW YORK, NY 10019
KLEIN, DENNIS	WRITER-PRODUCER	4915 SAN FELICIANO DR	WOODLAND HILLS, CA 91364
KLEIN, ELIZABETH ANN	ACTRESS	AMBROSE, 1466 BROADWAY	NEW YORK, NY 10036
KLEIN, ILISSA E	NEWS CORRESPONDENT	400 N CAPITOL ST, NW	WASHINGTON, DC 20001
KLEIN, JAIME B	SCREENWRITER	8955 BEVERLY BLVD	LOS ANGELES, CA 90048
KLEIN, JONATHAN C	WRITER	555 W 57TH ST #1230	NEW YORK, NY 10019
KLEIN, JORDAN N	DIRECTOR	POST OFFICE BOX 1270	BELLEVIEW, FL 32620
KLEIN, JOSEPH M	CONDUCTOR	28 W 87TH ST	NEW YORK, NY 10024
KLEIN, KENNETH R	CONDUCTOR	1 FOREST AVE	GLEN COVE, NY 11542
KLEIN, LARRY	TV WRITER-PRODUCER	3003 W OLIVE AVE	BURBANK, CA 91505
KLEIN, LAUREN	ACTRESS	ABRAMS ARTISTS & ASSOCIATES	
		420 MADISON AVE, 14TH FLOOR	NEW YORK, NY 10017
KLEIN, MARK A	WRITER	8955 BEVERLY BLVD	LOS ANGELES, CA 90048
KLEIN, MARTY	TALENT AGENT	9000 SUNSET BLVD #1200	LOS ANGELES, CA 90069
KLEIN, MARY L	NEWS CORRESPONDENT	1226 "G" ST, NW	WASHINGTON, DC 20003
KLEIN, PAUL L	CABLE EXECUTIVE	PLAYBOY, 919 N MICHIGAN AVE	CHICAGO, IL 60611
KLEIN, RICHARD	COLUMNIST	VARIETY, 1400 N CAHUENGA BLVD	HOLLYWOOD, CA 90028
KLEIN, ROBERT	COMED-ACT-WRI	THE WILLIAM MORRIS AGENCY	
		1350 AVE OF THE AMERICAS	NEW YORK, NY 10019
KLEIN, ROD	VIDEO EDITOR	ENTERTAINMENT TONIGHT	
		PARAMOUNT TELEVISION	
		5555 MELROSE AVE	LOS ANGELES, CA 90038
KLEIN, ROLAND	FASION DESIGNER	23 BURTON PL	LONDON W1 ENGLAND
KLEIN, VIRGINIA DOODY	COLUMNIST	7720 EL CAMINO REAL #2-C	RANCHO LA COSTA, CA 92008
KLEINBAUM, ALFRED W	WRITER	555 W 57TH ST #1230	NEW YORK, NY 10019
KLEINER, HARRY	SCREENWRITER	258 S SPALDING DR	BEVERLY HILLS, CA 90212
KLEINER, HENRY E, JR	NEWS CORRESPONDENT	242 HILLSIDE CIR	VIENNA, VA 22180
KLEINERMAN, ISAAC	DIRECTOR-PRODUCER	11 SANDUSKY RD	NEW CITY, NY 10956
KLEINMAN, DAN	WRITER	8955 BEVERLY BLVD	LOS ANGELES, CA 90048
KLEINMAN, MARSHA	CASTING DIRECTOR	704 N GARDNER ST #2	LOS ANGELES, CA 90046
KLEINMUNTZ, MANNY	ACTOR	FELBER, 2126 N CAHUENGA BLVD	LOS ANGELES, CA 90068
KLEINSCHMITT, CARL	WRITER	2119 MORENO DR	LOS ANGELES, CA 90039
KLEISER, RANDAL	FILM WRITER-DIRECTOR	2233 NICHOLS CANYON RD	LOS ANGELES, CA 90046
KLEIT, RICK	ACTOR	1420 OCEAN DR	MANHATTAN BEACH, CA 90266
KLEMENS, SUSAN	PHOTOGRAPHER	7423 FOX LEIGH WY	ALEXANDRIA, VA 22310
KLEMMER, JOHN	SAXOPHONIST	ALIVE ENTERTAINMENT AGENCY	
		1775 BROADWAY, 7TH FLOOR	NEW YORK, NY 10019

KLEMPERER, WERNER	ACTOR	1229 HORN AVE	LOS ANGELES, CA	90069
KLENCK, MARGARET L	ACTRESS	ABRAMS ARTISTS & ASSOCIATES		
		420 MADISON AVE, 14TH FLOOR	NEW YORK, NY	10017
KLENDER, RICHARD	SINGER	805 FOREST RIDGE DR #108	BEDFORD, TX	76022
KLENHARD, WALTER	ACTOR	617 GRANT ST #4	SANTA MONICA, CA	90405
KLENMAN, NORMAN	WRITER	14993 VALLEY VISTA BLVD	SHERMAN OAKS, CA	91413
KLETTER, RICHARD C	SCREENWRITER	401 9TH ST	SANTA MONICA, CA	90402
KLEVEN, MAX	WRITER-PRODUCER	POST OFFICE BOX 2406	OLYMPIC VALLEY, CA	95730
KLIBONOFF, JON	PIANIST	AFFILIATE ARTISTS, INC		
		37 W 65TH ST, 6TH FLOOR	NEW YORK, NY	10023
KLICK, MICHAEL J	DIRECTOR	1711 S CREST DR	LOS ANGELES, CA	90035
KLIEN, WALTER	PIANIST	MARIEDL ANDERS ARTISTS MGMT		
		535 EL CAMINO DEL MAR ST	SAN FRANCISCO, CA	94121
KLINE, ANTON D	WRITER	6064 ROD AVE	WOODLAND HILLS, CA	91367
KLINE, DAVID	BASSO-BARITONE	CAMI, 165 W 57TH ST	NEW YORK, NY	10019
KLINE, HERBERT	WRITER-PRODUCER	1280 N LAUREL AVE #12	HOLLYWOOD, CA	90046
KLINE, J W	SINGER	LUTZ, 5625 "O" STREET BLDG	LINCOLN, NE	68510
KLINE, JAMES	ACTOR	8831 SUNSET BLVD #402	LOS ANGELES, CA	90069
KLINE, KEVIN	ACTOR	888 7TH AVE #1602	NEW YORK, NY	10019
KLINE, RICHARD	ACTOR	9200 SUNSET BLVD #414	LOS ANGELES, CA	90069
KLINE, RICHARD H	CINEMATOGRAPHER	POST OFFICE BOX 2230	HOLLYWOOD, CA	90078
KLINE, RICHARD S	DIRECTOR	DGA, 7950 SUNSET BLVD	LOS ANGELES, CA	90046
KLINE, ROBERT D	WRITER	8955 BEVERLY BLVD	LOS ANGELES, CA	90048
KLINE, ROBERT D	PRODUCER	101 OCEAN AVE #D-3	SANTA MONICA, CA	90402
KLINE, STEVE E	TV WRITER	8428 MELROSE PL #C	LOS ANGELES, CA	90069
KLINE, WAYNE	TV WRITER	7245 FRANKLIN AVE #14	LOS ANGELES, CA	90046
KLING, HEYWOOD	WRITER	160 N CLIFFWOOD AVE	LOS ANGELES, CA	90049
KLING, RENO	GUITARIST	2811 WESTWOOD AVE	NASHVILLE, TN	37212
KLING, WILLIAM H	NEWS CORRESPONDENT	5210 26TH RD N	ARLINGTON, VA	22207
KLING, WOODY	TV WRITER	8428 MELROSE PL #C	LOS ANGELES, CA	90069
KLINGENSMITH, REX	SINGER	PROCESS, 439 WILEY AVE	FRANKLIN, PA	16323
KLINGER, JUDSON	SCREENWRITER	8955 BEVERLY BLVD	LOS ANGELES, CA	90048
KLINGER, MICHAEL	FILM PRODUCER	19 WATFORD RD, RADLETT	HERTS	ENGLAND
KLINGER, TONY	WRITER-PRODUCER	GENESIS, REGENTS CLOSE		
		RADLETT	HERTS	ENGLAND
KLINTBERG, PATRICIA PEAK	NEWS CORRESPONDENT	2607 N QUINCY ST	ARLINGTON, VA	22207
KLIPPSTATER, KURT	CONDUCTOR	61 W 62ND ST #6-F	NEW YORK, NY	10023
KLIQUE	RHYTHM & BLUES TRIO	200 W 51ST ST #1410	NEW YORK, NY	10019
KLO, TONGA	WRESTLER	POST OFFICE BOX 3859	STAMFORD, CT	06905
KLOBUCAR, BERISLAV	CONDUCTOR	59 E 54TH ST #81	NEW YORK, NY	10022
KLOESS, JOE N	CONDUCTOR	17114 SADDLEHILL RD	COLBERT, WA	99005
KLOPPER, NANCY	CASTING DIRECTOR	POST OFFICE BOX 5718	SHERMAN OAKS, CA	91403
KLOSS, CARL W	DIRECTOR	RURAL DELIVERY #5		
		ECHO VALLEY RD	NEWTOWN, CT	06470
KLOUS, PATRICIA	ACTRESS	15301 VENTURA BLVD #345	SHERMAN OAKS, CA	91403
KLOVES, STEVEN	SCREENWRITER	8955 BEVERLY BLVD	LOS ANGELES, CA	90048
KLOZAK, STEPHEN	CASTING DIRECTOR	EMBASSY TELEVISON		
		100 UNIVERSAL CITY PLAZA	UNIVERSAL CITY, CA	91608
KLUETMEIER, HEINZ	SPORTS PHOTOGRAPHER	SPORTS ILLUSTRATED MAGAZINE		
		TIME & LIFE BUILDING		
		ROCKEFELLER CENTER	NEW YORK, NY	10020
KLUG, SCOTT L	NEWS CORRESPONDENT	4461 CONNECTICUT AVE, NW	WASHINGTON, DC	20008
KLUGE, JOHN	TV-RADIO EXECUTIVE	METROMEDIA, 205 E 67TH ST	NEW YORK, NY	10021
KLUGER, BARRY D	CABLE EXECUTIVE	USA CABLE NETWORK		
		208 HARRISTOWN RD	GLEN ROCK, NJ	07452
KLUGER, GARRY	ACTOR	11650 HAYNES AVE #4	NORTH HOLLYWOOD, CA	91606
KLUGER, STEVE	ACTOR	1255 N VAN NESS AVE #11	HOLLYWOOD, CA	90038
KLUGH, EARL	GUITARIST	24225 W 9 MILE ST	SOUTHFIELD, MI	48601
KLUGMAN, ADAM	ACTOR	22548 W PACIFIC COAST HWY #110	MALIBU, CA	90265
KLUGMAN, DEBORAH	TV WRITER	22548 W PACIFIC COAST HWY #110	MALIBU, CA	90265
KLUGMAN, DON B	WRITER-PRODUCER	1446 N WELLS ST	CHICAGO, IL	60610
KLUGMAN, JACK	ACTOR-WRITER	22548 W PACIFIC COAST HWY #110	MALIBU, CA	90265
KLUGMAN, LYNN	DIRECTOR-PRODUCER	2624 AVE "M"	BROOKLYN, NY	11210
KLUMPH, LEAH FACKOS	PHOTOGRAPHER	1220 BLAIR MILL RD	SILVER SPRING, MD	20910
KLUNIS, TOM	ACTOR	200 W 57TH ST #1303	NEW YORK, NY	10019
KLURFELD, JAMES M	NEWS CORRESPONDENT	10399 GREEN MOUNTAIN CIR	COLUMBIA, MD	21044
KLYMAXX	RHYTHM & BLUES GROUP	3580 WILSHIRE BLVD #1840	LOS ANGELES, CA	90011
KNAP, TED	NEWS CORRESPONDENT	1429 WOODACRE DR	MC LEAN, VA	22101
KNAPIK, MICHAEL	NEWS CORRESPONDENT	1809 N MONROE ST	ARLINGTON, VA	22207
KNAPP, CHARLES	ACTOR	8721 SUNSET BLVD #200	LOS ANGELES, CA	90069
KNAPP, DAVID	ACTOR	1662 MARMONT AVE	LOS ANGELES, CA	90069
KNAPP, FRANKLIN	SINGER-GUITARIST	232 WELCH RD	NASHVILLE, TN	37211
KNAPP, GREGORY	SCREENWRITER	8955 BEVERLY BLVD	LOS ANGELES, CA	90048
KNAPP, LILO	COMPOSER	570 N ROSSMORE AVE #605	LOS ANGELES, CA	90004
KNAPTON, ROBYN	TV WRITER	10390 WILSHIRE BLVD #707	LOS ANGELES, CA	90024
KNATZ, NIKITA	FILM DIRECTOR	11241 SUNSHINE TERR	STUDIO CITY, CA	91604
KNAUP, HENRY E	DIRECTOR	145 E 16TH ST	NEW YORK, NY	10003
KNEALE, NIGEL	SCREENWRITER	8955 BEVERLY BLVD	LOS ANGELES, CA	90048
KNEBEL, LEVI L	ACTOR	304 S JEFFERSON ST	DUNKERTON, IA	50626
KNEE, ALLEN	WRITER	19 W 44TH ST #1500	NEW YORK, NY	10036
KNEE DEEP IN GRASS	C & W GROUP	POST OFFICE BOX 25371	CHARLOTTE, NC	28212
KNEFF, HILDERGARD	ACTRESS-SINGER	SCHOENBERGER, 7164 MACAPA DR	LOS ANGELES, CA	90068
KNELL, CATALAINE	ACTRESS	1236 N FLORES ST	LOS ANGELES, CA	90069
KNELL, DAVID	ACTOR	9229 SUNSET BLVD #306	LOS ANGELES, CA	90069
KNICKERBOCKER, BRAD	NEWS CORRESPONDENT	1707 DREWLAINE DR	VIENNA, VA	22180

Name	Occupation	Address	City	ZIP/Country
KNIE, ROBERTA	SOPRANO	CAMI, 165 W 57TH ST	NEW YORK, NY	10019
KNIEVEL, EVIL	DAREDEVIL	9960 YORK ALPHA DR	N ROYALTON, OH	44133
KNIFE, DENNIS H	DIRECTOR	41-14 247TH ST	DOUGLASTON, NY	11363
KNIGHT, ADELINE	DIRECTOR	157-20 90TH ST	HOWARD BEACH, NY	11414
KNIGHT, ALEX	WRESTLER	POST OFFICE BOX 3859	STAMFORD, CT	06905
KNIGHT, ARTHUR	FILM CRITIC-HISTORIAN	22202 PACIFIC COAST HWY	MALIBU, CA	90265
KNIGHT, ATHELIA W	NEWS CORRESPONDENT	1535 "C" ST, SE	WASHINGTON, DC	20003
KNIGHT, DERRICK HAYNES	WRITER-PRODUCER	4 SOUTH MANSIONS		
		GONDAR GARDENS	LONDON NW6	ENGLAND
KNIGHT, DON	ACTOR	4721 LAUREL CANYON BLVD #211	NORTH HOLLYWOOD, CA	91607
KNIGHT, EDMUND	ACTOR	35 BYWATER ST, CHELSEA	LONDON SW3	ENGLAND
KNIGHT, EILEEN	CASTING DIRECTOR	POST OFFICE BOX 5718	SHERMAN OAKS, CA	91403
KNIGHT, ERIC	CONDUCTOR	3003 VAN NESS ST #W-205, NW	WASHINGTON, DC	20008
KNIGHT, GENE	ACTOR	ATA, 2437 E WASHINGTON BLVD	PASADENA, CA	91104
KNIGHT, GLADYS & THE PIPS	VOCAL GROUP	9200 SUNSET BLVD #PH-15	LOS ANGELES, CA	90069
KNIGHT, HOLLY	SINGER-SONGWRITER	CHRYSALIS RECORDS COMPANY		
		645 MADISON AVE	NEW YORK, NY	10022
KNIGHT, JACK	ACTOR	8019 1/2 MELROSE AVE #3	LOS ANGELES, CA	90046
KNIGHT, JAMES L	TRUMPETER	320 E STOCKER ST #305	GLENDALE, CA	91207
KNIGHT, JEAN	SINGER	POST OFFICE BOX 19004	NEW ORLEANS, LA	70179
KNIGHT, JUNE	ACTRESS	BUEHLER, 3760 EUREKA DR	STUDIO CITY, CA	91604
KNIGHT, PAUL	TV PRODUCER	12 GORDON AVE, STANMORE	MIDDLESEX	ENGLAND
KNIGHT, ROBERT M	COMPOSER-CONDUCTOR	2417 WELLINGTON ST	DENTON, TX	76201
KNIGHT, RONALD	ACTOR	WEBB, 7500 DEVISTA DR	LOS ANGELES, CA	90046
KNIGHT, ROSALIND	ACTRESS	FEAST, 43-A PRINCESS RD	LONDON NW1	ENGLAND
KNIGHT, SHIRLEY	ACTRESS	SEE - KNIGHT-HOPKINS, SHIRLEY		
KNIGHT, SONNY	SINGER	OLDIES, 5218 ALMONT ST	LOS ANGELES, CA	90032
KNIGHT, VICKI	SINGER	POST OFFICE BOX 171132	NASHVILLE, TN	37217
KNIGHT, VIVA	DIRECTOR-PRODUCER	9760 CHARLEVILLE BLVD	BEVERLY HILLS, CA	90212
KNIGHT, WILLIAM	ACTOR	15010 VENTURA BLVD #219	SHERMAN OAKS, CA	91403
KNIGHT-HOPKINS, SHIRLEY	ACTRESS	LIONEL LARNER, 130 W 57TH ST	NEW YORK, NY	10019
KNIGHTEN, DAVID	ACTOR	1800 EL CERRITO PL #50	HOLLYWOOD, CA	90068
KNIGHTON, ELIZABETH	SOPRANO	CAMI, 165 W 57TH ST	NEW YORK, NY	10019
KNIGHTON, KIMBERLY C	NEWS CORRESPONDENT	2411 MENOKIN DR	ALEXANDRIA, VA	22302
KNIGHTS, ROBERT	FILM-TV DIRECTOR	41 LANCASTER LN, TOP FLAT	HAMPSTEAD NW3 4HB	ENGLAND
KNIPE, V H	WRITER	8955 BEVERLY BLVD	LOS ANGELES, CA	90048
KNITTERS, THE	ROCK & ROLL GROUP	POST OFFICE BOX 48888	LOS ANGELES, CA	90048
KNOB, EDWARD	SAXOPHONIST	429 GOLDEN BEACH BLVD	VENICE, CA	33595
KNOB, NANCY	FRENCH HORNIST	429 GOLDEN BEACH BLVD	VENICE, FL	33595
KNOBLOCK, FRED	SINGER	151 S EL CAMINO DR	BEVERLY HILLS, CA	90212
KNOBLOCK, KEVIN	TV DIRECTOR	ENTERTAINMENT TONIGHT		
		PARAMOUNT TELEVISION		
		5555 MELROSE AVE	LOS ANGELES, CA	90038
KNOLES, DON	NEWS CORRESPONDENT	3611 39TH ST #E-329, NW	WASHINGTON, DC	20016
KNOLLER, MARK	NEWS CORRESPONDENT	1825 "K" ST, NW	WASHINGTON, DC	20006
KNOP, PATRICIA	SCREENWRITER	8955 BEVERLY BLVD	LOS ANGELES, CA	90048
KNOPF, CHRISTOPHER	WRITER	910 25TH ST	SANTA MONICA, CA	90403
KNOPS, THE	ACROBATIC DUO	HALL, 138 FROG HOLLOW RD	CHURCHVILLE, PA	18966
KNORR, FRIEDA	ACTRESS	SAINT JAMES MANAGEMENT		
		22 GROOM PL	LONDON SW1	ENGLAND
KNOTT, FREDERICK	WRITER	555 W 57TH ST #1230	NEW YORK, NY	10019
KNOTT, JOHN W, JR	NEWS CORRESPONDENT	ABC-TV, NEWS DEPARTMENT		
		1717 DE SALES ST, NW	WASHINGTON, DC	20036
KNOTT, ROBERT E	DIRECTOR-PRODUCER	133 WILLOW TURN #B	MOUNT LAUREL, NJ	08054
KNOTTS, DON	ACTOR	1854 S BEVERLY GLEN #402	LOS ANGELES, CA	90025
KNOWLES, JOHN	GUITARIST	141 HOLLY FOREST	NASHVILLE, TN	37221
KNOWLES, KATHY	CASTING DIRECTOR	9044 HOLLYWOOD HILLS RD	LOS ANGELES, CA	90046
KNOWLES, PATRIC	ACTOR	6243 RANDI AVE	WOODLAND HILLS, CA	91367
KNOX, ALEXANDER	ACTOR	ICM, 388-396 OXFORD ST	LONDON W1	ENGLAND
KNOX, BUDDY	SINGER-SONGWRITER	POST OFFICE BOX 10	ARNAUD, MAN	CANADA
KNOX, DONALD E	DIRECTOR	1770 MEADOWLARK RD	EAGAN, MN	55122
KNOX, ELYSE	ACTRESS	320 N GUNSTON AVE	LOS ANGELES, CA	90049
KNOX, JACALYN	ACTRESS	9250 WILSHIRE BLVD #208	BEVERLY HILLS, CA	90212
KNOX, MATTHEW	WRITER	7733 HAMPTON AVE #8	HOLLYWOOD, CA	90046
KNOX, RICHARD	TV DIRECTOR	226 NEWPORT AVE	TAPPAN, NY	10983
KNOX, TERENCE	ACTOR	INTERNATIONAL TALENT AGENCY		
		241 E ANGELENO AVE	BURBANK, CA	91502
KNUCKLEHEADS, THE	ROCK & ROLL GROUP	SEE - JERRY & THE KNUCKLEHEADS		
KNUDSON, HARLAN	ACTOR	5505 SHOREVIEW DR	RANCHO PALISADES, CA	90274
KNULL, KATE R	WRITER	555 W 57TH ST #1230	NEW YORK, NY	10019
KNUR, JOSIE	ACTRESS	6605 HOLLYWOOD BLVD #220	HOLLYWOOD, CA	90028
KNUTSON, LAWRENCE L	NEWS CORRESPONDENT	214 9TH ST, SE	WASHINGTON, DC	20003
KOBA, ALEX	ACTOR	10000 SANTA MONICA BLVD #305	LOS ANGELES, CA	90067
KOBAL, JOHN C	WRITER	38 DRAYTON CT		
		DRAYTON GARDENS	LONDON SW10	ENGLAND
KOBAL, PETER "SUNDOWN"	SINGER-GUITARIST	POST OFFICE BOX 22988	NASHVILLE, TN	37202
KOBART, RUTH	ACTRESS	400 S BEVERLY DR #216	BEVERLY HILLS, CA	90212
KOBAYASHI, FUMIAKI	NEWS CORRESPONDENT	427 NATIONAL PRESS BLDG		
		529 14TH ST, NW	WASHINGTON, DC	20045
KOBAYASHI, KATZ	GUITARIST	304 PITT RD	SCOTT, LA	70583
KOBE, GAIL	TV PRODUCER	CBS TELEVISION NETWORK		
		"THE BOLD & THE BEAUTIFUL"		
		7800 BEVERLY BLVD	LOS ANGELES, CA	90036
KOBER, CHARLES M	TV DIRECTOR	361 MIRA MAR AVE	LONG BEACH, CA	90803
KOBER, MARTA	ACTRESS	183 N MARTEL AVE #260	LOS ANGELES, CA	90036

WERNER KLEMPERER

KEVIN KLINE

JACK KLUGMAN

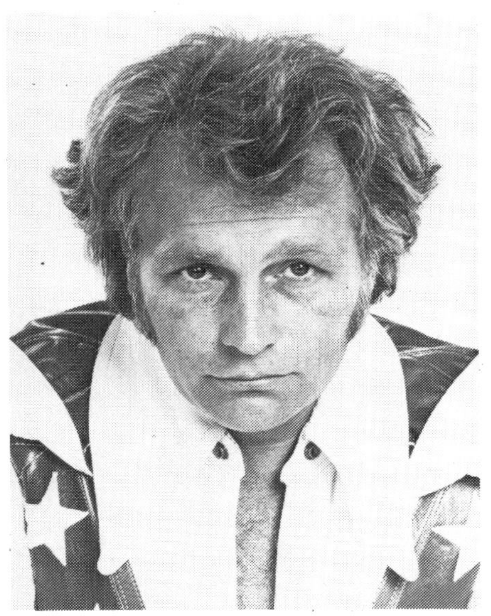
EVIL KNIEVEL

GLADYS KNIGHT

SHIRLEY KNIGHT

DON KNOTTS

ALICE KRIGE

SYLVIA KRISTEL

Name	Occupation	Address	City	Zip
KOBIALKA, DANIEL	VIOLINIST	1182 MARKET ST #311	SAN FRANCISCO, CA	94102
KOBLASA, GEORGE	DIRECTOR	POST OFFICE BOX 7116	MAMMOTH LAKES, CA	93546
KOBOR, EMERY S	NEWS CORRESPONDENT	1755 S JEFFERSON DAVIS HWY	ARLINGTON, VA	22202
KOBYLINSKI, LESLIE	NEWS CORRESPONDENT	NBC-TV, NEWS DEPARTMENT		
		4001 NEBRASKA AVE, NW	WASHINGTON, DC	20016
KOCH, ED	MAYOR-AUTHOR	CITY HALL, GRACIE MANSION	NEW YORK, NY	10007
KOCH, EDDIE B	COMPOSER	7009 JUMILLA AVE	CANOGA PARK, CA	91306
KOCH, HOWARD W	WRITER	8955 BEVERLY BLVD	LOS ANGELES, CA	90048
KOCH, HOWARD W, JR	FILM PRODUCER	1156 BEVERWILL DR	LOS ANGELES, CA	90035
KOCH, HOWARD W, SR	DIRECTOR-PRODUCER	704 N CRESCENT DR	BEVERLY HILLS, CA	90212
KOCH, JON C	NEWS CORRESPONDENT	2039 HUIDEKOPER PL, NW	WASHINGTON, DC	20007
KOCH, KATHLEEN L	NEWS CORRESPONDENT	8064 INVERNESS RIDGE RD	POTOMAC, MD	20854
KOCH, KENNETH	DIRECTOR	32100 BEACHFRONT LN	WESTLAKE VILLAGE, CA	91361
KOCH, SALLY	NEWS CORRESPONDENT	5130 CONNECTICUT AVE #409, NW	WASHINGTON, DC	20008
KOCH, THOMAS F	WRITER	8955 BEVERLY BLVD	LOS ANGELES, CA	90048
KOCHAN, JOHN R	DIRECTOR	300 N STATE ST	CHICAGO, IL	60610
KOCHANSKI, WLADIMER JAN	PIANIST	KOMAR, 1122 WEST ST	OCEANSIDE, CA	92054
KOCHMAN, ROBERT D	TV PRODUCER	CBS-TV, "THE GUIDING LIGHT"		
		51 W 52ND ST	NEW YORK, NY	10019
KOCSIS, ZOLTAN	PIANIST	ICM, 40 W 57TH ST	NEW YORK, NY	10019
KODA, DOROTHY	WRITER	555 W 57TH ST #1230	NEW YORK, NY	10019
KODALY DUO	MUSICAL DUO	IAPR, KINCORA, BEER RD		
		SEATON	DEVON	ENGLAND
KOECHL, PENELOPE	TV WRITER	CBS-TV, "AS THE WORLD TURNS"		
		51 W 52ND ST	NEW YORK, NY	10019
KOEHLER, MAURICE T L	CONDUCTOR	140 BAYONA DR	SANTA CRUZ, CA	95060
KOEMPEL, MICHAEL L	NEWS CORRESPONDENT	6612 ALLEGHENY AVE	TAKOMA PARK, MD	20912
KOENEKAMP, FRED J	CINEMATOGRAPHER	9756 SHOSHINE AVE	NORTHRIDGE, CA	91324
KOENIG, DAVID L	NEWS CORRESPONDENT	1527-2A CAMERON CRESCENT DR	RESTON, VA	22090
KOENIG, DENNIS	TV WRITER	8955 BEVERLY BLVD	LOS ANGELES, CA	90048
KOENIG, LAIRD	SCREENWRITER	1429 TIGERTAIL RD	LOS ANGELES, CA	90049
KOENIG, MARI JANE	NEWS CORRESPONDENT	1755 S JEFFERSON DAVIS HWY	ARLINGTON, VA	22202
KOENIG, PAUL N	PHOTOJOURNALIST	6925 WILLOW ST	FALLS CHURCH, VA	22046
KOENIG, RAYMOND	WRITER	1516 OCEAN PARK BLVD #2	SANTA MONICA, CA	90405
KOENIG, TOMMY	ACTOR	7285 FRANKLIN AVE #E	LOS ANGELES, CA	90046
KOENIG, WALTER	ACTOR-WRITER	5658 BECK AVE	NORTH HOLLYWOOD, CA	91601
KOENIGES, THOMAS R	PHOTOGRAPHER	167 ANCHORAGE DR	WEST ISLIP, NY	11795
KOENING, MARTIN P	NEWS CORRESPONDENT	2139 WISCONSIN AVE, NW	WASHINGTON, DC	20007
KOEPP, STEPHEN	WRITER-EDITOR	TIME/TIME & LIFE BLDG		
		ROCKEFELLER CENTER	NEW YORK, NY	10020
KOERNER, KENNETH	TV WRITER-DIRECTOR	4311 ENSENADA DR	WOODLAND HILLS, CA	91364
KOFFMAN, MOE, QUINTET	JAZZ QUINTET	5720 MOSHOLU AVE #300	RIVERDALE, NY	10471
KOGEN, ARNOLD	TV WRITER	4250 BONAVITA DR	ENCINO, CA	91436
KOGEN, BONNI D	WRITER	555 W 57TH ST #1230	NEW YORK, NY	10019
KOHAN, ALAN BUZ	TV WRITER-LYRICIST	2095 LOMA VISTA DR	BEVERLY HILLS, CA	90210
KOHAN, RHEA ARNOLD	WRITER	2095 LOMA VISTA DR	BEVERLY HILLS, CA	90210
KOHAN, SILVIA	SINGER-GUITARIST	POST OFFICE BOX 9388	STANFORD, CA	94305
KOHL, TERRY	ACTOR	ABC-TV, "ALL MY CHILDREN"		
		1330 AVE OF THE AMERICAS	NEW YORK, NY	10019
KOHLER, IRENE	PIANIST	28 CASTELNAU	LONDON SW13 9RU	ENGLAND
KOHLER, PAUL	COMEDIAN	10404 GREENHAVEN PARKWAY	BRECKSVILLE, OH	44141
KOHLRUST, ROBERT	DIRECTOR-PRODUCER	19625 SUNNYSIDE	SAINT CLAIR SHORES, MI	48080
KOHN, DANIEL F	DIRECTOR	47 HITCHING POST LN	GLEN COVE, NY	11542
KOHN, HOWARD	SCREENWRITER	8955 BEVERLY BLVD	LOS ANGELES, CA	90048
KOHN, JONATHAN	SCREENWRITER	8955 BEVERLY BLVD	LOS ANGELES, CA	90048
KOHN, JONATHAN	FILM EXECUTIVE	1354 N WETHERLY DR	LOS ANGELES, CA	90069
KOHN, JOSEPH R	DIRECTOR	29 W 64TH ST	NEW YORK, NY	10023
KOHN, KARL G	COMPOSER-CONDUCTOR	674 W 10TH ST	CLAREMONT, CA	91711
KOHN, ROSE SIMON	WRITER	1415 OCEAN AVE #704	SANTA MONICA, CA	90401
KOHNER, PANCHO	FILM WRITER-PRODUCER	901 STONE CANYON RD	LOS ANGELES, CA	90077
KOHNER, PASHE	FILM PRODUCER	1527 TIGERTAIL RD	LOS ANGELES, CA	90049
KOHNER, PAUL	TALENT AGENT	KOHNER, 9169 SUNSET BLVD	LOS ANGELES, CA	90069
KOHNER, SUSAN	ACTRESS	JOHN WEITZ, 710 PARK AVE	NEW YORK, NY	10021
KOHNHORST, ALLEN	GUITARIST	1716 ASHWOOD DR	NASHVILLE, TN	37212
KOHORST, KARL-HEINZ	NEWS CORRESPONDENT	7725 DESDEMONA CT	MC LEAN, VA	22102
KOHUT, ANNE H	NEWS CORRESPONDENT	2500 WISCONSIN AVE #430, NW	WASHINGTON, DC	20007
KOIZUMI, LUCI S	NEWS CORRESPONDENT	2162 GOLD COURSE DR	RESTON, VA	22091
KOJIAN, VARUJAN	CONDUCTOR	COLBERT, 111 W 57TH ST	NEW YORK, NY	10019
KOKICH, KIM A	NEWS CORRESPONDENT	2025 "M" ST, NW	WASHINGTON, DC	20036
KOKO POP	SINGER	PERLE, 4475 VINELAND AVE	STUDIO CITY, CA	91602
KOKUBO, CHRISTINA	ACTRESS	2318 DUANE ST	LOS ANGELES, CA	90039
KOLB, KEN	WRITER	10100 SANTA MONICA BLVD #1600	LOS ANGELES, CA	90067
KOLB, MINA	ACTRESS	9200 SUNSET BLVD #1210	LOS ANGELES, CA	90069
KOLBE, WINRICH	TV DIRECTOR	23012 LEONORA DR	WOODLAND HILLS, CA	91367
KOLBY, ALAN	GUITARIST	270 TAMPA DR #J-20	NASHVILLE, TN	37211
KOLE, JOHN W	NEWS CORRESPONDENT	2542 N 23RD RD	ARLINGTON, VA	22207
KOLE, NELSON	COMPOSER	2412 VISTA COLINA ST	HENDERSON, NV	89015
KOLIMA, LEE	ACTOR	1350 N HIGHLAND AVE #24	HOLLYWOOD, CA	90028
KOLKO, JOEL	NEWS CORRESPONDENT	1613 TILTON DR	SILVER SPRING, MD	20902
KOLLER, FRED	SINGER-SONGWRITER	5100 NEVADA AVE	NASHVILLE, TN	37209
KOLLO, RENE	TENOR	MARIEDL ANDERS ARTISTS MGMT		
		535 EL CAMINO DEL MAR ST	SAN FRANCISCO, CA	94121
KOLOFF, IVAN	WRESTLER	NATIONAL WRESTLING ALLIANCE		
		JIM CROCKETT PROMOTIONS		
		421 BRIARBEND DR	CHARLOTTE, NC	28209

KOLOFF, NIKITA	WRESTLER	NATIONAL WRESTLING ALLIANCE		
		JIM CROCKETT PROMOTIONS		
		421 BRIARBEND DR	CHARLOTTE, NC	28209
KOLOMYJEC, JOANNE	SOPRANO	CAMI, 165 W 57TH ST	NEW YORK, NY	10019
KOLUNDZIJA, JOVAN	VIOLINIST	GERSHUNOFF, 502 PARK AVE	NEW YORK, NY	10022
KOLZAK, STEPHEN F	CASTING DIRECTOR	EMBASSY TV, 1438 N GOWER ST	LOS ANGELES, CA	90028
KOMACK, JAMES	ACT-WRI-DIR	617 N BEVERLY DR	BEVERLY HILLS, CA	90210
KOMAROW, STEVEN	NEWS CORRESPONDENT	4519 N 18TH ST	ARLINGTON, VA	22207
KOMATSUBARA, HISAO	NEWS CORRESPONDENT	1639 SENECA AVE	MC LEAN, VA	22101
KOMISAROW, JOEL H	WRITER	555 W 57TH ST #1230	NEW YORK, NY	10019
KOMRADA, JOHN, JR	MUSIC ARRANGER	920 FOREST ACRES CT	NASHVILLE, TN	37220
KOMRADA, JUDITH	PIANIST	920 FOREST ACRES CT	NASHVILLE, TN	37220
KONDAZIAN, KAREN	ACTRESS	6310 SAN VICENTE BLVD #407	LOS ANGELES, CA	90048
KONDO, KEN	NEWS CORRESPONDENT	11710 DEVILWOOD CT	POTOMAC, MD	20854
KONDRACKE, MORTON M	NEWS CORRESPONDENT	7405 RIDGEWOOD AVE	CHEVY CHASE, MD	20815
KONE, RUSSELL J	DIRECTOR	18 LINCOLN AVE	ARDSLEY, NY	10502
KONG, VENICE	MODEL	MODELS & PROMOTIONS AGENCY		
		8560 SUNSET BLVD, 10TH FLOOR	LOS ANGELES, CA	90069
KONGA, KING	WRESTLER	SEE - KONGA THE BARBARIAN		
KONGA THE BARBARIAN	WRESTLER	NATIONAL WRESTLING ALLIANCE		
		JIM CROCKETT PROMOTIONS		
		421 BRIARBEND DR	CHARLOTTE, NC	28209
KONIG, KLAUS	TENOR	CAMI, 165 W 57TH ST	NEW YORK, NY	10019
KONNER, JOAN	TV WRITER-DIRECTOR	SNEDENS LANDING	PALISADES, NY	10964
KONNER, LAWRENCE M	SCREENWRITER	514 PALISADES AVE	SANTA MONICA, CA	90402
KONRAD, DOROTHY	ACTRESS	10650 MISSOURI AVE	LOS ANGELES, CA	90025
KONSTANTINOV, TZVETAN	PIANIST	FROTHINGHAM, 40 GROVE ST	WESSESLEY, MA	02181
KONTCHALOVSKY, ANDREI	WRITER	8955 BEVERLY BLVD	LOS ANGELES, CA	90048
KONTER, DARRYL J	WRITER	555 W 57TH ST #1230	NEW YORK, NY	10019
KONVITZ, JEFFREY	SCREENWRITER	12660 MULHOLLAND DR	BEVERLY HILLS, CA	90210
KOOCK, GUICH	ACTOR	9255 SUNSET BLVD #603	LOS ANGELES, CA	90069
KOOIMAN, DIRK	ACTOR	7469 MELROSE AVE #30	LOS ANGELES, CA	90046
KOOL & THE GANG	SOUL GROUP	WORLDWIDE ENTERTAINMENT COMP		
		GERALD DELET MANAGEMENT		
		641 LEXINGTON AVE	NEW YORK, NY	10022
KOON, DEAN	SINGER-GUITARIST	1101 PRESIDENT	TUPELO, MS	38801
KOONCE, KEN	WRITER	8955 BEVERLY BLVD	LOS ANGELES, CA	90048
KOONS, SHAYNE	GUITARIST	9006 FORESTLAWN DR		
		RURAL ROUTE #5	BRENTWOOD, TN	37027
KOONSE, JOHNNY	GUITARIST	201 STERRY CT	ANTIOCH, TN	37013
KOONTZ, DAVID	SCREENWRITER	4630 MIRADOR PL	TARZANA, CA	91356
KOONTZ, DEAN R	WRITER	8955 BEVERLY BLVD	LOS ANGELES, CA	90048
KOONTZ, ROD	BODYBUILDER	POST OFFICE BOX 2288	WESTMINISTER, CA	92683
KOOPER-BOEHM DUO	MUSICAL DUO	MUGDAN, 84 PROSPECT AVE	DOUGLASTON, NY	11363
KOOPMAN, TON	HARPSICHORDIST	BYERS-SCHWALBE, 1 5TH AVE	NEW YORK, NY	10003
KOOPMANN, WERNER	DIRECTOR	220 E 23RD ST	NEW YORK, NY	10010
KOPCHA, MIKE	ACTOR	1821 BENEDICT CANYON RD	BEVERLY HILLS, CA	90210
KOPEL, HAL	DIRECTOR	3312 N 28TH ST	MC ALLEN, TX	78501
KOPELAN, AMY DORN	TV EXECUTIVE	ABC TELEVISION NETWORK		
		1330 AVE OF THE AMERICAS	NEW YORK, NY	10019
KOPELL, BERNIE	ACTOR-WRITER	19413 OLIVOS DR	TARZANA, CA	91356
KOPF, BEVERLY	WRITER	8955 BEVERLY BLVD	LOS ANGELES, CA	90048
KOPINS, KAREN	ACTRESS	3907 W ALAMEDA AVE #101	BURBANK, CA	91505
KOPINSKI, MARKETTA	NEWS CORRESPONDENT	3727 ALBEMARLE ST, NW	WASHINGTON, DC	20016
KOPINSKI, THADDEUS C	NEWS CORRESPONDENT	3727 ALBEMARLE ST, NW	WASHINGTON, DC	20016
KOPIT, ARTHUR	TV WRITER	555 W 57TH ST #1230	NEW YORK, NY	10019
KOPLIK, JIM	TALENT AGENT	310 MADISON AVE #804	NEW YORK, NY	10017
KOPLIN, MERT	TV WRITER-PRODUCER	THE CORPORATION FOR		
		ENTERTAINMENT & LEARNING		
		515 MADISON AVE	NEW YORK, NY	10022
KOPLOVITZ, KAY	CABLE EXECUTIVE	USA CABLE NETWORK		
		208 HARRISTOWN RD	GLEN ROCK, NJ	07452
KOPP, FREDERICK E	COMPOSER-CONDUCTOR	102 N GARFIELD PL #D	MONROVIA, CA	91016
KOPPEL, DEBORAH	ACTRESS	348 E OLIVE AVE #K	BURBANK, CA	91502
KOPPEL, TED	BROADCAST JOURNALIST	ABC-TV, NEWS DEPARTMENT		
		1717 DE SALES ST, NW	WASHINGTON, DC	20036
KOPPELMAN, JANE ANNE	NEWS CORRESPONDENT	740 9TH ST, SE	WASHINGTON, DC	20003
KOPPELMAN, MITCHELL A	PHOTOGRAPHER	4521 PARK RD	ALEXANDRIA, VA	22312
KOPPERUD, JEAN	CLARINETIST	ROSENFIELD, 714 LADD RD	BRONX, NY	10471
KOPPLE, BARBARA J	DIRECTOR-PRODUCER	CABIN, 58 E 11TH ST	NEW YORK, NY	10003
KOPPY, MICHAEL	DIRECTOR	138 8TH ST	SAN FRANCISCO, CA	94103
KOPRULU, TUNA	NEWS CORRESPONDENT	5112 WESTPATH WY	BETHESDA, MD	20816
KOPTCHAK, SERGEI	BASS	61 W 62ND ST #6-F	NEW YORK, NY	10023
KORAL, GIAN	BARITONE	225 W 34TH ST #1012	NEW YORK, NY	10001
KORANSKY, KENNETH	TENOR	PERLS, 7 W 96TH ST	NEW YORK, NY	10025
KORD, KAZIMIERZ	CONDUCTOR	ICM, 40 W 57TH ST	NEW YORK, NY	10019
KORDA, DAVID	FILM PRODUCER	1-11 HAY HILL, BERKELEY SQ	LONDON W1H 7LF	ENGLAND
KORDA, MICHAEL	WRITER	555 W 57TH ST #1230	NEW YORK, NY	10019
KORDA, MURRAY	ACTOR	8721 SUNSET BLVD #200	LOS ANGELES, CA	90069
KORDA, RONALD	TV EXECUTIVE	NBC TELEVISION NETWORK		
		30 ROCKEFELLER PLAZA	NEW YORK, NY	10112
KORDUS, RICHARD	CASTING DIRECTOR	166 E SUPERIOR ST #412	CHICAGO, IL	60611

Name	Occupation	Address	City	Zip/Country
KORF, KERRY	ACTRESS	749 1/2 N LA FAYETTE PARK PL	LOS ANGELES, CA	90026
KORMAN, HARVEY	ACTOR-DIRECTOR	1136 STRADELLA RD #302	LOS ANGELES, CA	90077
KORMATES, THE	HIGHPOLE ACT	POST OFFICE BOX 87	WEST LEBANON, NY	12195
KORN, ARTUR	SINGER	NEIDHAUDP 22	A-3W KLOSTERNEULUNG	AUSTRIA
KORN, DAVID	WRITER	8955 BEVERLY BLVD	LOS ANGELES, CA	90048
KORN, HAL	CONDUCTOR	987 SCHUMACHER DR	LOS ANGELES, CA	90048
KORN, MICHAEL	CONDUCTOR	59 E 54TH ST #81	NEW YORK, NY	10022
KORN, PETER JONA	COMPOSER	GABRIEL-MAX STRASSE 9	8000 MUNCHEN 90	WEST GERMANY
KORNAU, JONATHAN	GUITARIST	550 HARDING PL #A-114	NASHVILLE, TN	37211
KORNELL, LORELEI	NEWS CORRESPONDENT	338 N COLUMBUS ST #2	ALEXANDRIA, VA	22314
KORNHEISER, ANTHONY I	WRITER-NEWS CORRES	2905 RITTENHOUSE ST	WASHINGTON, DC	20015
KORNMAN, CAM	ACTRESS	161 W 72ND ST	NEW YORK, NY	10023
KOROTKIN, JUDITH	TV WRITER	8955 BEVERLY BLVD	LOS ANGELES, CA	90048
KOROTKIN, KENNETH	PHOTOGRAPHER	5 FIRELIGHT CT	DIX HILLS, NY	11746
KORPORAAL, GLENDA	NEWS CORRESPONDENT	3801 CONNECTICUT AVE #711, NW	WASHINGTON, DC	20008
KORR, DAVID	WRITER	555 W 57TH ST #1230	NEW YORK, NY	10019
KORROS, ROBERT N	WRITER	527 VENICE WY #A	VENICE, CA	90291
KORT, DENNIS	ACTOR	427 N CANON DR #205	BEVERLY HILLS, CA	90210
KORTNER, PETER	WRITER	8231 DE LONGPRE AVE #6	LOS ANGELES, CA	90046
KORTY, JOHN	FILM DIRECTOR	200 MILLER AVE	MILL VALLEY, CA	94941
KOS, JEFREY A	TV DIRECTOR	7842 W OAKTON	NILES, IL	60648
KOS, MARTIN A	NEWS CORRESPONDENT	307 BROADWOOD DR	ROCKVILLE, MD	20851
KOSAR, SUSAN M	WRITER	446 W AVE 44	LOS ANGELES, CA	90065
KOSBERG, ROBERT A	TV WRITER	8955 BEVERLY BLVD	LOS ANGELES, CA	90048
KOSBERG, ROBERT J	TV WRITER	8955 BEVERLY BLVD	LOS ANGELES, CA	90048
KOSCINA, SYLVIA	ACTRESS	NICOLO DEL SASSOME 10, CIAMPINO	ROME	ITALY
KOSHNER, KAREN	WRITER	555 W 57TH ST #1230	NEW YORK, NY	10019
KOSINSKI, JERRY	WRITER-ACTOR	60 W 57TH ST	NEW YORK, NY	10019
KOSKE, BENNY	HUMAN BOMB	HALL, 138 FROG HOLLOW RD	CHURCHVILLE, PA	18966
KOSLICK, MARTIN	ACTOR	1026 N LAUREL AVE	LOS ANGELES, CA	90046
KOSLOW, LAUREN	ACTRESS	FARRELL, 10500 MAGNOLIA BLVD	NORTH HOLLYWOOD, CA	91601
KOSLOW, MARC	NEWS CORRESPONDENT	NBC-TV, NEWS DEPARTMENT		
		4001 NEBRASKA AVE, NW	WASHINGTON, DC	20016
KOSLOW, PAUL	ACTOR	17539 ELIZABETH LAKE RD	LAKE HUGHHES, CA	93532
KOSLOW, RON	SCREENWRITER	8955 BEVERLY BLVD	LOS ANGELES, CA	90048
KOSMALA, JERZY	VIOLIST	GREAT LAKES PERFORMING		
		310 E WASHINGTON ST	ANN ARBOR, MI	48104
KOSNETT, JEFFREY	NEWS CORRESPONDENT	8958 SKYROCK CT	COLUMBIA, MD	21046
KOSOWICZ, EDWARD S	DIRECTOR	35 W DEERHAVEN RD	MAHWAH, NJ	07430
KOSS, ALAN	ACTOR	8015 VARNA AVE	VAN NUYS, CA	91402
KOSS, ALLEN	TV PRODUCER	1888 CENTURY PARK E #1100	LOS ANGELES, CA	90067
KOSS, LEONARD L	WRITER	8955 BEVERLY BLVD	LOS ANGELES, CA	90048
KOSSLYN, JACK	ACTOR	1275 N SWEETZER AVE #112	LOS ANGELES, CA	90069
KOSSOFF, DAVID	ACTOR-WRITER	45 ROE GREEN CLOSE		
		COLLEGE LN, HATFIELD	HERTS	ENGLAND
KOSTAL, IRWIN J	CONDUCTOR	3149 DONA SUSANA DR	STUDIO CITY, CA	91604
KOSTE, WALTER	DIRECTOR	2541 MEADE CT	ANN ARBOR, MI	48105
KOSTER, DENNIS	GUITARIST	AFFILIATE ARTISTS, INC		
		37 W 65TH ST, 6TH FLOOR	NEW YORK, NY	10023
KOSTER, DOROTHY	CASTING DIRECTOR	THE S PAUL COMPANY		
		8776 SUNSET BLVD	LOS ANGELES, CA	90069
KOSTER, HENRY	DIRECTOR-PRODUCER	3101 VILLAGE #3	CAMARILLO, CA	93010
KOSTMAYER, JOHN H	TV WRITER	555 W 57TH ST #1230	NEW YORK, NY	10019
KOSTOVE, ROBERTA	WRITER	8955 BEVERLY BLVD	LOS ANGELES, CA	90048
KOSTROFF, LARRY	DIRECTOR	2210 3RD ST	SANTA MONICA, CA	90405
KOSTYK, DENNIS M	DIRECTOR	6636 BROOKMONT TERR	NASHVILLE, TN	37205
KOSUGI, SHO	ACTOR	6605 HOLLYWOOD BLVD #220	HOLLYWOOD, CA	90028
KOTAR, SUSAN L	WRITER	13416 RAMONA PARKWAY	BALDWIN PARK, CA	91706
KOTCHEFF, TED	FILM DIRECTOR	13451 FIRTH DR	BEVERLY HILLS, CA	90210
KOTERO, APOLLONIA	ACTRESS	9000 SUNSET BLVD #1112	LOS ANGELES, CA	90069
KOTERO, PATTY	ACTRESS	9000 SUNSET BLVD #801	LOS ANGELES, CA	90069
KOTLENKO, SVETLANA	SOPRANO	CAMI, 165 W 57TH ST	NEW YORK, NY	10019
KOTLER, JOHN D	NEWS CORRESPONDENT	4403 GLENRIDGE ST	KENSINGTON, MD	20895
KOTLOWITZ, ROBERT	TV EXECUTIVE	WNET-TV, 356 W 58TH ST	NEW YORK, NY	10019
KOTT, GARY	TV WRITER	8955 BEVERLY BLVD	LOS ANGELES, CA	90048
KOTTKE, LEO	SINGER-GUITARIST	POST OFFICE BOX 7308	CARMEL, CA	93923
KOTTO, YAPHET	ACTOR	1930 CENTURY PARK W #303	LOS ANGELES, CA	90067
KOTTON, STEVE A	DIRECTOR	1947 GLENDON AVE #4	LOS ANGELES, CA	90025
KOTZKY, ALEX	CARTOONIST-ARTIST	NEWS AMERICA SYNDICATE		
		1703 KAISER AVE	IRVINE, CA	92714
KOTZWINKLE, WILLIAM	AUTHOR	THE BERKELEY PRESS		
		200 MADISON AVE	NEW YORK, NY	10016
KOUF, M JAMES, JR	WRITER-PRODUCER	2161 BASIL LN	LOS ANGELES, CA	90077
KOUGHAN, MARTIN J	WRITER	555 W 57TH ST #1230	NEW YORK, NY	10019
KOURIS, PETER C	DIRECTOR-PRODUCER	9 IVY TRAIL	ATLANTA, GA	30342
KOURY, REX	COMPOSER-CONDUCTOR	5370 HAPPY PINES DR	FORESTHILL, CA	95631
KOUT, JIRI	CONDUCTOR	MARIEDL ANDERS ARTISTS MGMT		
		535 EL CAMINO DEL MAR ST	SAN FRANCISCO, CA	94121
KOUT, WENDY	TV WRITER	842 N BEVERLY GLEN BLVD	LOS ANGELES, CA	90077
KOVACH, BILL	NEWS CORRESPONDENT	5504 PARK ST	CHEVY CHASE, MD	20815
KOVACH, STEVE	WRITER	8955 BEVERLY BLVD	LOS ANGELES, CA	90048
KOVACIC, ERNST	VIOLINIST	111 W 57TH ST #1203	NEW YORK, NY	10019
KOVACK MEHTA, NANCY	ACTRESS	SEE - METHA, NANCY KOVACK		
KOVACS, ESTHER	SOPRANO	111 W 57TH ST #1209	NEW YORK, NY	10019

Name	Occupation	Address	City/State	Zip
KOVACS, MARK G	CONDUCTOR	1364 PARK AVE	LONG BEACH, CA	90804
KOVAL, HENRY	WRITER	8955 BEVERLY BLVD	LOS ANGELES, CA	90048
KOVALCIK, JANET C	WRITER	555 W 57TH ST #1230	NEW YORK, NY	10019
KOVAR, RUDOLF	ACTOR	10000 RIVERSIDE DR #12-14	TOLUCA LAKE, CA	91602
KOVATS, KOLOS	BASS	1182 MARKET ST #311	SAN FRANCISCO, CA	94102
KOVE, MARTIN	ACTOR	2150 SUNSET CREST DR	LOS ANGELES, CA	90046
KOVEN, STANLEY A	WRITER	555 W 57TH ST #1230	NEW YORK, NY	10019
KOWAL, STEFANIE S	WRITER	8955 BEVERLY BLVD	LOS ANGELES, CA	90048
KOWALL, RONALD	ACTOR-TV WRITER	4544 LAUREL GROVE AVE	STUDIO CITY, CA	91604
KOWALSKI, FRANCIS LOUIS	WRITER-PRODUCER	7847 RANCHITO AVE	PANORAMA CITY, CA	91402
KOWALSKI, L BERNARD	TV DIRECTOR-PRODUCER	17524 COMMUNITY ST	NORTHRIDGE, CA	91324
KOZA, PATRICIA A	NEWS CORRESPONDENT	8608 LEONARD DR	SILVER SPRING, MD	20910
KOZAK, HARLEY	ACTOR	NBC-TV, 3000 W ALAMEDA AVE	BURBANK, CA	91523
KOZAK, RICHARD E	PHOTOGRAPHER	91 CATHEDRAL ST	ANNAPOLIS, MD	21401
KOZICHAROW, EUGENE	NEWS CORRESPONDENT	2202 CEDAR COVE CT	RESTON, VA	22091
KOZINSKI, SUSAN J	WRITER	555 W 57TH ST #1230	NEW YORK, NY	10019
KOZLOSKY, ANTHONY	GUITARIST	189 WALLACE RD #C-95	NASHVILLE, TN	37211
KOZLOWSKA, JOANNA	SOPRANO	CAMI, 165 W 57TH ST	NEW YORK, NY	10019
KOZOLL, MICHAEL	TV WRITER	1726 CRISLER WY	LOS ANGELES, CA	90069
KRACAUER, HANS	TV WRITER	8955 BEVERLY BLVD	LOS ANGELES, CA	90048
KRACHMALNICK, SAMUEL J	CONDUCTOR	11944 BRIARVALE LN	STUDIO CITY, CA	91604
KRAFT, JEAN	MEZZO-SOPRANO	CAMI, 165 W 57TH ST	NEW YORK, NY	10019
KRAFT, WILLIAM	COMPOSER	6957 CAMROSE DR	LOS ANGELES, CA	90068
KRAFTOWITZ, LARRY	NEWS CORRESPONDENT	40007 CONNECTICUT AVE, NW	WASHINGTON, DC	20009
KRAFTWERK	ROCK & ROLL GROUP	MARVIN KATZ MANAGEMENT		
		75 ROCKEFELLER PLAZA	NEW YORK, NY	10019
KRAGEN, KEN	TALENT AGENT	1112 N SHERBOURNE DR	LOS ANGELES, CA	90069
KRAININ, JULIAN	WRITER-PRODUCER	67-38 FLEET ST	FOREST HILLS, NY	11375
KRAJACIC, MICHAEL	ACTOR	1717 N HIGHLAND AVE #614	LOS ANGELES, CA	90028
KRAKAUER, DAVID	CLARINETIST	AFFILIATE ARTISTS, INC		
		37 W 65TH ST, 6TH FLOOR	NEW YORK, NY	10023
KRAKOW, GARY S	WRITER	555 W 57TH ST #1230	NEW YORK, NY	10019
KRAKOW, HOWARD	DIRECTOR	3267 LEDGEWOOD DR	HOLLYWOOD, CA	90068
KRAKOWER, GARY	ACTOR	823 N GENESEE AVE	LOS ANGELES, CA	90046
KRAKOWSKY, IRWIN	WRITER	555 W 57TH ST #1230	NEW YORK, NY	10019
KRAL, ROY	SINGER	ROSENFIELD, 714 LADD RD	BRONX, NY	10471
KRAMER, BERT	ACTOR	STONE, 1052 CAROL DR	LOS ANGELES, CA	90069
KRAMER, BRUCE	BASS	POST OFFICE BOX 884	NEW YORK, NY	10023
KRAMER, CARL	PHOTOGRAPHER	3414 PARKHILL PL	FAIRFAX, VA	22030
KRAMER, CECILE	WRITER	8955 BEVERLY BLVD	LOS ANGELES, CA	90048
KRAMER, DANIEL	DIRECTOR	110 W 86TH ST	NEW YORK, NY	10024
KRAMER, DAVID F	NEWS CORRESPONDENT	4850 CONNECTICUT AVE #1226, NW	WASHINGTON, DC	20006
KRAMER, ERWIN	DIRECTOR	5 N CLOVER DR	GREAT NECK, NY	11021
KRAMER, GENE	NEWS CORRESPONDENT	2144 CALIFORNIA ST, NW	WASHINGTON, DC	20008
KRAMER, JACK	TENNIS	231 N GLENROY PL	LOS ANGELES, CA	90049
KRAMER, JAMES G	TV DIRECTOR	167 CROSBY ST	NEW YORK, NY	10012
KRAMER, KENNETH L	WRITER-PRODUCER	8955 BEVERLY BLVD	LOS ANGELES, CA	90048
KRAMER, LAWRENCE S	NEWS CORRESPONDENT	5314 32ND ST, NW	WASHINGTON, DC	20015
KRAMER, LISBETH	WRITER	555 W 57TH ST #1230	NEW YORK, NY	10019
KRAMER, LOUIS	DIRECTOR	333 CABRILLO ST #D	COSTA MESA, CA	92627
KRAMER, MICHAEL	NEWS CORRESPONDENT	2911 OLIVE ST, NW	WASHINGTON, DC	20007
KRAMER, MICHAEL ERIC	ACTOR	1801 CENTURY PARK E #1415	LOS ANGELES, CA	90067
KRAMER, NORMAN	WRITER	555 W 57TH ST #1230	NEW YORK, NY	10019
KRAMER, R B	GUITARIST	226 WOODMONT CIR	NASHVILLE, TN	37205
KRAMER, REMI	FILM WRITER-DIRECTOR	ROUTE #2, BOX 262-B	SANDPOINT, ID	83864
KRAMER, RICHARD L	SCREENWRITER	8495 FOUNTAIN AVE E #1	LOS ANGELES, CA	90069
KRAMER, RICHARD M	WRITER	555 W 57TH ST #1230	NEW YORK, NY	10019
KRAMER, ROBERT	SINGER-GUITARIST	452 MOSS TRAIL RD #I-24	GOODLETTSVILLE, TN	37072
KRAMER, RONALD H	TV DIRECTOR	103 HIGH ST	ASHLAND, OR	97520
KRAMER, SEARLE	WRITER	277 S SPALDING DR #R-4	BEVERLY HILLS, CA	90212
KRAMER, STANLEY	FILM DIRECTOR	12386 RIDGE CIR	LOS ANGELES, CA	90049
KRAMER, STEPFANIE	ACTRESS-DIRECTOR	STEPHEN J CANNELL PRODS		
		7083 HOLLYWOOD BLVD	HOLLYWOOD, CA	90028
KRAMER, STEVEN	ACTOR	4150 RIVERSIDE DR #204	BURBANK, CA	91505
KRAMER, SUSAN J	DIRECTOR	DGA, 110 W 57TH ST	NEW YORK, NY	10019
KRAMER, TERRY ALLEN	THEATER PRODUCER	711 5TH AVE	NEW YORK, NY	10022
KRANE, JONATHAN	FILM PRODUCER	1888 CENTURY PARK E #1616	LOS ANGELES, CA	90067
KRANISH, ARTHUR	NEWS CORRESPONDENT	3611 TAYLOR ST	CHEVY CHASE, MD	20815
KRANITZ, IAN D	COMPOSER	6400 FRANKLIN AVE #115	LOS ANGELES, CA	90028
KRANKIES, THE	COMEDY DUO	266 BROAD ST	BIRMINGHAM	ENGLAND
KRANTZ, ALLEN	GUITARIST	333 TAYLOR AVE N #202	SEATTLE, WA	98109
KRANTZ, HOWARD	TV WRITER	8955 BEVERLY BLVD	LOS ANGELES, CA	90048
KRANTZ, RICHARD S	NEWS CORRESPONDENT	5151 WISCONSIN AVE, NW	WASHINGTON, DC	20016
KRANTZ, ROBERT	ACTOR	11726 SAN VICENTE BLVD #300	LOS ANGELES, CA	90049
KRANZ, PATRICIA	NEWS CORRESPONDENT	813 PHILADELPHIA AVE	SILVER SPRING, MD	20910
KRASNAPOLSKY, YURI	CONDUCTOR	GURTMAN, 162 W 56TH ST	NEW YORK, NY	10019
KRASNER, JEFFREY	DIRECTOR	55 HICKS ST #22	BROOKLYN, NY	11201
KRASNOW, IRIS	NEWS CORRESPONDENT	2800 WISCONSIN AVE, NW	WASHINGTON, DC	20005
KRASNY, PAUL	TV DIRECTOR	3620 GOODLAND DR	STUDIO CITY, CA	91604
KRATOCHVIL, FRANK	DIRECTOR	15935 BENT TREE FOREST CIR	DALLAS, TX	75248
KRAUS, ALFREDO	TENOR	61 W 62ND ST #6-F	NEW YORK, NY	10023
KRAUS, DEBORAH	WRITER	555 W 57TH ST #1230	NEW YORK, NY	10019
KRAUS, DETLEF	PIANIST	243 W END AVE #907	NEW YORK, NY	10023
KRAUS, ELKE	ACTRESS	3151 W CAHUENGA BLVD #310	LOS ANGELES, CA	90068
KRAUS, JOE	PUBLISHER-EDITOR	POST OFFICE BOX 55328	STOCKTON, CA	95205

Name	Occupation	Address	City	Zip
KRAUS, LILI	PIANIST	CAMI, 165 W 57TH ST	NEW YORK, NY	10019
KRAUS, MARY JO	NEWS CORRESPONDENT	11928 VALLEYWOOD DR	WHEATON, MD	20902
KRAUS, PHILIP	BARITONE	431 S DEARBORN ST #1504	CHICAGO, IL	60605
KRAUS, RICHARD S	PHOTOGRAPHER	354 OLD BRIDGE RD	EAST NORTHPORT, NY	11731
KRAUSE, CAROLYN	ACTRESS	10845 LINDBROOK DR #3	LOS ANGELES, CA	90024
KRAUSE, KENNETH	MUSIC ARRANGER	8209 BRENTVIEW CT	BRENTWOOD, TN	37027
KRAUSE, TOM	BARITONE	CAMI, 165 W 57TH ST	NEW YORK, NY	10019
KRAUSS, MARVIN A	THEATER PRODUCER	250 W 52ND ST	NEW YORK, NY	10019
KRAUSS, MITCHELL	NEWS CORRESPONDENT	CBS NEWS HEADQUARTERS #6		
		18 SHARIA SAHEL GHELEL	CAIRO	EGYPT
KRAUSS, PERRY	DIRECTOR-PRODUCER	22460 KEARNY ST	WOODLAND HILLS, CA	91364
KRAVETZ, WALTER	DIRECTOR	DGA, 110 W 57TH ST	NEW YORK, NY	10019
KRAVITZ, BOB	SPORTS WRITER-EDITOR	SPORTS ILLUSTRATED MAGAZINE		
		TIME & LIFE BUILDING		
		ROCKEFELLER CENTER	NEW YORK, NY	10020
KRAVITZ, ROBERT N	NEWS CORRESPONDENT	1822 COLUMBIA RD #306, NW	WASHINGTON, DC	20009
KRAVITZ, SY	ACTOR	4061 S CLOVERDALE AVE	LOS ANGELES, CA	90008
KRAY, WALTER	ACTOR	1528 ENSLEY AVE	LOS ANGELES, CA	90024
KRAYER, JIM	WRITER-PRODUCER	12 DAILEY DR	CROTON-ON-HUDSON, NY	10520
KREBS, DAVID	THEATER PRODUCER	65 W 55TH ST #306	NEW YORK, NY	10019
KREBS, JOE	NEWS CORRESPONDENT	17125 FOUNDER'S MILL DR	ROCKVILLE, MD	20855
KREBS, LAWRENCE	PHOTOJOURNALIST	4400 JENIFER ST, NW	WASHINGTON, DC	20015
KREBS, NANCY	ACTRESS	8004 LONG HILL RD	PASADENA, MD	21122
KREBS, SUSAN	ACTRESS	2709 1/2 STRONGS DR	VENICE, CA	90291
KREDENSER, PETER	PHOTOGRAPHER	2551 ANGELO DR	LOS ANGELES, CA	90077
KREEK, BOB	CABLE EXECUTIVE	HBO, 1100 AVE OF THE AMERICAS	NEW YORK, NY	10036
KREFTING, MARK	WRITER	555 W 57TH ST #1230	NEW YORK, NY	10019
KREGER, JAMES	CELLIST	157 W 57TH ST #1100	NEW YORK, NY	10019
KREIDER, PAUL	BARITONE	CAMI, 165 W 57TH ST	NEW YORK, NY	10019
KREIN, CATHERINE C	WRITER	555 W 57TH ST #1230	NEW YORK, NY	10019
KREINBERG, STEVE	TV WRITER	1645 COURTNEY AVE #10	LOS ANGELES, CA	90046
KREINDEL, MITCH	WRITER	1322 3/4 N LUCILE AVE	LOS ANGELES, CA	90026
KREISHER, OTTO	NEWS CORRESPONDENT	2708 N KENSINGTON ST	ARLINGTON, VA	22207
KREISMAN, STUART GLENN	TV WRITER	672 KELTON AVE #4	LOS ANGELES, CA	90024
KREIT, ALICE	WRITER	555 W 57TH ST #1230	NEW YORK, NY	10019
KREITSEK, HOWARD B	TV WRITER	6740 HILLPARK DR #203	LOS ANGELES, CA	90068
KREKEL, TIM & THE SLUGGERS	ROCK & ROLL GROUP	2308 21ST AVE S #9	NASHVILLE, TN	37212
KREKEL, TIMOTHY	GUITARIST	2311 BERNARD AVE	NASHVILLE, TN	37212
KREMENLIEV, BORIS A	COMPOSER-CONDUCTOR	10507 TROON AVE	LOS ANGELES, CA	90064
KREMER, GIDON	VIOLINIST	ICM, 40 W 57TH ST	NEW YORK, NY	10019
KREMER, SELMAN M	CABLE EXECUTIVE	8252 S HARVARD AVE	TULSA, OK	74136
KREMPEL, PETER W	DIRECTOR	18865 RIVERSIDE DR	BIRMINGHAM, MI	48009
KREPPEL, KATE WRIGHT	ACTRESS-DANCER	15300 KILLION ST	VAN NUYS, CA	91401
KREPPEL, PAUL	ACTOR	138 S REEVES DR #A	BEVERLY HILLS, CA	90212
KREPS, WILLIAM H	DIRECTOR	4200 LAND GREEN ST	ROCKVILLE, MD	20853
KRESH, PAUL	WRITER	555 W 57TH ST #1230	NEW YORK, NY	10019
KRESKI, CONNIE	ACTRESS-MODEL	MODELS & PROMOTIONS AGENCY		
		8560 SUNSET BLVD, 10TH FLOOR	LOS ANGELES, CA	90069
KRESKIN	PSYCHIC	201 N ROBERTSON BLVD #A	BEVERLY HILLS, CA	90211
KRESKY, CAROLYN	WRITER-PRODUCER	207 W 106TH ST	NEW YORK, NY	10025
KRESSEN, SAM	ACTOR	311 S 13TH ST	PHILADELPHIA, PA	19107
KRETCHMER, JOHN TED	DIRECTOR	4833 WILLOWCREST AVE	NORTH HOLLYWOOD, CA	91601
KRETMAN, LESTER A	NEWS CORRESPONDENT	NBC-TV, NEWS DEPARTMENT		
		4001 NEBRASKA AVE, NW	WASHINGTON, DC	20016
KRETZ, ROBERT OLDS	PHOTOGRAPHER	11001 FARMWOOD DR	RALEIGH, NC	27612
KREVAT, DAVID	ACTOR	350 W 51ST ST	NEW YORK, NY	10019
KRICHEFSKI, BERNARD	TV PRODUCER	JERICHO, 25 FIRS AVE	LONDON N10 3LY	ENGLAND
KRICHMAR, ANITA J	WRITER	555 W 57TH ST #1230	NEW YORK, NY	10019
KRIEGER, BARBARA A	NEWS CORRESPONDENT	14211 CATAMOUNT CT	WHEATON, MD	20906
KRIEGER, HAROLD	FILM DIRECTOR	1090 FIREPLACE RD	EAST HAMPTON, NY	11937
KRIEGER, NORMAN	PIANIST	AFFILIATE ARTISTS, INC		
		37 W 65TH ST, 6TH FLOOR	NEW YORK, NY	10023
KRIEGER, ROBBY	GUITARIST-SONGWRITER	2548 HUTTON DR	BEVERLY HILLS, CA	90210
KRIEGER, ROBIN	ACTRESS	CASSELL, 843 N SYCAMORE AVE	LOS ANGELES, CA	90038
KRIEGER, STU	SCREENWRITER	3650 MEIER ST	LOS ANGELES, CA	90066
KRIEGLER, PHILIP	TV EXECUTIVE	ABC-TV, 4151 PROSPECT AVE	LOS ANGELES, CA	90027
KRIEGMAN, MITCHELL	TV WRITER	555 W 57TH ST #1230	NEW YORK, NY	10019
KRIESA, CHRISTOPHER	ACTOR	1706 BROCKTON AVE	LOS ANGELES, CA	90025
KRIGE, ALICE	ACTRESS	9255 SUNSET BLVD #505	LOS ANGELES, CA	90069
KRIKES, PETER	WRITER	736 SANCHEZ ST	MONTEBELLO, CA	90640
KRIKHAM, WILLARD E	DIRECTOR	3549 N KNOLL DR	HOLLYWOOD, CA	90068
KRILOVICI, MARINA	SOPRANO	CAMI, 165 W 57TH ST	NEW YORK, NY	10019
KRIM, ARTHUR B	FILM EXECUTIVE	1875 CENTURY PARK E #300	LOS ANGELES, CA	90067
KRIMER, WORTHAM	ACTOR	11726 SAN VICENTE BLVD #300	LOS ANGELES, CA	90049
KRIMS, MILTON	WRITER	2155 RIDGEMONT DR	LOS ANGELES, CA	90046
KRINSKI, SANFORD	TV WRITER	674 VIA SANTA YNEZ	PACIFIC PALISADES, CA	90272
KRISCH, JEFFREY W	WRITER	555 W 57TH ST #1230	NEW YORK, NY	10019
KRISH, JOHN	FILM WRITER-DIRECTOR	ICM, 388-396 OXFORD ST	LONDON W1	ENGLAND
KRISKA, SHANNON	ACTRESS	427 N CANON DR #205	BEVERLY HILLS, CA	90210
KRISS, RONALD	WRITER-EDITOR	TIME/TIME & LIFE BLDG		
		ROCKEFELLER CENTER	NEW YORK, NY	10020
KRISTEN, ILENE	ACTRESS	1650 BROADWAY #302	NEW YORK, NY	10019
KRISTEN, LIDIA	ACTRESS	208 S BEVERLY DR #4	BEVERLY HILLS, CA	90212
KRISTEN, MARTA	ACTRESS	3800 BARHAM BLVD #303	LOS ANGELES, CA	90068
KRISTOF, EMORY, JR	PHOTOGRAPHER	5705 N 15TH RD	ARLINGTON, VA	22207

KRISTOFFERSON, KRIS	SINGER-ACTOR-WRITER	3179 SUMACRIDGE DR	MALIBU, CA	90265
KRISTYL	C & W GROUP	POST OFFICE BOX 113	HAYS, KS	67601
KRIVEN, ALBERT	TV EXECUTIVE	METROMEDIA, 205 E 67TH ST	NEW YORK, NY	10021
KRIVICKAS, ERAZINA	NEWS CORRESPONDENT	5808 KING ARTHUR WY	GLEN DALE, MD	20769
KRIVITZ, JANE	ACTRESS	4731 LAUREL CANYON BLVD #5	NORTH HOLLYWOOD, CA	91607
KRIZ, MARGARET E	NEWS CORRESPONDENT	4534 MIDDLETON LN	BETHESDA, MD	20814
KROFFT, SID	PUPPETEER-PRODUCER	7710 WOODROW WILSON DR	LOS ANGELES, CA	90046
KROFINA, SHARON L	COMPOSER	10342 LINDLEY AVE #331	NORTHRIDGE, CA	91326
KROFT, STEVE	NEWS CORRESPONDENT	CBS NEWS, 3111 ONE MAIN PL	DALLAS, TX	75250
KROH, ERIC	ACTOR	NBC-TV, 4151 PROSPECT AVE	LOS ANGELES, CA	90027
KROKUS	ROCK & ROLL GROUP	THE PRESS OFFICE, LTD		
		83 RIVERSIDE DR	NEW YORK, NY	10024
KROLL, GERRY	TV WRITER	8955 BEVERLY BLVD	LOS ANGELES, CA	90048
KROLL, JACK	FILM CRITIC	NEWSWEEK, 444 MADISON AVE	NEW YORK, NY	10022
KROLL, NATHAN	DIRECTOR-PRODUCER	201 E 77TH ST	NEW YORK, NY	10021
KROMPIER, PENNY	ACTRESS	5058 FOUNTAIN AVE	LOS ANGELES, CA	90029
KRONE, HELMUT	DIRECTOR	1 E 62ND ST	NEW YORK, NY	10021
KRONEMEYER, SANDRA	ACTRESS	9744 WILSHIRE BLVD #206	BEVERLY HILLS, CA	90212
KRONEN, BEN	ACTOR	4227 WHITSETT AVE #2	STUDIO CITY, CA	91604
KRONHOLM, WILLIAM C	NEWS CORRESPONDENT	1324 MASSACHUSETTS AVE, SE	WASHINGTON, DC	20003
KRONHOLZ, KENNETH	TRUMPETER	2019 MONTGOMERY PARKWAY	CLARKSVILLE, TN	37040
KRONICK, WILLIAM	WRITER-PRODUCER	950 N KINGS RD #115	LOS ANGELES, CA	90069
KRONISH, STEPHEN DAVID	WRITER	11922 KLING ST #103	NORTH HOLLYWOOD, CA	91607
KRONSBERG, JEREMY JOE	WRITER-PRODUCER	POST OFFICE BOX 683	MALIBU, CA	90265
KRONZUCKER, DIETER	NEWS CORRESPONDENT	3540 ORDWAY ST, NW	WASHINGTON, DC	20016
KROON, JERRY	DRUMMER	255 GRAYMONT DR	NASHVILLE, TN	37217
KROOPF, STANFORD J	WRITER	1744 CANFIELD AVE	LOS ANGELES, CA	90035
KROSNICK, JOEL	CELLIST	COLBERT, 111 W 57TH ST	NEW YORK, NY	10019
KROSS, KATHRYN J	WRITER	555 W 57TH ST #1230	NEW YORK, NY	10019
KROSS, RONALD	ACTOR	342 E 49TH ST	NEW YORK, NY	10017
KROST, BARRY	FILM PRODUCER	415 N CRESCENT DR	BEVERLY HILLS, CA	90212
KROUSE, IAN	COMPOSER	328 N WOODS AVE	FULLERTON, CA	92632
KROWN, RICHARD	DIRECTOR-PRODUCER	3906 BON HOMME RD	WOODLAND HILLS, CA	91364
KROYER, BILL	WRITER	6561 DENSMORE AVE	VAN NUYS, CA	91406
KRPAN, VLADIMIR	PIANIST	FINELL, 155 W 68TH ST	NEW YORK, NY	10023
KRUEGER, DANA	MEZZO-SOPRANO	CONE, 221 W 57TH ST	NEW YORK, NY	10019
KRUEGER, RANDALL B	WRITER	8955 BEVERLY BLVD	LOS ANGELES, CA	90048
KRUG, FRED	DIRECTOR-PRODUCER	5911 MC DONIE AVE	WOODLAND HILLS, CA	91367
KRUGER, HARDY	ACTOR	HOHE BLEICHEN 5	D-200 HAMBURG 36	WEST GERMANY
KRUGER, JACK	WRESTLER	POST OFFICE BOX 3859	STAMFORD, CT	06905
KRUGER, JEFFREY S	ENTERTAINMENT EXEC	POST OFFICE BOX 130, HOVE	EAST SUSSEX BN3 6QU	ENGLAND
KRUGER, PAMELA	WRITER-EDITOR	US MAGAZINE COMPANY		
		1 DAG HAMMARSKJOLD PLAZA	NEW YORK, NY	10017
KRUGMAN, LOU	ACTOR	2444 N PARISH PL	BURBANK, CA	91504
KRULWICH, SARA	PHOTOGRAPHER	45 W 10TH ST	NEW YORK, NY	10011
KRUMHOLZ, CHESTER	TV WRITER	3953 BON HOMME RD	WOODLAND HILLS, CA	91364
KRUPP, ROSEMARY H	WRITER	8955 BEVERLY BLVD	LOS ANGELES, CA	90048
KRUSCHE, LUTZ	NEWS CORRESPONDENT	GELMWOOD CT	ROCKVILLE, MD	20850
KRUSCHEN, JACK	ACTOR	4874 WINNETKA AVE	WOODLAND HILLS, CA	91364
KRUSE, JOHN	TV WRITER-DIRECTOR	THE OLD RECTORY		
		UPTON HELLIONS, CREDITON	DEVON	ENGLAND
KRUZE	ROCK & ROLL GROUP	POST OFFICE BOX 11283	RICHMOND, VA	23230
KRYSLUR, JULIE	TALENT AGENT	118 RIVERWAY ST #7	BOSTON, MA	02215
KRYSTOL	RHYTHM & BLUES GROUP	200 W 51ST ST #1410	NEW YORK, NY	10019
KRZEMIEN, DEE K	TV WRITER	8955 BEVERLY BLVD	LOS ANGELES, CA	90048
KSYNIAK, JOE	ACTOR	508 RAYMOND AVE #2	SANTA MONICA, CA	90405
KUBEK, TONY	SPORTSCASTER	3311 N MC DONALD	APPLETON, WI	54911
KUBERT, ADAM	CARTOONIST	THE NATIONAL LAMPOON		
		635 MADISON AVE	NEW YORK, NY	10022
KUBETIN, W RANDY	NEWS CORRESPONDENT	2120 18TH ST, NW	WASHINGTON, DC	20037
KUBICHAN, JON	WRITER	3878 BEVERLY RIDGE DR	SHERMAN OAKS, CA	91423
KUBIK, ALEX	ACTOR-WRITER	2305 LORENZO DR	LOS ANGELES, CA	90068
KUBIK, LAWRENCE	FILM WRITER-PRODUCER	9834 WANDA PARK DR	BEVERLY HILLS, CA	90210
KUBO, SHINTARO	NEWS CORRESPONDENT	6305 MAIDEN LN	BETHESDA, MD	20817
KUBOTA, ELIZABETH REIKO	ACTRESS	8235 SANTA MONICA BLVD #202	LOS ANGELES, CA	90046
KUBRICK, STANLEY	FILM WRITER-DIRECTOR	BOX 123, BOREHAMWOOD	HERTS	ENGLAND
KUBY, BERNIE	ACTOR	10445 EASTBORNE AVE #107	LOS ANGELES, CA	90024
KUCENIC, PAMELA	SOPRANO	61 W 62ND ST #6-F	NEW YORK, NY	10023
KUCHARO, J MICHAEL	DIRECTOR	5848 N 44TH ST	PHOENIX, AZ	85018
KUCHEROV, ALEXANDRIA	NEWS CORRESPONDENT	5033 N 35TH ST	ARLINGTON, VA	22207
KUCKRO, ROD W	NEWS CORRESPONDENT	216 E WINDSOR AVE	ALEXANDRIA, VA	22301
KUDLOW, MARK J	WRITER	8955 BEVERLY BLVD	LOS ANGELES, CA	90048
KUEBLER, DAVID	TENOR	CAMI, 165 W 57TH ST	NEW YORK, NY	10019
KUEHL, JOAN A	WRITER	555 W 57TH ST #1230	NEW YORK, NY	10019
KUEHN, ANDREW J, JR	DIRECTOR	8003 HOLLYWOOD BLVD	HOLLYWOOD, CA	90046
KUEHN, JOHN	DIRECTOR	2 PEMBROOK DR	STONY BROOK, NY	11790
KUERTI, ANTON	PIANIST	5720 MOSHOLU AVE #300	RIVERDALE, NY	10471
KUFF, LINKOLN	SINGER	POST OFFICE BOX 308	BURKEVILLE, VA	23922
KUGEL, CARL	TV DIRECTOR	658 HAVERFORD AVE	PACIFIC PALISADES, CA	90272
KUHL, MARGARET	MEZZO-SOPRANO	200 W 70TH ST #7-F	NEW YORK, NY	10023
KUHN, BOWIE	BASEBALL EXECUTIVE	320 N MURRAY AVE	RIDGEWOOD, NJ	07450
KUHN, KATHY	FIDDLER	135 BRINKHAVEN AVE #F-76	MADISON, TN	37115
KUHN, MARK A	NEWS CORRESPONDENT	36 CONCORD DR	BRUNSWICK, MD	21716
KUHN, MARTIN	NEWS CORRESPONDENT	4601 N PARK AVE	CHEVY CHASE, MD	20815
KUHN, RICHARD	DIRECTOR	1155 BROADWAY	NEW YORK, NY	10001

KRIS KRISTOFFERSON

STANLEY KUBRICK

HEDY LA MARR

JAKE LA MOTTA

LAURA LA PLANTE

LASH LA RUE

MATTHEW LA BORTEAUX

CHERYL LADD

LORENZO LAMAS

Name	Occupation	Address	City	Zip/Country
KUHN, STEVE	PIANIST	2490 CHANNING WY #406	BERKELEY, CA	94704
KUKOFF, BERNIE	WRITER-PRODUCER	1428 WARNER AVE	LOS ANGELES, CA	90024
KUKURUGYA, GIULIO	BASSO-BARITONE	111 W 57TH ST #1209	NEW YORK, NY	10019
KULCSAR, MIKE	ACTOR	17160 NORDHOFF ST	NORTHRIDGE, CA	91325
KULIK, BUZZ	DIRECTOR-PRODUCER	10425 CHARING CROSS RD	LOS ANGELES, CA	90024
KULIK, KAROL	WRITER-PRODUCER	42 BLOOMSBURY ST	LONDON WC1	ENGLAND
KULLER, SID	WRITER	8955 BEVERLY BLVD	LOS ANGELES, CA	90048
KULOK, SCOTT	DIRECTOR	DGA, 110 W 57TH ST	NEW YORK, NY	10019
KULOK, WINSTON	WRITER	555 W 57TH ST #1230	NEW YORK, NY	10019
KULP, NANCY	ACTRESS	TUSCAROLA FARM	PORT ROYAL, PA	17082
KULUVA, WILL	ACTOR	6243 TAPIA DR	MALIBU, CA	90265
KUM, KRISTOPHER	ACTOR	OCA, 34 GRAFTON TERR	LONDON NW5 4HY	ENGLAND
KUMAGAI, DENICE	ACTRESS	KELMAN, 7813 SUNSET BLVD	LOS ANGELES, CA	90046
KUMAKI, MARGO	NEWS CORRESPONDENT	4400 JENIFER ST, NW	WASHINGTON, DC	20015
KUNDE, GREGORY	TENOR	61 W 62ND ST #6-F	NEW YORK, NY	10023
KUNDERA, MILAN	NOVELIST	RUE SEBASTIEN BOTIN	PARIS	FRANCE
KUNEN, JAMES S	WRITER	TIME & PEOPLE MAGAZINE		
		TIME & LIFE BUILDING		
		ROCKEFELLER CENTER	NEW YORK, NY	10020
KUNES, STEVEN	WRITER	8428 MELROSE PL #C	LOS ANGELES, CA	90069
KUNEY, JACK	DIRECTOR	79 W 12TH ST	NEW YORK, NY	10011
KUNHARDT, PETER W	TV PRODUCER	ABC NEWS, 7 W 66TH ST	NEW YORK, NY	10023
KUNKEL, SHERMAN	CINEMATOGRAPHER	7715 SUNSET BLVD #150	LOS ANGELES, CA	90046
KUNTRY, H J	MUSICIAN	POST OFFICE BOX 4311	TALLAHASSEE, FL	32303
KUNTZ, JOHN	TV WRITER	CBS-TV, "THE GUIDING LIGHT"		
		51 W 52ND ST	NEW YORK, NY	10019
KUNZEL, ERICH	CONDUCTOR	500 5TH AVE #2050	NEW YORK, NY	10110
KUPCINET, IRV	COLUMNIST-TV HOST	5400 N SAINT LOUIS AVE	CHICAGO, IL	60625
KUPCINET, JERRY	TV DIRECTOR	16631 NANBERRY RD	ENCINO, CA	91436
KUPERBERG, HOWARD J	WRITER	608 LINCOLN BLVD #D	SANTA MONICA, CA	90402
KUPERMAN, ROBERT	DIRECTOR	2032 BALMER DR	LOS ANGELES, CA	90039
KUPFER, MARVIN	WRITER-PRODUCER	1037 5TH ST #6	SANTA MONICA, CA	90403
KUPPERMAN, ALVIN	ACTOR	119 N SWALL DR #3	LOS ANGELES, CA	90048
KUPPERSTEIN, GORDON	ACTOR	355 RIVERSIDE DR	NEW YORK, NY	10025
KUR, BOB	NEWS CORRESPONDENT	NBC-TV, NEWS DEPARTMENT	WASHINGTON, DC	20016
		4001 NEBRASKA AVE, NW	WASHINGTON, DC	20016
KURALT, CHARLES	NEWS CORRESPONDENT	CBS NEWS, 51 W 52ND ST	NEW YORK, NY	10019
KUREISHI, HANIF	SCREENWRITER	10000 SANTA MONICA BLVD #305	LOS ANGELES, CA	90067
KURETSKI, PHILIP	WRITER	1419 MAPLE ST #A	SANTA MONICA, CA	90405
KURI, JOHN ANTHONY	DIRECTOR-PRODUCER	9300 WILSHIRE BLVD #410	BEVERLY HILLS, CA	90212
KURIGAMI, KAZUMI	FILM DIRECTOR	CAMEL, INC, VILLA SERENA 302		
		2-33-18 JINGUMARE SHIBUYA-KU	TOKOYO	JAPAN
KURLAND, BARBARA	PIANIST	1805 KINGSBURY DR	NASHVILLE, TN	37215
KURLAND, SHELLY	VIOLINIST	1805 KINGSBURY DR	NASHVILLE, TN	37064
KURLAND, WENDY	MUSICIAN	2422 N BERRY'S CHAPEL RD	FRANKLIN, TN	37064
KUROIWA, TORU	NEWS CORRESPONDENT	11612 MILBERN DR	POTOMAC, MD	20854
KUROSAWA, AKIRA	FILM DIRECTOR	MATSUBARA-CHO, SETAGAYA-KU	TOYKO	JAPAN
KURSAR, ROBERT J	NEWS CORRESPONDENT	5642 INDEPENDENCE CIR	ALEXANDRIA, VA	22302
KURSAWE CYCLING TRIO	CYCLING TRIO	HALL, 138 FROG HOLLOW RD	CHURCHVILLE, PA	18966
KURTIS, BILL	NEWS CORRESPONDENT	CBS NEWS, 51 W 52ND ST	NEW YORK, NY	10019
KURTIS, KEN	ACTOR	5330 LANKERSHIM BLVD #210	NORTH HOLLYWOOD, CA	91601
KURTIS, STAN	SINGER	POST OFFICE BOX 255	SCARSDALE, NY	10583
KURTIS BLOW	RAPPER-RAPWRITER	SEE - BLOW, KURTIS		
KURTZ, BOB	SPORTSCASTER	CNN, 10 COLUMBUS CIR	NEW YORK, NY	10019
KURTZ, DAVID M	COMPOSER-CONDUCTOR	1500 N BEVERLY DR	BEVERLY HILLS, CA	90210
KURTZ, GARY	FILM PRODUCER	EMI STUDIOS, BOREHAMWOOD	HERTS	ENGLAND
KURTZ, HOWARD	NEWS CORRESPONDENT	2711 ORDWAY ST, NW	WASHINGTON, DC	20008
KURTZ, JENNIFER BURTON	TV WRITER	8383 WILSHIRE BLVD #923	BEVERLY HILLS, CA	90211
KURTZ, KATHERINE	WRITER	8840 WHEATLAND PL	SUN VALLEY, CA	91352
KURTZ, MARCIA JEAN	ACTRESS	888 7TH AVE #201	NEW YORK, NY	10019
KURTZ, SWOOZIE	ACTRESS	10100 SANTA MONICA BLVD #1600	LOS ANGELES, CA	90067
KURTZMAN, ANDREW	WRITER	555 W 57TH ST #1230	NEW YORK, NY	10019
KURZ, RON	SCREENWRITER	BERNSTEIN, 119 W 57TH ST	NEW YORK, NY	10019
KURZFELD, STEPHEN	TV WRITER	8955 BEVERLY BLVD	LOS ANGELES, CA	90048
KUSATSU, CLYDE	ACTOR	3364 LARGA AVE	LOS ANGELES, CA	90039
KUSHNER, DONALD	TV PRODUCER	1119 N MC CADDEN PL	HOLLYWOOD, CA	90038
KUSHNER, TRUUSJE	WRITER	555 W 57TH ST #1230	NEW YORK, NY	10019
KUSLEY, MICHAEL	DIRECTOR	1208-A THE STRAND	MANHATTAN BEACH, CA	90266
KUSS, RICHARD	ACTOR	POST OFFICE BOX 5617	BEVERLY HILLS, CA	90210
KUSSACK, ELAINE	TV WRITER	10 E 44TH ST #700	NEW YORK, NY	10017
KUST-BLAZIE DUO	MUSICAL DUO	431 S DEARBORN ST #1504	CHICAGO, IL	60605
KUTASH, JEFF	SINGER	1901 AVE OF THE STARS #1240	LOS ANGELES, CA	90067
KUTCHER, JACK	ACTOR	6605 HOLLYWOOD BLVD #220	HOLLYWOOD, CA	90028
KUTCHUKIAN, SYLVIA	SOPRANO	111 W 57TH ST #1209	NEW YORK, NY	10019
KUTEE	ACTRESS	8019 1/2 MELROSE AVE #3	LOS ANGELES, CA	90046
KUTER, KAY E	ACTOR	5331 DENNY AVE	NORTH HOLLYWOOD, CA	91601
KUTNER, EDWARD W	WRITER	710 PIER AVE	SANTA MONICA, CA	90405
KUTNER, MICHAEL	BARITONE	756 7TH AVE #67	NEW YORK, NY	10019
KUTNER, STEVE	CABLE EXECUTIVE	UNITED SATELLIE COMMUNICATIONS		
		1345 AVE OF THE AMERICAS	NEW YORK, NY	10105
KUTRZEBA, JOSEPH S	DIRECTOR-PRODUCER	229 E 79TH ST	NEW YORK, NY	10021
KUYPER, MARCIA	DIRECTOR	DGA, 110 W 57TH ST	NEW YORK, NY	10019
KUZELL, CHRISTOPHER	COMPOSER-CONDUCTOR	907 E EL CAMINO	SANTA MARIA, CA	93454
KUZNETSOV, DONALD J	WRITER	2332 PORTLAND ST	LOS ANGELES, CA	90007
KUZYK, MIMI	ACTRESS	870 N VINE ST #G	LOS ANGELES, CA	90038

Name	Occupation	Address	City	Zip
KWAK, SUNG	CONDUCTOR	1776 BROADWAY #504	NEW YORK, NY	10019
KWAN, NANCY	ACTRESS	CED, 261 S ROBERTSON BLVD	BEVERLY HILLS, CA	90211
KWAPIS, KENNETH W	TV DIRECTOR	2307 1/2 ECHO PARK AVE	LOS ANGELES, CA	90026
KWARTIN, LESLIE	TV PRODUCER	CBS-TV, 51 W 52ND ST	NEW YORK, NY	10019
KWASMAN, SAM	ACTOR	4331 VENTURA CANYON AVE #1	SHERMAN OAKS, CA	91423
KWELLA, PATRIZIA	SOPRANO	BYERS-SCHWALBE, 1 5TH AVE	NEW YORK, NY	10003
KWESKIN, JIM	SINGER-MUSICIAN	THE MOUNTAIN RAILROAD		
		3602 ATWOOD AVE	MADISON, WI	53714
KWESKIN, RONALD LEE	WRITER	308 S CANON DR	BEVERLY HILLS, CA	90212
KWONG, DIANA N	TV WRITER	8955 BEVERLY BLVD	LOS ANGELES, CA	90048
KWONG, JOSEPH C	SCREENWRITER	9100 SUNSET BLVD #360	LOS ANGELES, CA	90069
KWONG, PETER	ACTOR	8235 SANTA MONICA BLVD #202	LOS ANGELES, CA	90046
KWOUK, BURT	ACTOR	LONDON MANAGEMENT, LTD		
		235-241 REGENT ST	LONDON W1A 2JT	ENGLAND
KYLE, JOE	ACTOR	1612 SUNSET PLAZA DR	LOS ANGELES, CA	90069
KYLE, ROBERT G	TV DIRECTOR	POST OFFICE BOX 18052	DENVER, CO	80218
KYLIAN, JIRI	CHOREOGRAPHER	KONINGSSTRAAT 118	THE HAGUE	NETHERLANDS
KYNASTON, NICOLAS	ORGANIST	15 HIGH ST #621	HARTFORD, CT	06103
KYNE, TERRY	TV DIRECTOR	950 WILSON ST	LAGUNA BEACH, CA	92651
KYRIAKIS, WILLIAM C	DIRECTOR	FILMSMITH CO, 122 E 42ND ST	NEW YORK, NY	10017
KYUN, TA	HIGH WIRE ACT	POST OFFICE BOX 87	WEST LEBANON, NY	12195

Name	Occupation	Address	City	Zip
L A DREAM TEAM	SOUL GROUP	3610 W 6TH ST #536	LOS ANGELES, CA	90020
L'AMOUR, LOUIS	AUTHOR	100 LORING AVE	LOS ANGELES, CA	90024
LA BAR, ARTHUR	FRENCH HORNIST	ROUTE #3, BOX 20-A-2	BAXTER, TN	38544
		336 SUFFIELD RD	BIRMINGHAM, MI	48009
LA BEEF, SLEEPY	SINGER	PENNY, 30 GUINAN ST	WALTHAM, MA	02154
LA BELLA, VINCENZO	WRITER-PRODUCER	521 SWARTHMORE AVE	PACIFIC PALISADES, CA	90272
LA BELLE, PATTI	SINGER-ACTRESS	8730 SUNSET BLVD #PH-W	LOS ANGELES, CA	90069
LA BEQUE, KATIA & MARIELLE	PIANO DUO	ICM, 40 W 57TH ST	NEW YORK, NY	10019
LA BOUNTY, BILL	SINGER	9454 WILSHIRE BLVD #309	BEVERLY HILLS, CA	90212
LA BOUR, FREDERICK	GUITARIST	4001 GRAYSPOINT RD	JOELTON, TN	37080
LA BOW, HILARY	ACTRESS	STONE, 1052 CAROL DR	LOS ANGELES, CA	90069
LA BRECQUE, REBECCA	PIANIST	AIA, 60 E 42ND ST	NEW YORK, NY	10165
LA CAVA, WILLIAM	DIRECTOR	313 CENTRAL PARKWAY	MOUNT VERON, NY	10552
LA CENTRA-STEWART, PEG	ACTRESS	8272 MARMONT LN	LOS ANGELES, CA	90069
LA CIVITA, RICHARD P	DIRECTOR	INTERNATIONAL VISION, INC		
		9 W 57TH ST, 49TH FLOOR	NEW YORK, NY	10128
LA COSTA	MUSIC GROUP	1ST AMERICAN CENTER, 21ST FLOOR	NASHVILLE, TN	37203
LA CROIX, LEONARD A	CONDUCTOR	25445 VIA ESCOVAR	VALENCIA, CA	91355
LA FAYETTE, JOHN	ACTOR	9165 SUNSET BLVD #202	LOS ANGELES, CA	90069
LA FLEUR, ART	ACTOR	9165 SUNSET BLVD #202	LOS ANGELES, CA	90069
LA FOND, BERNADETTE	TV DIRECTOR	155 E 37TH ST	NEW YORK, NY	10016
LA FONTAINE, BARBARA	SPORTS WRITER-EDITOR	SPORTS ILLUSTRATED MAGAZINE		
		TIME & LIFE BUILDING		
		ROCKEFELLER CENTER	NEW YORK, NY	10020
LA FONTAINE, CHRISTOPHER	TV DIRECTOR	BBC-TV, KENSINGTON HOUSE		
		RICHMOND WY	LONDON W14	ENGLAND
LA FOSSE, LEOPOLD	VIOLINIST	KAY, 58 W 58TH ST	NEW YORK, NY	10019
LA FRENAIS, IAN	FILM WRITER-PRODUCER	WITZEND PRODUCTIONS		
		4 QUEENSBOROUGH STUDIOS	LONDON W2 3SQ	ENGLAND
LA FRENIERE, CELINE M	SCREENWRITER	2317 KIMRIDGE RD	BEVERLY HILLS, CA	90210
LA GOYA, ALEXANDRE	GUITARIST	COLBERT, 111 W 57TH ST	NEW YORK, NY	10019
LA GREGA, ROBERT	WRITER	555 W 57TH ST #1230	NEW YORK, NY	10019
LA GUARDIA, MICHAEL	ACTOR	76 PELHAM LN	WILTON, CT	06897
LA HENDRO, ROBERT	TV DIRECTOR	15446 SHERMAN WY	VAN NUYS, CA	91406
LA JOIE, ROGER	ACTOR	125 N AVON ST #C	BURBANK, CA	91505
LA LANNE, JACK	EXERCISE INSTRUCTOR	POST OFFICE BOX 2	HOLLYWOOD, CA	90078
LA LENA, ANNE F	NEWS CORRESPONDENT	3040 IDAHO AVE, NW	WASHINGTON, DC	20016
LA MAR, EVERETTE	ACTOR	POST OFFICE BOX 11749	MARINA DEL REY, CA	90295
LA MAR, LIN	GUITARIST	POST OFFICE BOX 183	ROGERSVILLE, AL	35652
LA MARCA	ROCK & ROLL GROUP	SCOTTI BROS, 2128 PICO BLVD	SANTA MONICA, CA	90405
LA MARCA, LOUIS	NEWS CORRESPONDENT	6620 POTOMAC AVE	ALEXANDRIA, VA	22307
LA MARR, CINNIMIN	SINGER	POST OFFICE BOX 11321		
		FLAGLER STATION	MIAMI, FL	33101
LA MARR, HEDY	ACTRESS	THE NORTH BAY VILLAGE		
		7915 EAST DR #2-L	MIAMI, FL	33141
LA MAY, ROGER C	WRITER	555 W 57TH ST #1230	NEW YORK, NY	10019
LA MOND, BILL	TV WRITER	2605 ASTRAL DR	LOS ANGELES, CA	90046
LA MOND, JO	TV WRITER	2605 ASTRAL DR	LOS ANGELES, CA	90046
LA MOTTA, JAKE	BOXER	357 E 57TH ST	NEW YORK, NY	10022
LA MOTTA, JOHN	ACTOR	6380 WILSHIRE BLVD #1600	LOS ANGELES, CA	90048
LA MOTTA, VICKI	MODEL	520 EAST AVE	NORTH MIAMI, FL	10022
LA MOUR, DOROTHY	ACTRESS	5309 GOODLAND AVE	NORTH HOLLYWOOD, CA	91607
LA MURA, MARK	ACTOR	888 7TH AVE #1800	NEW YORK, NY	10019
LA PIERE, GEORGANNE	ACTRESS	4555 FULTON AVE #111	SHERMAN OAKS, CA	91423
LA PIERRE, JOHN	TENOR	HILLYER, 250 W 57TH ST	NEW YORK, NY	10107

Name	Occupation	Address	City
LA PLANTE, ANDRE	PIANIST	CAMI, 165 W 57TH ST	NEW YORK, NY 10019
LA PLANTE, LAURA	ACTRESS	58 LA RONDA DR	RANCHO MIRAGE, CA 92270
LA ROCCA, SONNY	ACTOR	10716 MOORPARK ST	NORTH HOLLYWOOD, CA 91602
LA ROCQUE, STEPHEN E	WRITER	8955 BEVERLY BLVD	LOS ANGELES, CA 90048
LA ROSA, JULIUS	ACTOR-SINGER	19 W 44TH ST #1500	NEW YORK, NY 10036
LA RUE, D C	SINGER	111 W 57TH ST #1204	NEW YORK, NY 10019
LA RUE, DANNY	ACTOR	ZAHL, 57 GREAT CUMBERLAND PL	LONDON W1H 7LJ ENGLAND
LA RUE, FLORENCE	SINGER	POST OFFICE BOX 10307	BEVERLY HILLS, CA 90213
LA RUE, LASH	ACTOR	POST OFFICE BOX 219	CONWAY, AK 72032
LA RUSCH, SUZANNE	ACTRESS	1133 N CEDAR ST	GLENDALE, CA 91207
LA RUSSA, ADRIENNE	ACTRESS	6430 SUNSET BLVD #1203	LOS ANGELES, CA 90028
LA RUSSO, LOUIS, III	WRITER	555 W 57TH ST #1230	NEW YORK, NY 10019
LA SAGE, CAROL	MEZZO-SOPRANO	431 S DEARBORN ST #1504	CHICAGO, IL 60605
LA SALLE, JOHN T	COMPOSER	11049 KLING ST	NORTH HOLLYWOOD, CA 91602
LA SALLE, RICHARD	COMPOSER	POST OFFICE BOX 4679	CARMEL, CA 93921
LA SALLE, RON	SINGER	41 BRITAIN ST #200	TORONTO, ONT CANADA
LA SALLE, RON & THE TWIN BULLET	ROCK & ROLL GROUP	POST OFFICE BOX 4087	MISSOULA, MT 59806
LA SCOLA, VINCENZO	TENOR	CAMI, 165 W 57TH ST	NEW YORK, NY 10019
LA TORRE, TONY	ACTOR	3575 W CAHUENGA BLVD #320	LOS ANGELES, CA 90068
LA TOURNEAUX, ROBERT	ACTOR	1155 3RD AVE	NEW YORK, NY 10021
LA VALLEY, DOUG	SINGER	ACE, 3407 GREEN RIDGE DR	NASHVILLE, TN 37214
LA VETTE, MAUREEN	ACTRESS	10587 CUSHDON AVE	LOS ANGELES, CA 90064
LA ZELLE, JAMES	ACTOR	1343 MALTMAN AVE #6	LOS ANGELES, CA 90026
LAARZ, WILLIAM	TRUMPETER	600 WHISPERING HILLS DR #K-9	NASHVILLE, TN 37211
LAAZ ROCKET	ROCK & ROLL GROUP	POST OFFICE BOX 1616	NOVATO, CA 94948
LABAN	ROCK & ROCK DUO	MEGA RECORDS SCANDINAVIA	
		FREDERIKSBORGGARDE 31	DK-1360 COPENHAGEN DENMARK
LABICH, RICHARD A	PUBLISHING EXECUTIVE	TV-CABLE WEEK, 123 MAIN ST	WHITE PLAINS, NY 10601
LABINE, CLAIRE	WRITER	555 W 57TH ST #1230	NEW YORK, NY 10019
LABOE, ART	RADIO PERSONALITY	KRLA, 1401 S OAK KNOLL AVE	PASADENA, CA 91109
LABORTEAUX, FRANCIS	ACTRESS	13111 VENTURA BLVD #204	STUDIO CITY, CA 91604
LABORTEAUX, PATRICK	ACTOR	POST OFFICE BOX 1399	BURBANK, CA 91507
LABRADA, LEE	BODYBUILDER	POST OFFICE BOX 690971	HOUSTON, TX 77269
LABUNSKI, STEPHEN B	RADIO EXECUTIVE	IRTS, 420 LEXINGTON AVE	NEW YORK, NY 10170
LACEY, DEBORAH	ACTRESS	6310 SAN VICENTE BLVD #407	LOS ANGELES, CA 90048
LACEY, RONALD	ACTOR	EDWARDS, 275 KENNINGTON RD	LONDON SE11 6BY ENGLAND
LACEY, RONALD	ACTOR	9255 SUNSET BLVD #505	LOS ANGELES, CA 90069
LACEYS, THE	GOSPEL GROUP	4305 S 70TH ST	TAMPA, FL 33619
LACHICA, EDUARDO	NEWS CORRESPONDENT	1301 20TH ST #410, NW	WASHINGTON, DC 20036
LACHMAN, BRAD	TV WRITER	8955 BEVERLY BLVD	LOS ANGELES, CA 90048
LACHMAN, CLIFFORD NEIL	DIRECTOR	2652 N BEACHWOOD DR	LOS ANGELES, CA 90068
LACHMAN, MORT	TV WRITER-PRODUCER	1356 LAUREL WY	BEVERLY HILLS, CA 90210
LACK, ANDREW	TV WRITER-PRODUCER	CBS-TV, 524 W 57TH ST	NEW YORK, NY 10019
LACK, FREDELL	VIOLINIST	KAY, 58 W 58TH ST	NEW YORK, NY 10019
LACKEY, JIM	NEWS CORRESPONDENT	2840 RAYMOND CT	FALLS CHURCH, VA 22042
LACY, CAROLYNE	WRITER	3476 TROY DR	LOS ANGELES, CA 90068
LACY, CLAY	DIRECTOR	DGA, 7950 SUNSET BLVD	LOS ANGELES, CA 90048
LACY, DON & COUNTRY SPECIAL	C & W GROUP	POST OFFICE BOX 82	GREENBRIER, TN 37073
LACY, JERRY	ACT-WRI-DIR	870 N VINE ST #G	LOS ANGELES, CA 90038
LACY, N LEE	DIRECTOR	8446 MELROSE PL	LOS ANGELES, CA 90069
LACY, PAOLI	CLOWN	2701 COTTAGE WY #14	SACRAMENTO, CA 95825
LACY, WILLIAM	DIRECTOR	819 N BEVERLY BLVD	LOS ANGELES, CA 90077
LADD, ALAN, JR	FILM EXECUTIVE	706 N ELM DR	BEVERLY HILLS, CA 90210
LADD, CHERYL	ACTRESS-SINGER	9051 ORIOLE WY	LOS ANGELES, CA 90069
LADD, DAVID	ACTOR	1234 N MAPLETON DR	LOS ANGELES, CA 90069
LADD, DIANE	ACTRESS	10351 SANTA MONICA BLVD #211	LOS ANGELES, CA 90025
LADD, LESLIE	MUSICIAN	1501 EASTLAND AVE	NASHVILLE, TN 37206
LADD, MARGARET	ACTRESS	444 21ST ST	SANTA MONICA, CA 90402
LADENDORFF, MARCIA	NEWS CORRESPONDENT	TBS, 1050 TECHWOOD DR, NW	ATLANTA, GA 30318
LADERMAN, EZRA	COMPOSER	POST OFFICE BOX 689	TEANECK, NJ 07666
LADMAN, CATHY	ACTRESS	8075 W 3RD ST #303	LOS ANGELES, CA 90048
LADY BROWN SUGAR BELL	C & W GROUP	PROCESS, 439 WILEY AVE	FRANKLIN, PA 16323
LAEMMLE, NINA	WRITER	8955 BEVERLY BLVD	LOS ANGELES, CA 90048
LAFFERTY, MARTIN C	TV PRODUCER	219 PERIMETER CENTER PARKWAY	ATLANTA, GA 30346
LAFFERTY, PERRY	TV EXECUTIVE	335 S BRISTOL AVE	LOS ANGELES, CA 90049
LAFFERTY, STEVE	CABLE EXECUTIVE	SHOWTIME, 1633 BROADWAY	NEW YORK, NY 10019
LAFFONT, JEAN-PIERRE	PHOTOGRAPHER	322 W 72ND ST	NEW YORK, NY 10023
LAGANA, JOSEPH T	WRITER	8955 BEVERLY BLVD	LOS ANGELES, CA 90048
LAGG, FREDERICK S	WRITER	2112 PERRY AVE	REDONDO BEACH, CA 90278
LAGIOS, MARIA	SOPRANO	431 S DEARBORN ST #1504	CHICAGO, IL 60605
LAGLER, RENE	ART DIRECTOR	151 S EL CAMINO DR	BEVERLY HILLS, CA 90212
LAGNADO, LUCETTE	NEWS CORRESPONDENT	1718 "P" ST, NW	WASHINGTON, DC 20036
LAGOMARSINO, RON	TV DIRECTOR	36 W 84TH ST	NEW YORK, NY 10024
LAGRUS, ALBERT R	TV WRITER	8955 BEVERLY BLVD	LOS ANGELES, CA 90048
LAH, MICHAEL R	DIRECTOR-PRODUCER	12211 HUSTON ST	NORTH HOLLYWOOD, CA 91607
LAHTI, CHRISTINE	ACTRESS	10100 SANTA MONICA BLVD #1600	LOS ANGELES, CA 90067
LAHTI, GARY	ACTOR	10100 SANTA MONICA BLVD #1600	LOS ANGELES, CA 90067
LAI, SINTING	NEWS REPORTER	TIME/TIME & LIFE BLDG	
		ROCKEFELLER CENTER	NEW YORK, NY 10020
LAID BACK	ROCK & ROLL GROUP	POST OFFICE BOX 1074	DK-1008 COPENHAGEN DENMARK
LAIDMAN, HARVEY	TV DIRECTOR	4923 ENCINO TERR	ENCINO, CA 91316
LAIFFER, DONALD M	WRITER	7250 FRANKLIN AVE #A-215	LOS ANGELES, CA 90046
LAIKIN, PAUL	TV WRITER	555 W 57TH ST #1230	NEW YORK, NY 10019

Name	Occupation	Address	City	Zip
LAIMAN, LEAH	TV WRITER	8955 BEVERLY BLVD	LOS ANGELES, CA	90048
LAINE, CLEO	SINGER	THE OLD RECTORY WAVENDON	MILTON KEYNES MK17 8LT	ENGLAND
LAINE, FRANKIE	SINGER-ACTOR	352 SAN GORGONIO ST	SAN DIEGO, CA	92106
LAINE & DANKWORTH	JAZZ DUO	10100 SANTA MONICA BLVD #1600	LOS ANGELES, CA	90067
LAIRD, BOB	CARTOONIST	POST OFFICE BOX 500	WASHINGTON, DC	20044
LAIRD, JACK	WRITER-PRODUCER	MCA/UNIVERSAL STUDIOS, INC		
		100 UNIVERSAL CITY PLAZA #422	UNIVERSAL CITY, CA	91608
LAIRD, JOYCE ANNE	ACTRESS	13207 WENTWORTH ST	ARLETA, CA	91331
LAIRD, MARLENA	TV DIRECTOR	2729 WESTSHIRE DR	HOLLYWOOD, CA	90068
LAKE, GREG	SINGER-GUITARIST	ATI, 888 7TH AVE, 21ST FLOOR	NEW YORK, NY	10106
LAKE, OLIVER & JUMP UP	JAZZ GROUP	FAST LN PRODUCTIONS		
		4590 MAC ARTHUR BLVD, NW	WASHINGTON, DC	20007
LAKE, PETER A	WRITER-EXECUTIVE	27 OUTRIGGER ST	MARINA DEL REY, CA	90292
LAKELAND, CHRISTINE	SINGER-GUITARIST	POST OFFICE BOX 8882	UNIVERSAL CITY, CA	91608
LAKES, GARY	TENOR	ICM, 40 W 57TH ST	NEW YORK, NY	10019
LAKESIDE	RHYTHM & BLUES GROUP	THE GRIFF COMPANY		
		1635 N CAHUENGA BLVD	LOS ANGELES, CA	90028
LAKI, KRISZTINA	SOPRANO	CAMI, 165 W 57TH ST	NEW YORK, NY	10019
LAKIN, HOWARD	TV WRITER	4751 DON PIO DR	WOODLAND HILLS, CA	91364
LAKIN, RITA	WRITER	1435 LINDACREST DR	BEVERLY HILLS, CA	90210
LAKSO, EDWARD	TV WRITER	2075 BENEDICT CANYON RD	BEVERLY HILLS, CA	90210
LAKSO, LAURIE	TV WRITER	8955 BEVERLY BLVD	LOS ANGELES, CA	90048
LAL, BRIJENDRA B	WRITER	555 W 57TH ST #1230	NEW YORK, NY	10019
LALA, JOE	ACTOR	1741 N IVAR AVE #221	LOS ANGELES, CA	90028
LALLEMAND, IRINA D	WRITER	555 W 57TH ST #1230	NEW YORK, NY	10019
LALLY, MICHAEL DAVID	ACTOR	3800 BARHAM BLVD #303	LOS ANGELES, CA	90068
LALLY, ROBERT J	TV DIRECTOR	4224 BLUEBELL AVE	BURBANK, CA	91505
LALLY, WILLIAM	ACTOR	8721 SUNSET BLVD #200	LOS ANGELES, CA	90069
LALLY-KNOWLES, ROSE MARIE	NEWS CORRESPONDENT	8717 DEBORAH ST	CLINTON, MD	20735
LAMAR, JACOB V, JR	WRITER-EDITOR	TIME/TIME & LIFE BLDG		
		ROCKEFELLER CENTER	NEW YORK, NY	10020
LAMAS, LORENZO	ACTOR	7850 WOODROW WILSON DR	LOS ANGELES, CA	90046
LAMB, ANNABEL	SINGER	BARRY DICKINS, ITB HAMMERHOUSE	LONDON W1	ENGLAND
LAMB, BILL	GUITARIST	4215 SNEED RD	NASHVILLE, TN	37211
LAMB, BRIAN P	NEWS CORRESPONDENT	400 N CAPITOL ST, NW	WASHINGTON, DC	20001
LAMB, CHARLES	ACTOR	37 CHISWICK LN #1, CHISWICK	LONDON W4	ENGLAND
LAMB, DR LAWRENCE	COLUMNIST	NEWS AMERICA SYNDICATE		
		1703 KAISER AVE	IRVINE, CA	92714
LAMB, GILL	ACTOR	6476 SAN MARCO CIR	HOLLYWOOD, CA	90068
LAMB, JULIA	SPORTS WRITER-EDITOR	SPORTS ILLUSTRATED MAGAZINE		
		TIME & LIFE BUILDING		
		ROCKEFELLER CENTER	NEW YORK, NY	10020
LAMB, LARRY	ACTOR	LONDON MANAGEMENT, LTD		
		235-241 REGENT ST	LONDON W1A 2JT	ENGLAND
LAMB, MARGARET	TALENT AGENT	6605 HOLLYWOOD BLVD #220	HOLLYWOOD, CA	90028
LAMBACK, JANICE A	WRITER	555 W 57TH ST #1230	NEW YORK, NY	10019
LAMBERT, DENNIS	MUSICIAN	15625 VANDORF PL	ENCINO, CA	91316
LAMBERT, EDWARD	RECORD EXECUTIVE	23445 LOS ENCINOS WY	WOODLAND HILLS, CA	91367
LAMBERT, GARLAND & THE STONEY C	BLUEGRASS GROUP	POST OFFICE BOX 25371	CHARLOTTE, NC	28212
LAMBERT, GAVIN	SCREENWRITER	8955 BEVERLY BLVD	LOS ANGELES, CA	90048
LAMBERT, HORACE M	PHOTOGRAPHER	7313 MAPLE AVE	CHEVY CHASE, MD	20015
LAMBERT, JERRY	SINGER	POST OFFICE BOX 25371	CHARLOTTE, NC	28212
LAMBERT, L W & BLUE RIVER BOYS	C & W GROUP	ROUTE #1	OLIN, NC	28860
LAMBERT, LAWRENCE A	PHOTOGRAPHER	232 6TH ST, SE	WASHINGTON, DC	20003
LAMBERT, MARK	MUSICIAN	180 WALLACE RD #U-13	NASHVILLE, TN	37211
LAMBERT, MARK ROBERT	DIRECTOR	DGA, 7950 SUNSET BLVD	LOS ANGELES, CA	90046
LAMBERT, PAUL	ACTOR	2806 BARRY AVE	LOS ANGELES, CA	90064
LAMBERT, ROBERT	DIRECTOR	16941 BOLLINGER ST	SEPULVEDA, CA	91343
LAMBERT, VERITY	TV PRODUCER	365 EUSTON RD	LONDON NW1	ENGLAND
LAMBIDAKIS, STEPHANIE E	NEWS CORRESPONDENT	2133 WISCONSIN AVE, NW	WASHINGTON, DC	20007
LAMBIE, JOE	ACTOR	SF & A, 121 N SAN VICENTE BLVD	BEVERLY HILLS, CA	90211
LAMBLE, LLOYD	ACTOR	55 GRENCROFT GARDENS	LONDON NW6	ENGLAND
LAMBRECHT, IRVING	TV DIRECTOR	4307 DON ARELLANES DR	LOS ANGELES, CA	90008
LAMBRECHT, WILLIAM	NEWS CORRESPONDENT	327 "C" ST, SE	WASHINGTON, DC	20003
LAMBRINOS, VASSILI	ACTOR	19 W 44TH ST #1500	NEW YORK, NY	10036
LAMBRO, DONALD	NEWS CORRESPONDENT	6605 GREENVIEW LN	SPRINGFIELD, VA	22152
LAMBRO, PHILLIP	COMPOSER-CONDUCTOR	1888 CENTURY PARK E #10	LOS ANGELES, CA	90067
LAMBROS, HELEN	ACTRESS	10850 RIVERSIDE DR #501	NORTH HOLLYWOOD, CA	91602
LAMENSDORF, LEONARD R	SCREENWRITER	8955 BEVERLY BLVD	LOS ANGELES, CA	90048
LAMEY, JUDY A	WRITER	555 W 57TH ST #1230	NEW YORK, NY	10019
LAMEY, T K	ACTOR	6125 GLEN OAK ST #5	LOS ANGELES, CA	90068
LAMKIN, KEN	DIRECTOR-PRODUCER	6876 ANGLEBUFF CIR	DALLAS, TX	75248
LAMM, KAREN	ACTRESS	3907 W ALAMEDA AVE #101	BURBANK, CA	91505
LAMM, ROBERT	MUSICIAN-SONGWRITER	1526 N BEVERLY DR	BEVERLY HILLS, CA	90210
LAMMERS, PAUL	TV DIRECTOR	DGA, 110 W 57TH ST	NEW YORK, NY	10019
LAMNECK, JOSEPH D	DIRECTOR	DGA, 110 W 57TH ST	NEW YORK, NY	10019
LAMOLINARA, GUY V	NEWS CORRESPONDENT	419 OLD TOWN CT	ALEXANDRIA, VA	22314
LAMONT, DUNCAN	ACTOR	SALEHURST FARM, BLACKHAM		
		NEAR TUNBRIDGE, WELLS	KENT	ENGLAND
LAMONT, JOHN	ACTOR	9145 SUNSET BLVD #228	LOS ANGELES, CA	90069
LAMONT, PEGGY	TV EXECUTIVE	TOMORROW ENTERTAINMENT		
		405 LEXINGTON AVE	NEW YORK, NY	10174
LAMONT, ROBERT C	GUITARIST	ROUTE #5, BOX 264		
		SOUTH HARPETH RD	NASHVILLE, TN	37221
LAMOREAUX, E S, III "BUD"	TV PRODUCER	CBS-TV, 524 W 57TH ST	NEW YORK, NY	10019

LAKESIDE
Tiemeyer McCain • Mark Wood • Fred Alexander • Marvin Craig
Steven Shockley • Fred Lewis • Otis Stokes • Thomas Shelby • Norman Beavers

HUEY LEWIS & THE NEWS
Sean Hopper • Billy Gibson • Johnny Colla • Huey Lewis • Mario Cipollina • Chris Hayes

Name	Occupation	Address	City	Zip
LAMOREAUX, ERNEST S	WRITER	555 W 57TH ST #1230	NEW YORK, NY	10019
LAMOT, DENISE G	NEWS CORRESPONDENT	1735 NEW HAMPSHIRE AVE, NW		
		SUITE #101	WASHINGTON, DC	20009
LAMPARSKI, RICHARD	AUTHOR	3289 CARSE DR	LOS ANGELES, CA	90068
LAMPE, ROY	WRITER	555 W 57TH ST #1230	NEW YORK, NY	10019
LAMPELL, MILLARD	TV WRITER	ICM, 8899 BEVERLY BLVD	LOS ANGELES, CA	90048
LAMPELL, ROMONA	TV WRITER	8955 BEVERLY BLVD	LOS ANGELES, CA	90048
LAMPERT, AL	ACTOR	42 NEW RD, BRENTFORD	MIDDLESEX	ENGLAND
LAMPERT, JEFFREY	ACTOR	3151 W CAHUENGA BLVD #310	LOS ANGELES, CA	90068
LAMPERT, RACHEL	DANCER	AFFILIATE ARTIST, INC		
		37 W 65TH ST, 6TH FLOOR	NEW YORK, NY	10023
LAMPERT, ZOHRA	ACTRESS	ICM, 8899 BEVERLY BLVD	LOS ANGELES, CA	90048
LAMPKIN, CHARLES	ACTOR	8721 SUNSET BLVD #104	LOS ANGELES, CA	90069
LAMPL, HANS	CONDUCTOR	12631 ROMAINE WY	GARDEN GROVE, CA	92645
LAMY, CATHERINE	SOPRANO	MUNRO, 334 W 72ND ST	NEW YORK, NY	10023
LANCASTER, BURT	ACTOR-DIRECTOR	2220 AVE OF THE STARS #1805	LOS ANGELES, CA	90067
LANCASTER, JOAN	ACTRESS	CED, 261 S ROBERTSON BLVD	BEVERLY HILLS, CA	90211
LANCASTER, JOANNA	FILM PRODUCER	2220 AVE OF THE STARS #1805	LOS ANGELES, CA	90067
LANCASTER, LUCIE	ACTRESS	30 W 60TH ST	NEW YORK, NY	10023
LANCASTER, STUART	ACTOR	3096 LAKE HOLLYWOOD DR	LOS ANGELES, CA	90068
LANCE, MAJOR	SINGER	FONTANA, 161 W 54TH ST	NEW YORK, NY	10019
LANCE, PETER	COMPOSER	5302 LAUREL CANYON BLVD	NORTH HOLLYWOOD, CA	91607
LANCELLOTTI, JOHN	WRITER	555 W 57TH ST #1230	NEW YORK, NY	10019
LANCHBERY, JOHN	CONDUCTOR	ICM, 40 W 57TH ST	NEW YORK, NY	10019
LAND, DAVID	FILM PROD-EXEC	STIGWOOD, 118 WARDOUR ST	LONDON W1	ENGLAND
LAND, EDWARD W	WRITER-DIRECTOR	11645 KIOWA AVE #4	LOS ANGELES, CA	90049
LAND, PETER	ACTOR	LONDON MANAGEMENT, LTD		
		235-241 REGENT ST	LONDON W1A 2JT	ENGLAND
LAND, PETER W	CONDUCTOR	26 VIA MEDIA	TUSTIN, CA	92680
LAND, RALPH	DRUMMER	128 ELNORA DR	HENDERSONVILLE, TN	37075
LANDA, DENNIS G	WRITER	4701 BALBOA AVE	ENCINO, CA	91316
LANDAKER, GREGG	SOUND ENGINEER	7131 DEVERON RIDGE RD	CANOGA PARK, CA	91307
LANDAU, EDIE	FILM PRODUCER	2029 CENTURY PARK E #460	LOS ANGELES, CA	90067
LANDAU, ELY	FILM PRODUCER	2276 CENTURY HILL	LOS ANGELES, CA	90067
LANDAU, JUDY	CASTING DIRECTOR	568 N LARCHMONT BLVD	LOS ANGELES, CA	90004
LANDAU, LUCY	ACTRESS	83-80 118TH ST	KEW GARDENS, NY	11415
LANDAU, MARTIN	ACTOR	12725 VENTURA BLVD #E	STUDIO CITY, CA	91604
LANDAU, RICHARD	SCREENWRITER	10377 W OLYMPIC BLVD	LOS ANGELES, CA	90064
LANDAU, SHELLY	WRITER	8955 BEVERLY BLVD	LOS ANGELES, CA	90048
LANDAU, SIEGFRIED	CONDUCTOR	26 OGDEN RD	SCARSDALE, NY	10583
LANDAU, TERRY	TV WRITER	8462 WYNDHAM RD	LOS ANGELES, CA	90046
LANDAU, VIVIEN	ACTRESS	MOUNT HOLLY RD E	KATONAH, NY	10536
LANDAY, ADDIE	ACTRESS	4731 LAUREL CANYON BLVD #5	NORTH HOLLYWOOD, CA	91607
LANDAY, JERRY M	NEWS CORRESPONDENT	CBS NEWS, 524 W 57TH ST	NEW YORK, NY	10019
LANDAY, JONATHAN	NEWS CORRESPONDENT	2125 NEWPORT PL, NW	WASHINGTON, DC	20037
LANDE, ART	PIANIST	2490 CHANNING WY #406	BERKELEY, CA	94704
LANDE, NATHANIEL	WRITER-DIRECTOR	25 CENTRAL PARK W	NEW YORK, NY	10023
LANDECK, PHILIP C	DIRECTOR-PRODUCER	420 LEXINGTON AVE	NEW YORK, NY	10017
LANDELL, BUDDY "NATURE BOY"	WRESTLER	NATIONAL WRESTLING ALLIANCE		
		JIM CROCKETT PROMOTIONS		
		421 BRIARBEND DR	CHARLOTTE, NC	28209
LANDEN, DINSDALE	ACTOR	15 GLENLOCH RD	LONDON NW36	ENGLAND
LANDER, DAVID L	ACTOR-WRITER	7009 SENALDA RD	LOS ANGELES, CA	90068
LANDER, DIANE	ACTRESS	10901 WHIPPLE ST #26	NORTH HOLLYWOOD, CA	91602
LANDER, JONN	ACTOR	8484 WILSHIRE BLVD #235	BEVERLY HILLS, CA	90211
LANDERS, ALAN	ACTOR	9040 HARRATT ST #5	LOS ANGELES, CA	90069
LANDERS, ANN	COLUMNIST	THE CHICAGO TRIBUNE		
		TRIBUNE TOWER		
		435 N MICHIGAN AVE	CHCIAGO, IL	60611
LANDERS, AUDREY	ACTRESS-SINGER	1913 N BEVERLY DR	BEVERLY HILLS, CA	90210
LANDERS, HAL	FILM WRITER-PRODUCER	1721 MONTE CIELO DR	BEVERLY HILLS, CA	90210
LANDERS, JIM	NEWS CORRESPONDENT	11928 ESCALANTE CT	RESTON, VA	22091
LANDERS, JUDY	ACTRESS-MODEL	1913 N BEVERLY DR	BEVERLY HILLS, CA	90210
LANDERS, MATT	ACTOR	11726 SAN VICENTE BLVD #300	LOS ANGELES, CA	90049
LANDERS, ROBERT	DIRECTOR	7240 ESTRELLA DE MAR	CARLSBAD, CA	92008
LANDERS, SUSAN	NEWS CORRESPONDENT	5408 N 27TH RD	ARLINGTON, VA	22207
LANDESBERG, RICHARD	NEWS CORRESPONDENT	1755 S JEFFERSON DAVIS HWY	ARLINGTON, VA	22202
LANDESBERG, STEVE	COMEDIAN-ACTOR	151 S EL CAMINO DR	BEVERLY HILLS, CA	90212
LANDHAM, SONNY	ACTOR	10000 SANTA MONICA BLVD #305	LOS ANGELES, CA	90067
LANDI, SAL	ACTOR	8721 SUNSET BLVD #202	LOS ANGELES, CA	90069
LANDIS, JOE	WRITER-DIRECTOR	2400 WEIDLAKE PL	HOLLYWOOD, CA	90068
LANDIS, JOHN	FILM WRITER-DIRECTOR	DGA, 7950 SUNSET BLVD	HOLLYWOOD, CA	90046
LANDIS, JOSEPH	DIRECTOR	2400 WEID PL	LOS ANGELES, CA	90068
LANDIS, MONTE	ACTOR	FELBER, 2126 N CAHUENGA BLVD	LOS ANGELES, CA	90068
LANDO, BARRY	WRITER	555 W 57TH ST #1230	NEW YORK, NY	10019
LANDOLFI, TONY	ACTOR	2 GARDEN ST	NORTH RANDOLPH, MA	02368
LANDON, HAL F	ACTOR	4150 RIVERSIDE DR #204	BURBANK, CA	91505
LANDON, HAL, JR	ACTOR	6430 SUNSET BLVD #701	LOS ANGELES, CA	90028
LANDON, JOSEPH S	TV WRITER	PLESHETTE, 2700 N BEACHWOOD DR	HOLLYWOOD, CA	90028
LANDON, KAY D	WRITER	8955 BEVERLY BLVD	LOS ANGELES, CA	90048
LANDON, LAURENE	ACTRESS	ICM, 8899 BEVERLY BLVD	LOS ANGELES, CA	90048
LANDON, LESLIE	ACTRESS	3800 BARHAM BLVD #303	LOS ANGELES, CA	90068
LANDON, MICHAEL	ACT-WRI-DIR-PROD	117 MALIBU COLONY RD	MALIBU, CA	90265
LANDON, SUSAN P	WRITER	8955 BEVERLY BLVD	LOS ANGELES, CA	90048
LANDON, TRISHA	ACTRESS	13111 VENTURA BLVD #204	STUDIO CITY, CA	91604
LANDOR, ROSALYN	ACTRESS	151 S EL CAMINO DR	BEVERLY HILLS, CA	90212

MARTIN LANDAU

MICHAEL LANDON

DIANE LANE

PRISCILLA LANE

JESSICA LANGE

TED LANGE

LISA LANGLOIS

ANGELA LANSBURY

NICOLETTE LARSON

Name	Occupation	Address	City	Zip
LANDREAUX, KENNY	BASEBALL	1840 S MARENGO AVE #56	ALHAMBRA, CA	91803
LANDRES, MORRIS	FILM EXECUTIVE	10501 WILSHIRE BLVD #2111	LOS ANGELES, CA	90024
LANDRES, PAUL	TV DIRECTOR	5343 AMESTOY AVE	ENCINO, CA	91316
LANDRUM, TERI	ACTRESS	6310 SAN VICENTE BLVD #407	LOS ANGELES, CA	90048
LANDRY, GAIL	ACTRESS	14017 SYLVAN ST	VAN NUYS, CA	91401
LANDRY, JOHN F	ACTOR-DIRECTOR	76 RANDOLPH AVE #GF	LONDON W9	ENGLAND
LANDRY, RON L	RADIO PERSONALITY	28980 CLIFFSIDE DR	MALIBU, CA	90265
LANDRY, WADE	GUITARIST	452 MOSS TRAIL #I-14	GOODLETTSVILLE, TN	37072
LANDSBERG, DAVID	ACTOR-WRITER	25809 VIA CANDICE	VALENCIA, CA	91355
LANDSBURG, ALAN	WRITER-PRODUCER	22432 PACIFIC COAST HWY	MALIBU, CA	90265
LANDSBURG, DAVID	ACTOR	15301 VENTURA BLVD #345	SHERMAN OAKS, CA	91403
LANDSBURG, VALERIE	ACTRESS	SF & A, 121 N SAN VICENTE BLVD	BEVERLY HILLS, CA	90211
LANDSLIDE	ROCK & ROLL GROUP	VARIETY ARTISTS INTL, INC		
		9073 NEMO ST, 3RD FLOOR	LOS ANGELES, CA	90069
LANDSTEIN-LANE, KATHERINE	WRITER	554 S SAN VICENTE BLVD #3	LOS ANGELES, CA	90048
LANDY, LEONARD	ACTOR	2100 BLYTHE ST	CANOGA PARK, CA	91304
LANDZATT, ANDRE	ACTOR	427 N CANON DR #205	BEVERLY HILLS, CA	90210
LANE, A E	WRITER	555 W 57TH ST #1230	NEW YORK, NY	10019
LANE, ANDREW	FILM PRODUCER	9220 SUNSET BLVD #212	LOS ANGELES, CA	90069
LANE, ANDREW J	SCREENWRITER	8955 BEVERLY BLVD	LOS ANGELES, CA	90048
LANE, BETTY	SOPRANO	260 W END AVE #7-A	NEW YORK, NY	10023
LANE, BRIAN ALAN	TV WRITER	8955 BEVERLY BLVD	LOS ANGELES, CA	90048
LANE, CHARLES	ACTOR	321 GRETNA GREEN WY	LOS ANGELES, CA	90049
LANE, CHRISTOPHER J	NEWS CORRESPONDENT	428 N ARMSTEAD ST	ALEXANDRIA, VA	22132
LANE, CRISTY	SINGER	1225 APACHE LN	MADISON, TN	37115
LANE, DANNY	DRUMMER	2717 ELM HILL PIKE	NASHVILLE, TN	37214
LANE, DIANE	ACTRESS	210 W 55TH ST #1103	NEW YORK, NY	10019
LANE, EARL	NEWS CORRESPONDENT	6907 STRATA ST	MC LEAN, VA	22101
LANE, IVA	ACTRESS	1752 FEDERAL AVE #5	LOS ANGELES, CA	90025
LANE, IVAN	COMPOSER	1085 CAROLYN WY	BEVERLY HILLS, CA	90210
LANE, JEFFREY S	TV WRITER	555 W 57TH ST #1230	NEW YORK, NY	10019
LANE, JENNIFER	ACTRESS	9025 WILSHIRE BLVD #309	BEVERLY HILLS, CA	90211
LANE, LENITA	ACTRESS	WILBUR, 4279 CLYBOURN AVE	NORTH HOLLYWOOD, CA	91602
LANE, LINDA	SCREENWRITER	8955 BEVERLY BLVD	LOS ANGELES, CA	90048
LANE, LOUIS	CONDUCTOR	1776 BROADWAY #504	NEW YORK, NY	10019
LANE, MARIE	ACTRESS	101-41 132ND ST	RICHMOND HILL, NY	11419
LANE, MC GUFFY	SINGER	ENTERTAINMENT ARTS, INC		
		819 18TH AVE S	NASHVILLE, TN	37203
LANE, MIKE	CARTOONIST	POST OFFICE BOX 1377	BALTIMORE, MD	21278
LANE, MIKE	CARTOONIST	POST OFFICE BOX 1377	BALTIMORE, MD	21278
LANE, NANCY	ACTRESS	3907 W ALAMEDA AVE #101	BURBANK, CA	91505
LANE, NANCY	WRITER	8955 BEVERLY BLVD	LOS ANGELES, CA	90048
LANE, NICHOLAS J	COMPOSER	3659 EDENHURST AVE	LOS ANGELES, CA	90039
LANE, PRISCILLA	ACTRESS	RURAL ROUTE #1, NORTH SHORE RD	DERRY, NH	03038
LANE, RED	GUITARIST	JACKSON & ASSOCIATES		
		901 18TH AVE S	NASHVILLE, TN	37212
LANE, REESE	ACTOR	17613 CALVERT ST	ENCINO, CA	91316
LANE, ROBERT	TV WRITER	555 W 57TH ST #1230	NEW YORK, NY	10019
LANE, ROBIN	SINGER	25 HUNTINGTON AVE #420	BOSTON, MA	02116
LANE, SCOTT	GUITARIST	221 N HIGHLAND AVE	MURFREESBORO, TN	37130
LANE, SCOTT EDWARD	ACTOR	727 ASHLAND AVE #8	SANTA MONICA, CA	90405
LANE, STANLEY	NEWS CORRESPONDENT	13319 OLD CHAPEL RD	BOWIE, MD	20715
LANE, WILLIAM	DIRECTOR	10427 VARIEL AVE	CHATSWORTH, CA	91311
LANE-BLOCK, SHANA	ACTRESS	1717 N HIGHLAND AVE #414	LOS ANGELES, CA	90028
LANEUVILLE, ERIC	ACTOR	4814 VICTORIA AVE	LOS ANGELES, CA	90043
LANG, ARCHIE	ACTOR	6736 LAUREL CANYON BLVD #306	NORTH HOLLYWOOD, CA	91606
LANG, DANIEL	GUITARIST	ROUTE #8, BOX 631-A	PENSACOLA, FL	32506
LANG, DAVID	WRITER	8955 BEVERLY BLVD	LOS ANGELES, CA	90048
LANG, JENNINGS	FILM PRODUCER	MCA/UNIVERSAL STUDIOS, INC		
		100 UNIVERSAL CITY PLAZA	UNIVERSAL CITY, CA	91608
LANG, JOHN S	NEWS CORRESPONDENT	2921 N 24TH ST	ARLINGTON, VA	22207
LANG, JUNE	ACTRESS	MORGAN, 12756 KAHLENBERG LN	NORTH HOLLYWOOD, CA	91607
LANG, K D	SINGER	41 BRITAIN ST #200	TORONTO, ONT	CANADA
LANG, KATHERINE KELLY	ACTRESS	10000 SANTA MONICA BLVD #305	LOS ANGELES, CA	90067
LANG, KELLY	SINGER	POST OFFICE BOX 121089	NASHVILLE, TN	37212
LANG, MIKE	SINGER	3012 STONEHENGE LN	CARROLLTON, TX	75006
LANG, MIREK	DIRECTOR-PRODUCER	15-C BUCKLAND CRESCENT	LONDON NW3	ENGLAND
LANG, OTTO	FILM DIRECTOR	15454 S MOUNTAIN RD	SANTA PAULA, CA	93060
LANG, PETER	ANIM-WRITER	60 HOLSWORTHY SQ, ELM ST	LONDON WC1	ENGLAND
LANG, RICHARD	TV DIRECTOR	1901 AVE OF THE STARS #840	LOS ANGELES, CA	90067
LANG, ROBERT	ACTOR	LEADING ARTISTS, LTD		
		60 SAINT JAMES'S ST	LONDON SW1	ENGLAND
LANG, ROCKY	FILM DIRECTOR	606 MOUNTAIN DR	BEVERLY HILLS, CA	90210
LANG, STAN	DIRECTOR	250 GEORGE RD #21-J	CLIFFSIDE PARK, NJ	07010
LANG, TED	WRITER	8955 BEVERLY BLVD	LOS ANGELES, CA	90048
LANG, TONY	WRITER	555 W 57TH ST #1230	NEW YORK, NY	10019
LANG, W RICHARD, JR	DIRECTOR	1901 AVE OF THE STARS #840	LOS ANGELES, CA	90067
LANGAN, KEVIN	SINGER	CAMI, 165 W 57TH ST	NEW YORK, NY	10019
LANGAN, TOM	TV PRODUCER	CBS-TV, 7800 BEVERLY BLVD	LOS ANGELES, CA	90036
LANGDON, DOLLY	NEWS CORRESPONDENT	1628 29TH ST, NW	WASHINGTON, DC	20007
LANGDON, HARRY	PHOTOGRAPHER	181 N MC CADDEN PL	LOS ANGELES, CA	90004
LANGDON, JERRY	NEWS CORRESPONDENT	9405 WOODEN BRIDGE RD	POTOMAC, MD	20854
LANGDON, SUE ANN	ACTRESS	7060 HOLLYWOOD BLVD #610	LOS ANGELES, CA	90028
LANGE, CHRISTINA	ACTRESS	6430 SUNSET BLVD #1203	LOS ANGELES, CA	90028
LANGE, DAVID R	WRITER-PRODUCER	8955 BEVERLY BLVD	LOS ANGELES, CA	90048

GEORGIA TERRY AUTOGRAPHS

We work actively from your WANT lists.

840 N.E. COCHRAN AVENUE
GRESHAM, OREGON 97030

FREE CATALOG

REASONABLE PRICES

Specializing in the ENTERTAINMENT field.

FAST, FRIENDLY SERVICE

Member U.A.C.C.

Collector since 1952
Dealer since 1978

LIGHTS!
CAMERA!
ACTION!

(503) 667-0950

LIGHTS!
CAMERA!
ACTION!

Name	Occupation	Address	City	Zip
LANGE, HENRY J, JR	DIRECTOR	2276 BOWMONT DR	BEVERLY HILLS, CA	90210
LANGE, HOPE	ACTRESS	320 SKYEWIAY RD	LOS ANGELES, CA	90049
LANGE, JESSICA	ACTRESS	ICM, 8899 BEVERLY BLVD	LOS ANGELES, CA	90048
LANGE, JIM	RADIO-TV PERSONALITY	KMPC, 5858 SUNSET BLVD	LOS ANGELES, CA	90028
LANGE, MICHAEL R	TV DIRECTOR	14021 MARQUESAS WY	MARINA DEL REY, CA	90292
LANGE, STEVEN T	WRITER	555 W 57TH ST #1230	NEW YORK, NY	10019
LANGE, TED	ACT-WRI-DIR	19305 REDWING ST	TARZANA, CA	91356
LANGE, TRICIA	ACTRESS-MODEL	MODELS & PROMOTIONS AGENCY		
		8560 SUNSET BLVD, 10TH FLOOR	LOS ANGELES, CA	90069
LANGELLA, FRANK	ACTOR	ICM, 40 W 57TH ST	NEW YORK, NY	10019
LANGENKAMP, HEATHER	ACTRESS	10100 SANTA MONICA BLVD #1600	LOS ANGELES, CA	90067
LANGFORD, BONNIE	ACTRESS-SINGER	BURNETT, 42 GRAFTON HOUSE		
		2-3 GOLDEN SQ	LONDON W1	ENGLAND
LANGFORD, FRANCES	SINGER	POST OFFICE BOX 96	JENSEN BEACH, FL	33457
LANGLAND, LIANE	ACTRESS	10 E 44TH ST #700	NEW YORK, NY	10017
LANGLEY, DAVID	DIRECTOR	536 W 50TH ST	NEW YORK, NY	10019
LANGLEY, NORMA	NEWS CORRESPONDENT	625 SMALLWOOD RD	ROCKVILLE, MD	20850
LANGLEY, ROGER	NEWS CORRESPONDENT	625 SMALLWOOD RD	ROCKVILLE, MD	20850
LANGLOIS, LISA	ACTRESS	10000 SANTA MONICA BLVD #305	LOS ANGELES, CA	90067
LANGLOIS, LORRAINE	FASHION DESIGNER	85 MOWAT AVE	TORONTO, ONT M6K 3E3	CANADA
LANGNER, PHILIP	THEATER PRODUCER	THEATRE GUILD PRODS		
		226 W 47TH ST	NEW YORK, NY	10036
LANGON, TOM	TV PRODUCER	CBS TELEVISION NETWORK		
		"THE YOUNG & THE RESTLESS"		
		7800 BEVERLY BLVD	LOS ANGELES, CA	90036
LANGONE, JOHN	WRITER-EDITOR	DISCOVER/TIME & LIFE BLDG		
		ROCKEFELLER CENTER	NEW YORK, NY	10020
LANGS, RUTH G	NEWS CORRESPONDENT	8207 RIDGE RD	SPRINGFIELD, VA	22153
LANGSCHWADT, ROSA	ACTRESS	ABC-TV, "ALL MY CHILDREN"		
		1330 AVE OF THE AMERICAS	NEW YORK, NY	10019
LANGSDON, MAL	PHOTOGRAPHER	2730 WISCONSIN AVE	WASHINGTON, DC	20007
LANGSTON, MURRAY	COMEDIAN-ACTOR	9034 SUNSET BLVD #200	LOS ANGELES, CA	90069
LANGSTON, SIMON	FILM DIRECTOR	CBS-TV, 1 CRAVEN HILL	LONDON W2	ENGLAND
LANGTON, BASIL	ACTOR-DIRECTOR	41 W 69TH ST	NEW YORK, NY	10023
LANGTON, DAVID	ACTOR	GREEN, 110 JERMYN ST		
		SAINT JAMES'S SQ	LONDON SW1	ENGLAND
LANGTON, SIMON	TV DIRECTOR	C BROWN, 162 REGENT ST	LONDON W1	ENGLAND
LANGTRY, LINDA	ACTRESS	5330 LANKERSHIM BLVD #210	NORTH HOLLYWOOD, CA	91601
LANHAM, MARTY	BANJOIST	4309 BURRUS ST	NASHVILLE, TN	37216
LANIER, CHRISTOPHER C	WRITER	8955 BEVERLY BLVD	LOS ANGELES, CA	90048
LANIER, HAL	BASEBALL	2365 WOODLAWN CIR E	SAINT PETERSBURG, FL	33704
LANIER, MARVIN	GUITARIST	555 DUPONT AVE #A-16	MADISON, TN	37115
LANKESTER, MICHAEL	CONDUCTOR	61 W 62ND ST #6-F	NEW YORK, NY	10023
LANKFORD, KIM	ACTRESS	3200 COLDWATER CANYON AVE	STUDIO CITY, CA	91604
LANKOVA, BISTRA	WRITER-PRODUCER	165 W 46TH ST #409	NEW YORK, NY	10036
LANNING, JACK	BASS	LIEBERMAN, 11 RIVERSIDE DR	NEW YORK, NY	10023
LANNING, JERRY	ACTOR	APA, 888 7TH AVE, 6TH FLOOR	NEW YORK, NY	10106
LANNING, ROBERT H	TV DIRECTOR	ABC-TV, 1330 AVE OF AMERICAS	NEW YORK, NY	10019
LANNOM, LES	ACTOR	11512 EMELITA ST	NORTH HOLLYWOOD, CA	91601
LANPHEAR, WILLIAM	ACTOR	KELMAN, 7813 SUNSET BLVD	LOS ANGELES, CA	90046
LANSBURGH, LARRY	WRITER-PRODUCER	POST OFFICE BOX 559	EAGLE POINT, OR	97524
LANSBURY, ANGELA	ACTRESS	HOTEL MANHATTAN PLAZA		
		484 W 43RD ST	NEW YORK, NY	10036
LANSBURY, CORAL	WRITER	555 W 57TH ST #1230	NEW YORK, NY	10019
LANSBURY, EDGAR	THEATER PRODUCER	1650 BROADWAY	NEW YORK, NY	10019
LANSBURY, WILLIAM	WRITER	10847 VICENZA WY	LOS ANGELES, CA	90077
LANSFORD, CARNEY	BASEBALL	821 REDWOOD DR	DANVILLE, CA	94526
LANSFORD, WILLIAM	TV WRITER	6953 TROLLEY WY	PLAYA DEL REY, CA	90291
LANSING, MICHAEL	ACTOR	FELBER, 2126 N CAHUENGA BLVD	LOS ANGELES, CA	90068
LANSING, ROBERT	ACTOR-DIRECTOR	1165 PARK AVE	NEW YORK, NY	10028
LANSING, SHERRY	FILM EXECUTIVE	1500 SAN YSIDRO DR	BEVERLY HILLS, CA	90210
LANSKY, KAREN	WRITER	3940 SAPPHIRE DR	ENCINO, CA	91436
LANSKY, SOPHIA	ACTRESS	JAYMES, 327 N LAUREL AVE	LOS ANGELES, CA	90048
LANTEAU, WILLIAM	ACTOR	2294 ALCYONA DR	LOS ANGELES, CA	90068
LANTIERI, ALBERT	ACTOR	11154 AQUA VISTA ST #2	NORTH HOLLYWOOD, CA	91602
LANTZ, JERE	CONDUCTOR	1776 BROADWAY #504	NEW YORK, NY	10019
LANTZ, LOUIS	WRITER	1071 S LA CIENEGA BLVD #309	LOS ANGELES, CA	90035
LANTZ, ROBERT	LITERARY-TALENT AGENT	9255 SUNSET BLVD #505	LOS ANGELES, CA	90069
LANTZ, WALTER	CARTOONIST	1715 CARLA RIDGE	BEVERLY HILLS, CA	90210
LANZARONE, BENJAMIN A	COMPOSER-CONDUCTOR	11455 SUNSHINE TERR	STUDIO CITY, CA	91604
LANZILLO, PAT	BODYBUILDER	CHAMPIONS TRAINING COMPLEX		
		22 4TH ST	TROY, NY	12180
LANZILLOTTI, LEONORE	MEZZO-SOPRANO	LIEBERMAN, 11 RIVERSIDE DR	NEW YORK, NY	10023
LAPENIEKS, VILIS M	CINEMATOGRAPHER	POST OFFICE BOX 2230	HOLLYWOOD, CA	90078
LAPIDESE, JONATHAN E	WRITER	1008 14TH ST #A	SANTA MONICA, CA	90403
LAPIN, MAUREEN	ACTOR	157 S MANSFIELD AVE	LOS ANGELES, CA	90036
LAPOTAIRE, JANE	ACTRESS	92-C OXFORD GARDENS	LONDON W10	ENGLAND
LAPOTEN, GARY	FILM DIRECTOR	POST OFFICE BOX 2222	BEVERLY HILLS, CA	90213
LAPPIN-THEMELIS, MARCIA	DIRECTOR	114 W 70TH ST	NEW YORK, NY	10023
LARABEE, COL LUCKY	RINGMASTER	HALL, 138 FROG HOLLOW RD	CHURCHVILLE, PA	18966
LARABEE, LOUISE	ACTRESS	HOTEL MANHATTAN PLAZA		
		400 W 43RD ST	NEW YORK, NY	10036
LARANGEIRA, CRISPIN	WRITER	555 W 57TH ST #1230	NEW YORK, NY	10019
LARBEY, BOB	TV WRITER	LEMON, 24 POTTERY LN	LONDON W11	ENGLAND
LARCH, JOHN	ACTOR	4506 VARNA AVE	SHERMAN OAKS, CA	91423

LARDNER, GEORGE E, JR	NEWS CORRESPONDENT	5604 32ND ST, NW	WASHINGTON, DC	20015
LARDNER, RING, JR	WRITER	55 CENTRAL PARK W	NEW YORK, NY	10023
LAREDO, JAIME	VIOLINIST	CAMI, 165 W 57TH ST	NEW YORK, NY	10019
LAREDO, RUTH	PIANIST	SHAW CONCERTS, 1995 BROADWAY	NEW YORK, NY	10023
LARGE, ARLEN J	NEWS CORRESPONDENT	120 1/2 RUMSEY CT, SE	WASHINGTON, DC	20003
LARGE, BRIAN	FILM-OPERA DIRECTOR	QUAVERS HOUSE, THE AVE		
		WHYTELEAFE SOUTH, CATERAM	SURREY CR30 AQ	ENGLAND
LARICK, DWIGHT	ACTOR	3041 W AVE 35 #1	LOS ANGELES, CA	90065
LARIOS, STEPHEN	GUITARIST	ROUTE #4, LINDERMAN AVE EXT	KINGSTON, NY	12401
LARKE, JAMES KENELM	DIRECTOR-PRODUCER	NORFOLK, 107 LONG ACRE	LONDON WC2E 9NT	ENGLAND
LARKEN, JOHN DAVID	DIRECTOR	16 E 72ND ST	NEW YORK, NY	10021
LARKEN, SHEILA	ACTRESS	9255 SUNSET BLVD #510	LOS ANGELES, CA	90069
LARKIN, BILL	TV WRITER	6725 SUNSET BLVD #506	HOLLYWOOD, CA	90028
LARKIN, BILLY	GUITARIST	ROUTE #1	BELVIDERE, TN	37306
LARKIN, NELSON	GUITARIST	2318 HEMMINGWAY DR	NASHVILLE, TN	37215
LARKIN, WILLIAM M	WRITER	8955 BEVERLY BLVD	LOS ANGELES, CA	90048
LARMORE, PHOEBE	WRITER	8955 BEVERLY BLVD	LOS ANGELES, CA	90048
LARNELLE	SINGER	POST OFFICE BOX 1776	LONGWOOD, FL	32750
LARNER, ESTHER	ACTRESS	3330 BARHAM BLVD #103	LOS ANGELES, CA	90068
LARNER, JEREMY	SCREENWRITER	8955 BEVERLY BLVD	LOS ANGELES, CA	90048
LARNER, STEVAN	CINEMATOGRAPHER	3872 LAS FLORES CANYON RD #1	MALIBU, CA	90265
LARON, ELAINE	WRITER	7367 HOLLYWOOD BLVD #206	HOLLYWOOD, CA	90046
LARRATT, IRIS	SINGER	4680 ELK LAKE DR #304	VICTORIA, BC V8Z 5M1	CANADA
LARROQUETTE, ELIZABETH	CASTING DIRECTOR	3970 OVERLAND AVE #700	CULVER CITY, CA	90232
LARROQUETTE, JOHN	ACTOR	POST OFFICE BOX 6303	MALIBU, CA	90265
LARRY, SHELDON	FILM DIRECTOR	143 W 21ST ST	NEW YORK, NY	10011
LARSEN, CARL, JR	PHOTOJOURNALIST	2600 CHILCOTT CT	VIENNA, VA	22180
LARSEN, ERIC	ACTOR	ACC, 890 W END AVE	NEW YORK, NY	10025
LARSEN, GAYLORD	TV WRITER	8955 BEVERLY BLVD	LOS ANGELES, CA	90048
LARSEN, GREGORY	PHOTOJOURNALIST	1931 N CLEVELAND ST	ARLINGTON, VA	22201
LARSEN, KATHY CAROLIN	NEWS CORRESPONDENT	1629 COLUMBIA RD, NW	WASHINGTON, DC	20009
LARSEN, LEONARD	NEWS CORRESPONDENT	4301 WILLOW WOODS DR	ANNANDALE, VA	22003
LARSEN, MILT	TV WRITER	929 LONGWOOD AVE	LOS ANGELES, CA	90019
LARSEN, PATRICIA	WRITER	8955 BEVERLY BLVD	LOS ANGELES, CA	90048
LARSEN, WILLIAM	ACTOR	7469 MELROSE AVE #30	LOS ANGELES, CA	90046
LARSON, BOB	FILM PRODCUER	1888 CENTURY PARK E #1400	LOS ANGELES, CA	90067
LARSON, CATHY	ACTRESS	ABC-TV, "RYAN'S HOPE"		
		1330 AVE OF THE AMERICAS	NEW YORK, NY	10019
LARSON, CHARLES	WRITER	8955 BEVERLY BLVD	LOS ANGELES, CA	90048
LARSON, DARRELL	ACTOR	2210 WILSHIRE BLVD #473	SANTA MONICA, CA	90403
LARSON, DON	BASEBALL	17090 COPPER HILL DR	MORGAN HILL, CA	95037
LARSON, ERIC	PUBLISHING EXECUTIVE	TV GUIDE WEEKLY MAGAZINE		
		4 RADNOR CORPORATION CENTER	RADNOR, PA	19088
LARSON, GARY	CARTOONIST	UNIVERSAL PRESS SYNDICATE		
		4900 MAIN ST, 9TH FLOOR	KANSAS CITY, MO	62114
LARSON, GLEN	TV WRITER-PRODUCER	351 DELFERN DR	LOS ANGELES, CA	90077
LARSON, JACK	ACTOR	449 SKYEWIAY RD N	LOS ANGELES, CA	90049
LARSON, JACK W	ACTOR	8721 SUNSET BLVD #203	LOS ANGELES, CA	90069
LARSON, JILL	ACTRESS	CBS-TV, "AS THE WORLD TURNS"		
		51 W 52ND ST	NEW YORK, NY	10019
LARSON, JOHN T	WRITER	8955 BEVERLY BLVD	LOS ANGELES, CA	90048
LARSON, KEITH	WRESTLER	SEE - KERNODLE, ROCKY		
LARSON, LISBY	ACTRESS	CBS-TV, "THE GUIDING LIGHT"		
		51 W 52ND ST	NEW YORK, NY	10019
LARSON, LISSER FORST	BODYBUILDER	SEE - FORST-LARSON, LISSER		
LARSON, NICOLETTE	SINGER-SONGWRITER	POST OFFICE BOX 4087	MISSOULA, MT	59806
LARSON, PAUL	ACTOR	3312 MENTONE AVE	LOS ANGELES, CA	90034
LARSON, RICHARD W	NEWS REPORTER	POST OFFICE BOX 70	SEATTLE, WA	98111
LARSON, SOPHIA	SOPRANO	CAMI, 165 W 57TH ST	NEW YORK, NY	10019
LARSON, STEPHEN E	PHOTOGRAPHER	5238 SHERIER PL, NW	WASHINGTON, DC	20016
LARSON, SUSAN	SOPRANO	AARON, 25 HUNTINGTON AVE	BOSTON, MA	02116
LASELL, JOHN	ACTOR	1350 N HIGHLAND AVE #24	HOLLYWOOD, CA	90028
LASER BOY	ROCK & ROLL GROUP	POST OFFICE BOX 1909	MILL VALLEY, CA	94942
LASHENDOCK-LINDQUIST, LINDA	NEWS CORRESPONDENT	3846 LYNDHURST DR	FAIRFAX, VA	22031
LASHER, MELANIE	ACTRESS	1450 BELFAST DR	LOS ANGELES, CA	90069
LASKA, RAY	ACTOR	1122 WILSHIRE BLVD	LOS ANGELES, CA	90017
LASKAY, JASON	ACTOR	9300 WILSHIRE BLVD #410	BEVERLY HILLS, CA	90212
LASKER, ALEX	SCREENWRITER	20032 PACIFIC COAST HWY	MALIBU, CA	90265
LASKER, JAY	RECORD EXECUTIVE	16021 ROYAL OAK RD	ENCINO, CA	91436
LASKER, LAWRENCE	SCREENWRITER	ICM, 8899 BEVERLY BLVD	LOS ANGELES, CA	90048
LASKER, PHILIP JAYSON	WRITER	8955 BEVERLY BLVD	LOS ANGELES, CA	90048
LASKEY, DAVID	SINGER	POST OFFICE BOX 5880	SHERMAN OAKS, CA	91413
LASKIN, MICHAEL	ACTOR	151 N SAN VICENTE BLVD #208	BEVERLY HILLS, CA	90211
LASKO, GENE	DIRECTOR-PRODUCER	12 E 86TH ST	NEW YORK, NY	10028
LASKOS, ANDREW	SCREENWRITER	BLOOM, 800 S ROBERTSON BLVD	LOS ANGELES, CA	90035
LASKY, GILBERT	SCREENWRITER	10969 WELLWORTH AVE #325	LOS ANGELES, CA	90024
LASKY, JESSE L	SCREENWRITER	MANN, 1 OLD COMPTON ST	LONDON W1	ENGLAND
LASKY, MARK	ACTOR	5330 LANKERSHIM BLVD #210	NORTH HOLLYWOOD, CA	91601
LASKY, ROBERT	ACTOR	5000 CENTINELA AVE #334	LOS ANGELES, CA	90068
LASORDA, TOMMY	BASEBALL	1473 W MAXZIM AVE	FULLERTON, CA	92633
LASSALLY, PETER	TV PROCUDER	NBC-TV, 3000 W ALAMEDA AVE	BURBANK, CA	91523
LASSALLY, WALTER	LIGHTING DIRECTOR	THE ABBEY, EYE	SUFFOLK	ENGLAND
LASSAN, ED	GUITARIST	806 46TH AVE	NASHVILLE, TN	37209

LASSER, LOUISE	ACTRESS-WRITER	200 E 71ST ST #20-C	NEW YORK, NY	10021
LASSICK, SYDNEY	ACTOR	439 S LA CIENEGA BLVD #120	LOS ANGELES, CA	90048
LASSITER, STANLEY	GUITARIST	505 NEELY'S BEND RD	MADISON, TN	37115
LASSON, LAWRENCE	VIOLINIST	9 MILLWOOD DR	NASHVILLE, TN	37217
LASSWELL, FRED	CARTOONIST	KING FEATURES SYNDICATE		
		235 E 45TH ST	NEW YORK, NY	10017
LAST DRIVE, THE	ROCK & ROLL GROUP	HITCH-HYKE RECORDS		
		5 KOSMA BALANOU	ATHENS 116-36	GREECE
LAST TANGO	ROCK & ROCK DUO	119 W 57TH ST #901	NEW YORK, NY	10019
LASTER, OWEN	TALENT AGENT	151 S EL CAMINO DR	BEVERLY HILLS, CA	90212
LASTING, RICHARD	ACTOR	3245 PRIMERA AVE	LOS ANGELES, CA	90068
LASZLO, ANDREW	CINEMATOGRAPHER	2766 CARMAR DR	LOS ANGELES, CA	90046
LATE NITE	ROCK & ROLL GROUP	BROTHERS, 141 DUNBAR AVE	FORDS, NJ	08863
LATEEF, AHMED	TV DIRECTOR	4163 MURIETTA AVE	SHERMAN OAKS, CA	91423
LATEEF, YUSEF	MUSICIAN	527 MADISON AVE #1012	NEW YORK, NY	10022
LATEINER, JACOB	PIANIST	TORNAY, 127 W 72ND ST	NEW YORK, NY	10023
LATELLA, DENISE	ACTRESS	1999 N SYCAMORE AVE #15	LOS ANGELES, CA	90068
LATER, TERRY	ACTOR	259 25TH ST	SANTA MONICA, CA	90402
LATESSA, DICK	ACTOR	250 W 57TH ST #2317	NEW YORK, NY	10107
LATHAM, AARON	SCREENWRITER	8955 BEVERLY BLVD	LOS ANGELES, CA	90048
LATHAM, KENNETH D	COMPOSER	1801 LONGHILL DR	MONTEREY PARK, CA	91754
LATHAM, LOUISE	ACTRESS	516 HANLEY PL	LOS ANGELES, CA	90049
LATHAM, LYNN	ACTRESS	PACIFIC ARTS, LTD		
		515 N LA CIENEGA BLVD	LOS ANGELES, CA	90048
LATHAM, LYNN M	TV WRITER	PLESHETTE, 2700 N BEACHWOOD DR	LOS ANGELES, CA	90068
LATHAM, MICHAEL	TV PRODUCER	12 DEALTRY RD	LONDON SW15	ENGLAND
LATHAM, PHILIP	ACTOR	BRYAN DREW, LTD		
		80-82 REGENT ST	LONDON W1	ENGLAND
LATHAN, BOBBI JO	ACTRESS	870 N VINE ST #G	LOS ANGELES, CA	90038
LATHAN, STAN	TV DIRECTOR	9200 SUNSET BLVD #423	LOS ANGELES, CA	90069
LATHEM, NILES RICHARD	NEWS CORRESPONDENT	6330 UTAH AVE, NW	WASHINGTON, DC	20015
LATHROP, PHILLIP	CINEMATOGRAPHER	POST OFFICE BOX 2230	HOLLYWOOD, CA	90078
LATIMER, JAMES	COMPOSER-CONDUCTOR	FROTHINGHAM, 40 GROVE ST	WESSESLEY, MA	02181
LATIN QUARTER	ROCK & ROLL GROUP	TONY MEILANDT MANAGEMENT		
		1312 N LA BREA AVE	LOS ANGELES, CA	90028
LATSIS, MARY J	WRITER	555 W 57TH ST #1230	NEW YORK, NY	10019
LATT, DANIEL R	NEWS CORRESPONDENT	NBC-TV, NEWS DEPARTMENT		
		4001 NEBRASKA AVE, NW	WASHINGTON, DC	20016
LATTANZI, MATT	ACTOR	9300 WILSHIRE BLVD #410	BEVERLY HILLS, CA	90212
LATTER, ILENE	ACTRESS	4789 VINELAND AVE #100	NORTH HOLLYWOOD, CA	91602
LATTIMORE, MICHAEL	DRUMMER	POST OFFICE BOX 23008	NASHVILLE, TN	37202
LATTIMORE, REUBEN M	NEWS CORRESPONDENT	412 TENNESSEE AVE #2, NE	WASHINGTON, DC	20003
LATTISAW, STACY	SINGER	65 W 55TH ST #6-C	NEW YORK, NY	10019
LATU, LESINI	BODYGUARD	2801 MEADOW LARK DR	SAN DIEGO, CA	92123
LAU, JOHN-SZICHENG	CONDUCTOR	PERLS, 7 W 96TH ST	NEW YORK, NY	10025
LAU, LAURENCE	ACTOR	NBC-TV, "ANOTHER WORLD"		
		30 ROCKEFELLER PLAZA	NEW YORK, NY	10112
LAUBER, KEN M	COMPOSER	244 N BOWLING GREEN WY	LOS ANGELES, CA	90049
LAUDER, ESTEE	COSMETIC EXECUTIVE	767 5TH AVE	NEW YORK, NY	10022
LAUER, DARRELL	TENOR	200 W 70TH ST #7-F	NEW YORK, NY	10023
LAUFER, DAVID G	WRITER	555 W 57TH ST #1230	NEW YORK, NY	10019
LAUFER, PETER D	NEWS CORRESPONDENT	1333 "H" ST, NW	WASHINGTON, DC	20005
LAUFFER, JOHNNY	MUSICIAN	1012 BRENTWOOD LN	BRENTWOOD, TN	37027
LAUFMAN, LAURIEN	CELLIST	POST OFFICE BOX U	REDDING, CT	06875
LAUFMAN DUO	MUSICAL DUO	IAM, 10572 JASON LN	COLUMBIA, MD	21044
LAUGHING DOGS, THE	ROCK & ROLL GROUP	3 E 54TH ST #1400	NEW YORK, NY	10022
LAUGHLIN, FRANK	DIRECTOR	12953 MARLBORO ST	LOS ANGELES, CA	90049
LAUGHLIN, TOM	ACTOR-FILM PRODUCER	12953 MARLBORO ST	LOS ANGELES, CA	90049
LAUGHTON, ROGER	TV EXECUTIVE	BBC, 12 CAVENDISH PL	LONDON W1	ENGLAND
LAUNER, BETH	CASTING DIRECTOR	749 N LA BREA AVE	LOS ANGELES, CA	90038
LAUNER, S JOHN	ACTOR	4415 ROMERO DR	TARZANA, CA	91356
LAUPER, CYNDI	SINGER-SONGWRITER	65 W 55TH ST #4-G	NEW YORK, NY	10019
LAURANCE, MATTHEW	ACTOR	3855 LANKERSHIM BLVD #818	NORTH HOLLYWOOD, CA	91604
LAURANCE, MITCHELL	ACTOR	POST OFFICE BOX 2350	HOLLYWOOD, CA	90078
LAURANCE, MITCHELL J	ACTOR	141 S EL CAMINO DR #205	BEVERLY HILLS, CA	90212
LAURANCE, TAMIE	MEZZO-SOPRANO	45 W 60TH ST #4-K	NEW YORK, NY	10023
LAURELS, THE	VOCAL GROUP	RUDY KARDOS, 1107 ADA DR	NORTH HUNTINGTON, PA	15642
LAUREN, BARBARA	CASTING DIRECTOR	7135 HOLLYWOOD BLVD	LOS ANGELES, CA	90046
LAUREN, JOAN	ACTRESS	9040 HARRATT ST #5	LOS ANGELES, CA	90069
LAUREN, JOE	WRESTLER	SEE - ROAD WARRIOR ANIMAL		
LAUREN, RALPH	FASHION DESIGNER	550 7TH AVE	NEW YORK, NY	10018
LAURENA, MISS	TRAPEZE ARTIST	HALL, 138 FROG HOLLOW RD	CHURCHVILLE, PA	18966
LAURENCE, ASHLEY	ACTRESS	3575 W CAHUENGA BLVD #320	LOS ANGELES, CA	90068
LAURENCE, JOHN	NEWS CORRESPONDENT	ABC NEWS, 8 CARBURTON ST	LONDON W1P 7DT	ENGLAND
LAURENCE, MICHAEL	ACTOR	4105 CRISP CYN RD	SHERMAN OAKS, CA	91403
LAURENCE, MICHAEL	WRITER	555 W 57TH ST #1230	NEW YORK, NY	10019
LAURENCE, ROBERT P	TV CRITIC	POST OFFICE BOX 191	SAN DIEGO, CA	92112
LAURENS, RICHARD	TV WRITER	8955 BEVERLY BLVD	LOS ANGELES, CA	90048
LAURENSON, AMELIA	ACTRESS	1717 N HIGHLAND AVE #414	LOS ANGELES, CA	90028
LAURENSON, JAMES	ACTOR	EDWARDS, 275 KENNINGTON RD	LONDON SE11	ENGLAND
LAURENT, ARTHUR H	NEWS CORRESPONDENT	2707 OCCIDENTAL DR	VIENNA, VA	22180
LAURENTS, ARTHUR	WRITER	8955 BEVERLY BLVD	LOS ANGELES, CA	90048
LAURIE, JIM	TV EXECUTIVE	ABC NEWS, 7 W 66TH ST	NEW YORK, NY	10023
LAURIE, PIPER	ACTRESS	907 12TH ST	SANTA MONICA, CA	90403
LAURIN, MARIE	ACTRESS	1901 AVE OF THE STARS #840	LOS ANGELES, CA	90067

CYNDI LAUPER

DALIAH LAVI

CAROL LAWRENCE

KELLY LE BROCK

FRANCIS LEDERER

CHRISTOPHER LEE

JOHNNY LEE

PINKY LEE

RON LEIBMAN

Name	Occupation	Address	City	Zip
LAURIN, TANYA	ACTRESS	9441 WILSHIRE BLVD #620-D	BEVERLY HILLS, CA	90210
LAURINIDAS, JOE	WRESTLER	SEE - ROAD WARRIOR ANIMAL		
LAUTER, DAVID	NEWS CORRESPONDENT	1726 NEWTON ST, NW	WASHINGTON, DC	20010
LAUTER, ED	ACTOR	11747 SUNSET BLVD #106	LOS ANGELES, CA	90049
LAUTER, HARRY	ACTOR	POST OFFICE BOX 119	OJAI, CA	93023
LAUTERSTEIN, DOROTHY	WRITER	555 W 57TH ST #1230	NEW YORK, NY	10019
LAVDANSKI, RICHARD M	CONDUCTOR	BOX 72, PINE ST	MOUNTAINHOME, PA	18342
LAVEN, ARNOLD	DIRECTOR-PRODUCER	15954 VALLEY VISTA BLVD	ENCINO, CA	91436
LAVENBURG, JOSEPH D	PHOTOGRAPHER	4200 DAMASCUS RD	LAYTONSVILLE, MD	20878
LAVENDER, IAN	ACTOR	THE RICHARD STONE AGENCY		
		18-20 YORK BUILDINGS. ADELPHI	LONDON WC2	ENGLAND
LAVER, WILLIAM	ACTOR	1418 N HIGHLAND AVE #102	LOS ANGELES, CA	90028
LAVERY, CHARLES V	TV EXECUTIVE	ABC TELEVISION NETWORK		
		1330 AVE OF THE AMERICAS	NEW YORK, NY	10019
LAVI, DALIAH	ACTRESS-MODEL	5900 SW 117TH ST	MIAMI, FL	33156
LAVIE, EFRAT	ACTRESS	6605 HOLLYWOOD BLVD #220	HOLLYWOOD, CA	90028
LAVIES, BIANCA	PHOTOGRAPHER	1 WAGNER ST	ANNAPOLIS, MD	21401
LAVIN, CHERYL	COLUMNIST-CRITIC	TRIBUNE MEDIA SERVICES		
		64 E CONCORD ST	ORLANDO, FL	32801
LAVIN, CHRISTINE	SINGER-GUITARIST	ROUNDER RECORDS, 1 CAMP ST	CAMBRIDGE, MA	02140
LAVIN, LINDA	ACTRESS-DIRECTOR	20781 BIG ROCK RD	MALIBU, CA	90265
LAVINE, FRED	CLOWN	2701 COTTAGE WY #14	SACRAMENTO, CA	95825
LAVINE, MELVIN S	WRITER	555 W 57TH ST #1230	NEW YORK, NY	10019
LAVUT, MARTIN H	WRITER	8955 BEVERLY BLVD	LOS ANGELES, CA	90048
LAW, ALEX	COMPOSER-CONDUCTOR	3105 S HUGHES AVE	FRESNO, CA	93706
LAW, CHRISTOPHER	ACTOR	326 N AVON ST	BURBANK, CA	91505
LAW, GENE H	TV DIRECTOR	DGA, 7950 SUNSET BLVD	LOS ANGELES, CA	90046
LAW, JOHN PHILLIP	ACTOR	1339 MILLER DR	LOS ANGELES, CA	90069
LAW, LINDSAY E	TV EXECUTIVE	356 W 58TH ST	NEW YORK, NY	10019
LAW, MARY	MUSICIAN	4601 PACKARD DR #C-288	NASHVILLE, TN	37211
LAWBAUGH, DAVID	DRUMMER	879 KIPLING DR	NASHVILLE, TN	37217
LAWHERN, TIMOTHY	GUITARIST	165 DELLWAY DR	NASHVILLE, TN	37207
LAWLER, MIKE	PIANIST	418 E THOMPSON LN	NASHVILLE, TN	37211
LAWLER, THOMAS W	WRITER	555 W 57TH ST #1230	NEW YORK, NY	10019
LAWLER, WILLIAM	TV DIRECTOR	OREGON RD #96	ASHLAND, MA	01721
LAWLES, JACK	SINGER	ROUTE #1, BOX 327	NASHVILLE, IN	47448
LAWLESS, LOUIE	WRITER-PRODUCER	634 E WALNUT AVE	BURBANK, CA	91501
LAWLOR, JOHN H	ACTOR	10351 SANTA MONICA BLVD #211	LOS ANGELES, CA	90025
LAWLOR, KATHLEEN J	TV WRITER	555 W 57TH ST #1230	NEW YORK, NY	10019
LAWMAN	WRESTLER	SEE - MUSTARD, PRESTON "LAWMAN"		
LAWN, CONSTANCE E	NEWS CORRESPONDENT	6130 BEACHWAY DR	FALLS CHURCH, VA	22041
LAWNDALE	ROCK & ROLL GROUP	POST OFFICE BOX 1	LAWNDALE, CA	90260
LAWNER, MORDECAI	ACTOR	309 E 76TH ST	NEW YORK, NY	10021
LAWRENCE, ALAN	DIRECTOR-PRODUCER	TALCO, 279 E 44TH ST	NEW YORK, NY	10017
LAWRENCE, ANTHONY	WRITER-PRODUCER	10100 SANTA MONICA BLVD #1600	LOS ANGELES, CA	90067
LAWRENCE, CAROL	ACTRESS-SINGER	POST OFFICE BOX 1895	STUDIO CITY, CA	91604
LAWRENCE, CAROL M	WRITER	8955 BEVERLY BLVD	LOS ANGELES, CA	90048
LAWRENCE, DAVID	TV WRITER-PRODUCER	4142 BENEDICT CANYON DR	SHERMAN OAKS, CA	91423
LAWRENCE, DIARMUID	TV DIRECTOR	DAISH, 83 EASTBOURNE MEWS	LONDON W2	ENGLAND
LAWRENCE, DONALD L	DIRECTOR-PRODUCER	12250 N 64TH ST	SCOTTSDALE, AZ	85254
LAWRENCE, DONNA	NEWS CORRESPONDENT	1200 N PIERCE ST #506	ARLINGTON, VA	22209
LAWRENCE, DOUGLAS	BARITONE	IMG ARTISTS, 22 E 71ST ST	NEW YORK, NY	10021
LAWRENCE, ELIZABETH	ACTRESS	200 W 57TH ST #1303	NEW YORK, NY	10019
LAWRENCE, ELNA	CASTING DIRECTOR	749 N LA BREA AVE	LOS ANGELES, CA	90038
LAWRENCE, ERNEST	ACTOR	4731 LAUREL CANYON BLVD #5	NORTH HOLLYWOOD, CA	91607
LAWRENCE, EVAN	TV WRITER	8955 BEVERLY BLVD	LOS ANGELES, CA	90048
LAWRENCE, GARY	GUITARIST	1100 PENNOCK	NASHVILLE, TN	37207
LAWRENCE, HAP JAMES	WRITER-PRODUCER	18948 CANTLAY ST	RESEDA, CA	91335
LAWRENCE, HENRY	COMEDIAN	EAI, 2211 INDUSTRIAL BLVD	SARASOTA, FL	33580
LAWRENCE, JAMES	TV WRITER	ROBERTS CO, 427 N CANON DR	BEVERLY HILLS, CA	90210
LAWRENCE, JEROME	SCREENWRITER	21056 LAS FLORES MESA DR	MALIBU, CA	90265
LAWRENCE, JILL D	NEWS CORRESPONDENT	5346 32ND ST, NW	WASHINGTON, DC	20015
LAWRENCE, JOEL	ACTOR	435 S LA CIENEGA BLVD #108	LOS ANGELES, CA	90048
LAWRENCE, KEVIN	BODYBUILDER	POST OFFICE BOX 3671	NEWPORT BEACH, CA	92663
LAWRENCE, KIVA	ACTRESS	109 1/2 S CLARK DR	LOS ANGELES, CA	90048
LAWRENCE, LINDA	ACTRESS	870 N VINE ST #G	LOS ANGELES, CA	90038
LAWRENCE, MARC	ACTOR-DIRECTOR	4444 VIA MARINA WY	MARINA DEL REY, CA	90292
LAWRENCE, N GAIL	TV WRITER	CBS-TV, "THE GUIDING LIGHT"		
		51 W 52ND ST	NEW YORK, NY	10019
LAWRENCE, NANCY	TV WRITER	8955 BEVERLY BLVD	LOS ANGELES, CA	90048
LAWRENCE, NANCY GAIL	TV WRITER	555 W 57TH ST #1230	NEW YORK, NY	10019
LAWRENCE, PATRICIA	ACTRESS	33 SAINTT LUKE'S ST	LONDON SW3	ENGLAND
LAWRENCE, RICHARD	NEWS CORRESPONDENT	8512 HOWELL RD	BETHESDA, MD	20817
LAWRENCE, ROBERT	CONDUCTOR	140 E 28TH ST	NEW YORK, NY	10016
LAWRENCE, ROBERT L	DIRECTOR	DGA, 110 W 57TH ST	NEW YORK, NY	10019
LAWRENCE, STEVE	SINGER-WRITER	POST OFFICE BOX 5140	BEVERLY HILLS, CA	90210
LAWRENCE, VERNON	TV DIRECTOR-PRODUCER	174 BALLARDS WY, CROYDON	SURREY	ENGLAND
LAWRENCE, VICKI	ACTRESS-SINGER	151 S EL CAMINO DR	BEVERLY HILLS, CA	90212
LAWRENCE, WILLIAM	GUITARIST	ROUTE #15, BOX 61	BOWLING GREEN, KY	42101
LAWRY, JOHN	PIANIST	LOT 168, FRANKLIN N I H EST	FRANKLIN, TN	37064
LAWS, HUBERT	FLUTIST	JOHN MASON, 9200 SUNSET BLVD	LOS ANGELES, CA	90069
LAWS, ROBERTA	SOPRANO	254 W 93RD ST #8	NEW YORK, NY	10025
LAWS, RONNIE	SAXOPHONIST	MR I MOUSE, LTD		
		920 DICKSON ST	MARINA DEL REY, CA	90292
LAWSKY, DAVID	NEWS CORRESPONDENT	5470 30TH ST, NW	WASHINGTON, DC	20015

Name	Occupation	Address	City/State	Zip
LAWSON, DENIS	ACTOR	CONWAY, EAGLE HOUSE		
		109 JERMYN ST	LONDON SW1	ENGLAND
LAWSON, DOYLE	GUITARIST	POST OFFICE BOX 145	CONCORD, VA	24538
LAWSON, LEE	ACTRESS	ICM, 40 W 57TH ST	NEW YORK, NY	10019
LAWSON, LEIGH	ACTRESS	ICM, 388-396 OXFORD ST	LONDON W1	ENGLAND
LAWSON, LEN	ACTOR	7466 BEVERLY BLVD #205	LOS ANGELES, CA	90036
LAWSON, MAGGIE L	NEWS CORRESPONDENT	4500 S FOUR MILE RUN DR #426	ARLINGTON, VA	22204
LAWSON, PATRICIA A	NEWS CORRESPONDENT	NBC-TV, NEWS DEPARTMENT		
		4001 NEBRASKA AVE, NW	WASHINGTON, DC	20016
LAWSON, RICHARD	ACTOR	MUCHNICK, 432 S OGDEN DR	LOS ANGELES, CA	90036
LAWSON, STEVE	TV WRITER	ROSENSTONE, 3 E 48TH ST	NEW YORK, NY	10017
LAWTON, DAVID	CONDUCTOR	254 W 93RD ST #8	NEW YORK, NY	10025
LAX, BERNARD	TALENT AGENT	9105 CARMELITA AVE	BEVERLY HILLS, CA	90210
LAX, SUZANNE	TALENT AGENT	9105 CARMELITA AVE #1	BEVERLY HILLS, CA	90210
LAY, RODNEY & THE WILD WEST	C & W GROUP	POST OFFICE BOX 107	COFFEYVILLE, KS	67337
LAY, SUSAN	TV WRITER	555 W 57TH ST #1230	NEW YORK, NY	10019
LAYE, EVELYN	ACTRESS	60 DORSET HOUSE, GLOUCESTER PL	LONDON NW1	ENGLAND
LAYMAN, ROMONA K	WRITER	555 W 57TH ST #1230	NEW YORK, NY	10019
LAYNE, BARRY C	NEWS CORRESPONDENT	1825 "K" ST, NW	WASHINGTON, DC	20006
LAYNE, JERRY	ACTOR	9538 WYSTONE AVE	NORTHRIDGE, CA	91324
LAYNE, JOSEPH	MUSIC ARRANGER	101 BEAR TRACK	NASHVILLE, TN	37221
LAYNE, PATRICIA	WRITER	555 W 57TH ST #1230	NEW YORK, NY	10019
LAYNG, LISSA	ACTRESS	8281 MELROSE AVE #305	LOS ANGELES, CA	90046
LAYTON, BILLY	COMPOSER	4 JOHN'S RD	SETAUKET, NY	11733
LAYTON, CARLA	ACTRESS	LIGHT, 113 N ROBERTSON BLVD	LOS ANGELES, CA	90048
LAYTON, GEORGE	ACTOR-WRITER	UNNA & DURBRIDGE, LTD		
		24-32 POTTERY LN		
		HOLLAND PARK	LONDON W11	ENGLAND
LAYTON, JOE	DIRECTOR	DGA, 7950 SUNSET BLVD	LOS ANGELES, CA	90046
LAZAR, IRVING	TALENT AGENT	1840 CARLA RIDGE	BEVERLY HILLS, CA	90210
LAZAR, JOEL	CONDUCTOR	SHAW CONCERTS, 1995 BROADWAY	NEW YORK, NY	10023
LAZAR, JOHN	ACTOR	439 S LA CIENEGA BLVD #117	LOS ANGELES, CA	90048
LAZAR, KAREN P	WRITER	555 W 57TH ST #1230	NEW YORK, NY	10019
LAZAR, MARK	ACTOR	3920 LONGRIDGE AVE	SHERMAN OAK, CA	91423
LAZAREVIC, JORDANKA L	NEWS CORRESPONDENT	5213 WESTBARD AVE	BETHESDA, MD	20816
LAZARUS, ERNA	WRITER	8955 BEVERLY BLVD	LOS ANGELES, CA	90048
LAZARUS, JERRY	SCREENWRITER	555 W 57TH ST #1230	NEW YORK, NY	10019
LAZARUS, LISA	WRITER	8955 SUNSET BLVD	LOS ANGELES, CA	90069
LAZARUS, MEL	CARTOONIST	NEWS AMERICA SYNDICATE		
		1703 KAISER AVE	IRVINE, CA	92714
LAZARUS, PAUL N, III	FILM PRODUCER	26172 PACIFIC COAST HWY	MALIBU, CA	90265
LAZARUS, TOM	TV WRITER	8955 BEVERLY BLVD	LOS ANGELES, CA	90048
LAZENBY, GEORGE	ACTOR	514 EULCID ST	SANTA MONICA, CA	90402
LAZO, JOY	ACTRESS	1605 CAHUENGA BLVD N #202	LOS ANGELES, CA	90028
LAZY COWGIRLS, THE	ROCK & ROLL GROUP	POST OFFICE BOX 1116	CULVER CITY, CA	90232
LAZY RACER	ROCK & ROLL GROUP	5 W 86TH ST #156	NEW YORK, NY	10024
LE BLANC, KATHY	MODEL	5524 GREGORY AVE	WHITTIER, CA	90601
LE BLANC, LENNY	SINGER	HEARTLAND, 660 DOUGLAS AVE	ALTAMONTE SPRINGS, FL	32714
LE BLANC, RENA D	WRITER	8955 BEVERLY BLVD	LOS ANGELES, CA	90048
LE BLANC, WHITNEY J	DIRECTOR	DGA, 7950 SUNSET BLVD	LOS ANGELES, CA	90046
LE BORG, REGINALD	FILM DIRECTOR	1304 N HAYWORTH AVE	HOLLYWOOD, CA	90046
LE BROCK, KELLY	ACTRESS-MODEL	FORD MODELS, 344 E 59TH ST	NEW YORK, NY	10022
LE BRON, LARRY J	WRITER	1800 MONTANA AVE	SANTA MONICA, CA	90403
LE CARRE, JOHN	WRITER	TREGIFFIAN, SAINT BURYAN		
		PEMZANCE	CORNWALL	ENGLAND
LE CLAIR, ANDRE R J	NEWS CORRESPONDENT	1705 DE SALES ST, NW	WASHINGTON, DC	20036
LE CLAIR, MICHAEL	ACTOR	12517 PARAMOUNT BLVD	DOWNEY, CA	90242
LE CLERC, JEAN	ACTOR	19 W 44TH ST #1500	NEW YORK, NY	10036
LE COMTE, MICHELLE C	NEWS CORRESPONDENT	1866 WYOMING AVE, NW	WASHINGTON, DC	20009
LE COVER, LISA	ACTRESS	115 N DOHENY DR #316	LOS ANGELES, CA	90046
LE DIZES, MARYVONNE	VIOLINIST	1182 MARKET ST #311	SAN FRANCISCO, CA	94102
LE DONNE, ROBERT J	WRITER	555 W 57TH ST #1230	NEW YORK, NY	10019
LE DOUX, HAROLD	CARTOONIST	NEWS AMERICA SYNDICATE		
		1703 KAISER AVE	IRVINE, CA	92714
LE FEVER, KIT	ACTRESS	200 W 57TH ST #1303	NEW YORK, NY	10019
LE FORT, DOMINIQUE	CLOWN	2701 COTTAGE WY #14	SACRAMENTO, CA	95825
LE GALLIENNE, EVA	ACTRESS	HILLSIDE RD	WESTON, CT	06880
LE GAULT, LANCE	ACTOR	8721 SUNSET BLVD #200	LOS ANGELES, CA	90069
LE GUIN, URSULA K	WRITER	8955 BEVERLY BLVD	LOS ANGELES, CA	90048
LE HERE, S SHANNON	NEWS CORRESPONDENT	4400 EAST-WEST HWY	BETHESDA, MD	20814
LE JUGE, ANGELICA	WRITER	555 W 57TH ST #1230	NEW YORK, NY	10019
LE MASSENA, WILLIAM	ACTOR	132 W 11TH ST	NEW YORK, NY	10011
LE MASTERS, KIM	TV EXECUTIVE	CBS-TV, 7800 BEVERLY BLVD	LOS ANGELES, CA	90036
LE MAT, PAUL	ACTOR	1100 N ALTA LOMA RD	LOS ANGELES, CA	90069
LE MESURIER, JOHN	ACTOR	56 BARON'S KEEP	LONDON W14	ENGLAND
LE PERRIERE, GAETAN	BARITONE	CAMI, 165 W 57TH ST	NEW YORK, NY	10019
LE PORE, FRANK	WRITER	555 W 57TH ST #1230	NEW YORK, NY	10019
LE ROI BROTHERS, THE	ROCK & ROLL GROUP	RICE, 6908 CHERRY MEADOW DR	AUSTIN, TX	78745
LE ROSE, NICHOLAS	WRITER	8955 BEVERLY BLVD	LOS ANGELES, CA	90048
LE ROUX	ROCK & ROLL GROUP	POST OFFICE BOX U	TARZANA, CA	91356
LE ROY, GEN	WRITER	555 W 57TH ST #1230	NEW YORK, NY	10019
LE ROY, GLORIA	ACTRESS	12725 VENTURA BLVD #E	STUDIO CITY, CA	91604
LE SAGE, JONI M	NEWS CORRESPONDENT	1111 18TH ST, NW	WASHINGTON, DC	20036
LE SUEUR, JOSEPH	WRITER	555 W 57TH ST #1230	NEW YORK, NY	10019
LE VAUX, MILDRED	WRITER	201 OCEAN AVE #1204-B	SANTA MONICA, CA	90402

LE VEILLE, STEVEN G	WRITER	555 W 57TH ST #1230	NEW YORK, NY 10019
LE VEQUE, EDWARD	ACTOR	541 N LUCERNE BLVD	LOS ANGELES, CA 90004
LE VEQUE, JOHN FRANCIS	SCREENWRITER	9027 GIBSON ST	LOS ANGELES, CA 90034
LE WINTER, JACQUELINE	TALENT AGENT	4051 RADFORD AVE #A	STUDIO CITY, CA 91604
LE WITT, SOL	SCULPTOR-ARTIST	SUSANNE SINGER, 308 E 79TH ST	NEW YORK, NY 10021
LEA, CHANELLE	ACTRESS	6310 SAN VICENTE BLVD #407	LOS ANGELES, CA 90048
LEA, SHARAN	ACTRESS	15010 VENTURA BLVD #219	SHERMAN OAKS, CA 91403
LEACH, BRITT	ACTOR	12725 VENTURA BLVD #E	STUDIO CITY, CA 91604
LEACH, BUDDY	WRITER	8955 BEVERLY BLVD	LOS ANGELES, CA 90048
LEACH, ROBIN	TV HOST	875 3RD AVE #1800	NEW YORK, NY 10022
LEACH, ROSEMARY	ACTRESS	MORRIS, 147-149 WARDOUR ST	LONDON W1V 3TB ENGLAND
LEACHMAN, CLORIS	ACTRESS	13127 BOCA DE CANON LN	LOS ANGELES, CA 90049
LEACOCK, PHILIP	DIRECTOR-PRODUCER	914 BIENVENEDA AVE	PACIFIC PALISADES, CA 90272
LEADER, JOSEPH	ACTOR	1418 N HIGHLAND AVE #102	LOS ANGELES, CA 90028
LEADER, TONY	TV DIRECTOR	112 S LA JOLLA AVE	LOS ANGELES, CA 90048
LEADON, BERNIE	SINGER	2016 MOUNT PROSPECT DR	TOPANGA CANYON, CA 90290
LEAF, MADONNA	NEWS CORRESPONDENT	6736 BARON RD	MC LEAN, VA 22101
LEAF, PAUL	WRI-DRI-PROD	2800 NEILSON WY #408	SANTA MONICA, CA 90405
LEAGAN, RICHARD W	NEWS CORRESPONDENT	NBC-TV, NEWS DEPARTMENT	
		4001 NEBRASKA AVE, NW	WASHINGTON, DC 20016
LEAHY, THOMAS F	TV EXECUTIVE	CBS-TV, 51 W 52ND ST	NEW YORK, NY 10019
LEAK, JENNIFER	ACTRESS	19 W 44TH ST #1500	NEW YORK, NY 10036
LEAKE, CRAIG	WRITER-PRODUCER	CBS-TV, 524 W 57TH ST	NEW YORK, NY 10019
LEAKE, CYNTHIA	ACTRESS	LIGHT, 113 N ROBERTSON BLVD	LOS ANGELES, CA 90048
LEAN, SIR DAVID	FILM DIRECTOR	FILM PRODUCERS ASSOCIATION	
		162 WARDOUR ST	LONDSON W1V 3AT ENGLAND
LEAPING LANNY	WRESTLER	SEE - POFFO, LEAPING LANNY	
LEAR, AMANDA	SINGER-ACTRESS	POSTFACH 800149	D-8000 MUNICH 80 WEST GERMANY
LEAR, EVELYN	SOPRANO	CAMI, 165 W 57TH ST	NEW YORK, NY 10019
LEAR, NORMAN	TV WRITER-PRODUCER	255 CHADBOURNE AVE	LOS ANGELES, CA 90049
LEAR, ROBERT	NEWS CORRESPONDENT	3724 MOUNT AIREY LN	ANNANDALE, VA 22003
LEARMAN, RICHARD	DIRECTOR	11920 SIERRA LN	NORTHRIDGE, CA 91326
LEARNED, MICHAEL	ACTRESS	145 CENTRAL PARK W	NEW YORK, NY 10023
LEARY, BRIANNE	ACTRESS	10390 SANTA MONICA BLVD #310	LOS ANGELES, CA 90025
LEARY, DR TIMOTHY	AUTHOR-LECTURER	3828 WILLAT AVE	CULVER CITY, CA 90230
LEARY, MARGARET	ACTRESS	46 GRANDVIEW AVE	GLEN ROCK, NJ 07452
LEARY, NOLAN	ACTOR	8721 SUNSET BLVD #103	LOS ANGELES, CA 90069
LEARY, ROBIN	ACTOR	DMI, 250 W 57TH ST	NEW YORK, NY 10107
LEARY, TIMOTHY	AUTHOR	3828 WILLAT AVE	CULVER CITY, CA 90230
LEARY, WARREN E	NEWS CORRESPONDENT	313 "T" ST, NW	WASHINGTON, DC 20001
LEASURE, JAN	COLUMNIST	UNIVERSAL PRESS SYNDICATE	
		4900 MAIN ST, 9TH FLOOR	KANSAS CITY, MO 62114
LEATH, RON	ACTOR	LOCKWOOD, 10845 LINDBROOK DR	LOS ANGELES, CA 90024
LEATHERWOLF	ROCK & ROLL GROUP	POST OFFICE BOX 9555	MARINA DEL REY, CA 90295
LEAVELL	ROCK & ROLL GROUP	VARIETY ARTISTS INTL, INC	
		9073 NEMO ST, 3RD FLOOR	LOS ANGELES, CA 90069
LEAVER, DON	TV DIRECTOR	22 FREWIN RD	LONDON SW18 ENGLAND
LEAVITT, RON	TV WRITER	8955 BEVERLY BLVD	LOS ANGELES, CA 90048
LEBE, ARLEEN C	WRITER	555 W 57TH ST #1230	NEW YORK, NY 10019
LEBE, MITCHELL S	WRITER	555 W 57TH ST #1230	NEW YORK, NY 10019
LEBER, STEVE	THEATER PROD-AGENT	65 W 55TH ST #306	NEW YORK, NY 10019
LEBHERZ, LOUIS	BASS	61 W 62ND ST #6-F	NEW YORK, NY 10023
LEBI, MARK	WRITER	555 W 57TH ST #1230	NEW YORK, NY 10019
LEBLING, ROBERT W, JR	NEWS CORRESPONDENT	11529 FENCHURCH CT	GERMANTOWN, MD 20874
LEBOVITZ, AMY	RECORD EXECUTIVE	AIM RECORDS, 6733 GLEEN	WHITTIER, CA 90601
LEBOW, MARTEE	SINGER	RAW MGMT, 48 W 37TH ST	NEW YORK, NY 10018
LEBOWITZ, MURRAY	ACTOR	10845 LINDBROOK DR #3	LOS ANGELES, CA 90024
LEBOWITZ, NEIL	TV WRITER	211 S BEVERLY DR #206	BEVERLY HILLS, CA 90212
LEBRECHT, THELMA J M	NEWS CORRESPONDENT	1825 "K" ST, NW	WASHINGTON, DC 20006
LEBSOCK, JACK	SINGER-GUITARIST	103 DANA DR	HENDERSONVILLE, TN 37075
LECHMAN, DON	FILM CRITIC	THE DAILY BREEZE	
		5215 TORRANCE BLVD	TORRANCE, CA 90509
LECHNER, SANFORD	WRITER	555 W 57TH ST #1230	NEW YORK, NY 10019
LECHOWICK, BERNARD	WRITER-PRODUCER	PLESHETTE, 2700 N BEACHWOOD DR	LOS ANGELES, CA 90068
LECKEY, ANDREW	COLUMNIST	TRIBUNE MEDIA SERVICES	
		64 E CONCORD ST	ORLANDO, FL 32801
LECLAIR, DENISE	CABLE EXECUTIVE	CNN, 1050 TECHWOOD DR, NW	ATLANTA, GA 30318
LECOMTE, FABRICE	COMPOSER	FINELL, 155 W 68TH ST	NEW YORK, NY 10023
LECROY, J BEVERLY	MUSICIAN	404 BELLENGRATH DR	NASHVILLE, TN 37211
LEDDING, EDWARD	DIRECTOR-PRODUCER	6384 LA PUHTA DR	LOS ANGELES, CA 90068
LEDDY, CRAIG W	NEWS CORRESPONDENT	2827 28TH ST #23, NW	WASHINGTON, DC 20008
LEDER, HERBERT JAY	WRITER-PRODUCER	90 RIVERSIDE DR	NEW YORK, NY 10024
LEDER, REUBEN A	TV WRITER-PRODUCER	1731 N VISTA ST	LOS ANGELES, CA 90046
LEDERER, FRANCIS	ACTOR-DIRECTOR	23134 SHERMAN WY	CANOGA PARK, CA 91307
LEDERER, RICHARD	FILM EXECUTIVE	17026 AVE SANTA YNEZ	PACIFIC PALISADES, CA 90272
LEDERER, SUZANNE	ACTRESS	13400 CHANDLER BLVD	VAN NUYS, CA 91401
LEDERGERBER, SONJA	ACTRESS	1029 HANOVER DR	BEVERLY HILLS, CA 90210
LEDERMANN, MARK	NEWS CORRESPONDENT	3052 PATRICK HENRY DR	FALLS CHURCH, VA 22044
LEDOUX, CHRIS	SINGER-GUITARIST	POST OFFICE BOX 253	SUMNER, IA 50674
LEDROIT, HENRI	TENOR	1182 MARKET ST #311	SAN FRANCISCO, CA 94102
LEE, ALAN S	WRITER-PRODUCER	5334 DONNA AVE	TARZANA, CA 91356
LEE, ALBERT	SINGER-GUITARIST	6399 WILSHIRE BLVD #PH	LOS ANGELES, CA 90048
LEE, ANDREW L	TV DIRECTOR	310 S HAMEL RD	LOS ANGELES, CA 90048
LEE, ANNA	ACTRESS	NATHAN, 1240 N DOHENY DR	LOS ANGELES, CA 90069
LEE, ARIEL	ACTRESS	COMAND, 1540 BROADWAY	NEW YORK, NY 10036

LEE, BARBARA	SINGER	POST OFFICE BOX 171132	NASHVILLE, TN	37217
LEE, BETH E	COMPOSER	20533 ARCHWOOD ST	CANOGA PARK, CA	91306
LEE, BILLY	ACTOR	POST OFFICE BOX 3217	BEAUMONT, CA	92223
LEE, BOB	JUMBLE WRITER	TRIBUNE MEDIA SERVICES		
		64 E CONCORD ST	ORLANDO, FL	32801
LEE, BRENDA	SINGER	POST OFFICE BOX 110033	NASHVILLE, TN	37222
LEE, BRUCE	MUSICIAN	7430 E 71ST ST	INDIANAPOLIS, IN	46256
LEE, CASSANDRA	SAXOPHONIST	910 WOODMONT BLVD #M-7	NASHVILLE, TN	37204
LEE, CECILIA	SINGER	RITA HEBREW, 8659 PINE CT	YPSILANTI, MI	48197
LEE, CHAI	ACTRESS	8235 SANTA MONICA BLVD #202	LOS ANGELES, CA	90046
LEE, CHAI	ACTRESS	BROWN, 47 WEST SQ	LONDON SE11	ENGLAND
LEE, CHARLES	TV WRITER	8955 BEVERLY BLVD	LOS ANGELES, CA	90048
LEE, CHINA	ACTRESS-MODEL	SAHL, 2325 SAN YSIDRO DR	BEVERLY HILLS, CA	90210
LEE, CHRISTOPHER	ACTOR	9000 SUNSET BLVD #315	LOS ANGELES, CA	90069
LEE, CYNTHIA	ACTRESS	ABC-TV, "ALL MY CHILDREN"		
		1330 AVE OF THE AMERICAS	NEW YORK, NY	10019
LEE, DANA	ACTOR	400 S BEVERLY DR #216	BEVERLY HILLS, CA	90212
LEE, DARIN	GUITARIST	131 SAVELY DR	HENDERSONVILLE, TN	37075
LEE, DAVID	TV WRITER	1650 WESTWOOD BLVD #201	LOS ANGELES, CA	90024
LEE, DAVID	GUITARIST	POST OFFICE BOX 1	EAGLEVILLE, TN	37060
LEE, DAVID CLARK	TV WRITER-PRODUCER	8955 BEVERLY BLVD	LOS ANGELES, CA	90048
LEE, DEAN	PHOTOGRAPHER	8 GUY CT	ROCKVILLE, MD	20850
LEE, DICKIE	SINGER-SONGWRITER	941 FORREST ACRES CT	NASHVILLE, TN	37220
LEE, DONALD A	NEWS CORRESPONDENT	2918 S BUCHANAN ST	ARLINGTON, VA	22206
LEE, DONALD RAY	GUITARIST	409 MALVIN ST	GALLATIN, TN	37066
LEE, DONNA	TV WRITER	8955 BEVERLY BLVD	LOS ANGELES, CA	90048
LEE, EDWARD P	PHOTOGRAPHER	2614 S ARLINGTON MILL DR #C	ARLINGTON, VA	22206
LEE, ELEANOR	ACTRESS	ICM, 8899 BEVERLY BLVD	LOS ANGELES, CA	90048
LEE, EUNICE	VIOLINIST	CAMI, 165 W 57TH ST	NEW YORK, NY	10019
LEE, FRANCES	ACTRESS	BENNETT, 1290 BLUE SKY DR	CARDIFF, CA	92007
LEE, GARY	TV WRITER	JEOPARDY, 1541 N VINE ST	HOLLYWOOD, CA	90028
LEE, GILBERT	TV WRITER	8955 BEVERLY BLVD	LOS ANGELES, CA	90048
LEE, GRACIA	ACTRESS	8350 SANTA MONICA BLVD #206-A	LOS ANGELES, CA	90069
LEE, HAROLD	GUITARIST	646 LARCHWOOD DR	NASHVILLE, TN	37214
LEE, HYAPATHA	ACTRESS-MODEL	POST OFFICE BOX 1924	INDIANAPOLIS, IN	46206
LEE, IRVING ALLEN	ACTOR	ABC-TV, "RYAN'S HOPE"		
		1330 AVE OF THE AMERICAS	NEW YORK, NY	10019
LEE, JACK	GUITARIST	5467 TILDEN AVE	VAN NUYS, CA	91401
LEE, JAMES	TV EXECUTIVE	51 HOLLAND ST, KENSINGTON	LONDON W8 7JB	ENGLAND
LEE, JAMES H	TV WRITER	8955 BEVERLY BLVD	LOS ANGELES, CA	90048
LEE, JARED	CARTOONIST	POST OFFICE BOX 4203	NEW YORK, NY	10017
LEE, JAY	WRITER	8955 BEVERLY BLVD	LOS ANGELES, CA	90048
LEE, JAY	SCREENWRITER	POST OFFICE BOX 626	BEVERLY HILLS, CA	90213
LEE, JENNIFER CLAYTON	ACTRESS	14471 SPA DR	HUNTINGTON BEACH, CA	92647
LEE, JESSICA	NEWS CORRESPONDENT	501 17TH ST, SE	WASHINGTON, DC	20003
LEE, JIM	DIRECTOR	DGA, 110 W 57TH ST	NEW YORK, NY	10019
LEE, JIMMY	GUITARIST	581 BLAKE MOORE DR	LA VERGNE, TN	37086
LEE, JOANNA	WRITER-PRODUCER	135 S CARMELINA AVE	LOS ANGELES, CA	90049
LEE, JOHNNY	SINGER-SONGWRITER	9255 SUNSET BLVD #706	LOS ANGELES, CA	90069
LEE, JONNA	ACTRESS	8721 SUNSET BLVD #103	LOS ANGELES, CA	90069
LEE, JUDY	GUITARIST	17 ELSDON ST	ROCHESTER, NY	14606
LEE, KAAREN	ACTRESS	9300 WILSHIRE BLVD #410	BEVERLY HILLS, CA	90212
LEE, KATHRYNE	WRITER	555 W 57TH ST #1230	NEW YORK, NY	10019
LEE, KEN NEAL	WRITER	8955 BEVERLY BLVD	LOS ANGELES, CA	90048
LEE, LARRY	GUITARIST	ROUTE #1	ASHLAND CITY, TN	37015
LEE, LESLIE	WRITER	555 W 57TH ST #1230	NEW YORK, NY	10019
LEE, LUAINE	FILM CRITIC	PASADENA STAR NEWS		
		525 E COLORADO BLVD	PASADENA, CA	91109
LEE, LUANN L	MODEL	MODELS & PROMOTIONS AGENCY		
		8560 SUNSET BLVD, 10TH FLOOR	LOS ANGELES, CA	90069
LEE, LYNN	WRITER	555 W 57TH ST #1230	NEW YORK, NY	10019
LEE, MACK L	NEWS CORRESPONDENT	2626 EAST-WEST HWY	CHEVY CHASE, MD	20815
LEE, MADELINE	ACTRESS	1435 LEXINGTON AVE	NEW YORK, NY	10028
LEE, MARGARET	WRITER	8955 BEVERLY BLVD	LOS ANGELES, CA	90048
LEE, MARK	WRITER	ICM, 8899 BEVERLY BLVD	LOS ANGELES, CA	90048
LEE, MICHELE	ACTRESS-SINGER	830 BIRCHWOOD DR	LOS ANGELES, CA	90024
LEE, MIKE	NEWS CORRESPONDENT	ABC NEWS, 7 W 66TH ST	NEW YORK, NY	10023
LEE, MOONHEE	NEWS CORRESPONDENT	3195 READSBOROUGH CT	FAIRFAX, VA	22031
LEE, MYRNA	SINGER	POST OFFICE BOX 171132	NASHVILLE, TN	37217
LEE, NAMKYU	NEWS CORRESPONDENT	3507 PENCE CT	ANNANDALE, VA	22003
LEE, NELLE HARPER	AUTHOR	MC INTOSH, 18 E 41ST ST	NEW YORK, NY	10017
LEE, PALMER	ACTOR	SEE - PALMER, GREGG		
LEE, PAT	TV PRODUCER	1438 N GOWER ST #250	LOS ANGELES, CA	90028
LEE, PATTI R	ACTRESS	9220 SUNSET BLVD #202	LOS ANGELES, CA	90069
LEE, PEGGY	SINGER-ACTRESS	11404 BELLAGIO RD	LOS ANGELES, CA	90049
LEE, PINKY	ACTOR	430 S BURNSIDE AVE #10-C	LOS ANGELES, CA	90036
LEE, RANDY	SINGER	CUDE, 519 N HALIFAX AVE	DAYTONA BEACH, FL	32018
LEE, REBEL	SINGER-SONGWRITER	KAREN STANFORD		
		ROUTE #1, BOX 114-A	BINGER, OK	73009
LEE, RENATA	ACTRESS	6640 SUNSET BLVD #203	LOS ANGELES, CA	90028
LEE, RICHARD E	NEWS CORRESPONDENT	1301 15TH ST #519, NW	WASHINGTON, DC	20005
LEE, ROBERT E	PLAYWRIGHT	15725 ROYAL OAK RD	ENCINO, CA	91316
LEE, ROBERT E	TRUMPETER	5124 KESTER AVE	SHERMAN OAKS, CA	91403
LEE, ROBIN	SINGER	TAYLOR, 2401 12TH AVE S	NASHVILLE, TN	37204

Cecilia Lee

For Fan Club information, contact

CE-TA PRODUCTIONS
8659 Pine Court
Ypsilanti, Michigan 48198

LEE, ROBIN	COMPOSER	1111 E RAMON RD #10	PALM SPRINGS, CA 92262
LEE, ROBIN BETH	ACTRESS	1717 N HIGHLAND AVE #414	LOS ANGELES, CA 90028
LEE, RONNIE	SINGER	BARBARUS, 110 BOYLSTON AVE N	SEATTLE, WA 98102
LEE, ROSA	SINGER-SONGWRITER	SEE - MARTIN, ROSA LEE	
LEE, RUTA	ACTRESS	7060 HOLLYWOOD BLVD #610	LOS ANGELES, CA 90028
LEE, SCOOTER	SINGER	311 CHURCH ST #300	NASHVILLE, TN 37201
LEE, SCOTTY	SINGER	38 MUSIC SQUARE E #216	NASHVILLE, TN 37203
LEE, SHIRLEY	SINGER	OLDIES, 5218 ALMONT ST	LOS ANGELES, CA 90032
LEE, STAGGER	WRESTLER	SEE - WARE, KOKO B	
LEE, STAN	CARTOONIST	THE COWLES SYNDICATE	
		715 LOCUST ST	DES MOINES, IA 50304
LEE, STEPHEN	ACTOR	KOHNER, 9169 SUNSET BLVD	LOS ANGELES, CA 90069
LEE, SUNG-JU	VIOLINIST	GEWALD, 58 W 58TH ST	NEW YORK, NY 10019
LEE, TERRI	SINGER-GUITARIST	VILLA-ADRIAN, 2955 FRANKLIN RD	NASHVILLE, TN 37215
LEE, THELMA	ACTRESS	2 LINCOLN AVE	RYE BROOK, NY 10573
LEE, TIGER CHUNG	WRESTLER	POST OFFICE BOX 3859	STAMFORD, CT 06905
LEE, TONY	ACTOR	WOSK, 435 S LA CIENEGA BLVD	LOS ANGELES, CA 90048
LEE, VELMA	SINGER	POST OFFICE BOX 25371	CHARLOTTLE, NC 28212
LEE, VINECE	ACTRESS	1141 19TH ST #125	SANTA MONICA, CA 90403
LEE, WANDA	SINGER	POST OFFICE BOX 6025	NEWPORT NEWS, IA 23606
LEE, ZONA	COMPOSER	16154 GILMORE ST	VAN NUYS, CA 91406
LEE-SUNG, RICHARD	ACTOR	8235 SANTA MONICA BLVD #202	LOS ANGELES, CA 90046
LEE-WRIGHT, JENNY	ACTRESS	PETER CHARLESWORTH, LTD	
		68 OLD BROMPTON RD	LONDON SW7 3LQ ENGLAND
LEECH, BEVERLY	ACTRESS	247 S BEVERLY DR #102	BEVERLY HILLS, CA 90210
LEECH, ELIZABETH J	MUSIC ARRANGER	4501 ALCOTT DR	NASHVILLE, TN 37215
LEECH, IAN M	DIRECTOR	DGA, 7950 SUNSET BLVD	LOS ANGELES, CA 90046
LEECH, MICHAEL A	MUSIC ARRANGER	4501 ALCOTT DR	NASHVILLE, TN 37215
LEECH, RICHARD	TENOR	59 E 54TH ST #81	NEW YORK, NY 10022
LEECH, RICHARD	ACTOR	27 CLAYLANDS RD	LONDON SW8 1NX ENGLAND
LEEDS, ELISSA	ACTRESS	151 N SAN VICENTE BLVD #208	BEVERLY HILLS, CA 90211
LEEDS, HOWARD	TV WRITER-PRODUCER	8955 BEVERLY BLVD	LOS ANGELES, CA 90048
LEEDS, JAN JULINE	SOPRANO	CAMI, 165 W 57TH ST	NEW YORK, NY 10019
LEEDS, PETER	ACTOR	626 N SCREENLAND DR	BURBANK, CA 91505
LEEDS, PHIL	ACTOR	1422 N SWEETZER AVE #309	LOS ANGELES, CA 90069
LEEDS, REGINA	ACTRESS	8721 SUNSET BLVD #103	LOS ANGELES, CA 90069
LEEDS, ROBERT	TV DIRECTOR	DGA, 7950 SUNSET BLVD	LOS ANGELES, CA 90046
LEEDS, STUART	CARTOONIST	POST OFFICE BOX 4203	NEW YORK, NY 10017
LEEKLEY, JOHN	TV WRITER-PRODUCER	5732 VESPER AVE	VAN NUYS, CA 91411
LEEN, TAMMY & JOHN & LEEN TWO	C & W GROUP	WOOD, 2901 EPPERLY DR	DEL CITY, OK 73115
LEEPSON, MARC	NEWS CORRESPONDENT	13741 MINNIEVILLE RD	WOODBRIDGE, VA 22193
LEES, BENJAMIN	COMPOSER	28 CAMBRIDGE RD	GREAT NECK, NY 11023
LEES, MICHAEL	ACTOR	908 CHELSEA CLOISTERS	
		SLOANE AVE	LONDON SW3 ENGLAND
LEES, ROBERT	WRITER	1600 COURTNEY AVE	LOS ANGELES, CA 90046
LEESON, MICHAEL	SCREENWRITER	3725 ALOMAR DR	SHERMAN OAKS, CA 91405
LEETCH, THOMAS	WRITER-PRODUCER	14593 DEERVALE PL	SHERMAN OAKS, CA 91403
LEEWOOD, JACK	DIRECTOR-PRODUCER	6220 OWENSMOUTH AVE #310	WOODLAND HILLS, CA 91367
LEFCOURT, PETER	TV WRITER-PRODUCER	5605 GREEN OAK DR	LOS ANGELES, CA 90068
LEFEBVRE, ANNE-CATHERINE	MODEL	POST OFFICE BOX 7211	MOUNTAIN VIEW, CA 94043
LEFEBVRE, JIM	ACTOR	15010 VENTURA BLVD #219	SHERMAN OAKS, CA 91403
LEFEVRE, MYLON & BROKEN HEART	GOSPEL GROUP	POST OFFICE BOX 723591	ATLANTA, GA 30339
LEFFER, WARREN K	PHOTOGRAPHER	11412 GRAYLING LN	ROCKVILLE, MD 20853
LEFFERTS, GEORGE	WRITER-PRODUCER	ROBBINS REST	FIRE ISLAND, NY 11776
LEFKOW, DAVID C	NEWS CORRESPONDENT	1824 BELMONT RD, NW	WASHINGTON, DC 20009
LEFKOWITZ, MISCHA	VIOLINIST	253 W 73RD ST #7-M	NEW YORK, NY 10023
LEFLER, DOUGLAS	WRITER	8955 BEVERLY BLVD	LOS ANGELES, CA 90048
LEFT, THE	ROCK & ROLL GROUP	POST OFFICE BOX 185	RED LION, PA 17356
LEFTWICH, ED H	DIRECTOR	DGA, 110 W 57TH ST	NEW YORK, NY 10019
LEGACY	ROCK & ROLL GROUP	POST OFFICE BOX 25654	RICHMOND, VA 23260
LEGAL WEAPON	ROCK & ROLL GROUP	1626 N WILCOX ST #722	HOLLYWOOD, CA 90078
LEGANTSOV, VLADISLAV	NEWS CORRESPONDENT	1850 COLUMBIA PIKE #511	ARLINGTON, VA 22204
LEGARD, JOHN B	FILM EDITOR	75 HOLLAND PARK	LONDON W11 ENGLAND
LEGEND	ROCK & ROLL GROUP	POST OFFICE BOX 1909	MILL VALLEY, CA 94942
LEGENDARY GOLDEN VAMPIRES, THE	ROCK & ROLL GROUP	LINTRUPER STR 39	1000 BERLIN 49 WEST GERMANY
LEGENDARY STARDUST COWBOY	SINGER	POST OFFICE BOX 26265	FORT WORTH, CA 76116
LEGG, JOHN EMMETT	HARPSICHORDIST	12622 CHANDLER LN	BOWIE, MD 20715
LEGGETT, KAREN L	NEWS CORRESPONDENT	4400 JENIFER ST, NW	WASHINGTON, DC 20015
LEGGETT, LAVRIAN	WRITER	LAKE, 1103 GLENDON AVE	LOS ANGELES, CA 90024
LEGNITTO, JANICE	WRITER	555 W 57TH ST #1230	NEW YORK, NY 10019
LEGRAND, MICHEL	PIANIST-COMPOSER	4146 LANKERSHIM BLVD #300	NORTH HOLLYWOOD, CA 91602
LEGS DIAMOND	VOCAL GROUP	POST OFFICE BOX 1816	BURBANK, CA 91507
LEH, ROBERT	ACTOR	410 N ROSSMORE AVE #302	LOS ANGELES, CA 90004
LEHANE, GREGORY	DIRECTOR	334 W 87TH ST #9-C	NEW YORK, NY 10024
LEHMAN, ERNEST	WRITER-PRODUCER	11759 CHENAULT ST	LOS ANGELES, CA 90049
LEHMAN, GLADYS C	WRITER	8955 BEVERLY BLVD	LOS ANGELES, CA 90048
LEHMAN, H JANE	NEWS CORRESPONDENT	11510 BUCKNELL DR #201	WHEATON, MD 20902
LEHMAN, LILLIAN	ACTRESS	14850 PARTHENIA ST #3	PANORAMA CITY, CA 91402
LEHMAN, ORIN	THEATER PRODUCER	67 E 82ND ST	NEW YORK, NY 10028
LEHMAN, ROBERT	DIRECTOR	14401 HARTSOOK ST	SHERMAN OAKS, CA 91403
LEHMANN, TED	ACTOR	1617 GRIFFITH PARK BLVD	LOS ANGELES, CA 90026
LEHNE, JOHN	ACTOR	9220 SUNSET BLVD #625	LOS ANGELES, CA 90069
LEHNING, KYLE	MUSICIAN	116 SKYVIEW DR	HENDERSONVILLE, TN 37075
LEHR, GEORGE	TV DIRECTOR-PRODUCER	3134 VETERAN AVE	LOS ANGELES, CA 90034

REBEL LEE

REBEL LEE FAN CLUB
C/O KAREN STANFORD
ROUTE #1, BOX 114-A, BINGER, OK 73009
$7.00 per year

BENEFITS ARE: 8 X 10 PHOTO, NEWSLETTER, BUTTON, BIOGRAPHY, ALBUM, AND BUMPER STICKERS.

SINGLES AVAILABLE:
"LOVE GAMES," "WHEN YOU TRY," "IN THE MIDDLE OF A MEMORY," "STRAIGHT FROM THE HEART," AND "LEAVIN' ON YOUR MIND."
$2.00 EACH

Name	Occupation	Address	City	Zip/Country
LEHR, KENETTE	TV WRITER	10901 WHIPPLE ST #27	NORTH HOLLYWOOD, CA	91602
LEHR, ZELLA	SINGER	38 MUSIC SQUARE E #300	NASHVILLE, TN	37203
LEHRER, GAEL	WRITER	8955 BEVERLY BLVD	LOS ANGELES, CA	90048
LEHRER, JIM	TV HOST-PLAYWRIGHT	POST OFFICE BOX 2626	WASHINGTON, DC	20013
LEHRMAN, MARGARET	NEWS CORRESPONDENT	NBC-TV, NEWS DEPARTMENT		
		4001 NEBRASKA AVE, NW	WASHINGTON, DC	20016
LEHRMAN, PHILLIP A	CONDUCTOR	4417 77TH ST	LUBBOCK, TX	79424
LEHRMAN, STEVEN	WRITER-PRODUCER	107-40 QUEENS BLVD	FOREST HILLS, NY	11375
LEHWALDER, HEIDI	HARPIST	59 E 54TH ST #81	NEW YORK, NY	10022
LEIB, GIL	CONDUCTOR	9725 CHARNOCK AVE #2	LOS ANGELES, CA	90034
LEIBERT, PHYLLIS R	TV EXECUTIVE	NBC TELEVISION NETWORK		
		30 ROCKEFELLER PLAZA	NEW YORK, NY	10112
LEIBMAN, RON	ACTOR-WRITER	10530 STRATHMORE DR	LOS ANGELES, CA	90024
LEIBOW, RUTH I	COMPOSER	11105 ROSE AVE #209	LOS ANGELES, CA	90034
LEIBOWITZ, NEIL H	NEWS CORRESPONDENT	1755 S JEFFERSON DAVIS HWY	ARLINGTON, VA	22202
LEIBU, DOLLEE	COMPOSER	1247 N SWEETZER AVE #2	LOS ANGELES, CA	90069
LEICHT, ALLAN	TV WRITER-PRODUCER	THE WILLIAM MORRIS AGENCY		
		1350 AVE OF THE AMERICAS	NEW YORK, NY	10019
LEIDER, JERRY	FILM PRODUCER	ITC PRODS, 12711 VENTURA BLVD	STUDIO CITY, CA	91604
LEIFER, NEIL	PHOTOGRAPHER	TIME/TIME & LIFE BLDG		
		ROCKEFELLER CENTER	NEW YORK, NY	10020
LEIFF, PHILIP	TV DIRECTOR-PRODUCER	702 FORDHAM RD	BALA-CYNWYD, PA	19004
LEIGH, A NORMAN	DIRECTOR	19 NIRVANA AVE	GREAT NECK, NY	11023
LEIGH, CARRIE	MODEL	HEFNER, 10236 CHARING CROSS RD	LOS ANGELES, CA	90024
LEIGH, DEVON	ACTRESS	CARPENTER, 1516-W REDWOOD ST	SAN DIEGO, CA	92101
LEIGH, GILBERT	ACTOR	300 W 49TH ST	NEW YORK, NY	10019
LEIGH, JANET	ACTRESS	BRANDT, 1625 SUMMITRIDGE DR	BEVERLY HILLS, CA	90210
LEIGH, JENNIFER JASON	ACTRESS	EDRICK, 8957 NORMA PL	LOS ANGELES, CA	90069
LEIGH, LINDY	GUITARIST	DOUBLE L RANCH, ROUTE #2		
		LEWISBURG PIKE	FRANKLIN, TN	37064
LEIGH, MIKE	FILM WRITER-DIRECTOR	8 EARLHAM GROVE	LONDON N22	ENGLAND
LEIGH, NORMAN	DIRECTOR	19 NIRVANA AVE	GREAT NECK, NY	11023
LEIGH, TERRI	ACTRESS	SCHOEMAN, 2600 W VICTORY BLVD	BURBANK, CA	91505
LEIGH-HUNT, BARBARA	ACTRESS	LEADING ARTISTS, LTD		
		60 SAINT JAMES'S ST	LONDON SW1	ENGLAND
LEIGH-HUNT, RONALD	ACTOR	LEADING PLAYERS, 31 KINGS RD	LONDON SW3	ENGLAND
LEIGHTON, DYAN	TV WRITER	6725 SUNSET BLVD #506	HOLLYWOOD, CA	90028
LEIGHTON, MERRILL	ACTRESS	8721 SUNSET BLVD #202	LOS ANGELES, CA	90069
LEIGHTON, ROBERTA	ACTRESS	CBS TELEVISION NETWORK		
		"THE YOUNG & THE RESTLESS"		
		7800 BEVERLY BLVD	LOS ANGELES, CA	90036
LEIGHTON, TED	TV WRITER	8955 BEVERLY BLVD	LOS ANGELES, CA	90048
LEIGHTOPN, FRANCES SPATZ	NEWS CORRESPONDENT	3636 16TH ST, NW	WASHINGTON, DC	20010
LEISER, ERNEST	TV PRODUCER	CBS-TV, 51 W 52ND ST	NEW YORK, NY	10019
LEISER, ROLAND B	NEWS CORRESPONDENT	2215 MONTGOMERY ST	SILVER SPRING, MD	20910
LEISER, SCOTT C	DIRECTOR	4489 HARVARD RD	DETROIT, MI	48224
LEISNER, DAVID	GUITARIST-COMPOSER	AFFILIATE ARTISTS, INC		
		37 W 65TH ST, 6TH FLOOR	NEW YORK, NY	10023
LEISSNER, JANET R	NEWS CORRESPONDENT	CBS NEWS, 2020 "M" ST, NW	WASHINGTON, DC	20036
LEISURE, DAVID	ACTOR	6430 SUNSET BLVD #1203	LOS ANGELES, CA	90028
LEITCH, CHRISTOPHER L	WRITER	8955 BEVERLY BLVD	LOS ANGELES, CA	90048
LEITERMAN, DOUGLAS	PRODUCER-EXECUTIVE	MOTION PICTURE GUARANTORS		
		43 BRITAIN ST	TORONTO, ONT M5A 1R7	CANADA
LEITNER, IRVING	WRITER	555 W 57TH ST #1230	NEW YORK, NY	10019
LEITNER, TED	SPORTSCASTER	KFMB-TV, 7677 ENGINEER RD	SAN DIEGO, CA	92111
LEKAS, TED T	WRITER	1720 CAMDEN AVE #9	LOS ANGELES, CA	90025
LELAND, ROBERT	DIRECTOR-PRODUCER	2105 ROBINSON ST #A	REDONDO BEACH, CA	90278
LELLE, WERNER	NEWS CORRESPONDENT	1551 BRUTON CT	MC LEAN, VA	22101
LELOUCH, CLAUDE	FILM DIRECTOR	15 AVE HOCHE	PARIS 75008	FRANCE
LEM, CAROL	TV EXECUTIVE	CBS-TV, 6121 SUNSET BLVD	LOS ANGELES, CA	90028
LEMARR, HEATHER	ACTRESS	BUSH & ROSS, 4942 VINELAND AVE	NORTH HOLLYWOOD, CA	91601
LEMAY, HARDING	WRITER	555 W 57TH ST #1230	NEW YORK, NY	10019
LEMAY, STEPHEN	WRITER	555 W 57TH ST #1230	NEW YORK, NY	10019
LEMBECK, HELAINE	ACTRESS	1251 N CRESCENT HGTS BLVD #B	LOS ANGELES, CA	90046
LEMBECK, MICHAEL	ACTOR	150 E HIGHLAND AVE #H	SIERRA MADRE, CA	91024
LEMBI, FRANCINE	ACTRESS	211 S BEVERLY BLVD	BEVERLY HILLS, CA	90212
LEMMO, JOAN	ACTRESS	11752 MAGNOLIA BLVD	NORTH HOLLYWOOD, CA	91607
LEMMON, CHRISTOPHER	ACTOR	7734 LEXINGTON AVE	HOLLYWOOD, CA	90046
LEMMON, DAVE	SINGER	SCA, 46 E HERBERT AVE	SALT LAKE CITY, UT	84111
LEMMON, JACK	ACTOR-DIRECTOR	141 S EL CAMINO DR #201	BEVERLY HILLS, CA	90212
LEMOINE, JACQUES	DIRECTOR	THE SUN GROUP COMPANY		
		505 5TH AVE, 11TH FLOOR	NEW YORK, NY	10017
LEMOINES, LES	AERIAL TROUPE	SEE - LES LEMOINES		
LEMON, BOB	BASEBALL	1141 CLAIBORNE DR	LONG BEACH, CA	90807
LEMON, MEADOWLARK	ACTOR-BASKETBALL	POST OFFICE BOX 398	SIERRA VISTA, AZ	85635
LEMON, MICHAEL	ACTOR	9255 SUNSET BLVD #510	LOS ANGELES, CA	90069
LEMON, RICHARD C	WRITER-EDITOR	PEOPLE/TIME & LIFE BLDG		
		ROCKEFELLER CENTER	NEW YORK, NY	10020
LEMON DROPS, THE	ROCK & ROLL GROUP	POST OFFICE BOX 791551	DALLAS, TX	75379
LEMON DROPS, THE MIGHTY	ROCK & ROLL GROUP	SEE - MIGHTY LEMON DROPS, THE		
LEMONICK, MICHAEL D	WRITER-EDITOR	TIME/TIME & LIFE BLDG		
		ROCKEFELLER CENTER	NEW YORK, NY	10020
LEMONRANDE, RUSTY	SCREENWRITER	8955 BEVERLY BLVD	LOS ANGELES, CA	90048
LEMONT, JOHN V	WRITER-PRODUCER	84 SUTHERLAND AVE	LONDON W9 2QS	ENGLAND
LEMPERT, LARRY	NEWS CORRESPONDENT	4300 EDGEHURST RD	BALTIMORE, MD	21209

JANET LEIGH

JACK LEMMON

MICHAEL LEON

RAMSEY LEWIS

JERRY LEE LEWIS

JUDITH LIGHT

GORDON LIGHTFOOT

VIVICA LINDFORS

VIRNA LISI

Name	Occupation	Address	City	Zip
LEMPERT, PETER	ACTOR	8951 KEITH AVE	LOS ANGELES, CA	90069
LEMS, KRISTIN	SINGER-PIANIST	FLYING FISH RECORDS		
		1304 W CHUBERT AVE	CHICAHO, IL	60614
LENA, VINCENT	DIRECTOR	910 ALMOND HILL CT	MANCHESTER, MO	63033
LENARD, ELISSA	DIRECTOR	6056 BEEMAN AVE	NORTH HOLLYWOOD, CA	91606
LENARD, KATHRYN	TV EXECUTIVE	NBC TELEVISION NETWORK		
		30 ROCKEFELLER PLAZA	NEW YORK, NY	10112
LENARD, KAY	WRITER	8955 BEVERLY BLVD	LOS ANGELES, CA	90048
LENARD, MARK	ACTOR	845 VIA DE LA PAZ #A-243	PACIFIC PALISADES, CA	90272
LENCH, KATHERINE	ACTRESS	9414 GOTHIC AVE	SEPULVEDA, CA	91343
LENDROTH, SHERRIE	ACTRESS	1234 N HAYWORTH AVE #A	LOS ANGELES, CA	90046
LENEHAN, NANCY	ACTRESS	1901 AVE OF THE STARS #840	LOS ANGELES, CA	90067
LENIADO-CHIRA, JOSEPH	COMPOSER-CONDUCTOR	POST OFFICE BOX U	REDDING, CT	06875
LENK, PAULy A	SAXOPHONIST	2127 BERNARD AVE	NASHVILLE, TN	37212
LENNANE, BRIAN	TV DIRECTOR	29 PRIMROSE MANSIONS		
		PRINCE OF WLAES DR	LONDON SW11	ENGLAND
LENNARD, AMY	SPORTS REPORTER	SPORTS ILLUSTRATED MAGAZINE		
		TIME & LIFE BUILDING		
		ROCKEFELLER CENTER	NEW YORK, NY	10020
LENNIE, ANGUS	ACTOR	DRYSDALE, 15 PEMBROKE GARDENS	LONDON W8	ENGLAND
LENNON, JANET	SINGER	BAHLER, 27943 KIT CARSON RD	HIDDEN HILLS, CA	91302
LENNON, JULIAN	SINGER-COMPOSER	200 W 57TH ST #1403	NEW YORK, NY	10019
LENNON, KIPP	ACTOR	944 HARDING AVE	VENICE, CA	90291
LENNON, PAUL	COMEDIAN	32500 CONCORD DR #221	MADISON HEIGHTS, MI	48071
LENNON, THOMAS F	WRITER	555 W 57TH ST #1230	NEW YORK, NY	10019
LENNON SISTERS, THE	VOCAL GROUP	3230 CORINTH AVE	LOS ANGELES, CA	90066
LENNOX, ANNIE	SINGER	10100 SANTA MONICA BLVD #1600	LOS ANGELES, CA	90067
LENNY, JACK	THEATER PRODUCER	140 W 58TH ST	NEW YORK, NY	10019
LENO, JAY	COMEDIAN-ACTOR	7419 DEL ZURO DR	LOS ANGELES, CA	90046
LENORE, RUBY	MUSICIAN	LCS, 1627 16TH AVE S	NASHVILLE, TN	37212
LENOX, JOHN THOMAS	DIRECTOR-PRODUCER	6603 MAMMOTH AVE	VAN NUYS, CA	91405
LENSKA, RULA	ACTRESS-MODEL	306-16 EUSTON RD	LONDON NW13	ENGLAND
LENSKI, KATHLEEN	VIOLINIST	CCS, 4478 PURDUE AVE	CULVER CITY, CA	90230
LENSKI, ROBERT W	TV WRITER	222 N GLENROY AVE	LOS ANGELES, CA	90049
LENSKY, LEIB	ACTOR	280 9TH AVE #7-E	NEW YORK, NY	10001
LENTINI, SUSAN	ACTRESS	445 N BEDFORD DR #PH	BEVERLY HILLS, CA	90210
LENTZ, PAT	ACTRESS	13740 RUNNYMEDE ST	VAN NUYS, CA	91405
LENTZ, STEVEN E	FLUTIST	720 ROOSEVELT AVE	YORK, PA	17404
LENYOUN, LORELEI	DIRECTOR	19303 WEXFORD ST	DETROIT, MI	48234
LENZ, KAY	ACTRESS	9229 SUNSET BLVD #306	LOS ANGELES, CA	90069
LENZ, RICK	ACTOR	8350 SANTA MONICA BLVD #206	LOS ANGELES, CA	90069
LENZER, NORMAN	WRITER-PRODUCER	12303 2ND HELENA DR	LOS ANGELES, CA	90049
LEO, JOHN	WRITER-EDITOR	TIME/TIME & LIFE BLDG		
		ROCKEFELLER CENTER	NEW YORK, NY	10020
LEO, MALCOLM	WRITER-PRODUCER	10048 CIELO DR	BEVERLY HILLS, CA	90210
LEODAS, GUS	DIRECTOR	LEODAS, 333 E 49TH ST	NEW YORK, NY	10017
LEOGRAND, BARBARA	SINGER	POST OFFICE BOX 171132	NASHVILLE, TN	37217
LEOKUM, ARKADY	WRITER-COLUMNIST	UNIVERSAL PRESS SYNDICATE		
		4900 MAIN ST, 9TH FLOOR	KANSAS CITY, MO	62114
LEOKUM, LEONARD	DIRECTOR	DGA, 110 W 57TH ST	NEW YORK, NY	10019
LEON, DOROTHY	ACTRESS	124 W 87TH ST	NEW YORK, NY	10024
LEON, FERDINAND	WRITER	8955 BEVERLY BLVD	LOS ANGELES, CA	90048
LEON, JOSEPH	ACTOR	257 W 39TH ST	NEW YORK, NY	10018
LEON, JUDY A	NEWS CORRESPONDENT	400 N CAPITOL ST, NW	WASHINGTON, DC	20001
LEON, MICHAEL	ACTOR	8721 SUNSET BLVD #102	LOS ANGELES, CA	90069
LEON, STEPHEN	ACTOR	2800 PELHAM PL	LOS ANGELES, CA	90068
LEON, VALERIE	ACTRESS	PRINCESS HOUSE #409		
		190 PICCADILLY	LONDON W1	ENGLAND
LEONARD, ADA	CONDUCTOR	BERNSTEIN, 11408 BERWICK ST	LOS ANGELES, CA	90049
LEONARD, BILL	TV PRODUCER	CBS-TV, 524 W 57TH ST	NEW YORK, NY	10019
LEONARD, BUCK	BASEBALL	605 ATLANTIC AVE	ROCKY MOUNT, NC	27801
LEONARD, DENNIS	BASEBALL	4102 EVERGREEN LN	BLUE SPRINGS, MO	64015
LEONARD, DONALD M	WRITER	2549 THAMES ST	LOS ANGELES, CA	90046
LEONARD, ELMORE	AUTHOR-SCREENWRITER	476 FAIRFAX	BIRMINGHAM, MI	48009
LEONARD, GAIL	ACTRESS	10850 RIVERSIDE DR #505	NORTH HOLLYWOOD, CA	91602
LEONARD, GARY	BODYBUILDER	POST OFFICE BOX 1459	CLOVIS, CA	93613
LEONARD, GLENN	SINGER	PERLE, 4475 VINELAND AVE	STUDIO CITY, CA	91602
LEONARD, GLORIA	ACTRESS-PUB EXEC	HIGH SOCIETY, 801 2ND AVE	NEW YORK, NY	10017
LEONARD, HERBERT	DIRECTOR-PRODUCER	5300 FULTON AVE	VAN NUYS, CA	91401
LEONARD, HUGH	PLAYWRIGHT	THEROS, COLIEMORE RD, DALKEY	DUBLIN	IRELAND
LEONARD, JACK	GUITARIST	ROUTE #1, FRANKLIN	GALLATIN, TN	37066
LEONARD, LU	ACTRESS	4959 DENNY AVE	NORTH HOLLYWOOD, CA	91601
LEONARD, MARY	NEWS CORRESPONDENT	513 "A" ST, SE	WASHINGTON, DC	20003
LEONARD, PETER	CONDUCTOR	SHAW CONCERTS, 1995 BROADWAY	NEW YORK, NY	10023
LEONARD, RAY	BOXER	SEE - LEONARD, SUGAR RAY		
LEONARD, SHELDON	ACTOR-DIRECTOR	1141 LOMA VISTA DR	BEVERLY HILLS, CA	90210
LEONARD, SUGAR RAY	BOXER-ACTOR	1505 BRADY CT	MITCHELLVILLE, MD	20716
LEONARD, TERRY JAMES	DIRECTOR	11074 OSO	CHATSWORTH, CA	91011
LEONARD, WILLIAM R	DIR-PROD-NEWS CORRES	2935 LEGATION ST, NW	WASHINGTON, DC	20015
LEONDOPOULOS, JORDAN	WRITER	555 W 57TH ST #1230	NEW YORK, NY	10019
LEONE, JOHN J	WRITER-PRODUCER	DGA, 7950 SUNSET BLVD	HOLLYWOOD, CA	90046
LEONE, LARRY	MUSICIAN	24530 HWY 74	PERRIS, CA	92370
LEONE, SERGIO	FILM DIRECTOR	MINISTRY OF TOURISM		
		VIA DELLA FERRA TELLA	ROME	ITALY
LEONETTI, CINDY	TV WRITER	8955 BEVERLY BLVD	LOS ANGELES, CA	90048

Name	Occupation	Address	City	Zip
LEONETTI, MATTHEW R	CINEMATOGRAPHER	POST OFFICE BOX 2230	HOLLYWOOD, CA	90078
LEONG, EUGENE	TV DIRECTOR	1947 N HARDING AVE	ALTADENA, CA	91001
LEONI, TONY	WRESTLER	AMERICAN WRESTLING ASSOC		
		MINNEAPLOIS WRESTLING		
		10001 WAYZATA BLVD	MINNETONKA, MN	55345
LEONSKAJA, ELISABETH	PIANIST	SHAW CONCERTS, 1995 BROADWAY	NEW YORK, NY	10023
LEONTI, CINCY	SINGER	PROCESS, 439 WILEY AVE	FRANKLIN, PA	16323
LEONTOVICH, EUGENIE	ACTRESS	45 W 81ST ST #609	NEW YORK, NY	10024
LEOPOLD, GLENN I	SCREENWRITER	8955 BEVERLY BLVD	LOS ANGELES, CA	90048
LEOPOLD, THOMAS	TV WRITER	8955 BEVERLY BLVD	LOS ANGELES, CA	90048
LEOZ, YOLANDA	DANCER	KOPELL, 19413 OLIVOS DR	TARZANA, CA	91356
LEPARD, JEREMY	CINEMATOGRAPHER	3975 WITZEL DR	SHERMAN OAKS, CA	91423
LEPAW, HELEN E	WRITER	555 W 57TH ST #1230	NEW YORK, NY	10019
LEPKOWSKI, WIL	NEWS CORRESPONDENT	1783 IVY OAK SQ	RESTON, VA	22090
LEPORSKA, ZOYA	ACTRESS	40 W 86TH ST #3-A	NEW YORK, NY	10024
LEPPARD, RAYMOND	CONDUCTOR	COLBERT, 111 W 57TH ST	NEW YORK, NY	10019
LERER, GAYLE	WRITER	242 S REXFORD DR	BEVERLY HILLS, CA	90212
LERMAN, LIZ	DANCER	AFFILIATE ARTISTS, INC		
		37 W 65TH ST, 6TH FLOOR	NEW YORK, NY	10023
LERMAN, RHODA	WRITER	555 W 57TH ST #1230	NEW YORK, NY	10019
LERNER, ALBERT	COMPOSER	4223 VANTAGE AVE	STUDIO CITY, CA	91604
LERNER, BENNETT	PIANIST	POST OFFICE BOX 1515	NEW YORK, NY	10023
LERNER, DAVID	TV WRITER	656 CRESTMOORE PL	VENICE, CA	90291
LERNER, ERIC	TV WRITER	8955 BEVERLY BLVD	LOS ANGELES, CA	90048
LERNER, FRED	TV DIRECTOR	14639 BLEDSOE ST	SYLMAR, CA	91342
LERNER, JOSEPH	DIRECTOR	2502 ANTIGUA TERR #M-4	CONONUT CREEK, FL	33066
LERNER, KAREN G	TV WRITER-PRODUCER	ABC-TV, 7 W 66TH ST	NEW YORK, NY	10023
LERNER, LARRY	DIRECTOR	328 W 11TH ST #1-B	NEW YORK, NY	10014
LERNER, MARC	NEWS CORRESPONDENT	1126 PARK ST, NE	WASHINGTON, DC	20002
LERNER, MICHAEL	ACTOR	POST OFFICE BOX 5617	BEVERLY HILLS, CA	90210
LERNER, MICHELINE M	WRITER	8955 BEVERLY BLVD	LOS ANGELES, CA	90048
LERNER, MIMI	MEZZO-SOPRANO	LEW, 204 W 10TH ST	NEW YORK, NY	10014
LERNER, MURRAY	WRITER-PRODUCER	630 9TH AVE	NEW YORK, NY	10036
LEROUX, ANNE	NEWS CORRESPONDENT	3114 WISCONSIN AVE #803, NW	WASHINGTON, DC	20016
LEROY, MERVYN	DIRECTOR-PRODUCER	615 N CAMDEN DR	BEVERLY HILLS, CA	90210
LERSKY, LESTER	FILM PRODUCER	485 MADISON AVE	NEW YORK, NY	10022
LES CHRISSENS	AERIAL CRADLE DUO	SEE - CHRISSENS, LES		
LES LEMOINES	AERIAL TROUPE	HALL, 138 FROG HOLLOW RD	CHURCHVILLE, PA	18966
LESAR, JOHN	NEWS CORRESPONDENT	5815 REXFORD DR #C	SPRINGFIELD, VA	22152
LESCHIN, DEBORAH	TV WRITER	13002 DICKENS ST	NORTH HOLLYWOOD, CA	91604
LESCHIN, LUISA	ACTRESS	536 N ORANGE DR	LOS ANGELES, CA	90036
LESCO, KENNETH R	DIRECTOR	DGA, 7950 SUNSET BLVD	LOS ANGELES, CA	90046
LESCOULIE, JACK	TV PERSONALITY	345 S WESTGATE AVE	LOS ANGELES, CA	90049
LESEMANN, FREDERICK	COMPOSER	216 S OCCIDENTAL BLVD #203	LOS ANGELES, CA	90057
LESH, CAROLYN	NEWS CORRESPONDENT	2500 "Q" ST #436, NW	WASHINGTON, DC	20007
LESHAY, JERRY	TV DIRECTOR	4149 FARMDALE AVE	STUDIO CITY, CA	91604
LESHNER, MARTIN	TV WRITER	840 N LARABEE ST #4-217	LOS ANGELES, CA	90069
LESKE, GISELA	NEWS CORRESPONDENT	2008 N KENMORE ST	ARLINGTON, VA	22207
LESLIE, ALEEN	WRITER	1700 LEXINGTON RD	BEVERLY HILLS, CA	90210
LESLIE, BETHEL	ACTRESS-WRITER	10100 SANTA MONICA BLVD #310	LOS ANGELES, CA	90027
LESLIE, EDWARD	WRESTLER	SEE - BEEFCAKE, BRUTUS		
LESLIE, JOAN	ACTRESS	CALDWELL, 2228 N CATALINA ST	LOS ANGELES, CA	90027
LESLIE, PHIL	WRITER	8955 BEVERLY BLVD	LOS ANGELES, CA	90048
LESLIE, WARREN	WRITER	8955 BEVERLY BLVD	LOS ANGELES, CA	90048
LESLIE-LYTTLE, KAREN	ACTRESS	19 W 44TH ST #1500	NEW YORK, NY	10036
LESNER, LESLIE	ACTRESS	7466 BEVERLY BLVD #205	LOS ANGELES, CA	90036
LESNIAK, EMILIA	ACTRESS	6515 SUNSET BLVD #401	LOS ANGELES, CA	90028
LESPERANCE, JACQUELINE	SOPRANO	253 W 73RD ST #7-M	NEW YORK, NY	10023
LESSAC, ARTHUR	ACTOR	11726 SAN VICENTE BLVD #300	LOS ANGELES, CA	90049
LESSAC, MICHAEL	TV DIRECTOR	1742 NICHOLS CANYON RD	LOS ANGELES, CA	90046
LESSER, DIANE	OBOIST	AFFILIATE ARTISTS, INC		
		37 W 65TH ST, 6TH FLOOR	NEW YORK, NY	10023
LESSER, ELANA	TV WRITER	17158 GERMAIN ST	GRANADA HILLS, CA	91344
LESSER, GEORGE H	NEWS CORRESPONDENT	2616 CATHEDRAL AVE, NW	WASHINGTON, DC	20008
LESSER, HOWARD M	NEWS CORRESPONDENT	9209 THREE OAKS	SILVER SPRING, MD	20901
LESSER, LEN	ACTOR	934 N EVERGREEN ST	BURBANK, CA	91505
LESSER, SEYMOUR H	CABLE EXECUTIVE	HEARST/ABC-TV		
		555 5TH AVE	NEW YORK, NY	10017
LESSING, NORMAN	TV WRITER	663 HIGHTREE RD	SANTA MONICA, CA	90402
LESTER, FRANK	ACTOR	9165 SUNSET BLVD #202	LOS ANGELES, CA	90069
LESTER, GENE	DIRECTOR-PRODUCER	4918 ALCOVE AVE	NORTH HOLLYWOOD, CA	91607
LESTER, JACK	ACTOR	9220 SUNSET BLVD #218	LOS ANGELES, CA	90069
LESTER, KITTY	ACTRESS	5931 COMEY AVE	LOS ANGELES, CA	90034
LESTER, LARRY	DIRECTOR	3965 WITZEL DR	SHERMAN OAKS, CA	91423
LESTER, MARIANNE	NEWS CORRESPONDENT	4112 EMERY PL, NW	WASHINGTON, DC	20016
LESTER, MARK	DIRECTOR-PRODUCER	7932 MULHOLLAND DR	LOS ANGELES, CA	90046
LESTER, RICHARD	FILM DIR-COMP	RIVER LN, PETERSHAM	SURREY	ENGLAND
LESTER, SEELEG	WRITER-PRODUCER	6228 RIVIERA CIR	LONG BEACH, CA	90815
LESTER, SUSAN C	DIRECTOR	14 HORATIO ST	NEW YORK, NY	10014
LESTER, TERRY	ACTOR	10000 SANTA MONICA BLVD #305	LOS ANGELES, CA	90067
LESTER, TOM	ACTOR	POST OFFICE BOX 1854	BEVERLY HILLS, CA	90213
LET'S ACTIVE	ROCK & ROLL GROUP	37 LEE ST	WATERBURY, CT	06708
LETELLIER, JACQUES	DIRECTOR	1160 5TH AVE	NEW YORK, NY	10029
LETHERMAN, MARK	ACTOR	10662 WILKINS AVE	LOS ANGELES, CA	90024
LETHIEC, MICHEL	CLARINETIST	POST OFFICE BOX 27539	PHILADELPHIA, PA	19118

Name	Occupation	Address	City	ZIP
LETHIN, LORI	ACTRESS	1801 CENTURY PARK E #1415	LOS ANGELES, CA	90067
LETNER, KEN	ACTOR	5706 FAIR AVE #211	NORTH HOLLYWOOD, CA	91601
LETTERIE, KATHLEEN	CASTING DIRECTOR	704 N GARDNER ST #2	LOS ANGELES, CA	90046
LETTERMAN, DAVID	COMEDIAN	30 ROCKEFELLER PLAZA #1410-W	NEW YORK, NY	10112
LETTERMEN, THE	VOCAL TRIO	LETTERMEN PRODUCTIONS		
		4318 BEN AVE	STUDIO CITY, CA	91604
LETTS, BARRY	TV DIRECTOR-PRODUCER	2 QUEENS AVE	LONDON N20 OJE	ENGLAND
LETTVIN, THEODORE	PIANIST	POST OFFICE BOX 27539	PHILADELPHIA, PA	19118
LEUBSDORF, CARL P	NEWS CORRESPONDENT	3408 "N" ST, NW	WASHINGTON, DC	20007
LEUDESDORF, BETH	WRITER	555 W 57TH ST #1230	NEW YORK, NY	10019
LEUGER, JOHN	ACTOR	3917 E PAULINE ST	COMPTON, CA	90221
LEUSTIG, ELISABETH	CASTING DIRECTOR	POST OFFICE BOX 69277	LOS ANGELES, CA	90069
LEUZINGER, CHRISTOPHER	GUITARIST	4911 TANGLEWOOD DR #C	NASHVILLE, TN	37216
LEVANT, BRIAN	TV WRITER	9528 DALEGROVE DR	BEVERLY HILLS, CA	90210
LEVASSEUR, DIANE	WRITER	555 W 57TH ST #1230	NEW YORK, NY	10019
LEVEL 42	ROCK & ROLL GROUP	OUTLAW MGMT, 145 OXFORD ST	LONDON W1	ENGLAND
LEVEN, BORIS	ART DIRECTOR	527 HANLEY PL	LOS ANGELES, CA	90049
LEVEN, JEREMY	WRITER	8955 BEVERLY BLVD	LOS ANGELES, CA	90048
LEVEN, MELVILLE A	COMPOSER-CONDUCTOR	11577 DILLING ST	STUDIO CITY, CA	91604
LEVENBACK, PAULA	WRITER	12930 CHANDLER BLVD	VAN NUYS, CA	91401
LEVENE, CAROL L	WRITER-PRODUCER	8955 BEVERLY BLVD	LOS ANGELES, CA	90048
LEVENS, PHILIP J	TV EXECUTIVE	ABC TELEVISION NETWORK		
		1330 AVE OF THE AMERICAS	NEW YORK, NY	10019
LEVENSON, JEFFREY	CELLIST	SAN DIEGO STATE UNIVERSITY		
		MUSIC DEPARTMENT		
		5402 COLLEGE AVE	SAN DIEGO, CA	92082
LEVENSON, ROBERT	DIRECTOR	125 OAK ST	TENAFLY, NJ	07670
LEVENSTEIN, JOHN S	WRITER	8955 BEVERLY BLVD	LOS ANGELES, CA	90048
LEVENTHAL, MICHAEL L	WRITER	555 W 57TH ST #1230	NEW YORK, NY	10019
LEVERENZ, JAN	ACTRESS	1973 CHEREMOYA AVE	LOS ANGELES, CA	90068
LEVERING, FRANK G	SCREENWRITER	11002 OPHIR DR #B	LOS ANGELES, CA	90024
LEVERINGTON, SHELBY	ACTRESS	1808 SHELL AVE	VENICE, CA	90291
LEVEY, ED	ACTOR	216 SAN JUAN AVE	VENICE, CA	90291
LEVEY, JEFFREY R	NEWS CORRESPONDENT	1855 CALVERT ST, NW	WASHINGTON, DC	20009
LEVEY, WILLIAM A	FILM WRITER-DIRECTOR	838 N DOHENY DR #904	LOS ANGELES, CA	90069
LEVI, ALAN J	WRITER-PRODUCER	3951 LONGRIDGE AVE	SHERMAN OAKS, CA	91423
LEVI, PAUL ALAN	COMPOSER	105 W 73RD ST	NEW YORK, NY	10023
LEVI, YOEL	CONDUCTOR	SHAW CONCERTS, 1995 BROADWAY	NEW YORK, NY	10023
LEVI-HARRY DUO	MUSICAL DUO	KAY, 58 W 58TH ST	NEW YORK, NY	10019
LEVIAN, LAUREN	ACTRESS	10000 RIVERSIDE DR #3	TOLUCA LAKE, CA	91602
LEVIEN, PHILIP	ACTOR	1202 N POINSETTIA DR	LOS ANGELES, CA	90046
LEVIEV, MILCHO I	COMPOSER	12027 CALIFA ST	NORTH HOLLYWOOD, CA	91607
LEVIN, ALAN	TV EXECUTIVE	CBS-TV, 7800 BEVERLY BLVD	LOS ANGELES, CA	90036
LEVIN, ALAN M	WRITER-PRODUCER	88 CLAREMONT AVE	MAPLEWOOD, NJ	07040
LEVIN, ALVIN IRVING	COMPOSER-CONDUCTOR	8612 JELLICO AVE	NORTHRIDGE, CA	91325
LEVIN, AMY B	WRITER	555 W 57TH ST #1230	NEW YORK, NY	10019
LEVIN, ARNIE	CARTOONIST	POST OFFICE BOX 4203	NEW YORK, NY	10017
LEVIN, AUDREY DAVIS	TV WRITER	2751 MOTOR AVE	LOS ANGELES, CA	90064
LEVIN, CHARLES	ACTOR	1357 3/4 N ALTA VISTA BLVD	LOS ANGELES, CA	90046
LEVIN, DAN	SPORTS WRITER-EDITOR	SPORTS ILLUSTRATED MAGAZINE		
		TIME & LIFE BUILDING		
		ROCKEFELLER CENTER	NEW YORK, NY	10020
LEVIN, ELIZABETH	TV WRITER	555 W 57TH ST #1230	NEW YORK, NY	10019
LEVIN, ERIC	WRITER-EDITOR	TIME & PEOPLE MAGAZINE		
		TIME & LIFE BUILDING		
		ROCKEFELLER CENTER	NEW YORK, NY	10020
LEVIN, GERALD M	CABLE EXECUTIVE	TIME VIDEO COMAPNY, INC		
		1271 AVE OF THE AMERICAS	NEW YORK, NY	10020
LEVIN, HERMAN	THEATER PRODUCER	424 MADISON AVE	NEW YORK, NY	10019
LEVIN, IDA	VIOLINIST	CAMI, 165 W 57TH ST	NEW YORK, NY	10019
LEVIN, IRA	AUTHOR	HAROLD OBER, 40 E 49TH ST	NEW YORK, NY	10017
LEVIN, IRVING H	FILM PRODUCER	1175 N HILLCREST RD	BEVERLY HILLS, CA	90210
LEVIN, JEFFREY	TV WRITER	8955 BEVERLY BLVD	LOS ANGELES, CA	90048
LEVIN, JERRY	WRITER	555 W 57TH ST #1230	NEW YORK, NY	10019
LEVIN, JOHN	WRITER	8955 BEVERLY BLVD	LOS ANGELES, CA	90048
LEVIN, LEAR	WRITER-PRODUCER	16 W 88TH ST	NEW YORK, NY	10024
LEVIN, LEONARD T	DIRECTOR	114 W 25TH ST	BALTIMORE, MD	21218
LEVIN, LISSA	TV WRITER	ICM, 8899 BEVERLY BLVD	LOS ANGELES, CA	90048
LEVIN, M D	WRITER	555 W 57TH ST #1230	NEW YORK, NY	10019
LEVIN, MARLIN	NEWS CORRESPONDENT	DISCOVER/TIME & LIFE BLDG		
		ROCKEFELLER CENTER	NEW YORK, NY	10020
LEVIN, MICHAEL	ACTOR	ABC-TV, "RYAN'S HOPE"		
		1330 AVE OF THE AMERICAS	NEW YORK, NY	10019
LEVIN, MOSHE	CINEMATOGRAPHER	3224 DURAND DR	LOS ANGELES, CA	90068
LEVIN, PETER	TV DIRECTOR	TIVOLI, 10313 W PICO BLVD	LOS ANGELES, CA	90064
LEVIN, SIDNEY	FILM DIRECTOR	3872 LAS FLORES CANYON RD #1	MALIBU, CA	90265
LEVIN, STU	ACTOR	11030 VENTURA BLVD #3	STUDIO CITY, CA	91604
LEVIN-EPSTEIN, MICHAEL	NEWS CORRESPONDENT	7530 CODDLE HARBOR LN	POTOMAC, MD	20854
LEVINE, ALEXANDRA	ACTRESS	1607 N EL CENTRO AVE #22	HOLLYWOOD, CA	90028
LEVINE, AMY B	NEWS CORRESPONDENT	2139 WISCONSIN AVE, NW	WASHINGTON, DC	20007
LEVINE, ANNA	ACTRESS	211 S BEVERLY BLVD #201	BEVERLY HILLS, CA	90212
LEVINE, ARNOLD	DIRECTOR	420 MARION ST	OCEANSIDE, NY	11572
LEVINE, DAVID	PIANIST	KAY, 58 W 58TH ST	NEW YORK, NY	10019
LEVINE, EMILY	TV WRITER	6547 CAHUENGA TERR	LOS ANGELES, CA	90068

Name	Occupation	Address	City/State	Zip
LEVINE, FLOYD	ACTOR	LIGHT, 113 N ROBERTSON BLVD	LOS ANGELES, CA	90048
LEVINE, GILBERT	CONDUCTOR	ICM, 40 W 57TH ST	NEW YORK, NY	10019
LEVINE, HANK	MUSIC ARRANGER	POST OFFICE BOX 532	HENDERSONVILLE, TN	37075
LEVINE, IRVING R	NEWS CORRESPONDENT	4342 WARREN ST, NW	WASHINGTON, DC	20016
LEVINE, JEFF	ACTOR	1901 AVE OF THE STARS #840	LOS ANGELES, CA	90067
LEVINE, JOSEPH E	FILM PRODUCER	277 PARK AVE	NEW YORK, NY	10017
LEVINE, KEN NEIL	WRITER-PRODUCER	829 THAYER AVE	LOS ANGELES, CA	90024
LEVINE, LAURA	TV WRITER	1756 MIDVALE AVE	LOS ANGELES, CA	90024
LEVINE, LOUIS P	DIRECTOR	2677 HIGH RIDGE RD	STANFORD, CT	06903
LEVINE, MICHAEL A	TV EXECUTIVE	NBC-TV, 3000 W ALAMEDA AVE	BURBANK, CA	91523
LEVINE, RICHARD	ACTOR	AFFILIATE ARTISTS, INC		
		37 W 65TH ST, 6TH FLOOR	NEW YORK, NY	10023
LEVINE, RICHARD DAVID	DIRECTOR	DGA, 110 W 57TH ST	NEW YORK, NY	10019
LEVINE, RICHARD I	TV EXECUTIVE	ABC TELEVISION NETWORK		
		1330 AVE OF THE AMERICAS	NEW YORK, NY	10019
LEVINE, RICK	FILM DIRECTOR	DGA, 7950 SUNSET BLVD	LOS ANGELES, CA	90046
LEVINE, ROBERT E	WRITER	8955 BEVERLY BLVD	LOS ANGELES, CA	90048
LEVINE, RON	GUITARIST	121 HAZELWOOD DR #K-112	NASHVILLE, TN	37075
LEVINE, SAM	MUSIC ARRANGER	5013 MANUEL DR	NASHVILLE, TN	37211
LEVINE, SOLOMON	NEWS CORRESPONDENT	2133 WISCONSIN AVE, NW	WASHINGTON, DC	20007
LEVINE, SPENCER	WRITER	555 W 57TH ST #1230	NEW YORK, NY	10019
LEVINE, STANLEY M	COMPOSER	13508 DEBELL ST	PACOIMA, CA	91331
LEVINE, TED	ACTOR	1509 N CRESCENT HGTS BLVD #7	LOS ANGELES, CA	90069
LEVINE, WANDA L	WRITER	555 W 57TH ST #1230	NEW YORK, NY	10019
LEVINSON, AMY	DIRECTOR	1338 PRINCETON ST #E	SANTA MONICA, CA	90404
LEVINSON, BARRY	FILM WRITER-DIRECTOR	10880 WILSHIRE BLVD #2110	LOS ANGELES, CA	90024
LEVINSON, BARRY	FILM PRODUCER	105 MOUNT ST	LONDON W1	ENGLAND
LEVINSON, DAVID	TV WRITER	3115 DEEP CANYON DR	BEVERLY HILLS, CA	90210
LEVINSON, FRED F	DIRECTOR	12 1/2 E 82ND ST	NEW YORK, NY	10028
LEVINSON, GREGORY	ACTOR	12725 VENTURA BLVD #E	STUDIO CITY, CA	91604
LEVINSON, JANE M	WRITER	555 W 57TH ST #1230	NEW YORK, NY	10019
LEVINSON, LARRY	SCREENWRITER	8955 BEVERLY BLVD	LOS ANGELES, CA	90048
LEVINSON, MARK	FILM PRODUCER	151 S EL CAMINO DR	BEVERLY HILLS, CA	90212
LEVINSON, ROBERT S	PRODUCER	650 N BRONSON AVE #250	LOS ANGELES, CA	90004
LEVINSON, SHELLEY	WRITER	8955 BEVERLY BLVD	LOS ANGELES, CA	90048
LEVINSON, WILLIAM G	WRITER	555 W 57TH ST #1230	NEW YORK, NY	10019
LEVISOHN, DAVID	CINEMATOGRAPHER	7715 SUNSET BLVD #150	LOS ANGELES, CA	90046
LEVIT, LAURIE	WRITER	8955 SUNSET BLVD	LOS ANGELES, CA	90048
LEVITCH, LEON	COMPOSER	13107 KELOWNA ST	PACOIMA, CA	91331
LEVITSKA, ANNA	SOPRANO	111 W 57TH ST #1209	NEW YORK, NY	10019
LEVITT, ALFRED L	WRITER	4124 STANSBURY AVE	SHERMAN OAKS, CA	91423
LEVITT, BEVERLY D	WRITER	8955 BEVERLY BLVD	LOS ANGELES, CA	90048
LEVITT, GENE	TV WRITER-DIRECTOR	315 GRAND CANAL	BALBOA ISLAND, CA	92662
LEVITT, HELEN SLOTE	WRITER	4124 STANSBURY AVE	SHERMAN OAKS, CA	91423
LEVITT, JUDY	ACTRESS	KOENIG, 5658 BECK AVE	NORTH HOLLYWOOD, CA	91606
LEVITT, STEPHEN I	DIRECTOR	330 8TH AVE	NEW YORK, NY	10001
LEVY, ALAN	CABLE EXECUTIVE	HBO, 1100 AVE OF THE AMERICAS	NEW YORK, NY	10036
LEVY, BRUCE	SONGWRITER	6921 PASEO DEL SERRA	LOS ANGELES, CA	90068
LEVY, DANIEL S	NEWS REPORTER	TIME/TIME & LIFE BLDG		
		ROCKEFELLER CENTER	NEW YORK, NY	10020
LEVY, DAVID	WRITER	8955 BEVERLY BLVD	LOS ANGELES, CA	90048
LEVY, DAVID A	WRITER	555 W 57TH ST #1230	NEW YORK, NY	10019
LEVY, EDMOND	TV WRITER-DIRECTOR	135 CENTRAL PARK W	NEW YORK, NY	10023
LEVY, EUGENE	ACT-WRI-COMED	9000 SUNSET BLVD #1200	LOS ANGELES, CA	90069
LEVY, FRANKLIN R	TV PRODUCER	ICPR, 9255 SUNSET BLVD		
		8TH FLOOR	LOS ANGELES, CA	90069
LEVY, GARY	ACTOR-DIRECTOR	4316 ALLOTT AVE	SHERMAN OAKS, CA	91423
LEVY, JANEL M	NEWS CORRESPONDENT	3215 19TH ST, NW	WASHINGTON, DC	20010
LEVY, JEFERY L	SCREENWRITER	8955 BEVERLY BLVD	LOS ANGELES, CA	90048
LEVY, JOANNA	MEZZO-SOPRANO	CAMI, 165 W 57TH ST	NEW YORK, NY	10019
LEVY, JOHN R	PHOTOJOURNALIST	6002 KING ARTHUR WY	GLENN DALE, MD	20769
LEVY, JULES	WRITER-PRODUCER	10128 EMPYREAN WY	LOS ANGELES, CA	90067
LEVY, LAWRENCE	DIRECTOR	DGA, 7950 SUNSET BLVD	LOS ANGELES, CA	90046
LEVY, LAWRENCE H	TV WRITER	8955 BEVERLY BLVD	LOS ANGELES, CA	90048
LEVY, LEW	TV WRITER	8428 MELROSE PL #C	LOS ANGELES, CA	90069
LEVY, MARTY	ACTOR	7469 MELROSE AVE #30	LOS ANGELES, CA	90046
LEVY, MARVIN DAVID	CONDUCTOR	SOFFER, 130 W 56TH ST	NEW YORK, NY	10019
LEVY, NORMAN B	FILM EXECUTIVE	4965 QUEEN FLORENCE LN	WOODLAND HILLS, CA	91364
LEVY, PAUL F	NEWS EDITOR	THE NATIONAL ENQUIRER		
		600 SE COAST AVE	LANTANA, FL	33464
LEVY, RALPH L	WRITER-PRODUCER	206 MC KENZIE ST	SANTE FE, NM	87501
LEVY, ROBERT J	DIRECTOR	DGA, 110 W 57TH ST	NEW YORK, NY	10019
LEVY, ROBERT L	FILM WRITER-PRODUCER	10128 EMPYREAN WY #204	LOS ANGELES, CA	90067
LEVY, THOMAS P	FILM PRODUCER	11680 LAURELWOOD DR	STUDIO CITY, CA	91604
LEVY, VIVIAN	TALENT AGENT	1717 N HIGHLAND AVE #414	LOS ANGELES, CA	90028
LEW, JOYCELYN	ACTRESS	WEBB, 7500 DEVISTA DR	LOS ANGELES, CA	90046
LEW, JOYCELYNE	ACTRESS	1976 N BRONSON AVE	LOS ANGELES, CA	90068
LEWENSTEIN, ABRAHAM M	WRITER	232 N CLARK DR #8	BEVERLY HILLS, CA	90211
LEWERTH, MARGARET	WRITER	555 W 57TH ST #1230	NEW YORK, NY	10019
LEWIN, ALBERT E	TV WRITER	4104 STANSBURY AVE	SHERMAN OAKS, CA	91423
LEWIN, DENNIS	TV PRODUCER	ABC-TV, SPORTS DEPARTMENT		
		1330 AVE OF THE AMERICAS	NEW YORK, NY	10019
LEWIN, HAROLD	PIANIST	61 W 62ND ST #6-F	NEW YORK, NY	10023

Name	Occupation	Address	City/State	Zip
LEWIN, NICHOLAS SPENCER	DIRECTOR	JENNIE, 127 W 79TH ST	NEW YORK, NY	10024
LEWIN, NICK	COMEDIAN	13906 VENTURA BLVD #156	SHERMAN OAKS, CA	91423
LEWIN, RHONDA	ACTRESS	NBC-TV, "ANOTHER WORLD"		
		30 ROCKEFELLER PLAZA	NEW YORK, NY	10112
LEWIN, ROBERT C	WRITER	11363 ALBATA ST	LOS ANGELES, CA	90049
LEWINE, FRANCES L	NEWS CORRESPONDENT	1702 37TH ST, NW	WASHINGTON, DC	20007
LEWINE, PETER E	WRITER	555 W 57TH ST #1230	NEW YORK, NY	10019
LEWINGTON, JENNIFER	NEWS CORRESPONDENT	411-4200 CATHEDRAL AVE, NW	WASHINGTON, DC	20016
LEWIS, ARNOLD M, JR	NEWS CORRESPONDENT	603 GALVESTON RD	FREDERICKSBURG, VA	22405
LEWIS, CARL	TRACK & FIELD	1801 OCEAN PARK BLVD #112	SANTA MONICA, CA	90405
LEWIS, CHARLES J	NEWS CORRESPONDENT	2338 RIVIERA DR	VIENNA, VA	22180
LEWIS, DAVID	ACTOR	9165 SUNSET BLVD #202	LOS ANGELES, CA	90069
LEWIS, DIANA	ACTRESS	POWELL, 383 W VERDE NORTE	PALM SPRINGS, CA	92262
LEWIS, EDWARD	FILM-TV PRODUCER	MCA/UNIVERSAL STUDIOS, INC		
		100 UNIVERSAL CITY PLAZA	UNIVERSAL CITY, CA	91608
LEWIS, EMANUEL	ACTOR	518 N LA CIENEGA BLVD	LOS ANGELES, CA	90048
LEWIS, FINDLAY	NEWS CORRESPONDENT	2727 CHESAPEAKE ST, NW	WASHINGTON, DC	20008
LEWIS, HARRY	ACTOR	THE HAMBURGER HAMLET		
		44 E WALTON ST	CHICAGO, IL	60611
LEWIS, HUEY & THE NEWS	ROCK & ROLL GROUP	POST OFFICE BOX 818	MILL VALLEY, CA	94942
LEWIS, JAY S	NEWS CORRESPONDENT	1201 CONNECTICUT AVE, NW	WASHINGTON, DC	20036
LEWIS, JENNY	ACTRESS	POST OFFICE BOX 1380	SANTEE, CA	92071
LEWIS, JERRY	COMED-ACT-DIR	3305 W SPRING MOUNTAIN RD #1	LAS VEGAS, NV	89102
LEWIS, JERRY D	WRITER	15757 SUNSET BLVD	PACIFIC PALISADES, CA	90272
LEWIS, JERRY LEE	SINGER-COMPOSER	LEWIS FARMS	NESBIT, MS	38651
LEWIS, JONATHAN	FILM WRITER-DIRECTOR	GREAT WESTERN FILMS		
		6 LYMINGTON MANSIONS		
		LYMINGTON RD	LONDON NW6	ENGLAND
LEWIS, JOSEPH	DIRECTOR	13900 PALAWAN WY	MARINA DEL REY, CA	90292
LEWIS, JUDY	ACTRESS	113 N SAN VICENTE BLVD #202	BEVERLY HILLS, CA	90211
LEWIS, KATHERINE	NEWS CORRESPONDENT	1753 "Q" ST #D, NW	WASHINGTON, DC	20009
LEWIS, KEITH	TENOR	119 W 57TH ST #1505	NEW YORK, NY	10019
		BAYVIEW DR	GALLATIN, TN	37066
LEWIS, KENNETH	GUITARIST	ROUTE #3, BOX 210		
		BAYVIEW DR	GALLATIN, TN	37066
LEWIS, LEONARD	TV WRITER-DIRECTOR	40 CROSS DEEP, TWICKENHAM	MIDDLESEX TW1 4RA	ENGLAND
LEWIS, LIDJ	WRITER	555 W 57TH ST #1230	NEW YORK, NY	10019
LEWIS, MARCIA	WRITER	8955 BEVERLY BLVD	LOS ANGELES, CA	90048
LEWIS, MARCIA	ACTRESS	9229 SUNSET BLVD #306	LOS ANGELES, CA	90069
LEWIS, MARK	ACTOR	CBS-TV, 51 W 52ND ST	NEW YORK, NY	10019
LEWIS, MARY MARGARET	ACTRESS	9165 SUNSET BLVD #202	LOS ANGELES, CA	90069
LEWIS, MARY RIO	ACTRESS	1026 E 219TH ST	BRONX, NY	10469
LEWIS, MATT	PHOTOGRAPHER	18740 TANTERRA WY	BROOKVILLE, MD	20729
LEWIS, MEL	DRUMMER	WILLARD ALEXANDER, INC		
		660 MADISON AVE	NEW YORK, NY	10021
LEWIS, MICHAEL J	COMPOSER-CONDUCTOR	FIRST COMPOSERS COMPANY		
		14 NEW BURLINGTON ST	LONDON W1X 2LR	ENGLAND
LEWIS, MIKE	MUSIC ARRANGER	908 HOLLY FOREST	NASHVILLE, TN	37221
LEWIS, MILDRED	PRODUCER	MCA/UNIVERSAL STUDIOS, INC		
LEWIS, MILDRED	WRITER	8955 BEVERLY BLVD	LOS ANGELES, CA	90048
		100 UNIVERSAL CITY PLAZA #507	UNIVERSAL CITY, CA	91608
LEWIS, MORT R	WRITER	14016 BORA BORA WY	MARINA DEL REY, CA	90292
LEWIS, MORTON	DIRECTOR-PRODUCER	MEADWAY, 70 WARDOUR ST	LONDON W1	ENGLAND
LEWIS, MYRON	FILM DIRECTOR	5228 FERNWOOD AVE #6	LOS ANGELES, CA	90028
LEWIS, NEIL	NEWS CORRESPONDENT	2936 PORTER ST, NW	WASHINGTON, DC	20008
LEWIS, PATRICIA A	WRITER	555 W 57TH ST #1230	NEW YORK, NY	10019
LEWIS, PHILIP	DIRECTOR	13 HUBBARD DR	WHITE PLAINS, NY	10605
LEWIS, RAMSEY	PIANIST-COMPOSER	10100 SANTA MONICA BLVD #1600	LOS ANGELES, CA	90067
LEWIS, RANDY	MUSIC CRITIC	L A TIMES NEWSPAPER		
		TIMES MIRROR SQUARE	LOS ANGELES, CA	90053
LEWIS, RICHARD	COMEDIAN-ACTOR	POST OFFICE BOX 5617	BEVERLY HILLS, CA	90210
LEWIS, RICHARD P	TV WRITER	334 N OAKHURST DR #4	BEVERLY HILLS, CA	90210
LEWIS, RICHARD W	WRITER	863 N BEVERLY GLEN BLVD	LOS ANGELES, CA	90077
LEWIS, ROBERT D G	NEWS CORRESPONDENT	2828 CONNECTICUT AVE, NW	WASHINGTON, DC	20008
LEWIS, ROBERT MICHAEL	TV DIRECTOR	DGA, 7950 SUNSET BLVD	HOLLYWOOD, CA	90046
LEWIS, ROBERT Q	TV PERSONALITY	2032 N BEVERLY DR	BEVERLY HILLS, CA	90210
LEWIS, ROGER	GUITARIST	1108 COLLINS ST	CONWAY, SC	29526
LEWIS, SAGAN	ACTRESS	11726 SAN VICENTE BLVD #300	LOS ANGELES, CA	90049
LEWIS, SHARI	VENTRILOQUIST	603 N ALTA DR	BEVERLY HILLS, CA	90210
LEWIS, STEPHEN	ACTOR	29 KINGS RD	LONDON SW3	ENGLAND
LEWIS, STEPHEN L	DIRECTOR-PRODUCER	11328 BRILL DR	STUDIO CITY, CA	91604
LEWIS, SUNNY	PIANIST	501 BLOOMFIELD AVE #7-B	CALDWELL, NJ	07006
LEWIS, TERRY	SONGWRITER-PRODUCER	FLYTE TYME PRODUCTIONS		
		4330 NICOLLET AVE	MINNEAPOLIS, MN	55409
LEWIS, TIMOTHY P	WRITER	8955 BEVERLY BLVD	LOS ANGELES, CA	90048
LEWIS, TOM	WRITER	8955 BEVERLY BLVD	LOS ANGELES, CA	90048
LEWIS, WILLIAM	TENOR	61 W 62ND ST #6-F	NEW YORK, NY	10023
LEWIS, WILLIAM W	WRITER	555 W 57TH ST #1230	NEW YORK, NY	10019
LEWIS/SHAFFER BAND	ROCK & ROLL GROUP	POST OFFICE BOX 18368	DENVER, CO	80218
LEWISTON, DENIS	FILM DIRECTOR	SUN CHARIOT FILM / TV, LTD		
		61 TATTENHAM CRESCENT, EPSOM	SURREY	ENGLAND
LEWTHWAITE, BILL	WRITER-PRODUCER	CAIRN COTTAGE, WOODHAM PARK WY		
		WOODHAM	SURREY KT15 3SD	ENGLAND
LEWTHWAITE, GILBERT A	NEWS CORRESPONDENT	10610 AUGUST LIGHT CT	COLUMBIA, MD	21044

Name	Occupation	Address	City	Zip/Country
LEWYN, SANDRA	ACTRESS	14315 SUMMERTIME LN	CULVER CITY, CA	90230
LEY, ROBERT	NEWS CORRESPONDENT	ESPN, ESPN PLAZA	BRISTOL, CT	06010
LEYLAND, RICHARD	TV DIRECTOR-PRODUCER	22-A FINBOROUGH RD	LONDON SW10	ENGLAND
LEYSHON, EMRYS	ACTOR	97 ALBERT PALACE MAN		
		LURLINE GARDENS	LONDON SW11	ENGLAND
LEYTON, JOHN	ACTOR	73 GROSVENOR ST	LONDON S1A 4SA	ENGLAND
LEYTON, SAUL	DIRECTOR-PRODUCER	150 E 52ND ST	NEW YORK, NY	10022
LEYTUS, DAVID	ACTOR	REFLECTIONS, 8961 SUNSET BLVD	LOS ANGELES, CA	90069
LEYTUS, JEANNE	ACTRESS	REFLECTIONS, 8961 SUNSET BLVD	LOS ANGELES, CA	90069
LEZHNEV, VSEVOLOD	CELLIST	FROTHINGHAM, 40 GROVE ST	WESSESLEY, MA	02181
LI, JIN	VIOLINIST	ANGLO-SWISS ARTISTS MGMT		
		16 MUSWELL HILL RD, HIGHGATE	LONDON N6 5UG	ENGLAND
LI, PAT	ACTRESS	8235 SANTA MONICA BLVD #202	LOS ANGELES, CA	90046
LIAPIS, PETER	ACTOR	9300 WILSHIRE BLVD #410	BEVERLY HILLS, CA	90212
LIBAEK, SVEN E	COMPOSER-CONDUCTOR	12513 MARTHA ST	NORTH HOLLYWOOD, CA	91607
LIBBY, BRIAN	ACTOR	8485 MELROSE PL #E	LOS ANGELES, CA	90069
LIBERMAN, HOWARD	WRITER	555 W 57TH ST #1230	NEW YORK, NY	10019
LIBERTI, JOHN A	TV DIRECTOR	4301 COLFAX AVE #214	STUDIO CITY, CA	91604
LIBERTI-BERGMANN, GAIL	DIRECTOR	14040 SUNSET BLVD	PACIFIC PALISADES, CA	90272
LIBERTINI, RICHARD	ACTOR	29235 HEATHERCLIFF RD #1	MALIBU, CA	90265
LIBERTY, JOHN	CLOWN	2701 COTTAGE WY #14	SACRAMENTO, CA	95825
LIBERTY SILVER	ROCK & ROLL GROUP	41 BRITAIN ST #200	TORONTO, ONT	CANADA
LIBIN, PAUL	THEATER PRODUCER	CIRCLE IN THE SQUARE		
		1633 BROADWAY	NEW YORK, NY	10019
LIBIN, SCOTT M	NEWS CORRESPONDENT	400 N CAPITOL ST, NW	WASHINGTON, DC	20001
LIBOV, MORTON	DIRECTOR	8787 SHOREHAM DR #710	LOS ANGELES, CA	90069
LIBOVE & LUGOVOY	MUSICAL DUO	POST OFFICE BOX U	REDDING, CT	06875
LIBRETTO, JOHN C	TV DIRECTOR	20 W 64TH ST	NEW YORK, NY	10023
LICAD, CECILE	PIANIST	CAMI, 165 W 57TH ST	NEW YORK, NY	10019
LICATA, KENNETH	DIRECTOR	331 ROBERTS LN	SCOTCH PLAINS, NJ	07076
LICHAK, MARY FRANCES	WRITER	555 W 57TH ST #1230	NEW YORK, NY	10019
LICHT, ANDY	FILM PRODUCER	4000 WARNER BLVD	BURBANK, CA	91522
LICHTENBERGER, JIM	MUSICIAN	920 DRUMMOND DR	NASHVILLE, TN	37211
LICHTER, GEORGE S	WRITER	8955 BEVERLY BLVD	LOS ANGELES, CA	90048
LICHTI, DANIEL	BARITONE	200 W 70TH ST #7-F	NEW YORK, NY	10023
LICHTMAN, JAMES	DIRECTOR	4444 WOODMAN AVE #28	SHERMAN OAKS, CA	91423
LICHTMAN, MYLA R	SCREENWRITER	8955 BEVERLY BLVD	LOS ANGELES, CA	90048
LICHTMAN, PAUL	ACT-WRI-PROD	4001 VAN NOORD AVE	STUDIO CITY, CA	91604
LICINI, CHUCK	ACTOR	15120 VICTORY BLVD #40	VAN NUYS, CA	91411
LICU, MARIO	ACTOR	14801 SHERMAN WY #1204	VAN NUYS, CA	91405
LIDDELL, GERALD	WRITER	555 W 57TH ST #1230	NEW YORK, NY	10019
LIDDLE, DWIGHT H	FILM DIRECTOR	999 N DOHENY DR #403	LOS ANGELES, CA	90069
LIDDY, G GORDON	AUTHOR	9310 IVANHOE RD	OXON HILL, MD	20010
LIDEKS, MARA	TV WRITER	3616 MOUNTAIN VIEW AVE	LOS ANGELES, CA	90066
LIDZ, FRANK	SPORTS WRITER-EDITOR	SPORTS ILLUSTRATED MAGAZINE		
		TIME & LIFE BUILDING		
		ROCKEFELLER CENTER	NEW YORK, NY	10020
LIEB, ROBERT P	ACTOR	4428 WORSTER AVE	NORTH HOLLYWOOD, CA	91604
LIEBER, ERIC	WRITER-PRODUCER	1200 N DOHENY DR	LOS ANGELES, CA	90069
LIEBER, JILL	SPORTS WRITER-EDITOR	SPORTS ILLUSTRATED MAGAZINE		
		TIME & LIFE BUILDING		
		ROCKEFELLER CENTER	NEW YORK, NY	10020
LIEBER, MICHAEL	WRITER	8955 BEVERLY BLVD	LOS ANGELES, CA	90048
LIEBER, PAUL	ACTOR	10000 SANTA MONICA BLVD #305	LOS ANGELES, CA	90067
LIEBERMAN, AMY	CASTING DIRECTOR	THE MARK TAPER FORUM		
		135 N GRAND AVE	LOS ANGELES, CA	90012
LIEBERMAN, HAL D	WRITER	8955 BEVERLY BLVD	LOS ANGELES, CA	90048
LIEBERMAN, JACK H	WRITER-PRODUCER	3995 PROSPECT AVE	LOS ANGELES, CA	90027
LIEBERMAN, JEFF	DIRECTOR	51 WARREN ST	HASTINGS-ON-HUDSON, NY	10706
LIEBERMAN, LORI	SINGER-SONGWRITER	J LENNER, 3 W 57TH ST	NEW YORK, NY	10019
LIEBERMAN, MARTIN R	DIRECTOR	488 WILLITS ST	BIRMINGHAM, MI	48009
LIEBERMAN, MEG	CASTING DIRECTOR	MGM, 10202 W WASHINGTON BLVD	CULVER CITY, CA	90230
LIEBERMAN, RHONDA A	NEWS CORRESPONDENT	1755 S JEFFERSON DAVIS HWY	ARLINGTON, VA	22202
LIEBERMAN, RICK	ACTOR	200 W 57TH ST #1303	NEW YORK, NY	10019
LIEBERMAN, ROBERT MITCHELL	TV DIRECTOR	10590 WILSHIRE BLVD #1103	LOS ANGELES, CA	90024
LIEBERMAN, RON	ACTOR	15535 HUSTON ST	ENCINO, CA	91436
LIEBERSON, SANFORD	FILM PRODUCER	51 HOLLAND ST, KENSINGTON	LONDON W8 7JB	ENGLAND
LIEBERT, PATRICIA L	WRITER	555 W 57TH ST #1230	NEW YORK, NY	10019
LIEBERTHAL, GARY B	TV EXECUTIVE	1901 AVE OF THE STARS #666	LOS ANGELES, CA	90067
LIEBHART, CYNTHIA L	NEWS CORRESPONDENT	3820 TUNLAW RD #304, NW	WASHINGTON, DC	20007
LIEBL, BRAD	BARITONE	AFFILIATE ARTISTS, INC		
		37 W 65TH ST, 6TH FLOOR	NEW YORK, NY	10023
LIEBLER, MARTHA A	NEWS CORRESPONDENT	2133 WISCONSIN AVE, NW	WASHINGTON, DC	20007
LIEBLER, PAUL E	NEWS CORRESPONDENT	CBS NEWS, 2020 "M" ST, NW	WASHINGTON, DC	20036
LIEBLING, HOWARD	TV WRITER	8955 BEVERLY BLVD	LOS ANGELES, CA	90048
LIEBLING, TERRY	CASTING DIRECTOR	POST OFFICE BOX 5718	SHERMAN OAKS, CA	91403
LIEBMANN, NORMAN	TV WRITER	8955 BEVERLY BLVD	LOS ANGELES, CA	90048
LIEGH, RONNIE & ALLIANCE	ROCK & ROLL GROUP	DMR, 117 HIGHBRIDGE ST	FAYETTEVILLE, NY	13066
LIEN, ARTHUR E	NEWS CORRESPONDENT	NBC-TV, NEWS DEPARTMENT		
		4001 NEBRASKA AVE, NW	WASHINGTON, DC	20016
LIEN, MICHAEL	CASTING DIRECTOR	336 N FOOTHILL RD #8	BEVERLY HILLS, CA	90210
LIENHARD, TONI	NEWS CORRESPONDENT	3508 GARFIELD ST, NW	WASHINGTON, DC	20007
LIFE	MUSICAL GROUP	CEE, 193 KONHAUS RD	MECHANICSBURG, PA	17055
LIFEBOAT	ROCK & ROLL GROUP	POST OFFICE BOX 326	BOSTON, MA	02101
LIFFORD, TINA	ACTRESS	15010 VENTURA BLVD #219	SHERMAN OAKS, CA	91403

LIGERMAN, NATHAN	WRITER	5235 SUNNYSLOPE AVE	VAN NUYS, CA	91401
LIGHT, GEORGE A	DIRECTOR	4305 JOPLIN DR	ROCKVILLE, MD	20853
LIGHT, JUDITH	ACTRESS	3410 WRIGHTVIEW DR	STUDIO CITY, CA	91604
LIGHT, KARL	ACTOR	11 ALEXANDER ST	PRINCETON, NJ	08540
LIGHT, LARRY	ACCORDIONIST	POST OFFICE BOX 110498	NASHVILLE, TN	37211
LIGHT, RONNY	MUSIC ARRANGER	POST OFFICE BOX 121145	NASHVILLE, TN	37212
LIGHTBODY, ANDY R	NEWS CORRESPONDENT	1225 JEFFERSON DAVIS HWY	ARLINGTON, VA	22202
LIGHTFOOT, GORDON	SINGER-SONGWRITER	1365 YONGE ST #207	TORONTO, ONT M4T 2P7	CANADA
LIGHTFOOT, LEONARD	ACTOR	10859 FRUITLAND DR #3	STUDIO CITY, CA	91604
LIGHTFOOT, PETER	BARITONE	ICM, 40 W 57TH ST	NEW YORK, NY	10019
LIGHTFOOT, TERRY	JAZZ MUSICIAN	THE THREE HORSESHOES, HARPENDEN	HERTS	ENGLAND
LIGHTFOOT-EILAND, LINDA	ACTRESS	6706 LEMP AVE	NORTH HOLLYWOOD, CA	91606
LIGHTHILL, BRIAN	FILM DIRECTOR	SEIFERT, 8-A BRUNSWICK GARDENS	LONDON W8 5EN	ENGLAND
LIGHTMAN, DAVID	NEWS CORRESPONDENT	16 SUNNYMEADE CT	ROCKVILLE, MD	20854
LIGHTMAN, HERB	DIRECTOR	POST OFFICE BOX 8272	UNIVERSAL CITY, CA	91608
LIGHTMAN, JULES	DIRECTOR	1825 SHELL AVE	VENICE, CA	90291
LIGHTNING	SOUL-DISCO GROUP	INHERIT PRODS, 1776 BROADWAY	NEW YORK, NY	10019
LIGHTSTONE, BARBARA G	WRITER	8955 BEVERLY BLVD	LOS ANGELES, CA	90048
LIGHTSTONE, MARILYN	ACTRESS	8380 MELROSE AVE #207	LOS ANGELES, CA	90069
LIGHTSTONE, RONALD	CABLE EXECUTIVE	VIACOM INTERNATIONAL, INC		
		1211 AVE OF THE AMERICAS	NEW YORK, NY	10036
LIGI, JOSELLA	SOPRANO	CAMI, 165 W 57TH ST	NEW YORK, NY	10019
LIGON, TOM	ACTOR	227 WAVERLY PL	NEW YORK, NY	10014
LILE, FORD	ACTOR	1735 N FULLER AVE	LOS ANGELES, CA	90046
LILLO, MARIE	ACTRESS	840 N LARRABEE ST #2-102	LOS ANGELES, CA	90069
LILLY, BRENDA	ACTRESS	331 N KENWOOD ST	BURBANK, CA	91505
LILLY, EVERETT	SINGER	ROUTE #1, BOX 161-E	BECKLEY, WV	25801
LILLY, LOU	DIRECTOR	2528 MANDEVILLE CANYON RD	LOS ANGELES, CA	90049
LIM, PIK-SEN	ACTRESS	OCA, 34 GRAFTON TERR	LONDON NW5 4HY	ENGLAND
LIM, STEPHEN	DIRECTOR	842 N STANLEY AVE	HOLLYWOOD, CA	90046
LIMA, LUIS	TENOR	CAMI, 165 W 57TH ST	NEW YORK, NY	10019
LIMBACH, FRANCIS J	NEWS CORRESPONDENT	1825 "K" ST, NW	WASHINGTON, DC	20006
LIMELITERS, THE	VOCAL GROUP	17530 VENTURA BLVD #108	ENCINO, CA	91316
LIMERICK, PAUL D	NEWS CORRESPONDENT	4820 S 29TH ST	ARLINGTON, VA	22206
LIMITED WARRANTY	ROCK & ROLL GROUP	POST OFFICE BOX 437	EXCELSIOR, MN	55331
LIMOR, ROBERTA	CELLIST	3715 RICHLAND AVE	NASHVILLE, TN	37205
LIN, CHO-LIANG	VIOLINIST	ICM, 40 W 57TH ST	NEW YORK, NY	10019
LINARES, RONALD	ACTOR	6542 FULCHER AVE	NORTH HOLLYWOOD, CA	91606
LINARES DE HOUSEIN, DELLA	NEWS CORRESPONDENT	6308 THOMAS DR	SPRINGFIELD, VA	22150
LINARI, NANCY	ACTRESS	8485 MELROSE PL #E	LOS ANGELES, CA	90069
LINCER, ARTHUR	PHOTOGRAPHER	435 W 57TH ST	NEW YORK, NY	10019
LINCOLN, ANINA	ACTRESS	NEW, 300 E GLENOAKS BLVD	GLENDALE, CA	91207
LINCOLN, FRAN	COMPOSER	5827 ERNEST ST	LOS ANGELES, CA	90034
LINCOLN, NINA G	ACTRESS	400 N OGDEN DR	LOS ANGELES, CA	90036
LINCOLN, SCOTT	ACTOR	15010 VENTURA BLVD #219	SHERMAN OAKS, CA	91403
LINCOLN COUNTY	C & W GROUP	SCA, 46 E HERBERT AVE	SALT LAKE CITY, UT	84111
LINCOLN COUNTY PARTNERS	BLUEGRASS GROUP	POST OFFICE BOX 25371	CHARLOTTE, NC	28212
LIND, BRITT	ACTRESS	1901 AVE OF THE STARS #1774	LOS ANGELES, CA	90067
LIND, DE DE	MODEL	MODELS & PROMOTIONS AGENCY		
		8560 SUNSET BLVD, 10TH FLOOR	LOS ANGELES, CA	90069
LIND, EVA	SOPRANO	MARIEDL ANDERS ARTISTS MGMT		
		535 EL CAMINO DEL MAR ST	SAN FRANCISCO, CA	94121
LIND, GRETCHEN	ACTRESS	10845 LINDBROOK DR #3	LOS ANGELES, CA	90024
LIND, KAREN	ACTRESS	4789 VINELAND AVE #100	NORTH HOLLYWOOD, CA	91602
LINDAHL, HAL	WRITER	1468 FOREST GLEN DR #20	HACIENDA HEIGHTS, CA	91745
LINDAUER, JERRY D	CABLE EXECUTIVE	T M CABLE TELEVISION		
		2381 MORSE AVE	IRVINE, CA	92714
LINDBERG, LAWRENCE	TV DIRECTOR	91 CENTRAL PARK W	NEW YORK, NY	10023
LINDBERGH, ANN MORROW	AVIATRIX-AUTHORESS	SCOTT'S COVE	DARIEN, CT	06820
LINDBLOM, RON	ACTOR	9025 WILSHIRE BLVD #309	BEVERLY HILLS, CA	90211
LINDE, DENNIS	GUITARIST	ROUTE #1, LAKEVIEW RD	HERMITAGE, TN	37076
LINDEMAN, BARD	COLUMNIST	TRIBUNE MEDIA SERVICES		
		64 E CONCORD ST	ORLANDO, FL	32801
LINDEMAN, ERIC D	NEWS CORRESPONDENT	1618 "S" ST, NW	WASHINGTON, DC	20009
LINDEMANN, CARL, JR	TV EXECUTIVE	CBS-TV, 51 W 52ND ST	NEW YORK, NY	10019
LINDEN, HAL	ACTOR-DIRECTOR	9200 SUNSET BLVD #808	LOS ANGELES, CA	90069
LINDEN, STEVEN	WRITER	555 W 57TH ST #1230	NEW YORK, NY	10019
LINDEN, V CAESAR	CONDUCTOR	POST OFFICE BOX 2645	LOS ANGELES, CA	90028
LINDEN, WILLIAM E, JR	TV DIRECTOR	2716 FOX MILL RD	HERNDON, VA	22071
LINDENSTRAND, SYLVIA	MEZZO-SOPRANO	CAMI, 165 W 57TH ST	NEW YORK, NY	10019
LINDER, CEC	ACTOR	LONDON MANAGEMENT, LTD		
		235-241 REGENT ST	LONDON W1A 2JT	ENGLAND
LINDER, DIANE	ACTRESS	6430 SUNSET BLVD #1203	LOS ANGELES, CA	90028
LINDER, KATE	ACTRESS	6430 SUNSET BLVD #1203	LOS ANGELES, CA	90028
LINDFORS, VIVECA	ACTRESS	172 E 95TH ST	NEW YORK, NY	10028
LINDHEIM, RICHARD	TV WRITER	166 N CARSON RD	BEVERLY HILLS, CA	90211
LINDINE, JACK	ACTOR	8485 MELROSE PL #E	LOS ANGELES, CA	90069
LINDLEY, AUDRA	ACTRESS	145 S CANON DR	BEVERLY HILLS, CA	90212
LINDLEY, LAURIE	ACTRESS	495 MAR VISTA DR	MONTEREY, CA	93940
LINDNER, SUSAN JANE	TV WRITER	10970 ASHTON AVE #307	LOS ANGELES, CA	90024
LINDROTH, LLOYD	COMPOSER	10113 RIVERSIDE DR	NORTH HOLLYWOOD, CA	91602
LINDSAY, CYNTHIA	WRITER	24932 MALIBU RD	MALIBU, CA	90265
LINDSAY, DIANE	SINGER	POST OFFICE BOX 4114	SYLMAR, CA	91342
LINDSAY, GRAHAM	TV PRODUCER	29 WINDMILL ST, BUSHEY HILL	HERTS	ENGLAND

Name	Occupation	Address	City	Zip/Country
LINDSAY, JOHN J	NEWS CORRESPONDENT	7322 14TH ST, NW	WASHINGTON, DC	20012
LINDSAY, JON	FILM PRODUCER	5 KENDAL STEPS		
		SAINT GEORGES FIELDS	LONDON WC2	ENGLAND
LINDSAY, MARK	SINGER-COMPOSER	9595 WILSHIRE BLVD #400	BEVERLY HILLS, CA	90212
LINDSAY, POWELL SMITH	NEWS CORRESPONDENT	5306 BLAKEFORD CT, NW	WASHINGTON, DC	20816
LINDSAY, ROBERT	ACTOR	FELIX DE WOLFE, 1 ROBERT ST		
		ADELPHI	LONDON WC2N 6BH	ENGLAND
LINDSAY-HOGG, MICHAEL	FILM DIRECTOR	CHATTO & LINNIT, LTD		
		PRINCE OF WALES THEATRE		
		COVENTRY ST	LONDON WC2	ENGLAND
LINDSEY, ALEX J	WRITER	8955 BEVERLY BLVD	LOS ANGELES, CA	90048
LINDSEY, CHARLES	TENOR	200 W 70TH ST #7-F	NEW YORK, NY	10023
LINDSEY, ELIZABETH	ACTRESS	6310 SAN VICENTE BLVD #407	LOS ANGELES, CA	90048
LINDSEY, GEORGE	ACT-SING-COMED	6310 SAN VICENTE BLVD #407	LOS ANGELES, CA	90048
LINDSEY, GEORGE S	WRITER	8955 BEVERLY BLVD	LOS ANGELES, CA	90048
LINDSEY, GEORGE T	WRITER-PRODUCER	13535 VALERIO ST #223	VAN NUYS, CA	91405
LINDSEY, JASON	FILM DIRECTOR	7 LINDEN GARDENS	LONDON W2 4HA	ENGLAND
LINDSEY, KEITH	ACTOR	5118 BAKMAN AVE #10	NORTH HOLLYWOOD, CA	91601
LINDSEY, MINNIE S	ACTRESS	334 VERNON AVE	VENICE, CA	90291
LINDSEY, MORT	COMPOSER-CONDUCTOR	6970 FERNHILL DR	MALIBU, CA	90265
LINDSLEY, CELINA	SOPRANO	59 E 54TH ST #81	NEW YORK, NY	10022
LINDSLEY, CLARKE	ACTOR	CASSELL, 843 N SYCAMORE AVE	LOS ANGELES, CA	90038
LINDSLEY, WILLIAM C	DIRECTOR	28362 FORESTBROOK ST	FARMINGTON HILLS, MI	48018
LINDSTROM, JON	ACTOR	208 S BEVERLY DR #4	BEVERLY HILLS, CA	90212
LINDSTROM, PIA	FILM CRITIC	WNBC-TV, 30 ROCKEFELLER PLAZA	NEW YORK, NY	10112
LINE, WILLIAM J	NEWS CORRESPONDENT	4461 CONNECTICUT AVE, NW	WASHINGTON, DC	20008
LINEBACK, RICHARD	ACTOR	2525 LYRIC AVE	LOS ANGELES, CA	90027
LINEBERGER, JAMES L	SCREENWRITER	555 W 57TH ST #1230	NEW YORK, NY	10019
LINEHAN, BARRY	ACTOR	15 BRECHIN PL	LONDON SW7	ENGLAND
LINEHAN, JOYCE	TALENT AGENT	POST OFFICE BOX 817	JAMAICA PLAIN, MA	02130
LINERO, JEANNIE	ACTRESS	9601 WILSHIRE BLVD #GL-11	BEVERLY HILLS, CA	90210
LING, EUGENE F	WRITER	808 ADELAIDE PL	SANTA MONICA, CA	90402
LING, PETER	TV WRITER	13 HIGH WICKHAM	HASTINGS	ENGLAND
LING, SHIRLEY	PIANIST	POST OFFICE BOX 27539	PHILADELPHIA, PA	19118
LING, SYDNEY	ACTOR-DIRECTOR	BROUWERSGRACHT, 68-1013 GX	AMSTERDAM	NETHERLANDS
LINK, JOSEPH L	NEWS CORRESPONDENT	6035 WILMINGTON DR	BURKE, VA	22105
LINK, KURT	BASS	LEW, 204 W 10TH ST	NEW YORK, NY	10014
LINK, ROBERT L	DIRECTOR	600 N MC CLURG CT	CHICAGO, IL	60611
LINK, WILLIAM	TV WRITER-PRODUCER	1501 SKYLARK LN	LOS ANGELES, CA	90069
LINKE, BETTINA BRENNA	ACTRESS	4098 ELMER AVE	NORTH HOLLYWOOD, CA	91602
LINKE, PAUL	ACTOR	3925 MICHAEL AVE	LOS ANGELES, CA	90066
LINKE, RICHARD O	TV PROD-TALENT AGT	4445 CARTWRIGHT AVE #110	NORTH HOLLYWOOD, CA	91602
LINKER, AMY	ACTRESS	1243 WELLESLEY AVE	LOS ANGELES, CA	90025
LINKLETTER, ART	TV PERSONALITY	1100 BEL AIR RD	LOS ANGELES, CA	90077
LINKLETTER, JACK	TV PERSONALITY	1100 BEL AIR RD	LOS ANGELES, CA	90077
LINKOLN KUFF	COMEDIAN	POST OFFICE BOX 308	BURKEVILLE, VA	23922
LINN, DENNIS R	DIRECTOR	BIG ORANGE PRODUCTIONS		
		2791 BIRD AVE	MIAMI, FL	33133
LINN, RAY L, JR	COMPOSER	POST OFFICE BOX 475	HOMEWOOD, CA	95718
LINN, ROBERT T	COMPOSER	3275 DE WITT DR	LOS ANGELES, CA	90068
LINN, ROBERTA	SINGER	HEINECKE'S, 8961 SUNSET BLVD	LOS ANGELES, CA	90069
LINN, TERI ANN	ACTRESS	CBS TELEVISION NETWORK		
		"THE BOLD & THE BEAUTIFUL"		
		7800 BEVERLY BLVD	LOS ANGELES, CA	90036
LINNEMAN, HORSE	GUITARIST	902 NEW DUE WEST AVE	MADISON, TN	37115
LINNETTE, SHERI	SINGER	POST OFFICE BOX 171132	NASHVILLE, TN	37217
LINNEY, ROMULUS	WRITER	555 W 57TH ST #1230	NEW YORK, NY	10019
LINSAY, GEORGE T	WRITER-DIRECTOR	13535 VALERIO ST #223	VAN NUYS, CA	91405
LINSON, ART	DIRECTOR-PRODUCER	DGA, 110 W 57TH ST	NEW YORK, NY	10019
LINTERMANS, GLORIA	COLUMNIST	UNIVERSAL PRESS SYNDICATE		
		4900 MAIN ST, 9TH FLOOR	KANSAS CITY, MO	62114
LINVILLE, ALBERT	ACTOR	7 W 81ST ST	NEW YORK, NY	10024
LINVILLE, JOANNE	ACTRESS	3148 FRYMAN RD	STUDIO CITY, CA	91604
LINVILLE, LARRY	ACTOR	12750 VENTURA BLVD #102	STUDIO CITY, CA	91604
LION, HAROLD H	PHOTOGRAPHER	8012 GOSPORT LN	SPRINGFIELD, VA	22151
LIOTTA, CHARLES	TV DIRECTOR	2492 WELLESLEY AVE	LOS ANGELES, CA	90064
LIOTTA, JERRY I	DIRECTOR	11 GAYLORD DR	WILTON, CT	06897
LIPACK, MICHAEL	PHOTOGRAPHER	253-26 61ST AVE	LITTLE NECK, NY	11362
LIPIN, CAROL	ACTRESS	1607 N EL CENTRO AVE #22	HOLLYWOOD, CA	90028
LIPKIN, SEYMOUR	PIANIST-CONDUCTOR	420 W END AVE	NEW YORK, NY	10024
LIPKIN, SHELLY	ACTOR	9255 SUNSET BLVD #510	LOS ANGELES, CA	90069
LIPMAN, DANIEL	TV WRITER	620 VIA DE LA PAZ	PACIFIC PALISADES, CA	90272
LIPMAN, DAVID	ACTOR	301 ORIENTAL BLVD #5-A	BROOKLYN, NY	11235
LIPMAN, HAROLD	DIRECTOR	35 E 35TH ST	NEW YORK, NY	10016
LIPMAN, LARRY	NEWS CORRESPONDENT	10226 EDGEWOOD AVE	SILVER SPRING, MD	20901
LIPMAN, MAUREEN	ACTRESS	SARABAND ASSOCIATES AGENCY		
		153 PETHERTON RD, HIGHBURY	LONDON N5	ENGLAND
LIPNICK, EDWARD	WRITER	20608 PACIFIC COAST HWY	MALIBU, CA	90265
LIPOVETSKY, LEONIDAG	PIANIST	POST OFFICE BOX 12403		
		NORTHSIDE STATION	ATLANTA, GA	30355
LIPOVSEK, MARJANA	MEZZO-SOPRANO	59 E 54TH ST #81	NEW YORK, NY	10022
LIPPERT, NORMAN E	DIRECTOR	15640 W TIMBER LN	LIBERTYVILLE, IL	60048
LIPPIN, ROBIN	CASTING DIRECTOR	1041 N FORMOSA TRAILER #45	HOLLYWOOD, CA	90046
LIPPMAN, MICHAEL	WRITER	555 W 57TH ST #1230	NEW YORK, NY	10019
LIPPS, INC	VOCAL GROUP	200 W 51ST ST #1410	NEW YORK, NY	10019

LIPPSTONE, LAURA	NEWS CORRESPONDENT	1316 NEW HAMPSHIRE AVE, NW	WASHINGTON, DC	20036
LIPSCOMB, DENNIS	ACTOR	247 S BEVERLY DR #102	BEVERLY HILLS, CA	90210
LIPSCOMB, JAMES	TV WRITER	555 W 57TH ST #1230	NEW YORK, NY	10019
LIPSKI, RICHARD A	PHOTOGRAPHER	900 BANKS PL	ALEXANDRIA, VA	22312
LIPSKY, ELEAZAR	WRITER	555 W 57TH ST #1230	NEW YORK, NY	10019
LIPSKY, JONATHAN	WRITER	555 W 57TH ST #1230	NEW YORK, NY	10019
LIPSKY, ROBIN	NEWS CORRESPONDENT	211 N WAYNE ST	ARLINGTON, VA	22201
LIPSON, G ROBERT	DIRECTOR	1565 OLD CHATHAM DR	BLOOMFIELD HILLS, MI	48013
LIPSON, GERALD	NEWS CORRESPONDENT	8023 PARK LN	BETHESDA, MD	20814
LIPSON-GRUZEN, BERENICE	PIANIST	POST OFFICE BOX U	REDDING, CT	06875
LIPSTONE, HOWARD	WRITER	3555 VALLEY MEADOW RD	SHERMAN OAKS, CA	91403
LIPSTONE, HOWARD	TV EXECUTIVE	11811 W OLYMPIC BLVD	LOS ANGELES, CA	90064
LIPSTONE, JANE	TV EXECUTIVE	11811 W OLYMPIC BLVD	LOS ANGELES, CA	90064
LIPSYTE, ROBERT M	NEWS CORRES-WRITER	CBS NEWS, 524 W 57TH ST	NEW YORK, NY	10019
LIPTAK, GREGORY J	CABLE EXECUTIVE	T M CABLE TELEVISION		
		2381 MORSE AVE	IRVINE, CA	92714
LIPTON, CELIA	SINGER	POST OFFICE BOX 15011	PLANTATION, FL	33318
LIPTON, DANIEL	CONDUCTOR	225 W 34TH ST #1012	NEW YORK, NY	10001
LIPTON, JAMES	THEATER WRI-PROD	2 PENNSYLVANIA PLAZA	NEW YORK, NY	10001
LIPTON, LARRY	FILM DIRECTOR	3006 BELLEVUE AVE	LOS ANGELES, CA	90026
LIPTON, LEONARD	TV DIRECTOR	ABC-TV, 7 W 66TH ST	NEW YORK, NY	10023
LIPTON, MICHAEL	ACTOR	250 W 57TH ST #2317	NEW YORK, NY	10019
LIPTON, MICHAEL A	WRITER-EDITOR	TV GUIDE, 100 MATSONFORD RD	RADNOR, PA	19088
LIPTON, PEGGY	ACTRESS	10880 WILSHIRE BLVD #2110	LOS ANGELES, CA	90024
LIPTON, ROBERT	ACTOR	10 E 44TH ST #700	NEW YORK, NY	10017
LIPTON, ROCHELLE	WRITER	555 W 57TH ST #1230	NEW YORK, NY	10019
LIPTON, SANDY	ACTRESS	8322 BEVERLY BLVD #202	LOS ANGELES, CA	90048
LISA, MISS	AERIALIST	SEE - MISS LISA		
LISA LISA & JAM CULT	SOUL GROUP	STEVE SALEM & COMPANY		
		FULL FORCE PRODUCTIONS		
		217 LAFAYETTE AVE	BROOKLYN, NY	11238
LISAK, STEVE	ACTOR	11235 AMESTOY AVE	GRANADA HILLS, CA	91344
LISANBY, CHARLES	ART DIRECTOR	151 S EL CAMINO DR	BEVERLY HILLS, CA	90212
LISANTI, MICHELLE P	TV WRITER	4730 BEN AVE #23	NORTH HOLLYWOOD, CA	91607
LISBERGER, STEVEN	WRITER-PRODUCER	838 WELLESLEY AVE	LOS ANGELES, CA	90049
LISBIN, SHELLEY	ACTRESS	9600 VANALDEN AVE	NORTHRIDGE, CA	91324
LISCHETTI, ROBERT	TENOR	CONE, 221 W 57TH ST	NEW YORK, NY	10019
LISCIANDRO, FRANK J	WRITER	8955 BEVERLY BLVD	LOS ANGELES, CA	90048
LISCIO, JOHN M	ACTOR	LENZ, 1456 E CHARLESTOWN BLVD	LAS VEGAS, NV	89104
LISHAWA, CHESTER	TV DIRECTOR	90 SURREY LN	TENAFLY, NJ	07670
LISI, GAETANO	DIRECTOR	225 E 88TH ST	NEW YORK, NY	10028
LISI, VIRNA	ACTRESS	VIA DI FILOMARINO 4	ROME	ITALY
LISNER DOU & DANUSKA	HEADBALANCERS	HALL, 138 FROG HOLLOW RD	CHURCHVILLE, PA	18966
LISS, BENNETT	ACTOR	1650 BROADWAY #302	NEW YORK, NY	10019
LISS, STEPHENIE A	WRITER	4941 WHITSETT AVE	NORTH HOLLYWOOD, CA	91607
LISSON, MARK	WRITER	1961 HOLMBY AVE	LOS ANGELES, CA	90025
LIST, RONALD	WRITER	555 W 57TH ST #1230	NEW YORK, NY	10019
LIST, SHELLEY P	TV WRITER	2919 STRONGS PL	VENICE, CA	90291
LISTER, WALTER	WRITER	555 W 57TH ST #1230	NEW YORK, NY	10019
LISTON, DENYCE	ACTRESS	15980 VALLEY WOOD RD	SHERMAN OAKS, CA	91403
LISTON, IAN	ACTOR	HISS & BOO, 24 W GROVE		
		WALTON ON THAMES	SURREY KT12 5NX	ENGLAND
LITHGOW, JOHN	ACTOR	1319 WARNALL AVE	LOS ANGELES, CA	90024
LITHGOW, WILLIAM	ACTOR	3330 BARHAM BLVD #103	LOS ANGELES, CA	90068
LITKE, MARK	WRITER	8955 BEVERLY BLVD	LOS ANGELES, CA	90048
LITT, LARRY	COMEDIAN	POST OFFICE BOX 3574	MIAMI BEACH, FL	33152
LITTELL, ROBERT	SCREENWRITER	8955 BEVERLY BLVD	LOS ANGELES, CA	90048
LITTLE, BENILDE	REPORTER	TIME & PEOPLE MAGAZINE		
		TIME & LIFE BUILDING		
		ROCKEFELLER CENTER	NEW YORK, NY	10020
LITTLE, BIG TINY	SINGER-SONGWRITER	FROST, W 3985 TAFT DR	SPOKANE, WA	99208
LITTLE, CLEAVON	ACTOR	SF & A, 121 N SAN VICENTE BLVD	BEVERLY HILLS, CA	90211
LITTLE, FRANK	TENOR	COLBERT, 111 W 57TH ST	NEW YORK, NY	10019
LITTLE, JAMES E	NEWS CORRESPONDENT	4461 CONNECTICUT AVE, NW	WASHINGTON, DC	20008
LITTLE, JOYCE	ACTRESS	LIGHT, 113 N ROBERTSON BLVD	LOS ANGELES, CA	90048
LITTLE, MICHELE	ACTRESS	POST OFFICE BOX 5617	BEVERLY HILLS, CA	90210
LITTLE, RICH	ACTOR-COMEDIAN	10100 SANTA MONICA BLVD #1600	LOS ANGELES, CA	90067
LITTLE, TAWNY	TV HOST	KABC-TV, 4151 PROSPECT AVE	HOLLYWOOD, CA	90027
LITTLE & LARGE	COMEDY DUO	LONDON MANAGEMENT, LTD		
		235-241 REGENT ST	LONDON W1A 2JT	ENGLAND
LITTLE ANTHONY	SINGER	SEE - GOURDINE, LITTLE ANTHONY		
LITTLE ANTHONY & THE IMPERIALS	VOCAL GROUP	8033 SUNSET BLVD #222	LOS ANGELES, CA	90046
LITTLE CAESAR & THE ROMANS	VOCAL GROUP	OLDIES, 5218 ALMONT ST	LOS ANGELES, CA	90032
LITTLE FIJI	WRESTLER	GORGEOUS LADIES OF WRESTLING		
		RIVIERA HOTEL & CASINO		
		DAVID B MC LANE PRODS		
		2901 S LAS VEGAS BLVD	LAS VEGAS, NV	89109
LITTLE JOE & THE THRILLERS	VOCAL GROUP	OLDIES, 5218 ALMONT ST	LOS ANGELES, CA	90032
LITTLE RICHARD	SINGER-SONGWRITER	8383 WILSHIRE BLVD #900	BEVERLY HILLS, CA	90211
LITTLE RIVER BAND	ROCK & ROLL GROUP	87-91 PALMERSTIN CRESCENT		
		ALBERT PARK	MELBOURNE U1C 3206	AUSTRALIA
LITTLE STEVEN & DISCIPLES OF SO	ROCK & ROLL GROUP	9200 SUNSET BLVD #915	LOS ANGELES, CA	90069
LITTLE TOYOKO	WRESTLER	POST OFFICE BOX 3859	STAMFORD, CT	06905
LITTLEBROOK, LORD	WRESTLER	POST OFFICE BOX 3859	STAMFORD, CT	06905
LITTLEFIELD, WARREN	TV EXECUTIVE	NBC-TV, 3000 W ALAMEDA AVE	BURBANK, CA	91523

CLEAVON LITTLE

RICH LITTLE

LITTLE RICHARD

BOB LIVINGSTON

SONDRA LOCKE

ANNE LOCKHART

HEATHER LOCKLEAR

ROBERT LOGAN

GINA LOLLABRIGIDA

LITTLEHALES, BATES W	PHOTOGRAPHER	4426 N DITTMAR RD	ARLINGTON, VA	22207
LITTLER, CRAIG	ACTOR	5488 ROUND MEADOW RD	HIDDEN HILLS, CA	91302
LITTLER, GENE	GOLFER	POST OFFICE BOX 1949	RANCHO SANTE FE, CA	92067
LITTLETON, CAROL	FILM EDITOR	ACE, 4416 1/2 FINLEY AVE	LOS ANGELES, CA	90027
LITTLETON, TWYLA	ACTRESS	141 S EL CAMINO DR #205	BEVERLY HILLS, CA	90212
LITTLETON, WILLIAM	GUITARIST	2508 PLEASANT GREEN RD	NASHVILLE, TN	37214
LITTMAN, GREGG	ACTOR	54 1/2 PALOMA AVE	VENICE, CA	90291
LITTMAN, LYNNE	TV DIRECTOR-PRODUCER	6620 CAHUENGA TERR	LOS ANGELES, CA	90068
LITTO, GEORGE	FILM PRODUCER	215 S BEVERLY BLVD #202	BEVERLY HILLS, CA	90212
LITVACK, JOHN ALAN	TV DIR-EXEC	1741 PIER AVE	SANTA MONICA, CA	90405
LITVACK, NEAL	CABLE EXECUTIVE	HOME BOX OFFICE PICTURES		
		1100 AVE OF THE AMERICAS	NEW YORK, NY	10036
LITZINGER, SAMUEL M	NEWS CORRESPONDENT	1825 "K" ST, NW	WASHINGTON, DC	20006
LIVE	RHYTHM & BLUES GROUP	PERLE, 4475 VINELAND AVE	STUDIO CITY, CA	91602
LIVELY-MEKKA, DELYSE	ACTRESS	WEBB, 7500 DEVISTA DR	LOS ANGELES, CA	90046
LIVENGOOD, VICTORIA	MEZZO-SOPRANO	1776 BROADWAY #504	NEW YORK, NY	10019
LIVERMORE, GARET	WRITER	555 W 57TH ST #1230	NEW YORK, NY	10019
LIVESAY, KENNETH R	TV WRITER	8955 BEVERLY BLVD	LOS ANGELES, CA	90048
LIVINGS, GEORGE	TENOR	CONE, 221 W 57TH ST	NEW YORK, NY	10019
LIVINGSTON, ALAN W	WRITER-PRODUCER	945 N ALPINE DR	BEVERLY HILLS, CA	90210
LIVINGSTON, BARRY	ACTOR	11310 BLIX ST	NORTH HOLLYWOOD, CA	91602
LIVINGSTON, BOB	ACTOR	5910 YOLANDA AVE #5	TARZANA, CA	91356
LIVINGSTON, DAVID W	MUSIC ARRANGER	2325 BELLEVUE DR	BOWLING GREEN, KY	42101
LIVINGSTON, HAROLD	SCREENWRITER	8955 BEVERLY BLVD	LOS ANGELES, CA	90048
LIVINGSTON, J A	COLUMNIST	NEWS AMERICA SYNDICATE		
		1703 KAISER AVE	IRVINE, CA	92714
LIVINGSTON, JAY	COMPOSER-LYRICIST	ASCAP, 1 LINCOLN PLAZA	NEW YORK, NY	10023
LIVINGSTON, ROBERT C	DIRECTOR	46 LARIAT RD	PALM SPRINGS, CA	92262
LIVINGSTON, ROBERT H	TV DIRECTOR	347 W 39TH ST	NEW YORK, NY	10018
LIVINGSTON, RUTH	ACTRESS	203 W 81ST ST	NEW YORK, NY	10024
LIVINGSTON, STAN	ACTOR	3575 W CAHUENGA BLVD #320	LOS ANGELES, CA	90068
LIVINGSTON, TONI	CASTING DIRECTOR	869 N SAN VICENTE BLVD	LOS ANGELES, CA	90048
LIVINGSTON, ULYSSES G	COMPOSER	27027 WHITESTONE RD	ROLLING HILLS, CA	90274
LIVINGSTON, WILLIAM	TENOR	61 W 62ND ST #6-F	NEW YORK, NY	10023
LIVINGSTONE, DAVID	GUITARIST	2325 BELLEVUE DR	BOWLING GREEN, KY	42101
LIVINGSTONE, DOUGLAS	TV WRITER-DIRECTOR	UNNA & DURBRIDGE, LTD		
		24-32 POTTERY LN		
		HOLLAND PARK	LONDON W11	ENGLAND
LIVNEH, SAMUEL	ACTOR	10809 FORBES AVE	GRANADA HILLS, CA	91344
LIVTYI, ALEXANDER G	NEWS CORRESPONDENT	1402 N BEAUREGARD ST #201	ALEXANDRIA, VA	22311
LIZER, KARI	ACTRESS	9229 SUNSET BLVD #607	LOS ANGELES, CA	90069
LIZZI, JOAN	ACTOR	13040 DRONFIELD AVE #26	SYLMAR, CA	91342
LIZZY BORDEN	ROCK & ROLL GROUP	POST OFFICE BOX 2428	EL SEGUNDO, CA	90245
LKER, DRAKE	WRITER	555 W 57TH ST #1230	NEW YORK, NY	10019
LLACE, DONALD T	TV WRITER	555 W 57TH ST #1230	NEW YORK, NY	10019
LLE, LOUIS	FILM DIRECTOR	LE COUEL, 46260 LIMOGNE	EN QUERCY	FRANCE
LLEN, ELIZABETH	ACTRESS	247 S BEVERLY DR #102	BEVERLY HILLS, CA	90212
LLEWELLYN, JOANNE	ACTRESS	FISHER-REYNOLDS ORGANISATION		
		50 SERVITE HOUSE, RECTORY RD		
		BECKINGHAM	KENT	ENGLAND
LLEWELYN, DOUG	ACTOR	23416 CANZONET ST	WOODLAND HILLS, CA	91367
LLORCA, ADOLFO	TENOR	61 W 62ND ST #6-F	NEW YORK, NY	10023
LLOYD, ALICE	VIOLINIST	840 MURFREESBORO RD #O-1	NASHVILLE, TN	37217
LLOYD, BENJAMIN	VIOLINIST	860 MURFREESBORO RD #O-1	NASHVILLE, TN	37217
LLOYD, CHARLES F	COMPOSER	ROUTE #1, BOX 63	BIG SUR, CA	93920
LLOYD, CHRISTOPHER	ACTOR	POST OFFICE BOX 5617	BEVERLY HILLS, CA	90210
LLOYD, CONSTANCE J	WRITER	555 W 57TH ST #1230	NEW YORK, NY	10019
LLOYD, DAVID	TV WRITER	8955 BEVERLY BLVD	LOS ANGELES, CA	90048
LLOYD, EDLYNE "PAT"	TV PRODUCER	KNBC-TV, "SANTA BARBARA"		
		3000 W ALAMEDA AVE	BURBANK, CA	91523
LLOYD, EUAN	FILM PRODUCER	NICHOLAS, 81 PICCADILLY	LONDON W1	ENGLAND
LLOYD, IAN	SINGER	1790 BROADWAY #PH	NEW YORK, NY	10019
LLOYD, INNES	TV PRODUCER	89 QUEEN'S RD, RICHMOND	SURREY	ENGLAND
LLOYD, JAN R	FILM DIRECTOR	15 QUARTERDECK ST	MARINA DEL REY, CA	90292
LLOYD, KARI	ACTRESS	3151 W CAHUENGA BLVD #310	LOS ANGELES, CA	90068
LLOYD, KATHLEEN	ACTRESS	9229 SUNSET BLVD #306	LOS ANGELES, CA	90069
LLOYD, LAUREN	CASTING DIRECTOR	4000 WARNER BLVD	BURBANK, CA	91522
LLOYD, LELAND	SINGER-GUITARIST	654 HARDING PL	NASHVILLE, TN	37211
LLOYD, LINDA BEATSON	ACTRESS	1467 N DOHENY DR	LOS ANGELES, CA	90069
LLOYD, MIKE	TV DIRECTOR-PRODUCER	1 THE CROFT, PARK HILL		
		EALING	LONDON W5 2JW	ENGLAND
LLOYD, NORMAN	ACTOR-DIRECTOR	1813 OLD RANCH RD	LOS ANGELES, CA	90049
LLOYD, NORMAN	MUSICIAN	82 RICHMOND HILL RD	GREENWICH, CT	06830
LLOYD, PATRICK	TV WRITER	8955 BEVERLY BLVD	LOS ANGELES, CA	90048
LLOYD, ROBERT	SINGER	CAMI, 165 W 57TH ST	NEW YORK, NY	10019
LLOYD, ROBIN	NEWS CORRESPONDENT	1666 79TH ST CROSSWAY #610	MIAMI, FL	33141
LLOYD, ROBIN	NEWS CORRESPONDENT	NBC-TV, NEWS DEPARTMENT		
		4001 NEBRASKA AVE, NW	WASHINGTON, DC	20016
LLOYD, SHERMAN	ACTOR	433 W 46TH ST	NEW YORK, NY	10036
LLOYD, TED	TV PRODUCER	CROFT HAM, KEWFERRY DR		
		NORTHWOOD	MIDDLESEX	ENGLAND
LLYNNE, BOBBE	SINGER	TERRY, 909 PARKVIEW AVE	LODI, CA	95240
LO, ROBERT H C	NEWS CORRESPONDENT	6402 WINNEPEG RD	BETHESDA, MD	20817
LO BIANCO, TONY	ACT-WRI-DIR	ICM, 8899 BEVERLY BLVD	LOS ANGELES, CA	90048
LO CICERO, THOMAS V	DIRECTOR	13730 HART	OAK PARK, MI	48237

Name	Occupation	Address	City	Zip
LO DICO, JOHN A	NEWS CORRESPONDENT	1709 1/2 21ST ST #23, NW	WASHINGTON, DC	20009
LO PINTO, DORIAN	ACTRESS	9744 WILSHIRE BLVD #206	BEVERLY HILLS, CA	90212
LO PINTO, JOHN	CABLE EXECUTIVE	TIME VIDEO INFORMATION SERVICE		
		1271 AVE OF THE AMERICAS	NEW YORK, NY	10020
LO PORTO, LINDA	ACTRESS	1605 N CAHUENGA BLVD #202	LOS ANGELES, CA	90028
LOACH, KENNETH	TV DIRECTOR	GOODWIN, 19 LONDON ST	LONDON W2	ENGLAND
LOBEL, MIKE	WRITER	8955 BEVERLY BLVD	LOS ANGELES, CA	90048
LOBELL, MIKE	FILM PRODUCER	MCA/UNIVERSAL STUDIOS, INC		
		100 UNIVERSAL CITY PLAZA	UNIVERSAL CITY, CA	91608
LOBER, LIONEL	WRITER	17449 ARMINTA ST	NORTHRIDGE, CA	91325
LOBL, VICTOR	TV DIRECTOR	137 S WESTGATE AVE	LOS ANGELES, CA	90049
LOBO	SINGER-SONGWRITER	DENIS VAUGHAN MANAGEMENT		
		HEATHCOAT HOUSE		
		19-20 SAVILE RD	LONDON W1	ENGLAND
LOBO, EL	WRESTLER	SEE - EL LOBO		
LOBSENZ, GEORGE P	NEWS CORRESPONDENT	216 3RD ST, SE	WASHINGTON, DC	20003
LOBUE, ANGE	ACTOR	5330 LANKERSHIM BLVD #210	NORTH HOLLYWOOD, CA	91601
LOBUE, J D	DIRECTOR	12304 ADDISON ST	NORTH HOLLYWOOD, CA	91607
LOCANTE, SAM G	ACTOR	235 W END AVE	NEW YORK, NY	10023
LOCATELL, CAROL	ACTRESS	4153 WOODMAN AVE	SHERMAN OAKS, CA	91423
LOCHER, DICK	CARTOONIST	THE CHICAGO TRIBUNE		
		TRIBUNE TOWER		
		435 N MICHIGAN AVE	CHICAGO, IL	60611
LOCHHEAD, LEE	DIRECTOR	4039 CAMELLIA AVE	STUDIO CITY, CA	91604
LOCHNER, DON	ACTOR	19 STUYVESANT ST	NEW YORK, NY	10003
LOCHTE, RICHARD S	WRITER	2700 NEILSON WY	SANTA MONICA, CA	90405
LOCK-ELLIOTT, SUMNER	WRITER	555 W 57TH ST #1230	NEW YORK, NY	10019
LOCKE, PETER	TV PRODUCER	1119 N MC CADDEN PL	HOLLYWOOD, CA	90038
LOCKE, RANDOLPH	TENOR	LEW, 204 W 10TH ST	NEW YORK, NY	10014
LOCKE, RICHARD B	TV DIRECTOR	2940 COTTONWOOD CT	NEWBURY PARK, CA	91320
LOCKE, RICHARD E	TV DIRECTOR	948 WINFIELD ST	NEWBURY PARK, CA	91320
LOCKE, SAM D	TV WRITER	3043 NICHOLS CANYON RD	HOLLYWOOD, CA	90046
LOCKE, SONDRA	ACTRESS	POST OFFICE BOX 69865	LOS ANGELES, CA	90069
LOCKER, KENNETH A	FILM WRITER-DIRECTOR	1607 N VISTA ST	LOS ANGELES, CA	90046
LOCKERMAN, BRADLEY	ACTOR	CBS-TV, 7800 BEVERLY BLVD	LOS ANGELES, CA	90036
LOCKETT, BRIAN	NEWS CORRESPONDENT	1114 SOUTH CAROLINA AVE, SE	WASHINGTON, DC	20003
LOCKHART, ANNE	ACTRESS	2045 STRADELLA RD	LOS ANGELES, CA	90077
LOCKHART, JUNE	ACTRESS	2045 STRADELLA RD	LOS ANGELES, CA	90077
LOCKHART, LAUREL	ACTRESS	8285 SUNSET BLVD #12	LOS ANGELES, CA	90046
LOCKHART, RAY	DIRECTOR	DGA, 110 W 57TH ST	NEW YORK, NY	10019
LOCKHART, RAY	TV EXECUTIVE	NBC TELEVISION NETWORK		
		30 ROCKEFELLER PLAZA	NEW YORK, NY	10112
LOCKLEAR, HEATHER	ACTRESS-MODEL	9200 SUNSET BLVD #931	LOS ANGELES, CA	90069
LOCKLIN, HANK	SINGER-SONGWRITER	ROUTE #1, BOX 123	MILTON, FL	32570
LOCKMAN, BRIAN	NEWS CORRESPONDENT	400 N CAPITOL ST, NW	WASHINGTON, DC	20001
LOCKWOOD, ALEXANDER	ACTOR	9000 SUNSET BLVD #1200	LOS ANGELES, CA	90069
LOCKWOOD, DIDIER	VIOLINIST	JEAN-MARIE SHALHANI		
		3 RUE CESAR FRANCK	PARIS 75015	FRANCE
LOCKWOOD, E GREY	DIRECTOR	DGA, 7950 SUNSET BLVD	LOS ANGELES, CA	90046
LOCKWOOD, GARY	ACTOR	3083 1/2 RAMBLA PACIFICA	MALIBU, CA	90265
LOCKWOOD, JULIA	ACTRESS	112 CASTLENAN	LONDON SW13	ENGLAND
LOCKWOOD, LESTER	THEATER PRODUCER	325 W END AVE	NEW YORK, NY	10023
LOCKWOOD, WALTER L	WRITER	10100 SANTA MONICA BLVD #1600	LOS ANGELES, CA	90067
LOCKYER, PAUL J	NEWS CORRESPONDENT	4858 LOUGHBORO RD, NW	WASHINGTON, DC	20016
LOCONTO, FRANK X	SINGER	7766 NW 44TH ST	SUNRISE, FL	33321
LODDER, SASKIA	ACTRESS	9025 WILSHIRE BLVD #309	BEVERLY HILLS, CA	90211
LODER, JOHN	ACTOR	BUCKS CLUB, 18 CLIFFORD ST	LONDON W1	ENGLAND
LODGE, DAVID	ACTOR	8 SYDNEY RD, RICHMOND	SURREY	ENGLAND
LODGE, J C	SINGER	POST OFFICE BOX 42517	WASHINGTON, DC	20015
LODGE, LINDA	ACTRESS	1429 N HAVENHURST DR #2	LOS ANGELES, CA	90046
LODGE, ROBERT W	NEWS CORRESPONDENT	9638 PARKWOOD DR	BETHESDA, MD	20814
LODGE, STEPHAN	ACTOR-WRITER	8955 BEVERLY BLVD	LOS ANGELES, CA	90048
LODGIC	ROCK & ROLL GROUP	7250 BEVERLY BLVD #200	LOS ANGELES, CA	90036
LODINE, EMILY	MEZZO-SOPRANO	431 S DEARBORN ST #1504	CHICAGO, IL	60605
LODOVICHETTI, ART	PHOTOGRAPHER	POST OFFICE BOX 682	KILL DEVIL HILLS, NC	27948
LOE, EDWARD A, JR	COMPOSER-CONDUCTOR	6245 GOODLAND PL	NORTH HOLLYWOOD, CA	91606
LOE, JUDY	ACTRESS	SARABAND ASSOCIATES AGENCY		
		153 PETHERTON RD, HIGHBURY	LONDON N5	ENGLAND
LOE, LINDA	ACTRESS	121 N ROBERTSON BLVD #B	BEVERLY HILLS, CA	90211
LOEB, MARSHA	TALENT AGENT	AVNET MANAGEMENT AGENCY		
		3805 MAGNOLIA BLVD	BURBANK, CA	91505
LOENGARD, JOHN	PHOTO EDITOR	LIFE/TIME & LIFE BLDG		
		ROCKEFELLER CENTER	NEW YORK, NY	10020
LOESCHER, SKIP	NEWS CORRESPONDENT	13 3RD ST, NE	WASHINGTON, DC	20002
LOEW, RICHARD	DIRECTOR	217 E 49TH ST	NEW YORK, NY	10017
LOEWE, FREDERICK	COMPOSER	815 PANORAMA RD	PALM SPRINGS, CA	92262
LOEWENWATER, PAUL L	WRITER	555 W 57TH ST #1230	NEW YORK, NY	10019
LOFARO, STEPHEN	TV DIRECTOR	DGA, 7950 SUNSET BLVD	LOS ANGELES, CA	90046
LOFARO, THOMAS	DIRECTOR	913 EUCLID ST #3	SANTA MONICA, CA	90403
LOFGREN, DENNIS	DIRECTOR	2600 10TH ST	BERKELEY, CA	94710
LOFGREN, NILS	SINGER-GUITARIST	1801 CENTURY PARK E #1132	LOS ANGELES, CA	90067
LOFT, ABRAM	VIOLINIST	EASTERN SCHOOL OF MUSIC		
		26 GIBBS ST	ROCHESTER, NY	14604
LOFTIN, CAREY	STUNTMAN	4249 RHODES AVE	STUDIO CITY, CA	91604

Name	Occupation	Address	City, State	ZIP
LOFTIN, WILLIAM	FILM DIRECTOR	22041 JONESPORT LN	HUNTINGTON BEACH, CA	92646
LOFTING, MORGAN	ACTRESS	8350 SANTA MONICA BLVD #103	LOS ANGELES, CA	90067
LOFTON, CHRIS	WRITER	4826 AGNES AVE	NORTH HOLLYWOOD, CA	91607
LOGAN, BOB	WRITER	8955 BEVERLY BLVD	LOS ANGELES, CA	90048
LOGAN, BRUCE	DIRECTOR	9601 WILSHIRE BLVD #506	BEVERLY HILLS, CA	90210
LOGAN, EUGENE	WRITER	8955 BEVERLY BLVD	LOS ANGELES, CA	90048
LOGAN, JACK DALE	GUITARIST	ROUTE #1, FLAT RIDGE RD	GOODLETTSVILLE, TN	37072
LOGAN, JOSHUA	WRITER-PRODUCER	435 E 52ND ST	NEW YORK, NY	10022
LOGAN, PATRICIA A	NEWS CORRESPONDENT	6303 FRENCHMAN DR #301	ALEXANDRIA, VA	22312
LOGAN, PHYLLIS	ACTRESS	9255 SUNSET BLVD #505	LOS ANGELES, CA	90069
LOGAN, ROBERT	ACTOR	9000 SUNSET BLVD #1112	LOS ANGELES, CA	90069
LOGAN, ROBERT T	COMPOSER	11825 SNELLING ST	SUN VALLEY, CA	91352
LOGAN, STEVEN	MUSICIAN	ROUTE #1, BOX 422-B	GOODLETTSVILLE, TN	37072
LOGAN, TOMMY	GUITARIST	1605 WAGGONER AVE	GRAND PRAIRIE, TX	75051
LOGE, MARC	ACTOR	96 HIGHLAND AVE	MANHATTAN BEACH, CA	90266
LOGGIA, ROBERT	ACTOR-DIRECTOR	2175 RIDGE DR	LOS ANGELES, CA	90049
LOGGINS, DAVE	SINGER	CALHOUN, 1609 CUMBERLAND ST	LITTLE ROCK, AK	72206
LOGGINS, DAVID	SINGER-SONGWRITER	POST OFFICE BOX 120475	NASHVILLE, TN	37212
LOGGINS, KENNY	SINGER-SONGWRITER	16869 ENCINO HILLS DR	ENCINO, CA	91436
LOHFELDT, HEINZ P	NEWS CORRESPONDENT	4501 "Q" LN, NW	WASHINGTON, DC	20007
LOHITE MOUNTAIN BLUEGRASS	BLUEGRASS GROUP	POST OFFICE BOX 4585	PORTSMOUTH, NH	03801
LOHMAN, AL	RADIO PERSONALITY	5403 JED SMITH RD	HIDDEN HILLS, CA	91302
LOIACONO, NICHOLAS P	WRITER	555 W 57TH ST #1230	NEW YORK, NY	10019
LOIEDERMAN, ROBERTO C	WRITER	6471 LANGDON AVE	VAN NUYS, CA	91406
LOJESKI, EDWARD, JR	CONDUCTOR	24905 EL DORADO MEADOW RD	CALABASAS, CA	91302
LOKEY, BEN	ACTOR	1326 STANFORD ST #C	SANTA MONICA, CA	90404
LOLLOBRIDGIDA, GINA	ACTRESS-PHOTOGRAPHER	VIA APPIA AUTICA 223	ROME 1-00178	ITALY
LOLLOS, JOHN S	VIDEO EXECUTIVE	VIDEO PROP, 33 E 68TH ST	NEW YORK, NY	10021
LOM, HERBERT	ACTOR	MORRIS, 147-149 WARDOUR ST	LONDON W1V 3TB	ENGLAND
LOMAN, MICHAEL	TV WRITER-PRODUCER	12034 OTSEGO ST	NORTH HOLLYWOOD, CA	91607
LOMAX, JOHN, III	MUSIC CRITIC	COUNTRY SOUNDS, 700 E STATE ST	IOLA, WI	54990
LOMBARD, MICHAEL	ACTOR	200 W 57TH ST #1303	NEW YORK, NY	10019
LOMBARD, RON	ACTOR	18350 HATTERAS ST #218	TARZANA, CA	91356
LOMBARDI, LEIGH	ACTRESS	9255 SUNSET BLVD #603	LOS ANGELES, CA	90069
LOMBARDI, STEVE	WRESTLER	POST OFFICE BOX 3859	STAMFORD, CT	06905
LOMBARDI, VITO F	WRITER	8955 BEVERLY BLVD	LOS ANGELES, CA	90048
LOMBARDO, JOSEPH, JR	ACTOR	439 S LA CIENEGA BLVD #117	LOS ANGELES, CA	90048
LOMBARDO, LOUIS J	FILM DIRECTOR	5455 LONGRIDGE AVE	VAN NUYS, CA	91401
LOMBARDO, NINA	ACTRESS	3800 BARHAM BLVD #303	LOS ANGELES, CA	90068
LOMBARDO, PHILIP J	DIRECTOR	24 MASTERTON RD	BRONXVILLE, NY	10708
LOMBARG, MICHAEL	ACTOR	ABC-TV, "ALL MY CHILDREN"		
		1330 AVE OF THE AMERICAS	NEW YORK, NY	10019
LOMBROSO, LINDA	WRITER-EDITOR	US MAGAZINE COMPANY		
		1 DAG HAMMARSKJOLD PLAZA	NEW YORK, NY	10017
LOMOND, BRITT	DIRECTOR	4155 BELLAIRE AVE	STUDIO CITY, CA	91604
LOMOND, DIANE	CASTING DIRECTOR	NBC-TV, 3000 W ALAMEDA AVE	BURBANK, CA	91523
LOMPALL & THE CHASER BROTHERS	C & W GROUP	POST OFFICE BOX 40484	NASHVILLE, TN	37212
LON, BILL	WRITER	555 W 57TH ST #1230	NEW YORK, NY	10019
LONCRAINE, RICHARD	FILM DIRECTOR	SEIFERT, 8-A BRUNSWICK GARDENS	LONDON W8	ENGLAND
LONDON, BARBARA	WRITER	8955 BEVERLY BLVD	LOS ANGELES, CA	90048
LONDON, BOBBY	CARTOONIST	KING FEATURES SYNDICATE		
		235 E 45TH ST	NEW YORK, NY	10017
LONDON, CHARLES S	DIRECTOR	641 LEXINGTON AVE	NEW YORK, NY	10022
LONDON, DAMIAN	ACTOR	659 1/4 N HUNTLEY DR	LOS ANGELES, CA	90069
LONDON, EDDIE	GUITARIST	3417 LEBANON RD #B-104	HERMITAGE, TN	37076
LONDON, HELYN S	WRITER	8955 BEVERLY BLVD	LOS ANGELES, CA	90048
LONDON, JERRY	WRITER-PRODUCER	1888 CENTURY PARK E #1400	LOS ANGELES, CA	90067
LONDON, JULIE	ACTRESS-SINGER	16074 ROYAL OAK RD	ENCINO, CA	91316
LONDON, LISA	CASTING DIRECTOR	9911 W PICO BLVD #1580	LOS ANGELES, CA	90038
LONDON, LISA	ACTRESS-MODEL	MARTEL, 7813 SUNSET BLVD	LOS ANGELES, CA	90046
LONDON, MARC	TV WRITER	8955 BEVERLY BLVD	LOS ANGELES, CA	90048
LONDON, MEL	DIRECTOR	170 2ND AVE	NEW YORK, NY	10003
LONDON, ROBBY	WRITER	8955 BEVERLY BLVD	LOS ANGELES, CA	90048
LONDON, ROY	WRITER-ACTOR	449 1/2 N SYCAMORE AVE	LOS ANGELES, CA	90036
LONDONER, CARROLL	CONDUCTOR	3751 NELLIS BLVD #404	LAS VEGAS, NV	89121
LONE, JOHN	ACTOR	10100 SANTA MONICA BLVD #1600	LOS ANGELES, CA	90067
LONE COWBOYS	ROCK & ROLL TRIO	CAROLINE RECORDS CO		
		5 BROSBY ST	NEW YORK, NY	10013
LONE JUSTICE	ROCK & ROLL GROUP	ARTISTES & THEATRICAL		
		SERVICES LTD, LEEDS	YORKSHIRE LS1 6LS	ENGLAND
LONESOME STRANGERS, THE	C & W GROUP	6520 SELMA AVE #443	LOS ANGELES, CA	90028
LONG, BEVERLY	CASTING DIRECTOR	8615 SHERWOOD DR	LOS ANGELES, CA	90069
LONG, CAROLINE M	NEWS CORRESPONDENT	11 S CONOCOCHEAGUE ST	WILLIAMSPORT, MD	21795
LONG, DEBORAH L	NEWS CORRESPONDENT	5151 WISCONSIN AVE, NW	WASHINGTON, DC	20016
LONG, GENE	DIRECTOR	316-B STEVENSON LN	BALTIMORE, MD	21204
LONG, GILBERT	GUITARIST	135 FOREST RETREAT	HENDERSONVILLE, TN	37075
LONG, HOWIE	FOOTBALL	151 S EL CAMINO DR	BEVERLY HILLS, CA	90212
LONG, JANET	CABLE EXECUTIVE	HOME BOX OFFICE PICTURES		
		1100 AVE OF THE AMERICAS	NEW YORK, NY	10036
LONG, JANICE R	NEWS CORRESPONDENT	2246 N BURLINGTON ST	ARLINGTON, VA	22207
LONG, JIM	MUSIC ARRANGER	751 HARPETH BEND DR	NASHVILLE, TN	37221
LONG, JOSEPH	WRITER	8955 BEVERLY BLVD	LOS ANGELES, CA	90048
LONG, KATHERINE A	NEWS CORRESPONDENT	4836 RESERVOIR RD, NW	WASHINGTON, DC	20007
LONG, KENNY	ACTOR	10850 RIVERSIDE DR #501	NORTH HOLLYWOOD, CA	91602
LONG, LORETTA	ACTRESS	CHILDREN'S TV WORKSHOP		
		1 LINCOLN PLAZA	NEW YORK, NY	10023

Name	Occupation	Address	City/State	Zip
LONG, NATE	TV DIRECTOR	5580 VILLAGE GREEN ST	LOS ANGELES, CA	90016
LONG, PAT	GUITARIST	2322 RIVERSIDE DR	NASHVILLE, TN	37216
LONG, RUFUS	SAXOPHONIST	278 LAKE TERR	HENDERSONVILLE, TN	37075
LONG, SHELLEY	ACTRESS	329 N WETHERLY DR #205	BEVERLY HILLS, CA	90211
LONG, STANLEY	DIRECTOR-PRODUCER	13 ARCHER ST	LONDON W1	ENGLAND
LONG, SUMNER A	TV WRITER	1268 S CAMDEN DR	LOS ANGELES, CA	90035
LONG, T A	WRITER	4605 LANKERSHIM BLVD #213	NORTH HOLLYWOOD, CA	91602
LONG, TODD	MODEL	4030 DEERVALE DR	SHERMAN OAKS, CA	91403
LONG, WAYNE	ACTOR	10920 WILSHIRE BLVD #220	LOS ANGELES, CA	90024
LONG, WILLIAM, JR	ACTOR	6736 LAUREL CANYON BLVD #306	NORTH HOLLYWOOD, CA	91606
LONG, WINONA M	CONDUCTOR	1292 S CITRUS AVE	LOS ANGELES, CA	90019
LONG RYDERS, THE	ROCK & ROLL GROUP	7523 HOLLYWOOD BLVD #313	HOLLYWOOD, CA	90046
LONGACRE, SARAH	WRITER	555 W 57TH ST #1230	NEW YORK, NY	10019
LONGDEN, JOHNNY	ACTOR	247 W LEMON AVE	ARCADIA, CA	91006
LONGDON, TERENCE	ACTOR	10 EMBANKMENT GARDENS	LONDON SW3	ENGLAND
LONGENECKER, JOHN O	FILM EXECUTIVE	13610 S GRAMERCY PL	GARDENA, CA	90249
LONGENECKER, JOHN W	FILM DIRECTOR	124 S ELM DR #3	BEVERLY HILLS, CA	90212
LONGENECKER, ROBERT	CINEMATOGRAPHER	16040 WYANDOTTE ST	VAN NUYS, CA	91406
LONGIN, GILBERT J	WRITER	555 W 57TH ST #1230	NEW YORK, NY	10019
LONGLEY, TAMARA	ACTRESS	9333 OSO AVE #1	CHATSWORTH, CA	91311
LONGO, BILLY	ACTOR	116 E MOSHOLU PARKWAY S	BRONX, NY	10471
LONGO, CRISTOFOR	WRITER	8955 BEVERLY BLVD	LOS ANGELES, CA	90048
LONGO, DICK	DIRECTOR	11636 PALA MESA DR	NORTHRIDGE, CA	91326
LONGO, EDWARD	ACTOR	542 E 79TH ST	NEW YORK, NY	10021
LONGO, TONY	ACTOR	STONE, 1052 CAROL DR	LOS ANGELES, CA	90069
LONGOS, LYNN	ACTRESS	3800 BARHAM BLVD #303	LOS ANGELES, CA	90068
LONGSTREET, HARRY S	WRITER	4024 DAVANA RD	SHERMAN OAKS, CA	91423
LONGSTREET, RENEE	WRITER	4024 DAVANA RD	SHERMAN OAKS, CA	91423
LONGSTREET, STEPHEN	SCREENWRITER	1133 MIRADERO RD	BEVERLY HILLS, CA	90210
LONGSTRETH, EMILY	ACTRESS	211 S BEVERLY DR #201	BEVERLY HILLS, CA	90212
LONNEN, RAY	ACTOR	CCA MGMT, 4 CT LODGE 48 SLOANE SQ	LONDON SW1W 8AT	ENGLAND
LONOW, CLAUDIA	ACTRESS	8285 SUNSET BLVD #12	LOS ANGELES, CA	90046
LONOW, MARK	ACTOR	15010 VENTURA BLVD #219	SHERMAN OAKS, CA	91403
LONOW, MARK	ENTERTAINMENT EXEC	IMPROV, 8162 MELROSE AVE	LOS ANGELES, CA	90046
LONOW, MARK M	WRITER	915 S OGDEN DR	LOS ANGELES, CA	90036
LONSDALE, PAMELA	TV PRODUCER	HOLLY COTTAGE, THE HIGHLANDS EAST HORSLEY	SURREY KT24 5BG	ENGLAND
LONZO & OSCAR	BLUEGRASS GROUP	1300 DIVISION ST #103	NASHVILLE, TN	37203
LOOK, THE	ROCK & ROLL GROUP	ICM, 40 W 57TH ST	NEW YORK, NY	10019
LOOK ONE LOOK	ROCK & ROLL GROUP	25 HUNTINGTON AVE #420	BOSTON, MA	02116
LOOK UP	ROCK & ROLL GROUP	2055 MOUNT PARAN RD, NW	ATLANTA, GA	30327
LOOKABILL, LAGENA	ACTRESS	3518 W CAHUENGA BLVD #204	LOS ANGELES, CA	90068
LOOKABILL, TOM	ACTOR	10929 1/2 WHIPPLE ST	NORTH HOLLYWOOD, CA	91602
LOOMIS, ARTHUR	PUBLISHING EXECUTIVE	US MAGAZINE COMPANY 1 DAG HAMMARSKJOLD PLAZA	NEW YORK, NY	10017
LOOMIS, ROD	ACTOR	12600 MIRADA ST	NORTH HOLLYWOOD, CA	91607
LOONEY, D O	GUITARIST	1925 CROMWELL DR	NASHVILLE, TN	37215
LOOS, ANNE	ACTRESS	1221 N GOWER ST #129	LOS ANGELES, CA	90038
LOOS, MARY	WRITER	335 AMALFI DR	SANTA MONICA, CA	90402
LOOS, ROB	WRITER	8955 BEVERLY BLVD	LOS ANGELES, CA	90048
LOOSE, WILLIAM G	COMPOSER	POST OFFICE BOX 53	BALBOA ISLAND, CA	92662
LOOSE ENDS	ROCK & ROLL GROUP	MANNA MANAGEMENT AGENCY 9 CARNABY ST, 4TH FLOOR	LONDON W1	ENGLAND
LOPARDO, FRANK	TENOR	CAMI, 165 W 57TH ST	NEW YORK, NY	10019
LOPATA, MOLLY	CASTING DIRECTOR	4024 RADFORD AVE	STUDIO CITY, CA	91604
LOPER, GEORGE	DIRECTOR	151 N CARONDELET ST	LOS ANGELES, CA	90026
LOPER, JAMES L	COMMUNICATIONS CONSUL	735 HOLLADAY RD	PASADENA, CA	91106
LOPERT, TANYA	ACTRESS	ARTMEDIA, 10 AVE GEORGE V	PARIS 75008	FRANCE
LOPEZ, AL	BASEBALL	3601 BEACH DR	TAMPA, FL	33609
LOPEZ, ARTHUR J	WRITER	8955 BEVERLY BLVD	LOS ANGELES, CA	90048
LOPEZ, LISA	SINGER	ALAMO TALENT & PRODS 217 ARDEN GROVE	SAN ANTONIO, TX	78215
LOPEZ, MARIO	ACTOR	6515 SUNSET BLVD #401	LOS ANGELES, CA	90028
LOPEZ, MICHAEL	TV DIRECTOR	301 E 73RD ST #2-A	NEW YORK, NY	10021
LOPEZ, NANCY	GOLFER	3203 COUNTRY CLUB RD	STAFFORD, TX	77477
LOPEZ, PAUL R	COMPOSER	12115 MAGNOLIA BLVD #143	NORTH HOLLYWOOD, CA	91607
LOPEZ, RAMON L	NEWS CORRESPONDENT	3000 SPOUT RUN PARKWAY #D-412	ARLINGTON, VA	22201
LOPEZ, RICARDO	ACTOR	FELBER, 2126 N CAHUENGA BLVD	LOS ANGELES, CA	90068
LOPEZ, ROBERT	DIRECTOR-PRODUCER	222 BEACH 97TH ST	ROCKAWAY BEACH, NY	11693
LOPEZ, SYLVIA T	WRITER	8955 BEVERLY BLVD	LOS ANGELES, CA	90048
LOPEZ, TRINI	SINGER-ACTOR	POST OFFICE 1987	STUDIO CITY, CA	91604
LOPEZ-CEPERO	TV DIRECTOR	131 W PARK AVE	LINDENWOOD, NJ	08021
LOPEZ-COBOS, JESUS	CONDUCTOR	ICM, 40 W 57TH ST	NEW YORK, NY	10019
LOPEZ-KABAYAO, MARCELITA	PIANIST	KAY, 58 W 58TH ST	NEW YORK, NY	10019
LOPIPARO, MICHAEL	WRITER	555 W 57TH ST #1230	NEW YORK, NY	10019
LOPRIENO, JOHN	ACTOR	ABC-TV, "ONE LIFE TO LIVE" 1330 AVE OF THE AMERICAS	NEW YORK, NY	10019
LORANGE, NICOLE	SOPRANO	CAMI, 165 W 57TH ST	NEW YORK, NY	10019
LORANGO, THOMAS	PIANIST	CAMI, 165 W 57TH ST	NEW YORK, NY	10019
LORBER, JEFF	MUSICIAN	LEFT BANK MANAGEMENT 2519 CARMEN CREST DR	LOS ANGELES, CA	90068
LORD, ALBERT	ACTOR	1327 1/2 N KINGSLEY DR	LOS ANGELES, CA	90027
LORD, ARTHUR A	TV WRITER-PRODUCER	NBC-TV, 3000 W ALAMEDA AVE	BURBANK, CA	91523
LORD, DON	SINGER	POST OFFICE BOX 11276	ROCHESTER, NY	14611

SHELLEY LONG

JACK LORD

SOPHIA LOREN

GLORIA LORING

MYRNA LOY

SUSAN LUCCI

IDA LUPINO

SUE LYON

SIMON MAC CORKINDALE

LORD, ERIC	ACTOR	1607 N EL CENTRO AVE #2	LOS ANGELES, CA	90028
LORD, JACK	ACTOR-DIRECTOR	4999 KAHALA AVE	HONOLULU, HI	96816
LORD, JUSTIN	ACTOR	2255 N CAHUENGA BLVD	LOS ANGELES, CA	90068
LORD, LEWIS	NEWS CORRESPONDENT	7221 CAROL LN	FALLS CHURCH, VA	22042
LORD, MARJORIE	ACTRESS	1110 MAYTOR PL	BEVERLY HILLS, CA	90210
LORD, ROBERT	GUITARIST	POST OFFICE BOX 887	PALM CITY, FL	33490
LORD, STEPHEN	TV WRITER	2049 CENTURY PARK E #1320	LOS ANGELES, CA	90067
LORD, VIVIANE	ACTRESS	6380 WILSHIRE BLVD #1600	LOS ANGELES, CA	90048
LORD, WILLIAM E	TV EXECUTIVE	ABC-TV, 7 W 66TH ST	NEW YORK, NY	10023
LORD VOLK, MARJORIE	ACTRESS	1110 MAYTOR PL	BEVERLY HILLS, CA	90210
LORDAN, FRANCES	ACTRESS	6404 WILSHIRE BLVD #800	LOS ANGELES, CA	90048
LORDS OF THE NEW CHURCH	ROCK & ROLL GROUP	FRONTIER BOOKING INTERNATIONAL		
		1776 BROADWAY, 6TH FLOOR	NEW YORK, NY	10019
LOREA, TONY	ACTOR	5672 LEMONA AVE	VAN NUYS, CA	91411
LOREDO, ARMANDO	COMPOSER	2117 VESTAL AVE	LOS ANGELES, CA	90026
LOREK, STANLEY	PHOTOGRAPHER	14832 LAKE TERR	ROCKVILLE, MD	20853
LORELEI, MISS	AERIALIST	SEE - MISS LORELEI		
LOREN, SOPHIA	ACTRESS	6 RUE CHARLES BONNET	GENEVA	SWITZERLAND
LORENGAR, PILAR	SOPRANO	119 W 57TH ST #1505	NEW YORK, NY	10019
LORENTZEN, ROBERT	DIRECTOR-PRODUCER	1508 82ND ST, NW	BRADENTON, FL	33529
LORENZ, LEE	CARTOONIST	POST OFFICE BOX 131	EASTON, CT	06425
LORENZ, MIKE & JUMP STREET	C & W GROUP	TGI, 1957 KILBURN DR	ATLANTA, GA	30324
LORENZO, CHRISTOPHER M	NEWS CORRESPONDENT	3344 HEWITT AVE	SILVER SPRING, MD	20906
LORENZO, LEONORA D	NEWS CORRESPONDENT	340 NATIONAL PRESS BLDG		
		529 14TH ST, NW	WASHINGTON, DC	20045
LORESCH, GARY	BODYBUILDER	THE GROVE GYM		
		5008 FAIRVIEW AVE	DOWNERS GROVE, IL	60515
LORIMER, JIM	BODYBUILDER	425 LONGFELLOW AVE	WORTHINGTON, OH	43085
LORIMER, LOUISE	ACTRESS	11 COPLEY ST	NEWTON, MA	02158
LORIMORE, ALEC	WRITER	1593 MANNING AVE	LOS ANGELES, CA	90024
LORIN, WILL	TV WRITER	10701 WILSHIRE BLVD #1801	LOS ANGELES, CA	90024
LORING, ANN	ACTRESS	303 W 66TH ST	NEW YORK, NY	10023
LORING, GLORIA	SINGER-ACTRESS	14755 VENTURA BLVD #1-744	SHERMAN OAKS, CA	91403
LORING, LYNN	ACTRESS-TV PRODUCER	THINNES, 2641 NICHOLS CANYON RD	LOS ANGELES, CA	90046
LORIOD, YVONNE	PIANIST	119 W 57TH ST #1505	NEW YORK, NY	10019
LORRAINE, LOCKE	CLOWN	2701 COTTAGE WY #14	SACRAMENTO, CA	95825
LORRAINE, LOUISE	ACTRESS	4832 THOR WY	CARMICHAEL, CA	95608
LORRE, LINDA	ACTRESS	5330 LANKERSHIM BLVD #210	NORTH HOLLYWOOD, CA	91601
LORRIMER, VERE	TV DIRECTOR	85 CARTHEW RD	LONDON W6	ENGLAND
LORRING, JOAN	ACTRESS	345 E 68TH ST	NEW YORK, NY	10021
LORRY, RED & YELLOW	ROCK & ROCK DUO	THE COACH HOUSE, FETTER LN	YORKSKIRE	ENGLAND
LORSUNG, THOMAS N	NEWS CORRESPONDENT	5367 IRON PEN PL	COLUMBIA, MD	21044
LORTEL, LUCILLE	ACTRESS-PRODUCER	60 W 57TH ST	NEW YORK, NY	10019
LORTIE, LOUIS	PIANIST	SHAW CONCERTS, 1995 BROADWAY	NEW YORK, NY	10023
LOS, NANCY	CELLIST	2703 NODYNE DR	NASHVILLE, TN	37214
LOS ILLEGALS	ROCK & ROLL GROUP	ICM, 40 W 57TH ST	NEW YORK, NY	10019
LOS LOBOS	ROCK & ROLL GROUP	POST OFFICE BOX 210103	SAN FRANCISCO, CA	94121
LOSAK, STANLEY	DIRECTOR-PRODUCER	11 W 81ST ST	NEW YORK, NY	10024
LOSEY, GAVRIK	FILM PRODUCER	12-A SPRING ST	LONDON W2	ENGLAND
LOSHIN, MICHAEL S	WRITER	478 DANIELS DR	BEVERLY HILLS, CA	90212
LOSK, RENEE	ACTRESS	5056 FAIR AVE	NORTH HOLLYWOOD, CA	91601
LOSSO, ERNEST A	DIRECTOR	DGA, 110 W 57TH ST	NEW YORK, NY	10019
LOTAS, JOHN	THEATER PRODUCER	355 LEXINGTON AVE	NEW YORK, NY	10017
LOTT, FELICITY	SOPRANO	MARIEDL ANDERS ARTISTS MGMT		
		535 EL CAMINO DEL MAR ST	SAN FRANCISCO, CA	94121
LOTT, LAWRENCE	ACTOR	9165 SUNSET BLVD #202	LOS ANGELES, CA	90069
LOTTIMER, EB	ACTOR	2121 AVE OF THE STARS #410	LOS ANGELES, CA	90067
LOTTMAN, EVAN	FILM EDITOR	ACE, 4416 1/2 FINLEY AVE	LOS ANGELES, CA	90027
LOTZE, GERD	NEWS CORRESPONDENT	1000 WILSON BLVD	ARLINGTON, VA	22209
LOU & JACOB	TRAPEZE ACT	POST OFFICE BOX 87	WEST LEBANON, NY	12195
LOUDEN, IAN KENNETH	NEWS CORRESPONDENT	318 E BELLEFONTE AVE	ALEXANDRIA, VA	22301
LOUDEN, VERNON R	DIRECTOR	400 CANAL ST #329	SAN RAFAEL, CA	94901
LOUDERMILK, JOHN D	SINGER-SONGWRITER	3000 HILLSBORO RD #66	NASHVILLE, TN	37215
LOUDIN, ROBERT	DIRECTOR	2260 CAHUENGA BLVD #307	LOS ANGELES, CA	90069
LOUDON, DOROTHY	ACTRESS	101 CENTRAL PARK W	NEW YORK, NY	10023
LOUGANIS, GREG	DIVER	POST OFFICE BOX 4068	MALIBU, CA	90265
LOUGHERY, DAVID	SCREENWRITER	8955 BEVERLY BLVD	LOS ANGELES, CA	90048
LOUGHLIN, LORI	ACTRESS	151 S EL CAMINO DR	BEVERLY HILLS, CA	90212
LOUGHLIN, MARY ANNE	CABLE PRODUCER	WTBS, 1050 TECHWOOD DR, NW	ATLANTA, GA	30318
LOUIE, BEBE	ACTRESS	FELBER, 2126 N CAHUENGA BLVD	LOS ANGELES, CA	90068
LOUIE, DIANE M	CONDUCTOR	8633 W KNOLL DR #306	LOS ANGELES, CA	90069
LOUIE, GARY	SAXOPHONIST	3003 VAN NESS ST #W-205, NW	WASHINGTON, DC	20008
LOUIE, JANET BEBE	ACTRESS	SEE - LOUIE, BEBE		
LOUIE, JOHN	ACTOR	8235 SANTA MONICA BLVD #202	LOS ANGELES, CA	90046
LOUIS, C E	TV WRITER	8955 BEVERLY BLVD	LOS ANGELES, CA	90048
LOUISE, TINA	ACTRESS	9565 LIME ORCHARD RD	BEVERLY HILLS, CA	90210
LOUISIANA	RHYTHM & BLUES GROUP	KINGSLAND, 108 SHARON DR	WEST MONROE, LA	71291
LOUISIANA HOT SAUCE	C & W GROUP	POST OFFICE BOX 9104	SHREVEPORT, LA	71139
LOUISIANA PURCHASE	RHYTHM & BLUES GROUP	POST OFFICE BOX 19066	NEW ORLEANS, LA	70179
LOUP, FRANCOIS	BASSO-BARITONE	CAMI, 165 W 57TH ST	NEW YORK, NY	10019
LOURIE, EUGENE	DIRECTOR	1737 N GARDNER ST	HOLLYWOOD, CA	90046
LOUSSIER, JACQUES	COMPOSER-MUSICIAN	ALMA, 8 SWIFT ST	LONDON SW6	ENGLAND
LOUVIN, CHARLIE	SINGER	102 JACKSTAFF DR	HENDERSONVILLE, TN	37075
LOUVIN, CHARLIE, JR	SINGER	120 ANDERSON LN	HENDERSONVILLE, TN	37075
LOVE, GEOFF	BANDLEADER	NGA, 24 DENMARK ST	LONDON WC2H 8NJ	ENGLAND

Name	Occupation	Address	City	Zip
LOVE, JERI L	WRITER	8955 BEVERLY BLVD	LOS ANGELES, CA	90048
LOVE, MIKE	SINGER-SONGWRITER	101 MESA LN	SANTA BARBARA, CA	91309
LOVE, PETER	ACTOR	ABC-TV, "RYAN'S HOPE" 1330 AVE OF THE AMERICAS	NEW YORK, NY	10019
LOVE, ROBERT	TV PRODUCER	FRASER, 91 REGENT ST	LONDON W1R 8RU	ENGLAND
LOVE, SHIRLEY	MEZZO-SOPRANO	59 E 54TH ST #81	NEW YORK, NY	10022
LOVE & MONEY	ROCK & ROLL GROUP	POLYGRAM RECORDS CO 810 7TH AVE	NEW YORK, NY	10019
LOVE & ROCKETS	ROCK & ROLL GROUP	BIG TIME RECORDS COMPANY 6777 HOLLYWOOD BLVD	LOS ANGELES, CA	90028
LOVE RELATION	MUSICAL GROUP	LUTZ, 5625 "O" STREET BLDG	LINCOLN, NE	68510
LOVE TRACTOR	ROCK & ROLL GROUP	BIG TIME RECORDS COMPANY 6777 HOLLYWOOD BLVD	HOLLYWOOD, CA	90028
LOVEJOY, FAITH	ACTRESS	5006 WEBSTER ST	OAKLAND, CA	94609
LOVELACE, KENNETH	GUITARIST	2921 BRANTLEY DR	ANTIOCH, TN	37013
LOVELESS, DAVID	COSTUME DESIGNER	CBS-TV, "THE GUIDING LIGHT" 51 W 52ND ST	NEW YORK, NY	10019
LOVELESS, WILLIAM E	NEWS CORRESPONDENT	1603 PRESTON RD	ALEXANDRIA, VA	22320
LOVELL, DYSON	FILM PRODUCER	1585 SUNSET PLAZA DR	LOS ANGELES, CA	90069
LOVELL, ROSEMARY	ACTRESS	5830 MORELLA AVE	NORTH HOLLYWOOD, CA	91607
LOVELY ELIZABETH, THE	WRESTLING VALET-MGR	SEE - MISS ELIZABETH		
LOVENHEIM, ROBERT	WRITER	667 KELTON AVE	LOS ANGELES, CA	90024
LOVER, ANTHONY	DIRECTOR-PRODUCER	LIBERTY, 238 E 26TH ST	NEW YORK, NY	10010
LOVERBOY	ROCK & ROLL GROUP	406-68 WATER ST #406	VANCOUVER, BC V6B 1A4	CANADA
LOVERDE, CAROL	SOPRANO	431 S DEARBORN ST #1504	CHICAGO, IL	60605
LOVESIN, JOHNNY	SINGER	41 BRITAIN ST #200	TORONTO, ONT	CANADA
LOVETT, JOSEPH F	TV PRODUCER	ABC-TV, "20/20," 11 5TH AVE	NEW YORK, NY	10003
LOVETT, JULIA	SOPRANO	POST OFFICE BOX 27539	PHILADELPHIA, PA	19118
LOVICH, LENE	SINGER	ATI, 888 7TH AVE, 21ST FLOOR	NEW YORK, NY	10106
LOVING, CANDY	MODEL	MODELS & PROMOTIONS AGENCY 8560 SUNSET BLVD, 10TH FLOOR	LOS ANGELES, CA	90069
LOVINGER, JEFFREY	DIRECTOR	DGA, 110 W 57TH ST	NEW YORK, NY	10019
LOVULLO, SAM	TV PRODUCER	POST OFFICE BOX 140400	NASHVILLE, TN	37214
LOWDEN, JOAN	NEWS CORRESPONDENT	7001 BRADWOOD CT	SPRINGFIELD, VA	22151
LOWDER, AARON	SINGER	POST OFFICE BOX 25371	CHARLOTTE, NC	28212
LOWDES, JAY C	NEWS CORRESPONDENT	5428 TREE LINE DR	CENTERVILLE, VA	22020
LOWE, BARRY	ACTOR	31 S AUDLEY ST	LONDON W1	ENGLAND
LOWE, CHAD	ACTOR	6968 DUNE RD	MALIBU, CA	90265
LOWE, CHAN	CARTOONIST	POST OFFICE BOX 14430	FORT LAUDERDALE, FL	33302
LOWE, DAVID, JR	DIRECTOR-PRODUCER	151 S EL CAMINO DR	BEVERLY HILLS, CA	90212
LOWE, EDWIN S	THEATER PRODUCER	375 PARK AVE	NEW YORK, NY	10022
LOWE, GWEN HILLIER	ACTRESS	122 S PARISH PL	BURBANK, CA	91506
LOWE, HEATHER	ACTRESS	6310 SAN VICENTE BLVD #407	LOS ANGELES, CA	90048
LOWE, JACK	PIANIST	CAMI, 165 W 57TH ST	NEW YORK, NY	10019
LOWE, JOHN H, III	ACTOR	122 S PARISH PL	BURBANK, CA	91506
LOWE, MALCOLM	VIOLINIST	AARON, 25 HUNTINGTON AVE	BOSTON, MA	02116
LOWE, MATTHEW	PHOTOGRAPHER	7803 GLENISTER DR	SPRINGFIELD, VA	22152
LOWE, MATTHEW A	NEWS CORRESPONDENT	CBS NEWS, 2020 "M" ST, NW	WASHINGTON, DC	20036
LOWE, NICK	SINGER	ICM, 40 W 57TH ST	NEW YORK, NY	10019
LOWE, RACHAEL M	NEWS CORRESPONDENT	1755 S JEFFERSON DAVIS HWY	ARLINGTON, VA	22202
LOWE, ROB	ACTOR	WOOD, 8672 LOOKOUT MOUNTAIN AVE	LOS ANGELES, CA	90046
LOWE, RUDY	ACTOR	1617 N POINSETTIA PL #305	LOS ANGELES, CA	90046
LOWE, TOM ROY	ACTOR	3800 BARHAM BLVD #303	LOS ANGELES, CA	90068
LOWELL, BOBBY	SINGER-SONGWRITER	IRON PONY RECORDS 3345 "R" ST	LINCOLN, IL	68503
LOWELL, ROSS	DIRECTOR	421 W 54TH ST	NEW YORK, NY	10019
LOWELL, WILLIAM F	DIRECTOR	201 GLEN ST	SOUTH NATICK, MA	01760
LOWENHAUPT, ALICE	MEZZO-SOPRANO	756 7TH AVE #67	NEW YORK, NY	10019
LOWENS, CURT	ACTOR	130 N FLORES ST	LOS ANGELES, CA	90048
LOWENSTEIN, AL	TV PRODUCER	EMBASSY TV, 1438 N GOWER ST	LOS ANGELES, CA	90028
LOWENTHAL, JEROME	PIANIST	CAMI, 165 W 57TH ST	NEW YORK, NY	10019
LOWERY, MELVIN	TENOR	SARDOS, 180 W END AVE	NEW YORK, NY	10023
LOWREY, FREDERIC D	NEWS CORRESPONDENT	1755 S JEFFERSON DAVIS HWY	ARLINGTON, VA	22202
LOWRIS, HELEN	WRITER	555 W 57TH ST #1230	NEW YORK, NY	10019
LOWRY, ARNOLDA	ACTRESS	9056 SANTA MONICA BLVD #201	LOS ANGELES, CA	90069
LOWRY, DICK	TV DIRECTOR	704 N GARDNER ST #5	LOS ANGELES, CA	90046
LOWRY, GARY	GUITARIST	613 HILLSBORO RD EXECUTIVE HOUSE #A-27	FRANKLIN, TN	37064
LOWRY, JIM	GUITARIST	125 MILLWOOD DR	NASHVILLE, TN	37217
LOWRY, JUNIE	CASTING DIRECTOR	WARNER-HOLLYWOOD STUDIOS 1041 N FORMOSA AVE	LOS ANGELES, CA	90046
LOWRY, LYNN	ACTRESS	4721 LAUREL CANYON BLVD #211	NORTH HOLLYWOOD, CA	91607
LOWRY, SYLVIA	SINGER	125 MILLWOOD DR	NASHVILLE, TN	37217
LOWTHER, WILLIAM A	NEWS CORRESPONDENT	5309 SLIPPER CT	COLUMBIA, MD	21045

Name	Occupation	Address	City	Zip/Country
LOXTON, DAVID R	TV DIRECTOR	935 PARK AVE	NEW YORK, NY	10028
LOY, MYRNA	ACTRESS	425 E 63RD ST	NEW YORK, NY	10021
LOYND, RAY	THEATER CRITIC	1400 N CAHUENGA BLVD	HOLLYWOOD, CA	90028
LOZ NETTO	ROCK & ROLL GROUP	POST OFFICE BOX 1318	BEVERLY HILLS, CA	90213
LU PONE, PATTI	ACTRESS	119 W 57TH ST #710	NEW YORK, NY	10019
LUBA	ROCK & ROLL GROUP	POST OFFICE BOX 641 STATION ABUNTSIC	MONTREAL H3L 3P2	CANADA
LUBAR, JEFFREY S	NEWS CORRESPONDENT	POST OFFICE BOX 2424	SPRINGFIELD, VA	22152
LUBART, THOMAS M	WRITER	555 W 57TH ST #1230	NEW YORK, NY	10019
LUBER, KEN	WRITER-PRODUCER	1052 KAGAWA ST	PACIFIC PALISADES, CA	90272
LUBIN, ARTHUR	FILM DIRECTOR	2881 SEATTLE DR	HOLLYWOOD, CA	90046
LUBIN, JEAN	ACTRESS	8721 SUNSET BLVD #103	LOS ANGELES, CA	90069
LUBIN, LOIS PHYLLIS	WRITER	11744 DARLINGTON AVE #103	LOS ANGELES, CA	90049
LUBIN, ROBERT	WRITER	8955 BEVERLY BLVD	LOS ANGELES, CA	90048
LUBLIN, JOANN S	NEWS CORRESPONDENT	9906 PARKWOOD DR	BETHESDA, MD	20814
LUBOFF, NORMAN	COMPOSER-CONDUCTOR	35 WEST SHORE DR	PORT WASHINGTON, NY	11050
LUBOV, SHERRI	ACTRESS	1032 S HAYWORTH AVE	LOS ANGELES, CA	90035
LUBOVITCH, LAR	DANCER-CHOREO	853 BROADWAY #1114	NEW YORK, NY	10003
LUBY, EARLE	WRITER	555 W 57TH ST #1230	NEW YORK, NY	10019
LUCA, SERGIU	VIOLINIST	POST OFFICE BOX 1515	NEW YORK, NY	10023
LUCARELLI, BERT	OBOIST	GURTMAN, 162 W 56TH ST	NEW YORK, NY	10019
LUCARELLI, JACK	ACTOR	13111 VENTURA BLVD #204	STUDIO CITY, CA	91604
LUCAS, A GAR	DIRECTOR	DGA, 110 W 57TH ST	NEW YORK, NY	10019
LUCAS, BERNIE T	ACTOR	1741 N IVAR AVE #221	LOS ANGELES, CA	90028
LUCAS, CARRIE	SINGER	200 W 51ST ST #1410	NEW YORK, NY	10019
LUCAS, GEORGE	WRI-DIR-PROD	POST OFFICE BOX 2009	SAN RAFAEL, CA	94912
LUCAS, GUS	TV EXECUTIVE	ABC-TV, 4151 PROSPECT AVE	LOS ANGELES, CA	90027
LUCAS, HUGH	NEWS CORRESPONDENT	3110 MOUNT VERNON AVE #1409	ALEXANDRIA, VA	22305
LUCAS, J FRANK	ACTOR	400 W 43RD ST #40-G	NEW YORK, NY	10036
LUCAS, JOHN MEREDYTH	WRITER-PRODUCER	16241 MEADOW RIDGE WY	ENCINO, CA	91436
LUCAS, JONATHAN	ACTOR	208 S BEVERLY DR #4	BEVERLY HILLS, CA	90212
LUCAS, JONATHAN	TV DIRECTOR	8690 FRANKLIN AVE	LOS ANGELES, CA	90069
LUCAS, MARK H	DIRECTOR	337 E 50TH ST #2-A	NEW YORK, NY	10022
LUCAS, MATT	SINGER	POST OFFICE BOX 1830	GRETNA, LA	70053
LUCAS, ROBERT	WRITER	555 W 57TH ST #1230	NEW YORK, NY	10019
LUCAS, RONN	VENTRILOQUIST	11355 W OLYMPIC BLVD #555	LOS ANGELES, CA	90064
LUCAS, STEVE	CLOWN	2701 COTTAGE WY #14	SACRAMENTO, CA	95825
LUCAS, WILLIAM	ACTOR	7 W EATON PL, MEWS	LONDON SW1	ENGLAND
LUCATORTO, TONY	ACTOR	14355 HUSTON ST #255	SHERMAN OAKS, CA	91423
LUCCHESI, DEBBIE	CASTING DIRECTOR	9336 W WASHINGTON BLVD BUILDING #H	CULVER CITY, CA	90230
LUCCHESI, JEANNINE L	WRITER	8955 BEVERLY BLVD	LOS ANGELES, CA	90048
LUCCHESI, VINCENT	ACTOR	1930 CENTURY PARK W #303	LOS ANGELES, CA	90067
LUCCHESINI, ANDREA	PIANIST	CAMI, 165 W 57TH ST	NEW YORK, NY	10019
LUCCI, MIKE	WRESTLER	POST OFFICE BOX 3859	STAMFORD, CT	06905
LUCCI, SUSAN	ACTRESS	122 E 42ND ST #210	NEW YORK, NY	10168
LUCE, CLAIRE BOOTH	ACTRESS-WRITER	4 SUTTON PL	NEW YORK, NY	10023
LUCE, JANICE	COMPOSER	23124 JONATHAN ST	CANOGA PARK, CA	91304
LUCE, RALPH	FILM PRODUCER	7840 LAUREL CANYON BLVD	NORTH HOLLYWOOD, CA	91605
LUCEY, PAUL EDWARD	WRITER	415 MARGUERITA AVE	SANTA MONICA, CA	90402
LUCHENBILL, GLORIA	ACTRESS	415 S SHIRLEY PL	BEVERLY HILLS, CA	90212
LUCHETTI, VERIANO	TENOR	61 W 62ND ST #6-F	NEW YORK, NY	10023
LUCIA, CHIP	ACTOR	12750 VENTURA BLVD #102	STUDIO CITY, CA	91604
LUCIANO, MICHAEL	FILM EDITOR	ACE, 4416 1/2 FINLEY AVE	LOS ANGELES, CA	90027
LUCKA, KLAUS	DIRECTOR	DGA, 110 W 57TH ST	NEW YORK, NY	10019
LUCKHAM, CYRIL	ACTOR	70 HEMPSTEAD WY	LONDON NW11	ENGLAND
LUCKINBILL, LAURENCE	ACTOR	10000 SANTA MONICA BLVD #305	LOS ANGELES, CA	90067
LUCKING, BILL	ACTOR	12750 VENTURA BLVD #102	STUDIO CITY, CA	91604
LUCKLY, ROBERT	PHOTOGRAPHER	19 BALFOUR LN	STONY BROOK, NY	11790
LUCKWELL, MIKE	TV-FILM PRODUCER	25 NOEL ST	LONDON WC1	ENGLAND
LUCKWITH, MARK	WRITER	555 W 57TH ST #1230	NEW YORK, NY	10019
LUCKY, CHRIS	TV WRITER	8955 BEVERLY BLVD	LOS ANGELES, CA	90048
LUCKY LOOK	C & W GROUP	POST OFFICE BOX 156	ROSELLE, NJ	07203
LUCRAFT, HOWARD	COMPOSER-CONDUCTOR	POST OFFICE BOX 91	LOS ANGELES, CA	90078
LUDDY, TOM	FILM PRODUCER	ZOETROPE, 916 KEARNY ST	SAN FRANCISCO, CA	94133
LUDEL, WILLIAM	DIRECTOR	170 W 74TH ST	NEW YORK, NY	10023
LUDGIN, CHESTER	BARITONE	59 E 54TH ST #81	NEW YORK, NY	10022
LUDLAM, HELEN	ACTOR	542 E 79TH ST	NEW YORK, NY	10021
LUDLOW, GRAHAM	ACTOR	6380 WILSHIRE BLVD #1600	LOS ANGELES, CA	90048
LUDLUM, MICHAEL	WRITER	555 W 57TH ST #1230	NEW YORK, NY	10019
LUDLUM, ROBERT	AUTHOR	H MORRISON, 58 W 10TH ST	NEW YORK, NY	10011
LUDWIG, CHRISTA	MEZZO-SOPRANO	COLBERT, 111 W 57TH ST	NEW YORK, NY	10019
LUDWIG, FORREST	TV EXECUTIVE	NBC-TV, 3000 W ALAMEDA AVE	BURBANK, CA	91523
LUDWIG, JERROLD L	FILM EDITOR	10860 KLING ST	NORTH HOLLYWOOD, CA	91602
LUDWIG, JERRY	TV WRITER-PRODUCER	11262 HOMEDALE ST	LOS ANGELES, CA	90049
LUDWIG, PAMELA	ACTRESS	6422 SUNNY SLOPE AVE	VAN NUYS, CA	91401
LUDWIG, SALEM	ACTOR	80 LA SALLE ST	NEW YORK, NY	10027
LUDWIG, WILLIAM	WRITER	8955 BEVERLY BLVD	LOS ANGELES, CA	90048
LUDWIN, RICHARD A	WRITER-PRODUCER	616 VETERAN AVE #117	LOS ANGELES, CA	90024
LUEDTKE, KURT M	SCREENWRITER	DISKANT, 1033 GAYLEY AVE	LOS ANGELES, CA	90024
LUENEBURG, CAL	BODYBUILDER	THE ACE PROMOTER 24531 O'LINDA TRAIL N	SCANDIA, MN	55073
LUENING, OTTO	COMPOSER-CONDUCTOR	460 RIVERSIDE DR	NEW YORK, NY	10027
LUESCHER, CHRISTINA	SCREENWRITER	8955 BEVERLY BLVD	LOS ANGELES, CA	90048

LUEVANO, ROSALVA	WRITER	8955 BEVERLY BLVD	LOS ANGELES, CA	90048
LUFT, HERBERT	FILM PRODUCER	1271 S BEDFORD DR	LOS ANGELES, CA	90035
LUFT, LORNA	ACTRESS	POST OFFICE BOX 5617	BEVERLY HILLS, CA	90210
LUFTIG, DON	WRITER-PRODUCER	119 MILLBURN AVE	MILLBURN, NJ	07041
LUGAR, LEX	WRESTLER	NATIONAL WRESTLING ALLIANCE		
		JIM CROCKETT PROMOTIONS		
		421 BRIARBEND DR	CHARLOTTE, NC	28209
LUGGIERO, GARY	NEWS CORRESPONDENT	3601 S 5TH ST #412	ARLINGTON, VA	22204
LUIESE	SINGER	SKEPNER, 7 MUSIC SQUARE N	NASHVILLE, TN	37203
LUISA	HOOP SPINNER	HALL, 138 FROG HOLLOW RD	CHURCHVILLE, PA	18966
LUISI, ED	TV DIRECTOR	21-24 CRESCENT ST	ASTORIA, NY	11105
LUISI, JAMES	ACTOR	4319 IRVINE AVE	STUDIO CITY, CA	91604
LUJAN, JESSE	BODYBUILDER	6514 LAKE ASHMERE CT	SAN DIEGO, CA	92119
LUJIA, SHI	NEWS CORRESPONDENT	2200 "S" ST, NW	WASHINGTON, DC	20008
LUKAS, CHRISTOPHER W	DIRECTOR-PRODUCER	159 RIVER RD	GRANDVIEW, NY	10960
LUKAS, ERNEST A	DIRECTOR	2833 SHERIDAN PL	EVANSTON, IL	60201
LUKAS, KARL	ACTOR	8721 SUNSET BLVD #103	LOS ANGELES, CA	90069
LUKATHER, PAUL	ACTOR	14185 SKYLINE DR	HACIENDA HEIGHTS, CA	91745
LUKE, ERIC N	WRITER	8955 BEVERLY BLVD	LOS ANGELES, CA	90048
LUKE, KEYE	ACTOR	10363 LUNDENE DR	WHITTIER, CA	90601
LUKEMAN, ROBERT M	NEWS CORRES-WRITER	ABC NEWS, 1717 DE SALES ST, NW	WASHINGTON, DC	20036
LUKENS, LINDA S	WRITER	8955 BEVERLY BLVD	LOS ANGELES, CA	90048
LUKES, JACK	TV WRITER	8955 BEVERLY BLVD	LOS ANGELES, CA	90048
LULABEL & SCOTTIE	VOCAL GROUP	POST OFFICE BOX 171132	NASHVILLE, TN	37217
LULU	SINGER-ACTRESS	12 RICHMOND BUILDINGS		
		DEAN ST	LONDON W1	ENGLAND
LUM, BENJAMIN	ACTOR	8235 SANTA MONICA BLVD #202	LOS ANGELES, CA	90046
LUM, JO ANN	NEWS REPORTER	TIME/TIME & LIFE BLDG		
		ROCKEFELLER CENTER	NEW YORK, NY	10020
LUMB, JACQUELINE	NEWS CORRESPONDENT	1420 "N" ST, NW	WASHINGTON, DC	20005
LUMBLY, CARL	ACTOR	5875 CAROLUS DR	LOS ANGELES, CA	90068
LUMET, BARUCH	ACTOR	7969 W NORTON AVE #A-8	LOS ANGELES, CA	90046
LUMET, SIDNEY	FILM WRITER-DIRECTOR	1380 LEXINGTON AVE	NEW YORK, NY	10028
LUMLEY, JOANNA	ACTRESS	WEST KENSINGTON	LONDON W14	ENGLAND
LUMMIS, DAYTON	ACTOR	POST OFFICE BOX 1091	SANTA MONICA, CA	90406
LUMPKIN, BEVERLEY C	NEWS CORRESPONDENT	ABC-TV, NEWS DEPARTMENT		
		1717 DE SALES ST, NW	WASHINGTON, DC	20036
LUMPKIN, GARY	GUITARIST	26 CAMEO DR	NASHVILLE, TN	37211
LUNA, BARBARA	ACTRESS	ABC-TV, "ONE LIFE TO LIVE"		
		1330 AVE OF THE AMERICAS	NEW YORK, NY	10019
LUNA, KATHERINE	SOPRANO	CAMI, 165 W 57TH ST	NEW YORK, NY	10019
LUND, ART	ACTOR	15216 SUTTON ST	SHERMAN OAKS, CA	91403
LUND, DEANNA	ACTRESS	6310 SAN VICENTE BLVD #407	LOS ANGELES, CA	90048
LUND, DONALD H	NEWS CORRESPONDENT	2400 "N" ST, NW	WASHINGTON, DC	20037
LUND, LICILLE	ACTRESS	HIGGINS, 3424 SHORE HGTS DR	MALIBU, CA	90265
LUND, MARTIN C	COMPOSER	3891 CLAYTON AVE	LOS ANGELES, CA	90027
LUND, PATRICIA	WRITER	555 W 57TH ST #1230	NEW YORK, NY	10019
LUNDBERG, DAN	WRITER	3347 BONNIE HILL DR	LOS ANGELES, CA	90068
LUNDBLOM, HOKAN	NEWS CORRESPONDENT	1233 NATIONAL PRESS BLDG		
		529 14TH ST, NW	WASHINGTON, DC	20045
LUNDE, JOHN L	NEWS CORRESPONDENT	5520 LEE HWY	ARLINGTON, VA	22207
LUNDE, MARTY	WRESTLER	SEE - ANDERSON, ARN		
LUNDEN, JOAN	TV HOST	ABC TELEVISION NETWORK		
		"GOOD MORNING AMERICA"		
		1330 AVE OF THE AMERICAS	NEW YORK, NY	10019
LUNDGREN, DOLF	BODYBUILDER-ACTOR	2079 MOUNT OLYMPUS DR	LOS ANGELES, CA	90046
LUNDIN, VICTOR R	WRITER	8955 BEVERLY BLVD	LOS ANGELES, CA	90048
LUNDSTROM, LINDA	FASHION DESIGNER	462 WELLINGTON ST W	TORONTO, ONT M5V 1E3	CANADA
LUNDY, CARMEN	SINGER	BRIDGE, 106 FORT GREENE PL	BROOKLYN, NY	11217
LUNDY, CURTIS	MUSICIAN	SEE - WATSON, BOBBY &		
		.... CURTIS LUNDY		
LUNDY, ROGER J	WRITER-PRODUCER	142 ASHLAND AVE	RIVER FOREST, IL	60305
LUNGHI, CHERIE	ACTRESS	CONWAY, EAGLE HOUSE		
		109 JERMYN ST	LONDON SW1	ENGLAND
LUNHAM, LLOYD R	COMPOSER-CONDUCTOR	6423 WILBUR AVE	RESEDA, CA	91335
LUNN, GARY	GUITARIST	6652 CLEARBROOK DR	NASHVILLE, TN	37205
LUNSFORD, ALICE N	WRITER	KLAUSNER, 71 PARK AVE	NEW YORK, NY	10016
LUNSFORD, MIKE	GUITARIST	2999 SMITH SPRINGS RD #E-88	NASHVILLE, TN	37217
LUPINO, IDA	ACTRESS-WRITER	MARY ANN ANDERSON		
		13451 ERWIN ST	VAN NUYS, CA	91401
LUPINO, RICHARD	ACTOR	19 W 44TH ST #1500	NEW YORK, NY	10036
LUPINSKI, ED	ACTOR	6239 ETHEL AVE	VAN NUYS, CA	91401
LUPO, FRANK	TV WRITER-PRODUCER	STEPHEN J CANNELL PRODS		
		7083 HOLLYWOOD BLVD	LOS ANGELES, CA	90028
LUPONE, PATTI	SINGER	ICM, 8899 BEVERLY BLVD	LOS ANGELES, CA	90048
LUPTON, JOHN	ACTOR	2528 TILDEN AVE	LOS ANGELES, CA	90064
LUPU, RADU	PIANIST	ICM, 40 W 57TH ST	NEW YORK, NY	10019
LUPUS, PETER	ACTOR	11375 DONA LISA DR	STUDIO CITY, CA	91604
LUREAU, BERTRAND J	NEWS CORRESPONDENT	5600 39TH AVE	HYATTSVILLE, MD	20781
LURIA, MICHAEL S	WRITER	555 W 57TH ST #1230	NEW YORK, NY	10019
LURIE, GEORGIE	COLUMNIST	POST OFFICE BOX 500	WASHINGTON, DC	20044
LURIE, RANAN	NEWS CORRESPONDENT	3520 OVERLOOK LN, NW	WASHINGTON, DC	20016
LURIE, RANAN	CARTOONIST	UNIVERSAL PRESS SYNDICATE		
		4900 MAIN ST, 9TH FLOOR	KANSAS CITY, MO	62114

Name	Occupation	Address	City	Zip/Country
LUSHUS DAIM & THE PRETTY VAIN	SOUL GROUP	CONCEITED/MOTOWN RECORDS		
		6255 SUNSET BLVD	HOLLYWOOD, CA	90028
LUSK, JOHN	WRESTLER	SEE - MANTELL, JOHNNY		
LUSMANN, STEPHEN	BARITONE	61 W 62ND ST #6-F	NEW YORK, NY	10023
LUSSIER, LYNNE S	WRITER	8955 BEVERLY BLVD	LOS ANGELES, CA	90048
LUSSIER, ROBERT	ACTOR	2126 SUNSET CREST DR	LOS ANGELES, CA	90046
LUSTIG, JO	PRODUCER-TALENT AGENT	POST OFFICE BOX 472	LONDON SW7 2QB	ENGLAND
LUSTIG, MILTON	COMPOSER	6708 MAMMOTH AVE	VAN NUYS, CA	91405
LUSTIG, RAY	PHOTOGRAPHER	4509 CLARK PL, NW	WASHINGTON, DC	20007
LUTHER, JAMES W	NEWS CORRESPONDENT	8603 ARLEY DR	SPRINGFIELD, VA	22152
LUTHRINGER, ANDREW	WRITER	555 W 57TH ST #1230	NEW YORK, NY	10019
LUTKINS, LARVE N	WRITER	555 W 57TH ST #1230	NEW YORK, NY	10019
LUTOSLAWSKI, WITOLD	COMPOSER	81-523 WARSZAWA		
		UL SMIALA NR 39	WARSAW	POLAND
LUTTON, CASEY	GUITARIST	POST OFFICE BOX 24325	NASHVILLE, TN	37202
LUTTON, WILLIAM	DRUMMER	968 SNEED RD	FRANKLIN, TN	37064
LUTTRELL, MARTHA	TALENT AGENT	ICM, 8899 BEVERLY BLVD	LOS ANGELES, CA	90048
LUTZ, ELLSWORTH M, JR	NEWS CORRESPONDENT	6265 DAWN DAY DR	COLUMBIA, MD	21045
LUTZ, JOHN	TRUMPETER	POST OFFICE BOX 1070	HENDERSONVILLE, TN	37075
LUVISI, LEE	PIANIST	1776 BROADWAY #504	NEW YORK, NY	10019
LUXON, BENJAMIN	BARITONE	SHAW CONCERTS, 1995 BROADWAY	NEW YORK, NY	10023
LUZ, FRANC	ACTOR	10100 SANTA MONICA BLVD #1600	LOS ANGELES, CA	90067
LYALL, MAX	PIANIST	GOLDEN GATE BAPTIST SEMINARY		
		STRAWBERRY POINT	MILL VALLEY, CA	94941
LYALL, ROBERT	CONDUCTOR	SARDOS, 180 W END AVNUE	NEW YORK, NY	10023
LYDON, JAMES	ACTOR-DIRECTOR	2746 BELDEN DR	LOS ANGELES, CA	90068
LYDON, THOMAS P	NEWS CORRESPONDENT	4850 CONNECTICUT AVE, NW	WASHINGTON, DC	20008
LYELL, WES	DRUMMER	3526 "T" ST	PANAMA CITY, FL	32404
LYKES, JOHN	ACTOR	8721 SUNSET BLVD #202	LOS ANGELES, CA	90069
LYLE, FREDERICK J	TV WRITER	8955 BEVERLY BLVD	LOS ANGELES, CA	90048
LYLE, ROBERT	CONDUCTOR	POST OFFICE BOX 131	SPRINGFIELD, VA	22150
LYLE, ROBERT H	NEWS CORRESPONDENT	1201 CONNECTICUT AVE, NW	WASHINGTON, DC	20036
LYLES, A C	WRITER-PRODUCER	2115 LINDA FLORA DR	LOS ANGELES, CA	90077
LYLES, FRED	PRODUCER	MCA/UNIVERSAL STUDIOS, INC		
		100 UNIVERSAL CITY PLAZA #69	UNIVERSAL CITY, CA	91608
LYLES, TRACEE	ACTRESS	7469 MELROSE AVE #30	LOS ANGELES, CA	90046
LYMAN, DOROTHY	ACTRESS	14 W 44TH ST #1500	NEW YORK, NY	10036
LYMPANY, MOURA	PIANIST	1776 BROADWAY #504	NEW YORK, NY	10019
LYN, DAVID	ACTOR	9 PAGET TERR, PENARTH	SOUTH GLAM CF6 1DR	ENGLAND
LYN, DAVID	TV WRITER	8955 BEVERLY BLVD	LOS ANGELES, CA	90048
LYNCH, ANN	PIANIST	1915 WARFIELD DR	NASHVILLE, TN	37215
LYNCH, BILL	NEWS CORRESPONDENT	CBS NEWS, 2020 "M" ST, NW	WASHINGTON, DC	20036
LYNCH, DAVID	FILM WRITER-DIRECTOR	DGA, 7950 SUNSET BLVD	LOS ANGELES, CA	90046
LYNCH, DAVID E	NEWS CORRESPONDENT	3850 TUNLAW RD, NW	WASHINGTON, DC	20007
LYNCH, DAVID J	NEWS CORRESPONDENT	1234 MASSACHUSETTS AVE, NW	WASHINGTON, DC	20005
LYNCH, DAVID KEITH	DIRECTOR	1888 CENTURY PARK E #1400	LOS ANGELES, CA	90067
LYNCH, DENISE	REPORTER	TIME & PEOPLE MAGAZINE		
		TIME & LIFE BUILDING		
		ROCKEFELLER CENTER	NEW YORK, NY	10020
LYNCH, DON	ACTOR	8721 SUNSET BLVD #200	LOS ANGELES, CA	90069
LYNCH, JOHN F	WRITER	555 W 57TH ST #1230	NEW YORK, NY	10019
LYNCH, KEN	ACTOR	10434 WOODBRIDGE ST	NORTH HOLLYWOOD, CA	91602
LYNCH, PATRICIA	TV PRODUCER	NBC TELEVISION NETWORK		
		30 ROCKEFELLER PLAZA	NEW YORK, NY	10112
LYNCH, PAUL	FILM DIRECTOR	33 HARBOUR SQ #3223	TORONTO, ONTARIO	CANADA
LYNCH, REBECCA	VIOLINIST	POST OFFICE BOX 150906	NASHVILLE, TN	37215
LYNCH, RICHARD	ACTOR	9000 SUNSET BLVD #1112	LOS ANGELES, CA	90069
LYNCH, SHEILA J	WRITER	8955 BEVERLY BLVD	LOS ANGELES, CA	90048
LYNCH, THOMAS W	TV WRITER	8955 BEVERLY BLVD	LOS ANGELES, CA	90048
LYNCH, WILLIAM D, JR	NEWS CORRESPONDENT	CBS NEWS, 2020 "M" ST, NW	WASHINGTON, DC	20036
LYNDE, JANICE	ACTRESS	200 W 57TH ST #1303	NEW YORK, NY	10019
LYNDHURST, NICHOLAS	ACTOR	CHATTO & LINNIT, LTD		
		PRINCE OF WALES THEATRE		
		COVENTRY ST	LONDON W1	ENGLAND
LYNE, ADRIAN	FILM DIRECTOR	2825 SEATTLE DR	LOS ANGELES, CA	90046
LYNGSTAD, FRIDA	SINGER-SONGWRITER	POST OFFICE BOX 26072		
		S-100 41	STOCKHOLM	SWEDEN
LYNLEY, CAROL	ACTRESS	POST OFFICE BOX 2190	MALIBU, CA	90265
LYNN, ANN	ACTRESS	SARABAND ASSOCIATES AGENCY		
		153 PETHERTON RD, HIGHBURY	LONDON N5	ENGLAND
LYNN, BETSY	SINGER	830 GLASTONBURY RD #614	NASHVILLE, TN	37217
LYNN, BETTY	ACTRESS	10424 TENNESSEE AVE	LOS ANGELES, CA	90064
LYNN, CHERYL	ACTRESS	6430 SUNSET BLVD #701	LOS ANGELES, CA	90028
LYNN, CHERYL	SINGER	200 W 51ST ST #1410	NEW YORK, NY	10019
LYNN, DAME VERA	ACTRESS	4 SANDHURST AVE, BISPHAM		
		BLACKPOOL	LANCASHIRE FY2 9AV	ENGLAND
LYNN, DIANNA & THE CALICO BAND	C & W GROUP	PENNY, 30 GUINAN ST	WALTHAM, MA	02154
LYNN, ERIC	COLUMNIST	TRIBUNE MEDIA SERVICES		
		64 E CONCORD ST	ORLANDO, FL	32801
LYNN, GARY	NEWS CORRESPONDENT	2139 WISCONSIN AVE, NW	WASHINGTON, DC	20007
LYNN, JEFFREY	ACTOR	11600 ACAMA ST	STUDIO CITY, CA	91604
LYNN, JONATHAN	ACTOR-WRITER	36 MEADWAY	LONDON NW11 6PJ	ENGLAND
LYNN, LORETTA	SINGER	7 MUSIC CIRCLE N	NASHVILLE, TN	37203

LYNN, MICHAEL D	WRITER	555 W 57TH ST #1230	NEW YORK, NY 10019
LYNN, RITA	ACTRESS	9021 MELROSE AVE #304	LOS ANGELES, CA 90069
LYNN, SHERRY	ACTRESS	POST OFFICE BOX 360	BEVERLY HILLS, CA 90213
LYNNE, GILLIAN	CHOREO-DIR	LONDON MANAGEMENT, LTD	
		235-241 REGENT ST	LONDON W1A 2JT ENGLAND
LYNTON, STEPHEN J	NEWS CORRESPONDENT	4207 37TH ST, NW	WASHINGTON, DC 20008
LYON, EARLE R	WRITER	8955 BEVERLY BLVD	LOS ANGELES, CA 90048
LYON, FRANCIS D	DIRECTOR	312 PLACITA ELEGANCIA	GREEN VALLEY, AZ 85614
LYON, FRITZ	WRITER	555 W 57TH ST #1230	NEW YORK, NY 10019
LYON, JANE D	WRITER	555 W 57TH ST #1230	NEW YORK, NY 10019
LYON, LESLIE	ACTRESS	8721 SUNSET BLVD #200	LOS ANGELES, CA 90069
LYON, LISA	BODYBUILDER-MODEL	POST OFFICE BOX 585	SANTA MONICA, CA 90406
LYON, NELSON	WRITER	555 W 57TH ST #1230	NEW YORK, NY 10019
LYON, ROBERT	TENOR	JCB, 155 W 68TH ST	NEW YORK, NY 10023
LYON, RON	WRITER	8955 BEVERLY BLVD	LOS ANGELES, CA 90048
LYON, RONALD	WRI-DIR-PROD	ABC TELEVISION NETWORK	
		2040 AVE OF THE STARS	LOS ANGELES, CA 90067
LYON, SUE	ACTRESS	9000 SUNSET BLVD #1112	LOS ANGELES, CA 90069
LYONS, C J	CASTING DIRECTOR	PEGASUS, 116 S LA BREA AVE	LOS ANGELES, CA 90035
LYONS, IVAN & NAN	WRITER	555 W 57TH ST #1230	NEW YORK, NY 10019
LYONS, JACK	WRITER	569 N ROSSMORE AVE #104	LOS ANGELES, CA 90004
LYONS, JEFFREY	FILM CRITIC	WPIX-TV, 11 WPIX PLAZA	NEW YORK, NY 10017
LYONS, PAUL	PHOTOGRAPHER	603 UPHAM PL, NW	VIENNA, VA 22180
LYONS, ROBERT F	ACTOR	10949 FRUITLAND DR #7	STUDIO CITY, CA 91604
LYONS, STEWART A	WRITER	8955 BEVERLY BLVD	LOS ANGELES, CA 90048
LYONS, STUART	FILM PRODUCER	29 SUNBURY COURT ISLAND	
		SUNBURY-ON-THAMES	MIDDLESEX ENGLAND
LYONS, TED	BASEBALL	1401 LOREE ST	VINTON, LA 70668
LYRAS, DEAN S	FILM DIRECTOR	4518 KRAFT AVE	NORTH HOLLYWOOD, CA 91602
LYRAS, PANAYIS	PIANIST	JCB, 155 W 68TH ST	NEW YORK, NY 10023
LYRES, THE	ROCK & ROLL GROUP	611 BROADWAY #526	NEW YORK, NY 10012
LYRIQUE TRIO	MUSICAL TRIO	ACC, 890 W END AVE	NEW YORK, NY 10025
LYSAK, MICHAEL J	WRITER	555 W 57TH ST #1230	NEW YORK, NY 10019
LYSDAHL, TORI	ACTRESS	9441 WILSHIRE BLVD #620-D	BEVERLY HILLS, CA 90210
LYSTAD, ROBERT D	NEWS CORRESPONDENT	4900 SCARSDALE RD	BETHESDA, MD 20816
LYTHGOE, NIGEL	CHOREO-PROD	5 BACONS DR, CUFFLEY	HERTS ENGLAND
LYTLE, ALEV N	SCREENWRITER	8955 BEVERLY BLVD	LOS ANGELES, CA 90048
LYTLE, CECIL	PIANIST	FROTHINGHAM, 40 GROVE ST	WESSESLEY, MA 02181
LYTLE, DAVID F	NEWS CORRESPONDENT	1905 N ODE ST	ARLINGTON, VA 22209
LYTTHANS, JAMES D	CONDUCTOR	302 VISTA DEL CANON	ANAHEIM, CA 92807
LYTTON, DEBBIE	ACTRESS	8831 SUNSET BLVD #402	LOS ANGELES, CA 90069
LYX	ROCK & ROLL GROUP	LUTZ, 5625 "O" STREET BLDG	LINCOLN, NE 68510

M, MAGNIFICENT	WRESTLER	SEE - MURACO, DON "MAGNIFICENT"	
M & M	ROCK & ROLL GROUP	41 BRITAIN ST #200	TORONTO, ONT CANADA
M C 5	MUSICAL GROUP	POST OFFICE BOX 82	GREAT NECK, NY 11021
M D C	ROCK & ROLL GROUP	SEE - MILLION DEAD KIDS	
M F Q	FOLK QUARTET	POST OFFICE BOX 2050	MALIBU, CA 90265
MA, CHRISTOPHER YI-WEN	NEWS CORRESPONDENT	1750 PENNSYLVANIA AVE, NW	WASHINGTON, DC 20006
MA, YO-YO	CELLIST	ICM, 40 W 57TH ST	NEW YORK, NY 10019
MAALOUF, BERTA LAUN	NEWS CORRESPONDENT	2727 29TH ST #226, NW	WASHINGTON, DC 20006
MAALOUF, RAFIC K	NEWS CORRESPONDENT	2727 29TH ST #226, NW	WASHINGTON, DC 20008
MAAS, JON	TV EXECUTIVE	NBC TELEVISION NETWORK	NEW YORK, NY 10112
MABE, RON	PIANIST	3550 PARADISE RD #203	LAS VEGAS, NV 89109
MAC, BOBBY & THE BREAKWAY	C & W GROUP	POST OFFICE BOX 8305	HOUSTON, TX 77004
MAC ALLEN, JAMES	DIRECTOR	246 E 46TH ST	NEW YORK, NY 10019
MAC ARTHUR, JAMES	ACTOR	3003 KALAKAUA AVE #5-B	HONOLULU, HI 96815
MAC BIRD, BONNIE	SCREENWRITER	CE & H, 9465 WILSHIRE BLVD	BEVERLY HILLS, CA 90212
MAC BRIDE, DAVID	COMPOSER	FINELL, 155 W 68TH ST	NEW YORK, NY 10023
MAC BRIDE, THOMAS, JR	PHOTOJOURNALIST	7318 FLOWER AVE	TAKOMA PARK, MD 20012
MAC CLOSKEY, YSABEL	ACTRESS	5821 MORELLA AVE	NORTH HOLLYWOOD, CA 91607
MAC COLL, CATRIONA	ACTRESS	CCA MGMT, 4 CT LODGE	
		48 SLOANE SQ	LONDON SW1 8AT ENGLAND
MAC CORKINDALE, SIMON	ACTOR	1640 LEXINGTON RD	BEVERLY HILLS, CA 90210
MAC DERMOT, GALT	COMPOSER	ASCAP, 1 LINCOLN PLAZA	NEW YORK, NY 10020
MAC DONALD, BRUCE-BRIGHT	COMPOSER	3230 ROWENA AVE	LOS ANGELES, CA 90027
MAC DONALD, DENISE	ACTRESS	5330 LANKERSHIM BLVD #210	NORTH HOLLYWOOD, CA 91601
MAC DONALD, DONALD J	WRITER	8955 BEVERLY BLVD	LOS ANGELES, CA 90048
MAC DONALD, GUS	TV WRITER-PRODUCER	GRANADA-TV, 3 UPPER JAMES ST	LONDON W1 ENGLAND
MAC DONALD, JOHN N	COMPOSER	400-A AVE "F"	REDONDO BEACH, CA 90277
MAC DONALD, MARCY	ACTRESS	123 N MAPLE ST #D	BURBANK, CA 91505
MAC DONALD, MARY	WRITER-EDITOR	US MAGAZINE COMPANY	
		1 DAG HAMMARSKJOLD PLAZA	NEW YORK, NY 10017
MAC DONALD, MICHAEL B	WRITER	8955 BEVERLY BLVD	LOS ANGELES, CA 90048

Name	Occupation	Address	City	Zip
MAC DONALD, SUSAN	ACTRESS	445 N BEDFORD DR #PH	BEVERLY HILLS, CA	90210
MAC DONNEIL, DENNIS	TALENT AGENT	POST OFFICE BOX 1616	NOVATO, CA	94948
MAC DONNELL, RAY	ACTOR	ABC-TV, "ALL MY CHILDREN"		
		1330 AVE OF THE AMERICAS	NEW YORK, NY	10019
MAC DOUGALL, ROGER	WRITER	8955 BEVERLY BLVD	LOS ANGELES, CA	90048
MAC FARLANE, LOUELLA	WRITER	8955 BEVERLY BLVD	LOS ANGELES, CA	90048
MAC GILLIVRAY, GREG A	DIRECTOR	POST OFFICE BOX 205	SOUTH LAGUNA, CA	92677
MAC GRAW, ALI	ACTRESS-MODEL	31108 BROAD BEACH RD	MALIBU, CA	90265
MAC GREEVY, THOMAS	ACTOR	3518 W CAHUENGA BLVD #316	LOS ANGELES, CA	90068
MAC GREGOR, DOUG	CARTOONIST	THE NORWICH BULLETIN		
MAC GREGOR, MARY	SINGER	151 S EL CAMINO DR	BEVERLY HILLS, CA	90212
MAC GUIRE, DOROTHY	ACTRESS	121 COPLEY PL	BEVERLY HILLS, CA	90210
MAC INTOSH, CATHLEEN	ACTRESS	8831 SUNSET BLVD #402	LOS ANGELES, CA	90069
MAC INTOSH, JAY W	ACTRESS	POST OFFICE BOX 605	PACIFIC PALISADES, CA	90272
MAC INTYRE, HAROLD	SINGER	2464 BRASILIA CIR	MISSISS, ONT L5N 2G1	CANADA
MAC KAILL, DOROTHY	ACTRESS	THE ROYAL HAWAIIAN		
		2259 KALAKAUA AVE #253	HONOLULU, HI	96815
MAC KAY, FULTON	ACTOR	LEADING PLAYERS, 31 KINGS RD	LONDON SW3	ENGLAND
MAC KAY, JEFF	ACTOR	9220 SUNSET BLVD #625	LOS ANGELES, CA	90069
MAC KAYE, DOROTHY	NEWS CORRESPONDENT	2512 "Q" ST, NW	WASHINGTON, DC	20007
MAC KELVIE, JOCK	WRITER	24901 EL DORADO MEADOW RD	CALABASAS, CA	91302
MAC KENZIE, GISELE	ACTRESS	15824 WOODVALE RD	ENCINO, CA	91416
MAC KENZIE, JOHN	FILM-TV DIRECTOR	A D PETERS & CO, LTD		
		10 BUCKINGHAM ST	LONDON WC2	ENGLAND
MAC KENZIE, KEITH	DIRECTOR	BBC NETWORK PRODUCTION CENTER		
		NEW BROADCAST HOUSE		
		OXFORD HOUSE	MANCHESTER M60 1SJ	ENGLAND
MAC KENZIE, MARY BETH	ACTRESS	1328 N SCREENLAND DR	BURBANK, CA	91505
MAC KENZIE, MIDGE	WRITER	555 W 57TH ST #1230	NEW YORK, NY	10019
MAC KENZIE, MURDO	DIRECTOR-PRODUCER	POST OFFICE BOX 6767	BEND, OR	97701
MAC KENZIE, PATCH	ACTRESS	9744 WILSHIRE BLVD #306	BEVERLY HILLS, CA	90212
MAC KENZIE, ROBERT	TRUMPETER	107 TIMBERCREST RD	BRENTWOOD, TN	37027
MAC KENZIE, ROCK	ACTOR	8961 SUNSET BLVD #B	LOS ANGELES, CA	90069
MAC KENZIE, WILL	ACTOR	13109 CHANDLER BLVD	VAN NUYS, CA	91401
MAC KENZIE, WILL	TV DIRECTOR	3955 ALOMAR ST	SHERMAN OAKS, CA	91423
MAC KERRON, CONRAD B	NEWS CORRESPONDENT	1842 KALORAMA RD, NW	WASHINGTON, DC	20037
MAC KEY, BOBBY	SINGER	SEIFERT, 1407 KENOVA AVE	CINCINNATI, OH	45237
MAC LACHLAN, JANET	ACTRESS	1919 N TAFT AVE	LOS ANGELES, CA	90068
MAC LAINE, SHIRLEY	ACTRESS	PARKER, 25200 OLD MALIBU RD	MALIBU, CA	90265
MAC LEAN, ALISTAIR	WRITER	4 W HALKIN ST	LONDON SW1	ENGLAND
MAC LEAN, DON	COMEDIAN	VAUGHAN ASSOC, 100 PARK ST	LONDON W1	ENGLAND
MAC LEAN, JEAN	DIRECTOR	240 E 76TH ST	NEW YORK, NY	10021
MAC LEAN, JOHN N	NEWS CORRESPONDENT	3604 PORTER ST, NW	WASHINGTON, DC	20016
MAC LEAN, PETER	ACTOR	742 PORTOLA TERR	LOS ANGELES, CA	90042
MAC LEAN, RORY H	SCREENWRITER	7 HOLLYWOOD MEWS	LONDON SW10	ENGLAND
MAC LEAN & MAC LEAN	ROCK & ROLL GROUP	41 BRITAIN ST #200	TORONTO, ONT	CANADA
MAC LEARN, R D	SINGER	4680 ELK LAKE DR #304	VICTORIA, BC V8Z 5M1	CANADA
MAC LEISCH, RODERICK	WRITER	555 W 57TH ST #1230	NEW YORK, NY	10019
MAC LENNAN, ALFRED	WRITER	555 W 57TH ST #1230	NEW YORK, NY	10019
MAC LEOD, GAVIN	ACTOR	151 S EL CAMINO DR	BEVERLY HILLS, CA	90212
MAC LEOD, MARGARET I	WRITER	555 W 57TH ST #1230	NEW YORK, NY	10019
MAC LEOD, MURRAY	ACTOR	533 18TH ST	SANTA MONICA, CA	90402
MAC LEOD, PATTI	ACTRESS	9842 CARDIGAN PL	BEVERLY HILLS, CA	90210
MAC MAHAON, ALINE	ACTRESS	KLINE, 517 N ROXBURY DR	BEVERLY HILLS, CA	90210
MAC MILLAN, ANDREW	ACTOR	220 W 93RD ST #6-C	NEW YORK, NY	10025
MAC MILLAN, KEITH	DIRECTOR	1961 N VAN NESS AVE	HOLLYWOOD, CA	90068
MAC MILLAN, NORMA	ACTRESS	400 S BEVERLY DR #216	BEVERLY HILLS, CA	90212
MAC MILLAN, STEPHANIE K	DIRECTOR	DGA, 7950 SUNSET BLVD	LOS ANGELES, CA	90046
MAC MURRAY, FRED	ACTOR	485 HALVERN DR	LOS ANGELES, CA	90049
MAC MURRAY, KATHERINE	ACTRESS	485 HALVERN DR	LOS ANGELES, CA	90049
MAC NAIR, ROBERT	ACTOR	6605 HOLLYWOOD BLVD #220	HOLLYWOOD, CA	90028
MAC NAIR, SUSAN	THEATER PRODUCER	QUAD PRODS, 890 BROADWAY	NEW YORK, NY	10003
MAC NAUGHTAN, ALAN	ACTOR	19 ARUNDEL CT, ARUNDEL GARDENS	LONDON W11 2LP	ENGLAND
MAC NAUGHTON, IAN	TV DIRECTOR	PERCHAER WEG 3	8137 BERG 1	WEST GERMANY
MAC NAUGHTON, ROBERT	ACTOR	ICM, 8899 BEVERLY BLVD	LOS ANGELES, CA	90048
MAC NAUGHTON, ROBERT	ACTOR	MAX NAUGHTON LOWE		
		200 FULHAM RD	LONDON SW1	ENGLAND
MAC NEE, PATRICK	ACTOR	REDWAY, 16 BERNERS ST	LONDON W1	ENGLAND
MAC NEIL, CORNELL	BARITONE	CAMI, 165 W 57TH ST	NEW YORK, NY	10019
MAC NEIL, NEIL	NEWS CORRESPONDENT	8110 LILLY STONE DR	BETHESDA, MD	20037
MAC NEIL, ROBERT	NEWS CORRESPONDENT	GENE NICHOLS, 1650 BROADWAY	NEW YORK, NY	10019
MAC NEIL, WALTER	TENOR	CAMI, 165 W 57TH ST	NEW YORK, NY	10019
MAC NELLY, JEFFREY	CARTOONIST	333 E GRACE ST	RICHMOND, VA	23219
MAC PHAIL, ALEXANDER L	WRITER	555 W 57TH ST #1230	NEW YORK, NY	10019
MAC PHAIL, WILLIAM C	CABLE EXECUTIVE	CNN, 1050 TECHWOOD DR, NW	ATLANTA, GA	30318
MAC PHERSON, KAREN A	NEWS CORRESPONDENT	3900 TUNLAW RD, NW	WASHINGTON, DC	20007
MAC PHERSON, PETER	ACTOR	ATA, 2437 E WASHINGTON BLVD	PASADENA, CA	91104
MAC QUEEN, CHIP	ACTOR	10850 RIVERSIDE DR #505	NORTH HOLLYWOOD, CA	91602
MAC RAE, CARMEN	SINGER	2200 SUMMITRIDGE DR	BEVERLY HILLS, CA	90210
MAC RAE, ELIZABETH	ACTRESS	TALENT REP, 20 E 53RD ST	NEW YORK, NY	10022
MAC RAE, HEATHER	ACTRESS	4430 HAYVENHURST AVE	ENCINO, CA	91436
MAC RAE, MEREDITH	ACTRESS	9243 1/2 DOHENY RD	LOS ANGELES, CA	90069
MAC RAE, MICHAEL	ACTOR	10390 SANTA MONICA BLVD #310	LOS ANGELES, CA	90025
MAC RAE, SHEILA	SINGER-ACTRESS	205 W 57TH ST #11-C	NEW YORK, NY	10019
MAC VALLEY'S GLOBE OF DEATH	MOTORCYCLISTS	HALL, 138 FROG HOLLOW RD	CHURCHVILLE, PA	18966

ALI MAC GRAW

SHIRLEY MAC LAINE

GAVIN MAC LEOD

FRED MAC MURRAY

RALPH MACCHIO

GUY MADISON

GEORGE MAHARIS

JOCK MAHONEY

NORMAN MAILOR

Name	Occupation	Address	City/State	ZIP
MACAL, ZDENEK	CONDUCTOR	ICM, 40 W 57TH ST	NEW YORK, NY	10019
MACARAEG, JEFFREY J	SINGER-SONGWRITER	2801 MEADOW LARK DR	SAN DIEGO, CA	92123
MACAULAY, CHARLES	ACTOR	208 S BEVERLY DR #4	BEVERLY HILLS, CA	90212
MACCHIO, RALPH	ACTOR	972 NICHOLS RD	DEER PARK, NY	11729
MACE, DON	NEWS CORRESPONDENT	12587 MC INTIRE DR	WOODBRIDGE, VA	22192
MACE, RAY	COMPOSER-CONDUCTOR	1306 WARNER AVE	LOS ANGELES, CA	90024
MACELHINNEY, ANDREW J	WRITER	555 W 57TH ST #1230	NEW YORK, NY	10019
MACERO, TED	MUSICIAN	DOCTOR JAZZ RECORDS COMPANY		
		1414 AVE OF THE AMERICAS	NEW YORK, NY	10019
MACHACEK, JOHN W	NEWS CORRESPONDENT	5631 ROCKY RUN DR	CENTREVILLE, VA	22060
MACHADO, MARIO J	ACTOR	5750 BRIARCLIFF RD	LOS ANGELES, CA	90068
MACHINES, THE	WRESTLING TAG TEAM	POST OFFICE BOX 3859	STAMFORD, CT	06905
MACHON, KAREN	ACTRESS	8150 BEVERLY BLVD #303	LOS ANGELES, CA	90048
MACHOVER, TOD	COMPOSER	FINELL, 155 W 68TH ST	NEW YORK, NY	10023
MACHT, STEPHEN	ACTOR	248 S RODEO DR	BEVERLY HILLS, CA	90212
MACK, BERNARD BURNELL	TV WRITER	3214 HIGHLAND AVE #A	SANTA MONICA, CA	90405
MACK, BRICE	CINEMATOGRAPHER	10941 1/2 BLOOMFIELD ST	NORTH HOLLYWOOD, CA	91602
MACK, BRICE	FILM DIRECTOR	10841 WRIGHTWOOD LN	NORTH HOLLYWOOD, CA	91604
MACK, GILBERT	ACTOR	11 BAYLIS PL	LYNBROOK, L I, NY	11563
MACK, GUY	ACTOR	ABC-TV, "GENERAL HOSPITAL"		
		1438 N GOWER ST	LOS ANGELES, CA	90028
MACK, JIMMIE	SINGER	TWM MGMT, 641 LEXINGTON AVE	NEW YORK, NY	10022
MACK, JONATHAN	TENOR	61 W 62ND ST #6-F	NEW YORK, NY	10023
MACK, LINDA E	NEWS CORRESPONDENT	1920 "S" ST, NW	WASHINGTON, DC	20009
MACK, LONNIE	SINGER-GUITARIST	POST OFFICE BOX 20043		
		COLUMBUS CIRCLE STATION	NEW YORK, NY	10023
MACK, MARION	ACTRESS	1323 STONEFIELD ST	COSTA MESA, CA	92626
MACK, ROY	CONDUCTOR	7506 HESPERIA AVE	RESEDA, CA	91335
MACK, WARNER	SINGER-GUITAR	118 HICKORY TRACE DR	NASHVILLE, TN	37211
MACK & JAMIE	COMEDY DUO	151 S EL CAMINO DR	BEVERLY HILLS, CA	90212
MACKAY, ROBERT	NEWS CORRESPONDENT	5732 READING AVE	ALEXANDRIA, VA	22311
MACKER, JOHN J	WRITER-PRODUCER	DGA, 7950 SUNSET BLVD	LOS ANGELES, CA	90046
MACKERRAS, SIR CHARLES	COMPOSER-CONDUCTOR	10 HAMILTON TERR	LONDON NW8 9UG	ENGLAND
MACKEY, MARTIN	DIRECTOR-PRODUCER	11038 LANDALE ST	NORTH HOLLYWOOD, CA	91602
MACKEY, MARY L	TV WRITER	8955 BEVERLY BLVD	LOS ANGELES, CA	90048
MACKIE, BOB	COSTUME DESIGNER	8636 MELROSE AVE	LOS ANGELES, CA	90069
MACONSAW	ROCK & ROLL GROUP	POST OFFICE BOX 448	RADFORD, VA	24141
MACY, BILL	ACTOR	10130 ANGELO CIR	BEVERLY HILLS, CA	90210
MACY, LILY TANNER	ACTRESS	1607 N EL CENTRO AVE #2	LOS ANGELES, CA	90028
MACY, W H	ACTOR	ABRAMS ARTIST & ASSOCIATES		
		420 MADISON AVE, 14TH FLOOR	NEW YORK, NY	10017
MAD DADDY'S, THE	ROCK & ROLL GROUP	JEM RECORDS, 3619 KENNEDY RD	SOUTH PLAINFIELD, NJ	07080
MAD DOG	WRESTLER	SEE - SAWYER, BUZZ "MAD DOG"		
MAD LADS, THE	RHYTHM & BLUES GROUP	UPS, 781 EUGENE RD	MEMPHIS, TN	38116
MAD MAX	ROCK & ROLL GROUP	POST OFFICE BOX 2896	TORRANCE, CA	90509
MADALA, LENORA	ACTRESS	SCHOEMAN, 2600 W VICTORY BLVD	BURBANK, CA	91505
MADALIN, CAROL	MEZZO-SOPRANO	MUNRO, 334 W 72ND ST	NEW YORK, NY	10023
MADDALENA, JAMES	BARITONE	254 W 93RD ST #8	NEW YORK, NY	10025
MADDALENA, JULIE	ACTRESS	12115 HOFFMAN ST	STUDIO CITY, CA	91604
MADDEN, DAVE	ACTOR	BENSON, 518 TOLUCA PARK DR	BURBANK, CA	91505
MADDEN, JEANNE	ACTRESS	MARTIN, RFD #5, BOX 246	MOSCOW, PA	18444
MADDEN, JENNIFER J	WRITER	555 W 57TH ST #1230	NEW YORK, NY	10019
MADDEN, JERRY	TV DIRECTOR-PRODUCER	7060 HOLLYWOOD BLVD #610	LOS ANGELES, CA	90028
MADDEN, JOHN	SPORTSCASTER	CBS-TV, 7800 BEVERLY BLVD	LOS ANGELES, CA	90036
MADDEN, JOHN PHILIP	DIRECTOR	DGA, 110 W 57TH ST	NEW YORK, NY	10019
MADDEN, LEE	DIRECTOR	16918 MARQUEZ AVE	PACIFIC PALISADES, CA	90272
MADDEN, MIMI	NEWS CORRESPONDENT	8903 HOOES RD	LORTON, VA	22079
MADDEN, PATRICK E	WRITER	555 W 57TH ST #1230	NEW YORK, NY	10019
MADDEN, ROBERT W	PHOTOGRAPHER	1822 GLADE CT	ANNAPOLIS, MD	21404
MADDEN, ROBIN	WRITER	8955 BEVERLY BLVD	LOS ANGELES, CA	90048
MADDEN, SHARON	ACTRESS	870 N VINE ST #G	LOS ANGELES, CA	90038
MADDEN, TOMMY	ACTOR	9255 SUNSET BLVD #603	LOS ANGELES, CA	90069
MADDEN, WILLIAM JAMES	ACTOR	10700 BLUFFSIDE DR #1	STUDIO CITY, CA	91604
MADDERN, VICTOR	ACTOR	J & W, 78 NEW BOND ST	LONDON W1	ENGLAND
MADDOCK, GLORIA	ACTRESS	6430 SUNSET BLVD #1203	LOS ANGELES, CA	90028
MADDOW, BEN	WRITER	2781 WESTSHIRE DR	LOS ANGELES, CA	90068
MADDOX, DIANA	WRITER-PRODUCER	211 S BEVERLY DR #206	BEVERLY HILLS, CA	90212
MADDOX, JOHNNY	PIANIST	LL PORT RESTAURANT		
		121 KING ST	ALEXANDRIA, VA	22314
MADDOX, LOUIS C	PHOTOGRAPHER	46-210 AHUI NANI PL	KANEOHE, HI	96744
MADDUX, R LEE	WRITER	2402 4TH ST #15	SANTA MONICA, CA	90405
MADER, B WILLIAM	NEWS CORRESPONDENT	TIME/TIME & LIFE BLDG		
		ROCKEFELLER CENTER	NEW YORK, NY	10020
MADIGAN, AMY	ACTRESS	8335 SUNSET BLVD #200	LOS ANGELES, CA	90069
MADIGAN, CHARLES M	NEWS CORRESPONDENT	516 N JACKSON ST	ARLINGTON, VA	22201
MADILL, KEVIN	PIANIST	820 SUTTON HILL RD	NASHVILLE, TN	37204
MADISON, ALFREDA	NEWS CORRESPONDENT	700 7TH ST #729, SW	WASHINGTON, DC	20024
MADISON, CHRISTOPHER	NEWS CORRESPONDENT	520 PHILADELPHIA AVE	TAKOMA PARK, MD	20912
MADISON, GUY	ACTOR	35022 1/2 AVE "H"	YUCAIPA, CA	92399
MADISON, JOEL	COMEDIAN	POST OFFICE BOX 9532	MADISON, WI	53715
MADISON, LAURA	ACTRESS	9220 SUNSET BLVD #218	LOS ANGELES, CA	90069
MADLOCK, BILL	BASEBALL	453 E DECATUR ST	DECATUR, IL	62521
MADNESS	ROCK & ROLL GROUP	STERLING ARTISTES MGMT		
		167 CALEDONIAN RD	LONDON N1 OSL	ENGLAND
MADOC, PHILIP	ACTOR	WATERSIDE HOUSE, LONDON COLONY	HERTS	ENGLAND

Name	Occupation	Address	City/State	Zip/Country
MADOC, RUTH	ACTRESS	BRAMBLE COTTAGE, GAWTRY	CAMBS	ENGLAND
MADONNA	SINGER-ACTRESS	PENN, 22271 CARBON MESA RD	MALIBU, CA	90265
MADRA, BARBARA	SOPRANO	ICM, 40 W 57TH ST	NEW YORK, NY	10019
MADRICK, MILLIE ROSE	PHOTOGRAPHER	POST OFFICE BOX 283	SOUTHPORT, CT	06490
MADRID, LANCE, III	TV WRITER	8955 BEVERLY BLVD	LOS ANGELES, CA	90048
MADSEN, DAVID W	WRITER	8955 BEVERLY BLVD	LOS ANGELES, CA	90048
MADSEN, KENNETH KORT	DIRECTOR	DGA, 110 W 57TH ST	NEW YORK, NY	10019
MADSEN, MICHAEL	ACTOR	ICM, 8899 BEVERLY LN	LOS ANGELES, CA	90048
MADSEN, THEODORE	VIOLINIST	5643 MEADOWCREST LN	NASHVILLE, TN	37209
MADSEN, VIRGINIA	ACTRESS	1888 CENTURY PARK E #1400	LOS ANGELES, CA	90067
MADURGA, GONZALO	ACTOR	807 RIVERSIDE DR #5-G	NEW YORK, NY	10032
MAEKANE, NACHIKO	MARIMBIST	AFFILIATE ARTISTS, INC		
		37 W 65TH ST, 6TH FLOOR	NEW YORK, NY	10023
MAER, PETER	NEWS CORRESPONDENT	1755 S JEFFERSON DAVIS HWY	ARLINGTON, VA	22202
MAESTRO, JOHNNY & BROOKLYN BRID	ROCK & ROLL GROUP	KNIGHT, 185 CLINTON AVE	STATEN ISLAND, NY	10301
MAFFETT, DEBRA SUE	ACTRESS-MODEL	1717 N HIGHLAND AVE #414	LOS ANGELES, CA	90028
MAGAHA, MACK	GUITARIST	501 BROADMOOR DR	NASHVILLE, TN	37216
MAGAR, GUY	FILM-TV DIRECTOR	8329 RIDPATH DR	LOS ANGELES, CA	90046
MAGARRELL, JACK	NEWS CORRESPONDENT	2131 TUNLAW RD, NW	WASHINGTON, DC	20007
MAGEE, JAMES E	WRITER	8955 BEVERLY BLVD	LOS ANGELES, CA	90048
MAGEE, KEN	ACTOR	12244 CALIFA ST	NORTH HOLLYWOOD, CA	91607
MAGEE, KEVIN A	WRITER	555 W 57TH ST #1230	NEW YORK, NY	10019
MAGEE, SANDRA LEE HENVILLE	ACTRESS	5314 MARMION WY	LOS ANGELES, CA	90042
MAGEEAN, WILLIAM	TV WRITER	8955 BEVERLY BLVD	LOS ANGELES, CA	90048
MAGELOF, PETER M	WRITER	555 W 57TH ST #1230	NEW YORK, NY	10019
MAGISTRETTI, PAUL	WRITER	10535 WYTON DR	LOS ANGELES, CA	90024
MAGIT, DEBRA	ACTRESS	730 N BEVERLY GLEN BLVD	LOS ANGELES, CA	90077
MAGNE, MICHEL	COMPOSER	20 RUE MOUFFELTARD	PARIS 75005	FRANCE
MAGNER, MARTIN	TV DIRECTOR	1282 S BURNSIDE AVE	LOS ANGELES, CA	90019
MAGNESS, CLIFF	WRITER-PRODUCER	4935 TOPEKA DR	TARZANA, CA	91356
MAGNIFICENT, MR	WRESTLER	SEE - KELLY, KEVIN		
		"MR MAGNIFICENT"		
MAGNIFICENT M	WRESTLER	SEE - MURACO, DON "MAGNIFICENT"		
MAGNIFICENT MURACO, THE	WRESTLER	SEE - MURACO, DON "MAGNIFICENT"		
MAGNOLI, ALBERT	FILM DIRECTOR	852 1/2 SANBORN AVE	LOS ANGELES, CA	90029
MAGNUM T A	WRESTLER	NATIONAL WRESTLING ALLIANCE		
		JIM CROCKETT PROMOTIONS		
		421 BRIARBEND DR	CHARLOTTE, NC	28209
MAGNUSON, ED	WRITER-EDITOR	TIME/TIME & LIFE BLDG		
		ROCKEFELLER CENTER	NEW YORK, NY	10020
MAGNUSSON, PAUL C	NEWS CORRESPONDENT	2415 20TH ST, NW	WASHINGTON, DC	20009
MAGUIRE, HUGH	ACTOR	8322 BEVERLY BLVD #202	LOS ANGELES, CA	90048
MAGUIRE, JEFFREY P	SCREENWRITER	8955 BEVERLY BLVD	LOS ANGELES, CA	90048
MAGUIRE, MARY	TV WRITER	8955 BEVERLY BLVD	LOS ANGELES, CA	90048
MAGUIRE, THOMAS P	FILM DIRECTOR	342 CULVER BLVD #4	PLAYA DEL REY, CA	90293
MAGWOOD, HOWARD	DIRECTOR-PRODUCER	23852 CASSANDRA BAY	LAGUNA NIGUEL, CA	92677
MAGWOOD, PAUL	FILM DIRECTOR	27176 GARZA DR	SAUGUS, CA	91350
MAGYAR, DEZSO D	DIRECTOR	1539 CALMAR CT	LOS ANGELES, CA	90024
MAGYAR, GABRIEL	CELLIST	708 DOVER PL	CHAMPAIGN, IL	61820
MAHADY, JIM	ACTOR	1265 BEVERLY GLEN DR	BEVERLY HILLS, CA	90212
MAHAFFEY, LORRIE	ACTRESS	WILLIAMS, 750 GALAXY HGTS DR	LA CANADA, CA	91011
MAHAN, BILLY	ACTOR	11670 SUNSET BLVD #108	LOS ANGELES, CA	90049
MAHAN, JAMES B	PHOTOGRAPHER	302 SAINT IVES ST	SEVERNA PARK, MD	21146
MAHAR, JOSEPH	ACTOR	11726 SAN VICENTE BLVD #300	LOS ANGELES, CA	90049
MAHARIS, GEORGE	ACTOR	13150 MULHOLLAND DR	BEVERLY HILLS, CA	90210
MAHER, BILL	ACTOR	10350 SANTA MONICA BLVD #210	LOS ANGELES, CA	90025
MAHER, PATRICIA	ACTRESS-PRODUCER	12243 SHETLAND LN	LOS ANGELES, CA	90049
MAHLER, BRUCE	TV WRITER	8955 BEVERLY BLVD	LOS ANGELES, CA	90048
MAHOGANY RUSH	ROCK & ROLL GROUP	65 W 55TH ST #306	NEW YORK, NY	10019
MAHON, JOHN	ACTOR	3518 W CAHUENGA BLVD #316	LOS ANGELES, CA	90068
MAHONEY, BOB	FILM DIRECTOR	5 D'ARBLAY ST	LONDON W1V 3FD	ENGLAND
MAHONEY, JAMES A	DIRECTOR	DGA, 110 W 57TH ST	NEW YORK, NY	10019
MAHONEY, JOCK	ACTOR	13332 HUSTON ST #A	SHERMAN OAKS, CA	91423
MAHONY, JOHN	FILM EXECUTIVE	NATIONAL SCREEN SERVICE, LTD		
		15 WADSWORTH RD, PERIVALE		
		GREENFORD	MIDDLESEX	ENGLAND
MAHR-GORDON DUO	MUSICAL DUO	POST OFFICE BOX 131	SPRINGFIELD, VA	22150
MAI TAI	VOCAL TRIO	CRITIQUE RECORDS, 400 MAIN ST	READING, MA	01867
MAIBAUM, PAUL	WRITER	1557 N STANLEY AVE	LOS ANGELES, CA	90046
MAIBAUM, RICHARD	WRITER-PRODUCER	826 GREENTREE RD	PACIFIC PALISADES, CA	90272
MAIER, FRANCIS X	WRITER	9249 1/2 BURTON WY	BEVERLY HILLS, CA	90210
MAIER, MAYLOU	ACTRESS	3564 MANDEVILLE CANYON RD	LOS ANGELES, CA	90049
MAIER, STEVEN PERRY	TV EXECUTIVE	ABC-TV, 4151 PROSPECT AVE	LOS ANGELES, CA	90027
MAIER, THOMAS	ACTOR	5350 LANKERSHIM BLVD #210	NORTH HOLLYWOOD, CA	91601
MAILER, LEV	ACTOR	6680 WHITLEY TERR	LOS ANGELES, CA	90068
MAILER, NORMAN	AUTHOR	142 COLUMBIA HGTS PL	BROOKLYN, NY	11201
MAILLAN, JACQUELINE	ACTRESS	M BRU, 33 CHAMPS-ELYSEES	PARIS 75008	FRANCE
MAILLET, PAUL	PIANIST	SPRINGER, 1001 ROLANDVUE RD	BALTIMORE, MD	21204
MAIN, DAVID	TV WRITER-PRODUCER	QUADRANT, 950 TONGE ST	TORONTO, ONTARIO	CANADA

Name	Occupation	Address	City	Zip
MAIN, LAURIE	ACTOR	3518 W CAHUENGA BLVD #316	LOS ANGELES, CA	90068
MAIN ATTRACTION, THE	ROCK & ROLL GROUP	2600 NONCONNAH BLVD #390	MEMPHIS, TN	38132
MAINEGRA, RICHARD	GUITARIST	4416 GERALD PL	NASHVILLE, TN	37205
MAINIERI, MIKE	ACTOR	C MARTIN, 242 W 30TH ST	NEW YORK, NY	10001
MAINSTREAM	MUSIC GROUP	NBA, 2605 NORTHRIDGE DR	GARLAND, TX	75043
MAINSTREET	MUSICAL GROUP	32500 CONCORD DR #211	MADISON HEIGHTS, MI	48071
MAIO, FRED	TV WRITER	8955 BEVERLY BLVD	LOS ANGELES, CA	90048
MAIO, PATRICK	NEWS CORRESPONDENT	22721 FREDERICK RD	CLARKSBURG, MD	20871
MAIR, AL	RECORD EXECUTIVE	ATTIC, 624 KING ST W	TORONTO, ONT M5V 1M7	CANADA
MAIR, GEORGE	WRITER	8895 BEVERLY BLVD	LOS ANGELES, CA	90048
MAIR, GEORGE I	NEWS CORRESPONDENT	3437 S UTAH ST	ARLINGTON, VA	22206
MAISEL, IVAN	SPORTS WRITER	SPORTS ILLUSTRATED MAGAZINE		
		TIME & LIFE BUILDING		
		ROCKEFELLER CENTER	NEW YORK, NY	10020
MAISEL, SALLY J	WRITER	10514 NATIONAL BLVD #330	LOS ANGELES, CA	90034
MAISENBERG, OLEG	PIANIST	LEISER, DORCHESTER TOWERS		
		155 W 68TH ST	NEW YORK, NY	10023
MAISNIK, KATHY	ACTRESS	9300 WILSHIRE BLVD #410	BEVERLY HILLS, CA	90212
MAISONETTE, HECTOR	ACTOR	3712 ARBOLADA RD	LOS ANGELES, CA	90027
MAITLAND, BETH	ACTRESS	6310 SAN VICENTE BLVD #407	LOS ANGELES, CA	90048
MAITLAND, SCOTTR	CINEMATOGRAPHER	622 E PALM AVE #A	BURBANK, CA	91501
MAIZE, RICHARD	TV WRITER	8955 BEVERLY BLVD	LOS ANGELES, CA	90048
MAJCHRZYK, MARIANNA	WRITER	555 W 57TH ST #1230	NEW YORK, NY	10019
MAJESKI, BILL	WRITER	555 W 57TH ST #1230	NEW YORK, NY	10019
MAJOR, NORMAN S	COMPOSER	2009 N GREENLEAF ST	SANTA ANA, CA	92706
MAJOROS, DAVID	BARITONE	SULLIVAN, 390 W END AVE	NEW YORK, NY	10024
MAJORS, BUFORD	SAXOPHONIST	1712 UNDERWOOD ST	NASHVILLE, TN	37208
MAJORS, LEE	ACTOR-DIRECTOR	23826 MALIBU RD	MALIBU, CA	90265
MAJORS, LEE, II	ACTOR	23826 MALIBU RD	MALIBU, CA	90265
MAJORS, STEVE	ACTOR-DIRECTOR	QUEENSDALE CRESCENT	LONDON W11	ENGLAND
MAK, MARII	ACTRESS	KOHNER, 9169 SUNSET BLVD	LOS ANGELES, CA	90069
MAKEPEACE, CHRIS	ACTOR	15 CLEVELAND ST	TORONTO, ONTARIO	CANADA
MAKIN' TIME	ROCK & ROLL GROUP	34-38 PROVOST ST	LONDON N1	ENGLAND
MAKKAWY, MOHAMED	BODYBUILDER	SUPER FITNESS CENTER		
		2110 DUNDAS ST E	MISSISS, ONT L4X 1L9	CANADA
MAKO	ACTOR	6310 SAN VICENTE BLVD #407	LOS ANGELES, CA	90048
MAKOTO OZONE	JAZZ GROUP	KURLAND, 173 BRIGHTON AVE	BOSTON, MA	02134
MAKOUL, RUDY	WRITER	3435 VINTON AVE #6	LOS ANGELES, CA	90034
MAKSYMIUK, KERZY	CONDUCTOR	SHAW CONCERTS, 1995 BROADWAY	NEW YORK, NY	10023
MALAGNINI, MARIO	TENOR	CAMI, 165 W 57TH ST	NEW YORK, NY	10019
MALAKOVA, PETRA	MEZZO-SOPRANO	111 W 57TH ST #1209	NEW YORK, NY	10019
MALAMED, DENNIS A	NEWS CORRESPONDENT	1707 COLUMBIA RD #211, NW	WASHINGTON, DC	20009
MALANDRO, KRISTINA	ACTRESS	9000 SUNSET BLVD #1200	LOS ANGELES, CA	90069
MALARA, ANTHONY C	TV EXECUTIVE	CBS-TV, 51 W 52ND ST	NEW YORK, NY	10019
MALAS, SPRIO	BASSO-BARITONE	CAMI, 165 W 57TH ST	NEW YORK, NY	10019
MALAVASI, RAY	FOOTBALL COACH	10131 THESUS DR	HUNTINGTON BEACH, CA	92646
MALBIN, ELAINE	SOPRANO	GERSHUNOFF, 502 PARK AVE	NEW YORK, NY	10022
MALBIN, MICHAEL J	NEWS CORRESPONDENT	500 DARTMOUTH AVE	SILVER SPRING, MD	20910
MALCOLM, GEORGE	HARPSICHORDIST	HILLYER, 250 W 57TH ST	NEW YORK, NY	10107
MALCOLM, ROBERT	TV DIRECTOR-PRODUCER	86 TALGARTH MANSIONS		
		BARONS CT	LONDON W14 9DE	ENGLAND
MALCOLM, WILLIAM J	TV DIRECTOR	NBC TELEVISION NETWORK	NEW YORK, NY	10112
MALDEN, KARL	ACTOR	1845 MANDEVILLE CANYON RD	LOS ANGELES, CA	90049
MALEK, LEONARD	FILM EDITOR	3650 S BENTLEY AVE	LOS ANGELES, CA	90034
MALENA, DON	SINGER	POST OFFICE BOX 1104	HARVEY, LA	70059
MALERSTEIN, SUSAN	ACTRESS	1252 N HAVENHURST DR #10	LOS ANGELES, CA	90046
MALESKA, EUGENE	CROSSWORD WRITER	N Y TIMES, 229 W 43RD ST	NEW YORK, NY	10036
MALET, ARTHUR	ACTOR-PRODUCER	419 HILL ST #2	SANTA MONICA, CA	90405
MALFITANO, CATHERINE	SOPRANO	CAMI, 165 W 57TH ST	NEW YORK, NY	10019
MALFITANO, JOSEPH	VIOLINIST	251 W 92ND ST	NEW YORK, NY	10025
MALICK, TERRENCE	WRITER-PRODUCER	2265 NICHOLS CANYON RD	LOS ANGELES, CA	90046
MALICK, WENDIE	ACTRESS	11726 SAN VICENTE BLVD #300	LOS ANGELES, CA	90049
MALIN, KYM	ACTRESS-MODEL	MODELS & PROMOTIONS AGENCY		
		8560 SUNSET BLVD, 10TH FLOOR	LOS ANGELES, CA	90069
MALINA, DAVID	TV WRITER	8955 BEVERLY BLVD	LOS ANGELES, CA	90048
MALINDA, JIM	ACTOR	1930 TAMARIND AVE #3	LOS ANGELES, CA	90068
MALINDA, RAY	ACTOR	10729 NEW HAVEN ST #21	SUN VALLEY, CA	91352
MALINOVA, MARGARITA & OLGA	PIANO DUO	POST OFFICE BOX U	REDDING, CT	06875
MALIPONTE, ADRIANA	SOPRANO	CAMI, 165 W 57TH ST	NEW YORK, NY	10019
MALIS, CLAIRE	ACTRESS	2121 AVE OF THE STARS #410	LOS ANGELES, CA	90067
MALIS, DAVID	BARITONE	HILLYER, 250 W 57TH ST	NEW YORK, NY	10107
MALIS, MARK	CASTING DIRECTOR	MCA/UNIVERSAL STUDIOS, INC		
		100 UNIVERSAL CITY PLAZA #463	UNIVERSAL CITY, CA	91608
MALIS-MOREY, ADELE	ACTRESS	470 S SAN VICENTE BLVD	LOS ANGELES, CA	90048
MALKO, GEORGE	TV WRITER	555 W 57TH ST #1230	NEW YORK, NY	10019
MALKOVICH, JOHN	ACTOR	151 S EL CAMINO DR	BEVERLY HILLS, CA	90212
MALLA, ALI	BODYBUILDER	125 STRAND AVE #C	SANTA MONICA, CA	90405
MALLARD, STEVE	SINGER	581-D OLD HICKORY BLVD	JACKSON, TN	38301
MALLE, LOUIS	FILM DIRECTOR	222 CENTRAL PARK S	NEW YORK, NY	10019
MALLER, JONATHAN	DIRECTOR	3 EDGEWOOD AVE	GLEN HEAD, NY	11545
MALLEY, HOWARD G	DIRECTOR	11523 DUQUE DR	STUDIO CITY, CA	91604
MALLIE, JOANNE P	WRITER	555 W 57TH ST #1230	NEW YORK, NY	10019
MALLIK, PROVASH	SCREENWRITER	MOLLIKO, 16 NEW BRIDGE ST	LONDON EC4	ENGLAND
MALLIK, UMESH	SCREENWRITER	MOLLIKO, 16 NEW BRIDGE ST	LONDON EC4	ENGLAND
MALLORY, BARBARA	ACTRESS	SCHWARTZ, 12800 MILBANK ST	STUDIO CITY, CA	91604

Name	Occupation	Address	City	Zip
MALLORY, CAROLYN	SOPRANO	POST OFFICE BOX 188		
		STATION A	TORONTO, ONT	CANADA
MALLORY, DRUE	ACTRESS	HEINZ, 43 HAY'S MEWS, BERKELEY SQ	LONDON W1X 7RU	ENGLAND
		BERKELEY SQ	LONDON W1X 7RU	ENGLAND
MALLORY, EDWARD	TV DIRECTOR	3158 OAKSHIRE DR	HOLLYWOOD, CA	90068
MALLORY, VICTORIA	ACTRESS	10351 SANTA MONICA BLVD #211	LOS ANGELES, CA	90025
MALLOW, THOMAS W	THEATER PRODUCER	AMERICAN THEATER PRODUCTIONS		
		1500 BROADWAY	NEW YORK, NY	10036
MALLOY, LARKIN	ACTOR	ABC-TV, "ALL MY CHILDREN"		
		1330 AVE OF THE AMERICAS	NEW YORK, NY	10019
MALLOY, MERRIT	WRITER	14144 VENTURA BLVD #200	SHERMAN OAKS, CA	91423
MALLOY, ROBERT	TV WRITER	555 W 57TH ST #1230	NEW YORK, NY	10019
MALMET, BARBARA	WRITER	555 W 57TH ST #1230	NEW YORK, NY	10019
MALMSTEEN, YNGWIE & RISING FORC	ROCK & ROLL GROUP	24514 CALVERT ST #210	WOODLAND HILLS, CA	91367
MALMUTH, BRUCE	FILM WRITER-DIRECTOR	9981 ROBBINS DR	BEVERLY HILLS, CA	90212
MALOCHE, LESLIE	CONDUCTOR	1838 ALDER DR	LOS ANGELES, CA	90065
MALONE, FRED	NEWS CORRESPONDENT	NBC-TV, NEWS DEPARTMENT		
		4001 NEBRASKA AVE, NW	WASHINGTON, DC	20016
MALONE, H ADRIAN	WRITER-PRODUCER	1901 AVE OF THE STARS	LOS ANGELES, CA	90067
MALONE, J C	ACTRESS	752 MARCO PL	VENICE, CA	90291
MALONE, JO JO	ACTRESS	10850 RIVERSIDE DR #505	NORTH HOLLYWOOD, CA	91602
MALONE, JOANN	NEWS CORRESPONDENT	3325 CHAUNCEY PL	MOUNT RAINIER, MD	20712
MALONE, JOEL	WRITER-PRODUCER	4455 ETHEL AVE	NORTH HOLLYWOOD, CA	91604
MALONE, JULIA L	NEWS CORRESPONDENT	4570 MAC ARTHUR BLVD, NW	WASHINGTON, DC	20007
MALONE, KENNETH	DRUMMER	2805 LINCOYA DR	NASHVILLE, TN	37214
MALONE, KITTY	ACTRES	2586 N BEACHWOOD DR	LOS ANGELES, CA	90068
MALONE, LAURA	ACTRESS	9200 SUNSET BLVD #1210	LOS ANGELES, CA	90069
MALONE, MOSES	BASKETBALL	POST OFFICE BOX 25040	PHILADELPHIA, PA	19147
MALONE, NANCY	ACTRESS-DIRECTOR	LILAC PRODS, 4507 AUCKLAND AVE	NORTH HOLLYWOOD, CA	91602
MALONE, WILL	SAXOPHONIST	RAY WARDEN, 162 8TH AVE	NASHVILLE, TN	37203
MALONEY, COLEEN	ACTRESS	8285 SUNSET BLVD #12	LOS ANGELES, CA	90046
MALONEY, JAMES B	WRITER	555 W 57TH ST #1230	NEW YORK, NY	10019
MALONEY, LAWRENCE D	NEWS CORRESPONDENT	7817 SNEAD LN	FALLS CHURCH, VA	22043
MALONEY, PATY	ACTRESS	10000 RIVERSIDE DR #3	TOLUCA LAKE, CA	91602
MALONEY, PETER	ACTOR	11726 SAN VICENTE BLVD #300	LOS ANGELES, CA	90049
MALONSON, KEITH, BAND	JAZZ GROUP	9777 HARWIN ST #101	HOUSTON, TX	77036
MALOOLY, MAGGIE	ACTRESS	4411 LOS FELIZ BLVD #906	LOS ANGELES, CA	90027
MALOY, RICHARD J	NEWS CORRESPONDENT	8313 MEADOWLARK LN	BETHESDA, MD	20817
MALTIN, LEONARD	FILM CRITIC-CORRES	200 W 79TH ST #5-L	NEW YORK, NY	10024
MALVIN, ARTHUR	TV PRODUCER	622 N LINDEN DR	BEVERLY HILLS, CA	90210
MALZBERG, BARRY	WRITER	948 GARRISON AVE	TEANECK, NJ	07666
MAMAKOS, PETER	ACTOR-WRITER	4653 FULTON AVE #4	SHERMAN OAKS, CA	91423
MAMAS & THE PAPAS, THE	ROCK & ROLL GROUP	DAVID FISHOF PRODUCTIONS		
		1775 BROADWAY	NEW YORK, NY	10019
MAMAS BOYS	ROCK & ROLL GROUP	ICM, 40 W 57TH ST	NEW YORK, NY	10019
MAMET, DAVID	SCREENWRITER	555 W 57TH ST #1230	NEW YORK, NY	10019
MAMEY, NORMAN	COMPOSER-CONDUCTOR	716 BALBOA AVE	GLENDALE, CA	91206
MAN MOUNTAIN DARSO	WRESTLER	SEE - KHRUSHCHEV, KHRUSHER		
MANAGO, CAROL E	WRITER	555 W 57TH ST #1230	NEW YORK, NY	10019
MANALE, SHIZUMI	DANCER	AFFILIATE ARTISTS, INC		
		37 W 65TH ST, 6TH FLOOR	NEW YORK, NY	10023
MANARD, BIFF	TV WRITER	8955 BEVERLY BLVD	LOS ANGELES, CA	90048
MANASSE, GEORGE	DIRECTOR	200 W 10TH ST	NEW YORK, NY	10014
MANBER, DAVID	SCREENWRITER	555 W 57TH ST #1230	NEW YORK, NY	10019
MANBY, C ROBERT	FILM EXECUTIVE	RKO-NEDERLANDER		
		1440 BROADWAY	NEW YORK, NY	10018
MANCHESTER, MELISSA	SINGER-SONGWRITER	3181 N BEACHWOOD DR	LOS ANGELES, CA	90068
MANCHESTER, WILLIAM	AUTHOR	POST OFFICE BOX 329		
		WESLEYAN STATION	MIDDLETON, CT	06457
MANCINI, ALBERT	CONDUCTOR	1949 CARMEN AVE	LOS ANGELES, CA	90068
MANCINI, ANTOINETTA	COMPOSER	1999 SANTA ANA AVE	COSTA MESA, CA	92627
MANCINI, HENRY	PIANIST-COMPOSER	261 BARODA DR	LOS ANGELES, CA	90077
MANCINI, MARIO	WRESTLER	POST OFFICE BOX 3859	STAMFORD, CT	06905
MANCINI, RIC	ACTOR	20148 CLARK ST	WOODLAND HILLS, CA	91367
MANCINI, THOMAS E	COMPOSER	1999 SANTA ANA AVE	COSTA MESA, CA	92627
MANCUSO, JAMES	TV DIRECTOR	KINGSTON CANYON	AUSTIN, NV	89310
MANCUSO, NICK	ACTOR	2121 AVE OF THE STARS #410	LOS ANGELES, CA	90067
MAND, JOHN	DRUMMER	3720 RICHLAND AVE	NASHVILLE, TN	37205
MANDALA, ANDREW R	NEWS CORREPONDENT	11 GRAFTON ST	CHEVY CHASE, MD	20815
MANDALA, CHERYL	NEWS CORRESPONDENT	11 GRAFTON ST	CHEVY CHASE, MD	20815
MANDALA, MARK	TV EXECUTIVE	ABC TELEVISION NETWORK		
		1330 AVE OF THE AMERICAS	NEW YORK, NY	10020
MANDAN, ROBERT	ACTOR	11726 SAN VICENTE BLVD #300	LOS ANGELES, CA	90049
MANDEL, ALAN R	SCREENWRITER	490 SIERRA KEYS DR	SIERRA MADRE, CA	91024
MANDEL, BABALOO	SCREENWRITER	1888 CENTURY PARK E #1400	LOS ANGELES, CA	90067
MANDEL, DENIS	ACTOR	9837 TABOR ST	LOS ANGELES, CA	90034
MANDEL, ELIZABETH	DIRECTOR	1268 CLAYTON ST	SAN FRANCISCO, CA	94114
MANDEL, HOWIE	ACTOR-COMEDIAN	10100 SANTA MONICA BLVD #1600	LOS ANGELES, CA	90067
MANDEL, JOHNNY	COMPOSER-CONDUCTOR	28946 CLIFFSIDE DR	MALIBU, CA	90265
MANDEL, LORING	SCREENWRITER	555 W 57TH ST #1230	NEW YORK, NY	10019
MANDEL, MARC	WRITER	5121 VANALDEN AVE	TARZANA, CA	91356
MANDEL, MIKE	SINGER	41 BRITAIN ST #200	TORONTO, ONT	CANADA
MANDEL, ROBERT	DIRECTOR	12129 TRAVIS ST	LOS ANGELES, CA	90049
MANDEL, SUZY	ACTRESS	8721 SUNSET BLVD #200	LOS ANGELES, CA	90069
MANDELBAUM, ART	WRITER	8955 BEVERLY BLVD	LOS ANGELES, CA	90048

HOWIE MANDEL

BARBARA MANDRELL

BARRY MANILOW

ROUBEN MAMOULIAN

MARCEL MARCEAU

JANET MARGOLIN

TEENA MARIE

MARION MARSH

ANNE-MARIE MARTIN

Name	Occupation	Address	City	Zip
MANDELBAUM, LEONARD	DIRECTOR	165 W END AVE	NEW YORK, NY	10023
MANDELBERG, CYNTHIA	TV WRITER	743 DAWSON AVE	LONG BEACH, CA	90804
MANDELIK, GIL	ACTOR	1607 N EL CENTRO AVE #23	LOS ANGELES, CA	90028
MANDELL, ALAN	ACTOR	721 N LA BREA AVE #201	LOS ANGELES, CA	90038
MANDELL, HANS E	DIRECTOR	3900 GREYSTONE AVE	RIVERDALE, NY	10463
MANDELL, JAMES E	COMPOSER	1839 N MARIPOSA AVE	LOS ANGELES, CA	90027
MANDLIN, HARVEY	DIRECTOR	250 W 99TH ST	NEW YORK, NY	10025
MANDRELL, BARBARA	SINGER-MUSICIAN	POST OFFICE BOX 332	HENDERSONVILLE, TN	37075
MANDRELL, ERLINE	ACTRESS-DRUMMER	POST OFFICE BOX 332	HENDERSONVILLE, TN	37075
MANDRELL, LOUISE	SINGER-MUSICIAN	POST OFFICE BOX 332	HENDERSONVILLE, TN	37075
MANDUKE, JOSEPH	DIRECTOR	236 S CLARK DR	BEVERLY HILLS, CA	90211
MANDY, JANE	ACTRESS	1717 N HIGHLAND AVE #414	LOS ANGELES, CA	90028
MANELLI, DONALD	WRITER	8955 BEVERLY BLVD	LOS ANGELES, CA	90048
MANERA, JO ANN	WRITER	555 W 57TH ST #1230	NEW YORK, NY	10019
MANES, FRITZ	FILM PRODUCER	MALPASO, 4000 WARNER BLVD	BURBANK, CA	91522
MANES, STEPHEN	TV WRITER	8955 BEVERLY BLVD	LOS ANGELES, CA	90048
MANES, STEPHEN	PIANIST	ROSENFIELD, 714 LADD RD	BRONX, NY	10471
MANESS, JAY DEE	GUITARIST	10125 GLORIA AVE	SEPULVEDA, CA	91343
MANESS, RICHARD	GUITARIST	130 DENISE DR	ANTIOCH, TN	37013
MANET, GEORGE	ACTOR	5330 LANKERSHIM BLVD #210	NORTH HOLLYWOOD, CA	91601
MANETTA, JOSEPH D	TV WRITER	CBS-TV, "THE GUIDING LIGHT"		
		51 W 52ND ST	NEW YORK, NY	10019
MANETTI, LARRY	ACTOR	4615 WINNETKA AVE	WOODLAND HILLS, CA	91364
MANFORD, BARBARA	CONTRALTO	KAY, 58 W 58TH ST	NEW YORK, NY	10019
MANFREDINI, HARRY	COMPOSER	LIVE MUSIC PUBLISHING		
		793 BINGHAM RD	RIDGEWOOD, NJ	07450
MANGANO, MICHAEL	DIRECTOR	400 E 54TH ST	NEW YORK, NY	10022
MANGIN, NOEL	SINGER	1776 BROADWAY #504	NEW YORK, NY	10019
MANGIONE, CHUCK	FLUEGELHORNIST	DI MARIA, GATES MUSIC		
		1845 CLINTON AVE N	ROCHESTER, NY	14621
MANGO, ALEC	ACTOR	27-A PARK MANSIONS	LONDON SW1	ENGLAND
MANGRAVITE, TOM	DIRECTOR	DGA, 110 W 57TH ST	NEW YORK, NY	10019
MANGRUM, DAWN	ACTRESS	208 S BEVERLY DR #8	BEVERLY HILLS, CA	90212
MANHATTAN TRANSFER, THE	VOCAL GROUP	AVNET MANAGEMENT AGENCY		
		3805 MAGNOLIA BLVD	BURBANK, CA	91505
MANHATTAN WOODWIND TRIO	WOODWIND TRIO	756 7TH AVE #67	NEW YORK, NY	10019
MANHATTANS, THE	VOCAL GROUP	WORLDWIDE ENTERTAINMENT COMPLEX		
		641 LEXINGTON AVE	NEW YORK, NY	10022
MANHEIM, CHRISTOPHER W	WRITER	2134 BEACHWOOD TERR	LOS ANGELES, CA	90068
MANHEIM, EMANUEL	WRITER	17020 SUNSET BLVD	PACIFIC PALISADES, CA	90272
MANHEIM, HET	WRITER	8955 BEVERLY BLVD	LOS ANGELES, CA	90048
MANHEIM, MICHAEL	WRITER-PRODUCER	8171 BAIRD RD	LOS ANGELES, CA	90046
MANHEIM, RICHARD	ACTOR	2134 BEACHWOOD TERR	LOS ANGELES, CA	90068
MANIAC, THE	WRESTLER	SEE - BORNE, MATT		
MANICHELLO, RICHARD	DIRECTOR	142 E 16TH ST	NEW YORK, NY	10003
MANIFOLD, GEOFFREY W	NEWS CORRESPONDENT	5033 BRADLEY BLVD	CHEVY CHASE, MD	20815
MANILOW, BARRY	SINGER-COMPOSER	P O BOX 69180	LOS ANGELES, CA	90069
MANINGS, ALAN	TV PRODUCER	CBS-TV, 7800 BEVERLY BLVD	LOS ANGELES, CA	90036
MANINGS, ALLAN S	WRITER	510 ARKELL DR	BEVERLY HILLS, CA	90210
MANION, JIM	BODYBUILDER	POST OFFICE BOX 442	CARNEGIE, PA	15106
MANISCO, GEORGE	ACTOR	315 1/2 N PALM AVE	ALHAMBRA, CA	91801
MANKIEWICZ, CAROL B	WRITER	8955 BEVERLY BLVD	LOS ANGELES, CA	90048
MANKIEWICZ, DON	TV WRITER	8955 BEVERLY BLVD	LOS ANGELES, CA	90048
MANKIEWICZ, JOSEPH L	WRITER-PRODUCER	RURAL FARM DELIVERY #2, BOX 82	BEDFORD, NY	10506
MANKIEWICZ, THOMAS F	WRITER-PRODUCER	1609 MAGNETIC TERR	LOS ANGELES, CA	90069
MANKOFF, BOB	CARTOONIST	POST OFFICE BOX 4203	NEW YORK, NY	10017
MANKOFSKY, ISIDORE	CINEMATOGRAPHER	1734 N ORANGE GROVE AVE	LOS ANGELES, CA	90046
MANLEY, CYNTHIA	SINGER	9000 SUNSET BLVD #611	LOS ANGELES, CA	90069
MANLEY, JEROLD H	PHOTOJOURNALIST	1123 ARTIC QUILL RD	HERNDON, VA	22070
MANLEY, RON	ACTOR	6736 LAUREL CANYON BLVD #306	NORTH HOLLYWOOD, CA	91606
MANLEY, STEPHEN	ACTOR	9000 SUNSET BLVD #801	LOS ANGELES, CA	90069
MANN, ABBY	WRITER-PRODUCER	1240 LA COLLINA RD	BEVERLY HILLS, CA	90210
MANN, ALLAN	DIRECTOR	DGA, 7950 SUNSET BLVD	LOS ANGELES, CA	90046
MANN, BRIAN	ACTOR	8350 SANTA MONICA BLVD #103	LOS ANGELES, CA	90069
MANN, CHRISTOPHER	ACTOR	304 W 90TH ST	NEW YORK, NY	10024
MANN, DANIEL GERARD	DIRECTOR	6328 FRONDOSA DR	MALIBU, CA	90265
MANN, DANNY	WRITER-PRODUCER	DGA, 7950 SUNSET BLVD	LOS ANGELES, CA	90046
MANN, DELBERT	DIRECTOR-PRODUCER	401 S BURNSIDE AVE #11-D	LOS ANGELES, CA	90036
MANN, DOLORES	ACTRESS	8350 SANTA MONICA BLVD #103	LOS ANGELES, CA	90069
MANN, EARL F	DIRECTOR	1900 N VINE ST #219	LOS ANGELES, CA	90068
MANN, EDWARD	DIRECTOR	DGA, 7950 SUNSET BLVD	LOS ANGELES, CA	90046
MANN, EDWARD ASHER	AUTHOR	2251 BOWMONT DR	BEVERLY HILLS, CA	90210
MANN, HERBIE	FLUTIST	119 W 57TH ST #818	NEW YORK, NY	10019
MANN, HOWARD	ACTOR	400 E 56TH ST	NEW YORK, NY	10022
MANN, HUMMIE	COMPOSER-CONDUCTOR	1238 BARRY AVE #3	LOS ANGELES, CA	90025
MANN, JODIE	ACTRESS	9300 WILSHIRE BLVD #410	BEVERLY HILLS, CA	90212
MANN, JOHNNY	COMPOSER-CONDUCTOR	19764 CORBIN DR	CHATSWORTH, CA	91311
MANN, JOHNNY	WRESTLER	POST OFFICE BOX 3859	STAMFORD, CT	06905
MANN, JONATHAN A	PHOTOGRAPHER	10679 OAK THRUSH CT	BURKE, VA	22015
MANN, LARRY D	ACTOR	15010 VENTURA BLVD #234	SHERMAN OAKS, CA	91403
MANN, LEONARD	ACTOR	9200 SUNSET BLVD #531	LOS ANGELES, CA	90069
MANN, LORENE	GUITARIST	399 ANNEX AVE	NASHVILLE, TN	37209
MANN, MICHAEL	WRITER-PRODUCER	7939 HILLSIDE AVE	LOS ANGELES, CA	90046
MANN, PAUL S	NEWS CORRESPONDENT	3743 INGALLS AVE	ALEXANDRIA, VA	22203

Name	Occupation	Address	City	ZIP
MANN, SHARON	FILM DIRECTOR	644 1/2 WOODLAWN AVE	VENICE, CA	90291
MANN, STANLEY	FILM WRITER-PRODUCER	1431 N STANLEY AVE	LOS ANGELES, CA	90046
MANN, TED	DIRECTOR-PRODUCER	9255 DOHENY RD #2906	LOS ANGELES, CA	90069
MANN, TED	TV WRITER	555 W 57TH ST #1230	NEW YORK, NY	10019
MANN, THOMAS LEW	ACTOR	750 E 5TH ST #71	AZUSA, CA	91702
MANN, ZANE B	WRITER	8955 BEVERLY BLVD	LOS ANGELES, CA	90048
MANN'S, MANFRED, EARTH BAND	ROCK & ROLL GROUP	LLOYD SEGAL, 1116 N CORY AVE	LOS ANGELES, CA	90069
MANNERS, DAVID	ACTOR	1725 DE LA VINA ST #6	SANTA BARBARA, CA	93101
MANNERS, DOROTHY	ACTRESS	744 N DOHENY DR	LOS ANGELES, CA	90069
MANNERS, KIM I	DIRECTOR	DGA, 7950 SUNSET BLVD	LOS ANGELES, CA	90046
MANNERS, MICKEY	COMEDIAN	8350 SANTA MONICA BLVD #206	LOS ANGELES, CA	90069
MANNERS, MISSY	ACTRESS	SEE - MISSY		
MANNERS, SAM B	DIRECTOR	4201 VANALDEN AVE	TARZANA, CA	91356
MANNERS, SCOTT	ACTOR	304 N LA PEER DR #4	BEVERLY HILLS, CA	90211
MANNERS, TERRY	DRUMMER	409 FAIRVIEW AVE	LEBANON, TN	37087
MANNES, ELENA S	WRITER-PRODUCER	DGA, 110 W 57TH ST	NEW YORK, NY	10019
MANNES, MICHAEL LAWRENCE	DIRECTOR	10 E 13TH ST #PH-D	NEW YORK, NY	10003
MANNIES, JO	NEWS CORRESPONDENT	3113 LEE ST	SILVER SPRING, MD	20910
MANNING, AMELIA	NEWS CORRESPONDENT	4506 DALTON RD	CHEVY CHASE, MD	20815
MANNING, GORDON	TV EXECUTIVE	NBC-TV, 30 ROCKEFELLER PLAZA	NEW YORK, NY	10112
MANNING, HUGH	ACTOR	29 PARLIAMENT HILL	LONDON NW3	ENGLAND
MANNING, JACK	ACTOR	26815 BASSWOOD AVE	PALOS VERDES, CA	90274
MANNING, KATE	WRITER	555 W 57TH ST #1230	NEW YORK, NY	10019
MANNING, MARK	ACTOR	JARRETT, 220 E 63RD ST	NEW YORK, NY	10021
MANNING, MARY-BETH	ACTRESS	SHUKAT CO, 340 W 55TH ST	NEW YORK, NY	10019
MANNING, MICHAEL	GUITARIST	POST OFFICE BOX 9388	STANFORD, CA	94305
MANNING, MONROE	WRITER	9161 HILLSBORO DR	LOS ANGELES, CA	90034
MANNING, ROBERT	ACTOR	105 MARON ST	SAINT PETERSBURG, FL	33704
MANNING, ROBERT A	NEWS CORRESPONDENT	2000 KLINGLE RD, NW	WASHINGTON, DC	20010
MANNING, RON	GUITARIST	304 BROWNING RD	NASHVILLE, TN	37211
MANNING, RUTH	ACTRESS	1250 N LAUREL AVE #A	LOS ANGELES, CA	90046
MANNING, SHEILA	CASTING DIRECTOR	470 S SAN VICENTE BLVD	LOS ANGELES, CA	90048
MANNING, SUZANNE ELAM	NEWS CORRESPONDENT	8204 TOWNSEND ST #10	FAIRFAX, VA	22031
MANNINO, FRANCO	CONDUCTOR	SHAW CONCERTS, 1995 BROADWAY	NEW YORK, NY	10023
MANNINO, VINCE	PHOTOGRAPHER	423 HAMPTON CT	FALLS CHURCH, VA	22046
MANNIX, JULIE H	WRITER	CONGDON, 177 E 70TH ST	NEW YORK, NY	10022
MANNIX, PEGGY	ACTRESS	6310 SAN VICENTE BLVD #407	LOS ANGELES, CA	90048
MANNO, CHARLES	DIRECTOR-PRODUCER	342 E 67TH ST	NEW YORK, NY	10021
MANNS, EVELYN C	WRITER	8955 BEVERLY BLVD	LOS ANGELES, CA	90048
MANOFF, DINAH	ACTRESS	913 AMOROSO PL	VENICE, CA	90291
MANON, GLORIA	ACTRESS	4230 STANSBURY AVE #201	SHERMAN OAKS, CA	91423
MANOUCHEHRY, FARHAD	WRITER-PRODUCER	1330 N CRESCENT HGTS BLVD #14	LOS ANGELES, CA	90046
MANOWITZ, STEVEN	WRITER	555 W 57TH ST #1230	NEW YORK, NY	10019
MANRIQUE, ROBERT	COMPOSER	130 CATAMARAN #4	MARINA DEL REY, CA	90292
MANS, JOSEPH L	WRITER	555 W 57TH ST #1230	NEW YORK, NY	10019
MANSBACH, ROBERT H	WRITER-PRODUCER	DGA, 110 W 57TH ST	NEW YORK, NY	10019
MANSELL, CAROL	ACTRESS	15010 VENTURA BLVD #219	SHERMAN OAKS, CA	91403
MANSELL, JOHN M, JR	NEWS CORRESPONDENT	6001 ARLINGTON BLVD #521	FALLS CHURCH, VA	22044
MANSELL, LILENE	ACTRESS	1650 BROADWAY #302	NEW YORK, NY	10019
MANSFIELD, MIKE	TV DIRECTOR	9 GREAT CHAPEL ST	LONDON W1	ENGLAND
MANSFIELD, PETER	DIRECTOR	DGA, 110 W 57TH ST	NEW YORK, NY	10019
MANSFIELD, ROBERT B	WRITER	8955 BEVERLY BLVD	LOS ANGELES, CA	90048
MANSKER, ERIC	ACTOR	11625 MAYFIELD AVE #6	LOS ANGELES, CA	90049
MANSON, ALAN	ACTOR	200 W 57TH ST #1303	NEW YORK, NY	10019
MANSON, EDDY	COMPOSER-CONDUCTOR	7245 HILLSIDE AVE #216	LOS ANGELES, CA	90046
MANSON, MAURICE	ACTOR	8811 CANOGA AVE #361	CANOGA PARK, CA	91304
MANSON, PAMELA	ACTRESS	20 HIGHTREES HOUSE		
		NIGHTINGALE LN	LONDON SW12	ENGLAND
MANSUR, CEM	CONDUCTOR	ANGLO-SWISS ARTISTS MGMT		
		16 MUSWELL HILL RD, HIGHGATE	LONDON N6 5UG	ENGLAND
MANTEE, PAUL	ACTOR	24632 MALIBU RD	MALIBU, CA	90265
MANTEGNA, JOE	ACTOR	4108 TUJUNGA AVE #7	STUDIO CITY, CA	91604
MANTEL, DUTCH	WRESTLER	NATIONAL WRESTLING ALLIANCE		
		JIM CROCKETT PROMOTIONS		
		421 BRIARBEND DR	CHARLOTTE, NC	28209
MANTEL, KEN	WRESTLING REFEREE	UNIVERSAL WRESTLING FEDERATION		
		MID SOUTH SPORTS, INC		
		5001 SPRING VALLEY RD	DALLAS, TX	75244
MANTELL, HAROLD	WRITER	555 W 57TH ST #1230	NEW YORK, NY	10019
MANTELL, JAMES	ACTOR	2054 PARAMOUNT DR	HOLLYWOOD, CA	90068
MANTELL, JOE	ACTOR	4919 ENCINO AVE	ENCINO, CA	91316
MANTELL, JOHNNY	WRESTLER	WORLD CLASS WRESTLING		
		SOUTHWEST SPORTS, INC		
		DALLAS SPORTATORIUM		
		1000 S INDUSTRIAL BLVD	DALLAS, TX	75207
MANTELL, PAUL	ACTOR	675 HUDSON ST	NEW YORK, NY	10014
MANTHEY, MARLENE	NEWS CORRESPONDENT	3019 CAMBRIDGE PL, NW	WASHINGTON, DC	20007
MANTLEY, JOHN	SCREENWRITER	4121 LONGRIDGE AVE	SHERMAN OAKS, CA	91423
MANTOOTH, DON	ACTOR	9021 MELROSE AVE #304	LOS ANGELES, CA	90069
MANTOOTH, RANDOLPH	ACTOR	9220 SUNSET BLVD #202	LOS ANGELES, CA	90069
MANUEL, ABRAHAM, SR	GUITARIST	ROUTE #2, BOX 128-B		
		BIG SPRINGS RD	CHRISTIANA, TN	37037
MANUEL, ANNE	NEWS CORRESPONDENT	505 5TH ST, NE	WASHINGTON, DC	20002

Name	Occupation	Address	City	Zip/Country
MANUEL, JOSEPH	GUITARIST	ROUTE #2, BOX 128-B		
		BIG SPRINGS RD	CHRISTIANA, TN	37037
MANUEL, LUIS	ACTOR	SHERMAN, 348 S REXFORD DR	BEVERLY HILLS, CA	90212
MANUEL, SAMUEL	COLUMNIST	POST OFFICE BOX 500	WASHINGTON, DC	20044
MANUEL, STEVEN	NEWS CORRESPONDENT	3709 GUNSTON RD	ALEXANDRIA, VA	22302
MANUGUERRA, MATTEO	BARITONE	61 W 62ND ST #6-F	NEW YORK, NY	10023
MANULIS, MARTIN	TV PRODUCER	242 COPA DE ORO RD	LOS ANGELES, CA	90077
MANUS, WILLARD	TV WRITER	248 S LASKY DR	BEVERLY HILLS, CA	90212
MANVELL, ROGER	AUTHOR	BOSTON UNIVERSITY		
		COMMUNICATIONS DEPARTMENT		
		640 COMMONWEALTH AVE	BOSTON, MA	02215
MANVILLE, DORIS	SOPRANO	61 W 62ND ST #6-F	NEW YORK, NY	10023
MANZA, RALPH	ACTOR	550 HYGEIA AVE	LEUCADIA, CA	92024
MANZANERA, PHIL	SINGER	E G RECORDS, 242 E 62ND ST	NEW YORK, NY	10021
MANZANO, SONIA	WRITER	555 W 57TH ST #1230	NEW YORK, NY	10019
MANZAREK, RAY	KEYBOARDIST	3011 LEDGEWOOD DR	HOLLYWOOD, CA	90068
MANZATT, RUSSELL V	SCREENWRITER	19904 SUMMIT DR	TOPANGA, CA	90290
MANZELLA, RAY	ACTOR	6430 SUNSET BLVD #1203	LOS ANGELES, CA	90028
MANZINI, MARIO	ESCAPE ARTIST	POST OFFICE BOX 87	WEST LEBANON, NY	12195
MAPHIS, ROSE LEE	GUITARIST	POST OFFICE BOX 1111		
		MADISON COLLEGE STATION	MADISON, TN	37115
MAR, JEFFREY K	CONDUCTOR	12304 MARSHALL ST	CULVER CITY, CA	90230
MARAIS, JEAN	ACTOR	JEAN NAINCHRIK AGENCE		
		31 AVE CHAMPS-ELYSEES	PARIS 75008	FRANCE
MARAIS, MARC	WRITER	8955 BEVERLY BLVD	LOS ANGELES, CA	90048
MARANNE, ANDRE	ACTOR	SIMONS, 9 NEAL ST	LONDON WC2H 9PU	ENGLAND
MARANTO, GINA	WRITER-EDITOR	DISCOVER/TIME & LIFE BLDG		
		ROCKEFELLER CENTER	NEW YORK, NY	10020
MARANTZ, MICHAEL S	NEWS CORRESPONDENT	5151 WISCONSIN AVE, NW	WASHINGTON, DC	20016
MARASCO, ROBERT	WRITER	555 W 57TH ST #1230	NEW YORK, NY	10019
MARAYNES, ALLAN L	WRITER	555 W 57TH ST #1230	NEW YORK, NY	10019
MARBLE, ALICE	TENNIS	77300 INDIANA	PALM DESERT, CA	92260
MARC, ALESSANDRA	SOPRANO	119 W 57TH ST #1505	NEW YORK, NY	10019
MARC, PETER	ACTOR	141 S EL CAMINO DR #205	BEVERLY HILLS, CA	90212
MARCEAU, MARCEL	PANTOMINIST	THEATRE DES CHAMPS-ELYSES		
		15 AVE MONTAIGNE	PARIS 75008	FRANCE
MARCEAU, SOPHIE	ACTRESS	30 AVE CHARLES DE GAULLE	NEUILLY 92200	FRANCE
MARCEL, JAMES	ACTOR	POST OFFICE BOX 8741	UNIVERSAL CITY, CA	91608
MARCEL, JOY M	NEWS CORRESPONDENT	3980 NORTHGATE PL	WALDORF, MD	20601
MARCEL, TERRY	WRITER-PRODUCER	GASTON BELL CLOSE, RICHMOND	SURREY	ENGLAND
MARCELINO, JAMES	ACTOR	8721 SUNSET BLVD #103	LOS ANGELES, CA	90069
MARCELINO, MARIO	ACTOR-WRITER	1418 N HIGHLAND AVE #102	LOS ANGELES, CA	90028
MARCELLINO, MUZZY	COMPOSER	14633 ROUND VALLEY DR	SHERMAN OAKS, CA	91403
MARCH, ALEX	DIRECTOR-PRODUCER	DGA, 7950 SUNSET BLVD	HOLLYWOOD, CA	90046
MARCH, JACK	TV WRITER	8955 BEVERLY BLVD	LOS ANGELES, CA	90048
MARCH, JUDY	ACTRESS	6605 HOLLYWOOD BLVD #220	HOLLYWOOD, CA	90028
MARCH, LORI	ACTRESS	19 W 44TH ST #1500	NEW YORK, NY	10036
MARCH, MELISAND	WRITER	555 W 57TH ST #1230	NEW YORK, NY	10019
MARCH, PAULA	ACTRESS	6380 WILSHIRE BLVD #1600	LOS ANGELES, CA	90048
MARCHAND, CORINE	ACTRESS	ARTMEDIA, 10 AVE GEORGE V	PARIS 75008	FRANCE
MARCHAND, GUY	ACTOR	DOMAINE DE CLAIRE CT		
		LA TRUCHE	GROSROUVRE 78125	FRANCE
MARCHAND, NANCY	ACTRESS	250 W 57TH ST #803	NEW YORK, NY	10019
MARCHAND-DOMAINE, GUY	ACTOR	DE CLAIRE CT, LA TRUCHE	GROSROUVRE 78125	FRANCE
MARCHESE, JOSEPH V	DIRECTOR	45-15 170TH ST	FLUSHING, NY	11358
MARCHESE, SUSAN M	COMPOSER	28242 REY DE COPAS LN	MALIBU, CA	90265
MARCHETTA, CAMILLE	TV WRITER	11501 HUSTON ST	NORTH HOLLYWOOD, CA	91601
MARCHIANO, SAL	SPORTSCASTER	ESPN, ESPN PLAZA	BRISTOL, CT	06010
MARCHIONE, MARK A	NEWS CORRESPONDENT	5420 31ST ST, NW	WASHINGTON, DC	20016
MARCHITTO, J THOMAS	NEWS CORRESPONDENT	ABC-TV, NEWS DEPARTMENT		
		1717 DE SALES ST, NW	WASHINGTON, DC	20036
MARCIANO, LINDA	ACTRESS	120 ENTERPRISE	SECAUCUS, NY	07094
MARCIL, ALLAN J	TV PRODUCER	ICM, 8899 BEVERLY BLVD	LOS ANGELES, CA	90048
MARCIONA, GENE	WRITER	555 W 57TH ST #1230	NEW YORK, NY	10019
MARCIONE, GENE	TV WRITER-DIRECTOR	7993 SANGAMON AVE	SUN VALLEY, CA	91352
MARCIONE, JAMES	DIRECTOR	19805 NEEDLES ST	CHATSWORTH, CA	91311
MARCO, PAUL	ACTOR	8820 SUNSET BLVD #ANB	LOS ANGELES, CA	90069
MARCOTT, MIGUEL	ACTOR	1605 N CAHUENGA BLVD #202	LOS ANGELES, CA	90028
MARCOVICCI, ANDREA	ACTRESS-SINGER	STONE, 1052 CAROL DR	LOS ANGELES, CA	90069
MARCOVICI, SILVIA	VIOLINIST	MARIEDL ANDERS ARTISTS MGMT		
		535 EL CAMINO DEL MAR ST	SAN FRANCISCO, CA	94121
MARCROFT, RONALD	ACTOR	1443 HILCREST AVE	GLENDALE, CA	91202
MARCUS, ALAN R	WRITER	8955 BEVERLY BLVD	LOS ANGELES, CA	90048
MARCUS, ANN	TV WRITER	EISENBACH-GREENE, INC		
		760 N LA CIENEGA BLVD	LOS ANGELES, CA	90069
MARCUS, DEVERA	ACTRESS-WRITER	7461 BEVERLY BLVD #400	LOS ANGELES, CA	90036
MARCUS, DIANA KOPALD	WRITER	8955 BEVERLY BLVD	LOS ANGELES, CA	90048
MARCUS, ELLIS	WRITER-PRODUCER	15660 WOODFIELD PL	SHERMAN OAKS, CA	91403
MARCUS, JERRY	CARTOONIST	KING FEATURES SYNDICATE		
		235 E 45TH ST	NEW YORK, NY	10017
MARCUS, KEN	PHOTOGRAPHER	6916 MELROSE AVE	LOS ANGELES, CA	90038
MARCUS, LAWRENCE B	TV WRITER	ICM, 8899 BEVERLY BLVD	LOS ANGELES, CA	90048
MARCUS, LYDIA	COMPOSER	2019 STANLEY HILLS DR	LOS ANGELES, CA	90046

Name	Occupation	Address	City	Zip/Country
MARCUS, MICHAEL A	NEWS CORRESPONDENT	400 N CAPITOL ST, NW	WASHINGTON, DC	20001
MARCUS, MIKE	TALENT AGENT	1888 CENTURY PARK E #1400	LOS ANGELES, CA	90067
MARCUS, RALPH J	NEWS CORRESPONDENT	2139 WISCONSIN AVE, NW	WASHINGTON, DC	20007
MARCUS, RICHARD	ACTOR	11726 SAN VICENTE BLVD #300	LOS ANGELES, CA	90049
MARCUS, RICHARD	ACTOR	9220 SUNSET BLVD #301	LOS ANGELES, CA	90069
MARCUS, RICHARD L	TV WRITER	8955 BEVERLY BLVD	LOS ANGELES, CA	90048
MARCUS, ROBERT	WRITER	8955 BEVERLY BLVD	LOS ANGELES, CA	90048
MARCUS, ROBERT L	WRITER	555 W 57TH ST #1230	NEW YORK, NY	10019
MARCY, STEVEN K	NEWS CORRESPONDENT	629 E CAPITOL ST, NW	WASHINGTON, DC	20003
MARDEN, MARY CARROLL	PHOTO EDITOR	PEOPLE/TIME & LIFE BLDG		
		ROCKEFELLER CENTER	NEW YORK, NY	10020
MARDEN, MICHAEL	TV EXECUTIVE	CBS-TV, 7800 BEVERLY BLVD	LOS ANGELES, CA	90036
MARDER, JEFF	COMEDIAN	EAI, 2211 INDUSTRIAL BLVD	SARASOTA, FL	33580
MARDER, MURRAY	NEWS CORRESPONDENT	711 6TH ST, SW	WASHINGTON, DC	20024
MARDIS, BOBBY	ACTOR	8484 WILSHIRE BLVD #235	BEVERLY HILLS, CA	90211
MARDONES, BENNY	SINGER	PANACEA, 132 NASSAU ST	NEW YORK, NY	10038
MAREK, MARK	CARTOONIST	THE NATIONAL LAMPOON		
		635 MADISON AVE	NEW YORK, NY	10022
MAREK'S, LOU SQUEEZE PLAY	MUSICAL GROUP	3928 SHRINE PARK	LEAVENWORTH, KS	66048
MAREVIL, PHILLIPPE	ACTOR	28 RUE DES SABLONS	PARIS 75116	FRANCE
MARFIELD, DWIGHT H	ACTOR	45 W 74TH ST	NEW YORK, NY	10023
MARGALIT, ISRAELA	PIANIST	CAMI, 165 W 57TH ST	NEW YORK, NY	10019
MARGARETTE, SUSAN	CASTING DIRECTOR	6815 WILLOUGHBY AVE #105	LOS ANGELES, CA	90038
MARGASAK, LAWRENCE N	NEWS CORRESPONDENT	10306 BRUNSWICK AVE	SILVER SPRING, MD	20902
MARGEY, JACKIE	CASTING DIRECTOR	THE CASTING CONNECTION		
		9903 SANTA MONICA BLVD	BEVERLY HILLS, CA	90212
MARGINAL MAN	ROCK & ROLL GROUP	POST OFFICE BOX 2428	EL SEGUNDO, CA	90245
MARGO, LARRY	ACTOR	14526 1/2 DICKENS ST	SHERMAN OAKS, CA	91403
MARGO, PHILIP F	TV WRITER	8955 BEVERLY BLVD	LOS ANGELES, CA	90048
MARGOLESE, E M	ACTOR	4721 LAUREL CANYON BLVD #211	NORTH HOLLYWOOD, CA	91607
MARGOLIES, MARJORIE	NEWS CORRESPONDENT	NBC-TV, NEWS DEPARTMENT		
		4001 NEBRASKA AVE, NW	WASHINGTON, DC	20016
MARGOLIN, ARNOLD	WRITER-PRODUCER	3411 LA FALDA PL	HOLLYWOOD, CA	90068
MARGOLIN, JAMES	ACTOR	9465 WILSHIRE BLVD #616	BEVERLY HILLS, CA	90212
MARGOLIN, JANET	ACTRESS	7667 SEATTLE PL	LOS ANGELES, CA	90046
MARGOLIN, STUART	ACTOR-DIRECTOR	2809 2ND ST #1	SANTA MONICA, CA	90405
MARGOLIS, ESTHER	WRITER	555 W 57TH ST #1230	NEW YORK, NY	10019
MARGOLIS, HERB	PRODUCER	MCA/UNIVERSAL STUDIOS, INC		
		100 UNIVERSAL CITY PLAZA #473	UNIVERSAL CITY, CA	91608
MARGOLIS, HERBERT F	STORY EDITOR	5409 KATHERINE AVE	VAN NUYS, CA	91401
MARGOLIS, JACK S	WRITER	1331 MILLER DR	LOS ANGELES, CA	90069
MARGOLIS, JEFF	TV DIRECTOR	1339 SCHUYLER RD	BEVERLY HILLS, CA	90210
MARGOLIS, JONATHAN C	NEWS CORRESPONDENT	14 CRESCENT PL	TAKOMA PARK, MD	20012
MARGOLIS, PAUL B	TV WRITER	8955 BEVERLY BLVD	LOS ANGELES, CA	90048
MARGOLYES, MIRIAM	ACTRESS	FEAST, 43-A PRINCESS RD	LONDON NW1	ENGLAND
MARGULIES, HARRIET	TV WRITER	8955 BEVERLY BLVD	LOS ANGELES, CA	90048
MARGULIES, HOWARD	CARTOONIST	THE HOUSTON POST		
		4747 SOUTHWEST FREEWAY	HOUSTON, TX	77001
MARGULIES, LEE	NEWS WRITER	L A TIMES NEWSPAPER		
		TIMES MIRROR SQUARE	LOS ANGELES, CA	90053
MARGULIES, STAN	TV PRODUCER	16965 STRAWBERRY DR	ENCINO, CA	91316
MARIANO, ANN B	NEWS CORRESPONDENT	3355 18TH ST, NW	WASHINGTON, DC	20010
MARIANO, IRENE	CASTING DIRECTOR	3970 OVERLAND AVE #700	CULVER CITY, CA	90230
MARIANO, PATTI	ACTRESS	6538 FOUNTAIN AVE #5	LOS ANGELES, CA	90028
MARIAS, MARK	ACTRESS	6380 WILSHIRE BLVD #1600	LOS ANGELES, CA	90048
MARICHAL, JUAN	BASEBALL	ED HACHE 3, PISO ESTE		
		KENNEDY AVE	SANTA DOMINGO	DOM REP
MARIE, ANNE	SINGER	SEE - ANNE MARIE		
MARIE, ANNE	ACTRESS-MODEL	SEE - ANNE-MARIE		
MARIE, DIANE	ACTRESS	8831 SUNSET BLVD #402	LOS ANGELES, CA	90069
MARIE, KRISTEN	ACTRESS	NBC-TV, "ANOTHER WORLD"		
		30 ROCKEFELLER PLAZA	NEW YORK, NY	10112
MARIE, LISA	ACTRESS	LIGHT, 113 N ROBERTSON BLVD	LOS ANGELES, CA	90048
MARIE, ROSE	ACTRESS	6916 CHISOLM AVE	VAN NUYS, CA	91406
MARIE, TEENA	SINGER	GTI, 1700 BROADWAY, 10TH FLOOR	NEW YORK, NY	10019
MARIE, TINA	ACTRESS	1450 BELFAST DR	LOS ANGELES, CA	90069
MARIELL, JEANE-PIERRE	ACTOR	FRANCE DEGAND AGENCE		
		94 RUE LAURISTON	PARIS 95116	FRANCE
MARIENBERG, EVELYN S	TV WRITER	8955 BEVERLY BLVD	LOS ANGELES, CA	90048
MARILLION	ROCK & ROLL GROUP	THE STATION AGENCY		
		132 LIVERPOOL RD	LONDON N1 1LA	ENGLAND
MARILYN	SINGER	33-34 CLEVELAND ST	LONDON W1	ENGLAND
MARIN, ANDREW PETER	SCREENWRITER	525 24TH ST	SANTA MONICA, CA	90402
MARIN, MINDY	CASTING DIRECTOR	4000 WARNER BLVD #104-E	BURBANK, CA	91522
MARIN, RICHARD "CHEECH"	ACTOR-COMEDIAN	21625 WOODLAND CREST DR	WOODLAND HILLS, CA	91364
MARIN, RIKKI	ACTRESS	21625 WOODLAND CREST DR	WOODLAND HILLS, CA	91365
MARIN, RUSS	ACTOR	6430 SUNSET BLVD #701	LOS ANGELES, CA	90028
MARINARO, ED	ACTOR-FOOTBALL	1466 N DOHENY DR	LOS ANGELES, CA	90069
MARINO, AMERIGO	COMPOSER	POST OFFICE BOX 2125	BIRMINGHAM, AL	35201
MARINO, FRANK	SINGER	POST OFFICE BOX 836	NYACK, NY	10960
MARION, RICHARD	ACTOR	149 N GRAMERCY PL	LOS ANGELES, CA	90004
MARIOTTI, DEBORAH	GUITARIST	IAPR, KINCORA, BEER RD, SEATON	DEVON	ENGLAND
MARIS, ADA	ACTRESS	11726 SAN VICENTE BLVD #300	LOS ANGELES, CA	90049
MARIUCCI, JOHN	DIRECTOR	DGA, 110 W 57TH ST	NEW YORK, NY	10019
MARK, DANIEL J	COMPOSER	POST OFFICE BOX 1206	STUDIO CITY, CA	91604

Name	Occupation	Address	City	Zip
MARK, DAVID	WRITER	555 W 57TH ST #1230	NEW YORK, NY	10019
MARK, PETER A	CONDUCTOR	OPERA, 261 W BUTE ST	NORFOLK, VA	23510
MARK, ROSS F	NEWS CORRESPONDENT	2039 NEW HAMPSHIRE AVE #103, NW	WASHINGTON, DC	20009
MARK, TAMARA	ACTRESS	2121 AVE OF THE STARS #410	LOS ANGELES, CA	90067
MARKEL, BRAD EDWARD	PHOTOGRAPHER	1341 SOUTH CAROLINA AVE, SE	WASHINGTON, DC	20003
MARKELL, DAVID	ACTOR	225 N CORDOVA ST #A	BURBANK, CA	91505
MARKELL, ROBERT	TV EXECUTIVE	CBS-TV, 6121 SUNSET BLVD	LOS ANGELES, CA	90028
MARKELL, ROBERT	TV PRODUCER	28 SIDNEY PL	BROOKLYN, NY	11201
MARKEN, KRISTINA G	WRITER	555 W 57TH ST #1230	NEW YORK, NY	10019
MARKES, DIANA	ACTRESS	3860 BERRY CT	STUDIO CITY, CA	91604
MARKES, LARRY W, JR	TV WRITER	3860 BERRY CT	STUDIO CITY, CA	91604
MARKEY, JUDY	HUMORIST-COLUMNIST	NEWS AMERICA SYNDICATE		
		1703 KAISER AVE	IRVINE, CA	92714
MARKHAM, DANIEL C	WRITER	555 W 57TH ST #1230	NEW YORK, NY	10019
MARKHAM, MONTE	ACTOR	POST OFFICE BOX 4200	MALIBU, CA	90265
MARKHAM, PORK CHOP	DRUMMER	510 HERITAGE DR #168	MADISON, TN	37115
MARKHAM & BROADWAY	COMEDY DUO	CAMI, 165 W 57TH ST	NEW YORK, NY	10019
MARKLE, FLETCHER	WRITER-PRODUCER	351 CONGRESS PL	PASADENA, CA	91105
MARKLIN, JEANNE	PHOTOGRAPHER	2411 N ROOSEVELT ST	ARLINGTON, VA	22207
MARKLIN, PETER	ACTOR	100 W 9TH ST	NEW YORK, NY	10011
MARKMAN, PACY	TV WRITER	8955 BEVERLY BLVD	LOS ANGELES, CA	90048
MARKO, LARRY	ACTOR	6380 WILSHIRE BLVD #1600	LOS ANGELES, CA	90048
MARKO, VICTOR	ACTOR	721 N LA BREA AVE #200	LOS ANGELES, CA	90038
MARKOE, MERRILL	TV WRITER	ICM, 40 W 57TH ST	NEW YORK, NY	10019
MARKOV, ALBERT	VIOLINIST	11 W 57TH ST #1203	NEW YORK, NY	10019
MARKOV, ALEXANDER	VIOLINIST	CAMI, 165 W 57TH ST	NEW YORK, NY	10019
MARKOVA, JIRINA	SOPRANO	61 W 62ND ST #6-F	NEW YORK, NY	10023
MARKOVA, JULIANNA	PIANIST	201 W 54TH ST #4-C	NEW YORK, NY	10019
MARKOWITZ, BRAD B	TV WRITER	835 4TH ST #309	SANTA MONICA, CA	90403
MARKOWITZ, GARY L	SCREENWRITER	110 S WESTGATE AVE	LOS ANGELES, CA	90049
MARKOWITZ, MITCHELL	TV WRITER	428 3/4 N ALTA VISTA BLVD	LOS ANGELES, CA	90036
MARKOWITZ, RICHARD	COMPOSER-CONDUCTOR	POST OFFICE BOX 24309	LOS ANGELES, CA	90024
MARKOWITZ, ROBERT L	WRITER-PRODUCER	3037 FRANKLIN CANYON DR	BEVERLY HILLS, CA	90210
MARKOWSKI & CEDRONE	PIANO DUO	GEWALD, 58 W 58TH ST	NEW YORK, NY	10019
MARKS, ALAN	PIANIST	SHAW CONCERTS, 1995 BROADWAY	NEW YORK, NY	10023
MARKS, ALFRED	COMEDIAN	BURNETT, 42 GRAFTON HOUSE		
		2-3 GOLDEN SQ	LONDON W1	ENGLAND
MARKS, ARTHUR	WRITER-PRODUCER	20010 WELLS DR	WOODLAND HILLS, CA	91364
MARKS, BARBARA J	WRITER	8955 BEVERLY BLVD	LOS ANGELES, CA	90048
MARKS, BEAU E	FILM DIRECTOR	5439 AMIGO AVE	TARZANA, CA	91356
MARKS, BRAD	TV WRITER	8955 BEVERLY BLVD	LOS ANGELES, CA	90048
MARKS, DAVE	TV DIRECTOR	1470 S BEVERLY DR	LOS ANGELES, CA	90035
MARKS, DENNIS G	WRITER	8955 BEVERLY BLVD	LOS ANGELES, CA	90048
MARKS, GERTRUDE ROSS	WRITER	11822 KEARSARGE ST	LOS ANGELES, CA	90049
MARKS, GUY	ACTOR	9000 SUNSET BLVD #502	LOS ANGELES, CA	90069
MARKS, JAMES WHIPPLE	PHOTOGRAPHER	1737 HARVARD ST, NW	WASHINGTON, DC	20009
MARKS, JOAN	TV WRITER	8955 BEVERLY BLVD	LOS ANGELES, CA	90048
MARKS, JOEY	ACTOR	KELMAN, 7813 SUNSET BLVD	LOS ANGELES, CA	90046
MARKS, LARRY B	TV DIRECTOR	248 N HEWLETT AVE	MERRICK, NY	11566
MARKS, LAURENCE	WRITER	5950 ROD AVE	WOODLAND HILLS, CA	91367
MARKS, LOUIS	TV WRITER-PRODUCER	MORRIS, 147-149 WARDOUR ST	LONDON W1V 3TB	ENGLAND
MARKS, MARIANNE	ACTRESS-MODEL	KOHNER, 9169 SUNSET BLVD	LOS ANGELES, CA	90069
MARKS, MICHAEL J	TV WRITER	8955 BEVERLY BLVD	LOS ANGELES, CA	90048
MARKS, PAUL D	WRITER	8955 BEVERLY BLVD	LOS ANGELES, CA	90048
MARKS, RICHARD	FILM EDITOR	648 ASHLAND AVE	SANTA MONICA, CA	90405
MARKS, S N	WRITER	8955 BEVERLY BLVD	LOS ANGELES, CA	90048
MARKS, WALTER	WRITER	555 W 57TH ST #1230	NEW YORK, NY	10019
MARKS, WILLIAM	WRITER	8955 BEVERLY BLVD	LOS ANGELES, CA	90048
MARKUS, DANIEL S	TALENT AGENT	ALIVE ENTERTAINMENT AGENCY		
		1775 BROADWAY, 7TH FLOOR	NEW YORK, NY	10019
MARKUS, JERRY	TV DIRECTOR-PRODUCER	12969 GREENLEAF ST	STUDIO CITY, CA	91604
MARKUS, JOHN	TV WRITER-PRODUCER	445 BEDFORD DR #PH	BEVERLY HILLS, CA	90210
MARKUS, JOHN A	TV WRITER	855 19TH ST	SANTA MONICA, CA	90403
MARKUS, LEAH	TV WRITER	9200 SUNSET BLVD #PH-25	LOS ANGELES, CA	90069
MARKUS, MARK J	COMPOSER	12969 GREENLEAF ST	STUDIO CITY, CA	91604
MARKUS & ROSITA	STRONG MAN ACT	HALL, 138 FROG HOLLOW RD	CHURCHVILLE, PA	18966
MARKUSON, STEPHEN	BASSO-BARITONE	45 W 60TH ST #4-K	NEW YORK, NY	10023
MARLAND, DOUGLAS	TV WRITER-DIRECTOR	CBS-TV, "AS THE WORLD TURNS"		
		51 W 52ND ST	NEW YORK, NY	10019
MARLAS, DENNIS C	DIRECTOR	447 SUNSET RD	WINNETKA, IL	60093
MARLBOROUGH, DEBRA	ACTRESS	4043 N NORA AVE	COVINA, CA	91722
MARLENS, NEAL	TV WRITER	3621 LANKERSHIM BLVD	LOS ANGELES, CA	90068
MARLER, RALPH W	NEWS CORRESPONDENT	1417 N INGLEWOOD ST	ARLINGTON, VA	22205
MARLES, BILL	COMPOSER	14748 MAGNOLIA BLVD #C	SHERMAN OAKS, CA	91403
MARLETTE, DOUG	CARTOONIST	POST OFFICE BOX 32188	CHARLOTTE, NC	28232
MARLIN, CAL A	NEWS CORRESPONDENT	CBS NEWS, 2020 "M" ST, NW	WASHINGTON, DC	20036
MARLIN-JONES, DAVEY	DIRECTOR	DGA, 110 W 57TH ST	NEW YORK, NY	10019
MARLOW, JEAN	ACTRESS	HAMILTON, 21 GOODGE ST	LONDON W1	ENGLAND
MARLOW, JESS	NEWS CORRESPONDENT	KNXT-TV, 6121 SUNSET BLVD	LOS ANGELES, CA	90028
MARLOW, LORRI	ACTRESS	122 S MAPLE DR #A	BEVERLY HILLS, CA	90212
MARLOW, NANCY	ACTRESS	11030 VENTURA BLVD #3	STUDIO CITY, CA	91604
MARLOW, RUTH L	NEWS CORRESPONDENT	COMMERCIAL DR	SPRINGFIELD, VA	22159
MARLOWE, CHRIS	ACTOR	1930 CENTURY PARK W #303	LOS ANGELES, CA	90067
MARLOWE, CURTISS	ACTOR	3800 BARHAM BLVD #303	LOS ANGELES, CA	90068
MARLOWE, DAVID	WRITER	8955 BEVERLY BLVD	LOS ANGELES, CA	90048

Name	Occupation	Address	City	Zip
MARLOWE, GENE	NEWS CORRESPONDENT	2301 N STAFFORD ST	ARLINGTON, VA	22207
MARLOWE, JONAS	ACTOR	3800 BARHAM BLVD #303	LOS ANGELES, CA	90068
MARLOWE, LOUIS J	DIRECTOR	2398 VIA MARIPOSA #3-C W	LAGUNA HILLS, CA	92653
MARLOWE, LOUISE S	PHOTOGRAPHER	1400 S JOYCE ST	ARLINGTON, VA	22202
MARLOWE, PAT	ACTRESS	3130 ELLINGTON DR	LOS ANGELES, CA	90068
MARLOWE, SCOTT	ACTOR	11032 MOORPARK ST #12	NORTH HOLLYWOOD, CA	91602
MARLOWE, WILLIAM	ACTOR	POST OFFICE BOX 130, HOWE	EAST SUSSEX BN3 6QU	ENGLAND
MARMELSTEIN, LINDA	WRITER	555 W 57TH ST #1230	NEW YORK, NY	10019
MARMER, MIKE	TV WRITER	8955 BEVERLY BLVD	LOS ANGELES, CA	90048
MARMON, LUCRETIA	NEWS CORRESPONDENT	4921 CUMBERLAND AVE	CHEVY CHASE, MD	20815
MARMOR, HELEN	TV PRODUCER	NBC TELEVISION NETWORK		
		30 ROCKEFELLER PLAZA	NEW YORK, NY	10112
MARMOREK, EILEEN	ACTRESS	9047 LANGDON AVE #23	SEPULVEDA, CA	91343
MARMORSTEIN, MALCOLM	WRITER	2350 HOLLYRIDGE DR	LOS ANGELES, CA	90068
MARMY, MAE	ACTRESS	435 S LA CIENEGA BLVD #108	LOS ANGELES, CA	90048
MARNER, EUGENE	WRITER-PRODUCER	141 BERGEN ST	BROOKLYN, NY	11217
MAROCCO, FRANK	COMPOSER	7063 WHITAKER AVE	VAN NUYS, CA	91406
MAROLAKOS, JOHN	ACTOR	707 SANFORD AVE	NEWARK, NJ	07106
MARON, ALFRED	ACTOR	50 LANGHAM ST #1	LONDON W1	ENGLAND
MARONEY, KELLI	ACTRESS	1930 CENTURY PARK W #303	LOS ANGELES, CA	90067
MAROON, FRED J	PHOTOGRAPHER	2725 "P" ST, NW	WASHINGTON, DC	20007
MAROONEY, JAMES J	DIRECTOR	DGA, 110 W 57TH ST	NEW YORK, NY	10019
MAROSS, JOE	ACTOR	336 S DOHENY DR #5	BEVERLY HILLS, CA	90211
MAROTTA, MONICA JUNG	WRITER	23049 LEONORA DR	WOODLAND HILLS, CA	91367
MARQUAND, CHRISTIAN	ACTOR	45 RUE DE BELLE CHASSE	PARIS 75007	FRANCE
MARQUAND, RICHARD	FILM DIRECTOR	A D PETERS & CO, LTD		
		10 BUCKINGHAM ST	LONDON WC2	ENGLAND
MARQUAND, SERGE	ACTOR	47 RUE VIELLE DU TEMPLE	PARIS 75004	FRANCE
MARQUES, DANNY	GUITARIST	230 ROCKLAND RD	HENDERSONVILLE, TN	37075
MARQUETTE, JACQUES	DIRECTOR	DGA, 7950 SUNSET BLVD	LOS ANGELES, CA	90046
MARQUETTE, JOSEPH C	PHOTOGRAPHER	REUTERS NEWS PICTURES		
		1333 "H" ST, NW	WASHINGTON, DC	20005
MARQUEZ, HUDSON	WRITER	8955 BEVERLY BLVD	LOS ANGELES, CA	90048
MARR, OCEANA	ACTRESS	721 N LA BREA AVE #200	LOS ANGELES, CA	90038
MARR, SALLY K	ACTRESS	8485 MELROSE PL #E	LOS ANGELES, CA	90069
MARRANT, ALEXANDER	WRITER	8955 BEVERLY BLVD	LOS ANGELES, CA	90048
MARRAZZO, RANDI	SOPRANO	CONE, 221 W 57TH ST	NEW YORK, NY	10019
MARRERO, FRANK	DIRECTOR-PRODUCER	236 W 52ND ST	NEW YORK, NY	10019
MARRIOTT, MICHAEL E	PHOTOJOURNALIST	737 LAWTON ST	MC LEAN, VA	22101
MARRIS, WEBB R	WRITER	17841 PORTO MARINA WY	PACIFIC PALISADES, CA	90272
MARROW, MARLETA	ACTRESS	247 S BEVERLY DR #102	BEVERLY HILLS, CA	90210
MARRS, DUANE	GUITARIST	1258 SIOUX TERR	MADISON, TN	37115
MARRS, LARRY	GUITARIST	1258 SIOUX TERR	MADISON, TN	37115
MARS, KENNETH	ACTOR	9000 SUNSET BLVD #801	LOS ANGELES, CA	90069
MARSAC, MAURICE	ACTOR	3972 SUNSWEPT DR	STUDIO CITY, CA	91604
MARSALIS, BRANFORD	SAXOPHONIST	POST OFFICE BOX 55398	WASHINGTON, DC	20040
MARSALIS, DELFEAYO	RECORD PRODUCER	BRAWYNN MUSIC COMPANY		
		8318 HICKORY ST	NEW ORLEANS, LA	70118
MARSALIS, ELLIS	PIANIST	POST OFFICE BOX 19004		
		MID CITY STATION	NEW ORLEANS, LA	70118
MARSALIS, WYNTON	TRUMPETER	POST OFFICE BOX 55398	WASHINGTON, DC	20040
MARSCH, LINDA-ANN	SPORTS REPORTER	SPORTS ILLUSTRATED MAGAZINE		
		TIME & LIFE BUILDING		
		ROCKEFELLER CENTER	NEW YORK, NY	10020
MARSDEN, ROY	ACTOR	DAWSON, 31 KINGS RD	LONDON SW3 4RP	ENGLAND
MARSEE, SUSANNE	MEZZO-SOPRANO	61 W 62ND ST #6-F	NEW YORK, NY	10023
MARSELLS, THE	ROCK & ROLL GROUP	25 HUNTINGTON AVE #420	BOSTON, MA	02116
MARSH, BRENDA	NEWS CORRESPONDENT	DISCOVER/TIME & LIFE BLDG		
		ROCKEFELLER CENTER	NEW YORK, NY	10020
MARSH, DONALD T	MUSIC ARRANGER	526 FOX HUNT CIR	HIGHLANDS RANCH, CO	80126
MARSH, EARLE F	AUTHOR	SHOWTIME, 1633 BROADWAY	NEW YORK, NY	10019
MARSH, JEAN	ACTRESS	THE PHEASANT, CHINNOR HILL	OXFORDSHIRE OX9 4BN	ENGLAND
MARSH, JOAN	ACTRESS	1329 PLAZA DE SONADORES	MONTECITO, CA	93108
MARSH, KEITH	ACTOR	BRYAN DREW, LTD		
		MEZZANINE QUADRANT HOUSE		
		80-82 REGENT ST	LONDON W1	ENGLAND
MARSH, LINDA	ACTRESS	4041 ALTA MESA DR	STUDIO CITY, CA	91604
MARSH, LINDA	TV WRITER	8955 BEVERLY BLVD	LOS ANGELES, CA	90048
MARSH, MARIAN	ACTRESS	POST OFFICE BOX 1	PALM DESERT, CA	92260
MARSH, MICHELE	ACTRESS	10920 WILSHIRE BLVD #220	LOS ANGELES, CA	90024
MARSH, RAY	TV DIRECTOR-PRODUCER	4721 GREENBUSH AVE	SHERMAN OAKS, CA	91423
MARSH, ROBERT	MUSIC CRITIC	1825 N LINCOLN PLAZA	CHICAGO, IL	60614
MARSH, RONALD	TV PRODUCER	BBC-TV CENTRE, WOOD LN		
		SHEPHERDS BUSH	LONDON W12	ENGLAND
MARSH, SIDNEY C	TV WRITER	8955 BEVERLY BLVD	LOS ANGELES, CA	90048
MARSH, TERENCE	SCREENWRITER	8955 BEVERLY BLVD	LOS ANGELES, CA	90048
MARSHACK, MEGAN R	WRITER	555 W 57TH ST #1230	NEW YORK, NY	10019
MARSHAK, DARRYL A	TALENT AGENT	3800 BARHAM BLVD #303	LOS ANGELES, CA	90068
MARSHAL, JOHN R	NEWS CORRESPONDENT	2139 WISCONSIN AVE, NW	WASHINGTON, DC	20007
MARSHALL, ALAN	ACTOR	6625 SUNSET BLVD #525-A	HOLLYWOOD, CA	90068
MARSHALL, ARMINA	PROD-ACT-WRI	THEATRE GUILD PRODUCTIONS		
		226 W 47TH ST	NEW YORK, NY	10036
MARSHALL, BRYAN	ACTOR	ROSE COTTAGE, MILTON FIELDS		
		CHALFONT SAINT GILES	BUCKS	ENGLAND

Name	Occupation	Address	City	Zip/Country
MARSHALL, BURT	ACTOR	6145 GLEN TOWER ST	LOS ANGELES, CA	90068
MARSHALL, DAVID B	DIRECTOR	146 CENTRAL PARK W #22-E	NEW YORK, NY	10023
MARSHALL, DON	ACTOR	9021 MELROSE AVE #304	LOS ANGELES, CA	90069
MARSHALL, E G	ACTOR	BRYAN LAKE RD & OREGON ROAD		
		RURAL FARM DELIVERY #2	MOUNT KISCO, NY	10549
MARSHALL, EMILY PURDUM	TV WRITER	8955 BEVERLY BLVD	LOS ANGELES, CA	90048
MARSHALL, FRANK	FILM PRODUCER	AMBLIN ENTERPRISES		
		100 UNIVERSAL CITY PLAZA	UNIVERSAL CITY, CA	91608
MARSHALL, GARRY	WRITER-PRODUCER	4055 TUJUNGA AVE	STUDIO CITY, CA	91604
MARSHALL, GEORGE E	FILM DIRECTOR	554 WESTBOURNE DR	LOS ANGELES, CA	90048
MARSHALL, GEORGE LEE	WRITER	8955 BEVERLY BLVD	LOS ANGELES, CA	90048
MARSHALL, JAMES ARTHUR	CELLIST	4000 ANDERSON RD #38	NASHVILLE, TN	37217
MARSHALL, JILL A	PIANIST	111 WHITSETT RD	NASHVILLE, TN	37211
MARSHALL, LARRY P	CONDUCTOR	4470 VENTURA CANYON AVE	SHERMAN OAKS, CA	91423
MARSHALL, MELORA	ACTRESS	1419 N TOPANGA CANYON BLVD	TOPANGA, CA	90290
MARSHALL, MIKE	ACTOR	11 AVE D'EYLAU	PARIS 75116	FRANCE
MARSHALL, MORT	ACTOR	363 E 76TH ST	NEW YORK, NY	10021
MARSHALL, NEAL WILLIAM	TV WRITER-PRODUCER	4115 WOODCLIFF RD	SHERMAN OAKS, CA	91403
MARSHALL, PENNY	ACTRESS	1849 SAWTELLE BLVD #500	LOS ANGELES, CA	90025
MARSHALL, PETER	ACTOR-TV HOST	16714 OAK VIEW DR	ENCINO, CA	91436
MARSHALL, PETER	MUSICIAN	3530 GRAND VIEW BLVD	LOS ANGELES, CA	90066
MARSHALL, RAY	TV WRITER-PRODUCER	OPIX, 5 CARLISLE ST	LONDON W1	ENGLAND
MARSHALL, ROB DOYLE	ACTOR	1 GLENWOOD RD	SCARSDALE, NY	10583
MARSHALL, ROGER	SCREENWRITER	20 MARCHMONT RD, RICHMOND	SURREY	ENGLAND
MARSHALL, SANDRA	ACTRESS	FERRIS, 5915 METROPLITAN PLAZA	LOS ANGELES, CA	90036
MARSHALL, SANDRA J	ACTRESS	427 N CANON DR #205	BEVERLY HILLS, CA	90210
MARSHALL, SARAH	ACTRESS	7466 BEVERLY BLVD #205	LOS ANGELES, CA	90036
MARSHALL, STEVE	TV WRITER	10100 SANTA MONICA BLVD #348	LOS ANGELES, CA	90067
MARSHALL, TIM	TV DIRECTOR	12-B KINGS GARDENS		
		WEST END LN	LONDON NW6 4PU	ENGLAND
MARSHALL, TRUDY	ACTRESS	343 N LA BREA AVE	LOS ANGELES, CA	90036
MARSHALL, WILLIAM	FILM PRODUCER	11351 DRONFIELD AVE	PACOIMA, CA	91331
MARSHALL TUCKER BAND	ROCK & ROLL GROUP	SEE - TUCKER, MARSHALL, BAND		
MARSICO, FRANK N	NEWS CORRESPONDENT	2139 WISCONSIN AVE, NW	WASHINGTON, DC	20007
MARSILII, PEGGY C	NEWS CORRESPONDENT	1805 S QUINCY ST	ARLINGTON, VA	22204
MARSLAND, KEVIN	TV DIRECTOR	112 WARDOUR ST	LONDON W1V 3LD	ENGLAND
MARSTON, JOEL	ACTOR	9424 LA TUNA CYN RD	SUN VALLEY, CA	91352
MARSTON, MERLIN	ACTOR	6721 LEXINGTON AVE #7	LOS ANGELES, CA	90038
MARTEL, EDMOND J	COMPOSER-CONDUCTOR	5136 TOPANGA CANYON BLVD	WOODLAND HILLS, CA	91367
MARTEL, GENE	DIRECTOR	108 LAWN TERR	MAMARONECK, NY	10543
MARTEL, LINDA	SINGER	BROWN, 3011 WOODWAY LN	COLUMBIA, SC	29206
MARTEL, RAY	ACTOR	5330 LANKERSHIM BLVD #210	NORTH HOLLYWOOD, CA	91601
MARTEL, RICK	WRESTLER	POST OFFICE BOX 3859	STAMFORD, CT	06905
MARTEL, SHERRI	WRESTLING VALET	AMERICAN WRESTLING ASSOC		
		MINNEAPLOIS WRESTLING		
		10001 WAYZATA BLVD	MINNETONKA, MN	55345
MARTEL, WILLIAM	ACTOR	10000 RIVERSIDE DR #3	TOLUCA LAKE, CA	91602
MARTELL, DONNA	ACTRESS	8721 SUNSET BLVD #200	LOS ANGELES, CA	90069
MARTELL, GREGG	ACTOR	8644 CAVEL ST	DOWNEY, CA	90242
MARTELL, LINDA	SINGER	POST OFFICE BOX 5702	COLUMBIA, SC	29206
MARTENS, RICA	ACTRESS	325 E 57TH ST	NEW YORK, NY	10022
MARTENSON, LESLIE H	TV DIRECTOR	2288 COLDWATER CANYON DR	BEVERLY HILLS, CA	90210
MARTER, IAN	ACTOR	74 NEW BOND ST	LONDON W1Y 9DA	ENGLAND
MARTH, FRANK	ACTOR	8538 EASTWOOD RD	LOS ANGELES, CA	90046
MARTIKA	ACTRESS	11350 VENTURA BLVD #206	STUDIO CITY, CA	91604
MARTIN, ALAN	WRESTLER	NATIONAL WRESTLING ALLIANCE		
		JIM CROCKETT PROMOTIONS		
		421 BRIARBEND DR	CHARLOTTE, NC	28209
MARTIN, ALEXANDER D	TV WRITER	8955 BEVERLY BLVD	LOS ANGELES, CA	90048
MARTIN, AMANDA	ACTRESS-WRITER	14211 DICKENS ST #14	SHERMAN OAKS, CA	91403
MARTIN, ANDREA	ACTRESS	1888 CENTURY PARK E #1400	LOS ANGELES, CA	90067
MARTIN, ANNE-MARIE	ACTRESS	211 S BEVERLY DR #107	BEVERLY HILLS, CA	90212
MARTIN, BARBARA	SOPRANO	CAMI, 165 W 57TH ST	NEW YORK, NY	10019
MARTIN, BARNEY	ACTOR	12750 VENTURA BLVD #102	STUDIO CITY, CA	91604
MARTIN, BEN	PHOTOGRAPHER	TIME/TIME & LIFE BLDG		
		ROCKEFELLER CENTER	NEW YORK, NY	10020
MARTIN, BENNY	MANDOLINIST	POST OFFICE BOX 60424	NASHVILLE, TN	37206
MARTIN, BILLY	BASEBALL	417 S BROAD ST	NEW ORLEANS, LA	70119
MARTIN, BOB	SINGER	ZACK, 234 POTTERS AVE	WARWICK, RI	02886
MARTIN, BRUCE S	WRITER	8955 BEVERLY BLVD	LOS ANGELES, CA	90048
MARTIN, CHARLES E	WRITER-PRODUCER	304 S ELM DR	BEVERLY HILLS, CA	90212
MARTIN, CHERYL L	NEWS CORRESPONDENT	NBC-TV, NEWS DEPARTMENT		
		4001 NEBRASKA AVE, NW	WASHINGTON, DC	20016
MARTIN, CLIFFORD HAROLD, JR	DRUMMER	5621 REGENCY PARK CT #6	SUITLAND, MD	20746
MARTIN, DANA C	NEWS CORRESPONDENT	1315 S WALTER REED #204	ARLINGTON, VA	22204
MARTIN, DAVID	NEWS CORRESPONDENT	CBS NEWS, 2020 "M" ST, NW	WASHINGTON, DC	20036
MARTIN, DAVID C	NEWS CORRESPONDENT	4700 DRUMMOND AVE	CHEVY CHASE, MD	20815
MARTIN, DEAN	ACTOR-SINGER	2002 LOMA VISTA DR	BEVERLY HILLS, CA	90210
MARTIN, DEANA	ACTRESS	8949 SUNSET BLVD #203	LOS ANGELES, CA	90069
MARTIN, DEREK	ACTOR	GARROD MANAGEMENT		
		SAINT MARTINS		
		SANDHILLS MEADOWS		
		SHEPPERTON	MIDDLESEX	ENGLAND
MARTIN, DEWEY	ACTOR	1430 STONEWOOD CT	SAN PEDRO, CA	90732
MARTIN, DICK	ACT-WRI-DIR-COMED	11030 CHALON RD	LOS ANGELES, CA	90077

DEAN MARTIN

JARED MARTIN

PAMELA SUE MARTIN

MARY MARTIN

STEVE MARTIN

ANDREW MASSET

KATHY MATTEA

WALTER MATTHAU

JOHN MATUSAK

Name	Occupation	Address	City	ZIP
MARTIN, DOC	PIANIST	POST OFFICE BOX 884	HENDERSONVILLE, TN	37075
MARTIN, DOLLY READ	ACTRESS-MODEL	11030 CHALON RD	LOS ANGELES, CA	90077
MARTIN, DON	CARTOONIST	MAD MAGAZINE, INC		
		485 MADISON AVE	NEW YORK, NY	10022
MARTIN, EDWARD R	CINEMATOGRAPHER	7667 MULHOLLAND DR	LOS ANGELES, CA	90046
MARTIN, ELLIOT	THEATER PRODUCER	152 W 58TH ST	NEW YORK, NY	10019
MARTIN, ERNEST	THEATER PRODUCER	THE MARK TAPOR FORUM		
		135 N GRAND AVE	LOS ANGELES, CA	90012
MARTIN, FOWLER W	NEWS CORRESPONDENT	3556 BRANDYWINE ST, NW	WASHINGTON, DC	20008
MARTIN, FRANCES	ACTRESS	LINDEN, 416 S BRISTOL AVE	LOS ANGELES, CA	90049
MARTIN, GINA	ACTRESS	9911 W PICO BLVD #560	LOS ANGELES, CA	90035
MARTIN, GLENN M	PIANIST	810 N CUMBERLAND	LEBANON, TN	37087
MARTIN, GREGORY	ACTOR	10845 LINDBROOK DR #3	LOS ANGELES, CA	90024
MARTIN, GREGORY G	GUITARIST	POST OFFICE BOX 795	GLASGOW, KY	42141
MARTIN, HENRY	CARTOONIST	TRIBUNE MEDIA SERVICES		
		64 E CONCORD ST	ORLANDO, FL	32801
MARTIN, HERBERT E	WRITER	555 W 57TH ST #1230	NEW YORK, NY	10019
MARTIN, IAN ROBERT	TV PRODUCER	THAMES TELEVISION		
		149 TOTTENHAM CT RD	LONDON W1	ENGLAND
MARTIN, J D	PIANIST	2101 BELMONT BLVD #604	NASHVILLE, TN	37212
MARTIN, JACK L	MUSIC ARRANGER	1906 SOUTH ST #301	NASHVILLE, TN	37212
MARTIN, JAMES M	CONDUCTOR	1532 YALE ST	SANTA MONICA, CA	90404
MARTIN, JAMES M	TV DIRECTOR	141 SAINT MARKS PL	MASSAPEQUA, NY	11758
MARTIN, JAMES O'DELL	BANJOIST	7591 RIDGEWOOD RD	GOODLETTSVILLE, TN	37072
MARTIN, JAMES T, JR	PHOTOJOURNALIST	1916 AUTUMN CHASE CT	FALLS CHURCH, VA	22043
MARTIN, JARED	ACTOR	8400 LOOKOUT MOUNTAIN AVE	LOS ANGELES, CA	90046
MARTIN, JIMMY	GUITARIST	BOX 46, CHANDLER RD	HERMITAGE, TN	37076
MARTIN, JIMMY & SUNNY MOUNTAIN	BLUEGRASS GROUP	POST OFFICE BOX 809	GOODLETTSVILLE, TN	37072
MARTIN, JOE	CARTOONIST	NEWS AMERICA SYNDICATE		
		1703 KAISER AVE	IRVINE, CA	92714
MARTIN, JOHN	ACTOR	ABC-TV, "ONE LIFE TO LIVE"		
		1330 AVE OF THE AMERICAS	NEW YORK, NY	10019
MARTIN, JOHN	NEWS CORRESPONDENT	ABC-TV, NEWS DEPARTMENT		
		1717 DE SALES ST, NW	WASHINGTON, DC	20036
MARTIN, JOHN	TV EXECUTIVE	ABC TELEVISION NETWORK		
		1330 AVE OF THE AMERICAS	NEW YORK, NY	10019
MARTIN, JOHN E	WRITER	555 W 57TH ST #1230	NEW YORK, NY	10019
MARTIN, JOHN J	ACTOR-WRITER	61 FULTON ST	WEEHAWKEN, NJ	07087
MARTIN, JOHN JAMES	DIRECTOR	DGA, 110 W 57TH ST	NEW YORK, NY	10019
MARTIN, JONATHAN	TV PRODUCER	ARKLE, 15 VALENTINE WY		
		CHALFONT SAINT GILES	BUCKS	ENGLAND
MARTIN, KIEL	ACTOR	10000 SANTA MONICA BLVD #305	LOS ANGELES, CA	90067
MARTIN, LORI	ACTRESS	BREITENBUCHER, 16512 GILMORE ST	VAN NUYS, CA	91406
MARTIN, LUCY	ACTRESS	250 W 57TH ST #2317	NEW YORK, NY	10107
MARTIN, LYLE	WRITER	8955 BEVERLY BLVD	LOS ANGELES, CA	90048
MARTIN, MARDIK	SCREENWRITER	2837 LA CASTANA DR	LOS ANGELES, CA	90046
MARTIN, MARGARET S	WRITER	8955 BEVERLY BLVD	LOS ANGELES, CA	90048
MARTIN, MARILYN	SINGER	HIT & RUN MUSIC, LTD		
		81-83 WALTON ST	LONDON SW3 2HR	ENGLAND
MARTIN, MARJI	ACTRESS	208 S BEVERLY DR #4	BEVERLY HILLS, CA	90212
MARTIN, MARVIS	SOPRANO	CAMI, 165 W 57TH ST	NEW YORK, NY	10019
MARTIN, MARY	ACTRESS	62 PRINCETON	RANCHO MIRAGE, CA	92270
MARTIN, MARY S	NEWS CORRESPONDENT	CBS NEWS, 2020 "M" ST, NW	WASHINGTON, DC	20036
MARTIN, MARYA	FLUTIST	1776 BROADWAY #504	NEW YORK, NY	10019
MARTIN, MELODY J	WRITER	8955 BEVERLY BLVD	LOS ANGELES, CA	90048
MARTIN, MICHAEL	SINGER	TMG, 14 MUSIC SQUARE E	NASHVILLE, TN	37203
MARTIN, MIHAELA	VIOLINIST	CAMI, 165 W 57TH ST	NEW YORK, NY	10019
MARTIN, MILLICENT	SINGER-ACTRESS	THE WESTBURY HOTEL		
		MADISON AVE AT 69TH ST	NEW YORK, NY	10019
MARTIN, NAN	ACTRESS	10100 SANTA MONICA BLVD #1600	LOS ANGELES, CA	90067
MARTIN, NANCY	PUBISHING EXECUTIVE	PLAYGIRL, 801 2ND AVE	NEW YORK, NY	10017
MARTIN, NORMAN L	TV WRITER	8955 BEVERLY BLVD	LOS ANGELES, CA	90048
MARTIN, PAMELA SUE	ACTRESS-PRODCUER	16130 VENTURA BLVD #210	ENCINO, CA	91436
MARTIN, PAUL L	CONDUCTOR	24630 PARK ST #5	TORRANCE, CA	90505
MARTIN, PAULINE	PIANIST	IAM, 10572 JASON LN	COLUMBIA, MD	21044
MARTIN, PEPPER	ACTOR	3518 W CAHUENGA BLVD #316	LOS ANGELES, CA	90068
MARTIN, QUINN	TV PRODUCER	POST OFFICE BOX 8986	RANCHO SANTE FE, CA	92067
MARTIN, RALPH G	WRITER	555 W 57TH ST #1230	NEW YORK, NY	10019
MARTIN, RICCI	ACTRESS	9911 W PICO BLVD #560	LOS ANGELES, CA	90035
MARTIN, RICHARD A	NEWS CORRESPONDENT	1420 W ABINGDON DR	ALEXANDRIA, VA	22314
MARTIN, ROBERT E	WRITER	555 W 57TH ST #1230	NEW YORK, NY	10019
MARTIN, ROSA LEE	SINGER-SONGWRITER	POST OFFICE BOX 101	KIRKSVILLE, MO	63501
MARTIN, SANDY	ACTRESS	4721 LAUREL CANYON BLVD #211	NORTH HOLLYWOOD, CA	91607
MARTIN, STEPHEN G	DIRECTOR-PRODUCER	420 E 55TH ST	NEW YORK, NY	10022
MARTIN, STEVE	ACTOR	9000 SUNSET BLVD #1200	LOS ANGELES, CA	90069
MARTIN, TED	CARTOONIST	UNIVERSAL PRESS SYNDICATE		
		4900 MAIN ST, 9TH FLOOR	KANSAS CITY, MO	62114
MARTIN, TIM	SINGER	216 TAYLOR RD	COLLINSVILLE, VA	24078
MARTIN, TODD	ACTOR	10391 ALMAYO AVE	LOS ANGELES, CA	90064
MARTIN, TONY	ACTOR-SINGER	2328 CENTURY HILL	LOS ANGELES, CA	90067
MARTIN, VIVIAN	SOPRANO	POST OFFICE BOX U	REDDING, CT	06875
MARTIN, WILLIAM	WRITER	8955 BEVERLY BLVD	LOS ANGELES, CA	90048
MARTIN, WILLIAM B	DIRECTOR	POST OFFICE BOX 3388	HOLLYWOOD, CA	90028
MARTIN, WILLIAM K	WRITER	8955 BEVERLY BLVD	LOS ANGELES, CA	90048
MARTIN, WILLIAM T	ACTOR	5000 LANKERSHIM BLVD #5	NORTH HOLLYWOOD, CA	91601

Nashville recording artist and songwriter Rosa Lee Martin

Name	Occupation	Address	City, State	Zip
MARTINDALE, ROBERT L	NEWS CORRESPONDENT	400 N CAPITOL ST, NW	WASHINGTON, DC	20001
MARTINDALE, WINK	GAME SHOW HOST	3211 RETREAT CT	MALIBU, CA	90265
MARTINEAU, GERALD H	PHOTOGRAPHER	300 S HARRISON ST	ARLINGTON, VA	22204
MARTINEZ, A	ACTOR	4721 LAUREL CANYON BLVD #211	NORTH HOLLYWOOD, CA	91607
MARTINEZ, AL	TV WRITER	1900 AVE OF THE STARS #2375	LOS ANGELES, CA	90067
MARTINEZ, ALMA	ACTRESS	SHERMAN, 348 S REXFORD DR	BEVERLY HILLS, CA	90212
MARTINEZ, BILL JOHN	DRUMMER	1758 HUNTERS POINT	GALLATIN, TN	37066
MARTINEZ, JAMES	ACTOR	1418 N HIGHLAND AVE #102	LOS ANGELES, CA	90028
MARTINEZ, JOAQUIN	ACTOR	4103 FARMDALE AVE	STUDIO CITY, CA	91604
MARTINEZ, JOSE E	WRITER	555 W 57TH ST #1230	NEW YORK, NY	10019
MARTINEZ, JOSUE D	NEWS CORRESPONDENT	444 N CAPITOL ST, NW	WASHINGTON, DC	20001
MARTINEZ, PATRICE	ACTRESS	1607 N EL CENTRO AVE #23	LOS ANGELES, CA	90028
MARTINO, AL	SINGER	927 N REXFORD DR	BEVERLY HILLS, CA	90210
MARTINO, EDWARD	TV WRITER	8955 BEVERLY BLVD	LOS ANGELES, CA	90048
MARTINO, LAURENCE	BASS	61 W 62ND ST #6-F	NEW YORK, NY	10023
MARTINO, NICK	TV DIRECTOR	ENTERTAINMENT TONIGHT		
		PARAMOUNT TELEVISION		
		5555 MELROSE ST	LOS ANGELES, CA	90038
MARTINO, RUSS N	COMPOSER-CONDUCTOR	208 N TORREY PINES DR	LAS VEGAS, NV	89107
MARTINOVIC, BORIS	BASS	61 W 62ND ST #6-F	NEW YORK, NY	10023
MARTINS, PETER	BALLET DANCER	LINCOLN CENTER PLAZA	NEW YORK, NY	10023
MARTINSON, LESLIE	TV DIRECTOR	2288 COLDWATER CANYON DR	BEVERLY HILLS, CA	90210
MARTINUS, DEREK	DIRECTOR-ACTOR	16 GRANTHAM RD	LONDON W4 2RS	ENGLAND
MARTON, ANDREW	DIRECTOR-PRODUCER	8856 APPIAN WY	LOS ANGELES, CA	90046
MARTON, EVA	SOPRANO	111 W 57TH ST #1209	NEW YORK, NY	10019
MARTON, RUTH	WRITER	555 W 57TH ST #1230	NEW YORK, NY	10019
MARTORANO, MICHAEL	ACTOR	5 TUDOR CITY PL	NEW YORK, NY	10017
MARTUCCI, RAY	ACTOR	POST OFFICE BOX 129		
		F D ROOSEVELT STATION	NEW YORK, NY	10150
MARTY, JEAN-PIERRE	CONDUCTOR	61 W 62ND ST #6-F	NEW YORK, NY	10023
MARTYN, JOHN	SINGER-SONGWRITER	ISLAND RECORDS COMPANY		
		444 MADISON AVE	NEW YORK, NY	10022
MARTYN, LARRY	ACTOR	47 STONEYDEEP, TWICKENHAM RD	TEDDINGTON	ENGLAND
MARTZ, STEFFANY A	WRITER	555 W 57TH ST #1230	NEW YORK, NY	10019
MARTZKE, RUDY	SPORTS WRITER	POST OFFICE BOX 500	WASHINGTON, DC	20044
MARUCCI, MAT	COMPOSER	POST OFFICE BOX 8464	UNIVERSAL CITY, CA	91608
MARUCCI, MICHAEL S	PHOTOGRAPHER	5250 VALLEY FORGE DR #705	ALEXANDRIA, VA	22304
MARUEL, LARRY	GUITARIST	5137 LANA RENEE DR	HERMITAGE, TN	37076
MARVEL, ANDY	RECORD EXECUTIVE	ALYSSA RECORDS, 8 PASTORE LN	ROSLYN HEIGHTS, NY	11577
MARVEL, JAMES	SINGER	POST OFFICE BOX 110423	NASHVILLE, TN	37211
MARVELETTES, THE	VOCAL GROUP	BROTHERS, 141 DUNBAR AVE	FORDS, NJ	08863
MARVELLS, THE	VOCAL GROUP	POST OFFICE BOX 22707	NASHVILLE, TN	37203
MARVIN, EDGAR	WRITER	555 W 57TH ST #1230	NEW YORK, NY	10019
MARVIN, GEORGE	DIRECTOR	5904 NW 81ST AVE	TAMARAC, FL	33321
MARVIN, IRA	WRITER-PRODUCER	33 W 67TH ST	NEW YORK, NY	10023
MARVIN, LEE	ACTOR	5055 N CALLE LA VELA	TUCSON, AZ	85718
MARVIN, MIKE	SCREENWRITER	14144 VENTURA BLVD #200	SHERMAN OAKS, CA	91423
MARVIN, MITZI	TV WRITER	8955 BEVERLY BLVD	LOS ANGELES, CA	90048
MARVIN, WILLIAM	CARTOONIST	POST OFFICE BOX 2416		
		TERMINAL ANNEX STATION	LOS ANGELES, CA	90051
MARVIN & JOHNNY	VOCAL DUO	OLDIES, 5218 ALMONT ST	LOS ANGELES, CA	90032
MARX, ARTHUR	PLAYWRIGHT	1244 BEL AIR RD	LOS ANGELES, CA	90077
MARX, CHRISTY L	SCREENWRITER	8955 BEVERLY BLVD	LOS ANGELES, CA	90048
MARX, GERTRUDE	ACTRESS	3800 BARHAM BLVD #303	LOS ANGELES, CA	90068
MARX, GREGG	ACTOR	6430 SUNSET BLVD #701	LOS ANGELES, CA	90069
MARX, JOHN	TALENT AGENT	10100 SANTA MONICA BLVD #1600	LOS ANGELES, CA	90067
MARX, KERRY	GUITARIST	248 CEDARCREEK DR	NASHVILLE, TN	37211
MARX, LLOYD	DIRECTOR	364 W 18TH ST	NEW YORK, NY	10011
MARX, PATRICIA A	WRITER	555 W 57TH ST #1230	NEW YORK, NY	10019
MARX, RICHARD H	CONDUCTOR	101 E ONTARIO	CHICAGO, IL	60611
MARX, SAMUEL	WRITER-PRODUCER	430 S BURNSIDE AVE #3-G	LOS ANGELES, CA	90036
MARY JANE GIRLS, THE	VOCAL GROUP	SEIDMAN & SEIDMAN AGENCY		
		135 DELAWARE AVE	BUFFALO, NY	14202
MARYMONT, JERRY	ACTOR	8025 GONZAGA AVE	LOS ANGELES, CA	90045
MARZ, RICHARD	GUITARIST	406 AVOCA AVE #A-6	NASHVILLE, TN	37203
MASAK, RON	ACTOR	5440 SHIRLEY AVE	TARZANA, CA	91356
MASCARINO, PIERRINO	ACTOR	953 S PARK VIEW ST	LOS ANGELES, CA	90006
MASCHLER, TIM	TV WRITER	8955 BEVERLY BLVD	LOS ANGELES, CA	90048
MASCOLO, JOSEPH	ACTOR	3818 BLUE CANYON DR	STUDIO CITY, CA	91604
MASEKELA, HUGH	TRUMPETER	ICM, 40 W 57TH ST	NEW YORK, NY	10019
MASER, GERHARD A	DIRECTOR	POST OFFICE BOX 715	ONELO, FL	33558
MASHEK, JOHN W	NEWS CORRESPONDENT	2400 "N" ST, NW	WASHINGTON, DC	20037
MASHORE, PAULA M	NEWS CORRESPONDENT	NBC-TV, NEWS DEPARTMENT		
		4001 NEBRASKA AVE, NW	WASHINGTON, DC	20016
MASI, NICHOLAS, JR	ACTOR	1351 N ORANGE DR #218	LOS ANGELES, CA	90028
MASINI, GIANFRANCO	CONDUCTOR	61 W 62ND ST #6-F	NEW YORK, NY	10023
MASIUS, JOHN	TV WRITER-PRODUCER	14100 SUNSET BLVD	PACIFIC PALISADES, CA	90272
MASK, MARILYN	ACTRESS	1414 1/2 S SIERRA BONITA AVE	LOS ANGELES, CA	90019
MASK MAN, THE	WRESTLER	WORLD CLASS WRESTLING		
		SOUTHWEST SPORTS, INC		
		DALLAS SPORTATORIUM		
		1000 S INDUSTRIAL BLVD	DALLAS, TX	75207

MARY JANE GIRLS

Candi • Cherri • Maxi • Jo Jo

MASON DIXON

Name	Occupation	Address	City	Zip
MASKED AVENGER	WRESTLER	SEE - ADAMS, CHRIS "GENTLEMAN"		
MASKED EXECUTIONER, THE	WRESTLER	SEE - ROSE, PLAYBOY BUDDY		
MASKED SUPERSTAR, THE	WRESTLER	POST OFFICE BOX 3859	STAMFORD, CT	06905
MASLANSKY, PAUL	DIRECTOR-PRODUCER	22852 PACIFIC COAST HWY #B	MALIBU, CA	90265
MASLOW, SOPHIE	CHOREOGRAPHER	POST OFFICE BOX 884	NEW YORK, NY	10023
MASLOW, STEVE	SOUNG ENGINEER	17235 TENNYSON PL	GRANADA HILLS, CA	91344
MASLOW, WALTER	ACTOR	8397 FOUNTAIN AVE #306	LOS ANGELES, CA	90069
MASOFF, MYRNA	EDITOR-WRITER	10 COLUMBUS CIR #1300	NEW YORK, NY	10019
MASON, BARBARA	SINGER	WMOT MGMT, 1228 SPRUCE ST	PHILADELPHIA, PA	19107
MASON, BILL	FILM DIRECTOR	DELL QUAY HOUSE, DELL QUAY		
		CHICHESTER	SUSSEX PO20 7EE	ENGLAND
MASON, BRENT	GUITARIST	301 KATE ST	MADISON, TN	37115
MASON, DAVE	SINGER-SONGWRITER	MARCOTTE, 16121 SUNSET BL #3	PACIFIC PALISADES, CA	90272
MASON, ELLEN B	WRITER	555 W 57TH ST #1230	NEW YORK, NY	10019
MASON, GEOFFREY	TV PRODUCER	NBC TELEVISION NETWORK		
		30 ROCKEFELLER PLAZA	NEW YORK, NY	10112
MASON, JACKIE	COMEDIAN	151 S EL CAMINO DR	BEVERLY HILLS, CA	90212
MASON, JANE	ACTRESS	13111 VENTURA BLVD #102	STUDIO CITY, CA	91604
MASON, LOLA	ACTRESS	913 S SPALDING AVE	LOS ANGELES, CA	90036
MASON, MADISON	ACTOR	15010 VENTURA BLVD #219	SHERMAN OAKS, CA	91403
MASON, MARGARET	ACTRESS	12345 VENTURA BLVD #X	STUDIO CITY, CA	91604
MASON, MARGERY	ACTRESS	27 COLLEGE CRESCENT	LONDON NW3	ENGLAND
MASON, MARLYN	ACTRESS-SINGER	8242 HILLSIDE AVE	LOS ANGELES, CA	90069
MASON, MARSHA	ACTRESS	1016 RIDGEDALE DR	BEVERLY HILLS, CA	90210
MASON, MARSHALL W	TV DIRECTOR	165 CHRISTOPHER ST	NEW YORK, NY	10014
MASON, MARTY	DRUMMER	441 WELCHWOOD DR #B-25	NASHVILLE, TN	37211
MASON, NAN	ACTRESS	8383 WILSHIRE BLVD #1024	BEVERLY HILLS, CA	90211
MASON, PAMELA	ACTRESS	1018 PAMELA DR	BEVERLY HILLS, CA	90210
MASON, PAUL	TV WRITER	13355 MULHOLLAND DR	BEVERLY HILLS, CA	90210
MASON, PAUL E	WRITER	8955 BEVERLY BLVD	LOS ANGELES, CA	90048
MASON, RANDY	DRUMMER	301 KATE ST	MADISON, TN	37115
MASON, ROBERT	ACTOR	FROTHINGHAM, 40 GROVE ST	WESSESLEY, MA	02181
MASON, ROBERT FINLAY	CELLIST	5510 BON AIR CIR	NASHVILLE, TN	37209
MASON, SEAN O	WRITER	555 W 57TH ST #1230	NEW YORK, NY	10019
MASON, THOMAS C	NEWS CORRESPONDENT	2546 N GREENBRIER ST	ARLINGTON, VA	22207
MASON, TODD Q	COMPOSER-CONDUCTOR	612 E MAPLE AVE	EL SEGUNDO, CA	90245
MASON, TOM	ACTOR	853 7TH AVE #9-A	NEW YORK, NY	10019
MASON, VICTORIA A	NEWS CORRESPONDENT	4132 S 36TH ST	ARLINGTON, VA	22206
MASON, VIVIEN	SINGER	1776 N SYCAMORE AVE #216	HOLLYWOOD, CA	90028
MASON, WILLIAM	DIRECTOR	230 RIVERSIDE DR	NEW YORK, NY	10025
MASON, WILLIAM B	NEWS CORRESPONDENT	4338 CARMELO DR #104	ANNANDALE, VA	22003
MASON DIXON	C & W GROUP	POST OFFICE BOX 57291	DALLAS, TX	75207
MASQUERADERS, THE	MUSICAL GROUP	COOKIN MUSIC, 120 W 25TH ST	NEW YORK, NY	10001
MASQUERES, EL	WRESTLING TAG TEAM	SEE - MASQUERES, THE		
MASS PRODUCTION	ROCK & ROLL GROUP	PEPPER PRODS, 200 W 72ND ST	NEW YORK, NY	10023
MASSAHOS, ACHILLES	ACTOR	4780 HUB ST	LOS ANGELES, CA	90042
MASSALAS, VALORIE	CASTING DIRECTOR	20TH CENTURY-FOX TV		
		10201 W PICO BLVD	LOS ANGELES, CA	90035
MASSARI, JOHN	COMPOSER-CONDUCTOR	5913 WILLOUGHBY AVE	LOS ANGELES, CA	90038
MASSARI, MARK ELLIOTT	WRITER-PRODUCER	227 S MADISON AVE	PASADENA, CA	91101
MASSARO, RUTH	TV WRITER	8955 BEVERLY BLVD	LOS ANGELES, CA	90048
MASSARUEH, ABDULSALAM Y	NEWS CORRESPONDENT	2301 15TH ST #101, NW	WASHINGTON, DC	20009
MASSELINK, BEN	WRITER	570 ERSKINE DR	PACIFIC PALISADES, CA	90272
MASSENKOFF, NIKOLAI	BASSO-BARITONE	GEWALD, 58 W 58TH ST	NEW YORK, NY	10019
MASSET, ANDREW	ACTOR	11635 HUSTON ST	NORTH HOLLYWOOD, CA	91601
MASSEY, ANDREW	CONDUCTOR	POST OFFICE BOX 1515	NEW YORK, NY	10023
MASSEY, ANNA	ACTRESS	ICM, 388-396 OXFORD ST	LONDON W1	ENGLAND
MASSEY, BARRY B	NEWS CORRESPONDENT	5453 CALVIN CT	SPRINGFIELD, VA	22151
MASSEY, CURT	ACTOR	76-383 FAIRWAY DR	INDIANA WELLS, CA	92260
MASSEY, GENE	WRITER-PRODUCER	550 S BARRINGTON AVE #2209	LOS ANGELES, CA	90049
MASSEY, GEORGE	BARITONE	MUNRO, 334 W 72ND ST	NEW YORK, NY	10023
MASSEY, JAMILA	ACTRESS	OCA, 34 GRAFTON TERR	LONDON NW5 4HY	ENGLAND
MASSEY, JANET LEE	PHOTOJOURNALIST	7033 BRADWOOD CT	SPRINGFIELD, VA	22151
MASSEY, KEN	WRESTLER	UNIVERSAL WRESTLING FEDERATION		
		MID SOUTH SPORTS, INC		
		5001 SPRING VALLEY RD	DALLAS, TX	75244
MASSEY, PERRY E, JR	TV EXECUTIVE	22525 DARDENNE ST	WOODLAND HILLS, CA	91364
MASSEY, TOBY	PHOTOGRAPHER	13523 ELLENDALE DR	CHANTILLY, VA	22021
MASSEY, WAYNE	ACTOR-SINGER	POST OFFICE BOX 2757	NASHVILLE, TN	37219
MASSION, RIVI	ACTRESS	13722 ALBERS ST	VAN NUYS, CA	91401
MASSMANN, KERRI	ACTRESS	14575 VALLEY VISTA BLVD	SHERMAN OAKS, CA	91403
MAST, MARTHA B	NEWS CORRESPONDENT	8902 MANCHESTER RD #106	SILVER SPRING, MD	20901
MASTER, WILLIAM J	FILM DIRECTOR	8146 BILLOW VISTA	PLAYA DEL REY, CA	90293
MASTER GEE	WRESTLER	SEE - WELLES, GEORGE		
MASTER JOHN	ACROBATIC ACT	POST OFFICE BOX 87	WEST LEBANON, NY	12195
MASTER'S FIVE	GOSPEL GROUP	POST OFFICE BOX 17272	MEMPHIS, TN	38187
MASTEROFF, JOE	PLAYWRIGHT	2 HORATIO ST	NEW YORK, NY	10014
MASTERS, BEN	ACTOR	10100 SANTA MONICA BLVD #1600	LOS ANGELES, CA	90067
MASTERS, FRANKIE	CONDUCTOR	132 TURKEY HILL RD	CARY, IL	60013
MASTERS, MICHAEL	ACTOR	9744 WILSHIRE BLVD #306	BEVERLY HILLS, CA	90212
MASTERS, QUENTIN	FILM DIRECTOR	GARRETT, 5 QUEEN ST	LONDON W1X 8LA	ENGLAND
MASTERS, WILLIAM H, III	WRITER-PRODUCER	155 E 88TH ST #6-B	NEW YORK, NY	10028
MASTERSON, PETER	FILM WRITER-DIRECTOR	9255 SUNSET BLVD #1122	LOS ANGELES, CA	90069
MASTERSON, SEAN	ACTOR	8721 SUNSET BLVD #200	LOS ANGELES, CA	90069

Name	Occupation	Address	City	Zip
MASTERSON, VALERIE	SOPRANO	CAMI, 165 W 57TH ST	NEW YORK, NY	10019
MASTIN, MIKK	PERCUSSIONIST	141 NEESE DR #DD-553	NASHVILLE, TN	37211
MASTIN, PAUL M	WRITER	8955 BEVERLY BLVD	LOS ANGELES, CA	90048
MASTORAKIS, NICO	WRITER-PRODUCER	POST OFFICE BOX 5617	BEVERLY HILLS, CA	90210
MASTRIANNI, NICK	DRUMMER	BOX 23-A, HICKORY HOLLOW RD	PESRAM, TN	37143
MASTRICOLO, CAROL A	PHOTOGRAPHER	45 W 81ST ST #1004	NEW YORK, NY	10024
MASTROGEORGE, HARRY	FILM DIRECTOR	10619 LANDALE ST	NORTH HOLLYWOOD, CA	91602
MASTROIANNI, MARCELLO	ACTOR	VIA DI PORTA, SAN SEBASTIANO 15	ROME 00179	ITALY
MASTROMEI, GIAMPIERO	BARITONE	61 W 62ND ST #6-F	NEW YORK, NY	10023
MASTY, STEPHEN J	NEWS CORRESPONDENT	718 NORTH CAROLINA AVE, SE	WASHINGTON, DC	20003
MASU, MAKATO	NEWS CORRESPONDENT	1452 DEWBERRY CT	MC LEAN, VA	22101
MASUCCI, TONY	TV DIRECTOR	CBS-TV, 6121 SUNSET BLVD	LOS ANGELES, CA	90028
MASUD, S A	NEWS CORRESPONDENT	1333 "H" ST, NW	WASHINGTON, DC	20005
MASUKO, TSUTOMU	BARITONE	200 W 70TH ST #7-F	NEW YORK, NY	10023
MASUOKA, MARK STEPHEN	TV WRITER	1233 KENISTON AVE	LOS ANGELES, CA	90019
MASUR, RICHARD	ACTOR-WRITER	2847 MANDEVILLE CANYON RD	LOS ANGELES, CA	90049
MATA, EDUARDO	CONDUCTOR	ICM, 40 W 57TH ST	NEW YORK, NY	10019
MATALON, VIVIAN	FILM DIRECTOR	888 7TH AVE #201	NEW YORK, NY	10019
MATASEJE, VERONICA	RECORD EXECUTIVE	ACCLAIM RECORDS, 1426 LUDBROOK	MISSISSOULA, ONT L5J 3	CANADA
MATCHA, JACK	WRITER	8955 BEVERLY BLVD	LOS ANGELES, CA	90048
MATCHINGA, CARYN L	WRITER	8955 BEVERLY BLVD	LOS ANGELES, CA	90048
MATEJKO, JOHN J	PHOTOGRAPHER	9652 SCOTCH HAVEN	VIENNA, VA	22180
MATER, BOB	MUSIC ARRANGER	1441 LEBANON RD #E-36	NASHVILLE, TN	37210
MATER, GENE PAUL	TV EXECUTIVE	CBS-TV, 51 W 52ND ST	NEW YORK, NY	10019
MATERA, FRAN	CARTOONIST	NEWS AMERICA SYNDICATE		
		1703 KAISER AVE	IRVINE, CA	92714
MATERA, JOSEPH A	PHOTOGRAPHER	17670 HORIZON PL	DERWOOD, MD	20855
MATERIAL	MUSICAL GROUP	GEORGIAKARAKOS, 45 W 81ST ST	NEW YORK, NY	10024
MATERNA, GARY S	ACTOR	6605 HOLLYWOOD BLVD #220	HOLLYWOOD, CA	90028
MATHAI, EAPEN	ACTOR	3005 1/2 BAGLEY AVE	LOS ANGELES, CA	90034
MATHENY, R NORMAN	PHOTOGRAPHER	7820 FRIARS CT	ALEXANDRIA, VA	22306
MATHER, GEORGE E	DIRECTOR	12330 HUSTON ST	NORTH HOLLYWOOD, CA	91607
MATHERS, JERRY	ACTOR	19640 GREEN MOUNTAIN DR	NEWHALL, CA	91321
MATHES, COLONEL DAVE	GUITARIST	POST OFFICE BOX 22653	NASHVILLE, TN	37202
MATHES, RACHEL	SOPRANO	SARDOS, 180 W END AVE	NEW YORK, NY	10023
MATHESON, DON	ACTOR	10000 RIVERSIDE DR #3	TOLUCA LAKE, CA	91602
MATHESON, MEGAN MURPHY	BALLERINA	3099 ELLINGTON DR	LOS ANGELES, CA	90068
MATHESON, RICHARD B	WRITER	24900 EL DORADO MEADOW RD	CALABASAS, CA	91302
MATHESON, RICHARD C, JR	WRITER	24900 EL DORADO MEADOW RD	CALABASAS, CA	91302
MATHESON, TIM	ACTOR	3099 ELLINGTON DR	LOS ANGELES, CA	90068
MATHEWS, CARMEN S	ACTRESS	400 E 52ND ST	NEW YORK, NY	10022
MATHEWS, CAROL	COLUMNIST	NEWS AMERICA SYNDICATE		
		1703 KAISER AVE	IRVINE, CA	92714
MATHEWS, CAROLE	ACTRESS	6316 ALONZO AVE	RESEDA, CA	91335
MATHEWS, DAVID	WRITER	8955 BEVERLY BLVD	LOS ANGELES, CA	90048
MATHEWS, EDDIE	BASEBALL	13744 RECUERDO DR	DEL MAR, CA	92014
MATHEWS, JOHN	NEWS CORRESPONDENT	NBC-TV, NEWS DEPARTMENT		
		4001 NEBRASKA AVE, NW	WASHINGTON, DC	20016
MATHEWS, ONZY D	COMPOSER	5114 EDGEWOOD PL	LOS ANGELES, CA	90019
MATHEWS, PATRICK J	TV WRITER	8955 BEVERLY BLVD	LOS ANGELES, CA	90048
MATHEWS, PATRICK M	MUSISICAN-WRITER	13126 HART ST	NORTH HOLLYWOOD, CA	91605
MATHEWS, WALTER	ACTOR	4326 BELLAIRE AVE	STUDIO CITY, CA	91604
MATHIAS, ANNA	ACTRESS	1930 WEEPAH WY	LOS ANGELES, CA	90046
MATHIAS, BOB	ACTOR-ATHELETE	3400 W 86TH ST	INDIANAPOLIS, IN	46268
MATHIAS, JOHNNY	SINGER	1469 STEBBINS TERR	LOS ANGELES, CA	90069
MATHIAS, SONNY	WRITER	211 S BEVERLY DR #201	BEVERLY HILLS, CA	90212
MATHIESON, GREG E	PHOTOGRAPHER	8308 TOBIN RD	ANNANDALE, MD	22003
MATHIEU, ALLAUDIN	MUSICIAN	POST OFFICE BOX 9388	STANFORD, CA	94305
MATHIEU, MIRIELLE	SINGER	122 AVE DE WAGRAM	PARIS 75017	FRANCE
MATHIS, EDITH	SOPRANO	59 E 54TH ST #81	NEW YORK, NY	10022
MATHISEN, CHRISTIAN	ACTOR	5330 LANKERSHIM BLVD #210	NORTH HOLLYWOOD, CA	91601
MATHISON, MELISSA	SCREENWRITER	POST OFFICE BOX 49344	LOS ANGELES, CA	90049
MATHOT, OLIVER	ACTOR	42 BIS RUE BOURDIGNON	SAINT MAUR 94100	FRANCE
MATICKA, JERRY M	DIRECTOR	404 E 66TH ST	NEW YORK, NY	10021
MATILDA	WRESTLING DOG	POST OFFICE BOX 3859	STAMFORD, CT	06905
MATILDA THE HUN	WRESTLER	GORGEOUS GIRLS OF WRESTLING		
		DAVID B MC LANE PRODS		
		RIVIERA HOTEL & CASINO		
		2901 S LAS VEGAS BLVD	LAS VEGAS, NV	89109
MATKIN, KIRK	VIDEO EDITOR	ENTERTAINMENT TONIGHT		
		PARAMOUNT TELEVISION		
		5555 MELROSE AVE	LOS ANGELES, CA	90038
MATLACK, CAROL	NEWS CORRESPONDENT	1611 CORCORAN ST, NW	WASHINGTON, DC	20009
MATLICK, ELDON	GUITARIST	813 SHA-WA CIR	MURRAY, KY	42071
MATLIN, MARLEE	ACTRESS	SF & A, 121 N SAN VICENTE BLVD	BEVERLY HILLS, CA	90211
MATLOCK, TONY	SINGER-GUITARIST	314 BRIDGEWAY CIR	NASHVILLE, TN	37211
MATOUSEK, CAROLYN	MUSICIAN	2610 COUCHVILLE PIKE	NASHVILLE, TN	37214
MATOUSEK, DANNY	GUITARIST	2610 COUCHVILLE PIKE	NASHVILLE, TN	37214
MATRIX	ROCK & ROLL GROUP	8465 KEYSTONE CROSSING #204	INDIANAPOLIS, IN	46240
MATSON, DONNA M	TV DIRECTOR	4418 AVOCADO ST	LOS ANGELES, CA	90027
MATSON, DONNA MARIE	WRITER	2261 EARL ST	LOS ANGELES, CA	90039
MATSON, JOHNNY	COMEDIAN	7221 OAK AVE, MILLER BEACH	GARY, IN	46403
MATSUSHITA, FUMIO	NEWS CORRESPONDENT	7788 HEATHERTON LN	POTOMAC, MD	20854
MATSUURA, TOSHIAKI	DIRECTOR	CREATIVE ENTERPRISE INTL		
		6630 SUNSET BLVD	HOLLYWOOD, CA	90028

MATTEA, KATHY	SINGER	POST OFFICE BOX 24475	NASHVILLE, TN 37202
MATTER, ALEX	SCREENWRITER	8955 BEVERLY BLVD	LOS ANGELES, CA 90048
MATTESON, PAMELA	ACTRESS	38 PATTON BLVD	NEW HYDE PARK, NY 11040
MATTHAU, WALTER	ACTOR	10100 SANTA MONICA BLVD #2200	LOS ANGELES, CA 90067
MATTHEWS, AL	ACTOR	9 MANATON CRES, SOUTHALL	MIDDLESEX UB1 2SY ENGLAND
MATTHEWS, ANDREA	SOPRANO	59 E 54TH ST #81	NEW YORK, NY 10022
MATTHEWS, ART, JAZZ TRIO	JAZZ TRIO	FROTHINGHAM, 40 GROVE ST	WESSESLEY, MA 02181
MATTHEWS, BENJAMIN	BASSO-BARITONE	200 W 70TH ST #7-F	NEW YORK, NY 10023
MATTHEWS, BRIAN	ACTOR	9255 SUNSET BLVD #1105	LOS ANGELES, CA 90069
MATTHEWS, CLAUDE	NEWS CORRESPONDENT	2805 31ST PL, NW	WASHINGTON, DC 20018
MATTHEWS, FRANCIS	ACTOR	THE RICHARD STONE AGENCY	
		18-20 YORK BLDGS, ADELPHI	LONDON WC2N 6JY ENGLAND
MATTHEWS, GUERRY	GUITARIST	2649 MIAMI AVE	NASHVILLE, TN 37214
MATTHEWS, HALE	THEATER PRODUCER	1088 PARK AVE	NEW YORK, NY 10028
MATTHEWS, JIM, FAMILY	GOSPEL GROUP	POST OFFICE BOX 342	BAILEY, MS 39320
MATTHEWS, JOHN	BARITONE	1182 MARKET ST #311	SAN FRANCISCO, CA 94102
MATTHEWS, JOY	ACTRESS	CED, 261 S ROBERTSON BLVD	BEVERLY HILLS, CA 90211
MATTHEWS, KATHLEEN C	NEWS CORRESPONDENT	4461 CONNECTICUT AVE, NW	WASHINGTON, DC 20008
MATTHEWS, KERWIN	ACTOR	76-A BUENA VISTA TERR	SAN FRANCISCO, CA 94117
MATTHEWS, LAWRENCE C, JR	NEWS CORRESPONDENT	1243 ELBEN ST	HERNDON, VA 22070
MATTHEWS, LLEWELLYN E	COMPOSER	13528 CURTIS & KING RD	NORWALK, CA 90650
MATTHEWS, MARK H	NEWS CORRESPONDENT	830 11TH ST, NE	WASHINGTON, DC 20002
MATTHEWS, NEAL, JR	MANDOLINIST	1900 ROSEWOOD VALLEY DR	BRENTWOOD, TN 37027
MATTHEWS, PAIGE	ACTRESS	9200 SUNSET BLVD #1210	LOS ANGELES, CA 90069
MATTHEWS, PATRICIA P	NEWS CORRESPONDENT	2158 ALICE AVE	OXON HILL, MD 20745
MATTHEWS, RANDY	SINGER-GUITARIST	POST OFFICE BOX 9004	CANTON, OH 44711
MATTHEWS, SIDNEY W	NEWS CORRESPONDENT	1322 DE WITT AVE	ALEXANDRIA, VA 22301
MATTHEWS, THOM	ACTOR	10390 SANTA MONICA BLVD #310	LOS ANGELES, CA 90025
MATTHEWS, WILLIAM	GUITARIST	GERSHUNOFF, 502 PARK AVE	NEW YORK, NY 10022
MATTHEWS, WILLIAM ROBERT	DIRECTOR	DGA, 110 W 57TH ST	NEW YORK, NY 10019
MATTHEY, HARRIET	ACTRESS	1259 N FLORES ST	LOS ANGELES, CA 90069
MATTHIESSEN, PETER	WRITER	555 W 57TH ST #1230	NEW YORK, NY 10019
MATTHIUS, GAIL	COMEDIAN	ICM, 8899 BEVERLY BLVD	LOS ANGELES, CA 90048
MATTICK, PATRICIA	ACTRESS	4115 BERENICE PL	LOS ANGELES, CA 90031
MATTICKS, DON	DIRECTOR	815 YORKTOWN RD	TURNERSVILLE, NJ 08012
MATTILA, KARITA	SOPRANO	CAMI, 165 W 57TH ST	NEW YORK, NY 10019
MATTINGLY, HEDLEY	ACTOR	4111 STONE CANYON AVE	SHERMAN OAKS, CA 91403
MATTIS-RUSSIN, LILLIAN	LYRICIST	6130 COLDWATER CANYON AVE #7	NORTH HOLLYWOOD, CA 91606
MATTISON, HARRY	PHOTOGRAPHER	TIME/TIME & LIFE BLDG	
		ROCKEFELLER CENTER	NEW YORK, NY 10020
MATTS, ANDY	DRUMMER	100 HAVEN ST	HENDERSONVILLE, TN 37075
MATTSON, ROBIN	ACTRESS	1339 HOLMBY AVE	LOS ANGELES, CA 90024
MATULAVICH, PETER	DIRECTOR	1414 PASEO MANZANA	SAN DIMAS, CA 91773
MATURO, MIMI O'BRIEN	TV DIRECTOR	3480 BARHAM BLVD	LOS ANGELES, CA 90068
MATUSZAK, JOHN	ACTOR-FOOTBALL	9220 SUNSET BLVD #218	LOS ANGELES, CA 90069
MATUTE, RAUL	COMPOSER	20933 TOMLEE AVE	TORRANCE, CA 90503
MATZ, PETER S	COMPOSER-CONDUCTOR	18926 PACIFIC COAST HWY	MALIBU, CA 90265
MATZA, JOSEPH	DIRECTOR	26729 LATIGO SHORE DR	MALIBU, CA 90265
MAUCH, BILLY	ACTOR	23427 CANZONET ST	WOODLAND HILLS, CA 91364
MAUCH, BOBBY	ACTOR	23427 CANZONET ST	WOODLAND HILLS, CA 91364
MAUCLAIR, JACQUES	ACTOR	17 RUE DES ARCHIVES	PARIS 75004 FRANCE
MAUGHAN, SHARON	ACTRESS	HEATH, PARAMOUNT HOUSE	
		162-170 WARDOUR ST	LONDON W1V 3AT ENGLAND
MAULDIN, BILL	CARTOONIST	NEWS AMERICA SYNDICATE	
		1703 KAISER AVE	IRVINE, CA 92714
MAULDIN, JOE B	GUITARIST	POST OFFICE BOX 210216	NASHVILLE, TN 37221
MAULDIN, NAT	TV WRITER	7050 PACIFIC VIEW DR	LOS ANGELES, CA 90068
MAULDIN, STEVE W	MUSIC ARRANGER	1905 STRATFORD AVE	NASHVILLE, TN 37216
MAULE, BRAD	ACTOR	151 S EL CAMINO DR	BEVERLY HILLS, CA 90212
MAULE, COREY	ACTOR	ABC-TV NETWORK, "LOVING"	
		1330 AVE OF THE AMERICAS	NEW YORK, NY 10019
MAUNDER, WAYNE	ACTOR	9000 SUNSET BLVD #801	LOS ANGELES, CA 90069
MAUPIN, SAMUEL	ACTOR	200 W 57TH ST #304	NEW YORK, NY 10019
MAURER, JOHN	ACTOR	11048 OTSEGO ST	NORTH HOLLYWOOD, CA 91601
MAURER, LINUS	PUZZLE WRITER	7720 EL CAMINO REAL #2-C	RANCHO LA COSTA, CA 92008
MAURER, MICHAEL	TV WRITER	8955 BEVERLY BLVD	LOS ANGELES, CA 90048
MAURER, NORMAN	WRITER-PRODUCER	3100 CAVENDISH DR	LOS ANGELES, CA 90064
MAUREY, DERREL	ACTOR	6380 WILSHIRE BLVD #910	LOS ANGELES, CA 90048
MAUREY, NICOLE	ACTRESS	3 SQUAIR-GERMAIN	MARLY LE ROY 78160 FRANCE
MAURIER, CLAIRE	ACTRESS	GEORGES LAMBERT AGENCE	
		13 BIS AVE LA MOTTE PIQUET	PARIS 75007 FRANCE
MAURIN, YVES-MARIE	ACTRESS	61 RUE CAULAINCOURT	PARIS 75018 FRANCE
MAURO, ANTHONY E	NEWS CORRESPONDENT	6 W LURAY AVE	ALEXANDRIA, VA 22301
MAURO, ERMANNO	TENOR	CAMI, 165 W 57TH ST	NEW YORK, NY 10019
MAURO, RALPH	ACTOR	8009 W NORTON AVE	HOLLYWOOD, CA 90046
MAUTI-NUNZIATA, ELENA	SOPRANO	61 W 62ND ST #6-F	NEW YORK, NY 10023
MAVEN, MAX	MINDREADER	POST OFFICE BOX 3819	LA MESA, CA 92044
MAX, HEINZ G	NEWS CORRESPONDENT	3132 "M" ST, NW	WASHINGTON, DC 20007
MAX, RON	ACTOR	324 S BEDFORD DR #1	BEVERLY HILLS, CA 90212
MAX CHEER	ROCK & ROLL GROUP	POST OFFICE BOX 198	COLLINSVILLE, CT 06022
MAXA, RUDY	NEWS CORRESPONDENT	2841 29TH ST, NW	WASHINGTON, DC 20008
MAXEY, LINDA	MARIMBIST	CAMI, 165 W 57TH ST	NEW YORK, NY 10019
MAXFIELD, B R	TV WRITER	8955 BEVERLY BLVD	LOS ANGELES, CA 90048
MAXTED, ELLEN	ACTRESS	141 S EL CAMINO DR #205	BEVERLY HILLS, CA 90212

Name	Occupation	Address	City	Zip
MAXWELL, BOB	ACTOR	9200 SUNSET BLVD #1210	LOS ANGELES, CA	90069
MAXWELL, DALE	ACTOR	10937 FRUITLAND DR #5	STUDIO CITY, CA	91604
MAXWELL, DAPHNE	ACTRESS	REID, 16540 ADLON RD	ENCINO, CA	91436
MAXWELL, DON	ACTOR	1350 N HIGHLAND AVE #24	HOLLYWOOD, CA	90028
MAXWELL, FRANK	ACTOR	446 SAN VICENTE BLVD #301	SANTA MONICA, CA	90402
MAXWELL, JAMES	ACTOR	AFFILIATE ARTISTS, LTD		
		37 W 65TH ST, 6TH FLOOR	NEW YORK, NY	10023
MAXWELL, JAMES	ACTOR	FRENCH'S, 26 BINNEY ST	LONDON W1	ENGLAND
MAXWELL, LINN	MEZZO-SOPRANO	SOFFER, 130 W 56TH ST	NEW YORK, NY	10019
MAXWELL, MORRIS J	COMPOSER	2219 BAXTER ST	LOS ANGELES, CA	90039
MAXWELL, RICHARD	SCREENWRITER	555 W 57TH ST #1230	NEW YORK, NY	10019
MAXWELL, ROBERT	CABLE EXECUTIVE	HOME BOX OFFICE PICTURES		
		1100 AVE OF THE AMERICAS	NEW YORK, NY	10036
MAXWELL, ROBERTA	ACTRESS	236 W 45TH ST	NEW YORK, NY	10036
MAXWELL, ROBIN	WRITER	247 S BEVERLY DR #102	BEVERLY HILLS, CA	90210
MAXWELL, RONALD F	FILM DIRECTOR	ICM, 8899 BEVERLY BLVD	LOS ANGELES, CA	90048
MAXX, THE	RHYTHM & BLUES GROUP	POST OFFICE BOX 11283	RICHMOND, VA	23230
MAY, ALBERT L, III	NEWS CORRESPONDENT	142 11TH ST, NE	WASHINGTON, DC	20002
MAY, ANDREW J	PHOTOGRAPHER	1920 356TH ST, NW	WASHINGTON, DC	20007
MAY, ANGELA	ACTRESS	6380 WILSHIRE BLVD #1600	LOS ANGELES, CA	90048
MAY, ARKIE	SINGER-GUITARIST	RURAL ROUTE #2, BOX 78-A5		
		PATES FORD RD	SMITHVILLE, TN	37166
MAY, BILLY	COMPOSER	22852 VIA CORDOVA	LAGUNA NIGUEL, CA	92677
MAY, BRIAN	COMPOSER	POST OFFICE BOX 562	BEVERLY HILLS, CA	90213
MAY, DEBORAH	ACTRESS	ICM, 8899 BEVERLY BLVD	LOS ANGELES, CA	90048
MAY, DONALD	ACTOR	TALENT REP, 20 E 53RD ST	NEW YORK, NY	10022
MAY, ELAINE	ACT-WRI-DIR	146 CENTRAL PARK W #4-E	NEW YORK, NY	10023
MAY, JACK	ACTOR	24 GLENLYON RD, ELTHAM	LONDON SE9	ENGLAND
MAY, JACK T	DIRECTOR	520 N MICHIGAN AVE #436	CHICAGO, IL	60611
MAY, JANET	ACTRESS	10845 LINDBROOK DR #3	LOS ANGELES, CA	90024
MAY, LEE	NEWS CORRESPONDENT	8809 VERNON VIEW DR	ALEXANDRIA, VA	22308
MAY, LENORA	ACTRESS	211 S BEVERLY DR #107	BEVERLY HILLS, CA	90212
MAY, PHIL & THE FALLEN ANGELS	ROCK & ROLL GROUP	105 EMLYN RD	LONDON W12 9TG	ENGLAND
MAY, PHILIP	WRITER-PRODUCER	12078 MOUND VIEW PL	STUDIO CITY, CA	91604
MAY, REX	CARTOONIST	POST OFFICE BOX 4203	NEW YORK, NY	10017
MAYALL, RIK	ACTOR-WRITER	BRUNSKILL, 169 QUEENSGATE #8	LONDON SW7	ENGLAND
MAYALL'S, JOHN, BLUESBREAKERS	RHYTHM & BLUES GROUP	POST OFFICE BOX 210103	SAN FRANCISCO, CA	94121
MAYAMA, MIKO	ACTRESS	9255 SUNSET BLVD #1105	LOS ANGELES, CA	90069
MAYBERRY, ROBERT	TV DIRECTOR	23957 VIA ONDA	VALENCIA, CA	91355
MAYBERRY, RUSSELL	TV DIRECTOR	DGA, 7950 SUNSET BLVD	LOS ANGELES, CA	90046
MAYEHOFF, EDDIE	ACTOR	369 PASEO DE PLAYA #411	VENTURA, CA	93001
MAYENZET, MARIA	ACTRESS	9165 SUNSET BLVD #202	LOS ANGELES, CA	90069
MAYER, ALLAN J	WRITER	555 W 57TH ST #1230	NEW YORK, NY	10019
MAYER, ARNO	NEWS CORRESPONDENT	4747 FULTON ST, NW	WASHINGTON, DC	20007
MAYER, CAROLINE E	NEWS CORRESPONDENT	3849 N UPLAND ST	ARLINGTON, VA	22207
MAYER, CHARLES	ACTOR	135 CENTRAL PARK W	NEW YORK, NY	10023
MAYER, CHRISTOPHER	ACTOR	329 N WETHERLY DR #205	BEVERLY HILLS, CA	90211
MAYER, DOE	FILM DIRECTOR	2510 4TH ST #C	SANTA MONICA, CA	90405
MAYER, DR JEAN	COLUMNIST	THE WASHINGTON POST		
		WRITERS GROUP		
		1150 15TH ST, NW	WASHINGTON, DC	20071
MAYER, GERALD	DIRECTOR-PRODUCER	104 S GLENROY AVE	LOS ANGELES, CA	90049
MAYER, HAROLD	DIRECTOR-PRODUCER	50 FERRISS ESTATE	NEW MILFORD, CT	06776
MAYER, HERBERT	CONDUCTOR	201 W 86TH ST	NEW YORK, NY	10024
MAYER, JANE M	NEWS CORRESPONDENT	2021 KALORAMA RD, NW	WASHINGTON, DC	20009
MAYER, JERRY	ACTOR	400 W 43RD ST #33-G	NEW YORK, NY	10036
MAYER, JERRY	TV WRITER-PRODUCER	POST OFFICE BOX 732	PACIFIC PALISADES, CA	90272
MAYER, KEN	ACTOR	5017 COLFAX AVE #A-19	NORTH HOLLYWOOD, CA	91601
MAYER, MIRIAM	COMPOSER	1500 S SHERBOURNE DR	LOS ANGELES, CA	90035
MAYER, PAUL A	TV WRITER	555 W 57TH ST #1230	NEW YORK, NY	10019
MAYER, PAULA	NEWS CORRESPONDENT	NBC-TV, NEWS DEPARTMENT		
		4001 NEBRASKA AVE, NW	WASHINGTON, DC	20016
MAYER, PIETER	DIRECTOR	DGA, 7950 SUNSET BLVD	LOS ANGELES, CA	90046
MAYER, RICHARD	ACTOR	10850 RIVERSIDE DR #505	NORTH HOLLYWOOD, CA	91602
MAYER, STEVE	PIANIST	R NAPAL, 340 W 23RD ST	NEW YORK, NY	10011
MAYER, URI	CONDUCTOR	SHAW CONCERTS, 1995 BROADWAY	NEW YORK, NY	10023
MAYERSBERG, PAUL	SCREENWRITER	409 N CAMDEN DR #105	BEVERLY HILLS, CA	90210
MAYERSON, MARC	WRITER	EISENBACH-GREENE, INC		
		760 N LA CIENEGA BLVD	LOS ANGELES, CA	90069
MAYES, DOROTHY	NEWS CORRESPONDENT	9810 WILLIAMSBURG DR	UPPER MARLBORO, MD	20772
MAYES, WENDELL	SCREENWRITER	1504 BEL AIR RD	LOS ANGELES, CA	90077
MAYEUR, ROBERT G	COMPOSER	838 BARRINGTON AVE #101	LOS ANGELES, CA	90049
MAYFIELD, CURTIS	SINGER-SONGWRITER	THE WILLIAM MORRIS AGENCY		
		1350 AVE OF THE AMERICAS	NEW YORK, NY	10019
MAYFIELD, LARRY	PIANIST	1905 ROSEWOOD VALLEY DR	BRENTWOOD, TN	37027
MAYFIELD, SAMMY	MUSICIAN	POST OFFICE BOX 18368	DENVER, CO	80218
MAYHALL, JACK	ACTOR	439 S LA CIENEGA BLVD #120	LOS ANGELES, CA	90048
MAYLAM, TONY	DIRECTOR	9000 SUNSET BLVD #1200	LOS ANGELES, CA	90069
MAYLE, MIKE "MACHO MAN"	WRESTLER	CAPITOL INTERNATIONAL		
		11844 MARKET ST	NORTH LIMA, OH	44452
MAYNARD, BILL	ACTOR	THE RICHARD STONE AGENCY		
		18-20 YORK BLDGS, ADELPHI	LONDON WC2N 6JY	ENGLAND
MAYNARD, EARL	BODYBUILDER	SPORTS WORLD RACQUETBALL		
		AND FITNESS CENTER		
		6666 GREEN VALLEY CIR	CULVER CITY, CA	90230

VIRGINIA MAYO

WILLIE MAYS

TONY MARTIN

IRISH MC CALLA

DAVID MC CALLUM

KEVIN MC CARTHY

PAUL MC CARTNEY

LEIGH MC CLOSKEY

PATTI MC CORMACK

MAYNARD, JIMMY	GUITARIST	325-A HICKORY RIDGE RD		
		ROUTE #5	LEBANON, TN	37087
MAYNARD, JOYCE	COLUMNIST	N Y TIMES SYNDICATION		
		130 5TH AVE	NEW YORK, NY	10011
MAYNARD, MIMI	ACTRESS	9300 WILSHIRE BLVD #410	BEVERLY HILLS, CA	90212
MAYNARD, ROBERT C	JOURNALIST-COLUMNIST	UNIVERSAL PRESS SYNDICATE		
		4900 MAIN ST, 9TH FLOOR	KANSAS CITY, MO	62114
MAYNARD, VINCENT	WRITER-PRODUCER	2293 W 20TH ST	NEW YORK, NY	10018
MAYNE, BOBBY	WRESTLER	SEE - JAGGERS, BOBBY		
MAYNE, FERDINAND	ACTOR	9807 PORTOLA DR	BEVERLY HILLS, CA	90210
MAYNES, CHARLES WILLIAM	COLUMNIST	N Y TIMES SYNDICATION		
		130 5TH AVE	NEW YORK, NY	10011
MAYNOR, ASA	ACTRESS-PRODUCER	POST OFFICE BOX 1641	BEVERLY HILLS, CA	90213
MAYNOR, KEVIN	SINGER	1776 BROADWAY #504	NEW YORK, NY	10019
MAYO, GEOFFREY M	DIRECTOR	58 W 15TH ST	NEW YORK, NY	10011
MAYO, JENNIFER	ACTRESS	1901 AVE OF THE STARS #840	LOS ANGELES, CA	90067
MAYO, VIRGINIA	ACTRESS	109 EAST AVE DES LAS ABOLES	THOUSAND OAKS, CA	91360
MAYO, WHITMAN	ACTOR	3210 W 80TH ST	INGLEWOOD, CA	90305
MAYOH, ROYSTON	TV DIRECTOR-PRODUCER	35 PHEASANT'S WY, RICKMANSWORTH	HERTS	ENGLAND
MAYORGA, LINCOLN	PIANIST	CCS, 4478 PURDUE AVE	CULVER CITY, CA	90230
MAYOTTE, FRANCE	ACTRESS	11350 VENTURA BLVD #206	STUDIO CITY, CA	91604
MAYRON, MELANIE	ACTRESS-WRITER	1317 N ORANGE GROVE AVE	LOS ANGELES, CA	90046
MAYS, DAWSON	ACTOR	3907 W ALAMEDA AVE #101	BURBANK, CA	91505
MAYS, DEBORAH	ACTRESS-MODEL	SEE - NAMATH, DEBORAH MAYS		
MAYS, DOROTHY	ACTRESS-MODEL	9200 SUNSET BLVD #1210	LOS ANGELES, CA	90069
MAYS, JOE	ACTOR	1723 1/2 N KINGSLEY DR	LOS ANGELES, CA	90027
MAYS, JOHN	GUITARIST	3261 NEW TOWNE RD	ANTIOCH, TN	37013
MAYS, LYLE	PIANIST	KURLAND, 173 BRIGHTON AVE	BOSTON, MA	02134
MAYS, MELINDA	ACTRESS-MODEL	1901 AVE OF THE STARS #840	LOS ANGELES, CA	90067
MAYS, ROD	ACTOR	348 E OLIVE AVE #K	BURBANK, CA	91502
MAYS, WILLIE	BASEBALL	51 MOUNT VERNON LN	ATHERTON, CA	94025
MAZE	RHYTHM & BLUES GROUP	V JONES, 805 MORAGA RD	LAFAYETTE, CA	94549
MAZE, RICHARD E	NEWS CORRESPONDENT	28 HAWTHORNE CT, NW	WASHINGTON, DC	20017
MAZE, STEPHANIE	PHOTOGRAPHER	1820 KALORAMA RD, NW	WASHINGTON, DC	20009
MAZER, IRA	DIRECTOR	DGA, 110 W 57TH ST	NEW YORK, NY	10019
MAZER, SUSAN & DALLAS SMITH	JAZZ DUO	HOFFER, 233 1/2 E 48TH ST	NEW YORK, NY	10017
MAZER, VIRGINIA	WRITER	555 W 57TH ST #1230	NEW YORK, NY	10019
MAZES, MICHAEL	ACTOR	1815 1/2 N EDGEMONT ST	LOS ANGELES, CA	90027
MAZIE, DAVID M	NEWS CORRESPONDENT	9115 LE VELLE DR	CHEVY CHASE, MD	20815
MAZIN, STAN	ACTOR	5506 LEGHORN AVE	VAN NUYS, CA	91401
MAZMAN, MELONIE	ACTRESS	12750 VENTURA BLVD #102	STUDIO CITY, CA	91604
MAZMANIAN, MARIUS	ACTOR	2446 1/2 N GOWER ST	HOLLYWOOD, CA	90068
MAZOTTI, PASCAL	ACTOR	19 PL DU MARCHE SAINT HONORE	PARIS 75001	FRANCE
MAZUER, MERRILL M	DIRECTOR	GOODMAN, 8909 OLYMPIC BLVD	BEVERLY HILLS, CA	90211
MAZURA, FRANZ	BASSO-BARITONE	CAMI, 165 W 57TH ST	NEW YORK, NY	10019
MAZURKEVICH, YURI	VIOLINIST	GEWALD, 58 W 58TH ST	NEW YORK, NY	10019
MAZURKI, MIKE	ACTOR	356 N CLYBOURN AVE	BURBANK, CA	91505
MAZUROK, YURI	BARITONE	MARIEDL ANDERS ARTISTS MGMT		
		535 EL CAMINO DEL MAR ST	SAN FRANCISCO, CA	94121
MAZURSKY, PAUL	WRITER-PRODUCER	707 N ALPINE DR	BEVERLY HILLS, CA	90210
MAZZATENTA, O LOUIS	PHOTOGRAPHER	4904 N CENTAUR ST	ANNANDALE, VA	22003
MAZZUCA, JOSEPH	TV DIRECTOR	22856 COVELLO ST	CANOGA PARK, CA	91307
MC ABEE, DENNIS	GUITARIST	ROUTE #4, BOX 51, DAVIS PL	COLUMBIA, TN	38401
MC ABEE, KATHRYN J	NEWS CORRESPONDENT	1755 S JEFFERSON DAVIS HWY	ARLINGTON, VA	22202
MC ADAMS, JAMES D	TV WRITER-PRODUCER	15980 VALLEY WOOD RD	SHERMAN OAKS, CA	91403
MC ALLISTER, KEITH	BASSMASTER	2801 MEADOW LARK DR	SAN DIEGO, CA	92123
MC ALPINE, DONALD	CINEMATOGRAPHER	POST OFFICE 2230	HOLLYWOOD, CA	90078
MC ALPINE, JAMES	ACTOR	AIMEE, 13743 VICTORY BLVD	VAN NUYS, CA	91401
MC ANALLY, MAC	SINGER	POST OFFICE BOX 2831	MUSCLE SHOALS, AL	35660
MC ANDREW, JACK	TV WRITER	8955 BEVERLY BLVD	LOS ANGELES, CA	90048
MC ANDREW, MARIANNE	ACTRESS	9220 SUNSET BLVD #202	LOS ANGELES, CA	90069
MC ANENY, PATRICIA	ACTRESS	7471 MELROSE AVE #11	LOS ANGELES, CA	90046
MC ANINCH, THOMAS	FRENCH HORNIST	1420 E CEDAR LN	MADISON, TN	37115
MC ANUFF, DES	THEATER DIRECTOR	THE WILLIAM MORRIS AGENCY		
		1350 AVE OF THE AMERICAS	NEW YORK, NY	10019
MC ARDLE, ANDREA	ACTRESS	1501 BROADWAY #1806-A	NEW YORK, NY	10036
MC ARDLE, JUDELLE A	NEWS CORRESPONDENT	10611 VALE RD	OAKTON, VA	22124
MC ARTHUR, GEORGE	NEWS CORRESPONDENT	4633 ROCKWOOD PARKWAY, NW	WASHINGTON, DC	20016
MC AVITY, HELEN	WRITER	1700 LEXINGTON RD	BEVERLY HILLS, CA	90210
MC AVOY, EUGENE T	DIRECTOR	DGA, 7950 SUNSET BLVD	LOS ANGELES, CA	90046
MC AVOY, KIM	NEWS CORRESPONDENT	1099 S FOREST DR	ARLINGTON, VA	22204
MC BAIN, DIANE	ACTRESS	15010 VENTURA BLVD #234	SHERMAN OAKS, CA	91403
MC BEE, SUSANNA	NEWS CORRESPONDENT	3834 "T" ST, NW	WASHINGTON, DC	20007
MC BRIDE, DICK	WRITER	555 W 57TH ST #1230	NEW YORK, NY	10019
MC BRIDE, HARLEE	ACTRESS	705 WESTMOUNT DR #302	LOS ANGELES, CA	90069
MC BRIDE, JAMES M	WRITER-PRODUCER	DGA, 7950 SUNSET BLVD	LOS ANGELES, CA	90046
MC BRIDE, JEFF	COMEDIAN	ICM, 8899 BEVERLY BLVD	LOS ANGELES, CA	90048
MC BRIDE, JOSEPH	FILM CRITIC	117 N KINGS RD	LOS ANGELES, CA	90048
MC BRIDE, MICHAEL	GUITARIST	121 HAZELWOOD DR #B-7	HENDERSONVILLE, TN	37075
MC BRIDE, MICHELE	SOPRANO	HILLYER, 250 W 57TH ST	NEW YORK, NY	10107
MC BRIDE, PATRICIA	ACTRESS	330 E 57TH ST	NEW YORK, NY	10022
MC BRIDE, ROBERT J	NEWS CORRESPONDENT	NBC-TV, NEWS DEPARTMENT		
		4001 NEBRASKA AVE, NW	WASHINGTON, DC	20016

MAZE

Top Row: Ron Smith • Frankie Beverly • McKinley Williams
Bottom Row: Sam Porter • Roame Lowry • Billy "Shoes" Johnson • Robin Duhe

MIAMI SOUND MACHINE

Emilo Estefan • Marcos Avila • Gloria Estefan • Kiki Garcia

Name	Occupation	Address	City/State	Zip
MC BROOM, AMANDA	SINGER-SONGWRITER	22903 MARIANO ST	WOODLAND HILLS, CA	91367
MC BROOM, BRUCE V	ACTOR	829 1/2 N FULLER AVE	LOS ANGELES, CA	90046
MC BRYDE, THOMAS R	PIANIST	3101 WEST END AVE #216	NASHVILLE, TN	37203
MC CABE, JOHN	COMPOSER	49 BURNS AVE, SOUTHALL	MIDDLESEX	ENGLAND
MC CABE, LEE	WRITER	555 W 57TH ST #1230	NEW YORK, NY	10019
MC CABE, ROBIN	PIANIST	1776 BROADWAY #504	NEW YORK, NY	10019
MC CABE, RON	ACTOR	14570 BENEFIT ST	SHERMAN OAKS, CA	91403
MC CABE, SANDRA	ACTRESS	1228 HILLDALE AVE	LOS ANGELES, CA	90069
MC CABE, SHANE	ACTOR	6380 WILSHIRE BLVD #1600	LOS ANGELES, CA	90048
MC CAFFERTY, JOHN J	ACTOR	8721 SUNSET BLVD #202	LOS ANGELES, CA	90069
MC CAFFERTY, JOHN W	FILM EDITOR	3123 BARRY AVE	LOS ANGELES, CA	90066
MC CAFFERTY, SUZANNE	FILM PRODUCER	ASTA PRODS, 126 S ORLANDO AVE	LOS ANGELES, CA	90048
MC CAFFERY, GREGORY C	NEWS CORRESPONDENT	826 "D" ST, NW	WASHINGTON, DC	20003
MC CAFFREY, PATRICEA	MEZZO-SOPRANO	CAMI, 165 W 57TH ST	NEW YORK, NY	10019
MC CAIN, FRANCES LEE	ACTRESS	POST OFFICE BOX 5617	BEVERLY HILLS, CA	90210
MC CALL, BRONWYN N	NEWS CORRESPONDENT	5416 55TH PL #203	RIVERDALE, MD	20737
MC CALL, C W	SINGER-SONGWRITER	OFFICE OF THE MAYOR, BILL FRIES	OURAY, CO	81427
MC CALL, CHERYL	WRITER-EDITOR	LIFE/TIME & LIFE BLDG		
		ROCKEFELLER CENTER	NEW YORK, NY	10020
MC CALL, CHUCK	GUITARIST	641 BEACH ST	KANSAS CITY, KS	66113
MC CALL, DARRELL	GUITARIST	7675 SAWYER BROWN RD	NASHVILLE, TN	37221
MC CALL, JADE	ACTOR	1351 N ORANGE DR #105	HOLLYWOOD, CA	90028
MC CALL, JAMES R	WRITER	555 W 57TH ST #1230	NEW YORK, NY	10019
MC CALL, JOAN	WRITER	9022 SUNSET BLVD #531	LOS ANGELES, CA	90069
MC CALL, LAURIE	WRITER	555 W 57TH ST #1230	NEW YORK, NY	10019
MC CALL, MARY ANN	ACTOR	1546 N GORDON ST	HOLLYWOOD, CA	90028
MC CALL, MITZI	ACTRESS-WRITER	6310 SAN VICENTE BLVD #407	LOS ANGELES, CA	90048
MC CALL, MONA	GUITARIST	7675 SAWYER BROWN RD	NASHVILLE, TN	37221
MC CALL, SHALANE	ACTRESS	POST OFFICE BOX 7088	BURBANK, CA	91510
MC CALLA, DEIDRE	SINGER	OLIVIA RECORDS COMPANY		
		4400 MARKET ST	OAKLAND, CA	94608
MC CALLA, IRISH	ACTRESS	MC INTYRE, 920 OAK TERR	PRESCOTT, AZ	86301
MC CALLION, JAMES	ACTOR	12303 EMELITA ST	NORTH HOLLYWOOD, CA	91607
MC CALLISTER, GEORGE	ACTOR	4141 WHITSETT AVE	STUDIO CITY, CA	91604
MC CALLISTER, LON	ACTOR	POST OFFICE BOX 396	LITTLE RIVER, CA	95456
MC CALLUM, DAVID	ACTOR	40 E 62ND ST	NEW YORK, NY	10021
MC CALLUM, JACK	SPORTS WRITER-EDITOR	SPORTS ILLUSTRATED MAGAZINE		
		TIME & LIFE BUILDING		
		ROCKEFELLER CENTER	NEW YORK, NY	10020
MC CALLY, DAVID	ACTOR	8831 SUNSET BLVD #402	LOS ANGELES, CA	90069
MC CALMAN, MACON	ACTOR	SF & A, 121 N SAN VICENTE BLVD	BEVERLY HILLS, CA	90211
MC CAMBRIDGE, MERCEDES	ACTRESS	MICHAEL HARTIG, 114 E 28TH ST	NEW YORK, NY	10016
MC CANDLESS, EARL R	COMPOSER	POST OFFICE BOX 828	SOLANA BEACH, CA	92075
MC CANLIES, TIMOTHY B	WRITER	8955 BEVERLY BLVD	LOS ANGELES, CA	90048
MC CANN, CHUCK	ACTOR-COMEDIAN	STONE, 1052 CAROL DR	LOS ANGELES, CA	90069
MC CANN, DANIEL	ACTOR	1411 S DETROIT ST	LOS ANGELES, CA	90046
MC CANN, DAVID DE WITT	TV DIRECTOR	POST OFFICE BOX 4325	DIAMOND BAR, CA	91765
MC CANN, ELIZABETH	THEATER PRODUCER	1501 BROADWAY	NEW YORK, NY	10036
MC CANN, HANK	CASTING DIRECTOR	POST OFFICE BOX 6020	BEVERLY HILLS, CA	90212
MC CANN, JOAN	SOPRANO	260 W END AVE #7-A	NEW YORK, NY	10023
MC CANN, JOHN	ACTOR	9255 SUNSET BLVD #603	LOS ANGELES, CA	90069
MC CANN, JULIE	ACTRESS	GOLDEN GATE BUIDLING		
		PACIFIC HIGHWAY		
		SURFERS PARADISE	QUEENSLAND	AUSTRALIA
MC CANN, KATHLEEN JOE	VIOLINIST	2121 BLAIR BLVD	NASHVILLE, TN	37212
MC CANN, LES	MUSICIAN-COMPOSER	315 S BEVERLY DR #207	BEVERLY HILLS, CA	90212
MC CANTS, REID	COMEDIAN	POST OFFICE BOX 82	GREAT NECK, NY	11022
MC CAREN, JOSEPH	ACTOR	400 W 43RD ST #35-F	NEW YORK, NY	10036
MC CARGAR, GEORGE L	NEWS CORRESPONDENT	2139 WISCONSIN AVE, NW	WASHINGTON, DC	20007
MC CARREN, FRED	ACTOR	364 S CLOVERDALE AVE #104	LOS ANGELES, CA	90036
MC CARROLL, THOMAS	NEWS CORRESPONDENT	TIME/TIME & LIFE BLDG		
		ROCKEFELLER CENTER	NEW YORK, NY	10020
MC CARTHY, ANDREW	ACTOR	317 W 12TH ST #3	NEW YORK, NY	10014
MC CARTHY, ANNETTE	ACTRESS	10100 SANTA MONICA BLVD #1600	LOS ANGELES, CA	90067
MC CARTHY, BARNETTA	ACTRESS	18653 VENTURA BLVD #349	TARZANA, CA	91356
MC CARTHY, DENNIS J	CONDUCTOR	535 BIRMINGHAM RD	BURBANK, CA	91504
MC CARTHY, ELIZABETH	WRITER	555 W 57TH ST #1230	NEW YORK, NY	10019
MC CARTHY, FRANCIS X	WRITER	8955 BEVERLY BLVD	LOS ANGELES, CA	90048
MC CARTHY, FRANK	ACTOR	10351 SANTA MONICA BLVD #211	LOS ANGELES, CA	90025
MC CARTHY, FRANK	FILM PRODUCER	1455 SEABRIGHT PL	BEVERLY HILLS, CA	90210
MC CARTHY, FRED	CARTOONIST	NEWS AMERICA SYNDICATE		
		1703 KAISER AVE	IRVINE, CA	92714
MC CARTHY, JULIANNA	ACTRESS	STONE, 1052 CAROL DR	LOS ANGELES, CA	90069
MC CARTHY, JULIE M	NEWS CORRESPONDENT	2325 ASHMEAD PL, NW	WASHINGTON, DC	20009
MC CARTHY, KEVIN	ACTOR	14854 SUTTON ST	SHERMAN OAKS, CA	91403
MC CARTHY, KEVIN D	TV DIRECTOR	12425 SARAH ST	STUDIO CITY, CA	91604
MC CARTHY, KYLE S	DIRECTOR	121 W 72ND ST	NEW YORK, NY	10023
MC CARTHY, LARK V	NEWS CORRESPONDENT	CBS NEWS, 2020 "M" ST, NW	WASHINGTON, DC	20036
MC CARTHY, LINWOOD	ACTOR	233 N SWALL DR	BEVERLY HILLS, CA	90211
MC CARTHY, MATT	TV DIRECTOR	16 RAMILLIES ST	LONDON W1V 1DL	ENGLAND
MC CARTHY, MIKE	CLOWN	2701 COTTAGE WY #14	SACRAMENTO, CA	95825
MC CARTHY, NEIL	ACTOR	61 OGLANDER RD	LONDON SE15	ENGLAND

MC CARTHY, RICHARD	TV DIRECTOR	2 OSWALD ST, CREMORNE	SYDNEY NSW	AUSTRALIA
MC CARTHY, RICHARD D MAX	NEWS CORRESPONDENT	1825 UHLE ST	ARLINGTON, VA	22201
MC CARTHY, ROBERT E	WRITER	8955 BEVERLY BLVD	LOS ANGELES, CA	90048
MC CARTHY, SEAN J	VIDEO EXECUTIVE	TIME VIDEO INFORMATION SERVICE		
		1271 AVE OF THE AMERICAS	NEW YORK, NY	10020
MC CARTHY, SHERYL	NEWS CORRESPONDENT	ABC-TV, 7 W 66TH ST	NEW YORK, NY	10023
MC CARTHY, VANCE	NEWS CORRESPONDENT	4511 SLEAFORD RD	BETHESDA, MD	20814
MC CARTNEY, JAMES H	NEWS CORRESPONDENT	4456 SPRINGDALE ST, NW	WASHINGTON, DC	20016
MC CARTNEY, LINDA	MUSICIAN-PHOTOGRAPHER	WATERFALL ESTATE, NEAR PEAMARCH		
		SAINT LEONARD-ON-THE-SEA	SUSSEX	ENGLAND
MC CARTNEY, PAUL	SINGER-COMPOSER	WATERFALL ESTATE, NEAR PEAMARCH		
		SAINT LEONARD-ON-THE-SEA	SUSSEX	ENGLAND
MC CARTNEY, PAUL & WINGS	ROCK & ROLL GROUP	MPL COMMUNICATIONS		
		1 SOHO SQ	LONDON W1F 6BQ	ENGLAND
MC CARTY, PATRICIA	VIOLIST	AARON, 25 HUNTINGTON AVE	BOSTON, MA	02116
MC CARTY, ROBERT	FILM WRITER-DIRECTOR	222 W 83RD ST	NEW YORK, NY	10024
MC CARTY, VICKI	ACTRESS-MODEL	MODELS & PROMOTIONS AGENCY		
		8560 SUNSET BLVD, 10TH FLOOR	LOS ANGELES, CA	90069
MC CARVER, HOLLY	ACTRESS	8568 SHERWOOD DR	LOS ANGELES, CA	90069
MC CARVER, SEAN	WRITER	8955 BEVERLY BLVD	LOS ANGELES, CA	90048
MC CARVER, TIM	SPORTSCASTER	RURAL ROUTE #1	MILLINGTON, TN	38053
MC CARY, ROD	ACTOR	12750 VENTURA BLVD #102	STUDIO CITY, CA	91604
MC CASH, DOUGLAS L	PHOTOJOURNALIST	217 E LURAY AVE	ALEXANDRIA, VA	22301
MC CASHIN, CONSTANCE	ACTRESS	10490 SELKIRK LN	LOS ANGELES, CA	90077
MC CASKEY, GEORGE H	WRITER	555 W 57TH ST #1230	NEW YORK, NY	10019
MC CASKILL, RODERICK C	ACTOR	7401 VARIEL AVE	CANOGA PARK, CA	91303
MC CASLIN, JOHN L	NEWS CORRESPONDENT	1016 PRINCE ST #5	ALEXANDRIA, VA	22314
MC CASLIN, MARY & JIM RINGER	VOCAL DUO	1671 APPIAN WY	SANTA MONICA, CA	90401
MC CASLIN, MAYLO	ACTRESS	9255 SUNSET BLVD #1105	LOS ANGELES, CA	90069
MC CAUGHEY, WILLIAM L	SOUND ENGINEER	5604 SARA DR	TORRANCE, CA	90503
MC CAULEY, BARRY	TENOR	CAMI, 165 W 57TH ST	NEW YORK, NY	10019
MC CAULEY, PAUL G	COMEDY WRITER	4401 KLING ST #16	BURBANK, CA	91505
MC CAVITT, T J	ACTOR	4600 KESTER AVE #A	SHERMAN OAKS, CA	91403
MC CAY, PEGGY	ACTRESS	8811 WONDERLAND AVE	LOS ANGELES, CA	90046
MC CHESNEY, JOANNE W	NEWS CORRESPONDENT	1751 LANIER PL, NW	WASHINGTON, DC	20009
MC CHESNEY, JOHN	NEWS CORRESPONDENT	1753 SWANN ST, NW	WASHINGTON, DC	20009
MC CLAIN, CHARLY	SINGER	POST OFFICE BOX 2757	NASHVILLE, TN	37219
MC CLAIN, GARETH	ACTOR	8949 SUNSET BLVD #203	LOS ANGELES, CA	90069
MC CLAIN, JACK S	WRITER	8955 BEVERLY BLVD	LOS ANGELES, CA	90048
MC CLAIN, JOHN D	NEWS CORRESPONDENT	3307 N TRINIDAD ST	ARLINGTON, VA	22213
MC CLAIN, KATIE	ACTRESS	1450 BELFAST DR	LOS ANGELES, CA	90069
MC CLAIN, SHEILAH	MODEL	POST OFFICE BOX 7211	MOUNTAIN VIEW, CA	94043
MC CLAIN, WALLIS	NEWS CORRESPONDENT	3100 CONNECTICUT AVE, NW	WASHINGTON, DC	20008
MC CLANAHAN, RUE	ACTRESS	10894 WILLOW CREST PL	STUDIO CITY, CA	91604
MC CLEAF, RICHARD	NEWS CORRESPONDENT	8534 GWYNEDD WY	SPRINGFIELD, VA	22153
MC CLEERY, KATHLEEN D	NEWS CORRESPONDENT	POST OFFICE BOX 2626	WASHINGTON, DC	20013
MC CLELLAN, MAX	TV WRITER	8955 BEVERLY BLVD	LOS ANGELES, CA	90048
MC CLELLAND, BILLY EARL	DOBROIST	POST OFFICE BOX 1273	NASHVILLE, TN	37202
MC CLENAHEN, JOHN S	NEWS CORRESPONDENT	2300 PIMMIT DR #1207	FALLS CHURCH, VA	22043
MC CLENDON, DEBBIE	SINGER	POST OFFICE BOX 2341	PASADENA, CA	91102
MC CLENDON, ERNESTINE	ACTRESS	8721 SUNSET BLVD #200	LOS ANGELES, CA	90069
MC CLENDON, SARAH	NEWS CORRESPONDENT	2933 28TH ST, NW	WASHINGTON, DC	20008
MC CLINTON, DELBERT	SINGER-GUITARIST	POST OFFICE BOX 2689	DANBURY, CT	06813
MC CLINTON, DENNIS	NEWS CORRESPONDENT	1301 7TH ST, NW	WASHINGTON, DC	20001
MC CLINTON, O B	SINGER	TESSIER, 505 CANTON PASS	MADISON, TN	37115
MC CLORY, SEAN	ACTOR-DIRECTOR	6612 WHITLEY TERR	LOS ANGELES, CA	90068
MC CLOSKEY, BILL	NEWS CORRESPONDENT	4709 OVERBROOK RD	BETHESDA, MD	20816
MC CLOSKEY, KRISTIN L	WRITER	555 W 57TH ST #1230	NEW YORK, NY	10019
MC CLOSKEY, LEIGH	ACTOR	6032 PHILIP AVE	MALIBU, CA	90265
MC CLOSKEY, PAUL	NEWS CORRESPONDENT	701 NORTH CAROLINA AVE, SE	WASHINGTON, DC	20003
MC CLURE, DOUG	ACTOR	14936 STONESBORO PL	SHERMAN OAKS, CA	91403
MC CLURE, ERIC	DRUMMER	371 WALLACE RD #H-54	NASHVILLE, TN	37209
MC CLURE, HARRY K	TV DIRECTOR	KMOX-TV, 1 MEMORIAL DR	SAINT LOUIS, MO	63102
MC CLURE, MARC	ACTOR	6310 SAN VICENTE BLVD #407	LOS ANGELES, CA	90048
MC CLURE, PAULA	NEWS REPORTER	ENTERTAINMENT TONIGHT		
		PARAMOUNT TELEVISION		
		5555 MELROSE AVE	LOS ANGELES, CA	90038
MC CLURE-WHITE, LINDA	ACTRESS	13111 VENTURA BLVD #102	STUDIO CITY, CA	91604
MC CLURG, BOB	ACTOR	643 N KILKEA DR	LOS ANGELES, CA	90048
MC CLURG, EDIE	ACTRESS	2065 HIGHTOWER DR	LOS ANGELES, CA	90068
MC COID, KATIE	ACTRESS	1629 RODNEY DR #2	LOS ANGELES, CA	90027
MC COLL, WILLIAM G	WRITER	555 W 57TH ST #1230	NEW YORK, NY	10019
MC COLLISTER, CHARLIE	ACTOR	4442 PRESIDIO DR	SIMI VALLEY, CA	93063
MC COLLISTER, RICK	PERCUSSIONIST	6436 FLEETWOOD DR	NASHVILLE, TN	37209
MC COLLUM, JESSE EARL	VIOLINIST	ROUTE #6, BOX 109	DICKSON, TN	37055
MC COLM, MATT	STUNTMAN	3518 W CAHUENGA BLVD #300	LOS ANGELES, CA	90068
MC COMBIE, J A S	SCREENWRITER	8955 BEVERLY BLVD	LOS ANGELES, CA	90048
MC CONNACHIE, BRIAN	TV WRITER	555 W 57TH ST #1230	NEW YORK, NY	10019
MC CONNELL, DAVID F	NEWS CORRESPONDENT	6031 UTAH AVE, NW	WASHINGTON, DC	20015
MC CONNELL, JAMES A	WRITER	8955 BEVERLY BLVD	LOS ANGELES, CA	90048
MC CONNELL, JOHN	WRITER	555 W 57TH ST #1230	NEW YORK, NY	10019
MC CONNELL, JUDITH	ACTRESS	9000 SUNSET BLVD #801	LOS ANGELES, CA	90069
MC CONNELL, KEITH	ACTOR	9165 SUNSET BLVD #202	LOS ANGELES, CA	90069
MC CONNELL, MAUREEN	ACTRESS	406 E WAPELLO ST	ALTADENA, CA	91001
MC CONNELL, THOMAS	TV WRITER-DIRECTOR	8401 BROADACRE DR	SUN VALLEY, CA	91332

Name	Occupation	Address	City	Zip
MC CONNELL, WILLIAM A	WRITER	555 W 57TH ST #1230	NEW YORK, NY	10019
MC CONNOCHIE, JOY	ACTRESS	6605 HOLLYWOOD BLVD #220	HOLLYWOOD, CA	90028
MC CONNOHIE, MICHAEL	ACTOR	568 1/2 E VERDUGO AVE	BURBANK, CA	91501
MC COO, MARILYN	SINGER-ACTRESS	DAVIS, 1017 RIDGEDALE DR	BEVERLY HILLS, CA	90210
MC COO & DAVIS	VOCAL DUO	1017 RIDGEDALE DR	BEVERLY HILLS, CA	90210
MC COOK, JOHN	ACT-SING-COND	4154 COLBATH AVE	SHERMAN OAKS, CA	91413
MC COOK, NANCY	CASTING DIRECTOR	3855 LANKERSHIM BLVD	NORTH HOLLYWOOD, CA	91604
MC COPPIN, PETER	CONDUCTOR	GERSHUNOFF, 502 PARK AVE	NEW YORK, NY	10022
MC CORD, CHARLES	WRITER	555 W 57TH ST #1230	NEW YORK, NY	10019
MC CORD, JONAS	WRITER	555 W 57TH ST #1230	NEW YORK, NY	10019
MC CORD, KENT	ACTOR	1738 N ORANGE GROVE AVE	LOS ANGELES, CA	90046
MC CORKINDALE, SIMON	ACTOR	WAGG, 78 NEW BOND ST	LONDON SW1	ENGLAND
MC CORKLE, PAT	CASTING DIRECTOR	240 W 44TH ST	NEW YORK, NY	10036
MC CORMAC, CYNDI	ACTRESS	2266 EDENDALE PL	LOS ANGELES, CA	90039
MC CORMACK, JAN	WRITER	8955 BEVERLY BLVD	LOS ANGELES, CA	90048
MC CORMACK, LISA P	NEWS CORRESPONDENT	105 9TH ST #302, SE	WASHINGTON, DC	20003
MC CORMACK, PATTY	ACTRESS	3870 AVENIDA DEL SOL	STUDIO CITY, CA	91604
MC CORMALLY, KEVIN	NEWS CORRESPONDENT	161 "D" ST, SE	WASHINGTON, DC	20003
MC CORMALLY, SEAN	NEWS CORRESPONDENT	120 DUDDINGTON PL, SE	WASHINGTON, DC	20003
MC CORMICK, BRIAN	TV WRITER	8955 BEVERLY BLVD	LOS ANGELES, CA	90048
MC CORMICK, CAROLYN	ACTRESS	15760 VENTURA BLVD #1730	ENCINO, CA	91436
MC CORMICK, GEORGE	GUITARIST	ROUTE #1, BOX 14453	SILVERPOINT, TN	38582
MC CORMICK, GERALD LEE	GUITARIST	123 MEADOWLAKE DR	HENDERSONVILLE, TN	37075
MC CORMICK, GILMER	ACTRESS	SF & A, 121 N SAN VICENTE BLVD	BEVERLY HILLS, CA	90211
MC CORMICK, HASKEL	BANJOIST	ROUTE #2	BETHPAGE, TN	37022
MC CORMICK, HENRY KELLY	MUSICIAN	ROUTE #2	BETHPAGE, TN	37022
MC CORMICK, JAMES LLOYD	GUITARIST	ROUTE #3	WESTMORELAND, TN	37186
MC CORMICK, KEVIN	CARTOONIST	NEWS AMERICA SYNDICATE		
		1703 KAISER AVE	IRVINE, CA	92714
MC CORMICK, MAUREEN	ACTRESS	10501 WILSHIRE BLVD #709	LOS ANGELES, CA	90024
MC CORMICK, NANCE	TV WRITER	8955 BEVERLY BLVD	LOS ANGELES, CA	90048
MC CORMICK, NEAL	GUITARIST	ROUTE #4, BOX 288-C	DEFUNIAK SPRINGS, FL	32433
MC CORMICK, PAT	ACT-WRI-COMED	4303 KLUMP AVE	NORTH HOLLYWOOD, CA	91602
MC CORMICK, PAT	SWIMMER	POST OFFICE BOX 250	SEAL BEACH, CA	90740
MC CORMICK, RANDY LYN	PIANIST	2112 TIMERWOOD PL	NASHVILLE, TN	37215
MC CORMICK, SUZANNE	PIANIST	GURTMAN, 162 W 56TH ST	NEW YORK, NY	10019
MC CORMICK, WILLIAM HAROLD	GUITARIST	ROUTE #2, BOX 66	BETHPAGE, TN	37022
MC CORTNEY, TERESA	ACTRESS	110 1/2 S ORANGE DR	LOS ANGELES, CA	90036
MC COURT, MALACHY	ACTOR	19 W 44TH ST #1500	NEW YORK, NY	10017
MC COURT, MICHAEL	NEWS CORRESPONDENT	ABC-TV, POST OFFICE BOX 4516	JOHANNESBURG 2000	SOUTH AFRICA
MC COURY, DELANO	GUITARIST	RURAL DELIVERY #1, BOX 94	GLEN ROCK, PA	17327
MC COVEY, WILLIE	BASEBALL	220 CREST RD	WOODSIDE, CA	94062
MC COWAN, GEORGE	TV DIRECTOR	409 N CANON DR #202	BEVERLY HILLS, CA	90210
MC COWEN, ALEC	ACTOR	CONWAY, EAGLE HOUSE		
		109 JERMYN ST	LONDON SW1	ENGLAND
MC COWIN, MARY P	NEWS CORRESPONDENT	1611 BALTIMORE RD	ALEXANDRIA, VA	22308
MC COWN, WILLIAM, JR	WRESTLING MANAGER	SEE - COSTELLO, J D		
MC COY, BILLY W	DIRECTOR	316 DALZELL AVE	PITTSBURGH, PA	15202
MC COY, CHARLIE	SINGER-GUITARIST	2314 SPRING BRANCH DR	MADISON, TN	37115
MC COY, CLYDE	MUSICIAN-COMPOSER	1631 SEA ISLE RD	MEMPHIS, TN	38117
MC COY, ELEANOR	ACTRESS	15010 VENTURA BLVD #219	SHERMAN OAKS, CA	91403
MC COY, JAY & THE RENAGADES	ROCK & ROLL GROUP	STRICKLAND, 1407 N 14TH AVE	OMAHA, NE	68102
MC COY, LARRY	PIANIST	ROUTE #2, LAKE MARIE RD	GALLATIN, TN	37210
MC COY, MARK	ACTOR	ABC-TV, "ALL MY CHILDREN"		
		1330 AVE OF THE AMERICAS	NEW YORK, NY	10019
MC COY, MATT	ACTOR	10000 SANTA MONICA BLVD #305	LOS ANGELES, CA	90067
MC COY, SETH	TENOR	1776 BROADWAY #504	NEW YORK, NY	10019
MC COY, SID	TV DIRECTOR	1221 OCEAN AVE	SANTA MONICA, CA	90401
MC CRACKEN, JAMES	TENOR	CAMI, 165 W 57TH ST	NEW YORK, NY	10019
MC CRAE, GEORGE	SINGER-SONGWRITER	495 SE 10TH CT	HIALEAH, FL	33010
MC CRAE, GWEN	SINGER-SONGWRITER	495 SE 10TH CT	HIALEAH, FL	33010
MC CRANE, PAUL	ACTOR	9200 SUNSET BLVD #1210	LOS ANGELES, CA	90069
MC CRARY'S, THE	VOCAL GROUP	1021 N CRESCENT HGTS BLVD #302	HOLLYWOOD, CA	90046
MC CRAW, SPENCER	DRUMMER	249-B LISA LN	NASHVILLE, TN	37210
MC CRAY, JAMES	TENOR	61 W 62ND ST #6-F	NEW YORK, NY	10023
MC CRAY, KEN	PRODUCER	LANDON, 10202 W WASHINGTON BLVD	CULVER CITY, CA	90230
MC CREA, JODY	ACTOR	RURAL ROUTE #1	CAMARILLO, CA	93010
MC CREA, JOEL	ACTOR	RURAL ROUTE #1	CAMARILLO, CA	93010
MC CREARY, LEW	COMPOSER	8437 WHITE OAK BLVD	NORTHRIDGE, CA	91324
MC CREE, CREE	WRITER-EDITOR	US MAGAZINE COMPANY		
		1 DAG HAMMARSKJOLD PLAZA	NEW YORK, NY	10017
MC CREEDY, SHARON	ACTRESS	18 18TH AVE #A	VENICE, CA	90291
MC CRINDLE, ALEX	ACTOR	MC LEAN, 236 DEODAR RD	LONDON SW15 2NP	ENGLAND
MC CRORY, MARTHA	CELLIST	MISSISSIPPI AVE	SEWANEE, TN	37375
MC CUAIG, DONALD M	DIRECTOR	4208 FARMDALE AVE	STUDIO CITY, CA	91604
MC CUBBIN, RUSS	ACTOR	439 S LA CIENEGA BLVD #117	LOS ANGELES, CA	90048
MC CUE, LISA J	NEWS CORRESPONDENT	6539 N 28TH ST	ARLINGTON, VA	22213
MC CUE, RICHARD T	DIRECTOR	57 PINE TREE LN	TAPPAN, NY	10983
MC CULLAN, JIM	ACTOR	STONE, 1052 CAROL DR	LOS ANGELES, CA	90069
MC CULLEN, KATHY	ACTRESS	7160 ASMAN AVE	CANOGA PARK, CA	91307
MC CULLOCH, IAN	ACTOR-WRITER	DUTTON, 24 ORMOND RD, RICHMOND	SURREY	ENGLAND
MC CULLOUGH, ANDREW	DIRECTOR	550 S BARRINGTON AVE #2301	LOS ANGELES, CA	90049
MC CULLOUGH, BRIAN	DIRECTOR	53 PRINCETON PL	WAYNE, NJ	07470
MC CULLOUGH, DARYL	ACTOR	5959 FRANKLIN AVE	LOS ANGELES, CA	90028
MC CULLOUGH, DENNY	GUITARIST	1031 NORTH "E" ST	LAKE WORTH, FL	33460

Name	Occupation	Address	City	Zip
MC CULLOUGH, ED	NEWS CORRESPONDENT	547 14TH ST, SE	WASHINGTON, DC	20003
MC CULLOUGH, JULIE	MODEL	MODELS & PROMOTIONS AGENCY		
		8560 SUNSET BLVD, 10TH FLOOR	LOS ANGELES, CA	90069
MC CULLOUGH, KEVIN P	NEWS CORRESPONDENT	400 N CAPITOL ST, NW	WASHINGTON, DC	20001
MC CULLOUGH, KIMBERLY	ACTRESS	3575 W CAHUENGA BLVD #320	LOS ANGELES, CA	90068
MC CULLOUGH, ROBERT L	TV WRITER	1888 CENTURY PARK E #1400	LOS ANGELES, CA	90067
MC CULLOUGH, RON	GUITARIST	1150 VULTEE BLVD #M-103	NASHVILLE, TN	37217
MC CULLOUGH, SHANA	ACTRESS	CABALLERO, 7920 ALABAMA AVE	CANOGA PARK, CA	91304
MC CULLOUGH, THOMAS	DRUMMER	2328 DENNYWOOD DR	NASHVILLE, TN	37214
MC CUNE, GREG A	NEWS CORRESPONDENT	1127 S EDISON ST	ARLINGTON, VA	22204
MC CURDY, JEAN H	TV EXECUTIVE	WARNER BROTHERS, INC		
		4000 WARNER BLVD	BURBANK, CA	91522
MC CURDY, JEANNE E	WRITER	555 W 57TH ST #1230	NEW YORK, NY	10019
MC CURDY, JOHN G	PHOTOGRAPHER	5309 BRILEY PL	BETHESDA, MD	20316
MC CURDY, RICHARD C	WRITER	8955 BEVERLY BLVD	LOS ANGELES, CA	90048
MC CURRY, ANN	ACTRESS	9300 WILSHIRE BLVD #410	BEVERLY HILLS, CA	90212
MC CURRY, DAN C	NEWS CORRESPONDENT	ROUTE #2	KEMPTON, PA	19529
MC CURRY, JOHN	ACTOR	109 W 85TH ST	NEW YORK, NY	10024
MC CUSKER, MARY	ACTRESS	870 N VINE ST #G	LOS ANGELES, CA	90038
MC CUTCHEN, DICK	WRITER	555 W 57TH ST #1230	NEW YORK, NY	10019
MC CUTCHEON, BILL	ACTOR	65 PARK TERR W	NEW YORK, NY	10034
MC DANIEL, ANN L	NEWS CORRESPONDENT	4114 DAVIS PL, NW	WASHINGTON, DC	20007
MC DANIEL, CHARLES	ACTOR	7466 BEVERLY BLVD #205	LOS ANGELES, CA	90036
MC DANIEL, CHIEF WAHOO	WRESTLER-FOOTBALL	NATIONAL WRESTLING ALLIANCE		
		JIM CROCKETT PROMOTIONS		
		421 BRIARBEND DR	CHARLOTTE, NC	28209
MC DANIEL, COEBURN "COPE"	GUITARIST	ROUTE #2, BOX 466-M	GOODLETTSVILLE, TN	37072
MC DANIEL, DONNA	ACTRESS	14853 SYLVAN ST #5	VAN NUYS, CA	91411
MC DANIEL, DOUGLAS P	NEWS CORRESPONDENT	10031 DALLAS AVE	SILVER SPRING, MD	20901
MC DANIEL, ED	WRESTLER	SEE - MC DANIEL, CHIEF WAHOO		
MC DANIEL, GEORGE	ACTOR	1419 N TOPANGA CANYON BLVD	TOPANGA CANYON, CA	90240
MC DANIEL, JAN M	NEWS CORRESPONDENT	ROUTE #1, BOX 457	LEESBURG, VA	22075
MC DANIEL, MEL	SINGER	106 CRANWELL DR	HENDERSONVILLE, TN	37075
MC DANIEL, RUSSELL	NEWS CORRESPONDENT	ROUTE #1, BOX 457	LEESBURG, VA	22075
MC DANIEL, WAHOO	WRESTLER	SEE - MC DANIEL, CHIEF WAHOO		
MC DANIEL, WANDA	ACTRESS	RUDDY, 1601 CLEAR VIEW DR	BEVERLY HILLS, CA	90210
MC DANIELS, GENE	SINGER	POST OFFICE BOX 82	GREAT NECK, NY	11021
MC DAVIT, CAROL	SOPRANO	45 W 60TH ST #4-K	NEW YORK, NY	10023
MC DERMID, FINLAY	WRITER	23388 MULHOLLAND DR	WOODLAND HILLS, CA	91364
MC DERMIT, MICKEY	SINGER	PROCESS, 439 WILEY AVE	FRANKLIN, PA	16323
MC DERMOTT, BARRY	SPORTS WRITER-EDITOR	SPORTS ILLUSTRATED MAGAZINE		
		TIME & LIFE BUILDING		
		ROCKEFELLER CENTER	NEW YORK, NY	10020
MC DERMOTT, BRIAN	ACTOR	GRANARY COTTAGE, BLAXHALL		
		WOODBRIDGE	SUFFOLK	ENGLAND
MC DERMOTT, COLLEEN	ACTRESS	6605 HOLLYWOOD BLVD #220	HOLLYWOOD, CA	90028
MC DERMOTT, FRANK D, JR	NEWS CORRESPONDENT	3426 S STAFFORD ST	ARLINGTON, VA	22206
MC DERMOTT, HUGH J	TV DIRECTOR	1806 "B" ST	BELMAR, NJ	07719
MC DERMOTT, JACK	ACTOR	10701 RIVERSIDE DR #13	TOLUCA LAKE, CA	91602
MC DERMOTT, KEITH	ACTOR	1746 N GRAMERCY PL #4	LOS ANGELES, CA	90028
MC DERMOTT, RICHARD	NEWS CORRESPONDENT	1333 "H" ST, NW	WASHINGTON, DC	20005
MC DERMOTT, THOMAS J	DIRECTOR	DGA, 7950 SUNSET BLVD	LOS ANGELES, CA	90048
MC DIVITT, JAMES A	ASTRONAUT	2349 IROQUOIS RD	WILMETTE, IL	60091
MC DONAGH, JUNE	FILM EDITOR	42 KINGFISHER DR, HAM		
		RICHMOND	SURREY	ENGLAND
MC DONAGH, PAT	FASHION DESIGNER	312 ADELAIDE ST W	TORONTO, ONT M5V 1R2	CANADA
MC DONALD, BARRY L	MUSIC ARRANGER	322 GREENWAY AVE	NASHVILLE, TN	37205
MC DONALD, BETTY	MUSICIAN	3821 WHITLAND AVE	NASHVILLE, TN	37205
MC DONALD, CHRIS	MUSIC ARRANGER	4809 LYNN DR	NASHVILLE, TN	37211
MC DONALD, CHRISTOPHER	ACTOR	9200 SUNSET BLVD #414	LOS ANGELES, CA	90069
MC DONALD, DANIEL	ACTOR	211 S BEVERLY DR #201	BEVERLY HILLS, CA	90212
MC DONALD, GRAEME	TV DIRECTOR-PRODUCER	BBC-TV, TV CENTRE, WOOD LN	LONDON W12	ENGLAND
MC DONALD, GREG	NEWS CORRESPONDENT	2500 "Q" ST #329	WASHINGTON, DC	20007
MC DONALD, JAMES B	COMPOSER	13907 JUDAH AVE	HAWTHORNE, CA	90250
MC DONALD, JOHN E	WRITER-PRODUCER	1548 OAK GROVE DR	LOS ANGELES, CA	90041
MC DONALD, KIM ANTHONY	NEWS CORRESPONDENT	6252 HILLSIDE RD	SPRINGFIELD, VA	22152
MC DONALD, LE ROY	DIRECTOR	318 N BEVERLY DR #156	BEVERLY HILLS, CA	90210
MC DONALD, LEE	ACTOR	8961 SUNSET BLVD #B	LOS ANGELES, CA	90069
MC DONALD, MARCIA	NEWS CORRESPONDENT	3420 PROSPECT ST, NW	WASHINGTON, DC	20007
MC DONALD, MARK	CINEMATOGRAPHER	RIVERSDALE, 264 HOOK RD		
		CHESSINGTON	SURREY	ENGLAND
MC DONALD, MAUREEN	COLUMNIST	POST OFFICE BOX 500	WASHINGTON, DC	20044
MC DONALD, MICHAEL	SINGER-SONGERWITER	6420 WILSHIRE BLVD #425	LOS ANGELES, CA	90048
MC DONALD, MIKE	COMEDIAN	ECI, 29 COMMONWEATH AVE	BOSTON, MA	02116
MC DONALD, ROBERT	DIRECTOR	45 GRAMERCY PARK N	NEW YORK, NY	10010
MC DONALD, ROBIN	WRITER-REPORTER	POST OFFICE BOX 820	WICHITA, KS	67201
MC DONALD, TOM	ACTOR	9465 WILSHIRE BLVD #616	BEVERLY HILLS, CA	90212
MC DONNELL, ELLEN	NEWS CORRESPONDENT	8713 MAYWOOD AVE	SILVER SPRING, MD	20910
MC DONNELL, JAMES	ACTOR	ABRAMS ARTISTS & ASSOCIATES		
		420 MADISON AVE, 14TH FLOOR	NEW YORK, NY	10017
MC DONNELL, JOHN	PHOTOGRAPHER	2010 4TH ST S	ARLINGTON, VA	22204
MC DONNELL, M J	TV DIRECTOR	16 W 64TH ST	NEW YORK, NY	10023
MC DONNELL, MARY	ACTRESS	11726 SAN VICENTE BLVD #300	LOS ANGELES, CA	90049
MC DONNELL, TERRENCE	TV WRITER	6430 SUNSET BLVD #1203	LOS ANGELES, CA	90028
MC DONNELL, VIRGINIA B	WRITER	CURTIS, 164 64TH ST	NEW YORK, NY	10021

Name	Occupation	Address	City/State	Zip
MC DONOUGH, JOSEPH F	DIRECTOR	1000 W SADDLE RIVER RD	HO-HO-KUS, NJ	07423
MC DONOUGH, KIT	ACTRESS	9744 WILSHIRE BLVD #206	BEVERLY HILLS, CA	90212
MC DONOUGH, MARY	ACTRESS	STONE, 1052 CAROL DR	LOS ANGELES, CA	90069
MC DONOUGH, RICHARD J	DIRECTOR	9454 WILSHIRE BLVD #805	BEVERLY HILLS, CA	90212
MC DONOUGH, WILL	COLUMNIST	THE BOSTON GLOBE		
		135 MORRISSEY BLVD	BOSTON, MA	02107
MC DOUGALL, BABETTE	WRITER	8955 BEVERLY BLVD	LOS ANGELES, CA	90048
MC DOUGALL, CALLUM	FILM DIRECTOR	HERONS CT, HERONSGATE		
		RICKMANSWORTH	HERTS	ENGLAND
MC DOUGALL, DON	DIRECTOR	DGA, 7950 SUNSET BLVD	LOS ANGELES, CA	90046
MC DOUGALL, WILLIAM E, JR	NEWS CORRESPONDENT	9 GUY CT	ROCKVILLE, MD	20850
MC DOWALL, RODDY	ACTOR	3110 BROOKDALE RD	STUDIO CITY, CA	91604
MC DOWELL, CHARLES	NEWS CORRESPONDENT	1300 NAMASSIN RD	ALEXANDRIA, VA	22308
MC DOWELL, JEANNE	NEWS CORRESPONDENT	TIME/TIME & LIFE BLDG		
		ROCKEFELLER CENTER	NEW YORK, NY	10020
MC DOWELL, MALCOLM	ACTOR	2501 OUTPOST DR	LOS ANGELES, CA	90068
MC DOWELL, RONNIE	SINGER	POST OFFICE BOX 452	PORTLAND, TN	37148
MC DUFFEE, JERRY	SAXOPHONIST	315 LAWNDALE DR	NASHVILLE, TN	37217
MC DUFFEE, RICHARD	DRUMMER	205 HANKINS DR	SMYRNA, TN	37167
MC DUFFIE, JAMES E	COMPOSER-CONDUCTOR	1826 JEWETT DR	LOS ANGELES, CA	90046
MC DUFFIE, ROBERT	VIOLINIST	CAMI, 165 W 57TH ST	NEW YORK, NY	10019
MC EDWARD, JOHN GORDON	WRITER	1860 BLUE NEIGHTS DR	LOS ANGELES, CA	90069
MC ELHINEY, BILL	MUSIC ARRANGER	1319 BURTON VALLEY RD	NASHVILLE, TN	37215
MC ELHINNEY, SUSAN T	PHOTOGRAPHER	3526 N 3RD ST	ARLINGTON, VA	22201
MC ELROY-BUTLER, DEBRA	NEWS CORRESPONDENT	POST OFFICE BOX 2626	WASHINGTON, DC	20013
MC ELWAIN, MITCH	DRUMMER	2318 RICHMOND AVE	MURFREESBORO, TN	37130
MC ENERY, PETER	ACTOR	32 LUPUS ST	LONDON SW1	ENGLAND
MC ENERY, RED RIVER DAVE	ACTOR-MUSICIAN	5760 WHITSETT AVE #A	NORTH HOLLYWOOD, CA	91607
MC ENNAN, JAIME	ACTOR	KELMAN, 7813 SUNSET BLVD	LOS ANGELES, CA	90046
MC ENROE, ANNIE	ACTRESS	15760 VENTURA BLVD #1730	ENCINO, CA	91436
MC ENROE, JOHN	TENNIS	22240 PACIFIC COAST HWY	MALIBU, CA	90265
MC ENTIRE, REBA	SINGER	HALSEY, 1111 16TH AVE S	NASHVILLE, TN	37212
MC EUEN, JOHN	SINGER	9000 SUNSET BLVD #1200	LOS ANGELES, CA	90069
MC EVEETY, DERNARD	TV DIRECTOR	4420 HASKELL AVE	ENCINO, CA	91436
MC EVEETY, VINCENT	TV DIRECTOR	14561 MULHOLLAND DR	LOS ANGELES, CA	90077
MC EVER, GEORGIA	SOPRANO	111 W 57TH ST #1209	NEW YORK, NY	10019
MC EVOY, ANNE MARIE	ACTRESS	6640 SUNSET BLVD #203	LOS ANGELES, CA	90028
MC EVOY-RICHARDSON, CAROL	WRITER	8955 BEVERLY BLVD	LOS ANGELES, CA	90048
MC EWAN, GERALDINE	ACTRESS	LARRY DALZELL ASSOCIATES		
		126 KENNINGTON PARK RD	LONDON SE11 4DJ	ENGLAND
MC EWEN, KENNETH	TV DIRECTOR	35 SUNRISE DR	MONTVALE, NJ	07645
MC EWEN, MARY	SAXOPHONIST	5919 MAXON ST	NASHVILLE, TN	37209
MC EWEN, RED	TRUMPETER	1901 OAKHILL DR	NASHVILLE, TN	37206
MC FADDEN, BARNEY	ACTOR	9744 WILSHIRE BLVD #306	BEVERLY HILLS, CA	90212
MC FADDEN, CYRA	TV WRITER	8955 BEVERLY BLVD	LOS ANGELES, CA	90048
MC FADDEN, MARY	FASHION DESIGNER	264 W 35TH ST	NEW YORK, NY	10001
MC FADDEN & WHITEHEAD	VOCAL DUO	200 W 51ST ST #1410	NEW YORK, NY	10019
MC FARLAND, ROBERT	BARITONE	CAMI, 165 W 57TH ST	NEW YORK, NY	10019
MC FARLAND, ROBERT D	TV EXEC-NEWS CORRES	NBC-TV, NEWS DEPARTMENT		
		4001 NEBRASKA AVE, NW	WASHINGTON, DC	20016
MC FARLAND, RON	COMPOSER	243 W END AVE #907	NEW YORK, NY	10023
MC FARLAND, SPANKY	ACTOR	POST OFFICE BOX 80202	FORT WORTH, TX	76180
MC FARLANE, JOHN I	WRITER	555 W 57TH ST #1230	NEW YORK, NY	10019
MC FEATTERS, ANN C	NEWS CORRESPONDENT	5 W LENOX ST	CHEVY CHASE, MD	20815
MC FEATTERS, DALE B	NEWS CORRESPONDENT	5 W LENOX ST	CHEVY CHASE, MD	20815
MC GANN, MARK	FILM DIRECTOR	22 KING ST #19	NEW YORK, NY	10014
MC GARRIGLE, KATE & ANNA	VOCAL GROUP	2067 BROADWAY #B	NEW YORK, NY	10023
MC GARVIN, DICK	ACTOR	3800 BARHAM BLVD #303	LOS ANGELES, CA	90068
MC GAVIN, DARREN	ACTOR	223 BONHILL RD	LOS ANGELES, CA	90049
MC GAVIN, GRAEM	ACTRESS	POST OFFICE BOX 2958	BEVERLY HILLS, CA	90213
MC GEARY, JOHANNA	NEWS CORRESPONDENT	1424 LONGFELLOW ST, NW	WASHINGTON, DC	20011
MC GEE, HENRY	ACTOR	1257-A FALCONERS HOUSE		
		SAINT JAMES CT	BUCKINGHAM GATE SW1	ENGLAND
MC GEE, IRISH PAT	WRESTLER	SEE - MC GHEE, SCOTT		
MC GEE, KIRK	SINGER	POST OFFICE BOX 626	FRANKLIN, TN	37064
MC GEE, KIRK	VIOLINIST	112 WILLIAMSBURG PL	FRANKLIN, TN	37064
MC GEE, MATT	GUITARIST	2936 IRONWOOD DR	NASHVILLE, TN	37214
MC GEE, PARKER	GUITARIST	1313 CLIFF AVE	FILLMORE, CA	93015
MC GEE, RONALD	WRITER	555 W 57TH ST #1230	NEW YORK, NY	10019
MC GEE, VONETTA	ACTRESS	9744 WILSHIRE BLVD #206	BEVERLY HILLS, CA	90212
MC GEEHAN, BERNICE	WRITER	13457 INWOOD DR	SHERMAN OAKS, CA	91423
MC GEEHAN, MARY KATE	ACTRESS	151 N SAN VICENTE BLVD #208	BEVERLY HILLS, CA	90211
MC GEEHAN, PAT	ACTOR	13457 INWOOD DR	SHERMAN OAKS, CA	91423
MC GEGAN, NICHOLAS	CONDUCTOR	BYERS-SCHWALBE, 1 5TH AVE	NEW YORK, NY	10003
MC GHEE, JAMES W	DIRECTOR-PRODUCER	ROUTE #4, BOX 318, NICHOLS RD	LENOIR CITY, TN	37771
MC GHEE, SCOTT	WRESTLER	POST OFFICE BOX 3859	STAMFORD, CT	06905
MC GHEE-ANDERSON, KATHLEEN	TV WRITER	9200 SUNSET BLVD #431	LOS ANGELES, CA	90069
MC GIBBON, DUNCAN SCOTT	TV WRITER	860 S WESTGATE AVE #205	LOS ANGELES, CA	90049
MC GILL, TONY	SINGER	POST OFFICE BOX 23262	NASHVILLE, TN	37202
MC GILLIS, KELLY	ACTRESS	9595 WILSHIRE BLVD #505	BEVERLY HILLS, CA	90212
MC GILLIVRAY, DAVID	TV WRITER	22-A BIRCHINGTON RD	LONDON NW6	ENGLAND
MC GILVRAY, ROBERT D	NEWS CORRESPONDENT	1225 NOYES DR	SILVER SPRING, MD	20910
MC GINLEY, CHERIE J	TV DIRECTOR-PRODUCER	432 N OAKHURST DR #B	BEVERLY HILLS, CA	90210
MC GINLEY, LAURIE	NEWS CORRESPONDENT	3133 CONNECTICUT AVE #711	WASHINGTON, DC	20008
MC GINLEY, LORI	ACTRESS	ICM, 8899 BEVERLY BLVD	LOS ANGELES, CA	90048

Name	Occupation	Address	City	ZIP
MC GINLEY, TED	ACTOR	1717 N HIGHLAND AVE #901	LOS ANGELES, CA	90028
MC GINN, JAMES T	TV WRITER	8955 BEVERLY BLVD	LOS ANGELES, CA	90048
MC GINNIS, DON	MUSICIAN	567 LOCKWOOD CT	NASHVILLE, TN	37214
MC GINNIS, SCOTT	ACTOR	3830 FRANKLIN AVE	LOS ANGELES, CA	90027
MC GIVENEY, MAURA	ACTRESS	3330 BARHAM BLVD #103	LOS ANGELES, CA	90068
MC GLAUGHLIN, BRUCE	ACTOR	1217 N GOWER ST #233	HOLLYWOOD, CA	90038
MC GLAUGHLIN, WILLIAM	CONDUCTOR	AIA, 60 E 42ND ST	NEW YORK, NY	10165
MC GLINCY, JAMES F	NEWS CORRES-WRITER	6113 N 22ND ST	ARLINGTON, VA	22205
MC GLOIN, DAVID	NEWS CORRESPONDENT	2133 WISCONSIN AVE, NW	WASHINGTON, DC	20007
MC GONAGILL, DANNY	DRUMMER	1423 PHILLIPS	CLEBURNE, TX	76031
MC GONAGLE, RICHARD	ACTOR	15010 VENTURA BLVD #234	SHERMAN OAKS, CA	91403
MC GOOHAN, PATRICK	ACT-WRI-DIR	16808 BOLLINGER DR	PACIFIC PALISADES, CA	90272
MC GOUGH, DORIN	ACTRESS	1239 N SWEETZER AVE #12	LOS ANGELES, CA	90069
MC GOUGH, THOMAS J	WRITER	8955 BEVERLY BLVD	LOS ANGELES, CA	90048
MC GOVERN, ELIZABETH	ACTRESS	17319 MAGNOLIA BLVD	ENCINO, CA	91316
MC GOVERN, GEORGE	POLITICIAN	2029 CONNECTICUT AVE, NW	WASHINGTON, DC	20008
MC GOVERN, MAUREEN	SINGER	529 W 42ND ST #7-F	NEW YORK, NY	10036
MC GOVERN, TERENCE	ACTOR	12725 VENTURA BLVD #E	STUDIO CITY, CA	91604
MC GOVERN, TERRY	ACTOR	10363 LOUISIANA AVE	LOS ANGELES, CA	90025
MC GOVERN, TODD	WRITER	THE NATIONAL LAMPOON		
		635 MADISON AVE	NEW YORK, NY	10022
MC GOVERN, WILLIAM	WRITER	8955 BEVERLY BLVD	LOS ANGELES, CA	90048
MC GOWAN, ANNIE	BANJOIST	POST OFFICE BOX 560	MARTIN, TN	38237
MC GOWAN, KEVIN	NEWS CORRESPONDENT	237 N GEORGE MASON DR	ARLINGTON, VA	22203
MC GOWAN, STUART E	TV WRITER-DIRECTOR	12133 HUSTON ST	NORTH HOLLYWOOD, CA	91607
MC GOWAN, TOM	ACTOR-WRITER	8955 BEVERLY BLVD	LOS ANGELES, CA	90048
MC GOWAN, WILLIAM G	COMM EXECUTIVE	1275 SUMMER ST	STAMFORD, CT	06204
MC GOWAN, WILLIAM J, II	WRITER	555 W 57TH ST #1230	NEW YORK, NY	10019
MC GOY, NEAL	SINGER	3198 ROYAL LN #204	DALLAS, TX	75229
MC GRADY, PHYLLIS	DIRECTOR	649 W DEMING PL #2-W	CHICAGO, IL	60614
MC GRAIL, DAVID L	DIRECTOR	1545 CANTERBURY LN	GLENVIEW, IL	60025
MC GRAIL, KATHERINE	NEWS CORRESPONDENT	4420 TANEY AVE #404	ALEXANDRIA, VA	22304
MC GRATH, BOB	SINGER	GREENGRASS, 16 E 48TH ST	NEW YORK, NY	10017
MC GRATH, DEREK	ACTOR-WRITER	11726 SAN VICENTE BLVD #300	LOS ANGELES, CA	90049
MC GRATH, DOUGLAS	ACTOR	1274 N HARPER AVE	LOS ANGELES, CA	90046
MC GRATH, DOUGLAS	TV WRITER	555 W 57TH ST #1230	NEW YORK, NY	10019
MC GRATH, GEORGE	ACTOR	10390 SANTA MONICA BLVD #310	LOS ANGELES, CA	90025
MC GRATH, JOHN	TV WRITER-DIRECTOR	MARGARET RAMSAY, LTD		
		14-A GOODWINS CT		
		SAINT MARTINS LN	LONDON WC2N 4LL	ENGLAND
MC GRATH, JOSEPH	TV WRITER-DIRECTOR	ICM, 388-396 OXFORD ST	LONDON W1	ENGLAND
MC GRATH, PATRICK E	NEWS CORRESPONDENT	5151 WISCONSIN AVE, NW	WASHINGTON, DC	20016
MC GRAW, CHARLES	ACTOR	POST OFFICE BOX 4796	NORTH HOLLYWOOD, CA	91607
MC GRAW, CHRISTINE	ACTRESS	427 N CANON DR #205	BEVERLY HILLS, CA	90210
MC GRAW, TUG	BASEBALL	COLESHILL ROSE VALLEY RD	MEDIA, PA	19063
MC GREEVEY, JOHN	TV WRITER	14144 VENTURA BLVD #200	SHERMAN OAKS, CA	91423
MC GREEVEY, MICHAEL S	TV WRITER	25603 ALMENDRA DR	VALENCIA, CA	91355
MC GREEVEY, TOM	ACTOR	9250 WILSHIRE BLVD #208	BEVERLY HILLS, CA	90212
MC GREGOR, JAMES L	NEWS CORRESPONDENT	416 10TH ST, SE	WASHINGTON, DC	20003
MC GREGOR, KEITH	GUITARIST	303 RACHEL RD	NASHVILLE, TN	37214
MC GREGOR-STEWART, KATE	ACTRESS	9200 SUNSET BLVD #1210	LOS ANGELES, CA	90069
MC GRORY, MARY	NEWS REPORTER	UNIVERSAL PRESS SYNDICATE		
		4900 MAIN ST, 9TH FLOOR	KANSAS CITY, MO	62114
MC GUANE, THOMAS	WRITER-PRODUCER	HOFFMAN ROUTE	LIVINGSTON, MT	59047
MC GUFFEE, JOE	GUITARIST	7006 BONNAVENT DR	HERMITAGE, TN	37076
MC GUFFEY, DANIEL	MUSICIAN	2131 ELM HILL PIKE #F-132	NASHVILLE, TN	37210
MC GUFFEY, MICHAEL	TRUMPETER	2123 SPRUCE ST #13	PHILADELPHIA, PA	19103
MC GUFFEY, PATRICK	TRUMPETER	2131 ELM HILL PIKE #F-132	NASHVILLE, TN	37210
MC GUIGAN, PATRICIA	WRITER	555 W 57TH ST #1230	NEW YORK, NY	10019
MC GUINN, JUDITH E	WRITER	8955 BEVERLY BLVD	LOS ANGELES, CA	90048
MC GUINN, ROGER	SINGER-SONGWRITER	POST OFFICE BOX 1265	MORRO BAY, CA	93442
MC GUIRE, AL	GUITARIST	810 BELLEVUE RD #123	NASHVILLE, TN	37221
MC GUIRE, AL	SPORTSCASTER	NBC-TV, SPORTS DEPARTMENT		
		30 ROCKEFELLER PLAZA	NEW YORK, NY	10112
MC GUIRE, BARRY	SINGER-EVANGLIST	POST OFFICE BOX 320	LINDALE, TX	75771
MC GUIRE, BETTY	ACTRESS	12725 VENTURA BLVD #E	STUDIO CITY, CA	91604
MC GUIRE, BIFF	ACTOR	1650 BROADWAY #406	NEW YORK, NY	10019
MC GUIRE, BILL	SINGER	3125 19TH ST #217	BAKERSFIELD, CA	93301
MC GUIRE, DON	SCREENWRITER	8955 BEVERLY BLVD	LOS ANGELES, CA	90048
MC GUIRE, DOROTHY	ACTRESS	211 S BEVERLY DR #201	BEVERLY HILLS, CA	90212
MC GUIRE, FRANCIS G	NEWS CORRESPONDENT	1495 NEWTON ST #201, NW	WASHINGTON, DC	20010
MC GUIRE, JAMES MICHAEL	BARITONE	CAMI, 165 W 57TH ST	NEW YORK, NY	10019
MC GUIRE, MAEVE	ACTRESS	10100 SANTA MONICA BLVD #1600	LOS ANGELES, CA	90067
MC GUIRE, MICHAEL	ACTOR	10000 SANTA MONICA BLVD #305	LOS ANGELES, CA	90067
MC GUIRE, MICHAEL D	TV WRITER	8955 BEVERLY BLVD	LOS ANGELES, CA	90048
MC GUIRE, MICKEY	DIRECTOR	7309 FRANKLIN AVE #102	LOS ANGELES, CA	90046
MC GUIRE, PATRICK D	ACTOR	10662 1/2 EASTBORNE AVE	LOS ANGELES, CA	90024
MC GUIRE, PHYLLIS	SINGER	100 RANCHO CIR	LAS VEGAS, NV	89119
MC GUIRE SISTERS, THE	VOCAL TRIO	5455 WILSHIRE BLVD #2200	LOS ANGELES, CA	90036
MC HATTIE, STEPHEN	ACTOR	274 MOUNTAIN AVE	WILTON, CT	06897
MC HUGH, ANTHONY	ACTOR	8150 BEVERLY BLVD #303	LOS ANGELES, CA	90048
MC HUGH, FRANK	ACTOR	FAMOUS ACTOR	COS COB, CT	06807
MC HUGH, JUDY	TALENT AGENT	8601 WILSHIRE BLVD #1000	BEVERLY HILLS, CA	90211

RONNIE MC DOWELL

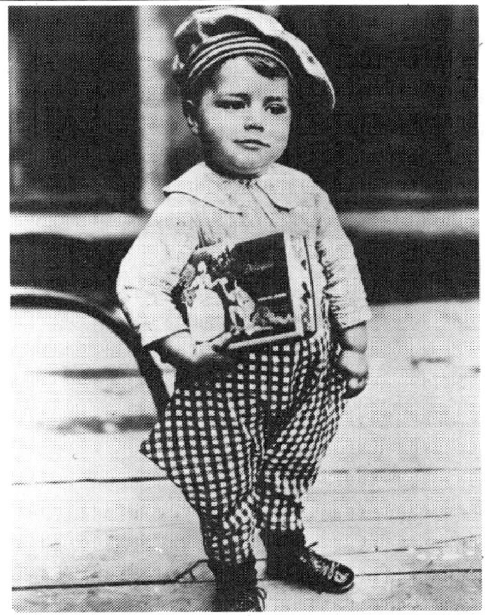

SPANKY MC FARLAND

DARREN MC GAVIN

TED MC GINLEY

ELIZABETH MC GOVERN

DOUG MC KEON

JIMMY MC NICHOL

BUTTERFLY MC QUEEN

CHRISTINE MC VIE

Name	Occupation	Address	City	Zip
MC INERNEY, PAT	GUITARIST	5907 KINSDALE DR	NASHVILLE, TN	37211
MC INNES, JAMES	ACTOR	11240 MAGNOLIA BLVD #202	NORTH HOLLYWOOD, CA	91601
MC INTIRE, JOHN	ACTOR	1417 SAMOA WY	LAGUNA BEACH, CA	92651
MC INTIRE, THOMAS	MUSIC ARRANGER	622-A ERMAC DR	NASHVILLE, TN	37210
MC INTOSH, DOUGLAS L	WRITER	8955 BEVERLY BLVD	LOS ANGELES, CA	90048
MC INTOSH, TOBY	NEWS CORRESPONDENT	917 N IRVING ST	ARLINGTON, VA	22201
MC INTURFF, BILLY	DRUMMER	621 BRENTLAWN RD	NASHVILLE, TN	37220
MC INTYRE, BILL	ACTOR	SF & A, 121 N SAN VICENTE BLVD	BEVERLY HILLS, CA	90211
MC INTYRE, DENNIS	WRITER	555 W 57TH ST #1230	NEW YORK, NY	10019
MC INTYRE, DONALD	BARITONE	1776 BROADWAY #504	NEW YORK, NY	10019
MC INTYRE, JAMES J	NEWS CORRESPONDENT	9426 GENTLE CIR	GAITHERSBURG, MD	20879
MC INTYRE, JOSEPH	PERCUSSIONIST	AFFILIATE ARTISTS, INC		
		37 W 65TH ST, 6TH FLOOR	NEW YORK, NY	10023
MC INTYRE, KEVIN	GUITARIST	1363 NORTHVIEW AVE, NE	ATLANTA, GA	30306
MC INTYRE, MARILYN	ACTRESS	10 E 44TH ST #700	NEW YORK, NY	10017
MC INTYRE, MARVIN J	ACTOR	10000 SANTA MONICA BLVD #305	LOS ANGELES, CA	90067
MC INTYRE, REBA	SINGER	CARTER-WOODS, 1026-A 18TH AVE S	NASHVILLE, TN	37212
MC IVER, MICHAEL D	WRITER	8955 BEVERLY BLVD	LOS ANGELES, CA	90048
MC KANNA, WILLIAM R	DIRECTOR	1 UNION SQUARE W	NEW YORK, NY	10003
MC KAY, BRIAN M	TV WRITER	8955 BEVERLY BLVD	LOS ANGELES, CA	90048
MC KAY, COLIN	WRITER	8955 BEVERLY BLVD	LOS ANGELES, CA	90048
MC KAY, GARDNER	ACTOR	9301 CHEROKEE LN	BEVERLY HILLS, CA	90210
MC KAY, HUGH D	WRITER	8955 BEVERLY BLVD	LOS ANGELES, CA	90048
MC KAY, JIM	SPORTS HOST	ABC-TV, SPORTS DEPARTMENT		
		1330 AVE OF THE AMERICAS	NEW YORK, NY	10019
MC KAY, JOHN	CLOWN	2701 COTTAGE WY #14	SACRAMENTO, CA	95825
MC KAY, MARION	COMPOSER-CONDUCTOR	220 COLLINGWOOD AVE	DAYTON, OH	45419
MC KAY, PEGGY	ACTRESS	NBC-TV, "DAYS OF OUR LIVES"		
		3000 W ALAMEDA AVE	BURBANK, CA	91523
MC KAY, RICHARD	PHOTOGRAPHER	2910 VILLAGE SPRING LN	VIENNA, VA	22180
MC KAY, SCOTT	ACTOR	9 W 46TH ST #3-R	NEW YORK, NY	10036
MC KAY, THERESA	SINGER	4680 ELK LAKE DR #304	VICTORIA, BC	CANADA
MC KAY, WANDA	ACTRESS	POST OFFICE BOX Y	RANCHO MIRAGE, CA	92270
MC KAY, WINNIW	TRAPEZE ACT	POST OFFICE BOX 87	WEST LEBANON, NY	12195
MC KEAN, KEVIN	WRITER-EDITOR	DISCOVER/TIME & LIFE BLDG		
		ROCKEFELLER CENTER	NEW YORK, NY	10020
MC KEAN, MICHAEL	ACTOR	10100 SANTA MONICA BLVD #1600	LOS ANGELES, CA	90067
MC KEAN, MICHAEL JOHN	TV WRITER-DIRECTOR	12143 MAXWELLTON RD	STUDIO CITY, CA	91604
MC KEAN, SUE ANN	BODYBUILDER	POST OFFICE BOX 4466	MOUNTAIN VIEW, CA	94040
MC KEAND, CAROL EVAN	TV WRITER-PRODUCER	507 N ALTA DR	BEVERLY HILLS, CA	90210
MC KEAND, MARTIN	TV PRODUCER	56 FITZJOHNS AVE	LONDON NW3	ENGLAND
MC KEAND, NIGEL	TV WRITER-PRODUCER	507 N ALTA DR	BEVERLY HILLS, CA	90210
MC KECHNIE, DONNA	ACTRESS	710 PARK AVE #7-B	NEW YORK, NY	10021
MC KECHNIE, DONNA	ACTRESS	151 S EL CAMINO DR	BEVERLY HILLS, CA	90212
MC KEE, CHARLES J	NEWS CORRESPONDENT	1414 17TH ST #314, NW	WASHINGTON, DC	20036
MC KEE, JOHNNY MAX	MANDOLINIST	1370 S LAFAYETTE ST	SHELBY, NC	28150
MC KEE, JOSEPH	BASSO-BARITONE	CAMI, 165 W 57TH ST	NEW YORK, NY	10019
MC KEE, LONETTE	ACTRESS	9255 SUNSET BLVD #505	LOS ANGELES, CA	90069
MC KEE, MICHAEL S	NEWS CORRESPONDENT	400 N CAPITOL ST, NW	WASHINGTON, DC	20001
MC KEE, PAMELA	ACTRESS	616 W 7TH ST	COLUMBIA, TN	38401
MC KEE, ROBERT C, JR	NEWS CORRESPONDENT	9540 GODWIN DR	MANASSAS, VA	22110
MC KEE, ROBERT O	TV WRITER	9022 SUNSET BLVD #531	LOS ANGELES, CA	90069
MC KEE, TODD	ACTOR	3151 W CAHUENGA BLVD #310	LOS ANGELES, CA	90068
MC KEEFE, ELLEN	TV EXECUTIVE	NBC TELEVISION NETWORK		
		30 ROCKEFELLER PLAZA	NEW YORK, NY	10112
MC KEITHENS, THE	C & W GROUP	POST OFFICE BOX 8078	NASHVILLE, TN	37207
MC KELLEN, IAN	ACTOR	25 EARLS TERR	LONDON W8	ENGLAND
MC KENNA, ALICE V	NEWS CORRESPONDENT	7539 SPRINGLAKE DR	BETHESDA, MD	20817
MC KENNA, BRIAN	ACTOR	15102 MARTHA ST	VAN NUYS, CA	91411
MC KENNA, JAMES	TV EXECUTIVE	CBS-TV, 51 W 52ND ST	NEW YORK, NY	10019
MC KENNA, PATRICK	NEWS CORRESPONDENT	NBC-TV, NEWS DEPARTMENT		
		4001 NEBRASKA AVE, NW	WASHINGTON, DC	20016
MC KENNA, THOMAS PATRICK	ACTOR	LEADING ARTISTS, LTD		
		60 SAINT JAMES'S ST	LONDON SW1	ENGLAND
MC KENNA, VIRGINIA	ACTRESS	67 GLEBE PL	LONDON SW3	ENGLAND
MC KENZIE, JULIA	ACTRESS	YOUNG, 31 KINGS RD	LONDON SN3 4RP	ENGLAND
MC KENZIE, KATIE	SINGER	4540 KEARNY VILLA RD #114	SAN DIEGO, CA	92123
MC KENZIE, MADORA	TV WRITER	8955 BEVERLY BLVD	LOS ANGELES, CA	90048
MC KENZIE, RICHARD	ACTOR	9744 WILSHIRE BLVD #206	BEVERLY HILLS, CA	90212
MC KENZIE WALDMAN, FAY	ACTRESS	WALDMAN, 4325 REDWOOD AVE #2	MARINA DEL REY, CA	90292
MC KEON, DOUG	ACTOR	1801 CENTURY PARK E #1415	LOS ANGELES, CA	90067
MC KEON, NANCY	ACTRESS	POST OFFICE BOX 6778	BURBANK, CA	91510
MC KEON, PHILIP	ACTOR	POST OFFICE BOX 1271	STUDIO CITY, CA	91604
MC KERN, LEO	ACTOR	12 SUMMERHILL RD	OXFORD OX2 7JY	ENGLAND
MC KIERNAN, KEVIN B	WRITER	8955 BEVERLY BLVD	LOS ANGELES, CA	90048
MC KIM, HARRY	ACTOR	1012 WASHINGTON PL	SAN DIEGO, CA	92103
MC KIM, SAMMY	ACTOR	WED ENTERPRISES, 1401 FLOWER ST	GLENDALE, CA	91201
MC KINLEY, J EDWARD	ACTOR	1632 SAN YSIDRO DR	BEVERLY HILLS, CA	90210
MC KINNEY, BILL	ACTOR	427 N CANON DR #205	BEVERLY HILLS, CA	90210
MC KINNEY, EUGENE	WRITER	555 W 57TH ST #1230	NEW YORK, NY	10019
MC KINNEY, JOAN	NEWS CORRESPONDENT	6010 TRAIL SIDE DR	SPRINGFIELD, VA	22150
MC KINNEY, PAT	SINGER	TAYLOR, 2401 12TH AVE S	NASHVILLE, TN	37204
MC KINNEY, THOMAS H, III	BANJOIST	POST OFFICE BOX 8403	ASHEVILLE, NC	28804
MC KINNEY, W R	WRITER	8955 BEVERLY BLVD	LOS ANGELES, CA	90048
MC KINNON, FRED	CINEMATOGRAPHER	7715 SUNSET BLVD #150	LOS ANGELES, CA	90046

Name	Occupation	Address	City / Zip
MC KINNON, ROBERT	TV DIRECTOR	1365 YORK AVE #20-H	NEW YORK, NY 10021
MC KINSEY, BEVERLEE	ACTRESS	888 7TH AVE #201	NEW YORK, NY 10019
MC KINSEY, DALE D	NEWS CORRESPONDENT	1260 21ST ST, NW	WASHINGTON, DC 20036
MC KITTERICK, MARY C	NEWS CORRESPONDENT	3307 QUESADA ST, NW	WASHINGTON, DC 20015
MC KNIGHT, DAVID	ACTOR	1607 N EL CENTRO AVE #22	HOLLYWOOD, CA 90028
MC KNIGHT, FRED J	TV WRITER	8955 BEVERLY BLVD	LOS ANGELES, CA 90048
MC KNIGHT, MARIAN	ACTRESS	8350 SANTA MONICA BLVD #206	LOS ANGELES, CA 90069
MC KNIGHT, SHARON	SINGER-DIRECTOR	MITCHELL BROTHERS THEATER 875 O'FARRELL ST	SAN FRANCISCO, CA 94209
MC KNIGHT, THOMAS	TV DIRECTOR	25547 VIA JARDIN	VALENCIA, CA 91355
MC KRELL, JIM	ACTOR	6055 JUMILLA AVE	WOODLAND HILLS, CA 91364
MC KUEN, ROD	SINGER-POET	1155 ANGELO DR	BEVERLY HILLS, CA 90210
MC LAGAN, IAN	SINGER	POST OFFICE BOX 2276	GARDEN GROVE, CA 92642
MC LAGLEN, ANDREW	FILM DIRECTOR	POST OFFICE BOX 1056	FRIDAY HARBOR, WA 98250
MC LAGLEN, ANDREW	TV EXECUTIVE	CBS-TV, 7800 BEVERLY BLVD	LOS ANGELES, CA 90036
MC LAIN, CHUCK	TV EXECUTIVE	WARNER BROTHERS, INC 4000 WARNER BLVD	BURBANK, CA 91522
MC LAIN, DENNY	BASEBALL	KOMETS, 4000 PARNELL AVE	FT WAYNE, IN 46805
MC LAIN, ELLEN	SOPRANO	POST OFFICE BOX 884	NEW YORK, NY 10023
MC LAIN, TOMMY	SINGER	MEAUX, 566 BROCK ST	HOUSTON, TX 77023
MC LARTY, GARY	STUNTMAN	9901 FOOTHILL BLVD	LAKE VIEW, CA 91342
MC LARTY, KAREN	STUNTWOMAN	3518 W CAHUENGA BLVD #206-A	LOS ANGELES, CA 90068
MC LAUGHLIN, BILL	NEWS CORRESPONDENT	CBS NEWS, 2020 "M" ST, NW	WASHINGTON, DC 20036
MC LAUGHLIN, CARROL	HARPIST	CAMI, 165 W 57TH ST	NEW YORK, NY 10019
MC LAUGHLIN, EMILY	ACTRESS	13451 ERWIN ST	VAN NUYS, CA 91405
MC LAUGHLIN, JAMES M	WRITER	555 W 57TH ST #1230	NEW YORK, NY 10019
MC LAUGHLIN, JOHN	ACTOR	10100 SANTA MONICA BLVD #1600	LOS ANGELES, CA 90067
MC LAUGHLIN, JOHN	NEWS CORRESPONDENT	2918 GARFIELD ST, NW	WASHINGTON, DC 20008
MC LAUGHLIN, JOHN	SINGER-SONGWRITER	KURLAND, 173 BRIGHTON AVE	BOSTON, MA 02134
MC LAUGHLIN, JOHN C	ACTOR	14932 GREENLEAF ST	SHERMAN OAKS, CA 91403
MC LAUGHLIN, LEE	ACTOR	6380 WILSHIRE BLVD #1600	LOS ANGELES, CA 90048
MC LAUGHLIN, MARIE	SOPRANO	CAMI, 165 W 57TH ST	NEW YORK, NY 10019
MC LAUGHLIN, WILLIAM J	NEWS CORRESPONDENT	CBS NEWS, 2020 "M" ST, NW	WASHINGTON, DC 20036
MC LEAN, BILL	ACTOR	6430 SUNSET BLVD #1203	LOS ANGELES, CA 90028
MC LEAN, BOB	ACTOR	2427 CENTINELA AVE #K	SANTA MONICA, CA 90405
MC LEAN, DODIE	CASTING DIRECTOR	8033 SUNSET BLVD #810	LOS ANGELES, CA 90046
MC LEAN, DON	SINGER-SONGWRITER	OLD MANITOU RD	GARRISON, NY 10524
MC LEAN, ELIZABETH C	NEWS CORRESPONDENT	4545 CONNECTICUT AVE, NW	WASHINGTON, DC 20008
MC LEAN, JAMES	TENOR	200 W 70TH ST #7-F	NEW YORK, NY 10023
MC LEAN, JIM	ACTOR	WRIGHT, 8422 MELROSE PL	LOS ANGELES, CA 90069
MC LEAN, MICHAEL	CASTING DIRECTOR	8272 SUNSET BLVD	LOS ANGELES, CA 90046
MC LEAN, MICHAEL	PRODUCER	WARNER BROTHERS, INC 4000 WARNER BLVD	BURBANK, CA 91522
MC LEAN, MICHAEL	TV DIRECTOR	4200 HAYVENHURST AVE	ENCINO, CA 91436
MC LEAN, W W	SAXOPHONIST	MADISON TOWERS #900 591 N DUPONT	MADISON, TN 37115
MC LEAN-IBSCOE, ELY	ILLUSTRATOR	POST OFFICE BOX 500	WASHINGTON, DC 20044
MC LEAREN, JOHN	ACTOR	48 PARKER PL	SHREWSBURY, NJ 07701
MC LELLAN, KENNY	PIANIST	POST OFFICE BOX 120914	NASHVILLE, TN 37212
MC LEOD, CATHERINE	ACTRESS	4146 ALLOTT AVE	VAN NUYS, CA 91423
MC LEOD, DONALD E	NEWS CORRESPONDENT	7928 CENTRAL PARK CIR	ALEXANDRIA, VA 22309
MC LEOD, DUNCAN	ACTOR	FARRELL, 10500 MAGNOLIA BLVD	NORTH HOLLYWOOD, CA 91601
MC LEOD, JACK M	NEWS CORRESPONDENT	7223 RESERVOIR RD	SPRINGFIELD, VA 22150
MC LESKEY, MICHAEL P	NEWS CORRESPONDENT	20412 ALDERLEAF TERR	GERMANTOWN, MD 20874
MC LIAM, JOHN	ACTOR	4721 LAUREL CANYON BLVD #211	NORTH HOLLYWOOD, CA 91607
MC LISH, RACHEL	BODYBUILDER	POST OFFICE BOX 11	SANTA MONICA, CA 90406
MC LOUGHLIN, TOMMY	WRITER	9220 SUNSET BLVD #202	LOS ANGELES, CA 90069
MC LURE, JAMES M	WRITER	555 W 57TH ST #1230	NEW YORK, NY 10019
MC MACKIN, MARK CONAN	PHOTOGRAPHER	406 HANSON LN	ALEXANDRIA, VA 22302
MC MAHAN, JANET	PIANIST	914 EVANS RD	NASHVILLE, TN 37204
MC MAHON, ANDREW	PIANIST	POST OFFICE BOX 517	DICKSON, TN 37055
MC MAHON, ED	TV HOST-ACTOR	NBC-TV, 3000 W ALAMEDA AVE	BURBANK, CA 91523
MC MAHON, JENNA	WRITER-PRODUCER	1888 CENTURY PARK E #1400	LOS ANGELES, CA 90067
MC MAHON, JOHN	TV PRODUCER	CARSON, 10045 RIVERSIDE DR	TOLUCA LAKE, CA 91602
MC MAHON, LEO J	WRITER	6501 CAMELLIA AVE	NORTH HOLLYWOOD, CA 91606
MC MAHON, THELMA	NEWS CORRESPONDENT	12410 SHADOW LN	BOWIE, MD 20715
MC MAHON, THOMAS A	WRITER	8955 BEVERLY BLVD	LOS ANGELES, CA 90048
MC MAHON, VINCE, JR	WRESTLING PROMOTER	POST OFFICE BOX 3859	STAMFORD, CT 06905
MC MAKIN, PATRICK	GUITARIST	4011 VAILWOOD DR	NASHVILLE, TN 37215
MC MANUS, DOYLE	NEWS CORRESPONDENT	7605 MARBURY RD	BETHESDA, MD 20814
MC MANUS, JASON	WRITER-EDITOR	TIME/TIME & LIFE BLDG ROCKEFELLER CENTER	NEW YORK, NY 10020
MC MANUS, KEVIN	WRESTLING WRITER	POST OFFICE BOX 48	ROCKVILLE CENTRE, NY 11571
MC MANUS, KEVIN A	NEWS CORRESPONDENT	122 "C" ST, NW	WASHINGTON, DC 20001
MC MANUS, MICHAEL L	ACTOR-WRITER	5127 GREENBUSH AVE	SHERMAN OAKS, CA 91423
MC MANUS, SEAN	TV EXECUTIVE	NBC-TV, SPORTS DEPARTMENT 30 ROCKEFELLER PLAZA	NEW YORK, NY 10112
MC MARTIN, JOHN	ACTOR	1650 BROADWAY #302	NEW YORK, NY 10019
MC MASTERS, THERESA	NEWS CORRESPONDENT	5275 WATSON ST, NW	WASHINGTON, DC 20016
MC MEEL, JOHN P	PUBLISHING EXECUTIVE	UNIVERSAL PRESS SYNDICATE 4900 MAIN ST, 9TH FLOOR	KANSAS CITY, MO 62114
MC MENAMIN, PATRIC ALAN	SCREENWRITER	7279 WOODROW WILSON DR	LOS ANGELES, CA 90068
MC MILLAN, KENNETH	ACTOR	12636 RYE ST	STUDIO CITY, CA 91604
MC MILLAN, KEVIN	BARITONE	59 E 54TH ST #81	NEW YORK, NY 10022
MC MILLAN, RONNIE	ACTOR	611 N HOWARD ST #107	GLENDALE, CA 91206

MC MILLAN, SUZANNE B	WRITER	8955 BEVERLY BLVD	LOS ANGELES, CA	90048
MC MILLAN, TERRY	SINGER	113 SHACKLETT LN CT	ANTIOCH, TN	37013
MC MILLEN, LIZ	NEWS CORRESPONDENT	820 S ARLINGTON MILL DR #104	ARLINGTON, VA	22204
MC MILLIAN, GERALDINE	SOPRANO	SOFFER, 130 W 56TH ST	NEW YORK, NY	10019
MC MILLIN, DUTCH	SAXOPHONIST	ROUTE #2, HARPETH RIDGE DR	FRANKLIN, TN	37064
MC MILLON, DORIS E	NEWS CORRESPONDENT	4461 CONNECTICUT AVE, NW	WASHINGTON, DC	20008
MC MULLAN, JIM	ACTOR	515 MOUNT HOLYOKE AVE	PACIFIC PALISADES, CA	90272
MC MULLEN, DAVID W	WRITER	555 W 57TH ST #1230	NEW YORK, NY	10019
MC MULLEN, JAY	WRITER-PRODUCER	DGA, 110 W 57TH ST	NEW YORK, NY	10019
MC MURPHY, DANNY	ACTOR	KELMAN, 7813 SUNSET BLVD	LOS ANGELES, CA	90046
MC MURRY, MURRY	ACTOR	922 N CORDOVA ST	BURBANK, CA	91505
MC MURTRY, LARRY	SCREENWRITER	8955 BEVERLY BLVD	LOS ANGELES, CA	90048
MC MYLER, PAMELA	ACTRESS	9229 SUNSET BLVD #306	LOS ANGELES, CA	90069
MC NAIR, SYLVIA	SOPRANO	COLBERT, 111 W 57TH ST	NEW YORK, NY	10019
MC NALLY, STEPHEN	ACTOR	624 N HILLCREST RD	BEVERLY HILLS, CA	90210
MC NALLY, TERRENCE	ACTOR	9220 SUNSET BLVD #202	LOS ANGELES, CA	90069
MC NALLY, TERRENCE	PLAYWRIGHT	218 W 10TH ST	NEW YORK, NY	10014
MC NAMARA, DERMOT	ACTOR	556 MAIN ST	ROOSEVELT ISLAND, NY	10044
MC NAMARA, ED	ACTOR	6736 LAUREL CANYON BLVD #306	NORTH HOLLYWOOD, CA	91606
MC NAMARA, EILEEN	NEWS CORRESPONDENT	2030 "F" ST #708, NW	WASHINGTON, DC	20037
MC NAMARA, J PATRICK	ACTOR	400 S BEVERLY DR #216	BEVERLY HILLS, CA	90212
MC NAMARA, JULIANNE	ACTRESS	12725 VENTURA BLVD #E	STUDIO CITY, CA	91604
MC NAMARA, PAT	ACTOR	11726 SAN VICENTE BLVD #300	LOS ANGELES, CA	90049
MC NAMARA, PATRICK	ACTOR	27350 ESCONDIDO BEACH RD #114	MALIBU, CA	90265
MC NAMARA, ROBERT	NEWS CORRESPONDENT	CBS NEWS, 524 W 57TH ST	NEW YORK, NY	10019
MC NAMEE, WALLY	PHOTOGRAPHER	3654 VACATION LN	ARLINGTON, VA	22207
MC NAUGHTAN, ALAN	ACTOR	19 ARUNDEL CT, ARUNDEL GARDENS	LONDON W11 2LP	ENGLAND
MC NEELY, BIG JAY	SAXOPHONIST	843 S MARIPOSA AVE #5	LOS ANGELES, CA	90005
MC NEELY, JERRY	WRITER-PRODUCER	4240 GAYLE DR	TARZANA, CA	91356
MC NEELY, LARRY	BANJOIST	17530 VENTURA BLVD #108	ENCINO, CA	91316
MC NEIL, BRYAN	BARITONE	POST OFFICE BOX 20548	NEW YORK, NY	10025
MC NEIL, LESLIE	DIRECTOR	299 RIVERSIDE DR	NEW YORK, NY	10024
MC NEIL, LESLIE	WRITER	555 W 57TH ST #1230	NEW YORK, NY	10019
MC NEIL, ROBERT B	NEWS CORRESPONDENT	8361 ORANGE CT	ALEXANDRIA, VA	22309
MC NEIL, ROBERT S	NEWS CORRESPONDENT	2919 TALLOW LN	BOWIE, MD	20715
MC NEILL, DON	TV-RADIO HOST	110 DE WINDT	WINNETKA, IL	60093
MC NEILL, DONALD	NEWS CORRESPONDENT	AMERICAN EMBASSY "M"	HELSINKI	FINLAND
MC NEILL, HARRY J	ACTOR	8446 LANGDON AVE #4	SEPULVEDA, CA	91343
MC NEILL, HARRY J	TV DIRECTOR	30 NEW HOLLAND VILLAGE #3	NAUET, NY	10954
MC NELIS, JAMES R	NEWS CORRESPONDENT	44 E LAKE DR	ANNAPOLIS, MD	21402
MC NEW, JULIE	BODYBUILDER	POST OFFICE BOX 86	SANTA MONICA, CA	90406
MC NICHOL, KRISTY	ACTRESS	14355 MILLBROOK DR	SHERMAN OAKS, CA	91423
MC NICHOL, TOMMY	ACTOR-SINGER	1717 N HIGHLAND AVE #414	LOS ANGELES, CA	90028
MC NULTY, FRANK	PUBLISHING EXECUTIVE	PARADE, 750 3RD AVE	NEW YORK, NY	10017
MC NULTY, RED	WRESTLER	SEE - KOLOFF, IVAN		
MC PEAK, SANDY	ACTOR	SF & A, 121 N SAN VICENTE BLVD	BEVERLY HILLS, CA	90211
MC PEAKE, WILLIAM	GUITARIST	ROUTE #6, GUILL RD	MOUNT JULIET, TN	37122
MC PEAKE BROTHERS, THE	C & W GROUP	1215 W NORTH ST	WYTHEVILLE, VA	24382
MC PHARLIN, J JAMES	TV DIRECTOR	ABC-TV, 190 N STATE ST	CHICAGO, IL	60601
MC PHEE, GEORGE	ORGANIST	15 HIGH ST #121	HARTFORD, CT	06103
MC PHEE, JOHN	WRITER	475 DRAKE'S CORNER RD	PRINCETON, NJ	08540
MC PHERSON, CRAIG	ARTIST	112 E 19TH ST #3-F	NEW YORK, NY	10003
MC PHERSON, DON	DIRECTOR	EGGERS, 6345 FOUNTAIN AVE	HOLLYWOOD, CA	90028
MC PHERSON, JAMES	GUITARIST	POST OFFICE BOX 153	HEALY, AK	99743
MC PHERSON, JOHN A	FILM DIRECTOR	8428 MELROSE PL #C	LOS ANGELES, CA	90069
MC PHERSON, PATRICIA	ACTRESS	9200 SUNSET BLVD #931	LOS ANGELES, CA	90069
MC PHERSON, STEPHEN F	TV WRITER-DIRECTOR	8225 LINCOLN TERR	LOS ANGELES, CA	90069
MC PHERSON, WARNER H	SINGER-GUITARIST	SEE - MACK, WARNER		
MC PHERSON, WILLIAM	NEWS CORRESPONDENT	1741 "Q" ST, NW	WASHINGTON, DC	20009
MC PHIE, TERU	ACTRESS	4721 LAUREL CANYON BLVD #211	NORTH HOLLYWOOD, CA	91607
MC PHILLIPS, HUGH	TV DIRECTOR	4256 CAHUENGA BLVD	NORTH HOLLYWOOD, CA	91602
MC QUADE, CHANCE	WRESTLER	NATIONAL WRESTLING ALLIANCE		
		JIM CROCKETT PROMOTIONS		
		421 BRIARBEND DR	CHARLOTTE, NC	28209
MC QUAKER, LYNNE	ACTRESS	430 S CLOVERDALE AVE #22	LOS ANGELES, CA	90036
MC QUEEN, BUTTERFLY	ACTRESS	470 W 144TH ST #A	NEW YORK, NY	10031
MC QUEEN, CHAD	ACTOR	6419 SURFSIDE DR	MALIBU, CA	90265
MC QUEEN, NEILE	ACTRESS	TOFFEL, 2323 BOWMONT DR	BEVERLY HILLS, CA	90210
MC QUILLAN, LAURANCE	NEWS CORRESPONDENT	2720 ARVIN ST	WHEATON, MD	20902
MC QUIRE, BILL	SINGER	3125 19TH ST #217	BAKERSFIELD, CA	93301
MC RAE, CARMEN	ACTRESS	2200 SUMMITRIDGE DR	BEVERLY HILLS, CA	90210
MC RAE, FRANK	ACTOR	10351 SANTA MONICA BLVD #211	LOS ANGELES, CA	90025
MC RAE, HAMILTON	ACTOR	14314 BURBANK BLVD #H-2031	VAN NUYS, CA	91401
MC RAE, HILTON	ACTOR	21 1ST AVE	LONDON SW14	ENGLAND
MC RAE, MARY A	NEWS CORRESPONDENT	2133 WISCONSIN AVE, NW	WASHINGTON, DC	20007
MC RAE, PAUL ANTHONY	CONDUCTOR	POST OFFICE BOX 160	HIGHLAND PARK, IL	60035
MC RAE, VIVIAN	CASTING DIRECTOR	POST OFFICE BOX 1351	BURBANK, CA	91507
MC RANEY, GERALD	ACTOR-DIRECTOR	6738 FERNHILL RD	MALIBU, CA	90265
MC RAVEN, DALE	TV WRITER	8955 BEVERLY BLVD	LOS ANGELES, CA	90048
MC REYNOLDS, JAMES	SINGER-GUITARIST	POST OFFICE BOX 304	GALLATIN, TN	37066

MC REYNOLDS, JESSE	SINGER-GUITARIST	POST OFFICE BOX 304	GALLATIN, TN	37066
MC REYNOLDS, JESSE KEITH	SINGER-GUITARIST	ROUTE #2, BOX 60-D	GALLATIN, TN	37066
MC REYNOLDS, JIM & JESSE	VOCAL DUO	POST OFFICE BOX BOX 304	GALLATIN, TN	37066
MC ROBBIE, PETER	ACTOR	ABRAMS ARTISTS & ASSOCIATES		
		420 MADISON AVE, 14TH FLOOR	NEW YORK, NY	10017
MC ROBERTS, BRIONY	ACTRESS	BURNETT, 42 GRAFTON HOUSE		
		2-3 GOLDEN SQ	LONDON W1	ENGLAND
MC ROBERTS, ROBERT	PIANIST	111 OLD HICKORY BLVD #231-W	NASHVILLE, TN	37221
MC SHANE, IAN	ACTOR	10100 SANTA MONICA BLVD #1600	LOS ANGELES, CA	90067
MC SHANE, JOHN D	DIRECTOR	15 CHRISTOPHER ST	NEW YORK, NY	10014
MC SHARRY, CARMEL	ACTRESS	J & W, 78 NEW BOND ST	LONDON W1	ENGLAND
MC TEAGUE, MICHELLE	CELLIST	2401 BELMONT BLVD	NASHVILLE, TN	37212
MC TIERNAN, JOHN	WRITER	8955 BEVERLY BLVD	LOS ANGELES, CA	90048
MC TYRE, ROBERT S	WRITER	10840 FULLBRIDGT AVE	CHATSWORTH, CA	91311
MC VAY, JARED	ACTOR	4789 VINELAND AVE #100	NORTH HOLLYWOOD, CA	91602
MC VAY, LEWIS	SINGER	HEARTLAND, 660 DOUGLAS AVE	ALTAMONTE SPRINGS, FL	32714
MC VEA, JACK	CLARINETIST	116 E 68TH ST	LOS ANGELES, CA	90003
MC VEAGH, EVE	ACTRESS	3518 W CAHUENGA BLVD #316	LOS ANGELES, CA	90068
MC VEY, DICK	GUITARIST	830 GLASTONBURY RD #827	NASHVILLE, TN	37217
MC VEY, TYLER	ACTOR	9220 SUNSET BLVD #218	LOS ANGELES, CA	90069
MC VIE, CHRISTINE	SINGER-SONGWRITER	9744 LLOYDCREST DR	BEVERLY HILLS, CA	90210
MC VIE, JOHN	SINGER-SONGWRITER	13486 FIRTH DR	BEVERLY HILLS, CA	90210
MC VITIE, J DOUGLAS	NEWS CORRESPONDENT	2827 S WAKEFIELD ST #C	ARLINGTON, VA	22206
MC WETHY, JOHN F	NEWS CORRESPONDENT	ABC-TV, NEWS DEPARTMENT		
		1717 DE SALES ST, NW	WASHINGTON, DC	20036
MC WHINNEY, COURTENAY	ACTRESS	2450 BEVERLY AVE #4	SANTA MONICA, CA	90405
MC WHIRTER, JULIE	ACTRESS	427 N CANON DR #205	BEVERLY HILLS, CA	90210
MC WHIRTER, MACK	TRUMPETER	1166 GREENLAND AVE	NASHVILLE, TN	37216
MC WILLIAMS, CAROLINE	ACTRESS	8500 WILSHIRE BLVD #506	BEVERLY HILLS, CA	90211
MC WILLIAMS, CHERYL	ACTRESS	10000 RIVERSIDE DR #12-14	TOLUCA LAKE, CA	91602
MC WILLIAMS, FLEMING	SINGER	POST OFFICE BOX 211	EAST PRAIRIE, MO	63845
MC WILLIAMS, KEN & THE SOUTHERN	C & W GROUP	POST OFFICE BOX 4234	PANORAMA CITY, CA	91412
MC WILLIAMS, RITA M	NEWS CORRESPONDENT	14135 CASTLE BLVD #302	SILVER SPRING, MD	20904
MC WILLIAMS, TIM	NEWS CORRESPONDENT	12700 YATES FORD RD	CLIFTON, VA	22024
MCC FERNANDEZ, MARY	NEWS REPORTER	TIME/TIME & LIFE BLDG		
		ROCKEFELLER CENTER	NEW YORK, NY	10020
MCD CHASE, NANCY	NEWS REPORTER	TIME/TIME & LIFE BLDG		
		ROCKEFELLER CENTER	NEW YORK, NY	10020
MDC	ROCK & ROLL GROUP	SEE - MILLION DEAD KIDS		
MEACHAM, PAUL	ACTOR	ANN WRIGHT, 136 E 57TH ST	NEW YORK, NY	10022
MEAD, MARY K	WRITER	555 W 57TH ST #1230	NEW YORK, NY	10019
MEAD, TERRY M	MUSIC ARRANGER	704 HERITAGE SQ DR	MADISON, TN	37115
MEADE, JULIA	ACTRESS	1010 5TH AVE	NEW YORK, NY	10028
MEADE, SUSANNA F	WRITER	555 W 57TH ST #1230	NEW YORK, NY	10019
MEADE, TIMOTHY E	NEWS CORRESPONDENT	7755 HERITAGE SQ #102	NEW CARROLLTON, MD	20784
MEADOR, JOE	GUITARIST	146 LAKE TERR DR	HENDERSONVILLE, TN	37075
MEADOW, BARRY	TV WRITER	9000 SUNSET BLVD #1200	LOS ANGELES, CA	90069
MEADOW, HERB	FILM-TV WRITER	6551 COMMODORE SLOAT DR	LOS ANGELES, CA	90048
MEADOW, LYNNE	THEATER DIRECTOR	321 E 73RD ST	NEW YORK, NY	10021
MEADOWS, AUDREY	ACTRESS	350 TROUSDALE PL	BEVERLY HILLS, CA	90210
MEADOWS, JAMES	DRUMMER	ROUTE #1	BUMPUS MILLS, TN	37028
MEADOWS, JAYNE	ACTRESS	16185 WOODVALE RD	ENCINO, CA	91436
MEADOWS, KRISTIN	ACTRESS	15301 VENTURA BLVD #345	SHERMAN OAKS, CA	91403
MEAGHER, KEVIN M	WRITER-PRODUCER	110 WORTH ST #3	NEW YORK, NY	10013
MEALING, PENNY	SINGER	9200 SUNSET BLVD #621	LOS ANGELES, CA	90069
MEALS, SYLVIA	ACTRESS	3940 PACHECO DR	SHERMAN OAKS, CA	91403
MEALY, BARBARA	ACTRESS	1418 N HIGHLAND AVE #102	LOS ANGELES, CA	90028
MEAN GENE	WRESTLING ANNOUNCER	POST OFFICE BOX 3859	STAMFORD, CT	06905
MEANEY, DONALD V	TV EXECUTIVE	NBC NEWS, 4001 NEBRASKA AVE, NW	WASHINGTON, DC	20016
MEANS, HOWARD	COMMENTATOR	KING FEATURES SYNDICATE		
		235 E 45TH ST	NEW YORK, NY	10017
MEANS, HOWARD B	NEWS CORRESPONDENT	6709 PYLE RD	BETHESDA, MD	20817
MEANS, JOHN	ACTOR	ABRAMS ARTISTS & ASSOCIATES		
		420 MADISON AVE, 14TH FLOOR	NEW YORK, NY	10017
MEANS, JOHN A	TV DIRECTOR	4707 LA VILLA MARINA #H	MARINA DEL REY, CA	90292
MEANS, MARIANNE	NEWS CORRESPONDENT	1521 31ST ST, NW	WASHINGTON, DC	20007
MEARA, ANNE	COMEDIENNE-ACTRESS	118 RIVERSIDE DR	NEW YORK, NY	10024
MEAT LOAF	SINGER-COMPOSER	POST OFFICE BOX 68		
		STOCKPORT	CHESIRE SK30 JY	ENGLAND
MEAT PUPPETS, THE	ROCK & ROLL GROUP	POST OFFICE BOX 110	TEMPE, AZ	85281
MEATHELY, DEBORAH	CASTING DIRECTOR	4820 N CLEON AVE	NORTH HOLLYWOOD, CA	91601
MECCHI, IRENE M	TV WRITER	8955 BEVERLY BLVD	LOS ANGELES, CA	90048
MECEY, DAVID	PHOTOGRAPHER	MODELS & PROMOTIONS AGENCY		
		8560 SUNSET BLVD, 10TH FLOOR	LOS ANGELES, LA	90069
MECHAM, MICHAEL R	NEWS CORRESPONDENT	2525 N 10TH ST	ARLINGTON, VA	22201
MECHEM, DAN	NEWS CORRESPONDENT	122 "C" ST, NW	WASHINGTON, DC	20001
MECHETTI, FABIO	CONDUCTOR	AFFILIATE ARTIST, INC		
		37 W 65TH ST, 6TH FLOOR	NEW YORK, NY	10023
MECHLING, THOMAS B	NEWS CORRESPONDENT	1608 19TH ST #4, NW	WASHINGTON, DC	20009
MECO	MUSICAL GROUP	RANDALL, 9340 DAVANA RD	SHERMAN OAKS, CA	91403
MEDAK, PETER	FILM DIRECTOR	142 S BEDFORD DR	BEVERLY HILLS, CA	90212
MEDALIS, JOSEPH G	ACTOR	1242 1/2 N HAVENHURST DR	LOS ANGELES, CA	90046

JAYNE MEADOWS

RALPH MEEKER

JOHN C. MELLENCAMP

MEN AT WORK

HEATHER MENZIES

BURGESS MEREDITH

JIM MESSINA

BETTE MIDLER

VERA MILES

Name	Occupation	Address	City	Zip
MEDAUGH, CLIFF	ACTOR	2482 MAINE AVE	LONG BEACH, CA	90806
MEDAVOY, MIKE	FILM EXECUTIVE	9262 OAKMERE RD	LOS ANGELES, CA	90035
MEDCALF, VIRGIL	SAXOPHONIST	POST OFFICE BOX 326	THOMASTON, GA	30286
MEDDICK, JIM	CARTOONIST	UNITED FEATURE SYNDICATE		
		200 PARK AVE	NEW YORK, NY	10166
MEDECIN, ILENE GRAHAM	ACTRESS	9855 WHITWELL DR	BEVERLY HILLS, CA	90210
MEDEIROS, GINNY	ACTRESS	200 W 57TH ST #1303	NEW YORK, NY	10019
MEDFORD, DON	FILM DIRECTOR	1 DRIFTWOOD ST #6	MARINA DEL REY, CA	90292
MEDFORD, JODY	ACTRESS	ICM, 8899 BEVERLY BLVD	LOS ANGELES, CA	90048
MEDFORD, LISA	DIRECTOR	4240 VIA MARINA #33	MARINA DEL REY, CA	90292
MEDICI, JOHN	ACTOR	AIMEE, 13743 VICTORY BLVD	VAN NUYS, CA	91401
MEDIEVAL STEEL	ROCK & ROLL GROUP	1254 LAMAR AVE #312	MEMPHIS, TN	38114
MEDIN, HARRIET	ACTRESS	235 W 76TH ST	NEW YORK, NY	10023
MEDINA, HAZEL	ACTRESS	8722 SKYLINE DR	LOS ANGELES, CA	90046
MEDINA, PATRICIA	ACTRESS	1993 MESA DR	PALM SPRINGS, CA	92264
MEDINA, SARA C	WRITER-EDITOR	TIME/TIME & LIFE BLDG		
		ROCKEFELLER CENTER	NEW YORK, NY	10020
MEDLEY, BILL	SINGER-SONGWRITER	17835 VENTURA BLVD #207	ENCINO, CA	91316
MEDLIN, JAMES E	SCREENWRITER	8955 BEVERLY BLVD	LOS ANGELES, CA	90048
MEDLINSKY, HARVEY	DIRECTOR	9555 W OLYMPIC BLVD	BEVERLY HILLS, CA	90212
MEDNICK, MURRAY M	WRITER	8955 BEVERLY BLVD	LOS ANGELES, CA	90048
MEDOWAY, CARY C	WRITER-PRODUCER	859 N FULLER AVE	LOS ANGELES, CA	90046
MEDUSA	MUSICAL GROUP	50 MUSIC SQUARE W #102	NASHVILLE, TN	37203
MEDVED, MICHAEL	WRITER-FILM CRITIC	1224 ASHLAND AVE	SANTA MONICA, CA	90405
MEDVEE, DENNIS D	NEWS CORRESPONDENT	2025 "M" ST, NW	WASHINGTON, DC	20036
MEDWAY, ELIZABETH	TV WRITER	8955 BEVERLY BLVD	LOS ANGELES, CA	90048
MEDWIN, MICHAEL	ACT-WRI-PROD	LEADING ARTISTS, LTD		
		60 SAINT JAMES'S ST	LONDON SW1	ENGLAND
MEEHAN, ELIZABETH A	WRITER	555 W 57TH ST #1230	NEW YORK, NY	10019
MEEHAN, JANE C	WRITER	555 W 57TH ST #1230	NEW YORK, NY	10019
MEEHAN, JOHN	CHOREOGRAPHER	AMERICAN BALLET, 888 7TH AVE	NEW YORK, NY	10019
MEEHAN, MARY	NEWS CORRESPONDENT	23 2ND ST #18, NE	WASHINGTON, DC	20002
MEEHAN, THOMAS E	SCREENWRITER	555 W 57TH ST #1230	NEW YORK, NY	10019
MEEKER, KEN	ACTOR	ABC-TV, "ONE LIFE TO LIVE"		
		1330 AVE OF THE AMERICAS	NEW YORK, NY	10019
MEEKER, RALPH	ACTOR	POST OFFICE BOX 4020	BEVERLY HILLS, CA	90213
MEEKS, ORRIE	TV WRITER	8955 BEVERLY BLVD	LOS ANGELES, CA	90048
MEENA, JAMES	CONDUCTOR	253 W 73RD ST #7-M	NEW YORK, NY	10023
MEERBAUM, NORA	ACTRESS	5741 EL CANON AVE	WOODLAND HILLS, CA	91367
MEERSON, STEVEN R	WRITER	14072 DAVANA TERR	SHERMAN OAKS, CA	91423
MEETINGS, THE	ROCK & ROLL GROUP	ROCKFEVER, 535 BROADWAY	LAWRENCE, MA	01841
MEGA MAHARISHI I AM ED	WRESTLER	SEE - DE BEERS, COLONEL		
MEGAHEY, LESLIE	TV WRITER-DIRECTOR	3 HOLLY VILLAS, WELLESLEY AVE	LONDON W6	ENGLAND
MEGAHY, FRANCIS	WRITER-PRODUCER	BEDFORD, 13 CHURCH ST	LONDON NW8	ENGLAND
MEGGS, BROWN	SCREENWRITER	1450 EL MIRADOR DR	PASADENA, CA	91103
MEGLIN, NICK	EDITOR-WRITER	MAD MAGAZINE, INC		
		485 MADISON AVE	NEW YORK, NY	10022
MEGNA, JOHN	ACTOR	507 CRANE BLVD	LOS ANGELES, CA	90065
MEGNOT, ROYA	ACTRESS	ABC-TV NETWORK, "LOVING"		
		1330 AVE OF THE AMERICAS	NEW YORK, NY	10019
MEGREMIS, YEORYIA	CONTRALTO	45 W 60TH ST #4-K	NEW YORK, NY	10023
MEHLER, EDWARD	ACTOR	8831 SUNSET BLVD #402	LOS ANGELES, CA	90069
MEHLING, HAROLD	WRITER	555 W 57TH ST #1230	NEW YORK, NY	10019
MEHTA, MEHLI	CONDUCTOR	321 TILDEN AVE	LOS ANGELES, CA	90049
MEHTA, NANCY KOVACK	ACTRESS	301 OCEANO DR	LOS ANGELES, CA	90049
MEHTA, NAUSHAD S	NEWS REPORTER	TIME/TIME & LIFE BLDG		
		ROCKEFELLER CENTER	NEW YORK, NY	10020
MEHTA, ZUBIN	CONDUCTOR	301 OCEANO DR	LOS ANGELES, CA	90049
MEIER, DON	WRITER-PRODUCER	320 LOCUST RD, BOX 279	WINNETKA, IL	60093
MEIER, JOHANNA	SOPRANO	CAMI, 165 W 57TH ST	NEW YORK, NY	10019
MEIER, WALTRAUD	MEZZO-SOPRANO	CAMI, 165 W 57TH ST	NEW YORK, NY	10019
		ROCKEFELLER CENTER	NEW YORK, NY	10020
MEIGHER, S CHRISTOPHER, III	PUBLISHING EXECUTIVE	LIFE/TIME & LIFE BLDG		
MEIKLEJOHN, DON D	NEWS CORRESPONDENT	501 SLATERS LN #103	ALEXANDRIA, VA	22314
MEILANDT, TONY	TALENT AGENT	AGM MGMT, 1312 N LA BREA AVE	HOLLYWOOD, CA	90028
MEILEN, BILL	WRITER	8955 BEVERLY BLVD	LOS ANGELES, CA	90048
MEISELAS, SUSAN	PHOTOGRAPHER	236 ELIZABETH ST	NEW YORK, NY	10012
MEISENBACH, MEGAN	FLUTIST	POST OFFICE BOX U	REDDING, CT	06875
MEISENBACH, PEARCE	CELLIST	POST OFFICE BOX U	REDDING, CT	06875
MEISER, EDITH	ACTRESS	484 W 43RD ST	NEW YORK, NY	10036
MEISLER, BESS	ACTRESS	938 S ORANGE GROVE AVE #2	LOS ANGELES, CA	90036
MEISNER, GUNTER	ACTOR	STARKMAN, 1501 BROADWAY	NEW YORK, NY	10036
MEISNER, RANDY	SINGER-SONGWRITER	2565 ZORADA DR	LOS ANGELES, CA	90046
MEISSNER, ARNOLD	WRITER	8955 BEVERLY BLVD	LOS ANGELES, CA	90048
MEISSNER, JOE	COMPOSER	5015 BILOXI AVE	NORTH HOLLYWOOD, CA	91601
MEISSNER, STAN	SINGER	41 BRITAIN ST #200	TORONTO, ONT	CANADA
MEISTER, DAVID L	CABLE EXECUTIVE	HOME BOX OFFICE PICTURES		
		1100 AVE OF THE AMERICAS	NEW YORK, NY	10036
MEISTER & BENDER	VOCAL DUO	GERSHUNOFF, 502 PARK AVE	NEW YORK, NY	10022
MEKKA, DELYSE LIVELY	ACTRESS	SEE - LIVELY-MEKKA, DELYSE		
MEKKA, EDDIE	ACTOR	WEBB, 7500 DEVISTA DR	LOS ANGELES, CA	90046
MEKLER, MANI	SOPRANO	61 W 62ND ST #6-F	NEW YORK, NY	10023
MEKLER, OSCAR	CONDUCTOR	386 HUNTLEY DR	LOS ANGELES, CA	90048
MEKONS, THE	ROCK & ROLL GROUP	6 CLIFTON MANSIONS		
		COLDHARBOR LN, BRIXTON	LONDON SW9 8LL	ENGLAND

Name	Occupation	Address	City/State	Zip
MELANIE	SINGER	DENIS VAUGHAN MANAGEMENT		
		HEATHCOAT HOUSE		
		18-20 SAVILE RD	LONDON W1	ENGLAND
MELCHIOR, IB J	WRITER-PRODUCER	8228 MARMONT LN	LOS ANGELES, CA	90069
MELDRUM, WENDEL	ACTRESS	11726 SAN VICENTE BLVD #300	LOS ANGELES, CA	90049
MELE, ARTHUR	DIRECTOR	3387 N KNOLL DR	LOS ANGELES, CA	90068
MELE, NICHOLAS	ACTOR	12725 VENTURA BLVD #E	STUDIO CITY, CA	91604
MELENDEZ, BILL	ANIMATION DIRECTOR	438 N LARCHMONT BLVD	LOS ANGELES, CA	90004
MELENDEZ, MARIA	ACTRESS	15010 VENTURA BLVD #219	SHERMAN OAKS, CA	91403
MELENDY, DAVID R	NEWS CORRESPONDENT	1825 "K" ST, NW	WASHINGTON, DC	20006
MELGAR, GABRIEL	ACTOR	10000 RIVERSIDE DR #3	TOLUCA LAKE, CA	91602
MELHAM, RICHARD	NEWS CORRESPONDENT	5418 CROSSRAIL DR	BURKE, VA	22015
MELIA, JOE	ACTOR	64 ORMONDE TERR	LONDON NW8	ENGLAND
		MAIDSTONE	KENT	ENGLAND
MELIORA QUARTET	MUSIC ENSEMBLE	ICM, 40 W 57TH ST	NEW YORK, NY	10019
MELITO, NICK A	WRITER	555 W 57TH ST #1230	NEW YORK, NY	10019
MELLE, GIL	COMPOSER	6404 WILSHIRE BLVD #800	LOS ANGELES, CA	90048
MELLEN, CHASE, III	WRITER	8955 BEVERLY BLVD	LOS ANGELES, CA	90048
MELLENCAMP, JOHN COUGAR	SINGER-SONGWRITER	ROUTE #1, BOX 361	NASHVILLE, IN	47448
MELLINGER, LEONIE	ACTRESS	LONDON MANAGEMENT, LTD		
		235-241 REGENT ST	LONDON W1A 2JT	ENGLAND
MELLINGER, MICHAEL	ACTOR	THE OLD VICARAGE		
		BOUGHTON MONCHELSEA		
		MAIDSTONE	KENT	ENGLAND
MELLINI, SCOTT	ACTOR	6430 SUNSET BLVD #1203	HOLLYWOOD, CA	90028
MELLISH, PAMELA	SOPRANO	45 W 60TH ST #4-K	NEW YORK, NY	10023
MELLORS, PARKIN	WRITER	8955 BEVERLY BLVD	LOS ANGELES, CA	90048
MELLOW, DICK	MUSIC ARRANGER	921 KIRKWOOD AVE	NASHVILLE, TN	37204
MELLOWES, MARILYN R	WRITER	555 W 57TH ST #1230	NEW YORK, NY	10019
MELMAN, JEFFREY	DIRECTOR-PRODUCER	3694 BUENA PARK DR	STUDIO CITY, CA	91604
MELMED, JERRY	DIRECTOR	45 5TH AVE	NEW YORK, NY	10003
MELNICK, DANIEL	FILM PRODUCER	1123 SUNSET HILLS DR	LOS ANGELES, CA	90069
MELNICK, MARK	WRITER	8955 BEVERLY BLVD	LOS ANGELES, CA	90048
MELO, NIELS	DIRECTOR-PRODUCER	POST OFFICE BOX 1116	BELMONT, CA	94002
MELONAS, EMILIE	ACTRESS	1241 1/2 N JUNE ST	LOS ANGELES, CA	90038
MELSTED, LINDA	VIOLINIST	333 TAYLOR AVE N #202	SEATTLE, WA	98109
MELTON, BARRY "THE FISH"	SINGER-SONGWRITER	17337 VENTURA BLVD #300-C	ENCINO, CA	91316
MELTON, FRANKLIN	TV DIRECTOR	13950 NW PASSAGE	MARINA DEL REY, CA	90292
MELTON, ROY	GUITARIST	400 TINNIN RD	GOODLETTSVILLE, TN	37072
MELTON, SID	ACTOR	5347 CEDROS AVE	VAN NUYS, CA	91410
MELTON, TYLER C	NEWS CORRESPONDENT	317 WHITTIER ST, NW	WASHINGTON, DC	20012
MELTZER, BERNARD	COLUMNIST	NEWS AMERICA SYNDICATE		
		1703 KAISER AVE	IRVINE, CA	92714
MELTZER, DANIEL	WRITER	555 W 57TH ST #1230	NEW YORK, NY	10019
MELTZER, MARTHA	TV WRITER	17525 LORNE ST	NORTHRIDGE, CA	91325
MELTZER, NEWTON	WRITER-PRODUCER	67 YALE ST	ROSLYN HEIGHTS, NY	11577
MELVILLE, SAM	ACTOR	9050 HOLLYWOOD HILLS RD	LOS ANGELES, CA	90046
MELVIN, ALLAN	ACTOR	271 N BOWLING GREEN WY	LOS ANGELES, CA	90049
MELVIN, DONNIE	SINGER	45 OVERLOOK TERR	NEW YORK, NY	10033
MELVIN, MURRAY	ACTOR	JJ LTD, 7 W EATON PLACE MEWS	LONDON SW4	ENGLAND
MELVOIN, JEFF	TV WRITER	153 GRETA GREEN WY	LOS ANGELES, CA	90049
MELVOIN, MICHAEL	COMPOSER	5638 CARLTON WY	LOS ANGELES, CA	90028
MEMMOTT, MARK	COLUMNIST	POST OFFICE BOX 500	WASHINGTON, DC	20044
MEMORIES, THE	VOCAL TRIO	FENCHEL, 2104 S JEFFERSON AVE	MASON CITY, IA	50401
MEMPHIS SLIM	SINGER-PIANIST	R & B, 8959 S OGLESBY AVE	CHICAGO, IL	60617
MEN AT WORK	ROCK & ROLL GROUP	575 MADISON AVE #600	NEW YORK, NY	10022
MEN WITHOUT HATS	ROCK & ROLL GROUP	41 BRITAIN ST #200	TORONTO, ONT	CANADA
MENCHEL, DONALD	TV EXECUTIVE	445 PARK AVE	NEW YORK, NY	10022
MENCHER, HY	ACTOR	325 W 86TH ST	NEW YORK, NY	10024
MENDEL, STEPHEN	ACTOR	9000 SUNSET BLVD #910	LOS ANGELES, CA	90069
MENDELSOHN, ALFRED	DIRECTOR	129 E 82ND ST	NEW YORK, NY	10028
MENDELSOHN, JACK	TV WRITER	14066 ROBLAR RD	SHERMAN OAKS, CA	91423
MENDELSOHN, ROBERT	ACTOR	8230 BEVERLY BLVD #23	BEVERLY HILLS, CA	90048
MENDELSOHN, ROBYN	WRITER	555 W 57TH ST #1230	NEW YORK, NY	10019
MENDELSON, LEE	WRITER-PRODUCER	1408 CHAPIN AVE	BURLINGAME, CA	94010
MENDELSSOHN, VLADIMIR	VIOLIST	SHAW CONCERTS, 1995 BROADWAY	NEW YORK, NY	10023
MENDELSSOHN PIANO TRIO	PIANO TRIO	POST OFFICE BOX U	REDDING, CT	06875
MENDELSSOHN STRING QUARTET	STRING QUARTET	KAPLAN, 115 COLLEGE ST	BURLINGTON, VT	05401
MENDELUK, GEORGE	DIRECTOR-PRODUCER	6263 TOPIA DR	MALIBU, CA	90265
MENDENHALL, DAVID	ACTOR	8721 SUNSET BLVD #200	LOS ANGELES, CA	90069
MENDENHALL, IRENA	ACTRESS	6407 DIX ST	LOS ANGELES, CA	90068
MENDENHALL, JAMES	ACTOR	5860 VERDUN AVE	LOS ANGELES, CA	90043
MENDENHALL, MATT	BODYBUILDER	POST OFFICE BOX 934	SANTA MONICA, CA	90406
MENDES, SERGIO	PIANIST-SONGWRITER	4849 ENCINO AVE	ENCINO, CA	91436
MENDEZ, GENE	HIGH WIRE ACT	POST OFFICE BOX 87	WEST LEBANON, NY	12195
MENDEZ, JOHN	DRUMMER	SEE - MAND, JOHN		
MENDEZ & ELEANOR	HIGH WIRE DUO	POST OFFICE BOX 87	WEST LEBANON, NY	12195
MENDLESON, ANTHONY	COSTUME DESIGNER	37 CROMWELL RD	LONDON SW7	ENGLAND
MENDOZA, ERNESTO J	WRITER	555 W 57TH ST #1230	NEW YORK, NY	10019
MENDOZA, JOE	WRITER-PRODUCER	42 MURRAY MEWS	LONDON NW1 9RJ	ENGLAND
MENDOZA, NICOLAS OLIVEROS	DIRECTOR	DGA, 7950 SUNSET BLVD	LOS ANGELES, CA	90046
MENDOZA, VINCENT J	COMPOSER	12300 PACIFIC AVE	LOS ANGELES, CA	90066
MENEES, TIM	CARTOONIST	UNIVERSAL PRESS SYNDICATE		
		4900 MAIN ST, 9TH FLOOR	KANSAS CITY, MO	62114
MENESES, ANTONIO	CELLIST	ICM, 40 W 57TH ST	NEW YORK, NY	10019

Name	Occupation	Address	City	Zip
MENGATTI, JOHN	ACTOR	4621 COUNCIL ST #5	LOS ANGELES, CA	90004
MENGER, WILLIAM H	WRITER	1862 S NEWELL RD	MALIBU, CA	90265
MENGERS, SUE	TALENT AGENT	938 BEL AIR RD	LOS ANGELES, CA	90077
MENGLE, KLINE H	NEWS CORRESPONDENT	1927 BRIGHTLEAF CT	SILVER SPRING, MD	20902
MENKEN, ROBIN	ACTRESS-WRITER	1208 HILLDALE AVE	LOS ANGELES, CA	90069
MENKEN, SHEPARD	ACTOR	3401 S COAST VIEW DR	MALIBU, CA	90265
MENKIN, LAWRENCE	WRITER-PRODUCER	SAN FRANCISCO LITERARY AGENCY		
		899 E FRANCISCO BLVD	SAN RAFAEL, CA	94901
MENMUIR, RAYMOND	TV DIRECTOR-PRODUCER	CCA MGMT, 4 CT LODGE		
		48 SLOANE SQ	LONDON SW1W 8AT	ENGLAND
MENNIN, PETER	COMPOSER	JUILLIARD SCHOOL OF MUSIC		
		LINCOLN CENTER	NEW YORK, NY	10023
MENON, VIJAYA	RECORD EXECUTIVE	CAPITOL RECORDS CO		
		1750 N VINE ST	HOLLYWOOD, CA	90028
MENOTTI, GARY	TV DIRECTOR	1503 1/2 W 10TH ST	AUSTIN, TX	78703
MENOTTI, GIAN CARLO	COMPOSER	27 E 62ND ST	NEW YORK, NY	10021
MENS, ESTELLE	ACTRESS	39 W 95TH ST	NEW YORK, NY	10025
MENSCHEL, NEAL JOSEPH	PHOTOGRAPHER	340 E FOSTER ST	MELROSE, MA	02176
MENTAL AS ANYTHING	ROCK & ROLL GROUP	OLD SOUTH HEAD RD #17-79	BONDI JUNCTION NSW	AUSTRALIA
MENTEER, DAVID	TV DIRECTOR	4104 MAGNA CARTA RD	WOODLAND HILLS, CA	91364
MENTEER, GARY	WRITER-PRODUCER	1907 N CURSON AVE	LOS ANGELES, CA	90046
MENTION, MICHEL H	COMPOSER	21747 CANON DR	TOPANGA, CA	90290
MENTORS, THE	ROCK & ROLL GROUP	POST OFFICE BOX 2428	EL SEGUNDO, CA	90245
MENTZER, SUSANNE	MEZZO-SOPRANO	CAMI, 165 W 57TH ST	NEW YORK, NY	10019
MENUDO	ROCK & ROLL GROUP	PADOSA HATO REY		
		157 PONCE DE LEON	SAN JUAN	PUERTO RICO
MENUHIN, JEREMY	PIANIST	CAMI, 165 W 57TH ST	NEW YORK, NY	10019
MENUHIN, YEHUDI	VIOLINIST	19750 ALMA BRIDGE RD	LOS GATOS, CA	95030
MENVILLE, CHARLES	TV WRITER	31833 BROAD BEACH RD	MALIBU, CA	90265
MENZA, DONALD J	COMPOSER	12328 MAGNOLIA BLVD	NORTH HOLLYWOOD, CA	91607
MENZIES, HEATHER	ACTRESS	URICH, 3637 LONGRIDGE AVE	SHERMAN OAKS, CA	91403
MENZIES, JAMES C	TV WRITER	15925 KITTRIDGE ST	VAN NUYS, CA	91406
MENZIES, TIM	GUITARIST	5101 LINBAR DR #G-203	NASHVILLE, TN	37211
MENZIES, VICTOR	TV WRITER-PRODUCER	LISTER WELCH, LTD		
		3 GOLDBEATERS HOUSE		
		MARETTE ST	LONDON W1V 5LD	ENGLAND
MEPHITIS, PAT	SCREENWRITER	555 W 57TH ST #1230	NEW YORK, NY	10019
MEPPEN, ADRIAN J	WRITER	555 W 57TH ST #1230	NEW YORK, NY	10019
MERCADIER, MARTHE	ACTRESS	1 RUE PAUL DELAROCHE	PARIS 75016	FRANCE
MERCADO, HECTOR JAIME	ACTOR	9255 SUNSET BLVD #510	LOS ANGELES, CA	90069
MERCEDES, JON, III	WRITER	8955 BEVERLY BLVD	LOS ANGELES, CA	90048
MERCER, BILL	WRESTLING EMCEE	WORLD CLASS WRESTLING		
		SOUTHWEST SPORTS, INC		
		DALLAS SPORTATORIUM		
		1000 S INDUSTRIAL BLVD	DALLAS, TX	75207
MERCER, BOB	FILM EXECUTIVE	30 GOLDEN SQ	LONDON W1	ENGLAND
MERCER, ERNESTINE	ACTRESS	7469 MELROSE AVE #30	LOS ANGELES, CA	90046
MERCER, FRANCES	ACTRESS	561 S ORANGE GROVE AVE	LOS ANGELES, CA	90036
MERCER, JANE	WRITER	27 WESTCROFT SQ	LONDON W6 OTD	ENGLAND
MERCER, MARIAN	ACTRESS	3800 BARHAM BLVD #303	LOS ANGELES, CA	90068
MERCER, ROBERT PIERCE	TALENT AGENT	POST OFFICE BOX 2458	TOLUCA LAKE, CA	91602
MERCEY BROTHERS, THE	C & W GROUP	4680 ELK LAKE DR #304	VICTORIA, BC V8Z 5M1	CANADA
MERCHANT, ISMAIL	FILM PRODUCER	4 MORNINGTON PL	LONDON NW1	ENGLAND
MERCOURI, MELINA	ACTRESS	ANAGNOSTROPOULON 25	ATHENS	GREECE
MERCURIO, MICOLE	ACTRESS	8075 W 3RD ST #305	LOS ANGELES, CA	90048
MERCURY, FREDDIE	SINGER-SONGWRITER	5 CAMPDEN ST	LONDON W8	ENGLAND
MERCY RIVER BOYS, THE	C & W GROUP	6750 W 75TH ST, MARKADE 75		
		BUILDING #2-A	OVERLAND PARK, KS	66212
MERCYFUL FATE	ROCK & ROLL GROUP	328 HVIDOREVEJ	3TV 2650 HVIDOVRE	DENMARK
MERDIN, JONATHAN L	DIRECTOR	DGA, 110 W 57TH ST	NEW YORK, NY	10019
MEREDITH, BURGESS	ACT-WRI-DIR	25 MALIBU COLONY RD	MALIBU, CA	90265
MEREDITH, DON	ACTOR	POST OFFICE BOX 597	SANTE FE, NM	87504
MEREDITH, JO ANNE	ACTRESS	7060 HOLLYWOOD BLVD #610	LOS ANGELES, CA	90028
MEREDITH, LUCILLE	ACTRESS	6310 SAN VICENTE BLVD #407	LOS ANGELES, CA	90048
MEREDITH, SUSAN, AARON RUSSELL	C & W GROUP	TESSIER, 505 CANTON PASS	MADISON, TN	37115
MERHOLZ, B J	WRITER	2514 3RD ST	SANTA MONICA, CA	90405
MERIL, MACHA	ACTRESS	AG ALPHA ARTISTS AGENCE		
		27 RUE DE LA POMPE	PARIS 75016	FRANCE
MERIMS, H GREG	ACTOR	1730 3RD AVE	SAN DIEGO, CA	92101
MERIN, EDA REISS	ACTRESS	870 N VINE ST #G	LOS ANGELES, CA	90038
MERIWETHER, LEE	ACTRESS	POST OFFICE BOX 402	ENCINO, CA	91316
MERK, RON	TV WRITER	8955 BEVERLY BLVD	LOS ANGELES, CA	90048
MERL, JUDY	TV WRITER	8955 BEVERLY BLVD	LOS ANGELES, CA	90048
MERLIN, BARBARA	WRITER	3044 MOTOR AVE	LOS ANGELES, CA	90064
MERLIN, JAN	ACTOR-WRITER	9016 WONDERLAND AVE	LOS ANGELES, CA	90046
MERLIN, MILTON	WRITER	3044 MOTOR AVE	LOS ANGELES, CA	90064
MERLIN-JONES, SALLY B	WRITER	9708 BEVERLYWOOD ST	LOS ANGELES, CA	90034
MERLIS, GEORGE	TV PRODUCER	PARAMOUNT TELEVISION		
		ENTERTAINMENT TONIGHT		
		5555 MELROSE AVE	LOS ANGELES, CA	90038
MERMELSTEIN, PAUL	WRITER	555 W 57TH ST #1230	NEW YORK, NY	10019
MERNIT, JOHN M	WRITER	555 W 57TH ST #1230	NEW YORK, NY	10019
MERRELL, MURIEL L	COMPOSER	823 LAUREL AVE	LOS ANGELES, CA	90046

Name	Occupation	Address	City
MERRELL, RICHARD	ACTOR	110 W 40TH ST #2401	NEW YORK, NY 10018
MERRFIELD, DAVID	HELICOPTER TRAPEZE	HALL, 138 FROG HOLLOW RD	CHURCHVILLE, PA 18966
MERRICK, DAVID	THEATER PRODUCER	246 W 44TH ST	NEW YORK, NY 10036
MERRICK, DAWN	ACTRESS	ABC-TV, "GENERAL HOSPITAL"	
		1438 N GOWER ST	LOS ANGELES, CA 90028
MERRICK, GEORGE	DRUMMER	3609 HAMPTON AVE	NASHVILLE, TN 37215
MERRICK, JIM	CASTING DIRECTOR	POST OFFICE BOX 5718	SHERMAN OAKS, CA 91403
MERRICK, MIKE	THEATER PRODUCER	9000 SUNSET BLVD	LOS ANGELES, CA 90069
MERRILL, BOB	COMPOSER	ASCAP, 1 LINCOLN PLAZA	NEW YORK, NY 10023
MERRILL, CAROL	MODEL	29800 W CUTHBERT RD	MALIBU, CA 90265
MERRILL, CLAIRE B	WRITER	555 W 57TH ST #1230	NEW YORK, NY 10019
MERRILL, DINA	ACTRESS	325 DUNEMERE DR	LA JOLLA, CA 92037
MERRILL, GARY	ACTOR	THORNHURST RD	FALMOUTH FORESIDE, MA 04105
MERRILL, HOWARD	TV WRITER	136 S PALM DR	BEVERLY HILLS, CA 90212
MERRILL, KATHRYN	ACTRESS	1717 N HIGHLAND AVE #414	LOS ANGELES, CA 90028
MERRILL, KIETH	WRITER-PRODUCER	11930 RHUS RIDGE RD	LOS ALTOS, CA 94022
MERRILL, PAUL	ACTOR	230 W 107TH ST	NEW YORK, NY 10025
MERRILL, RICHARD	WRITER	555 W 57TH ST #1230	NEW YORK, NY 10019
MERRILL, ROBERT	BARITONE	79 OXFORD DR	NEW ROCHELLE, NY 10801
MERRILL, SAMUEL	WRITER	555 W 57TH ST #1230	NEW YORK, NY 10019
MERRILL, SI	DIRECTOR	DGA, 110 W 57TH ST	NEW YORK, NY 10019
MERRIMAN, CATHY	ACTRESS	ABC-TV, "ALL MY CHILDREN"	
		1330 AVE OF THE AMERICAS	NEW YORK, NY 10019
MERRION, PAUL	NEWS CORRESPONDENT	419 N NELSON ST	ARLINGTON, VA 22203
MERRITT, CHRIS	TENOR	CAMI, 165 W 57TH ST	NEW YORK, NY 10019
MERRITT, JERRY	SINGER	STUDIO ONE, 4009 E 18TH ST	VANCOUVER, WA 98661
MERRITT, JOSEPH MYERS	PIANIST	117 N POINTE DR	AUBURNDALE, FL 33873
MERRITT, STANLEY S	WRITER-PRODUCER	DGA, 110 W 57TH ST	NEW YORK, NY 10019
MERRITT, THERESA	ACTRESS	9220 SUNSET BLVD #202	LOS ANGELES, CA 90069
MERRITTS, EUGENE L	MUSICIAN	202 BONNACLIFF CT	HERMITAGE, TN 37076
MERRITTS, GARY	FLUTIST	107 LAKEVIEW DR	ASHLAND CITY, TN 37015
MERROW, JANE	ACTRESS	SHARKEY, 90 REGENT ST	LONDON W1 ENGLAND
MERRY, ROBERT W	NEWS CORRESPONDENT	1313 MERRIE RIDGE RD	MC LEAN, VA 22101
MERSON, MARC	ACTOR	9200 SUNSET BLVD #PH-25	LOS ANGELES, CA 90069
MERSON, MELISSA	NEWS CORRESPONDENT	4508 CHESAPEAKE ST, NW	WASHINGTON, DC 20016
MERSON, RICHARD	ACTOR	208 S BEVERLY DR #4	BEVERLY HILLS, CA 90212
MERSON, SUSAN	ACTRESS	15010 VENTURA BLVD #219	SHERMAN OAKS, CA 91403
MERTINS, PATRICIA	ACTRESS	315 E 70TH ST	NEW YORK, NY 10023
MERTON, ALICE	ACTRESS	26 CORNELIA ST	NEW YORK, NY 10014
MERTON, ZENIA	ACTRESS	POST OFFICE BOX 130, HOVE	EAST SUSSEX BN3 6QU ENGLAND
MERWALD, FRANK	TV DIRECTOR-PRODUCER	3734 CLARINGTON AVE #5	LOS ANGELES, CA 90034
MERWAN, NANCY	ACTRESS	7718 W NORTON AVE #17	LOS ANGELES, CA 90046
MERY-CLARK, LAURENCE	FILM EDITOR	34 KENSINGTON SQ	LONDON W8 5HH ENGLAND
MES, ERICA	BODYBUILDER	BETTER BODIES MODEL &	
		SPORTS MANAGEMENT COMPANY	
		12 W 21ST ST	NEW YORK, NY 10010
MESE, JOHN	BODYBUILDER	NPC, 170 NE 99TH ST	MIAMI SHORES, FL 33138
MESHINSKY, JEFFREY M	NEWS CORRESPONDENT	11920 LEDGEROCK CT	POTOMAC, MD 20854
MESPLE, MADY	SOPRANO	1182 MARKET ST #311	SAN FRANCISCO, CA 94102
MESSENGER SERVICE	ROCK & ROLL GROUP	FPM, 1256 JAMAICA PLAIN STATION	BOSTON, MA 02130
MESSIAEN, OLIVER	COMPOSER	119 W 57TH ST #1505	NEW YORK, NY 10019
MESSICK, DALE	CARTOONIST	TRIBUNE MEDIA SERVICES	
		64 E CONCORD ST	ORLANDO, FL 32801
MESSICK, DON	ACTOR	9220 SUNSET BLVD #218	LOS ANGELES, CA 90069
MESSIER, LISE	SOPRANO	ROSENFIELD, 714 LADD RD	BRONX, NY 10471
MESSINA, DIANNE	TV WRITER	14413 COLLINS ST	VAN NUYS, CA 91401
MESSINA, JIM	SINGER-SONGWRITER	2110 E VALLEY RD	SANTA BARBARA, CA 93108
MESSINA, LOU	TV WRITER	14413 COLLINS ST	VAN NUYS, CA 91401
MESSINA, PHILLIP	FILM WRITER-DIRECTOR	358 S CITRUS AVE	LOS ANGELES, CA 90036
MESSINA, SAL	WRITER	555 W 57TH ST #1230	NEW YORK, NY 10019
MESSINA, TONY	ACTOR	11805 LAURELWOOD DR #3	STUDIO CITY, CA 91604
MESSING, CAROL	ACTRESS	1509 N CRESCENT HGTS BLVD #7	LOS ANGELES, CA 90069
MESSING, HAROLD	DIRECTOR	61 W 62ND ST	NEW YORK, NY 10023
MESSINGER, DOMINIC A	COMPOSER-CONDUCTOR	12000 RHODE ISLAND AVE #4	LOS ANGELES, CA 90025
MESSMER, JACK L	NEWS CORRESPONDENT	1825 "K" ST, NW	WASHINGTON, DC 20006
MESSURI, ANTHONY C	DIRECTOR	16 FAIRVIEW AVE	TARRYTOWN, NY 10591
MESTER, JORGE	CONDUCTOR	ICM, 40 W 57TH ST	NEW YORK, NY 10019
MESZOLY, ROBIN D	NEWS CORRESPONDENT	5909 PLAINVIEW RD	BETHESDA, MD 20817
METCALF, CHARLES W	TV WRITER	8955 BEVERLY BLVD	LOS ANGELES, CA 90048
METCALF, RORY	WRITER	555 W 57TH ST #1230	NEW YORK, NY 10019
METCALF, WILLIAM	BARITONE	59 E 54TH ST #81	NEW YORK, NY 10022
METCALFE, BURT	TV WRITER-DIRECTOR	POST OFFICE BOX 900	BEVERLY HILLS, CA 90213
METCALFE, GORDON	ACTOR	2523 IVAN HILL TERR	LOS ANGELES, CA 90039
METCALFE, TIMOTHY J	WRITER	8955 BEVERLY BLVD	LOS ANGELES, CA 90048
METH, MYRNA	CASTING DIRECTOR	4421 1/2 N OGDEN DR	LOS ANGELES, CA 90036
METHA, NANCY KOVACK	ACTRESS	240 E 72ND ST	NEW YORK, NY 10021
METHA, ZUBIN	COMPOSER-CONDUCTOR	240 E 72ND ST	NEW YORK, NY 10021
METHENY, MIKE, QUARTET	JAZZ GROUP	KURLAND, 173 BRIGHTON AVE	BOSTON, MA 02134
METHENY, PAT, GROUP	JAZZ GROUP	KURLAND, 173 BRIGHTON AVE	BOSTON, MA 02134
METHVIN, EUGENE H	NEWS CORRESPONDENT	8111 OLD GEORGETOWN PIKE	MC LEAN, VA 22102
METRAL, SOPHIE	ACTRESS	20 RUE SAUFFREY	PARIS 75017 FRANCE
METRANO, ART	ACTOR	1330 N DOHENY DR	LOS ANGELES, CA 90069
METROS, THE	ROCK & ROLL GROUP	MTM RECORDS, 21 MUSIC SQUARE E	NASHVILLE, TN 37203
METROV, DOUGLAS A	WRITER	8955 BEVERLY BLVD	LOS ANGELES, CA 90048
METTER, ALAN	FILM WRITER-DIRECTOR	8315 MARMONT LN	LOS ANGELES, CA 90069

Name	Occupation	Address	City	Zip/Country
METTEY, LYNNETTE	ACTRESS	942 N MARTEL AVE	LOS ANGELES, CA	90046
METZ, BELINDA	SINGER	41 BRITAIN ST #200	TORONTO, ONT	CANADA
METZGER, DOUGLAS	TV DIRECTOR	718 RANCHO RD	THOUSAND OAKS, CA	91362
METZGER, ED	ACTOR	14350 ADDISON ST #111-W	SHERMAN OAKS, CA	91423
METZGER, MIKE	TV WRITER	8955 BEVERLY BLVD	LOS ANGELES, CA	90048
METZLER, ROBERT F	WRITER-PRODUCER	10971 SAVONA RD	LOS ANGELES, CA	90077
METZNER, JEFFREY	DIRECTOR	295 5TH AVE	NEW YORK, NY	10016
MEUNIER, JACQUES	TV WRITER	8955 BEVERLY BLVD	LOS ANGELES, CA	90048
MEURISSE, PAUL	ACTOR	4 BLVD JEAN MERMOZ	92 NEUILLY-S-SEINE	FRANCE
MEVORACH, LINDA	DIRECTOR	DGA, 110 W 57TH ST	NEW YORK, NY	10019
MEWS, MARVIN	DIRECTOR	1209 PARLIAMENT CT	LIBERTYVILLE, IL	60048
MEYER, BARRY M	TV EXECUTIVE	WARNER BROTHERS TV		
		4000 WARNER BLVD	BURBANK, CA	91522
MEYER, BEN F	NEWS CORRESPONDENT	2632 S GRANT ST	ARLINGTON, VA	22202
MEYER, BERN	TV DIRECTOR	170 AVE "C"	NEW YORK, NY	10009
MEYER, CHRISTOPHER A	NEWS CORRESPONDENT	4902 GREENWAY DR	BETHESDA, MD	20816
MEYER, CORD	COLUMNIST	NEWS AMERICA SYNDICATE		
		1703 KAISER AVE	IRVINE, CA	92714
MEYER, DEBORAH G	NEWS CORRESPONDENT	2761 STONE HOLLOW DR	VIENNA, VA	22180
MEYER, EDWIN	NEWS CORRESPONDENT	10933 MONTROSE AVE	GARRETT PARK, MD	20896
MEYER, ELLEN	CASTING DIRECTOR	POST OFFICE BOX 2147	MALIBU, CA	90265
MEYER, EMILE	ACTOR	2016 MEHLE AVE	ARABI, LA	70032
MEYER, GEORGE A	WRITER	555 W 57TH ST #1230	NEW YORK, NY	10019
MEYER, JACK	DIRECTOR	PACIFIC, 809 N CAHUENGA BLVD	LOS ANGELES, CA	90038
MEYER, JEFFREY M	TV WRITER	8955 BEVERLY BLVD	LOS ANGELES, CA	90048
MEYER, KERRY L	NEWS CORRESPONDENT	9437 MAYFLOWER CT	LAUREL, MD	20707
MEYER, KERSTIN	MEZZO-SOPRANO	59 E 54TH ST #81	NEW YORK, NY	10022
MEYER, LAWRENCE R	NEWS CORRESPONDENT	3311 ROSS PL, NW	WASHINGTON, DC	20008
MEYER, LINDA	WRITER	555 W 57TH ST #1230	NEW YORK, NY	10019
MEYER, MARCIA	SINGER-GUITARIST	POST OFFICE BOX 86183	NORTH VANCOUVER, BC	CANADA
MEYER, MARIANNE	WRITER	555 W 57TH ST #1230	NEW YORK, NY	10019
MEYER, MARIUS	ACTOR	10351 SANTA MONICA BLVD #211	LOS ANGELES, CA	90025
MEYER, MARK	PHOTOGRAPHER	TIME/TIME & LIFE BLDG		
		ROCKEFELLER CENTER	NEW YORK, NY	10020
MEYER, MARK F	PHOTOGRAPHER	19 VILLAGE SQ	SMYRNA, DE	19977
MEYER, NICHOLAS	WRITER-PRODUCER	2109 STANLEY HILLS DR	LOS ANGELES, CA	90046
MEYER, RICK	ACTOR	JARRETT, 220 E 63RD ST	NEW YORK, NY	10021
MEYER, RONALD C	WRITER	555 W 57TH ST #1230	NEW YORK, NY	10019
MEYER, ROY F	TV EXECUTIVE	NBC-TV, NEWS DEPARTMENT		
		4001 NEBRASKA AVE, NW	WASHINGTON, DC	20016
MEYER, RUSS	FILM WRITER-PRODUCER	POST OFFICE BOX 3748	HOLLYWOOD, CA	90078
MEYER, STEVE	ACTOR	9021 MELROSE AVE #304	LOS ANGELES, CA	90069
MEYER, TARO	ACTRESS	165 W 46TH ST #409	NEW YORK, NY	10036
MEYER, THOMAS J	NEWS CORRESPONDENT	2800 QUEBEC ST #546	WASHINGTON, DC	20008
MEYER, TOM	CARTOONIST	SAN FRANCISCO CHRONICLE		
		901 MISSION ST	SAN FRANCISCO, CA	94119
MEYERING, RALPH, JR	ACTOR	8350 SANTA MONICA BLVD #103	LOS ANGELES, CA	90069
MEYEROWITZ, RICK	CARTOONIST	THE NATIONAL LAMPOON		
		635 MADISON AVE	NEW YORK, NY	10022
MEYERS, ALFRED	DIRECTOR	253 EVERETT PL	ENGLEWOOD, NJ	07631
MEYERS, ARI	ACTRESS	VINER, 2630 EDEN PL	BEVERLY HILLS, CA	90210
MEYERS, GAYANNE	ACTRESS	12926 RIVERSIDE DR #C	SHERMAN OAKS, CA	91423
MEYERS, HOWARD	TV WRITER	8383 WILSHIRE BLVD #923	BEVERLY HILLS, CA	90211
MEYERS, JANET M	NEWS CORRESPONDENT	5410 CONNECTICUT AVE, NW	WASHINGTON, DC	20015
MEYERS, JOHN A	PUBLISHING EXECUTIVE	LIFE & PEOPLE MAGAZINES		
		TIME & LIFE BUILDING		
		ROCKEFELLER CENTER	NEW YORK, NY	10020
MEYERS, JOHN F	WRITER-PRODUCER	1221 OCEAN AVE #PH-4	SANTA MONICA, CA	90401
MEYERS, MARSHA	ACTRESS	1333 WATERLOO ST	LOS ANGELES, CA	90026
MEYERS, MARTIN	ACTOR	145 W 86TH ST	NEW YORK, NY	10024
MEYERS, NANCY	FILM WRITER-PRODUCER	8955 BEVERLY BLVD	LOS ANGELES, CA	90048
MEYERS, RON	TV PRODUCER	1438 N GOWER ST	LOS ANGELES, CA	90028
MEYERS, WARREN B	CONDUCTOR	8440 FOUNTAIN AVE #108	LOS ANGELES, CA	90069
MEYERS, WILLIAM K	COMPOSER	5677 SPREADING OAK DR	LOS ANGELES, CA	90068
MEYERSHON, JON	WRITER	555 W 57TH ST #1230	NEW YORK, NY	10019
MEYERSON, JANICE	MEZZO-SOPRANO	ICM, 40 W 57TH ST	NEW YORK, NY	10019
MEYERSON, PETER A	WRITER-PRODUCER	8778 WONDERLAND AVE	LOS ANGELES, CA	90046
MEYJES, MENNO	SCREENWRITER	8955 BEVERLY BLVD	LOS ANGELES, CA	90048
MEYRINK, MICHELLE	ACTRESS	10100 SANTA MONICA BLVD #1600	LOS ANGELES, CA	90067
MEZZACAPPA, DALE	NEWS CORRESPONDENT	3116 WELLINGTON RD	ALEXANDRIA, VA	22302
MEZZROW, MEZZ	CLARINETIST	SWING & DRG RECORDS CO		
		157 W 57TH ST	NEW YORK, NY	10019
MFQ	FOLK QUARTET	SEE - M F Q		
MIADES, JAMES	TV DIRECTOR	106 COLBERG AVE	ROSLINDALE, MA	02131
MIANO, ROBERT	ACTOR	400 N DOHENY DR #12-B	LOS ANGELES, CA	90048
MIANOWANY, JOSEPH	NEWS CORRESPONDENT	5147 N 10TH RD	ARLINGTON, VA	22205
MICALE, PAUL J	ACTOR	6614 COSTELLO AVE	VAN NUYS, CA	91405
MICHAEL, EARL	CIRCUS RINGMASTER	HALL, 138 FROG HOLLOW RD	CHURCHVILLE, PA	18966
MICHAEL, GEORGE	SINGER-COMPOSER	IXWORTH PLACE, 1ST FLOOR	LONDON SW3 3PU	ENGLAND
MICHAEL, JO LYNNE	TV WRITER	8955 BEVERLY BLVD	LOS ANGELES, CA	90048
MICHAEL, MARY E	NEWS CORRESPONDENT	2250 WASHINGTON AVE #301	SILVER SPRING, MD	20910
MICHAEL, RALPH	ACTOR	POST OFFICE BOX 130, HOVE	EAST SUSSEX BN3 6QU	ENGLAND
MICHAEL, STEPHEN	FILM EDITOR	4355 MC CONNELL BLVD	LOS ANGELES, CA	90066
MICHAEL, WERNER	TV EXECUTIVE	MGM-TV, 10202 W WASHINGTON BL	CULVER CITY, CA	90230
MICHAELI, JOHN E	ENTER EXECUTIVE	1800 CENTURY PARK E #1100	LOS ANGELES, CA	90067

Name	Occupation	Address	City	Zip
MICHAELIAN, KATHRYN	TV WRITER	22500 MAC FARLANE DR	WOODLAND HILLS, CA	91364
MICHAELIAN, MICHAEL	SCREENWRITER	11421 CANTON DR	STUDIO CITY, CA	91604
MICHAELS, AL	SPORTSCASTER	ABC SPORTS, 524 W 57TH ST	NEW YORK, NY	10019
MICHAELS, CABERT	MAGICIAN	FROTHINGHAM, 40 GROVE ST	WESSESLEY, MA	02181
MICHAELS, DAVID	DIRECTOR	DGA, 110 W 57TH ST	NEW YORK, NY	10019
MICHAELS, DIANA MADDOX	WRITER	1614 THAYER AVE	LOS ANGELES, CA	90024
MICHAELS, DREW	ACTOR	3601 DELLVALE PL	ENCINO, CA	91436
MICHAELS, DWIGHT	FIDDLER	1809 HILLMONT #TH-B3	NASHVILLE, TN	37215
MICHAELS, GREGORY	ACTOR	7469 MELROSE AVE #30	LOS ANGELES, CA	90046
MICHAELS, JIM	NEWS CORRESPONDENT	2059 HUNTINGTON AVE	ALEXANDRIA, VA	22303
MICHAELS, JOEL B	FILM PRODUCER	214 KING ST W #600	TORONTO, ONT M5H 1K4	CANADA
MICHAELS, JOSEPH	WRITER	555 W 57TH ST #1230	NEW YORK, NY	10019
MICHAELS, JOSEPH E	DIRECTOR	334 E 49TH ST #2-B	NEW YORK, NY	10017
MICHAELS, KERRY L	ACTRESS	1350 N HIGHLAND AVE #24	HOLLYWOOD, CA	90028
MICHAELS, LARRY H	WRITER	555 W 57TH ST #1230	NEW YORK, NY	10019
MICHAELS, LORI	ACTRESS	439 S LA CIENEGA BLVD #120	LOS ANGELES, CA	90048
MICHAELS, LORNE	TV WRITER-PRODUCER	88 CENTRAL PARK W	NEW YORK, NY	10023
MICHAELS, LORRAINE	ACTRESS	5330 LANKERSHIM BLVD #210	NORTH HOLLYWOOD, CA	91601
MICHAELS, MARGARET	ACTRESS	1717 N HIGHLAND AVE #414	LOS ANGELES, CA	90028
MICHAELS, MARILYN	COMEDIENNE	185 W END AVE	NEW YORK, NY	10023
MICHAELS, MARK	DIRECTOR	DGA, 7950 SUNSET BLVD	LOS ANGELES, CA	90046
MICHAELS, NORMA	ACTRESS	3330 BARHAM BLVD #103	LOS ANGELES, CA	90068
MICHAELS, PATRICE	COLORATURA	431 S DEARBORN ST #1504	CHICAGO, IL	60605
MICHAELS, PETER J	NEWS CORRESPONDENT	1807 N KEY BLVD	ARLINGTON, VA	20001
MICHAELS, RICHARD	FILM DIRECTOR	1934 WESTRIDGE RD	LOS ANGELES, CA	90049
MICHAELS, ROBERT, BAND	ROCK & ROLL GROUP	BISHOP, 2505 PLAINVIEW AVE	PITTSBURGH, PA	15226
MICHAELS, ROSALIND	WRITER	555 W 57TH ST #1230	NEW YORK, NY	10019
MICHAELS, SAL	TALENT AGENT	200 W 51ST ST #1410	NEW YORK, NY	10019
MICHAELS, SHAWN	ACTOR	10920 WILSHIRE BLVD #220	LOS ANGELES, CA	90024
MICHAELS, SHAWN	WRESTLER	SEE - MIDNIGHT ROCKERS, THE		
MICHAELS, SIDNEY	WRITER	8955 BEVERLY BLVD	LOS ANGELES, CA	90048
MICHAELS, STEPHEN	ACTOR	25801 LOCHMOOR RD	VALENCIA, CA	91355
MICHAELS, TIMOTHY	SINGER	LUTZ, 5625 "O" STREET BLDG	LINCOLN, NE	68510
MICHAELSON, KARI	ACTRESS	1717 N HIGHLAND AVE #414	LOS ANGELES, CA	90028
MICHAELSON, MIKE	NEWS CORRESPONDENT	C-SPAN, 400 N CAPITOL ST, NW	WASHINGTON, DC	20001
MICHAU, SIMON	NEWS CORRESPONDENT	2711 ORDWAY ST, NW	WASHINGTON, DC	20008
MICHAUD, DAN	CONDUCTOR	20165 SEAGULL WY	SARATOGA, CA	95070
MICHAUD, MICHAEL	ACTOR	207 W ALAMEDA AVE #202	BURBANK, CA	91502
MICHAUD, RUDI	WRITER	555 W 57TH ST #1230	NEW YORK, NY	10019
MICHEAL, JAY	ACTOR	1607 N EL CENTRO AVE #23	LOS ANGELES, CA	90028
MICHEL, GENEVIEVE L	WRITER	555 W 57TH ST #1230	NEW YORK, NY	10019
MICHEL, JEAN	ACTOR	4731 LAUREL CANYON BLVD #5	NORTH HOLLYWOOD, CA	91607
MICHEL, ODILE	ACTRESS	14 RUE LOUIS BRAILLE	MAIS-ALF 94700	FRANCE
MICHELANGELI, ARTURO BENEDETTI	PIANIST	CAMI, 165 W 57TH ST	NEW YORK, NY	10019
MICHELE & DAVID	VOCAL DUO	LUTZ, 5625 "O" STREET BLDG	LINCOLN, NE	68510
MICHELET, MICHEL	COMPOSER	1624 N COURTNEY AVE	LOS ANGELES, CA	90046
MICHELIS, JAY	TV EXECUTIVE	NBC-TV, 3000 W ALAMEDA AVE	BURBANK, CA	91523
MICHELL, KEITH	ACTOR	LIONEL LARNER, 130 W 57TH ST	NEW YORK, NY	10019
MICHELLE, MARGUERITE	HAIR SUSPENSIONIST	HALL, 138 FROG HOLLOW RD	CHURCHVILLE, PA	18966
MICHELLE, STEVEN	TV WRITER	8955 BEVERLY BLVD	LOS ANGELES, CA	90048
MICHELMORE, CLIFF	TV HOST	WHITE HOUSE, REIGATE	SURREY	ENGLAND
MICHELS, DAVID ALLEN	ACTOR	3389 TARECO DR	HOLLYWOOD, CA	90068
MICHELSEN, EDWARD J	NEWS CORRESPONDENT	2153 FLORIDA AVE, NW	WASHINGTON, DC	20008
MICHENER, JAMES A	WRITER	POST OFFICE BOX 125	PIPERSVILLE, PA	18947
MICHON, CHRIS	NEWS CORRESPONDENT	NBC-TV, NEWS DEPARTMENT		
		4001 NEBRASKA AVE, NW	WASHINGTON, DC	20016
MICHU, CLEMENT	ACTOR	4 RUE GASTON COUTE	PARIS 75018	FRANCE
MICKELBURY, PENNY	NEWS CORRESPONDENT	4461 CONNECTICUT AVE, NW	WASHINGTON, DC	20008
MICKEY, PATTI	ACTRESS	427 N CANON DR #205	BEVERLY HILLS, CA	90210
MICKEY & SYLVIA	VOCAL DUO	OLDIES, 5218 ALMONT ST	LOS ANGELES, CA	90032
MICRODISNEY	ROCK & ROLL GROUP	TIGER WARD MANAGEMENT		
		40 WHITTINGTON CT		
		AYLMER RD	LONDON N2 OBT	ENGLAND
MICUCCI, BUDDY	ACTOR	819 1/4 N SWEETZER AVE	LOS ANGELES, CA	90069
MIDDLEBROOKS, FELICIA	WRITER	555 W 57TH ST #1230	NEW YORK, NY	10019
MIDDLEBROOKS, HARRY	ACTOR	19013 COMMUNITY ST	NORTHRIDGE, CA	91324
MIDDLETON, DREW	NEWS CORRES-COLUMNIST	N Y TIMES, 229 W 43RD ST	NEW YORK, NY	10036
MIDDLETON, GREGORY E	COMPOSER	406 W MARIPOSA AVE	ALTADENA, CA	91001
MIDDLETON, MARGARET	ACTRESS	121 N ROBERTSON BLVD #B	BEVERLY HILLS, CA	90211
MIDDLETON, MARTHA	NEWS CORRESPONDENT	817 DAVIS AVE	TAKOMA PARK, MD	20912
MIDDLETON, THOMAS H	ACTOR	337 MEDIO DR	LOS ANGELES, CA	90049
MIDGLEY, ELIZABETH	NEWS CORRESPONDENT	2715 36TH PL, NW	WASHINGTON, DC	20007
MIDGLEY, JOHN	NEWS CORRESPONDENT	2715 36TH PL, NW	WASHINGTON, DC	20007
MIDGLEY, LESLIE	TV CONSULTANT	400 E 56TH ST	NEW YORK, NY	10022
MIDLER, BETTE	SING-ACT-COMED	POST OFFICE BOX 46703	LOS ANGELES, CA	90046
MIDLER, ROBERT A	NEWS CORRESPONDENT	6407 N 29TH ST	ARLINGTON, VA	22207
MIDNEY, BARBARA	OBOIST	1031 NORFLEET DR	NASHVILLE, TN	37220
MIDNIGHT RIDER	WRESTLER	SEE - RHODES, DUSTY		
MIDNIGHT ROCKERS, THE	WRESTLING TAG TEAM	AMERICAN WRESTLING ASSOC		
		MINNEAPLOIS WRESTLING		
		10001 WAYZATA BLVD	MINNETONKA, MN	55345
MIDNIGHT STAR	RHYTHM & BLUES GROUP	POST OFFICE BOX 9481	COLUMBUS, OH	43209
MIDNITERS, THE	ROCK & ROLL GROUP	OLDIES, 5218 ALMONT ST	LOS ANGELES, CA	90032
MIELCHE, PAUL E	WRITER	3390 SAN MARINO ST	LOS ANGELES, CA	90006

Name	Occupation	Address	City	Zip/Country
MIFELOW, ALVIN R	DIRECTOR	ALMIF, 853 7TH AVE	NEW YORK, NY	10019
MIFUNE, TOSHIRO	ACTOR	9-30-7, SEIJYO, SETAGAYAKU	TOKYO	JAPAN
MIGDAIL, CARL J	NEWS CORRESPONDENT	7301 CONNECTICUT AVE	CHEVY CHASE, MD	20815
MIGHTY CLOUDS OF JOY, THE	GOSPEL GROUP	10100 SANTA MONICA BLVD #1600	LOS ANGELES, CA	90067
MIGHTY DIAMONDS, THE	REGGAE GROUP	POST OFFICE BOX 42517	WASHINGTON, DC	20015
MIGHTY FIRE	ROCK & ROLL GROUP	222 S FIGUEROA ST #921	LOS ANGELES, CA	90012
MIGHTY FLYERS, THE	ROCK & ROLL GROUP	POST OFFICE BOX 2458	TOLUCA LAKE, CA	91602
MIGHTY IGOR, THE	WRESTLER	CAPITOL INTERNATIONAL		
		11844 MARKET ST	NORTH LIMA, OH	44452
MIGHTY LEMON DROPS, THE	ROCK & ROLL GROUP	SIRE RECORDS COMPANY		
		75 ROCKEFELLER PLAZA	NEW YORK, NY	10019
MIGHTY MOFOS, THE	ROCK & ROLL GROUP	POST OFFICE BOX 18481	MINNEAPOLIS, MN	55418
MIGLIORE, TONY	PERCUSSIONIST	POST OFFICE BOX 12612	NASHVILLE, TN	37212
MIHALKA, GEORGE	FILM DIRECTOR	2030 CLOSSE #4	MONTREAL, QUE H3H 1Z9	CANADA
MIHO	ACTRESS	400 W 43RD ST #30-R	NEW YORK, NY	10036
MIHOCES, GARY	SPORTS WRITER	POST OFFICE BOX 500	WASHINGTON, DC	20044
MIHOK, KATHERINE	NEWS REPORTER	TIME/TIME & LIFE BLDG		
		ROCKEFELLER CENTER	NEW YORK, NY	10020
MIKALS, TYKIN	ACTOR	938 N HARPER AVE	HOLLYWOOD, CA	90046
MIKELL, GEORGE	ACTOR	CCA MGMT, 4 CT LODGE		
		48 SLOANE SQ	LONDON SW1W 8AT	ENGLAND
MIKKELSEN, DWIGHT B	COMPOSER	2208 W PEYTON AVE	BURBANK, CA	91504
MIKLASZEWSKI, JAMES A	NEWS CORRESPONDENT	18111 QUEEN ELIZABETH DR	OLNEY, MD	20832
MILAN, TED	DIRECTOR	315 E 68TH ST	NEW YORK, NY	10021
MILANA, VINCENT DUKE	ACTOR	11422 RUGGIERO AVE	LAKE VIEW TERRACE, CA	91342
MILANDER, STAN	TALENT AGENT	4146 LANKERSHIM BLVD #300	NORTH HOLLYWOOD, CA	91602
MILANOVA, VANYA	VIOLINIST	SOFFER, 130 W 56TH ST	NEW YORK, NY	10019
MILAVSKY, J RONALD	TV EXECUTIVE	NBC TELEVISION NETWORK		
		30 ROCKEFELLER PLAZA	NEW YORK, NY	10112
MILBERG, S ALAN	TV WRITER	555 W 57TH ST #1230	NEW YORK, NY	10019
MILBURN, SUE	TV WRITER	3811 SUNSHINE CT	STUDIO CITY, CA	91604
MILCH, DAVID	TV WRITER-PRODUCER	ICM, 8899 BEVERLY BLVD	LOS ANGELES, CA	90048
MILCHAN, ARNON	FILM PRODUCER	REGENCY FILMS, 57 W 57TH ST	NEW YORK, NY	10019
MILCHEVA, ALEXANDRINA	MEZZO-SOPRANO	CAMI, 165 W 57TH ST	NEW YORK, NY	10019
MILENIC, ALEXANDER M	PHOTOJOURNALIST	8506 SALEM WY	BETHESDA, MD	20814
MILES, AUSTIN	CIRCUS RINGMASTER	HALL, 138 FROG HOLLOW RD	CHURCHVILLE, PA	18966
MILES, BUDDY	MUSICIAN	13719 VENTURA BLVD #H	SHERMAN OAKS, CA	91423
MILES, CHRISTOPHER	FILM WRITER-DIRECTOR	10 SELWOOD PL	LONDON SW7	ENGLAND
MILES, DALLAS	TV HOST-ACTOR	10000 RIVERSIDE DR #12-14	TOLUCA LAKE, CA	91602
MILES, DAVID K	WRITER	8955 BEVERLY BLVD	LOS ANGELES, CA	90048
MILES, DOUGLAS K	WRITER-PRODUCER	27 SOMMER AVE	GLEN RIDGE, NJ	07028
MILES, JOANNA	ACTRESS	2062 N VINE ST	LOS ANGELES, CA	90028
MILES, KELLY	ACTRESS	10624 BLOOMFIELD ST	NORTH HOLLYWOOD, CA	91602
MILES, LARRY	CABLE EXECUTIVE	T M CABLE TELEVISION		
		2381 MORSE AVE	IRVINE, CA	92714
MILES, LINDA	ACTRESS	6331 HOLLYWOOD BLVD #924	LOS ANGELES, CA	90028
MILES, PETER	ACTOR-AUTHOR	268 N BOWLING GREEN WY	LOS ANGELES, CA	90049
MILES, RICHARD	WRITER	8955 BEVERLY BLVD	LOS ANGELES, CA	90048
MILES, SARAH	ACTRESS	409 N CAMDEN DR #105	BEVERLY HILLS, CA	90210
MILES, SYLVIA	ACTRESS	240 CENTRAL PARK S	NEW YORK, NY	10024
MILES, T J	TV WRITER	8955 BEVERLY BLVD	LOS ANGELES, CA	90048
MILES, VERA	ACTRESS	POST OFFICE BOX 1704	BIG BEAR LAKE, CA	92315
MILES, WALTER O	ACTOR	3318 W BURBANK BLVD	BURBANK, CA	91505
MILFORD, JOHN	ACTOR	15010 VENTURA BLVD #234	SHERMAN OAKS, CA	91403
MILFORD, PENELOPE	ACTRESS	219 MARKET ST	VENICE, CA	90291
MILIANO, RUGIERO L	WRITER	555 W 57TH ST #1230	NEW YORK, NY	10019
MILICEVIC, DJORDJE	SCREENWRITER	8955 BEVERLY BLVD	LOS ANGELES, CA	90048
MILITO, SEBASTIAN	TV WRITER	6619 MATILIJA AVE	VAN NUYS, CA	91405
MILIUS, JOHN	WRITER-PRODUCER	888 LINDA FLORA DR	LOS ANGELES, CA	90049
MILIUS, PETER	NEWS CORRESPONDENT	3224 RITTENHOUSE ST, NW	WASHINGTON, DC	20015
MILKEE, HARRY	COMEDIAN	2211 INDUSTRIAL BLVD	SARASOTA, FL	33580
MILKIS, EDWARD K	TV-FILM DIR-PROD	609 N CRESCENT DR	BEVERLY HILLS, CA	90210
MILKLER, MINDI	ACTRESS	9200 SUNSET BLVD #909	LOS ANGELES, CA	90069
MILLAN, ASHLEY NICOLE	ACTRESS	CBS TELEVISION NETWORK		
		"THE YOUNG & THE RESTLESS"		
		7800 BEVERLY BLVD	LOS ANGELES, CA	90036
MILLAN, MANNY	SPORTS PHOTOGRAPHER	SPORTS ILLUSTRATED MAGAZINE		
		TIME & LIFE BUILDING		
		ROCKEFELLER CENTER	NEW YORK, NY	10020
MILLAN, ROBYN	ACTRESS	9300 WILSHIRE BLVD #410	BEVERLY HILLS, CA	90212
MILLAN, VICTOR	ACTOR	120 S VICTORY BLVD #104	BURBANK, CA	91502
MILLAR, GAVIN	TV WRITER-DIRECTOR	DAISH, 83 EASTBOURNE MEWS	LONDON W2 6LQ	ENGLAND
MILLAR, JEFF	CARTOONIST	UNIVERSAL PRESS SYNDICATE		
		4900 MAIN ST, 9TH FLOOR	KANSAS CITY, MO	62114
MILLAR, STUART	WRITER-PRODUCER	300 CENTRAL PARK W #15-G	NEW YORK, NY	10024
MILLARD, DAVID	TV DIRECTOR-PRODUCER	LITTLE SPLINTERS		
		YEW TREE GARDENS		
		PANNAL ASH, HARROGATE	HERTS	ENGLAND
MILLARD, OSCAR	WRITER	13717 ROMANY DR	PACIFIC PALISADES, CA	89272
MILLARD, WILLIAM J, III	DIRECTOR	30 RIVERSIDE PLAZA	NEW YORK, NY	10010
MILLAWAY, JAMES B	WRITER	8955 BEVERLY BLVD	LOS ANGELES, CA	90048
MILLCHIP, ROY	WRITER	8955 BEVERLY BLVD	LOS ANGELES, CA	90048
MILLER, AL	SINGER	POST OFFICE BOX 5701	LINCOLN, NE	68505
MILLER, ALDEN	WRITER-PRODUCER	13272 CHELTENHAM DR	SHERMAN OAKS, CA	91423
MILLER, ALLAN	ACTOR	13340 VALLEY VISTA BLVD	SHERMAN OAKS, CA	91423

MILLER, ALLAN	FILM DIRECTOR	194 RIVERSIDE DR	NEW YORK, NY	10025
MILLER, ALLAN W	GUITARIST	ROUTE #2, BOX 126	BROWN'S SUMMIT, NC	27214
MILLER, ANDREW C	NEWS CORRESPONDENT	5617 NEWINGTON RD	BETHESDA, MD	20816
MILLER, ANN	ACTRESS-DANCER	151 AINSLIE ST	BROOKLYN, NY	11211
MILLER, ANNA MARIA	PIANIST	600 WHISPERING HILLS DR #G-11	NASHVILLE, TN	37211
MILLER, ANNETTE	NEWS CORRESPONDENT	POST OFFICE BOX 2626	WASHINGTON, DC	20013
MILLER, ARNOLD	DIRECTOR-PRODUCER	GLOBEL, 143 WARDOUR ST	LONDON W1	ENGLAND
MILLER, ARTHUR	AUTHOR-PLAYWRIGHT	TOPHET RD	ROXBURY, CT	06783
MILLER, BARBARA	CASTING DIRECTOR	3970 OVERLAND AVE #700	CULVER CITY, CA	90230
MILLER, BEBE	DANCER	AFFILIATE ARTIST, INC		
		37 W 65TH ST, 6TH FLOOR	NEW YORK, NY	10023
MILLER, BERWYN L	NEWS CORRESPONDENT	5012 HAMPDEN LN	BETHESDA, MD	20014
MILLER, BILL	NEWS CORRESPONDENT	813 S ALFRED ST	ALEXANDRIA, VA	22314
MILLER, BOB	DRUMMER	5016 MANUEL DR	NASHVILLE, TN	37211
MILLER, BRUCE	NEWS CORRESPONDENT	8101-A LEE HWY	FALLS CHURCH, VA	22042
MILLER, BRUCE PHILLIP	ACTOR	13233 HESBY ST	SHERMAN OAKS, CA	91423
MILLER, BRUCE W	COMPOSER-CONDUCTOR	21136 TULSA ST	CHATSWORTH, CA	91311
MILLER, BUZZ	ACTOR	8 W 9TH ST	NEW YORK, NY	10011
MILLER, CARL	NEWS CORRESPONDENT	3161 W 34TH AVE	DENVER, CO	80211
MILLER, CARL T	SINGER	851-D OLD HICKORY BLVD	JACKSON, TN	38301
MILLER, CAROLYN HANDLER	TV WRITER	554 S SAN VICENTE BLVD #3	LOS ANGELES, CA	90048
MILLER, CHARLES	ACTOR	470 S VAN VICENTE BLVD #104	LOS ANGELES, CA	90048
MILLER, CHARLOTTE RUTH	TV WRITER	9000 SUNSET BLVD #1200	LOS ANGELES, CA	90069
MILLER, CHERYL	ACTRESS	8322 BEVERLY BLVD #202	LOS ANGELES, CA	90048
MILLER, CHRIS	TV WRITER	8955 BEVERLY BLVD	LOS ANGELES, CA	90048
MILLER, CHRISTOPHER D	DIRECTOR	424 ASHLAND AVE	SANTA MONICA, CA	90405
MILLER, CLAY	ACTOR	10845 LINDBROOK DR #3	LOS ANGELES, CA	90024
MILLER, DANIEL W	RECORD EXECUTIVE	POST OFFICE BOX 8604	MADISON, WI	53708
MILLER, DAVID	FILM DIRECTOR	1843 THAYER AVE #1	LOS ANGELES, CA	90025
MILLER, DAVID	GRAPHIC IMPRESSIONIST	NEWS AMERICA SYNDICATE		
		1703 KAISER AVE	IRVINE, CA	92714
MILLER, DAVID ALAN	CONDUCTOR	SOFFER, 130 W 56TH ST	NEW YORK, NY	10019
MILLER, DEAN	ACTOR-BROADCASTER	POST OFFICE BOX 608	SIDNEY, OH	45365
MILLER, DEAN	DRUMMER	1010 16TH AVE S	NASHVILLE, TN	37212
MILLER, DEBORAH A	DIRECTOR	6636 VESPER AVE	VAN NUYS, CA	91405
MILLER, DENISE	ACTRESS	10351 SANTA MONICA BLVD #211	LOS ANGELES, CA	90025
MILLER, DENNY	ACTOR	1104 FOOTHILL RD	OJAI, CA	93023
MILLER, DOROTHY G	NEWS CORRESPONDENT	6726 SULKY LN	ROCKVILLE, MD	20852
MILLER, DOUG	ACTOR	8721 SUNSET BLVD #200	LOS ANGELES, CA	90069
MILLER, DOUGLAS	SINGER	10100 SANTA MONICA BLVD #1600	LOS ANGELES, CA	90067
MILLER, ED	DIRECTOR	7221 E SUTTON DR	SCOTTSDALE, AZ	85260
MILLER, ELIZABETH	NEWS CORRESPONDENT	2030 "M" ST, NW	WASHINGTON, DC	20036
MILLER, ERNIE	GUITARIST	200 TYLER DR	HERMITAGE, TN	37076
MILLER, FRANK R	TV PRODUCER	GROUP W PRODUCTIONS		
		70 UNIVERSAL CITY PLAZA	UNIVERSAL CITY, CA	91608
MILLER, FRANK R	TV DIRECTOR	18772 CANASTA ST	TARZANA, CA	91356
MILLER, FRANK, DVM	COLUMNIST	THE CHRONICLE FEATURES		
		870 MARKET ST	SAN FRANCISCO, CA	94102
MILLER, FRED	ACTOR	350 W 55TH ST	NEW YORK, NY	10010
MILLER, FRED L	WRITER	8955 BEVERLY BLVD	LOS ANGELES, CA	90048
MILLER, GARY H	TV WRITER	8955 BEVERLY BLVD	LOS ANGELES, CA	90048
MILLER, GARY L	MUSICIAN	600 WHISPERING HILLS DR #G-11	NASHVILLE, TN	37211
MILLER, GENE	GUITARIST	4771 TRENTON DR	HERMITAGE, TN	37076
MILLER, GEORGE	FILM DIRECTOR	AUSTRALIAN FILM COMM		
		9229 SUNSET BLVD	LOS ANGELES, CA	90069
MILLER, HARVEY	SCREENWRITER	8955 BEVERLY BLVD	LOS ANGELES, CA	90048
MILLER, HARVEY	TV DIRECTOR	151 S EL CAMINO DR	BEVERLY HILLS, CA	90212
MILLER, HENRY R	DIRECTOR	35-10 168TH ST	FLUSHING, NY	11358
MILLER, HERMAN	WRITER	9022 SUNSET BLVD #531	LOS ANGELES, CA	90069
MILLER, HOPE RIDINGS	NEWS CORRESPONDENT	1868 COLUMBIA RD, NW	WASHINGTON, DC	20009
MILLER, HOWARD W	TV WRITER	9000 SUNSET BLVD #1200	LOS ANGELES, CA	90069
MILLER, IRA	SCREENWRITER	8955 BEVERLY BLVD	LOS ANGELES, CA	90048
MILLER, IRVING	COMPOSER	7259 HILLSIDE AVE #101	LOS ANGELES, CA	90046
MILLER, J P	TV WRITER	555 W 57TH ST #1230	NEW YORK, NY	10019
MILLER, J PHILIP	TV DIRECTOR-PRODUCER	11 EXETER ST	BOSTON, MA	02116
MILLER, JAMES A	NEWS CORRESPONDENT	CBS NEWS, 2020 "M" ST, NW	WASHINGTON, DC	20036
MILLER, JAMES F, JR	TROMBONIST	39 CHARLES ST #4	NEW YORK, NY	10014
MILLER, JAMES M	WRITER-PRODUCER	9300 WILSHIRE BLVD #410	BEVERLY HILLS, CA	90212
MILLER, JAN	WRITER	8955 BEVERLY BLVD	LOS ANGELES, CA	90048
MILLER, JASON	ACT-WRI-DIR	7089 BIRDVIEW AVE	MALIBU, CA	90265
MILLER, JAY	TV DIRECTOR-PRODUCER	NBC TELEVISION NETWORK		
		30 ROCKEFELLER PLAZA	NEW YORK, NY	10112
MILLER, JEANETTE	ACTRESS	3151 W CAHUENGA BLVD #310	LOS ANGELES, CA	90068
MILLER, JENNIFER A	TV WRITER	8955 BEVERLY BLVD	LOS ANGELES, CA	90048
MILLER, JIM	CABLE EXECUTIVE	SHOWTIME, 1633 BROADWAY	NEW YORK, NY	10019
MILLER, JOANNE	NEWS CORRESPONDENT	122 "C" ST, NW	WASHINGTON, DC	20001
MILLER, JODY	SINGER	HALSEY, 3225 S NORWOOD AVE	TULSA, OK	74135
MILLER, JOHN L	WRITER	555 W 57TH ST #1230	NEW YORK, NY	10019
MILLER, JOHN S	SAXOPHONIST	POST OFFICE BOX 331	ISLAND NEIGHTS, NJ	08732
MILLER, JONATHAN	NEWS CORRESPONDENT	6140 N 12TH RD	ARLINGTON, VA	22205
MILLER, JONATHAN WRIGHT	FILM DIRECTOR	MURPHY, CURTIS BROWN, LTD		
		162-168 REGENT ST	LONDON W1	ENGLAND
MILLER, JOSHUA	WRITER	8955 BEVERLY BLVD	LOS ANGELES, CA	90048
MILLER, JULIE	ACTRESS-SINGER	9200 SUNSET BLVD #620	LOS ANGELES, CA	90069
MILLER, KARL	TV WRITER	555 W 57TH ST #1230	NEW YORK, NY	10019

STEVE MILLER

TAYLOR MILLER

HAYLEY MILLS

RONNIE MILSAP

YVETTE MIMIEUX

DON MITCHELL

ROBERT MITCHUM

TOSHIRO MIFUME

MOODY BLUES

MILLER, KARYL	TV WRITER	14455 DUNBAR PL	SHERMAN OAKS, CA	91423
MILLER, KATHLYN A	WRITER	555 W 57TH ST #1230	NEW YORK, NY	10019
MILLER, LAJOS	BARITONE	CAMI, 165 W 57TH ST	NEW YORK, NY	10019
MILLER, LARRY	WRITER	8955 BEVERLY BLVD	LOS ANGELES, CA	90048
MILLER, LEE	TV DIRECTOR-PRODUCER	137 N CARMELINA AVE	LOS ANGELES, CA	90049
MILLER, LINDA G	ACTRESS	10 E 44TH ST #700	NEW YORK, NY	10017
MILLER, LINDSAY M	WRITER	555 W 57TH ST #1230	NEW YORK, NY	10019
MILLER, LOUISE D	NEWS CORRESPONDENT	2219 HALL PL, NW	WASHINGTON, DC	20007
MILLER, MARK	TV & THEATER PRODUCER	DRYBANK HOUSE, BRAILES		
		NEAR BANBURY	OXON	ENGLAND
MILLER, MARK C	TV WRITER	8383 WILSHIRE BLVD #923	BEVERLY HILLS, CA	90211
MILLER, MARK JAY	GUITARIST	1627 GLEN ECHO RD	NASHVILLE, TN	37215
MILLER, MARK K	NEWS CORRESPONDENT	1122 1/2 "E" ST, SE	WASHINGTON, DC	20003
MILLER, MARKHAM	NEWS CORRESPONDENT	4701 WILLARD AVE #817	CHEVY CHASE, MD	20815
MILLER, MARY	TV WRITER	8955 BEVERLY BLVD	LOS ANGELES, CA	90048
MILLER, MARY LOUISE	ACTRESS	1234 N MAPLE ST	BURBANK, CA	91505
MILLER, MAX	WRITER-PRODUCER	3130 DONA MARIA DR	STUDIO CITY, CA	91604
MILLER, MELISAA	SCREENWRITER	8955 BEVERLY BLVD	LOS ANGELES, CA	90048
MILLER, MICHAEL J	TV DIRECTOR	433 COCHRAN AVE #201	LOS ANGELES, CA	90038
MILLER, MICHAEL K	TRUMPETER	620 STONE CANYON RD	LOS ANGELES, CA	90024
MILLER, MICHAEL L	WRITER-PRODUCER	9100 WILSHIRE BLVD #517	BEVERLY HILLS, CA	90210
MILLER, MIKE	TV WRITER	555 W 57TH ST #1230	NEW YORK, NY	10019
MILLER, MITCH	MUSICIAN-COMPOSER	345 W 58TH ST	NEW YORK, NY	10019
MILLER, MOLLIE D	WRITER	8955 BEVERLY BLVD	LOS ANGELES, CA	90048
MILLER, NANCY ANN	WRITER	8955 BEVERLY BLVD	LOS ANGELES, CA	90048
MILLER, PATRICIA	MEZZO-SOPRANO	59 E 54TH ST #81	NEW YORK, NY	10022
MILLER, PAUL D	TV DIRECTOR	4249 WOODCLIFF RD	SHERMAN OAKS, CA	91403
MILLER, PETER	ACTOR	LIGHT, 113 N ROBERTSON BLVD	LOS ANGELES, CA	90048
MILLER, PETER	FILM WRITER-PRODUCER	THE LINES, CHARFIELD	GLOS	ENGLAND
MILLER, RICHARD "DICK"	ACTOR	8852 WONDERLAND AVE	LOS ANGELES, CA	90046
MILLER, RICHARD M	DIRECTOR	333 PARK AVE	NEW YORK, NY	10010
MILLER, ROBERT ELLIS	FILM-TV DIRECTOR	1901 AVE OF THE STARS #1040	LOS ANGELES, CA	90067
MILLER, ROBERT J	WRITER-NEWS CORRES	ABC-TV, NEWS DEPARTMENT		
		1717 DE SALES ST, NW	WASHINGTON, DC	20036
MILLER, ROBERT JOHN	TV PRODUCER	TVS, TELEVISION CENTRE	SOUTHHAMPTON	ENGLAND
MILLER, ROBERT L	PUBLISHING EXECUTIVE	TIME & LIFE MAGAZINES		
		TIME & LIFE BUILDING		
		ROCKEFELLER CENTER	NEW YORK, NY	10020
MILLER, ROGER	SINGER-SONGWRITER	411 LARKWOOD DR	SAN ANTONIO, TX	78209
MILLER, ROGER DEAN	GUITARIST	211 E 51ST ST #8-E	NEW YORK, NY	10022
MILLER, ROGER L	TV DIRECTOR	520 N MICHIGAN AVE #436	CHICAGO, IL	60611
MILLER, RON	FILM PROD-EXEC	500 S BUENA VISTA ST	BURBANK, CA	91521
MILLER, RON	NEWS CORRESPONDENT	ABC NEWS, 7 W 66TH ST	NEW YORK, NY	10023
MILLER, SANDI	SINGER	POST OFFICE BOX 17472	NASHVILLE, TN	37217
MILLER, SCOTT	TV WRITER	8955 BEVERLY BLVD	LOS ANGELES, CA	90048
MILLER, SIDNEY	ACTOR-DIRECTOR	3284 BARHAM BLVD #304	LOS ANGELES, CA	90068
MILLER, SIGMUND	WRITER	555 W 57TH ST #1230	NEW YORK, NY	10019
MILLER, SKEDGE	ACTOR	326 E 74TH ST	NEW YORK, NY	10021
MILLER, SNUFFY	DRUMMER	6001 OLD HICKORY BLVD #415	HERMITAGE, TN	37076
MILLER, SONNY	DRUMMER	6223 SELMA AVE #101	HOLLYWOOD, CA	90028
MILLER, STANLEY	FILM-TV WRITER	88 LEXHAM GARDENS	LONDON W8	ENGLAND
MILLER, STEPHEN A	TV WRITER	9300 WILSHIRE BLVD #410	BEVERLY HILLS, CA	90212
MILLER, STEPHEN C	WRITER	555 W 57TH ST #1230	NEW YORK, NY	10019
MILLER, STEVE	SINGER-SONGWRITER	POST OFFICE BOX 4127	BELLEVUE, WA	98004
MILLER, STEVE	TV DIRECTOR	5530 COLBATH AVE	VAN NUYS, CA	91401
MILLER, SUSAN	TV WRITER	8955 BEVERLY BLVD	LOS ANGELES, CA	90048
MILLER, TAYLOR	ACTRESS	STONE, 1052 CAROL DR	LOS ANGELES, CA	90069
MILLER, TERRY	TV DIRECTOR-PRODUCER	7 WAPPING RD		
		MERCHANTS LANDING	BRISTOL BS1 4RH	ENGLAND
MILLER, TERRY, BAND	C & W GROUP	POST OFFICE BOX O	EXCELSIOR, MN	55331
MILLER, THOMAS	PRODUCER	3970 OVERLAND AVE	CULVER CITY, CA	90230
MILLER, THOMAS LEE	TV WRITER	8955 BEVERLY BLVD	LOS ANGELES, CA	90048
MILLER, TONY	ACTOR	10000 RIVERSIDE DR #3	TOLUCA LAKE, CA	91602
MILLER, VICTOR	TV WRITER	CBS-TV, "THE GUIDING LIGHT"		
		51 W 52ND ST	NEW YORK, NY	10019
MILLER, VICTOR B	SCREENWRITER	555 W 57TH ST #1230	NEW YORK, NY	10019
MILLER, WALTER C	WRITER-PRODUCER	2401 CREST VIEW DR	LOS ANGELES, CA	90046
MILLER, WARREN	ACTOR	1241 1/2 N HAVENHURST DR	LOS ANGELES, CA	90046
MILLER, WARREN	CARTOONIST	POST OFFICE BOX 4203	NEW YORK, NY	10017
MILLER, WARREN I	WRITER	8955 BEVERLY BLVD	LOS ANGELES, CA	90048
MILLER, WILLIAM H	NEWS CORRESPONDENT	4411 S 36TH ST	ARLINGTON, VA	22206
MILLER, WINSTON	WRITER-PRODUCER	727 N RODEO DR	BEVERLY HILLS, CA	90210
MILLERICK, KERRY	DIRECTOR	7300 FRANKLIN AVE	LOS ANGELES, CA	90046
MILLET, ANNE L	NEWS CORRESPONDENT	657 "C" ST, SE	WASHINGTON, DC	20003
MILLETAIRE, CARL	ACTOR	1025 N FAIRFAX AVE #117	LOS ANGELES, CA	90046
MILLIAN, ANDRA	ACTRESS	8235 SANTA MONICA BLVD #302	LOS ANGELES, CA	90046
MILLIGAN, MIKE	TV WRITER	8955 BEVERLY BLVD	LOS ANGELES, CA	90048
MILLIGAN, SPENCER	ACTOR	JTM, 9243 1/2 DOHENY RD	LOS ANGELES, CA	90069
MILLIGAN, SPIKE	ACTOR-DIRECTOR	9 ORME CT	LONDON W2	ENGLAND
MILLIGAN, SUSAN E	NEWS CORRESPONDENT	1500 "T" ST, NW	WASHINGTON, DC	20009
MILLIKEN, CARL E, JR	WRITER	8955 BEVERLY BLVD	LOS ANGELES, CA	90048
MILLIKEN, SUE	FILM PRODUCER	119 PYRMONT ST	PYRMONT NSW 2009	AUSTRALIA
MILLIN, DAVID	CINEMATOGRAPHER	POST OFFICE 2230	HOLLYWOOD, CA	90078

Name	Occupation	Address	City	Zip
MILLMAN, JOEL A	WRITER	555 W 57TH ST #1230	NEW YORK, NY	10019
MILLO, APRILE	SOPRANO	CAMI, 165 W 57TH ST	NEW YORK, NY	10019
MILLOT, CHARLES	ACTOR	18 RUE DE FG SAINT HONORE	PARIS 75008	FRANCE
MILLS, ALLEN	TALENT AGENT	POST OFFICE BOX K-350	TARZANA, CA	91356
MILLS, ALLEY	ACTRESS	211 S BEVERLY DR #201	BEVERLY HILLS, CA	90212
MILLS, ALVIN M	COMPOSER-CONDUCTOR	2916 SAINT GEORGE ST #110	LOS ANGELES, CA	90027
MILLS, ANDREW	WRITER-EDITOR	TV GUIDE, 100 MATSONFORD RD	RADNOR, PA	19088
MILLS, ARNOLD	TALENT AGENT	8721 SUNSET BLVD	LOS ANGELES, CA	90069
MILLS, ARTHUR R	THEATER PRODUCER	47 W 68TH ST	NEW YORK, NY	10023
MILLS, BERT	NEWS CORRESPONDENT	310 BEVERLY DR	ALEXANDRIA, VA	22305
MILLS, BETTY	NEWS CORRESPONDENT	POST OFFICE BOX 1042	WASHINGTON, DC	20013
MILLS, BUNNIE	SINGER	POST OFFICE BOX 8074	BOSSIER CITY, LA	71113
MILLS, CASSANDRA	TALENT AGENT	POST OFFICE BOX K-350	TARZANA, CA	91356
MILLS, CYNTHIA J	NEWS CORRESPONDENT	120 DUDDINGTON PL, SE	WASHINGTON, DC	20003
MILLS, DON C	DRUMMER	117 BURRUS AVE	HENDERSONVILLE, TN	37075
MILLS, DONN LAURENCE	COMPOSER-CONDUCTOR	4213 CALLE ABRIL	SAN CLEMENTE, CA	92672
MILLS, DONNA	ACTRESS-MODEL	LORIMAR-TELEPICTURES		
		3970 OVERLAND DR	CULVER CITY, CA	90230
MILLS, DOUGLAS	PHOTOGRAPHER	5002 COLUMBIA PIKE #5	ARLINGTON, VA	22204
MILLS, ERIE	SOPRANO	ICM, 40 W 57TH ST	NEW YORK, NY	10019
MILLS, FRANK	PIANIST	4881 YONGE ST #412	TORONTO, ONTARIO	CANADA
MILLS, HAYLEY	ACTRESS	SHARKEY, 90 REGENT ST	LONDON W1	ENGLAND
MILLS, JED	ACTOR	6430 SUNSET BLVD #1203	LOS ANGELES, CA	90028
MILLS, JEFFREY	NEWS CORRESPONDENT	1010 13TH ST, SE	WASHINGTON, DC	20003
MILLS, JOHN & DONALD	VOCAL DUO	9454 WILSHIRE BLVD #206	BEVERLY HILLS, CA	90212
MILLS, JULIET	ACTRESS	4036 FOOTHILL RD	CARPINTERIA, CA	93013
MILLS, KEITH	ACTOR	3330 BARHAM BLVD #103	LOS ANGELES, CA	90068
MILLS, LEEANN	ACTRESS	12023 VENTURA BLVD	STUDIO CITY, CA	91604
MILLS, MARGARET	PIANIST	SIMONDS, 30 HEWLETT ST	WATERBURY, CT	06710
MILLS, MICHAEL	TV PRODUCER	PCL, 68 OLD BROMPTON RD	LONDON SW7 3LQ	ENGLAND
MILLS, MONA P	NEWS CORRESPONDENT	2828 CONNECTICUT AVE, NW	WASHINGTON, DC	20008
MILLS, ROBERT L	TV WRITER	4241 BECK AVE	STUDIO CITY, CA	91604
MILLS, STEPHANIE	SINGER	POST OFFICE BOX K-350	TARZANA, CA	91356
MILLS, STEVE	TV DIRECTOR-PRODUCER	CBS-TV, 4024 RADFORD ST	STUDIO CITY, CA	91604
MILLS BROTHERS, THE	VOCAL GROUP	ICM, 8899 BEVERLY BLVD	LOS ANGELES, CA	90048
MILLSAP, BOB	GUITARIST	POST OFFICE BOX 564	HOLLISTER, MO	65672
MILLSTEIN, GREG	STILTWALKER	HALL, 138 FROG HOLLOW RD	CHURCHVILLE, PA	18966
MILNER, MARTIN	ACTOR-RADIO PERS	1846 OCEAN FRONT WALK	DEL MAR, CA	91014
MILNES, DAVID	CONDUCTOR	AFFILIATE ARTISTS, INC		
		37 W 65TH ST, 6TH FLOOR	NEW YORK, NY	10023
MILNES, SHERRILL	BARITONE	1776 BROADWAY #504	NEW YORK, NY	10019
MILO, JANA	ACTRESS	13549 HAYNES ST	VAN NUYS, CA	91401
MILRAD, ABRAHAM	WRITER-PRODUCER	10833 MASSACHUSETTS AVE	LOS ANGELES, CA	90024
MILSAP, RONNIE	SINGER-SONGWRITER	12 MUSIC CIRCLE S	NASHVILLE, TN	37203
MILSOM, DEBORAH	MEZZO-SOPRANO	MUNRO, 334 W 72ND ST	NEW YORK, NY	10023
MILSTEAD, HARRIS GLENN	ACTOR-ACTRESS	SEE - DEVINE		
MILSTEIN, NATHAN	VIOLINIST	SHAW CONCERTS, 1995 BROADWAY	NEW YORK, NY	10023
MILSTEIN, SIDNEY	DIRECTOR	6 WINDROSE WY	GREENWICH, CT	06830
MILSTEIN, WILLIAM B	WRITER	555 W 57TH ST #1230	NEW YORK, NY	10019
MILT, VICTOR	DIRECTOR	300 LAKE FRONT RD	PUTNAM VALLEY, NY	10579
MILTON, CHARLES H	TV PRODUCER	CBS-TV, 51 W 52ND ST	NEW YORK, NY	10019
MILTON, CHERILYN	ACTRESS	10845 LINDBROOK DR #3	LOS ANGELES, CA	90024
MILTON, DAVID SCOTT	TV WRITER	1235 24TH ST #1	SANTA MONICA, CA	90404
MILTON, RICHARD	WRITER-PRODUCER	1137 S SHENANDOAH ST	LOS ANGELES, CA	90035
MIMIEUX, YVETTE	ACTRESS-WRITER	DONEN, 9626 OAK PASS RD	BEVERLY HILLS, CA	90210
MIMS, WILLIAM	ACTOR	10000 RIVERSIDE DR #3	TOLUCA LAKE, CA	91602
MINCHENBURG, RICHARD	ACTOR	211 S BEVERLY DR #107	BEVERLY HILLS, CA	90212
MINCHEV, MINCHO	VIOLINIST	CAMI, 165 W 57TH ST	NEW YORK, NY	10019
MINDE, STEFAN	CONDUCTOR	61 W 62ND ST #6-F	NEW YORK, NY	10023
MINDLIN, MICHAEL, JR	TV WRITER	8955 BEVERLY BLVD	LOS ANGELES, CA	90048
MINDWARP, ZODIAC & THE LOVE REA	ROCK & ROLL GROUP	145 OXFORD ST	LONDON W1	ENGLAND
MINEO, SAMUEL H	COMPOSER	4348 SEPULVEDA BLVD	SHERMAN OAKS, CA	91403
MINER, ALLEN	WRITER-PRODUCER	644 TUALLITAN RD	LOS ANGELES, CA	90049
MINER, JAN	ACTRESS	300 E 46TH ST #9-J	NEW YORK, NY	10017
MINER, RICHARD A	WRITER	8955 BEVERLY BLVD	LOS ANGELES, CA	90048
MINER, STEVE	FILM DIRECTOR	9200 SUNSET BLVD #601	LOS ANGELES, CA	90069
MINER, TONY	THEATER-TV EXECUTIVE	145 W 58TH ST #12-J	NEW YORK, NY	10019
MINER, W PETER	TV DIRECTOR	315 W 106TH ST	NEW YORK, NY	10025
MINERY, VINCENT	DRUMMER	519 GLEN PARK DR	NASHVILLE, TN	37217
MINEVA, STEFKA	MEZZO-SOPRANO	61 W 62ND ST #6-F	NEW YORK, NY	10023
MINGARELLI, ORLANDO J	PHOTOJOURNALIST	5103 LAWTON DR	WASHINGTON, DC	20816
MINGER, JERRY	GUITARIST	2407 ROCKY CLIFF CT	BLOOMINGTON, IN	47401
MINGUS, CHARLES	BASSIST	484 W 43RD ST #435	NEW YORK, NY	10036
MINIMAL MAN	ROCK & ROLL GROUP	49R ELLIS ST #1842	SAN FRANCISCO, CA	94102
MINIS, WEVONNEDA	NEWS CORRESPONDENT	9228 PINEY BRANCH RD	SILVER SPRING, MD	20903
MINK DEVILLE	ROCK & ROLL GROUP	STEVENS ENTERPRISES		
		240 CENTRAL PARK S	NEW YORK, NY	10019
MINKUS, BARBARA	ACTRESS	15010 VENTURA BLVD #219	SHERMAN OAKS, CA	91403
MINN, HAUNANI	ACTRESS	721 N LA BREA AVE #200	LOS ANGELES, CA	90038
MINNELLI, LIZA	ACTRESS-SINGER	BLACK, 150 E 69TH ST #21-G	NEW YORK, NY	10021
MINNER, RICHARD L	NEWS CORRESPONDENT	1333 "H" ST, NW	WASHINGTON, DC	20005
MINNIX, BRUCE M	WRITER-DIRECTOR	20 JACKSON ST	CAPE MAY, NJ	08204
MINOFF, LEE	WRITER	555 W 57TH ST #1230	NEW YORK, NY	10019
MINOFF, MARVIN	WRITER	15745 ROYAL OAK RD	ENCINO, CA	91436
MINOR, BOB	ACTOR	10401 7TH AVE	INGLEWOOD, CA	90303

Name	Occupation	Address	City	Zip
MINOR, DALE	WRITER	555 W 57TH ST #1230	NEW YORK, NY	10019
MINOR, PHILIP	DIRECTOR	229 E 21ST ST	NEW YORK, NY	10010
MINOSO, MINNIE	BASEBALL	4250 MARIN DR	CHICAGO, IL	60613
MINOT, ANNA S	ACTRESS	226 W 10TH ST	NEW YORK, NY	10014
MINOT, CHRIS	CLOWN	2701 COTTAGE WY #14	SACRAMENTO, CA	95825
MINS, PETER	ACTOR	917 N LARRABEE ST #18	LOS ANGELES, CA	90069
MINSKOFF, JEROME	THEATER PRODUCER	1350 AVE OF THE AMERICAS	NEW YORK, NY	10019
MINSKY, MEIR	CONDUCTOR	59 E 54TH ST #81	NEW YORK, NY	10022
MINTER, DREW	COUNTERTENOR	61 W 62ND ST #6-F	NEW YORK, NY	10023
MINTER, GORDON	DIRECTOR	181 MONTCLAIR DR	SANTA CRUZ, CA	95060
MINTER, NIKI MOORE	DIRECTOR	7330 PYRAMID DR	LOS ANGELES, CA	90046
MINTON, JOHN	WRESTLER-ACTOR	SEE - STUDD, BIG JOHN		
MINTON, JULES	TV WRITER	JEOPARDY, 1541 N VINE ST	HOLLYWOOD, CA	90028
MINTON, MIGHTY	WRESTLER-ACTOR	SEE - STUDD, BIG JOHN		
MINTON, SANFORD	TV WRITER	8955 BEVERLY BLVD	LOS ANGELES, CA	90048
MINTZ, ART	PHOTOGRAPHER	245 W 99TH ST	NEW YORK, NY	10025
MINTZ, ELI	ACTOR	86-11 KINGSTON PL	JAMAICA, NY	11423
MINTZ, GEORGE JACOB	PIANIST	200 W 70TH ST #7-F	NEW YORK, NY	10023
MINTZ, LARRY	WRITER-PRODUCER	1323 S BENTLEY AVE #C	LOS ANGELES, CA	90025
MINTZ, MELANIE I	TV WRITER	555 W 57TH ST #1230	NEW YORK, NY	10019
MINTZ, MORTON	NEWS CORRESPONDENT	3022 MACOMB ST, NW	WASHINGTON, DC	20008
MINTZ, MURRAY	FILM DIRECTOR	717 HAMPSHIRE ST	SAN FRANCISCO, CA	94110
MINTZ, ROBERT	TV WRITER-PRODUCER	2777 GLENDOWER AVE	LOS ANGELES, CA	90027
MINTZ, SHLOMO	VIOLINIST	ICM, 40 W 57TH ST	NEW YORK, NY	10019
MINUTEMEN	ROCK & ROLL GROUP	POST OFFICE BOX 1	LAWNDALE, CA	90260
MINZESHEIMER, ROBERT	NEWS CORRESPONDENT	1904 37TH ST, NW	WASHINGTON, DC	20007
MIR	C & W GROUP	POST OFFICE BOX 25371	CHARLOTTE, NC	28212
MIRACHI, JOE	CARTOONIST	POST OFFICE BOX 4203	NEW YORK, NY	10017
MIRACLE, BARBARA	NEWS CORRESPONDENT	420 N THOMAS ST #4	ARLINGTON, VA	22203
MIRACLES, THE	VOCAL GROUP	PICHINSON, 518 N LA CIENEGA BL	LOS ANGELES, CA	90048
MIRANADA, NOEL	TV DIRECTOR	POST OFFICE BOX 55294	VALENCIA, CA	91355
MIRANDA, A J, III	DIRECTOR	853 N LARRABEE ST #4	LOS ANGELES, CA	90069
MIRANDA, BILLY	SINGER	POST OFFICE BOX 11321		
		FLAGLER STATION	MIAMI, FL	33101
MIRANDA, JOHN M	ACTOR	1245 N ORANGE DR #17	HOLLYWOOD, CA	90038
MIRANDA, ROBERT	ACTOR	3800 BARHAM BLVD #303	LOS ANGELES, CA	90068
MIRATTI, TONY	ACTOR	5881 1/2 LOCKSLEY PL	HOLLYWOOD, CA	90068
MIRELEZ, TONY	ACTOR	4218 EFFIE ST	LOS ANGELES, CA	90029
MIRGA, TOMAS	NEWS CORRESPONDENT	3314 PROSPECT ST, NW	WASHINGTON, DC	20007
MIRICIOIU, NELLY	SOPRANO	CAMI, 165 W 57TH ST	NEW YORK, NY	10019
MIRISCH, ANDREW	TV WRITER-PRODUCER	MCA/UNIVERSAL STUDIOS, INC		
		100 UNIVERSAL CITY PLAZA #507	UNIVERSAL CITY, CA	91608
MIRISCH, MARVIN	FILM PRODUCER	723 N CRESCENT DR	BEVERLY HILLS, CA	90210
MIRISCH, WALTER	FILM EXEC-PROD	647 WARNER AVE	LOS ANGELES, CA	90024
MIRKIN, DAVID	WRITER	8955 BEVERLY BLVD	LOS ANGELES, CA	90048
MIRKIN, DR GENE	COLUMNIST-AUTHOR	N Y TIMES SYNDICATION		
		130 5TH AVE	NEW YORK, NY	10011
MIRREN, HELEN	ACTRESS	AL PARKER, 55 PARK LN	LONDON W1	ENGLAND
MIRRORS BAND, THE	MUSICIAL GROUP	POST OFFICE BOX 25371	CHARLOTTE, NC	28212
MIRTO, JOE	WRESTLER	POST OFFICE BOX 3859	STAMFORD, CT	06905
MIRZA, FRED	COMPOSER	13506 HARTLAND ST	VAN NUYS, CA	91405
MIRZOEFF, EDWARD	TV PRODUCER	BBC-TV, KENSINGTON HOUSE		
		RICHMOND WAY	LONDON W14	ENGLAND
MISCH, DAVID	TV WRITER	8955 BEVERLY BLVD	LOS ANGELES, CA	90048
MISCHER, DON	TV DIRECTOR-PRODUCER	14951 ALVA RD	PACIFIC PALISADES, CA	90272
MISHKIN, CHARLES M	WRITER	1900 AVE OF THE STARS #2375	LOS ANGELES, CA	90067
MISHKIN, JUDITH	WRITER	3844 RIDGEMOOR DR	STUDIO CITY, CA	91604
MISHKIN, MEYER	TALENT AGENT	2355 BENEDICT CANYON DR	BEVERLY HILLS, CA	90210
MISHKIN, PHILIP	TV WRITER	3844 RIDGEMOOR DR	STUDIO CITY, CA	91604
MISHOE, PHILIP B, JR	PHOTOJOURNALIST	1907 N WOODLEY ST	ARLINGTON, VA	22207
MISING LINK, THE	WRESTLER	UNIVERSAL WRESTLING FEDERATION		
		MID SOUTH SPORTS, INC		
		5001 SPRING VALLEY RD	DALLAS, TX	75244
MISIOROWSKI, ROBERT A	TV WRITER	1885 VETERAN AVE #206	LOS ANGELES, CA	90025
MISITA, MICHAEL	ACTOR	108 N SYCAMORE AVE #6	LOS ANGELES, CA	90036
MISLOVE, MICHAEL	SCREENWRITER	1302 N SWEETZER AVE #601	LOS ANGELES, CA	90069
MISRAKI, PAIL	COMPOSER	35 AVE BUGEAUD	PARIS 75018	FRANCE
MISS ELIZABETH	WRESTLING VALET-MGR	POST OFFICE BOX 3859	STAMFORD, CT	06905
MISS LAURENA	TRAPEZE ARTIST	SEE - LAURENA, MISS		
MISS LISA	AERIALIST	HALL, 138 FROG HOLLOW RD	CHURCHVILLE, PA	18966
MISS LORELEI	AERIALIST	HALL, 138 FROG HOLLOW RD	CHURCHVILLE, PA	18966
MISS WENDY	AERIALIST	HALL, 138 FROG HOLLOW RD	CHURCHVILLE, PA	18966
MISSING PERSONS	ROCK & ROLL GROUP	9903 SANTA MONICA BLVD #129	BEVERLY HILLS, CA	90212
MISSION	ROCK & ROLL GROUP	FRANTIC RECORDS COMPANY		
		2105 MARYLAND AVE	BALTIMORE, MD	21218
MISSISSIPPI BAND	C & W GROUP	OBA, 5601 ODANA RD	MADISON, WI	53719
MISSY	ACTRESS	MITCHELL BROTHERS THEATER		
		875 O'FARRELL ST	SAN FRANCISCO, CA	94209
MIST	MUSIC GROUP	BENNETT, 4630 DEEPDALE DR	CORPUS CHRISTI, TX	78413
MISTER, MISTER	ROCK & ROLL GROUP	SEE - MR MISTER		
MISTER, MR	ROCK & ROLL GROUP	SEE - MR MISTER		
MISTER MISTER	ROCK & ROLL GROUP	SEE - MR MISTER		
MISTRESSES, THE	ROCK & ROLL GROUP	9777 HARWIN ST #101	HOUSTON, TX	77036
MITACEK, MICHAEL	COMPOSER	178-H CASUDA CANYON DR	MONTEREY PARK, CA	91754
MITCHELL, ALISON	NEWS CORRESPONDENT	1625 15TH ST #5, NW	WASHINGTON, DC	20009

Name	Occupation	Address	City	Zip
MITCHELL, ANDREA	NEWS CORRESPONDENT	CBS NEWS, 2020 "M" ST, NW	WASHINGTON, DC	20036
MITCHELL, ANDREW	FILM PRODUCER	THORN-EMI ELSTREE STUDIOS LTD	BOREHAMWOOD	ENGLAND
MITCHELL, ANN	ACTRESS	CBS-TV, "AS THE WORLD TURNS"		
		51 W 52ND ST	NEW YORK, NY	10019
MITCHELL, ARTIE	FILM PRODUCER	MITCHELL BROTHERS THEATER		
		875 O'FARRELL ST	SAN FRANCISCO, CA	94209
MITCHELL, BILL	TV WRITER	8955 BEVERLY BLVD	LOS ANGELES, CA	90048
MITCHELL, BRIAN	ACTOR	14980 VALLEY VISTA BLVD	SHERMAN OAKS, CA	91403
MITCHELL, CAMERON	ACTOR	CONTEMPORARY ARTISTS		
		132 S LASKY DR	BEVERLY HILLS, CA	90212
MITCHELL, CASEY T	TV WRITER	8955 BEVERLY BLVD	LOS ANGELES, CA	90048
MITCHELL, CEBUM	GUITARIST	18 LUTIE ST #B	NASHVILLE, TN	37210
MITCHELL, CHUCK "PORKY"	ACTOR	LEONETTI, 6526 SUNSET BLVD	HOLLYWOOD, CA	90028
MITCHELL, COLEMAN "CHICK"	WRITER-PRODUCER	151 S EL CAMINO DR	BEVERLY HILLS, CA	90212
MITCHELL, DANNY J	GUITARIST	POST OFFICE BOX 17737	NASHVILLE, TN	37217
MITCHELL, DAVID A, SR	GUITARIST	106 GEORGETOWN DR	HENDERSONVILLE, TN	37075
MITCHELL, DEAN	WRITER	555 W 57TH ST #1230	NEW YORK, NY	10019
MITCHELL, DEBORAH	WRITER-EDITOR	US MAGAZINE COMPANY		
		1 DAG HAMMARSKJOLD PLAZA	NEW YORK, NY	10017
MITCHELL, DON	ACTOR	4139 CLOVERDALE AVE	LOS ANGELES, CA	90008
MITCHELL, DR CLAUDE W	WRITER	8955 BEVERLY BLVD	LOS ANGELES, CA	90048
MITCHELL, ELIZABETH	WRITER	8955 BEVERLY BLVD	LOS ANGELES, CA	90048
MITCHELL, EMILY	HARPIST	CAMI, 165 W 57TH ST	NEW YORK, NY	10019
MITCHELL, EMILY	NEWS REPORTER	TIME/TIME & LIFE BLDG		
		ROCKEFELLER CENTER	NEW YORK, NY	10020
MITCHELL, ESTHER O	TV WRITER	4770 BREWSTER DR	TARZANA, CA	91356
MITCHELL, GLORIA CARBONE	TV WRITER	10303 VALLEY SPRING LN	NORTH HOLLYWOOD, CA	91602
MITCHELL, GORDON B	TV WRITER	19525 BRAEWOOD DR	TARZANA, CA	91356
MITCHELL, HENRY	NEWS CORRESPONDENT	4511 DAVENPORT ST	WASHINGTON, DC	20016
MITCHELL, IAN	ACTOR	BOX 400, WEST DO	EDINBURGH	SCOTLAND
MITCHELL, JAMES	ACTOR	APA, 888 7TH AVE, 6TH FLOOR	NEW YORK, NY	10106
MITCHELL, JOHN H	TV EXECUTIVE	1801 AVE OF THE STARS #312	LOS ANGELES, CA	90067
MITCHELL, JOHN W	TV WRITER-DIRECTOR	9926 WOODLEY AVE	SEPULVEDA, CA	91343
MITCHELL, JONI	SINGER-SONGWRITER	624 FUNCHAL RD	LOS ANGELES, CA	90024
MITCHELL, JUDITH P	TV WRITER	8955 BEVERLY BLVD	LOS ANGELES, CA	90048
MITCHELL, KENNETH B	NEWS CORRESPONDENT	NBC-TV, NEWS DEPARTMENT		
		4001 NEBRASKA AVE, NW	WASHINGTON, DC	20016
MITCHELL, KIM	SINGER-GUITARIST	POST OFFICE BOX 9		
		STATION J	TORONTO, ONT M4L 4Y8	ENGLAND
MITCHELL, LARRY	TV WRITER	8955 BEVERLY BLVD	LOS ANGELES, CA	90048
MITCHELL, LAUREN	ACTRESS	AFFILIATE ARTISTS, INC		
		37 W 65TH ST, 6TH FLOOR	NEW YORK, NY	10023
MITCHELL, LAWRENCE E	DIRECTOR	11524 LAURELCREST DR	STUDIO CITY, CA	91604
MITCHELL, LEONA	SOPRANO	CAMI, 165 W 57TH ST	NEW YORK, NY	10019
MITCHELL, LOFTEN	PLAYWRIGHT	ANN ELMO, 60 E 42ND ST	NEW YORK, NY	10017
MITCHELL, MARCUS J	MUSIC ARRANGER	4501 PACKARD DR #E-3	NASHVILLE, TN	37211
MITCHELL, MAURICE PETE	ACTOR	8961 SUNSET BLVD #B	LOS ANGELES, CA	90069
MITCHELL, NORMAN	ACTOR-WRITER	FIR GRANGE LODGE		
		FIR GRANGE AVE		
		WEYBRIDGE	SURREY	ENGLAND
MITCHELL, ODELL PATRICK	PHOTOGRAPHER	2315 KIRBY DR	TEMPLE HILLS, MD	20748
MITCHELL, PAT	TV HOST	GROUP W PRODUCTIONS		
		70 UNIVERSAL CITY PLAZA	UNIVERSAL CITY, CA	91608
MITCHELL, PATRICIA PICONE	NEWS CORRESPONDENT	6823 BARRETT RD	FALLS CHURCH, VA	22042
MITCHELL, PETE	GUITARIST	142 SAUNDERS FERRY #23	HENDERSONVILLE, TN	37075
MITCHELL, RAYMOND	ACTOR	POST OFFICE BOX 670	CATHEDRAL CITY, CA	92234
MITCHELL, ROBERT J	TV WRITER	8721 SUNSET BLVD #104	LOS ANGELES, CA	90069
MITCHELL, ROBERT JAMES	DIRECTOR	6611 SANTA MONICA BLVD	HOLLYWOOD, CA	90038
MITCHELL, ROBIN	RECORD EXECUTIVE	SCOTTI BROS, 2128 W PICO BLVD	SANTA MONICA, CA	90405
MITCHELL, RUTH	THEATER PRODUCER	1270 AVE OF THE AMERICAS	NEW YORK, NY	10020
MITCHELL, SCOEY	COMEDIAN-ACTOR	5850 HOLLYWOOD BLVD	LOS ANGELES, CA	90028
MITCHELL, SHELLY	WRITER	8955 BEVERLY BLVD	LOS ANGELES, CA	90048
MITCHELL, SHIRLEY	ACTRESS	133 S OAKHURST DR	BEVERLY HILLS, CA	90212
MITCHELL, SKIP	GUITARIST	329 ROCKLAND RD #1	HENDERSONVILLE, TN	37075
MITCHELL, WARREN	ACTOR	28 SHELDON AVE	LONDON N6	ENGLAND
MITCHELL, WILL	PIANIST	POST OFFICE BOX 1128	NATCHITOCHES, LA	71457
MITCHELL-RUDD DUO, THE	MUSICAL DUO	POST OFFICE BOX 12403		
		NORTHSIDE STATION	ATLANTA, GA	30355
MITCHELSON, MARVIN	TALENT AGENT	1801 CENTURY PARK E #1900	LOS ANGELES, CA	90067
MITCHUM, CARRIE	ACTRESS	CBS TELEVISION NETWORK		
		"THE BOLD & THE BEAUTIFUL"		
		7800 BEVERLY BLVD	LOS ANGELES, CA	90036
MITCHUM, JIM	ACTOR	1482 E VALLEY RD #629	MONTECITO, CA	93108
MITCHUM, JOHN	ACTOR	9744 WILSHIRE BLVD #306	BEVERLY HILLS, CA	90212
MITCHUM, ROBERT	ACTOR	860 SAN YSIDRO RD	SANTA BARBARA, CA	93108
MITNICK, PATRICE R	WRITER	555 W 57TH ST #1230	NEW YORK, NY	10019
MITTELMAN, STEVE	COMEDIAN	ICM, 8899 BEVERLY BLVD	LOS ANGELES, CA	90048
MITTLEMAN, RICHARD "RICK"	TV WRITER	3945 VALLEY MEADOW RD	ENCINO, CA	91436
MITTOO, JACKIE	KEYBOARDIST	DON RON PRODUCTIONS		
		555 POST ST	SAN FRANCISCO, CA	94102
MITTY, NOMI	ACTRESS	13111 VENTURA BLVD #102	STUDIO CITY, CA	91604
MITWELL, JILL B	TV DIRECTOR	221 W 26TH ST #51	NEW YORK, NY	10001
MITZ, RICK	TV WRITER-PRODUCER	8955 BEVERLY BLVD	LOS ANGELES, CA	90048
MITZMAN, NEWT	WRITER-PRODUCER	663 N BROADWAY	HASTINGS-ON-HUDSON, NY	10706
MIXON, ALAN	ACTOR	210 W 16TH ST	NEW YORK, NY	10011

Name	Occupation	Address	City	Zip
MIYAKE, PERRY Y, JR	WRITER	8955 BEVERLY BLVD	LOS ANGELES, CA	90048
MIYAMA, HIDEAKI	NEWS CORRESPONDENT	1066 CARPER ST	MC LEAN, VA	22101
MIYORI, KIM	ACTRESS	8033 SUNSET BLVD #770	LOS ANGELES, CA	90046
MIZE, JOHNNY	BASEBALL	POST OFFICE BOX 112	DEMOREST, GA	30535
MIZIKER, RON	TV PRODUCER	500 S BUENA VISTA ST	BURBANK, CA	91521
MJOSETH, MARCIA	NEWS CORRESPONDENT	2217 40TH ST, NW	WASHINGTON, DC	20007
MOAR, ANDREA	ACTRESS	3800 BARHAM BLVD #303	LOS ANGELES, CA	90068
MOBLEY, GEORGE F	PHOTOGRAPHER	ROUTE #1, BOX 54	MAURERTOWN, VA	22644
MOBLEY, MARY ANN	ACTRESS	COLLINS, 2751 HUTTON DR	BEVERLY HILLS, CA	90210
MOBY GRAPE	ROCK & ROLL GROUP	MATTHEW KATZ PRODS		
		555 POST ST	SAN FRANCISCO, CA	94102
MOCCIO, FRANK	FILM DIRECTOR	321 E 69TH ST #5-C	NEW YORK, NY	10021
MOCHIDA, NAOTAKE	NEWS CORRESPONDENT	444 N CAPITOL ST, NW	WASHINGTON, DC	20001
MOCK, FREIDA LEE	WRITER	339 ADELAIDE DR	SANTA MONICA, CA	90402
MOCK, PAT	CASTING DIRECTOR	MCA/UNIVERSAL STUDIOS, INC		
		100 UNIVERSAL CITY PLAZA #473	UNIVERSAL CITY, CA	91608
MOCKRIDGE, JEANNE	ACTRESS	3800 BARHAM BLVD #303	LOS ANGELES, CA	90068
MOD SQUAD, THE	WRESTLING TAG TEAM	NATIONAL WRESTLING ALLIANCE		
		JIM CROCKETT PROMOTIONS		
		421 BRIARBEND DR	CHARLOTTE, NC	28209
MODEAN, JAYNE	ACTRESS	151 S EL CAMINO DR	BEVERLY HILLS, CA	90212
MODELS, THE	ROCK & ROLL GROUP	GEFFEN RECORDS COMPANY		
		9130 SUNSET BLVD	LOS ANGELES, CA	90069
MODER, DICK	DIRECTOR	22435 PAUL REVERE DR	WOODLAND HILLS, CA	91364
MODERN JAZZ QUARTET, THE	JAZZ QUARTET	KURLAND, 173 BRIGHTON AVE	BOSTON, MA	02134
MODERN ROMANCE	ROCK & ROLL GROUP	TOPLAND LIMITED		
		30 GREAT PORTLAND ST	LONDON W1	ENGLAND
MODERNAIRES, THE	VOCAL GROUP	17752 SKYPARK BLVD #265	IRVINE, CA	92714
MODES, SONIA	SINGER	COVER, 1425 N STAR RD	COLUMBUS, OH	43212
MOECK, WALTER F	CONDUCTOR	14209 CHANDLER BLVD	VAN NUYS, CA	91401
MOELLER, GUNNAR	ACTOR	42 GURNEY DR	LONDON N2	ENGLAND
MOELLER, RICHARD	TV DIRECTOR	345 W 55TH ST	NEW YORK, NY	10019
MOENNING, WILDA	MUSICIAN	3 VALLEY FORGE	NASHVILLE, TN	37205
MOER, PAUL E	COMPOSER	9323 KESTER AVE	PANORAMA CITY, CA	91402
MOERKE, GARY	ACTOR	13970 PEACH GROVE ST	SHERMAN OAKS, CA	91423
MOERSCH, WILLIAM	MARIMBIST	157 W 57TH ST #1100	NEW YORK, NY	10019
MOESER, MARION V	NEWS CORRESPONDENT	1825 "K" ST, NW	WASHINGTON, DC	20006
MOESSINGER, DAVID	WRITER-PRODUCER	3861 KINGSWOOD RD	SHERMAN OAKS, CA	91405
MOFFAT, DONALD	ACTOR	10100 SANTA MONICA BLVD #1608	LOS ANGELES, CA	90067
MOFFAT, IVAN	WRITER	12101 MULHOLLAND DR	BEVERLY HILLS, CA	90210
MOFFAT, KATHERINE	ACTRESS	6310 SAN VICENTE BLVD #407	LOS ANGELES, CA	90048
MOFFATT, JOHN	ACTOR	59-A WARRINGTON ST	LONDON W9	ENGLAND
MOFFATT, KATY	SINGER-GUITARIST	3122 SALE ST	DALLAS, TX	75219
MOFFATT, PETER	TV DIRECTOR	MURPHY, CURTIS BROWN, LTD		
		162-168 REGENT ST	LONDON W1	ENGLAND
MOFFET, JORDAN H	TV WRITER	157 S MARTEL AVE	LOS ANGELES, CA	90036
MOFFET, SALLY	ACTRESS	KELLIN, 23 CLINTON AVE	NYACK, NY	10960
MOFFETT, ANNE	NEWS CORRESPONDENT	7706 ELBA RD	ALEXANDRIA, VA	22306
MOFFETT, GEORGE D, III	NEWS CORRESPONDENT	1606 34TH ST, NW	WASHINGTON, DC	20007
MOFFITT, JOHN	PRODUCER	1438 N GOWER ST #250	LOS ANGELES, CA	90028
MOFFITT, WILLIAM	DIRECTOR-PRODUCER	785 NEW YORK DR	ALTADENA, CA	91001
MOFFLY, JOE REB	TV WRITER	8955 BEVERLY BLVD	LOS ANGELES, CA	90048
MOFFO, ANNA	SOPRANO	4 E 66TH ST	NEW YORK, NY	10019
MOFOS, THE	ROCK & ROLL GROUP	SEE - MIGHTY MOFOS, THE		
MOGELL, LEZLIE	ACTRESS	3908 1/2 LAUREL CANYON BLVD	STUDIO CITY, CA	91604
MOGULL, ARTHUR	RECORD EXECUTIVE	2720 BENEDICT CANYON DR	BEVERLY HILLS, CA	90210
MOHR, CHARLES H	NEWS CORRESPONDENT	4329 LELAND ST	CHEVY CHASE, MD	20815
MOHR, MAJ GEN HENRY	COLUMNIST-ARMY GEN	SAINT LOUIS GLOBE-DEMOCRAT		
		710 N TUCKER BLVD	SAINT LOUIS, MO	63101
MOHR, MARCIA	ACTRESS	SEA COLONY DR #42	SANTA MONICA, CA	90405
MOHR, MARGIT	COMPOSER	5067 TOPANGA CANYON BLVD	WOODLAND HILLS, CA	91364
MOHS, MAYO	WRITER-EDITOR	DISCOVER/TIME & LIFE BLDG		
		ROCKEFELLER CENTER	NEW YORK, NY	10020
MOIO, JOHN	TV DIRECTOR	11708 CANTON PL	STUDIO CITY, CA	91604
MOIR, JAMES	TV PRODUCER	BBC-TV CENTRE, WOOD LN		
		SHEPHERDS BUSH	LONDON W12	ENGLAND
MOIR, MICHAEL	DIRECTOR	DGA, 110 W 57TH ST	NEW YORK, NY	10019
MOISY, CLAUDE	NEWS CORRESPONDENT	4316 WESTOVER PL, NW	WASHINGTON, DC	20016
MOJAVE	C & W GROUP	VP, 2779 MIRADA RD	HIGHLAND, CA	92346
MOJO	RHYTHM & BLUES GROUP	3401 S ONEIDA WY #D	DENVER, CO	80224
MOLCHAN, DENNIS	VIOLINIST	5109 W CONCORD RD	BRENTWOOD, TN	37027
MOLCHAN, MARTHA	VIOLINIST	5109 W CONCORD RD	BRENTWOOD, TN	37027
MOLDEN, PRENTISS	ACTOR	24105 WILLOW CREEK RD	DIAMOND BAR, CA	91765
MOLDOVAN, DEBRA	WRITER	555 W 57TH ST #1230	NEW YORK, NY	10019
MOLDOVEANU, EUGENIA	SOPRANO	61 W 62ND ST #6-F	NEW YORK, NY	10023
MOLDOVEANU, VASILE	TENOR	CAMI, 165 W 57TH ST	NEW YORK, NY	10019
MOLE, RALPH	DIRECTOR-PRODUCER	156 MYRTLE ST	HAWORTH, NJ	07641
MOLE, ROBERT	PHOTOGRAPHER	15219 NOBELWOOD LN	BOWIE, MD	20716
MOLEON, ARY	NEWS CORRESPONDENT	4708 RESERVOIR RD, NW	WASHINGTON, DC	20007
MOLER, RON	FILM PRODUCER	3393 BENNETT DR	LOS ANGELES, CA	90068
MOLIN, BUD	TV DIRECTOR	557 E VERDUGO AVE	BURBANK, CA	91501
MOLINA, ALFRED	ACTOR	COULSON, 37 BERWICK ST	LONDON W1	ENGLAND
MOLINARE, RICHARD	ACTOR	205 WASHINGTON AVE #8	SANTA MONICA, CA	90403
MOLINARO, AL	ACTOR	POST OFFICE BOX 9303	GLENDALE, CA	91206
MOLINSKI, DAN	NEWS CORRESPONDENT	1201 CONNECTICUT AVE, NW	WASHINGTON, DC	20036

Name	Occupation	Address	City	Zip
MOLL, ELICK	WRITER	9322 READCREST DR	BEVERLY HILLS, CA	90210
MOLL, KURT	SINGER	MARIEDL ANDERS ARTISTS MGMT		
		535 EL CAMINO DEL MAR ST	SAN FRANCISCO, CA	94121
MOLL, RICHARD	ACTOR	6430 SUNSET BLVD #1203	LOS ANGELES, CA	90028
MOLLICA, JAMES J	WRITER	555 W 57TH ST #1230	NEW YORK, NY	10019
MOLLICA, MAE	BODYBUILDER	1106 2ND ST #116	ENCINITAS, CA	92024
MOLLICONE, HENRY	CONDUCTOR	SULLIVAN, 390 W END AVE	NEW YORK, NY	10024
MOLLIN, LARRY	TV WRITER	10960 WILSHIRE BLVD #922	LOS ANGELES, CA	90024
MOLLISON, ANDREW	NEWS CORRESPONDENT	4891 POTOMAC AVE, NW	WASHINGTON, DC	20007
MOLLO, DICK	SINGER	POST OFFICE BOX 171132	NASHVILLE, TN	37217
MOLLOT, LAWRENCE	DIRECTOR	MRC FILMS & TAPE CO		
		71 W 23RD ST	NEW YORK, NY	10010
MOLLY HATCHET	ROCK & ROLL GROUP	POST OFFICE BOX 6600	MACON, GA	51215
MOLONEY, DARREN	ACTOR	4345 LEMP AVE	STUDIO CITY, CA	91604
MOLONEY, ROBERT	ACTOR-WRITER	4007 VAN NOORD AVE	STUDIO CITY, CA	91604
MOLONEY, SEAN	ACTOR	4345 LEMP AVE	STUDIO CITY, CA	91604
MOLOTSKY, IRVIN D	NEWS CORRESPONDENT	1725 "T" ST, NW	WASHINGTON, DC	20009
MOLPUS, DAVID L	NEWS CORRESPONDENT	9505 SEMINOLE ST	SILVER SPRING, MD	20901
MOLYNEAUX, LAURA S	VIOLINIST	ROUTE #1, BOX 284	COLLEGE GROVE, TN	37046
MOMARY, DOUGLAS R	WRITER	8955 BEVERLY BLVD	LOS ANGELES, CA	90048
MOMENT OF TRUTH	VOCAL GROUP	BERGEN, 159 W 53RD ST	NEW YORK, NY	10019
MOMENTS, THE	VOCAL GROUP	POST OFFICE BOX 82	GREAT NECK, NY	11021
MON PERE, CAROL J	TV WRITER	8955 BEVERLY BLVD	LOS ANGELES, CA	90048
MON TOY, MARY	ACTRESS	66 W 88TH ST #1-G	NEW YORK, NY	10024
MONACELLA, ALFRED	TV WRITER	615 N CANON DR	BEVERLY HILLS, CA	90210
MONACO, LAWRENCE	ACTOR	357 S REXFORD DR #203	BEVERLY HILLS, CA	90212
MONAGHAN, EDWARD V	WRITER	1931 N WILCOX AVE #1	LOS ANGELES, CA	90068
MONAGHAN, NANCY	NEWS EDITOR	POST OFFICE BOX 500	WASHINGTON, DC	20044
MONAGHAN, PAUL	NEWS CORRESPONDENT	POST OFFICE BOX 1042	WASHINGTON, DC	20013
MONAGHAN, PETER	NEWS CORRESPONDENT	2122 MASSACHUSETTS AVE #2, NW	WASHINGTON, DC	20037
MONAHAN, BOB	CASTING DIRECTOR	6509 W 6TH ST	LOS ANGELES, CA	90048
MONAHAN, DAN	ACTOR	STONE, 1052 CAROL DR	LOS ANGELES, CA	90069
MONASH, PAUL	WRITER-PRODUCER	9121 ALTO CEDRO DR	BEVERLY HILLS, CA	90210
MONASTER, NATE	TV WRITER	826 N KINGS RD	LOS ANGELES, CA	90069
MONBERG, HELENE C	NEWS CORRESPONDENT	123 6TH ST, SE	WASHINGTON, DC	20003
MONCION, FRANCISCO J	ACTOR	410 CENTRAL PARK W	NEW YORK, NY	10025
MONDAY, DICK	CLOWN	2701 COTTAGE WY #14	SACRAMENTO, CA	95825
MONDE, ARTHUR	ACTOR	358 W ALAMEDA AVE	BURBANK, CA	91506
MONDEAUX, JOEL	DIRECTOR	2033 CHEREMOYA AVE	HOLLYWOOD, CA	90068
MONDI, LAWRENCE	NEWS REPORTER	TIME/TIME & LIFE BLDG		
		ROCKEFELLER CENTER	NEW YORK, NY	10020
MONDO, PEGGY	ACTRESS	7060 HOLLYWOOD BLVD #610	LOS ANGELES, CA	90028
MONDY, PIERRE	ACTOR	ARTMEDIA, 10 AVE GEORGE V	PARIS 75008	FRANCE
MONDY, RONALD	SINGER-SAXOPHONIST	158 CUMBERLAND DR	HENDERSONVILLE, TN	37075
MONET, BRIDGETTE	ACTRESS	CABALLERO, 7920 ALABAMA AVE	CANOGA PARK, CA	91304
MONETTE, PAUL	WRITER	1500 N KINGS RD	LOS ANGELES, CA	90069
MONEY, EDDIE	ROCK & ROLL GROUP	POST OFFICE BOX 1994	SAN FRANCISCO, CA	94101
MONGIARDO-COOPER DUO	MUSICAL DUO	FINELL, 155 W 68TH ST	NEW YORK, NY	10023
MONGOL, BEPPO	WRESTLER	SEE - VOLKOFF, NIKOLAI		
MONGOL, BOLO	WRESTLER	SEE - MASKED SUPERSTAR, THE		
MONICA, CORBETT	COMEDIAN-ACTOR	101 W 57TH ST #11-E	NEW YORK, NY	10019
MONICK, SUSIE	MANDOLINIST	125 TAGGART AVE #B	NASHVILLE, TN	37207
MONIQUE, CARMEN	MODEL	MODELS & PROMOTIONS AGENCY		
		8560 SUNSET BLVD, 10TH FLOOR	LOS ANGELES, CA	90069
MONJONYA	ROCK & ROLL GROUP	POST OFFICE BOX 82	GREAT NECK, NY	11022
MONK, ISABELL	ACTRESS	211 S BEVERLY DR #201	BEVERLY HILLS, CA	90212
MONK, JULIUS	DIRECTOR-PRODUCER	VENDOME, 350 W 57TH ST	NEW YORK, NY	10019
MONK, KERMIT & HIS STONE MOUNTA	C & W GROUP	POST OFFICE BOX 316	CHUCKEY, TN	37641
MONK, MEREDITH	CHOREO-COMP-MUS	THE HOUSE FOUNDATION FOR		
		THE PERFORMING ARTS		
		325 SPRING ST	NEW YORK, NY	10013
MONK, TERENCE	ACTOR	7469 MELROSE AVE #30	LOS ANGELES, CA	90046
MONKHOUSE, BOB	ACTOR-WRITER	PRICHARD, 19 W EATON PL	LONDON SW1X 8LT	ENGLAND
MONKOVICH, GEORGE J	ACTOR	442 S OAKHURST DR #6	BEVERLY HILLS, CA	90212
MONKS, JAMES	ACTOR	23 E 39TH ST	NEW YORK, NY	10016
MONKS, JOHN, JR	ACTOR-WRITER	1058 NAPOLI DR	PACIFIC PALISADES, CA	90272
MONOD, JACQUES	ACTOR	16 RUE THIBAUD	PARIS 75014	FRANCE
MONOSON, LAWRENCE	ACTOR	151 S EL CAMINO DR	BEVERLY HILLS, CA	90212
MONROE, BILL	NEWS CORRESPONDENT	28 WESTPATH WY	FORT SUMNER, MD	20816
MONROE, BILL	SINGER-GUITARIST	3819 DICKERSON RD	NASHVILLE, TN	37207
MONROE, BILL & THE BLUEGRASS BO	BLUEGRASS GROUP	38 MUSIC SQUARE E #300	NASHVILLE, TN	37203
MONROE, JAMES & TENNESSEE THUND	C & W GROUP	TESSIER, 505 CANTON PASS	MADISON, TN	37115
MONROE, JAMES W	GUITARIST	3819 DICKERSON RD	NASHVILLE, TN	37207
MONROE, MICHAEL	ACTOR	1161 N DOHENY DR	LOS ANGELES, CA	90069
MONROE, ROBERT	WRITER	8955 BEVERLY BLVD	LOS ANGELES, CA	90048
MONROE, WILLIAM B, JR	NEWS CORRESPONDENT	NBC-TV, NEWS DEPARTMENT		
		4001 NEBRASKA AVE, NW	WASHINGTON, DC	20016
MONSKY, MARK	TV EXECUTIVE	METROMEDIA TV, 205 E 67TH ST	NEW YORK, NY	10021
MONSON, WILLIAM N	WRITER	8955 BEVERLY BLVD	LOS ANGELES, CA	90048
MONSOON, GORILLA	WRESTLING ANNOUNCER	POST OFFICE BOX 3859	STAMFORD, CT	06905
MONSTER EIFFEL TOWER	WRESTLER	SEE - ANDRE THE GIANT		
MONSTER ROUSIMOFF	WRESTLER	SEE - ANDRE THE GIANT		
MONTAGNE, EDWARD	WRITER-PRODUCER	8955 BEVERLY BLVD	LOS ANGELES, CA	90048
MONTAGUE, BRUCE	ACTOR-WRITER	LEADING PLAYERS, 31 KING'S RD	LONDON SW3	ENGLAND

EDDIE MONEY

GEORGE MONTGOMERY

ARCHIE MOORE

CLAYTON MOORE

COLLEEN MOORE

DEMI MOORE

GARY MOORE

MARY TYLER MOORE

ROGER MOORE

Name	Occupation	Address	City/State	ZIP
MONTAGUE, CARRIE	NEWS CORRESPONDENT	3201 WISCONSIN AVE #101, NW	WASHINGTON, DC	20016
MONTAGUE, DIANA	MEZZO-SOPRANO	CAMI, 165 W 57TH ST	NEW YORK, NY	10019
MONTAGUE, FRED	PHOTOJOURNALIST	5813 MARBURY RD	BETHESDA, MD	20034
MONTAGUE, LEE	ACTOR	5 KEATS CLOSE	LONDON NW3	ENGLAND
MONTAGUE, NATHANIEL	WRITER	8955 BEVERLY BLVD	LOS ANGELES, CA	90048
MONTAGUE, WILLIAM	NEWS CORRESPONDENT	1202 S WASHINGTON ST	ALEXANDRIA, VA	22314
MONTAIGNE, LAWRENCE	WRITER	8955 BEVERLY BLVD	LOS ANGELES, CA	90048
MONTALBAN, CARLOS J	ACTOR	58 W 58TH ST	NEW YORK, NY	10019
MONTALBAN, RICARDO	ACTOR-DIRECTOR	9256 ROBIN DR	LOS ANGELES, CA	90069
MONTALBO, JOSEPH	ACTOR	81 GRAND ST	NEW YORK, NY	10013
MONTANA	C & W GROUP	POST OFFICE BOX O	EXCELSIOR, MN	55331
MONTANA, JOE	FOOTBALL	711 NEVADA ST	REDWOOD CITY, CA	94061
MONTANA, MONTIE	ACTOR	10234 ESCONDIDO CYN RD	AQUA DULCE, CA	91350
MONTANA, PATSY	SINGER	4950 CASTANA	LAKEWOOD, CA	90712
MONTANA SKY	C & W GROUP	POST OFFICE BOX O	EXCELSIOR, MN	55331
MONTAND, YVES	ACTOR	15 PLACE DAUPHINE		
		ILE DE LA CITE	PARIS 75001	FRANCE
MONTANE, CARLOS	TENOR	61 W 62ND ST #6-F	NEW YORK, NY	10023
MONTANINO, GENNARDO	FILM WRITER-DIRECTOR	5639 SATSUMA AVE	NORTH HOLLYWOOD, CA	91601
MONTARSOLO, PAOLO	BASSO-BARITONE	61 W 62ND ST #6-F	NEW YORK, NY	10023
MONTE, DON	NEWS REPORTER	THE NATIONAL ENQUIRER		
		600 SE COAST AVE	LANTANA, FL	33464
MONTE, ERIC	ACT-WRI-PROD	19664 TRULL BROOK DR	TARZANA, CA	91356
MONTEFIORE, APRILE	SOPRANO	45 W 60TH ST #4-K	NEW YORK, NY	10023
MONTEFIORE, DAVID	TENOR	GEWALD, 58 W 58TH ST	NEW YORK, NY	10019
MONTEFIORE, GENE	TV DIRECTOR	LINCOLN TOWERS, 142 W END AVE	NEW YORK, NY	10023
MONTEITH, KELLY	COMED-WRI	19200 PACIFIC COAST HWY	MALIBU, CA	90265
MONTEL, JOAN	SINGER	KCA, 928 MOSS ST	NEW ORLEANS, LA	70119
MONTEL, MICHAEL	DIRECTOR	9000 SUNSET BLVD #1200	LOS ANGELES, CA	90069
MONTELFIORE, DAVID	TENOR	GEWALD, 58 W 58TH ST	NEW YORK, NY	10019
MONTEUX, CLAUDE	FLUTIST	KAY, 58 W 58TH ST	NEW YORK, NY	10019
MONTEVECCHI, LILIANE	SINGER	ICM, 8899 BEVERLY BLVD	LOS ANGELES, CA	90048
MONTGOMERY, BABY PEGGY	ACTRESS	CARY, 7220 DURANGO CIR	CARLSBAD, CA	92008
MONTGOMERY, BELINDA J	ACTRESS	15301 VENTURA BLVD #345	SHERMAN OAKS, CA	91403
MONTGOMERY, BOB	GUITARIST	POST OFFICE BOX 120967	NASHVILLE, TN	37212
MONTGOMERY, BRIAN	BARITONE	CAMI, 165 W 57TH ST	NEW YORK, NY	10019
MONTGOMERY, CAMILLE	VIOLINIST	1502 WOODMONT BLVD	NASHVILLE, TN	37215
MONTGOMERY, CEC	ACTOR	8230 BEVERLY BLVD #23	LOS ANGELES, CA	90048
MONTGOMERY, CHARLES	NEWS REPORTER	THE NATIONAL ENQUIRER		
		600 SE COAST AVE	LANTANA, FL	33464
MONTGOMERY, CHUCK	FILM EDITOR	ACE, 4416 1/2 FINLEY AVE	LOS ANGELES, CA	90027
MONTGOMERY, DAVID J	NEWS CORRESPONDENT	6826 WILD ROSE CT	SPRINGFIELD, VA	21285
MONTGOMERY, DILLARD	PIANIST	2605 BUCHANAN ST	NASHVILLE, TN	37208
MONTGOMERY, EARL	ACTOR	13029 GLADSTONE AVE	SYLMAR, CA	91342
MONTGOMERY, ELIZABETH	ACTRESS	1230 BENEDICT CANYON DR	BEVERLY HILLS, CA	90210
MONTGOMERY, GEORGE	ACTOR	16531 SATICOY ST	VAN NUYS, CA	91406
MONTGOMERY, HALE	NEWS CORRESPONDENT	4208 N 23RD ST	ARLINGTON, VA	22207
MONTGOMERY, JO	WRITER	8955 BEVERLY BLVD	LOS ANGELES, CA	90048
MONTGOMERY, JOHNNY T	GUITARIST	ROUTE #3, BOX 367	LEBANON, TN	37087
MONTGOMERY, JOSEPH, JR	WRITER	555 W 57TH ST #1230	NEW YORK, NY	10019
MONTGOMERY, JULIE	ACTRESS	211 S BEVERLY DR #201	BEVERLY HILLS, CA	90212
MONTGOMERY, KATHRYN	FILM-TV WRITER	2937 WESTBROOK AVE	LOS ANGELES, CA	90046
MONTGOMERY, LEE	ACTOR	15301 VENTURA BLVD #345	SHERMAN OAKS, CA	91403
MONTGOMERY, LESLIE	WRITER	555 W 57TH ST #1230	NEW YORK, NY	10019
MONTGOMERY, LYNN P	WRITER	8955 BEVERLY BLVD	LOS ANGELES, CA	90048
MONTGOMERY, MARIAN B	WRITER	8955 BEVERLY BLVD	LOS ANGELES, CA	90048
MONTGOMERY, MELBA	SINGER	1300 DIVISION ST #103	NASHVILLE, TN	37203
MONTGOMERY, MICHAEL T	TV WRITER	8955 BEVERLY BLVD	LOS ANGELES, CA	90048
MONTGOMERY, PHIL	ACTOR	1200 N LAS PALMAS AVE	HOLLYWOOD, CA	90038
MONTGOMERY, ROBERT	WRITER	555 W 57TH ST #1230	NEW YORK, NY	10019
MONTGOMERY, SUZANNE	NEWS CORRESPONDENT	150 N MUHLENBERG ST	WOODSTOCK, VA	22664
MONTGOMERY, TANNIS	ACTRESS	STONE, 1052 CAROL DR	LOS ANGELES, CA	90069
MONTGOMERY-MEISSNER, KATHRYN	SOPRANO	STANDSTR #93	5303 BORNHEIM 4	WEST GERMANY
MONTI, CARLOTTA	ACTRESS-WRITER	7946 FOUNTAIN AVE	LOS ANGELES, CA	90046
MONTI, JERRY	WRESTLER	POST OFFICE BOX 3859	STAMFORD, CT	06905
MONTIAGUE, JOSEF	WRITER	8955 BEVERLY BLVD	LOS ANGELES, CA	90048
MONTONE, JOHN F	WRITER	555 W 57TH ST #1230	NEW YORK, NY	10019
MONTOYA, CARLOS	GUITARIST	345 W 58TH ST	NEW YORK, NY	10019
MONTOYA, JULIA	ACTRESS	2223 HEPWORTH AVE	COMMERCE, CA	90040
MONTROSE, JACK	COMPOSER	2236 HACIENDA AVE	LAS VEGAS, NV	89119
MONTROSE/FROOM	ROCK & ROLL GROUP	3 E 54TH ST #1400	NEW YORK, NY	10022
MONTROSS, CHRISTOPHER	TV DIRECTOR	6310 FRANKLIN RD	BIRMINGHAM, MI	48010
MONTWIELER, NANCY H	NEWS CORRESPONDENT	3939 MILITARY RD, NW	WASHINGTON, DC	20015
MONTY, EVA	ACTRESS	7938 DRISCOLL AVE	VAN NUYS, CA	91406
MONTY, GLORIA	TV DIRECTOR-PRODUCER	16065 JEANNE LN	ENCINO, CA	91316
MONTY, JERRY	WRESTLER	POST OFFICE BOX 3859	STAMFORD, CT	06905
MONTY, NORMA	TV WRITER	ABC-TV, "GENERAL HOSPITAL"		
		1438 N GOWER ST	LOS ANGELES, CA	90028
MONTY PYTHON	COMEDY GROUP	20 FITZROY SQ	LONDON W1P 6BB	ENGLAND
MONZON DUO	MUSICAL DUO	POST OFFICE BOX 131	SPRINGFIELD, VA	22150
MOO-YOUNG, IAN	ANIMATION DIRECTOR	26 GREAT SUTTON ST	LONDON	ENGLAND
MOOD EXPRESS	C & W GROUP	POST OFFICE BOX 5563	ROCKFORD, IL	61125
MOODY, CARLTON & THE MOODY BROT	C & W GORUP	POST OFFICE BOX 25371	CHARLOTTE, NC	28212
MOODY, CLYDE	SINGER	RRT, 827 MERIDIAN ST	NASHVILLE, TN	37207
MOODY, DAVID	ACTOR	6640 SUNSET BLVD #203	LOS ANGELES, CA	90028

Name	Occupation	Address	City/State	Zip/Country
MOODY, JOHN W	DIRECTOR	100 KINGS POINT DR #810	NORTH MIAMI BEACH, FL	33160
MOODY, KING	ACTOR	6041 CALVIN AVE	TARZANA, CA	91356
MOODY, MICHAEL D	WRITER	8955 BEVERLY BLVD	LOS ANGELES, CA	90048
MOODY, PAULA	STUNTWOMAN	3518 W CAHUENGA BLVD #206-A	LOS ANGELES, CA	90068
MOODY, PHILIP T	COMPOSER	4179 HAZELTINE AVE	SHERMAN OAKS, CA	91403
MOODY, RON	ACTOR	GLASS, 28 BERKELEY SQ	LONDON W1X 6HD	ENGLAND
MOODY, SUSET	ACTRESS	439 S LA CIENEGA BLVD #120	LOS ANGELES, CA	90048
MOODY BLUES, THE	ROCK & ROLL GROUP	WEINTRAUB ENTERTAINMENT GROUP		
		11111 SANTA MONICA BLVD		
		20TH FLOOR	LOS ANGELES, CA	90025
MOON, EDWARD	GUITARIST	POST OFFICE BOX 1232	DURHAM, NC	27702
MOON, FRANK	ACTOR	13111 VENTURA BLVD #102	STUDIO CITY, CA	91604
MOON, JULIE	NEWS CORRESPONDENT	3443 N RANDOLPH ST	ARLINGTON, VA	22207
MOON, MYUNG-HO	NEWS CORRESPONDENT	3176 BORGE ST	OAKTON, VA	22124
MOON, ROBERT L	NEWS CORRESPONDENT	1003 DORSET DR	SAINT CHARLES, MD	20601
MOON, SARAH	DIRECTOR	DGA, 7950 SUNSET BLVD	LOS ANGELES, CA	90046
MOONDOG SPOT	WRESTLER	POST OFFICE BOX 3859	STAMFORD, CT	06905
MOONEY, DAVID	ACTOR	6565 SUNSET BLVD #525-A	HOLLYWOOD, CA	90068
MOONEY, DEBRA	ACTRESS	9229 SUNSET BLVD #306	LOS ANGELES, CA	90069
MOONEY, GAVIN	ACTOR	6570 DE LONGPRE AVE	LOS ANGELES, CA	90028
MOONEY, JOHN CHARLES	ACTOR	15 CATAMARAN ST #4	MARINA DEL REY, CA	90292
MOONEY, PAUL	TV WRITER	8955 BEVERLY BLVD	LOS ANGELES, CA	90048
MOONEY, WILLIAM	ACTOR	SCHUMER-OUBRE, 1697 BROADWAY	NEW YORK, NY	10019
MOONGLOWS, THE	VOCAL GROUP	5300 POWERLINE RD #202	FORT LAUDERDALE, FL	33309
MOONJEAN, HANK	FILM PRODUCER	292 S LA CIENEGA BLVD #205	BEVERLY HILLS, CA	90211
MOONLIGHT DRIVE	ROCK & ROLL GROUP	41 BRITAIN ST #200	TORONTO, ONT	CANADA
MOONSHINE CLOGGERS, THE	C & W GROUP	POST OFFICE BOX 418	BRENTWOOD, TN	37027
MOOR, BILL	ACTOR	9200 SUNSET BLVD #1210	LOS ANGELES, CA	90069
MOORE, ALAN	MUSIC ARRANGER	4909 GRANNY WHITE PIKE	NASHVILLE, TN	37220
MOORE, ALVY	ACTOR	8546 AMESTOY AVE	NORTHRIDGE, CA	91324
MOORE, ARCHIE	BOXER	3517 EAST ST	SAN DIEGO, CA	92102
MOORE, BOB	GUITARIST	POST OFFICE BOX 15291	NASHVILLE, TN	37215
MOORE, BRIAN	WRITER	8955 BEVERLY BLVD	LOS ANGELES, CA	90048
MOORE, CHARLOTTE	ACTRESS	211 S BEVERLY DR #201	BEVERLY HILLS, CA	90212
MOORE, CLARENCE W	NEWS CORRESPONDENT	2022 COLUMBIA RD, NW	WASHINGTON, DC	20009
MOORE, CLAYTON	ACTOR	4720 PARK OLIVO	CALABASAS, CA	91302
MOORE, CLIFTON H	NEWS CORRESPONDENT	4461 CONNECTICUT AVE, NW	WASHINGTON, DC	20008
MOORE, COLLEEN	ACTRESS	RURAL ROUTE #1, BOX 207-A	TEMPLETON, CA	93456
MOORE, CONSTANCE	ACTRESS	1661 FERRARI DR	BEVERLY HILLS, CA	90210
MOORE, CRAIG & MOORE COUNTRY BA	C & W GROUP	JOYCE, 2028 CHESTNUT ST	PHILADELPHIA, PA	19103
MOORE, DAVID LEON	SPORTS WRITER	POST OFFICE BOX 500	WASHINGTON, DC	20044
MOORE, DEBORAH	ACTRESS	427 N CANON DR #205	BEVERLY HILLS, CA	90210
MOORE, DEMI	ACTRESS	1888 CENTURY PARK E #1400	LOS ANGELES, CA	90067
MOORE, DENA	ACTRESS	6116 FULTON AVE #315	VAN NUYS, CA	91401
MOORE, DENNIS "MICKEY"	DIRECTOR	26706 LATIGO SHORE DR	MALIBU, CA	90265
MOORE, DERICK C	NEWS CORRES-WRITER	53 "D" ST, SE	WASHINGTON, DC	20003
MOORE, DICKEY	ACTOR	165 W 46TH ST #907	NEW YORK, NY	10036
MOORE, DOUGLAS G	NEWS CORRESPONDENT	1801-A LEE HWY	FALLS CHURCH, VA	22042
MOORE, DUDLEY	ACTOR-WRITER	5505 OCEAN FRONT WALK	MARINA DEL REY, CA	90292
MOORE, ED	ACTOR	ABC-TV NETWORK, "LOVING"		
		1330 AVE OF THE AMERICAS	NEW YORK, NY	10019
MOORE, EDWARD J	ACTOR	ICM, 8899 BEVERLY BLVD	LOS ANGELES, CA	90048
MOORE, ERNEST L	NEWS CORRESPONDENT	400 N CAPITOL ST, NW	WASHINGTON, DC	20001
MOORE, EVELYN W	WRITER	555 W 57TH ST #1230	NEW YORK, NY	10019
MOORE, FREDERICK P	DIRECTOR	DGA, 7950 SUNSET BLVD	LOS ANGELES, CA	90046
MOORE, G PHIL	PIANIST-CONDUCTOR	8949 SUNSET BLVD #202	LOS ANGELES, CA	90069
MOORE, GARY	SINGER-SONGWRITER	PARK ROCK MANAGEMENT		
MOORE, GARY	TV HOST	12 S CALIBOQUE CAY	HILTON HEAD ISLAND, SC	29928
		4 MONTAGU ROW, 71 BAKER ST	LONDON W1H 1AB	ENGLAND
MOORE, GRADY	GUITARIST	504 RICHMAR DR	NASHVILLE, TN	37211
MOORE, H THOMAS	DIRECTOR	DGA, 7950 SUNSET BLVD	LOS ANGELES, CA	90046
MOORE, IRVING	TV DIRECTOR	5126 RANCHITO AVE	SHERMAN OAKS, CA	91423
MOORE, IVANA	ACTRESS	15010 VENTURA BLVD #219	SHERMAN OAKS, CA	91403
MOORE, JACKIE	SINGER	200 W 51ST ST #1410	NEW YORK, NY	10019
MOORE, JAMES W	DIRECTOR	38 E 19TH ST	NEW YORK, NY	10003
MOORE, JOHN F	TV DIRECTOR	984 ESPLANADE	PELHAM, NY	10803
MOORE, JOHN L	NEWS CORRESPONDENT	807 COTTONWOOD DR	SEVERNA PARK, MD	21146
MOORE, JONATHAN	ACTOR	200 W 57TH ST #1303	NEW YORK, NY	10019
MOORE, JOSEPH PAUL	FILM DIRECTOR	5720 OWENSMOUTH AVE #129	WOODLAND HILLS, CA	91367
MOORE, JUANITA	ACTRESS	856 W 42ND PL	LOS ANGELES, CA	90037
MOORE, JULIANNE	ACTRESS	CBS-TV, "AS THE WORLD TURNS"		
		51 W 52ND ST	NEW YORK, NY	10019
MOORE, KATHY	WRITER	8955 BEVERLY BLVD	LOS ANGELES, CA	90048
MOORE, KATHY	BODYBUILDER	16088 GREEN VALLEY HGTS RD	RAMONA, CA	92065
MOORE, KEITH	GUITARIST	601 OLD NASHVILLE HWY		
		ROUTE #10	MURFREESBORO, TN	37130
MOORE, KELLY	SINGER-GUITARIST	3724 TIBBS DR	NASHVILLE, TN	37211
MOORE, KEN	PIANIST	POST OFFICE BOX 121413	NASHVILLE, TN	37212
MOORE, KENNETH J	COMPOSER-CONDUCTOR	843 MALTMAN AVE	LOS ANGELES, CA	90026
MOORE, KENNY	SPORTS WRITER-EDITOR	SPORTS ILLUSTRATED MAGAZINE		
		TIME & LIFE BUILDING		
		ROCKEFELLER CENTER	NEW YORK, NY	10020
MOORE, KINGMAN	TV DIRECTOR	2750 MARKET ST #202	SAN FRANCISCO, CA	94114
MOORE, LAWRENCE	TV DIRECTOR-PRODUCER	NEW MEDIA, 79 PARKWAY	LONDON NW1 7PP	ENGLAND
MOORE, LESLI NOBLES	TV DIRECTOR	18415 "J" COLLINS ST	TARZANA, CA	91356

MOORE, LEWIS	SINGER	POST OFFICE BOX 383	WEST POINT, GA	31833
MOORE, MARY TYLER	ACTRESS	POST OFFICE BOX 49032	LOS ANGELES, CA	90049
MOORE, MAUREEN	ACTRESS	1650 BROADWAY #302	NEW YORK, NY	10019
MOORE, MELBA	SINGER	HUSH PRODS, 231 W 58TH ST	NEW YORK, NY	10019
MOORE, MICKEY	FILM DIRECTOR	26706 LATIGO SHORE DR	MALIBU, CA	90265
MOORE, MILES DAVID	NEWS CORRESPONDENT	4419 4TH RD #3	ARLINGTON, VA	22203
MOORE, MILLIE	FILM EDITOR	ACE, 4416 1/2 FINLEY AVE	LOS ANGELES, CA	90027
MOORE, MONICA T	NEWS CORRESPONDENT	4507 N WASHINGTON BLVD #B	ARLINGTON, VA	22201
MOORE, NANCY	TV WRITER	555 W 57TH ST #1230	NEW YORK, NY	10019
MOORE, PETER R	FRENCH HORNIST	6250 HILLSBORO RD	NASHVILLE, TN	37215
MOORE, RANDY C	GUITARIST	407 OAKWOOD RD	FRANKLIN, TN	37064
MOORE, RICHARD	CINEMATOGRAPHER	887 CHATTANOOGA AVE	PACIFIC PALISADES, CA	90272
MOORE, RICK	NEWS CORRESPONDENT	CNN, 1050 TECHWOOD DR, NW	ATLANTA, GA	30318
MOORE, ROBERT L, JR	WRITER	555 W 57TH ST #1230	NEW YORK, NY	10019
MOORE, ROBIN	ACTOR	100 W 57TH ST	NEW YORK, NY	10019
MOORE, ROGER	ACTOR	CHALET FENIL	GRUND BEI GSTAAD	SWITZERLAND
MOORE, RONNIE	BANJOIST	ROUTE #9, AMANDA WY	MURFREESBORO, TN	37130
MOORE, RUSSELL T	NEWS CORRESPONDENT	2248 N QUEBEC ST	ARLINGTON, VA	22207
MOORE, SAMUEL	WRITER	555 W 57TH ST #1230	NEW YORK, NY	10019
MOORE, STEVE	CARTOONIST	TRIBUNE MEDIA SERVICES		
		64 E CONCORD ST	ORLANDO, FL	32801
MOORE, SUSAN D	ACTRESS	8721 SUNSET BLVD #202	LOS ANGELES, CA	90069
MOORE, TERRY	ACTRESS	833 OCEAN AVE #104	SANTA MONICA, CA	90403
MOORE, THOMAS	TV PRODUCER-EXECUTIVE	91 DORCHESTER RD	DARIEN, CT	06820
MOORE, THOMAS J	NEWS CORRESPONDENT	18 10TH ST, NE	WASHINGTON, DC	20002
MOORE, THOMAS, JR	TV WRITER	8955 BEVERLY BLVD	LOS ANGELES, CA	90048
MOORE, TIM	SINGER	POST OFFICE BOX 669	WOODSTOCK, NY	12498
MOORE, TOM	TV DIRECTOR	VINCENT ANDREWS MGMT		
		488 MADISON AVE	NEW YORK, NY	10022
MOORE, W JOHN	NEWS CORRESPONDENT	4815 S 28TH ST #B	ARLINGTON, VA	22206
MOORE, WENDELL	SINGER	439 GAINESVILLE AVE	MEMPHIS, TN	38109
MOORE, WINFIELD SCOTT, III	GUITARIST	1609 MC GAVOCK ST #A	NASHVILLE, TN	37203
MOORES, JAMES	PRODUCER	641 CALIFORNIA AVE	VENICE, CA	90291
MOORMAN, JEFFREY R	PHOTOJOURNALIST	11556 ROLLING GREEN CT #300	RESTON, VA	22901
MOOSEKIAN, VAHAN	ACTOR	1321 WELLESLEY AVE #3	LOS ANGELES, CA	90025
MOOVES, LESLIE	ACTOR	3624 MOUNDVIEW AVE	STUDIO CITY, CA	91604
MOOY, LEN	ACTOR	10000 RIVERSIDE DR #3	TOLUCA LAKE, CA	91602
MORA, PHILIPPE	FILM DIRECTOR	409 N CAMDEN DR #105	BEVERLY HILLS, CA	90210
MORABITO, BRUCE D	CONDUCTOR	7609 HINDS AVE	NORTH HOLLYWOOD, CA	91605
MORAGA, PETER	WRITER	3752 MOORE ST	LOS ANGELES, CA	90066
MORAHAN, CHRISTOPHER	DIRECTOR-PRODUCER	LEADING ARTISTS, LTD		
		60 SAINT JAMES'S ST	LONDON SW1	ENGLAND
MORALES, ABRAM	TENOR	CAMI, 165 W 57TH ST	NEW YORK, NY	10019
MORALES, CHRISTOPHER L	NEWS CORRESPONDENT	923 VEIRS MILLS RD	ROCKVILLE, MD	20851
MORALES, ESAI	ACTOR	ICM, 8899 BEVERLY BLVD	LOS ANGELES, CA	90048
MORALES, PEDRO	WRESTLER	POST OFFICE BOX 3859	STAMFORD, CT	06905
MORALES, SANTOS	ACTOR	3907 W ALAMEDA AVE #101	BURBANK, CA	91505
MORALES, SYLVIA	WRITER-PRODUCER	DGA, 7950 SUNSET BLVD	LOS ANGELES, CA	90046
MORALS, DEL	AERIAL CRADLE DUO	HALL, 138 FROG HOLLOW RD	CHURCHVILLE, PA	18966
MORAN, ERIN	ACTRESS	3224 OAKDELL RD	STUDIO CITY, CA	91604
MORAN, GAYLE	SINGER	COREA, 2635 GRIFFITH PARK BLVD	LOS ANGELES, CA	90039
MORAN, LOIS	ACTRESS	POST OFFICE BOX 1088	SEDONA, AZ	86336
MORAN, MARK	NEWS CORRESPONDENT	10414 PARTHENON CT	BETHESDA, MD	20817
MORAN, MICHAEL	NEWS CORRESPONDENT	3941 LANGLEY CT, NW	WASHINGTON, DC	20016
MORAN, PATRICIA RAE	TV WRITER	8955 BEVERLY BLVD	LOS ANGELES, CA	90048
MORAN, SEAN	ACTOR	807 HYPERION AVE #7	LOS ANGELES, CA	90029
MORAN, THOMAS	GUITARIST	POST OFFICE BOX 359	LAKESHORE, MS	39558
MORAN, WILLIAM H	WRITER	555 W 57TH ST #1230	NEW YORK, NY	10019
MORAND, TIMOTHY	ACTOR	THOMAS & BENDA, 361 EDGWARE RD	LONDON W2 1BS	ENGLAND
MORANIS, RICK	ACTOR	9000 SUNSET BLVD #1200	LOS ANGELES, CA	90069
MORANVILLE, JOHN B	DIRECTOR	4624 CAHUENGA BLVD	TOLUCA LAKE, CA	91602
MORATH, INGE	PHOTOGRAPHER	RURAL ROUTE #1, BOX 320	ROXBURY, CT	06783
MORATH, MAX	SINGER	CAMI, 165 W 57TH ST	NEW YORK, NY	10019
MORAVEC, IVAN	PIANIST	IMG ARTISTS, 22 E 71ST ST	NEW YORK, NY	10021
MORDANA, MICHELE	ACTRESS	303 E 71ST ST	NEW YORK, NY	10021
MORDENTE, TONY	DIRECTOR	4541 COMBER AVE	ENCINO, CA	91316
MORDENTI, PHILIP	NEWS CORRESPONDENT	3904 HOLLYVIEW ST	OLNEY, MD	20832
MORE, ALEXANDRA	ACTRESS	5330 LANKERSHIM BLVD #210	NORTH HOLLYWOOD, CA	91601
MORE, CAMILLA	ACTRESS	445 N BEDFORD DR #PH	BEVERLY HILLS, CA	90210
MOREAU, FREDERICK DANIEL	NEWS CORRESPONDENT	403 ELM ST	TAKOMA PARK, MD	20912
MOREHART, DEBORAH	ACTRESS	ABC-TV, "ALL MY CHILDREN"		
		1330 AVE OF THE AMERICAS	NEW YORK, NY	10019
MOREHEAD, FRANK	ACTOR	10032 COLLETT AVE	SEPULVEDA, CA	91343
MOREHEAD, MARTHA B	TV WRITER	8955 BEVERLY BLVD	LOS ANGELES, CA	90048
MOREIN, DONNA	MEZZO-SOPRANO	61 W 62ND ST #6-F	NEW YORK, NY	10023
MOREL, JACQUES	ACTOR	45 BLVD SAINT-JACQUES	PARIS 75014	FRANCE
MORELL, ALBERT BENDER	WRITER	5305 E 2ND ST #201	LONG BEACH, CA	90803
MORELLI, CARL J	BODYBUILDER	605 3RD AVE	NEW YORK, NY	10158
MORENO, AIDA	WRITER	555 W 57TH ST #1230	NEW YORK, NY	10019
MORENO, BELITA	ACTRESS	11726 SAN VICENTE BLVD #300	LOS ANGELES, CA	90049
MORENO, HILDA	DANCER	THE ACTOR'S FUND HOME		
		155 W HUDSON AVE	ENGLEWOOD, NJ	07631
MORENO, JAIME	NEWS CORRESPONDENT	444 N CAPITOL ST, NW	WASHINGTON, DC	20001
MORENO, MARK C	NEWS CORRES-WRITER	ABC NEWS, 1717 DE SALES ST, NW	WASHINGTON, DC	20036
MORENO, RITA	ACTRESS	1620 AMALFI DR	PACIFIC PALISADES, CA	90272

RITA MORENO

JAYE P. MORGAN

MICHAEL MORIARTY

ROBERT MORLEY

GARY MORRIS

GREG MORRIS

BARRY MORSE

MARTIN MULL

CAROLINE MUNRO

Name	Occupation	Address	City	Zip
MORENO, RUBEN	ACTOR	10000 RIVERSIDE DR #3	TOLUCA LAKE, CA	91602
MORESS, STAN	TALENT AGENT	SCOTTI BROS, 2128 PICO BLVD	SANTA MONICA, CA	90405
MOREY, ARTHUR	WRITER	555 W 57TH ST #1230	NEW YORK, NY	10019
MOREY, BILL	ACTOR	6310 SAN VICENTE BLVD #407	LOS ANGELES, CA	90048
MOREY, SEAN	COMEDIAN	2828 3RD ST #17	SANTA MONICA, CA	90405
MORFOGEN, ANN	TV EXECUTIVE	CBS-TV, 524 W 57TH ST	NEW YORK, NY	10019
MORFOGEN, GEORGE J	ACTOR	700 COLUMBUS AVE	NEW YORK, NY	10025
MORGAN, ALEXANDRA	ACTRESS	19710 PACIFIC COAST HWY	MALIBU, CA	90265
MORGAN, ANDRE E	FILM WRITER-PRODUCER	120 S EL CAMINO DR #204	BEVERLY HILLS, CA	90212
MORGAN, ANDREW	TV DIRECTOR	28 WYNDHAM ST	LONDON W1H 1DD	ENGLAND
MORGAN, BARRY	TALENT AGENT	7250 BEVERLY BLVD #200	LOS ANGELES, CA	90036
MORGAN, BEVERLY	SOPRANO	CAMI, 165 W 57TH ST	NEW YORK, NY	10019
MORGAN, CASS	ACTRESS	9229 SUNSET BLVD #306	LOS ANGELES, CA	90069
MORGAN, CHARLENE	SINGER	ROUTE #7, BOX 52-C	MURFREESBORO, TN	37130
MORGAN, CHARLES	WRITER	8955 BEVERLY BLVD	LOS ANGELES, CA	90048
MORGAN, CHRISTINE	NEWS REPORTER	TIME/TIME & LIFE BLDG		
		ROCKEFELLER CENTER	NEW YORK, NY	10020
MORGAN, CHRISTOPHER	WRITER-PRODUCER	10437 SARAH ST	NORTH HOLLYWOOD, CA	91602
MORGAN, CINDY	ACTRESS	9220 SUNSET BLVD #625	LOS ANGELES, CA	90069
MORGAN, DANNY	SINGER	POST OFFICE BOX 6507	CINCINNATI, OH	45206
MORGAN, DEBBI	ACTRESS	ABC-TV, "ALL MY CHILDREN"		
		1330 AVE OF THE AMERICAS	NEW YORK, NY	10019
MORGAN, DENNIS	ACTOR-SINGER	POST OFFICE BOX 3036	AHWAHNEE, CA	93601
MORGAN, DENNIS	GUITARIST	397 LAKEWOOD DR, ROUTE #2	FAIRVIEW, TN	37062
MORGAN, DICK	WRITER	8955 BEVERLY BLVD	LOS ANGELES, CA	90048
MORGAN, DONALD MAXWELL	DIRECTOR	DGA, 7950 SUNSET BLVD	LOS ANGELES, CA	90046
MORGAN, ED	ACTOR	121 N ROBERTSON BLVD #B	BEVERLY HILLS, CA	90211
MORGAN, EDWARD P	NEWS CORRESPONDENT	1211 CREST LN	MC LEAN, VA	22101
MORGAN, ELAINE	PLAYWRIGHT	24 ABERFFRWD RD, MOUNTAIN ASH	GLAMORGAN	ENGLAND
MORGAN, GARY	ACTOR	8444 MAGNOLIA DR	LOS ANGELES, CA	90046
MORGAN, HARRY	ACTOR-DIRECTOR	13172 BOCA DE CANON LN	LOS ANGELES, CA	90049
MORGAN, JACK	COMPOSER	6902 TEXHOMA AVE	VAN NUYS, CA	91406
MORGAN, JANE	ACTRESS	WEINTRAUB, 661 DOHENY RD	BEVERLY HILLS, CA	90210
MORGAN, JAYE P	SINGER-ACTRESS	30130 CUTHBERT	MALIBU, CA	90265
MORGAN, JEFFREY PAUL	ACTOR	5258 CAHUENGA BLVD	NORTH HOLLYWOOD, CA	91601
MORGAN, JINX	WRITER	8955 BEVERLY BLVD	LOS ANGELES, CA	90048
MORGAN, JOHN B	NEWS CORRESPONDENT	529 14TH STREE, NW	WASHINGTON, DC	20045
MORGAN, JOHN W	COMPOSER	18445 COLLINS ST #113	TARZANA, CA	91356
MORGAN, JON	SINGER	LUTZ, 5625 "O" STREET BLDG	LINCOLN, NE	68510
MORGAN, JUSTIN	DIRECTOR-PRODUCER	28525 TRAILRIDERS DR	PALOS VERDES, CA	90274
MORGAN, LORRIE	SINGER	TESSIER, 505 CANTON PASS	MADISON, TN	37115
MORGAN, LYNN MARIE	TV DIRECTOR	8333 COLUMBUS AVE #23	SEPULVEDA, CA	91343
MORGAN, MARGARET	NEWS CORRESPONDENT	1703 DEWITT AVE	ALEXANDRIA, VA	22301
MORGAN, MARSHALL	GUITARIST	703 CANEBRAKE DR	NASHVILLE, TN	37209
MORGAN, MICHAEL D	RECORD EXECUTIVE	POST OFFICE BOX 2388	PRESCOTT, AZ	86302
MORGAN, MICHAEL D	CONDUCTOR	SOFFER, 130 W 56TH ST	NEW YORK, NY	10019
MORGAN, MICHELE	ACTRESS	OLGA HOISTG-PRIMUZ		
		76 CHAMPS-ELYSEES	PARIS 75008	FRANCE
MORGAN, MILES	FILM DIRECTOR	129 E 74TH ST	NEW YORK, NY	10021
MORGAN, NANCY	ACTRESS	9220 SUNSET BLVD #202	LOS ANGELES, CA	90069
MORGAN, PATRICK	DIRECTOR	DGA, 110 W 57TH ST	NEW YORK, NY	10019
MORGAN, PAUL C	DIRECTOR	2705 GLENDOWER AVE	LOS ANGELES, CA	90027
MORGAN, PAULA	WRITER	8955 BEVERLY BLVD	LOS ANGELES, CA	90048
MORGAN, PRISCILLA	ACTRESS	31 NASSAU RD	LONDON SW13	ENGLAND
MORGAN, READ	ACTOR	12524 CULVER BLVD #17	LOS ANGELES, CA	90066
MORGAN, RICHARD W	TV WRITER	8955 BEVERLY BLVD	LOS ANGELES, CA	90048
MORGAN, ROBERT W	RADIO-TV PERSONAILTY	3559 KNOBHILL DR	SHERMAN OAKS, CA	91423
MORGAN, ROBERT W	WRITER	555 W 57TH ST	NEW YORK, NY	10019
MORGAN, RONALD E	ACTOR	5667 PACKARD ST	LOS ANGELES, CA	90019
MORGAN, SEAN	ACTOR	55710 YALE RD	SPOKANE, WA	99203
MORGAN, SHELLEY TAYLOR	ACTRESS	LIGHT, 113 N ROBERTSON BLVD	LOS ANGELES, CA	90048
MORGAN, STAFFORD	ACTOR	1605 N CAHUENGA BLVD #202	LOS ANGELES, CA	90028
MORGAN, THE	MUSIC GROUP	276 CAMBRIDGE ST #4	BOSTON, MA	02134
MORGAN, TONY L	GUITARIST	157 GATONE DR	HENDERSONVILLE, TN	37075
MORGAN, TRACY	ACTRESS	10000 RIVERSIDE DR #3	TOLUCA LAKE, CA	91602
MORGAN-WITTS, MAX	AUTHOR-PRODUCER	CLOWES, 22 PRINCE ALBERT RD	LONDON NW1 7ST	ENGLAND
MORGANSTERN, DANIEL	CELLIST	ACC, 890 W END AVE	NEW YORK, NY	10025
MORGANSTERN, HOWARD	WRITER	8955 BEVERLY BLVD	LOS ANGELES, CA	90048
MORGENROTH, BARBARA A	WRITER	555 W 57TH ST #1230	NEW YORK, NY	10019
MORGENSTERN, MARC	WRITER	555 W 57TH ST #1230	NEW YORK, NY	10019
MORGROVE, RONALD E	TV WRITER	8955 BEVERLY BLVD	LOS ANGELES, CA	90048
MORGULIS, DEBORAH	WRITER	555 W 57TH ST #1230	NEW YORK, NY	10019
MORHAIM, JOSEPH	TV WRITER	2511 ANGELO DR	LOS ANGELES, CA	90077
MORHEIM, LOU	TV WRITER	2511 ANGELO DR	LOS ANGELES, CA	90077
MORI, MITSUTOSHI	NEWS CORRESPONDENT	2500 WISCONSIN AVE, NW	WASHINGTON, DC	20007
MORIARTY, JAY	WRITER	10100 SANTA MONICA BLVD #1600	LOS ANGELES, CA	90067
MORIARTY, MICHAEL	ACTOR	200 W 58TH ST #3-B	NEW YORK, NY	10019
MORICK, DAVE	ACTOR	4851 BEEMAN AVE	NORTH HOLLYWOOD, CA	91607
MORIHARA, KIMITOSHI	NEWS CORRESPONDENT	2062 "O" ST #22, NW	WASHINGTON, DC	20036
MORILINO, JIM	ACTOR	CARPENTER, 1516-W REDWOOD ST	SAN DIEGO, CA	92101
MORIN, ALBERTO	ACTOR	1901 AVE OF THE STARS #840	LOS ANGELES, CA	90067
MORIN, JIM	CARTOONIST	THE MIAMI HERALD		
		1 HERALD PLAZA	MIAMI, FL	33101
MORIN, MICHAEL	ACTOR	AFFILIATE ARTIST, LTD		
		37 W 65TH ST, 6TH FLOOR	NEW YORK, NY	10023

Name	Occupation	Address	City	Zip
MORINA, TONY	TV DIRECTOR	ABC-TV, "ALL MY CHILDREN"		
		1330 AVE OF THE AMERICAS	NEW YORK, NY	10019
MORING, JO	TV EXECUTIVE	NBC TELEVISION NETWORK		
		30 ROCKEFELLER PLAZA	NEW YORK, NY	10112
MORISHIGE, KYOSUKE	NEWS CORRESPONDENT	10516 TYLER TERR	POTOMAC, MD	20854
MORISON, PATRICIA	ACTRESS-SINGER	400 S HAUSER BLVD #9-L	LOS ANGELES, CA	90036
MORISON, ROBERT F	NEWS CORRESPONDENT	7913 BAINBRIDGE RD	ALEXANDRIA, VA	22308
MORITA, AKIHIKO	NEWS CORRESPONDENT	1173 NATIONAL PRESS BLDG		
		529 14TH ST, NW	WASHINGTON, DC	20045
MORITA, NORIYUKI "PAT"	ACTOR -COMEDIAN	CONTEMPORARY ARTISTS		
		132 S LASKY DR	BEVERLY HILLS, CA	90212
MORITZ, LOUISA	ACTRESS-MODEL	2354 JUPITER DR	LOS ANGELES, CA	90046
MORLEY, ANGELA	COMPOSER-CONDUCTOR	23624 DEL CERRO CIR	CANOGA PARK, CA	91304
MORLEY, DONALD	ACTOR	LEADING PLAYERS, 31 KINGS RD	LONDON SW3	ENGLAND
MORLEY, KAREN	ACTRESS	GOUGH, 4411 MATILIJA AVE	SHERMAN OAKS, CA	91423
MORLEY, PETER	DIRECTOR-PRODUCER	81 HILLWAY, HIGHGATE	LONDON N6	ENGLAND
MORLEY, ROBERT	ACTOR	FAIRMANS, WARGRAVE	BERKSHIRE	ENGLAND
MORNING	C & W GROUP	1515 ALMEADA WY #107	SAN JOSE, CA	95126
MOROAICA, HORIA	CONDUCTOR	3332 CALIFORNIA ST	HUNTINGTON PARK, CA	90255
MORODER, GIORGIO	COMPOSER-PRODUCER	4162 LANKERSHIM BLVD	UNIVERSAL CITY, CA	91602
MOROF, RICHARD	ACTOR	7471 MELRSOE AVE #11	LOS ANGELES, CA	90046
MORONES, BOB	CASTING DIRECTOR	733 N SEWARD ST	LOS ANGELES, CA	90038
MORONEY, E J	ACTOR	1150 HOBART AVE	NEW YORK, NY	10461
MORPHET, DAVID	WRITER-PRODUCER	GREENPARK, 101 HONOR OAK PARK	LONDON SE23 3LB	ENGLAND
MORRELL, DAVID	AUTHOR	1805 W BENTON ST	IOWA CITY, IA	52240
MORRELL, STEPHEN	ACTOR	1605 N CAHUENGA BLVD #202	LOS ANGELES, CA	90028
MORRIN, JOHN	WRITER	555 W 57TH ST #1230	NEW YORK, NY	10019
MORRING, FRANK, JR	NEWS CORRESPONDENT	713 "A" ST, NE	WASHINGTON, DC	20002
MORRIS, ANITA	ACTRESS	10100 SANTA MONICA BLVD #1600	LOS ANGELES, CA	90067
MORRIS, BAILEY U	NEWS CORRESPONDENT	5155 MACOMB ST, NW	WASHINGTON, DC	20016
MORRIS, BOB	TV DIRECTOR-PRODUCER	322 E 84TH ST	NEW YORK, NY	10028
MORRIS, BOBBI	CASTING DIRECTOR	439 S LA CIENEGA BLVD	LOS ANGELES, CA	90048
MORRIS, CHRIS	BODYGUARD-MODEL	2801 MEADOW LARK DR	SAN DIEGO, CA	92123
MORRIS, COLIN	PLAYWRIGHT	75 HILLWAY	LONDON N6	ENGLAND
MORRIS, CRAIG D	GUITARIST	158 EVERGREEN CIR	HENDERSONVILLE, TN	37075
MORRIS, DALE CECIL	GUITARIST	816 19TH AVE S	NASHVILLE, TN	37203
MORRIS, DELORES	TV EXECUTIVE	ABC TELEVISION NETWORK		
		1330 AVE OF THE AMERICAS	NEW YORK, NY	10019
MORRIS, DONALD D	FLUTIST	437 ROCKWOOD DR	HERMITAGE, TN	37076
MORRIS, DUANE	ACTOR	484 W 43RD ST #30-L	NEW YORK, NY	10036
MORRIS, EDMUND	WRITER	8955 BEVERLY BLVD	LOS ANGELES, CA	90048
MORRIS, FARRELL	DRUMMER	726 VOSSWOOD DR	NASHVILLE, TN	37205
MORRIS, GARRETT	ACTOR	9200 SUNSET BLVD #1210	LOS ANGELES, CA	90069
MORRIS, GARY	ACTOR-SINGER	MORRIS, 2325 CRESTMOOR RD	NASHVILLE, TN	37215
MORRIS, GARY	GUITARIST	ROUTE #3, HUNTING CREEK RD	FRANKLIN, TN	37064
MORRIS, GEORGIA S	WRITER	555 W 57TH ST #1230	NEW YORK, NY	10019
MORRIS, GREG	ACTOR	6310 SAN VICENTE BLVD #407	LOS ANGELES, CA	90048
MORRIS, HAVILAND	ACTRESS	151 S EL CAMINO DR	BEVERLY HILLS, CA	90212
MORRIS, HOWARD	ACTOR-DIRECTOR	9300 WILSHIRE BLVD #410	BEVERLY HILLS, CA	90212
MORRIS, JAMES	BASSO-BARITONE	COLBERT, 111 W 57TH ST	NEW YORK, NY	10019
MORRIS, JAMES B, JR	WRITER	555 W 57TH ST #1230	NEW YORK, NY	10019
MORRIS, JEFF	ACTOR	15760 VENTURA BLVD #1730	ENCINO, CA	91436
MORRIS, JEREMIAH	TV DIRECTOR	3677 MEADVILLE DR	SHERMAN OAKS, CA	91403
MORRIS, JIM	WRESTLER	SEE - HILLBILLY JIM		
MORRIS, JOHN	CARTOONIST	177 E HARTSDALE AVE	HARTSDALE, NY	10530
MORRIS, KENNETH J	TV WRITER-PRODUCER	1125 N CLARK ST #D	LOS ANGELES, CA	90069
MORRIS, KERRY	PHOTOGRAPHER	MODELS & PROMOTIONS AGENCY		
		8560 SUNSET BLVD, 10TH FLOOR	LOS ANGELES, CA	90069
MORRIS, KIM	MODEL	MODELS & PROMOTIONS AGENCY		
		8560 SUNSET BLVD, 10TH FLOOR	LOS ANGELES, CA	90069
MORRIS, KYLE	TV WRITER	8955 BEVERLY BLVD	LOS ANGELES, CA	90048
MORRIS, LARRY	PHOTOGRAPHER	THE WASHINGTON POST		
		PHOTO DEPARTMENT		
		1150 15TH ST, NW	WASHINGTON, DC	20071
MORRIS, LINDA	TV WRITER	8955 BEVERLY BLVD	LOS ANGELES, CA	90048
MORRIS, LINDA K	SONGWRITER	2920 NEILSON WY #103	SANTA MONICA, CA	90405
MORRIS, MALCOLM	TV DIRECTOR-PRODUCER	25 ROEHAMPTON CLOSE		
		ROEHAMPTON LN	LONDON SW15	ENGLAND
MORRIS, MARK B	DRUMMER	POST OFFICE BOX 12275	NASHVILLE, TN	37212
MORRIS, MARTIN	TV DIRECTOR	4256 CAMELLIA AVE	STUDIO CITY, CA	91604
MORRIS, MARY	ACTRESS	26 COPE PL, KENSINGTON	LONDON W8 6AA	ENGLAND
MORRIS, MICHAEL	TV WRITER	8955 BEVERLY BLVD	LOS ANGELES, CA	90048
MORRIS, NORMAN S	WRITER	555 W 57TH ST #1230	NEW YORK, NY	10019
MORRIS, OSWALD	CINEMATOGRAPHER	HOLBROOK, CHURCH ST		
		FONTMELL MAGNA	DORSET	ENGLAND
MORRIS, PHIL	ACTOR	11909 WEDDINGTON #303	NORTH HOLLYWOOD, CA	91607
MORRIS, RICHARD	ORGANIST	CAMI, 165 W 57TH ST	NEW YORK, NY	10019
MORRIS, RICHARD	SINGER	ICM, 8899 BEVERLY BLVD	LOS ANGELES, CA	90048
MORRIS, RICHARD H	WRITER	3828 CODY RD	SHERMAN OAKS, CA	91403
MORRIS, ROBERT F	TV DIRECTOR	332 E 84TH ST	NEW YORK, NY	10028
MORRIS, ROBERT T	COMPOSER	POST OFFICE BOX 11103	BEVERLY HILLS, CA	90213
MORRIS, RODGER D	PIANIST	4757 KENNYSAW DR	OLD HICKORY, TN	37138
MORRIS, ROY J	TV WRITER-DIRECTOR	1718 SUNSET PLAZA DR	LOS ANGELES, CA	90069
MORRIS, SHERYL	NEWS CORRESPONDENT	1679 31ST ST, NW	WASHINGTON, DC	20007
MORRIS, THOMAS W, JR	NEWS CORRESPONDENT	529 14TH ST, NW	WASHINGTON, DC	20045

Name	Occupation	Address	City	ZIP
MORRIS, VERNON	FIDDLER	POST OFFICE BOX 391	LITTLE ELM, TX	75068
MORRIS, WOLFE	ACTOR	HATTON, 18 JERMYN ST	LONDON SW1Y 6HN	ENGLAND
MORRISON, BOB	GUITARIST	11 VALLEY CT	BRENTWOOD, TN	37027
MORRISON, BUD	DIRECTOR	8383 WILSHIRE BLVD #610	BEVERLY HILLS, CA	90211
MORRISON, C B	NEWS CORRESPONDENT	1015 "E" ST, SE	WASHINGTON, DC	20003
MORRISON, DON	FILM WRITER-DIRECTOR	2 GROSVENOR CT, SLOANE ST	LONDON SW1	ENGLAND
MORRISON, DONALD	WRITER-EDITOR	TIME/TIME & LIFE BLDG		
		ROCKEFELLER CENTER	NEW YORK, NY	10020
MORRISON, ERNIE "SUNSHINE SAMMY	ACTOR	3315 W ADAMS BLVD #3	LOS ANGELES, CA	90018
MORRISON, HAROLD	GUITARIST	226 MORRIS ST	HENDERSONVILLE, TN	37075
MORRISON, HOBBY	DIRECTOR	DGA, 7950 SUNSET BLVD	LOS ANGELES, CA	90046
MORRISON, J S	WRITER	555 W 57TH ST #1230	NEW YORK, NY	10019
MORRISON, JAMES	ACTOR	10100 SANTA MONICA BLVD #1600	LOS ANGELES, CA	90067
MORRISON, JIM	WRESTLER	SEE - HILLBILLY JIM		
MORRISON, MARK	WRITER-EDITOR	US MAGAZINE COMPANY		
		1 DAG HAMMARSKJOLD PLAZA	NEW YORK, NY	10017
MORRISON, MARK L	WRITER	8955 BEVERLY BLVD	LOS ANGELES, CA	90048
MORRISON, MICHAEL D	ACTOR	5626 DE LONGPRE AVE #207	HOLLYWOOD, CA	90028
MORRISON, PAMELA	TV WRITER	8955 BEVERLY BLVD	LOS ANGELES, CA	90048
MORRISON, RAND L	WRITER	555 W 57TH ST #1230	NEW YORK, NY	10019
MORRISON, TONI	WRITER	555 W 57TH ST #1230	NEW YORK, NY	10019
MORRISON, VAN	SINGER-SONGWRITER	12304 SANTA MONICA BLVD #300	LOS ANGELES, CA	90025
MORRISON, WILLIAM C	ACTOR	1418 N HIGHLAND AVE #102	LOS ANGELES, CA	90028
MORRISS, FRANK	FILM EDITOR	10100 SANTA MONICA BLVD #1600	LOS ANGELES, CA	90067
MORRISSEAU, RONALD D	WRITER	555 W 57TH ST #1230	NEW YORK, NY	10019
MORRISSETTE, WALTER E, JR	NEWS CORRESPONDENT	6 E NELSON AVE #308-A	ALEXANDRIA, VA	22301
MORRISSEY, GLENN	ACTOR	8380 MELROSE AVE #310	LOS ANGELES, CA	90069
MORRISSEY, PAUL	WRITER	8955 BEVERLY BLVD	LOS ANGELES, CA	90048
MORROW, BARRY	TV WRITER	8955 BEVERLY BLVD	LOS ANGELES, CA	90048
MORROW, BRYON	ACTOR	8350 SANTA MONICA BLVD #206-A	LOS ANGELES, CA	90069
MORROW, COUSIN BRUCIE	RADIO PERSONALITY	WCBS-FM, 51 W 52ND ST	NEW YORK, NY	10019
MORROW, DAN	BODYBUILDER	POST OFFICE BOX 11883	FRESNO, CA	93775
MORROW, DON	WRESTLER	SEE - MURACO, MAGNIFICENT		
MORROW, DOUGLAS	WRITER	8955 BEVERLY BLVD	LOS ANGELES, CA	90048
MORROW, JEFF	ACTOR	4828 BALBOA AVE #B	ENCINO, CA	91316
MORROW, JO	ACTRESS	DRAPER, 37 W 57TH ST	NEW YORK, NY	10019
MORROW, KAREN	ACTRESS	4231 FAIR AVE	NORTH HOLLYWOOD, CA	91602
MORROW, LANCE	WRITER-EDITOR	TIME/TIME & LIFE BLDG		
		ROCKEFELLER CENTER	NEW YORK, NY	10020
MORROW, MAXWELL	ACTOR	823 S SYCAMORE AVE	LOS ANGELES, CA	90036
MORROW, PAUL DAVID	ACTOR-WRITER	7422 HAZELTINE AVE #1	VAN NUYS, CA	91405
MORROW, TODD	SINGER	XHRM-FM, 4183 M L KING WY	SAN DIEGO, CA	92102
MORROW, WILLIE	RADIO EXECUTIVE	XHRM-FM, 4183 M L KING WY	SAN DIEGO, CA	92112
MORSE, BARRY	ACTOR	POST OFFICE BOX 1572	JASPER, ALBERTA TOE IE	CANADA
MORSE, CARLTON E	WRITER	POST OFFICE BOX 50, STAR ROUTE	REDWOOD CITY, CA	94062
MORSE, JACK	WRITER	3160 HOLLYCREST DR #4	LOS ANGELES, CA	90068
MORSE, JOHN HOLLINGSWORTH	DIRECTOR	3219 OAKDELL LN	STUDIO CITY, CA	91604
MORSE, MAT	DRUMMER	233 WILLOW LN	NASHVILLE, TN	37211
MORSE, RALPH	PHOTOGRAPHER	TIME/TIME & LIFE BLDG		
		ROCKEFELLER CENTER	NEW YORK, NY	10020
MORSE, RICHARDSON	ACTOR	8350 SANTA MONICA BLVD #103	LOS ANGELES, CA	90069
MORSE, ROBERT	ACTOR	STERLING-WINTER COMPANY		
		2040 AVE OF THE STARS	LOS ANGELES, CA	90067
MORSE, ROBERT J	NEWS CORRESPONDENT	224 FOREST DR	FALLS CHRUCH, VA	22046
MORSE, SIDNEY	TV WRITER	8955 BEVERLY BLVD	LOS ANGELES, CA	90048
MORSE, STEVE, BAND	ROCK & ROLL GROUP	ICM, 40 W 57TH ST	NEW YORK, NY	10019
MORSELL, FRED	ACTOR	800 W END AVE	NEW YORK, NY	10025
MORSS, ANTHONY	CONDUCTOR	1199 PARK AVE #1-E	NEW YORK, NY	10028
MORTIMER, CAROLINE	ACTRESS	BRYAN DREW, LTD		
		MEZZANINE QUADRANT HOUSE		
		80-82 REGENT ST	LONDON W1	ENGLAND
MORTIMER, JOHN	PLAYWRIGHT	TURVILLE HEATH COTTAGE		
		HENLEY-ON-THAMES	OXFORDSHIRE	ENGLAND
MORTON, BILL	TV PRODUCER	BBC-TV, KENSINGTON HOUSE		
		RICHMOND WY	LONDON W14	ENGLAND
MORTON, BILLIE	WRITER	8955 BEVERLY BLVD	LOS ANGELES, CA	90048
MORTON, BRUCE A	NEWS CORRESPONDENT	CBS NEWS, 2020 "M" ST, NW	WASHINGTON, DC	20036
MORTON, DAVID	COMPOSER	2254 S WELLESLEY AVE	LOS ANGELES, CA	90064
MORTON, DEBRA S	WRITER	555 W 57TH ST #1230	NEW YORK, NY	10019
MORTON, ERIGI	WRESTLER	POST OFFICE BOX 3859	STAMFORD, CT	06905
MORTON, GARY	COMEDIAN	1000 N ROXBURY DR	BEVERLY HILLS, CA	90210
MORTON, HOWARD	ACTOR	6310 SAN VICENTE BLVD #407	LOS ANGELES, CA	90048
MORTON, JACK	WRITER	8955 BEVERLY BLVD	LOS ANGELES, CA	90048
MORTON, JOE	ACTOR	35 W 92ND ST	NEW YORK, NY	10025
MORTON, JOHN	ACTOR-WRITER	KLAUSNER, 71 PARK AVE	NEW YORK, NY	10016
MORTON, JOSEPH B	DIRECTOR-PRODUCER	212 N GROVE #1-N	OAK PARK, IL	60302
MORTON, JOSHUA DILL	CINEMATOGRAPHER	9 OAK KNOLL GARDEN	PASADENA, CA	91106
MORTON, LAWRENCE	COMPOSER	1113 N SWEETZER AVE	LOS ANGELES, CA	90069
MORTON, LEONARD HUGH, SR	MUSIC ARRANGER	4120 W HAMILTON RD	NASHVILLE, TN	37218
MORTON, LEONARD, JR	PIANIST	810 BLUE RIDGE DR	NASHVILLE, TN	37207
MORTON, MICKEY	ACTOR	10433 WILSHIRE BLVD #120	LOS ANGELES, CA	90024
MORTON, RICHARD	WRESTLER	SEE - MORTON, RICKY		
MORTON, RICKY	WRESTLER	NATIONAL WRESTLING ALLIANCE		
		JIM CROCKETT PROMOTIONS		
		421 BRIARBEND DR	CHARLOTTE, NC	28209

Name	Occupation	Address	City	Zip
MORTON, ROB	SCREENWRITER	8955 BEVERLY BLVD	LOS ANGELES, CA	90048
MORTON, ROBERT E	WRITER	555 W 57TH ST #1230	NEW YORK, NY	10019
MORTON, WAYNE	ACTOR	6535 HASKELL AVE #112	VAN NUYS, CA	91406
MORWOOD, JOEL	WRITER	403 N MARIPOSA ST	BURBANK, CA	91506
MOSCHEO, JOE	PIANIST	BMI, 10 MUSIC SQUARE E	NASHVILLE, TN	37203
MOSCHITTA, JOHN, JR	ACTOR	11726 SAN VICENTE BLVD #300	LOS ANGELES, CA	90049
MOSCONI, WILLIE	BILLARDS	1804 PROSPECT RIDGE	HIDDEN HEIGHTS, NJ	08035
MOSCOW, LARRY	NEWS CORRESPONDENT	2133 WISCONSIN AVE, NW	WASHINGTON, DC	20007
MOSEL, TAD	PLAYWRIGHT	400 E 57TH ST	NEW YORK, NY	10022
MOSER, EDDA	SOPRANO	61 W 62ND ST #6-F	NEW YORK, NY	10023
MOSER, JAMES	WRITER-PRODUCER	24620 MALIBU RD	MALIBU, CA	90265
MOSER, RHONDA	ACTRESS	AMBROSE, 1466 BROADWAY	NEW YORK, NY	10018
MOSER, THOMAS	TENOR	MARIEDL ANDERS ARTISTS MGMT		
		535 EL CAMINO DEL MAR ST	SAN FRANCISCO, CA	94121
MOSES, ALBERT	ACTOR	12 PICKERING CT, GRANVILLE RD	LONDON N22 4EL	ENGLAND
MOSES, BEN	DIRECTOR-PRODUCER	9220 SUNSET BLVD #202	LOS ANGELES, CA	90069
MOSES, BURKE	ACTOR	ABC-TV NETWORK, "LOVING"		
		1330 AVE OF THE AMERICAS	NEW YORK, NY	10019
MOSES, DAVID	ACTOR	10528 CIMARRON ST	LOS ANGELES, CA	90047
MOSES, EDWIN	TRACK & FIELD	20 MIBERLY CIR	DAYTON, OH	45408
MOSES, GAVIN	REPORTER	TIME & PEOPLE MAGAZINE		
		TIME & LIFE BUILDING		
		ROCKEFELLER CENTER	NEW YORK, NY	10020
MOSES, GILBERT	FILM DIRECTOR	449 N HIGHLAND AVE	LOS ANGELES, CA	90036
MOSES, HARRY	ACTOR	13424 GALEWOOD ST	SHERMAN OAKS, CA	91423
MOSES, HARRY	TV PRODUCER	CBS-TV, 524 W 57TH ST	NEW YORK, NY	10019
MOSES, HARRY	WRITER-PRODUCER	103 E 84TH ST	NEW YORK, NY	10028
MOSES, JUDITH	TV PRODUCER-REPORTER	ABC-TV NEWS, "20-20"		
		7 W 66TH ST	NEW YORK, NY	10023
MOSES, KATHRYN	SINGER	GATES, 1845 CLINTON AVE N	ROCHESTER, NY	14621
MOSES, RICK	ACTOR-SINGER	3637 WOODHILL CANYON RD	STUDIO CITY, CA	91604
MOSES, SAM	SPORTS WRITER-EDITOR	SPORTS ILLUSTRATED MAGAZINE		
		TIME & LIFE BUILDING		
		ROCKEFELLER CENTER	NEW YORK, NY	10020
MOSES, SENTA	ACTRESS	8322 BEVERLY BLVD #202	LOS ANGELES, CA	90048
MOSES, WILLIAM R	ACTOR	9200 SUNSET BLVD #931	LOS ANGELES, CA	90069
MOSESON, RICHARD S	WRITER	555 W 57TH ST #1230	NEW YORK, NY	10019
MOSIMAN, MARNIE	ACTRESS	LIGHT, 113 N ROBERTSON BLVD	LOS ANGELES, CA	90048
MOSKOFF, JOHN	ACTOR	6032 WILKINSON AVE	NORTH HOLLYWOOD, CA	91606
MOSKOWITZ, ALAN	TV WRITER	8955 BEVERLY BLVD	LOS ANGELES, CA	90048
MOSKOWITZ, DANIEL B	NEWS CORREPOPNDENT	5026 CATHEDRAL AVE, NW	WASHINGTON, DC	20016
MOSKOWITZ, KEN	NEWS CORRESPONDENT	3235 RITTENHOUSE ST, NW	WASHINGTON, DC	20015
MOSKOWITZ, LARRY	ACTOR	10845 LINDBROOK DR #3	LOS ANGELES, CA	90024
MOSLEY, DAVID L	FRENCH HORNIST	4025 SAINT GERMAINE CT	LOUISVILLE, KY	40207
MOSLEY, IRVIN	ACTOR	3778 6TH AVE	LOS ANGELES, CA	90018
MOSLEY, LEIGH H	PHOTOGRAPHER	1811 WYOMING AVE, NW	WASHINGTON, DC	20009
MOSLEY, ROBERT	BASSO-BARITONE	PERLS, 7 W 96TH ST	NEW YORK, NY	10025
MOSLEY, ROGER E	ACTOR	3756 PRESTWICK DR	LOS ANGELES, CA	90027
MOSNER, MARIANNE	WRITER	11611 MONTANA AVE #2	LOS ANGELES, CA	90049
MOSS, ARNOLD	ACT-WRI-DIR	301 E 66TH ST	NEW YORK, NY	10021
MOSS, BARRY	CASTING DIRECTOR	311 W 43RD ST	NEW YORK, NY	10036
MOSS, CHARLES A	WRITER	555 W 57TH ST #1230	NEW YORK, NY	10019
MOSS, FRANCIS CHANDLER	TV WRITER	8955 BEVERLY BLVD	LOS ANGELES, CA	90048
MOSS, FRANK	FILM WRITER-PRODUCER	12512 CHANDLER BLVD #105	NORTH HOLLYWOOD, CA	91607
MOSS, GENE	ACTOR-WRITER	3429 BONNIE HILL DR	LOS ANGELES, CA	90068
MOSS, GEOFFREY	CARTOONIST	315 E 68TH ST	NEW YORK, NY	10021
MOSS, IRA	RECORD EXECUTIVE	176 BEACH	NEPOSNIT QUEENS, NY	11694
MOSS, JEFFREY	TV WRITER-PRODUCER	CHILDREN'S TV WORKSHOP		
		1 LINCOLN PLAZA	NEW YORK, NY	10023
MOSS, LARRY	ACTOR	6605 HOLLYWOOD BLVD #220	HOLLYWOOD, CA	90028
MOSS, LEONARD L	COMPOSER	POST OFFICE BOX 3448	SANTA MONICA, CA	90403
MOSS, MARSHALL	COMPOSER-CONDUCTOR	1840 DEER HILL TRIAL	TOPANGA, CA	90290
MOSS, RONN	ACTOR	CBS TELEVISION NETWORK		
		"THE BOLD & THE BEAUTIFUL"		
		7800 BEVERLY BLVD	LOS ANGELES, CA	90036
MOSS, STERLING	ACTOR	46 SHEPHERD ST, MAYFAIR	LONDON W1Y 8JN	ENGLAND
MOSS, STEWART	ACTOR	9744 WILSHIRE BLVD #206	BEVERLY HILLS, CA	90212
MOSS, STEWART	TV WRITER	8955 BEVERLY BLVD	LOS ANGELES, CA	90048
MOSS, WAYNE	GUITARIST	1108 CINDERELLA ST	MADISON, TN	37115
MOSS, WINSTON	TV WRITER	4714 RODEO LN #3	LOS ANGELES, CA	90016
MOSS BACK MULE BAND	MUSICAL GROUP	306 S SALINA ST #316	SYRACUSE, NY	13202
MOSS-TRENTON, TONI	ACTRESS	436 N ALTA VISTA BLVD	LOS ANGELES, CA	90036
MOSSBERG, WALTER S	NEWS CORRESPONDENT	5314 41ST ST, NW	WASHINGTON, DC	20015
MOSSIN, RICHARD E	NEWS CORRESPONDENT	4515 WILLARD AVE #619	CHEVY CHASE, MD	20815
MOSSLER, HELEN	TV EXECUTIVE	5555 MELROSE AVE	LOS ANGELES, CA	90038
MOSSMAN, TOM	TV DIRECTOR	24043 W AVE CRESCENTA	VALENCIA, CA	91355
MOST, ABE	COMPOSER	17030 OTSEGO ST	ENCINO, CA	91316
MOST, DONALD	ACTOR	208 S BEVERLY DR #4	BEVERLY HILLS, CA	90212
MOSTEL, JOSHUA	ACTOR	10100 SANTA MONICA BLVD #1600	LOS ANGELES, CA	90067
MOTCH, JACK	COMPOSER	3439 FOWLER AVE	SANTA CLARA, CA	95051
MOTE, THOMAS D	NEWS CORRESPONDENT	2139 WISCONSIN AVE, NW	WASHINGTON, DC	20007

Name	Occupation	Address	City/State	Zip
MOTELS, THE	ROCK & ROLL GROUP	GARAY, 13849 VENTURA BLVD	SHERMAN OAKS, CA	91423
MOTHERSBAUGH, MARK A	WRITER	8955 BEVERLY BLVD	LOS ANGELES, CA	90048
MOTLEY CRUE	ROCK & ROLL GROUP	DOC MC GHEE MANAGEMENT		
		240 CENTRAL PARK S	NEW YORK, NY	10019
MOTORHEAD	ROCK & ROLL GROUP	GWR/PROFILE RECORDS		
		740 BROADWAY	NEW YORK, NY	10003
MOTT, ROBERT L	WRITER	8955 BEVERLY BLVD	LOS ANGELES, CA	90048
MOTTAZ, PHILIPPE-JEAN	NEWS CORRESPONDENT	3721 "R" ST, NW	WASHINGTON, DC	20007
MOTTOLA, LORRAINE	WRITER	555 W 57TH ST #1230	NEW YORK, NY	10019
MOTTOLA, TOMMY	TALENT AGENT	130 W 57TH ST #2-A	NEW YORK, NY	10019
MOULD, DAVID	NEWS CORRESPONDENT	1325 15TH ST #403, NW	WASHINGTON, DC	20005
MOULTON, HERBERT L	WRITER	8955 BEVERLY BLVD	LOS ANGELES, CA	90048
MOULTON, LESLIE	TV DIRECTOR	11732 NE 102ND PL	KIRKLAND, WA	98033
MOULTON, PAUL LEE	PHOTOJOURNALIST	5234 LEEWARD LN	ALEXANDRIA, VA	22310
MOUNT, PEGGY	ACTRESS	THE RICHARD STONE AGENCY		
		18-20 YORK BOULDING, ADELPHI	LONDON WC2N 6JY	ENGLAND
MOUNT FUJI	WRESTLER	GORGEOUS LADIES OF WRESTLING		
		RIVIERA HOTEL & CASINO		
		DAVID B MC LANE PRODS		
		2901 S LAS VEGAS BLVD	LAS VEGAS, NV	89109
MOUNTAIN	ROCK & ROLL GROUP	310 MADISON AVE #804	NEW YORK, NY	10017
MOUNTAIN, SALLY	SINGER	POST OFFICE DRAWER 160	HENDERSONVILLE, TN	37075
MOUNTAIN, STEVE	TALENT AGENT	CORNERSTONE MANAGEMENT		
		23 E LANCASTER AVE	ARDMORE, PA	19003
MOUSKOURI, NANA	SINGER	10100 SANTA MONICA BLVD #1600	LOS ANGELES, CA	90067
MOVING PICTURES, THE	MUSIC GROUP	10100 SANTA MONICA BLVD #1600	LOS ANGELES, CA	90067
MOVING TARGETS	ROCK & ROLL GROUP	195 HIGH ST	IPSWICH, MA	01938
MOVITA	ACTRESS	2766 MOTOR AVE	LOS ANGELES, CA	90064
MOWER, BERNARD H	NEWS CORRESPONDENT	1318 22ND ST #502, NW	WASHINGTON, DC	20037
MOWER, JOAN	NEWS CORRESPONDENT	4034 N 21ST ST	ARLINGTON, VA	22207
MOWER, PATRICK	ACTOR	LONDON MANAGEMENT, LTD		
		235-241 REGENT ST	LONDON W1A 2JT	ENGLAND
MOWERY, CARRIE	ACTRESS	439 S LA CIENEGA BLVD #120	LOS ANGELES, CA	90048
MOWERY, CHARLES	DRUMMER	POST OFFICE BOX 35	WHITES CREEK, TN	37189
MOWERY, JAMES WILLIAM	TV DIRECTOR	1517 E GARFIELD AVE #114	GLENDALE, CA	91205
MOXEY, JOHN LLEWELLYN	DIRECTOR	22313 CARBON MESA RD	MALIBU, CA	90265
MOYA, ANGELA	ACTRESS	8230 BEVERLY BLVD #23	LOS ANGELES, CA	90048
MOYE, MICHAEL	TV WRITER-PRODUCER	EMBASSY TV, 1438 N GOWER ST	LOS ANGELES, CA	90028
MOYER, FREDERICK	PIANIST	AFFILIATE ARTISTS, INC		
		37 W 65TH ST, 6TH FLOOR	NEW YORK, NY	10023
MOYER, ROBIN	PHOTOGRAPHER	TIME/TIME & LIFE BLDG		
		ROCKEFELLER CENTER	NEW YORK, NY	10020
MOYER, TAWNY	ACTRESS	9200 SUNSET BLVD #931	LOS ANGELES, CA	90069
MOYER, TOM	FILM PRODUCER	6464 HOLISTER AVE	GOLETA, CA	93117
MOYERS, BILL	NEWS CORRESPONDENT	CBS NEWS, 51 W 52ND ST	NEW YORK, NY	10019
MOYERS, WALLY	GUITARIST	3009 45TH ST	LUBBOCK, TX	79413
MOYLE, ALLAN	WRITER-PRODUCER	49 PARK AVE	NEW YORK, NY	10016
MOZART ON FIFTH	JAZZ TRIO	MAINSTAGE MANAGEMENT		
		976 CAPTAIN'S WALK	ANNAPOLIS, MD	21403
MOZART STRING TRIO	STRING TRIO	SHAW CONCERTS, 1995 BROADWAY	NEW YORK, NY	10023
MR ATLANTA	WRESTLER	SEE - MC DANIEL, CHIEF WAHOO		
		SEE - BLACKWELL, EARL "MR"		
MR CPR	BODYGUARD-BODYBUILDER	SEE - BELL, DAVID "MR CPR"		
MR ELECTRICITY	WRESTLER	SEE - REGAL, STEVE		
		"MR ELECTRICITY"		
MR EXCITEMENT	COMEDIAN-ACTOR	SEE - RICKLES, DON		
MR FUJI	WRESTLER-MANAGER	SEE - FUJI, MR		
MR MAGNIFICENT	WRESTLER	SEE - KELLY, KEVIN		
		"MR MAGNIFICENT"		
MR MISTER	ROCK & ROLL GROUP	POST OFFICE BOX 69343	LOS ANGELES, CA	90069
MR T	ACTOR	SEE - T, MR		
MR USA	WRESTLER	SEE - ATLAS, TONY		
MR W	WRESTLER	SEE - ORNDORFF, PAUL		
		"MR WONDERFUL"		
MR WIZARD	TV PERSONALITY	SEE - HERBERT, DON "MR WIZARD"		
MR WONDERFUL	WRESTLER	SEE - ORNDORFF, PAUL		
		"MR WONDERFUL"		
MR WRESTLING	WRESTLER	SEE - FUNK, JIMMY JACK		
MR WRESTLING #2	WRESTLER	SEE - HERNANDEZ, HERCULES		
MR X	WRESTLER	SEE - X, MR		
MUCKEY, BILL	WRESTLER	NATIONAL WRESTLING ALLIANCE		
		JIM CROCKETT PROMOTIONS		
		421 BRIARBEND DR	CHARLOTTE, NC	28209
MUCKEY, RANDY	WRESTLER	NATIONAL WRESTLING ALLIANCE		
		JIM CROCKETT PROMOTIONS		
		421 BRIARBEND DR	CHARLOTTE, NC	28209
MUDD, ROGER	NEWS CORRESPONDENT	7167 OLD DOMINION DR	MC LEAN, VA	22101
MUELLER, DON RUSSELL	ACTOR	432 S NORTON AVE #305	LOS ANGELES, CA	90020
MUELLER, ELAINE	TV WRITER	8955 BEVERLY BLVD	LOS ANGELES, CA	90048
MUELLER, INGOLF	NEWS CORRESPONDENT	3132 "M" ST	WASHINGTON, DC	20007
MUELLER, JEFF	PRODUCER	LICHT, 4000 WARNER BLVD	BURBANK, CA	91522
MUELLER, JOHN W, JR	NEWS CORRESPONDENT	1301 PENNSYLVANIA AVE, NW	WASHINGTON, DC	20004
MUELLER, JUDY	ACTRESS	1126 N FORMOSA AVE #4	LOS ANGELES, CA	90046
MUELLER, LEO	CONDUCTOR	SCHWEIZERTALSTRASSE, S I 20	A-1130 VIENNA	AUSTRIA
MUELLER, PETE	CARTOONIST	THE READER, 635 STATE ST	SAN DIEGO, CA	92101

Name	Occupation	Address	City
MUELLER, ZIZI	FLUTIST	ALLIED ARTISTS, 170 W 74TH ST	NEW YORK, NY 10023
MUELLER-STAHL, ARMIN	ACTOR	KOHNER, 9169 SUNSET BLVD	LOS ANGELES, CA 90069
MUENSTER, PETRA	NEWS CORRESPONDENT	2103 ELLIOTT AVE	MC LEAN, VA 22101
MUENSTER, WINFRED P	NEWS CORRESPONDENT	2103 ELLIOTT AVE	MC LEAN, VA 22101
MUGHAN, SHARON	ACTRESS	HEATH, PARAMOUNT HOUSE	
		162-170 WARDOUR ST	LONDON W1V 3AT ENGLAND
MUGLESTONS, THE	ROCK & ROLL GROUP	MUGS, 10336 PARISE DR	WHITTIER, CA 90604
MUHAMMAD, BURNELL	BODYBUILDER	POST OFFICE BOX FLOOR 374	FLATS 3 BERMUDA
MUHAMMAD, MARGARET	BODYBUILDER	POST OFFICE BOX FLOOR 374	FLATS 3 BERMUDA
MUHAMMAD, OZIER	PHOTOGRAPHER	89-15 PARSONS BLVD	JAMAICA, NY 11432
MUHEIM, HARRY	WRITER	555 W 57TH ST #1230	NEW YORK, NY 10019
MUIR, ALLAN L	DIRECTOR	DGA, 7950 SUNSET BLVD	LOS ANGELES, CA 90046
MUIR, DAVID	ACTOR	8350 SANTA MONICA BLVD #103	LOS ANGELES, CA 90069
MUIR, FRANK	TV EXECUTIVE	YOUNG, 31 KINGS RD	LONDON SW3 4RP ENGLAND
MUIR, GRAEME	TV PRODUCER	MENDIP COTTAGE, RENFEW RD	
		COOMBE, KINGSTON-UPON-THAMES	SURREY ENGLAND
MUIR, JEAN	ACTRESS	UNIVERSITY OF NEW MEXICO	
		THEATER ARTS DEPARTMENT	
		CENTRAL & UNIVERSITY	ALBUQUERQUE, NM 87131
MUIR, JEAN	FASHION DESIGNER	22 BRUTON ST	LONDON W1 ENGLAND
MULA, FRANK C	TV WRITER	5043 BUFFALO AVE #3	SHERMAN OAKS, CA 91423
MULCAHEY, PATRICK	TV WRITER	KNBC-TV, "SANTA BARBARA"	
		3000 W ALAMEDA AVE	BURBANK, CA 91523
MULCAHY, RUSSELL	FILM DIRECTOR	SEIFERT, 8-A BRUNSWICK GARDENS	LONDON W8 4AJ ENGLAND
MULCAHY, TERENCE	WRITER	8955 BEVERLY BLVD	LOS ANGELES, CA 90048
MULDAUR, DIANA	ACTRESS	259 QUADRO VECCHIO ST	PACIFIC PALISADES, CA 90272
MULDAUR, MARIA	SINGER-SONGWRITER	POST OFFICE BOX 5535	MILL VALLEY, CA 94942
MULDOON, THOMAS L	NEWS REPORTER	THE NATIONAL ENQUIRER	
		600 SE COAST AVE	LANTANA, FL 33464
MULE DEER, GARY	COMEDIAN	POST OFFICE BOX 4003	BEVERLY HILLS, CA 90213
MULERS, JOHN	NEWS CORRESPONDENT	NBC-TV, NEWS DEPARTMENT	
		4001 NEBRASKA AVE, NW	WASHINGTON, DC 20016
MULFORD, LOU	ACTRESS	6310 SAN VICENTE BLVD #407	LOS ANGELES, CA 90048
MULGREW, KATE	ACTRESS	9220 SUNSET BLVD #625	LOS ANGELES, CA 90069
MULHALL, JOHN ANTHONY	WRITER	8955 BEVERLY BLVD	LOS ANGELES, CA 90048
MULHARE, EDWARD	ACTOR	606 WILSHIRE BLVD #614	SANTA MONICA, CA 90401
MULHERN, SCOTT E	WRITER	8955 BEVERLY BLVD	LOS ANGELES, CA 90048
MULHOLLAND, BARRY	ACTOR	5950 CARLTON WY #1	HOLLYWOOD, CA 90028
MULHOLLAND, BRIAN	ACTOR	5950 CARLTON WY #1	HOLLYWOOD, CA 90028
MULHOLLAND, JAMES C	TV WRITER	8955 BEVERLY BLVD	LOS ANGELES, CA 90048
MULHOLLAND, KEVIN M	TV WRITER	8955 BEVERLY BLVD	LOS ANGELES, CA 90048
MULHOLLAND, ROBERT E	TV EXECUTIVE	NBC TELEVISION NETWORK	
		30 ROCKEFELLER PLAZA	NEW YORK, NY 10112
MULIN, DENNIS	NEWS CORRESPONDENT	1200 23RD ST, NW	WASHINGTON, DC 20037
MULKEY, ABE	GUITARIST	10 BRENTFORD CIR	SACRAMENTO, CA 95823
MULKEY, CHRIS	ACTOR	918 VENEZIA AVE	VENICE, CA 90291
MULL, MARTIN	ACT-WRI-COMED	9000 SUNSET BLVD #1200	LOS ANGELES, CA 90069
MULLALLY, DONN	WRITER	8955 BEVERLY BLVD	LOS ANGELES, CA 90048
MULLALLY, FREDERIC	WRITER	8955 BEVERLY BLVD	LOS ANGELES, CA 90048
MULLALLY, MICHAEL F	DIRECTOR	11292 CANTON DR	STUDIO CITY, CA 91604
MULLARD, ARTHUR	ACTOR	2 MANNING HOUSE	
		FIELDING CRESCENT	LONDON N5 ENGLAND
MULLARD, IAN	TALENT AGENT	BOXERCARE MUSIC LTD	
		21 WIGMORE ST	LONDON W1 ENGLAND
MULLAVEY, GREG	ACTOR	4430 HAYVENHURST AVE	ENCINO, CA 91436
MULLEN, GREGG	WRITER	555 W 57TH ST #1230	NEW YORK, NY 10019
MULLEN, MARJORIE	TV DIRECTOR	9203 SUMMERTIME LN	CULVER CITY, CA 90230
MULLENDORE, JOS	COMPOSER	1590 PLEASANT WY	PASADENA, CA 91105
MULLER, ALFRED	DIRECTOR	NEXUS, 10 E 40TH ST	NEW YORK, NY 10011
MULLER, HENRY	WRITER-EDITOR	TIME & LIFE MAGAZINES	
		TIME & LIFE BUILDING	
		ROCKEFELLER CENTER	NEW YORK, NY 10020
MULLER, HERB	ACTOR	6472 SANTA MONICA BLVD #206	HOLLYWOOD, CA 90038
MULLER, LILLIAN	ACTRESS-MODEL	SEE - RUVAL, YULIIS	
MULLER, ROBERT	SCREENWRITER	2 CAMDEN SQ	LONDON NW1 ENGLAND
MULLER, ROMERO, JR	TV WRITER	555 W 57TH ST #1230	NEW YORK, NY 10019
MULLER-LORENZ, WOLFGANG	TENOR	CAMI, 165 W 57TH ST	NEW YORK, NY 10019
MULLIGAN, BLACK JACK	WRESTLER	POST OFFICE BOX 3859	STAMFORD, CT 06905
MULLIGAN, BLACKJACK	WRESTLER	POST OFFICE BOX 3859	STAMFORD, CT 06905
MULLIGAN, GERARD A	TV WRITER	ICM, 40 W 57TH ST	NEW YORK, NY 10019
MULLIGAN, JAMES	CARTOONIST	POST OFFICE BOX 4203	NEW YORK, NY 10017
MULLIGAN, JAMES M	TV WRITER	30507 RHONE DR	RANCHO PALISADES, CA 90274
MULLIGAN, RICHARD	ACTOR	145 S BEACHWOOD DR	LOS ANGELES, CA 90004
MULLIGAN, ROBERT	DIRECTOR-PRODUCER	1120 STONE CANYON RD	LOS ANGELES, CA 90077
MULLIKEN, STEPHANIE	WRITER	555 W 57TH ST #1230	NEW YORK, NY 10019
MULLIKIN, BILL	ACTOR	9630 CEDROS AVE	PANORAMA CITY, CA 91402
MULLINGS, PETER	TV DIRECTOR-PRODUCER	2 PENRITH, SALE	CHESHIRE ENGLAND
MULLINS, CAM	MUSIC ARRANGER	1409 WINTHORNE DR	NASHVILLE, TN 37217
MULLINS, DUNCAN	GUITARIST	1614 18TH AVE S	NASHVILLE, TN 37212
MULLINS, GENE A	MUSICIAN	6417 THUNDERBIRD DR	NASHVILLE, TN 37209
MULLINS, JAMES E	WRITER	555 W 57TH ST #1230	NEW YORK, NY 10019
MULLINS, JOE	NEWS REPORTER	THE NATIONAL ENQUIRER	
		600 SE COAST AVE	LANTANA, FL 33464
MULLINS, KENNY	SINGER	POST OFFICE BOX 1084	NEWARK, DE 19175
MULLINS, MARCY ECKROTH	CARTOONIST	POST OFFICE BOX 500	WASHINGTON, DC 20044

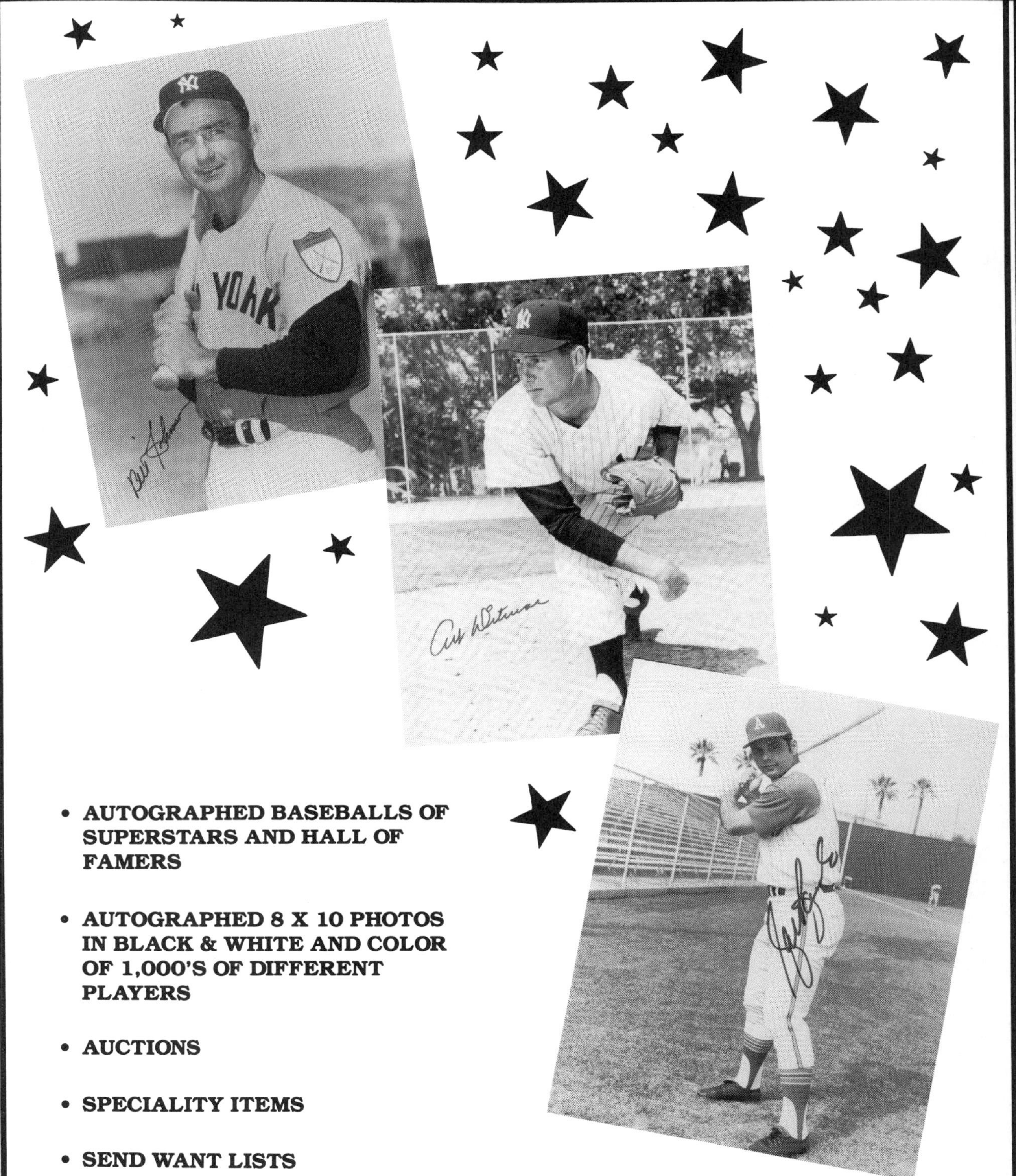

THE NATIONAL PASTIME
93 ISELIN DRIVE, NEW ROCHELLE, NY 10804
(Tel: (914) 576-1755 OR (718) 224-1795)
SEND A S.A.S.E. FOR A COMPLETE LIST OF AVAILABLE PHOTOS AND BASEBALLS.

Name	Occupation	Address	City
MULLINS, MICHAEL	ACTOR	1850 N WHITLEY AVE #706	HOLLYWOOD, CA 90028
MULLINS, PETER	ART DIRECTOR	11 WARWICK GARDENS	LONDON W14 ENGLAND
MULLOVA, VIKTORIA	VIOLINIST	CAMI, 165 W 57TH ST	NEW YORK, NY 10019
MULLOWNEY, DEBORAH	ACTRESS	151 S EL CAMINO DR	BEVERLY HILLS, CA 90212
MULVOY, MARK	WRITER-EDITOR	SPORTS ILLUSTRATED MAGAZINE	
		TIME & LIFE BUILDING	
		ROCKEFELLER CENTER	NEW YORK, NY 10020
MUMFORD, THAD	TV WRITER	3130 OAKSHIRE DR	LOS ANGELES, CA 90068
MUMMERT, EDWARD	PERCUSSIONIST	1024 DRUMMOND DR #A	NASHVILLE, TN 37211
MUMMERT, ROBERT	DRUMMER	1024 DRUMMOND DR #A	NASHVILLE, TN 37211
MUMMY CALLS	ROCK & ROLL GROUP	GEFFEN RECORDS COMPANY	
		9130 SUNSET BLVD	LOS ANGELES, CA 90069
MUMOLO, TONY	ACTOR	2133 1/2 HOLLY DR	LOS ANGELES, CA 90068
MUMY, BILL	ACTOR	2419 LAUREL PASS AVE	LOS ANGELES, CA 90046
MUNDAHL, MITCHELL	ACTOR	7800 MC LAREN AVE	CANOGA PARK, CA 91304
MUNDAY, MARY	WRITER	8955 BEVERLY BLVD	LOS ANGELES, CA 90048
MUNDE, ALAN	BANJOIST	2701 WALNUT RD	NORMAN, OK 73069
MUNDEN, SHARON	MEZZO-SOPRANO	LEW, 204 W 10TH ST	NEW YORK, NY 10014
MUNE, IAN	ACTOR-WRITER	8955 BEVERLY BLVD	LOS ANGELES, CA 90048
MUNFORD, MABEL	NEWS CORRESPONDENT	1353 KENNEDY ST, NW	WASHINGTON, DC 20011
MUNGER, WILLIAM	TV WRITER	8955 BEVERLY BLVD	LOS ANGELES, CA 90048
MUNISTERI, MARY R	TV WRITER	555 W 57TH ST #1230	NEW YORK, NY 10019
MUNNOCH, PHILIP	TV WRITER	1 MILE END RD	LONDON E1 ENGLAND
MUNOZ, DANIEL	TENOR	LIEBERMAN, 11 RIVERSIDE DR	NEW YORK, NY 10023
MUNOZ, CHRISTOPHER	HUMAN CANNONBALL	POST OFFICE BOX 87	WEST LEBANON, NY 12195
MUNRO, CAROLINE	ACTRESS-MODEL	ICM, 388-396 OXFORD ST	LONDON W1N 9HE ENGLAND
MUNRO, DAVID I	TV DIRECTOR	19 CHEYNE ROW	LONDON SW3 5HW ENGLAND
MUNRO, J RICHARD	PUBLISHING EXECUTIVE	TIME/TIME & LIFE BLDG	
		ROCKEFELLER CENTER	NEW YORK, NY 10020
MUNRO, LEIGH	SOPRANO	61 W 62ND ST #6-F	NEW YORK, NY 10023
MUNRO, ROSS H	NEWS CORRESPONDENT	2711 N UPSHUR ST	ARLINGTON, VA 22207
MUNRO, STEPHEN P	NEWS CORRESPONDENT	1737 "U" ST, NW	WASHINGTON, DC 20009
MUNROE, LORNE	CELLIST	GERSHUNOFF, 502 PARK AVE	NEW YORK, NY 10022
MUNROE, WILLIAM	WRITER	555 W 57TH ST #1230	NEW YORK, NY 10019
MUNSEL, PATRICE	ACTRESS-SINGER	337 LATTINGTOWN RD	LOCUST VALLEY, LI, NY 11560
MUNSHOWER, THOMAS PAUL	DIRECTOR	1380 E SAHARA BLVD	LAS VEGAS, NV 81904
MUNSON, SARA	MODEL	POST OFFICE BOX 7211	MOUNTAIN VIEW, CA 94043
MUNTNER, SIMON	TV WRITER	9200 SUNSET BLVD #431	LOS ANGELES, CA 90069
MUNZER, CYNTHIA	MEZZO-SOPRANO	CAMI, 165 W 57TH ST	NEW YORK, NY 10019
MUPPETS, THE	PUPPETS	227 E 67TH ST	NEW YORK, NY 10021
MURACO, DON	WRESTLER	SEE - MURACO, "DON" MAGNIFICENT	
MURACO, DON "MAGNIFICENT"	WRESTLER	POST OFFICE BOX 3859	STAMFORD, CT 06905
MURACO, MAGNIFICENT	WRESTLER	SEE - MURACO, DON "MAGNIFICENT"	
MURAD, MAURICE	TV WRITER-DIRECTOR	3 TRAILSIDE CT	NEW YORK, NY 10956
MURADIAN, VAZGEN	COMPOSER	260 W END AVE #7-A	NEW YORK, NY 10023
MURAKOSHI, SUZEN HARUE	ACTRESS	337 E 18TH ST #4-B	NEW YORK, NY 10003
MURARI, TIMERI	WRITER	555 W 57TH ST #1230	NEW YORK, NY 10019
MURCELO, KARMIN	ACTRESS	211 S BEVERLY DR #201	BEVERLY HILLS, CA 90212
MURCH, WALTER S	WRITER	8955 BEVERLY BLVD	LOS ANGELES, CA 90048
MURCHISON, WILLIAM	COLUMNIST	POST OFFICE BOX 225237	DALLAS, TX 75265
MURCOTT, DEREK	ACTOR	D EISEN, 154 E 61ST ST	NEW YORK, NY 10021
MURDICH, BIG DADDY	WRESTLER	SEE - MURDICH, DICK	
MURDICH, DICK	WRESTLER	NATIONAL WRESTLING ALLIANCE	
		JIM CROCKETT PROMOTIONS	
		421 BRIARBEND DR	CHARLOTTE, NC 28209
MURDOCH, HART DICK	WRESTLER	SEE - MURDOCH, DICK	
MURDOCH, RICHARD	ACTOR	THE END COTTAGE, HURST DR	
		WALTON-ON-THE-HILL, TADWORTH	SURREY KT20 7QT ENGLAND
MURDOCK, ALEC	ACTOR	1208 BROADWAY #5	SANTA MONICA, CA 90404
MURDOCK, ALLAN R	DIRECTOR	26751 SIMONE	DEARBORN HEIGHTS, MI 48127
MURDOCK, GEORGE	ACTOR	9255 SUNSET BLVD #603	LOS ANGELES, CA 90069
MURDOCK, JACK	ACTOR	11726 SAN VICENTE BLVD #300	LOS ANGELES, CA 90049
MURDOCK, KIM	ACTRESS	9230 OLYMPIC BLVD #203	BEVERLY HILLS, CA 90212
MURDOCK, LYDIA	SINGER	MALAMUD, MEDIA CONSULTANTS	
		14923 CYPRESS HILLS	DALLAS, TX 75248
MURDOCK, RUPERT	PUBLISHING EXECUTIVE	660 WHITE PLAINS RD	TARRYTOWN, NY 10591
MURGU, CORNELIU	TENOR	CAMI, 165 W 57TH ST	NEW YORK, NY 10019
MURLEY, ALLAN	ACTOR	19 W 44TH ST #1500	NEW YORK, NY 10036
MUROVICH, LUCILLE	DIRECTOR	DGA, 110 W 57TH ST	NEW YORK, NY 10019
MURPHEY, DEE	WRITER	8955 BEVERLY BLVD	LOS ANGELES, CA 90048
MURPHEY, DENISE M	WRITER	4265 COLFAX AVE #20	STUDIO CITY, CA 91604
MURPHY	C & W GROUP	TM, 1019 17TH AVE S	NASHVILLE, TN 37212
MURPHY, BEN	ACTOR	23906 DE VILLE WY	MALIBU, CA 90265
MURPHY, BETTY	ACTRESS	SCHOEMAN, 2600 W VICTORY BLVD	BURBANK, CA 91505
MURPHY, BRIAN	ACTOR	35 GILDEN RD	LONDON NW5 ENGLAND
MURPHY, CHARLES THOMAS	ACTOR	247 S BEVERLY DR #102	BEVERLY HILLS, CA 90210
MURPHY, CULLEN	CARTOONIST	KING FEATURES SYNDICATE	
		235 E 45TH ST	NEW YORK, NY 10017
MURPHY, DALE	BASEBALL	12055 HOUZE RD	ROSWELL, GA 30076
MURPHY, DANIEL C	NEWS CORRESPONDENT	1825 "K" ST, NW	WASHINGTON, DC 20006
MURPHY, DELWYN B	SAXOPHONIST	ROUTE #1, BOX 42	ADAMS, TN 37010
MURPHY, DOUGLAS	NEWS CORRESPONDENT	1607-A CORCORAN ST, NW	WASHINGTON, DC 20009
MURPHY, E DANNY	ACTOR	9441 WILSHIRE BLVD #620-D	BEVERLY HILLS, CA 90210
MURPHY, EDDIE	ACT-COMED-WRI	ENTERTAINMENT MGMT ASSOC	
		232 E 63RD ST	NEW YORK, NY 10021

MURPHY, EDWARD D	NEWS CORRESPONDENT	4409 DUKE ST #204	ALEXANDRIA, VA	22304
MURPHY, EMMETT	WRITER	555 W 57TH ST #1230	NEW YORK, NY	10019
MURPHY, GARY	TV WRITER	8955 BEVERLY BLVD	LOS ANGELES, CA	90048
MURPHY, GEORGE	ACTOR-POLITICIAN	100 WORTH AVE #419	PALM BEACH, FL	33480
MURPHY, J AUSTIN	SPORTS REPORTER	SPORTS ILLUSTRATED MAGAZINE		
		TIME & LIFE BUILDING		
		ROCKEFELLER CENTER	NEW YORK, NY	10020
MURPHY, JAMES T	WRITER	555 W 57TH ST #1230	NEW YORK, NY	10019
MURPHY, JAMES W	GUITARIST	5300 VANDERBILT RD	MOUNT JULIET, TN	37122
MURPHY, JAMIE	WRITER-EDITOR	TIME/TIME & LIFE BLDG		
		ROCKEFELLER CENTER	NEW YORK, NY	10020
MURPHY, JEREMIAH	SINGER	3426 CROFFUT PL, SE	WASHINGTON, DC	20019
MURPHY, JEREMIAH & UNLIMITED PR	GOSPEL GROUP	3426 CROFFUT PL, SE	WASHINGTON, DC	20019
MURPHY, JOHN B "JACK"	DIRECTOR	2133 NE 19TH AVE	FORT LAUDERDALE, FL	33305
MURPHY, JOHN CULLEN	ILLUSTRATOR	14 MEAD AVE	COS COB, CT	06807
MURPHY, JOHN L	PHOTOGRAPHER	2206 MARTHAS RD	ALEXANDRIA, VA	22307
MURPHY, JOHN P	TV DIRECTOR	DGA, 7950 SUNSET BLVD	LOS ANGELES, CA	90046
MURPHY, JOHN W	DIRECTOR	17400 BURBANK BLVD #221	ENCINO, CA	91316
MURPHY, KATHLEEN C	WRITER	8955 BEVERLY BLVD	LOS ANGELES, CA	90048
MURPHY, LYLE "SPUD"	COMPOSER-CONDUCTOR	817 N VINE ST	LOS ANGELES, CA	90038
MURPHY, M P	ACTOR	11030 VENTURA BLVD #3	STUDIO CITY, CA	91604
MURPHY, MARVIN	NEWS CORRESPONDENT	6038 RICHMOND HWY #503	ALEXANDRIA, VA	22303
MURPHY, MAUREEN	COMEDIENNE	6310 SAN VICENTE BLVD #407	LOS ANGELES, CA	90048
MURPHY, MAUREEN P	TV WRITER	8955 BEVERLY BLVD	LOS ANGELES, CA	90048
MURPHY, MEGAN	BALLERINA	SEE - MATHESON, MEGAN MURPHY		
MURPHY, MICHAEL	ACTOR	1888 CENTURY PARK E #1400	LOS ANGELES, CA	90067
MURPHY, MICHAEL	PHOTOGRAPHER	8817 HUNTING LN	LAUREL, MD	20708
MURPHY, MICHAEL M	NEWS CORRESPONDENT	611 49TH ST, NE	WASHINGTON, DC	20019
MURPHY, MICHAEL MARTIN	SINGER-GUITARIST	POST OFFICE BOX FFF	TAOS, NM	87571
MURPHY, PATRICIA A	NEWS CORRESPONDENT	6807 WOODLAND AVE	TAKOMA PARK, MD	20912
MURPHY, PATRICIA C	WRITER	555 W 57TH ST #1230	NEW YORK, NY	10019
MURPHY, RED	GUITARIST	1508 DICKERSON RD #C-13	NASHVILLE, TN	37207
MURPHY, RICHARD	WRITER-PRODUCER	8428 MELROSE PL #C	LOS ANGELES, CA	90069
MURPHY, ROBERT	WRITER	8955 BEVERLY BLVD	LOS ANGELES, CA	90048
MURPHY, ROBERT J	TV WRITER-DIRECTOR	109 W BROAD ST	BERGENFIELD, NJ	07621
MURPHY, ROSEMARY	ACTRESS	220 E 73RD ST	NEW YORK, NY	10021
MURPHY, SUZANNE	SOPRANO	COLBERT, 111 W 57TH ST	NEW YORK, NY	10019
MURPHY, TAB	WRITER	151 S EL CAMINO DR	BEVERLY HILLS, CA	90212
MURPHY, TERENCE S	NEWS CORRESPONDENT	400 N CAPITOL ST, NW	WASHINGTON, DC	20001
MURPHY, THOMAS	ACTOR	10920 WILSHIRE BLVD #220	LOS ANGELES, CA	90024
MURPHY, TIM	GUITARIST	3327 PARK AVE	NASHVILLE, TN	37209
MURPHY, TIMOTHY	PHOTOGRAPHER	5210 LIGHTHORNE RD	BURKE, VA	22015
MURPHY, TIMOTHY PATRICK	ACTOR	KOHNER, 9169 SUNSET BLVD	LOS ANGELES, CA	90069
MURPHY, TOM	CLOWN	2701 COTTAGE WY #14	SACRAMENTO, CA	95825
MURRAY, ALAN S	NEWS CORRESPONDENT	4631 "Q" ST, NW	WASHINGTON, DC	20007
MURRAY, ANN	MEZZO-SOPRANO	COLBERT, 111 W 57TH ST	NEW YORK, NY	10019
MURRAY, ANNE	SINGER	4881 YONGE ST #412	TORONTO, ONT M2N 5X3	CANADA
MURRAY, ARTHUR	DANCE INSTRUCTOR	2877 KALAKAUA AVE	HONOLULU, HI	96815
MURRAY, BERT	WRITER	11175 HUSTON ST	NORTH HOLLYWOOD, CA	91601
MURRAY, BILL	ACTOR	RURAL FARM DELIVERY #1		
		WASHINGTON SPRINGS RD		
		BOX 250-A	PALISADES, NY	10964
MURRAY, BONNIE	SOPRANO	GEWALD, 58 W 58TH ST	NEW YORK, NY	10019
MURRAY, BRIAN	ACTOR	169 QUEEN'S GATE #8	LONDON SW7 5EH	ENGLAND
MURRAY, COLLEEN	ACTRESS-MODEL	410 SANTA ROSA AVE	SANTA BARBARA, CA	93108
MURRAY, DAROLD O	DIRECTOR	DGA, 110 W 57TH ST	NEW YORK, NY	10019
MURRAY, DENNIS	WRITER	555 W 57TH ST #1230	NEW YORK, NY	10019
MURRAY, DON	ACT-WRI-DIR	2121 AVE OF THE STARS #410	LOS ANGELES, CA	90067
MURRAY, EDDIE	BASEBALL	711 40TH ST #450	BALTIMORE, MD	21211
MURRAY, JAN	ACTOR-COMEDIAN	1157 CALLE VISTA DR	BEVERLY HILLS, CA	90210
MURRAY, JANE	CASTING DIRECTOR	EMBASSY TELEVEISION		
		100 UNIVERSAL CITY PLAZA	UNIVERSAL CITY, CA	91608
MURRAY, JOE	COMEDIAN	POST OFFICE BOX 830	ALBANY, NY	12201
MURRAY, JOHN FENTON	WRITER	15651 DICKENS ST #205	ENCINO, CA	91436
MURRAY, KATHERINE	DANCE INSTRUCTOR	2877 KALAKAUA AVE	HONOLULU, HI	96815
MURRAY, KEN	ACTOR	2370 BOWMONT DR	BEVERLY HILLS, CA	90210
MURRAY, LARRY	WRITER	8955 BEVERLY BLVD	LOS ANGELES, CA	90048
MURRAY, LELAND	ACTOR	BERZON, 336 E 17TH ST	COSTA MESA, CA	92627
MURRAY, LINDA DIANNE	GUITARIST	97 WHITE BRIDGE RD #A-15	NASHVILLE, TN	37205
MURRAY, LU	TV DIRECTOR	ENTERTAINMENT TONIGHT		
		PARAMOUNT TELEVISION		
		5555 MELROSE AVE	LOS ANGELES, CA	90038
MURRAY, LYN	CONDUCTOR	3603 WESTFALL DR	ENCINO, CA	91436

Name	Occupation	Address	City	Zip/Country
MURRAY, MICHAEL	ORGANIST	15 HIGH ST #621	HARTFORD, CT	06103
MURRAY, MILDRED	ACTRESS	2 SUTTON PL S	NEW YORK, NY	10022
MURRAY, PEG	ACTRESS	41 GREENWICH AVE	NEW YORK, NY	10014
MURRAY, PHILIP W	DIRECTOR	1609 CENTRAL AVE	WILMETTE, IL	60091
MURRAY, ROBERT J	WRITER	8955 BEVERLY BLVD	LOS ANGELES, CA	90048
MURRAY, RUBY	SINGER	10-A VICTORIA PARADE, TORQUAY	DEVON	ENGLAND
MURRAY, SEAN	COMPOSER	410 SANTA ROSA AVE	SANTA BARBARA, CA	93108
MURRAY, WARREN	WRITER-PRODUCER	GENERAL DELIVERY	DORSET, VT	05251
MURRAY, WARREN S	TV WRITER	8955 BEVERLY BLVD	LOS ANGELES, CA	90048
MURRAY, WILLIAM	WRITER	8955 BEVERLY BLVD	LOS ANGELES, CA	90048
MURRAY, WILLIAM	BARITONE	POST OFFICE BOX 188		
		STATION A	TORONTO, ONT	CANADA
MURRELL, JIMMY	GUITARIST	279 OLD SHACKLE ISLAND RD	HENDERSONVILLE, TN	37075
MURRELL, RICHARD	MANDOLINIST	POST OFFICE BOX 1164	HENDERSONVILLE, TN	37075
MURRILL, MILTON	ACTOR	13600 CALIFA ST	VAN NUYS, CA	91401
MURTAGH, KATE	ACTRESS	15146 MOORPARK ST	SHERMAN OAKS, CA	91403
MURTAUGH, JAMES	ACTOR	6640 SUNSET BLVD #203	LOS ANGELES, CA	90028
MUSANTE, TONY	ACTOR-WRITER	10000 SANTA MONICA BLVD #305	LOS ANGELES, CA	90067
MUSBURGER, BRENT	SPORTSCASTER	CBS SPORTS, 51 W 52ND ST	NEW YORK, NY	10019
MUSCARELLA, STEVE	TV WRITER-DIRECTOR	830 WARREN AVE	VENICE, CA	90291
MUSCATINE, ALISON	NEWS CORRESPONDENT	1150 15TH ST, NW	WASHINGTON, DC	20071
MUSE, MARGARET	ACTRESS	1418 N HIGHLAND AVE #102	LOS ANGELES, CA	90028
MUSE, REYNELDA W	NEWS CORRESPONDENT	1739 E 29TH AVE	DENVER, CO	80205
MUSER, WOLFGANG	ACTOR	3905 EUREKA DR	STUDIO CITY, CA	91604
MUSIAL, STAN	BASEBALL	85 TRENT DR	LADUE, MO	63124
MUSIC, LORENZO	WRITER	1717 N HIGHLAND AVE #414	LOS ANGELES, CA	90028
MUSICAL YOUTH	RHYTHM & BLUES GROUP	200 W 51ST ST #1410	NEW YORK, NY	10019
MUSICK, PAT	ACTRESS	ICM, 8899 BEVERLY BLVD	LOS ANGELES, CA	90048
MUSILLI, JOHN	DIRECTOR	CAMERA THREE PRODUCTIONS		
		555 W 57TH ST	NEW YORK, NY	10019
MUSKRATS, THE	MUSICAL DUO	SUBTERRANEAN RECORDS		
		577 VALENCIA ST	SAN FRANCISCO, CA	94110
MUSSELWHITE, DAPHINE W	NEWS CORRESPONDENT	2039 N BRANDYWINE ST	ARLINGTON, VA	22207
MUSSOLENO, ROSEMARY	SOPRANO	CAMI, 165 W 57TH ST	NEW YORK, NY	10019
MUSTAFA, DEMETRA	ACTRESS	FELBER, 2126 N CAHUENGA BLVD	LOS ANGELES, CA	90068
MUSTAIN, MINOR	WRITER	8955 BEVERLY BLVD	LOS ANGELES, CA	90048
MUSTANG, SALLY	SINGER	2028 CHESTNUT ST	PHILADELPHIA, PA	19103
MUSTARD, PRESTON "LAWMAN"	WRESTLER	CAPITOL INTERNATIONAL		
		11844 MARKET ST	NORTH LIMA, OH	44452
MUSTO, MICHAEL J	WRITER	555 W 57TH ST #1230	NEW YORK, NY	10019
MUTCHIE, MARJORIE JANE	ACTRESS	DE LONY, 1169 MARY CIR	LA VERNE, CA	91750
MUTI, ORNELLA	ACTRESS	17-A N MARTELLI 3	ROME	ITALY
MUTINY	SOUL-DISCO GROUP	FAST FORWARD, 110 W 57TH ST	NEW YORK, NY	10019
MUTO, ALFONSO A	PHOTOGRAPHER	3443 COURTLAND DR	BAILEY'S CROSS RDS, VA	22041
MUTRUX, CHARLES FLOYD	WRITER-PRODUCER	DGA, 7950 SUNSET BLVD	LOS ANGELES, CA	90046
MUTSCHLER, HARRY R	DIRECTOR	DGA, 110 W 57TH ST	NEW YORK, NY	10019
MUTTER, ANNE-SOPHIE	VIOLINIST	CAMI, 165 W 57TH ST	NEW YORK, NY	10019
MUTU, ORNELLA	ACTRESS	VIA N MARTELLI 3	ROME	ITALY
MYDANS, CARL	PHOTOGRAPHER	TIME/TIME & LIFE BLDG		
		ROCKEFELLER CENTER	NEW YORK, NY	10020
MYER, BOB	TV WRITER	8955 BEVERLY BLVD	LOS ANGELES, CA	90048
MYERS, ADOLYN	NEWS CORRESPONDENT	NBC-TV, NEWS DEPARTMENT		
		4001 NEBRASKA AVE, NW	WASHINGTON, DC	20016
MYERS, BARBARA	CABLE EXECUTIVE	HOME BOX OFFICE PICTURES		
		1100 AVE OF THE AMERICAS	NEW YORK, NY	10036
MYERS, BEVERLY	SOPRANO	HILLYER, 250 W 57TH ST	NEW YORK, NY	10107
MYERS, BUD	TV DIRECTOR	84-09 35TH AVE #4-E	JACKSON HEIGHTS, NY	11372
MYERS, CARRELL	ACTOR	ABC-TV, "RYAN'S HOPE"		
		1330 AVE OF THE AMERICAS	NEW YORK, NY	10019
MYERS, E MICHAEL	NEWS CORRESPONDENT	1400 "I" ST, 8TH FLOOR, NW	WASHINGTON, DC	20045
MYERS, FRANCES	WRITER	555 W 57TH ST #1230	NEW YORK, NY	10019
MYERS, FRANK JOSEPH	GUITARIST	4501 PACKARD DR #H-11	NASHVILLE, TN	37211
MYERS, GEORGE	GUITARIST	ROUTE #1, BOX 6		
		PRIEST LAKE MOBILE HOME PARK	SMYRNA, TN	37167
MYERS, GINGER	ACTRESS	13111 VENTURA BLVD #102	STUDIO CITY, CA	91604
MYERS, IDA N	WRITER	8955 BEVERLY BLVD	LOS ANGELES, CA	90048
MYERS, JOHN	TENOR	111 W 57TH ST #1209	NEW YORK, NY	10019
MYERS, JORDAN	ACTOR	5330 LANKERSHIM BLVD #210	NORTH HOLLYWOOD, CA	91601
MYERS, LAURENCE	ENTERTAINMENT EXEC	27-A QUEENS TERR		
		SAINT JOHN'S WOOD	LONDON NW8	ENGLAND
MYERS, LISA M	NEWS CORRESPONDENT	NBC-TV, NEWS DEPARTMENT		
		4001 NEBRASKA AVE, NW	WASHINGTON, DC	20016
MYERS, LORNA	MEZZO-SOPRANO	POST OFFICE BOX 1515	NEW YORK, NY	10023
MYERS, LOU	CARTOONIST	POST OFFICE BOX 4203	NEW YORK, NY	10017
MYERS, MICHAEL	TENOR	CAMI, 165 W 57TH ST	NEW YORK, NY	10019
MYERS, MYRON	BASS	431 S DEARBORN ST #1504	CHICAGO, IL	60605
MYERS, PAMELA	ACTRESS	9300 WILSHIRE BLVD #410	BEVERLY HILLS, CA	90212
MYERS, PAMELA	SOPRANO	SARDOS, 180 W END AVE	NEW YORK, NY	10023
MYERS, PAUL ERIC	TV WRITER	8955 BEVERLY BLVD	LOS ANGELES, CA	90048
MYERS, PETER	COMPOSER	4146 LANKERSHIM BLVD #300	NORTH HOLLYWOOD, CA	91602
MYERS, PETER S	FILM EXECUTIVE	1711 ALTA MURA RD	PACIFIC PALISADES, CA	90272
MYERS, ROBERT	GRAPHIC IMPRESSIONIST	NEWS AMERICA SYNDICATE		
		1703 KAISER AVE	IRVINE, CA	92714
MYERS, RUSSELL	CARTOONIST	TRIBUNE MEDIA SERVICES		
		64 E CONCORD ST	ORLANDO, FL	32801

EDDIE MURPHY

BILL MURRAY

DON MURRAY

JAN MURRAY

ORNELLA MUTI

GEORGE NADER

NAKED EYES

JOE NAMATH

PATRICIA NEAL

Name	Occupation	Address	City	Zip
MYERS, SARALYN	ACTRESS	1605 N CAHUENGA BLVD #202	LOS ANGELES, CA	90028
MYERS, SIDNEY	DIRECTOR	2 W 45TH ST	NEW YORK, NY	10036
MYERS, STANLEY	COMPOSER	44 REDCLIFFE RD	LONDON SW10	ENGLAND
MYERS, STANLEY A	COMPOSER-CONDUCTOR	215 W 1ST ST #204	TUSTIN, CA	92680
MYERS, WAYNE E	NEWS CORRESPONDENT	2822 JERMANTOWN RD	OAKTON, VA	22124
MYERSON, ALAN	FILM-TV DIRECTOR	POST OFFICE BOX 5617	BEVERLY HILLS, CA	90210
MYERSON, BESS	COLUMNIST-ADVOCATE	2 E 71ST ST	NEW YORK, NY	10021
MYERSON, ROBERT	WRITER-PRODUCER	17 W 67TH ST	NEW YORK, NY	10023
MYHERS, JOHN	ACTOR-WRITER	8841 EVANVIEW DR	LOS ANGELES, CA	90069
MYHRUM, ROBERT	TV DIRECTOR	POST OFFICE BOX 99	PERU, VT	05152
MYLES, GARRETT	WRITER	8955 BEVERLY BLVD	LOS ANGELES, CA	90048
MYLES, JOHN M	CONDUCTOR	11458 SWINTON AVE	GRANADA HILLS, CA	91344
MYLES, LYNDA	TV WRITER	KNBC-TV, "SANTA BARBARA"		
		3000 W ALAMEDA AVE	BURBANK, CA	91523
MYLES, STAN	TV EXECUTIVE	CBS-TV, 7800 BEVERLY BLVD	LOS ANGELES, CA	90036
MYRE, JOHN G	NEWS CORRESPONDENT	3310 PROSPECT ST, NW	WASHINGTON, DC	20007
MYRICK, GARY & THE FIGURES	ROCK & ROLL GROUP	POST OFFICE BOX 7308	CARMEL, CA	93921
MYRICK, WELDON	DOBROIST	7927 HOOTEN HOWS RD	NASHVILLE, TN	37221
MYRON, THOMAS J, III	NEWS CORRESPONDENT	529 14TH ST, NW	WASHINGTON, DC	20045
MYROW, FREDRIC E	COMPOSER-CONDUCTOR	208 S SAINT ANDREWS PL	LOS ANGELES, CA	90004
MYROW, JEFFREY B	TV WRITER-DIRECTOR	1209 TURQUESA LN	PACIFIC PALISADES, CA	90272
MYROW, JOSEF	COMPOSER	1254 SUNSET PLAZA DR	LOS ANGELES, CA	90069
MYSTICS, THE	VOCAL GROUP	CONTRERA, 88 ANADOR ST	STATEN ISLAND, NY	10303

Name	Occupation	Address	City	Zip
N, JANIS	SINGER-SONGWRITER	629 S LUCERNE BLVD	LOS ANGELES, CA	90020
N R B O	C & W GROUP	ROUNDER RECORDS, 1 CAMP ST	CAMBRIDGE, MA	02140
N'DOUR, YOUSSOU	SINGER	VERNA GILLIS, SOUNDSCAPE		
		500 W 52ND ST	NEW YORK, NY	10019
NAAR, JOSEPH THOMAS	WRITER	244 MEDIO DR	LOS ANGELES, CA	90049
NABBIE, JIM	SINGER	5300 POWERLINE RD #202	FORT LAUDERDALE, FL	33309
NABEL, WILLIAM	TENOR	756 7TH AVE #67	NEW YORK, NY	10019
NABER, THOMAS M	NEWS CORRESPONDENT	11005 GLUECK LN	KENSINGTON, MD	20895
NABLO, JAN P	TV WRITER	8955 BEVERLY BLVD	LOS ANGELES, CA	90048
NABORS, JIM	ACTOR-SINGER	215 KALUMANU	HONOLULU, HI	96816
NACHBAR, AMY	ACTRESS	303 N LA PEER DR #302	BEVERLY HILLS, CA	90211
NACHMAN, JERRY	TV EXECUTIVE	NBC TELEVISION NETWORK		
		30 ROCKEFELLER PLAZA	NEW YORK, NY	10112
NACHTIGALL, ANDREW	ACTOR	26665 SEAGULL WY #A-104	MALIBU, CA	90265
NACHTWEY, JAMES	PHOTOGRAPHER	TIME/TIME & LIFE BLDG		
		ROCKEFELLER CENTER	NEW YORK, NY	10020
NACK, WILLIAM	SPORTS WRITER-EDITOR	SPORTS ILLUSTRATED MAGAZINE		
		TIME & LIFE BUILDING		
		ROCKFELLER CENTER	NEW YORK, NY	10020
NADDER, ROBERT	ACTOR	1329 N VISTA ST #105	LOS ANGELES, CA	90046
NADEL, ARTHUR H	WRITER-PRODUCER	10450 WILSHIRE BLVD #8-B	LOS ANGELES, CA	90024
NADEL, BRUCE	DIRECTOR	BROOK TRAIL	CROTON-ON-HUDSON, NY	10520
NADEL, LAUREL	WRITER	555 W 57TH ST #1230	NEW YORK, NY	10019
NADEL, PAUL J	WRITER	8955 BEVERLY BLVD	LOS ANGELES, CA	90048
NADEL, ROGER S	WRITER	5348 ALLOTT AVE	VAN NUYS, CA	91401
NADELL, EDMUND	TV DIRECTOR	RURAL ROUTE #1		
		SPRING LAKE RD	SHERMAN, CT	06784
NADER, GEORGE	ACTOR	42-520 STARDUST PL	BERMUNDA DUNES, CA	92201
NADER, MICHAEL	ACTOR	329 N WETHERLY DR #205	BEVERLY HILLS, CA	90211
NADER, RALPH	CONSUMER ADVOCATE	POST OFFICE BOX 19267	WASHINGTON, DC	20036
NADER, SAMIR N	NEWS CORRESPONDENT	1410 N MC KINLEY RD	ARLINGTON, VA	22205
NADLER, HARVEY "BUDDY"	DIRECTOR	3770 DUNN DR #14	LOS ANGELES, CA	90034
NADLER, MARTY	WRITER	8955 BEVERLY BLVD	LOS ANGELES, CA	90048
NADLER, PAUL	CONDUCTOR	POST OFFICE BOX 131	SPRINGFIELD, VA	22150
NADLER, SHEILA	MEZZO-SOPRANO	CAMI, 165 W 57TH ST	NEW YORK, NY	10019
NADLIN, MARK	PIANIST	1608 18TH AVE S	NASHVILLE, TN	37212
NADOR, MAGDA	SOPRANO	CAMI, 165 W 57TH ST	NEW YORK, NY	10019
NAFE, ALICIA	MEZZO-SOPRANO	CAMI, 165 W 57TH ST	NEW YORK, NY	10019
NAFF, LYCIA	ACTRESS	12725 VENTURA BLVD #E	STUDIO CITY, CA	91604
NAFIE, CAROL LEE	TV DIRECTOR	861 10TH ST	MANHATTAN BEACH, CA	90266
NAGAN, SEYMOUR PETER	NEWS CORRESPONDENT	9308 INGLEWOOD CT	POTOMAC, MD	20854
NAGANO, KENT	CONDUCTOR	AFFILIATE ARTISTS, INC		
		37 W 65TH ST, 6TH FLOOR	NEW YORK, NY	10023
NAGATA, DAVID	DIRECTOR	56 E 66TH ST	NEW YORK, NY	10021
NAGAZUMI, YASUKO	ACTRESS	OCA, 34 GRAFTON TERR	LONDON NW5 4HY	ENGLAND
NAGEL, DON	ACTOR	14155 MAGNOLIA BLVD #110	VAN NUYS, CA	91423
NAGEL, ROBERT	TRUMPETER	POST OFFICE BOX U	REDDING, CT	06875
NAGESH, INDIRA	DIRECTOR-PRODUCER	15758 STARE ST	SEPULVEDA, CA	91343
NAGLER, BARNEY	WRITER	555 W 57TH ST #1230	NEW YORK, NY	10019
NAGLER, HARVEY	WRITER	555 W 57TH ST #1230	NEW YORK, NY	10019
NAGURKA, STUART C	NEWS CORRESPONDENT	2800 QUEBEC ST, NW	WASHINGTON, DC	20008
NAGY, ANNA	WRITER	555 W 57TH ST #1230	NEW YORK, NY	10019
NAGY, ISABEL	WRITER	8955 BEVERLY BLVD	LOS ANGELES, CA	90048

Name	Occupation	Address	City	Zip
NAGY, IVAN	WRITER-PRODUCER	10128 EMPYREAN WY	CENTURY CITY, CA	90067
NAGY, JANOS	TENOR	111 W 57TH ST #1209	NEW YORK, NY	10019
NAGY, JOHN DAVID	NEWS CORRESPONDENT	9311 WINBOURNE RD	BURKE, VA	22015
NAHAN, STU	SPORTSCASTER	11274 CANTON DR	STUDIO CITY, CA	91604
NAHARIN, OHAD	DANCER	AFFILIATE ARTRISTS, INC		
		37 W 65TH ST, 6TH FLOOR	NEW YORK, NY	10023
NAIL, DAWSON B	NEWS CORRESPONDENT	6509 ORLAND ST	FALLS CHURCH, VA	22043
NAIL, JOANNE	ACTRESS	4261 TROOST AVE #2	STUDIO CITY, CA	91604
NAILL, JERRY & THE ARMADILLO EX	C & W GROUP	POST OFFICE BOX 1373	LEWISVILLE, TX	75067
NAILS, THE	ROCK & ROLL GROUP	TERRY DUNE MGMT		
		125 E 15TH ST	NEW YORK, NY	10003
NAISBITT, JOHN	COLUMNIST	UNIVERSAL PRESS SYNDICATE		
		4900 MAIN ST, 9TH FLOOR	KANSAS CITY, MO	62114
NAISH, PHILIP	GUITARIST	POST OFFICE BOX 111581	NASHVILLE, TN	37211
NAJEE-ULLAH, MANSOOR	ACTOR	175 W 90TH ST	NEW YORK, NY	10024
NAKAHARA, KELLYE	ACTRESS	3906 SUNBEAM DR	LOS ANGELES, CA	90065
NAKAJIMA, KENICHIRO	NEWS CORRESPONDENT	9719 HOLMHURST RD	BETHESDA, MD	20817
NAKAMOTO, ED	ACTOR	8235 SANTA MONICA BLVD #202	LOS ANGELES, CA	90046
NAKANO, DESMOND	SCREENWRITER	3554 LAURELVALE DR	STUDIO CITY, CA	91604
NAKANO, GEORGE H	DIRECTOR	UNO, 119 W 22ND ST	NEW YORK, NY	10011
NAKED EYES	ROCK & ROCK DUO	KRAGEN, 8 CADMAN PLAZA W	BROOKLYN, NY	11201
NAKED PREY, THE	ROCK & ROLL GROUP	POST OFFICE BOX 22	SUN VALLEY, CA	91353
NALEPINSKI, BRUCE A	DIRECTOR	5 KARLSRUHE LN	EAST HAMPTON, NY	11937
NALL, CECILY	SOPRANO	61 W 62ND ST #6-F	NEW YORK, NY	10023
NALL, NAN	SOPRANO	ROSENFIELD, 714 LADD RD	BRONX, NY	10471
NALL, STEPHANIE L	NEWS CORRESPONDENT	500 HAZLETT AVE	BALTIMORE, MD	21229
NALTCHAYAN, HARRY N	PHOTOGRAPHER	4027 HONEY LN	ANNANDALE, VA	22003
NAM, RICHARD S	NEWS CORRESPONDENT	640 LINCOLN ST	ROCKVILLE, MD	20850
NAMATH, DEBORAH MAYS	ACTRESS-MODEL	906 N HILLCREST DR	BEVERLY HILLS, CA	90210
NAMATH, JOE	ACTOR-FOOTBALL	906 N HILLCREST DR	BEVERLY HILLS, CA	90210
NAMEI, FRANK D	WRITER	8955 BEVERLY BLVD	LOS ANGELES, CA	90048
NANAS, HERB	TALENT AGENT	SCOTTI BROS, 2128 PICO BLVD	SANTA MONICA, CA	90405
NANAS, HERB A	FILM PRODUCER	4915 TYRONE AVE #230	SHERMAN OAKS, CA	91423
NANAS, JOSEPH M	COMPOSER	306 WALDON DR	VENTNOR CITY, NJ	08406
NANCE, ROSCOE	SPORTS WRITER	POST OFFICE BOX 500	WASHINGTON, DC	20044
NANKANO, DESMOND L	SCREENWRITER	8955 BEVERLY BLVD	LOS ANGELES, CA	90048
NANKIN, MICHAEL	WRITER-PRODUCER	336 S COCHRAN AVE #4	LOS ANGELES, CA	90036
NANTUCKET	ROCK & ROLL GROUP	CMC PRODS, 3924 BROWNING PL	RALEIGH, NC	27609
NANUS, SUSAN	WRITER	555 W 57TH ST #1230	NEW YORK, NY	10019
NAOUMOFF, EMILE	PIANIST	MARIEDL ANDERS ARTISTS MGMT		
		535 EL CAMINO DEL MAR ST	SAN FRANCISCO, CA	94121
NAPACH, BERNICE F	NEWS CORRESPONDENT	3201 WALBRIDGE PL, NW	WASHINGTON, DC	20010
NAPIER, ALAN	ACTOR	17919 PORTO MARINA WY	PACIFIC PALISADES, CA	90272
NAPIER, CHARLES	ACTOR	3151 W CAHUENGA BLVD #310	LOS ANGELES, CA	90068
NAPIER, MARITA	SOPRANO	61 W 62ND ST #6-F	NEW YORK, NY	10023
NAPIER, PAUL	ACTOR	3800 BARHAM BLVD #303	LOS ANGELES, CA	90068
NAPLES, PHILLIP J	TV WRITER	8955 BEVERLY BLVD	LOS ANGELES, CA	90048
NAPLES, TONI	ACTRESS	3151 W CAHUENGA BLVD #310	LOS ANGELES, CA	90068
NAPOLEON, ARTHUR D	WRITER	8955 BEVERLY BLVD	LOS ANGELES, CA	90048
NAPOLEON, JO	WRITER	432 S CURSON AVE #1-D	LOS ANGELES, CA	90036
NAPOLI, MICHAEL A	ACTOR	6565 SUNSET BLVD #525-A	HOLLYWOOD, CA	90068
NARDINO, GARY	FILM-TV PROD-EXEC	NARDINO PRODS, 5555 MELROSE AVE	LOS ANGELES, CA	90038
NARDO, PATRICIA	TV WRITER	4020 PACHECO DR	SHERMAN OAKS, CA	91403
NARIZZANO, DINO	TV DIRECTOR	465 W BROADWAY	NEW YORK, NY	10012
NARIZZANO, SILVIO	TV-FILM DIRECTOR	AL PARKER, 55 PARK LN	LONDON	ENGLAND
NARZ, JACK	TV HOST	1905 BEVERLY PL	BEVERLY HILLS, CA	90210
NASCHEL, LARRY	ACTOR	1512 MARLAY DR	LOS ANGELES, CA	90069
NASCO, PETER	TV WRITER	8955 BEVERLY BLVD	LOS ANGELES, CA	90048
NASELLA, JIM	FILM DIRECTOR	1423 WINCHESTER AVE	GLENDALE, CA	91201
NASET, MARTHA	PIANIST	POST OFFICE BOX U	REDDING, CT	06875
NASH, ALDEN	WRITER	6212 LA MIRADA AVE #121	HOLLYWOOD, CA	90038
NASH, CHRIS	ACTOR	8730 SUNSET BLVD #PH-W	LOS ANGELES, CA	90069
NASH, FRANKLIN M	DIRECTOR	202 W 10TH ST	NEW YORK, NY	10014
NASH, GRAHAM	SINGER-SONGWRITER	SIDDONS & ASSOCIATES		
		1588 CROSSROADS OF WORLD	HOLLYWOOD, CA	90028
NASH, JOHNNY	SINGER-SONGWRITER	ICM, 40 W 57TH ST	NEW YORK, NY	10019
NASH, KATHLEEN	NEWS CORRESPONDENT	906 CONSTITUTION AVE, NE	WASHINGTON, DC	20002
NASH, N RICHARD	SCREENWRITER	8955 BEVERLY BLVD	LOS ANGELES, CA	90048
NASH, RICHARD	COMPOSER	19323 OXNARD ST	TARZANA, CA	91356
NASH, ROBIN	TV PRODUCER	BBC-TV CENTRE, WOOD LN		
		SHEPHERDS BUSH	LONDON W12	ENGLAND
NASH, SARAH	SINGER	1680 N VINE ST #214	HOLLYWOOD, CA	90028
NASH, VILL	SINGER	PAM, 815 18TH AVE S	NASHVILLE, TN	37203
NASH THE SLASH	ROCK & ROLL GROUP	41 BRITAIN ST #200	TORONTO, ONT	CANADA
NASHOBA, NUCHIE	ACTRESS	1717 N HIGHLAND AVE #414	LOS ANGELES, CA	90028
NASHVILLE BLUEGRASS BAND	BLUEGRASS GROUP	POST OFFICE BOX 1487	MILWAUKEE, WI	53201
NASHVILLE SOUNDS OF DALLAS	C & W GROUP	SODP, 29 HUDSON ST	WATERFORD, NY	12188
NASHVILLE TEENS, THE	ROCK & ROLL GROUP	AMBER HOUSE MANAGEMENT		
		278 SEVEN SISTERS RD	LONDON	ENGLAND
NASKIEWICZ, JOHN	CONDUCTOR	AIA, 60 E 42ND ST	NEW YORK, NY	10165
NASSIF, CHRISTOPHER	TALENT AGENT	8721 SUNSET BLVD #102	LOS ANGELES, CA	90069
NAT, MARIE-JOSE	ACTRESS	GEORGES BEAUME AGENCE		
		3 QUAI MALAQUAIS	PARIS 75006	FRANCE
NATALE, RICHARD	WRITER	8955 BEVERLY BLVD	LOS ANGELES, CA	90048
NATANSON, AGATHE	ACTRESS	31 AVE FELIX FAURE	PARIS 75015	FRANCE

Name	Occupation	Address	City/State	Zip
NATASHA DUO	SKCYCLE ACT	HALL, 138 FROG HOLLOW RD	CHURCHVILLE, PA	18966
NATH, STEPHEN	DRUMMER	117 CONNOR DR	GOODLETTSVILLE, TN	37072
NATHAN, JOHN	WRITER	1888 CENTURY PARK E #1400	LOS ANGELES, CA	90067
NATHAN, MORT	WRITER	8955 BEVERLY BLVD	LOS ANGELES, CA	90048
NATHAN, NANCY B	NEWS CORRESPONDENT	7807 STRATFORD RD	BETHESDA, MD	20814
NATHAN, STEPHEN	ACTOR-WRITER	8685 CRESCENT DR	LOS ANGELES, CA	90046
NATHAN, STEVEN	PIANIST	3550 HELTON DR #G-7	FLORENCE, AL	35630
NATHANS, RHODA R	WRITER	555 W 57TH ST #1230	NEW YORK, NY	10019
NATHANSON, EDWARD	TV DIRECTOR-PRODUCER	POST OFFICE BOX 64	FAIRFIELD, CT	06430
NATHANSON, GREG	CABLE EXECUTIVE	SHOWTIME ENTERTAINMENT		
		1633 BROADWAY	NEW YORK, NY	10019
NATHANSON, TED	TV DIRECTOR-PRODUCER	NBC-TV, 30 ROCKEFELLER PLAZA	NEW YORK, NY	10112
NATHKIN, RICK	SCREENWRITER	3249 CORINTH AVE	LOS ANGELES, CA	90066
NATION, JOHN	TV WRITER	8955 BEVERLY BLVD	LOS ANGELES, CA	90048
NATION, TERRY	TV WRITER-PRODUCER	LYNSTED PARK, LYNSTED	KENT	ENGLAND
NATIVIDAD, KITTEN	ACTRESS-MODEL	CABALLERO, 7920 ALABAMA AVE	CANOGA PARK, CA	91304
NATOLA-GINASTERA, AURORA	CELLIST	111 W 57TH ST #1203	NEW YORK, NY	10019
NATURAL, THE	WRESTLER	SEE - REED, BUTCH "THE NATURAL"		
NATURE BOY	WRESTLING MASCOT	GORGEOUS LADIES OF WRESTLING		
		RIVIERA HOTEL & CASINO		
		DAVID B MC LANE PRODS		
		2901 S LAS VEGAS BLVD	LAS VEGAS, NV	89109
NATWICK, MILDRED	ACTRESS	1001 PARK AVE	NEW YORK, NY	10028
NATWICK, MYRON	ACTOR	15140 MORRISON ST	SHERMAN OAKS, CA	91403
NAUD, MELINDA	ACTRESS	12330 VIEWCREST RD	STUDIO CITY, CA	91604
NAUD, THOMAS HAROLD, JR	WRITER	12330 VIEWCREST RD	STUDIO CITY, CA	91604
NAUGHTON, DAVID	ACTOR-SINGER	2750 N BEACHWOOD DR	LOS ANGELES, CA	90068
NAUGHTON, JAMES	ACTOR	211 S BEVERLY DR #201	BEVERLY HILLS, CA	90212
NAUGHTON, MIKE	CLOWN	2701 COTTAGE WY #14	SACRAMENTO, CA	95825
NAUMANN, OSCAR E	NEWS CORRESPONDENT	2722 CORTLAND PL, NW	WASHINGTON, DC	20008
NAVA, GREGORY JAMES	FILM WRITER-DIRECTOR	10541 BLYTHE AVE	LOS ANGELES, CA	90064
NAVA, JOSE MANUEL	NEWS CORRESPONDENT	1234 MASSACHUSETTS AVE #819, NW	WASHINGTON, DC	20005
NAVARRA, ANDRE	CELLIST	POST OFFICE BOX U	REDDING, CT	06875
NAVARRA, JACK J	COMPOSER	5802 S ADELE AVE	WHITTIER, CA	90606
NAVARRA & D'ARCO	MUSICAL DUO	POST OFFICE BOX U	REDDING, CT	06875
NAVARRO, AL	WRESTLER	POST OFFICE BOX 3859	STAMFORD, CT	06905
NAVARRO, GARCIA	CONDUCTOR	MARIEDL ANDERS ARTISTS MGMT		
		535 EL CAMINO DEL MAR ST	SAN FRANCISCO, CA	94121
NAVARRO, NELSON	TV DIRECTOR	78-08 WOODSIDE AVE	ELMHURST, NY	11373
NAVARRO DA COSTA, MARIO	NEWS CORRESPONDENT	4301 COLUMBIA PIKE #405	ARLINGTON, VA	22204
NAVARROS, THE	CYCLING TROUPE	HALL, 138 FROG HOLLOW RD	CHURCHVILLE, PA	18966
NAVE, MARIA LUISA	MEZZO-SOPRANO	61 W 62ND ST #6-F	NEW YORK, NY	10023
NAVE, STEVE	ACTOR	4789 VINELAND AVE #100	NORTH HOLLYWOOD, CA	91602
NAVERT, RANDY	TALENT AGENT	3465 ENCINAL CANYON RD	MALIBU, CA	90265
NAVIES, JEROME C	WRITER	4385 EL PRIETO RD	ALTADENA, CA	91001
		ROCKEFELLER CENTER	NEW YORK, NY	10020
NAVON, ADRIANNE JUCIUS	NEWS REPORTER	TIME/TIME & LIFE BLDG		
NAYLOR, BARTLETT	NEWS CORRESPONDENT	1216 S GLEBE RD	ARLINGTON, VA	22204
NAYLOR, CAL	TV DIRECTOR	17606 POSETANO RD	PACIFIC PALISADES, CA	90272
NAYTHONS, MATTHEW	PHOTOGRAPHER	TIME/TIME & LIFE BLDG		
		ROCKEFELLER CENTER	NEW YORK, NY	10020
NAYTHONS, MATTHEW EDWARD	PHOTOGRAPHER	POST OFFICE BOX 356	SAUSALITO, CA	94965
NAZARETH	ROCK & ROLL GROUP	3101 E EISENHOWER HWY #3	ANN ARBOR, MI	48104
NAZARETH, DANIEL	CONDUCTOR	SHAW CONCERTS, 1995 BROADWAY	NEW YORK, NY	10023
NAZARIO, JOE	BODYBUILDER	9157 RESEDA BLVD	NORTHRIDGE, CA	91324
NAZARRO, RAY	FILM DIRECTOR	10965 BLUFFSIDE DR #15	STUDIO CITY, CA	91604
NDI, JAMES	MAGICIAN	51 LUNNOX AVE	RUNSEN, NJ	07760
NEAL, COOPER	ACTOR	3575 W CAHUENGA BLVD #320	LOS ANGELES, CA	90068
NEAL, KELLY	FILM EXECITIVE	SKOURAS, 415 N CRESCENT DR	BEVERLY HILLS, CA	90210
NEAL, PATRICIA	ACTRESS	POST OFFICE BOX 1043	EDGARTOWN, MA	02539
NEAL, WILLIAM	SAXOPHONIST	ROUTE #2, BOX 142-DD	LEWES, DE	19958
NEALE, L FORD	TV WRITER	8955 BEVERLY BLVD	LOS ANGELES, CA	90048
NEALON, KEVIN	COMEDIAN	5039 1/2 ROSEWOOD AVE	LOS ANGELES, CA	90004
NEAME, CHRISTOPHER	ACTOR	5 BELLSIZE SQ #2	LONDON NW3	ENGLAND
NEAME, CHRISTOPHER	FILM PRODUCER	9 KENSINGTON CT MEWS	LONDON W8 5DR	ENGLAND
NEAME, RONALD	DIRECTOR	2317 KIMRIDGE RD	BEVERLY HILLS, CA	90210
NEAPOLITANS, THE	C & W GROUP	PROCESS, 439 WILEY AVE	FRANKLIN, PA	16323
NEAR, HOLLY	SINGER-GUITARIST	REDWOOD RECORDS COMPANY		
		476 W MAC ARTHUR BLVD	OAKLAND, CA	94609
NEARY, BRIAN F	WRITER	8955 BEVERLY BLVD	LOS ANGELES, CA	90048
NEARY, JACK	BODYBUILDER	190 SUTHERLAND DR	TORONTO, ONT M4G 1J2	CANADA
NEARY, JUDY	ACTRESS	10850 RIVERSIDE DR #505	NORTH HOLLYWOOD, CA	91602
NEARY, KATHLEEN	WRITER	555 W 57TH ST #1230	NEW YORK, NY	10019
NEARY, LYNN	NEWS CORRESPONDENT	2719 36TH PL, NW	WASHINGTON, DC	20007
NEARY, R PATRICK	TV WRITER	1642 MANKATO CT	CLAREMONT, CA	91711
NEBBIA, MICHAEL	TV DIRECTOR	330 E 71ST ST	NEW YORK, NY	10021
NEBBIA, THOMAS	DIRECTOR	911 9TH ST #202	SANTA MONICA, CA	90403
NEBENZAL, HAROLD	WRITER-PRODUCER	2024 COLDWATER CANYON DR	BEVERLY HILLS, CA	90210
NEBLETT, CAROL	SOPRANO	CAMI, 165 W 57TH ST	NEW YORK, NY	10019
NEBSETH, AMY	DIRECTOR	DGA, 7950 SUNSET BLVD	LOS ANGELES, CA	90046
NECHES, ROBERT	ACTOR	11726 SAN VICENTE BLVD #300	LOS ANGELES, CA	90049
NECKELS, BRUCE	ACTOR	4410 CAHUENGA BLVD	NORTH HOLLYWOOD, CA	91602
NEDERLANDER, JAMES M	PRODUCER	RKO-NEDERLANDER PRODS		
		1440 BROADWAY	NEW YORK, NY	10018

NEDERLANDER, ROBERT E	PRODUCER	RKO-NEDERLANDER PRODS		
		1440 BROADWAY	NEW YORK, NY	10018
NEDWELL, ROBIN	ACTOR	ICM, 388-396 OXFORD ST	LONDON W1	ENGLAND
NEE, PHILIP	WRITER	555 W 57TH ST #1230	NEW YORK, NY	10019
NEEDELL, BENJAMIN	PUBLISHING EXECUTIVE	US MAGAZINE COMPANY		
		1 DAG HAMMARSKJOLD PLAZA	NEW YORK, NY	10017
NEEDHAM, CLARENCE	GUITARIST	POST OFFICE BOX 1054	DETROIT LAKES, MN	56501
NEEDHAM, CONNIE	ACTRESS	8075 W 3RD ST #303	LOS ANGELES, CA	90048
NEEDHAM, HAL	WRITER-PRODUCER	2220 AVE OF THE STARS #2803	LOS ANGELES, CA	90067
NEEDHAM, LARRY	DRUMMER	POST OFFICE BOX 1054	DETROIT LAKES, MN	56501
NEEDLE, ANDREW	DIRECTOR	1122 18TH ST #109	SANTA MONICA, CA	90403
NEEDLEMAN, LAWRENCE	WRITER	8955 BEVERLY BLVD	LOS ANGELES, CA	90048
NEEL, MICHAEL	DRUMMER	1441 LEBANON RD #M-126	NASHVILLE, TN	37210
NEELEY, NORMAN	VIOLINIST	4821 SAN MATEO LN #391, NE	ALBUQUERQUE, NM	87109
NEELEY, TED	ACTOR-SINGER	12744 SARAH ST	STUDIO CITY, CA	91604
NEELY, KENNETH "DOC"	BODYBUILDER	POST OFFICE BOX 490338	COLLEGE PARK, GA	30349
NEELY, PHILLIP	TV DIRECTOR	DGA, 7950 SUNSET BLVD	LOS ANGELES, CA	90046
NEELY, PRENELLA	NEWS CORRESPONDENT	4461 CONNECTICUT AVE, NW	WASHINGTON, DC	20008
NEELY, SAM	SINGER	POST OFFICE BOX 1373	LEWISVILLE, TN	65067
NEER, JUDIE	TV WRITER	5714 TROOST AVE	NORTH HOLLYWOOD, CA	91601
NEFF, BILL	DIRECTOR	1103 N CEDARVIEW	BOZEMAN, MT	59715
NEFF, CAROLYN	ACTRESS	6605 HOLLYWOOD BLVD 3220	HOLLYWOOD, CA	90028
NEFF, CRAIG	SPORTS WRITER-EDITOR	SPORTS ILLUSTRATED MAGAZINE		
		TIME & LIFE BUILDING		
		ROCKEFELLER CENTER	NEW YORK, NY	10020
NEFF, HILDEGARD	ACTRESS	KOHNER, 9169 SUNSET BLVD	LOS ANGELES, CA	90069
NEFF, JESSE	ACTRESS	9165 SUNSET BLVD #202	LOS ANGELES, CA	90069
NEFF, JOHN	SAXOPHONIST	2116 WESTWOOD AVE	NASHVILLE, TN	37212
NEFF, WILLIAM	ACTOR	17050 SUNSET BLVD	PACIFIC PALISADES, CA	90272
NEFT, ANN	TV WRITER	3620 GLENRIDGE DR	SHERMAN OAKS, CA	91423
NEGATIVE FIX	ROCK & ROLL GROUP	39 POPLAR ST	MELROSE, MA	02176
NEGELE, JIM	ACTOR	3726 LAUREL CANYON BLVD	STUDIO CITY, CA	91604
NEGRI, ADELAIDE	SOPRANO	CAMI, 165 W 57TH ST	NEW YORK, NY	10019
NEGRI, CYNTHIA	ACTRESS	3 CREST RD W	ROLLING HILLS, CA	90274
NEGRI, PATTI	ACTRESS	15010 VENTURA BLVD #234	SHERMAN OAKS, CA	91403
NEGRI, VITTORIO	CONDUCTOR	COLBERT, 111 W 57TH ST	NEW YORK, NY	10019
NEGRIN, SOL	TV DIRECTOR	873 CUSTER ST	VALLEY STREAM, NY	11580
NEGRINI, GUALTIERO	TENOR	CAMI, 165 W 57TH ST	NEW YORK, NY	10019
NEGRON, TAYLOR	ACTOR	ICM, 8899 BEVERLY BLVD	LOS ANGELES, CA	90048
NEGULESCO, JEAN	DIRECTOR-PRODUCER	904 N BEDFORD DR	BEVERLY HILLS, CA	90210
NEHLS, ALLYN R	TV DIRECTOR	ABC-TV, 190 N STATE ST	CHICAHO, IL	60601
NEIDHART, JIM "THE ANVIL"	WRESTLER	POST OFFICE BOX 3859	STAMFORD, CT	06905
NEIERS, MIKE	CINEMATOGRAPHER	7715 SUNSET BLVD #150	LOS ANGELES, CA	90046
NEIGHBORHOODS, THE	ROCK & ROLL GROUP	25 HUNTINGTON AVE #420	BOSTON, MA	02116
NEIGHER, GEOFFREY MARK	TV WRITER	342 N MC CADDEN PL	LOS ANGELES, CA	90004
NEIGHER, STEPHEN	STORY EDITOR	147 N MARTEL AVE	LOS ANGELES, CA	90036
NEIKIRK, WILLIAM	NEWS CORRESPONDENT	5121 N 38TH ST	ARLINGTON, VA	22207
NEIL, DIANE THOMPSON	ACTRESS	9200 SUNSET BLVD #1210	LOS ANGELES, CA	90069
NEIL, HILDEGARD	ACTRESS	CONWAY, EAGLE HOUSE		
		109 JERMYN ST	LONDON SW1	ENGLAND
NEIL, JAY	NEWS CORRESPONDENT	531-D LAKE VISTA CIR	COCKEYVILLE, MD	21030
NEIL, JOSEPH H	PHOTOGRAPHER	9746 HEDIN DR	SILVER SPRING, MD	20903
NEILL, NOEL	ACTRESS	POST OFFICE BOX 1370	STUDIO CITY, CA	91604
NEILL, SAM	ACTOR	AL PARKER, 55 PARK LN	LONDON W1	ENGLAND
NEILL, WILLIAM	TENOR	59 E 54TH ST #81	NEW YORK, NY	10022
NEILSEN, CATHERINE A	NEWS CORRESPONDENT	400 N CAPITOL ST, NW	WASHINGTON, DC	20001
NEILSEN, INGA	ACTRESS	BENSON, 518 TOLUCA PARK DR	BURBANK, CA	91505
NEILSON, CATHERINE	ACTRESS	LEADING PLAYERS, 31 KINGS RD	LONDON SW3	ENGLAND
NEILSON, DOUGLAS J	NEWS CORRESPONDENT	4461 CONNECTICUT AVE, NW	WASHINGTON, DC	20008
NEILSON, JOHN	ACTOR-WRITER	4501 VISTA DEL MONTE AVE #8	SHERMAN OAKS, CA	91403
NEIMAN, IRVING G	WRITER	555 W 57TH ST #1230	NEW YORK, NY	10019
NEIMAN, LE ROY	ARTIST	1 W 67TH ST	NEW YORK, NY	10023
NEIMAND, STEVEN M	WRITER	5453 KESTER AVE #1	VAN NUYS, CA	91411
NEIPRIS, JANET	TV WRITER	555 W 57TH ST #1230	NEW YORK, NY	10019
NELAN, BRUCE	NEWS CORRESPONDENT	9231 CHAPEL HILL TERR	FAIRFAX, VA	22031
NELBERT, SHELLEY	WRITER	8955 BEVERLY BLVD	LOS ANGELES, CA	90048
NELKIN, STACEY	ACTRESS	BOSTWICK, 2770 HUTTON DR	BEVERLY HILLS, CA	90210
NELLIGAN, KATE	ACTRESS	CHATTO & LINNIT, LTD		
		PRINCE OF WALES THEATRE		
		COVENTRY ST	LONDON WC2	ENGLAND
NELSON, ANN	ACTRESS	7469 MELROSE AVE #30	LOS ANGELES, CA	90046
NELSON, B J	WRITER	8955 BEVERLY BLVD	LOS ANGELES, CA	90048
NELSON, BABY FACE	WRESTLER	SEE - VALENTINE, GREG		
		"THE HAMMER"		
NELSON, BARRY	ACTOR	1101 OCEAN FRONT WALK	VENICE, CA	90291
NELSON, BILL	SINGER-GUITARIST	POST OFFICE BOX 134-A		
		THAMES DITTON	SURREY	ENGLAND
NELSON, BONNIE	SINGER	TRIANGLE TALENT, INC		
		9701 TAYLORSVILLE RD	LOUISVILLE, KY	40299
NELSON, BYRON	GOLFER	ROUTE #2, FAIRWAY RANCH	ROANOKE, TX	76262

Name	Occupation	Address	City	Zip
NELSON, CARLYLE	CONDUCTOR	215 CHAPIN LN	BURLINGAME, CA	94010
NELSON, CHRISTOPHER ALAN	DIRECTOR	DGA, 7950 SUNSET BLVD	LOS ANGELES, CA	90046
NELSON, CRAIG E	GUITARIST	109 RIDGEWOOD LN	FRANKLIN, TN	37064
NELSON, CRAIG R	DIRECTOR	1900 AVE OF THE STARS #2535	LOS ANGELES, CA	90067
NELSON, CRAIG RICHARD	ACTOR	9100 SUNSET BLVD #200	LOS ANGELES, CA	90069
NELSON, CRAIG T	ACTOR-WRITER	1472 RISING GLEN RD	LOS ANGELES, CA	90024
NELSON, DAVID	ACTOR-DIRECTOR	WESTERN INTERNATIONAL MEDIA		
		8732 SUNSET BLVD	LOS ANGELES, CA	90038
NELSON, DONALD R	TV WRITER	8955 BEVERLY BLVD	LOS ANGELES, CA	90048
NELSON, DOYLE	GUITARIST	414 E FORREST AVE	LEBANON, TN	37087
NELSON, FRANK	ACTOR	8906 EVANVIEW DR	LOS ANGELES, CA	90069
NELSON, GARY	DIRECTOR	1888 CENTURY PARK E #1400	LOS ANGELES, CA	90067
NELSON, GENE	ACTOR-DIRECTOR	3431 VINTON AVE #1	LOS ANGELES, CA	90034
NELSON, GREGORY A	CELLIST	9233 QUEENSBORO CT	BRENTWOOD, TN	37027
NELSON, HELEN V	DIRECTOR	350 E 52ND ST	NEW YORK, NY	10022
NELSON, JACK	NEWS CORRESPONDENT	4528 VAN NESS ST, NW	WASHINGTON, DC	20016
NELSON, JAMES	NEWS REPORTER	THE NATIONAL ENQUIRER		
		600 SE COAST AVE	LANTANA, FL	33464
NELSON, JAY	GUIATRIST	440 HENRY DR	NASHVILLE, TN	37214
NELSON, JESSICA	ACTRESS	445 BEDFORD DR #PH	BEVERLY HILLS, CA	90210
NELSON, JIM	WRESTLER	SEE - ZHUKOV, BORIS		
NELSON, JOHN ALLEN	ACTOR	10390 SANTA MONICA BLVD #310	LOS ANGELES, CA	90025
NELSON, JUDD	ACTOR	1888 CENTURY PARK E #1400	LOS ANGELES, CA	90067
NELSON, KAM	ACTRESS-MODEL	SEE - NELSON-SEAGREN, BOB		
NELSON, KATHY F	NEWS CORRESPONDENT	403 DREAMS LANDING	ANNAPOLIS, MD	21401
NELSON, KENNETH	ACTOR	720 GREENWICH ST	NEW YORK, NY	10014
NELSON, KRISTIN	ACTRESS	209 S CARMELINA AVE	LOS ANGELES, CA	90049
NELSON, LARRY	WRESTLING ANNOUNCER	AMERICAN WRESTLING ASSOC		
		MINNEAPLOIS WRESTLING		
		10001 WAYZATA BLVD	MINNETONKA, MN	55345
NELSON, LARS-ERIK	NEWS CORRESPONDENT	6020 BROAD ST	BROOKMONT, MD	20816
NELSON, LINDSEY	SPORTSCASTER	CBS SPORTS, 51 W 52ND ST	NEW YORK, NY	10019
NELSON, LISA	DRUMMER	79 MILLWOOD DR #P-79	NASHVILLE, TN	37217
NELSON, MARGERY	ACTRESS	13111 VENTURA BLVD #204	STUDIO CITY, CA	91604
NELSON, MARK E	NEWS CORRESPONDENT	1115 "C" ST, SE	WASHINGTON, DC	20003
NELSON, NELDA	MEZZO-SOPRANO	1776 BROADWAY #504	NEW YORK, NY	10019
NELSON, PETER	ACTOR	9000 SUNSET BLVD #1200	LOS ANGELES, CA	90069
NELSON, PETER	TV WRITER	8955 BEVERLY BLVD	LOS ANGELES, CA	90048
NELSON, PRINCE ROGERS	SINGER-SONGWRITER	SEE - PRINCE & THE REVOLUTION		
NELSON, PRIVATE JIM	WRESTLER	SEE - ZHUKOV, BORIS		
NELSON, RALPH	FILM WRITER-DIRECTOR	DGA, 7950 SUNSET BLVD	LOS ANGELES, CA	90046
NELSON, RICHARD H	TV WRITER	22715 CALVERT ST	WOODLAND HILLS, CA	91367
NELSON, ROBERT	COMEDIAN	POST OFFICE BOX 1556	GAINESVILLE, FL	32602
NELSON, SANDY	DRUMMER	2911 CARDIFF AVE	LOS ANGELES, CA	90034
NELSON, STEPHEN	NEWS CORRESPONDENT	1734 19TH ST, NW	WASHINGTON, DC	20009
NELSON, SUSIE	SINGER	TESSIER, 505 CANTON PASS	MADISON, TN	37115
NELSON, TRACY	ACTRESS	3100 TORREYSON PL	LOS ANGELES, CA	90046
NELSON, TRACY	SINGER	POST OFFICE BOX 1343	MARIETTA, GA	30061
NELSON, W DALE	NEWS CORRESPONDENT	8725 STOCKTON PARKWAY	ALEXANDRIA, VA	22308
NELSON, WILLIAM J	WRITER	8955 BEVERLY BLVD	LOS ANGELES, CA	90048
NELSON, WILLIE	SINGER-SONGWRITER	6600 BASELINE RD	LITTLE ROCK, AK	72209
NELSON-HORCHLER, JOANI M	NEWS CORRESPONDENT	805 INDEPENDENCE AVE, SE	WASHINGTON, DC	20003
NELSON-SEAGREN, KAM	ACTRESS	120 S THURSTON AVE	LOS ANGELES, CA	90049
NELSOVA, ZARA	CELLIST	1776 BROADWAY #504	NEW YORK, NY	10019
NEMEC, DENNIS MICHAEL	TV WRITER	8955 BEVERLY BLVD	LOS ANGELES, CA	90048
NEMEC, RUTH B	WRITER	555 W 57TH ST #1230	NEW YORK, NY	10019
NEMEROV, BRUCE	GUITARIST	ROUTE #1, BRUSH CREEK RD	FAIRVIEW, TN	37062
NEMERSON, ROY E	WRITER	J MICHAEL BLOOM AGENCY		
		233 PARK AVE S, 10TH FLOOR	NEW YORK, NY	10017
NEMES, SCOTT	ACTOR	8322 BEVERLY BLVD #202	LOS ANGELES, CA	90048
NEMIR, HELEN	ACTRESS	FARRELL, 10500 MAGNOLIA BLVD	NORTH HOLLYWOOD, CA	91601
NEMIROFF, PAUL R	DIRECTOR	152 COLD SPRING RD	SYOSSET, NY	11791
NEMITZ, DONALD J	COMPOSER	20716 LULL ST	CANOGA PARK, CA	91306
NENNO, STEPHEN K	TV EXECUTIVE	ABC TELEVISION NETWORK		
		1330 AVE OF THE AMERICAS	NEW YORK, NY	10019
NENTWIG, FRANZ-FERDINAND	BARITONE	CAMI, 165 W 57TH ST	NEW YORK, NY	10019
NEPTUNE, KING & THE SEA SERPENT	ROCK & ROLL GROUP	OLDIES, 5218 ALMONT ST	LOS ANGELES, CA	90032
NEPUS, RIA	SCREENWRITER	418 N MAPLE DR #E	BEVERLY HILLS, CA	90210
NERENBERG, SUSAN A	TV EXECUTIVE	ABC TELEVISION NETWORK		
		1330 AVE OF THE AMERICAS	NEW YORK, NY	10019
NERO, FRANCO	ACTOR	VIA MARGUTTA LA	ROME 00187	ITALY
NERO, PETER	PIANIST	4114 ROYAL CREST PL	ENCINO, CA	91436
NERO, TONI	ACTRESS	8350 SANTA MONICA BLVD #103	LOS ANGELES, CA	90069
NERVOUS EATERS	ROCK & ROLL GROUP	POST OFFICE BOX 579		
		KENMORE STATION	BOSTON, MA	02215
NERYDA	EXOTIC DANCER	THE ACTOR'S FUND HOME		
		155 W HUDSON AVE	ENGLEWOOD, NJ	07631
NESBIT, JEFFERY ASHER	NEWS CORRESPONDENT	10217 RAIDER LN	FAIRFAX, CA	22030
NESBIT, PAT	ACTRESS	250 W 57TH ST #2317	NEW YORK, NY	10107
NESBITT, BILL	ACTOR	3630 S SEPULVEDA BLVD #1-140	LOS ANGELES, CA	90034
NESI, THOMAS	WRITER	11621 CHENAULT ST #5	LOS ANGELES, CA	90049
NESMITH, EUGENE	ACTOR	444 W 49TH ST #2-B	NEW YORK, NY	10019
NESMITH, JEFF	NEWS CORRESPONDENT	100 LONGVIEW DR	ALEXANDRIA, VA	20009
NESNOW, JOE	ACTOR	1350 N HIGHLAND AVE #24	HOLLYWOOD, CA	90028
NESOR, AL	ACTOR	2780 NE 183RD ST #603-C	NORTH MIAMI BEACH, FL	33160

NOEL NEILL

KATE NELLIGAN

BARRY NELSON

WILLIE NELSON

FRANCO NERO

LOIS NETTLETON

ANTHONY NEWLEY

JULIE NEWMAR

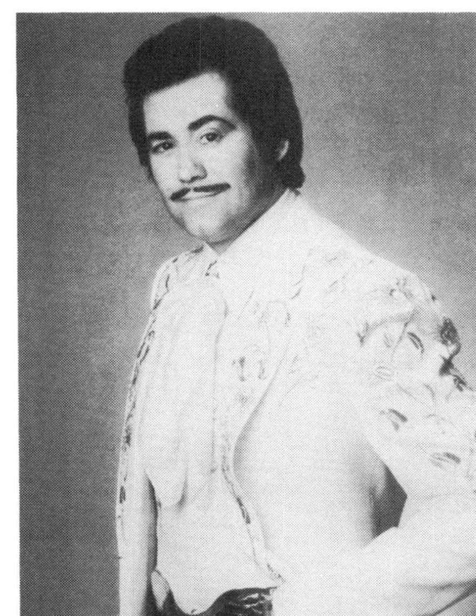
WAYNE NEWTON

Name	Occupation	Address	City	Zip
NESSEN, RONALD H	NEWS CORRESPONDENT	1755 S JEFFERSON DAVIS HWY	ARLINGTON, VA	22202
NESTER, JOHN J	NEWS CORRESPONDENT	148 "G" ST, NW	WASHINGTON, DC	20024
NESTICO, SAMUEL L	COMPOSER	12230 SINTONTE CT	SAN DIEGO, CA	92128
NESTOR, GREGG	GUITARIST	CPS, 34-66TH PL	LONG BEACH, CA	90803
NETHERCOTT, GEOFFREY	DIRECTOR-PRODUCER	CINEVENTURE, 95 FRAMPTON ST	LONDON NW8	ENGLAND
NETTLETON, JOHN	ACTOR	24 THE AVE, SAINT MARGARETS		
		TWICKENHAM	MIDDLESEX	ENGLAND
NETTLETON, LOIS	ACTRESS	1263 N FLORES AVE	LOS ANGELES, CA	90069
NEU, CYNTHIA	NEWS CORRESPONDENT	6705 WEAVER RD	MC LEAN, VA	22101
NEUBAUER, JOHN	PHOTOGRAPHER	1522 S ARLINGTON RIDGE RD	ARLINGTON, VA	22202
NEUBAUER, LEONARD	SCREENWRITER	340 S OAKHURST DR	BEVERLY HILLS, CA	90212
NEUBAUER, PAUL	VIOLIST	59 E 54TH ST #81	NEW YORK, NY	10022
NEUBECKER, ROBERT	CARTOONIST	THE NATIONAL LAMPOON		
		635 MADISON AVE	NEW YORK, NY	10022
NEUFELD, JOHN A	WRITER	1203 N SWEETZER AVE #115	LOS ANGELES, CA	90069
NEUFELD, MACE	DIRECTOR-PRODUCER	624 N ARDEN DR	BEVERLY HILLS, CA	90210
NEUFELD, SIGMUND, JR	FILM DIRECTOR	1867 RISING GLEN RD	LOS ANGELES, CA	90069
NEUFER, LYNNE L	WRITER	555 W 57TH ST #1230	NEW YORK, NY	10019
NEUGOLD, KATHLEEN M	NEWS CORRESPONDENT	CBS NEWS, 2020 "M" ST, NW	WASHINGTON, DC	20036
NEUHARTH, ALLEN H	PUBLISHING EXECUTIVE	POST OFFICE BOX 500	WASHINGTON, DC	20044
NEUHOLD, GUNTER	CONDUCTOR	61 W 62ND ST #6-F	NEW YORK, NY	10023
NEUKUM, JOHN E	DIRECTOR	430 S FULLER AVE #2-M	LOS ANGELES, CA	90036
NEUMAN, DAVID	SCREENWRITER	8955 BEVERLY BLVD	LOS ANGELES, CA	90048
NEUMAN, DEANNE E	NEWS CORRESPONDENT	1738 IRVING ST, NW	WASHINGTON, DC	20010
NEUMAN, E JACK	WRITER-PRODUCER	1849 RISING GLEN RD	LOS ANGELES, CA	90069
NEUMAN, JOHANNA	NEWS CORRESPONDENT	1880 COLUMBIA RD, NW	WASHINGTON, DC	20009
NEUMAN, MATT	TV WRITER	8955 BEVERLY BLVD	LOS ANGELES, CA	90048
NEUMAN, SAM WILLIAM	WRITER-PRODUCER	9300 CREBS AVE	NORTHRIDGE, CA	91324
NEUMANN, DOROTHY	ACTRESS	10860 KINGSLAND ST	LOS ANGELES, CA	90034
NEUMANN, E JACK	TV WRITER	1900 AVE OF THE STARS #2535	LOS ANGELES, CA	90067
NEUMANN, JENNY	ACTRESS	8322 BEVERLY BLVD #202	LOS ANGELES, CA	90048
NEUMANN, ROGER L	COMPOSER-CONDUCTOR	4940 CAHUENGA BLVD	NORTH HOLLYWOOD, CA	91601
NEUMANN, SUSAN L	RECORD EXECUTIVE	BEE HIVE, 1130 COLFAX	EVANSTON, IL	60201
NEUMAYER, INGRID	WRITER	8955 BEVERLY BLVD	LOS ANGELES, CA	90048
NEUMNA, ALAN	WRITER-PRODUCER	6725 SUNSET BLVD #505	LOS ANGELES, CA	90028
NEUSTADT, JAMES J	NEWS CORRESPONDENT	NBC-TV, NEWS DEPARTMENT		
		4001 NEBRASKA AVE, NW	WASHINGTON, DC	20016
NEUSTEIN, JOSEPH	TV WRITER	834 PEARL ST	SANTA MONICA, CA	90405
NEUWIRTH, BEBE	ACTRESS	1650 BROADWAY #406	NEW YORK, NY	10019
NEVE, ANDRE	CONDUCTOR	POST OFFICE BOX 131	SPRINGFIELD, VA	22150
NEVE, PAT	BODYBUILDER	5031 N 35TH AVE	PHOENIX, AZ	85016
NEVENS, PAUL	ACTOR	360 W 55TH ST	NEW YORK, NY	10019
NEVIL, STEVE	ACTOR	10914 NATIONAL BLVD #201	LOS ANGELES, CA	90064
NEVILL, HUGH G	NEWS CORRESPONDENT	3230 "P" ST, NW	WASHINGTON, DC	20007
NEVILLE, DANIEL A	PHOTOGRAPHER	453 NEW YORK AVE	HUNTINGTON, NY	11743
NEVILLE BROTHERS, THE	RHYTHM & BLUES GROUP	POST OFFICE BOX 24752	NEW ORLEANS, LA	70184
NEVINS, PHYLLIS	WRITER	555 W 57TH ST #1230	NEW YORK, NY	10019
NEVINS, SHEILA	WRITER	555 W 57TH ST #1230	NEW YORK, NY	10019
NEVINSON, NANCY	ACTRESS	23 MILL CLOSE, FISHBOURNE	CHICHESTER	ENGLAND
NEW, DEREK	COMPOSER	99 GREENHILL, PRINCE ARTHUR RD	LONDON NW3	ENGLAND
NEW BREED, THE	ROCK & ROLL GROUP	POST OFFICE BOX 791551	DALLAS, TX	75379
NEW CHRISTY MINSTRELS, THE	VOCAL	8467 BEVERLY BLVD #100	LOS ANGELES, CA	90048
NEW COUNTRY IMAGE	C & W GROUP	STM, 1311 CANDLELIGHT AVE	DALLAS, TX	75216
NEW EDITION	RHYTHM & BLUES GROUP	200 W 51ST ST #1410	NEW YORK, NY	10019
NEW ENGLAND	ROCK & ROLL GROUP	AUCION MGMT, 645 MADISON AVE	NEW YORK, NY	10021
NEW GRASS REVIVAL	C & W GROUP	POST OFFICE BOX 4003	BEVERLY HILLS, CA	90213
NEW KIDS ON THE BLOCK, THE	ROCK & ROLL GROUP	POST OFFICE BOX 39	BOSTON, MA	02122
NEW MATH	ROCK & ROLL GROUP	POST OFFICE BOX 14563	SAN FRANCISCO, CA	94114
NEW MODELS, THE	ROCK & ROLL GROUP	POST OFFICE BOX 36		
		ANSONIA STATION	NEW YORK, NY	10023
NEW ORDER	ROCK & ROLL GROUP	QWEST RECORDS COMPANY		
		7250 BEVERLY BLVD	LOS ANGELES, CA	90036
NEW PRESIDENTS, THE	ROCK & ROLL GROUP	LOST KINGDOM RECORDS		
		4729 SARATOGA AVE	SAN DIEGO, CA	92107
NEW REGIME	ROCK & ROLL GROUP	41 BRITAIN ST #200	TORONTO, ONT	CANADA
NEW RELATIONS, THE	C & W GROUP	POST OFFICE BOX O	EXCELSIOR, MN	55331
NEW RIDERS OF THE PURPLE SAGE	ROCK & ROLL GROUP	150 5TH AVE #1103	NEW YORK, NY	10011
NEW SEEKERS, THE	VOCAL GROUP	CAPITOL, 11844 MARKET ST	NORTH LIMA, LA	44452
NEW VIRGINIANS, THE	VOCAL GROUP	VA TECH, 321 PATTON HALL	BLACKSBURG, VA	24061
NEW WORLD BRASS QUINTET, THE	BRASS QUINTET	POST OFFICE BOX 20548	NEW YORK, NY	10025
NEW YORK HARP ENSEMBLE	HARP ENSEMBLE	POST OFFICE BOX 20548	NEW YORK, NY	10025
NEW YORK SAMBA BAND, THE	SAMBA BAND	HOFFER, 233 1/2 E 48TH ST	NEW YORK, NY	10017
NEWALL, GEORGE	DIRECTOR	DGA, 110 W 57TH ST	NEW YORK, NY	10019
NEWARK, DEREK	ACTOR	JULIA MAC DERMOT		
		14 LEAMORE ST	LONDON W6	ENGLAND
NEWBORN, IRA	COMPOSER	3524 VERDUGO TERR	LOS ANGELES, CA	90065
NEWBOUND, LAURIE	TV WRITER	8955 BEVERLY BLVD	LOS ANGELES, CA	90048
NEWBROOK, PETER	CINEMATOGRAPHER	APPLECROSS MANAGEMENT		
		185-A NEWMARKET RD		
		NORWICH	NORFOLK NR4 6AP	ENGLAND
NEWBURY, MICKEY	SINGER-SONGWRITER	POST OFFICE BOX 40427	NASHVILLE, TN	37204
NEWBY, JEFFREY	DIRECTOR	6026 WILKINSON AVE	NORTH HOLLYWOOD, CA	91606
NEWCLEUS	RHYTHM & BLUES GROUP	200 W 51ST ST #1410	NEW YORK, NY	10019
NEWCOMBE, RICHARD S	PUBLISHING EXECUTIVE	NEWS AMERICA SYNDICATE		
		1703 KAISER AVE	IRVINE, CA	92714

Name	Occupation	Address	City	Zip/Country
NEWELL, BROOKE	GUITARIST	ROUTE #3, TELECASTER HILL		
		OLD HILLSBORO RD	FRANKLIN, TN	37064
NEWELL, FRED	GUITARIST	ROUTE #3, TELECASTER HILL		
		OLD HILLSBORO RD	FRANKLIN, TN	37064
NEWELL, GEORGE M, JR	DIRECTOR	14 INNESS PL	GLEN RIDGE, NJ	07028
NEWELL, MIKE	FILM-TV DRIECTOR	HEATH, PARAMOUNT HOUSE		
		162-170 WARDOUR ST	LONDON W1V 3AT	ENGLAND
NEWELL, NORMAN	SONGWRITER	GOLDEN HOUSE #52		
		29 GREAT PULTENEY ST	LONDON W1	ENGLAND
NEWELL, PATRICK	ACTOR	CROUCH, 59 FRITH ST	LONDON W1	ENGLAND
NEWHALL, PATRICIA	ACTRESS	360 E 55TH ST	NEW YORK, NY	10022
NEWHART, BOB	ACTOR-COMEDIAN	215 STRADA CORTA RD	LOS ANGELES, CA	90077
NEWHOUSE, DAVID	WRITER	17616 CANTARA ST	NORTHRIDGE, CA	91325
NEWHOUSE, RUDOLPH R	WRITER	8955 BEVERLY BLVD	LOS ANGELES, CA	90048
NEWHUMET, CHRIS	NEWS CORRESPONDENT	2101 DAYTON ST	SILVER SPRING, MD	20902
NEWLAND, JEANNE	CROSSWORD WRITER	NEWS AMERICA SYNDICATE		
		1703 KAISER AVE	IRVINE, CA	92714
NEWLAND, JOHN	DIRECTOR-PRODUCER	1901 AVE OF THE STARS #840	LOS ANGELES, CA	90067
NEWLAND, MICHAEL	ACTOR	8721 SUNSET BLVD #202	LOS ANGELES, CA	90069
NEWLEY, ANTHONY	SING-ACT-WRI	4419 VAN NUYS BLVD #304-B	SHERMAN OAKS, CA	91403
NEWMAN, ALAN	COMPOSER	28904 CLIFFSIDE DR	MALIBU, CA	90265
NEWMAN, ANTHONY	ORGANIST	119 W 57TH ST #1505	NEW YORK, NY	10019
NEWMAN, BARRY	ACTOR	425 N OAKHURST DR	BEVERLY HILLS, CA	90210
NEWMAN, BRUCE	SPORTS WRITER-EDITOR	SPORTS ILLUSTRATED MAGAZINE		
		TIME & LIFE BUILDING		
		ROCKEFELLER CENTER	NEW YORK, NY	10020
NEWMAN, CHARLES M	GUITARIST	615 LONGHUNTER CT	NASHVILLE, TN	37217
NEWMAN, COLIN	SINGER	POST OFFICE BOX 2428	EL SEGUNDO, CA	90245
NEWMAN, DAISY	SOPRANO	SHAW CONCERTS, 1995 BROADWAY	NEW YORK, NY	10023
NEWMAN, DAVID	SCREENWRITER	555 W 57TH ST #1230	NEW YORK, NY	10019
NEWMAN, EDWIN	NEWS CORRESPONDENT	NBC-TV, NEWS DEPARTMENT		
		30 ROCKEFELLER PLAZA	NEW YORK, NY	10112
NEWMAN, ELAINE	TV WRITER	8955 BEVERLY BLBD	LOS ANGELES, CA	90048
NEWMAN, GARY W	SINGER-GUITARIST	220 N SAINT JULIEN RD	BROUSSARD, LA	70518
NEWMAN, HAL	PIANIST	ROUTE #1, WARREN RD	FRANKLIN, TN	37064
NEWMAN, HARRY S	ACTOR	1605 N CAHUENGA BLVD #202	LOS ANGELES, CA	90028
NEWMAN, HOWIE	COMEDIAN	276 CAMBRIDGE ST #4	BOSTON, MA	02134
NEWMAN, JACK	TV WRITER-PRODUCER	NBC-TV, 3000 W ALAMEDA AVE	BURBANK, CA	91523
NEWMAN, JIMMY C	SINGER-SONGWRITER	ROUTE #2	CHRISTINA, TN	37037
NEWMAN, JOSEPH	FILM DIRECTOR	10900 WINNETKA AVE	CHATSWORTH, CA	91311
NEWMAN, LARAINE	ACTRESS	10480 ASHTON AVE	LOS ANGELES, CA	90024
NEWMAN, LAUNA JANE	WRITER	11945 ADDISON ST	STUDIO CITY, CA	91607
NEWMAN, LEE	COMPOSER	1400 N FAIRFAX AVE #13	LOS ANGELES, CA	90046
NEWMAN, LESLIE	SCREENWRITER	555 W 57TH ST #1230	NEW YORK, NY	10019
NEWMAN, LIONEL	COMPOSER-CONDUCTOR	POST OFFICE BOX 900	BEVERLY HILLS, CA	90213
NEWMAN, LOIS	ACTRESS	5711 1/2 LEXINGTON AVE	LOS ANGELES, CA	90038
NEWMAN, MICHAEL	GUITARIST	SOFFER, 130 W 56TH ST	NEW YORK, NY	10019
NEWMAN, MILTON	SAXOPHONIST	5 ACADEMY CT	COLUMBIA, TN	38401
NEWMAN, NANCY	NEWS REPORTER	TIME/TIME & LIFE BLDG		
		ROCKEFELLER CENTER	NEW YORK, NY	10020
NEWMAN, NANETTE	ACTRESS	ICM, 388-396 OXFORD ST	LONDON W1	ENGLAND
NEWMAN, PAMELA	ACTRESS	6310 SAN VICENTE BLVD #407	LOS ANGELES, CA	90048
NEWMAN, PAUL	ACTOR-DIRECTOR	711 5TH AVE #401	NEW YORK, NY	10022
NEWMAN, PHYLLIS	ACTRESS	529 W 42ND ST #7-F	NEW YORK, NY	10036
NEWMAN, RANDY	SINGER-SONGWRITER	601 HIGHTREE RD	SANTA MONICA, CA	90402
NEWMAN, ROBERT	ACTOR	9200 SUNSET BLVD #1210	LOS ANGELES, CA	90069
NEWMAN, ROGER S	WRITER	555 W 57TH ST #1230	NEW YORK, NY	10019
NEWMAN, STEPHEN	ACTOR	10100 SANTA MONICA BLVD #1600	LOS ANGELES, CA	90067
NEWMAN, STEVEN B	NEWS CORRESPONDENT	6232 WILLIAMSBURG BLVD	ARLINGTON, VA	22207
NEWMAN, THOMAS	ACTOR	9220 SUNSET BLVD #202	LOS ANGELES, CA	90069
NEWMAN, TIM D	DIRECTOR	1711 N OGDEN DR	LOS ANGELES, CA	90046
NEWMAN, TONY	DRUMMER	3919 BRIGHTON RD	NASHVILLE, TN	37205
NEWMAN, WALTER BROWN	WRITER	4021 STONE CANYON AVE	SHERMAN OAKS, CA	91403
NEWMAN-MANTEE, ANNE	ACTRESS	24632 MALIBU RD	MALIBU, CA	90265
NEWMAN-MINSON, LAUNA	TV EXECUTIVE	ABC-TV ENTERTAINMENT CENTER		
		2040 AVE OF THE STARS	LOS ANGELES, CA	90067
NEWMAR, JULIE	ACTRESS-MODEL	204 S CARMELINA AVE	LOS ANGELES, CA	90049
NEWTON, JOHN	ACTOR	34 W 65TH ST	NEW YORK, NY	10023
NEWTON, JUICE	SINGER-SONGWRITER	R LANDIS, 6856 LOS ALTOS PL	HOLLYWOOD, CA	90068
NEWTON, LINDA	WRESTLING VALET	SEE - DARK JOURNEY		
NEWTON, RICHARD	WRITER-PRODUCER	14637 VALLEY VISTA BLVD	SHERMAN OAKS, CA	91403
NEWTON, RICHARD	ACTOR	721 N LA BREA AVE #200	LOS ANGELES, CA	90038
NEWTON, SANDI	ACTRESS-TV HOST	10751 WILSHIRE BLVD #505	LOS ANGELES, CA	90024
NEWTON, WAYNE	SING-ACT	6629 S PECOS	LAS VEGAS, NV	89120
NEWTON, WILLIAM M	DIRECTOR-PRODUCER	4340 45TH ST S	SAINT PETERSBURG, FL	33711
NEWTON-JOHN, OLIVIA	SINGER-ACTRESS	3575 W CAHUENGA BLVD #580	LOS ANGELES, CA	90068
NEY, RICHARD	ACTOR	800 S SAN RAFAEL AVE	PASADENA, CA	91105
NGOR, DR HAING S	ACTOR	9255 SUNSET BLVD #505	LOS ANGELES, CA	90069
NGUYEN, DUSTIN	ACTOR	8230 BEVERLY BLVD #23	LOS ANGELES, CA	90048
NIBLEY, A SLOAN	WRITER	3760 WRIGHTWOOD DR	NORTH HOLLYWOOD, CA	91604
NIBLEY, ANDREW M	NEWS CORRESPONDENT	2250 WASHINGTON AVE	SILVER SPRING, MD	20910
NICASTRO, MICHELLE	ACTRESS	15301 VENTURA BLVD #345	SHERMAN OAKS, CA	91403
NICAUD, PHILIPPE	ACTOR	26 RUE DES PLANTES	PARIS 75014	FRANCE
NICE, CARTER	CONDUCTOR	GERSHUNOFF, 502 PARK AVE	NEW YORK, NY	10022
NICELY, TIMOTHY	ACTOR	18819 CALVERT ST	RESEDA, CA	91335

OLIVIA NEWTON-JOHN

NICK NOLTE

KIM NOVAK

MARGARET O'BRIEN

HELEN O'CONNELL

RYAN O'NEAL

MAUREEN O'SULLIVAN

BILLY OCEAN

JEFF OSBORNE

Name	Occupation	Address	City	Zip
NICHLAUS, JACK	GOLFER	1208 UNITED STATES HWY #1	NORTH PALM BEACH, FL	33408
NICHOL, ALEX	ACTOR-DIRECTOR	10601 OHIO AVE	LOS ANGELES, CA	90024
NICHOLAS, DENISE	ACTRESS	HILL, 932 LONGWOOD AVE	LOS ANGELES, CA	90019
NICHOLAS, JAMES D	WRITER-PRODUCER	1922 GRIFFITH PARK BLVD	LOS ANGELES, CA	90039
NICHOLAS, JOHN GEORGE	DIRECTOR	1 BROOKSIDE CIR	BRONXVILLE, TN	10708
NICHOLAS, JOHN P	DIRECTOR	431 N FULTON AVE	MOUNT VERNON, NY	10552
NICHOLAS, LESLIE	SAXOPHONIST	21850 COOLIDGE #103-B	OAK PARK, MI	48237
NICHOLAS, N J, JR	PUBLISHING EXECUTIVE	TIME & LIFE MAGAZINES		
		TIME & LIFE BUILDING		
		ROCKEFELLER CENTER	NEW YORK, NY	10020
NICHOLAS, PAUL	ACTOR-SINGER	HEATH, PARAMOUNT HOUSE		
		162-170 WARDOUR ST	LONDON W1V 3AT	ENGLAND
NICHOLAS, SARAH	PIANIST	207 CRAIGHEAD AVE	NASHVILLE, TN	37205
NICHOLLS, ALLAN	ACTOR	11726 SAN VICENTE BLVD #300	LOS ANGELES, CA	90069
NICHOLLS, ALLAN F	WRITER	8955 BEVERLY BLVD	LOS ANGELES, CA	90048
NICHOLS, BOB	COMPOSER	1633 W 81ST ST	LOS ANGELES, CA	90047
NICHOLS, CHARLES	FILM DIRECTOR	1890 EUCLID AVE	SAN MARINO, CA	91108
NICHOLS, JAMES	ACTOR	10850 RIVERSIDE DR #501	NORTH HOLLYWOOD, CA	91602
NICHOLS, JOHN	WRITER	8955 BEVERLY BLVD	LOS ANGELES, CA	90048
NICHOLS, JON	DRUMMER	5099 LINBAR DR #D-42	NASHVILLE, TN	37211
NICHOLS, JOSEPHINE	ACTRESS	200 W 57TH ST #304	NEW YORK, NY	10019
NICHOLS, MICHELE	ACTRESS	23281 LEONORA DR	WOODLAND HILLS, CA	91367
NICHOLS, MIKE	FILM WRITER-DIRECTOR	POST OFFICE BOX 7419	THOUSAND OAKS, CA	91359
NICHOLS, NICHELLE	ACTRESS	23281 LEONORA DR	WOODLAND HILLS, CA	91367
NICHOLS, PETER	SCREENWRITER	MARGARET RAMSAY, LTD		
		14-A GOODWINS CT		
		SAINT MARTINS LN		
NICHOLS, ROBERT	ACTOR	19 W 44TH ST #1500	NEW YORK, NY	10036
NICHOLS, ROGER S	COMPOSER	4105 DUNDEE DR	LOS ANGELES, CA	90027
NICHOLS, STEPHEN	ACTOR	KNBC-TV, "DAYS OF OUR LIVES"		
		3000 W ALAMEDA AVE	BURBANK, CA	91523
NICHOLSON, ADELLE	MEZZO-SOPRANO	254 W 93RD ST #8	NEW YORK, NY	10025
NICHOLSON, BRADLEY	SINGER	CUDE, 519 N HALIFAX AVE	DAYTONA BEACH, FL	32018
NICHOLSON, ERWIN W	TV DIRECTOR	333 E 58TH ST	NEW YORK, NY	10022
NICHOLSON, GARY	GUITARIST	307 PARK CIR	NASHVILLE, TN	37205
NICHOLSON, J D & HIS SOUL BENDE	SOUL GROUP	OLDIES, 5218 ALMONT ST	LOS ANGELES, CA	90032
NICHOLSON, JACK	ACTOR-DIRECTOR	12850 MULHOLLAND DR	BEVERLY HILLS, CA	90210
NICHOLSON, JAMES R	FILM DIRECTOR	1248 N CRESCENT HGTS BLVD	LOS ANGELES, CA	90046
NICHOLSON, JOHN D	ACTOR	2338 CLEMENT AVE	VENICE, CA	90291
NICHOLSON, JOHN J	DIRECTOR	10000 SANTA MONICA BLVD #305	LOS ANGELES, CA	90067
NICHOLSON, JOHN J	WRITER	8955 BEVERLY BLVD	LOS ANGELES, CA	90048
NICHOLSON, KARYN B	NEWS CORRESPONDENT	7805 ALBERTA CT	SPRINGFIELD, VA	22152
NICHOLSON, MARCIA	ACTRESS	760 MONTEREY BLVD	HERMOSA BEACH, CA	90254
NICHOLSON, NICK	TV PRODUCER	ABC TELEVISION NETWORK		
		1330 AVE OF THE AMERICAS	NEW YORK, NY	10019
NICHOLSON, ROBERT A	DIRECTOR	4120 NW 26TH TERR	LIGHTHOUSE POINT, FL	33064
NICHTERN, CLAIRE	THEATER PRODUCER	75 ROCKEFELLER PLAZA	NEW YORK, NY	10019
NICIPHOR, NICK	WRITER	8955 BEVERLY BLVD	LOS ANGELES, CA	90048
NICITA, WALLY	CASTING DIRECTOR	TBS, 4000 WARNER BLVD	BURBANK, CA	91505
NICKELL, JOHN PAUL	DIRECTOR	DGA, 110 W 57TH ST	NEW YORK, NY	10019
NICKELS, THE	ROCK & ROLL GROUP	VARIETY ARTISTS INTL, INC		
		9073 NEMO ST, 3RD FLOOR	LOS ANGELES, CA	90069
NICKENS, DARYL G	TV WRITER	CONTEMPORARY ARTISTS		
		132 S LASKY DR	BEVERLY HILLS, CA	90212
NICKENS, SAM	ACTOR	1632 S FAIRFAX AVE	LOS ANGELES, CA	90019
NICKERSON, CHELSEA	TV WRITER	8955 BEVERLY BLVD	LOS ANGELES, CA	90048
NICKERSON, IRA	WRITER	8955 BEVERLY BLVD	LOS ANGELES, CA	90048
NICKERSON, JOHN PAUL	ACTOR	1270 1ST AVE	NEW YORK, NY	10021
NICKERSON, LEE	ACTOR	357 S REXFORD DR #203	BEVERLY HILLS, CA	90212
NICKERSON, ROBERT	DRUMMER	312 SNOPPE CT	ANTIOCH, TN	37013
NICKOLAOU, VELLO	TV DIRECTOR	ENTERTAINMENT TONIGHT		
		PARAMOUNT TELEVISION		
		5555 MELROSE AVE	LOS ANGELES, CA	90038
NICKS, STEVIE	SINGER-SONGWRITER	FRONT LINE MANAGEMENT		
		80 UNIVERSAL CITY PLAZA	UNIVERSAL CITY, CA	91608
NICKSAY, DAVID	DIRECTOR-PRODUCER	POST OFFICE BOX 7210	VENTURA, CA	93006
NICKSON, JULIA	ACTRESS	500 S SEPULVEDA BLVD #510	LOS ANGELES, CA	90049
NICOL, ALEXANDER	ACTOR-DIRECTOR	10601 OHIO AVE	LOS ANGELES, CA	90024
NICOL, LESSLIE	ACTRESS	136 N HAMPTON DR	WHITE PLAINS, NY	10603
NICOLA, ION	WRITER	555 W 57TH ST #1230	NEW YORK, NY	10019
NICOLAYSON, F BRUCE	WRITER	8955 BEVERLY BLVD	LOS ANGELES, CA	90048
NICOLE COMISSIONG, LYDIA	ACTRESS	8322 BEVERLY BLVD #202	LOS ANGELES, CA	90048
NICOLESCO, MARIANA	SOPRANO	CAMI, 165 W 57TH ST	NEW YORK, NY	10019
NICOLSON, JAMES	HARPSICHORDIST	FROTHINGHAM, 40 GROVE ST	WESSESLEY, MA	02181
NIECHNIEDOWICZ, PAUL M	DIRECTOR	DGA, 7950 SUNSET BLVD	LOS ANGELES, CA	90046
NIEDERMAN, MICHAEL	ACTOR	9046 W 24TH ST	LOS ANGELES, CA	90034
NIEHAUS, LENNIE	COMPOSER	24201 GILMORE ST	CANOGA PARK, CA	91307
NIEKRO, PHIL	BASEBALL	4781 CASTLEWOOD DR	LILBURN, GA	30247
NIELSEN, BRIGITTE	ACTRESS	STALLONE, 1570 AMALFI DR	PACIFIC PALISADES, CA	90272
NIELSEN, CHRIS	SINGER	POST OFFICE BOX 8768		
		STATION L	EDMONTON, ALT T6E OB7	CANADA
NIELSEN, DENNIS L	NEWS CORRESPONDENT	2025 "M" ST, NW	WASHINGTON, DC	20036
NIELSEN, GILBERT L	WRITER	555 W 57TH ST #1230	NEW YORK, NY	10019
NIELSEN, JOHN WARD	DIRECTOR	DGA, 7950 SUNSET BLVD	LOS ANGELES, CA	90046
NIELSEN, JUDITH ANNE	TV WRITER	8955 BEVERLY BLVD	LOS ANGELES, CA	90048

Name	Occupation	Address	City	Zip
NIELSEN, LESLIE	ACTOR	1622 VIEWMONT DR	LOS ANGELES, CA	90069
NIELSEN, SEAN	PIANIST	600 WHISPERING HILLS DR #Q-11	NASHVILLE, TN	37211
NIELSEN, SHAUN	SINGER	POST OFFICE BOX 25083	NASHVILLE, TN	37202
NIELSEN, THOR	ACTOR	3330 BARHAM BLVD #103	LOS ANGELES, CA	90068
NIELSEN, TOM	ACTOR	254 PARK AVE S #10-F	NEW YORK, NY	10010
NIENDORFF, JOHN	WRITER	8780 SHOREHAM DR #311	LOS ANGELES, CA	90069
NIERENBERG, ALVIN	WRITER	8955 BEVERLY BLVD	LOS ANGELES, CA	90048
NIERENBERG, ROGER	CONDUCTOR	1776 BROADWAY #504	NEW YORK, NY	10019
NIERO, NANCY ELLEN	NEWS CORRESPONDENT	1449 "A" ST #A, NE	WASHINGTON, DC	20002
NIESEN, BARBARA	ACTRESS	851 S MANSFIELD AVE #202	LOS ANGELES, CA	90036
NIGGEMEYER, AL	DIRECTOR	23 SCOTLAND ST	SAN FRANCISCO, CA	94133
NIGHSWANDER, LARRY	PHOTOGRAPHER	877 LANCASTER DR	MEDINA, OH	44256
NIGHT CROSSING	ROCK & ROLL GROUP	FASTFIRE RECORDS		
		220 E 42ND ST	NEW YORK, NY	10017
NIGHT RANGER	ROCK & ROLL GROUP	POST OFFICE BOX 7308	CARMEL, CA	93923
NIGHT RIDER	ROCK & ROLL GROUP	POST OFFICE BOX O	EXCELSIOR, MN	55331
NIGHTHAWKS, THE	RHYTHM & BLUES GROUP	POST OFFICE BOX 210103	SAN FRANCISCO, CA	94121
NIGHTINGALE, EARL CLIFFORD	RADIO PERS-WRI-PROD	8074 LAKE PL	CARMEL, CA	93923
NIGHTINGALE, MICHAEL	ACTOR-WRITER	FILM RIGHTS COMPANY		
		4 BURLINGTON PL		
		REGENT ST	LONDON W1X 2AS	ENGLAND
NIGITA, SALVATORE	DIRECTOR	DGA, 110 W 57TH ST	NEW YORK, NY	10019
NIGRO, ROBERT	TV DIRECTOR	317 W 103RD ST	NEW YORK, NY	10025
NIGRO-CHACON, GIOVANNA	TV WRITER-DIRECTOR	1341 SINALOA DR	GLENDALE, CA	91207
NIJA	WRESTLER	SEE - HEADHUNTERS, THE		
NILE, WILLIE	SINGER	THE WILLIAM MORRIS AGENCY		
		1350 AVE OF THE AMERICAS	NEW YORK, NY	10019
NILES, FRED A	WRITER-PRODUCER	1125 LONG VALLEY RD	GLENVIEW, IL	60025
NILES, SUZANNE	SINGER	2701 COTTAGE WY #14	SACRAMENTO, CA	95825
NILES, WENDELL	ANNOUNCER	10357 VALLEY SPRING LN	NORTH HOLLYWOOD, CA	91602
NILSON, LOY	TV DIRECTOR	1275 15TH ST	FORT LEE, NJ	07024
NILSSON, BOB	WRITER-PRODUCER	8955 BEVERLY BLVD	LOS ANGELES, CA	90048
NILSSON, BRIGIT	SOPRANO	111 W 57TH ST #1209	NEW YORK, NY	10019
NILSSON, HARRY	SINGER-SONGWRITER	10549 ROCCA PL	LOS ANGELES, CA	90024
NIMCHUK, MICHAEL J	WRITER	8955 BEVERLY BLVD	LOS ANGELES, CA	90048
NIMESGERN, JOHN	PHILOSOPHER-COACH	2801 MEADOW LARK DR	SAN DIEGO, CA	92123
NIMMO, DEREK	ACTOR	GARRICK CLUB	LONDON WC2	ENGLAND
NIMNICHT, DARREN	BARITONE	829 9TH AVE #5-C	NEW YORK, NY	10019
NIMOY, LEONARD	ACT-WRI-DIR	409 N CAMDEN AVE #202	BEVERLY HILLS, CA	90210
NIMSGERN, SIEGMUND	BARITONE	CAMI, 165 W 57TH ST	NEW YORK, NY	10019
NINA	WRESTLER	SEE - HEADHUNTERS, THE		
NINGA, SUPER	WRESTLER	SEE - SUPER NINGA		
NIP DIVERS, THE	ROCK & ROLL GROUP	22714 SUSANA CT	TORRANCE, CA	90505
NIPAR, YVETTE	ACTRESS	ABC-TV, "GENERAL HOSPITAL"		
		1438 N GOWER ST	LOS ANGELES, CA	90028
NIRVANA, YANA	ACTRESS	1000 N OGDEN DR #7	LOS ANGELES, CA	90046
NIRVANA DEVILS, THE	ROCK & ROLL GROUP	LINTRUPER STR 39	1000 BERLIN 49	WEST GERMANY
NISBET, LINDY	ACTRESS	4721 LAUREL CANYON BLVD #211	NORTH HOLLYWOOD, CA	91607
NISBET, STUART	ACTOR	1443 DOROTHY DR	GLENDALE, CA	91202
NISBETH, JOANNE F	WRITER	555 W 57TH ST #1230	NEW YORK, NY	10019
NISHI, KUNIO	NEWS CORRESPONDENT	635 NATIONAL PRESS BLDG		
		529 14TH ST, NW	WASHINGTON, DC	20045
NISSEN, GRETA	ACTRESS	ECKERT, 2114 FORGE RD	MONTECITO, CA	93108
NISSENSON, MARILYN	WRITER	555 W 57TH ST #1230	NEW YORK, NY	10019
NISSMAN, BARBARA	PIANIST	59 E 54TH ST #81	NEW YORK, NY	10022
NISSMAN, MICHAEL	ACTOR	3012 VISTA CREST DR	HOLLYWOOD, CA	90068
NIST, JOHN A	WRITER	8955 BEVERLY BLVD	LOS ANGELES, CA	90048
NITECAPS, THE	ROCK & ROLL GROUP	3 E 54TH ST #1400	NEW YORK, NY	10022
NITTY GRITTY DIRT BAND	C & W GROUP	FEYLINE, 2175 S CHERRY ST	DENVER, CO	80222
NIVEN, KIP	ACTOR	20781 BIG ROCK DR	MALIBU, CA	90265
NIVEN, LARRY	WRITER	3961 VANALDEN AVE	TARZANA, CA	91356
NIVER, JAMES	TV DIRECTOR	3878 FREDONIA DR	LOS ANGELES, CA	90068
NIX, MARTHA	ACTRESS	JTM, 9243 1/2 DOHENY RD	LOS ANGELES, CA	90069
NIXON, AGNES	TV WRITER-PRODUCER	774 CONESTOGA RD	ROSEMONT, PA	19010
NIXON, BEBE	WRITER	555 W 57TH ST #1230	NEW YORK, NY	10019
NIXON, CHARLIE	GUITARIST	1507 LETHIA DR	NASHVILLE, TN	37206
NIXON, JAMES	SINGER-GUITARIST	2830 BRONTE AVE	NASHVILLE, TN	37216
NIXON, MARNI	ACTRESS	9000 SUNSET BLVD #1200	LOS ANGELES, CA	90069
NIXON, MARNI	SOPRANO	GERSHUNOFF, 502 PARK AVE	NEW YORK, NY	10022
NIXON, MIKE	NEWS CORRESPONDENT	1820 ONTARIO PL, NW	WASHINGTON, DC	20009
NIXON, MODO & SKID ROPER	ROCK & ROCK DUO	611 BROADWAY #526	NEW YORK, NY	10012
NIXON, RICHARD	PRESIDENT-AUTHOR	26 FEDERAL PLAZA #1300	NEW YORK, NY	10007
NOACK, DIANE	ACTRESS	CARPENTER, 1516-W REDWOOD ST	SAN DIEGO, CA	92101
NOAH, PETER R	TV WRITER	523 PACIFIC ST	SANTA MONICA, CA	90405
NOAH, ROBERT	TV WRITER-PRODUCER	1023 BENEDICT CANYON DR	BEVERLY HILLS, CA	90210
NOBLE, ANITA	ACTRESS	12 26TH AVE	VENICE, CA	90291
NOBLE, EULALIE	ACTRESS	300 RIVERSIDE DR	NEW YORK, NY	10025
NOBLE, GIL	TV PROD-NEWS CORRES	WABC-TV, 7 LINCOLN SQ	NEW YORK, NY	10023
NOBLE, JAMES	ACTOR	4249 AGNES AVE	STUDIO CITY, CA	91604
NOBLE, JEFFREY S	NEWS CORRESPONDENT	2139 WISCONSIN AVE, NW	WASHINGTON, DC	20007
NOBLE, JON	FILM WRITER-DIRECTOR	RAFFLES HOTEL #185		
		1 BEACH RD	SINGAPORE 0718	CHINA
NOBLE, KARA	ACTRESS-SINGER	SONGBIRD, 60 GOLDNEY RD	LONDON W9	ENGLAND
NOBLE, KATINA	ACTRESS	86 HOLMLEIGH RD	LONDON N16	ENGLAND
NOBLE, KENNETH B	NEWS CORRESPONDENT	1709 "P" ST, NW	WASHINGTON, DC	20036

THE NITTY GRITTY DIRT BAND

Jeff Hanna • Bob Carpenter • Jimmie Fadden • Jim Ibbotson • John McEven

OHIO PLAYERS

NOBLE, MICHAEL	BANJOIST	4907 NEVADA AVE	NASHVILLE, TN	37209
NOBLE, PAUL	TV PRODUCER	WNEW-TV, 205 E 67TH ST	NEW YORK, NY	10021
NOBLE, THOM	FILM EDITOR	POST OFFICE BOX 5617	BEVERLY HILLS, CA	90210
NOBLE, TIMOTHY	BARITONE	CAMI, 165 W 57TH ST	NEW YORK, NY	10019
NOBLE, TOM	WRITER	8955 BEVERLY BLVD	LOS ANGELES, CA	90048
NOBLE, TRISHA	ACTRESS	211 S BEVERLY DR #107	BEVERLY HILLS, CA	90212
NOBLES, VERNON	FILM DIRECTOR	10390 SANTA MONICA BLVD #310	LOS ANGELES, CA	90025
NOBOA, RAFAEL	NEWS CORRESPONDENT	4224 40TH ST, NW	WASHINGTON, DC	20016
NOBY-ARDEN	TRAPEZE AERIALIST	HALL, 138 FROG HOLLOW RD	CHURCHVILLE, PA	18966
NOCK, BELLO	LOW WIRE ACT	HALL, 138 FROG HOLLOW RD	CHURCHVILLE, PA	18966
NOCK, TONY & RENE	SWAYPOLE DUO	HALL, 138 FROG HOLLOW RD	CHURCHVILLE, PA	18966
NOCKS, ARNOLD J	DIRECTOR	RURAL DELIVERY #1, BOX 103	KINTERSVILLE, PA	18930
NODA, KEN	PIANIST	CAMI, 165 W 57TH ST	NEW YORK, NY	10019
NODDIN, CONRAD	MUSICIAN	126 CLOVERCROFT RD	FRANKLIN, TN	37064
NODELLA, BURT	WRITER	13534 BALI WY #F-402	MARINA DEL REY, CA	90292
NOE, RANDALL	GUITARIST	1809 HILLMONT DR #TH-B3	NASHVILLE, TN	37215
NOEL, ARNOLD	PHOTOGRAPHER	ROUTE #1, BOX 127	BROWNTOWN, VA	22610
NOEL, DENISE	ACTRESS	GEORGE LAMBERT AGENCE		
		13 BIS AVE LA MOTTE PIQUET	PARIS 75007	FRANCE
NOEL, GARY	CLOWN	2701 COTTAGE WY #14	SACRAMENTO, CA	95825
NOEL, LAURA	ACTRESS	3907 W ALAMEDA AVE #101	BURBANK, CA	91505
NOEL, MAGALI	ACTRESS	4 RUE VALENTIN HAVY	PARIS 75015	FRANCE
NOEL, RICHARD	COMPOSER	864 AMBER DR	CAMARILLO, CA	93010
NOEL, RITA	MEZZO-SOPRANO	POST OFFICE BOX U	REDDING, CT	06875
NOFTE, DONAVAN MERLE	DIRECTOR	DGA, 7950 SUNSET BLVD	LOS ANGELES, CA	90046
NOGALES, ALEX	WRITER	8955 BEVERLY BLVD	LOS ANGELES, CA	90048
NOGULICH, NATALIA	ACTRESS	247 S BEVERLY DR #102	BEVERLY HILLS, CA	90210
NOJIMA, MINORU	PIANIST	HILLYER, 250 W 57TH ST	NEW YORK, NY	10107
NOKES, R GREGORY	NEWS CORRESPONDENT	802 CHALFONTE DR	ALEXANDRIA, VA	22305
NOLAN, BUCK	CLOWN	2701 COTTAGE WY #14	SACRAMENTO, CA	95825
NOLAN, JEANETTE	ACTRESS	9255 SUNSET BLVD #1105	LOS ANGELES, CA	90069
NOLAN, KATHLEEN	ACTRESS	ICM, 8899 BEVERLY BLVD	LOS ANGELES, CA	90048
NOLAN, KENNY	SINGER-SONGWRITER	BENNETT, 211 S BEVERLY DR	BEVERLY HILLS, CA	90219
NOLAN, MARGARET	ACTRESS	7 WELL RD	LONDON NW3	ENGLAND
NOLAN, PATRICK J	TV WRITER	8955 BEVERLY BLVD	LOS ANGELES, CA	90048
NOLAN, PHILIP	ACTOR	134 W 58TH ST #102	NEW YORK, NY	10019
NOLAN, RODNEY	TENOR	59 E 54TH ST #81	NEW YORK, NY	10022
NOLAN, ROGER	ACTOR	11225 CAMARILLO ST	NORTH HOLLYWOOD, CA	91602
NOLAN, TOM	WRITER	8955 BEVERLY BLVD	LOS ANGELES, CA	90048
NOLAN, WILLIAM F	TV WRITER	5301 JOHN DODSON DR	AGOURA HILLS, CA	91301
NOLEN, TIMOTHY	BARITONE	CAMI, 165 W 57TH ST	NEW YORK, NY	10019
NOLIN, MICHAEL FARRELL	WRITER-PRODUCER	7890 WILLOW GLEN RD	LOS ANGELES, CA	90046
NOLTE, CHARLES	ACTOR	1927 E RIVER TERR	MINNEAPOLIS, MN	55414
NOLTE, NICK	ACTOR	29555 RAINSFORD PL	MALIBU, CA	90265
NOLTING, MARK	ACTOR	4040 VINELAND AVE #225	STUDIO CITY, CA	91604
NOMAD, MIKE	ACTOR	313 CHURCH LN	LOS ANGELES, CA	90049
NONO, CLARE	ACTRESS	12725 VENTURA BLVD #E	STUDIO CITY, CA	91604
NOOMIN, DIANE	WRITER	8955 BEVERLY BLVD	LOS ANGELES, CA	90048
NOONAN, BARTHOLOMEW V	NEWS CORRESPONDENT	317 "E" ST, SE	WASHINGTON, DC	20007
NOONAN, JOHN FORD	TV WRITER	555 W 57TH ST #1230	NEW YORK, NY	10019
NOONAN, LUCY K	WRITER	555 W 57TH ST #1230	NEW YORK, NY	10019
NOONAN, MARGARET	WRITER	555 W 57TH ST #1230	NEW YORK, NY	10019
NOONAN, SUSAN H	WRITER	555 W 57TH ST #1230	NEW YORK, NY	10019
NOONAN, TOM	ACTOR	POST OFFICE BOX 5617	BEVERLY HILLS, CA	90210
NOONE, KATHLEEN	ACTRESS	ABC-TV, "ALL MY CHILDREN"		
		1330 AVE OF THE AMERICAS	NEW YORK, NY	10019
NOONE, PETER	SINGER-ACTOR	9200 SUNSET BLVD #1210	LOS ANGELES, CA	90069
NOONOO, BOB	TV WRITER	9528 BOLTON RD	LOS ANGELES, CA	90034
NOOSE, TED	ACTOR	10000 RIVERSIDE DR #3	TOLUCA LAKE, CA	91602
NORCROSS, CLAYTON	ACTOR	CBS TELEVISION NETWORK		
		"THE BOLD & THE BEAUTIFUL"		
		7800 BEVERLY BLVD	LOS ANGELES, CA	90036
NORD, JOANIE	ACTRESS	SEE - KJAR, JOAN		
NORD THE BARBARIAN	WRESTLER	AMERICAN WRESTLING ASSOC		
		MINNEAPLOIS WRESTLING		
		10001 WAYZATA BLVD	MINNETONKA, MN	55345
NORDEN, CHRISTER	COMPOSER	POST OFFICE BOX 4663	PANORAMA CITY, CA	91412
NORDEN, DENIS	ACTOR-WRITER	YOUNG, 31 KING'S RD	LONDON SW3 4RP	ENGLAND
NORDLINGER, STEPHEN E	NEWS CORRESPONDENT	3307 SHEPHERD ST	CHEVY CHASE, MD	20815
NORELL, JUDITH	HARPSICHORDIST	IMG ARTISTS, 22 E 71ST ST	NEW YORK, NY	10021
NORIN, BIL	ACTOR	1607 N EL CENTRO AVE #2	LOS ANGELES, CA	90028
NORKETT, DONALD	PHOTOGRAPHER	28 N BABYLON TURNPIKE	MERRICK, NY	11566
NORLAND, DEAN E	NEWS CORRESPONDENT	ABC-TV, NEWS DEPARTMENT		
		1717 DE SALES ST, NW	WASHINGTON, DC	20036
NORLING, RICHARD A	NEWS CORRESPONDENT	10082 DUDLEY DR	IJAMSVILLE, MD	21754
NORLING, RICHARD V	PHOTOJOURNALIST	8809 TALLEYHO TRAIL	POTOMAC, MD	20854
NORLUND, EVY	ACTRESS	2375 KIMRIDGE RD	BEVERLY HILLS, CA	90210
NORMAN, BARRY	TV WRITER	10 BURY LN, DATCHWORTH	HERTS	ENGLAND
NORMAN, BEN	DIRECTOR	1221 SUNSET PLAZA DR #11	LOS ANGELES, CA	90069
NORMAN, BRUCE	WRITER-PRODUCER	14 THE RYDE, HATFIELD	HERTS	ENGLAND
NORMAN, DAVID	DIRECTOR	258 BROADWAY	NEW YORK, NY	10007
NORMAN, DON	ACTOR	8831 SUNSET BLVD #402	LOS ANGELES, CA	90069
NORMAN, HAL JON	ACTOR	5330 LANKERSHIM BLVD #210	NORTH HOLLYWOOD, CA	91601
NORMAN, JEROLD	TENOR	59 E 54TH ST #81	NEW YORK, NY	10022
NORMAN, JESSYE	SOPRANO	SHAW CONCERTS, 1995 BROADWAY	NEW YORK, NY	10023
NORMAN, JIM ED	MUSIC ARRANGER	22110 CLARENDON ST #101	WOODLAND HILLS, CA	91367
NORMAN, JOHN T	NEWS CORRESPONDENT	9420 COLUMBIA BLVD	SILVER SPRING, MD	20910
NORMAN, JUNIOR	SINGER	PROCESS, 439 WILEY AVE	FRANKLIN, PA	16323
NORMAN, MAIDIE	ACTRESS	15010 VENTURA BLVD #219	SHERMAN OAKS, CA	91403

Name	Occupation	Address	City	Zip
NORMAN, MARC B	WRITER-PRODUCER	28 LATIMER RD	SANTA MONICA, CA	90402
NORMAN, MARSHA W	TV WRITER	555 W 57TH ST #1230	NEW YORK, NY	10019
NORMAN, PETER RIES	DIRECTOR	WEST HEBRON RD	SALEM, NY	12865
NORMAN, THEODORE	COMPOSER	451 WESTMOUNT DR	LOS ANGELES, CA	90048
NORMAN, ZACK	ACTOR	STONE, 1052 CAROL DR	LOS ANGELES, CA	90069
NORMENT, JOHN	CARTOONIST	POST OFFICE BOX 4203	NEW YORK, NY	10017
NORMINGTON, JOHN	ACTOR	BROWNE, 13 SAINT MARTINS RD	LONDON SW9	ENGLAND
NORR, CARL	DIRECTOR	DGA, 110 W 57TH ST	NEW YORK, NY	10019
NORRIS, CHARLENE	PIANIST	636 TOBY LYNN CT	NASHVILLE, TN	37211
NORRIS, CHRISTOPHER	ACTRESS	10000 SANTA MONICA BLVD #305	LOS ANGELES, CA	90067
NORRIS, CHUCK	ACTOR	7 W EMPTY SADDLE RD	ROLLING HILLS, CA	90274
NORRIS, JANE	VIOLINIST	4021 SUNNYBROOK DR	NASHVILLE, TN	37205
NORRIS, LESLIE	ACTRESS	3800 BARHAM BLVD #303	LOS ANGELES, CA	90068
NORRIS, MIKE	ACTOR	7 W EMPTY SADDLE RD	ROLLING HILLS, CA	90274
NORRIS, PAMELA	WRITER	555 W 57TH ST #1230	NEW YORK, NY	10019
NORRIS, RUFUS	ACTOR	27 W 9TH ST	NEW YORK, NY	10011
NORTE, RUBEN	TV DIRECTOR	ENTERTAINMENT TONIGHT		
		PARAMOUNT TELEVISION		
		5555 MELROSE AVE	LOS ANGELES, CA	90038
NORTH, ALAN	ACTOR	POST OFFICE BOX 5617	BEVERLY HILLS, CA	90210
NORTH, ALEX	COMPOSER	630 RESOLANO DR	PACIFIC PALISADES, CA	90272
NORTH, BARBARA	ACTRESS	19133 OXNARD ST	TARZANA, CA	91356
NORTH, DAVID	NEWS CORRESPONDENT	332 CLUB VIEW DR	GREAT FALLS, VA	22206
NORTH, EDMUND H	SCREENWRITER	212 N CARMELINA AVE	LOS ANGELES, CA	90049
NORTH, HOPE	ACTRESS	9441 WILSHIRE BLVD #620-D	BEVERLY HILLS, CA	90210
NORTH, JAY	ACTOR	12214 VIEWCREST RD	STUDIO CITY, CA	91604
NORTH, KIM	ACTRESS	247 S BEVERLY DR #102	BEVERLY HILLS, CA	90210
NORTH, LT COL OLIVER	LIEUTENANT COLONEL	839 17TH ST, NW	WASHINGTON, DC	20006
NORTH, NOELLE	ACTRESS	13335 CHANDLER BLVD	VAN NUYS, CA	91401
NORTH, REX	GUITARIST	ROUTE #2	BON AQUA, TN	37025
NORTH, SHEREE	ACTRESS	10100 SANTA MONICA BLVD #1600	LOS ANGELES, CA	90067
NORTH, STEVEN	ACTOR-WRITER	19133 OXNARD ST	TARZANA, CA	91356
NORTHERN PIKES	ROCK & ROLL GROUP	41 BRITAIN ST #200	TORONTO, ONT	CANADA
NORTHINGTON, DAVID	PIANIST	1182 MARKET ST #311	SAN FRANCISCO, CA	94102
NORTHROP, ANN E	WRITER	555 W 57TH ST #1230	NEW YORK, NY	10019
NORTHROP, WAYNE	ACTOR	21919 W CANON DR	TOPANGA CANYON, CA	90290
NORTHRUP, STEPHEN	PHOTOGRAPHER	TIME/TIME & LIFE BLDG		
		ROCKEFELLER CENTER	NEW YORK, NY	10020
NORTHSHIELD, ROBERT	TV WRITER-PRODUCER	CBS-TV, 524 W 57TH ST	NEW YORK, NY	10019
NORTHUP, HARRY E	ACTOR	1239 3/4 N HAVENHURST DR	LOS ANGELES, CA	90046
NORTON, BILL W L	FILM WRITER-DIRECTOR	151 S EL CAMINO DR	BEVERLY HILLS, CA	90210
NORTON, CHARLES	TV DIRECTOR	2403 CRESTVIEW DR	HOLLYWOOD, CA	90046
NORTON, CLARK R	WRITER	8955 BEVERLY BLVD	LOS ANGELES, CA	90048
NORTON, CLIFF	ACTOR	211 S REEVES DR	BEVERLY HILLS, CA	90212
NORTON, DON W	DIRECTOR	5332 S SHONE DR	CHICAGO, IL	60637
NORTON, ELEANOR ELIAS	SCREENWRITER	8955 BEVERLY BLVD	LOS ANGELES, CA	90048
NORTON, KEN	ACTOR-BOXER	5511 BEDFORD AVE	LOS ANGELES, CA	90056
NORTON, MARY E	NEWS CORRESPONDENT	5151 WISCONSIN AVE, NW	WASHINGTON, DC	20016
NORTON, RANDY	ACTOR	8350 SANTA MONICA BLVD #103	LOS ANGELES, CA	90069
NORTON, WILLIAM LLOYD	FILM WRITER-DIRECTOR	2509 OCEAN FRONT WALK	VENICE, CA	90291
NORTON BUFFALO STAMPEDE	ROCK & ROLL GROUP	POST OFFICE BOX 2489	SAN RAFAEL, CA	94901
NORTON-TAYLOR, JUDY	ACTRESS-MODEL	4926 REDFORMA RD	WOODLAND HILLS, CA	91367
NORUM, ROGER	WRITER	555 W 57TH ST #1230	NEW YORK, NY	10019
NORVET, ROBERT W	FILM EXECUTIVE	534 AVONDALE AVE	LOS ANGELES, CA	90049
NORWOOD, AUDRIANNE	ACTRESS	357 S REXFORD DR #203	BEVERLY HILLS, CA	90212
NORWOOD, FRANK	TV WRITER	8955 BEVERLY BLVD	LOS ANGELES, CA	90048
NOSSECK, NOEL	WRITER-PRODUCER	20406 SEABOARD RD	MALIBU, CA	90265
NOSTRO, CAYSTANO	OBOIST	3607 MAYFLOWER PL #A	NASHVILLE, TN	37204
NOTEY, JANET COLE	ACTRESS	27 FLEET ST #20	MARINA DEL REY, CA	90292
NOTO, CLAIRE B	WRITER	8955 BEVERLY BLVD	LOS ANGELES, CA	90048
NOTO, LORE	THEATER PRODUCER	181 SULLIVAN ST	NEW YORK, NY	10012
NOURI, MICHAEL	ACTOR	10100 SANTA MONICA BLVD #1600	LOS ANGELES, CA	90067
NOVACK, SHELLY	ACTRESS	390 VANCE ST	PACIFIC PALISADES, CA	90272
NOVAK, BLAINE	WRITER	555 W 57TH ST #1230	NEW YORK, NY	10019
NOVAK, JANE	ACTRESS	4172 STANSBURY AVE	SHERMAN OAKS, CA	91423
NOVAK, KIM	ACTRESS	445 N BEDFORD DR #PH	BEVERLY HILLS, CA	90210
NOVAK, MARY E	WRITER	555 W 57TH ST #1230	NEW YORK, NY	10019
NOVAK, RALPH	WRITER-EDITOR	PEOPLE/TIME & LIFE BLDG		
		ROCKEFELLER CENTER	NEW YORK, NY	10020
NOVAK, ROBERT	NEWS REPORTER	NEWS AMERICA SYNDICATE		
		1703 KAISER AVE	IRVINE, CA	92714
NOVAK, THOMAS M	NEWS CORRESPONDENT	ROUTE #1, BOX 1170-A	PORT TOBACCO, MD	20677
NOVAKOVICH, ALEX	ACTRESS-MODEL	2118 CALIFORNIA AVE	SANTA MONICA, CA	90403
NOVECK, FIMA	TV DIRECTOR-PRODUCER	161 E 61ST ST	NEW YORK, NY	10021
NOVELLO, DON	ACT-WRI-COMED	ICM, 8899 BEVERLY BLVD	LOS ANGELES, CA	90048
NOVELLO, JOSEPH	TV DIRECTOR	84 MIDVALE AVE	MILLINGTON, NJ	07946
NOVER, NAOMI	NEWS CORRESPONDENT	3001 VEAZEY TERR, NW	WASHINGTON, DC	20008
NOVIK, M S	DIRECTOR	300 W 23RD ST	NEW YORK, NY	10011
NOVITSKAYA, EKATERINA	PIANIST	GERSHUNOFF, 502 PARK AVE	NEW YORK, NY	10022
NOVOA, SALVADOR	TENOR	45 W 60TH ST #4-K	NEW YORK, NY	10023
NOVOSON, SHERMAN	CELLIST	2201 25TH AVE S	NASHVILLE, TN	37212
NOWAK, MICHAEL	CONDUCTOR	16733 BOLLINGER DR	PACIFIC PALISADES, CA	90272
NOWELL, DAVID	CINEMATOGRAPHER	7715 SUNSET BLVD #150	LOS ANGELES, CA	90046
NOWINSON, DAVID	WRITER	11051 MISSOURI AVE #A-4	LOS ANGELES, CA	90025
NOXON, NICOLAS L	WRITER-PRODUCER	11139 HORTENSE ST	NORTH HOLLYWOOD, CA	91602

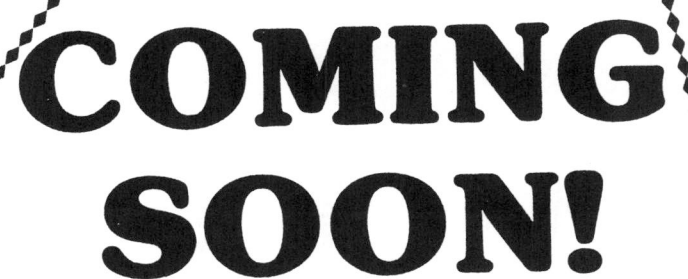

Name	Occupation	Address	City	ZIP
NOYCE, PHILLIP	FILM DIRECTOR	AUSTRALIAN FILM COMM		
		9229 SUNSET BLVD	LOS ANGELES, CA	90069
NOYCE, RICHARD	ACTOR	FELBER, 2126 N CAHUENGA BLVD	LOS ANGELES, CA	90068
NOYCE, ROBERT	INVENTER	3200 LAKESIDE DR	SANTA CLARA, CA	95051
NOYES, DANIEL P	NEWS CORRESPONDENT	4849 CONNECTICUT AVE, NW	WASHINGTON, DC	20008
NOYES, HELEN	ACTRESS	1271 BOYNTON ST #10	GLENDALE, CA	91205
NOYES, TIMOTHY	ACTOR	752 N EDINBURGH AVE #1/2	LOS ANGELES, CA	90046
NRBO	C & W GROUP	SEE - N R B O		
NRBQ & THE WHOLE WHEAT HORNS	RHYTHM & BLUES GROUP	POST OFFICE BOX 210103	SAN FRANCISCO, CA	94121
NSKY, ROBERT	VIOLINIST	3003 VAN NESS ST #W-205, NW	WASHINGTON, DC	20008
NU SHOOZ	ROCK-JAZZ DUO	GTI, 1700 BROADWAY, 10TH FLOOR	NEW YORK, NY	10019
NUCCI, DANNY	ACTOR	12725 VENTURA BLVD #E	STUDIO CITY, CA	91604
NUCCI, LEO	BARITONE	CAMI, 165 W 57TH ST	NEW YORK, NY	10019
NUCKLES, WILLIAM PAUL	DIRECTOR	CONDOR CRAG STUNT RD	CALABASAS, CA	91302
NUCLEAR ASSAULT	ROCK & ROLL GROUP	POST OFFICE BOX 4164	OSBORNVILLE, NJ	08723
NUDELL, SAM	ACTOR	14721 PARTHENIA ST	PANORAMA CITY, CA	91402
NUELL, DAVID	TV DIRECTOR	ENTERTAINMENT TONIGHT		
		PARAMOUNT TELEVISION		
		5555 MELROSE AVE	LOS ANGELES, CA	90038
NUGENT, EDWARD	ACTOR	419 DEVONSHIRE ST	SAN ANTONIO, TX	78209
NUGENT, JO	WRITER	8955 BEVERLY BLVD	LOS ANGELES, CA	90048
NUGENT, JOHN PEER	WRITER	1322 2ND ST #35	SANTA MONICA, CA	90401
NUGENT, KELBE	ACTRESS	6430 SUNSET BLVD #701	LOS ANGELES, CA	90028
NUGENT, NELLE	THEATER PRODUCER	1501 BROADWAY	NEW YORK, NY	10036
NUGENT, TED	SINGER-GUITARIST	3101 E EISENHOWER #3	ANN ARBOR, MI	48104
NUISANCE	ROCK & ROLL GROUP	VARIETY ARTISTS INTL, INC		
		9073 NEMO ST, 3RD FLOOR	LOS ANGELES, CA	90069
NUMAN, GARY	SINGER-SONGWRITER	BEGGAR'S, 8 HOGARTH RD	LONDON SW5	ENGLAND
NUNLEY, LOUIS	MUSIC ARRANGER	POST OFFICE BOX 2112	NASHVILLE, TN	37214
NUNLEY, LOUISE	SINGER	POST OFFICE BOX 2112	NASHVILLE, TN	37214
NUNN, ALICE	ACTRESS	976 N LARRABEE ST #228	LOS ANGELES, CA	90069
NUNN, RAY	TV PRODUCER	ABC TELEVISION NETWORK		
		1330 AVE OF THE AMERICAS	NEW YORK, NY	10019
NUNN, TREVOR	TV DIRECTOR	BARBICAN THEATRE, SILK ST	LONDON EC2	ENGLAND
NUNS, THE	ROCK & ROLL GROUP	JEM RECORDS COMPANY		
		3619 KENNEDY RD	SOUTH PLAINFIELD, NJ	07080
NUREYEV, RUDOLPH	DANCER	GORLINSKY, 35 DOVER ST	LONDON W1	ENGLAND
NURSE, KARL	DIRECTOR	294 SHAWMUT AVE	BOSTON, MA	02116
NUSS, WILLIAM M	WRITER	8955 BEVERLY BLVD	LOS ANGELES, CA	90048
NUSSBAUM, AL	WRITER	8955 BEVERLY BLVD	LOS ANGELES, CA	90048
NUSSBAUM, GAIL	REPORTER	TIME & PEOPLE MAGAZINE		
		TIME & LIFE BUILDING		
		ROCKEFELLER CENTER	NEW YORK, NY	10020
NUSSBAUM, STANLEY	COMPOSER	2051 BENTLEY AVE #104	LOS ANGELES, CA	90025
NUTTER, MAYF	ACTOR	1930 CENTURY PARK W #303	LOS ANGELES, CA	90067
NUTTER, TARAH	ACTRESS	10351 SANTA MONICA BLVD #211	LOS ANGELES, CA	90025
NUTTING, BRIAN	NEWS CORRESPONDENT	14906 LAUREL OAKS LN	LAUREL, MD	20707
NUTZLE, FUTZIE	CARTOONIST	POST OFFICE BOX 325	AROMAS, CA	95004
NUYEN, FRANCE	ACTRESS	MORELL, 1800 FRANKLIN CYN TERR	BEVERLY HILLS, CA	90210
NUZUM, ROBERT	ACTOR	6565 SUNSET BLVD #218	HOLLYWOOD, CA	90028
NUZZI, ROBYN	MODEL	POST OFFICE BOX 7211	MOUNTAIN VIEW, CA	94043
NYBERG, CHRISTINA	ACTRESS	439 S LA CIENEGA BLVD #117	LOS ANGELES, CA	90048
NYBERG, PETER	WRITER	8955 BEVERLY BLVD	LOS ANGELES, CA	90048
NYBY, CHRISTIAN, III	DIRECTOR	1030 GREEN LN	LA CANADA, CA	91011
NYE, ANITA	SONGWRITER	1241 CORSICA DR	PACIFIC PALISADES, CA	90272
NYE, BARRY D	TV DIRECTOR	11317 BLIX ST	NORTH HOLLYWOOD, CA	91602
NYE, CARRIE	ACTRESS	109 E 79TH ST	NEW YORK, NY	10019
NYE, DAVID	GUITARIST	830 GLASTONBURY RD #804	NASHVILLE, TN	37217
NYE, DOROTHY	WRITER-PRODUCER	POST OFFICE BOX 7141	CARMEL, CA	93921
NYE, HARRY F	WRITER	555 W 57TH ST #1230	NEW YORK, NY	10019
NYE, LOUIS	ACTOR-COMEDIAN	1241 CORSICA DR	PACIFIC PALISADES, CA	90272
NYE, PETER J	NEWS CORRESPONDENT	5780 DUNSTER CT #173	ALEXANDRIA, VA	22311
NYGAARD, JENS	PIANIST	JCB, 155 W 68TH ST	NEW YORK, NY	10023
NYKANEN, ANN	WRITER	555 W 57TH ST #1230	NEW YORK, NY	10019
NYKANEN, MARK	NEWS CORRESPONDENT	NBC-TV, NEWS DEPARTMENT		
		30 ROCKEFELLER PLAZA	NEW YORK, NY	10112
NYKVIST, SVEN	CINEMATOGRAPHER	7715 SUNSET BLVD #150	LOS ANGELES, CA	90046
NYLONS, THE	ROCK & ROLL GROUP	366 ADELAIDE ST E #436	TORONTO, ONT M5A 3X9	CANADA
NYPE, RUSSELL	ACTOR	170 E 78TH ST	NEW YORK, NY	10021
NYRO, LAURA	SINGER-SONGWRITER	POST OFFICE BOX 186	SHOREHAM, NY	11786
NYROP, SIRI	NEWS CORRESPONDENT	3132 "M" ST, NW	WASHINGTON, DC	20007

Name	Occupation	Address	City	ZIP
O, BARRY	WRESTLER	SEE - BARRY O		
O, GARY	SINGER-SONGWRITER	SEE - GARY O		
O'BANION, JOHN	SINGER	433 N CAMDEN DR #950	BEVERLY HILLS, CA	90210
O'BANION, JOHN	ACTOR	7469 MELROSE AVE #30	LOS ANGELES, CA	90046

Name	Occupation	Address	City	Zip
O'BANNON, DAN	FILM WRITER-DIRECTOR	MORTON AGY, 1105 GLENDON AVE	LOS ANGELES, CA	90024
O'BRIAN, HUGH	ACTOR	3195 BENEDICT CANYON DR	BEVERLY HILLS, CA	90210
O'BRIEN, BOB	TV WRITER	8955 BEVERLY BLVD	LOS ANGELES, CA	90048
O'BRIEN, BRIAN	ACTOR	9220 SUNSET BLVD #202	LOS ANGELES, CA	90069
O'BRIEN, CUBBY	ACTOR	11274 DULCET AVE	NORTHRIDGE, CA	91324
O'BRIEN, ELLEN	ACTRESS	9220 SUNSET BLVD #218	LOS ANGELES, CA	90069
O'BRIEN, FRANK	ACTOR	1520 YORK AVE	NEW YORK, NY	10028
O'BRIEN, JACK	DIRECTOR	POST OFFICE BOX 2171	SAN DIEGO, CA	92112
O'BRIEN, JEAN	WRITER	8955 BEVERLY BLVD	LOS ANGELES, CA	90048
O'BRIEN, JOAN	WRITER	8955 BEVERLY BLVD	LOS ANGELES, CA	90048
O'BRIEN, LAURIE	ACTRESS	10000 SANTA MONICA BLVD #305	LOS ANGELES, CA	90067
O'BRIEN, LIAM	WRITER	2259 SAN YSIDRO DR	BEVERLY HILLS, CA	90210
O'BRIEN, MARGARET	ACTRESS	1250 LA PERESA DR	THOUSAND OAKS, CA	91362
O'BRIEN, MARIA	ACTRESS	1930 CENTURY PARK W #303	LOS ANGELES, CA	90067
O'BRIEN, PATRICIA	NEWS CORRESPONDENT	5318 MC ARTHUR BLVD, NW	WASHINGTON, DC	20016
O'BRIEN, PETER	FILM PRODUCER	264 SEATON ST	TORONTO, ONT M5A 2T4	CANADA
O'BRIEN, ROBERT	NEWS CORRESPONDENT	1851 COLUMBIA RD #302, NW	WASHINGTON, DC	20009
O'BRIEN, TIM	NEWS CORRESPONDENT	ABC-TV, NEWS DEPARTMENT		
		1717 DE SALES ST, NW	WASHINGTON, DC	20036
O'BRIEN, TIM	SINGER	POST OFFICE BOX 6025	NEWPORT NEWS, VA	23606
O'BRYAN	SINGER-SONGWRITER	POST OFFICE BOX 48306	LOS ANGELES, CA	90048
O'BRYAN, FRAN	TALENT AGENT	9085 W 3RD ST #303	LOS ANGELES, CA	90048
O'BRYANT, ALAN	GUITARIST	POST OFFICE BOX 11	KINGSTON SPRINGS, TN	37082
O'BYRNE, BRYAN	ACTOR	9200 SUNSET BLVD #801	LOS ANGELES, CA	90069
O'CALLAGHAN, RICHARD	ACTOR	HEATH, PARAMOUNT HOUSE		
		162-170 WARDOUR ST	LONDON W1V 3AT	ENGLAND
O'CHRISTOPHER, C R	TV WRITER	8955 BEVERLY BLVD	LOS ANGELES, CA	90048
O'CON, PAULINE	CASTING DIRECTOR	ABC-TV ENTERTAINMENT CENTER		
		2040 AVE OF THE STARS	LOS ANGELES, CA	90067
O'CONNELL, BOB	ACTOR	334 E 90TH ST	NEW YORK, NY	10028
O'CONNELL, FRANCES	WRITER	555 W 57TH ST #1230	NEW YORK, NY	10019
O'CONNELL, HELEN	SINGER	1260 S BEVERLY GLEN BLVD	LOS ANGELES, CA	90024
O'CONNELL, MARY ANN	NEWS CORRESPONDENT	10905 PAYNES CHURCH DR	FAIRFAX, VA	22032
O'CONNELL, RAYMOND T	TV EXECUTIVE	NBC TELEVISION NETWORK		
		30 ROCKEFELLER PLAZA	NEW YORK, NY	10112
O'CONNELL, RICHARD J	NEWS CORRESPONDENT	10905 PAYNES CHURCH DR	FAIRFAX, VA	22032
O'CONNELL, SUSAN	WRITER	555 W 57TH ST #1230	NEW YORK, NY	10019
O'CONNELL, SUSAN MARY	NEWS CORRESPONDENT	10905 PAYNES CHURCH DR	FAIRFAX, VA	22032
O'CONNELL, TAAFFE	ACTRESS	8019 1/2 MELROSE AVE #3	LOS ANGELES, CA	90046
O'CONNELL, WILLIAM	ACTOR	8150 BEVERLY BLVD #303	LOS ANGELES, CA	90048
O'CONNOR, CARROLL	ACT-WRI-DIR	30826 BROAD BEACH RD	MALIBU, CA	90265
O'CONNOR, CHUCK	WRESTLER-ACTOR	SEE - STUDD, BIG JOHN		
O'CONNOR, DANIEL P	TV EXECUTIVE	NBC TELEVISION NETWORK		
		30 ROCKEFELLER PLAZA	NEW YORK, NY	10112
O'CONNOR, DES	SINGER	235 REGENT ST	LONDON W1	ENGLAND
O'CONNOR, DONALD	ACTOR-DIRECTOR	3715 ALOMAR DR	SHERMAN OAKS, CA	91423
O'CONNOR, GEORGE W	NEWS CORRESPONDENT	1755 S JEFFERSON DAVIS HWY	ARLINGTON, VA	22202
O'CONNOR, GLYNNIS	ACTRESS	853 7TH AVE #9-A	NEW YORK, NY	10019
O'CONNOR, JOHN J	TV CRITIC	N Y TIMES, 229 W 43RD ST	NEW YORK, NY	10036
O'CONNOR, KEVIN	ACTOR	CHELSEA HOTEL, 222 W 23RD ST	NEW YORK, NY	10011
O'CONNOR, KEVIN J	ACTOR	666 5TH AVE	NEW YORK, NY	10019
O'CONNOR, LANA	ACTRESS	8350 SANTA MONICA BLVD #104	LOS ANGELES, CA	90069
O'CONNOR, MARILYN	ACTRESS	6430 SUNSET BLVD #1203	LOS ANGELES, CA	90028
O'CONNOR, MARK	MUSICIAN	KEITH CASE COMPANY		
O'CONNOR, MARK	NEWS CORRESPONDENT	POST OFFICE BOX 2741	WASHINGTON, DC	20057
		1016 16TH AVE S	NASHVILLE, TN	37212
O'CONNOR, PHILIP	NEWS CORRESPONDENT	3000 SPOUT RUN PARKWAY	ARLINGTON, VA	22201
O'CONNOR, RICHARD	PIANIST	FROTHINGHAM, 40 GROVE ST	WESSESLEY, MA	02181
O'CONNOR, RICHARD L	DIRECTOR	7247 WHITSETT AVE #1	STUDIO CITY, CA	91604
O'CONNOR, RICHARD L	TV PRODUCER	14937 VENTURA BLVD #201	SHERMAN OAKS, CA	91403
O'CONNOR, TERRENCE	ACTRESS	1418 N HIGHLAND AVE #102	LOS ANGELES, CA	90028
O'CONNOR, THOMAS P	WRITER	555 W 57TH ST #1230	NEW YORK, NY	10019
O'CONNOR, TIM	ACTOR	10000 SANTA MONICA BLVD #305	LOS ANGELES, CA	90067
O'CONNOR, TOM	COMEDIAN	TY GWYN, TITE HILL		
O'CONOR, JOHN	PIANIST	CAMI, 165 W 57TH ST	NEW YORK, NY	10019
		229 W 43RD ST	NEW YORK, NY	10036
		EDGEFIELD GREEN	SURREY	ENGLAND
O'DAY, ALAN	SINGER	9200 SUNSET BLVD #222	LOS ANGELES, CA	90069
O'DAY, MOLLY	ACTRESS	V O KENASTON		
		POST OFFICE BOX458	AVILA, CA	93424
O'DAY, NELL	ACTRESS	450 S GRAND VIEW ST #1101	LOS ANGELES, CA	90057
O'DAY, TOMMY	GUITARIST	10015 W 8 MILE RD	FRANKSVILLE, WI	53126
O'DELL, HOLLY	SINGER	1711 18TH AVE S #C-1	NASHVILLE, TN	37212
O'DELL, KENNY	SINGER-GUITARIST	GELFAND / BRESLAUER		
		7 MUSIC CIRCLE N	NASHVILLE, TN	37203
O'DELL, PAUL	TV DIRECTOR	35 NORMANDY AVE, HIGH BARNET	HERTFORDSHIRE	ENGLAND
O'DELL, TONY	ACTOR	3575 W CAHUENGA BLVD #320	LOS ANGELES, CA	90068
O'DETTE, PAUL	LUTENIST	AARON, 25 HUNTINGTON AVE	BOSTON, MA	02116
O'DONNELL, BOB	GUITARIST	920 DUE WEST AVE	MADISON, TN	37115

Name	Occupation	Address	City	Zip
O'DONNELL, CLAUDE	VIOLINIST	6231 BRESSLYN RD	NASHVILLE, TN	37205
O'DONNELL, JAYNE ELLEN	NEWS CORRESPONDENT	1415 RHODE ISLAND AVE #704, NW	WASHINGTON, DC	20005
O'DONNELL, KAREN J	NEWS CORRESPONDENT	1020 N QUINCY ST	ARLINGTON, VA	22201
O'DONNELL, MARK P	TV WRITER	555 W 57TH ST #1230	NEW YORK, NY	10019
O'DONNELL, MAUREEN	NEWS CORRESPONDENT	8750 GEORGIA AVE #821-A, NW	WASHINGTON, DC	20910
O'DONNELL, RICHARD	NEWS CORRESPONDENT	5151 WISCONSIN AVE, NW	WASHINGTON, DC	20016
O'DONNELL, ROBERT H	DIRECTOR	28 W 120 ROBIN LN	WEST CHICAGO, IL	60185
O'DONNELL, STEPHEN M	WRITER	555 W 57TH ST #1230	NEW YORK, NY	10019
O'DONNELL, TIMOTHY J	TV WRITER	1620 VISTA DR	GLENDALE, CA	91201
O'DONOGHUE, MICHAEL	WRITER-PRODUCER	1619 BROADWAY #915	NEW YORK, NY	10019
O'DONOUGHUE, BRIAN	TALENT AGENT	TOPLAND COMPANY, LTD		
		30 GREAT PORTLAND ST	LONDON W1	ENGLAND
O'DRISCOLL, MARTHA	ACTRESS	APPLETON, 22 INDIAN CIRCLE DR		
		INDIAN CREEK VILLAGE	MIAMI BEACH, FL	33154
O'DWYER, PATRICIA	NEWS CORRESPONDENT	1862 CALIFORNIA ST, NW	WASHINGTON, DC	20009
O'FARRELL, LEO FRANCIS	TV DIRECTOR	1713 N NORTH PARK AVE #4	CHICAGO, IL	60614
O'FLAHERTY, DENNIS M	SCREENWRITER	8955 BEVERLY BLVD	LOS ANGELES, CA	90048
O'FLANAGAN, J P	WRITER	8955 BEVERLY BLVD	LOS ANGELES, CA	90048
O'GARA, MIKE	TV PRODUCER	ENTERTAINMENT TONIGHT		
		PARAMOUNT TELEVISION		
		5555 MELROSE AVE	LOS ANGELES, CA	90038
O'GRADY, GAIL	ACTRESS	247 S BEVERLY DR #102	BEVERLY HILLS, CA	90210
O'GRADY, JACK T	WRITER	555 W 57TH ST #1230	NEW YORK, NY	10019
O'GRADY, LANI	ACTRESS	3800 BARHAM BLVD #303	LOS ANGELES, CA	90068
O'GUINNE, MICHAEL	ACTOR	400 S BEVERLY DR #216	BEVERLY HILLS, CA	90212
O'HAGAN, TIMOTHY	ACTOR	400 S BEVERLY DR #216	BEVERLY HILLS, CA	90212
O'HALLAREN, WILLIAM	WRITER	30071 ANDROMEDA LN	MALIBU, CA	90265
O'HALLORAN, THOMAS, JR	PHOTOGRAPHER	3531 DUKE ST	COLLEGE PARK, MD	20740
O'HARA, CATHERINE	ACTOR-WRITER	SCTV, 110 LOMBARD ST	TORONTO, ONT M5C IM3	CANADA
O'HARA, GERRY	FILM WRITER-DIRECTOR	51 ELM PARK GARDENS #K	LONDON SW10	ENGLAND
O'HARA, J G	WRITER	555 W 57TH ST #1230	NEW YORK, NY	10019
O'HARA, JENNY	ACTRESS	8663 WONDERLAND AVE	LOS ANGELES, CA	90046
O'HARA, MARGARET	NEWS CORRESPONDENT	6202 BEACHWAY DR	FALLS CHURCH, VA	22041
O'HARA, MAUREEN	ACTRESS	POST OFFICE BOX 1400		
		CHRISTEANSTED	SAINT CROIX, VI	00820
O'HARA, MEG	WRITER	555 W 57TH ST #1230	NEW YORK, NY	10019
O'HARA, MICHAEL	WRITER	8955 BEVERLY BLVD	LOS ANGELES, CA	90048
O'HARA, PATRICK J	WRITER	555 W 57TH ST #1230	NEW YORK, NY	10019
O'HARA-FORSTER, BRIGID	NEWS REPORTER	TIME/TIME & LIFE BLDG		
		ROCKEFELLER CENTER	NEW YORK, NY	10020
O'HARE, BRIAN	SINGER	LUTZ, 5625 "O" STREET BLDG	LINCOLN, NE	68510
O'HARE, MICHAEL	ACTOR	10 E 44TH ST #700	NEW YORK, NY	10017
O'HEARN, KATHERINE I	WRITER	555 W 57TH ST #1230	NEW YORK, NY	10019
O'HEARN, KATHY	PHOTOJOURNALIST	1522 31ST ST, NW	WASHINGTON, DC	20007
O'HERLIHY, DAN	ACTOR	31016 BROAD BEACH RD	MALIBU, CA	90265
O'HERLIHY, GAVAN	ACTOR	IAR, 235-241 REGENT ST	LONDON W1A 2JT	ENGLAND
O'HERLIHY, MICHAEL	DIRECTOR	1659 N KINGS RD	LOS ANGELES, CA	90069
O'HORGAN, THOMAS FOSTER	DIRECTOR	DGA, 110 W 57TH ST	NEW YORK, NY	10019
O'JAYS, THE	VOCAL TRIO	200 W 51ST ST #1410	NEW YORK, NY	10019
O'KEEFE, DENNIS GERARD	PHOTOJOURNALIST	201 MASSACHUSETTS AVE, NW		
		ROOM #117-A	WASHINGTON, DC	20002
O'KEEFE, DONALD	ACTOR	4521 SUNSET BLVD #104	LOS ANGELES, CA	90027
O'KEEFE, JAMES	MUSIC ARRANGER	1609 1/2 S BENTLEY AVE	LOS ANGELES, CA	90025
O'KEEFE, PAUL	ACTOR	18 W 86TH ST	NEW YORK, NY	10024
O'KEEFFE, MILES	ACTOR	POST OFFICE BOX 69365	LOS ANGELES, CA	90069
O'KELLY, BARBARA E	WRITER	8955 BEVERLY BLVD	LOS ANGELES, CA	90048
O'KUN, LAN	TV WRITER	8955 BEVERLY BLVD	LOS ANGELES, CA	90048
O'LEARY, DERRY	COMPOSER-CONDUCTOR	801 E KENSINGTON RD	LOS ANGELES, CA	90026
O'LEARY, JACK	ACTOR	726 GLADYS AVE	LONG BEACH, CA	90807
O'LEARY, JAMES "REBEL"	SINGER-SONGWRITER	POST OFFICE BOX 3525	YORK, PA	17402
O'LEARY, JEREMIAH	NEWS CORRESPONDENT	405 PRINCE ST	ALEXANDRIA, VA	22314
O'LEARY, JOHN	ACTOR	365 W END AVE	NEW YORK, NY	10024
O'LEARY, JOHN F	PHOTOGRAPHER	7518 INZER ST	SRPINGFIELD, VA	22151
O'LEARY, MICHAEL	ACTOR	CBS-TV, "THE GUILDING LIGHT		
		51 W 52ND ST	NEW YORK, NY	10019
O'LEARY, PAT	COLUMNIST	TRIBUNE MEDIA SERVICES		
		64 E CONCORD ST	ORLANDO, FL	32801
O'LEARY, RICHARD A	TV CONSULTANT	1 E 57TH ST	NEW YORK, NY	10022
O'LOUGHLIN, GERALD S	ACTOR-DIRECTOR	13907 RAYEN ST	ARLETA, CA	91331
O'LOUGHLIN, JIM	TALENT AGENT	11833 LAUREL WOOD DR #8	STUDIO CITY, CA	91604
O'LOUGHLIN, MERYL	CASTING DIRECTOR	COLUMBIA PICTURES		
		COLUMBIA PLAZA E	BURBANK, CA	91505
O'MAHONEY, PRINCESS	ACTRESS	5838 BUSCH DR	MALIBU, CA	90265
O'MALLEY, DAVE	SCREENWRITER	11726 SAN VICENTE BLVD #300	LOS ANGELES, CA	90049
O'MALLEY, KATHLEEN	ACTRESS	9165 SUNSET BLVD #202	LOS ANGELES, CA	90069
O'MALLEY, KATHY	COLUMNIST-CRITIC	TRIBUNE MEDIA SERVICES		
		64 E CONCORD ST	ORLANDO, FL	32801
O'MALLEY, SUZANNE	SCREENWRITER	9000 SUNSET BLVD #1200	LOS ANGELES, CA	90069
O'MARA, KATE	ACTRESS	BURNETT, 42 GRAFTON HOUSE		
		2-3 GOLDEN SQ	LONDON W1	ENGLAND
O'MEARA, SUSAN	WRITER	555 W 57TH ST #1230	NEW YORK, NY	10019
O'MEARA, WILLIAM J	WRITER	555 W 57TH ST #1230	NEW YORK, NY	10019
O'MELLA, JOSEPH	ACTOR	200 N ROBERTSON BLVD #308	BEVERLY HILLS, CA	90210
O'NEAL, CHARLES E	WRITER	741 CHAPALA DR	PACIFIC PALISADES, CA	90272

KING OF COUNTRY MUSIC

THE MAN — THE LEGEND

JAMES "REBEL" O'LEARY

Awards

1987	***LIVING LEGEND AWARD*** *Presented by Melvin Bittner Sr., President Country Musicians, Green Mountain Jubilee*
1986	***COMMISSIONED CAPTAIN NASHVILLE TENN. METRO POLICE*** ***Country Music Hall of Fame Foundation Library, Nashville, TN*** ***United Way Community Spirit — Certificate of Appreciation, U.S. Jaycees***
1985	***VIDEO: THE MAN...THE LEGEND*** *Producer Ned Lightner, Cable TV* *Country Musicians Hall of Fame, Green Mountain Jubilee*
1985–87	***Salute to Ernest Tubb • Midnight Jamboree • Fan Fair • Nashville, Tennessee***
1984	***INTERNATIONAL ENTERTAINER OF THE YEAR*** ***Blue Rooster Award —*** *Country Musicians Green Mountain Jubilee* ***Ohio State Fair Certificate of Appreciation,*** *Ohio Country Music Association*
1983	***Easter Seals Appreciation Award, Sunshine Foundation Award***
1982	***C.M.E. MALE ENTERTAINER, K.C.Z.T. MALE VOCALIST***
1981	***M.A.F.C. HONARY OF THE YEAR***
1979 '80, '81	***K.C.Z.T. KING OF COUNTRY MUSIC***
1978	***TEXAS PROUD HILLBILLY HEART AWARD***

James "Rebel" O'Leary International Fan Club
P.O. BOX 3525 York, PA 17402 (717) 792-3060

Barbara Hope, Director
J.E. Christiner, Manager

Name	Occupation	Address	City	Zip
O'NEAL, FREDERICK	ACTOR-DIRECTOR	41 CONVENT AVE	NEW YORK, NY	10027
O'NEAL, GRIFFIN	ACTOR	21368 PACIFIC COAST HWY	MALIBU, CA	90265
O'NEAL, KEVIN	SCREENWRITER	12320 BURBANK BLVD #112	NORTH HOLLYWOOD, CA	91607
O'NEAL, PATRICK	ACTOR-DIRECTOR	DGA, 110 W 57TH ST	NEW YORK, NY	10019
O'NEAL, PATRICK	WRITER	555 W 57TH ST #1230	NEW YORK, NY	10019
O'NEAL, RON	ACTOR-DIRECTOR	12750 VENTURA BLVD #102	STUDIO CITY, CA	91604
O'NEAL, RYAN	ACTOR	21368 PACIFIC COAST HWY	MALIBU, CA	90265
O'NEAL, TATUM	ACTRESS	22240 PACIFIC COAST HWY	MALIBU, CA	90265
O'NEIL, DENNY E	WRITER	8955 BEVERLY BLVD	LOS ANGELES, CA	90048
O'NEIL, EMMITT-LEON	FILM DIRECTOR	1345 N HAYWORTH AVE #209	LOS ANGELES, CA	90046
O'NEIL, ROBERT VINCENT	SCREENWRITER	8955 BEVERLY BLVD	LOS ANGELES, CA	90048
O'NEIL, ROGER	NEWS CORRESPONDENT	NBC-TV, NEWS DEPARTMENT		
		30 ROCKEFELLER PLAZA	NEW YORK, NY	10112
O'NEIL, SHANE	FILM EXECUTIVE	RKO-GENERAL, 1440 BROADWAY	NEW YORK, NY	10018
O'NEIL, TERENCE G	WRITER	555 W 57TH ST #1230	NEW YORK, NY	10019
O'NEIL, TERRY	TV PRODUCER	CBS-TV, 51 W 52ND ST	NEW YORK, NY	10019
O'NEIL, TONY	ACTOR	8230 BEVERLY BLVD #23	LOS ANGELES, CA	90048
O'NEIL, TRICIA	ACTRESS	15201 VENTURA BLVD #345	SHERMAN OAKS, CA	91403
O'NEILL, ANNIE	ACTRESS	9220 SUNSET BLVD #625	LOS ANGELES, CA	90069
O'NEILL, CATHARINE	CARTOONIST	POST OFFICE BOX 4203	NEW YORK, NY	10017
O'NEILL, DENNIS	TENOR	CAMI, 165 W 57TH ST	NEW YORK, NY	10019
O'NEILL, DENNIS R	WRITER	555 W 57TH ST #1230	NEW YORK, NY	10019
O'NEILL, DICK	ACTOR	ICM, 8899 BEVERLY BLVD	LOS ANGELES, CA	90048
O'NEILL, EILEEN	WRITER	9654 HIGH RIDGE DR	BEVERLY HILLS, CA	90210
O'NEILL, EILEEN	ACTRESS	9056 SANTA MONICA BLVD #201	LOS ANGELES, CA	90069
O'NEILL, FREDERICK R	TV DIRECTOR	492 WAYNE AVE	SPRINGFIELD, PA	19064
O'NEILL, GREY	ACTOR	3104 W BALL RD	ANAHEIM, CA	92804
O'NEILL, JENNIFER	ACTRESS-MODEL	2121 AVE OF THE STARS #410	LOS ANGELES, CA	90067
O'NEILL, JULIET	NEWS CORRESPONDENT	1920 35TH PL, NW	WASHINGTON, DC	20007
O'NEILL, KATIE	ACTRESS	3575 W CAHUENGA BLVD #320	LOS ANGELES, CA	90068
O'NEILL, KEN	TV DIRECTOR	ROSEMAN, 8 POLAND ST	LONDON W1	ENGLAND
O'NEILL, MICHAEL G	DIRECTOR	DGA, 110 W 57TH ST	NEW YORK, NY	10019
O'NEILL, PATRICIA	SOPRANO	61 W 62ND ST #6-F	NEW YORK, NY	10023
O'NEILL, REMY	ACTRESS	BUSH & ROSS, 4942 VINELAND AVE	NORTH HOLLYWOOD, CA	91601
O'NEILL, ROBERT F	TV WRITER-PRODUCER	22855 PAUL REVERE DR	CALABASAS, CA	91302
O'REILLY, CYRIL	ACTOR	151 S EL CAMINO DR	BEVERLY HILLS, CA	90212
O'REILLY, DANIEL PATRICK	WRITER	8955 BEVERLY BLVD	LOS ANGELES, CA	90048
O'REILLY, ERIN	ACTRESS	9255 SUNSET BLVD #1105	LOS ANGELES, CA	90069
O'REILLY, JANE	WRITER	555 W 57TH ST #1230	NEW YORK, NY	10019
O'REILLY, KATHRYN	ACTRESS	113 N SAN VICENTE BLVD #202	BEVERLY HILLS, CA	90211
O'RILEY, CHRISTOPHER	PIANIST	59 E 54TH ST #81	NEW YORK, NY	10022
O'ROURKE, HEATHER	ACTRESS	CED, 261 S ROBERTSON BLVD	BEVERLY HILLS, CA	90211
O'ROURKE, JOSEPH J	DIRECTOR	5 HOLLY DR	FAIRFIELD, NJ	07006
O'ROURKE, LAWRENCE M	NEWS CORRESPONDENT	3904 ROSEMARY ST	CHEVY CHASE, MD	20815
O'ROURKE, MIKE	TV DIRECTOR	1626 N WILCOX AVE #315	LOS ANGELES, CA	90028
O'ROURKE, P J	SCREENWRITER	555 W 57TH ST #1230	NEW YORK, NY	10019
O'SHEA, JAMES E	NEWS CORRESPONDENT	3739 MILITARY RD, NW	WASHINGTON, DC	20015
O'SHEA, MILO	ACTOR	THE BANCROFT HOTEL		
		40 W 72ND ST #17-A	NEW YORK, NY	10023
O'SHEA, PEGGY	TV WRITER	ABC-TV, "ONE LIFE TO LIVE"		
		1330 AVE OF THE AMERICAS	NEW YORK, NY	10019
O'SHEA, ROBERT	ACTOR	LEONETTI, 6526 SUNSET BLVD	HOLLYWOOD, CA	90028
O'STEEN, SAM	TV WRITER-DIRECTOR	190 N CANON DR #202	BEVERLY HILLS, CA	90210
O'SULLAVAN, MAUREEN	ACTRESS	1839 UNION ST	SCHENECTATY, NY	12309
O'SULLIVAN, GILBERT	SINGER	SAINT GEORGE'S HILL	WEYBRIDGE	ENGLAND
O'SULLIVAN, JIM	ACTOR	ABC-TV, "ONE LIFE TO LIVE"		
		1330 AVE OF THE AMERICAS	NEW YORK, NY	10019
O'SULLIVAN, RICHARD	ACTOR	MITCHELL, 7 GARRICK ST	LONDON WC2	ENGLAND
O'TOOLE, ANNETTE	ACTRESS	151 S EL CAMINO DR	BEVERLY HILLS, CA	90212
O'TOOLE, JAMES	NEWS CORRESPONDENT	1753 "Q" ST #B, NW	WASHINGTON, DC	20009
O'TOOLE, JOHN	WRITER	555 W 57TH ST #1230	NEW YORK, NY	10019
O'TOOLE, MAUREEN	ACTRESS	3330 BARHAM BLVD #103	LOS ANGELES, CA	90068
O'TOOLE, OLLIE	ACTOR	10000 RIVERSIDE DR #3	TOLUCA LAKE, CA	91602
O'TOOLE, PETER	ACTOR	98 HEATH ST	LONDON NW3	ENGLAND
O'TOOLE, STANLEY	FILM PRODUCER	TREWOLFE ORCHARD, LAMORNA		
		NEAR PENZANCE	CORNWALL	ENGLAND
OAK RIDGE BOYS, THE	C & W GROUP	329 ROCKLAND RD	HENDERSONVILLE, TN	37075
OAKES, BETTY	ACTRESS	170 2ND AVE	NEW YORK, NY	10003
OAKES, BOB	PIANIST	2131 ELM HILL PIKE #P-295	NASHVILLE, TN	37210
OAKES, RANDI	ACTRESS	15509 BRIARWOOD DR	SHERMAN OAKS, CA	91403
OAKES, ROBERT S	PHOTOGRAPHER	11110 KENNELWORTH AVE	GARRET PARK, MD	20766
OAKES, RODNEY H	COMPOSER	228 EL MOLINO AVE	PASADENA, CA	91101
OAS-HEIM, GORDON	ACTOR	14556 MAGNOLIA BLVD #103	SHERMAN OAKS, CA	91403
OASIS	GOSPEL GROUP	POST OFFICE BOX 28082	COLUMBUS, OH	43228
OASIS HILLBILLY BAND, THE	BLUEGRASS GROUP	POST OFFICE BOX 25371	CHARLOTTE, NC	28212
OATES, DIANE M	DIRECTOR	DGA, 110 W 57TH ST	NEW YORK, NY	10019
OATES, ED	DIRECTOR	137 HERITAGE VILLAGE #A	SOUTHBURY, CT	06488
OATES, MARTY	WRESTLER	SEE - JANNETTY, MARTY		
OATES, RONG	MUSIC ARRANGER	113 BEAR TRACK	NASHVILLE, TN	37221
OATES, WALTER	PHOTOGRAPHER	8837 BROOKVALE CT	SPRINGFIELD, VA	22153
OATES, WENDY	ACTRESS	CONTEMPORARY ARTISTS		
		132 S LASKY DR	BEVERLY HILLS, CA	90212
OATTES VAN SCHAIK	ROCK & ROCK DUO	POST OFFICE BOX 470309	BROOKLYN, NY	11247
OBER, ARLON L E	COMPOSER	1253 19TH ST	SANTA MONICA, CA	90404
OBER, EUGENE W	FRENCH HORNIST	737 N CATALINA AVE	PASADENA, CA	91104

OBER, GENE	ACTOR-MODEL	6523 WOODMAN AVE #3	VAN NUYS, CA	91401
OBERDORFER, DON	NEWS CORRESPONDENT	4630 30TH ST, NW	WASHINGTON, DC	20008
OBERGON, ANA	ACTRESS	KOHNER, 9169 SUNSET BLVD	LOS ANGELES, CA	90069
OBERHOLTZER, NELLIE	NEWS CORRESPONDENT	2534 N GRANADA ST	ARLINGTON, VA	22207
OBERLEY, CHARLET	ACTRESS	340 W 28TH ST	NEW YORK, NY	10011
OBERMAN, MARGARET	TV WRITER	8955 BEVERLY BLVD	LOS ANGELES, CA	90048
OBERMAYER, BETTY NAN L	PHOTOGRAPHER	4114 N RIDGEVIEW RD	ARLINGTON, VCA	22207
OBERMAYER, HERMAN JOSEPH	NEWS CORRESPONDENT	4114 N RIDGEVIEW RD	ARLINGTON, VA	22207
OBERSCHALL, FRANK	ACTOR	610 S KENMORE AVE #109	LOS ANGELES, CA	90005
OBOLER, ARCH	WRITER-PRODUCER	32436 W MULHOLLAND HWY	MALIBU, CA	90265
OBRAZTSOVA, ELENA	MEZZO-SOPRANO	ICM, 40 W 57TH ST	NEW YORK, NY	10019
OBSESSION	ROCK & ROLL GROUP	POST OFFICE BOX 9591	NEW HAVEN, CT	06535
OBST, LYNDA	FILM PRODUCER	PARAMOUNT PICTURES CORP		
		HILL/OBST PRODUCTIONS		
		5555 MELROSE AVE	LOS ANGELES, CA	90038
OCAMPO, PEDRO E	ACTOR	1646 IST AVE	NEW YORK, NY	10028
OCASEK, RIC	SINGER-SONGWRITER	LOOKOUT, 9120 SUNSET BLVD	LOS ANGELES, CA	90069
OCASIO, JOE	ACTOR	715 W 180TH ST	NEW YORK, NY	10033
OCEAN, BILLY	SINGER-COMPOSER	5 MONMOUTH PL	LONDON W2	ENGLAND
OCHMAN, WIESLAW	TENOR	CAMI, 165 W 57TH ST	NEW YORK, NY	10019
OCHOA, BETH N	COMPOSER	866 LEE HALL	SAN ANTONIO, TX	78212
OCHOA, BUDDY	WRITER	8955 BEVERLY BLVD	LOS ANGELES, CA	90048
OCHOA, KAREN F	WRITER	8955 BEVERLY BLVD	LOS ANGELES, CA	90048
OCHS, DAVID R	NEWS CORRESPONDENT	1825 "K" ST, NW	WASHINGTON, DC	20006
OCHS, MICHAEL	ROCK HISTORIAN	520 VICTORIA AVE	VENICE, CA	90291
OCKER, DAVID A	COMPOSER	4313 FINLEY AVE	LOS ANGELES, CA	90027
OCKO, DANIEL	ACTOR	484 W 43RD ST	NEW YORK, NY	10036
OCNOFF, EDWARD E	COMPOSER-CONDUCTOR	505 DORADO CT	AGOURA, CA	91301
ODA, TAKAHIRO	NEWS CORRESPONDENT	10607 CROSSING CREEK RD	POTOMAC, MD	20854
ODAM, NORMAN	SINGER	POST OFFICE BOX 26265	FORT WORTH, TX	76116
ODDIE, WILLIAM	ACTOR-WRITER	8 CHALCOT RD	LONDON NW1	ENGLAND
ODDIS, KELLIE A	WRITER	555 W 57TH ST #1230	NEW YORK, NY	10019
ODELL, DAVID B	WRITER	8955 BEVERLY BLVD	LOS ANGELES, CA	90048
ODEN, HENRY	NEWS CORRESPONDENT	23 W CEDAR ST	ALEXANDRIA, VA	22301
ODYSSEY	SOUL GROUP	60 EVERGREEN PL #200	EAST ORANGE, NJ	07018
OEHLER, DALE D	COMPOSER	4298 BAKMAN AVE	NORTH HOLLYWOOD, CA	91602
OERMANN, ROBERT K	MUSIC CRITIC	NASHVILLE TENNESSEAN		
		1100 BROADWAY	NASHVILLE, TN	37202
OESTREICHER, GERARD	THEATER PRODUCER	680 MADISON AVE	NEW YORK, NY	10021
OFFENDERS, THE	ROCK & ROLL GROUP	805 NORWALK LN	AUSTIN, TX	78703
OFFER, THOMAS R	WRITER	555 W 57TH ST #1230	NEW YORK, NY	10019
OFFS, THE	ROCK & ROLL GROUP	1230 GRANT AVE #531	SAN FRANCISCO, CA	94133
OFIELD, JACK	DIRECTOR-PRODUCER	POST OFFICE BOX 12792	SAN DIEGO, CA	92112
OGANESOFF, IGOR	WRITER-PRODUCER	140 W END AVE	NEW YORK, NY	10023
OGDIN, ROBERT	PIANIST	119 MAPLEHURST LN	NASHVILLE, TN	37204
OGG, JAMES H	WRITER	8955 BEVERLY BLVD	LOS ANGELES, CA	90048
OGIENS, MICHAEL	TV EXECUTIVE	CBS-TV, 51 W 52ND ST	NEW YORK, NY	10019
OGILVY, IAN	ACTOR	17 GREAT CUMBERLAND PLAZA	LONDON W1A 146	ENGLAND
OGURO, KUNIJI	NEWS CORRESPONDENT	1938 MC FALL ST	MC LEAN, VA	22101
OGUST, RICHARD J	WRITER	555 W 57TH ST #1230	NEW YORK, NY	10019
OH, HAE KYUNG "HELEN"	NEWS CORRESPONDENT	122 "C" ST, NW	WASHINGTON, DC	20001
OH, SOON-TECK	ACTOR	8235 SANTA MONICA BLVD #202	LOS ANGELES, CA	90046
OHANIAN, NANCY	CARTOONIST	NEWS AMERICA SYNDICATE		
		1703 KAISER AVE	IRVINE, CA	92714
OHATA, TOSHIO	NEWS CORRESPONDENT	6209 STARDUST LN	BETHESDA, MD	20817
OHER, JOSEPH	DIRECTOR	1314 W WRIGHTWOOD AVE	CHICAGO, IL	60614
OHIO EXPRESS, THE	SOUL GROUP	810 ABE LINCOLN AVE #3-B	CARTERET, NJ	07008
OHIO PLAYERS, THE	SOUL GROUP	888 8TH AVE #1-F	NEW YORK, NY	10019
OHLMEYER, DONALD W, JR	TV DIRECTOR-PRODUCER	9744 WILSHIRE BLVD, 4TH FLOOR	BEVERLY HILLS, CA	90212
OHLSSON, GARRICK	PIANIST	SHAW CONCERTS, 1995 BROADWAY	NEW YORK, NY	10023
OHMAN, JACK	CARTOONIST	PORTLAND OREGONIAN		
		1320 SW BROADWAY	PORTLAND, OR	97201
OHMER, TOM	ACTOR	9255 SUNSET BLVD #603	LOS ANGELES, CA	90069
OHTA, BENNETT	ACTOR	3151 W CAHUENGA BLVD #310	LOS ANGELES, CA	90068
OILY RAGS	ROCK & ROLL GROUP	SIGNATURE RECORDS COMPANY		
		1414 AVE OF THE AMERICAS	NEW YORK, NY	10019
OINGO BOINGO	ROCK & ROLL GROUP	L A PERSONAL DIRECTION		
		633 N LA BREA AVE	LOS ANGELES, CA	90036
OISTRAKH, IGOR	VIOLINIST	CAMI, 165 W 57TH ST	NEW YORK, NY	10019
OJALA, ARVO	ACTOR	KELMAN, 7813 SUNSET BLVD	LOS ANGELES, CA	90046
OJEDA, FRANCISCO	NEWS CORRESPONDENT	815 NATIONAL PRESS BLDG		
		529 14TH ST, NW	WASHINGTON, DC	20045
OKABE, TORU	NEWS CORRESPONDENT	444 N CAPITOL ST, NW	WASHINGTON, DC	20001
OKERLUND, MEAN GENE	WRESTLING ANNOUNCER	POST OFFICE BOX 3859	STAMFORD, CT	06905
OKIE, RICHARD	WRITER	2049 CENTURY PARK E #1320	LOS ANGELES, CA	90067
OKIE, RICHARD C	TV EXECUTIVE	NBC-TV, 3000 W ALAMEDA AVE	BURBANK, CA	91523
OKON, THEODORE	DIRECTOR	16 CENTER DR	MALBA, NY	11357
OLANDER, JIM	GUITARIST	2131 ELM HILL PIKE #J-180	NASHVILLE, TN	37210
OLANDT, KEN	ACTOR	12725 VENTURA BLVD #E	STUDIO CITY, CA	91604
OLAR, SUSAN	ACTRESS	3151 W CAHUENGA BLVD #310	LOS ANGELES, CA	90068
OLBERMANN, KEITH	SPORTS CORRESPONDENT	CNN, 1050 TECHWOOD DR, NW	ATLANTA, GA	30318
OLD MAN FROM THE MOUNTAIN BAND	C & W GROUP	POST OFFICE BOX 11276	ROCHESTER, NY	14611
OLDFIELD, BRUCE	FASHION DESIGNER	27 BEAUCHAMP PL	LONDON SW3	ENGLAND
OLDFIELD, MIKE	MUSICIAN-COMPOSER	LITTLE HALINGS, TILEHOUSE LN		
		DENHA	BUCKS	ENGLAND

Name	Occupation	Address	City	Zip/Country
OLDFIELD, SALLY	SINGER	BRONZE, 100 CHALK FARM RD	LONDON NW1	ENGLAND
OLDFIELD, W ALAN	COMPOSER-CONDUCTOR	4454 SIMPSON AVE	NORTH HOLLYWOOD, CA	91607
OLDHAM, ANNE	VIOLINIST	1346 OTTER CREEK RD	NASHVILLE, TN	37215
OLDHAM, BRUCE	CINEMATOGRAPHER	7715 SUNSET BLVD #150	LOS ANGELES, CA	90046
OLDHAM, R WAYNE	PIANIST	POST OFFICE BOX 48	NASHVILLE, TN	37202
OLDHAM, SPOONER	GUITARIST	3143 STEVENS ST	LA CRESCENTA, CA	91214
OLDS, GERRY C	COMPOSER	POST OFFICE BOX 1033	BOLINAS, CA	94924
OLEFSKY, PAUL	CELLIST	111 W 57TH ST #1209	NEW YORK, NY	10019
OLEK, HENRY	ACTOR-TV WRITER	10850 RIVERSIDE DR #501	NORTH HOLLYWOOD, CA	91602
OLEMBERT, THEODORA	FILM WRITER-PRODUCER	15 OSLO CT, PRINCE ALBERT RD	LONDON NW8	ENGLAND
OLENICOFF, SERGE	WRITER	3834 ALOHA ST	LOS ANGELES, CA	90027
OLESEN, WINSTRUP H	CONDUCTOR	8215 JAMIESON AVE	RESEDA, CA	91335
OLEVSKY, JULIAN	VIOLINIST	68 BLUE HILL RD	AMHERST, MA	01002
OLFSON, KEN	ACTOR	6720 HILLPARK DR #301	LOS ANGELES, CA	90068
OLGIN, HOWARD A, MD	WRITER	8955 BEVERLY BLVD	LOS ANGELES, CA	90048
OLHAVA, JODY LEE	ACTRESS	11956 COLLINS ST	NORTH HOLLYWOOD, CA	91607
OLIAN, CATHERINE	WRITER	555 W 57TH ST #1230	NEW YORK, NY	10019
OLIANSKY, JOEL	WRITER-PRODUCER	1320 MILLER DR #11	LOS ANGELES, CA	90069
OLIGARIO, CAROLE	WRITER	1276 N HARPER AVE	LOS ANGELES, CA	90046
OLIM, DOROTHY	THEATER PRODUCER	1540 BROADWAY	NEW YORK, NY	10036
OLIN, DIRK	NEWS CORRESPONDENT	1640 19TH ST, NW	WASHINGTON, DC	20009
OLINEY, ALAN	TV DIRECTOR	6725 SHERBOURNE DR	LOS ANGELES, CA	90056
OLINKA, SETH L	WRITER	8955 BEVERLY BLVD	LOS ANGELES, CA	90048
OLIPHANT, JOHN L	NEWS CORRESPONDENT	4816 "W" ST, NW	WASHINGTON, DC	20007
OLIPHANT, PATRICK	CARTOONIST	UNIVERSAL PRESS SYNDICATE		
		4900 MAIN ST, 9TH FLOOR	KANSAS CITY, MO	62114
OLIPHANT, THOMAS NEWTON	NEWS CORRESPONDENT	2910 "Q" ST #A-31	WASHINGTON, DC	20036
OLITZKY, STEVEN L	COMPOSER	2301 23RD ST	SANTA MONICA, CA	90405
OLIVA, SAM	GUITARIST	POST OFFICE BOX 335	MADISON, TN	37115
OLIVA, SERGIO	BODYBUILDER	OLIVIA'S GYM, 7383 ROGERS AVE	CHICAGO, IL	60626
OLIVARES, CARLOTTA G	WRITER	555 W 57TH ST #1230	NEW YORK, NY	10019
OLIVAS, CONRAD, III	CINEMATOGRAPHER	7715 SUNSET BLVD #150	LOS ANGELES, CA	90046
OLIVE, DIEGO	WRITER	555 W 57TH ST #1230	NEW YORK, NY	10019
OLIVEIRA, DONA	BODYBUILDER	POST OFFICE BOX M47	HOBOKEN, NJ	07030
OLIVEIRA, ELMAR	VIOLINIST	CAMI, 165 W 57TH ST	NEW YORK, NY	10019
OLIVER, BARRET	ACTOR	10100 SANTA MONICA BLVD #1600	LOS ANGELES, CA	90067
OLIVER, DON	NEWS CORRESPONDENT	NBC TELEVISION NETWORK		
		30 ROCKEFELLER PLAZA	NEW YORK, NY	10112
OLIVER, EDITH	THEATER CRITIC	N Y MAGAZINE, 25 W 43RD ST	NEW YORK, NY	10036
OLIVER, GEORGE V	CONDUCTOR	5845 LANCASTER DR	SAN DIEGO, CA	92120
OLIVER, GORDON	ACTOR-DIRECTOR	237 N ALMONT DR	BEVERLY HILLS, CA	90211
OLIVER, JACK	TV DIRECTOR	4802 NORWICH AVE	SHERMAN OAKS, CA	91403
OLIVER, JOHN	COMPOSER	BOSTON SYMPHONY ORCHESTRA		
		SYMPHONY HALL	BOSTON, MA	02115
OLIVER, RAYMOND	ACTOR	3575 CAHUENGA BLVD #125	LOS ANGELES, CA	90068
OLIVER, RICHARD	TV WRITER	8955 BEVERLY BLVD	LOS ANGELES, CA	90048
OLIVER, ROBIN R	DIRECTOR	22307 MAC FARLANE DR	WOODLAND HILLS, CA	91364
OLIVER, STAN	WRITER	8955 BEVERLY BLVD	LOS ANGELES, CA	90048
OLIVER, STEPHEN	COMPOSER	44 QUEEN'S GATE	LONDON SW7	ENGLAND
OLIVER, SUSAN	ACTRESS	STONE, 1052 CAROL DR	LOS ANGELES, CA	90069
OLIVIER, DAVID	ACTOR	721 N LA BREA AVE #201	LOS ANGELES, CA	90038
OLIVIER, DEANNA	ACTRESS	WEBB, 7500 DEVISTA DR	LOS ANGELES, CA	90046
OLIVIER, SIR LAURENCE	ACTOR-DIRECTOR	33 CHANCERY LN	LONDON WC2 1EN	ENGLAND
OLIVO, FRANK	TV DIRECTOR	333 E 23RD ST	NEW YORK, NY	10010
OLIVO, ROCCO	ACTOR	8721 SUNSET BLVD #200	LOS ANGELES, CA	90069
OLIVOR, JANE	SINGER	10100 SANTA MONICA BLVD #1600	LOS ANGELES, CA	90067
OLKEN, JONATHAN	TV EXECUTIVE	130 W 75TH ST	NEW YORK, NY	10023
OLKEWICZ, WALTER	ACTOR	ICM, 8899 BEVERLY BLVD	LOS ANGELES, CA	90048
OLLIE & JERRY	VOCAL DUO	200 W 51ST ST #1410	NEW YORK, NY	10019
OLLMANN, KURT	BARITONE	CAMI, 165 W 57TH ST	NEW YORK, NY	10019
OLLSTEIN, MARTY	WRITER	427 N CANON DR #212	BEVERLY HILLS, CA	90210
OLMOS, EDWARD JAMES	ACTOR	10000 SANTA MONICA BLVD #305	LOS ANGELES, CA	90067
OLMSTEAD, NELSON	ACTOR	9255 SUNSET BLVD #610	LOS ANGELES, CA	90069
OLMSTED, MAXINE	ACTRESS	8484 WILSHIRE BLVD #235	BEVERLY HILLS, CA	90211
OLNEY, DAVID	GUITARIST	POST OFFICE BOX 121612	NASHVILLE, TN	37212
OLOFSON, DARWIN R	NEWS CORRESPONDENT	10828 ADMIRALS WY	POTOMAC, MD	20854
OLSEN, ALFA-BETTY	WRITER	555 W 57TH ST #1230	NEW YORK, NY	10019
OLSEN, CHUCK	ACTOR	1350 N HIGHLAND AVE #24	HOLLYWOOD, CA	90028
OLSEN, DANA	SCREENWRITER	8955 BEVERLY BLVD	LOS ANGELES, CA	90048
OLSEN, KEITH	TENOR	CAMI, 165 W 57TH ST	NEW YORK, NY	10019
OLSEN, KELLY R	WRITER	8955 BEVERLY BLVD	LOS ANGELES, CA	90048
OLSEN, MARK	ACTOR-MINE	GREAT LAKES PERFORMING		
		310 E WASHINGTON ST	ANN ARBOR, MI	48104
OLSEN, MERLIN	ACTOR-SPORTSCASTER	1080 LORAIN RD	SAN MARINO, CA	91108
OLSEN, MERRITT	ACTOR	LEONETTI, 6526 SUNSET BLVD	HOLLYWOOD, CA	90028
OLSEN, MICKEY	PIANIST	FARRIS, 821 19TH AVE S	NASHVILLE, TN	37203
OLSEN, PATRICIA	WRITER	555 W 57TH ST #1230	NEW YORK, NY	10019
OLSEN, PEARL	WRITER	8955 BEVERLY BLVD	LOS ANGELES, CA	90048
OLSEN, STANLEY B	DIRECTOR	WINGS, 825 ADMORE DR	SIDNEY, BC V81 351	CANADA
OLSEN-FISHER, MARQUITA	WRITER	8955 BEVERLY BLVD	LOS ANGELES, CA	90048
OLSHANSKY, LUDWIG	PIANIST	GEWALD, 58 W 58TH ST	NEW YORK, NY	10019
OLSHEFSKI, NORBERT S	PHOTOGRAPHER	12703 KRAMER LN	BOWIE, MD	20715
OLSHER, LAURA	TV WRITER	8955 BEVERLY BLVD	LOS ANGELES, CA	90048
OLSMAN, PHIL	DIRECTOR	2051 STANLEY HILLS DR	LOS ANGELES, CA	90046
OLSON, CANDY	ACTRESS	3575 W CAHUENGA BLVD #320	LOS ANGELES, CA	90068

Name	Occupation	Address	City	Zip
OLSON, ELIZABETH G	NEWS CORRESPONDENT	2943 TILDEN ST, NW	WASHINGTON, DC	20008
OLSON, GLEN	TV WRITER	1650 WESTWOOD BLVD #201	LOS ANGELES, CA	90024
OLSON, JAMES	ACTOR	9220 SUNSET BLVD #202	LOS ANGELES, CA	90069
OLSON, LYNN	NEWS CORRESPONDENT	6900 STRATHMORE ST #222	CHEVY CHASE, MD	20815
OLSON, NANCY	ACTRESS	945 N ALPINE DR	BEVERLY HILLS, CA	90210
OLSON, PAM E	NEWS CORRESPONDENT	3232 PROSPECT ST, NW	WASHINGTON, DC	20007
OLSSON, NIGEL	DRUMMER-SINGER	PICHINSON-BABCOCK MGMT		
		518 N LA CIENEGA BLVD	LOS ANGELES, CA	90048
OLSTEIN, JUDY	TV WRITER	555 W 57TH ST #1230	NEW YORK, NY	10019
OLYMPIA	WRESTLER	GORGEOUS GIRLS OF WRESTLING		
		RIVIERA HOTEL & CASINO		
		DAVID B MC LANE PRODS		
		2901 S LAS VEGAS BLVD	LAS VEGAS, NV	89109
OLYMPICS, THE	VOCAL GROUP	MONACH PRODUCTIONS		
		9227 BELLFLOWER ST	BELLFLOWER, CA	90706
OMAN, MARK	WRITER	8955 BEVERLY BLVD	LOS ANGELES, CA	90048
OMANG, JOANNE	NEWS CORRESPONDENT	524 6TH ST, SE	WASHINGTON, DC	20003
OMARR, SYDNEY	WRITER	201 OCEAN AVE #1706-B	SANTA MONICA, CA	90402
OMEGA'S PROMISE	VOCAL GROUP	LUTZ, 5625 "O" STREET BLDG	LICNOLN, NE	68510
OMEN	ROCK & ROLL GROUP	POST OFFICE BOX 2428	EL SEGUNDO, CA	90245
OMEN, JUDD	ACTOR	208 S BEVERLY BLVD #4	BEVERLY HILLS, CA	90212
OMENS, SHERWOOD WOODY	CINEMATOGRAPHER	POST OFFICE BOX 2230	HOLLYWOOD, CA	90078
OMMERLE, JEANNE	SOPRANO	HILLYER, 250 W 57TH ST	NEW YORK, NY	10107
ONASSIS, CHRISTINA	CELEBRITY	88 AVE FOCH	PARIS 75016	FRANCE
ONCZAY, CSABA	CELLIST	POST OFFICE BOX 27539	PHILADELPHIA, PA	19118
ONE, MIK	ACTOR	10920 WILSHIRE BLVD #220	LOS ANGELES, CA	90024
ONE, YOKO	SINGER-SONGWRITER	THE DAKOTA, 1 W 72ND ST	NEW YORK, NY	10023
ONE MAN GANG	WRESTLER	POST OFFICE BOX 3859	STAMFORD, CT	06905
ONE TO ONE	ROCK & ROLL GROUP	41 BRITAIN ST #200	TORONTO, ONT	CANADA
ONE WAY	RHYTHM & BLUES GROUP	PERK'S MUSIC COMPANY		
		1866 PENOBSCOT BLVD	DETROIT, MI	48226
ONES, THE	ROCK & ROLL GROUP	9777 HARWIN ST #101	HOUSTON, TX	77036
ONG, BENNY	FASHION DESIGNER	3 BENTINCK MEWS	LONDON W1	ENGLAND
ONG, JACK	ACTOR	2431 3RD ST #3	SANTA MONICA, CA	90405
ONOFRIO, MICHAEL, JR	DIRECTOR	1 CYPRESS LN	RIDGEFIELD, CT	06877
ONORATO, AL	CASTING DIRECTOR	8480 BEVERLY BLVD #165	LOS ANGELES, CA	90048
ONTIVEROS, LUPE M	ACTRESS	9402 HOLBROOK ST	PICO RIVERA, CA	90660
ONTKEAN, MICHAEL	ACTOR	7120 GRASSWOOD AVE	MALIBU, CA	90265
OONK, MILDRED	VIOLINIST	741 DARDEN PL	NASHVILLE, TN	37205
OORE, GARY	TV HOST	12 S CALIBOQUE CAY	HILTON HEAD ISLAND, SC	29928
OPATOSHU, DAN	SCREENWRITER	8201 MANNIX DR	LOS ANGELES, CA	90046
OPATOSHU, DAVID	ACTOR-WRITER	4161 DIXIE CANYON AVE	SHERMAN OAKS, CA	91423
OPENDEN, LORI	CASTING DIRECTOR	18648 STARE ST	NORTHRIDGE, CA	91324
OPIE, EVERETT	CARTOONIST	POST OFFICE BOX 4203	NEW YORK, NY	10017
OPIE, WINFIELD	DIRECTOR	9426 VIA MONIQUE	BURBANK, CA	91504
OPKINS, ANTHONY	ACTOR	1672 CLEARVIEW DR	BEVERLY HILLS, CA	90210
OPOTOWSKY, STAN	TV EXECUTIVE-AUTHOR	ABC-TV, 7 W 66TH ST	NEW YORK, NY	10023
OPPENHEIMER, ALAN	ACTOR	6987 LOS TILOS RD	LOS ANGELES, CA	90068
OPPENHEIMER, JERRY	NEWS REPORTER	THE NATIONAL ENQUIRER		
		600 SE COAST AVE	LANTANA, FL	33464
OPPENHEIMER, JESS	WRITER-PRODUCER	549 MORENO AVE	LOS ANGELES, CA	90049
OPPENHEIMER, JOEL	WRITER-POET	WESTBETH, 463 WEST ST	NEW YORK, NY	10019
OPPENHEIMER, PEER J	WRITER	3971 ROYAL OAK PL	ENCINO, CA	91436
OPPENS, URSULA	PIANIST	COLBERT, 111 W 57TH ST	NEW YORK, NY	10019
OPPERMAN, DOUGLAS	PHOTOGRAPHER	5941 WILLIAMSBURG RD	ALEXANDRIA, VA	22303
OPPITZ, GERHARD	PIANIST	CAMI, 165 W 57TH ST	NEW YORK, NY	10019
OPTEKMAN, BONNIE	WRITER	555 W 57TH ST #1230	NEW YORK, NY	10019
OPTHOF, CORNELIS	BARITONE	SARDOS, 180 W END AVE	NEW YORK, NY	10023
OPUS	ROCK & ROLL GROUP	330 W 58TH ST #5-P	NEW YORK, NY	10019
ORAGGS, JULIAN	DIRECTOR	1419 DAUPHINE ST	NEW ORLEANS, LA	70116
ORAM, BOB	ACTOR	10480 SUNLAND BLVD #56	SUNLAND, CA	91040
ORANGE, BUZZY	GUITARIST	4028 GENERAL BATES DR	NASHVILLE, TN	37204
ORANTES, CESAR A	NEWS CORRESPONDENT	8907 BATTERY RD	ALEXANDRIA, VA	22308
ORBACH, JERRY	ACTOR	301 W 53RD ST	NEW YORK, NY	10019
ORBELIAN, CONSTANTINE	PIANIST	CAMI, 165 W 57TH ST	NEW YORK, NY	10019
ORBEN, ROBERT	WRITER	1200 N NASH ST #1122	ARLINGTON, VA	22209
ORBISON, ROY	SINGER-SONGWRITER	5414 BLACKWELL RD	MEMPHIS, TN	38134
ORCHARD, THOMAS	WRITER	555 W 57TH ST #1230	NEW YORK, NY	10019
ORDOVENSKY, PATRICK	NEWS CORRESPONDENT	5650 HIGH TOR HILL	COLUMBIA, MD	21045
ORDUNG, WYOTT	DIRECTOR	11920 CHANDLER BLVD #218	NORTH HOLLYWOOD, CA	91607
ORDWAY, GIRARD L	NEWS CORRESPONDENT	3913 VIRGINIA ST	CHEVY CHASE, MD	20815
OREKMOV, NIKOLAY F	NEWS CORRESPONDENT	5683 DERBY CT #102	ALEXANDRIA, VA	22311
ORENSTEIN, BERNARD	TV WRITER	12366 RIDGE CIR	LOS ANGELES, CA	90049
ORENSTEIN, LARRY	COMPOSER	4050 STANSBURY AVE	SHERMAN OAKS, CA	91423
ORENTREICH, BRIAN D	TV DIRECTOR-PRODUCER	111 E 75TH ST #9-C	NEW YORK, NY	10021
ORFORD QUARTET, THE	STRING QUARTET	5720 MOSHOLU AVE #300	RIVERDALE, NY	10471
ORGEL, LEE	WRITER	421 S VAN NESS AVE #39	LOS ANGELES, CA	90020
ORGOLINI, ARNOLD H	WRITER-PRODUCER	12717 MARLBORO ST	LOS ANGELES, CA	90049
ORICK, GEORGE T	WRITER	555 W 57TH ST #1230	NEW YORK, NY	10019
ORIGINAL CAMELLIA JAZZ BAND, TH	JAZZ BAND	POST OFFICE BOX 19004	NEW ORLEANS, LA	70179
ORIGINAL DRIFTERS, THE	VOCAL GROUP	CAROLINA ATTRACTIONS		
		203 CULVER AVE	CHARLESTON, SC	29407
ORIGINAL EXCITERS, THE	VOCAL GROUP	JAMES EVANS, 200 W 57TH ST	NEW YORK, NY	10019
ORIGINAL FLAMINGOS, THE	VOCAL GROUP	POST OFFICE BOX 262	CARTERET, NJ	07008
ORIGINAL MIRRORS, THE	VOCAL GROUP	1790 BROADWAY #PH	NEW YORK, NY	10019

Name	Occupation	Address	City	Zip
ORIGINAL RIVER ROAD BOYS, THE	VOCAL GROUP	STAR ATTRACTIONS		
		2039 ANTOINE DR	HOUSTON, TX	77055
ORIGINAL SIN	ROCK & ROLL GROUP	POST OFFICE BOX 836	NYACK, NY	10960
ORIGINALS, THE	VOCAL GROUP	ROY JAY'S, 12340 NW MARSHALL ST	PORTLAND, OR	97229
ORIN-HAGUE, RENEE	WRITER	9300 WILSHIRE BLVD #410	BEVERLY HILLS, CA	90212
ORINGER, ANNIE	ACTRESS	11350 VENTURA BLVD #206	STUDIO CITY, CA	91604
ORINGER, BARRY	WRITER-PRODUCER	8955 BEVERLY BLVD	LOS ANGELES, CA	90048
ORION	VOCAL GROUP	POST OFFICE BOX 40686	NASHVILLE, TN	37204
ORKIN, RICHARD	TV WRITER	8955 BEVERLY BLVD	LOS ANGELES, CA	90048
ORKOW, BEN HARRISON	WRITER	14934 DICKENS ST	SHERMAN OAKS, CA	91403
ORLAND, JOHN W	WRITER	2810 KELTON AVE	LOS ANGELES, CA	90064
ORLANDI, FELICE	ACTRESS-WRITER	3800 REDLAW DR	NORTH HOLLYWOOD, CA	91604
ORLANDO, ELEANOR	ACTRESS	10234 ESCONDIDO CANYON RD	AQUA DULCE, CA	91350
ORLANDO, KAT & THE REACTIONS	ROCK & ROLL GROUP	POST OFFICE BOX 18368	DENVER, CO	80218
ORLANDO, RAFFAELLO	CLARINETIST	ROSENFIELD, 714 LADD RD	BRONX, NY	10471
ORLANDO, TONY	SINGER	151 S EL CAMINO DR	BEVERLY HILLS, CA	90212
ORLEANS	ROCK & ROLL GROUP	POST OFFICE BOX 120308	NASHVILLE, TN	37212
ORLIKOFF, SUSAN D	DIRECTOR	15239 RAYNETA DR	SHERMAN OAKS, CA	91403
ORLOFF, ARTHUR E	WRITER	2318 COLDWATER CANYON DR	BEVERLY HILLS, CA	90210
ORLOFF, JOHN	DIRECTOR	1193 SUMMIT DR	BEVERLY HILLS, CA	90210
ORLONS, THE	VOCAL GROUP	2011 FERRY AVE #U-19	CAMDEN, NJ	08104
ORMENY, TOM	ACTOR	12833 LANDALE ST	NORTH HOLLYWOOD, CA	91604
ORMES, MARGO	ACTRESS	11030 VENTURA BLVD #3	STUDIO CITY, CA	91604
ORMSBY, ALAN	SCREENWRITER	8955 BEVERLY BLVD	LOS ANGELES, CA	90048
ORNADEL, CYRIL	COMPOSER-CONDUCTOR	THE RICHARD STONE AGENCY		
		18-20 YORK BLDGS, ADELPHI	LONDON WC2N 6JY	ENGLAND
ORNDORFF, PAUL "MR WONDERFUL"	WRESTLER	POST OFFICE BOX 3859	STAMFORD, CT	06905
ORNSTEIN, MICHAEL	FILM EDITOR	633 CRESTMOORE PL	VENICE, CA	90291
OROOP, JOSEPH	COMPOSER	7826 LAUREL CANYON BLVD #6	NORTH HOLLYWOOD, CA	91605
OROZCO, RAFAEL	PIANIST	CAMI, 165 W 57TH ST	NEW YORK, NY	10019
ORPHAN	ROCK & ROLL GROUP	POST OFFICE BOX 141		
		STATION C	WINNIPEG, MAN R3M 3S3	CANADA
ORR, BENJAMIN	SINGER-SONGWRITER	LOOKOUT, 9120 SUNSET BLVD	LOS ANGELES, CA	90069
ORR, DAVID H	DIRECTOR	6214 DANBURY ST	DALLAS, TX	75214
ORR, J SCOTT	NEWS CORRESPONDENT	506 2ND ST, SE	WASHINGTON, DC	20003
ORR, JOHN	GUITARIST	844 MARTHA AVE	LANCASTER, PA	17601
ORR, PHILIP	MUSICIAN	3621 MEADOWBROOK AVE	NASHVILLE, TN	37205
ORR, RACHEL	ACTRESS	11240 MAGNOLIA BLVD #202	NORTH HOLLYWOOD, CA	91601
ORR, SAMUEL	TV WRITER	2612 ELM AVE	MANHATTAN BEACH, CA	90266
ORR, WAYNE	CINEMATOGRAPHER	7715 SUNSET BLVD #150	LOS ANGELES, CA	90046
ORRALL, ROBERT ELLIS	SINGER	3 E 54TH ST #1400	NEW YORK, NY	10022
ORRISON, BRAD	STUNTMAN	3518 W CAHUENGA BLVD #300	LOS ANGELES, CA	90068
ORRISON, MARK	STUNTMAN	3518 W CAHUENGA BLVD #300	LOS ANGELES, CA	90068
ORSATTI, FRANK	TV DIRECTOR	3518 W CAHUENGA BLVD #106	HOLLYWOOD, CA	90068
ORSATTI, NOON	STUNTMAN	3518 W CAHUENGA BLVD #300	LOS ANGELES, CA	90068
ORSHANSKY, BORIS	NEWS CORRESPONDENT	1201 CONNECTICUT AVE, NW	WASHINGTON, DC	20036
ORTELLI, DYANA	ACTRESS	1717 N HIGHLAND AVE #414	LOS ANGELES, CA	90028
ORTEZ, GEORGE	PHOTOGRAPHER	NEWS, 13013 224TH ST E	GRAHAM, WA	98338
ORTH, PETER	PIANIST	SHAW CONCERTS, 1995 BROADWAY	NEW YORK, NY	10023
ORTH, PETER	TV EXECUTIVE	ABC-TV, 4151 PROSPECT AVE	LOS ANGELES, CA	90027
ORTH, ROBERT	BARITONE	CAMI, 165 W 57TH ST	NEW YORK, NY	10019
ORTIZ, ALBERTO R	WRITER	555 W 57TH ST #1230	NEW YORK, NY	10019
ORTIZ, ANTONIO G	WRITER	8955 BEVERLY BLVD	LOS ANGELES, CA	90048
ORTIZ, CARMELLA	WRITER	8955 BEVERLY BLVD	LOS ANGELES, CA	90048
ORTIZ, CRISTINA	PIANIST	ICM, 40 W 57TH ST	NEW YORK, NY	10019
ORTIZ, FRANCISCO	TENOR	225 W 34TH ST #1012	NEW YORK, NY	10001
ORTIZ-GIL, LEON	FILM EDITOR	ACE, 4416 1/2 FINLEY AVE	LOS ANGELES, CA	90027
ORTON, ACE	WRESTLER	SEE - ORTON, COWBOY BOB		
ORTON, BARRY	WRESTLER	SEE - O, BARRY		
ORTON, COWBOY BOB	WRESTLER	POST OFFICE BOX 3859	STAMFORD, CT	06905
ORTON, DAVID	FILM PRODUCER	CHILVERS COTON, 20 MIDWAY		
		SAINT ALBAN'S	HERTFORDSHIRE	ENGLAND
ORTON, JAMES	ACTOR	7561 1/2 SUNSET BLVD #5	LOS ANGELES, CA	90046
ORTON, PETER Z	SCREENWRITER	29025 MALIBU DR	AGOURA, CA	91301
ORTON, ROBERT, JR	WRESTLER	SEE - ORTON, COWBOY BOB		
ORTUSO, DOMINICK	TV DIRECTOR	893 BLUE SPRING DR	WESTLAKE VILLAGE, CA	91359
ORTWIN, ROBERT	ACTOR	973 GRETNA GREEN WY	LOS ANGELES, CA	90049
ORZECHOWSKI, ROBERT	CARTOONIST	THE NATIONAL LAMPOON		
		635 MADISON AVE	NEW YORK, NY	10022
OSAWA, SANDRA V	WRITER	8955 BEVERLY BLVD	LOS ANGELES, CA	90048
OSAWA, YUZO	NEWS CORRESPONDENT	6909 STRATA ST	MC LEAN, VA	22101
OSBON, BRUCE	GUITARIST	142 BROOKRIDGE DR	LAVERGNE, TN	37086
OSBORN, DAVID	DRUMMER	ROUTE #2, BOX 30-B	DICKSON, TN	37055
OSBORN, JOE	GUITARIST	ROUTE #2, BOX 30-B	DICKSON, TN	37055
OSBORN, JOHN JAY, JR	TV WRITER	8955 BEVERLY BLVD	LOS ANGELES, CA	90048
OSBORN, PAUL	PLAYWRIGHT	1165 PARK AVE	NEW YORK, NY	10028
OSBORN, RONALD E	SCREENWRITER	8955 BEVERLY BLVD	LOS ANGELES, CA	90048
OSBORN, THOMAS M	CONDUCTOR	20349 DELITA DR	WOODLAND HILLS, CA	91364
OSBORNE, ANGELA	WRITER-PRODUCER	75 E END AVE	NEW YORK, NY	10028
OSBORNE, BOBBY VAN	GUITARIST	838 STEPHANIE DR	GALLATIN, TN	37066
OSBORNE, DONALD	BARITONE	61 W 62ND ST #6-F	NEW YORK, NY	10023
OSBORNE, JEFFREY	SINGER-SONGWRITER	NELSON, 5800 VALLEY OAK DR	LOS ANGELES, CA	90068
OSBORNE, JOHN	PLAYWRIGHT	11 HANNOVER ST	LONDON W1	ENGLAND
OSBORNE, LAWRENCE	TV DIRECTOR	142 SUTTON MANOR	NEW ROCHELLE, NY	10805
OSBORNE, MARIE	ACTRESS	YEATS, 110 CALLE BELLA LOMA	SAN CLEMENTE, CA	92672

Name	Occupation	Address	City	Zip
OSBORNE, MATTHEW	WRESTLER	SEE - BORNE, MATT		
OSBORNE, ROBBY	GUITARIST	159 GATONE DR	HENDERSONVILLE, TN	37075
OSBORNE, ROBERT	FILM CRITIC	KTTV-TV, 5746 SUNSET BLVD	LOS ANGELES, CA	90028
OSBORNE, RUDY	GUITARIST	9005 WOODFORD DR	LITTLE ROCK, AR	72209
OSBORNE, SCOTT	NEW REPORTER	ENTERTAINMENT TONIGHT		
		PARAMOUNT TELEVISION		
		5555 MELROSE AVE	LOS ANGELES, CA	90038
OSBORNE, SONNY	BANJOIST	POST OFFICE BOX 647	HENDERSONVILLE, TN	37075
OSBORNE, STEVEN	WRITER	555 W 57TH ST #1230	NEW YORK, NY	10019
OSBORNE, WYNN	GUITARIST	POST OFFICE BOX 141	HENDERSONVILLE, TN	37075
OSBOURNE, OZZY	SINGER-SONGWRITER	34 WINDMILL ST	LONDON W1	ENGLAND
OSBURN, CYNTHIA L	WRITER	555 W 57TH ST #1230	NEW YORK, NY	10019
OSCARSON, SEIEROE DIANE	ACTRESS	560 S MAIN ST #6-W	LOS ANGELES, CA	90013
OSER, HELEN A	WRITER	8955 BEVERLY BLVD	LOS ANGELES, CA	90048
OSGOOD, CHARLES	NEWS CORRESPONDENT	CBS NEWS, 51 W 52ND ST	NEW YORK, NY	10019
OSHEN, JEFFREY	CASTING DIRECTOR	1438 N GOWER ST #432	LOS ANGELES, CA	90028
OSHIMA, NAGISA	DIRECTOR	2-15-7 AKASAKA, MINATO-KU	TOKYO	JAPAN
OSHRY, SUZANNE	WRITER	555 W 57TH ST #1230	NEW YORK, NY	10019
OSIECKI, JOHN J	CONDUCTOR	32017 KINGSPARK CT	WESTLAKE VILLAGE, CA	91361
OSINCHUK, JULIANA	PIANIST	POST OFFICE BOX U	REDDING, CT	06875
OSKAR, LEE	MUSICIAN	FAR OUT, 7417 SUNSET BLVD	LOS ANGELES, CA	90046
OSMENT, BILL	FIDDLER	3628 BRUSH HILL RD	NASHVILLE, TN	37216
OSMOND, CLIFF	ACTOR	KOHNER, 9169 SUNSET BLVD	LOS ANGELES, CA	90069
OSMOND, CLIFF	SCREENWRITER	2049 CENTURY PARK E #1320	LOS ANGELES, CA	90067
OSMOND, DONNY	SINGER	3 CORPORATE PLAZA #220	NEWPORT BEACH, CA	92664
OSMOND, JIMMY	SINGER	10331 RIVERSIDE DR #203	NORTH HOLLYWOOD, CA	91602
OSMOND, KEN	ACTOR	1221 N KINGS RD #PH-405	LOS ANGELES, CA	90069
OSMOND, MARIE	SINGER-ACTRESS	POST OFFICE BOX 6000	PROVO, UT	84603
OSMOND BROTHERS, THE	VOCAL GROUP	KARL ENGEMANN MANAGEMENT		
		1799 N STATE ST	OREM, UT	84057
OSORIO, PANCSO	HIGH WIRE ACT	POST OFFICE BOX 87	WEST LEBANON, NY	12195
OSTBERG, ROBERT	TV DIRECTOR	1222 SHARON RD	SANTA ANA, CA	92706
OSTENDORF, JOHN	SINGER	59 E 54TH ST #81	NEW YORK, NY	10022
OSTER, JERRY	WRITER	555 W 57TH ST #1230	NEW YORK, NY	10019
OSTERGREN, EDUARDO	CONDUCTOR	ROSENFIELD, 714 LADD RD	BRONX, NY	10471
OSTERHAGE, JEFF	ACTOR	3720 BARHAM BLVD #A-209	LOS ANGELES, CA	90068
OSTERMAN, LESTER	THEATER PRODUCER	1650 BROADWAY	NEW YORK, NY	10019
OSTERWALD, BIBI	ACTRESS	4219 WARNER BLVD	BURBANK, CA	91505
OSTLING, RICHARD N	WRITER-EDITOR	TIME/TIME & LIFE BLDG		
		ROCKEFELLER CENTER	NEW YORK, NY	10020
OSTLUND, RICHARD	ACTOR	432 S NORTON AVE #305	LOS ANGELES, CA	90020
OSTRAWSKI, KRISTIN	NEWS CORRESPONDENT	60 S VAN DORN ST	ALEXANDRIA, VA	22304
OSTROFF, HOWARD	TV WRITER	10789 OHIO AVE #2	LOS ANGELES, CA	90024
OSTROFF, JAMES J	NEWS CORRESPONDENT	4859 S 28TH ST #B, NW	ARLINGTON, VA	22206
OSTROFF, ROBERTA JOAN	WRITER	8955 BEVERLY BLVD	LOS ANGELES, CA	90048
OSTROW, ABE	COMPOSER-CONDUCTOR	13427 RIVERSIDE DR #A	SHERMAN OAKS, CA	91423
OSTROW, RONALD	NEWS CORRESPONDENT	6401 81ST ST	CABIN JOHN, MD	20818
OSTROW, STUART	THEATER PRODUCER	POST OFFICE BOX 188	POUND RIDGE, NY	10576
OSTROWIDZKI, VICTOR	NEWS CORRESPONDENT	1408 "C" ST, SE	WASHINGTON, DC	20003
OSTRYNIEC, JAMES	OBOIST	MUGDAN, 84 PROSPECT AVE	DOUGLASTON, NY	11363
OSUNA, JESS	ACTOR	247 S BEVERLY DR #102	BEVERLY HILLS, CA	90210
OSWALD, GERD	DIRECTOR	237 SPALDING DR #A	BEVERLY HILLS, CA	90212
OSWALD, PETE	GUITARIST	603 GRAYCROFT RD	MADISON, TN	37115
OSWALT, RANDY	DRUMMER	551 HIGHCREST DR	NASHVILLE, TN	37211
OTAKA, TADAAKI	CONDUCTOR	SHAW CONCERTS, 1995 BROADWAY	NEW YORK, NY	10023
OTCHIS, ALLAN	ACTOR	6533 HOLLYWOOD BLVD #201	HOLLYWOOD, CA	90028
OTEY, JAMES	GUITARIST	244 HAYNES PARK DR	NASHVILLE, TN	37218
OTEY, LOUIS	BARITONE	CAMI, 165 W 57TH ST	NEW YORK, NY	10019
OTIS, BRENDA W	NEWS CORRESPONDENT	3138 VALENTINO CT	OAKTON, VA	22124
OTIS, DONALD G	DIRECTOR	KHJ-TV, 5515 MELROSE AVE	HOLLYWOOD, CA	90038
OTIS, JOHNNY	SINGER-GUITARIST	POST OFFICE BOX 6024	CHICAGO, IL	60660
OTRIN, JOHN	ACTOR	8383 WILSHIRE BLVD #1024	BEVERLY HILLS, CA	90211
OTSUKI, TAMAYO	COMEDIENNE	8235 SANTA MONICA BLVD	LOS ANGELES, CA	90046
OTT, JAMES	NEWS CORRESPONDENT	1411 WOODSIDE PARKWAY	SILVER SPRING, MD	20910
OTT-WORROW, KAREN	NEWS CORRESPONDENT	7710 MAPLE AVE #608	TAKOMA PARK, MD	20912
OTTALINI, DAVID G	NEWS CORRESPONDENT	906 ROBIN RD	SILVER SPRING, MD	20901
OTTAVIANO, FRED	ACTOR	23777 W MULHOLLAND HWY	CALABASAS, CA	91302
OTTEN, ALAN L	NEWS CORRESPONDENT	6601 RIVERCREST CT	BETHESDA, MD	20816
OTTEN, DANIEL	VIOLINIST	POST OFFICE BOX U	REDDING, CT	06875
OTTENAD, THOMAS W	NEWS CORRESPONDENT	4021 EVERETT ST	KENSINGTON, MD	20795
OTTENSTEIN, STANLEY M	TV WRITER	8955 BEVERLY BLVD	LOS ANGELES, CA	90048
OTTH, JOHN A	NEWS CORRESPONDENT	2139 WISCONSIN AVE, NW	WASHINGTON, DC	20007
OTTO, GREG	COMEDIAN	3800 BARHAM BLVD #303	LOS ANGELES, CA	90068
OTTO, HENRY B	WRITER	25161 MALIBU RD	MALIBU, CA	90265
OTTO, JORG	NEWS CORRESPONDENT	4701 WILLARD AVE	CHEVY CHASE, MD	20815
OTTO, LINDA	DIRECTOR	DGA, 7950 SUNSET BLVD	LOS ANGELES, CA	90046
OTWELL, JENIFER	NEWS CORRESPONDENT	2906 S 13TH RD	ARLINGTON, VA	22204
OU, CHUN-LIN	NEWS CORRESPONDENT	4738 LAFITTE CT	ALEXANDRIA, VA	22312
OUELLET, JO	PUZZLE WRITER	UNIVERSAL PRESS SYNDICATE		
		4900 MAIN ST, 9TH FLOOR	KANSAS CITY, MO	62114
OULMANN, RENE	DIRECTOR	300 E 51ST ST	NEW YORK, NY	10022
OULTON, BRIAN	ACTOR	43 CHESTER CLOSE N		
		REGENT'S PARK	LONDON NW1	ENGLAND
OUMANSKY, ANDRE	ACTOR	3 RUE ETEX	PARIS 75018	FRANCE

DONNY OSMOND

MARIE OSMOND

CATHERINE OXENBERG

JACK PAAR

AL PACINO

JACK PALANCE

BARBARA PARKINS

DOLLY PARTON

BILLY PAUL

Name	Occupation	Address	City	Zip
OUSSET, CECILE	PIANIST	CAMI, 165 W 57TH ST	NEW YORK, NY	10019
OUT BACK JACK	WRESTLER	POST OFFICE BOX 3859	STAMFORD, CT	06905
OUTCRY	ROCK & ROLL GROUP	6112 KELLOGG AVE	MINNEAPOLIS, MN	55424
OUTFIELD, THE	ROCK & ROLL TRIO	SCARF, UNIT E-1, BOW WORKS		
		REGENT'S PARK	LONDON E3	ENGLAND
OUTLAND, RANDALL	TENOR	KAZAKO HILLYER, 250 W 57TH ST	NEW YORK, NY	10107
OUTLAWS, THE	ROCK & ROLL GROUP	WOMACK, 217 SMOKE RISE CIR	MARIETTA, GA	30067
OVE, HORACE	TV DIRECTOR	5-A GREENCROFT GARDENS	LONDON NW6	ENGLAND
OVER, W H	TV WRITER	8955 BEVERLY BLVD	LOS ANGELES, CA	90048
OVERBYE, DENNIS	WRITER-EDITOR	DISCOVER/TIME & LIFE BLDG		
		ROCKEFELLER CENTER	NEW YORK, NY	10020
OVERHOLT, SHERRY	SOPRANO	CONE, 221 W 57TH ST	NEW YORK, NY	10019
OVERMAN, ANTHONY J	WRITER	8955 BEVERLY BLVD	LOS ANGELES, CA	90048
OVERMAN, STEPHANIE	NEWS CORRESPONDENT	2000 N ADAMS ST #331	ARLINGTON, VA	22201
OVERSHINER	C & W GROUP	POST OFFICE BOX 25371	CHARLOTTE, NC	28212
OVERSTREET, TOMMY	SINGER-GUITARIST	POST OFFICE BOX 455	BRENTWOOD, TN	37027
OVERTON, BILL	ACTOR	9105 CARMELITA AVE #1	BEVERLY HILLS, CA	90210
OVERTON, JAMES L	WRITER	555 W 57TH ST #1230	NEW YORK, NY	10019
OVERTON, JULIE ANN	NEWS CORRESPONDENT	CBS NEWS, 2020 "M" ST, NW	WASHINGTON, DC	20036
OVERTON, RICK	COMEDIAN	ICM, 8899 BEVERLY BLVD	LOS ANGELES, CA	90048
OVERWISE, JESSICA	CASTING DIRECTOR	7471 MELROSE AVE #12	LOS ANGELES, CA	90046
OWEN, BARRY	WRESTLER	POST OFFICE BOX 3859	STAMFORD, CT	06905
OWEN, BETHANY	ACTRESS	11240 MAGNOLIA BLVD #202	NORTH HOLLYWOOD, CA	91601
OWEN, BILL	ACTOR	THE RICHARD STONE AGENCY		
		18-20 YORK BLDGS, ADELPHI	LONDON WC2N 6JY	ENGLAND
OWEN, CLIFF	TV DIRECTOR	20 MARLBOROUGH PL	LONDON NW8	ENGLAND
OWEN, D W	WRITER	8955 BEVERLY BLVD	LOS ANGELES, CA	90048
OWEN, JOHN STEVEN	TV WRITER	8955 BEVERLY BLVD	LOS ANGELES, CA	90048
OWEN, LAWRENCE	DIRECTOR	323 N CALIFORNIA ST	BURBANK, CA	91505
OWEN, LYNN	SOPRANO	21 CLAREMONT AVE	NEW YORK, NY	10027
OWEN, PAT	ACTOR	6736 LAUREL CANYON BLVD #306	NORTH HOLLYWOOD, CA	91606
OWEN, STEPHEN	BASSO-BARITONE	CONE, 221 W 57TH ST	NEW YORK, NY	10019
OWEN-THOMAS, GAVIN	TV DIRECTOR	3390 CREATWOOD TRAIL	SMYRNA, GA	30080
OWENS, ANN	SINGER	TRENDA, 18747 SHERMAN WY	RESEDA, CA	91335
OWENS, BUCK	SINGER-SONGWRITER	1225 N CHESTER AVE	BAKERSFIELD, CA	93308
OWENS, CORKY	GUITARIST	3132 SHADY TRAIL	TYLER, TX	75702
OWENS, CYNTHIA	NEWS CORRESPONDENT	1523 CORCORAN ST, NW	WASHINGTON, DC	20009
OWENS, EDWIN	ACTOR	5050 AMESTOY AVE	ENCINO, CA	91316
OWENS, GARY	RADIO PERSONALITY	POST OFFICE BOX 76860	LOS ANGELES, CA	90076
OWENS, GRANT	ACTOR	13403 CANTARA ST	VAN NUYS, CA	91402
OWENS, HARRY R	COMPOSER-ORCH LEADER	POST OFFICE BOX 5454	EUGENE, OR	97405
OWENS, JAMES L	COMPOSER-CONDUCTOR	ROUTE #2, BOX 171-J	LINDALE, TX	75771
OWENS, JIM	SINGER	POST OFFICE BOX 418	BRENTWOOD, TN	37027
OWENS, JOAN D	WRITER	8955 BEVERLY BLVD	LOS ANGELES, CA	90048
OWENS, MARIE	SINGER	2401 12TH AVE S	NASHVILLE, TN	37204
OWENS, MEL	PERCUSSIONIST	21 VAUGHNS GAP RD #C-39	NASHVILLE, TN	37205
OWENSBY, EARL	DIRECTOR-PRODUCER	POST OFFICE BOX 184	SHELBY, NC	28150
OWNBY, JOHN	MUSICIAN	2502 WOODYHILL DR	NASHVILLE, TN	37207
OWSLEY, LYNN	GUITARIST	417 BROADWAY	NASHVILLE, TN	37203
OXENBERG, CATHERINE	ACTRESS-MODEL	9228 HAZEN DR	BEVERLY HILLS, CA	90210
OXFORD, VERNON	SINGER-GUITARIST	POST OFFICE BOX 50	HERMITAGE, TN	37076
OYSTER, DAVID	DIRECTOR	4437 FINLEY AVE	LOS ANGELES, CA	90027
OYSTERS, THE	ROCK & ROLL GROUP	611 BROADWAY #526	NEW YORK, NY	10012
OZ	ROCK & ROLL GROUP	COMBAT RECORDS COMPANY		
		149-03 GUY BREWER BLVD	JAMAICA, NY	11454
OZ, FRANK	PUPPETEER	117 E 69TH ST	NEW YORK, NY	10024
OZARCHUK, JOYCE	WRITER	1112 MAPLE ST	SANTA MONICA, CA	90405
OZARK MOUNTAIN DAREDEVILS	C & W GROUP	POST OFFICE BOX 437	EXCELSIOR, MN	55331
OZICK, CYNTHIA	WRITER	KNOPF, 201 E 50TH ST	NEW YORK, NY	10022
OZIMEK, KENNETH H	SINGER-GUITARIST	300 BERKLEY DR #R-2	MADISON, TN	37115
OZMAN, BOB	ACTOR	10000 RIVERSIDE DR #3	TOLUCA LAKE, CA	91602
OZNOWICZ, FRANK RICHARD	DIRECTOR	DGA, 7950 SUNSET BLVD	LOS ANGELES, CA	90046
OZOLINS, ARTHUR	PIANIST	411 DUPLEX AVE #2018	TORONTO, ONT M4R 1V2	CANADA
OZONE	SOUL-DISCO GROUP	GAMI, 6255 SUNSET BLVD	LOS ANGELES, CA	90028
OZONE, MAKOTO	PIANIST	KURLAND, 173 BRIGHTON AVE	BOSTON, MA	02134
OZZ KNOZZ	C & W GROUP	4615 SOUTHWEST FREEWAY #475	HOUSTON, TX	77027
OZZELLO, MARK	ACTOR	8075 W 3RD ST #303	LOS ANGELES, CA	90048

Name	Occupation	Address	City	Zip
P Y T #1	WRESTLER	SEE - WARE, KOKO B		
PABLO CRUISE	ROCK & ROLL GROUP	POST OFFICE BOX 779	MILL VALLEY, CA	94941
PACE, IRENE	TV DIRECTOR	POST OFFICE BOX 206	WARWICK, NY	10990
PACE, JUDY	ACTRESS	4139 CLOVERDALE AVE	LOS ANGELES, CA	90008
PACE, RALPH	DRUMMER	1806-B 15TH AVE S	NASHVILLE, TN	37212
PACELLI, FRANK T	TV DIRECTOR	POST OFFICE BOX 69191	LOS ANGELES, CA	90069
PACHECO, FERDIE	WRITER	555 W 57TH ST #1230	NEW YORK, NY	10019
PACINO, AL	ACTOR	9 E 68TH ST	NEW YORK, NY	10021
PACK, CHARLES LLOYD	ACTOR	25 NEVILLE ST	LONDON SW7	ENGLAND

Name	Occupation	Address	City	ZIP/Country
PACK, JACKIE	SINGER	RAINBOW, 124 W BALTIMORE AVE	LANSDOWNE, PA	19050
PACK, ROBERT	NEWS CORRESPONDENT	7702 OLD CHESTER RD	BETHESDA, MD	20817
PACK, ROGER LOYD	ACTOR	11 DOYNTON ST	LONDON N19	ENGLAND
PACKARD, FRANK E, III	WRITER	8955 BEVERLY BLVD	LOS ANGELES, CA	90048
PACKARD, VANCE	AUTHOR	87 MILL RD	NEW CANAAN, CT	06840
PACKER, JULIET	TV WRITER	555 W 57TH ST #1230	NEW YORK, NY	10019
PACOME, MARIA	ACTRESS	2 TER RUE SAINT-SAVEUR		
		BALLAINVILLI	LONGJUMEAU 91160	FRANCE
PADDEN, EUGENE	TRUMPETER	2518 TIMWOOD DR	NASHVILLE, TN	37214
PADDOCK, JAMES F	WRITER	555 W 57TH ST #1230	NEW YORK, NY	10019
PADGETT, JIMMY	DRUMMER	ROUTE #1, BOX 5		
		PRIEST LAKE MOBILE	SMYRNA, TN	37167
PADGETT, MICHAEL	DRUMMER	31 CAMEO DR	NASHVILLE, TN	37211
PADILLA, DANNY	BODYBUILDER	WORLD GYM, 2210 MAIN ST	SANTA MONICA, CA	90405
PADILLA, MANUEL, JR	ACTOR	242 S LAMAR ST	BURBANK, CA	91506
PADLOCK	ROCK & ROLL GROUP	ISLAND TRADING COMPANY		
		14 E 4TH ST	NEW YORK, NY	10012
PADNICK, GLENN A	TV WRITER	2158 BEVERWIL DR	LOS ANGELES, CA	90034
PADWE, SANDY	SPORTS WRITER-EDITOR	SPORTS ILLUSTRATED MAGAZINE		
		TIME & LIFE BUILDING		
		ROCKEFELLER CENTER	NEW YORK, NY	10020
PAFTERY, J PATRICK	BARITONE	CAMI, 165 W 57TH ST	NEW YORK, NY	10019
PAGAN, ANNA L	ACTRESS	2649 N BEACHWOOD DR #1	HOLLYWOOD, CA	90068
PAGANO, CAIO	PIANIST	3003 VAN NESS ST #W-205, NW	WASHINGTON, DC	20008
PAGANO, PENNY	NEWS CORRESPONDENT	4701 BERKELEY TERR, NW	WASHINGTON, DC	20007
PAGANO, RICHARD	CASTING DIRECTOR	THE MARK TAPER FORUM		
		601 W TEMPLE ST	LOS ANGELES, CA	90012
PAGE, ANITA	ACTRESS	717 "A" AVE	CORONADO, CA	92118
PAGE, ANTHONY	FILM DIRECTOR	MORRIS, 147-149 WARDOUR ST	LONDON W1V 3TB	ENGLAND
PAGE, CAROLANN	SOPRANO	61 W 62ND ST #6-F	NEW YORK, NY	10023
PAGE, CHRIS	COMPOSER	1611 RIVERSIDE DR	GLENDALE, CA	91201
PAGE, ELIZABETH	TV WRITER	ABC-TV, "ALL MY CHILDREN"		
		1330 AVE OF THE AMERICAS	NEW YORK, NY	10019
PAGE, HARRISON	ACTOR	3800 BARHAM BLVD #303	LOS ANGELES, CA	90068
PAGE, HOLLIS	ACTRESS	KOHNER, 9169 SUNSET BLVD	LOS ANGELES, CA	90069
PAGE, JAMES O	WRITER	8955 BEVERLY BLVD	LOS ANGELES, CA	90048
PAGE, JIM	SINGER-GUITARIST	FLYING FISH RECORDS		
		1304 W SCHUBERT ST	CHICAGO, IL	60614
PAGE, JIMMY	SINGER-GUITARIST	PHIL CARSON, ATLANTIC RECORDS		
		75 ROCKEFELLER PLAZA	NEW YORK, NY	10019
PAGE, KEN	SINGER	GLOBENFELT, 1205 FRANKLIN AVE	GARDEN CITY, NY	11530
PAGE, LAUREL	ACTRESS	BOWEN, 11216 HORTENSE ST	NORTH HOLLYWOOD, CA	91602
PAGE, LE WANDA	ACTRESS	1607 N EL CENTRO AVE #22	HOLLYWOOD, CA	90028
PAGE, MAX C	NEWS CORRESPONDENT	400 N CAPITOL ST, NW	WASHINGTON, DC	20001
PAGE, NATHEN	GUITARIST	3003 VAN NESS ST #W-205, NW	WASHINGTON, DC	20008
PAGE, PATTI	SINGER	POST OFFICE BOX 1105	RANCHO SANTE FE, CA	92067
PAGE, PAUL B	NEWS CORRESPONDENT	2844 WISCONSIN AVE, NW	WASHINGTON, DC	20007
PAGE, ROBERT	CONDUCTOR	POST OFFICE BOX 1515	NEW YORK, NY	10023
PAGE, ROBERT E	PUBLISHING EXECUTIVE	NEWS AMERICA SYNDICATE		
		1703 KAISER AVE	IRVINE, CA	92714
PAGE, SUSAN	NEWS CORRESPONDENT	3408 "N" ST, NW	WASHINGTON, DC	20007
PAGE, THOMAS	WRITER	8955 BEVERLY BLVD	LOS ANGELES, CA	90048
PAGES, THE	ROCK & ROLL GROUP	CHIZ, 7031 WOODROW WILSON DR	LOS ANGELES, CA	90068
PAGES, THE FLYING	TRAPEZE ACT	HALL, 138 FROG HOLLOW RD	CHURCHVILLE, PA	18966
PAGET, PORTMAN	TV DIRECTOR	44 W END AVE	NEW YORK, NY	10028
PAGET, ROBERT	WRITER-PRODUCER	MANHATAN FILMS COMPANY		
		217 BROMPTON RD	LONDON SW3	ENGLAND
PAGETT, GARY	ACTOR	3518 W CAHUENGA BLVD #316	LOS ANGELES, CA	90068
PAGETT, NICOLA	ACTRESS	22 VICTORIA RD	LONDON SW14	ENGLAND
PAGLIALUNGA, AUGUSTO	TENOR	111 W 57TH ST #1209	NEW YORK, NY	10019
PAGLIARO, JOANNE M	WRITER	605 31ST ST	MANHATTAN BEACH, CA	90266
PAI-RITCHIE, DAVID S	WRITER	3673 BERRY DR	STUDIO CITY, CA	91604
PAICH, DAVID F	COMPOSER-CONDUCTOR	POST OFFICE BOX 6008	SHERMAN OAKS, CA	91413
PAICH, MARTIN	COMPOSER	24157 LUPIN HILL RD	CALABASAS, CA	91302
PAID VACATION	ROCK & ROLL GROUP	POST OFFICE BOX 390		
		OLD CHELSEA STATION	NEW YORK, NY	10113
PAIGE, ELAINE	ACTRESS	196 SHAFTESBURY AVE	LONDON WC2	ENGLAND
PAIGE, JANIS	ACTRESS	GILBERT, 1700 RISING GLEN RD	LOS ANGELES, CA	90069
PAIGE, KYMBERLY	MODEL	MODELS & PROMOTIONS AGENCY		
		8560 SUNSET BLVD, 10TH FLOOR	LOS ANGELES, CA	90069
PAIGE, MARVIN	CASTING DIRECTOR	SUNSET-GOWER, 1438 N GOWER ST	LOS ANGELES, CA	90028
PAIGE, MICHAEL	CONDUCTOR	9876 WILSHIRE BLVD #GS-1	BEVERLY HILLS, CA	90210
PAIGE, ROBERT	ACTOR	12606 MOORPARK ST	STUDIO CITY, CA	91604
PAIK, K KENNETH	PHOTOGRAPHER	5541 SUFFIELD CT	COLUMBIA, MD	21044
PAIK, KUN-WOO	PIANIST	BYERS-SCHWALBE, 1 5TH AVE	NEW YORK, NY	10003
PAIK, NAM JUNE	COMPOSER-VIDEO ARTIST	BONINO, 48 GREAT JONES ST	NEW YORK, NY	10012
PAILLARD, JEAN-FRANCOIS	CONDUCTOR	MARIEDL ANDERS ARTISTS MGMT		
		535 EL CAMINO DEL MAR ST	SAN FRANCISCO, CA	94121
PAINE, BARRY E	DIRECTOR-PRODUCER	BRAESIDE COTTAGE		
		RHODYATE BLAGDON	BRISTOL	ENGLAND
PAINE, CATHEY	ACTRESS	8721 SUNSET BLVD #202	LOS ANGELES, CA	90069
PAINE, JEFFREY THOMAS	WRITER	1869 VERDUGO LOMA DR	GLENDALE, CA	91208
PAINE, KEN	DIRECTOR	1 WINDSOR ST	LARCHMONT, NY	10538
PAINE, ROLAND D	NEWS CORRESPONDENT	3915 BENTON ST, NW	WASHINGTON, DC	20007
PAINTED WILLIE	ROCK & ROLL GROUP	10649 BURBANK BLVD	NORTH HOLLYWOOD, CA	91601

Name	Occupation	Address	City/State	Zip/Country
PAINTER, PATRICIA A	ACTRESS	19305 ENTRADERO AVE #I	TORRANCE, CA	90503
PAINTER, SAMUEL E	NEWS CORRESPONDENT	448 NEW JERSEY AVE, SE	WASHINGTON, DC	20003
PAINTERS & DOCKERS	ROCK & ROLL GROUP	POST OFFICE BOX 38		
PAINTON, PEGGY	ACTRESS	4065 GLENALBYN DR	LOS ANGELES, CA	90065
PAISER, DINA	ACTRESS	119 BANK ST	NEW YORK, NY	10014
PAISLEY, BOB & SOUTHERN GRASS	C & W GROUP	POST OFFICE BOX 156	ROSELLE, NJ	07203
PAISNER, BRUCE	ENTERTAINMENT EXEC	KING FEATURE ENTERPRISES		
		235 E 45TH ST	NEW YORK, NY	10017
PAKALINI, JACKSON J	CONDUCTOR	1024 N STANLEY AVE #1	LOS ANGELES, CA	90046
PAKCHANIAN, KOURKEN	DIRECTOR	DGA, 110 W 57TH ST	NEW YORK, NY	10019
PAKULA, ALAN	WRITER-PRODUCER	730 PARK AVE #5-A	NEW YORK, NY	10021
PALACE	ROCK & ROLL GROUP	POST OFFICE BOX 1909	MILL VALLEY, CA	94942
PALANCE, BROOKE	ACTRESS	2451 HOLLY DR	LOS ANGELES, CA	90068
PALANCE, HOLLY	ACTRESS	1636 N BEVERLY DR	BEVERLY HILLS, CA	90210
PALANCE, JACK	ACTOR-DIRECTOR	15301 VENTURA BLVD #345	SHERMAN OAKS, CA	91403
PALANCE, VIRGINIA	PRODUCER	1438 N GOWER ST #31	LOS ANGELES, CA	90038
PALANCE, VIRGINIA BAKER	ACTRESS	2170 CENTURY PARK E #711	LOS ANGELES, CA	90067
PALAO, GELSA T	COMPOSER	6541 KESTER AVE #205	VAN NUYS, CA	91411
PALEY, PETRONIA	ACTRESS	NBC-TV, "ANOTHER WORLD"		
		30 ROCKEFELLER PLAZA	NEW YORK, NY	10112
PALEY, PHILLIP	ACTOR	400 S BEVERLY DR #216	BEVERLY HILLS, CA	90212
PALEY, SARAH C	TV WRITER	555 W 57TH ST #1230	NEW YORK, NY	10019
PALEY, STANLEY	WRITER	350 S FULLER AVE #8-L	LOS ANGELES, CA	90036
PALEY, WILLIAM S	TV EXECUTIVE	CBS-TV, 51 W 52ND ST	NEW YORK, NY	10019
PALFI-ANDOR, LOTTA	ACTRESS	123 W 93RD ST	NEW YORK, NY	10025
PALFREYMAN, RICHARD D	NEWS CORRESPONDENT	4181 WOODWAY LN, NW	WASHINGTON, DC	20016
PALIES, CHRIS	WRESTLER	SEE - BUNDY, KING KONG		
PALIFOX	C & W GROUP	FIELDS, 3753 VINEYARD CT	MARIETTA, GA	30062
PALILLO, RON	ACTOR	9220 SUNSET BLVD #202	LOS ANGELES, CA	90069
PALIN, MICHAEL	ACTOR-WRITER	6 CAMBRIDGE GATE	LONDON NW1 4JR	ENGLAND
PALL, LAWRENCE	FILM DIRECTOR	RURAL ROUTE #2	ERIN, ONT NOB ITO	CANADA
PALLADIN, ALEXANDER, JR	NEWS CORRESPONDENT	4701 WILLARD AVE #704, NW	WASHINGTON, DC	20815
PALLARDY, THOMAS P	MUSIC ARRANGER	ROUTE #1, BOX 257	NOLENSVILLE, TN	37135
PALLATTO, DOMINICK	ACTOR	224 W 16TH ST #12	NEW YORK, NY	10011
PALLENBERG, ROSPO	SCREENWRITER	9021 BURROUGHS RD	LOS ANGELES, CA	90046
PALLO, IMRE	CONDUCTOR	HILLYER, 250 W 57TH ST	NEW YORK, NY	10107
PALM, SIEGFRIED	CELLIST	59 E 54TH ST #81	NEW YORK, NY	10022
PALMER, ANTHONY	TV WRITER	8955 BEVERLY BLVD	LOS ANGELES, CA	90048
PALMER, ARNOLD	GOLFER	POST OFFICE BOX 616	LATROBE, PA	15650
PALMER, BETSY	ACTRESS	721 N LA BREA AVE #200	LOS ANGELES, CA	90038
PALMER, BYRON	ACTOR-SINGER	7044 LOS TILOS RD	HOLLYWOOD, CA	90068
PALMER, DON	COMPOSER-CONDUCTOR	3048 CLOUDCREST	LA CRESCENTA, CA	91214
PALMER, FELICITY	MEZZO-SOPRANO	ICM, 40 W 57TH ST	NEW YORK, NY	10019
PALMER, GENE	DIRECTOR	MCA/UNIVERSAL STUDIOS, INC		
		100 UNIVERSAL CITY PLAZA	UNIVERSAL CITY, CA	91608
PALMER, GRETCHEN F	ACTRESS	427 N CANON DR #205	BEVERLY HILLS, CA	90210
PALMER, JAY D	WRITER-EDITOR	TIME/TIME & LIFE BLDG		
		ROCKEFELLER CENTER	NEW YORK, NY	10020
PALMER, JIM	BASEBALL-ANNOUNCER	POST OFFICE BOX 145	BROOKLANDVILLE, MD	21022
PALMER, JIMMY A	FIDDLER	ROUTE #1	SPRINGFIELD, TN	37172
PALMER, KEITH	PIANIST	5101 LINBAR DR #A-101	NASHVILLE, TN	37211
PALMER, MARK	DETECTIVE	2801 MEADOW LARK DR	SAN DIEGO, CA	92123
PALMER, MAVIS NEAL	ACTRESS	11153 VALLEY SPRING PL	NORTH HOLLYWOOD, CA	91602
PALMER, MICHAEL	CONDUCTOR	SHAW CONCERTS, 1995 BROADWAY	NEW YORK, NY	10023
PALMER, MORRIS	DRUMMER	1217 1ST AVE S	NASHVILLE, TN	37210
PALMER, NICHOLAS	WRITER-PRODUCER	FRASER, 91 REGENT ST	LONDON W1	ENGLAND
PALMER, NORMAN	FILM EDITOR	9549 ENCINO AVE	NORTHRIDGE, CA	91325
PALMER, PATRICK	FILM PRODUCER	YORKTOWN, 9336 W WASHINGTON BLVD	CULVER CITY, CA	90230
PALMER, PETER	ACTOR	12428 HESBY ST	NORTH HOLLYWOOD, CA	91607
PALMER, RENZO	ACTOR	FRANCE DEGAND AGENCE		
		94 RUE LAURISTON	PARIS 75116	FRANCE
PALMER, ROBERT	SINGER-SONGWRITER	2-A CHELSEA MANOR, BLOOD ST	LONDON SW3	ENGLAND
PALMER, SCOTT	ACTOR	247 S BEVERLY DR #102	BEVERLY HILLS, CA	90210
PALMER, STACY E	NEWS CORRESPONDENT	2801 QUEBEC ST, NW	WASHINGTON, DC	20008
PALMER, T STEVEN	TV DIRECTOR	4336 BEEMAN AVE	STUDIO CITY, CA	91604
PALMER, TOM	CASTING DIRECTOR	CBS-TV, 7800 BEVERLY BLVD	LOS ANGELES, CA	90036
PALMER, TOM	ACTOR	151 N SAN VICENTE BLVD #208	BEVERLY HILLS, CA	90211
PALMER, TOM	TV WRITER	8955 BEVERLY BLVD	LOS ANGELES, CA	90048
PALMER, TONY	WRITER-PRODUCER	4 KENSINGTON PARK GARDENS	LONDON W11	ENGLAND
PALMERIO, ANTHONY J	TV WRITER	SCOTT MEREDITH, 845 3RD AVE	NEW YORK, NY	10022
PALMERTON, JEAN	ACTRESS	7469 MELROSE AVE #30	LOS ANGELES, CA	90046
PALMISANO, CONRAD	FILM DIRECTOR	13346 GLENOAKS BLVD	SYLMAR, CA	91342
PALOMBI, DAVID R	NEWS CORRESPONDENT	3901 LANGLEY CT #E, NW	WASHINGTON, DC	20016
PALOMBI, RICK	PIANIST	2019 BERNARD CIR #1	NASHVILLE, TN	37212
PALOMINO, CARLOS	BOXER	6501 OXFORD DR	HUNTINGTON BEACH, CA	92647
PALTER, LEW	ACTOR	3800 BARHAM BLVD #303	LOS ANGELES, CA	90068
PALTROW, BRUCE W	WRITER-PRODUCER	304 21ST ST	SANTA MONICA, CA	90402
PALUMBO, DENNIS	SCREENWRITER	4942 RADFORD AVE	NORTH HOLLYWOOD, CA	91607

Name	Occupation	Address	City	Zip
PALUMBO, GENE	TV WRITER	555 W 57TH ST #1230	NEW YORK, NY	10019
PALUMBO, THOMAS	DIRECTOR	211 SPORTSMAN AVE	FREEPORT, L I, NY	11520
PALUZZI, LUCIANA	ACTRESS	SOLOMAN, 200 OLD PALISADE RD	FORT LEE, NJ	07024
PALYO, CATHEY	BODYBUILDER	GOLD'S GYM, 510 LEWIS RD	SANTA ROSA, CA	95401
PAMER, ERIC H	NEWS CORRESPONDENT	301 POPLAR CHURCH	FALLS CHURCH, VA	22046
PAMPLIN, RUSHTON	ACTOR	8485 MELROSE PL #E	LOS ANGELES, CA	90069
PAN, HERMES	CHOREOGRAPHER	9550 CHEROKEE LN	BEVERLY HILLS, CA	90210
PANAMA, NORMAN	WRITER-PRODUCER	1721 STONE CANYON RD	LOS ANGELES, CA	90077
PANCAKE, ROGER	ACTOR	5850 CANOGA AVE #110	WOODLAND HILLS, CA	91367
PANDEMONIUM	ROCK & ROLL GROUP	POST OFFICE BOX 2428	EL SEGUNDO, CA	90245
PANDORAS	ROCK & ROLL GROUP	POST OFFICE BOX 49217	LOS ANGELES, CA	90049
PANETTIERE, VINCENT P	WRITER	1841 N FULLER AVE #206	HOLLYWOOD, CA	90046
PANG, KIMBERLEY	ACTRESS	SCHOEMAN, 2600 W VICTORY BLVD	BURBANK, CA	91505
PANITT, MERRILL	PUBLISHING EXECUTIVE	TV GUIDE, 4 CORPORATE CENTER	RADNOR, PA	19088
PANKIN, JOY	ACTRESS	8831 SUNSET BLVD #402	LOS ANGELES, CA	90049
PANKIN, STUART	ACTOR	15010 VENTURA BLVD #219	SHERMAN OAKS, CA	91403
PANKOW, JAMES	MUSICIAN-COMPOSER	9301 WILSHIRE BLVD #212	BEVERLY HILLS, CA	90210
PANKOW, JOHN	ACTOR	10100 SANTA MONICA BLVD #1600	LOS ANGELES, CA	90067
PANNO, CARLO	TV WRITER	1541 N VINE ST	HOLLYWOOD, CA	90028
PANSING, SALLY	ACTRESS	WILLIAMSON, 932 N LA BREA AVE	LOS ANGELES, CA	90038
PANSKY, MIROSLAV	CONDUCTOR	KAY, 58 W 58TH ST	NEW YORK, NY	10019
PANSULLO, EDDIE	ACTOR	10850 RIVERSIDE DR #505	NORTH HOLLYWOOD, CA	91602
PANTHER	ROCK & ROLL GROUP	GREENWALD PRODUCTIONS		
		20445 GRAMMERCY PL	TORRANCE, CA	90501
PANTING, DEANNA	BODYBUILDER	POST OFFICE BOX 2669	WINNIPEG, MAN R3C 4B3	CANADA
PANTOLIANO, JOE	ACTOR	1514 ELECTRIC AVE #F	VENICE, CA	90291
PANUFNIK, ANDRZEJ	CONDUCTOR	SOFFER, 130 W 56TH ST	NEW YORK, NY	10019
PANZER, CHESTER V	PHOTOGRAPHER	8409 GOLDEN ASPEN CT	SPRINGFIELD, VA	22153
PANZER, WILLIAM	FILM PRODUCER	1438 N GOWER ST #401	LOS ANGELES, CA	90038
PAOLANTONIO, BILL	PRODUCER	ALAN LANDSBURG PRODUCTIONS		
		11811 OLYMPIC BLVD	LOS ANGELES, CA	90064
PAOLANTONIO, WILLIAM J, JR	WRITER	18645 HATTERAS ST #176	TARZANA, CA	91356
PAOLUCCI, ANNE	PLAYWRIGHT	SAINT JOHN'S UNIVERSITY		
		81-10 UTOPA PARKWAY &		
		GRAND CENTRAL	JAMAICA, NY	11439
PAONESSA, DONALD J	SCREENWRITER	8955 BEVERLY BLVD	LOS ANGELES, CA	90048
PAPA, PATRICIA	NEWS CORRESPONDENT	19025 JERICHO DR	GAITHERSBURG, MD	20879
PAPA DOO RUN RUN	ROCK & ROLL GROUP	POST OFFICE BOX 255	CUPERTINO, CA	95015
PAPA-OOM-MOW-MOW	ROCK & ROLL GROUP	OLDIES, 5218 ALMONT ST	LOS ANGELES, CA	90032
PAPAI, RAY A	COMPOSER-CONDUCTOR	501 E PROVIDENCE RD	PALATINE, IL	60067
PAPANEK, JOHN	SPORTS WRITER-EDITOR	SPORTS ILLUSTRATED MAGAZINE		
		TIME & LIFE BUILDING		
		ROCKEFELLER CENTER	NEW YORK, NY	10020
PAPANICOLAS, YVONNE	ACTRESS	5645 TOPANGA CANYON BLVD #316-A	WOODLAND HILLS, CA	91367
PAPAS, IRENE	ACTRESS	XENOKRATOUS 39	ATHENS-KOLONAKI	GREECE
PAPAZIAN, AROUTIAN	PIANIST	SHAW CONCERTS, 1995 BROADWAY	NEW YORK, NY	10023
PAPAZIAN, ROBERT A	WRITER-PRODUCER	DGA, 7950 SUNSET BLVD	LOS ANGELES, CA	90046
PAPELL, STAN	WRITER	203 MONTANA AVE #204	SANTA MONICA, CA	90403
PAPIN, RALPH L	DIRECTOR	DGA, 7950 SUNSET BLVD	LOS ANGELES, CA	90046
PAPP, FRANK	TV DIRECTOR	404 E 55TH ST	NEW YORK, NY	10022
PAPP, JOSEPH	DIRECTOR-PRODUCER	N Y SHAKESPEARE FESTIVAL		
		425 LA FAYETTE ST	NEW YORK, NY	10003
PAPPALARDI, FELIX	SINGER	3 E 54TH ST #1400	NEW YORK, NY	10022
PAPPAS, IKE	NEWS CORRESPONDENT	1531 FOREST LN	MC LEAN, VA	22101
PARACHUTE CLUB, THE	ROCK & ROLL GROUP	41 BRITAIN ST #200	TORONTO, ONT	CANADA
PARADISE, MITCH	TV WRITER	8955 BEVERLY BLVD	LOS ANGELES, CA	90048
PARADISE, RICHARD	ACTOR	22842 WYANDOTTE ST	CANOGA PARK, CA	91307
PARADISE EXPRESS	ROCK & ROLL GROUP	HECHT/HARMON MANAGEMENT		
		1032 HILLDALE AVE	LOS ANGELES, CA	90069
PARADY, RON	ACTOR	9220 SUNSET BLVD #202	LOS ANGELES, CA	90069
PARAGON, JOHN	WRITER	1262 N FLORES ST	LOS ANGELES, CA	90069
PARASURAM, T V	NEWS CORRESPONDENT	3723 EMILY ST	KENSINGTON, MD	20895
PARATORE, ANTHONY & JOSEPH	PIANO DUO	COLBERT, 111 W 57TH ST	NEW YORK, NY	10019
PARAZAIDER, WALTER	MUSICIAN	9301 WILSHIRE BLVD #212	BEVERLY HILLS, CA	90210
PARCE, ERICH	BARITONE	61 W 62ND ST #6-F	NEW YORK, NY	10023
PARCELL, JAMES A	PHOTOGRAPHER	THE WASHINGTON POST		
		PHOTO DEPARTMENT		
		1150 15TH ST, NW	WASHINGTON, DC	20071
PARCELLS, ELIZABETH	SOPRANO	59 E 54TH ST #81	NEW YORK, NY	10022
PARCHER, WILLIAM	BARITONE	CONE, 221 W 57TH ST	NEW YORK, NY	10019
PARE, MICHAEL	ACTOR	17352 SUNSET BLVD #303-D	PACIFIC PALISADES, CA	90272
PARENT, GAIL	SCREENWRITER	2001 MANDEVILLE CANYON RD	LOS ANGELES, CA	90049
PARENTI, ROSE	ACTRESS	8721 SUNSET BLVD #200	LOS ANGELES, CA	90069
PARESA, DENNIS E	ACTOR	216 S MAPLE DR	BEVERLY HILLS, CA	90212
PARETZKY, YVONNE R	NEWS CORRESPONDENT	1703 CRESTVIEW DR	POTOMAC, MD	20854
PARFITT, JUDY	ACTRESS	CONWAY, EAGLE HOUSE		
		109 JERMYN ST	LONDON SW1	ENGLAND
PARGAS, NATALIE	NEWS CORRESPONDENT	11500 HEATHSTONE CT	RESTON, VA	22091
PARIMOO, JAGAN N	NEWS CORRESPONDENT	4500 CONNECTICUT AVE, NW	WASHINGTON, DC	20008
PARIOT, BARBARA	ACTRESS	721 N LA BREA AVE #200	LOS ANGELES, CA	90038
PARIS	ROCK & ROLL GROUP	POST OFFICE BOX 682	LEBANON, IN	46052
PARIS, BOB	BODYBUILDER	8033 SUNSET BLVD #238	LOS ANGELES, CA	90046
PARIS, DUKE	SINGER-GUITARIST	141 EDGEWOOD DR	HENDERSONVILLE, TN	37075
PARIS, JEFF	SINGER-GUITARIST	2519 CARMEN CREST DR	LOS ANGELES, CA	90068
PARIS, JOHNNY & THE HURRICANES	ROCK & ROLL GROUP	1764 PARKWAY DR	SOUTH MAUMEE, OH	43537

Name	Occupation	Address	City	Zip
PARISH SISTERS, THE	VOCAL GROUP	WOOD, 2901 EPPERLY DR	DEL CITY, OK	73115
PARISI, LUKE	ACTOR	8831 SUNSET BLVD #402	LOS ANGELES, CA	90069
PARITZ, JACK	TV WRITER	8955 BEVERLY BLVD	LOS ANGELES, CA	90048
PARK, JEANNIE	NEWS REPORTER	TIME/TIME & LIFE BLDG		
		ROCKEFELLER CENTER	NEW YORK, NY	10020
PARK, NICHOLAS	TENOR	JCB, 155 W 68TH ST	NEW YORK, NY	10023
PARK, W B	CARTOONIST	UNITED FEATURES SYNDICATE		
		200 PARK AVE	NEW YORK, NY	10017
PARKE, DOROTHY	ACTRESS	9220 SUNSET BLVD #625	LOS ANGELES, CA	90069
PARKE, LAWRENCE	ACTOR	8721 SUNSET BLVD #200	LOS ANGELES, CA	90069
PARKENING, CHRISTOPHER	GUITARIST	CAMI, 165 W 57TH ST	NEW YORK, NY	10019
PARKER, ALAN	FILM WRITER-DIRECTOR	MORRIS, 147-149 WARDOUR ST	LONDON W1V 3TB	ENGLAND
PARKER, ALAN C	CONDUCTOR	13839 BURTON ST	PANORAMA CITY, CA	91402
PARKER, ANTHONY	DIRECTOR-PRODUCER	IAR, 235-241 REGENT ST	LONDON W1A 2JT	ENGLAND
PARKER, BILL	SINGER-GUITARIST	ROUTE #7, BOX 669	BROKEN ARROW, OK	74012
PARKER, BONNIE	ACTRESS	10100 SANTA MONICA BLVD #1600	LOS ANGELES, CA	90067
PARKER, BRANT	CARTOONIST	NEWS AMERICA SYNDICATE		
		1703 KAISER AVE	IRVINE, CA	92714
PARKER, BRIAN	TV DIRECTOR	5 DEERHURST RD	LONDON SW16 2AN	ENGLAND
PARKER, CARL D	ACTOR	6736 LUAREL CYN BLVD #302	NORTH HOLLYWOOD, CA	91606
PARKER, CECELIA	ACTRESS	450 S EVERGREEN DR	VENTURA, CA	93003
PARKER, CHARLIE & HIS ORCHESTRA	ORCHESTRA LEADER	BILL POTTS, 731 MONROE ST	ROCKVILLE, MD	20850
PARKER, CLIFFORD	GUITARIST	4828 SIERRA DR	OLD HICKORY, TN	37138
PARKER, COLONIAL TOM	TALENT AGENT	1166 VISTA VESPERO	PALM SPRINGS, CA	92262
PARKER, DANIEL	CONDUCTOR	SOFFER, 130 W 56TH ST	NEW YORK, NY	10019
PARKER, DAVE	BASEBALL	CINCINNATI REDS BB CLUB		
		100 RIVERFRONT STADIUM		
		RIVERFRONT STADIUM	CINCINNATI, OH	45202
PARKER, DAVID E	RECORD EXECUTIVE	AMHERST RECORDS CO		
		1800 MAIN ST	BUFFALO, NY	14208
PARKER, DENNIS F	COMPOSER-CONDUCTOR	POST OFFICE BOX 4102	NORTH HOLLYWOOD, CA	91607
PARKER, DIAMOND JIM	CLOWN	2701 COTTAGE WY #14	SACRAMENTO, CA	95825
PARKER, ED	KARATE INSTRUCTOR	1705 E WALNUT ST	PASADENA, CA	91106
PARKER, ELEANOR	ACTRESS	2195 LA PAZ WY	PALM SPRINGS, CA	92262
PARKER, ELLEN	ACTRESS	CBS-TV, "THE GUIDING LIGHT"		
		51 W 52ND ST	NEW YORK, NY	10019
PARKER, EVERETT C	PUBLISH EXECUTIVE	CHANNELS MAGAZINE		
		131 N CHATSWORTH	LARCHMONT, NY	10538
PARKER, F WILLIAM	ACTOR	9000 SUNSET BLVD #801	LOS ANGELES, CA	90069
PARKER, FESS	ACTOR	100 N HOPE #5	SANTA BARBARA, CA	93111
PARKER, FRANCINE	TV DIRECTOR-PRODUCER	847 N ALEXANDRIA AVE	LOS ANGELES, CA	90029
PARKER, FRANK	ACTOR	9441 WILSHIRE BLVD #620-D	BEVERLY HILLS, CA	90210
PARKER, GEORGE A	DIRECTOR	529 W 42ND ST	NEW YORK, NY	10036
PARKER, GLORIA	MEZZO-SOPRANO	253 W 73RD ST #7-M	NEW YORK, NY	10023
PARKER, GRAHAM	SINGER-GUITARIST	ICM, 40 W 57TH ST	NEW YORK, NY	10019
PARKER, INA	ACTRESS	4789 VINELAND AVE #100	NORTH HOLLYWOOD, CA	91602
PARKER, J STANFORD	TV WRITER	9100 SUNSET BLVD #200	LOS ANGELES, CA	90069
PARKER, JAMES A	TV WRITER	8955 BEVERLY BLVD	LOS ANGELES, CA	90048
PARKER, JAMESON	ACTOR	10100 SANTA MONICA BLVD #1600	LOS ANGELES, CA	90067
PARKER, JANET LEE	ACTRESS	1895 N AVE 52	LOS ANGELES, CA	90042
PARKER, JEAN	ACTRESS	1750 CANADA BLVD	GLENDALE, CA	91208
PARKER, JOHN C	COMPOSER-CONDUCTOR	3036 NICHOLS CANYON RD	LOS ANGELES, CA	90046
PARKER, JOLENNON	VIOLINIST	3818 CENTRAL AVE	NASHVILLE, TN	37205
PARKER, JON KIMURA	PIANIST	ICM, 40 W 57TH ST	NEW YORK, NY	10019
PARKER, JUDITH	TV WRITER	8955 BEVERLY BLVD	LOS ANGELES, CA	90048
PARKER, KAY	ACTRESS-WRITER	POST OFFICE BOX 407	SANTA MONICA, CA	90406
PARKER, LARA	ACTRESS	7469 MELROSE AVE #30	LOS ANGELES, CA	90046
PARKER, LINDA R	ACTRESS	4054 WITZEL DR	SHERMAN OAKS, CA	91423
PARKER, MARION	TALENT AGENT	POST OFFICE BOX 74368	HOUSTON, TX	77274
PARKER, MARTIN	GUITARIST	2639 PENNINGTON BEND RD	NASHVILLE, TN	37214
PARKER, MARY KATHRYN	VIOLINIST	3818 CENTRAL AVE	NASHVILLE, TN	37205
PARKER, MAYNARD	PUBLISHING EXECUTIVE	NEWSWEEK, 444 MADISON AVE	NEW YORK, NY	10022
PARKER, MONICA S	WRITER	427 N CANON DR #213	BEVERLY HILLS, CA	90210
PARKER, MORTEN	WRITER-PRODUCER	1457 BROADWAY #801	NEW YORK, NY	10036
PARKER, NORMA JEAN	SINGER	POST OFFICE BOX 390	PONTOTOC, MS	38863
PARKER, NORMAN	ACTOR	SF & A, 121 N SAN VICENTE BLVD	BEVERLY HILLS, CA	90211
PARKER, O'HARA	ACTRESS	ABC-TV NETWORK, "LOVING"		
		1330 AVE OF THE AMERICAS	NEW YORK, NY	10019
PARKER, RANDY	DRUMMER	3603 CALDWELL CT	NASHVILLE, TN	37204
PARKER, RAY	ACTOR	36 AVONDALE RD	HARRISON, NY	10528
PARKER, RAY, JR	SINGER-GUITARIST	11355 W OLYMPIC BLVD #555	LOS ANGELES, CA	90064
PARKER, ROCHELLE	ACTRESS	200 W 57TH ST #1303	NEW YORK, NY	10019
PARKER, ROD	TV WRITER	8955 BEVERLY BLVD	LOS ANGELES, CA	90048
PARKER, RON	TV PRODUCER	ABC-TV ENTERTAINMENT CENTER		
		2040 AVE OF THE STARS	LOS ANGELES, CA	90067
PARKER, SARAH JESSICA	ACTRESS	POST OFFICE BOX 611	ENGLEWOOD, NJ	07631
PARKER, SCOTT	SCREENWRITER	8955 BEVERLY BLVD	LOS ANGELES, CA	90048
PARKER, SUSAN G	NEWS CORRESPONDENT	DANIEL ST	ARLINGTON, VA	22201
PARKER, SUZY	ACTRESS	770 HOT SPRINGS RD	SANTA BARBARA, CA	93103
PARKER, TOM	TALENT AGENT	SEE - PARKER, COLONEL TOM		
PARKER, VIVECA	ACTRESS	165 W 46TH ST #409	NEW YORK, NY	10036
PARKER, WES	ACTOR	1237 VILLA WOODS DR	PACIFIC PALISADES, CA	90272
PARKER, WILLIAM	BARITONE	CAMI, 165 W 57TH ST	NEW YORK, NY	10019
PARKER, WILLIAM	TV WRITER	8955 BEVERLY BLVD	LOS ANGELES, CA	90048
PARKERS, WALTER F	SCREENWRITER	8955 BEVERLY BLVD	LOS ANGELES, CA	90048

Name	Occupation	Address	City/State	ZIP
PARKES, ROGER	TV WRITER	CARTLANDS COTTAGE, KINGS LN		
		COOKHAM DEAN	BERKS SL6 9AY	ENGLAND
PARKES, WALTER F	SCREENWRITER	1619 THAYER AVE	LOS ANGELES, CA	90024
PARKEY, MONTY	PIANIST	142 HILLSDALE DR	HENDERSONVILLE, TN	37075
PARKHURST, MICHAEL	WRITER-PRODUCER	7753 DENSMORE AVE	VAN NUYS, CA	91406
PARKIN, JUDD	TV EXECUTIVE	NBC-TV, 3000 W ALAMEDA AVE	BURBANK, CA	91523
PARKINS, BARBARA	ACTRESS	MORRIS, 147-149 WARDOUR ST	LONDON W1V 3TB	ENGLAND
PARKINSON, ANDREW	CINEMATOGRAPHER	THE GATEHOUSE, 4 ELLERTON RD		
		WIMBLEDON	LONDON SW20	ENGLAND
PARKINSON, BOB	TV WRITER-PRODUCER	1717 N HIGHLAND AVE #814	HOLLYWOOD, CA	90028
PARKINSON, DIAN	MODEL-ACTRESS	CBS TELEVISION NETWORK		
		"THE PRICE IS RIGHT"		
		7800 BEVERLY BLVD	LOS ANGELES, CA	90036
PARKINSON, MICHAEL	WRITER	58 QUEEN ANNE ST	LONDON W1	ENGLAND
PARKINSON, ROBIN	ACTOR	20 KINGSTON LN, TEDDINGTON	MIDDLESEX	ENGLAND
PARKINSON, ZAIDEE	PIANIST	ALPHA, 685 W END AVE	NEW YORK, NY	10025
PARKS, ANDREW	ACTOR	3231 OAKDELL RD	STUDIO CITY, CA	91604
PARKS, BERT	ENTERTAINER	SKYRIDGE RD	GREENWICH, CT	06830
PARKS, C CARSON	GUITARIST	6001 KENWOOD DR	NASHVILLE, TN	37215
PARKS, CATHERINE	ACTRESS	500 S SEPULVEDA BLVD #510	LOS ANGELES, CA	90049
PARKS, CHARLES	ACTOR	5967 W 3RD ST #205	LOS ANGELES, CA	90036
PARKS, FREEMAN	ACTOR	40 E 64TH ST	NEW YORK, NY	10023
PARKS, GEOFF	ACTOR	1418 N HIGHLAND AVE #102	LOS ANGELES, CA	90028
PARKS, GORDON	FILM WRITER-DIRECTOR	860 UNITED NATIONS PLAZA	NEW YORK, NY	10017
PARKS, HILDY	PROD-WRI-ACT	225 W 44TH ST	NEW YORK, NY	10036
PARKS, KIMI	ACTRESS	CBS-TV, "THE GUIDING LIGHT"		
		51 W 52ND ST	NEW YORK, NY	10019
PARKS, MICHAEL	ACTOR	9744 WILSHIRE BLVD #306	BEVERLY HILLS, CA	90212
PARKS, REGGIE	WRESTLER	POST OFFICE BOX 3859	STAMFORD, CT	06905
PARKS, TOM	COMEDIAN	CARLIN, 901 BRINGHAM AVE	LOS ANGELES, CA	90049
PARKS, VAN DYKE	COMPOSER	POST OFFICE BOX 1207	STUDIO CITY, CA	91604
PARLET	SOUL-DISCO GROUP	9000 SUNSET BLVD #711	LOS ANGELES, CA	90069
PARLIAMENT	VOCAL GROUP	200 W 51ST ST #1410	NEW YORK, NY	10019
PARLOFF, MICHAEL	FLUTIST	METROPOLITAN OPERA		
		LINCOLN CENTER	NEW YORK, NY	10023
PARLY, TICHO	TENOR	GEWALD, 58 W 58TH ST	NEW YORK, NY	10019
PARMAN, CLIFF	MUSIC ARRANGER	POST OFFICE BOX 70	PULASKI, TN	38478
PARNAS, LESLIE	CELLIST	59 E 54TH ST #81	NEW YORK, NY	10022
PARNELL, BARRY ROSS	WRITER	3328 OAK GLEN DR	LOS ANGELES, CA	90068
PARNELL, CHIC	COMPOSER	812 N KILKEA DR	LOS ANGELES, CA	90046
PARNELLE, PETER	TV WRITER	555 W 57TH ST #1230	NEW YORK, NY	10019
PARNELLO, JOE	CONDUCTOR	POST OFFICE BOX 854	CHATSWORTH, CA	91311
PARNES, JULES	ACTOR	11690 MONTANA AVE #207	LOS ANGELES, CA	90049
PARNES, RICHARD	ACTOR	11030 VENTURA BLVD #3	STUDIO CITY, CA	91604
PARONE, EDWARD	TV DIRECTOR	1336 N HARPER AVE N	LOS ANGELES, CA	90046
PAROUTAUD, FRED C	COMPOSER	1316 BARRY AVE #9	LOS ANGELES, CA	90025
PARR, JOHN	SINGER-SONGWRITER	THE PRESS OFFICE, LTD		
		83 RIVERSIDE DR	NEW YORK, NY	10024
PARR, ROBERT	ACTOR	8230 BEVERLY BLVD #23	LOS ANGELES, CA	90048
PARR, STEPHEN	ACTOR	9000 SUNSET BLVD #1200	LOS ANGELES, CA	90069
PARRENT, JOANNE E	WRITER	1835 PANDORA AVE #3	LOS ANGELES, CA	90025
PARRIOTT, JAMES D	WRITER-PRODUCER	2340 CANYON DR	HOLLYWOOD, CA	90068
PARRIS, FRED & THE SATINS	VOCAL GROUP	MARS, 168 ORCHID DR	PEARL RIVER, NY	10965
PARRIS, GEORGE	SINGER-GUITARIST	2732 MC KEIGE ST	NASHVILLE, TN	37214
PARRIS, PATRICIA E	ACTRESS	8659 LOOKOUT MOUNTAIN AVE	LOS ANGELES, CA	90046
PARRISH, CHERYL	SOPRANO	HILLYER, 250 W 57TH ST	NEW YORK, NY	10107
PARRISH, DAWN	ACTRESS	6430 SUNSET BLVD #1203	LOS ANGELES, CA	90028
PARRISH, DOROTHY	ACTRESS	9744 WILSHIRE BLVD #306	BEVERLY HILLS, CA	90212
PARRISH, JULIE	ACTRESS	6310 SAN VICENTE BLVD #407	LOS ANGELES, CA	90048
PARRISH, MOLLY R	NEWS CORRESPONDENT	635 MISSISSIPPI AVE	SILVER SPRING, MD	20910
PARRISH, ROBERT R	DIRECTOR-PRODUCER	HUTTON, 200 FULHAM RD	LONDON SW10 9PN	ENGLAND
PARROS, PETER	ACTOR	8485 MELROSE PL #E	LOS ANGELES, CA	90069
PARROTT, ANDREW	CONDUCTOR	WENTWORTH, 5 LOCKWOOD RD	SCARSDALE, NY	10583
PARRY, KEN	ACTOR	54 MYDDLETON SQ #1	LONDON EC1	ENGLAND
PARRY, ROBERT	NEWS CORRESPONDENT	130 S HIGHLAND ST	ARLINGTON, VA	22204
PARSHALL, GERALD	NEWS CORRESPONDENT	851 N KENSINGTON ST	ARLINGTON, VA	22205
PARSLEY, REED	TV WRITER-DIRECTOR	1701 35TH AVE	SEATTLE, WA	98122
PARSLOW, PHILIP	DIRECTOR	3535 LOADSTONE DR	SHERMAN OAKS, CA	91403
PARSONS, ALAN, PROJECT	ROCK & ROCK DUO	WOOLSONGS COMPANY		
		30 THE AVE MUSWELL HILL	LONDON N10	ENGLAND
PARSONS, CLIVE	FILM PRODUCER	10 PEMBRIDGE PL	LONDON W2	ENGLAND
PARSONS, DAVID	BARITONE	COLBERT, 111 W 57TH ST	NEW YORK, NY	10019
PARSONS, ESTELLE	ACTRESS	241 E 75TH ST	NEW YORK, NY	10021
PARSONS, HARRIET	WRITER-PRODUCER	2253 COLDWATER CANYON DR	BEVERLY HILLS, CA	90210
PARSONS, ICEMAN KING	WRESTLER	UNIVERSAL WRESTLING FEDERATION		
		MID SOUTH SPORTS, INC		
		5001 SPRING VALLEY RD	DALLAS, TX	75244
PARSONS, LINDSLEY, III	FILM DIRECTOR	8618 ORION AVE	SEPULVEDA, CA	91343
PARSONS, MEREDITH	MEZZO-SOPRANO	SULLIVAN, 390 W END AVE	NEW YORK, NY	10024
PARSONS, MICHAEL	ACTOR	CONTEMPORARY ARTISTS		
		132 S LASKY DR	BEVERLY HILLS, CA	90212
PARSONS, NANCY	ACTRESS	SF & A, 121 N SAN VICENTE BLVD	BEVERLY HILLS, CA	90211
PARSONS, NICHOLAS	ACTOR-COMEDIAN	THE RICHARD STONE AGENCY		
		18-20 YORK BLDGS, ADELPHI	LONDON WC2N 6JY	ENGLAND

Name	Occupation	Address	City
PARSONS, SHELLY	ACTRESS	1736 1/4 GRIFFITH PARK BLVD	LOS ANGELES, CA 90026
PARSONS, TERRY	CLOWN	HALL, 138 FROG HOLLOW RD	CHURCHVILLE, PA 18966
PARSONS, WAYNE	TV DIRECTOR	13380 GOLDEN VALLEY LN	GRANADA HILLS, CA 91344
PART, JENNIFER JACKSON	CASTING DIRECTOR	4000 WARNER BLVD	BURBANK, CA 91505
PARTLOW, RICHARD	ACTOR	15010 VENTURA BLVD #219	SHERMAN OAKS, CA 91403
PARTLOW, WAYNE	PHOTOGRAPHER	7701 SURACI CT	ANNANDALE, VA 22003
PARTON, DOLLY	SINGER-ACTRESS	POST OFFICE BOX 1976	NOLENSVILLE, TN 37135
PARTON, RANDLE	GUITARIST	POST OFFICE BOX 314	ANTIOCH, TN 37013
PARTON, RANDY	SINGER	POST OFFICE BOX 82	GREENBRIER, TN 37073
PARTON, REGIS	DIRECTOR	DGA, 7950 SUNSET BLVD	LOS ANGELES, CA 91311
PARTON, STELLA	SINGER	POST OFFICE BOX 120295	NASHVILLE, TN 37212
PARTRIDGE, DEREK	ACTOR	7616 HOLLYWOOD BLVD	LOS ANGELES, CA 90046
PARTRIDGE, IAN	TENOR	BYERS-SCHWALBE, 1 5TH AVE	NEW YORK, NY 10003
PARUCHA, ROBERT CARL	ACTOR	329 N WETHERLY DR #205	BEVERLY HILLS, CA 90211
PASATIERI, THOMAS	COMPOSER	500 W END AVE	NEW YORK, NY 10024
PASCAL, DAVID	CARTOONIST	POST OFFICE BOX 4203	NEW YORK, NY 10017
PASCAL, FRANCOISE	ACTRESS	89 RIVERVIEW GARDENS	LONDON SW13 ENGLAND
PASCAL, GISELLE	ACTRESS	AGENCE M ETIENNE	
		78 CHAMPS-ELYSEES	PARIS 75008 FRANCE
PASCAL, JEAN-CLAUDE	ACTOR	139 BLVD EXELMANS	PARIS 75016 FRANCE
PASCAL, MARY ANN	ACTRESS	3151 W CAHUENGA BLVD #310	LOS ANGELES, CA 90068
PASCHAL, KAY	SOPRANO	CONE, 221 W 57TH ST	NEW YORK, NY 10019
PASCHOLCZYK, DAVID A	NEWS CORRESPONDENT	15 CANTERBURY SQ #101	ALEXANDRIA, VA 22304
PASCO, RICHARD	ACTOR	LEADING ARTISTS, LTD	
		60 SAINT JAMES'S ST	LONDON SW1 ENGLAND
PASEKOFF, MARILYN	ACTRESS	123 S KENMORE AVE	LOS ANGELES, CA 90004
PASEORNEK, MICHAEL	SCREENWRITER	555 W 57TH ST #1230	NEW YORK, NY 10019
PASETTA, MARTIN A, JR	TV DIRECTOR	10615 BELLAGIO RD	LOS ANGELES, CA 90077
PASETTA, MARTIN A, SR	TV DIRECTOR-PRODUCER	10615 BELLAGIO RD	LOS ANGELES, CA 90077
PASHDAG, JOHN A	TV WRITER	8955 BEVERLY BLVD	LOS ANGELES, CA 90048
PASKAY, STEVE	TV WRITER	ENTERTAINMENT TONIGHT	
		PARAMOUNT TELEVISION	
		5555 MELROSE AVE	LOS ANGELES, CA 90038
PASKO, MARTIN J	TV WRITER	8955 BEVERLY BLVD	LOS ANGELES, CA 90048
PASKOSKI, SUSAN	DIRECTOR	1 UNIVERSITY PL	NEW YORK, NY 10003
PASQUALINA, ROBERT	DIRECTOR	1900 AVE OF THE STARS #800	LOS ANGELES, CA 90067
PASQUETTO, GIANCARLO	BARITONE	CAMI, 165 W 57TH ST	NEW YORK, NY 10019
PASQUIN, JOHN R	DIRECTOR	DGA, 110 W 57TH ST	NEW YORK, NY 10019
PASS, JOE	GUITARIST	SALLE, 451 N CANON DR	BEVERLY HILLS, CA 90210
PASSARELLA, JOSEPH	DIRECTOR-PRODUCER	88 KEMPSHALL TERR	FANWOOD, NJ 07023
PASSARELLI, KENNETH	MUSICIAN	POST OFFICE BOX 919	LYONS, CO 80540
PASSARIELLO, KEN	BODYBUILDER	POST OFFICE BOX 761	ORANGE, CT 06477
PASSAS, PETER	DIRECTOR	44 CIRCLE DR E	RIDGEFIELD, CT 06877
PASSENGER	C & W GROUP	1209 BAYLOR ST	AUSTIN, TX 78703
PASSION STORY	ROCK & ROLL GROUP	41 BRITAIN ST #200	TORONTO, ONT CANADA
PASSON, SAMUEL	NEWS CORRESPONDENT	1825 "T" ST #501, NW	WASHINGTON, DC 20009
PASSPORT	JAZZ GROUP	KONZERTBUERO CLAUS SCHREINER	
		POSTFACH 2230, MARKET 22	MARBURG/LAHN WEST GERMANY
PASTNER, ROBERT	ACTOR	166 E 63RD ST	NEW YORK, NY 10021
PASTORELLI, ROBERT	ACTOR	9229 SUNSET BLVD #306	LOS ANGELES, CA 90069
PASTORIUS, JACO	MUSICIAN	KURLAND, 173 BRIGHTON AVE	BOSTON, MA 02134
PASZTOR, ANDREW G	NEWS CORRESPONDENT	4850 CRESCENT ST	BETHESDA, MD 20816
PATAKI, MICHAEL	ACTOR	STONE, 1052 CAROL DR	LOS ANGELES, CA 90069
PATAKI, MICHAEL	DIRECTOR	4068 KRAFT AVE	STUDIO CITY, CA 91604
PATANE, GIUSEPPE	CONDUCTOR	61 W 62ND ST #6-F	NEW YORK, NY 10023
PATCHELL, LINDA	ACTRESS	369 S CRESCENT DR	BEVERLY HILLS, CA 90212
PATCHES	CLOWN	2701 COTTAGE WY #14	SACRAMENTO, CA 95825
PATCHETT, TOM	WRITER-PRODUCER	1043 FRANKLIN ST	SANTA MONICA, CA 90403
PATE, MICHAEL	ACTOR	21 BUKDARRA RD	BELLVUE HILL 2023 AUSTRALIA
PATEL, SHARAD	DIRECTOR-PRODUCER	SFA, 14 GLEBE HOUSE, FITZ MEWS	LONDON W1P 5DP ENGLAND
PATEMAN, MICHAEL	DIRECTOR	155 E 35TH ST	NEW YORK, NY 10016
PATENAUDE-YARNELL, JOAN	SOPRANO	POST OFFICE BOX 27539	PHILADELPHIA, PA 19118
PATERSON, ALLEN	DIRECTOR-PRODUCER	422 VIEW PARK CT	MILL VALLEY, CA 94941
PATES, CHARLES W	ART DIRECTOR	LIFE/TIME & LIFE BLDG	
		ROCKEFELLER CENTER	NEW YORK, NY 10020
PATIK, VICKIE	TV WRITER	ICM, 8899 BEVERLY BLVD	LOS ANGELES, CA 90048
PATIN, BOB	PIANIST	5274 EDMONDSON PIKE #813	NASHVILLE, TN 37211
PATINKIN, MANDY	ACTRESS	200 W 90TH ST	NEW YORK, NY 10024
PATNODE, HAROLD	TV DIRECTOR	6294 OCCOQUAN FOREST DR	MANASSA, VA 22111
PATRICK, DENNIS	ACTOR	208 S BEVERLY DR #4	BEVERLY HILLS, CA 90212
PATRICK, DICK	SPORTS WRITER	POST OFFICE BOX 500	WASHINGTON, DC 20044
PATRICK, JOHN	PLAYWRIGHT	FORTUNA HILL ESTATE, BOX 2386	SAINT THOMAS, VI 00801
PATRICK, JOHNNY, SR	GUITARIST	196 SPRUCE ST	ALCOA, TN 37701
PATRICK, JULIAN	BARITONE	59 E 54TH ST #81	NEW YORK, NY 10022
PATRICK, LOUGENIA	TV WRITER	14955 DICKENS ST #12	SHERMAN OAKS, CA 91403
PATRICK, LYN	ACTRESS	KOHNER, 9169 SUNSET BLVD	LOS ANGELES, CA 90069

Name	Occupation	Address	City/State	Zip
PATRICK, PAT	GUITARIST	POST OFFICE BOX 120516	NASHVILLE, TN	37212
PATRICK, ROBERT	PLAYWRIGHT	LA MAMA, 74-A E 4TH ST	NEW YORK, NY	10003
PATRICK, VINCENT	SCREENWRITER	555 W 57TH ST #1230	NEW YORK, NY	10019
PATRIOT	C & W GROUP	POST OFFICE BOX O	EXCELSIOR, MN	55331
PATRON, VIRGILIO HOMERO	CONDUCTOR	5055 UNION PACIFIC AVE	LOS ANGELES, CA	90022
PATTA, JOAN	ACTRESS	24301 BESSEMER ST	WOODLAND HILLS, CA	91367
PATTARSON, DAN	ACTOR	POST OFFICE BOX 1955	HOLLYWOOD, CA	90078
PATTEN, LUANA	ACTRESS	SMITH, 13266 RELIANCE	ARLETA, CA	91331
PATTEN, MOULTRIE	ACTOR	484 W 43RD ST #20-K	NEW YORK, NY	10036
PATTEN, PATRICIA A	NEWS CORRESPONDENT	400 N CAPITOL ST, NW	WASHINGTON, DC	20001
PATTEN, ROBERT	ACTOR	24932 MALIBU RD	MALIBU, CA	90265
PATTERSON, CASANDRA	ACTRESS	PANACEA, 2705 GLENDOWER AVE	LOS ANGELES, CA	90027
PATTERSON, DAVID J	FILM PRODUCER	360 PLACE ROYALE	MONTREAL, QUE H2Y 2V1	CANADA
PATTERSON, DICK	ACTOR	10525 STRATHMORE DR	LOS ANGELES, CA	90024
PATTERSON, DOROTHY	ACTRESS	6310 SAN VICENTE BLVD #407	LOS ANGELES, CA	90048
PATTERSON, FLOYD	BOXER	SPRINGFIELD RD #336	NEW PALTZ, NY	12561
PATTERSON, GEORGE F	PHOTOGRAPHER	14316 WATERY MOUNTAIN CT	CENTERVILLE, VA	22020
PATTERSON, JAMES	OPERA SINGER	ICM, 40 W 57TH ST	NEW YORK, NY	10019
PATTERSON, JEFFREY L	CONDUCTOR	1525 AMHERST AVE #209	LOS ANGELES, CA	90025
PATTERSON, JOHN T	TV DIRECTOR	508 N GLEN TRAIL	TOPANGA, CA	90290
PATTERSON, KATHRYN B	PHOTOGRAPHER	6831-D WASHINGTON BLVD	ARLINGTON, VA	22213
PATTERSON, KENNETH G	ACTOR	9021 MELROSE AVE #304	LOS ANGELES, CA	90069
PATTERSON, LARRY	ACTOR	CED, 261 S ROBERTSON BLVD	BEVERLY HILLS, CA	90211
PATTERSON, LAURA J	TV DIRECTOR	5310 CIRCLE DR #107	SHERMAN OAKS, CA	91401
PATTERSON, LEE	ACTOR	1221 N KINGS RD #PH-405	LOS ANGELES, CA	90069
PATTERSON, LORNA	ACTRESS	4023 GOODLAND PL	STUDIO CITY, CA	91604
PATTERSON, MELODY	ACTRESS	GRIFFITH, 1884 LAUREL CYN BLVD	LOS ANGELES, CA	90046
PATTERSON, MICHAEL	COMPOSER	4342 SAINT CLAIR AVE	STUDIO CITY, CA	91604
PATTERSON, NEVA	ACTRESS	210 W 90TH ST #7-B	NEW YORK, NY	10024
PATTERSON, RICHARD	WRITER-PRODUCER	135 MEDIO DR	LOS ANGELES, CA	90049
PATTERSON, RICHARD E	COMPOSER	2406 CAMINITO OCEAN COVE	CARDIFF BY THE SEA, CA	92007
PATTERSON, RUSSELL	CONDUCTOR	GERSHUNOFF, 502 PARK AVE	NEW YORK, NY	10022
PATTERSON, TIM	WRESTLER	POST OFFICE BOX 3859	STAMFORD, CT	06905
PATTI, SANDI	SINGER	HELVERING, 530 GRAND AVE	ANDERSON, IN	46012
PATTIE, JOSEPH DELTON	NEWS CORRESPONDENT	819 COPLEY LN	SILVER SPRING, MD	20904
PATTON, CHARLOTTE	ACTRESS	8322 BEVERLY BLVD #202	LOS ANGELES, CA	90048
PATTON, DAVID W	MUSIC ARRANGER	126 GRAPEVINE RD	HENDERSONVILLE, TN	37075
PATTON, DAVID, BAND	C & W GROUP	POST OFFICE BOX 1373	LEWISVILLE, TX	75067
PATTON, DONALD	DIRECTOR	9538 JELLICO AVE	NORTHRIDGE, CA	91324
PATTON, DONALD K	GUITARIST	106-A MEADOWBROOK DR		
PATTON, JOHNNY	SINGER	POST OFFICE BOX 418	BRENTWOOD, TN	37027
PATTON, LYNDI	ACTRESS	ABC-TV, "ALL MY CHILDREN"		
		1330 AVE OF THE AMERICAS	NEW YORK, NY	10019
PATTON, RITA LYNN	MUSICIAN	1604 PORTER AVE	NASHVILLE, TN	37206
PAUK, GYORGY	VIOLINIST	1776 BROADWAY #504	NEW YORK, NY	10019
PAUKEN, ADAM "CHIP"	VIDEO EDITOR	ENTERTAINMENT TONIGHT		
		PARAMOUNT TELEVISION		
		5555 MELROSE AVE	LOS ANGELES, CA	90038
PAUL, ADRIAN	ACTOR	9000 SUNSET BLVD #801	LOS ANGELES, CA	90069
PAUL, ALEXANDRA	ACTRESS	8370 WILSHIRE BLVD #310	BEVERLY HILLS, CA	90211
PAUL, ANGUS H	NEWS CORRESPONDENT	1727 MASSACHUSETTS AVE #812, NW	WASHINGTON, DC	20036
PAUL, BYRON	ACTOR-DIRECTOR	103 S ROCKINGHAM AVE	LOS ANGELES, CA	90049
PAUL, DEANNE	ACTRESS	5850 CANOGA AVE #110	WOODLAND HILLS, CA	91367
PAUL, EDDIE	STUNTMAN	STUNTS, 124 NEVADA ST	EL SEGUNDO, CA	90245
PAUL, ESTHER JANE	TV WRITER	8955 BEVERLY BLVD	LOS ANGELES, CA	90048
PAUL, GEORGE	DIRECTOR	THE WILLIAM MORRIS AGENCY		
		1350 AVE OF THE AMERICAS	NEW YORK, NY	10019
PAUL, GEORGIE	ACTRESS	8350 SANTA MONICA BLVD #103	LOS ANGELES, CA	90069
PAUL, HENRY	PIANIST	728 HAYSTACK LN	ANTIOCH, TN	37013
PAUL, HENRY, BAND	C & W GROUP	210 25TH AVE N #N-101	NASHVILLE, TN	37203
PAUL, JAMES	CONDUCTOR	SHAW CONCERTS, 1995 BROADWAY	NEW YORK, NY	10023
PAUL, JODY	COMPOSER	1321 S KENISTON AVE	LOS ANGELES, CA	90019
PAUL, JOHN	ACTOR	THE OLD DUKE'S HEAD		
		BUCKLAND VILLA		
		NEAR AYLESBURY	BUCKS	ENGLAND
PAUL, LEE	ACTOR	9255 SUNSET BLVD #603	LOS ANGELES, CA	90069
PAUL, LES	GUITARIST	78 DEERHAVEN RD	MAHWAH, NJ	07430
PAUL, NANCY	ACTRESS	9200 SUNSET BLVD #1210	LOS ANGELES, CA	90069
PAUL, RICHARD	ACTOR	6380 WILSHIRE BLVD #910	LOS ANGELES, CA	90048
PAUL, SOL J	PUBLISH EXECUTIVE	TELEVISON/RADIO AGE MAGAZINE		
		1270 AVE OF THE AMERICAS	NEW YORK, NY	10020
PAUL, STEVE	FILM DIRECTOR	8776 SUNSET BLVD	LOS ANGELES, CA	90069
PAUL, THOMAS	SINGER	COLBERT, 111 W 57TH ST	NEW YORK, NY	10019
PAUL, VAUGHN	DIRECTOR	4344 PROMENDE WY	MARINA DEL REY, CA	90292
PAULA & RUTH	FLUTE/PIANO DUO	SHAW CONCERTS, 1995 BROADWAY	NEW YORK, NY	10023
PAULEY, JANE	TV HOST	271 CENTRAL PARK W #10-E	NEW YORK, NY	10024
PAULIN, SCOTT	ACTOR	211 S BEVERLY DR #201	BEVERLY HILLS, CA	90212
PAULL, MORGAN	ACTOR	4104 CAMELLIA AVE	NORTH HOLLYWOOD, CA	91604
PAULSEN, ALBERT	ACTOR	CONTEMPORARY ARTISTS		
		132 S LASKY DR	BEVERLY HILLS, CA	90212
PAULSEN, DAVID	TV WRITER-DIRECTOR	15652 WOODFIELD PL	SHERMAN OAKS, CA	91403
PAULSEN, PAT	COMEDIAN-ACTOR	113 N ROBERTSON BLVD #2	LOS ANGELES, CA	90048
PAULSON, DAVID R	NEWS CORRESPONDENT	4461 CONNECTICUT AVE, NW	WASHINGTON, DC	20008
PAULSON, MORTON C	NEWS CORRESPONDENT	14801 PEBBLESTONE DR	SILVER SPRING, MD	20904
PAULSON, S LAWRENCE	NEWS CORRESPONDENT	4215 JEFFERSON ST	HYATTSVILLE, MD	20781

GOLDEN
TREASURES
P.O. BOX 601
BENTONVILLE, AR. 72712
© 1983 - Golden Treasures

PAULSON, WILLIAM C	NEWS CORRESPONDENT	4409 FARADAY PL, NW	WASHINGTON, DC 20016
PAUNOVA, MARIANA	CONTRALTO	111 W 57TH ST #1209	NEW YORK, NY 10019
PAVAN, MARISA	ACTRESS	LORCASTER LOLA MOULOUDJI	
		27 RUE DE RICHELIEU	PARIS 75001 FRANCE
PAVAROTTI, LUCIANO	TENOR	941 VIA GIARDINI	
		41040 SALICETA SOUTH	
		GULIANO	MODENA ITALY
PAVEK, JANET	SOPRANO	LIEBERMAN, 11 RIVERSIDE DR	NEW YORK, NY 10023
PAVUK, ANNE	NEWS CORRESPONDENT	3725 MACOMB ST, NW	WASHINGTON, DC 20016
PAWLAWSKI, RITA	SAXOPHONIST	865 BELLEVUE RD #E-18	NASHVILLE, TN 37221
PAXTON, BILL	ACTOR	ICM, 8899 BEVERLY BLVD	LOS ANGELES, CA 90048
PAXTON, GLENN	CONDUCTOR	913 MARCO PL	MARINA DEL REY, CA 90292
PAXTON, ROBERT	GUITARIST	1224 GRANDVIEW DR	NASHVILLE, TN 37215
PAXTON, TOM	SINGER-GUITARIST	PRODUCERS, 5109 OAK HAVEN LN	TAMPA, FL 33617
PAYCHECK, JOHNNY	SINGER	50 MUSIC SQUARE W #905	NASHVILLE, TN 37203
PAYLOW, CLARK	DIRECTOR	4938 RUBIO AVE	ENCINO, CA 91436
PAYMER, DAVID	ACTOR	1150 1/2 N FULLER AVE	LOS ANGELES, CA 90046
PAYNE, ARTHUR J	NEWS CORRESPONDENT	2139 WISCONSIN AVE, NW	WASHINGTON, DC 20007
PAYNE, CLARENCE	GUITARIST	ROUTE #2, KINNY'S RD	SPRINGFIELD, TN 37172
PAYNE, DEVIN	PRODUCER	3700 VENTURA CANYON AVE	SHERMAN OAKS, CA 91423
PAYNE, ETHEL L	NEWS CORRESPONDENT	6101 16TH ST, NW	WASHINGTON, DC 20011
PAYNE, FREDA	SINGER	1505 BLUE JAY WY	LOS ANGELES, CA 90069
PAYNE, GARELD G	COMPOSER-CONDUCTOR	1306 W 1ST ST	COFFEYVILLE, KS 67337
PAYNE, GORDON	GUITARIST	ROUTE #1, BOX 224-B	COLLEGE GROVE, TN 37046
PAYNE, HARRIET P	COMPOSER	3254-A SAN AMADEO	LAGUNA HILLS, CA 92653
PAYNE, JULIE	ACTRESS	SEE - PAYNE TOWNE, JULIE	
PAYNE, PATRICIA	MEZZO-SOPRANO	CAMI, 165 W 57TH ST	NEW YORK, NY 10019
PAYNE, PATRICIA	TV WRITER	8955 BEVERLY BLVD	LOS ANGELES, CA 90048
PAYNE, ROBERT W	COMPOSER	27506 DIANE MARIE CIR	SAUGUS, CA 91350
PAYNE, SCHERRIE	SINGER	8544 EASTWOOD RD	LOS ANGELES, CA 90046
PAYNE, SETH T	NEWS CORRESPONDENT	7006 OAK FOREST LN	BETHESDA, MD 20817
PAYNE, STEPHEN J	WRITER	8306 WILSHIRE BLVD #58	BEVERLY HILLS, CA 90211
PAYNE TOWNE, JULIE	ACTRESS	9744 WILSHIRE BLVD #206	BEVERLY HILLS, CA 90212
PAYNTER, ROBERT	CINEMATOGRAPHER	55 WORTHING RD, HORSHAM	SUSSEX ENGLAND
PAYOLA$, THE	ROCK & ROLL GROUP	41 BRITAIN ST #200	TORONTO, ONT CANADA
PAYTON, DOUGLAS	ACTOR	730 ASHLAND AVE #A	SANTA MONICA, CA 90405
PAYTON, ED	DRUMMER	212 CHERRY DR	FRANKLIN, TN 37064
PAYTON, WALTER	FOOTBALL	55 E JACKSON BLVD	CHICAGO, IL 60604
PAYTON-WRIGHT, PAMELA	ACTRESS	21 E 93RD ST	NEW YORK, NY 10028
PEACE, LYNCH	SINGER	TRENDA, 18747 SHERMAN WY	RESEDA, CA 91335
PEACE CORPSE	ROCK & ROLL GROUP	POST OFFICE BOX 242	POMONA, CA 91769
PEACE ON EARTH	GOSPEL GROUP	POST OFFICE BOX 337	HEMET, CA 92343
PEACOCK, CHIARA	ACTRESS	370 LEXINGTON AVE #2008	NEW YORK, NY 10017
PEAK, CHRISTOPHER	DRUMMER	4872 SHASTA DR	OLD HICKORY, TN 37138
PEAKER, E J	ACTRESS	JAYMES, 327 N LAUREL AVE	LOS ANGELES, CA 90048
PEALE, DR NORMAN VINCENT	EVANGELIST-AUTHOR	1030 5TH AVE	NEW YORK, NY 10028
PEAR, ROBERT	NEWS CORRESPONDENT	425 "D" ST, SE	WASHINGTON, DC 20003
PEARCE, JACQUELINE	ACTRESS	HEATH, PARAMOUNT HOUSE	
		162-170 WARDOUR ST	LONDON W1V 3AT ENGLAND
PEARCE, JOHN	ACTOR	3330 BARHAM BLVD #103	LOS ANGELES, CA 90068
PEARCE, KATHLEEN D	NEWS CORRESPONDENT	4420 CONNECTICUT AVE, NW	WASHINGTON, DC 20008
PEARCE, RICHARD	DIRECTOR	767 PASEO MIRAMAR	PACIFIC PALISADES, CA 90271
PEARCY, STEVE	SINGER	1818 ILLION ST	SAN DIEGO, CA 92110
PEARL, BARRY	ACTOR	9255 SUNSET BLVD #603	LOS ANGELES, CA 90069
PEARL, BILL	BODYBUILDER	POST OFFICE BOX 1080	PHOENIX, OR 97535
PEARL, LESLIE	SINGER	1101 N KING'S HWY #107	CHERRY HILL, NJ 08034
PEARL, MINNIE	SINGER-ACTRESS	HALSEY, 1111 16TH AVE S	NASHVILLE, TN 37212
PEARL, REBECCA	NEWS CORRESPONDENT	11 E CUSTIS AVE	ALEXANDRIA, VA 22301
PEARL, RENEE	ACTRESS	BRAMSON, 240 CENTRAL PARK S	NEW YORK, NY 10019
PEARLBERG, IRVING	WRITER	11829 SUNSHINE TERR	STUDIO CITY, CA 91604
PEARLBERG, NANCY	ACTRESS	11829 SUNSHINE TERR	STUDIO CITY, CA 91604
PEARLMAN, NANCY	NEWS CORRESPONDENT	10617 HIGH BEAM CT	COLUMBIA, MD 21044
PEARLMAN, STEPHEN	ACTOR	5224 RIVERTON AVE	NORTH HOLLYWOOD, CA 91601
PEARLMAN, SY	TV PRODUCER	NBC TELEVISION NETWORK	
		30 ROCKEFELLER PLAZA	NEW YORK, NY 10112
PEARLSTEIN, DAVID B	COMPOSER	2147 HOLLY DR	LOS ANGELES, CA 90068
PEARRE, LARRY	GUITARIST	1416 WILDWOOD CT	FRANKLIN, TN 37064
PEARSON, BARBARA	SOPRANO	SHAW CONCERTS, 1995 BROADWAY	NEW YORK, NY 10023
PEARSON, BRUCE	GUITARIST	810 BELLEVUE RD #236	NASHVILLE, TN 37221
PEARSON, DURK	SCIENTIST-AUTHOR	POST OFFICE BOX 1067	HOLLYWOOD, FL 33022
PEARSON, DURK J	TV WRITER	8955 BEVERLY BLVD	LOS ANGELES, CA 90048
PEARSON, GARRET	ACTOR	14238 HAMLIN ST	VAN NUYS, CA 91401
PEARSON, GLENN	TV DIRECTOR	15810 KENTFIELD ST	DETROIT, MI 48223
PEARSON, GREG W	NEWS CORRESPONDENT	1225 EUCLID ST, NW	WASHINGTON, DC 20009
PEARSON, JEROLD	ACTOR	2032 VISTA DEL MAR AVE	LOS ANGELES, CA 90068
PEARSON, MARSHALL	DRUMMER	40 W BEL AIR BLVD	CLARKSVILLE, TN 37040
PEARSON, MICHAEL	GUITARIST	1114 SUNNYMEADE DR	NASHVILLE, TN 37216
PEARSON, PAULETTE	SINGER-ACTRESS	WASHINGTON, 4604 PLACIDIA AVE	TOLUCA LAKE, CA 91602
PEARSON, RICHARD	ACTOR	EDWARDS, 275 KENNINGTON RD	LONDON SE11 ENGLAND
PEARSON, RONALD	TV DIRECTOR	41793 SYCAMORE DR	NOVI, MI 48050
PEARSON, TONY	BODYBUILDER	POST OFFICE BOX 299	NORTHRIDGE, CA 91328
PEART, PAULINE	ACTRESS	LMA, 213 EDGEWARE RD	LONDON W2 ENGLAND
PEASE, PATRICIA	ACTRESS	KNBC-TV, "DAYS OF OUR LIVES"	
		3000 W ALAMEDA AVE	BURBANK, CA 91523
PEATMAN, LEIGHTON	WRITER	667 LACHMAN LN	PACIFIC PALISADES, CA 90272

FREDA PAYNE

GREGORY PECK

ANTHONY PERKINS

CARL PERKINS

GIGI PERREAU

STEVE PERRY

DONNA PESCOW

BERNADETTE PETERS

JIM PHOTOGLO

Name	Occupation	Address	City	Zip
PEATTIE, YVONNE	ACTRESS	11240 MAGNOLIA BLVD #202	NORTH HOLLYWOOD, CA	91601
PECCHIO, CARMEN	ACTOR	1436 S SHENANDOAH ST #305	LOS ANGELES, CA	90035
PECCHIOLI, BENEDETTA	MEZZO-SOPRANO	61 W 62ND ST #6-F	NEW YORK, NY	10023
PECHIN, CHRISTOPHER	TV DIRECTOR	11565 ADDISON ST	NORTH HOLLYWOOD, CA	91601
PECK, BRIAN	ACTOR	ROSE COTTAGE, 102 HIGH ST		
		WOKING	SURREY	ENGLAND
PECK, CLAIRE	ACTRESS	7469 MELROSE AVE #30	LOS ANGELES, CA	90046
PECK, CLARE	ACTRESS	703 9TH ST #3	SANTA MONICA, CA	90402
PECK, DONALD	FLUTIST	POST OFFICE BOX 160	HIGHLAND PARK, IL	60035
PECK, DOROTHY	ACTRESS	ARNOLD, 73193 TRAILS CIR	PALM DESERT, CA	92260
PECK, ED	ACTOR	9000 SUNSET BLVD #801	LOS ANGELES, CA	90069
PECK, GREGORY	ACTOR	POST OFFICE BOX 837	BEVERLY HILLS, CA	90213
PECK, KIMI ZAN	SCREENWRITER	8955 BEVERLY BLVD	LOS ANGELES, CA	90048
PECK, LOUIS M	NEWS CORRESPONDENT	125 5TH ST, NE	WASHINGTON, DC	20002
PECK, RAY	SINGER	POST OFFICE BOX 256577	CHICAGO, IL	60625
PECK, ROBERT NEWTON	AUTHOR	500 SWEETWATER CLUB CIR	LONGWOOD, FL	32779
PECK, STEPHEN	DIRECTOR-PRODUCER	1039 MAPLE ST	SANTA MONICA, CA	90405
PECK, STEVEN	ACTOR	3800 BARHAM BLVD #303	LOS ANGELES, CA	90068
PECKARSKY, PETER	NEWS CORRESPONDENT	950 25TH ST, NW	WASHINGTON, DC	20037
PECKHAM, JACK	NEWS CORRESPONDENT	2500 WISCONSIN AVE #405, NW	WASHINGTON, DC	20007
PECKINPAH, DAVID E	WRITER	4643 CERRILLOS DR	WOODLAND HILLS, CA	91364
PECORARO, TONY	ACTOR	5330 LANKERSHIM BLVD #210	NORTH HOLLYWOOD, CA	91601
PECORELLA, LARRY	PIANIST	6700 CABOT DR #0-14	NASHVILLE, TN	37209
PEDEN, JOHN H B	DIRECTOR	168 5TH AVE	NEW YORK, NY	10010
PEDERSEN, TED	TV WRITER	2620 OAKWOOD AVE	VENICE, CA	90291
PEDERSON, MILLIE	ACTRESS	FELBER, 2126 N CAHUENGA BLVD	LOS ANGELES, CA	90068
PEDERSON, RUFUS J, JR	TV DIRECTOR	45 CREEK RD	FAIRFAX, CA	93930
PEDI, TOM	ACTOR	FORMAN, 2845 UNIVERSITY AVE	BRONX, NY	10468
PEDICIN, MICHAEL, JR	SAXOPHONIST	ZANE MANAGEMENT AGENCY		
		1529 WALNUT ST, 6TH FLOOR	PHILADELPHIA, PA	19102
PEDRIANA, LESA ANN	MAKE-UP ARTIST-MODEL	KEN MARCUS STUDIOS		
		6916 MELROSE AVE	LOS ANGELES, CA	90038
PEDROTTI, MARK	BARITONE	59 E 54TH ST #81	NEW YORK, NY	10022
PEEBLES, ANN	SINGER	TRENDA, 18747 SHERMAN WY	RESEDA, CA	91335
PEEBLES, VICTORIA LYNN	NEWS CORRESPONDENT	POST OFFICE BOX 1042	WASHINGTON, DC	20013
PEELER, GARY	FIDDLER	POST OFFICE BOX 571	DICKSON, TN	37055
PEELER, H ELMO	COMPOSER-CONDUCTOR	2646 WOODSTOCK RD	LOS ANGELES, CA	90046
PEEPLES, NIA	ACTRESS	9255 SUNSET BLVD #1115	LOS ANGELES, CA	90069
PEEPLES, SAMUEL A	WRITER-PRODUCER	11371 QUAIL CREEK RD	NORTHRIDGE, CA	91326
PEER, RACHEL	MUSICIAN	5105 COCHRAN DR	NASHVILLE, TN	37220
PEER, REX	MUSICIAN	5105 COCHRAN DR	NASHVILLE, TN	37220
PEERCE, LARRY	FILM DIRECTOR	7731 FIRENZE AVE	LOS ANGELES, CA	90046
PEERS, JOHNNY	CLOWN	POST OFFICE BOX 87	WEST LEBANON, NY	12195
PEET, STEPHEN	DIRECTOR-PRODUCER	16 LANGBOURNE AVE	LONDON N6	ENGLAND
PEETE, N GARLAND	TV DIRECTOR	67 W 68TH ST	NEW YORK, NY	10023
PEETE, ROBERT L	TV WRITER	3850 CRESTWAY DR	LOS ANGELES, CA	90043
PEETERS, BARBARA	DIRECTOR	11600 SAN VICENTE BLVD	LOS ANGELES, CA	90049
PEGASUS	MUSICAL DUO	LUTZ, 5625 "O" STREET BLDG	LINCOLN, NE	68510
PEGASUS	ROCK & ROLL GROUP	41 BRITAIN ST #200	TORONTO, ONT	CANADA
PEGGY SUE & SONNY WRIGHT	VOCAL DUO	TAYLOR, 2401 12TH AVE S	NASHVILLE, TN	37204
PEINEMANN, EDITH	VIOLINIST	CAMI, 165 W 57TH ST	NEW YORK, NY	10019
PEIRCE, NEAL	COLUMNIST	THE WASHINGTON POST		
		WRITERS GROUP		
		1150 15TH ST, NW	WASHINGTON, DC	20071
PEKINEL SISTERS, THE	PIANO DUO	ANGLO-SWISS ARTISTS MGMT		
		16 MUSWELL HILL RD, HIGHGATE	LONDON N6 5UG	ENGLAND
PEKKONEN, DONNA	TV WRITER	13518 CONTOUR DR	SHERMAN OAKS, CA	91423
PEKOW, CHARLES	NEWS CORRESPONDENT	1024 WISCONSIN AVE, NW	WASHINGTON, DC	20007
PEKURNY, ROBERT G	WRITER	1117 9TH ST	SANTA MONICA, CA	90403
PELGRIFT, KATHRYN C	TV EXECUTIVE	NBC-TV, 30 ROCKEFELLER PLAZA	NEW YORK, NY	10112
PELI, WILLIAM	TENOR	225 W 34TH ST #1012	NEW YORK, NY	10001
PELIKAN, LISA	ACTRESS	8531 BRIER DR	LOS ANGELES, CA	90046
PELISSIE, JEAN-MARIE	DIRECTOR	333 E 34TH ST	NEW YORK, NY	10016
PELL, JOHN	GUITARIST	1810 NATCHEZ TRACE	NASHVILLE, TN	37212
PELL BROTHERS, THE	GOSPEL GROUP	CEE, 193 KONHAUS RD	MECHANICSBURG, PA	17055
PELLE, NADIA	SOPRANO	59 E 54TH ST #81	NEW YORK, NY	10022
PELLECCHIA, JOSEPH	GUITARIST	1603 STOKES LN	NASHVILLE, TN	37215
PELLEGRIN, RAYMOND	ACTOR	EUROP' ACTEURS AGENCE		
		35 RUE DE RIVOLI	PARIS 75004	FRANCE
PELLEGRINI, EUGENE	ACTOR	140 W 79TH ST	NEW YORK, NY	10024
PELLEGRINI, MARIA	SOPRANO	61 W 62ND ST #6-F	NEW YORK, NY	10023
PELLEGRINI, MARIO	FILM DIRECTOR	1601 HOLLINDALE DR	ALEXANDRA, VA	22306
PELLEGRINO, NICK	ACTOR	10351 SANTA MONICA BLVD #211	LOS ANGELES, CA	90025
PELLER, CLARA "WHERE'S THE BEEF	ACTRESS	33 N DEARBORN ST #1515	CHICAGO, IL	60602
PELLER, RICK	MUSICIAN	POST OFFICE BOX 9388	STANFORD, CA	94305
PELLOW, CLIFFORD A	ACTOR	1850 RIVERSIDE DR	GLENDALE, CA	91201
PELT, CHERYL	WRITER	1206 MEADOWBROOK AVE	LOS ANGELES, CA	90019
PELUCE, MEENO	ACTOR	10390 SANTA MONICA BLVD #310	LOS ANGELES, CA	90025
PELUSO, ANTHONY D	CONDUCTOR	246 ARON PL	ANAHEIM, CA	92804
PELUSO, LISA	ACTRESS	KOHNER, 9169 SUNSET BLVD	LOS ANGELES, CA	90069
PELUZA	CLOWN	2701 COTTAGE WY #14	SACRAMENTO, CA	95825
PELZIG, DANIEL	CHOREOGRAPHER	LEW, 204 W 10TH ST	NEW YORK, NY	10014
PEMBER, RON	ACTOR	DAWSON, 31 KINGS RD	LONDON SW3	ENGLAND
PEMBLETON, ARTHUR	DIRECTOR	423 "G" ST	SALT LAKE CITY, UT	84103
PEMSTEIN, RONALD	NEWS CORRESPONDENT	330 INDEPENDENCE AVE, SW	WASHINGTON, DC	20547

Name	Occupation	Address	City	Zip
PENA, PACO	GUITARIST	SHAW CONCERTS, 1995 BROADWAY	NEW YORK, NY	10023
PENBERTHY, BEVERLY	ACTRESS	ABRAMS ARTISTS & ASSOCIATES		
		420 MADISON AVE, 14TH FLOOR	NEW YORK, NY	10017
PENCE, DENISE	ACTRESS	165 W 46TH ST #710	NEW YORK, NY	10036
PENCE, RUSTY	GUITARIST	116 CURTIS CROSS RD #64	HENDERSONVILLE, TN	37075
PENDERECKI, KRZYSZTOF	COMPOSER-CONDUCTOR	ICM, 40 W 57TH ST	NEW YORK, NY	10019
PENDERGRAPH, RICHARD	BARITONE	CAMI, 165 W 57TH ST	NEW YORK, NY	10019
PENDERGRASS, TEDDY	SINGER-SONGWRITER	57 CROSLEY BROWN RD	GLADWYN, PA	19035
PENDERS, MAURA	TV WRITER	KNBC-TV, "SANTA BARBARA"		
		3000 W ALAMEDA AVE	BURBANK, CA	91523
PENDLE, FRANK	ACTOR	17197 SIERRA HWY 36	CANYON COUNTRY, CA	91351
PENDLEBURY, L J	NEWS CORRESPONDENT	1042 N STUART ST	ARLINGTON, VA	22201
PENDLEBURY, STEPHEN T	NEWS CORRESPONDENT	1825 "K" ST, NW	WASHINGTON, DC	20006
PENDLETON, AUSTIN	COMEDIAN	155 E 76TH ST	NEW YORK, NY	10021
PENDLETON, WYMAN	ACTOR	36 BEDFORD ST	NEW YORK, NY	10014
PENDRELL, ERNEST	DIRECTOR	POST OFFICE BOX 7218	GLENDALE, CA	91205
PENGHLIS, THAAO	ACTOR	7187 MACAPA DR	LOS ANGELES, CA	90068
PENGUINS, THE	VOCAL GROUP	MARS, 168 ORCHID DR	PEARL RIVER, NY	10965
PENHALIGAN, SUSAN	ACTRESS	CONWAY, EAGLE HOUSE		
		109 JERMYN ST	LONDON SW1	ENGLAND
PENHALL, BRUCE	ACTOR	319 36TH ST #A	MANHATTAN BEACH, CA	90266
PENIN, JEAN-PAUL	CONDUCTOR	ICM, 40 W 57TH ST	NEW YORK, NY	10019
PENLAND, ROY TIMOTHY	DIRECTOR	133 VIRGINIA AVE	GLENDALE, CA	91202
PENN, ARTHUR	DIRECTOR	FLORIN PRODS, 1860 BROADWAY	NEW YORK, NY	10023
PENN, CHRISTOPHER	ACTOR	6728 ZUMIREZ DR	MALIBU, CA	90265
PENN, DAN	GUITARIST	1100 BATEY DR	NASHVILLE, TN	37204
PENN, EDWARD	ACTOR	1350 N HIGHLAND AVE #24	HOLLYWOOD, CA	90028
PENN, IRVING	PHOTOGRAPHER	POST OFFICE BOX 934		
		F D ROOSEVELT STATION	NEW YORK, NY	10150
PENN, LEO	FILM WRITER-DIRECTOR	6728 ZUMIREZ DR	MALIBU, CA	90265
PENN, MADONNA	SINGER-ACTRESS	SEE - MADONNA		
PENN, MARINA	ACTRESS	1270 N HAVENHURST DR #12-B	LOS ANGELES, CA	90046
PENN, RICHARD	TV WRITER	8955 BEVERLY BLVD	LOS ANGELES, CA	90048
PENN, SEAN	ACTOR	22271 CARBON MESA RD	MALIBU, CA	90265
PENNARIO, LEONARD	PIANIST-COMPOSER	1140 CALLE VISTA DR	BEVERLY HILLS, CA	90210
PENNELL, ELIZABETH	RADIO WRITER	555 W 57TH ST #1230	NEW YORK, NY	10019
PENNEY, EDMUND F	ACTOR	8721 SUNSET BLVD #200	LOS ANGELES, CA	90069
PENNEY, EDMUND F	WRITER-DIRECTOR	2144 ROCKLEDGE RD	LOS ANGELES, CA	90068
PENNEY, SCOTT	TALENT AGENT	10390 SANTA MONICA BLVD #310	LOS ANGELES, CA	90025
PENNIMAN, JUDITH M	NEWS CORRESPONDENT	525 WILKES ST	ALEXANDRIA, VA	22314
PENNINGROTH, PHIL	TV WRITER	8955 BEVERLY BLVD	LOS ANGELES, CA	90048
PENNINGTON, ANN	ACTRESS-MODEL	1801 AVE OF THE STARS #911	LOS ANGELES, CA	90067
PENNINGTON, BILL	MUSIC ARRANGER	190 TOWNSHIP DR	HENDERSONVILLE, TN	37075
PENNINGTON, JANICE	MODEL-ACTRESS	CBS TELEVISION NETWORK		
		"THE PRICE IS RIGHT"		
		7800 BEVERLY BLVD	LOS ANGELES, CA	90036
PENNINGTON, MARLA	ACTRESS	3800 BARHAM BLVD #303	LOS ANGELES, CA	90068
PENNINGTON, MICHAEL	ACTOR	3 WESTBOURNE GARDENS	LONDON W2	ENGLAND
PENNINGTON, ROGER	FILM WRITER-DIRECTOR	DINNAGES FARM, BROAD OAK		
		HEATHFIELD	SUSSEX	ENGLAND
PENNINO, JOHNNY	SINGER	POST OFFICE BOX 1830	GRETNA, LA	70053
PENNISI, ELIZABETH	WRITER-EDITOR	DISCOVER/TIME & LIFE BLDG		
		ROCKEFELLER CENTER	NEW YORK, NY	10020
PENNOCK, CHRISTOPHER	ACTOR	25150 1/2 MALIBU RD	MALIBU, CA	90265
PENNY, JOE	ACTOR	MORESS, 2128 W PICO BLVD	SANTA MONICA, CA	90405
PENNY, JOHN	RECORD EXEC-TAL AGENT	30 GUINAN ST	WALTHAM, MA	02154
PENNY, JOHN, BAND	C & W GROUP	30 GUINAN ST	WALTHAM, MA	02154
PENNY, SYDNEY	ACTRESS	15301 VENTURA BLVD #345	SHERMAN OAKS, CA	91403
PENROD, JUDITH	ACTRESS	10000 RIVERSIDE DR #3	TOLUCA LAKE, CA	91602
PENROD, JUDITH	ACTRESS	6736 LAUREL CANYON BLVD #306	NORTH HOLLYWOOD, CA	91606
PENTAGON	MUSIC GROUP	CEE, 193 KONHAUS RD	MECHANICSBURG, PA	17055
PENTECOST, GEORGE	ACTOR	211 S BEVERLY DR #201	BEVERLY HILLS, CA	90212
PENVERN, ANDRE	ACTOR	7 RUE NEUVE NOTRE DAME	VERSAILLES 78000	FRANCE
PENYA, ANTHONY	ACTOR	9165 SUNSET BLVD #202	LOS ANGELES, CA	90069
PENYCATE, JOHN	TV DIRECTOR-PRODUCER	BBC-TV, LIME GROVE	LONDON W12 7RJ	ENGLAND
PENZNER, SEYMOUR	ACTOR	680 W END AVE	NEW YORK, NY	10012
PEOPLES, BOB	ACTOR	8831 SUNSET BLVD #402	LOS ANGELES, CA	90069
PEOPLES, DAVID	SCREENWRITER	SHAPIRO, 8827 BEVERLY BLVD	LOS ANGELES, CA	90048
PEPPARD, GEORGE	ACTOR-DIRECTOR	1643 LINDACREST DR	BEVERLY HILLS, CA	90210
PEPPER, BUDDY	ACTOR-COMPOSER	JAREST, 4516 LENNOX AVE	SHERMAN OAKS, CA	91423
PEPPER, PAUL	ACTOR	2697 N BEACHWOOD DR	HOLLYWOOD, CA	90068
PEPPERMAN, PAUL E	SCREENWRITER	8955 BEVERLY BLVD	LOS ANGELES, CA	90048
PEPPERMAN, RICHARD	TV DIRECTOR	215 W 75TH ST	NEW YORK, NY	10023
PEPPIATT, FRANK	TV WRITER	9579 1/2 LIME ORCHARD RD	BEVERLY HILLS, CA	90210
PEPPLER, JAMES H	PHOTOGRAPHER	80 W JERICHO TURNPIKE	SYOSSET, NY	11791
PERA, LISA	ACTRESS	7475 FRANKLIN AVE	LOS ANGELES, CA	90046
PERAGINE, FRANCES	CABLE EXECUTIVE	THE CINEMAX CORPORATION		
		1271 AVE OF THE AMERICAS	NEW YORK, NY	10020
PERAGINE, KENNETH F	TV WRITER	8955 BEVERLY BLVD	LOS ANGELES, CA	90048
PERAHIA, MURRAY	PIANIST	201 W 54TH ST #4-C	NEW YORK, NY	10019
PERAK, JOHN	ACTOR	11323 DANUBE AVE	GRANADA HILLS, CA	91344
PERALTA, CRAIG	ACTOR	3609 OCEAN VIEW AVE	LOS ANGELES, CA	90066
PERANI, STEPHEN	WRITER	5805 VENICE BLVD	LOS ANGELES, CA	90019
PERAULT, ROBERT	ACTOR	108 N SYCAMORE AVE #5	LOS ANGELES, CA	90036
PERCELAY, DAVID	TV EXECUTIVE	CBS-TV, 524 W 57TH ST	NEW YORK, NY	10019

PERCEVAL, DAVID	ACTOR	10845 LINDBROOK DR #3	LOS ANGELES, CA	90024
PERCIVAL, LANCE	TV PERSONALITY	THE RICHARD STONE AGENCY		
		18-20 YORK BLDGS, ADELPHI	LONDON WC2N 6JY	ENGLAND
PERE UBU	ROCK & ROLL GROUP	ROUGH TRADE RECORDS		
		61-71 COLLIER	LONDON N1	ENGLAND
PEREL, DAVID	NEWS REPORTER	THE NATIONAL ENQUIRER		
		600 SE COAST AVE	LANTANA, FL	33464
PERENCHIO, ANDREW	FILM-TV EXECUTIVE	23526 MALIBU COLONY DR #77	MALIBU, CA	90265
PERENYI, MIKLOS	CELLIST	CAMI, 165 W 57TH ST	NEW YORK, NY	10019
PERESS, GILLES	PHOTOGRAPHER	RICHARDSON, 304 BOWERY ST	NEW YORK, NY	10012
PERESS, MAURICE	CONDUCTOR	GERSHUNOFF, 502 PARK AVE	NEW YORK, NY	10022
PEREW, THOMAS JOHN	TV WRITER	1327 N LAUREL AVE #16	LOS ANGELES, CA	90046
PEREZ, BOBBY	WRESTLER	UNIVERSAL WRESTLING FEDERATION		
		MID SOUTH SPORTS, INC		
		116 W BRECKINRIDGE	BIXBY, OK	74008
PEREZ, DAUD	COMPOSER	1022 S STANLEY AVE	LOS ANGELES, CA	90019
PEREZ, JOSE	ACTOR	10100 SANTA MONICA BLVD #1600	LOS ANGELES, CA	90067
PEREZ, LIVIA E	DIRECTOR	DGA, 110 W 57TH ST	NEW YORK, NY	10019
PEREZ, PHILIP J	DIRECTOR	408 8TH ST	MANHATTAN BEACH, CA	90266
PEREZ, TONY	ACTOR	8721 SUNSET BLVD #202	LOS ANGELES, CA	90069
PEREZ, TONY	BASEBALL	LOS FLORES #113	SANTURCE, PR	00911
PERFECT TIMIN'	RHYTHM & BLUES GROUP	9777 HARWIN ST #101	HOUSTON, TX	77036
PERGOLA, NICHOLAS J	PHOTOGRAPHER	18 RIDGE RD #V	GREENBELT, MD	20770
PERICK, CHRISTOF	CONDUCTOR	SHAW CONCERTS, 1995 BROADWAY	NEW YORK, NY	10023
PERILLI, FRANK RAY	WRITER	1159 1/2 GREENACRE AVE	LOS ANGELES, CA	90046
PERILLO, VICTOR	TALENT AGENT	9229 SUNSET BLVD #611	LOS ANGELES, CA	90069
PERINA, GEORGE	ACTOR	20880 VENTURA BLVD #23	WOODLAND HILLS, CA	91364
PERINE, PARKE	WRITER-PRODUCER	13370 CONTOUR DR	SHERMAN OAKS, CA	91423
PERINI, DANIEL J	COMPOSER	5821 WHEELHOUSE LN	AGOURA, CA	91301
PERISIC, ZORAN	WRITER-PRODUCER	SMITH, 10 WYNDHAM PL	LONDON W1H 1AS	ENGLAND
PERITO, JENNIFER	ACTRESS	1231 9TH ST #6	SANTA MONICA, CA	90401
PERITO, NICK	CONDUCTOR	5798 PENLAND RD	CALABASAS, CA	91302
PERKINS, ANTHONY	ACTOR-WRITER	2840 SEATTLE DR	LOS ANGELES, CA	90046
PERKINS, BUDD	ACTOR	13111 VENTURA BLVD #102	STUDIO CITY, CA	91604
PERKINS, CARL	SINGER-SONGWRITER	459 COUNTRY CLUB LN	JACKSON, TN	38301
PERKINS, CHRISTOPHER	ACTOR	10845 LINDBROOK DR #3	LOS ANGELES, CA	90024
PERKINS, ELIZABETH	ACTRESS	151 S EL CAMINO DR	BEVERLY HILLS, CA	90212
PERKINS, FRANK S	COMPOSER	3057 PATRICIA AVE	LOS ANGELES, CA	90064
PERKINS, GIL	ACTOR	1841 FAIRBURN AVE	LOS ANGELES, CA	90025
PERKINS, JACK	ACTOR	19620 WELLS DR	TARZANA, CA	91356
PERKINS, JAMES N	CABLE EXECUTIVE	6 E 68TH ST	NEW YORK, NY	10021
PERKINS, KENT	ACTOR	721 N LA BREA AVE #200	LOS ANGELES, CA	90038
PERKINS, LUCIAN	PHOTOGRAPHER	1609 "S" ST, NW	WASHINGTON, DC	20009
PERKINS, MILLIE	ACTRESS	SF & A, 121 N SAN VICENTE BLVD	BEVERLY HILLS, CA	90211
PERKINS, REBECCA B	NEWS CORRESPONDENT	108 W HOWELL AVE	ALEXANDRIA, VA	22301
PERKINS, RICHARD	DIRECTOR	729 MUSKINGUM AVE	PACIFIC PALISADES, CA	90272
PERKINS, RON	ACTOR	400 W 43RD ST #45-G	NEW YORK, NY	10036
PERKINS, ROWLAND	TALENT AGENT	1888 CENTURY PARK E #1400	LOS ANGELES, CA	90067
PERKINS, STEVE	SPORTS WRITER	UNIVERSAL PRESS SYNDICATE		
		4900 MAIN ST, 9TH FLOOR	KANSAS CITY, MO	62114
PERKINS, SUZANNE	ACTRESS	853 1/2 N FULLER AVE	LOS ANGELES, CA	90046
PERKINS, TONY	ACTOR-DIRECTOR	SEE - PERKINS, ANTHONY		
PERKINS, TONY	COMEDIAN	EAI, 2211 INDUSTRIAL BLVD	SARASOTA, FL	33580
PERKINS, TONY	GUITARIST	1011 BROADMOOR DR A	NASHVILLE, TN	37216
PERKINS, WALTER	CINEMATOGRAPHER	1428 TIGERTAIL RD	LOS ANGELES, CA	90049
PERL, PETER	NEWS CORRESPONDENT	2006 GLEN ROSE RD	SILVER SPRING, MD	20910
PERLAKY, BELA	NEWS CORRESPONDENT	3132 "M" ST, NW	WASHINGTON, DC	20007
PERLE, REBECCA	ACTRESS	CONTEMPORARY ARTISTS		
		132 S LASKY DR	BEVERLY HILLS, CA	90212
PERLEE, CHARLES R	CONDUCTOR	463 W RIVERSIDE DR #A	BURBANK, CA	91506
PERLMAN, BARBARA K	TV WRITER	555 W 57TH ST #1230	NEW YORK, NY	10019
PERLMAN, CINDY	ACTRESS	8949 SUNSET BLVD #203	LOS ANGELES, CA	90069
PERLMAN, HEIDE	TV WRITER	8955 BEVERLY BLVD	LOS ANGELES, CA	90048
PERLMAN, ITZHAK	VIOLINIST	ICM, 40 W 57TH ST	NEW YORK, NY	10019
PERLMAN, RHEA	ACTRESS	1746 COURTNEY AVE	LOS ANGELES, CA	90046
PERLMAN, RON	ACTOR	9255 SUNSET BLVD #505	LOS ANGELES, CA	90069
PERLMUTTER, ALVIN	TV-FILM PRODUCER	27 W 86TH ST	NEW YORK, NY	10024
PERLOVE, PAUL	TV WRITER-PRODUCER	211 S BEVERLY DR #206	BEVERLY HILLS, CA	90212
PERLOW, ROBERT	TV WRITER	447 1/2 KELTON AVE	LOS ANGELES, CA	90024
PERNER, JOHN	GUITARIST	ROUTE #3, BOX 128	LEBANON, TN	37087
PERONE, ANTHONY	TV DIRECTOR	4541 NW 9TH AVE	POMPANO, FL	33064
PEROPAT, GLORIA	DIRECTOR	55 MORTON ST	NEW YORK, NY	10014
PERREAU, GIGI	ACTRESS	4258 BEEMAN AVE	STUDIO CITY, CA	91604
PERREN, FREDERICK J	COMPOSER	4028 COLFAX AVE	STUDIO CITY, CA	91604
PERRET, ANNE	MEZZO-SOPRANO	KAY, 58 W 58TH ST	NEW YORK, NY	10019
PERRET, GENE	TV WRITER	1485 W HAVEN RD	SAN MARINO, CA	91108
PERRET-DE ZAYAS DUO	MUSICAL DUO	KAY, 58 W 58TH ST	NEW YORK, NY	10019
PERRI, MICHAEL J	NEWS CORRESPONDENT	2139 WISCONSIN AVE, NW	WASHINGTON, DC	20007
PERRIE, GREGG	ACTOR	3832 LOMINA AVE	LONG BEACH, CA	90808
PERRIN, JACQUES	ACTOR	REGGANE FILMS, 38 RUE LEON	PARIS 75018	FRANCE
PERRIN, SAM	TV WRITER	8955 BEVERLY BLVD	LOS ANGELES, CA	90048
PERRIN, VIC	ACTOR	4218 TROOST AVE #17	STUDIO CITY, CA	91604
PERRINE, VALERIE	ACTRESS-MODEL	14627 VALLEY VISTA BLVD	SHERMAN OAKS, CA	91403
PERRIS, JIM	WRESTLER	SEE - KOLOFF, IVAN		
PERRY, ALFRED	CONDUCTOR	13900 TAHITI WY #129	MARINA DEL REY, CA	90292

PERRY, BARBARA	ACTRESS	208 S BEVERLY DR #4	BEVERLY HILLS, CA	90212
PERRY, CELIA ANN	ACTRESS	13111 VENTURA BLVD #102	STUDIO CITY, CA	91604
PERRY, DEBRA VENAY	ACTRESS	7918 PEACHTREE AVE	VAN NUYS, CA	91402
PERRY, DON	ACTOR	STACEY LANE MANAGEMENT		
		13455 VENTURA BLVD	SHERMAN OAKS, CA	91423
PERRY, DOUGLAS	TENOR	CAMI, 165 W 57TH ST	NEW YORK, NY	10019
PERRY, FELTON	ACTOR	2516 S SYCAMORE AVE	LOS ANGELES, CA	90016
PERRY, FRANK	DIRECTOR-PRODUCER	655 PARK AVE	NEW YORK, NY	10021
PERRY, GAYLORD	BASEBALL	RURAL ROUTE #3, BOX 565	WILLIAMSTON, NC	27892
PERRY, GREGORY	MUSIC ARRANGER	POST OFFICE BOX 50939	NASHVILLE, TN	37205
PERRY, HERBERT	BASSO-BARITONE	CAMI, 165 W 57TH ST	NEW YORK, NY	10019
PERRY, HERBERT O	COMPOSER-CONDUCTOR	POST OFFICE BOX 664	RANCHO SANTE FE, CA	92067
PERRY, HOWARD G	COMPOSER-CONDUCTOR	2729 E 58TH ST	HUNTINGTON PARK, CA	90255
PERRY, JIMMY	ACT-WRI-DIR	THE RICHARD STONE AGENCY		
		18-20 YORK BLDGS, ADELPHI	LONDON WC2N 6JY	ENGLAND
PERRY, JOE	SINGER	POST OFFICE BOX 703	ALLSTON, MA	02134
PERRY, JOHN	TV PRODUCER	LORIMAR, 4024 RADFORD AVE	STUDIO CITY, CA	91604
PERRY, JOHN BENNETT	ACTOR	10100 SANTA MONICA BLVD #1600	LOS ANGELES, CA	90067
PERRY, JOYCE	TV WRITER	2250 N GOWER ST	HOLLYWOOD, CA	90068
PERRY, LEMUEL	COMPOSER	6140 CANTERBURY DR #6-202	CULVER CITY, CA	90230
PERRY, MARLENE	TV WRITER	8955 BEVERLY BLVD	LOS ANGELES, CA	90048
PERRY, MORRIS	ACTOR	14 PETHERTON RD	LONDON N5	ENGLAND
PERRY, PENNY	CASTING DIRECTOR	2049 CENTURY PARK E #4100	LOS ANGELES, CA	90067
PERRY, ROGER	ACTOR	4363 LEDGE AVE	TOLUCA LAKE, CA	91602
PERRY, SCOTT	MUSIC EDITOR	7637 CAPISTRANO AVE	CANOGA PARK, CA	91304
PERRY, SIMON	WRITER-PRODUCER	UMBRELLA, 111-A WARDOUR ST	LONDON W1V 3TD	ENGLAND
PERRY, STEVE	SINGER-COMPOSER	POST OFFICE BOX 5952	SAN FRANCISCO, CA	94101
PERRY, WILLIAM "REFRIGERATOR"	FOOTBALL	250 N WASHINGTON RD	LAKE FOREST, IL	60045
PERRYMAN, CLARA	ACTRESS	10000 SANTA MONICA BLVD #305	LOS ANGELES, CA	90067
PERRYMAN, MACK	CABLE EXECUTIVE	HOME BOX OFFICE PICTURES		
		1100 AVE OF THE AMERICAS	NEW YORK, NY	10036
PERSCHMANN, PAUL	WRESTLER	SEE - ROSE, PLAYBOY BUDDY		
PERSHING, D'VAUGHN E	CONDUCTOR	19142 SYLVAN ST	RESEDA, CA	91335
PERSIAN WOLF	ROCK & ROLL GROUP	1419 8TH AVE #4-N	BROOKLYN, NY	11215
PERSINA, ELLEN M	NEWS CORRESPONDENT	500 NATIONAL PRESS BLDG		
		529 14TH ST, NW	WASHINGTON, DC	20045
PERSKY, LISA JANE	ACTRESS	9229 SUNSET BLVD #306	LOS ANGELES, CA	90069
PERSKY, WILLIAM	WRITER-DIRECTOR	7450 PALO VISTA DR	LOS ANGELES, CA	90046
PERSOFF, NEHEMIAH	ACTOR	5847 TAMPA AVE	TARZANA, CA	91356
PERSUADERS, THE	VOCAL GROUP	1500 BROADWAY #160	NEW YORK, NY	10036
PERSUASIONS, THE	VOCAL GROUP	101 W 57TH ST #2-A	NEW YORK, NY	10019
PERTMAN, ADAM	NEWS CORRESPONDENT	1791 LANIER PL #43, NW	WASHINGTON, DC	20009
PERTUSI, MICHELE	SINGER	CAMI, 165 W 57TH ST	NEW YORK, NY	10019
PERTWEE, BILL	ACTOR	THE RICHARD STONE AGENCY		
		18-20 YORK BLDGS, ADELPHI	LONDON WC2N 6JY	ENGLAND
PERTWEE, JON	ACTOR-COMEDIAN	26 SEATON CLOSE, LYNDEN GATE		
		PUTNEY HEATH	LONDON SW15 3JJ	ENGLAND
PERTWEE, MICHAEL	ACTOR-WRITER	34 AYLESTONE AVE	LONDON NW6	ENGLAND
PERUZOVIC, JOSIP	WRESTLER	SEE - VOLKOFF, NIKOLAI		
PERZIGIAN, JERRY	TV WRITER-PRODUCER	948 14TH ST #5	SANTA MONICA, CA	90403
PESCI, JOE	ACTOR	19423 TWIN HILLS PL	NORTHRIDGE, CA	91326
PESCOW, DONNA	ACTRESS	4331 VENTURA CANYON AVE	SHERMAN OAKS, CA	91423
PESEK, LIBOR	CONDUCTOR	SHAW CONCERTS, 1995 BROADWAY	NEW YORK, NY	10023
PESETSKY, ALAN	WRITER-PRODUCER	185 W END AVE	NEW YORK, NY	10023
PESKANOV, ALEXANDER	PIANIST	CAMI, 165 W 57TH ST	NEW YORK, NY	10019
PESKANOV, MARK	VIOLINIST	ICM, 40 W 57TH ST	NEW YORK, NY	10019
PESKO, ZOLTAN	CONDUCTOR	61 W 62ND ST #6-F	NEW YORK, NY	10023
PET SHOP BOYS, THE	ROCK & ROLL GROUP	MASSIVE, 47-B WELBECK ST	LONDON W1	ENGLAND
PETALE, ALEXANDER	ACTOR	11015 AQUA VISTA ST	NORTH HOLLYWOOD, CA	91602
PETARA, KEN	WRESTLER	POST OFFICE BOX 3859	STAMFORD, CT	06905
PETER, FRANCIS J	PHOTOJOURNALIST	8701 BRIERLY CT	CHEVY CHASE, MD	20815
PETER, GEORGE E	NEWS CORRESPONDENT	1801 N QUINN ST #201	ARLINGTON, VA	22209
PETER, LAURENCE J	AUTHOR-EDUCATOR	2332 VIA ANACAPA	PALOS VERDES, CA	90274
PETER, PAUL & MARY	VOCAL TRIO	FRITZ/TURNER MANAGEMENT		
		648 S ROBERTSON BLVD	LOS ANGELES, CA	90069
PETERMAN, DON	CINEMATOGRAPHER	POST OFFICE BOX 2230	HOLLYWOOD, CA	90078
PETERMAN, ROY	GUITARIST	406 BRINKLEY LN	WHITE HOUSE, TN	38188
PETERMAN, STEVEN	ACTOR	2314 N BEACHWOOD DR	LOS ANGELES, CA	90068
PETERMANN, FRED	DIRECTOR	2115 CASTILIAN DR	HOLLYWOOD, CA	90068
PETERS, ARLEN S	WRITER	2847 NICHOLS CANYON PL	LOS ANGELES, CA	90046
PETERS, AUDREY	ACTRESS	200 W 57TH ST #1303	NEW YORK, NY	10019
PETERS, BARBARA	TV DIRECTOR	4243 BAKMAN AVE	NORTH HOLLYWOOD, CA	91602
PETERS, BEN	PIANIST	900 OLD HICKORY BLVD		
		ROUTE #6	BRENTWOOD, TN	37027
PETERS, BETH	ACTRESS-SINGER	POST OFFICE BOX 38641	VAN NUYS, CA	90038
PETERS, BROCK	ACT-WRI-PROD	POST OFFICE BOX 8156	NORTH HOLLYWOOD, CA	91608
PETERS, CHARLIE	SCREENWRITER	151 S EL CAMINO DR	BEVERLY HILLS, CA	90212
PETERS, CRAIG	WRESTLING WRITER	POST OFFICE BOX 48	ROCKVILLE CENTRE, NY	11571
PETERS, DAN C	DIRECTOR	201 E 60TH ST	NEW YORK, NY	10021
PETERS, DOC	GUITARIST	126 MC ARTHUR DR	MADISON, TN	37115
PETERS, DONALD A	WRITER	12801 CHANDLER BLVD	NORTH HOLLYWOOD, CA	91607
PETERS, GORDON	ACTOR	20 ELM TREE AVE, ESTER	SURREY	ENGLAND
PETERS, HOUSE, JR	ACTOR	999 DONALD ST, OLD HARBOR	WHEDLKY ISLAND, WA	98277
PETERS, JAN	ACTOR	6736 LAUREL CANYON BLVD #306	NORTH HOLLYWOOD, CA	91606

THE PERSUASIONS

THE PRETENDERS

Blair Cunningham • Robbie McIntosh • Chrissie Hynde • Rupert Black • Malcom Foster

Name	Occupation	Address	City	Zip/Country
PETERS, JEAN	ACTRESS	507 N PALM DR	BEVERLY HILLS, CA	90210
PETERS, JON	FILM PRODUCER	9348 SANTA MONICA BLVD	BEVERLY HILLS, CA	90210
PETERS, KATHARYN WELLS	ACTRESS	1252 1/2 S RIDGELEY DR	LOS ANGELES, CA	90019
PETERS, KATHLEEN N	NEWS CORRESPONDENT	444 N CAPITOL ST, NW	WASHINGTON, DC	20001
PETERS, KELLY JEAN	ACTRESS	1717 N BEVERLY GLEN BLVD	LOS ANGELES, CA	90024
PETERS, LANCE	SCREENWRITER	25 JEYMER DR, GREENFIELD	MIDDLESEX	ENGLAND
PETERS, LUAN	ACTRESS	POST OFFICE BOX 130, HOVE	EAST SUSSEX BN3 6QU	ENGLAND
PETERS, MARGIE	SINGER	PERLE, 4475 VINELAND AVE	STUDIO CITY, CA	91602
PETERS, MARJORIE	TV WRITER	1027 23RD ST	SANTA MONICA, CA	90403
PETERS, MICHAEL	CARTOONIST	1421 COOLWOOD CT	XENIA, OH	45385
PETERS, MICHAEL	DIRECTOR	DGA, 110 W 57TH ST	NEW YORK, NY	10019
PETERS, MIKE	CARTOONIST	POST OFFICE BOX 1061	DAYTON, OH	45401
PETERS, PAMELA	ACTRESS	CASSELL, 843 N SYCAMORE AVE	LOS ANGELES, CA	90038
PETERS, REINHARD	CONDUCTOR	59 E 54TH ST #81	NEW YORK, NY	10022
PETERS, ROBERTA	SINGER	FIELDS, 64 GARDEN RD	SCARSDALE, NY	10583
PETERS, SUSAN ALBERT	CONDUCTOR	254 W 93RD ST #8	NEW YORK, NY	10025
PETERS, SUZANNA	ACTRESS	9200 SUNSET BLVD #620	LOS ANGELES, CA	90069
PETERS, TOM	COLUMNIST	TRIBUNE MEDIA SERVICES		
		64 E CONCORD ST	ORLANDO, FL	32801
PETERS, VICTORIA	ACTRESS-MODEL	MARX, 11130 HUSTON ST	NORTH HOLLYWOOD, CA	91601
PETERS, VIRGINIA	ACTRESS	10000 RIVERSIDE DR #3	TOLUCA LAKE, CA	91602
PETERS, WILLIAM	WRITER-PRODUCER	166 BANK ST #4-A	NEW YORK, NY	10014
PETERSEN, CHRIS	DIRECTOR	10520 LE CONTE AVE	LOS ANGELES, CA	90024
PETERSEN, DENNIS	TENOR	45 W 60TH ST #4-K	NEW YORK, NY	10023
PETERSEN, DONALD G	SCREENWRITER	8955 BEVERLY BLVD	LOS ANGELES, CA	90048
PETERSEN, MARK	TV DIRECTOR	8 CHOLMELEY PARK	LONDON N6	ENGLAND
PETERSEN, PAT	ACTOR	9229 SUNSET BLVD #607	LOS ANGELES, CA	90069
PETERSEN, PAUL	ACTOR	205 S BEVERLY DR #210	BEVERLY HILLS, CA	90212
PETERSEN, WOLFGANG	FILM DIRECTOR	BAVARIA ATELIER		
		8022 GEISELGASTEIG	MUNICH	GERMANY
PETERSMANN, DIRK	TV DIRECTOR	2950 BELDEN DR	HOLLYWOOD, CA	90068
PETERSON, ARTHUR	ACTOR	9255 SUNSET BLVD #610	LOS ANGELES, CA	90069
PETERSON, BONNIE	TV WRITER	8955 BEVERLY BLVD	LOS ANGELES, CA	90048
PETERSON, CASSANDRA	ACTRESS	POST OFFICE BOX 38246	HOLLYWOOD, CA	90038
PETERSON, CHRISTINE A	NEWS CORRESPONDENT	5604 ASBURY CT	ALEXANDRIA, VA	22312
PETERSON, CLAUDETTE	SOPRANO	CAMI, 165 W 57TH ST	NEW YORK, NY	10019
PETERSON, DAN	ACTOR	6310 SAN VICENTE BLVD #407	LOS ANGELES, CA	90048
PETERSON, DENISE	NEWS CORRESPONDENT	3620 WARREN ST, NW	WASHINGTON, DC	20008
PETERSON, DIANE	STUNTWOMAN	LIGHT, 113 N ROBERTSON BLVD	LOS ANGELES, CA	90048
PETERSON, DIANE	ACTRESS	870 N VINE ST #G	LOS ANGELES, CA	90038
PETERSON, DICK	TV DIRECTOR	2030 CASA GRANDE ST	PASADENA, CA	91104
PETERSON, HERB	ACTOR	201 CLUB DR	WOODMERE, NY	11598
PETERSON, JOHN E	NEWS CORRESPONDENT	2614 QUINCY ADAMS DR	HERNDON, VA	22071
PETERSON, JULIE	MODEL	MODELS & PROMOTIONS AGENCY		
		8560 SUNSET BLVD, 10TH FLOOR	LOS ANGELES, CA	90069
PETERSON, LYNNE F	NEWS CORRESPONDENT	POST OFFICE BOX 55361	FORT WASHINGTON, MD	20744
PETERSON, MAURICE	SCREENWRITER	555 W 57TH ST #1230	NEW YORK, NY	10019
PETERSON, OSCAR	PIANIST	SALLE, 451 N CANON DR	BEVERLY HILLS, CA	90210
PETERSON, PAUL	ACTOR	3151 W CAHUENGA BLVD #310	LOS ANGELES, CA	90068
PETERSON, RICHARD	TV DIRECTOR	2080 CASA GRANDE ST	PASADENA, CA	91104
PETERSON, ROBERT J	PHOTOGRAPHER	10501 S GLEN RD	POTOMAC, MD	20854
PETERSON, ROBERTA	TV DIRECTOR	252 JACKSON ST	NEWTON CENTRE, MA	02159
PETERSON, ROBYN	ACTRESS	9220 SUNSET BLVD #202	LOS ANGELES, CA	90069
PETERSON, ROD	TV PRODUCER	LORIMAR, 4024 RADFORD AVE	STUDIO CITY, CA	91604
PETERSON, RODERICK	TV WRITER	4451 BEN AVE	NORTH HOLLYWOOD, CA	91607
PETERSON, ROGER	NEWS CORRESPONDENT	ABC-TV, NEWS DEPARTMENT		
		1717 DE SALES ST, NW	WASHINGTON, DC	20036
PETERSON, SUSAN	SOPRANO	CONE, 221 W 57TH ST	NEW YORK, NY	10019
PETERSON, TED	ACTOR	BERZON, 336 E 17TH ST	COSTA MESA, CA	92627
PETERSON, THEODORE R	COMPOSER	18565 ARMINTA ST	RESEDA, CA	91335
PETERSON, VINCENT R	NEWS REPORTER	TIME & PEOPLE MAGAZINE		
		ROCKEFELLER CENTER	NEW YORK, NY	10020
PETERSON, VINCENT R **	NEWS REPORTER	TIME & LIFE BUILDING		
PETERSON, WILLIAM R	NEWS CORRESPONDENT	304 W MYRTLE ST	ALEXANDRIA, VA	22301
PETHERBRIDGE, EDWARD	ACTOR	HEATH, PARAMOUNT HOUSE		
		162-170 WARDOUR ST	LONDON W1V 3AT	ENGLAND
PETIT, PASCALE	ACTOR	ART SERVICE MANAGEMENT		
		78 CHAMPS-ELYSEES	PARIS 75008	FRANCE
PETIT, TOM	TV EXECUTIVE	NBC TELEVISION NETWORK		
		30 ROCKEFELLER PLAZA	NEW YORK, NY	10112
PETITCLERC, DEANE B	SCREENWRITER	445 N BEDFORD DR #PH	BEVERLY HILLS, CA	90210
PETITTO, DAVE	TV WRITER	21919 GALVEZ ST	WOODLAND HILLS, CA	91364
PETLOCK, JOHN	ACTOR	5451 BECK AVE	NORTH HOLLYWOOD, CA	91601
PETRA	GOSPEL GROUP	POST OFFICE BOX 50358	NASHVILLE, TN	37205
PETRACCHI, FRANCO	SINGER	MARIEDL ANDERS ARTISTS MGMT		
		535 EL CAMINO DEL MAR ST	SAN FRANCISCO, CA	94121
PETRANTO, RUSSELL	TV DIRECTOR	8428 MELROSE PL #C	LOS ANGELES, CA	90069
PETRAS, WILLIAM	PHOTOGRAPHER	4227 ISBELL ST	SILVER SPRING, MD	20906
PETRE, CARL	TV DIRECTOR	309 BOOTHBAY CT	SAINT CHARLES, MO	63301
PETRI, MICHALA	SOPRANO	ICM, 40 W 57TH ST	NEW YORK, NY	10019
PETRI, MICHALA, TRIO	MUSIC ENSEMBLE	ICM, 40 W 57TH ST	NEW YORK, NY	10019
PETRICK, JACK	TV EXECUTIVE	PUBLIC BROADCASTING		
		1111 16TH ST, NW	WASHINGTON, DC	20036
PETRICONE, ARTHUR	FILM DIRECTOR	9 CACCAMO TRAIL	WESTPORT, CT	06880
PETRIE, ANN	WRITER-PRODUCER	225 W 106TH ST #PH-K	NEW YORK, NY	10025

Name	Occupation	Address	City	Zip
PETRIE, DANIEL	TV DIRECTOR	1509 N CRESCENT HGTS BLVD #7	LOS ANGELES, CA	90069
PETRIE, DONALD	ACTOR	13201 HANEY PL	LOS ANGELES, CA	90049
PETRIE, DOROTHEA G	WRITER	13201 HANEY PL	LOS ANGELES, CA	90049
PETRIE, GEORGE O	ACTOR	9229 SUNSET BLVD #306	LOS ANGELES, CA	90069
PETRILLI, MARIO	ACTOR	120 S VICTORY BLVD #104	BURBANK, CA	91502
PETROFF, PAUL	DIRECTOR	20 GUTHEIL LN	GREAT NECK, NY	11024
PETROS, EVELYN	SOPRANO	CAMI, 165 W 57TH ST	NEW YORK, NY	10019
PETROU, DAVID MICHAEL	WRITER-PRODUCER	2739 "O" ST, NW	WASHINGTON, DC	20007
PETROVNA, SONIA	ACTRESS	LANTZ, 888 7TH AVE, 25TH FLOOR	NEW YORK, NY	10106
PETROW, VLADIMER	WRESTLER	NATIONAL WRESTLING ALLIANCE		
		JIM CROCKETT PROMOTIONS		
		421 BRIARBEND DR	CHARLOTTE, NC	28209
PETROWSKI, ALLEN	CONDUCTOR	16306 BLACKHAWK ST	GRANADA HILLS, CA	91344
PETRUCELLI, ANTHONY J	DIRECTOR	103 5TH AVE	NEW YORK, NY	10003
PETRY, GEDDA	ACTRESS	175 W 72ND ST	NEW YORK, NY	10023
PETRYNI, MICHAEL	TV WRITER	17817 SAN FERNANDO MISS BLVD	GRANADA HILLS, CA	91344
PETTIFER, JULIAN	TV DIRECTOR	9 ROLAND GARDENS	LONDON SW7 3PE	ENGLAND
PETTIT, DEBRA	NEWS CORRESPONDENT	NBC-TV, NEWS DEPARTMENT		
		4001 NEBRASKA AVE, NW	WASHINGTON, DC	20016
PETTIT, JOANNA	ACTRESS	7387 WOODROW WILSON DR	LOS ANGELES, CA	90046
PETTIT, TOM	TV CORRESPONDENT	NBC-TV, NEWS DEPARTMENT		
		30 ROCKEFELLER PLAZA	NEW YORK, NY	10112
PETTUS, ALAN	GUITARIST	714 NEW DUE WEST AVE #G-104	MADISON, TN	37115
PETTUS, KEN	TV WRITER	8955 BEVERLY BLVD	LOS ANGELES, CA	90048
PETTY, RICHARD	AUTO RACER	ROUTE #3, BOX 631	RANDLEMAN, NC	27317
PETTY, ROSS	ACTOR	24 KING ST	NEW YORK, NY	10014
PETTY, TOM & THE HEARTBREAKERS	ROCK & ROLL GROUP	LOOKOUT, 9120 SUNSET BLVD	LOS ANGELES, CA	90069
PETWAY, ALVA	ACTRESS	13412 CARNABY ST	CERRITOS, CA	90701
PEVNEY, JOSEPH	TV DIRECTOR	11829 MAYFIELD AVE #303	LOS ANGELES, CA	90049
PEVSNER, DONALD L	COLUMNIST	UNIVERSAL PRESS SYNDICATE		
		4900 MAIN ST, 9TH FLOOR	KANSAS CITY, MO	62114
PEVSNER, THOMAS	FILM PRODUCER	11 WILDWOOD GROVE, NORTH END	LONDON NW3	ENGLAND
PEYRONNIN, JOSEPH F, III	NEWS CORRESPONDENT	CBS NEWS, 2020 "M" ST, NW	WASHINGTON, DC	20036
PEYSER, ANTHONY L	WRITER	415 N SYCAMORE AVE	LOS ANGELES, CA	90036
PEYSER, ARNOLD	TV WRITER	141 TIGERTAIL RD	LOS ANGELES, CA	90049
PEYSER, JOHN	WRITER-PRODUCER	19721 REDWING ST	WOODLAND HILLS, CA	91364
PEYSER, LOIS	TV WRITER	141 TIGERTAIL RD	LOS ANGELES, CA	90049
PEYSER, MICHAEL	DIRECTOR	DGA, 110 W 57TH ST	NEW YORK, NY	10019
PEYSER, PENNY	ACTRESS	7319 BEVERLY BLVD #7	LOS ANGELES, CA	90036
PEYSON, ROBERT	DIRECTOR	333 PEARL ST	NEW YORK, NY	10038
PEYTON, PHILIP	DIRECTOR	138 E 78TH ST	NEW YORK, NY	10021
PEYTON, ROBERT	ACTOR	8949 SUNSET BLVD #203	LOS ANGELES, CA	90069
PEYTON, STEVE	PRODUCER	20249 BLYTHE ST	CANOGA PARK, CA	91306
PFEIFER, HOWARD R	CONDUCTOR	911 N KINGS RD #103	LOS ANGELES, CA	90069
PFEIFFER, CONSTANCE	ACTRESS-WRITER	16124 SUNSET BLVD #B	PACIFIC PALISADES, CA	90272
PFEIFFER, FRANK	DIRECTOR	1629 N 24TH AVE	MELROSE PARK, IL	60160
PFEIFFER, MICHELLE	ACTRESS	13794 BEACH BLVD	WESTMINISTER, CA	92683
PFENNING, WESLEY	ACTRESS	6106 GLEN OAK	HOLLYWOOD, CA	90068
PFISTER, WALTER C	NEWS CORRESPONDENT	400 N CAPITOL ST, NW	WASHINGTON, DC	20001
PFIZER, BERYL	WRITER-PRODUCER	349 E 62ND ST	NEW YORK, NY	10021
PFLEIDERER, STEPHEN D	NEWS CORRESPONDENT	4977 MAC ARTHUR BLVD, NW	WASHINGTON, DC	20007
PFLIEGER, JEAN	ACTRESS	1441 S SHENANDOAH ST #2	LOS ANGELES, CA	90035
PFLUG, JO ANN	ACTRESS	POST OFFICE BOX 491075	LOS ANGELES, CA	90049
PHALEN, ROBERT	ACTOR	247 S BEVERLY DR #102	BEVERLY HILLS, CA	90212
PHAM, CUONG G	NEWS CORRESPONDENT	2209 S BUCHANAN ST	ARLINGTON, VA	22206
PHANTOM LIMBS, THE	ROCK & ROLL GROUP	1230 GRANT AVE #531	SAN FRANCISCO, CA	94133
PHANTOM, ROCKER & SLICK	ROCK & ROLL TRIO	POST OFFICE BOX 38246	HOLLYWOOD, CA	90038
PHANTOMS, THE	VOCAL GROUP	POST OFFICE BOX 830	ALBANY, NY	12201
PHANTON OPERA	ROCK & ROLL GROUP	POST OFFICE BOX 21	SAN PEDRO, CA	90733
PHELAN, ANNA HAMILTON	SCREENWRITER	10100 SANTA MONICA BLVD #1600	LOS ANGELES, CA	90067
PHELAN, JOSEPH	ACTOR	10845 LINDBROOK DR #3	LOS ANGELES, CA	90024
PHELPS, ALAN	SINGER-GUITARIST	ROUTE #1, BOX 520	MOUNT VERNON, TX	75457
PHELPS, DAVID M	NEWS CORRESPONDENT	8803 MELWOOD RD	BETHESDA, MD	20817
PHELPS, DOUG	MUSICIAN	158 EVERGREEN CIR	HENDERSONVILLE, TN	37075
PHELPS, ELEANOR	ACTRESS	145 W 79TH ST	NEW YORK, NY	10024
PHELPS, JACK A, JR	GUITARIST	2305 OXFORD RD	NASHVILLE, TN	37215
PHELPS, JACKIE	GUITARIST	1351 CARDINAL DR	NASHVILLE, TN	37216
PHELPS, JILL FARREN	TV PRODUCER	KNBC-TV, "SANTA BARBARA"		
		3000 W ALAMEDA AVE	BURBANK, CA	91523
PHELPS, JULIA LA BELLA	GUITARIST	ROUTE #1, BOX 520	MOUNT VERNON, TX	75457
PHELPS, PAULA	SPORTS REPORTER	SPORTS ILLUSTRATED MAGAZINE		
		TIME & LIFE BUILDING		
		ROCKEFELLER CENTER	NEW YORK, NY	10020
PHELPS, RICK	GUITARIST	142 SAUNDERS FERRY RD #12	HENDERSONVILLE, TN	37075
PHELPS, STAN	MUSICIAN	821 HERITAGE CIR	MADISON, TN	37115
PHELPS, STUART	DIRECTOR	3617 CODY RD	SHERMAN OAKS, CA	91403
PHEROMONES, THE	ROCK & ROCK DUO	POST OFFICE BOX 5765	BETHESDA, MD	20814
PHILBIN, BILL	CINEMATOGRAPHER	7715 SUNSET BLVD #150	LOS ANGELES, CA	90046
PHILBIN, JOHN	ACTOR	KOHNER, 9169 SUNSET BLVD	LOS ANGELES, CA	90069
PHILBIN, MARY	ACTRESS	1332 N FAIRFAX AVE	HOLLYWOOD, CA	90046
PHILBIN, REGIS	TV HOST	LIFETIME MEDICAL TV NETWORK		
		1211 AVE OF THE AMERICAS	NEW YORK, NY	10036
PHILIPPS, PETER	NEWS CORRESPONDENT	8904 HONEYBEE LN	BETHESDA, MD	20817
PHILIPS, EMO	COMEDIAN	1780 BROADWAY #1201	NEW YORK, NY	10019
PHILIPS, LEE	TV DIRECTOR	11939 GORHAM AVE #104	LOS ANGELES, CA	90049

PHILIPSON, NEIL	TV DIRECTOR	52 W 87TH ST	NEW YORK, NY	10024
PHILLIPS, ANDY	COMPOSER-CONDUCTOR	2475 TIERRA DR	LOS OSOS, CA	93402
PHILLIPS, BARNEY	ACTOR	721 N LA BREA AVE #201	LOS ANGELES, CA	90038
PHILLIPS, BILL	GUITARIST	ROUTE #1, COOKE RD	MOUNT JULIET, TN	37122
PHILLIPS, BILLY G	GUITARIST	3848 SAM BONEY DR	NASHVILLE, TN	37211
PHILLIPS, BUSTER	DRUMMER	3214 MC GAVOCK PIKE	NASHVILLE, TN	37214
PHILLIPS, CHARLES H	PHOTOGRAPHER	8744 OXWELL LN	LAUREL, MD	20810
PHILLIPS, CHYNNA	ACTRESS	10557 TROON AVE	LOS ANGELES, CA	90064
PHILLIPS, CLYDE B	FILM PRODUCER	13395 CONTOUR DR	SHERMAN OAKS, CA	91423
PHILLIPS, CLYDE W	GUITARIST	812 HAMBLEN DR	MADISON, TN	37115
PHILLIPS, DANIEL	VIOLINIST	1776 BROADWAY #504	NEW YORK, NY	10019
PHILLIPS, DON	NEWS CORRESPONDENT	5603 DERBY CT	ALEXANDRIA, VA	22311
PHILLIPS, ETHAN	ACTOR	11726 SAN VICENTE BLVD #300	LOS ANGELES, CA	90049
PHILLIPS, HARVEY	TUBIST	CAMI, 165 W 57TH ST	NEW YORK, NY	10019
PHILLIPS, IRVING H	PHOTOGRAPHER	2029 MADISON AVE	BALTIMORE, MD	21217
PHILLIPS, JAMES C	COMPOSER	10963 WHIPPLE ST #6	NORTH HOLLYWOOD, CA	91602
PHILLIPS, JEFFREY	TROMBONIST	202 HURST DR	OLD HICKORY, TN	37138
PHILLIPS, JOBYNA	ACTRESS	6211 AFTON PL	HOLLYWOOD, CA	90028
PHILLIPS, JOHN	ACTOR	MARMONT MANAGEMENT		
		LANGHAM HOUSE		
		302 REGENT ST	LONDON W1	ENGLAND
PHILLIPS, JOHN A	COMPOSER	22110 CLARENDON ST #101	WOODLAND HILLS, CA	91367
PHILLIPS, JOHN C	NEWS CORRESPONDENT	2615 42ND ST #205, NW	WASHINGTON, DC	20007
PHILLIPS, JOHN DAVID	GUITARIST	7207 SHEFFIELD SQ	NASHVILLE, TN	37221
PHILLIPS, JOSEPH PETER	POET	POST OFFICE BOX 968	BANNING, CA	92220
PHILLIPS, JOSEPH RILEY	SINGER-GUITARIST	213 S MAIN ST	CROSSVILLE, TN	38555
PHILLIPS, JULIA	FILM PRODUCER	2534 BENEDICT CANYON DR	BEVERLY HILLS, CA	90210
PHILLIPS, JULIANNE	ACTRESS-MODEL	POST OFFICE BOX 5617	BEVERLY HILLS, CA	90210
PHILLIPS, LANCE	ACTOR	953 17TH ST #E	SANTA MONICA, CA	90403
PHILLIPS, LARRY	HARPSICHORDIST	KAY, 58 W 58TH ST	NEW YORK, NY	10019
PHILLIPS, LESLIE	ACTOR-DIRECTOR	HATTON, 18 JERMYN ST	LONDON SW1	ENGLAND
PHILLIPS, LESLIE	COLUMNIST	POST OFFICE BOX 500	WASHINGTON, DC	20044
PHILLIPS, MAC KENZIE	ACTRESS-SINGER	AIMEE, 13743 VICTORY BLVD	VAN NUYS, CA	91401
PHILLIPS, MICHAEL	FILM PRODUCER	1501 GILCREST DR	BEVERLY HILLS, CA	90210
PHILLIPS, MICHELLE	ACTRESS-SINGER	10557 TROON AVE	LOS ANGELES, CA	90064
PHILLIPS, MIKE & TRICIA	ILLUSIONISTS	HALL, 138 FROG HOLLOW RD	CHURCHVILLE, PA	18966
PHILLIPS, MONISA	PIANIST	39 GRACELAWN DR	BRENTWOOD, TN	37027
PHILLIPS, NIC	TV DIRECTOR	4 VICTORIA RD, WEYBRIDGE	SURREY	ENGLAND
PHILLIPS, RALPH	TV WRITER	8383 WILSHIRE BLVD #923	BEVERLY HILLS, CA	90211
PHILLIPS, ROBERT	ACTOR	15301 VENTURA BLVD #345	SHERMAN OAKS, CA	91403
PHILLIPS, RONALD	DIRECTOR	1317 EL HITO CT	PACIFIC PALISADES, CA	90272
PHILLIPS, SHAWN	SINGER-SONGWRITER	TWM MGMT, 641 LEXINGTON AVE	NEW YORK, NY	10022
PHILLIPS, SIAN	ACTRESS	SARABAND ASSOCIATES AGENCY		
		153 PETHERTON RD, HIGHBURY	LONDON N5	ENGLAND
PHILLIPS, STU	GUITARIST	1001 FRANKLIN RD	BRENTWOOD, TN	37027
PHILLIPS, TEDDY S, SR	CONDUCTOR	6252 1/2 NITA AVE	WOODLAND HILLS, CA	91364
PHILLIPS, TOMMY	GUITARIST	3604 GOLF ST	NASHVILLE, TN	37216
PHILLIPS, WILLIAM F	WRITER-PRODUCER	9255 SUNSET BLVD #510	LOS ANGELES, CA	90069
PHILLIPS, WOOLF	COMPOSER-CONDUCTOR	16319 VILLAGE 16	CAMARILLO, CA	93010
PHILLISTEENS, THE	ROCK & ROLL GROUP	VARIETY ARTISTS INTL, INC		
		9073 NEMO ST, 3RD FLOOR	LOS ANGELES, CA	90069
PHILPOT, MARK	ACTOR	ABC-TV, "ONE LIFE TO LIVE"		
		1330 AVE OF THE AMERICAS	NEW YORK, NY	10019
PHILPOTT, THOMAS R	NEWS CORRESPONDENT	14404 COACHWAY DR	CENTREVILLE, VA	22020
PHINNEY, DAVID	FILM DIRECTOR	3629 CORINTH AVE	LOS ANGELES, CA	90066
PHIPPS, TONY R	PIANIST	2929 SELENA DR #D-68	NASHVILLE, TN	37211
PHIPPS, WILLIAM EDWARD	ACTOR	4721 LAUREL CANYON BLVD #211	NORTH HOLLYWOOD, CA	91607
PHLEGAR, BEN F	NEWS CORRESPONDENT	4740 CONNECTICUT AVE #806, NW	WASHINGTON, DC	20008
PHOENIX, PAT	ACTRESS	SUNNY PL COTTAGE	CHESHIRE	ENGLAND
PHOENIX, RIVER	ACTOR	1450 BELFAST DR	LOS ANGELES, CA	90069
PHOENIX, ROGER	TV DIRECTOR	ROUTE #1, BOX 404	STONY POINT, NY	10980
PHOTOGLO, JIM	SINGER-SONGWRITER	1453 YALE ST #B	SANTA MONICA, CA	90404
PIANIN, ERIC S	NEWS CORRESPONDENT	6007 33RD ST, NW	WASHINGTON, DC	20015
PIANTINI, CARLOS	CONDUCTOR	45 W 60TH ST #4-K	NEW YORK, NY	10023
PIATT, JEAN	ACTOR	9 PL VAUBAN	PARIS 75007	FRANCE
PIAZZA, BEN	ACTOR	3914 CUMBERLAND AVE	LOS ANGELES, CA	90027
PIAZZI, JIM	ACTOR	120 E 7TH ST	NEW YORK, NY	10009
PICARD, FRANK	ACTOR	5330 LANKERSHIM BLVD #210	NORTH HOLLYWOOD, CA	91601
PICARD, PAUL	TV PRODUCER	4000 WARNER BLVD	BURBANK, CA	91522
PICARDO, ROBERT	ACTOR	10100 SANTA MONICA BLVD #1600	LOS ANGELES, CA	90067
PICCIRILLO, CHARLES	DIRECTOR	18 PARSONAGE RD	GREENWICH, CT	06830
PICCOLI, MICHEL	ACTOR	5 AVE MAC-MAHON	PARIS 75017	FRANCE
PICCOLO, JOHN D	DIRECTOR	4 E 89TH ST	NEW YORK, NY	10028
PICCOLODEON	MUSICAL DUO	157 W 57TH ST #1100	NEW YORK, NY	10019
PICERNI, CHARLES F	DIRECTOR	5113 TOPEKA DR	TARZANA, CA	91356
PICERNI, PAUL	ACTOR	19119 WELLS DR	TARZANA, CA	91356
PICHINSON, MARTY	TALENT AGENT	518 N LA CIENEGA BLVD	LOS ANGELES, CA	90048
PICHIRALLO, JOE	NEWS CORRESPONDENT	1739 19TH ST #3, NW	WASHINGTON, DC	20009
PICK, MARK	FILM PRODUCER	PICNIC ENTS, 1438 N GOWER ST	LOS ANGELES, CA	90028
PICK, ROBERT	ACTOR	1605 N CAHUENGA BLVD #202	LOS ANGELES, CA	90028
PICKENS, CHEROKEE WATIE RILEY	SINGER	CUDE, 519 N HALIFAX AVE	DAYTON BEACH, FL	32018
PICKENS, JAMES, JR	ACTOR	NBC-TV, "ANOTHER WORLD"		
		30 ROCKEFELLER PLAZA	NEW YORK, NY	10112
PICKENS, PIC	SINGER	CUDE, 519 N HALIFAX AVE	DAYTONA BEACH, FL	32018
PICKERELL, JAMES H	PHOTOGRAPHER	8104 CINDY LN	BETHESDA, MD	20817

Name	Occupation	Address	City	Zip/Country
PICKERING, BILL	SINGER	1522 28TH ST	LUBBOCK, TX	79405
PICKERING, DONALD	ACTOR	FIR TREE COTTAGE, ALBURY	SURREY	ENGLAND
PICKETT, CHARLIE	SINGER-GUITARIST	TWIN TONE RECORDS CO		
		44 NORTHWEST AVE	MIAMI, FL	33169
PICKETT, CINDY	ACTRESS	151 S EL CAMINO DR	BEVERLY HILLS, CA	90212
PICKETT, WILSON	SINGER	200 W 57TH ST #907	NEW YORK, NY	10019
PICKING, KEN	SPORTS WRITER	POST OFFICE BOX 500	WASHINGTON, DC	20044
PICKLES, CAROLYN	ACTRESS	CONWAY, EAGLE HOUSE		
		109 JERMYN ST	LONDON SW1	ENGLAND
PICKLES, CHRISTINA	ACTRESS	137 S WESTGATE AVE	LOS ANGELES, CA	90049
PICKLES, VIVIAN	ACTRESS	FRASER, 91 REGENT ST	LONDON W1R 8RU	ENGLAND
PICKREN, STACEY	ACTRESS	3291 TARECO DR	LOS ANGELES, CA	90068
PICKUP, RONALD	ACTOR	54 CROUCH HALL RD	LONDON N8	ENGLAND
PICON, MOLLY	ACTRESS	1 LINCOLN PLAZA #35-E	NEW YORK, NY	10023
PICON-BOREL, RAYMOND	PHOTOGRAPHER	16 RUE CASSINI	PARIS 75014	FRANCE
PIECES OF A DREAM	ROCK & ROLL GROUP	HARMON, 1127 E HORTTER ST	PHILADELPHIA, PA	19138
PIECKA, ANDREW	ACTOR	1605 N MARTEL AVE #35	LOS ANGELES, CA	90046
PIED PIPERS, THE	VOCAL GROUP	32500 CONCORD DR #221	MADISON HEIGHTS, MI	48071
PIEDMONT, LEON	SCREENWRITER	8955 BEVERLY BLVD	LOS ANGELES, CA	90048
PIELLISCH, RICHARD	NEWS CORRESPONDENT	1831 WYOMING AVE, NW	WASHINGTON, DC	20009
PIELMEIER, JOHN	TV WRITER	555 W 57TH ST #1230	NEW YORK, NY	10019
PIERAULD, GUY	ACTOR	145 RUE DU GAL LECLERC	SAINT-LEU-LA-FORET 953	FRANCE
PIERCE, ARTHUR C	TV WRITER	8955 BEVERLY BLVD	LOS ANGELES, CA	90048
PIERCE, BILL	PHOTOGRAPHER	TIME/TIME & LIFE BLDG		
		ROCKEFELLER CENTER	NEW YORK, NY	10020
PIERCE, CHARLES	IMPERSONATOR	4445 CARTWRIGHT AVE #309	NORTH HOLLYWOOD, CA	91602
PIERCE, FREDERICK S	TV EXECUTIVE	ABC TELEVISION NETWORK		
		1330 AVE OF THE AMERICAS	NEW YORK, NY	10019
PIERCE, JIM	PIANIST	POST OFFICE BOX 158	MADISON, TN	37115
PIERCE, NAT	COMPOSER	446 1/2 S WILTON PL	LOS ANGELES, CA	90020
PIERCE, NEAL R	NEWS CORRESPONDENT	610 "G" ST, SW	WASHINGTON, DC	20024
PIERCE, RICHARD K	TV WRITER	8955 BEVERLY BLVD	LOS ANGELES, CA	90048
PIERCE, ROBERT	ACTOR	1901 AVE OF THE STARS #840	LOS ANGELES, CA	90067
PIERCE, ROGER LAWRENCE	ACTOR	4438 MURIETTA AVE #17	SHERMAN OAKS, CA	91423
PIERCE, STACK	ACTOR	8721 SUNSET BLVD #200	LOS ANGELES, CA	90069
PIERCE, WEBB	SINGER	JOYCE, 2028 CHESTNUT ST	PHILADELPHIA, PA	19103
PIERCE, WILLIAM	GUITARIST	111 WHITSETT RD	NASHVILLE, TN	37211
PIERCY, ANDY	SINGER	3 E 54TH ST #1400	NEW YORK, NY	10022
PIEROBON, JAMES R	NEWS CORRESPONDENT	1816 NEW HAMPSHIRE AVE, NW		
		ROOM #908	WASHINGTON, DC	20009
PIEROTTI, JOHN	CARTOONIST	2004 OCEAN AVE	BRIGANTINE, NJ	08203
PIERPOINT, ERIC	ACTOR	110 W 40TH ST #2401	NEW YORK, NY	10018
PIERPOINT, ROBERT C	NEWS CORRESPONDENT	CBS NEWS, 2020 "M" ST, NW	WASHINGTON, DC	20036
PIERRAT, SIMONE	CELLIST	KAY, 58 W 58TH ST	NEW YORK, NY	10019
PIERSON, FRANK	FILM WRITER-DIRECTOR	1223 AMALFI DR	PACIFIC PALISADES, CA	90272
PIERSON, GEOFF	ACTOR	BRET ADAMS, 448 W 44TH ST	NEW YORK, NY	10036
PIES, JUDY	ACTRESS	11687 MONTANA AVE #101	LOS ANGELES, CA	90049
PIESTRUP, DONALL J	COMPOSER	4425 CLYBOURN AVE	NORTH HOLLYWOOD, CA	91602
PIFER, ALICE	TV PRODUCER	ABC-TV, 7 W 66TH ST	NEW YORK, NY	10023
PIGAUT, ROGER	ACTOR	ARTMEDIA, 10 AVE GEORGE V	PARIS 75008	FRANCE
PIGG, DE WAYNE	SAXOPHONIST	2044 BERNARD CIR #1	NASHVILLE, TN	37212
PIGOTT-SMITH, TIM	ACTOR	CONWAY, EAGLE HOUSE		
		109 JERMYN ST	LONDON SW1	ENGLAND
PIKE, ANDREA	ACTRESS	4225 ETHEL AVE #6	STUDIO CITY, CA	91604
PIKE, DAVE	SINGER	PENNY, 30 GUINAN ST	WALTHAM, MA	02154
PIKE, DON	FILM DIRECTOR	DGA, 7950 SUNSET BLVD	LOS ANGELES, CA	90046
PIKE, DON	STUNTMAN	3518 W CAHUENGA BLVD #300	LOS ANGELES, CA	90068
PIKE, GREGORY ALLEN	DIRECTOR	8787 SHOREHAM DR #101	LOS ANGELES, CA	90069
PIKE, JOHN S	TV EXECUTIVE	PARAMOUNT TELEVISION		
		5555 MELROSE AVE	LOS ANGELES, CA	90038
PIKE, SIDNEY	CABLE EXECUTIVE	TBS, 1050 TECHWOOD, NW	ATLANTA, GA	30318
PILAND, JEANNE	MEZZO-SOPRANO	MARIEDL ANDERS ARTISTS MGMT		
		535 EL CAMINO DEL MAR ST	SAN FRANCISCO, CA	94121
PILAR, BONNIE	ACTRESS	208 S BEVERLY DR #4	BEVERLY HILLS, CA	90212
PILAVIN, BARBARA	ACTRESS	208 S BEVERLY DR #4	BEVERLY HILLS, CA	90212
PILCHER, SALLY	TV DIRECTOR	1313 N RITCHIE CT #2602	CHICAGO, IL	60610
PILEDRIVER	ROCK & ROLL GROUP	POST OFFICE BOX 249		
		STATION M	TORONTO, ONT M6S 4T3	CANADA
PILGRIM, NEVA	SOPRANO	POST OFFICE BOX 884	NEW YORK, NY	10023
PILLER, MICHAEL B	TV WRITER-PRODUCER	737 N ORANGE DR	LOS ANGELES, CA	90038
PILLOW	BODYBUILDER	POST OFFICE BOX 1076	VENICE, CA	90294
PILLOW, DARYL	SINGER	TAYLOR, 2401 12TH AVE S	NASHVILLE, TN	37204
PILLOW, RAY	SINGER	ROUTE #4, NEW HWY 96 W	FRANKLIN, TN	37064
PILLSBURY, DREW	ACTOR	9220 SUNSET BLVD #202	LOS ANGELES, CA	90069
PILLSBURY, GARTH	ACTOR-PHOTOGRAPHER	2219 N BEACHWOOD DR	HOLLYWOOD, CA	90068
PILOF, JUDY	DIRECTOR	235 W 75TH ST	NEW YORK, NY	10023
PILON, DANIEL	ACTOR	10100 SANTA MONICA BLVD #1600	LOS ANGELES, CA	90067
PILOT	JAZZ GROUP	POST OFFICE BOX 19004	NEW ORLEANS, LA	70179
PILOU, JEANNETTE	SOPRANO	CAMI, 165 W 57TH ST	NEW YORK, NY	10019
PILSON, NEAL H	TV EXECUTIVE	CBS-TV, 51 W 52ND ST	NEW YORK, NY	10019
PIMBLE, WILLIAM H, JR	NEWS CORRESPONDENT	1755 S JEFFERSON DAVIS HWY	ARLINGTON, VA	22202
PIMENTA-NEVES, ANTONIO M	NEWS CORRESPONDENT	3306 MILLER HGTS RD	OAKTON, VA	22124
PINASSI, KEVIN	ACTOR	332 S ROXBURY DR	BEVERLY HILLS, CA	90212
PINCHOT, BRONSON	ACTOR	11726 SAN VICENTE BLVD #300	LOS ANGELES, CA	90049
PINCHUK, SHELDON	WRITER	4506 EL CABALLERO DR	TARZANA, CA	91356

Name	Occupation	Address	City	Zip/Country
PINCUS, WALTER H	NEWS CORRESPONDENT	3202 KLINGLE RD, NW	WASHINGTON, DC	20008
PINDER, RODNEY	NEWS CORRESPONDENT	8222 FORT HUNT RD	ALEXANDRIA, VA	22308
PINE, ANGEL	ACTRESS	22915 HATTERAS ST	WOODLAND HILLS, CA	91367
PINE, ART	NEWS CORRESPONDENT	3211 RITTENHOUSE ST, NW	WASHINGTON, DC	20015
PINE, DAVE	SINGER	PENNY, 30 GUINAN ST	WALTHAM, MA	02154
PINE, GRANVILLE	DIRECTOR	3975 VAN NOORD AVE	STUDIO CITY, CA	91604
PINE, PHILLIP	ACTOR	7034 COSTELLO AVE	VAN NUYS, CA	91405
PINE, ROBERT	ACTOR-DIRECTOR	3975 VAN NOORD AVE	STUDIO CITY, CA	91604
PINE, TINA	SCREENWRITER	8955 BEVERLY BLVD	LOS ANGELES, CA	90048
PINEDA, RENE	COMPOSER	309 MONTEREY RD	SOUTH PASADENA, CA	91030
PINELLA, LOU, SR	BASEBALL	57 SHERI DR	ALLENDALE, NJ	07401
PINETUCKETT	C & W GROUP	POST OFFICE BOX 25371	CHARLOTTE, NC	28212
PINHEIRO, VICTOR	ACTOR	525 S GRAMERCY PL #103	LOS ANGELES, CA	90020
PINK FLOYD	ROCK & ROLL GROUP	43 PORTLAND RD	LONDON W11	ENGLAND
PINKARD, FRED	ACTOR	4721 LAUREL CANYON BLVD #211	NORTH HOLLYWOOD, CA	91607
PINKARD, RON	ACTOR	1722 LAUREL CANYON BLVD	LOS ANGELES, CA	90046
PINKARD, SANDY	GUITARIST	1009 17TH AVE S	NASHVILLE, TN	37212
PINKSON, RAY	PHOTOGRAPHER	10709 KESWICK ST	GARRETT PARK, MD	20896
PINKY	ROCK & ROLL GROUP	ICM, 40 W 57TH ST	NEW YORK, NY	10019
PINNEY, PATRICK	ACTOR	11936 BURBANK BLVD #12	NORTH HOLLYWOOD, CA	91607
PINNOCK, TREVOR	CONDUCTOR	ICM, 40 W 57TH ST	NEW YORK, NY	10019
PINOTEAU, CLAUDE	FILM DIRECTOR	21 RUE MADELEINE-MICHELIS	NEUILLY 92200	FRANCE
PINSKER, JUDITH	TV WRITER	555 W 57TH ST #1230	NEW YORK, NY	10019
PINSKER, LEWIS H	TV WRITER	555 W 57TH ST #1230	NEW YORK, NY	10019
PINSKER, SETH	FILM DIRECTOR	461 1/2 N SIERRA BONITA AVE	LOS ANGELES, CA	90036
PINTAR, JUDITH	HARPIST	SONA GAIA PRODS, POSTBUS 6037	2001 HA HAARLEM	HOLLAND
PINTER, HAROLD	SCREENWRITER	ACTAC, 16 CADOGAN LN	LONDON SW1	ENGLAND
PINTER, JOHN	FLUTIST	POST OFFICE BOX 770		
		WESLEYAN STATION	MIDDLETON, CT	06457
PINTER, MARK	ACTOR	CBS-TV, "AS THE WORLD TURNS"		
		51 W 52ND ST	NEW YORK, NY	10019
PINTO, DAVID H	COMPOSER	410 S OAK AVE	PASADENA, CA	91107
PINTO, JESUS	TENOR	CAMI, 165 W 57TH ST	NEW YORK, NY	10019
PINTOFF, ERNEST	FILM DIRECTOR	1842 OUTPOST DR	LOS ANGELES, CA	90068
PINZOLAS, JOSE MARIA	PIANIST	GURTMAN, 162 W 56TH ST	NEW YORK, NY	10019
PIOLI, JUDY	TV WRITER	129 FLEET ST	MARINA DEL REY, CA	90292
PIPE, G RUSSELL	NEWS CORRESPONDENT	13349 FELDMAN PL	HERNDON, VA	22070
PIPER, KELLY	ACTRESS	8350 SANTA MONICA BLVD #206	LOS ANGELES, CA	90069
PIPER, PATRICK M	NEWS CORRESPONDENT	1755 S JEFFERSON DAVIS HWY	ARLINGTON, VA	22202
PIPER, ROWDY RODDY	WRESTLER	POST OFFICE BOX 3859	STAMFORD, CT	06905
PIPER, WILLIAM	TV DIRECTOR	ABC-TV, 4151 PROSPECT AVE	HOLLYWOOD, CA	90027
PIPER ROAD SPRING BAND	BLUEGRASS GROUP	POST OFFICE BOX 138	BLACK EARTH, WI	53515
PIPKIN, LEO	TV WRITER	8955 BEVERLY BLVD	LOS ANGELES, CA	90048
PIPPIN, WILLIAM	GUITARIST	849 FLORENCE CIR	MADISON, TN	37115
PIPS, THE	VOCAL GROUP	SEE - KNIGHT, GLADYS &		
		THE PIPS		
PIRANHA	RHYTHM & BLUES GROUP	KINGSLAND, 108 SHARON DR	WEST MONROE, LA	71291
PIRARO, DAN	CARTOONIST	CHRONICLE FEATURES		
		870 MARKET ST	SAN FRANCISCO, CA	94102
PIRES, GERARD	DIRECTOR	19 RUE CLEMENT MAROT	PARIS 75008	FRANCE
PIRES, MARIA JOAO	PIANIST	CAMI, 165 W 57TH ST	NEW YORK, NY	10019
PIRIE, DR LYNNE	BODYBUILDER	NORTH PHOENIX HEATH INSTITUTE		
		750 E THUNDERBIRD RD	PHOENIX, AZ	85022
PIRILLO, VINCENT	ACTOR	1633 VISTA DEL MAR ST #201	LOS ANGELES, CA	90028
PIRKO, THOMAS R	WRITER	426 S NORTON AVE #210	LOS ANGELES, CA	90020
PIROSH, ROBERT	SCREENWRITER	133 S BEDFORD DR #C	BEVERLY HILLS, CA	90212
PISCOPO, JOE	ACT-WRI-COMED	122 E 42ND ST #210	NEW YORK, NY	10168
PISTOLE, GREGORY	TV WRITER	8955 BEVERLY BLVD	LOS ANGELES, CA	90048
PISTONE, KIMBERLEY	ACTRESS	SHERMAN, 348 S REXFORD DR	BEVERLY HILLS, CA	90212
PITCHFORD, DEAN	LYRICIST-PRODUCER	1880 CENTURY PARK E #900	LOS ANGELES, CA	90067
PITHEY, WENSLEY	ACTOR	10 DOWNSIDE	LONDON SW15 2AE	ENGLAND
PITILLO, MARIA	ACTRESS	ABC-TV, "ALL MY CHILDREN"		
		1330 AVE OF THE AMERICAS	NEW YORK, NY	10019
PITKIN, LEMUEL	TV WRITER	8955 BEVERLY BLVD	LOS ANGELES, CA	90048
PITLIK, DAVID	ACTOR-TV WRITER	8955 BEVERLY BLVD	LOS ANGELES, CA	90048
PITLIK, NOAM	ACTOR-TV DIRECTOR	2838 NICHOLS CANYON PL	LOS ANGELES, CA	90046
PITNEY, GENE	SINGER	6046 37TH AVE	KENOSHA, WI	53142
PITONIAK, ANN	ACTRESS	8901 6 MILE RD	CALEDONIA, WI	53108
PITSIS, TED	ACTOR	6217 AFTON PL #6	LOS ANGELES, CA	90028
PITSS, JOHN	SPORTS WRITER	POST OFFICE BOX 500	WASHINGTON, DC	20044
PITT, INGRID	ACTRESS	ROGER HANCOCK MAGANEMENT		
		8 WATERLOO PL, PALL MALL	LONDON SW1	ENGLAND
PITT, PETER	FILM EDITOR	4 FAIR CLOSE, BUSHEY	HERTS	ENGLAND
PITT, STEFFANIE	ACTRESS	ICM, 388-396 OXFORD ST	LONDON W1	ENGLAND
PITTEL, HARVEY	SAXOPHONIST	CAMI, 165 W 57TH ST	NEW YORK, NY	10019
PITTELLI, PATRICK	DIRECTOR	DGA, 110 W 57TH ST	NEW YORK, NY	10019
PITTENGER, MEL	ACTOR	POST OFFICE BOX 247	ACTON, CA	93510
PITTENGER, RICHARD	TV DIRECTOR	ABC-TV, 7 W 66TH ST	NEW YORK, NY	10023
PITTMAN, BRUCE	DIRECTOR	PLESHETTE, 2700 N BEACHWOOD DR	LOS ANGELES, CA	90068
PITTMAN, REBECCA S	NEWS CORRESPONDENT	1514 17TH ST, NW	WASHINGTON, DC	20036
PITTS, CARY	ACTOR	208 S BEVERLY DR #4	BEVERLY HILLS, CA	90212
PITTS, DON	VOICE SPECIALIST	7461 BEVERLY BLVD #400	LOS ANGELES, CA	90068
PITTS, ROSS	GUITARIST	601 N DUPONT AVE #C-53	MADISON, TN	37115
PITTSBURG	C & W GROUP	4680 ELK LAKE DR #304	VICTORIA, BC V8Z 5M1	CANADA
PIUCCI, MATT & TIM LEE	ROCK & ROCK DUO	POST OFFICE BOX 2428	EL SEGUNDO, CA	90245

Name	Occupation	Address	City	Zip
PIVEN, BYRNE	ACTOR	1509 N CRESCENT HGTS BLVD #7	LOS ANGELES, CA	90069
PIZZA, PATT	ACTOR	95 CHRISTOPHER ST	NEW YORK, NY	10014
PIZZI, DONNA L	TV WRITER	GLORIA SAFIER MGMT		
		667 MADISON AVE	NEW YORK, NY	10021
PIZZI, JOHN R	NEWS CORRESPONDENT	2025 "M" ST, NW	WASHINGTON, DC	20036
PIZZI, RAY M	COMPOSER	POST OFFICE BOX 8137	VAN NUYS, CA	91406
PIZZOLI, ANNE F	NEWS CORRESPONDENT	5706 BROAD BRANCH RD, NW	WASHINGTON, DC	20015
PLACE, MARY KAY	ACTOR-WRITER	2739 MOTOR AVE	LOS ANGELES, CA	90064
PLAIN WRAP	ROCK & ROLL GROUP	POST OFFICE BOX 2428	EL SEGUNDO, CA	90245
PLAKINGER, TINA	BODYBUILDER	21100 ERWIN ST	WOODLAND HILLS, CA	91367
PLAN 9	ROCK & ROLL GROUP	POST OFFICE BOX 817	JAMAICA PLAIN, MA	02130
PLANA, TONY	ACTOR	KOHNER, 9169 SUNSET BLVD	LOS ANGELES, CA	90069
PLANCO, LOIS	CASTING DIRECTOR	233 W 16TH ST	NEW YORK, NY	10011
PLANET	ROCK & ROLL GROUP	STERLING, 10020 PIONEER BLVD #104	SANTA FE SPRINGS, CA	90670
PLANET 10	ROCK & ROLL GROUP	FAST LANE PRODUCTIONS		
		4590 MAC ARTHUR BLVD, NW	WASHINGTON, DC	20007
PLANET PATROL	ROCK & ROLL GROUP	FUTURE BEAT ALLIANCE		
		1747 1ST AVE	NEW YORK, NY	10128
PLANT, ROBERT	SINGER-SONGWRITER	PHIL CARSON, ATLANTIC RECORDS		
		75 ROCKEFELLER PLAZA	NEW YORK, NY	10019
PLANTE, JAMES F	TV EXECUTIVE	NBC TELEVISION NETWORK		
		30 ROCKEFELLER PLAZA	NEW YORK, NY	10112
PLANTE, LOUIS R	ACTOR	5330 LANKERSHIM BLVD #210	NORTH HOLLYWOOD, CA	91601
PLANTE, WILLIAM M	NEWS CORRESPONDENT	CBS NEWS, 2020 "M" ST, NW	WASHINGTON, DC	20036
PLANTT-WINSTON, SUSAN	ACTRESS	113 N SAN VICENTE BLVD #202	BEVERLY HILLS, CA	90211
PLASCHKES, OTTO	FILM PRODUCER	ARIEL, 162-170 WARDOUR ST	LONDON W1V 3AT	ENGLAND
PLASSCHAERT, KELLYN	ACTRESS	7466 BEVERLY BLVD #205	LOS ANGELES, CA	90036
PLASTICLAND	ROCK & ROLL GROUP	POST OFFICE BOX 2896	TORRANCE, CA	90509
PLATER, ALAN	SCREENWRITER	5 HULL RD, COTTINGHAM	HUMBERSIDE HU16 4PA	ENGLAND
PLATINUM	ROCK & ROLL GROUP	JIMMY ALLEN ARTIST MGMT		
		1548 ASHLAND AVE	SAINT PAUL, MN	55104
PLATINUM BLONDE	ROCK & ROLL GROUP	82 GERRARD ST E #2-F	TORONTO, ONT M5B 2J1	CANADA
PLATNICK, JONATHAN	TV WRITER	51 7TH AVE S	NEW YORK, NY	10014
PLATO, DANA	ACTRESS	6640 SUNSET BLVD #203	LOS ANGELES, CA	90028
PLATON, DON R	NEWS CORRESPONDENT	6631 WAKEFIELD DR	ALEXANDRIA, VA	22307
PLATT, HOWARD	ACTOR	22828 PACIFIC COAST HWY #C	MALIBU, CA	90265
PLATT, POLLY	WRITER-AUTHORESS	142 ADELAIDE DR	SANTA MONICA, CA	90402
PLATTERS, THE	VOCAL GROUP	8033 SUNSET BLVD #222	LOS ANGELES, CA	90046
PLATTNER, ANDREW	NEWS CORRESPONDENT	2326 COLUMBINE CT	GAMBRILLS, MD	21054
PLATTS-MILLS, BARNEY	WRITER-PRODUCER	SIEFERT, 8-A BRUNSWICK GARDENS	LONDON W8 4AJ	ENGLAND
PLATZ, TOM	BODYBUILDER	POST OFFICE BOX 1262	SANTA MONICA, CA	90406
PLAVNICK, JUDITH	NEWS CORRESPONDENT	918 16TH ST, NW	WASHINGTON, DC	20006
PLAWIN, PAUL	NEWS CORRESPONDENT	2329 N OAK ST	FALLS CHURCH, VA	22046
PLAYBOY, THE	WRESTLER	SEE - ROSE, PLAYBOY BUDDY		
PLAYER	ROCK & ROLL GROUP	PALMER/ROSWELL, 1307 BERRY DR	LOS ANGELES, CA	90025
PLAYER, GARY	GOLFER	1 ERIE VIEW PLAZA #1300	CLEVELAND, OH	44114
PLAYER, SUSAN	ACTRESS	SEE - PLAYER-JARREAU, SUSAN		
PLAYER-JARREAU, SUSAN	ACTRESS	11752 LA MAIDA ST	NORTH HOLLYWOOD, CA	91607
PLAYGROUND SLAP, THE	ROCK & ROLL GROUP	3246 VIA CALIENTE DEL SOL	JAMUL, CA	92035
PLAYMATES, THE	VOCAL GROUP	JOYCE AGENCY, 435 E 79TH ST	NEW YORK, NY	10021
PLAYTEN-WHITE, ALICE	ACTRESS	33 5TH AVE	NEW YORK, NY	10003
PLEASANTS, EDWIN A	COMPOSER	1879 CLOVERDALE AVE	LOS ANGELES, CA	90019
PLEASANTS-MACLEAY, ELLEN	PIANIST	ALPHA, 685 W END AVE	NEW YORK, NY	10025
PLEASENCE, DONALD	ACTOR	11 STRAND ON THE GREEN	LONDON W4	ENGLAND
PLEASURE	SOUL GROUP	POST OFFICE BOX 601	PORTRLAND, OR	97207
PLEDGER, COURTNEY	ACTRESS	8285 SUNSET BLVD #12	LOS ANGELES, CA	90046
PLEITGEN, FRITZ	NEWS CORRESPONDENT	3132 "M" ST, NW	WASHINGTON, DC	20007
PLESHETTE, JOHN	ACTOR-WRITER	2643 CRESTON DR	LOS ANGELES, CA	90068
PLESHETTE, LYNN	LITERARY AGENT	2643 CRESTON DR	LOS ANGELES, CA	90068
PLESHETTE, SUZANNE	ACTRESS	POST OFFICE BOX 1492	BEVERLY HILLS, CA	90213
PLESKOW, ERIC	FILM EXECUTIVE	1875 CENTURY PARK E #300	LOS ANGELES, CA	90067
PLETCHER, ELDON	CARTOONIST	331 TIFFANY ST	SLIDELL, LA	70458
PLETTS, TOM	ACTOR	8921 SUNSET BLVD #B	LOS ANGELES, CA	90069
PLEVEN, PATRICK A	TV EXECUTIVE	1160 5TH AVE	NEW YORK, NY	10029
PLIMPTON, GEORGE	AUTHOR	541 E 72ND ST	NEW YORK, NY	10021
PLIMSOULS, THE	ROCK & ROLL GROUP	6515 SUNSET BLVD #202	LOS ANGELES, CA	90028
PLISHKA, PAUL	SINGER	CAMI, 165 W 57TH ST	NEW YORK, NY	10019
PLISSNER, MARTIN	NEWS CORRES-WRITER	CBS NEWS, 2020 "M" ST, NW	WASHINGTON, DC	20036
PLMOUR, DEIDRA	MEZZO-SOPRANO	HILLYER, 250 W 57TH ST	NEW YORK, NY	10107
PLOG, ANTHONY	TRUMPETER	CCS, 4478 PURDUE AVE	CULVER CITY, CA	90230
PLONE, ALLEN LEE	DIRECTOR	317 N ORANGE DR	LOS ANGELES, CA	90036
PLOWDEN, JULIAN	WRITER	11660 TERRY HILL PL	LOS ANGELES, CA	90049
PLOWRIGHT, JOAN	ACTRESS	70 ROEBUCK HOUSE, PALACE ST	LONDON SW1	ENGLAND
PLOWRIGHT, ROSALIND	SOPRANO	CAMI, 165 W 57TH ST	NEW YORK, NY	10019
PLOZET, THOMAS P	NEWS CORRESPONDENT	NBC-TV, NEWS DEPARTMENT		
		4001 NEBRASKA AVE, NW	WASHINGTON, DC	20016
PLUMB, EVE	ACTRESS	10845 LINDBROOK DR #3	LOS ANGELES, CA	90024
PLUMB, FLORA	ACTRESS	9200 SUNSET BLVD #909	LOS ANGELES, CA	90069
PLUMB, NEELY	COMPOSER	6463 FIRMAMENT AVE	VAN NUYS, CA	91406
PLUMB, SUSAN	ACTRESS	9220 SUNSET BLVD #202	LOS ANGELES, CA	90069
PLUMER, AMY	ACTRESS	295 CENTRAL PARK W #10-C	NEW YORK, NY	10024
PLUMLEY, DON	ACTOR	415 CENTRAL PARK W	NEW YORK, NY	10025
PLUMMER, AMANDA	ACTRESS	1650 BROADWAY #302	NEW YORK, NY	10019
PLUMMER, BRIAN	SINGER	41 BRITAIN ST #200	TORONTO, ONT	CANADA
PLUMMER, CHRISTOPHER	ACTOR	49 WAMPUM HILL RD	WESTON, CT	06883

Name	Occupation	Address	City/State	Zip/Country
PLUMMER, KATHRYN	MUSICIAN	1625 STOKES LN	NASHVILLE, TN	37215
PLUMMER, SCOTTY	SINGER	TERRY, 909 PARKVIEW AVE	LODI, CA	95240
PLUMMER, STEPHEN	TENOR	LEW, 204 W 10TH ST	NEW YORK, NY	10014
PLUMMER, WILLIAM	WRITER-EDITOR	TIME & PEOPLE MAGAZINE		
		TIME & LIFE BUILDING		
		ROCKEFELLER CENTER	NEW YORK, NY	10020
PLUNKETT, JIM	FOOTBALL	51 KILROY WY	ATHERTON, CA	94025
PLUTE, THEODORE M	CONDUCTOR	6728 HILLPARK DR #407	LOS ANGELES, CA	90068
PLYTAS, STEVE	ACTOR	70 LANSBURY AVE, FELTHAM	MIDDLESEX TW14 OJR	ENGLAND
POCHET, JOHN C	NEWS CORRESPONDENT	2121 COLUMBIA PIKE	ARLINGTON, VA	22204
POCHNA, JOHN	ACTOR	6626 FRANKLIN AVE #302	HOLLYWOOD, CA	90028
POCKET FIRE	ROCK & ROLL GROUP	VARIETY ARTISTS INTL, INC		
		9073 NEMO ST, 3RD FLOOR	LOS ANGELES, CA	90069
POCO	ROCK & ROLL GROUP	POST OFFICE BOX 24475	NASHVILLE, TN	37202
PODDANY, EUGENE	COMPOSER	2036 GRIFFITH PARK BLVD	LOS ANGELES, CA	90039
PODE, DONNA	TV WRITER	ABC-TV, "GENERAL HOSPITAL"		
		1438 N GOWER ST	LOS ANGELES, CA	90028
PODELL, RICK	ACTOR	1100 N ALTA LOMA RD #707	LOS ANGELES, CA	90069
PODHORETZ, NORMAN	AUTHOR-EDITOR	AMERICAN JEWISH COMMUNITY		
		COMMENTARY MAGAZINE		
		165 E 56TH ST	NEW YORK, NY	10022
PODIS-JACOBS, VICKI	PIANIST	CEDARWOOD APARTMENTS #C-42	LEBANON, TN	37087
PODLES, EWA	MEZZO-SOPRANO	LEISER, DORCHESTER TOWERS		
		155 W 68TH ST	NEW YORK, NY	10023
POE, EDGAR A	NEWS CORRESPONDENT	2615 S LYNN ST	ARLINGTON, VA	22202
POE, WILLIAM	GUITARIST	7385 W SUNRISE BLVD	PLANTATION, FL	33313
POFFO, ELIZABETH	WRESTLING VALET	SEE - MISS ELIZABETH		
POFFO, LEAPING LANNY	WRESTLER	POST OFFICE BOX 3859	STAMFORD, CT	06905
POFFO, RANDY	WRESTLER	SEE - SAVAGE, RANDY		
		"MACHO MAN"		
POGACNIK, MIHA	VIOLINIST	AARON, 25 HUNTINGTON AVE	BOSTON, MA	02116
POGORELICH, IVO	PIANIST	ANGLO-SWISS ARTISTS MGMT		
		16 MUSWELL HILL RD, HIGHGATE	LONDON N6 5UG	ENGLAND
POGUE, CHARLES E, JR	ACTOR-WRITER	8955 BEVERLY BLVD	LOS ANGELES, CA	90048
POGUES, THE	ROCK & ROLL GROUP	POST OFFICE BOX 2428	EL SEGUNDO, CA	90245
POINDEXTER, JOSEPH B	WRITER-EDITOR	LIFE/TIME & LIFE BLDG		
		ROCKEFELLER CENTER	NEW YORK, NY	10020
POINDEXTER, LARRY	ACTOR	721 N LA BREA AVE #200	LOS ANGELES, CA	90038
POINT BLANK	ROCK & ROLL GROUP	ATI, 888 7TH AVE, 21ST FLOOR	NEW YORK, NY	10106
POINTER, BONNIE	SINGER	1680 N VINE ST #214	HOLLYWOOD, CA	90028
POINTER, JOE	GUITARIST	803 GWYNN DR	NASHVILLE, TN	37216
POINTER, NOEL	MUSICIAN	KEWLEY, 11 BAILEY AVE	RIDGEFIELD, CT	06877
POINTER, PRISCILLA	ACTRESS	10100 SANTA MONICA BLVD #1600	LOS ANGELES, CA	90067
POINTER, SIDNEY	ACT-WRI-DIR	9350 WILSHIRE BLVD #310	BEVERLY HILLS, CA	90212
POINTER SISTERS, THE	VOCAL TRIO	10100 SANTA MONICA BLVD #1600	LOS ANGELES, CA	90067
POIRE, ALAIN	FILM PRODUCER	13 RUE MADELEINE MICHELIS	NEUILLY 92200	FRANCE
POISON	ROCK & ROLL GROUP	POST OFFICE BOX 2428	EL SEGUNDO, CA	90245
POISON GIRLS	ROCK & ROLL GROUP	ALLIED AGENCY & MANAGEMENT		
		76 TOTTENHAM COURT RD	LONDON W1P 9PA	ENGLAND
POITRENAUD, JACQUEST	FILM DIRECTOR	72 RUE SAINT DENIS	PARIS 75001	FRANCE
POKRESS, DAVID L	PHOTOGRAPHER	98 STAPLES ST	FARMINGDALE, NY	11735
POKRESS, JACKSON	PHOTOGRAPHER	508 ATLANTA AVE	N MASSAPEQUA, NY	11758
POLACK, REBECCA	ACTRESS	11990 LAURELWOOD DR #24	STUDIO CITY, CA	91604
POLAKOFF, JAMES	DIRECTOR	POST OFFICE BOX 8205	NEWPORT BEACH, CA	92660
POLAKOFF, JOSEPH	NEWS CORRESPONDENT	2712 CORTLAND PL, NW	WASHINGTON, DC	20008
POLAN, LOIS ANNE	DIRECTOR	DGA, 7950 SUNSET BLVD	LOS ANGELES, CA	90046
POLAN, NINA	ACTRESS	16 W 64TH ST	NEW YORK, NY	10023
POLANSKI, ROMAN	ACT-WRI-DIR-PROD	43 AVE MONTAIGNE	PARIS 75008	FRANCE
POLASKI, DEBORAH	SOPRANO	CAMI, 165 W 57TH ST	NEW YORK, NY	10019
POLE, FRANCIS	ACTRESS	400 W 43RD ST	NEW YORK, NY	10036
POLEDOURIS, BASIL	COMPOSER	4549 ALONZO AVE	ENCINO, CA	91316
POLEVOY, ROY	TV EXECUTIVE	ABC-TV, 4151 PROSPECT AVE	LOS ANGELES, CA	90027
POLGAR, LASZLO	BASS	61 W 62ND ST #6-F	NEW YORK, NY	10023
POLIC, HENRY, III	ACTOR	5307 WILKERSON AVE #20	LOS ANGELES, CA	90046
POLICH, JOHN	TV DIRECTOR	1612 RANDALL ST	GLENDALE, CA	91201
POLIER, DAN	WRITER	13926 MAGNOLIA BLVD	SHERMAN OAKS, CA	91423
POLIFRONI, PAM	CASTING DIRECTOR	14755 VENTURA BLVD #1529	SHERMAN OAKS, CA	91403
POLIKOFF, GERALD	TV DIRECTOR	533 WOODMERE BLVD	WOODMERE, NY	11598
POLING, DOUG	NEWS CORRESPONDENT	CBS NEWS, 51 W 52ND ST	NEW YORK, NY	10019
POLING, WILLIAM	NEWS CORRESPONDENT	114 SUNNYSIDE RD	SILVER SPRING, MD	20910
POLINSKI, JOHN J	COMPOSER-CONDUCTOR	13170 BRACKEN ST	PACOIMA, CA	91331
POLINSKY, JOEL	ACTOR	BENSON, 518 TOLUCA PARK DR	BURBANK, CA	91505
POLINSKY-LAV, ALEXANDER	NEWS CORRESPONDENT	2601 PARK CENTER DR #C-1111	ALEXANDRIA, VA	22302
POLISHCHUK, ARKADY	NEWS CORRESPONDENT	1201 CONNECTICUT AVE, NW	WASHINGTON, DC	20036
POLITE, CHARLENE	ACTRESS	CARPENTER, 1516-W REDWOOD ST	SAN DIEGO, CA	92101
POLITO, GENE	CINEMATOGRAPHER	4701 ABBEYVILLE AVE	WOODLAND HILLS, CA	91364
POLIVNICK, PAUL	CONDUCTOR	GERSHUNOFF, 502 PARK AVE	NEW YORK, NY	10022
POLIZZI, JOSEPH	TV WRITER	8955 BEVERLY BLVD	LOS ANGELES, CA	90048
POLK, BETTY	PIANIST	2131 ELM HILL PIKE #G-144	NASHVILLE, TN	37210
POLK, JACKSON H	NEWS CORRESPONDENT	340 NATIONAL PRESS BLDG		
		529 14TH ST, NW	WASHINGTON, DC	20045
POLK, JAMES E	CONDUCTOR	POST OFFICE BOX 19345-A	LOS ANGELES, CA	90019
POLK, JAMES R	NEWS CORRESPONDENT	NBC-TV, NEWS DEPARTMENT		
		4001 NEBRASKA AVE, NW	WASHINGTON, DC	20016
POLK, LEE	WRITER-PRODUCER	150 E 69TH ST	NEW YORK, NY	10021

ROBERT PLANT

SUZANNE PLESHETTE

POINTER SISTERS

SIDNEY POITIER

ROMAN POLANSKI

STEPHANIE POWERS

VINCENT PRICE

CHARLEY PRIDE

PRIME TIME

Name	Occupation	Address	City	Zip
POLK, RANDY	ACTOR	SCHOEMAN, 2600 W VICTORY BLVD	BURBANK, CA	91505
POLL, MARTIN	FILM PRODUCER	919 3RD AVE	NEW YORK, NY	10019
POLL, MELVYN	TENOR	59 E 54TH ST #81	NEW YORK, NY	10022
POLLACK, BARRY HOWARD	TV WRITER	8955 BEVERLY BLVD	LOS ANGELES, CA	90048
POLLACK, BRIAN	ACTOR-TV WRITER	7608 WILLOW GLEN RD	LOS ANGELES, CA	90046
POLLACK, DANIEL	PIANIST	SOFFER, 130 W 56TH ST	NEW YORK, NY	10019
POLLACK, DARRYLE	WRITER	1706 N DOHENY DR	LOS ANGELES, CA	90069
POLLACK, SYDNEY	WRITER-PRODUCER	1067 CORSICA DR	PACIFIC PALISADES, CA	90272
POLLAN, TRACY	ACTRESS	10100 SANTA MONICA BLVD #1600	LOS ANGELES, CA	90067
POLLARD, DAVID E	NEWS CORRESPONDENT	2400 "N" ST, NW	WASHINGTON, DC	20037
POLLARD, JOHN	SINGER	POST OFFICE BOX 25371	CHARLOTTE, NC	28212
POLLARD, MICHAEL J	ACTOR	9255 SUNSET BLVD #510	LOS ANGELES, CA	90069
POLLICK, MICHAEL	NEWS CORRESPONDENT	2922 WOODSTOCK AVE	SILVER SPRING, MD	20910
POLLICK, TENO	ACTOR	7733 HAMPTON AVE #1	LOS ANGELES, CA	90046
POLLINI, MAURIZIO	PIANIST	CAMI, 165 W 57TH ST	NEW YORK, NY	10019
POLLNER, FRAN	NEWS CORRESPONDENT	510 PHILADELPHIA AVE	TAKOMA PARK, MD	20912
POLLOCK, ALAN M	TV DIRECTOR	4428 SEDGWICK ST, NW	WASHINGTON, DC	20016
POLLOCK, BERNARD	ACTOR	53 LEROY ST	NEW YORK, NY	10014
POLLOCK, DAVID M	TV WRITER	11019 AMERY AVE	SOUTH GATE, CA	90280
POLLOCK, EILEEN	TV WRITER	8955 BEVERLY BLVD	LOS ANGELES, CA	90048
POLLOCK, MICHAEL A	NEWS CORRESPONDENT	9906 PARKWOOD DR	BETHESDA, MD	20814
POLLOCK, NANCY R	ACTRESS	98 RIVERSIDE DR	NEW YORK, NY	10024
POLLOCK, ROBERT MASON	TV WRITER	8955 BEVERLY BLVD	LOS ANGELES, CA	90048
POLLON, DAPHNE	TV WRITER	8955 BEVERLY BLVD	LOS ANGELES, CA	90048
POLONSKY, ABRAHAM	FILM WRITER-DIRECTOR	135 S MC CARTHY DR	BEVERLY HILLS, CA	90212
POLONSKY, HANK V	FILM DIRECTOR	DGA, 7950 SUNSET BLVD	LOS ANGELES, CA	90046
POLOWICHAK, NICHOLAS	TV DIRECTOR	ABC TELEVISION NETWORK 1330 AVE OF THE AMERICAS	NEW YORK, NY	10019
POLSON, BETH	TV DIRECTOR-PRODUCER	2020 AVE OF THE STARS #560	LOS ANGELES, CA	90067
POLSON, SAMUEL E	NEWS CORRESPONDENT	427 6TH ST, NE	WASHINGTON, DC	20002
POMASANOFF, ALEX	WRITER	129 OCEAN WY	SANTA MONICA, CA	90402
POMERANCE, DIANE	ACTRESS	18310 KAREN DR	TARZANA, CA	91356
POMERANTS, DANA	VIOLINIST	GEWALD, 58 W 58TH ST	NEW YORK, NY	10019
POMERANTZ, EARL	TV WRITER	320 PACIFIC ST	SANTA MONICA, CA	90405
POMERANTZ, EDWARD	TV WRITER	555 W 57TH ST #1230	NEW YORK, NY	10019
POMERANTZ, JEFFREY	ACTOR-WRITER	5930 FRANKLIN AVE	LOS ANGELES, CA	90028
POMERANTZ, MARK J	COMPOSER-CONDUCTOR	14415 MAGNOLIA BLVD	SHERMAN OAKS, CA	91423
POMMIER, JEAN-BERNARD	PIANIST	ICM, 40 W 57TH ST	NEW YORK, NY	10019
POMPADUR, MARTIN	PUBLISHING EXECUTIVE	ZIFF CORPORATION, 1 PARK AVE	NEW YORK, NY	10016
POMPIAN, PAUL	TV WRITER-PRODUCER	425 N OAKHURST DR #101	BEVERLY HILLS, CA	90210
POMUS, JEROME "DOC"	SONGWRITER	253 W 72ND ST	NEW YORK, NY	10023
PONAZECKI, JOE	ACTOR	10 E 44TH ST #700	NEW YORK, NY	10017
POND, SHERRI	SINGER	POST OFFICE BOX 208	GOODLETTSVILLE, TN	37072
POND, STANLEY S	NEWS CORRESPONDENT	2021 LANIER DR	SILVER SPRING, MD	20910
PONDER, JIMMY	SINGER	POST OFFICE BOX 82	GREAT NECK, NY	11022
PONE, BOB	ACTOR	9437 GLADE AVE	CHATSWORTH, CA	91311
PONICSAN, DARRYL	SCREENWRITER	8955 BEVERLY BLVD	LOS ANGELES, CA	90048
PONS, JUAN	BARITONE	CAMI, 165 W 57TH ST	NEW YORK, NY	10019
PONTI, CARLO	FILM PRODUCER	PALAZZO COLONNA VIDES PIAZZA PITAG	ROME	ITALY
PONTI, MICHAEL	PIANIST	3003 VAN NESS ST #W-205, NW	WASHINGTON, DC	20008
PONTIAC BROTHERS, THE	ROCK & ROLL GROUP	POST OFFICE BOX 22	SUN VALLEY, CA	91353
PONZINI, ANTHONY	ACTOR	ABC-TV, "ALL MY CHILDREN" 1330 AVE OF THE AMERICAS	NEW YORK, NY	10019
POOLE, DUANE E	COMPOSER-WRITER	7974 WOODROW WILSON DR	LOS ANGELES, CA	90046
POOLE, GEORGE E	COMPOSER	801 W WARD #128	RIDGECREST, CA	93555
POOLE, MARCUS LLOYD	CABLE EXECUTIVE	DIASPORA, 175 ADAMS ST	BROOKLYN, NY	11201
POOLE, ROY	ACTOR	10100 SANTA MONICA BLVD #310	LOS ANGELES, CA	90067
POOLE, STEPHEN	GUITARIST	15 ROGERS PL	HYDE PARK, NY	12538
POOLE, THOMAS	TENOR	SULLIVAN, 390 W END AVE	NEW YORK, NY	10024
POOLEY, OLAF	ACTOR-WRITER	3456 ALANA DR	SHERMAN OAKS, CA	91403
POON, ANNA MARIA	ACTRESS	9021 MELROSE AVE #304	LOS ANGELES, CA	90069
POOR, PETER	TV WRITER-PRODUCER	1150 5TH AVE	NEW YORK, NY	10028
POP, IGGY	SINGER	250 W 57TH ST #603	NEW YORK, NY	10107
POP, THE	MUSICAL GROUP	6430 SUNSET BLVD #1516	LOS ANGELES, CA	90028
POP ART	ROCK & ROLL GROUP	STONEGARDEN RECORDS 12436 MARVA AVE	GRANADA HILLS, CA	91344
POP RIVETS, THE	ROCK & ROLL GROUP	JIM'S RECORDS 4526 LIBERTY AVE	PITTSBURGH, PA	15224
POP-O-PIES, THE	ROCK & ROLL GROUP	POST OFFICE BOX 14563	SAN FRANCISCO, CA	94114
POPE, DONNA	SINGER	POST OFFICE BOX 25371	CHARLOTTE, NC	28212
POPE, ELAINE	TV WRITER	8955 BEVERLY BLVD	LOS ANGELES, CA	90048
POPE, KEVIN	CARTOONIST	TRIBUNE MEDIA SERVICES 64 E CONCORD ST	ORLANDO, FL	32801
POPE, PEGGY	ACTRESS	9220 SUNSET BLVD #625	LOS ANGELES, CA	90069
POPE, THOMAS	SCREENWRITER	8955 BEVERLY BLVD	LOS ANGELES, CA	90048
POPE JOHN PAUL II	POPE	PALAZZO APOSTOLICO VATICANO	VATICAN CITY	ITALY
POPESCU, PETRU	WRITER	1349 LONDONDERRY PL	LOS ANGELES, CA	90069
POPKIN, LEO	DIRECTOR	9970 SUNSET BLVD	BEVERLY HILLS, CA	90210
POPOV, VLADIMER	TENOR	CAMI, 165 W 57TH ST	NEW YORK, NY	10019
POPOVA, NINA	BALLERINA	33 ADAMS	SEA CLIFF, NY	11579
POPOVA, VALERI	SOPRANO	61 W 62ND ST #6-F	NEW YORK, NY	10023
POPP, LUCIA	SOPRANO	MARIEDL ANDERS ARTISTS MGMT 535 EL CAMINO DEL MAR ST	SAN FRANCISCO, CA	94121
POPPE, HARRY H, JR	WRITER	11818 MOORPARK ST #P	STUDIO CITY, CA	91604

Name	Occupation	Address	City	Zip
POPPE, HERMAN	ACTOR	13436 CANTARA ST	VAN NUYS, CA	91402
POPPENGER, CAROL	ACTRESS	465 W 23RD ST	NEW YORK, NY	10011
POPPER, JAN	CONDUCTOR	UCLA MUSIC DEPARTMENT		
		405 HILGARD AVE	LOS ANGELES, CA	90024
POPPICK, ERIC	ACTOR	CED, 261 S ROBERTSON BLVD	BEVERLY HILLS, CA	90211
POPSTIN, S LEE	FILM WRITER-DIRECTOR	1030 TOWER RD	BEVERLY HILLS, CA	90210
POPWELL, ALBERT	ACTOR	1830 N BRONSON AVE #317	LOS ANGELES, CA	90028
PORCELLI, KARINA	NEWS CORRESPONDENT	1738 CHURCH ST, NW	WASHINGTON, DC	20036
PORETZ, CAROL	ACTRESS	837 1/4 N ALFRED ST	LOS ANGELES, CA	90069
PORGES, PAUL PETER	ARTIST-WRITER	MAD MAGAZINE, INC		
		485 MADISON AVE	NEW YORK, NY	10022
PORGES, WALTER	TV PRODUCER	ABC-TV, 7 W 66TH ST	NEW YORK, NY	10023
PORIZKOVA, PAULINA	MODEL	ELITE MODELS, 150 E 58TH ST	NEW YORK, NY	10022
PORK & THE HAVANA DUCKS	C & W GROUP	POST OFFICE BOX 1771	CHAMPAIGN, IL	61820
PORTER, BEN E, JR	CONDUCTOR	POST OFFICE BOX 320	MC CLOUD, CA	96057
PORTER, BETH	ACTRESS	MARSHALL, 44 PERRYN RD	LONDON W3	ENGLAND
PORTER, BEVERLY A	PIANIST	909 FOREST DALE	HERMITAGE, TN	37076
PORTER, BRETT	ACTOR	1930 CENTURY PARK W #303	LOS ANGELES, CA	90067
PORTER, CATHERINE E	NEWS CORRESPONDENT	NBC-TV, NEWS DEPARTMENT		
		4001 NEBRASKA AVE, NW	WASHINGTON, DC	20016
PORTER, CLAIRE	DANCER	GREAT LAKES PERFORMING		
		310 E WASHINGTON ST	ANN ARBOR, MI	48104
PORTER, DEAN	MANDOLINIST	638 SUNSET DR	CLAREMORE, OK	74017
PORTER, DON	ACTOR-DIRECTOR	1900 AVE OF THE STARS #2270	LOS ANGELES, CA	90067
PORTER, DONALD J	NEWS CORRESPONDENT	NBC-TV, NEWS DEPARTMENT		
		4001 NEBRASKA AVE, NW	WASHINGTON, DC	20016
PORTER, EDDIE RAY	SINGER-GUITARIST	MOD LANG MANAGEMENT		
		48 SHATTLUCK SQ #138	BERKELEY, CA	94704
PORTER, ERIC	ACTOR	LONDON MANAGEMENT, LTD		
		235-241 REGENT ST	LONDON W1A 2JT	ENGLAND
PORTER, FRED H	DIRECTOR	7 W 16TH ST #4	NEW YORK, NY	10011
PORTER, H DALE	CONDUCTOR	4432 CANDLEBERRY AVE	SEAL BEACH, CA	90740
PORTER, HALE	ACTOR	8484 WILSHIRE BLVD #235	BEVERLY HILLS, CA	90211
PORTER, JAMES F	CONDUCTOR	1062 HANLEY AVE	LOS ANGELES, CA	90049
PORTER, JEAN	ACTRESS	8729 LOOKOUT MOUNTAIN AVE	LOS ANGELES, CA	90046
PORTER, MADISON T	ACTOR	4918 W MARTIN L KING BLVD #4	LOS ANGELES, CA	90016
PORTER, NYREE DAWN	ACTRESS	LONDON MANAGEMENT, LTD		
		235-241 REGENT ST	LONDON W1A 2JT	ENGLAND
PORTER, RALPH	WRITER-PRODUCER	251 E 61ST ST	NEW YORK, NY	10021
PORTER, ROBERT	FILM PRODUCER	50 GLENAGEARY LODGE		
		GLENAGEARY COUNTY	DUBLIN	IRELAND
PORTER, ROBERT G	COMPOSER-CONDUCTOR	9825 MELINDA DR	BEVERLY HILLS, CA	90210
PORTER, ROBERT M	COMPOSER	350 VASSAR AVE	BERKELEY, CA	94708
PORTER, ROD	ACTOR	BERZON, 336 E 17TH ST	COSTA MESA, CA	92627
PORTER, ROYCE	PIANIST	19 SHORESIDE DR	HENDERSONVILLE, TN	37075
PORTER, STEPHEN G	NEWS CORRESPONDENT	1413 TRAP RD	VIENNA, VA	22180
PORTER, STEPHEN W	DIRECTOR	DGA, 110 W 57TH ST	NEW YORK, NY	10019
PORTER, SYLVIA	ACTRSESS	2 5TH AVE	NEW YORK, NY	10011
PORTER, SYLVIA	COLUMNIST	UNIVERSAL PRESS SYNDICATE		
		4900 MAIN ST, 9TH FLOOR	KANSAS CITY, MO	62114
PORTER, WILEY THOMAS	BANJOIST	518 HUNTING HILLS DR	MOUNT JULIET, TN	37122
PORTER-ARNOLD, PAMELA	SOPRANO	61 W 62ND ST #6-F	NEW YORK, NY	10023
PORTERFIELD, CHRISTOPHER	WRITER-EDITOR	TIME/TIME & LIFE BLDG		
		ROCKEFELLER CENTER	NEW YORK, NY	10020
PORTERFIELD, JOHN M	TV WRITER	8955 BEVERLY BLVD	LOS ANGELES, CA	90048
PORTILLO, ROSE	ACTRESS	957 TULAROSA DR	LOS ANGELES, CA	90026
PORTNEY, ROBERT	VIOLINIST	GURTMAN, 162 W 56TH ST	NEW YORK, NY	10019
PORTUGUES, GLADYS	BODYBUILDER	POST OFFICE BOX 69-A-05	HOLLYWOOD, CA	90069
PORTZ, GEOFF SCOTT, JR	WRESTLER	SEE - MC GHEE, SCOTT		
PORYES, MICHAEL D	WRITER	1659 VETERAN AVE	LOS ANGELES, CA	90024
POSAR, POMPEO	PHOTOGRAPHER	MODELS & PROMOTIONS AGENCY		
		8560 SUNSET BLVD, 10TH FLOOR	LOS ANGELES, CA	90069
POSEY, SANDY	SINGER	430 OAK GROVE #110	MINNEAPOLIS, MN	55403
POSNAK, PAUL	PIANIST	333 TAYLOR AVE N #202	SEATTLE, WA	98109
POSNER, IRINA	WRITER-PRODUCER	DGA, 110 W 57TH ST	NEW YORK, NY	10019
POSNER, MARLA R	NEWS CORRESPONDENT	1600 S JOYCE ST #C-1104	ARLINGTON, VA	22202
POSNER, MICHAEL	NEWS CORRESPONDENT	3500 36TH ST, NW	WASHINGTON, DC	20016
POSNER, NEIL B	CONDUCTOR	4261 TROOST AVE #3	STUDIO CITY, CA	91604
POSSANNER, GEORGE	NEWS CORRESPONDENT	7008 HOPEWOOD ST	BETHESDA, MD	20817
POSSELT, LEE	TV DIRECTOR	40968 FOREST HOME BLVD	FOREST FALLS, CA	92339
POSSO BROTHERS, THE	HIGH WIRE TROUPE	HALL, 138 FROG HOLLOW RD	CHURCHVILLE, PA	18966
POST, MARKIE	ACTRESS	ICM, 8899 BEVERLY BLVD	LOS ANGELES, CA	90048
POST, MIKE	COMPOSER	10453 KLING ST	NORTH HOLLYWOOD, CA	91602
POST, ROBERT	MIME	AFFILIATE ARTISTS, INC		
		37 W 65TH ST, 6TH FLOOR	NEW YORK, NY	10023
POST, TED	FILM DIRECTOR	T P FILMS, BLUMENTHAL & LEVIN		
		3250 OCEAN PARK BLVD	SANTA MONICA, CA	90405
POSTAL, JULIUS B	TV DIRECTOR	POST OFFICE BOX 46	RIDGEWOOD, NY	11385
POSTER, TOM	COLUMNIST-CRITIC	TRIBUNE MEDIA SERVICES		
		64 E CONCORD ST	ORLANDO, FL	32801
POSTIL, ADAM	ACTOR	10424 VALLEY VIEW AVE	WHITTIER, CA	90604
POSTIL, LELAND	COMPOSER	4507 CARPENTER AVE	NORTH HOLLYWOOD, CA	91607
POSTON, TOM	ACTOR	415 GREENCRAIG RD	LOS ANGELES, CA	90049
POTASNIK, DAVID C	PHOTOGRAPHER	6759 SURREYWOOD LN	BETHESDA, MD	20817
POTEETE, JESSE	GUITARIST	POST OFFICE BOX 52	COLLEGE GROVE, TN	37046

Name	Occupation	Address	City	ZIP
POTTER, ALLEN DALE	FIDDLER	2503 BOYD ST	DALLAS, TX	75224
POTTER, ALLEN M	ACTOR-TV PRODUCER	NBC TELEVISION NETWORK		
		30 ROCKEFELLER PLAZA	NEW YORK, NY	10112
POTTER, ANTHONY ROSS	WRITER-PRODUCER	DGA, 110 W 57TH ST	NEW YORK, NY	10019
POTTER, CAROL	ACTRESS	THE WILLIAM MORRIS AGENCY		
		1350 AVE OF THE AMERICAS	NEW YORK, NY	10019
POTTER, CURTIS	SINGER	4047 NACO-PERRIN BLVD #110	SAN ANTONIO, TX	78217
POTTER, DEBORAH A	NEWS CORRESPONDENT	CBS NEWS, 2020 "M" ST, NW	WASHINGTON, DC	20036
POTTER, DENNIS	SCREENWRITER	8955 BEVERLY BLVD	LOS ANGELES, CA	90048
POTTER, DON	ACTOR	6310 SAN VICENTE BLVD #407	LOS ANGELES, CA	90048
POTTER, DON	GUITARIST	1101 BELVEDERE DR	NASHVILLE, TN	37204
POTTER, DUKE	ACTOR	214 RIVERSIDE DR #415	NEW YORK, NY	10025
POTTER, EMILY	TV WRITER	8955 BEVERLY BLVD	LOS ANGELES, CA	90048
POTTER, JERRY	ACTOR	3518 W CAHUENGA BLVD #316	LOS ANGELES, CA	90068
POTTER, JERRY	SPORTS WRITER	POST OFFICE BOX 500	WASHINGTON, DC	20044
POTTER, JESSICA	ACTRESS	3061 N BEACHWOOD DR	LOS ANGELES, CA	90068
POTTER, JOAN	ACTOR	9400 READCREAST DR	BEVERLY HILLS, CA	90210
POTTER, JOHN	NEWS CORRESPONDENT	744 6TH ST #111, SW	WASHINGTON, DC	20024
POTTER, KEN	NEWS REPORTER	THE NATIONAL ENQUIRER		
		600 SE COAST AVE	LANTANA, FL	33464
POTTER, LOUIS A	TV WRITER	555 W 57TH ST #1230	NEW YORK, NY	10019
POTTER, MARK	NEWS CORRESPONDENT	ABC TELEVEISION NETWORK		
		2801 PONCE DE LEON BLVD #82	CORAL CABLES, FL	33134
POTTER, MARTIN	ACTOR	PLANT & FROGGATT, LTD		
		JULIAN HOUSE		
		4 WINDMILL ST	LONDON W1	ENGLAND
POTTER, MICHAEL	ACTOR	208 S BEVERLY DR #4	BEVERLY HILLS, CA	90212
POTTER, RICK, JR	DIRECTOR	910 DIABLO RD	DANVILLE, CA	94526
POTTER, SUZANNE	VIOLINIST	2004 20TH AVE S	NASHVILLE, TN	37212
POTTER, THOMAS	GUITARIST	2004 20TH AVE S	NASHVILLE, TN	37212
POTTS, ANNIE	ACTRESS	4211 HOLLY KNOLL DR	LOS ANGELES, CA	90027
POTTS, CLIFF	ACTOR	POST OFFICE BOX 131	TOPANGA CANYON, CA	90290
POTTS, DONALD	GUITARIST	5099 LINBAR DR #G-122	NASHVILLE, TN	37211
POTTS, NELL	ACTOR	NEWMAN, 59 COLLEYTOWN RD	WESTPORT, CT	06880
POULIOT, STEPHEN	WRITER-PRODUCER	1223 CABRILLO AVE	VENICE, CA	90291
POULSON, GERALD	FILM DIRECTOR	CHEQUERS, LITTLE BARDFIELD	ESSEX	ENGLAND
POUND, EDWARD T	NEWS CORRESPONDENT	5305 GLENWOOD RD	BETHESDA, MD	20814
POUND, LESLIE	FILM EXECUTIVE	322 W 57TH ST #44-M	NEW YORK, NY	10019
POUNDER, C C H	ACTRESS	870 N VINE ST #G	LOS ANGELES, CA	90038
POUNDSTONE, PAULA	COMEDIENNE	9000 SUNSET BLVD #1200	LOS ANGELES, CA	90069
POUSETTE-DART BAND, THE	ROCK & ROLL GROUP	3 E 54TH ST #1400	NEW YORK, NY	10022
POUSSAINT, RENEE F	NEWS CORRESPONDENT	6104 29TH ST, NW	WASHINGTON, DC	20015
POVICH, ELAINE S	NEWS CORRESPONDENT	8150 IMPERIAL DR	LAUREL, MD	20708
POVILL, JONATHAN	TV WRITER	1503 BAINUM DR	TOPANGA, CA	90290
POWELL, ADAM	WRITER	POST OFFICE BOX 1058	LA MESA, CA	92044
POWELL, ADAM	SINGER-SONGWRITER	POST OFFICE BOX 1058	LA MESA, CA	92044
POWELL, ADDISON	ACTOR	334 W 86TH ST	NEW YORK, NY	10024
POWELL, ANTHONY	COSTUME DESIGNER	10 THE GLEBE #2	LONDON SE3 9TG	ENGLAND
POWELL, BARBARA	TV DIRECTOR	12070 MOUND VIEW PL	STUDIO CITY, CA	91604
POWELL, BOOG	BASEBALL	U S ANGLERS MARINE	KEY WEST, FL	33040
POWELL, BRADLEY R	COMPOSER	POST OFFICE BOX 8891	UNIVERSAL CITY, CA	91608
POWELL, DONALD L	MUSICIAN	2430 N BRAZOS AVE	HOBBS, NM	88240
POWELL, DREXEL	CARTOONIST	215 S MC DOWELL ST	RALEIGH, NC	27602
POWELL, ELEANOR	FILM EXECUTIVE	10 THE GLEBE #2	LONDON SE3 9TG	ENGLAND
POWELL, FORREST	COMPOSER	1150 E 56TH ST	LOS ANGELES, CA	90011
POWELL, HARLAND W	GUITARIST	117 W CELESTE	GARLAND, TX	75041
POWELL, HELEN M	NEWS CORRESPONDENT	13025 BLUHILL RD	SILVER SPRING, MD	20906
POWELL, HOLLY	ACTRESS	223 W 14TH ST	NEW YORK, NY	10011
POWELL, HOMER	DIRECTOR	1413 N KINGSLEY DR	LOS ANGELES, CA	90029
POWELL, JANE	ACTRESS	230 W 55TH ST	NEW YORK, NY	10019
POWELL, JERRY D	SINGER	121 HAZELWOOD DR #J-74	HENDERSONVILLE, TN	37075
POWELL, JIMMY R	DOBROIST	ROUTE #3, BOX 163-A	WESTVILLE, FL	32464
POWELL, JOSEPH L, JR	NEWS CORRESPONDENT	4501 LOWELL ST, NW	WASHINGTON, DC	20016
POWELL, KATHRYN J	NEWS CORRESPONDENT	3159 18TH ST, NW	WASHINGTON, DC	20010
POWELL, LARRY	DIRECTOR	17270 DEVONSHIRE ST	NORTHRIDGE, CA	91325
POWELL, LEE	REPORTER	TIME & PEOPLE MAGAZINE		
		TIME & LIFE BUILDING		
		ROCKEFELLER CENTER	NEW YORK, NY	10020
POWELL, MAX	GUITARIST	380 HARDING PL #T-3	NASHVILLE, TN	37211
POWELL, MICHAEL	WRITER-PRODUCER	LONDON MANAGEMENT, LTD		
		235-241 REGENT ST	LONDON W1A 2JT	ENGLAND
POWELL, NORMAN S	TV EXECUTIVE	CBS-TV, 6121 SUNSET BLVD	LOS ANGELES, CA	90028
POWELL, NORMAN S	WRITER-PRODUCER	12070 MOUND VIEW PL	STUDIO CITY, CA	91604
POWELL, PETER W	CINEMATOGRAPHER	3 EVERGLADES AVE, COWPLAIN	HAMPSHIRE PO8 8NA	ENGLAND
POWELL, RANDOLPH	ACTOR	2644 HIGHLAND AVE	SANTA MONICA, CA	90405
POWELL, REGINALD G	COMPOSER	POST OFFICE BOX 1518	STUDIO CITY, CA	91604
POWELL, RICHARD M	TV WRITER	24554 MALIBU RD	MALIBU, CA	90265
POWELL, ROBERT	ACTOR	ICM, 388-396 OXFORD ST	LONDON W1	ENGLAND
POWELL, ROGER	SINGER	POST OFFICE BOX 135	BEARSVILLE, NY	12409
POWELL, ROLAND A	NEWS CORRESPONDENT	13025 BLUHILL RD	SILVER SPRING, MD	20906
POWELL, SANDI	SINGER	3198 ROYAL LN #204	DALLAS, TX	75229
POWELL, SUE	SINGER	38 MUSIC SQUARE E #300	NASHVILLE, TN	37203
POWELL, SUSAN	ACTRESS	6333 BRYN MAWR DR	LOS ANGELES, CA	90068
POWELL, SUSAN	SOPRANO	CAMI, 165 W 57TH ST	NEW YORK, NY	10019
POWELL, TERRY	SINGER	LUTZ, 5625 "O" STREET BLDG	LINCOLN, NE	68510

☆ MOVIE POSTERS
☆ LOBBY CARDS
☆ OUT-OF-PRINT BOOKS
☆ 8 x 10 PHOTOS
☆ MOVIE MAGAZINES
☆ PAPERBACK MOVIE TIE-INS

COME VISIT US IN BEAUTIFUL
DOWNTOWN BURBANK
WE ARE LOCATED IN THE HEART
OF THE MOVIE-ENTERTAINMENT
INDUSTRY. MINUTES FROM
WARNER, COLUMBIA,
DISNEY, AND UNIVERSAL!

"...ANOTHER SATISFIED CUSTOMER"

MOVIE WORLD
212 N. GOLDEN MALL
BURBANK, CA 91502
(818) 845-1563

OPEN 7 DAYS
11a.m.-6 p.m.

Name	Occupation	Address	City/State	ZIP/Country
POWELL, TOM	COMEDIAN	32500 CONCORD DR #221	MADISON HGTS, MI	48071
POWELL, TRISTRAM	TV PRODUCER	DOUGLAS RAE MANAGEMENT		
		28 CHARING CROSS RD	LONDON WC2	ENGLAND
POWELL, WILLIAM C	PHOTOJOURNALIST	6301 RIDGE DR	BETHESDA, MD	20816
POWELSON, DAVID	GUITARIST	2258 CASTLEMAN DR	NASHVILLE, TN	37215
POWELSON, MARK	GUITARIST	122 CLINE AVE	HENDERSONVILLE, TN	37075
POWELSON, RICHARD S	NEWS CORRESPONDENT	2000 S EADS ST #402	ARLINGTON, VA	22202
POWER, ALEXA	ACTRESS	10000 RIVERSIDE DR #12-14	TOLUCA LAKE, CA	91602
POWER, CHRIS	CHOREOGRAPHER	22 GREENWOOD RD		
		THAMES DITTON	SURREY	ENGLAND
POWER, EDWARD	ACTOR	19 W 44TH ST #1500	NEW YORK, NY	10036
POWER, ROMINA	ACTRESS	CELLINO SAN MARCO	PROVINZ BRINDISE	ITALY
POWER, TARYN	ACTRESS	9255 SUNSET BLVD #510	LOS ANGELES, CA	90069
POWER, UDANA	ACTRESS	838 N DOHENY DR #1402	LOS ANGELES, CA	90069
POWER PLAY	RHYTHM & BLUES GROUP	POST OFFICE BOX 11283	RICHMOND, VA	23230
POWERPLAY	ROCK & ROLL GROUP	BROTHERS, 141 DUNBAR AVE	FORDS, NJ	08863
POWERS, ALEX	ACTOR	5330 LANKERSHIM BLVD #210	NORTH HOLLYWOOD, CA	91601
POWERS, ALFRED	ACTOR	8230 BEVERLY BLVD #23	LOS ANGELES, CA	90048
POWERS, BILLY	GUITARIST	ROUTE #3, BOX 280	DICKSON, TN	37055
POWERS, CAROL T	PHOTOGRAPHER	1024 MASSACHUSETTS AVE #9, NE	WASHINGTON, DC	20002
POWERS, GEORGE A, JR	DIRECTOR	DGA, 7950 SUNSET BLVD	LOS ANGELES, CA	90046
POWERS, JERRY	SINGER-SONGWRITER	POST OFFICE BOX 1058	LA MESA, CA	92044
POWERS, JULIE	NEWS CORRESPONDENT	1811 KEY BLVD	ARLINGTON, VA	22201
POWERS, KATHERINE	DIRECTOR	DGA, 110 W 57TH ST	NEW YORK, NY	10019
POWERS, MALA	ACTRESS	MILLER, 4317 FORMAN AVE	NORTH HOLLYWOOD, CA	91602
POWERS, MARTHA C	NEWS CORRESPONDENT	2805 SAINT PAUL ST	BALTIMORE, MD	21218
POWERS, RAY	ACTOR	2100 N BEACHWOOD DR #307	LOS ANGELES, CA	90068
POWERS, RON	MEDIA CRITIC	GELLER MGMT, 250 W 57TH ST	NEW YORK, NY	10019
POWERS, SALLY	CASTING DIRECTOR	POST OFFICE BOX 5718	SHERMAN OAKS, CA	91403
POWERS, STEFANIE	ACTRESS	2661 HUTTON DR	BEVERLY HILLS, CA	90210
POWERS, UDANA	ACTRESS	12725 VENTURA BLVD #E	STUDIO CITY, CA	91604
POYNER, JIM	ACTOR	DMI, 250 W 57TH ST	NEW YORK, NY	10019
POZEN, PAT	COMPOSER	133 S CROFT AVE #9	LOS ANGELES, CA	90048
PRAED, MICHAEL	ACTOR	LONDON MANAGEMENT, LTD		
		235-241 REGENT ST	LONDON W1A 2JT	ENGLAND
PRAGER, KARSTEN	WRITER-EDITOR	TIME/TIME & LIFE BLDG		
		ROCKEFELLER CENTER	NEW YORK, NY	10020
PRAIRIE FIRE	C & W GROUP	OME, 233 W WOODLAND AVE	OTTUMWA, IA	52501
PRAISER, IAN R	SCREENWRITER	5020 TILDEN AVE #C	SHERMAN OAKS, CA	91423
PRALGO, MEL	ACTOR	FARRELL, 10500 MAGNOLIA BLVD	NORTH HOLLYWOOD, CA	91601
PRAML, JOE	ACTOR	8350 SANTA MONICA BLVD #103	LOS ANGELES, CA	90069
PRANGE, LAURIE	ACTRESS	3468 OAK GLEN DR #15	HOLLYWOOD, CA	90068
PRATHER, DAVID B	ACTOR	1002 N LARRABEE ST	LOS ANGELES, CA	90069
PRATHER, JOAN	ACTRESS	26033 W MULHOLLAND HWY	CALABASAS, CA	91302
PRATT, CHARLES A, JR	FILM EXECUTIVE	15725 WOODVALE RD	ENCINO, CA	91436
PRATT, DANNY P	ACCORDIONIST	SEE - WALLABY JACK		
PRATT, DEBORAH	ACTRESS	5065 ENCINO AVE	ENCINO, CA	91316
PRATT, DENNIS A	ACTOR	3518 W CAHUENGA BLVD #316	LOS ANGELES, CA	90068
PRATT, DENNIS M	PIANIST	302 VILLAGE GREEN DR	NASHVILLE, TN	37217
PRATT, JUDSON	ACTOR	8745 OAK PARK AVE	NORTHRIDGE, CA	91325
PRATT, SUSAN	ACTRESS	CBS-TV, "THE GUILDING LIGHT"		
		51 W 52ND ST	NEW YORK, NY	10019
PREBBLE, SIMON	ACTOR	12 BEDFORD HOUSE, THE AVE	LONDON W4	ENGLAND
PRECHT, ROBERT	DIRECTOR	803 N LINDEN DR	BEVERLY HILLS, CA	90210
PRECIOUS	WRESTLING VALET	NATIONAL WRESTLING ALLIANCE		
		JIM CROCKETT PROMOTIONS		
		421 BRIARBEND DR	CHARLOTTE, NC	28209
PRECIOUS PAUL	WRESTLER	SEE - ELLERING, PRECIOUS PAUL		
PREECE, MICHAEL	TV DIRECTOR	12233 EVERGLADE ST	LOS ANGELES, CA	90066
PREJAN, PATRICT	ACTOR	103 RUE DU MAL JOFFRE	COLOMBE 92700	FRANCE
PRELL, JERRY	ACTOR	206 3RD AVE	VENICE, CA	90291
PRELOH, ANNE M	NEWS CORRESPONDENT	400 N CAPITOL ST, NW	WASHINGTON, DC	20001
PRELUTSKY, BURT	ACTOR-WRITER	POST OFFICE BOX 5617	BEVERLY HILLS, CA	90210
PREMINGER, MIKE	COMEDIAN-WRITER	11613 OTSEGO ST	NORTH HOLLYWOOD, CA	91601
PRENDERGAST, FRANK	DIRECTOR	8748 HOLLOWAY DR	LOS ANGELES, CA	90069
PRENDERGAST, GERARD	ACTOR	209 COPA DE ORO RD	LOS ANGELES, CA	90077
PRENDERGAST, JAMES	GUITARIST	2709 W LINDEN AVE	NASHVILLE, TN	37212
PRENSKY, YARON	VIOLINIST	484 BRENTLAWN DR	NASHVILLE, TN	37220
PRENTICE, JOHN	CARTOONIST	KING FEATURES SYNDICATE		
		235 E 45TH ST	NEW YORK, NY	10017
PRENTISS, ANN	ACTRESS	719 N FOOTHILL RD	BEVERLY HILLS, CA	90210
PRENTISS, ED	ACTOR	267 TOYOPA DR	PACIFIC PALISADES, CA	90272
PRENTISS, PAULA	ACTRESS	BENJAMIN, 719 N FOOTHILL RD	BEVERLY HILLS, CA	90210
PRENTNIEKS, ERIK P	PHOTOGRAPHER	4408 BURLINGTON PL	WASHINGTON, DC	20016
PRESBY, SHANNON	ACTOR	1901 AVE OF THE STARS #840	LOS ANGELES, CA	90067
PRESCOTT, ELEANOR	TV PRODUCER	ABC-TV, "20/20", 7 W 66TH ST	NEW YORK, NY	10023
PRESLE, MICHELINE	ACTRESS	S VATINET, 41 RUE DU TEMPLE	PARIS 75004	FRANCE
PRESLEY, LISA MARIE	ACTRESS	1167 SUMMIT DR	BEVERLY HILLS, CA	90210
PRESLEY, MARK	PERCUSSIONIST	830 GLASTONBURY RD #521	NASHVILLE, TN	37217
PRESLEY, PRISCILLA BEAULIEU	ACTRESS-MODEL	1167 SUMMIT DR	BEVERLY HILLS, CA	90210
PRESLEY, VESPER	ELVIS'S DAD	3764 ELVIS PRESLEY BLVD	MEMPHIS, TN	38116
PRESS, LINDA	SINGER	POST OFFICE 1764	LAKE ARROWHEAD, CA	92352

Name	Occupation	Address	City	Zip/Country
PRESSBURGER, FRED	DIRECTOR	SPECTRA, 140 W 57TH ST	NEW YORK, NY	10025
PRESSLER, MENAHEM	PIANIST	KAPLAN, 115 COLLEGE ST	BURLINGTON, VT	05401
PRESSMAN, DAVID	DIRECTOR	333 CENTRAL PARK W	NEW YORK, NY	10025
PRESSMAN, EDWARD R	FILM PRODUCER	4000 WARNER BLVD	BURBANK, CA	91522
PRESSMAN, LAWRENCE	ACTOR	15033 ENCANTO DR	SHERMAN OAKS, CA	91403
PRESSMAN, MICHAEL	FILM WRITER-DIRECTOR	8635 LOOKOUT MOUNTAIN AVE	LOS ANGELES, CA	90046
PRESSMAN, STEVEN	NEWS CORRESPONDENT	1897 INGLESIDE TERR, NW	WASHINGTON, DC	20015
PRESSON, JASON	ACTOR	3800 BARHAM BLVD #303	LOS ANGELES, CA	90068
PRESTIA, SHIRLEY	ACTRESS	LIGHT, 113 N ROBERTSON BLVD	LOS ANGELES, CA	90048
PRESTON, BILLY	SINGER-SONGWRITER	1680 N VINE ST #214	HOLLYWOOD, CA	90028
PRESTON, J A	ACTOR	211 S BEVERLY DR #201	BEVERLY HILLS, CA	90212
PRESTON, JAMES LEONARD	PHOTOGRAPHER	14462 E WAGONTRAIL DR	AURORA, CO	80014
PRESTON, KELLY	ACTRESS	10390 SANTA MONICA BLVD #310	LOS ANGELES, CA	90025
PRESTON, MARILYN	TV CRITIC	THE CHICAGO TRIBUNE		
		TRIBUNE TOWER		
		435 N MICHIGAN AVE	CHICAGO, IL	60611
PRESTON, RICHARD L	NEWS CORRESPONDENT	1755 S JEFFERSON DAVIS HWY	ARLINGTON, VA	22202
PRESTON, WAYDE	ACTOR	POST OFFICE BOX 8713	UNIVERSAL CITY, CA	91608
PRESTON, WILLIAM	ACTOR	219 E 32ND ST #3-D	NEW YORK, NY	10016
PRETENDERS, THE	ROCK & ROLL GROUP	CHEVAL MUSIC LIMITED		
PRETENDERS, THE	ROCK & ROLL GROUP	5 DEAN ST, 3RD FLOOR	LONDON W1T 5RN	ENGLAND
PRETO, MARTIN	SINGER-GUITARIST	17634 COKE AVE	BELLFLOWER, CA	90706
PRETTY BOY	WRESTLER	SEE - SOMERS, DOUG		
		"PRETTY BOY"		
PRETTYBOY	ROCK & ROLL TRIO	POST OFFICE BOX 197	ROSEDALE, NY	11422
PREUCIL, WILLIAM	VIOLINIST	2109 HERITAGE DR, NE	ATLANTA, GA	30345
PREUSS, GORDON A	TV DIRECTOR	WLS-TV, 190 N STATE ST	CHICAGO, IL	60601
PREVIEW	ROCK & ROLL GROUP	3 E 54TH ST #1400	NEW YORK, NY	10022
PREVIN, ANDRE	COMPOSER-CONDUCTOR	304 S BEDFORD DR	BEVERLY HILLS, CA	90212
PREVIN, DORY	COMPOSER-SINGER	BAKER, 2533 ZORADA DR	LOS ANGELES, CA	90046
PREVIN, STEVE	DIRECTOR	10960 WILSHIRE BLVD #922	LOS ANGELES, CA	90024
PREVIN, STEVE	FILM EXECUTIVE	487 S HAMEL RD	LOS ANGELES, CA	90048
PREVITO, DOUG	GUITARIST	3720 CHARLOTTE ST	MOBILE, AL	36605
PREVOST, FRANCOIS	ACTOR	5 RUE BREZIN	PARIS 75014	FRANCE
PREVOT, SUSAN	NEWS CORRESPONDENT	1629 "K" ST, NW	WASHINGTON, DC	20006
PREWITT, MELISSA	SINGER	LIMELITERS, 50 MUSIC SQUARE W	NASHVILLE, TN	37212
PREY, HERMANN	BARITONE	SHAW CONCERTS, 1995 BROADWAY	NEW YORK, NY	10023
PREZIA, BENITO	ACTOR	1315 N JUNE ST #205	LOS ANGELES, CA	90028
PRIAULX, ROBERT	DIRECTOR	90 E CHESTER RD	NEW ROCHELLE, NY	10801
PRICE, ALAN	SINGER-SONGWRITER	CROMWELL MANAGEMENT AGENCY		
		THE COACH HOUSE		
		9A THE BROADWAY		
		HUNTINGDON	CAMBS PE17 4BX	ENGLAND
PRICE, BILLY & THE KEYSTONE RHY	RHYTHM & BLUES GROUP	CORNERSTONE MANAGEMENT		
		23 E LANCASTER AVE	ARDMORE, PA	19003
PRICE, BRYAN	ACTOR	3575 W CAHUENGA BLVD #320	LOS ANGELES, CA	90068
PRICE, CHRIS	PIANIST	POST OFFICE BOX 101	FOSS, OK	73647
PRICE, DAN	GUITARIST	POST OFFICE BOX 101	FOSS, OK	73647
PRICE, DARIA	SCREENWRITER	555 W 57TH ST #1230	NEW YORK, NY	10019
PRICE, DEBORAH JANE	NEWS CORRESPONDENT	8814 RIDGE RD	BETHESDA, MD	20817
PRICE, DENISE	SINGER	POST OFFICE BOX 17087	NASHVILLE, TN	37217
PRICE, E HOFFMAN	WRITER	POST OFFICE BOX 406	REDWOOD CITY, CA	94604
PRICE, ERICK	PERCUSSIONIST	POST OFFICE BOX 101	FOSS, OK	73647
PRICE, EUGENE	TV WRITER	8955 BEVERLY BLVD	LOS ANGELES, CA	90048
PRICE, GERI LYNN	ACTRESS	10701 RANCH RD	CULVER CITY, CA	90230
PRICE, HENRY	TENOR	1776 BROADWAY #504	NEW YORK, NY	10019
PRICE, ISABEL	ACTRESS	230 CENTRAL PARK S	NEW YORK, NY	10019
PRICE, JANELLE	ACTRESS	CONTEMPORARY ARTISTS		
		132 S LASKY DR	BEVERLY HILLS, CA	90212
PRICE, JEFFREY L	SCREENWRITER	8955 BEVERLY BLVD	LOS ANGELES, CA	90048
PRICE, JOEL	GUITARIST	ROUTE #1	LAVONIA, GA	30553
PRICE, JUDY	TV EXECUTIVE	CBS-TV, 7800 BEVERLY BLVD	LOS ANGELES, CA	90036
PRICE, KENNY	SINGER-SONGWRITER	19 LA CRESTA DR	FLORENCE, KY	41042
PRICE, LEONTYNE	SOPRANO	CAMI, 165 W 57TH ST	NEW YORK, NY	10019
PRICE, LLOYD	SINGER	MARS, 185 CLINTON AVE	STATEN ISLAND, NY	10301
PRICE, LORIN E	THEATER PRODUCER	1501 BROADWAY	NEW YORK, NY	10036
PRICE, MARGARET	SOPRANO	BAYERISCHE STAATSOPER MUNCHEN		
		MAX JOSEF PLATZ 2	8000 MUNICH 22	WEST GERMANY
PRICE, MIKE H	FILM CRITIC	POST OFFICE BOX 1870	FORT WORTH, TX	76101
PRICE, PATRICIAN	ACTRESS	3205 LOS FELIZ BLVD #6-110	LOS ANGELES, CA	90039
PRICE, PAUL B	TV WRITER	8955 BEVERLY BLVD	LOS ANGELES, CA	90048
PRICE, PENNY	BODYBUILDER	POST OFFICE BOX 1490		
		RADIO CITY STATION	NEW YORK, NY	10101
PRICE, PERRY	TENOR	45 W 60TH ST #4-K	NEW YORK, NY	10023
PRICE, RAY	SINGER	POST OFFICE BOX 1986	MOUNT PLEASANT, TX	75230
PRICE, RAYMOND	JOURNALIST-COLUMNIST	N Y TIMES SYNDICATION		
		130 5TH AVE	NEW YORK, NY	10011
PRICE, REGI	PIANIST	POST OFFICE BOX 101	FOSS, OK	73647
PRICE, REYNOLDS	TV WRITER	555 W 57TH ST #1230	NEW YORK, NY	10019
PRICE, RICHARD S	FILM EXECUTIVE	SEYMOUR MEWS HOUSE		
		SEYMOUR MEWS		
		WIGMORE ST	LONDON W1	ENGLAND
PRICE, RICK	SINGER	JP, 600 NEVAN RD	VIRGINIA BEACH, VA	23451
PRICE, RON	GUITARIST	POST OFFICE BOX 101	FOSS, OK	73647
PRICE, SAMANTHA	ACTRESS	4624 TOBIAS AVE	SHERMAN OAKS, CA	91403

Name	Occupation	Address	City / ZIP
PRICE, SARI	ACTRESS	8721 SUNSET BLVD #103	LOS ANGELES, CA 90069
PRICE, STANLEY	SCREENWRITER	17 CRANLEY GARDENS	LONDON N6 ENGLAND
PRICE, STEVEN A	NEWS CORRESPONDENT	1624 27TH ST #204, SE	WASHINGTON, DC 20020
PRICE, TIM ROSE	TV WRITER	LONDON MANAGEMENT, LTD	
		235-241 REGENT ST	LONDON W1A 2JT ENGLAND
PRICE, TOM	NEWS CORRESPONDENT	5204 41ST ST, NW	WASHINGTON, DC 20015
PRICE, VINCENT	ACTOR	9255 SWALLOW DR	LOS ANGELES, CA 90069
PRICE SISTERS, THE	VOCAL DUO	MBA, 8914 GEORGIAN DR	AUSTIN, TX 78753
PRICEMAN, GEORGE	ACTOR	6968 DUME DR	MALIBU, CA 90265
PRICHARD, PETER	EDITORIAL DIRECTOR	POST OFFICE BOX 500	WASHINGTON, DC 20044
PRICOPIE, SORIN S	ACTOR	517 HIGHLAND AVE	MANHATTAN BEACH, CA 90266
PRIDDY, NANCY	ACTRESS	6736 LAUREL CANYON BLVD #306	NORTH HOLLYWOOD, CA 91606
PRIDE, CHARLEY	SINGER	3198 ROYAL LN #204	DALLAS, TX 75229
PRIDEAUX, JAMES	TV WRITER	840 N LARRABEE ST #4-123	LOS ANGELES, CA 90069
PRIDESMEN, THE	C & W GROUP	3198 ROYAL LN #204	DALLAS, TX 75229
PRIDONOFF, EUGENE & ELIZABETH	PIANO DUO	AIA, 60 E 42ND ST	NEW YORK, NY 10165
PRIEST, DAN	ACTOR-WRITER	8618 AQUEDUCT AVE	SEPULVEDA, CA 91343
PRIEST, NATALIE	ACTRESS	27 W 96TH ST	NEW YORK, NY 10025
PRIEST, ROBERT	ART DIRECTOR	US MAGAZINE COMPANY	
		1 DAG HAMMARSKJOLD PLAZA	NEW YORK, NY 10017
PRIEST, ROBERT M	DIRECTOR	5937 HILLVIEW PARK AVE	VAN NUYS, CA 91401
PRIESTLEY, THOMAS A	DIRECTOR	DGA, 110 W 57TH ST	NEW YORK, NY 10019
PRIETO, CARLOS	CELLIST	GURTMAN, 162 W 56TH ST	NEW YORK, NY 10019
PRIM, GARY	PIANIST	520 MOSS LANDING DR	ANTIOCH, TN 37013
PRIME TIME	VOCAL GROUP	TOTAL EXPERIENCE RECORDS	
		1800 N ARGYLE AVE	HOLLYWOOD, CA 90028
PRIME TYME	ROCK & ROLL GROUP	POST OFFICE BOX 448	RADFORD, VA 24141
PRIMUS, BARRY	ACTOR-DIRECTOR	2526 VASANTA WY	HOLLYWOOD, CA 90068
PRINA, L EDGAR	NEWS CORRESPONDENT	4813 QUEBEC ST, NW	WASHINGTON, DC 20016
PRINCE	SING-SONGWRI-ACT-DIR	11355 W OLMMPIC BLVD #555	LOS ANGELES, CA 90064
PRINCE, BRUCE	PIANIST	57 CHOWNING SQ	NASHVILLE, TN 37205
PRINCE, FAITH	ACTRESS	9220 SUNSET BLVD #202	LOS ANGELES, CA 90069
PRINCE, HAROLD S	DIRECTOR-PRODUCER	1270 AVE OF THE AMERICAS	NEW YORK, NY 10020
PRINCE, JOHN H	COMPOSER-CONDUCTOR	2050 VOLK AVE	LONG BEACH, CA 90815
PRINCE, JONATHAN	ACTOR	151 S EL CAMINO DR	BEVERLY HILLS, CA 90212
PRINCE, MICHAEL	ACTOR	9220 SUNSET BLVD #202	LOS ANGELES, CA 90069
PRINCE, PAM	TALENT AGENT	151 S EL CAMINO DR	BEVERLY HILLS, CA 90212
PRINCE, ROBERT H	COMPOSER-CONDUCTOR	2246 MANDEVILLE CANYON RD	LOS ANGELES, CA 90049
PRINCE, TOM	GUITARIST	601 N DUPONT AVE #C-51	MADISON, TN 37115
PRINCE, WILLIAM	ACTOR	9061 KEITH AVE #305	LOS ANGELES, CA 90069
PRINCE, WINTHROP	CARTOONIST	THE CHRONICLE FEATURES	
		870 MARKET ST	SAN FRANCISCO, CA 94102
PRINCE & THE REVOLUTION	ROCK & ROLL GROUP	11355 W OLYMPIC BLVD #555	LOS ANGELES, CA 90064
PRINCI, ELAINE	ACTRESS	4906 LEDGE AVE	NORTH HOLLYWOOD, CA 91601
PRINCIPAL, VICTORIA	ACTRESS-AUTHORESS	9755 OAK PASS RD	BEVERLY HILLS, CA 90210
PRINCZ, GARY	DIRECTOR	4 SPUR DR	NANUET, NY 10954
PRINDLE, KAREN	TV DIRECTOR	629 W FULLERTON PARKWAY	CHICAGO, IL 60614
PRINE, ANDREW	ACTOR	3264 LONGRIDGE AVE	SHERMAN OAKS, CA 91423
PRINE, JOHN	SINGER-SONGWRITER	4121 WILSHIRE BLVD #215	LOS ANGELES, CA 90010
PRING, ROBERT E	COMPOSER	230 W 54TH ST #511	NEW YORK, NY 10019
PRINGEL, PERCY	WRESTLING MANAGER	WORLD CLASS WRESTLING	
		SOUTHWEST SPORTS, INC	
		DALLAS SPORTATORIUM	
		1000 S INDUSTRIAL BLVD	DALLAS, TX 75207
PRINGLE, AILEEN	ACTRESS	300 E 57TH ST	NEW YORK, NY 10022
PRINGLE, BRYAN	ACTOR	PLANT & FROGGATT, LTD	
		JULIAN HOUSE	
		WINDMILL ST	LONDON W1 ENGLAND
PRINGLE, JOAN	ACTRESS	23938 HAMLIN ST	CANOGA PARK, CA 91307
PRINGLE, PETER J	NEWS CORRESPONDENT	4221 ARGYLE TERR, NW	WASHINGTON, DC 20011
PRINGLE, RENEE M	NEWS CORRESPONDENT	2025 "M" ST, NW	WASHINGTON, DC 20036
PRIOR, ALLAN	NOVELIST	MAX NAUGHTON LOWE	
		200 FULHAM RD	LONDON SW10 9PN ENGLAND
PRIOR, BENIAMINO	TENOR	CAMI, 165 W 57TH ST	NEW YORK, NY 10019
PRIOR, PENNY	ACTRESS	10000 RIVERSIDE DR #12-14	TOLUCA LAKE, CA 91602
PRISM	ROCK & ROLL GROUP	68 WATER ST #406	VANCOUVER, BC V6B 1A4 CANADA
PRISONER	MUSICAL GROUP	2130 E CRAWFORD ST #309	SALINA, KS 67401
PRISONERS, THE	ROCK & ROLL GROUP	BIG BEAT RECORDS CO	
		134 GRAFTON RD	
		KENTISH TOWN	LONDON NW5 4BA ENGLAND
PRITCHARD, WILLIAM ROSE	NEWS CORRESPONDENT	5521 4TH ST S	ARLINGTON, VA 22204
PRITCHETT, JAMES	ACTOR	53 W 74TH ST	NEW YORK, NY 10023
PRITCHETT, JIM	GUITARIST	5101 LINBAR DR #J-301	NASHVILLE, TN 37211
PRITCHETT, RODNEY	TROMBONIST	6333 MONTPELIER RD	CHARLOTTE, NC 28210
PRITCHETT, TONY	SINGER-SONGWRITER	POST OFFICE BOX 110423	NASHVILLE, TN 37211
PRITIKIN, CAROL	ACTRESS	151 S EL CAMINO DR	BEVERLY HILLS, CA 90212
PRITZKER, STEVEN	TV WRITER-PRODUCER	8071 WOODROW WILSON DR	LOS ANGELES, CA 90046
PRIVATE LIGHTING	ROCK & ROLL GROUP	FRED HELLER ENTERPRISES	
		1756 BROADWAY	NEW YORK, NY 10019
PRIVITELLI, GREGORY	ACTOR	1413 OCEAN PARK BLVD #4	SANTA MONICA, CA 90405
PRO ARTE QUARTET	STRING QUARTET	LEISER, DORCHESTER TOWERS	
		155 W 68TH ST	NEW YORK, NY 10023
PROCESS AND THE DOO RAGS	VOCAL GROUP	COLUMBIA RECORDS CO	
		51 W 52ND ST	NEW YORK, NY 10019
PROCTOR, MARLAND	ACTOR	11548 MAGNOLIA BLVD #112	NORTH HOLLYWOOD, CA 91601

PRINCE

VICTORIA PRINCIPAL

DOROTHY PROVINE

RICHARD PRYOR

SARAH PURCELL

LINDA PURL

DENVER PYLE

DENNIS QUAID

ANTHONY QUINN

Name	Occupation	Address	City	Zip/Country
PROCTOR, PHILIP	ACTOR-WRITER	9824 WANDA PARK DR	BEVERLY HILLS, CA	90210
PRODIGAL	ROCK & ROLL GROUP	POST OFFICE BOX 1254	MOUNT DORA, FL	32757
PROFFITT, DONALD	ACTOR	POST OFFICE BOX 141	RESCUE, CA	95672
PROFT, PATRICK	TV WRITER	841 BIENVENEDA AVE	PACIFIC PALISADES, CA	90272
PROKOP, JAN	SOPRANO	LEW, 204 W 10TH ST	NEW YORK, NY	10014
PRONZINI, BILL	WRITER	POST OFFICE BOX 27368	SAN FRANCISCO, CA	94127
PROPHET, MELISSA	ACTRESS	3907 W ALAMEDA AVE #101	BURBANK, CA	91505
PROPHET, RONNIE	SINGER-SONGWRITER	1227 SAXON DR	NASHVILLE, TN	37215
PROPHET, TONY	SINGER	1227 SAXON DR	NASHVILLE, TN	37215
PROPS, BABETTE	ACTRESS	3800 BARHAM BLVD #303	LOS ANGELES, CA	90068
PROPST, JOHN	PIANIST	211 CLIFFDALE RD	NASHVILLE, TN	37214
PROSER, CHIP	SCREENWRITER	9255 SUNSET BLVD #1122	LOS ANGELES, CA	90069
PROSER, MICHAEL	PHOTOGRAPHER	5325 TUSCARAWAS RD	BETHESDA, MD	20816
PROSKY, ROBERT	ACTOR	SF & A, 121 N SAN VICENTE BLVD	BEVERLY HILLS, CA	90211
PROVAL, DAVID	ACTOR	10000 SANTA MONICA BLVD #305	LOS ANGELES, CA	90067
PROVENCE, DENIS	ACTOR	57 AVE PAUL DOUMER	PARIS 75016	FRANCE
PROVENZA, PAUL	ACTOR	22 NAVY ST #303	VENICE, CA	90291
PROWSE, DAVE	ACTOR	7 CARLYLE RD	CROYDON CRO 7HN	ENGLAND
PROWSE, JOHN	TV DIRECTOR	FRITH COTTAGE, PAINSWICK	GLOS	ENGLAND
PROWSE, JULIET	ACTRESS-DANCER	MC COOK, 343 S BEVERLY GLEN BL	LOS ANGELES, CA	90046
PRUDEN, JAMES WESLEY, JR	NEWS CORRESPONDENT	2070 BELMONT RD, NW	WASHINGTON, DC	20009
PRUDHOMME, PAUL	CHEF-AUTHOR	406 CHARTES ST #2	NEW ORLEANS, LA	70130
PRUEITT, GERALD	WRITER-PRODUCER	50 E 42ND ST	NEW YORK, NY	10017
PRUETT, ELIZABETH	SOPRANO	119 W 57TH ST #1505	NEW YORK, NY	10019
PRUETT, JACK H, JR	GUITARIST	397 BONNAVALE DR	HERMITAGE, TN	37076
PRUETT, JACK HOUSTON, SR	GUITARIST	397 BONNAVALE DR	HERMITAGE, TN	37076
PRUETT, JEANNE	SINGER	1300 DIVISION ST #102	NASHVILLE, TN	37203
PRUETT, SAM	GUITARIST	5103 WILLIAMSBURG RD	BRENTWOOD, TN	37027
PRYDE, JOAN A	NEWS CORRESPONDENT	3945 CONNECTICUT AVE, NW	WASHINGTON, DC	20008
PRYOR, AINSLIE	ACTRESS	3634 DIXIE CYN PL	SHERMAN OAKS, CA	91423
PRYOR, JAMES	GUITARIST	729 MORTON AVE	MARTINSVILLE, IN	46151
PRYOR, NICHOLAS	ACTOR	ICM, 8899 BEVERLY BLVD	LOS ANGELES, CA	90048
PRYOR, RAY	GUITARIST	285 WILLAMONT AVE	GALLATIN, TN	37066
PRYOR, RICHARD	ACTOR-COMEDIAN	17267 PARTHENIA ST	NORTHRIDGE, CA	91324
PRYOR, THOMAS M	NEWS EDITOR	VARIETY, 1400 N CAHUENGA BLVD	HOLLYWOOD, CA	90028
PRYSOCK, ARTHUR	SINGER	D PALMER, 211 W 53RD ST	NEW YORK, NY	10019
PRYTHERCH, ERIC	TV DIRECTOR-PRODUCER	GRANADA TV CENTRE	MANCHESTER M60 9EA	ENGLAND
PSALTERY, THE	FOLK DUO	FROTHINGHAM, 40 GROVE ST	WESSESLEY, MA	02181
PSANOS, MIKE	DRUMMER	712 LEMONT DR	NASHVILLE, TN	37216
PSYCHEDELIC FURS, THE	ROCK & ROLL GROUP	AMANITA, 1 CATHEDRAL ST	LONDON SE1	ENGLAND
PUBLIC IMAGE, LTD	ROCK & ROLL GROUP	ICM, 40 W 57TH ST	NEW YORK, NY	10019
PUCKETT, DWIGHT	DRUMMER	ROUTE #3, B-312	MT JULIET, TN	37122
PUCKETT, GARY	SINGER-SONGWRITER	7817 BACKER RD	SAN DIEGO, CA	92126
PUCKETT, ROLLAND	PIANIST	300 KATE ST	MADISON, TN	37115
PUDNEY, GARY LAURENCE	TV EXEC-CAST DIR	ABC-TV ENTERTAINMENT CENTER		
		2040 AVE OF THE STARS	LOS ANGELES, CA	90067
PUENTE, TITO & LATIN/JAZZ SEXTE	JAZZ SEXTET	200 W 51ST ST #1410	NEW YORK, NY	10019
PUERTAS, JOSE ANTONIO	NEWS CORRESPONDENT	6715 GREYSWOOD RD	BETHESDA, MD	20817
PUETT, BILLY	FLUTIST	2001 BLAIR BLVD	NASHVILLE, TN	37212
PUGH, WILLARD E	ACTOR	9220 SUNSET BLVD #202	LOS ANGELES, CA	90069
PUGLISI, ROBERT	ACTOR	8570 WONDERLAND AVE	LOS ANGELES, CA	90046
PUKKA ORCHESTRA	ROCK & ROLL GROUP	41 BRITAIN ST #200	TORONTO, ONT	CANADA
PULICE, SHAR	ACTRESS	2624 LETICIA DR	HACIENDA HEIGHTS, CA	91745
PULLEN, DON	FLUTIST	705 LEDFORD DR	NASHVILLE, TN	37207
PULLEN, DON & GEORGE ADAMS	JAZZ DUO	BRIDGE, 106 FORT GREENE PL	BROOKLYN, NY	11217
PULLEN, DON, QUARTET	JAZZ QUARTET	POST OFFICE BOX 201	WAGENINGEN	HOLLAND
PULTZ, ALAN	TV DIRECTOR	3583 WOODCLIFF RD	SHERMAN OAKS, CA	91403
PULVER, LISELOTTE	ACTRESS	VILLA BIP	PERROY KANTON VAUDOIS	SWITZERLAND
PULZ, DONALD E	NEWS CORRESPONDENT	340 NATIONAL PRESS BLDG		
		529 14TH ST, NW	WASHINGTON, DC	20045
PUMPIAN, PAUL	TV WRITER	10711 WHEATLAND AVE	SUNLAND, CA	91040
PUNSLEY, BERNARD	ACTOR	1415 GRANVIA ALTAMIRA	PALOS VERDES, CA	90274
PUOPOLO, LOUIS A	DIRECTOR	381 PARK AVE S	NEW YORK, NY	10016
PURBAUGH, MARVIN W	PHOTOJOURNALIST	1708 CODY DR	SILVER SPRING, MD	20902
PURCELL, ERIC	ACTOR	SHERMAN, 348 S REXFORD DR	BEVERLY HILLS, CA	90212
PURCELL, EVELYN	FILM DIRECTOR	1355 MILLER PL	LOS ANGELES, CA	90069
PURCELL, JAMES	ACTOR	4324 FINLEY AVE	LOS ANGELES, CA	90027
PURCELL, JOSEPH	TV DIRECTOR	1760 HILLCREST AVE	GLENDALE, CA	91202
PURCELL, LEE	ACTRESS	9220 SUNSET BLVD #625	LOS ANGELES, CA	90069
PURCELL, ROSEMARY	NEWS CORRESPONDENT	6449 ROCKSHIRE ST	ALEXANDRIA, VA	22310
PURCELL, SARAH	ACTRESS	ICM, 8899 BEVERLY BLVD	LOS ANGELES, CA	90048
PURCELL STRING QUARTET	STRING QUARTET	333 TAYLOR AVE N #202	SEATTLE, WA	98109
PURCILL, KAREN	ACTRESS	6736 LAUREL CANYON BLVD #306	NORTH HOLLYWOOD, CA	91606
PURDEE, NATHAN	ACTOR	1776 N SYCAMORE AVE #110	HOLLYWOOD, CA	90028
PURDHAM, DAVID	ACTOR	ABC-TV, "ALL MY CHILDREN"		
		1330 AVE OF THE AMERICAS	NEW YORK, NY	10019
PURDUM, E J	TV WRITER	8955 BEVERLY BLVD	LOS ANGELES, CA	90048
PURDUM, HERBERT R	TV WRITER	1301 N SPARKS ST	BURBANK, CA	91506
PURDY, DONALD A, JR	NEWS CORRESPONDENT	1224 N MEADE ST	ARLINGTON, VA	22209
PURE PRAIRIE LEAGUE	ROCK & ROLL GROUP	VARIETY ARTISTS INTL, INC		
		9073 NEMO ST, 3RD FLOOR	LOS ANGELES, CA	90069
PURGASON, HOWARD	ACTOR	6605 HOLLYWOOD BLVD #220	HOLLYWOOD, CA	90028
PURIM, FLORA	SINGER	SEE - AIRTO & FLORA PURIM		
PURL, LINDA	ACTRESS	9540 LANIA LN	BEVERLY HILLS, CA	90212
PURPLE THINGS, THE	ROCK & ROLL GROUP	36 HANWAY ST	LONDON W1	ENGLAND

Name	Occupation	Address	City / Country	Zip
PURPUS, TIMOTHY	WRITER	POST OFFICE BOX 432	HERMOSA BEACH, CA	90254
PURSE, WILLIAM E	COMPOSER-CONDUCTOR	5531 PATTILAR AVE	WOODLAND HILLS, CA	91367
PURSELL, TERRY & SUSAN WRIGHT	VOCAL DUO	GOOD, 2500 NW 39TH ST	OKLAHOMA CITY, OK	73112
PURSELL, WILLIAM W	MUSIC ARRANGER	895 S CURTISWOOD LN	NASHVILLE, TN	37204
PURSER, DOROTHY ANN	TV WRITER	ABC-TV, "ONE LIFE TO LIVE"		
		1330 AVE OF THE AMERICAS	NEW YORK, NY	10019
PURVES, PETER	ACTOR	ARLINGTON, 1 CHARLOTTE ST	LONDON W1	ENGLAND
PUSH COMES TO SHOVE	ROCK & ROLL GROUP	25 HUNTINGTON AVE #420	BOSTON, MA	02116
PUSH PUSH	ROCK & ROLL GROUP	25 HUNTINGTON AVE #420	BOSTON, MA	02116
PUSHMAN, TERENCE	ACTOR	8261 W NORTON AVE #6	LOS ANGELES, CA	90046
PUTCH, JOHN P	ACTOR	1714 STONER AVE	LOS ANGELES, CA	90025
PUTCH, PAMELA	ACTRESS	9220 SUNSET BLVD #202	LOS ANGELES, CA	90069
PUTMAN, FRED	TV WRITER	8955 BEVERLY BLVD	LOS ANGELES, CA	90048
PUTMAN, WILLIAM	TV WRITER	8955 BEVERLY BLVD	LOS ANGELES, CA	90048
PUTNAM, NORBERT	GUITARIST-PRODUCER	134 4TH AVE N	FRANKLIN, TN	37064
PUTNAM, PAT	SPORTS WRITER-EDITOR	SPORTS ILLUSTRATED MAGAZINE		
		TIME & LIFE BUILDING		
		ROCKEFELLER CENTER	NEW YORK, NY	10020
PUTTKAMER, RICHARD K	DIRECTOR	6 PEACEDALE RD	NEEDHAM, MA	02192
PUTTNAM, DAVID T	FILM PRODCUER	ENIGMA PRODUCTIONS		
		15 QUEENS GATE PL, MEWS	LONDON SW7 5BG	ENGLAND
PUTZEL, MICHAEL	NEWS CORRESPONDENT	4938 QUEBEC ST, NW	WASHINGTON, DC	20016
PUYANA, RAFAEL	HARPSICHORDIST	KAY, 58 W 58TH ST	NEW YORK, NY	10019
PUZO, MARIO	AUTHOR-SCREENWRITER	866 MANOR LN	BAY SHORE, NY	11706
PUZZO, PETER	TENOR	MUNRO, 334 W 72ND ST	NEW YORK, NY	10023
PYATT, RUDOLPH A, JR	NEWS CORRESPONDENT	403 RIVER WOOD DR	FORT WASHINGTON, MD	20744
PYE, CHRIS B	DIRECTOR	STONE, 1052 CAROL DR	LOS ANGELES, CA	90069
PYKE, HY	ACTOR	8230 BEVERLY BLVD #23	LOS ANGELES, CA	90048
PYLANT, ROY	MUSICIAN	3962 DICKERSON RD	NASHVILLE, TN	37207
PYLE, DENVER	ACT-WRI-DIR	10614 WHIPPLE ST	NORTH HOLLYWOOD, CA	91602
PYLE, PETE	GUITARIST	3230 MAYOR LN	NASHVILLE, TN	37218
PYLE, RICHARD C	TV DIRECTOR	CHEYNEY RD	CHEYNEY, PA	19319
PYNDELL, JOANNE E	NEWS CORRESPONDENT	6615 PEPIN DR	UPPER MARLBORO, MD	20772
PYNE, DANIEL J	TV WRITER	8955 BEVERLY BLVD	LOS ANGELES, CA	90048
PYNE, FREDERICK	ACTOR	LAMBETH, 22 ACOL RD	LONDON NW6	ENGLAND
PYNE, NATASHA	ACTRESS	FEAST, 43-A PRINCESS RD		
		REGENTS	LONDON NW1	ENGLAND
PYT #1	WRESTLER	SEE - WARE, KOKO B		
PYTKA, JOHN A	DIRECTOR	520 N MICHIGAN AVE #436	CHICAGO, IL	60611
PYTKA, JOSEPH	DIRECTOR	520 N MICHIGAN AVE #436	CHICAGO, IL	60611

Name	Occupation	Address	City / Country	Zip
Q, STACY	SINGER	SEE - STACY Q		
Q T HUSH	SOUL GROUP	POST OFFICE BOX 10161	DETROIT, MI	48210
QUABIUS, FAITH	ACTRESS	9165 CORDELL DR	LOS ANGELES, CA	90069
QUADLING, LEW	COMPOSER-CONDUCTOR	POST OFFICE BOX 482	LAGUNA, CA	92677
QUAID, DAVID L	DIRECTOR	POST OFFICE BOX 1617	DUXBURY, MA	02332
QUAID, DENNIS	ACTOR	POST OFFICE 5617	BEVERLY HILLS, CA	90210
QUAID, DIANE	TV DIRECTOR	17 SEAMAN AVE	NEW YORK, NY	10034
QUAID, RANDY	ACTOR	15760 VENTURA BLVD #1730	ENCINO, CA	91436
QUALEN, JOHN	ACTOR	22903 NADINE CIR #A	TORRANCE, CA	90505
QUANT, MARY	FASHION DESIGNER	3 IVES ST	LONDON SW3	ENGLAND
QUARLES, NORMA	NEWS CORRESPONDENT	NBC-TV, NEWS DEPARTMENT		
		30 ROCKEFELLER PLAZA	NEW YORK, NY	10112
QUARLES, RANDALL DEAN	NEWS CORRESPONDENT	2828 CONNECTICUT AVE #701, NW	WASHINGTON, DC	20008
QUARRY, ROBERT	ACTOR	11032 MOORPARK ST #A-3	NORTH HOLLYWOOD, CA	91602
QUART, JULIE	PUZZLES WRITER	UNIVERSAL PRESS SYNDICATE		
		4900 MAIN ST, 9TH FLOOR	KANSAS CITY, MO	62114
QUARTERFLASH	ROCK & ROLL GROUP	POST OFFICE BOX 8231	PORTLAND, OR	97207
QUASARANO, JOSEPH R	DIRECTOR	16835 BIRCHER ST	GRANADA HILLS, CA	91344
QUASSARS, THE	AERIAL ROCKETSHIP ACT	HALL, 138 FROG HOLLOW RD	CHURCHVILLE, PA	18966
QUATEMAN, BILL	SINGER	14302 COLLINS ST	VAN NUYS, CA	91401
QUATRO, SUZI	SINGER	ATI, 888 7TH AVE, 21ST FLOOR	NEW YORK, NY	10106
QUAYLE, ANNA	ACTRESS	GREEN & UNDERWOOD, LTD		
		3 THE BROADWAY		
		GUNNERSBURY LN	LONDON W3 8HR	ENGLAND
QUAYLE, ANTHONY	ACTOR	498 ELYSTAN PL	LONDON SW3 3JY	ENGLAND
QUEEN	ROCK & ROLL GROUP	46 PEMBRIDGE RD	LONDON W11 3HN	ENGLAND
QUEENSRYCHE	ROCK & ROLL GROUP	HARRIS MANAGEMENT AGENCY		
		4801 BEACH DR, SW	SEATTLE, WA	98116
QUELER, EVE	CONDUCTOR	1776 BROADWAY #504	NEW YORK, NY	10019
QUELLO, JAMES H	COMMUNICATIONS EXEC	FCC, 1919 "M" ST, NW	WASHINGTON, DC	20554
QUELYN, ANN	ACTRESS	10000 RIVERSIDE DR #12-14	TOLUCA LAKE, CA	91602
QUENNESSEN, VALERIE	ACTRESS	151 S EL CAMINO DR	BEVERLY HILLS, CA	90212
QUENTIN, CHRISTOPHER	ACTOR	PARSONAGE CT, PALATINZ RD		
		WITHINGTON, MANCHESTER	LANCSHIRE	ENGLAND
QUESADA, PETER A	CONDUCTOR	2125 COVE AVE	LOS ANGELES, CA	90026
QUEST	JAZZ GROUP	1560 BROADWAY #507	NEW YORK, NY	10036

QUESTED, JOHN	DIRECTOR-PRODUCER	BRENT WALKER MANAGEMENT		
		9 CHESTERFIELD ST	LONDON W1	ENGLAND
QUESTEL, MAE	ACTRESS	27 E 65TH ST	NEW YORK, NY	10021
QUICHE	C & W GROUP	BAR, 158 S BROADWAY	LAWRENCE, MA	01843
QUICK, DIANA	ACTRESS	39 SEYMOUR WALK	LONDON SW10	ENGLAND
QUICK, ELDON	ACTOR	2312 CHEREMOYA AVE	LOS ANGELES, CA	90068
QUICK, SARAH	MODEL	MODELS & PROMOTIONS AGENCY		
		8560 SUNSET BLVD, 10TH FLOOR	LOS ANGELES, CA	90069
QUICK, SUSAN	ACTRESS	7461 BEVERLY BLVD #400	LOS ANGELES, CA	90036
QUICK CHANCE	C & W GROUP	TESSIER, 505 CANTON PASS	MADISON, TN	37115
QUICKSILVER, ELIZABETH J	TV WRITER	9310 AIRDROME ST	LOS ANGELES, CA	90035
QUIET RIOT	ROCK & ROLL GROUP	3208 W CAHUENGA BLVD #107	LOS ANGELES, CA	90068
QUIGLEY, LINNEA	ACTRESS-MODEL	1717 N HIGHLAND AVE #414	LOS ANGELES, CA	90028
QUIGLEY, ROBERT E	ACTOR	12062 1/4 HOFFMAN ST	STUDIO CITY, CA	91604
QUILICO, GINO	BARITONE	CAMI, 165 W 57TH ST	NEW YORK, NY	10019
QUILICO, LOUIS	BARITONE	CAMI, 165 W 57TH ST	NEW YORK, NY	10019
QUILL, MICHAEL	ACTOR	408 W 46TH ST, 3RD FLOOR	NEW YORK, NY	10036
QUILLAN, EDDIE	ACTOR	12607 EMELITA ST	NORTH HOLLYWOOD, CA	91607
QUILLEY, DENIS	ACTOR-SINGER	22 WILLOW RD	LONDON NW3	ENGLAND
QUILLING, BRENDA	SOPRANO	59 E 54TH ST #81	NEW YORK, NY	10022
QUINE, RICHARD	ACTOR-DIRECTOR	DGA, 7950 SUNSET BLVD	LOS ANGELES, CA	90046
QUINETTE, RICHARD R	DIRECTOR	DGA, 110 W 57TH ST	NEW YORK, NY	10019
QUINLAN, KATHLEEN	ACTRESS	POST OFFICE BOX 2465	MALIBU, CA	90265
QUINLAN, MARY KAY	NEWS CORRESPONDENT	9675 BRASSIE WY	GAITHERSBURG, MD	20879
QUINLAN, PETER FRANCIS	SINGER	4680 ELK LAKE DR #304	VICTORIA, BC V8Z 5M1	CANADA
QUINN, AIDAN	ACTOR	POST OFFICE BOX 2149	SANTA MONICA, CA	90406
QUINN, AILEEN	ACTRESS	400 MADISON AVE #20	NEW YORK, NY	10007
QUINN, ANTHONY	ACTOR-DIRECTOR	2 E 86TH ST	NEW YORK, NY	10028
QUINN, BILL	ACTOR	9744 WILSHIRE BLVD #306	BEVERLY HILLS, CA	90212
QUINN, DIANA	NEWS CORRESPONDENT	6324 WASHINGTON BLVD	ARLINGTON, VA	22205
QUINN, EILEEN P	NEWS CORRESPONDENT	400 N CAPITOL ST, NW	WASHINGTON, DC	20001
QUINN, GARY	TV WRITER	8955 BEVERLY BLVD	LOS ANGELES, CA	90048
QUINN, GARY N	NEWS CORRESPONDENT	5151 WISCONSIN AVE, NW	WASHINGTON, DC	20016
QUINN, GLORIA J	NEWS CORRESPONDENT	1329 "E" ST, SE	WASHINGTON, DC	20003
QUINN, HENRY J	ACTOR	11 TANGLE LN	WANTAGH, NY	11793
QUINN, HOWARD	TV DIRECTOR	6703 PORTSHEAD RD	MALIBU, CA	90265
QUINN, J C	ACTOR	11726 SAN VICENTE BLVD #300	LOS ANGELES, CA	90049
QUINN, JAMES	FILM PRODUCER	108 MARINE PARADE	BRIGHTON	ENGLAND
QUINN, JANE BRYANT	COLUMNIST	NEWSWEEK, 444 MADISON AVE	NEW YORK, NY	10022
QUINN, JOHN	NEWS CORRESPONDENT	NBC NEWS, 4001 NEBRASKA AVE, NW	WASHINGTON, DC	20016
QUINN, JOHN C	NEWS EDITOR	POST OFFICE BOX 500	WASHINGTON, DC	20044
QUINN, MARTHA	VIDEO JOCKEY	POST OFFICE BOX 1370	NEW YORK, NY	10101
QUINN, MATTHEW C	NEWS CORRESPONDENT	652 E CAPITOL ST, NE	WASHINGTON, DC	20003
QUINN, MICHAEL	NEWS REPORTER	TIME/TIME & LIFE BLDG		
		ROCKEFELLER CENTER	NEW YORK, NY	10020
QUINN, PATRICK	ACTOR	10000 SANTA MONICA BLVD #305	LOS ANGELES, CA	90067
QUINN, ROBERT J	TV DIRECTOR	12152 MOORPARK ST #303	STUDIO CITY, CA	91604
QUINN, ROBERT JOSEPH	TV DIRECTOR	35 WENDT AVE	LARCHMONT, NY	10538
QUINN, ROBERT L	WRITER-PRODUCER	4731 VINELAND AVE #2-A	NORTH HOLLYWOOD, CA	91602
QUINN, SALLY	JOURNALIST	1150 15TH ST, NW	WASHINGTON, DC	20005
QUINN, STANLEY J, JR	DIRECTOR	36 CHURCH ST	NOANK, CT	06340
QUINONES, JOHN	NEWS CORRESPONDENT	ABC NEWS, 7 W 66TH ST	NEW YORK, NY	10023
QUINTERO, JOSE	DIRECTOR	LANTZ, 888 7TH AVE, 25TH FLOOR	NEW YORK, NY	10106
QUINTOS, MARISSA Y	NEWS CORRESPONDENT	400 N CAPITOL ST, NW	WASHINGTON, DC	20001
QUIRT, JOHN H	NEWS CORRESPONDENT	1529 HARWOOD LN	MC LEAN, VA	22101
QUISENBERRY, BYRON	DIRECTOR-PRODUCER	7501 ASMAN AVE	CANOGA PARK, CA	91307
QUIST, JACK	SINGER	50 MUSIC SQUARE W #905	NASHVILLE, TN	37203
QUITTMEYER, SUSAN	MEZZO-SOPRANO	COLBERT, 111 W 57TH ST	NEW YORK, NY	10019
QUIVAR, FLORENCE	MEZZO-SOPRANO	CAMI, 165 W 57TH ST	NEW YORK, NY	10019

R & B CADETS	RHYTHM & BLUES GROUP	611 BROADWAY #526	NEW YORK, NY	10012
R O A R	ROCK & ROLL GROUP	11833 LAUREL WOOD DR #8	STUDIO CITY, CA	91604
RABB, CHARLES	NEWS CORRESPONDENT	800 AZALEA DR	ROCKVILLE, MD	20850
RABB, ELLIS	DIRECTOR	20 W 64TH ST #27-R	NEW YORK, NY	10023
RABBITT, EDDIE	SINGER-SONGWRITER	SCOTTI BROS, 2128 W PICO BLVD	SANTA MONICA, CA	90405
RABE, DAVID	PLAYWRIGHT	440 W END AVE #16-B	NEW YORK, NY	10024
RABE, ERIC W	NEWS CORRESPONDENT	5151 WISCONSIN AVE, NW	WASHINGTON, DC	20016
RABEL, ED	NEWS CORRESPONDENT	CBS NEWS, 524 W 57TH ST	NEW YORK, NY	10019
RABER, PATRICIA	NEWS CORRESPONDENT	4700 CONNECTICUT AVE #304	WASHINGTON, DC	20008
RABER, RICHARD A	NEWS CORRESPONDENT	433 3RD ST, NE	WASHINGTON, DC	20002
RABIN, ALVIN	TV DIRECTOR-PRODUCER	4455 GAYLE DR	TARZANA, CA	91356
RABIN, ARTHUR	WRITER	401 S HARVARD BLVD #304	LOS ANGELES, CA	90020
RABIN, TREVOR	SINGER	330 W 58TH ST #7	NEW YORK, NY	10019
RABINOVITCH, DAVID	WRITER-PRODUCER	150 MADRONE AVE	LARKSPUR, CA	94939
RABINOVITSJ, MAX	CONDUCTOR	157 W 57TH ST #1100	NEW YORK, NY	10019
RABINOWITZ, DOROTHY	COLUMNIST	NEWS AMERICA SYNDICATE		
		1703 KAISER AVE	IRVINE, CA	92714

EDDIE RABBITT

GILDA RADNER

DEBORAH RAFFIN

ELLA RAINES

BARTON RANDALL

TONY RANDALL

EDDY RAVEN

LOU RAWLS

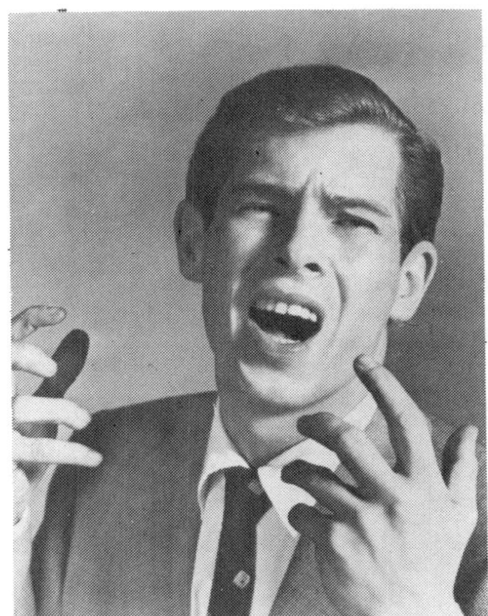
JOHNNY RAY

Name	Occupation	Address	City / Country	Zip
RABINOWITZ, HARRY	COMPOSER-CONDUCTOR	HONOR MUSIC, HOPE END		
		HOLMBURY SAINT MARY, DORKING	SURREY RH5 6PE	ENGLAND
RABWIN, PAUL HARTLEY	TV PRODUCER	HARTLEY'S, 5509 LA JOLLA BLVD	LA JOLLA, CA	92037
RACE, HANDSOME HARLEY	WRESTLER	POST OFFICE BOX 3859	STAMFORD, CT	06905
RACE, ROGER	TV PRODUCER	44 RITHERDOM RD	LONDON SW17	ENGLAND
RACERS, THE	ROCK & ROLL GROUP	POST OFFICE BOX 2095	PHILADELPHIA, PA	19103
RACHFORD, THOMAS G	ACTOR	9173 WOOLLEY ST	TEMPLE CITY, CA	91780
RACHINS, ALAN	ACT-WRI-DIR	1124 N LARRABEE ST	LOS ANGELES, CA	90069
RACHMANINOFF PIANO TRIO	PIANO TRIO	POST OFFICE BOX U	REDDING, CT	06875
RACHOR, DAVID	SAXOPHONIST	1007 S WASHINGTON ST	BLOOMINGTON, IN	47401
RACIMO, VICTORIA	ACTRESS	9255 SUNSET BLVD #505	LOS ANGELES, CA	90069
RACINA, THOM	AUTHOR	BANTAM BOOKS, 414 E GOLF RD	DES PLAINES, IL	60016
RACKMIL, GLADYS	THEATER PRODUCER	250 W 52ND ST	NEW YORK, NY	10019
RACY, ALI JIHAD	COMPOSER	3570 TILDEN AVE	LOS ANGELES, CA	90034
RADCLIFFE, REDONIA	NEWS CORRESPONDENT	1920 VALLEY WOOD RD	MC LEAN, VA	22101
RADER, JACK	ACTOR	20251 ARCHWOOD ST	CANOGA PARK, CA	91306
RADFORD, MARSHA	BODYBUILDER	1017 STEVENS CREEK RD #208-J	AUGUSTA, GA	30907
RADFORD, MICHAEL	FILM DIRECTOR	3-B RICKERING MEWS	LONDON W2 5AD	ENGLAND
RADICE, FRANCIS J	NEWS CORRESPONDENT	NBC-TV, NEWS DEPARTMENT		
		4001 NEBRASKA AVE, SW	WASHINGTON, DC	20016
RADIN, PAUL	TV PRODUCER	1606 GILCREST DR	BEVERLY HILLS, CA	90210
RADNER, GILDA	ACTRESS-COMEDIENNE	9200 SUNSET BLVD #428	LOS ANGELES, CA	90069
RADNITZ, BRAD	TV WRITER	2049 CENTURY PARK E #1320	LOS ANGELES, CA	90067
RADNITZ, ROBERT B	FILM WRITER-PRODUCER	19728 PACIFIC COAST HWY	MALIBU, CA	90265
RADNOFSKY, KENNETH	SAXOPHONOST	AFFILIATE ARTISTS, INC		
		37 W 65TH ST, 6TH FLOOR	NEW YORK, NY	10023
RADO, JAN	ACTRESS	8230 BEVERLY BLVD #23	LOS ANGELES, CA	90048
RADOSTA, JACK	ACTOR	1350 N HIGHLAND AVE #24	HOLLYWOOD, CA	90028
RADOVSKY, DAN	NEWS CORRESPONDENT	CBS NEWS, 2020 "M" ST, NW	WASHINGTON, DC	20036
RADWASTE	ROCK & ROLL GROUP	POST OFFICE BOX 94565	PASADENA, CA	91109
RAE, BARBRA	ACTRESS	9601 WILSHIRE BLVD #GL-11	BEVERLY HILLS, CA	90210
RAE, CHARLOTTE	ACTRESS	9220 SUNSET BLVD #625	LOS ANGELES, CA	90069
RAE, DOUGLAS	LITERARY-TALENT AGENT	28 CHARING CROSS RD	LONDON WC2	ENGLAND
RAE, DOUGLAS	TV PRODUCER	ROSEMAN, 8 POLAND ST	LONDON W1	ENGLAND
RAEBURN, MICHAEL	WRITER-PRODUCER	10 SPENCER PARK	LONDON SW18 2SX	ENGLAND
RAFANELLI, FLORA	MEZZO-SOPRANO	61 W 62ND ST #6-F	NEW YORK, NY	10023
RAFEL, LISA	ACTRESS	15010 VENTURA BLVD #219	SHERMAN OAKS, CA	91403
RAFELSON, ROBERT	FILM WRITER-DIRECTOR	8222 MARMONT LN	LOS ANGELES, CA	90069
RAFFANTI, DANO	TENOR	CAMI, 165 W 57TH ST	NEW YORK, NY	10019
RAFFELL, DONALD H	COMPOSER	3757 WOODCLIFF RD	SHERMAN OAKS, CA	91403
RAFFENSPERGER, KAREN E	NEWS CORRESPONDENT	2727 29TH ST, NW	WASHINGTON, DC	20008
RAFFERTY, FRANCES	ACTRESS	BAKER, 411 N PALM DR	BEVERLY HILLS, CA	90210
RAFFERTY, GERRY	SINGER-SONGWRITER	MICHAEL GRAY MANAGEMENT		
		51 PADDINGTON ST	LONDON W1	ENGLAND
RAFFETY, SUE	WRITER-EDITOR	TIME/TIME & LIFE BLDG		
		ROCKEFELLER CENTER	NEW YORK, NY	10020
RAFFIL, STEWART	WRITER-PRODUCER	DGA, 7950 SUNSET BLVD	LOS ANGELES, CA	90046
RAFFIN, DEBORAH	ACTRESS	VINER, 2630 EDEN PL	BEVERLY HILLS, CA	90210
RAFKIN, ALAN	TV WRITER-DIRECTOR	1008 SAINT BIMINI CIR	PALM SPRINGS, CA	92262
RAFNER, LEE	FILM DIRECTOR	13554 HAMLIN ST	VAN NUYS, CA	91401
RAFT, WALTER R	DIRECTOR	8569 RAMBLEWOOD DR	CORAL SPRINGS, FL	33065
RAGAIN, JANICE	BODYBUILDER	POST OFFICE BOX 34541	LOS ANGELES, CA	90034
RAGAINS, DIANE	SOPRANO	431 S DEARBORN ST #1504	CHICAGO, IL	60605
RAGAN, JAMES	FILM PRODUCER	3342 OAK GLEN DR	LOS ANGELES, CA	90068
RAGAWAY, MARTIN A	TV WRITER	8625 HOLLOWAY DR	LOS ANGELES, CA	90069
RAGGIO, LISA	ACTRESS	9220 SUNSET BLVD #306	LOS ANGELES, CA	90069
RAGIN, DEREK LEE	SINGER	COLBERT, 111 W 57TH ST	NEW YORK, NY	10019
RAGIN, JOHN S	ACTOR	5708 BRIARCLIFF RD	LOS ANGELES, CA	90068
RAGIN' BULL	WRESTLER	SEE - FERNANDEZ, MANNY		
RAGIR, MARSHALL B	WRITER-PRODUCER	2920 11TH ST #4	SANTA MONICA, CA	90405
RAGLAND, GARY	ACTOR	1054 17TH ST	SANTA MONICA, CA	90403
RAGLAND, ROBERT O	COMPOSER-PIANIST	9931 YOUNG DR #A	BEVERLY HILLS, CA	90212
RAGONESE, ANTHONY S	ACTOR	380 N SAN VICENTE BLVD	LOS ANGELES, CA	90048
RAGOTZY, JACK	DIRECTOR	2057 CASTILIAN DR	HOLLYWOOD, CA	90068
RAGSDALE, CARL VAN DYKE	DIRECTOR-PRODUCER	4725 STILLBROOKE DR	HOUSTON, TX	77035
RAGSDALE, JOHN W	MUSIC ARRANGER	2805 27TH AVE S	NASHVILLE, TN	37212
RAGSDALE, WARNER B, JR	NEWS CORRESPONDENT	12605 EASTBOURNE DR	SILVER SPRING, MD	20904
RAHAL, CARL	ACTOR	11265 PALMS BLVD #B	LOS ANGELES, CA	90066
RAHN, EDUARDO	CONDUCTOR	1776 BROADWAY #504	NEW YORK, NY	10019
RAIA, ALEXANDER	PHOTOGRAPHER	128 WELLINGTON RD	GARDEN CITY, NY	11530
RAIDER, THE	WRESTLER	POST OFFICE BOX 3859	STAMFORD, CT	06905
RAIL	VOCAL GROUP	J BAUER, 2500 116TH AVE, NE	BELLEVUE, WA	98004
RAILSBACK, STEVE	ACTOR	10050 CIELO DR	BEVERLY HILLS, CA	90210
RAIM, CYNTHIA	PIANIST	BYERS-SCHWALBE, 1 5TH AVE	NEW YORK, NY	10003
RAIMONDI, RUGGERO	BASSO-BARITONE	CAMI, 165 W 57TH ST	NEW YORK, NY	10019
RAIMUNDO, JEFFERY M	NEWS CORRESPONDENT	3612 N MONROE ST	ARLINGTON, VA	22207
RAINBOLT, SHEREE	ACTRESS	10845 LINDBROOK DR #3	LOS ANGELES, CA	90024
RAINBOLT, WILLIAM	ACTOR-DIRECTOR	6818 CAHUENGA PARK TERR	LOS ANGELES, CA	90068
RAINBOW	C & W GROUP	2701 COTTAGE WY #14	SACRAMENTO, CA	95825
RAINBOW EXPRESS	C & W GROUP	BENNETT, 4630 DEEPDALE DR	CORPUS CHRISTI, TX	78413
RAINE, GILLIAN	ACTRESS	13 BILLING RD	LONDON SW10	ENGLAND
RAINER, LUISE	ACTRESS	KNITTEL, VICO MORCOTE	LUGANO 6911	SWITZERLAND
RAINER, PETER	WRITER	1323 9TH ST	SANTA MONICA, CA	90401
RAINES, CRISTINA	ACTRESS	15301 VENTURA BLVD #345	SHERMAN OAKS, CA	91403
RAINES, EARL E	CONDUCTOR	2835 N HIGHVIEW	ALTADENA, CA	91001

Name	Occupation	Address	City	Zip
RAINES, ELLA	ACTRESS	13114 HESBY ST	SHERMAN OAKS, CA	91423
RAINES, GENE	GUITARIST	207 ROBIN HOOD DR	CLARKSVILLE, TN	37040
RAINES, HOWELL	NEWS CORRESPONDENT	4844 LANGDRUM LN	CHEVY CHASE, MD	20815
RAINES, TIM	BASEBALL	2316 AIRPORT BLVD	SANFORD, FL	32771
RAINEY, FORD	ACTOR	3821 CARBON CYN RD	MALIBU, CA	90265
RAINIE, HARRISON	NEWS CORRESPONDENT	5006 N 25TH ST	ARLINGTON, VA	22207
RAINONE, LOUIS J	TV DIRECTOR	9480 BLUEWING TERR	CINCINNATI, OH	45241
RAINSFORD, WILLIE	PIANIST	1285 OLD HICKORY BLVD	NASHVILLE, TN	37207
RAISON, ROBERT	TALENT AGENT	1930 CENTURY PARK W #403	LOS ANGELES, CA	90067
RAITT, BONNIE	SINGER	7323 WOODROW WILSON DR	LOS ANGELES, CA	90046
RAITT, JOHN	ACTOR	7060 HOLLYWOOD BLVD #610	LOS ANGELES, CA	90028
RAITZ, JEFF	WRESTLER	UNIVERSAL WRESTLING FEDERATION		
		MID SOUTH SPORTS, INC		
		5001 SPRING VALLEY RD	DALLAS, TX	75244
RAITZIN, MISHA	TENOR	SARDOS, 180 W END AVE	NEW YORK, NY	10023
RAK, KAREN	NEWS CORRESPONDENT	SCIENTIST'S CLIFFS	PORT REPUBLIC, MD	20676
RAKER, FRED	TV WRITER	8955 BEVERLY BLVD	LOS ANGELES, CA	90048
RAKI, LAYA	ACTRESS	KOHNER, 9169 SUNSET BLVD	LOS ANGELES, CA	90069
RAKITA, BOB	CARTOONIST	THE NATIONAL LAMPOON		
		635 MADISON AVE	NEW YORK, NY	10022
RAKOFF, ALVIN	FILM DIRECTOR	JARA, 1 THE ORCHARD		
		CHISWICK	LONDON W41 JZ	ENGLAND
RAKSIN, DAVID	COMPOSER-CONDUCTOR	6519 ALDEA AVE	VAN NUYS, CA	91406
RAKUSIN, FREDDA	MEZZO-SOPRANO	61 W 62ND ST #6-F	NEW YORK, NY	10023
RALEIGH, SUSAN	NEWS CORRESPONDENT	3707 WOODLEY RD, NW	WASHINGTON, DC	20016
RALFE, DON	COMPOSER	POST OFFICE BOX 1223	STUDIO CITY, CA	91604
RALKE, CLIFF D	WRITER	13343 BARBARA ANN ST	NORTH HOLLYWOOD, CA	91605
RALLING, ANTONY C	TV DIRECTOR-PRODUCER	THE COACH HOUSE, TANKERVILLE		
		KINGSTON HILL	SURREY	ENGLAND
RALLO, TONY & THE MIDNIGHT BAND	SOUL-DISCO GROUP	9701 WILSHIRE BLVD #1000	BEVERLY HILLS, CA	90212
RALOFF, JANET	NEWS CORRESPONDENT	9704 BRUNETT AVE	SILVER SPRING, MD	20901
RALPH & JANICE	VOCAL DUO	POST OFFICE BOX C	RIVER EDGE, NJ	07661
RALSTON, ALFRED	COMPOSER-CONDUCTOR	14 W HATCH MANOR, RUISLIP	MIDDLESEX HA4 8QT	ENGLAND
RALSTON, ESTHER	ACTRESS	35 HEATHER WY	VENTURA, CA	93003
RALSTON, JAMES	ACTOR	13111 VENTURA BLVD #102	STUDIO CITY, CA	91604
RALSTON, ROBERT	ORGANIST	17027 TENNYSON PL	GRANADA HILLS, CA	91344
RALSTON, TERI	ACTRESS	9300 WILSHIRE BLVD #410	BEVERLY HILLS, CA	90212
RALSTON, VERA HRUBA	ACTRESS	4121 CRESCIENTE DR	SANTA BARBARA, CA	93110
RAM, BUCK	SONGWRITER-PROUCER	POST OFFICE BOX 39	LAS VEGAS, NV	89125
RAM, ELIMELECH	NEWS CORRESPONDENT	4701 WILLARD AVE	CHEVY CHASE, MD	20815
RAM'S, BUCK, PLATTERS	VOCAL GROUP	SEE - PLATTERS, THE		
RAMADAN, WAFIK	NEWS CORRESPONDENT	1045 31ST ST, NW	WASHINGTON, DC	20007
RAMATI, ALEXANDER	WRITER	4151 DAVANA RD	SHERMAN OAKS, CA	91423
RAMBALDI, CARLO	DESIGN-SCLUPTOR	3831 HAYVENHURST AVE	ENCINO, CA	91436
RAMBO, CARROLL A	NEWS CORRESPONDENT	NBC-TV, NEWS DEPARTMENT		
		4001 NEBRASKA AVE, NW	WASHINGTON, DC	20016
RAMBO, DACK	ACTOR	RAMBO HORSE RANCH	EARLIMART, CA	93219
RAMEAU, INGRID	ACTRESS	6605 HOLLYWOOD BLVD #220	HOLLYWOOD, CA	90028
RAMEY, SAMUEL	BASSO-BARITONE	CAMI, 165 W 57TH ST	NEW YORK, NY	10019
RAMIN, MANFRED	CONDUCTOR	61 W 62ND ST #6-F	NEW YORK, NY	10023
RAMIN, RONALD B	COMPOSER-CONDUCTOR	969 HILGARD AVE	LOS ANGELES, CA	90024
RAMIREZ, ALEJANDRO	TENOR	CAMI, 165 W 57TH ST	NEW YORK, NY	10019
RAMIREZ, FRANK	ACTOR	9220 SUNSET BLVD #202	LOS ANGELES, CA	90069
RAMIREZ, HECTOR	CINEMATOGRAPHER	7715 SUNSET BLVD #150	LOS ANGELES, CA	90046
RAMIREZ, JANIE C & THE CACTUS C	C & W GROUP	ALAMO, 217 ARDEN GROVE	SAN ANTONIO, TX	78215
RAMIREZ, OLGA G	NEWS CORRESPONDENT	409 SCHUYLER RD	SILVER SPRING, MD	20910
RAMIREZ DE ARELLANO, SUSANNE	NEWS CORRESPONDENT	1425 17TH ST, NW	WASHINGTON, DC	20006
RAMIS, ANNE J	WRITER	456 15TH ST	SANTA MONICA, CA	90402
RAMIS, HAROLD	ACT-WRI-DIR	456 15TH ST	SANTA MONICA, CA	90402
RAMM, EBERHARD	FRENCH HORNIST	2503 BELMONT BLVD	NASHVILLE, TN	37212
RAMONE, KAREN	SINGER	GARY KURFIRST, OVERLAND PRODS		
		1775 BROADWAY, 7TH FLOOR	NEW YORK, NY	10019
RAMONES, THE	ROCK & ROLL GROUP	GARY FURFIRST, OVERLAND PRODS		
		1775 BROADWAY, 7TH FLOOR	NEW YORK, NY	10019
RAMOS, LOYDA	ACTRESS	11030 AQUA VISTA ST #52	STUDIO CITY, CA	91602
RAMOS, RICHARD	ACTOR	265 RIVERSIDE DR	NEW YORK, NY	10025
RAMOS, ROBERT R	NEWS CORRESPONDENT	6147 LEESBURG PIKE #101	WASHINGTON, DC	22041
RAMOS FAMILY, THE	HIGH WIRE ACT	POST OFFICE BOX 87	WEST LEBANON, NY	12195
RAMPAL, JEAN-PIERRE	FLUTIST	COLBERT, 111 W 57TH ST	NEW YORK, NY	10019
RAMPLING, CHARLOTTE	ACTRESS	OLGA HORSTIG-PRIMUZ		
		76 CHAMPS ELYS	PARIS 75008	FRANCE
RAMRUS, ALVIN	SCREENWRITER	15254 EARLHAM ST	PACIFIC PALISADES, CA	90272
RAMSAY, W NEAL	FLUTIST	755 WINTHORNE DR	NASHVILLE, TN	37217
RAMSAY, WES	MUSIC ARRANGER	4402 UTAH AVE	NASHVILLE, TN	37209
RAMSBROCK, GERD	NEWS CORRESPONDENT	1077 31ST ST, NW	WASHINGTON, DC	20007
RAMSEN, BOBBY	ACTOR	ICM, 8899 BEVERLY BLVD	LOS ANGELES, CA	90048
RAMSEUR, DAVID	NEWS CORRESPONDENT	738 9TH ST, SE	WASHINGTON, DC	20003
RAMSEY, AL	CONDUCTOR	2205 FRONTIER AVE	LAS VEGAS, NV	89106
RAMSEY, ANNE	ACTRESS	12923 KILLION ST	VAN NUYS, CA	91401
RAMSEY, DONALD A	WRITER	2280 THE TERR	LOS ANGELES, CA	90049
RAMSEY, DOUG	GUITARIST	1245 RUGBY DR	NASHVILLE, TN	37207
RAMSEY, ELMER H	COMPOSER-CONDUCTOR	3648 MOUNTCLEF BLVD	THOUSAND OAKS, CA	91360
RAMSEY, GORDON	ACTOR	90 MARION AVE	STATEN ISLAND, NY	10304
RAMSEY, JOANNE	SINGER	POST OFFICE BOX 171132	NASHVILLE, TN	37217
RAMSEY, LOGAN	ACTOR	12923 KILLION ST	VAN NUYS, CA	91401

THE RAMONES

Johnny • Richie • Joey • Dee Dee

RUSH

Geddy Lee • Neil Pert • Alex Lifeson

Name	Occupation	Address	City	Zip
RAMSEY, SHEILA	ACTRESS	AFFILIATE ARTIST, INC		
		37 W 65TH ST, 6TH FLOOR	NEW YORK, NY	10023
RAMSEY, STEVE	PIANIST	200 MILL CREEK CT	ANTIOCH, TN	37013
RAMSHAW, GREGG W	NEWS CORRESPONDENT	513-A ST, SE	WASHINGTON, DC	20003
RAMUNO, PHILIP	TV DIRECTOR	26045 FARMFIELD RD	CALABASAS, CA	91302
RAMUS, NICK	ACTOR	3907 W ALAMEDA AVE #101	BURBANK, CA	91505
RANBOM, SHEPPARD J	NEWS CORRESPONDENT	3937 DAVIS PL #2, NW	WASHINGTON, DC	20007
RANCATORE, STEVE	CLOWN	2701 COTTAGE WY #14	SACRAMENTO, CA	95825
RAND, GARY & THE STRANGERS	GOSPEL GROUP	POST OFFICE BOX 723591	ATLANTA, GA	30339
RAND, JOSEPH E	COMPOSER	1813 SCOTT RD #F	BURBANK, CA	91504
RAND, LINDA L	ACTRESS	4569 FINLEY AVE #1	LOS ANGELES, CA	90027
RAND, ROBERT	NEWS CORRESPONDENT	1201 CONNECTICUT AVENUE. NW	WASHINGTON, DC	20036
RAND, RONALD	TENOR	POST OFFICE BOX 188		
		STATION A	TORONTO, ONT	CANADA
RANDAL, JUDITH	NEWS CORRESPONDENT	815 3RD ST, SW	WASHINGTON, DC	20024
RANDALL, ANITA L	NEWS CORRESPONDENT	NBC-TV, NEWS DEPARTMENT		
		4001 NEBRASKA AVE, NW	WASHINGTON, DC	20016
RANDALL, ANNE	ACTRESS	7461 BEVERLY BLVD #400	LOS ANGELES, CA	90036
RANDALL, ANNE T	ACTRESS	SEE - RANDALL, ANNE		
RANDALL, BARTON	ACTOR-SCREENWRITER	901 LEVERING AVE #24	LOS ANGELES, CA	90024
RANDALL, BOB	SCREENWRITER	555 W 57TH ST #1230	NEW YORK, NY	10019
RANDALL, BOBBY	SAXOPHONIST	625 HICKORY VIEW DR	NASHVILLE, TN	37211
RANDALL, CHARLES	ACTOR	484 W 43RD ST #6-P	NEW YORK, NY	10036
RANDALL, DICK	FILM PRODUCER	113 WARDOUR ST	LONDON W1	ENGLAND
RANDALL, GENE	NEWS CORRESPONDENT	7342 GREENTREE RD	BETHESDA, MD	20817
RANDALL, GEORGE	ACTOR	FELBER, 2126 N CAHUENGA BLVD	LOS ANGELES, CA	90068
RANDALL, GLENN H, JR	DIRECTOR	DGA, 7950 SUNSET BLVD	LOS ANGELES, CA	90046
RANDALL, HARRY	DIRECTOR	POST OFFICE BOX 220	PEQUANNOCK, NJ	07440
RANDALL, LAURA J	NEWS CORRESPONDENT	1705 DE SALES ST, NW	WASHINGTON, DC	20036
RANDALL, LYNNE	ACTRESS	ICM, 8899 BEVERLY BLVD	LOS ANGELES, CA	90048
RANDALL, RUSS	TV DIRECTOR	704 N ARDEN DR	BEVERLY HILLS, CA	90210
RANDALL, STEVE	ACTOR-WRITER	1912 COMSTOCK AVE	LOS ANGELES, CA	90025
RANDALL, TONY	ACTOR-WRITER	145 CENTRAL PARK W #6-C	NEW YORK, NY	10023
RANDAZZO, TEDDY	SINGER	BROWN, 29 CEDAR ST	CRESSKILL, NJ	07626
RANDELL, TON	ACTOR	19 W 44TH ST #1500	NEW YORK, NY	10036
RANDLE, JIM	NEWS CORRESPONDENT	2725 MANOR HAVEN CT	ALEXANDRIA, VA	22306
RANDLES, WILLIAM	CABLE EXECUTIVE	CABLENTERTAINMENT		
		295 MADISON AVE	NEW YORK, NY	10017
RANDOLPH, BOOTS	SAXOPHONIST	4798 LICKTON PIKE	WHITES CREEK, TN	37189
RANDOLPH, DONALD	ACTOR	1825 N KINGSLEY DR	LOS ANGELES, CA	90027
RANDOLPH, JOHN	ACTOR	561 W 163RD ST	NEW YORK, NY	10032
RANDOLPH, JOYCE	ACTRESS	295 CENTRAL PARK W	NEW YORK, NY	10024
RANDOLPH, MARGE	ACTRESS	8721 SUNSET BLVD #200	LOS ANGELES, CA	90069
RANDOVA, EVA	MEZZO-SOPRANO	61 W 62ND ST #6-F	NEW YORK, NY	10023
RANDY, ANTHONY	COMPOSER	1162 S MOSCADA AVE	WALNUT, CA	91789
RANDY, RICKY	ACTOR	POST OFFICE BOX 3142	HOLLYWOOD, CA	90028
RANDY & THE RAINBOWS	VOCAL GROUP	POST OFFICE BOX 499	QUEENS, NY	11365
RANEY, JANET	ACTRESS	419 N LARCHMONT BLVD #245	LOS ANGELES, CA	90004
RANEY, THOMAS D	COMPOSER	3957 BRILLIANT DR	LOS ANGELES, CA	90065
RANGEL, MARIA	ACTRESS	ABC-TV, "GENERAL HOSPITAL"		
		1438 N GOWER ST	LOS ANGELES, CA	90028
RANGERS, THE	C & W GROUP	TAYLOR, 2401 12TH AVE S	NASHVILLE, TN	37204
RANIER, THOMAS J	COMPOSER	282 LONGBRANCH CIR	BREA, CA	92621
RANK & FILE	C & W GROUP	611 BROADWAY #526	NEW YORK, NY	10012
RANKI, DEZSO	PIANIST	LEISER, DORCHESTER TOWERS		
		155 W 68TH ST	NEW YORK, NY	10023
RANKIN, BILLY	SINGER	3101 E EISENHOWER HWY #3	ANN ARBOR, MI	48104
RANKIN, JAY	ACTOR	2121 N HOBART BLVD	LOS ANGELES, CA	90027
RANKIN, KENNETH E	NEWS CORRESPONDENT	17735 STRILEY DR	ASHTON, MD	20861
RANKIN, KENNY	SINGER-SONGWRITER	POST OFFICE BOX 7308	CARMEL, CA	93923
RANKIN, MOIRA K	NEWS CORRESPONDENT	7005 23RD PL	ADELPHI, MD	20783
RANKIN, WILLIAM	NEWS CORRESPONDENT	2254 CATHEDRAL AVE, NW	WASHINGTON, DC	20008
RANN, GROVER	GUITARIST	200 PARAGON MILLS RD #E-18	NASHVILLE, TN	37211
RANNELLS, ROBERT	GUITARIST	212 CLIPPER CT	NASHVILLE, TN	37211
RANNOW, JERRY	TV WRITER	9250 WARBLER WY	LOS ANGELES, CA	90069
RANSLEY, PETER	TV WRITER	LEMON, 24 POTTERY LN	LONDON W11	ENGLAND
RANSOHOFF, MARTIN	WRITER-PRODUCER	210 N CAROLWOOD DR	LOS ANGELES, CA	90077
RANSOM, GLENN	ACTOR	3330 BARHAM BLVD #103	LOS ANGELES, CA	90068
RANSOM, NORMA	ACTRESS	9255 SUNSET BLVD #610	LOS ANGELES, CA	90069
RANSOM, ROBERT V, JR	MUSIC ARRANGER	616 MALTA DR	NASHVILLE, TN	37207
RANSOM, RONALD SCOTT	FILM DIRECTOR	POST OFFICE BOX 1100	TELLURIDE, CO	81435
RANSOME, PRUNELLA	ACTRESS	CROUCH, 59 FRITH ST	LONDON W1	ENGLAND
RANSON, GERALD W	DIRECTOR	171 W 79TH ST	NEW YORK, NY	10024
RANTZEN, ESTHER	TV PRODUCER	GAY, 24 DENMARK ST	LONDON W2	ENGLAND
RAPELYE, MARY LINDA	ACTRESS	THE WILLIAM MORRIS AGENCY		
		1350 AVE OF THE AMERICAS	NEW YORK, NY	10019
RAPER, BRET	MUSICIAN	446 TANGLEWOOD CT	NASHVILLE, TN	37211
RAPF, MATTHEW W	SCREENWRITER	120 MALIBU COLONY DR	MALIBU, CA	90265
RAPF, MAURICE	WRITER-PRODUCER	6 CONANT RD	HANOVER, NH	03755
RAPHAEL	SINGER	THE WILLIAM MORRIS AGENCY		
		1350 AVE OF THE AMERICAS	NEW YORK, NY	10019
RAPHAEL, ALISON	NEWS CORRESPONDENT	507 ALBANY AVE	TAKOMA PARK, MD	20912
RAPHAEL, FRED	DIRECTOR	2 BEEKMAN PL	NEW YORK, NY	10022
RAPHAEL, FREDERIC	SCREENWRITER	8955 BEVERLY BLVD	LOS ANGELES, CA	90048
RAPHAEL, SALLY JESSY	TV HOST	KSDK-TV, 1000 MARKET ST	SAINT LOUIS, MO	63101

Name	Occupation	Address	City	Zip
RAPHEL, JEROME	ACTOR	53 W 83RD ST	NEW YORK, NY	10024
RAPISARDA, TONY	ACTOR	12423 STANWOOD PL	LOS ANGELES, CA	90066
RAPOPORT, DANIEL	NEWS CORRESPONDENT	3804 JENIFER ST, NW	WASHINGTON, DC	20015
RAPOPORT, I C	TV WRITER	559 MUSKINGUM AVE	PACIFIC PALISADES, CA	90272
RAPP, PAUL	FILM WRITER-DIRECTOR	301 N ALPINE DR	BEVERLY HILLS, CA	90210
RAPP, RICHARD	ACTOR	327 CENTRAL PARK W	NEW YORK, NY	10025
RAPP, WILLIAM	DIRECTOR	2203 HASTINGS DR #3	BELMONT, CA	94002
RAPPAPORT, JOHN H	TV WRITER	15946 WOODVALE RD	ENCINO, CA	91436
RAPPER, IRVING	FILM DIRECTOR	10777 WILSHIRE BLVD #16	LOS ANGELES, CA	90024
RAPPORT, LOUISE	ACTRESS	10845 LINDBROOK DR #3	LOS ANGELES, CA	90024
RARE EARTH	ROCK & ROLL GROUP	NORTHERN INTL TALENT		
		5224 S LOGAN ST	LANSING, MI	48910
RARE SILK	JAZZ GROUP	2888 BLUFF ST #115	BOULDER, CO	80301
RASCHE, DAVID	ACTOR	10100 SANTA MONICA BLVD #1600	LOS ANGELES, CA	90067
RASCHELLA, CAROLE P	TV WRITER	8736 OAKDALE AVE	NORTHRIDGE, CA	91324
RASCHKE, JAMES	WRESTLER	SEE - VON RASCHKE, BARON		
RASCOE, JUDITH E	SCREENWRITER	8955 BEVERLY BLVD	LOS ANGELES, CA	90048
RASER, BOB	DIRECTOR	4400 YORKFIELD CT	WESTLAKE VILLAGE, CA	91361
RASEY, JEAN	ACTRESS	870 N VINE ST #G	LOS ANGELES, CA	90038
RASH, STEVE	DIRECTOR	3742 LOWER MOUNTAIN RD	FOREST GROVE, PA	18922
RASHAD, AHMAD	FOOTBALL	30 ROCKEFELLER PLAZA #1411	NEW YORK, NY	10112
RASHAD, PHYLICIA	ACTRESS	BRET ADAMS, 448 W 44TH ST	NEW YORK, NY	10036
RASHID, ROBERT D	DIRECTOR	6620 STEADMAN ST	DEARBORN, MI	48126
RASKIN, CAROLYN	WRITER-PRODUCER	4112 WOODCLIFF RD	SHERMAN OAKS, CA	91403
RASKING, KAREN W	WRITER	11008 AYRES AVE	LOS ANGELES, CA	90064
RASKING, RICHARD A	WRITER	8306 WILSHIRE BLVD #429	BEVERLY HILLS, CA	90211
RASKY, HARRY	WRITER-PRODUCER	POST OFFICE BOX 500		
		STATION A	TORONTO, ONT M5W 1E6	CANADA
RASKY, SUSAN F	NEWS CORRESPONDENT	1627 IRVING ST, NW	WASHINGTON, DC	20010
RASMUSSEN, JOSEPH	PERCUSSIONIST	ROUTE #2, BOX 149	BAXTER, TN	38544
RASMUSSEN, LISA A	NEWS CORRESPONDENT	NBC-TV, NEWS DEPARTMENT		
		4001 NEBRASKA AVE, NW	WASHINGTON, DC	20016
RASMUSSEN, R J "ACE"	STUD	2801 MEADOW LARK DR	SAN DIEGO, CA	92123
RASMUSSEN, WILLIAM F	CABLE EXECUTIVE	8252 S HARVARD ST	TULSA, OK	74136
RASPBERRY, LARRY	SINGER	POST OFFICE BOX O	MINNEAPOLIS, MN	55331
RASPBERRY, WILLIAM	NEWS CORRESPONDENT	1150 15TH ST, NW	WASHINGTON, DC	20071
RAST, CAROLYN A	PHOTOGRAPHER	6503 RED TOP RD	HYATTSVILLE, MD	20783
RAST, REYNOLDS R	NEWS CORRESPONDENT	3486 FORESTDALE AVE	WOODBRIDGE, VA	22193
RASULALA, THALMUS	ACTOR	9255 SUNSET BLVD #603	LOS ANGELES, CA	90069
RATCLIFF, CHARLES	PIANIST	5319 NOLENSVILLE RD #B-304	NASHVILLE, TN	37211
RATCLIFFE, SAMUEL D	TV WRITER	ICM, 40 W 57TH ST	NEW YORK, NY	10019
RATESH, NESTOR	NEWS CORRESPONDENT	1201 CONNECTICUT AVE, NW	WASHINGTON, DC	20036
RATH, EARL	CINEMATOGRAPHER	6063 SUNSET BLVD	LOS ANGELES, CA	90028
RATHBUN, BENJAMIN, JR	NEWS CORRESPONDENT	3711 UPTON ST, NW	WASHINGTON, DC	20016
RATHER, DAN	NEWS CORRESPONDENT	10 COLUMBUS CIR	NEW YORK, NY	10019
RATIONAL YOUTH	ROCK & ROLL GROUP	41 BRITAIN ST #200	TORONTO, ONT	CANADA
RATNER, MARC	ACTOR	18518 MAYALL ST #J	NORTHRIDGE, CA	91324
RATNER, VIC	NEWS CORRESPONDENT	ABC-TV, NEWS DEPARTMENT		
		1717 DE SALES ST, NW	WASHINGTON, DC	20036
RATT	ROCK & ROLL GROUP	6253 HOLLYWOOD BLVD #1128	HOLLYWOOD, CA	90028
RATTLE, SIMON	CONDUCTOR	201 W 54TH ST #4-C	NEW YORK, NY	10019
RATTLEY, SANDRA C	NEWS CORRESPONDENT	2025 "M" ST, NW	WASHINGTON, DC	20036
RATZENBERGER, JOHN	ACTOR	10445 VALLEY SPRING LN	NORTH HOLLYWOOD, CA	91602
RATZLAFF, DAVID	TV DIRECTOR	1306 S FINLEY RD #3-B	LOMBARD, IL	60148
RATZLAFF, LESLIE A	NEWS CORRESPONDENT	3832 COLUMBIA PIKE #202	ARLINGTON, VA	22204
RAUCH, EARL M	SCREENWRITER	5900 CLOVER HGTS AVE	MALIBU, CA	90265
RAUCH, ELLEN	FILM DIRECTOR	333 E 79TH ST	NEW YORK, NY	10021
RAUCH, JONATHAN C	NEWS CORRESPONDENT	2829 CONNECTICUT AVE, NW	WASHINGTON, DC	20008
RAUCH, MICHAEL	TV DIRECTOR	333 E 79TH ST	NEW YORK, NY	10021
RAUCH, PAUL	TV PRODUCER	ABC-TV, "ONE LIFE TO LIVE"		
		1330 AVE OF THE AMERICAS	NEW YORK, NY	10019
RAUCHER, HERMAN	SCREENWRITER	555 W 57TH ST #1230	NEW YORK, NY	10019
RAULLERSON, KEVIN G	NEWS CORRESPONDENT	2139 WISCONSIN AVE, NW	WASHINGTON, DC	20007
RAUM, THOMAS	NEWS CORRESPONDENT	6463 FENESTRA CT	BURKE, VA	22015
RAUNCH HANDS	ROCK & ROLL GROUP	POST OFFICE BOX 1558		
		MADISON SQUARE STATION	NEW YORK, NY	10159
RAUSCH, LEON	SINGER	1300 DIVISION ST #102	NASHVILLE, TN	37203
RAUSEO, VICTOR	WRITER-PRODUCER	2920 NEILSON WY #103	SANTA MONICA, CA	90405
RAVE	VOCAL GROUP	8831 SUNSET BLVD #200	LOS ANGELES, CA	90069
RAVE-UPS, THE	ROCK & ROLL GROUP	POST OFFICE BOX 1818	BEVERLY HILLS, CA	90213
RAVEN	ROCK & ROLL GROUP	K J DOUGHTON MANAGEMENT		
		2225 PACIFIC COAST HIGHWAY	MALIBU, CA	90265
RAVEN, EDDY	SINGER-GUITARIST	POST OFFICE BOX 1402	HENDERSONVILLE, TN	37075
RAVEN, ELSA	ACTRESS	1297 3RD AVE	NEW YORK, NY	10021
RAVENS, RUPERT	ACTOR	250 W 57TH ST #2317	NEW YORK, NY	10107
RAVENSCROFT, RONALD A	COMPOSER-CONDUCTOR	1960 N VERMONT AVE	LOS ANGELES, CA	90027
RAVETCH, HARRIET FRANK, JR	WRITER	8277 SKYLINE DR	LOS ANGELES, CA	90046
RAVETCH, IRVING	SCREENWRITER	8277 SKYLINE DR	LOS ANGELES, CA	90046
RAVIER, CLAUDE	TALENT AGENT	BRB, 666 N ROBERTSON BLVD	LOS ANGELES, CA	90060
RAVIN'	ROCK & ROLL GROUP	POST OFFICE BOX 448	RADFORD, VA	24141
RAVISHING ONE, THE	WRESTLER	NATIONAL WRESTLING ALLIANCE		
		JIM CROCKETT PROMOTIONS		
		421 BRIARBEND DR	CHARLOTTE, NC	28209
RAVYNS, THE	ROCK & ROLL GROUP	ATI, 888 7TH AVE, 21ST FLOOR	NEW YORK, NY	10106
RAW POWER	ROCK & ROLL GROUP	POST OFFICE BOX 242	PONOMA, CA	91769

Name	Occupation	Address	City	Zip/Country
RAW-KUS ROCK-A-BILLY	ROCK & ROLL GROUP	OLDIES, 5218 ALMONT ST	LOS ANGELES, CA	90032
RAWCLIFFE, MARY	SOPRANO	61 W 62ND ST #6-F	NEW YORK, NY	10023
RAWI, OUSAMA	CINEMATOGRAPHER	49 BELSIZE LN	LONDON NW3	ENGLAND
RAWLE, JEFF	ACTOR	NEMS, 31 KINGS RD	LONDON SW3	ENGLAND
RAWLEY, DONALD	ACTOR	10000 RIVERSIDE DR #12-14	TOLUCA LAKE, CA	91602
RAWLEY, JAMES	ACTOR	CASSELL, 843 N SYCAMORE AVE	LOS ANGELES, CA	90038
RAWLEY, PETER	TALENT AGENT	ICM, 8899 BEVERLY BLVD	LOS ANGELES, CA	90048
RAWLINGS, RICHARD, SR	CINEMATOGRAPHER	7715 SUNSET BLVD #150	LOS ANGELES, CA	90046
RAWLINS, DAVID	DIRECTOR	1999 N SYCAMORE AVE #19	HOLLYWOOD, CA	90068
RAWLINS, JOHN	DIRECTOR	DGA, 7950 SUNSET BLVD	LOS ANGELES, CA	90046
RAWLS, LOU	SINGER	109 FREMONT PL W	LOS ANGELES, CA	90005
RAWNSLEY, JOHN	BARITONE	CAMI, 165 W 57TH ST	NEW YORK, NY	10019
RAY, ALDO	ACTOR	1765 N HIGHLAND AVE #127	HOLLYWOOD, CA	90028
RAY, ANDREW	ACTOR	WHITE, 31 KINGS RD	LONDON SW3	ENGLAND
RAY, GENE ANTHONY	ACTOR	104-60 QUEENS BLVD #1-D	FOREST HILLS, NY	11375
RAY, JACKI	ACTRESS-MODEL	11381 HOMEDALE ST	LOS ANGELES, CA	90049
RAY, JAMES	ACTOR	11726 SAN VICENTE BLVD #300	LOS ANGELES, CA	90049
RAY, JEFFREY	TV WRITER	8955 BEVERLY BLVD	LOS ANGELES, CA	90048
RAY, JOHANNA	CASTING DIRECTOR	332 N OAKHURST DR #A	BEVERLY HILLS, CA	90210
RAY, JOHNNIE	SINGER	POST OFFICE BOX C	RIVER EDGE, NJ	07661
RAY, MALCOLM W	DIRECTOR	DGA, 7950 SUNSET BLVD	LOS ANGELES, CA	90046
RAY, MARC B	WRITER	23369 OSTRONIC DR	WOODLAND HILLS, CA	91367
RAY, MARGUERITE	ACTRESS	9744 WILSHIRE BLVD #306	BEVERLY HILLS, CA	90212
RAY, NORMAN	SAXOPHONIST	ROUTE #10, CHURCHILL RD	FRANKLIN, TN	37064
RAY, OLA	ACTRESS-MODEL	3800 BARHAM BLVD #303	LOS ANGELES, CA	90068
RAY, ROBIN	ACTOR-WRITER	WILKINSON MANAGEMENT		
		8 WATERLOO PL, PALL MALL	LONDON SW1	ENGLAND
RAY, SATYAJIT	DIRECTOR	1/1 BISHOP LEFROY RD #8	CALCUTTA 20	INDIA
RAY, WADE	GUITARIST	ROUTE #3	SPARTA, IL	62286
RAY, GOODMAN & BROWN	VOCAL TRIO	HUSH PRODS, 231 W 58TH ST	NEW YORK, NY	10019
RAYAM, CURTIS	TENOR	61 W 62ND ST #6-F	NEW YORK, NY	10023
RAYBORN, C D	ACTOR	6605 HOLLYWOOD BLVD #220	HOLLYWOOD, CA	90028
RAYBOULD, HARRY	ACTOR	BENSON, 518 TOLUCA PARK DR	BURBANK, CA	91505
RAYBURN, GENE	TV HOST	SEAVIEW AVE	OSTERVILLE, ME	02655
RAYBURN, JOEANNA	ACTRESS	10850 RIVERSIDE DR #410	NORTH HOLLYWOOD, CA	91609
RAYE, BOBBY	COMEDIAN	CEE, 193 KONHAUS RD	MECHANICSBURG, PA	17055
RAYE, KATHY	SINGER	POST OFFICE BOX 6025	NEWPORT NEWS, VA	23606
RAYE, MARTHA	ACT-SING-DAN-COMED	1153 ROSCOMARE RD	LOS ANGELES, CA	90024
RAYE, MICHAEL	ACTOR	3330 BARHAM BLVD #103	LOS ANGELES, CA	90068
RAYE, SUSAN	SINGER	17530 VENTURA BLVD #108	ENCINO, CA	91316
RAYFIEL, DAVID	SCREENWRITER	555 W 57TH ST #1230	NEW YORK, NY	10019
RAYMER, STEVEN	PHOTOGRAPHER	NATIONAL GEOGRAPHIC		
		PHOTO DEPARTMENT		
		17TH & "M" STS, NW	WASHINGTON, DC	20036
RAYMOND, GARY	ACTOR	4 SAINT PETER'S SQ	LONDON W6	ENGLAND
RAYMOND, GENE	ACTOR	250 TRINO WY	PACIFIC PALISADES, CA	90272
RAYMOND, GUY	ACTOR	151 N SAN VICENTE BLVD #208	BEVERLY HILLS, CA	90211
RAYMOND, GUY MICHAEL	DIRECTOR	6 RIDENOUR CT	TOWSON, MD	21204
RAYMOND, JACK	TV WRITER	8955 BEVERLY BLVD	LOS ANGELES, CA	90048
RAYMOND, JOHN A	WRITER	3113 OAKCREST DR	HOLLYWOOD, CA	90068
RAYMOND, LINA	ACTRESS	12725 VENTURA BLVD #E	STUDIO CITY, CA	91604
RAYMOND, PAULA	ACTRESS	POST OFFICE BOX 86	BEVERLY HILLS, CA	90213
RAYMOND, ROBIN	ACTRESS	10390 WILSHIRE BLVD #302	LOS ANGELES, CA	90024
RAYMOND, SID	ACTOR	19380 COLLINS AVE #927	MIAMI BEACH, FL	33160
RAYMOND, SUSAN CULLINAN	TV DIRECTOR	VIDEO VERITE, 927 MADISON AVE	NEW YORK, NY	10021
RAYNER, GORDON	DIRECTOR	7722 VENTURA CANYON AVE	PANORAMA CITY, CA	91402
RAYNER, HANSEL M	CONDUCTOR	14711 COBALT ST	SYLMAR, CA	91342
RAYNOR, SHEILA	ACTRESS	SLAUGHDEN END, ALDEBURGH	SUFFOLK	ENGLAND
RAYNOR, TED	PRODUCER	8480 W BEVERLY BLVD #133	LOS ANGELES, CA	90048
RAYNOR, WILLIAM E	TV WRITER	8955 BEVERLY BLVD	LOS ANGELES, CA	90048
RAYS, THE	VOCAL GROUP	OLDIES, 5218 ALMONT ST	LOS ANGELES, CA	90032
RAYSON, BENJAMIN	ACTOR	8285 SUNSET BLVD #12	LOS ANGELES, CA	90046
RAYVID, JAY	TV EXECUTIVE	WQED-TV, 4802 5TH AVE	PITTSBURGH, PA	15213
RAZ, KAVI	ACTOR	8831 SUNSET BLVD #402	HOLLYWOOD, CA	90069
RAZNICK, DEBORAH	TV WRITER	15215 MAGNOLIA BLVD #108	SHERMAN OAKS, CA	91403
REA, DAVID C	WRITER-PRODUCER	20 BREWSTER GARDENS	LONDON W10	ENGLAND
REA, KAREN	CASTING DIRECTOR	POST OFFICE BOX 1303	SANTA MONICA, CA	90406
REA, PEGGY	ACTRESS	8835 DORRINGTON AVE	LOS ANGELES, CA	90048
REA, SEAN	BASS	61 W 62ND ST #6-F	NEW YORK, NY	10023
REA, STEPHEN	ACTOR	HOPE & LYNE, 5 MILNER PL	LONDON N1	ENGLAND
REACH, STEPHANIE	SINGER	9744 WILSHIRE BLVD #400	BEVERLY HILLS, CA	90212
REACTIONS, THE	ROCK & ROLL GROUP	POST OFFICE BOX 570	ROCKVILLE CENTRE, NY	11571
READ, ANTHONY	WRITER-PRODUCER	7 CEDAR CHASE, TAPLOW		
		MAIDENHEAD	BERKS	ENGLAND
READ, DOLLY	ACTRESS-MODEL	SEE - MARTIN, DOLLY READ		
READ, JAMES	ACTOR	SF & A, 121 N SAN VICENTE BLVD	BEVERLY HILLS, CA	90211
READ, JOHN	FILM WRITER-PRODUCER	123 HAVERSTOCK HILL #9	LONDON NW3	ENGLAND
READY FOR THE WORLD	RHYTHM & BLUES GROUP	A M I PRODUCTIONS		
		1776 BROADWAY, 10TH FLOOR	NEW YORK, NY	10019
REAGAN, MAUREEN	ACTRESS	1255 S BEVERLY GLEN BLVD	LOS ANGELES, CA	90024
REAGAN, NANCY	ACTRESS-FIRST LADY	1600 PENNSYLVANIA AVE, NW	WASHINGTON, DC	20006
REAGAN, ROBERT B	DIRECTOR	2200 JEFFERSONIA WY	LOS ANGELES, CA	90049
REAGAN, RONALD	ACTOR-PRESIDENT	1600 PENNSYLVANIA AVE, NW	WASHINGTON, DC	20006
REAGAN, RONALD, JR	DANCER	1283 DEVON AVE	LOS ANGELES, CA	90024
REAL LIFE	ROCK & ROLL GROUP	POST OFFICE BOX 214		
		ALBERT PARK	VICTORIA 3206	AUSTRALIA

GENE RAYBURN

RONALD REAGAN

PETER RECKELL

HELEN REDDY

ROBERT REDFORD

ANN REINKING

LEE REMICK

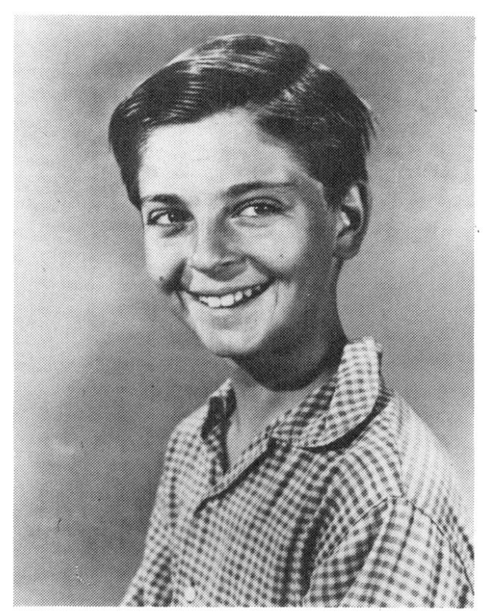
TOMMY RETTIG

BURT REYNOLDS

Name	Occupation	Address	City
REALMAN, KENNETH	TV WRITER	8955 BEVERLY BLVD	LOS ANGELES, CA 90048
REALS, GARY J	NEWS CORRESPONDENT	4461 CONNECTICUT AVE, NW	WASHINGTON, DC 20008
REAM, L MICHAEL	DIRECTOR	DGA, 110 W 57TH ST	NEW YORK, NY 10019
REAP, PATRICK T	NEWS CORRESPONDENT	2133 WISCONSIN AVE, NW	WASHINGTON, DC 20007
REARDON, JOHN	BARITONE	3003 VAN NESS ST #W-205, NW	WASHINGTON, DC 20008
REARDON, JOHN	TV DIRECTOR	APPLE TREE HOUSE	
		26 DOWER PARK	
		SAINT LEONARD'S HILL	
		WINDSOR	BERKS ENGLAND
REASMAN, BRUCE	TV WRITER	8955 BEVERLY BLVD	LOS ANGELES, CA 90048
REASON, LIONEL I	CONDUCTOR	3012 NEWTON ST	BATON ROUGE, LA 70802
REASON, REX	ACTOR	20105 RHAPSODY RD	WALNUT, CA 91789
REASON, RHODES	ACTOR	409 WINCHESTER AVE	GLENDALE, CA 91201
REASONER, EDDIE	PIANIST	POST OFFICE BOX 363	HENDERSONVILLE, TN 37075
REASONER, HARRY	NEWS JOURNALIST	CBS NEWS, 524 W 57TH ST	NEW YORK, NY 10019
REAVES, GARY	NEWS CORRESPONDENT	CBS NEWS, 524 W 57TH ST	NEW YORK, NY 10019
REAVES, J MICHAEL	TV WRITER	841 1/2 N VENDOME ST	LOS ANGELES, CA 90026
REAVES-PHILLIPS, SANDRA	SINGER	SHAFMAN, 723 7TH AVE	NEW YORK, NY 10019
REAVEY, MARGARET	WRITER	2513 RALSTON LN	REDONDO BEACH, CA 90278
REBACK, KATHERINE JAY	WRITER	1269 N FLORES ST #B-2	LOS ANGELES, CA 90069
REBEL, THE	WRESTLER	SEE - SLATER, DICK "THE REBEL"	
REBEL, THE	WRESTLER	SEE - ROBERTS, BUDDY "JACK"	
REBELS, THE	C & W GROUP	POST OFFICE BOX 1830	GRETNA, LA 70053
REBETA-BURDITT, JOYCE	WRITER	1009 E WALNUT AVE	BURBANK, CA 91501
RECHIN, BILL	CARTOONIST	NEWS AMERICA SYNDICATE	
		1703 KAISER AVE	IRVINE, CA 92714
RECIO, MARIA E	NEWS CORRESPONDENT	1517 RED OAK DR	SILVER SPRING, MD 20910
RECKELL, PETER	ACTOR	12750 VENTURA BLVD #102	STUDIO CITY, CA 91604
RECTOR, RICKY RAY	SINGER-GUITARIST	2022 20TH AVE S	NASHVILLE, TN 37212
RECTOR, ROBERT	DRUMMER	1232 LOIS ST	KERRVILLE, TX 78028
RED, SPANISH	WRESTLER	SEE - SPANISH RED	
RED 7	ROCK & ROLL GROUP	POST OFFICE BOX 2210	NOVATO, CA 94948
RED DEMON, THE	WRESTLER	POST OFFICE BOX 3859	STAMFORD, CT 06905
RED GARTER BANJO BAND, THE	BANJO BAND	MUSKRAT PRODUCTIONS, INC	
		44 N CENTRAL AVE	ELSMFORD, NY 10523
RED HOT CHILI PEPPERS	ROCK & ROLL GROUP	11116 AQUA VISTA ST #39	STUDIO CITY, CA 91602
RED LESTERS, THE	ROCK & ROLL GROUP	VARIETY ARTISTS INTL, INC	
		9073 NEMO ST, 3RD FLOOR	LOS ANGELES, CA 90069
RED LETTER	ROCK & ROLL GROUP	41 BRITAIN ST #200	TORONTO, ONT CANADA
RED LOUISIANA	ROCK & ROLL GROUP	DENIS VAUGHAN MGMT	
		HEATHCOAT HOUSE	
		19-20 SAVILE ROW	LONDON W1 ENGLAND
RED NOUVEAU	ROCK & ROLL GROUP	VARIETY ARTISTS INTL, INC	
		9073 NEMO ST, 3RD FLOOR	LOS ANGELES, CA 90069
RED RIDER	ROCK & ROLL GROUP	41 BRITAIN ST #200	TORONTO, ONT CANADA
RED ROCKERS, THE	ROCK & ROLL GROUP	ICM, 40 W 57TH ST	NEW YORK, NY 10019
RED RUCKERS, THE	ROCK & ROLL GROUP	3740 RUE DENISE	NEW ORLEANS, LA 70114
RED SHADOW, THE	WRESTLER	UNIVERSAL WRESTLING FEDERATION	
		MID SOUTH SPORTS, INC	
		5001 SPRING VALLEY RD	DALLAS, TX 75244
RED STAR, KEVIN	ARTIST	340 READ ST	SANTA FE, NM 87501
REDA, LOUIS J	AUTHOR-PRODUCER	44 N 2ND ST	EASTON, PA 18042
REDACK, JAY	TV WRITER	1991 STRADELLA RD	LOS ANGELES, CA 90077
REDBONE	ROCK & ROLL GROUP	FAR OUT MGMT, 7417 SUNSET BLVD	LOS ANGELES, CA 90046
REDBONE, LEON	SINGER-GUITARIST	HANDLER, 179 AQUETONG RD	NEW HOPE, PA 18938
REDBURN, THOMAS	NEWS CORRESPONDENT	2748 STEPHENSON LN, NW	WASHINGTON, DC 20015
REDD, MARY-ROBIN	ACTRESS	515 N SIERRA DR	BEVERLY HILLS, CA 90210
REDDING, BOBBY	DRUMMER	2433 VALE LN #A	NASHVILLE, TN 37214
REDDING, WILLIAM	PHOTOJOURNALIST	600 WATER ST #2-16, SW	WASHINGTON, DC 20024
REDDING HUTNER, JULI	ACTRESS	115 N CAROLWOOD DR	LOS ANGELES, CA 90024
REDDY, HELEN	SINGER	820 STANFORD ST	SANTA MONICA, CA 90403
REDEKER, BILL	NEWS CORRESPONDENT	ABC NEWS, 7 W 66TH ST	NEW YORK, NY 10023
REDEKER, QUINN	ACTOR-WRITER	10 TOLUCA ESTATES DR	NORTH HOLLYWOOD, CA 91602
REDENBACHER, ORVILLE	POPCORN ENTREPRENEUR	1780 AVE DEL MUNDO #704	CORONADO, CA 92118
REDFEARN, LINDA	ACTRESS	9744 WILSHIRE BLVD #306	BEVERLY HILLS, CA 90212
REDFIELD, DENNIS	ACTOR	9744 WILSHIRE BLVD #206	BEVERLY HILLS, CA 90212
REDFORD, J A C	COMPOSER	11318 MAYBROOK AVE	WHITTIER, CA 90603
REDFORD, JEFF	ACTOR	3912 WILLOW CREST AVE	NORTH HOLLYWOOD, CA 91604
REDFORD, ROBERT	ACTOR-DIRECTOR	POST OFFICE BOX 837	PROVO, UT 84601
REDGRAVE, LYNN	ACTRESS	21342 COLINA DR	TOPANGA CANYON, CA 90290
REDGRAVE, VANESSA	ACTRESS	1 RAVENSCOURT RD	LONDON W6 ENGLAND
REDING, GERALD F	COMPOSER-CONDUCTOR	808 S CURSON AVE #2	LOS ANGELES, CA 90036
REDLIN, JOEL	ACTOR	1258 N FAIRFAX AVE #4	LOS ANGELES, CA 90046
REDLINE	ROCK & ROLL GROUP	KASTLE, 213 N MAIN ST	ANN ARBOR, MI 48104
REDMAN, AMANDA	ACTRESS	CROUCH, 59 FRITH ST	LONDON W1 ENGLAND
REDMAN, CHRISTOPHER J	NEWS CORRESPONDENT	4135 W WOODBINE ST	CHEVY CHASE, MD 20815
REDMANN, KIRK	TENOR	CAMI, 165 W 57TH ST	NEW YORK, NY 10019
REDMOND, MARGE	ACTRESS	101 CENTRAL PARK W	NEW YORK, NY 10023
REDMOND, MOIRA	ACTRESS	COMBE, 17 RICHMOND HILL	
		RICHMOND	SURREY ENGLAND
REDNECK, CAPTAIN	WRESTLER	SEE - MURDOCH, DICK	
REDPATH, JEAN	SINGER	243 W END AVE #907	NEW YORK, NY 10023
REDRIDER BAND, THE	C & W GROUP	TESSIER, 505 CANTON PASS	MADISON, TN 37115
REDUCERS, THE	ROCK & ROLL GROUP	RAVE ON/CAROLINE RECORDS	
		5 CROSBY ST	NEW YORK, NY 10013

Name	Occupation	Address	City	Zip
REECE, DAVID	PIANIST	612 FEDDERS DR	MADISON, TN	37115
REECE, LEON	BANJOIST	ROUTE #1	GORDONSVILLE, TN	37083
REECE, RICKY	GUITARIST	ROUTE #1, BOX 206-A	HARTSVILLE, TN	37074
REED, ALAINA	ACTRESS	14 W 44TH ST #1500	NEW YORK, NY	10036
REED, ALEXANDER	ACTOR	6 W 87TH ST	NEW YORK, NY	10024
REED, ANDRE L	COMPOSER	624 N HOWARD AVE #127	MONTEBELLO, CA	90640
REED, ANN	SINGER-GUITARIST	788 FULLER AVE	SAINT PAUL, MN	55104
REED, BARBIE	ACTRESS	SCHOEMAN, 2600 W VICTORY BLVD	BURBANK, CA	91505
REED, BRUCE	TENOR	LEW, 204 W 10TH ST	NEW YORK, NY	10014
REED, BRUCE	ACTOR	5330 LANKERSHIM BLVD #210	NORTH HOLLYWOOD, CA	90212
REED, BRUCE	WRESTLER	SEE - REED, BUTCH "THE NATURAL"		
REED, BUTCH "THE NATURAL"	WRESTLER	POST OFFICE BOX 3859	STAMFORD, CT	06905
REED, CLAY	BODYGUARD-MODEL	2801 MEADOW LARK DR	SAN DIEGO, CA	92123
REED, DIANA	SOPRANO	45 W 60TH ST #4-K	NEW YORK, NY	10023
REED, ELLIS C	PHOTOGRAPHER	1956 15TH ST	SAN FRANCISCO, CA	94114
REED, ERNIE	VIOLINIST	240 ROCKLAND RD #A	HENDERSONVILLE, TN	37075
REED, EVERETT L	COMPOSER	11729 RIVERSIDE DR #5	NORTH HOLLYWOOD, CA	91607
REED, HACKSAW BUTCH	WRESTLER	SEE - REED, BUTCH "THE NATURAL"		
REED, HADEN	SINGER	PAL'S, 120 MIKEL DR	SUMMERVILLE, SC	29483
REED, J D	WRITER-EDITOR	TIME/TIME & LIFE BLDG		
		ROCKEFELLER CENTER	NEW YORK, NY	10020
REED, JACKSON	ACTOR	348 E OLIVE AVE #K	BURBANK, CA	91502
REED, JERRY	SINGER-ACTOR-SONGWRI	POST OFFICE BOX 38	THOMPSONS STATION, TN	37179
REED, JIMMY & BLUES FAN CLUB	DED-TRIB GROUP	OLDIES, 5218 ALMONT ST	LOS ANGELES, CA	90032
REED, LOU	SINGER-SONGWRITER	ATI, 888 7TH AVE, 21ST FLOOR	NEW YORK, NY	10106
REED, MARGARET	ACTRESS	CBS-TV, "AS THE WORLD TURNS"		
		51 W 52ND ST	NEW YORK, NY	10019
REED, MICHAEL	CINEMATOGRAPHER	THE BRAMBLINGS, SPEEN		
		NEAR AYLESBURY	BUCKS	ENGLAND
REED, NIGEL	ACTOR	165 W 46TH ST #409	NEW YORK, NY	10036
REED, OLIVER	ACTOR	DAVID REED, 314 HIGH ST		
		DORKING	SURREY RH4 1QX	ENGLAND
REED, PAMELA	ACTRESS	10100 SANTA MONICA BLVD #1600	LOS ANGELES, CA	90067
REED, PETER	FILM EXECUTIVE	2 W END CT, PRIORY RD	LONDON NW6	ENGLAND
REED, PHIL	PERCUSSIONIST	7011 CORTEZ CT	HERMITAGE, TN	37076
REED, PHILIP	ACTOR	969 BEL AIR RD	LOS ANGELES, CA	90077
REED, REX	FILM CRITIC	1 W 72ND ST #86	NEW YORK, NY	10023
REED, ROBERT	ACTOR	2121 AVE OF THE STARS #410	LOS ANGELES, CA	90067
REED, SHANNA	ACTRESS	247 S BEVERLY DR #102	BEVERLY HILLS, CA	90210
REED, SUSAN K	WRITER-EDITOR	PEOPLE/TIME & LIFE BLDG		
		ROCKEFELLER CENTER	NEW YORK, NY	10020
REED, SUSANNE	ACTRESS	9021 MELROSE AVE #304	LOS ANGELES, CA	90069
REED, TRACY	ACTRESS	113 N SAN VICENTE BLVD #202	BEVERLY HILLS, CA	90211
REED, VAUGHAN	GUITARIST	135 BRINKHAVEN #B-20	MADISON, TN	37115
REED, VIVIAN	ACTRESS	201 W 70TH ST	NEW YORK, NY	10023
REEDER, CARLOS A	DIRECTOR	9025 WILSHIRE BLVD #301	BEVERLY HILLS, CA	90212
REEDER, DAVID F	NEWS CORRESPONDENT	908 PHEASANT RUN DR	GAITHERSBURG, MD	20878
REEDER, DON	NEWS CORRESPONDENT	11009 DEL MAR CT	FAIRFAX, VA	22030
REEDER, GORDON H	COMPOSER	11315 PLAYA ST	CULVER CITY, CA	90230
REEDER, PHILIP W	TV WRITER	8955 BEVERLY BLVD	LOS ANGELES, CA	90048
REEDER, THOMAS	TV WRITER	8955 BEVERLY BLVD	LOS ANGELES, CA	90048
REEDY, BRUCE W	PHOTOGRAPHER	POST OFFICE BOX 9414	WASHINGTON, DC	20016
REELEY, RON	SINGER	FIELDS, 3753 VINEYARD CT	MARIETTA, GA	30062
REELLY, ANN L	NEWS CORRESPONDENT	CBS NEWS, 2020 "M" ST, NW	WASHINGTON, DC	20036
REEMS, HARRY	ACTOR	19900 PACIFIC COAST HWY	MALIBU, CA	90265
REES, CARLYLE W	DIRECTOR	2927 CROOKS RD	ROYAL OAK, MI	48073
REES, DAVID	ACT-WRI-PROD	30 STEELES RD, HAMPSTEAD	LONDON NW3	ENGLAND
REES, JOHN	NEWS CORRESPONDENT	2805 SAINT PAUL ST	BALTIMORE, MD	21218
REES, ROGER	ACTOR	ICM, 388-396 OXFORD ST	LONDON W1	ENGLAND
REESE, CHARLEY	COMMENTATOR	KING FEATURES SYNDICATE		
		235 E 45TH ST	NEW YORK, NY	10017
REESE, DELLA	SINGER-ACTRESS	1910 BEL AIR RD	LOS ANGELES, CA	90077
REESE, GILBERT	CELLIST	CPS, 34 66TH PL	LONG BEACH, CA	90803
REESE, JOHN	PIANIST	311 54TH AVE N	NASHVILLE, TN	37209
REESE, JOHN D	GUITARIST	119 EDGEWOOD DR	HENDERSONVILLE, TN	37075
REESE, MICHELLE	ACTRESS	3151 W CAHUENGA BLVD #310	LOS ANGELES, CA	90068
REESE, PEE WEE	BASEBALL	POST OFFICE BOX 35700		
		MAIN OFFICE STATION	LOUISVILLE, KY	40232
REESE, RALPH	CARTOONIST	THE NATIONAL LAMPOON		
		635 MADISON AVE	NEW YORK, NY	10022
REESE, ROXANNE	ACTRESS	620 N BEACHWOOD DR	LOS ANGELES, CA	90004
REESE, SARAH	SOPRANO	CAMI, 165 W 57TH ST	NEW YORK, NY	10019

REESE, TOM	ACTOR	10000 RIVERSIDE DR #3	TOLUCA LAKE, CA	91602
REEVE, CHRISTOPHER	ACTOR	100 W 78TH ST #5-A	NEW YORK, NY	10024
REEVE, GEOFFREY JAMES	DIRECTOR-PRODUCER	ELMBROOK, MARSH, AYLESBURY	BUCKS	ENGLAND
REEVE, SCOTT	BARITONE	CAMI, 165 W 57TH ST	NEW YORK, NY	10019
REEVES, ALAN DAVID	COMPOSER	9000 SUNSET BLVD #1115	LOS ANGELES, CA	90069
REEVES, DEL	SINGER	991 HWY #100	CENTERVILLE, TN	37033
REEVES, GEORGE	TV WRITER	8955 BEVERLY BLVD	LOS ANGELES, CA	90048
REEVES, KARI	SINGER	POST OFFICE BOX 242	HORSESHOE BEND, AR	72512
REEVES, PAMELA	NEWS CORRESPONDENT	1003 HEATHER HILL CT	MC LEAN, VA	22101
REEVES, RICHARD	COLUMNIST-REPORTER	UNIVERSAL PRESS SYNDICATE		
		4900 MAIN ST, 9TH FLOOR	KANSAS CITY, MO	62114
REEVES, STEVE	ACTOR-BODYBUILDER	POST OFFICE BOX 807	VALLEY CENTER, CA	92082
REFF, KENNETH E	NEWS CORRESPONDENT	2133 WISCONSIN AVE, NW	WASHINGTON, DC	20007
REFUGEE	ROCK & ROLL GROUP	FALCON PRODUCTIONS		
REFUGEE	ROCK & ROLL GROUP	3080 LENWORTH DR	MISSISSAUGA, ONT L4X 2	CANADA
REGA, WILLIAM J	WRITER	8306 SKYLINE DR	LOS ANGELES, CA	90046
REGAL, STEVE	WRESTLER	POST OFFICE BOX 3859	STAMFORD, CT	06905
REGALBUTO, JOE	ACTOR	817 18TH ST #2	SANTA MONICA, CA	90403
REGAN, DENNIS	MUSICIAN-WRITER	23427 FRIAR ST	WOODLAND HILLS, CA	91367
REGAN, KEN	PHOTOGRAPHER	6 W 20TH ST	NEW YORK, NY	10011
REGAN, PATRICK	WRITER-PRODUCER	3680 WILL ROGERS ST	SANTA MONICA, CA	90403
REGAN, PATTY	ACTOR	121 N ROBERTSON BLVD #B	BEVERLY HILLS, CA	90211
REGAN, TOM	ACTOR	120 S VICTORY BLVD #104	BURBANK, CA	91502
REGARD, SUZANNE	ACTRESS-MODEL	THE ATHLETES REGISTRY		
		2221 S BARRY AVE	LOS ANGELES, CA	90064
REGAS, JACK	DIRECTOR	20518 SAN JOSE ST	CHATSWORTH, CA	91311
REGATTA	ROCK & ROLL GROUP	41 BRITAIN ST #200	TORONTO, ONT	CANADA
REGEHR, DUNCAN	ACTOR	9200 SUNSET BLVD #1210	LOS ANGELES, CA	90069
REGEIMBAL, NEIL R	NEWS CORRESPONDENT	13811 MARIANNA DR	ROCKVILLE, MD	20853
REGENTS, THE	ROCK & ROLL GROUP	MARS, 168 ORCHID DR	PEARL RIVER, NY	10965
REGER, JOHN PATRICK	ACTOR	9230 OLYMPIC BLVD #203	BEVERLY HILLS, CA	90212
REGINA	SINGER	BELKIN MANAGEMENT		
		28001 CHARGIN BLVD	CINCINNATI, OH	44122
REGINA, PAUL	ACTOR	9200 SUNSET BLVD #1210	LOS ANGELES, CA	90069
REGINALD, REX	ACTOR	2051 HERCULES DR	LOS ANGELES, CA	90046
REGISTER, BILL	BODYBUILDER	4530 NE 74TH ST	PORTLAND, OR	97218
REGULAR GUYS, THE	ROCK & ROLL GROUP	POST OFFICE BOX 3278	LONG BEACH, CA	90803
REHAK, BRIAN	WRITER	POST OFFICE BOX 430	BURBANK, CA	91503
REHAK, KANDY	WRITER	2324 N KENNETH RD	BURBANK, CA	91504
REHFELD, BARRY	NEWS REPORTER	TIME/TIME & LIFE BLDG		
		ROCKEFELLER CENTER	NEW YORK, NY	10020
REHM, BARBARA	NEWS CORRESPONDENT	2737 DEVONSHIRE PL #410, NW	WASHINGTON, DC	20008
REHR, DARRYL	TV DIRECTOR	2227 PARNELL AVE	LOS ANGELES, CA	90064
REHRIG, WILLIAM	GUITARIST	2445 WALBERT AVE	ALLENTOWN, PA	18104
REICH, GUNTER	BASSO-BARITONE	CAMI, 165 W 57TH ST	NEW YORK, NY	10019
REICH, JOE	CASTING DIRECTOR	MCA/UNIVERSAL STUDIOS, INC		
		100 UNIVERSAL CITY PLAZA		
		BUILDING #463-104	UNIVERSAL CITY, CA	91608
REICH, STEVE	COMPOSER	LYNN GARON, 1199 PARK AVE	NEW YORK, NY	10028
REICHARD, JOHN P	NEWS CORRESPONDENT	9505 CAROLINE AVE	SILVER SPRING, MD	20901
REICHARDT, TEMPE L	NEWS CORRESPONDENT	122 "C" ST, NW	WASHINGTON, DC	20001
REICHEG, RICHARD	ACTOR	1416 N SYRACUSE AVE	LOS ANGELES, CA	90028
REICHENBACH, WILLIAM F	COMPOSER	14181 CLARETTA ST	PACOIMA, CA	91331
REICHLER, JOSEPH	AUTHOR	1212 6TH AVE	NEW YORK, NY	10036
REICHLINE, NEIL	WRITER	5448 ALLOTT AVE	VAN NUYS, CA	91401
REICHMAN, LOREN	TV WRITER	8955 BEVERLY BLVD	LOS ANGELES, CA	90048
REID, ALASTAIR	FILM DIRECTOR	THE OLD STORES, CURLOAD		
		STOKE, NEAR TAUNTON	SOMERSET	ENGLAND
REID, BERYL	ACTOR-COMEDIAN	HONEYPOT COTTAGE, WRAYSBURY		
		NEAR STAINES	MIDDLESEX	ENGLAND
REID, BRIAN M	NEWS CORRESPONDENT	4461 CONNECTICUT AVE, NW	WASHINGTON, DC	20008
REID, DON	ACTOR	POST OFFICE BOX 8589	UNIVERSAL CITY, CA	91608
REID, DONALD	COMPOSER	POST OFFICE BOX 2703	STAUNTON, VA	24401
REID, ELLIOTT	ACTOR-WRITER	6310 SAN VICENTE BLVD #407	LOS ANGELES, CA	90048
REID, FRANCES	ACTRESS	400 S BEVERLY DR #216	BEVERLY HILLS, CA	90212
REID, GEORGE	SINGER	CAMI, 165 W 57TH ST	NEW YORK, NY	10019
REID, GORDON	BANJOIST	122 TWO VALLEY RD	HENDERSONVILLE, TN	37075
REID, GREGORY D	DIRECTOR	DGA, 110 W 57TH ST	NEW YORK, NY	10019
REID, HAROLD	SINGER	POST OFFICE BOX 2703	STAUNTON, VA	24401
REID, HARVEY	SINGER-GUITARIST	POST OFFICE BOX 4585	PORTSMOUTH, NH	03801
REID, JERRY LAYNE	SINGER-ACTOR-SONGWRI	SEE - REED, JERRY		
REID, JOAN	ACTRESS	1418 N HIGHLAND AVE #102	LOS ANGELES, CA	90028
REID, JOHN R	TRUMPETER	2707 BLUEFIELD AVE #B	NASHVILLE, TN	37214
REID, LAUREN	MODEL	POST OFFICE BOX 7211	MOUNTAIN VIEW, CA	94043
REID, MARY	ACTRESS	10850 RIVERSIDE DR #505	NORTH HOLLYWOOD, CA	91602
REID, MAX	FILM WRITER-DIRECTOR	2512 4TH ST	SANTA MONICA, CA	90405
REID, MIKE	SINGER	POST OFFICE BOX 1556	GAINESVILLE, FL	32602
REID, SHEILA	ACTRESS	29 RYLETT RD	LONDON W12	ENGLAND
REID, TIM	ACTOR	16540 ADLON RD	ENCINO, CA	91436
REID, WILLIAM J	WRITER-PRODUCER	500 S BUENA VISTA ST	BURBANK, CA	91521
REIDY, CHRISTOPHER G	NEWS CORRESPONDENT	2701 CONNECTICUT AVE, NW	WASHINGTON, DC	20008
REIG, JUNE	TV WRITER-DIRECTOR	454 W 46TH ST	NEW YORK, NY	10036
REIHER, JAMES	WRESTLER	SEE - SNUKA, JIMMY "SUPERFLY"		
REIHLE, JAMES E	NEWS CORRESPONDENT	5151 WISCONSIN AVE, NW	WASHINGTON, DC	20016
REIKER, DON	PRODUCER	MGM, 10202 W WASHINGTON BLVD	CULVER CITY, CA	90230

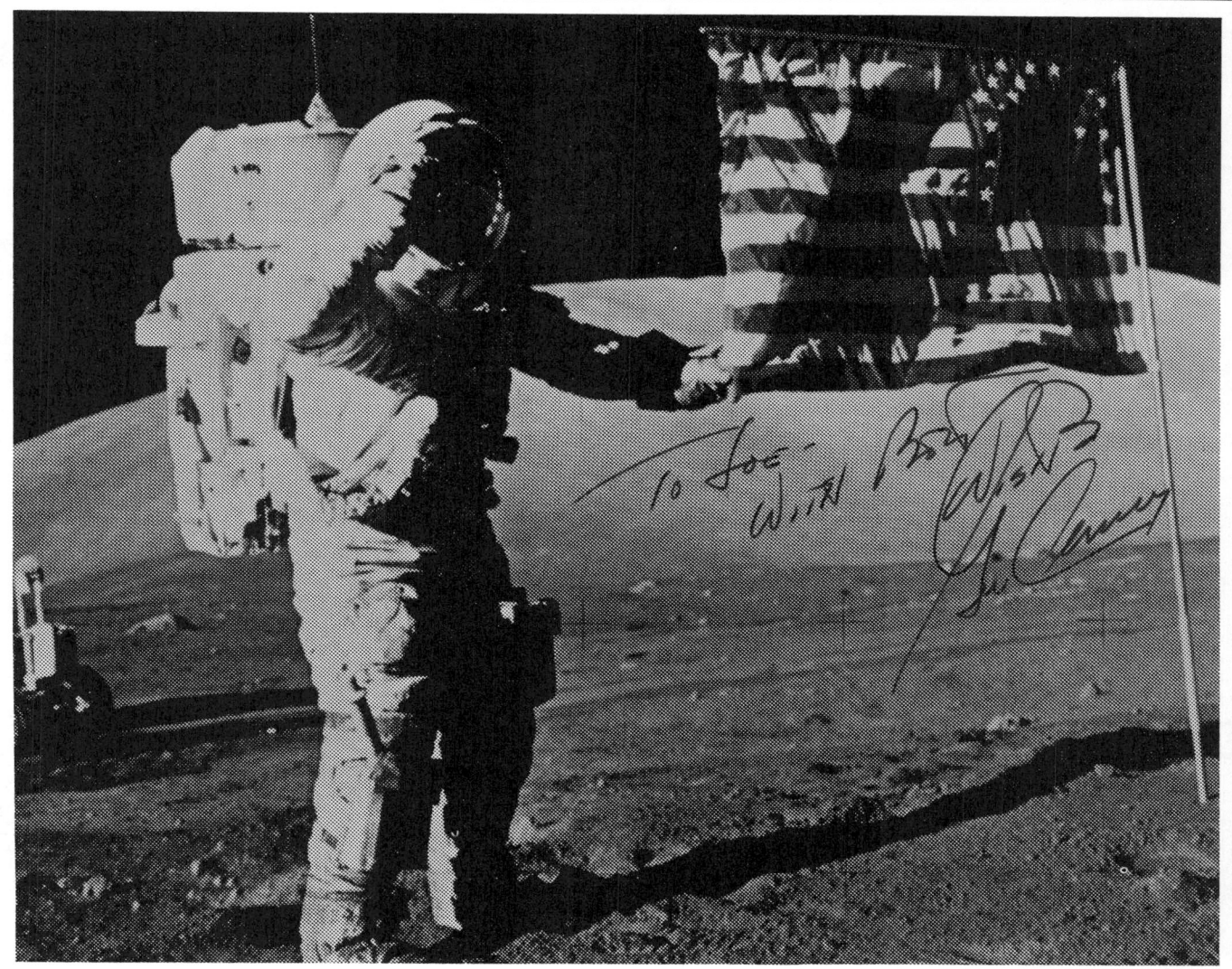

REIKER, DONALD	TV WRITER	3695 SHANNON RD	LOS ANGELES, CA	90027
REIKES, ANDREW	TV DIRECTOR	287 HARVARD ST #23	CAMBRIDGE, MA	02139
REILLY, ANN MARIE	NEWS CORRESPONDENT	3120 "R" ST #104, NW	WASHINGTON, DC	20007
REILLY, CHARLES NELSON	ACTOR	2341 GLOAMING WY	BEVERLY HILLS, CA	90210
REILLY, DEIRDRE	DIRECTOR	RIVER RD	LUMBERVILLE, PA	18933
REILLY, DONALD	CARTOONIST	POST OFFICE BOX 4203	NEW YORK, NY	10017
REILLY, JACK	TV PRODUCER	ENTERTAINMENT TONIGHT		
		PARAMOUNT TELEVISION		
		5555 MELROSE AVE	LOS ANGELES, CA	90038
REILLY, JAMES E	TV WRITER	ABC-TV, "GENERAL HOSPITAL"		
		1438 N GOWER ST	LOS ANGELES, CA	90028
REILLY, JOHN	ACTOR	POST OFFICE BOX 5617	BEVERLY HILLS, CA	90210
REILLY, JOHN M	TV DIRECTOR	322 W 57TH ST	NEW YORK, NY	10019
REILLY, PAUL A	NEWS CORRESPONDENT	1825 "K" ST, NW	WASHINGTON, DC	20006
REILLY, RICK	SPORTS WRITER-EDITOR	SPORTS ILLUSTRATED MAGAZINE		
		TIME & LIFE BUILDING		
		ROCKEFELLER CENTER	NEW YORK, NY	10020
REILLY, TOM	ACTOR	9220 SUNSET BLVD #625	LOS ANGELES, CA	90069
REILLY, WALTER N	WRITER	5928 LINDENHURST AVE	LOS ANGELES, CA	90036
REIMUELLER, ROSS C	CONDUCTOR	1647 ANGELUS AVE	LOS ANGELES, CA	90026
REIN, HAL	DIRECTOR	33 5TH AVE	NEW YORK, NY	10003
REINA, JAMES L	TV EXECUTIVE	ABC TELEVISION NETWORK		
		1330 AVE OF THE AMERICAS	NEW YORK, NY	10019
REINBOLT, JEREMY SCOTT	ACTOR	1450 BELFAST DR	LOS ANGELES, CA	90069
REINBOLT, TIFFANY	ACTRESS	1450 BELFAST DR	LOS ANGELES, CA	90069
REINER, CARL	ACTOR-DIRECTOR	714 N RODEO DR	BEVERLY HILLS, CA	90210
REINER, ESTELLE	SINGER	714 N RODEO DR	BEVERLY HILLS, CA	90210
REINER, ROB	ACT-WRI-DIR	9161 HAZEN DR	BEVERLY HILLS, CA	90210
REINER, STEVEN D	NEWS CORRESPONDENT	NBC-TV, NEWS DEPARTMENT		
		4001 NEBRASKA AVE, NW	WASHINGTON, DC	20016
REINHARD, RICK	PHOTOGRAPHER	1910 PARK RD, NW	WASHINGTON, DC	20010
REINHARD, WILLIAM	NEWS CORRESPONDENT	9725-P COVERED WAGON DR	LAUREL, MD	20707
REINHART, RICHARD	TV WRITER	16000 VALERIO ST	VAN NUYS, CA	91406
REINHOLD, GADY	TV DIRECTOR	70 RIVERSIDE DR	NEW YORK, NY	10024
REINHOLD, JUDGE	ACTOR	3855 LANKERSHIM BLVD #818	NORTH HOLLYWOOD, CA	91601
REINKING, ANN	ACTRESS	1888 CENTURY PARK E #1400	LOS ANGELES, CA	90067
REINSTEIN, MARK S	PHOTOGRAPHER	7926 INVERNESS RIDGE RD	POTOMAC, MD	20854
REIS, ALEXANDER JOHN	NEWS CORRESPONDENT	236 MASSACHUSETTS AVE, NE	WASHINGTON, DC	20002
REIS, DIANE M	NEWS CORRESPONDENT	1600 28TH ST, NW	WASHINGTON, DC	20007
REISBERG, RICHARD S	TV EXECUTIVE	15915 WOODVALE RD	ENCINO, CA	91436
REISCH, STEVEN D	ACTOR	3151 W CAHUENGA BLVD #310	LOS ANGELES, CA	90068
REISER, ALOIS	COMPOSER-CONDUCTOR	1542 COURTNEY AVE	LOS ANGELES, CA	90046
REISER, HAROLD L	DIRECTOR	9256 SWINTON AVE	SEPULVEDA, CA	91343
REISER, PAUL	ACTOR	1888 CENTURY PARK E #1400	LOS ANGELES, CA	90067
REISER, ROBERT S	TV WRITER	8955 BEVERLY BLVD	LOS ANGELES, CA	90048
REISFELD, BERT	COMPOSER	POST OFFICE BOX 390	BEVERLY HILLS, CA	90213
REISHER, PAUL	COMEDIAN	1888 S CENTURY PARK E #1400	LOS ANGELES, CA	90067
REISIG, ANNE	SPINTO	431 S DEARBORN ST #1504	CHICAGO, IL	60605
REISMAN, DAVID	DIRECTOR	70 E 10TH ST	NEW YORK, NY	10003
REISMAN, DEL	WRITER	14411 RIVERSIDE DR #21	SHERMAN OAKS, CA	91423
REISMAN, JAY	WRITER	4808 LA VILLA MARINA #D	MARINA DEL REY, CA	90292
REISMAN, JOE	COMPOSER-CONDUCTOR	4337 CLYBOURNE AVE	NORTH HOLLYWOOD, CA	91602
REISMAN, MARK A	SCREENWRITER	8955 BEVERLY BLVD	LOS ANGELES, CA	90048
REISMAN, PHILIP H, JR	TV WRITER	555 W 57TH ST #1230	NEW YORK, NY	10019
REISNER, ALLEN	DIRECTOR	9165 CORDELL DR	LOS ANGELES, CA	90069
REISS, ANDRE	GUITARIST	329 VALERIA ST	NASHVILLE, TN	37210
REISS, DAVID	TV WRITER	8955 BEVERLY BLVD	LOS ANGELES, CA	90048
REISS, JEFFREY C	CABLE EXECUTIVE	CABLE HEALTH NETWORK		
		1211 AVE OF THE AMERICAS	NEW YORK, NY	10020
REISTER, FREDRICK	DIRECTOR	6426 WOODARD BAY RD, NE	OLYMPIA, WA	98506
REISZ, KAREL	FILM DIRECTOR	FILM CONTRACTS, LTD		
		2 LOWER JAMES ST	LONDON W1R 3PN	ENGLAND
REITEL, ENN	ACTOR	16 SWYNCOMBE AVE	EALING W5	ENGLAND
REITER, ANDREA	DIRECTOR	400 E 85TH ST #15-L	NEW YORK, NY	10028
REITER, JOHN	NEWS CORRESPONDENT	816 N LINCOLN ST	ARLINGTON, VA	22201
REITMAN, IVAN	DIRECTOR-PRODUCER	1426 STONE CANYON RD	LOS ANGELES, CA	90077
REJJO, PETER	CELLIST	CCS, 4478 PURDUE AVE	CULVER CITY, CA	90230
REJTO, GABOR	CELLIST	POST OFFICE BOX 20548	NEW YORK, NY	10025
REKERT, WINSTON	ACTOR	11726 SAN VICENTE BLVD #300	LOS ANGELES, CA	90049
RELAY	MUSICAL GROUP	POST OFFICE BOX 6568	CINCINNATI, OH	45206
RELLAS, CHRIS P	WRITER	6739 LARAMIE AVE	CANOGA PARK, CA	91306
RELPH, MICHAEL	WRITER-PRODUCER	PRIMOSE HILL STUDIOS		
		THE LODGES	LONDON NW1	ENGLAND
RELPH, SIMON	FILM PRODUCER	338 LIVERPOOL RD	LONDON N7	ENGLAND
RELYEA, ROBERT	DIRECTOR	12950 BLAIRWOOD DR	STUDIO CITY, CA	91604
REMAR, JAMES	ACTOR	ICM, 8899 BEVERLY BLVD	LOS ANGELES, CA	90048
REMEDIOS, ALBERTO	TENOR	SARDOS, 180 W END AVE	NEW YORK, NY	10023
REMICK, LEE	ACTRESS-PRODUCER	570 N BUNDY DR	LOS ANGELES, CA	90049
REMICK, PATRICIA J	NEWS CORRESPONDENT	3524 S 7TH ST	ARLINGTON, VA	22204
REMON, CESAR	ACTOR	2404 KANSAS AVE #A	SANTA MONICA, CA	90404
REMSEN, ANN	CASTING DIRECTOR	RALEIGH, 650 N BRONSON AVE	LOS ANGELES, CA	90004
REMSEN, BARBARA	CASTING DIRECTOR	RALEIGH, 650 N BRONSON AVE	LOS ANGELES, CA	90004
REMSEN, BERT	ACTOR	5722 MAMMOTH AVE	VAN NUYS, CA	91401
REMSEN, GUY	ACTOR	8721 SUNSET BLVD #103	LOS ANGELES, CA	90069
REMUS, ROBERT	WRESTLER	SEE - SLAUGHTER, SGT		

Name	Occupation	Address	City	Zip
RENAISSANCE	ROCK & ROLL GROUP	POST OFFICE BOX 1333	MONTCLAIR, NJ	07042
RENALDO AND THE LOAF	ROCK & ROLL GROUP	109 MINNA ST #391	SAN FRANCISCO, CA	94105
RENASCENCE TRIO	C & W GROUP	PROCESS, 439 WILEY AVE	FRANKLIN, PA	16323
RENAUD, LINE	ACTRESS	1417 N SPAULDING AVE	LOS ANGELES, CA	90046
RENAY, LIZ	BURLESQUE	3708 SAN ANGELO AVE	LAS VEGAS, NV	89102
RENBOURN, JOHN	SINGER-GUITARIST	FOLKLORE PRODS, 1671 APPIAN WY	SANTA MONICA, CA	90401
RENDALL, DAVID	TENOR	CAMI, 165 W 57TH ST	NEW YORK, NY	10019
RENDELY, RICHARD R	DIRECTOR	POST OFFICE BOX 231	GREENWICH, CT	06830
RENDINA, VICTOR	ACTOR	141 N KENWOOD ST	GLENDALE, CA	91206
RENE, HENRI	CONDUCTOR	1081 LIGHTHOUSE AVE #214	PACIFIC GROVE, CA	93950
RENE, JOSEPH	COMPOSER	220 GREGORY PL	WEST PALM BEACH, FL	33405
RENE & ANGELA	SOUL DUO	200 W 51ST ST #1410	NEW YORK, NY	10019
RENEE, MADELYN	SOPRANO	119 W 57TH ST #1505	NEW YORK, NY	10019
RENEGADE	ROCK & ROLL GROUP	10020 PIONEER BLVD #104	SANTA FE SPRINGS, CA	90670
RENEGADES, THE	ROCK & ROLL GROUP	POST OFFICE BOX 57291	DALLAS, TX	75207
RENELLA, PAT	ACTOR	1825 N WHITLEY AVE #505	LOS ANGELES, CA	90028
RENICK, JEANE	TV EXECUTIVE	CBS-TV, 51 W 52ND ST	NEW YORK, NY	10019
RENNARD, DEBORAH	ACTRESS	POST OFFICE BOX 5617	BEVERLY HILLS, CA	90210
RENNERT, LEO	NEWS CORRESPONDENT	5914 ROLSTON RD	BETHESDA, MD	20817
RENO, JACK	SINGER	POST OFFICE BOX 201	CINCINNATI, OH	45201
RENO, JEFF	TV WRITER	8955 BEVERLY BLVD	LOS ANGELES, CA	90048
RENO, RONNIE	SINGER-GUITARIST	135 CHIROC RD	HENDERSONVILLE, TN	37075
RENOIR, JEAN	FILM DIRECTOR	1273 LEONA DR	BEVERLY HILLS, CA	90210
RENOUDET, PETE	ACTOR	1532 N LIMA ST	BURBANK, CA	91505
RENSBERGER, BOYCE	NEWS CORRESPONDENT	3110 THURSTON RD	FREDERICK, MD	21701
RENSLOW, RICK	WRESTLER	POST OFFICE BOX 3859	STAMFORD, CT	06905
RENZ, FREDERICK	CONDUCTOR	HILLYER, 250 W 57TH ST	NEW YORK, NY	10107
RENZI, MAGGIE	ACTRESS	5850 CANOGA AVE #110	WOODLAND HILLS, CA	91367
RENZI, MAGGIE	FILM PRODUCER	RED DOG FILMS, 306 W 38TH ST	NEW YORK, NY	10018
REO, DAVID R	TV WRITER	8955 BEVERLY BLVD	LOS ANGELES, CA	90048
REO, DON	TV WRITER-PRODUCER	8042 WOODROW WILSON DR	LOS ANGELES, CA	90046
REO SPEEDWAGON	ROCK & ROLL GROUP	BARUCK, 1046 CAROL DR	LOS ANGELES, CA	90069
REOLIN, WILLIAM J	NEWS CORRESPONDENT	2232 GUNSMITH SQ	RESTON, VA	22091
REPARATA & THE DELRONS	ROCK & ROLL GROUP	MARS, 168 ORCHID DR	PEARL RIVER, NY	10965
REPCZYNSKI, JOHN	DIRECTOR	13458 FRIAR ST	VAN NUYS, CA	91401
REPPERT, CHARLES BARTON	NEWS CORRESPONDENT	1616 18TH ST #1008, NW	WASHINGTON, DC	20009
RESCH, PAMELA	PIANIST	ALPHA, 685 W END AVE	NEW YORK, NY	10025
RESCHER, DEE DEE	ACTRESS	1901 AVE OF THE STARS #840	LOS ANGELES, CA	90067
RESCHER, GAYNE	CINEMATOGRAPHER	939 N WETHERLY DR	LOS ANGELES, CA	90069
RESCIGNO, JOSEPH	CONDUCTOR	61 W 62ND ST #6-F	NEW YORK, NY	10023
RESETAR, ROBERT J	COMPOSER	2135 N BEACHWOOD DR #4	LOS ANGELES, CA	90068
RESIDENTS, THE	ROCK & ROLL GROUP	109 MINNA ST #391	SAN FRANCISCO, CA	94105
RESIN, DAN	ACTOR	LIZANDRA, 115 HUBER ST	SECAUCUS, NJ	07094
RESING, GEORGE	TV EXECUTIVE	GROUP W PRODUCTIONS		
		100 UNIVERSAL CITY PLAZA	UNIVERSAL CITY, CA	91608
RESKE, HENRY J	NEWS CORRESPONDENT	441 1/2 22ND ST, SE	WASHINGTON, DC	20003
RESNAIS, ALAIN	DIRECTOR	70 RUE DES PLANTES	PARIS 75014	FRANCE
RESNER, LAWRENCE	WRITER	11618 KIOWA AVE #115	LOS ANGELES, CA	90049
RESNICK, NOEL	TV EXECUTIVE	ABC-TV ENTERTAINMENT CENTER		
		2040 AVE OF THE STARS	LOS ANGELES, CA	90067
RESNICK, PATRICIA	SCREENWRITER	8955 BEVERLY BLVD	LOS ANGELES, CA	90048
RESNICOFF, ETHEL	WRITER	14002 PALAWAN WY #3111	MARINA DEL REY, CA	90292
RESNIKOFF, ROBERT D	WRITER	861 CHATTANOOGA AVE	PACIFIC PALISADES, CA	90272
RESS, GARY L	TV WRITER	8955 BEVERLY BLVD	LOS ANGELES, CA	90048
RESTANI, PAOLO	PIANIST	POST OFFICE BOX 27539	PHILADELPHIA, PA	19118
RESTER, GINA L	TV WRITER	8955 BEVERLY BLVD	LOS ANGELES, CA	90048
RESTIVO, JOE	ACTOR-TV WRITER	6640 SUNSET BLVD #203	LOS ANGELES, CA	90028
RESTIVO, JOEY	ACTOR	3330 BARHAM BLVD #103	LOS ANGELES, CA	90068
RESTIVO, STEVE	ACTOR	3330 BARHAM BLVD #103	LOS ANGELES, CA	90068
RESTON, JAMES	NEWS CORRESPONDENT	1804 KALORAMA SQ, NW	WASHINGTON, DC	20008
RETHWISCH, GUS	ACTOR	1836 REYNOSA DR	TORRANCE, CA	90501
RETTIG, RICHARD	TV EXECUTIVE	NBC-TV, 3000 W ALAMEDA AVE	BURBANK, CA	91523
RETTIG, TOMMY	ACTOR	9300 WILSHIRE BLVD #470	BEVERLY HILLS, CA	90212
RETURN TO FOREVER	JAZZ GROUP	KURLAND, 173 BRIGHTON AVE	BOSTON, MA	02134
REUBENS, PAUL "PEE WEE HERMAN"	COMEDIAN-ACTOR	6640 SUNSET BLVD #203	LOS ANGELES, CA	90028
REV, THE	ROCK & ROLL GROUP	25 HUNTINGTON AVE #420	BOSTON, MA	02116
REVARD, JAMES	TV EXECUTUVE	CBS-TV, 7800 BEVERLY BLVD	LOS ANGELES, CA	90036
REVERE, ANNE	ACTRESS	9 FOX LN	LOCUST VALLEY, NY	11560
REVERE, PAUL & THE RAIDERS	ROCK & ROLL GROUP	9044 MELROSE AVE #200	LOS ANGELES, CA	90069
REVILL, CLIVE	ACTOR	15029 ENCANTO DR	SHERMAN OAKS, CA	91403
REVILO	CARTOONIST	POST OFFICE BOX 4203	NEW YORK, NY	10017
REVIVAL BROTHERS, THE	C & W GROUP	4047 NACO-PERRIN BLVD #110	SAN ANTONIO, TX	78217
REVOLUTION, THE	ROCK & ROLL GROUP	SEE - PRINCE & THE REVOLUTION		
REVZON, JOEL	CONDUCTOR	5720 MOSHOLU AVE #300	RIVERDALE, NY	10471
REX, CHARLES	VIOLINIST	HILLYER, 250 W 57TH ST	NEW YORK, NY	10107
REX, CHRISTOPHER	CELLIST	HILLYER, 250 W 57TH ST	NEW YORK, NY	10107
REX, JEFF	SINGER-GUITARIST	734 TURF RD	NORTH WOODMERE, NY	11581
REXSTEINER, ROB	WRESTLER	SEE - STEINER, RICK		
REY, ANTONIA	ACTRESS	523 W 112TH ST #31	NEW YORK, NY	10025
REY, FERNANDO	ACTOR	ORENSE 62	MADRID 20	SPAIN
REY, MARGO	ACTRESS	439 S LA CIENEGA BLVD #117	LOS ANGELES, CA	90048
REYES, ANGEL	SPORTS REPORTER	SPORTS ILLUSTRATED MAGAZINE		
		TIME & LIFE BUILDING		
		ROCKEFELLER CENTER	NEW YORK, NY	10020
REYES, ERNIE	ACTOR	ICM, 8899 BEVERLY BLVD	LOS ANGELES, CA	90069

Name	Occupation	Address	City	Zip
REYES, ERNIE, JR	ACTOR	ICM, 8899 BEVERLY BLVD	LOS ANGELES, CA	90048
REYES, KERRY LEE	BODYBUILDER	WORLD OF FITNESS, 2110 WHITSON	SELMA, CA	93662
REYES, LUIS	WRITER-PRODUCER	4540 LAUREL CANYON BLVD	NORTH HOLLYWOOD, CA	91607
REYNOLDS, AL	TV WRITER	8955 BEVERLY BLVD	LOS ANGELES, CA	90048
REYNOLDS, BILLY RAY	SINGER-GUITARIST	ROUTE #1, BOX 176	PRIMM SPRINGS, TN	38476
REYNOLDS, BURT	ACTOR-DIRECTOR	245 N CAROLWOOD DR	LOS ANGELES, CA	90024
REYNOLDS, CINDY	MUSICIAN	3110 W END CIR	NASHVILLE, TN	37203
REYNOLDS, CLARKE E	WRITER-PRODUCER	4139 VIA MARINA #1106-8	MARINA DEL REY, CA	90292
REYNOLDS, DALE	ACTOR	1538 N DETROIT ST #6	LOS ANGELES, CA	90046
REYNOLDS, DAVID	TV DIRECTOR	PENCOB HOUSE, SCOTTON		
		KNARESBOROUG	NORTH YORKS	ENGLAND
REYNOLDS, DEAN	NEWS CORRESPONDENT	ABC-TV, NEWS DEPARTMENT		
		1717 DE SALES ST, NW	WASHINGTON, DC	20036
REYNOLDS, DEBBIE	ACTRESS	11595 LA MAIDA ST	NORTH HOLLYWOOD, CA	91602
REYNOLDS, GENE	ACTOR-DIRECTOR	2034 CASTILIAN DR	LOS ANGELES, CA	90068
REYNOLDS, JACK	DIRECTOR	93 SHERWOOD DR	WESTLAKE VILLAGE, CA	91361
REYNOLDS, JACK	NEWS CORRESPONDENT	NBC-TV, NEWS DEPARTMENT		
		30 ROCKEFELLER PLAZA	NEW YORK, NY	10112
REYNOLDS, JAMES E	NEWS CORRESPONDENT	4105 GALLATIN ST	HYATTSVILLE, MD	20781
REYNOLDS, JAMES V	ACTOR	5348 1/2 ABBOTT PL	LOS ANGELES, CA	90042
REYNOLDS, JODY	SINGER	OLDIES, 5218 ALMONT ST	LOS ANGELES, CA	90032
REYNOLDS, JOHN J	NEWS CORRESPONDENT	NBC-TV, NEWS DEPARTMENT		
		4001 NEBRASKA AVE, NW	WASHINGTON, DC	20016
REYNOLDS, JOHN M	NEWS CORRESPONDENT	902 KERWIN RD	SILVER SPRING, MD	20015
REYNOLDS, JOSEPH J	TV DIRECTOR	POST OFFICE BOX 904	MARY ESTHER, FL	32569
REYNOLDS, LARRY	GUITARIST	3601 MEADOWBROOK AVNUE	NASHVILLE, TN	37205
REYNOLDS, LEE	DIRECTOR	2980 WILSON AVE	OAKTON, VA	22124
REYNOLDS, LEE	SINGER	POST OFFICE BOX 21322	SAN ANTONIO, TX	78221
REYNOLDS, LEE ALLEN	SINGER-GUITARIST	POST OFFICE BOX 120657	NASHVILLE, TN	37212
REYNOLDS, LEE D	SCREENWRITER	8955 BEVERLY BLVD	LOS ANGELES, CA	90048
REYNOLDS, LISA	VIOLINIST	POST OFFICE BOX 120464	NASHVILLE, TN	37212
REYNOLDS, MARIE	ACTRESS	10 E 44TH ST #700	NEW YORK, NY	10017
REYNOLDS, MIKE	ACTOR	5000 LANKERSHIM BLVD #5	NORTH HOLLYWOOD, CA	91601
REYNOLDS, R T	WRESTLER	SEE - KIRCHNER, CORPORAL		
REYNOLDS, RICHARD E	CONDUCTOR	4332 AGNES AVE	STUDIO CITY, CA	91604
REYNOLDS, RICK	ACTOR	141 S EL CAMINO DR #205	BEVERLY HILLS, CA	90212
REYNOLDS, ROBERT J	NEWS CORRESPONDENT	2133 WISCONSIN AVE, NW	WASHINGTON, DC	20007
REYNOLDS, STERLING TOM	DIRECTOR	7141 N 16TH ST	PHOENIX, AZ	85020
REYNOLDS, TED	GUITARIST	1801 GOLF CLUB RD	OLD HICKORY, TN	37138
REYNOLDS, VERA	ACTRESS	BIRCH, PALM HILL COUNTRY CLUB		
		62 SABAL PLAM DR	LARGO, FL	33540
REYNOLDS, WILLIAM	ACTOR	11215 JELLICO AVE	GRANADA HILLS, CA	91344
REYNOLDS, WILLIAM F	NEWS CORRESPONDENT	5803 DEVONSHIRE DR	BETHESDA, MD	20816
REZNICK, SIDNEY	TV WRITER	8955 BEVERLY BLVD	LOS ANGELES, CA	90048
RHAPSODY	MUSICAL GROUP	LUTZ, 5625 "O" STREET BLDG	LINCOLN, NE	68510
RHEA, FREDDY K	MUSICIAN-WRITER	290 S 5TH ST E	MOUNTAIN HOME, ID	83647
RHEA, JOHN	NEWS CORRESPONDENT	220 CEDAR LN	VEINNA, VA	22180
RHEIN, REGINALD, JR	NEWS CORRESPONDENT	6102 PRINCETON AVE	GLEN ECHO, MD	20812
RHEINGANS, BRAD	WRESTLER	AMERICAN WRESTLING ASSOC		
		MINNEAPLOIS WRESTLING		
		10001 WAYZATA BLVD	MINNETONKA, MN	55345
RHEINSTEIN, FREDERIC	DIRECTOR	6335 HOMEWOOD AVE	LOS ANGELES, CA	90028
RHETT, ALICIA	ACTRESS	50 TRADD ST	CHARLESTON, SC	29401
RHINE, LARRY	TV WRITER	567 CRESTLINE DR	LOS ANGELES, CA	90049
RHINES, MARIE	VIOLIST	FROTHINGHAM, 40 GROVE ST	WESSESLEY, MA	02181
RHOADES, BARBARA	ACTRESS	12366 RIDGE CIR	LOS ANGELES, CA	90049
RHOADS, DEBORAH	AUTO HARPIST	1101 MORROW AVE	NASHVILLE, TN	37204
RHOADS, MARJORIE	PIANIST	1101 MORROW AVE	NASHVILLE, TN	37204
RHODES, ALBURTT	TENOR	LIEBERMAN, 11 RIVERSIDE DR	NEW YORK, NY	10023
RHODES, BETTY JANE	ACTRESS	BROWN, 10693 CHALON RD	LOS ANGELES, CA	90024
RHODES, CURLY	GUITARIST	4603 LOG CABIN RD	NASHVILLE, TN	37216
RHODES, CYNTHIA	ACTRESS-DANCER	15 LIGHTHOUSE ST	MARINA DEL REY, CA	90292
RHODES, DAVID	COMPOSER-CONDUCTOR	4848 COLLETT AVE	ENCINO, CA	91436
RHODES, DONNELLY	ACTOR	9744 WILSHIRE BLVD #206	BEVERLY HILLS, CA	90212
RHODES, DUSTY	WRESTLER	NATIONAL WRESTLING ALLIANCE		
		JIM CROCKETT PROMOTIONS		
		421 BRIARBEND DR	CHARLOTTE, NC	28209
RHODES, ERIC AARON	FILM EXECUTIVE	CURZON CINEMA, LANGNEY RD		
		EASTBORNE	EAST SUSSEX	ENGLAND
RHODES, ERIK	ACTOR	405 E 54TH ST	NEW YORK, NY	10022
RHODES, GRANDON	ACTOR	5168 YARMOUTH AVE	ENCINO, CA	91316
RHODES, GREG	ACTOR	2501 W BURBANK BLVD #304	BURBANK, CA	91505
RHODES, HARI	ACTOR	CONTEMPORARY ARTISTS		
		132 S LASKY DR	BEVERLY HILLS, CA	90212
RHODES, JAMES W	PHOTOGRAPHER	3700 N CAPITOL ST, NW	WASHINGTON, DC	20317
RHODES, JENNIFER	ACTRESS	9255 SUNSET BLVD #603	LOS ANGELES, CA	90069
RHODES, LEE	ACTOR	3330 BARHAM BLVD #103	LOS ANGELES, CA	90068
RHODES, LEON	GUITARIST	2227 AUBREY CT	NASHVILLE, TN	37214
RHODES, LISA	SINGER-GUITARIST	SPINDLETOP RECORDS		
		1 CAMP ST	CAMBRIDGE, MA	02140
RHODES, MICHAEL	WRITER-PRODUCER	2672 HUTTON DR	BEVERLY HILLS, CA	90210
RHODES, MICHAEL R	DIRECTOR	17564 CASTELLAMMARE DR	PACIFIC PALISADES, CA	90272
RHODES, MICHAEL W	GUITARIST	177 STEWARTS FERRY PIKE	HERMITAGE, TN	37076
RHODES, NORMAN	MUSICIAN	2715 PRIEST LAKE DR	NASHVILLE, TN	37217
RHODES, SAMUEL	VIOLIST	240 W 98TH ST #13-A	NEW YORK, NY	10025

DEBBIE REYNOLDS

LIONEL RICHIE

DON RICKLES

DIANA RIGG

CATHY RIGBY

JEANNINE RILEY

JIM RINGER

LEE RITENOUR

HAL ROACH, SR.

Name	Occupation	Address	City/State	Zip/Country
RHODES, SPECK	FIDDLER	1201 EASTDALE AVE	NASHVILLE, TN	37216
RHODES, STEVE, BAND	ROCK & ROLL GROUP	GOOD, 2500 NW 39TH ST	OKLAHOMA CITY, OK	73112
RHODES, VIVIAN	ACTRESS	110 W END AVE	NEW YORK, NY	10023
RHODES, ZANDRA	FASHION DESIGNER	85-87 RICHFORD ST		
		HAMMERSMITH	LONDON W6	ENGLAND
RHOTON, HOWARD	GUITARIST	4836 ASTER DR	NASHVILLE, TN	37211
RHOTON, MICHAEL	ACTOR	KNBC-TV, "DAYS OF OUR LIVES"		
		3000 W ALAMEDA AVE	BURBANK, CA	91523
RHUE, MADLYN	ACTRESS	148 S MAPLE DR #D	BEVERLY HILLS, CA	90212
RHYMES, CASS	NEWS CORRESPONDENT	6612 DEARBORN DR	FALLS CHURCH, VA	22044
RHYS-DAVIS, JOHN	ACTOR	10100 SANTA MONICA BLVD #1600	LOS ANGELES, CA	90067
RHYTHM & NOISE	ROCK & ROLL GROUP	109 MINNA ST #391	SAN FRANCISCO, CA	94105
RHYTHM CORPS, THE	ROCK & ROLL GROUP	POST OFFICE BOX 37044	DETROIT, MI	48237
RHYTHM PALS, THE	C & W GROUP	4680 ELK LAKE DR #304	VICTORIA, BC V8Z 5M1	CANADA
RHYTHM PIGS, THE	ROCK & ROLL GROUP	POST OFFICE BOX 988	SAN FRANCISCO, CA	94101
RIBERI, PETER	TENOR	45 W 60TH ST #4-K	NEW YORK, NY	10023
RIBMAN, RONALD	PLAYWRIGHT	DRAMA GUILD, 234 W 44TH ST	NEW YORK, NY	10036
RICARD, ADRIAN	ACTRESS	1307 S STANLEY AVE	LOS ANGELES, CA	90019
RICARDO, DON	CONDUCTOR	964 HILLSIDE TERR	PASADENA, CA	91105
RICCI, JOSEPH	GUITARIST	2405 CRESTMOOR DR	NASHVILLE, TN	37215
RICCI, PHYLLIS	CASTING DIRECTOR	446 N GOLDEN MALL	BURBANK, CA	91502
RICCI, RUGGIERO	VIOLINIST	SHAW CONCERTS, 1995 BROADWAY	NEW YORK, NY	10023
RICCIARELLI, KATIA	SOPRANO	CAMI, 165 W 57TH ST	NEW YORK, NY	10019
RICE, ALAN B	NEWS CORRESPONDENT	9419 EAGLETON LN	GAITHERSBURG, MD	20760
RICE, ALLAN L	WRITER	19400 SHENANGO DR	TARZANA, CA	91356
RICE, ALLAN LEONARD	TV EXECUTIVE	10201 W PICO BLVD	LOS ANGELES, CA	90064
RICE, ANNEKA	ACTRESS	ARLINGTON, 1-3 CHARLOTTE ST	LONDON W1A 1HD	ENGLAND
RICE, BILL	PIANIST	POST OFFICE BOX 25267	NASHVILLE, TN	37202
RICE, BOBBY	SINGER	124 NATHAN FORREST DR	HENDERSONVILLE, TN	37075
RICE, DONNA	ACTRESS-MODEL	ERICKSON MODELING AGENCY		
		1483 CHAIN BRIDGE RD	MC LEAN, VA	22101
RICE, DOROTHY	ACTRESS	427 N CANON DR #205	BEVERLY HILLS, CA	90210
RICE, JAMES GOODWIN	ACTOR	280 RIVERSIDE DR #12-E	NEW YORK, NY	10025
RICE, JIM	BASEBALL	RURAL ROUTE #8, BOX 686	ANDERSON, SC	29621
RICE, JOHN	GUITARIST	309 ALTA LOMA RD	MADISON, TN	37115
RICE, KEVIN R	NEWS CORRESPONDENT	2025 "M" ST, NW	WASHINGTON, DC	20036
RICE, LAURA BROOKS	MEZZO-SOPRANO	COLBERT, 111 W 57TH ST	NEW YORK, NY	10019
RICE, NORMAN	ACTOR	24236 WELBY WY	CANOGA PARK, CA	91307
RICE, STORMY	SINGER	POST OFFICE BOX 138	BLACK EARTH, WI	53515
RICE, SUSAN	WRITER	151 S EL CAMINO DR	BEVERLY HILLS, CA	90212
RICE, SYLVESTER	MUSICIAN	4023 W 28TH ST	LOS ANGELES, CA	90018
RICE, TIM	LYRICIST	LAND, 118 WARDOUR ST	LONDON W1	ENGLAND
		NEAR CHICHESTER	SUSSEX	ENGLAND
RICH, ADAM	ACTOR	6640 SUNSET BLVD #203	LOS ANGELES, CA	90028
RICH, ALLAN	ACTOR	225 E 57TH ST	NEW YORK, NY	10022
RICH, ANDREA GILES	TV DIRECTOR	CBS-TV, "THE GUIDING LIGHT"		
		51 W 52ND ST	NEW YORK, NY	10019
RICH, BARBARA	ACTRESS	429 N OGDEN DR #3	LOS ANGELES, CA	90036
RICH, BUDDY	DRUMMER	660 MADISON AVE #1700	NEW YORK, NY	10021
RICH, CHARLIE	SINGER-SONGWRITER	8229 ROCKCREEK PARKWAY	CORDOVA, TN	38018
RICH, CHRISTOPHER	ACTOR	15760 VENTURA BLVD #1730	ENCINO, CA	91436
RICH, DAVID LOWELL	FILM-TV DIRECTOR	465 LORING AVE	LOS ANGELES, CA	90024
RICH, ELAINE	TV PRODUCER	WARNER-HOLLYWOOD STUDIOS		
		1041 N FORMOSA AVE	LOS ANGELES, CA	90046
RICH, JACKIE M	TV WRITER	8955 BEVERLY BLVD	LOS ANGELES, CA	90048
RICH, JOHN	WRITER-PRODUCER	1575 CARLA RIDGE DR	BEVERLY HILLS, CA	90210
RICH, JOHN L, JR	MUSICIAN	4406 UTAH AVE	NASHVILLE, TN	37209
RICH, JUDY	TALENT AGENT	9255 SUNSET BLVD #603	LOS ANGELES, CA	90069
RICH, KATIE	ACTOR	8721 SUNSET BLVD #202	LOS ANGELES, CA	90069
RICH, KENNY	TV WRITER	8955 BEVERLY BLVD	LOS ANGELES, CA	90048
RICH, LARRY	RINGMASTER	POST OFFICE BOX 206	EPHRATA, PA	17522
RICH, LEE	TV PRODUCER	703 N BEVERLY DR	BEVERLY HILLS, CA	90212
RICH, MERT	ACTOR-WRITER	429 N OGDEN DR #3	LOS ANGELES, CA	90026
RICH, MERT	ACTOR	12345 VENTURA BLVD #X	STUDIO CITY, CA	91604
RICH, MICKEY	TV WRITER-DIRECTOR	DGA, 7950 SUNSET BLVD	HOLLYWOOD, CA	90046
RICH, PETE R	TV WRITER	CBS-TV, "THE GUIDING LIGHT"		
		51 W 52ND ST	NEW YORK, NY	10019
RICH, PETER D L	TV DIRECTOR	21515 MARCHENA ST	WOODLAND HILLS, CA	91364
RICH, PETER T	TV WRITER	555 W 57TH ST #1230	NEW YORK, NY	10019
RICH, RICHARD	FILM WRITER-DIRECTOR	500 S BUENA VISTA ST	BURBANK, CA	91521
RICH, SHIRLEY	CASTING DIRECTOR	POST OFFICE BOX 5718	SHERMAN OAKS, CA	91403
RICH, SPENCER	NEWS CORRESPONDENT	3301 NEWARK ST, NW	WASHINGTON, DC	20008
RICH, SPIDER	GUITARIST	POST OFFICE BOX 642	WINCHESTER, TN	37398
RICHARD, CLIFF	SINGER-ACTOR	POST OFFICE BOX 46-C, ESHER	SURREY KT10 9AF	ENGLAND
RICHARD, DICK	PRODUCER	RICHARDS, 4000 WARNER BLVD	BURBANK, CA	91522
RICHARD, EMILY	ACTRESS	MARMONT, LANGHAM HOUSE		
		302 REGENT ST	LONDON W1	ENGLAND
RICHARD, MICHAEL	COMPOSER	841 1/2 N FORMOSA AVE	LOS ANGELES, CA	90046
RICHARD, WENDY	ACTRESS	326 MUMBLES RD, SWANSEA	WALES	ENGLAND
RICHARDE, PAMELA	ACTRESS	10100 SANTA MONICA BLVD #1600	LOS ANGELES, CA	90067

Name	Occupation	Address	City	Zip
RICHARDE, TESSA	ACTRESS	12725 VENTURA BLVD #E	STUDIO CITY, CA	91604
RICHARDS, ANN	FLUTIST	2115 ASHWOOD AVE	NASHVILLE, TN	37212
RICHARDS, BEAH	ACTRESS	9255 SUNSET BLVD #1105	LOS ANGELES, CA	90069
RICHARDS, CAROL R	NEWS CORRESPONDENT	511 7TH ST, SE	WASHINGTON, DC	20003
RICHARDS, CAROL R	WRITER-EDITOR	POST OFFICE BOX 500	WASHINGTON, DC	20044
RICHARDS, CLAY F	NEWS CORRESPONDENT	511 7TH ST, SE	WASHINGTON, DC	20003
RICHARDS, CLAYTON	TV WRITER	8955 BEVERLY BLVD	LOS ANGELES, CA	90048
RICHARDS, DAVID T	RECORD EXECUTIVE	POST OFFICE BOX 411	MAYWOOD, CA	90270
RICHARDS, DEKE	COMPOSER	9911 W PICO BLVD #610	LOS ANGELES, CA	90035
RICHARDS, DICK	ACTOR	5712 RIVERTON AVE	NORTH HOLLYWOOD, CA	91601
RICHARDS, DICK	DIRECTOR	151 S EL CAMINO DR	BEVERLY HILLS, CA	90212
RICHARDS, DOUGLAS DORMAN	NEWS CORRESPONDENT	1916 "R" ST, NW	WASHINGTON, DC	20009
RICHARDS, DR RENEE	TENNIS	1604 UNION ST	SAN FRANCISCO, CA	94123
RICHARDS, EVAN	ACTOR	9220 SUNSET BLVD #625	LOS ANGELES, CA	90069
RICHARDS, GEOFFREY H	NEWS CORRESPONDENT	1705 DE SALES ST, NW	WASHINGTON, DC	20036
RICHARDS, JANICE K	NEWS CORRESPONDENT	5151 WISCONSIN AVE, NW	WASHINGTON, DC	20007
RICHARDS, JOHN	SINGER	POST OFFICE BOX 29543	ATLANTA, GA	30359
RICHARDS, JON F	ACTOR	257 W 99TH ST	NEW YORK, NY	10025
RICHARDS, KARLA	ACTRESS	8230 BEVERLY BLVD #23	LOS ANGELES, CA	90048
RICHARDS, KEITH	ACTOR	1124 N LA CIENEGA BLVD #304	LOS ANGELES, CA	90069
RICHARDS, KEN H	ACTOR	444 E 82ND ST	NEW YORK, NY	10028
RICHARDS, KENNETH N	DIRECTOR	DGA, 110 W 57TH ST	NEW YORK, NY	10019
RICHARDS, KIM	ACTRESS	POST OFFICE BOX 5617	BEVERLY HILLS, CA	90210
RICHARDS, LARRY	SAXOPHONIST	1921 MORAN DR	NASHVILLE, TN	37216
RICHARDS, LAURENCE	TV WRITER	8955 BEVERLY BLVD	LOS ANGELES, CA	90048
RICHARDS, LESLIE	MEZZO-SOPRANO	1182 MARKET ST #311	SAN FRANCISCO, CA	94102
RICHARDS, LISA BLAKE	ACTRESS	9744 WILSHIRE BLVD #308	BEVERLY HILLS, CA	90212
RICHARDS, LLOYD	TV DIRECTOR	90 YORK SQ	NEW HAVEN, CT	06511
RICHARDS, MARC	TV WRITER	17910 ACRE ST	NORTHRIDGE, CA	91325
RICHARDS, MARTIN	PRODUCER	PRODUCERS CIRCLE COMPANY		
		1350 AVE OF THE AMERICAS	NEW YORK, NY	10019
RICHARDS, MICHAEL	SINGER	ICM, 8899 BEVERLY BLVD	LOS ANGELES, CA	90048
RICHARDS, MICHAEL	TV WRITER	8955 BEVERLY BLVD	LOS ANGELES, CA	90048
RICHARDS, MICHAEL W	NEWS CORRESPONDENT	1446 "Q" ST, NW	WASHINGTON, DC	20009
RICHARDS, MIKE	WRESTLER	POST OFFICE BOX 3859	STAMFORD, CT	06905
RICHARDS, R M "DICK"	DIRECTOR	151 S EL CAMINO DR	BEVERLY HILLS, CA	90212
RICHARDS, RON	WRITER-PRODUCER	15151 ENADIA WY	VAN NUYS, CA	91405
RICHARDS, TED	ACTOR	29051 1/2 PACIFIC COAST HWY	MALIBU, CA	90265
RICHARDS, VIKKI	ACTRESS	RJPM, 59 KNIGHTSBRIDGE	LONDON SW1X 7RA	ENGLAND
RICHARDSON, CINDY	SINGER	HEARTLAND, 660 DOUGLAS AVE	ALTAMONTE SPRINGS, FL	32714
RICHARDSON, CLIVE	COMPOSER	398 WIMBLEDON PARK RD	LONDON SW19 6PN	ENGLAND
RICHARDSON, DON	TV DIRECTOR	14352 MIRANDA ST	VAN NUYS, CA	91401
RICHARDSON, HENRY	FILM EDITOR	178 ALBURY DR, PINNER	MIDDLESEX	ENGLAND
RICHARDSON, IAN	ACTOR	LONDON MANAGEMENT, LTD		
		235-241 REGENT ST	LONDON W1A 2JT	ENGLAND
RICHARDSON, JIM	PHOTOGRAPHER	1652 NIAGARA ST	DENVER, CO	80220
RICHARDSON, JOEL M	PHOTOGRAPHER	5731 NEVADA ST	BERWYN HEIGHTS, MD	20740
RICHARDSON, LEE	ACTOR	244 REDDING RD	WESTON, CT	06883
RICHARDSON, LINDA	WRITER-PRODUCER	ELKAR, 11 SANDUSKY RD	NEW YORK, NY	10956
RICHARDSON, MARTHA	NEWS CORRESPONDENT	1687 32ND ST, NW	WASHINGTON, DC	20007
RICHARDSON, MIRANDA	ACTRESS	GARDNER, 15 KENNINGTON HIGH ST	LONDON W8 5NP	ENGLAND
RICHARDSON, NATASHA	ACTRESS	30 BRACKENBURY RD	LONDON W6	ENGLAND
RICHARDSON, PATRICIA	ACTRESS	10000 SANTA MONICA BLVD #305	LOS ANGELES, CA	90067
RICHARDSON, PEGGY L	NEWS CORRESPONDENT	POST OFFICE BOX 314	WHITE PLAINS, MD	20695
RICHARDSON, PETER	DIRECTOR	4510 BLACKFRIAR RD	WOODLAND HILLS, CA	91364
RICHARDSON, SUSAN	ACTRESS	6331 HOLLYWOOD BLVD #924	LOS ANGELES, CA	90028
RICHARDSON, TONY	FILM WRITER-DIRECTOR	1478 N KINGS RD	LOS ANGELES, CA	90069
RICHBURG, KEITH BERNARD	NEWS CORRESPONDENT	5519 MAC ARTHUR BLVD, NW	WASHINGTON, DC	20016
RICHE, WENDY	WRITER-PRODUCER	215 N FOOTHILL RD	BEVERLY HILLS, CA	90210
RICHEY, B J	NEWS CORRESPONDENT	5 COLEMAN LN	STERLING, VA	22170
RICHEY, GEORGE	PIANIST-COMPOSER	6 MUSIC CIRCLE N	NASHVILLE, TN	37203
RICHIE, LIONEL, JR	SINGER-SONGWRITER	1112 N SHERBOURNE DR	LOS ANGELES, CA	90069
RICHLIN, MAURICE	WRITER	1295 BIENVENEDA AVE	PACIFIC PALISADES, CA	90272
RICHMAN, ALAN	WRITER-EDITOR	TIME/TIME & LIFE BLDG		
		ROCKEFELLER CENTER		
RICHMAN, DON C	WRITER	8707 SAINT IVES DR	LOS ANGELES, CA	90069
RICHMAN, JEFFREY	TV WRITER	8955 BEVERLY BLVD	LOS ANGELES, CA	90048
RICHMAN, JOAN	TV EXECUTIVE	CBS-TV, 524 W 57TH ST	NEW YORK, NY	10019
RICHMAN, JONATHAN & THE MODERN	ROCK & ROLL GROUP	EPSTEIN, 644 N DOHENY DR	LOS ANGELES, CA	90069
RICHMAN, PETER MARK	ACTOR	5114 DEL MORENO DR	WOODLAND HILLS, CA	91364
RICHMAN, PHYLLIS C	COLUMNIST	THE WASHINGTON POST		
		WRITERS GROUP		
		1150 15TH ST, NW	WASHINGTON, DC	20071
RICHMAN, ROGER	ACTOR	8574 APPIAN WY	LOS ANGELES, CA	90046
RICHMAN, SHELDON B	NEWS CORRESPONDENT	2741 CARTER FARM CT	ALEXANDRIA, VA	22306
RICHMAN, STELLA	TV PRODUCER	28 CURZON ST	LONDON W1Y 8EA	ENGLAND
RICHMOND, ANTHONY	CINEMATOGRAPHER	CANNON, 167 WARDOUR ST	LONDON W1	ENGLAND
RICHMOND, ANTHONY B	DIRECTOR	DGA, 7950 SUNSET BLVD	LOS ANGELES, CA	90046
RICHMOND, BILL	TV WRITER-PRODUCER	11812 MOORPARK ST #A	STUDIO CITY, CA	91604
RICHMOND, BOBBY	SINGER	OME, 233 W WOODLAND AVE	OTTUMWA, IA	52501
RICHMOND, BRANSCOMBE	ACTOR	5738 ENCINO AVE #E	ENCINO, CA	91316
RICHMOND, JANE	TV WRITER	555 W 57TH ST #1230	NEW YORK, NY	10019
RICHMOND, KIM	COMPOSER	12800 MARTHA ST	NORTH HOLLYWOOD, CA	91607
RICHMOND, STEVE	ACTOR	137 HOLLISTER AVE	SANTA MONICA, CA	90405

RICHNER, THOMAS	PIANIST	15 HIGH ST #621	HARTFORD, CT	06103
RICHTER, BELLE	ACTRESS	CED, 261 S ROBERTSON BLVD	BEVERLY HILLS, CA	90211
RICHTER, DEBI	ACTRESS	11726 SAN VICENTE BLVD #300	LOS ANGELES, CA	90049
RICHTER, EILEEN	SINGER	EAI, 2211 INDUSTRIAL BLVD	SARASOTA, FL	33580
RICHTER, ELIZABETH	PHOTOGRAPHER	2130 "P" ST, NW	WASHINGTON, DC	20037
RICHTER, JAY	NEWS CORRESPONDENT	2209 MARTHA'S RD	ALEXANDRIA, VA	22307
RICHTER, M J	NEWS CORRESPONDENT	1333 "H" ST, NW	WASHINGTON, DC	20005
RICHTER, MISCHA	CARTOONIST	POST OFFICE BOX 4203	NEW YORK, NY	10017
RICHTER, RICHARD	TV PRODUCER	ABC-TV, 7 W 66TH ST	NEW YORK, NY	10023
RICHTER, ROBERT	WRITER-PRODUCER	472 HAZEL AVE	GLENCOE, IL	60022
RICHTER, ROBERT	WRITER-PRODUCER	330 W 42ND ST	NEW YORK, NY	10036
RICHTER, ROBERT J	NEWS CORRESPONDENT	1946 SEMINARY RD	SILVER SPRING, MD	20910
RICHTER, ROMONA	ACTRESS	SEE - TOPPING, LYNNE		
RICHTER, WALTER D	SCREENWRITER	2049 CENTURY PARK E #1320	LOS ANGELES, CA	90067
RICHTERS, CHRISTINE	MODEL	MODELS & PROMOTIONS AGENCY		
		8560 SUNSET BLVD, 10TH FLOOR	LOS ANGELES, CA	90069
RICHTERS, THE	ACROBATIC TROUPE	HALL, 138 FROG HOLLOW RD	CHURCHVILLE, PA	18966
RICHWINE, MARIA	ACTRESS	160 S SYCAMORE AVE	LOS ANGELES, CA	90036
RICKARD, THOMAS O	TV DIRECTOR	1826 OVERLOOK LN	SANTA BARBARA, CA	93103
RICKARDS, JOCELYN	COSTUME DESIGNER	6 MEDINA PL	LONDON NW8	ENGLAND
RICKARDS, STEVEN	TENOR	1182 MARKET ST #311	SAN FRANCISCO, CA	94102
RICKENBACHER, KARL ANTON	CONDUCTOR	111 W 57TH ST #1203	NEW YORK, NY	10019
RICKER, CYNTHIA HELLER	VIOLINIST	233 37TH AVE N	NASHVILLE, TN	37209
RICKER, RICHARD	FRENCH HORNIST	233 37TH AVE N	NASHVILLE, TN	37209
RICKERT, WILLIAM	ACTOR	3513 N LINCOLN AVE	ALTADENA, CA	91001
RICKETT, FRANCES	TV WRITER	555 W 57TH ST #1230	NEW YORK, NY	10019
RICKEY, CARRIE	FILM CRITIC	NEW WOMAN, 215 LEXINGTON AVE	NEW YORK, NY	10016
RICKEY, CHARLES ED	TV DIRECTOR	518 N KENWOOD ST #206	GLENDALE, CA	91206
RICKLES, DON	COMEDIAN-ACTOR	925 N ALPINE DR	BEVERLY HILLS, CA	90210
RICKMAN, THOMAS	FILM WRITER-DIRECTOR	1888 CENTURY PARK E #1400	LOS ANGELES, CA	90067
RIDDER, WALTER	NEWS CORRESPONDENT	1219 CREST LN	MC LEAN, VA	22101
RIDDINGTON, KEN	TV PRODUCER	BBC-TV CENTRE, WOOD LN		
		SHEPHERDS BUSH	LONDON W12	ENGLAND
RIDDLE, GEORGE	ACTOR	225 E 11TH ST	NEW YORK, NY	10003
RIDDLE, GEORGE	SINGER-GUITARIST	POST OFFICE BOX 8288	NASHVILLE, TN	37207
RIDDLE, HAL	ACTOR	339 S DETROIT ST #102	LOS ANGELES, CA	90036
RIDDLE, SAMUEL	TV PRODUCER	2536 ANGELO DR	LOS ANGELES, CA	90077
RIDDLE, STEVE	DRUMMER	1717 MARSDEN AVE	NASHVILLE, TN	37216
RIDDLE, WAIDE	ACTOR	1605 N CAHUENGA BLVD #202	LOS ANGELES, CA	90028
RIDEOUT, CHRISTINA L	ACTRESS	9601 WILSHIRE BLVD #GL-11	BEVERLY HILLS, CA	90210
RIDER, MICHAEL	ACTOR	9601 WILSHIRE BLVD #GL-11	BEVERLY HILLS, CA	90210
RIDER, MIDNIGHT	WRESTLER	SEE - RHODES, DUSTY		
RIDER, RAYMOND	GUITARIST	428 MILLWOOD DR	NASHVILLE, TN	37217
RIDER, RED	ROCK & ROLL GROUP	SEE - RED RIDER		
RIDERS IN THE SKY	C & W GROUP	SKEPNER & BUCKSKIN CO		
		7 MUSIC CIRCLE N	NASHVILLE, TN	37203
RIDGE, CLYDE H	COMPOSER	1400 E RENO AVE #45	LAS VEGAS, NV	89119
RIDGELEY, ANDREW	SINGER-COMPOSER	17 GOSFIELD ST	LONDON W1	ENGLAND
RIDGEWAY, FRANK	CARTOONIST	KING FEATURES SYNDICATE		
		235 E 45TH ST	NEW YORK, NY	10017
RIDGEWAY, JAMES	NEWS CORRESPONDENT	3103 MACOMB ST, NW	WASHINGTON, DC	20008
RIDGEWAY-GRETZ	MUSICAL DUO	SPRINGER, 1001 ROLANDVUE RD	BALTIMORE, MD	21204
RIDGWAY, GENE & BLACK KETTLE CO	C & W GROUP	POST OFFICE BOX 4234	PANORAMA CITY, CA	91412
RIDLEY, JULIE	ACTRESS	DMI, 250 W 57TH ST	NEW YORK, NY	10107
RIDLEY, ROBERT	GUITARIST	2203 PENNINGTON BEND RD	NASHVILLE, TN	37214
RIDLEY, ROY	GUITARIST	J H EARLS, 933 GLENDALE LN	NASHVILLE, TN	37204
RIEBL, THOMAS	VIOLIST	POST OFFICE BOX 1515	NEW YORK, NY	10023
RIEFENSTAHL, LENI	FILM DIRECTOR	TENGSTRASSE 20	8000 MUNICH 40	WEST GERMANY
RIEGEL, KENNETH	TENOR	59 E 54TH ST #81	NEW YORK, NY	10022
RIEHL, KATE	ACTRESS	10402 BLOOMFIELD ST	NORTH HOLLYWOOD, CA	91602
RIEHLE, LARRY	GUITARIST	231 NEW SHACKLE ISLAND RD #103	HENDERSONVILLE, TN	37075
RIEHLE, THOMAS	NEWS CORRESPONDENT	1614 OAK ST, NW	WASHINGTON, DC	20010
RIEMAN, RICHARD	NEWS CORRESPONDENT	1776 "G" ST, NW	WASHINGTON, DC	20006
RIEMER, BLANCA	NEWS CORRESPONDENT	2320 ASHMEAD PL, NW	WASHINGTON, DC	20009
RIES, BARBARA	PHOTOGRAPHER	3601 WISCONSIN AVE, NW	WASHINGTON, DC	20016
RIESEL, VICTOR	COLUMINIST	NEWS AMERICA SYNDICATE		
		1703 KAISER AVE	IRVINE, CA	92714
RIEUF, GLENN	GUITARIST	114 17TH AVE S	NASHVILLE, TN	37203
RIFKIN, ARNOLD	TALENT AGENT	10100 SANTA MONICA BLVD #1600	LOS ANGELES, CA	90067
RIFKIN, IVA	ACTRESS	5604 HOLLY OAK DR	LOS ANGELES, CA	90068
RIFKIN, JOSHUA	CONDUCTOR	AIA, 60 E 42ND ST	NEW YORK, NY	10165
RIFKIN, LEO	WRITER	815 S LORRAINE BLVD	LOS ANGELES, CA	90005
RIFKIN, RON	ACTOR	5604 HOLLY OAK DR	LOS ANGELES, CA	90068
RIFKINSON, JAN S	DIRECTOR	DGA, 110 W 57TH ST	NEW YORK, NY	10019
RIGACCI, BRUNO	CONDUCTOR	225 W 34TH ST #1012	NEW YORK, NY	10001
RIGACCI, SUZANNA	SOPRANO	225 W 34TH ST #1012	NEW YORK, NY	10001
RIGAI, AMIRAM	PIANIST	POST OFFICE BOX U	REDDING, CT	06875
RIGAMONTI, ROBERT A	DIRECTOR	400 W 43RD ST #45-F	NEW YORK, NY	10036
RIGBY, CATHY	TV PERSONALITY	POST OFFICE BOX 387	BLUE JAY, CA	92317
RIGBY, PAUL	CARTOONIST	531 MAIN ST #621	NEW YORK, NY	10044
RIGBY, TERENCE	ACTOR	LONDON MANAGEMENT, LTD		
		235-241 REGENT ST	LONDON W1A 2JT	ENGLAND
RIGBY, WILL	DRUMMER	EGON RECORDS, 719 GARDENS ST	HOBOKEN, NJ	07030
RIGER, ELEANOR	WRITER-PRODUCER	DGA, 110 W 57TH ST	NEW YORK, NY	10019
RIGER, ROBERT	WRITER-PRODUCER	2 CHARLTON ST	NEW YORK, NY	10014

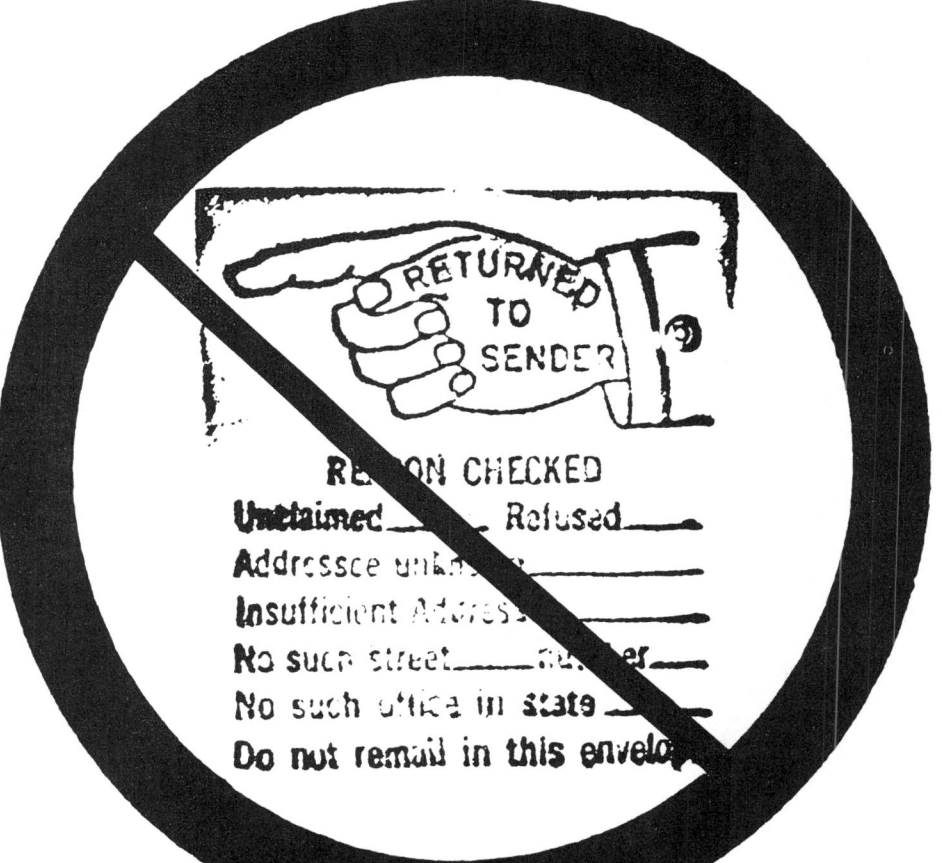

Name	Occupation	Address	City
RIGG, DIANA	ACTRESS	LONDON MANAGEMENT, LTD	
		235-241 REGENT ST	LONDON W1A 2JT ENGLAND
RIGGAN, DALLAS H	NEWS CORRESPONDENT	1755 S JEFFERSON DAVIS HWY	ARLINGTON, VA 22202
RIGGINS, ROSE	TV DIRECTOR	392 CENTRAL PARK W #15-E	NEW YORK, NY 10025
RIGGS, BOBBY	TENNIS	508 EAST AVE	CORONADO, CA 92118
RIGGS, JAMES W	NEWS CORRESPONDENT	529 14TH ST, NW	WASHINGTON, DC 20045
RIGGS, ROBERT S	NEWS CORRESPONDENT	444 N CAPITOL ST, NW	WASHINGTON, DC 20001
RIGGS, SYLVIA	NEWS CORRESPONDENT	357 N GRANADA ST	ARLINGTON, VA 22203
RIGGS, TERRY ANN	DIRECTOR	917 N BEVERLY GLEN BLVD	LOS ANGELES, CA 90077
RIGGS-HALL, CARLA	SINGER-SONGWRITER	POST OFFICE BOX 473	RADCLIFFE, KY 40160
RIGHT, ROBIN	SINGER	PENNY, 30 GUINAN ST	WALTHAM, MA 02154
RIGHT TIME	ROCK & ROLL GROUP	29 COMMONWEALTH AVE #705	BOSTON, MA 02116
RIGHTEOUS BROTHERS, THE	VOCAL DUO	RILLERA, 9841 HOT SPRINGS DR	HUNTINGTON BEACH, CA 92646
RIGSBY, GORDON	TV DIRECTOR	117 S SWEETZER AVE	HOLLYWOOD, CA 90048
RIISNA, ENE	TV DIRECTOR-PRODUCER	14 W 10TH ST	NEW YORK, NY 10011
RIKER, ROBIN	ACTRESS	1711 N CURSON AVE	LOS ANGELES, CA 90046
RIKLIS, MESHULAM	PRODUCER	23720 MALIBU COLONY DR	MALIBU, CA 90265
RIKLIS, PIA ZADORA	ACTRESS-SINGER	SEE - ZADORA, PIA	
RILEY, ANGELA W	NEWS CORRESPONDENT	230 VARNUM ST, NE	WASHINGTON, DC 20011
RILEY, BILLIE LEE	SINGER	RURAL DELIVERY #1, BOX 104	NEWPORT, AR 72112
RILEY, BOB	SINGER	PENNY, 30 GUINAN ST	WALTHAM, MA 02154
RILEY, BROOKS	WRITER	10000 SANTA MONICA BLVD #305	LOS ANGELES, CA 90067
RILEY, JACK	ACTOR-WRITER	1440 QUEENS RD	LOS ANGELES, CA 90069
RILEY, JEANNIE C	SINGER	POST OFFICE BOX 454	BRENTWOOD, TN 37027
RILEY, JEANNINE	ACTRESS	POST OFFICE BOX 11789	MARINA DEL REY, CA 90295
RILEY, JOHN	TV WRITER	9255 SUNSET BLVD #1122	LOS ANGELES, CA 90069
RILEY, KAREN	NEWS CORRESPONDENT	3411 CYPRESS DR	FALLS CHURCH, VA 22042
RILEY, LARRY	ACTOR	10100 SANTA MONICA BLVD #1600	LOS ANGELES, CA 90067
RILEY, LEN	TV WRITER	8955 BEVERLY BLVD	LOS ANGELES, CA 90048
RILEY, MICHAEL	BASSO-BARITONE	200 W 70TH ST #7-F	NEW YORK, NY 10023
RILEY, PATRICK	TENOR	243 W END AVE #907	NEW YORK, NY 10023
RILLA, WOLF	FILM WRITER-DIRECTOR	12 DAGMAR TERR	LONDON N1 2BN ENGLAND
RILLERA, BARRY	GUITARIST-AGENT	9841 HOT SPRINGS DR	HUNTINGTON BEACH, CA 92646
RILLING, HELMUTH	CONDUCTOR	STUTTGARRER MUSIKFREUND	
		EV D-7000	HASENBERGSTEIGE 3 WEST GERMANY
RIMMER, GERALD	TV DIRECTOR	14131 ARTESIAN ST	DETROIT, MI 48223
RIMMER, SHANE	ACTOR	CROUCH, 59 FRITH ST	LONDON W1 ENGLAND
RINEHART, ELAINE	ACTRESS	400 W 43RD ST #42-L	NEW YORK, NY 10036
RINELL, SUSAN	ACTRESS	445 N BEDFORD DR #PH	BEVERLY HILLS, CA 90210
RING, BUDDY	GUITARIST	POST OFFICE BOX 1014	LEBANON, TN 37087
RINGE, LINDA	NEWS CORRESPONDENT	4461 CONNECTICUT AVE, NW	WASHINGTON, DC 20008
RINGEL, ELEANOR	FILM CRITIC	POST OFFICE 4689	ATLANTA, GA 30302
RINGER, JIM & MARY MC CASLIN	MUSICAL DUO	FOLKLORE, 1671 APPIAN WY	SANTA MONICA, CA 90401
RINGLE, KENNETH A	NEWS CORRESPONDENT	204 9TH ST, SE	WASHINGTON, DC 20003
RINGLE, WILLIAM	NEWS CORRESPONDENT	6900 STRATA ST	MC LEAN, VA 22101
RINGO, JENNIFER	SOPRANO	CAMI, 165 W 57TH ST	NEW YORK, NY 10019
RINGO, MARILYN	TV DIRECTOR-PRODUCER	TBS, 1050 TECHWOOD DR, NW	ATLANTA, GA 30318
RINGO, SHARON	ACTRESS	10850 RIVERSIDE DR #505	NORTH HOLLYWOOD, CA 91602
RINGOLD, STEPHEN	JUGGLER	SPOTFIELD PRODUCTIONS	
		84 ELM ST	WESTFIELD, NJ 07090
RINGOLSBY, TRACY	SPORTS COLUMNIST	TRIBUNE MEDIA SERVICES	
		64 E CONCORD ST	ORLANDO, FL 32801
RINGWALD, KIMMER	TV WRITER	900 SUNSET BLVD #611	LOS ANGELES, CA 90069
RINGWALD, MOLLY	ACTRESS	120 S EL CAMINO DR #104	BEVERLY HILLS, CA 90212
RINSLER, DENNIS	WRITER	7320 LENNOX AVE #I-15	VAN NUYS, CA 91405
RINTELS, DAVID W	TV WRITER-PRODUCER	2002 OLD RANCH RD	LOS ANGELES, CA 90049
RINTELS, JONATHAN B, JR	TV WRITER	330 S BARRINGTON AVE #306	LOS ANGELES, CA 90049
RINTZLER, MARIUS	SINGER	59 E 54TH ST #81	NEW YORK, NY 10022
RIO	C & W GROUP	LUTZ, 5625 "O" STREET BLDG	LINCOLN, NE 68510
RIO	ROCK & ROLL GROUP	41 BRITAIN ST #200	TORONTO, ONT CANADA
RIOLO, VAL	TV DIRECTOR	ENTERTAINMENT TONIGHT	
		PARAMOUNT TELEVISION	
		5555 MELROSE AVE	LOS ANGELES, CA 90038
RIOLO, VALENTE	TV DIRECTOR	1250 N KINGS RD #414	LOS ANGELES, CA 90069
RIORDAN, RETTA M	NEWS CORRESPONDENT	2626 41ST ST, NW	WASHINGTON, DC 20007
RIPANI, RICHARD JAY	MUSIC ARRANGER	204 THEODORE RD	NASHVILLE, TN 37214
RIPKEN, CAL, JR	BASEBALL	410 CLOVER ST	ABERDEEN, MD 21001
RIPKEN, CAL, SR	BASEBALL	410 CLOVER ST	ABERDEEN, MD 21001
RIPLEY, JAY	ACTOR	WOOD, 5730 LANKERSHIM BLVD	NORTH HOLLYWOOD, CA 91601
RIPPON, MICHAEL	BARITONE	SOFFER, 130 W 56TH ST	NEW YORK, NY 10019
RIPPS, LEONARD ALLEN	TV WRITER	3380 CAMINO DE LA CUMBRE	SHERMAN OAKS, CA 91423
RIPPY, ROBERT	GUITARIST	3604 LEILA AVE	TAMPA, FL 33611
RIPPY, RODNEY ALLEN	ACTOR	6430 SUNSET BLVD #1203	LOS ANGELES, CA 90028
RIPROCK, DASH & THE DRAGONS	ROCK & ROLL GROUP	NBA, 2605 NORTHRIDGE DR	GARLAND, TX 75043
RIPS, MARTIN	TV WRITER-PRODUCER	12196 LAUREL TERRACE DR	STUDIO CITY, CA 91604
RISCH, GREGORY C	NEWS CORRESPONDENT	1111 18TH ST, NW	WASHINGTON, DC 20036
RISCOE, JOHNNIE	COMEDIAN	3 CANNING CRESCENT	
		WOOD GREEN	LONDON N22 5SR ENGLAND
RISENEFELD, ED	ACTOR	3168 MOUNTAIN VIEW AVE	LOS ANGELES, CA 90066
RISHER, TOM	DRUMMER	1722 BECKMAN DR	FLORENCE, AL 35630
RISK, VICTORIA	ACTRESS	6736 LAUREL CANYON BLVD #306	NORTH HOLLYWOOD, CA 91606
RISKIN, RALPH	TV DIRECTOR	1344 N WETHERLY DR	LOS ANGELES, CA 90069
RISO, ADRIAN A	DIRECTOR	47 BARLOW LN	RYE, NY 10580
RISSIEN, EDWARD L	FILM PRODUCER	760 N LA CIENEGA BLVD	LOS ANGELES, CA 90069
RIST, ROBBIE	ACTOR	CED, 261 S ROBERTSON BLVD	BEVERLY HILLS, CA 90211
RITCHIE, CLINT	ACTOR	9744 WILSHIRE BLVD #306	BEVERLY HILLS, CA 90212

RITCHIE, JEAN	SINGER	BENSON EAST #B-10	JENKINTOWN, PA	19046
RITCHIE, MICHAEL	DIRECTOR-PRODUCER	1801 AVE OF THE STARS #911	LOS ANGELES, CA	90067
RITCHIE FAMILY, THE	VOCAL GROUP	65 E 55TH ST #302	NEW YORK, NY	10022
RITELIS, VIKTORS	TV-FILM DIRECTOR	38 NITON RD, RICHMOND	SURREY	ENGLAND
RITENOUR, LEE	GUITARIST	POST OFFICE BOX 3122	BURBANK, CA	91504
RITMANIS, LOLITA L	COMPOSER	13033 LANDALE ST	STUDIO CITY, CA	91604
RITT, MARTIN	DIRECTOR-PRODUCER	13515 ROMANY DR	PACIFIC PALISADES, CA	90272
RITT, MARTINA SUE	DIRECTOR	DGA, 110 W 57TH ST	NEW YORK, NY	10019
RITTER, BIG DADDY	WRESTLER	SEE - JUNKYARD DOG, THE		
RITTER, HOWARD	TV DIRECTOR	4633 VENTURA CANYON AVE	SHERMAN OAKS, CA	91423
RITTER, JAMES	WRITER	1713 EWING ST	LOS ANGELES, CA	90026
RITTER, JOHN	ACTOR	236 TIGERTAIL RD	LOS ANGELES, CA	90049
RITTER, SYLVESTER	WRESTLER	SEE - JUNKYARD DOG, THE		
RITZ, BEVERLY M	COMPOSER	19 COPRA LN	PACIFIC PALISADES, CA	90272
RITZ, JAMES J	SCREENWRITER	8955 BEVERLY BLVD	LOS ANGELES, CA	90048
RIVA, J MICHAEL	ART DIRECTOR	10100 SANTA MONICA BLVD #1600	LOS ANGELES, CA	90067
RIVAS, CARLOS	ACTOR	8831 SUNSET BLVD #402	LOS ANGELES, CA	90069
RIVAS, RAMON J	DIRECTOR	1001 POINSETTIA PL	HOLLYWOOD, CA	90024
RIVCHUN, STUART L	NEWS CORRESPONDENT	4461 CONNECTICUT AVE, NW	WASHINGTON, DC	20008
RIVE, KENNETH	FILM PRODUCER	CANNON, 167 WARDOUR ST	LONDON W1V 3TA	ENGLAND
RIVEIRE, GEORGE M, JR	NEWS CORRESPONDENT	6820 OREGON AVE, NW	WASHINGTON, DC	20015
RIVELLI, TOMMY	DRUMMER	5500 VANDERBILT RD	OLD HICKORY, TN	37138
RIVENQ, NICOLAS	BARITONE	ANGLO-SWISS ARTISTS MGMT		
		16 MUSWELL HILL RD, HIGHGATE	LONDON N6 5UG	ENGLAND
RIVER STREET BAND	ROCK & ROLL GROUP	41 BRITAIN ST #200	TORONTO, ONT	CANADA
RIVERA, GERALDO	NEWS JOURNALIST	28283 VIA ACERO	MALIBU, CA	90265
RIVERA, HENRY M	COMMUNICATIONS EXEC	FCC, 1919 "M" ST, NW	WASHINGTON, DC	20554
RIVERA, JOSE	TV WRITER	8955 BEVERLY BLVD	LOS ANGELES, CA	90048
RIVERA, JOSE LUIS	WRESTLER	POST OFFICE BOX 3859	STAMFORD, CT	06905
RIVERO, JORGE	ACTOR	SALVADOR NOVO 71	COYOACAN 21 DF	MEXICO
RIVERS, JERRY	MANDOLINIST	ROUTE #1, BOX 20	GOODLETTSVILLE, TN	37072
RIVERS, JOAN	COMED-DIR-TV HOST	POST OFFICE BOX 49774	LOS ANGELES, CA	90049
RIVERS, JOHNNY	SINGER-SONGWRITER	3141 COLDWATER CANYON LN	BEVERLY HILLS, CA	90210
RIVETT-RIVER, JACKIE	WRITER-PRODUCER	LIFE STYLE PRODUCTIONS		
		2500 N LAKEVIEW AVE	CHICAGO, IL	60614
RIVETTI, JAMES J	COMPOSER	15159 HAMLIN ST	VAN NUYS, CA	91401
RIVITUSO, JO ANN	TV DIRECTOR	CBS-TV, "THE GUIDING LIGHT"		
		51 W 52ND ST	NEW YORK, NY	10019
RIVKIN, ALLEN	SCREENWRITER	8980 LLOYD PL	LOS ANGELES, CA	90069
RIX, COLIN	ACTOR	37 CHURCH LN	TEDDINGTON	ENGLAND
RIZO, MARCO	COMPOSER-CONDUCTOR	310 LEXINGTON AVE	NEW YORK, NY	10016
RIZZO, JEFFREY J	COMPOSER-CONDUCTOR	144 N VALLEY ST	BURBANK, CA	91505
RIZZO, TONY	SINGER	LUTZ, 5625 "O" STREET BLDG	LINCOLN, NE	68510
RIZZUTO, PHIL	BASEBALL	912 WESTMINISTER AVE	HILLSIDE, NJ	07205
RJ'S LATEST ARRIVAL	ROCK & ROLL GROUP	DOUGLASS, 2600 BOOK BUILDING	DETROIT, MI	48226
ROACH, DARYL	ACTOR	ABC-TV, "ONE LIFE TO LIVE"		
		1330 AVE OF THE AMERICAS	NEW YORK, NY	10019
ROACH, HAL, SR	PRODUCER	1183 STRADELLA RD	LOS ANGELES, CA	90077
ROACH, JANET	WRITER-PRODUCER	511 E 80TH ST	NEW YORK, NY	10021
ROACH, MAX	MUSICIAN-COMPOSER	415 CENTRAL PARK W	NEW YORK, NY	10025
ROACHE, WILLIAM	ACTOR	GRANAD TV CENTRE	MANCHESTER M60 9EA	ENGLAND
ROAD, MIKE	ACTOR	11180 VALLEY SPRING PL	NORTH HOLLYWOOD, CA	91602
ROAD WARRIOR ANIMAL	WRESTLER	SEE - ROAD WARRIORS, THE		
ROAD WARRIOR HAWK	WRESTLER	SEE - ROAD WARRIORS, THE		
ROAD WARRIORS, THE	WRESTLING TAG TEAM	NATIONAL WRESTLING ALLIANCE		
		JIM CROCKETT PROMOTIONS		
		421 BRIARBEND DR	CHARLOTTE, NC	28209
ROADHOUSE RIDERS, THE	C & W GROUP	LST, 2138 FLAGMARSH RD	MOUNT AIRY, MD	21771
ROADMASTER	ROCK & ROLL GROUP	6325 GUILFORD AVE #4	INDIANAPOLIS, IN	46220
ROAR	ROCK & ROLL GROUP	SEE - R O A R		
ROARING, THE	ROCK & ROLL GROUP	POST OFFICE BOX 4307	HOLLYWOOD, CA	90078
ROARK-STRUMMER, LINDA	SOPRANO	61 W 62ND ST #6-F	NEW YORK, NY	10023
ROARKE, ADAM	ACTOR	4520 AIDA PL	WOODLAND HILLS, CA	91364
ROARKE, JOHN	ACTOR	8322 BEVERLY BLVD #202	LOS ANGELES, CA	90048
ROAT, RICHARD	ACTOR	247 S BEVERLY DR #102	BEVERLY HILLS, CA	90210
ROBAK, EDWARD	WRITER	1263 N FLORES ST	LOS ANGELES, CA	90069
ROBARDS, GLENN	ACTOR	11249 VICTORY BLVD	NORTH HOLLYWOOD, CA	91606
ROBARDS, JASON	ACTOR	888 7TH AVE #201	NEW YORK, NY	10019
ROBARDS, SAM	ACTOR	211 S BEVERLY DR #201	BEVERLY HILLS, CA	90212
ROBB, DAVID	ACTOR	MORRIS, 147-149 WARDOUR ST	LONDON W1V 3TB	ENGLAND
ROBB, GREGORY A	NEWS CORRESPONDENT	1332 MASSACHUSETTS AVE, SE	WASHINGTON, DC	20003
ROBB, LARRY	ACTOR	4137 1/2 WARNER BLVD	BURBANK, CA	91505
ROBB, SANDY	SINGER	POST OFFICE BOX 29262	INDIANAPOLIS, IN	46229
ROBB, TOM	GUITARIST	251 CEDAR VIEW DR	ANTIOCH, TN	37013
ROBBIE, SEYMOUR	TV DIRECTOR	9980 LIEBE DR	BEVERLY HILLS, CA	90210
ROBBIN, IRVING	DIRECTOR	GIBSON HILL RD	CHESTER, NY	10918
ROBBIN, PETER	ACTOR	CAPRI, 8227 FOUNTAIN AVE #2	LOS ANGELES, CA	90046
ROBBINS, CARLA	NEWS CORRESPONDENT	4813 DAVENPORT ST, NW	WASHINGTON, DC	20016
ROBBINS, DEANNA	ACTRESS	1830 HILTON DR	BURBANK, CA	91504
ROBBINS, DENNIS	SINGER	PORTER & ROUSSELL MGMT		
		9 MUSIC SQUARE W	NASHVILLE, TN	37203
ROBBINS, HARGUS	PIANIST	1206 HABER DR	BRENTWOOD, TN	37027
ROBBINS, HAROLD	NOVELIST	1501 TOWER GROVE DR	BEVERLY HILLS, CA	90210
ROBBINS, JEROME	CHOREOGRAPHER	117 E 81ST ST	NEW YORK, NY	10028
ROBBINS, JULIEN	BASSO-BARITONE	CAMI, 165 W 57TH ST	NEW YORK, NY	10019

Name	Occupation	Address	City	Zip/Country
ROBBINS, LOIS	ACTRESS	STONE, 1052 CAROL DR	LOS ANGELES, CA	90069
ROBBINS, MATTHEW	WRITER-PRODUCER	DGA, 7950 SUNSET BLVD	HOLLYWOOD, CA	90046
ROBBINS, MICHAEL	ACTOR	65 QUEENS RD, WIMBLEDON	LONDON SW19	ENGLAND
ROBBINS, RANDY	TV DIRECTOR	CBS TELEVISION NETWORK		
		"THE YOUNG & THE RESTLESS"		
		7800 BEVERLY BLVD	LOS ANGELES, CA	90036
ROBBINS, REX	ACTOR	ASTOR, 119 W 57TH ST	NEW YORK, NY	10019
ROBBINS, RICHARD P	SCREENWRITER	3202 LONGRIDGE AVE	SHERMAN OAKS, CA	91423
ROBBINS, ROCKIE	SINGER	THE WILLIAM MORRIS AGENCY		
		1350 AVE OF THE AMERICAS	NEW YORK, NY	10019
ROBBINS, RONNY	SINGER	407 RAINTREE PL	HERMITAGE, TN	37076
ROBBINS, TIM	ACTOR	9229 SUNSET BLVD #306	LOS ANGELES, CA	90069
ROBE, MIKE	TV WRITER-PRODUCER	8955 BEVERLY BLVD	LOS ANGELES, CA	90048
ROBERSON, BOBBIE	SINGER-GUITARIST	POST OFFICE BOX 98	FOREST HILLS, NY	11375
ROBERSON, PEGGY	NEWS CORRESPONDENT	2234 WILLIAM & MARY DR	ALEXANDRIA, VA	22308
ROBERT & JOHNNY	VOCAL DUO	OLDIES, 5218 ALMONT ST	LOS ANGELES, CA	90032
ROBERTS, ARTHUR	ACTOR	7461 BEVERLY BLVD #400	LOS ANGELES, CA	90036
ROBERTS, AUSTIN	GUITARIST	221 COUNTRYSIDE DR	FRANKLIN, TN	37064
ROBERTS, BEVERLY	ACTRESS	30912 ARIANA LN	LAGUNA NIGUEL, CA	92677
ROBERTS, BRIAN KENDALL	DIRECTOR	DGA, 7950 SUNSET BLVD	LOS ANGELES, CA	90046
ROBERTS, BUDDY "JACK"	WRESTLER	UNIVERSAL WRESTLING FEDERATION		
		MID SOUTH SPORTS, INC		
		5001 SPRING VALLEY RD	DALLAS, TX	75244
ROBERTS, CINDY	ACTRESS	15010 VENTURA BLVD #234	SHERMAN OAKS, CA	91403
ROBERTS, CORINNE B	NEWS CORRESPONDENT	5315 BRADLEY BLVD	BETHESDA, MD	20814
ROBERTS, DALE	WRESTLER	SEE - ROBERTS, BUDDY "JACK"		
ROBERTS, DANNY	SINGER	45 TUDOR CITY PL #911	NEW YORK, NY	10017
ROBERTS, DAVIS	ACTOR	7466 BEVERLY BLVD #205	LOS ANGELES, CA	90036
ROBERTS, DICK	BODYBUILDER	POST OFFICE BOX 110	NEWALLA, OK	74857
ROBERTS, DORIS	ACTRESS-DIRECTOR	277 W END AVE	NEW YORK, NY	10023
ROBERTS, ELLIOT	TALENT AGENT	LOOKOUT, 9120 SUNSET BLVD	LOS ANGELES, CA	90069
ROBERTS, ERIC	ACTOR	853 7TH AVE #9-A	NEW YORK, NY	10019
ROBERTS, ERIC L	TV WRITER	CBS TELEVISION NETWORK		
		"THE YOUNG & THE RESTLESS"		
		7800 BEVERLY BLVD	LOS ANGELES, CA	90036
ROBERTS, EVE	ACTRESS	9255 SUNSET BLVD #603	LOS ANGELES, CA	90069
ROBERTS, FRANCESCA	ACTRESS	2037 S SHERBOURNE DR	LOS ANGELES, CA	90034
ROBERTS, GENE	NEWS CORRESPONDENT	1333 "H" ST, NW	WASHINGTON, DC	20005
ROBERTS, GEORGE E	ACTOR	13575 BORDEN AVE	SYLMAR, CA	91342
ROBERTS, HUNTER	ACTOR	8484 WILSHIRE BLVD #235	BEVERLY HILLS, CA	90211
ROBERTS, JAKE "THE SNAKE"	WRESTLER	POST OFFICE BOX 3859	STAMFORD, CT	06905
ROBERTS, JERRY MICHAEL	GUITARIST	3825 W END AVE	NASHVILLE, TN	37205
ROBERTS, JOAN	ACTRESS	15010 VENTURA BLVD #219	SHERMAN OAKS, CA	91403
ROBERTS, JOHN M	NEWS CORRESPONDENT	8812 MELWOOD RD	BETHESDA, MD	20817
ROBERTS, JOHN S	NEWS CORRESPONDENT	826 S ROYAL ST	ALEXANDRIA, VA	22314
ROBERTS, JONATHAN	SCREENWRITER	8955 BEVERLY BLVD	LOS ANGELES, CA	90048
ROBERTS, JOSEPH B	PHOTOGRAPHER	716 AMERICANA DR #A-5	ANNAPOLIS, MD	21403
ROBERTS, JUDITH ANNA	ACTRESS	9200 SUNSET BLVD #1210	LOS ANGELES, CA	90069
ROBERTS, JUDY	SINGER	845 VIA DE LA PAZ #365	PACIFIC PALISADES, CA	90272
ROBERTS, JUDY HARRISON	PIANIST	POST OFFICE BOX 1273	NASHVILLE, TN	37202
ROBERTS, JULIE	NEWS CORRESPONDENT	122 "C" ST, NW	WASHINGTON, DC	20001
ROBERTS, KATHY	ACTRESS	9021 MELROSE AVE #207	LOS ANGELES, CA	90069
ROBERTS, KAYTON A	GUITARIST	BROAD ST, ROUTE #2, HWY 41	GREENBRIER, TN	37073
ROBERTS, KENNY	SINGER	KEARNEY, 16 FARM LN	WASHINGTONVILLE, NY	10992
ROBERTS, KIMBERLEY A	NEWS CORRES-WRITER	1705 DE SALES ST, NW	WASHINGTON, DC	20036
ROBERTS, LES	WRITER	5761 OSTIN AVE	WOODLAND HILLS, CA	91367
ROBERTS, LOUIE E	SINGER-GUITARIST	POST OFFICE BOX 180	GREENBRIER, TN	37073
ROBERTS, MARGARET	NEWS CORRESPONDENT	1818 19TH ST, NW	WASHINGTON, DC	20009
ROBERTS, MARY	BODYBUILDER	POST OFFICE BOX 10493	SANTA ANA, CA	92711
ROBERTS, MICHAEL	TALENT AGENT	POST OFFICE BOX 216		
		ALBERT PARK	VICTORIA 3206	AUSTRALIA
ROBERTS, MICHAEL D	ACTOR	10825 CAMARILLO ST	NORTH HOLLYWOOD, CA	91602
ROBERTS, MIKE	GUITARIST	210 BRITTAIN CT	BRENTWOOD, TN	37027
ROBERTS, NANCI	ACTRESS	8949 SUNSET BLVD #203	LOS ANGELES, CA	90069
ROBERTS, NICKLA	WRESTLING VALET	SEE - BABY DOLL		
ROBERTS, PAULA	ACTRESS	307 MARINE ST #B	SANTA MONICA, CA	90405
ROBERTS, PENNANT	TV DIRECTOR	67 BURLINGTON RD		
		ISLEWORTH	MIDDLESEX	ENGLAND
ROBERTS, PERNELL	ACTOR	20395 SEABOARD RD	MALIBU, CA	90265
ROBERTS, RANDOLPH	ACTOR	CARPENTER, 1516-W REDWOOD ST	SAN DIEGO, CA	92101
ROBERTS, RAY	SINGER	POST OFFICE BOX 25371	CHARLOTTE, NC	28212
ROBERTS, ROBIN	BASEBALL	504 TERRACE HILL DR	TEMPLE TERRACE, FL	33617
ROBERTS, ROY	TV PRODUCER	GRANADA, 36 GOLDEN SQ	LONDON W1	ENGLAND
ROBERTS, STANLEY	ACTOR	7466 BEVERLY BLVD #205	LOS ANGELES, CA	90036
ROBERTS, STEPHEN	ACTOR	16701 MORRISON ST	ENCINO, CA	91436
ROBERTS, STEPHEN	DIRECTOR	4328 VALLEY MEADOW RD	ENCINO, CA	91436
ROBERTS, STEVE	FILM WRITER-DIRECTOR	4 STEELES STUDIOS		
		HAVERSTOCK HILL	LONDON NW3	ENGLAND
ROBERTS, STEVEN V	NEWS CORRESPONDENT	5315 BRADLEY BLVD	BETHESDA, MD	20814
ROBERTS, SUSAN	BODYBUILDER	ROBERTS HEALTH CLUB		
		930-B CARPENTER RD	MODESTO, CA	95351
ROBERTS, TANYA	ACTRESS	9000 SUNSET BLVD #1112	LOS ANGELES, CA	90069
ROBERTS, TEAL	ACTRESS	4121 VIA MARINA #102	MARINA DEL REY, CA	90292
ROBERTS, TONY	ACTOR	970 PARK AVE #8-N	NEW YORK, NY	10028
ROBERTS, WARD	ACTOR	6736 LAUREL CANYON BLVD #306	NORTH HOLLYWOOD, CA	91606

TANYA ROBERTS

CLIFF ROBERTSON

EUGENE ROCHE

ROBERT ROCKWELL

JIMMIE RODGERS

GILBERT ROLAND

YVONNE ROMAIN

LINA ROMAY

CESAR ROMERO

Name	Occupation	Address	City	Zip
ROBERTS, WILLIAM S	WRITER	KOHNER, 9169 SUNSET BLVD	LOS ANGELES, CA	90069
ROBERTS, WILSON K	GUITARIST	4700 HUMBER DR #G-10	NASHVILLE, TN	37211
ROBERTSHAW, IVAN E	WRITER	10014 AMANITA AVE	TUJUNGA, CA	91042
ROBERTSHAW, NICKY	NEWS CORRESPONDENT	1705 "P" ST #1, NW	WASHINGTON, DC	20036
ROBERTSON, ALAN	MUSICIAN	4022 LEALAND LN	NASHVILLE, TN	37204
ROBERTSON, ALLEN B	TV DIRECTOR	59 W 69TH ST	NEW YORK, NY	10023
ROBERTSON, ANGUS	NEWS CORRESPONDENT	2220 N ILLINOIS ST	ARLINGTON, VA	22205
ROBERTSON, BAXTER, BAND	ROCK & ROLL GROUP	1888 CENTURY PARK E #1400	LOS ANGELES, CA	90067
ROBERTSON, CAROLINE W	NEWS CORRESPONDENT	STAR ROUTE #231	SAINT GEORGE ISLAND, M	20674
ROBERTSON, CLIFF	ACT-WRI-DIR	325 DUNEMERE DR	LA JOLLA, CA	92037
ROBERTSON, CLIFFORD E	CONDUCTOR	6701 YOLANDA DR	RESEDA, CA	91335
ROBERTSON, DALE	ACTOR	POST OFFICE BOX 226	YUKON, OK	73099
ROBERTSON, DENNIS	ACTOR	4704 TOBIAS AVE	SHERMAN OAKS, CA	91403
ROBERTSON, DON I	COMPOSER	POST OFFICE BOX 4122	THOUSAND OAKS, CA	91359
ROBERTSON, HARRY	FILM PRODUCER	PINEWOOD STUDIOS, IVER HEATH	BUCKINGHAMSHIRE	ENGLAND
ROBERTSON, HUGH A	FILM DIRECTOR	208-A TERRACE VALE RD		
		GOOD WOOD PARK	TRINIDAD	WEST INDIES
ROBERTSON, JACK	NEWS CORRESPONDENT	2317 N STUART ST	ARLINGTON, VA	22207
ROBERTSON, KATHY	SINGER	3125 19TH ST #217	BAKERSFIELD, CA	93301
ROBERTSON, KIMMY	ACTRESS	400 S BEVERLY DR #216	BEVERLY HILLS, CA	90212
ROBERTSON, OSCAR	BASKETBALL	6 E 4TH ST	CINCINNATI, OH	45202
ROBERTSON, PAT	EVANGELIST	CHRISTIAN BROADCASTING		
		NETWORK CENTER	VIRGINIA BEACH, VA	23463
ROBERTSON, RICHARD T	PUBLISHING EXECUTIVE	US MAGAZINE COMPANY		
		1 DAG HAMMARSKJOLD PLAZA	NEW YORK, NY	10017
ROBERTSON, STANLEY GERALD	PRODUCER	11398 THURSTON CIR	LOS ANGELES, CA	90049
ROBERTSON, WILLIAM J, JR	HARMONICIST	3816 HARDING PL	NASHVILLE, TN	37215
ROBICHEAUX, VIRGINIA	NEWS CORRESPONDENT	POST OFFICE BOX 25824	WASHINGTON, DC	20005
ROBIN, CARYN	SINGER	SEE - RAVE		
ROBIN, DIANE	ACTRESS	1330 N CRESCENT HGTS BLVD	LOS ANGELES, CA	90046
ROBINS, BUTCH	GUITARIST	1906 5TH ST	RADFORD, VA	24141
ROBINS, CHRIS & THE COUNTRYMEN	C & W GROUP	POST OFFICE BOX 208	GOODLETTSVILLE, TN	37072
ROBINS, ISOBEL	THEATER PRODUCER	248 E 68TH ST	NEW YORK, NY	10021
ROBINS, JOHN	FILM-TV PRODUCER	ROGER HANCOCK MANAGEMENT		
		8 WATERLOO PL, PALL MALL	LONDON SW1Y 4AW	ENGLAND
ROBINS, JOHN M	TV DIRECTOR	18203 COASTLINE DR #4	MALIBU, CA	90265
ROBINS, LAWRENCE LEE	DIRECTOR	DGA, 7950 SUNSET BLVD	LOS ANGELES, CA	90046
ROBINS, LISA	ACTRESS	4176 ARCH DR #314	STUDIO CITY, CA	91604
ROBINS, OLIVER	ACTOR	11726 SAN VICENTE BLVD #300	LOS ANGELES, CA	90049
ROBINSON, ANDREW	ACTOR	10000 SANTA MONICA BLVD #305	LOS ANGELES, CA	90067
ROBINSON, ANGELA	ACTRESS	3907 W ALAMEDA AVE #101	BURBANK, CA	91505
ROBINSON, ANGELA Y	NEWS CORRESPONDENT	5151 WISCONSIN AVE, NW	WASHINGTON, DC	20016
ROBINSON, BARRY	NEWS CORRESPONDENT	1513 MOUNT EAGLE PL	ALEXANDRIA, VA	22302
ROBINSON, BILLY	GUITARIST	ROUTE #2, BOX 140	WHITE HOUSE, TN	37188
ROBINSON, BROOKS	BASEBALL	1506 SHERBROOK RD	LUTHERVILLE, MD	21093
ROBINSON, BRUCE	SCREENWRITER	1888 CENTURY PARK E #1400	LOS ANGELES, CA	90067
ROBINSON, BUDD	SCREENWRITER	6815 SHOUP AVE	CANOGA PARK, CA	91309
ROBINSON, BUMPER	ACTOR	SAVAGE, 6212 BANNER AVE	LOS ANGELES, CA	90038
ROBINSON, CARDEW	ACTOR-COMEDIAN	14 THE GROVE, SAINT MARGARET'S	TWICKENHAM	ENGLAND
ROBINSON, CHARLES KNOX	ACTOR	427 N CANON DR #205	BEVERLY HILLS, CA	90210
ROBINSON, CHARLIE	ACTOR	10000 SANTA MONICA BLVD #305	LOS ANGELES, CA	90067
ROBINSON, CHRIS	ACTOR-DIRECTOR	6235 HOLLYMONT DR	LOS ANGELES, CA	90068
ROBINSON, CLIFFORD H	COMPOSER	14251 JUDD ST	PACOIMA, CA	91331
ROBINSON, CLYDE W	PHOTOJOURNALIST	512 HIGHLAND ST	VIENNA, VA	22180
ROBINSON, DOUGLAS	ACTOR	9255 SUNSET BLVD #603	LOS ANGELES, CA	90069
ROBINSON, DOUGLAS	TENOR	200 W 70TH ST #7-F	NEW YORK, NY	10023
ROBINSON, EARL	COMP-WRI-COND	3937 BLEDSOE AVE	LOS ANGELES, CA	90066
ROBINSON, EARL H	COMPOSER	3929 CALLE CITA	SANTA BARBARA, CA	93110
ROBINSON, FAYE	SOPRANO	CAMI, 165 W 57TH ST	NEW YORK, NY	10019
ROBINSON, FENTON	SINGER	THE ROOSTER BLUES		
		2615 N WILTON AVE	CHICAGO, IL	60614
ROBINSON, FLOYD	GUITARIST	2436 EASTLAND AVE	NASHVILLE, TN	37206
ROBINSON, FRANK	BASEBALL	15557 AQUA VERDE DR	LOS ANGELES, CA	90024
ROBINSON, GAIL	SOPRANO	61 W 62ND ST #6-F	NEW YORK, NY	10023
ROBINSON, HARRY	COMPOSER	MUSICAL ASSOCIATES		
		11 TOWNSEND HOUSE		
		22-25 DEAN ST	LONDON SW10	ENGLAND
ROBINSON, HARRY A	GUITARIST	ROUTE# 1, BOX 157-B	CHARLOTTE, TN	37036
ROBINSON, JAMIE	PHOTOGRAPHER	222 W 23RD ST #105	NEW YORK, NY	10011
ROBINSON, JAY	ACTOR	15010 VENTURA BLVD #219	SHERMAN OAKS, CA	91403
ROBINSON, JONATHAN	ACTOR	25 CLEVELAND TERR #4	LONDON WC2	ENGLAND
ROBINSON, JOSHUA	NEWS CORRESPONDENT	2139 WISCONSIN AVE, NW	WASHINGTON, DC	20007
ROBINSON, JOYCE	CASTING DIRECTOR	2049 CENTURY PARK E #4100	LOS ANGELES, CA	90067
ROBINSON, KENNETH N	NEWS CORRESPONDENT	1400 "I" ST, NW	WASHINGTON, DC	20005
ROBINSON, LEON	ACTOR	8230 BEVERLY BLVD #23	LOS ANGELES, CA	90048
ROBINSON, LEROY	TV WRITER	8955 BEVERLY BLVD	LOS ANGELES, CA	90048
ROBINSON, LISA	ACTRESS	3575 W CAHUENGA BLVD #320	LOS ANGELES, CA	90068
ROBINSON, LISA	ROCK WRITER-CRITIC	N Y TIMES SYNDICATION		
		130 5TH AVE	NEW YORK, NY	10011
ROBINSON, MARGARET L	NEWS CORRESPONDENT	POST OFFICE BOX 2626	WASHINGTON, DC	20013

ROBINSON, MARILYN L	NEWS CORRESPONDENT	CBS NEWS, 2020 "M" ST, NW	WASHINGTON, DC	20036
ROBINSON, MARVIN W	TV WRITER	8955 BEVERLY BLVD	LOS ANGELES, CA	90048
ROBINSON, MATTHEW	TV DIRECTOR	48 SEYMOUR WALK	LONDON SW10	ENGLAND
ROBINSON, MATTHEW T, JR	TV WRITER	555 W 57TH ST #1230	NEW YORK, NY	10019
ROBINSON, MAX	BROADCAST JOURNALIST	ABC-TV, 190 N STATE ST	CHICAGO, IL	60601
ROBINSON, MAX W	CONDUCTOR	2821 ROSETTE ST	SIMI VALLEY, CA	93065
ROBINSON, MC NEIL	ORGANIST	15 HIGH ST #621	HARTFORD, CT	06103
ROBINSON, MICHELE L	NEWS CORRESPONDENT	6151 30TH ST, NW	WASHINGTON, DC	20015
ROBINSON, MIRIAM "MITZI"	TV WRITER	8955 BEVERLY BLVD	LOS ANGELES, CA	90048
ROBINSON, PAULETTE J	NEWS CORRESPONDENT	2133 WISCONSIN AVE, NW	WASHINGTON, DC	20007
ROBINSON, PHIL ALDEN	SCREENWRITER	151 S EL CAMINO DR	BEVERLY HILLS, CA	90212
ROBINSON, RICHARD R	SCREENWRITER	FLA IFC, 100 W SOUTH ST	ORLANDO, FL	32801
ROBINSON, RICKY & THE BAYOU BOY	C & W GROUP	PENNY, 30 GUINAN ST	WALTHAM, MA	02154
ROBINSON, ROBERT	TV PERSONALITY	BBC-TV CENTRE, WOOD LN		
		SHEPHERDS BUSH	LONDON W12	ENGLAND
ROBINSON, ROBERT D	TV WRITER	8955 BEVERLY BLVD	LOS ANGELES, CA	90048
ROBINSON, ROBERT L	GUITARIST	500 CHEYENNE BLVD #118	MADISON, TN	37115
ROBINSON, ROBERTA	ACTRESS	4721 LAUREL CANYON BLVD #211	NORTH HOLLYWOOD, CA	91607
ROBINSON, ROGER	ACTOR	7116 HILLSIDE AVE	LOS ANGELES, CA	90046
ROBINSON, SALLY B	TV WRITER	8955 BEVERLY BLVD	LOS ANGELES, CA	90048
ROBINSON, SHARON	CELLIST	SHAW CONCERTS, 1995 BROADWAY	NEW YORK, NY	10023
ROBINSON, SMOKEY	SINGER-SONGWRITER	631 N OAKHURST DR	BEVERLY HILLS, CA	90210
ROBINSON, STEPHEN	GUITARIST	3003 VAN NESS ST #W-205, NW	WASHINGTON, DC	20008
ROBINSON, STEVE	SPORTS WRITER-EDITOR	SPORTS ILLUSTRATED MAGAZINE		
		TIME & LIFE BUILDING		
		ROCKEFELLER PLAZA	NEW YORK, NY	10020
ROBINSON, STU	TALENT AGENT	8428 MELROSE PL #C	LOS ANGELES, CA	90069
ROBINSON, STUART K	ACTOR	2000 N BEACHWOOD DR	LOS ANGELES, CA	90068
ROBINSON, SUGAR RAY	BOXER-ACTOR	1060 CRENSHAW BLVD #101	LOS ANGELES, CA	90019
ROBINSON, SYLVIA	SINGER-RECORD EXEC	SUGARHILL RECORDS		
		96 WEST ST	ENGLEWOOD, NJ	07631
ROBINSON, TERI	NEWS CORRESPONDENT	1700 17TH ST #209, NW	WASHINGTON, DC	20009
ROBINSON, TERRY JEAN	SINGER-DANCER	22200 CRAGGYVIEW ST	CHATSWORTH, CA	91311
ROBINSON, THOMAS S	NEWS CORRESPONDENT	1010 PRINCE ST	ALEXANDRIA, VA	22314
ROBINSON, VALERIE C	ACTRESS	CONTEMPORARY ARTISTS		
		132 S LASKY DR	BEVERLY HILLS, CA	90212
ROBINSON, VICKI SUE	SINGER	1650 BROADWAY #611	NEW YORK, NY	10019
ROBINSON, VIRGINIA	ACTRESS	321 W 55TH ST	NEW YORK, NY	10019
ROBINSON, VIRGINIA	NEWS CORRESPONDENT	221 ORONOCO ST	ALEXANDRIA, VA	22314
ROBINSON, WALTER V	NEWS CORRESPONDENT	1750 PENNSYLVANIA AVE #318, NW	WASHINGTON, DC	20006
ROBINSON, WAYNE E	COMPOSER-CONDUCTOR	20147 GRESHAM ST	CANOGA PARK, CA	91306
ROBINSON, WILLIAM E	NEWS CORRESPONDENT	4216 WILLOW WOOD DR	ANNANDALE, VA	22003
ROBINSON'S, TOM, SECTOR 27	MUSICAL GROUP	250 W 57TH ST #603	NEW YORK, NY	10107
ROBISON, PAULA	FLUTIST	SHAW CONCERTS, 1995 BROADWAY	NEW YORK, NY	10023
ROBLEE, STERLING	ACTOR	6605 HOLLYWOOD BLVD #220	HOLLYWOOD, CA	90028
ROBMAN, MARK	ACTOR	5330 LANKERSHIM BLVD #210	NORTH HOLLYWOOD, CA	91601
ROBMAN, STEVEN	TV DIRECTOR	201 W 85TH ST	NEW YORK, NY	10024
ROBOTHAM, GEORGE	DIRECTOR	9840 WANDA PARK DR	BEVERLY HILLS, CA	90210
ROBOTHAM, ROSEMARIE A	NEWS REPORTER	LIFE/TIME & LIFE BLDG		
		ROCKEFELLER CENTER	NEW YORK, NY	10020
ROBY, LAVELLE	ACTRESS	806 N SYCAMORE AVE #1	LOS ANGELES, CA	90038
ROBYNS, ANNETTE	ACTRESS	10850 RIVERSIDE DR #505	NORTH HOLLYWOOD, CA	91602
ROCA, JOHN	PHOTOGRAPHER	1742 64TH ST	BROOKLYN, NY	11204
ROCCO, ALEX	ACTOR	1755 OCEAN OAKS RD	CARPINTERIA, CA	93013
ROCCO, MARY	ACTRESS	5 RIVERSIDE DR	NEW YORK, NY	10023
ROCCUZZO, MARIO	ACTOR	870 N VINE ST #G	LOS ANGELES, CA	90038
ROCHA, VICTORIA	ACTRESS	1710 LAUREL CANYON BLVD #4	LOS ANGELES, CA	90046
ROCHE, EUGENE	ACTOR	451 1/2 KELTON AVE	LOS ANGELES, CA	90024
ROCHEFORT, JEAN	ACTRESS	LE CHENE ROGNEAUX	GROSVRE F078125	FRANCE
ROCHELLE, CARL	NEWS CORRESPONDENT	4618 N 41ST ST	ARLINGTON, VA	22207
ROCHES, THE	ROCK & ROLL GROUP	POST OFFICE BOX 1333	MONTCLAIR, NJ	07042
ROCHIN, AARON	SOUND ENGINEER	15421 VISTA HAVEN PL	SHERMAN OAKS, CA	91403
ROCHLEN, KENDIS	TV WRITER	8955 BEVERLY BLVD	LOS ANGELES, CA	90048
ROCK, FELIPPA	ACTRESS	MICHAEL PATE, 21 BUKDARRA RD	BELLVUE HILL 2023	AUSTRALIA
ROCK, MELANI	NEWS CORRESPONDENT	1100 17TH ST, NW	WASHINGTON, DC	20036
ROCK, MONTI, III	SINGER-ACTOR	MOSMAN, 395 NE 21ST ST	MIAMI, FL	33137
ROCK, PHILLIP	WRITER	3519 STONE CANYON AVE	SHERMAN OAKS, CA	91403
ROCK, PHILLIP M	DIRECTOR	626 ACORN DR	SAINT LOUIS, MO	63126
ROCK 'N 'ROLL AMERICANA	ROCK & ROLL GROUP	OLDIES, 5218 ALMONT ST	LOS ANGELES, CA	90032
ROCK 'N' ROLL EXPRESS, THE	WRESTLING TAG TEAM	NATIONAL WRESTLING ALLIANCE		
		JIM CROCKETT PROMOTIONS		
		421 BRIARBEND DR	CHARLOTTE, NC	28209
ROCK GODDESS	ROCK & ROLL TRIO	JOHN TURNER MANAGEMENT		
		118 WANDSWORTH HIGH ST	LONDON SW18	ENGLAND
ROCKEFELLER, KEN	DIRECTOR	104 NORTHAMPTON DR	WHITE PLAINS, NY	10603
ROCKETS, THE	ROCK & ROLL GROUP	LAZAR, 3222 BELINDA DR	STERLING HEIGHTS, MI	48077
ROCKIN' 50'S BIG BEAT	ROCK & ROLL GROUP	OLDIES, 5218 ALMONT ST	LOS ANGELES, CA	90032
ROCKIN' REBELS, THE	ROCK & ROLL GROUP	OLDIES, 5218 ALMONT ST	LOS ANGELES, CA	90032
ROCKLEN, GARY S	WRITER	1222 PRESTON WY	VENICE, CA	90291
ROCKPILE	ROCK & ROLL GROUP	ICM, 40 W 57TH ST	NEW YORK, NY	10019
ROCKWELL	SINGER-SONGWRITER	GORDY, 801 SARBONNE RD	LOS ANGELES, CA	90077
ROCKWELL, DONNA	NEWS CORRESPONDENT	2133 WISCONSIN AVE, NW	WASHINGTON, DC	20007
ROCKWELL, JEFFREY	ACTOR-COMPOSER	1515 1/2 N HAYWORTH AVE	LOS ANGELES, CA	90046
ROCKWELL, L MARK	NEWS CORRESPONDENT	3028 WISCONSIN AVE, NW	WASHINGTON, DC	20016
ROCKWELL, ROBERT	ACTOR	650 TOYOPA DR	PACIFIC PALISADES, CA	90272

Name	Occupation	Address	City	Zip
ROCKWOOD, JERRY	MIME	ARTHUR SHAFMAN, 723 7TH AVE	NEW YORK, NY	10019
ROCKWOOD, NORMA	MIME	ARTHUR SHAFMAN, 723 7TH AVE	NEW YORK, NY	10019
ROCKY HILL BAND	RHYTHM & BLUES GROUP	9777 HARWIN ST #101	HOUSTON, TX	94925
ROCOS, CLEO	ACTRESS	ICM, 8899 BEVERLY BLVD	LOS ANGELES, CA	90048
RODBY, JOHN L	CONDUCTOR	5351 PENFIELD AVE	WOODLAND HILLS, CA	91364
RODD, MARCIA	ACTRESS	251 W 71ST ST	NEW YORK, NY	10023
RODDAM, FRANC	FILM DIRECTOR	ICM, 388-396 OXFORD ST	LONDON W1	ENGLAND
RODDAM, FRANCIS G	DIRECTOR	DGA, 7950 SUNSET BLVD	LOS ANGELES, CA	90046
RODDENBERRY, EUGENE	WRITER-PRODUCER	9147 LEANDER PL	BEVERLY HILLS, CA	90210
RODDY, PATRICK M	PHOTOGRAPHER	13958 TRIADELPHIA MILLS RD	DAYTON, MD	21036
RODERICK, KYLE	WRITER-EDITOR	US MAGAZINE COMPANY		
		1 DAG HAMMARSKJOLD PLAZA	NEW YORK, NY	10017
RODERICK, LEE	NEWS CORRESPONDENT	12812 CIRCLE DR	ROCKVILLE, MD	20850
RODESCU, JULIAN	SINGER	POST OFFICE BOX 188		
		STATION A	TORONTO, ONT	CANADA
RODGERS, AGGIE GUERARD	COSTUME DESIGNER	10100 SANTA MONICA BLVD #1600	LOS ANGELES, CA	90067
RODGERS, ANTON	ACTOR	THE WHITE HOUSE		
		LOWER BASILDON	BERKSHIRE	ENGLAND
RODGERS, BEVERLY D	TV DIRECTOR	KGO-TV, 277 GOLDEN GATE AVE	SAN FRANCISCO, CA	94102
RODGERS, FOREST	BANJOIST	970 W JUNIATA ST	CLERMONT, FL	32711
RODGERS, HARRY H	COMPOSER-CONDUCTOR	11 WILLOWBROOK LN #204	DELRAY BEACH, FL	33446
RODGERS, JIMMIE	SINGER-SONGWRITER	20224 SHERMAN WY #56	CANOGA PARK, CA	91306
RODGERS, JOAN	SOPRANO	CAMI, 165 W 57TH ST	NEW YORK, NY	10019
RODGERS, JOHN	MUSICIAN	5308 STALLWORTH DR	NASHVILLE, TN	37220
RODGERS, JONATHAN	TV PRODUCER	CBS-TV, 524 W 57TH ST	NEW YORK, NY	10019
RODGERS, MARK	TV WRITER	8955 BEVERLY BLVD	LOS ANGELES, CA	90048
RODGERS, MARY	SCREENWRITER	8955 BEVERLY BLVD	LOS ANGELES, CA	90048
RODGERS, PAMELA	ACTRESS	8721 SUNSET BLVD #200	LOS ANGELES, CA	90069
RODINE, ALEX	ACTOR	FARRELL, 10500 MAGNOLIA BLVD	NORTH HOLLYWOOD, CA	91601
RODMAN, ADAM	TV WRITER	8955 BEVERLY BLVD	LOS ANGELES, CA	90048
RODMAN, ELLEN	TV EXECUTIVE	NBC TELEVISION NETWORK		
		30 ROCKEFELLER PLAZA	NEW YORK, NY	10112
RODMAN, JOHN	MUSICIAN	1106 HOLLY HILL DR	FRANKLIN, TN	37064
RODMAN, JUDY	SINGER	MTM MUSIC GROUP, INC		
		21 MUSIC SQUARE E	NASHVILLE, TN	37203
RODOMISTA, ROD H	TV EXECUTIVE	ABC TELEVISION NETWORK		
		1330 AVE OF THE AMERICAS	NEW YORK, NY	10020
RODRIGUES, CHARLES	CARTOONIST	THE NATIONAL LAMPOON		
		635 MADISON AVE	NEW YORK, NY	10022
RODRIGUES, PERCY	ACTOR	2121 AVE OF THE STARS #410	LOS ANGELES, CA	90067
RODRIGUES, STEVE	TV DIRECTOR	10707 CAMARILLO ST #111	NORTH HOLLYWOOD, CA	91602
RODRIGUEZ, JOHNNY	SINGER-SONGWRITER	240 WILSON PIKE CIR	NASHVILLE, TN	37203
RODRIGUEZ, JOSE LUIS	SINGER	151 S EL CAMINO DR	BEVERLY HILLS, CA	90212
RODRIGUEZ, PAUL	COMEDIAN-ACTOR	9255 SUNSET BLVD #1115	LOS ANGELES, CA	90069
RODRIGUEZ, PAUL	NEWS CORRESPONDENT	12106 FOLEY ST	WHEATON, MD	20902
RODRIGUEZ, SANTIAGO	PIANIST	SHAW CONCERTS, 1995 BROADWAY	NEW YORK, NY	10023
RODRIGUEZ-LARA, JOSE I	NEWS CORRESPONDENT	6901 VALLEY BROOK DR	FALLS CHURCH, VA	22042
RODRIQUES, CHARLIE	CARTOONIST	TRIBUNE MEDIA SERVICES		
		64 E CONCORD ST	ORLANDO, FL	32801
RODRIQUEZ, ANDY	WRESTLING WRITER	POST OFFICE BOX 48	ROCKVILLE CENTRE, NY	11571
RODS, THE	ROCK & ROLL GROUP	605 3RD ST #1501	NEW YORK, NY	10016
RODWAY, NORMAN	ACTOR	MARTIN, 7 WINDMILL ST	LONDON W1	ENGLAND
RODZIANKO, ANNA	ACTRESS	4412 MARIOTA AVE	NORTH HOLLYWOOD, CA	91602
ROE, TOMMY	SINGER-SONGWRITER	HOFFMAN TALENT MANAGEMENT		
		1011 TWELVE OAKS CENTER		
		15500 WAYZATA BLVD	WAYZATA, MN	55391
ROE, WILLY	DIRECTOR-PRODUCER	18 GREEK ST	LONDON W1	ENGLAND
ROEBUCK, GREGG	ACTOR	8961 SUNSET BLVD #B	LOS ANGELES, CA	90069
ROECA, SAMUEL F	TV WRITER	5461 ENCINO AVE	ENCINO, CA	91316
ROEDER, EDWARD	NEWS CORRESPONDENT	1220 "G" ST, SE	WASHINGTON, DC	20003
ROEG, NICOLAS	FILM DIRECTOR	2-E OXFORD & CAMBRIDGE MANSIONS		
		OLD MARYLEBONE RD	LONDON NW1	ENGLAND
ROEHM, CAROLYNE	FASHION DESIGNER	550 7TH AVE	NEW YORK, NY	10018
ROELOFSEN, HANS	DOUBLE BASS	ROSENFIELD, 714 LADD RD	BRONX, NY	10471
ROEMER, LARRY	TV DIRECTOR-PRODUCER	63 E 9TH ST	NEW YORK, NY	10003
ROEMER, RACHEL	VIOLINIST	2150 SMALLHOUSE RD	BOWLING GREEN, KY	42101
ROEMHELD, HEINZ	COMPOSER	2950 LOS FELIZ BLVD #204	LOS ANGELES, CA	90039
ROERICK, WILLIAM	ACTOR	145 W 79TH ST	NEW YORK, NY	10024
ROEVES, MAURICE	ACTOR-WRITER-DIRECTOR	LONDON MANAGEMENT, LTD		
		235-241 REGENT ST	LONDON W1A 2JT	ENGLAND
ROFFIS, JANE D	WRITER	311 MONTANA AVE #202	SANTA MONICA, CA	90403
ROGAN, GEORGE	ACTOR	1605 N CAHUENGA BLVD #202	LOS ANGELES, CA	90028
ROGAN, JOSH	SCREENWRITER	8955 BEVERLY BLVD	LOS ANGELES, CA	90048
ROGAN, WILLIAM	FRENCH HORNIST	POST OFFICE BOX 131	SPRINGFIELD, VA	22150
ROGE, PASCAL	PIANIST	SHAW CONCERTS, 1995 BROADWAY	NEW YORK, NY	10023
ROGELL, ALBERT S	FILM DIRECTOR	10120 EMPYREAN WY	LOS ANGELES, CA	90067
ROGER	SINGER	TROUTMAN, 2010 SALEM AVE	DAYTON, OH	45406
ROGER & ROGER	COMEDY DUO	BRB, 666 N ROBERTSON BLVD	LOS ANGELES, CA	90060
ROGERS, ADRIANE	ACTRESS	5330 LANKERSHIM BLVD #210	NORTH HOLLYWOOD, CA	91601
ROGERS, ALBERT S	TV WRITER	8955 BEVERLY BLVD	LOS ANGELES, CA	90048
ROGERS, ANNE	ACTRESS	CONTEMPORARY ARTISTS		
		132 S LASKY DR	BEVERLY HILLS, CA	90212
ROGERS, BIG BUBBA	WRESTLER	NATIONAL WRESTLING ALLIANCE		
		JIM CROCKETT PROMOTIONS		
		421 BRIARBEND DR	CHARLOTTE, NC	28209

Name	Occupation	Address	City	ZIP
ROGERS, BRUCE A	COMPOSER	13037 MOORPARK ST	STUDIO CITY, CA	91604
ROGERS, CHARLES "BUDDY"	ACTOR	1147 PICKFAIR WY	BEVERLY HILLS, CA	90210
ROGERS, D J	SINGER	GOLDEN, 788 MONTECITO ST	LOS ANGELES, CA	90031
ROGERS, DAVID	GUITARIST	556 AUGUSTA DR	HERMITAGE, TN	37076
ROGERS, DAVID	SINGER	ACE, 3407 GREEN RIDGE DR	NASHVILLE, TN	37204
ROGERS, DAVID R	NEWS CORRESPONDENT	7412 TAKOMA AVE	SILVER SPRING, MD	20910
ROGERS, DINAH ANNE	ACTRESS	11300 EMELITA ST	NORTH HOLLYWOOD, CA	91601
ROGERS, DOUG	DIRECTOR	5514 PACIFIC AVE	MARINA DEL REY, CA	90292
ROGERS, DOUGLAS G	PERCUSSIONIST	141 NEESE DR #C-8	NASHVILLE, TN	37211
ROGERS, DUSTY	SINGER	POST OFFICE BOX 1507	APPLE VALLEY, CA	92307
ROGERS, EDMUND H, JR	DIRECTOR	928 CHANTILLY RD	LOS ANGELES, CA	90077
ROGERS, EDWIN A	NEWS CORRESPONDENT	4411 PENWOOD DR	ALEXANDRIA, VA	22310
ROGERS, ELIE S	PHOTOGRAPHER	10 WATERGATE CT	SILVER SPRING, MD	20904
ROGERS, EVAN	SINGER-GUITARIST	16130 VENTURA BLVD #640	ENCINO, CA	91436
ROGERS, FRED	TV HOST	4802 5TH AVE	PITTSBURGH, PA	15213
ROGERS, GAMBLE	SINGER	POST OFFICE BOX 1556	GAINESVILLE, FL	32602
ROGERS, GERALD T	WRITER-PRODUCER	5225 OLD ORCHARD RD	SKOKIE, IL	60077
ROGERS, GIL	ACTOR	40 5TH AVE	NEW YORK, NY	10011
ROGERS, GINGER	ACTRESS-DANCER	ROGERS ROGUE RIVER RANCH		
		18745 CRATER LAKE HWY	EAGLE POINT, OR	97524
ROGERS, HARLAN DALE	COMPOSER	3301 S BEAR RD #51-A	SANTA ANA, CA	92704
ROGERS, JACK	COMPOSER	POST OFFICE BOX 404	HILLSBORO, OH	45133
ROGERS, JAMIE JUAN	DIRECTOR	6514 LANKERSHIM BLVD	NORTH HOLLYWOOD, CA	91606
ROGERS, JEAN	ACTRESS	14743 OTSEGO ST	SHERMAN OAKS, CA	91403
ROGERS, JIM	TV WRITER	14144 VENTURA BLVD #200	SHERMAN OAKS, CA	91423
ROGERS, JIM R	DIRECTOR	4348 BECK AVE	STUDIO CITY, CA	91604
ROGERS, JOY	ACTRESS	12016 MOORPARK ST #3	STUDIO CITY, CA	91604
ROGERS, JULIE	ACTRESS	1001 N VISTA ST	LOS ANGELES, CA	90046

Name	Occupation	Address	City	Zip/Country
ROGERS, KEITH	ACTRESS	8322 BEVERLY BLVD #202	LOS ANGELES, CA	90048
ROGERS, KENNY	SINGER-SONGWRITER	KRAGEN, 1112 N SHERBOURNE DR	LOS ANGELES, CA	90069
ROGERS, LAURA ANN	NEWS CORRESPONDENT	2730 WISCONSIN AVE #26, NW	WASHINGTON, DC	20007
ROGERS, LESLEY	ACTRESS	211 S BEVERLY BLVD #201	BEVERLY HILLS, CA	90212
ROGERS, MELODY	ACTRESS-TV HOST	200 N ROBERTSON BLVD #219	BEVERLY HILLS, CA	90211
ROGERS, MICHAEL	SCREENWRITER	8955 BEVERLY BLVD	LOS ANGELES, CA	90048
ROGERS, MICHELE	ACTRESS	15010 VENTURA BLVD #219	SHERMAN OAKS, CA	91403
ROGERS, MIMI	ACTRESS	9744 WILSHIRE BLVD #206	BEVERLY HILLS, CA	90212
ROGERS, NEIL PATTON	SINGER-GUITARIST	ROUTE #1, BOX 464		
		SHACKLE ISLAND RD	HENDERSONVILLE, TN	37075
ROGERS, NIGEL	TENOR	AARON, 25 HUNTINGTON AVE	BOSTON, MA	02116
ROGERS, NOELLE	SOPRANO	61 W 62ND ST #6-F	NEW YORK, NY	10023
ROGERS, NORMA	FLUTIST	7298 CAVALIER DR	NASHVILLE, TN	37221
ROGERS, PATRICK J	NEWS CORRESPONDENT	7106 SYCAMORE AVE	TAKOMA PARK, MD	20912
ROGERS, PAUL	ACTOR	9 HILLSIDE GARDENS	LONDON N6 5SU	ENGLAND
ROGERS, PAULINE B	WRITER	920 N KINGS RD #229	LOS ANGELES, CA	90069
ROGERS, PEE WEE	GUITARIST	716 WILLOWVIEW DR	LAVERGNE, TN	37086
ROGERS, PETER	FILM WRITER-PRODUCER	DRUMMERS YARD, AMERSHAM RD		
		BEACONSFIELD	BUCKS	ENGLAND
ROGERS, R F "BUDDY"	DRUMMER	ROUTE #7, 101 BROOKSIDE DR	FRANKLIN, TN	37064
ROGERS, RITA	DIRECTOR	4337 RHODES AVE	STUDIO CITY, CA	91604
ROGERS, ROBERT FRANCIS	TV WRITER-PRODUCER	NBC-TV, NEWS DEPARTMENT		
		4001 NEBRASKA AVE, NW	WASHINGTON, DC	20016
ROGERS, RONNIE	SINGER-GUITARIST	ROUTE #6	FRANKLIN, TN	37064
ROGERS, ROSEMARY	NOVELIST	AVON BOOKS, 959 8TH AVE	NEW YORK, NY	10019
ROGERS, ROSWELL	WRITER	4500 CAMPUS DR #316	NEWPORT BEACH, CA	92660
ROGERS, ROY	ACTOR-SINGER	15650 SENECA RD	VICTORVILLE, CA	92392
ROGERS, ROY "DUSTY," JR	SINGER-GUITARIST	POST OFFICE BOX 1507	APPLE VALLEY, CA	92307
ROGERS, SHEILA	ACTRESS	8019 1/2 MELROSE AVE #3	LOS ANGELES, CA	90046
ROGERS, SHEILA	WRITER-EDITOR	US MAGAZINE COMPANY		
		1 DAG HAMMARSKJOLD PLAZA	NEW YORK, NY	10017
ROGERS, STEVE	BASEBALL	2718 S UTICA	TULSA, OK	74114
ROGERS, SUZANNE	ACTRESS	3800 BARHAM BLVD #303	LOS ANGELES, CA	90068
ROGERS, TED	ACTOR	2121 VALDERAS DR #46	GLENDALE, CA	91208
ROGERS, TIMMIE	COMEDIAN	1911 GARTH AVE	LOS ANGELES, CA	90034
ROGERS, TRISTAN	ACTOR	9220 SUNSET BLVD #625	LOS ANGELES, CA	90069
ROGERS, WAYNE	ACTOR-WRITER-DIRECTOR	916 N BEVERLY DR	BEVERLY HILLS, CA	90210
ROGERS, WILL, JR	ACTOR		TUBAC, AZ	85640
ROGERS, WILLIAM DAVID	GUITARIST	6107 HENRY FORD DR	NASHVILLE, TN	37209
ROGIN, GILBERT	WRITER-EDITOR	DISCOVER/TIME & LIFE BLDG		
		ROCKEFELLER CENTER	NEW YORK, NY	10020
ROGLER, HELEN	ACTRESS	7015 LANEWOOD AVE #A-2	LOS ANGELES, CA	90028
ROGOFF, LYNN	WRITER	THE WILLIAM MORRIS AGENCY		
		1350 AVE OF THE AMERICAS	NEW YORK, NY	10019
ROGOSIN, JOEL	WRITER-PRODUCER	6034 PENFIELD AVE	WOODLAND HILLS, CA	91367
ROGOSIN, ROY M	TV WRITER-CONDUCTOR	11488 HUSTON ST	NORTH HOLLYWOOD, CA	91601
ROGOWSKI, AL	WRESTLER	SEE - ANDERSON, OLE		
ROGOWSKI, LEONARD J	COMPOSER	6532 KELVIN AVE	CANOGA PARK, CA	91306
ROGOWSKI, PHYLLIS LEE	WRITER	5700 CANNONSIDE RD	LA CRESCENTA, CA	91214
ROGOWSKI, ROCK	WRESTLER	SEE - ANDERSON, OLE		
ROHA, RONALEEN R	NEWS CORRESPONDENT	4201 MASSACHUSETTS AVE, NW	WASHINGTON, DC	20016
ROHDE, BARRY C	WRITER	13637 CREWE ST	VAN NUYS, CA	91405
ROHDE, DAVID	NEWS CORRESPONDENT	201 "I" ST #630, SW	WASHINGTON, DC	20024
ROHMER, ERIC	DIRECTOR	26 AVE PIERRE-LER-DE-SERBIE	PARIS 75116	FRANCE
ROHMER, PATRICE	ACTRESS	POST OFFICE BOX 49335	LOS ANGELES, CA	90049
ROHNER, CLAYTON	ACTOR	9100 SUNSET BLVD #200	LOS ANGELES, CA	90069
ROHNER, MARK F	NEWS CORRESPONDENT	8706 MILFORD AVE	SILVER SPRING, MD	20910
ROIZMAN, OWEN	CINEMATOGRAPHER	17533 MAGNOLIA BLVD	ENCINO, CA	91436
ROKER, ROXIE	ACTRESS	6380 WILSHIRE BLVD #910	LOS ANGELES, CA	90048
ROKETENETZ, ANNEMARIE	NEWS CORRESPONDENT	2228 OBSERVATORY PL, NW	WASHINGTON, DC	20007
ROLAND, FRITZ	DIRECTOR	2419 N RANDOLPH ST	ARLINGTON, VA	22207
ROLAND, GILBERT	ACTOR	518 N ROXBURY DR	BEVERLY HILLS, CA	90210
ROLAND, KATHLEEN	ACTRESS	320 W 75TH ST	NEW YORK, NY	10023
ROLAND, NEIL	NEWS CORRESPONDENT	2124 "I" ST #702, NW	WASHINGTON, DC	20037
ROLAND, SANDRA W	SCREENWRITER	8955 BEVERLY BLVD	LOS ANGELES, CA	90048
ROLAND, STEVE	ACTOR	175 W 72ND ST	NEW YORK, NY	10023
ROLANDI, GIANNA	SOPRANO	CAMI, 165 W 57TH ST	NEW YORK, NY	10019
ROLAPP, THOMAS	ACTOR	3426 LONDON ST	LOS ANGELES, CA	90026
ROLEN, L FELTON	NEWS CORRESPONDENT	3453 WARNER RD	RICHMOND, VA	23225
ROLEY, LIDDY	ACTRESS	777 ARDEN RD	PASADENA, CA	91106
ROLEY, SUTTON	TV WRITER-DIRECTOR	777 ARDEN RD	PASADENA, CA	91106
ROLF, TOM	FILM EDITOR	9046 SUNSET BLVD #202	LOS ANGELES, CA	90069
ROLFE, DAVID	FILM DIRECTOR	5 MEARD ST	LONDON W1	ENGLAND
ROLFE, HILDA N	WRITER	400 N CARMELINA AVE	LOS ANGELES, CA	90049
ROLFE, MICHAEL	TV DIRECTOR	PANTECHNICON FILMS, LTD		
		8 LABURNHAM GROVE, MOSELEY	BIRMINGHAM B13 8EL	ENGLAND
ROLFE, SAM H	TV WRITER	400 N CARMELINA AVE	LOS ANGELES, CA	90049
ROLIN, JUDI	ACTRESS	ANN WRIGHT, 136 E 57TH ST	NEW YORK, NY	10022
ROLL, DONNA	SOPRANO	POST OFFICE BOX 27539	PHILADELPHIA, PA	19118
ROLLE, ESTHER	ACTRESS	4421 DON FELIPE DR	LOS ANGELES, CA	90008
ROLLE, GREG	SINGER-KEYBOARDIST	POST OFFICE BOX 5952	SAN FRANCISCO, CA	94101
ROLLER, CLEVE	ACTRESS	1501 BROADWAY	NEW YORK, NY	10036

Name	Occupation	Address	City	Zip
ROLLER, CLYDE LEE	PHOTOGRAPHER	2816 HENDERSON CT	WHEATON, MD	20902
ROLLING STONES, THE	ROCK & ROLL GROUP	ROLLING STONES RECORDS		
		75 ROCKEFELLER PLAZA	NEW YORK, NY	10019
ROLLINS, BERNARD	TV WRITER	5443 OVERDALE DR	LOS ANGELES, CA	90043
ROLLINS, BETTY	NEWS CORRESPONDENT	ABC-TV, NEWS DEPARTMENT		
		1330 AVE OF THE AMERICAS	NEW YORK, NY	10020
ROLLINS, BONNIE S	NEWS CORRESPONDENT	NBC-TV, NEWS DEPARTMENT		
		4001 NEBRASKA AVE, NW	WASHINGTON, DC	20016
ROLLINS, BYRON H	PHOTOGRAPHER	4421 BUTTERWORTH PL, NW	WASHINGTON, DC	20016
ROLLINS, HAROLD E, JR	ACTOR	1501 BROADWAY #1510	NEW YORK, NY	10036
ROLLINS, JACK	FILM-TV PRODUCER	ROLLINS/JOFFE, 130 W 57TH ST	NEW YORK, NY	10019
ROLLINS, SONNY	SAXOPHONIST	ROUTE #9-G	GERMANTOWN, NY	12526
ROLOFF, ROGER	BARITONE	CONE, 221 W 57TH ST	NEW YORK, NY	10019
ROLSTON, SHAUNA	CELLIST	5720 MOSHOLU AVE #300	RIVERDALE, NY	10471
ROM, NATALIA	SOPRANO	61 W 62ND ST #6-F	NEW YORK, NY	10023
ROMA, PAUL	WRESTLER	POST OFFICE BOX 3859	STAMFORD, CT	06905
ROMA, TONY	ACTOR	9930 BEVERLY GROVE DR	BEVERLY HILLS, CA	90210
ROMAGNOLA, RICHARD	DIRECTOR	210 HIGHLAND RD	SOUTH ORANGE, NJ	07079
ROMAGUERA, JOAQUIN	CHARACTER TENOR	SARDOS, 180 W END AVE	NEW YORK, NY	10023
ROMAN, FREDDIE	COMEDIAN	JONAS, 101 W 57TH ST	NEW YORK, NY	10019
ROMAN, JOSEPH	ACTOR	9200 SUNSET BLVD #909	LOS ANGELES, CA	90069
ROMAN, LAWRENCE	SCREENWRITER	4097 SAPPHIRE DR	ENCINO, CA	91436
ROMAN, LULU	ACTRESS	POST OFFICE BOX 1092	BRANSON, MO	65616
ROMAN, RUTH	ACTRESS	1225 CLIFF DR	LAGUNA BEACH, CA	92651
ROMAN, VINCENT N	TV DIRECTOR	KGO-TV, 277 GOLDEN GATE AVE	SAN FRANCISCO, CA	94102
ROMAN HOLLIDAY	ROCK & ROLL GROUP	POST OFFICE BOX 475	LONDON	ENGLAND
ROMANEK, JAMES GERARD	TROMBONIST	115 NORWAY ST #2	BOSTON, MA	02115
ROMANO, ANDY	ACTOR	10390 SANTA MONICA BLVD #310	LOS ANGELES, CA	90025
ROMANO, BRUNO	WRESTLER-ANNOUNCER	SEE - SAMMARTINO, BRUNO		
ROMANO, DEANE LOUIS	WRITER	4612 FERN PL	LOS ANGELES, CA	90032
ROMANOUSKY & PHILLIPS	VOCAL DUO	2269 MARKET ST #301	SAN FRANCISCO, CA	94114
ROMANTICS, THE	VOCAL GROUP	POST OFFICE BOX 133-LV	LATHROP VILLAGE, MI	48076
ROMANUS, RICHARD	ACTOR	1840 CAMINO PALMERO ST	LOS ANGELES, CA	90046
ROMANUS, ROBERT	ACTOR	1840 CAMINO PALMERO ST	LOS ANGELES, CA	90046
ROMAY, LINA	ACTRESS	8019 1/2 MELROSE AVE #3	LOS ANGELES, CA	90046
ROMBOLA, FERDE	WRITER	4026 SEQUOIA ST	LOS ANGELES, CA	90039
ROME, SYDNE	ACTRESS	VIA DI PORTA, PINCIANA 14	ROME 1-00100	ITALY
ROMEO VOID	ROCK & ROLL GROUP	ICM, 40 W 57TH ST	NEW YORK, NY	10019
ROMER, DANIELLE	ACTRESS	8831 SUNSET BLVD #402	LOS ANGELES, CA	90069
ROMER, DENNIS	ACTOR	340 W 72ND ST #3-B	NEW YORK, NY	10023
ROMER, LINDA	ACTRESS	3151 W CAHUENGA BLVD #310	LOS ANGELES, CA	90068
ROMERO, ANGEL	GUITARIST	CAMI, 165 W 57TH ST	NEW YORK, NY	10019
ROMERO, CARLOS	ACTOR	7812 COLDWATER CANYON AVE	NORTH HOLLYWOOD, CA	91605
ROMERO, CELEDONIO	GUITARIST	CAMI, 165 W 57TH ST	NEW YORK, NY	10019
ROMERO, CELIN	GUITARIST	CAMI, 165 W 57TH ST	NEW YORK, NY	10019
ROMERO, CESAR	ACTOR	12115 SAN VICENTE BLVD #302	LOS ANGELES, CA	90049
ROMERO, GABE	NEWS CORRESPONDENT	CBS NEWS, 2020 "M" ST, NW	WASHINGTON, DC	20036
ROMERO, GEORGE A	DIRECTOR-PRODUCER	247 FORT PITT BLVD	PITTSBURGH, PA	15222
ROMERO, GUSTAVO	PIANIST	CAMI, 165 W 57TH ST	NEW YORK, NY	10019
ROMERO, LAURIE	SOPRANO	CAMI, 165 W 57TH ST	NEW YORK, NY	10019
ROMERO, NED	ACTOR	19438 LASSEN ST	NORTHRIDGE, CA	91324
ROMERO, PEPE	GUITARIST	CAMI, 165 W 57TH ST	NEW YORK, NY	10019
ROMILLY, GEORGE P	NEWS CORRESPONDENT	4334 "P" ST, NW	WASHINGTON, DC	20007
ROMMEL, JOHN	TRUMPETER	180 WALLACE RD #F-17	NASHVILLE, TN	37211
ROMSEY, LORD	FILM PRODUCER	BROADLANDS	ROMSEY SO5 9ZD	ENGLAND
RONA, ANTHONY LASZLO	ACTOR	200 N ROBERTSON BLVD #308	BEVERLY HILLS, CA	90210
RONAN, DAN	NEWS CORRESPONDENT	1755 S JEFFERSON DAVIS HWY	ARLINGTON, VA	22202
RONARD, JASON	ACTOR	1328 N FORMOSA AVE	LOS ANGELES, CA	90046
RONDEAU, CHARLES	FILM DIRECTOR	4251 FULTON AVE	SHERMAN OAKS, CA	91423
RONDELL, RIC	DIRECTOR	4062 WITZEL DR	SHERMAN OAKS, CA	91423
RONDELL, RONALD A	DIRECTOR	DGA, 7950 SUNSET BLVD	LOS ANGELES, CA	90046
RONDELL, RONNIE	ACTOR-STUNTMAN	4631 ENSENADA DR	WOODLAND HILLS, CA	91364
RONDINI, DINI	GUITARIST	3832 LAKE AIRE DR	NASHVILLE, TN	37217
RONET, MAURICE	ACTOR	1 BIS AVE DE LOWENDAL	PARIS 75007	FRANCE
RONETTES, THE	VOCAL GROUP	OLDIES, 5218 ALMONT ST	LOS ANGELES, CA	90032
RONKA, ILMARI	COMPOSER-CONDUCTOR	6217 ELMER AVE	NORTH HOLLYWOOD, CA	91606
RONN, GARY T	NEWS CORRESPONDENT	ABINGDON ST	ARLINGTON, VA	22203
RONNIE, JULIE	ACTRESS	12725 VENTURA BLVD #E	STUDIO CITY, CA	91604
RONNINGEN, GRETA	ACTRESS	9601 OAK PASS RD	BEVERLY HILLS, CA	90210
RONNY & THE DAYTONAS	VOCAL GROUP	ROBERT J MC KENZIE MGMT		
		114 PRINCE GEORGE DR	HAMPTON, VA	23669
RONSTADT, LINDA	SINGER	ASHER, 644 N DOHENY DR	LOS ANGELES, CA	90069
RONZIO, FRANK	ACTOR	6430 SUNSET BLVD #1203	LOS ANGELES, CA	90028
ROOD, MICK	NEWS CORRESPONDENT	133 7TH ST #202	WASHINGTON, DC	20003
ROOD, RICK	WRESTLER	SEE - RUDE, RAVISHING RICK		
ROOK, THOMAS	DIRECTOR	302 S MANSFIELD AVE	LOS ANGELES, CA	90036
ROOLEY, ANTHONY	LUTIST	BYERS-SCHWALBE, 1 5TH AVE	NEW YORK, NY	10003
ROOM OF FOOLS	ROCK & ROLL GROUP	41 BRITAIN ST #200	TORONTO, ONT	CANADA
ROOMFUL OF BLUES	BLUES GROUP	CHICKLES, 15 MANSFIELD ST	BOSTON, MA	02134
ROONEY, ANDY	ACTOR-WRITER-DIRECTOR	254 ROWAYTON AVE	ROWAYTON, CT	06853
ROONEY, JAMES	GUITARIST	1906 SOUTH ST #401	NASHVILLE, TN	37212
ROONEY, JAN CHAMBERLIN	ACTRESS	7500 DEVISTA DR	LOS ANGELES, CA	90046
ROONEY, MICKEY	ACTOR	7500 DEVISTA DR	LOS ANGELES, CA	90046
ROONEY, ROGER H	RADIO WRI-DIR	9600 RESEDA BLVD #119	NORTHRIDGE, CA	91324
ROONEY, SHERRY	ACTRESS	8285 SUNSET BLVD #12	LOS ANGELES, CA	90046

LINDA RONSTADT

MICKEY ROONEY

DIANA ROSS

KATHARINE ROSS

MISTY ROWE

GENE ROWLANDS

JANICE RULE

BARBARA RUSH

PATRICE RUSHEN

Name	Occupation	Address	City	Zip
ROONEY, WALLACE	ACTOR	14 STUYVESANT OVAL	NEW YORK, NY	10009
ROOP, RICHARD	GUITARIST	POST OFFICE BOX 533	LAVERGNE, TN	37086
ROOS, DONALD P	TV WRITER	3815 W OLIVE AVE #202	BURBANK, CA	91505
ROOS, FREDERICK	FILM PRODUCER	10020 WESTWANDA DR	BEVERLY HILLS, CA	90210
ROOSEVELT, PHIL	COLUMNIST	POST OFFICE BOX 500	WASHINGTON, DC	20044
ROOT, ROBERT	ACTOR	12808 INDIANAPOLIS ST	LOS ANGELES, CA	90066
ROOT, WELLS	WRITER	701 HAMPDEN PL	PACIFIC PALISADES, CA	90272
ROOTERING, JAN-HENDRICK	SINGER	CAMI, 165 W 57TH ST	NEW YORK, NY	10019
ROOTERS, JOHNNY	DRUMMER	5099 LINBAR DR #J-178	NASHVILLE, TN	37211
ROOTH, LASZLO	CONDUCTOR	45 W 60TH ST #4-K	NEW YORK, NY	10023
ROOY, ROBERT	FILM DIRECTOR	819 SUPERBA AVE	VENICE, CA	90291
ROPELEWSKI, ROBERT R	NEWS CORRESPONDENT	910 CANTLE LN	GREAT FALLS, VA	22066
ROPER, BOB	RECORD EXECUTIVE	WEA MUSIC, 180 BIRCHMONT RD	SCARBOROUGH, ONT M1P 2	CANADA
ROPER, CAROL	TV WRITER	2370 GLENDON AVE	LOS ANGELES, CA	90064
ROPER, JAMES E	NEWS CORRESPONDENT	6640 OLD DOMINION DR	MC LEAN, VA	22101
ROPER, JAY M	DIRECTOR	18340 KINZIE ST	NORTHRIDGE, CA	91325
ROPER, JOE	SINGER	214 OLD HICKORY BLVD #194	NASHVILLE, TN	37221
ROPER, JOY	PIANIST	210 OLD HICKORY BLVD #194	NASHVILLE, TN	37221
ROPER, LESLIE ANN	NEWS CORRESPONDENT	40 S VAN DORN ST #D-409	ALEXANDRIA, VA	22304
ROPER, STEVE	GUITARIST	400 FORREST PARK RD B-S #6	MADISON, TN	37115
ROPIAK, DEREK	RECORD EXECUTIVE	APEXTON, 44-27 PURVES ST	LONG ISLAND CITY, NY	11101
ROREM, NED	COMPOSER	BOOSEY & HAWKES, 30 W 57TH ST	NEW YORK, NY	10019
RORKE, HAYDEN	ACTOR	12816 HORTENSE ST	STUDIO CITY, CA	91604
ROSALES, RACHEL	SOPRANO	CAMI, 165 W 57TH ST	NEW YORK, NY	10019
ROSAND, AARON	VIOLINIST	LEISER, DORCHESTER TOWERS 155 W 68TH ST	NEW YORK, NY	10023
ROSARIO, BERT	ACTOR	10850 RIVERSIDE DR #501	NORTH HOLLYWOOD, CA	91602
ROSARIO, JOE	ACTOR	6736 LAUREL CANYON BLVD #306	NORTH HOLLYWOOD, CA	91606
ROSATI, MARK S	NEWS CORRESPONDENT	8750 GEORGIA AVE #821	SILVER SPRING, MD	20910
ROSATO, TONY	TV WRITER	555 W 57TH ST #1230	NEW YORK, NY	10019
ROSBURG, ROBERT	DIRECTOR	DGA, 110 W 57TH ST	NEW YORK, NY	10019
ROSE, ADELE	TV WRITER	LONDON MANAGEMENT, LTD 235-241 REGENT ST	LONDON W1A 2JT	ENGLAND
ROSE, ALEX	FILM PRODUCER	1630 S GREENFIELD AVE	LOS ANGELES, CA	90025
ROSE, CLIFF	DIRECTOR	1423 S ROSEWOOD ST	SANTA ANA, CA	92707
ROSE, CLIFFORD	ACTOR	ICM, 388-396 OXFORD ST	LONDON W1	ENGLAND
ROSE, DAVID	COMPOSER	4020 LONGRIDGE AVE	SHERMAN OAKS, CA	91423
ROSE, DAVID	GRAPHIC IMPRESSIONIST	NEWS AMERICA SYNDICATE 1703 KAISER AVE	IRVINE, CA	92714
ROSE, FLOYD	NEWS CORRESPONDENT	230 E CAPITOL ST, NE	WASHINGTON, DC	20003
ROSE, FRANK	WRESTLER	POST OFFICE BOX 3859	STAMFORD, CT	06905
ROSE, JACK	SCREENWRITER	8955 BEVERLY BLVD	LOS ANGELES, CA	90048
ROSE, JAMIE	ACTRESS	7550 WOODROW WILSON DR	LOS ANGELES, CA	90046
ROSE, JEROME	PIANIST	KAPLAN, 115 COLLEGE ST	BURLINGTON, VT	05401
ROSE, JIM	DIRECTOR	435 N OAKHURST DR	BEVERLY HILLS, CA	90210
ROSE, JOHN	ORGANIST	15 HIGH ST #621	HARTFORD, CT	06103
ROSE, JUDD	NEWS CORRESPONDENT	ABC-TV ENTERTAINMENT CENTER NEWS DEPARTMENT 2040 AVE OF THE STARS	LOS ANGELES, CA	90067
ROSE, KRISTI AND MIDNIGHT WALKE	ROCK & ROLL GROUP	ROUNDER RECORDS 1 CAMP ST	CAMBRIDGE, MA	02140
ROSE, LES	FILM DIRECTOR	17 MAPLE AVE	TORONTO, ONT	CANADA
ROSE, MARGOT	ACTRESS	9200 SUNSET BLVD #1210	LOS ANGELES, CA	90069
ROSE, MICHAEL PAUL	COMPOSER-CONDUCTOR	1226 1/4 N OGDEN DR	LOS ANGELES, CA	90046
ROSE, PAULA	FILM CRITIC	VARIETY, 154 W 46TH ST	NEW YORK, NY	10036
ROSE, PETE	BASEBALL	1203 NEEB RD	CINCINNATI, OH	45238
ROSE, PHILIP	THEATER PRODUCER	157 W 57TH ST	NEW YORK, NY	10019
ROSE, PLAYBOY BUDDY	WRESTLER	AMERICAN WRESTLING ASSOC MINNEAPLOIS WRESTLING 10001 WAYZATA BLVD	MINNETONKA, MN	55345
ROSE, RALPH	CONDUCTOR	1105 W OLIVE AVE #14	SUNNYVALE, CA	94086
ROSE, REGINALD	SCREENWRITER	20 WEDGEWOOD RD	WESTPORT, CT	06880
ROSE, REVA	ACTRESS	1570 S REXFORD DR	LOS ANGELES, CA	90035
ROSE, ROBERT L	NEWS CORRESPONDENT	2831 PARK CENTER DR	ALEXANDRIA, VA	22302
ROSE, ROBIN PEARSON	ACTRESS	6910 WOODROW WILSON DR	LOS ANGELES, CA	90068
ROSE, ROGER	ACTOR	11744 MOORPARK ST	STUDIO CITY, CA	91604
ROSE, SHARON	ACTRESS	SF & A, 121 N SAN VICENTE BLVD	BEVERLY HILLS, CA	90211
ROSE, SIMON	TV WRITER	12350 VIEWCREST RD	NORTH HOLLYWOOD, CA	91604
ROSE, STEWART	ACTOR	2501 W BURBANK BLVD #304	BURBANK, CA	91505
ROSE, SYDNEY	FILM PRODUCER	9 CLIFFORD ST	LONDON W1	ENGLAND
ROSE BROTHERS, THE	SOUL GROUP	SHIRLEY A MORGAN MGMT 127 S KENTER AVE	LOS ANGELES, CA	90049
ROSE MARIE	ACTRESS	6918 CHISOLM AVE	VAN NUYS, CA	91406
ROSE ROYCE	VOCAL GROUP	7751 ALABAMA AVE #13	CANOGA PARK, CA	91304
ROSE-MARIE	SINGER	PROCESS, 439 WILEY AVE	FRANKLIN, PA	16323
ROSEBROOK, JEB J	SCREENWRITER	12301 COLLINS ST	NORTH HOLLYWOOD, CA	91607
ROSEFELD, MIKE	TV PRODUCER	1888 CENTURY PARK E #1400	LOS ANGELES, CA	90067
ROSELLI, H MICHAEL	NEWS CORRESPONDENT	2133 WISCONSIN AVE, NW	WASHINGTON, DC	20007
ROSEMAN, RALPH	THEATER PRODUCER	THEATRE NOW, 1515 BROADWAY	NEW YORK, NY	10036
ROSEMOND, PERRY	DIRECTOR	11928 KIOWA AVE #103	LOS ANGELES, CA	90049
ROSEMONT, NORMAN	TV PRODUCER	VIACOM INTERNATIONAL, INC 1211 AVE OF THE AMERICAS	NEW YORK, NY	10036
ROSEN, AL	ACTOR	8831 SUNSET BLVD #402	LOS ANGELES, CA	90069
ROSEN, ALAN	TV WRITER-DIRECTOR	14964 GREENLEAF ST	SHERMAN OAKS, CA	91403
ROSEN, BARRY M	SCREENWRITER	8955 BEVERLY BLVD	LOS ANGELES, CA	90048

ROSEN, CHARLES	PIANIST	CAMI, 165 W 57TH ST	NEW YORK, NY	10019
ROSEN, ERWIN	TV DIRECTOR	3675 DIXIE CANYON AVE	SHERMAN OAKS, CA	91423
ROSEN, J & THE K-PROS	ROCK & ROLL GROUP	LCS, 1627 16TH AVE S	NASHVILLE, TN	37212
ROSEN, JACK	TV DIRECTOR	56 EBERLING DR	NEW YORK, NY	10956
ROSEN, LAWRENCE R	TV WRITER-PRODUCER	17025 COTTER PL	ENCINO, CA	91436
ROSEN, MILT	TV WRITER	8955 BEVERLY BLVD	LOS ANGELES, CA	90048
ROSEN, MILTON S	COMPOSER	12030 IREDELL ST	STUDIO CITY, CA	91604
ROSEN, NATHANIEL	CELLIST	SHAW CONCERTS, 1995 BROADWAY	NEW YORK, NY	10023
ROSEN, NEIL	TV WRITER	8955 BEVERLY BLVD	LOS ANGELES, CA	90048
ROSEN, NORMAN I	COMPOSER	8501 S SEPULVEDA BLVD #305-A	LOS ANGELES, CA	90045
ROSEN, PERRY	ACTOR	85 PUTNAM BLVD	ATLANTIC CITY, NY	11509
ROSEN, PETER	DIRECTOR	114 E 71ST ST	NEW YORK, NY	10021
ROSEN, ROB	ACTOR	11030 VENTURA BLVD #3	STUDIO CITY, CA	91604
ROSEN, ROBERT L	DIRECTOR-PRODUCER	MARTIN WEISS MANAGEMENT		
		12301 WILSHIRE BLVD	LOS ANGELES, CA	90025
ROSEN, SAM	WRITER	1846 1/2 N NEW HAMPSHIRE AVE	LOS ANGELES, CA	90027
ROSEN, STEVEN M	DIRECTOR	DGA, 110 W 57TH ST	NEW YORK, NY	10019
ROSEN, STUART	TV PRODUCER	7631 LEXINGTON AVE	LOS ANGELES, CA	90046
ROSEN, SY	TV WRITER	1650 WESTWOOD BLVD #201	LOS ANGELES, CA	90024
ROSENBAUM, DAVID	WRESTLING WRITER	POST OFFICE BOX 48	ROCKVILLE CENTRE, NY	11571
ROSENBAUM, DAVID E	NEWS CORRESPONDENT	3824 HARRISON ST, NW	WASHINGTON, DC	20016
ROSENBAUM, HENRY	SCREENWRITER	8955 BEVERLY BLVD	LOS ANGELES, CA	90048
ROSENBAUM, JOEL H	COMPOSER	6049 VAN NOORD AVE	VAN NUYS, CA	91401
ROSENBAUM, MARCUS D	NEWS CORRESPONDENT	2025 "M" ST, NW	WASHINGTON, DC	20036
ROSENBAUM, R ROBERT	TV EXECUTIVE	PARAMOUNT TELEVISION		
		5555 MELROSE AVE	LOS ANGELES, CA	90038
ROSENBAUM, RICHARD D	NEWS CORRESPONDENT	5101 RIVER RD	BETHESDA, MD	20816
ROSENBAUM, RUSSELL ROBERT	DIRECTOR	11169 OPHIR DR	LOS ANGELES, CA	90024
ROSENBAUM, THEA	NEWS CORRESPONDENT	3132 "M" ST, NW	WASHINGTON, DC	20007
ROSENBERG, ANDREW B	NEWS CORRESPONDENT	2025 "M" ST, NW	WASHINGTON, DC	20036
ROSENBERG, ANDREW L	TV DIRECTOR	30 BIG OAK CIR	STAMFORD, CT	06903
ROSENBERG, ARTHUR	ACTOR	17706 DUNCAN ST	RESEDA, CA	91335
ROSENBERG, BENJY	TV DIRECTOR	7172 HAWTHORN AVE #310	HOLLYWOOD, CA	90046
ROSENBERG, DAVID	ACTOR	1208 N POINSETTIA PL	LOS ANGELES, CA	90046
ROSENBERG, FRANK	FILM WRITER-PRODUCER	140 N BRISTOL AVE	LOS ANGELES, CA	90049
ROSENBERG, FRED D	TV WRITER	8955 BEVERLY BLVD	LOS ANGELES, CA	90048
ROSENBERG, GARY	PHOTOGRAPHER	1335 FORTY OAKS DR	HERNDON, VA	22070
ROSENBERG, GRANT	TV EXECUTIVE	5451 MARATHON ST	HOLLYWOOD, CA	90038
ROSENBERG, HOWARD	TV CRITIC-WRITER	5859 LARBOARD LN	AGOURA HILLS, CA	91301
ROSENBERG, JEANNE	SCREENWRITER	119 MUERDAGO RD	TOPANGA CANYON, CA	90290
ROSENBERG, JERRERY A	NEWS CORRESPONDENT	2025 "M" ST, NW	WASHINGTON, DC	20036
ROSENBERG, LEE	TALENT AGENT	10100 SANTA MONICA BLVD #1600	LOS ANGELES, CA	90067
ROSENBERG, META	DIRECTOR	1126 SAN YSIDRO DR	BEVERLY HILLS, CA	90210
ROSENBERG, META	TV WRITER-PRODUCER	9255 SUNSET BLVD #1122	LOS ANGELES, CA	90069
ROSENBERG, MORRIS W	NEWS CORRESPONDENT	4000 MASSACHUSETTS AVE, NW	WASHINGTON, DC	20016
ROSENBERG, NORMA	WRITER	18423 COLLINS ST #A	TARZANA, CA	91356
ROSENBERG, PHILIP	TV WRITER	555 W 57TH ST #1230	NEW YORK, NY	10019
ROSENBERG, RICHARD	TALENT AGENT	10100 SANTA MONICA BLVD #1600	LOS ANGELES, CA	90067
ROSENBERG, STUART	WRITER-PRODUCER	1984 COLDWATER CANYON DR	BEVERLY HILLS, CA	90210
ROSENBERG, VICKI	CASTING DIRECTOR	9220 SUNSET BLVD #306	LOS ANGELES, CA	90069
ROSENBERGER, CAROL	PIANIST	CONE, 221 W 57TH ST	NEW YORK, NY	10019
ROSENBERGER, JAMES	TV DIRECTOR	7907 CROYDON AVE	LOS ANGELES, CA	90045
ROSENBLATT, DEBORAH	ACTRESS	14735 VICTORY BLVD #10	VAN NUYS, CA	91411
ROSENBLATT, DENNIS	DIRECTOR	DGA, 7950 SUNSET BLVD	LOS ANGELES, CA	90046
ROSENBLATT, ROBERT	NEWS CORRESPONDENT	3356 TALEEN CT	ALEXANDRIA, VA	22003
ROSENBLATT, ROGER	WRITER-EDITOR	TIME/TIME & LIFE BLDG		
		ROCKEFELLER CENTER	NEW YORK, NY	10020
ROSENBLATT, SELMA	ACTRESS	79-11 256TH ST	FLORAL PARK, NY	11004
ROSENBLATT, STEPHEN M	NEWS CORRESPONDENT	2213 N VAN DORN ST	ALEXANDRIA, VA	22304
ROSENBLOOM, DAVID L	DIRECTOR	3237 BENDA ST	LOS ANGELES, CA	90068
ROSENBLOOM, RICHARD M	TV EXECUTIVE	1875 CENTURY PARK E #300	LOS ANGELES, CA	90067
ROSENBLUM, ARTHUR	DIRECTOR	DGA, 7950 SUNSET BLVD	LOS ANGELES, CA	90046
ROSENBLUM, DANIEL	NEWS CORRESPONDENT	404 SEWARD SQ #2, SE	WASHINGTON, DC	20003
ROSENBLUM, RALPH B	TV DIRECTOR	344 W 84TH ST	NEW YORK, NY	10024
ROSENCRANS, ROBERT M	CABLE EXECUTIVE	ROGERS UA CABLESYSTEMS		
		315 POST RD W	WESTPORT, CT	06881
ROSENDO, JOEY	ACTOR	12375 HERBERT ST	LOS ANGELES, CA	90066
ROSENFELD, JEROME E	DIRECTOR	1349 LEXINGTON AVE	NEW YORK, NY	10028
ROSENFELD, STEPHEN S	NEWS CORRESPONDENT	7308 RIPPON RD	ALEXANDRIA, VA	22307
ROSENFELDER, MICHAEL J	NEWS CORRESPONDENT	1705 DE SALES ST, NW	WASHINGTON, DC	20036
ROSENFELT, FRANK	FILM EXECUTIVE	MGM, 10202 W WASHINGTON BLVD	CULVER CITY, CA	90239
ROSENKRANTZ, LUCY	ACTRESS	11402 E FLORENCE AVE	SANTA FE, CA	90670
ROSENMAN, HOWARD	FILM PRODUCER	PARAMOUNT PICTURES CORP		
		5555 MELROSE AVE	LOS ANGELES, CA	90038
ROSENMAN, JON	ACTOR	4916 BEN AVE	NORTH HOLLYWOOD, CA	91607
ROSENMAN, LEONARD	COMPOSER-ARRANGER	23333 W PALM CYN LN	MALIBU, CA	90265
ROSENSCHEIN, WARNER	DIRECTOR	DGA, 110 W 57TH ST	NEW YORK, NY	10019
ROSENSHEIN, NEIL	TENOR	CAMI, 165 W 57TH ST	NEW YORK, NY	10019
ROSENSTEIN, DONNA	CASTING DIRECTOR	PARAMOUNT PICTURES CORP		
		DIRECTOR'S BUILDING #401		
		5555 MELROSE AVE	LOS ANGELES, CA	90038
ROSENSTEIN, GERTRUDE	DIRECTOR	650 PARK AVE	NEW YORK, NY	10021
ROSENSTEIN, JAY	NEWS CORRESPONDENT	3 W MYRTLE ST	ALEXANDRIA, VA	22301
ROSENSTOCK, RICH	PRODUCER	MTM, 4024 RADFORD AVE	STUDIO CITY, CA	91604
ROSENSTOCK, RICHARD	TV WRITER	8955 BEVERLY BLVD	LOS ANGELES, CA	90048

Name	Occupation	Address	City	Zip
ROSENTHAL, A M "ABE"	COLUMNIST	N Y TIMES, 229 W 43RD ST	NEW YORK, NY	10036
ROSENTHAL, ALAN	DIRECTOR	DGA, 110 W 57TH ST	NEW YORK, NY	10019
ROSENTHAL, ARNIE	TV PRODUCER	TELEFRANCE USA, LTD		
		1966 BROADWAY	NEW YORK, NY	10023
ROSENTHAL, ARNOLD H	DIRECTOR	DGA, 110 W 57TH ST	NEW YORK, NY	10019
ROSENTHAL, HARRY F	NEWS CORRESPONDENT	14101 BLAZER LN	ASPEN HILL, MD	20906
ROSENTHAL, JACK	TV WRITER	124 DUKE'S AVE	LONDON N10	ENGLAND
ROSENTHAL, JANE	TV EXECUTIVE	CBS-TV, 6121 SUNSET BLVD	LOS ANGELES, CA	90028
ROSENTHAL, LAURENCE	COMPOSER	3815 W OLIVE AVE #202	BURBANK, CA	91505
ROSENTHAL, MARK DAVID	TV WRITER	8955 BEVERLY BLVD	LOS ANGELES, CA	90048
ROSENTHAL, RICHARD L, JR	TV WRITER	8904 WONDERLAND AVE	LOS ANGELES, CA	90046
ROSENTHAL, RICK	FILM DIRECTOR	7471 MELROSE AVE #17	LOS ANGELES, CA	90046
ROSENTHAL, ROBERT J	SCREENWRITER	8955 BEVERLY BLVD	LOS ANGELES, CA	90048
ROSENWINK, KATHERINE	SCREENWRITER	8955 BEVERLY BLVD	LOS ANGELES, CA	90048
ROSENZWEIG, AARON B	CONDUCTOR	637 S BRADSHAWE	MONTEREY PARK, CA	91754
ROSENZWEIG, BARNEY	TV WRITER-PRODUCER	146 S BEACHWOOD DR	LOS ANGELES, CA	90004
ROSIE & THE ORIGINALS	VOCAL GROUP	OLDIES, 5218 ALMONT ST	LOS ANGELES, CA	90032
ROSIN, CHARLES	TV WRITER-PRODUCER	6131 BARROWS DR	LOS ANGELES, CA	90048
ROSIN, MARK B	WRITER	ICM, 8899 BEVERLY BLVD	LOS ANGELES, CA	90048
ROSLOFF, WENDY SUE	ACTRESS	248 N IRVING BLVD	LOS ANGELES, CA	90004
ROSNER, GEORGE	COMPOSER	1541 W PALMAIRE AVE	PHOENIX, AZ	85021
ROSNER, PAUL	WRITER	7596 MULHOLLAND DR	LOS ANGELES, CA	90046
ROSNER, RICHARD	TV WRITER	8955 BEVERLY BLVD	LOS ANGELES, CA	90048
ROSNER, RICK	TV PRODUCER	NBC-TV, 3000 W ALAMEDA AVE	BURBANK, CA	91523
ROSQUI, TOM	ACTOR	14950 VICTORY BLVD #205	VAN NUYS, CA	91411
ROSS, AL	CARTOONIST	POST OFFICE BOX 4203	NEW YORK, NY	10017
ROSS, ALAN	ACTOR	400 W 43RD ST #38-O	NEW YORK, NY	10036
ROSS, ALAN	DIRECTOR-PRODUCER	40 THE MEAD, BECKENHAM	KENT	ENGLAND
ROSS, ALAN J	ACTOR	6331 HOLLYWOOD BLVD #924	LOS ANGELES, CA	90028
ROSS, ALVIN	ACTOR	8949 SUNSET BLVD #203	LOS ANGELES, CA	90069
ROSS, ARNOLD	COMPOSER	1720 PACIFIC AVE #322	MARINA DEL REY, CA	90292
ROSS, ARTHUR	ACTOR	5330 LANKERSHIM BLVD #210	NORTH HOLLYWOOD, CA	91601
ROSS, ARTHUR A	TV WRITER	8955 BEVERLY BLVD	LOS ANGELES, CA	90048
ROSS, BILL	GUITARIST	13720 KENDALE LAKE DR	MIAMI, FL	33183
ROSS, BOB	ACTOR	1227 N HORN AVE	LOS ANGELES, CA	90069
ROSS, BRIAN	NEWS CORRESPONDENT	NBC-TV, NEWS DEPARTMENT		
		30 ROCKEFELLER PLAZA	NEW YORK, NY	10112
ROSS, DANNY J	TV DIRECTOR	7942 S COLFAX AVE	CHICAGO, IL	60617
ROSS, DEBBIE A	DIRECTOR	251 W 30TH ST #14-E	NEW YORK, NY	10001
ROSS, DIANA	SINGER-ACTRESS	7250 BEVERLY BLVD #208	LOS ANGELES, CA	90036
ROSS, DICK	DIRECTOR	4230 STANSBURY AVE	SHERMAN OAKS, CA	91403
ROSS, DON	ACTOR	1810 N BRONSON AVE #301	HOLLYWOOD, CA	90028
ROSS, DON	BODYBUILDER	POST OFFICE BOX 981	VENICE, CA	90294
ROSS, DONALD H	TV WRITER	151 S EL CAMINO DR	BEVERLY HILLS, CA	90212
ROSS, DUNCAN	ACTOR	3319 WRIGHTWOOD DR	STUDIO CITY, CA	91604
ROSS, GENE	ACTOR	3800 BARHAM BLVD #303	LOS ANGELES, CA	90068
ROSS, GEORGE; III	DIRECTOR	55 W 11TH ST	NEW YORK, NY	10011
ROSS, GORDON	ACTOR	6736 LAUREL CANYON BLVD #306	NORTH HOLLYWOOD, CA	91606
ROSS, HERBERT	DIRECTOR-PRODUCER	30900 BROAD BEACH RD	MALIBU, CA	90265
ROSS, HOWARD	TV DIRECTOR-PRODUCER	15 LARKFIELD RD, RICHMOND	SURREY	ENGLAND
ROSS, IRVING	DIRECTOR	9611 ARBY DR	BEVERLY HILLS, CA	90210
ROSS, JEREMY	ACTOR	1605 N CAHUENGA BLVD #202	LOS ANGELES, CA	90028
ROSS, JERRY	TV WRITER	141 S EL CAMINO DR #205	BEVERLY HILLS, CA	90212
ROSS, JIM	WRESTLING ANNOUNCER	UNIVERSAL WRESTLING FEDERATION		
		MID SOUTH SPORTS, INC		
		5001 SPRING VALLEY RD	DALLAS, TX	75244
ROSS, JOE	ACTOR	208 S BEVERLY DR #4	BEVERLY HILLS, CA	90212
ROSS, JONATHAN	ACTOR	12725 VENTURA BLVD #E	STUDIO CITY, CA	91604
ROSS, JUDITH	SCREENWRITER	8955 BEVERLY BLVD	LOS ANGELES, CA	90048
ROSS, KATHARINE	ACTRESS	33050 PACIFIC COAST HWY	MALIBU, CA	90265
ROSS, KEN	CARTOONIST	UNIVERSAL PRESS SYNDICATE		
		4900 MAIN ST, 9TH FLOOR	KANSAS CITY, MO	62114
ROSS, KENNETH	SCREENWRITER	1610 N CRESCENT HGTS BLVD	LOS ANGELES, CA	90069
ROSS, KIMBERLY	ACTRESS	13111 VENTURA BLVD #204	STUDIO CITY, CA	91604
ROSS, LYNN	NEWS CORRESPONDENT	400 N CAPITOL ST, NW	WASHINGTON, DC	20001
ROSS, MARC	TV WRITER	8955 BEVERLY BLVD	LOS ANGELES, CA	90048
ROSS, MARCIA	CASTING DIRECTOR	8265 SUNSET BLVD #207	LOS ANGELES, CA	90046
ROSS, MARION	ACTRESS	14159 RIVERSIDE DR #101	SHERMAN OAKS, CA	91423
ROSS, MARK	DIRECTOR	338 E 30TH ST	NEW YORK, NY	10016
ROSS, MERRIE LYNN	ACTRESS	3814 GLENRIDGE DR	SHERMAN OAKS, CA	91423
ROSS, MICHAEL	DIRECTOR	9350 WILSHIRE BLVD #400	BEVERLY HILLS, CA	90049
ROSS, MICHAEL	PRODUCER	NRW CO, 5746 SUNSET BLVD	LOS ANGELES, CA	90028
ROSS, MICHAEL	WRITER-PRODUCER	ELLIOTT WAX MANAGEMENT		
		9255 SUNSET BLVD	LOS ANGELES, CA	90069
ROSS, MICHAEL ALAN	ACTOR	9744 WILSHIRE BLVD #206	BEVERLY HILLS, CA	90212
ROSS, NANCY L	NEWS CORRESPONDENT	1150 15TH ST, NW	WASHINGTON, DC	10071
ROSS, NATALIE	ACTRESS	ABC-TV, "ALL MY CHILDREN"		
		1330 AVE OF THE AMERICAS	NEW YORK, NY	10019
ROSS, NICK	TV DIRECTOR-PRODUCER	38 WILLES RD	LONDON NW5 3DL	ENGLAND
ROSS, NORMAN	DIRECTOR	DGA, 110 W 57TH ST	NEW YORK, NY	10019
ROSS, PAUL L	ACTOR	30 CHARLTON ST	NEW YORK, NY	10014
ROSS, PHILIP	TV WRITER	555 W 57TH ST #1230	NEW YORK, NY	10019
ROSS, RICHARD	CABLE EXECUTIVE	USA CABLE NETWORK		
		208 HARRISTOWN RD	GLEN ROCK, NJ	07452
ROSS, RICHARD JACK	GUITARIST	564 JANICE DR	ANTIOCH, TN	37211

ROSS, SHELLEY Z	TV WRITER	8955 BEVERLY BLVD	LOS ANGELES, CA	90048
ROSS, STAN	ACTOR	8721 SUNSET BLVD #103	LOS ANGELES, CA	90069
ROSS, STANLEY RALPH	WRITER	451 BEVERWIL DR	BEVERLY HILLS, CA	90212
ROSS, TRACEY	ACTRESS	ABC-TV, "RYAN'S HOPE"		
		1330 AVE OF THE AMERICAS	NEW YORK, NY	10019
ROSS, WENDY	ACTRESS	8306 WILSHIRE BLVD #158	BEVERLY HILLS, CA	90211
ROSS, WILLIAM K	COMPOSER-CONDUCTOR	4642 SANTA LUCIA DR	WOODLAND HILLS, CA	91364
ROSS-LEMING, EUGENIE	ACTOR-WRITER-PRODUCER	5041 AMBROSE AVE	LOS ANGELES, CA	90027
ROSSALL, KERRY	STUNTMAN	3518 W CAHUENGA BLVD #300	LOS ANGELES, CA	90068
ROSSE, RICHARD A	NEWS CORRESPONDENT	1755 S JEFFERSON DAVIS HWY	ARLINGTON, VA	22202
ROSSELLINI, ISABELLA	ACTRESS	10100 SANTA MONICA BLVD	LOS ANGELES, CA	90067
ROSSEN, CAROL	ACTRESS	14238 SUNSET BLVD	PACIFIC PALISADES, CA	90272
ROSSEN, ELLEN	TV PRODUCER	ABC-TV, 7 W 66TH ST	NEW YORK, NY	10023
ROSSEN, STEPHEN	WRITER	2010 GLENDON AVE	LOS ANGELES, CA	90025
ROSSER, JACKIE	SINGER	STM, 1311 CANDLELIGHT AVE	DALLAS, TX	75206
ROSSETTER, KATHY	ACTRESS	10 E 44TH ST #700	NEW YORK, NY	10017
ROSSETTI, DOMINICK J	DIRECTOR	171 E 62ND ST	NEW YORK, NY	10021
ROSSI, AL	ACTOR	3050 W 7TH ST #200	LOS ANGELES, CA	90005
ROSSINGTON, NORMAN	ACTOR	27 PARLIAMENT HILL	LONDON NW3	ENGLAND
ROSSITER, ALEXANDER H, JR	NEWS CORRESPONDENT	5448 THUNDER HILL RD	COLUMBIA, MD	21045
ROSSNER, DICK	ACTOR-WRITER	8645 LANGDON AVE	SEPULVEDA, CA	91343
ROSSO, FRANCO	FILM DIRECTOR	SEIFERT, 8-A BRUNSWICK GARDENS	LONDON W8	ENGLAND
ROSSO, HENRY DAVID	NEWS CORRESPONDENT	2203 S 2ND ST #8	ARLINGTON, VA	22204
ROSSOV, NANCI	WRITER-DIRECTOR	7224 HILLSIDE AVE #34	LOS ANGELES, CA	90046
ROSSOVICH, RICK	ACTOR	ICM, 8899 BEVERLY BLVD	LOS ANGELES, CA	90069
ROSSOVICH, TIM	ACTOR	9744 WILSHIRE BLVD #306	BEVERLY HILLS, CA	90212
ROSTAL & SCHAEFER	PIANO DUO	CAMI, 165 W 57TH ST	NEW YORK, NY	10019
ROSTEN, IRWIN	WRITER-PRODUCER	2217 CHELAN DR	LOS ANGELES, CA	90068
ROSTEN, PETER D	WRITER	3445 TARECO DR	LOS ANGELES, CA	90068
ROSTON, RONALD	DIRECTOR	129 AMITY ST	BROOKLYN, NY	11201
ROSTROPOVICH, OLGA	CELLIST	CAMI, 165 W 57TH ST	NEW YORK, NY	10019
ROSTROPVICH, MSTISLAV	CELLIST	CAMI, 165 W 57TH ST	NEW YORK, NY	10019
ROSU, FRANCES L	CONDUCTOR	9722 3RD AVE	INGLEWOOD, CA	90305
ROSWELL, MAGGIE	ACTRESS	245 S VAN NESS AVE	LOS ANGELES, CA	90004
ROSZA, MIKLOS	COMPOSER	4146 LANKERSHIM BLVD #300	NORTH HOLLYWOOD, CA	91602
ROTBERG, ALBERT	COMPOSER	17084 ESCALON DR	ENCINO, CA	91436
ROTBLATT, JANET	ACTRESS	6605 HOLLYWOOD BLVD #220	HOLLYWOOD, CA	90028
ROTCOP, J KENNETH	WRITER	616 VETERAN AVE #112	LOS ANGELES, CA	90024
ROTELLA, JOHNNY	COMPOSER	6654 ALLOTT AVE	VAN NUYS, CA	91401
ROTENBERG, SHELDON	VIOLINIST	60 BROWNE ST	BROOKLINE, MA	02146
ROTH, ANDY	ACTOR	6660 W 5TH ST	LOS ANGELES, CA	90048
ROTH, BOBBY	WRITER-PRODUCER	7957 FAREHOLM DR	LOS ANGELES, CA	90068
ROTH, DAVID G	DIRECTOR	134 GLENWOOD AVE	LEONIA, NJ	07605
ROTH, DAVID LEE	SINGER-SONGWRITER	3960 LAUREL CANYON BLVD #430	STUDIO CITY, CA	91604
ROTH, DONALD	GUITARIST	608 HICKS RD	NASHVILLE, TN	37221
ROTH, ENID	DIRECTOR	165 W END AVE	NEW YORK, NY	10023
ROTH, GEOFFREY A	NEWS CORRESPONDENT	4461 CONNECTICUT AVE, NW	WASHINGTON, DC	20008
ROTH, JOHNIE	PHOTOGRAPHER	19104 TREADWAY RD	BROOKEVILLE, MD	20729
ROTH, JOYCE	ACTRESS	5917 CHULA VISTA WY #5	LOS ANGELES, CA	90068
ROTH, LYNN	WRITER-PRODUCER	448 N PALM DR #B	BEVERLY HILLS, CA	90210
ROTH, MARTIN	TV WRITER	8955 BEVERLY BLVD	LOS ANGELES, CA	90048
ROTH, PAULA A	TV WRITER	3848 VANTAGE AVE	STUDIO CITY, CA	91604
ROTH, PHIL	ACTOR	1252 N HAVENHURST DR #16	LOS ANGELES, CA	90046
ROTH, RICHARD	FILM PRODUCER	1741 COLDWATER CANYON DR	BEVERLY HILLS, CA	90210
ROTH, RICHARD	NEWS CORRESPONDENT	CBS-TV, 524 W 57TH ST	NEW YORK, NY	10019
ROTH, STAN	ACTOR	844 N GENESEE AVE	LOS ANGELES, CA	90046
ROTH, STEVE	FILM PRODUCER	ICM, 8899 BEVERLY BLVD	LOS ANGELES, CA	90048
ROTH, THEODORE P	NEWS REPORTER	TIME/TIME & LIFE BLDG		
		ROCKEFELLER CENTER	NEW YORK, NY	10020
ROTH, ULI	SINGER	ICM, 40 W 57TH ST	NEW YORK, NY	10019
ROTHBERG, DONALD M	NEWS CORRESPONDENT	3232 WOODLEY RD, NW	WASHINGTON, DC	20008
ROTHBERG, HAL	WRITER-PRODUCER	22450 DOMINGO RD	WOODLAND HILLS, CA	91364
ROTHBERG, HOWARD	TALENT AGENT	1706 N DOHENY DR	LOS ANGELES, CA	90069
ROTHBERG, LEE	DIRECTOR	985 5TH AVE	NEW YORK, NY	10021
ROTHENBERG, FAY WRAY	ACTRESS	2080 CENTURY PARK E #406	LOS ANGELES, CA	90067
ROTHENBERG, MARVIN	DIRECTOR	405 E 54TH ST	NEW YORK, NY	10022
ROTHLEIN, LEWIS	COLUMNIST	CHRONICLE FEATURES		
		870 MARKET ST	SAN FRANCISCO, CA	94102
ROTHLISBERGER, KENNETH	DRUMMER	682 HUNTINGTON PARKWAY	NASHVILLE, TN	37211
ROTHMAN, BERNARD	TV WRITER	8955 BEVERLY BLVD	LOS ANGELES, CA	90048
ROTHMAN, JOHN	ACTOR	211 S BEVERLY DR #201	BEVERLY HILLS, CA	90212
ROTHMAN, JOSEPH	DIRECTOR	530 E 72ND ST	NEW YORK, NY	10021
ROTHMAN, MARK	WRITER-PRODUCER	9930 LANCASTER-CIRCLEVILLE RD	AMANDA, OH	43102
ROTHMAN, MOSES	FILM EXECUTIVE	4 RED LION YARD, WAVERTON ST	LONDON W1X 7FL	ENGLAND
ROTHMAN, ROBERT	NEWS CORRESPONDENT	1927 17TH ST #3, NW	WASHINGTON, DC	20009
ROTHMAN, STEPHANIE	WRITER-PRODUCER	11925 MAYFIELD AVE #4	LOS ANGELES, CA	90049
ROTHSCHILD, LOUIS, JR	NEWS CORRESPONDENT	3025 CLEVELAND AVE, NW	WASHINGTON, DC	20008
ROTHSCHILD, RICHARD	FILM DIRECTOR	2021 WHITLEY TERR STEPS	LOS ANGELES, CA	90068
ROTHSCHILD, SONIA	NEWS CORRESPONDENT	3025 CLEVELAND AVE, NW	WASHINGTON, DC	20008
ROTHSTEIN, DEBBIE	ACTRESS	FELBER, 2126 N CAHUENGA BLVD	LOS ANGELES, CA	90068
ROTHSTEIN, NORMAN	THEATER PRODUCER	1515 BROADWAY	NEW YORK, NY	10036
ROTHSTEIN, RICHARD	SCREENWRITER	201 S WINDSOR BLVD	LOS ANGELES, CA	90004
ROTHSTEIN, SIDNEY	CONDUCTOR	POST OFFICE BOX 1515	NEW YORK, NY	10023
ROTHWELL, ROBERT	ACTOR	8350 SANTA MONICA BLVD #103	LOS ANGELES, CA	90069
ROTMAN, KEITH	FILM EXECUTIVE	4 RED LION YARD, WAVERTON ST	LONDON W1X 7FL	ENGLAND

Name	Occupation	Address	City	Zip
ROTONDI, EDWARD J	DIRECTOR	DGA, 110 W 57TH ST	NEW YORK, NY	10019
ROTONDI, JOE P, SR	COMPOSER	2260 BRONSON HILL DR	LOS ANGELES, CA	90068
ROTUNDA, MARJORIE N	TV DIRECTOR	3778 BALBOA TERR #A	SAN DIEGO, CA	92117
ROTUNDO, MIKE	WRESTLER	POST OFFICE BOX 3859	STAMFORD, CT	06905
ROTUNNO, GIUSEPPE	CINEMATOGRAPHER	POST OFFICE BOX 2230	HOLLYWOOD, CA	90078
ROTWEIN, RANDI	ACTRESS	19355 SHERMAN WY #35	RESEDA, CA	91335
ROUDEBUSH, EVERETT	ACTOR	348 W 56TH ST	NEW YORK, NY	10019
ROUGAS, MICHAEL	ACTOR	1036 N CRESCENT HGTS BLVD #6	LOS ANGELES, CA	90046
ROUGEAU, JACQUES	WRESTLER	POST OFFICE BOX 3859	STAMFORD, CT	06905
ROUGEAU, RAYMOND	WRESTLER	POST OFFICE BOX 3859	STAMFORD, CT	06905
ROUGEAU BROTHERS, THE	WRESTLING TAG TEAM	POST OFFICE BOX 3859	STAMFORD, CT	06905
ROUGH, MATT	TV CRITIC	POST OFFICE BOX 500	WASHINGTON, DC	20044
ROUGH CUTT	ROCK & ROLL GROUP	18653 VENTURA BLVD #307	TARZANA, CA	91356
ROULEAU, JOSEPH	BASSO	SARDOS, 180 W END AVE	NEW YORK, NY	10023
ROULETTES, THE	VOCAL GROUP	9100 SUNSET BLVD #220	HOLLYWOOD, CA	90069
ROUMANIS, GEORGE Z	COMPOSER-CONDUCTOR	2332 CENTURY HILL	LOS ANGELES, CA	90067
ROUNDTREE, RICHARD	ACTOR	4528 CAMELLIA AVE	NORTH HOLLYWOOD, CA	91602
ROURA, PHIL	COLUMNIST-CRITIC	TRIBUNE MEDIA SERVICES		
		64 E CONCORD ST	ORLANDO, FL	32801
ROURKE, MICKEY	ACTOR	400 S BEVERLY DR #216	BEVERLY HILLS, CA	90212
ROUS, JOHN	PHOTOGRAPHER	100 BLUFF VIEW DR #202-B	BELL AIR BLUFFS, FL	33540
ROUSE, RUSSELL	DIRECTOR-PRODUCER	16632 OLDHAM ST	ENCINO, CA	91436
ROUSH, EDD J	BASEBALL	122 39TH STREET CT NW	BRADENTON, FL	33505
ROUSIMOFF, ANDRE	WRESTLER	SEE - ANDRE THE GIANT		
ROUSIMOFF, MONSTER	WRESTLER	SEE - ANDRE THE GIANT		
ROUSSELIN, PIERRE	NEWS CORRESPONDENT	4912 44TH ST, NW	WASHINGTON, DC	20016
ROUSTABOUTS, THE	BLUEGRASS GROUP	POST OFFICE BOX 25371	CHARLOTTE, NC	28212
ROUTCH, ROBERT	FRENCH HORN	POST OFFICE BOX 30	TENAFLY, NJ	07670
ROUTLEDGE, PATRICIA	ACTRESS	LARRY DALZELL ASSOCIATES		
		126 KENNINGTON PARK RD	LONDON SE11 4FJ	ENGLAND
ROUTON, JOE	VIOLINIST	POST OFFICE BOX 684	PARIS, TN	38242
ROUTT, RANDOLPH J	PHOTOGRAPHER	303 LEXINGTON DR		
		WOODMORE	SILVER SPRING, MD	20901
ROVEN, BRANDY	ACTRESS	910 N ALPINE DR	BEVERLY HILLS, CA	90210
ROVENSKY, SUSAN	NEWS CORRESPONDENT	4701 WILLARD AVE #1236	CHEVY CHASE, MD	20815
ROVERS, THE	VOCAL GROUP	UNICORN, 547 HOMER ST	VANCOUVER, BC V6B 2V7	CANADA
ROVETA, SANDY	ACTRESS	247 S BEVERLY DR #102	BEVERLY HILLS, CA	90210
ROVIT, SAM	NEWS CORRESPONDENT	1515 16TH ST #4-B, NW	WASHINGTON, DC	20036
ROVNER, NAOMI S	NEWS CORRESPONDENT	6308 OWEN PL	BETHESDA, MD	20817
ROW, RICHARD	ACTOR	7915 W NORTON AVE	LOS ANGELES, CA	90046
ROWADER, DARRELL	TENOR	431 S DEARBORN ST #1504	CHICAGO, IL	60605
ROWAN, BRENT	GUITARIST	POST OFFICE BOX 120665	NASHVILLE, TN	37212
ROWAN, CARL	COLUMNIST	NEWS AMERICA SYNDICATE		
		1703 KAISER AVE	IRVINE, CA	92714
ROWAN, DAN	COMEDIAN	792 N MANASOTA KEY	ENGLEWOOD, FL	33533
ROWAN, FRANK	ACTOR	THE ACTOR'S FUND HOME		
		155 W HUDSON AVE	ENGLEWOOD, NJ	07631
ROWAN, GAY	ACTRESS	427 N CANON DR #205	BEVERLY HILLS, CA	90210
ROWAND, NADA	ACTRESS	ABC-TV NETWORK, "LOVING"		
		1330 AVE OF THE AMERICAS	NEW YORK, NY	10019
ROWE, ALAN	ACTOR	8 SHERWOOD CLOSE	LONDON SW13	ENGLAND
ROWE, ARTHUR	TV WRITER	325 S CANON DR	BEVERLY HILLS, CA	90212
ROWE, DEAN	TV DIRECTOR	6201 EDGEWOOD RD	CRYSTAL LAKE, IL	60014
ROWE, EARL	ACTOR	80 SAINT NICHOLAS PL	NEW YORK, NY	10026
ROWE, FANNY	ACTRESS	WHITE, 31 KINGS RD	LONDON SW3	ENGLAND
ROWE, GORDON A	TV DIRECTOR	12415 RIVERSIDE DR #1	NORTH HOLLYWOOD, CA	91607
ROWE, HANSFORD	ACTOR	215 W 91ST ST	NEW YORK, NY	10024
ROWE, JAMES L, JR	NEWS CORRESPONDENT	3051 LEGATION ST, NW	WASHINGTON, DC	20015
ROWE, JO ANN	NEWS CORRESPONDENT	9 MISTY DALE WY	GAITHERSBURG, MD	20877
ROWE, MISTY	ACTRESS	9000 SUNSET BLVD #1112	LOS ANGELES, CA	90069
ROWE, NANCY J	NEWS CORRESPONDENT	618 CONSTITUTION AVE, NE	WASHINGTON, DC	20002
ROWE, PAMELA	NEWS CORRESPONDENT	3026 WISCONSIN AVE #C-107	WASHINGTON, DC	20016
ROWE, ROSEMARIE	ACTRESS	SEE - STACK, ROSEMARIE		
ROWE, S ROBERT	WRITER-PRODUCER	2680 TIMBERCREEK CIR	BOCA RATON, FL	33431
ROWE, TOM	SCREENWRITER	8955 BEVERLY BLVD	LOS ANGELES, CA	90048
ROWELL, ERNIE	GUITARIST	210 DIANE DR	MADISON, TN	37115
ROWEN, HOBART	NEWS CORRESPONDENT	5701 WARWICK PL	CHEVY CHASE, MD	20815
ROWICKI, WITOLD	CONDUCTOR	HILLYER, 250 W 57TH ST	NEW YORK, NY	10107
ROWLAND, BETTY	BURLESQUE	MR B'S, 217 BROADWAY	SANTA MONICA, CA	90405
ROWLAND, DAVE	SINGER	POST OFFICE BOX 120021	NASHVILLE, TN	37212
ROWLAND, GEOFFREY	FILM EDITOR	2630 LACY ST	LOS ANGELES, CA	90031
ROWLAND, ROY	FILM DIRECTOR	DGA, 7950 SUNSET BLVD	HOLLYWOOD, CA	90046
ROWLANDS, DAVID	ACTOR	7917 WOODROW WILSON DR	LOS ANGELES, CA	90046
ROWLANDS, GENA	ACTRESS	7917 WOODROW WILSON DR	LOS ANGELES, CA	90046
ROWLANDS, PATSY	ACTRESS	WHITE, 31 KINGS RD	LONDON SW3	ENGLAND
ROWLES, JIMMY	COMPOSER	520 N BEL AIRE DR	BURBANK, CA	91501
ROWLES, KENNETH F	TV DIRECTOR-PRODUCER	60 WARDOUR ST	LONDON W1	ENGLAND
ROWLES, POLLY	ACTRESS	29 W 10TH ST	NEW YORK, NY	10011
ROWLEY, BILL	ACTOR	527 MADISON AVE #820	NEW YORK, NY	10022
ROWLEY, JAMES C	NEWS CORRESPONDENT	8801 RIDGE RD	BETHESDA, MD	20817
ROWLEY, JIM	DIRECTOR	4430 WILDWOOD RD	DALLAS, TX	75209
ROWLEY, STORER H	NEWS CORRESPONDENT	2500 "Q" ST #436, NW	WASHINGTON, DC	20007
ROWSE, ARTHUR E	NEWS CORRESPONDENT	4012 VIRGINIA ST	CHEVY CHASE, MD	20815
ROXTON, STEVE	ACTOR	6 THORNTON RD, LEYTONSTONE	LONDON E11	ENGLAND

ROY, JACK	COMEDIAN-ACTOR	SEE - DANGERFIELD, RODNEY		
ROY, RICHARD FRANCIS	DIRECTOR	15 RAMSAY RD	MONTCLAIR, NJ	07042
ROY, RON	ACTOR	5856 VESPER AVE	VAN NUYS, CA	91411
ROY, WILL	BASS	45 W 60TH ST #4-K	NEW YORK, NY	10023
ROYAL, BILLY JOE	SINGER-SONGWRITER	ENTERTAINMENT ARTISTS		
		819 18TH AVE S	NASHVILLE, TN	37203
ROYAL, DANIEL C	DIRECTOR	1283 FRANKLIN CIR, NE	ATLANTA, GA	30324
ROYAL, GARY	WRESTLER	NATIONAL WRESTLING ALLIANCE		
		JIM CROCKETT PROMOTIONS		
		421 BRIARBEND DR	CHARLOTTE, NC	28209
ROYAL, TED	MUSICIAN	9777 HARWIN ST #101	HOUSTON, TX	77036
ROYALTONES, THE	VOCAL GROUP	OLDIES, 5218 ALMONT ST	LOS ANGELES, CA	90032
ROYCE, KENNETH	AUTHOR	3 ABBOTTS CLOSE		
		ABBOTTS ANN, ANDOVER	HANTS SP11 7NP	ENGLAND
ROYCE, KNUT S	NEWS CORRESPONDENT	2111 JEFFERSON DAVIS HWY #620-N	ALEXANDRIA, VA	22202
ROYCE, RICHARD	ACTOR	10000 RIVERSIDE DR #3	TOLUCA LAKE, CA	91602
ROYER, ROBB	WRITER-COMPOSER	6255 SUNSET BLVD #1214	LOS ANGELES, CA	90028
ROYKO, GAYLE	SOPRANO	431 S DEARBORN ST #1504	CHICAGO, IL	60605
ROYKO, MIKE	COLUMNIST	THE CHICAGO TRIBUNE		
		TRIBUNE TOWER		
		435 N MICHIGAN AVE	CHICAGO, IL	60611
ROYLANCE, PAMELA	ACTRESS	7411 OSTROM AVE	VAN NUYS, CA	91406
ROYLE, CAROL	ACTRESS	LEADING PLAYERS, 31 KINGS RD	LONDON SW3	ENGLAND
ROYSTER, WILLIAM V	NEWS CORRESPONDENT	134 "E" ST, NW	WASHINGTON, DC	20003
ROZAKIS, GREGORY	ACTOR	OPPENHEIM, 565 5TH AVE	NEW YORK, NY	10017
ROZARIO, COLLIN	PIANIST	698 SNEED RD	FRANKLIN, TN	37064
ROZARIO, ROBERT V	COMPOSER-CONDUCTOR	5850 EL CANON AVE	WOODLAND HILLS, CA	91367
ROZE, CHEYENNE	ACTOR	CARPENTER, 1516-W REDWOOD ST	SAN DIEGO, CA	92101
ROZELLE, PETE	FOOTBALL COMMISIONER	410 PARK AVE	NEW YORK, NY	10022
ROZENBERG, BERNARD	TV DIRECTOR	3671 HUDSON MANOR TERR	RIVERDALE, NY	10463
ROZENZWEIG, BARNEY	TV PRODUCER	615 S ROSSMORE AVE	LOS ANGELES, CA	90005
RROCKK	ROCK & ROLL GROUP	POST OFFICE BOX 18368	DENVER, CO	80218
RUBANOFF, JAYE	CONDUCTOR	13200 HARTSOOK ST	SHERMAN OAKS, CA	91423
RUBAUM, IRENE	ACTRESS	1225 CORSICA DR	PACIFIC PALISADES, CA	90272
RUBBER, VIOLA	THEATER PRODUCER	400 W 43RD ST	NEW YORK, NY	10036
RUBBER RODEO	ROCK & ROLL GROUP	FAT ARTISTS AGENCY		
		400 ESSEX ST	SALEM, MA	01970
RUBEL, MARC REID	WRITER	1670 MICHAEL LN	PACIFIC PALISADES, CA	90272
RUBELL, MARIA	ACTRESS	721 N LA BREA AVE #200	LOS ANGELES, CA	90038
RUBEN, AARON	WRITER-PRODUCER	576 CHALETTE DR	BEVERLY HILLS, CA	90210
RUBEN, AL	TV WRITER	555 W 57TH ST #1230	NEW YORK, NY	10019
RUBEN, ANDY	FILM-TV WRITER	8955 BEVERLY BLVD	LOS ANGELES, CA	90048
RUBEN, JOSEPH P	WRITER-PRODUCER	2680 WOODSTOCK RD	LOS ANGELES, CA	90046
RUBEN, KATT SHEA	ACTRESS-WRITER	SEE - SHEA RUBEN, KATT		
RUBENS, WILLIAM S	TV EXECUTIVE	NBC TELEVISION NETWORK		
		30 ROCKEFELLER PLAZA	NEW YORK, NY	10112
RUBENSTEIN, BERNARD	CONDUCTOR	1776 BROADWAY #504	NEW YORK, NY	10019
RUBENSTEIN, LARRY	PHOTOGRAPHER	4711 S 29TH ST	ARLINGTON, VA	22206
RUBENSTEIN, PHIL	ACTOR	9229 SUNSET BLVD #306	LOS ANGELES, CA	90069
RUBENSTEIN, SCOTT IAN	TV WRITER	10940 WESTWOOD BLVD	CULVER CITY, CA	90230
RUBIN, ALBERT	TV EXECUTIVE	ABC TELEVISION NETWORK		
		1330 AVE OF THE AMERICAS	NEW YORK, NY	10019
RUBIN, BERNARD	DIRECTOR	2295 S OCEAN BLVD	PALM BEACH, FL	33480
RUBIN, BLANCHE	ACTRESS	1741 N IVAR AVE #221	LOS ANGELES, CA	90028
RUBIN, BOB	TV DIRECTOR	999 N DOHENY DR #1210	LOS ANGELES, CA	90069
RUBIN, BRADY	ACTRESS	6605 HOLLYWOOD BLVD #220	HOLLYWOOD, CA	90028
RUBIN, BRUCE	SCREENWRITER	8955 BEVERLY BLVD	LOS ANGELES, CA	90048
RUBIN, CYMA	THEATER PRODUCER	170 E 77TH ST	NEW YORK, NY	10021
RUBIN, DAVID	CASTING DIRECTOR	9911 W PICO BLVD #1580	LOS ANGELES, CA	90035
RUBIN, DOROTHY	AUTHOR-TV HOST	TRENTON STATE COLLEGE		
		HILLWOOD LAKES	TRENTON, NJ	08625
RUBIN, FRED	TV WRITER-PRODUCER	1900 N VINE ST #209	LOS ANGELES, CA	90068
RUBIN, GAIL	NEWS CORRESPONDENT	400 N CAPITOL ST, NW	WASHINGTON, DC	20001
RUBIN, JAMES H	NEWS CORRESPONDENT	4350 ALTON PL, NW	WASHINGTON, DC	20016
RUBIN, JAY	PUBLISHING EXECUTIVE	CABLEVISION COMPANY		
		101 PARK AVE, 4TH FLOOR	NEW YORK, NY	10178
RUBIN, KATT	ACTRESS	SEE - SHEA RUBIN, KATT		
RUBIN, LANCE M	COMPOSER	416 SAN VICENTE BLVD #112	SANTA MONICA, CA	90402
RUBIN, MANN	SCREENWRITER	11975 FOXBORO DR	LOS ANGELES, CA	90049
RUBIN, MARC D	TV WRITER	8955 BEVERLY BLVD	LOS ANGELES, CA	90048
RUBIN, MARK J	TV WRITER	8955 BEVERLY BLVD	LOS ANGELES, CA	90048
RUBIN, MAURY R	TV DIRECTOR	424 E 85TH ST	NEW YORK, NY	10028
RUBIN, MURRAY	ACTOR	1350 N HIGHLAND AVE #24	HOLLYWOOD, CA	90028
RUBIN, PHILLIP S	TV DIRECTOR	290 UNDERWOOD ST	HOLLISTON, MA	01746
RUBIN, ROBERT H	TV EXECUTIVE	GROUP W PRODUCTIONS		
		645 MADISON AVE	NEW YORK, NY	10022
RUBIN, RON	TV WRITER	8955 BEVERLY BLVD	LOS ANGELES, CA	90048
RUBIN, RONALD	ORCHESTRA LEADER	1207 EL MEDIO AVE	PACIFIC PALISADES, CA	90272
RUBIN, SAM	NEWS REPORTER	THE NATIONAL ENQUIRER		
		600 SE COAST AVE	LANTANA, FL	33464
RUBIN, STANLEY	WRITER-PRODUCER	8818 RISING GLEN PL	LOS ANGELES, CA	90069
RUBINEK, SAUL	ACTOR	9200 SUNSET BLVD #1210	LOS ANGELES, CA	90069
RUBINFIER, JAMES J	TV WRITER	1155 HACIENDA PL #205	LOS ANGELES, CA	90069
RUBINGER, DAVID	PHOTOGRAPHER	TIME/TIME & LIFE BLDG		
		ROCKEFELLER CENTER	NEW YORK, NY	10020

Name	Occupation	Address	City, State	ZIP
RUBINI, JAN	CONDUCTOR	8 RUE VILLARS	NEWPORT BEACH, CA	92660
RUBINI, MICHEL	COMPOSER	1646 S LA CIENEGA BLVD	LOS ANGELES, CA	90035
RUBINO, GEORGE	TV WRITER	8955 BEVERLY BLVD	LOS ANGELES, CA	90048
RUBINOOS, THE	ROCK & ROLL GROUP	POST OFFICE BOX 134	EL CERRITO, CA	94530
RUBINOWITZ, BARRY	TV WRITER	627 WESTMOUNT DR	LOS ANGELES, CA	90069
RUBINSTEIN, DEBRA	CASTING DIRECTOR	EMBASSY TV, 1438 N GOWER AVE	LOS ANGELES, CA	90028
RUBINSTEIN, JOHN	ACTOR	10420 SCENARIO LN	LOS ANGELES, CA	90024
RUBINSTEIN, JOHN A	COMPOSER-CONDUCTOR	1900 AVE OF THE STARS #1630	LOS ANGELES, CA	90067
RUBINSTEIN, RICHARD P	FILM EXECUTIVE	LAUREL, 928 BROADWAY	NEW YORK, NY	10010
RUBINSTEIN, SHOLOM	TV DIRECTOR	ABC-TV, 31 E 28TH ST	NEW YORK, NY	10016
RUBINSTEIN, ZELDA	ACTRESS	1850 SILVER LAKE BLVD	LOS ANGELES, CA	90026
RUBINTON, ERIC	TV WRITER	555 W 57TH ST #1230	NEW YORK, NY	10019
RUBIO, HELEN	ACTRESS	3800 BARHAM BLVD #303	LOS ANGELES, CA	90068
RUBY, CLIFF	TV WRITER	8955 BEVERLY BLVD	LOS ANGELES, CA	90048
RUBY, ELVERA	NEWS CORRESPONDENT	2480 16TH ST, NW	WASHINGTON, DC	20009
RUBY, JOSEPH C	WRITER-PRODUCER	9147 ENCINO AVE	NORTHRIDGE, CA	91325
RUCKER, ALLEN	PRODUCER	MCA/UNIVERSAL STUDIOS, INC 100 UNIVERSAL CITY PLAZA #473	UNIVERSAL CITY, CA	91608
RUCKER, BOB	NEWS CORRESPONDENT	74 CRESTLINE DR	SAN FRANICSCO, CA	94131
RUCKER, CLINTON A	TV WRITER	8955 BEVERLY BLVD	LOS ANGELES, CA	90048
RUCKER, DICK	CINEMATOGRAPHER	641 N WILCOX AVE #3-F	LOS ANGELES, CA	90004
RUCKER, MARK	BARITONE	HILLYER, 250 W 57TH ST	NEW YORK, NY	10107
RUDD, ENID	TV WRITER	555 W 57TH ST #1230	NEW YORK, NY	10019
RUDD, HUGHES	NEWS CORRESPONDENT	ABC NEWS, 7 W 66TH ST	NEW YORK, NY	10023
RUDD, PAUL K	ACTOR	145 W 55TH ST	NEW YORK, NY	10019
RUDDY, ALBERT S	FILM WRITER-PRODUCER	1601 CLEARVIEW DR	BEVERLY HILLS, CA	90210
RUDE, RAVISHING RICK	WRESTLER	WORLD CLASS WRESTLING SOUTHWEST SPORTS, INC DALLAS SPORTATORIUM 1000 S INDUSTRIAL BLVD	DALLAS, TX	75207
RUDEEN, KENNETH	WRITER-EDITOR	SPORTS ILLUSTRATED MAGAZINE TIME & LIFE BUILDING ROCKEFELLER CENTER	NEW YORK, NY	10020
RUDEL, JULIUS	CONDUCTOR	ICM, 40 W 57TH ST	NEW YORK, NY	10019
RUDELSON, ROBERT	SCREENWRITER	15459 WYANDOTTE ST	VAN NUYS, CA	91406
RUDENSKY, MARIA	NEWS CORRESPONDENT	13 6TH ST, NE	WASHINGTON, DC	20002
RUDESILL, MIKE	SINGER	POST OFFICE DRAWER 20146	SAINT PETERSBURG, FL	33742
RUDICH, RACHEL	FLUTIST	AFFILIATE ARTISTS, INC 37 W 65TH ST, 6TH FLOOR	NEW YORK, NY	10023
RUDIN, ANDREW	COMPOSER	FINELL, 155 W 68TH ST	NEW YORK, NY	10023
RUDIN, HURRICANE SAM	SINGER-PIANIST	FROTHINGHAM, 40 GROVE ST	WESSESLEY, MA	02181
RUDLEY, HERBERT	ACTOR	13056 MAXELLA AVE #1	MARINA DEL REY, CA	90292
RUDMAN, KAL	WRESTLING CORRES	WORLD WRESTLING FEDERATION TITAN SPORTS PUBLICATIONS 1055 SUMMER ST	STAMFORD, CT	06905
RUDNYTSKY, ROMAN	PIANIST	POST OFFICE BOX U	REDDING, CT	06875
RUDOLF, MAX	CONDUCTOR	ICM, 40 W 57TH ST	NEW YORK, NY	10019
RUDOLPH, ALAN	FILM WRITER-DIRECTOR	1020 S CARMELINA AVE	LOS ANGELES, CA	90049
RUDOLPH, BARBARA	WRITER-EDITOR	TIME/TIME & LIFE BLDG ROCKEFELLER CENTER	NEW YORK, NY	10020
RUDOLPH, LOUIS	PRODUCER	2001 WILSHIRE BLVD #301	SANTA MONICA, CA	90403
RUDOLPH, OSCAR	TV DIRECTOR	16739 OCTAVIA PL	ENCINO, CA	91436
RUDY, MARTIN	ACTOR	439 S LA CIENEGA BLVD #120	LOS ANGELES, CA	90048
RUDY, MIKHAIL	PIANIST	CAMI, 165 W 57TH ST	NEW YORK, NY	10019
RUEL, SUSAN	NEWS CORRESPONDENT	1816 NEW HAMPSHIRE AVE #406, NW	WASHINGTON, DC	20009
RUFFALO, JOSEPH F	TALENT AGENT	11340 W OLYMPIC BLVD #357	LOS ANGELES, CA	90064
RUFFIANS, THE	ROCK & ROLL GROUP	2560 BANCROFT WY #33	BERKELEY, CA	94704
RUFFIN, BOBBY	SINGER	5300 POWERLINE RD #202	FORT LAUDERDALE, FL	33309
RUFFIN, DAVID	SINGER	200 W 51ST ST #1410	NEW YORK, NY	10019
RUFFIN, DAVID C	NEWS CORRESPONDENT	501 12TH ST #3, NE	WASHINGTON, DC	20002
RUFFIN, JIMMY	SINGER-SONGWRITER	RSO RECORDS, 1775 BROADWAY	NEW YORK, NY	10019
RUFUS	SOUL GROUP	7250 BEVERLY BLVD #200	LOS ANGELES, CA	90036
RUGA, ELLIOT	TV DIRECTOR	SAND SPRING RD	MORRISTOWN, NJ	07960
RUGE, GEORGE MARSHALL	ACTOR	872 S WESTGATE AVE #2	LOS ANGELES, CA	90049
RUGENSTEIN, DAVE	DRUMMER	POST OFFICE BOX 121141	NASHVILLE, TN	37212
RUGG, HAROLD	GUITARIST	8306 TERRY LN	HERMITAGE, TN	37076
RUGGEDY ANNES, THE	ROCK & ROLL GROUP	TABB RECORDS COMPANY 6201 SANTA MONICA BLVD	HOLLYWOOD, CA	90038
RUGGLES, DERYA	ACTRESS	KNBC-TV, "DAYS OF OUR LIVES" 3000 W ALAMEDA AVE	BURBANK, CA	91523
RUGH, PHIL	PIANIST	POST OFFICE BOX 90702	NASHVILLE, TN	37209
RUHMANN, HEINZ	ACTOR	ROBERT-KOCH-STRASSE 20	8022 GEISELGASTEIG ...WEST GERMANY	
RUIZ, JOSE LUIS	WRITER-PRODUCER	POST OFFICE BOX 27788	LOS ANGELES, CA	90027
RUKEYSER, BUD, JR	TV EXECUTIVE	NBC-TV, 30 ROCKEFELLER PLAZA	NEW YORK, NY	10112
RUKEYSER, LOUIS	TV HOST-JOURNALIST	306 TACONIC RD	GREENWICH, CT	06830
RULE, ELTON H	TV EXECUTIVE	706 N LINDEN DR	BEVERLY HILLS, CA	90210
RULE, JANICE	ACTRESS	1122 BERKELEY ST	SANTA MONICA, CA	94030
RUMANES, GEORGE N	WRITER	143 N HAMEL DR	BEVERLY HILLS, CA	90211
RUMBAUGH, DON	TV DIRECTOR	27522 RONDELL ST	AGOURA, CA	91301
RUMMAGE, J REID	DIRECTOR	DGA, 7950 SUNSET BLVD	HOLLYWOOD, CA	90046
RUMOUR, THE	ROCK & ROLL GROUP	157 W 57TH ST PH #A	NEW YORK, NY	10019
RUMSHINSKY, MURRAY	COMPOSER-CONDUCTOR	1200 RIVERSIDE DR #233	BURBANK, CA	91506
RUN-D M C	RAP GROUP	1133 BROADWAY #907	NEW YORK, NY	10010

Name	Occupation	Address	City	Code
RUNACRE, JENNY	ACTRESS	LEADING PLAYERS, 31 KINGS RD	LONDON SW3	ENGLAND
RUNAWAYS, THE	ROCK & ROLL GROUP	FOWLEY, 6000 SUNSET BLVD	LOS ANGELES, CA	90028
RUNDGREN, TODD & UTOPIA	ROCK & ROLL GROUP	PANACEA ENTERTAINMENT		
		2705 GLENDOWER RD	LOS ANGELES, CA	90027
RUNDLE, CIS	ACTRESS	9744 WILSHIRE BLVD #306	BEVERLY HILLS, CA	90212
RUNNELS, VIRGIL RILEY, JR	WRESTLER	SEE - RHODES, DUSTY		
RUNNER	ROCK & ROLL GROUP	PROLOGUE RECORDS, 1674 BROADWAY	NEW YORK, NY	10019
RUNNINGEN, ROGER D	NEWS CORRESPONDENT	5409 RICHENBACHER AVE	ALEXANDRIA, VA	22304
RUNNION, MARGE	REPORTER	TIME & PEOPLE MAGAZINE		
		TIME & LIFE BUILDING		
		ROCKEFELLER CENTER	NEW YORK, NY	10020
RUNYEON, RANDALL D	MUSICIAN	116 HARDING PL #A-6	NASHVILLE, TN	37205
RUNYON, ARTHUR L	TV DIRECTOR	3839 WEDDELL ST	DEARBORN, MI	48124
RUNYON, JENNIFER	ACTRESS	10100 SANTA MONICA BLVD #1600	LOS ANGELES, CA	90067
RUNYON, KEN R	COMPOSER	CMS, 26690 SAND CYN RD	CANYON COUNTRY, CA	91351
RUPLINGER, DALE	BODYBUILDER	4611 WASHINGTON ST	DAVENPORT, IA	52806
RUPRECHT, DAVID	ACTOR	9744 WILSHIRE BLVD #206	BEVERLY HILLS, CA	90212
RUSCH, GLORIA	ACTRESS	5000 LANKERSHIM BLVD #5	NORTH HOLLYWOOD, CA	91601
RUSCHA, EDWARD	ACTOR	13775 VALLEY VISTA BLVD	SHERMAN OAKS, CA	91423
RUSCIO, AL	ACTOR	5722 HESPERIA AVE	ENCINO, CA	91316
RUSH	ROCK & ROLL GROUP	41 BRITAIN ST #200	TORONTO, ONT	CANADA
RUSH, ALAN	GUITARIST	POST OFFICE BOX 56	MOUNT JULIET, TN	37122
RUSH, ALVIN	TV EXECUTIVE	MCA-TV, 445 PARK AVE	NEW YORK, NY	10022
RUSH, BARBARA	ACTRESS	1708 TROPICAL AVE	BEVERLY HILLS, CA	90210
RUSH, BEVERLY	SINGER	POST OFFICE BOX 16	HILLSBORO, NH	03244
RUSH, CHRIS	SINGER	61-45 98TH ST #12-B	REGO PARK, NY	11374
RUSH, DAVID L	NEWS CORRESPONDENT	15330 MANOR VILLAGE LN	ROCKVILLE, MD	20853
RUSH, DEBORAH	ACTRESS	10100 SANTA MONICA BLVD #1600	LOS ANGELES, CA	90067
RUSH, HERMAN	TV EXECUTIVE	1984 STRADELLA RD	LOS ANGELES, CA	90077
RUSH, JAMES J	DIRECTOR	35-17 162ND ST	FLUSHING, NY	11358
RUSH, JENNIFER	SINGER	CBS SONGS COMPANY		
		BLEICHSTRASSE 64-66A	6000 FRANKFURT-MAIN	WEST GERMANY
RUSH, LETTY	ACTRESS	6155 COLGATE AVE	LOS ANGELES, CA	90036
		7300 E CAMELBACK RD	SCOTTSDALE, AZ	85251
RUSH, RICHARD	WRITER-PRODUCER	821 STRADELLA RD	LOS ANGELES, CA	90077
RUSH, SARAH	ACTRESS	1132 N VISTA ST #2	LOS ANGELES, CA	90046
RUSH, TOM	SINGER-SONGWRITER	POST OFFICE BOX 16	HILLSBORO, NH	03244
RUSHEN, PATRICE	SINGER	CLASS ACT, 1090 S LA BREA AVE	LOS ANGELES, CA	90010
RUSHLOW, PAUL M	NEWS CORRESPONDENT	4646 40TH ST, NW	WASHINGTON, DC	20016
RUSHMORE, KAREN	ACTRESS	9000 SUNSET BLVD #1112	LOS ANGELES, CA	90069
RUSHNELL, SQUIRE D	TV EXECUTIVE	ABC TELEVISION NETWORK		
		1330 AVE OF THE AMERICAS	NEW YORK, NY	10019
RUSHTON, DONALD A	DIRECTOR	520 N MICHIGAN AVE #436	CHICAGO, IL	60611
RUSHTON, MATTHEW	TV PRODUCER	15301 VENTURA BLVD #221	SHERMAN OAKS, CA	91403
RUSHTON, SHARON	ACTRESS	11618 GORHAM AVE #4	LOS ANGELES, CA	90049
RUSKIN, COBY	TV DIRECTOR	10035 HILLGROVE DR	BEVERLY HILLS, CA	90210
RUSKIN, JEANNE	ACTRESS	10000 SANTA MONICA BLVD #305	LOS ANGELES, CA	90067
RUSKIN, JOSEPH	ACTOR	13840 KITTRIDGE ST	VAN NUYS, CA	91405
RUSKIN, PHIL	DIRECTOR	4418 PRATT	LINCOLNWOOD, IL	60646
RUSOFF, GARRY	SCREENWRITER	620 MILWOOD AVE	VENICE, CA	90291
RUSS, KAREL	FILM PRODUCER	ROSEMAN, 8 POLAND ST	LONDON W1	ENGLAND
RUSSEL, TONY	ACTOR	10000 RIVERSIDE DR #3	TOLUCA LAKE, CA	91602
RUSSELL, AARON	SINGER	TESSIER, 505 CANTON PASS	MADISON, TN	37115
RUSSELL, ALAN	TV DIRECTOR-PRODUCER	109 THE AVE	LONDON W13	ENGLAND
RUSSELL, ANNA	MUSICIAN	ARTHUR SHAFMAN, 723 7TH AVE	NEW YORK, NY	10019
RUSSELL, ANTHONY	ACTOR	LIGHT, 113 N ROBERTSON BLVD	LOS ANGELES, CA	90048
RUSSELL, ARLAND	ACTOR	244 RIVERSIDE DR #4-H	NEW YORK, NY	10025
RUSSELL, BETSY	ACTRESS	6310 SAN VICENTE BLVD #407	LOS ANGELES, CA	90048
RUSSELL, BILL	SPORTSCASTER	POST OFFICE BOX 58	MERCER ISLAND, WA	98040
RUSSELL, BILL	MUSICIAN	ROUTE #1, BOX 208	DICKSON, TN	37055
RUSSELL, BING	ACTOR	229 E GAINSBOROUGH RD	THOUSAND OAKS, CA	91360
RUSSELL, BRENDA	SINGER	POST OFFICE BOX 3875	HOLLYWOOD, CA	90028
RUSSELL, BRUCE ALAN	ACTOR	3814 LORADO WY	LOS ANGELES, CA	90043
RUSSELL, CHRISTINE	NEWS CORRESPONDENT	4914 30TH PL, NW	WASHINGTON, DC	20008
RUSSELL, CHUCK	FILM PRODUCER	8961 SUNSET BLVD #A	LOS ANGELES, CA	90069
RUSSELL, CRAIG	SINGER	HAAS, 8329 SALOMA AVE	VAN NUYS, CA	91402
RUSSELL, DAVID	FIDDLER	2632 MT VIEW	DALLAS, TX	75234
RUSSELL, DIANE F	NEWS CORRESPONDENT	NBC-TV, NEWS DEPARTMENT		
		4001 NEBRASKA AVE, NW	WASHINGTON, DC	20016
RUSSELL, FORBESY	ACTRESS	9200 SUNSET BLVD #1210	LOS ANGELES, CA	90069
RUSSELL, GEORGE	WRITER-EDITOR	TIME/TIME & LIFE BLDG		
		ROCKEFELLER CENTER	NEW YORK, NY	10020
RUSSELL, GEORGE H	COMPOSER	31423 COAST HWY #36	LAGUNA NIGUEL, CA	92677
RUSSELL, JANE	ACTRESS	2934 LORITA RD	SANTA BARBARA, CA	93108
RUSSELL, JOHN	ACTOR	8831 SUNSET BLVD #402	LOS ANGELES, CA	90069
RUSSELL, JOHN	STILTWALKER	HALL, 138 FROG HOLLOW RD	CHURCHVILLE, PA	18966
RUSSELL, JOHN MICHAEL	BARITONE	LIEBERMAN, 11 RIVERSIDE DR	NEW YORK, NY	10023
RUSSELL, JOHNNY	SINGER-SONGWRITER	TAYLOR, 2401 12TH AVE S	NASHVILLE, TN	37204
RUSSELL, KEN	FILM DIRECTOR	7 BELLMOUNT WOOD LN	WATFORD, HERTS	ENGLAND
RUSSELL, KURT	ACTOR	229 E GAINSBOROUGH RD	THOUSAND OAKS, CA	91360
RUSSELL, LEON	SINGER-SONGWRITER	POST OFFICE BOX 1006	HENDERSONVILLE, TN	37077
RUSSELL, LISA	REPORTER	TIME & PEOPLE MAGAZINE		
		TIME & LIFE BUILDING		
		ROCKEFELLER CENTER	NEW YORK, NY	10020
RUSSELL, MARK	SATIRIST-COMEDIAN	2828 WISCONSIN AVE, NW	WASHINGTON, DC	20007

HAROLD RUSSELL

JANE RUSSELL

JOHN RUSSELL

LEON RUSSELL

ANN RUTHERFORD

BOBBY RYDELL

EVA MARIE SAINT

SUSAN SAINT JAMES

EMMA SAMMS

Name	Occupation	Address	City	Zip/Country
RUSSELL, MARVIN	GUITARIST	422 N HOUSTON ST	MARYVILLE, TN	37801
RUSSELL, MICHAEL	TV WRITER	8955 BEVERLY BLVD	LOS ANGELES, CA	90048
RUSSELL, NIPSEY	COMED-WRI-DIR	353 W 57TH ST	NEW YORK, NY	10021
RUSSELL, PADDY	TV DIRECTOR	27 FERRYMOOR, HAM, RICHMOND	SURREY	ENGLAND
RUSSELL, RANDEE	SCREENWRITER	8955 BEVERLY BLVD	LOS ANGELES, CA	90048
RUSSELL, ROBERT BRUCE	NEWS CORRESPONDENT	8621 RAYBURN RD	BETHESDA, MD	20817
RUSSELL, ROXANNE	NEWS CORRESPONDENT	1900 "S" ST, NW	WASHINGTON, DC	20009
RUSSELL, ROY	TV WRITER	UNNA & DURBRIDGE, LTD		
		24-32 POTTERY LN		
		HOLLAND PARK	LONDON W11	ENGLAND
RUSSELL, S FRANK, JR	PHOTOGRAPHER	ASSOCIATED PRESS		
		2021 "K" ST, NW	WASHINGTON, DC	20006
RUSSELL, THERESA	ACTRESS	9255 SUNSET BLVD #505	LOS ANGELES, CA	90069
RUSSELL, TOM	SINGER-SONGWRITER	GOLDMINE, 700 E STATE ST	IOLA, WI	54990
RUSSIA	ROCK & ROLL GROUP	3 E 54TH ST #1400	NEW YORK, NY	10022
RUSSNOW, MICHAEL A	TV WRITER	12952 RIVERSIDE DR	SHERMAN OAKS, CA	91423
RUSSO, AARON	FILM PRODUCER	1145 GAYLEY AVE #301	LOS ANGELES, CA	90024
RUSSO, AL	ACTOR	8383 WILSHIRE BLVD #923	BEVERLY HILLS, CA	90211
RUSSO, GARY	TV DIRECTOR	288 NOME AVE	STATEN ISLAND, NY	10314
RUSSO, GIANNI	ACTOR	400 S BEVERLY DR #216	BEVERLY HILLS, CA	90212
RUSSO, HOWARD	TV DIRECTOR	327 10TH ST	SANTA MONICA, CA	90402
RUSSO, JOHN DUKE	ACTOR	1333 TALMADGE ST	LOS ANGELES, CA	90027
RUSSO, LILLIAN	TV DIRECTOR	9 TULIP LN	PORT WASHINGTON, NY	11050
RUSTHOVEN, MADELYN	ACTRESS	1745 CAMINO PALMERO ST #312	LOS ANGELES, CA	90046
RUTAN, CARL M	NEWS CORRESPONDENT	400 N CAPITOL ST, NW	WASHINGTON, DC	20001
RUTH, NORMA	ACTRESS	SCHOEMAN, 2600 W VICTORY BLVD	BURBANK, CA	91505
RUTH, PETER "MADCAT"	SINGER-GUITARIST	POST OFFICE BOX 8125	ANN ARBOR, MI	48107
RUTH, RICHARD	ACTOR	33 GOLD ST #415	NEW YORK, NY	10038
RUTH ANN	SINGER-GUITARIST	IN TUNE MANAGEMENT		
		276 CAMBRIDGE ST #4	BOSTON, MA	02134
RUTHERFORD, ANN	ACTRESS	DOZIER, 826 GREENWAY DR	BEVERLY HILLS, CA	90210
RUTHERFORD, JOHN H	NEWS CORRESPONDENT	NBC-TV, NEWS DEPARTMENT		
		4001 NEBRASKA AVE, NW	WASHINGTON, DC	20016
RUTHERFORD, MEGAN	NEWS REPORTER	TIME/TIME & LIFE BLDG		
		ROCKEFELLER CENTER	NEW YORK, NY	10020
RUTHSTEIN, ROY	TV EXECUTIVE	ABC-TV, 7 W 66TH ST	NEW YORK, NY	10023
RUTLEDGE, JAMES A, JR	NEWS CORRESPONDENT	3714 WARREN ST, NW	WASHINGTON, DC	20007
RUTLEDGE, RUSTY	DRUMMER	5370 EDMONDSON PIKE #A-12	NASHVILLE, TN	37211
RUTLEDGE, THOMAS	GUITARIST	3905 BRADLEY CT	ANTIOCH, TN	37013
RUTMAN, PAUL	PIANIST	CAMI, 165 W 57TH ST	NEW YORK, NY	10019
RUTTER, JOYCE	EDITOR-WRITER	10 COLUMBUS CIR #1300	NEW YORK, NY	10019
RUTTER, SHANNON	NEWS CORRESPONDENT	5653 DERBY CT	ALEXANDRIA, VA	22311
RUVAL, YULIIS	ACTRESS-MODEL	3907 W ALAMEDA AVE #101	BURBANK, CA	91505
RUXIN, JAMES	WRITER-PRODUCER	221 N BUNDY DR	LOS ANGELES, CA	90049
RUYMEN, AYN	ACTRESS	211 S BEVERLY DR #107	BEVERLY HILLS, CA	90212
RYAL, DICK	ACTOR	1633 VISTA DEL MAR ST #201	LOS ANGELES, CA	90028
RYAN, ALBERT J	NEWS CORRESPONDENT	2302 CHEVERLY AVE	CHEVERLY, MD	20785
RYAN, BILL	DRUMMER	170 EDGEWATER CIR	GALLATIN, TN	37066
RYAN, CHARLES	TALENT AGENT	6671 SUNSET BLVD #1574	LOS ANGELES, CA	90028
RYAN, DAN	TALENT AGENT	7250 BEVERLY BLVD #200	LOS ANGELES, CA	90036
RYAN, DEBORAH	ACTRESS	247 S BEVERLY DR #102	BEVERLY HILLS, CA	90210
RYAN, DEDE	NEWS CORRESPONDENT	7011 SYCAMORE AVE	TAKOMA PARK, MD	20912
RYAN, DESMOND	FILM CRITIC	PHILADELPHIA INQUIRER		
		400 N BROAD ST	PHILADELPHIA, PA	19101
RYAN, FRAN	ACTRESS	15010 VENTURA BLVD #219	SHERMAN OAKS, CA	91403
RYAN, FRANKLIN P, JR	DIRECTOR	392 CENTRAL PARK W	NEW YORK, NY	10025
RYAN, JAMES F	WRITER	17106 CANTARA ST	VAN NUYS, CA	91406
RYAN, JEFF	WRESTLING WRITER	POST OFFICE BOX 48	ROCKVILLE CENTRE, NY	11571
RYAN, JENNIFER Q	NEWS CORRESPONDENT	1838 MONROE ST, NW	WASHINGTON, DC	20010
RYAN, JOHN J	CELLIST	2301 ELLISTON PL #B-3	NASHVILLE, TN	37203
RYAN, JOHN P	ACTOR	1422 N SIERRA BONITA AVE	LOS ANGELES, CA	90046
RYAN, KATHLEEN	MODER-ACTRESS	7060 HOLLYWOOD BLVD #1010	LOS ANGELES, CA	90028
RYAN, LEE	ACTOR	9165 SUNSET BLVD #202	LOS ANGELES, CA	90069
RYAN, MADGE	ACTRESS	54 BLENHEIM TERR	LONDON NW8	ENGLAND
RYAN, MARGARET	NEWS CORRESPONDENT	5108 CHEROKEE AVE	ALEXANDRIA, VA	22312
RYAN, MARTY	TV PRODUCER	NBC-TV, 3000 W ALAMEDA AVE	BURBANK, CA	91523
RYAN, MICHAEL M	ACTOR	48 E 3RD ST	NEW YORK, NY	10003
RYAN, MITCHELL	ACTOR	30355 MULHOLLAND DR	CORNELL, CA	91301
RYAN, NOLAN	BASEBALL	POST OFFICE BOX 409	ALVIN, TX	77511
RYAN, PAMELA	TV WRITER	8955 BEVERLY BLVD	LOS ANGELES, CA	90048
RYAN, PATRICIA	EDITOR-EXECUTIVE	PEOPLE/TIME & LIFE BLDG		
		ROCKEFELLER CENTER	NEW YORK, NY	10020
RYAN, RICHARD A	NEWS CORRESPONDENT	505 GOLDSBOROUGH DR	ROCKVILLE, MD	20850
RYAN, SANDRA	ACTRESS	345 S ELM DR #402	BEVERLY HILLS, CA	90212
RYAN, TED	ACTOR	9220 SUNSET BLVD #218	LOS ANGELES, CA	90069
RYAN, TERRY	DIRECTOR-PRODUCER	OPIX, 5 CARLISLE ST	LONDON W1	ENGLAND
RYAN, THOMAS	ACTOR	9255 SUNSET BLVD #510	LOS ANGELES, CA	90069
RYAN, THOMAS K	CARTOONIST	NEWS AMERICA SYNDICATE		
		1703 KAISER AVE	IRVINE, CA	92714
RYDBECK, WHITNEY	ACTOR	9780 VIA ZIBELLO	BURBANK, CA	91504
RYDELL, BOBBY	SINGER	917 BRYN MAWR AVE	NARBERTH, PA	19072
RYDELL, CHRISTOPHER	ACTOR	1369 BOBOLINK PL	LOS ANGELES, CA	90069
RYDELL, MARK	ACTOR-FILM DIRECTOR	1369 BOBOLINK PL	LOS ANGELES, CA	90069
RYDER, BUDDY	WRESTLER	POST OFFICE BOX 3859	STAMFORD, CT	06905

RYDER, EDDIE	ACTOR	151 S EL CAMINO DR	BEVERLY HILLS, CA 90212
RYDER, JEFFREY C	TV EXECUTIVE	NBC TELEVISION NETWORK	
		30 ROCKEFELLER PLAZA	NEW YORK, NY 10112
RYDER, RICHARD	ACTOR	17010 KNAPP ST	NORTHRIDGE, CA 91325
RYDER, THOMAS A	DIRECTOR	DGA, 110 W 57TH ST	NEW YORK, NY 10019
RYDL, KURT	SINGER	CAMI, 165 W 57TH ST	NEW YORK, NY 10019
RYECART, PATRICK	ACTOR-PRODUCER	HEATH, PARAMOUNT HOUSE	
		162-170 WARDOUR ST	LONDON W1V 3AT ENGLAND
RYERSON, ANN	ACTRESS	870 N VINE ST #G	LOS ANGELES, CA 90038
RYERSON, GEORGE S	MUSIC ARRANGER	4615 MARIA ST	CHATTANOOGA, TN 37411
RYERSON, GREG	SINGER	COLBERT, 111 W 57TH ST	NEW YORK, NY 10019
RYHLICK, FRANK	WRITER	2320 THE STRAND	MANHATTAN BEACH, CA 90266
RYLES, JOHN WESLEY	SINGER	POST OFFICE BOX 1470	HENDERONVILLE, TN 37075
RYMER, GEORGE	FILM EXECUTIVE	CANNON FILMS, 167 WARDOUR ST	LONDON W1V 3TA ENGLAND
RYNOTT, JULIE K	NEWS CORRESPONDENT	6621 WAKEFIELD DR	ALEXANDRIA, VA 22307
RYPKS, DON	PHOTOGRAPHER	2506 LESLIE AVE	ALEXANDRIA, VA 22301
RYSAK, F DAVID	NEWS CORRESPONDENT	7514 NEVIS RD	BETHESDA, MD 20817
RYSANEK, LEONIE	SOPRANO	119 W 57TH ST #1505	NEW YORK, NY 10019
RYSK	ROCK & ROLL GROUP	POST OFFICE BOX 1578	SIOUX FALLS, SD 57101
RYSKIND, ALLAN H	NEWS CORRESPONDENT	3340 ALABAMA AVE, SE	WASHINGTON, DC 20020

SAAD, MOHAMMED	WRESTLER	CAPITOL INTERNATIONAL	
		11844 MARKET ST	NORTH LIMA, OH 44452
SAAR, JOHN	WRITER-EDITOR	PEOPLE/TIME & LIFE BLDG	
		ROCKEFELLER CENTER	NEW YORK, NY 10020
SAARINEN, GLORIA	PIANIST	200 W 70TH ST #7-F	NEW YORK, NY 10023
SABAROFF, ROBERT	WRITER	11847 KIOWA AVE #8	LOS ANGELES, CA 90049
SABATINO, ANTHONY	ART DIRECTOR	151 S EL CAMINO DR	BEVERLY HILLS, CA 90212
SABATINO, CHUCK	FILM DIRECTOR	85 SUTTON MANOR	NEW ROCHELLE, NY 10805
SABATINO, MICHAEL	ACTOR	9720 REGENT ST #8	LOS ANGELES, CA 90034
SABATO, BO	ACTOR	SCHOEMAN, 2600 W VICTORY BLVD	BURBANK, CA 91505
SABBAGH, DORIS	CASTING DIRECTOR	COLUMBIA PICTURES TV	
		COLUMBIA PLAZA	BURBANK, CA 91505
SABELLA, ERNIE	ACTOR	1145 GAYLEY AVE #309	LOS ANGELES, CA 90024
SABELLA, GUS	ACTOR	11 LOCUST AVE	OAKDALE, NY 11769
SABICAS	GUITARIST	1776 BROADWAY #504	NEW YORK, NY 10019
SABINSON, ALLEN C	TV EXECUTIVE	NBC-TV, 3000 W ALAMEDA AVE	BURBANK, CA 91523
SABLE, KENNETH S	DIRECTOR	CBS-TV, 524 W 57TH ST	NEW YORK, NY 10019
SABULIS, TOM	FILM CRITIC	DALLAS TIMES HERALD	
		1101 PACIFIC AVE	DALLAS, TX 75202
SACCHARINE TRUST	ROCK & ROLL GROUP	POST OFFICE BOX 1	LAWNDALE, CA 90260
SACCHI, ROBERT	ACTOR	3151 W CAHUENGA BLVD #310	LOS ANGELES, CA 90068
SACHA, KENNY	COMEDIAN	RITCH, 6201 QUEBEC DR	HOLLYWOOD, CA 90068
SACHS, ALICE H	ACTRESS	13017 SUNSET BLVD	LOS ANGELES, CA 90049
SACHS, ANDREA	NEWS REPORTER	TIME/TIME & LIFE BLDG	
		ROCKEFELLER CENTER	NEW YORK, NY 10020
SACHS, ANDREW	ACTOR	THE RICHARD STONE AGENCY	
		18-20 YORK BLDGS, ADELPHI	LONDON WC2N 6JY ENGLAND
SACHS, ARNOLD	PHOTOGRAPHER	411 WINSLOW RD	OXON HILL, MD 20021
SACHS, HOWARD	PHOTOGRAPHER	411 WINSLOW RD	OXON HILL, MD 20021
SACHS, LLOYD	FILM CRITIC	THE CHICAGO SUN-TIMES	
		401 N WABASH AVE	CHICAGO, IL 60611
SACHS, MARK	NEWS CORRESPONDENT	415 SILVER SPRING AVE	SILVER SPRING, MD 20910
SACHS, ROBIN	ACTOR	MARTIN, 7 WINDMILL ST	LONDON W1 ENGLAND
SACHS, WILLIAM	FILM WRITER-DIRECTOR	8955 BEVERLY BLVD	LOS ANGELES, CA 90048
SACHSE, SALLI	ACTRESS	233 ASHLAND AVE #G	SANTA MONICA, CA 90405
SACK, JOHN	TV WRITER	2005 LA BREA TERR	LOS ANGELES, CA 90046
SACK, JOHN	ACTOR	439 S LA CIENEGA BLVD #117	LOS ANGELES, CA 90048
SACK, STEVE	CARTOONIST	MINNEAPOLIS STAR & TRIBUNE	
		425 PORTLAND AVE	MINNEAPOLIS, MN 55488
SACKETT, NANCY L	TV WRITER	8955 BEVERLY BLVD	LOS ANGELES, CA 90048
SACKHEIM, JERRY	WRITER	3901 ETHEL AVE	NORTH HOLLYWOOD, CA 91604
SACKHEIM, WILLIAM	TV-FILM WRI-PROD	1118 TOWER RD	BEVERLY HILLS, CA 90210
SACKS, ALAN	WRITER-PRODUCER	20655 SHERMAN WY #51	CANOGA PARK, CA 91306
SACKS, EZRA M	SCREENWRITER	8955 BEVERLY BLVD	LOS ANGELES, CA 90048
SACKS, MICHAEL	ACTOR	151 S EL CAMINO DR	BEVERLY HILLS, CA 90212
SACKS, STEVEN R	CONDUCTOR	POST OFFICE BOX 6041	WOODLAND HILLS, CA 91365
SACRED, BILL	GUITARIST	311 SUMPTER AVE	BOWLING GREEN, KY 42101
SACRED FIRE	GOSPEL GROUP	POST OFFICE BOX 723591	ATLANTA, GA 30339
SACRED RITE	ROCK & ROLL GROUP	GREENWALD, 20445 GRAMERCY PL	TORRANCE, CA 90501
SACRIFICE	ROCK & ROLL GROUP	POST OFFICE BOX 2428	EL SEGUNDO, CA 90245
SAD CAFE	ROCK & ROLL GROUP	3 E 54TH ST #1400	NEW YORK, NY 10022
SADA, RALPH J	NEWS CORRESPONDENT	1000 WILSON BLVD	ALEXANDRIA, VA 22209
SADAKA, NEIL	SINGER-SONGWRITER	10 COLUMBUS CIR	NEW YORK, NY 10019
SADANE, MARC	SINGER	1697 BROADWAY #600	NEW YORK, NY 10019
SADDLER, JEANNE E	NEWS CORRESPONDENT	313 "T" ST, NW	WASHINGTON, DC 20001
SADE	SINGER-SONGWRITER	103 NORTIMER ST	LONDON W1 ENGLAND

Name	Occupation	Address	City/State	Zip/Country
SADEK, OSAMA	NEWS CORRESPONDENT	3802-A STEPPER CT	FALLS CHURCH, VA	22041
SADER, LUKE	TV DIRECTOR	ENTERTAINMENT TONIGHT		
		PARAMOUNT TELEVISION		
		5555 MELROSE AVE	LOS ANGELES, CA	90038
SADJADI, HADI	ACTOR	SCHOEMAN, 2600 W VICTORY BLVD	BURBANK, CA	91505
SADLER, BETH	WRITER-EDITOR	US MAGAZINE COMPANY		
		1 DAG HAMMARSKJOLD PLAZA	NEW YORK, NY	10017
SADLER, WILLIAM	ACTOR	9220 SUNSET BLVD #625	LOS ANGELES, CA	90069
SADOFF, FRED	ACTOR	CED, 261 S ROBERTSON BLVD	BEVERLY HILLS, CA	90211
SADOFF, ROBERT	FILM-TV PRODUCER	G B PLAYS, 50 HANS CRESCENT	LONDON SW1	ENGLAND
SADOVNIKOFF, MARY	FORTEPIANIST	ROSENFIELD, 714 LADD RD	BRONX, NY	10471
SADWITH, JAMES S	WRITER	2752 HALSEY RD	TOPANGA CANYON, CA	90290
SAETA, EDDIE	FILM DIRECTOR	DGA, 7950 SUNSET BLVD	HOLLYWOOD, CA	90046
SAETA, STEVEN	TV DIRECTOR	6628 E BUTTONWOOD AVE	AGOURA, CA	91301
SAFER, MORLEY	NEWS JOURNALIST	CBS NEWS, 51 W 52ND ST	NEW YORK, NY	10019
SAFFRON, JOHN	TV WRITER	555 W 57TH ST #1230	NEW YORK, NY	10019
SAFIR, LAWRENCE	FILM EXECUTIVE	TOWNSEND HOUSE, 22 DEAN ST	LONDON W1V 5AL	ENGLAND
SAFIR, SIDNEY	FILM EXECUTIVE	TOWNSEND HOUSE, 22 DEAN ST	LONDON W1V 5AL	ENGLAND
SAFIRE, WILLIAM	COLUMNIST-NEWS CORRES	6200 ELMWOOD RD	CHEVY CHASE, MD	20815
SAFRAN, DON	SCREENWRITER	8955 BEVERLY BLVD	LOS ANGELES, CA	90048
SAGA	ROCK & ROLL GROUP	41 BRITAIN ST #200	TORONTO, ONT	CANADA
SAGAL, BORIS	DIRECTOR	POST OFFICE BOX 889		
		PROSPECT HILLS STATION	STOCKBRIDGE, MA	01262
SAGAL, JEAN	ACTRESS	3800 BARHAM BLVD #303	LOS ANGELES, CA	90068
SAGAL, JOEY	ACTOR	17250 SUNSET BLVD #202	PACIFIC PALISADES, CA	90272
SAGAL, LIZ	ACTRESS	400 S BEVERLY DR #216	BEVERLY HILLS, CA	90212
SAGAN, CARL	ASTRONOMER-WRITER	BEN KUBASIK, 30 E 42ND ST	NEW YORK, NY	10017
SAGANSKY, JEFF	TV EXECUTIVE	NBC-TV, 3000 W ALAMEDA AVE	BURBANK, CA	91523
SAGE, DE WITT L, JR	WRITER-PRODUCER	271 CENTRAL PARK W	NEW YORK, NY	10024
SAGE, GREG	SINGER	POST OFFICE BOX 2896	TORRANCE, CA	90509
SAGE, LIZ	TV WRITER-PRODUCER	WITT/THOMAS PRODUCTIONS		
		1438 N GOWER ST, 4TH FLOOR	LOS ANGELES, CA	90028
SAGE, ROBERT	DIRECTOR	41523 MAY CREEK RD	SULTAN, WA	98294
SAGEBRUSH	VOCAL GROUP	POST OFFICE BOX O	EXCELSIOR, MN	55331
SAGENDORF, BUD	CARTOONIST	KING FEATURES SYNDICATE		
		235 E 45TH ST	NEW YORK, NY	10017
SAGER, CAROLE BAYER	SINGER-SONGWRITER	BACHARACH, 1465 DONHILL DR	BEVERLY HILLS, CA	90210
SAGER, CRAIG	SPORTSCASTER	3064 SPRING HILL RD	SMYRNA, GA	30080
SAGLE, CHARLES H	MUSIC ARRANGER	POST OFFICE BOX 41012	NASHVILLE, TN	37204
SAGOES, KEN	ACTOR	3151 W CAHUENGA BLVD #310	LOS ANGELES, CA	90068
SAGON, PATRICIA	NEWS CORRESPONDENT	4101 CATHEDRAL AVE, NW	WASHINGTON, DC	20016
SAHA, MARK	WRITER	2129 OCEAN AVE #5	SANTA MONICA, CA	90405
SAHL, MORT	COMEDIAN-WRITER	2325 SAN YSIDRO DR	BEVERLY HILLS, CA	90210
SAIDENBERG, DANIEL	CELLIST	980 5TH AVE	NEW YORK, NY	10021
SAIGER, SUSAN	ACTRESS	291 S LA CIENEGA BLVD	BEVERLY HILLS, CA	90211
SAIKOWSKI, CHARLOTTE	NEWS CORRESPONDENT	3101 NEW MEXICO AVE, NW	WASHINGTON, DC	20016
SAILER	VOCAL GROUP	GOOD, 2500 NW 39TH ST	OKLAHOMA CITY, OK	73112
SAILOR, CHARLES	AUTHOR	1474 QUEENS RD	LOS ANGELES, CA	90069
SAINT, EVA MARIE	ACTRESS	10590 WILSHIRE BLVD #408	LOS ANGELES, CA	90024
SAINT CLAIR, BARRIE	FILM PRODUCER	GOLD CRYSTAL INTERNATIONL		
		NBS BUILDING, 1ST FLOOR		
		PIETERMARITZBURG 3201	NATAL	SOUTH AFRICA
SAINT JAMES, SUSAN	ACTRESS	MS MARLENE FAIT		
		854 N GENESEE AVE	LOS ANGELES, CA	90046
SAINT TROPEZ	ROCK & ROLL GROUP	PERLE, 4475 VINELAND AVE	STUDIO CITY, CA	91602
SAINT VITUS	ROCK & ROLL GROUP	POST OFFICE BOX 1	LAWNDALE, CA	90260
SAINT-PIERRE, RAYMOND	NEWS CORRESPONDENT	1667 34TH ST, NW	WASHINGTON, DC	20016
SAINTE-MARIE, BUFFY	SINGER-SONGWRITER	RURAL ROUTE #1, BOX 368	KAPAA, KAUAI, HI	96746
SAINTS, THE	RHYTHM & BLUES GROUP	TAYLOR, 2501 TALBOT AVE	LOUISVILLE, KY	40205
SAIRE, REBECCA	ACTRESS	LONDON MANAGEMENT, LTD		
		235-241 REGENT ST	LONDON W1A 2JT	ENGLAND
SAITO, BILL	ACTOR	8235 SANTA MONICA BLVD #202	LOS ANGELES, CA	90046
SAITO, JAMES	ACTOR	8235 SANTA MONICA BLVD #202	LOS ANGELES, CA	90046
SAJAK, PAT	TV HOST	MERV GRIFFIN PRODUCTIONS		
		"THE WHEEL OF FORTUNE"		
		1541 N VINE ST	HOLLYWOOD, CA	90028
SAJEM, JOHNNY	CARTOONIST	NEWS AMERICA SYNDICATE		
		1703 KAISER AVE	IRVINE, CA	92714
SAJNOVIC, JOVAN	CONDUCTOR	IAPR, KINCORA, BEER RD		
		SEATON	DEVON	ENGLAND
SAKAI, KOSUKE	NEWS CORRESPONDENT	5304 BANGOR DR	KENSINGTON, MD	20895
SAKAMOTO, DENNIS	ACTOR	121 N ROBERTSON BLVD #B	BEVERLY HILLS, CA	90211
SAKAMOTO, MASAAKI	NEWS CORRESPONDENT	18 TRAIL RIDGE CT	POTOMAC, MD	20854
SAKELLARIOU, GEORGE	GUITARIST	1182 MARKET ST #311	SAN FRANCISCO, CA	94102
SAKER, ANNE P	NEWS CORRESPONDENT	1629 COLUMBIA RD #210, NW	WASHINGTON, DC	20009
SAKI, EILEEN	ACTRESS	LIGHT, 113 N ROBERTSON BLVD	LOS ANGELES, CA	90048
SAKS, GENE	DIRECTOR-ACTOR	DGA, 110 W 57TH ST	NEW YORK, NY	10019
SAKS, GIDON	BARITONE	JCB, 155 W 68TH ST	NEW YORK, NY	10023
SAKS, SOL	WRITER	14623 SUTTON ST	SHERMAN OAKS, CA	91403
SAKS, STUART M	WRESTLING WRITER	POST OFFICE BOX 48	ROCKVILLE CENTRE, NY	11571
SAKUMA, TOSHIYUKI	NEWS CORRESPONDENT	1633 WRIGHTSON DR	MC LEAN, VA	22101
SALA, SUSAN J	NEWS CORRESPONDENT	2605 39TH ST #102, NW	WASHINGTON, DC	20007
SALAMON, JULIE	FILM CRITIC	THE WALL ST JOURNAL		
		200 LIBERTY ST	NEW YORK, NY	10281
SALAMON, OTTO	TV WRITER	555 W 57TH ST #1230	NEW YORK, NY	10019

Name	Occupation	Address	City	Zip/Country
SALAND, RONALD	DIRECTOR	THE FILM COMPANY		
		9000 SUNSET BLVD	LOS ANGELES, CA	90069
SALANT, RICHARD	TV EXECUTIVE	NBC TELEVISION NETWORK		
		30 ROCKEFELLER PLAZA	NEW YORK, NY	10112
SALAS, HANK	ACTOR	247 S BEVERLY DR #102	BEVERLY HILLS, CA	90212
SALATA, GREGORY	ACTOR	10 E 44TH ST #700	NEW YORK, NY	10017
SALAZAR, ZORAYDA	SOPRANO	CAMI, 165 W 57TH ST	NEW YORK, NY	10019
SALCIDO, MICHAEL A	ACTOR	2936 YEARLING ST	LAKEWOOD, CA	90712
SALDANA, THERESA	ACTRESS	9229 SUNSET BLVD #611	LOS ANGELES, CA	90069
SALDITCH, MARTIN	NEWS CORRESPONDENT	14 10TH ST, NE	WASHINGTON, DC	20002
SALE, RICHARD	WRITER-PRODUCER	138 S CAMDEN DR #A	BEVERLY HILLS, CA	90212
SALE, RICHARD T	NEWS CORRESPONDENT	2123 CALIFORNIA ST, NW	WASHINGTON, DC	20008
SALE, VIRGINIA	ACTRESS	23388 MULHOLLAND DR	WOODLAND HILLS, CA	91364
SALEM, MURRAY	ACTOR	733 N KINGS RD #147	LOS ANGELES, CA	90069
SALEM, PAMELA	ACTRESS	MARTIN, 7 WINDMILL ST	LONDON W1P 1HF	ENGLAND
SALEM, RICHARD	ACTOR	14343 ADDISON ST #219	SHERMAN OAKS, CA	91423
SALEMNO, LOUIS	CONDUCTOR	CONE, 221 W 57TH ST	NEW YORK, NY	10019
SALERNO-SONNENBERG, NADJA	VIOLINIST	CAMI, 165 W 57TH ST	NEW YORK, NY	10019
SALES, SOUPY	ACT-COMED-WRI	245 E 35TH ST	NEW YORK, NY	10016
SALES, VICTORIA	NEWS REPORTER	TIME/TIME & LIFE BLDG		
		ROCKEFELLER CENTER	NEW YORK, NY	10020
SALINAS, ISAAC	TENOR	45 W 60TH ST #4-K	NEW YORK, NY	10023
SALINGER, DIANE	ACTRESS	211 S BEVERLY DR #201	BEVERLY HILLS, CA	90212
SALINGER, PIERRE	NEWS CORRESPONDENT	ABC-TV, 7 W 66TH ST	NEW YORK, NY	10023
SALINGER, PIERRE	NEWS CORRES-AUTHOR	248 RUE DE RIVOLI	PARIS 75001	FRANCE
SALISBURY, FRANK P	TV WRITER	3631 DIXIE CANYON PL	SHERMAN OAKS, CA	91423
SALK, DR JONAS	SCIENTIST	2444 ELLENTOWN RD	LA JOLLA, CA	92037
SALKIN, JAMES	TV DIRECTOR	209 E 25TH ST #4-C	NEW YORK, NY	10010
SALKIN, LEO	WRITER	3584 MULTIVIEW DR	LOS ANGELES, CA	90068
SALKIND, ALEXANDER	FILM PRODUCER	PINEWOOD STUDIOS, PINEWOOD RD		
		IVER HEATH	BUCKS SLO ONH	ENGLAND
SALKIND, ILYA	FILM PRODUCER	PINEWOOD STUDIOS, PINEWOOD RD		
		IVER HEATH	BUCKS SLO ONH	ENGLAND
SALKOW, SIDNEY	WRITER-PRODUCER	12336 ADDISON ST	NORTH HOLLYWOOD, CA	91607
SALKOWITZ, JOEL	DIRECTOR	DGA, 110 W 57TH ST	NEW YORK, NY	10019
SALKOWITZ, SY	WRITER-PRODUCER	21632 PACIFIC COAST HWY	MALIBU, CA	90265
SALLAN, BRUCE	TV PRODUCER	ABC-TV, 4151 PROSPECT AVE	LOS ANGELES, CA	90027
SALLE, DAVID	PAINTER	MARY BOONE GALLERY		
		417 W BROADWAY	NEW YORK, NY	10012
SALLEY, JERRY	SINGER-GUITARIST	320 MAPLE AVE	MADISON, TN	37115
SALLEY, RONALD	ACTOR	510 PACIFIC AVE #4	VENICE, CA	90291
SALLIN, ROBERT	DIRECTOR	1345 N WETHERLY DR	LOS ANGELES, CA	90069
SALLINGER, MATT	ACTOR	15760 VENTURA BLVD #1730	ENCINO, CA	91436
SALLIS, PETER	ACTOR	LONDON MANAGEMENT, LTD		
		235-241 REGENT ST	LONDON W1A 2JT	ENGLAND
SALLY & THE SOPHISTICATZ	ROCK & ROLL GROUP	25 HUNTINGTON AVE #420	BOSTON, MA	02116
SALLY THE FARMER'S DAUGHTER	WRESTLER	GORGEOUS GIRLS OF WRESTLING		
		DAVID B MC LANE PRODS		
		RIVIERA HOTEL & CASINO		
		2901 S LAS VEGAS BLVD	LAS VEGAS, NV	89109
SALMI, ALBERT	ACTOR	6310 SAN VICENTE BLVD #407	LOS ANGELES, CA	90048
SALMINEN, MATTI	SINGER	MARIEDL ANDERS ARTISTS MGMT		
		535 EL CAMINO DEL MAR ST	SAN FRANCISCO, CA	94121
SALMON, JOHN	PIANIST	ALPHA, 685 W END AVE	NEW YORK, NY	10025
SALMONS, JANE LEE	ACTRESS-MODEL	9255 SUNSET BLVD #510	LOS ANGELES, CA	90069
SALMORE, CHARLES	WRITER	828 7TH ST #A	SANTA MONICA, CA	90403
SALOB, LORIN	TV DIRECTOR	3819 MANDEVILLE CANYON RD	LOS ANGELES, CA	90049
SALOMON STRING QUARTET	STRING QUARTET	KAPLAN, 115 COLLEGE ST	BURLINGTON, VT	05401
SALONEN, ESA-PEKKA	CONDUCTOR	ICM, 40 W 57TH ST	NEW YORK, NY	10019
SALSOUL ORCHESTRA, THE	SOUL-DISCO ORCH	JOYCE AGENCY, 435 E 79TH ST	NEW YORK, NY	10021
SALT, JENNIFER	ACTRESS	10000 SANTA MONICA BLVD #305	LOS ANGELES, CA	90067
SALT CREEK	VOCAL GROUP	POST OFFICE BOX O	EXCELSIOR, MN	55331
SALTER, HANS J	COMPOSER-CONDUCTOR	3658 WOODHILL CYN RD	STUDIO CITY, CA	91604
SALTER, IVOR	ACTOR	PATRICK FREEMAN MANAGEMENT		
		4 CROMWELL GROVE, HAMMERSMITH	LONDON W6 7RG	ENGLAND
SALTER, JAMES	SCREENWRITER	8955 BEVERLY BLVD	LOS ANGELES, CA	90048
SALTER, JOYCE K	SCREENWRITER	8955 BEVERLY BLVD	LOS ANGELES, CA	90048
SALTHOUSE, JOHN	ACTOR	MC REDDIE, 4 PADDINGTON ST	LONDON W1	ENGLAND
SALTZMAN, ERIC F	DIRECTOR	155 RIVERSIDE DR	NEW YORK, NY	10024
SALTZMAN, HARRY	FILM PRODUCER	H M TENNENT, GLOBE THEATRE		
		SHAFTESBURY AVE, CONDON	LONDON W1	ENGLAND
SALTZMAN, JOSEPH	TV WRITER-PRODUCER	2116 VIA ESTUDILLO	PALOS VERDES, CA	90274
SALTZMAN, PHILIP	TV WRITER-PRODUCER	10530 GARWOOD PL	LOS ANGELES, CA	90024
SALUGA, BILL	ACTOR	230 S LUCERNE BLVD	LOS ANGELES, CA	90004
SALVADORI, ANTONIO	BARITONE	CAMI, 165 W 57TH ST	NEW YORK, NY	10019
SALVESEN, ARTHUR H	TV DIRECTOR	254 PARK AVE S #7-R	NEW YORK, NY	10010
SALVI, DELIA	ACTRESS	1132 N VISTA ST	LOS ANGELES, CA	90046
SALYER, RICK	GUITARIST	4701 LEBANON RD #130-D	HERMITAGE, TN	37076
SALZANO, CARLO J	NEWS CORRESPONDENT	5220 N CARLIN SPRINGS RD	ARLINGTON, VA	22203
SALZER, ALBERT J	DIRECTOR	DGA, 7950 SUNSET BLVD	LOS ANGELES, CA	90046
SALZMAN, BERTRAM	WRITER-PRODUCER	RUE DES PETITS PAS	PONTLEVOY 41400	FRANCE
SALZMAN, DAVID E	PUBLISHING EXECUTIVE	US MAGAZINE COMPANY		
		1 DAG HAMMARSKJOLD PLAZA	NEW YORK, NY	10017
SAM & DAVE	VOCAL DUO	J D BROWN, 300 W 55TH ST	NEW YORK, NY	10019
SAM THE SHAM	SINGER-SONGWRITER	SEE - SHAMUDO, SAM "THE SHAM"		

Name	Occupation	Address	City	Zip
SAMET, NORMAN	TV DIRECTOR	60 SUTTON PL S #7-BN	NEW YORK, NY	10022
SAMETH, JACK R	TV DIRECTOR-PRODUCER	220 E 73RD ST #1-C	NEW YORK, NY	10021
SAMGHABADI, RAJI	NEWS CORRESPONDENT	TIME/TIME & LIFE BLDG		
		ROCKEFELLER CENTER	NEW YORK, NY	10020
SAMMARTINO, BRUNO	WRESTLER-ANNOUNCER	POST OFFICE BOX 3859	STAMFORD, CT	06905
SAMMETH, BARBARA	ACTRESS	1508 GREENFIELD AVE	LOS ANGELES, CA	90025
SAMMETH, BILL	TV PRODUCER	KTTV-TV, 5746 SUNSET BLVD	HOLLYWOOD, CA	90028
SAMMS, EMMA	ACTRESS	POST OFFICE BOX 339	TUJUNGA, CA	91042
SAMMY, SCREAMING	COMEDIAN-ACTOR	SEE - KINISON, SCREAMING SAMMY		
SAMOAN, THE	WRESTLER	SEE - AFI, SIVA		
SAMPLE, JOE	MUSICIAN	8467 BEVERLY BLVD #100	LOS ANGELES, CA	90048
SAMPLER, PHILECE	ACTRESS	BLAISDELL, 641 N NAOMI ST	BURBANK, CA	91505
SAMPSELL, DAVE	PIANIST	420 WELSHWOOD DR #47	NASHVILLE, TN	37211
SAMPSON, DON	GUITARIST	ROUTE #4, BOYD MILL PIKE	FRANKLIN, TN	37064
SAMPSON, DON	SINGER	POST OFFICE BOX 84088	LOS ANGELES, CA	90073
SAMPSON, PAUL	NEWS CORRESPONDENT	4338 ALTON PL, NW	WASHINGTON, DC	20016
SAMPSON, R J "PADDY"	DIRECTOR	33 WOOD ST #1005	TORONTO, ONT	CANADA
SAMPSON, ROBERT	ACTOR	9255 SUNSET BLVD #1105	LOS ANGELES, CA	90069
SAMPSON & DELILAH	BODYBUILDERS	SEE - EVERSON, CORY & JEFF		
SAMPSON-PARR, MARY ANN	ACTRESS	3138 GRIFFITH PARK BLVD	LOS ANGELES, CA	90027
SAMPY, DAVID	PHOTOGRAPHER	2206 WINTERGREEN AVE	DISTRICT HEIGHTS, MD	20747
SAMROCK, VICTOR	THEATER PRODUCER	745 5TH AVE	NEW YORK, NY	10022
SAMSON, KURT J	NEWS CORRESPONDENT	10708 LESTER ST	SILVER SPRING, MD	20902
SAMUELS, PETER	TV WRITER	555 W 57TH ST #1230	NEW YORK, NY	10019
SAMUELS, RON	TALENT AGENT	120 S EL CAMINO DR #212	BEVERLY HILLS, CA	90212
SAMUELS, STEVE	PIANIST	9110 BROADWAY ST #M-101	SAN ANTONIO, TX	78217
SAMUELS, STU	TV EXECUTIVE	ABC-TV, 4151 PROSPECT AVE	LOS ANGELES, CA	90027
SAMUELSON, BETTY JEAN	ACTRESS	8721 SUNSET BLVD #103	LOS ANGELES, CA	90069
SAMUELSON, DAVID	FILM DIRECTOR	303-315 CRICKLEWOOD BRWY	LONDON NW2	ENGLAND
SAMUELSON, MICHAEL	FILM EXECUTIVE	4 ROXBOROUGH PARK		
		HARROW-ON-THE-HILL	MIDDLESEX	ENGLAND
SAMUELSON, PETER	FILM PRODUCER	10900 WILSHIRE BLVD #1400	LOS ANGELES, CA	90024
SAMUELSON, SYDNEY W	FILM EXECUTIVE	303 CRICKLEWOOD BROADWAY	LONDON NW2 6PQ	ENGLAND
SAMUL, JOSEPH	DIRECTOR	824 15TH ST #4	SANTA MONICA, CA	90403
SAN ANDRES, LUIS	WRITER-PRODUCER	28 CADMAN PLAZA W	BROOKLYN, NY	11201
SAN JOAQUIN	GUITARIST	1612 CITATION DR	NASHVILLE, TN	37212
SANAT, TERESA	NEWS CORRESPONDENT	4201 S 31ST ST #215	ARLINGTON, VA	22206
SANBORN, DAVID	SAXOPHONIST	9034 SUNSET BLVD #250	LOS ANGELES, CA	90069
SANBORN, KRISTINA	ACTRESS	2501 W BURBANK BLVD #304	BURBANK, CA	91505
SANCHEZ, CLARK	BODYBUILDER	PRO GYM FITNESS CENTER		
		322 MURIEL ST, NE	ALBUQUERQUE, NM	87123
SANCHEZ, JAIME	ACTOR	9255 SUNSET BLVD #510	LOS ANGELES, CA	90069
SANCHEZ, PATTY JOHNSON	BODYBUILDER	SEE - JOHNSON, PATTY-SANCHEZ		
SANCHEZ-LUNA, ALFREDO	TENOR	260 W END AVE #7-A	NEW YORK, NY	10023
SANCTON, THOMAS A	WRITER-EDITOR	TIME/TIME & LIFE BLDG		
		ROCKEFELLER CENTER	NEW YORK, NY	10020
SAND, ARLENE R	TV WRITER	8955 BEVERLY BLVD	LOS ANGELES, CA	90048
SAND, BARRY	TV PRODUCER	151 S EL CAMINO DR	BEVERLY HILLS, CA	90212
SAND, BARRY	TV PRODUCER	NBC TELEVISION NETWORK		
		30 ROCKEFELLER PLAZA	NEW YORK, NY	10112
SAND, FROMA	WRITER	1263 N HAYWORTH AVE #11	LOS ANGELES, CA	90046
SAND, H BARRY	WRITER	1145 LONGWOOD AVE	LOS ANGELES, CA	90019
SAND, LAUREN JOY	TV WRITER	12000 SALTAIR PL	LOS ANGELES, CA	90049
SAND, PAUL	ACTOR-COMEDIAN	2409 PANORAMA TERR	LOS ANGELES, CA	90039
SAND, ROBERT L	TV WRITER	2236 OVERLAND AVE #7	LOS ANGELES, CA	90064
SANDBAND, HENRY	PHOTOGRAPHER	24 NUTMEG DR	GREENWICH, CT	06830
SANDBANK, HENRY	DIRECTOR	105 E 16TH ST	NEW YORK, NY	10003
SANDBERG, BRENDA	NEWS CORRESPONDENT	1221 EDGEVALE RD	SILVER SPRING, MD	20919
SANDCASTLE	MUSICAL GROUP	POST OFFICE BOX 11283	RICHMOND, VA	23230
SANDEEN, DARRELL	ACTOR	12345 HUSTON ST	NORTH HOLLYWOOD, CA	91607
SANDEFUR, B W	TV WRITER	11166 VALLEY SPRING LN	NORTH HOLLYWOOD, CA	91602
SANDEFUR, DONALD DAVID	WRITER	11166 VALLEY SPRING LN	NORTH HOLLYWOOD, CA	91602
SANDEFUR, JAMES	GUITARIST	900 JONES ST	OLD HICKORY, TN	37138
SANDER, CASEY	ACTOR	13111 VENTURA BLVD #102	STUDIO CITY, CA	91604
SANDERFORD, JOHN	ACTOR	LIGHT, 113 N ROBERTSON BLVD	LOS ANGELES, CA	90048
SANDERLING, KURT	CONDUCTOR	MARIEDL ANDERS ARTISTS MGMT		
		535 EL CAMINO DEL MAR ST	SAN FRANCISCO, CA	94121
SANDERLING, THOMAS	CONDUCTOR	ICM, 40 W 57TH ST	NEW YORK, NY	10019
SANDERS, ALAIN L	NEWS REPORTER	TIME/TIME & LIFE BLDG		
		ROCKEFELLER CENTER	NEW YORK, NY	10020
SANDERS, BARBARA	ACTRESS	9040 HARRATT ST #5	LOS ANGELES, CA	90069
SANDERS, BEVERLY	ACTRESS	9220 SUNSET BLVD #202	LOS ANGELES, CA	90069
SANDERS, BILL	CARTOONIST	POST OFFICE BOX 661	MILWAUKEE, WI	53201
SANDERS, CHUCK	GUITARIST	4700 HUMBER DR #D-9	NASHVILLE, TN	37211
SANDERS, DENIS	FILM WRITER-DIRECTOR	5033 CAMPANILE DR	SAN DIEGO, CA	92115
SANDERS, DONALD	SAXOPHONIST	POST OFFICE BOX 270	NASHVILLE, TN	37221
SANDERS, DOUG	GOLFER	8828 SANDRINGHAM DR	HOUSTON, TX	77024
SANDERS, ELIZABETH	ACTRESS	15010 VENTURA BLVD #234	SHERMAN OAKS, CA	91403
SANDERS, HENRY G	ACTOR	15010 VENTURA BLVD #219	SHERMAN OAKS, CA	91403
SANDERS, JACQUELINE	ACTRESS	20 RESIDENCES DE LA COTE	MORGES 1110	SWITZERLAND
SANDERS, JAY O	ACTOR	165 W 46TH ST #409	NEW YORK, NY	10036
SANDERS, KELLY	ACTRESS	2151 GUTHRIE DR	LOS ANGELES, CA	90034
SANDERS, LINDA	ACTRESS	9000 SUNSET BLVD #1200	LOS ANGELES, CA	90069
SANDERS, MARILYN R	ACTRESS	5318 VANTAGE AVE #4	NORTH HOLLYWOOD, CA	91607
SANDERS, MARLENE	TV WRITER-DIRECTOR	175 RIVERSIDE DR	NEW YORK, NY	10024

BETTY JEAN SAMUELSON

TOMMY SANDS

CHRIS SARANDON

FATHER GUIDO SARDUCCI

BEVERLY SASSOON

JACK SCALIA

NATALIE SCHAFER

ROY SCHEIDER

MAXIMILIAN SCHELL

Name	Occupation	Address	City	Zip
SANDERS, NORMAN	NEWS REPORTER	THE NATIONAL ENQUIRER		
		600 SE COAST AVE	LANTANA, FL	33464
SANDERS, PHAROAH	SAXOPHONIST	KURLAND, 173 BRIGHTON AVE	BOSTON, MA	02134
SANDERS, RICHARD	ACTOR-WRITER	4954 STROHM AVE	NORTH HOLLYWOOD, CA	91601
SANDERS, RICHARD	WRITER	TIME & PEOPLE MAGAZINE		
		TIME & LIFE BUILDING		
		ROCKEFELLER CENTER	NEW YORK, NY	10020
SANDERS, RUBY TAYLOR	VIOLINIST	MERCURY MANOR #25, MERCURY BLVD	MURFREESBORO, TN	37130
SANDERS, TERRY B	FILM WRITER-DIRECTOR	339 ADELAIDE DR	SANTA MONICA, CA	90402
SANDERS, WAYNE	CARTOONIST	NEWS AMERICA SYNDICATE		
		1703 KAISER AVE	IRVINE, CA	92714
SANDERSON, JIM	COLUMNIST	7720 EL CAMINO REAL #2-C	RANCHO LA COSTA, CA	92008
SANDERSON, WILLIAM	ACTOR	10390 SANTA MONICA BLVD #310	LOS ANGELES, CA	90025
SANDESON, WILLIAM	CARTOONIST	119 W SHERWOOD TERR	FORT WAYNE, IN	46807
SANDFORD, CHRISTOPHER	ACTOR-SINGER	HOBO, 14 BREWER ST, 1ST FLOOR	LONDON W1	ENGLAND
SANDIN, CARL H	DIRECTOR	5857 N KENMORE AVE	CHICAGO, IL	60660
SANDLER, BARRY	SCREENWRITER	515 N HUNTLEY DR	LOS ANGELES, CA	90048
SANDLER, ELLEN	TV WRITER	8955 BEVERLY BLVD	LOS ANGELES, CA	90048
SANDLER, MALLORY	ACTRESS	1440 23RD ST #317	SANTA MONICA, CA	90404
SANDLER, ROGER	PHOTOGRAPHER	15963 VALLEY VISTA BLVD	ENCINO, CA	91436
SANDMANN, JEFFREY R	NEWS CORRESPONDENT	537 4TH ST, SE	WASHINGTON, DC	20003
SANDOR, GYORGY	PIANIST	GERSHUNOFF, 502 PARK AVE	NEW YORK, NY	10022
SANDOR, STEVE	ACTOR	9744 WILSHIRE BLVD #306	BEVERLY HILLS, CA	90212
SANDORA, SAM P	WRITER	7061 WHITSETT AVE #205	NORTH HOLLYWOOD, CA	91605
SANDOVAL, JOSE	PIANIST	POST OFFICE BOX 131	SPRINGFIELD, VA	22150
SANDOZ, DOLORES	ACTRESS	402 N PALM DR	BEVERLY HILLS, CA	90210
SANDRETTI, MARYANNE	NEWS CORRESPONDENT	400 N CAPITOL ST, NW	WASHINGTON, DC	20001
SANDRI, THOMAS	BASS	431 S DEARBORN ST #1504	CHICAGO, IL	60605
SANDRICH, JAY	ACTOR-DIRECTOR	1 NORTHSTAR ST #205	MARINA DEL REY, CA	90292
SANDS, B EDWIN	TV WRITER	8955 BEVERLY BLVD	LOS ANGELES, CA	90048
SANDS, BARBARA	ACTRESS	11030 VENTURA BLVD #3	STUDIO CITY, CA	91604
SANDS, HALLI	ACTRESS	12926 RIVERSIDE DR #C	SHERMAN OAKS, CA	91423
SANDS, JOHNNY	ACTOR	2333 KAPIOLANI BLVD	HONOLULU, HI	96814
SANDS, LANA	TV WRITER	8955 BEVERLY BLVD	LOS ANGELES, CA	90048
SANDS, PEGGY	MODEL	MODELS & PROMOTIONS AGENCY		
		8560 SUNSET BLVD, 10TH FLOOR	LOS ANGELES, CA	90069
SANDS, TOMMY	ACTOR-SINGER	511 HAHAIONE PL	HONOLULU, HI	96825
SANDS, TRACY B, JR	COMPOSER	1201 N LADERA VISTA DR	FULLERTON, CA	92631
SANDY, GARY	ACTOR	12810 WADDELL ST	NORTH HOLLYWOOD, CA	91607
SANDY, JERRY L	TV DIRECTOR	644 DARTMOUTH AVE	SAN CARLOS, CA	94070
SANDY, KEVEN M	NEWS CORRESPONDENT	4214 SELKIRK DR	FAIRFAX, VA	20032
SANFORD, ALAN H	TV DIRECTOR	524 HALSEY AVE	FOREST HILLS, PA	15221
SANFORD, ARLENE	TV WRITER-DIRECTOR	1425 STANFORD ST #9	SANTA MONICA, CA	90404
SANFORD, BILLY	GUITARIST	2616 PENNINGTON BEND RD	NASHVILLE, TN	37214
SANFORD, CHARLES	FILM DIRECTOR	430 N ORANGE DR	LOS ANGELES, CA	90036
SANFORD, DONALD S	TV WRITER	11515 AMANDA DR	NORTH HOLLYWOOD, CA	91604
SANFORD, GERALD	TV WRITER	9300 WILSHIRE BLVD #410	BEVERLY HILLS, CA	90212
SANFORD, GUYLAINE	ACTRESS	1605 N CAHUENGA BLVD #202	LOS ANGELES, CA	90028
SANFORD, ISABEL	ACTRESS	707 N ALTA DR	BEVERLY HILLS, CA	90210
SANFORD, MARK	CINEMATOGRAPHER	7715 SUNSET BLVD #150	LOS ANGELES, CA	90046
SANG, SAMANTHA	SINGER	200 W 51ST ST #1410	NEW YORK, NY	10019
SANGSTER, JIMMY	WRITER-PRODUCER	2049 CENTURY PARK E #1320	LOS ANGELES, CA	90067
SANK, LESLIE ALEXIS	ACTRESS	9255 SUNSET BLVD #510	LOS ANGELES, CA	90069
SANOFF, ALVIN P	NEWS CORRESPONDENT	5510 JOHNSON AVE	BETHESDA, MD	20817
SANOFF, JOEL R	WRITER	13429 MOORPARK ST #L	SHERMAN OAKS, CA	91423
SANSBURY, TIMOTHY	NEWS CORRESPONDENT	710-A S 15TH ST	ARLINGTON, VA	22202
SANSOM, ART	CARTOONIST	1050 EIRE CLIFF DR	CLEVELAND, OH	44107
SANSOM, KEN	ACTOR	10000 RIVERSIDE DR #3	TOLUCA LAKE, CA	91602
SANTA ESMERALDA	ROCK & ROLL GROUP	AMUSEX, 970 O'BRIEN DR	MENLO PARK, CA	94025
SANTA MARIA, MONGO	CONGO DRUMMER	HOOKE, 78-08 223RD ST	BAYSIDE, NY	11364
SANTANA	ROCK & ROLL GROUP	POST OFFICE BOX 1994	SAN FRANCISCO, CA	94101
SANTANA, TITO	WRESTLER	POST OFFICE BOX 3859	STAMFORD, CT	06905
SANTEE, CLARK K	DIRECTOR-PRODUCER	774 VILLAGE RD W	LAWRENCEVILLE, NJ	08648
SANTERS, THE	ROCK & ROLL GROUP	41 BRITAIN ST #200	TORONTO, ONT	CANADA
SANTI, NELLO	CONDUCTOR	61 W 62ND ST #6-F	NEW YORK, NY	10023
SANTIAGO, ERNIE	BODYBUILDER	67-658 KUHE PL	WAIALUA, HI	96791
SANTILLAN, ANTONIO	DIRECTOR-PRODUCER	425 N ALFRED ST	LOS ANGELES, CA	90048
SANTING, MATHILDE	SINGER-PIANIST	GRAMAVISION RECORDS		
		260 W BROADWAY	NEW YORK, NY	10013
SANTINI, JEAN-LOUIS	NEWS CORRESPONDENT	4400 EAST-WEST HWY	BETHESDA, MD	20814
SANTINI, MAUREEN	NEWS CORRESPONDENT	3900 TUNLAW RD #513, NW	WASHINGTON, DC	20007
SANTO, MARK	WRITER	9220 SUNSET BLVD #202	LOS ANGELES, CA	90069
SANTO & JOHNNY	VOCAL DUO	OLDIES, 5218 ALMONT ST	LOS ANGELES, CA	90032
SANTON, PENNY	ACTRESS	1918 N EDGEMONT ST	LOS ANGELES, CA	90027
SANTONI, RENI	ACTOR	802 N SWEETZER AVE #102	LOS ANGELES, CA	90069
SANTOS, JOE	ACTOR	12750 VENTURA BLVD #102	STUDIO CITY, CA	91604
SANTOS, LORI	NEWS CORRESPONDENT	417 "A" ST, NE	WASHINGTON, DC	20002
SANTOS, MISHAY	BODYBUILDER	GOLD'S GYM, 360 HAMPTON DR	VENICE, CA	90291
SANTOS, MOACIR	COMPOSER	1946 LAYTON ST	PASADENA, CA	91104
SANTOS, STEVEN J	DIRECTOR	900 HIGHLAND AVE #7	MANHATTAN BEACH, CA	90266
SANTOS, TURIBIO	GUITARIST	BYERS-SCHWALBE, 1 5TH AVE	NEW YORK, NY	10003
SANUCCI, FRANK	COMPOSER	226 N NAOMI ST	BURBANK, CA	91505
SANZ, MARIA	NEWS CORRESPONDENT	1612 "K" ST #400, NW	WASHINGTON, DC	20006
SAPERSTEIN, DAVID A	DIRECTOR	16 CALTON LN	NEW ROCHELLE, NY	10804
SAPERSTEIN, HENRY	FILM-TV PRODUCER	545 ARKELL DR	BEVERLY HILLS, CA	90210

SAPHIER, PETER	FILM PRODUCER	1800 CENTURY PARK E #1100	LOS ANGELES, CA	90067
SAPINSLEY, ALVIN	TV WRITER	15029 GREENLEAF ST	SHERMAN OAKS, CA	91403
SAPINSLEY, BARBARA	TV WRITER	555 W 57TH ST #1230	NEW YORK, NY	10019
SAPIRSTEIN, LISBETH	NEWS CORRESPONDENT	1308 27TH ST, NW	WASHINGTON, DC	20007
SAPPHO, FRED	SCREENWRITER	8955 BEVERLY BLVD	LOS ANGELES, CA	90048
SARACENO, CAROL	TV WRITER	1900 AVE OF THE STARS #2535	LOS ANGELES, CA	90067
SARAFIAN, RICHARD C	ACTOR	10000 SANTA MONICA BLVD #305	LOS ANGELES, CA	90067
SARAFIAN, RICHARD C	DIRECTOR	11901 SUNSET BLVD #203	LOS ANGELES, CA	90049
SARANDON, CHRIS	ACTOR	147 W 79TH ST #16-B	NEW YORK, NY	10024
SARANDON, SUSAN	ACTRESS	25 E 9TH ST	NEW YORK, NY	10019
SARASOHN, CAROL	TV WRITER	30603 RAYO DEL SOL DR	MALIBU, CA	90265
SARASOHN, LANE	TV WRITER	30603 RAYO DEL SOL DR	MALIBU, CA	90265
SARASTE, JUKKA-PEKKA	CONDUCTOR	SHAW CONCERTS, 1995 BROADWAY	NEW YORK, NY	10023
SARAZAN, GENE	GOLFER	EMERALD BEACH, BOX 677	MARCO, FL	33937
SARAZIN, KALI	MODEL	POST OFFICE BOX 7211	MOUNTAIN VIEW, CA	94043
SARDINERO, VICENTE	BARITONE	61 W 62ND ST #6-F	NEW YORK, NY	10023
SARGENT, ALVIN	WRITER	2950 NEILSON WY #504-A	SANTA MONICA, CA	90405
SARGENT, ANTHONY H	NEWS CORRESPONDENT	ABC-TV, NEWS DEPARTMENT		
		1717 DE SALES ST, NW	WASHINGTON, DC	20036
SARGENT, BEN	CARTOONIST	UNIVERSAL PRESS SYNDICATE		
		4900 MAIN ST, 9TH FLOOR	KANSAS CITY, MO	62114
SARGENT, BILL	THEATER PRODUCER	SPECIAL EVENTS ENTS		
		502 PARK AVE	NEW YORK, NY	10022
SARGENT, DICK	ACTOR	7422 PALO VISTA DR	LOS ANGELES, CA	90046
SARGENT, EDWARD D	NEWS CORRESPONDENT	2215 BUNKER HILL RD, NE	WASHINGTON, DC	20018
SARGENT, HERB	TV WRITER	555 W 57TH ST #1230	NEW YORK, NY	10019
SARGENT, JOSEPH	DIRECTOR-PRODUCER	33740 PACIFIC COAST HWY	MALIBU, CA	90265
SARGENT, MICHAEL DUANE	PHOTOGRAPHER	10636 MONTROSE AVE	BETHESDA, MD	20814
SARGENT, ROBERT	GUITARIST	908 DAVIDSON DR B	NASHVILLE, TN	37205
SARGOUS, HARRY	OBOIST	200 W 70TH ST #7-F	NEW YORK, NY	10023
SARIEGO, RALPH	DIRECTOR-PRODUCER	25682 MONTE NIDO DR	CALABASAS, CA	91302
SARLATTE, BOB	NEW CORRESPONDENT	ENTERTAINMENT THIS WEEK		
		PARAMOUNT TELEVISION		
		5555 MELROSE AVE	LOS ANGELES, CA	90038
SARNE, MICHAEL	ACT-WRI-DIR	61 CAMPDEN HILL TOWERS	LONDON W11	ENGLAND
SARNO, JOHN	ACTOR	427 N CANON DR #205	BEVERLY HILLS, CA	90210
SARNO, JOHNNY	ACTOR	8741 ROSEWOOD AVE	LOS ANGELES, CA	90048
SARNO, ROBERT A	SCREENWRITER	8955 BEVERLY BLVD	LOS ANGELES, CA	90048
SAROYAN, HANK D	DIRECTOR	DGA, 7950 SUNSET BLVD	LOS ANGELES, CA	90046
SAROYAN, LUCY	ACTRESS	11915 KLING ST #15	NORTH HOLLYWOOD, CA	91607
SARRACINO, ERNEST	ACTOR	9601 WILSHIRE BLVD #GL-11	BEVERLY HILLS, CA	90210
SARRADET, RICHARD	ACTOR	142 SAN VICENTE BLVD #C	SANTA MONICA, CA	90402
SARRAZIN, MICHAEL	ACTOR	9920 BEVERLY GROVE DR	BEVERLY HILLS, CA	90210
SARRIS, ANDREW	FILM CRITIC	19 E 88TH ST	NEW YORK, NY	10028
SARRY, CHRISTINE	BALLERINA	890 BROADWAY	NEW YORK, NY	10003
SARSON, CHRISTOPHER	WRITER-PRODUCER	223 TENAFLY RD	ENGLEWOOD, NJ	07631
SARTAIN, GAILARD	ACTOR-WRITER	9255 SUNSET BLVD #610	LOS ANGELES, CA	90069
SARTAIN, GRADY	BANJOIST	1005 IVERSON ST	NASHVILLE, TN	37216
SASAKI, KEN	PIANIST	POST OFFICE BOX U	REDDING, CT	06875
SASDY, PETER	FILM-TV DIRECTOR	REDWAY, 16 BERNERS ST	LONDON W1	ENGLAND
SASE, MORIYOSHI	NEWS CORRESPONDENT	1831 RUPERT ST	MC LEAN, VA	22101
SASS, SYLVIA	SOPRANO	CAMI, 165 W 57TH ST	NEW YORK, NY	10019
SASSER, LARRY	GUITARIST	249 LOOKOUT DR	OLD HICKORY, TN	37138
SASSON, DEBORAH	SOPRANO	CAMI, 165 W 57TH ST	NEW YORK, NY	10019
SASSON, MICHAEL	CONDUCTOR	305 DEAN RD	BROOKLINE, MA	02146
SASSOON, BEVERLY ADAMS	ACTRESS-MODEL	738 N HOLMBY AVE	LOS ANGELES, CA	90024
SASSOON, CATYA	ACTRESS	738 N HOLMBY AVE	LOS ANGELES, CA	90024
SASSOON, VIDAL	HAIR STYLIST	279 S BEVERLY DR #1066	BEVERLY HILLS, CA	90212
SATANI DEMON	FIRE JUMPER	POST OFFICE BOX 87	WEST LEBANON, NY	12195
SATLOFF, RONALD	TV DIRECTOR-PRODUCER	15301 VENTURA BLVD #345	SHERMAN OAKS, CA	91403
SATO, KINYA	NEWS CORRESPONDENT	6000 CHATSWORTH LN	BETHESDA, MD	20814
SATTERFIELD, FRED	DRUMMER	243 IRIS DR	HENDERSONVILLE, TN	37075
SATTERLEE, RICHARD	ACTOR	4253 SHEPHERDS LN	LA CANADA, CA	91011
SATURDAY NIGHT BAND, THE	VOCAL GROUP	GOOD, 2500 NW 39TH ST	OKLAHOMA CITY, OK	73112
SAUER, ERNEST G	DIRECTOR	330 W 42ND ST		
		PENTHOUSE FLOOR	NEW YORK, NY	10036
SAUER, LEO	ACTOR	2832 WAVERLY DR	LOS ANGELES, CA	90039
SAUER, RICHARD C	SCREENWRITER	8955 BEVERLY BLVD	LOS ANGELES, CA	90048
SAUERS, CHARLES	CARTOONIST	POST OFFICE BOX 4203	NEW YORK, NY	10017
SAUL, OSCAR	SCREENWRITER	448 HILGARD AVE	LOS ANGELES, CA	90024
SAUNDERS, BARBARA	NEWS CORRESPONDENT	3209 N NOTTINGHAM ST	ARLINGTON, VA	22207
SAUNDERS, CARL R	COMPOSER	6506 BEN AVE	NORTH HOLLYWOOD, CA	91606
SAUNDERS, HERMAN S	TV PRODUCER	3551 VISTA HAVEN RD	SHERMAN OAKS, CA	91403
SAUNDERS, JAMES	PLAYWRIGHT	MARGARET RAMSAY, LTD		
		14-A GOODWINS CT		
		SAINT MARTINS LN	LONDON WC2N 4LL	ENGLAND
SAUNDERS, JOHN	CARTOONIST	NEWS AMERICA SYNDICATE		
		1703 KAISER AVE	IRVINE, CA	92714
SAUNDERS, JUDITH	DIRECTOR	DGA, 7950 SUNSET BLVD	LOS ANGELES, CA	90046
SAUNDERS, LANNA	ACTRESS	15033 ENCANTO DR	SHERMAN OAKS, CA	91403
SAUNDERS, NICHOLAS	ACTOR	175 W 72ND ST	NEW YORK, NY	10023
SAUNDERS, PAMELA ANNE	MODEL	MODELS & PROMOTIONS AGENCY		
		8560 SUNSET BLVD, 10TH FLOOR	LOS ANGELES, CA	90069
SAUNDERS, PATRICIA	NEWS CORRESPONDENT	4616 SEDGWICK ST, NW	WASHINGTON, DC	20016
SAUNDERS, TOM	TV WRITER	8955 BEVERLY BLVD	LOS ANGELES, CA	90048

Name	Occupation	Address	City/State	Zip
SAUNDERS, WYN	ACTRESS	6404 HOLLYWOOD BLVD #800	LOS ANGELES, CA	90048
SAUNDERS & ZIEGLER	CARTOONISTS	NEWS AMERICA SYNDICATE		
		1703 KAISER AVE	IRVINE, CA	92714
SAURO, WILLIAM E	PHOTOGRAPHER	217 KENDALL RD	KENDALL PARK, NJ	08824
SAUTER, JOHN, BAND	ROCK & ROLL GROUP	VARIETY ARTISTS INTL, INC		
		9073 NEMO ST, 3RD FLOOR	LOS ANGELES, CA	90069
SAUTER, VAN GORDON	TV EXECUTIVE	CBS NEWS, 51 W 52ND ST	NEW YORK, NY	10019
SAUTTER, CARL G	TV WRITER	2151 N BEACHWOOD DR	LOS ANGELES, CA	90068
SAUTTER, WILLIAM H	NEWS CORRESPONDENT	1919 WESTMORELAND ST	MC LEAN, VA	22101
SAUVAGNARUES, PHILIPPE	NEWS CORRESPONDENT	4711 ELLICOTT ST, NW	WASHINGTON, DC	20016
SAVADOVE, LAURENCE	WRITER-PRODUCER	7420 FRANKLIN AVE	LOS ANGELES, CA	90046
SAVAGE, CLARK	ACTOR	6237 CARPENTIER AVE	NORTH HOLLYWOOD, CA	91606
SAVAGE, DOMINIC	ACTOR-DIRECTOR	21 EATON RD, MARGATE	KENT CT9 1XB	ENGLAND
SAVAGE, GAIL, BAND	ROCK & ROLL GROUP	POST OFFICE BOX 1600	HAVERHILL, MA	01831
SAVAGE, JOHN	ACTOR	ICM, 8899 BEVERLY BLVD	LOS ANGELES, CA	90048
SAVAGE, JUDITH	AGENT	6212 BANNER AVE	LOS ANGELES, CA	90038
SAVAGE, KIM	ACTRESS	6605 HOLLYWOOD BLVD #220	HOLLYWOOD, CA	90028
SAVAGE, NICK	ACTOR	13111 VENTURA BLVD #102	STUDIO CITY, CA	91604
SAVAGE, PAUL	TV WRITER	8955 BEVERLY BLVD	LOS ANGELES, CA	90048
SAVAGE, PETER	WRITER-PRODUCER	2803 WEEKS AVE	OCEANSIDE, NY	11572
SAVAGE, RANDY "MACHO MAN"	WRESTLER	POST OFFICE BOX 1438	GREENWICH, CT	06830
SAVAGE, TRACIE	ACTRESS	6212 BANNER AVE	LOS ANGELES, CA	90038
SAVAGE, YVONNE	UNICYCLE JUMPER	HALL, 138 FROG HOLLOW RD	CHURCHVILLE, PA	18966
SAVAGE GRACE	ROCK & ROLL GROUP	232 S REEVES DR #101	BEVERLY HILLS, CA	90212
SAVAGLIO, TED C	WRITER	538 S LA JOLLA AVE	LOS ANGELES, CA	90048
SAVALAS, CANDACE	ACTRESS	6605 HOLLYWOOD BLVD #220	HOLLYWOOD, CA	90028
SAVALAS, TELLY	ACT-WRI-DIR	SHERATON UNIVERSAL HOTEL		
		333 UNIVERSAL CITY PLAZA	UNIVERSAL CITY, CA	91608
SAVANNAH JACK	WRESTLER	UNIVERSAL WRESTLING FEDERATION		
		MID SOUTH SPORTS, INC		
		5001 SPRING VALLEY RD	DALLAS, TX	75244
SAVANT, DOUG	ACTOR	9601 WILSHIRE BLVD #GL-11	BEVERLY HILLS, CA	90210
SAVASTANO, ANTONIO	TENOR	61 W 62ND ST #6-F	NEW YORK, NY	10023
SAVATAGE	ROCK & ROLL GROUP	ROBERT ZEMSKY, AMI PRODUCTIONS		
		1776 BROADWAY, 10TH FLOOR	NEW YORK, NY	10019
SAVENICK, PHILLIP ADAM	TV WRITER	8064 WILLOW GLEN RD	LOS ANGELES, CA	90046
SAVIANO, PAT	DIRECTOR	7901 W BLOOMINGDALE	ELMWOOD PARK, IL	60635
SAVIDGE, JENNIFER	ACTRESS	2108 N BEVERLY GLEN BLVD	LOS ANGELES, CA	90077
SAVILLE, DAVID	ACTOR	55 GOODHALL ST	LONDON NW10 6TT	ENGLAND
SAVILLE, PHILIP	TV WRITER-DIRECTOR	DOUGLAS RAE MANAGEMENT		
		28 CHARING CROSS RD	LONDON WC2	ENGLAND
SAVITZ, CHARLOTTE	PRODUCER	7800 BEVERLY BLVD #3371	LOS ANGELES, CA	90036
SAVOLDI, JUMPING JOE	WRESTLER	UNIVERSAL WRESTLING FEDERATION		
		MID SOUTH SPORTS, INC		
		116 W BRECKINRIDGE	BIXBY, OK	74008
SAVOVA, GALINA	SOPRANO	CAMI, 165 W 57TH ST	NEW YORK, NY	10019
SAVOY BROWN	ROCK & ROLL GROUP	DMA, 17650 W 12 MILE RD	SOUTHFIELD, MI	48076
SAWAYA, GEORGE C	ACTOR	4041 GOODLAND AVE	STUDIO CITY, CA	91604
SAWAYA, GEORGE R	ACTOR	5648 RIVERTON AVE	NORTH HOLLYWOOD, CA	91601
SAWISLAK, ARNOLD B	NEWS CORRESPONDENT	1414 17TH ST #803, NW	WASHINGTON, DC	20036
SAWMILL CREEK	VOCAL GROUP	LST, 2138 FLAG MARSH RD	MOUNT AIRY, MD	21771
SAWYER, BEVERLY M	FILM EDITOR	1523 CRENSHAW BLVD	LOS ANGELES, CA	90019
SAWYER, CONNIE	ACTRESS	AIMEE, 13743 VICTORY BLVD	VAN NUYS, CA	91401
SAWYER, DEL	MUSIC ARRANGER	4400 BELMONT PARK TERR #204	NASHVILLE, TN	37215
SAWYER, DIANE	BROADCAST JOURNALIST	CBS NEWS, 524 W 57TH ST	NEW YORK, NY	10019
SAWYER, FORREST	TV HOST	CBS MORNING NEWS		
		51 W 52ND ST	NEW YORK, NY	10019
SAWYER, JON M	NEWS CORRESPONDENT	2915 PORTER ST, NW	WASHINGTON, DC	20008
SAWYER, KATHY	NEWS CORRESPONDENT	820 "A" ST, SE	WASHINGTON, DC	20003
SAWYER, LESLIE	NEWS CORRESPONDENT	1825 "K" ST, NW	WASHINGTON, DC	20006
SAWYER, THOMAS B	WRITER-PRODUCER	25301 MALIBU RD	MALIBU, CA	90265
SAWYER, TONI	ACTRESS	6736 LAUREL CANYON BLVD #306	NORTH HOLLYWOOD, CA	91606
SAX, GEOFFREY	TV DIRECTOR	4 KINGS-WELL, HEATH ST	LONDON NW3	ENGLAND
SAX, STEVE	BASEBALL	11 WESTPORT	MANHATTAN BEACH, CA	90266
SAXON	ROCK & ROLL GROUP	POST OFFICE BOX 69	WOLVERHAMPTON WV6 9AQ	ENGLAND
SAXON, CHARLES	CARTOONIST	POST OFFICE BOX 4203	NEW YORK, NY	10017
SAXON, ERIC	SINGER	1209 BAYLOR ST	AUSTIN, TX	78703
SAXON, JOHN	ACTOR-WRITER	2432 BANYAN DR	LOS ANGELES, CA	90049
SAXON, SKY "SUNLIGHT"	SINGER-GUITARIST	POST OFFICE BOX 1984	KAILUA, HI	96734
SAXON, STEPHEN	BASSO-BARITONE	ICM, 40 W 57TH ST	NEW YORK, NY	10019
SAXTON, BOB	GUITARIST	POST OFFICE BOX 1258	HENDERSONVILLE, TN	37075
SAXTON, JOHN C	SCREENWRITER	8955 BEVERLY BLVD	LOS ANGELES, CA	90048
SAYEGH, JAMES N	DIRECTOR	563 5TH ST	BROOKLYN, NY	11215
SAYER, CYNTHIA & THE NEW YORK B	BANJO ENSEMBLE	POST OFFICE BOX 12403		
		NORTHSIDE STATION	ATLANTA, GA	30355
SAYER, LEO	SINGER-SONGWRITER	151 S EL CAMINO DR	BEVERLY HILLS, CA	90212
SAYERS, GALE	FOOTBALL	624 BUCH RD	NORTHBROOK, IL	60062
SAYERS, PETER	GUITARIST	ROSEWOOD HOUSE, WOODITTON RD		
		NEWMARKET	SUFFOLK CB8 9BQ	ENGLAND
SAYLE, ALEXEL	ACT-WRI-COMED	ICM, 388-396 OXFORD ST	LONDON W1	ENGLAND
SAYLES, JOHN T	WRITER-PRODUCER	DGA, 110 W 57TH ST	NEW YORK, NY	10019
SAYLOR, LAURA	ACTRESS	8230 BEVERLY BLVD #23	LOS ANGELES, CA	90048
SAYLOR, ROGER	BARITONE	POST OFFICE BOX 884	NEW YORK, NY	10023
SAYLOR, STEPHEN	ACTOR	6331 HOLLYWOOD BLVD #924	LOS ANGELES, CA	90028
SAYRE, DAVID	NEWS CORRESPONDENT	3434 SURREY LN	FALLS CHRUCH, VA	22042

Name	Occupation	Address	City	ZIP
SBARDELLATI, JIM	PRODUCER	2246 EDENDALE PL	LOS ANGELES, CA	90039
SCACCHI, GRETA	ACTRESS	HEATH, PARAMOUNT HOUSE 162-170 WARDOUR ST	LONDON W1V 3AT	ENGLAND
SCADUTO, AL	CARTOONIST	KING FEATURES SYNDICATE 235 E 45TH ST	NEW YORK, NY	10017
SCAGGS, BOZ	SINGER-SONGWRITER	FRONT LINE MANAGEMENT 80 UNIVERSAL CITY PLAZA	UNIVERSAL CITY, CA	91608
SCALA, TINA	ACTRESS	915 ARIZONA AVE #7	SANTA MONICA, CA	90401
SCALERA, MICHAEL	ACTOR	ABC-TV, "ALL MY CHILDREN" 1330 AVE OF THE AMERICAS	NEW YORK, NY	10019
SCALES, HARVEY	SINGER	8467 BEVERLY BLVD #112	LOS ANGELES, CA	90048
SCALES, PRUNELLA	ACTRESS	46 NORTHSIDE, WANDSWORTH COMMON	LONDON SW18 2SL	ENGLAND
SCALES, TOM	TV CRITIC	THE WASHINGTON POST 1150 15TH ST, NW	WASHINGTON, DC	20071
SCALETTA, SUE ELLYN	NEWS CORRESPONDENT	8934 CENTRAL PARK DR	ALEXANDRIA, VA	22309
SCALIA, JACK T	ACTOR	1888 CENTURY PARK E #1400	LOS ANGELES, CA	90067
SCALICI, JACK	ACTOR	7215 HILLSIDE AVE #27	HOLLYWOOD, CA	90046
SCALLY, WILLIAM F	NEWS CORRESPONDENT	2918 LEGATION ST, NW	WASHINGTON, DC	20015
SCANCARELLI, JIM	CARTOONIST	TRIBUNE MEDIA SERVICES 64 E CONCORD ST	ORLANDO, FL	32801
SCANLAN, DANIEL O	NEWS CORRESPONDENT	1755 S JEFFERSON DAVIS HWY	ARLINGTON, VA	22202
SCANLAN, JOSEPH L	DIRECTOR	14004 PALAWAN WY #314	MARINA DEL REY, CA	90292
SCANLAN, MARY ANN & KRISTY ANN	ACROBATIC DUO	HALL, 138 FROG HOLLOW RD	CHURCHVILLE, PA	18966
SCANLON, JAMES	ACTOR	1521 N SIERRA BONITA AVE	LOS ANGELES, CA	90046
SCANLON, JOHN G	ACTOR	247 S BEVERLY DR #102	BEVERLY HILLS, CA	90210
SCANNELL, KEVIN	ACTOR	11726 SAN VICENTE BLVD #300	LOS ANGELES, CA	90049
SCANNELL, SUSAN	ACTRESS	113 N SAN VICENTE BLVD #202	BEVERLY HILLS, CA	90211
SCANTLIN, CLIFFORD R	WRITER	3747 LATROBE ST	LOS ANGELES, CA	90031
SCARABELLI, ADELINA	SOPRANO	CAMI, 165 W 57TH ST	NEW YORK, NY	10019
SCARABELLI, MICHELLE	ACTRESS	HENDERSON, 405 W 44TH ST	NEW YORK, NY	10036
SCARBER, SAM	ACTOR	12209 CREWE ST	NORTH HOLLYWOOD, CA	91605
SCARBOROUGH, CHARLES	BROADCAST JOURNALIST	NBC TELEVISION NETWORK 30 ROCKEFELLER PLAZA	NEW YORK, NY	10112
SCARBOROUGH, JOHN	FILM EXECUTIVE	61 CONDUIT ST	LONDON W1R 9FD	ENGLAND
SCARBURY, JOEY	SINGER-SONGWRITER	LAVENDER, 444 2ND AVE	SEASIDE, OR	97138
SCARDINO, DON	ACTOR	NBC TELEVISION NETWORK 30 ROCKEFELLER PLAZA	NEW YORK, NY	10112
SCARPACI, PHIL	ACTOR	6909 LASAINE AVE	VAN NUYS, CA	91406
SCARPELLI, GLENN	ACTOR	9220 SUNSET BLVD #625	LOS ANGELES, CA	90069
SCARWID, DIANA	ACTRESS	POST OFFICE BOX 3614	SAVANNAH, GA	31404
SCARZA, VINCENT J	DIRECTOR-PRODUCER	FADO, 145 E 15TH ST	NEW YORK, NY	10003
SCATES, JOE	RECORD EXECUTIVE	POST OFFICE BOX 12353	SAN ANTONIO, TX	78212
SCATMAN, THE	GOLFER-STUD	SEE - THOMPSON, SCOTT "THE SCATMAN"		
SCATTERDAY, PAUL	ACTOR	6040 CARLOS AVE #5	LOS ANGELES, CA	90028
SCATTINI, BEN	ACTOR	6461 KESTER AVE #11	VAN NUYS, CA	91411
SCAVULLO, FRANCESCO	PHOTOGRAPHER	212 E 63RD ST	NEW YORK, NY	10021
SCHAAD, DR MICHAEL	PHILOSOPHER	2801 MEADOW LARK DR	SAN DIEGO, CA	92123
SCHAADT, JAMES G	DIRECTOR	POST OFFICE BOX 173	COTUIT, MA	02635
SCHAAF, EDWARD	ACTOR	1350 N HIGHLAND AVE #24	HOLLYWOOD, CA	90028
SCHAAL, RICHARD	ACT-WRI-DIR	8721 SUNSET BLVD #200	LOS ANGELES, CA	90069
SCHAAL, WENDY	ACTRESS	POST OFFICE BOX 5617	BEVERLY HILLS, CA	90210
SCHACHT, ROSE A	TV WRITER	8955 BEVERLY BLVD	LOS ANGELES, CA	90048
SCHACHTER, JANINE	ACTRESS	SUZELLE, 182-06 MIDLAND PKWY	JAMAICA, NY	11432
SCHACHTER, SIMONE	ACTRESS	SUZELLE, 182-06 MIDLAND PKWY	JAMAICA, NY	11432
SCHACTER, FELICE	ACTRESS	POST OFFICE BOX 6547	FRESH MEADOWS, NY	11365
SCHAEFER, EDWARD A	NEWS CORRESPONDENT	1600 S EADS ST #924-N	ALEXANDRIA, VA	22202
SCHAEFER, GEORGE	TV DIRECTOR-PRODUCER	1040 WOODLAND DR	BEVERLY HILLS, CA	90210
SCHAEFER, HAL	COMPOSER	11 DERBY RD	PORT WASHINGTON, NY	11050
SCHAEFER, LUCINDA A	NEWS CORRESPONDENT	1746 EUCLID ST, NW	WASHINGTON, DC	20009
SCHAEFER, TERI	NEWS CORRESPONDENT	3446 MILDRED DR	FALLS CHURCH, VA	22042
SCHAEFER, WILLIS H	COMPOSER-CONDUCTOR	10850 RIVERSIDE DR #505	NORTH HOLLYWOOD, CA	91602
SCHAEFFER, CHARLES	NEWS CORRESPONDENT	6036 CHATSWORTH LN	BETHESDA, MD	20014
SCHAEFFER, PHYLLIS	NEWS CORRESPONDENT	19633 CLUB LAKE RD	GAITHERSBURG, MD	20879
SCHAEHNER, RUSSELL K	PUBLISHING EXECUTIVE	US MAGAZINE COMPANY 1 DAG HAMMARSKJOLD PLAZA	NEW YORK, NY	10017
SCHAENEN, LEE	CONDUCTOR	61 W 62ND ST #6-F	NEW YORK, NY	10023
SCHAERTEL, ALAN R	NEWS CORRESPONDENT	1825 "K" ST, NW	WASHINGTON, DC	20006
SCHAETZLE, BUD	DIRECTOR	3855 LANKERSHIM BLVD #122	NORTH HOLLYWOOD, CA	91604
SCHAEUFELE, BENNY	GUITARIST	10 MUSIC CIRCLE E	NASHVILLE, TN	37203

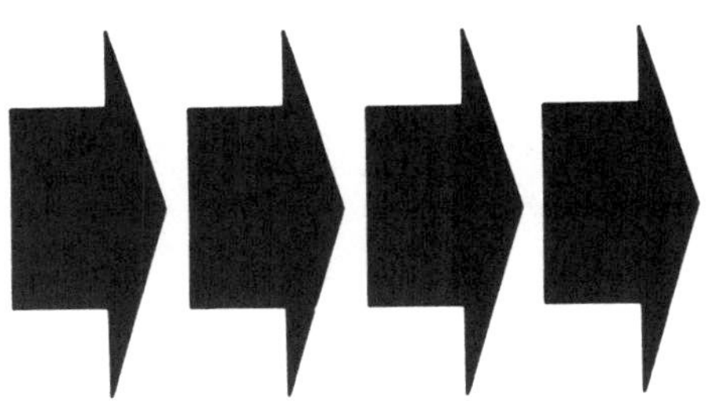

REMINDER:

Always be sure to enclose a self-addressed stamped envelope when writing any celebrity or advertiser.

Name	Occupation	Address	City	Zip
SCHAFER, CHRISTOPHER	GUITARIST	3241 CLOVERWOOD DR	NASHVILLE, TN	37214
SCHAFER, DAN	GUITARIST	3236 CLOVERWOOD DR	NASHVILLE, TN	37214
SCHAFER, NATALIE	ACTRESS	514 N RODEO DR	BEVERLY HILLS, CA	90210
SCHAFER, REUBEN	ACTOR	175 W 87TH ST #25-F	NEW YORK, NY	10024
SCHAFER, RUBE	SINGER	PROCESS, 439 WILEY AVE	FRANKLIN, PA	16323
SCHAFER, SUSANNE M	NEWS CORRESPONDENT	8048 INVERNESS RIDGE RD	POTOMAC, MD	20854
SCHAFF, MICHAEL L	NEWS CORRESPONDENT	1000 WILSON BLVD	ARLINGTON, VA	22209
SCHAFFEL, BETH	ACTRESS	17211 OROZCO ST	GRANADA HILLS, CA	91344
SCHAFFEL, ROBERT	FILM PRODCUER	TRI-STAR PICTURES COMPANY		
		1875 CENTURY PARK E	LOS ANGELES, CA	90067
SCHAFFER, PETER	VIOLINIST	31 COLLIER AVE, KARORI	WELLINGTON 5-764536	NEW ZEALAND
SCHAFFER, SHARON	ACTRESS	FARRELL, 10500 MAGNOLIA BLVD	NORTH HOLLYWOOD, CA	91601
SCHAFFER, STEPHEN	GUITARIST	POST OFFICE BOX 150254	NASHVILLE, TN	37215
SCHAFFNER, FRANKLIN	DIRECTOR	2158 LA MESA DR	SANTA MONICA, CA	90402
SCHAIN, DONALD	WRITER-PRODUCER	1865 N FULLER AVE #203	LOS ANGELES, CA	90046
SCHAKNE, ROBERT	NEWS CORRESPONDENT	CBS NEWS, 2020 "M" ST, NW	WASHINGTON, DC	20036
SCHALLERT, WILLIAM	ACTOR	14920 RAMOS PL	PACIFIC PALISADES, CA	90272
SCHANZER, BEVERLY	TV WRITER	555 W 57TH ST #1230	NEW YORK, NY	10019
SCHAPPI, JOHN V	NEWS CORRESPONDENT	5023 ESKRIDGE TERR, NW	WASHINGTON, DC	20016
SCHARF, WALTER	COMPOSER-CONDUCTOR	814 AMHERST AVE #102	LOS ANGELES, CA	90049
SCHARFMAN, MORT	TV WRITER	1616 PANDORA AVE	LOS ANGELES, CA	90024
SCHARLACH, ED	TV WRITER	3570 VISTA HAVEN RD	SHERMAN OAKS, CA	91403
SCHATZ, MARK	GUITARIST	8506 DENSON AVE	MADISON, TN	37115
SCHATZ, WILLIE	NEWS CORRESPONDENT	4451 ALBERMARLE ST, NW	WASHINGTON, DC	20016
SCHATZBERG, JERRY	FILM WRITER-DIRECTOR	BARD & KASS, 551 5TH AVE	NEW YORK, NY	10176
SCHAUER, SUSAN M	NEWS CORRESPONDENT	1404 N 12TH ST #32	ARLINGTON, VA	22209
SCHAUSEIL, ROBIN DALE	NEWS CORRESPONDENT	6704-E LEE HWY	ARLINGTON, VA	22205
SCHEAR, MICHAEL A	DIRECTOR	98 EMWOOD DR	EMERSON, NJ	07630
SCHECKWITZ, AL	ACTOR	5330 LANKERSHIM BLVD #210	NORTH HOLLYWOOD, CA	91601
SCHECTER, LES	THEATER PRODUCER	1501 BROADWAY	NEW YORK, NY	10036
SCHEDEEN, ANNE	ACTRESS	11227 HORTENSE ST	NORTH HOLLYWOOD, CA	91602
SCHEERER, ROBERT	WRITER-PRODUCER	4951 CARPENTER AVE	NORTH HOLLYWOOD, CA	91607
SCHEFF, MICHAEL	TV WRITER	10400 SUMMER HOLLY CIR	LOS ANGELES, CA	90077
SCHEFFER, RON	DIRECTOR	88 LEXINGTON AVE	NEW YORK, NY	10016
SCHEIBEL, KENNETH M	NEWS CORRESPONDENT	1325 18TH ST, NW	WASHINGTON, DC	20036
SCHEIBLA, SHIRLEY	NEWS CORRESPONDENT	6630 TANSEY DR	FALLS CHURCH, VA	22042
SCHEID, JON F	NEWS CORRESPONDENT	5707 INDIAN CT #1-B	ALEXANDRIA, VA	22303
SCHEIDER, ROY	ACTOR	11 E 73RD ST #2-B	NEW YORK, NY	10021
SCHEIFFER, BOB L	NEWS CORRESPONDENT	CBS NEWS, 2020 "M" ST, NW	WASHINGTON, DC	20036
SCHEIMER, LOUIS	TV PRODUCER	18918 LA MONTANA PL	TARZANA, CA	91356
SCHEINE, RAYNOR	ACTOR	188 E 93RD ST #M	NEW YORK, NY	10028
SCHELL, CATHERINE	ACTRESS	FRENCH, 26 BINNEY ST	LONDON W1	ENGLAND
SCHELL, MARIA	ACTRESS	D08094 HEBERTHAL	BEI WASSERBURG-INN	WEST GERMANY
SCHELL, MAXIMILIAN	ACTOR	2 KEPLER STRASSE	MUNICH 27	WEST GERMANY
SCHELL, RONNIE	COMEDIAN-ACTOR	1888 CENTURY PARK E #622	LOS ANGELES, CA	90067
SCHELLA, MICHAEL	TV WRITER	8736 OAKDALE AVE	NORTHRIDGE, CA	91324
SCHEMMER, BENJAMIN F	NEWS CORRESPONDENT	1318 22ND ST #306, NW	WASHINGTON, DC	20037
SCHENCK, GEORGE	WRITER-PRODUCER	17949 KAREN DR	ENCINO, CA	91316
SCHENET, ROBERT A	NEWS CORRESPONDENT	609 FONTAINE ST	ALEXANDRIA, VA	22302
SCHENKEL, CHRIS	SPORTSCASTER	ABC-TV, SPORTS DEPARTMENT		
		1330 AVE OF THE AMERICAS	NEW YORK, NY	10019
SCHENKEL, RICHARD	DIRECTOR	162 PEACEABLE ST	RIDGEFIELD, CT	06877
SCHEPISI, FREDERIC	FILM WRITER-DIRECTOR	1326 DAWN RIDGE DR	BEVERLY HILLS, CA	90210
SCHER, CYNTHIA D	NEWS CORRESPONDENT	10301 45TH PL #202	BELTSVILLE, MD	20705
SCHERER, DAVID	NEWS CORRESPONDENT	2139 WISCONSIN AVE, NW	WASHINGTON, DC	20007
SCHERER, GENE	ACTOR	15010 VENTURA BLVD #234	SHERMAN OAKS, CA	91403
SCHERER, MARION	ACTRESS	13111 VENTURA BLVD #204	STUDIO CITY, CA	91604
SCHERF, MARGARET	NEWS CORRESPONDENT	938 N DANVILLE ST	ARLINGTON, VA	22201
SCHERICK, EDGAR	FILM PRODUCER	10960 WILSHIRE BLVD #2230	LOS ANGELES, CA	90024
SCHERMAN-STEIN, RONI	DIRECTOR	93 COUNTRY RIDGE DR		
		RYE BROOK	NEW YORK, NY	10573
SCHERR, KENNETH	ACTOR	439 S LA CIENEGA BLVD #117	LOS ANGELES, CA	90048
SCHERSCHEL, JOSEPH J	PHOTOGRAPHER	ROUTE #1, BOX 112	FLINT HILL, VA	22627
SCHERSCHEL, PATRICIA M	NEWS CORRESPONDENT	3306 PORTER ST, NW	WASHINGTON, DC	20008
SCHEXNAYDER, BRIAN	BARITONE	CAMI, 165 W 57TH ST	NEW YORK, NY	10019
SCHIAVELLI, VINCENT	ACTOR	KOHNER, 9169 SUNSET BLVD	LOS ANGELES, CA	90069
SCHIAVONE, LOUISE L	NEWS CORRESPONDENT	4201 CATHEDRAL AVE, NW	WASHINGTON, DC	20016
SCHIAVONE, TONY	WRESTLING ANNOUNCER	NATIONAL WRESTLING ALLIANCE		
		JIM CROCKETT PROMOTIONS		
		421 BRIARBEND DR	CHARLOTTE, NC	28209
SCHIBI, MARGARET J	TV WRITER	2030 OAKSTONE WY	LOS ANGELES, CA	90046
SCHICK, ELLIOT	DIRECTOR-PRODUCER	2175 CASTILIAN DR	LOS ANGELES, CA	90068
SCHICK, STEVEN	PERCUSSIONIST	AFFILIATE ARTISTS, INC		
		37 W 65TH ST, 6TH FLOOR	NEW YORK, NY	10023
SCHICKEL, RICHARD	FILM WRITER-PRODUCER	33 HARRISON ST	NEW YORK, NY	10013
SCHIEFFER, BOB	BROADCAST JOURNALIST	CBS NEWS, 524 W 57TH ST	NEW YORK, NY	10019
SCHIFF, ANDRAS	PIANIST	CAMI, 165 W 57TH ST	NEW YORK, NY	10019
SCHIFF, ANDREA	ACTRESS	2160 S BEVERLY GLEN BLVD #357	LOS ANGELES, CA	90025
SCHIFF, DAVID	TALENT AGENT	ICM, 8899 BEVERLY BLVD	LOS ANGELES, CA	90048
SCHIFF, ERIC	ACTOR	3800 BARHAM BLVD #303	LOS ANGELES, CA	90068
SCHIFF, HEINRICH	CELLIST	CAMI, 165 W 57TH ST	NEW YORK, NY	10019
SCHIFF, STEPHEN	FILM CRITIC	VANITY FAIR, 350 MADISON AVE	NEW YORK, NY	10017
SCHIFFMAN, GLENN	SCREENWRITER	10328 LEOLANG AVE	SUNLAND, CA	91040
SCHIFFRES, FRANCINE	ACTRESS	1337 BERKELEY ST #7	SANTA MONICA, CA	90404
SCHIFFRES, MANUEL	NEWS CORRESPONDENT	3110 WISCONSIN AVE #702, NW	WASHINGTON, DC	20016

Name	Occupation	Address	City	ZIP
SCHIFRIN, LALO	COMPOSER-CONDUCTOR	710 N HILLCREST RD	BEVERLY HILLS, CA	90210
SCHILLER, BOB	ACTOR	1607 N EL CENTRO AVE #23	LOS ANGELES, CA	90028
SCHILLER, CRAIG	TV DIRECTOR-PRODUCER	4522 WOODMAN AVE #C-210	SHERMAN OAKS, CA	91423
SCHILLER, FRED	WRITER	149 S WETHERLY DR	LOS ANGELES, CA	90048
SCHILLER, LAWRENCE J	DIRECTOR-PRODUCER	POST OFFICE BOX 5784	SHERMAN OAKS, CA	91413
SCHILLER, RHODA K	TV DIRECTOR	1741 "T" ST #303, NW	WASHINGTON, DC	20009
SCHILLER, ROBERT A	WRITER-PRODUCER	1661 CASALE RD	PACIFIC PALISADES, CA	90272
SCHILLER, THOMAS	WRITER-PRODUCER	DGA, 110 W 57TH ST	NEW YORK, NY	10019
SCHILLER, ULRICH	NEWS CORRESPONDENT	8205 BEECHTREE RD	BETHESDA, MD	20817
SCHILLER, WILTON	WRITER	11756 MOORPARK ST #D	STUDIO CITY, CA	91604
SCHILLING, PETER	SINGER	ABANDA MUSIKUNTERNEHEM		
		39 ZENETTI ST	8000 MUNICH 2	WEST GERMANY
SCHILLING, WILLIAM	ACTOR	6310 SAN VICENTE BLVD #407	LOS ANGELES, CA	90048
SCHILLIO, EMILE J	COMPOSER	106 S KINGS RD	LOS ANGELES, CA	90048
SCHILZ, TED G, JR	DIRECTOR	4714 ARCOLA AVE	NORTH HOLLYWOOD, CA	91602
SCHILZ, TED N, JR	ACTOR	5187 LLANO DR	WOODLAND HILLS, CA	91364
SCHIMMEL, PAULA	WRITER	2007 SELBY AVE	LOS ANGELES, CA	90025
SCHINDEHETTE, SUSAN	NEWS CORRESPONDENT	3726 HARRISON ST, NW	WASHINGTON, DC	20015
SCHINDLER, MAX A	DIRECTOR-NEWS CORRES	904 S BELGRADE RD	SILVER SPRING, MD	20902
SCHINDLER, MAX J	NEWS CORRESPONDENT	NBC-TV, NEWS DEPARTMENT		
		4001 NEBRASKA AVE, NW	WASHINGTON, DC	20016
SCHIPPER, HENRY	COLUMNIST	VARIETY, 1400 N CAHUENGA BLVD	HOLLYWOOD, CA	90028
SCHIRMER, GUS	CASTING DIRECTOR	1403 N ORANGE GROVE	LOS ANGELES, CA	90046
SCHIRRA, WALTER M, JR	ASTRONAUT	GO WEST TRAIL	MORRISON, MO	80465
SCHISGAL, MURRAY	SCREENWRITER	555 W 57TH ST #1230	NEW YORK, NY	10019
SCHLAFLY, PHYLLIS	NEWS CORRESPONDENT	68 FAIRMONT	ALTON, IL	62002
SCHLAMME, THOMAS D	TV DIRECTOR	123 W 88TH ST	NEW YORK, NY	10024
SCHLATTER, GEORGE	WRITER-PRODUCER	615 N ARDEN DR	BEVERLY HILLS, CA	90210
SCHLEETER, TIMOTHY R	NEWS CORRESPONDENT	1214 "A" S THOMAS ST #A	ARLINGTON, VA	22204
SCHLEGEL, BARRY C	PHOTOJOURNALIST	406 CIR AVE	TAKOMA PARK, MD	20912
SCHLEIN, ALAN M	NEWS CORRESPONDENT	314 E CAPITOL ST, NE	WASHINGTON, DC	20003
SCHLENKER, MARVIN F	DIRECTOR	23 KRISTIN PL	OLD TAPPAN, NJ	07675
SCHLESINGER, JOHN R	DIRECTOR	10 VICTORIA RD	LONDON W8 5RD	ENGLAND
SCHLESINGER, JOSEPH	NEWS CORRESPONDENT	5236 LOUGHBORO RD, NW	WASHINGTON, DC	20016
SCHLISSEL, JACK	THEATER PRODUCER	234 W 44TH ST	NEW YORK, NY	10036
SCHLITT, ROBERT	TV WRITER-PRODUCER	8955 BEVERLY BLVD	LOS ANGELES, CA	90048
SCHLITZ, DON	GUITARIST	POST OFFICE BOX 120594	NASHVILLE, TN	37212
SCHLOEMER, HANS-PETER	NEWS CORRESPONDENT	3132 "M" ST, NW	WASHINGTON, DC	20007
SCHLOSS, HANK	CINEMATOGRAPHER	149 S MAPLE DR	BEVERLY HILLS, CA	90212
SCHMALSTIEG, ROXANNE	NEWS CORRESPONDENT	5550 FRIENDSHIP BLVD	CHEVY CHASE, MD	20815
SCHMECHEL, ROLF H	NEWS CORRESPONDENT	3132 "M" ST, NW	WASHINGTON, DC	20007
SCHMELING, MAX	BOXER	2115 HALLENSTEDT	HAMBURG	WEST GERMANY
SCHMERER, JAMES	TV WRITER	15321 KINGSWOOD LN	SHERMAN OAKS, CA	91403
SCHMERTZ, HERB	COLUMNIST	HERITAGE FEATURES SYNDICATE		
		214 MASSACHUSETTS AVE, NE	WASHINGTON, DC	20002
SCHMICK, PAUL A	PHOTOGRAPHER	7117 WHETSTONE RD	ALEXANDRIA, VA	22306
SCHMICK, PAUL M	PHOTOGRAPHER	1319 PRINCE RD	SAINT AUGUSTINE, FL	32086
SCHMICK, WILLIAM F, III	NEWS CORRESPONDENT	440 ARGYLE DR	ALEXANDRIA, VA	22305
SCHMID, RANDOLPH F	NEWS CORRESPONDENT	5814 FLAXTON PL	ALEXANDRIA, VA	22303
SCHMID, SHARON L	NEWS CORRESPONDENT	1840 MACON ST	MC LEAN, VA	22101
SCHMIDLAPP, F L	ACTOR	7 JANE ST	NEW YORK, NY	10014
SCHMIDT, ANN D	NEWS CORRESPONDENT	115 5TH ST, SE	WASHINGTON, DC	20003
SCHMIDT, ARTHUR L	TV WRITER	8955 BEVERLY BLVD	LOS ANGELES, CA	90048
SCHMIDT, CLAUDINE	CLOWN	2701 COTTAGE WY #14	SACRAMENTO, CA	95825
SCHMIDT, DOV	CONDUCTOR	POST OFFICE BOX 131	SPRINGFIELD, VA	22150
SCHMIDT, FELIX	CELLIST	ANGLO-SWISS ARTISTS MGMT		
		16 MUSWELL HILL RD, HIGHGATE	LONDON N6 5UG	ENGLAND
SCHMIDT, HARVEY	WRITER-COMPOSER	313 W 74TH ST	NEW YORK, NY	10023
SCHMIDT, JOE	CARTOONIST	POST OFFICE BOX 1207	CHULA VISTA, CA	92011
SCHMIDT, MIKE	BASEBALL	24 LAKEWOOD DR	MEDIA, PA	19063
SCHMIDT, TRUDELIESE	MEZZO-SOPRANO	MARIEDL ANDERS ARTISTS MGMT		
		535 EL CAMINO DEL MAR ST	SAN FRANCISCO, CA	94121
SCHMIDT/VERDERY DUO	MUSICAL DUO	SIMONDS, 30 HEWLETT ST	WATERBURY, CT	06710
SCHMIETH, MARY T	CARTOONIST	TRIBUNE MEDIA SERVICES		
		64 E CONCORD ST	ORLANDO, FL	32801
SCHMIT, TIMOTHY B	SINGER-GUITARIST	2416 CARMAN CREST DR	LOS ANGELES, CA	90068
SCHMOELLER, DAVID	FILM WRITER-DIRECTOR	2244 STANLEY HILLS DR	LOS ANGELES, CA	90046
SCHNABEL, KARL	PIANIST	305 W END AVE	NEW YORK, NY	10023
SCHNAUT, GABRIELE	SOPRANO	CAMI, 165 W 57TH ST	NEW YORK, NY	10019
SCHNECK, STEPHEN	SCREENWRITER	1628 N GARDNER ST	LOS ANGELES, CA	90046
SCHNEER, CHARLES H	FILM PRODUCER	ANDOR, 8 ILCHESTER PL	LONDON W14 8AA	ENGLAND
SCHNEIDER, ALEXANDER	VIOLINIST-CONDUCTOR	201 W 54TH ST #4-C	NEW YORK, NY	10019
SCHNEIDER, ANDREW	ACTOR	1509 N CRESCENT HGTS BLVD #7	LOS ANGELES, CA	90069
SCHNEIDER, ANDREW	TV WRITER	3148 WAVERLY DR	LOS ANGELES, CA	90027
SCHNEIDER, ANDY	TV PRODUCER	LARSON, 10201 W PICO BLVD	LOS ANGELES, CA	90035
SCHNEIDER, ARTHUR	VIDEO EDITOR	27044 HELMOND DR	AGOURA, CA	91301
SCHNEIDER, BARRY	WRITER-DRUMMER	4110 STONE CANYON AVE	SHERMAN OAKS, CA	91403
SCHNEIDER, JAMES A	PHOTOGRAPHER	10 HILLYER CT	WASHINGTON, DC	20008
SCHNEIDER, JOHN	ACT-WRI-SING	9255 SUNSET BLVD #1115	LOS ANGELES, CA	90069
SCHNEIDER, MARK	ACTOR	7060 HOLLYWOOD BLVD #610	LOS ANGELES, CA	90028
SCHNEIDER, MARK D	DIRECTOR	258 BROADWAY #7-F	NEW YORK, NY	10007
SCHNEIDER, MARNI	TV DIRECTOR-PRODUCER	KCET-TV, 4401 SUNSET BLVD	LOS ANGELES, CA	90027
SCHNEIDER, PAUL	TV WRITER	8955 BEVERLY BLVD	LOS ANGELES, CA	90048
SCHNEIDER, RICHARD	DIRECTOR	139 E 35TH ST	NEW YORK, NY	10016

NAME	OCCUPATION	ADDRESS	CITY	ZIP
SCHNEIDER, SASCHA	TV PRODUCER	8480 BEVERLY BLVD #117	LOS ANGELES, CA	90048
SCHNEIDER, TAWNY	TV HOST	SEE - LITTLE, TAWNY		
SCHNEIDER, TOM	COLUMNIST	CHRONICLE FEATURES		
		870 MARKET ST	SAN FRANCISCO, CA	94102
SCHNEIDER, WILLIAM	NEWS CORRESPONDENT	2646 1/2 WOODLEY PL, NW	WASHINGTON, DC	20008
SCHNESSEL, S MICHAEL	TV WRITER	ABC-TV, "ONE LIFE TO LIVE"		
		1330 AVE OF THE AMERICAS	NEW YORK, NY	10019
SCHNETZER, STEPHEN	ACTOR	BRET ADAMS, 448 W 44TH ST	NEW YORK, NY	10036
SCHNIEDER, BARRY	TV WRITER	14144 VENTURA BLVD #200	SHERMAN OAKS, CA	91423
SCHNITZER, GERALD	WRITER-PRODUCER	1155 N LA CIENEGA BLVD #1203	LOS ANGELES, CA	90069
SCHNITZLER, PETER A	WRITER	2913 HIGHLAND AVE	SANTA MONICA, CA	90405
SCHNORF, ROBERT	TV DIRECTOR	KMOX-TV, 1 MEMORIAL DR	ST LOUIS, MO	63102
SCHNUR, JEROME	TV DIRECTOR-PRODUCER	135 CENTRAL PARK W	NEW YORK, NY	10023
SCHNURER, TONY	WRITER	8347 CARMAR PL	LOS ANGELES, CA	90046
SCHOEFFLING, MICHAEL	ACTOR	POST OFFICE BOX 2563	CANYON CITY, CA	91351
SCHOELEN, JILL	ACTRESS	POST OFFICE BOX 1168-173	STUDIO CITY, CA	91604
SCHOEN, VIC	COMPOSER-CONDUCTOR	11403 80TH AVE, NE	KIRKLAND, WA	98033
SCHOENBAUM, BERNARD	CARTOONIST	POST OFFICE BOX 4203	NEW YORK, NY	10017
SCHOENBERG, ALBERT	ACTOR	3330 BARHAM BLVD #103	LOS ANGELES, CA	90068
SCHOENBERG, JEREMY	ACTOR	1717 N HIGHLAND AVE #414	HOLLYWOOD, CA	90028
SCHOENBERG, STEVEN	PIANIST	KURLAND, 173 BRIGHTON AVE	BOSTON, MA	02134
SCHOENBRUN, JOSEF	COMPOSER-CONDUCTOR	316 SAN VICENTE BLVD #104	SANTA MONICA, CA	90402
SCHOENBURG, STUART	PRODUCER	RANDOM, 5437 LAUREL CYN BLVD	NORTH HOLLYWOOD, CA	91607
SCHOENDIENST, ALFRED "RED"	BASEBALL	331 LADUE WOODS CT	CREVE COEUR, MO	63141
SCHOENE, WOLFGANG	BARITONE	CAMI, 165 W 57TH ST	NEW YORK, NY	10019
SCHOENFELD, GERALD	THEATER PRODUCER	225 W 44TH ST	NEW YORK, NY	10036
SCHOENMANN, DONALD E	PHOTOGRAPHER	19229 WARRIOR BROOK DR	GERMANTOWN, MD	10767
SCHOFFMAN, STUART	WRITER	2899 RAMBLA PACIFICO	MALIBU, CA	90265
SCHOFIELD, KATHARINE	ACTRESS	AL PARKER, 55 PARK LN	LONDON W1	ENGLAND
SCHOLL, ARTHUR	DIRECTOR	1041 MOFFATT ST	RIALTO, CA	92376
SCHONBERG, HAROLD	MUSIC CRITIC	118 RIVERSIDE DR	NEW YORK, NY	10024
SCHONWANDT, MICHAEL	CONDUCTOR	ICM, 40 W 57TH ST	NEW YORK, NY	10019
SCHOPPA, KELLY & THE AMARILLO B	VOCAL GROUP	POST OFFICE BOX 1373	LEWISVILLE, TX	75067
SCHOPPE, JAMES	ART DIRECTOR	3872 LAS FLORES CANYON RD #1	MALIBU, CA	90265
SCHOR, LORI M	NEWS CORRESPONDENT	2800 QUEBEC ST #827, NW	WASHINGTON, DC	20008
SCHOR, LOUIS	WRITER-PRODUCER	5003 MAMMOTH AVE	VAN NUYS, CA	91423
SCHORR, BILL	CARTOONIST	POST OFFICE BOX 2416		
		TERMINAL ANNEX	LOS ANGELES, CA	90051
SCHORR, BURT	NEWS CORRESPONDENT	113 OXFORD ST	CHEVY CHASE, MD	20815
SCHORR, DANIEL	BROADCAST JOURNALIST	3113 WOODLEY RD	WASHINGTON, DC	20008
SCHOTT, BOB	ACTOR	3151 W CAHUENGA BLVD #310	LOS ANGELES, CA	90068
SCHOTT, SUZI	MODEL	MODELS & PROMOTIONS AGENCY		
		8560 SUNSET BLVD, 10TH FLOOR	LOS ANGELES, CA	90069
SCHOTTEN & COLLIER	MUSICAL DUO	CCS, 4478 PURDUE AVE	CULVER CITY, CA	90230
SCHOTTENFELD, MATTHEW A	COMPOSER	2005 BEACHWOOD CYN RD	LOS ANGELES, CA	90068
SCHOTZ, ERIC R	TV DIRECTOR	105 1/2 S CLARK DR	LOS ANGELES, CA	90048
SCHOUMACHER, DAVID E	NEWS CORRESPONDENT	4461 CONNECTICUT AVE, NW	WASHINGTON, DC	20008
SCHRADER, PAUL	WRITER-PRODUCER	DGA, 7950 SUNSET BLVD	LOS ANGELES, CA	90046
SCHREDER, CAROL	TV WRITER-PRODUCER	21021 WAVEVIEW DR	TOPANGA CANYON, CA	90290
SCHREIBER, AVERY	ACTOR-COMEDIAN	4420 LOS FELIZ BLVD #201	LOS ANGELES, CA	90027
SCHREIBER, CATHERINE	ACTRESS	9744 WILSHIRE BLVD #306	BEVERLY HILLS, CA	90212
SCHREIBMAN, MYRL A	DIRECTOR	15913 ENADIA WY	VAN NUYS, CA	91406
SCHREIER, PETER	TENOR	MARIEDL ANDERS ARTISTS MGMT		
		535 EL CAMINO DEL MAR ST	SAN FRANCISCO, CA	94121
SCHREIER, RICHARD LEE	DIRECTOR	DGA, 7950 SUNSET BLVD	LOS ANGELES, CA	90046
SCHREINER, WILLIAM	ACTOR	427 N CANON DR #205	BEVERLY HILLS, CA	90210
SCHREMMER, ROBERT	FLUTIST	7209 BIRCH BARK DR	NASHVILLE, TN	37221
SCHRIENER, DENISE LYNN	DIRECTOR	DGA, 110 W 57TH ST	NEW YORK, NY	10019
SCHRIMPF, MIKE	PIANIST	143 FORREST RETREAT DR	HENDERSONVILLE, TN	37075
SCHRODER, RICKY	ACTOR	POST OFFICE BOX 140		
		FT HAMILTON STATION	BROOKLYN, NY	11209
SCHRODER, SUSAN	ACTRESS	POST OFFICE BOX 491340	LOS ANGELES, CA	90049
SCHROEDER, MICHAEL	DIRECTOR-PRODUCER	30825 WHIM DR	WESTLAKE VILLAGE, CA	91362
SCHROEDER, RICHARD C	NEWS CORRESPONDENT	9111 CORONADO TERR	FAIRFAX, VA	22031
SCHROEDER, RUSSELL	DRUMMER	1010 16TH AVE N	NASHVILLE, TN	37202
SCHROEDER, WALTER K	DIRECTOR	2318 MOTOR PARKWAY	RONKONKOMA, NY	11779
SCHROER, RICHARD	DIRECTOR	14539 VALLEY VISTA BLVD	SHERMAN OAKS, CA	91403
SCHROM, MICHAEL STUART	DIRECTOR	DGA, 110 W 57TH ST	NEW YORK, NY	10019
SCHRUERS, FRED	WRITER-EDITOR	US MAGAZINE COMPANY		
		1 DAG HAMMARSKJOLD PLAZA	NEW YORK, NY	10017
SCHUB, ANDRE-MICHEL	PIANIST	ICM, 40 W 57TH ST	NEW YORK, NY	10019
SCHUBACK, THOMAS	CONDUCTOR	59 E 54TH ST #81	NEW YORK, NY	10022
SCHUBB, MARK	ACTOR	1525 1/2 HI POINT ST	LOS ANGELES, CA	90035
SCHUBERT, BERNARD	WRITER	1036 N LAUREL AVE	LOS ANGELES, CA	90046
SCHULBERG, BUDD	TV WRITER	555 W 57TH ST #1230	NEW YORK, NY	10019
SCHULBERG, PETER C	NEWS CORRESPONDENT	4600 CONNECTICUT AVE, NW	WASHINGTON, DC	20008
SCHULE, JAMES R	NEWS CORRESPONDENT	2139 WISCONSIN AVE, NW	WASHINGTON, DC	20007
SCHULER, ANNIE CAROLINE	SCREENWRITER	1255 N HARPER AVE #109	LOS ANGELES, CA	90046
SCHULER, LAUREN	FILM PRODUCER	500 S BUENA VISTA ST	BURBANK, CA	91521
SCHULER, RICHARD	TENOR	CAMI, 165 W 57TH ST	NEW YORK, NY	10019
SCHULLER, DR ROBERT	EVANGELIST	464 S ESPLANADE ST	ORANGE, CA	92669
SCHULLER, FRANK	ACTOR	9220 SUNSET BLVD #625	LOS ANGELES, CA	90069
SCHULLER, GUNTHER	CONDUCTOR	POST OFFICE BOX 1515	NEW YORK, NY	10023
SCHULMAN, ARNOLD	WRITER-PRODUCER	8755 SHOREHAM DR #402	LOS ANGELES, CA	90069
SCHULMAN, HEIDI	TV WRITER	470 SHERMAN CANAL #4	VENICE, CA	90291

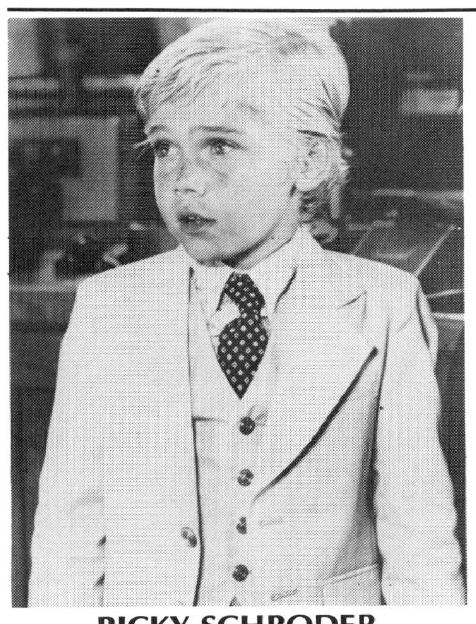
RICKY SCHRODER

FRED SCOTT

MARTHA SCOTT

JOHN SEBASTIAN

NEIL SEDAKA

GEORGE SEGAL

BOB SEGAR

CONNIE SELLECA

TOM SELLECK

Name	Occupation	Address	City	Zip
SCHULMAN, JESSE	NEWS CORRESPONDENT	499 S CAPITOL ST, SW	WASHINGTON, DC	20003
SCHULTZ, DWIGHT	ACTOR	7224 HILLSIDE AVE #5	LOS ANGELES, CA	90046
SCHULTZ, IVY	TV WRITER	8955 BEVERLY BLVD	LOS ANGELES, CA	90048
SCHULTZ, JACK	PHOTOGRAPHER	1-C SOUTHWAY	GREENBELT, MD	20770
SCHULTZ, JACQUELINE	ACTRESS	ANN WRIGHT, 136 E 57TH ST	NEW YORK, NY	10022
SCHULTZ, JAMES J	NEWS CORRESPONDENT	2133 WISCONSIN AVE, NW	WASHINGTON, DC	20007
SCHULTZ, MICHAEL	FILM DIRECTOR	POST OFFICE BOX 8659	SAN MARINO, CA	91108
SCHULTZ, PHIL	DIRECTOR	2 PETER COOPER RD	NEW YORK, NY	10010
SCHULTZ, ROBERT	DIRECTOR-PRODUCER	4711 BIZET PL	WOODLAND HILLS, CA	91364
SCHULTZE, ANDREW	BASSO-BARITONE	111 W 57TH ST #1209	NEW YORK, NY	10019
SCHULTZE, RALF	NEWS CORRESPONDENT	1111 ARMY-NAVY DR	ARLINGTON, VA	22202
SCHULZ, CHARLES	CARTOONIST	1 SNOOPY PL	SANTA ROSA, CA	95401
SCHULZ, DAVID	ACTOR	CARPENTER, 1516-W REDWOOD ST	SAN DIEGO, CA	92101
SCHULZ, KLAUS-ROLAND	NEWS CORRESPONDENT	4701 WILLARD AVE	CHEVY CHASE, MD	20815
SCHULZ, WILLIAM	NEWS CORRESPONDENT	5000 HAWTHORNE PL, NW	WASHINGTON, DC	20016
SCHUMACHER, JOEL	WRITER-PRODUCER	10051 CIELO DR	BEVERLY HILLS, CA	90210
SCHUMACHER, JOSEPH S, JR	DIRECTOR	1262 BRIARWOOD LN	LIBERTYVILLE, IL	60048
SCHUMACHER, KARL H	PHOTOGRAPHER	1453 MC LEAN MEWS CT	MC LEAN, VA	22101
SCHUMAN, PATRICIA	SOPRANO	CAMI, 165 W 57TH ST	NEW YORK, NY	10019
SCHUMAN, WILLIAM	COMPOSER	RICHMOND HILL RD	GREENWICH, CT	06830
SCHUMANN, MARIE	PHOTO REPORTER	LIFE/TIME & LIFE BLDG		
		ROCKEFELLER CENTER	NEW YORK, NY	10020
SCHUNK, ROBERT	TENOR	CAMI, 165 W 57TH ST	NEW YORK, NY	10019
SCHURMAN, KARL NELSON	TV DIRECTOR	POST OFFICE BOX 14	GERTON, NC	28735
SCHUSTACK, HELEN	ACTRESS	1816 N STANLEY AVE	LOS ANGELES, CA	90046
SCHUSTER, GARY F	NEWS CORRESPONDENT	2908 BLUE ROBIN CT	HERNDON, VA	22071
SCHUSTER, HAROLD	DIRECTOR	31620 BROAD BEACH RD	MALIBU, CA	90265
SCHUSTER, MARK H	NEWS CORRESPONDENT	2133 WISCONSIN AVE, NW	WASHINGTON, DC	20007
SCHUYLER, RICHARD	GUITARIST	205 S CLIFFDALE DR	WINSTON SALEM, NC	27104
SCHWAB, AARON	TV PRODUCER	MMA, 8484 WILSHIRE BLVD	BEVERLY HILLS, CA	90212
SCHWAB, DON	DIRECTOR	10333 ASHTON AVE	LOS ANGELES, CA	90024
SCHWAB, FAYE	TV PRODUCER	MMA, 8484 WILSHIRE BLVD	BEVERLY HILLS, CA	90212
SCHWAB, LANA	ACTRESS	5000 LANKERSHIM BLVD #5	NORTH HOLLYWOOD, CA	91601
SCHWADEL, RICHARD ALAN	DIRECTOR	2456 BEVERLY AVE #B	SANTA MONICA, CA	90405
SCHWARTZ, AL	TV PRODUCER	CLARK PRODUCTIONS		
		3003 W OLIVE AVE	BURBANK, CA	91505
SCHWARTZ, AL	TV WRITER	8955 BEVERLY BLVD	LOS ANGELES, CA	90048
SCHWARTZ, ALLEN	TV DIRECTOR	9707 ARBY DR	BEVERLY HILLS, CA	90210
SCHWARTZ, BERL	NEWS CORRESPONDENT	2053 PARK RD, NW	WASHINGTON, DC	20010
SCHWARTZ, BERNIE	PRODUCER	MCA/UNIVERSAL STUDIOS, INC		
		100 UNIVERSAL CITY PLAZA		
		BUILDING #507-3-G	UNIVERSAL CITY, CA	91608
SCHWARTZ, BOB	DIRECTOR	501 E 79TH ST	NEW YORK, NY	10028
SCHWARTZ, BOB	TV DIRECTOR	CBS-TV, "AS THE WORLD TURNS"		
		51 W 52ND ST	NEW YORK, NY	10019
SCHWARTZ, CHARLES L	TV DIRECTOR-PRODUCER	223 E 61ST ST	NEW YORK, NY	10021
SCHWARTZ, DEBORAH	SOPRANO	756 7TH AVE #67	NEW YORK, NY	10019
SCHWARTZ, DON	NEWS EDITOR	THE NATIONAL ENQUIRER		
		600 SE COAST AVE	LANTANA, FL	33464
SCHWARTZ, DOUGLAS N	FILM WRITER-PRODUCER	8955 BEVERLY BLVD	LOS ANGELES, CA	90048
SCHWARTZ, ELROY	TV WRITER	8955 BEVERLY BLVD	LOS ANGELES, CA	90048
SCHWARTZ, GERHARD	ACTOR-WRITER	2000 HAMBURG 60	POSTFACH 60-24-51	WEST GERMANY
SCHWARTZ, HOWARD	CINEMATOGRAPHER	7715 SUNSET BLVD #150	LOS ANGELES, CA	90046
SCHWARTZ, JOHN D	DIRECTOR-PRODUCER	10488 EASTBOURNE AVE	LOS ANGELES, CA	90024
SCHWARTZ, JONATHAN M	DIRECTOR	36 RIVERSIDE DR	NEW YORK, NY	10023
SCHWARTZ, LELAND	NEWS CORRESPONDENT	304 SOUTH CAROLINA AVE, SE	WASHINGTON, DC	20003
SCHWARTZ, LLOYD	WRITER-PRODUCER	12800 MILBANK ST	STUDIO CITY, CA	91604
SCHWARTZ, LLOYD M	NEWS CORRESPONDENT	1905 COURTLAND RD	ALEXANDRIA, VA	22306
SCHWARTZ, MARC	CASTING DIRECTOR	9911 W PICO BLVD #1580	LOS ANGELES, CA	90035
SCHWARTZ, MARTIN N	DIRECTOR	DGA, 7950 SUNSET BLVD	LOS ANGELES, CA	90046
SCHWARTZ, MICHAEL M	NEWS CORRESPONDENT	107 N IRVING ST	ARLINGTON, VA	22201
SCHWARTZ, MICHAEL WILLIAM	ACTOR	11 W 84TH ST #5	NEW YORK, NY	10024
SCHWARTZ, MURRAY	FILM DIRECTOR	4015 PATRICK HENRY PL	AGOURA, CA	91301
SCHWARTZ, MURRAY	TV EXECUTIVE	1541 N VINE ST	HOLLYWOOD, CA	90028
SCHWARTZ, NAN L	COMPOSER	4410 SAINT CLAIR AVE	STUDIO CITY, CA	91604
SCHWARTZ, NEIL J	ACTOR	9200 SUNSET BLVD #1210	LOS ANGELES, CA	90069
SCHWARTZ, RHONDA	NEWS CORRESPONDENT	NBC-TV, NEWS DEPARTMENT		
		4001 NEBRASKA AVE, NW	WASHINGTON, DC	20016
SCHWARTZ, SERGIU	VIOLINIST	POST OFFICE BOX 27539	PHILADELPHIA, PA	19118
SCHWARTZ, SHELDON D	NEWS CORRESPONDENT	2139 WISCONSIN AVE, NW	WASHINGTON, DC	20007
SCHWARTZ, SHERWOOD	TV WRITER-PRODUCER	1865 CARLA RIDGE	BEVERLY HILLS, CA	90210
SCHWARTZ, STEPHEN	COMPOSER-LYRICIST	PARAMOUSE ASSOCIATES		
		1414 AVE OF THE AMERICAS	NEW YORK, NY	10019
SCHWARTZ, STEPHEN	DIRECTOR	DGA, 110 W 57TH ST	NEW YORK, NY	10019
SCHWARTZ, STEPHEN	TV WRITER	8955 BEVERLY BLVD	LOS ANGELES, CA	90048
SCHWARTZ, TED	ACTOR	4603 ETHEL AVE	SHERMAN OAKS, CA	91423
SCHWARTZ, TONY	DIRECTOR	455 W 56TH ST	NEW YORK, NY	10019
SCHWARTZ, VICTOR J	WRITER	2101 MALCOLM AVE	LOS ANGELES, CA	90025
SCHWARTZ, WILLIAM	TV WRITER	8955 BEVERLY BLVD	LOS ANGELES, CA	90048
SCHWARTZ, WILLIAM J	DIRECTOR-PRODUCER	212 S BEMISTON AVE	SAINT LOUIS, MO	63105
SCHWARY, RONALD L	FILM PRODUCER	19950 GREENBRIAR DR	TARZANA, CA	91356
SCHWARZ, HANNA	MEZZO-SOPRANO	CAMI, 165 W 57TH ST	NEW YORK, NY	10019
SCHWARZ, HANS-HELMUT	PIANIST	111 W 57TH ST #1209	NEW YORK, NY	10019
SCHWARZ, IRA	PHOTOGRAPHER	2514 "K" ST, NW	WASHINGTON, DC	20037
SCHWARZ, MILTON MICKEY	DIRECTOR	14-A WEAVERS HILL	GREENWICH, CT	06830

SCHWARZ, ROBERT S	DIRECTOR	LILLA LN	EAST HAMPTON, NY	11937
SCHWARZ, TED	NOVELIST	8955 BEVERLY BLVD	LOS ANGELES, CA	90048
SCHWARZENEGGER, ARNOLD	ACTOR-BODYBUILDER	POST OFFICE BOX 1234	SANTA MONICA, CA	90406
SCHWARZWALD, H ARNOLD	COMPOSER	5636 COSTELLO AVE	VAN NUYS, CA	91401
SCHWED, PAULA	NEWS CORRESPONDENT	1700 PENNSYLVANIA AVE, NW	WASHINGTON, DC	20006
SCHWEDE, WALTER	VIOLINIST	5102 PRINCE PHILIP COVE	BRENTWOOD, TN	37027
SCHWEDT, HERMAN	ACTOR	63-42 253RD ST	LITTLE NECK, NY	11362
SCHWEI, BARBARA	THEATER PRODUCER	1501 BROADWAY	NEW YORK, NY	10036
SCHWEID, BARRY	NEWS CORRESPONDENT	1272 NEW HAMPSHIRE AVE, NW	WASHINGTON, DC	20036
SCHWEITZ, ROBERT E	NEWS CORRESPONDENT	3808 HAYNSWORTH PL	FAIRFAX, VA	22031
SCHWEITZER, MURRAY H	NEWS CORRESPONDENT	2206 PINNEBERG AVE	ROCKVILLE, MD	20851
SCHWERIN, JULES VICTOR	DIRECTOR	317 W 83RD ST	NEW YORK, NY	10024
SCHWERZLER, NANCY J	NEWS CORRESPONDENT	2601 WOODLEY PL #112, NW	WASHINGTON, DC	20008
SCHWISOW, JAMES	TENOR	CAMI, 165 W 57TH ST	NEW YORK, NY	10019
SCHYGULLA, HANNA	ACTRESS	GEORGES BEAUME AGENCE		
		3 QUAI MALAQUAIS	PARIS 75008	FRANCE
SCINTO, MARIE	ACTRESS	8350 SANTA MONICA BLVD #206	LOS ANGELES, CA	90069
SCINTO, ROBERT L	TV DIRECTOR	POST OFFICE BOX 343	RINGWOOD, NJ	07456
SCOFFIELD, JON	TV DIRECTOR-PRODUCER	CENTRAL INDEPENDENT TV		
		LENTON LN	NOTTINGHAM NG7 2NA	ENGLAND
SCOFIELD, DINO	ACTOR	3330 BARHAM BLVD #103	LOS ANGELES, CA	90068
SCOFIELD, PAUL	ACTOR	THE GABLES, BALCOMBE	SUSSEX	ENGLAND
SCOGGINS, TRACY	ACTRESS-MODEL	445 N BEDFORD DR #PH	BEVERLY HILLS, CA	90210
SCOLARI, PETER	ACTOR	11726 SAN VICENTE BLVD #300	LOS ANGELES, CA	90049
SCOOTERS, THE	ROCK & ROLL GROUP	RINGE, 15190 ENCANTO DR	SHERMAN OAKS, CA	91403
SCOPELITIS, JOHN	ACTOR	514 N AVE #54	LOS ANGELES, CA	90042
SCORCHERS, THE	ROCK & ROLL GROUP	SEE - JASON AND THE SCORCHERS		
SCORER, IAN	FILM-TV EXECUTIVE	8 NAPIER AVE	LONDON SW6	ENGLAND
SCORPIO	ROCK & ROLL GROUP	BORSA PRODS, 112 4TH AVE	NORWOOD, MA	02062
SCORPIO, JAY	ACTOR	12725 VENTURA BLVD #E	STUDIO CITY, CA	91604
SCORPIONS, THE	ROCK & ROLL GROUP	POST OFFICE BOX 5220	3000 HANNOVER 1	GERMANY
SCORSESE, MARTIN	FILM WRITER-DIRECTOR	165 DUANE ST #9-A	NEW YORK, NY	10013
SCORTIA, THOMAS N	WRITER	7177 BRYDON RD	LA VERNE, CA	91750
SCORZA, PHILIP A	WRITER	14133 ARCHWOOD ST	VAN NUYS, CA	91405
SCOT, JOHN ANTONY	CONDUCTOR	POST OFFICE BOX 4638	LONG BEACH, CA	90804
SCOT, MARGARET W	DIRECTOR	4424 MOORPARK WY	NORTH HOLLYWOOD, CA	91602
SCOTFORD, SYBIL	ACTRESS	4155 CAMELLIA AVE	STUDIO CITY, CA	91604
SCOTT, ALLAN	TV WRITER-PRODUCER	16-A THE BOLTONS	LONDON SW10	ENGLAND
SCOTT, ALLAN G	SCREENWRITER	1441 S BEVERLY GLEN BLVD	LOS ANGELES, CA	90024
SCOTT, ANNIE	TV WRITER	8955 BEVERLY BLVD	LOS ANGELES, CA	90048
SCOTT, ASHLEY	MODEL	EILEEN FORD, 334 E 59TH ST	NEW YORK, NY	10022
SCOTT, BILLY	SINGER	POST OFFICE BOX 25371	CHARLOTTE, NC	28212
SCOTT, BRENDA	ACTRESS	902 TIVERTON AVE	LOS ANGELES, CA	90024
SCOTT, CAROL E	TV DIRECTOR	DGA, 7950 SUNSET BLVD	LOS ANGELES, CA	90046
SCOTT, CHARLES R, JR	DIRECTOR	10820 PEACHGROVE ST	NORTH HOLLYWOOD, CA	91601
SCOTT, DEAN	SINGER	4615 SOUTHWEST FREEWAY #475	HOUSTON, TX	77027
SCOTT, DEBORAH K	TV WRITER	8955 BEVERLY BLVD	LOS ANGELES, CA	90048
SCOTT, DEBRALEE	ACTRESS	11726 SAN VICENTE BLVD #300	LOS ANGELES, CA	90049
SCOTT, DICK	TALENT AGENT	159 W 53RD ST	NEW YORK, NY	10019
SCOTT, DONOVAN	ACTOR	9200 SUNSET BLVD #1210	LOS ANGELES, CA	90069
SCOTT, DOUG	ACTOR	3575 W CAHUENGA BLVD #320	LOS ANGELES, CA	90068
SCOTT, DOUGLAS F	ACTOR	2325 PANORAMIC DR	CONCORD, CA	94520
SCOTT, DR GENE	TV HOST-TEACHER	POST OFFICE BOX 1	LOS ANGELES, CA	90053
SCOTT, DUNCAN M	DIRECTOR-PRODUCER	90-50 UNION TURNPIKE	GLENDALE, NY	11385
SCOTT, DWIGHT	PIANIST	2109 BERNARD AVE	NASHVILLE, TN	37212
SCOTT, EDWARD	TV PRODUCER	CBS TELEVISION NETWORK		
		"THE YOUNG & THE RESTLESS"		
		7800 BEVERLY BLVD	LOS ANGELES, CA	90036
SCOTT, EDWARD J	DIRECTOR	13220 INGRES AVE	GRANADA HILLS, CA	91344
SCOTT, EINAR PERRY	ACTOR	140 W 57TH ST	NEW YORK, NY	10019
SCOTT, EVELYN	ACTRESS	9021 MELROSE AVE #304	LOS ANGELES, CA	90069
SCOTT, F M, III	COMPOSER	POST OFFICE BOX 2107	RANCHO SANTE FE, CA	92067
SCOTT, FRED	ACTOR	1716 CAMINO PAROCELA	PALM SPRINGS, CA	92262
SCOTT, FRED DANIEL	ACTOR	2028 N BEACHWOOD DR #304	LOS ANGELES, CA	90068
SCOTT, GAREN	TV WRITER	8955 BEVERLY BLVD	LOS ANGELES, CA	90048
SCOTT, GARY	DRUMMER	787 BELLEVUE RD	NASHVILLE, TN	37221
SCOTT, GARY	COMPOSER	5128 GAVIOTA AVE	ENCINO, CA	91436
SCOTT, GENE	TV HOST-TEACHER	SEE - SCOTT, DR GENE		
SCOTT, GEOFFREY	ACTOR	3464 PRIMERA AVE	LOS ANGELES, CA	90068
SCOTT, GEORGE C	ACTOR-DIRECTOR	JANE DEACY AGENCY		
		181 REVOLUTIONARY DR	SCARSBOROUGH, NY	10510
SCOTT, GEORGE W	ACTOR	5701 SAN VICENTE BLVD	LOS ANGELES, CA	90019
SCOTT, GERRY S	NEWS CORRESPONDENT	1776 "C" ST, NW	WASHINGTON, DC	20006
SCOTT, GORDON L T	TV PRODUCER	BURTON HILL, GRENFELL RD		
		BEACONS	BUCKS	ENGLAND
SCOTT, HERBERT J	TV DIRECTOR	WCAU TELEVISION STATION		
		CITY LINE & MONUMENT RDS	PHILADEPHIA, PA	19131
SCOTT, IVAN	COMPOSER-CONDUCTOR	1420 QUUENS RD	LOS ANGELES, CA	90069
SCOTT, JACK	SINGER-SONGWRITER	ATTIC RECORDS COMPANY		
SCOTT, JACK ALBERT	TV DIRECTOR	4411 LOS FELIZ BLVD #901	LOS ANGELES, CA	90027
SCOTT, JACQUELINE	ACTRESS	POST OFFICE BOX 69405	LOS ANGELES, CA	90069
SCOTT, JAMES	FILM DIRECTOR	FLAMINGO, 47 LONSDALE SQ	LONDON N1 1EW	ENGLAND
SCOTT, JEAN BRUCE	ACTRESS	10390 SANTA MONICA BLVD #310	LOS ANGELES, CA	90025
SCOTT, JEF	SINGER-GUITARIST	POST OFFICE BOX 2601	HOLLYWOOD, CA	90078

Name	Occupation	Address	City/State	Zip
SCOTT, JEFFREY	WRITER-PRODUCER	STEPHEN J CANNELL PRODS		
		7083 HOLLYWOOD BLVD	HOLLYWOOD, CA	90028
SCOTT, JEFFREY ALAN	TV WRITER	8955 BEVERLY BLVD	LOS ANGELES, CA	90048
SCOTT, JERRY	CARTOONIST	POST OFFICE BOX 1315	NIPOMA, CA	93444
SCOTT, JOAN	WRITER	9100 SUNSET BLVD #340	LOS ANGELES, CA	90069
SCOTT, JOHN	ACTOR	9255 SUNSET BLVD #510	LOS ANGELES, CA	90069
SCOTT, JOHN	COMPOSER	2 QUEENS GATE PLACE MEWS		
		SOUTH KENNINGTON	LONDON SW7 5BQ	ENGLAND
SCOTT, JOHN	GUITARIST	ROUTE #1, BOX 181-L	MOBILE, AL	36601
SCOTT, JOHN	ORGANIST	15 HIGH ST #621	HARTFORD, CT	06103
SCOTT, JUD	TV WRITER	8955 BEVERLY BLVD	LOS ANGELES, CA	90048
SCOTT, JUDSON	ACTOR	1650 BROADWAY #302	NEW YORK, NY	10019
SCOTT, KAREN LYNN	ACTRESS	8961 SUNSET BLVD #B	LOS ANGELES, CA	90069
SCOTT, KARYL M	NEWS CORRESPONDENT	2122 19TH ST	ARLINGTON, VA	22201
SCOTT, KATHRYN J	NEWS CORRESPONDENT	1330 NEW HAMPSHIRE AVE, NW	WASHINGTON, DC	20036
SCOTT, KATHRYN LEIGH	ACTRESS	3236 BENNETT DR	LOS ANGELES, CA	90068
SCOTT, KEN	ACTOR	208 S BEVERLY DR #4	BEVERLY HILLS, CA	90212
SCOTT, LARRY	BODYBUILDER	POST OFFICE BOX 162	NO SALT LAKE CITY, UT	84054
SCOTT, LINDA J	NEWS CORRESPONDENT	5151 WISCONSIN AVE, NW	WASHINGTON, DC	20016
SCOTT, LIZABETH	ACTRESS	8277 HOLLYWOOD BLVD	VAN NUYS, CA	91401
SCOTT, MARILYN	SINGER	VISION, 2112 N CAHUENGA BLVD	LOS ANGELES, CA	90068
SCOTT, MARK EDWARD	NEWS CORRESPONDENT	1528 N WAKEFIELD ST	ARLINGTON, VA	22207
SCOTT, MARTHA	ACTRESS	10000 SANTA MONICA BLVD #305	LOS ANGELES, CA	90067
SCOTT, MELODY THOMAS	ACTRESS	CBS TELEVISION NETWORK		
		"THE YOUNG & THE RESTLESS"		
		7800 BEVERLY BLVD	LOS ANGELES, CA	90036
SCOTT, MICHAEL	TV DIRECTOR	13261 1/2 BLOOMFIELD ST	SHERMAN OAKS, CA	91423
SCOTT, MICHAEL JAMES FOLEY	DIRECTOR-PRODUCER	84 QUEENSTON ST	WINNIPEG, MB	CANADA
SCOTT, MICHAEL T	COMPOSER	4401 KRAFT AVE #8	NORTH HOLLYWOOD, CA	91602
SCOTT, MIKE	BASEBALL	5417 W 134TH PL	HAWTHORNE, CA	90250
SCOTT, NATHAN G	COMPOSER	14222 WEDDINGTON ST	VAN NUYS, CA	91401
SCOTT, OZ	TV DIRECTOR	6645 ALLOTT AVE	VAN NUYS, CA	91401
SCOTT, PAUL J	NEWS CORRESPONDENT	6516 ELMHURST ST	DISTRICT HEIGHTS, MD	20747
SCOTT, PETER GRAHAM	TV DIRECTOR-PRODUCER	HIGH PINES, WINDLESHAM	SURREY	ENGLAND
SCOTT, PIPPA	ACTRESS	1474 3RD AVE	NEW YORK, NY	10028
SCOTT, RENA	SINGER	BUDDAH RECORDS CO		
		810 7TH AVE	NEW YORK, NY	10019
SCOTT, RIDLEY	FILM DIRECTOR	1888 CENTURY PARK E #1400	LOS ANGELES, CA	90067
SCOTT, RITA	DIRECTOR	12244 EMELITA ST	NORTH HOLLYWOOD, CA	91607
SCOTT, ROBERT	ACTOR	SEE - ROBERTS, MARK		
SCOTT, SARAH	NEWS CORRESPONDENT	NBC NEWS, 4001 NEBRASKA AVE, NW	WASHINGTON, DC	20016
SCOTT, SHERI LEE	ACTRESS	244 MADISON AVE #10-D	NEW YORK, NY	10016
SCOTT, SIMON	ACTOR	9255 SUNSET BLVD #610	LOS ANGELES, CA	90069
SCOTT, SIR PETER	TV PERSONALITY	NEW GROUNDS, SLIMBRIDGE	GLOSGLOW	ENGLAND
SCOTT, SYDNA	ACTRESS	9200 SUNSET BLVD #909	LOS ANGELES, CA	90069
SCOTT, TERRY	ACTOR	GREENACRE, GASDEN COPSE		
		WITLEY	SURREY	ENGLAND
SCOTT, THOMAS W	COMPOSER-CONDUCTOR	JESS MORGAN COMPANY		
		6420 WILSHIRE BLVD, 19TH FLOOR	LOS ANGELES, CA	90048
SCOTT, TIMOTHY	ACTOR	SF & A, 121 N SAN VICENTE BLVD	BEVERLY HILLS, CA	90211
SCOTT, TOM	SAXOPHONIST	10100 SANTA MONICA BLVD #1600	LOS ANGELES, CA	90067
SCOTT, TOM	SINGER	11 BAILEY AVE	RIDGEFIELD, CT	06877
SCOTT, TOMMY "DOC" & REAL MEDIC	C & W GROUP	POST OFFICE BOX 100	TOCCOA, GA	30577
SCOTT, TONY	FILM DIRECTOR	BILL UNGER, 422 N HAYWORTH AVE	LOS ANGELES, CA	90048
SCOTT, WALTER	COLUMNIST	PARADE MAGAZINE, 750 3RD AVE	NEW YORK, NY	10017
SCOTT, WALTER E	DIRECTOR	14543 BLEDSOE ST	SYLMAR, CA	91342
SCOTT, WILLARD	WEATHERPERSON	NBC TELEVISION NETWORK		
		30 ROCKEFELLER PLAZA #304	NEW YORK, NY	10112
SCOTT-HERON, GIL	SINGER-PIANIST	POST OFFICE BOX 1417-838	ALEXANDRIA, VA	22313
SCOTTI, DIANA	ACTRESS	1504 BERKELEY ST	SANTA MONICA, CA	90404
SCOTTI, VITO	ACTOR	5456 VANALDEN AVE	TARZANA, CA	91356
SCOTTO, RENATA	SOPRANO	61 W 62ND ST #6-F	NEW YORK, NY	10023
SCOTTY, JERRY	CARTOONIST	KING FEATURES SYNDICATE		
		235 E 45TH ST	NEW YORK, NY	10017
SCOURBY, HELEN	ACTRESS	23 E 11TH ST	NEW YORK, NY	10003
SCRANTON, PETER	ACTOR	2084 LEWIS TERR	LOS ANGELES, CA	90046
SCRAWS	CARTOONIST	KING FEATURES SYNDICATE		
		235 E 45TH ST	NEW YORK, NY	10017
SCREAMING BLUE MESSIAHS, THE	ROCK & ROLL GROUP	JOHN DUMMER, 17 CRESCENT WY	LONDON SE4 1QL	ENGLAND
SCREAMING SAMMY	COMEDIAN-ACTOR	SEE - KINISON, SCREAMING SAMMY		
SCRIMA, VINCENT P	COMPOSER	4232 TORREON DR	WOODLAND HILLS, CA	91364
SCRUFFY THE CAT	ROCK & ROLL GROUP	78 HILLSIDE ST #3	ROXBURY, MA	02120
SCRUGGS, EARL	BANJOIST-SONGWRITER	POST OFFICE BOX 66	MADISON, TN	37115
SCRUGGS, GARY	GUITARIST	774 ELYSIAN FIELDS RD	NASHVILLE, TN	37204
SCRUGGS, NOEL	FIDDLER	POST OFFICE BOX 153	HARTSVILLE, TN	37074
SCRUGGS, RANDY	BANJOIST	808 GLEN LEVEN DR	NASHVILLE, TN	37204
SCUDDAY, MARY R	WRITER	1636 N VERDUGO RD #208	GLENDALE, CA	91208
SCULLY, JOE	CASTING DIRECTOR	POST OFFICE BOX 5718	SHERMAN OAKS, CA	91403
SCULLY, MALCOLM G	NEWS CORRESPONDENT	321 FOREST DR	FALLS CHURCH, VA	22046
SCULLY, VIN	SPORTSCASTER	1555 CAPRI DR	PACIFIC PALISADES, CA	90272
SEA LEVEL	ROCK & ROLL GROUP	119 W 57TH ST #901	NEW YORK, NY	10019
SEABERRY, JANE A	NEWS CORRESPONDENT	5420 S 4TH ST	ARLINGTON, VA	22204
SEABOLD, ELIZABETH	WRITER	11580 BLIX ST	NORTH HOLLYWOOD, CA	91602
SEABRIDGE, JUDY A	TV DIRECTOR	68 PARK AVE	ALBANY, NY	12202
SEABRIGHT	HIGH WIRE ACT	POST OFFICE BOX 87	WEST LEBANON, NY	12195

SEABURY, JOHN	BARITONE	JCB, 155 W 68TH ST	NEW YORK, NY	10023
SEACAT, SANDRA	ACTRESS	10100 SANTA MONICA BLVD #1600	LOS ANGELES, CA	90067
SEADER, RICHARD	THEATER PRODUCER	344 W 72ND ST	NEW YORK, NY	10023
SEAFORTH-HAYES, SUSAN	ACTRESS	4528 BECK AVE	NORTH HOLLYWOOD, CA	91602
SEAGO, DAVID A	TV DIRECTOR	23970 23 MILE RD	MOUNT CLEMENS, MI	48043
SEAGRAVE, MALCOLM R	COMPOSER	915 DOUGLAS ST	LOS ANGELES, CA	90026
SEAGREN, BOB	ACTOR	120 S THURSTON AVE	LOS ANGELES, CA	90049
SEAGROVE, JENNY	ACTRESS	10-A HIGHBURY, NEW PARK		
		GARDEN FLAT	LONDON N5 2DB	ENGLAND
SEAGULL, BARBARA	ACTRESS	SEE - HERSHEY, BARBARA		
SEALE, DAMON	PIANIST	2936 DONNA HILL DR	NASHVILLE, TN	37214
SEALE, JOHN	CINEMATOGRAPHER	3872 LAS FLORES CANYON RD #1	MALIBU, CA	90265
SEALE, STANLEY M	COMPOSER	POST OFFICE BOX 951	POINT ANGELES, WA	98362
SEALES, FRANKLYN	ACTOR	10100 SANTA MONICA BLVD #1600	LOS ANGELES, CA	90067
SEALS, DAN	SINGER-SONGWRITER	POST OFFICE BOX 1770	HENDERSONVILLE, TN	37077
SEALS, ED	PIANIST	223 LAKE TERR DR	HENDERSONVILLE, TN	37075
SEALS, JAY R	DRUMMER	250 DONNA DR #5-B	HENDERSONVILLE, TN	37075
SEALS, TROY	GUITARIST	POST OFFICE BOX 1446	HENDERSONVILLE, TN	37075
SEAMAN, A BARRETT	NEWS CORRESPONDENT	5307 ELLIOTT RD	BETHESDA, MD	20816
SEAMAN, PETER S	SCREENWRITER	8955 BEVERLY BLVD	LOS ANGELES, CA	90048
SEAMANS, ANDY	EDITOR-COLUMNIST	HERITAGE FEATURES SYNDICATE		
		214 MASSACHSUETTS AVE, NE	WASHINGTON, DC	20002
SEARCHERS, THE	VOCAL GROUP	POST OFFICE BOX 262	CARTARET, NJ	07008
SEARCHINGER, GENE	FILM DIRECTOR	200 W 72ND ST #46	NEW YORK, NY	10023
SEARLE, HUMPHREY	COMPOSER	44 ORDNANCE HILL	LONDON NW8	ENGLAND
SEARLE, JUDITH	ACTRESS	6310 SAN VICENTE BLVD #407	LOS ANGELES, CA	90048
SEARLES, DAN	GUIATRIST	RUNYEON, 108 TAGGERT AVE	NASHVILLE, TN	37205
SEARLS, HANK	WRITER	10100 SANTA MONICA BLVD #1600	LOS ANGELES, CA	90067
SEARS, DAVID R	COMPOSER-CONDUCTOR	5846 4TH AVE	LOS ANGELES, CA	90043
SEARS, KENNETH	VIOLINIST	ROUTE #4, BOX 179-AA	GALLATIN, TN	37066
SEARS, SALLY	THEATER PRODUCER	PRIM PRODS, 387 1/2 BLEEKER ST	NEW YORK, NY	10014
SEATON, EULA	SCREENWRITER	8955 BEVERLY BLVD	LOS ANGELES, CA	90048
SEATON, JOHNNY	SINGER-GUITARIST	ROUNDER RECORDS		
SEAVER, TOM	BASEBALL	LARKSPUR LN	GREENWICH, CT	06830
SEAVERNS, CHARLES	ACTOR	8927 SAINT IVES DR	LOS ANGELES, CA	90069
SEAVERS, VICKY LYNNE	ACTRESS	3700 BAGLEY AVE #213	LOS ANGELES, CA	90034
SEAVEY, DAVID	CARTOONIST	POST OFFICE BOX 500	WASHINGTON, DC	20044
SEAWIND	ROCK & ROLL GROUP	200 W 51ST ST #1410	NEW YORK, NY	10019
SEAY, LINDA	SOPRANO	LIEBERMAN, 11 RIVERSIDE DR	NEW YORK, NY	10023
SEBASTIAN, BRUNO	TENOR	KAY, 58 W 58TH ST	NEW YORK, NY	10019
SEBASTIAN, JOHN	SINGER-SONGWRITER	BENDETT, 2431 BRIARCREST RD	BEVERLY HILLS, CA	90210
SEBASTIAN, MARK	ACTOR	6310 SAN VICENTE BLVD #407	LOS ANGELES, CA	90048
SEBASTIAN, PAUL EDWIN	ACTOR	1741 N IVAR AVE #221	LOS ANGELES, CA	90028
SEBASTIAN, STUART	CHOREOGRAPHER	61 W 62ND ST #6-F	NEW YORK, NY	10023
SEBRING, DAVID	GUIATRIST	2001 BEECHWOOD AVE	NASHVILLE, TN	37212
SECKLER, CURLY	MANDOLINIST	320 EDWIN ST	NASHVILLE, TN	37207
SECOMBE, SIR HARRY	ACTOR-SINGER	46 SAINT JAMES'S ST	LONDON SW1	ENGLAND
SECONDARI, HELEN JEAN	DIRECTOR	1148 5TH AVE	NEW YORK, NY	10028
SECOR, KYLE	ACTOR	KNBC-TV, "SANTA BARBARA"		
		3000 W ALAMEDA AVE	BURBANK, CA	91523
SECOTA, ELENA	ACTRESS	427 N CANON DR #205	BEVERLY HILLS, CA	90210
SECREST, JAMES F	ACTOR	484 W 43RD ST	NEW YORK, NY	10036
SECRET LIVES	ROCK & ROLL GROUP	41 BRITAIN ST #200	TORONTO, ONT	CANADA
SECUNDA, AL	ACTOR	1360 N LAUREL AVE #3	LOS ANGELES, CA	90046
SECUNDE, NADINE	SOPRANO	CAMI, 165 W 57TH ST	NEW YORK, NY	10019
SEDAKA, DARA	SINGER	910 5TH AVE	NEW YORK, NY	10019
SEDAKA, NEIL	SINGER-SONGWRITER	330 W 58TH ST #4-A	NEW YORK, NY	10019
SEDAN	ROCK & ROLL GROUP	SANTINO PRODUCTIONS		
		10097 GRANDVIEW	WOODLAWN, OH	45215
SEDAWIE, NORMAN W	WRITER-PRODUCER	5352 TOPEKA DR	TARZANA, CA	91356
SEDELMAIER, JOHN JOSEF	DIRECTOR	520 N MICHIGAN AVE #436	CHICAGO, IL	60611
SEDERHOLM, DAVID	ACTOR	ABC TELEVISION NETWORK		
		1330 AVE OF THE AMERICAS	NEW YORK, NY	10019
SEDGWICK, EILEEN	ACTRESS	10792 WELLWORTH AVE	LOS ANGELES, CA	90024
SEDGWICK, TOD	NEWS CORRESPONDENT	3100 45TH ST, NW	WASHINGTON, DC	20016
SEDLAK, JOHN E	TV WRITER	555 W 57TH ST #1230	NEW YORK, NY	10019
SEDWICK, CAROL	TV DIRECTOR	317 W 54TH ST #3-A	NEW YORK, NY	10019
SEDWICK, JO ANNE	TV DIRECTOR	CBS-TV, "THE GUIDING LIGHT"		
		51 W 52ND ST	NEW YORK, NY	10019
SEDWICK, JOHN W	DIRECTOR	56 WILLOW ST	BROOKLYN, NY	11201
SEE, CAROLYN	TV WRITER	8955 BEVERLY BLVD	LOS ANGELES, CA	90048
SEE, CHARLES E	COMPOSER	2464 W 1ST AVE #102	VANCOUVER, BC V6K 1G6	CANADA
SEEBER, IRV	BANJOIST	POST OFFICE BOX 121204	NASHVILLE, TN	37212
SEEGAR, SARA	ACTRESS	STONE MEADOWS FARM		
		BUCKS COUNTY	NEWTON, PA	18940
SEEGER, PETE	SINGER-SONGWRITER	DUCHESS JUNCTION	BEACON, NY	12508
SEEGER, SANFORD	ACTOR	545 W 126TH ST	NEW YORK, NY	10027
SEEGER, SUSAN	TV WRITER	8955 BEVERLY BLVD	LOS ANGELES, CA	90048
SEELY, EILEEN	ACTRESS	1930 CENTURY PARK W #303	LOS ANGELES, CA	90067
SEELY, JEANNIE	SINGER	38 MUSIC SQUARE E #300	NASHVILLE, TN	37203
SEELY, SCOTT B	COMPOSER	39 BELMONT AVE	RANCHO MIRAGE, CA	92270
SEFF, RICHARD	ACTOR	260 S WETHERLY DR	BEVERLY HILLS, CA	90211
SEFLINGER, CAROL ANNE	ACTRESS	8025 RESEDA BLVD #42	RESEDA, CA	91335
SEFSIK, STEPHEN	SAXOPHONIST	6616 SUSSEX CIR	NASHVILLE, TN	37205
SEGAL, A DAVID	DIRECTOR	DGA, 110 W 57TH ST	NEW YORK, NY	10019

Name	Occupation	Address	City/State	Zip/Country
SEGAL, BARBARA	SOPRANO	111 W 57TH ST #1209	NEW YORK, NY	10019
SEGAL, DANIEL	WRITER	19433 PACIFIC COAST HWY	MALIBU, CA	90265
SEGAL, ELLEN	DIRECTOR-PRODUCER	210 E 73RD ST	NEW YORK, NY	10021
SEGAL, ERICH	AUTHOR	53 THE PRYORS, EAST HEATH RD	LONDON NW3 1BP	ENGLAND
SEGAL, GEORGE	ACTOR	ICM, 8899 BEVERLY BLVD	LOS ANGELES, CA	90048
SEGAL, JEFFREY	ACTOR	MC LEAN, 23-B DEODAR RD	LONDON SW15 2NP	ENGLAND
SEGAL, JERRY	SCREENWRITER	8955 BEVERLY BLVD	LOS ANGELES, CA	90048
SEGAL, JOEL B	FILM DIRECTOR	2757 BENTLEY PL	MARIETTA, GA	30067
SEGAL, JOHN	ACTOR	MALONE, 89 RIVERVIEW, BARNES	LONDON SW13	ENGLAND
SEGAL, JONATHAN	ACTOR	600 RADCLIFFE AVE	PACIFIC PALISADES, CA	90272
SEGAL, MICHAEL	ACTOR	27 CYPRUS AVE, FINCHLEY	LONDON N3 1SS	ENGLAND
SEGAL, PETER	GUITARIST	POST OFFICE BOX 27539	PHILADELPHIA, PA	19118
SEGAL, STANLEY	TV HOST	POST OFFICE BOX 11985	SAN DIEGO, CA	92111
SEGAL, STEPHANIE	ACTRESS	9744 WILSHIRE BLVD #306	BEVERLY HILLS, CA	90212
SEGAL, URI	CONDUCTOR	SHAW CONCERTS, 1995 BROADWAY	NEW YORK, NY	10023
SEGAL, VIVIENNE	SINGER-ACTRESS	ROBINSON, 152 N LE DOUX RD	BEVERLY HILLS, CA	90211
SEGALL, DONALD	TV WRITER-PRODUCER	156 S ALMONT DR	BEVERLY HILLS, CA	90211
SEGALL, PAMELA	ACTRESS	POST OFFICE BOX 5617	BEVERLY HILLS, CA	90210
SEGALL, RICK	ACTOR	4006 YANKEE DR	AGOURA HILLS, CA	91301
SEGALL, STUART	TV PRODUCER	STEPHEN J CANNELL PRODS		
		7083 HOLLYWOOD BLVD	LOS ANGELES, CA	90028
SEGAR, KATHLEEN	MEZZO-SOPRANO	SULLIVAN, 390 W END AVE	NEW YORK, NY	10024
SEGAR, MAX	ACTOR	8831 SUNSET BLVD #402	LOS ANGELES, CA	90069
SEGEL, RUSSELL	DIRECTOR	10311 RIVERSIDE DR #302	TOLUCA LAKE, CA	91602
SEGELIN, BERNARD	FILM EXECUTIVE	523 CASHMERE TERR	LOS ANGELES, CA	90049
SEGELSKA, ELIZABETH	MEZZO-SOPRANO	PERLS, 7 W 96TH ST	NEW YORK, NY	10025
SEGER, BOB & THE SILVER BULLET	ROCK & ROLL GROUP	PUNCH ENTERPRISES		
		567 PURDY ST	BIRMINGHAM, MI	48009
SEGERBERG, OSBORN C	TV WRITER	555 W 57TH ST #1230	NEW YORK, NY	10019
SEGERS, FRANK	COLUMNIST	VARIETY, 1400 N CAHUENGA BLVD	HOLLYWOOD, CA	90028
SEGHERS, FRANCES	NEWS CORRESPONDENT	3701 MASSACUSETTS AVE #301, NW	WASHINGTON, DC	20016
SEGRERAS, THE FLYING	AERIAL ACT	HALL, 138 FROG HOLLOW RD	CHURCHVILLE, PA	18966
SEGURA, PANCHO	TENNIS	RANCHO LA COSTA HOTEL & SPA		
		COSTA DEL MAR RD	CARLSBAD, CA	92008
SEGURSON, HOWARD J	COMPOSER	6648 BOBBYBOYAR AVE	CAONGA PARK, CA	91307
SEHRES, BILL	ACTOR	BERZON, 336 E 17TH ST	COSTA MESA, CA	92627
SEHULSTER, TONI	GUITARIST	2109 BERNARD AVE	NASHVILLE, TN	37212
SEIBEL, LYNN	ACTOR	4625 VARNA AVE	SHERMAN OAKS, CA	91423
SEIBERT, L H	COMPOSER	1102 E VINE AVE	WEST COVINA, CA	91790
SEIDELMAN, ARTHUR	FILM-TV DIRECTOR	618 MIDVALE AVE #A	LOS ANGELES, CA	90024
SEIDELMAN, SUSAN	FILM DIRECTOR	DGA, 110 W 57TH ST	NEW YORK, NY	10019
SEIDEMAN, DAVID	NEWS REPORTER	TIME/TIME & LIFE BLDG		
		ROCKEFELLER CENTER	NEW YORK, NY	10020
SEIDLER, DAVID	TV WRITER	8955 BEVERLY BLVD	LOS ANGELES, CA	90048
SEIDMAN, ERIC	ART DIRECTOR	DISCOVER/TIME & LIFE BLDG		
		ROCKEFELLER CENTER	NEW YORK, NY	10020
SEIGEL, DONALD L	TV WRITER-DIRECTOR	10350 SANTA MONICA BLVD #250	LOS ANGELES, CA	90025
SEIGEL, ROBERT C	NEWS CORRESPONDENT	3489 S UTAH ST	ARLINGTON, VA	22206
SEIGENTHALER, JOHN	EDITORIAL DIRECTOR	POST OFFICE BOX 500	WASHINGTON, DC	20044
SEIGHMAN, BILL	GUITARIST	4128 COLERIDGE DR	ANTIOCH, TN	37013
SEINFELD, JERRY	COMEDIAN	141 S EL CAMINO DR #205	BEVERLY HILLS, CA	90212
SEIPT, VIRGINIA GAIL	DIRECTOR	NBC TELEVISION NETWORK		
		30 ROCKEFELLER PLAZA #1455	NEW YORK, NY	10112
SEITER, CHRISTOPHER	TV DIRECTOR-PRODUCER	645 S EUCLID AVE	PASADENA, CA	91106
SEITZ, GEORGE B, JR	WRITER-PRODUCER	10375 WILSHIRE BLVD #5-F	LOS ANGELES, CA	90024
SEITZ, MICHAEL	WRESTLER	SEE - HAYES, MICHAEL "P S"		
SEKA	ACTRESS-MODEL	840 N MICHIGAN AVE #408	CHICAGO, IL	60611
SELBY, DAVID	ACTOR	151 S EL CAMINO DR	BEVERLY HILLS, CA	90212
SELBY, KATHRYN	PIANIST	SHAW CONCERTS, 1995 BROADWAY	NEW YORK, NY	10023
SELBY, TONY	ACTOR	99 RECTORY LN	LONDON SW17	ENGLAND
SELBY-WRIGHT, SONYA	DIRECTOR	DGA, 110 W 57TH ST	NEW YORK, NY	10019
SELDEN, ALBERT W	THEATER PRODUCER	246 W 44TH ST	NEW YORK, NY	10036
SELDEN, FRED	SAXOPHONIST	11561 DECENTE DR	STUDIO CITY, CA	91604
SELDEN, JOSEPH H, III	NEWS CORRESPONDENT	201 "I" ST, SW	WASHINGTON, DC	20024
SELDIN, ERIC A	NEWS CORRESPONDENT	3320 MOUNT PLEASANT ST, NW	WASHINGTON, DC	20010
SELDON, JOIE	ACTRESS	810 N DOHENY DR	LOS ANGELES, CA	90069
SELDON, SUICIDE	HUMAN BOMB	HALL, 138 FROG HOLLOW RD	CHURCHVILLE, PA	18966
SELF, EDWIN B	TV WRITER	8955 BEVERLY BLVD	LOS ANGELES, CA	90048
SELF, WILLIAM	DIRECTOR	975 SOMERA RD	LOS ANGELES, CA	90077
SELFE, RAY	ACTOR-DIRECTOR	126 THRONLAW RD, WEST NORWOOD	LONDON SE27	ENGLAND
SELIGMAN, ADAM	WRITER	9255 SUNSET BLVD #1122	LOS ANGELES, CA	90069
SELIK, LILA	CASTING DIRECTOR	4117 MC LAUGHLIN AVE #9	LOS ANGELES, CA	90066
SELIN, MARGO	BODYBUILDER	POST OFFICE BOX 9560		
		FRIENDSHIP STATION	WASHINGTON, DC	20016
SELINGER, MARK	ACTOR	3518 W CAHUENGA BLVD #316	LOS ANGELES, CA	90068
SELKIRK, FRANCENE	ACTRESS	2041 HIGH TOWER DR	LOS ANGELES, CA	90068
SELL, LORETTA	SINGER	SEE - HILDEGARDE		
SELL, RICHARD	GUITARIST	500 FESSLERS LN #J-2	NASHVILLE, TN	37210
SELLARS, BILL	TV PRODUCER	KENSINGTON HIGH ST		
		55 KENTON CT	LONDON W14	ENGLAND
SELLECA, CONNIE	ACTRESS	POST OFFICE BOX 60257	LOS ANGELES, CA	90060
SELLECK, JACQUELYN RAY	ACTRESS-MODEL	11385 HOMEDALE ST	LOS ANGELES, CA	90049
SELLECK, TOM	ACTOR	510 18TH ST	HONOLULU, HI	96816
SELLERS, ARLENE	FILM PRODUCER	9720 WILSHIRE BLVD #706	BEVERLY HILLS, CA	90212

DOC SEVERINSON

JANE SEYMOUR

TED SHACKELFORD

OMAR SHARIF

RAY SHARKEY

JULES SHEAR

CHARLIE SHEEN

SHEILA E.

MARK SHERA

Name	Occupation	Address	City/State	ZIP
SELLERS, ARTHUR D	SCREENWRITER	6144 GLEN OAK ST	LOS ANGELES, CA	90068
SELLERS, DALE	GUITARIST	ROUTE #2, BOX 475	BURNS, TN	37029
SELLERS, DAVID A	NEWS CORRESPONDENT	846 N JEFFERSON ST	ARLINGTON, VA	22205
SELLERS, KEVIN S	TV WRITER	8955 BEVERLY BLVD	LOS ANGELES, CA	90048
SELLERS, OLIVIA J	NEWS CORRESPONDENT	2133 WISCONSIN AVE, NW	WASHINGTON, DC	20007
SELLIN, NANCY	ACTRESS	675 W END AVE	NEW YORK, NY	10025
SELLINGER, MARGERY B	NEWS CORRESPONDENT	3903 VIRGINIA ST	CHEVY CHASE, MD	20815
SELLZ, RON B	WRITER	21808 KINGSBURY ST	CHATSWORTH, CA	91311
SELMA, REGINALD G	PHOTOJOURNALIST	601 FOUR-MILE RUN #218	ALEXANDRIA, VA	22305
SELOVER, JAMES R	CONDUCTOR	2283 TERMINO AVE	LONG BEACH, CA	90815
SELPH, JAMES	GUITARIST	420 WALTON LN #B-5	MADISON, TN	37115
SELSBY, HARV	ACTOR	1050 E ELMWOOD AVE	BURBANK, CA	91501
SELTZER, JODY	ACTRESS	SCHOEMAN, 2600 W VICTORY BLVD	BURBANK, CA	91505
SELTZER, LEO	WRITER-PRODUCER	368 E 69TH ST	NEW YORK, NY	10021
SELTZER, RICHARD J	NEWS CORRESPONDENT	13816 TURNMORE RD	SILVER SPRING, MD	20906
SELTZER, WILL	ACTOR	1547 MURRAY DR	LOS ANGELES, CA	90026
SELWART, TONIO	ACTOR	130 W 57TH ST	NEW YORK, NY	10019
SELWYN-GILBERT, JOHN	TV DIRECTOR-PRODUCER	166 GLOUCESTER TERR	LONDON W2 6HR	ENGLAND
SELZER, MILTON	ACTOR	21042 RIOS ST	WOODLAND HILLS, CA	91364
SEMBELLO, MICHAEL	SINGER-COMPOSER	BRIAN AVNET MANAGEMENT		
		3805 W MAGNOLIA BLVD	BURBANK, CA	91505
SEMEDO, BARBARA	NEWS CORRESPONDENT	5315 CONNECTICUT AVE, NW	WASHINGTON, DC	20015
SEMENCHUK, K ANATOLE	DIRECTOR	10660 W GLENNON DR	LAKEWOOD, CO	80226
SEMKOFF, OLEG NICHOLAS	TV DIRECTOR	4620 N PARK AVE #PH 2-E	CHEVY CHASE, MD	20815
SEMKOW, JERZY	CONDUCTOR	ICM, 40 W 57TH ST	NEW YORK, NY	10019
SEMLING, HAROLD V, JR	NEWS CORRESPONDENT	1600 S EADS ST #818	ARLINGTON, VA	22202
SEMPLE, LORENZO, JR	SCREENWRITER	8955 BEVERLY BLVD	LOS ANGELES, CA	90048
SEN, BACHOO	DIRECTOR-PRODUCER	6 WOODLAND WY, PETTS WOOD	KENT BR5 1ND	ENGLAND
SENDAK, MAURICE	ILLUSTRATOR-ARTIST	200 CHESTNUT HILL RD	RIDGEFIELD, CT	06877
SENDLER, DAVID	EDITOR-WRITER	TV GUIDE, 100 MATSONFORD RD	RADNOR, PA	19088
SENDREY, ALBERT R	COMPOSER	1377 MILLER PL	LOS ANGELES, CA	90069
SENESKY, RALPH	DIRECTOR	1714 SUNSET PLAZA DR	LOS ANGELES, CA	90069
SENIA, PAUL A	COMPOSER-CONDUCTOR	2207 WEST AVE #N-8	PALMDALE, CA	93550
SENIOR, WILLIAM C	NEWS CORRESPONDENT	2400 OLD TRACE LN	RESTON, VA	22091
SENN, MARTA	MEZZO-SOPRANO	CAMI, 165 W 57TH ST	NEW YORK, NY	10019
SENN, RUDOLF	DOUBLE BASS	ROSENFIELD, 714 LADD RD	BRONX, NY	10471
SENNA, LORRAINE	DIRECTOR	DGA, 7950 SUNSET BLVD	LOS ANGELES, CA	90046
SENSATIONAL LEIGHS, THE	AERIAL ACT	HALL, 138 FROG HOLLOW RD	CHURCHVILLE, PA	18966
SENSE, JEAN-LOUIS	NEWS CORRESPONDENT	1807 19TH ST, NW	WASHINGTON, DC	20009
SENTER, LESTER	MEZZO-SOPRANO	GERSHUNOFF, 502 PARK AVE	NEW YORK, NY	10022
SENTINEL BEAST	ROCK & ROLL GROUP	POST OFFICE BOX 2428	EL SEGUNDO, CA	90245
SENTRY, FRANK	WRITER-PRODUCER	7471 MELROSE AVE	HOLLYWOOD, CA	90046
SEPPA, NATHAN	NEWS CORRESPONDENT	1736 COLUMBIA RD #406, NW	WASHINGTON, DC	20009
SEPPY, TOM	NEWS CORRESPONDENT	1502 ANDERSON CT	ALEXANDRIA, VA	22312
SERAFIN, MICHAEL G	WRITER	14521 BENEFIT ST #102	SHERMAN OAKS, CA	91403
SERAPHINE, DANNY	DRUMMER	32371 LAKE PLEASANT DR	THOUSAND OAKS, CA	91360
SERAREID, MICHAEL	ACT-WRI-EXEC	15419 GREENLEAF ST	SHERMAN OAKS, CA	91403
SERBO, RICO	TENOR	61 W 62ND ST #6-F	NEW YORK, NY	10023
SEREBRIER, JOSE	CONDUCTOR	GERSHUNOFF, 502 PARK AVE	NEW YORK, NY	10022
SERENDIPITY SINGERS, THE	VOCAL GROUP	POST OFFICE BOX 142	WAUCONDA, IL	60084
SERENSITS, JOSEPH S	NEWS CORRESPONDENT	6510 FAIRBANKS ST	NEW CARROLLTON, MD	20784
SERESIN, MICHAEL S	DIRECTOR	BFCS, 218 E 50TH ST	NEW YORK, NY	10022
SERETAN, STEPHAN H	COMPOSER-CONDUCTOR	1317 12TH ST #9	SANTA MONICA, CA	90401
SERKIN, PETER	PIANIST	S KIRSHBAUM, 711 WEST END AVE	NEW YORK, NY	10025
SERNA, GIL	ACTOR	11240 MAGNOLIA BLVD #202	NORTH HOLLYWOOD, CA	91601
SERNA, PEPE	ACTOR	2321 HILL DR	LOS ANGELES, CA	90041
SEROTOFF, NAOMI	ACTRESS	10727 MC CUNE AVE #3	LOS ANGELES, CA	90034
SERRA, LUCIANA	SOPRANO	CAMI, 165 W 57TH ST	NEW YORK, NY	10019
SERRA, RAYMOND	ACTOR	19 W 44TH ST #1500	NEW YORK, NY	10036
SERRANO, CARLOS	BARITONE	CAMI, 165 W 57TH ST	NEW YORK, NY	10019
SERRILL, MICHAEL S	WRITER-EDITOR	TIME/TIME & LIFE BLDG		
		ROCKEFELLER CENTER	NEW YORK, NY	10020
SERRY, JOHN	SINGER	YAHM, 2593 BEACHWOOD DR	LOS ANGELES, CA	90068
SERTNER, MORT	ACTOR	1350 N HIGHLAND AVE #24	HOLLYWOOD, CA	90028
SERTNER, ROBERT M	TV PRODUCER	1827 NICHOLS CANYON RD	LOS ANGELES, CA	90046
SERVANT	GOSPEL GROUP	POST OFFICE BOX 669	WILDERVILLE, OR	97543
SERVER, ERIC	ACTOR	1139 N ONTARIO ST	BURBANK, CA	91505
SERVICE, THE	ROCK & ROLL GROUP	POST OFFICE BOX 268043	CHICAGO, IL	60626
SESNO, FRANK W	NEWS CORRESPONDENT	1310 ROBINSON PL	FALLS CHURCH, VA	22046
SESSIONS, RONNIE	SINGER-SONGWRITER	POST OFFICE BOX 4966	LITTLE ROCK, AK	72214
SESTO, CAMILO	SINGER	151 S EL CAMINO DR	BEVERLY HILLS, CA	90212
SETLOWE, BEVERLY J	WRITER	4602 CARTWRIGHT AVE	NORTH HOLLYWOOD, CA	91602
SETLOWE, RICHARD	WRITER	4602 CARTWRIGHT AVE	NORTH HOLLYWOOD, CA	91602
SETON, MIMI	ACTRESS	15010 VENTURA BLVD #219	SHERMAN OAKS, CA	91403
SETTLE, MIKE	SINGER	RNJ PRODS, 11514 CALVERT ST	NORTH HOLLYWOOD, CA	91606
SETTLES, RICHARD	ACTOR	11002 ROSE AVE #202	LOS ANGELES, CA	90034
SEUSS, DR	AUTHOR	SEE - GEISEL, TED		
SEVAREID, ERIC	NEWS JOURNALIST	CBS NEWS, 2020 "M" ST, NW	WASHINGTON, DC	20036
SEVEN, JOHNNY	ACTOR-DIRECTOR	11024 BALBOA BLVD	GRANADA HILLS, CA	91344
SEVEREID, SUSANNE	ACTRESS-MODEL	POST OFFICE BOX 4171	MALIBU, CA	90265
SEVERINSEN, DOC	TRUMPETER	1100 ALTA LOMA RD #707	LOS ANGELES, CA	90069
SEVERINSEN, DOC & XEBRON	JAZZ GROUP	1100 ALTA LOMA RD #707	LOS ANGELES, CA	90069
SEVERN, MAIDA	ACTRESS	151 N SAN VICENTE BLVD #208	BEVERLY HILLS, CA	90211
SEVERS, MICHAEL	GUITARIST	5008 YORKTOWN RD	NASHVILLE, TN	37205
SEVERS, PATRICK	GUITARIST	417 BOWLING AVE	NASHVILLE, TN	37205

Name	Occupation	Address	City/State	Zip
SEVORG, JON	TV WRITER	8955 BEVERLY BLVD	LOS ANGELES, CA	90048
SEWELL, GEORGE	ACTOR	26 WORCESTER CRESCENT		
		WOODFORD GREEN	ESSEX	ENGLAND
SEWELL, JOE	BASEBALL	1618 DEARING PL	TUSCALOOSA, AL	35401
SEWELL, LESLIE	NEWS CORRESPONDENT	NBC NEWS, 4001 NEBRASKA AVE, NW	WASHINGTON, DC	20016
SEXTON, DANIEL	ACTOR	330 N MAPLE ST #P	BURBANK, CA	91505
SEXTON, DREW	MUSICIAN	104 EVERGREEN CIR	HENDERSONVILLE, TN	37075
SEXTON, GARY	ACTOR	909 N GARDNER ST	LOS ANGELES, CA	90046
SEXTON, RON	WRESTLER	UNIVERSAL WRESTLING FEDERATION		
		MID SOUTH SPORTS, INC		
		5001 SPRING VALLEY RD	DALLAS, TX	75244
SEYMORE, DENNIS	SINGER	ACE, 3407 GREEN RIDGE DR	NASHVILLE, TN	37214
SEYMORE, JAMES	WRITER-EDITOR	PEOPLE/TIME & LIFE BLDG		
		ROCKEFELLER CENTER	NEW YORK, NY	10020
SEYMOUR, ANNE	ACTRESS	4219 LAUREL GROVE AVE	STUDIO CITY, CA	91604
SEYMOUR, BOBBE	PIANIST	POST OFFICE BOX 611	HENDERSONVILLE, TN	37075
SEYMOUR, CAROLYN	ACTRESS	9000 SUNSET BLVD #801	LOS ANGELES, CA	90069
SEYMOUR, DAN	ACTOR	1839 HILLSBORO AVE	LOS ANGELES, CA	90035
SEYMOUR, JANE	ACTRESS-MODEL	SAINT CATHERINE'S CT		
		BATHEASTON, BATH	AVON	ENGLAND
SEYMOUR, JOHN D	ACTOR	25 MINETA AVE	NEW YORK, NY	10012
SEYMOUR, MARK	PIANIST	849 WALNUT ST	MADISON, TN	37115
SEYMOUR, RALPH	ACTOR	14967 SUTTON ST	SHERMAN OAKS, CA	91403
SEYRIG, DELPHINE	ACTRESS	21 PL DES VOSGES	PARIS 3	FRANCE
SGARLATE, CARMEN	CLOWN	POST OFFICE BOX 87	WEST LEBANON, NY	12195
SGARRO, NICHOLAS	DIRECTOR	174 S ORANGE DR	LOS ANGELES, CA	90036
SGOUROS, DIMITRIS	PIANIST	ANGLO-SWISS ARTISTS MGMT		
		16 MUSWELL HILL RD, HIGHGATE	LONDON N6 5UG	ENGLAND
SHA NA NA	ROCK & ROLL GROUP	POST OFFICE BOX 92326	MILWAUKEE, WI	53202
SHABAREKH, ROBERT	GUITARIST	3913 BRADLEY CT	ANTIOCH, TN	37013
SHABECOFF, PHILIP	NEWS CORRESPONDENT	30 GRAFTON ST	CHEVY CHASE, MD	20815
SHABER, DAVID	SCREENWRITER	555 W 57TH ST #1230	NEW YORK, NY	10019
SHABTAI, SABI H	WRITER	POST OFFICE BOX 9906	MARINA DEL REY, CA	90292
SHACHT, LIBA	VIOLINIST	AFFILIATE ARTISTS, INC		
		37 W 65TH ST, 6TH FLOOR	NEW YORK, NY	10023
SHACHTMAN, TOM	WRITER	THE WILLIAM MORRIS AGENCY		
		1350 AVE OF THE AMERICAS	NEW YORK, NY	10019
SHACKLEFORD, TED	ACTOR	1973 CHEREMOYA AVE	LOS ANGELES, CA	90049
SHADDEN, TIMOTHY	ACTOR	3330 BARHAM BLVD #103	LOS ANGELES, CA	90068
SHADE, ELLEN	SOPRANO	CAMI, 165 W 57TH ST	NEW YORK, NY	10019
SHADE, NANCY	SOPRANO	59 E 54TH ST #81	NEW YORK, NY	10022
SHADOWFAX	JAZZ GROUP	VARIETY ARTISTS INTL, INC		
		9073 NEMO ST, 3RD FLOOR	LOS ANGELES, CA	90069
SHAFER, HAL	ACTOR	439 S LA CIENEGA BLVD #117	LOS ANGELES, CA	90048
SHAFER, RONALD G	NEWS CORRESPONDENT	1807 BALDWIN DR	MC LEAN, VA	22101
SHAFER, SANGER	GUITARIST	151 ROBERTA DR	HENDERSONVILLE, TN	37075
SHAFFER, ANTHONY	SCREENWRITER	8955 BEVERLY BLVD	LOS ANGELES, CA	90048
SHAFFER, GARY	CASTING DIRECTOR	WARNER-HOLLYWOOD STUDIOS		
		1041 N FORMOSA AVE	LOS ANGELES, CA	90046
SHAFFER, LLOYD	COMPOSER-CONDUCTOR	16295 AVENIDA NOBLEZA	SAN DIEGO, CA	92128
SHAFFER, LOUISE	ACTRESS	8285 SUNSET BLVD #12	LOS ANGELES, CA	90046
SHAFFER, NICHOLAS	ACTOR	POST OFFICE BOX 69405	LOS ANGELES, CA	90069
SHAFFER, PETER	SCREENWRITER	9255 SUNSET BLVD #505	LOS ANGELES, CA	90069
SHAFTER, BERT	ACTOR	42 HORATIO ST	NEW YORK, NY	10014
SHAGAN, STEVE	WRITER-PRODUCER	614 N CAMDEN DR	BEVERLY HILLS, CA	90210
SHAH, KRISHNA	WRITER-PRODUCER	POST OFFICE BOX 64515	LOS ANGELES, CA	90064
SHAIN, CARL	CASTING DIRECTOR	921 S CURSON AVE	HOLLYWOOD, CA	90036
SHAINMAN, LAWRENCE	NEWS CORRESPONDENT	NBC-TV, NEWS DEPARTMENT		
		4001 NEBRASKA AVE, NW	WASHINGTON, DC	20016
SHAKER, TED	TV EXECUTIVE	CBS SPORTS, 51 W 52ND ST	NEW YORK, NY	10019
SHAKOCIUS, SANDY	TV WRITER	8955 BEVERLY BLVD	LOS ANGELES, CA	90048
SHAKTMAN, BEN	TV WRITER-DIRECTOR	140 W 55TH ST	NEW YORK, NY	10019
SHALAMAR	SOUL GROUP	200 W 51ST ST #1410	NEW YORK, NY	10019
SHALET, DIANA	ACTRESS	7466 BEVERLY BLVD #205	LOS ANGELES, CA	90036
SHALIT, GENE	FILM CRITIC	NBC TELEVISION NETWORK		
		30 ROCKEFELLER PLAZA	NEW YORK, NY	10112
SHALLCROSS, ALAN	TV PRODUCER	BBC-TV CENTRE, WOOD LN		
		SHEPHERDS BUSH	LONDON W12	ENGLAND
SHALLECK, ALAN	DIRECTOR-PRODUCER	84 MORNINGSIDE DR	OSSINING, NY	10562
SHALLON, DAVID	CONDUCTOR	ICM, 40 W 57TH ST	NEW YORK, NY	10019
SHALNEV, ALEXANDER A	NEWS CORRESPONDENT	5631 DERBY CT	ALEXANDRIA, VA	22311
SHAMBERG, MICHAEL	FILM WRITER-PRODUCER	3328 MANDEVILLE CANYON RD	LOS ANGELES, CA	90049
SHAMES, JONATHAN	PIANIST	GREAT LAKES PERFORMING		
		310 E WASHINGTON ST	ANN ARBOR, MI	48104
SHAMRAY, GERRY	CARTOONIST	NEWS AMERICA SYNDICATE		
		1703 KAISER AVE	IRVINE, CA	92714
SHAMUDO, SAM "THE SHAM"	SINGER-SONGWRITER	3667 TETWILER AVE	MEMPHIS, TN	38122
SHAMVILL, REGINA	PIANIST	1182 MARKET ST #311	SAN FRANCISCO, CA	94102
SHANAHAN, J MICHAEL	NEWS CORRESPONDENT	1629 COLUMBIA RD #600, NW	WASHINGTON, DC	20009
SHANAHAN, RICHARD M	TV DIRECTOR-PRODUCER	744 FLORENCE DR	PARK RIDGE, IL	60068
SHAND, FRIEDA	ACTRESS	SAINT JAMES MGMT		
		22 GROOM PL	LONDON SW1	ENGLAND
SHAND, IAN	ACT-WRI-DIR	ROSEHILL HOUSE, ROSE HILL		
		BURNHAM	BUCKS	ENGLAND
SHANDEL, PAMELA	ACTRESS	937 1/2 N HARPER AVE	LOS ANGELES, CA	90046

SHANDLING, GARRY	COMED-ACT-WRI	151 S EL CAMINO DR	BEVERLY HILLS, CA	90212
SHANER, JOHN HERMAN	SCREENWRITER	151 S EL CAMINO DR	BEVERLY HILLS, CA	90212
SHANG, RUBY	DANCER	AFFILIATE ARTISTS, INC		
		37 W 65TH ST, 6TH FLOOR	NEW YORK, NY	10023
SHANGHAI DOG	ROCK & ROLL GROUP	550 W 6TH AVE	VANCOUVER, BC	CANADA
SHANK	ROCK & ROLL GROUP	SPINDLETOP RECORDS		
		1500 SUMMIT ST	AUSTIN, TX	78741
SHANKAR, RAVI	SITARIST	6 PAVLOVA, LITTLE GIBBS RD	BOMBAY	INDIA
SHANKLIN, DOUGLAS ALAN	ACTOR	6640 SUNSET BLVD #203	LOS ANGELES, CA	90028
SHANKS, ANN	DIRECTOR-PRODUCER	2237 N NEW HAMPSHIRE AVE	LOS ANGELES, CA	90027
SHANKS, BILL	ACTOR	CBS-TV, "AS THE WORLD TURNS"		
		51 W 52ND ST	NEW YORK, NY	10019
SHANKS, BOB	TV WRITER	ICM, 8899 BEVERLY BLVD	LOS ANGELES, CA	90048
SHANKS, JEFF	ACTOR	9220 SUNSET BLVD #202	LOS ANGELES, CA	90069
SHANKS, JERRY	DIRECTOR	4 QUARTERDECK ST #102	MARINA DEL REY, CA	90292
SHANNON	SINGER	POST OFFICE BOX 395	MERRICK, NY	11566
SHANNON	SINGER	POST OFFICE BOX 395	MERRICK, NY	11566
SHANNON, DEL	SINGER-SONGWRITER	WESTOVER, 26825 GWENALDA LN	CANYON COUNTRY, CA	91351
SHANNON, DONALD	NEWS CORRESPONDENT	1068 30TH ST, NW	WASHINGTON, DC	20007
SHANNON, DONALD, III	DIRECTOR	WFLD-TV, 300 N STATE ST	CHICAGO, IL	60610
SHANNON, ELAINE	NEWS CORRESPONDENT	1424 MADISON ST, NW	WASHINGTON, DC	20011
SHANNON, MICHAEL	ACTOR	9255 SUNSET BLVD #1105	LOS ANGELES, CA	90069
SHANNON, MICHAEL J	ACTOR	CONWAY, EAGLE HOUSE		
		109 JERMYN ST	LONDON SW1	ENGLAND
SHANNON, RAY D	NEWS CORRESPONDENT	ABC-TV, NEWS DEPARTMENT		
		1717 DE SALES ST, NW	WASHINGTON, DC	20036
SHANNON, SCOTT	WRESTLER	SEE - MC GHEE, SCOTT		
SHANNON, SOPHIA	ACTRESS	9025 WILSHIRE BLVD #309	BEVERLY HILLS, CA	90211
SHANOV, ELIZABETH	WRITER	330 S MENTOR AVE #223	PASADENA, CA	91106
SHAPER, HAL	LYRICIST	41-A ONSLOW SQ	LONDON SW7	ENGLAND
SHAPIRO, ALBERT	FILM DIRECTOR	14623 ROUND VALLEY DR	SHERMAN OAKS, CA	91403
SHAPIRO, ALLAN M	TV DIRECTOR	DGA, 110 W 57TH ST	NEW YORK, NY	10019
SHAPIRO, ARNOLD J	PRODUCER-EXECUTIVE	839 MALCOLM AVE	LOS ANGELES, CA	90024
SHAPIRO, BERT	WRITER-PRODUCER	196 E 75TH ST	NEW YORK, NY	10021
SHAPIRO, CONSTANTINE	COMPOSER-CONDUCTOR	3231 LOWRY RD	LOS ANGELES, CA	90027
SHAPIRO, DAN	TV WRITER	8955 BEVERLY BLVD	LOS ANGELES, CA	90048
SHAPIRO, DAVID	NEWS CORRESPONDENT	13515 APPLE BARREL CT	HERNDON, VA	22071
SHAPIRO, DAVID	NEWS CORRESPONDENT	43 LONG GREEN CT	SILVER SPRING, MD	20906
SHAPIRO, DAVID J	COMPOSER-CONDUCTOR	1135 ONTARIO ST	BURBANK, CA	91505
SHAPIRO, DAVID T	NEWS CORRESPONDENT	POST OFFICE BOX 2626	WASHINGTON, DC	20013
SHAPIRO, ERIC	TV DIRECTOR	19 ROCKFORD DR	W NYACK, NY	10994
SHAPIRO, ESTHER	TV WRITER-PRODUCER	617 N ALTA DR	BEVERLY HILLS, CA	90210
SHAPIRO, HARRIET	WRITER-EDITOR	TIME & PEOPLE MAGAZINE		
		TIME & LIFE BUILDING		
		ROCKEFELLER CENTER	NEW YORK, NY	10020
SHAPIRO, HELEN	SINGER-ACTRESS	BURNETT, 42 GRAFTON HOUSE		
		2-3 GOLDEN SQ	LONDON W1	ENGLAND
SHAPIRO, HOWARD S	TV DIRECTOR	9211 WASHINGTON	MORTON GROVE, IL	60053
SHAPIRO, JOSEPH P	NEWS CORRESPONDENT	109 "C" ST #1, SE	WASHINGTON, DC	20003
SHAPIRO, JOSHUA J	FILM DIRECTOR	110 W END AVE	NEW YORK, NY	10023
SHAPIRO, KENNETH R	FILM DIRECTOR	2044 STANLEY HILLS DR	LOS ANGELES, CA	90036
SHAPIRO, KENNETH S	TV WRITER-PRODUCER	13035 MAGNOLIA BLVD	SHERMAN OAKS, CA	91423
SHAPIRO, LEONARD	FILM PRODUCER	3884 FREDONIA DR #B-14	LOS ANGELES, CA	90068
SHAPIRO, MARGARET	NEWS CORRESPONDENT	3624 VAN NESS ST, NW	WASHINGTON, DC	20008
SHAPIRO, MICHAEL JOEL	ACTOR-FILM PRODUCER	1815 N CRESCENT HGTS BLVD	LOS ANGELES, CA	90069
SHAPIRO, RICHARD ALLEN	TV WRITER-PRODUCER	617 N ALTA DR	BEVERLY HILLS, CA	90210
SHAPIRO, ROBERT	FILM PRODUCER	4000 WARNER BLVD	BURBANK, CA	91522
SHAPIRO, ROBERT W	FILM EXECUTIVE	607 N OAKHURST DR	BEVERLY HILLS, CA	90210
SHAPIRO, RUBIN	DIRECTOR	500 2ND AVE	NEW YORK, NY	10016
SHAPIRO, SARI	CASTING DIRECTOR	POST OFFICE BOX 69277	LOS ANGELES, CA	90069
SHAPIRO, STANLEY	WRITER-PRODUCER	9938 ROBBINS DR	BEVERLY HILLS, CA	90212
SHAPS, CYRIL	ACTOR	MARR, 32 WIGMORE ST	LONDON W1H 5ZB	ENGLAND
SHARGO, BECKY	COMPOSER	3815 W OLIVE AVE #202	BURBANK, CA	91505
SHARIF, OMAR	ACTOR	MORRIS, 147-149 WARDOUR ST	LONDON W1V 3TB	ENGLAND
SHARKEY, BILLY RAY	ACTOR	SCHOEMAN, 2600 W VICTORY BLVD	BURBANK, CA	91505
SHARKEY, RAY	ACTOR	SCOTTI BROTHERS, 2128 W PICO BLVD	SANTA MONICA, CA	90405
SHARKS, THE	ROCK & ROLL GROUP	2109 W RIDGE AVE	LANCASTER, PA	17603
SHARLAND, MIKE	PLAYWRIGHT	53 ALWYN AVE, CHISWICK	LONDON W4	ENGLAND
SHARMA, BARBARA	ACTRESS	4445 1/2 CLARISSA AVE	LOS ANGELES, CA	90027
SHARNIK, JOHN S	TV WRITER-DIRECTOR	125 HICKS ST	BROOKLYN, NY	11201
SHARON, RALPH	CONDUCTOR	4858 FULTON AVE	SHERMAN OAKS, CA	91423
SHARP, ALEX	WRITER	4567 NAGLE AVE	SHERMAN OAKS, CA	91423
SHARP, CAL	GUITARIST	231 NEW SHACKLE ISLAND RD #H-64	HENDERSONVILLE, TN	37075
SHARP, CHRIS	FILM DIRECTOR	49 SAINT MARKS RD	LONDON W11 1RE	ENGLAND
SHARP, DON	TV WRITER-DIRECTOR	80 CASTELNAU, BARNES	LONDON SW13 9EX	ENGLAND
SHARP, HENRY ENOCH	WRITER	16839 ADLON RD	ENCINO, CA	91436
SHARP, IAN	FILM DIRECTOR	22 WESTBERE RD	LONDON NW2	ENGLAND
SHARP, JON	TV DIRECTOR	2006 N HOBART BLVD	LOS ANGELES, CA	90027
SHARP, JUDY	ACTRESS	1717 N HIGHLAND AVE #414	LOS ANGELES, CA	90028
SHARP, KIYO GLEN	CASTING DIRECTOR	4567 NAGLE AVE	SHERMAN OAKS, CA	91423
SHARP, SAUNDRA	TV WRITER	8955 BEVERLY BLVD	LOS ANGELES, CA	90048
SHARP, TODD	SINGER-GUITARIST	POST OFFICE BOX 2413	HOLLYWOOD, CA	90078
SHARP, WILLIAM	BARITONE	1776 BROADWAY #504	NEW YORK, NY	10019
SHARPE, IRON MIKE	WRESTLER	POST OFFICE BOX 3859	STAMFORD, CT	06905
SHARPE, ROBERT K	WRITER-PRODUCER	765 N BROADWAY, DUPLEX #15-E	HASTING-ON-HUDSON, NY	10706

Name	Occupation	Address	City
SHARPLES, DICK	TV WRITER	28 MAKEPEACE AVE, HIGHGATE	LONDON N6 ENGLAND
SHARRAD, JOHN S	FILM DIRECTOR	THE PRODUCTION COMPANY	
		35 LITTLE RUSSELL ST	LONDON WC1 ENGLAND
SHARRETT, MICHAEL	ACTOR	12200 RIVERSIDE DR #2	NORTH HOLLYWOOD, CA 91607
SHASKY, JIM	DIRECTOR	DGA, 110 W 57TH ST	NEW YORK, NY 10019
SHATNER, MARCY LAFFERTY	ACTRESS	3674 BERRY AVE	STUDIO CITY, CA 91604
SHATNER, WILLIAM	ACTOR-DIRECTOR	3674 BERRY AVE	STUDIO CITY, CA 91604
SHATTUCK, SHARI	ACTRESS	3907 W ALAMEDA AVE #101	BURBANK, CA 91505
SHAUGHNESSY, ALFRED	TV WRITER	WARE, 19-C JOHN SPENCER SQ	CANONBURY N1 2LZ ENGLAND
SHAUGHNESSY, CHARLES	ACTOR	STONE, 1052 CAROL DR	LOS ANGELES, CA 90069
SHAUGHNESSY, ED & ENERGY FORCE	JAZZ GROUP	WILLARD ALEXANDER, INC	
		660 MADISON AVE	NEW YORK, NY 10021
SHAUGHNESSY, MARY	REPORTER	TIME & PEOPLE MAGAZINE	
		TIME & LIFE BUILDING	
		ROCKEFELLER CENTER	NEW YORK, NY 10020
SHAUN, JACQUELYNE	BROADCAST JOURNALIST	428 N PALM DR	BEVERLY HILLS, CA 90210
SHAVELSON, MELVILLE	WRITER-PRODUCER	11947 SUNSHINE TERR	NORTH HOLLYWOOD, CA 91604
SHAVER, BOB	ACTOR	333 W 57TH ST	NEW YORK, NY 10019
SHAVER, HELEN	ACTRESS	10100 SANTA MONICA BLVD #1600	LOS ANGELES, CA 90067
SHAW, ADRIANA	ACTRESS	7047 FRANKLIN AVE #221	LOS ANGELES, CA 90028
SHAW, ARTIE	ORCHESTRA LEADER	2127 W PALOS CT	NEWBURY PARK, CA 91320
SHAW, DAVID	TV WRITER	8955 BEVERLY BLVD	LOS ANGELES, CA 90048
SHAW, HELEN	ACTRESS	8721 SUNSET BLVD #200	LOS ANGELES, CA 90069
SHAW, J LISTER	ACTOR	LEONETTI, 6526 SUNSET BLVD	HOLLYWOOD, CA 90028
SHAW, JEAN	MUSICIAN-SONGWRITER	11972 KIOWA AVE #102	LOS ANGELES, CA 90049
SHAW, JEROME	WRITER-PRODUCER	16 ESTRELLA	RANCHO MIRAGE, CA 92276
SHAW, KENNETH	BARITONE	JCB, 155 W 68TH ST	NEW YORK, NY 10023
SHAW, LOU	PRODUCER	10201 W PICO BLVD	LOS ANGELES, CA 90035
SHAW, LOUIS	TV WRITER	12170 IREDELL ST	STUDIO CITY, CA 91604
SHAW, MARLENA	SINGER	POST OFFICE BOX 82	GREAT NECK, NY 11021
SHAW, MARTIN	ACTOR	219 LIVERPOOL RD	LONDON N1 ENGLAND
SHAW, MICHAEL P	ACTOR	8831 SUNSET BLVD #402	LOS ANGELES, CA 90069
SHAW, PETER	TV PRODUCER	32 PORCHESTER TERR	LONDON W2 ENGLAND
SHAW, REBECCA	ACTRESS	2017 N HOOVER ST #2	LOS ANGELES, CA 90027
SHAW, RICHARD "RICK"	TV WRITER	8955 BEVERLY BLVD	LOS ANGELES, CA 90048
SHAW, ROBERT	CONDUCTOR	SHAW CONCERTS, 1995 BROADWAY	NEW YORK, NY 10023
SHAW, ROBERT D, JR	NEWS CORRESPONDENT	7233 TIMBER LN	FALLS CHURCH, VA 22046
SHAW, ROBERT J	TV WRITER	1515 N DOHENY DR	LOS ANGELES, CA 90069
SHAW, STAN	ACTOR	9220 SUNSET BLVD #625	LOS ANGELES, CA 90069
SHAW, STEPHEN J	NEWS CORRESPONDENT	1701 18TH ST, NW	WASHINGTON, DC 20009
SHAW, SUSAN	TV DIRECTOR	101 STRAND ST #A	SANTA MONICA, CA 90405
SHAW, SUSAN	CASTING DIRECTOR	COLUMBIA PICTURES INDUSTRIES	
		COLUMBIA PLAZA #149	BURBANK, CA 91505
SHAW, SYDNEY	NEWS CORRESPONDENT	206 11TH ST, SE	WASHINGTON, DC 20003
SHAW, TOMMY	SINGER-SONGWRITER	E S "BUD" PRAGER MANAGEMENT	
		1790 BROADWAY, PENTHOUSE	NEW YORK, NY 10019
SHAW-STRAMONDO, JAN RENE	TV DIRECTOR	1503 REPUBLIC ST	SAN DIEGO, CA 92114
SHAWLEE, JOAN	ACTRESS-WRITER	STONE, 1052 CAROL DR	LOS ANGELES, CA 90069
SHAWN, WALLACE	ACTOR	10100 SANTA MONICA BLVD #1600	LOS ANGELES, CA 90067
SHAWNN, REA	ACTRESS	4800 HALIFAX RD	TEMPLE CITY, CA 91780
SHAWYER, DAVID	ACTOR	16 RYLETT RD	LONDON W12 ENGLAND
SHAY, LARRY	COMPOSER	2201 CHANNEL RD	BALBOA, CA 92661
SHAYE, LIN	ACTRESS	15010 VENTURA BLVD #219	SHERMAN OAKS, CA 91403
SHAYNE, ALAN	FILM WRITER-EXECUTIVE	9371 BEVERLYCREST DR	BEVERLY HILLS, CA 90210
SHAYNE, BOB	TV WRITER	8955 BEVERLY BLVD	LOS ANGELES, CA 90048
SHAYNE, EDWARD R	WRITER	4658 ATOLL AVE	SHERMAN OAKS, CA 91423
SHAYNE, LINDA	ACTRESS	2460 BEVERLY AVE	SANTA MONICA, CA 90405
SHAYNE, ROBERT	ACTOR	10707 CAMARILLO ST #118	NORTH HOLLYWOOD, CA 91602
SHEA, D MICHAEL	NEWS CORRESPONDENT	1200 N NASH ST	ARLINGTON, VA 22209
SHEA, GEORGE BEVERLY	SINGER	1300 HARMON PL	MINNEAPOLIS, MN 55403
SHEA, JACK	ACTOR	8350 SANTA MONICA BLVD #103	LOS ANGELES, CA 90069
SHEA, JOHN	ACTOR	ICM, 8899 BEVERLY BLVD	LOS ANGELES, CA 90048
SHEA, JOHN P "JACK"	WRITER-PRODUCER	1128 16TH ST #B	SANTA MONICA, CA 90403
SHEA, MARGARET L	NEWS CORRESPONDENT	2025 "M" ST, NW	WASHINGTON, DC 20036
SHEA, MIKE & RAZORTALK	ROCK & ROLL GROUP	POST OFFICE BOX 4429	AUSTIN, TX 78765
SHEA, PATT	TV WRITER	8428 MELROSE PL #C	LOS ANGELES, CA 90069
SHEA, ROGER M	TV DIRECTOR-PRODUCER	1930 W GATE AVE	LARGO, FL 33540
SHEA, TERENCE F	NEWS CORRESPONDENT	15025 BUTTERCHURN LN	SILVER SPRING, MD 20904
SHEA RUBIN, KATT	ACTRESS-WRITER	THOMAS, 9243 1/2 DOHENY RD	LOS ANGELES, CA 90069
SHEAFE, ALEX	ACTOR	208 S BEVERLY DR #4	BEVERLY HILLS, CA 90212
SHEAR, GREG	ACTOR	8949 SUNSET BLVD #203	LOS ANGELES, CA 90069
SHEAR, JULES	SINGER-SONGWRITER	POST OFFICE BOX 7451	NEW YORK, NY 10022
SHEAR, PEARL	ACTRESS	13549 CONTOUR DR	SHERMAN OAKS, CA 91403
SHEAR, RHONDA	ACTRESS-MODEL	POST OFFICE BOX 67838	LOS ANGELES, CA 90068
SHEARE, THADDEUS	CARTOONIST	ROUTE #1, BOX 21, TATUMUCK RD	POUND RIDGE, NY 10576
SHEARER, CAREY	ACTOR	8350 SANTA MONICA BLVD #103	LOS ANGELES, CA 90069
SHEARER, CODY P	NEWS CORRESPONDENT	2708 CATHEDRAL AVE, NW	WASHINGTON, DC 20008
SHEARER, HANNAH L	WRITER	4321 GREENBUSH AVE	SHERMAN OAKS, CA 91423
SHEARER, HARRY	TV WRITER-DIRECTOR	11726 SAN VICENTE BLVD #300	LOS ANGELES, CA 90049
SHEARER, MARY	SOPRANO	59 E 54TH ST #81	NEW YORK, NY 10022
SHEARIN, JOHN	ACTOR	9100 SUNSET BLVD #200	LOS ANGELES, CA 90069
SHEARING, GEORGE	PIANIST	10100 SANTA MONICA BLVD #1600	LOS ANGELES, CA 90067
SHEARMAN, ALAN	TV WRITER	8955 BEVERLY BLVD	LOS ANGELES, CA 90048
SHEARS, DAVID J A	NEWS CORRESPONDENT	6525 32ND ST, NW	WASHINGTON, DC 20015

Name	Occupation	Address	City	Zip/Country
SHEARS, ROBIN L	NEWS CORRESPONDENT	8101-A LEE HWY	FALLS CHURCH, VA	22042
SHEASBY, JOHN S	DIRECTOR	1640 RIDGEWOOD E	GLENVIEW, IL	60025
SHEATER, CODY	COLUMNIST	NEWS AMERICA SYNDICATE		
		1703 KAISER AVE	IRVINE, CA	92714
SHEAVER, TED	CARTOONIST	KING FEATURES SYNDICATE		
		235 E 45TH ST	NEW YORK, NY	10017
SHEBIB, DONALD	FILM DIRECTOR	EUDON, 312 WRIGHT AVE	TORONTO, ONT W6R 1L9	CANADA
SHEDD, BEN A	FILM DIRECTOR	2009 N BRONSON AVE	LOS ANGELES, CA	90068
SHEDDAN, MARYLIN	ASTROLOGER	UNIVERSAL PRESS SYNDICATE		
		4900 MAIN ST, 9TH FLOOR	KANSAS CITY, MO	62114
SHEDDAN, THOMAS	GUITARIST	POST OFFICE BOX 390	LAWTEY, FL	32058
SHEEDY, ALLY	ACTRESS	10100 SANTA MONICA BLVD #1600	LOS ANGELES, CA	90067
SHEEHAN, ANTHONY	TV WRITER-DIRECTOR	2000 NICHOLS CANYON RD	LOS ANGELES, CA	90046
SHEEHAN, DAVID	FILM CRITIC	7310 MULHOLLAND DR	HOLLYWOOD, CA	90046
SHEEHAN, DOUGLAS	ACTOR	6126 MELVIN AVE	TARZANA, CA	91356
SHEEHAN, MICHAEL	ACTOR	9110 SUNSET BLVD #140	LOS ANGELES, CA	90069
SHEEHAN, NORA	ART DIRECTOR	LIFE/TIME & LIFE BLDG		
		ROCKEFELLER CENTER	NEW YORK, NY	10020
SHEEN, CHARLIE	ACTOR	6916 DUNE DR	MALIBU, CA	90265
SHEEN, MARTIN	ACTOR-TV DIRECTOR	6916 DUNE DR	MALIBU, CA	90265
SHEERAN, JOSETTE A	NEWS CORRESPONDENT	115 8TH ST, NW	WASHINGTON, DC	20003
SHEETS, CHAD	ACTOR	12725 VENTURA BLVD #E	STUDIO CITY, CA	91604
SHEETS, KENNETH R	NEWS CORRESPONDENT	9115 SANTAYANA DR	FAIRFAX, VA	22031
SHEFFIELD, DAVID	TV WRITER	555 W 57TH ST #1230	NEW YORK, NY	10019
SHEFFIELD, DON, JR	TRUMPETER	634 SHADOW WOOD AVE	NASHVILLE, TN	37205
SHEFFIELD, JOHNNY	ACTOR	834 1ST AVE	CHULA VISTA, CA	92011
SHEFFIELD, SHEF	DRUMMER	1312 PENNOCK AVE	NASHVILLE, TN	37207
SHEFLIN, DAN	ACTOR	269 N FLORENCE ST	BURBANK, CA	91505
SHEFTER, BERT A	COMPOSER-CONDUCTOR	1737 BEL AIR RD	LOS ANGELES, CA	90077
SHEFTER, MILTON R	WRITER	512 N WALDEN DR	BEVERLY HILLS, CA	90210
SHEIK, THE	WRESTLER	CAPITOL INTERNATIONAL		
		11844 MARKET ST	NORTH LIMA, OH	44452
SHEIL, MARTHA	SOPRANO	CONE, 221 W 57TH ST	NEW YORK, NY	10019
SHEILA E	SINGER-PERCUSSIONIST	1888 CENTURY PARK E #1400	LOS ANGELES, CA	90067
SHEINER, DAVID S	ACTOR	8143 W 4TH ST	LOS ANGELES, CA	90048
SHEINER, MARY DAVID	WRITER	8143 W 4TH ST	LOS ANGELES, CA	90048
SHELBY, JEFF	PIANIST	2611 QUENBY ST	HOUSTON, TX	77005
SHELDON, COURTNEY	NEWS CORRESPONDENT	7704 HACKAMORE DR	POTOMAC, MD	20854
SHELDON, DAVID	WRITER-PRODUCER	1437 RISING GLEN RD	LOS ANGELES, CA	90069
SHELDON, DAVID	WRESTLER	UNIVERSAL WRESTLING FEDERATION		
		MID SOUTH SPORTS, INC		
		5001 SPRING VALLEY RD	DALLAS, TX	75244
SHELDON, ELISABETH	SOPRANO	POST OFFICE BOX 20548	NEW YORK, NY	10025
SHELDON, GARY	CONDUCTOR	POST OFFICE BOX 1515	NEW YORK, NY	10023
SHELDON, JAMES	TV DIRECTOR	9428 LLOYDCREST DR	BEVERLY HILLS, CA	90210
SHELDON, JEROME M	ACTOR	11512 DONA TERESA DR	STUDIO CITY, CA	91604
SHELDON, JIMMY	COMPOSER-CONDUCTOR	BLUE ECHOES BY THE SEA	HARMONY, CA	93435
SHELDON, KENNY	CONDUCTOR	1420 N FULLER AVE #304	LOS ANGELES, CA	90046
SHELDON, LEE	TV WRITER-PRODUCER	STEPHEN J CANNELL PRODS		
		7083 HOLLYWOOD BLVD	LOS ANGELES, CA	90028
SHELDON, RALPH	FILM EDITOR	8 PLOUGH FARM CLOSE	RUISLIP HA4 7GH	ENGLAND
SHELDON, RON	CINEMATOGRAPHER	7715 SUNSET BLVD #150	LOS ANGELES, CA	90046
SHELDON, RONALD D	DIRECTOR	2201 LOMA VISTA	VICTORIA, TX	77901
SHELDON, SIDNEY	WRITER	10250 SUNSET BLVD	LOS ANGELES, CA	90024
SHELER, JEFFERY L	NEWS CORRESPONDENT	11354 BAROQUE RD	SILVER SPRING, MD	20901
SHELL, LARRY	GUITARIST	371 WALLACE RD #1	NASHVILLE, TN	37211
SHELLE, LORI	ACTRESS	230 E 87TH ST	NEW YORK, NY	10028
SHELLEN, STEPHEN	ACTOR	9000 SUNSET BLVD #1200	LOS ANGELES, CA	90069
SHELLEY, CAROLE	ACTRESS	LIONEL LARNER, 130 W 57TH ST	NEW YORK, NY	10019
SHELLEY, DAVE	ACTOR	5800 FAIRHAVEN AVE	WOODLAND HILLS, CA	91367
SHELLEY, DICK	GUITARIST	2922 DOBBS AVE	NASHVILLE, TN	37211
SHELLEY, JOSHUA	DIRECTOR	1919 N BEVERLY GLEN BLVD	LOS ANGELES, CA	90077
SHELLEY, KATHLEEN A	TV WRITER	8425 MELROSE PL #C	LOS ANGELES, CA	90069
SHELLEY, PAUL	ACTOR	CONWAY, EAGLE HOUSE		
		109 JERMYN ST	LONDON SW1	ENGLAND
SHELLY, BRUCE	TV WRITER	SCHALLERT, 9350 WILSHIRE BLVD	BEVERLY HILLS, CA	90212
SHELLY, NORMAN	ACTOR	467 CENTRAL PARK W	NEW YORK, NY	10025
SHELMERDINE, MARK	FILM PRODUCER	44-A FLORAL ST	LONDON WC2E 9DA	ENGLAND
SHELSTAD, KIRBY	PERCUSSIONIST	3434 LOVE CIR	NASHVILLE, TN	37212
SHELTON, ABIGAIL	ACTRESS	6331 HOLLYWOOD BLVD #924	LOS ANGELES, CA	90028
SHELTON, ANNE	SINGER	15 ATHERTON PL, LOUGFORD AVE		
		SOUTHALL	MIDDLESEX	ENGLAND
SHELTON, DEBORAH	ACTRESS	LEVY, 1251 LAGO VISTA DR	BEVERLY HILLS, CA	90210
SHELTON, LESLEY	ACTRESS	953 DEXTER ST	LOS ANGELES, CA	90042
SHELTON, LUCY	SOPRANO	IMG ARTISTS, 22 E 71ST ST	NEW YORK, NY	10021
SHELTON, MIKE	CARTOONIST	POST OFFICE BOX 11626	SANTA ANA, CA	92711
SHELTON, RAYMOND ALLEN	BANJOIST	ROUTE #2, BOX 184	BETHPAGE, TN	37022
SHELTON, REID	ACTOR	9229 SUNSET BLVD #306	LOS ANGELES, CA	90069
SHELTON, RONALD W	WRITER-PRODUCER	DGA, 7950 SUNSET BLVD	LOS ANGELES, CA	90046
SHELTON, SLOANE	ACTRESS	49 GROVE ST	NEW YORK, NY	10014
SHELTON, TIMOTHY	ACTOR	DULCINA EISEN, 154 E 61ST ST	NEW YORK, NY	10021
SHELTON, WILLIAM R	WRITER	9255 SUNSET BLVD #1122	LOS ANGELES, CA	90069
SHENAR, PAUL	ACTOR	10390 SANTA MONICA BLVD #310	LOS ANGELES, CA	90025
SHENDAL, MARGARET	ACTRESS	11726 SAN VICENTE BLVD #300	LOS ANGELES, CA	90049
SHENSON, WALTER	FILM PRODUCER	419 SAINT CLOUD RD	LOS ANGELES, CA	90077

Name	Occupation	Address	City/State	Zip/Country
SHEPARD, BILL	CASTING DIRECTOR	POST OFFICE BOX 5718	SHERMAN OAKS, CA	91403
SHEPARD, CHARLES S	NEWS CORRESPONDENT	4127 S FOUR MILE RUN DR #104	ARLINGTON, VA	22204
SHEPARD, ELLEN	TV WRITER	8955 BEVERLY BLVD	LOS ANGELES, CA	90048
SHEPARD, GERALD	FILM EDITOR	11628 CHENAULT ST #6	LOS ANGELES, CA	90049
SHEPARD, GERALD S	WRITER-PRODUCER	14144 VENTURA BLVD #200	SHERMAN OAKS, CA	91423
SHEPARD, JACK	TV DIRECTOR-PRODUCER	500 S SUNSET CANYON DR	BURBANK, CA	91501
SHEPARD, JEAN	SINGER	TESSIER, 505 CANTON PASS	MADISON, TN	37115
SHEPARD, JEWEL	ACTRESS-MODEL	FELBER, 2126 N CAHUENGA BLVD	LOS ANGELES, CA	90068
SHEPARD, RICHMOND	ACTOR	5330 LANKERSHIM BLVD #210	NORTH HOLLYWOOD, CA	91601
SHEPARD, ROBERT W	NEWS CORRESPONDENT	4805 MANION ST	ANNANDALE, VA	22003
SHEPARD, SUSAN	ACTRESS	CARPENTER, 1516-W REDWOOD ST	SAN DIEGO, CA	92101
SHEPHERD, CYBILL	ACTRESS-MODEL	11842 MOORPARK ST #F	STUDIO CITY, CA	91604
SHEPHERD, DAVID	GUITARIST	108 THOMPSON LN #E-10	NASHVILLE, TN	37211
SHEPHERD, ELIZABETH	ACTRESS	10744 STEPHON TERR	CULVER CITY, CA	90230
SHEPHERD, JACK	ACTOR-WRITER	GREEN & UNDERWOOD, LTD		
		GUNNERSBURY LN	LONDON W3 8HR	ENGLAND
SHEPHERD, JEAN P	TV WRITER	555 W 57TH ST #1230	NEW YORK, NY	10019
SHEPHERD, JOHN	ACTOR	6310 SAN VICENTE BLVD #407	LOS ANGELES, CA	90048
SHEPHERD, JOHN A	GUITARIST	POST OFFICE BOX 23336	NASHVILLE, TN	37202
SHEPHERD, PEGGY	PIANIST	5039 HILLSBORO RD #121	NASHVILLE, TN	37215
SHEPHERD, SAM	ACTOR-DIRECTOR	240 W 44TH ST	NEW YORK, NY	10036
SHEPHERD, SANDRA	TV WRITER	8955 BEVERLY BLVD	LOS ANGELES, CA	90048
SHEPHERD, SCOTT	TV WRITER	8955 BEVERLY BLVD	LOS ANGELES, CA	90048
SHEPHERD, SHERRIE	CARTOONIST	UNITED FEATURE SYNDICATE		
		200 PARK AVE	NEW YORK, NY	10017
SHEPPARD, BOBBY	SINGER	PENNY, 30 GUINAN ST	WALTHAM, MA	02154
SHEPPARD, CAROLE S	DIRECTOR	DGA, 110 W 57TH ST	NEW YORK, NY	10019
SHEPPARD, COLLEEN	SINGER	GOOD, 2500 NW 39TH ST	OKLAHOMA CITY, OK	73112
SHEPPARD, GORDON	WRITER-PRODUCER	3449 PEEL ST	MONTREAL, QUE	CANADA
SHEPPARD, JILL	TV DIRECTOR	28 MURRAY MEWS	LONDON NW1 9RJ	ENGLAND
SHEPPARD, LEE	NEWS CORRESPONDENT	1111 ARLINGTON BLVD	ARLINGTON, VA	22209
SHEPPARD, R Z	WRITER-EDITOR	TIME/TIME & LIFE BLDG		
		ROCKEFELLER CENTER	NEW YORK, NY	10020
SHEPPARD, T G	SINGER	SCOTTI BROS, 2128 PICO BLVD	SANTA MONICA, CA	90405
SHEPPHIRD, CARROLL	FILM DIRECTOR	3008 CLUBHOUSE CIR	COSTA MESA, CA	92626
SHER, ANTONY	ACTOR	HOPE & LYNE, 5 MILNER PL	LONDON N1	ENGLAND
SHER, JACK	WRITER-PRODUCER	9520 DALEGROVE DR	BEVERLY HILLS, CA	90210
SHERA, MARK	ACTOR	211 S BEVERLY DR #201	BEVERLY HILLS, CA	90212
SHERBELL, SCHEPHERD	PHOTOGRAPHER	1514 COLUMBIA RD, NW	WASHINGTON, DC	20009
SHERBOW, ROBERT E	PHOTOGRAPHER	POST OFFICE BOX 35	MOUNT RAINER, MD	20822
SHERDEMAN, TED	WRITER	23388 MULHOLLAND DR	WOODLAND HILLS, CA	91364
SHERER, MEL	TV WRITER	9209 WHITWORTH DR	BEVERLY HILLS, CA	90212
SHERIDAN, JAMEY	ACTOR	1650 BROADWAY #302	NEW YORK, NY	10019
SHERIDAN, JAY	TV DIRECTOR	155 N HARBOR DR #5402	CHICAGO, IL	60601
SHERIDAN, LIZ	ACTRESS	9229 SUNSET BLVD #306	LOS ANGELES, CA	90069
SHERIDAN, NICOLLETTE	ACTRESS	1444 QUEENS RD	LOS ANGELES, CA	90069
SHERIFF	ROCK & ROLL GROUP	ICM, 40 W 57TH ST	NEW YORK, NY	10019
SHERIFF, JAIME	SINGER	JAY LANDERS, 9255 SUNSET BLVD	LOS ANGELES, CA	90069
SHERIN, EDWIN	FILM DIRECTOR	ROAD #2, GORDON RD	CARMEL, NY	10512
SHERMAN, BOB	ACTOR	5330 LANKERSHIM BLVD #210	NORTH HOLLYWOOD, CA	91601
SHERMAN, BOB	ACTOR	31 BRECON RD	LONDON	ENGLAND
SHERMAN, BOB	PHOTOGRAPHER	1166 NE 182ND ST	NORTH MIAMI BEACH, FL	33162
SHERMAN, BOB	PRODUCER	LAYTON PRODUCTIONS		
		4000 WARNER BLVD	BURBANK, CA	91522
SHERMAN, BOBBY	SINGER-ACTOR	1870 SUNSET PLAZA DR	LOS ANGELES, CA	90069
SHERMAN, DARYL	MUSICIAN	POST OFFICE BOX C	RIVER EDGE, NJ	07661
SHERMAN, DON	ACTOR	7461 BEVERLY BLVD #400	LOS ANGELES, CA	90036
SHERMAN, GARY ARON	WRITER-PRODUCER	4501 CEDROS AVE #328	SHERMAN OAKS, CA	91403
SHERMAN, GEOFFREY	DIRECTOR	10 E 44TH ST #700	NEW YORK, NY	10017
SHERMAN, GEORGE	DIRECTOR	4314 MARINA CITY DR #316	MARINA DEL REY, CA	90292
SHERMAN, GRADY	ACTOR	ATA, 2437 E WASHINGTON BLVD	PASADENA, CA	91104
SHERMAN, JENNY LEE	ACTRESS-MODEL	POST OFFICE BOX 73	LOS ANGELES, CA	90078
SHERMAN, JILL	TV WRITER	8955 BEVERLY BLVD	LOS ANGELES, CA	90048
SHERMAN, JULIE	WRITER	CURTIS BROWN MANAGEMENT		
		86 WILLIAM ST	PADDINGTON NSW 2021	AUSTRALIA
SHERMAN, KERRY	ACTRESS	12750 VENTURA BLVD #102	STUDIO CITY, CA	91604
SHERMAN, LENORE	ACTRESS	112-39 68TH RD	FOREST HILLS, NY	11375
SHERMAN, PAUL	ACTOR	CASSELL, 843 N SYCAMORE AVE	LOS ANGELES, CA	90038
SHERMAN, RALPH	COMEDIAN	ATTRACTIONS TALENT AGENCY		
		6525 N FRANCISCO AVE	CHICAGO, IL	60645
SHERMAN, RICHARD	COMPOSER-LYRICIST	712 HILLCREST RD	BEVERLY HILLS, CA	90210
SHERMAN, ROBERT	DIRECTOR	999 N DOHENY DR #403	LOS ANGELES, CA	90069
SHERMAN, ROBERT B	SONGWRITER	808 N CRESCENT DR	BEVERLY HILLS, CA	90210
SHERMAN, RUSSELL	PIANIST	COLBERT, 111 W 57TH ST	NEW YORK, NY	10019
SHERMAN, SAMUEL	DIRECTOR	DGA, 7950 SUNSET BLVD	LOS ANGELES, CA	90046
SHERMAN, STANFORD L	SCREENWRITER	36 SUNSET AVE	VENICE, CA	90291
SHERMAN, SYLVAN ROBERT	ACTOR	170 W END AVE	NEW YORK, NY	10023
SHERMAN, VINCENT	FILM DIRECTOR	6355 SYCAMORE MEADOWS DR	MALIBU, CA	90265
SHEROHMAN, THOMAS K	SCREENWRITER	3534 DAHLIA AVE	LOS ANGELES, CA	90026
SHERRILL, BILLY NORRIS	PIANIST-ARRANGER	3631 WOODLAWN DR	NASHVILLE, TN	37215
SHERRILL, CHARLES L	NEWS CORRESPONDENT	1125 MOOREFIELD HILL CT	VIENNA, VA	22180
SHERRILL, MARK	GUITARIST	114 CUMBERLAND SHORES DR	HENDERSONVILLE, TN	37075
SHERRILL, WILLIAM D	PIANIST	1708 GRAND AVE	NASHVILLE, TN	37212
SHERRIN, NED	WRITER-PRODUCER	19 WELLINGTON SQ	LONDON SW3	ENGLAND
SHERROD, JOHN	STUNTMAN	3518 W CAHUENGA BLVD #300	LOS ANGELES, CA	90068

SAM SHEPPARD

BROOKE SHIELDS

RICHARD SHOBERG

LONNIE SHORR

SYLVIA SIDNEY

PAUL SIMON

RICHARD SIMMONS

O.J. SIMPSON

FRANK SINATRA

Name	Occupation	Address	City	Zip/Country
SHERRY, DAN	PIANIST	5845 BRENTWOOD TRACE	BRENTWOOD, TN	37027
SHERRY, DIANE	ACTRESS	6736 LAUREL CANYON BLVD #306	NORTH HOLLYWOOD, CA	91606
SHERRY, FRED	CELLIST	ALLIED ARTISTS, 170 W 74TH ST	NEW YORK, NY	10023
SHERWIN, DAVID N	SCREENWRITER	8955 BEVERLY BLVD	LOS ANGELES, CA	90048
SHERWIN, DERRICK	ACT-WRI-PROD	3 MARYON MEWS	LONDON NW3	ENGLAND
SHERWOOD, DEBORAH	TV WRITER	8955 BEVERLY BLVD	LOS ANGELES, CA	90048
SHERWOOD, JAMES SHAMUS	ACTOR	10605 MOORPARK ST #2	NORTH HOLLYWOOD, CA	91602
SHERWOOD, MADELEINE	ACTRESS	32 LEROY ST	NEW YORK, NY	10014
SHERWOOD, MELANIE	CASTING DIRECTOR	6305 YUCCA ST, 6TH FLOOR	LOS ANGELES, CA	90028
SHERWOOD, ROB	WRITER	8428 MELROSE PL #C	LOS ANGELES, CA	90069
SHERWOOD, ROBERTA	SINGER-ACTRESS	SCHOEMAN, 2600 W VICTORY BLVD	BURBANK, CA	91505
SHERWOOD, ROBIN	ACTRESS	FRASER, 91 REGENT ST	LONDON W1	ENGLAND
SHERWOOD, ROBIN	ACTRESS	1931 BENEDICT CANYON DR	BEVERLY HILLS, CA	90210
SHERWOOD, THOMAS R	NEWS CORRESPONDENT	1150 15TH ST, NW	WASHINGTON, DC	20071
SHESLOW, STUART M	WRITER	123 N OAKHURST DR	BEVERLY HILLS, CA	90210
SHETENVAN, DAN	NEWS CORRESPONDENT	1100 NATIONAL PRESS BLDG 529 14TH ST, NW	WASHINGTON, DC	20045
SHETLER ZIPORYN DUO	MUSICAL DUO	KAY, 58 W 58TH ST	NEW YORK, NY	10019
SHEVITT, AVA	CASTING DIRECTOR	4424 FORMAN AVE	TOLUCA LAKE, CA	91602
SHEVLIN, JEAN	ACTRESS	5 STUYVESANT OVAL	NEW YORK, NY	10009
SHEYBAL, VLADEK	ACTOR-DIRECTOR	CCA MGMT, 4 CT LODGE 48 SLOANE SQ	LONDON SW1W 8AT	ENGLAND
SHEYNKMAN, EMANUIL	MANDOLINIST	903 W SEPULVEDA ST	SAN PEDRO, CA	90731
SHIBATA, YUTAKA	NEWS CORRESPONDENT	7011 SEA CLIFF RD	MC LEAN, VA	22101
SHIC, NOOR	ACTRESS	427 N CANON DR #205	BEVERLY HILLS, CA	90210
SHICOFF, NEIL	TENOR	119 W 57TH ST #1505	NEW YORK, NY	10019
SHIELDS, BROOKE	ACTRESS-MODEL	POST OFFICE BOX B	HAWORTH, NJ	07641
SHIELDS, EDWARD J	NEWS CORRESPONDENT	319 5TH ST, SE	WASHINGTON, DC	20003
SHIELDS, EILEEN	NEWS CORRESPONDENT	3335 RESERVOIR RD, NW	WASHINGTON, DC	20007
SHIELDS, JOHN E	NEWS CORRESPONDENT	19128 ROMAN WY	GAITHESBURG, MD	20879
SHIELDS, LORAINE	ACTRESS	159 N CLARK DR #4	BEVERLY HILLS, CA	90211
SHIELDS, MEL	TV WRITER	8955 BEVERLY BLVD	LOS ANGELES, CA	90048
SHIELDS, PAT R	DIRECTOR	2575 GARDNER PL #A-41	GLENDALE, CA	91206
SHIELDS, ROBERT	MIME-WRITER	8955 BEVERLY BLVD	LOS ANGELES, CA	90048
SHIELDS, THE	VOCAL GROUP	OLDIES, 5218 ALMONT ST	LOS ANGELES, CA	90032
SHIFFLETT, FORREST N	NEWS CORRESPONDENT	8226 BRITTAINY DR	ANNANDALE, VA	22003
SHIFRIN, CAROLE A	NEWS CORRESPONDENT	3013 STEPHENSON PL, NW	WASHINGTON, DC	20015
SHIFRIN, DAVID	CLARINETIST	IMG ARTISTS, 22 E 71ST ST	NEW YORK, NY	10021
SHIGETA, JAMES	ACTOR	8917 CYNTHIA ST #1	LOS ANGELES, CA	90069
SHIH, COMET K M	NEWS CORRESPONDENT	8539 W HOWELL RD	BETHESDA, MD	20817
SHILAKOWSKY, HARRIS	PIANIST	4000 AUBURN LN #A	NASHVILLE, TN	37215
SHILS, JUDI A	DIRECTOR	DGA, 110 W 57TH ST	NEW YORK, NY	10019
SHILTON, GILBERT	TV DIRECTOR	5011 WESTPARK DR	NORTH HOLLYWOOD, CA	91601
SHIMADA, TOSHIYUKI	CONDUCTOR	500 5TH AVE #2050	NEW YORK, NY	10110
SHIMADA, YOKO	ACTRESS	7245 HILLSDALE AVE #415	LOS ANGELES, CA	90046
SHIMER, PORTER	COLUMNIST	UNIVERSAL PRESS SYNDICATE 4900 MAIN ST, 9TH FLOOR	KANSAS CITY, MO	62114
SHIMERMAN, ARMIN	ACTOR	5833 MELVIN AVE	TARZANA, CA	91356
SHIMIZU, YOSHIRO	NEWS CORRESPONDENT	444 N CAPITOL ST, NW	WASHINGTON, DC	20001
SHIMKUS, JOANNA	ACTRESS	9350 WILSHIRE BLVD #310	BEVERLY HILLS, CA	90212
SHIMOKAWA, GARY K	DIRECTOR	2029 CENTURY PARK E #1300	LOS ANGELES, CA	90067
SHIMONO, SAB	ACTOR	3332 DESCANSO DR	LOS ANGELES, CA	90026
SHINDLER, COLIN	TV PRODUCER	HEATH, PARAMOUNT HOUSE 162-170 WARDOUR ST	LONDON W1V 3AT	ENGLAND
SHINDO, TAK	COMPOSER	1322 W CAMINO DEL SUR	SAN DIMAS, CA	91773
SHINE, THOMAS A	NEWS CORRES-WRITER	ABC-TV, NEWS DEPARTMENT 1717 DE SALES ST, NW	WASHINGTON, DC	20036
SHINER, MERVIN	GUITARIST	3933 EDEN ROC CIR E	TAMPA, FL	33614
SHINES, JOHNNY	SINGER	CHICKLES, 15 MANSFIELD ST	BOSTON, MA	02134
SHINKAI, BILL	TV WRITER	18408 COLTMAN AVE	CARSON, CA	90746
SHIPLEY, DAVID	GUITARIST	315 THUSS AVE	NASHVILLE, TN	37211
SHIPLEY, DON	SINGER	POST OFFICE BOX 42466	TUCSON, AZ	85733
SHIPLEY, ELLEN	SINGER	3 E 54TH ST #1400	NEW YORK, NY	10022
SHIPMAN, BARRY	WRITER	3055 N ARROWHEAD AVE	SAN BERNARDINO, CA	92405
SHIPMAN, GRETA	ACTRESS	1418 N HIGHLAND AVE #102	LOS ANGELES, CA	90028
SHIPMAN, NINA	ACTRESS	8721 SUNSET BLVD #200	LOS ANGELES, CA	90069
SHIPP, JOHN WESLEY	ACTOR	J MICHAEL BLOOM AGENCY 233 PARK AVE S, 10TH FLOOR	NEW YORK, NY	10017
SHIPPY, KENNETH ROBERT	ACTOR	1925 FOX HILLS DR	LOS ANGELES, CA	90025
SHIPSTON, B G	ACTRESS	406 E RANDOLPH ST	GLENDALE, CA	91207
SHIRAI, MITSUKO	SOPRANO	POST OFFICE BOX 1515	NEW YORK, NY	10023
SHIRAN, ORA	VIOLINIST	ROSENFIELD, 714 LADD RD	BRONX, NY	10471
SHIRE, DAVID	COMPOSER	14820 VALLEY VISTA BLVD	SHERMAN OAKS, CA	91403
SHIRE, NOEL	ACTOR	17730 POSETANO RD	PACIFIC PALISADES, CA	90272
SHIRE, RAY	WRESTLER	SEE - STEVENS, RAY "THE CRIPPLER"		
SHIRE, SANFORD	CONDUCTOR	1550 N LAUREL AVE #305	LOS ANGELES, CA	90046
SHIRE, TALIA	ACTRESS	SCHWARTZMAN, 10730 BELLAGIO RD	LOS ANGELES, CA	90024
SHIRELLES, THE	VOCAL GROUP	MARS, 168 ORCHID DR	PEARL RIVER, NY	10965
SHIRK, RICHARD	PIANIST	POST OFFICE BOX U	REDDING, CT	06875
SHIRLEY, ALEISA	ACTRESS	9200 SUNSET BLVD #414	LOS ANGELES, CA	90069
SHIRLEY, ANNE	ACTRESS	LEDERER, 7416 ROSEWOOD AVE	LOS ANGELES, CA	90036
SHIRLEY, PEG	ACTRESS	8721 SUNSET BLVD #103	LOS ANGELES, CA	90069
SHIRLEY, RICHARD MARVIN	DIRECTOR	610 N FAIRBANKS CT	CHICAGO, IL	60611
SHIRLEY-QUIRK, JOHN	BASSO-BARITONE	CAMI, 165 W 57TH ST	NEW YORK, NY	10019

Name	Occupation	Address	City/State	ZIP
SHIRRIFF, CATHIE	ACTRESS-MODEL	6310 SAN VICENTE BLVD #407	LOS ANGELES, CA	90048
SHIRTS, THE	ROCK & ROLL GROUP	SPHINX MANAGEMENT AGENCY		
		2 UNITY PL, WESTGATE		
		ROTHERHAM	SOUTH YORKS S60 1AR	ENGLAND
SHITTONS, THE	VOCAL GROUP	POST OFFICE BOX 4585	PORTSMOUTH, NH	03801
SHIVAS, MARK	TV DIRECTOR-PRODUCER	LIMEHOUSE, 43 WHITFIELD ST	LONDON W1	ENGLAND
SHKOLNIK, SHELDON	PIANIST	157 W 57TH ST #1100	NEW YORK, NY	10019
SHOBERG, RICHARD	ACTOR	ABC-TV, "ALL MY CHILDREN"		
		1330 AVE OF THE AMERICAS	NEW YORK, NY	10019
SHOCK	ROCK & ROLL GROUP	DOUBLE TEE, 712 SW SALMON ST	PORTLAND, OR	97214
SHOCKEY, SUZIE	ACTRESS	138 N MANSFIELD AVE	LOS ANGELES, CA	90036
SHOCKLEY, KAREN	NEWS CORRESPONDENT	7128 ORA GLEN CT	GREENBELT, MD	20770
SHOE, BOB & THE CAROLINA MOUNTA	C & W GROUP	POST OFFICE BOX 25371	CHARLOTTE, NC	28212
SHOEL, MICHAEL J	ACTOR	296 S EL MOLINO AVE #A	PASADENA, CA	91101
SHOEL, MICHAEL J	ACTOR	3772 OAKDALE AVE	PASADENA, CA	91107
SHOEMAKER, CHARLES	SAXOPHONIST	707 OMANDALE DR	NASHVILLE, TN	37204
SHOEMAKER, EMILY	TV WRITER	8955 BEVERLY BLVD	LOS ANGELES, CA	90048
SHOEMAKER, PAMELA	ACTRESS	130 W 42ND ST #1804	NEW YORK, NY	10036
SHOEMAKER, RANDALL	NEWS CORRESPONDENT	2123 N EARLY ST	ALEXANDRIA, VA	22302
SHOEMAKER, VAUGHN	CARTOONIST	POST OFFICE DRAWER V	CARMEL, CA	93921
SHOENMAN, ELLIOT	WRITER-PRODUCER	10530 TENNESSEE AVE	LOS ANGELES, CA	90064
SHOGAN, ROBERT	NEWS CORRESPONDENT	3513 RAYMOND ST	CHEVY CHASE, MD	20815
SHOLEM, LEE	DIRECTOR	2346 ASTRAL DR	LOS ANGELES, CA	90046
SHONTEEF, LINDSAY	FILM DIRECTOR	10 KERRIS WY		
		WILLOWDALE ESTATE		
		LOWER EARLEY	BERKSHIRE RG6 2UW	ENGLAND
SHOOB, MICHAEL	SCREENWRITER	908 14TH ST #1	SANTA MONICA, CA	90403
SHOOK, JACK	GUITARIST	2503 STINSON RD	NASHVILLE, TN	37214
SHOOK, JERRY	GUITARIST	802 18TH AVE S	NASHVILLE, TN	37203
SHOOK, SHAWN	GUITARIST	309 CARRILLON DR	NASHVILLE, TN	37217
SHOOP, PAMELA SUSAN	ACTRESS	454 N PALM DR #A	BEVERLY HILLS, CA	90210
SHOOTING STAR	ROCK & ROLL GROUP	POST OFFICE BOX 32431	KANSAS CITY, MO	64111
SHOPE, ROGER H	DIRECTOR	51 RICHARDS RD	PT WASHINGTON, LI, NY	11050
SHOPPE	C & W GROUP	POST OFFICE BOX 973	BEDFORD, TX	76021
SHOR PATROL	ROCK & ROLL GROUP	ICM, 40 W 57TH ST	NEW YORK, NY	10019
SHORE, BENJAMIN	NEWS CORRESPONDENT	6038 N 28TH ST	ARLINGTON, VA	22207
SHORE, DINAH	SINGER-TV HOST	916 OXFORD WY	BEVERLY HILLS, CA	90210
SHORE, FREDRIC R	FILM WRITER-PRODUCER	ICM, 8899 BEVERLY BLVD	LOS ANGELES, CA	90048
SHORE, JEROME	DIRECTOR	330 E 33RD ST	NEW YORK, NY	10016
SHORE, MITZI	TV WRITER	8955 BEVERLY BLVD	LOS ANGELES, CA	90048
SHORE, RICHARD	TV DIRECTOR	711 W END AVE	NEW YORK, NY	10025
SHORE, SAMMY	COMEDIAN	151 S EL CAMINO DR	BEVERLY HILLS, CA	90212
SHORE, SAMUEL R	TV DIRECTOR-PRODUCER	1939 VIRGINIA ST	BERKELEY, CA	94709
SHORES, RICHARD W	COMPOSER-CONDUCTOR	16644 CHAPLIN AVE	ENCINO, CA	91316
SHORR, LONNIE	COMEDIAN	141 S EL CAMINO DR #205	BEVERLY HILLS, CA	90212
SHORR, RICHARD	WRITER-PRODUCER	8463 UTICA DR	LOS ANGELES, CA	90046
SHORT, BOBBY	ACTOR-SINGER	205 W 57TH ST	NEW YORK, NY	10019
SHORT, KEVIN	BASS	SPRINGER, 1001 ROLANDVUE RD	BALTIMORE, MD	21204
SHORT, MARTIN	ACTOR	ROLLINS/JOFFE MANAGEMENT		
		801 WESTMOUNT DR	LOS ANGELES, CA	90069
SHORT, MICHAEL	TV WRITER	8955 BEVERLY BLVD	LOS ANGELES, CA	90048
SHORT STUFF	MUSICAL GROUP	MAC MGMT, 2222 N FARWELL AVE	MILWAUKEE, WI	53202
SHORTE, DINO	ACTOR	10850 RIVERSIDE DR #501	NORTH HOLLYWOOD, CA	91602
SHORTLAND, ELLEN	ACTRESS	7461 BEVERLY BLVD #400	LOS ANGELES, CA	90036
SHORTRIDGE, STEPHEN	ACTOR	15301 VENTURA BLVD #345	SHERMAN OAKS, CA	91403
SHOSTAC, DAVID	FLUTIST	CCS, 4478 PURDUE AVE	CULVER CITY, CA	90230
SHOTEL, BARBARA	WRITER	2812 MONTANA AVE #A	SANTA MONICA, CA	90403
SHOTGUN	SOUL-DISCO GROUP	PICHINSON, 518 LA CIENEGA BLVD	LOS ANGELES, CA	90048
SHOUP, DAVID W	CONDUCTOR	2204 OAKDALE RD	CLEVELAND HGTS, OH	44118
SHOUSE, WILLIAM N	PIANIST	POST OFFICE BOX 1323	HENDERSONVILLE, TN	37075
SHOW, GRANT	ACTOR	THE WILLIAM MORRIS AGENCY		
		1350 AVE OF THE AMERICAS	NEW YORK, NY	10019
SHOWALTER, MAX	ACTOR	7953 HOLLYWOOD BLVD	LOS ANGELES, CA	90046
SHOWDOWN	C & W GROUP	POST OFFICE BOX 156	ROSELLE, NJ	07203
SHOWER, KATHY	ACTRESS-MODEL	9744 WILSHIRE BLVD #306	LOS ANGELES, CA	90212
SHRADER, JAMES	TENOR	GREAT LAKES PERFORMING		
		310 E WASHINGTON ST	ANN ARBOR, MI	48104
SHRADER, ROBERT E	NEWS CORRESPONDENT	2139 WISCONSIN AVE, NW	WASHINGTON, DC	20007
SHRAKE, EDWIN "BUD"	WRITER	ICM, 8899 BEVERLY BLVD	LOS ANGELES, CA	90048
SHRAPNEL, JOHN	ACTOR	64 RICHMOND AVE	LONDON N1	ENGLAND
SHREEVE, CRAIG	ACTOR	5743 RADFORD AVE	NORTH HOLLYWOOD, CA	91607
SHREEVE, LARRY	WRESTLER	SEE - ABDULLAH THE BUTCHER		
SHREEVE, LAURIE	ACTRESS	5743 RADFORD AVE	NORTH HOLLYWOOD, CA	91607
SHREWSBURY, ALAINE	ACTRESS	6940 PACIFIC VIEW DR	HOLLYWOOD, CA	90068
SHREWSBURY, ROBERT	ACTOR	380 RIVERSIDE DR #5-C	NEW YORK, NY	10025
SHRIBMAN, DAVID M	NEWS CORRESPONDENT	4321 VERPLANCK PL, NW	WASHINGTON, DC	20016
SHRICKBACK	ROCK & ROLL GROUP	WORD SERVICE AGENCY		
		235 UPPER RICHMOND RD	LONDON SW15 6SN	ENGLAND
SHRIMPTON, JEAN "COX"	ACTRESS	ABBEY HOTEL, PENZANCE	CORNWALL	ENGLAND
SHRINER, CATHY	ACTRESS	14833 VALLEY VISTA BLVD	SHERMAN OAKS, CA	91403
SHRINER, INDY	ACTRESS	8721 SUNSET BLVD #202	LOS ANGELES, CA	90069
SHRINER, KIN	ACTOR	2655 N BEVERLY GLEN BLVD	LOS ANGELES, CA	90077
SHRINER, WIL	ACT-WRI-COMED	14833 VALLEY VISTA BLVD	SHERMAN OAKS, CA	91403
SHROG, MAURICE	ACTOR	473 F D ROOSEVELT DR	NEW YORK, NY	10009
SHROPSHIRE, ANNE	ACTRESS	31 MORTON ST	NEW YORK, NY	10014

Name	Occupation	Address	City	Zip
SHROYER, SONNY	ACTOR	3800 BARHAM BLVD #303	LOS ANGELES, CA	90068
SHRYACK, DENNIS R	SCREENWRITER	12192 LAUREL TERR DR	STUDIO CITY, CA	91604
SHTRUM, HAIM	COMPOSER	1434 COMSTOCK AVE	LOS ANGELES, CA	90024
SHUANG, GEORGE K	NEWS CORRESPONDENT	1121 NATIONAL PRESS BLDG		
		529 14TH ST, NW	WASHINGTON, DC	20045
SHUBIK, IRENE	TV WRITER-PRODUCER	HIGHAM, 5 LOWER JOHN ST	LONDON W1R 4HA	ENGLAND
SHUCK, JIM	ACTOR	305 CORONADO AVE #1	LONG BEACH, CA	90814
SHUE, BOB & THE CAROLINA MOUNTA	BLUEGRASS GROUP	POST OFFICE BOX 25371	CHARLOTTE, NC	28212
SHUE, ELISABETH	ACTRESS	76 S ORANGE AVE	SOUTH ORANGE, NJ	07079
SHUFORD, ANDY	ACTOR	POST OFFICE BOX 119	EAGLEVILLE, TN	37060
SHULENBERGER, JON	GUITARIST	5850 MERRIMAR DR	NASHVILLE, TN	37215
SHULER, LAUREN D	TV PRODUCER	1619 MARMONT AVE	LOS ANGELES, CA	90069
SHULKIN, JOE	TV WRITER	1888 CENTURY PARK E #1400	LOS ANGELES, CA	90067
SHULL, JENNIFER	CASTING DIRECTOR	COLUMBIA PICTURES INDUSTRIES		
		COLUMBIA PLAZA #212	BURBANK, CA	91506
SHULL, JOHN	ACTOR	439 S LA CIENEGA BLVD #120	LOS ANGELES, CA	90048
SHULL, RICHARD B	ACTOR	THE PLAYERS, 16 GRAMERCY PARK	NEW YORK, NY	10003
SHULMAN, LAWRENCE G	TV DIRECTOR	905 S WOOSTER ST	LOS ANGELES, CA	90035
SHULMAN, MAX	TV WRITER	1100 N ALTA LOMA RD #1505	LOS ANGELES, CA	90069
SHULTZ, JAN	STUNTMAN	3518 W CAHUENGA BLVD #300	LOS ANGELES, CA	90068
SHUMAN, ERIC	SAXOPHONIST	1501 BERNARD AVE	NASHVILLE, TN	37212
SHUMAN, PAUL	ACTOR	8961 SUNSET BLVD #B	LOS ANGELES, CA	90069
SHUMLIN, DIANA	THEATER PRODUCER	150 E 77TH ST	NEW YORK, NY	10021
SHUMSKY, OSCAR	VIOLINIST	GERSHUNOFF, 502 PARK AVE	NEW YORK, NY	10022
SHURE, ABNEY	ACTRESS	10850 RIVERSIDE DR #505	NORTH HOLLYWOOD, CA	91602
SHURE, JON	NEWS CORRESPONDENT	1844 COLUMBIA RD #306, NW	WASHINGTON, DC	20009
SHURE, TAMARA	ACTRESS	1901 AVE OF THE STARS #1040	LOS ANGELES, CA	90067
SHURLEY, BRUCE L	DIRECTOR	7950 SUNSET BLVD	LOS ANGELES, CA	90046
SHUSETT, RONALD	SCREENWRITER	8955 BEVERLY BLVD	LOS ANGELES, CA	90048
SHUST, WILLIAM	ACTOR-MIME	ARTHUR SHAFMAN, 723 7TH AVE	NEW YORK, NY	10019
SHUSTER, RACHEL	SPORTS WRITER	POST OFFICE BOX 500	WASHINGTON, DC	20044
SHUTAN, JAN	ACTRESS	3115 DEEP CANYON DR	BEVERLY HILLS, CA	90210
SHUTT, CHARLES E	PHOTOGRAPHER	1145 RIVERBANK RD	STANFORD, CT	06903
SHY TALK	ROCK & ROLL GROUP	NEMPEROR ARTISTS, LTD		
		870 7TH AVE, 30TH FLOOR	NEW YORK, NY	10019
SHYDNER, RITCH	COMEDIAN	10100 SANTA MONICE BLVD #1600	LOS ANGELES, CA	90067
SHYER, CHARLES R	FILM WRITER-DIRECTOR	4040 STANSBURY AVE	SHERMAN OAKS, CA	91423
SHYLO	VOCAL GROUP	SHOWTIME, 50 MUSIC SQUARE W	NASHVILLE, TN	37203
SHYMAN, JIM	ACTOR	4622 GLENCOE AVE #5	MARINA DEL REY, CA	90292
SHYRE, PAUL	TV WRITER	LUCY KROLL, 390 W END AVE	NEW YORK, NY	10024
SI, CHEN	NEWS CORRESPONDENT	2200 "S" ST, NW	WASHINGTON, DC	20008
SIAMIS, KORBY	TV WRITER	8955 BEVERLY BLVD	LOS ANGELES, CA	90048
SIBBETT, JANE	ACTRESS	KNBC-TV, "SANTA BARBARA"		
		3000 W ALAMEDA AVE	BURBANK, CA	91523
SIBERRY, JANE	SINGER-GUITARIST	POST OFFICE BOX 9388	STANFORD, CA	94305
SIBERT, JOHN NEIL	GUITARIST	2570 MURFREESBORO RD		
		PRIEST LAKE MANOR #24-D	NASHVILLE, TN	37217
SICARI, JOSEPH R	ACTOR	2177 N ARGYLE AVE	LOS ANGELES, CA	90068
SICILIANI, ALESSANDRO	CONDUCTOR	ICM, 40 W 57TH ST	NEW YORK, NY	10019
SIDARIS, ANDREW	WRITER-PRODUCER	1891 CARLA RIDGE	BEVERLY HILLS, CA	90210
SIDARIS, ARLENE TERRY	WRITER-PRODUCER	1891 CARLA RIDGE	BEVERLY HILLS, CA	90210
SIDDALL, TEDDI	ACTRESS	636 1/2 N ORANGE DR	LOS ANGELES, CA	90036
SIDE EFFECT	VOCAL GROUP	HAMILTON, 9022 HAMILTON PL	LOS ANGELES, CA	90069
SIDES, GARY	PIANIST	114 SPRINGDALE DR	MOUNT JULIET, TN	37122
SIDES, GREG	MUSICIAN	321 FAULKNER PL	NASHVILLE, TN	37211
SIDES, PATRICIA A	WRITER-PRODUCER	55 E 67TH ST	NEW YORK, NY	10021
SIDLIN, MURRY	CONDUCTOR	SHAW CONCERTS, 1995 BROADWAY	NEW YORK, NY	10023
SIDNEY, GEORGE	DIRECTOR-PRODUCER	910 N REXFORD DR	BEVERLY HILLS, CA	90210
SIDNEY, HUGH	WRITER-EDITOR	TIME/TIME & LIFE BLDG		
		ROCKEFELLER CENTER	NEW YORK, NY	10020
SIDNEY, P JAY	ACTOR	19 MAPLE ST	BROOKLYN, NY	11225
SIDNEY, ROBERT	DIRECTOR-CHOREO	1129 CORY AVE	LOS ANGELES, CA	90069
SIDNEY, SYLVIA	ACTRESS	9744 WILSHIRE BLVD #308	BEVERLY HILLS, CA	90212
SIEBELS, DAVID J	CONDUCTOR	7105 OWENS ST	TUJUNGA, CA	91042
SIEBERT, CHARLES	ACTOR-DIRECTOR	1038 CHAUTAUQUA BLVD	PACIFIC PALISADES, CA	90272
SIEBERT, GLENN	TENOR	59 E 54TH ST #81	NEW YORK, NY	10022
SIEBERT, HORST A	NEWS CORRESPONDENT	7301 RADNOR RD	BETHESDA, MD	20817
SIEBERT, STEVEN J	WRITER	2029 CENTURY PARK E #1330	LOS ANGELES, CA	90067
SIECK, MARGARET	SPORTS WRITER-EDITOR	SPORTS ILLUSTRATED MAGAZINE		
		TIME & LIFE BUILDING		
		ROCKEFELLER CENTER	NEW YORK, NY	10020
SIEDEN, CYNDIA	SOPRANO	CAMI, 165 W 57TH ST	NEW YORK, NY	10019
SIEG, CHARLES W	DIRECTOR	NBC TELEVISION NETWORK		
		30 ROCKEFELLER PLAZA	NEW YORK, NY	10112
SIEGEL, BARRY MARTIN	SCREENWRITER	1045 OCEAN AVE #6	SANTA MONICA, CA	90403
SIEGEL, DAN	SINGER	TDA MGMT, 1672 E 23RD ST	EUGENE, OR	97403
SIEGEL, DANIEL C	COMPOSER	8383 WILSHIRE BLVD #546	BEVERLY HILLS, CA	90211
SIEGEL, DONALD	DIRECTOR	4030 SUMAC DR	SHERMAN OAKS, CA	91403

Name	Occupation	Address	City	Zip
SIEGEL, ELWOOD "WOODY"	DIRECTOR	317 W 89TH ST	NEW YORK, NY	10024
SIEGEL, ERIC B	TV DIRECTOR	127 W 81ST ST	NEW YORK, NY	10024
SIEGEL, GERALD K	WRITER	ICM, 8899 BEVERLY BLVD	LOS ANGELES, CA	90048
SIEGEL, JEFFREY	PIANIST	CAMI, 165 W 57TH ST	NEW YORK, NY	10019
SIEGEL, JEROME M	DIRECTOR	619 N CRESCENT DR	BEVERLY HILLS, CA	90210
SIEGEL, JOEL	FILM CRITIC-WRITER	WABC-TV, 7 LINCOLN SQ	NEW YORK, NY	10023
SIEGEL, LAUREN	TV DIRECTOR	311 E 75TH ST	NEW YORK, NY	10021
SIEGEL, LAURENCE	CONDUCTOR	POST OFFICE BOX 131	SPRINGFIELD, VA	22150
SIEGEL, LAWRENCE H	WRITER	11724 CHENAULT ST	LOS ANGELES, CA	90049
SIEGEL, LIONEL E	WRITER-PRODUCER	30 DORVAL RD	TORONTO, ONT M6P 2B4	CANADA
SIEGEL, MARC	WRITER-PRODUCER	75 CENTRAL PARK W	NEW YORK, NY	10023
SIEGEL, MORT	TV DIRECTOR	WABC-TV, 7 LINCOLN SQ	NEW YORK, NY	10023
SIEGEL, PETER	BODYBUILDER	444 LINCOLN BLVD #308	VENICE, CA	90291
SIEGEL, ROBERT J	DIRECTOR	DGA, 110 W 57TH ST	NEW YORK, NY	10019
SIEGEL, SANDRA KAY	TV WRITER	5003 TILDEN AVE #202	SHERMAN OAKS, CA	91423
SIEGEL, WILLIAM H	TV WRITER	8955 BEVERLY BLVD	LOS ANGELES, CA	90048
SIEGFRIED & ROY	CIRCUS ACT	2535 LAS VEGAS BLVD	LAS VEGAS, NV	89109
SIEGLER, ROBERT	DIRECTOR	DGA, 110 W 57TH ST	NEW YORK, NY	10019
SIEGLER, SCOTT	TV WRITER-EXECUTIVE	135 PALISADES AVE	SANTA MONICA, CA	90402
SIEMASZKO, CASEY	ACTOR	11726 SAN VICENTE BLVD #300	LOS ANGELES, CA	90049
SIENNA, BRIDGET	ACTRESS	11726 SAN VICENTE BLVD #300	LOS ANGELES, CA	90049
SIEPI, CESARE	SINGER	CAMI, 165 W 57TH ST	NEW YORK, NY	10019
SIERING, JAMES	ACTOR	1418 N HIGHLAND AVE #102	LOS ANGELES, CA	90028
SIERRA	VOCAL GROUP	38 MUSIC SQUARE E #217	NASHVILLE, TN	37203
SIERRA, GREGORY	ACTOR	9200 SUNSET BLVD #808	LOS ANGELES, CA	90069
SIFF, HELEN J	ACTRESS	10650 DESPLAIN PL	CHATSWORTH, CA	91311
SIGALL, EDWARD	NEWS EDITOR	THE NATIONAL ENQUIRER		
		600 SE COAST AVE	LANTANA, FL	33464
SIGGINS, JERRY	ACTOR	859 N JUNE ST	LOS ANGELES, CA	90038
SIGHELE, MIETTA	SOPRANO	61 W 62ND ST #6-F	NEW YORK, NY	10023
SIGLER, BUNNY	SINGER-MUSICIAN	1515 MARKET ST #700	PHILADELPHIA, PA	19102
SIGMUND FROG	BARREL CONTORTIONIST	HALL, 138 FROG HOLLOW RD	CHURCHVILLE, PA	18966
SIGNORELLI, JAMES	DIRECTOR	DGA, 110 W 57TH ST	NEW YORK, NY	10019
SIKA	WRESTLER	POST OFFICE BOX 3859	STAMFORD, CT	06905
SIKES, CYNTHIA	ACTRESS	805 N CRESCENT DR	BEVERLY HILLS, CA	90210
SIKI, BELA	PIANIST	333 TAYLOR AVE N #202	SEATTLE, WA	98109
SIKKING, JAMES B	ACTOR	258 S CARMELINA AVE	LOS ANGELES, CA	90049
SIKORSKY, BOB	COLUMNIST-AUTHOR	N Y TIMES SYNDICATION		
		130 5TH AVE	NEW YORK, NY	10011
SILAGYI, CHRIS	ACTOR	6342 IVARENE AVE	LOS ANGELES, CA	90068
SILANO, GEORGE	DIRECTOR	1641 3RD AVE	NEW YORK, NY	10028
SILBAR, ADAM	ACTOR	1865 N FULLER AVE #310	HOLLYWOOD, CA	90046
SILBER, BARBARA D	TV DIRECTOR	ABC-TV, 1926 BROADWAY	NEW YORK, NY	10023
SILBERG, ROBERT A	WRITER	6419 DEMPSEY AVE	VAN NUYS, CA	91406
SILBERMAN, PETER H	NEWS CORRESPONDENT	5337 28TH ST, NW	WASHINGTON, DC	20015
SILBERSHER, MARVIN	TV WRITER-DIRECTOR	797 AVE OF THE AMERICAS	NEW YORK, NY	10001
SILBERSTANG, EDWIN	WRITER	12836 BLOOMFIELD ST	STUDIO CITY, CA	91604
SILENT MOVIES	ROCK & ROLL GROUP	BRINSLEY, TALENT BANK MGMT		
		194 KENSINGTON PARK RD	LONDON W11 2ES	ENGLAND
SILENT RUNNING	ROCK & ROLL GROUP	3 E 54TH ST #1400	NEW YORK, NY	10022
SILER, W CAROLE	NEWS CORRESPONDENT	3220 MORRISON ST, NW	WASHINGTON, DC	20015
SILIMEO, DEBRA J	NEWS CORRESPONDENT	4533 S 28TH RD #B	ARLINGTON, VA	22206
SILJA, ANJA	SOPRANO	COLBERT, 111 W 57TH ST	NEW YORK, NY	10019
SILK, THE	ROCK & ROLL GROUP	POST OFFICE BOX 8125	ANN ARBOR, MI	48107
SILKE, JAMES R	SCREENWRITER	18200 GRESHAM ST	NORTHRIDGE, CA	91325
SILKOSKY, RONALD	WRITER	1345 N ORANGE DR #14	LOS ANGELES, CA	90028
SILLER, RAYMOND D	TV WRITER	1373 MONUMENT ST	PACIFIC PALISADES, CA	90272
SILLIMAN, JULIE	ACTRESS	8721 SUNSET BLVD #202	LOS ANGELES, CA	90069
SILLIPHANT, STIRLING	FILM WRITER-PRODUCER	815 N CAMDEN AVE	BEVERLY HILLS, CA	90210
SILLS, BEVERLY	SOPRANO	RURAL FARM DELIVERY		
		OFF LAMBERT'S COVE RD	VINEGARD HAVEN, MA	02568
SILLS, GREGORY	DIRECTOR	DGA, 7950 SUNSET BLVD	LOS ANGELES, CA	90046
SILLS, PAUL	DIRECTOR	1356 LUCILE AVE	LOS ANGELES, CA	90026
SILLS, THEODORE B	WRITER	8911 CYNTHIA ST #12	LOS ANGELES, CA	90069
SILMAN, JAMES, JR	DIRECTOR	7700 HEMLOCK ST	BETHESDA, MD	20817
SILO, SUSAN	ACTRESS	1350 N HIGHLAND AVE #24	HOLLYWOOD, CA	90028
SILOS, THE	ROCK & ROLL GROUP	POST OFFICE BOX 20895	NEW YORK, NY	10019
		TOMPKINS SQUARE STATION		
SILVA, GENO	ACTOR	8325 RIDPATH DR	LOS ANGELES, CA	90046
SILVA, HENRY	ACTOR	POST OFFICE BOX 5617	BEVERLY HILLS, CA	90210
SILVA, STELLA	MEZZO-SOPRANO	225 W 34TH ST #1012	NEW YORK, NY	10001
SILVA, TRINIDAD, JR	ACTOR	7471 MELROSE AVE #11	LOS ANGELES, CA	90046
SILVEIRA, RUTH	ACTRESS	149 N GRAMERCY PL	LOS ANGELES, CA	90004
SILVER, ARTHUR	FILM WRITER-DIRECTOR	8955 BEVERLY BLVD	LOS ANGELES, CA	90048
SILVER, BARRY E	TV WRITER	5740 ETIWANDA AVE #3	TARZANA, CA	91356
SILVER, BORAH	ACTOR	1832 EL CERRITO PL #1	LOS ANGELES, CA	90068
SILVER, DANIEL S	NEWS CORRESPONDENT	1801 PARK RD #10, NW	WASHINGTON, DC	20010
SILVER, DIANE	WRITER-PRODUCER	1239 N SWEETZER AVE	LOS ANGELES, CA	90069
SILVER, ERIC	GUITARIST	189 WALLACE RD #A-49	NASHVILLE, TN	37211
SILVER, FRANELLE	WRITER	1650 WESTWOOD BLVD #201	LOS ANGELES, CA	90024
SILVER, HARTLEY	ACTOR	1350 N HIGHLAND AVE #24	HOLLYWOOD, CA	90028
SILVER, HORACE, QUINTET	JAZZ GROUP	BRIDGE, 106 FORT GREENE PL	BROOKLYN, NY	11217
SILVER, JOAN MICKLIN	FILM WRITER-DIRECTOR	MIDWEST FILM PRODUCTIONS		
		600 MADISON AVE, 18TH FLOOR	NEW YORK, NY	10022
SILVER, JOE	ACTOR	300 CENTRAL PARK W	NEW YORK, NY	10024

Name	Occupation	Address	City, State	Zip
SILVER, JOE	SINGER	POST OFFICE BOX 211	EAST PRAIRIE, MO	63845
SILVER, JOEL	FILM PRODUCER	SILVER PICTURES COMPANY		
		10201 W PICO BLVD	LOS ANGELES, CA	90035
SILVER, JOHNNY	ACTOR	1350 N HIGHLAND AVE #24	HOLLYWOOD, CA	90028
SILVER, LEO	TV DIRECTOR	5727 W OLYMPIC BLVD	LOS ANGELES, CA	90036
SILVER, LOUIS	NEWS CORRESPONDENT	9530 MIRANDA CT	FAIRFAX, VA	22031
SILVER, MARC	ACTOR	9165 SUNSET BLVD #202	LOS ANGELES, CA	90069
SILVER, RAPHAEL D	TV WRITER-DIRECTOR	MIDWEST FILM PRODUCTIONS		
		600 MADISON AVE, 10TH FLOOR	NEW YORK, NY	10022
SILVER, RON	ACTOR	3855 WOODCLIFF RD	SHERMAN OAKS, CA	91403
SILVER, SPIKE	STUNTMAN	3518 W CAHUENGA BLVD #300	LOS ANGELES, CA	90068
SILVER, STEPHANIE	ACTRESS	5643 RHODES AVE	NORTH HOLLYWOOD, CA	91607
SILVER, STUART	TV WRITER	8955 BEVERLY BLVD	LOS ANGELES, CA	90048
SILVER, STUART BRANDT	TV DIRECTOR	106 PERRY ST	NEW YORK, NY	10014
SILVER, SUSAN A	TV WRITER	8955 BEVERLY BLVD	LOS ANGELES, CA	90048
SILVER, TONY	DIRECTOR	325 W END AVE #3-B	NEW YORK, NY	10023
SILVER CONDOR	JAZZ GROUP	3 E 54TH ST #1400	NEW YORK, NY	10022
SILVER CONNECTION	VOCAL GROUP	200 W 51ST ST #1410	NEW YORK, NY	10019
SILVER CREEK	ROCK & ROLL GROUP	POST OFFICE BOX 448	RADFORD, VA	24141
SILVER STREET	MUSICAL GROUP	POST OFFICE BOX 1808	ASHEVILLE, NC	28802
SILVERADO	ROCK & ROLL GROUP	MAHLER, 29 LEXINGTON AVE	WATERBURY, CT	06710
SILVERBERG, DAVID	NEWS CORRESPONDENT	1317 "F" ST, NW	WASHINGTON, DC	20004
SILVERBERG, SUSAN	DIRECTOR	2918 1/2 GRAND CANAL	VENICE, CA	90291
SILVERMAN, BARTON	PHOTOGRAPHER	6 SIGNAL CT	DIX HILLS, NY	11745
SILVERMAN, DAVID	TV WRITER	8955 BEVERLY BLVD	LOS ANGELES, CA	90048
SILVERMAN, EDWIN ELLIS	DIRECTOR	DGA, 110 W 57TH ST	NEW YORK, NY	10019
SILVERMAN, FAYE-ELLEN	COMPOSER	FINELL, 155 W 68TH ST	NEW YORK, NY	10023
SILVERMAN, FRED	TV PRODUCER-EXECUTIVE	101 CENTRAL PARK W #10-E	NEW YORK, NY	10023
SILVERMAN, IRA N	NEWS CORRESPONDENT	NBC-TV, NEWS DEPARTMENT	WASHINGTON, DC	20016
SILVERMAN, JEFF	WRITER-EDITOR	US MAGAZINE COMPANY		
		1 DAG HAMMARSKJOLD PLAZA	NEW YORK, NY	10017
SILVERMAN, LYNNE	SOPRANO	111 W 57TH ST #1209	NEW YORK, NY	10019
SILVERMAN, PETER	TV WRITER	11726 SAN VICENTE BLVD #300	LOS ANGELES, CA	90049
SILVERMAN, PETER H	DIRECTOR	80 WARREN ST #15	NEW YORK, NY	10007
SILVERMAN, STANLEY H	TV WRITER	555 W 57TH ST #1230	NEW YORK, NY	10019
SILVERMAN, STUART	TV WRITER	2049 CENTURY PARK E #1320	LOS ANGELES, CA	90067
SILVERMAN, SYD	PUBLISHING EXECUTIVE	VARIETY, 1400 N CAHUENGA BLVD	HOLLYWOOD, CA	90028
SILVERN, BEA	ACTRESS	5681 SPREADING OAK DR	LOS ANGELES, CA	90068
SILVERS, CATHY	ACTRESS	9220 SUNSET BLVD #625	LOS ANGELES, CA	90069
SILVERS, HERB	CONDUCTOR	3839 ROYAL WOODS DR	SHERMAN OAKS, CA	91403
SILVERSTEIN, ELLIOT	FILM DIRECTOR	DGA, 7950 SUNSET BLVD	HOLLYWOOD, CA	90046
SILVERSTEIN, JOSEPH	VIOLINIST	SHAW CONCERTS, 1995 BROADWAY	NEW YORK, NY	10023
SILVERSTEIN, KARIN	PHOTO EDITOR	US MAGAZINE COMPANY		
		1 DAG HAMMARSKJOLD PLAZA	NEW YORK, NY	10017
SILVERSTEIN, MIKE D	NEWS CORRESPONDENT	1301 20TH ST, NW	WASHINGTON, DC	20036
SILVERSTEIN, MORTON	WRITER-PRODUCER	DGA, 110 W 57TH ST	NEW YORK, NY	10019
SILVERSTONE, KENNETH J	NEWS CORRESPONDENT	11405 LOVEJOY ST	SILVER SPRING, MD	20902
SILVERSTONE, LOU	WRITER	MAD MAGAZINE, INC		
		485 MADISON AVE	NEW YORK, NY	10022
SILVERTON, DORIS	TV WRITER	1900 AVE OF THE STARS #2375	LOS ANGELES, CA	90067
SILVERWIND	GOSPEL GROUP	POST OFFICE BOX 1441	TACOMA, WA	98401
SILVESTRE, EDDIE	BODYBUILDER	POST OFFICE BOX 176	SAN YSIDRO, CA	92073
SILWA, LISA	MODEL	ELITE MODELS, 150 E 58TH ST	NEW YORK, NY	10022
SIM, GERALD	ACTOR	MARR, 32 WIGMORE ST	LONDON W1H 9DF	ENGLAND
SIMAK, CLIFFORD D	AUTHOR	5823 SCENIC CT	MINNETONKA, MN	55343
SIMMON, LISA MARIE	ACTRESS	3800 BARHAM BLVD #303	LOS ANGELES, CA	90068
SIMMONDS, STANLEY	ACTOR	888 8TH AVE	NEW YORK, NY	10019
SIMMONS, ANN	SINGER	902 PINECONE TRAIL	ANDERSON, SC	29621
SIMMONS, ANTHONY	WRITER-PRODUCER	WEST ONE FILM PRODUCTIONS		
		2 LOWER JAMES ST	LONDON W1R 3PN	ENGLAND
SIMMONS, CAROL L	WRITER	1411 MC COLLUM ST	LOS ANGELES, CA	90026
SIMMONS, CRAIG	ACTOR	14350 ADDISON ST #214	SHERMAN OAKS, CA	91423
SIMMONS, DAVID	SINGER	WMOT MGMT, 1228 SPRUCE ST	PHILADELPHIA, PA	19107
SIMMONS, DICK	ACTOR	5500 EL CAMINO REAL	CARLSBAD, CA	92008
SIMMONS, ED	TV WRITER	8955 BEVERLY BLVD	LOS ANGELES, CA	90048
SIMMONS, EDWARD L	WRITER-PRODUCER	133 STONECREST RD	RIDGEFIELD, CT	06877
SIMMONS, GARNER	SCREENWRITER	10010 SANTA MONICA BLVD #1600	LOS ANGELES, CA	90067
SIMMONS, GARY A	TV WRITER	8955 BEVERLY BLVD	LOS ANGELES, CA	90048
SIMMONS, GENE	SING-ACT-COMP	427 N CANON DR #205	BEVERLY HILLS, CA	90210
SIMMONS, JEAN	ACTRESS	636 ADELAIDE WY	SANTA MONICA, CA	90402
SIMMONS, JOAN	CASTING DIRECTOR	5224 TOPEKA DR	TARZANA, CA	91356
SIMMONS, JOHN	WRITER-PRODUCER	3 BATEMAN ST	LONDON W1V 5TT	ENGLAND
SIMMONS, MATTY	FILM WRITER-PRODUCER	715 N CANON DR	BEVERLY HILLS, CA	90210
SIMMONS, MATTY	PUBLISHING EXECUTIVE	THE NATIONAL LAMPOON		
		635 MADISON AVE	NEW YORK, NY	10022
SIMMONS, NANCY F	NEWS CORRESPONDENT	5817 BRUNSWICK ST	SPRINGFIELD, VA	22150
SIMMONS, PATRICK	SINGER-SONGWRITER	POST OFFICE BOX 7308	CARMEL, CA	93923
SIMMONS, PAUL	SINGER	POST OFFICE BOX 11321		
		FLAGLER STATION	MIAMI, FL	33101
SIMMONS, RICHARD	EXERCISE INSTRUCTOR	1334 LONDONDERRY PL	LOS ANGELES, CA	90069
SIMMONS, RICHARD ALAN	SCREENWRITER	514 N BEVERLY DR	BEVERLY HILLS, CA	90210
SIMMONS, RICHARD D	PUBLISH EXECUTIVE	NEWSWEEK, 444 MADISON AVE	NEW YORK, NY	10022
SIMMONS, ROBIN	TV PRODUCER	1438 N GOWER ST #31	LOS ANGELES, CA	90038
SIMMONS, ROGER	SINGER	902 PINECONE TRAIL	ANDERSON, SC	29621

SIMMONS, SARAH	ACTRESS	4647 WILLIS AVE	SHERMAN OAKS, CA	91403
SIMMONS, TOMMY	GUITARIST	POST OFFICE BOX 204	LAKELAND, NC	28451
SIMMS, EARL EDWARD, JR	WRITER	4226 TOLUCA LAKE LN	BURBANK, CA	91505
SIMMS, GINNY	ACTRESS	EASTVOLD, 1578 MURRAY CANYON DR	PALM SPRINGS, CA	92262
SIMMS, LARRY	ACTOR	1043 KEEHI MARINA	HONOLULU, HI	96819
SIMMS, MICHAEL DAVID	ACTOR	6736 LAUREL CANYON BLVD #306	NORTH HOLLYWOOD, CA	91606
SIMMS, OLGA PALSSON	WRITER	4226 TOLUCA LAKE LN	BURBANK, CA	91505
SIMON, ABBEY	PIANIST	GURTMAN, 162 W 56TH ST	NEW YORK, NY	10019
SIMON, BARRY E	TV DIRECTOR	3775 ROBERTA ST	LOS ANGELES, CA	90031
SIMON, BOB	NEWS CORRESPONDENT	CBS NEWS, 2020 "M" ST, NW	WASHINGTON, DC	20036
SIMON, CARLY	SINGER-SONGWRITER	145 CENTRAL PARK W	NEW YORK, NY	10023
SIMON, COURTNEY S	TV WRITER	555 W 57TH ST #1230	NEW YORK, NY	10019
SIMON, DANIEL	WRITER-PRODUCER	15233 MAGNOLIA BLVD #302	SHERMAN OAKS, CA	91403
SIMON, DARREN	CLOWN	2701 COTTAGE WY #14	SACRAMENTO, CA	95825
SIMON, DAVID S	TV WRITER	8955 BEVERLY BLVD	LOS ANGELES, CA	90048
SIMON, DYANNE ASIMOW	WRITER	8071 WILLOW GLEN RD	LOS ANGELES, CA	90046
SIMON, JACK	DIRECTOR	MADISON SQ GARDEN NETWORK		
		4 PENNSYLVANUA PLAZA	NEW YORK, NY	10001
SIMON, JEFF	TV DIRECTOR	162 CROSS RD	OAKLAND, CA	94618
SIMON, JOANNA	MEZZO-SOPRANO	SHAW CONCERTS, 1995 BROADWAY	NEW YORK, NY	10023
SIMON, JOE	SINGER	POST OFFICE BOX 82	GREAT NECK, NY	11021
SIMON, JOEL	ACTOR	168 W 86TH ST	NEW YORK, NY	10024
SIMON, LAUREN	ACTRESS	5904 CARLTON WY	LOS ANGELES, CA	90028
SIMON, LISA D	DIRECTOR	20 E 9TH ST	NEW YORK, NY	10003
SIMON, MAYO	WRITER	574 CHAPALA DR	PACIFIC PALISADES, CA	90272
SIMON, NEIL	PLAYWRIGHT	700 PARK AVE #PH	NEW YORK, NY	10021
SIMON, PAUL	SCREENWRITER	555 W 57TH ST #1230	NEW YORK, NY	10019
SIMON, PAUL	SINGER-SONGWRI-ACTOR	88 CENTRAL PARK W	NEW YORK, NY	10022
SIMON, PETER	ACTOR	CBS-TV, "THE GUIDING LIGHT"		
		51 W 52ND ST	NEW YORK, NY	10019
SIMON, ROBERT D	FILM DIRECTOR	536 E 79TH ST #3-N	NEW YORK, NY	10021
SIMON, ROGER L	SCREENWRITER	21458 RAMBLA VISTA	MALIBU, CA	90265
SIMON, SAM	TV WRITER	8955 BEVERLY BLVD	LOS ANGELES, CA	90048
SIMON, SIMONE	ACTRESS	5 RUE DE TILSITT	PARIS 75008	FRANCE
SIMON, SUSAN ORLIKOFF	TV WRITER-DIRECTOR	15239 RAYNETA DR	SHERMAN OAKS, CA	91403
SIMON, TODD H	TV DIRECTOR	11744 1/8 MAYFIELD AVE	LOS ANGELES, CA	90049
SIMON, TOM M	TV DIRECTOR-PRODUCER	114 W 16TH ST #3-G	NEW YORK, NY	10011
SIMONE, JULIE	MODEL	MODELS & PROMOTIONS AGENCY		
		8560 SUNSET BLVD, 10TH FLOOR	LOS ANGELES, CA	90069
SIMONE, NINA	SINGER-PIANIST	ASSOCIATED BOOKING CORP		
SIMONE, SERGIA	ACTRESS	9250 WILSHIRE BLVD #208	BEVERLY HILLS, CA	90212
SIMONELLI, GEORGE	ACTOR	439 S LA CIENEGA BLVD #110	LOS ANGELES, CA	90069
SIMONS, DAVID	NEWS CORRESPONDENT	4638 ELLICOTT ST, NW	WASHINGTON, DC	20016
SIMONS, DAVID A	ACTOR	6252 LUBAO AVE	WOODLAND HILLS, CA	91367
SIMONS, JOHN B	NEWS CORRESPONDENT	2139 WISCONSIN AVE, NW	WASHINGTON, DC	20007
SIMONS, MARY	WRITER-EDITOR	LIFE/TIME & LIFE BLDG		
		ROCKEFELLER CENTER	NEW YORK, NY	10020
SIMONSON, NANCEE	NEWS CORRESPONDENT	2108 HUIDEKOPER PL, NW	WASHINGTON, DSC	20007
SIMOUN, HENRI	TV WRITER	8955 BEVERLY BLVD	LOS ANGELES, CA	90048
SIMPLE MINDS	ROCK & ROLL GROUP	SCHOOLHOUSE MGMT		
		63 FREDERICK ST	EDINBURGH EH2 1LH	SCOTLAND
SIMPLY RED	ROCK & ROLL GROUP	36 ATWOOD RD, DIDSBURY	MANCHESTER 20	ENGLAND
SIMPSON, ALAN	ACTOR-WRITER	LE BARS, 18 QUEEN ANNE ST	LONDON W1	ENGLAND
SIMPSON, CAROLE	NEWS CORRESPONDENT	ABC-TV, NEWS DEPARTMENT		
		1717 DE SALES ST, NW	WASHINGTON, DC	20036
SIMPSON, DON	FILM PROD-EXEC	9472 CHEROKEE LN	BEVERLY HILLS, CA	90210
SIMPSON, FRANCIS R	DIRECTOR	84-09 35TH AVE	JACKSON HEIGHTS, NY	11372
SIMPSON, FRANK	FILM DIRECTOR	POST OFFICE BOX 852	STOCKBRIDGE, MA	01262
SIMPSON, GARRY	TV DIRECTOR	RURAL DELIVERY #3, KELLOGG RD	VERGENNES, VT	05491
SIMPSON, GARY	GUITARIST	65 STARROWBUSH RD	MAHWAH, NJ	07430
SIMPSON, GEORGE E	WRITER	9000 SUNSET BLVD #1200	LOS ANGELES, CA	90069
SIMPSON, JIM	RECORD EXECUTIVE	BIG BEAR RECORDS		
		190 MONUMENT	BIRMINGHAM B16 8UU	ENGLAND
SIMPSON, JOY	SOPRANO	JCB, 155 W 68TH ST	NEW YORK, NY	10023
SIMPSON, MARIETTA	MEZZO-SOPRANO	JCB, 155 W 68TH ST	NEW YORK, NY	10023
SIMPSON, O J	ACTOR-FOOTBALL	360 N ROCKINGHAM AVE	LOS ANGELES, CA	90049
SIMPSON, PEGGY A	NEWS CORRESPONDENT	1719 SWANN ST, NW	WASHINGTON, DC	20009
SIMPSON, RED	SINGER	POST OFFICE BOX 4234	PANORAMA CITY, CA	91412
SIMPSON, RICHIE	DRUMMER	3806 EDWARDS AVE	NASHVILLE, TN	37216
SIMPSON, ROSS W	NEWS CORRESPONDENT	1755 S JEFFERSON DAVIS HWY	ARLINGTON, VA	22202
SIMPSON, ROY	DIRECTOR-PRODUCER	PINEWOOD STUDIOS, IVER HEATH	BUCKS SLO ONH	ENGLAND
SIMPSON, SANDY	ACTOR	400 S BEVERLY DR #216	BEVERLY HILLS, CA	90212
SIMPSON, SCOTT	WRESTLER	SEE - KOLOFF, NIKITA		
SIMPSON, STEVE	WRESTLER	WORLD CLASS WRESTLING		
		SOUTHWEST SPORTS, INC		
		DALLAS SPORTATORIUM		
		1000 S INDUSTRIAL BLVD	DALLAS, TX	75207
SIMS, JERRY	DIRECTOR	3765 W CAHUENGA BLVD	STUDIO CITY, CA	91604
SIMS, JOAN	ACTRESS	17 ESMOND CT, THACKERY ST	LONDON W8	ENGLAND
SIMS, MARLEY	TV WRITER	8955 BEVERLY BLVD	LOS ANGELES, CA	90048
SIMS, SYLVIA	ACTRESS	135 E 63RD ST	NEW YORK, NY	10021
SINATRA, FRANK	SINGER-ACTOR	70588 FRANK SINATRA BLVD	RANCHO MIRAGE, CA	92270
SINATRA, FRANK, JR	SINGER	2211 FLORIAN PL	BEVERLY HILLS, CA	90210
SINATRA, NANCY	SINGER-ACTOR	LAMBERT, 9817 HYTHE CT	BEVERLY HILLS, CA	90210
SINATRA, RAY	COMPOSER-CONDUCTOR	1234 S 8TH PL	LAS VEGAS, NV	89104

NANCY SINATRA

PEGGY SINGLETON

RED SKELTON

GRACE SLICK

BUFFALO BOB SMITH

JACLYN SMITH

MAGGIE SMITH

JAN SMITHERS

HANK SNOW

Name	Occupation	Address	City	Zip
SINBAD	COMEDIAN	7319 BEVERLY BLVD #7	LOS ANGELES, CA	90036
SINCEROS	ROCK & ROLL GROUP	LIVE MGMT, 25 BULIVER ST		
		SHEPHERDS BUSH	LONDON W12 8AR	ENGLAND
SINCLAIR, BETTY	ACTRESS	871 1ST AVE	NEW YORK, NY	10017
SINCLAIR, ERIC	ACTOR	7735 ATLANTIC AVE #13	CUDAHY, CA	90201
SINCLAIR, GABRIELLE	ACTRESS	326 E 74TH ST #15	NEW YORK, NY	10021
SINCLAIR, MADGE	ACTRESS	8035 BRIAR SUMMIT DR	LOS ANGELES, CA	90046
SINCLAIR, MOLLY K	NEWS CORRESPONDENT	4456 SPRINGDALE ST, NW	WASHINGTON, DC	20016
SINCLAIR, NANCY	ACTRESS	6380 WILSHIRE BLVD #1600	LOS ANGELES, CA	90048
SINCLAIR, WARD	NEWS CORRESPONDENT	5604 ASBURY CT	ALEXANDRIA, VA	22312
SINDELL, JANE	TALENT AGENT	ICM, 8899 BEVERLY BLVD	LOS ANGELES, CA	90048
SINDEN, DONALD	ACTOR	60 TEMPLE FORTUNE LN	LONDON NW11	ENGLAND
SINDEN, JEREMY	ACTOR	ICM, 388-396 OXFORD ST	LONDON W1	ENGLAND
SINDEN, LEON	ACTOR	70 OVERSTRAND MANSIONS		
		PRINCE OF WALES DR	LONDON SW11	ENGLAND
SINDEN, MARC	ACTOR	LONDON MANAGEMENT, LTD		
		235-241 REGENT ST	LONDON W1A 2JT	ENGLAND
SINER, ROBERT C	NEWS CORRESPONDENT	420 FAIRTREE DR	SEVERNA PARK, MD	21146
SINGER, ABBY	TV PRODUCER	MTM, 4024 RADFORD AVE	STUDIO CITY, CA	91604
SINGER, ALEXANDER	TV DIRECTOR	989 BLUEGRASS LN	LOS ANGELES, CA	90049
SINGER, BRUCE F	TV WRITER	8955 BEVERLY BLVD	LOS ANGELES, CA	90048
SINGER, CARLA	TV PRODUCER	WARNER BROTHERS PICTURES		
		4000 WARNER BLVD	BURBANK, CA	91522
SINGER, JUDITH	TV WRITER	989 BLUEGRASS LN	LOS ANGELES, CA	90049
SINGER, LES	BANJOIST	834 GALLAVISTA #A	MADISON, TN	37115
SINGER, LORI	ACTRESS	330 W 72ND ST #10-B	NEW YORK, NY	10023
SINGER, MARC	ACTOR	11218 CANTON DR	STUDIO CITY, CA	91604
SINGER, RAYMOND	ACTOR	211 S BEVERLY DR #107	BEVERLY HILLS, CA	90212
SINGER, RAYMOND B	ACTOR	121 N SYCAMORE AVE	LOS ANGELES, CA	90036
SINGER, RAYMOND E	ACTOR-PRODUCER	1711 COLDWATER CANYON DR	BEVERLY HILLS, CA	90210
SINGER, ROBERT	FILM PRODUCER	4000 WARNER BLVD #32-28	BURBANK, CA	91522
SINGER, ROBERT S	DIRECTOR	DGA, 7950 SUNSET BLVD	LOS ANGELES, CA	90046
SINGER, STEPHEN	ACTOR	66 E 7TH ST #7	NEW YORK, NY	10003
SINGLE, ERIC	HIGH WIRE ACT	POST OFFICE BOX 87	WEST LEBANON, NY	12195
SINGLETARY, MICHAEL	TV DIRECTOR	375 HAWTHORNE TERR	MOUNT VERNON, NY	10552
SINGLETARY, TONY	TV DIRECTOR-PRODUCER	1218 S SYCAMORE AVE	LOS ANGELES, CA	90019
SINGLETON, CHARLIE	SINGER-GUITARIST	200 W 51ST ST #1410	NEW YORK, NY	10019
SINGLETON, DORIS	ACTRESS	9255 SUNSET BLVD #603	LOS ANGELES, CA	90069
SINGLETON, MARJORIE	SINGER-GUITARIST	POST OFFICE BOX 567	HENDERSONVILLE, TN	37075
SINGLETON, PENNY	ACTRESS	POST OFFICE BOX 174	VAN NUYS, CA	91401
SINGLETON, SHELBY	GUITARIST	1152 CRATER HILL RD	NASHVILLE, TN	37215
SINGLETON, VALERIE	ACTRESS	ARLINGTON, 1 CHARLOTTE ST	LONDON W1	ENGLAND
SINK, KITTY	ACTRESS	8075 W 3RD ST #303	LOS ANGELES, CA	90048
SINKS, HENRY EARL	GUITARIST	POST OFFICE BOX 3555	RIDGETOP, TN	37152
SINKS, RITA FAYE	AUTO HARPIST	POST OFFICE BOX 3555	RIDGETOP, TN	37152
SINKYS, ALBERT	ACTOR	465 W END AVE	NEW YORK, NY	10024
SINN, PATRICIA	NEWS CORRESPONDENT	1434 PERRY PL, NW	WASHINGTON, DC	20010
SINNOTT, PATRICIA	ACTRESS	4 PARK AVE	NEW YORK, NY	10016
SIODMAK, CURT	WRITER-PRODUCER	43422 S FORK DR	THREE RIVERS, CA	93271
SIOLI, FRANCO	BARITONE	61 W 62ND ST #6-F	NEW YORK, NY	10023
SIPE, WELDON S	ACTOR	20146 SEPTO ST	CHATSWORTH, CA	91311
SIPES, MARILYN	WRITER	929 N REXFORD DR	BEVERLY HILLS, CA	90210
SIPORIN, RALPH	DIRECTOR	21880 GLENMORRA ST	SOUTHFIELD, MI	48076
SIRIANNE, MARY FRANCES	TV DIRECTOR	WETA-TV, 3620 S 27TH ST	ARLINGTON, VA	22206
SIRINSKY, MARC	WRITER-PRODUCER	1483 N OCCIDENTAL BLVD	LOS ANGELES, CA	90026
SIROLA, JOSEPH	ACTOR	9200 SUNSET BLVD #1210	LOS ANGELES, CA	90069
SIROTA, JOSEPH	TV WRITER	8955 BEVERLY BLVD	LOS ANGELES, CA	90048
SIRULNICK, LEON	DIRECTOR	18 WHITTIER DR	ENGLISHTOWN, NJ	07726
SISCO, PAUL C	PHOTOJOURNALIST	8207 BRYANT DR	BETHESDA, MD	20817
SISK, GENE	MUSIC ARRANGER	721 DUE WEST AVE #F-302	MADISON, TN	37115
SISK, KATHLEEN	ACTRESS	ABC-TV NETWORK, "LOVING"		
		1330 AVE OF THE AMERICAS	NEW YORK, NY	10019
SISK, ROSS, JR	GUITARIST	137 S SUNSET	HOPKINSVILLE, KY	42240
SISKEL, GENE	FILM CRITIC	THE CHICAGO TRIBUNE		
		TRIBUNE TOWER		
		435 N MICHIGAN AVE	CHICAGO, IL	60611
SISLEN, MYRNA	VIHUELIST-GUITARIST	LINDY S MARTIN MGMT		
		GENERAL DELIVERY	PINEHURST, NC	28374
SISON, RAMON	ACTOR	200 S LINDEN DR	BEVERLY HILLS, CA	90212
SISSON, ROBERT	PHOTOGRAPHER	5307 POTOMAC AVE, NW	WASHINGTON, DC	20016
SISSON, ROSEMARY ANNE	TV WRITER	ANDREW MANN, 1 OLD COMPTON ST	LONDON W1	ENGLAND
SISTER SLEDGE	VOCAL GROUP	A M I PRODUCTIONS		
		1776 BROADWAY, 10TH FLOOR	NEW YORK, NY	10019
SISTERS OF MERCY, THE	ROCK & ROLL GROUP	MERCIFUL RELEASE		
		19 ALL SAINTS RD	LONDON W11	ENGLAND
SITA, YING	REPORTER	TIME & PEOPLE MAGAZINE		
		TIME & LIFE BUILDING		
		ROCKEFELLER CENTER	NEW YORK, NY	10020
SITBON, NADJA	MODEL	POST OFFICE BOX 7211	MOUNTAIN VIEW, CA	94043
SITKA, EMIL	ACTOR	18124 VILLAGE #18	CAMARILLO, CA	93010
SITKOVETSKY, DMITRY	VIOLINIST	CAMI, 165 W 57TH ST	NEW YORK, NY	10019
SITOWITZ, HAL	WRITER-PRODUCER	207 N ELM DR	BEVERLY HILLS, CA	90210
SITTENFIELD, JOAN	CASTING DIRECTOR	MCA/UNIVERSAL STUDIOS, INC		
		100 UNIVERSAL CITY PLAZA		
		BUILDING #426-1	UNIVERSAL CITY, CA	91608

SISTER SLEDGE
Joni • Kim • Kathy • Debbie

S.O.S. BAND

Name	Occupation	Address	City	Zip
SITTON, RUTH	ACTRESS	10000 RIVERSIDE DR #12-14	TOLUCA LAKE, CA	91602
SIUKOLA, HEIKKI	TENOR	CAMI, 165 W 57TH ST	NEW YORK, NY	10019
SIVERO, FRANK	ACTOR	6736 LAUREL CANYON BLVD #306	NORTH HOLLYWOOD, CA	91606
SIVITZ, LARRY	WRITER	7432 HAZELTINE AVE #2	VAN NUYS, CA	91405
SIWOLOP, SANA	WRITER-EDITOR	DISCOVER/TIME & LIFE BLDG		
		ROCKEFELLER CENTER	NEW YORK, NY	10020
SIX, JIM & CITY LIMITS	MUSICAL GROUP	POST OFFICE BOX 592	KING OF PRUSSIA, PA	19406
SIXTA, GEORGE	CARTOONIST	NEWS AMERICA SYNDICATE		
		1703 KAISER AVE	IRVINE, CA	92714
SIZEMORE, HERSHEL	GUITARIST	5720 BARNS AVE, NW	ROANOKE, VA	24019
SJOMAN, VILGOT	FILM DIRECTOR	POST OFFICE BOX 27126	S-10252 STOCKHOLM	SWEDEN
SKAFF, GEORGE	ACTOR	208 S BEVERLY DR #4	BEVERLY HILLS, CA	90212
SKAFISH	ROCK & ROLL GROUP	CAMERON, 822 HILLGROVE AVE	WESTERN SPRINGS, IL	60558
SKAGGS, OPAL	PIANIST	ROUTE #4, BOX 5298	GOODLETTSVILLE, TN	37072
SKAGGS, RICKY	SINGER-GUITARIST	380 FOREST RETREAT	HENDERSONVILLE, TN	37075
SKAGGS, SHARON WHITE	SINGER-GUITARIST	380 FOREST RETREAT	HENDERSONVILLE, TN	37075
SKALA, LILIA	ACTRESS	42-02 LAYTON ST	ELMHURST, NY	11373
SKALAK, WILLIAM	COMPOSER	6017 FAWN AVE	LAS VEGAS, NV	89107
SKANE, WILLIAM J	NEWS CORRESPONDENT	CBS NEWS, 2020 "M" ST, NW	WASHINGTON, DC	20036
SKATT BROTHERS, THE	SOUL GROUP	AUCION MGMT, 645 MADISON AVE	NEW YORK, NY	10022
SKATULA, KATHRYN	ACTRESS	9856 1/2 VIDOR DR	LOS ANGELES, CA	90035
SKEGGS, ROY	FILM PRODUCER	3 OAK TREE CT, BARNET LN		
		ELSTRE	HERTS	ENGLAND
SKEHAN, MICHAEL E	NEWS CORRESPONDENT	1705 DE SALES ST, NW	WASHINGTON, DC	20036
SKEHAN, PATRICK D	NEWS CORRESPONDENT	1705 DE SALES ST, NW	WASHINGTON, DC	20036
SKELLY, JOHN T	NEWS CORRESPONDENT	POST OFFICE BOX 1227	ARLINGTON, VA	22209
SKELTON, GEORGE	NEWS CORRESPONDENT	10617 GREENE DR	LORTON, VA	22079
SKELTON, JUDITH A	WRITER	11989 1/2 LAURELWOOD DR	STUDIO CITY, CA	91604
SKELTON, PATRICK	ACTOR	200 N ROBERTSON BLVD #219	BEVERLY HILLS, CA	90211
SKELTON, RED	ACTOR-COMEDIAN	37801 THOMSON RD	RANCHO MIRAGE, CA	92270
SKENE, GORDON D	WRITER	11747 MAYFIELD AVE #6	LOS ANGELES, CA	90049
SKENE, PATRICIA T	WRITER	11747 MAYFIELD AVE #8	LOS ANGELES, CA	90049
SKERNICK, LINDA	HARPSICHORDIST	AFFILIATE ARTISTS, LTD		
		37 W 65TH ST, 6TH FLOOR	NEW YORK, NY	10023
SKERRITT, TOM	ACTOR	25711 CLINE RD	CALABASAS, CA	91302
SKID ROW JOE	SINGER	POST OFFICE BOX 211	EAST PRAIRIE, MO	63845
SKIDMORE, HAROLD	DRUMMER	1005 SAM DAVIS RD	SMYRNA, TN	37167
SKILES, KENNETH	TV DIRECTOR	4511 COLBATH AVE #8	SHERMAN OAKS, CA	91423
SKILES & HENDERSON	COMEDIANS	4421 RIVERSIDE DR #211	BURBANK, CA	91505
SKILLEN, CATHERANE	ACTRESS	1607 N EL CENTRO AVE #22	HOLLYWOOD, CA	90028
SKILLEN, JANIECE	ACTRESS	3163 BARBARA CT #C	LOS ANGELES, CA	90068
SKILLING, KENNETH	NEWS CORRESPONDENT	1209 PRISCILLA LN	ALEXANDRIA, VA	22308
SKIN & BONES	CLOWN DUO	2701 COTTAGE WY #14	SACRAMENTO, CA	95825
SKINNELL, ROBERT G	COMPOSER-CONDUCTOR	4004 ORANGEDALE AVE	MONTROSE, CA	91020
SKINNER, ANN	PRODUCER	SKREBA, 145-C SAINT GEORGE'S RD	LONDON SE1 6HY	ENGLAND
SKINNER, DAVID	TV WRITER	8955 BEVERLY BLVD	LOS ANGELES, CA	90048
SKINNER, JAMES	NEWS CORRESPONDENT	1941 SHIVER DR	ALEXANDRIA, VA	22307
SKIP & LINDA	VOCAL DUO	38 MUSIC SQUARE E #217	NASHVILLE, TN	37203
SKIPPER, BUDDY	MUSIC ARRANGER	324 WILLOW BOUGH LN	OLD HICKORY, TN	37138
SKIPPER, THE	BUSINESS AGENT	SEE - BERES, PETER		
		"THE SKIPPER"		
SKIPWORTH & TURNER	RHYTHM & BLUES GROUP	200 W 51ST ST #1410	NEW YORK, NY	10019
SKLAR, ALBERT	ACTOR	3330 BARHAM BLVD #103	LOS ANGELES, CA	90068
SKOFF, MELISSA	CASTING DIRECTOR	11684 VENTURA BLVD #5141	STUDIO CITY, CA	91604
SKOG, ALAN	DIRECTOR	140 W 79TH ST #3-C	NEW YORK, NY	10024
SKOGLUND, CLIFF	MODEL	WILHELMINA, 9 E 37TH ST	NEW YORK, NY	10016
SKOLIMOWSKI, JERZY	FILM DIRECTOR	FILM POLASKI, U1 MAZOWIECKA 618	990947 WARSAW	POLAND
SKOLNEK, MORLEY	DIRECTOR-PRODUCER	10610 ROCHESTER AVE	LOS ANGELES, CA	90024
SKOMAL, PEGGY	ACTRESS	1418 N HIGHLAND AVE #102	LOS ANGELES, CA	90028
SKOOFGORS, LEIF	PHOTOGRAPHER	WOODFIN CAMP, 925 1/2 "F" ST	WASHINGTON, DC	20004
SKOPP, HARRY	CONDUCTOR	18930 CITRONIA ST	NORTHRIDGE, CA	91324
SKORODIN, ELAINE	VIOLINIST	157 W 57TH ST #1100	NEW YORK, NY	10019
SKOURAS, SPYROS	TALENT AGENT	1901 AVE OF THE STARS #840	LOS ANGELES, CA	90067
SKOVALD, FLORENCE	COMPOSER	138 N 2ND ST, BOX 621	BAYFIELD, WI	54814
SKOW, LEE	GUITARIST	POST OFFICE BOX 237	MC EWEN, TN	37101
SKREBNESKI, VICTOR	DIRECTOR	1350 N LA SALLE ST	CHICAGO, IL	60610
SKRENTNY, JAN E	TV DIRECTOR	7029 TROLLEY WY	PLAYA DEL REY, CA	90291
SKROWACZEWSKI, STANISLAW	CONDUCTOR	ICM, 40 W 57TH ST	NEW YORK, NY	10019
SKRZYCKI, CINDY	NEWS CORRESPONDENT	6697 FAIRFAX RD	CHEVY CHASE, MD	20815
SKUBINNA, MARTIN L	NEWS CORRESPONDENT	16 3RD ST, NE	WASHINGTON, DC	20002
SKUTCH, IRA, JR	DIRECTOR-PRODUCER	3656 GLENRIDGE DR	SHERMAN OAKS, CA	91423
SKY KING	ROCK & ROLL GROUP	POST OFFICE BOX 18368	DENVER, CO	80218
SKYBOYS, THE	VOCAL GROUP	FAR WEST, 110 BOYLSTON AVE E	SEATTLE, WA	98102
SKYLER, WILLIAM	ACTOR	200 N ROBERTSON BLVD #308	BEVERLY HILLS, CA	90210
SKYLES, LINDY	ACTOR	439 S LA CIENEGA BLVD #120	LOS ANGELES, CA	90048
SKYLINE	BLUEGRASS GROUP	POST OFFICE BOX 53201	MILWAUKEE, WI	53201
SKYLINERS, THE	VOCAL GROUP	MARS, 168 ORCHID DR	PEARL RIVER, NY	10965
SKYWALK	JAZZ-ROCK GROUP	1560 BROADWAY #507	NEW YORK, NY	10036
SKYY	RHYTHM & BLUES GROUP	POST OFFICE BOX 846	NEW YORK, NY	10101
SLACK, BEN	ACTOR	870 N VINE ST #G	LOS ANGELES, CA	90038
SLADE	ROCK & ROLL GROUP	ICM, 40 W 57TH ST	NEW YORK, NY	10019
SLADE, BERNARD	SCREENWRITER	345 N SALTAIR AVE	LOS ANGELES, CA	90049
SLADE, BETSY	ACTRESS	8285 SUNSET BLVD #12	LOS ANGELES, CA	90046
SLADE, JON	ACTOR	2435 OSWEGO ST	PASADENA, CA	91107
SLADE, JON C	ACTOR	10920 WILSHIRE BLVD #220	LOS ANGELES, CA	90024

Name	Occupation	Address	City	Code
SLADE, MARK	ACTOR	2247 LINDA FLORA DR	LOS ANGELES, CA	90077
SLADE, MELINDA	WRITER	2247 LINDA FLORA DR	LOS ANGELES, CA	90077
SLADEN, ELIZABETH	ACTRESS	2 TAVENERS CLOSE	LONDON W11	ENGLAND
SLAIGHT, BRADLEY C	ACTOR	835 4TH ST #102	SANTA MONICA, CA	90403
SLASH, THE	ROCK & ROLL GROUP	SEE- NASH THE SLASH		
SLATE, BARBARA	ACTRESS	9858 1/2 W OLYMPIC BLVD	BEVERLY HILLS, CA	90212
SLATE, HENRY	ACTOR	6310 SAN VICENTE BLVD #407	LOS ANGELES, CA	90048
SLATE, JEREMY	ACTOR	STONE, 1052 CAROL DR	LOS ANGELES, CA	90069
SLATE, LANE	WRITER-PRODUCER	1169 AMALFI DR	PACIFIC PALISADES, CA	90272
SLATE, STEVE	GUITARIST	127 CHIROC RD	HENDERSONVILLE, TN	37075
SLATER, DERRICK	ACTOR-WRITER	1 WILLINGTON CT		
		THE TRIANGLE		
		LOWER WILLINGTON		
		EASTBOURNE	EAST SUSSEX	ENGLAND
SLATER, DICK "THE REBEL"	WRESTLER	POST OFFICE BOX 3859	STAMFORD, CT	06905
SLATER, FONTELLE	WRITER	446 MOUNT WASHINGTON DR	LOS ANGELES, CA	90065
SLATER, HELEN	ACTRESS	J MICHAEL BLOOM AGENCY		
		233 PARK AVE S, 10TH FLOOR	NEW YORK, NY	10017
SLATER, SANDY	ACTRESS	12926 RIVERSIDE DR #C	SHERMAN OAKS, CA	91423
SLATER, SHIRLEY	ACTRESS	1418 N HIGHLAND AVE #102	LOS ANGELES, CA	90028
SLATER, SHIRLEY	ACTRESS	920 1/2 S SERRANO AVE	LOS ANGELES, CA	90006
SLATER, SUZEE	ACTRESS-MODEL	8831 SUNSET BLVD #402	LOS ANGELES, CA	90069
SLATER, VAN RICHARD	WRESTLER	SEE - SLATER, DICK "THE REBEL"		
SLATER-WILSON, MARY JO	CASTING DIRECTOR	ABC-TV, 56 W 66TH ST	NEW YORK, NY	10023
SLATINARU, MARIA	SOPRANO	CAMI, 165 W 57TH ST	NEW YORK, NY	10019
SLATKIN, LEONARD	CONDUCTOR	ICM, 40 W 57TH ST	NEW YORK, NY	10019
SLATTERY, RICHARD X	ACTOR	POST OFFICE BOX 2410	AVALON, CA	90704
SLATZER, ROBERT	WRITER-PRODUCER	7171 PACIFIC VIEW DR	HOLLYWOOD, CA	90068
SLAUGHTER, BOB	WRESTLER	SEE - SLAUGHTER, SGT		
SLAUGHTER, ENOS	BASEBALL	RURAL ROUTE #2	ROXBORO, NC	27573
SLAUGHTER, HENRY	PIANIST	105 OAK VALLEY DR	NASHVILLE, TN	37207
SLAUGHTER, JACK	TRUMPETER	1773 THERESA DR	CLARKSVILLE, TN	37040
SLAUGHTER, MIKE	DRUMMER	105 OAK VALLEY DR	NASHVILLE, TN	37207
SLAUGHTER, SGT	WRESTLER	AMERICAN WRESTLING ASSOC		
		MINNEAPOLIS WRESTLING		
		10001 WAYZATA BLVD	MINNETONKA, MN	55345
SLAVE	SOUL-DISCO GROUP	200 W 51ST ST #1410	NEW YORK, NY	10019
SLAVIN, GEORGE F	WRITER	527 LATIMER RD	SANTA MONICA, CA	90402
SLAVIN, MILLIE	ACTRESS	KOHNER, 9169 SUNSET BLVD	LOS ANGELES, CA	90069
SLAYEN, SARA	ACTRESS	LEONETTI, 6526 SUNSET BLVD	HOLLYWOOD, CA	90028
SLAYER	ROCK & ROLL GROUP	GEFFEN RECORDS COMPANY		
		9130 SUNSET BLVD	LOS ANGELES, CA	90069
SLAYMAN, DON	VIOLINIST	516 ROOSEVELT DR	MADISON, TN	37115
SLEDD, DALE	BANJOIST	POST OFFICE BOX 537	WARSAW, MO	65355
SLEDGE, LARRY	GUITARIST	GENERAL DELIVERY	REEDS SPRINGS, MO	65737
SLEDGE, PERCY	SINGER	POST OFFICE BOX 82	GREAT NECK, NY	11021
SLEEP, WAYNE	DANCER	PINEAPPLE DANCE CENTRE		
		7 LANGLEY ST	LONDON WC2	ENGLAND
SLEET, JACKSON	ACTOR	439 S LA CIENEGA BLVD #117	LOS ANGELES, CA	90048
SLEETER, BILL	PIANIST	6820 PENNYWELL DR	NASHVILLE, TN	37205
SLESAR, HENRY	TV WRITER-COMPOSER	SIEGEL, 8733 SUNSET BLVD	LOS ANGELES, CA	90069
SLESIN, AVIVA	DIRECTOR	DGA, 110 W 57TH ST	NEW YORK, NY	10019
SLESS, CONNY	ACTOR	1160 N OGDEN DR #211	LOS ANGELES, CA	90046
SLEVIN, JOSPEH R	NEWS CORRESPONDENT	16 E MELROSE ST	CHEVY CHASE, MD	20815
SLEZAK, ERIKA	ACTRESS	ICM, 40 W 57TH ST	NEW YORK, NY	10019
SLICK, EARL	SINGER	3 E 54TH ST #1400	NEW YORK, NY	10022
SLICK, GRACE	SINGER-SONGWRITER	STARSHIP INC, 1319 BRIDGEWAY	SAUSALITO, CA	94965
SLICK "THE DOCTOR OF STYLE"	WRESTLING MANAGER	POST OFFICE BOX 3859	STAMFORD, CT	06905
SLICKEE BOYS, THE	ROCK & ROLL GROUP	POST OFFICE BOX 5073	FALMOUTH, VA	22403
SLIFE, JOSEPH M	NEWS CORRESPONDENT	1825 "K" ST, NW	WASHINGTON, DC	20006
SLIGHT, NIKKE	TALENT AGENT	MASSIVE, 47-B WELBECK ST	LONDON W1	ENGLAND
SLIM, UVALDE	WRESTLER	SEE - RHODES, DUSTY		
SLIM HARPO	SINGER	OLDIES, 5218 ALMONT ST	LOS ANGELES, CA	90032
SLINGLAND, FRANK D	DIRECTOR	DGA, 110 W 57TH ST	NEW YORK, NY	10019
SLINGSHOT	ROCK & ROLL GROUP	POST OFFICE BOX 448	RADFORD, VA	24141
SLIPPERY ROCK TOWN MEETING	BLUEGRASS GROUP	CEE, 193 KONHAUS RD	MECHANICSBURG, PA	17055
SLOAN, BARRY	STILTWALKER	HALL, 138 FROG HOLLOW RD	CHURCHVILLE, PA	18966
SLOAN, JOHN R	FILM PRODUCER	LONDON MANAGEMENT, LTD		
		235-241 REGENT ST	LONDON W1A 2JT	ENGLAND
SLOAN, JUDITH E	PHOTOGRAPHER	1210 N TAFT ST	ARLINGTON, VA	22201
SLOAN, KAREN L	NEWS CORRESPONDENT	600 N HUDSON ST	ARLINGTON, VA	22201
SLOAN, LISA	ACTRESS	SF & A, 121 N SAN VICENTE BLVD	BEVERLY HILLS, CA	90211
SLOAN, MICHAEL	TV WRITER-PRODUCER	20722 PACIFIC COAST HWY #227	MALIBU, CA	90265
SLOAN, NANCY	ACTRESS	CBS TELEVISION NETWORK		
		"THE YOUNG & THE RESTLESS"		
		7800 BEVERLY BLVD	LOS ANGELES, CA	90036
SLOAN, RANDEL	PRODUCER	MARVIN PRODS, 658 OZONE ST	SANTA MONICA, CA	90405
SLOAN, TINA	ACTRESS	CBS-TV, "THE GUIDING LIGHT"		
		51 W 52ND ST	NEW YORK, NY	10019
SLOANE, LANCE	ACTOR	11350 VENTURA BLVD #206	STUDIO CITY, CA	91604
SLOANE, PEGGY	TV WRITER	ABC-TV, "ALL MY CHILDREN"		
		1330 AVE OF THE AMERICAS	NEW YORK, NY	10019
SLOANE, WARD C	NEWS CORRESPONDENT	1754 KILBOURNE PL, NW	WASHINGTON, DC	20010
SLOCOMBE, DOUGLAS	CINEMATOGRAPHER	24 HEREFORD SQ	LONDON SW7	ENGLAND
SLOCUM, FRANK	TV WRITER	555 W 57TH ST #1230	NEW YORK, NY	10019

Name	Occupation	Address	City/State	Zip/Country
SLOMAN, ROGER	ACTOR	10 KINGS COURT MANSIONS		
		FULHAM RD	LONDON SW6	ENGLAND
SLOSSER, R JOHN	DIRECTOR	1116 S ALVIRA ST	LOS ANGELES, CA	90035
SLOTE, RICHARD	TV WRITER-DIRECTOR	SIGNET PRODS, 200 W 58TH ST	NEW YORK, NY	10019
SLOVACEK, ALOIS, JR	CONDUCTOR	961 N CYPRESS	LA HABRA, CA	90631
SLOVENLY	ROCK & ROLL GROUP	POST OFFICE BOX 21	SAN PEDRO, CA	90733
SLOVER, TANYA D	WRITER	11819 KLING ST	NORTH HOLLYWOOD, CA	91607
SLOWINSKI, FRANCIS HILL	NEWS CORRESPONDENT	313 N WEST ST	FALLS CHURCH, VA	22046
SLOYAN, JAMES	ACTOR	3709 LONGVIEW VALLEY RD	SHERMAN OAKS, CA	91423
SLUGGERS, THE	ROCK & ROLL GROUP	POST OFFICE BOX 120235	NASHVILLE, TN	37204
SLUHAN, ELLIOTT D	DIRECTOR	4285 DEEPWOOD LN	TOLEDO, OH	43614
SLY DOG	ROCK & ROLL GROUP	POST OFFICE BOX 18368	DENVER, CO	80218
SLYTER BROTHERS, THE	C & W GROUP	PENNY, 30 GUINAN ST	WALTHAM, MA	02154
SMACK	ROCK & ROLL GROUP	POST OFFICE BOX 2428	EL SEGUNDO, CA	90245
SMALL, CLIVE D	NEWS CORRESPONDENT	2030 "M" ST, NW	WASHINGTON, DC	20036
SMALL, EMILIE	TV WRITER	8955 BEVERLY BLVD	LOS ANGELES, CA	90048
SMALL, HASKEL	PIANIST	GURTMAN, 162 W 56TH ST	NEW YORK, NY	10019
SMALL, JENNIFER	NEWS CORRESPONDENT	2737 DEVONSHIRE PL #414, NW	WASHINGTON, DC	20008
SMALL, MARY	ACTRESS	165 W 66TH ST	NEW YORK, NY	10023
SMALL, MERRYA	ACTRESS	445 N BEDFORD DR #PH	BEVERLY HILLS, CA	90210
SMALL, MICHAEL	WRITER-EDITOR	TIME & PEOPLE MAGAZINE		
		TIME & LIFE BUILDING		
		ROCKEFELLER CENTER	NEW YORK, NY	10020
SMALL, NORMA	SINGER	POST OFFICE BOX 171132	NASHVILLE, TN	37217
SMALL, ROBERT	DANCER	AFFILIATE ARTISTS, INC		
		37 W 65TH ST, 6TH FLOOR	NEW YORK, NY	10023
SMALLEY, JACK	COMPOSER	3762 ALTA MESA DR	STUDIO CITY, CA	91604
SMALLEY, STEVEN SCOTT	COMPOSER	4385 ALLOTT AVE	SHERMAN OAKS, CA	91423
SMALLWOOD, BILL	SINGER	POST OFFICE BOX 228	FREDERICKSBURG, TX	78624
SMALLWOOD, LOUIS	TV WRITER	8955 BEVERLY BLVD	LOS ANGELES, CA	90048
SMALLWOOD, RICHARD, SINGERS	GOSPEL GROUP	10100 SANTA MONICA BLVD #1600	LOS ANGELES, CA	90067
SMARDZ, ZOFIA	NEWS CORRESPONDENT	2619 "O" ST, NW	WASHINGTON, DC	20007
SMARR, BOBBY W	NEWS CORRESPONDENT	12411 HICKORY TREE WY #G	GERMANTOWN, MD	20874
SMARR, ROD	GUITARIST	613 GLEN PARK CT	NASHVILLE, TN	37217
SMART, DOUGLAS W	TV DIRECTOR	4183 FAIR AVE	NORTH HOLLYWOOD, CA	91602
SMART, GRAHAM	DIRECTOR-PRODUCER	470 GREEN LANES	LONDON N13 5XF	ENGLAND
SMART, JEAN	ACTRESS	ICM, 8899 BEVERLY BLVD	LOS ANGELES, CA	90048
SMART, NANCY E	NEWS CORRESPONDENT	330 INDEPENDENCE AVE, NW	WASHINGTON, DC	20547
SMART, PATSY	ACTRESS	46-A PRIMROSE MANSIONS		
		PRINCE OF WALES DR	LONDON SW11	ENGLAND
SMART, WILLIAM	NEWS CORRESPONDENT	ROUTE #2, LONGEVITY FARM	LA PLATA, MD	20646
SMARTIES, THE	ROCK & ROLL GROUP	JENS GALLMEYER, ROSEGGERSTR 5	3000 HANOVER 1	WEST GERMANY
SMASH	WRESTLER	SEE - DEMOLITION		
SMATHERS, BEN & THE STONEY MOUN	C & W GROUP	38 MUSIC SQUARE E #300	NASHVILLE, TN	37203
SMEAL, LUCIA	NEWS CORRESPONDENT	5225 11TH RD N	ARLINGTON, VA	22205
SMEDLEY-ASTON, BRIAN	FILM EDITOR	8 CONNAUGHT SQ	LONDON W2	ENGLAND
SMEDVIG, ROLF	TRUMPETER	CAMI, 165 W 57TH ST	NEW YORK, NY	10019
SMEE, PHIL	RECORD EXECUTIVE	BAM-CARUSO, 4 LIVERPOOL	HERTS	ENGLAND
SMET, JON	ACTOR	9255 SUNSET BLVD #510	LOS ANGELES, CA	90069
SMET, JONATHAN B	TV WRITER	2101 N BEACHWOOD DR	HOLLYWOOD, CA	90068
SMETHHURST, JACK	ACTOR	IAR, 235-241 REGENT ST	LONDON W1A 2JT	ENGLAND
SMIETAN, BOB	COMPOSER	3412 LANTANA LN	COSTA MESA, CA	92626
SMIGHT, ALEC	ACTOR	11061 MISSOURI AVE #4	LOS ANGELES, CA	90025
SMIGHT, JACK	DIRECTOR	255 TIGERTAIL RD	LOS ANGELES, CA	90049
SMILDSIN, KURT	ACTOR	828 1/2 N LAS PALMAS AVE	LOS ANGELES, CA	90038
SMILE	ROCK & ROLL GROUP	POST OFFICE BOX 69210	LOS ANGELES, CA	90069
SMILER	ROCK & ROLL GROUP	VARIETY ARTISTS INTL, INC		
		9073 NEMO ST, 3RD FLOOR	LOS ANGELES, CA	90069
SMILEY, JIM	GUITARIST	129 LUCILLE ST	NASHVILLE, TN	37207
SMILEY, TISH	ACTRESS	5000 LANKERSHIM BLVD #5	NORTH HOLLYWOOD, CA	91601
SMILGIS, MARTHA	WRITER-EDITOR	TIME/TIME & LIFE BLDG		
		ROCKEFELLER CENTER	NEW YORK, NY	10020
SMILLIE, BILL	ACTOR	10502 ILONA AVE	LOS ANGELES, CA	90064
SMILLIE, JAMES	ACTOR	LONDON MANAGEMENT, LTD		
		235-241 REGENT ST	LONDON W1A 2JT	ENGLAND
SMILOW, DAVID H	SCREENWRITER	22 19TH AVE #1	VENICE, CA	90291
SMIRNOFF, BRUCE	COMEDIAN	7400 FOUNTAIN AVE	LOS ANGELES, CA	90046
SMIRNOFF, YAKOV	COMEDIAN-ACTOR	221 W 57TH ST #900	NEW YORK, NY	10019
SMIRNOW, VIRGIL	NEWS CORRESPONDENT	POST OFFICE BOX 34425	BETHESDA, MD	20817
SMITH, ALAN ABRAHAM	NEWS REPORTER	THE NATIONAL ENQUIRER		
		600 SE COAST AVE	LANTANA, FL	33464
SMITH, ALBERT F, III	DRUMMER	POST OFFICE BOX 120684	NASHVILLE, TN	37212
SMITH, ALEXIS	ACTRESS	1308 N FLORES ST	LOS ANGELES, CA	90069
SMITH, AMOS H, JR	PIANIST	BULL RUN RD, ROUTE #3	ASHLAND CITY, TN	37015
SMITH, ANDREW	BARITONE	61 W 62ND ST #6-F	NEW YORK, NY	10023
SMITH, ANDREW	SCREENITER	8955 BEVERLY BLVD	LOS ANGELES, CA	90048
SMITH, ANTHONY L	MUSICIAN	860 MURFREESBORO RD #N-1	NASHVILLE, TN	37217
SMITH, APRIL	TV WRITER	427 7TH ST	SANTA MONICA, CA	90402
SMITH, ARCHIE	ACTOR	417 W 118TH ST	NEW YORK, NY	10027
SMITH, ARLANDO	TV DIRECTOR	9176 ONEIDA AVE	SUN VALLEY, CA	91352
SMITH, ARLENE & THE CHANTELLS	VOCAL GROUP	TRUMBALL PRODUCTIONS		
		60 SEAMAN AVE	BROOKLYN, NY	11222
SMITH, AURELIAN, JR	WRESTLER	SEE - ROBERTS, JAKE "THE SNAKE"		
SMITH, BARBARA	NEWS CORRESPONDENT	6621 WILSON LN	BETHESDA, MD	20817
SMITH, BARBARA E	SCREENWRITER	8955 BEVERLY BLVD	LOS ANGELES, CA	90048

Name	Occupation	Address	City	Zip
SMITH, BERNARD	TV WRITER-DIRECTOR	30512 ABINGTON CT	LAGUNA NIGUEL, CA	92677
SMITH, BILL	BODYBUILDER	POST OFFICE BOX 11883	FRESNO, CA	93775
SMITH, BILLY B	GUITARIST	130 PORT DR	MADISON, TN	37115
SMITH, BILLY RAY	DIRECTOR	STAR ROUTE #3, BOX 6-CC	TEHACHAPI, CA	93561
SMITH, BOBBY C	GUITARIST	BOX 199, ROUTE #2	WATERTOWN, TN	37184
SMITH, BUBBA	DRUMMER	1900 ROSEWOOD AVE #A-2	NASHVILLE, TN	37212
SMITH, BUBBA	ACTOR	1828 PRUESS RD	LOS ANGELES, CA	90035
SMITH, BUFFALO BOB	ACTOR	BIG LAKE	PRINCETON, ME	04619
SMITH, BUFFY	SINGER	4822 ALBEMARLE RD	CHARLOTTE, NC	28205
SMITH, C M	SCREENWRITER	8955 BEVERLY BLVD	LOS ANGELES, CA	90048
SMITH, CAL	SINGER	POST OFFICE BOX 121089	NASHVILLE, TN	37212
SMITH, CAMERON	ACTOR	ABC-TV, "GENERAL HOSPITAL"		
		1438 N GOWER ST	LOS ANGELES, CA	90028
SMITH, CARL	SINGER	2510 FRANKLIN RD	NASHVILLE, TN	37204
SMITH, CARL M	GUITARIST	ROUTE #7, BERRY CHAPEL RD	FRANKLIN, TN	37064
SMITH, CAROLINE	ACTRESS	427 N CANON DR #205	BEVERLY HILLS, CA	90210
SMITH, CARY	MODEL	2400 ASPEN DR	HOLLYWOOD, CA	90068
SMITH, CECIL	DRAMA CRITIC	L A TIMES NEWSPAPER		
		TIMES MIRROR SQUARE	LOS ANGELES, CA	90053
SMITH, CHARLES C	GUITARIST	1418 HOLLY ST	NASHVILLE, TN	37206
SMITH, CHARLES L	DIRECTOR	43 W ELFIN GREEN	PORT HUENEME, CA	93041
SMITH, CHARLES M, III	GUITARIST	POST OFFICE BOX 1371	LEESBURG, VA	22075
SMITH, CHARLES MARTIN	ACTOR	146 N ALMONT DR #8	LOS ANGELES, CA	90048
SMITH, CHIP	BANJOIST	510-B N 17TH ST	NASHVILLE, TN	37206
SMITH, CLAY	TV PRODUCER	ENTERTAINMENT TONIGHT		
		PARAMOUNT TELEVISION		
		5555 MELROSE AVE	LOS ANGELES, CA	90038
SMITH, CONNIE	SINGER	1300 DIVISION ST #103	NASHVILLE, TN	37203
SMITH, COTTER	ACTOR	11726 SAN VICENTE BLVD #300	LOS ANGELES, CA	90049
SMITH, CRYSTAL	TV HOST-MODEL	PLAYBOY, 8560 SUNSET BLVD	LOS ANGELES, CA	90069
SMITH, DALE	TENOR	45 W 60TH ST #4-K	NEW YORK, NY	10023
SMITH, DALLAS	MUSICIAN	SEE - MAZER, SUSAN &		
		DALLAS SMITH		
SMITH, DALLAS S	GUITARIST	ROUTE #2, BOX 199	WATERTOWN, TN	37184
SMITH, DAN FRANKLIN	PIANIST	254 W 93RD ST #8	NEW YORK, NY	10025
SMITH, DAN FREDERICK	TV DIRECTOR	2101 CASTILIAN DR	HOLLYWOOD, CA	90068
SMITH, DAVEY BOY	WRESTLER	SEE - BRITISH BULLDOGS, THE		
SMITH, DAVID	WRESTLER	SEE - BRITISH BULLBOGS, THE		
SMITH, DAVID	HUMAN CANNONBALL	HALL, 138 FROG HOLLOW RD	CHURCHVILLE, PA	18966
SMITH, DAVID "WALTER"	GUITARIST	ROUTE #3, BOX 247	SPRINGFIELD, TN	37172
SMITH, DAVID A	GUITARIST	POST OFFICE BOX 8321	NASHVILLE, TN	37207
SMITH, DAVID MARK	TV DIRECTOR	715 PACIFIC ST #B	SANTA MONICA, CA	90405
SMITH, DAVID RAE	BASSO-BARITONE	SARDOS, 180 W END AVE	NEW YORK, NY	10023
SMITH, DAYNA	PHOTOGRAPHER	623 "C" ST, NW	WASHINGTON, DC	20002
SMITH, DEBRA ZIMMER	TV DIRECTOR	380 VALLEJO ST	SAN FRANCISCO, CA	94133
SMITH, DELOS V	ACTOR	420 RIVERSIDE DR	NEW YORK, NY	10025
SMITH, DENNIS	SINGER	POST OFFICE BOX 25083	NASHVILLE, TN	37202
SMITH, DEREK	ACTOR	63 ELSTREE RD, BUSHEY HEATH	HERTS WD2 3QX	ENGLAND
SMITH, DONALD	PHOTOGRAPHER	17109 HOSKINSON RD	POOLESVILLE, MD	20837
SMITH, DONALD R	NEWS CORRESPONDENT	23 LOGAN CIR, NW	WASHINGTON, DC	20005
SMITH, DONEGAN	ACTOR	LIGHT, 113 N ROBERTSON BLVD	LOS ANGELES, CA	90048
SMITH, DONNA	MODEL	MODELS & PROMOTIONS AGENCY		
		8560 SUNSET BLVD, 10TH FLOOR	LOS ANGELES, CA	90069
SMITH, DONNA	NEWS CORRESPONDENT	4418 DUKE ST	ALEXANDRIA, CA	22304
SMITH, DOUG	SPORTS WRITER	POST OFFICE BOX 500	WASHINGTON, DC	20044
SMITH, DOUGLAS ALAN	GUITARIST	POST OFFICE BOX 38831	GERMANTOWN, TN	38138
SMITH, DUNCAN R	SCREENWRITER	8955 BEVERLY BLVD	LOS ANGELES, CA	90048
SMITH, ESSEX	ACTOR	15010 VENTURA BLVD #219	SHERMAN OAKS, CA	91403
SMITH, EVE	ACTRESS	12725 VENTURA BLVD #E	STUDIO CITY, CA	91604
SMITH, EVELYNE	ACTRESS	1607 N EL CENTRO AVE #23	LOS ANGELES, CA	90028
SMITH, FRANK OWEN	ACTOR	9025 WILSHIRE BLVD #309	BEVERLY HILLS, CA	90211
SMITH, G WARREN	TV DIRECTOR	4219 W OLIVE AVE #136	BURBANK, CA	91505
SMITH, GAIL A	ACTRESS	8831 SUNSET BLVD #402	LOS ANGELES, CA	90069
SMITH, GARNETT	ACTOR	208 S BEVERLY DR #4	BEVERLY HILLS, CA	90212
SMITH, GARY	SINGER	4615 SW FREEWAY #475	HOUSTON, TX	77027
SMITH, GARY WAYNE	PIANIST	6001 OLD HICKORY BLVD #323	HERMITAGE, TN	37076
SMITH, GRAYSMITH	CARTOONIST	901 MISSION ST	SAN FRANCISCO, CA	94103
SMITH, GREG	TV PRODUCER	ELSTREE PRODUCTION COMPANY		
		EMI STUDIOS, BOREHAMWOOD	HERTS	ENGLAND
SMITH, GREGG	MUSICIAN	171 W 71ST ST	NEW YORK, NY	10023
SMITH, GREGORY P	DIRECTOR	8922 RANGELY AVE	LOS ANGELES, CA	90048
SMITH, HAL	ACTOR	3907 W ALAMEDA AVE #101	BURBANK, CA	91505
SMITH, HEDRICK I	NEWS CORRESPONDENT	3502 SHEPHERD ST	CHEVY CHASE, MD	20815
SMITH, HENRY C	DIRECTOR	201 FRONT ST	BROOKLYN, NY	11201
SMITH, HERB	ACTOR	1607 N EL CENTRO AVE #22	HOLLYWOOD, CA	90028
SMITH, HERBE	SINGER	1582 W DOROTHY LN #A	DAYTON, OH	45409
SMITH, HILLARY BAILEY	ACTRESS	CBS-TV, "AS THE WORLD TURNS"		
		51 W 52ND ST	NEW YORK, NY	10019
SMITH, HOLLY	ACTRESS	9332 W OLYMPIC BLVD	BEVERLY HILLS, CA	90212
SMITH, HOPE H	TV PRODUCER	CBS TELEVISION NETWORK		
		"THE BOLD & THE BEAUTIFUL"		
		7800 BEVERLY BLVD	LOS ANGELES, CA	90036
SMITH, HOWARD	DIRECTOR	VILLAGE VOICE, 842 BROADWAY	NEW YORK, NY	10003
SMITH, HOWARD	SINGER	9200 SUNSET BLVD #PH-15	LOS ANGELES, CA	90069
SMITH, HOWARD K	NEWS CORRESPONDENT	6450 BROOKS LN, NW	WASHINGTON, DC	20016

SMITH, HUBERT W	SCREENWRITER	8955 BEVERLY BLVD	LOS ANGELES, CA 90048
SMITH, HUEY "PIANO," & THE CLOW	MUSIC GROUP	OLDIES, 5218 ALMONT ST	LOS ANGELES, CA 90032
SMITH, HY	FILM EXECUTIVE	VIP HOUSE, 45 BEADON RD	
		HAMMERSMITH	LONDON W6 OEG ENGLAND
SMITH, JACK	TV DIRECTOR-PRODUCER	48 DEAN RD, HANDFORTH	CHESHIRE ENGLAND
SMITH, JACK	NEWS CORRESPONDENT	CBS NEWS, 2020 "M" ST, NW	WASHINGTON, DC 20036
SMITH, JACK D	GUITARIST	3850 OLD HICKORY BLVD	OLD HICKORY, TN 37138
SMITH, JACK P	NEWS CORRESPONDENT	ABC-TV, NEWS DEPARTMENT	
		1717 DE SALES ST, NW	WASHINGTON, DC 20036
SMITH, JACLYN	ACTRESS-MODEL	773 STRADELLA RD	LOS ANGELES, CA 90077
SMITH, JAKE "GRIZZLY"	WRESTLER	UNIVERSAL WRESTLING FEDERATION	
		MID SOUTH SPORTS, INC	
		5001 SPRING VALLEY RD	DALLAS, TX 75244
SMITH, JAMES H	TV DIRECTOR	8527 WALNUT DR	LOS ANGELES, CA 90046
SMITH, JAMES HARRELL	VIOLINIST	JACKSONVILLE RD #4	GOODLETTSVILLE, TN 37072
SMITH, JAMES RUSSELL, JR	PIANIST	PINE PARK #F-94	
		1210 HAZELWOOD DR	MURFREESBORO, TN 37130
SMITH, JAMES S	NEWS CORRESPONDENT	3607 LONGFELLOW	HYATTSVILLE, MD 20782
SMITH, JAN	NEWS CORRESPONDENT	1125 CREST LN	MC LEAN, VA 22101
SMITH, JEFFREY J	TV WRITER	8955 BEVERLY BLVD	LOS ANGELES, CA 90048
SMITH, JEREMY	ACTOR	20718 PACIFIC COAST HWY #2	MALIBU, CA 90265
SMITH, JEROME A	NEWS CORRESPONDENT	205 YOAKUM PARKWAY	ALEXANDRIA, VA 22304
SMITH, JERRY DEAN	PIANIST	POST OFFICE BOX 24206	NASHVILLE, TN 37202
SMITH, JERRY STEVE	GUITARIST	213 PANAMINT DR	ANTIOCH, TN 37013
SMITH, JIMMY, TRIO	JAZZ TRIO	HOFFER, 233 1/2 E 48TH ST	NEW YORK, NY 10017
SMITH, JOE	RECORD EXECUTIVE	962 N LA CIENEGA BLVD	LOS ANGELES, CA 90069
SMITH, JOHN	TV WRITER	8955 BEVERLY BLVD	LOS ANGELES, CA 90048
SMITH, JOHN F	TV WRITER	555 W 57TH ST #1230	NEW YORK, NY 10019
SMITH, JOHN J	DIRECTOR	16519 CALAHAN ST	SEPULVEDA, CA 91343
SMITH, JOHN V, JR	TV DIRECTOR	1009 COLLINGS AVE	WEST COLLINGSWOOD, NJ 08107
SMITH, JOHN WALTON	ACTOR	119 N SAN VICENTE BLVD #203	BEVERLY HILLS, CA 90211
SMITH, JON M	NEWS CORRESPONDENT	4800 FAIRFAX DR	ARLINGTON, VA 22203
SMITH, JOSEPH	PIANIST	POST OFFICE BOX U	REDDING, CT 06875
		235 E 45TH ST	NEW YORK, NY 10017
SMITH, JOSEPH KINGSBURY	COMMENTATOR	KING FEATURES SYNDICATE	
SMITH, JOSEPH L	TV DIRECTOR	1032 BRUSSELS ST	SAN FRANCISCO, CA 94134
SMITH, JULIA	DIRECTOR-PRODUCER	6 QUEEN ANNE'S GROVE	LONDON W4 ENGLAND
SMITH, KARYN	ACTRESS	3151 W CAHUENGA BLVD #310	LOS ANGELES, CA 90068
SMITH, KATHI	ACTRESS	8721 SUNSET BLVD #200	LOS ANGELES, CA 90069
SMITH, KATHY	AEROBICS INSTRUCTOR	JCI VIDEO COMPANY	
		5308 DERRY AVE	AGOURA HILLS, CA 91301
SMITH, KEITH	ACTOR	29 CLAVERING AVE	LONDON SW13 9DX ENGLAND
SMITH, KENNETH M	GUITARIST	3718 SENTINEL DR	NASHVILLE, TN 37209
SMITH, KENNETH O	GUITARIST	115 CHOCTAW	HENDERSONVILLE, TN 37075
SMITH, KENNETH S	NEWS CORRESPONDENT	7045 WILSON LN	BETHESDA, MD 20817
SMITH, KURTWOOD	ACTOR	400 S BEVERLY DR #216	BEVERLY HILLS, CA 90212
SMITH, L KIM	NEWS CORRESPONDENT	5606 CHEVY CHASE PARKWAY, NW	WASHINGTON, DC 20015
SMITH, LANE	ACTOR	10390 SANTA MONICA BLVD #310	LOS ANGELES, CA 90025
SMITH, LARRY	ORGANIST	15 HIGH ST #621	HARTFORD, CT 06103
SMITH, LARRY K	GUITARIST	1161 N HIGHLAND AVE	LOS ANGELES, CA 90038
SMITH, LARRY W	MUSICIAN	POST OFFICE BOX 24815	NASHVILLE, TN 37202
SMITH, LAWRENCE LEIGHTON	CONDUCTOR	ICM, 40 W 57TH ST	NEW YORK, NY 10019
SMITH, LEO	COMPOSER	39 DORCHESTER RD	BUFFALO, NY 14222
SMITH, LESLIE	SINGER	4121 WILSHIRE BLVD #215	LOS ANGELES, CA 90010
SMITH, LEWIS	ACTOR	9100 SUNSET BLVD #300	LOS ANGELES, CA 90069
SMITH, LITTLEFIELD & SMITH	C & W GROUP	POST OFFICE BOX 121542	NASHVILLE, TN 37212
SMITH, LIZ	FILM CRITIC	THE N Y DAILY NEWS	
		220 E 42ND ST	NEW YORK, NY 10017
SMITH, LOIS	ACTRESS	BRET ADAMS, 448 W 44TH ST	NEW YORK, NY 10036
SMITH, LONNIE LISTON	KEYBOARDIST	FONTANA, 161 W 54TH ST	NEW YORK, NY 10019
SMITH, LORI ROBIN	GUITARIST	409 ELLEN DR	GOODLETTSVILLE, TN 37072
SMITH, LYNNETTE H	COMPOSER	4291 COUNTRY CLUB DR	LONG BEACH, CA 90807
SMITH, MADELINE	ACTRESS	JOAN GRAY MANAGEMENT	
		SUNBURY CT ISLAND	
		SUNBURY ON THAMES	MIDDLESEX ENGLAND
SMITH, MADOLYN	ACTRESS	POST OFFICE BOX 5617	BEVERLY HILLS, CA 90210
SMITH, MAGGIE	ACTRESS	ICM, 388-396 OXFORD ST	LONDON W1 ENGLAND
SMITH, MALCOLM	SINGER	59 E 54TH ST #81	NEW YORK, NY 10022
SMITH, MARCUS J	NEWS CORRESPONDENT	8750 GEORGIA AVE #1007-B	SILVER SPRING, MD 20910
SMITH, MARGO	SINGER	38 MUSIC SQUARE #300	NASHVILLE, TN 37203
SMITH, MARILYN KAY	VIOLINIST	15645 GULF BLVD	REDINGTON BEACH, FL 33708
SMITH, MARK H	GUITARIST	115 DONALD ST	NASHVILLE, TN 37207
SMITH, MARK LANE	PERCUSSIONIST	922 POTTER LN	NASHVILLE, TN 37206
SMITH, MARTHA	ACTRESS-MODEL	9690 HEATHER RD	BEVERLY HILLS, CA 90210
SMITH, MARTIN	TV WRITER-DIRECTOR	242 LAFAYETTE ST	NEW YORK, NY 10012
SMITH, MARTIN "BUD"	FILM DIRECTOR	234 N CORDOVA ST	BURBANK, CA 91505
SMITH, MARTIN C	SCREENWRITER	555 W 57TH ST #1230	NEW YORK, NY 10019
SMITH, MARTIN J	SCREENWRITER	8955 BEVERLY BLVD	LOS ANGELES, CA 90048
SMITH, MICHAEL	WRESTLER	SEE - HOUSTON, SAM	
SMITH, MICHAEL GLEN	GUITARIST	254 CEDAR VIEW DR	ANTIOCH, TN 37013
SMITH, MICHAEL W	GUITARIST	857 BRESSLYN RD	NASHVILLE, TN 37205
SMITH, MIGNON C	NEWS CORRESPONDENT	2500 VIRGINIA AVE, NW	WASHINGTON, DC 20037
SMITH, MIKE	TV-RADIO PERSONALITY	BAGENAL HARVEY ORGANIZATION	
		1-A CAVENDISH SQ	LONDON W1 ENGLAND
SMITH, MILTON W	PIANIST	1857 FABER ST	FAYETTEVILLE, NC 28304

Name	Occupation	Address	City	Zip/Country
SMITH, MIRIAM S	PIANIST	3207 ACKLEN AVE	NASHVILLE, TN	37212
SMITH, MR & MRS GEORGE	CARTOONISTS	UNIVERSAL PRESS SYNDICATE		
		4900 MAIN ST, 9TH FLOOR	KANSAS CITY, MO	62114
SMITH, MURRAY	SCREENWRITER	THE WHITE HOUSE, NONNINGTON LN		
		GRAFTON	WEST SUSSEX GU28 OPX	ENGLAND
SMITH, NEIL B	TV DIRECTOR	38 VERANDAH PL	BROOKLYN, NY	11201
SMITH, NICHOLAS	ACTOR	IAR, 235-241 REGENT ST	LONDON W1A 2JT	ENGLAND
SMITH, NORWOOD	ACTOR	1730 CAMINO PALMERO ST #215	LOS ANGELES, CA	90046
SMITH, O C	SINGER	14621 LEADWELL ST	VAN NUYS, CA	91405
SMITH, OLIVER H	NEWS CORRESPONDENT	1755 S JEFFERSON DAVIS HWY	ARLINGTON, VA	22202
SMITH, OSCAR WILLIAM	SAXOPHONIST	321 WALTON LN #D-59	MADISON, TN	37115
SMITH, OZZIE	BASEBALL	SAINT LOUIS CARDINALS		
		250 STADIUM PLAZA		
		BUSCH STADIUM		
SMITH, PATRICIA F	TV WRITER	8955 BEVERLY BLVD	LOS ANGELES, CA	90048
SMITH, PATTI, GROUP	ROCK & ROLL GROUP	3 E 54TH ST #1400	NEW YORK, NY	10022
SMITH, PAUL	TV DIRECTOR-PRODUCER	MORRIS, 147-149 WARDOUR ST	LONDON W1V 3TB	ENGLAND
SMITH, PAUL	FASHION DESIGNER	44 FLORAL ST	LONDON WC2	ENGLAND
SMITH, PAUL L	ACTOR	ICM, 8899 BEVERLY BLVD	LOS ANGELES, CA	90048
SMITH, PAUL S	TV DIRECTOR	23250 GILMORE ST	CANOGA PARK, CA	91307
SMITH, PERRY N	DIRECTOR	136 NYAC AVE	PELHAM, NY	10807
SMITH, PETER K	DIRECTOR-CHOREO	POST OFFICE BOX 208	ARMONK, NY	10504
SMITH, PHILIP A	NEWS CORRESPONDENT	727 S LEE ST	ALEXANDRIA, VA	22314
SMITH, R C	EDITOR-WRITER	TV GUIDE, 100 MATSONFORD RD	RADNOR, PA	19088
SMITH, R HARLAN	SINGER	POST OFFICE BOX 8768		
		STATION L	EDMONDTON, ALTA T6E	CANADA
SMITH, RALPH	CARTOONIST	KING FEATURES SYNDICATE		
		235 E 45TH ST	NEW YORK, NY	10017
SMITH, RAY	ACTOR	5 ROBIN HILL, DINAS POWIS		
		SOUTH GLAM	WALES	ENGLAND
SMITH, REID	ACTOR	9744 WILSHIRE BLVD #206	BEVERLY HILLS, CA	90212
SMITH, REX	ACTOR-SINGER	STEPHEN WEISS, 177 E 75TH ST	NEW YORK, NY	10021
SMITH, RICHARD	TV WRITER	8955 BEVERLY BLVD	LOS ANGELES, CA	90048
SMITH, RICHARD JON	SINGER	ZOMBA, 165 WILLESDEN HIGH RD	LONDON NW10	ENGLAND
SMITH, RICHARD M	PUBLISHING EXECUTIVE	NEWSWEEK, 444 MADISON AVE	NEW YORK, NY	10022
SMITH, RICKY & VINCE	C & W DUO	POST OFFICE BOX 1221	POTTSVILLE, PA	17901
SMITH, ROBERT	TV WRITER	FRIEDMANN, 24 BLOOMSBURY ST	LONDON WC1	ENGLAND
SMITH, ROBERT D	NEWS CORRESPONDENT	1233 N VAN DORN ST	ALEXANDRIA, VA	22304
SMITH, ROBERT D	TV WRITER	8955 BEVERLY BLVD	LOS ANGELES, CA	90048
SMITH, ROBERT EDWARD	HARPSICHORDIST	15 HIGH ST #621	HARTFORD, CT	06103
SMITH, ROBERT G	NEWS CORRESPONDENT	4847 BAYARD BLVD	BETHESDA, MD	20816
SMITH, ROBIN A	NEWS CORRESPONDENT	3420 16TH ST #106, NW	WASHINGTON, DC	20010
SMITH, ROGER	ACTOR-WRITER	2707 BENEDICT CANYON DR	BEVERLY HILLS, CA	90210
SMITH, ROGER P	NEWS CORRESPONDENT	301 "G" ST #323, SW	WASHINGTON, DC	20024
SMITH, RUSSELL	SINGER	MSS, 1000 ALABAMA AVE	SHEFFIELD, AL	35660
SMITH, RUSSELL	GUITARIST	POST OFFICE BOX 58	COLLEGE GROVE, TN	37046
SMITH, SAMMI	SINGER	TAYLOR, 2401 12TH AVE S	NASHVILLE, TN	37204
SMITH, SAMMY	ACTOR	888 8TH AVE	NEW YORK, NY	10019
SMITH, SANDRA C	NEWS CORRESPONDENT	232-A 14TH ST, NE	WASHINGTON, DC	20002
SMITH, SANDY	NEWS CORRESPONDENT	804 HOLLY DR	ANNAPOLIS, MD	21401
SMITH, SARAH	ACTRESS	12345 VENTURA BLVD #X	STUDIO CITY, CA	91604
SMITH, SAVANNAH	ACTRESS	SEE - SMITH BOUCHER, SAVANNAH		
SMITH, SHAWNEE	ACTRESS	151 S EL CAMINO AVE	BEVERLY HILLS, CA	90212
SMITH, SHEAMUS	TV EXECUTIVE	PAVANNE, QUILL RD		
		KILMACANOGUE	CO WICKLOW	IRELAND
SMITH, SHEILA	ACTRESS	9229 SUNSET BLVD #306	LOS ANGELES, CA	90069
SMITH, SHEILA	MEZZO-SOPRANO	CONE, 221 W 57TH ST	NEW YORK, NY	10019
SMITH, SHELDON	COMPOSER	1395 UNION ST #1	SAN FRANCISCO, CA	94109
SMITH, SHELLEY	ACTRESS-MODEL	9145 SUNSET BLVD #228	LOS ANGELES, CA	90069
SMITH, SHIRLEY A	NEWS CORRESPONDENT	1755 S JEFFERSON DAVIS HWY	ARLINGTON, VA	22202
SMITH, SIDNEY F R	DIRECTOR-PRODUCER	240 CENTRAL PARK S	NEW YORK, NY	10019
SMITH, STEPHEN	PUBLISHING EXECUTIVE	NEWSWEEK, 444 MADISON AVE	NEW YORK, NY	10022
SMITH, STEVE & VITAL INFORMATIO	JAZZ GROUP	3 E 54TH ST #1400	NEW YORK, NY	10022
SMITH, STEVE A	NEWS CORRESPONDENT	529 14TH ST, NW	WASHINGTON, DC	20045
SMITH, STEVEN LYNN	MUSICIAN	861 HERITAGE CIR	MADISON, TN	37115
SMITH, STEVEN PHILLIP	SCREENWRITER	C LAKE, 1103 GLENDON AVE	LOS ANGELES, CA	90024
SMITH, STROUBE J	NEWS CORRESPONDENT	1822 TAYLOR AVE, NW	FORT WASHINGTON, DC	20744
SMITH, SUKEY	ACTRESS	11240 MAGNOLIA BLVD #202	NORTH HOLLYWOOD, CA	91601
SMITH, SYLVIA L	DIRECTOR	HOBBS RD	WAYLAND, MA	01778
SMITH, TAYLOR	ACTRESS	8230 BEVERLY BLVD #23	LOS ANGELES, CA	90048
SMITH, TERENCE F	NEWS CORRESPONDENT	1309 29TH ST, NW	WASHINGTON, DC	20007
SMITH, TERRY	SINGER-SONGWRITER	1404 HUFFINE ST	NASHVILLE, TN	37216
SMITH, TERRY K	GUITARIST	130 PORT DR	MADISON, TN	37115
SMITH, THOMAS EDWARD	GUITARIST	ROUTE #6, GIBBS RD	ASHLAND CITY, TN	37015
SMITH, TIM	MUSIC ARRANGER	340 CANE RIDGE RD #302	ANTIOCH, TN	37013
SMITH, TIMOTHY K	NEWS CORRESPONDENT	816 "D" ST, NE	WASHINGTON, DC	20002
SMITH, TODD	SINGER	POST OFFICE BOX 70	BUCKLEY, WA	98321
SMITH, TOM	PIANIST	1202 16TH AVE S	NASHVILLE, TN	37212
SMITH, TRACY N	ACTRESS	9300 WILSHIRE BLVD #410	BEVERLY HILLS, CA	90212
SMITH, VARLEY R	SCREENWRITER	8955 BEVERLY BLVD	LOS ANGELES, CA	90048
SMITH, VELMA ELIZABETH	GUITARIST	ROUTE #4, JACKSON RD	GOODLETTSVILLE, TN	37072
SMITH, VINCE	SINGER-SONGWRITER	POST OFFICE BOX 1221	POTTSVILLE, PA	17901
SMITH, WALTER A	SAXOPHONIST	POST OFFICE BOX 24206	NASHVILLE, TN	37202
SMITH, WALTER E	TV WRITER	8955 BEVERLY BLVD	LOS ANGELES, CA	90048
SMITH, WENDY	ACTRESS	7060 HOLLYWOOD BLVD #610	LOS ANGELES, CA	90028

Name	Occupation	Address	City	Zip
SMITH, WILLIAM	ACTOR	9255 SUNSET BLVD #610	LOS ANGELES, CA	90069
SMITH, WILLIAM A, III	GUITARIST	1050 PLEASANT HILL RD #M-146	NASHVILLE, TN	37214
		ROCKEFELLER CENTER	NEW YORK, NY	10020
SMITH, WILLIAM E	WRITER-EDITOR	TIME/TIME & LIFE BLDG		
SMITH, WILLIAM JAMES	DRUMMER	POST OFFICE BOX 40686	NASHVILLE, TN	37204
SMITH, WILLIAM O	GUITARIST	829 KIRKWOOD LN	NASHVILLE, TN	37204
SMITH, WILSON	ACTOR	6533 HOLLYWOOD BLVD #201	HOLLYWOOD, CA	90028
SMITH, WONDERFUL	ACTOR	6515 SUNSET BLVD #300-A	LOS ANGELES, CA	90028
SMITH, ZANE	WRESTLER	NATIONAL WRESTLING ALLIANCE		
		JIM CROCKETT PROMOTIONS		
		421 BRIARBEND DR	CHARLOTTE, NC	28209
SMITH & CHONG	MUSICAL DUO	POST OFFICE BOX 131	SPRINGFIELD, VA	22150
SMITH BOUCHER, SAVANNAH	ACTRESS	SF & A, 121 N SAN VICENTE BLVD	BEVERLY HILLS, CA	90211
SMITH STREET SOCIETY JAZZ BAND,	JAZZ GROUP	POST OFFICE BOX C	RIVER EDGE, NJ	07661
SMITH-NICHOLS, WILSON	TENOR	260 W END AVE #7-A	NEW YORK, NY	10023
SMITHEREENS, THE	ROCK & ROLL GROUP	POST OFFICE BOX 1665	NEW YORK, NY	10009
SMITHERS, JAN	ACTRESS	8741 SAINT IVES DR	LOS ANGELES, CA	90069
SMITHERS, WILLIAM	ACTOR	11664 LAURELCREST DR	STUDIO CITY, CA	91604
SMITHS, THE	ROCK & ROLL GROUP	FRONTIER BOOKING INTERNATIONAL		
		1776 BROADWAY, 6TH FLOOR	NEW YORK, NY	10019
SMITMAN, SUSAN E	DIRECTOR	1 BANK ST	NEW YORK, NY	10014
SMITNOV, DIANA	PIANIST	482 FORT WASHINGTON AVE #1-H	NEW YORK, NY	10033
SMITROVICH, BILL	ACTOR	10 E 44TH ST #700	NEW YORK, NY	10017
SMITS, JIMMY	ACTOR	SHERMAN, 348 S REXFORD DR	BEVERLY HILLS, CA	90212
SMITS, SONJA	ACTRESS	10000 SANTA MONICA BLVD #305	LOS ANGELES, CA	90067
SMOLANOFF, MICHAEL	COMPOSER	20-A BROUN PL	BRONX, NY	10475
SMOLLETT, MOLLY	TV DIRECTOR	41-23 HAMPTON ST	ELMHURST, NY	11373
SMOLLINS, MICHAEL J	WRITER	937 N LAUREL AVE	LOS ANGELES, CA	90046
SMOLOWE, JILL	WRITER-EDITOR	TIME/TIME & LIFE BLDG		
		ROCKEFELLER CENTER	NEW YORK, NY	10020
SMOTHERMAN, MICHAEL	SINGER	8467 BEVERLY BLVD #100	LOS ANGELES, CA	90048
SMOTHERS, DICK	COMEDIAN-ACTOR	2317 VINE HILL DR	SANTA CRUZ, CA	95065
SMOTHERS, TOM	COMED-ACT-DIR	1976 WARM SPRINGS RD	KENWOOD, CA	95452
SMOTHERS BROTHERS, THE	COMEDY-MUSICAL DUO	SEE - SMOTHERS, DICK & TOM		
SMOYER, MONTANA	ACTRESS	16079 YARNELL ST #1-B	SYLMAR, CA	91342
SMUIN, MICHAEL	DANCER-CHOREOGRAPHER	SAN FRANCISCO BALLET		
		378 18TH AVE	SAN FRANCISCO, CA	94121
SMYLIE, DENNIS	CLARINETIST	FINELL, 155 W 68TH ST	NEW YORK, NY	10023
SMYTH, JOSEPH, III	DRUMMER	106 ARSENAL CT	FRANKLIN, TN	37064
SMYTHE, MARCUS	ACTOR	250 W 74TH ST	NEW YORK, NY	10023
SMYTHE, REGGIE	CARTOONIST	WHITEGATES CALEDONIAN RD		
		HARTLEP	CLEVELAND	ENGLAND
SNAILS, THE	ROCK & ROLL GROUP	RED RUN RECORDS CO		
		8861 ZENCARD AVE	SAN DIEGO, CA	92123
SNAKE OUT	ROCK & ROLL GROUP	GARAGELAND STUDIOS		
		19620 WAHRMAN	NEW BOSTON, MI	48164
SNASDELL, DAVID	FILM DIRECTOR	369-A UXBRIDGE RD		
		HATCH END, PIN	MIDDLESEX	ENGLAND
SNAZELLE, E E GREGG	DIRECTOR	7 STRAWBERRY LANDING		
		413 E STRAWBERRY DR	MILL VALLEY, CA	94941
SNEAD, BILL	PHOTOGRAPHER	THE WASHINGTON POST		
		PHOTO DEPARTMENT		
		1150 15TH ST, NW	WASHINGTON, DC	20071
SNEAD, EARL THOMAS	BANJOIST	1001 N JOHNSON ST	AMARILLO, TX	79107
SNEAK PREVIEW	ROCK & ROLL GROUP	VARIETY ARTISTS INTL, INC		
		9073 NEMO ST, 3RD FLOOR	LOS ANGELES, CA	90069
SNEAKER	SINGER	POST OFFICE BOX 7308	CARMEL, CA	93921
SNEDDON, PHYLLIS	FLUTIST	1206 STRATFORD AVE	NASHVILLE, TN	37216
SNEDDON, STEVE	SPORTS WRITER	POST OFFICE BOX 500	WASHINGTON, DC	20044
SNEDDON, WILLIAM	OBOIST	1206 STRATFORD AVE	NASHVILLE, TN	37216
SNEE, DENNIS	WRITER	MAD MAGAZINE, INC		
		485 MADISON AVE	NEW YORK, NY	10022
SNEED, MAURICE	ACTOR	3800 BARHAM BLVD #303	LOS ANGELES, CA	90068
SNEED, MICHAEL	COLUMNIST	TRIBUNE MEDIA SERVICES		
		64 E CONCORD ST	ORLANDO, FL	32801
SNELL, DIETRICH	CELLIST	406 AVOCA ST #A-8	NASHVILLE, TN	37203
SNELL, GEORGE	TV DIRECTOR	366 NEW PROVIDENCE RD	MOUNTAINSIDE, NJ	07092
SNELL, PETER R E	FILM PRODUCER	PINEWOOD STUDIOS, IVER HEATH	BUCKS	ENGLAND
SNIDER, DEE	SINGER-SONGWRITER	POST OFFICE BOX 360	MERRICK, NY	11561
SNIDER, DUKE	BASEBALL	3037 LAKEMONT DR	FALLBROOK, CA	92028
SNIDER, MIKE	WRITER	MAD MAGAZINE, INC		
		485 MADISON AVE	NEW YORK, NY	10022
SNIDER, MIKE & CROSS COUNTRY	BLUEGRASS GROUP	BEACHAM, 1012 16TH AVE S	NASHVILLE, TN	37212
SNIFFEN, MICHAEL J	NEWS CORRESPONDENT	401 4TH ST, SE	WASHINGTON, DC	20003
SNIVELY, ROBERT	ACTOR	8721 SUNSET BLVD #200	LOS ANGELES, CA	90069
SNOAD, HAROLD	TV DIRECTOR-PRODUCER	FIR TREE COTTAGE, HAWKEWOOD RD		
		SUNBURY-ON-THAMES	MIDDLESEX	ENGLAND
SNODDY, JON	NEWS CORRESPONDENT	2025 "M" ST, NW	WASHINGTON, DC	20036
SNODGRASS, QUINCY	SINGER	POST OFFICE BOX 4234	PANORAMA CITY, CA	91412
SNODGRESS, CARRIE	ACTRESS	16650 SCHOENBORN	SEPULVEDA, CA	91343
SNORTLAND, ELLEN	ACTRESS	10000 RIVERSIDE DR #3	TOLUCA LAKE, CA	91602
SNOW, GRANT	ACTOR	ABC-TV, "RYAN'S HOPE"		
		1330 AVE OF THE AMERICAS	NEW YORK, NY	10019

VINCE SMITH

Country and Western recording artist **Vince Smith** has just recorded a single entitled *''My Annette''* which was dedicated to his idol, Annette Funicello. Vince will be recording his first solo album in June. Vince is also with the MFN Agency, Rt. 1 Box 187-F, Whitney, Texas 76692.

You can also write Vince c/o his fan club at P.O. Box 1221, Pottsville, PA 17901

The album, *Old Country Love Songs''* is still available. It is also on cassette.

Name	Occupation	Address	City/State	Zip
SNOW, HANK	SINGER-SONGWRITER	POST OFFICE BOX 1084	NASHVILLE, TN	37202
SNOW, JIMMIE ROGERS	GUITARIST	POST OFFICE BOX 245	MADISON, TN	37115
SNOW, JONATHON G	NEWS CORRESPONDENT	1705 DE SALES ST, NW	WASHINGTON, DC	20036
SNOW, MARK	COMPOSER	4146 LANKERSHIM BLVD #300	NORTH HOLLYWOOD, CA	91602
SNOW, MICHAEL	TV DIRECTOR	THE FORGE, LITTLE SNORING		
		FAKEHAM	NORFOLK	ENGLAND
SNOW, NICHOLAS J	NEWS CORRESPONDENT	7013 JEFFERSON AVE	FALLS CHURCH, VA	22042
SNUFF	C & W GROUP	1180 INDIAN AVE	VIRGINIA BEACH, VA	23451
SNUKA, BIG	WRESTLER	SEE - SNUKA, JIMMY "SUPERFLY"		
SNUKA, GREAT	WRESTLER	SEE - SNUKA, JIMMY "SUPERFLY"		
SNUKA, JIMMY "SUPERFLY"	WRESTLER	AMERICAN WRESTLING ASSOC		
		MINNEAPLOIS WRESTLING		
		10001 WAYZATA BLVD	MINNETONKA, MN	55345
SNUKA, TAMI	WRESTLER	SEE - SNUKA, JIMMY "SUPERFLY"		
SNYDER, ANNE	TV WRITER	8955 BEVERLY BLVD	LOS ANGELES, CA	90048
SNYDER, ARLEN DEAN	ACTOR	10100 SANTA MONICA BLVD #1600	LOS ANGELES, CA	90067
SNYDER, CHARLES	NEWS CORRESPONDENT	4902 CRESCENT ST	BETHESDA, MD	20816
SNYDER, CLIFF	MUSICIAN-EXECUTIVE	SEE - STONE, CLIFFIE		
SNYDER, DARREL	TV DIRECTOR	25 ENTERPRISE DR	CORTE MADERA, CA	94925
SNYDER, DREW	ACTOR	1930 CENTURY PARK W #303	LOS ANGELES, CA	90067
SNYDER, JAMES J	NEWS CORRESPONDENT	1755 S JEFFERSON DAVIS HWY	ARLINGTON, VA	22202
SNYDER, JIM	SINGER	POST OFFICE BOX 25371	CHARLOTTE, NC	28212
SNYDER, JIMMY "THE GREEK"	ODDSMAKER	NEWS AMERICA SYNDICATE		
		1703 KAISER AVE	IRVINE, CA	92714
SNYDER, JOHN	CARTOONIST	L A TIMES NEWSPAPER		
		TIMES MIRROR SQUARE	LOS ANGELES, CA	90053
SNYDER, PETER B	TV DIRECTOR	310 W 56TH ST	NEW YORK, NY	10019
SNYDER, ROBERT	FILM DIRECTOR	1431 OCEAN AVE #1400	SANTA MONICA, CA	90401
SNYDER, SUZANNE	ACTRESS	10390 SANTA MONICA BLVD #310	LOS ANGELES, CA	90025
SNYDER, TOM	TV HOST	2801 HUTTON DR	BEVERLY HILLS, CA	90210
SOBEL, CURT E	COMPOSER	14001 PALAWAN WY PH #14	MARINA DEL REY, CA	90292
SOBEL, MARK S	TV DIRECTOR	POST OFFICE BOX 8601	UNIVERSAL CITY, CA	91608
SOBER, ERROL	TALENT AGENT	6671 SUNSET BLVD #1574	LOS ANGELES, CA	90028
SOBIESKI, CAROL	SCREENWRITER	541 LATIMER RD	SANTA MONICA, CA	90402
SOBLE, RON	ACTOR	8322 BEVERLY BLVD #202	LOS ANGELES, CA	90048
SOBOLOFF, ARNOLD	ACTOR	145 W 55TH ST	NEW YORK, NY	10019
SOBRAN, JOSEPH	COLUMNIST	UNIVERSAL PRESS SYNDICATE		
		4900 MAIN ST, 9TH FLOOR	KANSAS CITY, MO	62114
SOCCIO, GINO	SINGER	ROBERT CAVIANO, CAPITOL TOWERS		
		254 W 51ST ST	NEW YORK, NY	10019
SOCIAL DISTORTION	ROCK & ROLL GROUP	POST OFFICE BOX 6246	FULLERTON, CA	92634
SOCIETY OF SEVEN	MUSIC GROUP	PDQ DIRECTION, 1474 N KINGS RD	LOS ANGELES, CA	90069
SOCKWELL, SHEILA GAIL	NEWS CORRESPONDENT	2800 QUEBEC ST #535, NW	WASHINGTON, DC	20008
SOCOL, GARY	ACTOR	939 N ALFRED ST #4	LOS ANGELES, CA	90069
SOCOL, GARY	TV PRODUCER	METROMEDIA, 5746 SUNSET BLVD	LOS ANGELES, CA	90028
SODA, RALPH	COLUMNIST	POST OFFICE BOX 500	WASHINGTON, DC	20044
SODERBERG, NOEL	NEWS CORRESPODENT	400 N CAPITOL ST, NW	WASHINGTON, DC	20001
SODERBERG, ROBERT W	TV WRITER	ABC-TV, "GENERAL HOSPITAL"		
		1438 N GOWER ST	LOS ANGELES, CA	90028
SODERSTROM, ELISABETH	SOPRANO	CAMI, 165 W 57TH ST	NEW YORK, NY	10019
SODERSTROM, KENNETH	MUSICIAN	213-B DONNA DR	MADISON, TN	37115
SOFAER, ABRAHAM	ACTOR	23388 MULHOLLAND DR	WOODLAND HILLS, CA	91364
SOFFEL, DORIS	MEZZO-SOPRANO	COLBERT, 111 W 57TH ST	NEW YORK, NY	10019
SOFFER, SHELDON	IMPRESSARIO	130 W 56TH ST	NEW YORK, NY	10019
SOFGE, CHARLES	PIANIST	901 WOODMONT BLVD	NASHVILLE, TN	37204
SOFT CELL	ROCK & ROCK DUO	BIZARRE, 17 SAINT ANNE'S CT	LONDON W1	ENGLAND
SOGARD, PHILIP	TV DIRECTOR	32370 LAKE PLEASANT DR	WESTLAKE VILLAGE, CA	91361
SOGORKA, CHRISTINE	SOPRANO	756 7TH AVE #67	NEW YORK, NY	10019
SOHL, CHRIS	TV PRODUCER	1888 CENTURY PARK E #1100	LOS ANGELES, CA	90067
SOHL, JERRY	WRITER	150 W 87TH ST #60	NEW YORK, NY	10024
SOHMER, STEVE	TV DIRECTOR	2625 LARMAR RD	LOS ANGELES, CA	90068
SOKOLOW, ANNA	DANCER-CHOREOGRAPHER	1 CHRISTOPHER ST	NEW YORK, NY	10014
SOKOLSKY, MELVIN	TV DIRECTOR	SUNLIGHT, 322 E 39TH ST	NEW YORK, NY	10018
SOLARI, RUDY	ACTOR	6915 ETHEL AVE	NORTH HOLLYWOOD, CA	91605
SOLBERG, STEVEN	ACTOR	9165 SUNSET BLVD #202	LOS ANGELES, CA	90069
SOLDO, CHRIS	FILM DIRECTOR	5121 WESTPARK DR	NORTH HOLLYWOOD, CA	91601
SOLE, ALFRED	FILM WRITER-DIRECTOR	1641 N KINGS RD	LOS ANGELES, CA	90069
SOLEATHER, JON	SINGER	130 W 42ND ST #1106	NEW YORK, NY	10036
SOLEE, DENIS HARVEY	FLUTIST	ROUTE #2, BEACH HILL ROAD	PEGRAM, TN	37143
SOLES, P J	ACTRESS	870 N VINE ST #G	LOS ANGELES, CA	90038
SOLIN, HARVEY	ACTOR	9021 MELROSE AVE #304	LOS ANGELES, CA	90069
SOLIS, MERCED	WRESTLER	SEE - SANTANA, TITO		
SOLMS, KENNY	ACTOR-WRITER	8484 HAROLD WY	LOS ANGELES, CA	90049
SOLO, ROBERT H	FILM PRODUCER	1121 OLIVE DR #113	LOS ANGELES, CA	90069
SOLOFF, DANA	TV WRITER	8955 BEVERLY BLVD	LOS ANGELES, CA	90048
SOLOMAN, CINDY	NEWS REPORTER	THE NATIONAL ENQUIRER		
		600 SE COAST AVE	LANTANA, FL	33464
SOLOMON, AUBREY	TV WRITER	8833 SUNSET BLVD #202	LOS ANGELES, CA	90069
SOLOMON, BOB	DRUMMER	808 RICHARDS RD	ANTIOCH, TN	37013
SOLOMON, DAVID	DIRECTOR	DGA, 110 W 57TH ST	NEW YORK, NY	10019
SOLOMON, EDWARD J	TV WRITER	8955 BEVERLY BLVD	LOS ANGELES, CA	90048
SOLOMON, GEORGE	ACTOR	1335 N DETROIT ST #207	LOS ANGELES, CA	90046
SOLOMON, JACK	GUITARIST	8449 MERRY MOUNT DR	KINGSTON SPRINGS, TN	37082

SOLOMON, JEAN THORNTON	DIRECTOR	6255 SUNSET BLVD #1005	LOS ANGELES, CA	90028
SOLOMON, MARK	WRITER	8428 MELROSE PL #C	LOS ANGELES, CA	90069
SOLOMON, MARK B	NEWS CORRESPONDENT	3110 WISCONSIN AVE #301, NW	WASHINGTON, DC	20016
SOLOMON, MELBA	GUITARIST	8449 MERRYMOUNT DR	KINGSTON SPRINGS, TN	37082
SOLOMON, MICHAEL	PUBLISHING EXECUTIVE	US MAGAZINE COMPANY		
		1 DAG HAMMARSKJOLD PLAZA	NEW YORK, NY	10017
SOLOMON, NICHOLAS	BASSO-BARITONE	SULLIVAN, 390 W END AVE	NEW YORK, NY	10024
SOLOMONOW, RAMI	VIOLIST	ACC, 890 W END AVE	NEW YORK, NY	10025
SOLORZANO, LUCIA	NEWS CORRESPONDENT	4600 CONNECTICUT AVE #514, NW	WASHINGTON, DC	20008
SOLOV, ZACHARY	CHOREOGRAPHER	200 W 58TH ST	NEW YORK, NY	10019
SOLOW, HERBERT F	WRITER-PRODUCER	29060 CLIFFSIDE DR	MALIBU, CA	90265
SOLOW, JEFFREY	CELLIST	AFFILIATE ARTISTS, INC		
		37 W 65TH ST, 6TH FLOOR	NEW YORK, NY	10023
SOLOWAY, LEONARD	THEATER PRODUCER	230 CENTRAL PARK S	NEW YORK, NY	10019
SOLT, ANDREW	TV PRODUCER	151 S EL CAMINO DR	BEVERLY HILLS, CA	90212
SOLT, ANDREW W	WRITER-PRODUCER	1252 SHADYBROOK DR	BEVERLY HILLS, CA	90210
SOLTI, SIR GEORGE	CONDUCTOR	COLBERT, 111 W 57TH ST	NEW YORK, NY	10019
SOLYOM-NAGY, SANDOR	BARITONE	1182 MARKET ST #311	SAN FRANCISCO, CA	94102
SOMACH, BEVERLY	VIOLINIST	POST OFFICE BOX U	REDDING, CT	06875
SOMERS, BRETT	ACTRESS	1650 BROADWAY #406	NEW YORK, NY	10019
SOMERS, DOUG "PRETTY BOY"	WRESTLER	AMERICAN WRESTLING ASSOC		
		MINNEAPLOIS WRESTLING		
		10001 WAYZATA BLVD	MINNETONKA, MN	55345
SOMERS, KRISTI	ACTRESS	POST OFFICE BOX 69407	LOS ANGELES, CA	90069
SOMERS, PAUL, JR	WRITER	THE NATIONAL LAMPOON		
		635 MADISON AVE	NEW YORK, NY	10022
SOMERS, SUZANNE	ACTRESS-SINGER	10342 MISSISSIPPI AVE	LOS ANGELES, CA	90025
SOMERSON, DOUG	WRESTLER	SEE - SOMERS, DOUG "PRETTY BOY"		
SOMERVILLE, WARREN	DIRECTOR	DGA, 110 W 57TH ST	NEW YORK, NY	10019
SOMMARS, JULIE	ACTRESS	12959 WOODBRIDGE ST	STUDIO CITY, CA	91604
SOMMER, ELKE	ACTRESS	540 N BEVERLY GLEN BLVD	LOS ANGELES, CA	90024
SOMMER, HANS	COMPOSER-CONDUCTOR	569 MOUNT HOLYOKE AVE	PACIFIC PALISADES, CA	90272
SOMMER, JOSEF	ACTOR	10100 SANTA MONICA BLVD #1600	LOS ANGELES, CA	90067
SOMMERFIELD, DIANE	ACTRESS	1726 1/2 N WILTON PL	LOS ANGELES, CA	90026
SOMMERKAMP, ANNETTE L	NEWS CORRESPONDENT	3614 CONNECTICUT AVE, NW	WASHINGTON, DC	20008
SOMMERS, JULIE	ACTRESS	16031 ROYAL OAK RD	ENCINO, CA	91316
SOMMERSCHIELD, BENGT	DIRECTOR	333 E 30TH ST	NEW YORK, NY	10016
SOMMESE, DON	ACTOR	4313 1/2 OCEAN DR	MANHATTAN BEACH, CA	90266
SOMOGYI, LIZ	NEWS CORRESPONDENT	2030 "M" ST, NW	WASHINGTON, DC	22036
SOMOROFF, BENJAMIN	CINEMATOGRAPHER	MILL RIVER RD	SOUTH SALEM, NY	10590
SONDHEIM, STEPHEN	COMPOSER-LYRICIST	246 E 49TH ST	NEW YORK, NY	10017
SONNEBORN, DANIEL A	COMPOSER	7870 CAMINO GLORITA	SAN DIEGO, CA	92122
SONNENBERG, MELANIE	MEZZO-SOPRANO	AFFILIATE ARTISTS, INC		
		37 W 65TH ST, 6TH FLOOR	NEW YORK, NY	10023
SONNETT, SHERRY	SCREENWRITER	3413 1/2 ADINA DR	LOS ANGELES, CA	90068
SONNIER, JOEL	MUSICIAN	12019 VAN OWEN ST #102	LOS ANGELES, CA	91605
SONS OF THE PIONEERS	C & W GROUP	PARKER, 12403 W GREEN MTN CIR	LAKEWOOD, CO	80228
SONSKY, STEVE	TV CRITIC	THE MIAMI HERALD		
		1 HERALD PLAZA	MIAMI, FL	33101
SONTAG, DAVID B	WRITER	211 S BEVERLY DR #201	BEVERLY HILLS, CA	90212
SONTAG, SUSAN	AUTHOR-DIRECTOR	FARRAR, STRAUSS & GIROUX		
		19 UNION SQUARE W	NEW YORK, NY	10003
SOODIK, TRISH	ACTRESS-WRITER	2460 BEVERLY AVE	SANTA MONICA, CA	90405
SOOTER, EDWARD	TENOR	59 E 54TH ST #81	NEW YORK, NY	10022
SOPANEN, JERI	DIRECTOR	110 RIVERSIDE DR	NEW YORK, NY	10024
SOPKO, ANDREW S	COMPOSER-CONDUCTOR	POST OFFICE BOX 218473	HOUSTON, TX	77218
SORANNO, ALEX	TV DIRECTOR	6278 QUARTZ PL	NEWARK, CA	94560
SORBO, RON	DRUMMER	420 ELYSIAN FIELDS RD #A-1	NASHVILLE, TN	37211
SORCSEK, JEROME P	COMPOSER	9585 RESEDA BLVD #214	NORTHRIDGE, CA	91324
SOREL, CLAUDETTE	PIANIST	333 W END AVE	NEW YORK, NY	10023
SOREL, GUY	ACTOR	152 E 94TH ST	NEW YORK, NY	10028
SOREL, LOUISE	ACTRESS	9229 SUNSET BLVD #306	LOS ANGELES, CA	90069
SOREL, TED	ACTOR	9220 SUNSET BLVD #202	LOS ANGELES, CA	90069
SORELLE, SKIP	GUITARIST	1501 HOLLY ST	NASHVILLE, TN	37206
SORENSEN, DICKSON P	DIRECTOR	DGA, 110 W 57TH ST	NEW YORK, NY	10019
SORENSEN, JACKI	EXERCISE INSTRUCTOR	19420 MERRIDY ST	NORTHRIDGE, CA	91324
SORENSEN, PAUL	ACTOR	11802 HESBY ST	NORTH HOLLYWOOD, CA	91607
SORGE, HELMUT	NEWS CORRESPONDENT	4201 FORDHAM RD, NW	WASHINGTON, DC	20016
SORIAN, JACK	ACTOR	314 W 104TH ST	NEW YORK, NY	10025
SORIAN, RICHARD M	NEWS CORRESPONDENT	1815 18TH ST #201, NW	WASHINGTON, DC	20009
SORIANELLO, FRANCESCO	ACTOR	18926 WYANDOTTE ST	RESEDA, CA	91335
SORIANO, CARMEN	SINGER	POST OFFICE BOX 63	ORINDA, CA	94563
SORIANO, JOAQUIN	PIANIST	GERSHUNOFF, 502 PARK AVE	NEW YORK, NY	10022
SORKIN, ARLA	WRITER-PRODUCER	1557 COURTNEY AVE	LOS ANGELES, CA	90046
SORKIN, ARLEEN	ACTRESS	9000 SUNSET BLVD #1200	LOS ANGELES, CA	90069
SOROCA, KAREN	ACTRESS	3208 DOS PALOS DR	HOLLYWOOD, CA	90068
SOROKIN, NIKOLAI	NEWS CORRESPONDENT	118 W TAYLOR RUN PARKWAY	ALEXANDRIA, VA	22314
SORRELL, MAURICE B	PHOTOGRAPHER	5700 NEW HAMPSHIRE AVE, NW	WASHINGTON, DC	20011
SORRELLS, BILL	ACTOR	8019 1/2 MELROSE AVE #3	LOS ANGELES, CA	90046
SORRELLS, JOHN H, JR	NEWS CORRESPONDENT	25 W GLEBE RD #A-23	ALEXANDRIA, VA	22305
SORRELLS, ROBERT D	ACTOR	8721 SUNSET BLVD #103	LOS ANGELES, CA	90069
SORVINO, PAUL	ACTOR	4 BOULDER RD	TENAFLY, NJ	07630
SOS BAND	ROCK BAND	119 W 57TH ST #901	NEW YORK, NY	10019
SOSENKO, ALAN	NEWS CORRESPONDENT	301 "G" ST, SW	WASHINGTON, DC	20024
SOSKIN, CAROL	CASTING DIRECTOR	POST OFFICE BOX 480106	LOS ANGELES, CA	90048

SUZANNE SOMERS

JOANNIE SOMMERS

ARLEEN SORKIN

ANN SOUTHERN

DAVID SOUL

CATHERINE SPAAK

CAMILLA SPARV

SISSY SPACEK

BILLY JO SPEARS

Name	Occupation	Address	City	Zip
SOSNIK, HARRY	COMPOSER-CONDUCTOR	215 E 68TH ST	NEW YORK, NY	10023
SOTERO, PAULO	NEWS CORRESPONDENT	4823 CUMBERLAND AVE	CHEVY CHASE, MD	20815
SOTHERN, ANN	ACTRESS	POST OFFICE BOX 2285	KETCHUM, ID	83340
SOTIN, HANS	SINGER	COLBERT, 111 W 57TH ST	NEW YORK, NY	10019
SOTIRAKIS, DIMITRI	DIRECTOR	DGA, 7950 SUNSET BLVD	LOS ANGELES, CA	90046
SOTIROPULOS, KOPI	ACTOR	4941 ELMWOOD AVE	LOS ANGELES, CA	90004
SOTKIN, MARC	TV WRITER	25 FLEET ST	MARINA DEL REY, CA	90292
SOTO, LUIS	DIRECTOR	54 W 57TH ST	NEW YORK, NY	10019
SOTOMAYOR, JOHN	PHOTOGRAPHER	31 CENTRAL AVE	EAST BRUNSWICK, NJ	08816
SOUCHERAY, PHILIP H	NEWS CORRESPONDENT	1825 "K" ST, NW	WASHINGTON, DC	20006
SOUCY, PEGGY	NEWS CORRESPONDENT	2133 WISCONSIN AVE, NW	WASHINGTON, DC	20007
SOUDANT, HUBERT	CONDUCTOR	SHAW CONCERTS, 1995 BROADWAY	NEW YORK, NY	10023
SOUL, DAVID	ACT-SING-DIR	4201 HUNT CLUB LN	WESTLAKE VILLAGE, CA	91361
SOUL, KAREN	ACTRESS	4220 ALLOTT AVE	SHERMAN OAKS, CA	91403
SOUL ASYLUM	ROCK & ROLL GROUP	611 BROADWAY #526	NEW YORK, NY	10012
SOUL CHILDREN	SOUL-DISCO GROUP	DORTCH, 2272 DEADRICK AVE	MEMPHIS, TN	38114
SOUL QUEEN OF NEW ORLEANS	SINGER	SEE - THOMAS, IRMA		
SOUL SONIC FORCE	RHYTHM & BLUES GROUP	GTI, 1700 BROADWAY, 10TH FLOOR	NEW YORK, NY	10019
SOUL YEARS, THE	SOUL GROUP	OLDIES, 5218 ALMONT ST	LOS ANGELES, CA	90032
SOULES, DALE	ACTOR	AFFILIATE ARTISTS, INC		
		37 W 65TH ST, 6TH FLOOR	NEW YORK, NY	10023
SOULS, THE	ROCK & ROLL GROUP	25 HUNTINGTON AVE #420	BOSTON, MA	02116
SOUND BARRIER	ROCK & ROLL GROUP	POST OFFICE BOX 35897	LOS ANGELES, CA	90035
SOUTENDIJK, RENEE	ACTRESS	9255 SUNSET BLVD #505	LOS ANGELES, CA	90069
SOUTH, JOE	SINGER-SONGWRITER	POST OFFICE BOX 121557	NASHVILLE, TN	37212
SOUTH, JOHN	NEWS REPORTER	THE NATIONAL ENQUIRER		
		600 SE COAST AVE	LANTANA, FL	33464
SOUTHAN, MALCOLM	TV PRODUCER	LONDON WEEKEND TV, SOUTH BANK	LONDON SE1	ENGLAND
SOUTHERLAND, CRAIG	SINGER	POST OFFICE BOX 17272	MEMPHIS, TN	38187
SOUTHERLAND, JIM	PHOTOGRAPHER	SAINT CROIX 127, BOX 158		
		CHRISTENS	SAINT CROIX, VI	00820
SOUTHERLAND, ROBERT	ACTOR	ATA, 2437 E WASHINGTON BLVD	PASADENA, CA	91104
SOUTHERN, COL HAL	SINGER	POST OFFICE BOX 4234	PANORAMA CITY, CA	91412
SOUTHERN, RICHARD	ACTOR	430 E 63RD ST #9-J	NEW YORK, NY	10021
SOUTHERN, TERRY	TV WRITER	8955 BEVERLY BLVD	LOS ANGELES, CA	90048
SOUTHERN BELLE, THE	WRESTLER	SEE - SCARLET THE SOUTHERN BELLE		
SOUTHERN BELLES, THE	WRESTLING TAG TEAM	GORGEOUS LADIES OF WRESTLING		
		RIVIERA HOTEL & CASINO		
		DAVID B MC LANE PRODS		
		2901 S LAS VEGAS BLVD	LAS VEGAS, NV	89109
SOUTHERN BREEZE	C & W GROUP	POST OFFICE BOX 9393	PENSACOLA, FL	32513
SOUTHERN CONNECTION	SOUL-DISCO GROUP	LIONEL JOB, 17 KENT RD	WHITE PLAINS, NY	10603
SOUTHERN HIGH	C & W GROUP	POST OFFICE BOX 25371	CHARLOTTE, NC	28212
		CRESTON STATION	PORTLAND, OR	97206
SOUTHERN PACIFIC	ROCK 'N' GROUP	POST OFFICE BOX 6906		
SOUTHROAD CONNECTION	SOUL-DISCO GROUP	LIONEL JOB, 17 KENT RD	WHITE PLAINS, NY	10603
SOUTHSIDE JOHNNY & THE JUKES	ROCK & ROLL GROUP	POST OFFICE BOX 405	BOGOTA, NJ	07603
SOUTHWICK, SHAWN	ACTRESS	POST OFFICE BOX 5617	BEVERLY HILLS, CA	90210
SOUZAY, GERARD	BARITONE	SHAW CONCERTS, 1995 BROADWAY	NEW YORK, NY	10023
SOVIAK, GEORGE	ACTOR	1321 N FAIRVIEW AVE #4	LOS ANGELES, CA	90046
SOVIERO, DIANA	SOPRANO	CAMI, 165 W 57TH ST	NEW YORK, NY	10019
SOWARDS, JACK B	TV WRITER-PRODUCER	4428 CARPENTER AVE	NORTH HOLLYWOOD, CA	91607
SPACAGNA, MARIA	SOPRANO	61 W 62ND ST #6-F	NEW YORK, NY	10023
SPACEK, SISSY	ACTRESS	FISK, BEAU VAL FARM, BOX #7	COBHAM, VA	22929
SPADACENE, KAREN L	NEWS CORRESPONDENT	2131 N KENTUCKY ST	ARLINGTON, VA	22205
SPADER, JAMES	ACTOR	151 S EL CAMINO DR	BEVERLY HILLS, CA	90212
SPAHN, WARREN	BASEBALL	RURAL ROUTE #2	HARTSHORNE, OK	74547
SPAHNI, WALTER E	NEWS CORRESPONDENT	8607 EWING DR	BETHESDA, MD	20817
SPAIN, THOMAS	WRITER-PRODUCER	POST OFFICE BOX 230	SKILLMAN, NJ	08558
SPALDING, HARRY	SCREENWRITER	3936 GLENRIDGE DR	SHERMAN OAKS, CA	91423
SPANDAU BALLET	ROCK & ROLL GROUP	REFORMATION MANAGEMENT		
		89 GREAT PORTLAND	LONDON W1	ENGLAND
SPANDRI, JENNIFER	ACTRESS	SCHOEMAN, 2600 W VICTORY BLVD	BURBANK, CA	91505
SPANG, LAURETTE	ACTRESS	MC COOK, 4154 COLBATH AVE	SHERMAN OAKS, CA	91413
SPANGLER, LARRY G	FILM PRODUCER	1289 N CRESCENT HGTS BLVD	LOS ANGELES, CA	90046
SPANISH RED	WRESTLER	GORGEOUS LADIES OF WRESTLING		
		RIVIERA HOTEL & CASINO		
		DAVID B MC LANE PRODS		
		2901 S LAS VEGAS BLVD	LAS VEGAS, NV	89109
SPANKO, JOHN	ACTOR	4441 TUJUNGA AVE #2	NORTH HOLLYWOOD, CA	91602
SPANKY & OUR GANG	ROCK & ROLL GROUP	208 E MARCY ST #7	SANTE FE, NM	87501
SPANO, JOE	ACTOR	SF & A, 121 N SAN VICENTE BLVD	BEVERLY HILLS, CA	90211
SPANO, VINCENT	ACTOR	49 W 9TH ST	NEW YORK, NY	10011
SPARER, PAUL	ACTOR	205 W 89TH ST	NEW YORK, NY	10024
SPARKS	ROCK & ROCK DUO	POST OFFICE BOX 1710	BEVERLY HILLS, CA	90213
SPARKS, PAM	CASTING DIRECTOR	12725 VENTURA BLVD #E	STUDIO CITY, CA	91604
SPARKS, RANDY & THE PATCH FAMIL	VOCAL GROUP	2701 COTTAGE WY #21	SACRAMENTO, CA	95825
SPARKS, THE	ROCK & ROLL GROUP	10100 SANTA MONICA BLVD #1600	LOS ANGELES, CA	90067
SPARKS, ZONA	NEWS REPORTER	TIME/TIME & LIFE BLDG		
		ROCKEFELLER CENTER	NEW YORK, NY	10020
SPARROW, CAROL	SOPRANO	HILLYER, 250 W 57TH ST	NEW YORK, NY	10107
SPARTON, JOE	TV WRITER	555 W 57TH ST #1230	NEW YORK, NY	10019
SPARV, CAMILLA	ACTRESS	HOOVER, 2854 ROSCOMARE RD	LOS ANGELES, CA	90077
SPEAR, JOSEPH C	NEWS CORRESPONDENT	4840 ALBEMARLE ST, NW	WASHINGTON, DC	20016
SPEARMAN, DAVE	WRESTLER	NATIONAL WRESTLING ALLIANCE		
		JIM CROCKETT PROMOTIONS		
		421 BRIARBEND DR	CHARLOTTE, NC	28209
SPEARMANS, THE	GOSPEL GROUP	DYER ROUTE	COWEN, WV	26206
SPEARS, BEE	GUITARIST	ROUTE #1, BOX 160	BUFFALO VALLEY, TN	38548
SPEARS, BILLIE JO	SINGER	POST OFFICE BOX 23470	NASHVILLE, TN	37202
SPEARS, HAZEL	ACTRESS-ANNOUNCER	512 S HOBART BLVD #607	LOS ANGELES, CA	90020
SPEARS, ROBERT	TV WRITER	8955 BEVERLY BLVD	LOS ANGELES, CA	90048

Name	Occupation	Address	City	Zip/Country
SPEARS, STEPHEN W	TV WRITER	8955 BEVERLY BLVD	LOS ANGELES, CA	90048
SPEARS, WILLIS	GUITARIST	ROUTE #1, BOX 60	SUMMERTOWN, TN	38483
SPECHT, DON	COMPOSER-CONDUCTOR	11740 EL CERRO LN	STUDIO CITY, CA	91604
SPECHT, MICHAEL R	PHOTOJOURNALIST	2901 MEADOW LARK DR	SAN DIEGO, CA	92123
SPECHT, ROBERT	TV WRITER	8955 BEVERLY BLVD	LOS ANGELES, CA	90048
SPECIAL CONSENSUS	BLUEGRASS GROUP	ATTRACTIONS TALENT AGENCY		
		6525 N FRANCISCO AVE	CHICAGO, IL	60645
SPECIAL DELIVERY	WRESTLER	SEE - JONES, S D		
SPECIAL FORCES	ROCK & ROLL GROUP	8306 WILSHIRE BLVD #1531	BEVERLY HILLS, CA	90211
SPECK, B ALAN	NEWS CORRESPONDENT	ABC-TV, NEWS DEPARTMENT		
		1717 DE SALES ST, NW	WASHINGTON, DC	20036
SPECK, JOSEPH M	CONDUCTOR	5454 ZELZAH AVE	ENCINO, CA	91316
SPECTOR, DAVID	WRITER	1413 OCEAN PARK BLVD #5	SANTA MONICA, CA	90405
SPECTOR, LEE	GUITARIST	111 ACKLEN PARK DR #C-110	NASHVILLE, TN	37203
SPECTOR, PHIL	RECORD PRODUCER	POST OFFICE BOX 69529	LOS ANGELES, CA	90069
SPECTOR, RONNIE	SINGER	710 W END AVE #7-A	NEW YORK, NY	10025
SPEDDING, CHRIS	SINGER-GUITARIST	225 CENTRAL PARK W	NEW YORK, NY	10024
SPEECHLEY, DAVID	FILM DIRECTOR	VISNEWS, CUMBERLAND AVE	LONDON NW10 7EH	ENGLAND
SPEED, DORIS	ACTRESS	SIBSON RD, CHORLTON		
		MANCHESTER	LANCSHIRE	ENGLAND
SPEER, BEN LACY	PIANIST	POST OFFICE BOX 40201	NASHVILLE, TN	37204
SPEER, BROCK	GUITARIST	5318 ANCHORAGE DR #9201	NASHVILLE, TN	37220
SPEER, KATHY	TV WRITER	8955 BEVERLY BLVD	LOS ANGELES, CA	90048
SPEER, MARC	GUITARIST	5318 ANCHORAGE DR	NASHVILLE, TN	37220
SPEER, MARTIN	ACTOR	10000 SANTA MONICA BLVD #305	LOS ANGELES, CA	90067
SPEER FAMILY, THE	GOSPEL GROUP	LIGHT, 1100 17TH AVE S	NASHVILLE, TN	37212
SPEHAR, KATHIE	ACTRESS	5330 LANKERSHIM BLVD #210	NORTH HOLLYWOOD, CA	91601
SPEIGHT, JOHNNY	TV WRITER	LE BARS, 18 QUEEN ST	LONDON W1	ENGLAND
SPEIGHTS, ERIC V	PHOTOJOURNALIST	4226 3RD ST, NW	WASHINGTON, DC	20011
SPEILBERG, DAVID	ACTOR	10000 SANTA MONICA BLVD #305	LOS ANGELES, CA	90067
SPEIR, DONA	ACTRESS-MODEL	MODELS & PROMOTIONS AGENCY		
		8560 SUNSET BLVD, 10TH FLOOR	LOS ANGELES, CA	90069
SPEIRS, JACK	WRITER-PRODUCER	7 OAKS, 56 LOWER LAKE RD	THOUSAND OAKS, CA	91360
SPEIZER, IRWIN	NEWS CORRESPONDENT	1616-C BELMONT ST, NW	WASHINGTON, DC	20009
SPELIUS, SUSAN	MUSICIAN	2528 W JEROME AVE #A	CHICAGO, IL	60645
SPELL, GEORGE	ACTOR	809 5TH AVE	LOS ANGELES, CA	90005
SPELL, WINSTON	ACTOR	809 5TH AVE	LOS ANGELES, CA	90005
SPELLER, ROBERT, JR	ACTOR	343 W 14TH ST	NEW YORK, NY	10014
SPELLING, AARON	TV WRITER-PRODUCER	594 MAPLETON DR	LOS ANGELES, CA	90024
SPELMAN, SHARON	ACTRESS	11592 SUNSHINE TERR	STUDIO CITY, CA	91604
SPENCE, LEW	COMPOSER	215 E 68TH ST #17-K	NEW YORK, NY	10021
SPENCE, SAMUEL L	COMPOSER	MENZINGERSTR 118	8 MUNICH 50	GERMANY 811
SPENCER, ALAN C	TV WRITER-PRODUCER	8955 BEVERLY BLVD	LOS ANGELES, CA	90048
SPENCER, BUD	ACTOR	AVE MICHELE PIETRAVILLE		
		VIALE BRUNO BUOZZI 51	ROME 00197	ITALY
SPENCER, DIANE	ACTRESS	12211 WIXOM ST	NORTH HOLLYWOOD, CA	91605
SPENCER, GILLIAN	ACTRESS-WRITER	305 MADISON AVE #4419	NEW YORK, NY	10165
SPENCER, LARRY M	WRITER	211 S BEVERLY DR #206	BEVERLY HILLS, CA	90212
SPENCER, PATRICIA	FLUTIST	425 RIVERSIDE DR #5-G	NEW YORK, NY	10025
SPENCER, PATRICIA	NEWS CORRESPONDENT	21 WATKINS PARK DR	UPPER MARLSBORO, MD	20772
SPENCER, RONALD CHARLES	WRITER-PRODUCER	PACESETTER PRODUCTIONS		
		NEW BARN HOUSE		
		LEITH HILL LN	SURREY RH5 5PH	ENGLAND
SPENCER, SALLY	ACTRESS	NBC-TV, "ANOTHER WORLD"		
		30 ROCKEFELLER PLAZA	NEW YORK, NY	10112
SPENCER, SCOTT	SCREENWRITER	555 W 57TH ST #1230	NEW YORK, NY	10019
SPENCER, SUSAN	NEWS CORRESPONDENT	CBS NEWS, 2020 "M" ST, NW	WASHINGTON, DC	20036
SPENCER, WILLIAM M	CINEMATOGRAPHER	POST OFFICE 2230	HOLLYWOOD, CA	90078
SPENGLER, PIERRE	FILM PRODUCER	14 RUE DES VOLONTAIRES	PARIS 15	FRANCE
SPENTON-FOSTER, GEORGE	TV PRODUCER	8 ROEHAMPTON CT		
		QUEENS RIDE, BATH	LONDON SW13	ENGLAND
SPERBER, WENDIE JO	ACTRESS	4110 WITZEL DR	SHERMAN OAKS, CA	91423
SPERDAKOS, GEORGE	ACTOR	5958 SAINT CLAIR AVE	NORTH HOLLYWOOD, CA	91607
SPERLING, GODFREY, JR	NEWS CORRESPONDENT	8101 CONNECTICUT AVE	CHEVY CHASE, MD	20815
SPERLING, KAREN JO	WRITER	13701 RIVERSIDE DR #400	SHERMAN OAKS, CA	91423
SPERLING, NEAL J	TV WRITER	8955 BEVERLY BLVD	LOS ANGELES, CA	90048
SPERO, ROBERTA	ACTRESS	10850 RIVERSIDE DR #505	NORTH HOLLYWOOD, CA	91602
SPERRY, PAUL	TENOR	POST OFFICE BOX 1515	NEW YORK, NY	10023
SPERY, JOSEPH C	DIRECTOR-PRODUCER	47 GARFIELD ST	OAK PARK, IL	60304
SPEVACK, MELODEE M	ACTRESS	4731 LAUREL CANYON BLVD #5	NORTH HOLLYWOOD, CA	91607
SPHERE	JAZZ GROUP	240 W 98TH ST #13-A	NEW YORK, NY	10025
SPICER, MARIANNA CHASE	DIRECTOR	8947 TAMAR DR #301	COLUMBIA, MD	21045
SPICER, PHILIP X	NEWS CORRESPONDENT	2139 WISCONSIN AVE, NW	WASHINGTON, DC	20007
SPICHER, BUDDY	FIDDLER	ROUTE #6, BOX 280-A	FRANKLIN, TN	37064
SPIEGEL, BARBARA	ACTRESS	534 MADISON AVE	NEW YORK, NY	10022
SPIEGEL, DENNIS	ACTOR-WRITER	6923 PASEO DEL SERRA	LOS ANGELES, CA	90068
SPIEGEL, EDWARD	WRITER-PRODUCER	2739 NICHOLS CANYON RD	LOS ANGELES, CA	90046
SPIEGEL, LARRY J	WRITER-PRODUCER	2029 CENTURY PARK E #1850	LOS ANGELES, CA	90067

Name	Occupation	Address	City	Zip
SPIEGL, STEVE H	COMPOSER	2816 SHADY GLEN LN	ORANGE, CA	92667
SPIELBERG, ANNE	WRITER	ICM, 8899 BEVERLY BLVD	LOS ANGELES, CA	90048
SPIELBERG, DAVID	ACTOR	150 W 82ND ST	NEW YORK, NY	10024
SPIELBERG, STEVEN	DIRECTOR-PRODUCER	MCA/UNIVERSAL STUDIOS, INC		
		100 UNIVERSAL CITY PLAZA #477	UNIVERSAL CITY, CA	91608
SPIELMAN, EARL V	MUSICIAN	4305 BRUSH HILL RD	NASHVILLE, TN	37216
SPIELMAN, EDWARD	TV WRITER	8955 BEVERLY BLVD	LOS ANGELES, CA	90048
SPIELMAN, FRED	COMPOSER	710 WEST END AVE #16-B	NEW YORK, NY	10025
SPIES, ADRIAN	TV WRITER	11937 SUNSET BLVD	LOS ANGELES, CA	90049
SPIKE	WRESTLER	SEE - MOD SQUAD, THE		
SPIKES, THE	ROCK & ROLL GROUP	JANET MILLS, 83 MORIAH ST	CLAYTON 3168, VICTORIA	AUSTRALIA
SPIKINGS, BARRY	FILM EXECUTIVE	56 MALIBU COLONY DR	MALIBU, CA	90265
SPIKOL, ALLEN	DIRECTOR	11 W 17TH ST #11	NEW YORK, NY	10011
SPILKER, SUSAN	ACTRESS	12365 LAUREL TERR DR	STUDIO CITY, CA	91604
SPILLANE, MICKEY	WRITER	2049 CENTURY PARK E #2350	LOS ANGELES, CA	90067
SPILLANE, SHERRI	ACTRESS	2049 CENTURY PARK E #2350	LOS ANGELES, CA	90067
SPILLMAN, HERNDON	ORGANIST	15 HIGH ST #621	HARTFORD, CT	06103
SPILLMAN, SANDY	ACTOR	6430 SUNSET BLVD #1203	LOS ANGELES, CA	90028
SPILLMAN, SANFORD	DIRECTOR	DGA, 7950 SUNSET BLVD	LOS ANGELES, CA	90046
SPILMAN, CAROL	ACTRESS	1531 CABRILLO AVE #2	VENICE, CA	90291
SPILSBURY, KLINTON	ACTOR	329 N WETHERLY DR #205	BEVERLY HILLS, CA	90211
SPINA, HAROLD	COMPOSER-CONDUCTOR	2232 VISTA DEL MAR PL	LOS ANGELES, CA	90068
SPINELLI, MARTIN J	DIRECTOR	12 E 86TH ST	NEW YORK, NY	10028
SPINKS, DANNY	GUITARIST	112 WONDER VALLEY DR	HENDERSONVILLE, TN	37075
SPINKS, LEON	BOXER	19300 BRITTON DR	DETROIT, MI	48224
SPINKS, MICHAEL	BOXER	20284 ARCHDALE ST	DETROIT, MI	48235
SPINNER, ANTHONY	WRITER-PRODUCER	1223 MANNING AVE	LOS ANGELES, CA	90024
SPINNERS, THE	VOCAL GROUP	65 W 55TH ST #6-C	NEW YORK, NY	10019
SPINRAD, NAOMI	NEWS CORRESPONDENT	NBC-TV, NEWS DEPARTMENT		
		4001 NEBRASKA AVE, SW	WASHINGTON, DC	20016
SPINRAD, NORMAN	WRITER	2017 ROSILLA PL	LOS ANGELES, CA	90046
SPIRIT, SUZIE	WRESTLER	SEE - CHEERLEADERS, THE		
SPIRO, MICHAEL	PERCUSSIONIST	POST OFFICE BOX 9388	STANFORD, CA	94305
SPIRO, STANLEY JEROME	DIRECTOR	44 WOOD LN	WOODSBURGH, NY	11598
SPIROPOULOS, JOHN	NEWS CORRESPONDENT	9115 CROSBY RD	SILVER SPRING, MD	20910
SPITKOVA, JELA	VIOLINIST	POST OFFICE BOX U	REDDING, CT	06875
SPITZ, KATHY	ACTRESS	15010 VENTURA BLVD #219	SHERMAN OAKS, CA	91403
SPITZ, MARK	SWIMMER	383 DALEHURST AVE	LOS ANGELES, CA	90024
SPIVA, HUBERT T	WRITER	10066 VALLEY SPRING LN	NORTH HOLLYWOOD, CA	91602
SPIVACK, MIRANDA S	NEWS CORRESPONDENT	1730 RHODE ISLAND AVE, NW	WASHINGTON, DC	20036
SPIVAK, ALICE	ACTRESS	247 W 4TH ST	NEW YORK, NY	10014
SPIVAK, LAWRENCE	TV-RADIO PRODUCER	2600 WOODLEY RD, NW	WASHINGTON, DC	20008
SPIVEY, CHRISTOPHER W	PHOTOGRAPHER	8205 ADENLEE AVE	FAIRFAX, VA	22031
SPIVEY, DANIEL "GOLDEN BOY"	WRESTLER	POST OFFICE BOX 3859	STAMFORD, CT	06905
SPLAVER, RICHARD	WRITER	430 N MAPLE DR #203	BEVERLY HILLS, CA	90210
SPLIT ENZ	ROCK & ROLL GROUP	E N Z MANAGEMENT		
		138 NELSON RD		
		SOUTH MELBOURNE	VICTORIA	AUSTRALIA
SPLITTGERBER, DOUG	BODYBUILDER	NAUTILUS FITNESS CENTER		
		150 NICOLET DR	APPLETON, WI	54914
SPLITTGERBER, JEANNE	BODYBUILDER	NAUTILUS FITNESS CENTER		
		150 NICOLET DR	APPLETON, WI	54914
SPOILER, THE	WRESTLER	POST OFFICE BOX 3859	STAMFORD, CT	06905
SPONSELLER, GAIL W	CONDUCTOR	POST OFFICE BOX 2235	ORANGE, CA	92669
SPOONER, BILL	SINGER-GUITARIST	109 MINNA ST #391	SAN FRANCISCO, CA	94105
SPOONER, DENNIS	WRITER	ROGER HANCOCK MANAGEMENT		
		8 WATERLO PL, PALL MALL	LONDON SW1Y 4AW	ENGLAND
SPOONS	ROCK & ROLL GROUP	41 BRITAIN ST #200	TORONTO, ONT	CANADA
SPOT, MOONDOG	WRESTLER	SEE - MOONDOG SPOT		
SPOTTISWOODE, ROGER	DIRECTOR	2451 HOLLY DR	LOS ANGELES, CA	90068
SPOTTS, ROGER HAMILTON	COMPOSER	1362 LONGWOOD AVE #6	LOS ANGELES, CA	90019
SPOUND, MICHAEL	ACTOR	1814 THAYER AVE #6	LOS ANGELES, CA	90025
SPRADLIN, G D	ACTOR-DIRECTOR	MISHKIN, 2355 BENEDICT CANYON	BEVERLY HILLS, CA	90210
SPRAGER, HART	ACTOR	CASSELL, 843 N SYCAMORE AVE	LOS ANGELES, CA	90038
SPRAGUE, DEAN	NEWS CORRESPONDENT	11113 ARDWICK DR	RICKVILLE, MD	20852
SPRATLEY, TOM	ACTOR	POST OFFICE BOX 1105	PACIFIC PALISADES, CA	90272
SPRIGGS, C MICHAEL	GUITARIST	134 MEADOWGREEN DR	FRANKLIN, TN	37064
SPRING, BETH	NEWS CORRESPONDENT	4983 MC FARLAND DR	FAIRFAX, VA	22032
SPRING, SALLY	SINGER	276 CAMBRIDGE ST #4	BOSTON, MA	02134
SPRINGER, ASHTON	THEATER PRODUCER	240 W 44TH ST	NEW YORK, NY	10036
SPRINGER, LENNY	FIDDLER	644 WHISPERING OAKS PL	NASHVILLE, TN	37211
SPRINGER, PHILIP	COMPOSER-CONDUCTOR	POST OFFICE BOX 1174	PACIFIC PALISADES, CA	90272
SPRINGER, REED	DIRECTOR-PRODUCER	23 ACACIA AVE	BELVEDERE, CA	94920
SPRINGFIELD, BOBBY	GUITARIST	CHAPPELL MUSIC COMPANY		37203
		11 MUSIC CIRCLE S	NASHVILLE, TN	37203
SPRINGFIELD, RICK	SINGER-GUITARIST	POST OFFICE BOX 9518	NORTH HOLLYWOOD, CA	91609
SPRINGSTEEN, BRUCE & THE E STRE	ROCK & ROLL GROUP	3 E 54TH ST #1400	NEW YORK, NY	10022
SPRINGSTEEN, JULIANNE PHILLIPS	ACTRESS-MODEL	SEE - PHILLIPS, JULIANNE		
SPRINGSTEEN, R G	DIRECTOR	401 "C" AVE	CORONADO, CA	92118
SPROAT, RON	WRITER	ICM, 40 W 57TH ST	NEW YORK, NY	10019
SPROSTY, PAUL J	COMPOSER	2126 MANNING AVE	LOS ANGELES, CA	90025
SPROUL, ROBIN	NEWS CORRESPONDENT	ABC-TV, NEWS DEPARTMENT		
		1717 DE SALES ST, NW	WASHINGTON, DC	20036
SPROUSE, BLAINE	FIDDLER	212 WOODMONT CIR #A	NASHVILLE, TN	37205
SPRUCE, MARY F	PHOTOGRAPHER	4849 CONNECTICUT AVE, NW	WASHINGTON, DC	20008

MICKEY SPILLANE

BRUCE SPRINGSTEEN

ROBERT STACK

FRANK STALLONE

SYLVESTER STALLONE

JOE STAMPLEY

MAUREEN STAPLETON

EDWIN STARR

BOB STEELE

NAME	OCCUPATION	ADDRESS	CITY/STATE	ZIP
SPRUNG, SANDY	ACTRESS-WRITER	1738 CANYON DR #318	LOS ANGELES, CA	90028
SPRY, ROBIN	FILM DIRECTOR	5330 DUROCHER	MONTREAL, QUE H2V 3Y1	CANADA
SPURLOCK, ESTELLE	DANCER	236 E 8TH AVE	ROSELLE, NJ	07203
SPURRLOWS, THE	GOSPEL	32500 CONCORD DR #221	MADISON HEIGHTS, MI	48071
SPYRO GYRA	JAZZ GROUP	POST OFFICE BOX 239	TALLMAN, NY	10982
SQUARE, JEFFREY L	TV DIRECTOR	4750 BEDFORD AVE	BROOKLYN, NY	11235
SQUEEZE	ROCK & ROLL GROUP	SQUEEZE 85 MANAGEMENT		
		40 GREENWICH MARKET	LONDON SE10	ENGLAND
SQUIER, BILLY	SINGER-GUITARIST	DELOTE MGMT, PETER LUBIN		
		850 7TH AVE	NEW YORK, NY	10019
SQUIER, ROBERT	TV DIRECTOR	THE COMMUNICATIONS COMPANY		
		514 SEWARD SQ, SE	WASHINGTON, DC	20003
SQUIRE, ANTHONY	WRITER-PRODUCER	MAX NAUGHTON LOWE		
		200 FULHAM RD	LONDON SW10 9PN	ENGLAND
SQUIRE, JANIE	ACTRESS	2929 COLORADO AVE #18	SANTA MONICA, CA	90404
SQUIRE, ROBIN	TV WRITER	212 FRANCIS RD, HARROW	MIDDLESEX HA1 2RB	ENGLAND
SQUIRE, SYDNEY	ACTRESS	1930 CENTURY PARK W #303	LOS ANGELES, CA	90067
SQUIRES, EMILY H	TV DIRECTOR	250 W 94TH ST	NEW YORK, NY	10025
SQUIRES, SALLY	NEWS CORRESPONDENT	3524 "S" ST, NW	WASHINGTON, DC	20007
SQUITIERI, TOM	NEWS CORRESPONDENT	1100 6TH ST #501, SW	WASHINGTON, DC	20024
ST ALIX, ALAIN	ACTOR	ABC-TV, "GENERAL HOSPITAL"		
		1438 N GOWER ST	LOS ANGELES, CA	90028
ST ANDREW, TARA	ACTRESS	1327 N VISTA ST	LOS ANGELES, CA	90046
ST CLAIR, ELIZABETH	ACTRESS	1314 HILL ST	SANTA MONICA, CA	90405
ST CLAIR, ISLA	ACTRESS	73-A DE BEAUVOIR RD		
		ISLINGTON	LONDON N1	ENGLAND
ST CLAIR, MIKE	GUITARIST	OLD HICKORY ESTATES		
		500 CHEYENNE BLVD #179	MADISON, TN	37115
ST CLAIRE, BONWITT	ACTRESS	4721 LAUREL CANYON BLVD #211	NORTH HOLLYWOOD, CA	91607
ST CYR, LILI	BURLESQUE	624 N PLYMOUTH BLVD #7	LOS ANGELES, CA	90004
ST DAVID, MARTYN	ACTRESS	8721 SUNSET BLVD #200	LOS ANGELES, CA	90069
ST ELWOOD, JON	ACTOR	12725 VENTURA BLVD #E	STUDIO CITY, CA	91604
ST GEORGE, CATHY	ACTRESS-MODEL	MODELS & PROMOTIONS AGENCY		
		8560 SUNSET BLVD, 10TH FLOOR	LOS ANGELES, CA	90069
ST GEORGE, DAVID	SINGER	MALACO RECORDS COMPANY		
		3023 W NORTHSIDE DR	JACKSON, MS	39213
ST JACQUES, RAYMOND	ACTOR-DIRECTOR	9440 READCREST DR	BEVERLY HILLS, CA	90210
ST JAMES, LARRY	ACTOR	10841 WHIPPLE ST #217	NORTH HOLLYWOOD, CA	91602
ST JAMES, PHYLLIS	ACTRESS	7001 NAGLE AVE	NORTH HOLLYWOOD, CA	91605
ST JOHN, ANN	DIRECTOR	DGA, 7950 SUNSET BLVD	LOS ANGELES, CA	90046
ST JOHN, JILL	ACTRESS	10390 SANTA MONICA BLVD #310	LOS ANGELES, CA	90025
ST JOHN, KRISTOFF	ACTOR	12725 VENTURA BLVD #E	STUDIO CITY, CA	91604
ST JOHN, MARCO	ACTOR	870 N VINE ST #G	LOS ANGELES, CA	90038
ST JOHN, RALPH	GUITARIST	9316 OLD SMYRNA RD	BRENTWOOD, TN	37027
ST JOHNS, ADELA ROGERS	WRITER	32504 PACIFIC COAST HWY	MALIBU, CA	90265
ST JOHNS, KATHLEEN	TV EXECUTIVE	COLUMBIA PICTURES TV		
		COLUMBIA PLAZA	BURBANK, CA	91505
ST JOHNS, RICHARD	PRODUCER	MGM, 10202 W WASHINGTON BLVD	CULVER CITY, CA	90230
ST JOHNS, RICHARD	FILM-TV EXECUTIVE	9091 ALTO CEDRO DR	BEVERLY HILLS, CA	90210
ST JOHNS, RICHARD	FILM PRODUCER	MGM, 10202 W WASHINGTON BLVD	CULVER CITY, CA	90230
ST LAURENT, YVES	FASHION DESIGNER	15 COLUMBUS CIR	NEW YORK, NY	10023
ST MARIE, SUSAN	SINGER	POST OFFICE BOX 418	BRENTWOOD, TN	37027
ST PIERRE, MONIQUE	ACTRESS-MODEL	GARAY, 13200 CHELTENHAM DR	SHERMAN OAKS, CA	91413
ST ROMAIN, KIRBY	COMEDIAN	2701 COTTAGE WY #14	SACRAMENTO, CA	95825
STAAB, REBECCA	ACTRESS	CBS-TV, "THE GUIDING LIGHT"		
		51 W 52ND ST	NEW YORK, NY	10019
STAAHL, JIM	ACTOR-WRITER	7611 W NORTON AVE	LOS ANGELES, CA	90046
STABILIZERS, THE	ROCK & ROLL GROUP	MGMT III, 4570 ENCINO AVE	ENCINO, CA	91316
STABLER, BENJAMIN G	CONDUCTOR	3201 NEW MEXICO AVE, NW	WASHINGTON, DC	20016
STABLER, ROBERT	TV WRITER	8955 BEVERLY BLVD	LOS ANGELES, CA	90048
STACEY, ERIC, JR	WRITER-PRODUCER	2022 1/2 N ARGYLE AVE	LOS ANGELES, CA	90068
STACEY, JOHN	DRUMMER	1538 CAMPBELL RD	GOODLETTSVILLE, TN	37072
STACK, PAT	ACTOR	8375 FOUNTAIN AVE	LOS ANGELES, CA	90069
STACK, PATRICK	ACTOR	870 N VINE ST #G	LOS ANGELES, CA	90038
STACK, ROBERT	ACTOR	321 SAINT PIERRE RD	LOS ANGELES, CA	90077
STACK, ROSEMARIE	ACTRESS	321 SAINT PIERRE RD	LOS ANGELES, CA	90077
STACK, TIMOTHY	ACTOR	ICM, 8899 BEVERLY BLVD	LOS ANGELES, CA	90048
STACKS, JOHN F	NEWS CORRESPONDENT	TIME/TIME & LIFE BLDG		
		ROCKEFELLER CENTER	NEW YORK, NY	10020
STACY, JAMES	ACTOR	POST OFFICE BOX 610	OJAI, CA	93023
STACY, NEIL	ACTOR	FRASER, 91 REGENT ST	LONDON W1R 8RU	ENGLAND
STACY, SUSAN	ACTRESS	8949 SUNSET BLVD #203	LOS ANGELES, CA	90069
STACY, TIM	GUITARIST	3210 WINGATE AVE	NASHVILLE, TN	37211
STACY Q	SINGER	641 S PALM ST #D	LA HABRA, CA	90631
STADD, ARLENE	WRITER	1541 1/2 N SIERRA BONITA AVE	LOS ANGELES, CA	90046
STADER, PAUL B	FILM DIRECTOR	25266 MALIBU RD	MALIBU, CA	90265
STADLEN, LEWIS J	ACTOR	10 E 44TH ST #700	NEW YORK, NY	10017
STAFFORD, CHARLES L	NEWS CORRESPONDENT	6812 BELLAMY AVE	SPRINGFIELD, VA	22152
STAFFORD, DAVID HUNT	ACTOR	7266 FOUNTAIN AVE	HOLLYWOOD, CA	90046
STAFFORD, GRACE	ACTRESS	9255 SUNSET BLVD #505	LOS ANGELES, CA	90069
STAFFORD, GRACE	ACTRESS	LANTZ, 1715 CARLA RIDGE	BEVERLY HILLS, CA	90212
STAFFORD, JIM	SINGER	151 S EL CAMINO DR	BEVERLY HILLS, CA	90212
STAFFORD, JO	SINGER	2339 CENTURY HILL	LOS ANGELES, CA	90067
STAFFORD, MARILYN	ACTRESS	9229 SUNSET BLVD #611	LOS ANGELES, CA	90069
STAFFORD, NANCY	ACTRESS	9220 SUNSET BLVD #625	LOS ANGELES, CA	90069

Name	Occupation	Address	City	Zip
STAFFORD, STEVE	DIRECTOR	1901 AVE OF THE STARS #1040	LOS ANGELES, CA	90067
STAFFORD, SUSAN	ACTRESS	1250 S BEVERLY GLEN BLVD #104	LOS ANGELES, CA	90067
STAFFORD, TAMARA	DIRECTOR	DGA, 7950 SUNSET BLVD	LOS ANGELES, CA	90046
STAFFORD, WILLIAM L	COMPOSER	4561 REEVES AVE	RIDGECREST, CA	93555
STAFFORD-CLARK, NIGEL	TV PRODUCER	25 NOEL ST	LONDON W1	ENGLAND
STAGGER LEE	WRESTLER	SEE - WARE, KOKO B		
STAHL, DAVID	CONDUCTOR	COLBERT, 111 W 57TH ST	NEW YORK, NY	10019
STAHL, LESLEY	JOURNALIST	CBS-TV, NEWS DEPARTMENT		
		40TH & BRANDYWINE STS, NW	WASHINGTON, DC	20016
STAHL, RICHARD	ACTOR	9255 SUNSET BLVD #603	LOS ANGELES, CA	90069
STAHL, STANLEY	THEATER PRODUCER	277 PARK AVE	NEW YORK, NY	10017
STAIN, STEVE	SINGER-GUITARIST	1800 BAILEY DR	TORRANCE, CA	90504
STAINS, THE	ROCK & ROLL GROUP	POST OFFICE BOX 448	RADFORD, VA	24141
STAIRCASE	ROCK & ROLL GROUP	POST OFFICE BOX 11283	RICHMOND, VA	23230
STAIRWELL	ROCK & ROLL GROUP	POST OFFICE BOX 448	RADFORD, VA	24141
STALEY, CHUCK	TV DIRECTOR	2027 N CURSON AVE	LOS ANGELES, CA	90046
STALEY, JAMES	ACTOR	19425 LEMARSH ST	NORTHRIDGE, CA	91324
STALEY, JOAN	ACTRESS	439 S LA CIENEGA BLVD #120	LOS ANGELES, CA	90048
STALEY, LORA	ACTRESS	11726 SAN VICENTE BLVD #300	LOS ANGELES, CA	90049
STALEY, MARILYN	ACTRESS	10350 SANTA MONICA BLVD #210	LOS ANGELES, CA	90067
STALEY, TINA	ACTRESS	8350 SANTA MONICA BLVD #206	LOS ANGELES, CA	90069
STALLION	C & W GROUP	POST OFFICE BOX 1373	LEWISVILLE, TX	75067
STALLMAN, ROBERT	FLUTIST	GEWALD, 58 W 58TH ST	NEW YORK, NY	10019
STALLONE, FRANK	ACTOR	10100 SANTA MONICA BLVD #1600	LOS ANGELES, CA	90067
STALLONE, JACQUELINE	WRESTLER	GORGEOUS GIRLS OF WRESTLING		
		RIVIERA HOTEL & CASINO		
		DAVID B MC LANE PRODS		
		2901 S LAS VEGAS BLVD	LAS VEGAS, NV	89109
STALLONE, SASHA	PERSONALITY	253 S ROCKINGHAM AVE	LOS ANGELES, CA	90049
STALLONE, SYLVESTER	ACT-WRI-DIR	1570 AMALFI DR	PACIFIC PALISADES, CA	90272
STALMASTER, HAL	ACTOR	5506 BLUEBELL AVE	NORTH HOLLYWOOD, CA	91607
STALMASTER, LYNN	CASTING DIRECTOR	POST OFFICE BOX 3282	BEVERLY HILLS, CA	90212
STALVEY, DORRANCE	COMPOSER-CONDUCTOR	2145 MANNING AVE	LOS ANGELES, CA	90025
STAMAS, VICKEY J	NEWS CORRESPONDENT	3701 MASSACHUSETTS AVE, NW	WASHINGTON, DC	20016
STAMBERG, SUSAN L	NEWS CORRESPONDENT	2025 "M" ST, NW	WASHINGTON, DC	20036
STAMM, JEFFREY	TENOR	59 E 54TH ST #81	NEW YORK, NY	10022
STAMOS, JOHN	ACTOR	151 S EL CAMINO DR	BEVERLY HILLS, CA	90212
STAMOS, NICHOLAS PETER	DIRECTOR	1756 N VAN NESS AVE	HOLLYWOOD, CA	90028
STAMOS, THEO	NEWS CORRESPONDENT	1603 19TH ST, NW	WASHINGTON, DC	20009
STAMP, TERENCE	ACTOR	HEATH, PARAMOUNT HOUSE		
		162-170 WARDOUR ST	LONDON W1V 3AT	ENGLAND
STAMPER, PHIL	DRUMMER	906 JONES AVE	OLD HICKORY, TN	37138
STAMPFEL, PETER & THE BOTTLECAP	ROCK & ROLL GROUP	ROUNDER RECORDS, 1 CAMP ST	CAMBRIDGE, MA	02140
STAMPLEY, JOE	SINGER	ENCORE, 2137 ZERCHER RD	SAN ANTONIO, TX	78209
STAMPS QUARTET, THE	VOCAL GROUP	POST OFFICE BOX 17272	MEMPHIS, TN	38187
STANDELLS, THE	ROCK & ROLL GROUP	OLDIES, 5218 ALMONT ST	LOS ANGELES, CA	90032
STANDER, LIONEL	ACTOR	13176 BOCA DE CANON LN	LOS ANGELES, CA	90049
STANDING, JOHN	ACTOR	MORRIS, 147-149 WARDOUR ST	LONDON W1V 3TB	ENGLAND
STANDRIDGE, RICHARD	DIRECTOR	125 TRUMAN PL	CENTERPORT, NY	11721
STANFIELD, JAMES L	PHOTOGRAPHER	3606 N ABINGDON ST	ARLINGTON, VA	22207
STANFIELD, ROBERT I	NEWS CORRESPONDENT	2667 CARROLLTON RD	ANNAPOLIS, MD	21403
STANFIELD, ROCHELLE L	NEWS CORRESPONDENT	1724 "Q" ST, NW	WASHINGTON, DC	20009
STANFILL, JAMES "POLY"	SINGER	851 OLD HICKORY BLVD #D	JACKSON, TN	38301
STANFORD-TUCK, ANTHONY	TV WRITER-PRODUCER	HOSKINS, 10 CONNAUGHT SQ	LONDON W2 2HG	ENGLAND
STANG, ARNOLD	ACTOR	439 S LA CIENEGA BLVD #120	LOS ANGELES, CA	90048
STANGEL, EDWARD M	WRITER	7415 NITA AVE	CANOGA PARK, CA	91303
STANGER, BARBARA	ACTRESS	208 S BEVERLY DR #4	BEVERLY HILLS, CA	90212
STANGER, HUGO L	ACTOR	8230 BEVERLY BLVD #23	LOS ANGELES, CA	90048
STANGER, RUSSELL	CONDUCTOR	1776 BROADWAY #504	NEW YORK, NY	10019
STANHOPE, WARREN	ACTOR	LEONETTI, 6526 SUNSET BLVD	HOLLYWOOD, CA	90028
STANIS, BERNADETTE	ACTRESS	1607 N EL CENTRO AVE #2	LOS ANGELES, CA	90028
STANISLAVSKY, MICHAEL	DIRECTOR	8977 SAINT IVES DR	LOS ANGELES, CA	90069
STANKUS, TOM "T-BONE"	SINGER	POST OFFICE BOX 93	BROAD BROOK, CT	06016
STANLEIGH, KATHRYN	ACTRESS	13111 VENTURA BLVD #204	STUDIO CITY, CA	91604
STANLEY, ALESSANDRA	NEWS CORRESPONDENT	1050 CONNECTICUT AVE, NW	WASHINGTON, DC	20036
STANLEY, ALLAN	DIRECTOR	DOLPHIN, 140 E 80TH ST	NEW YORK, NY	10021
STANLEY, FRANK	CINEMATOGRAPHER	POST OFFICE BOX 2230	HOLLYWOOD, CA	90078
STANLEY, HARRY	VAUDEVILLIAN	THE ACTOR'S FUND HOME		
		155 W HUDSON AVE	ENGLEWOOD, NJ	07631
STANLEY, JAMES LEE	SINGER	POST OFFICE BOX 1556	GAINESVILLE, FL	32602
STANLEY, KIM	ACTRESS	888 7TH AVE #2500	NEW YORK, NY	10106
STANLEY, PAMELA	SINGER	15775 N HILLCREST RD #508	DALLAS, TX	75248
STANLEY, PAUL	DIRECTOR	15301 VENTURA BLVD #345	SHERMAN OAKS, CA	91403
STANLEY, PAUL N	PUBLISHING EXECUTIVE	ARCATA GRAPHICS COMPANY		
		GREAT AMERICAN BUILDING		
		600 "B" ST #1137	SAN DIEGO, CA	92101
STANLEY, RALPH & THE CLINCH MOU	C & W GROUP	380 LEXINGTON AVE #1119	NEW YORK, NY	10017
STANLEY, REBECCA	ACTRESS	10413 BLOOMFIELD ST	NORTH HOLLYWOOD, CA	91602
STANLEY, ROB	GUITARIST	POST OFFICE BOX 90813	NASHVILLE, TN	37209
STANNARD, NICK	ACTOR	484 W 43RD ST #30-A	NEW YORK, NY	10036
STANTON, HARRY DEAN	ACTOR	14527 MULHOLLAND DR	LOS ANGELES, CA	90077
STANTON, MARY	PIANIST	POST OFFICE BOX U	REDDING, CT	06875
STANTON, MICHAEL	GUITARIST	792 EDWARDS DR	FRANKLIN, TN	37064
STANTON, MOOK	SINGER	POST OFFICE BOX 1385	MERCHANTVILLE, NJ	08109
STANWYCK, BARBARA	ACTRESS	1055 LOMA VISTA DR	BEVERLY HILLS, CA	90210

Name	Occupation	Address	City	Zip
STANZA	ROCK & ROLL GROUP	VARIETY ARTISTS INTL, INC		
		9073 NEMO ST, 3RD FLOOR	LOS ANGELES, CA	90069
STAPLES, THE	GOSPEL-VOCAL GROUP	200 W 57TH ST #901	NEW YORK, NY	10019
STAPLETON, JEAN	ACTRESS	635 PERUGIA WY	LOS ANGELES, CA	90024
STAPLETON, MAUREEN	ACTRESS	15 W 70TH ST	NEW YORK, NY	10023
STAPLETON, WILLIAM J	COMPOSER	POST OFFICE BOX 1168-S-5105	STUDIO CITY, CA	91604
STAPP, GREGORY	BASS	CONE, 221 W 57TH ST	NEW YORK, NY	10019
STAPP, OLIVIA	SOPRANO	CAMI, 165 W 57TH ST	NEW YORK, NY	10019
STARBECKER, GENE	WRITER-PRODUCER	SLIGO CREEK PARKWAY	SILVER SPRING, MD	20901
STARCHER, BUDDY	GUITARIST	POST OFFICE BOX 57	CRAIGVILLE, WV	26225
STAREK, JIRI	CONDUCTOR	KAY, 58 W 58TH ST	NEW YORK, NY	10019
STARETSKI, JOSEPH	TV WRITER-PRODUCER	146 FRASER AVE	SANTA MONICA, CA	90405
STARGARDTER, ANN	NEWS CORRESPONDENT	1400 S JOYCE ST	ARLINGTON, VA	22202
STARGELL, WILLIE	BASEBALL	7232 THOMAS BLVD	PITTSBURGH, PA	15208
STARGER, MARTIN	FILM PRODUCER	21404 PACIFIC COAST HWY	MALIBU, CA	90265
STARIN, STEFANI	FLUTIST	AFFILIATE ARTISTS, INC		
		37 W 65TH ST, 6TH FLOOR	NEW YORK, NY	10023
STARK, CHARLES M	DIRECTOR	1212-D WESTLAKE BLVD	WESTLAKE VILLAGE, CA	91361
STARK, DON	ACTOR	8350 SANTA MONICA BLVD #103	LOS ANGELES, CA	90069
STARK, DOUGLAS	ACTOR	6290 SUNSET BLVD #326	LOS ANGELES, CA	90028
STARK, GRAHAM	ACTOR-DIRECTOR	53 ATHENAEUM RD	LONDON N20	ENGLAND
STARK, JOHN	WRITER-EDITOR	TIME & LIFE MAGAZINES		
		TIME & LIFE BUILDING		
		ROCKEFELLER CENTER	NEW YORK, NY	10020
STARK, NED	TV DIRECTOR	SNEDENS LANDING	PALISADES, NY	10964
STARK, RAY	FILM PRODUCER	232 S MAPLETON DR	LOS ANGELES, CA	90024
STARK, RONALD	DIRECTOR-PRODUCER	357 N SPRUCEWOOD AVE	AGOURA, CA	91301
STARK, SHELDON	WRITER	16401 AKRON ST	PACIFIC PALISADES, CA	90272
STARK, STEVE	CASTING DIRECTOR	8687 MELROSE AVE #M-20	LOS ANGELES, CA	90069
STARK, WILBUR	DIRECTOR-PRODUCER	3712 BAREDON BLVD #C-203	LOS ANGELES, CA	90068
STARKE, ROLAND	TV WRITER	8955 BEVERLY BLVD	LOS ANGELES, CA	90048
STARKER, GWEN A	VIOLINIST	2109 HERITAGE DR, NE	ATLANTA, GA	30345
STARKER, JANOS	CELLIST	COLBERT, 111 W 57TH ST	NEW YORK, NY	10019
STARKES, JAISON	SCREENWRITER	4077 S CLOVERDALE AVE	LOS ANGELES, CA	90008
STARKEY, RICHARD	GUITARIST	RURAL FARM DELIVERY #1		
		STEELE RD, BOX 349	NEW HARTFORD, CT	06057
STARKS, WILLIAM O	NEWS CORRESPONDENT	NBC-TV, NEWS DEPARTMENT		
		4001 NEBRASKA AVE, NW	WASHINGTON, DC	20016
STARLITE RAMBLERS	C & W GROUP	8119 WCR 48 1/2	JOHNSTOWN, CO	80534
STARPOINT	SOUL GROUP	POST OFFICE BOX 224	CROWNSVILLE, MD	21032
STARR, BARBARA	NEWS CORRESPONDENT	2500 WISCONSIN AVE #533, NW	WASHINGTON, DC	20007
STARR, BEAU	ACTOR	12725 VENTURA BLVD #E	STUDIO CITY, CA	91604
STARR, BEN	TV WRITER	1506 S BENTLEY AVE	LOS ANGELES, CA	90025
STARR, BILLY	GUITARIST	4 GORDON AVE	ROSSVILLE, GA	30741
STARR, DON	ACTOR	151 N SAN VICENTE BLVD #208	BEVERLY HILLS, CA	90211
STARR, EDWIN	SINGER	1680 N VINE ST #214	HOLLYWOOD, CA	90028
STARR, ELVIS	SINGER	POST OFFICE BOX 11276	ROCHESTER, NY	14611
STARR, ERROLL	SINGER	41 BRITAIN ST #200	TORONTO, ONT	CANADA
STARR, FREDDIE	ACTOR-COMEDIAN	CLIFFORD, 109 NEW BOND ST	LONDON W1	ENGLAND
STARR, JACK & BURNING STARR	ROCK & ROLL GROUP	POST OFFICE BOX 251	HUNTINGTON STATION, NY	11761
STARR, KAY	SINGER	223 ASHDALE PL	LOS ANGELES, CA	90069
STARR, KENNY	SINGER	POST OFFICE BOX 23470	NASHVILLE, TN	37202
STARR, LEONARD	CARTOONIST	TRIBUNE MEDIA SERVICES		
		64 E CONCORD ST	ORLANDO, FL	32801
STARR, MANYA	TV WRITER	555 W 57TH ST #1230	NEW YORK, NY	10019
STARR, MARK	CONDUCTOR	KAY, 58 W 58TH ST	NEW YORK, NY	10019
STARR, MAURICE	SINGER	POST OFFICE BOX 82	GREAT NECK, NY	11021
STARR, NADYA	ACTRESS	1015 BELLA VISTA AVE	PASADENA, CA	91107
STARR, PAUL	ACTOR	6533 HOLLYWOOD BLVD #201	HOLLYWOOD, CA	90028
STARR, RINGO	ACTOR-DRUMMER	TITTENHURST PARK, ASCOT	SURREY	ENGLAND
STARR, STEVEN	PHOTOGRAPHER	256 CARLISLE DR	MIAMI, FL	33166
STARR, SUSAN	PIANIST	1776 BROADWAY #504	NEW YORK, NY	10019
STARR, TONY	SINGER	POST OFFICE BOX 11276	ROCHESTER, NY	14611
STARRETT, AUDREY	TV DIRECTOR	76 MORTIMER CT, ABBEY RD	LONDON NW8	ENGLAND
STARRETT, JACK	ACT-WRI-DIR	STONE, 1052 CAROL DR	LOS ANGELES, CA	90069
STARRS, FRANKIE	GUITARIST	12834 N 29TH PL	PHOENIX, AZ	85032
STARSHIP, THE	ROCK & ROLL GROUP	STARSHIP INC, 1318 BRIDGEWAY	SAUSALITO, CA	94965
STARSHIP EAGLE	WRESTLER	SEE - SPIVEY, DANIEL		
		.... "GOLDEN BOY"		
START	ROCK & ROLL GROUP	GO NOW INC, 4108 BURBANK BLVD	BURBANK, CA	91505
STASIO, FRANK J, JR	NEWS CORRESPONDENT	3026 FENWICK RD	FALLS CHURCH, VA	22042
STASIO, JANETTA	SOPRANO	260 W END AVE #7-A	NEW YORK, NY	10023
STASIS, PATRICIA	SOPRANO	253 W 73RD ST #7-M	NEW YORK, NY	10023
STASIUNAS, CARL	TRUMPETER	672 LAKE TERR	NASHVILLE, TN	37217
STASKEL, JIM	ACTOR	1207 1/2 N CITRUS AVE	LOS ANGELES, CA	90038
STATE LINE BAND	C & W GROUP	POST OFFICE BOX 25371	CHARLOTTE, NC	28212
STATES, THE	ROCK & ROLL GROUP	POST OFFICE BOX 6231	NORFOLK, VA	23508
STATHIS, JIMMY	ACTOR	6380 WILSHIRE BLVD #1600	LOS ANGELES, CA	90048
STATHOPLOS, DEMMIE	SPORTS WRITER-EDITOR	SPORTS ILLUSTRATED MAGAZINE		
		TIME & LIFE BUILDING		
		ROCKEFELLER CENTER	NEW YORK, NY	10020
STATLER, ALEX	ACTOR	7466 BEVERLY BLVD #205	LOS ANGELES, CA	90036
STATLER, MARC T	DIRECTOR	9 CEDAR LANE TERR	OSSINING, NY	10562
STATLER BROTHERS, THE	VOCAL GROUP	POST OFFICE BOX 2703	STAUNTON, VA	24401
STATON, CANDI	SINGER	6 TERR CIR #2-A	GREAT NECK, NY	11021

THE STATLER BROTHERS
Harold • Jimmy • Don • Phil

TALKING HEADS
Chris Frantz • Jerry Harrison • Martina Weymouth • David Bryne

Name	Occupation	Address	City	ZIP / Country
STATUS QUO	ROCK & ROLL GROUP	HYDON GRANGE, HAMBLEDONE	SURREY	ENGLAND
STAUB, RUSTY	BASEBALL	1271 3RD AVE	NEW YORK, NY	10021
STAUBACH, ROGER	FOOTBALL	6750 L B JOHNSON FREEWAY #1100	DALLAS, TX	75240
STAUDIGL, HENRY	WRITER-PRODUCER	12909 HANOVER ST	LOS ANGELES, CA	90049
STAUFFER, JACK	ACTOR	4063 WOODCLIFF RD	SHERMAN OAKS, CA	91403
STAUGUS, JANE	CASTING DIRECTOR	4043 RADFORD AVE	STUDIO CITY, CA	91604
STAVEACRE, TONY	TV DIRECTOR-PRODUCER	CHANNEL VIEW BLAGDON	AVON	ENGLAND
STAVOLA, CHARLIE	ACTOR	12926 RIVERSIDE DR #C	SHERMAN OAKS, CA	91423
STAXX	ROCK & ROLL GROUP	POST OFFICE BOX 448	RADFORD, VA	24141
STAYSKAL, WAYNE	CARTOONIST	POST OFFICE BOX 191	TAMPA, FL	33601
STEAD, ARTHUR W	COMPOSER	69 S HAMILTON ST	POUGHKEEPSIE, NY	12601
STEADMAN, ALISON	ACTRESS	HORNE, 15 LITTLE NEWPORT ST	LONDON WC2	ENGLAND
STEADMAN, JOHN	ACTOR	8721 SUNSET BLVD #200	LOS ANGELES, CA	90069
STEAFEL, SHEILA	ACTRESS	CROUCH, 59 FRITH ST	LONDON W1	ENGLAND
STEAGALL, RED	SINGER	WILLIAMS-CIMINI AGENCY		
		816 N LA CIENEGA BLVD	LOS ANGELES, CA	90069
STEAKLEY, BARBARA	GUITARIST	1199 MURFREESBORO RD #K-6	NASHVILLE, TN	37217
STEAMBOAT, RICKY "THE DRAGON"	WRESTLER	POST OFFICE BOX 3859	STAMFORD, CT	06905
STEAMBOAT, SAMMY, JR	WRESTLER	SEE - STEAMBOAT, RICKY		
		"THE DRAGON"		
STEAMER, THE	WRESTLER	SEE - STEAMBOAT, RICKY		
		"THE DRAGON"		
STEARNS, DUNCAN	PIANIST	POST OFFICE BOX U	REDDING, CT	06875
STEARNS, JESSIE	NEWS CORRESPONDENT	100 5TH ST, SE	WASHINGTON, DC	20003
STEARNS, MICHAEL O	DIRECTOR	5871 CHABOT RD	OAKLAND, CA	94618
STEARNS, NEIL	LITERARY AGENCY	9300 WILSHIRE BLVD #410	BEVERLY HILLS, CA	90212
STEBBINS, DIANE	NEWS CORRESPONDENT	5500 FRIENDSHIP BLVD	CHEVY CHASE, MD	20815
STEBEL, SIDNEY L	WRITER	1963 MANDEVILLE CANYON RD	LOS ANGELES, CA	90049
STEBER, ELEANOR	SOPRANO	2109 BROADWAY	NEW YORK, NY	10023
STECHER & HOROWITZ	PIANO DUO	CAMI, 165 W 57TH ST	NEW YORK, NY	10019
STECK, HAZEL W	ACTRESS	58 SAINT MARKS PL	NEW YORK, NY	10003
STECKEL, NED	DIRECTOR	OGLEBAY PARK	WHEELING, WV	26003
STECKLER, DOUGLAS	ACTOR-WRITER	832 S NORTON AVE	LOS ANGELES, CA	90005
STECKLER, LEN	DIRECTOR	9530 HEATHER RD	BEVERLY HILLS, CA	90210
STECKLER, RALPH	DIRECTOR-PRODUCER	14159 DICKENS ST #308	SHERMAN OAKS, CA	91423
STEED, MAGGIE	ACTRESS	M MARTIN, 7 WINDMILL ST	LONDON W1	ENGLAND
STEEG, BRUCE	CONDUCTOR	6000 34TH AVE	HYATTSVILLE, MD	20782
STEEL, AMY	ACTRESS	10100 SANTA MONICA BLVD #1600	LOS ANGELES, CA	90067
STEEL, ROBERT	DIRECTOR	DGA, 110 W 57TH ST	NEW YORK, NY	10019
STEEL, TERRY	TV DIRECTOR	E WILLIAMS, 61 BECK ST	LONDON W1	ENGLAND
STEEL BREEZE	ROCK & ROLL GROUP	151 S EL CAMINO DR	BEVERLY HILLS, CA	90212
STEELE, BARBARA	ACTRESS	MONROE & ASSOCIATES		
		412 E 55TH ST	NEW YORK, NY	10022
STEELE, BILL	ACTOR	79 HORATIO ST	NEW YORK, NY	10014
STEELE, BOB	ACTOR	11524 MOORPARK ST	NORTH HOLLYWOOD, CA	91602
STEELE, CYNTHIA	ACTRESS	6736 LAUREL CANYON BLVD #306	NORTH HOLLYWOOD, CA	91606
STEELE, CYNTHIA K	NEWS CORRESPONDENT	2133 WISCONSIN AVE, NW	WASHINGTON, DC	20007
STEELE, GEORGE "THE ANIMAL"	WRESTLER	POST OFFICE BOX 3859	STAMFORD, CT	06905
STEELE, HAROLD K	NEWS CORRESPONDENT	4400 JENIFER ST, NW	WASHINGTON, DC	20015
STEELE, HAROLD M	NEWS CORRESPONDENT	4400 JENIFER ST, NW	WASHINGTON, DC	20015
STEELE, JADRIAN	ACTOR	JARRETT, 220 E 63RD ST	NEW YORK, NY	10021
STEELE, JON	COMPOSER	19481 ROSITA ST	TARZANA, CA	91356
STEELE, JON D	NEWS CORRESPONDENT	1705 DE SALES ST, NW	WASHINGTON, DC	20036
STEELE, KITTY	ACTRESS	319 AVE "C"	NEW YORK, NY	10009
STEELE, PHILIP	BASS	LIEBERMAN, 11 RIVERSIDE DR	NEW YORK, NY	10023
STEELE, SALLY	NEWS CORRESPONDENT	5004 JAMESTOWN RD	BETHESDA, MD	20816
STEELE, SAUNDRA	SINGER	PICALIC, 1204 16TH AVE S	NASHVILLE, TN	37212
STEELE, TOMMY	ACTOR-SINGER	TALENTS ARTISTS		
		37 HILL ST	LONDON W1X 8JY	ENGLAND
STEELEYE SPAN	ROCK & ROLL GROUP	ALLIED AGENCY & MANAGEMENT		
		76 TOTTENHAM CT RD	LONDON W10 9PA	ENGLAND
STEELSMITH, MARY	ACTRESS	5122 W 9TH ST	LOS ANGELES, CA	90036
STEEN, LINDA E	NEWS CORRESPONDENT	1508 21ST ST #4, NW	WASHINGTON, DC	20036
STEEN, NANCY	ACTRESS-WRITER	5127 GREENBUSH AVE	SHERMAN OAKS, CA	91423
STEENBURGEN, MARY	ACTRESS	ICM, 8899 BEVERLY BLVD	LOS ANGELES, CA	90048
STEENERSON, ROBERT	DIRECTOR	6025 W 86TH PL	LOS ANGELES, CA	90045
STEENSLAND, MELANIE	DIRECTOR	3952 BORA BORA WY	MARINA DEL REY, CA	90292
STEERE, CLIFTON	ACTOR	305 W 45TH ST	NEW YORK, NY	10036
STEFANO, JOE	ACTOR	4789 VINELAND AVE #100	NORTH HOLLYWOOD, CA	91602
STEFANO, JOHN	ACTOR	135 N KENWOOD ST	BURBANK, CA	91505
STEFANO, JOHN	SCREENWRITER	8721 SUNSET BLVD #202	LOS ANGELES, CA	90069
STEFANO, JOSEPH	WRITER-PRODUCER	10216 CIELO DR	BEVERLY HILLS, CA	90210
STEFFE, EDWIN	ACTOR	145 W 55TH ST	NEW YORK, NY	10019
STEFFEN, DON CARL	PHOTOGRAPHER	12806 GAFFNEY RD	SILVER SPRING, MD	20904
STEGALL, KEITH	GUITARIST	113 DEER RD	SMYRNA, TN	37167
STEGERS, BERNICE	ACTOR	30 CANFELOWES RD	LONDON NW1	ENGLAND
STEGNER, PHILLIP G	PIANIST	813 AIRWAYS CIR #M	NASHVILLE, TN	37214
STEHNEY, MICHAEL	DIRECTOR	25051 COSTEAU	LAGUNA HILLS, CA	92653
STEHR, HERBERT	NEWS CORRESPONDENT	3132 "M" ST, NW	WASHINGTON, DC	20007
STEIBEL, WARREN	DIRECTOR-PRODUCER	150 E 35TH ST	NEW YORK, NY	10022
STEIGELMAN, DAVID EARL	PHOTOGRAPHER	1145 W CAMINO REAL	BOCA RATON, FL	33432
STEIGER, JOEL	TV WRITER-PROUCER	ICM, 8899 BEVERLY BLVD	LOS ANGELES, CA	90048
STEIGER, ROD	ACTOR	23822 MALIBU COLONY RD	MALIBU, CA	90265
STEIN, ABBEY	COMEDIENNE	EAI, 2211 INDUSTRIAL BLVD	SARASOTA, FL	33580
STEIN, ARTHUR	PHOTOGRAPHER	1845 MAC ARTHUR DR	MC LEAN, VA	22101

The Stellar Unit

ON THE STAIRWAY TO STARDOM

THEIR UNIQUE SOUND IS REMINISCENT OF THE MANHATTAN TRANSFER, THE FOUR FRESHMEN, THE PIED PIPERS, BUT IS ALL *STELLAR*.

Webster's dictionary defines...STELLAR as...*"most important of, or pertaining to the stars."* **This quartet, each an accomplished singer and musician on multiple instruments, has put together shows that sound as if ten people were playing. Their variety in music spans Dixieland, Jazz, Country, Blues, Top 40, Rock and Roll, and Nostalgia of the '40s, '50s and '60s.**

So give yourself a treat...don't look to the heavens, just look here in Las Vegas to THE STELLAR UNIT.

Managed By
PERSONALITY PRODUCTIONS, INC.
P. O. Box 39, Las Vegas, NV 89125
(702) 648-3515

Name	Occupation	Address	City, State	Zip
STEIN, BENJAMIN	WRITER	7251 PACIFIC VIEW DR	LOS ANGELES, CA	90068
STEIN, DANIEL	MIME	AFFILIATE ARTISTS, INC		
		37 W 65TH ST, 6TH FLOOR	NEW YOEK, NY	10023
STEIN, HERBERT D	TV DIRECTOR	4233 GLENALBYN DR	LOS ANGELES, CA	90065
STEIN, HERMAN	COMPOSER	3787 AMESBURY RD	LOS ANGELES, CA	90027
STEIN, HORST	CONDUCTOR	MARIEDL ANDERS ARTISTS MGMT		
		535 EL CAMINO DEL MAR ST	SAN FRANCISCO, CA	94121
STEIN, JAMES RONALD	WRITER-PRODUCER	2765 BOTTLEBRUSH DR	LOS ANGELES, CA	90024
STEIN, JEFFREY A	FILM WRITER-PRODUCER	2870 BENEDICT CANYON DR	BEVERLY HILLS, CA	90210
STEIN, JEFFREY L	SCREENWRITER	8955 BEVERLY BLVD	LOS ANGELES, CA	90048
STEIN, JOSEPH	PLAYWRIGHT	1130 PARK AVE	NEW YORK, NY	10028
STEIN, KERRY	ACTOR	3124 YALE AVE	VENICE, CA	90291
STEIN, LEONARD D	COMPOSER	2635 CARMEN CREST DR	LOS ANGELES, CA	90068
STEIN, LISA A	NEWS CORRESPONDENT	216 3RD ST, SE	WASHINGTON, DC	20003
STEIN, MAX	TV DIRECTOR	5307 WILKINSON AVE #6	NORTH HOLLYWOOD, CA	91607
STEIN, NICHOLAS A	TV DIRECTOR-PRODUCER	2426 HOLLYRIDGE DR	HOLLYWOOD, CA	90068
STEIN, NORMAN	PHOTOGRAPHER	8437 JANDY AVE	LAUREL, MD	20707
STEIN, NORMAN S	NEWS CORRESPONDENT	CBS NEWS, 2020 "M" ST, NW	WASHINGTON, DC	20036
STEIN, ROBERT M	TV DIRECTOR	2546 GLEN GREEN ST	LOS ANGELES, CA	90068
STEIN, RON	FILM DIRECTOR	3518 W CAHUENGA BLVD	HOLLYWOOD, CA	90068
STEIN, RONALD	COMPOSER-CONDUCTOR	POST OFFICE BOX 2037	EVERGREEN, CO	80439
STEIN, SAM	ACTOR	8322 BEVERLY BLVD #202	LOS ANGELES, CA	90048
STEIN, SEYMOUR	RECORD EXECUTIVE	SIRE RECORDS COMPANY		
		75 ROCKEFELLER PLAZA	NEW YORK, NY	10019
STEIN, STEPHEN	CONDUCTOR	AFFILIATE ARTISTS, INC		
		37 W 65TH ST, 6TH FLOOR	NEW YORK, NY	10023
STEINBAUER, MARY YOUATT	EDITOR-PUBLISHER	LIFE/TIME & LIFE BLDG		
		ROCKEFELLER CENTER	NEW YORK, NY	10020
STEINBERG, ALBERT	CONDUCTOR	11918 KIOWA AVE #301	LOS ANGELES, CA	90049
STEINBERG, ANNE "HONEY"	SINGER	POST OFFICE BOX 11321		
		FLAGLER STATION	MIAMI, FL	33101
STEINBERG, BARRY	FILM DIRECTOR	3819 SEAHORN DR	MALIBU, CA	90265
STEINBERG, DAVID	COMED-ACT-WRI-DIR	4539 GLORIA AVE	ENCINO, CA	91346
STEINBERG, DAVID L	PHOTOJOURNALIST	3925 GARRISON ST, NW	WASHINGTON, DC	20016
STEINBERG, HARRIET	SCREENWRITER	555 W 57TH ST #1230	NEW YORK, NY	10019
STEINBERG, JEFFREY E	MUSIC ARRANGER	POST OFFICE BOX 121464	NASHVILLE, TN	37212
STEINBERG, LENORE J	DESIGNER	1802 ANGELO DR	BEVERLY HILLS, CA	90210
STEINBERG, MELISSA	ACTRESS	9220 SUNSET BLVD #625	LOS ANGELES, CA	90069
STEINBERG, NORMAN	WRITER-PRODUCER	2800 SEATTLE DR	LOS ANGELES, CA	90046
STEINBERG, PINCHAS	CONDUCTOR	61 W 62ND ST #6-F	NEW YORK, NY	10023
STEINBERG, ROY	ACTOR	45 CARMINE ST #4-B	NEW YORK, NY	10014
STEINBERG, SARI	TV DIRECTOR	2517 MAPLE AVE	MANHATTAN BEACH, CA	90266
STEINBERG, STEVEN J	WRITER-PRODUCER	POST OFFICE BOX 373	NEW YORK, NY	11374
STEINBERG, ZIGGY	TV WRITER	2038 BENEDICT CANYON DR	BEVERLY HILLS, CA	90210
STEINBERGER, BERT	TV EXECUTIVE	5460 WHITE OAK AVE #E-132	ENCINO, CA	91316
STEINEM, GLORIA	AUTHORESS	119 W 40TH ST	NEW YORK, NY	10018
STEINER, ARMIN	RECORDING ENGINEER	ERS, 4403 W MAGNOLIA BLVD	BURBANK, CA	91505
STEINER, BILL	WRESTLER	UNIVERSAL WRESTLING FEDERATION		
		MID SOUTH SPORTS, INC		
		5001 SPRING VALLEY RD	DALLAS, TX	75244
STEINER, EARL J	PHOTOGRAPHER	9708 MARSHALL AVE	SILVER SPRING, MD	20901
STEINER, FREDERICK	COMPOSER-CONDUCTOR	4455 GABLE DR	ENCINO, CA	91316
STEINER, GAIL	SOPRANO	225 W 34TH ST #1012	NEW YORK, NY	10001
STEINER, GEORGE	CONDUCTOR	POST OFFICE BOX 131	SPRINGFIELD, VA	22150
STEINER, GEORGE	WRITER	CHURCHHILL COLLEGE	CAMBRIDGE	ENGLAND
STEINER, GITTA	COMPOSER-PIANIST	71-81 244TH ST	DOUGLASTON, NY	11362
STEINER, OLIVER	VIOLINIST	POST OFFICE BOX U	REDDING, CT	06875
STEINER, PETER	CARTOONIST	POST OFFICE BOX 4203	NEW YORK, NY	10017
STEINER, RICK	WRESTLER	UNIVERSAL WRESTLING FEDERATION		
		MID SOUTH SPORTS, INC		
		5001 SPRING VALLEY RD	DALLAS, TX	75244
STEINFELD, JAKE	ACTOR-BODYBUILDER	LIGHT, 113 N ROBERTSON BLVD	LOS ANGELES, CA	90048
STEINHAUER, ROBERT BENNETT	TV WRITER-PRODUCER	8955 BEVERLY BLVD	LOS ANGELES, CA	90048
STEINHAUSER, BERT	DIRECTOR	126 E 36TH ST	NEW YORK, NY	10016
STEINKE, DR GREG	COMPOSER-CONDUCTOR	UNIVERSITY OF IDAHO		
		SCHOOL OF MUSIC	MOSCOW, ID	83843
STEINKE, MICHAEL	WRESTLING WRITER	POST OFFICE BOX 48	ROCKVILLE CENTRE, NY	11571
STEINMETZ, DENNIS	TV DIRECTOR	10546 DEERING AVE	CHATSWORTH, CA	91311
STEINMETZ, JOHN	DIRECTOR	315 W 70TH ST	NEW YORK, NY	10023
STEIS, BILL	ACTOR	2943 ESCONDIDO DR	MALIBU, CA	90265
STELFOX, SHIRLEY	ACTRESS	AIM, 142 CROMWELL RD	LONDON SW7 4EF	ENGLAND
STELLAR UNIT	VOCAL GROUP	POST OFFICE BOX 39	LAS VEGAS, NV	89125
STELLMAN, MARTIN	SCREENWRITER	SEIFERT, 8-A BRUNSWICK GARDENS	LONDON W8	ENGLAND
STEMBER, SOL	WRITER	14938 LEADWELL ST	VAN NUYS, CA	91405
STEMLER, DAVID	NEWS CORRESPONDENT	12008 AINTREE LN	RESTON, VA	22091
STEMPLEMAN, NEIL	NEWS CORRESPONDENT	1931 N CLEVELAND ST #607	ARLINGTON, VA	22201
STENBORG, HELEN	ACTRESS	165 W 46TH ST #710	NEW YORK, NY	10036
STENCEL, SANDRA	NEWS CORRESPONDENT	12130 QUORN LN	RESTON, VA	22091
STENDER, ERNST-ERICH	ORGANIST	15 HIGH ST #621	HARTFORD, CT	06103
STENGEL, RICHARD	WRITER-EDITOR	TIME/TIME & LIFE BLDG		
		ROCKEFELLER CENTER	NEW YORK, NY	10020
STENGER, FRED	FILM DIRECTOR	651-A QUEEN ST	TORONTO ONT M5V 1V3	CANADA
STENNETT, STAN	ACTOR-COMEDIAN	BARTRAM, 266 BROAD ST	BIRMINGHAM B1 2DS	ENGLAND

TOMMY STEELE

ROD STEIGER

LINDA STERLING

CAT STEVENS

RAY STEVENS

SHAKIN STEVENS

STELLA STEVENS

PARKER STEVENSON

AL STEWART

Name	Occupation	Address	City	Zip
STENSTROM, ODDVAR	NEWS CORRESPONDENT	1173 FOXHOUND CT	MC LEAN, VA	22102
STEPHANS, PAUL	GUITARIST	502 DOROTHY DR	GOODLETTSVILLE, TN	37072
STEPHANY, JAMES	GUITARIST	1150 VULTEE BLVD #G-4	NASHVILLE, TN	37217
STEPHEN, BEVERLY	COLUMNIST	N Y CITY DAILY NEWS		
		229 W 43RD ST	NEW YORK, NY	10036
STEPHENS, ANDREW R	NEWS CORRESPONDENT	1837 CALIFORNIA ST, NW	WASHINGTON, DC	20009
STEPHENS, GARN	ACTRESS	4538 WORSTER AVE	STUDIO CITY, CA	91604
STEPHENS, GARN	TV WRITER	8955 BEVERLY BLVD	LOS ANGELES, CA	90048
STEPHENS, JAMES	ACTOR-DIRCTOR	2121 AVE OF THE STARS #410	LOS ANGELES, CA	90067
STEPHENS, JAMES E, JR	GUITARIST	2841 EMERY DR	NASHVILLE, TN	37214
STEPHENS, JAMES N	ACTOR	1033 LAS PULGAS RD	PACIFIC PALISADES, CA	90272
STEPHENS, JOHN	BASSO-BARITONE	MUNRO, 334 W 72ND ST	NEW YORK, NY	10023
STEPHENS, JOHN	PRODUCER	MCA/UNIVERSAL STUDIOS, INC		
		100 UNIVERSAL CITY PLAZA #473	UNIVERSAL CITY, CA	91608
STEPHENS, JOHN D	COMPOSER	11782 GAGER ST	SYLMAR, CA	91342
STEPHENS, JOHN G	DIRECTOR	9300 WILSHIRE BLVD #410	BEVERLY HILLS, CA	90212
STEPHENS, JOHN M	DIRECTOR	10950 VENTURA BLVD	STUDIO CITY, CA	91604
STEPHENS, JOHN M	TV DIRECTOR	6744 HILLPARK DR	LOS ANGELES, CA	90068
STEPHENS, LARAINE	ACTRESS	GERBER, 10800 CHALON RD	LOS ANGELES, CA	90077
STEPHENS, LARRY	WRESTLER	NATIONAL WRESTLING ALLIANCE		
		JIM CROCKETT PROMOTIONS		
		421 BRIARBEND DR	CHARLOTTE, NC	28209
STEPHENS, LEWIS WARD	GUITARIST	816 MEADOWPARK DR	FORT WORTH, TX	76108
STEPHENS, MARTHA J	NEWS CORRESPONDENT	1073 CEDAR RIDGE CT	ANNAPOLIS, MD	21403
STEPHENS, PERRY	ACTOR	ABC-TV NETWORK, "LOVING"		
		1330 AVE OF THE AMERICAS	NEW YORK, NY	10019
STEPHENS, ROBERT	ACTOR	FILM RIGHTS, 113 WARDOUR ST	LONDON W1	ENGLAND
STEPHENS, SPENCER KEITH	NEWS CORRESPONDENT	5113 ALLAN TERR	BETHESDA, MD	20816
STEPHENSON, AL	PHOTOGRAPHER	1239 KENSINGTON RD	MC LEAN, VA	22101
STEPHENSON, JOHN	ACTOR	121 N ROBERTSON BLVD #B	BEVERLY HILLS, CA	90211
STEPHENSON, LARRY	MUSICIAN	1302 SAUNDERS AVE	MADISON, TN	37115
STEPHENSON, MALVINA	NEWS CORRESPONDENT	2111 JEFFERSON DAVIS HWY #203-S	ARLINGTON, VA	22202
STEPHENSON, MARGOT	ACTRESS	AVERY, 84 GROVE ST #19	NEW YORK, NY	10014
STEPHENSON, PAMELA	ACTRESS	1888 CENTURY PARK E #1400	LOS ANGELES, CA	90067
STEPHENSON, RON	CASTING DIRECTOR	MCA/UNIVERSAL STUDIOS, INC		
		100 UNIVERSAL CITY PLAZA		
		BUILDING #463-106	UNIVERSAL CITY, CA	91608
STEPHENSON, SKIP	COMEDIAN-ACTOR	3920 SUNNY OAK RD	SHERMAN OAKS, CA	91403
STEPIEN, CHRISTOPHER L	TV DIRECTOR-PRODUCER	6540 JONATHON ST	DEARBORN, MI	48126
STEPNER, DANIEL	VIOLINIST	AARON, 25 HUNTINGTON AVE	BOSTON, MA	02116
STEPPE BROTHERS, THE	C & W GROUP	BURCHAN, 129 TOBLER LN	KNOXVILLE, TN	37919
STEPS AHEAD	JAZZ GROUP	1501 BORADWAY #1506	NEW YORK, NY	10036
STERLING	SOUL-DISCO GROUP	LUTZ, 5625 "O" STREET BLDG	LINCOLN, NE	68510
STERLING, BRIAN	FIDDLER	3233 TOWNE VILLAGE RD	ANTIOCH, TN	37013
STERLING, DAVID-MICHAEL	ACTOR	4966 FRANKLIN AVE #1	LOS ANGELES, CA	90027
STERLING, MINDY	ACTRESS	8484 WILSHIRE BLVD #235	BEVERLY HILLS, CA	90211
STERLING, PHILIP	ACTOR	4114 BENEDICT CANYON DR	SHERMAN OAKS, CA	91423
STERLING, ROBERT	ACTOR	121 S BENTLEY AVE	LOS ANGELES, CA	90049
STERLING, RONNIE	COMEDIAN	CEE, 193 KONHAUS RD	MECHANICSBURG, PA	17055
STERLING, TISHA	ACTRESS	POST OFFICE BOX 903	TOPANGA, CA	90290
STERLING, WILLIAM	DIRECTOR-PRODUCER	9 HILLCREST		
		51-57 LADBROKE GROVE	LONDON W11	ENGLAND
STERN, BARRY	DIRECTOR-PRODUCER	8744 SKYLINE DR	LOS ANGELES, CA	90046
STERN, CARL	NEWS CORRESPONDENT	2956 DAVENPORT ST, NW	WASHINGTON, DC	20008
STERN, DANIEL	CONDUCTOR	GERSHUNOFF, 502 PARK AVE	NEW YORK, NY	10022
STERN, DAVID	DIRECTOR	ASSOCIATES & TOBACK		
		6532 SUNSET BLVD	HOLLYWOOD, CA	90028
STERN, DAVID B	TV DIRECTOR-PRODUCER	POST OFFICE BOX 10210	STAMFORD, CT	06904
STERN, DONALD H	DIRECTOR	11582 LONGACRE RD	GRANADA HILLS, CA	91344
STERN, ELLIOT	TV WRITER	3021 1/2 LAUREL CANYON BLVD	STUDIO CITY, CA	91604
STERN, ELLYN	ACTRESS	8721 SUNSET BLVD #103	LOS ANGELES, CA	90069
STERN, ERIK	ACTOR	337 N CRESCENT HGTS BLVD	LOS ANGELES, CA	90048
STERN, HENRY	TV WRITER	8955 BEVERLY BLVD	LOS ANGELES, CA	90048
STERN, HENRY M	TV WRITER	8955 BEVERLY BLVD	LOS ANGELES, CA	90048
STERN, ISAAC	VIOLINIST	211 CENTRAL PARK W	NEW YORK, NY	10024
STERN, JOHN L	TV WRITER	8955 BEVERLY BLVD	LOS ANGELES, CA	90048
STERN, LEONARD	WRITER-PRODUCER	1709 ANGELO DR	BEVERLY HILLS, CA	90210
STERN, LINDA S	NEWS CORRESPONDENT	14 HICKORY AVE	TAKOMA PARK, MD	20912
STERN, MARCUS A	NEWS CORRESPONDENT	1706 21ST ST, NW	WASHINGTON, DC	20009
STERN, PEGGY	MUSICIAN	POST OFFICE BOX 9388	STANFORD, CA	94305
STERN, PETER R	DIRECTOR	DGA, 110 W 57TH ST	NEW YORK, NY	10019
STERN, RICHARD A	DIRECTOR	DGA, 7950 SUNSET BLVD	LOS ANGELES, CA	90046
STERN, SANDOR	WRITER-PRODUCER	474 PECK DR	BEVERLY HILLS, CA	90212
STERN, STEVEN HILLIARD	WRITER-PRODUCER	4321 CLEAR VALLEY DR	ENCINO, CA	91436
STERN, STEWART	WRITER	1851 MANDEVILLE CANYON RD	LOS ANGELES, CA	90049
STERNBERG, JONATHAN	CONDUCTOR	POST OFFICE BOX U	REDDING, CT	06875
STERNBERG, KEN	NEWS CORRESPONDENT	807 N LINCOLN ST	ARLINGTON, VA	22201
STERNBERG, SCOTT	TV WRITER-PRODUCER	15030 MARBLE DR	SHERMAN OAKS, CA	91403
STERNBERG, WILLIAM	NEWS CORRESPONDENT	13 MARCUS CT	ROCKVILLE, MD	20850
STERNHAGEN, FRANCES	ACTRESS	10100 SANTA MONICA BLVD #1600	LOS ANGELES, CA	90067
STERNIG, BARBARA	NEWS REPORTER	THE NATIONAL ENQUIRER		
		600 SE COAST AVE	LANTANA, FL	33464
STERNIN, ROBERT	TV WRITER	6538 COSTELLO AVE	VAN NUYS, CA	91401
STERRITT, DORREESE	ACTRESS	10850 RIVERSIDE DR #505	NORTH HOLLYWOOD, CA	91602
STERTEN, BRUCE M	WRITER	1143 HIGHLAND AVE	MANHATTAN BEACH, CA	90266

Name	Occupation	Address	City	ZIP
STERTZ, MARC H	NEWS CORRESPONDENT	6013 MELVERN DR	BETHESDA, MD	20817
STETTIN, MONTE DAVID	TV WRITER	1231 9TH ST #4	SANTA MONICA, CA	90401
STEUART, ELIZABETH	NEWS CORRESPONDENT	2605 39TH ST, NW	WASHINGTON, DC	20007
STEUERMAN, JEAN-LOUIS	PIANIST	LEISER, DORCHESTER TOWERS		
		155 W 68TH ST	NEW YORK, NY	10023
STEVE, JAIME C	NEWS CORRESPONDENT	1862 PARK RD, NW	WASHINGTON, DC	20010
STEVENS, ANDREW	ACTOR	2049 CENTURY PARK E #3700	LOS ANGELES, CA	90067
STEVENS, APRIL	SINGER	19530 SUPERIOR ST	NORTHRIDGE, CA	91324
STEVENS, ART	DIRECTOR	500 S BUENA VISTA ST	BURBANK, CA	91521
STEVENS, BOB	WRITER	8428 MELROSE PL #C	LOS ANGELES, CA	90069
STEVENS, BRENT	TV WRITER	8955 BEVERLY BLVD	LOS ANGELES, CA	90048
STEVENS, BRINKE	ACTRESS-MODEL	8033 SUNSET BLVD #557	LOS ANGELES, CA	90046
STEVENS, CAT	SINGER-SONGWRITER	SEE - ISLAM, YUSUF		
STEVENS, CLARK	ACTOR	8721 SUNSET BLVD #200	LOS ANGELES, CA	90069
STEVENS, CONNIE	ACTRESS-SINGER	243 DELFERN DR	LOS ANGELES, CA	90077
STEVENS, CRAIG	ACTOR	1308 N FLORES ST	LOS ANGELES, CA	90069
STEVENS, DANIEL R	WRITER	O'CONNOR, 4654 BECK AVE	STUDIO CITY, CA	91602
STEVENS, DORIT	MODEL-ACTRESS	11524 AMANDA DR	STUDIO CITY, CA	91604
STEVENS, DUNCAN	NEWS CORRESPONDENT	2002 ERIE ST	ADELPHI, MD	20783
STEVENS, EDMOND MICHAEL	SCREENWRITER	6924 OAKWOOD AVE	LOS ANGELES, CA	90036
STEVENS, EVEN	GUITARIST	POST OFFICE BOX 140110	NASHVILLE, TN	37214
STEVENS, FRAN	ACTRESS	209 W 80TH ST	NEW YORK, NY	10024
STEVENS, GEORGE, JR	DIRECTOR-PRODUCER	THE AMERICAN FILM INSTITUTE		
		JOHN F KENNEDY CENTER	WASHINGTON, DC	20566
STEVENS, HERB	ACTOR	10845 LINDBROOK DR #3	LOS ANGELES, CA	90024
STEVENS, JEAN	SINGER-ACTRESS	8467 BEVERLY BLVD #100	LOS ANGELES, CA	90048
STEVENS, JEREMY	SCREENWRITER	613 EL MEDIO AVE	PACIFIC PALISADES, CA	90272
STEVENS, K T	ACTRESS	147 GRETNA GREEN WY	LOS ANGELES, CA	90069
STEVENS, LARRY	WRESTLER	NATIONAL WRESTLING ALLIANCE		
		JIM CROCKETT PROMOTIONS		
		421 BRIARBEND DR	CHARLOTTE, NC	28209
STEVENS, LEE	TALENT AGENT	151 S EL CAMINO DR	BEVERLY HILLS, CA	90212
STEVENS, LEIGH HOWARD	MARIMBIST	MARIMBA, 487 W END AVE	NEW YORK, NY	10024
STEVENS, LEON B	ACTOR	175 W 93RD ST	NEW YORK, NY	10025
STEVENS, MARK	ACTOR	1901 AVE OF THE STARS #840	LOS ANGELES, CA	90067
STEVENS, MAURICE W	DIRECTOR	37 SAINT SINIFREDS RD		
		TEDDINGTON	MIDDLESEX TW11 9JS	ENGLAND
STEVENS, MICK	CARTOONIST	POST OFFICE BOX 4203	NEW YORK, NY	10017
STEVENS, MORGAN	ACTOR	9220 SUNSET BLVD #202	LOS ANGELES, CA	90069
STEVENS, MORTON	COMPOSER	315 S BEVERLY DR #50	BEVERLY HILLS, CA	90212
STEVENS, NAOMI	ACTRESS	8721 SUNSET BLVD #200	LOS ANGELES, CA	90069
STEVENS, NICO	ACTOR	1605 N CAHUENGA BLVD #202	LOS ANGELES, CA	90028
STEVENS, PAT	ACTRESS	15010 VENTURA BLVD #219	SHERMAN OAKS, CA	91403
STEVENS, RAY	SINGER-SONGWRITER	1708 GRAND AVE	NASHVILLE, TN	37212
STEVENS, RAY "THE CRIPPLER"	WRESTLER	AMERICAN WRESTLING ASSOC		
		MINNEAPLOIS WRESTLING		
		10001 WAYZATA BLVD	MINNETONKA, MN	55345
STEVENS, RISE	MEZZO-SOPRANO	157 E 74TH ST	NEW YORK, NY	10021
STEVENS, ROBERT	DIRECTOR	DGA, 110 W 57TH ST	NEW YORK, NY	10019
STEVENS, ROBERT L	GUITARIST	3122 BOULDER PARK DR	NASHVILLE, TN	37214
STEVENS, ROGER L	THEATER PRODUCER	1501 BROADWAY	NEW YORK, NY	10036
STEVENS, RON	ACTOR-COMEDIAN	9665 WILSHIRE BLVD #400	BEVERLY HILLS, CA	90212
STEVENS, RONNIE	ACTOR	LARRY DALZELL ASSOCIATES		
		126 KENNINGTON PARK RD	LONDON SE11 4DJ	ENGLAND
STEVENS, SCOOTER	ACTOR	12725 VENTURA BLVD #E	STUDIO CITY, CA	91604
STEVENS, SHADOE	RADIO-TV PERS	9100 SUNSET BLVD #113	LOS ANGELES, CA	90069
STEVENS, SHAKIN'	SINGER	158 CAMDEN RD	LONDON NW1	ENGLAND
STEVENS, SHAWN	ACTOR	10055 RIVERSIDE DR	TOLUCA LAKE, CA	91602
STEVENS, STELLA	ACTRESS	POST OFFICE BOX 133	TWISP, WA	98856
STEVENS, WADE	TV WRITER	8955 BEVERLY BLVD	LOS ANGELES, CA	90048
STEVENS, WARREN	ACTOR	14324 KILLION ST	VAN NUYS, CA	91401
STEVENS, WESLEY	ACTRESS	5967 W 3RD ST #205	LOS ANGELES, CA	90036
STEVENS & GRDNIC	COMEDY DUO	2029 CENTURY PARK E #1670	LOS ANGELES, CA	90067
STEVENSON, B W	SINGER	NBA, 8517 SHAGROCK LN	DALLAS, TX	75238
STEVENSON, BOBBI	ACTRESS	10845 LINDBROOK DR #3	LOS ANGELES, CA	90024
STEVENSON, CHARLES C	ACTOR	6640 SUNSET BLVD #203	LOS ANGELES, CA	90028
STEVENSON, DELCINA	SOPRANO	POST OFFICE BOX 884	NEW YORK, NY	10023
STEVENSON, DOUGIE	RECORD EXECUTIVE	BGS PRODS, NEWTOWN ST		
		KILSYTH	GLASGOW G65 OJX	SCOTLAND
STEVENSON, DOUGLAS	ACTOR	151 S EL CAMINO DR	BEVERLY HILLS, CA	90212
STEVENSON, DOUGLAS	NEWS CORRESPONDENT	2022 37TH ST, NW	WASHINGTON, DC	20007
STEVENSON, DOUGLAS C	ACTOR	8350 SANTA MONICA BLVD #206	LOS ANGELES, CA	90069
STEVENSON, GUY	GUITARIST	ROUTE #2	PIEDMONT, MO	63957
STEVENSON, JEFF	ACTOR	MILLION DOLLAR MUSIC		
		12 PRAED MEWS	LONDON W2 1QY	ENGLAND
STEVENSON, JOY	TALENT AGENT	12725 VENTURA BLVD #E	STUDIO CITY, CA	91604
STEVENSON, MARGOT	ACTRESS	84 GROVE ST	NEW YORK, NY	10014
STEVENSON, MC LEAN	ACTOR-WRITER	POST OFFICE BOX 1668	STUDIO CITY, CA	91604
STEVENSON, PARKER	ACTOR	3715 AVENIDA DEL SOL	STUDIO CITY, CA	91604
STEVENSON, PHYLLIS M	NEWS CORRESPONDENT	1131 UNIVERSITY BLVD	WEST SILVER SPRING, MD	20902
STEVENSON, SCOTT MC KAY	ACTOR	2339 34TH ST #3	SANTA MONICA, CA	90405
STEVENSONS, THE	MUSIC GROUP	4728 W BROWN ST	GLENDALE, AZ	85302
STEVLINGSON, EDWARD	ACTOR	484 W 43RD ST #43-Q	NEW YORK, NY	10036

Name	Occupation	Address	City	Zip
STEWART, ALANA	ACTRESS	151 S EL CAMINO DR	BEVERLY HILLS, CA	90212
STEWART, ANNA	WRITER-EDITOR	LIFE/TIME & LIFE BLDG		
		ROCKEFELLER CENTER	NEW YORK, NY	10020
STEWART, ANNE RANDALL	ACTRESS-MODEL	SEE - RANDALL, ANNE		
STEWART, BENJAMIN	ACTOR	9300 WILSHIRE BLVD #410	BEVERLY HILLS, CA	90212
STEWART, BRUCE	DRUMMER	1509 17TH AVE S	NASHVILLE, TN	37212
STEWART, BRUCE	TV WRITER	UNNA & DURBRIDGE, LTD		
		24-32 POTTERY LN		
		HOLLAND PARK	LONDON W11	ENGLAND
STEWART, CATHERINE MARY	ACTRESS	9229 SUNSET BLVD #306	LOS ANGELES, CA	90069
STEWART, CHARLES	ACTOR	1418 N HIGHLAND AVE #102	LOS ANGELES, CA	90028
STEWART, CHARLES N, JR	TV WRITER	8955 BEVERLY BLVD	LOS ANGELES, CA	90048
STEWART, CHARLES N, SR	TV WRITER	8955 BEVERLY BLVD	LOS ANGELES, CA	90048
STEWART, CHUCK	SINGER	HOT, 306 W CHURCH ST	HORSESHOE BEND, AR	72512
STEWART, DALE	DIRECTOR	DCA PRODS, 285 MADISON AVE	NEW YORK, NY	10017
STEWART, DAVID	TALENT AGENT	1888 CENTURY PARK E #622	LOS ANGELES, CA	90067
STEWART, DEAN	ACTOR	8721 SUNSET BLVD #200	LOS ANGELES, CA	90069
STEWART, DENNIS	ACTOR	113 N ROBERTSON BLVD	LOS ANGELES, CA	90048
STEWART, DEREK	DIRECTOR-PRODUCER	15 BEACONSFIELD RD	LONDON NW10 2LE	ENGLAND
STEWART, DICK	ACTOR	3151 W CAHUENGA BLVD #310	LOS ANGELES, CA	90068
STEWART, DON	ACTOR	9255 SUNSET BLVD #603	LOS ANGELES, CA	90069
STEWART, DONALD E	DIRECTOR	151 S EL CAMINO DR	BEVERLY HILLS, CA	90212
STEWART, DONALD E	WRITER	6430 SUNSET BLVD #1203	LOS ANGELES, CA	90028
STEWART, DONALD L	SCREENWRITER	2500 4TH ST #5	SANTA MONICA, CA	90405
STEWART, DOUGLAS DAY	SCREENWRITER	8955 BEVERLY BLVD	LOS ANGELES, CA	90048
STEWART, DOUGLAS S	DIRECTOR	14150 HARTSOOK ST	SHERMAN OAKS, CA	91423
STEWART, DOUGLASS M, JR	TV DIRECTOR	2522 NELSON AVE #B	REDONDO BEACH, CA	90278
STEWART, FRED M	SCREENWRITER	555 W 57TH ST #1230	NEW YORK, NY	10019
STEWART, GARY	SINGER	POST OFFICE BOX 25371	CHARLOTTE, NC	28212
STEWART, J FRANK	ACTOR	8383 WILSHIRE BLVD #1024	BEVERLY HILLS, CA	90211
STEWART, JAMES D	NEWS CORRESPONDENT	2000 PENNSYLVANIA AVE #1000, NW	WASHINGTON, DC	20006
STEWART, JAMES O	CONDUCTOR	1953 REDESDALE AVE	LOS ANGELES, CA	90039
STEWART, JEFF	SINGER	213 N MAIN ST	ANN ARBOR, MI	48104
STEWART, JERMAINE	SINGER	I WRIGHT, TBA INTL, LTD		
		575 MADISON AVE	NEW YORK, NY	10022
STEWART, JIMMY	ACTOR-DIRECTOR	918 N ROXBURY DR	BEVERLY HILLS, CA	90210
STEWART, JOHN	SINGER-SONGWRITER	7247 BIRDVIEW AVE	MALIBU, CA	90265
STEWART, JOHN	TENOR	CONE, 221 W 57TH ST	NEW YORK, NY	10019
STEWART, LANE	SPORTS PHOTOGRAPHER	SPORTS ILLUSTRATED MAGAZINE		
		TIME & LIFE BUILDING		
		ROCKEFELLER CENTER	NEW YORK, NY	10020
STEWART, LARRY	DIRECTOR	9300 WILSHIRE BLVD #410	BEVERLY HILLS, CA	90212
STEWART, LARRY	TV WRITER	8955 BEVERLY BLVD	LOS ANGELES, CA	90048
STEWART, LINDA	WRITER	MORRISON, 58 W 10TH ST	NEW YORK, NY	10061
STEWART, LIZ	MODEL	9230 OLYMPIC BLVD #203	BEVERLY HILLS, CA	90212
STEWART, MARGARET	TV WRITER	8955 BEVERLY BLVD	LOS ANGELES, CA	90048
STEWART, MEL	ACTOR	7319 BEVERLY BLVD #7	LOS ANGELES, CA	90036
STEWART, PATRICK	ACTOR	BOYACK, 9 CORK ST	LONDON W1	ENGLAND
STEWART, PEG	ACTRESS	SEE - LA CENTRA STEWART, PEG		
STEWART, PEGGY	ACTRESS	11139 HORTENSE ST	NORTH HOLLYWOOD, CA	91602
STEWART, RAY	ACTOR	8721 SUNSET BLVD #202	LOS ANGELES, CA	90069
STEWART, REDD	SINGER	TESSIER, 505 CANTON PASS	MADISON, TN	37115
STEWART, RICHARD J	TV WRITER	11726 SAN VICENTE BLVD #300	LOS ANGELES, CA	90049
STEWART, ROD	SINGER-SONGWRITER	391 N CAROLWOOD DR	LOS ANGELES, CA	90077
STEWART, SCOTT	PHOTOGRAPHER	3009 GATEPOST LN	HERNDON, VA	22070
STEWART, SLAM	BASSIST	80 CHESTNUT ST	BINGHAMTON, NY	13905
STEWART, SUSAN MISTY	TV WRITER	2049 CENTURY PARK E #1320	LOS ANGELES, CA	90067
STEWART, SYLVESTER	SINGER-SONGWRITER	SEE - STONE, SLY		
STEWART, THOMAS	BARITONE	CAMI, 165 W 57TH ST	NEW YORK, NY	10019
STEWART, WILLIAM GLADSTONE	TV DIRECTOR-PRODUCER	REGENT PRODUCTIONS		
		235-241 REGENT ST	LONDON W1A 2JT	ENGLAND
STEWART, WILMOT I	ACTRESS	942 N GARDNER ST #206	LOS ANGELES, CA	90046
STEWART, YVONNE	ACTRESS	FARRELL, 10500 MAGNOLIA BLVD	NORTH HOLLYWOOD, CA	91601
STEWART & STEWART	VOCAL DUO	LUTZ, 5625 "O" STREET BLDG	LINCOLN, NE	68510
STEWART-LAING, PAUL	TV DIRECTOR-PRODUCER	29 KILDARE TERR, BAY'WTR	LONDON W2	ENGLAND
STEWER, DANIEL J	COMPOSER-CONDUCTOR	17401 SE 39TH ST #89	CAMAS, WA	98607
STICKNEY, DOROTHY	ACTRESS	13 E 94TH ST	NEW YORK, NY	10028
STICKNEY, SHAWN	DRUMMER	1618 JONES BLVD	MURFREESBORO, TN	37130
STIDHAM, BRUCE	ACTOR	8337 CASTANO PL	SUN VALLEY, CA	91352
STIDHAM, G STEVE	GUITARIST	4626 NOWAK AVE	DAYTON, OH	45424
STIEGLER, JACK	ACT-SING-WRI	7010 BIRDVIEW AVE	MALIBU, CA	90265
STIEGLITZ, PERRY J	NEWS CORRESPONDENT	4000 MASSACHUSETTS AVE, NW	WASHINGTON, DC	20016
STIENER, SALLY	CASTING DIRECTOR	1438 N GOWER ST	LOS ANGELES, CA	90028
STIERS, DAVID OGDEN	ACTOR-DIRECTOR	3827 RHONDA VISTA PL	LOS ANGELES, CA	90027
STIERWALT, WILLIAM L	DIRECTOR	22227 CAPULIN CT	WOODLAND HILLS, CA	91364
STIGWOOD, ROBERT	FILM-RECORD PROD	67 BROOK ST	LONDON W1Y 1YE	ENGLAND
STILES, NORMAN	WRITER	5550 TUXEDO TERR	LOS ANGELES, CA	90068
STILL, WILLIAM THOMAS	NEWS CORRESPONDENT	POST OFFCIE BOX 9	PURCELLVILLE, VA	22132
STILLE, ROBIN ROCHELLE	ACTRESS	7746 S BRIGHT AVE	WHITTIER, CA	90602
STILLER, JERRY	COMED-ACT-WRI	8500 WILSHIRE BLVD #506	BEVERLY HILLS, CA	90211
STILLMAN, WINSLOW	SINGER-GUITARIST	2824 AZALEA PL	NASHVILLE, TN	37204
STILLS, STEPHEN	SINGER-SONGWRITER	12077 WILSHIRE BLVD #745	LOS ANGELES, CA	90025
STILWELL, DIANE	ACTRESS	9620 HIGHLAND GORGE RD	BEVERLY HILLS, CA	90210
STILWELL, JEAN	MEZZO-SOPRANO	POST OFFICE BOX 188		
STILWELL, RICHARD	BARITONE	CAMI, 165 W 57TH ST	NEW YORK, NY	10019

JAMES STEWART

PEGGY STEWART

ROD STEWART

SLY STONE

GALE STORM

PETER STRAUSS

MERYL STREEP

WOODY STRODE

DON STROUD

Name	Occupation	Address	City	Zip
STIMSON, KEN	ACTOR	10249 TUJUNGA CYN BLVD #16	TUJUNGA, CA	91042
STING	ACT-SING-COMP	2 THE GROVE, HIGHGATE VILLAGE	LONDON N16	ENGLAND
STING, BLADE RUNNER	WRESTLER	UNIVERSAL WRESTLING FEDERATION		
		MID SOUTH SPORTS, INC		
		5001 SPRING VALLEY RD	DALLAS, TX	75244
STINGERS, THE	ROCK & ROLL GROUP	9514-9 RESEDA BLVD #429	NORTHRIDGE, CA	91324
STINSON, JAMES W	NEWS CORRESPONDENT	444 N CAPITOL ST, NW	WASHINGTON, DC	20001
STINSON, JOHN	ACTOR	1717 N HIGHLAND AVE #414	LOS ANGELES, CA	90028
STINSON, JOSEPH C	SCREENWRITER	11726 SAN VICENTE BLVD #300	LOS ANGELES, CA	90049
STIPANICH, MICHAEL	ACTOR	1144 N VISTA ST #4	LOS ANGELES, CA	90046
STIRDIVANT, MARC	WRITER-PRODUCER	8532 DA COSTA ST	DOWNEY, CA	90240
STIRLING, LINDA	ACTRESS	3760 WRIGHTWOOD DR	NORTH HOLLYWOOD, CA	91604
STITH, JAMES	BARITONE	61 W 62ND ST #6-F	NEW YORK, NY	10023
STITT, MILAN	TV WRITER	1888 CENTURY PARK E #1400	LOS ANGELES, CA	90067
STITZEL, ROBERT DEAN	FILM WRITER-DIRECTOR	4167 KLUMP AVE	NORTH HOLLYWOOD, CA	91602
STIVENDER, EDWARD	CONDUCTOR	170 W 81ST ST #3-A	NEW YORK, NY	10024
STIVERS, BARBARA	TV WRITER	1883 RISING GLEN RD	LOS ANGELES, CA	90069
STIVERS, CYNDI	WRITER-EDITOR	US MAGAZINE COMPANY		
		1 DAG HAMMARSKJOLD PLAZA	NEW YORK, NY	10017
STOBIE, RICHARD	ACTOR	8787 WONDERLAND AVE	LOS ANGELES, CA	90046
STOCK, ALAN	ACTOR	6333 LEXINGTON AVE #308	LOS ANGELES, CA	90038
STOCK, BARBARA	ACTRESS	5820 HAZELTINE AVE #11-A	VAN NUYS, CA	91401
STOCK, KEVIN	ACTOR	3318 ROWENA AVE #1	LOS ANGELES, CA	90027
STOCK, MORGAN	ACTOR	8721 SUNSET BLVD #200	LOS ANGELES, CA	90069
STOCKDALE, GARY W	COMPOSER	450 SAN VICENTE BLVD #104	SANTA MONICA, CA	90402
STOCKER, WALTER	ACTOR	16252 RAYEN ST	SEPULVEDA, CA	91343
STOCKFIELD, ROBERT	PHOTOGRAPHER	24 E MOUNT VERNON PL	BALTIMORE, MD	21202
STOCKHAUSEN, KARLHEINZ	COMPOSER	STOCKHAUSEN-VERLAG	5067 KURTEN	WEST GERMANY
STOCKWELL, DEAN	ACTOR	4700 SANDYLAND LN #28	CARPINTERIA, CA	93013
STOCKWELL, GUY	ACTOR	721 N LA BREA AVE #200	LOS ANGELES, CA	90038
STOCKWELL, JEREMY L	ACTOR	307 W 82ND ST	NEW YORK, NY	10024
STODDARD, BARRY	TV DIRECTOR	10447 MELVIN AVE	NORTHRIDGE, CA	91326
STODDARD, BRANDON	FILM-TV EXECUTIVE	240 N GLENROY AVE	LOS ANGELES, CA	90049
STODDARD, MALCOLM	ACTOR	CROUCH, 59 FRITH ST	LONDON W1	ENGLAND
STODDART, ALEXANDRA	TV WRITER	8955 BEVERLY BLVD	LOS ANGELES, CA	90048
STOFAN, RICHARD	ACTOR	5330 LANKERSHIM BLVD #210	NORTH HOLLYWOOD, CA	91601
STOFFEL, RONALD	CONDUCTOR	POST OFFICE BOX 131	SPRINGFIELD, VA	22150
STOFFEL, RONALD A	CONDUCTOR	1109 PEDEN ST #A	HOUSTON, TX	77006
STOHL, HANK	ACTOR	439 S LA CIENEGA BLVD #120	LOS ANGELES, CA	90048
STOIBER, EDMUND	ACTOR	427 N CANON DR #205	BEVERLY HILLS, CA	90210
STOJKA, ANDRE FRANCIS	WRITER	6229 COMMODORE SLOAT	LOS ANGELES, CA	90048
STOJKA, LESLIE	ACTRESS	6233 COMMODORE SLOAT	LOS ANGELES, CA	90048
STOKER, G ALAN	DRUMMER	1204 CLAYTON AVE	NASHVILLE, TN	37212
STOKER, GORDON	PIANIST	POST OFFICE BOX 121497	NASHVILLE, TN	37212
STOKES, BARBARA	VIOLINIST	4657 TARA DR	NASHVILLE, TN	37215
STOKES, BARRY	ACTOR	20 GARFIELD RD	LONDON SW11	ENGLAND
STOKES, BRUCE	NEWS CORRESPONDENT	660 MARYLAND AVE, NE	WASHINGTON, DC	20002
STOKES, GARY A	NEWS CORRESPONDENT	400 N CAPITOL ST, NW	WASHINGTON, DC	20001
STOKES, STANZI	CASTING DIRECTOR	11012 VENTURA BLVD #DD	STUDIO CITY, CA	91604
STOKES, TERRY	HYPNOTIST	POST OFFICE BOX 60845	SACRAMENTO, CA	95860
STOKEY, MICHAEL	ACTOR-PRODUCER	11924 RIVERSIDE DR #107	NORTH HOLLYWOOD, CA	91607
STOLER, SHIRLEY	ACTRESS	300 W 17TH ST	NEW YORK, NY	10011
STOLL, JOHN	ART DIRECTOR	39 ORNAN RD, HAMPSTEAD	LONDON NW3 4QD	ENGLAND
STOLLER, EZRA	PHOTOGRAPHER	KIRBY LN	NORTH RYE, NY	10580
STOLLERY, DAVID J	ACTOR	3208 BERN CT	LAGUNA BEACH, CA	92651
STOLLMACK, FRED	TV DIRECTOR	53 STONEBRIDGE RD	MONTCLAIR, NJ	07042
STOLOFF, VICTOR	TV WRITER-DIRECTOR	400 W 43RD ST #45-S	NEW YORK, NY	10036
STOLPER, DARRYL	ACTOR	950 KAGAWA ST	PACIFIC PALISADES, CA	90272
STOLTZ, ARNOLD T	ACTOR	10933 MAGNOLIA BLVD #2	NORTH HOLLYWOOD, CA	91607
STOLTZ, ERIC	ACTOR	6834 HOLLYWOOD BLVD #303	HOLLYWOOD, CA	90028
STOLTZ, RICHARD	NEWS CORRESPONDENT	972 PAULSBORO DR	ROCKVILLE, MD	20850
STOLZ, TRUDY	ACTRESS	16945 LIGGETT ST	SEPULVEDA, CA	91343
STOMPERS, THE	ROCK & ROLL GROUP	25 HUNTINGTON AVE #420	BOSTON, MA	02116
STONE, ALLEN	TV WRITER	9000 SUNSET BLVD #1200	LOS ANGELES, CA	90069
STONE, ANDREW	DIRECTOR-PRODUCER	10478 WYTON DR	LOS ANGELES, CA	90024
STONE, CHARLES M, JR	TV DIRECTOR	2720 CLARKE'S LANDING DR	OAKTON, VA	22124
STONE, CHRISTOPHER	ACTOR-WRITER	23035 CUMORAH CREST DR	WOODLAND HILLS, CA	91364
STONE, CLIFFIE	MUSICIAM-EXECUTIVE	6255 SUNSET BLVD #723	LOS ANGELES, CA	90028
STONE, CORDELIA	DIRECTOR	2006 N HOBART BLVD	LOS ANGELES, CA	90027
STONE, DANTON	ACTOR	151 S EL CAMINO DR	BEVERLY HILLS, CA	90212
STONE, DEE WALLACE	ACTRESS	23035 CUMORAH CREST DR	WOODLAND HILLS, CA	91364
STONE, DICK	DIRECTOR	381 PARK AVE S #612	NEW YORK, NY	10016
STONE, DOC	GUITARIST	307 BEL AIR DR	FRANKLIN, TN	37064
STONE, EZRA	ACTOR-DIRECTOR	STONE MEADOWS FARM		
		BUCKS COUNTY	NEWTOWN, PA	18940
STONE, FRED	DIRECTOR	5325 NEWCASTLE AVE #229	ENCINO, CA	91316
STONE, HAROLD F, JR	DIRECTOR	306 E GREENTREE LN	LAKE MARY, FL	32746
STONE, HAROLD J	ACTOR	427 N CANON DR #205	BEVERLY HILLS, CA	90210
STONE, IRVING	SCREENWRITER	1360 SUMMITRIDGE PL	BEVERLY HILLS, CA	90210
STONE, JACKIE	NEWS CORRESPONDENT	5151 WISCONSIN AVE, NW	WASHINGTON, DC	20016
STONE, JON	WRITER-PRODUCER	1 SHERMAN SQ #PH-A	NEW YORK, NY	10023
STONE, LEONARD	ACTOR	1901 AVE OF THE STARS #1774	LOS ANGELES, CA	90067
STONE, MARIANNE	ACTRESS	46 ABBEY RD	LONDON NW8	ENGLAND

Name	Occupation	Address	City	Zip
STONE, MARSHALL A	CINEMATOGRAPHER	STEPPINGSTONE FARM	SHERMAN, CT	06784
STONE, MARVIN L	NEWS CORRESPONDENT	6368 WATERBURY DR	FALLS CHURCH, VA	22044
STONE, MICHAEL B	TV WRITER	555 W 57TH ST #1230	NEW YORK, NY	10019
STONE, NOREEN	TV WRITER	12309 9TH HELENA DR	LOS ANGELES, CA	90049
STONE, OLIVER	FILM WRITER-DIRECTOR	POST OFFICE BOX 43	SAGADONACK, NY	11962
STONE, PATRICIA	SOPRANO	MUNRO, 334 W 72ND ST	NEW YORK, NY	10023
STONE, PETER	TV WRITER	ICM, 8899 BEVERLY BLVD	LOS ANGELES, CA	90048
STONE, PETER H	PLAYWRIGHT	160 E 71ST ST	NEW YORK, NY	10021
STONE, PHILIP	ACTOR	LONDON MANAGEMENT, LTD 235-241 REGENT ST	LONDON W1A 2JT	ENGLAND
STONE, RANDY	CASTING DIRECTOR	ALAN LANDSBURG PRODUCTIONS 11811 W OLYMPIC BLVD	LOS ANGELES, CA	90064
STONE, RICHARD	COMPOSER	20720 SCHOENBORN	CANOGA PARK, CA	91306
STONE, RICHARD A	ACTOR	1027 LINCOLN BLVD #A	SANTA MONICA, CA	90403
STONE, ROB	ACTOR	9200 SUNSET BLVD #1210	LOS ANGELES, CA	90069
STONE, ROCKY	SINGER	VISTONE, 6331 SANTA MONICA BLVD	HOLLYWOOD, CA	90038
STONE, SHARON	ACTRESS-MODEL	1717 N HIGHLAND AVE #901	LOS ANGELES, CA	90028
STONE, SLY	SINGER-SONGWRITER	6255 SUNSET BLVD #200	HOLLYWOOD, CA	90028
STONE, STEPHEN A	WRITER	103 S LAPEER DR	LOS ANGELES, CA	90048
STONE, SUZANNE	TV WRITER	MERV GRIFFIN PRODUCTIONS "JEOPARDY," 1541 N VINE ST	HOLLYWOOD, CA	90028
STONE, TRUDE	ACTRESS	372 CENTRAL PARK W	NEW YORK, NY	10025
STONE, VIRGINIA	DIRECTOR-PRODUCER	4248 VIA MARINA #83	MARINA DEL REY, CA	90292
STONE, WILLIAM	BARITONE	CAMI, 165 W 57TH ST	NEW YORK, NY	10019
STONE FURY	ROCK & ROCK DUO	POST OFFICE BOX 4006	NORTH HOLLYWOOD, CA	91607
STONE OAK	C & W GROUP	OBA, 5601 ODANA RD	MADISON, WI	53719
STONEBOLT	VOCAL GROUP	1 ALEXANDER ST #400	VANCOUVER, BC V6A 1B2	CANADA
STONEMAN, OSCAR	GUITARIST	POST OFFICE BOX 17044	NASHVILLE, TN	37217
STONEMAN, PATTIE	GUITARIST	POST OFFICE BOX 17044	NASHVILLE, TN	37217
STONEMAN, RONI	SINGER	TAYLOR, 2401 12TH AVE S	NASHVILLE, TN	37204
STONEMAN, VAN HADEN	MUSICIAN	POST OFFICE BOX 17044	NASHVILLE, TN	37217
STONEMAN FAMILY, THE	VOCAL GROUP	TAYLOR, 2401 12TH AVE S	NASHVILLE, TN	37204
STONER, SHERRI	ACTRESS	KELMAN, 7813 SUNSET BLVD	LOS ANGELES, CA	90046
STONESTREET, DANNY	PIANIST	287 W BARSTOW #141-B	CLOVIS, CA	93612
STONY RIDGE	BLUEGRASS GROUP	CEE, 193 KONHAUS RD	MECHANICSBURG, PA	17055
STOOKEY, NOEL PAUL	SINGER-SONGWRITER	NEWORLD, ROUTE #175	SOUTH BLUE HILL, ME	04615
STOONES, BOINEY	TV WRITER	8955 BEVERLY BLVD	LOS ANGELES, CA	90048
STOONES, HARRY	TV WRITER	8955 BEVERLY BLVD	LOS ANGELES, CA	90048
STOPAK, CHARLES	TV DIRECTOR	715 HORTON DR	SILVER SPRING, MD	20902
STOPPARD, TOM	PLAYWRIGHT	FRASER, 91 REGENT ST	LONDON W1R 8RU	ENGLAND
STORCH, ARTHUR	DIRECTOR	JEFFERSON TOWERS	SYRACUSE, NY	13203
STORCH, ARTHUR	ACTOR	820 E GENESEE ST	SYRACUSE, NY	13210
STORCH, LARRY	ACTOR	2419 ASTRAL DR	LOS ANGELES, CA	90046
STOREY, ALFRED J	PHOTOJOURNALIST	4001 S 7TH ST	ARLINGTON, VA	22204
STORM	MUSIC GROUP	POST OFFICE BOX 1385	MERCHANTVILLE, NJ	08109
STORM, GALE	ACTRESS-SINGER	103 MONARCH BAY	SOUTH LAGUNA, CA	91677
STORM, HOWARD	ACT-WRI-DIR	6224 WARNER DR	LOS ANGELES, CA	90048
STORM, JIM	ACTOR	10000 RIVERSIDE DR #	TOLUCA LAKE, CA	91602
STORM, MICHAEL	ACTOR	STARKMAN, 1501 BROADWAY	NEW YORK, NY	10036
STORM, TEMPEST	BURLESQUE	1714 NE 11TH ST	FORT LAUDERDALE, FL	33338
STORM, WARREN	SINGER	MEAUX, 566 BROCK ST	HOUSTON, TX	77023
STORM, WAYNE	ACTOR	16826 MAGNOLIA BLVD	ENCINO, CA	91436
STOROJEV, NIKITA	SINGER	CAMI, 165 W 57TH ST	NEW YORK, NY	10019
STORPER, CRAIG A	WRITER	613 MOUNTAIN DR	BEVERLY HILLS, CA	90210
STORY, BILL	ACTOR	159 E 55TH ST	NEW YORK, NY	10022
STORY, CARL	MUSICIAN	CEE, 193 KONHAUS RD	MECHANICSBURG, PA	17055
STORY, DONALD	SAXOPHONIST	504 OLIVE	MURRAY, KY	42071
STORY, LIZ	PIANIST	POST OFFICE BOX 9388	STANFORD, CA	94305
STORY, LIZ	SINGER	POST OFFICE BOX 9532	MADISON, WI	53715
STORY, MARK	DIRECTOR	DGA, 110 W 57TH ST	NEW YORK, NY	10019
STORY, RALPH	TV PERSONALITY	3425 WONDERVIEW DR	LOS ANGELES, CA	90068
STOSSEL, JOHN	BROADCAST JOURNALIST	ABC-TV, NEWS DEPARTMENT 1330 AVE OF THE AMERICAS	NEW YORK, NY	10019
STOUDEMIERE, DAVID	WRESTLER	POST OFFICE BOX 3859	STAMFORD, CT	06905
STOUGH, CHUCK	GUITARIST	135 BRINKHAVEN AVE #E-68	MADISON, TN	37115
STOUT, DAVID G	COMPOSER	7522 JAMIESON AVE	RESEDA, CA	91335
STOUT, WILLIAM	JOURNALIST	601 N CANON DR	BEVERLY HILLS, CA	90210
STOVALL, COUNT	ACTOR	CBS-TV, "AS THE WORLD TURNS" 51 W 52ND ST	NEW YORK, NY	10019
STOVER, DON	BANJOIST	15604 BRANDYWINE RD	BRANDYWINE, MD	20613
STOVER, JOHN	GUITARIST	MMM, 935 NW 19TH AVE	PORTLAND, OR	97209
STOVER, WARREN	ACTOR	8721 SUNSET BLVD #200	LOS ANGELES, CA	90069
STOWE, JOHN CHAPPELL	ORGANIST	15 HIGH ST #621	HARTFORD, CT	06103
STOWELL, ALAN M	NEWS CORRESPONDENT	8413 HUNT VALLEY DR	VIENNA, VA	22180
STRACCI, RAYMOND	DRUMMER	1001 NEELYS BEND RD	MADISON, TN	37115
STRACHAN, ALAN	FILM EDITOR	14 CLIFFORD GROVE, ASHFORD	MIDDLESEX	ENGLAND
STRADER, SCOTT	ACTOR	3907 W ALAMEDA AVE #101	BURBANK, CA	91505
STRADLING, HARRY, JR	CINEMATOGRAPHER	7715 SUNSET BLVD #150	LOS ANGELES, CA	90046
STRAIGHT, BEATRICE	ACTRESS	156 E 62ND ST	NEW YORK, NY	10021
STRAIGHT A'S	ROCK & ROLL GROUP	POST OFFICE BOX 448	RADFORD, VA	24141
STRAIT, GEORGE	SINGER-SONGWRITER	ERV WOOLSEY MANAGEMENT 1000 18TH AVE S	NASHVILLE, TN	37212
STRAIT, RALPH	ACTOR	2501 W BURBANK BLVD #304	BURBANK, CA	91505
STRALKA, BILL	ACTOR	5600 ROCK CREEK RD	AGOURA HILLS, CA	91301
STRAND, MANNY	CONDUCTOR	11045 CALIFA ST	NORTH HOLLYWOOD, CA	91601

STRAND, PETER	DIRECTOR	520 N MICHIGAN AVE #436	CHICAGO, IL	60611
STRAND, ROBIN	ACTOR	9806 PORTOLA DR	BEVERLY HILLS, CA	90210
STRANG, DAVID	TV WRITER	8955 BEVERLY BLVD	LOS ANGELES, CA	90048
STRANG, JOHN P	DIRECTOR	35 SUTTON PL	NEW YORK, NY	10022
STRANGE, BILLY	GUITARIST	1417 WILDCOURT CT	FRANKLIN, TN	37064
STRANGE ADVANCE	ROCK & ROLL GROUP	41 BRITAIN ST #200	TORONTO, ONT	CANADA
STRANGER	ROCK & ROLL GROUP	POST OFFICE BOX 7877		
		COLLEGE PARK STATION	ORLANDO, FL	32854
STRANGIS, GREGORY	TV WRITER-PRODUCER	14057 MARGATE ST	VAN NUYS, CA	91401
STRANGIS, JUDY	ACTRESS	11775 BELLAGIO RD	LOS ANGELES, CA	90049
STRANGIS, SAM J	TV DIRECTOR-PRODUCER	232 S BENTLEY AVE	LOS ANGELES, CA	90049
STRANGLERS, THE	VOCAL GROUP	FAST FORWARD, 110 W 57TH ST	NEW YORK, NY	10019
STRASBERG, SUSAN	ACTRESS	124 W 79TH ST #14-B	NEW YORK, NY	10024
STRASFOGEL, IAN	OPERA-STAGE DIRECTOR	915 W END AVE	NEW YORK, NY	10025
STRASSBURG, ROBERT	CONDUCTOR	5157 FRANKLIN AVE	LOS ANGELES, CA	90027
STRASSER, FRED J	NEWS CORRESPONDENT	208 9TH ST, NE	WASHINGTON, DC	20002
STRASSER, ROBIN	ACTRESS	152 E 82ND ST	NEW YORK, NY	10028
STRASSMAN, MARCIA	ACTRESS	1315 N WETHERLY DR	LOS ANGELES, CA	90069
STRASSNER, NORMAN H	TV DIRECTOR	1950 N NORMANDIE AVE	LOS ANGELES, CA	90027
STRATAS, TERESA	SOPRANO	MET OPERA, 186 S BROADWAY	NEW YORK, NY	10023
STRATTON, GIL	SPORTSCASTER	12527 HESBY ST	NORTH HOLLYWOOD, CA	91607
STRATTON, WILLIAM R	TV WRITER	9000 SUNSET BLVD #1200	LOS ANGELES, CA	90069
STRATTON & CHRISTOPHER	COMEDY DUO	SHANKS, 630 TANDY CT	CHICO, CA	95926
STRATTON-SMITH, TONY	FILM-RECORD PRODUCER	CHARISMA, 90 WARDOUR ST	LONDON W1	ENGLAND
STRAUB, TERRY L	PHOTOTJOURNALIST	122 11TH ST, SE	WASHINGTON, DC	20003
STRAUBING, HAROLD	WRITER	10722 BELMAR AVE	NORTHRIDGE, CA	91326
STRAULI, CHRISTOPHER	ACTOR	LADKIN, 11 GARRICK ST	LONDON WC2 9AR	ENGLAND
STRAUS, BARNARD	THEATER PRODUCER	LFR & CO, 666 5TH AVE	NEW YORK, NY	10019
STRAUS, RICHARD	NEWS CORRESPONDENT	9209 BARDON RD	BETHESDA, MD	20814
STRAUSS, HERBERT H	DIRECTOR	30 PARK AVE	NEW YORK, NY	10016
STRAUSS, JOHN L	CONDUCTOR	1134 N OGDEN DR #5	LOS ANGELES, CA	90046
STRAUSS, JOSEPH	TV DIRECTOR	5545 OSTIN AVE	WOODLAND HILLS, CA	91367
STRAUSS, LESLIE	REPORTER	TIME & PEOPLE MAGAZINE		
		ROCKEFELLER CENTER	NEW YORK, NY	10020
STRAUSS, PAUL	CONDUCTOR	36 RUS DU TRONE, BTE 45	1050 BRUSSELS	BELGIUM
STRAUSS, PETER	ACTOR	1096 WALLACE RIDGE	BEVERLY HILLS, CA	90210
STRAUSS, RICHARD S	TV WRITER	8955 BEVERLY BLVD	LOS ANGELES, CA	90048
STRAUSS, THEODORE	TV WRITER	8955 BEVERLY BLVD	LOS ANGELES, CA	90048
STRAW DOGS, THE	ROCK & ROLL GROUP	118 RIVERWAY ST #7	BOSTON, MA	02215
STRAWBERRY ALARM CLOCK	ROCK & ROLL GROUP	13719 VENTURA BLVD #H	SHERMAN OAKS, CA	91423
STRAWBERRY SWITCHBLADE, THE	ROCK & ROLL GROUP	BALFE KING MGMT		
		36-38 WEST ST	LONDON WC1	ENGLAND
STRAWBS, THE	ROCK & ROLL GROUP	ARNAKATA, 211 W 56TH ST	NEW YORK, NY	10019
STRAWN, ROBERT A	PHOTOGRAPHER	109 N GALVESTON ST	ARLINGTON, VA	22203
STRAWSER, NEIL E	NEWS CORRESPONDENT	CBS NEWS, 2020 "M" ST, NW	WASHINGTON, DC	20036
STRAWTHER, LARRY	TV WRITER	8180 MANITOBA ST #215	PLAYA DEL REY, CA	90293
STRAY CATS, THE	ROCK & ROLL TRIO	POST OFFICE BOX 38246	HOLLYWOOD, CA	90038
STREB, ELIZABETH	DANCER	AFFILIATE ARTISTS, LTD		
		37 W 65TH ST, 6TH FLOR	NEW YORK, NY	10023
STREEKY, ED	PHOTOGRAPHER	2300 S 24TH RD	ARLINGTON, VA	22207
STREEP, HARRY	DANCER	AFFILIATE ARTIST, INC		
		37 W 65TH ST, 6TH FLOOR	NEW YORK, NY	10023
STREEP, MERYL	ACTRESS	POST OFFICE BOX 105	TACONIC, CT	06079
STREET, ELLIOTT	ACTOR	427 N CANON DR #205	BEVERLY HILLS, CA	90210
STREET, LORI	ACTRESS	427 N CANON DR #205	BEVERLY HILLS, CA	90210
STREET, REBECCA	ACTRESS	247 S BEVERLY DR #102	BEVERLY HILLS, CA	90210
STREETER, MICHAEL	GUITARIST	232 SANTA ROSA CT	OLD HICKORY, TN	37138
STREETLIFE	ROCK & ROLL GROUP	NBA, 2605 NORTHRIDGE DR	GARLAND, TX	75043
STREETS, THE	ROCK & ROLL GROUP	ICM, 8899 BEVERLY BLVD	LOS ANGELES, CA	90048
STREICH, FRANK	TV DIRECTOR	25 CENTRAL PARK W #6-J	NEW YORK, NY	10023
STREISAND, BARBRA	SING-ACT-DIR	5775 RAMIREZ CYN RD	MALIBU, CA	90265
STREPP, MIKE	CARTOONIST	THE NATIONAL ENQUIRER		
		600 SE COAST AVE	LANTANA, FL	33464
STREULI, ANTHONY R	NEWS CORRESPONDENT	5132 BRADLEY BLVD	CHEVY CHASE, MD	20815
STRIAR, ROBERT	PHOTOGRAPHER	3311 FESSENDEN ST, NW	WASHINGTON, DC	20008
STRICK	C & W GROUP	POST OFFICE BOX 25371	CHARLOTTE, NC	28212
STRICK, JOSEPH	FILM DIRECTOR	266 RIVER RD	GRANDVIEW, NY	10960
STRICK, WESLEY E	SCREENWRITER	555 W 57TH ST #1230	NEW YORK, NY	10019
STRICKLAND, AMZIE	ACTRESS	9255 SUNSET BLVD #610	LOS ANGELES, CA	90069
STRICKLAND, GAIL	ACTRESS	POST OFFICE BOX 5617	BEVERLY HILLS, CA	90213
STRICKLAND, GREGORY L	NEWS CORRESPONDENT	5151 WISCONSIN AVE, NW	WASHINGTON, DC	20016
STRICKLIN, DEBRA	ACTRESS	10100 SANTA MONICA BLVD #1600	LOS ANGELES, CA	90067
STRICKLYN, RAY	ACTOR	852 N GENESEE AVE	LOS ANGELES, CA	90046
STRIDE, JOHN	ACTOR	HATTON, 18 JERMYN ST	LONDON SW1	ENGLAND
STRIGLOS, BILL	ACTOR	3642 FREDONIA DR	HOLLYWOOD, CA	90068
STRINGER, DEE WAYNE	GUITARIST	2641 PULLEY RD	NASHVILLE, TN	37214
STRINGER, HOWARD	TV WRITER-DIRECTOR	186 RIVERSIDE DR	NEW YORK, NY	10024
STRINGER, LOU	GUITARIST	2641 PULLEY RD	NASHVILLE, TN	37214
STRINGER, ROBERT W	DIRECTOR	SOUTH MOUNTAIN PASS	GARRISON, NY	10524
STRINGER, TONYA	MUSICIAN	2641 PULLEY RD	NASHVILLE, TN	37214
STRINGER, WYNNDALE	BANJOIST	2641 PULLEY RD	NASHVILLE, TN	37214
STRIPLING, MICKEY	GUITARIST	119 LOUANN DR	HENDERSONVILLE, TN	37075
STRIS, MARVIN A	ACTOR	4614 MALEZA PL	TARZANA, CA	91356
STRITCH, ELAINE	ACTRESS	THE SAVOY HOTEL	LONDON W1	ENGLAND
STROBEL, RALPH	OBOIST	2300 E MC GALLIARD RD	MUNCIE, IN	47303

Name	Occupation	Address	City	Zip
STROCK, HERBERT	WRITER-PRODUCER	1630 HILTS AVE #205	LOS ANGELES, CA	90024
STRODE, WOODY	ACTOR	1135 N GLENDORA AVE	GLENDORA, CA	91740
STROH, KANDICE	ACTRESS	9300 WILSHIRE BLVD #410	BEVERLY HILLS, CA	90212
STROHEIM, LEO	WRESTLER	POST OFFICE BOX 3859	STAMFORD, CT	06905
STROHMEYER, DONNA J	WRITER	14854 TAMARIX DR	HACIENDA HEIGHTS, CA	91745
STROLLER, LOU	PRODUCER	MCA/UNIVERSAL STUDIOS, INC		
		100 UNIVERSAL CITY PLAZA #507	UNIVERSAL CITY, CA	91608
STROMBERG, AMY	NEWS CORRESPONDENT	1718 "P" ST #220, NW	WASHINGTON, DC	20036
STROMBERG, GARY	FILM PRODUCER	4461 BABCOCK AVE	STUDIO CITY, CA	91604
STROME, EDWIN F	ACTOR	POST OFFICE BOX 623	NEW YORK, NY	10001
STROMQUIST, ROBERT W, JR	COMPOSER	7036 AURA AVE	RESEDA, CA	91335
STROMSOE, FRED	DIRECTOR	430 TUMBLE CREEK LN	FALLBROOK, CA	92028
STRONG, BRENDA	ACTRESS	6430 SUNSET BLVD #1203	LOS ANGELES, CA	90028
STRONG, COLIN	TV DIRECTOR	18 LADBROKE TERR		
		HOLLAND PARK	LONDON W11	ENGLAND
STRONG, JOHN C, III	WRITER-PRODUCER	8278 SUNSET BLVD #401	LOS ANGELES, CA	90046
STRONG, KEN	ACTOR	6565 SUNSET BLVD #525-A	HOLLYWOOD, CA	90068
STRONG, PATRICK	ACT-WRI-DIR	722 HILL ST #A	SANTA MONICA, CA	90405
STROOCK, GLORIA	ACTRESS	STERN, 4 LIGHTHOUSE ST #14	MARINA DEL REY, CA	90292
STROSSNER, MARY ANN	ACTRESS	2445 S BARRINGTON AVE #202	LOS ANGELES, CA	90064
STROUD, DON	ACTOR	15301 VENTURA BLVD #345	SHERMAN OAKS, CA	91403
STROUD, DUKE	ACTOR	NBC-TV, "ANOTHER WORLD"		
		30 ROCKEFELLER PLAZA	NEW YORK, NY	10112
STROUD, RICHARD	TV DIRECTOR	DAISH, 83 EASTBOURNE MEWS	LONDON W2	ENGLAND
STROUPE, RONALD	DRUMMER	ROUTE #1, BOX 426	CROSS PLAINS, TN	37049
STROUSE, CHARLES	COMPOSER	171 W 57TH ST	NEW YORK, NY	10019
STROUT, RICHARD L	NEWS CORRESPONDENT	4517 GARFIELD ST, NW	WASHINGTON, DC	20007
STROW-PICCOLO, LYNN	SOPRANO	61 W 62ND ST #6-F	NEW YORK, NY	10023
STROZZI, KAY	ACTRESS	687 LEXINGTON AVE	NEW YORK, NY	10022
STRUBLE, EDGAR M	MUSIC ARRANGER	333 INDIAN LAKE RD	HENDERSONVILLE, TN	37075
STRUCK, ARTHUR	DIRECTOR	70 BELDEN HILL RD	WILTON, CT	06897
STRUCK, MYRON	NEWS CORRESPONDENT	7433 FOXLEIGH WY	ALEXANDRIA, VA	22310
STRUDWICK, JANE	ACTRESS	POST OFFICE BOX 31	PALOS VERDES, CA	90274
STRUMMER, PETER	BASSO-BARITONE	61 W 62ND ST #6-F	NEW YORK, NY	10023
STRUNK, JUD	SINGER-MUSICIAN	38 MUSIC SQUARE E #300	NASHVILLE, TN	37203
STRUSS, JANE	MEZZO-SOPRANO	254 W 93RD ST #8	NEW YORK, NY	10025
STRUTHERS, IAN D	CINEMATOGRAPHER	7 ADDISON PL	LONDON W11 4RJ	ENGLAND
STRUTHERS, SALLY	ACTRESS	181 N SALTAIR AVE	LOS ANGELES, CA	90049
STRYDOM, GARY	BODYBUILDER	POST OFFICE BOX 2612	PEARLAND, TX	77588
STRYKER, JACK	ACTOR	6736 LAUREL CANYON BLVD #306	NORTH HOLLYWOOD, CA	91606
STRYPER	ROCK & ROLL GROUP	225 W 57TH ST #300	NEW YORK, NY	10019
STRZELECKI, HENRY	GUITARIST	3439 STOKESMONT RD	NASHVILLE, TN	37215
STRZELECKI, LARRY	DRUMMER	121 WOODWARD RD	BIRMINGHAM, AL	35228
STUART, ANNA	ACTRESS	200 W 57TH ST #304	NEW YORK, NY	10019
STUART, ARLEN	ACTRESS	9255 SUNSET BLVD #610	LOS ANGELES, CA	90069
STUART, BARBARA	ACTRESS	GAUTIER, 12747 ADDISON ST	NORTH HOLLYWOOD, CA	91607
STUART, CASSIE	ACTRESS	M MARTIN, 7 WINDMILL ST	LONDON W1	ENGLAND
STUART, ENZO	ACTOR	9200 SUNSET BLVD #621	LOS ANGELES, CA	90069
STUART, GLORIA	ACTRESS	SHEEKMAN, 884 S BUNDY DR	LOS ANGELES, CA	90049
STUART, JAN	ACTRESS	LEONETTI, 6526 SUNSET BLVD	HOLLYWOOD, CA	90028
STUART, JASON	ACTOR-COMEDIAN	JAYMES, 327 N LAUREL AVE	LOS ANGELES, CA	90048
STUART, JAY	TV WRITER	555 W 57TH ST #1230	NEW YORK, NY	10019
STUART, JEFF	TV WRITER	8955 BEVERLY BLVD	LOS ANGELES, CA	90048
STUART, JOHN	ACTOR	3330 BARHAM BLVD #103	LOS ANGELES, CA	90068
STUART, JOHN T, SR	ACTOR	18224 SUGARMAN ST	TARZANA, CA	91356
STUART, JOSEPH	TV DIRECTOR-PRODUCER	360 CONCORD DR	MAYWOOD, NJ	07607
STUART, JOSEPH E, JR	FIDDLER	1036 NEW DUE WEST	MADISON, TN	37115
STUART, LAIRD	TV WRITER	8955 BEVERLY BLVD	LOS ANGELES, CA	90048
STUART, LEN	EXEC-TV PRODUCER	10100 SANTA MONICA BLVD #348	LOS ANGELES, CA	90067
STUART, MARK	TV DIRECTOR	LONDON WEEKEND TV, SOUTH BANK	LONDON SE1	ENGLAND
STUART, MARTY	SINGER-SONGWRITER	120 STARURAL ROUTE BLVD	MADISON, TN	37115
STUART, MARY	ACTRESS	ICM, 40 W 57TH ST	NEW YORK, NY	10019
STUART, MAXINE	ACTRESS	9744 WILSHIRE BLVD #206	BEVERLY HILLS, CA	90212
STUART, MEL	FILM WRITER-DIRECTOR	11508 THURSTON CIR	LOS ANGELES, CA	90049
STUART, NICK	ACTOR	EBONY, 4720 W WASHINGTON BLVD	LOS ANGELES, CA	90016
STUART, PETER Z	DIRECTOR	DGA, 7950 SUNSET BLVD	LOS ANGELES, CA	90046
STUART, REGINALD A	NEWS CORRESPONDENT	13102 TAMARACK RD	SILVER SPRING, MD	20904
STUART, ROY	ACTOR	4948 RADFORD AVE	NORTH HOLLYWOOD, CA	91607
STUART, STEPHEN E	ACTOR	1326 N LAS PALMAS AVE	LOS ANGELES, CA	90028
STUART, WALKER	FILM DIRECTOR	TOWN LN	AMAGANSETT, NY	11930
STUART, WILLIAM L	WRITER	11692 CHENAULT ST	LOS ANGELES, CA	90049
STUARTI, ENZO	SINGER	2 BALFOUR LN	SCOTCH PLAINS, NJ	07076
STUBBS, JANET	MEZZO-SOPRANO	VKD INTERNATIONAL ARTISTS		
		220 SHEPPARD AVE E		
		WILLOWDALE	TORONTO, ONT 3A9	CANADA
STUCKER, LANNY	TV DIRECTOR	68-17 DOUGLASTON PARKWAY	DOUGLASTON, NY	11362
STUCKEY, NAT	SINGER-SONGWRITER	ROUTE #3, ASHLEY DR	BRENTWOOD, TN	37207
STUCKMANN, EUGENE	ACTOR	159 E 55TH ST	NEW YORK, NY	10022
STUDD, BIG JOHN	WRESTLER-ACTOR	POST OFFICE BOX 3859	STAMFORD, CT	06905
STUDER, CHERYL	SOPRANO	CAMI, 165 W 57TH ST	NEW YORK, NY	10019
STUDER, HAL	ACTOR	6 W 77TH ST	NEW YORK, NY	10024
STUDY, LOMAX	ACTOR	440 DENSLOW AVE	LOS ANGELES, CA	90049
STUFF	ROCK & ROLL GROUP	YANDOLINO, 1775 BROADWAY	NEW YORK, NY	10019
STUFF, HOT	WRESTLER	SEE - GILBERT, EDDIE "HOT STUFF"		
STULBERG, NEAL	CONDUCTOR	IMG ARTISTS, 22 E 71ST ST	NEW YORK, NY	10021

BOOK
CASTLE

Name	Occupation	Address	City	Zip/Country
STULCE, JEFF	SINGER-GUITARIST	300 BAKERTOWN RD #14-F	ANTIOCH, TN	37013
STUMP, MATT	NEWS CORRESPONDENT	11409 COMMONWEALTH DR #302	ROCKVILLE, MD	20852
STUNZI, ERIC	TV WRITER	8955 BEVERLY BLVD	LOS ANGELES, CA	90048
STURDIVANT, JOHNNY	GUITARIST	352 CUMBERLAND HILLS DR	MADISON, TN	37115
STURGES, ALLISUN	ACTRESS	3575 W CAHUENGA BLVD #320	LOS ANGELES, CA	90068
STURGES, JEFFREY A	CONDUCTOR	22270 DEL VALLE ST	WOODLAND HILLS, CA	91364
STURGES, JOHN	FILM WRITER-DIRECTOR	13063 VENTURA BLVD #202	NORTH HOLLYWOOD, CA	91604
STURGESS, RAY	CINEMATOGRAPHER	91 NAPIER CT, HURLINGHAM	LONDON SW6	ENGLAND
STURGESS, SIDNEY	ACTRESS	POST OFFICE BOX 1572	JASPER, ALTA TOE IEO	CANADA
STURGIS, WILLIAM	ACTOR	1558 E 19TH ST	BROOKLYN, NY	11230
STURHAHN, LAWRENCE C	TV DIRECTOR-PRODUCER	ODYSSEUS PRODUCTIONS		
		52 LOCUST AVE	MILL VALLEY, CA	94941
STURR, JIMMY & HIS BAND	POLKA BAND	POST OFFICE BOX 1	FLORIDA, NY	10921
STURRIDGE, CHARLES	TV DIRECTOR	10 BUCKINGHAM ST	LONDON WC2	ENGLAND
STURT, GEORGE	DIRECTOR-PRODUCER	10 STRATHRAY GARDENS	LONDON NW3	ENGLAND
STUTEVILLE, EDDIE RAY	GUITARIST	114 CHEROKEE CT	ANTIOCH, TN	37013
STUTZKE, CHERYL A	TV DIRECTOR	3033 W LOGAN BLVD	CHICAGO, IL	60647
STUYCK, JORIS	ACTOR	ABC-TV, "ONE LIFE TO LIVE"		
		1330 AVE OF THE AMERICAS	NEW YORK, NY	10019
STYLE COUNCIL, THE	ROCK & ROLL GROUP	THE TORCH SOCIETY		
		45-53 SINCLAIR RD	LONDON W14	ENGLAND
STYLER, ADELE	TV WRITER	12653 MILBANK ST	NORTH HOLLYWOOD, CA	91604
STYLER, BURT	WRITER	12653 MILBANK ST	NORTH HOLLYWOOD, CA	91604
STYLES, BEVERLY	COMPOSER	POST OFFICE BOX 615	JOSHUA TREE, CA	92252
STYLES, BOB & THE COUNTRY SWING	C & W GROUP	POST OFFICE BOX O	EXCELSIOR, MN	55331
STYLES, JULIAN H	NEWS CORRESPONDENT	2133 WISCONSIN AVE, NW	WASHINGTON, DC	20007
STYLISTICS, THE	VOCAL GROUP	POST OFFICE BOX 82	GREAT NECK, NY	11021
STYNE, BETH ANN	ACTRESS	220 S SWALL DR	BEVERLY HILLS, CA	90211
STYNE, JULE	SONGWRITER-ROCK PROD	237 W 51ST ST	NEW YORK, NY	10019
STYX	ROCK & ROLL GROUP	BOB GARCIA, A & M RECORDS		
		1416 N LA BREA AVE	HOLLYWOOD, CA	90028
SUAREZ, ANTONIO	PHOTOGRAPHER	TIME/TIME & LIFE BLDG		
		ROCKEFELLER CENTER	NEW YORK, NY	10020
SUAREZ, CESAR-ANTONIO	TENOR	CAMI, 165 W 57TH ST	NEW YORK, NY	10019
SUAREZ, PHILIP	DIRECTOR	DGA, 110 W 57TH ST	NEW YORK, NY	10019
SUAREZ, SANTIAGO F	DIRECTOR	DGA, 110 W 57TH ST	NEW YORK, NY	10019
SUAU, ANTHONY	PHOTOGRAPHER	1150 S CHERRY ST	DENVER, CO	80222
SUBARSKY, RANDI	TV PRODUCER	ABC-TV, "ALL MY CHILDREN"		
		1330 AVE OF THE AMERICAS	NEW YORK, NY	10019
SUBER, EDWARD	NEWS CORRESPONDENT	NBC-TV, NEWS DEPARTMENT		
		4001 NEBRASKA AVE, NW	WASHINGTON, DC	20016
SUBITZKY, ED	WRITER	THE NATIONAL LAMPOON		
		635 MADISON AVE	NEW YORK, NY	10022
SUBOTSKY, MILTON	SCREENWRITER	20 STRADELLA RD	LONDON SE24 9HA	ENGLAND
SUBURBAN NIGHTMARE	ROCK & ROLL GROUP	SEE - DWARVES, THE		
SUBURBS, THE	ROCK & ROLL GROUP	LEVY MANAGEMENT AGENCY		
		526 NICOLLET MALL, 2ND FLOOR	MINNEAPOLIS, MN	55402
SUCHER, HENRY	WRITER	6654 ETHEL AVE	NORTH HOLLYWOOD, CA	91606
SUCHET, DAVID	ACTOR	169 QUEEN'S GATE #8	LONDON SW7 5EH	ENGLAND
SUCHIN, MILTON B	TALENT AGENT	201 N ROBERTSON BLVD #A	BEVERLY HILLS, CA	90211
SUDDEN, NIKKI & DAVE KUSWORTH	ROCK & ROCK DUO	TWIN TONE RECORDS		
		2541 NICOLLET AVE	MINNEAPOLIS, MN	55404
SUDDETH, RICHARD W	NEWS CORRESPONDENT	428 JAMES CT	FALLS CHURCH, VA	22046
SUDEKUM, BOBBY	DRUMMER	116 SCOTCH ST	HENDERSONVILLE, TN	37075
SUDOL, KIM	ACTRESS	10000 RIVERSIDE DR #3	TOLUCA LAKE, CA	91602
SUES, ALAN	ACTOR	5645 FERWOOD AVE	LOS ANGELES, CA	90028
SUFFIN, JORDAN	ACTOR	7733 OAKWOOD AVE	LOS ANGELES, CA	90036
SUFIAN, VICKI	NEWS CORRESPONDENT	601 24TH ST, NW	WASHINGTON, DC	20007
SUGAR, JAMES E	PHOTOGRAPHER	1145 17TH ST, NW	WASHINGTON, DC	20036
SUGAR, SWEET BROWN	WRESTLER	SEE - WARE, KOKO B		
SUGAR HOLLOW	ROCK & ROLL GROUP	POST OFFICE BOX 448	RADFORD, VA	24141
SUGARAWARA, SANDRA	NEWS CORRESPONDENT	3815 WARREN ST, NW	WASHINGTON, DC	20016
SUGARHILL GANG	RAP GROUP	200 W 51ST ST #1410	NEW YORK, NY	10019
SUGARMAN, BURT	ROCK PRODUCER	400 TROUSDALE PL	BEVERLY HILLS, CA	90210
SUGARMAN, CARYN D	NEWS CORRESPONDENT	6204 ROBINWOOD RD	BETHESDA, MD	20817
SUGARMAN, PETER B	DIRECTOR	301 W 53RD ST #5-B	NEW YORK, NY	10019
SUGDEN, MOLLIE	ACTRESS	REDDIN, 2 TAVERNER'S CLOSE		
		HOLLAND PARK	LONDON W11 4SA	ENGLAND
SUGHRUE, JOHN J, JR	DIRECTOR	56 TENNIS PL	FOREST HILLS, NY	11375
SUGHRUE, KAREN M	NEWS CORRESPONDENT	1909 QUAKER LN	ALEXANDRIA, VA	22302
SUH, HAI-KYUNG	PIANIST	ICM, 40 W 57TH ST	NEW YORK, NY	10019
SUHOSKY, ROBERT A	FILM WRITER-PRODUCER	4544 COLBATH AVE #5	SHERMAN OAKS, CA	91423
SUICIDE SELDON	HUMAN BOMB	SEE - SELDON, SUICIDE		
SUK, JOSEF	VIOLINIST	MARIEDL ANDERS ARTISTS MGMT		
		535 EL CAMINO DEL MAR ST	SAN FRANCISCO, CA	94121
SUKMAN, SUSAN	CASTING DIRECTOR	MGM, 10202 W WASHINGTON BLVD	CULVER CITY, CA	90230
SUKONICK, ARNOLD	COMPOSER	1308 N POINSETTIA PL	LOS ANGELES, CA	90046
SULLIVAN, A	RECORD EXECUTIVE	AMIRON RECORDS COMPANY		
		20531 PLUMMER ST	CHATSWORTH, CA	91311
SULLIVAN, BARRY	ACTOR	14687 ROUND VALLEY DR	SHERMAN OAKS, CA	91403
SULLIVAN, BILL	ACTOR	ABC-TV, "ALL MY CHILDREN"		
		1330 AVE OF THE AMERICAS	NEW YORK, NY	10019
SULLIVAN, BRAD	ACTOR	247 S BEVERLY DR #102	BEVERLY HILLS, CA	90212
SULLIVAN, BRIAN E	NEWS CORRESPONDENT	1755 S JEFFERSON DAVIS HWY	ARLINGTON, VA	22202
SULLIVAN, CHARLES H	WRITER	14722 HUSTON ST	SHERMAN OAKS, CA	91403

SIDNEY STURGESS

DONNA SUMMER

JOE SUN

SALLY SUSSMAN

DONALD SUTHERLAND

SYLVESTER

SYLVIA

RUSS TAMBLYN

ELIZABETH TAYLOR

SULLIVAN, CORNELIUS	TENOR	CAMI, 165 W 57TH ST	NEW YORK, NY	10019
SULLIVAN, DAN	FILM-THEATER CRITIC	L A TIMES NEWSPAPER		
		TIMES MIRROR SQUARE	LOS ANGELES, CA	90053
SULLIVAN, DANIEL	BASSO-BARITONE	HILLYER, 250 W 57TH ST	NEW YORK, NY	10107
SULLIVAN, DAVID	DIRECTOR-PRODUCER	34 UPTON LN	LONDON E7	ENGLAND
SULLIVAN, GENE J	COMPOSER	300 E COAST HWY #262	NEWPORT BEACH, CA	92660
SULLIVAN, J CHRISTOPHER	ACTOR	3050 W 7TH ST #200	LOS ANGELES, CA	90005
SULLIVAN, JAMES A	DIRECTOR	1207 BEACON HILL	IRVING, TX	75061
SULLIVAN, JENNY	ACTRESS	9220 SUNSET BLVD #202	LOS ANGELES, CA	90069
SULLIVAN, JOHN FOX	NEWS CORRESPONDENT	1412 28TH ST, NW	WASHINGTON, DC	20007
SULLIVAN, JOHN L	WRESTLER-MANAGER	SEE - V, JOHNNY		
SULLIVAN, JOHN R	NEWS CORRESPONDENT	1012 14TH ST, NW	WASHINGTON, DC	20005
SULLIVAN, JOHN W	TV DIRECTOR	61 CLINTON RD	GLEN RIDGE, NJ	07028
SULLIVAN, JOHNNY	WRESTLER-MANAGER	SEE - V, JOHNNY		
SULLIVAN, JOSEPH H	TV DIRECTOR	1323 EUTAW PL	BALTIMORE, MD	21217
SULLIVAN, JOSEPH M	DIRECTOR	14 PARK ST CT	MEDFORD, MA	02155
SULLIVAN, JOSEPH T	NEWSWRITER	15952 KALISHER ST	GRANADA HILLS, CA	91344
SULLIVAN, K	DANCER	AMERICAN BALLET THEATRE		
		890 BROADWAY	NEW YORK, NY	10003
SULLIVAN, KATHIE	SINGER	6750 W 75TH ST		
		MARKADE 75 BUILDING #2-A	OVERLAND PARK, KS	66204
SULLIVAN, KERRY	TV WRITER-DIRECTOR	4409 STERN AVE	SHERMAN OAKS, CA	91423
SULLIVAN, KEVIN	ACTOR	950 N KINGS RD #254	LOS ANGELES, CA	90069
SULLIVAN, KEVIN	WRESTLER	NATIONAL WRESTLING ALLIANCE		
		JIM CROCKETT PROMOTIONS		
		421 BRIARBEND DR	CHARLOTTE, NC	28209
SULLIVAN, LIAM	ACTOR	6430 SUNSET BLVD #1203	LOS ANGELES, CA	90028
SULLIVAN, MAGGIE	ACTRESS	427 N CANON DR #205	BEVERLY HILLS, CA	90210
SULLIVAN, MARGUERITE H	NEWS CORRESPONDENT	4930 SEDGWICK ST, NW	WASHINGTON, DC	20016
SULLIVAN, MAUREEN	ACTRESS	7200 HOLLYWOOD BLVD #110	LOS ANGELES, CA	90046
SULLIVAN, MAXINE	SINGER	THE HOUSE THAT JAZZ BUILT		
		1312 STEBBINS AVE	BRONX, NY	10459
SULLIVAN, NIKI	SINGER-GUITARIST	517 LEE DR	BLUE SPRINGS, MO	64015
SULLIVAN, OSCAR	MANDOLINIST	ROUTE #3, BOX 262	CAVE CITY, KY	42127
SULLIVAN, PATRICIA M	TV DIRECTOR	832 O'DONNELL AVE	SCOTCH PLAINS, NJ	07076
SULLIVAN, RICK	WRESTLER	NATIONAL WRESTLING ALLIANCE		
		JIM CROCKETT PROMOTIONS		
		421 BRIARBEND DR	CHARLOTTE, NC	28209
SULLIVAN, ROBERT	SPORTS WRITER-EDITOR	SPORTS ILLUSTRATED MAGAZINE		
		TIME & LIFE BUILDING		
		ROCKEFELLER CENTER	NEW YORK, NY	10020
SULLIVAN, ROGER J	NEWS CORRESPONDENT	2139 WISCONSIN AVE, NW	WASHINGTON, DC	20007
SULLIVAN, SUSAN	ACTRESS	211 S BEVERLY DR #201	BEVERLY HILLS, CA	90212
SULLIVAN, THOMAS	WRESTLER-MANAGER	SEE - V, JOHNNY		
SULLIVAN, TIM	SINGER	GOOD, 2500 NW 39TH ST	OKLAHOMA CITY, OK	73112
SULLIVAN, TOM	SINGER-SONGWRI-ACTOR	2201 VIA ROSA	PALOS VERDES, CA	90274
SULLIVAN-STORPER, BETH	SCREENWRITER	8955 BEVERLY BLVD	LOS ANGELES, CA	90048
SULLIVANS, THE	C & W GROUP	GOOD, 2500 NW 39TH ST	OKLAHOMA CITY, OK	73112
SULLIVANT, CHUCK	ACTOR	4438 VISTA LARGO	TORRANCE, CA	90505
SULLIVANT, RICK	ACTOR	615 S CATALINA AVE #122	REDONDO BEACH, CA	90277
SUMARA, NATALIE	ACTRESS	2028 KENOMA ST	GLENDORA, CA	91740
SUMIDA, NAGAYOSHI	NEWS CORRESPONDENT	6504 EL NIDO DR	MC LEAN, VA	22101
SUMITRA	FOLK GROUP	276 CAMBRIDGE ST #4	BOSTON, MA	02134
SUMMER, DONNA	SINGER-ACTRESS	MUNAO, 1224 N VINE ST	LOS ANGELES, CA	90028
SUMMERFIELD, ELEANOR	ACTRESS	10 KILDARE TERR	LONDON W2	ENGLAND
SUMMERS, ANDY	SINGER-SONGWRITER	FIRSTIR MANAGEMENT, LTD		
		194 KENSINGTON PARK RD	LONDON W11	ENGLAND
SUMMERS, BILL & SUMMERS HEAT	ROCK & ROLL GROUP	199 CALIFORNIA ST #208	MILLBRAE, CA	94030
SUMMERS, BOB R	COMPOSER	2407 GRAND AVE	COVINA, CA	91723
SUMMERS, BUNNY	ACTRESS	15010 VENTURA BLVD #219	SHERMAN OAKS, CA	91403
SUMMERS, DANA	CARTOONIST	POST OFFICE BOX 2833	ORLANDO, FL	32802
SUMMERS, DIRK W	WRITER	4404 PETIT AVE	ENCINO, CA	91436
SUMMERS, DOUG	WRESTLER	SEE - SOMERS, DOUG "PRETTY BOY"		
SUMMERS, GENE	SINGER-SONGWRITER	3006 W NORTHWEST HWY	DALLAS, TX	75220
SUMMERS, GORDON "STING"	ACT-SING-COMP	SEE - STING		
SUMMERS, JARON	TV WRITER	9000 SUNSET BLVD #611	LOS ANGELES, CA	90069
SUMMERS, JEREMY	TV WRITER-DIRECTOR	SMITH LTD, 10 WYNDHAM PL	LONDON W2	ENGLAND
SUMMERS, JONATHAN	BARITONE	61 W 62ND ST #6-F	NEW YORK, NY	10023
SUMMERS, KAREN	ACTRESS	PENGUIN, 15015 VENTURA BLVD	VAN NUYS, CA	91403
SUMMERS, MARGARET T	NEWS CORRESPONDENT	925 13TH ST, NW	WASHINGTON, DC	20004
SUMMERS, STAN	COMPOSER	1729 JENNER ST	LANCASTER, CA	93534
SUMMERS, WALTER	GUITARIST	292 LAWNDALE DR	NASHVILLE, TN	37211
SUMMERS, YALE	ACTOR	9490 CHEROKEE LN	BEVERLY HILLS, CA	90210
SUMMERVILLE CREEK	C & W GROUP	POST OFFICE BOX O	EXCELSIOR, MN	55331
SUMNER, J D	SINGER-GUITARIST	POST OFFICE BOX 150592	NASHVILLE, TN	37215
SUMNER, J D & THE STAMPS	C & W GROUP	POST OFFICE BOX 17272	MEMPHIS, TN	38117
SUMPER, WILLIAM	ACTOR	6121 WOODMAN AVE #211	VAN NUYS, CA	91401
SUMPTER, SHARON	ACTRESS	8961 SUNSET BLVD #B	LOS ANGELES, CA	90069
SUMROY, JACK R	TV DIRECTOR	125 HUNTERS DR, MUTTONTOWN	SYOSSET PO, NY	11791
SUN	SOUL-DISCO GROUP	200 W 51ST ST #1410	NEW YORK, NY	10019
SUN, IRENE YAH-LING	ACTRESS	6736 LAUREL CANYON BLVD #202	NORTH HOLLYWOOD, CA	91606
SUN, JOE	SINGER-SONGWRITER	LEE WILLIAMS PROMOTIONS		
		6-A MARKET PL, WANTAGE	OXON OX1 28AB	ENGLAND
SUN, YUNG	ACTOR	8235 SANTA MONICA BLVD #202	LOS ANGELES, CA	90046
SUN MESSENGERS, THE	JAZZ GROUP	POST OFFICE BOX 8125	ANN ARBOR, MI	48107

Name	Occupation	Address	City	Zip
SUNDANCER	ROCK & ROLL GROUP	POST OFFICE BOX 942	RAPID CITY, SD	57709
SUNDBERG, CLINTON	ACTOR	827 21ST ST	SANTA MONICA, CA	90403
SUNDINE, STEPHANIE	SOPRANO	LEW, 204 W 10TH ST	NEW YORK, NY	10014
SUNDQUIST, GERRY	ACTOR	PLANT & FROGGATT, LTD		
		JULIAN HOUSE		
		4 WINDMILL ST	LONDON W1	ENGLAND
SUNDRUD, JACK	SINGER-GUITARIST	4700 HUMBER DR #G-10	NASHVILLE, TN	37211
SUNDSTROM, GEOFFREY L	NEWS CORRESPONDENT	314 ASHBY ST #A	ALEXANDRIA, VA	22305
SUNG, ALFRED	FASHION DESIGNER	720 KING ST #404	TORONTO, ONT M5V 2T3	CANADA
SUNGA, GEORGE	PRODUCER	NRW COMPANY, 5746 SUNSET BLVD	LOS ANGELES, CA	90028
		72 PARK AVE	WAKEFIELD, MA	01880
SUNNY COWBOYS, THE	C & W GROUP	OFF THE TRAIL PRODUCTIONS		
SUNSHINE	WRESTLING VALET	WORLD CLASS WRESTLING		
		SOUTHWEST SPORTS, INC		
		DALLAS SPORTATORIUM		
		1000 S INDUSTRIAL BLVD	DALLAS, TX	75207
SUNSHINE, MADELINE	TV WRITER-PRODUCER	11582 OTSEGO ST	NORTH HOLLYWOOD, CA	91601
SUNSHINE, STEVEN	TV WRITER-PRODUCER	11582 OTSEGO ST	NORTH HOLLYWOOD, CA	91601
SUNSHINE BOYS, THE	C & W GROUP	POST OFFICE BOX 973	BEDFORD, TX	76021
SUNSHINE COMPANY	ROCK & ROLL GROUP	POST OFFICE BOX 133	MANHATTAN, KS	66502
SUNSHINE EXPRESS, THE	MUSIC GROUP	CEE, 193 KONHAUS RD	MECHANICSBURG, PA	17055
SUNSTEAD, DAVID	PIANIST	4420 GRAYCROFT AVE	NASHVILLE, TN	37216
SUPER, GLENN	COMEDIAN	21229 PACIFIC COAST HWY #1042	MALIBU, CA	90265
SUPER DESTROYER	WRESTLER	SEE - SPOILER, THE		
SUPER DESTROYER #2	WRESTLER	SEE - IRWIN, WILD BILL		
SUPER DESTROYER MARK II	WRESTLER	SEE - SLAUGHTER, SGT		
SUPER GRIT COWBOY BAND	C & W GROUP	POST OFFICE BOX 1204	GREENVILLE, NC	27835
SUPER MACHINE	WRESTLER	SEE - MASKED SUPERSTAR, THE		
SUPER NINGA	WRESTLER	AMERICAN WRESTLING ASSOC		
		MINNEAPLOIS WRESTLING		
		10001 WAYZATA BLVD	MINNETONKA, MN	55345
SUPERFLY, THE	WRESTLER	SEE - AFI, SIVA		
SUPERIOR MOVEMENT	ROCK & ROLL GROUP	POST OFFICE BOX 14524	CHICAGO, IL	60614
SUPERSTAR #2, '	WRESTLER-ACTOR	SEE - STUDD, BIG JOHN		
SUPERTRAMP	ROCK & ROLL GROUP	16530 VENTURA BLVD #201	ENCINO, CA	91436
SUPINSKI, TERRY	WRESTLER	SEE - WARLORD, THE		
SUPIRAN, JERRY	ACTOR	6640 SUNSET BLVD #203	LOS ANGELES, CA	90028
SUPREMES, THE	VOCAL TRIO	11777 SAN VICENTE BLVD #700	LOS ANGELES, CA	90049
SURF RAIDERS, THE	ROCK & ROLL GROUP	OLDIES, 5218 ALMONT ST	LOS ANGELES, CA	90032
SURFACE	VOCAL TRIO	361 S CRESCENT DR	BEVERLY HILLS, CA	90212
SURFARIES, THE	ROCK & ROLL GROUP	MONARCH PRODUCTIONS		
		9227 NICHOLS ST	BELLFLOWER, CA	90706
SURGAL, JON	WRITER-PRODUCER	838 NW KNOLL DR	HOLLYWOOD, CA	90069
SURJAN, GIORGIO	SINGER	CAMI, 165 W 57TH ST	NEW YORK, NY	10019
SURNOW, JOEL KENNETH	WRITER	1421 S ROXBURY DR	LOS ANGELES, CA	90035
SUROVY, NICOLAS	ACTOR	ICM, 8899 BEVERLY BLVD	LOS ANGELES, CA	90048
SURTEES, BRUCE	CINEMATOGRAPHER	25535 HACIENDA PL	CARMEL, CA	93923
SURVIVOR	ROCK & ROLL GROUP	BARUCK, 1046 CAROL DR	LOS ANGELES, CA	90069
SUSCA, VITO	COMPOSER	1025 OLIVE LN	LA CANADA, CA	91011
SUSCHITZKY, WOLFGANG	CINEMATOGRAPHER	6 MAIDA AVE #11	LONDON W2	ENGLAND
SUSHANSKAYA, RIMMA	VIOLINIST	482 FORT WASHINGTON AVE #1-H	NEW YORK, NY	10033
SUSKA, ALAN	TRUMPETER	500 PARAGON MILLS #B-8	NASHVILLE, TN	37211
SUSMAN, ED	NEWS REPORTER	THE NATIONAL ENQUIRER		
		600 SE COAST AVE	LANTANA, FL	33464
SUSMAN, TODD	ACTOR	10340 KEOKUK AVE	CHATSWORTH, CA	91311
SUSSKIND, STEVE	ACTOR	9744 WILSHIRE BLVD #306	BEVERLY HILLS, CA	90212
SUSSMAN, BARRY	NEWS CORRESPONDENT	11016 GAINSBOROUGH RD	POTOMAC, MD	20854
SUSSMAN, GERALD	SCREENWRITER	555 W 57TH ST #1230	NEW YORK, NY	10019
SUSSMAN, SALLY	TV WRITER	CBS TELEVISION NETWORK		
		"THE YOUNG & THE RESTLESS"		
		7800 BEVERLY BLVD	LOS ANGELES, CA	90036
SUSSMAN, STANLEY B	CONDUCTOR	2109 BROADWAY #3157	NEW YORK, NY	10023
SUSSMAN, SUE	AUTHORESS-NOVELIST	927 NOYES ST	EVANSTON, IL	60201
SUSTAR, JAYNIE	ACTRESS	120 W VICTORY BLVD #104	BURBANK, CA	91502
SUSTARSIC, STEPHEN, II	TV WRITER	18645 HATTERAS ST #299	TARZANA, CA	91356
SUTER, ERIC	ACTOR	3846 S SYCAMORE AVE	LOS ANGELES, CA	90008
SUTER, WILLIAM A	COMPOSER	2535 LA MESA DR	SANTA MONICA, CA	90402
SUTHARD, JAMES R	NEWS CORRESPONDENT	1333 "F" ST, NW	WASHINGTON, DC	20005
SUTHERLAND, DAME JOAN	SOPRANO	COLBERT, 111 W 57TH ST	NEW YORK, NY	10019
SUTHERLAND, DONALD	ACTOR	1888 CENTURY PARK E #1400	LOS ANGELES, CA	90067
SUTHERLAND, JOAN	SOPRANO	CAMI, 111 W 57TH ST	NEW YORK, NY	10019
SUTHERLAND, KATHERINE LEIGH	TV DIRECTOR	3039 "Q" ST #42, NW	WASHINGTON, DC	20007
SUTHERLAND, KRISTINE	ACTRESS	211 S BEVERLY DR #107	BEVERLY HILLS, CA	90212
SUTHERLAND, TAYLOR	SCREENWRITER	8955 BEVERLY BLVD	LOS ANGELES, CA	90048
SUTORIUS, JAMES	ACTOR	SF & A, 121 N SAN VICENTE BLVD	BEVERLY HILLS, CA	90211
SUTT, JO	SINGER	POST OFFICE BOX 171132	NASHVILLE, TN	37217
SUTTER, DANIEL	DIRECTOR	DGA, 110 W 57TH ST	NEW YORK, NY	10019
SUTTERFIELD, ALAN	TV WRITER	2049 CENTURY PARK E #1320	LOS ANGELES, CA	90067
SUTTON, ALBERT H	COMPOSER	POST OFFICE BOX 11	ZEPHYR COVE, NV	89448
SUTTON, CHARLES J	TV WRITER	8955 BEVERLY BLVD	LOS ANGELES, CA	90048
SUTTON, CHRISTOPHER	FILM PRODUCER	17-A ADOLPHUS RD		
		FINSBURY PARK	LONDON N4 2AT	ENGLAND

Name	Occupation	Address	City	Zip
SUTTON, DON	BASEBALL	25542 GALLUP CIR	LAGUNA HILLS, CA	92653
SUTTON, DUDLEY	ACTOR	12 CARLYLE HOUSE		
		OLD CHURCH ST	LONDON SW3	ENGLAND
SUTTON, GLENN	GUITARIST	POST OFFICE BOX 23062	NASHVILLE, TN	37202
SUTTON, GRADY	ACTOR	1207 N ORANGE DR	LOS ANGELES, CA	90038
SUTTON, HENRY	ACTOR	1550 N HAYWORTH AVE #3	LOS ANGELES, CA	90046
SUTTON, HORACE	COLUMNIST	NEWS AMERICA SYNDICATE		
		1703 KAISER AVE	IRVINE, CA	92714
SUTTON, JOHN	DRUMMER	201 CANTRELL AVE	NASHVILLE, TN	37205
SUTTON, KAY	ACTRESS	ALGER, 1130 PARK AVE	NEW YORK, NY	10028
SUTTON, KAY	PIANIST	244 BRIDGEWAY CIR	NASHVILLE, TN	37211
SUTTON, KELSO F	PUBLISHING EXECUTIVE	LIFE & PEOPLE MAGAZINES		
		TIME & LIFE BUILDING		
		ROCKEFELLER CENTER	NEW YORK, NY	10020
SUTTON, LISA	ACTRESS	10000 SANTA MONICA BLVD #305	LOS ANGELES, CA	90067
SUTTON, LORI	ACTRESS	9250 WILSHIRE BLVD #208	BEVERLY HILLS, CA	90212
SUTTON, MICHAEL D	TV WRITER	8955 BEVERLY BLVD	LOS ANGELES, CA	90048
SUTTON, PHOEF	PLAYWRIGHT	BERMAN, 240 W 44TH ST	NEW YORK, NY	10036
SUTTON, ROBERT	ACTOR	6533 HOLLYWOOD BLVD #201	HOLLYWOOD, CA	90028
SUTTON, SARAH	ACTRESS	30 CHALFONT CT, BAKER ST	LONDON NW1 5RS	ENGLAND
SUTTON, THOMAS F	NEWS CORRESPONDENT	2139 WISCONSIN AVE, NW	WASHINGTON, DC	20007
SUVADA, STEVEN	GUITARIST	POST OFFICE BOX 160	HIGHLAND PARK, IL	60035
SUVALLE, RUTHIE	COMPOSER	15541 NORDHOFF ST #48	SEPULVEDA, CA	91343
SUVER, IRENE	CASTING DIRECTOR	280 S BEVERLY DR #501	BEVERLY HILLS, CA	90212
SUWOL, ROBINA	ACTRESS	8285 SUNSET BLVD #12	LOS ANGELES, CA	90046
SUZEAU, PATRICK	DANCER	AFFILIATE ARTISTS, INC		
		37 W 65TH ST, 6TH FLOOR	NEW YORK, NY	10023
SUZMAN, JANET	ACTRESS	MORRIS, 147-149 WARDOUR ST	LONDON W1V 3TB	ENGLAND
SUZUKI, SHIGERU	NEWS CORRESPONDENT	4615 N PARK AVE #1105	CHEVY CHASE, MD	20815
SUZUKI, YASUO	NEWS CORRESPONDENT	5205 RIDGEFIELD RD	BETHESDA, MD	20816
SVANOE, BILL	SCREENWRITER	9200 SUNSET BLVD #1009	LOS ANGELES, CA	90069
SVENSON, BO	ACTOR	801 GREENTREE RD	PACIFIC PALISADES, CA	90272
SVETLANOVA, NINA	PIANIST	CAMI, 165 W 57TH ST	NEW YORK, NY	10019
SVOBODA, WAYNE	WRITER-EDITOR	TIME/TIME & LIFE BLDG		
		ROCKEFELLER CENTER	NEW YORK, NY	10020
SWACKHAMER, E W	WRITER-PRODUCER	16671 OAK VIEW DR	ENCINO, CA	91436
SWACKHAMER, ELIZABETH	ACTRESS	9000 SUNSET BLVD #1200	LOS ANGELES, CA	90069
SWADOS, ELIZABETH	COMPOSER-LYRICIST	360 CENTRAL PARK W #16-G	NEW YORK, NY	10025
SWADOS, ROBIN	ACTOR	2642 2ND ST	SANTA MONICA, CA	90405
SWAGGERT, JIMMY	EVANGELIST	POST OFFICE BOX 2550	BATON ROUGE, LA	70821
SWAIM, CASKEY	ACTOR	8350 SANTA MONICA BLVD #103	LOS ANGELES, CA	90069
SWAIN, JACK	CINEMATOGRAPHER	POST OFFICE BOX 2230	HOLLYWOOD, CA	90078
SWAIN, SUSAN M	NEWS CORRESPONDENT	400 N CAPITOL ST, NW	WASHINGTON, DC	20001
SWALE, THOMAS BENJAMIN	WRITER-PRODUCER	7353 PACIFIC VIEW DR	LOS ANGELES, CA	90068
SWALLOW, NORMAN	TV WRITER-PRODUCER	GRANADA TV	MANCHESTER M60	ENGLAND
SWALLOW, WENDY W	NEWS CORRESPONDENT	5544 30TH PL, NW	WASHINGTON, DC	20015
SWAN, BILLY	SINGER	151 S EL CAMINO DR	BEVERLY HILLS, CA	90212
SWAN, JEREMY	TV DIRECTOR	17 ASHNESS RD	LONDON SW11	ENGLAND
SWAN, MICHAEL	ACTOR	CBS-TV, "AS THE WORLD TURNS"		
		51 W 52ND ST	NEW YORK, NY	10019
SWAN, RAYMOND H	NEWS CORRESPONDENT	3542 GUNSTON RD	ALEXANDRIA, VA	22302
SWAN, WILLIAM	ACTOR	81 PROSPECT PL	BROOKLYN, NY	11217
SWANN, ELAINE	ACTRESS	304 BLEECKER ST	NEW YORK, NY	10014
SWANN, JEFFREY	PIANIST	LEISER, DORCHESTER TOWERS		
		155 W 68TH ST	NEW YORK, NY	10023
SWANN, LYNN	FOOTBALL	12301 WILSHIRE BLVD #203	LOS ANGELES, CA	90025
SWANN, MONE	MODEL	MODELS & PROMOTIONS AGENCY		
		8560 SUNSET BLVD, 10TH FLOOR	LOS ANGELES, CA	90069
SWANN, MONICA	CASTING DIRECTOR	REUBEN CANNON & ASSOCIATES		
		CARSON TELEVISION PRODS		
		10045 RIVERSIDE DR	TOLUCA LAKE, CA	91602
SWANN, PHILLIP	NEWS CORRESPONDENT	631 ACKER ST, NE	WASHINGTON, DC	20002
SWANSON, GLEN OWEN	TV DIRECTOR	9800 VANALDEN ST	NORTHRIDGE, CA	91324
SWANSON, GLENWOOD J	DIRECTOR	DGA, 7950 SUNSET BLVD	LOS ANGELES, CA	90046
SWANSON, KRISTY	ACTRESS	LIGHT, 113 N ROBERTSON BLVD	LOS ANGELES, CA	90048
SWANSON, RICHARD L	PHOTOGRAPHER	6122 WISCASSET RD, NW	WASHINGTON, DC	20016
SWANSON, ROBERT E	TV WRITER	ICM, 8899 BEVERLY BLVD	LOS ANGELES, CA	90048
SWANSON, STERLING	ACTOR	12405 WEDDINGTON ST #9	NORTH HOLLYWOOD, CA	91607
SWANSTON, WALTERENE J	NEWS CORRESPONDENT	7604 RANGE RD	ALEXANDRIA, VA	22306
SWANTON, M H	WRITER	17232 NORDHOFF ST	NORTHRIDGE, CA	91325
SWANTON, SCOTT JAMES	TV WRITER	2715 6TH ST	SANTA MONICA, CA	90405
SWARBRICK, CAROL	ACTRESS	10913 FRUITLAND DR #308	STUDIO CITY, CA	91604
SWARD, ANNE	ACTRESS	10 E 44TH ST #700	NEW YORK, NY	10017
SWARDSON, ANNE	NEWS CORRESPONDENT	1100 "E" ST, SE	WASHINGTON, DC	20003
SWARTHOUT, MILES H	WRITER	29257 1/2 HEATHERCLIFF RD	MALIBU, CA	90265
SWATZELL, TOM	MUSICIAN	SHOWAY, 11623 OLD TELEGRAPH RD	HOUSTON, TX	77067
SWAYBILL, ROGER	SCREENWRITER	9200 SUNSET BLVD #808	LOS ANGELES, CA	90069
SWAYZE, PATRICK	ACTOR	10100 SANTA MONICA BLVD #1600	LOS ANGELES, CA	90067
SWEENEY, ALISON ANN	ACTRESS	6460 SUNSET BLVD #203	LOS ANGELES, CA	90028
SWEENEY, AURELIA	ACTRESS	1911 HARCOURT AVE	LOS ANGELES, CA	90016
SWEENEY, BOB	DIRECTOR-PRODUCER	5757 OWENSMITH AVE #5	WOODLAND HILLS, CA	91364
SWEENEY, DONALD P	CONDUCTOR	5000 WOODMAN AVE #9	SHERMAN OAKS, CA	91423
SWEENEY, EUGENE M	PHOTOGRAPHER	519 W PRATT ST	BALTIMORE, MD	21201
SWEENEY, JAMES D	NEWS CORRESPONDENT	4901 BATTERY LN #201	BETHESDA, MD	20814
SWEENEY, JOSEPH T	NEWS CORRESPONDENT	51 S EDISON ST	ARLINGTON, VA	22204

Name	Occupation	Address	City	Zip
SWEENEY, JOYCE	SOPRANO	KAY, 58 W 58TH ST	NEW YORK, NY	10019
SWEENEY, LOUISE	NEWS CORRESPONDENT	3413 PROSPECT ST, NW	WASHINGTON, DC	20007
SWEENEY, ROBERT E	TV DIRECTOR	135 CARL ST	SAN FRANCISCO, CA	94117
SWEENY, JOAN	ACTRESS	9220 SUNSET BLVD #306	LOS ANGELES, CA	90069
SWEET	ROCK & ROLL GROUP	9229 SUNSET BLVD #625	LOS ANGELES, CA	90069
SWEET, MATTHEW	SINGER	AGM MGMT, 6412 HOLLYWOOD BLVD	LOS ANGELES, CA	90028
SWEET, RACHEL	SINGER	STIFF/CBS RECORDS		
		51 W 52ND ST	NEW YORK, NY	10019
SWEET, SHARON LEIGH	SOPRANO	CAMI, 165 W 57TH ST	NEW YORK, NY	10019
SWEET BROWN SUGAR	WRESTLER	SEE - WARE, KOKO B		
SWEET G	RHYTHM & BLUES GROUP	POST OFFICE BOX 82	GREAT NECK, NY	11022
SWEET HONEY IN THE ROCK	ACAPPELLA QUINTET	ROADWORK MANAEMENT, INC		
		1475 HARVARD ST, NW	WASHINGTON, DC	20009
SWEET INSPIRATIONS, THE	VOCAL GROUP	SCHILLING, 6534 SUNSET BLVD	HOLLYWOOD, CA	90028
SWEET THUNDER	SOUL-DISCO GROUP	ROY JAY'S, 12340 NW MARSHALL ST	PORTLAND, OR	97229
SWEETS, FREDERIC F	PHOTOGRAPHER	3536 S GEORGE MASON DR	ALEXANDRIA, VA	22303
SWEETWATER	C & W GROUP	POST OFFICE BOX 475	MADISONVILLE, TN	37354
SWEETWATER EXPRESS	C & W GROUP	POST OFFICE BOX 4	LAKE LURE, NC	28746
SWEGLAR, NELSON	WRESTLING CORRES	WORLD WRESTLING FEDERATION		
		TITAN SPORTS PUBLICATIONS		
		1055 SUMMER ST	STAMFORD, CT	06905
SWEID, NANCY	WRITER-EDITOR	US MAGAZINE COMPANY		
		1 DAG HAMMARSKJOLD PLAZA	NEW YORK, NY	10017
SWENSEN, JOSEPH	VIOLINIST	ICM, 40 W 57TH ST	NEW YORK, NY	10019
SWENSON, GORDON	PHOTOGRAPHER	14 BISCAYNE PL	STERLING, VA	22170
SWENSON, INGA	ACTRESS	211 S BEVERLY DR #201	BEVERLY HILLS, CA	90212
SWENSON, LINDA L	ACTRESS	205 W 95TH ST	NEW YORK, NY	10025
SWENSON, RUTH ANN	SOPRANO	ICM, 40 W 57TH ST	NEW YORK, NY	10019
SWENSON, SWEN	ACTOR	16 MINETTA LN	NEW YORK, NY	10012
SWERDLOFF, ARTHUR	WRITER-DIRECTOR	4224 ELLENITA AVE	TARZANA, CA	91356
SWERDLOW, EZRA N	DIRECTOR	5400 FIELDSTON RD	RIVERDALE, NY	10471
SWERLING, JO, JR	WRITER-PRODUCER	5400 JED SMITH RD	CALABASAS, CA	91302
SWERTLOW, FRANK	COLUMNIST	UNIVERSAL PRESS SYNDICATE		
		4900 MAIN ST, 9TH FLOOR	KANSAS CITY, MO	62114
SWICKARD, RALPH	COMPOSER	169 LITTLE PARK LN	LOS ANGELES, CA	90049
SWICORD, ROBIN	SCREENWRITER	3014 3RD ST	SANTA MONICA, CA	90405
SWIDLER, HOWARD	TV DIRECTOR	413 WINSTON DR	DEERFIELD, IL	60601
SWIERSZ, STANLEY	WRITER	MAD MAGAZINE, INC		
		485 MADISON AVE	NEW YORK, NY	10022
SWIFT, CLIVE	ACTOR	ICM, 388-396 OXFORD ST	LONDON W1	ENGLAND
SWIFT, DAVID	WRITER-DIRECTOR	12831 HANOVER ST	LOS ANGELES, CA	90069
SWIFT, E M	SPORTS WRITER-EDITOR	SPORTS ILLUSTRATED MAGAZINE		
		TIME & LIFE BUILDING		
		ROCKEFELLER CENTER	NEW YORK, NY	10020
SWIFT, ELLIOTT	ACTOR	16 W 16TH ST	NEW YORK, NY	10011
SWIFT, JAMES A	CONDUCTOR	8741 WHITE OAK AVE	NORTHRIDGE, CA	91324
SWIFT, LELA	TV DIRECTOR	27 W 86TH ST	NEW YORK, NY	10024
SWIFT, RANDY	GUITARIST	415 TUSCULUM RD #G-16	NASHVILLE, TN	37211
SWIFT, SUSAN	ACTRESS	9105 CARMELITA AVE #1	BEVERLY HILLS, CA	90210
SWIFT, WENDON	TALENT AGENT	725 S BARRINGTON ST #202	LOS ANGELES, CA	90049
SWINBURNE, NORA	ACTRESS	EDMUND KNIGHT, 35 BYWATER ST		
		CHELSEA	LONDON SW3	ENGLAND
SWING, MARLIN GRAM	TV DIRECTOR	245 E 35TH ST	NEW YORK, NY	10016
SWIRNOFF, BRADLEY R	WRITER-PRODUCER	10564 CUSHDON AVE	LOS ANGELES, CA	90064
SWIRNOFF, MARY A	WRITER	10564 CUSHDON AVE	LOS ANGELES, CA	90064
SWIT, DAVID	NEWS CORRESPONDENT	2934 UPTON ST, NW	WASHINGTON, DC	20008
SWIT, LORETTA	ACTRESS	151 S EL CAMINO DR	BEVERLY HILLS, CA	90212
SWITCH	SOUL-DISCO GROUP	K S PRODUCTIONS		
		25 E WASHINGTON ST	CHICAGO, IL	60602
SWITZER, MICHAEL	TV DIRECTOR	130 MONTREAL ST	PLAYA DEL REY, CA	90291
SWOBODA, FRANK	NEWS CORRESPONDENT	4027 N STUART ST	ARLINGTON, VA	22207
SWOFFORD, KEN	ACTOR	9000 SUNSET BLVD #801	LOS ANGELES, CA	90069
SWOPE, MEL	TV DIRECTOR-PRODUCER	1900 AVE OF THE STARS #2375	LOS ANGELES, CA	90067
SWOPE, TOPO	ACTRESS	2255 BENEDICT CANYON DR	BEVERLY HILLS, CA	90210
SWOPE, TRACY BROOKS	ACTRESS	14455 DICKENS ST	SHERMAN OAKS, CA	90210
SWORDS, TRAVIS	ACTOR	1221 HORN AVE #1	LOS ANGELES, CA	90069
SWYER, ALAN M	WRITER	7239 PACIFIC VIEW DR	HOLLYWOOD, CA	90068
SYBERBERG, HANS-JURGEN	FILM DIRECTOR	BUNDESVERBAND DEUTSCHER		
		FILM PRODUZENTEN		
		LANGENBECK STR #9	6200 WIESBADEN	WEST GERMANY
SYDNOR, EARL	ACTOR	413 GRAND ST	NEW YORK, NY	10002
SYKES, BOBBY	GUITARIST	713 18TH AVE S	NASHVILLE, TN	37203
SYKES, ERIC	ACTOR-WRITER-DIRECTOR	ELLIOTT, 11 THE ALDWYCH #1	LONDON WC2	ENGLAND
SYKES, MICHAEL	GUITARIST	810 BELLEVUE RD #224	NASHVILLE, TN	37221
SYKES, PETER	WRITER-PRODUCER	ICM, 388-396 OXFORD ST	LONDON W1	ENGLAND
SYKES, TOM	SINGER	POST OFFICE BOX 29543	ATLANTA, GA	30359
SYLBERT, ANTHEA	FILM PRODUCER	HAWN-SYLBERT PRODUCTIONS		
		4000 WARNER BLVD		
		PRODUCERS BUILDING #2		
		ROOM 1101	BURBANK, CA	91522
SYLBERT, PAUL	FILM WRITER-DIRECTOR	52 E 64TH ST #3	NEW YORK, NY	10021
SYLVAN, PAUL	ACTOR	12725 VENTURA BLVD #E	STUDIO CITY, CA	91604
SYLVAN, SANFORD	BARITONE	AARON, 25 HUNTINGTON AVE	BOSTON, MA	02116
SYLVESTER	SINGER-SONGWRITER	BORZOI MUSIC, 222 DUNCAN ST	SAN FRANCISCO, CA	94131
SYLVESTER, DAVID S	COMPOSER	807 DEERFLATS DR	SAN DIMAS, CA	91773

Name	Occupation	Address	City	Zip
SYLVESTER, HAROLD	ACTOR	12343 CALVERT ST	NORTH HOLLYWOOD, CA	91606
SYLVESTER, MICHAEL	TENOR	HILLYER, 250 W 57TH ST	NEW YORK, NY	10107
SYLVESTER, ROBERT	CELLIST	59 E 54TH ST #81	NEW YORK, NY	10022
SYLVESTER, TERRY	SINGER	GOOD, 2500 NW 39TH ST	OKLAHOMA CITY, OK	73112
SYLVESTER, WILLIAM	ACTOR	9200 SUNSET BLVD #909	LOS ANGELES, CA	90069
SYLVIA	SINGER	POST OFFICE BOX 150912	NASHVILLE, TN	37215
SYME, DAVID	PIANIST	POST OFFICE BOX 27539	PHILADELPHIA, PA	19118
SYMES, BUDD	ACTOR	CASSELL, 843 N SYCAMORE AVE	LOS ANGELES, CA	90038
SYMON, JAMES G	DIRECTOR	351 ELM RD	BRIARCLIFF, NY	10510
SYMONDS, ROBERT	ACTOR	LIGHT, 113 N ROBERTSON BLVD	LOS ANGELES, CA	90048
SYMS, SYLVIA	ACTRESS	MARMONT MGMT, LANGHAM HOUSE		
		302 REGENT ST	LONDON W1R 5AL	ENGLAND
SYNES, ROBERT	TV WRITER	3325 BONNIE HILL DR	LOS ANGELES, CA	90068
SYSE, GLENNA	DRAMA CRITIC	THE CHICAGO SUN-TIMES		
		401 N WABASH ST	CHICAGO, IL	60611
SYSTEM, THE	ROCK & ROLL GROUP	AMI PRODUCTIONS COMPANY		
		1776 BROADWAY, 10TH FLOOR	NEW YORK, NY	10019
SZABO, ALBERT	ACTOR	KOHNER, 9169 SUNSET BLVD	LOS ANGELES, CA	90069
SZABO, GEZA	JUGGLER	POST OFFICE BOX 87	WEST LEBANON, NY	12195
SZABO, ISTVAN	FILM DIRECTOR	KOHNER, 9169 SUNSET BLVD	LOS ANGELES, CA	90069
SZABO, JOAN C	NEWS CORRESPONDENT	918 S 26TH PL	ARLINGTON, VA	22202
SZATHMARY, IRVING	COMPOSER-CONDUCTOR	DAVID LICHT, 9171 WILSHIRE BLVD	BEVERLY HILLS, CA	90210
SZEGO, LESLIE	COMPOSER	1530 DOGWOOD PL	LOS ANGELES, CA	90042
SZEKELY, PETER A	NEWS CORRESPONDENT	1809 NEWTON ST #2, NW	WASHINGTON, DC	20010
SZERYNG, HENRYK	VIOLINIST	SHAW CONCERTS, 1995 BROADWAY	NEW YORK, NY	10023
SZIGETI, CYNTHIA	ACTRESS	429 N OGDEN DR #4	LOS ANGELES, CA	90036
SZIGMOND, VILMOS	CINEMATOGRAPHER	POST OFFICE 2230	HOLLYWOOD, CA	90078
SZKAFAROWSKY, STEFAN	BASS	61 W 62ND ST #6-F	NEW YORK, NY	10023
SZOLLOSI, THOMAS E	TV WRITER	5127 STERN AVE	SHERMAN OAKS, CA	91423
SZWARC, JEANNOT	FILM DIRECTOR	2964 OKEAN PL	LOS ANGELES, CA	90046

Name	Occupation	Address	City	Zip
T, MR	ACTOR	333 E ONTARIO ST	CHICAGO, IL	60611
T S O L	ROCK & ROLL GROUP	6253 HOLLYWOOD BLVD #800	HOLLYWOOD, CA	90028
T T QUICK	ROCK & ROLL GROUP	POST OFFICE BOX 327	LEONIA, NJ	07605
T-CONNECTION	SOUL GROUP	9400 S DADELAND BLVD #220	MIAMI, FL	33156
TA KYUN	HIGH WIRE ACT	SEE - KYUN, TA		
TAAB, BILL	WRESTLER	NATIONAL WRESTLING ALLIANCE		
		JIM CROCKETT PROMOTIONS		
		421 BRIARBEND DR	CHARLOTTE, NC	28209
TAAFFE, WILLIAM	SPORTS WRITER-EDITOR	SPORTS ILLUSTRATED MAGAZINE		
		TIME & LIFE BUILDING		
		ROCKEFELLER CENTER	NEW YORK, NY	10020
TABACHNIK, MICHEL	CONDUCTOR	59 E 54TH ST #81	NEW YORK, NY	10022
TABATSKY & LARUSSO	JUGGLERS	HALL, 138 FROG HOLLOW RD	CHURCHVILLE, PA	18966
TABER, GEORGE M	WRITER-EDITOR	TIME/TIME & LIFE BLDG		
		ROCKEFELLER CENTER	NEW YORK, NY	10020
TABOR, MARTHA W	PHOTOGRAPHER	1854 WYOMING AVE, NW	WASHINGTON, DC	20009
TABORI, KRISTOFFER	ACTOR	172 E 95TH ST	NEW YORK, NY	10028
TABRIZI, ALEXANDER	ACTOR	16802 OUTRIGGER CIR	CERRITOS, CA	90701
TACHOIR, JERRY	MUSIC ARRANGER	145 TOWNSHIP DR	HENDERSONVILLE, TN	37075
TACHOIR, MARLENE	MUSIC ARRANGER	145 TOWNSHIP DR	HENDERSONVILLE, TN	37075
TACKETT, FREDDIE	GUITARIST	1229 ALPINE TRAIL	TOPANGA CANYON, CA	90290
TACKETT, ROGER	GUITARIST	112 CHAPMAN DR	LEBANON, TN	37087
TACO	SINGER-SONGWRITER	8124 W 3RD ST #204	LOS ANGELES, CA	90048
TACON, GARY	ACTOR	ABRAMS ARTISTS & ASSOCIATES		
		420 MADISON AVE, 14TH FLOOR	NEW YORK, NY	10017
TADDEI, GIUSEPPE	BASSO-BARITONE	61 W 62ND ST #6-F	NEW YORK, NY	10023
TADMAN, AUBREY	TV WRITER	20111 MAYALL ST	CHATSWORTH, CA	91311
TAFFET, MARC	CARTOONIST	THE NATIONAL LAMPOON		
		635 MADISON AVE	NEW YORK, NY	10022
TAFT, DALE R	NEWS CORRESPONDENT	1801 HORSEBACK TRAIL	VIENNA, VA	22180
TAFT, GENE	PRODUCER	185 N REXFORD DR	BEVERLY HILLS, CA	90210
TAFT, STEVEN GENE	WRITER-PRODUCER	DGA, 7950 SUNSET BLVD	LOS ANGELES, CA	90046
TAG-YR-IT	ROCK & ROLL GROUP	AFTERHOURS RECORDS		
		300 PROSPECT AVE	CLEVELAND, OH	44115
TAGGERT, BRIAN W	WRITER	5149 BABCOCK AVE	NORTH HOLLYWOOD, CA	91607
TAGLIAFERRO, MAGDA	PIANIST	GERSHUNOFF, 502 PARK AVE	NEW YORK, NY	10022
TAHIR, MUHAMMAD	NEWS CORRESPONDENT	101 "G" ST #A-619, SW	WASHINGTON, DC	20024
TAHSE, MARTIN	TV PRODUCER	11727 BARRINGTON CT	LOS ANGELES, CA	90049
TAILGATORS, THE	ROCK & ROLL GROUP	101 W 12TH ST #8-T	NEW YORK, NY	10011
TAIRA, LINDA M	NEWS CORRESPONDENT	400 N CAPITOL ST, NW	WASHINGTON, DC	20001
TAISHOFF, LAWRENCE B	NEWS CORRESPONDENT	4200 MASSACHUSETTS AVE #806, NW	WASHINGTON, DC	20016
TAIT, DONALD S	TV WRITER	7085 BIRDVIEW AVE	MALIBU, CA	90265
TAJ MAHAL	SINGER-SONGWRITER	FOLKLORE, 1671 APPIAN WY	SANTA MONICA, CA	90401
TAJO, ITALO	BASSIST	MET OPERA, 1865 BROADWAY	NEW YORK, NY	10023
TAKA, MIIKO	ACTRESS	BLONDHEIM, 14560 ROUND VLY RD	SHERMAN OAKS, CA	91403
TAKA BOOM	SINGER	SEE - BOOM, TAKA		

Name	Occupation	Address	City/State	Zip
TAKACS, KLARA	MEZZO-SOPRANO	61 W 62ND ST #6-F	NEW YORK, NY	10023
TAKAHASHI, YOSHIO	NEWS CORRESPONDENT	6641 WAKEFIELD DR #110	ALEXANDRIA, VA	22370
TAKEDA, YOSHIMI	CONDUCTOR	59 E 54TH ST #81	NEW YORK, NY	10022
TAKEI, DIANE	ACTRESS	1203 VICTORIA AVE	LOS ANGELES, CA	90019
TAKEI, GEORGE	ACTOR	4368 W 8TH ST	LOS ANGELES, CA	90005
TAKEMOTO, PAUL H	NEWS CORRESPONDENT	4719 SAUL RD	KENSINGTON, MD	20895
TALAS	ROCK & ROLL GROUP	STARSTRUCK PRODUCTIONS		
		2650 DELAWARE AVE	BUFFALO, NY	14216
TALBERT, DOUGLAS F	COMPOSER-CONDUCTOR	7250 FRANKLIN AVE #1108	LOS ANGELES, CA	90046
TALBERT, THOMAS	COMPOSER	1268 GLENNEYRE ST	LAGUNA BEACH, CA	92651
TALBOT, BRYAN	PERCUSSIONIST	6117 BRESSLYN RD	NASHVILLE, TN	37205
TALBOT, HELEN	ACTRESS	BAILEY, 7926 LASAINE AVE	NORTHRIDGE, CA	91325
TALBOT, JOSEPH	GUITARIST	6117 BRESSLYN RD	NASHVILLE, TN	37205
TALBOT, KATHY	ACTRESS-SINGER	1035 N CAHUENGA BLVD	LOS ANGELES, CA	90038
TALBOT, NITA	ACTRESS	3420 MERRIMAC RD	LOS ANGELES, CA	90049
TALBOT, OGDEN	ACTOR	1773 N SYCAMORE AVE #7	LOS ANGELES, CA	90028
TALBOT-MARTIN, ELIZABETH	ACTRESS	4418 YOUNG DR	MONTROSE, CA	91020
TALBOTT, MICHAEL	ACTOR	12758 MULHOLLAND DR	BEVERLY HILLS, CA	90210
TALBOTT, STROBE	NEWS CORRESPONDENT	2842 28TH ST, SW	WASHINGTON, DC	20008
TALESE, GAY	WRITER	154 E ATLANTIC BLVD	OCEAN CITY, NJ	08226
TALICH STRING QUARTET	STRING QUARTET	KAPLAN, 115 COLLEGE ST	BURLINGTON, VT	05401
TALISMAN, DAVID	TV WRITER	14144 VENTURA BLVD #200	SHERMAN OAKS, CA	91423
TALK TALK	ROCK & ROLL GROUP	ASPDEN, 121-A REVELSTONE N		
		WIMBLETON PL	LONDON W15	ENGLAND
TALKING HEADS, THE	ROCK & ROLL GROUP	GARY KURFIRST, OVERLAND PRODS		
		1775 BROADWAY, 7TH FLOOR	NEW YORK, NY	10019
TALL, TOM	SINGER	DOWN HOME MUSIC COMPANY		
		10341 SAN PABLO AVE	EL CERRITO, CA	94530
TALLCHIEF, MARIA	BALLERINA	LYRIC OPERA, 20 N WACKER DR	CHICAGO, IL	60606
TALLENT, CHARLES	PIANIST	4628 VILLA GREEN DR	NASHVILLE, TN	37215
TALLEY, DEBORAH ANN	TV DIRECTOR	4545 CONNECTICUT AVE, NW	WASHINGTON, DC	20008
TALLEY, GARY	GUITARIST	POST OFFICE BOX 121023	NASHVILLE, TN	37212
TALLEY, JAMES	GUITARIST	POST OFFICE BOX 120722	NASHVILLE, TN	37212
TALLICHET, MARGARET	ACTRESS	WYLER, 1121 SUMMIT DR	BEVERLY HILLS, CA	90210
TALLMAN, CLIFFORD P, JR	PUBLISHING EXECUTIVE	US MAGAZINE COMPANY		
		1 DAG HAMMARSKJOLD PLAZA	NEW YORK, NY	10017
TALLMER, JERRY	MOVIE CRITIC	N Y POST, 210 SOUTH ST	NEW YORK, NY	10002
TALMAN, ANN	ACTRESS	BIKOFF, 19 W 44TH ST	NEW YORK, NY	10036
TALMI, YOAV	CONDUCTOR	SHAW CONCERTS, 1995 BROADWAY	NEW YORK, NY	10023
TALVELA, MARTTI	BASS	119 W 57TH ST #1505	NEW YORK, NY	10019
TALYN, OLGA	ACTRESS	870 N VINE ST #G	LOS ANGELES, CA	90038
TAMAGAWA, TAKAMICHI	NEWS CORRESPONDENT	6663 TENNYSON DR	MC LEAN, VA	22101
TAMARIN, NATHAN	ACTOR	148 ROCKWOOD PL	ENGLEWOOD, NJ	07631
TAMBLING, RICHARD F	WRITER-PRODUCER	106 THE DR, BECKENHAM	KENT	ENGLAND
TAMBLYN, RUSS	ACTOR	2310 6TH ST #2	SANTA MONICA, CA	90405
TAMBOR, JEFFREY	ACTOR	4443 SAINT CLAIR AVE	STUDIO CITY, CA	91604
TAMBURRO, CHARLES	DIRECTOR	DGA, 7950 SUNSET BLVD	LOS ANGELES, CA	90046
TAMES, GEORGE	PHOTOGRAPHER	4215 YUMA ST, NW	WASHINGTON, DC	20016
TAMI SNUKA	WRESTLER	SEE - SNUKA, JIMMY "SUPERFLY"		
TAMKUS, DAMOE	SCREENWRITER	555 W 57TH ST #1230	NEW YORK, NY	10019
TAMM, MARY	ACTRESS	REDWAY, 16 BERNERS ST	LONDON W1	ENGLAND
TAMS, THE	ROCK & ROLL GROUP	CAROLINA ATTRACTIONS		
		203 CULVER AVE	CHARLESTON, SC	29407
TAMURA, HIDEO	NEWS CORRESPONDENT	8504 LYNWOOD PL	CHEVY CHASE, MD	20815
TANAKA, SEIJI	NEWS CORRESPONDENT	472 NATIONAL PRESS BLDG		
		529 14TH ST, NW	WASHINGTON, DC	20045
TANASESCU, GINO	DIRECTOR	DGA, 7950 SUNSET BLVD	LOS ANGELES, CA	90046
TANDY, JESSICA	ACTRESS	165 W 46TH ST #409	NEW YORK, NY	10036
TANDY & MORGAN	ROCK & ROLL GROUP	POST OFFICE BOX 2924	LAGUNA HILLS, CA	92654
TANEN, NED	FILM PROD-EXEC	PARAMOUNT TELEVISION		
		5555 MELROSE AVE	LOS ANGELES, CA	90038
TANENBAUM, DAVID	GUITARIST	AFFILIATE ARTISTS, INC		
		37 W 65TH ST, 6TH FLOOR	NEW YORK, NY	10023
TANENBAUM, MICHELLE	ACTRESS	11350 VENTURA BLVD #206	STUDIO CITY, CA	91604
TANGERINE DREAM	ROCK & ROLL GROUP	POST OFFICE BOX 303340	1000 BERLIN 30	WEST GERMANY
TANI, MASUO	NEWS CORRESPONDENT	8200 MAC ARTHUR BLVD	CABIN JOHN, MD	20818
TANIGUCHI, IKOU	NEWS CORRESPONDENT	9301 SINGLETON DR	BETHESDA, MD	20817
TANKER, JAMES E	TV DIRECTOR	4650 FORMAN AVE	TOLUCA LAKE, CA	91602
TANNEHILL, FRANCES	ACTRESS	175 W 79TH ST	NEW YORK, NY	10024
TANNEN, STEVE	ACTOR	682 1/2 S CLOVERDALE AVE	LOS ANGELES, CA	90036
TANNEN, WILLIAM P	DIRECTOR	129 FRASER AVE	SANTA MONICA, CA	90405
TANNENBAUM, ALLAN	PHOTOGRAPHER	182 DUANE ST	NEW YORK, NY	10013
TANNENBAUM, THOMAS D	TV PRODUCER	VIACOM, 10900 WILSHIRE BLVD	LOS ANGELES, CA	90024
TANNER, JEFFREY	ACTOR	1901 AVE OF THE STARS #840	LOS ANGELES, CA	90067
TANNER, JOSEPH	GUITARIST	1207 16TH AVE S #6	NASHVILLE, TN	37212
TANNER, JULIA	CELLIST	ROUTE #3, BOX 385-A	WOODBURY, TN	37190
TANNER, PETER	FILM EDITOR	LONDON MANAGEMENT, LTD		
		235-241 REGENT ST	LONDON W1A 2JT	ENGLAND
TANNER, ROBERT C	DIRECTOR	925 MICHIGAN AVE	EVANSTON, IL	60202
TANNER, TONY	THEATER DIRECTOR	ICM, 40 W 57TH ST	NEW YORK, NY	10019
TANNINEN, AARME J O	NEWS CORRESPONDENT	1077 PAPERMILL CT, NW	WASHINGTON, DC	20007
TANOUS, MARK	ACTOR	5329 SUNNYSLOPE AVE	VAN NUYS, CA	91401
TANTRUM, THE	ROCK & ROLL GROUP	RUFFIAN MANAGEMENT		
		6914 W NORTH AVE	CHICAGO, IL	60635
TANZ, BERNIE	TV WRITER	8955 BEVERLY BLVD	LOS ANGELES, CA	90048

Name	Occupation	Address	City	Zip
TANZER, LESTER	NEWS CORRESPONDENT	4859 N 30TH ST	ARLINGTON, VA	22207
TANZINI, PHILIP	ACTOR	1433 HONEYHILL DR	WALNUT, CA	91789
TANZY, KATHLEEN	NEWS CORRESPONDENT	5501 SEMINARY RD #2515-S	FALLS CHURCH, VA	22041
TAOGAGA, MAX	WRESTLER	SEE - AFI, SIVA		
TAPER, MARK	ACTOR	816 ALPINE DR	BEVERLY HILLS, CA	90210
TAPESTRY	MUSICAL GROUP	MARS, 168 ORCHID DR	PEARL RIVER, NY	10965
TAPP, GORDIE	SINGER-SONGWRITER	TAYLOR, 2401 12TH AVE S	NASHVILLE, TN	37204
TAPPAN, TIMOTHY	PIANIST	6625 UPTON LN	NASHVILLE, TN	37209
TAPPER, DAVID A	WRITER-PRODUCER	133 W 17TH ST #PH-B	NEW YORK, NY	10011
TAPPIS, JOEL	TV WRITER	5663 RUTHWOOD DR	CALABASAS, CA	91302
TAPSCOTT, MARK	ACTOR	8303 SKYLINE DR	LOS ANGELES, CA	90046
TARADASH, DANIEL	WRITER-PRODUCER	9140 HAZEN DR	BEVERLY HILLS, CA	90210
TARAN, CAROLE	SINGER	ADAM, 2501 S OCEAN DR	HOLLYWOOD, FL	33019
TARAS, JOHN	BALLET MASTER	NEW YORK STATE THEATRE		
		LINCOLN CENTER	NEW YORK, NY	10023
TARASENKOV, DMITRY	NEWS CORRESPONDENT	1201 CONNECTICUT AVE, NW	WASHINGTON, DC	20036
TARBUCK, BARBARA	ACTRESS	10810 1/4 LINDBROOK DR	LOS ANGELES, CA	90024
TARBUCK, JIMMY	COMEDIAN	PRICHARD, 118 BEAUFORT ST	LONDON SW3 6BU	ENGLAND
TARBUTTON, JAMES	GUITARIST	272 INDIAN LAKE RD	HENDERSONVILLE, TN	37075
TARDIO, NEIL	DIRECTOR	LOVINGER, 157 E 35TH ST	NEW YORK, NY	10016
TARGETS, THE	ROCK & ROLL GROUP	POST OFFICE BOX 34553	LOS ANGELES, CA	90034
TARKINGTON, FRAN	FOOTBALL	3345 PEACHTREE RD, NE	ATLANTA, GA	30326
TARKINGTON, ROCKNE	ACTOR	6736 LAUREL CANYON BLVD #306	NORTH HOLLYWOOD, CA	91601
TARLAU, ROBERT S	WRITER	5530 BEVIS AVE	VAN NUYS, CA	91411
TARLOFF, ERIK	TV WRITER	9596 SHIRLEY LN	BEVERLY HILLS, CA	90210
TARLOFF, FRANK	SCREENWRITER	9596 SHIRLEY LN	BEVERLY HILLS, CA	90210
TARPEY, TOM	ACTOR	15010 VENTURA BLVD #219	SHERMAN OAKS, CA	91403
TARPLEY, EDWARD	VIOLINIST	201 BOWLING AVE	NASHVILLE, TN	37205
TARPLEY, S P	RECORD EXECUTIVE	POST OFFICE BOX 78	FAIRVIEW, OH	43736
TARR, CYNTHIA	ACTRESS	7285 FRANKLIN AVE #E	LOS ANGELES, CA	90046
TARRANT, ALAN	TV PRODUCER	6 PARK CRESCENT, TWICKENHAM	MIDDLESEX	ENGLAND
TARRANT, ANDY	GUITARIST	312 CANE RIDGE RD #1218	ANTIOCH, TN	37013
TARSES, JAY	SCREENWRITER	20601 DUMONT ST	WOODLAND HILLS, CA	91364
TARSHIS, LAUREN	WRITER-EDITOR	US MAGAZINE COMPANY		
		1 DAG HAMMARSKJOLD PLAZA	NEW YORK, NY	10017
TARTAGLIA, JOHN ANDREW	COMPOSER-CONDUCTOR	500 S SEPULVEDA BLVD #510	LOS ANGELES, CA	90049
TARTAN, JAMES	TV DIRECTOR	1013 1/2 HANCOCK AVE	LOS ANGELES, CA	90069
TARTAN, JIM	ACTOR	15010 VENTURA BLVD #219	SHERMAN OAKS, CA	91403
TARTER, DALE	ACTOR	GRIFFITH, 1884 LAUREL CYN BLVD	LOS ANGELES, CA	90046
TARTIKOFF, BRANDON	TV EXECUTIVE	1648 N BEVERLY DR	BEVERLY HILLS, CA	90210
TARVER, MILT	ACTOR	9943 NOBLE AVE	MISSION HILLS, CA	91345
TASCO, RAI	ACTOR-DIRECTOR	12838 KLING ST	STUDIO CITY, CA	91604
TASH, MAX D	TV WRITER	1819 N SIERRA BONITA AVE	LOS ANGELES, CA	90046
TASH, STEVEN	ACTOR	CONTEMPORARY ARTISTS		
		132 S LASKY DR	BEVERLY HILLS, CA	90212
TASHIMA, TERRI LYNN	ACTRESS	3867 DEGNAN BLVD	LOS ANGELES, CA	90008
TASKER, KELLY	WRITER-EDITOR	DISCOVER/TIME & LIFE BLDG		
		ROCKEFELLER CENTER	NEW YORK, NY	10020
TASKER, WILLIAM D, JR	COMPOSER-CONDUCTOR	WILHELMSHOHER STR 26	BERLIN 4, 1000	WEST GERMANY
TASNADI, CHARLES	PHOTOGRAPHER	4534 ALBEMARLE ST, NW	WASHINGTON, DC	20016
TASTE OF HONEY, A	VOCAL GROUP	DENIS VAUGHAN MGMT		
		HEATHCOAT HOUSE		
		19-20 SAVILLE ROW	LONDON W1	ENGLAND
TASTY NICKEL	ROCK & ROLL GROUP	VARIETY ARTISTS INTL, INC		
		9073 NEMO ST, 3RD FLOOR	LOS ANGELES, CA	90069
TATA, JOE E	ACTOR	8538 HOLLYWOOD BLVD	LOS ANGELES, CA	90069
TATASCIORE, FRED	WRITER	1288 TOWER GROVE DR	BEVERLY HILLS, CA	90210
TATE, DANNY	SINGER-GUITARIST	914 WINTHORNE DR #A-8	NASHVILLE, TN	37217
TATE, JERRY	GUITARIST	POST OFFICE BOX 261	ANTIOCH, TN	37013
TATE, JUDY	ACTRESS	1650 BROADWAY #302	NEW YORK, NY	10019
TATE, LAURA	ACTRESS	1717 N HIGHLAND AVE #414	LOS ANGELES, CA	90028
TATE, LINCOLN	ACTOR	439 S LA CIENEGA BLVD #117	LOS ANGELES, CA	90048
TATE, NICK	ACTOR	JOSEPH, 78 NEW BOND ST	LONDON W1	ENGLAND
TATE, ROBERT	TENOR	2230 SACRAMENTO ST	SAN FRANCISCO, CA	94115
TATER, CLARENCE	FIDDLER	121 KEYSTONE LN	HENDERSONVILLE, TN	37075
TATOR, JOEL J	DIRECTOR	DGA, 7950 SUNSET BLVD	LOS ANGELES, CA	90046
TATRO, DUANE L	COMPOSER-CONDUCTOR	15705 SUPERIOR ST	SEPULVEDA, CA	91343
TATUM, ALAN	NEWS CORRESPONDENT	1755 S JEFFERSON DAVIS HWY	ARLINGTON, VA	22202
TATUM, JOHN "HOLLYWOOD"	WRESTLER	UNIVERSAL WRESTLING FEDERATION		
		MID SOUTH SPORTS, INC		
		5001 SPRING VALLEY RD	DALLAS, TX	75244
TATUM, MARK	SINGER	6750 W 75TH ST, MARKADE 75		
		BUILDING #2-A	OVERLAND PARK, KS	66212
TAUB, JUDITH P	NEWS CORRESPONDENT	4444 CONNECTICUT AVE, NW	WASHINGTON, DC	20008
TAUB, ROBERT	PIANIST	SHAW CONCERTS, 1995 BROADWAY	NEW YORK, NY	10023
TAUB, WILLIAM STEVEN	TV WRITER	1844 WESTHOLME AVE	LOS ANGELES, CA	90025
TAUBER, PETER	TV WRITER	8955 BEVERLY BLVD	LOS ANGELES, CA	90048
TAUBIN, WILLIAM	DIRECTOR	60 HICKORY DR	EAST HILLS, LI, NY	11576
TAUBMAN, PHILIP	NEWS CORRESPONDENT	2850 28TH ST, NW	WASHINGTON, DC	20008
TAULBEE, PAMELA D	NEWS CORRESPONDENT	1864 WYOMING AVE, NW	WASHINGTON, DC	20009
TAUPIN, BERNIE	LYRICIST	1320 N DOHENY DR	LOS ANGELES, CA	90069
TAUSINGER, YVETTE	PIANIST	POST OFFICE BOX 131	SPRINGFIELD, VA	22150
TAVERNIER, BERTRAND	FILM DIRECTOR	LITTLE BEAR PRODUCTIONS		
		66 BLVD, MALESHERDES	PARIS 75008	FRANCE
TAVIS, WARREN J	COMPOSER	1820 N GRACE AVE #6	LOS ANGELES, CA	90028

Name	Occupation	Address	City	Code
TAWEEL, GEORGE	WRITER-PRODUCER	5609 COLFAX AVE #250	NORTH HOLLYWOOD, CA	91601
TAXXI	ROCK & ROLL GROUP	POST OFFICE BOX 7308	CARMEL, CA	93923
TAYBACK, VIC	ACTOR-DIRECTOR	300 CUMBERLAND RD	GLENDALE, CA	91202
TAYLOE, JACK	ACTOR	YOUNG MODELS, 9124 SUNSET BLVD	LOS ANGELES, CA	90069
TAYLOR, ADRIAN C	NEWS CORRESPONDENT	2025 "M" ST, NW	WASHINGTON, DC	20036
TAYLOR, ANNE F	SCREENWRITER	8955 BEVERLY BLVD	LOS ANGELES, CA	90048
TAYLOR, B K	CARTOONIST	THE NATIONAL LAMPOON		
		635 MADISON AVE	NEW YORK, NY	10022
TAYLOR, BAZ	TV DIRECTOR-PRODUCER	17 ALEXANDER ST	LONDON W2	ENGLAND
TAYLOR, BENEDICT	ACTOR	35 HEDDEN ST	LONDON W1	ENGLAND
TAYLOR, BENJAMIN B	NEWS CORRESPONDENT	6805 6TH ST, NW	WASHINGTON, DC	20012
TAYLOR, BILLY	MUSICIAN	555 KAPPOCK ST	BRONX, NY	16463
TAYLOR, BILLY C	GUITARIST	ROUTE #2, MEADOWWOOD DR	MURFREESBORO, TN	37130
TAYLOR, BILLY, TRIO	JAZZ TRIO	500 5TH AVE #2050	NEW YORK, NY	10110
TAYLOR, BOB	CARTOONIST	DALLAS TIMES-HERALD		
		1101 PACIFIC AVE	DALLAS, TX	75202
TAYLOR, BOBBY G	MUSICIAN	1041 REDMOND CT	NASHVILLE, TN	37211
TAYLOR, BRIAN	ACTOR	APA, 888 7TH AVE	NEW YORK, NY	10106
TAYLOR, BRUCE	TV WRITER	8955 BEVERLY BLVD	LOS ANGELES, CA	90048
TAYLOR, BUCK	ACTOR	ROUTE #2, BOX 150	ENNIS, MT	59729
TAYLOR, CECIL	JAZZ MUSICIAN	BRIDGE, 106 FORT GREENE PL	BROOKLYN, NY	11217
TAYLOR, CHARLES	ACTOR	400 S BEVERLY DR #216	BEVERLY HILLS, CA	90212
TAYLOR, CHARLES W	NEWS CORRESPONDENT	1833 CORCORAN ST, NW	WASHINGTON, DC	20009
TAYLOR, DAVE	RECORD EXECUTIVE	POST OFFICE BOX 262	LIVINGSTON, NJ	07039
TAYLOR, DAVID C	NEWS CORRESPONDENT	4217 KINCAID CT	CHANTILLY, VA	22021
TAYLOR, DAVID C	SCREENWRITER	9200 SUNSET BLVD #PH-25	LOS ANGELES, CA	90069
TAYLOR, DAVID L	GUITARIST	139 CUMBERLAND SHORES DR	HENDERSONVILLE, TN	37075
TAYLOR, DELBERT C	CONDUCTOR	1266 MEADOWBROOK AVE	LOS ANGELES, CA	90019
TAYLOR, DELORES	ACTRESS	LAUGHLIN, 12953 MARLBORO ST	LOS ANGELES, CA	90049
TAYLOR, DON	FILM DIRECTOR	1111 SAN VICENTE BLVD	SANTA MONICA, CA	90402
TAYLOR, DUB	ACTOR	21417 GAONA ST	WOODLAND HILLS, CA	91364
TAYLOR, ELIZABETH	ACTRESS	700 NIMES RD	LOS ANGELES, CA	90024
TAYLOR, ERNEST J W	COMPOSER	11167 KLING ST	NORTH HOLLYWOOD, CA	91607
TAYLOR, ERNEST-FRANK	ACTOR	3857 TRACY ST	LOS ANGELES, CA	90027
TAYLOR, FEMI	ACTRESS-DANCER	6 AMYAND PARK GARDENS		
		SAINT MARGARETS, TWICKENHAM	MIDDLESEX	ENGLAND
TAYLOR, FRANK	TV DIRECTOR	4201 ARCH DR	STUDIO CITY, CA	91604
TAYLOR, FRANK THOMAS	NEWS CORRESPONDENT	2501 CALVERT ST, NW	WASHINGTON, DC	20008
TAYLOR, GLENHALL	WRITER	1603 GLENDON AVE #6	LOS ANGELES, CA	90024
TAYLOR, GREG "FINGERS"	HARMONICIST	RED LIGHTNIN, THE WHITE HOUSE		
		THE SAINT, NORTH LOPHAM, DISS	NORFOLK IP22 2LU	ENGLAND
TAYLOR, HAL	NEWS CORRESPONDENT	19013 SHANNON WY	POOLESVILLE, MD	20837
TAYLOR, HOLLAND	ACTRESS	POST OFFICE BOX 5617	BEVERLY HILLS, CA	90210
TAYLOR, JAMES	SINGER	ASHER, 644 N DOHENY DR	LOS ANGELES, CA	90069
TAYLOR, JANET	ACTRESS	2501 W BURBANK BLVD #304	BURBANK, CA	91505
TAYLOR, JANICE	MEZZO-SOPRANO	CAMI, 165 W 57TH ST	NEW YORK, NY	10019
TAYLOR, JEFFREY	PHOTOGRAPHER	ANTONIA LOPEZ DE BELLO		
		445 SANTIAGO, NORT	CHILE	SOUTH AFRICA
TAYLOR, JERI	TV WRITER-DIRECTOR	3861 KINGSWOOD RD	SHERMAN OAKS, CA	91403
TAYLOR, JOAN	TV WRITER	8955 BEVERLY BLVD	LOS ANGELES, CA	90048
TAYLOR, JODI	ACTRESS	151 S EL CAMINO DR	BEVERLY HILLS, CA	90212
TAYLOR, JOHN	TALENT AGENT	POST OFFICE BOX 272	LONDON N20 0B4	ENGLAND
TAYLOR, JOHNNIE	SINGER	POST OFFICE BOX 82	GREAT NECK, NY	11021
TAYLOR, JOSEPH	ACTOR	JAYMES, 327 N LAUREL AVE	LOS ANGELES, CA	90048
TAYLOR, JOSH	ACTOR	9744 WILSHIRE BLVD #308	BEVERLY HILLS, CA	90212
TAYLOR, JUD	DIRECTOR	16425 BOSQUE DR	ENCINO, CA	91436
TAYLOR, JUDY	CASTING DIRECTOR	FENTON, 10201 W PICO BLVD	LOS ANGELES, CA	90035
TAYLOR, JUDY E	GUITARIST	POST OFFICE BOX 558	ANTIOCH, TN	37013
TAYLOR, JULIET	CASTING DIRECTOR	130 W 57TH ST	NEW YORK, NY	10019
TAYLOR, JUNE	ACTRESS	35 W 45TH ST	NEW YORK, NY	10036
TAYLOR, JUNE WHITLEY	ACTRESS	615 OCEAN AVE #1	SANTA MONICA, CA	90402
TAYLOR, KATE	SINGER	POST OFFICE BOX 36	CHILMARK, MA	02535
TAYLOR, KEN	TV WRITER	17 CREIGHTON AVE	LONDON N10	ENGLAND
TAYLOR, KURT B	COMEDY WRITER	572 E LOMA ALTA DR	ALTADENA, CA	91001
TAYLOR, LARRY	ACTOR	45 ABERDEEN ST, WESTDENE	JOHANNESBURG 2092	SOUTH AFRICA
TAYLOR, LARRY	GUITARIST	POST OFFICE BOX 23233	NASHVILLE, TN	37202
TAYLOR, LAUREN-MARIE	ACTRESS	ABC-TV NETWORK, "LOVING"		
		1330 AVE OF THE AMERICAS	NEW YORK, NY	10019
TAYLOR, LES	COMPOSER	17000 LISETTE ST	GRANADA HILLS, CA	91344
TAYLOR, LIVINGSTON	SINGER-SONGWRITER	POST OFFICE BOX 16	HILLSBORO, NH	03244
TAYLOR, MALCOLM	TV DIRECTOR	46 WORMHOLT RD	LONDON W12	ENGLAND
TAYLOR, MARC S	TV WRITER	8955 BEVERLY BLVD	LOS ANGELES, CA	90048
TAYLOR, MARCIA Z	NEWS CORRESPONDENT	5104 BRADLEY BLVD	CHEVY CHASE, MD	20815
TAYLOR, MARK L	ACTOR	7919 W NORTON AVE	LOS ANGELES, CA	90046
TAYLOR, MARSHA G	NEWS CORRESPONDENT	2501 CALVERT ST, NW	WASHINGTON, DC	20008
TAYLOR, MARY CURTIS	VIOLINIST	ROUTE #7, BOX 21	MURRAY, KY	42071
TAYLOR, MEDFORD	PHOTOGRAPHER	POST OFFICE BOX 53117	WASHINGTON, DC	20009
TAYLOR, MICHAEL	FILM PRODUCER	MACK-TAYLOR PRODUCTIONS		
		595 MADISON AVE	NEW YORK, NY	10022
TAYLOR, MILLARD	CONCERT MASTER	26 GIBBS ST	ROCHESTER, NY	14604
TAYLOR, PAUL	CHOREOGRAPHER	YESSELMAN, 550 BROADWAY	NEW YORK, NY	10012
TAYLOR, PAUL K	TV WRITER	999 N DOHENY DR #403	LOS ANGELES, CA	90069
TAYLOR, PAUL KELLY	NEWS ED	8321 BURNET AVE #8	SEPULVEDA, CA	91343
TAYLOR, PHILIP JOHN	TV WRITER	9200 SUNSET BLVD #431	LOS ANGELES, CA	90069
TAYLOR, PRISCILLA	ACTRESS	1033 LAS PULGAS RD	PACIFIC PALISADES, CA	90272

JAMES TAYLOR

JOSH TAYLOR

TEARS FOR FEARS

LEIGH TAYLOR-YOUNG

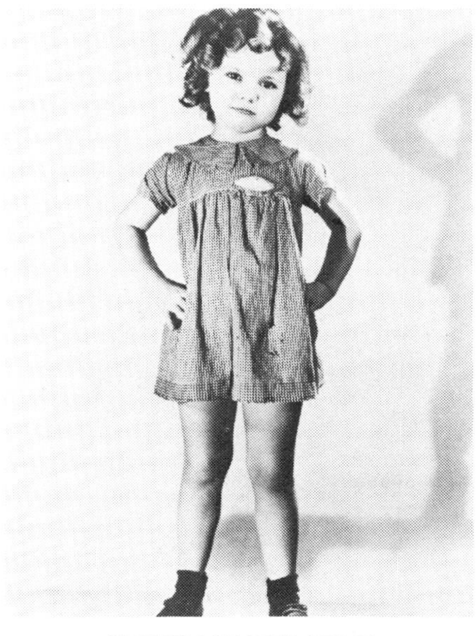
SHIRLEY TEMPLE

LAUREN TEWES

URSULA THEISS

ROY THINNES

B.J. THOMAS

Name	Occupation	Address	City/State	ZIP/Country
TAYLOR, RACHEL	ACTRESS	77 W 85TH ST	NEW YORK, NY	10024
TAYLOR, RAY L	PIANIST	303 MARKET ST, BOX 5	PORTLAND, TN	37148
TAYLOR, RENEE	ACTRESS-WRITER	BOLOGNA, 613 N ARDEN DR	BEVERLY HILLS, CA	90210
TAYLOR, RICHARD	NEWS REPORTER	THE NATIONAL ENQUIRER		
		600 SE COAST AVE	LANTANA, FL	33464
TAYLOR, RICHARD	WRITER-PRODUCER	5165 CANFIELD GARDENS	LONDON NW6	ENGLAND
TAYLOR, RICHARD L	NEWS CORRESPONDENT	1101 PENNSYLVANIA AVE, SE	WASHINGTON, DC	20003
TAYLOR, RICK S	DRUMMER	139 HILLSDALE DR	HENDERSONVILLE, TN	37075
TAYLOR, RIP	ACTOR	ICM, 8899 BEVERLY BLVD	LOS ANGELES, CA	90048
TAYLOR, ROBERT E	NEWS CORRESPONDENT	3417 QUESADA ST, NW	WASHINGTON, DC	20015
TAYLOR, ROD	ACTOR	2375 BOWMONT DR	BEVERLY HILLS, CA	90210
TAYLOR, RODERICK	SCREENWRITER	13233 STONERIDGE PL	SHERMAN OAKS, CA	91423
TAYLOR, RONALD A	NEWS CORRESPONDENT	105 ROCK CREEK CHURCH RD, NW	WASHINGTON, DC	20011
TAYLOR, ROSE	MEZZO-SOPRANO	POST OFFICE BOX 1515	NEW YORK, NY	10023
TAYLOR, SAM R, JR	NEWS CORRESPONDENT	1111 ARLINGTON BLVD	ARLINGTON, VA	22209
TAYLOR, SAMUEL A	WRITER	ICM, 8899 BEVERLY BLVD	LOS ANGELES, CA	90048
TAYLOR, SETH "FINGERS"	PIANIST	4774 TERRY RD	JACKSON, MS	39212
TAYLOR, SHARON	ACTRESS	LENZ, 1456 E CHARLESTON BLVD	LAS VEGAS, NV	89104
TAYLOR, STEVE	DRUMMER	641 TERESA DR	OLD HICKORY, TN	37138
TAYLOR, STUART S, JR	NEWS CORRESPONDENT	3816 JOCELYN ST, NW	WASHINGTON, DC	20015
TAYLOR, SUSAN	GUITARIST	2608 W 17TH ST	PLAINVIEW, TX	79072
TAYLOR, TAMMY	ACTRESS	KELMAN, 7813 SUNSET BLVD	LOS ANGELES, CA	90046
TAYLOR, TED	MUSICIAN	454 W 46TH ST #1B-N	NEW YORK, NY	10036
TAYLOR, TUT	GUITARIST	ROUTE #15, BOX 398	PIGEON FORGE, TN	37863
TAYLOR, WALLY	ACTOR	9255 SUNSET BLVD #1105	LOS ANGELES, CA	90069
TAYLOR, WILLIAM A, JR	DIRECTOR	34 ESSEX LN	DEERFIELD, IL	60015
TAYLOR, WILLIAM B	ACTOR	10845 LINDBROOK DR #3	LOS ANGELES, CA	90024
TAYLOR, WILLIAM J	TV WRITER	8955 BEVERLY BLVD	LOS ANGELES, CA	90048
TAYLOR-ALLAN, LEE	ACTRESS	11726 SAN VICENTE BLVD #300	LOS ANGELES, CA	90049
TAYLOR-CORBETT, LYNNE	CHOREOGRAPHER	POST OFFICE BOX 884	NEW YORK, NY	10023
TAYLOR-GOOD, KAREN	SINGER	ESSEX MANAGEMENT		
		1111 16TH AVE S	NASHVILLE, TN	37212
TAYLOR-MEAD, ELIZABETH	TV PRODUCER	METROPOLIS, 8 NEAL'S YARD	LONDON WC2	ENGLAND
TAYLOR-YOUNG, LEIGH	ACTRESS	702 N ELM DR	BEVERLY HILLS, CA	90210
TAZAKI, ETSKO	PIANIST	AIA, 60 E 42ND ST	NEW YORK, NY	10165
TCHERKASSKY, MICHAEL	PHOTOGRAPHER	10154 GOODIN CIR	COLUMBIA, MD	21046
TEAGAN	BODYBUILDER	POST OFFICE BOX 621	VENICE, CA	90294
TEAGUE, BOB	MUSICIAN	POST OFFICE BOX 110753	NASHVILLE, TN	37211
TEAGUE, JEFFREY	DRUMMER	2116 W LINDEN AVE	NASHVILLE, TN	37212
TEAGUE, LEWIS	FILM DIRECTOR	2190 N BEVERLY GLEN BLVD	LOS ANGELES, CA	90077
TEAGUE, MARSHALL	ACTOR	9200 SUNSET BLVD #1009	LOS ANGELES, CA	90069
TEAL, DONALD	VIOLINIST	3706 WOODMONT BLVD	NASHVILLE, TN	37215
TEARE, JACQUELINE K	NEWS CORRESPONDENT	4886 S 28TH ST #A	ARLINGTON, VA	22206
TEARE, JOHN H	NEWS CORRESPONDENT	4886 S 28TH ST #A	ARLINGTON, VA	22206
TEARS, THE	ROCK & ROLL GROUP	618 1/4 N DOHENY DR	LOS ANGELES, CA	90069
TEARS FOR FEARS	ROCK & ROCK DUO	POST OFFICE BOX 4ZN	LONDON W1A 4ZN	ENGLAND
TEAZ	ROCK & ROLL GROUP	VARIETY ARTISTS INTL, INC		
		9073 NEMO ST, 3RD FLOOR	LOS ANGELES, CA	90069
TEDE, MARGERY	MEZZO-SOPRANO	243 W END AVE #907	NEW YORK, NY	10023
TEDESCO, LOU	TV DIRECTOR	11666 MAYFIELD AVE	LOS ANGELES, CA	90049
TEDICK, FEODORE	ACTOR	POST OFFICE BOX 397	CLIFTON, NJ	07011
TEDROW, IRENE	ACTRESS	5763 CORTEEN PL	NORTH HOLLYWOOD, CA	91602
TEEFY, MAUREEN	ACTRESS	SCHUMER-OUBRE, 1697 BROADWAY	NEW YORK, NY	10019
TEEL, ROSS	TV WRITER	CONTEMPORARY ARTISTS		
		132 S LASKY DR	BEVERLY HILLS, CA	90212
TEEMS, DAVID & BLUE EAGLE	ROCK & ROLL GROUP	POST OFFICE BOX 723591	ATLANTA, GA	30339
TEENA MARIE	SINGER	151 S EL CAMINO DR	BEVERLY HILLS, CA	90212
TEENAGE HEAD	ROCK & ROLL GROUP	41 BRITAIN ST #200	TORONTO, ONT	CANADA
TEENAGERS, THE	VOCAL GROUP	JOEL WARSHAW MANAGEMENT		
		11 MIDDLE NECK RD	GREAT NECK, NY	11021
TEESDALE, CAROL	ACTRESS	2141 S BENTLEY AVE #201	LOS ANGELES, CA	90025
TEETER, ASA	ACTOR	23387 HARTLAND ST	CANOGA PARK, CA	91307
TEETERS, CLARENCE	DANCER	AFFILIATE ARTISTS, LTD		
		37 W 65TH ST, 6TH FLOOR	NEW YORK, NY	10023
TEEZE	ROCK & ROLL GROUP	POST OFFICE BOX 308	LANSDALE, PA	19446
TEFKIN, BLAIR	ACTRESS	11726 SAN VICENTE BLVD #300	LOS ANGELES, CA	90049
TEGLAND, A L	TV WRITER	554 S SAN VICENTE BLVD #3	LOS ANGELES, CA	90048
TEICHER, LOUIS	PIANIST	GLISS ENTERPRISES, INC		
		1180 AVE OF THE AMERICAS	NEW YORK, NY	10036
TEICHER, ROY	TV WRITER-PRODUCER	4415 PLACIDIA AVE	NORTH HOLLYWOOD, CA	91602
TEICHMANN, REINHARD	ACTOR	SCHOEMAN, 2600 W VICTORY BLVD	BURBANK, CA	91505
TEITELBAUM, IRVING	TV PRODUCER	23 HAMILTON GARDENS	LONDON WC2	ENGLAND
TEITLER, WILLIAM	DIRECTOR	434 GREENWICH ST	NEW YORK, NY	10013
TELANDER, RICK	SPORTS WRITER-EDITOR	SPORTS ILLUSTRATED MAGAZINE		
		TIME & LIFE BUILDING		
		ROCKEFELLER CENTER	NEW YORK, NY	10020
TELEP-EHRLICH, JUDITH	SOPRANO	LIEBERMAN, 11 RIVERSIDE DR	NEW YORK, NY	10023
TELESE, MARYANNE	SOPRANO	MUNRO, 334 W 72ND ST	NEW YORK, NY	10023
TELETUNES, THE	ROCK & ROLL GROUP	POST OFFICE BOX 427	BROOMFIELD, CO	80020
TELFORD, BOB F	ACTOR	10850 RIVERSIDE DR #505	NORTH HOLLYWOOD, CA	91602
TELFORD, ROBERT S	ACTOR-DIRECTOR	3925 E 14TH ST	LONG BEACH, CA	90804
TELGENHOF, PAM	ACTRESS	20652 LASSEN ST #70	CHATSWORTH, CA	91311
TELGENHOF, TAM	ACTRESS	20652 LASSEN ST #70	CHATSWORTH, CA	91311
TELL, ARTHUR	ACTOR	360 E 72ND ST	NEW YORK, NY	10021
TELSA	ROCK & ROLL GROUP	GEFFEN RECORDS COMPANY		
		9130 SUNSET BLVD	LOS ANGELES, CA	90069

Name	Occupation	Address	City	Zip / Country
TEMES, WILLARD	GUITARIST	ROUTE #4, BOX 349	COLUMBIA, TN	38401
TEMIANKA, HENRI	VIOLINIST	2915 PATRICIA AVE	LOS ANGELES, CA	90064
TEMPCHIN, JACK	SINGER-SONGWRITER	103 N HWY 101 #1013	ENCINITAS, CA	92008
TEMPE	C & W GROUP	POST OFFICE BOX 256577	CHICAGO, IL	60625
TEMPLE, CARLA	BODYBUILDER	1215 DAVIE ST #120	VANCOUVER, BC V6E 1N4	CANADA
TEMPLE, JULIEN	FILM DIRECTOR	MIDNIGHT, 1 SLINGSBY PL	LONDON WC2	ENGLAND
TEMPLE BLACK, SHIRLEY	ACTRESS	115 LAKEVIEW DR	WOODSIDE, CA	94062
TEMPLETON, BEN	CARTOONIST	TRIBUNE MEDIA SERVICES		
		64 E CONCORD ST	ORLANDO, FL	32801
TEMPLETON, CHRISTOPHER	ACTRESS	8485 MELROSE PL #E	LOS ANGELES, CA	90069
TEMPLETON, GARRY	BASEBALL	13552 DEL MONTE RD	POWAY, CA	92064
TEMPLETON, JO	DRUMMER	POST OFFICE BOX 583	GALLATIN, TN	37066
TEMPO, NINO	SINGER	19530 SUPERIOR ST	NORTHRIDGE, CA	91324
TEMPTATIONS, THE	VOCAL GROUP	STAR DIRECTION MGMT		
		605 N OAKHURST DR	BEVERLY HILLS, CA	90210
TEN TEN	ROCK & ROLL GROUP	POST OFFICE BOX 27983	RICHMOND, VA	23261
TENAN, JODY LYNN	ACTRESS	11339 1/2 HOMEDALE ST	LOS ANGELES, CA	90049
TENDETER, STACY	ACTRESS	27 THORNBY RD	LONDON E5	ENGLAND
TENDLER, BEA	ACTRESS	29 HURRICANE ST #1	MARINA DEL REY, CA	90292
TENENBAUM, HENRY L	NEWS CORRESPONDENT	NBC-TV, NEWS DEPARTMENT		
		4001 NEBRASKA AVE, NW	WASHINGTON, DC	20016
TENENBAUM, JERRY	VIDEO EDITOR	ENTERTAINMENT TONIGHT		
		PARAMOUNT TELEVISION		
		5555 MELROSE AVE	LOS ANGELES, CA	90038
TENKAY, DENA	ACTRESS-MODEL	MODELS & PROMOTIONS AGENCY		
		8560 SUNSET BLVD, 10TH FLOOR	LOS ANGELES, CA	90069
TENNANT, ANDY	ACTOR-WRITER	10807 ASHTON AVE	LOS ANGELES, CA	90024
TENNANT, VICTORIA	ACTRESS	HEATH, PARAMOUNT HOUSE		
		162-170 WARDOUR ST	LONDON W1V 3AT	ENGLAND
TENNENHOUSE, ROBERT	ACTOR	320 W 76TH ST #5-D	NEW YORK, NY	10023
TENNENT, LESLIE	BARITONE	45 W 60TH ST #4-K	NEW YORK, NY	10023
TENNESSEANS, THE	C & W GROUP	POST OFFICE BOX 17272	MEMPHIS, TN	38187
TENNESSEE JERRY	GUITARIST	GENERAL DELIVERY	RUTHERFORD, TN	38369
TENNESTEDT, KLAUS	CONDUCTOR	ROESELL 13, 2305 HEIKENDORF	HAMBURG	WEST GERMANY
TENNEY, CHRISTOPHER	ACTOR	1016 S BARRINGTON AVE	LOS ANGELES, CA	90049
TENNEY, MARTY	TV WRITER	8955 BEVERLY BLVD	LOS ANGELES, CA	90048
TENNILLE, TONI	SINGER	SEE - CAPTAIN & TENNILLE, THE		
TENNIS, CRAIG G	WRITER	4560 MARTSON DR	ENCINO, CA	91316
TENNSTEDT, KLAUS	CONDUCTOR	53 WELBECK ST	LONDON W1	ENGLAND
TENNYSON, LEONARD B	NEWS CORRESPONDENT	3801 FULTON ST, NW	WASHINGTON, DC	20007
TENOWICH, THOMAS F	TV WRITER	4936 GLORIA AVE	ENCINO, CA	91436
TENPENNY, LEE	GUITARIST	ROUTE #2	MURFREESBORO, TN	37130
TENSER, MARILYN	FILM PRODUCER	CROWN INTERNATIONAL, INC		
		8701 WILSHIRE BLVD	BEVERLY HILLS, CA	90211
TEPPER, ESTELLE	CASTING DIRECTOR	7033 SUNSET BLVD #208	LOS ANGELES, CA	90028
TEPPER, KIRBY	ACTOR	11508 CANTON DR	STUDIO CITY, CA	91604
TEPPER, ROBERT	SINGER-GUITARIST	SCOTTI BROS, 2128 PICO BLVD	SANTA MONICA, CA	90405
TEPPER, WILLIAM	ACTOR-WRITER	STONE, 1052 CAROL DR	LOS ANGELES, CA	90069
TEQUILA SUNRISE	C & W GROUP	BENNETT, 4630 DEEPDALE DR	CORPUS CHRISTI, TX	78413
TERADA, KAYO	NEWS CORRESPONDENT	444 N CAPITOL ST, NW	WASHINGTON, DC	20001
TERILLI, JOHN	BODYBUILDER	POST OFFICE BOX M47	HOBOKEN, NJ	07030
TERKEL, STUDS	NOVELIST	850 W CASTLEWOOD TERR	CHICAGO, IL	60640
TERMO, LEONARD	ACTOR	11908 DARLINGTON AVE	LOS ANGELES, CA	90049
TERPILOFF, ELIZABETH BARROWS	WRITER	1788 S HOLT AVE #202-A	LOS ANGELES, CA	90035
TERRANCE, MICHAEL	TV WRITER	8955 BEVERLY BLVD	LOS ANGELES, CA	90048
TERRANOVA, CAROLINE	VIOLINIST	1502 WOODMONT BLVD	NASHVILLE, TN	37215
TERRANOVA, DAN	ACTOR	18055 RANCHO ST	ENCINO, CA	91316
TERRANOVA, SAMUEL	VIOLINIST	1502 WOODMONT BLVD	NASHVILLE, TN	37215
TERRELL, IRENE	CASTING DIRECTOR	6331 HOLLYWOOD BLVD #273	LOS ANGELES, CA	90028
TERRENCE, PHILIP	TV DIRECTOR-PRODUCER	12214 IREDELL ST	STUDIO CITY, CA	91604
TERRI, VICKI	ACTRESS	6867 BABCOCK AVE	NORTH HOLLYWOOD, CA	91605
TERRILL, HOWARD	FILM EDITOR	ACE, 4416 1/2 FINLEY AVE	LOS ANGELES, CA	90027
TERRIO, DENEY	DANCER-TV HOST	8535 W KNOLL DR #311	LOS ANGELES, CA	90069
TERRIS, MALCOLM	ACTOR	14 ENGLAND'S LN	LONDON NW3	ENGLAND
TERRIS, NORMA	SINGER-ACTRESS	SEA RANCH CLUB		
		5100 N OCEAN BLVD #711	FORT LAUDERDALE, FL	33308
TERRY, ALICE	ACTRESS	INGRAM, 11566 KELSEY ST	NORTH HOLLYWOOD, CA	91608
TERRY, BILL	BASEBALL	POST OFFICE BOX 2177	JACKSONVILLE, FL	32202
TERRY, CLARK, BIG BAND	JAZZ BAND	WILLARD ALEXADNER, INC		
		660 MADISON AVE	NEW YORK, NY	10021
TERRY, GORDON	GUITARIST	1510 LETHIA DR	NASHVILLE, TN	37206
TERRY, JOE M	GUITARIST	1303 W 11TH ST	SHEFFIELD, AL	35660
TERRY, JOSEPH C	DIRECTOR	DGA, 110 W 57TH ST	NEW YORK, NY	10019
TERRY, KEN	COLUMNIST	VARIETY, 1400 N CAHUENGA BLVD	HOLLYWOOD, CA	90028
TERRY, MEGAN	PLAYWRIGHT	2309 HANSCOM BLVD	OMAHA, NE	68105
TERRY, NIGEL	ACTOR	KATE FEAST MANAGEMENT		
		43-A PRINCESS RD		
		REGENTS PARK	LONDON NW1 8JS	ENGLAND
TERRY & THE PIRATES	ROCK & ROLL GROUP	POST OFFICE BOX 4355	ARLINGTON, VA	22204
TERRY-THOMAS	ACTOR	15 BERKELEY ST #11	LONDON W1	ENGLAND
TERWILLIGER, TOM	BODYBUILDER	BETTER BODIES MODEL & SPORTS		
		12 W 21ST ST	NEW YORK, NY	10010
TESH, JOHN	TV HOST	ENTERTAINMENT TONIGHT		
		PARAMOUNT TELEVISION		
		5555 MELROSE AVE	LOS ANGELES, CA	90038

THE TEMPTATIONS

Richard Street • Dennis Edwards • Otis Williams • Melvin Franklin • Glenn Leonard

TOTO

Mike Porcaro • Joseph Williams • Bobby Kimball • Steve Porcaro • Steve Lukather • David Paich

Name	Occupation	Address	City	Zip
TESICH, STEVE	SCREENWRITER	ICM, 40 W 57TH ST	NEW YORK, NY	10019
TESLER, BRIAN	TV EXECUTIVE	89 PARK RD, CHISWICK	LONDON W4	ENGLAND
TESREAU, KRISTA	ACTRESS	CBS-TV, "THE GUIDING LIGHT"		
		51 W 52ND ST	NEW YORK, NY	10019
TESSENYI, JANOS	BASSO-BARITONE	KAY, 58 W 58TH ST	NEW YORK, NY	10019
TESSIER, ALBERT D	COMPOSER-CONDUCTOR	3926 ARLINGTON AVE	LOS ANGELES, CA	90008
TESSIER, ROBERT W	ACTOR	JAYMES, 327 N LAUREL AVE	LOS ANGELES, CA	90048
TESTA, ANN L	COMPOSER	1811 N PEPPER ST	BURBANK, CA	91505
TESTA, WALTER	COMPOSER	2120 STRAND	HERMOSA BEACH, CA	90254
TESTO, RUSS	BODYBUILDER	3 OXFORD RD	TROY, NY	12180
TETA, ROBERT L	ACTOR	17043 MIDWOOD DR	GRANADA HILLS, CA	91344
TETER, JAN	ACTRESS	9229 SUNSET BLVD #611	LOS ANGELES, CA	90069
TETER, JIM	COMEDIAN	ROHRBACH, 1525 CEDAR CLIFF DR	CAMP HILL, PA	17011
TETREAULT, STEPHAN R	NEWS CORRESPONDENT	5320 LA ROCHELLE CT	ALEXANDRIA, VA	22310
TETRICK, MICHAEL C	TV DIRECTOR	622 PRAIRIE	WILMETTE, IL	60091
TETZLAFF, TED	FILM DIRECTOR	DGA, 7950 SUNSET BLVD	HOLLYWOOD, CA	90046
TEUBER, JERRY	COMPOSER	POST OFFICE BOX 1193	DESERT HOT SPRINGS, CA	92240
TEUBER, JOHN	NEWS CORRESPONDENT	3624 WHITEHAVEN PARKWAY, NW	WASHINGTON, DC	20007
TEUFEL, RON	BODYBUILDER	THE UNIVERSE GYM		
		18763 W 107TH AVE	MIAMI, FL	33157
TEWES, LAUREN	ACTRESS	10509 CUSHDON AVE	LOS ANGELES, CA	90064
TEWKESBURY, JOAN	FILM WRITER-DIRECTOR	201 OCEAN AVE #1702-B	SANTA MONICA, CA	90402
TEWSON, JOSEPHINE	ACTRESS	IAR, 235-241 REGENT ST	LONDON W1A 2JT	ENGLAND
TEX AND THE HORSEHEADS	ROCK & ROLL GROUP	POST OFFICE BOX 2428	EL SEGUNDO, CA	90245
TEXAS LONG RIDER	WRESTLER	SEE - CASEY, SCOTT		
TEXAS RENEGADE	C & W GROUP	POST OFFICE BOX 57291	DALLAS, TX	75207
TEXAS THUNDER BAND	C & W GROUP	POST OFFICE BOX 171132	NASHVILLE, TN	37217
TEXAS TRADITION	C & W GROUP	POST OFFICE BOX 57291	DALLAS, TX	75207
TEXAS TWISTER, THE	WRESTLER	SEE - HOUSTON, SAM		
TEXAS VOCAL CO	C & W GROUP	3198 ROYAL LN #204	DALLAS, TX	75229
TEXAS WATER	C & W GROUP	1311 CANDLELIGHT AVE	DALLAS, TX	75216
TEXTER, GILDA	ACTRESS	3391 TROY DR	LOS ANGELES, CA	90068
TEXTONES, THE	ROCK & ROLL GROUP	151 S EL CAMINO DR	BEVERLY HILLS, CA	90212
TH' INBRED	MUSIC GROUP	POST OFFICE BOX 242	PONOMA, CA	91769
THACKER, ROCKY LANE	GUITARIST	721 NEW DUE WEST AVE #F-201	MADISON, TN	37115
THACKERY, BUD	CINEMATOGRAPHER	POST OFFICE BOX 2230	HOLLYWOOD, CA	90078
THADANI, JAYA	NEWS CORRESPONDENT	4701 WILLARD AVE #1724	CHEVY CHASE, MD	20815
THAI, TED	PHOTOGRAPHER	TIME/TIME & LIFE BLDG		
		ROCKEFELLER CENTER	NEW YORK, NY	10020
THALER, ALVIN	DIRECTOR	8 E 83RD ST	NEW YORK, NY	10028
THALER, FRED R	COMPOSER-CONDUCTOR	16169 SUNSET BLVD #306	PACIFIC PALISADES, CA	90272
THALER, ROBERT	ACTOR	KNBC-TV, "SANTA BARBARA"		
		3000 W ALAMEDA AVE	BURBANK, CA	91523
THAMES, ROBERT	DRUMMER	920 ALGONQUIN CT	ANTIOCH, TN	37013
THATCHER, GERALD T	CONDUCTOR	1134 E COLLINS AVE	ORANGE, CA	92667
THATCHER, JAMES W	COMPOSER	13521 TERR PL	WHITTIER, CA	90601
THAU, LINDA E	TV WRITER-PRODUCER	828 14TH ST #5	SANTA MONICA, CA	90403
THAW, JOHN	ACTOR	70 GROVE PARK RD, CHISWICK	LONDON W4	ENGLAND
THAW, MORT	WRITER	1263 N FLORES ST	LOS ANGELES, CA	90069
THAXTER, PHYLLIS	ACTRESS	716 RIOMAR DR	VERO BEACH, FL	32960
THAYARD, HARRY	TENOR	59 E 54TH ST #81	NEW YORK, NY	10022
THAYER, BRYNN	ACTRESS	888 7TH AVE #201	NEW YORK, NY	10019
THAYER, LORNA	ACTRESS	4055 TUJUNGA AVE #210	STUDIO CITY, CA	91604
THAYER, MAX	ACTOR	ICM, 8899 BEVERLY BLVD	LOS ANGELES, CA	90048
THE ACE	STUD	SEE - RASMUSSEN, R J "ACE"		
THE AMERICAN DREAM	WRESTLER	SEE - RHODES, DUSTY		
THE ANGEL OF DEATH	WRESTLER	SEE - SHELDON, DAVID		
THE ANIMAL	WRESTLER	SEE - STEELE, GEORGE		
		"THE ANIMAL"		
THE ANVIL	WRESTLER	SEE - NEIDHART, JIM "THE ANVIL"		
THE BARBARIAN	WRESTLER	SEE - KONGA THE BARBARIAN		
THE BEST	WRESTLER	SEE - ORTON, COWBOY BOB		
THE BIRDMAN	WRESTLER	SEE - WARE, KOKO B		
THE BLOCKS	SWORD BALANCERS	SEE - BLOCKS, THE		
THE BLONDE BOMBER	WRESTLER	SEE - STEVENS, RAY		
		"THE CRIPPLER "		
THE BODY	WRESTLER-ANNOUNCER	SEE - VENTURA, JESSE "THE BODY"		
THE BRAIN	WRESTLING MANAGER	SEE - HEENAN, BOBBY "THE BRAIN"		
THE BRANDON BULL	WRESTLER	SEE - ORNDORFF, PAUL		
		"MR WONDERFUL"		
THE CANADIAN BUMBLE BEE	WRESTLER	SEE - BLACKWELL, CRUSHER JERRY		
THE CANADIAN ROAD WARRIOR	WRESTLER	SEE - CANADIAN ROAD WARIOR, THE		
THE CENTRONS	AERIAL MOTORCYCLISTS	SEE - CENTRONS, THE		
THE CHEERLEADERS	WRESTLING TAG TEAM	SEE - CHEERLEADERS, THE		
THE CHIMES FAMILY	HARMONICA VIRTUOSOS	SEE - CHIMES FAMILY, THE		
THE CHRISSENS	AERIAL CRADLE DUO	SEE - CHRISSENS, LES		
THE COLONEL	WRESTLING MANAGER	SEE - HART, COLONEL JIMMY		
THE CRIPPLER	WRESTLER	SEE - STEVENS, RAY		
THE CRIPPLER	WRESTLER	SEE - BUNDY, KING KONG		
		"THE CRIPPLER"		
THE CRUSHER	WRESTLER	SEE - BLACKWELL, CRUSHER JERRY		
THE CYCLONIANS	UNICYCLISTS	SEE - CYCLONIANS, THE		
THE DOCTOR OF STYLE	WRESTLING MANAGER	SEE - SLICK "THE DOCTOR		
		OF STYLE "		

THE DOLLY SISTERS	AERIAL TRIO	SEE - DOLLY SISTERS, THE	
THE DRAGON	WRESTLER	SEE - STEAMBOAT, RICKY "THE DRAGON"	
THE DREAM TEAM	WRESTLING TAG TEAM	SEE - NEW DREAM TEAM, THE	
THE DYNAMITE KID	WRESTLER	SEE - BRITISH BULLDOGS, THE	
THE ENEMY WITHIN	ROCK & ROLL GROUP	SEE - ENEMY WITHIN, THE	
THE FABULOUS THUNDERBIRDS	ROCK & ROLL GROUP	SEE - FABULOUS THUNDERBIRDS, THE	
THE FARMER'S DAUGHTER	WRESTLER	SEE - SALLY THE FARMER'S DAUGHTER	
THE FIVE PLATTERS	VOCAL GROUP	SEE - PLATTERS, THE	
THE FLYING CORTEZ	TRAPEZE TROUPE	SEE - FLYING CIRTEZ, THE	
THE FLYING ESPANAS	TRAPEZE ACT	SEE - FLYING ESPANAS, THE	
THE FLYING IBARRAS	AERIAL ACT	SEE - IBARRAS, THE FLYING	
THE FLYING LA RAYS	TRAPEZE ACT	SEE - FLYING LA RAYS, THE	
THE FLYING LANES	FLYING TRAPEZE ACT	SEE - FLYING LANES, THE	
THE FLYING PAGES	TRAPEZE ACT	SEE - PAGES, THE FLYING	
THE FORNASARY FAMILY	ACROBATS	SEE - FORNASARY FAMILY, THE	
THE FOSSET FAMILY	SWAPOLE ACT	SEE - FOSSET FAMILY, THE	
THE FRANCONI DUO	TRAPEZE ACT	SEE - FRANCONI DUO, THE	
THE FREEBIRD	WRESTLER	SEE - HAYES, MICHAEL "P S"	
THE FRENCH GIANT	WRESTLER	SEE - ANDRE THE GIANT	
THE GIANT	WRESTLER	SEE - ANDRE THE GIANT	
THE GLORIONS	CRADLE-PERCH DUO	SEE - GLORIONS, THE	
THE GOLDEN BOY	WRESTLER	SEE - SPIVEY, DANIEL "GOLDEN BOY"	
THE GOLDEN SISTERS	ACROBATIC DUO	SEE - GOLDEN SISTERS, THE	
THE GRAPPLER	WRESTLER	SEE - GRAPPLER, THE	
THE GRAPPLER II	WRESTLER	SEE - GRAPPLER II	
THE GREAT HUBERTO	AERIAL ACT	SEE - HUBERTO, GREAT	
THE GREAT VENTURA	WRESTLER-ANNOUNCER	SEE - VENTURA, JESSE "THE BODY"	
THE GREAT WALLENDAS	HIGH WIRE ACT	SEE - WALLENDAS, THE GREAT	
THE GREAT WIRENGRAD	SWAYPOLIST	SEE - WIRENGRAD, GREAT	
THE GREAT WOJO	WRESTLER	SEE - GREAT WOJO, THE	
THE GREEK	ODDSMAKER	SEE - SNYDER, JIMMY "THE GREEK"	
THE GRIND	ROCK & ROLL GROUP	SEE - GRIND, THE	
THE HACKENSACK HAMMER	WRESTLER	SEE - WOLFE, BUDDY	
THE HAMMER	WRESTLER	SEE - VALENTINE, GREG "THE HAMMER"	
THE HANGMAN	WRESTLER	SEE - BLACK BART	
THE HART FOUNDATION	WRESTLING DUO	SEE - HART FOUNDATION, THE	
THE HEADHUNTERS	WRESTLING TAG TEAM	SEE - HEADHUNTERS, THE	
THE HEAVY METAL SISTERS	WRESTLING TAG TEAM	SEE - HEAVY METAL SISTERS, THE	
THE HIT MAN	WRESTLER	SEE - HART, BRET "HIT MAN"	
THE HOOD	WRESTLER	SEE - MANTELL, JOHNNY	
THE HOT ROD	WRESTLER	SEE - PIPER, ROWDY RODDY	
THE HULK	WRESTLER	SEE - HOGAN, HULK	
THE HULKSTER	WRESTLER	SEE - HOGAN, HULK	
THE HUMAN BOMB	HUMAN BOMB	SEE - KOSKE, BENNY	
THE HUMAN TORCH	HUMAN TORCH	SEE - GILBRIDE, JOE "THE HUMAN TORCH"	
THE INCREDIBLE HULK	WRESTLER	SEE - HOGAN, HULK	
THE INTELLIGENT MONSTER	WRESTLER	SEE - BRODY, BRUISER	
THE INVADER	WRESTLER	SEE - MURDICH, DICK	
THE ITALIAN STALLION	WRESTLER	SEE - ITALIAN STALLION, THE	
THE JAMAICAN KID	WRESTLER	SEE - JAMAICAN KID, THE	
THE KANSAS JAYHAWKS	WRESTLING TAG TEAM	SEE - KANSAS JAYHAWKS, THE	
THE KING OF WRESTLING	WRESTLER	SEE - RACE, HANDSOME HARLEY	
THE KNOPS	ACROBATIC DUO	SEE - KNOPS, THE	
THE KNUCKLEHEADS	ROCK & ROLL GROUP	SEE - JOHNNY & THE KNUCKLEHEADS	
THE KORMATES	HIGHPOLE ACT	SEE - KORMATES, THE	
THE LEFT	ROCK & ROLL GROUP	SEE - LEFT, THE	
THE LOVELY ELIZABETH	WRESTLING VALET-MGR	SEE - MISS ELIZABETH	
THE MAGNIFICENT MURACO	WRESTLER	SEE - MURACO, DON "MAGNIFICENT"	
THE MANIAC	WRESTLER	SEE - BORNE, MATT	
THE MASK MAN	WRESTLER	SEE - MASK MAN, THE	
THE MASKED AVENGER	WRESTLER	SEE - ADAMS, CHRIS "GENTLEMAN"	
THE MASKED EXECUTIONER	WRESTLER	SEE - ROSE, PLAYBOY BUDDY	
THE MASKED SUPERSTAR	WRESTLER	SEE - MASKED SUPERSTAR, THE	
THE MIDNIGHT ROCKERS	WRESTLING TAG TEAM	SEE - MIDNIGHT ROCKERS, THE	
THE MIGHTY IGOR	WRESTLER	SEE - MIGHTY IGOR, THE	
THE MISING LINK	WRESTLER	SEE - MISING LINK, THE	
THE MOUTH OF THE SOUTH	WRESTLING MANAGER	SEE - HART, COLONEL JIMMY	
THE NAKED PREY	ROCK & ROLL GROUP	SEE - NAKED PREY, THE	
THE NATURAL	WRESTLER	SEE - REED, BUTCH "THE NATURAL"	
THE NATURE BOY	WRESTLER	SEE - LANDELL, BUDDY "NATURE BOY"	
THE NAVARROS	SKYCYCLE ACT	SEE - NAVARROS, THE	
THE NEW DREAM TEAM	WRESTLING TAG TEAM	SEE - NEW DREAM TEAM, THE	
THE NEW YORK SAMBA BAND	SAMBA BAND	SEE - NEW YORK SAMBA BAND, THE	
THE PLAYBOY	WRESTLER	SEE - ROSE, PLAYBOY BUDDY	
THE POSSO BROTHERS	HIGH WIRE TROUPE	SEE - POSSO BROS, THE	
THE PROFESSIONAL	WRESTLER	SEE - THORNTON, LES	
THE QUASSARS	AERIAL ROCKETSHIP ACT	SEE - QUASSARS, THE	
THE RAIDER	WRESTLER	SEE - RAIDER, THE	
THE RAMOS FAMILY	HIGH WIRE ACT	SEE - RAMOS FAMILY, THE	

Name	Occupation	Address	City	Zip
THE RAVISHING ONE	WRESTLER	SEE - RAVISHING ONE, THE		
THE REBEL	WRESTLER	SEE - SLATER, DICK "THE REBEL"		
THE REBEL	WRESTLER	SEE - ROBERTS, BUDDY "JACK"		
THE RED DEMON	WRESTLER	SEE - RED DEMON, THE		
THE RED SHADOW	WRESTLER	SEE - RED SHADOW, THE		
THE REV	ROCK & ROLL GROUP	SEE - REV, THE		
THE REVOLUTION	ROCK & ROLL GROUP	SEE - PRINCE & THE REVOLUTION		
THE RICHTERS	ACROBATIC TROUPE	SEE - RICHTERS, THE		
THE ROAD WARRIOR	WERSTLER	SEE - ROAD WARRIOR ANIMAL		
THE ROARING	ROCK & ROLL GROUP	SEE - ROARING, THE		
THE SAMOAN	WRESTLER	SEE - AFI, SIVA		
THE SCATMAN	GOLFER-STUD	SEE - THOMPSON, SCOTT		
		"THE SCATMAN"		
THE SENSATIONAL LEIGHS	AERIAL ACT	SEE - SENSATIONAL LEIGHS, THE		
THE SHEIK	WRESTLER	SEE - SHEIK, THE		
THE SKIPPER	BUSINESS AGENT	SEE - BERES, PETER		
		"THE SKIPPER"		
THE SLASH	ROCK & ROLL GROUP	SEE - NASH THE SLASH		
THE SMARTIES	ROCK & ROLL GROUP	SEE - SMARTIES, THE		
THE SMITHEREENS	ROCK & ROLL GROUP	SEE - SMITHEREENS, THE		
THE SMITHS	ROCK & ROLL GROUP	SEE - SMITHS, THE		
THE SOUTHERN BELLE	WRESTLER	SEE - SCARLET THE SOUTHERN BELLE		
THE SOUTHERN BELLES	WRESTLING TAG TEAM	SEE - SOUTHERN BELLES, THE		
THE SPIDER GODDESS	AERIALIST	SEE - DANUTA, THE SPIDER		
THE SPIKES	ROCK & ROLL GROUP	SEE - SPIKES, THE		
THE SPOILER	WRESTLER	SEE - SPOILER, THE		
THE STEAMER	WRESTLER	SEE - STEAMBOAT, RICKY		
		"THE DRAGON"		
THE STUDENT	WRESTLER	SEE - STEELE, GEORGE		
		"THE ANIMAL"		
THE SUBURBS	ROCK & ROLL GROUP	SEE - SUBURBS, THE		
THE SUPER MACHINE	WRESTLER	SEE - MASKED SUPERSTAR, THE		
THE SUPER NINJA	WRESTLER	SEE - SUPER NINJA, THE		
THE SUPERFLY	WRESTLER	SEE - AFI, SIVA		
THE TAILGATORS	ROCK & ROLL GROUP	SEE - TAILGATORS, THE		
THE TEXAS LONG RIDER	WRESTLER	SEE - CASEY, SCOTT		
THE TEXAS TWISTER	WRESTLER	SEE - HOUSTON, SAM		
THE THREE O'CLOCK	ROCK & ROLL GROUP	SEE - THREE O'CLOCK, THE		
THE UGANDAN GIANT	WRESTLER	SEE - KIMALA		
THE UGANDON HEAD HUNTER	WRESTLER	SEE - KIMALA		
THE VAMPIRE	WRESTLER	SEE - SMITH, DAVEY BOY		
THE VEX	ROCK & ROLL GROUP	SEE - VEX, THE		
THE VIKING	WRESTLER	SEE - VIKING, THE		
THE WARLORD	WRESTLER	SEE - WARLORD, THE		
THE WEASEL	WRESTLING MANAGER	SEE - HEENAN, BOBBY "THE BRAIN"		
THE WONDEROUS WINNS	AERIAL TROUPE	SEE - WINNS, THE WONDEROUS		
THEIDOR, MARLON	SINGER-GUITARIST	1335 LOUREL AVE	TOLEDO, OH	43614
THEISS, WILLIAM WARE	COSTUME DESIGNER	3872 LAS FLORES CANYON RD #1	MALIBU, CA	90265
THEMMEN, HAROLD B	CONDUCTOR	10734 VALLEY SPRING LN	NORTH HOLLYWOOD, CA	91602
THEODORE, DONNA	SINGER	20121 VENTURA BLVD #343	WOODLAND HILLS, CA	91364
THEODORE, SONDRA	ACT-SING-MOD	MODELS & PROMOTIONS AGENCY		
		8560 SUNSET BLVD, 10TH FLOOR	LOS ANGELES, CA	90069
THERESA	SINGER	POST OFFICE BOX 4	LAKE LURE, NC	28746
THERON, J P	SWAYPOLE DUO	HALL, 138 FROG HOLLOW RD	CHURCHVILLE, PA	18966
THEUS, B J	ACTOR	PACIFIC, 515 N LA CIENEGA BLVD	LOS ANGELES, CA	90048
THIBAUDET, JEAN-YVES	PIANIST	IMG ARTISTS, 22 E 71ST ST	NEW YORK, NY	10021
THIBEAU, JACK	ACTOR	3800 BARHAM BLVD #303	LOS ANGELES, CA	90068
THIBODEAU, DAVID	DRUMMER	1226 SEARCY ST #47	MURFREESBORO, TN	37130
THIBODEAU, RUFUS	VIOLINIST	ROUTE #2, BOX 272-C	DUSON, LA	70301
THICKE, ALAN	TV HOST-SINGER	POST OFFICE BOX 724	ALTADENA, CA	91001
THIEL, NICK	TV WRITER-PRODUCER	8955 BEVERLY BLVD	LOS ANGELES, CA	90048
THIELE, CHRISTOPHER W	TV DIRECTOR-EDITOR	3156 COOLIDGE AVE	LOS ANGELES, CA	90066
THIELE, JOHN C	WRITER-PRODUCER	6255 LE SAGE AVE	WOODLAND HILLS, CA	91367
THIELMAN, TOOTS, QUARTET	JAZZ QUARTET	HOFFER, 233 1/2 E 48TH ST	NEW YORK, NY	10017
THIES, DONALD E	NEWS CORRESPONDENT	978 SUMMERHILL DR	GAMBRILLS, MD	21054
THIESS, URSULA	ACTRESS	SCHACKER, 1940 BEL AIR RD	LOS ANGELES, CA	90077
THIESSEN, CHERIE	TV WRITER	8955 BEVERLY BLVD	LOS ANGELES, CA	90048
THIGPEN, DAVID E	NEWS REPORTER	TIME/TIME & LIFE BLDG		
		ROCKEFELLER CENTER	NEW YORK, NY	10020
THIGPEN, LYNNE	ACTRESS	35 W 20TH ST	NEW YORK, NY	10011
THIMMESCH, NICK	NEWS CORRESPONDENT	6301 BROADBRANCH RD	CHEVY CHASE, MD	20815
THINGS, THE	ROCK & ROLL GROUP	POST OFFICE BOX 7112	BURBANK, CA	91510
THINNES, ROY	ACTOR	2641 NICHOLS CANYON RD	LOS ANGELES, CA	90046
THIRD FINGER UP	ROCK & ROLL GROUP	POST OFFICE BOX 48597	NILES, IL	60648
THIRD WORLD	REGGAE BAND	JAH'S MUSIC, 6 DUMFRIES RD	KINGSTON 10	JAMAICA
THODE, WILLIAM SCOTT	PHOTOGRAPHER	41 62ND ST #12 1/2	WEST NEW YORK, NJ	07093
THOLSTED, MIMI	ACTRESS	6430 SUNSET BLVD #701	LOS ANGELES, CA	90028
THOM, RUTH	ACTRESS	8961 SUNSET BLVD #B	LOS ANGELES, CA	90069
THOMA, MARALYN	TV WRITER	8955 BEVERLY BLVD	LOS ANGELES, CA	90048
THOMA, STEVE	COMPOSER-CONDUCTOR	548 1/2 W CALIFORNIA ST	GLENDALE, CA	91203
THOMANN, BERNIE	TV WRITER	8955 BEVERLY BLVD	LOS ANGELES, CA	90048
THOMAS, ANNA	SCREENWRITER	ICM, 8899 BEVERLY BLVD	LOS ANGELES, CA	90069

THOMAS, ANNIE	CASTING DIRECTOR	2049 CENTURY PARK E #4100	LOS ANGELES, CA 90067
THOMAS, B J	SINGER-SONGWRITER	STARBOUND, 128 VOLUNTEER DR	HENDERSONVILLE, TN 37075
THOMAS, BETTY	ACTRESS	12750 VENTURA BLVD #102	STUDIO CITY, CA 91604
THOMAS, BRIAN K	GUITARIST	583 BLAKE MOORE DR	LA VERGNE, TN 37086
THOMAS, BRUCE	GUITARIST	1719 ALLISON PL	NASHVILLE, TN 37203
THOMAS, BUBBA	MUSICIAN	9777 HARWIN ST #101	HOUSTON, TX 77036
THOMAS, CAL	COLUMNIST	L A TIMES NEWSPAPER	
		TIMES MIRROR SQUARE	NEW YORK, NY 90053
THOMAS, CHARLES MICHAEL	BANJOIST	18 VALLEY CT	BRENTWOOD, TN 37027
THOMAS, CHRISTOPHER	ACTOR	5967 W 3RD ST #205	LOS ANGELES, CA 90036
THOMAS, CHRISTOPHER	NEWS CORRESPONDENT	12216 RED CHURCH CT	POTOMAC, MD 20854
THOMAS, CHRISTOPHER P	NEWS CORRESPONDENT	9410 CHATTEROY PL	GAITHERSBURG, MD 20879
THOMAS, CLARENCE	COMPOSER	3908 DEGNAN BLVD	LOS ANGELES, CA 90008
THOMAS, DAMIEN	ACTOR	31 KINGS RD	LONDON SW3 4RD ENGLAND
THOMAS, DANNY	ACTOR-DIRECTOR	1187 N HILLCREST RD	BEVERLY HILLS, CA 90210
THOMAS, DARRELL, BAND	C & W GROUP	POST OFFICE BOX B	CARLISLE, IA 50047
THOMAS, DAVID	BASS	BYERS-SCHWALBE, 1 5TH AVE	NEW YORK, NY 10003
THOMAS, DAVID	SINGER	TWIN TONE RECORDS	
		2541 NICOLLET AVE	MINNEAPOLIS, MN 55404
THOMAS, DOUGLAS	FILM EXECUTIVE	127 WARDOUR ST	LONDON W1 ENGLAND
THOMAS, EDWARD DUFF	PHOTOGRAPHER	1101 ARLINGTON BLVD	ARLINGTON, VA 22209
THOMAS, ELVIN B	SINGER-GUITARIST	ROUTE #1	CASTALIAN SPRINGS, TN 37031
THOMAS, ERHARD	NEWS CORRESPONDENT	3132 "M" ST, NW	WASHINGTON, DC 20007
THOMAS, ERNEST	ACTOR	9021 MELROSE AVE #304	LOS ANGELES, CA 90069
THOMAS, FRANK M	ACTOR	4140 WARNER BLVD #210	BURBANK, CA 91505
THOMAS, FRANKIE, JR	ACTOR	4140 WARNER BLVD #210	BURNAK, CA 91505
THOMAS, GAVIN OWEN	DIRECTOR	DGA, 110 W 57TH ST	NEW YORK, NY 10019
THOMAS, GERALD	FILM DIRECTOR	PINEWOOD STUDIOS, IVER HEATH	BUCKS SLO ONH ENGLAND
THOMAS, GORMAN	BASEBALL	759 TALLWOOD RD	CHARLESTON, SC 29412
THOMAS, GUY	SCREENWRITER	8955 BEVERLY BLVD	LOS ANGELES, CA 90048
THOMAS, HEATHER	ACTRESS-MODEL	329 N WETHERLY DR #205	BEVERLY HILLS, CA 90211
THOMAS, HELEN	NEWS CORRESPONDENT	2501 CALVERT ST, NW	WASHINGTON, DC 20008
THOMAS, HOWARD	TV DIRECTOR-PRODUCER	OLD SHIP HOUSE, WHARFE LN	
		HENLEY-ON-THAMES	OXON ENGLAND
THOMAS, IAN	SINGER-SONGWRITER	41 BRITAIN ST #200	TORONTO, ONT CANADA
THOMAS, IRMA	SINGER	ROUNDER RECORDS, 1 CAMP ST	CAMBRIDGE, MA 02140
THOMAS, IVAN	BASSO-BARITONE	LIEBERMAN, 11 RIVERSIDE DR	NEW YORK, NY 10023
THOMAS, JACK W	WRITER	1961 N LOOKOUT DR	AGOURA, CA 91301
THOMAS, JANET E	NEWS CORRESPONDENT	1825 "K" ST, NW	WASHINGTON, DC 20006
THOMAS, JAY	SINGER-GUITARIST	510 HERITAGE DR #108	MADISON, TN 37115
THOMAS, JAY	SINGER-SONGWRITER	POST OFFICE BOX 110423	NASHVILLE, TN 37211
THOMAS, JEREMY	FILM PRODUCER	RECORDED PICTURE COMPANY	
		8-12 BROADWICK ST	LONDON W1 ENGLAND
THOMAS, JESS	TENOR	COLBERT, 111 W 57TH ST	NEW YORK, NY 10019
THOMAS, JOEL	ACTOR	16 STUYVESANT OVAL	NEW YORK, NY 10009
THOMAS, JOHN	DIRECTOR	91 W GAINSBOROUGH RD	THOUSAND OAKS, CA 91360
THOMAS, JONNETTA	ACTRESS	SAVAGE, 6212 BANNER AVE	LOS ANGELES, CA 90038
THOMAS, KATHY ANITA	NEWS CORRESPONDENT	2607 BRENTWOOD RD, NE	WASHINGTON, DC 20018
THOMAS, KEVIN	FILM CRITIC	L A TIMES NEWSPAPER	
		TIMES MIRROR SQUARE	LOS ANGELES, CA 90053
THOMAS, KURT	ACTOR-ATHLETIC	8431 N 75TH ST	SCOTTSDALE, AZ 85258
THOMAS, LEE	TV WRITER	8955 BEVERLY BLVD	LOS ANGELES, CA 90048
THOMAS, LILLO	SINGER	HUSH PRODS, 231 W 58TH ST	NEW YORK, NY 10019
THOMAS, LOWELL, JR	WRITER-PRODUCER	7022 TANAINA DR	ANCHORAGE, AK 99502
THOMAS, M MARTEZ	TV WRITER	8955 BEVERLY BLVD	LOS ANGELES, CA 90048
THOMAS, MARGARET	PHOTOGRAPHER	ROUTE 1, BELLEVIEW FARMS	WARRENTON, VA 22186
THOMAS, MARK	ACTOR	1221 N KINGS RD #PH-405	LOS ANGELES, CA 90069
THOMAS, MARLO	ACTRESS-WRITER	400 E 70TH ST #1103	NEW YORK, NY 10024
THOMAS, MELISSA A	NEWS CORRESPONDENT	3270 S UTAH ST	ARLINGTON, VA 22206
THOMAS, MELODY	ACTRESS	SEE - SCOTT, MELODY THOMAS	
THOMAS, MICHAEL TILSON	CONDUCTOR	24 W 57TH ST, 7TH FLOOR	NEW YORK, NY 10019
THOMAS, PEG	SINGER	RNJ, 11514 CALVERT ST	NORTH HOLLYWOOD, CA 91606
THOMAS, PHILIP MICHAEL	ACTOR	2501 W BURBANK BLVD #304	BURBANK, CA 91505
THOMAS, RALPH	FILM DIRECTOR	PINEWOOD STUDIOS, IVER HEATH	BUCKS SLO ONH ENGLAND
THOMAS, RALPH L	FILM DIRECTOR	365 MARKHAM ST	TORONTO, ONT M6G 2K8 CANADA
THOMAS, RICARDO	PHOTOGRAPHER	POST OFFICE BOX 6636	WASHINGTON, DC 20009
THOMAS, RICHARD	ACTOR-DIRECTOR	4834 BONVUE AVE	LOS ANGELES, CA 90027
THOMAS, RICHARD	NEWS CORRESPONDENT	1822 CORCORAN ST, NW	WASHINGTON, DC 20009
THOMAS, RICHARD	SINGER	611 BROADWAY #415	NEW YORK, NY 10012
THOMAS, RICHARD K	NEWS CORRESPONDENT	9801 SOTWEED DR	POTOMAC, MD 20854
THOMAS, ROBERT B	COMPOSER	22923 INGOMAR ST	CANOGA PARK, CA 91304
THOMAS, ROGER	TV DIRECTOR-PRODUCER	29 COURTNELL ST	LONDON W2 ENGLAND
THOMAS, RON	ACTOR	12725 VENTURA BLVD #E	STUDIO CITY, CA 91604
THOMAS, ROSS	TV WRITER	8955 BEVERLY BLVD	LOS ANGELES, CA 90048
THOMAS, ROY	SCREENWRITER	11726 SAN VICENTE BLVD #300	LOS ANGELES, CA 90049
THOMAS, RUFUS	SINGER	JOYCE AGENCY, 435 E 79TH ST	NEW YORK, NY 10021
THOMAS, RUSS	SINGER	POST OFFICE BOX 655	HUDSON, OH 44236
THOMAS, SHARON	ACTRESS	3800 BARHAM BLVD #303	LOS ANGELES, CA 90068
THOMAS, SONNY	GUITARIST	643 HERITAGE DR	MADISON, TN 37115
THOMAS, TALFRYN	ACTOR	DE WOLFE, 1 ROBERT ST	LONDON WC2N 6BH ENGLAND
THOMAS, THOM	TV WRITER	151 S EL CAMINO DR	BEVERLY HILLS, CA 90212
THOMAS, THOMAS D	DIRECTOR	16460 AKRON ST	PACIFIC PALISADES, CA 90272
THOMAS, TIMMY	SINGER-SONGWRITER	200 W 51ST ST #1410	NEW YORK, NY 10019
THOMAS, TONY	PRODUCER	WITT/THOMAS PRODUCTIONS	
		1438 N GOWER ST, 4TH FLOOR	LOS ANGELES, CA 90028

DANNY THOMAS

MARLO THOMAS

RICHARD THOMAS

CHERYL TIEGS

GENE TIERNEY

PAMELA TIFFIN

CHARLENE TILTON

MEL TILLIS

ANGEL TOMPKINS

Name	Occupation	Address	City	Code
THOMAS, TOWYNA	ACTRESS	7060 HOLLYWOOD BLVD #610	LOS ANGELES, CA	90028
THOMAS, TREVOR	ACTOR	OCS, 34 GRAFTON TERR	LONDON NW5 4HY	ENGLAND
THOMAS, VIVIANE	SOPRANO	CONE, 221 W 57TH ST	NEW YORK, NY	10019
THOMAS, WALTER L, JR	TV DIRECTOR	2600 PINE LAKE RD	WEST BLOOMFIELD, MI	48033
THOMAS, WAYNE	ACTOR	11030 VENTURA BLVD #3	STUDIO CITY, CA	91604
THOMASCHKE, THOMAS	SINGER	CAMI, 165 W 57TH ST	NEW YORK, NY	10019
THOMASON, HARRY Z	TV WRITER	8955 BEVERLY BLVD	LOS ANGELES, CA	90048
THOMASON, ROLLAND	DRUMMER	ROUTE #9, BOX 290	BOWLING GREEN, KY	42101
THOMASSON, DAN K	NEWS CORRESPONDENT	8300 NIGHTINGALE CT	ANNANDALE, VA	22003
THOME, JOEL	CONDUCTOR	POST OFFICE BOX 188		
		STATION A	TORONTO, ONT	CANADA
THOMERSON, TIM	ACTOR-COMEDIAN	9220 SUNSET BLVD #625	LOS ANGELES, CA	90069
THOMI, PATRICK P	COMPOSER	12814 PACIFIC AVE #3	LOS ANGELES, CA	90066
THOMOPOULOS, ANTHONY D	FILM EXECUTIVE	152 GRANVILLE AVE	LOS ANGELES, CA	90049
THOMPSON, ALAN R	NEWS CORRESPONDENT	201 S ABINGDON ST	ARLINGTON, VA	22204
THOMPSON, ALLAN	BANJOIST	901 18TH AVE S #B	NASHVILLE, TN	37212
THOMPSON, BOBBY	BANJOIST	POST OFFICE BOX 702	GOODLETTSVILLE, TN	37072
THOMPSON, BOYCE, JR	NEWS CORRESPONDENT	929 N KENMORE ST	ARLINGTON, VA	22201
THOMPSON, BRIAN	ACTOR	1901 AVE OF THE STARS #840	LOS ANGELES, CA	90067
THOMPSON, BRUCE	TV DIRECTOR-PRODUCER	BBC-TV CENTRE, WOOD LN		
		SHEPHERDS BUSH	LONDON W12	ENGLAND
THOMPSON, BUDDY	MUSIC ARRANGER	6807 PENNYWELL DR	NASHVILLE, TN	37205
THOMPSON, CARLOS	ACTOR	VILLA LA LOMA 8683	GOLDINGEN	SWITZERLAND
THOMPSON, CHARLES P	COMPOSER	6513 LANKERSHIM BLVD, BOX 126	NORTH HOLLYWOOD, CA	91606
THOMPSON, CHRISTIE	SINGER	POST OFFICE BOX 171132	NASHVILLE, TN	37217
THOMPSON, CHRISTOPHER N	WRITER-PRODUCER	3855 BERRY DR	STUDIO CITY, CA	91604
THOMPSON, CYNTHIA	ACTRESS	9200 SUNSET BLVD #414	LOS ANGELES, CA	90069
THOMPSON, CYNTHIA L	TV WRITER	1888 CENTURY PARK E #1400	LOS ANGELES, CA	90067
THOMPSON, DALEY	TRACK & FIELD	1 CHURCH ROW, WANDSWORTH PLAIN	LONDON SW18	ENGLAND
THOMPSON, DAMON	NEWS CORRESPONDENT	323 "E" ST, NE	WASHINGTON, DC	20002
THOMPSON, DONALD B	COMPOSER	12671 CHASE ST	GARDEN GROVE, CA	92641
THOMPSON, DONALD G	SCREENWRITER	8955 BEVERLY BLVD	LOS ANGELES, CA	90048
THOMPSON, E FRANCIS	DIRECTOR	310 E 51ST ST	NEW YORK, NY	10022
THOMPSON, EDWARD T	PUBLISHING EXECUTIVE	US MAGAZINE COMPANY		
		1 DAG HAMMARSKJOLD PLAZA	NEW YORK, NY	10017
THOMPSON, ERNEST	SCREENWRITER	8955 BEVERLY BLVD	LOS ANGELES, CA	90048
THOMPSON, FRANKLIN	SCREENWRITER	8955 BEVERLY BLVD	LOS ANGELES, CA	90048
THOMPSON, GEORGE	TV DIRECTOR	6701 COLGATE AVE	LOS ANGELES, CA	90048
THOMPSON, GREG	SINGER	JIMAK, 600 NEVAN RD	VIRGINIA BEACH, VA	23451
THOMPSON, HANK	SINGER-SONGWRITER	1300 DIVISION ST #102	NASHVILLE, TN	37203
THOMPSON, HILARY	ACTRESS	8485 MELROSE PL #E	LOS ANGELES, CA	90069
THOMPSON, J LEE	FILM DIRECTOR	DGA, 7950 SUNSET BLVD	LOS ANGELES, CA	90046
THOMPSON, J W	SINGER	POST OFFICE BOX 9104	SHREVEPORT, LA	71139
THOMPSON, JACK	ACTOR	SF & A, 121 N SAN VICENTE BLVD	BEVERLY HILLS, CA	90211
THOMPSON, JAMES E	DIRECTOR	4826 PATRAE ST	LOS ANGELES, CA	90066
THOMPSON, JIM	CARTOONIST	THE NATIONAL ENQUIRER		
		600 SE COAST AVE	LANTANA, FL	33464
THOMPSON, JOHN G	SCREENWRITER	8955 BEVERLY BLVD	LOS ANGELES, CA	90048
THOMPSON, KAY	ACTRESS	300 E 57TH ST	NEW YORK, NY	10022
THOMPSON, LARRY	FILM PRODUCER	1888 CENTURY PARK E, 6TH FLOOR	LOS ANGELES, CA	90067
THOMPSON, LARRY J	NEWS CORRESPONDENT	BULLS RUN PARKWAY	BETHESDA, MD	20817
THOMPSON, LEA	ACTRESS	POST OFFICE BOX 5617	BEVERLY HILLS, CA	90210
THOMPSON, LINDA	ACTRESS	SEE - THOMPSON JENNER, LINDA		
THOMPSON, LINDA	SINGER	MORRIS, 147-149 WARDOUR ST	LONDON W1V 3TB	ENGLAND
THOMPSON, MARCUS	VIOLIST	AIA, 60 E 42ND ST	NEW YORK, NY	10165
THOMPSON, MARK F	SINGER-GUITARIST	1420 OTTER CREEK RD	NASHVILLE, TN	37215
THOMPSON, MARK J	NEWS CORRESPONDENT	11006 STILLWATER AVE	KENSINGTON, MD	20895
THOMPSON, MARSHALL	DIRECTOR	9200 SUNSET BLVD #909	LOS ANGELES, CA	90069
THOMPSON, MARY HUGHES	TV WRITER	8955 BEVERLY BLVD	LOS ANGELES, CA	90048
THOMPSON, NEIL H	ACTOR-WRITER	5101 LEDGE AVE	NORTH HOLLYWOOD, CA	91601
THOMPSON, NEVILLE	FILM PRODUCER	HEATH, PARAMOUNT HOUSE		
		162-170 WARDOUR ST	LONDON W1V 3AT	ENGLAND
THOMPSON, PHILIPPA T	FLUTIST	1003 39TH AVE N	NASHVILLE, TN	37209
THOMPSON, RAY WALLACE	VIOLINIST	ROUTE #4, BOX 359	GREENSBURG, KY	42743
THOMPSON, RAYMOND W	ACTOR-WRITER	ICM, 388-396 OXFORD ST	LONDON W1	ENGLAND
THOMPSON, RICHARD	SINGER-GUITARIST	POST OFFICE BOX 7095	NEW YORK, NY	10116
THOMPSON, ROBERT C	DIRECTOR-PRODUCER	4536 MARY ELLEN AVE	SHERMAN OAKS, CA	91423
THOMPSON, ROBERT E	NEWS CORRESPONDENT	3601 CONNECTICUT AVE, NW	WASHINGTON, DC	20008
THOMPSON, ROBERT E	TV WRITER	8955 BEVERLY BLVD	LOS ANGELES, CA	90048
THOMPSON, ROBERT F	TV WRITER	8955 BEVERLY BLVD	LOS ANGELES, CA	90048
THOMPSON, ROCHELLE L	NEWS CORRESPONDENT	61 RHODE ISLAND AVE, NE	WASHINGTON, DC	20002
THOMPSON, ROCKY	SINGER	4047 NACO-PERRIN BLVD #110	SAN ANTONIO, TX	78217
THOMPSON, ROGER K	NEWS CORRESPONDENT	10747 MIST HAVE TERR	ROCKVILLE, MD	20852
THOMPSON, RON & THE RESISTORS	C & W GROUP	POST OFFICE BOX 1909	MILL VALLEY, CA	94942
THOMPSON, RON ALLEN	TV WRITER	8955 BEVERLY BLVD	LOS ANGELES, CA	90048
THOMPSON, SADA	ACTRESS	250 W 57TH ST #803	NEW YORK, NY	10019
THOMPSON, SCOTT "THE SCATMAN"	GOLFER-STUD	POST OFFICE BOX 1058	LA MESA, CA	92044
THOMPSON, SELMA R	TV WRITER	555 W 57TH ST #1230	NEW YORK, NY	10019
THOMPSON, SHAWN	ACTOR	CBS-TV, "THE GUIDING LIGHT"		
		51 W 52ND ST	NEW YORK, NY	10019
THOMPSON, TAZ	ACTRESS	9255 SUNSET BLVD #610	LOS ANGELES, CA	90069
THOMPSON, U S	VAUDEVILLIAN	402 W 153RD ST	NEW YORK, NY	10031
THOMPSON, VIRGIL	COMPOSER	222 W 23RD ST	NEW YORK, NY	10011
THOMPSON, WES	DIRECTOR	15619 W SOLEDAD CANYON RD	CANYON COUNTRY, CA	91351
THOMPSON, WESLEY	ACTOR	1930 CENTURY PARK W #303	LOS ANGELES, CA	90067

THOMPSON, WILLIAM J	NEWS CORRESPONDENT	4646 40TH ST, NW	WASHINGTON, DC	20016
THOMPSON JENNER, LINDA	ACTRESS	POST OFFICE BOX 665	MALIBU, CA	90265
THOMPSON TWINS, THE	ROCK & ROLL TRIO	TEEFAX, 9 ECCLESTON ST	LONDON SW1	ENGLAND
THOMSEN, MARK	TENOR	CAMI, 165 W 57TH ST	NEW YORK, NY	10019
THOMSON, BRENDA	ACTRESS	4704 CAHUENGA BLVD	NORTH HOLLYWOOD, CA	91602
THOMSON, DORRIE	ACTRESS	113 N SAN VICENTE BLVD #202	BEVERLY HILLS, CA	90211
THOMSON, GORDON	ACTOR	151 S EL CAMINO DR	BEVERLY HILLS, CA	90212
THOMSON, HEATHER	SOPRANO	SARDOS, 180 W END AVE	NEW YORK, NY	10023
THOMSON, PATRICIA	ACTRESS	9229 SUNSET BLVD #306	LOS ANGELES, CA	90069
THOMSON, R H	ACTOR	10100 SANTA MONICA BLVD #1600	LOS ANGELES, CA	90067
THOMSON, SCOTT	ACTOR	12725 VENTURA BLVD #E	STUDIO CITY, CA	91604
THOR, CAMERON	ACTOR	817 25TH ST	SANTA MONICA, CA	90403
THOR, DANNY	ACTOR	14714 FIRMONA AVE	LAWNDALE, CA	90260
THOR, JEROME	ACTOR	9200 SUNSET BLVD #909	LOS ANGELES, CA	90069
THOREAU, JEAN	ACTRESS	KOHNER, 9169 SUNSET BLVD	LOS ANGELES, CA	90069
THORN, TARA	ACTRESS	1605 N CAHUENGA BLVD #202	LOS ANGELES, CA	90028
THORNBER, THOMAS A	TV DIRECTOR	GENERAL DELIVERY	LITCHFIELD, CT	06759
THORNBURY, BILL	ACTOR	28231 DRIVER AVE	AGOURA, CA	91301
THORNDIKE, CHUCK	CARTOONIST	11660 CANAL DR	NORTH MIAMI, FL	33161
THORNE, C PATRICK	NEWS CORRESPONDENT	5810 RUNFORD DR	NEW CARROLLTON, MD	20784
THORNE, DONALD K	TV DIRECTOR	9255 DOHENY RD	LOS ANGELES, CA	90069
THORNE, FRANCIS	COMPOSER	116 E 66TH ST	NEW YORK, NY	10021
THORNE, FRED	DIRECTOR	4453 GENTRY AVE	NORTH HOLLYWOOD, CA	91604
THORNE, KENNETH R	COMPOSER	8040 BOBBY BOYAR AVE	CANOGA PARK, CA	91304
THORNE, WORLEY	TV WRITER	14144 VENTURA BLVD #200	SHERMAN OAKS, CA	91423
THORNELL, CYNTHIA	ACTRESS	6330 S GREEN VALLEY CIR #111	CULVER CITY, CA	90230
THORNELL, JACK	PHOTOGRAPHER	5236 UTICA ST	METAIRIE, LA	70002
THORNHILL, DAVID	GUITARIST	3223 CRISLYNNDALE DR	NASHVILLE, TN	37207
THORNLEY, STEVEN	SCREENWRITER	8955 BEVERLY BLVD	LOS ANGELES, CA	90048
THORNTON, FRANK	ACTOR	CLOUGH, 70-A GLOUCESTER AVE	LONDON NW1 8JD	ENGLAND
THORNTON, JEANNYE	NEWS CORRESPONDENT	6315 NAVAL AVE	LANHAM, MD	20706
THORNTON, LES	WRESTLER	POST OFFICE BOX 3859	STAMFORD, CT	06905
THORNTON, MARY E	NEWS CORRESPONDENT	7119 9TH ST, NW	WASHINGTON, DC	20012
THORNTON, PHILIP J	DIRECTOR	703 BELLEVUE AVE E #F-31	SEATTLE, WA	98102
THORNTON, WILLIAM J, JR	COMPOSER	347 SHARON DR	SAN ANTONIO, TX	78216
THORNTON-SHERWOOD, MADELEINE	ACTRESS	32 LEROY ST	NEW YORK, NY	10014
THOROGOOD, GEORGE & THE DESTROY	ROCK & ROLL GROUP	POST OFFICE BOX 210103		
		GEARY STATION	SAN FRANCISCO, CA	94121
THORPE, BILLY	SINGER-GUITARIST	PASHA, 5615 MELROSE AVE	HOLLYWOOD, CA	90038
THORPE, JERRY	DIRECTOR	865 S BUNDY DR	LOS ANGELES, CA	90049
THORPE, JOHN	GUITARIST	ROUTE #1, POST OFFICE BOX 250	CLIMAX, NC	27333
THORPE, RICHARD	DIRECTOR	1550 S CAMINO REAL #222	PALM SPRINGS, CA	92262
THORPE-BATES, PEGGY	ACTRESS	43 CHESTER CLOSE NORTH		
		REGENT'S PARK	LONDON NW1	ENGLAND
THORSON, LINDA	ACTRESS	200 W 57TH ST #1303	NEW YORK, NY	10019
THOUGHT	ROCK & ROLL GROUP	POST OFFICE BOX 2896	TORRANCE, CA	90509
THRASHER BROTHERS, THE	C & W GROUP	POST OFFICE BOX 22707	NASHVILLE, TN	37203
THREADGILL, HENRY, SEXTETT	JAZZ SEXTETT	BRIDGE, 106 FORT GREENE PL	BROOKLYN, NY	11217
THREE DEGREES, THE	VOCAL GROUP	1132 ROSEGLEN RD	LUDWYNE, PA	19035
THREE DOG NIGHT	ROCK & ROLL GROUP	151 S EL CAMINO DR	BEVERLY HILLS, CA	90212
THREE JOHNS, THE	ROCK & ROLL GROUP	ABSTRACT RECORDS COMPANY		
		10 TIVERTON RD	LONDON NW10	ENGLAND
THREE O'CLOCK, THE	ROCK & ROLL GROUP	POST OFFICE BOX 1018	SUN VALLEY, CA	91333
THRELFALL, DAVID	ACTOR	SHARKEY, 90 REGENT ST	LONDON W1	ENGLAND
THRESHER, JAMES	PHOTOGRAPHER	4766 N 21ST RD	ARLINGTON, VA	22207
THRONE, MALACHI	ACTOR	13067 GREENLEAF ST	STUDIO CITY, CA	91604
THRUST	ROCK & ROLL GROUP	FROTHINGHAM, 40 GROVE ST	WESSESLEY, MA	02181
THULIN, INGRID	ACTRESS	KEVINGESTRAND 7-B	DANDERYD	SWEDEN
THUMMA, BARRY	PHOTOGRAPHER	13152 PAVILION LN	FAIRFAX, VA	22030
THUNA, LEONORA	WRITER	2552 BENEDICT CANYON DR	BEVERLY HILLS, CA	90210
THUNDER, JOHNNY & LIGHTENING	RHYTHM & BLUES GROUP	9777 HARWIN ST #101	HOUSTON, TX	77036
THUNDER BAY	ROCK & ROLL GROUP	VARIETY ARTISTS INTL, INC		
		9073 NEMO ST, 3RD FLOOR	LOS ANGELES, CA	90069
THUNDER ROAD	C & W GROUP	JIMKA, 600 NEVAN RD	VIRGINIA BEACH, VA	23451
THUNDER ROAD	ROCK & ROLL GROUP	POST OFFICE BOX 448	RADFORD, VA	24141
THUNDERFOOT #1	WRESTLER	NATIONAL WRESTLING ALLIANCE		
		JIM CROCKETT PROMOTIONS		
		421 BRIARBEND DR	CHARLOTTE, NC	28209
THUNDERFOOT #2	WRESTLER	NATIONAL WRESTLING ALLIANCE		
		JIM CROCKETT PROMOTIONS		
		421 BRIARBEND DR	CHARLOTTE, NC	28209
THUNDERKLOUD, BILLY & THE CHIEF	C & W GROUP	1300 DIVISION ST #200	NASHVILLE, TN	37203
THURLEY, MARTIN	ACTOR	LONDON MANAGEMENT, LTD		
		235-241 REGENT ST	LONDON W1A 2JT	ENGLAND
THURM, JOEL	CASTING DIRECTOR	NBC-TV, 3000 W ALAMEDA AVE	BURBANK, CA	91523
THURMAN, JAMES F	TV WRITER	8955 BEVERLY BLVD	LOS ANGELES, CA	90048
THURSTON, MICHAEL R	COMPOSER	13910 SHERMAN OAKS #309	VAN NUYS, CA	91406
THURSTON, TED	ACTOR	564 W 52ND ST	NEW YORK, NY	10019
THYSSEN, CHARLOTT	ACTRESS	75-26 VLEIGH PL	FLUSHING, NY	11367
THYSSEN, GRETA	ACTRESS	444 E 82ND ST	NEW YORK, NY	10028
TIANO, LOU	ACTOR	12144 MOORPARK ST	STUDIO CITY, CA	91604
TIBBLES, CHRISTINE	TV WRITER	2160 CENTURY PARK E #711	LOS ANGELES, CA	90067
TIBORIS, PETER	CONDUCTOR	111 W 57TH ST #1209	NEW YORK, NY	10019
TICE, JIM	NEWS CORRESPONDENT	6161 EDSALL RD #805	ALEXANDRIA, VA	22304

Name	Occupation	Address	City	Zip/Country
TICHO, CHARLES J	TV DIRECTOR-PRODUCER	PERFORMANCE DESIGNS		
		100 5TH AVE	NEW YORK, NY	10011
TICOTIN, RACHEL	ACTRESS	3855 LANKERSHIM BLVD #818	NORTH HOLLYWOOD, CA	91604
TIDMORE, JAMES	ACTOR	2489 1/2 N GOWER ST	LOS ANGELES, CA	90068
TIDWELL, DIANE	FLUTIST	757 BROWNLEE DR	NASHVILLE, TN	37205
TIDWELL, GEORGE	TRUMPETER	757 BROWNLEE DR	NASHVILLE, TN	37205
TIDWELL, RICHARD WILLIAM	DIRECTOR	1262 LEAFWOOD HGTS	NOVATO, CA	94947
TIDYMAN, CHRIS-CLARK	SCREENWRITER	8955 BEVERLY BLVD	LOS ANGELES, CA	90048
TIEDMANN, KARL	TV WRITER	555 W 57TH ST #1230	NEW YORK, NY	10019
TIEFER, GREGORY H	WRITER	22820 MAC FARLANE DR	WOODLAND HILLS, CA	91364
TIEGS, CHERYL	MODEL	7060 HOLLYWOOD BLVD #1010	LOS ANGELES, CA	90028
TIEPPO, GIORGIO	TENOR	CAMI, 165 W 57TH ST	NEW YORK, NY	10019
TIERNAN, AUDREY C	PHOTOGRAPHER	99 EDWARD ST #2-C	ROSLYN HEIGHTS, NY	11577
TIERNEY, LAWRENCE	ACTOR	350 OLD COUNTRY RD	GARDEN CITY, NJ	11530
TIERNEY-LEE, GENE	ACTRESS	2200 WILLOWICK #5-A	HOUSTON, TX	77027
TIFFANY & CO	C & W GROUP	POST OFFICE BOX 2642	KALAMAZOO, MI	49003
TIFFIN, PAMELA	ACTRESS-MODEL	15 W 67TH ST	NEW YORK, NY	10023
TIFFIN, PETER	TV PRODUCER	FIRS, CERNEY WICK	GLOUCESTERSHIRE	ENGLAND
TIFFT, SUSAN	WRITER-EDITOR	TIME/TIME & LIFE BLDG		
		ROCKEFELLER CENTER	NEW YORK, NY	10020
TIGAR, KENNETH	ACTOR	225 WINDWARD AVE	VENICE, CA	90291
TIGER'S BAKU	JAZZ GROUP	KURLAND, 173 BRIGHTON AVE	BOSTON, MA	02134
TIGERT, SUZANNE	BODYBUILDER	POST OFFICE BOX 881	REDONDO BEACH, CA	90277
TIGHE, KEVIN	ACTOR	KOHNER, 9169 SUNSET BLVD	LOS ANGELES, CA	90069
TIL TUESDAY	ROCK & ROLL GROUP	SYMMETRY, 48 W 75TH ST	NEW YORK, NY	10023
TILL, ERIC	FILM DIRECTOR	62 CHAPLIN CRESCENT	TORONTO, ONT M5P 1A3	CANADA
TILL, LEROY P	TV DIRECTOR	3540 CARRIAGE HILL CIR #T-3	RANDALLSTOWN, MD	21133
TILLER, NADJA	ACTRESS	VIA TAMPORIVA 26	CH-6976 CASTAGNOLA	SWITZERLAND
TILLERY, LINDA "TUI"	SINGER	POST OFFICE BOX 3336	BERKELEY, CA	94703
TILLES, JACK H	DIRECTOR	4 DURHAM CT	LINCOLNSHIRE, IL	60045
TILLIS, MEL	SINGER	1520 DEMONBREUN ST	NASHVILLE, TN	37203
TILLMAN, FLOYD	SINGER	BAGATELLE, 400 SAN JACINTO	HOUSTON, TX	77002
TILLOTSON, JOHNNY	SINGER	17530 VENTURA BLVD #105	ENCINO, CA	91316
TILLOTSON, MARY	NEWS CORRESPONDENT	8212 CUSTER RD	BETHESDA, MD	20817
TILLY, JENNIFER	ACTRESS	15760 VENTURA BLVD #1730	ENCINO, CA	91436
TILLY, MEG	ACTRESS	1888 CENTURY PARK E #1400	LOS ANGELES, CA	90067
TILNEY, COLIN	HARPSICHORDIST	157 W 57TH ST #1100	NEW YORK, NY	10019
TILNEY & BAIRD	MUSICAL DUO	157 W 57TH ST #1100	NEW YORK, NY	10019
TILTON, CHARLENE	ACTRESS	2204 N BEVERLY DR	BEVERLY HILLS, CA	90211
TILTON, DEBORAH	ACTRESS	905 SANBORN AVE	LOS ANGELES, CA	90029
TILVERN, ALAN	ACTOR	12 GROSVENOR RD	LONDON N3	ENGLAND
TIM, TINY	SINGER-SONGWRITER	HOTEL OLCOTT, 27 W 72ND ST	NEW YORK, NY	10023
TIM & THE TURBOS	ROCK & ROLL GROUP	41 BRITAIN ST #200	TORONTO, ONT	CANADA
TIMBERG, ROBERT R	NEWS CORRESPONDENT	5607 GLOSTER RD	BETHESDA, MD	20816
TIMBERLAKE, MARY GAEL	NEWS CORRESPONDENT	1918 COLUMBIA PIKE	ARLINGTON, VA	22204
TIMBERMAN, ELEANOR B	TV WRITER	555 W 57TH ST #1230	NEW YORK, NY	10019
TIME	VOCAL GROUP	POST OFFICE BOX 10119	MINNEAPOLIS, MN	55401
TIMEX SOCIAL CLUB	ROCK & ROLL GROUP	1442-A WALNUT ST	BERKELEY, CA	94709
TIMKO, JOHNNY	ACTOR	8322 BEVERLY BLVD #202	LOS ANGELES, CA	90048
TIMM, ANDREA	NEWS CORRESPONDENT	4044 VACATION LN	ARLINGTON, VA	22201
TIMMINS, CALI	ACTRESS	ABC-TV, "RYAN'S HOPE"		
		1330 AVE OF THE AMERICAS	NEW YORK, NY	10019
TIMMONS, KIRBY	TV WRITER	4605 LANKERSHIM BLVD #213	NORTH HOLLYWOOD, CA	91602
TIMOTHY, CHRISTOPHER	ACTOR	PLANT & FROGGATT, LTD		
		JULIAN HOUSE		
		4 WINDMILL ST	LONDON W1	ENGLAND
TIMOTHY, MARJORY J	NEWS CORRESPONDENT	2107 N 18TH ST #1052	ARLINGTON, VA	22201
TINDALL, HILARY	ACTRESS	BRYAN DREW, LTD		
		MEZZANINE QUADRANT HOUSE		
		80-82 REGENT ST	LONDON W1	ENGLAND
TINDER, PAUL	ACTOR	10000 RIVERSIDE DR #3	TOLUCA LAKE, CA	91602
TINERINO, DENNIS	BODYBUILDER	POST OFFICE BOX 299	NORTHRIDGE, CA	91328
TING, ROBIN	NEWS CORRESPONDENT	300 INDEPENDENCE AVE, NW	WASHINGTON, DC	20547
TINKER, GRANT	TV EXECUTIVE	760 LAUSANNE RD	LOS ANGELES, CA	90077
TINKER, JOHN H	TV WRITER	8955 BEVERLY BLVD	LOS ANGELES, CA	90048
TINKER, MARK C	WRITER-PRODUCER	12335 OTSEGO ST	NORTH HOLLYWOOD, CA	91607
TINNEY, HUGH	PIANIST	CAMI, 165 W 57TH ST	NEW YORK, NY	10019
TINSLEY, PAULINE	SOPRANO	CAMI, 165 W 57TH ST	NEW YORK, NY	10019
TINSMAN, JIM	CLOWN	2701 COTTAGE WY #14	SACRAMENTO, CA	95825
TIO, MARIA M	NEWS CORRESPONDENT	4461 CONNECTICUT AVE, NW	WASHINGTON, DC	20008
TIPPET, CLARK	DANCER	AMERICAN BALLET, 890 BROADWAY	NEW YORK, NY	10003
TIPPETT, SIR MICHAEL	COMPOSER-CONDUCTOR	48 GREAT MARLBOROUGH	LONDON W1V 2BN	ENGLAND
TIPPIT, JACK	CARTOONIST	KING FEATURES SYNDICATE		
		235 E 45TH ST	NEW YORK, NY	10017
TIPPIT, WAYNE	ACTOR	8285 SUNSET BLVD #12	LOS ANGELES, CA	90046
TIPTON, BOBBY	DRUMMER	743 ALBAR DR	NASHVILLE, TN	37221
TIPTON, CARL	FIDDLER	POST OFFICE BOX 1074	MURFREESBORO, TN	37130
TIRA-ANDREA, MERCEDES A	NEWS CORRESPONDENT	600 ROOSEVELT BLVD #106	FALLS CHURCH, VA	22044
TIRCE, LEE	DIRECTOR	4147 DAVANA RD	SHERMAN OAKS, CA	91423
TIRELLI, JAMIE	ACTOR	ABC-TV, "ALL MY CHILDREN"		
		1330 AVE OF THE AMERICAS	NEW YORK, NY	10019
TIRRELL, BARBARA	ACTRESS	AFFILIATE ARTISTS, INC		
		37 W 65TH ST, 6TH FLOOR	NEW YORK, NY	10023
TISCH, STEVE	TV-FILM PRODUCER	515 N ROBERTSON BLVD	LOS ANGELES, CA	90048
TISCHLER, GAYE	TV DIRECTOR	WDIV-TV, 550 LAFAYETTE BLVD	DETROIT, MI	48231

Name	Occupation	Address	City	Zip/Country
TISDALE, JIM	TV WRITER	9300 WILSHIRE BLVD #410	BEVERLY HILLS, CA	90212
TITLE, SUSAN L	TV WRITER	8955 BEVERLY BLVD	LOS ANGELES, CA	90048
TITTLE, Y A	FOOTBALL	611 BURLESON ST	MARSHALL, TX	75670
TITUS, ALAN	BARITONE	CAMI, 165 W 57TH ST	NEW YORK, NY	10019
TIVERS, CYNTHIA	TV WRITER	1454 EDRIS DR	LOS ANGELES, CA	90035
TJEKNAVORIAN, LORIS	CONDUCTOR	59 E 54TH ST #81	NEW YORK, NY	10022
TKACH, JOHN R	SPORTS WRITER	POST OFFICE BOX 500	WASHINGTON, DC	20044
TNNDRILL	MUSIC GROUP	HOMEGROWN, 4412 WHISSETT AVE	STUDIO CITY, CA	91604
TNT	ROCK & ROLL GROUP	FREEFAL PRESENTATIONS		
		40 UNDERHILL BLVD	SYOSSET, NY	11791
TOBACK, JAMES	FILM WRITER-DIRECTOR	11 E 87TH ST	NEW YORK, NY	10028
TOBACK, NORMAN	DIRECTOR-PRODUCER	3234 OAKDELL RD	STUDIO CITY, CA	91604
TOBEY, BARNEY	CARTOONIST	POST OFFICE BOX 4203	NEW YORK, NY	10017
TOBEY, KENNETH	ACTOR	14155 MAGNOLIA BLVD #34	SHERMAN OAKS, CA	91423
TOBIAS, EDWARD L	NEWS CORRESPONDENT	1825 "K" ST, NW	WASHINGTON, DC	20006
TOBIAS, MARICE	FILM DIRECTOR	386 S BURNSIDE	LOS ANGELES, CA	90036
TOBIAS, OLIVER	ACTOR	MITCHELL, 7 GARRICK ST	LONDON WC2	ENGLAND
TOBIAS, PAUL	VIOLINIST	628 ST CLOUD DR	ANTIOCH, TN	37013
TOBIE, ELLEN	ACTRESS	9220 SUNSET BLVD #625	LOS ANGELES, CA	90069
TOBIN, DAN	ACTOR	919 RIVAS CYN RD	PACIFIC PALISADES, CA	90272
TOBIN, GENEVIEVE	ACTRESS	KEIGHLEY, 1025 5TH AVE	NEW YORK, NY	10028
TOBIN, JOHN H	DIRECTOR	3212 ANNRAE ST	SAN DIEGO, CA	92123
TOBIN, MATTHEW	ACTOR	CED, 261 S ROBERTSON BLVD	BEVERLY HILLS, CA	90211
TOBIN, MICHELLE	ACTRESS	3800 BARHAM BLVD #303	LOS ANGELES, CA	90068
TOCCO, JAMES	PIANIST	SHAW CONCERTS, 1995 BROADWAY	NEW YORK, NY	10023
TOCHI, BRIAN	ACTOR	9200 SUNSET BLVD #1210	LOS ANGELES, CA	90069
TOCZYSKA, STEFANIA	MEZZO-SOPRANO	CAMI, 165 W 57TH ST	NEW YORK, NY	10019
TODD, BEVERLY	ACTRESS	10100 SANTA MONICA BLVD #1600	LOS ANGELES, CA	90067
TODD, BOB	ACTOR	THE RICHARD STONE AGENCY		
		18-20 YORK BLDGS, ADELPHI	LONDON WC2N 6JY	ENGLAND
TODD, ERICA	ACTRESS	LEONETTI, 6526 SUNSET BLVD	HOLLYWOOD, CA	90028
TODD, HALLIE	ACTRESS	870 N VINE ST #G	LOS ANGELES, CA	90038
TODD, JOY	CASTING DIRECTOR	250 W 57TH ST #1813	NEW YORK, NY	10019
TODD, MICHAEL J	ACTOR	200 N ROBERTSON BLVD #308	BEVERLY HILLS, CA	90210
TODD, PAMELA	ACTRESS	320 E 72ND ST	NEW YORK, NY	10021
TODD, RACHEL	ACTRESS	6430 SUNSET BLVD #1203	LOS ANGELES, CA	90028
TODD, RICHARD	ACTOR	CHINHAM FARM, FARINGDON	OXFORDSHIRE	ENGLAND
TODD, RUSSELL	ACTOR	9229 SUNSET BLVD #306	LOS ANGELES, CA	90069
TODDS, WALTER	TV PRODUCER	17 PRINCE OF WALES TERR	LONDON W8	ENGLAND
TOFANI, LORETTA	NEWS CORRESPONDENT	2116 "O" ST, NW	WASHINGTON, DC	20037
TOGNAZZI, UGO	ACTOR	PIAZZA DELLI ORO N 3	ROME 00186	ITALY
TOGUCHI, MASANORI	WRESTLER	SEE - LEE, TIGER CHUNG		
TOIBIN, NIALL	ACTOR	15 WESTFIELD RD	DUBLIN 6	IRELAND
TOKATYAN, DIANA BELL	WRITER	8428 MELROSE PL #C	LOS ANGELES, CA	90069
TOKATYAN, LEON	TV WRITER	13958 STROUD ST	VAN NUYS, CA	91402
TOKODY, ILONA	SOPRANO	61 W 62ND ST #6-F	NEW YORK, NY	10023
TOKOFSKY, JERRY	FILM PRODUCER	11755 MONTANA AVE #302	LOS ANGELES, CA	90049
TOKUDA, MARILYN	ACTRESS	208 S BEVERLY DR #8	BEVERLY HILLS, CA	90212
TOLAN, MICHAEL	ACTOR	9200 SUNSET BLVD #1210	LOS ANGELES, CA	90069
TOLAND, DAVE	SINGER	POST OFFICE BOX O	EXCELSIOR, MN	55331
TOLAND, JOHN	AUTHOR	1 LONG RIDGE RD	DANBURY, CT	06810
TOLAND, MICHAEL	ACTOR	9200 SUNSET BLVD #1210	LOS ANGELES, CA	90069
TOLBERT, BELINDA	ACTRESS	ICM, 8899 BEVERLY BLVD	LOS ANGELES, CA	90048
TOLCHIN, MARTIN	NEWS CORRESPONDENT	5117 WICKETT TERR	BETHESDA, MD	20814
TOLEDO, JOSE	MODEL	FORD MODEL AGENCY		
		344 E 59TH ST	NEW YORK, NY	10022
TOLES, TOM	CARTOONIST	BUFFALO NEWS, 1 NEWS PLAZA	BUFFALO, NY	14240
TOLKAN, JAMES	ACTOR	9255 SUNSET BLVD #1105	LOS ANGELES, CA	90069
TOLKIN, MEL	TV WRITER-PRODUCER	2187 SUMMITRIDGE DR	BEVERLY HILLS, CA	90210
TOLKIN, MICHAEL LENNART	WRITER	539 N SYCAMORE AVE	LOS ANGELES, CA	90036
TOLKIN, STEPHEN M	WRITER	1322 1/2 N HARPER AVE	LOS ANGELES, CA	90046
TOLL, TED	ACTOR	CED, 261 S ROBERTSON BLVD	BEVERLY HILLS, CA	90211
TOLL, THEODORE	DIRECTOR	1074 CALLE CASTANO	THOUSAND OAKS, CA	91360
TOLMAN, KIMBERLY	VIOLINIST	2709 MERRIHILLS DR SW	ROCHESTER, MN	55901
TOLSKY, SUSAN	ACTRESS	10815 ACAMA ST	NORTH HOLLYWOOD, CA	91602
TOM TOM CLUB	ROCK & ROLL GROUP	GARY KURFIST, OVERLAND PRODS		
		1775 BROADWAY, 7TH FLOOR	NEW YORK, NY	10019
TOMA, DAVID	WRITER	POST OFFICE BOX 854	CLARK, NJ	07066
TOMAN, BONNIE	ACTRESS	6863 SUMMY COVE	HOLLYWOOD, CA	90068
TOMARKEN, PETER	ACT-WRI-DIR	337 S ALMONT DR	BEVERLY HILLS, CA	90211
TOMASELLI, DANIEL	TENOR	LIEBERMAN, 11 RIVERSIDE DR	NEW YORK, NY	10023
TOMASINA, JEANA	ACTRESS-MODEL	9000 SUNSET BLVD #1112	LOS ANGELES, CA	90069
TOMASSI, MALGOSIA	ACTRESS	KEACH, 27522 WINDING WY	MALIBU, CA	90265
TOMASSON, HELGI	DANCER	NEW YORK CITY BALLET		
		LINCOLN CENTER FOR		
		THE PERFORMING ARTS	NEW YORK, NY	10023
TOMBRAGEL, MAURICE	WRITER	6050 WHITSETT AVE #3	NORTH HOLLYWOOD, CA	91606
TOMEI, CONCETTA	ACTRESS	ICM, 8899 BEVERLY BLVD	LOS ANGELES, CA	90048
TOMEI, MARISA	ACTRESS	10 E 44TH ST #700	NEW YORK, NY	10017
TOMELTY, JOSEPH	ACTOR	SANDY LN, BLACKROCK, DUNDALK	CO LOUTH	IRELAND
TOMERLIN, JOHN E	TV WRITER	8955 BEVERLY BLVD	LOS ANGELES, CA	90048
TOMEY, TRICIA	ACTRESS	7612 FOUNTAIN AVE	HOLLYWOOD, CA	90046
TOMICH, NANCY E	NEWS CORRESPONDENT	5609 LAMAR RD	BETHESDA, MD	20816
TOMITA, TAMLYN	ACTRESS	6605 HOLLYWOOD BLVD #220	HOLLYWOOD, CA	90028
TOMIZAWA, HIDEKI	NEWS CORRESPONDENT	7701 SEBAGO RD	BETHESDA, MD	20817

Name	Occupation	Address	City	Zip/Country
TOMIZAWA, THOMAS M	DIRECTOR	DGA, 110 W 57TH ST	NEW YORK, NY	10019
TOMKO, JOSEPH J, JR	PHOTOJOUNRLIST	6604 96TH AVE	SEABROOK, MD	20706
TOMKO, JOSEPH S, III	PHOTOJOURNALIST	1737 LEISURE WY	CROFTON, MD	21114
TOMLIN, GARY D	DIRECTOR	DGA, 110 W 57TH ST	NEW YORK, NY	10019
TOMLIN, LILY	COMED-ACT-WRI	POST OFFICE BOX 27700	LOS ANGELES, CA	90027
TOMLIN, TRUMAN "PINKY"	COMP-ACT	279 S GLENROY AVE	LOS ANGELES, CA	90049
TOMLINSON, DAVID	ACTOR	BROOK COTTAGE, MURSLEY	BUCKS	ENGLAND
TOMLINSON, JOHN	SINGER	CAMI, 165 W 57TH ST	NEW YORK, NY	10019
TOMOWA-SINTOW, ANNA	SOPRANO	CAMI, 165 W 57TH ST	NEW YORK, NY	10019
TOMPKINS, ANGEL	ACTRESS	POST OFFICE BOX 5069	BEVERLY HILLS, CA	90210
TOMPKINS, JOAN	ACTRESS	8235 SANTA MONICA BLVD #315	LOS ANGELES, CA	90046
TONDO, JERRY S	ACTOR	3330 DESCANSO DR	LOS ANGELES, CA	90026
TONE, FLORENCE T	NEWS CORRESPONDENT	1300 ARMY NAVY DR #807	ARLINGTON, VA	22202
TONER, TOM	ACTOR	ICM, 8899 BEVERLY BLVD	LOS ANGELES, CA	90048
TONGA	WRESTLER	SEE - TONGA, KING		
TONGA, KING	WRESTLER	POST OFFICE BOX 3859	STAMFORD, CT	06905
TONGA, KING KONG	WRESTLER	SEE - TONGA, KING		
TONGA, PRINCE	WRESTLER	SEE - TONGA, KING		
TONGA, TAMA	WRESTLER	SEE - TONGA, KING		
TONGA JOHN	WRESTLER	SEE - KONGA THE BARBARIAN		
TONI, JOLENE	SINGER	MEAUX, 566 BROCK ST	HOUSTON, TX	77023
TONNER, WILLIAM	WRITER	5748 SILVA ST	LAKEWOOD, CA	90713
TONOGAI, KIMIKO	NEWS CORRESPONDENT	1016 NATIONAL PRESS BLDG		
		529 14TH ST, NW	WASHINGTON, DC	20045
TOOK, BARRY	TV-RADIO WRITER	17 HANOVER HOUSE		
		SAINT JOHN'S WOOD		
		HIGH ST	LONDON NW8	ENGLAND
TOOLE, MARY E	NEWS CORRESPONDENT	2727 CALKINS RD	HERNDON, VA	22071
TOOLEY, SIR JOHN	OPERA DIRECTOR	2 MART ST	LONDON WC2	ENGLAND
TOOMEY, REGIS	ACTOR	23388 MULHOLLAND DR	WOODLAND HILLS, CA	91364
TOOTS & THE MAYTALS	RAGGAE GROUP	POST OFFICE BOX 82	GREAT NECK, NY	11021
TOPAZ	ROCK & ROLL GROUP	POST OFFICE BOX 448	RADFORD, VA	24141
TOPHAM, EDWARD C	WRITER	9876 BEVERLY GROVE DR	BEVERLY HILLS, CA	90210
TOPOL, CHAIM	ACTOR-DIRECTOR	DOV HOZ ST	TEL AVIV	ISRAEL
TOPOROFF, RALPH M	DIRECTOR	219 W 81ST ST	NEW YORK, NY	10024
TOPPER, BURT	WRITER-PRODUCER	999 N DOHENY DR #403	LOS ANGELES, CA	90069
TOPPER, TIM	ACTOR	6533 TROOST AVE	NORTH HOLLYWOOD, CA	91606
TOPPING, LYNNE	ACTRESS	211 S BEVERLY DR #107	BEVERLY HILLS, CA	90212
TOPPINGS, ROBERT	GUITARIST	ROUTE #1, BOX 31	AYNOR, SC	29511
TORADZE, ALEXANDER	PIANIST	CAMI, 165 W 57TH ST	NEW YORK, NY	10019
TORDAY, PETER	NEWS CORRESPONDENT	2325 42ND ST #201, NW	WASHINGTON, DC	20007
TORGOV, SARAH	ACTRESS	10351 SANTA MONICA BLVD #211	LOS ANGELES, CA	90025
TORK, PETER	SINGER-ACTOR	SEE - MONKEES, THE		
TORKILDSON, TIM	CLOWN	2701 COTTAGE WY #14	SACRAMENTO, CA	95825
TORME, MEL	SING-ACT-WRI	3518 W CAHUENGA BLVD #206	HOLLYWOOD, CA	90068
TORME, TRACY	TV WRITER	8955 BEVERLY BLVD	LOS ANGELES, CA	90048
TORN, RIP	ACTOR-DIRECTOR	435 W 22ND ST	NEW YORK, NY	10011
TORNADO ON WHEELS	AERIAL THRILL ACT	HALL, 138 FROG HOLLOW RD	CHURCHVILLE, PA	18966
TORNBORG, KAY	ACTRESS	3800 BARHAM BLVD #303	LOS ANGELES, CA	90068
TOROKVEI, PETER	TV WRITER	8955 BEVERLY BLVD	LOS ANGELES, CA	90048
TORP, JONATHAN	SCREENWRITER	2049 CENTURY PARK E #1320	LOS ANGELES, CA	90067
TORRANCE, DONALD C	NEWS CORRESPONDENT	1050 PAPERMILL CT, NW	WASHINGTON, DC	20007
TORRE, RENE R	NEWS CORRESPONDENT	1610 BROOKSIDE RD	MC LEAN, VA	22101
TORRENCE, DEAN	SINGER-SONGWRITER	8912 BURTON WY	BEVERLY HILLS, CA	90211
TORRES	ACROBATIC TROUPE	HALL, 138 FROG HOLLOW RD	CHURCHVILLE, PA	18966
TORRES, ANGELO	CARTOONIST	MAD MAGAZINE, INC		
		485 MADISON AVE	NEW YORK, NY	10022
TORRES, CESAR A	DIRECTOR	DGA, 110 W 57TH ST	NEW YORK, NY	10019
TORRES, JOAN E	SCREENWRITER	2649 34TH ST #C	SANTA MONICA, CA	90405
TORRES, LIZ	SINGER-ACTRESS	525 N SYCAMORE AVE #432	LOS ANGELES, CA	90036
TORRES, RAQUEL	ACTRESS	POST OFFICE BOX 376	BEVERLY HILLS, CA	90213
TORREY, RICH	CARTOONIST	KING FEATURES SYNDICATE		
		235 E 45TH ST	NEW YORK, NY	10017
TORRILLO, SHERRI L	NEWS CORRESPONDENT	2139 WISCONSIN AVE, NW	WASHINGTON, DC	20007
TORTELIER, PAUL	CELLIST	MARIEDL ANDERS ARTISTS MGMT		
		535 EL CAMINO DEL MAR	SAN FRANCISCO, CA	94121
TORTELIER, YAN PASCAL	CONDUCTOR	ICM, 40 W 57TH ST	NEW YORK, NY	10019
TORTI, ROBERT	ACTOR	9704 LEV AVE	ARLETA, CA	91331
TORTORIELLO, DONALD	DIRECTOR	417 E 84TH ST	NEW YORK, NY	10028
TORVIK, SOLVEIG	NEWS CORRESPONDENT	2431 "I" ST, NW	WASHINGTON, DC	20037
TORZEWSKI, MAREK	TENOR	CAMI, 165 W 57TH ST	NEW YORK, NY	10019
TORZEWSKI, WARREN	CLOWN	2701 COTTAGE WY #14	SACRAMENTO, CA	95825
TOSCANI, PALMA	SOPRANO	243 W END AVE #907	NEW YORK, NY	10023
TOSCANO, MICHAEL	NEWS CORRESPONDENT	317 "C" ST, NE	WASHINGTON, DC	20002
TOSH, PETER	SINGER-SONGWRITER	EMI RECORDS COMPANY		
		20 MANCHESTER SQ	LONDON W1A 1ES	ENGLAND
TOSI, MARIO	CINEMATOGRAPHER	1512 MARLAY DR	LOS ANGELES, CA	90069
TOSTADO, E M	COMPOSER	360 AVENIDA OLANCHA	PALM SPRINGS, CA	92262
TOTENBERG, NINA	NEWS CORRESPONDENT	133 NORTH CAROLINA AVE, SE	WASHINGTON, DC	20003
TOTH, ALEX	ACTOR	2121 BROADVIEW TERR	HOLLYWOOD, CA	90068
TOTH, ANDOR	CELLIST	POST OFFICE BOX U	REDDING, CT	06875
TOTH, ROBERT	NEWS CORRESPONDENT	21 PRIMROSE ST	CHEVY CHASE, MD	20815
TOTO	ROCK & ROLL GROUP	7250 BEVERLY BLVD #200	LOS ANGELES, CA	90036
TOTTEN, ROBERT	ACT-WRI-DIR	13819 RIVERSIDE DR	SHERMAN OAKS, CA	91423
TOTTER, AUDREY	ACTRESS	1350 N HIGHLAND AVE #24	HOLLYWOOD, CA	90028

AUDREY TOTTER

CONSTANCE TOWERS

SIMON TOWNSHEND

PAT TRAVERS BAND

RANDY TRAVIS

ROBIN TROWER

KATHLEEN TURNER

LANA TURNER

TINA TURNER

Name	Occupation	Address	City	Zip
TOUBER, SELWYN	DIRECTOR	3546 LAURELVALE DR	STUDIO CITY, CA	91604
TOUCEDA, ENRIQUE	WRITER	3744 GOODLAND AVE	STUDIO CITY, CA	91604
TOUCH	SOUL-DISCO GROUP	8465 KEYSTONE CORSSING #204	INDIANAPOLIS, IN	46240
TOUCHSTONE	FOLK GROUP	POST OFFICE BOX 1487	MILWAUKEE, WI	53201
TOUCHSTONE, TOM	BODYBUILDER	POST OFFICE BOX 663	LAMONT, CA	93241
TOUFEXIS, ANASTASIA	WRITER-EDITOR	TIME/TIME & LIFE BLDG		
		ROCKEFELLER CENTER	NEW YORK, NY	10020
TOUMANOVA, TAMARA	DANCER-ACTRESS	305 N ELM DR	BEVERLY HILLS, CA	90210
TOUSSAINT, ALLEN	PROD-COMP-ARR	3809 CLEMATIS AVE	NEW ORLEANS, LA	70122
TOUVRON, GUY	TRUMPETER	MARIEDL ANDERS ARTISTS MGMT		
		535 EL CAMINO DEL MAR ST	SAN FRANCISCO, CA	94121
TOUZET, RENE	COMPOSER	7680 NW 4TH ST	MIAMI, FL	33126
TOVAR, LUPITA	ACTRESS	1527 TIGERTAIL RD	LOS ANGELES, CA	90049
TOVATT, PATRICK	ACTOR	BRET ADAMS, 448 W 44TH ST	NEW YORK, NY	10036
TOVEY, ARTHUR	ACTOR	12454 KLING ST	NORTH HOLLYWOOD, CA	91604
TOWB, HARRY	ACTOR	SAVAGE, 9 FITZMAURICE PL	LONDON W1	ENGLAND
TOWBIN, FREDI	TV WRITER	10550 LAURISTON AVE	LOS ANGELES, CA	90064
TOWELL, PATRICK	NEWS CORRESPONDENT	310 "G" ST, SW #832	WASHINGTON, DC	20024
TOWER OF POWER	ROCK & ROLL GROUP	151 S EL CAMINO DR	BEVERLY HILLS, CA	90212
TOWER SUITE	ROCK & ROLL GROUP	POST OFFICE BOX 397	MOUNT JULIET, TN	37122
TOWERS, CONSTANCE	ACTRESS	GAVIN, 2415 CENTURY HILL	LOS ANGELES, CA	90067
TOWERS, HARRY ALAN	FILM WRITER-PRODUCER	59 DEVONSHIRE ST #9	LONDON W1	ENGLAND
TOWLE, PATRICIA	NEWS REPORTER	THE NATIONAL ENQUIRER		
		600 SE COAST AVE	LANTANA, FL	33464
TOWLER, JOHN	ACTOR	464 S PALM DR	BEVERLY HILLS, CA	90212
TOWN, JOHN	ACTOR	1221 HORN AVE #9	LOS ANGELES, CA	90069
TOWNE, CHARLES W	NEWS CORRESPONDENT	4419 39TH ST, NW	WASHINGTON, DC	20016
TOWNE, EARLE	ACTOR	11709 ODESSA AVE	GRANADA HILLS, CA	91344
TOWNE, ROBERT	FILM WRITER-DIRECTOR	25036 MALIBU RD	MALIBU, CA	90265
TOWNE, ROGER	SCREENWRITER	8955 BEVERLY BLVD	LOS ANGELES, CA	90048
TOWNER, RALPH	GUITARIST	KURLAND, 173 BRIGHTON AVE	BOSTON, MA	02134
TOWNER & ABERCROMBIE	JAZZ DUO	KURLAND, 173 BRIGHTON AVE	BOSTON, MA	02134
TOWNES, HARRY	ACTOR	2476 W HORSESHOE CYN RD	LOS ANGELES, CA	90046
TOWNSEN & YOCKERS	CLOWN DUO	2701 COTTAGE WY #14	SACRAMENTO, CA	95825
TOWNSEND, BARBARA	ACTRESS	1930 CENTURY PARK W #303	LOS ANGELES, CA	90067
TOWNSEND, BUD	FILM DIRECTOR	5917 BLAIRSTONE DR	CULVER CITY, CA	90230
TOWNSEND, CLAIRE	ACTRESS	2424 LAUREL PASS	LOS ANGELES, CA	90046
TOWNSEND, ERNEST	ACTOR	10 E 44TH ST #700	NEW YORK, NY	10017
TOWNSEND, JIM	ACTOR	8075 W 3RD ST #303	LOS ANGELES, CA	90048
TOWNSEND, JULIAN C	DIRECTOR	65 ABERDEEN DR	TROY, MI	48098
TOWNSEND, K C	ACTRESS	200 W 58TH ST	NEW YORK, NY	10019
TOWNSEND, LEO	SCREENWRITER	25403 PINE CREEK LN	WILMINGTON, CA	90744
TOWNSEND, PATRICIA	ACTRESS	3800 BARHAM BLVD #303	LOS ANGELES, CA	90068
TOWNSEND, PRIMI	ACTRESS	90 KENTON AVE		
		SUNBURY-ON-THAMES	MIDDLESEX	ENGLAND
TOWNSEND, ROBERT	COMEDIAN	445 N BEDFORD DR #PH	BEVERLY HILLS, CA	90210
TOWNSEND, RON	SAXOPHONIST	1503 STELLA AVE	DALLAS, TX	75216
TOWNSEND, THORNTON L	NEWS CORRESPONDENT	4850 CONNECTICUT AVE, NW	WASHINGTON, DC	20008
TOWNSEND, VINCE MONROE, JR	ACTOR	3662 S ARLINGTON AVE	LOS ANGELES, CA	90018
TOWNSEND, WINSTON	PHOTOGRAPHER	5134 N 3RD ST	ARLINGTON, VA	22203
TOWNSEND-EVANS, COLLEEN	ACTRESS	NATIONAL PRESBYTERIAN CHURCH		
		4101 NEBRASKA AVE, SW	WASHINGTON, DC	20007
TOWNSHEND, PETER	SINGER-COMPOSER	120 PALL MALL	LONDON SW1	ENGLAND
TOWNSHEND, SIMON	SINGER	TRINFOLD, 112 WARDOUR ST	LONDON W1	ENGLAND
TOWNSHEND-ZELLNER, JOSH	ACTOR	10845 LINDBROOK DR #3	LOS ANGELES, CA	90024
TOYNE, CHRISTOPHER	FILM PRODUCER	56 BRONSART RD	LONDON SW6	ENGLAND
TOYNTON, IAN	TV DIRECTOR	1 PROSPECT COTTAGES		
		LEE COMMON		
		GREAT MISSENDEN	BUCKS HP16 9JP	ENGLAND
TOYOKO, LITTLE	WRESTLER	SEE - LITTLE TOYOKO		
TOZZI, GIORGIO	ACTOR	6263 EBBTIDE WY	MALIBU, CA	90265
TRABERT, TONY	TENNIS	2 TOJAN CT	RANCHO MIRAGE, CA	92270
TRABULUS, MARC F	WRITER	7523 MULHOLLAND DR	LOS ANGELES, CA	90046
TRACHTE, DON	CARTOONIST	KING FEATURES SYNDICATE		
		235 E 45TH ST	NEW YORK, NY	10017
TRACHTENBERG, LEO	DIRECTOR-PRODUCER	98 RIVERSIDE DR	NEW YORK, NY	10024
TRACI, DONNA	SINGER	POST OFFICE BOX 171132	NASHVILLE, TN	37217
TRACY, ARTHUR	ACTOR	350 W 57TH ST	NEW YORK, NY	10019
TRACY, DICK	SINGER	VARIETY ARTISTS INTL, INC		
		9073 NEMO ST, 3RD FLOOR	LOS ANGELES, CA	90069
TRACY, EMILY	TV WRITER	8955 BEVERLY BLVD	LOS ANGELES, CA	90048
TRACY, JEANIE	SINGER	BORZOI, 222 DUNIC ST	SAN FRANCISCO, CA	94131
TRACY, JOHN	TV DIRECTOR	3510 RIDGEFORD DR	WESTLAKE VILLAGE, CA	91361
TRACY, WOODY	ACTOR	1307 TAMARIND AVE #1	LOS ANGELES, CA	90028
TRAEGER, RICK	ACTOR	13838 VICTORY BLVD #26	VAN NUYS, CA	91401
TRAFFORD, ABIGAIL	NEWS CORRESPONDENT	2600 UPTON ST, NW	WASHINGTON, DC	20008
TRAIL	ROCK & ROLL GROUP	HOT RECORDS & ROUGH TRADE		
		326 6TH ST	SAN FRANCISCO, CA	94103
TRAIN, WIRE	ROCK & ROLL GROUP	SEE - WIRE TRAIN		
TRAINER, CYNTHIA	GUITARIST	799 BELLEVUE RD	NASHVILLE, TN	37221
TRAINER, DAVID	TV WRITER	555 W 57TH ST #1230	NEW YORK, NY	10019
TRAINOR, MARY ELLEN	ACTRESS	3800 BARHAM BLVD #303	LOS ANGELES, CA	90068
TRAKAS, CHRISTOPHER	BARITONE	CAMI, 165 W 57TH ST	NEW YORK, NY	10019
TRAMER, BENNETT	TV WRITER	418 9TH ST	SANTA MONICA, CA	90402
TRAMMPS, THE	SOUL GROUP	BROTHERS, 141 DUNBAR AVE	FORDS, NJ	08863

Name	Occupation	Address	City	Zip
TRAMONT, JEAN-CLAUDE	WRITER-DIR ECTOR	938 BEL AIR RD	LOS ANGELES, CA	90077
TRAMPOLINE GUYS, THE	TRAMPOLINE GROUP	HALL, 138 FROG HOLLOW RD	CHURCHVILLE, PA	18966
TRANELLI, DEBORAH	ACTRESS	9601 WILSHIRE BLVD #GL-11	BEVERLY HILLS, CA	90210
TRANG, H TU	NEWS CORRESPONDENT	9309 KILBY GLEN DR	VIENNA, VA	22180
TRANTHAM, RICK	BANJOIST	2360 ANTIOCH PIKE	ANTIOCH, TN	37013
TRAPEZOID	FOLK GROUP	POST OFFICE BOX 604	CONIFER, CO	80433
TRAPNELL, COLES	WRITER-PRODUCER	10577 ROCHESTER AVE	LOS ANGELES, CA	90024
TRASK, DIANA	SINGER	10889 WILSHIRE BLVD #1146	LOS ANGELES, CA	90024
TRAUM, ARTIE & PAT ALGER	VOCAL GROUP	49 W 96TH ST #5-C	NEW YORK, NY	10025
TRAUSCH, SUSAN R	NEWS CORRESPONDENT	2939 VAN NESS ST #518, NW	WASHINGTON, DC	20008
TRAUTMAN, ROBERT GEORGE	NEWS CORRESPONDENT	5903 WESTCHESTER ST	ALEXANDRIA, VA	22310
TRAVALENA, FRED	COMED-ACT-WRI	POST OFFICE BOX 171	ENCINO, CA	91316
TRAVANTI, DANIEL J	ACTOR	14205 SUNSET BLVD	PACIFIC PALISADES, CA	90272
TRAVELIN' BAND, THE	C & W GROUP	TM, 1019 17TH AVE S	NASHVILLE, TN	37212
TRAVER, NANCY	WRITER-EDITOR	TIME/TIME & LIFE BLDG		
		ROCKEFELLER CENTER	NEW YORK, NY	10020
TRAVERS, BILL	ACT-WRI-DIR-PROD	67 GLEBE PL	LONDON SW3 5JB	ENGLAND
TRAVERS, LINDEN	ACTOR	HOLMAN, LORAINE, SAINT IVES	CORWALL	ENGLAND
TRAVERS, PAT, BAND	ROCK & ROLL GROUP	POST OFFICE BOX 7877		
		COLLEGE PARK STATION	ORLANDO, FL	32854
TRAVERS, PETER	FILM CRITIC	PEOPLE/TIME & LIFE BLDG		
		ROCKEFELLER CENTER	NEW YORK, NY	10020
TRAVERS, SY	ACTOR	357 W 43RD ST	NEW YORK, NY	10036
TRAVIESO, JOHN J	NEWS CORRESPONDENT	NBC NEWS, 4001 NEBRASKA AVE, NW	WASHINGTON, DC	20016
TRAVILLA, WILLIAM	COSTUME DESIGNER	3241 N KNOLL DR	LOS ANGELES, CA	90068
TRAVIS, DIANNE TURLEY	ACTRESS	8350 SANTA MONICA BLVD #103	LOS ANGELES, CA	90069
TRAVIS, JIM	SINGER-GUITARIST	113 SCOTCH ST	HENDERSONVILLE, TN	37075
TRAVIS, LEE	ACTRESS	1741 N IVAR AVE #221	LOS ANGELES, CA	90028
TRAVIS, LEE	TV WRITER	8955 BEVERLY BLVD	LOS ANGELES, CA	90048
TRAVIS, MERLE	SINGER-GUITARIST	ROUTE #1, BOX 128	PARK HILL, OK	74451
TRAVIS, NANCY	ACTRESS	SHUKAT, 340 W 55TH ST	NEW YORK, NY	10019
TRAVIS, RANDY	SINGER-SONGWRITER	ELIZABETH HATCHER		
		1610 16TH AVE S	NASHVILLE, TN	37203
TRAVOLTA, ANN	ACTRESS	3151 W CAHUENGA BLVD #310	LOS ANGELES, CA	90068
TRAVOLTA, ELLEN	ACTRESS	1650 BROADWAY #406	NEW YORK, NY	10019
TRAVOLTA, JOEY	ACTOR	LIGHT, 113 N ROBERTSON BLVD	LOS ANGELES, CA	90048
TRAVOLTA, JOHN	ACTOR-SINGER	RANCHO TAJIGUAS		
		SUNBURST FARMS		
		HIGHWAY #101	SANTA BARBARA, CA	93103
TRAVOLTA, SAM	ACTOR	9300 WILSHIRE BLVD #410	BEVERLY HILLS, CA	90212
TRAYLOR, BILL	GUITARIST	3120 CEDARCROFT DR	ANTIOCH, TN	37013
TRAYLOR, WILLIAM	ACTOR	11610 BELLAGIO RD	LOS ANGELES, CA	90049
TRAYNE, JOHN	ACTOR	10850 RIVERSIDE DR #501	NORTH HOLLYWOOD, CA	91602
TRAYNHAM, PETER C	NEWS CORRESPONDENT	CBS NEWS, 2020 "M" ST, NW	WASHINGTON, DC	20036
TRAYNOR, PETER	DIRECTOR	20940 WAVE VIEW DR	TOPANGA CANYON, CA	90290
TRBOVICH, THOMAS	TV DIRECTOR	1369 EL HITO CIR	PACIFIC PALISADES, CA	90272
TREADWELL, DAVID	NEWS CORRESPONDENT	1545 18TH ST, NW	WASHINGTON, DC	20036
TREAS, TERRI	ACTRESS	9105 CARMELITIA AVE #1	BEVERLY HILLS, CA	90210
TREBEK, ALEX	TV HOST	2666 CARMER DR	LOS ANGELES, CA	90046
TREDANARI, LEE J	DIRECTOR	307 W 103RD ST	NEW YORK, NY	10025
TREE, MICHAEL	VIOLINIST	45 E 89TH ST	NEW YORK, NY	10028
TREEN, MARY	ACTRESS	7060 HOLLYWOOD BLVD #610	LOS ANGELES, CA	90028
TREGER, CHARLES	VIOLINIST	POST OFFICE BOX U	REDDING, CT	06875
TREGER, LISA	SOPRANO	HILLYER, 250 W 57TH ST	NEW YORK, NY	10107
TREGOE, WILLIAM	ACTOR	7270 FRANKLIN AVE #9	HOLLYWOOD, CA	90046
TREHY, ROBERT	BARITONE	GEWALD, 58 W 58TH ST	NEW YORK, NY	10019
TREIGLE, PHYLLIS	SOPRANO	CAMI, 165 W 57TH ST	NEW YORK, NY	10019
TREIMER, WINIFRED	STORY EDITOR	2300 VASANTA WY	LOS ANGELES, CA	90068
TRELA, MARK ANTHONY	WRITER	3011 MANHATTAN AVE	LA CRESCENTA, CA	91214
TREMAYNE, LES	ACTOR	901 S BARRINGTON AVE	LOS ANGELES, CA	90049
TREMBLAY, LUCIE BLUE	SINGER-GUITARIST	OLIVIA RECORDS COMPANY		
		4400 MARKET ST	OAKLAND, CA	94608
TREMONT STRING QUARTET	STRING QUARTET	FINELL, 155 W 68TH ST	NEW YORK, NY	10023
TRENCHARD-SMITH, BRIAN	WRITER-PRODUCER	26 MARANKA ST	HORNSBY NSW	AUSTRALIA
TRENGROVE, JAMES A	NEWS CORRESPONDENT	4461 CONNECTICUT AVE, NW	WASHINGTON, DC	20008
TRENIERS, THE	MUSIC GROUP	7060 HOLLYWOOD BLVD #1212	HOLLYWOOD, CA	90028
TRENNER, BARON "MICKEY"	DIRECTOR	DGA, 110 W 57TH ST	NEW YORK, NY	10019
TRENNER, DONN R	COMPOSER-CONDUCTOR	21418 SALAMANCA AVE	WOODLAND HILLS, CA	91364
TRENT, BUCK	SINGER-MUSICIAN	742-B LINDEN GREEN DR	HERMITAGE, TN	37076
TRENT, JACKIE	SINGER	M & M MUSIC, 32 SOUTHACRE		
		HYDE PARK CRESCENT	LONDON W2 2QB	ENGLAND
TRENT, JOHN	FILM DIRECTOR	50 DALE AVE	TORONTO, ONT	CANADA
TRENTHAM, BARBARA L	FILM DIRECTOR	82 LADBROKE RD	LONDON W11	ENGLAND
TRES HOMBRES	ROCK & ROLL GROUP	41 BRITAIN ST #200	TORONTO, ONT	CANADA
TRESS, DAVID	ACTOR	3456 WADE ST	LOS ANGELES, CA	90066
TRETICK, CLIFFORD	FLUTIST	200 W 70TH ST #7-F	NEW YORK, NY	10023
TRETICK, STAN	PHOTOGRAPHER	4365 EMBASSY PARK DR, NW	WASHINGTON, DC	20016
TRETTIN, HENRY	DIRECTOR	868 BROOKTREE RD	PACIFIC PALISADES, CA	90272
TRETYAKOV, VIKTOR	VIOLINIST	CAMI, 165 W 57TH ST	NEW YORK, NY	10019
TREUTELAAR, BARBARA	ACTRESS	ABC-TV, "ONE LIFE TO LIVE"		
		1330 AVE OF THE AMERICAS	NEW YORK, NY	10019
TREVES, FREDERICK	ACTOR-WRITER	YOUNG, 31 KING'S RD	LONDON SW3 4RP	ENGLAND
TREVEY, KENNETH E	WRITER	2663 LARMAR RD	LOS ANGELES, CA	90068
TREVILLION, DALE	WRITER	152 MORENO DR	BEVERLY HILLS, CA	90212
TREVINO, DAVE	TRUMPETER	201 E PALESTINE #F-27	MADISON, TN	37115

Name	Occupation	Address	City/State	Zip
TREVINO, JESUS SALVADOR	WRITER-PRODUCER	2358 YORKSHIRE DR	LOS ANGELES, CA	90065
TREVOR, CLAIRE	ACTRESS	THE PIERCE HOTEL		
		2 E 61ST ST & 5TH AVE	NEW YORK, NY	10021
TREVOR, DON M	DIRECTOR	1-3 POND BROOK RD	NEWTOWN, CT	06470
TREVOR, ELLESTON	WRITER	16122 OCOTILLO DR	FOUNTAIN HILLS, AZ	85268
TREVOR, JOHN	CARTOONIST	POST OFFICE BOX J	ALBUQUERQUE, NM	87103
TREVOR, KIRK	CONDUCTOR	1776 BROADWAY #504	NEW YORK, NY	10019
TREWHITT, HENRY L	NEWS CORRESPONDENT	3155 TENNYSON ST, NW	WASHINGTON, DC	20015
TREXLER, PAT	COLUMNIST	UNIVERSAL PRESS SYNDICATE		
		4900 MAIN ST, 9TH FLOOR	KANSAS CITY, MO	62114
TREYZ, RUSSELL L	TV DIRECTOR	107 BEDFORD ST	NEW YORK, NY	10014
TREZEVANT, JOHN G	PUBLISHING EXECUTIVE	NEWS AMERICA SYNDICATE		
		1703 KAISER AVE	IRVINE, CA	92714
TRIBOBOFF, DANIEL	NEWS CORRESPONDENT	604 ETHAN ALLEN AVE	TAKOMA PARK, MD	20912
TRICKER, GEORGE J	TV WRITER	22100 VICTORY BLVD	WOODLAND HILLS, CA	91367
TRICKS, THE	ROCK & ROLL GROUP	VARIETY ARTISTS INTL, INC		
		9073 NEMO ST, 3RD FLOOR	LOS ANGELES, CA	90069
TRICKSTER	ROCK & ROLL GROUP	2049 CENTURY PARK E #414	LOS ANGELES, CA	90067
TRIESAULT, JON	DIRECTOR	8562 CRESCENT DR	HOLLYWOOD, CA	90046
TRIFFIDS, THE	ROCK & ROLL GROUP	HOT RECORDS & ROUGH TRADE		
		326 6TH ST	SAN FRANCISCO, CA	94103
TRIGAUX, ROBERT	NEWS CORRESPONDENT	9 W LINDEN ST	ALEXANDRIA, VA	22301
TRIKILIS, MICHAEL	DIRECTOR-PRODUCER	493 LORING AVE	LOS ANGELES, CA	90024
TRIKONIS, GUS	TV DIRECTOR	1901 AVE OF THE STARS #840	LOS ANGELES, CA	90067
TRIKOSKO, MARION	PHOTOGRAPHER	2147 "O" ST, NW	WASHINGTON, DC	20037
TRILLIN, CALVIN	AUTHOR-REPORTER	KING FEATURES SYNDICATE		
		235 E 45TH ST	NEW YORK, NY	10017
TRILLION	ROCK & ROLL GROUP	TWOGETHER, 2137 LINDEN LN	PALATINE, IL	60067
TRIM, DAVID	ACTOR	ABC-TV, "ALL MY CHILDREN"		
		1330 AVE OF THE AMERICAS	NEW YORK, NY	10019
TRIMARCHI, DOMENICO	BASSO-BARITONE	CAMI, 165 W 57TH ST	NEW YORK, NY	10019
TRIMBLE, LESTER	COMPOSER	98 RIVERSIDE DR	NEW YORK, NY	10023
TRIMEL, SUZANNE M	NEWS CORRESPONDENT	2400 16TH ST, NW	WASHINGTON, DC	20006
TRIMIS, EDWARD A	COMPOSER	4629 LA CRESENTA AVE	LA CRESCENTA, CA	91214
TRIMPLE, CHUCK	GUITARIST	POST OFFICE BOX 8036	NASHVILLE, TN	37207
TRINGHAM, DAVID	FILM DIRECTOR	40 LANGTHORNE ST	LONDON SW6	ENGLAND
TRINIDAD, ARSENIO	ACTOR	5332 HOLLYWOOD BLVD	HOLLYWOOD, CA	90027
TRINTIGNANT, JEAN-LOUIS	ACTOR	30 RUE DES FRANCE-BOURGEOS	PARIS 75008	FRANCE
TRIO	ROCK & ROLL GROUP	REGENSTESTR 10-A	2907 GROBENKNETEN 2	WEST GERMANY
TRIPLETS, THE	ROCK & ROLL GROUP	MC DERMOTT, MEGA MANAGEMENT		
		71 W 23RD ST	NEW YORK, NY	10010
TRIPP, ALLEN	SINGER	111 OLD HICKORY BLVD #W-299	NASHVILLE, TN	37221
TRIPP, PAUL	ACTOR	2 5TH AVE	NEW YORK, NY	10011
TRIPPEL, RICHARD C "BUCK"	DIRECTOR	DGA, 7950 SUNSET BLVD	LOS ANGELES, CA	90046
TRIPPET, FRANK	WRITER-EDITOR	TIME/TIME & LIFE BLDG		
		ROCKEFELLER CENTER	NEW YORK, NY	10020
TRIPPETT, ROBERT	PHOTOGRAPHER	6634 HAZEL LN	MC LEAN, VA	22101
TRIPPLE A BAND	JAZZ GROUP	9777 HARWIN ST #101	HOUSTON, TX	77036
TRISCHKA, TONY & SKYLINE	BLUEGRASS GROUP	POST OFFICE BOX 1487	MILWAUKEE, WI	53201
TRISKA, JAN	ACTOR	9255 SUNSET BLVD #505	LOS ANGELES, CA	90069
TRISKA, KARLA	ACTRESS	9255 SUNSET BLVD #505	LOS ANGELES, CA	90069
TRISTAN	C & W GROUP	POST OFFICE BOX 29543	ATLANTA, GA	30359
TRISTAN, DOROTHY	ACTRESS-WRITER	POST OFFICE BOX 5617	BEVERLY HILLS, CA	90210
TRITT, WILLIAM	PIANIST	500 5TH AVE #2050	NEW YORK, NY	10110
TRIUMPH	ROCK & ROLL GROUP	3611 MAVIS RD #5	MISSISSAUGA, ONT L5C 1	CANADA
TRIVETTE, BUTCH	SINGER	POST OFFICE BOX 13584	ATLANTA, GA	30324
TROCCOLI'S DOG, TOM	ROCK & ROLL GROUP	POST OFFICE BOX 1	LAWNDALE, CA	90260
TRODD, KENITH	TV PRODUCER	188 GLOUCESTER TERR	LONDON W2	ENGLAND
TROGDON, MIRIAM	TV WRITER	8955 BEVERLY BLVD	LOS ANGELES, CA	90048
TROHA, JOHN	PHOTOGRAPHER	12258 SAINT JAMES RD	POTOMAC, MD	20854
TROIA/GRIER	ROCK & ROCK DUO	POST OFFICE BOX 8786	NEW HAVEN, CT	06532
TROMBERG, SHELDON	NEWS CORRESPONDENT	4200 RIVER RD, NW	WASHINGTON, DC	20016
TRONCATTY, RON	ACTOR	5312 CHESEBRO RD	AGOURA, CA	91301
TRONSON, ROBERT	FILM DIRECTOR	HEATH, PARAMOUNT HOUSE		
		162-170 WARDOUR ST	LONDON W1V 3AT	ENGLAND
TROOBNICK, EUGENE	ACTOR	211 S BEVERLY DR #107	BEVERLY HILLS, CA	90212
TROOPER	ROCK & ROLL GROUP	41 BRITAIN ST #200	TORONTO, ONT	CANADA
TROPIN, MITCHELL, JR	NEWS CORRESPONDENT	2939 VAN NESS ST #808, NW	WASHINGTON, DC	20008
TROSSMAN, JOAN	ACTRESS	4711 NATICK AVE #230	SHERMAN OAKS, CA	91403
TROST, CATHY	NEWS CORRESPONDENT	2415 20TH ST #16, NW	WASHINGTON, DC	20009
TROTT, LAURENCE	PICCOLO	157 W 57TH ST #1100	NEW YORK, NY	10019
TROTT, WILLIAMS C	NEWS CORRESPONDENT	1825 16TH ST, NW	WASHINGTON, DC	20009
TROUBLE BOYS	MUSIC TRIO	LUTZ, 5625 "O" STREET BLDG	LINCOLN, NE	68510
TROUGHTON, PATRICK	ACTOR	FILM RIGHTS COMPANY		
		4 NEW BURLINGTON PL		
		REGENT ST	LONDON W1	ENGLAND
TROUP, BOBBY	ACT-COMP-SING	16074 ROYAL OAK ST	ENCINO, CA	91316
TROUP, RONNE	ACTRESS	3800 BARHAM BLVD #303	LOS ANGELES, CA	90068
TROUPE, TOM	ACTOR	8829 ASHCROFT AVE	LOS ANGELES, CA	90048
TROWER, ROBIN	SINGER-GUITARIST	STARDUST ENTERPRISES		
		2650 GLENDOWER AVE	LOS ANGELES, CA	90027
TROXEL, JOHN P	FRENCH HORNIST	4716 HOSEY DR	BIRMINGHAM, AL	35243
TROY, BENNY & COMPANY	ROCK & ROLL GROUP	BROTHERS, 141 DUNBAR AVE	FORDS, NJ	08863
TROYANOS, TATIANA	MEZZO-SOPRANO	CAMI, 165 W 57TH ST	NEW YORK, NY	10019
TRUBE, IRENE	WRITER	LEHRMAN, 11937 SUNSET BLVD #C	LOS ANGELES, CA	90049

Name	Occupation	Address	City	Zip
TRUCKENBROD, PHILLIP	TALENT AGENT	15 HIGH ST #621	HARTFORD, CT	06103
TRUCKS, BUTCH	SINGER	POST OFFICE BOX 1566	MONTCLAIR, NJ	07042
TRUDEAU, GARY	CARTOONIST-WRITER	271 CENTRAL PARK W#10-E	NEW YORK, NY	10024
TRUE WEST	ROCK & ROLL GROUP	JEM RECORDS, 3619 KENNEDY RD	SOUTH PLAINFIELD, NJ	07080
TRUEBLOOD, GUERDON	WRITER-PRODUCER	DGA, 7950 SUNSET BLVD	HOLLYWOOD, CA	90046
TRUEMAN, ANDREW	TALENT AGENT	24514 CALBERT ST #210	WOODLAND HILLS, CA	91367
TRUEMAN, PAULA	ACTRESS	340 E 63RD ST	NEW YORK, NY	10021
TRULAND, BUDD	ACTOR	5161 COLLINS AVE	MIAMI BEACH, FL	33140
TRULL, TERESA	SINGER	OLIVIA RECORDS COMPANY		
		4400 MARKET ST	OAKLAND, CA	94608
TRULY, DAVID	GUITARIST	3010 SCHILLER ST	TAMPA, FL	33609
TRUMAN, EDWARD	COMPOSER-CONDUCTOR	1826 JEWETT DR	LOS ANGELES, CA	90046
TRUMAN, MARGARET	AUTHORESS	SEE - DANIEL, MARGARET TRUMAN		
TRUMBULL, BRAD	ACTOR	333 TIGERTAIL RD	LOS ANGELES, CA	90049
TRUMBULL, DOUGLAS	WRITER-PRODUCER	1133 GEORGINA AVE	SANTA MONICA, CA	90402
TRUMP, DONALD	SPORTS EXECUTIVE	725 5TH AVE	NEW YORK, NY	10022
TRUMP, JILL	TV WRITER	8955 BEVERLY BLVD	LOS ANGELES, CA	90048
TRUMPER, JOHN	FILM EDITOR	WAYSIDE, VINE RD	LONDON SW13 ONE	ENGLAND
TRUMPOWER, MAX	ACTOR	149 MUERDAGO RD	TOPANGA CANYON, CA	90290
TRUSCOTT, ALAN	BRIDGE ANALYST	N Y TIMES, 229 W 43RD ST	NEW YORK, NY	10036
TRUSEL, LISA	ACTRESS	9000 SUNSET BLVD #1200	LOS ANGELES, CA	90069
TRUSSEL, JACQUE	TENOR	CAMI, 165 W 57TH ST	NEW YORK, NY	10019
TRUSSELL, CHRISTOPHER M	COMPOSER-CONDUCTOR	1175 W BASELINE RD	CLAREMONT, CA	91711
TRUTH	MUSICAL GROUP	POST OFFICE BOX 8554	MOBILE, AL	36608
TRUTH, THE	ROCK & ROLL GROUP	194 KENSINGSTON PARK RD	LONDON W11 2ES	ENGLAND
TRYFLES, THE	ROCK & ROLL GROUP	POST OFFICE BOX 390		
		OLD CHELSEA STATION	NEW YORK, NY	10113
TRYON, THOMAS	ACTOR-NOVELIST	1266 SUNSET PLAZA DR	LOS ANGELES, CA	90069
TSAGARATOS, GEORGIA-ELLIE	NEWS CORRESPONDENT	4921 SEMINARY RD	ALEXANDRIA, VA	22311
TSCHAMMER, HANS	SINGER	CAMI, 165 W 57TH ST	NEW YORK, NY	10019
TSCHUDIN, RICHARD	DIRECTOR	POST OFFICE BOX 281	LAKE ARROWHEAD, CA	92352
TSE, MARIKO	ACTRESS	1711 FRANKLIN ST #D	SANTA MONICA, CA	90404
TSEITLIN, IRINA	VIOLINIST	POST OFFICE BOX 27539	PHILADELPHIA, PA	19118
TSEITLIN, VALENTINA	BALLERINA	14858 VIA DEL CANON	DEL MAR, CA	92014
TSENG, FLEURANCE	ACTRESS	POST OFFICE BOX 3741	GRANADA HILLS, CA	91344
TSOL	ROCK & ROLL GROUP	SEE - T S O L		
TSOUTSOUVAS, SAM	ACTOR	19 W 44TH ST #1500	NEW YORK, NY	10036
TSU, IRENE	ACTRESS	9744 WILSHIRE BLVD #306	BEVERLY HILLS, CA	90212
TSUMURA, MARI	VIOLINIST	CPS, 34 66TH PL	LONG BEACH, CA	90803
TSUTSUMI, TSUYOSHI	CELLIST	HILLYER, 250 W 57TH ST	NEW YORK, NY	10107
TUAN, LE	ACTOR	8235 SANTA MONICA BLVD #202	LOS ANGELES, CA	90046
TUBB, ERNEST	SINGER-GUITARIST	513 JANICE DR	ANTIOCH, TN	37013
TUBB, JUSTIN	SINGER-GUITARIST	POST OFFICE BOX 500	NASHVILLE, TN	37202
TUBBS, CONSTANCE	SPORTS WRITER-EDITOR	SPORTS ILLUSTRATED MAGAZINE		
		TIME & LIFE BUILDING		
		ROCKEFELLER CENTER	NEW YORK, NY	10020
TUBELLE, LARRY	WRITER	166 S PLYMOUTH BLVD	LOS ANGELES, CA	90004
TUBER, RICHARD J	WRITER	5445 LINDLEY AVE #30	TARZANA, CA	91356
TUBERT, MARC	ACTOR	1350 N HIGHLAND AVE #24	HOLLYWOOD, CA	90028
TUBERT, MARCELO	ACTOR	4349 BAKMAN AVE	NORTH HOLLYWOOD, CA	91602
TUBES, THE	ROCK & ROLL GROUP	POST OFFICE BOX 6894	SAN FRANCISCO, CA	94101
TUCCI, MICHAEL	ACTOR	ICM, 8899 BEVERLY BLVD	LOS ANGELES, CA	90048
TUCH, LAWRENCE BARTON	WRITER	5713 OSTIN AVE	WOODLAND HILLS, CA	91367
TUCHNER, MICHAEL	FILM DIRECTOR	4 KENT RD, E MOLESEY	SURREY	ENGLAND
TUCK, ANTHONY STANFORD	WRITER-PRODUCER	HOSKINS, 10 CONNAUGHT SQ	LONDON W2 2HG	ENGLAND
TUCK, MICHAEL	BROADCAST JOURNALIST	POST OFFICE BOX 85347	SAN DIEGO, CA	92138
TUCKER, ARLIN	SINGER	POST OFFICE BOX 25371	CHARLOTTE, NC	28212
TUCKER, COLIN	TV PRODUCER	A D PETERS & CO, LTD		
		10 BUCKINGHAM ST	LONDON WC2	ENGLAND
TUCKER, DONALD	GUITARIST	4952 CIMARRON WY	ANTIOCH, TN	37013
TUCKER, ELIZABETH	NEWS CORRESPONDENT	1651 FULLER ST #1, NW	WASHINGTON, DC	20009
TUCKER, GABE	TRUMPETER	2107 ANSBURY DR	HOUSTON, TX	77018
TUCKER, GENE	TENOR	3003 VAN NESS ST #W-205, NW	WASHINGTON, DC	20008
TUCKER, JAMES P, JR	NEWS CORRESPONDENT	208 4TH ST, SE	WASHINGTON, DC	20003
TUCKER, JOHN T	NEWS CORRESPONDENT	1012 14TH ST, NW	WASHINGTON, DC	20005
TUCKER, LA COSTA	SINGER	50 MUSIC SQUARE W #907	NASHVILLE, TN	37212
TUCKER, LARRY	FILM WRITER-PRODUCER	1888 CENTURY PARK E #1400	LOS ANGELES, CA	90067
TUCKER, LEMUEL	NEWS CORRESPONDENT	2127 CALIFORNIA ST, NW	WASHINGTON, DC	20008
TUCKER, MARSHALL, BAND	ROCK & ROLL GROUP	SUGAR PINE, 300 E HENRY ST	SPARTANBURG, SC	69302
TUCKER, MAUREEN	SINGER-GUITARIST	POST OFFICE BOX 22012	PHOENIX, AZ	85028
TUCKER, MELVILLE	FILM PRODUCER	2115 MANDEVILLE CANYON RD	LOS ANGELES, CA	90049
TUCKER, MICHAEL	ACTOR	11726 SAN VICENTE BLVD #300	LOS ANGELES, CA	90049
TUCKER, NANCY MEREDITH	NEWS CORRESPONDENT	4091 S FOUR MILE RUN #101	ARLINGTON, VA	22204
TUCKER, ORIN	CONDUCTOR	POST OFFICE BOX 1001	CATHEDRAL CITY, CA	92234
TUCKER, PATRICK	TV DIRECTOR	42-A WARRINGTON CRESCENT	LONDON W9 1EP	ENGLAND
TUCKER, PAULA MC KINNEY	WRITER-PRODUCER	26126 MEADOWCREST	HUNTINGTON WOODS, MI	48070
TUCKER, ROGER	TV DIRECTOR	HEATH, PARAMOUNT HOUSE		
		162-170 WARDOUR ST	LONDON W1V 4AB	ENGLAND
TUCKER, SANDRA	ACTRESS	8831 SUNSET BLVD #402	LOS ANGELES, CA	90069
TUCKER, TANYA	SINGER	POST OFFICE BOX 15245	NASHVILLE, TN	37215
TUCKER, VINCENT	ACTOR	LENZ, 1456 E CHARLESTON BLVD	LAS VEGAS, NV	89104
TUCKSON, COLEMAN REED	PHOTOGRAPHER	POST OFFICE BOX 1104	SILVER SPRING, MD	20910
TUCKWELL, BARRY	HORN	CAMI, 165 W 57TH ST	NEW YORK, NY	10019
TUDOR, CHRISTINE	ACTRESS	8220 GOULD AVE	LOS ANGELES, CA	90046
TUDOR, DAVID	MUSICIAN-COMPOSER	GATE HILL RD	STONY POINT, NY	10980

Name	Occupation	Address	City/State	Zip
TUDOR, THOMAS	COMPOSER	10960 HESBY ST	NORTH HOLLYWOOD, CA	91601
TUELL, JOHN	ACTOR	806 S CITRUS AVE	LOS ANGELES, CA	90036
TUERPE, PAUL	ACTOR	6328 GOODLAND PL	NORTH HOLLYWOOD, CA	91606
TUFELD, LYNN	ACTRESS	167 S SYCAMORE AVE	LOS ANGELES, CA	90036
TUFTY, BARBARA J	NEWS CORRESPONDENT	3812 LIVINGSTON ST, NW	WASHINGTON, DC	20015
TUFTY, ESTER VAN WAGONER	NEWS CORRESPONDENT	820 ARCTURUS ON POTOMAC	ALEXANDRIA, VA	23308
TUFTY, HAL	NEWS CORRESPONDENT	3812 LIVINGSTON ST, NW	WASHINGTON, DC	20015
TUGEND, ALINA	NEWS CORRESPONDENT	4101 DAVID PL, NW	WASHINGTON, DC	20007
TUGEND, HARRY	WRITER-PRODUCER	838 N DOHENY DR #100	LOS ANGELES, CA	90069
TUGEND, JAMES	WRITER	1618 S BARRINGTON AVE	LOS ANGELES, CA	90025
TUGGLE, RICHARD ALLAN	WRITER-PRODUCER	840 21ST ST #C	SANTA MONICA, CA	90403
TUHY, CARRIE	WRITER-EDITOR	LIFE/TIME & LIFE BLDG		
		ROCKEFELLER CENTER	NEW YORK, NY	10020
TUIDER, HERMAN	ACTOR	1236 N OGDEN DR #7	LOS ANGELES, CA	90046
TULCHIN, HAROLD M	DIRECTOR-PRODUCER	240 E 45TH ST	NEW YORK, NY	10017
TULIN, MARK	WRITER	20746 DOLOROSA ST	WOODLAND HILLS, CA	91367
TULIS, DAVID	PHOTOGRAPHER	10636 MONTROSE AVE	BETHESDA, MD	20814
TULL, JETHRO	ROCK & ROLL GROUP	SEE - JETHRO TULL		
TULLIS, KYLE	GUITARIST	BOX 214, LIBERTY PIKE	FRANKLIN, TN	37064
TULLY, JOHN	TV DIRECTOR	BUCKINGHAM FILMS, 139 HARROW RD	LONDON W2	ENGLAND
TUMAGIAN, EDUARD	BARITONE	CAMI, 165 W 57TH ST	NEW YORK, NY	10019
TUMULTY, KAREN	NEWS CORRESPONDENT	2601 WOODLEY PL, NW	WASHINGTON, DC	20008
TUNBERG, KARL	WRITER	29136 CRAGS DR	AGOURA, CA	91301
TUNE, TOMMY	DAN-DIR-CHOR	1501 BROADWAY #1508	NEW YORK, NY	10036
TUNG, LING	CONDUCTOR	1776 BROADWAY #504	NEW YORK, NY	10019
TUNICK, JONATHAN	CONDUCTOR	1776 BROADWAY #504	NEW YORK, NY	10019
TUNIE, TAMARIA	ACTRESS	CBS-TV, "AS THE WORLD TURNS"		
		51 W 52ND ST	NEW YORK, NY	10019
TUNNEY, DICK	ACCORDIONIST	592 BLAKE MOORE DR	LA VERGNE, TN	37086
TUNNEY, JACK	WRESTLING EXECUTIVE	POST OFFICE BOX 3859	STAMFORD, CT	06905
TURBINES, THE	ROCK & ROLL GROUP	33 MUSIC SQUARE W #100	NASHVILLE, TN	37203
TURBOS, THE	ROCK & ROLL GROUP	SEE - TIM & THE TURBOS		
TURBYVILLE, CHARLES W	NEWS CORRESPONDENT	8 COLUMBIA AVE	TAKOMA PARK, MD	20912
TURCI, LISA & CLUES '84	JAZZ GROUP	GOOD, 2500 NW 39TH ST	OKLAHOMA CITY, OK	73112
TUREAUD, LAWRENCE	ACTOR	SEE - T, MR		
TURECK, ROSALYN	PIANIST	CAMI, 165 W 57TH ST	NEW YORK, NY	10019
TURETSKY, ELI	DIRECTOR	49 BROOKLAWN TERR	FAIRFIELD, CT	06430
TURGEON, PETER B	ACTOR	320 E 53RD ST	NEW YORK, NY	10022
TURIEL, DANIEL E	COMPOSER-CONDUCTOR	441 8TH AVE S	NAPLES, FL	33940
TURK, CARL W	TV DIRECTOR	9100 MC VICKER	MORTON GROVE, IL	60053
TURK, TRAVIS	DRUMMER	513 GALESBURG CT	NASHVILLE, TN	37217
TURKATENKO, NIKOLAY	NEWS CORRESPONDENT	4615 N PARK AVE #909	CHEVY CHASE, MD	20045
TURKEL, ANN	ACTRESS	9877 BEVERLY GROVE	BEVERLY HILLS, CA	90210
TURKEL, JOSEPH	ACTOR	POST OFFICE BOX 819	MOSS BEACH, CA	94038
TURKNETT, CLIFFORD H	ACTOR	14646 DICKENS ST #21	SHERMAN OAKS, CA	91403
TURKOVIC, MILAN	BASSOONIST	AIA, 60 E 42ND ST	NEW YORK, NY	10165
TURLEY, JACK BRADFORD	TV WRITER	10072 WESTWANDA DR	BEVERLY HILLS, CA	90210
TURLEY, MICHELLE	ACTRESS	11350 VENTURA BLVD #206	STUDIO CITY, CA	91604
TURLEY, MYRA	ACTRESS	151 N SAN VICENTE BLVD #208	BEVERLY HILLS, CA	90211
TURMAN, GLYNN	ACTOR	STONE, 1052 CAROL DR	LOS ANGELES, CA	90069
TURMAN, LAWRENCE	FILM PRODUCER	21336 PACIFIC COAST HWY	MALIBU, CA	90265
TURNBULL, NICK	TV PRODUCER	ARCHERY HOUSE, NORTH RD, HALE	CHESHIRE	ENGLAND
TURNBULL, RAE	COLUMNIST	NEWS AMERICA SYNDICATE		
		1703 KAISER AVE	IRVINE, CA	92714
TURNBULL, WALTER	TENOR	SPRINGER, 1001 ROLANDVUE RD	BALTIMORE, MD	21204
TURNER, AL D	PHOTOJOURNALIST	7417 OSKALOOSA DR	DEERWOOD, MD	20855
TURNER, ARNOLD F	TV WRITER-PRODUCER	8955 BEVERLY BLVD	LOS ANGELES, CA	90048
TURNER, BARBARA	TV WRITER	8955 BEVERLY BLVD	LOS ANGELES, CA	90048
TURNER, BILL	TV DIRECTOR-PRODUCER	7 GREEN ST	LONDON W1	ENGLAND
TURNER, CHARLES L	DIRECTOR	33 N SOUND BEACH AVE	RIVERSIDE, CT	06878
TURNER, CLIFFORD	TV PRODUCER	49-B CHRISTCHURCH ST, CHELSEA	LONDON SW3 4AS	ENGLAND
TURNER, CONSTANCE	TV WRITER	8955 BEVERLY BLVD	LOS ANGELES, CA	90048
TURNER, DENNIS L	TV WRITER	8955 BEVERLY BLVD	LOS ANGELES, CA	90048
TURNER, DOUGLAS L	NEWS CORRESPONDENT	7923 SAINT GEORGE CT	SPRINGFIELD, VA	22153
TURNER, FRANCESCA	TV WRITER	8955 BEVERLY BLVD	LOS ANGELES, CA	90048
TURNER, GRANT	SINGER	POST OFFICE BOX 414	BRENTWOOD, TN	37027
TURNER, HARRY L	NEWS CORRESPONDENT	9920 CHERRY TREE LN	SILVER SPRING, MD	20901
TURNER, JAKE	ACTOR	ABRAMS ARTISTS & ASSOCIATES		
		420 MADISON AVE, 14TH FLOOR	NEW YORK, NY	10017
TURNER, JANINE	ACTRESS	2121 AVE OF THE STARS #410	LOS ANGELES, CA	90067
TURNER, JUDITH AXLER	NEWS CORRESPONDENT	2830 CALVERT ST, NW	WASHINGTON, DC	20008
TURNER, KATHLEEN	ACTRESS	POST OFFICE BOX 5617	BEVERLY HILLS, CA	90213
TURNER, LANA	ACTRESS	POST OFFICE BOX 69187	LOS ANGELES, CA	90069
TURNER, LEE	MUSIC ARRANGER	4263 SAN JOSE BLVD	JACKSONVILLE, FL	32207
TURNER, LEONARD O	ACTOR	1607 N EL CENTRO AVE #22	HOLLYWOOD, CA	90028
TURNER, MARY LOU	SINGER	TESSIER, 505 CANTON PASS	MADISON, TN	37204
TURNER, MORIA	ACTRESS	AIMEE, 13743 VICTORY BLVD	VAN NUYS, CA	91401
TURNER, MORRIE	CARTOONIST	NEWS AMERICA SYNDICATE		
		1703 KAISER AVE	IRVINE, CA	92714
TURNER, ROBIN K	NEWS CORRESPONDENT	3346 CURTIS DR #203	SUITLAND, MD	20746
TURNER, RONALD G	COMPOSER	938 E FAIRVIEW BLVD	INGLEWOOD, CA	90302
TURNER, RUSSELL	FILM-TV PRODUCER	RANK, 127 WARDOUR ST	LONDON W1V 4AD	ENGLAND
TURNER, SPYDER	SINGER	POST OFFICE BOX 1235	NEW ROCHELLE, NY	10802
TURNER, STEPHANIE	ACTRESS	LEADING ARTISTS, LTD		
		60 SAINT JAMES'S ST	LONDON SW1	ENGLAND

Name	Occupation	Address	City	Code
TURNER, TED	BROADCAST EXECUTIVE	1050 TECHWOOD DR, NW	ATLANTA, GA	30318
TURNER, TIERRE	ACTOR	16348 LAHEY ST	GRANADA HILLS, CA	91344
TURNER, TINA	SINGER-ACTRESS	10100 SANTA MONICA BLVD #1600	LOS ANGELES, CA	90067
TURNEY, EDGAR W	NEWS CORRESPONDENT	1611 SANFORD RD	SILVER SPRING, MD	20902
TURNLEY, PEGGY	ACTRESS	200 W 54TH ST	NEW YORK, NY	10019
TUROVSKY, YULI	CONDUCTOR	WENTWORTH, 5 LOCKWOOD RD	SCARSDALE, NY	10583
TURPIN, GEORGE	TV DIRECTOR-PRODUCER	2131 OAK KNOLL AVE	SAN MARINO, CA	91108
TURPIN, GERRY	CINEMATOGRAPHER	FRITH HILL FARM, FRITH HILL		
		GREAT MISSENDEN	BUCKS	ENGLAND
TURRE, MICHAEL J	COMPOSER	1548 CABRILLO AVE	VENICE, CA	90291
TURRENTINE, ROGERS	TV WRITER	PLESHETTE, 2700 N BEACHWOOD DR	HOLLYWOOD, CA	90028
TURTELTAUB, SAUL	WRITER-PRODUCER	1126 COLDWATER CANYON DR	BEVERLY HILLS, CA	90210
TURTLES, THE	ROCK & ROLL GROUP	DAVID FISHOF PRODS		
		1775 BROADWAY	NEW YORK, NY	10019
TUSHER, WILL	COLUMNIST	VARIETY, 1400 N CAHUENGA BLVD	HOLLYWOOD, CA	90028
TUSHER, WILLIAM	WRITER	9978 WHEATLAND AVE	SUNLAND, CA	91040
TUSHINGHAM, RITA	ACTRESS	LONDON MANAGEMENT, LTD		
		235-241 REGENT ST	LONDON W1A 2JT	ENGLAND
TUTEN, ALLEN	MUSIC ARRANGER	3008 HILLSIDE RD #B	NASHVILLE, TN	37207
TUTIN, DOROTHY	ACTRESS	BURNETT, 42 GRAFTON HOUSE		
		2-3 GOLDEN SQ	LONDON W1	ENGLAND
TUTMAN, DANIEL	PHOTOGRAPHER	1816 KALORAMA RD, NW	WASHINGTON, DC	20009
TUTONE, TOMMY	SINGER-DANCER	ICM, 40 W 57TH ST	NEW YORK, NY	10019
TUTTLE, GAYLE MC CRACKEN	NEWS CORRESPONDENT	104 W MASON AVE	ALEXANDRIA, VA	22301
TUTTLE, JERRY	SAXOPHONIST	ROUTE #2, BOX 450	MALDEN, MO	63863
TUTTLE, MARK	TV WRITER	10646 ART ST	SUNLAND, CA	91040
TUTTLE, RICHARD S	NEWS CORRESPONDENT	2601 SIGMONA ST	FALLS CHURCH, VA	24602
TUTTLE, STEVEN	NEWS CORRESPONDENT	104 W MASON AVE	ALEXANDRIA, VA	22301
TUTTMAN, PETER M	WRITER-PRODUCER	311 E 72ND ST	NEW YORK, NY	10021
TUTU, ARCH BISHOP DESMOND	ARCH BISHOP	POST OFFICE BOX 31190		
TUVIM, MARK	ACTOR	608 N BEACHWOOD DR	LOS ANGELES, CA	90004
TUXEDO JUNCTION	SOUL-DISCO GROUP	2029 CENTURY PARK E #3585	LOS ANGELES, CA	90067
TUXEDOMOON	ROCK & ROLL GROUP	POST OFFICE BOX 2428	EL SEGUNDO, CA	90245
TWEED, SHANNON	ACTRESS-MODEL	8380 MELROSE AVE #200	LOS ANGELES, CA	90069
TWEEDY, DONALD W	MUSIC ARRANGER	504 DORAL COUNTRY DR	NASHVILLE, TN	37221
TWEEDY, LLOYD F	DIRECTOR	498 MANOR LN	PELHAM, NY	10802
TWENTY CENTURY REBELS	ROCK & ROLL GROUP	41 BRITAIN ST #200	TORONTO, ONT	CANADA
TWIGGE, JENNY	ACTRESS	72-A SAINT JOHN'S		
		WOOD HIGH ST	LONDON NW8	ENGLAND
TWIGGS, BYRON	TV WRITER	8955 BEVERLY BLVD	LOS ANGELES, CA	90048
TWIGGY	MODEL-ACTRESS-DANCER	SHULMAN, 43 WELBECK ST	LONDON W1	ENGLAND
TWILIGHT	RHYTHM & BLUES GROUP	KINGSLAND, 108 SHARON DR	WEST MONROE, LA	71291
TWILLEY, DWIGHT	SINGER-SONGWRITER	8306 WILSHIRE BLVD #196	BEVERLY HILLS, CA	90211
TWISTED SISTER	ROCK & ROLL GROUP	ARNOLD FREEDMAN MANAGEMENT		
		1200 PROVIDENCE HWY	SHARON, MA	02067
TWITTY, CONWAY	SINGER-SONGWRITER	1 MUSIC VILLAGE BLVD	HENDERSONVILLE, TN	37075
TWITTY, MICHAEL	SINGER	POST OFFICE BOX 23470	NASHVILLE, TN	37202
TWO MINDS CRACK	ROCK & ROLL GROUP	HOWFREE MGMT, 31 NORFOLK PL	LONDON W2 1QH	ENGLAND
TWO ON THE TOWN	MUSIC DUO	ATTRACTIONS TALENT AGENCY		
		6525 N FRANCISCO AVE	CHICAGO, IL	60645
TWOHY, MIKE	CARTOONIST	POST OFFICE BOX 4203	NEW YORK, NY	10017
TYCOON	ROCK & ROLL GROUP	330 W 58TH ST #7-J	NEW YORK, NY	10019
TYLER, ANNE	NOVELIST	222 TURNBRIDGE RD	BALTIMORE, MD	21212
TYLER, BONNIE	SINGER-SONGWRITER	THE STATION AGENCY		
		132 LIVERPOOL RD	LONDON N1 1LA	ENGLAND
TYLER, CHARLES, JR	TV DIRECTOR	ABC-TV, NEWS DEPARTMENT		
		1717 DE SALES ST, NW	WASHINGTON, DC	20006
TYLER, GINNY	ACTRESS	4650 CAHUENGA BLVD #4	NORTH HOLLYWOOD, CA	91602
TYLER, JAMES	GUITARIST	BYERS-SCHWALBE, 1 5TH AVE	NEW YORK, NY	10003
TYLER, MARILYN	ACTRESS	SCHOEMAN, 2600 W VICTORY BLVD	BURBANK, CA	91505
TYLER, MARYFRAN	NEWS CORRESPONDENT	1601 OLD STAGE RD	ALEXANDRIA, VA	22308
TYLER, PATRICK EDWARD	NEWS CORRESPONDENT	1750 LAMONT ST, NW	WASHINGTON, DC	20010
TYLER, RANDY	DRUMMER	24 MARKWEST COVE	JACKSON, TN	38301
TYLER, ROBIN	SINGER-COMPOSER	13514 HART ST	VAN NUYS, CA	91405
TYLER, STEVEN K	CONDUCTOR	19638 HARTLAND ST	RESEDA, CA	91335
TYLER, SUSAN	CASTING DIRECTOR	446 N GOLDEN MALL	BURBANK, CA	91502
TYLER, WILLIE & LESTER	VENTRILOQUIST	MONDRUS, 1001 S CARMELINA AVE	LOS ANGELES, CA	90049
TYLO, MICHAEL	ACTOR	ABC-TV, "ALL MY CHILDREN"		
		1330 AVE OF THE AMERICAS	NEW YORK, NY	10019
TYNAN, WILLIAM	NEWS REPORTER	TIME/TIME & LIFE BLDG		
		ROCKEFELLER CENTER	NEW YORK, NY	10020
TYNDALL, KATHLEEN	NEWS CORRESPONDENT	1210 WALTER ST, SE	WASHINGTON, DC	20003
TYNE, ETHEL	WRITER	1449 BENEDICT CANYON DR	BEVERLY HILLS, CA	90210
TYNE, GEORGE	ACTOR-DIRECTOR	1449 BENEDICT CANYON DR	BEVERLY HILLS, CA	90210
TYNER, CHARLES	ACTOR	2325 KANSAS AVE #9	SANTA MONICA, CA	90404
TYNER, MC COY	PIANIST	HOFFER, 233 1/2 E 48TH ST	NEW YORK, NY	10017
TYRANT	ROCK & ROLL GROUP	POST OFFICE BOX 2428	EL SEGUNDO, CA	90245
TYREE, DAVID	COMEDIAN	9145 SUNSET BLVD #228	LOS ANGELES, CA	90069
TYRRELL, ELLIOTT L	DIRECTOR	12 CLARK ST	BROOKLYN, NY	11201
TYRRELL, LOU	TV DIRECTOR	300 E 34TH ST	NEW YORK, NY	10016
TYRRELL, R EMMETT	COMMENTATOR	KING FEATURES SYNDICATE		
		235 E 45TH ST	NEW YORK, NY	10017
TYRRELL, SUSAN	ACTRESS	9220 SUNSET BLVD #625	LOS ANGELES, CA	90069
TYSON, CICELY	ACTRESS	315 W 70TH ST	NEW YORK, NY	10023
TYSON, MIKE	BOXER	9 W 57TH ST #4800	NEW YORK, NY	10019

SHANNON TWEED

CONWAY TWITTY

CICELY TYSON

LESLIE UGGAMS

ROBERT URICH

ALAN URSILLO

PETER USTINOV

LEE VAN CLEEF

DICK VAN DYKE

Name	Occupation	Address	City	Zip/Country
TYSON, RAE J	NEWS CORRESPONDENT	13033 COMPTON RD	CLIFTON, VA	22034
TYTLA, PETER THOMAS	DIRECTOR-EDITOR	1138 1/2 POINSETTIA PL	HOLLYWOOD, CA	90046
TYTLE, HARRY	DIRECTOR-PRODUCER	1515 IRVING AVE	GLENDALE, CA	91201
TYZACK, MARGARET	ACTRESS	EDWARDS, 275 KENNINGTON RD	LONDON W1	ENGLAND

Name	Occupation	Address	City	Zip/Country
U F O	ROCK & ROLL GROUP	PERFORMING ART NETWORK		
		10 SUTHERLAND	LONDON W9 24Q	ENGLAND
U K	ROCK & ROLL GROUP	E G RECORDS, 246 E 62ND ST	NEW YORK, NY	10021
U S E	ROCK & ROLL GROUP	SEE - UNITED STATES OF EXISTENCE		
U S EXPRESS	WRESTLING TAG TEAM	WORLD CLASS WRESTLING		
		SOUTHWEST SPORTS, INC		
		DALLAS SPORTATORIUM		
		1000 S INDUSTRIAL BLVD	DALLAS, TX	75207
U-2	ROCK & ROLL GROUP	PRINCIPLE MANAGEMENT AGENCY		
		4 WINDMILL LN, DUBLIN 2	EIRE	IRELAND
UBELL, JANE	TV PRODUCER	ENTERTAINMENT TONIGHT		
		PARAMOUNT TELEVISION		
		5555 MELROSE AVE	LOS ANGELES, CA	90038
UCHIDA, MITSUKO	PIANIST	SHAW CONCERTS, 1995 BROADWAY	NEW YORK, NY	10023
UCHIMA, CHARLEY	NEWS CORRESPONDENT	5151 WISCONSIN AVE, NW	WASHINGTON, DC	20016
UDELL, ANN	TV WRITER	8955 BEVERLY BLVD	LOS ANGELES, CA	90048
UDOFF, YALE MAURICE	SCREENWRITER	3383 N KNOLL DR	LOS ANGELES, CA	90068
UDY, HELENE	ACTRESS	870 N VINE ST #B	LOS ANGELES, CA	90038
UEBERROTH, PETER	BASEBALL EXECUTIVE	61 EMERALD BAY	LAGUNA BEACH, CA	92651
UECKER, BOB	BASEBALL-ACTOR	NORTH 60 WEST 15734	MENOMONEE FALLS, WI	53051
UFLAND, HARRY	TALENT AGENT	7055 FERNHILL DR	MALIBU, CA	90265
UFLAND, LEN	DIRECTOR	4400 HILLCREST DR #901	HOLLYWOOD, FL	33021
UFO	ROCK & ROLL GROUP	SEE - U F O		
UGANDAN GIANT, THE	WRESTLER	SEE - KIMALA		
UGANDAN HEADHUNTER, THE	WRESTLER	SEE - KIMALA		
UGER, ALAN	TV WRITER-PRODUCER	4803 CROMWELL AVE	LOS ANGELES, CA	90027
UGGAMS, LESLIE	SINGER-ACTRESS	9255 SUNSET BLVD #404	LOS ANGELES, CA	90069
UGHI, UTO	VIOLINIST	LEISER, DORCHESTER TOWERS		
		155 W 68TH ST	NEW YORK, NY	10023
UHRIG, PAUL JACOB	GUITARIST	3003 FRANKLIN RD	NASHVILLE, TN	37204
UJLAKI, STEPHEN G	WRITER	103 STRAND ST	SANTA MONICA, CA	90405
ULENE, DR ART	TV DOCTOR	10810 VIA VERONA	LOS ANGELES, CA	90077
ULFUNG, RAGNAR	TENOR	CAMI, 165 W 57TH ST	NEW YORK, NY	10019
ULIANO, RICHARD J	NEWS CORRESPONDENT	1825 "K" ST, NW	WASHINGTON, DC	20006
ULICK, MICHAEL	FILM DIRECTOR	55 GREENE ST	NEW YORK, NY	10013
ULIUS, BETTY	WRITER	19791 GRAND VIEW DR	TOPANGA CANYON, CA	90290
ULLMAN, LIV	ACTRESS	HAFRS FJORDSGATE #7	OLSO 2	NORWAY
ULLMAN, TRACEY	ACTRESS-SINGER	COULSON, 37 BERWICK ST	LONDON W1	ENGLAND
ULLMAN, VALLIE	ACTRESS	7036 MIDDLESBURY RIDGE CIR	CANOGA PARK, CA	91307
ULLMANN, OWEN	NEWS CORRESPONDENT	5510 HOOVER ST	BETHESDA, MD	20817
ULRICH, BOBBI	SINGER-GUITARIST	509 CLEARWATER DR	NASHVILLE, TN	37217
ULRICH, RICHARD	COMPOSER	3009 ALLENTON AVE	HACIENDA HGTS, CA	91745
ULRICH, RICHARD L	ACTOR	PACIFIC, 515 N LA CIENEGA BLVD	LOS ANGELES, CA	90048
ULTRAVOX	ROCK & ROLL GROUP	O'DONNELL MANAGEMENT		
		9 DISRAELI RD	LONDON SW15	ENGLAND
UMARAN-DAVILA, JOACHIM	BARITONE	200 W 70TH ST #7-F	NEW YORK, NY	10023
UNCLE ELMER	WRESTLER	POST OFFICE BOX 3859	STAMFORD, CT	06905
UNDERGROUND RAILWAY THEATER	SHADOWIST-PUPPETEER	AARON, 25 HUNTINGTON AVE	BOSTON, MA	02116
UNDERWOOD, BETTY	ACTRESS	DEUTSCH, 715 N PALM DR	BEVERLY HILLS, CA	90210
UNDERWOOD, HANK	ACTOR	10000 RIVERSIDE DR #3	TOLUCA LAKE, CA	91602
UNDERWOOD, PATRICK	TV DIRECTOR-PRODUCER	WXYZ-TV, 20777 W 10 MILE RD	SOUTHFIELD, MI	48037
UNDERWOOD, RAY	ACTOR	9007 NORMA PL	LOS ANGELES, CA	90069
UNDERWOOD, TOM	WUZZLE WRITER	NEWS AMERICA SYNDICATE		
		1703 KAISER AVE	IRVINE, CA	92714
UNGEHEUER, FREDERICK	NEWS CORRESPONDENT	TIME/TIME & LIFE BLDG		
		ROCKEFELLER CENTER	NEW YORK, NY	10020
UNGER, ANTHONY B	FILM PRODUCER	1272 S BEVERLY GLEN BLVD	LOS ANGELES, CA	90024
UNGER, BILL	ACTOR	445 N BEDFORD DR #PH	BEVERLY HILLS, CA	90210
UNGER, DANIEL	FILM EXECUTIVE	6 BASIL MANSIONS, BASIL ST	LONDON SW3	ENGLAND
UNGER, JIM	CARTOONIST	UNIVERSAL PRESS SYNDICATE		
		4900 MAIN ST, 9TH FLOOR	KANSAS CITY, MO	62114
UNGER, JOE	ACTOR	6558 SANTA MONICA BLVD	LOS ANGELES, CA	90038
UNGER, KURT	FILM PRODUCER	6 BASIL MANSIONS, BASIL ST	LONDON SW3	ENGLAND
UNGER, LEANNE	SCREENWRITER	555 W 57TH ST #1230	NEW YORK, NY	10019
UNGER, MAURICE	DIRECTOR	6 NORTHSTAR ST #203	MARINA DEL REY, CA	90292
UNGER, STEPHEN A	FILM EXECUTIVE	11774 MOORPARK ST #G	STUDIO CITY, CA	91604
UNIDOS	RHYTHM & BLUES GROUP	POST OFFICE BOX 634	LAWRENCE, KS	66044
UNITAS, JOHNNY	FOOTBALL	6354 YORK RD	BALTIMORE, MD	21212
UNITED STATES OF EXISTENCE, THE	ROCK & ROLL GROUP	BAM CARUSO RECORDS COMPANY		
		9 RIDGEMONT RD, SAINT ALBANS	HERTSHIRE	ENGLAND
UNLAND, RAYMOND L	DRUMMER	ROUTE #4, LONGVIEW DR	MT JULIET, TN	37122
UNNA, WARREN W	NEWS CORRESPONDENT	121 6TH ST, NE	WASHINGTON, DC	20002

U - 2

Adam • Edge • Larry • Bono

Name	Occupation	Address	City	Zip/Country
UNTOLD FABLES, THE	ROCK & ROLL GROUP	POST OFFICE BOX 1975	BURBANK, CA	91507
UPCHURCH, PHIL	SINGER	WIRTZ, 86 S SIERRA MADRE BLVD	PASADENA, CA	91107
UPPMAN, THEODOR	BARITONE	CAMI, 165 W 57TH ST	NEW YORK, NY	10019
UPSHAW, JAMES R	NEWS CORRESPONDENT	NBC-TV, NEWS DEPARTMENT		
		4001 NEBRASKA AVE, NW	WASHINGTON, DC	20016
UPTON, DALE	SINGER	POST OFFICE BOX 25371	CHARLOTTE, NC	28212
UPTON, GABRIELLE	WRITER	ICM, 8899 BEVERLY BLVD	LOS ANGELES, CA	90048
UPTOWN	RAP GROUP	POST OFFICE BOX 1126	CORONA, NY	11373
URBAN, STUART	WRITER-PRODUCER	CYCLOPS, 20 SYDNEY ST	LONDON SW3 6PP	ENGLAND
URBAN RENEWAL BAND	ROCK & ROLL GROUP	25 HUNTINGTON AVE #420	BOSTON, MA	02116
URBAND, JEFF	ARRANGER-COMPOSER	8506 NORRIS AVE	SUN VALLEY, CA	91352
URBATIONS, THE	ROCK & ROLL GROUP	MSA, 442 E LAFAYETTE BLVD	DETROIT, MI	48226
URBISCI, ROCCO N	TV WRITER	10519 WILKINS AVE	LOS ANGELES, CA	90049
URETA, JUAN E	PHOTOGRAPHER	6106 CLEARBROOK DR	SPRINGFIELD, VA	22150
URIAH HEEP	ROCK & ROLL GROUP	HARRY MALONEY MANAGEMENT		
		18-19 WARWICK ST, 3RD FLOOR	LONDON W1R 5RB	ENGLAND
URICH, HEATHER MENZIES	ACTRESS	475 WESTERN AVE	BOSTON, MA	02135
URICH, ROBERT	ACTOR-WRITER	475 WESTERN AVE	BOSTON, MA	02135
URICH, TOM	ACTOR	250 W 57TH ST #2317	NEW YORK, NY	10107
URIE, JOHN	WRITER-PRODUCER	1415 INNES PL	VENICE, CA	90291
URIS, LEON	AUTHOR	POST OFFICE BOX 1559	ASPEN, CO	81611
URQUHART, ROBERT	ACTOR	BOYACK, 9 CORK ST	LONDON W1	ENGLAND
URQUHART, SIDNEY	NEWS REPORTER	TIME/TIME & LIFE BLDG		
		ROCKEFELLER CENTER	NEW YORK, NY	10020
URSILLO, ALAN	ACTOR	8075 W 3RD ST #303	LOS ANGELES, CA	90048
URSO, ROBERT	TV WRITER	8955 BEVERLY BLVD	LOS ANGELES, CA	90048
USA, MR	WRESTLER	SEE - ATLAS, TONY		
USCHER, NANCY	VIOLIST	61 W 62ND ST #6-F	NEW YORK, NY	10023
USE	ROCK & ROLL GROUP	SEE - UNITED STATES OF		
		.... EXISTENCE, THE		
USEN, SKIP	TV WRITER	8955 BEVERLY BLVD	LOS ANGELES, CA	90048
USHIODA, MASUKO	VIOLINIST	HILLYER, 250 W 57TH ST	NEW YORK, NY	10107
USTINOV, PETER	ACTOR-WRITER-DIRECTOR	11 RUE DE SILLY	BOULOGNE 92100	FRANCE
UTAL, MATTHEW	COMPOSER	POST OFFICE BOX 9864	GLENDALE, CA	91206
UTH, TONY	CARTOONIST	PHILADELPHIA INQUIRER		
		400 N BROAD ST	PHILADELPHIA, PA	19101
UTHE, MIC	SINGER	OME, 233 W WOODLAND AVE	OTTUMWA, IA	52501
UTLEY, GARRICK	NEWS CORRESPONDENT	12 HANOVER TERR	LONDON NW1	ENGLAND
UTLEY, JERRY	SINGER	YENOWINE, 10630 ST RENE	JEFFERSTOWN, KY	40299
UTMAN, BRYAN	ACTOR	3355 WILSHIRE BLVD #1009	LOS ANGELES, CA	90010
UTOPIA	ROCK & ROLL GROUP	PANACEA, 132 NASSAU ST	NEW YORK, NY	10038
UTVICH, MICHAEL JOHN	WRITER	519 WESTMOUNT DR	LOS ANGELES, CA	90048
UVALDE SLIM	WRESTLER	SEE - RHODES, DUSTY		

Name	Occupation	Address	City	Zip/Country
V, JOHNNY	WRESTLER-MANAGER	POST OFFICE BOX 3859	STAMFORD, CT	06905
VACCARINO, MAURICE	TV DIRECTOR	3593 BERRY DR	STUDIO CITY, CA	91604
VACCARO, BRENDA	ACTRESS	2627 BENEDICT CANYON DR	BEVERLY HILLS, CA	90210
VACCARO, TRACY	ACTRESS-MODEL	MODELS & PROMOTIONS AGENCY		
		8560 SUNSET BLVD, 10TH FLOOR	LOS ANGELES, CA	90069
VACIO, NATIVIDAD	ACTOR	931 N FORD ST	BURBANK, CA	91505
VACZY, RICHARD A	TV WRITER	2128 ASHLAND AVE	SANTA MONICA, CA	90405
VADEN, TOMMY	VIOLINIST	102 1/2 GLENROSE AVE	NASHVILLE, TN	37210
VADER, J E	SPORTS REPORTER	SPORTS ILLUSTRATED MAGAZINE		
		TIME & LIFE BUILDING		
		ROCKEFELLER CENTER	NEW YORK, NY	10020
VADIM, ROGER	FILM DIRECTOR	2429 BEVERLY AVE	SANTA MONICA, CA	90406
VAIL, EDMUND, SR	TV WRITER	8955 BEVERLY BLVD	LOS ANGELES, CA	90048
VAIL, KARY LYNN	ACTRESS	CARPENTER, 1516-W REDWOOD ST	SAN DIEGO, CA	92101
VAIL, LAWRENCE	TV WRITER	8955 BEVERLY BLVD	LOS ANGELES, CA	90048
VAIL, LORIN	MODEL	MODELS & PROMOTIONS AGENCY		
		8560 SUNSET BLVD, 10TH FLOOR	LOS ANGELES, CA	90069
VAILLANCOURT, ROD	PIANIST	4909 NEBRASKA AVE	NASHVILLE, TN	37209
VAINES, COLIN	WRITER	22 SOUTHAMPTON PL	LONDON WC1	ENGLAND
VAINSHTEIN, LEV	NEWS CORRESPONDENT	1201 CONNECTICUT AVE, NW	WASHINGTON, DC	20036
VAJDA, PETER	NEWS CORRESPONDENT	4701 WILLARD AVE	CHEVY CHASE, MD	20815
VAJNA, ANDREW	FILM PRODUCER	8810 MELROSE AVE #201	LOS ANGELES, CA	90069
VAL, STEVE	SINGER-GUITARIST	POST OFFICE BOX 44024	SYLMAR, CA	91342
VALADEZ, JORGE	COMPOSER	2813 MERRITT AVE	LAS VEGAS, NV	89102
VALCARCEL, TONY	MUSICIAN	ROUTE #4, OLD CARTER'S CREEK	FRANKLIN, TN	37064
VALDEZ, DANIEL	ACTOR-COMPOSER	11726 SAN VICENTE BLVD #300	LOS ANGELES, CA	90049
VALDEZ, JOE	BODYBUILDER	POST OFFICE BOX 5175	WHITTIER, CA	90607
VALDEZ, LUIS M	WRITER-PRODUCER	DGA, 7950 SUNSET BLVD	LOS ANGELES, CA	90046
VALDY	MUSICAL GROUP	4680 ELK LAKE DR #304	VICTORIA, BC	CANADA
VALDY, SIOUTH	SINGER	4680 ELK LAKE DR #304	VICTORIA, BC V8Z 5M1	CANADA
VALE, EUGENE	WRITER	9000 CYNTHIA ST	LOS ANGELES, CA	90069
VALE, JERRY	SINGER	621 N PALM DR	BEVERLY HILLS, CA	90210
VALEN, JIM	WRESTLER	SEE - VALIANT, JIMMY		

Name	Occupation	Address	City/State	ZIP
VALEN, NANCY	ACTRESS	ABC-TV, "RYAN'S HOPE"		
		1330 AVE OF THE AMERICAS	NEW YORK, NY	10019
VALENCIA	HIGH WIRE ACT	POST OFFICE BOX 87	WEST LEBANON, NY	12195
VALENTA, LEONARD	TV DIRECTOR	134 CAMPUS RD	STATEN ISLAND, NY	10301
VALENTE, BENITA	SOPRANO	CAMI, 165 W 57TH ST	NEW YORK, NY	10019
VALENTE, RENEE	FILM PRODUCER	PRODUCERS GUILD OF AMERICA		
		400 S BEVERLY DR	BEVERLY HILLS, CA	90212
VALENTE, RICK	BODYBUILDER	POST OFFICE BOX 11117	MARINA DEL REY, CA	90295
VALENTI, JACK	FILM EXECUTIVE	1600 "I" ST, NW	WASHINGTON, DC	20006
VALENTI, JOSEPH A	COMPOSER-CONDUCTOR	4417 LUCERA CIR	PALOS VERDES ESTATES,	90274
VALENTIN, DAVE	SINGER	3RD WAVE MGMT, 155 W 72ND ST	NEW YORK, NY	10023
VALENTINE, ANTHONY	ACTOR	LONDON MANAGEMENT, LTD		
		235-241 REGENT ST	LONDON W1A 2JT	ENGLAND
VALENTINE, BERNI	ACTRESS	622 N SPAULDING AVE	LOS ANGELES, CA	90036
VALENTINE, BOBBY	BASEBALL	791 NORTH ST	WHITE PLAINS, NY	10605
VALENTINE, DALE	WRESTLER	SEE - ROBERTS, BUDDY "JACK"		
VALENTINE, GREG "THE HAMMER"	WRESTLER	POST OFFICE BOX 3859	STAMFORD, CT	06905
VALENTINE, JOHNNY, JR	WRESTLER	SEE - VALENTINE, GREG		
		"THE HAMMER"		
VALENTINE, PAUL	ACTOR	208 S BEVERLY DR #4	BEVERLY HILLS, CA	90212
VALENTINE, PAUL W	NEWS CORRESPONDENT	5327 NEVADA LN, NW	WASHINGTON, DC	20015
VALENTINE, SCOTT	ACTOR	8370 WILSHIRE BLVD #310	BEVERLY HILLS, CA	90211
VALENTINE BROTHERS, THE	SOUL-DISCO GROUP	SOURCE, 1902 5TH AVE	LOS ANGELES, CA	90018
VALENTINI-TERRANI, LUCIA	MEZZO-SOPRANO	CAMI, 165 W 57TH ST	NEW YORK, NY	10019
VALENTINO	SINGER	POST OFFICE BOX 528	BRACKETTVILLE, TX	78832
VALENTINO, PATRICK M	COMPOSER-CONDUCTOR	91223 INDEX ST #4	NORTHRIDGE, CA	91326
VALENTINO & THE SHAHAN EXPRESS	C & W GROUP	POST OFFICE BOX 528	BRACKETTVILLE, TX	78832
VALENTY, LILI	ACTRESS	7717 HOLLYWOOD BLVD #1	LOS ANGELES, CA	90046
VALENZUELA, FERNANDO	BASEBALL	3004 N BEACHWOOD DR	LOS ANGELES, CA	90068
VALERIANI, RICHARD	NEWS JOURNALIST	3025 ARIZONA AVE, NW	WASHINGTON, DC	20016
VALERY, ANNE	TV WRITER	5 ABBOT'S PL	LONDON NW6	ENGLAND
VALERY, DANA	ACTRESS	19 W 44TH ST #1500	NEW YORK, NY	10036
VALIANT, JIMMY	WRESTLER	NATIONAL WRESTLING ALLIANCE		
		JIM CROCKETT PROMOTIONS		
		421 BRIARBEND DR	CHARLOTTE, NC	28209
VALIANT, JOHNNY	WRESTLER-MANAGER	SEE - V, JOHNNY		
VALINSKY, ERIC	COMPOSER	FINELL, 155 W 68TH ST	NEW YORK, NY	10023
VALL, SEYMOUR	THEATER PRODUCER	35 W 81ST ST	NEW YORK, NY	10024
VALLACHER, KITTY	ACTRESS	4570 W 1ST ST	LOS ANGELES, CA	90004
VALLANCE, LOUISE	ACTRESS	1930 CENTURY PARK W #303	LOS ANGELES, CA	90067
VALLELY, TANNIS	ACTRESS	151 N SAN VICENTE BLVD #208	BEVERLY HILLS, CA	90211
VALLI, FRANKIE	SINGER	1470 BLUE JAY WY	LOS ANGELES, CA	90069
VALLI, JUNE	SINGER	J D MERCHANT MGMT		
		1158 BRIAR WY	FORT LEE, NJ	07024
VALLIERE, RICHARD H	NEWS CORRESPONDENT	2613 KEY BLVD	ARLINGTON, VA	22201
VALTASAARI, MIKKO	NEWS CORRESPONDENT	3710 39TH ST, NW	WASHINGTON, DC	20016
VAMPIRE, THE	WRESTLER	SEE - SMITH, DAVEY BOY		
VAN, DOROTHY	TV WRITER	8955 BEVERLY BLVD	LOS ANGELES, CA	90048
VAN, GARWOOD	CONDUCTOR	341 DESERT INN RD	LAS VEGAS, NV	89109
VAN ALLAN, RICHARD	SINGER	CAMI, 165 W 57TH ST	NEW YORK, NY	10019
VAN ARK, JOAN	ACTRESS	10950 ALTA VIEW DR	STUDIO CITY, CA	91604
VAN ATTA, DALE	NEWS CORRESPONDENT	214 MEADOWLAND LN WEST	STERLING, VA	22170
VAN ATTA, DONALD	DIRECTOR-PRODUCER	4818 CORBIN AVE	TARZANA, CA	91356
VAN ATTA, THOMAS	PIANIST	ROUTE #4, SAUNDERS FERRY RD	MOUNT JULIET, TN	37122
VAN BIEMA, DAVID	WRITER-EDITOR	PEOPLE/TIME & LIFE BLDG		
		ROCKEFELLER CENTER	NEW YORK, NY	10020
VAN BREEMS, ARLENE	WRITER	5910 LOCKSLEY PL	LOS ANGELES, CA	90068
VAN BUREN, ABIGAIL	COLUMNIST-LECTURER	UNIVERSAL PRESS SYNDICATE		
		4900 MAIN ST, 9TH FLOOR	KANSAS CITY, MO	62114
VAN BUSKIRK, CHARLES	RINGMASTER	HALL, 138 FROG HOLLOW RD	CHURCHVILLE, PA	18966
VAN BUSKIRK, LESLIE	WRITER-EDITOR	US MAGAZINE COMPANY		
		1 DAG HAMMARSKJOLD PLAZA	NEW YORK, NY	10017
VAN CITTERS, JOEL	DIRECTOR	391-A NORMANDY DR	NORWOOD, MA	02062
VAN CLEEF, LEE	ACTOR	POST OFFICE BOX 16	TARZANA, CA	91356
VAN DAM, JEANIE	ACTRESS	8350 SANTA MONICA BLVD #206	LOS ANGELES, CA	90069
VAN DAM, JOSE	BASSO-BARITONE	COLBERT, 111 W 57TH ST	NEW YORK, NY	10019
VAN DE VEN, MONIQUE	ACTRESS	POST OFFICE BOX 5617	BEVERLY HILLS, CA	90210
VAN DEMARK, JAMES	DOUBLE BASS	5720 MOSHOLU AVE #300	RIVERDALE, NY	10471
VAN DEN ECKER, BEAU	DIRECTOR	DGA, 7950 SUNSET BLVD	LOS ANGELES, CA	90046
VAN DER FEER, TOM	DIRECTOR	160 W 46TH ST	NEW YORK, NY	10036
VAN DER LINDEN, FRANK	NEWS CORRESPONDENT	5312 BLACKSTONE RD	BETHESDA, MD	20816
VAN DER MEER, RUUD	BARITONE	SOFFER, 130 W 56TH ST	NEW YORK, NY	10019
VAN DER VELDE, NADINE	ACTRESS	6430 SUNSET BLVD #701	LOS ANGELES, CA	90028
VAN DER WOUDE, TERESA	ACTRESS	ABC-TV, "GENERAL HOSPITAL"		
		1438 N GOWER ST	LOS ANGELES, CA	90028
VAN DEVERE, TRISH	ACTRESS	9300 WILSHIRE BLVD #410	BEVERLY HILLS, CA	90212
VAN DOREN, MAMIE	ACTRESS-SINGER	EICHLER, 1524 LA BAIG AVE	LOS ANGELES, CA	90028
VAN DREELAN, JOHN	ACTOR	1636 ARTEIQUE RD	TOPANGA CANYON, CA	90290
VAN DRIESTEN, ROELOF	CONDUCTOR	KAY, 58 W 58TH ST	NEW YORK, NY	10019
VAN DUSEN, CRHIS	CARTOONIST	POST OFFICE BOX 4203	NEW YORK, NY	10017
VAN DYCK, ROLAND	GUITARIST	POST OFFICE BOX 998	GOODLETTSVILLE, TN	37072
VAN DYCKE, LOUIS	PIANIST	POST OFFICE BOX U	REDDING, CT	06875
VAN DYCKE, LOUIS, JAZZ TRIO	JAZZ TRIO	POST OFFICE BOX U	REDDING, CT	06875
VAN DYKE, BARRY	ACTOR	6301 PISCES ST	AGOURA, CA	91301
VAN DYKE, CHARLES E	NEWS CORRESPONDENT	1776 "C" ST, NW	WASHINGTON, DC	20006

Name	Occupation	Address	City, State	Zip
VAN DYKE, DICK	ACTOR-WRITER	151 S EL CAMINO DR	BEVERLY HILLS, CA	90212
VAN DYKE, JERRY	ACTOR-COMEDIAN	15010 VENTURA BLVD #234	SHERMAN OAKS, CA	91403
VAN DYKE, JOSEPH	PIANIST	1004 BEN ALLEN RD	NASHVILLE, TN	37216
VAN DYKE, LEROY	SINGER-SONGWRITER	POST OFFICE BOX 490	HENDERSONVILLE, TN	37075
VAN DYKE, RICHARD W	DIRECTOR	4335 MARINA CITY DR	MARINA DEL REY, CA	90292
VAN DYKE, WILLARD	FILM DIRECTOR	505 W END ST	NEW YORK, NY	10024
VAN EGMOND, MAX	BARITONE	BYERS-SCHWALBE, 1 5TH AVE	NEW YORK, NY	10003
VAN EMAN, CHARLES	ACTOR	8500 WILSHIRE BLVD #506	BEVERLY HILLS, CA	90211
VAN ENGER, DICK, JR	FILM EDITOR	ACE, 4416 1/2 FINLEY AVE	LOS ANGELES, CA	90027
VAN EPS, ROBERT	COMPOSER	1618 EL RITO AVE	GLENDALE, CA	91208
VAN EYKEN, RAYMOND	COMPOSER	15455 VANOWEN ST #4	VAN NUYS, CA	91406
VAN FLEET, JO	ACTRESS	54 RIVERSIDE DR	NEW YORK, NY	10024
VAN HALEN	ROCK & ROLL GROUP	9229 SUNSET BLVD #625	LOS ANGELES, CA	90069
VAN HAMEL, MARTINE	BALLERINA	AMERICAN BALLET THEATRE		
		890 BROADWAY	NEW YORK, NY	10003
VAN HEUSEN, JAMES	COMPOSER-PIANIST	POST OFFICE BOX 44	BRANT LAKE, NY	12815
VAN HORN, BUDDY	DIRECTOR	4409 PONCA AVE	TOLUCA LAKE, CA	91602
VAN HOY, RAFE	GUITARIST	4306 ESTES RD	NASHVILLE, TN	37215
VAN ITALLIE, JEAN C	TV WRITER	555 W 57TH ST #1230	NEW YORK, NY	10019
VAN KAMP, MARETE	ACTRESS	10390 SANTA MONICA BLVD #310	LOS ANGELES, CA	90025
VAN LEUVEN, HENDRIK W	WRITER	3181 LARGA AVE	LOS ANGELES, CA	90039
VAN NIEL, PIETER JAN	ACTOR	5252 BLUEMOND RD	ROLLING HILLS, CA	90274
VAN NORDEN, PETER	ACTOR	14133 COHASSET ST	VAN NUYS, CA	91405
VAN NOSTRAND, RON	PHOTOJOURNALSIT	9020 COPENHAVER DR	POTOMAC, MD	20854
VAN ORMAN, GARY	ACTOR	ROUTE #2, BOX 51	LYLE, WA	98635
VAN OSDALE, GARY	VIOLINIST	2703 VALLEY BROOK PL	NASHVILLE, TN	37215
VAN OSDALE, PAMELA	VIOLINIST	2703 VALLEY BROOK PL	NASHVILLE, TN	37215
VAN OSS, ALEX	NEWS CORRESPONDENT	2025 "M" ST, NW	WASHINGTON, DC	20036
VAN PALLANDT, NINA	ACTRESS	845 E 6TH ST	LOS ANGELES, CA	90021
VAN PATTEN, DICK	ACTOR	13920 MAGNOLIA BLVD	SHERMAN OAKS, CA	91423
VAN PATTEN, JAMES	ACTOR	13920 MAGNOLIA BLVD	SHERMAN OAKS, CA	91423
VAN PATTEN, JOYCE	ACTRESS	2041 GRACE AVE	LOS ANGELES, CA	90068
VAN PATTEN, NELS	ACTOR	6430 SUNSET BLVD #1203	LOS ANGELES, CA	90028
VAN PATTEN, PATRICIA	ACTRESS	13920 MAGNOLIA BLVD	SHERMAN OAKS, CA	91423
VAN PATTEN, TIM	ACTOR	400 S BEVERLY DR #216	BEVERLY HILLS, CA	90212
VAN PATTEN, VINCENT	ACTOR	409 N CAMDEN DR #105	BEVERLY HILLS, CA	90210
VAN PEEBLES, MARIO	ACTOR	130 W 42ND ST #1804	NEW YORK, NY	10036
VAN PEEBLES, MEGAN	ACTOR	353 W 56TH ST #10-F	NEW YORK, NY	10019
VAN PEEBLES, MELVIN	ACT-WRI-DIR	353 W 56TH ST #10-F	NEW YORK, NY	10019
VAN PRAAG, WILLIAM	DIRECTOR	135 E 55TH ST	NEW YORK, NY	10022
VAN RAVENSWAAY, THEODORE F	NEWS CORRESPONDENT	2139 WISCONSIN AVE, NW	WASHINGTON, DC	20007
VAN REES, JOOST	TV DIRECTOR	210 RIVERSIDE DR	NEW YORK, NY	10025
VAN RELLIM, TIM	FILM PRODUCER	22 WINDSOR CT, MOSCOW RD	LONDON W2	ENGLAND
VAN RIPER, FRANK A	NEWS CORRESPONDENT	3502 QUESADA ST, NW	WASHINGTON, DC	20015
VAN RONK, DAVE	SINGER-GUITARIST	FOLKLORE, 1671 APPIAN WY	SANTA MONICA, CA	90401
VAN SCOYK, ROBERT E	TV WRITER	1740 WESTRIDGE RD	LOS ANGELES, CA	90069
VAN TASSEL, JANE	NEWS REPORTER	TIME/TIME & LIFE BLDG		
		ROCKEFELLER CENTER	NEW YORK, NY	10020
VAN THAL, DENNIS	TV DIRECTOR	GLEBE LODGE, CROSS LN		
		GUILDFIELD	SURREY	ENGLAND
VAN VALKENBURGH, DEBORAH	ACTRESS	151 S EL CAMINO DR	BEVERLY HILLS, CA	90212
VAN VOGT, A E	WRITER	2850 BELDEN DR	LOS ANGELES, CA	90068
VAN VOOREN, MONIQUE	ACTRESS-SINGER	165 E 66TH ST	NEW YORK, NY	10021
VAN VOORHEES, RACHEL	HARPIST	AFFILIATE ARTISTS, INC		
		37 W 65TH ST, 6TH FLOOR	NEW YORK, NY	10023
VAN VOORST, L BRUCE	NEWS CORRESPONDENT	3003 VAN NESS ST #S-922, NW	WASHINGTON, DC	20008
VAN WINKLE, JOSEPH	SCREENWRITER	4836 STROHM AVE	NORTH HOLLYWOOD, CA	91601
VAN ZANT, JOHNNY, BAND	ROCK & ROLL GROUP	POST OFFICE BOX 4804	MACON, GA	31201
VAN-DELLS, THE	VOCAL GROUP	POST OFFICE BOX 40686	NASHVILLE, TN	37204
VANACORE, VICTOR A	CONDUCTOR	9712 SALOMA AVE	SEPULVEDA, CA	91343
VANAUD, MARCEL	BARITONE	CAMI, 165 W 57TH ST	NEW YORK, NY	10019
VANAUGH, RICHARD	BANJOIST	300 TAMPA DR	NASHVILLE, TN	37211
VANCE, AL	GUITARIST	1715 BLAIR BLVD #A	NASHVILLE, TN	37212
VANCE, DANA	ACTRESS	151 S EL CAMINO DR	BEVERLY HILLS, CA	90212
VANCE, KIRSTEN	ACTRESS	348 E OLIVE AVE #K	BURBANK, CA	91502
VANCE, LEIGH	WRITER-PRODUCER	1801 BEL AIR RD	LOS ANGELES, CA	90077
VANCE, RAY	WRESTLER	POST OFFICE BOX 3859	STAMFORD, CT	06905
VANCE, WILLIAM	NEWS CORRESPONDENT	4330 46TH ST, NW	WASHINGTON, DC	20016
VANDEMAN, STEVE	STUNTMAN	3518 W CAHUENGA BLVD #300	LOS ANGELES, CA	90068
VANDEMARK, JAMES	SINGER	59 E 54TH ST #81	NEW YORK, NY	10022
VANDENBERG	ROCK & ROLL GROUP	ICM, 40 W 57TH ST	NEW YORK, NY	10019
VANDENBURG, WILLIAM	CONDUCTOR	25281 LA ESTRADA	LAGUNA NIGUEL, CA	92677
VANDERBILT, GLORIA	FASHION DESIGNER	10 GRACIE SQ #PH	NEW YORK, NY	10018
VANDERBURG, NIKKI	MUSICIAN	LCS, 1627 16TH AVE S	NASHVILLE, TN	37212
VANDERKOOI, DAVID	CELLIST	1412 GRAYBAR LN	NASHVILLE, TN	37215
VANDERLINDE, DEBRA	SOPRANO	SOFFER, 130 W 56TH ST	NEW YORK, NY	10019
VANDERS, WARREN	ACTOR	9000 SUNSET BLVD #1112	LOS ANGELES, CA	90069
VANDERSCHMIDT, F SYDNOR	WRITER-EDITOR	DISCOVER/TIME & LIFE BLDG		
		ROCKEFELLER CENTER	NEW YORK, NY	10020
VANDERSPAR-SIMON, FIONA	VIOLINIST	61 W 62ND ST #6-F	NEW YORK, NY	10023
VANDERSTOCK, GEOFF	ACTOR	POST OFFICE BOX 9158	WHITTIER, CA	90601
VANDERVALK, BRUCE	COMPOSER-CONDUCTOR	1563 DEVONSHIRE AVE	WESTLAKE VILLAGE, CA	91361
VANDERVEEN, JOYCE	ACTRESS	13560 GAULT ST	VAN NUYS, CA	91405
VANDEVER, MICHAEL	ACTOR	4265 LEMP AVE	STUDIO CITY, CA	91604
VANDIS, TITOS	ACTOR	2238 JEFFERSONIA WY	LOS ANGELES, CA	90049

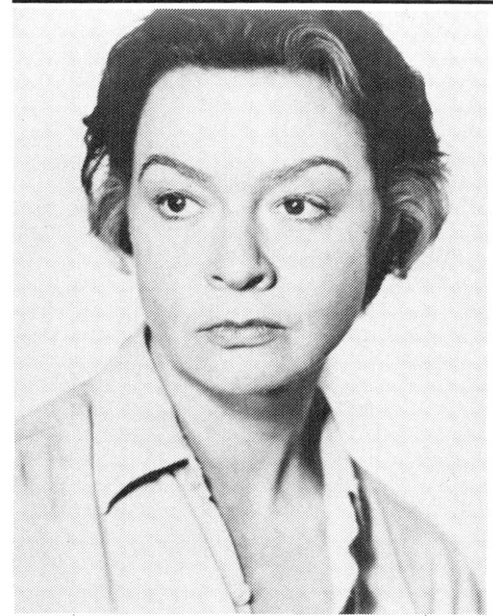
JO VAN FLEET

DICK VAN PATTEN

LUTHER VANDROSS

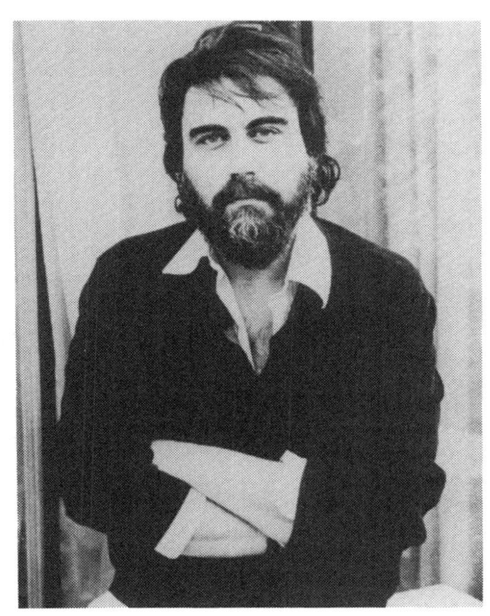
VANGELIS

VANITY

ROBERT VAUGHN

SARAH VAUGHAN

STEVE RAY VAUGHAN
& DOUBLE TROUBLE

BEN VEREEN

Name	Occupation	Address	City
VANDROSS, LUTHER	SINGER	POST OFFICE BOX 5880	SHERMAN OAKS, CA 91413
VANE, CHRISTOPHER L	TV WRITER	1844 THAYER AVE	LOS ANGELES, CA 90025
VANE, NORMAN THADDEUS	SCREENWRITER	1121 OLIVE DR #104	LOS ANGELES, CA 90069
VANEL, CHARLES	ACTOR	ARTMEDIA, 10 AVE GEORGE V	PARIS 75008 FRANCE
VANELLI, ADRIANA	SOPRANO	CAMI, 165 W 57TH ST	NEW YORK, NY 10019
VANELLI, GINO	SINGER-SONGWRITER	31270 LA BAYA DR #110	WESTLAKE VILLAGE, CA 91362
VANESS, CAROL	SOPRANO	119 W 57TH ST #1015	NEW YORK, NY 10019
VANGELIS	COMPOSER	YANUS ZOGRAPHON, NEMO STUDIOS HAMPDEN GURNEY ST	LONDON ENGLAND
VANITY	SINGER-ACTRESS	1400 KELTON AVE #302	LOS ANGELES, CA 90024
VANITY 6	VOCAL TRIO	POST OFFICE BOX 4499	NORTH HOLLYWOOD, CA 91607
VANOCUR, SANDOR	NEWS CORRESPONDENT	ABC-TV, NEWS DEPARTMENT 1330 AVE OF THE AMERICAS	NEW YORK, NY 10019
VANOFF, BORIS	RECORD-TV PRODUCER	8590 HOLLYWOOD BLVD	LOS ANGELES, CA 90069
VANOFF, ELAINE	ACTRESS	8590 HOLLYWOOD BLVD	LOS ANGELES, CA 90069
VANOFF, NICK	TV WRITER-PRODUCER	910 N FOOTHILL RD	BEVERLY HILLS, CA 90210
VANSELOW, BOB	ACTOR	4720 LOS FELIZ BLVD #1	LOS ANGELES, CA 90027
VANTI, LELA	ACTRESS	6605 HOLLYWOOD BLVD #220	HOLLYWOOD, CA 90028
VANTREASE, JAMES	PIANIST	904 RAMSEY DR	GALLATIN, TN 37066
VANWARMER, RANDY	SINGER-SONGWRITER	POST OFFICE BOX 135	BEARSVILLE, NY 12409
VANZANT, JAQUELINE	VIOLINIST	5716 VINE RIDGE DR	NASHVILLE, TN 37205
VAPORS, THE	ROCK & ROLL GROUP	MAYBURY MANAGEMENT WOKING	SURREY ENGLAND
VARADY, JULIA	SOPRANO	COLBERT, 111 W 57TH ST	NEW YORK, NY 10019
VARDAMAN, THOMAS	NEWS CORRESPONDENT	1755 S JEFFERSON DAVIS HWY	ARLINGTON, VA 22202
VARDY, MIKE	TV DIRECTOR	GLEBE LODGE, CROSS LN GUILDFORD	SURREY ENGLAND
VARELA, DANTE	COMPOSER	7725 GREENBUSH	PANORAMA CITY, CA 91402
VARELA, JAY F	TV WRITER	8955 BEVERLY BLVD	LOS ANGELES, CA 90048
VARELA, MIGDIA	ACTRESS-WRITER	1326 CORDOVA AVE	GLENDALE, CA 91207
VARELA, ROBERT	NEWS CORRESPONDENT	201 W MOUNT IDA AVE	ALEXANDRIA, VA 22305
VARELLA, MINDY	ACTRESS	6736 LAUREL CANYON BLVD #306	NORTH HOLLYWOOD, CA 91606
VARHOL, MICHAEL C	DIRECTOR	920 S WOOSTER ST	LOS ANGELES, CA 90035
VARI, JOHN	ACTOR	405 E 54TH ST	NEW YORK, NY 10022
VARNADO, DEBRA	ACTRESS	CED, 261 S ROBERTSON BLVD	BEVERLY HILLS, CA 90211
VARNEY, CARLETON	INTERIOR DESIGNER	N Y TIMES SYNDICATION 130 5TH AVE	NEW YORK, NY 10011
VARNEY, REG	ACTOR-COMEDIAN	LONDON MANAGEMENT, LTD 235-241 REGENT ST	LONDON W1A 2JT ENGLAND
VARON, DARVIN	ACTOR	17 E 7TH ST	NEW YORK, NY 10003
VARON, RUDY	CONDUCTOR	940 MALTMAN AVE	LOS ANGELES, CA 90026
VARVISO, SILVIO	CONDUCTOR	COLBERT, 111 W 57TH ST	NEW YORK, NY 10019
VASARI, KRISTINA	ACTRESS	439 S LA CIENEGA BLVD #117	LOS ANGELES, CA 90048
VASARY, TAMAS	CONDUCTOR-PIANIST	LEISER, DORCHESTER TOWERS 155 W 68TH ST	NEW YORK, NY 10023
VASELOPULOS, PETER G	NEWS CORRESPONDENT	340 NATIONAL PRESS BLDG 529 14TH ST, NW	WASHINGTON, DC 20045
VASEY, JOHN C	WRITER	10941 STRATHMORE DR #44	LOS ANGELES, CA 90024
VASGERSIAN, ED	ACTOR	3575 W CAHUENGA BLVD #243	LOS ANGELES, CA 90068
VASIRI, HOSSEIN KHOSROW	WRESTLER	SEE - IRON SHEIK, THE	
VASIRI, KHOSROW	WRESTLER	SEE - IRON SHEIK, THE	
VASQUEZ, ROBERTA	ACTRESS-MODEL	9229 SUNSET BLVD #306	LOS ANGELES, CA 90069
VASSAR, DAVID A	TV DIRECTOR	POST OFFICE BOX 43	VENICE, CA 90291
VASSER, RONALD T	TV DIRECTOR	929 MARGATE TERR	CHICAGO, IL 60657
VASSY, GLORIA JEAN	ACTRESS	620 1/2 N HUNTLEY DR	LOS ANGELES, CA 90069
VATH, RICHARD	ACTOR	208 S BEVERLY DR #4	BEVERLY HILLS, CA 90212
VAUGHAN, CHARLES	GUITARIST	143 HILLCREST DR	MADISON, TN 37115
VAUGHAN, CLIFFORD	CONDUCTOR	12700 ELLIOTT AVE #455	EL MONTE, CA 91732
VAUGHAN, ELIZABETH	SOPRANO	61 W 62ND ST #6-F	NEW YORK, NY 10023
VAUGHAN, ELIZABETH H	NEWS CORRESPONDENT	4000 TUNLAW RD	WASHINGTON, DC 20007
VAUGHAN, PETER	ACTOR	ICM, 388-396 OXFORD ST	LONDON W1 ENGLAND
VAUGHAN, SARAH	SINGER	24921 KIT CARSON	HIDDEN HILLS, CA 91302
VAUGHAN, SKEETER	ACTOR	11240 MAGNOLIA BLVD #202	NORTH HOLLYWOOD, CA 91601
VAUGHAN, STEVIE RAY & DOUBLE TR	ROCK & ROLL GROUP	POST OFFICE BOX DRAWER T	MANOR, TX 78653
VAUGHN, DELANE	ACTOR	6736 LAUREL CANYON BLVD #306	NORTH HOLLYWOOD, CA 91606
VAUGHN, HEIDI	ACTRESS	10000 RIVERSIDE DR #3	TOLUCA LAKE, CA 91602
VAUGHN, KEVIN	WRESTLER	SEE - VON ERICH, LANCE	
VAUGHN, LINDA RHYS	MODEL	MODELS & PROMOTIONS AGENCY 8560 SUNSET BLVD, 10TH FLOOR	LOS ANGELES, CA 90069
VAUGHN, PAUL	TV WRITER	8955 BEVERLY BLVD	LOS ANGELES, CA 90048
VAUGHN, RICKY	WRESTLER	SEE - VON ERICH, LANCE	

Name	Occupation	Address	City	Zip
VAUGHN, ROBERT	ACTOR-DIRECTOR	162 OLD W MOUNTAIN RD	RIDGEFIELD, CT	06877
VAUGHN, VINCENT RAY	MUSIC ARRANGER	608-A MC PHERSON CT S	NASHVILLE, TN	37221
VAUGHN COMBO, BEN	ROCK 'N' ROLL COMBO	POST OFFICE BOX 42684	PHILADELPHIA, PA	19101
VAUTROT, JAMES E	NEWS CORRESPONDENT	110 WATCH HILL LN	GAITHERSBURG, MD	20878
VAZAK, P H	SCREENWRITER	ICM, 8899 BEVERLY BLVD	LOS ANGELES, CA	90048
VAZIRI, ALI	WRESTLER	SEE - IRON SHEIK, THE		
VE SOTA, GENEVIEVE	ACTRESS	12541 MITCHELL AVE	LOS ANGELES, CA	90066
VECCHIA, CHRISTOPHER R, JR	TV DIRECTOR	7 BULLFINCH PL	BOSTON, MA	02114
VEE, BOBBY	SINGER-SONGWRITER	POST OFFICE BOX 41	SAUK RAPIDS, MN	56379
VEE, JOHN	WRESTLING MANAGER	SEE - V, JOHNNY		
VEE BAND, THE	ROCK & ROLL GROUP	3717 W 50TH ST #L-2	MINNEAPOLIS, MN	55410
VEERHOFF, ALFRED B	NEWS CORRESPONDENT	3408 BRADLEY LN	CHEVY CHASE, MD	20815
VEGA, ROBERT	ACTOR	9220 SUNSET BLVD #202	LOS ANGELES, CA	90069
VEGA BROTHERS, THE	ROCK & ROCK DUO	9255 SUNSET BLVD #1115	LOS ANGELES, CA	90069
VEGAS, MARGARITO	NEWS CORRESPONDENT	444 N CAPITOL ST, NW	WASHINGTON, DC	20001
VEHICLE	ROCK & ROLL GROUP	41 BRITAIN ST #200	TORONTO, ONT	CANADA
VEIGLE, ANNE J	NEWS CORRESPONDENT	813 N MONROE ST	ARLINGTON, VA	22201
VEIKLEY, STEVE, JAZZ QUINTET	JAZZ QUINTET	FROTHINGHAM, 40 GROVE ST	WESSESLEY, MA	02181
VEITCH, JOHN	FILM PRODUCER	COLUMBIA PICTURES INDUSTRIES		
		COLUMBIA PLAZA	BURBANK, CA	91505
VEITH, SANDY	PRODUCER	MCA/UNIVERSAL STUDIOS, INC		
		100 UNIVERSAL CITY PLAZA #507	BURBANK, CA	91505
VEJAR, LAURENCE	EDITOR	958 E AVE "Q"	PALMDALE, CA	93350
VEJAR, RUDOLPH L	DIRECTOR	640 PRISCILLA LN	BURBANK, CA	91505
VEJZOVIC, DUNJA	SOPRANO	CAMI, 165 W 57TH ST	NEW YORK, NY	10019
VEKSHTEIN, SEMYON	CONDUCTOR	500 5TH AVE #2050	NEW YORK, NY	10110
VELA, ROSIE	MODEL-SINGER	FORD MODEL AGENCY		
		344 E 59TH ST	NEW YORK, NY	10022
VELASCO, ENRIQUE	GUITARIST	KAY, 58 W 58TH ST	NEW YORK, NY	10019
VELASCO, JERRY	ACTOR	6515 SUNSET BLVD #300-A	LOS ANGELES, CA	90028
VELEZ, EDDIE	ACTOR	STONE, 1052 CAROL DR	LOS ANGELES, CA	90069
VELEZ, KAREN	MODEL	MODELS & PROMOTIONS AGENCY		
		8560 SUNSET BLVD, 10TH FLOOR	LOS ANGELES, CA	90069
VELLINE, BOBBY	SINGER-SONGWRITER	SEE - VEE, BOBBY		
VELONS, THE	VOCAL GROUP	POST OFFICE BOX 22372	SAN FRANCISCO, CA	94122
VELTRI, MICHELANGELO	CONDUCTOR	61 W 62ND ST #6-F	NEW YORK, NY	10023
VELTZ, LEE	BARITONE	HILLYER, 250 W 57TH ST	NEW YORK, NY	10107
VENDICE, WILLIAM	CONDUCTOR	61 W 62ND ST #6-F	NEW YORK, NY	10023
VENDIG, IRVING	TV WRITER	555 W 57TH ST #1230	NEW YORK, NY	10019
VENER, VICTOR	CONDUCTOR	265 S SIERRA BONITA AVE	PASADENA, CA	91106
VENET, NICK	RECORD PRODUCER	POST OFFICE BOX 638	MALIBU, CA	90265
VENETO, ANDY	ACTOR	1422 N SWEETZER AVE #203	LOS ANGELES, CA	90069
VENETO, TONY	ACTOR	8949 SUNSET BLVD #203	LOS ANGELES, CA	90069
VENGER, RICHARD R	COMPOSER	250 S OAK KNOLL #102	PASADENA, CA	91101
VENNELL, VICKI A	NEWS CORRESPONDENT	9011 MC NAIR DR	ALEXANDRIA, VA	22309
VENNEMA, JOHN C	ACTOR	BRET ADAMS, 448 W 44TH ST	NEW YORK, NY	10036
VENOCUR, JOHNNY	ACTOR	CONTEMPORARY ARTISTS		
		132 S LASKY DR	BEVERLY HILLS, CA	90212
VENOM	ROCK & ROLL GROUP	IRD, 149-03 GUY R BREWER BLVD	JAMAICA, NY	11434
VENTANTONIO, JOHN	ACTOR	1807 LUCILE AVE	LOS ANGELES, CA	90026
VENTHAM, WANDA	ACTOR	SAINT JAMES'S MGMT		
		22 GROOM PL	LONDON SW1	ENGLAND
VENTRIGLIA, FRANCO	BASS	61 W 62ND ST #6-F	NEW YORK, NY	10023
VENTURA, JESSE "THE BODY"	WRESTLER-ACTOR	POST OFFICE BOX 3859	STAMFORD, CT	06905
VENTURA, LENO	ACTOR	4 PARC DE MONTRETOUT	SAINT CLOUD 92210	FRANCE
VENTURA, MICHAEL V	WRITER	8955 BEVERLY BLBVD	LOS ANGELES, CA	90048
VENTURA, SAMUEL J	DIRECTOR	2128 N SEDGWICK ST #10	CHICAGO, IL	60614
VENTURE, RICHARD	ACTOR	9744 WILSHIRE BLVD #206	BEVERLY HILLS, CA	90212
VENTURELLI, DOUGLAS A	WRITER	10310 RIVERSIDE DR	NORTH HOLLYWOOD, CA	91602
VENTURES, THE	ROCK & ROLL GROUP	POST OFFICE BOX 1646	BURBANK, CA	91507
VENUTA, BENAY	ACTRESS	50 E 79TH ST	NEW YORK, NY	10021
VER DORN, JERRY	ACTOR	CBS-TV, "THE GUIDING LIGHT"		
		51 W 52ND ST	NEW YORK, NY	10019
VERA, ANA-MARIA	PIANIST	3003 VAN NESS ST #W-205, NW	WASHINGTON, DC	20008
VERA, BILLY	ACTOR	9000 SUNSET BLVD #1200	LOS ANGELES, CA	90069
VERA, BILLY & THE BEATERS	ROCK & ROLL GROUP	POST OFFICE BOX 82	GREAT NECK, NY	11022
VERBIT, HELEN	ACTRESS	8350 SANTA MONICA BLVD #103	LOS ANGELES, CA	90069
VERBIT, MARTHA	PIANIST	3003 VAN NESS ST #W-205, NW	WASHINGTON, DC	20008
VERDEAUX, CYRILLE	MUSICIAN	POST OFFICE BOX 9388	STANFORD, CA	94305
VERDERY, BENJAMIN	GUITARIST	SIMONDS, 30 HEWLETT ST	WATERBURY, CT	06710
VERDI, ANTHONY C	TV DIRECTOR	9900 AUTUMNWOOD WY	POTOMAC, MD	20854
VERDIER, PAUL	ACTOR	9229 SUNSET BLVD #306	LOS ANGELES, CA	90069
VERDON, GWEN	ACT-DAN-CHOREO	91 CENTRAL PARK W	NEW YORK, NY	10023
VERDUGO, ELENA	ACTRESS	208 S BEVERLY DR #4	BEVERLY HILLS, CA	90212
VERDY, VIOLETTE	BALLERINA	THE BOSTON BALLET		
		555 TREMONT ST	BOSTON, MA	02116
VERED, ILANA	PIANIST	CAMI, 165 W 57TH ST	NEW YORK, NY	10019
VEREECKE, AIME	COMPOSER	1474 CLYBOURN AVE	BURBANK, CA	91505
VEREEN, BEN	ACTOR-SINGER-DANCER	190 E SADDLE RIVER RD	SADDLE RIVER, NJ	07458
VEREEN, DIXIE D	PHOTOGRAPHER	8605 VILLAGE WY	ALEXANDRIA, VA	22309
VERGARA, VICTORIA	MEZZO-SOPRANO	CAMI, 165 W 57TH ST	NEW YORK, NY	10019
VERHAGEN, FRANS	NEWS CORRESPONDENT	2138 "O" ST, NW	WASHINGTON, DC	20037
VERHEY, EMMY	VIOLINIST	ICM, 40 W 57TH ST	NEW YORK, NY	10019
VERHOEVEN, PAUL	ACTOR	9255 SUNSET BLVD #505	LOS ANGELES, CA	90069
VERI & JAMANIS	PIANO DUO	CAMI, 165 W 57TH ST	NEW YORK, NHY	10019

Name	Occupation	Address	City/State	Zip
VERKKOLA, MATTI J	NEWS CORRESPONDENT	2821 OLIVE ST, NW	WASHINGTON, DC	20007
VERKKOLA, TUIJA	NEWS CORRESPONDENT	2821 OLIVE ST, NW	WASHINGTON, DC	20007
VERNA, GARY	WRITER	4141 KNOBHILL DR	SHERMAN OAKS, CA	91403
VERNA, TONY	DIRECTOR	500 OCAMPO DR	PACIFIC PALISADES, CA	90272
VERNA, TRESSA ANNE	PHOTOGRAPHER	809 WINDWARD CT	FORT WASHINGTON, MD	20744
VERNALI, JAY	PIANIST	2502 WOODYHILL DR	NASHVILLE, TN	37207
VERNON, DIANE	NEWS CORRESPONDENT	1012 14TH ST, NW	WASHINGTON, DC	20005
VERNON, HARVEY	ACTOR	12750 VENTURA BLVD #102	STUDIO CITY, CA	91604
VERNON, JOHN	ACTOR	15125 MULHOLLAND DR	LOS ANGELES, CA	90024
VERNON, KATE	ACTRESS	STONE, 1052 CAROL DR	LOS ANGELES, CA	90069
VERNON, RICHARD	ACTOR	LEADING ARTISTS, LTD		
		60 SAINT JAMES'S ST	LONDON SW1	ENGLAND
VERNON, RICHARD	BASSO-BARITONE	111 W 57TH ST #1209	NEW YORK, NY	10019
VERNON, WES	NEWS CORRESPONDENT	1605 BILLMAN LN	SILVER SPRING, MD	20902
VERONA, MICHAEL ROSS	ACTOR	956 PALM AVE	LOS ANGELES, CA	90069
VERONA, STEPHEN	WRITER-PRODUCER	1251 STONE CANYON RD	LOS ANGELES, CA	90024
VERONELLI, ERNESTO	TENOR	CAMI, 165 W 57TH ST	NEW YORK, NY	10019
VERRETT, SHIRLEY	SOPRANO	CAMI, 165 W 57TH ST	NEW YORK, NY	10019
VERROS, JOHN	ACTOR	10631 PINEWOOD AVE	TUJUNGA, CA	91042
VERSALLE, RICHARD	HELDENTENOR	PERLS, 7 W 96TH ST	NEW YORK, NY	10025
VERSHOTH, ANITA	SPORTS WRITER-EDITOR	SPORTS ILLUSTRATED MAGAZINE		
		TIME & LIFE BUILDING		
		ROCKEFELLER CENTER	NEW YORK, NY	10020
VERTELNEY, REED P	COMPOSER	511 RAYMOND AVE #4	SANTA MONICA, CA	90405
VERTUE, BERYL	FILM-TV PRODUCER	HARTSWOOD FILMS, STARLINGS		
		NEW HOUSE LN, SALFORDS	SURREY RH1 5RE	ENGLAND
VESAK, NORBERT	DIRECTOR-CHOREO	METROPOLITAN OPERA		
		LINCOLN CENTER	NEW YORK, NY	10023
VESEY, DAVID	NEWS CORRESPONDENT	2225 40TH PL, NW	WASHINGTON, DC	20007
VESPA, MARY	WRITER-EDITOR	PEOPLE/TIME & LIFE BLDG		
		ROCKEFELLER CENTER	NEW YORK, NY	10020
VEST, HAL	DRUMMER	1130 MURFREESBORO RD #121	NASHVILLE, TN	37217
VEST, JAKE	CARTOONIST	TRIBUNE MEDIA SERVICES		
		64 E CONCORD ST	ORLANDO, FL	32801
VEST, JIM	GUITARIST	ROUTE #2, HUNTERS LN	HENDERSONVILLE, TN	37075
VEST, KENNETH M	NEWS CORRESPONDENT	5323 MACOMB ST, NW	WASHINGTON, DC	20016
VESTAL, CHRISTINE	NEWS CORRESPONDENT	3701 MASSACHUSETTS AVE #5487, NW	WASHINGTON, DC	20016
VESTERMAN, HELENA	PIANIST	POST OFFICE BOX 131	SPRINGFIELD, VA	22150
VETO, TOMAS	CONDUCTOR	482 FORT WASHINGTON AVE #1-H	NEW YORK, NY	10033
VETRI, VICTORIA	ACTRESS-MODEL	13111 VENTURA BLVD #204	STUDIO CITY, CA	91604
VETTER, RICHARD H	FILM EXECUTIVE	17627 CAMINO YATASTO	PACIFIC PALISADES, CA	90272
VEX, THE	ROCK & ROLL GROUP	25 HUNTINGTON AVE #420	BOSTON, MA	02116
VEY, PETER	CARTOONIST	POST OFFICE BOX 4203	NEW YORK, NY	10017
VIALA, JEAN-LUC	TENOR	ANGLO-SWISS ARTISTS MGMT		
		16 MUSWELL HILL RD, HIGHGATE	LONDON N6 5UG	ENGLAND
VIATOR, CASEY	BODYBUILDER	POST OFFICE BOX 31616	TUSCON, AZ	85751
VIBRATIONS, THE	VOCAL GROUP	POST OFFICE BOX 262	CARTERET, NJ	07008
VICAR, JAMES F	DIRECTOR	600 W 111TH ST	NEW YORK, NY	10025
VICARIO, VIRGINIA ANN	PHOTOGRAPHER	1606 WOODMOOR LN	MC LEAN, VA	22101
VICAS, GEORGE A	WRITER-PRODUCER	4011 N 26TH ST	ARLINGTON, VA	22207
VICHI, GERRY	ACTOR	444 E 82ND ST	NEW YORK, NY	10028
VICINI, JAMES	NEWS CORRESPONDENT	9301 OCALA ST	SILVER SPRING, MD	20901
VICK, WANDA	GUITARIST	141 NEESE DR #U-421	NASHVILLE, TN	37211
VICKERS, MARC	GUITARIST	1510 NORVEL AVE #B	NASHVILLE, TN	37216
VICKERS, MIKE	COMPOSER	FIRST COMPOSERS COMPANY		
		14 NEW BURLINGTON ST	LONDON W1X 5LR	ENGLAND
VICKERS, YVETTE	ACTRESS	10021 WESTWANDA DR	BEVERLY HILLS, CA	90210
VICKERY, HUGH	NEWS CORRESPONDENT	7879 CONNECTICUT AVE, NW	WASHINGTON, DC	20008
VICKERY, MACK	SINGER	POST OFFICE BOX 6025	NEWPORT NEWS, VA	23606
VICKLAND, PAUL M	WRITER	8612 WYSTONE AVE	NORTHRIDGE, CA	91324
VICKSBURGS, THE	GOSPEL GROUP	CEE, 193 KONHAUS RD	MECHANICSBURG, PA	17055
VICTOR, DAVID	WRITER-PRODUCER	147 GROVERTON PL	LOS ANGELES, CA	90077
VICTOR, JAMES	ACTOR	POST OFFICE BOX 5617	BEVERLY HILLS, CA	90210
VICTOR, KATHRIN	ACTRESS	4731 LAUREL CANYON BLVD #5	NORTH HOLLYWOOD, CA	91607
VICTOR, KIRK	NEWS CORRESPONDENT	149 DUDDINGTON PL, SE	WASHINGTON, DC	20003
VICTOR, MARK A	SCREENWRITER	707 ALMA REAL DR	PACIFIC PALIADES, CA	90272
VICTOR, PAULA	ACTRESS	1346 1/2 N HAVENHURST DR	LOS ANGELES, CA	90046
VICTOR, RICHARD	DIRECTOR	520 N MICHIGAN AVE #436	CHICAGO, IL	60611
VICTORY, JACK	WRESTLER	UNIVERSAL WRESTLING FEDERATION		
		MID SOUTH SPORTS, INC		
		5001 SPRING VALLEY RD	DALLAS, TX	75244
VIDAL, EDWIN	NEWS CORRESPONDENT	2144 CALIFORNIA ST #901, NW	WASHINGTON, DC	20008
VIDAL, GORE	WRITER	2562 OUTPOST DR	LOS ANGELES, CA	90068
VIDAL, MARIA	SINGER	CATCH A RISING STAR, INC		
		157 W 57TH ST	NEW YORK, NY	10019
VIDEEO	ROCK & ROLL GROUP	HARVEY/LYNCH AGENCY		
		7600 W TIDWELL RD	HOUSTON, TX	77040
VIDOR, ZOLL	CINEMATOGRAPHER	124 S CANON DR	BEVERLY HILLS, CA	90212
VIEIRA, GEORGE D	DIRECTOR-PRODUCER	20032 PACIFIC COAST HWY	MALIBU, CA	90265
VIEIRA, PETER J	DIRECTOR	4331 TALOFA AVE	NORTH HOLLYWOOD, CA	91602
VIERTEL, PETER	SCREENWRITER	8955 BEVERLY BLVD	LOS ANGELES, CA	90048
VIETRO, ROBERT A	DIRECTOR	20 WESTMERE AVE	ROWAYTON, CT	06853
VIG, TOMMY	COMPOSER	8530 WILSHIRE BLVD #500	BEVERLY HILLS, CA	90211
VIGARD, KRISTEN	ACTRESS	9000 SUNSET BLVD #1200	LOS ANGELES, CA	90069
VIGIL, SHANNON	TALENT AGENT	725 S BARRINGTON #202	LOS ANGELES, CA	90049

VICTORIA VETRI

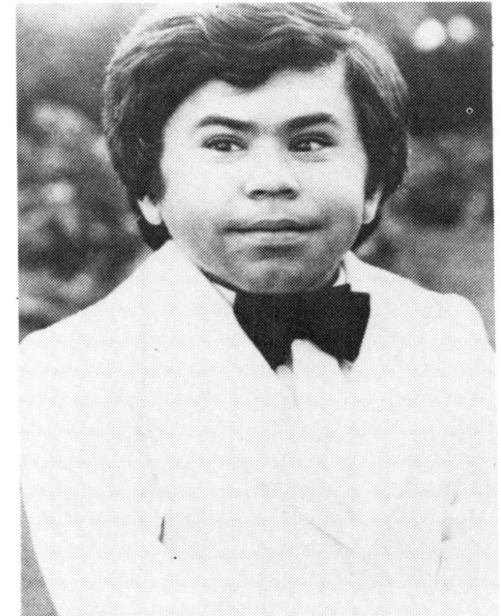
HERVE VILLECHAIZE

BOBBY VINTON

LINDSAY WAGNER

JOHN WAITE

CLINT WALKER

JIMMY WALKER

NANCY WALKER

JUNIOR WALKER

Name	Occupation	Address	City	Zip/Country
VIGNOLES, TIMOTHY	TV EXECUTIVE	19 WELLS ST	LONDON WI	ENGLAND
VIGODA, ABE	ACTOR	1215 BEVERLY VIEW DR	BEVERLY HILLS, CA	90210
VIGON, BARRY	TV WRITER	11812 SAN VICENTE BLVD #510	LOS ANGELES, CA	90049
VIGUS, LARRY	CASTING DIRECTOR	2021 N WESTERN AVE #10	LOS ANGELES, CA	90027
VIGUS, LARRY L, II	ACTOR	6550 ELDER ST	LOS ANGELES, CA	90042
VIHARO, ROBERT	ACTOR	1341 OCEAN AVE	SANTA MONICA, CA	90401
VIKING, THE	WRESTLER	UNIVERSAL WRESTLING FEDERATION		
		MID SOUTH SPORTS, INC		
		5001 SPRING VALLEY RD	DALLAS, TX	75244
VILANCH, BRUCE	WRITER	12417 MULHOLLAND DR	BEVERLY HILLS, CA	90210
VILAS, GUILLERMO	TENNIS	AVENUE FOCH #86	PARIS	FRANCE
VILLADESEN, M KURT	WRITER	20503 BIG ROCK DR	MALIBU, CA	90265
VILLAFANE, FEDERICO JIMENEZ	GUITARIST	POST OFFICE BOX 15445	SANTA FE, NM	87506
VILLAGE PEOPLE, THE	ROCK & ROLL GROUP	251 PARK AVE S	NEW YORK, NY	10010
VILLAIRE, DAVID A	WRITER	8720 SHOREHAM DR #403	LOS ANGELES, CA	90069
VILLALOBOS, ANI	ACTRESS	5330 LANKERSHIM BLVD #210	NORTH HOLLYWOOD, CA	91601
VILLARD, TOM	ACTOR	211 S BEVERLY DR #201	BEVERLY HILLS, CA	90212
VILLASENOR, VICTOR E	SCREENWRITER	445 N BEDFORD DR #PH	BEVERLY HILLS, CA	90210
VILLAVERDE, JOSE	CASTING DIRECTOR	POST OFFICE BOX 5718	SHERMAN OAKS, CA	91403
VILLECHAIZE, HERVE	ACTOR	POST OFFICE BOX 1305	BURBANK, CA	91507
VILLELLA, EDWARD	DIRECTOR-DANCER	129 W 69TH ST	NEW YORK, NY	10023
VILLIERS, JAMES	ACTOR	29 BELSIZE PARK	LONDON NW3	ENGLAND
VINAO, EZEQUIEL	PIANIST	POST OFFICE BOX U	REDDING, CT	06875
VINCENT, DON	COMPOSER	3591 ALGOQUIN DR	LAS VEGAS, NV	89109
VINCENT, E DUKE	WRITER-PRODUCER	9526 DALEGROVE DR	BEVERLY HILLS, CA	90210
VINCENT, ELMORE	ACTOR	8831 SUNSET BLVD #402	LOS ANGELES, CA	90069
VINCENT, JAN-MICHAEL	ACTOR	31339 PACIFIC COAST HWY	MALIBU, CA	90265
VINCENT, JOE MACK	GUITARIST	2411 PAFFORD DR	NASHVILLE, TN	37206
VINCENT, LARRY	DIRECTOR	DGA, 7950 SUNSET BLVD	LOS ANGELES, CA	90046
VINCENT, PAUL	ACTOR	1650 BROADWAY #302	NEW YORK, NY	10019
VINCENT, ROMO	ACTOR	1124 N SHERBOURNE DR #A-20	LOS ANGELES, CA	90006
VINCENT, RUSSEL	TV WRITER-DIRECTOR	7182 CHELAN WY	HOLLYWOOD, CA	90068
VINCENT, SAM	ACTOR	8350 SANTA MONICA BLVD #206	LOS ANGELES, CA	90069
VINCENT, VINNIE	SINGER-GUITARIST	CHRYSALIS RECORDS COMPANY		
		645 MADISON AVE	NEW YORK, NY	10022
VINCENT, VIRGINIA	ACTRESS	1001 HAMMOND ST	LOS ANGELES, CA	90069
VINCO, IVO	SINGER	CAMI, 165 W 57TH ST	NEW YORK, NY	10019
VINCZ, MELANIE	ACTRESS-MODEL	1151 3RD ST	MANHATTAN BEACH, CA	90266
VINCZE, ERNEST	CINEMATOGRAPHER	25 MARVILLE RD	LONDON SW6	ENGLAND
VINE, PATTI S	NEWS CORRESPONDENT	5151 WISCONSIN AVE, NW	WASHINGTON, DC	20016
VINER, JOHN	TV WRITER-PRODUCER	66 GAINSBOROUGH CT		
		WALTON-ON-THAMES	SURREY	ENGLAND
VINER, MICHAEL	SCREENWRITER	2630 EDEN PL	BEVERLY HILLS, CA	90210
VINES, ROBERT	DRUMMER	529 AMALIE CT #B	NASHVILLE, TN	37211
VINETT, JERRY	SAXOPHONIST	745 TAHLENA AVE	MADISON, TN	37115
VING, LEE	ACTOR	151 S EL CAMINO DR	BEVERLY HILLS, CA	90212
VINING, DANIEL	SCREENWRITER	8955 BEVERLY BLVD	LOS ANGELES, CA	90048
VINSON, DON	GUITARIST	ROUTE #2, BOX 114-B		
		WALKUP RD	PEGRAM, TN	37143
VINSON, HELEN	ACTRESS	HADDENBROOK, 2213 CAROL WOODS	CHAPEL HILL, NC	27514
VINSON, JAMES W	NEWS WRITER	4228 LOS FELIZ BLVD	LOS ANGELES, CA	90027
VINSON, LAURA & RED WYNG	C & W GROUP	POST OFFICE BOX 8768		
		STATION L	EDMONDTON, ALT	CANADA
VINSON, ROBERT	ACTOR	3575 W CAHUENGA BLVD #320	LOS ANGELES, CA	90068
VINT, ALAN	ACTOR	POST OFFICE BOX 8589	UNIVERSAL CITY, CA	91608
VINT, BILL	ACTOR	1901 AVE OF THE STARS #1774	LOS ANGELES, CA	90067
VINT, JESSE	ACTOR	5003 TYRONE AVE #1	SHERMAN OAKS, CA	91423
VINT, ROBERT	TV DIRECTOR	649 E 14TH ST	NEW YORK, NY	10009
VINTAS, GUSTAV	ACTOR	3800 BARHAM BLVD #303	LOS ANGELES, CA	90068
VINTON, BOBBY	SINGER	POST OFFICE BOX 906	MALIBU, CA	90265
VINZING, UTE	SOPRANO	CAMI, 165 W 57TH ST	NEW YORK, NY	10019
VIOLA, ALFRED F	MUSICIAN	4221 GOODLAND AVE	STUDIO CITY, CA	91604
VIOLA, ALFRED M	FILM DIRECTOR	2049 CENTURY PARK E #1320	LOS ANGELES, CA	90067
VIOLA, JOSEPH	WRITER-PRODUCER	926 N HARPER AVE	LOS ANGELES, CA	90046
VIOLENT FEMMES, THE	ROCK & ROLL GROUP	POST OFFICE BOX 1304	BURBANK, CA	91507
VIOLET, ULTRA	ACTRESS	1891 SCHIEFFELIN PL	BRONX, NY	10466
VIOLETTE, CHARLES H	NEWS CORRESPONDENT	ROUTE 1, BOX 750	GORE, VA	22614
VIOLINAIRES, THE	VIOLIN ENSEMBLE	SEE - FANTASTIC VIOLINAIRES, THE		
VIOTTI, D E	COMPOSER	2205 BUTTERFIELD RD #262	YAKIMA, WA	98901
VIPERS, THE	ROCK & ROLL GROUP	348 E 9TH ST #10	NEW YORK, NY	10003
VIRGIL, OZZIE, JR	BASEBALL	4316 W MERCAL ST	GLENDALE, AZ	85301
VIRGIN PRUNES, THE	ROCK & ROLL GROUP	POST OFFICE BOX 433	DEARBORN, MI	48121
VIRGINIA WOLF	ROCK & ROLL GROUP	PERFORMING ARTS NETWORK		
		10 SUTHERLAND AVE	LONDON W9	ENGLAND
VIRGO, PETER C, JR	ACTOR	1701 MORTON AVE	LOS ANGELES, CA	90026
VIRKHAUS, TAAVO	CONDUCTOR	POST OFFICE BOX 27539	PHILADELPHIA, PA	19118
VIRKLER, DENNIS	DIRECTOR	19730 VALLEY VIEW DR	TOPANGA CANYON, CA	90290
VIRSIS, PETER	DIRECTOR	DGA, 110 W 57TH ST	NEW YORK, NY	10019
VIRTANEN, MICHAEL	NEWS CORRESPONDENT	911 N BARTON ST	ARLINGTON, VA	22201
VIRTUES, THE	VOCAL GROUP	OLDIES, 5218 ALMONT ST	LOS ANGELES, CA	90032
VIRTUOSI QUINTET, THE	MUSIC ENSEMBLE	15 HIGH ST #621	HARTFORD, CT	06103
VIRZALADZE, ELIZO	PIANIST	MARIEDL ANDERS ARTISTS MGMT		
		535 EL CAMINO DEL MAR ST	SAN FRANCISCO, CA	94121
VISA	ROCK & ROLL GROUP	BRAD SIMON, 445 E 80TH ST	NEW YORK, NY	10021
VISCA, CLAUDIA	SOPRANO	59 E 54TH ST #81	NEW YORK, NY	10022

VISCA, DENNIS	ACTOR	909 6TH ST #10	SANTA MONICA, CA	90403
VISCONTI, PIERO	TENOR	CAMI, 165 W 57TH ST	NEW YORK, NY	10019
VISCUSO, SAL	ACTOR	6491 IVARENE AVE	LOS ANGELES, CA	90068
VISE, DAVID A	NEWS CORRESPONDENT	2939 VAN NESS ST #947, NW	WASHINGTON, DC	20008
VISELTEAR, MICHAEL	WRITER	9741 1/2 HELEN AVE	SUNLAND, CA	91040
VISHNEVSKAYA, GALINA	SOPRANO	CAMI, 165 W 57TH ST	NEW YORK, NY	10019
VISITOR, NANA	ACTRESS	8500 WILSHIRE BLVD #506	BEVERLY HILLS, CA	90211
VISKUPIC, GARY	CARTOONIST	NEWSDAY, 1500 BROADWAY	NEW YORK, NY	10036
VISONE, JUSTINE	ACTRESS	1605 N CAHUENGA BLVD #202	LOS ANGELES, CA	90028
VISSARI, VICTOR V	PHOTOGRAPHER	5101 MACON RD	ROCKVILLE, MD	20853
VISSER, DICK, GUITAR TRIO	GUITAR TRIO	POST OFFICE BOX U	REDDING, CT	06875
VIT & SALUTATIONS	VOCAL GROUP	POST OFFICE BOX 82	GREAT NECK, NY	11022
VITAL INFORMATION	JAZZ GROUP	SEE - SMITH, STEVE &		
		VITAL INFORMATION		
VITALE, CAROLE	ACTRESS-MODEL	KIQQ RADIO, 6430 SUNSET BLVD	LOS ANGELES, CA	90028
VITALE, JOE	ACTOR	POST OFFICE BOX 11749	MARINA DEL REY, CA	90295
VITAMIN Z	ROCK & ROLL GROUP	PETE SMITH MANAGEMENT		
		360 OXFORD ST	LONDON W1	ENGLAND
VITARELLI, ARTHUR J	DIRECTOR	200 1/2 EMERALD AVE	BALBOA ISLAND, CA	92662
VITARELLI, ROBERT E	TV DIRECTOR-PRODUCER	11104 GILCRIST CT	POTOMAC, MD	20854
VITELLO, DONALD	TV DIRECTOR	SUTTON TOWERS		
		908-A COLLINGS AVE	COLLINGSWOOD, NJ	08107
VITOUS, MIROSLAV	BASS	KURLAND, 173 BRIGHTON AVE	BOSTON, MA	02134
VITTES, MICHAEL	TV WRITER	2049 CENTURY PARK E #1320	LOS ANGELES, CA	90067
VITTI, MONICA	ACTRESS	VIA VICENZO TIBERIO 18	ROME	ITALY
VITTORI, EMILY LOVE	ACTRESS	124 W OAK AVE	EL SEGUNDO, CA	90245
VITTORINI, CARLO	PUBLISHING EXECUTIVE	PARADE, 750 3RD AVE	NEW YORK, NY	10017
VIXEN	ROCK & ROLL GROUP	VARIETY ARTISTS INTL, INC		
		9073 NEMO ST, 3RD FLOOR	LOS ANGELES, CA	90069
VLADY, MARINA	ACTRESS	10 AVE DE MARIVAUZ	MISSION LAFITTE 78800	FRANCE
VLAHOS, SAM	ACTOR	3124 1/4 HELMS AVE	LOS ANGELES, CA	90034
VLUDRICEK, LUZIAN	WRITER-PRODUCER	28 REGENT ST	LANCASTER LA1 1SQ	ENGLAND
VO, HUYNH	NEWS CORRESPONDENT	406 WINTERTHUR CT	SILVER SPRING, MD	20904
VODENICHAROV, BOYAN	PIANIST	KAY, 58 W 58TH ST	NEW YORK, NY	10019
VOGEL, ALLAN	OBOIST	IMG ARTISTS, 22 E 71ST ST	NEW YORK, NY	10021
VOGEL, CAROL	CASTING DIRECTOR	AKA CASTING, 6522 HAYES DR	LOS ANGELES, CA	90048
VOGEL, CAROL	ACTRESS	8400 LOOKOUT MOUNTAIN AVE	LOS ANGELES, CA	90046
VOGEL, HELEN	ACTRESS	8350 SANTA MONICA BLVD #102	LOS ANGELES, CA	90069
VOGEL, JULES	CONDUCTOR	17611 BASTANCHURY RD	YORBA LINDA, CA	92686
VOGEL, TONY	ACTOR	ICM, 388-396 OXFORD ST	LONDON W1	ENGLAND
VOGEL, VIRGIL	FILM DIRECTOR	5550 COLBATH AVE	VAN NUYS, CA	91401
VOGELSANG, JUDITH AYERS	TV DIRECTOR	5659 BECK AVE	NORTH HOLLYWOOD, CA	91601
VOGT, ROY	GUITARIST	638 EZELL RD	NASHVILLE, TN	37217
VOGUES, THE	VOCAL GROUP	POST OFFICE BOX 399	LISLE, IL	60532
VOHAR, DENNY	NEWS CORRESPONDENT	1211 AUTUMN PL	HERNDON, VA	22070
VOICU, ION	VIOLINIST	POST OFFICE BOX 131	SPRINGFIELD, VA	22150
VOICU, MADALIN	CONDUCTOR	POST OFFICE BOX 131	SPRINGFIELD, VA	22150
VOIGHT, JON	ACTOR	2260 BOWMONT DR	BEVERLY HILLS, CA	90210
VOIGHTLANDER, TED	CINEMATOGRAPHER	POST OFFICE BOX 2230	HOLLYWOOD, CA	90078
VOIGHTS, RICHARD	ACTOR	160 W END AVE	NEW YORK, NY	10023
VOISS, TOM	PRODUCER	THE BURBANK STUDIOS		
		4000 WARNER BLVD	BURBANK, CA	91522
VOKES, HOWARD	SINGER-GUITARIST	POST OFFICE BOX 12	NEW KENSINGTON, PA	15068
VOKETAITIS, ARNOLD	BASSO-BARITONE	1776 BROADWAY #504	NEW YORK, NY	10019
VOLCANO SUNS, THE	ROCK & ROLL TRIO	POST OFFICE BOX 570	ROCKVILLE CENTRE, NY	11571
VOLD, INGRID	ACTRESS	10000 RIVERSIDE DR #3	TOLUCA LAKE, CA	91602
VOLDSTAD, JOHN	ATCTOR	688 S HOBART BLVD	LOS ANGELES, CA	90005
VOLETTI, MICHAEL	ACTOR	FELBER, 2126 N CAHUENGA BLVD	LOS ANGELES, CA	90068
VOLKER, WILLIAM	HARPSICHORDIST	AFFILIATE ARTISTS, INC		
		37 W 65TH ST, 6TH FLOOR	NEW YORK, NY	10023
VOLKOFF, NIKOLAI	WRESTLER	POST OFFICE BOX 3859	STAMFORD, CT	06905
VOLLEN, RENEE	SCREENWRITER	2950 NEILSON WY #504-A	SANTA MONICA, CA	90405
VOLLENWEIDER, ANDREAS	HARPIST-COMPOSER	1501 BROADWAY #1506	NEW YORK, NY	10036
VOLPICELLI, LOUIS	DIRECTOR-PRODUCER	38 PHILLIPS LN	DARIEN, CT	06820
VOLTAGE BROTHERS, THE	RHYTHM & BLUES GROUP	POST OFFICE BOX 11283	RICHMOND, VA	23230
VOLTAGE BROTHERS, THE	SOUL GROUP	POST OFFICE BOX 11283	RICHMOND, VA	23230
VOLUMATIX	ROCK & ROLL GROUP	9777 HARWIN ST #101	HOUSTON, TX	77036
VOLZ, JOSEPH	NEWS CORRESPONDENT	15611 PASSAIE LN	BOWIE, MD	20716
VOLZ, NEDRA	ACTRESS	615 TULARE WY	UPLAND, CA	91786
VOLZ, WILLARD G	PHOTOGRAPHER	1006 HELENA DR	SILVER SPRING, MD	20901
VON ALPENHEIM, ILSE	PIANIST	MARIEDL ANDERS ARTISTS MGMT		
		535 EL CAMINO DEL MAR ST	SAN FRANCISCO, CA	94121
VON AROLDINGEN, KARIN	BALLERINA	NEW YORK CITY BALLET		
		LINCOLN CENTER PLAZA	NEW YORK, NY	10023
VON DOHNANYI, CHRISTOPH	CONDUCTOR	COLBERT, 111 W 57TH ST	NEW YORK, NY	10019
VON DUYKE, MORTON	NEWS CORRESPONDENT	1201 CONNECTICUT AVE, NW	WASHINGTON, DC	20036
VON ERICH, KERRY	WRESTLER	WORLD CLASS WRESTLING		
		SOUTHWEST SPORTS, INC		
		DALLAS SPORTATORIUM		
		1000 S INDUSTRIAL BLVD	DALLAS, TX	75207
VON ERICH, KEVIN	WRESTLER	WORLD CLASS WRESTLING		
		SOUTHWEST SPORTS, INC		
		DALLAS SPORTATORIUM		
		1000 S INDUSTRIAL BLVD	DALLAS, TX	75207

Name	Occupation	Address	City	Zip/Country
VON ERICH, LANCE	WRESTLER	WORLD CLASS WRESTLING		
		SOUTHWEST SPORTS, INC		
		DALLAS SPORTATORIUM		
		1000 S INDUSTRIAL BLVD	DALLAS, TX	75207
VON FREMD, JOHN G	NEWS CORRESPONDENT	3813 DECATUR AVE	KENSINGTON, MD	20895
VON FREMD, MIKE	SINGER	POST OFFICE BOX 6025	NEWPORT NEWS, VA	23606
VON FURSTENBERG, BETSY	ACTRESS	114 E 28TH ST #203	NEW YORK, NY	10016
VON FURSTENBERG, DIANE	FASHION DESIGNER	1407 BROADWAY	NEW YORK, NY	10018
VON GOGH, GENEVIEVE	ACTRESS	10666 1/2 BLUFFSIDE DR	NORTH HOLLYWOOD, CA	91604
VON HAIG, CRUSHER	WRESTLER	SEE - ROAD WARRIOR HAWK		
VON HALEM, VICTOR	SINGER	CAMI, 165 W 57TH ST	NEW YORK, NY	10019
VON HOELTKE, JERRY	ACTOR	8401 FOUNTAIN AVE	HOLLYWOOD, CA	90069
VON HOFFMAN, NICHOLAS	COMMENTATOR	KING FEATURES SYNDICATE		
		235 E 45TH ST	NEW YORK, NY	10017
VON KAENEL, JANE A	NEWS CORRESPONDENT	2556 MASSACHUSETTS AVE, NW	WASHINGTON, DC	20008
VON KANTOR, GEORGE	PHOTOGRAPHER	1014 TOTTENHAM CT	STERLING, VA	22170
VON KARAJAN, HERBERT	CONDUCTOR	FESTSPIELHAUS A-5010	SALZBURG	AUSTRIA
VON LEER, HUNTER	ACTOR	8322 BEVERLY BLVD #202	LOS ANGELES, CA	90048
VON LENNARTZ, PAULETTE	WRITER	821 3RD ST #105	SANTA MONICA, CA	90403
VON MOUILLARD, THOMAS	NEWS CORRESPONDENT	4717 LINNEAN AVE, NW	WASHINGTON, DC	20008
VON OTTER, ANNE SOFIE	MEZZO-SOPRANO	CAMI, 165 W 57TH ST	NEW YORK, NY	10019
VON RASCHKE, BARON	WRESTLER	NATIONAL WRESTLING ALLIANCE		
		JIM CROCKETT PROMOTIONS		
		421 BRIARBEND DR	CHARLOTTE, NC	28209
VON RHEIN, JOHN	MUSIC CRITIC	435 N MICHIGAN AVE	CHICAGO, IL	60611
VON ROTZ, RAYMOND	MUSICIAN	801 OAKWOOD TERR	ANTIOCH, TN	37013
VON SCHOELER, SASHA	ACTRESS	ABC-TV, "ALL MY CHILDREN"		
		1330 AVE OF THE AMERICAS	NEW YORK, NY	10019
VON STADE, FREDERICA	MEZZO-SOPRANO	CAMI, 165 W 57TH ST	NEW YORK, NY	10019
VON SYDOW, MAX	ACTOR	AVD C/G RISBERG, STRANDVEGEN B	114-56 STOCKHOLM	SWEDEN
VON ZEPPELIN, CHRISTINA LEESE	NEWS CORRESPONDENT	8729 HAYSHED LN	COLUMBIA, MD	21045
VON ZERNECK, DANIELLE	ACTRESS	151 S EL CAMINO DR	BEVERLY HILLS, CA	90212
VON ZERNECK, PETER	ACTOR	10311 RIVERSIDE DR	TOLUCA LAKE, CA	91602
VONN, VEOLA	ACTRESS	8906 EVANVIEW DR	LOS ANGELES, CA	90069
VONNEGUT, KURT, JR	WRITER	228 E 48TH ST	NEW YORK, NY	10017
VOODOO DOLLS	ROCK & ROLL GROUP	POST OFFICE BOX 139	447-00 VARGARDA	SWEDEN
VOORHEES, DEBISUE	ACTRESS	3151 W CAHUENGA BLVD #310	LOS ANGELES, CA	90068
VOORHEES, JOE	DIRECTOR	7606 GOODLAND AVE	NORTH HOLLYWOOD, CA	91605
VORGAN, GIGI	ACTRESS	3676 STONE CANYON AVE	SHERMAN OAKS, CA	91403
VORKAPICH, SLAVOMIR	DIRECTOR	DGA, 110 W 57TH ST	NEW YORK, NY	10019
VORNHOLT, JOHN	WRITER	4618 MAUBERT AVE	LOS ANGELES, CA	90027
VORTEX	RHYTHM & BLUES GROUP	KINGSLAND, 108 SHARON DR	WEST MONROE, LA	71291
VOSBURGH, DAVID	ACTOR	6638 ATOLL AVE	NORTH HOLLYWOOD, CA	91606
VOSBURGH, DICK	TV WRITER	18 COLLEGE CROSS	LONDON N1	ENGLAND
VOSBURGH, MARCY	ACTRESS	5040 TUJUNGA AVE #12	NORTH HOLLYWOOD, CA	91601
VOSBURGH, RICHARD	TV WRITER	8955 BEVERLY BLVD	LOS ANGELES, CA	90048
VOSS, ERIKA B	NEWS CORRESPONDENT	NBC-TV, NEWS DEPARTMENT		
		4001 NEBRASKA AVE, NW	WASHINGTON, DC	20016
VOSS, KENNETH JUDE	DIRECTOR	3 CIRCLE DR	HAWTHORNE WOODS, IL	60047
VOSS, ROBERT W	COMPOSER	68 BINNEY LN	OLD GREENWICH, CT	06870
VOTAPEK, RALPH	PIANIST	GERSHUNOFF, 502 PARK AVE	NEW YORK, NY	10022
VOTAW, KIM	PERCUSSIONIST	300 BERKLEY DR #S-11	MADISON, TN	37115
VOTE, ROBIN	TV WRITER	8955 BEVERLY BLVD	LOS ANGELES, CA	90048
VOTE, ROBIN	TV WRITER	8955 BEVERLY BLVD	LOS ANGELES, CA	90048
VOTH, CHARLES M	NEWS CORRESPONDENT	236 MASSACHUSETTS AVE, NE	WASHINGTON, DC	20002
VOUDOURIS, ROGER	SINGER	10100 SANTA MONICA BLVD #1600	LOS ANGELES, CA	90067
VOUTSAS, GEORGE	DIRECTOR	116 YANKEE POINT DR	CARMEL, CA	93923
VOWELL, DAVID	TV WRITER	11427 SUNSHINE TERR	STUDIO CITY, CA	91604
VOYER, LOU	TV WRITER	8955 BEVERLY BLVD	LOS ANGELES, CA	90048
VOYEUR	ROCK & ROLL GROUP	10100 SANTA MONICA BLVD #1600	LOS ANGELES, CA	90067
VOYTEK	TV DIRECTOR	12 THE VARONS #1		
		SAINT MARGARETS		
		TWICKENHAM	MIDDLESEX TW1 2AN	ENGLAND
VOZOFF, LORINNE	ACTRESS	9100 SUNSET BLVD #200	LOS ANGELES, CA	90069
VRBANCICH, E	CARTOONIST	4 PHYLLIS ST	DEE-WHY NSW 2099	AUSTRALIA
VRIEZELAAR, CLINT	ACTOR	305 W 45TH ST	NEW YORK, NY	10036
VROMAN, JERRY	GUITARIST	1159 PILGRAM AVE	DELTONA, FL	32725
VU, TU H	NEWS CORRESPONDENT	8101 LEE HWY	FALLS CHURCH, VA	22042
VUILLEUMIER, PIERRE	ACTOR	51 1/2 OZONE AVE	VENICE, CA	90291
VYPER	ROCK & ROLL GROUP	15 W 10TH ST #900	KANSAS CITY, MO	64105

Name	Occupation	Address	City	Zip/Country
W, MR	WRESTLER	SEE - ORNDORFF, PAUL		
		.... "MR WONDERFUL"		
W A S P	ROCK & ROLL GROUP	ICM, 40 W 57TH ST	NEW YORK, NY	10019
WACHTLER, JUNE	HARPIST	POST OFFICE BOX 131	SPRINGFIELD, VA	22150
WADDELL, H HUGH	DRUMMER	1154 W MAIN ST	HENDERSONVILLE, TN	37075
WADDELL, PATRICK	ACTOR	117 S ORCHARD DR	BURBANK, CA	91506
WADDELL, TERRY	MUSIC ARRANGER	1615 18TH AVE S	NASHVILLE, TN	37212

Name	Occupation	Address	City, State	Zip
WADE, ADAM	ACTOR-SINGER	11816 CHANDLER BLVD #11	NORTH HOLLYWOOD, CA	91607
WADE, ELVIS	SINGER	POST OFFICE BOX 22707	NASHVILLE, TN	37202
WADE, HARKER	TV PRODUCER	LARSON PRODS, 10201 W PICO BLVD	LOS ANGELES, CA	90035
WADE, JOHN THOMAS	TROMBONIST	1153 FERNBANK DR	MADISON, TN	37115
WADE, JOSEPH	NEWS CORRESPONDENT	301 "G" ST, SW	WASHINGTON, DC	20024
WADE, LINDA	ACTRESS	FELBER, 2126 N CAHUENGA BLVD	LOS ANGELES, CA	90068
WADE, MICHAEL BLAND	GUITARIST	433 ROLLING MILL RD	OLD HICKORY, TN	37138
WADE, PETE	GUITARIST	433 ROLLING MILL RD	OLD HICKORY, TN	37138
WADE, RUSSELL	ACTOR	47287 W EL DORADO DR	INDIAN WELLS, CA	92260
WADE, SALLY	SCREENWRITER	8955 BEVERLY BLVD	LOS ANGELES, CA	90048
WADE, WILLIS	SINGER-GUITARIST	POST OFFICE BOX 841	HENDERSONVILLE, TN	37075
WADER, DAVID	TV DIRECTOR	2153 N ROOSEVELT ST	ALTADENA, CA	91001
WADLEIGH, MICHAEL	FILM WRITER-DIRECTOR	DGA, 7950 SUNSET BLVD	LOS ANGELES, CA	90046
WADSWORTH	C & W GROUP	POST OFFICE BOX 25677	CHICAGO, IL	60625
WADSWORTH, CHARLES	PIANIST	TULLY HALL, 1941 BROADWAY	NEW YORK, NY	10021
WADSWORTH, L GLEN	NEWS CORRESPONDENT	529 14TH ST, NW	WASHINGTON, DC	20045
WAEGEL, JANET	ART DIRECTOR	US MAGAZINE COMPANY		
		1 DAG HAMMARSKJOLD PLAZA	NEW YORK, NY	10017
WAEKER, DUHHAINE	WRITER-PRODUCER	5030 TUJUNGA AVE	NORTH HOLLYWOOD, CA	91601
WAFFLE, JOAN	NEWS CORRESPONDENT	207 RAMSAY ALLEY	ALEXANDRIA, VA	23214
WAGERS, JILL	NEWS CORRESPONDENT	13532 VANDALIA DR	ROCKVILLE, MD	20853
WAGGONER, LYLE	ACTOR	4450 BALBOA AVE	ENCINO, CA	91316
WAGHORN, KERRY	CARICATURIST	CHRONICLE FEATURES		
		870 MARKET ST	SAN FRANCISCO, CA	94102
WAGLIN, ED	TV DIRECTOR	330 CARIBBEAN RD	KEY BISCAYNE, FL	33149
WAGMAN, ROBERT	NEWS CORRESPONDENT	8806 1ST AVE	SILVER SPRING, MD	20910
WAGMAN, SHAYNA J	WRITER	551 N GOWER ST	LOS ANGELES, CA	90004
WAGNER, ALAN CYRIL	FILM PRODUCER	950 3RD AVE	NEW YORK, NY	10022
WAGNER, BRUCE	SCREENWRITER	8955 BEVERLY BLVD	LOS ANGELES, CA	90048
WAGNER, CHUCK	ACTOR	9441 WILSHIRE BLVD #620-D	BEVERLY HILLS, CA	90210
WAGNER, DAVE	WRESTLER	POST OFFICE BOX 3859	STAMFORD, CT	06905
WAGNER, DENNIS DALE	GUITARIST	3887 SHAKER RD	FRANKLIN, OH	45005
WAGNER, ED	ACTOR	1605 N CAHUENGA BLVD #202	LOS ANGELES, CA	90068
WAGNER, FRED	CARTOONIST	TRIBUNE MEDIA SERVICES		
		64 E CONCORD ST	ORLANDO, FL	32801
WAGNER, GEORGE	FILM DIRECTOR	POST OFFICE BOX 5777	SANTA MONICA, CA	90405
WAGNER, HELEN	ACTRESS	CBS-TV, "AS THE WORLD TURNS"		
		51 W 52ND ST	NEW YORK, NY	10019
WAGNER, JACK P	ACTER-SINGER	10100 SANTA MONICA BLVD #1600	LOS ANGELES, CA	90067
WAGNER, JANE	WRITER-PRODUCER	POST OFFICE BOX 27700	LOS ANGELES, CA	90027
WAGNER, LINDSAY	ACTRESS	3371 COLDWATER CANYON AVE	NORTH HOLLYWOOD, CA	91604
WAGNER, LOU	ACTOR	8527 WONDERLAND AVE	LOS ANGELES, CA	90046
WAGNER, MADELINE D	TV WRITER	BLS & A, 800 S ROBERTSON BLVD	LOS ANGELES, CA	90025
WAGNER, MARIA	TV DIRECTOR	145 E 16TH ST	NEW YORK, NY	10003
WAGNER, MARY LOUISE	NEWS CORRESPONDENT	26 S PARK DR	ARLINGTON, VA	22204
WAGNER, MICHAEL	SCREENWRITER	8955 BEVERLY BLVD	LOS ANGELES, CA	90048
WAGNER, MICHAEL DAN	ACTOR	8961 SUNSET BLVD #B	LOS ANGELES, CA	90069
WAGNER, ROBERT	ACTOR	1500 OLD OAK RD	LOS ANGELES, CA	90077
WAGNER, ROBERT F	MAYOR	425 PARK AVE	NEW YORK, NY	10022
WAGNER, ROGER	CONDUCTOR	5930 PENFIELD AVE	WOODLAND HILLS, CA	91367
WAGNER, ROY	CINEMATOGRAPHER	21243 VENTURA BLVD #221	WOODLAND HILLS, CA	91364
WAGNER, ZACH	ACTOR	1633 VISTA DEL MAR #201	LOS ANGELES, CA	90028
WAGON, CHUCK & THE WHEELS	C & W GROUP	CMP, 5353 E FORT LOWELL RD	TUCSON, AZ	85712
WAGONER, PORTER	SINGER-SONGWRITER	POST OFFICE BOX 121089	NASHVILLE, TN	37212
WAGONER, RALPH W, JR	TV DIRECTOR	CUTTING ROOM FLOOR PRODS		
		1216 S CRESCENT	PARK RIDGE, IL	60068
WAGONHURST, ROCK	ACTOR	5134 CALENDA DR	WOODLAND HILLS, CA	91367
WAGREICH, HERBERT	DIRECTOR	9 ICHABOD LN	OSSINING, NY	10562
WAGY, NORMAN O	NEWS CORRESPONDENT	400 N CAPITOL ST, NW	WASHINGTON, DC	20001
WAHL, KEN	ACTOR	9100 WILSHIRE BLVD #517	BEVERLY HILLS, CA	90212
WAHLE, KIKKER	PIANIST	121 HAZELWOOD DR #L-122	HENDERSONVILLE, TN	37075
WAIGHER, PAUL	WRITER	2151 N BEACHWOOD DR	LOS ANGELES, CA	90068
WAIN, BEA	SINGER	BARUCH, 9955 DURANT DR #305	BEVERLY HILLS, CA	90212
WAIN, JOHN	SINGER	BMP, 732 BRANDON AVE, SW	ROANOKE, VA	24015
WAINWRIGHT, BETTY MEARS	TV WRITER-PRODUCER	8955 BEVERLY BLVD	LOS ANGELES, CA	90048
WAINWRIGHT, SUSAN M	TV DIRECTOR	750 N DEARBORN ST #3303	CHICAGO, IL	60601
WAISBREN, BRAD	ACTOR	3146 HUTTON DR	BEVERLY HILLS, CA	90210
WAISLREM, BRAD	TALENT AGENT	POST OFFICE BOX 8741	UNIVERSAL CITY, CA	91608
WAISSMAN, KENNETH	THEATER PRODUCER	1501 BROADWAY	NEW YORK, NY	10036
WAITE, RALPH	ACTOR-DIRECTOR	8060 MULHOLLAND DR	LOS ANGELES, CA	90046
WAJDA, ANDRZEJ	DIRECTOR	UL HAUKEGO 14	01-540 WARSAW	POLAND
WAKEFIELD, DAN	SCREENWRITER	939 N WETHERLY DR	LOS ANGELES, CA	90069
WAKEFIELD, FOSTER C	COMPOSER-CONDUCTOR	2828 ROWENA AVE	LOS ANGELES, CA	90039
WAKEHAM, DEBORAH	ACTRESS	9220 SUNSET BLVD #625	LOS ANGELES, CA	90069
WAKEMAN, RICK	SINGER	SUN ARTISTS, 9 HILLGATE ST	LONDON W8	ENGLAND
WALBERG, GARRY	ACTOR	7060 HOLLYWOOD BLVD #610	LOS ANGELES, CA	90028
WALBERG, PAUL L	COMPOSER-CONDUCTOR	POST OFFICE BOX 305	REDONDO BEACH, CA	90277
WALCOTT, GREGORY	ACTOR	9744 WILSHIRE BLVD #306	BEVERLY HILLS, CA	90212
WALCOTT, JOHN L	NEWS CORRESPONDENT	7905 FOXHOUND RD	MC LEAN, VA	22102
WALCUTT, JOHN	ACTOR	4265 COLFAX AVE #16	STUDIO CITY, CA	91604
WALCZAK, LEE	NEWS CORRESPONDENT	1517 RED OAK DR	SILVER SPRING, MD	20910
WALD, JEFF	TALENT AGENT	23844 MALIBU RD	MALIBU, CA	90265
WALD, MALVIN	TV WRITER-PRODUCER	4525 GREENBUSH AVE	VAN NUYS, CA	91423
WALDEN, JAMIE	GUITARIST	300 BAKERTOWN RD #5-E	ANTIOCH, TN	37013
WALDEN, JEAN HOUSTON	TV DIRECTOR	322 W 57TH ST	NEW YORK, NY	10019

WALDEN, LOIS	WRITER	ICM, 8899 BEVERLY BLVD	LOS ANGELES, CA	90048
WALDEN, NARADA MICHAEL	SINGER	POST OFFICE BOX 690	SAN FRANCISCO, CA	94101
WALDEN, ROBERT	ACTOR	3851 RHODES AVE	STUDIO, CA	91604
WALDEN, STANLEY	COMPOSER-CLARINET	ROUTE #3, BOX 438	HOPEWELL, NY	12533
WALDEN, SUSAN	ACTRESS	STONE, 1052 CAROL DR	LOS ANGELES, CA	90069
WALDER, ERNST A	ACTOR	17 MAIN ST, BRADLEY		
		NEAR SPEPTON	YORKS	ENGLAND
WALDERS, JOE	WRITER	POST OFFICE BOX 55732	VALENCIA, CA	91355
WALDHORN, GARY	ACTOR	9255 SUNSET BLVD #505	LOS ANGELES, CA	90069
WALDMAN, FRANK	SCREENWRITER	3836 MALIBU COLONY DR	MALIBU, CA	90265
WALDMAN, JULES	DIRECTOR	74 5TH AVE #2-A	NEW YORK, NY	10011
WALDMAN, LESLIE D	TV DIRECTOR	4369 BECK AVE	STUDIO CITY, CA	91604
WALDMAN, MYRON S	NEWS CORRESPONDENT	4309 DRESDEN ST	KENSINGTON, MD	20895
WALDMAN, RANDY B	CONDUCTOR	5634 CAMELLIA AVE	NORTH HOLLYWOOD, CA	91601
WALDMAN, STEVEN	NEWS CORRESPONDENT	1332 MASSACHUSETTS AVE, SE	WASHINGTON, DC	20003
WALDO, ELISABETH	COMPOSER	POST OFFICE BOX 101	NORTHRIDGE, CA	91324
WALDO, JANET	ACTRESS	15725 ROYAL OAK RD	ENCINO, CA	91316
WALDON, ROSEANNE KATON	ACTRESS-MODEL	SEE - KATON-WALDON, ROSEANNE		
WALDRON, GYNETH M	DIRECTOR	1900 AVE OF THE STARS #2270	LOS ANGELES, CA	90067
WALDROP, GIDEO	COMPOSER-CONDUCTOR	160 RIVERSIDE DR	NEW YORK, NY	10024
WALES, JIMMY	GUITARIST	ROUTE #4, QUAIL HOLLOW	COLUMBIA, TN	38401
WALK, JOE DONALD	SAXOPHONIST	318 7TH AVE, NW	DECATUR, AL	35601
WALK THE WEST	ROCK & ROLL GROUP	POST OFFICE BOX 150973	NASHVILLE, TN	37215
WALKEN, CHRISTOPHER	ACTOR	142 CEDAR RD	WILTON, CT	06897
WALKER, ALAN	CINEMATOGRAPHER	7715 SUNSET BLVD #150	LOS ANGELES, CA	90046
WALKER, ARNETIA	ACTRESS	CONTEMPORARY ARTISTS		
		132 S LASKY DR	BEVERLY HILLS, CA	90212
WALKER, BETTY	ACTRESS	3702 EUREKA DR	STUDIO CITY, CA	91604
WALKER, BILL	TV WRITER	8955 BEVERLY BLVD	LOS ANGELES, CA	90048
WALKER, BILLY	SINGER-GUITARIST	POST OFFICE BOX 618	HENDERSONVILLE, TN	37075
WALKER, CHARLES	ACTOR	8350 SANTA MONICA BLVD #206-A	LOS ANGELES, CA	90069
WALKER, CHARLES L, JR	GUITARIST	113 INLET DR	HENDERSONVILLE, TN	37075
WALKER, CHARLIE	SINGER	HOT, 306 W CHURCH ST	HORSHEHOE BEND, AR	72512
WALKER, DIANA H	PHOTOGRAPHER	3414 LOWELL ST, NW	WASHINGTON, DC	20016
WALKER, ERIC	ACTOR	6640 SUNSET BLVD #203	LOS ANGELES, CA	90028
WALKER, FIONA	ACTRESS	13 DESPARD RD	LONDON N9	ENGLAND
WALKER, FRANK W	SAXOPHONIST	306 ELMINGTON AVE	NASHVILLE, TN	37205
WALKER, JERRY JEFF	SINGER-SONGWRITER	NORTH LIGHT CONCERTS AGENCY		
		1775 BROADWAY, 7TH FLOOR	NEW YORK, NY	10019
WALKER, JIMMIE	ACTOR-COMEDIAN	9200 SUNSET BLVD #909	LOS ANGELES, CA	90069
WALKER, JOHN	ORGANIST	15 HIGH ST #621	HARTFORD, CT	06103
WALKER, JOHN H	GUITARIST	103 MAYME CT	MADISON, TN	37115
WALKER, JUNIOR & THE ALL STARS	SOUL GROUP	BROTHERS, 141 DUNBAR AVE	FORDS, NJ	08863
WALKER, KEITH	WRITER	151 S EL CAMINO DR	BEVERLY HILLS, CA	90212
WALKER, KENNETH	DIRECTOR	23147 FRESCA DR	VALENCIA, CA	91355
WALKER, LEIGH TAYLOR	ACTRESS	3575 W CAHUENGA BLVD #320	LOS ANGELES, CA	90068
WALKER, LUKE	ACTOR	6736 LAUREL CANYON BLVD #306	NORTH HOLLYWOOD, CA	91606
WALKER, MARCY	ACTRESS	KNBC-TV, "SANTA BARBARA"		
		3000 W ALAMEDA AVE	BURBANK, CA	91523
WALKER, MITCH	MUSIC ARRANGER	179 ROBINHOOD CIR	HENDERSONVILLE, TN	37075
WALKER, MORT	CARTOONIST	KING FEATURES SYNDICATE		
		235 E 45TH ST	NEW YORK, NY	10017
WALKER, NANCY	ACTRESS-DIRECTOR	9200 SUNSET BLVD #531	LOS ANGELES, CA	90069
WALKER, NICHOLAS	ACTOR	151 S EL CAMINO DR	BEVERLY HILLS, CA	90212
WALKER, PATRIC	COLUMNIST	NEWS AMERICA SYNDICATE		
		1703 KAISER AVE	IRVINE, CA	92714
WALKER, PETE	WRITER-PRODUCER	23 BENTINCK ST	LONDON W1	ENGLAND
WALKER, RAYMOND C, JR	GUITARIST	823 NESBITT LN	MADISON, TN	37115
WALKER, ROBERT E	GUITARIST	2920 MC CAMPBELL RD	NASHVILLE, TN	37214
WALKER, ROBERT, JR	ACTOR	767 PASEO MIRAMAR	PACIFIC PALISADES, CA	90272
WALKER, RUDOLPH	ACTOR	17 RICHMOND, RICHMOND	SURREY TW10 6RE	ENGLAND
WALKER, SAMUEL A	NEWS CORRESPONDENT	1301 PENNSYLVANIA AVE, NW	WASHINGTON, DC	20004
WALKER, SAMUEL R	NEWS CORRESPONDENT	3323 VALLEY DR	ALEXANDRIA, VA	22302
WALKER, SANDRA	MEZZO-SOPRANO	CAMI, 165 W 57TH ST	NEW YORK, NY	10019
WALKER, SARAH	MEZZO-SOPRANO	SOFFER, 130 W 56TH ST	NEW YORK, NY	10019
WALKER, SHIRLEY A	COMPOSER-CONDUCTOR	8509 CAPISTRANO AVE	CANOGA PARK, CA	91304
WALKER, STANLEY P	FILM PRODUCER	SWA, 147 VICTORIA RD	LEEDS LS6 1DU	ENGLAND
WALKER, SUSAN F	TV WRITER	8955 BEVERLY BLVD	LOS ANGELES, CA	90048
WALKER, THOMAS M	NEWS CORRESPONDENT	535 S FAIRFAX ST	ALEXANDRIA, VA	22314
WALKER, TONJA	ACTRESS	9255 SUNSET BLVD #603	LOS ANGELES, CA	90069
WALKER, TRICIA	MUSIC ARRANGER	2101 BELMONT BLVD #D-3	NASHVILLE, TN	37212
WALKER, TURNLEY	WRITER	3671 ALOMAR DR	VAN NUYS, CA	91403
WALKER, WENDY A	NEWS CORRESPONDENT	3100 DUMBARTON ST, NW	WASHINGTON, DC	20007
WALKER, WILLIAM ALFRED	MUSIC ARRANGER	POST OFFICE BOX 22224	NASHVILLE, TN	37202
WALKER, WILLIAM F	ACTOR-WRITER	350 S FULLER AVE #6-D	LOS ANGELES, CA	90036
WALKER, WILLIAM F	BASSO-BARITONE	431 S DEARBORN ST #1504	CHICAGO, IL	60605
WALKER, ZENA	ACTRESS	FRENCH'S, 26 BINNEY ST	LONDON W1	ENGLAND
WALL, ALISA J	MUSICAN	POST OFFICE BOX 491	MOUNTAIN VIEW, AR	72560
WALL, ERIC	DIRECTOR	4901 BEVERLY BLVD #24	LOS ANGELES, CA	90004
WALL, MICHAEL B	TV DIRECTOR	190 N STATE ST	CHICAGO, IL	60601
WALL STREET	ROCK & ROLL GROUP	9777 HARWIN ST #101	HOUSTON, TX	77036
WALLABY JACK	ACCORDIONIST	ROUTE #1, BOX 104	HOLLADAY, TN	38341
WALLACE, AMY	NEWS CORRESPONDENT	1418 "S" ST, NW	WASHINGTON, DC	20009
WALLACE, ART	ACTOR	9 E 96TH ST	NEW YORK, NY	10028
WALLACE, BILLY	ACTOR	1607 N EL CENTRO #22	HOLLYWOOD, CA	90028

JEAN WALLACE

ELI WALLACH

BURT WARD

RACHEL WARD

JACK WARDEN

FRAN WARREN

RUTH WARRICK

DONNA WASHINGTON

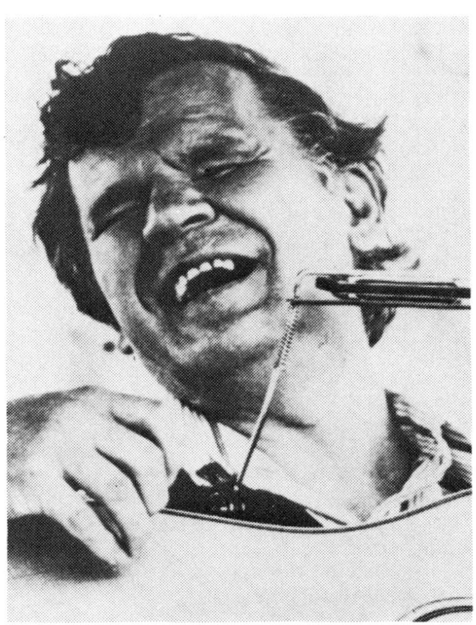
DOC WATSON

Name	Occupation	Address	City	Zip
WALLACE, BRIAN P	NEWS CORRESPONDENT	6308 9TH ST, NW	WASHINGTON, DC	20011
WALLACE, CAROL	WRITER-EDITOR	PEOPLE/TIME & LIFE BLDG		
		ROCKEFELLER CENTER	NEW YORK, NY	10020
WALLACE, CHRIS	ACTOR	257 1/2 S ELM DR	BEVERLY HILLS, CA	90212
WALLACE, DEE	ACTRESS	SEE - STONE, DEE WALLACE		
WALLACE, EARL W	SCREENWRITER	445 N BEDFORD DR #PH	BEVERLY HILLS, CA	90210
WALLACE, GEORGE	COMEDIAN	151 S EL CAMINO DR	BEVERLY HILLS, CA	90212
WALLACE, GEORGE	SINGER	9255 SUNSET BLVD #526	LOS ANGELES, CA	90069
WALLACE, GEORGE D	ACTOR	1766 N ORANGE GROVE AVE	LOS ANGELES, CA	90046
WALLACE, HEDGER	ACTOR	40 HOMEFIELD RD	LONDON W4	ENGLAND
WALLACE, HENDERSON R, III	NEWS CORRESPONDENT	6350 CROSS ST	MC LEAN, VA	22101
WALLACE, IAN	SINGER-ACTOR	GREENE, 91 REGENT ST	LONDON WIR 8RU	ENGLAND
WALLACE, IRVIN	DIRECTOR	5629 BABBIT AVE	ENCINO, CA	91316
WALLACE, IRVING	WRITER	308 S BRISTOL AVE	LOS ANGELES, CA	90049
WALLACE, JAMES N	NEWS CORRESPONDENT	9606 PODIUM DR	VIENNA, VA	22180
WALLACE, JANE	ACTRESS	113 N SAN VICENTE BLVD #202	BEVERLY HILLS, CA	90211
WALLACE, JEAN	ACTRESS	1003 WALLACE RIDGE	BEVERLY HILLS, CA	90210
WALLACE, JERRY	SINGER-COMPOSER	POST OFFICE BOX 17272	MEMPHIS, TN	38187
WALLACE, JOHN L, III	NEWS CORRESPONDENT	2139 WISCONSIN AVE, NW	WASHINGTON, DC	20007
WALLACE, KEVIN	POOL REPAIRMAN	2801 MEADOW LARK DR	SAN DIEGO, CA	92123
WALLACE, MARCIA	ACTRESS	8937 APPIAN WY	LOS ANGELES, CA	90046
WALLACE, MELISSA	MODEL	POST OFFICE BOX 7211	MOUNTAIN VIEW, CA	94043
WALLACE, MERVIN	TENOR	POST OFFICE BOX 27539	PHILADELPHIA, PA	19118
WALLACE, MIKE	BROADCAST JOURNALIST	CBS NEWS, 524 W 57TH ST	NEW YORK, NY	10019
WALLACE, RANDALL T	WRITER	4448 WORSTER AVE	STUDIO CITY, CA	91604
WALLACE, RICK	TV DIRECTOR	6041 GRACIOSA DR	LOS ANGELES, CA	90068
WALLACE, ROGER A	CONDUCTOR	7934 VANALDEN AVE	RESEDA, CA	91335
WALLACE, ROGER P	NEWS CORRESPONDENT	6180 GREENWOOD DR	FALLS CHURCH, VA	22044
WALLACE, ROYCE	ACTRESS	2442 W 18TH ST	LOS ANGELES, CA	90019
WALLACE, TOMMY LEE	FILM WRITER-DIRECTOR	POST OFFICE BOX 5617	BEVERLY HILLS, CA	90210
WALLACH, ALLAN	DRAMA CRITIC	64 LONG ST	HUNTINGTON STATION, NY	11746
WALLACH, ELI	ACTOR	90 RIVERSIDE DR	NEW YORK, NY	10024
WALLACH, GEORGE	TV DIRECTOR-PRODUCER	14 LAWRENCE ST	NEW HYDE PARK, NY	11040
WALLACH, IRA	SCREENWRITER	345 W 58TH ST	NEW YORK, NY	10019
WALLACH, JOHN P	NEWS CORRESPONDENT	2915 FOXHALL RD, NW	WASHINGTON, DC	20016
WALLAT, HANS	CONDUCTOR	PERLS, 7 W 96TH ST	NEW YORK, NY	10025
WALLEN, REBECCA BOYD	FLUTIST	2929 FERNBROOK LN	NASHVILLE, TN	37214
WALLENDA, CARLA	HIGHPOLE ACT	POST OFFICE BOX 87	WEST LEBANON, NY	12195
WALLENDA, DELILAH	HIGH WIRE ACT	HALL, 138 FROG HOLLOW RD	CHURCHVILLE, PA	18966
WALLENDA, ENRICO	HIGH WIRE ACT	HALL, 138 FROG HOLLOW RD	CHURCHVILLE, PA	18966
WALLENDA, RICKY STAR	HIGH WIRE ACT	HALL, 138 FROG HOLLOW RD	CHURCHVILLE, PA	18966
WALLENDA-ZOPPE	HIGH WIRE DUO	HALL, 138 FROG HOLLOW RD	CHURCHVILLE, PA	18966
WALLENDAS, THE GREAT	HIGH WIRE ACT	HALL, 138 FROG HOLLOW RD	CHURCHVILLE, PA	18966
WALLENGREN, ERNEST F	WRITER	231 S VALLEY ST	BURBANK, CA	91505
WALLENGREN, ERNIE	PRODUCER	CBS-MTM, 4024 RADFORD AVE	STUDIO CITY, CA	91604
WALLENSTEIN, JOSEPH B	WRITER-PRODUCER	13027 DELANO ST	VAN NUYS, CA	91401
WALLER, ALBERT C	WRITER-PRODUCER	300 E 74TH ST	NEW YORK, NY	10021
WALLER, DAVID	ACTOR	FRASER, 91 REGENT ST	LONDON W1	ENGLAND
WALLER, GRETA G	NEWS CORRESPONDENT	3133 CONNECTICUT AVE, NW	WASHINGTON, DC	20008
WALLER, KEN	BODYBUILDER	POST OFFICE BOX 212	SANTA MONICA, CA	90405
WALLER FAMILY, THE	RHYTHM & BLUES GROUP	POST OFFICE BOX 25654	RICHMOND, CA	23260
WALLERSTEIN, ROWE	DIRECTOR	2049 CENTURY PARK E #1320	LOS ANGELES, CA	90067
WALLETS, THE	ROCK & ROLL GROUP	VARIETY ARTISTS INTL, INC		
		9073 NEMO ST, 3RD FLOOR	LOS ANGELES, CA	90069
WALLEY, DEBORAH	ACTRESS	1923 OLIVERA DR	AGOURA, CA	91301
WALLEZ, JEAN-PIERRE	VIOLINIST	243 W END AVE #907	NEW YORK, NY	10023
WALLING, CHUCK	ACTOR	10845 LINDBROOK DR #3	LOS ANGELES, CA	90024
WALLING, STRATTON	ACTOR	445 PACIFIC ST	BROOKLYN, NY	11217
WALLIS, ALAN	DIRECTOR-PRODUCER	DAVIE, 37 HILL ST	LONDON W1X 8JY	ENGLAND
WALLIS, CLAUDIA	WRITER-EDITOR	TIME/TIME & LIFE BLDG		
		ROCKEFELLER CENTER	NEW YORK, NY	10020
WALLIS, DELIA	MEZZO-SOPRANO	CAMI, 165 W 57TH ST	NEW YORK, NY	10019
WALLIS, MARTHA HYER	ACTRESS-WRITER	515 S MAPLETON DR	LOS ANGELES, CA	90024
WALLIS, SHANI	ACTRESS	LIGHT, 113 N ROBERTSON BLVD	LOS ANGELES, CA	90048
WALLS, BOBBIE JOE	PIANIST	1555 NE 125 ST #6	NORTH MIAMI, FL	33161
WALLS, BYRON	SINGER	BIRDSONG, 2714 WESTWOOD DR	NASHVILLE, TN	37204
WALLS, ELIZABETH D	NEWS CORRESPONDENT	3025 ONTARIO RD, NW	WASHINGTON, DC	20009
WALLS, GEORGE	DIRECTOR	POST OFFICE BOX 523	DESERT HOT SPRINGS, CA	92240
WALN, RICK	ACTOR	2863 DURAND DR	HOLLYWOOD, CA	90068
WALSH, ADDIE	TV WRITER	555 W 57TH ST #1230	NEW YORK, NY	10019
WALSH, ALAN	TV DIRECTOR-PRODUCER	74 NEWMAN ST	LONDON W1	ENGLAND
WALSH, BOB	TV DIRECTOR-PRODUCER	1223 FILSON WY	PITTSBURGH, PA	15212
WALSH, DIANE	PIANIST	POST OFFICE BOX U	REDDING, CT	06875
WALSH, GEORGE	ACTOR	2790 STERNS ST	SIMI VALLEY, CA	93063
WALSH, HERB	CONDUCTOR	1637 N VINE ST #1006	LOS ANGELES, CA	90028
WALSH, J T	ACTOR	247 S BEVERLY DR #102	BEVERLY HILLS, CA	90210
WALSH, JAMES	DIRECTOR	HAVILAND HOLLOW RD	PATTERSON, NY	12563
WALSH, JAMES BARRY	PIANIST	1301 NEELYS BEND RD #G-57	MADISON, TN	37115
WALSH, JOE	SINGER-GUITARIST	9044 MELROSE AVE #306	LOS ANGELES, CA	90069
WALSH, JOHN	ACTOR	8075 W 3RD ST #303	LOS ANGELES, CA	90048
WALSH, JOHN J	TV WRITER	8955 BEVERLY BLVD	LOS ANGELES, CA	90048
WALSH, JOHN MATTHEW	NEWS CORRESPONDENT	708 E CAPITOL ST, NW	WASHINGTON, DC	20003
WALSH, JOSEPH P, JR	NEWS CORRESPONDENT	1755 S JEFFERSON DAVIS HWY	ARLINGTON, VA	22202
WALSH, KENNETH T	NEWS CORRESPONDENT	2547 HOLMAN AVE	SILVER SPRING, MD	20910
WALSH, LORY	ACTRESS	8485 MELROSE PL #E	LOS ANGELES, CA	90069
WALSH, M EMMET	ACTOR	POST OFFICE BOX 5617	BEVERLY HILLS, CA	90210

WALSH, MARY E	NEWS CORRESPONDENT	3528 S STAFFORD ST	ARLINGTON, VA	22206
WALSH, MAUREEN H	NEWS CORRESPONDENT	11533 LINKS DR	RESTON, VA	22090
WALSH, MICHAEL	WRITER-EDITOR	TIME/TIME & LIFE BLDG		
		ROCKEFELLER CENTER	NEW YORK, NY	10020
WALSH, PATRICK	DIRECTOR-PRODUCER	3919 W 8TH ST	LOS ANGELES, CA	90005
WALSH, RON	WRITER-PRODUCER	1211 HORN AVE #702	LOS ANGELES, CA	90069
WALSH, SEAN FALLON	ACTOR	8350 SANTA MONICA BLVD #206	LOS ANGELES, CA	90069
WALSH, SHELLY	FASHION DESIGNER	MODA CORPORATION, 65 DENSLEY	TORONTO, ONT M6M 2P8	CANADA
WALSTON, RAY	ACTOR	423 REXFORD DR #205	BEVERLY HILLS, CA	90212
WALTER, DOUGLAS E	CONDUCTOR	8312 KITTYHAWK AVE	LOS ANGELES, CA	90045
WALTER, E V	COMPOSER	15243 S PURDUE AVE	GARDENA, CA	90249
WALTER, JESSICA	ACTRESS	10530 STRATHMORE DR	LOS ANGELES, CA	90024
WALTER, JOHN W	NEWS EDITOR	POST OFFICE BOX 500	WASHINGTON, DC	20044
WALTER, PERLA	ACTRESS	8230 BEVERLY BLVD #23	LOS ANGELES, CA	90048
WALTER, RICHARD F	WRITER	2127 VESTAL AVE	LOS ANGELES, CA	90026
WALTER, TRACEY	ACTOR	8807 BURTON WY #12	LOS ANGELES, CA	90048
WALTER, UTE	MEZZO-SOPRANO	CAMI, 165 W 57TH ST	NEW YORK, NY	10019
WALTERS, BARBARA	NEWS JOURNALIST	33 W 60TH ST	NEW YORK, NY	10023
WALTERS, CASEY	ACTOR	783 8TH AVE	NEW YORK, NY	10036
WALTERS, GEORGE T	COMPOSER	419 N ORANGE AVE	MONTEREY PARK, CA	91754
WALTERS, HUGH	ACTOR	15 CHRISTCHURCH AVE	LONDON NW6 7QP	ENGLAND
WALTERS, JAMES D	GUITARIST	134 LAKESHORE DR	BELLINGHAM, MA	02019
WALTERS, JAMES M	FILM DIRECTOR	POST OFFICE BOX 8504	UNIVERSAL CITY, CA	91608
WALTERS, JULIE	ACTRESS	SARABAND ASSOCIATES AGENCY		
		153 PETHERTON RD, HIGHBURY	LONDON N5	ENGLAND
WALTERS, LAURIE	ACTRESS	21241 VENTURA BLVD #188	WOODLAND HILLS, CA	91364
WALTERS, MARK	VIDEO EDITOR	ENTERTAINMENT TONIGHT		
		PARAMOUNT TELEVISION		
		5555 MELROSE AVE	LOS ANGELES, CA	90038
WALTERS, NOEL	GUITARIST	124 HAVEN ST	HENDERSONVILLE, TN	37075
WALTERS, NOLAN	NEWS CORRESPONDENT	8 E OAK ST #A	ALEXANDRIA, VA	22308
WALTERS, NORBY	TALENT AGENT	200 W 51ST ST #1400	NEW YORK, NY	10019
WALTERS, ROBERT M	NEWS CORRESPONDENT	3550 CHESAPEAKE ST, NW	WASHINGTON, DC	20008
WALTERS, TERESA	PIANIST	KAY, 58 W 58TH ST	NEW YORK, NY	10019
WALTERS, THORLEY	ACTOR	808 KEYES HOUSE, DOLPHIN SQ	LONDON SW1	ENGLAND
WALTERS, VINCENT C	DIRECTOR	DGA, 110 W 57TH ST	NEW YORK, NY	10019
WALTHER, GERALDINE	VIOLIST	1182 MARKET ST #311	SAN FRANCISCO, CA	94102
WALTHER, UTE	MEZZO-SOPRANO	MARIEDL ANDERS ARTISTS MGMT		
		535 EL CAMINO DEL MAR ST	SAN FRANCISCO, CA	94121
WALTON, FREDERICK	DIRECTOR	2420 DETOUR DR	LOS ANGELES, CA	90068
WALTON, GLADYS	ACTRESS	HERBEL, 225 MAIN ST	MORRO BAY, CA	93442
WALTON, JEFF	WRESTLING CORRES	WORLD WRESTLING FEDERATION		
		TITAN SPORTS PUBLICATIONS		
		1055 SUMMER ST	STAMFORD, CT	06905
WALTON, JESS	ACTRESS	9000 SUNSET BLVD #801	LOS ANGELES, CA	90069
WALTON, KIP	TV DIRECTOR	11019 WRIGHTWOOD LN	STUDIO CITY, CA	91604
WALTON, SUNNI	ACTRESS	6612 CANTALOUPE AVE	VAN NUYS, CA	91405
WALTRIP, KIM	ACTRESS	9230 OLYMPIC BLVD #203	BEVERLY HILLS, CA	90212
WALWIN, KENT	DIRECTOR-PRODUCER	YELLOWBILL, 11 CROSS KEYS CLOSE	LONDON W1M 5FY	ENGLAND
WAMBAUGH, JOSEPH	NOVELIST	PERIGORD PRESS COMPANY		
		WILLIAM MORROW & CO		
		105 MADISON AVE	NEW YORK, NY	10016
WANAMAKER, EDITH	ACTRESS	8721 SUNSET BLVD #200	LOS ANGELES, CA	90069
WANAMAKER, SAM	ACTOR-DIRECTOR	PLAYHOUSE, 40 BANKSIDE	LONDON SE1	ENGLAND
WANAMAKER, ZOE	ACTRESS	CONWAY, EAGLE HOUSE		
		109 JERMYN ST	LONDON SW1	ENGLAND
WANDS, RANDOLPH H	TV DIRECTOR	64 KENSINGTON RD	BRONXVILLE, NY	10708
WANG, INGRID	ACTRESS	8235 SANTA MONICA BLVD #202	LOS ANGELES, CA	90046
WANG, JACK C	NEWS CORRESPONDENT	6161 EDSALL RD #1504	ALEXANDRIA, VA	22304
WANNBERG, KENNETH	MUSIC ED-COMP	10738 MOLONY RD	CULVER CITY, CA	90230
WANSLEY, JOYCE	WRITER-EDITOR	PEOPLE/TIME & LIFE BLDG		
		ROCKEFELLER CENTER	NEW YORK, NY	10020
WAPNER, PHYLLIS	TV WRITER	8955 BEVERLY BLVD	LOS ANGELES, CA	90048
WAR	ROCK-SOUL GROUP	8306 WILSHIRE BLVD #789	BEVERLY HILLS, CA	90211
WARBECK, DAVID	ACTOR	ICM, 388-396 OXFORD ST	LONDON W1	ENGLAND
WARD, AL C	TV WRITER-DIRECTOR	ALFA PRODUCTIONS, MGM STUDIOS		
		10202 W WADHINGTON BLVD	CULVER CITY, CA	90230
WARD, ANITA	SINGER	200 W 51ST ST #1410	NEW YORK, NY	10019
WARD, B J	ACTRESS	8322 BEVERLY BLVD #202	LOS ANGELES, CA	90048
WARD, BRUCE A	WRITER	2324 OCEAN PARK BLVD #B	SANTA MONICA, CA	90405
WARD, BURT	ACTOR	113-A ALTA LOMA RD #331	LOS ANGELES, CA	90069
WARD, DAVID	FILM WRITER-DIRECTOR	246 21ST ST	SANTA MONICA, CA	90402
WARD, DAVID P	COMPOSER	5619 AUCKLAND AVE	NORTH HOLLYWOOD, CA	91601
WARD, DICKSON	TV DIRECTOR-PRODUCER	710 WESTMOUNT DR	LOS ANGELES, CA	90069
WARD, DOUGLAS	ACTOR-PLAYWRIGHT	AEA, 165 W 46TH ST	NEW YORK, NY	10036
WARD, EDMUND	SCREENWRITER	FAIRVIEW, FITZWILLIAM RD		
		WICKLOW	EIRE	ENGLAND
WARD, FRED	ACTOR	211 S BEVERLY DR #201	BEVERLY HILLS, CA	90212
WARD, FRED	PHOTOGRAPHER	7106 SAUNDERS CT	BETHESDA, MD	20817
WARD, JACKY	SINGER	54 MUSIC SQUARE E #300	NASHVILLE, TN	37203
WARD, JANET	ACTRESS	43 W 73RD ST	NEW YORK, NY	10023
WARD, JANIS	ACTRESS	329 N WETHERLY DR #205	BEVERLY HILLS, CA	90211
WARD, JOHN	TV DIRECTOR	6933 CAMROSE DR	HOLLYWOOD, CA	90068
WARD, JOHN D	DIRECTOR	DGA, 110 W 57TH ST	NEW YORK, NY	10019
WARD, JON PARKER	DIRECTOR	DGA, 7950 SUNSET BLVD	LOS ANGELES, CA	90046

Name	Occupation	Address	City	Zip
WARD, JONATHAN	WRITER-NEWS CORRES	CBS NEWS, 2020 "M" ST, NW	WASHINGTON, DC	20036
WARD, KELLY	ACTOR	19338 ARCHWOOD ST	RESEDA, CA	91335
WARD, LALLA	ACTRESS	LONDON MANAGEMENT, LTD		
		235-241 REGENT ST	LONDON W1A 2JT	ENGLAND
WARD, LYMAN	ACTOR	1901 AVE OF THE STARS #840	LOS ANGELES, CA	90067
WARD, MARY B	ACTRESS	ABC-TV, "ONE LIFE TO LIVE"		
		1330 AVE OF THE AMERICAS	NEW YORK, NY	10019
WARD, MICHAEL	ACTOR	77-A RANDOLPH AVE	LONDON W9 1DW	ENGLAND
WARD, PHILIP SCOTT	TV DIRECTOR	2015 PHEASANT HILL RD	LANSDALE, PA	19446
WARD, PHYLLIS J	DIRECTOR	20 8TH ST, SE	WASHINGTON, DC	20003
WARD, RACHEL	ACTRESS	10100 SANTA MONICA BLVD #1600	LOS ANGELES, CA	90067
WARD, RICHARD D	GUITARIST	197 TOWNSHIP DR	HENDERSONVILLE, TN	37075
WARD, ROBERT M	SCREENWRITER	555 W 57TH ST #1230	NEW YORK, NY	10019
WARD, ROBIN	REPORTER	TIME & PEOPLE MAGAZINE		
		TIME & LIFE BUILDING		
		ROCKEFELLER CENTER	NEW YORK, NY	10020
WARD, RUSSELL H	NEWS CORRESPONDENT	1333 "H" ST, NW	WASHINGTON, DC	20005
WARD, SAM	ILLUSTRATOR	POST OFFICE BOX 500	WASHINGTON, DC	20044
WARD, SANDY	ACTOR	3800 BARHAM BLVD #303	LOS ANGELES, CA	90068
WARD, SELA	ACTRESS	ICM, 8899 BEVERLY BLVD	LOS ANGELES, CA	90048
WARD, SKIP	ACTOR	POST OFFICE BOX 755	BEVERLY HILLS, CA	90213
WARD, SKIP	PRODUCER	WARNER BROS, 4000 WARNER BLVD	BURBANK, CA	91522
WARD, WALLY	ACTOR	6430 SUNSET BLVD #1203	LOS ANGELES, CA	90028
WARD, WILLIAM	ACTOR	FELBER, 2126 N CAHUENGA BLVD	LOS ANGELES, CA	90068
WARD-GUIDRY, ANDREA M	NEWS CORRESPONDENT	400 N CAPITOL ST, NW	WASHINGTON, DC	20001
WARDA, ARNE	ACTOR	147 S ALMONT DR	BEVERLY HILLS, CA	90211
WARDELL, JOHN	ACTOR	165 W 46TH ST #710	NEW YORK, NY	10036
WARDELL, STEPHEN R	TV WRITER	555 W 57TH ST #1230	NEW YORK, NY	10019
WARDEN, DON	GUITARIST	POST OFFICE BOX 3065	BRENTWOOD, TN	37027
WARDEN, HUGH	ACTOR	8961 SUNSET BLVD #B	LOS ANGELES, CA	90069
WARDEN, JACK	ACTOR	23604 MALIBU COLONY DR	MALIBU, CA	90265
WARDEN, VERONICA FREDRICKS	ACTRESS	POST OFFICE BOX 68	SIERRA MADRE, CA	91024
WARE, CLYDE	WRITER-PRODUCER	1252 N LAUREL AVE #B	HOLLYWOOD, CA	90046
WARE, HERTA	ACTRESS	POST OFFICE BOX 151	TOPANGA CANYON, CA	90290
WARE, JAMES	ACTOR	19-C JOHN SPENCER SQ		
		CANONBURY	LONDON N1 2LZ	ENGLAND
WARE, KOKO B	WRESTLER	POST OFFICE BOX 3859	STAMFORD, CT	06905
WARE, PETER	COMPOSER	LIEBERMAN, 11 RIVERSIDE DR	NEW YORK, NY	10023
WARE, SUSAN	WRITER	4375 CAMELLIA AVE	STUDIO CITY, CA	91604
WARE, WALLACE	TV WRITER	8955 BEVERLY BLVD	LOS ANGELES, CA	90048
WARFIELD, KENNETH J	COMPOSER	4627 W 18TH ST	LOS ANGELES, CA	90019
WARFIELD, MARSHA	COMEDIENNE	6310 SAN VICENTE BLVD #407	LOS ANGELES, CA	90048
WARFIELD, POLLY	FILM CRITIC	DRAMA-LOGUE, 1456 N GORDON ST	HOLLYWOOD, CA	90028
WARFIELD, SANDRA	MEZZO-SOPRANO	CAMI, 165 W 57TH ST	NEW YORK, NY	10019
WARFIELD, WILLIAM	ACTOR-SINGER	706 PHOENIX DR	CHAMPAIGN, IL	61820
WARGA, WAYNE	TV WRITER	15320 KINGSWOOD LN	SHERMAN OAKS, CA	91403
WARHIT, DOUGLAS	ACTOR	1800 CAMDEN AVE #210	LOS ANGELES, CA	90025
WARINER, STEVE	SINGER-GUITARIST	DON LIGHT, 1100 17TH AVE S	NASHVILLE, TN	37212
WARINER, TERRY DALE	GUITARIST	ROUTE #3, BOX 290	RUSSELL SPRINGS, KY	42642
WARING, DEREK	ACTOR	BROWNE, 13 SAINT MARTINS RD	LONDON SW9	ENGLAND
WARING, RICHARD	TV WRITER	17 CHESTER CLOSE, BARNES	LONDON SW13	ENGLAND
WARK, MARTIN	WRITER	4169 VIA MARINA #214	MARINA DEL REY, CA	90292
WARLOCK	ROCK & ROLL GROUP	POLYGRAM RECORDS, 810 7TH AVE	NEW YORK, NY	10019
WARLOCK, BILLY	ACTOR	KNBC-TV, "DAYS OF OUR LIVES"		
		3000 W ALAMEDA AVE	BURBANK, CA	91523
WARLORD	ROCK & ROLL GROUP	POST OFFICE BOX 2896	TORRANCE, CA	90509
WARLORD, THE	WRESTLER	NATIONAL WRESTLING ALLIANCE		
		JIM CROCKETT PROMOTIONS		
		421 BRIARBEND DR	CHARLOTTE, NC	28209
WARNE, GARY	WRITER	14144 VENTURA BLVD #200	SHERMAN OAKS, CA	91423
WARNER, BYRON H, JR	GUITARIST	863 HIGHLAND CREST DR	NASHVILLE, TN	37205
WARNER, CHARLES E	PHOTOJOURNALIST	8002 DANIEL DR	FORESTVILLE, MD	20028
WARNER, CHERYL K	SINGER	NAOMI HATCHER MANAGEMENT		
		4601 BARKBRIDGE CT	CHESTERFIELD, VA	23832
WARNER, CRAIG	NEWS CORRESPONDENT	1755 S JEFFERSON DAVIS HWY	ARLINGTON, VA	22202
WARNER, DARYL	TV WRITER	554 S SAN VICENTE BLVD #3	LOS ANGELES, CA	90048
WARNER, DAVID	ACTOR	LEADING ARTISTS, LTD		
		60 SAINT JAMES'S ST	LONDON SW1	ENGLAND
WARNER, DON	SINGER-GUITARIST	DON LIGHT, 1100 17TH AVE S	NASHVILLE, TN	37212
WARNER, FREDERICK	SCREENWRITER	PINEWOOD STUDIOS, IVER HEATH	BUCKS SLO ONH	ENGLAND
WARNER, GLENN ALLYN, JR	WRITER	3662 BARHAM BLVD #M-223	LOS ANGELES, CA	90068
WARNER, HARVEY, JR	DRUMMER	5172 HILSON RD	NASHVILLE, TN	37211
WARNER, JERRY	TV WRITER-DIRECTOR	DGA, 7950 SUNSET BLVD	HOLLYWOOD, CA	90046
WARNER, KATHLEEN	PIANIST	5172 HILSON DR	NASHVILLE, TN	37211
WARNER, LAVINIA	TV DIRECTOR-PRODUCER	9 DANEMERE ST, PUTNEY	LONDON SW15	ENGLAND
WARNER, LESLIE O	DIRECTOR	POST OFFICE BOX 653	YUCCA VALLEY, CA	92284
WARNER, MALCOLM-JAMAL	ACTOR	8230 BEVERLY BLVD #23	LOS ANGELES, CA	90048
WARNER, MARGARET G	NEWS CORRESPONDENT	1843 MINTWOOD PL, NW	WASHINGTON, DC	20009
WARNER, MARSHA	ACTRESS	5738 WILLIS AVE	VAN NUYS, CA	91411
WARNER, RICHARD	ACTOR	ESSANAY, 75 HAMMERSMITH RD	LONDON W14	ENGLAND
WARNER, RICHARD W	ART DIRECTOR	SPORTS ILLUSTRATED MAGAZINE		
		TIME & LIFE BUILDING		
		ROCKEFELLER CENTER	NEW YORK, NY	10020
WARNER, ROBERT	DIRECTOR	7 E 78TH ST	NEW YORK, NY	10021
WARNER, ROBERT E	TV DIRECTOR	7 MAIN ST	FLANDERS, NJ	07836

WANG CHUNG

Nick Feldman • Jack Hues • Darren Costin

THE WHITES

Cheryl • Buck • Sharon

Name	Occupation	Address	City/Zip
WARNER, WYNN	CONDUCTOR	13131 MINDANAO WY #1	MARINA DEL REY, CA 90292
WARNES, JENNIFER	SINGER-SONGWRITER	GARY GEORGE, 3288 BENNETT DR	LOS ANGELES, CA 90068
WARNICK, ALLAN	ACTOR	2878 HUME RD	MALIBU, CA 90265
WARNIER, STEVE	SINGER-SONGWRITER	POST OFFICE BOX 120308	NASHVILLE, TN 37212
WARNKEN, RODNEY G	WRITER	8705 WONDERLAND PARK AVE	LOS ANGELES, CA 90046
WARREN, ALBERT	NEWS CORRESPONDENT	26 W KIRKE ST	CHEVY CHASE, MD 20816
WARREN, CHARLES	WRITER-PRODUCER	1130 TOWER RD	BEVERLY HILLS, CA 90210
WARREN, DANIEL	NEWS CORRESPONDENT	4547 GRANT RD, NW	WASHINGTON, DC 20016
WARREN, DAVID H	DRUMMER	469 ROCKWOOD DR	HERMITAGE, TN 37076
WARREN, ELLEN ANNE	NEWS CORRESPONDENT	3924 LEGATION ST, NW	WASHINGTON, DC 20015
WARREN, FRAN	ACTRESS-SINGER	STEINMAN, 15 CENTRAL PARK W	NEW YORK, NY 10023
WARREN, GENE	DIRECTOR-PRODUCER	9725 HENSAL RD	BEVERLY HILLS, CA 90210
WARREN, GLORIA	SINGER	16872 BOSQUE DR	ENCINO, CA 91316
WARREN, JEFF	ACTOR	2266 1/2 COVE AVE	LOS ANGELES, CA 90069
WARREN, JENNIFER	ACTRESS	1675 OLD OAK RD	LOS ANGELES, CA 90049
WARREN, JOHN GRANVILLE	GUITARIST	POST OFFICE BOX 158	ANTIOCH, TN 37013
WARREN, JOHN P	FIDDLER	114 LEOTA DR	HENDERSONVILLE, TN 37075
WARREN, JOSEPH	ACTOR	11726 SAN VICENTE BLVD #300	LOS ANGELES, CA 90049
WARREN, KATHY	MUSICAN	910 S TENNESSEE BLVD #N-2	MURFREESBORO, TN 37130
WARREN, KELLY	MUSICAN	2204 S 6TH ST	LA MESA, TX 79331
WARREN, L D	CARTOONIST	1815 WM H TAFT RD	CINCINNATI, OH 45206
WARREN, LESLEY ANN	ACTRESS	3619 MEADVILLE	SHERMAN OAKS, CA 91403
WARREN, LUCIAN C	NEWS CORRESPONDENT	557 BACHELORS HOPE CT	ISSUE, MD 20645
WARREN, MADELINE	FILM EXECUTIVE	10313 CHEVIOT DR	LOS ANGELES, CA 90064
WARREN, MARC	TV WRITER	1888 CENTURY PARK E #1400	LOS ANGELES, CA 90067
WARREN, MARK	TV DIRECTOR	1830 OUTPOST DR	HOLLYWOOD, CA 90028
WARREN, MARY LYNN	PIANIST	POST OFFICE BOX 373	HERMITAGE, TN 37076
WARREN, MICHAEL	PRODUCER	WARNER, 1041 N FORMOSA AVE	LOS ANGELES, CA 90046
WARREN, MICHAEL	ACTOR	1141 STEARNS DR	LOS ANGELES, CA 90035
WARREN, MICHAEL	ARRANGER-CONDUCTOR	12233 LAUREL TERRACE DR	STUDIO CITY, CA 91604
WARREN, MICHAEL R	TV WRITER	8428 MELROSE PL #C	LOS ANGELES, CA 90069
WARREN, NORMAN J	FILM-TV DIRECTOR	59 SHEPHERDS BUSH RD	
		HAMMERSMITH	LONDON W6 ENGLAND
WARREN, PATRICIA	TV WRITER	6 GARFIELD RD, TWICKENHAM	MIDDLESEX TW1 3JS ENGLAND
WARREN, PAUL & EXPLORER	ROCK & ROLL GROUP	COASTAL ARTISTS AGENCY	
		8744 WILSHIRE BLVD	BEVERLY HILLS, CA 90212
WARREN, RAYMOND	CONDUCTOR	POST OFFICE BOX 131	SPRINGFIELD, VA 22150
WARREN, ROBERT	WRESTLING REFEREE	AMERICAN WRESTLING ASSOC	
		MINNEAPOLIS WRESTLING	
		10001 WAYZATA BLVD	MINNETONKA, MN 55345
WARREN, ROBERT PENN	WRITER	2495 REDDING RD	FAIRCHILD, CT 06430
WARREN, SMOKEY	SINGER	116 PRINCETON RD	LINDEN, NJ 07036
WARREN, VICKI	NEWS CORRESPONDENT	1769 "T" ST, NW	WASHINGTON, DC 20009
WARREN-GREEN, CHRISTOPHER	VIOLINIST	CAMI, 165 W 57TH ST	NEW YORK, NY 10019
WARRICK, RUTH	ACTRESS	ABRAMS ARTISTS & ASSOCIATES	
		420 MADISON AVE, 14TH FLOOR	NEW YORK, NY 10017
WARRINGTON, DON	ACTOR	ICM, 388-396 OXFORD ST	LONDON W1 ENGLAND
WARRIOR, DINGO	WRESTLER	SEE - DINGO WARRIOR	
WARRIOR, JAMES	ACTOR	LADKIN, 11 ALDWYCH	LONDON WC2 ENGLAND
WARSHOFSKY, FRED	WRITER-PRODUCER	SCIENCE COMMUNICATION	
		4 PUMPKIN HILL	WESTPORT, CT 06880
WARWICK, DAVID	TV DIRECTOR-PRODUCER	GRANADA TV CENTRE	MANCHESTER M60 9EA ENGLAND
WARWICK, DIONNE	SINGER	6464 SUNSET BLVD #1030	HOLLYWOOD, CA 90028
WARWICK, JAMES	ACTOR	74 SAINT MARYS RD	LONDON W5 ENGLAND
WARWICK, RICHARD	ACTOR	ICM, 388-396 OXFORD ST	LONDON W1 ENGLAND
WAS (NOT WAS)	ROCK & ROLL GROUP	ICM, 8899 BEVERLY BLVD	LOS ANGELES, CA 90048
WASHAM, WISNER	TV WRITER	ABC-TV, "ALL MY CHILDREN"	
		1330 AVE OF THE AMERICAS	NEW YORK, NY 10019
WASHBOURNE, MONA	ACTRESS	15-A ALBERT ST	LONDON SW7 ENGLAND
WASHBROOK, JOHNNY	ACTOR	8356 CAPISTARNO AVE	CANOGA PARK, CA 91304
WASHBURN, CHARLES C	FILM WRITER-DIRECTOR	22034 TIARA ST	WOODLAND HILLS, CA 91367
WASHBURN, DERIC	SCREENWRITER	8955 BEVERLY BLVD	LOS ANGELES, CA 90048
WASHBURN, JAMES	DIRECTOR	6921 PASEO DEL SERRA	HOLLYWOOD, CA 90068
WASHBURN, MILTON	CONDUCTOR	9782 ROYAL PALM BLVD	GARDEN GROVE, CA 92641
WASHBURN, SUSANNE	NEWS REPORTER	TIME/TIME & LIFE BLDG	
		ROCKEFELLER CENTER	NEW YORK, NY 10020
WASHINGTON, ADRIENNE T	NEWS CORRESPONDENT	NBC-TV, NEWS DEPARTMENT	
		4001 NEBRASKA AVE, NW	WASHINGTON, DC 20016
WASHINGTON, ART	WRITER-PRODUCER	1870 PACIFIC AVE #601	SAN FRANCISCO, CA 94109
WASHINGTON, CLAUDELL	BASEBALL	12 CHARLES HILL RD	ORINDA, CA 94563
WASHINGTON, DENZEL	ACTOR	4604 PLACIDIA AVE	TOLUCA LAKE, CA 91602
WASHINGTON, DONNA	SINGER	DON DANIELS, 160 PARK AVE	BELMONT SHORES, CA 90803
WASHINGTON, ELSIE B	NEWS REPORTER	TIME/TIME & LIFE BLDG	
		ROCKEFELLER CENTER	NEW YORK, NY 10020
WASHINGTON, ERVIN S	NEWS CORRESPONDENT	744 GIRARD ST, NW	WASHINGTON, DC 20001
WASHINGTON, ERWIN	TV WRITER	CONNELL, 4605 LANKERSHIM BLVD	NORTH HOLLYWOOD, CA 91602
WASHINGTON, GROVER, JR	SAXOPHONIST	ZANE MANAGEMENT AGENCY	
		700 THREE PENN CENTER PL	PHILADELPHIA, PA 19102
WASHINGTON SQUARES, THE	ROCK & ROLL GROUP	ATI, 888 7TH AVE, 21ST FLOOR	NEW YORK, NY 10106
WASS, TED	ACTOR	2002 LA BREA TERR	LOS ANGELES, CA 90046
WASSEL, JOHN S	DIRECTOR	3961 SAPPHIRE DR	ENCINO, CA 91436
WASSERMAN, ALBERT	WRITER-PRODUCER	259 W 11TH ST	NEW YORK, NY 10014
WASSERMAN, CHARLES H	DIRECTOR	326 SAN VICENTE BLVD #C	SANTA MONICA, CA 90402
WASSERMAN, DALE	PLAYWRIGHT	DWK & C, 10 E 40TH ST	NEW YORK, NY 10016
WASSERMAN, LEW	FILM EXECUTIVE	911 N FOOTHILL RD	BEVERLY HILLS, CA 90210

WASSERMAN, WAYNE ROGER	ACTOR	11548 MAGNOLIA BLVD #155	NORTH HOLLYWOOD, CA	91601
WASSON, CRAIG	ACTOR	50 W 77TH ST #5-L	NEW YORK, NY	10024
WATANABE, GEDDE	ACTOR	10351 SANTA MONICA BLVD #211	LOS ANGELES, CA	90025
WATANABE, SADAO	MUSICAN	THE WILLIAM MORRIS AGENCY		
		1350 AVE OF THE AMERICAS	NEW YORK, NY	10019
WATANABE, YOKO	SOPRANO	CAMI, 165 W 57TH ST	NEW YORK, NY	10019
WATER, DENNIS	ACTOR	ICM, 388-396 OXFORD ST	LONDON	ENGLAND
WATERBOYS, THE	ROCK & ROLL GROUP	3 MONMOUTH PL		
		OFF MAMMOUTH RD	LONDON W2	ENGLAND
WATERFIELD, LARRY	NEWS CORRESPONDENT	8212 SPRINGFIELD VILLAGE DR	SPRINGFIELD, VA	22152
WATERFRONT	SINGER	BROTHERS, 141 DUNBAR AVE	FORDS, NJ	08863
WATERHOUSE, KEITH	TV WRITER	29 KENWAY RD	LONDON SW5	ENGLAND
WATERHOUSE, MATTHEW	ACTOR	JOHN MAHONEY MANAGEMENT		
		30 CHALFONT CT, BAKER ST	LONDON NW1	ENGLAND
WATERMAN, BRUCE	MUSICAN	209 LONDON LN	FRANKLIN, TN	37064
WATERMAN, DENNIS	ACTOR	ICM, 388-396 OXFORD ST	LONDON W1	ENGLAND
WATERMAN, WILLARD	ACTOR	10 E 44TH ST #700	NEW YORK, NY	10017
WATERS, ANDRE	ACTOR	807 N JUNE ST	LOS ANGELES, CA	90038
WATERS, BUNNY	ACTRESS	GREEN, 903 N BEDFORD DR	BEVERLY HILLS, CA	90210
WATERS, DONALD T	NEWS CORRESPONDENT	2300 PIMMIT DR, NW	WASHINGTON, DC	22043
WATERS, E S	TV WRITER	31537 VICTORIA POINT RD	MALIBU, CA	90265
WATERS, JOE & THE APPALACHIAN B	C & W GROUP	455 MASSIEVILLE RD #K	CHILICOTHE, OH	45601
WATERS, JOHN	WRITER	THE NATIONAL LAMPOON		
		635 MADISON AVE	NEW YORK, NY	10022
WATERS, LILA	ACTRESS	6464 GAYNOR AVE	VAN NUYS, CA	91406
WATERS, MARLON	ACTOR	20027 ENSLOW DR	CARSON, CA	90746
WATERS, SPURGIN M	NEWS CORRESPONDENT	1755 S JEFFERSON DAVIS HWY	ARLINGTON, VA	22202
WATERS, WILLIE ANTHONY	CONDUCTOR	225 W 34TH ST #1012	NEW YORK, NY	10001
WATERSTON, SAM	ACTRESS	RURAL ROUTE BOX 197, EAST ST	WEST CORNWALL, CT	06796
WATFORD, GWEN	ACTRESS	MILLER, 82 BROOM PARK		
		TEDDINGTON	SURREY	ENGLAND
WATKINS, BEVERLY T	NEWS CORRESPONDENT	2950 VAN NESS ST, NW	WASHINGTON, DC	20008
WATKINS, BRUCE	MUSICAN	110 WINDING WAR DR	HENDERSONVILLE, TN	37075
WATKINS, CARLENE	ACTRESS	15760 VENTURA BLVD #1730	ENCINO, CA	91436
WATKINS, JAMES P	GUITARIST	4007 KINGS LN	NASHVILLE, TN	37218
WATKINS, JOHN D	NEWS CORRESPONDENT	4646 40TH ST, NW	WASHINGTON, DC	20016
WATKINS, LAMAR	GUITARIST	MADISON SQ APARTMENTS #H-21	MADISON, TN	37115
WATKINS, MACK A	GUITARIST	POST OFFICE BOX 1345	HENDERSONVILLE, TN	37075
WATKINS, MARY	PIANIST	REDWOOD RECORDS COMPANY		
		476 W MAC ARTHUR BLVD	OAKLAND, CA	94609
WATKINS, RICHARD D	PHOTOGRAPHER	2826 SHAWN LEIGH DR	VIENNA, VA	22180
WATKINS, ROBIN RENEE	ACTRESS	POST OFFICE BOX 5617	BEVERLY HILLS, CA	90210
WATKINS, SARA	OBOIST	CAMI, 165 W 57TH ST	NEW YORK, NY	10019
WATKINS, TOM	TALENT AGENT	MASSIVE, 47-B WELBECK ST	LONDON W1	ENGLAND
WATKINS, WILLIAM	DIRECTOR	7038 WHITAKER AVE	VAN NUYS, CA	91406
WATKINSON, CAROLYN	MEZZO-SOPRANO	SOFFER, 130 W 56TH ST	NEW YORK, NY	10019
WATLING, DILYS	ACTRESS	LONDON MANAGEMENT, LTD		
		235-241 REGENT ST	LONDON W1A 2JT	ENGLAND
WATRUD, DONALD K, JR	NEWS CORRESPONDENT	5965 POWELLS LANDING RD	BURKE, VA	22015
WATSON, ALBERTA	ACTRESS	10100 SANTA MONICA BLVD #1600	LOS ANGELES, CA	90067
WATSON, ALEX NOEL	CARTOONIST	POST OFFICE BOX 4203	NEW YORK, NY	10017
WATSON, BILL	ACTOR	8484 WILSHIRE BLVD #235	BEVERLY HILLS, CA	90211
WATSON, BOBBY & CURTIS LUNDY	JAZZ DUO	HOFFER, 233 1/2 E 48TH ST	NEW YORK, NY	10017
WATSON, BOBS	ACTOR	29250 PIPING ROCK RD	SUN CITY, CA	92381
WATSON, DOC	SINGER-GUITARIST	FOLKLORE, 1671 APPIAN WY	SANTA MONICA, CA	90401
WATSON, DOUGLASS	ACTOR	345 E 57TH ST	NEW YORK, NY	10022
WATSON, GARRY A	ACTOR	608 N CATALINA ST	BURBANK, CA	91505
WATSON, GENE	SINGER	POST OFFICE BOX 22419	NASHVILLE, TN	37202
WATSON, JACK	ACTOR	JOSEPH, 78 NEW BOND ST	LONDON	ENGLAND
WATSON, JAMES A, JR	ACTOR-WRITER	5738 BURNET AVE	VAN NUYS, CA	91411
WATSON, JEROME R	NEWS CORRESPONDENT	5803 NAMAKAGA RD	BETHESDA, MD	20816
WATSON, JOHN	TV DIRECTOR	1915 COMSTOCK AVE	LOS ANGELES, CA	90025
WATSON, JOHNNY "GUITAR"	SINGER-GUITARIST	PDQ DIRECTIONS AGENCY		
		1474 N KINGS RD	LOS ANGELES, CA	90069
WATSON, LEON "LOUIE," JR	GUITARIST	110 GENERAL JACKSON LN	HERMITAGE, TN	37076
WATSON, MILLS	ACTOR	2824 DELL AVE	VENICE, CA	90291
WATSON, MORAY	ACTOR	UNDERWOOD HOUSE, ETCHINGHAM	EAST SUSSEX	ENGLAND
WATSON, PAUL	TV WRITER-DIRECTOR	103 GRANDISON RD	LONDON SW11	ENGLAND
WATSON, RICARDO	PHOTOGRAPHER	1718 CORCORAN ST, NW	WASHINGTON, DC	20009
WATSON, RICHARD	DRUMMER	1612 18TH AVE S #D	NASHVILLE, TN	37212
WATSON, SUSAN	ACTRESS	12725 VENTURA BLVD #E	STUDIO CITY, CA	91604
WATSON, THOMAS C	NEWS CORRESPONDENT	1640 19TH ST, NW	WASHINGTON, DC	20009
WATSON, WILLIAM	TENOR	431 S DEARBORN ST #1504	CHICAGO, IL	60605
WATSON, WILLIAM	ACTOR	STONE, 1052 CAROL DR	LOS ANGELES, CA	90069
WATT, BILLIE LOU	ACTRESS	6 W 77TH ST	NEW YORK, NY	10024
WATT, CHRISTOPHER	DIRECTOR	DGA, 7950 SUNSET BLVD	LOS ANGELES, CA	90046
WATT, JEREMY	FILM PRODUCER	KENDON, 8 BERWICK ST	LONDON W1	ENGLAND
WATTAM, ROGER	OBOIST	5831 PRESCOTT DR	BATON ROUGE, LA	70805
WATTER, JOHN C	ACTOR	80 S BALDWIN AVE	SIERRA MADRE, CA	91024
WATTERS, MARK E	COMPOSER-CONDUCTOR	415 BEIRUT AVE	PACIFIC PALISADES, CA	90272
WATTERS, SUSAN	NEWS CORRESPONDENT	3212 38TH ST, NW	WASHINGTON, DC	20016
WATTERSON, BILL	CARTOONIST	UNIVERSAL PRESS SYNDICATE		
		4900 MAIN ST, 9TH FLOOR	KANSAS CITY, MO	62114
WATTES, TOMAS G	ACTOR	ABC-TV, "ALL MY CHILDREN"		
		1330 AVE OF THE AMERICAS	NEW YORK, NY	10019

WATTS, CAROLINE	MODEL	FORD MODEL AGENCY		
		344 E 59TH ST	NEW YORK, NY	10022
WATTS, CHARLIE	DRUMMER	HALSDON HOUSE, NEAR BARNSTABLE	DEVON	ENGLAND
WATTS, ERNIE	SAXOPHONIST	KURLAND, 173 BRIGHTON AVE	BOSTON, MA	02134
WATTS, ERNIE	SINGER	7250 BEVERLY BLVD #207	LOS ANGELES, CA	90036
WATTS, HEATHER	BALLERINA	NEW YORK CITY BALLET		
		STATE THEATER		
		LINCOLN CENTER	NEW YORK, NY	10023
WATTS, KEITH	ACTOR	2462 VALENTINE AVE #51	BRONX, NY	10458
WATTS, MEL	DRUMMER	4801 NEBRASKA AVE	NASHVILLE, TN	37209
WATTS, ROBERT	FILM PRODUCER	HEATH, PARAMOUNT HOUSE		
		162-170 WARDOUR ST	LONDON W1V 4AB	ENGLAND
WATTS, ROBERT LEE	DRUMMER	711 VECUNA RD	ATLANTA BEACH, FL	32233
WATTS, ROGER PHILIP	PHOTOGRAPHER	1318 "A" ST, SE	WASHINGTON, DC	20003
WATTS, TALMAGE M	MUSICAN	235 37TH ST E #G-35	TUSCALOOSA, AL	35401
WATTS, TONY	FILM CRITIC	MEDIA TECHNIQUES, 112 WOODHILL	LONDON SE18 5JL	ENGLAND
WAUGH, FRED	STUNTMAN	33231 CYN QUAIL TRAIL	SAUGUS, CA	91350
WAUTERS, MELLICENT	ACTRESS	LEONETTI, 6526 SUNSET BLVD	HOLLYWOOD, CA	90028
WAX	SOUL-DISCO GROUP	DANCER PRODUCTIONS		
		1810 CALVERT ST, NW	WASHINGTON, DC	20009
WAXMAN, AL	ACTOR	211 S BEVERLY DR #201	BEVERLY HILLS, CA	90212
WAXMAN, MARK	DIRECTOR-PRODUCER	9725 CRESTA DR	LOS ANGELES, CA	90035
WAY, ANN	ACTRESS	PLANT & FROGGATT, LTD		
		JULIAN HOUSE		
		4 WINDMILL ST	LONDON W1	ENGLAND
WAYBORN, KRISTINA	ACTRESS-MODEL	409 N CAMDEN DR #105	BEVERLY HILLS, CA	90210
WAYDA, STEPHEN	PHOTOGRAPHER	MODELS & PROMOTIONS AGENCY		
		8560 SUNSET BLVD, 10TH FLOOR	LOS ANGELES, CA	90069
WAYLAND, LEN	ACTOR	6310 SAN VICENTE BLVD #407	LOS ANGELES, CA	90048
WAYLAND, NEWTON	CONDUCTOR	SHAW CONCERTS, 1995 BROADWAY	NEW YORK, NY	10023
WAYNE, BERNIE	COMPOSER	P SCHREIBMAN MANAGEMENT		
		1900 AVE OF THE STARS	LOS ANGELES, CA	90067
WAYNE, BRETT	WRESTLER	SEE - SAWYER, BRETT WAYNE		
WAYNE, DAVID	ACTOR	868 NAPOLI DR	PACIFIC PALISADES, CA	90272
WAYNE, ETHAN	ACTOR	CBS TELEVISION NETWORK		
		"THE BOLD & THE BEAUTIFUL"		
		7800 BEVERLY BLVD	LOS ANGELES, CA	90036
WAYNE, FRANK	TV PRODUCER	CBS-TV, "THE PRICE IS RIGHT"		
		7800 BEVERLY BLVD	LOS ANGELES, CA	90036
WAYNE, FRANK	WRITER	555 W 57TH ST #1230	NEW YORK, NY	10019
WAYNE, FREDD	ACTOR-WRITER	8955 BEVERLY BLVD	LOS ANGELES, CA	90048
WAYNE, GAYLON	GUITARIST	POST OFFICE BOX 140362	NASHVILLE, TN	37214
WAYNE, JEFF	COMEDIAN	BUSH & ROSS, 4942 VINELAND AVE	NORTH HOLLYWOOD, CA	91601
WAYNE, MICHAEL	FILM EXECUTIVE	10425 KLING ST	NORTH HOLLYWOOD, CA	91602
WAYNE, PATRICK	ACTOR	10502 WHIPPLE ST	NORTH HOLLYWOOD, CA	91602
WAYNE, PAUL	WRITER	2049 CENTURY PARK E	LOS ANGELES, CA	90067
WAYNE, PHILIP	TV PRODUCER	CBS-TV, "THE PRICE IS RIGHT"		
		7800 BEVERLY BLVD	LOS ANGELES, CA	90036
WAYNE, RICH	GUITARIST	POST OFFICE BOX 588	BRENTWOOD, TN	37027
WAYNE, WOODY	GUITARIST	2256 CABIN HILL RD #A	NASHVILLE, TN	37214
WAYNESMITH, GARY	ACTOR	1807 MARINE ST	SANTA MONICA, CA	90405
WAYSTED	ROCK & ROLL GROUP	ICM, 40 W 57TH ST	NEW YORK, NY	10019
WE THE PEOPLE	MUSICAL GROUP	POST OFFICE BOX 399	LISLE, IL	60532
WE'VE GOT A FUZZBOX & WE'RE GON	ROCK & ROLL GROUP	POST OFFICE BOX 235		
		BALSALL HEATH	BIRMINGHAM B1Z 9RZ	ENGLAND
WEAD, TIMOTHY	ACTOR	45 ROSE AVE #9	VENICE, CA	90291
WEAKLEY, HAROLD	DRUMMER	517 CAMDEN DR	NASHVILLE, TN	37211
WEASEL, THE	WRESTLING MANAGER	SEE - HEENAN, BOBBY "THE BRAIN"		
WEATHER, BRUCE	GUITARIST	125 QUEEN ANNE DR	MADISON, TN	37115
WEATHER REPORT	ROCK & ROLL GROUP	ICM, 8899 BEVERLY BLVD	LOS ANGELES, CA	90048
WEATHERLY, JIM	SINGER-GUITARIST	10351 SANTA MONICA BLVD #300	LOS ANGELES, CA	90025
WEATHERLY, SHAWN	ACTRESS-MODEL	151 S EL CAMINO DR	BEVERLY HILLS, CA	90212
WEATHERS, CARL	ACTOR	17352 SUNSET BLVD	PACIFIC PALAISADES, CA	90272
WEATHERS, DIANE	NEWS CORRESPONDENT	2915 CONNECTICUT AVE, NW	WASHINGTON, DC	20008
WEATHERS, JOHNNY & CROSS ROADS	C & W GROUP	POST OFFICE BOX 4	LAKE LURE, NC	28746
WEATHERS, JOHNNY E	FIDDLER	522 3RD ST	LAWRENCEBURG, TN	38464
WEATHERS, PATRICK	WRITER	THE NATIONAL LAMPOON		
		635 MADISON AVE	NEW YORK, NY	10022
WEATHERWAX, THOMAS P	DIRECTOR	2300 KIEL 14	LANGER REHM 7	GERMANY
WEATHERWX, BOB	ANIMAL TRAINER	16133 SOLEDAD CANYON RD	CANYON COUNTRY, CA	91351
WEAVER, ADRIAN	DRUMMER	1319 SCHOOL LN	NASHVILLE, TN	37217
WEAVER, DENNIS	ACTOR	25006 MALIBU RD	MALIBU, CA	90265

Name	Occupation	Address	City	Zip
WEAVER, EARL	BASEBALL	19016 W LAKE DR	HIALEAH, FL	33015
WEAVER, FRITZ	ACTOR	161 W 75TH ST	NEW YORK, NY	10023
WEAVER, GARY A	MUSIC ARRANGER	411 SENECA CT	NASHVILLE, TN	37214
WEAVER, HASCAL B	PHOTOGRAPHER	13303 CARTHAGE LN	DALLAS, TX	75243
WEAVER, JOHN D	WRITER	16314 MEADOW RIDGE RD	ENCINO, CA	91436
WEAVER, JOHN L, III	PIANIST	POST OFFICE BOX 140542	NASHVILLE, TN	37214
WEAVER, JOHNNY	WRESTLER	NATIONAL WRESTLING ALLIANCE		
		JIM CROCKETT PROMOTIONS		
		421 BRIARBEND DR	CHARLOTTE, NC	28209
WEAVER, KAY	PIANIST	CIRCLE RECORDS COMPANY		
		256 S ROBERTSON BLVD	BEVERLY HILLS, CA	90211
WEAVER, L G	TV WRITER	8955 BEVERLY BLVD	LOS ANGELES, CA	90048
WEAVER, LEE	ACTOR	10100 SANTA MONICA BLVD #1600	LOS ANGELES, CA	90067
WEAVER, PATTY	ACTRESS-SINGER	10000 SANTA MONICA BLVD #305	LOS ANGELES, CA	90067
WEAVER, RICK	PRODUCER	MCA/UNIVERSAL STUDIOS, INC		
		100 UNIVERSAL CITY PLAZA #105	UNIVERSAL CITY, CA	91608
WEAVER, ROBBY	ACTOR	1930 CENTURY PARK W #303	LOS ANGELES, CA	90067
WEAVER, RON	TV PRODUCER	CBS TELEVISION NETWORK		
		"THE BOLD & THE BEAUTIFUL"		
		7800 BEVERLY BLVD	LOS ANGELES, CA	90036
WEAVER, ROSIE CRUZ	DIRECTOR	520 N MICHIGAN AVE #436	CHICAGO, IL	60611
WEAVER, S MASON, JR	TV DIRECTOR	32210 FARMERSVILLE ST	FARMINGTON HILLS, MI	48018
WEAVER, SIGOURNEY	ACTRESS	12 W 72ND ST	NEW YORK, NY	10023
WEAVER, WARREN A, JR	NEWS CORRESPONDENT	1521 31ST ST, NW	WASHINGTON, DC	20007
WEAVER, WILLIAM	ACTOR	59 W 21ST ST	NEW YORK, NY	10010
WEBB, ALEXANDER	PHOTOGRAPHER	50 MANOR RD	STATEN ISLAND, NY	10310
WEBB, AMY	TV WRITER	8955 BEVERLY BLVD	LOS ANGELES, CA	90048
WEBB, ANITA	ACTRESS	400 W 43RD ST #23-F	NEW YORK, NY	10036
WEBB, BRIAN	CONDUCTOR	IAPR, KINCORA, BEER RD		
		SEATON	DEVON	ENGLAND
WEBB, DAVID A	PHOTOJOURNALIST	3420 16TH ST #209-S, NW	WASHINGTON, DC	20010
WEBB, ELLIOT	TALENT AGENT	10100 SANTA MONICA BLVD #348	LOS ANGELES, CA	90067
WEBB, JIMMY	SINGER-COMPOSER	1560 N LAUREL AVE #109	LOS ANGELES, CA	90046
WEBB, LENORE L	NEWS CORRESPONDENT	3-4819 N 16TH ST	ARLINGTON, VA	22205
WEBB, LONNIE	PIANIST	917 RICHARDS RD	ANTIOCH, TN	37013
WEBB, LUCY	ACTRESS-COMEDIENNE	11726 SAN VICENTE BLVD #300	LOS ANGELES, CA	90049
WEBB, MARIANNE	ORGANIST	15 HIGH ST #621	HARTFORD, CT	06103
WEBB, MARILYN	WRITER-EDITOR	US MAGAZINE COMPANY		
		1 DAG HAMMARSKJOLD PLAZA	NEW YORK, NY	10017
WEBB, RICHARD	ACTOR	13330 CHANDLER BLVD	VAN NUYS, CA	91401
WEBB, ROBERT DELANEY	DIRECTOR	13063 VENTURA BLVD #201	STUDIO CITY, CA	91604
WEBB, ROBERT H	CONDUCTOR	750 N KINGS RD #107	LOS ANGELES, CA	90069
WEBB, RON	COMPOSER	1819 WOLLAM ST	LOS ANGELES, CA	90065
WEBB, ROY	COMPOSER	865 COMSTOCK AVE	LOS ANGELES, CA	90024
WEBB, RUTH	ACTRESS-AGENT	7500 DEVISTA DR	LOS ANGELES, CA	90046
WEBB, WILLIAM H	DIRECTOR	164 BOONTON AVE	KINNELON, NJ	07405
WEBBER, ANDREW LLOYD	COMPOSER	20 GREEK ST	LONDON W1V 5LF	ENGLAND
WEBBER, CAROL	SOPRANO	1776 BROADWAY #504	NEW YORK, NY	10019
WEBBER, JULIAN LLOYD	CELLIST-VIOLIST	IBBSP TILLETT, 450 EDGWARE	LONDON W2 1EG	ENGLAND
WEBBER, MIKE	GUITARIST	1918 ASHWOOD AVE	NASHVILLE, TN	37212
WEBBER, PEGGY	ACTRESS	6612 WHITLEY TERR	LOS ANGELES, CA	90068
WEBBER, ROBERT	ACTOR	24908 MALIBU RD	MALIBU, CA	90265
WEBBER, SHARON	ACTRESS	5930 FRANKLIN AVE	LOS ANGELES, CA	90028
WEBBER, VALERIE	ACTRESS	121 N ROBERTSON BLVD #B	BEVERLY HILLS, CA	90211
WEBER, BOB, SR	CARTOONIST	KING FEATURES SYNDICATE		
		235 E 45TH ST	NEW YORK, NY	10017
WEBER, BRUCE	DIRECTOR	DGA, 110 W 57TH ST	NEW YORK, NY	10019
WEBER, EBERHARD	GUITARIST	KURLAND, 173 BRIGHTON AVE	BOSTON, MA	02134
WEBER, FRANK	SINGER	ED NEWMARK, 793 BINGHAM RD	RIDGEWOOD, NJ	07540
WEBER, JOHN ROY	COMPOSER-CONDUCTOR	203 CALLE DE ANZA	SAN CLEMENTE, CA	92672
WEBER, LARRY	ACTOR	35 W 64 TH ST	NEW YORK, NY	10023
WEBER, PATRICIA J	NEWS CORRESPONDENT	400 N CAPITOL ST, NW	WASHINGTON, DC	20001
WEBER, PAUL	ACTOR	WILLIAMSON, 932 N LA BREA AVE	LOS ANGELES, CA	90038
WEBER, PAUL	SINGER	NATA MANAGEMENT AGENCY		
		84 AMARANTH ST E		
		GRAND VALLEY	ONATRIO, ONT	CANADA
WEBER, RICHARD K	ACTOR	10 E 44TH ST #700	NEW YORK, NY	10017
WEBER, RICKY W	NEWS CORRESPONDENT	35 "E" ST, NW	WASHINGTON, DC	20001
WEBER, ROBERT	CARTOONIST	POST OFFICE BOX 4203	NEW YORK, NY	10017
WEBLEY, SCOTT	ACTOR	15029 WYANDOTTE ST	VAN NUYS, CA	91405
WEBSTER, ANTHONY C	WRITER	999 N DOHENY DR #1110	LOS ANGELES, CA	90069
WEBSTER, APRIL	CASTING DIRECTOR	MC LEAN, 8272 SUNSET BLVD	LOS ANGELES, CA	90046
WEBSTER, BYRON	ACTOR	4273 STERN AVE	SHERMAN OAKS, CA	91423
WEBSTER, CHARLES D	WRITER	21686 YUCATAN AVE	WOODLAND HILLS, CA	91364
WEBSTER, DANIEL J	NEWS CORRESPONDENT	6515 BELLAMINE CT	MC LEAN, VA	22101
WEBSTER, DIANA	TV WRITER	8955 BEVERLY BLVD	LOS ANGELES, CA	90048
WEBSTER, DIANA	ACTRESS	10000 RIVERSIDE DR #3	TOLUCA LAKE, CA	91602
WEBSTER, GENE	DIRECTOR	DGA, 7950 SUNSET BLVD	LOS ANGELES, CA	90046
WEBSTER, GENE	EDITORIALIST	12021 VALLEYHEART DR #206	STUDIO CITY, CA	91604
WEBSTER, JAMES C	NEWS CORRESPONDENT	6723 PINE CREEK CT	MC LEAN, VA	22101
WEBSTER, JOHN	SINGER	GOOD, 2500 NW 39TH ST	OKLAHOMA CITY, OK	73112
WEBSTER, NICHOLAS	WRITER-PRODUCER	4135 FULTON AVE	SHERMAN OAKS, CA	91423
WEBSTER, SKIP	TV WRITER-PRODUCER	8955 BEVERLY BLVD	LOS ANGELES, CA	90048
WEBSTER, SONJA	FILM DIRECTOR	121 E 31ST ST	NEW YORK, NY	10016
WEBSTER, SUSAN	NEWS CORRESPONDENT	2950 VAN NESS ST #210, NW	WASHINGTON, DC	20008

DAVID WAYNE

JEFF WAYNE

DENNIS WEAVER

SIGOURNEY WEAVER

TIM WEISBERG

RAQUEL WELCH

LISA WHELCHEL

ADAM WEST

DOTTIE WEST

Name	Occupation	Address	City/State	Zip
WECHSLER, JILL	NEWS CORRESPONDENT	7715 ROCTON AVE	CHEVY CHASE, MD	20815
WECHTER, DAVID J	TV WRITER-DIRECTOR	4508 FARMDALE AVE	NORTH HOLLYWOOD, CA	91602
WECHTER, ROBERT	NEWS CORRESPONDENT	NBC-TV, NEWS DEPARTMENT		
		4001 NEBRASKA AVE, NW	WASHINGTON, DC	20016
WECKERLY, SCOTT	DRUMMER	300 KATE ST #G-17	MADISON, TN	37115
WECKSLER, A N	NEWS CORRESPONDENT	2801 NEW MEXICO AVE, NW	WASHINGTON, DC	20007
WEDDELL, MIMI	ACTRESS	1349 LEXINGTON AVE	NEW YORK, NY	10028
WEDDLE, VERNON	ACTOR	18608 VINCENNES ST	NORTHRIDGE, CA	91324
WEDEL, RENEE	ACTRESS	4143 VIA MARINA #8-815	MARINA DEL REY, CA	90292
WEDGEWORTH, ANN	ACTRESS	329 N WETHERLY DR #205	BEVERLY HILLS, CA	90211
WEDLOCK, HUGH, JR	TV WRITER	11825 MAGNOLIA BLVD #205	NORTH HOLLYWOOD, CA	91607
WEDNER, ALAN	ACTOR	3153 WELDON AVE	LOS ANGELES, CA	90065
WEDNESDAY WEEK	ROCK & ROLL GROUP	POST OFFICE BOX 2428	EL SEGUNDO, CA	90245
WEED, GENE	WRITER-PRODUCER	13539 HARTLAND ST	VAN NUYS, CA	91405
WEED, MARLENE	WRITER	VIRGIRIA R WELLS		
		1540 WILSHIRE BLVD	LOS ANGELES, CA	90017
WEEDLE, VERDON	ACTOR	6736 LAUREL CANYON BLVD #306	NORTH HOLLYWOOD, CA	91606
WEEDMAN, SAM	GUITARIST	131 PAGE RD	NASHVILLE, TN	37205
WEEDON, RICHARD T	NEWS CORRESPONDENT	529 14TH ST, NW	WASHINGTON, DC	20045
WEEGE, REINHOLD	TV WRITER	4131 LONGRIDGE AVE	SHERMAN OAKS, CA	91423
WEEKS, CHRISTOPHER	ACTOR	9255 SUNSET BLVD #510	LOS ANGELES, CA	90069
WEEKS, STEPHEN	WRITER-PRODUCER	PENHOW CASTLE, NEAR NEWPORT	GWENT NP6 3AD	ENGLAND
WEEMS, PRISCILLA	ACTRESS	1450 BELFAST DR	LOS ANGELES, CA	90069
WEEZER, LILLIAN	TV WRITER	8955 BEVERLY BLVD	LOS ANGELES, CA	90048
WEGHER, BARBARA JEAN	TV WRITER	4329 BELLINGHAM AVE	STUDIO CITY, CA	91604
WEHEELER, ROMAYNE	PIANIST	KAY, 58 W 58TH ST	NEW YORK, NY	10019
WEHR, ELIZABETH	NEWS CORRESPONDENT	6028 CHESHIRE DR	BETHESDA, MD	20814
WEI, REX	ACTOR	OCA, 34 GRAFTON TERR	LONDON NW5 4HY	ENGLAND
WEICK, MELISSA	SOPRANO	260 W END AVE #7-A	NEW YORK, NY	10023
WEIDE, ROBERT B	TV PRODUCER	9110 SUNSET BLVD #120	LOS ANGELES, CA	90069
WEIDENBENNER, LEONARD	GUN EXPERT	2801 MEADOW LARK DR	SAN DIEGO, CA	92123
WEIDLINGER, TOM	TV DIRECTOR	1572 S GLENVILLE DR	LOS ANGELES, CA	90035
WEIDMAN, JEROME	TV WRITER	8955 BEVERLY BLVD	LOS ANGELES, CA	90048
WEIGALL, MICHAEL	WRITER-PRODUCER	53 KENSINGTON CT	LONDON W8 5DE	ENGLAND
WEIGEL, TERI	MODEL	MODELS & PROMOTIONS AGENCY		
		8560 SUNSET BLVD, 10TH FLOOR	LOS ANGELES, CA	90069
WEIHE, N FREDERICK	TV DIRECTOR	RURAL DELIVERY 2		
		BOX 125, MEKEEL ST	BATONAH, NY	10536
WEIK, DAVID P	PHOTOGRAPHER	2980 TREADWELL LN	HERNDON, VA	22071
WEIL, BRUNO	CONDUCTOR	SHAW CONCERTS, 1995 BROADWAY	NEW YORK, NY	10023
WEIL, BUD	DIRECTOR	3671 HUDSON MANOR TERR	RIVERDALE, NY	10463
WEIL, HERB	ACTOR	3297 TARECO DR	LOS ANGELES, CA	90068
WEIL, ROBERT E	ACTOR	484 W 43RD ST #29-D	NEW YORK, NY	10036
WEILERSTEIN DUO	MUSICAL DUO	FINELL, 155 W 68TH ST	NEW YORK, NY	10023
WEILL, CLAUDIA	FILM-TV DIRECTOR	1697 BROADWAY #1109	NEW YORK, NY	10019
WEIN, GEORGE	MUSIC PRODUCER	311 W 74TH ST	NEW YORK, NY	10023
WEINBACH, ROBERT D	WRITER-PRODUCER	12023 LORNE ST	NORTH HOLLYWOOD, CA	91605
WEINBERG, DICK	TV DIRECTOR	12959 VALLEYHEART DR	STUDIO CITY, CA	91604
WEINBERG, ROBERT ADAM	DIRECTOR	3025 HEWITT AVE #472	SILVER SPRING, MD	20906
WEINBERGER, EDWIN	TV WRITER-PRODUCER	1625 SUNSET PLAZA DR	LOS ANGELES, CA	90069
WEINBERGER, MICHAEL	TV WRITER	15319 DEL GADO DR	SHERMAN OAKS, CA	91403
WEINER, ARN	ACTOR	THE MANHATTAN PLAZA		
		400 W 43RD ST	NEW YORK, NY	10036
WEINER, DONALD J	DIRECTOR	DGA, 7950 SUNSET BLVD	LOS ANGELES, CA	90046
WEINER, ELLIS	TV WRITER	8955 BEVERLY BLVD	LOS ANGELES, CA	90048
WEINER, GENE	CLOWN	2701 COTTAGE WY #14	SACRAMENTO, CA	95825
WEINER, HYMAN	FILM DIRECTOR	245 E 19TH ST	NEW YORK, NY	10003
WEINER, JUDITH	CASTING DIRECTOR	1438 N GOWER ST, 4TH FLOOR	HOLLYWOOD, CA	90028
WEINER, KIM	VIOLINIST	4601 PACKARD DR #C-288	NASHVILLE, TN	37211
WEINER, ROBERT	THEATER PRODUCER	161 W 54TH ST	NEW YORK, NY	10019
WEINER, ROBERTA	NEWS CORRESPONDENT	3299 "K" ST, NW	WASHINGTON, DC	20007
WEINER, RON	TV DIRECTOR	412 CAROL CT	HIGHLAND PARK, IL	60035
WEINFELD, ANDRE	TV WRITER	8955 BEVERLY BLVD	LOS ANGELES, CA	90048
WEINFELD, MICHAEL P	NEWS CORRESPONDENT	1825 "K" ST, NW	WASHINGTON, DC	20006
WEINGART, ROBERT J	MUSIC ARRANGER	113 LAUDERDALE RD #A	NASHVILLE, TN	37205
WEINGARTEN, ARTHUR	WRITER	9900 DURANT DR #A	BEVERLY HILLS, CA	90212
WEINGEROFF, GEORGE	WRESTLER	UNIVERSAL WRESTLING FEDERATION		
		MID SOUTH SPORTS, INC		
		5001 SPRING VALLEY RD	DALLAS, TX	75244
WEINGROD, HERSCHEL	SCREENWRITER	1200 N BEVERLY GLEN BLVD	LOS ANGELES, CA	90077
WEINMAN, RICHARD C	DIRECTOR	3333 HENRY HUDSON PARKWAY	RIVERDALE, NY	10463
WEINRAUB, BERNARD	NEWS CORRESPONDENT	1000 CONNECTICUT AVE, NW	WASHINGTON, DC	20036
WEINRIB, LEONARD	WRITER	7321 CLINTON ST	LOS ANGELES, CA	90036
WEINSCHENKER, GREGORY J	DIRECTOR	BOX 176, TRAVIS RD	HYDE PARK, NY	12538
WEINSTEIN, DANIEL J	COMPOSER	13015 1/2 VENICE BLVD	LOS ANGELES, CA	90066
WEINSTEIN, DEBRA	NEWS CORRESPONDENT	330 INDEPENDENCE AVE, SW	WASHINGTON, DC	20547
WEINSTEIN, JACK	TV WRITER	8955 BEVERLY BLVD	LOS ANGELES, CA	90048
WEINSTEIN, MELVIN B	WRITER	11433 ROCHESTER AVE #102	LOS ANGELES, CA	90025
WEINSTEIN, PAULA	FILM EXECUTIVE	24016 MALIBU RD	MALIBU, CA	90265
WEINSTEIN, SOL	TV WRITER	5807 TOPANGA CANYON BLVD #M-105	WOODLAND HILLS, CA	91367
WEINSTOCK, KEN	TV PRODUCER	9533 MOONRIDGE TERR	BEVERLY HILLS, CA	90210

Name	Occupation	Address	City	Zip
WEINTRAUB, CARL	ACTOR	45 HORIZON AVE #D	VENICE, CA	90291
WEINTRAUB, FRED	FILM PRODUCER	11939 GORHAM AVE #305	LOS ANGELES, CA	90049
WEINTRAUB, JERRY	PRODUCER	661 DOHENY RD	BEVERLY HILLS, CA	90210
WEINTRAUB, SANDY	SINGER	6236 W 6TH ST	LOS ANGELES, CA	90048
WEINTRAUB ROLAND, SANDRA	SCREENWRITER	11939 GORHAM AVE #305	LOS ANGELES, CA	90049
WEINTRAUG, BERNIE	TALENT AGENT	8428 MELROSE PL #C	LOS ANGELES, CA	90069
WEIR, GILLIAN	ORGANIST	15 HIGH ST #621	HARTFORD, CT	06103
WEIR, PETER	FILM DIRECTOR	AUSTRALIAN FILM COMMISSION		
		9229 SUNSET BLVD	LOS ANGELES, CA	90069
WEIR, SANDRA L	DIRECTOR	ANCHOR PRODUCTIONS		
		2335 W BELDEN AVE	CHICAGO, IL	60647
WEIR, TOM	SPORTS WRITER	POST OFFICE BOX 500	WASHINGTON, DC	20044
WEIS, DON	FILM-TV DIRECTOR	400 CASTLE PL	BEVERLY HILLS, CA	90210
WEIS, JACK	WRITER-PRODUCER	6771 MARSHALL FOCH ST	NEW ORLEANS, LA	70124
WEISBARTH, MICHAEL L	TV PRODUCER	ICM, 8899 BEVERLY BLVD	LOS ANGELES, CA	90048
WEISBERG, ARTHUR	CONDUCTOR	POST OFFICE BOX U	REDDING, CT	06875
WEISBERG, ROGER E	TV DIRECTOR-PRODUCER	POST OFFICE BOX 548	PALISADES, NY	10964
WEISBERG, SHEILA JUDIS	WRITER	5155 BABCOCK AVE	NORTH HOLLYWOOD, CA	91607
WEISBERG, TIM	MUSICIAN	1145 SUNSET VALE AVE	LOS ANGELES, CA	90069
WEISBORD, SAM	TALENT EXECUTIVE	9255 DOHENY RD #2206	LOS ANGELES, CA	90069
WEISBURD, DAN E	WRITER	10260 MOORPARK ST	NORTH HOLLYWOOD, CA	91602
WEISENBORN, GORDON	TV WRITER-DIRECTOR	544 W WELLINGTON AVE	CHICAGO, IL	60657
WEISER, STANLEY	WRITER	2021 OCEAN AVE #223	SANTA MONICA, CA	90405
WEISER-FINLEY, SUSAN	SCREENWRITER	151 S EL CAMINO DR	BEVERLY HILLS, CA	90212
WEISGALL, HUGO	COMPOSER-CONDUCTOR	81 MAPLE DR	GREAT NECK, NY	11021
WEISHAUS, MARC	ACTOR	5023 VENTURA CANYON AVE	SHERMAN OAKS, CA	91423
WEISINGER, RALPH	TV DIRECTOR-PRODUCER	511 W 54TH ST	NEW YORK, NY	10019
WEISKOPF, HERM	WRITER-EDITOR	SPORTS ILLUSTRATED MAGAZINE		
		TIME & LIFE BUILDING		
		ROCKEFELLER CENTER	NEW YORK, NY	10020
WEISKOPF, KIM ROBERT	TV WRITER-DIRECTOR	4022 MADELIA AVE	SHERMAN OAKS, CA	91403
WEISKOPF, ROBERT	TV WRITER	21612 RAMBLA VISTA	MALIBU, CA	90265
WEISLOGEL, CYNTHIA	ACTRESS	11748 DOROTHY ST #4	LOS ANGELES, CA	90049
WEISMAN, BENJAMIN	COMPOSER	4527 ALLA RD #3	MARINA DEL REY, CA	90292
WEISMAN, BRICE	TV DIRECTOR-PRODUCER	ABC TELEVISION NETWORK		
		1330 AVE OF THE AMERICAS	NEW YORK, NY	10019
WEISMAN, JOEL M	DIRECTOR	939 MAYFIELD RD	WOODMERE, NY	11598
WEISMAN, JOHN	NEWS CORRESPONDENT	5329 SARATOGA AVE	CHEVY CHASE, MD	20815
WEISMAN, SAM	ACTOR	4448 TUJUNGA AVE	NORTH HOLLYWOOD, CA	91602
WEISMAN, SAM	TV DIRECTOR	10490 SELKIRK LN	LOS ANGELES, CA	90077
WEISMEIER, LYNDA	ACTRESS-MODEL	MODELS & PROMOTIONS AGENCY		
		8560 SUNSET BLVD, 10TH FLOOR	LOS ANGELES, CA	90069
WEISS, ADRIAN	DIRECTOR	5155 TERRAMAR WY	OXNARD SHORES, CA	93030
WEISS, ARNOLD	ACTOR	1759 N ORCHID AVE #210	HOLLYWOOD, CA	90028
WEISS, CAROL	CONDUCTOR	1415 N FORMOSA AVE	LOS ANGELES, CA	90046
WEISS, ELLEN R	NEWS CORRESPONDENT	2025 "M" ST, NW	WASHINGTON, DC	20036
WEISS, FREDRIC	TV WRITER	14144 VENTURA BLVD #200	SHERMAN OAKS, CA	91423
WEISS, GLENN P	NEWS CORRESPONDENT	2139 WISCONSIN AVE, NW	WASHINGTON, DC	20007
WEISS, HARRIETT	TV WRITER	18701 HATTERAS ST #16	TARZANA, CA	91356
WEISS, HARRY ALLAN	WRITER	1670 MARMONT AVE	LOS ANGELES, CA	90069
WEISS, HENRY J	TV DIRECTOR	12724 BYRON AVE	GRANADA HILLS, CA	91344
WEISS, JOEL	ACTOR	3340 BAILEY AVE #5	NEW YORK, NY	10463
WEISS, JOSEPH	COMPOSER	6142 MANTON AVE	WOODLAND HILLS, CA	91367
WEISS, KENNETH	NEWS CORRESPONDENT	3301 GEIGER AVE	KENSINGTON, MD	20895
WEISS, LARS A	NEWS CORRESPONDENT	4341 FOREST LN, NW	WASHINGTON, DC	20007
WEISS, MICHAEL	ACTOR	KNBC-TV, "DAYS OF OUR LIVES"		
		3000 W ALAMEDA AVE	BURBANK, CA	91523
WEISS, MICHAEL J	FILM PRODUCER	1735 NEW HAMPSHIRE AVE	WASHINGTON, DC	20009
WEISS, MICHAEL J	NEW CORRESPONDENT	1400 20TH ST #803, NW	WASHINGTON, DC	20036
WEISS, NEIL A	TV DIRECTOR	15 SPINNING WHEEL RD #7-A	MASSAPEQUA, NY	11758
WEISS, PETER	ACTOR-WRITER	3262 TILDEN AVE	LOS ANGELES, CA	90034
WEISS, ROBERT	BALLET DANCER	80 CENTRAL PARK W	NEW YORK, NY	10023
WEISS, ROBERT	PRODUCER	MCA/UNIVERSAL STUDIOS, INC		
		100 UNIVERSAL CITY PLAZA #448	UNIVERSAL CITY, CA	91608
WEISS, ROBERTA	ACTRESS	ABRAMS ARTISTS & ASSOCIATES		
		420 MADISON AVE, 14TH FLOOR	NEW YORK, NY	10017
WEISSBOURD, BURT	FILM PRODUCER	240 BENTLY CIR	LOS ANGELES, CA	90049
WEISSENBERG, ALEXIS	PIANIST	ANGLO-SWISS ARTISTS MGMT		
		16 MUSWELL HILL RD, HIGHGATE	LONDON N6 5UG	ENGLAND
WEISSER, GRAZIELLA	NEWS CORRESPONDENT	4817 LINNEAN AVE, NW	WASHINGTON, DC	20008
WEISSER, NORBERT	ACTOR	211 S BEVERLY DR #201	BEVERLY HILLS, CA	90212
WEISSMAN, BEN	FILM PRODUCER	4216 BEEMAN AVE	STUDIO CITY, CA	91604
WEISSMAN, BRADLEY	ACTOR	1418 N HIGHLAND AVE #102	LOS ANGELES, CA	90028
WEISSMAN, DENNIS W	NEWS CORRESPONDENT	709 "A" ST, NE	WASHINGTON, DC	20002
WEISSMAN, JERRY	WRITER-PRODUCER	DGA, 7950 SUNSET BLVD	LOS ANGELES, CA	90046
WEISSMAN, KAREN	FILM EDITOR	4216 BEEMAN AVE	STUDIO CITY, CA	91604
WEISSMAN, NORMAN	WRITER-PRODUCER	188 WHITFIELD ST	GUILFORD, CT	06437
WEISSMAN, SEYMOUR J	WRITER-PRODUCER	562 W END AVE	NEW YORK, NY	10024
WEISSMAN, STEVEN R	NEWS CORRESPONDENT	1249 33RD ST, NW	WASHINGTON, DC	20007
WEITHORN, MICHAEL J	TV WRITER-PRODUCER	653 HANLEY AVE	LOS ANGELES, CA	90049
WEITMAN, ROBERT M	FILM EXECUTIVE	1880 CARLA RIDGE	BEVERLY HILLS, CA	90210
WEITZ, BARRY JON	FILM WRITER-PRODUCER	13642 SUNSET BLVD	PACIFIC PALISADES, CA	90272
WEITZ, BRUCE	ACTOR	2385 CASTILIAN DR	LOS ANGELES, CA	90068
WEITZ, JOHN	FASHION DESIGNER	600 MADISON AVE	NEW YORK, NY	10022
WEITZ, KRISTINE	ACTRESS	LENZ, 1456 E CHARLESTON BLVD	LAS VEGAS, NV	89104

Name	Occupation	Address	City	Zip
WEITZEL, THOMAS A	DIRECTOR	308 PALMETTO AVE #24	PACIFICA, CA	94044
WEITZENHOFFER, A MAX	THEATER PRODUCER	70 E 77TH ST	NEW YORK, NY	10021
WEITZMAN, HARVEY	TV WRITER	8955 BEVERLY BLVD	LOS ANGELES, CA	90048
WEITZNER, DAVID A	FILM EXECUTIVE	22601 FEDERALIST RD	WOODLAND HILLS, CA	91364
WEKRE, FROYDIS REE	HORN	CCS, 4478 PURDUE AVE	CULVER CITY, CA	90230
WELCH, CHARLES C	ACTOR	610 W END AVE	NEW YORK, NY	10024
WELCH, ELIZABETH	ACTRESS-SINGER	4-A CAPENTERS CLOSE	LONDON SW1	ENGLAND
WELCH, JAKE	NEWS CORRESPONDENT	1910 NEW HAMPSHIRE AVE, NW	WASHINGTON, DC	20009
WELCH, KEN	COMPOSER-LYRICIST	9200 SUNSET BLVD #808	LOS ANGELES, CA	90069
WELCH, LENNY	SINGER	POST OFFICE BOX 82	GREAT NECK, NY	11021
WELCH, LISA	ACTRESS-MODEL	12021 WILSHIRE BLVD #454	LOS ANGELES, CA	90025
WELCH, LOUIS	ACTOR	11645 MONTANA AVE #136	LOS ANGELES, CA	90049
WELCH, MARILYN	TV WRITER	11506 ORUM RD	LOS ANGELES, CA	90049
WELCH, MITZI	COMPOSER-LYRICIST	9200 SUNSET BLVD #808	LOS ANGELES, CA	90069
WELCH, NELSON	ACTOR	275 S NEW HAMPSHIRE AVE #507	LOS ANGELES, CA	90004
WELCH, RAQUEL	ACT-SING-WRI	POST OFFICE BOX 26472	PRESCOTT, AZ	85253
WELCH, ROBERT	WRITER-PRODUCER	43 FLETCHER RD	BELMONT, MA	02178
WELCH, RUPERT	NEWS CORRESPONDENT	2045 N BRANDYWINE ST	ARLINGTON, VA	22207
WELCH, TAHNEE	ACTRESS	600 MADISON AVE	NEW YORK, NY	10077
WELCH, TIMOTHY E	PHOTOGRAPHER	11722 BUTLERS BRANCH RD	CLINTON, MD	20735
WELCH, TINA	SINGER	PENNY, 30 GUINAN ST	WALTHAM, MA	02154
WELCH, WAYNE M	NEWS CORRESPONDENT	5597 SEMINARY RD S #2516	FALLS CHURCH, VA	22041
WELCH, WILLIAM M	NEWS CORRESPONDENT	3013 GATEPOST LN	HERNDON, VA	22071
WELD, TUESDAY	ACTRESS	300 CENTRAL PARK W #5-E	NEW YORK, NY	10019
WELDON, ANN	ACTRESS	1935 WEEPAH WY	LOS ANGELES, CA	90046
WELDON, CHARLES	ACTOR	7466 BEVERLY BLVD #205	LOS ANGELES, CA	90036
WELDON, FAY	WRITER	ORCHARD LEIGH HOUSE		
		EAST COMPTON		
WELDON, HARRY L	PHOTOJOURNALIST	1927 BETTEN HOLLOW RD	VIENNA, VA	22180
WELFORD, NANCY	ACTRESS	810 GONZALES DR #3-D	SAN FRANCISCO, CA	94132
WELHASCH, IRENA	SOPRANO	CONE, 221 W 57TH ST	NEW YORK, NY	10019
WELK, LAWRENCE	MUSICAN	1221 OCEAN AVE #602	SANTA MONICA, CA	90401
WELK, TANYA	SINGER	10433 KLING ST	NORTH HOLLYWOOD, CA	91602
WELKER, FRANK	ACTOR-COMEDIAN	2405 SIERRA CREEK RD	AGOURA, CA	91301
WELKER, MARYANN	DIRECTOR	DGA, 7950 SUNSET BLVD	LOS ANGELES, CA	90046
WELLAND, COLIN	SCREENWRITER	PETER CHARLESWORTH, LTD		
		68 OLD BROMPTON RD	LONDON SW7 3LQ	ENGLAND
WELLBORN, STANLEY N	NEWS CORRESPONDENT	6001 UTAH AVE, NW	WASHINGTON, DC	20015
WELLER, DIETER	SINGER	59 E 54TH ST #81	NEW YORK, NY	10022
WELLER, FREDDY	SINGER-SONGWRITER	TAYLOR, 2401 12TH AVE S	NASHVILLE, TN	37204
WELLER, GEORGE	NEWS CORRESPONDENT	236 MASSACHUSETTS AVE, NE	WASHINGTON, DC	20002
WELLER, MARY LOUISE	ACTRESS	9300 WILSHIRE BLVD #410	BEVERLY HILLS, CA	90212
WELLER, MICHAEL	SCREENWRITER	555 W 57TH ST #1230	NEW YORK, NY	10019
WELLER, PETER	ACTOR	853 7TH AVE #9-A	NEW YORK, NY	10019
WELLER, ROB	TV HOST	ENTERTAINMENT THIS WEEK		
		PARAMOUNT TELEVISION		
		5555 MELROSE AVE	LOS ANGELES, CA	90038
WELLER, WALTER	CONDUCTOR	ICM, 40 W 57TH ST	NEW YORK, NY	10019
WELLES, GEORGE	WRESTLER	WORLD CLASS WRESTLING		
		SOUTHWEST SPORTS, INC		
		DALLAS SPORTATORIUM		
		1000 S INDUSTRIAL BLVD	DALLAS, TX	75207
WELLES, GWEN	ACTRESS	9000 SUNSET BLVD #1112	LOS ANGELES, CA	90069
WELLES, HALSTED	WRITER	10100 SANTA MONICA BLVD #1600	LOS ANGELES, CA	90067
WELLES, JOAN	ACTRESS	9200 SUNSET BLVD #1210	LOS ANGELES, CA	90069
WELLES, REBECCA	ACTRESS	WEIS, 400 CASTLE PL	BEVERLY HILLS, CA	90210
WELLES, TERRI	ACTRESS-MODEL	SIMMER, 20725 QUEDO DR	WOODLAND HILLS, CA	91364
WELLINGTON, SAMUEL	DRUMMER	407 MURFREESBORO RD	NASHVILLE, TN	37210
WELLMAN, MAGGIE	ACTRESS	427 N CANON DR #205	BEVERLY HILLS, CA	90210
WELLMAN, WENDELL	SCREENWRITER	1122 9TH ST #2	SANTA MONICA, CA	90403
WELLMAN, WILLIAM, JR	ACTOR	410 N BARRINGTON AVE	LOS ANGELES, CA	90049
WELLS, AARIKA	ACTRESS	8350 SANTA MONICA BLVD #206	LOS ANGELES, CA	90069
WELLS, BRANDI	SINGER	1125 ATLANTIC AVE #413	ATLANTIC CITY, NJ	08401
WELLS, CAROLE	ACTRESS	113 N SAN VICENTE BLVD #202	BEVERLY HILLS, CA	90211
WELLS, CARRIE	ACTRESS	1450 BELFAST DR	LOS ANGELES, CA	90069
WELLS, CLAUDETTE	ACTRESS	10401 WILSHIRE BLVD #415	LOS ANGELES, CA	90024
WELLS, CLAUDIA	ACTRESS	9220 SUNSET BLVD #202	LOS ANGELES, CA	90069
WELLS, CLYDE	CARTOONIST	POST OFFICE BOX 1928	AUGUSTA, GA	30913
WELLS, CORY	SINGER-SONGWRITER	POST OFFICE BOX 82	MALIBU, CA	90265
WELLS, DANNY	ACTOR	1930 CENTURY PARK W #303	LOS ANGELES, CA	90067
WELLS, DAVID	ACTOR	15010 VENTURA BLVD #219	SHERMAN OAKS, CA	91403
WELLS, DAVID	CELLIST	333 TAYLOR AVE N #202	SEATTLE, WA	98109
WELLS, DAWN	ACTRESS	206 CARDEN AVE	NASHVILLE, TN	37205
WELLS, EDWARD	TV DIRECTOR	309 CENTURY PARK W	DESTIN, FL	32541
WELLS, GEORGE	WRESTLER	POST OFFICE BOX 3859	STAMFORD, CT	06905
WELLS, GEORGE	WRITER	SWANSON, 8523 SUNSET BLVD	LOS ANGELES, CA	90069
WELLS, GEORGE T	NEWS CORRESPONDENT	2942 S COLUMBUS ST #A-2	ARLINGTON, DC	22206
WELLS, JACK	ACTOR	2268 COLDWATER CANYON DR	BEVERLY HILLS, CA	90210
WELLS, JAMES L	PHOTOGRAPHER	1333 "R" ST, NW	WASHINGTON, DC	20009
WELLS, JEFFREY	SOPRANO	HILLYER, 250 W 57TH ST	NEW YORK, NY	10107
WELLS, JIM	PHOTOGRAPHER	2809 S 20TH ST	ARLINGTON, VA	22204
WELLS, JOHN	ACTOR-WRITER	1-A SCARSDALE VILLAS	LONDON W8	ENGLAND
WELLS, KITTY	SINGER	352 CUMBERLAND HILLS DR	MADISON, TN	37115
WELLS, LLOYD	GUITARIST	119 W BROOKFIELD DR	NASHVILLE, TN	37205

Name	Occupation	Address	City	Zip
WELLS, MARIAN	NOVELIST	BETHANY HOUSE PUBLISHING		
		6820 AUTO CLUB RD	MINNEAPOLIS, MN	55438
WELLS, MARY	SINGER-AUTHORESS	1680 N VINE ST #214	HOLLYWOOD, CA	90028
WELLS, MARY K	TV WRITER	ABC-TV, "ALL MY CHILDREN"		
		1330 AVE OF THE AMERICAS	NEW YORK, NY	10019
WELLS, NINA	ACTRESS	8721 SUNSET BLVD #103	LOS ANGELES, CA	90069
WELLS, PATRICIA	SOPRANO	CAMI, 165 W 57TH ST	NEW YORK, NY	10019
WELLS, RALPH	BARITONE	MMM, 935 NW 19TH AVE	PORTLAND, OR	97209
WELLS, RICHARD A	DIRECTOR	DGA, 7950 SUNSET BLVD	LOS ANGELES, CA	90046
WELLS, RICHARD ALAN	PHOTOGRAPHER	10613 WEYMOUTH ST	BETHESDA, MD	20814
WELLS, RICHARD J	DIRECTOR	DGA, 7950 SUNSET BLVD	LOS ANGELES, CA	90046
WELLS, ROBERT	TV WRITER	8955 BEVERLY BLVD	LOS ANGELES, CA	90048
WELLS, SUSIE	PIANIST	2608 W 17TH ST	PLAINVIEW, TX	79072
WELLS, TOMMY	DRUMMER	2706 ACKLEN AVE #3	NASHVILLE, TN	37212
WELLS, VICTORIA	ACTRESS	11030 VENTURA BLVD #3	STUDIO CITY, CA	91604
WELLS DUO, THE	MUSICAL DUO	333 TAYLOR AVE N #202	SEATTLE, WA	98109
WELSCH, MICHELLE M	WRITER-NEWS CORRES	3010 S ABINGDON ST	ARLINGTON, VA	22206
WELSH, ANNE MARIE	ARTS CRITIC	POST OFFICE BOX 191	SAN DIEGO, CA	92112
WELSH, DONALD E	PUBLISHING EXECUTIVE	US MAGAZINE COMPANY		
		1 DAG HAMMARSKJOLD PLAZA	NEW YORK, NY	10017
WELSH, JOHN J	ACTOR	6720 HAYVENHURST AVE #56	VAN NUYS, CA	91406
WELSH, MICHAEL K	COMPOSER	8026 FOUNTAIN AVE #6	LOS ANGELES, CA	90046
WELTER, FRANCES	ACTRESS	5000 LANKERSHIM BLVD #5	NORTH HOLLYWOOD, CA	91601
WELTMAN, STU	ACTOR	FELBER, 2126 N CAHUENGA BLVD	LOS ANGELES, CA	90068
WELZ, JOEY	SINGER-GUITARIST	JOANNE VEE, 201 N MILDRED ST	RANSON, WV	25438
WENCE, JODY JIM	PIANIST	ROUTE #4, BOX 357	LEBANON, TN	37087
WENCES, SENOR	VENTRILIQUIST	204 W 55TH ST #701-A	NEW YORK, NY	10019
WENDEL, SAM	TV WRITER	8955 BEVERLY BLVD	LOS ANGELES, CA	90048
WENDELKEN-WILSON, CHARLES	CONDUCTOR	1776 BROADWAY #504	NEW YORK, NY	10019
WENDELL, ELMARIE	ACTRESS	2501 W BURBANK BLVD #304	BURBANK, CA	91505
WENDERS, WIM	TV DIRECTOR	KOHNER, 9169 SUNSET BLVD	LOS ANGELES, CA	90069
WENDKOS, PAUL	FILM DIRECTOR	DGA, 7950 SUNSET BLVD	LOS ANGELES, CA	90046
WENDLEY, RICHARD H	TV WRITER	8955 BEVERLY BLVD	LOS ANGELES, CA	90048
WENDLING, LIONEL R	GUITARIST	11 ALLEE DE LA ROBERTSAU	6700 STRASBOURG	FRANCE
WENDSCHUH, RONALD	ACTOR	27 SOUNDVIEW AVE	NORWALK, CT	06854
WENDT, GEORGE	ACTOR	11726 SAN VICENTE BLVD #300	LOS ANGELES, CA	90049
WENDY, MISS	AERIALIST	SEE - MISS WENDY		
WENGROD, LAWRENCE C	WRITER	820 N GENESEE AVE	LOS ANGELES, CA	90046
WENKEL, ORTRUN	CONTRALTO	119 W 57TH ST #1505	NEW YORK, NY	10019
WENKER-KONNER, RONNIE	TV WRITER	555 W 57TH ST #1230	NEW YORK, NY	10019
WENMAN, DIANA B	TV DIRECTOR	151 E 83RD ST	NEW YORK, NY	10028
WENNBLOM, RALPH D	NEWS CORRESPONDENT	11714 FARMLAND DR	ROCKVILLE, MD	20852
WENNER, JANN S	PUBLISHING EXECUTIVE	US MAGAZINE COMPANY		
		1 DAG HAMMARSKJOLD PLAZA	NEW YORK, NY	10017
WENSLOW, MICHAEL F	COMPOSER	1172 N KINGSLEY DR #103	LOS ANGELES, CA	90029
WENTZ, BILL	SINGER	POST OFFICE BOX 25371	CHARLOTTE, NC	28212
WENTZEL, ANDREW	SINGER	59 E 54TH ST #81	NEW YORK, NY	10022
WENTZEL, VOLKMAR KURT	PHOTOGRAPHER	2204 KALORAMA RD, NW	WASHINGTON, DC	20008
WENZEL, MARK	MINE	POST OFFICE BOX 3819	LA MESA, CA	92044
WENZELBERG, CHARLES	PHOTOGRAPHER	6802 21ST AVE	BROOKLYN, NY	11204
WERBLE, COLE PALMER	NEWS CORREPONDENT	4912 GREENWAY DR	BETHESDA, MD	20816
WERBLE, WALLACE, JR	NEWS CORRESPONDENT	9709 FALLS BRIDGE LN	POTOMAC, MD	20854
WERFELMAN, LINDA	NEWS CORRESPONDENT	2032 BELMONT RD, NW	WASHINGTON, DC	20009
WERLE, BARBARA	ACTRESS	7204 ESTRELLA DEL MAR RD	LA COSTA, CA	92008
WERMEIL, STEPHEN J	NEWS CORRESPONDENT	6301 OWEN PL	BETHESDA, MD	20817
WERNER, DANIEL J	NEWS CORRESPONDENT	POST OFFICE BOX 2626	WASHINGTON, DC	20013
WERNER, DAVID	SINGER	3 E 54TH ST #1400	NEW YORK, NY	10022
WERNER, JEFFREY L	DIRECTOR-PRODUCER	4212 TEESDALE AVE	STUDIO CITY, CA	91604
WERNER, LESLIE MAITLAND	NEWS CORRESPONDENT	7400 HELMSDALE RD	BETHESDA, MD	20817
WERNER, MICHAEL H	WRITER	11011 1/2 STRATHMORE DR	LOS ANGELES, CA	90024
WERNER, PETER	DIRECTOR-PRODUCER	359 20TH ST	SANTA MONICA, CA	90402
WERNER, TOM	TV PRODUCER	1438 N GOWER ST #376	LOS ANGELES, CA	90028
WERRENRATH, REINALD, JR	DIRECTOR	2108 PARK LN	HIGHLAND PARK, IL	60035
WERTH, PAUL	THEATER PRODUCER	223 S BRIGHTON ST	BURBANK, CA	91506
WERTHEIMER, LINDA C	NEWS CORRESPONDENT	1416 35TH ST, NW	WASHINGTON, DC	20007
WERTIMER, NED	ACTOR	7782 VIA RONALDO	SUN VALLEY, CA	91352
WERTZ, JAY	VIDEO EDITOR	ENTERTAINMENT TONIGHT		
		PARAMOUNT TELEVISION		
		5555 MELROSE AVE	LOS ANGELES, CA	90038
WESLEY, JAMES M	NEWS CORRESPONDENT	3426 16TH ST, NW	WASHINGTON, DC	20010
WESLEY, JOHN	ACTOR	247 S BEVERLY DR #102	BEVERLY HILLS, CA	90210
WESLEY, KASSIE	ACTRESS	CBS-TV, "THE GUIDING LIGHT"		
		51 W 52ND ST	NEW YORK, NY	10019
WESSELL, ROBERT, JR	PIANIST	40 JONES CIR	OLD HICKORY, TN	37138
WESSELS, HUGO L	PHOTOGRAPHER	2130 "P" ST #628, NW	WASHINGTON, DC	20037
WESSON, BERNARD C	DIRECTOR	465 W BROADWAY	NEW YORK, NY	10012
WESSON, CELESTE L	NEWS CORRESPONDENT	2025 "M" ST, NW	WASHINGTON, DC	20036
WESSON, DICK	ACTOR-WRITER	3575 W CAHUENGA BLVD #320	LOS ANGELES, CA	90068
WESSON, EILEEN	ACTRESS	12725 VENTURA BLVD #E	STUDIO CITY, CA	91604
WEST, ADAM	ACTOR	612 EL CERCO PL	PACIFIC PALISADES, CA	90272
WEST, ALVY	COMPOSER-CONDUCTOR	39 ANDOVER RD	ROSLYN HEIGHTS, NY	11577
WEST, BERNARD	TV WRITER	8955 BEVERLY BLVD	LOS ANGELES, CA	90048
WEST, BERNIE	PRODUCER	NRW COMP, 5746 SUNSET BLVD	LOS ANGELES, CA	90028
WEST, BROOKS	ACTOR	9066 SAINT IVES DR	LOS ANGELES, CA	90069
WEST, CARINTHIA	ACTRESS	9255 SUNSET BLVD #505	LOS ANGELES, CA	90069

Name	Occupation	Address	City
WEST, CARYN	ACTRESS	ABRAMS ARTISTS & ASSOCIATES	
		420 MADISON AVE, 14TH FLOOR	NEW YORK, NY 10017
WEST, DAN	SINGER	HOT, 306 W CHURCH ST	HORSESHOE BEND, AR 71512
WEST, DENNIS W	MUSICIAN	300 16TH ST	OLD HICKORY, TN 37138
WEST, DONALD	NEWS CORRESPONDENT	2122 MASSACHUSETTS AVE, NW	WASHINGTON, DC 20008
WEST, DOTTIE	SINGER	POST OFFICE BOX 120537	NASHVILLE, TN 37212
WEST, ELLIOT	NOVELIST	8955 BEVERLY BLVD	LOS ANGELES, CA 90048
WEST, ELVIS R, II	GUITARIST	431 GATES RD	GOODLETTSVILLE, TN 37072
WEST, JAMES D	WRITER	4112 SHADYGLADE AVE	STUDIO CITY, CA 91604
WEST, JON FREDERIC	TENOR	CAMI, 165 W 57TH ST	NEW YORK, NY 10019
WEST, LOCKWOOD	ACTOR	PORT HALL COTTAGE	
		170-A DYKE RD	
		BRIGHTON	SUSSEX ENGLAND
WEST, LOUISE C	AGENT-PRODUCER	1775 BROADWAY, 7TH FLOOR	NEW YORK, NY 10019
WEST, MARTIN	ACTOR	10035 KEOKUK AVE	CHATSWORTH, CA 91311
WEST, MARY	CASTING DIRECTOR	7319 BEVERLY BLVD #10	LOS ANGELES, CA 90036
WEST, NORMA	ACTRESS	BROWE, 13 SAINT MARTIN'S RD	LONDON SW9 ENGLAND
WEST, ORMAND J, JR	DIRECTOR	140 W END AVE	NEW YORK, NY 10023
WEST, PARKER	ACTOR	1301 N FULLER AVE	LOS ANGELES, CA 90046
WEST, PAUL	NEWS CORRESPONDENT	1202 NATIONAL PRESS BLDG	
		529 14TH ST, NW	WASHINGTON, DC 20045
WEST, PAUL	WRITER	8955 BEVERLY BLVD	LOS ANGELES, CA 90048
WEST, RED	ACTOR-AUTHOR	15301 VENTURA BLVD #345	SHERMAN OAKS, CA 91403
WEST, RON	PIANIST	300 BAKERTOWN RD #17-C	ANTIOCH, TN 37013
WEST, ROY	SINGER	PROCESS, 439 WILEY AVE	FRANKLIN, PA 16323
WEST, SHELLY	SINGER	MC FADDEN & ASSOCIATES	
		818 18TH AVE S	NASHVILLE, TN 37203
WEST, TEGAN	ACTOR	10000 SANTA MONICA BLVD #305	LOS ANGELES, CA 90067
WEST, TIMOTHY	ACTOR	46 NORTH SIDE	
		WANDSWORTH COMMON	LONDON SW18 ENGLAND
WEST, TOMMY	SINGER	POST OFFICE BOX 29543	ATLANTA, GA 30359
WEST, WALLY	ACTOR	12418 LAUREL TERR "D"	STUDIO CITY, CA 91604
WEST, WARREN	ACTOR	1607 N EL CENTRO AVE #23	LOS ANGELES, CA 90028
WEST, WILLIAM BILLY	DRUMMER	101 BLUE HILL CT	NASHVILLE, TN 37214
WEST, WOODY	NEWS CORRESPONDENT	3026 CREST AVE	CHEVERLY, MD 20785
WESTBERG, REBECCA	ACTRESS	4173 W 5TH AVE	LOS ANGELES, CA 90020
WESTBERRY, KENT	SINGER-GUITARIST	515 UTLEY DR	GOODLETTSVILLE, TN 37072
WESTBROOK, DAROL	ACTOR	120 S VICTORY BLVD #104	BURBANK, CA 91501
WESTBROOK-GEHA, MARY	MEZZO-SOPRANO	AARON, 25 HUNTINGTON AVE	BOSTON, MA 02116
WESTBROOKS, LOGAN	RECORD EXECUTIVE	15223 RAYNETA DR	SHERMAN OAKS, CA 91403
WESTBURY, KENNETH	CINEMATOGRAPHER	32 NELSON RD, WHITTON	
		TWICKINGHAM	MIDDLESEX TW2 7AU ENGLAND
WESTCHESTER WIND QUINTET	WIND QUINTET	756 7TH AVE #67	NEW YORK, NY 10019
WESTCOTT, DEXTER	WRESTLER	NATIONAL WRESTLING ALLIANCE	
		JIM CROCKETT PROMOTIONS	
		421 BRIARBEND DR	CHARLOTTE, NC 28209
WESTCOTT, RICHARD W	NEWS CORRESPONDENT	NBC-TV, NEWS DEPARTMENT	
		4001 NEBRASKA AVE, NW	WASHINGTON, DC 20016
WESTENBURG, RICHARD	CONDUCTOR	59 E 54TH ST #81	NEW YORK, NY 10022
WESTERMARK, VICTORIA	WRITER	1911 IDAHO AVE	SANTA MONICA, CA 90403
WESTERSCHULTE, RICHARD	TV WRITER	8955 BEVERLY BLVD	LOS ANGELES, CA 90048
WESTGATE, ROBERT D	NEWS CORRESPONDENT	1425 17TH ST #401, NW	WASHINGTON, DC 20036
WESTHEIMER, DAVID	TV WRITER	11722 DARLINGTON AVE	LOS ANGELES, CA 90049
WESTHEIMER, DR RUTH	SEX THERAPIST	LIFETIME MEDICAL TELEVISION	
		1211 AVE OF THE AMERICAS	NEW YORK, NY 10036
WESTIN, AVRAM ROBERT	TV DIRECTOR	ABC-TV, 7 W 66TH ST	NEW YORK, NY 10023
WESTLAKE, DONALD E	NOVELIST	555 W 57TH ST #1230	NEW YORK, NY 10019
WESTLEIN, PATRICIA	NEWS CORRESPONDENT	4301 MASSACHUSETTS AVE, NW	WASHINGTON, DC 20016
WESTMAN, JAMES A	DIRECTOR	4849 CASTLE RD	LA CANADA, CA 91011
WESTMORELAND, DICK	FOOTBALL	2801 MEADOW LARK DR	SAN DIEGO, CA 92123
WESTMORELAND, JAMES	ACTOR	8019 1/2 W NORTON AVE	LOS ANGELES, CA 90046
WESTMORELAND, JANET M	NEWS CORRESPONDENT	3137 BRADFORD WOOD CT	OAKTON, VA 22124
WESTNEY, WILLIAM	PIANIST	LIEBERMAN, 11 RIVERSIDE DR	NEW YORK, NY 10023
WESTON, ANN H	TV WRITER	8955 BEVERLY BLVD	LOS ANGELES, CA 90048
WESTON, CAROLYN	WRITER	505 OLYMPIC BLVD #49	SANTA MONICA, CA 90401
WESTON, CELIA	ACTRESS	10100 SANTA MONICA #1600	LOS ANGELES, CA 90067
WESTON, CHRIS	NEWS CORRESPONDENT	9506 SALUDA CT	LORTON, VA 22079
WESTON, DAVID	ACTOR	123-A GROSVENOR RD	LONDON SW 1 ENGLAND
WESTON, ELLEN	ACTRESS	10513 HOLMAN AVE	LOS ANGELES, CA 90024
WESTON, ERIC	DIRECTOR	DGA, 7950 SUNSET BLVD	LOS ANGELES, CA 90046
WESTON, GRACIE	ACTRESS	257 HAMPTON DR #1	VENICE, CA 90291
WESTON, JACK	ACTOR	A KOZAK, 468 PARK AVE S	NEW YORK, NY 10016
WESTON, JEFF	ACTOR	3151 W CAHUENGA BLVD #310	LOS ANGELES, CA 90068
WESTON, KIM	SINGER	614 CHRYSLER DR #304	DETROIT, MI 48207
WESTON, PAUL	MUSICIAN-COMPOSER	2339 CENTURY HILL	LOS ANGELES, CA 90067
WESTON, RICHARD	TALENT AGENT	1900 AVE OF THE STARS #2375	LOS ANGELES, CA 90067
WESTPHELING, ROBERT P, III	NEWS CORRESPONDENT	9011 EDGEPARK RD	VIENNA, VA 22180
WESTWOOD, BARRY	ACTOR-PRODUCER	231 WEST ST, FAREHAM	HANTS ENGLAND
WESTWOOD WIND QUINTET	WIND QUINTET	333 TAYLOR AVE N #202	SEATTLE, WA 98109
WET BEHIND THE EARS	C & W GROUP	OBA, 5601 ODANA RD	MADISON, WI 53719
WET WILLIE	ROCK & ROLL GROUP	210 25TH AVE N #N-101	NASHVILLE, TN 37203
WETHERBEE, DAN	FILM EDITOR	6464 SUNSET BLVD #1150	HOLLYWOOD, CA 90028
WETHERILL, LINDA	FLUTIST	333 TAYLOR AVE N #202	SEATTLE, WA 98109
WEVER, NED	ACTOR	355 AVENIDA SEVILLA	LAGUNA HILLS, CA 92653
WEVERKA, ROBERT	WRITER	317 S HOLLISTON AVE	PASADENA, CA 91106

Name	Occupation	Address	City	Zip
WEXLER, HASKELL	CINEMATOGRAPHER	26701 LATIGO SHORE DR	MALIBU, CA	90265
WEXLER, NORMAN	SCREENWRITER	8955 BEVERLY BLVD	LOS ANGELES, CA	90048
WEXLER, ROBERT	ACTOR	5628 BELLINGHAM AVE	NORTH HOLLYWOOD, CA	91607
WEXLER, STANLEY	BASSO-BARITONE	CAMI, 165 W 57TH ST	NEW YORK, NY	10019
WEXLER, YALE	PRODUCER	9360 WILSHIRE BLVD	BEVERLY HILLS, CA	90212
WEYMAN, ANDREW D	DIRECTOR	DAVIS/WEYMAN, 68 E END AVE	NEW YORK, NY	10028
WEYMAN, JUDITH	MEZZO-SOPRANO	756 7TH AVE #67	NEW YORK, NY	10019
WEYMAN, LEO "HAP"	DIRECTOR	DGA, 7950 SUNSET BLVD	LOS ANGELES, CA	90046
WEYR, THOMAS	NEWS CORRESPONDENT	2725 29TH ST, NW	WASHINGTON, DC	20008
WHALEN, JOHN M	NEWS CORRESPONDENT	1231 25TH ST, NW	WASHINGTON, DC	20037
WHALEN, WILLIAM	TV DIRECTOR	1346 MIDLAND AVE	BRONXVILLE, NY	10708
WHALEN, WILLIAM L	NEWS CORRESPONDENT	100 N NOTTINGHAM ST	ARLINGTON, VA	22203
WHALEY, PAT	WRITER-EDITOR	POST OFFICE BOX 500	WASHINGTON, DC	20044
WHALLON, EVAN	CONDUCTOR	1776 BROADWAY #504	NEW YORK, NY	10019
WHARTON, ANNIE	ACTRESS	434 N OAKHURST DR #11	BEVERLY HILLS, CA	90210
WHARTON, DENNIS	NEWS CORRESPONDENT	7020 STATENDAM CT	MC LEAN, VA	22101
WHARTON, PETER G	NEWS CORRESPONDENT	ABC-TV, NEWS DEPARTMENT		
		1717 DE SALES ST, NW	WASHINGTON, DC	20036
WHAT IS THIS	ROCK & ROLL GROUP	6520 SELMA AVE #211	HOLLYWOOD, CA	90028
WHATHAM, CLAUDE	TV DIRECTOR-PRODUCER	CAMP HOUSE, CAMP		
		MISERDEN, STROUD	GLOUSTER	ENGLAND
WHATLEY, MOP HEAD	WRESTLER	SEE - WHATLEY, PISTOL PEZ		
WHATLEY, PISTOL PEZ	WRESTLER	NATIONAL WRESTLING ALLIANCE		
		JIM CROCKETT PROMOTIONS		
		421 BRIARBEND DR	CHARLOTTE, NC	28209
WHATLEY, SHASKA	WRESTLER	SEE - WHATLEY, PISTOL PEZ		
WHDON, JOHN	WRITER	14144 VENTURA BLVD #200	SHERMAN OAKS, CA	91423
WHEAT, WARREN	WRITER-EDITOR	POST OFFICE BOX 500	WASHINGTON, DC	20044
WHEAT, WARREN D	NEWS CORRESPONDENT	7420 RIDGE RD	SPRINGFIELD, VA	22150
WHEATON, JACK W	CONDUCTOR	4469 VENTURA CANYON AVE #E-110	SHERMAN OAKS, CA	91423
WHEATON, KAHILL	ACTOR	6380 WILSHIRE BLVD #1600	LOS ANGELES, CA	90048
WHEATON, KEN	SINGER	POST OFFICE BOX 6025	NEWPORT NEWS, VA	23606
WHEATON, PAMELA	TV WRITER	ENTERTAINMENT TONIGHT		
		PARAMOUNT TELEVISION		
		5555 MELROSE AVE	LOS ANGELES, CA	90038
WHEATON, VIRGINIA	NEWS CORRESPONDENT	6744 2ND ST, NW	WASHINGTON, DC	20012
WHEATON, WIL	ACTOR	11350 VENTURA BLVD #206	STUDIO CITY, CA	91604
WHEDON, PEGGY	NEWS CORRESPONDENT	1012 14TH ST, NW	WASHINGTON, DC	20005
WHEDON, THOMAS	TV WRITER	1730 MICHAEL LN	PACIFIC PALISADES, CA	90272
WHEELER, BILLY EDD	SINGER	POST OFFICE BOX 7	SWANNONOA, NC	28778
WHEELER, DAVID F	DIRECTOR	DGA, 110 W 57TH ST	NEW YORK, NY	10019
WHEELER, DEBBIE	ACTRESS	17 RICHMOND HILL, RICHMOND	SURREY	ENGLAND
WHEELER, DONNA M	DIRECTOR	DGA, 7950 SUNSET BLVD	LOS ANGELES, CA	90046
WHEELER, GARY	ACTOR	9744 WILSHIRE BLVD #306	BEVERLY HILLS, CA	90212
WHEELER, HUGH C	SCREENWRITER	8955 BEVERLY BLVD	LOS ANGELES, CA	90048
WHEELER, JOHN	ACTOR	4741 LAUREL CANYON BLVD #109	STUDIO CITY, CA	91607
WHEELER, LINDA	PHOTOGRAPHER	1620 3RD ST, NW	WASHINGTON, DC	20001
WHEELER, MARGARET	ACTRESS	3546 MULTIVIEW DR	HOLLYWOOD, CA	90068
WHEELER, NANCY	ACTRESS	8019 1/2 MELROSE AVE #3	LOS ANGELES, CA	90046
WHEELER, ONIE	MUSICAN	POST OFFICE BOX 166	MOUNT JULIET, TN	37122
WHEELER, R W	ACTOR	1605 N CAHUENGA BLVD #202	LOS ANGELES, CA	90028
WHEELER, TIMOTHY L	NEWS CORRESPONDENT	816 BEAUMONT AVE	BALTIMORE, MD	21212
WHEELWRIGHT, JEFF	WRITER-EDITOR	LIFE/TIME & LIFE BLDG		
		ROCKEFELLER CENTER	NEW YORK, NY	10020
WHELAN, HELEN K	NEWS CORRESPONDENT	236 MASSACHUSETTS AVE, NW	WASHINGTON, DC	20002
WHELAN, JILL	ACTRESS	POST OFFICE BOX 1305	WOODLAND HILLS, CA	91364
WHELAN, JOHN W, JR	WRITER	445 N BEDFORD DR #PH	BEVERLY HILLS, CA	90210
WHELCHEL, LISA	ACTRESS	8500 WILSHIRE BLVD #506	BEVERLY HILLS, CA	90211
WHELEN, CHRISTOPHER	COMPOSER	55 CONRWALL GARDENS #12	LONDON SW7	ENGLAND
WHELPLEY, JOHN FRANCIS	TV WRITER	22561 CARBON MESA RD	MALIBU, CA	90265
WHETZELL, SUSAN	WRITER	1820 CANYON DR	LOS ANGELES, CA	90028
WHIPP, JOSEPH	ACTOR	1418 N HIGHLAND AVE #102	LOS ANGELES, CA	90028
WHIPPLE, CHRISTOPHER	WRITER-REPORTER	LIFE/TIME & LIFE BLDG		
		ROCKEFELLER CENTER	NEW YORK, NY	10020
WHIPPLE, SAM	ACTOR	9157 SUNSET BLVD #206	LOS ANGELES, CA	90069
WHIPPLE, SCOTT	GUITARIST	1420 OTTER CREEK RD	NASHVILLE, TN	37215
WHIPPLE, STERLING	GUITARIST	POST OFFICE BOX 437	RIDGETOP, TN	37152
WHIPPLE, WALLACE	ACTOR	LEONETTI, 6526 SUNSET BLVD	HOLLYWOOD, CA	90028
WHISKEY HOLLOW	C & W GROUP	PT & M, 2464 BRASILIA CIR	MISSISSAUGA, ONT	CANADA
WHISKEY RIVER	C & W GROUP	LST, 2138 FLAG MARSH RD	MOUNT AIRY, MD	21771
WHISPERINGS, THE	VOCAL GROUP	LUTZ, 5626 "O" ST BUILDING	LINCOLN, NE	68510
WHISPERS, THE	VOCAL GROUP	200 W 51ST ST #1410	NEW YORK, NY	10019
WHISTLE	RAP GROUP	SELECT RECORDS, 175 5TH AVE	NEW YORK, NY	10010
WHITAKER, CHRISTINA	ACTRESS	6380 WILSHIRE BLVD #1600	LOS ANGELES, CA	90048
WHITAKER, CLAIRE	TV WRITER	8955 BEVERLY BLVD	LOS ANGELES, CA	90048
WHITAKER, DAVID	COMPOSER	37 BUSHWOOD RD, KEW	SURREY TW9 3BG	ENGLAND
WHITAKER, LESLIE	NEWS REPORTER	TIME/TIME & LIFE BLDG		
		ROCKEFELLER CENTER	NEW YORK, NY	10020
WHITAKER, STEVEN	GUITARIST	1109 LIPSCOMB DR	NASHVILLE, TN	37204
WHITBREAD, PETER	ACTOR-WRITER	39 THE STREET, HINDOLVESTON		
		DEREHAM	NORFOLK NR20 5AS	ENGLAND
WHITCHURCH, MISSU	ACTRESS	417 W 56TH ST #4-A	NEW YORK, NY	10019
WHITCOMB, IAN	SING-ACT-PROD	POST OFFICE BOX 451	ALTADENA, CA	91001
WHITCOMB, KENNETH G	COMPOSER-CONDUCTOR	1423 W CHATEAU AVE	ANAHEIM, CA	92802
WHITE, AL	ACTOR	1930 CENTURY PARK W #303	LOS ANGELES, CA	90067

WHITE, BARRY	SINGER-SONGWRITER	6101 ATOLL AVE	VAN NUYS, CA	91401
WHITE, BETTY	ACTRESS	506 N CARLEINA AVE	LOS ANGELES, CA	90049
WHITE, BIZ	GUITARIST	145 50TH AVE N	NASHVILLE, TN	37209
WHITE, BUCK & THE DOWN HOME FOL	C & W GROUP	380 LEXINGTON AVE #1119	NEW YORK, NY	10017
WHITE, CALLAN	ACTRESS	ABC-TV NETWORK, "LOVING"		
		1330 AVE OF THE AMERICAS	NEW YORK, NY	10019
WHITE, CAROL	ACTRESS	8019 1/2 MELROSE AVE #3	LOS ANGELES, CA	90046
WHITE, CAROLE ITA	ACTRESS-WRITER	517 N REXFORD DR	BEVERLY HILLS, CA	90210
WHITE, CATHERINE	HARPIST	AFFILIATE ARTISTS, INC		
		37 W 65TH ST, 6TH FLOOR	NEW YORK, NY	10023
WHITE, CHARLES	ACTOR	2 STUYVESANT OVAL	NEW YORK, NY	10009
WHITE, CHARLES M	NEWS CORRESPONDENT	4812 DE RUSSEY PL	CHEVY CHASE, MD	20815
WHITE, D BERGEN	GUITARIST	2907 TYNE BLVD	NASHVILLE, TN	37215
WHITE, DAVID	ACTOR	7466 BEVERLY BLVD #205	LOS ANGELES, CA	90036
WHITE, DAVID	DIRECTOR	DGA, 7950 SUNSET BLVD	LOS ANGELES, CA	90046
WHITE, DEBORAH	ACTRESS	9300 WILSHIRE BLVD #410	BEVERLY HILLS, CA	90212
WHITE, DIANE	COLUMNIST	THE BOSTON GLOBE		
		135 MORRISSEY BLVD	BOSTON, MA	02107
WHITE, DONALD B	NEWS CORRESPONDENT	512 ETHAN ALLEN AVE	TAKOMA PARK, MD	20912
WHITE, DOUGLAS M	NEWS CORRESPONDENT	340 NATIONAL PRESS BLDG		
		529 14TH ST, NW	WASHINGTON, DC	20045
WHITE, DUCK	SINGER-GUITARIST	POST OFFICE BOX 15871	NASHVILLE, TN	37215
WHITE, DWIGHT L	COMPOSER-CONDUCTOR	1432 OLIVE ST	SAN BERNARDINO, CA	92410
WHITE, FRANCES	ACTRESS	BRYAN DREW, LTD		
		80-82 REGENT ST	LONDON W1	ENGLAND
		MEZZANINE QUADRANT HOUSE		
WHITE, GARRY MICHAEL	TV WRITER	7018 WOODROW WILSON DR	LOS ANGELES, CA	90068
WHITE, GORDON E	NEWS CORRESPONDENT	1502 STONEWALL RD, BOX 3067	ALEXANDRIA, VA	22302
WHITE, HOLLY	TV WRITER	8955 BEVERLY BLVD	LOS ANGELES, CA	90048
WHITE, HOWARD O, JR	GUITARIST	1301 NEELS BEND RD #B-17	MADISON, TN	37115
WHITE, HUBERT BILL	DIRECTOR	5907 W PICO BLVD	LOS ANGELES, CA	90035
WHITE, JALEEL	ACTRESS	1450 BELFAST DR	LOS ANGELES, CA	90069
WHITE, JAMES EARL	GUITARIST	POST OFFICE BOX 367	HENDERSONVILLE, TN	37075
WHITE, JESSE	ACTOR	1944 GLENDON AVE #304	LOS ANGELES, CA	90025
WHITE, JOHN	PHOTOGRAPHER	CHICAGO SUN-TIMES		
		401 N WABASH AVE	CHICAGO, IL	60611
WHITE, JOHN SYLVESTER	ACTOR	4717 CEDROS AVE	SHERMAN OAKS, CA	91403
WHITE, JOHNNY	C & W GROUP	PENNY, 30 GUINAN ST	WALTHAM, MA	02154
WHITE, JOSEPH JOHN	DIRECTOR	DGA, 110 W 57TH ST	NEW YORK, NY	10019
WHITE, JOSH, JR	SINGER	DAY PRODS, 300 W 55TH ST	NEW YORK, NY	10019
WHITE, JOSHUA W	DIRECTOR	33 5TH AVE	NEW YORK, NY	10003
WHITE, KENNETH	MUSIC ARRANGER	POST OFFICE BOX 22564	NASHVILLE, TN	37202
WHITE, LARRY	PRODUCER	COLUMBIA PICTURES TV		
		COLUMBIA PLAZA	BURBANK, CA	91505
WHITE, LARRY B	COMPOSER-CONDUCTOR	1628 N FAIRFAX AVE	LOS ANGELES, CA	90046
WHITE, LAWSON WAYNE	DRUMMER	416 HILLTOP DR	COLUMBIA, TN	38401
WHITE, LEON	WRESTLER	AMERICAN WRESTLING ASSOC		
		MINNEAPLOIS WRESTLING		
		10001 WAYZATA BLVD	MINNETONKA, MN	55345
WHITE, LEONARD	ACTOR-DIRECTOR	HIGHLANDS, 40 HILL CREST RD		
		NEWHAVEN	SUSSEX BN9 9EG	ENGLAND
WHITE, LESTER ALFRED	WRITER	2256 BAGLEY AVE	LOS ANGELES, CA	90034
WHITE, MAURICE	SINGER-COMPOSER	POST OFFICE BOX 5880	SHERMAN OAKS, CA	91413
WHITE, MICHAEL	FILM PRODUCER	13 DUKE ST, SAINT JAMES	LONDON SW1Y 6DB	ENGLAND
WHITE, MICHAEL ALLEN	TRUMPETER	2918 OAKLAND AVE	NASHVILLE, TN	37212
WHITE, MICHELE	SINGER	TALENT MANAGEMENT		
		2460 SPRING LAKE DR	MARIETTA, GA	30062
WHITE, NAOMI	ACTRESS	22660 PACIFIC COAST HWY #5-A	MALIBU, CA	90265
WHITE, NATHANIAL	ACTOR	250 E 113TH ST	NEW YORK, NY	10029
WHITE, NONI	ACTRESS	6430 SUNSET BLVD #1203	LOS ANGELES, CA	90028
WHITE, ONNA	CHOREOGRAPHER	SSD & C, 1501 BROADWAY	NEW YORK, NY	10036
WHITE, PATRICK	TV WRITER	8955 BEVERLY BLVD	LOS ANGELES, CA	90048
WHITE, PEREGRINE	NEWS CORRESPONDENT	NBC-TV, NEWS DEPARTMENT		
		4001 NEBRASKA AVE, NW	WASHINGTON, DC	20016
WHITE, PETER	ACTOR	9300 WILSHIRE BLVD #410	BEVERLY HILLS, CA	90212
WHITE, PETER V	TV DIRECTOR-PRODUCER	12433 MOORPARK ST #216	STUDIO CITY, CA	91604
WHITE, PHYLLIS	TV WRITER	8955 BEVERLY BLVD	LOS ANGELES, CA	90048
WHITE, ROBERT	TENOR	59 E 54TH ST #81	NEW YORK, NY	10022
WHITE, ROBERT	TV WRITER	8955 BEVERLY BLVD	LOS ANGELES, CA	90048
WHITE, ROBERT B	VIOLINIST	30011 OAKWOOD	MAGNOLIA, TX	77355
WHITE, ROBERT F	DIRECTOR	DGA, 7950 SUNSET BLVD	LOS ANGELES, CA	90046
WHITE, ROBERT G	DRUMMER	10701 MOORP[ARK ST #2	NORTH HOLLYWOOD, CA	91602
WHITE, ROY E	CONDUCTOR	13733 PHILADELPHIA ST	WHITTIER, CA	90601
WHITE, RUTH S	COMPOSER	POST OFFICE BOX 34485	LOS ANGELES, CA	90034
WHITE, SAM	DIRECTOR-PRODUCER	18579 BRASILIA DR	NORTHRIDGE, CA	91326
WHITE, SHARON SKAGGS	SINGER-GUITARIST	SEE - SKAGGS, SHARON WHITE		
WHITE, SHEILA	ACTRESS	PETER CHARLESWORTH, LTD		
		68 OLD BROMPTON RD	LONDON SW7 3LQ	ENGLAND
WHITE, SONNY	GUITARIST	7511 SE HENRY BLVD	PORTLAND, OR	97206
WHITE, STEPHEN W	WRITER	4915 AGNES AVE	NORTH HOLLYWOOD, CA	91607
WHITE, TONY	WRESTLER	SEE - ATLAS, TONY		
WHITE, TONY JOE	SINGER	35 MUSIC SQUARE E	NASHVILLE, TN	37203
WHITE, VANNA	LETTER TURNER-MODEL	MERV GRIFFIN PRODUCTIONS		
		"THE WHEEL OF FORTUNE"		
		1541 N VINE ST	HOLLYWOOD, CA	90028

TONY JOE WHITE

STUART WHITMAN

RICHARD WIDMARK

ROBERT J. WILKE

JUNE WILKINSON

BILLY DEE WILLIAMS

DENICE WILLIAMS

DON WILLIAMS

HANK WILLIAMS, JR.

Name	Occupation	Address	City	Zip
WHITE, VIRGINIA	ACTRESS	7 E 14TH ST	NEW YORK, NY	10003
WHITE, WENDY	MEZZO-SOPRANO	59 E 54TH ST #81	NEW YORK, NY	10022
WHITE, WENDY A	NEWS CORRESPONDENT	NBC-TV, NEWS DEPARTMENT		
		4001 NEBRASKA AVE, NW	WASHINGTON, DC	20016
WHITE, WILLARD	BASSO-BARITONE	CAMI, 165 W 57TH ST	NEW YORK, NY	10019
WHITE, WILLIAM	JOURNALIST	25860 W 14 MILE RD	FRANKLIN, MI	48025
WHITE BUFFALO BAND	MUSICAL GROUP	SOUTHERN TALENT INTL		
		2925 FALLOWRIDGE CT	SNELLVILLE, GA	30278
WHITE CHINA	ROCK & ROLL GROUP	41 BRITAIN ST #200	TORONTO, ONT	CANADA
WHITE LIGHTIN'	ROCK & ROLL GROUP	41 BRITAIN ST #200	TORONTO, ONT	CANADA
WHITEFORD, STEVEN	ACTOR	1638 1/4 EDGECLIFFE DR	LOS ANGELES, CA	90026
WHITEHALL, WAYNE	ACTOR	214 W 82ND ST	NEW YORK, NY	10024
WHITEHEAD, DENNIS RICHARD	PHOTOGRAPHER	1410 N NELSON ST	ARLINGTON, VA	22201
WHITEHEAD, GEOFFREY	ACTOR	BRYAN DREW, LTD		
		MEZZANINE QUADRANT HOUSE		
		80-82 REGENT ST	LONDON W1	ENGLAND
WHITEHEAD, O Z	ACTOR	45 UPPER LEESON ST		
		GROUND FLOOR FLAT	DUBLIN 4	IRELAND
WHITEHEAD, PAUL	PIANIST	1857 LAUREL RIDGE	NASHVILLE, TN	37215
WHITEHEAD, PAXTON	ACTOR	9255 SUNSET BLVD #505	LOS ANGELES, CA	90069
WHITEHEAD, ROBERT	THEATER PRODUCER	1501 BROADWAY	NEW YORK, NY	10036
WHITEHEAD, WILLIAM	TV WRITER	8955 BEVERLY BLVD	LOS ANGELES, CA	90048
WHITEHILL, LOU	WRITER	1020 N DOHENY DR #3	LOS ANGELES, CA	90069
WHITEHOUSE, BRIAN	TV DIRECTOR-PRODUCER	BBC-TV CENTRE, WOOD LN		
		SHEPHERDS BUSH	LONDON W12	ENGLAND
WHITEHURST, JERRY	PIANIST	1125 OMAN DR	BRENTWOOD, CA	37027
WHITELAW, ARTHUR	THEATER PRODUCER	132 E 38TH ST	NEW YORK, NY	10016
WHITELAW, BILLIE	ACTRESS	JOY JAMESON, LTD		
		7 W EATON PLACE MEWS	LONDON SW1	ENGLAND
WHITELEY, JOHN SCOTT	ORGANIST	15 HIGH ST #621	HARTFORD, CT	06103
WHITELEY, SANDY	TV DIRECTOR	2043 W FARWELL AVE #2-N	CHICAGO, IL	60645
WHITEMAN, FRANK	ACTOR	7230 ESTEPA DR	TUJUNGA, CA	91042
WHITEMIRE, RICHARD	NEWS CORRESPONDENT	4609 38TH ST, NW	WASHINGTON, DC	20016
WHITEMORE, HUGH	PLAYWRIGHT	DAISH, 83 EASTBOURNE MEWS	LONDON W2 6LQ	ENGLAND
WHITES, THE	C & W GROUP	POST OFFICE BOX 22419	NASHVILLE, TN	37202
WHITESELL, JOHN P, II	DIRECTOR	265 RIVERSIDE DR	NEW YORK, NY	10025
WHITESNAKE	ROCK & ROLL GROUP	CONCERT, 166-198 LIVERPOOL RD	LONDON N1	ENGLAND
WHITFIELD, BARBARA & THE SAVAGE	ROCK & ROLL GROUP	25 HUNTINGTON AVE #420	BOSTON, MA	02116
WHITFIELD, JUNE	ACTRESS	YOUNG, 31 KING'S RD	LONDON SW3 4RP	ENGLAND
WHITFIELD, LYNN	ACTRESS	SF & A, 121 N SAN VICENTE BLVD	BEVERLY HILLS, CA	90211
WHITFIELD, VANTILE E	TV DIRECTOR	1429 VARNUM ST, NW	WASHINGTON, DC	20011
WHITING, BARBARA	ACTRESS	SMITH, 1085 WADDINGTON ST	BIRMINGHAM, MI	48009
WHITING, JAMEY	GUITARIST	247 WELCH RD	NASHVILLE, TN	37211
WHITING, JOE	SINGER	POST OFFICE BOX 11276	ROCHESTER, NY	14611
WHITING, MARGARET	SINGER	41 W 58TH ST #5-A	NEW YORK, NY	10019
WHITLEY, BRIAN	ACTOR-DIRECTOR	POST OFFICE BOX 18512	LOS ANGELES, CA	90018
WHITLEY, KEITH	SINGER	POST OFFICE BOX 120308	NASHVILLE, TN	37212
WHITLEY, RICHARD FRANCIS	SCREENWRITER	172 N SYCAMORE AVE	LOS ANGELES, CA	90036
WHITLOW, JILL	ACTRESS	LIGHT, 113 N ROBERTSON BLVD	LOS ANGELES, CA	90048
WHITLOW, ZETTA	ACTRESS	11600 MONTANA AVE #210	LOS ANGELES, CA	90049
WHITMAN, JACK	TV DIRECTOR	14046 FENTON LN	SYLMAR, CA	91342
WHITMAN, JOHN	PHOTOGRAPHER	604 N JACKSON ST	ARLINGTON, VA	22201
WHITMAN, SLIM	SINGER	1300 DIVISION ST #103	NASHVILLE, TN	37203
WHITMAN, STUART	ACTOR	749 SAN YSIDRO RD	SANTA BARBARA, CA	93108
WHITMAN, WANDA	STORY ANALYST	1408 N DETROIT ST	LOS ANGELES, CA	90046
WHITMORE, JAMES	ACTOR	25 CENTRAL PARK W	NEW YORK, NY	10023
WHITMORE, JAMES, JR	ACTOR	7642 ETIWANDA AVE	RESEDA, CA	91335
WHITMORE, JANE	NEWS CORRESPONDENT	1400 29TH ST, NW	WASHINGTON, DC	20007
WHITMORE, STANFORD	WRITER	4816 GLORIA AVE	ENCINO, CA	91436
WHITMORE, STEPHEN	ACTOR	1324 MYRTLE ST #D	GLENDALE, CA	91203
WHITMORE, SUSAN	NEWS CORRESPONDENT	1310 N MEADE ST #203	ARLINGTON, VA	22209
WHITNEY, CECE	ACTRESS	840 N ODGEN DR	LOS ANGELES, CA	90046
WHITNEY, DAVID L	NEWS CORRESPONDENT	9405 ULYSEES CT	BURKE, VA	22015
WHITNEY, JOHN	WRITER-PRODUCER	IBA, 70 BROMPTON RD	LONDON SW3 1EY	ENGLAND
WHITNEY, KYLE C	NEWS CORRESPONDENT	1776 "G" ST, NW	WASHINGTON, DC	20006
WHITNEY, PHYLLIS	ACTRESS	2160 S BEVERLY GLEN BLVD #357	LOS ANGELES, CA	90025
WHITNEY, ROBERT	ACTOR	3792 HARRISON ST #36	OAKLAND, CA	94611
WHITNEY & ALVARADO	PIANO DUO	KAY, 58 W 58TH ST	NEW YORK, NY	10019
WHITROW, BENJAMIN	ACTOR	MC REDDIE, 91 REGENT ST	LONDON W1	ENGLAND
WHITSITT, JAMES E	COMPOSER	6609 HILLGROVE DR	SAN DIEGO, CA	92120
WHITTAKER, DONALD T	TV DIRECTOR	170 AMBERWOOD LN	WALNUT, CA	91789
WHITTAKER, RICHARD R	WRITER	POST OFFICE BOX 471	CORTE MADERA, CA	94925
WHITTAKER, ROGER	SINGER-SONGWRITER	IRENE COLLINS MANAGEMENT		
		50 REGENTS PARK RD		
		PRIMROSE HILL	LONDON NW1 7SX	ENGLAND
WHITTEMORE, JACK	TALENT AGENT	80 PARK AVE #2-G	NEW YORK, NY	10022
WHITTEMORE, L H	TV WRITER	555 W 57TH ST #1230	NEW YORK, NY	10019
WHITTEN, CHARLIE	GUITARIST	800 18TH AVE S	NASHVILLE, TN	37203
WHITTINGHAM, CHARLES A	PUBLISHING EXECUTIVE	LIFE/TIME & LIFE BLDG		
		ROCKEFELLER CENTER	NEW YORK, NY	10020
WHITTINGHILL, DICK	RADIO PERSONALITY	11310 VALLEY SPRING LN	TOLUCA LAKE, CA	91602
WHITTINGTON, KARL	GUITARIST	POST OFFICE BOX 6593	SAN JOSE, CA	95150
WHITTINGTON, MIKE	SINGER	POST OFFICE BOX 25371	CHARLOTTE, NC	28212
WHITTLE, JIM	ACTOR	3330 BARHAM BLVD #103	LOS ANGELES, CA	90068
WHITTLE, RICHARD	NEWS CORRESPONDENT	2129 FLORIDA AVE #304, NW	WASHINGTON, DC	20008

Name	Occupation	Address	City	Zip
WHITTON, BOBBY	GUITARIST	112 DONMOND DR	HENDERSONVILLE, TN	37075
WHITTON, MARGARET	ACTRESS	10100 SANTA MONICA BLVD #1600	LOS ANGELES, CA	90067
WHODINI	RAP GROUP	RUSH ARTISTS, 40 E 19TH ST	NEW YORK, NY	10003
WHOLIGANS, THE	ROCK & ROLL GROUP	41 BRITAIN ST #200	TORONTO, ONT	CANADA
WHORF, DAVID M	TV DIRECTOR	1326 GREENWICH ST	SAN FRANCISCO, CA	94109
WHYTE, PAUL T	PHOTOGRAPHER	9514 TINKER CT	BURKE, VA	22015
WIARD, WILLIAM O	FILM DIRECTOR	1142 LAS PULGAS PL	PACIFIC PALISADES, CA	90272
WICKER, IREENE	WRITER-SINGER	781 5TH AVE	NEW YORK, NY	10022
WICKERSHEIM, THEODORE J	COMPOSER	3716 MAINE	BALDWIN PARK, CA	91706
WICKES, DAVID	WRITER-PRODUCER	TWICKENHAM FILM STUDIOS		
		SAINT MARGARET'S, TWICKEHAM	MIDDLESEX TW1 2AW	ENGLAND
WICKES, MARY	ACTRESS	2160 CENTURY PARK E #503	LOS ANGELES, CA	90067
WICKETT, HELENE	PIANIST	POST OFFICE BOX U	REDDING, CT	06875
WICKI, BERNHARD	DIRECTOR	RESTELBERGSTRASSE 60	8 ZURICH	SWITZERLAND
WICKLUND, KAREN	SOPRANO	MUNRO, 334 W 72ND ST	NEW YORK, NY	10023
WIDDOES, KATHLEEN	ACTRESS	CBS-TV, "AS THE WORLD TURNS"		
		51 W 52ND ST	NEW YORK, NY	10019
WIDEL, ROSS	ACTOR	22744 CLARENDON ST	WOODLAND HILLS, CA	91367
WIDEMAN, M G	ACTOR	POST OFFICE BOX 491373	LOS ANGELES, CA	90014
WIDERBERG, BO	DIRECTOR	SVENSKA FILMINSTITUTET, KUNG	STOCKHOLM C	SWEDEN
WIDLAKE, BRIAN	ACTOR-WRITER	51 NASSAU RD, BARNES	LONDON SW13	ENGLAND
WIDMARK, RICHARD	ACTOR	ICM, 8899 BEVERLY BLVD	LOS ANGELES, CA	90048
WIDOFF, JOHN G	NEWS CORRESPONDENT	2888 S BUCHANAN ST	ARLINGTON, VA	22206
WIDOW	ROCK & ROLL GROUP	POST OFFICE BOX 66558	SEATTLE, WA	98166
WIEBERG, STEVE	SPORTS WRITER	POST OFFICE BOX 500	WASHINGTON, DC	20044
WIECK, PAUL R	NEWS CORRESPONDENT	3267 "P" ST, NW	WASHINGTON, DC	20007
WIEDERHORN, KEN	FILM DIRECTOR	9080 WONDERLAND PARK AVE	LOS ANGELES, CA	90046
WIEDMAN, JOHN	TV WRITER	555 W 57TH ST #1230	NEW YORK, NY	10019
WIEGERT, BOB	RECORD PRODUCER	POST OFFICE BOX 186	CEDARBURG, WI	53102
WIEGHART, JAMES G	NEWS CORRESPONDENT	4013 FESSENDEN ST, NW	WASHINGTON, DC	20016
WIEGMAN, DAVE, JR	PHOTOGRAPHER	3202 WAKE DR	KENSINGTON, MD	20895
WIELAND, DICK	ACTOR	13760 OXNARD ST #201	VAN NUYS, CA	91401
WIEMERS, DAVID	WRITER	918 1/2 N VERDUGO RD	GLENDALE, CA	91206
WIEN, IRWIN I	COMPOSER	1235 N KINGS RD #410	LOS ANGELES, CA	90069
WIENCEK, DAVID G	NEWS CORRESPONDENT	3133 CONNECTICUT AVE, NW	WASHINGTON, DC	20008
WIENER, CHARLIE	SINGER	GREG, 1686 CATALPA RD	CLEVELAND, OH	44112
WIENER, JON	AUTHOR	UNIV CALIF OF IRVINE		
		DEPARTMENT OF HISTORY	IRVINE, CA	92717
WIENER, LEONARD	NEWS CORRESPONDENT	5501 BURLING CT	BETHESDA, MD	20817
WIENER, WILLARD	WRITER	2600 CARMAN CREST DR	LOS ANGELES, CA	90068
WIENS, EDITH	SOPRANO	CAMI, 165 W 57TH ST	NEW YORK, NY	10019
WIER, RUSTY	SINGER	WATKINS, 3819 JEFFERSON ST	AUSTIN, TX	78703
WIERE, HARRY	COMEDIAN-ACTOR	14350 ADDISON ST	SHERMAN OAKS, CA	91423
WIERE, HERBERT	COMEDIAN-ACTOR	12360 MAGNOLIA BLVD	NORTH HOLLYWOOD, CA	91607
WIESE, NANETTE A	NEWS CORRESPONDENT	8212 LA FAYE CT	ALEXANDRIA, VA	22306
WIESEN, BERNARD	TV DIRECTOR-PRODUCER	2565 CRESTON DR	HOLLYWOOD, CA	90068
WIESMEYER, ROGER MICHAEL	OBOIST	205 WOODMONT CIR	NASHVILLE, TN	37205
WIESSLER, DAVID A	NEWS CORRESPONDENT	1123 E CAPITOL ST, NW	WASHINGTON, DC	20003
WIESSLER, JUDY B	NEWS CORRESPONDENT	1123 E CAPITOL ST, NW	WASHINGTON, DC	20003
WIGAN, GARETH	FILM PRODUCER	1902 COLDWATER CANYON DR	BEVERLY HILLS, CA	90210
WIGGINS, GERALD F	COMPOSER	20142 CLARK ST	WOODLAND HILLS, CA	91367
WIGGINS, ROY	GUITARIST	309 BONNACROFT DR	HERMITAGE, TN	37076
WIGGINS, RUSSELL	ACTOR	31656 TICK CYN RD	SAUGUS, CA	91350
WIGGINS, TUDI	ACTRESS	10 E 44TH ST #700	NEW YORK, NY	10017
WIGGINS, WILLIAM	DRUMMER	POST OFFICE BOX 120812	NASHVILLE, TN	37212
WIGGS, HILDRED A	TV DIRECTOR	1 GLENWOOD AVE #5-M	YONKERS, NY	10701
WIGHTMAN, RICHARD J	NEWS CORRESPONDENT	1711 MASSACHUSETTS AVE, NW	WASHINGTON, DC	20036
WIGLE, SHARI LYNN	TV WRITER	1411 KITTRIDGE ST #223	VAN NUYS, CA	91405
WIIK, CAROL A	NEWS CORRESPONDENT	2133 WISCONSIN AVE, NW	WASHINGTON, DC	20007
WIKE, CHARLES B	COMPOSER	3150 WELDON AVE #3	LOS ANGELES, CA	90065
WILAND, HARRY A	DIRECTOR	639 HILL ST #B	SANTA MONICA, CA	90405
WILBER, CAREY	TV DIRECTOR	8955 BEVERLY BLVD	LOS ANGELES, CA	90048
WILBORN, THOMAS L	NEWS CORRESPONDENT	1825 "K" ST, NW	WASHINGTON, DC	20006
WILBOURN, CLAUDIA	BODYBUILDER	POST OFFICE BOX 167	SANTA MONICA, CA	90406
WILBRANDT, THOMAS	CONDUCTOR	ANGLO-SWISS ARTISTS MGMT		
		16 MUSWELL HILL RD, HIGHGATE	LONDON N6 5UG	ENGLAND
WILBURN, LESLIE FLOYD	SINGER-GUITARIST	ROUTE #4, 225 DEVINS DR	BRENTWOOD, TN	37027
WILBURN, LESTER LLOYD	SINGER-GUITARIST	5042 MARCHANT DR	NASHVILLE, TN	37211
WILBURN, TEDDY	SINGER-GUITARIST	60 MUSIC SQUARE W	NASHVILLE, TN	37203
WILBURN BROTHERS, THE	C & W GROUP	ATLAS, 217 E CEDAR ST	GOODLETTSVILLE, TN	37072
WILCOX, DAN	TV PRODUCER	MTM, 4024 RADFORD AVE	STUDIO CITY, CA	91604
WILCOX, DANIEL HARRIS	TV WRITER	3610 LOWRY RD	LOS ANGELES, CA	90027
WILCOX, DAVE	SINGER	41 BRITAIN ST #200	TORONTO, ONT	CANADA
WILCOX, DESMOND JOHN	WRITER-PRODUCER	11 LICHFIELD RD, KEW GARDENS	SURREY	ENGLAND
WILCOX, DON	TV WRITER	1900 AVE OF THE STARS #1530	LOS ANGELES, CA	90067
WILCOX, LARRY	ACTOR-DIRECTOR	13 APPALOSA LN, BELL CYN	CANOGA PARK, CA	91305
WILCOX, MARY	ACTRESS-MODEL	SEE - WILCOX, SHANNON		
WILCOX, PAULA	ACTRESS	MARMONT, LANGHAM HOUSE		
		302 REGENT ST	LONDON W1R 5AL	ENGLAND
WILCOX, RALPH	ACTOR	CONTEMPORARY ARTISTS		
		132 S LASKY DR	BEVERLY HILLS, CA	90212
WILCOX, SHANNON	ACTRESS	SF & A, 121 N SAN VICENTE BLVD	BEVERLY HILLS, CA	90211

Name	Occupation	Address	City	Zip/Country
WILD, EARL	PIANIST	JCB, 155 W 68TH ST	NEW YORK, NY	10023
WILD, JACK	ACTOR	PETER CHARLESWORTH, LTD		
		68 OLD BROMPTON RD	LONDON SW7 3LQ	ENGLAND
WILD, TOMMY	GUITARIST	201 ACKLEN PARK DR #33	NASHVILLE, TN	37203
WILD BILL	WRESTLER	SEE - IRWIN, WILD BILL		
WILD BLUE	ROCK & ROLL GROUP	RB & CO, 504 W ARLINGTON PL	CHICAGO, IL	60614
WILD CHERRY	ROCK & ROLL GROUP	28001 CHARGRIN BLVD #205	CLEVELAND, OH	44122
WILDE, CORNEL	ACT-WRI-DIR	10433 WILSHIRE BLVD #809	LOS ANGELES, CA	90024
WILDE, EUGENE	SINGER	POST OFFICE BOX 11981	PHILADELPHIA, PA	19145
WILDE, JOHN K	WRITER-PRODUCER	264 CONWAY AVE	LOS ANGELES, CA	90024
WILDE, KIM	SINGER-SONGWRITER	MICKEY MOST MANAGEMENT		
		42-48 CHARLBERT ST	LONDON NW8	ENGLAND
WILDE, LOIS	ACTRESS	LENZ, 1456 E CHARLESTON BLVD	LAS VEGAS, NV	89104
WILDE, TIMOTHY	TV DIRECTOR	119 KINGS ROW	ARLINGTON, TX	76010
WILDE, WENDELL BLAKE	DRUMMER	519 CLIFFWOOD	NEWPORT, TN	37821
WILDER, ALEC V	ACTOR	25 MINETA LN	NEW YORK, NY	10012
WILDER, BILLY	WRITER-PRODUCER	10375 WILSHIRE BLVD	LOS ANGELES, CA	90024
WILDER, DON	CARTOONIST	NEWS AMERICA SYNDICATE		
		1703 KAISER AVE	IRVINE, CA	92714
WILDER, GENE	ACT-WRI-DIR	9350 WILSHIRE BLVD #400	BEVERLY HILLS, CA	90212
WILDER, GLENN R	DIRECTOR	STUNTS UNLIMITED ASSOC		
		3518 W CAHUENGA BLVD	LOS ANGELES, CA	90068
WILDER, KELLY	ACTRESS	12926 RIVERSIDE DR #C	SHERMAN OAKS, CA	91423
WILDER, MATTHEW	SINGER	10100 SANTA MONICA BLVD #1600	LOS ANGELES, CA	90067
WILDER, MYLES	PRODUCER	WARNER BROS, 4000 WARNER BLVD	BURBANK, CA	91522
WILDER, MYLES H	TV WRITER	280 HOMEWOOD RD	LOS ANGELES, CA	90049
WILDER, RALPH	TROMBONIST	422 SPRINGVIEW DR	NASHVILLE, TN	37214
WILDER, STELLA	CARTOONIST	NEWS AMERICA SYNDICATE		
		1703 KAISER AVE	IRVINE, CA	92714
WILDER, YVONNE	ACTRESS	5450 TOPEKA DR	TARZANA, CA	91356
WILDERMANN, WILLIAM	BASSO	SARDIS, 180 W END AVE	NEW YORK, NY	10023
WILDFLOWERS, THE	ROCK & ROLL GROUP	41 BRITAIN ST #200	TORONTO, ONT	CANADA
WILDING, MICHAEL	ACTOR	CBS-TV, "THE GUIDING LIGHT"		
		51 W 52ND ST	NEW YORK, NY	10019
WILDSTROM, STEPHEN H	NEWS CORRESPONDENT	10300 PARKWOOD DR	KENSINGTON, MD	20895
WILENSKY, STEWART	DIRECTOR	443 19TH ST	SANTA MONICA, CA	90402
WILENTZ, AMY	WRITER-EDITOR	TIME/TIME & LIFE BLDG		
		ROCKEFELLER CENTER	NEW YORK, NY	10020
WILES, GORDON	DIRECTOR	17123 ADLON RD	ENCINO, CA	91436
WILEY, BILL	ACTOR	9220 SUNSET BLVD #625	LOS ANGELES, CA	90069
WILEY, DARLENE	COLORATURA	ALPHA, 685 W END AVE	NEW YORK, NY	10025
WILEY, PETER	CELLIST	CAMI, 165 W 57TH ST	NEW YORK, NY	10019
WILEY, RALPH	SPORTS WRITER-EDITOR	SPORTS ILLUSTRATED MAGAZINE		
		TIME & LIFE BUILDING		
		ROCKEFELLER CENTER	NEW YORK, NY	10020
WILF, HOWLIN' & THE VEE-JAYS	ROCK & ROLL GROUP	ACE, 48-50 STEELE RD	LONDON NW10 7AS	ENGLAND
WILF, RUTH ANN	ACTRESS	9 ROLLING RD	PHILADELPHIA, PA	19151
WILHELM, HOYT	BASEBALL	POST OFFICE BOX 2217	SARASOTA, FL	33578
WILHELM, JOSEPH FRANKLIN	TV WRITER	3606 WOODHILL CYN RD	STUDIO CITY, CA	91604
WILHOITE, JIM J	GUITARIST	ROUTE #1, BOX 616	TRINITY, AL	35673
WILHOITE, JOHN	GUITARIST	ROUTE #1, BOX 616	TRINITY, AL	35673
WILHOITE, KATHLEEN	ACTRESS	POST OFFICE BOX 5617	BEVERLY HILLS, CA	90210
WILK, ANDREW CARL	TV WRITER-DIRECTOR	30 LINCOLN PLAZA #4-W	NEW YORK, NY	10023
WILK, BABETTE	TV WRITER	8955 BEVERLY BLVD	LOS ANGELES, CA	90048
WILK, DIANE E	TV WRITER	8955 BEVERLY BLVD	LOS ANGELES, CA	90048
WILK, MAX	TV WRITER	8955 BEVERLY BLVD	LOS ANGELES, CA	90048
WILKE, JOHN	NEWS CORRESPONDENT	1234 MASSACHUSETTS AVE #308, NW	WASHINGTON, DC	20005
WILKE, ROBERT J	ACTOR	12550 OTSEGO ST	NORTH HOLLYWOOD, CA	91607
WILKES, BECKY	ACTRESS	2160 S BEVERLY GLEN BLVD #357	LOS ANGELES, CA	90025
WILKES, DONNA	ACTRESS	7060 HOLLYWOOD BLVD #610	LOS ANGELES, CA	90028
WILKES, DOUGLAS H	NEWS CORRESPONDENT	5151 WISCONSIN AVE, NW	WASHINGTON, DC	20016
WILKIE, CURTIS C	NEWS CORRESPONDENT	7119 9TH ST, NW	WASHINGTON, DC	20012
WILKIN, BUCKY	GUITARIST	5856 BEAUREGARD DR	NASHVILLE, TN	37215
WILKIN, MARIJOHN	PIANIST	SCARRITT PL, 1022 18TH ST #A	NASHVILLE, TN	37212
WILKINS, ANN MARIE	TALENT AGENT	POST OFFICE BOX 55398	WASHINGTON, DC	20040
WILKINS, CHRISTOPHER	CONDUCTOR	AFFILIATE ARTISTS, INC		
		37 W 65TH ST, 6TH FLOOR	NEW YORK, NY	10023
WILKINS, DAVID	PIANIST	819 FONNIC DR	NASHVILLE, TN	37207
WILKINS, FRANK	BASSIST	INNER CITY RECORDS COMPANY		
		MMO MUSIC GROUP, INC		
		423 W 55TH ST	NEW YORK, NY	10019
WILKINS, FRASER B	NEWS CORRESPONDENT	3114 45TH ST, NW	WASHINGTON, DC	20016
WILKINS, LITTLE DAVID	SINGER	ACE, 3407 GREEN RIDGE DR	NASHVILLE, TN	37204
WILKINS, RONALD STEPHEN	PIANIST	POST OFFICE BOX 4496	NORTH HOLLYWOOD, CA	91607
WILKINS, WILLIAM H, JR	TV DIRECTOR	607 TEXAS ST	SAN FRANCISCO, CA	94107
WILKINSON, ANN E	ACTRESS	870 N VINE ST #G	LOS ANGELES, CA	90038
WILKINSON, CHRISTOPHER G	DIRECTOR	DGA, 7950 SUNSET BLVD	LOS ANGELES, CA	90046
WILKINSON, F CLYDE	PHOTOGRAPHER	6323 N 25TH ST	ARLINGTON, VA	22207
WILKINSON, HARRY	DRUMMER	5009 WYOMING AVE	NASHVILLE, TN	37209
WILKINSON, JUNE	ACTRESS	5151 TYRONE AVE	SHERMAN OAKS, CA	91423
WILKINSON, KRISTIN	MUSIC ARRANGER	905 CANTRELL AVE	NASHVILLE, TN	37215
WILKINSON, LISA	ACTRESS	870 N VINE ST #G	LOS ANGELES, CA	90038
WILKINSON, MARC	COMPOSER-CONDUCTOR	31 BELSIZE PARK	LONDON NW3	ENGLAND
WILKINSON, WENDLA	PHOTOJOURNALIST	10215 RIDGELINE DR	GAITHERSBURG, MD	20879
WILKMAN, JON K	WRITER	6160 RODGERTON DR	HOLLYWOOD, CA	90068

Name	Occupation	Address	City/State	Zip
WILKOMIRSKA, WANDA	VIOLINIST	JCB, 155 W 68TH ST	NEW YORK, NY	10023
WILKOSZ, JUSUP	BODYBUILDER	JUSUP'S GALAXY FITNESS		
		BRUCKSTRASSE	D-7012 FELLBACH	WEST GERMANY
WILL, EDWARD JACOB	BASSO-BARITONE	AFFILIATE ARTISTS, INC		
		37 W 65TH ST, 6TH FLOOR	NEW YORK, NY	10023
WILL, GEORGE F	WRITER-COLUMNIST	THE WASHINGTON POST		
		WRITERS GROUP		
		1150 15TH ST, NW	WASHINGTON, DC	20071
WILL, SANDRA	ACTRESS	2105 N BEVERLY GLEN BLVD	LOS ANGELES, CA	90077
WILL, STU	SINGER	POST OFFICE BOX 6025	NEWPORT NEWS, VA	23606
WILLARD, FRED C	ACTOR	12318 19TH HELENA DR	LOS ANGELES, CA	90049
WILLEN, MARK M	NEWS CORRESPONDENT	2025 "M" ST, NW	WASHINGTON, DC	20036
WILLENS, MICHELE	TV WRITER	3870 RAMBLA ORIENTA	MALIBU, CA	90265
WILLENS, SHELDON MILES	TV WRITER	3140 CHANDELLE RD	LOS ANGELES, CA	90046
WILLENSON, KIM	NEWS CORRESPONDENT	205 N EMERSON ST	ARLINGTON, VA	22203
WILLES, JEAN	ACTRESS	COWHIG, 14244 CALIFA ST	VAN NUYS, CA	91401
WILLETTE, JOANN	ACTRESS	ICM, 8899 BEVERLY BLVD	LOS ANGELES, CA	90048
WILLEY, WALT	ACTOR	ABC-TV, "RYAN'S HOPE"		
		1330 AVE OF THE AMERICAS	NEW YORK, NY	10019
WILLIAM, JOELLE	NEWS CORRESPONDENT	1615 TILTON DR	SILVER SPRING, MD	20902
WILLIAMS, ALLEN	TV WRITER-DIRECTOR	2049 CENTURY PARK E #1320	LOS ANGELES, CA	90067
WILLIAMS, ANDY	SINGER-ACTOR	9000 SUNSET BLVD #1200	LOS ANGELES, CA	90069
WILLIAMS, ANSON	ACTOR-SINGER	750 GALAXY HGTS DR	LA CANADA, CA	91011
WILLIAMS, ANTHONY	FILM PRODUCER	PINEWOOD STUDIOS, IVER HEATH	BUCKS SLO ONH	ENGLAND
WILLIAMS, ANTHONY V	DIRECTOR	1436 WINDSOR PARK LN	HAVERTOWN, PA	19083
WILLIAMS, BARRY	ACTOR	21006 PACIFIC COAST HWY	MALIBU, CA	90265
WILLIAMS, BART	ACTOR	10742 1/2 CAMARILLO ST	NORTH HOLLYWOOD, CA	91602
WILLIAMS, BERNADETTE	ACTRESS	4721 LAUREL CANYON BLVD #211	NORTH HOLLYWOOD, CA	91607
WILLIAMS, BERNARD T	FILM PRODUCER	4027 HAYVENHURST DR	ENCINO, CA	91436
WILLIAMS, BERT	ACTOR	4731 LAUREL CANYON BLVD #5	NORTH HOLLYWOOD, CA	91607
WILLIAMS, BILL	ACTOR	9744 WILSHIRE BLVD #306	BEVERLY HILLS, CA	90212
WILLIAMS, BILLIE JO	SINGER	POST OFFICE BOX 783	MADISON, TN	37115
WILLIAMS, BILLY	CINEMATOGRAPHER	THE COACH HOUSE		
		HAWKSHILL PL, ESHER	SURREY KT10 9HY	ENGLAND
WILLIAMS, BILLY DEE	ACTOR	605 N OAKHURST DR	BEVERLY HILLS, CA	90210
WILLIAMS, BLAKE	MUSICAN	ROUTE #1, BOX 54-A	SPARTA, TN	38583
WILLIAMS, BOB	COMPOSER	4513 MORSE AVE	STUDIO CITY, CA	91604
WILLIAMS, BRIAN D	NEWS CORRESPONDENT	5151 WISCONSIN AVE, NW	WASHINGTON, DC	20016
WILLIAMS, BUTCH	DRUMMER	623 MAYVIEW DR	MADISON, TN	37115
WILLIAMS, CAMILLA	SOPRANO	UNIVERSITY OF INDIANA		
		SCHOOL OF MUSIC	BLOOMINGTON, IN	47401
WILLIAMS, CARA	ACTRESS	DANN, 209 N CANON DR	BEVERLY HILLS, CA	90210
WILLIAMS, CAROL ANN	ACTRESS	8484 WILSHIRE BLVD #235	BEVERLY HILLS, CA	90211
WILLIAMS, CHUCK	BODYBUILDER	POST OFFICE BOX 8421	FOUNTAIN VALLEY, CA	92728
WILLIAMS, CINDY	ACTRESS	10100 SANTA MONICA BLVD #1600	LOS ANGELES, CA	90067
WILLIAMS, CLARENCE, III	ACTOR	9255 SUNSET BLVD #706	LOS ANGELES, CA	90069
WILLIAMS, CLARK	GUITARIST	ROUTE #1, BOX 434		
		INDIANA SPRINGS	PEGRAM, TN	37143
WILLIAMS, CLIFFORD	BARITONE	CAMI, 165 W 57TH ST	NEW YORK, NY	10019
WILLIAMS, CRYSTAL L	NEWS CORRESPONDENT	5523 HALWIS ST	ALEXANDRIA, VA	22303
WILLIAMS, CURT	ACTOR	305 CONVENT AVE	NEW YORK, NY	10031
WILLIAMS, CYNTHIA A	NEWS CORRESPONDENT	1840 MINTWOOD PL, NW	WASHINGTON, DC	20009
WILLIAMS, DANA KEITH	GUITARIST	110 SAVELY DR	HENDERSONVILLE, TN	37075
WILLIAMS, DANIEL C	NEWS CORRESPONDENT	3110 MOUNT VERNON AVE #301	ALEXANDRIA, VA	22305
WILLIAMS, DARNELL	ACTOR	400 MADISON AVE #2000	NEW YORK, NY	10017
WILLIAMS, DAVID	NEWS CORRESPONDENT	4710 BETHESDA AVE #1105	BETHESDA, MD	20814
WILLIAMS, DAVID A	NEWS CORRESPONDENT	400 N CAPITOL ST, NW	WASHINGTON, DC	20001
WILLIAMS, DEBBIE	SINGER	888 8TH AVE #1-F	NEW YORK, NY	10019
WILLIAMS, DENIECE	SINGER	ALIVE ENTERTAINMENT		
		8271 MELROSE AVE	LOS ANGELES, CA	90046
WILLIAMS, DENNIS	ACTOR	FERRIS, 5915 METROPOLITAN PLAZA	LOS ANGELES, CA	90036
WILLIAMS, DENNIS E	COMPOSER	1133 CAMPBELL ST #1	GLENDALE, CA	91207
WILLIAMS, DICK ANTHONY	ACTOR	ICM, 8899 BEVERLY BLVD	LOS ANGELES, CA	90048
WILLIAMS, DON	SINGER-SONGWRITER	HALLMARK DIRECTION		
		15 MUSIC SQUARE W	NASHVILLE, TN	37203
WILLIAMS, DWIGHT J	FILM DIRECTOR	POST OFFICE BOX 746	NEW YORK, NY	10150
WILLIAMS, ED	ACTOR	120 W VICTORY BLVD #104	BURBANK, CA	91501
WILLIAMS, EDY	ACTRESS-MODEL	1717 SUNSET PLAZA DR	LOS ANGELES, CA	90069
WILLIAMS, ELMO	FILM EXECUTIVE	9255 SUNSET BLVD #800	LOS ANGELES, CA	90069
WILLIAMS, EMLYN	PLAYWRIGHT-ACTRESS	123 DOVEHOUSE ST	LONDON SW 3	ENGLAND
WILLIAMS, ESTHER	ACTRESS	9377 READCREST DR	BEVERLY HILLS, CA	90210
WILLIAMS, FLORENCE	ACTRESS	POST OFFICE BOX 307	ROCKPORT, ME	04856
WILLIAMS, FRANCE E	ACTRESS	10850 RIVERSIDE DR #501	NORTH HOLLYWOOD, CA	91602
WILLIAMS, FRANK	ACTOR	31 MANOR PARK CRESCENT	EDGEWARE	ENGLAND
WILLIAMS, GARY	CELLIST	P E GARRETT, 4212 MURPHY RD	NASHVILLE, TN	37209
WILLIAMS, GILBERT	WRITER-PRODUCER	16 NORMAN PL	TENAFLY, NJ	07670
WILLIAMS, GRAHAM	TV PRODUCER	A D PETERS & CO, LTD		
		10 BUCKINGHAM ST	LONDON WC2	ENGLAND
WILLIAMS, GRAHAM C	TV DIRECTOR	BLATT, 1-A LARPENT AVE	PUTNEY SW15	ENGLAND
WILLIAMS, HAL	ACTOR	8322 BEVERLY BLVD #202	LOS ANGELES, CA	90048
WILLIAMS, HANK, JR	SINGER-GUITARIST	POST OFFICE BOX 790	CULLMAN, AL	35055
WILLIAMS, HOWARD F	NEWS CORRESPONDENT	5725 N KINGS HWY	ALEXANDRIA, VA	22303
WILLIAMS, JACK	COLUMNIST	POST OFFICE BOX 500	WASHINGTON, DC	20044
WILLIAMS, JACK	NEWS CORRESPONDENT	52 S FRENCH ST	ALEXANDRIA, VA	22304
WILLIAMS, JACK	GUITARIST	2626 WAYLAND CT	NASHVILLE, TN	37215

WILLIAMS, JACKIEE LEE	SINGER	PENNY, 30 GUINAN ST	WALTHAM, MA 02154
WILLIAMS, JAMES	WRESTLER	SEE - GARVIN, GORGEOUS JIMMY	
WILLIAMS, JAMES E	FILM EXEC-DIR	956 CORSICA DR	PACIFIC PALISADES, CA 90272
WILLIAMS, JAN WARREN	FILM PRODUCER	2264 LAUGHLIN ST	LA CANADA, CA 91011
WILLIAMS, JENNIFER	ACTRESS	135 EASTERN PARKWAY #2	BROOKLYN, NY 11238
WILLIAMS, JERRY	PIANIST	795 N 700 EAST	PROVO, UT 84601
WILLIAMS, JO BETH	ACTRESS	5743 SPRING OAK RD	LOS ANGELES, CA 90068
WILLIAMS, JOE	SINGER	3337 KNOLLWOOD CT	LAS VEGAS, NV 89121
WILLIAMS, JOHN	GUITARIST	HOLT, 31 SINCLAIR RD	LONDON W14 ENGLAND
WILLIAMS, JOHN C	DIRECTOR	1008 PRINCE ST	ALEXANDRIA, VA 22314
WILLIAMS, JOHN T	COMPOSER-CONDUCTOR	301 MASSACHUSETTS AVE	BOSTON, MA 02115
WILLIAMS, JOHN WARNER	ACTOR	5967 W 3RD ST #205	LOS ANGELES, CA 90036
WILLIAMS, JORDON	ACTOR	ABC-TV, "ALL MY CHILDREN"	
		1330 AVE OF THE AMERICAS	NEW YORK, NY 10019
WILLIAMS, JUAN	NEWS CORRESPONDENT	2113 2ND ST, NW	WASHINGTON, DC 20001
WILLIAMS, JUNE H	MUSICAN	1725 LINDEN AVE	NASHVILLE, TN 37212
WILLIAMS, KAREN	PHOTOJOURNALIST	1823 "Q" ST, NW	WASHINGTON, DC 20009
WILLIAMS, KEITH	COMP	POST OFFICE BOX 6	PACIFIC PALISADES, CA 90272
WILLIAMS, KEITH R	COMPOSER-CONDUCTOR	13349 WENTWORTH ST	PACOIMA, CA 91331
WILLIAMS, KENNETH	ACTOR	ICM, 388-396 OXFORD ST	LONDON W1 ENGLAND
WILLIAMS, KENNY	ACTOR-DIRECTOR	18 ANTIGUA CT	CORONADO, CA 92118
WILLIAMS, KIT	GUITARIST	422 ACKLEN PARK DR	NASHVILLE, TN 37205
WILLIAMS, LARRY	SINGER	OLDIES, 5218 ALMONT ST	LOS ANGELES, CA 90032
WILLIAMS, LAWRENCE	SONGWRITER	306 N SAINT CRISPEN	BREA, CA 92621
WILLIAMS, LAWRENCE E, JR	DIRECTOR	RURAL DELIVERY #2, BOX 409	
		SCOTCHTOWN RD	MONTGOMERY, NY 12549
WILLIAMS, LENNY	SINGER	1326 N FLORES ST #26	LOS ANGELES, CA 90069
WILLIAMS, LINDA	NEWS REPORTER	TIME/TIME & LIFE BLDG	
		ROCKEFELLER CENTER	NEW YORK, NY 10020
WILLIAMS, LOU	ACTOR	16661 VENTURA BLVD #400	ENCINO, CA 91436
WILLIAMS, LOUISE	NEWS CORRESPONDENT	1020 N QUINCY ST #816	ARLINGTON, VA 22201
WILLIAMS, LUMP	GUITARIST	1395 GOLDEN GATE AVE #203	SAN FRANCISCO, CA 94115
WILLIAMS, MACK RAY, JR	DIRECTOR	1674 CHIMNEY HOUSE RD	RESTON, VA 22090
WILLIAMS, MARCELYN ANN	ACTRESS	6605 HOLLYWOOD BLVD #220	HOLLYWOOD, CA 90028
WILLIAMS, MARION	SINGER	POST OFFICE BOX 884	NEW YORK, NY 10023
WILLIAMS, MARSHALL L	TV WRITER	157 HART AVE	SANTA MONICA, CA 90405
WILLIAMS, MARY LOU	PIANIST	POST OFFICE BOX 6695	
		COLLEGE STATION	DURHAM, NC 27708
WILLIAMS, MASON	SINGER-SONGWRITER	D ROSS PRODUCTIONS	
		3097 FLORAL HILL RD	EUGENE, OR 97403
WILLIAMS, MAURICE & THE ZODIACS	VOCAL GROUP	INSIGHT, 2300 E INDEPENDENCE BL	CHARLOTTE, NC 28205
WILLIAMS, MICHAEL	ACTOR	4 PROSPECT WALK, HOLLY WALK	LONDON NW3 ENGLAND
WILLIAMS, MILTON	PHOTOGRAPHER	1660 LANIER PL #208, NW	WASHINGTON, DC 20009
WILLIAMS, NANCY	TV WRITER	CBS-TV, "THE GUIDING LIGHT"	
		51 W 52ND ST	NEW YORK, NY 10019
WILLIAMS, OSCAR	FILM WRITER-DIRECTOR	856 S SAINT ANDREWS PL	LOS ANGELES, CA 90005
WILLIAMS, PAGE	COMPOSER-CONDUCTOR	POST OFFICE BOX 325	ALHAMBRA, CA 91802
WILLIAMS, PAT	BODYBUILDER	POST OFFICE BOX 6100	ROSEMEAND, CA 91770
WILLIAMS, PATRICIA NOEL	NEWS CORRESPONDENT	1954 COLUMBIA RD #107, NW	WASHINGTON, DC 20007
WILLIAMS, PATRICK	COMPOSER	532 17TH ST	SANTA MONICA, CA 90402
WILLIAMS, PATTY	WRESTLING VALET	SEE - PRECIOUS	
WILLIAMS, PAUL	SINGER-SONGWRITER	645 SAND POINT RD	CARPINTERIA, CA 93013
WILLIAMS, PAUL W	DIRECTOR	40101 PACIFIC COAST HWY	MALIBU, CA 90265
WILLIAMS, RICHARD	CONDUCTOR	SULLIVAN, 390 W END AVE	NEW YORK, NY 10024
WILLIAMS, RICHARD	FILM ANIMATOR	13 SOHO SQ	LONDON W1V 5FB ENGLAND
WILLIAMS, RICHARD E	TV DIRECTOR	3193 WADE ST	LOS ANGELES, CA 90066
WILLIAMS, ROBERT F	SCREENWRITER	8955 BEVERLY BLVD	LOS ANGELES, CA 90048
WILLIAMS, ROBERT H	NEWS CORRESPONDENT	16096 RADBURN	WOODBRIDGE, VA 22191
WILLIAMS, ROBERT H	NEWS CORRESPONDENT	1615 TILTON DR	SILVER SPRING, MD 20902
WILLIAMS, ROBIN	COMED-ACT-WRI	1100 WALL RD	NAPA, CA 94550
WILLIAMS, ROBIN & LINDA	VOCAL DUO	POST OFFICE BOX 8753	ALBANY, NY 12208
WILLIAMS, ROBIN M	DIRECTOR	POST OFFICE BOX 48516	LOS ANGELES, CA 90048
WILLIAMS, ROGER	PIANIST	VIRTUOSO, 5710 WALLIS LN	WOODLAND HILLS, CA 91364
WILLIAMS, ROGER C	FLUTIST	4105 HOME HAVEN DR	NASHVILLE, TN 37218
WILLIAMS, SAMM-ART	PLAYWRIGHT-WRITER	THE WILLIAM MORRIS AGENCY	
		1350 AVE OF THE AMERICAS	NEW YORK, NY 10019
WILLIAMS, SHANNON	SOPRANO	756 7TH AVE #67	NEW YORK, NY 10019
WILLIAMS, SIMON	ACTOR	BURNETT, 42 GRAFTON HOUSE	
		2-3 GOLDEN SQ	LONDON W1 ENGLAND
WILLIAMS, SPICE	ACTRESS	427 N CANON DR #205	BEVERLY HILLS, CA 90210
WILLIAMS, STEPHANIE	ACTRESS	6380 WILSHIRE BLVD #1600	LOS ANGELES, CA 90048
WILLIAMS, STEVE	GUITARIST	2305 BRITTANY DR	NASHVILLE, TN 37206
WILLIAMS, STEVE "DR DEATH"	WRESTLER	UNIVERSAL WRESTLING FEDERATION	
		MID SOUTH SPORTS, INC	
		5001 SPRING VALLEY RD	DALLAS, TX 75244
WILLIAMS, STEVEN H	DIRECTOR	1142 MANHATTAN AVE #232-CP	MANHATTAN BEACH, CA 90266
WILLIAMS, TED	BASEBALL	POST OFFICE BOX 481	ISLAMORADA, FL 33036
WILLIAMS, TERENCE PAUL	DIRECTOR-PRODUCER	SMITH, 10 WYNDHAM PL	LONDON W1 ENGLAND
WILLIAMS, TERRY WAYNE	MUSICIAN	4502 GRANNY WHITE PIKE	NASHVILLE, TN 37204
WILLIAMS, TOM	ACTOR	3800 BARHAM BLVD #303	LOS ANGELES, CA 90068
WILLIAMS, TOMMY	GUITARIST	1617 CROCKETT HILLS	BRENTWOOD, TN 37027
WILLIAMS, TONY	DRUMMER	KURLAND, 173 BRIGHTON AVE	BOSTON, MA 02134
WILLIAMS, TREAT	ACTOR	APA, 888 7TH AVE, 6TH FLOOR	NEW YORK, NY 10106
WILLIAMS, VAN	ACTOR	14723 ORACLE PL	PACIFIC PALISADES, CA 90272

ROBIN WILLIAMS

BRUCE WILLIS

DAVID WILLS

NANCY WILSON

WILLIAM WINDOM

PENELOPE WINDUST

HENRY WINKLER

PAUL WINFIELD

JOHNNY WINTERS

Name	Occupation	Address	City	Zip
WILLIAMS, VANESSA	ACT-SING-MOD	POST OFFICE BOX 40	MILLWOOD, NY	10546
WILLIAMS, VICKI	COMMENTATOR	KING FEATURES SYNDICATE		
		235 E 45TH ST	NEW YORK, NY	10017
WILLIAMS, WALTER C	TV WRITER	555 W 57TH ST #1230	NEW YORK, NY	10019
WILLIAMS, WALTER E	COLUMNIST	HERITAGE FEATURES SYNDICATE		
		214 MASSACHUSETTS AVE, NE	WASHINGTON, DC	20002
WILLIAMS, WENDY	ACTRESS	CAREY, 126 KENNINGTON PARK	LONDON SE11 4DJ	ENGLAND
WILLIAMS, WENDY O	SINGER-ACTRESS	POST OFFICE BOX 837	NEW YORK, NY	10013
WILLIAMS & REE	VOCAL DUO	HALSEY, 3225 S NORWOOD AVE	TULSA, OK	74135
WILLIAMS-JONES, MICHAEL	FILM EXECUTIVE	UIP HOUSE, 45 BEADON RD		
		HAMMERSMITH	LONDON W6 OEG	ENGLAND
WILLIAMSON, BRUCE	FILM CRITIC	PLAYBOY, 8560 SUNSET BLVD	LOS ANGELES, CA	90069
WILLIAMSON, CHRIS	SINGER	OLIVIA RECORDS CO		
		4400 MARKET ST	OAKLAND, CA	94608
WILLIAMSON, DONNIE	PIANIST	ROUTE #2, BOX 265-4	ALVATON, KY	42122
WILLIAMSON, ERMAL	ACTOR	BERZON, 336 E 17TH ST	COSTA MESA, CA	92627
WILLIAMSON, FRED	ACTOR-DIRECTOR	9220 SUNSET BLVD #202	LOS ANGELES, CA	90069
WILLIAMSON, FRED W, JR	GUITARIST	1600 16TH AVE S #6	NASHVILLE, TN	37212
WILLIAMSON, GRAHAM	GUITARIST	ROUTE #8, PEARCE PL	MURFREESBORO, TN	37130
WILLIAMSON, JACK	WRITER	POST OFFICE BOX 761	PORTALES, NM	88130
WILLIAMSON, JAMES E	COMPOSER	8444 HILLROSE ST	SUNLAND, CA	91040
WILLIAMSON, JAMES W	PIANIST	423 LYNN CT	NASHVILLE, TN	37211
WILLIAMSON, MYKEL T	ACTOR	LIGHT, 113 N ROBERTSON BLVD	LOS ANGELES, CA	90048
WILLIAMSON, NANCY PIERCE	WRITER-NEWS REPORTER	PEOPLE/TIME & LIFE BLDG		
		ROCKEFELLER CENTER	NEW YORK, NY	10023
WILLIAMSON, NICOL	ACTOR	ICM, 388-396 OXFORD ST	LONDON W1	ENGLAND
WILLIAMSON, TONY	TV WRITER	MAX NAUGHTON LOWE		
		200 FULHAM RD	LONDON SW10 9PN	ENGLAND
WILLINGHAM, CALDER	PLAYWRIGHT	THE VANGUARD PRESS		
		424 MADISON AVE	NEW YORK, NY	10017
WILLIS, ANITA	NEWS CORRESPONDENT	8407 11TH AVE	SILVER SPRING, MD	20903
WILLIS, AUSTIN	ACTOR	427 N CANON DR #205	BEVERLY HILLS, CA	90210
WILLIS, BRUCE	ACTOR-SINGER	10100 SANTA MONICA BLVD #1600	LOS ANGELES, CA	90067
WILLIS, BRYNJA	ACTRESS	3800 BARHAM BLVD #303	LOS ANGELES, CA	90068
WILLIS, CHUCK	SINGER-GUITARIST	VELVET PRODS, 517 W 57TH ST	LOS ANGELES, CA	90037
WILLIS, GARRY	COLUMNIST	UNIVERSAL PRESS SYNDICATE		
		4900 MAIN ST, 9TH FLOOR	KANSAS CITY, MO	62114
WILLIS, GORDON	CINEMATOGRAPHER	7715 SUNSET BLVD #150	LOS ANGELES, CA	90046
WILLIS, HENRY	TV DIRECTOR	7449 RUFFNER AVE	VAN NUYS, CA	91406
WILLIS, HERB	ACTOR-DIRECTOR	8721 SUNSET BLVD #203	LOS ANGELES, CA	90069
WILLIS, JACK	WRITER	151 EL CAMINO DR	BEVERLY HILLS, CA	90212
WILLIS, JOE	DRUMMER	247 BURNING TREE DR	HERMITAGE, TN	37076
WILLIS, JOHN	TV DIRECTOR	BLACKBERRY, 52 LADY SOMERSET RD	LONDON NW5	ENGLAND
WILLIS, JOSEPH E	GUITARIST	1002 S COLLEGE	NEVEDA, MO	64772
WILLIS, LISA	ACTRESS	120 W VICTORY BLVD #104	BURBANK, CA	91501
WILLIS, LYNN	COMPOSER	24736 SEASHELL WY	DANA POINT, CA	92629
WILLIS, MARY PLESHETTE	WRITER	14144 VENTURA BLVD #200	SHERMAN OAKS, CA	91423
WILLIS, S C	DRUMMER	951 MAXWELL AVE	NASHVILLE, TN	37206
WILLIS, SCOTT	CARTOONIST	POST OFFICE BOX 5533	SAN JOSE, CA	95190
WILLIS, SUSAN C	ACTRESS	37 CHARLES ST	NEW YORK, NY	10014
WILLIS, TED	WRITER-PRODUCER	5 SHEPHERDS GREEN		
		CHISLEHURST	KENT	ENGLAND
WILLIS, VIC	ACCORDIONIST	POST OFFICE BOX 158554	NASHVILLE, TN	37215
WILLMORE, JOE	TV PRODUCER	CBS-TV, "THE GUIDING LIGHT"		
		51 W 52ND ST	NEW YORK, NY	10019
WILLOCK, MARGARET	ACTRESS	15010 VENTURA BLVD #219	SHERMAN OAKS, CA	91403
WILLOUGHBY, LARRY	SINGER	POST OFFICE BOX 121542	NASHVILLE, TN	37212
WILLS, DAVID	SINGER	4047 NACO-PERRIN BLVD #110	SAN ANTONIO, TX	78217
WILLS, LISA	ACTRESS	6380 WILSHIRE BLVD #1600	LOS ANGELES, CA	90048
WILLS, LOU	ACTOR	11240 MAGNOLIA BLVD #202	NORTH HOLLYWOOD, CA	91601
WILLS, MAURY	BASEBALL	245 FOWLING	PLAYA DEL REY, CA	90291
WILLS, TERRY	ACTRESS	15010 VENTURA BLVD #219	SHERMAN OAKS, CA	91403
WILLS, TOMMY	SINGER-SAXOPHONIST	THE TOWN & COUNTRY		
		10319 BARIBEAU LN	INDIANAPOLIS, IN	46229
WILLSHIRE, MAUREEN	ACTRESS	484 W 43RD ST #40-J	NEW YORK, NY	10036
WILLSON, PAUL	ACTOR	401 N CURSON AVE #5	LOS ANGELES, CA	90036
WILLSON, PAUL	TV WRITER	8955 BEVERLY BLVD	LOS ANGELES, CA	90048
WILMER, DOUGLAS	ACTOR	LEADING ARTISTS, LTD		
		60 SAINT JAMES'S ST	LONDON SW1	ENGLAND
WILMINGTON, MICHAEL	FILM CRITIC	L A TIMES NEWSPAPER		
		TIMES MIRROR SQUARE	LOS ANGELES, CA	90053
WILMONT, HARRY	ACTOR	VAMP, 715 E LA LOMA AVE #1	CAMARILLO, CA	93010
WILMOT, MICHAEL D	DIRECTOR	727 MIRAMONTES ST	HALF MOON BAY, CA	94019
WILSON, AL	SINGER	POST OFFICE BOX 82	GREAT NECK, NY	11021
WILSON, ALBERT P	FILM EDITOR	ACE, 4416 1/2 FINLEY AVE	LOS ANGELES, CA	90027
WILSON, BILLY BUN	DRUMMER	1330 FORT CAMPBELL BLVD	CLARKSVILLE, TN	37040
WILSON, BRENDA L	WRITER-NEWS CORRES	3420 16TH ST	WASHINGTON, DC	20010
WILSON, BRIAN	MUSICIAN	1317 CLUB VIEW DR	LOS ANGELES, CA	90024
WILSON, BRUCE P	NEWS CORRESPONDENT	5328 SHERRILL AVE	CHEVY CHASE, MD	20815
WILSON, CARL	SINGER-SONGWRITER	8860 EVAN VIEW DR	LOS ANGELES, CA	90069
WILSON, CHARLES O	NEWS CORRESPONDENT	13123 HOLDRIDGE RD	WHEATON, MD	20906
WILSON, CHRISTOPHER D	NEWS CORRESPONDENT	529 14TH ST, NW	WASHINGTON, DC	20045
WILSON, CHUCK	SINGER	SODP, 29 HUDSON ST	WATERFORD, NY	12188
WILSON, DAVE	TV DIRECTOR	NBC TELEVISION NETWORK		
		30 ROCKEFELLER PLAZA	NEW YORK, NY	10112

Name	Occupation	Address	City/State/Zip
WILSON, DAVID E	DIRECTOR	2207 LINDEN DR, SE	CEDAR RAPIDS, IA 52403
WILSON, DENNIS	PIANIST-COMPOSER	CARTHAGENA LODGE	
		SUTTON, SANDY	BEDS SG19 2NQ ENGLAND
WILSON, DENNIS W	GUITARIST	POST OFFICE BOX 193	HENDERSONVILLE, TN 37075
WILSON, DICK	ACTOR	3518 W CAHUENGA BLVD #316	LOS ANGELES, CA 90068
WILSON, DOUG	TV DIRECTOR	LEWIS RD	IRVING-ON-HUDSON, NY 10533
WILSON, EDDIE	PIANIST	300 BAKERTOWN RD #33-H	ANTIOCH, TN 37013
WILSON, ELEANOR	ACTRESS	32 MORNINGSIDE AVE	NEW YORK, NY 10026
WILSON, ELIZABETH	ACTRESS	211 S BEVERLY DR #201	BEVERLY HILLS, CA 90212
WILSON, ELIZABETH	TV WRITER	8955 BEVERLY BLVD	LOS ANGELES, CA 90048
WILSON, ERICA	COLUMNIST	TRIBUNE MEDIA SERVICES	
		64 E CONCORD ST	ORLANDO, FL 32801
WILSON, FLIP	COMED-ACT-WRI	21970 PACIFIC COAST HWY	MALIBU, CA 90265
WILSON, GAHAN	CARTOONIST	POST OFFICE BOX 4203	NEW YORK, NY 10017
WILSON, GEORGE, III	NEWS CORRESPONDENT	843 BERKSHIRE DR	HYATTSVILLE, MD 20783
WILSON, GERALD S	TRUMPETER	4625 BRYNHURST AVE	LOS ANGELES, CA 90043
WILSON, GRAN	TENOR	LEW, 204 W 10TH ST	NEW YORK, NY 10014
WILSON, HUGH	WRITER-PRODUCER	4007 SUNSSWEPT DR	STUDIO CITY, CA 91604
WILSON, HULEN	SINGER-SONGWRITER	POST OFFICE BOX 655	HUDSON, OH 44236
WILSON, IAN	CINEMATOGRAPHER	40 CHARLTON KINGS RD	LONDON NW5 ENGLAND
WILSON, JAMES O	PHOTOGRAPHER	176 GARFIELD PL	BROOKLYN, NY 11215
WILSON, JEANNIE	ACTRESS	10100 SANTA MONICA BLVD #1600	LOS ANGELES, CA 90067
WILSON, JENNIFER	ACTRESS	ROSE COTTAGE, 102 HIGH ST	
		OLD WOKING	SURREY ENGLAND
WILSON, JOE L	GUITARIST	ROUTE #5, THALMAN DR	BRENTWOOD, TN 37027
WILSON, JOEMY	HAMMERED DULCIMER	POST OFFICE BOX 189	BURBANK, CA 91503
WILSON, JOHN A	GUITARIST	ROUTE #1	HERMITAGE, TN 37076
WILSON, JOHN C	DIRECTOR	DGA, 110 W 57TH ST	NEW YORK, NY 10019
WILSON, JOHN G	WRITER-PRODUCER	16188 MEADOWCREST RD	SHERMAN OAKS, CA 91403
WILSON, JOHN RICHARD	COMPOSER	21056 LAS FLORES MESA DR	MALIBU, CA 90265
WILSON, JUSTIN	SINGER	POST OFFICE BOX 267	FORT SETTLEMENT, LA 70733
WILSON, KENT	DIRECTOR	6961 SUNNYDELL TRAIL	HOLLYWOOD, CA 90068
WILSON, KITTY	GUITARIST	ROUTE #2, BOX 357-B	GOODLETTSVILLE, TN 37072
WILSON, LISA ANNE	TV WRITER	CBS-TV, "AS THE WORLD TURNS"	
		51 W 52ND ST	NEW YORK, NY 10019
WILSON, LON	DRUMMER	439 MOSS TRAIL	GOODLETTSVILLE, TN 37072
WILSON, MARY	SINGER-AUTHORESS	9200 SUNSET BLVD #1220	LOS ANGELES, CA 90069
WILSON, MESCAL	PIANIST	POST OFFICE BOX U	REDDING, CT 06875
WILSON, MICHAEL G	FILM WRITER-PRODUCER	EON FILMS, 2 S AUDLEY ST	LONDON W1 ENGLAND
WILSON, MIKE	WRESTLING ANNOUNCER	UNIVERSAL WRESTLING FEDERATION	
		MID SOUTH SPORTS, INC	
		5001 SPRING VALLEY RD	DALLAS, TX 75244
WILSON, MOOKIE	BASEBALL	NEW YORK METS BB CLUB	
		WILLIAM A SHEA STADIUM	FLUSHING, NY 11368
WILSON, NANCY	SINGER-ACTRESS	5455 WILSHIRE BLVD #1606	LOS ANGELES, CA 90036
WILSON, NEIL	TENOR	CAMI, 165 W 57TH ST	NEW YORK, NY 10019
WILSON, NORRIS D	PIANIST	3422 WOODMONT BLVD	NASHVILLE, TN 37215
WILSON, PAP	GUITARIST	ROUTE #2, BOX 150	DOVER, TN 37058
WILSON, PATRICIA L	NEWS CORRESPONDENT	5328 SHERRILL AVE	CHEVY CHASE, MD 20815
WILSON, PAUL E	WRITER-PRODUCER	9 OYSTER BAY DR	RUMSON, NJ 07760
WILSON, PEE WEE	GUITAIST	617 HIDDEN HILL RD	HERMITAGE, TN 37076
WILSON, PHIL	COMPOSER-MUSICIAN	8 HAMMOND RD	BELMONT, MA 02178
WILSON, RALPH GABY	SCREENWRITER	9022 SUNSET BLVD #531	LOS ANGELES, CA 90069
WILSON, RANSOM	FLUTIST	CAMI, 165 W 57TH ST	NEW YORK, NY 10019
WILSON, RICHARD L	CONDUCTOR	22623 MAPLE AVE	TORRANCE, CA 90505
WILSON, RICHARD W	TV WRITER	8955 BEVERLY BLVD	LOS ANGELES, CA 90048
WILSON, RICKY	DRUMMER	714 DUE WEST AVE #L-166	MADISON, TN 37115
WILSON, RIP	GUITARIST	907 BROADMOOR DR	NASHVILLE, TN 37216
WILSON, RITA	ACTRESS	7461 BEVERLY BLVD #400	LOS ANGELES, CA 90036
WILSON, ROBERT	ACTOR	9165 SUNSET BLVD #202	LOS ANGELES, CA 90069
WILSON, ROBIN E	NEWS CORRESPONDENT	1728 N QUEENS LN #178	ARLINGTON, VA 22201
WILSON, RONALD	TV DIRECTOR	CONWAY, EAGLE HOUSE	
		109 JERMYN ST	LONDON SW1 ENGLAND
WILSON, RONALD V	NEWS CORRESPONDENT	1545 18TH ST #310, NW	WASHINGTON, DC 20036
WILSON, ROWLAND BRAGG	CARTOONIST	33871 CALLE ACORDARSE	SAN JUAN CAPISTRANO, CA 92675
WILSON, SCOTT	ACTOR	CONTEMPORARY ARTISTS	
		132 S LASKY DR	BEVERLY HILLS, CA 90212
WILSON, SCOTT	BODYBUILDER	GOLD'S GYM, 35 NOTRE DAME AVE	SAN JOSE, CA 95113
WILSON, SHEREE J	ACTRESS	LIGHT, 113 N ROBERTSON BLVD	LOS ANGELES, CA 90048
WILSON, SMILEY	GUITARIST	ROUTE #2, BOX 357-B	GOODLETTSVILLE, TN 37072
WILSON, SPIDER	GUITARIST	243 FESCUE DR	MOUNT JULIET, TN 37122
WILSON, STANLEY E	NEWS CORRESPONDENT	6631 WAKEFIELD DR #110	ALEXANDRIA, VA 22307
WILSON, TARA	ACTRESS	NBC-TV, "ANOTHER WORLD"	
		30 ROCKEFELLER PLAZA	NEW YORK, NY 10112
WILSON, TEDDY	PIANIST	EDITH KIGGEN, 50 E 72ND ST	NEW YORK, NY 10021
WILSON, THEODORE R	ACTOR	1635 N FORMOSA AVE #105	LOS ANGELES, CA 90046
WILSON, THEODORE ROOSEVELT	ACTOR	649 S BURNSIDE AVE #108	LOS ANGELES, CA 90038
WILSON, TOM	CARTOONIST	12120 ELMWOOD AVE	CLEVELAND, OH 44111
WILSON, TREY	ACTOR	5954 GRACIOSA DR	LOS ANGELES, CA 90068
WILSON, WARREN D "BILLY"	CONDUCTOR	602 2ND AVE N	COLUMBUS, MS 39701
WILSON, WILLIAM D	PHOTOGRAPHER	4608 JOHN HANCOCK CT #103	ANNANDALE, VA 22003
WILSON, WOODROW	PHOTOGRAPHER	6211 ELMHURST ST	DISTRICT HEIGHTS, MD 20747
WILTON, PENELOPE	ACTRESS	46 ELSYNGE RD	LONDON SW18 ENGLAND
WILTSE, DAVID G	TV WRITER	555 W 57TH ST #1230	NEW YORK, NY 10019

Name	Occupation	Address	City	Zip
WIMBERGER, PETER	BASSO-BARITONE	61 W 62ND ST #6-F	NEW YORK, NY	10023
WIMBERLY, WILLIAM J	COMPOSER-CONDUCTOR	1552 LUCRETIA AVE	LOS ANGELES, CA	90026
WIMMER, RICHARD S	TV WRITER	10100 SANTA MONICA BLVD #1600	LOS ANGELES, CA	90067
WINANT, BRUCE	ACTOR	4864 1/2 TUJUNGA AVE	NORTH HOLLYWOOD, CA	91601
WINBERGH, GOESTA	TENOR	CAMI, 165 W 57TH ST	NEW YORK, NY	10019
WINBURN, GEORGE R, JR	DIRECTOR	DGA, 7950 SUNSET BLVD	LOS ANGELES, CA	90046
WINCELBERG, ANITA M	WRITER	301 S WETHERLY DR	BEVERLY HILLS, CA	90211
WINCELBERG, SIMON	WRITER	301 S WETHERLY DR	BEVERLY HILLS, CA	90211
WINCENC, CAROL	FLUTIST	IMG ARTISTS, 22 E 71ST ST	NEW YORK, NY	10021
WINCENC & LEHWALDER	MUSICAL DUO	IMG ARTISTS, 22 E 71ST ST	NEW YORK, NY	10021
WINCHELL, PAUL	ACTOR	14136 JANNA WY	SYLMAR, CA	91342
WINCHELL, PAUL	DIRECTOR-PRODUCER	2800 OLYMPIC BLVD	SANTA MONICA, CA	90404
WINCHESTER, JESSE	SINGER-SONGWRITER	POST OFFICE BOX 7308	CARMEL, CA	93921
WIND, THE	ROCK & ROLL GROUP	POST OFFICE BOX 390		
		OLD CHELSEA STATION	NEW YORK, NY	10113
WINDBREAKERS, THE	ROCK & ROLL GROUP	450 14TH ST #201	ATLANTA, GA	30318
WINDER, MICHAEL	SCREENWRITER	8955 BEVERLY BLVD	LOS ANGELES, CA	90048
WINDHAM, BARRY	WRESTLER	NATIONAL WRESTLING ALLIANCE		
		JIM CROCKETT PROMOTIONS		
		421 BRIARBEND DR	CHARLOTTE, NC	28209
WINDHAM, BIG BOB	WRESTLER	SEE - MULLIGAN, BLACKJACK		
WINDHAM, R CRAIG	NEWS CORRESPONDENT	1776 "G" ST, NW	WASHINGTON, DC	20006
WINDHAM, ROBERT	WRESTLER	SEE - MULLIGAN, BLACKJACK		
WINDING, VICTOR	ACTOR	CRICK FARM, LYDART, MONMOUTH	GWENT	ENGLAND
WINDOFFER, ROB	GUITARIST	1614 18TH AVE S	NASHVILLE, TN	37212
WINDOM, WILLIAM	ACTOR	6535 LANGDON AVE	VAN NUYS, CA	91406
WINDSOR, BARBARA	ACTRESS-SINGER	THE THE RICHARD STONE AGENCY		
		18-20 YORK BLDGS, ADELPHI	LONDON WC2N 6JY	ENGLAND
WINDSOR, BETH	ACTRESS	15760 VENTURA BLVD #1730	ENCINO, CA	91436
WINDSOR, FRANK	ACTOR	AMAL, 33 ROSARY GARDENS	LONDON SW7	ENGLAND
WINDSOR, GERI	CASTING DIRECTOR	MTM, 4042 RADFORD AVE	STUDIO CITY, CA	91604
WINDSOR, JANE	ACTRESS	8285 SUNSET BLVD #12	LOS ANGELES, CA	90046
WINDSOR, MARIE	ACTRESS	15010 VENTURA BLVD #234	SHERMAN OAKS, CA	91403
WINDSOR, TAMMY	CASTING DIRECTOR	14001 PEACH GROVE	SHERMAN OAKS, CA	91423
WINDUST, PENELOPE	ACTRESS	11726 SAN VICENTE BLVD #300	LOS ANGELES, CA	90049
WINE, NATHANIEL B	CONDUCTOR	12717 WEDDINGTON AVE	NORTH HOLLYWOOD, CA	91607
WINEBRENNER, JANE	NEWS CORRESPONDENT	3135 HIGHLAND PL, NW	WASHINGTON, DC	20008
WINER, HARRY S	TV DIRECTOR	1033 OCEAN AVE #204	SANTA MONICA, CA	90403
WINER, STEPHEN H	TV WRITER	555 W 57TH ST #1230	NEW YORK, NY	10019
WINES, MIKE	NEWS CORRESPONDENT	228 S WEST ST	ALEXANDRIA, VA	22314
WINFIELD, CHIP	GUITARIST	2732 ELM HILL PIKE	NASHVILLE, TN	37214
WINFIELD, DAVE	BASEBALL	367 W FOREST	TEANECK, NJ	07666
WINFIELD, JOHN	ACTOR	4228 AGNES AVE	STUDIO CITY, CA	91604
WINFIELD, PAUL	ACTOR	10000 SANTA MONICA BLVD #305	LOS ANGELES, CA	90067
WINFREY, OPRAH	ACTRESS-TV HOST	WLS-TV, 190 N STATE ST	CHICAGO, IL	60601
WING, LESLIE	ACTRESS	247 S BEVERLY DR #102	BEVERLY HILLS, CA	90210
WINGER, DEBRA	ACTRESS	POST OFFICE BOX 9078	VAN NUYS, CA	91409
WINGERT, DICK	CARTOONIST	KING FEATURES SYNDICATE		
		235 E 45TH ST	NEW YORK, NY	10017
WINGERT, MICHAEL	MUSICIAN	371 WALLACE RD #111	NASHVILLE, TN	37211
WINGFIELD, DON	PHOTOGRAPHER	3601 DANNY'S LN	ALEXANDRIA, VA	22311
WINGO, HAL	WRITER-EDITOR	PEOPLE/TIME & LIFE BLDG		
		ROCKEFELLER CENTER	NEW YORK, NY	10020
WINGO, WALTER S	NEWS CORRESPONDENT	4655 N 24TH ST	ARLINGTON, VA	22207
WINGREEN, JASON	ACTOR	4224 TEESDALE AVE	NORTH HOLLYWOOD, CA	91604
WINITSKY, ALEX	FILM PRODUCER	9720 WILSHIRE BLVD #704	BEVERLY HILLS, CA	90212
WINKER, JAMES R	ACTOR	2610 WAVERLY DR	LOS ANGELES, CA	90039
WINKLER, HENRY	ACTOR-PRODUCER	POST OFFICE BOX 1764	STUDIO CITY, CA	91604
WINKLER, IRWIN	FILM PRODUCER	10125 W WASHINGTON BLVD	CULVER CITY, CA	90230
WINKLER, K C	ACTRESS-MODEL	POST OFFICE BOX 3673	SANTA MONICA, CA	90403
WINKLER, KENNETH	GUITARIST	4425 WESTLAWN DR #C-303	NASHVILLE, TN	37209
WINKLESS, JEFF	ACTOR	15739 PLUMMER ST	SEPULVEDA, CA	91343
WINKLESS, NELSON	DIRECTOR	11745 LANDALE ST	NORTH HOLLYWOOD, CA	91607
WINKLESS, TERENCE H	WRITER	3174 DERONDA DR	HOLLYWOOD, CA	90068
WINN, DAVID	ACTOR	8961 MEGAN AVE	CANOGA PARK, CA	91304
WINN, HANS	HIGH WIRE ACT	POST OFFICE BOX 87	WEST LEBANON, NY	12195
WINN, KITTY	ACTRESS	10000 SANTA MONICA BLVD #305	LOS ANGELES, CA	90067
WINNER, CHRISTOPHER P	COLUMNIST	POST OFFICE BOX 500	WASHINGTON, DC	20044
WINNER, JEFFREY	ACTOR	7518 WILLOUGHBY AVE	LOS ANGELES, CA	90046
WINNER, MICHAEL	WRITER-PRODUCER	SCIMITAR, 6 SACKVILLE ST	LONDON W1X 1DD	ENGLAND
WINNICK, JERRY	TV WRITER	9300 WILSHIRE BLVD #410	BEVERLY HILLS, CA	90212
WINNINGHAM, MARE	ACTRESS	12256 LA MAIDA ST	NORTH HOLLYWOOD, CA	91607
WINNS, THE WONDEROUS	AERIAL TROUPE	HALL, 138 FROG HOLLOW RD	CHURCHVILLE, PA	18966
WINOKUR, MARC	SINGER	POST OFFICE BOX 98	FOREST HILLS, NY	11375
WINSEMAN, DANA D	ACTOR	8828 ZEILER AVE	ARLETA, CA	91331
WINSEMAN, DAVID E	ACTOR	8828 ZEILER AVE	ARLETA, CA	91331
WINSHIP, MICHAEL J	WRITER	135 W 50TH ST #1950	NEW YORK, NY	10019
WINSLOIW, STEPHANIE	SINGER	POST OFFICE BOX 1750	HOLLYWOOD, CA	90028
WINSLOW, BIRGIT	ACTRESS	1122 26TH ST	SANTA MONICA, CA	90403
WINSLOW, GEORGE "FOGHORN"	ACTOR	WALLY WENZLAFF		
		85 RAILROAD AVE	CAMP MEEKER, CA	95419
WINSLOW, MICHAEL	ACTOR-COMEDIAN	2121 AVE OF THE STARS #410	LOS ANGELES, CA	90067
WINSTEN, ARCHER	FILM CRITIC	425 W BROADWAY	NEW YORK, NY	10012
WINSTEN, FELIX H	NEWS CORRESPONDENT	129 3RD ST, NE	WASHINGTON, DC	20002
WINSTON, ELLEN M	JOURNALIST	10969 WELLWORTH AVE #311	LOS ANGELES, CA	90024

Name	Occupation	Address	City/State	Zip
WINSTON, GEORGE	PIANIST-COMPOSER	GREAT AMERICAN MUSIC HALL		
		859 O'FARRELL ST	SAN FRANCISCO, CA	94109
WINSTON, HATTIE	ACTRESS	13025 JARVIS AVE	LOS ANGELES, CA	90061
WINSTON, HELENE	ACTRESS	7466 BEVERLY BLVD #205	LOS ANGELES, CA	90036
WINSTON, JOHN	ACTOR	9165 SUNSET BLVD #202	LOS ANGELES, CA	90069
WINSTON, LESLIE	ACTRESS	5752 BUFFALO AVE	VAN NUYS, CA	91401
WINSTON, PAMELA W	NEWS CORRESPONDENT	221 CONSTITION AVE #22, NE	WASHINGTON, DC	20002
WINSTON, ROBERT	ACTOR	25 5TH AVE	NEW YORK, NY	10003
WINSTON, SHERIE	NEWS CORRESPONDENT	2456 20TH ST #306, NW	WASHINGTON, DC	20009
WINSTON, SUSAN	TV PRODUCER	LORIMAR-TELEPICTURES		
		3970 OVERLAND AVE	CULVER CITY, CA	90230
WINSTON, SUSAN B	DIRECTOR	310 W 72ND ST	NEW YORK, NY	10023
WINTER, CATHY	SINGER	POST OFFICE BOX 6380	ALBANY, NY	12206
WINTER, EDGAR	SINGER-GUITARIST	350 5TH AVE #5215	NEW YORK, NY	10018
WINTER, EDWARD	ACTOR	4359 HAYVENHURST AVE	ENCINO, CA	91316
WINTER, GARY	DIRECTOR	DGA, 7950 SUNSET BLVD	LOS ANGELES, CA	90046
WINTER, JACK	WRITER-PRODUCER	470 W END AVE	NEW YORK, NY	10024
WINTER, JOHNNY	SINGER-GUITARIST	POST OFFICE BOX 60234	CHICAGO, IL	60660
WINTER, LYNETTE	ACTRESS	CARPENTER, 1516-W REDWOOD ST	SAN DIEGO, CA	92101
WINTER, MICHAEL	TV DIRECTOR	437 N OAKHURST DR	BEVERLY HILLS, CA	90210
WINTER, PAUL	BASS	253 W 73RD ST #7-M	NEW YORK, NY	10023
WINTER, PAUL, CONSORT	JAZZ GROUP	2067 BROADWAY #PH-B	NEW YORK, NY	10023
WINTER, THOMAS S	NEWS CORRESPONDENT	16 4TH ST, SE	WASHINGTON, DC	20003
WINTER HOURS	ROCK & ROLL GROUP	AAM, 277 CHURCH ST	NEW YORK, NY	10013
WINTERS, BARBARA JO	MUSICIAN	3529 COLDWATER CANYON AVE	STUDIO CITY, CA	91604
WINTERS, BERNIE	COMEDIAN	50 REGENTS PARK	LONDON NW1 75X	ENGLAND
WINTERS, DAVID	DIRECTOR	13850 MULHOLLAND DR	BEVERLY HILLS, CA	90210
WINTERS, DEBORAH	ACTRESS	211 S BEVERLY DR #107	BEVERLY HILLS, CA	90212
WINTERS, DENNIS	GUITARIST	POST OFFICE BOX 2227	NOLENSVILLE, TN	37135
WINTERS, DON	GUITARIST	ROUTE #5, WILSON PIKE	FRANKLIN, TN	37064
WINTERS, DONALD L	GUITARIST	BOX 33-A, HICKORY HILL RD	PEGRAM, TN	37143
WINTERS, GLENN S	WRITER-PRODUCER	1855 FOOTHILL BLVD	LA CANADA, CA	91011
WINTERS, JERRY	DIRECTOR	11 PALM ISLAND	MIAMI BEACH, FL	33139
WINTERS, JONATHAN	COMEDIAN-ACTOR	4310 ARCOLA AVE	NORTH HOLLYWOOD, CA	91602
WINTERS, KAREN COLE	TV WRITER	1855 FOOTHILL BLVD	LA CANADA, CA	91011
WINTERS, RALPH E	FILM EDITOR	ACE, 4416 1/2 FINLEY AVE	LOS ANGELES, CA	90027
WINTERS, ROLAND	ACTOR	405 E 51ST ST	NEW YORK, NY	10022
WINTERS, SHELLEY	ACTRESS	POST OFFICE BOX 10269	BEVERLY HILLS, CA	90210
WINTERS, STEPHANIE	ACTRESS	ABC-TV, "ALL MY CHILDREN"		
		1330 AVE OF THE AMERICAS	NEW YORK, NY	10019
WINTERS, WENDEE	COMEDIENNE	1680 N VINE ST #214	HOLLYWOOD, CA	90028
WINTERSOLE, WILLIAM	ACTOR	1177 N ARDMORE AVE #6	LOS ANGELES, CA	90029
WINTHER, JORN	TV DIRECTOR-PRODUCER	7 GREENWOOD LN	WESTPORT, CT	06880
WINTHROP, DIANA R	NEWS CORRESPONDENT	1829 SUMMIT PL, NW	WASHINGTON, DC	20009
WINTON, WAYNE	ACTOR	6290 SUNSET BLVD	LOS ANGELES, CA	90028
WINWOOD, STEVE	SINGER-SONGWRITER	ISLAND RECORDS COMPANY		
		22 SAINT PETERS SQUARE	LONDON W6	ENGLAND
WIPERS, THE	ROCK & ROLL GROUP	POST OFFICE BOX 2428	EL SEGUNDO, CA	90245
WIRE TRAIN	ROCK & ROLL GROUP	POST OFFICE BOX 14563	SAN FRANCISCO, CA	94114
WIRENGARD	HIGH WIRE ACT	HALL, 138 FROG HOLLOW RD	CHURCHVILLE, PA	18966
WIRENGRAD, GREAT	SWAYPOLIST	HALL, 138 FROG HOLLOW RD	CHURCHVILLE, PA	18966
WIRTH, DONALD	MUSICIAN	636 HARPETH KNOLL RD	NASHVILLE, TN	37221
WIRTH, JOHN L	WRITER	1888 CENTURY PARK E #1107	LOS ANGELES, CA	90067
WISBERG, AUBREY	WRITER	KOHNER, 9169 SUNSET BLVD	LOS ANGELES, CA	90069
WISDOM, NORMAN	ACTOR	28 BERKELEY SQ	LONDON 6HD	ENGLAND
WISE, CHUBBY	GUITARIST	PLACID BAY ESTATES		
		400 FOREST GROVE	COLONIAL BEACH, VA	22443
WISE, DAVID	TV WRITER	8955 BEVERLY BLVD	LOS ANGELES, CA	90048
WISE, HERBERT	FILM-TV DIRECTOR	13 DESMOND RD	LONDON N19 5NP	ENGLAND
WISE, LEONARD	AUTHOR	2250 FOX HILLS DR	LOS ANGELES, CA	90064
WISE, PATRICIA	SOPRANO	CAMI, 165 W 57TH ST	NEW YORK, NY	10019
WISE, PAUL A	DIRECTOR	5993 WESTERN RUN DR	BALTIMORE, MD	21209
WISE, RICK	DIRECTOR	DGA, 7950 SUNSET BLVD	LOS ANGELES, CA	90046
WISE, ROBERT	DIRECTOR-PRODUCER	2222 AVE OF THE STARS #2303	LOS ANGELES, CA	90067
WISE, TIM	ACTOR	13111 VENTURA BLVD #204	STUDIO CITY, CA	91604
WISE, WAYNE	DRUMMER	ROUTE #2, BOX 474	KINGSTON SPRINGS, TN	37082
WISEMAN, BARRY	ACTOR	550 S BARRINGTON AVE #1119	LOS ANGELES, CA	90049
WISEMAN, JOSEPH	ACTOR	382 CENTRAL PARK W	NEW YORK, NY	10019
WISEMAN, MAC B	SINGER-GUITARIST	2732 MOSS DALE DR	NASHVILLE, TN	37217
WISEMAN, TEDDY D	PIANIST	POST OFFICE BOX 117	PORTLAND, TN	37148
WISENBERG, DINAH	NEWS CORRESPONDENT	1701 MASSACHUSETTS AVE #411, NW	WASHINGTON, DC	20005
WISER, BERNARD T	TV WRITER	11725 SUNSHINE TERR	STUDIO CITY, CA	91604
WISER, BUD	TV PRODUCER	EMBASSY TV, 1438 N GOWER ST	LOS ANGELES, CA	90028
WISH, JEROME W	WRITER	115 S SWALL DR #3	LOS ANGELES, CA	90068
WISHART, ROBERT H	NEWS CORRESPONDENT	3824 VAN NESS ST, NW	WASHINGTON, DC	20016
WISHBONE ASH	ROCK & ROLL GROUP	JOHN SHERRY, 65 E 55TH ST	NEW YORK, NY	10022
WISHNER, SUZANNE	ACTRESS	612 N SYCAMORE AVE	LOS ANGELES, CA	90036
WISKOSKI, ED	WRESTLER	SEE - DE BEERS, COLONEL		
WISLON, LOIS	ACTRESS	11579 HESBY ST	NORTH HOLLYWOOD, CA	91601
WISLON, RICHARD A	FILM WRITER-DIRECTOR	501 OCEAN FRONT WALK	SANTA MONICA, CA	90402
WISNISKI, JOHN ANTHONY, JR	WRESTLER	SEE - VALENTINE, GREG		
		"THE HAMMER"		
WISSINGER, DONNA	FLUTIST	111 W 57TH ST #1203	NEW YORK, NY	10019
WITANOWSKI, EDWARD S	DIRECTOR	116 WEEKS RD	EAST WILLISTON, NY	11596
WITCOVER, JULES	NEWS CORRESPONDENT	1516 INLET CT	RESTON, VA	22090

STEVE WINWOOD

STEVIE WONDER

LANA WOOD

JAMES WOODS

JOAN WOODBURY

FAY WRAY

GARY WRIGHT

JANE WYATT

JANE WYMAN

WITHERS, BILL	SINGER-SONGWRITER	2600 BENEDICT CANYON DR	BEVERLY HILLS, CA	90210
WITHERS, JANE	ACTRESS	2208 LIVE OAK DR	HOLLYWOOD, CA	90068
WITHERS, MARK	ACTOR	6426 BALCOM AVE	RESEDA, CA	91335
WITHERSPON, JIMMY	SINGER-MUSICIAN	HOFFER, 233 1/2 E 48TH ST	NEW YORK, NY	10017
WITHERSPOON, DANE	ACTOR	8485 MELROSE PL #E	LOS ANGELES, CA	90069
WITHROW, SCOTT S	PIANIST	4341 LITTLE RIVER RD	BIRMINGHAM, AL	35213
WITMAN, ROBERT KING	NEWS CORRESPONDENT	5 BENWAY CT	CATONSVILLE, MD	21228
WITNEY, WILLIAM N	DIRECTOR	DGA, 7950 SUNSET BLVD	LOS ANGELES, CA	90046
WITT, DAVID	TV PRODUCER	METROMEDIA, 5746 SUNSET BLVD	LOS ANGELES, CA	90028
WITT, ELDER	NEWS CORRESPONDENT	6001 UTAH AVE, NW	WASHINGTON, DC	20015
WITT, G EVANS	NEWS CORRESPONDENT	1754 KENYON ST, NW	WASHINGTON, DC	20010
WITT, HOLGER	NEWS CORRESPONDENT	3132 "M" ST, NW	WASHINGTON, DC	20007
WITT, HOWARD	ACTOR	1825 N GRAMERCY PL #309	LOS ANGELES, CA	90028
WITT, PAUL F	COMPOSER-CONDUCTOR	3322 MENTONE AVE #3	LOS ANGELES, CA	90034
WITT, PAUL, JR	WRITER-PRODUCER	16032 VALLEY VISTA BLVD	ENCINO, CA	91436
WITT, WILLIAM LEE	GUITARIST	315 MELPAR DR	NASHVILLE, TN	37211
WITTAN, SUSAN D	PHOTOGRAPHER	3003 VAN NESS ST, NW	WASHINGTON, DC	20008
WITTEN, FREDERICK G	DIRECTOR	3654 BARHAM BLVD #Q-213	LOS ANGELES, CA	90068
WITTEN, ROBERT H	NEWS CORRESPONDENT	1755 S JEFFERSON DAVIS HWY	ARLINGTON, VA	22202
WITTER, CHERIE	MODEL	MODELS & PROMOTIONS AGENCY		
		8560 SUNSET BLVD, 10TH FLOOR	LOS ANGELES, CA	90069
WITTER, JERE D	WRITER	POST OFFICE BOX 1525	BIG BEAR LAKE, CA	92315
WITTER, KAREN	ACTRESS-MODEL	MODELS & PROMOTIONS AGENCY		
		8560 SUNSET BLVD, 10TH FLOOR	LOS ANGELES, CA	90069
WITTER, WILLIS	NEWS CORRESPONDENT	224 3RD ST, SE	WASHINGTON, DC	20003
WITTHANS, ROBERT	ACTOR	NEW, 300 E GLENOAKS BLVD	GLENDALE, CA	91207
WITTLIFF, WILLIAM D	FILM WRITER-DIRECTOR	1301 KENT LN	AUSTIN, TX	78703
WITTMAN, ELLEN	TV WRITER-PRODUCER	2612 ELM AVE	MANHATTAN BEACH, CA	90266
WITTMAN, MALCOLM	ACTOR	8721 SUNSET BLVD #103	LOS ANGELES, CA	90069
WITTMAN, WILLIAM DONALD	PHOTOGRAPHER	6015 BELLA VISTA AVE	BALTIMORE, MD	21214
WITTY, JOHN	ACTOR-WRITER	22 N HILL	LONDON N6 4QA	ENGLAND
WITTY, RICHARD	DIRECTOR	327 CENTRAL PARK W	NEW YORK, NY	10025
WITUS, BARBARA	WRITER	1341 OCEAN AVE #323	SANTA MONICA, CA	90401
WIXEN, RANDALL	TALENT AGENT	POST OFFICE BOX 49217	LOS ANGELES, CA	90049
WIZAN, JOSEPH	FILM-TV PRODUCER	10751 WILSHIRE BLVD #PH-9	LOS ANGELES, CA	90024
WIZARD, MR	TV PERSONALITY	SEE - HERBERT, DON "MR HERBERT"		
WIZARD, THE	WRESTLING MANAGER	POST OFFICE BOX 3859	STAMFORD, CT	06905
WODWARD, DIANE	ACTRESS	4401 KLING ST #39	BURBANK, CA	91505
WOESSNER, FREDERICK T	COMPOSER-CONDUCTOR	952 N HUDSON AVE #2	LOS ANGELES, CA	90038
WOFF, WILLIAM	ACTOR	1251 N CRESCENT HGTS BLVD #B	LOS ANGELES, CA	90046
WOGAN, TERRY	TV HOST	GURNETT, 45 QUEEN'S GATE MEWS	LONDON SW7	ENGLAND
WOHL, ALFRED	COMPOSER	6122 GOODLAND AVE	NORTH HOLLYWOOD, CA	91606
WOHL, DAVID	ACTOR	9229 SUNSET BLVD #306	LOS ANGELES, CA	90069
WOHL, WALLY	ACTOR-DIRECTOR	345 S EL CAMINO DR	BEVERLY HILLS, CA	90212
WOHLAFKA, LOUISE	SOPRANO	254 W 93RD ST #8	NEW YORK, NY	10025
WOJCIK, LESZEK	NEWS CORRESPONDENT	11205 W MONTPELIER RD	GREAT FALLS, VA	22066
WOJNO, STAN, JR	ACTOR	8780 SHOREHAM DR #304	LOS ANGELES, CA	90069
WOLCOTT, CHARLES	COMPOSER	POST OFFICE BOX 155	HAIFA	ISRAEL
WOLF, CATHRINE	SPORTS REPORTER	SPORTS ILLUSTRATED MAGAZINE		
		TIME & LIFE BUILDING		
		ROCKEFELLER CENTER	NEW YORK, NY	10020
WOLF, DAVID M	SCREENWRITER	1162 N WETHERLY DR	LOS ANGELES, CA	90069
WOLF, GARIN	TV WRITER	CBS-TV, "AS THE WORLD TURNS"		
		51 W 52ND ST	NEW YORK, NY	10019
WOLF, GARY	SINGER-GUITARIST	POST OFFICE BOX 397	FRANKLIN, OH	45005
WOLF, GEORGE E	DIRECTOR	330 W 45TH ST #J	NEW YORK, NY	10036
WOLF, HARRY L	CINEMATOGRAPHER	502 N LA JOLLA AVE	LOS ANGELES, CA	90048
WOLF, JEANNE	TV REPORTER	ENTERTAINMENT TONIGHT		
		PARAMOUNT TELEVISION		
		5555 MELROSE AVE	LOS ANGELES, CA	90038
WOLF, JOHN C, III	DIRECTOR	87 STATE ST	BROOKLYN, NY	11201
WOLF, LEONARD	PIANIST	7300 WESTON WY	NASHVILLE, TN	37221
WOLF, MARCIA	ACTRESS	POST OFFICE BOX 2422	NORTH HOLLYWOOD, CA	91602
WOLF, MARY ANN	NEWS CORRESPONDENT	NBC-TV, NEWS DEPARTMENT		
		4001 NEBRASKA AVE, NW	WASHINGTON, DC	20016
WOLF, MICHAEL	ACTOR	41 LANSDOWNE RD	LONDON W11 2LQ	ENGLAND
WOLF, NORA	NEWS CORRESPONDENT	1825 "K" ST, NW	WASHINGTON, DC	20006
WOLF, PETER	SINGER-SONGWRITER	LIPPMAN, 9669 OAK PASS RD	BEVERLY HILLS, CA	90210
WOLF, PETER F	COMPOSER	1506 DOROTHY AVE	SIMI VALLEY, CA	93063
WOLF, RICHARD A	WRITER-PRODUCER	2393 CASTILIAN DR	LOS ANGELES, CA	90068
WOLF, SALLY	SOPRANO	CAMI, 165 W 57TH ST	NEW YORK, NY	10019
WOLF, SUSAN G	ACTRESS	681 LATIMER RD	SANTA MONICA, CA	90402
WOLF, THOMAS H	WRITER	13430 QUERY MILL	GATHERSBURG, MD	20879
WOLF, VIRGINIA	ROCK & ROLL GROUP	SEE - VIRGINIA WOLF		
WOLF, WILLIAM	FILM CRITIC	POST OFFICE BOX 7858	WASHINGTON, DC	20044
WOLFBERG, DENNIS	COMEDIAN	ICM, 8899 BEVERLY BLVD	LOS ANGELES, CA	90048
WOLFE, BUDDY	WRESTLER	AMERICAN WRESTLING ASSOC		
		MINNEAPLOIS WRESTLING		
		10001 WAYZATA BLVD	MINNETONKA, MN	55345
WOLFE, DIGBY	TV WRITER-PRODUCER	1642 N BEVERLY DR	BEVERLY HILLS, CA	90210
WOLFE, FLETCHER	CHOIR DIRECTOR	POST OFFICE BOX 8583	ATLANTA, GA	30306
WOLFE, IAN	ACTOR	4652 NOBLE AVE	SHERMAN OAKS, CA	91403
WOLFE, ISABEL	ACTRESS	1705 CARLA RIDGE	BEVERLY HILLS, CA	90210
WOLFE, JACKIE	NEWS CORRESPONDENT	4550 CONNECTICUT AVE #701, NW	WASHINGTON, DC	20008
WOLFE, JAMES DAVID	DRUMMER	1111 STRATFORD AVE	NASHVILLE, TN	37216

Name	Occupation	Address	City	ZIP
WOLFE, JOEL R	ACTOR	325 W 86TH ST	NEW YORK, NY	10024
WOLFE, JUNE	PIANIST	2166 BROOKVIEW DR	NASHVILLE, TN	37214
WOLFE, KEDRIC	ACTOR	POST OFFICE BOX 584	TOPANGA CANYON, CA	90290
WOLFE, KEITH	CASTING DIRECTOR	1040 N LAS PALMAS AVE	HOLLYWOOD, CA	90038
WOLFE, NANCY L	NEWS CORRESPONDENT	400 NATIONAL PRESS BLDG		
		529 14TH ST, NW	WASHINGTON, DC	20045
WOLFE, ROBERT L	FILM EDITOR	ACE, 4416 1/2 FINLEY AVE	LOS ANGELES, CA	90027
WOLFE, ROBERT T	DIRECTOR	175 E 74TH ST	NEW YORK, NY	10021
WOLFE, RONALD	WRITER-PRODUCER	1 GROSVENOR GARDENS	LONDON NW11 OHH	ENGLAND
WOLFE, STANLEY	COMPOSER	32 FERNDALE DR	HASTINGS-ON-HUDSON, NY	10706
WOLFE, WENDY	ACTRESS	18 MARY ANN LN	HARRINGTON PARK, NJ	07640
WOLFF, ALEXANDER	SPORTS WRITER-EDITOR	SPORTS ILLUSTRATED MAGAZINE		
		TIME & LIFE BUILDING		
		ROCKEFELLER CENTER	NEW YORK, NY	10020
WOLFF, ART	DIRECTOR	120 E 74TH ST	NEW YORK, NY	10021
WOLFF, ELIZABETH	PIANIST	POST OFFICE BOX U	REDDING, CT	06875
WOLFF, F ROGER	COMPOSER	340 N BEACHWOOD DR	LOS ANGELES, CA	90004
WOLFF, HUGH	CONDUCTOR	AFFILIATE ARTISTS, INC		
		37 W 65TH ST, 6TH FLOOR	NEW YORK, NY	10023
WOLFF, JURGEN M	TV WRITER	8955 BEVERLY BLVD	LOS ANGELES, CA	90048
WOLFF, RUTH	WRITER	165 W 46TH ST #409	NEW YORK, NY	10036
WOLFF, WILLIAM J	WRITER	1631 19TH ST	MANHATTAN BEACH, CA	90266
WOLFINGTON, IGGIE	ACTOR	11216 AQUA VISTA ST	NORTH HOLLYWOOD, CA	91602
WOLFMAN JACK	RADIO-TV PERSONALITY	1644 FERRARI DR	BEVERLY HILLS, CA	90210
WOLFRAM, WILLIAM	PIANIST	500 5TH AVE #2050	NEW YORK, NY	10110
WOLFREY, EDITH	ACTRESS	1319 S RIMPAU BLVD	LOS ANGELES, CA	90019
WOLFSON, AARON W	COMPOSER	8456 ALLENWOOD RD	LOS ANGELES, CA	90046
WOLFSON, CHARLES M	NEWS CORRESPONDENT	3916 LELAND ST	CHEVY CHASE, MD	20815
WOLFSON, ROBERT G	NEWS CORRESPONDENT	1101 S ARLINGTON RIDGE RD #310	ARLINGTON, VA	22202
WOLIN, KENNY	TV WRITER	8955 BEVERLY BLVD	LOS ANGELES, CA	90048
WOLITZER, HILMA	TV WRITER	555 W 57TH ST #1230	NEW YORK, NY	10019
WOLL, CYNTHIA	ACTRESS	2050 HIGH TOWER DR #2	HOLLYWOOD, CA	90068
WOLLERT, DAVE	TV DIRECTOR	6854 PACIFIC VIEW DR	HOLLYWOOD, CA	90068
WOLLET, MICHAEL	ACTOR	1329 N COLUMBUS AVE #D	GLENDALE, CA	91202
WOLLMAN, MARJORIE RECK	WRITER	8715 LOOKOUT MOUNTAIN AVE	LOS ANGELES, CA	90046
WOLMAN, DAN	FILM DIRECTOR	POST OFFICE BOX 229	JERUSALEM	ISRAEL
WOLMAN, JONATHAN P	NEWS CORRESPONDENT	2020 LANIER DR	SILVER SPRING, MD	20910
WOLMUTH, ROGER R	WRITER-EDITOR	PEOPLE/TIME & LIFE BLDG		
		ROCKEFELLER CENTER	NEW YORK, NY	10020
WOLPER, DAVID L	FILM-TV PRODUCER	10847 BELLAGIO DR	LOS ANGELES, CA	9007
WOLPERT, ROLAND	TV WRITER	6444 HAYES DR	LOS ANGELES, CA	90048
WOLPERT, STUART	TV WRITER-PRODUCER	EMBASSY TV, 1438 N GOWER ST	LOS ANGELES, CA	90028
WOLSK, EUGENE	THEATER PRODUCER	165 W 46TH ST	NEW YORK, NY	10036
WOLSTENHOLME, JOHN	WRITER-PRODUCER	13 FENTIMAN RD	LONDON SW8	ENGLAND
WOLSTENHOLME, KENNETH	TV HOST	106 MEADOW WALK, EWELL	SURREY	ENGLAND
WOLTER, SHERILYN	ACTRESS	11931 GOSHEN AVE #7	LOS ANGELES, CA	90049
WOLTERSTORFF, ROBERT A	TV WRITER	1267 MONUMENT ST	PACIFIC PALISADES, CA	90272
WOMACK, BOBBY	SINGER	TRUTH RECORDS COMPANY		
		2841 FIRENZE PL	LOS ANGELES, CA	90048
WOMACK, LEON	SINGER	3125 19TH ST #217	BAKERSFIELD, CA	93301
WOMACK, STEVE A	TV DIRECTOR	1315 GLADE DR	FRANKLIN, TN	37064
WOMACK & WOMACK	VOCAL DUO	1174 LONGWOOD AVE	LOS ANGELES, CA	90019
WON, KYUNG-SOO	CONDUCTOR	HIGHAM INTERNATIONAL ARTISTS		
		16 LAURISTON RD, WIMBLETON	LONDON SW19 4TQ	ENGLAND
WONDER, STEVIE	SINGER-SONGWRITER	BLACKBULL MUSIC COMPANY		
		4616 MAGNOLIA BLVD	BURBANK, CA	91505
WONG, ALAN LEE	ACTOR	623 NECTARINE ST #A	INGLEWOOD, CA	90301
WONG, JEFF	CARTOONIST	THE NATIONAL LAMPOON		
		635 MADISON AVE	NEW YORK, NY	10022
WONG, LEONARD	DIRECTOR	DGA, 110 W 57TH ST	NEW YORK, NY	10019
WOOD, ANDY	ACTOR	10390 SANTA MONICA BLVD #310	LOS ANGELES, CA	90025
WOOD, ANN P	NEWS CORRESPONDENT	11900 ESCALANTE CT	RESTON, VA	22091
WOOD, BARRY D	NEWS CORRESPONDENT	330 INDEPENDENCE AVE, SW	WASHINGTON, DC	20547
WOOD, BILL	TV WRITER	8955 BEVERLY BLVD	LOS ANGELES, CA	90048
WOOD, BOB	GUITARIST	115 AIRFLOAT DR	HENDERSONVILLE, TN	37075
WOOD, BOBBY R	PIANIST	ROUTE #4, LOT 2, SUNNY HILL RD	BRENWTOOD, TN	37027
WOOD, CHARLES	SCREENWRITER	FRASER, 91 REGENT ST	LONDON W1	ENGLAND
WOOD, CHARLES E	DRUMMER	2101 JONES CIR	NASHVILLE, TN	37207
WOOD, CHRISTOPHER	SCREENWRITER	VALENCE DE COLLONGES	MEYSSAS 19500	FRANCE
WOOD, DARYL	ACTRESS	CED, 261 S ROBERTSON BLVD	BEVERLY HILLS, CA	90211
WOOD, DAVID	ACTOR-WRITER	MILLER, 82 BROOM PARK		
		TEDDINGTON	MIDDLESEX TW11 9NY	ENGLAND
WOOD, DAVID B	NEWS CORRESPONDENT	9407 FERNWOOD RD	BETHESDA, MD	20817
WOOD, DEL	SINGER	POST OFFICE BOX 82	GREENBRIER, TN	37073
WOOD, DIANA PAGE	DIRECTOR	DGA, 110 W 57TH ST	NEW YORK, NY	10019
WOOD, DON	COMPOSER-CONDUCTOR	1329 WOODRUFF AVE	LOS ANGELES, CA	90024
WOOD, E RICHARD	RESTAURATEUR	THE OLD DEL MAR CAFE		
		2730 VIA DEL LA VALLE	DEL MAR, CA	92014
WOOD, FORREST	ACTOR	2056 RODNEY DR #4	LOS ANGELES, CA	90027
WOOD, JACK	TV WRITER	ABC-TV, "ALL MY CHILDREN"		
		1330 AVE OF THE AMERICAS	NEW YORK, NY	10019
WOOD, JACK K	TV WRITER-DIRECTOR	400 E 54TH ST #26-E	NEW YORK, NY	10022
WOOD, JAMES	GUITARIST	3109 POST OAK	ABILENE, TX	79606
WOOD, JAMES LESLIE	FIDDLER	POST OFFICE BOX 68	FAIRVIEW, TN	37062

WOOD, JANET	ACTRESS	427 N CANON DR #205	BEVERLY HILLS, CA 90210
WOOD, JANET	NEWS CORRESPONDENT	1313 TRINITY DR	ALEXANDRIA, VA 22314
WOOD, JOHN	ACTOR	ICM, 388-396 OXFORD ST	LONDON W1 ENGLAND
WOOD, JUDITH	ACTRESS	1300 1/4 N SYCAMORE AVE	HOLLYWOOD, CA 90028
WOOD, JUDY	COMPOSER	1237 N ORANGE GROVE	LOS ANGELES, CA 90046
WOOD, LANA	ACTRESS	SEE - WOOD-BALTER, LANA	
WOOD, LAUREN	SINGER	JACK DALEY, 825 LAS PALMAS RD	PASADENA, CA 91105
WOOD, LYNN	ACTRESS	9300 WILSHIRE BLVD #410	BEVERLY HILLS, CA 90212
WOOD, PETER	TV DIRECTOR	11 WARWICK AVE	LONDON W9 ENGLAND
WOOD, PRESTON	TV WRITER	8955 BEVERLY BLVD	LOS ANGELES, CA 90048
WOOD, RICK	WRESTLER	SEE - RUDE, RAVISHING RICK	
WOOD, ROBIN	SINGER	POST OFFICE BOX 171132	NASHVILLE, TN 37217
WOOD, WALTER	MUSICIAN	POST OFFICE BOX 129	PULASKI, TN 38478
WOOD, WALTER	PHOTOGRAPHER	5801 SAN JUAN DR	CLINTON, MD 20735
WOOD, WILLIAM	WRITER	10100 SANTA MONICA BLVD #1600	LOS ANGELES, CA 90067
WOOD, WINSTON S	NEWS CORRESPONDENT	1619 30TH ST, NW	WASHINGTON, DC 20007
WOOD-BALTER, LANA	ACTRESS	15610 MOORPARK ST #5	ENCINO, CA 91436
WOODALL, ANN	TV WRITER	1755 N ALEXANDRIA AVE	LOS ANGELES, CA 90027
WOODALL, THOMAS G	NEWS CORRESPONDENT	1854 MAC ARTHUR DR	MC LEAN, VA 22101
WOODARD, ALFRE	WRITER	2921 CREST DR	MANHATTAN BEACH, CA 90266
WOODARD, CHARLAINE	ACTRESS	777 W END AVE	NEW YORK, NY 10025
WOODARD, JIMMY DALE	PIANIST	524 BISCAYNE AVE	WEST PALM BEACH, FL 33401
WOODBECK, VICTORIA	ACTRESS	3607 PACIFIC AVE #3	VENICE, CA 90291
WOODBRIDGE, BILL	ACTOR	SP, 1226 SIERRA ALTA WY	LOS ANGELES, CA 90069
WOODBRIDGE, GEORGE	CARTOONIST	MAD MAGAZINE, INC	
		485 MADISON AVE	NEW YORK, NY 10022
WOODBURN, WILLIAM	DIRECTOR	5229 BALBOA BLVD #15	ENCINO, CA 91316
WOODBURY, JOAN	ACTRESS	MITCHELL, 43-155 PORTOLA #125	PALM DESERT, CA 92260
WOODCOCK, JOHN M	FILM EDITOR	ACE, 4416 1/2 FINLEY AVE	LOS ANGELES, CA 90027
WOODDELL, DAVID	PHOTOGRAPHER	3032 RODMAN ST, NW	WASHINGTON, DC 20009
WOODELL, WOODY	GUITARIST	POST OFFICE BOX 134	PRINCETON, KY 42445
WOODEN NICKEL	ROCK & ROLL GROUP	LUTZ, 5625 "O" STREET BLDG	LINCOLN, NE 68510
WOODFIELD, WILLIAM READ	TV WRITER-PRODUCER	1367 CASIANO RD	LOS ANGELES, CA 90049
WOODHOUSE, BARBARA	TV PERSONALITY	CAMPIONS, CROXLEY GREEN	
		RICKMANSWOOD	HERTS ENGLAND
WOODHOUSE, MARTIN	TV WRITER	COMMON SIDE, STOCK	INGATESTONE ENGLAND
WOODLAND, GLENN	PERCUSSIONIST	POST OFFICE BOX 121493	NASHVILLE, TN 37212
WOODLEY, ARTHUR	BASSO-BARITONE	CAMI, 165 W 57TH ST	NEW YORK, NY 10019
WOODLIEF, WAYNE	NEWS CORRESPONDENT	219 N COLUMBUS ST	ALEXANDRIA, VA 22314
WOODLOCK, JOAN	ACTRESS	POST OFFICE BOX 167	WOODLAND HILLS, CA 91364
WOODMAN, ELIZABETH R	CASTING DIRECTOR	222 E 44TH ST, 9TH FLOOR	NEW YORK, NY 10017
WOODMAN, THOMAS	BARITONE	119 W 57TH ST #1505	NEW YORK, NY 10019
WOODMAN, WILLIAM E	DIRECTOR	320 W END AVE #4-B	NEW YORK, NY 10023
WOODMERE, DEE	GUITARIST	ROUTE #1, BOX 210	HARTSVILLE, TN 37074
WOODROW, ALAN	TENOR	POST OFFICE BOX 188	
		STATION A	TORONTO, ONT CANADA
WOODRUFF, FRANK	DIRECTOR-PRODUCER	170 N CRESCENT DR	BEVERLY HILLS, CA 90210
WOODRUFF, JUDY	BROADCAST JOURNALIST	POST OFFICE BOX 2626	WASHINGTON, DC 20013
WOODRUFF, LES A	NEWS CORRESPONDENT	24001 SUGAR CANE LN	GAITHERSBURG, MD 20879
WOODS, AUBREY	ACTOR	21 GERRARD RD	LONDON SW13 ENGLAND
WOODS, BOB	EDITOR-WRITER	10 COLMBUS CIR #1300	NEW YORK, NY 10019
WOODS, CHRIS	ACTOR	8350 SANTA MONICA BLVD #104	LOS ANGELES, CA 90069
WOODS, DANNY	ACTOR	18 FISKE PL	BROOKLYN, NY 11215
WOODS, DARREN KEITH	TENOR	CONE, 221 W 57TH ST	NEW YORK, NY 10019
WOODS, EDDIE H	GUITARIST	125 LOOKOUT DR	LA VERGNE, TN 37086
WOODS, H DONALD	COMPOSER-CONDUCTOR	POST OFFICE BOX 311	LOS ANGELLS, CA 90078
WOODS, JAMES	ACTOR-DIRECTOR	1888 CENTURY PARK E #1400	LOS ANGELES, CA 90067
WOODS, LESLEY	ACTRESS	115 S ROSE ST	BURBANK, CA 91505
WOODS, MARIAN	ACTRESS	165 W 46TH ST #409	NEW YORK, NY 10036
WOODS, MICHAEL	ACTOR	9220 SUNSET BLVD #625	LOS ANGELES, CA 90069
WOODS, MICHAEL J	NEWS CORRESPONDENT	6248 DIAMOND DR	FALLS CHURCH, VA 22044
WOODS, PHIL	SAX-CLARINET	POST OFFICE BOX 278	DELAWARE WATER GAP, PA 18327
WOODS, PHIL, QUARTET	JAZZ QUARTET	HOFFER, 233 1/2 E 48TH ST	NEW YORK, NY 10017
WOODS, REN	SINGER	2372 W 29TH PL	LOS ANGELES, CA 90018
WOODS, RICHARD	SCREENWRITER	8955 BEVERLY BLVD	LOS ANGELES, CA 90048
WOODS, ROBERT	ACTOR	KNBC-TV, "DAYS OF OUR LIVES"	
		3000 W ALAMEDA AVE	BURBANK, CA 91523
WOODS, ROBERT S	ACTOR	9000 SUNSET BLVD #1200	LOS ANGELES, CA 90069
WOODS, ROZALIN	SINGER	ED MARTINEZ, 1344 COLVER PL	COVINA, CA 91724
WOODS, SHERYL	SOPRANO	MUNRO, 334 W 72ND ST	NEW YORK, NY 10023
WOODS, STEVIE	SINGER-MUSICIAN	151 S EL CAMINO DR	BEVERLY HILLS, CA 90212
WOODSMOKE	C & W GROUP	PROCESS, 439 WILEY AVE	FRANKLIN, PA 16323
WOODSON, WILLIAM	ACTOR	8322 BEVERLY BLVD #202	LOS ANGELES, CA 90048
WOODWARD, BRADLEY	NEWS CORRESPONDENT	1825 "T" ST #601, NW	WASHINGTON, DC 20009
WOODWARD, CHARLES	THEATER PRODUCER	226 W 47TH ST	NEW YORK, NY 10036
WOODWARD, EDWARD	ACTOR	10390 SANTA MONICA BLVD #310	LOS ANGELES, CA 90025
WOODWARD, JOANNE	ACTRESS-DIRECTOR	NEWMAN, 59 COLEYTOWN RD	WESTPORT, CT 00880
WOODWARD, LENORE	ACTRESS	3518 W CAHUENGA BLVD #316	LOS ANGELES, CA 90068
WOODWARD, MORGAN	ACTOR	2111 ROCKLEDGE RD	LOS ANGELES, CA 90068
WOODWARD, ROBERT	NEWS CORRESPONDENT	3027 "Q" ST, NW	WASHINGTON, DC 20007
WOODWARD, ROGER	PIANIST	CAMI, 165 W 57TH ST	NEW YORK, NY 10019
WOODWARD, STEVE	SPORTS WRITER	POST OFFICE BOX 500	WASHINGTON, DC 20044
WOODWARD, TIM	ACTOR	58 ASTBURY RD, PECKHAM	LONDON SE ENGLAND
WOODWARD, VAN	WRITER	555 W 578TH ST #1230	NEW YORK, NY 10019
WOODWARD, WOODY	GUITARIST	4821 CANE RUN RD	LOUISVILLE, KY 40216

Name	Occupation	Address	City	Zip
WOODWORTH, MARJORIE	ACTRESS	KOSTURICK, 807 N LA BREA DR	INGLEWOOD, CA	90301
WOODY, CHIP	PIANIST	2902 BELMONT BLVD	NASHVILLE, TN	37212
WOODY, DOUGLAS	GUITARIST	2907 LYNCREST DR	NASHVILLE, TN	37214
WOODY, RUSS	TV WRITER	8955 BEVERLY BLVD	LOS ANGELES, CA	90048
WOOLARD, GREG	MUSIC ARRANGER	300 BAKERTOWN RD #26-A	ANTIOCH, TN	37013
WOOLERY, CHUCK	TV HOST	114 S GLENROY AVE	LOS ANGELES, CA	90049
WOOLEY, SHEB	SINGER	TESSIER, 505 CANTON PASS	MADISON, TN	37115
WOOLF, ALAN	ACTOR	128 CHARLES ST #11	NEW YORK, NY	10014
WOOLF, CHARLES	ACTOR	1418 N HIGHLAND AVE #102	LOS ANGELES, CA	90028
WOOLF, LESLIE	ACTRESS	457 W 57TH ST	NEW YORK, NY	10019
WOOLF, SIR JOHN	FILM-TV PRODUCER	BROOK HOUSE, PARK LN	LONDON W1Y 4JN	ENGLAND
WOOLF, STEPHANIE	VIOLINIST	3615 HOODS HILL RD	NASHVILLE, TN	37215
WOOLFORD, STANLEY	DIRECTOR-PRODUCER	127 WARDOUR ST	LONDON W1V 4AD	ENGLAND
WOOLLARD, TONY	ART DIRECTOR	24 RAYNERS RD	LONDON SW15	ENGLAND
WOOLLEN, SUSAN L	WRITER	23239 COMMUNITY ST	CANOGA PARK, CA	91304
WOOLLEY, JAMES A	DIRECTOR	41-41 51ST ST	WOODSIDE, NY	11377
WOOLLEY, STEPHEN	PRODUCER	PALACE PICTURES, LTD		
		36 BERWICK ST	LONDON W1	ENGLAND
WOOLSEY, CHARLES	NEWS CORRESPONDENT	6234 VALLEY RD	BETHESDA, MD	20817
WOOLSEY, JAMES P	NEWS CORRESPONDENT	7728 SHOOTING STAR	SPRINGFIELD, VA	22152
WOOLSTON-SMITH, PAUL	FILM DIRECTOR	FILM AUSTRALIA, LINDFIELD	SYDNEY NSW 2070	AUSTRALIA
WOOMER, BILLY	ACTOR	3967 EUREKA DR	STUDIO CITY, CA	91604
WOOS, KURT	CONDUCTOR	HILLYER, 250 W 57TH ST	NEW YORK, NY	10107
WOOSTER, ARTHUR G	FILM-TV DIRECTOR	KINGHAMS MEADOWS		
		LITTLE GADDESDON		
		BERSHAMSTED	HERTS	ENGLAND
WOOSTER, MARTIN MORSE	NEWS CORRESPONDENT	8624 FLOWER AVE #101	TOKOMA PARK, MD	20912
WOOTEN, GENE	DOBROIST	860 MURFREESBORO RD #C-23	NASHVILLE, TN	37217
WOOTTEN, LAWRENCE	COMPOSER	9836 KALE ST	SOUTH EL MONTE, CA	91733
WOOTTEN, ROBERT	GUITARIST	216 FRIENDSHIP DR	GOODLETTSVILLE, TN	37072
WOOTTON, ANITA	GUITARIST	311 DRAPER CIR	GOODLETTSVILLE, TN	37072
WOPAT, TOM	ACTOR-DIRECTOR	12245 MORRISON ST	NORTH HOLLYWOOD, CA	91607
WORCHESTER, MARJORIE	TV DIRECTOR	8955 BEVERLY BLVD	LOS ANGELES, CA	90048
WORDEN, HANK	ACTOR	208 S BEVERLY DR #4	BEVERLY HILLS, CA	90212
WOREN, DAN	ACTOR	12723 RIVERSIDE DR	NORTH HOLLYWOOD, CA	91607
WORF, GLENN	GUITARIST	114 GLENHAVEN DR	FAIRVIEW, TN	37062
WORF, NEIL	MUSICIAN	114 GLENHAVEN DR	FAIRVIEW, TN	37062
WORK, CLEMENS P	NEWS CORRESPONDENT	3721 MOMMOUTH PL	LAUREL, MD	20707
WORKMAN, C LINDSAY	ACTOR	1717 N HIGHLAND AVE #414	LOS ANGELES, CA	90028
WORKMAN, CARL	FILM WRITER-DIRECTOR	711 N OLD TOPANGA CANYON RD	TOPANGA CANYON, CA	90290
WORKMAN, CHUCK	CLERGYMAN	7171 ALVARADO RD #A	LA MESA, CA	92041
WORKMAN, ELLYEEN	ACTRESS	626 WONDERVIEW DR	CALABASAS, CA	91302
WORKMAN, WILLIAM	BARITONE	CONE, 221 W 57TH ST	NEW YORK, NY	10019
WORLD CLASS WRECKING CRU	ROCK-SOUL GROUP	8306 WILSHIRE BLVD #381	BEVERLY HILLS, CA	90211
WORLEY, JO ANNE	ACTRESS	4363 LEDGE AVE	NORTH HOLLYWOOD, CA	91602
WORLEY, PAUL N	SINGER-GUITARIST	210 OLD HICKORY BLVD #178	NASHVILLE, TN	37221
WORMSER, GERRIE	CASTING DIRECTOR	341 N MAPLE DR	BEVERLY HILLS, CA	90210
WOROBEC, MARY R	NEWS CORRESPONDENT	900 NEW MARK ESPLANADE	ROCKVILLE, MD	20850
WORONOV, MARY	ACTRESS	STONE, 1052 CAROL DR	LOS ANGELES, CA	90069
WORRELL, ERNEST P	ACTOR-COMEDIAN	POST OFFICE BOX 23325	NASHVILLE, TN	37202
WORRELL, MARY	TV WRITER	8955 BEVERLY BLVD	LOS ANGELES, CA	90048
WORSHAM, BRANCH	MIME	AFFILIATE ARTISTS, INC		
		37 W 65TH ST, 6TH FLOOR	NEW YORK, NY	10023
WORSNOP, RICHARD L	NEWS CORRESPONDENT	333 11TH ST, SE	WASHINGTON, DC	20003
WORTH, BARBARA	NEWS CORRESPONDENT	1825 "K" ST, NW	WASHINGTON, DC	20006
WORTH, FRANK J	COMPOSER-CONDUCTOR	20101 VILLAGE #20	CAMARILLO, CA	93010
WORTH, HOWARD	DIRECTOR	1393 ROSE ST	VENICE, CA	90291
WORTH, MARTIN	SCREENWRITER	MBA LITERARY AGENCY		
		118 TOTTENHAM RD	LONDON W1	ENGLAND
WORTH, MARVIN	FILM WRITER-PRODUCER	9784 DRAKE LN	BEVERLY HILLS, CA	90210
WORTH, MERLE	TV DIRECTOR-PRODUCER	390 RIVERSIDE DR	NEW YORK, NY	10025
WORTH, NICHOLAS	ACTOR	4041 ARCH DR #214	STUDIO CITY, CA	91604
WORTHINGTON, CAL	CAR DEALER	3962 KENWAY AVE	LOS ANGELES, CA	90008
WORTHINGTON, CATHY	ACTRESS	KRAGEN, 1112 N SHERBOURNE DR	LOS ANGELES, CA	90069
WORTHINGTON, JANET W	TV WRITER	555 W 57TH ST #1230	NEW YORK, NY	10019
WORTHY, CARDOZAR	NEWS CORRESPONDENT	4661 CONNECTICUT AVE, NW	WASHINGTON, DC	20008
WOTRING, JAMES D	DIRECTOR	322 N KENMORE AVE	CHICAGO, IL	60657
WOUK, HERMAN	AUTHOR	3255 "N" ST, NW	WASHINGTON, DC	20007
WOW II	MUSICAL GROUP	POST OFFICE BOX 1235	NEW ROCHELLE, NY	10802
WPHL, JACK	WRITER-PRODUCER	711 N ROXBURY DR	BEVERLY HILLS, CA	90210
WRATH	ROCK & ROLL GROUP	POST OFFICE BOX 466	WAUKEGAN, IL	60079
WRATHER, BONITA GRANVILLE	ACTRESS-DIRECTOR	172 DELFERN DR	LOS ANGELES, CA	90077
WRAY, BOB	GUITARIST	1014 CALDWELL LN #B	NASHVILLE, TN	37204
WRAY, FAY	ACTRESS	2080 CENTURY PARK E #406	LOS ANGELES, CA	90067
WRAY, JOHN	DIRECTOR	511 CIRCLE DR #C21-2	HUDSON, NC	28638
WRAY, MARGARET JANE	MEZZO-SOPRANO	CAMI, 165 W 57TH ST	NEW YORK, NY	10019
WRECKING CREW	ROCK & ROLL GROUP	ATI, 888 7TH AVE, 21ST FLOOR	NEW YORK, NY	10106
WREN, CLARE	ACTRESS	6430 SUNSET BLVD #701	LOS ANGELES, CA	90028
WRESTLING, MR	WRESTLER	SEE - FUNK, JIMMY JACK		
WRIGHT, BEN	ACTOR	7454 VISTA DEL MONTE	VAN NUYS, CA	91405
WRIGHT, BERNARD	SINGER	POST OFFICE BOX 38	SAINT ALBANS, NY	11412
WRIGHT, BOBBY	GUITARIST	824 N SUMMERFIELD DR	MADISON, TN	37115
WRIGHT, CARTER	COMPOSER	1607 TALMADGE ST	LOS ANGELES, CA	90027
WRIGHT, CHRISTOPHER B	NEWS CORRESPONDENT	ABC-TV, NEWS DEPARTMENT		
		1717 DE SALES ST, NW	WASHINGTON, DC	20036

Name	Occupation	Address	City	Zip
WRIGHT, CHUCK	GUITARIST	ROUTE #1, BOX 632	GROVE, OK	74344
WRIGHT, CLAUDIA	NEWS CORRESPONDENT	4643 KENMORE DR, NW	WASHINGTON, DC	20007
WRIGHT, COBINA, JR	ACTRESS	BEAUDETTE, 1326 DOVE MEADOW RD	SOLVANG, CA	93463
WRIGHT, DAVID	NEWS REPORTER	THE NATIONAL ENQUIRER		
		600 SE COAST AVE	LANTANA, FL	33464
WRIGHT, DAVID T	MUSICIAN	812 18TH AVE S #10	NASHVILLE, TN	37203
WRIGHT, DON	CARTOONIST	THE MIAMI NEWS		
		1 HERALD PLAZA	MIAMI, FL	33101
WRIGHT, DR JAMES	BODYBUILDER	7863 GRASS HOLLOW	SAN ANTONIO, CA	78233
WRIGHT, ED	ACTOR	7461 BEVERLY BLVD #400	LOS ANGELES, CA	90036
WRIGHT, ELIZABETH ANN	NEWS CORRESPONDENT	HA, 1921 KALORAMA RD, NW	WASHINGTON, DC	20009
WRIGHT, EUGENIA	ACTRESS	8831 SUNSET BLVD #402	LOS ANGELES, CA	90069
WRIGHT, GARY	SINGER-SONGWRITER	3 E 54TH ST #1400	NEW YORK, NY	10022
WRIGHT, GEORGE	CONDUCTOR	6565 SUNSET BLVD #315	LOS ANGELES, CA	90028
WRIGHT, GIL	MUSICIAN	137 HARPETH TRACE DR	NASHVILLE, TN	37221
WRIGHT, HERBERT J	WRITER-PRODUCER	2069 WATSONIA TERR	LOS ANGELES, CA	90068
WRIGHT, JAMES R	DIRECTOR	DGA, 110 W 57TH ST	NEW YORK, NY	10019
WRIGHT, JENNY LEE	ACTRESS	SEE - LEE-WRIGHT, JENNY		
WRIGHT, JERRY	DRUMMER	POST OFFICE BOX 363	LAKE WACCAMAW, NC	28450
WRIGHT, JOHNNIE	SINGER-GUITARIST	1302 SAUNDERS AVE	MADISON, TN	37115
WRIGHT, LENORE A	SCREENWRITER	8955 BEVERLY BLVD	LOS ANGELES, CA	90048
WRIGHT, LEONARD A	CELLIST	954 GRAYBAR LN	NASHVILLE, TN	37204
WRIGHT, MAGIE	ACTRESS	78 PORTSEA HALL, PORTSEA PL	LONDON W2	ENGLAND
WRIGHT, MAURICE	DIRECTOR	1210 PARK NEWPORT #410	NEWPORT BEACH, CA	92660
WRIGHT, MAX	ACTOR	15760 VENTURA BLVD #1730	ENCINO, CA	91436
WRIGHT, MILLIE	ACTRESS	5330 LANKERSHIM BLVD #210	NORTH HOLLYWOOD, CA	91601
WRIGHT, NORMAN HALL	TV WRITER-DIRECTOR	16661 PARADISE MOUNTAIN RD	VALLEY CENTER, CA	92082
WRIGHT, NORTON W	TV DIRECTOR	3639 SHADY OAK RD	STUDIO CITY, CA	91604
WRIGHT, PATRICK	ACTOR	3907 W ALAMEDA AVE #101	BURBANK, CA	91505
WRIGHT, PEGGY SUE	GUITARIST	160 LUNA LN	HENDERSONVILLE, TN	37075
WRIGHT, RANDY J	GUITARIST	4000 ANDERSON RD #42	NASHVILLE, TN	37217
WRIGHT, RANDY NEAL	PIANIST	3516 LAKESIDE DR	BIRMINGHAM, AL	35243
WRIGHT, RICHARD D	NEWS CORRESPONDENT	4570 LYNN FOREST DR, NW	WASHINGTON, DC	22065
WRIGHT, ROBERT	TV EXECUTIVE	NBC TELEVISION NETWORK	NEW YORK, NY	10112
		30 ROCKEFELLER PLAZA	NEW YORK, NY	10112
WRIGHT, ROBERT VINCENT	WRITER	3462 STANDISH DR	ENCINO, CA	91436
WRIGHT, RUDY R	DIRECTOR	POST OFFICE BOX 19519	SAN DIEGO, CA	92119
WRIGHT, SEAN	TV WRITER	1541 N VINE ST	HOLLYWOOD, CA	90028
WRIGHT, SONNY	GUITARIST	160 LUNA LN	HENDERSONVILLE, TN	37075
WRIGHT, STEPHEN	ACTOR	MANHATTAN PLAZA, 400 W 43RD ST	NEW YORK, NY	10036
WRIGHT, STEVE	SINGER	PROCESS, 439 WILEY AVE	FRANKLIN, PA	16323
WRIGHT, STEVEN	COMEDIAN	9000 SUNSET BLVD #1200	LOS ANGELES, CA	90069
WRIGHT, TERESA	ACTRESS	340 HARBOUR VILLAGE	BRANFORD, CT	06405
WRIGHT, THOMAS	DIRECTOR	2143 SUNNYBANK DR	LA CANADA, CA	91011
WRIGHT, TOM	ACTOR	ABRAMS ARTISTS & ASSOCIATES		
		420 MADISON AVE, 14TH FLOOR	NEW YORK, NY	10017
WRIGHT, TOM	TV WRITER	UNNA & DURBRIDGE, LTD		
		HOLLAND PARK	LONDON W11	ENGLAND
WRIGHT, WINK	DRUMMER	3206 ROBB PL #D	CORPUS CHRISTI, TX	78415
WRIGHT BROTHERS, THE	C & W GROUP	214 OLD HICKORY BLVD #198	NASHVILLE, TN	37205
WRIGHT MILLER, JONATHAN	TV DIRECTOR	SPOKESMEN / BROWN, LTD		
		162 REGENT ST	LONDON W1	ENGLAND
WRIGLEY, BEN	COMEDIAN	DOWNING, 3038 E BURNSIDE ST	PORTLAND, OR	97214
WRIXON, MARIS	ACTRESS	3410 LA SOMBRA DR	LOS ANGELES, CA	90068
WRYE, DONALD	WRITER-PRODUCER	6101 CAVALLERI RD	MALIBU, CA	90265
WUGUTOW, DANIEL	TV PRODUCER	ICM, 8899 BEVERLY BLVD	LOS ANGELES, CA	90048
WUHL, ROBERT	COMED-ACT-WRI	10590 HOLMAN AVE	LOS ANGELES, CA	90024
WULF, STEVE	SPORTS WRITER-EDITOR	SPORTS ILLUSTRATED MAGAZINE		
		TIME & LIFE BUILDING		
		ROCKEFELLER CENTER	NEW YORK, NY	10020
WULFF, JOHN W	PHOTOGRAPHER	3019 S BUCHANAN ST #B-1	ARLINGTON, VA	22206
WULFF, KAI	ACTOR	8350 SANTA MONICA BLVD #206	LOS ANGELES, CA	90069
WULKOPF, CORNELIA	CONTRALTO	MARIEDL ANDERS ARTISTS MGMT		
		535 EL CAMINO DEL MAR ST	SAN FRANCISCO, CA	94121
WUNTCH, PHILIP	FILM CRITIC	POST OFFICE BOX 225237	DALLAS, TX	75265
WURL, TOM	ACTOR	ABC-TV, "ALL MY CHILDREN"		
		1330 AVE OF THE AMERICAS	NEW YORK, NY	10019
WUSSLER, ROBERT	DIRECTOR	DGA, 110 W 57TH ST	NEW YORK, NY	10019
WUSSLER, ROBERT J	CABLE EXECUTIVE	TBS, 1050 TECHWOOD DR, NW	ATLANTA, GA	30318
WYATT, ALAN WILL	TV EXECUTIVE	38 ABINGER RD	LONDON W4	ENGLAND
WYATT, ALLAN	DIRECTOR	DGA, 7950 SUNSET BLVD	LOS ANGELES, CA	90046
WYATT, ANDY	CARTOONIST	POST OFFICE BOX 4203	NEW YORK, NY	10017
WYATT, CHARLES	FLUTIST	510 BASSWOOD DR #7	NASHVILLE, TN	37209
WYATT, IAN	TV DIRECTOR	6 PARKE RD	LONDON SW13 9NE	ENGLAND
WYATT, JANE	ACTRESS	651 SIENA WY	LOS ANGELES, CA	90024
WYATT, MICHAEL	DRUMMER	832 HERMITAGE RIDGE	HERMITAGE, TN	37076
WYATT, ROBERT	DRUMMER-SINGER	GRAMAVISION RECORDS		
		260 W BROADWAY	NEW YORK, NY	10013
WYATT, SHARON	ACTRESS	ROUTE #11, BOX 43	CROSSVILLE, TN	38555
WYATT, TESSA	ACTRESS	ST JAMES'S, 22 GROOM PL	LONDON SW1	ENGLAND
WYATT, WILL	TV PRODUCER	38 ABINGER RD	LONDON W4	ENGLAND
WYCKOFF, LOU ANN	SOPRANO	61 W 62ND ST #6-F	NEW YORK, NY	10023
WYCOFF, MICHAEL	SINGER	151 S EL CAMINO DR	BEVERLY HILLS, CA	90212
WYENN, THAN	ACTOR	12719 JIMENO AVE	GRANADA HILLS, CA	91344
WYETH, ANDREW	ARTIST	POSTMASTER/GENERAL DELIVERY	CHADDS FORD, PA	19317

Name	Occupation	Address	City	Zip
WYETH, SANDY BROWN	ACTRESS	SHERMAN, 348 S REXFORD DR	BEVERLY HILLS, CA	90212
WYLE, GEORGE	CONDUCTOR	4212 ELLENITA AVE	TARZANA, CA	91356
WYLER, GRETCHEN	ACTRESS	11515 LAURELCREST DR	STUDIO CITY, CA	91604
WYLER, JOHN	ACTOR	721 N LA BREA AVE #200	LOS ANGELES, CA	90038
WYLES, DOUG	DIRECTOR	160 W 87TH ST	NEW YORK, NY	10024
WYLES, J DAVID	WRITER	2904 STRONGS DR	VENICE, CA	90291
WYLIE, PATRICIA	ACTRESS	7515 DE LONGPRE AVE	LOS ANGELES, CA	90046
WYLLIE, MEG	ACTRESS	1316 IRVING AVE	GLENDALE, CA	91201
WYLLY, PHILLIPS	TV DIRECTOIR	4900 MATULA DR	TARZANA, CA	91356
WYMAN, DANIEL N	COMPOSER	17760 VISTA AVE	LOS GATOS, CA	95030
WYMAN, DOUGLAS	TV WRITER	12358 CANTURA ST	STUDIO CITY, CA	91604
WYMAN, IRA	PHOTOGRAPHER	14 CRANE AVE	WEST PEABODY, MA	01960
WYMAN, JANE	ACTRESS	POST OFFICE BOX 4499	NORTH HOLLYWOOD, CA	91607
WYMAN, STEPHEN J	TV DIRECTOR	20 CONTINENTAL AVE #3-T	FOREST HILLS, CA	11375
WYMAN, THOMAS H	TV EXECUTIVE	CBS-TV, 51 W 52ND ST	NEW YORK, NY	10019
WYMORE, PATRICE	ACTRESS	PORT ANTONIO	JAMAICA, BRITISH	WEST INDIES
WYNANT, H M	ACTOR	1021 N BEVERLY GLEN BLVD	LOS ANGELES, CA	90077
WYNDHAM, ANNE	ACTRESS	3518 W CHAUNEGA BLVD #316	LOS ANGELES, CA	90068
WYNDHAM, VICTORIA	ACTRESS	19 W 44TH ST #1500	NEW YORK, NY	10036
WYNDHAM-DAVIES, JUNE	TV DIRECTOR	HEATH, PARAMOUNT HOUSE		
		162-170 WARDOUR ST	LONDON W1V 3AT	ENGLAND
WYNER, GEORGE	ACTOR	3450 LAURIE PL	STUDIO CITY, CA	91604
WYNETTE, TAMMY	SINGER-ACTRESS	RICHEY, 6 MUSIC CIRCLE N	NASHVILLE, TN	37203
WYNN, BOB	PRODUCER	SCHLATTER, 8321 BEVERLY BLVD	LOS ANGELES, CA	90048
WYNN, DAN	TV DIRECTOR	170 E 73 RD ST	NEW YORK, NY	10021
WYNN, EARLY	BASEBALL	POST OFFICE BOX 218	NOKOMIS, FL	33551
WYNN, NED K	ACTOR-WRITER	937 19TH ST #6	SANTA MONICA, CA	90403
WYNN, RANDALL L	NEWS CORRESPONDENT	214 12TH ST, SE	WASHINGTON, DC	20003
WYNN, ROBERT	TV DIRECTOR-PRODUCER	3115 W OLIVE AVE	BURBANK, CA	91505
WYNN JONES, STUART	ANIMATION DIRECTOR	23 SAINT JAMES AVE		
		EWELL, EPSON	SURREY	ENGLAND
WYNNE, JONATHAN	ACTOR	4904 PRESIDIO DR	LOS ANGELES, CA	90043
WYNNE, WAYNE	CASTING DIRECTOR	POST OFFICE BOX 2459	TOLUCA LAKE, CA	91602
WYNOCKER, DIANE L	NEWS CORRESPONDENT	4450 S PARK AVE	CHEVY CHASE, MD	20815
WYNSTON, MARY	SOPRANO	45 W 60TH ST #4-K	NEW YORK, NY	10023
WYNTER, DANA	ACTRESS	9206 MONTE MAR DR	LOS ANGELES, CA	90035
WYNTER, LEON	NEWS CORRESPONDENT	1836 METZEROTT RD	ADELPHI, MD	20783
WYRICK, BOB	NEWS CORRESPONDENT	1760 EUCLID AVE, NW	WASHINGTON, DC	20009
WYSE, BILL R	DIRECTOR	12021 VALLEYHEART DR	STUDIO CITY, CA	91604
WYSS, AMANDA	ACTRESS	10100 SANTA MONICA BLVD #1600	LOS ANGELES, CA	90067
WYSS, MEGAN	ACTRESS	8721 SUNSET BLVD #202	LOS ANGELES, CA	90069
WYSS, REBECCA	VIOLINIST	364 MELPAR DR	NASHVILLE, TN	37211

Name	Occupation	Address	City	Zip
X	ROCK & ROLL GROUP	10100 SANTA MONICA BLVD #1600	LOS ANGELES, CA	90067
X, MR	WRESTLER	POST OFFICE BOX 3859	STAMFORD, CT	06905
X T C BAND	ROCK & ROLL GROUP	MID-ATLANTIC PRODUCTIONS		
		501 JARMAN ST	JACKSONVILLE, NC	28540
X Y Z	ROCK & ROLL GROUP	POST OFFICE BOX 448	RADFORD, VA	24141
XEREXS	ROCK & ROLL GROUP	POST OFFICE BOX 448	RADFORD, VA	24141
XIFARAS, TEX	SINGER	6215 SHELTER CREEK #144	SAN BRUNO, CA	94066
XKE	ROCK & ROLL GROUP	4407 MEDICAL PARKWAY #2	AUSTIN, TX	78756
XL	ROCK & ROLL GROUP	PEGASUS PRODUCTIONS, INC		
		306 S WEBSTER AVE	INDIANPOLIS, IN	46219
XTC	ROCK & ROLL GROUP	FRONTIER BOOKING INTERNATIONAL		
		1776 BROADWAY, 6TH FLOOR	NEW YORK, NY	10019
XYZ	ROCK & ROLL GROUP	POST OFFICE BOX 448	RADFORD, VA	24141

Name	Occupation	Address	City	Zip
Y & T	ROCK & ROLL GROUP	845 VIA DE LA PAZ #365	PACIFIC PALISADES, CA	90272
YABLANS, FRANK	FILM WRITER-PRODUCER	MGM, 10202 W WASHINGTON BLVD	CULVER CITY, CA	90230
YABLANS, IRWIN	FILM PRODUCER	706 N PALM DR	BEVERLY HILLS, CA	90210
YABLONSKAYA, OXANA	PIANIST	JCB, 155 W 68TH ST	NEW YORK, NY	10023
YABLONSKY, DMITRY	CELLIST	JCB, 155 W 68TH ST	NEW YORK, NY	10023
YABLONSKY, LEWIS	WRITER	14010 CAPTAINS ROW DR #250	MARINA DEL REY, CA	90292
YABLONSKY, YABO	WRITER-PRODUCER	10960 WILSHIRE BLVD #922	LOS ANGELES, CA	90024
YACKEE, SUSAN K	NEWS CORRESPONDENT	330 INDEPENDENCE AVE, SW	WASHINGTON, DC	20547
YAEGERMANN, KELLY	ACTRESS	6430 SUNSET BLVD #1203	LOS ANGELES, CA	90028
YAGEMANN, WILLIAM F	DIRECTOR	1818 POINT ABBEY PL	NEWPORT BEACH, CA	92660
YAGEMANN, WILLIAM SCOTT	DIRECTOR	3928 BLUE CANYON DR	STUDIO CITY, CA	91604
YAGHER, JEFF	ACTOR	4510 MURIETTA AVE #5	SHERMAN OAKS, CA	91423

PATRICE WYMORE

WEIRD AL YANKOVIC

DICK YORK

JESSE COLIN YOUNG

ROBERT YOUNG

JACKLYN ZEMAN

ANTHONY ZERBE

WARREN ZEVON

EFFREM ZIMBALIST, JR.

Name	Occupation	Address	City/State	ZIP
YAHR, BETTY	WRITER	459 S ELM DR	BEVERLY HILLS, CA	90212
YAHR, CAROL	MEZZO-SOPRANO	LEW, 204 W 10TH ST	NEW YORK, NY	10014
YAJIMA, HIROKO	VIOLINIST	240 W 98TH ST #13-A	NEW YORK, NY	10025
YAJIMA & RHODES	VIOLIN-VIOLA DUO	240 W 98TH ST #13-A	NEW YORK, NY	10025
YAKAR, RACHEL	SOPRANO	CAMI, 165 W 57TH ST	NEW YORK, NY	10019
YALEM, RICHARD	TV WRITER	11168 ACAMA ST #4	NORTH HOLLYWOOD, CA	91602
YALOR, MICK	SINGER-SONGWRITER	150 5TH AVE #1103	NEW YORK, NY	10011
YALOWITZ, GERSON	NEWS CORRESPONDENT	8004 CINDY LN	BETHESDA, MD	20817
YAMA, MICHAEL	ACTOR	8235 SANTA MONICA BLVD #202	LOS ANGELES, CA	90046
YAMAZAKI, SANAE	ART DIRECTOR	PEOPLE/TIME & LIFE BLDG		
		ROCKEFELLER CENTER	NEW YORK, NY	10020
YAMPOLSKY, VICTOR	CONDUCTOR	SOFFER, 130 W 56TH ST	NEW YORK, NY	10019
YANCEY, MATT	NEWS CORRESPONDENT	5215 N WASHINGTON BLVD	ARLINGTON, VA	22205
YANCY, EMILY	ACTRESS	247 S BEVERLY DR #102	BEVERLY HILLS, CA	90210
YANDELL, PAUL	GUITARIST	2813 FORTLAND DR	NASHVILLE, TN	37206
YANE, JOHN, BAND	ROCK & ROLL GROUP	25 HUNTINGTON AVE #420	BOSTON, MA	02116
YANG, JOHN E	NEWS CORRESPONDENT	3100 CONNECTICUT AVE #241, NW	WASHINGTON, DC	20008
YANKEE, ALAN L	COMPOSER	12022 POUTOUS CT	SUNNYMEAD, CA	92388
YANKOVIC, WEIRD AL	SINGER-SONGWRITER	925 WESTMOUNT DR	LOS ANGELES, CA	90069
YANKS, THE	ROCK & ROLL GROUP	POST OFFICE BOX 22129	SAN FRANCISCO, CA	94122
YANNING, LI	NEWS CORRESPONDENT	2200 "S" ST, NW	WASHINGTON, DC	20008
YANOK, GEORGE	TV WRITER-PRODUCER	EL-DON PRODS, 5746 SUNSET BLVD	LOS ANGELES, CA	90028
YAP, DIOSDADO M	NEWS CORRESPONDENT	5306 BELT RD, NW	WASHINGTON, DC	20015
YARBOROUGH & PEOPLES	VOCAL DUO	200 W 51ST ST #1410	NEW YORK, NY	10019
YARBROUGH, GLENN	SINGER	2835 WOODSTOCK RD	LOS ANGELES, CA	90046
YARBROUGH, JAMES	GUITARIST	113 COARSEY BLVD	HENDERSONVILLE, TN	37075
YARBROUGH, RUAL HOLT	GUITARIST	ROUTE #2, BOX 533	KILLEN, AL	35645
YARBROUGH & COWAN	PIANO DUO	GERSHUNOFF, 502 PARK AVE	NEW YORK, NY	10022
YARDLEY, SCOTT	ART DIRECTOR	US MAGAZINE COMPANY		
		1 DAG HAMMARSKJOLD PLAZA	NEW YORK, NY	10017
YARIN, ROBERT M	WRITER	1620 FEDERAL AVE #3	LOS ANGELES, CA	90025
YARLETT, CLAIRE	ACTRESS	DYNASTY II: THE COLBYS		
		1041 N FORMOSA AVE	LOS ANGELES, CA	90046
YARMAS, MICHAEL	NEWS CORRESPONDENT	400 N CAPITOL ST, NW	WASHINGTON, DC	20001
YARMY, DICK	ACTOR	16815 OAK VIEW DR	ENCINO, CA	91436
YARNELL, CELESTE	ACTRESS	7060 HOLLYWOOD BLVD #1010	LOS ANGELES, CA	90028
YARNELL, LORENE	ACTRESS	201 N ROBERTSON BLVD #A	BEVERLY HILLS, CA	90211
YARO, BORIS A	WRITER	17042 CALAHAN ST	NORTHRIDGE, CA	91325
YARROW, ARNOLD	ACTOR-WRITER	2 PERRY CT COTTAGES		
		BROGDALE RD, FAVERSHAM	KENT	ENGLAND
YARWOOD, MIKE	COMEDIAN	DEREK BLOCK AGENCY		
		RICHMOND HOUSE		
		12 RICHMOND BUILDINGS		
		DEAN ST	LONDON W1	ENGLAND
YARWOOD, RICHARD	PHOTOGRAPHER	7 FRONTIER LN	EAST NORTHPORT, NY	11731
YASTRZEMSKI, CARL	BASEBALL	4621 S OCEAN BLVD	HIGHLAND BEACH, FL	33431
YATES, BILL	GUITARIST	6905 ALPINE DR	ANNANDALE, VA	22003
YATES, BILL	CARTOONIST-COMICS ED	KING FEATURES SYNDICATE		
		235 E 45TH ST	NEW YORK, NY	10017
YATES, BROCK	SCREENWRITER	ICM, 8899 BEVERLY BLVD	LOS ANGELES, CA	90048
YATES, CASSIE	ACTRESS	151 S EL CAMINO DR	BEVERLY HILLS, CA	90212
YATES, DEVON	ACTRESS	CARPENTER, 1516-W REDWOOD ST	SAN DIEGO, CA	92101
YATES, H WILLIAM, II	NEWS CORRESPONDENT	1 LOPA CT	GAITHERSBURG, MD	20878
YATES, HAROLD R	DIRECTOR	DGA, 110 W 57TH ST	NEW YORK, NY	10019
YATES, JIMMY H	GUITARIST	POST OFFICE BOX 878	HENDERSONVILLE, TN	37075
YATES, JOHN	ACTOR	9825 SHADOW ISLAND DR	SUNLAND, CA	91040
YATES, KEN	PRODUCER	1112 N SHERBOURNE DR	LOS ANGELES, CA	90069
YATES, PAULINE	ACTRESS	FEAST, 43-A PRINCESS RD	LONDON NW1	ENGLAND
YATES, PETER	FILM DIRECTOR	190 N CANON DR #201	BEVERLY HILLS, CA	90210
YAU, STEPHEN Y	NEWS CORRESPONDENT	4210 ASPEN HILL RD	ROCKVILLE, MD	20853
YAUGER, MARGARET	MEZZO-SOPRANO	59 E 54TH ST #81	NEW YORK, NY	10022
YAUK, MEL	CARTOONIST	POST OFFICE BOX 4203	NEW YORK, NY	10017
YAVNEH, CYRUS	ACTOR-DIRECTOR	254 S ROBERTSON BLVD #204	BEVERLY HILLS, CA	90210
YAVUZ, TURAN	NEWS CORRESPONDENT	202 NATIONAL PRESS BLDG		
		529 14TH ST, NW	WASHINGTON, DC	20045
YAWN, OTTICE	SINGER	POST OFFICE BOX 344	NOLENSVILLE, TN	37135
YDSTIE, JOHN E	NEWS CORRESPONDENT	2025 "M" ST, NW	WASHINGOTN, DC	20036
YEAGER, BIFF	ACTOR	120 W VICTORY BLVD #104	BURBANK, CA	91501
YEAGER, JEANA	AVAITRIX	VOYAGER AIRCRAFT INC, HANGER 77	MOJAVE, CA	93501
YEAGER, WARREN P	NEWS CORRESPONDENT	4305 BURKE STATION RD	FAIRFAX, VA	22032
YEE, MARILYNN K	PHOTOGRAPHER	870 OCEAN AVE	BROOKLYN, NY	11226
YEH, TSUNG	CONDUCTOR	AFFILIATE ARTISTS, INC		
		37 W 65TH ST, 6TH FLOOR	NEW YORK, NY	10023
YELDHAM, PETER	TV WRITER	2 FLORENCE ST, CREMORNE	SYDNEY 2090	AUSTRALIA
YELLEN, LINDA	WRITER-PRODUCER	3 SHERIDAN SQ	NEW YORK, NY	10014
YELLEN, SHERMAN	TV WRITER	445 N BEDFORD DR #PH	BEVERLY HILLS, CA	90210
YELLON, ALVIN H	TV DIRECTOR	516 WEST BRIAR #2-D	CHICAGO, IL	60601
YELLOW MAGIC ORCHESTRA	ROCK & ROLL GROUP	151 S EL CAMINO DR	BEVERLY HILLS, CA	90212
YELLOWJACKETS, THE	JAZZ GROUP	KURLAND, 173 BRIGHTON AVE	BOSTON, MA	02134
YELTON, ROY LEE	SINGER	POST OFFICE BOX 25371	CHARLOTTE, NC	28212
YENTOB, ALAN	TV DIRECTOR-PRODUCER	99 BLENHEIM CRESCENT	LONDON W11	ENGLAND
YEOMAN, BRIAN	FILM EXECUTIVE	PARAMOUNT, 162-170 WARDOUR ST	LONDON W1V 3AT	ENGLAND
YEPES, NARCISO	GUITARIST	MARIEDL ANDERS ARTISTS MGMT		
		535 EL CAMINO DEL MAR ST	SAN FRANCISCO, CA	94121
YERKOVICH, ANTHONY HENDEN	TV WRITER-PRODUCER	1802 ASHLAND AVE	SANTA MONICA, CA	90405

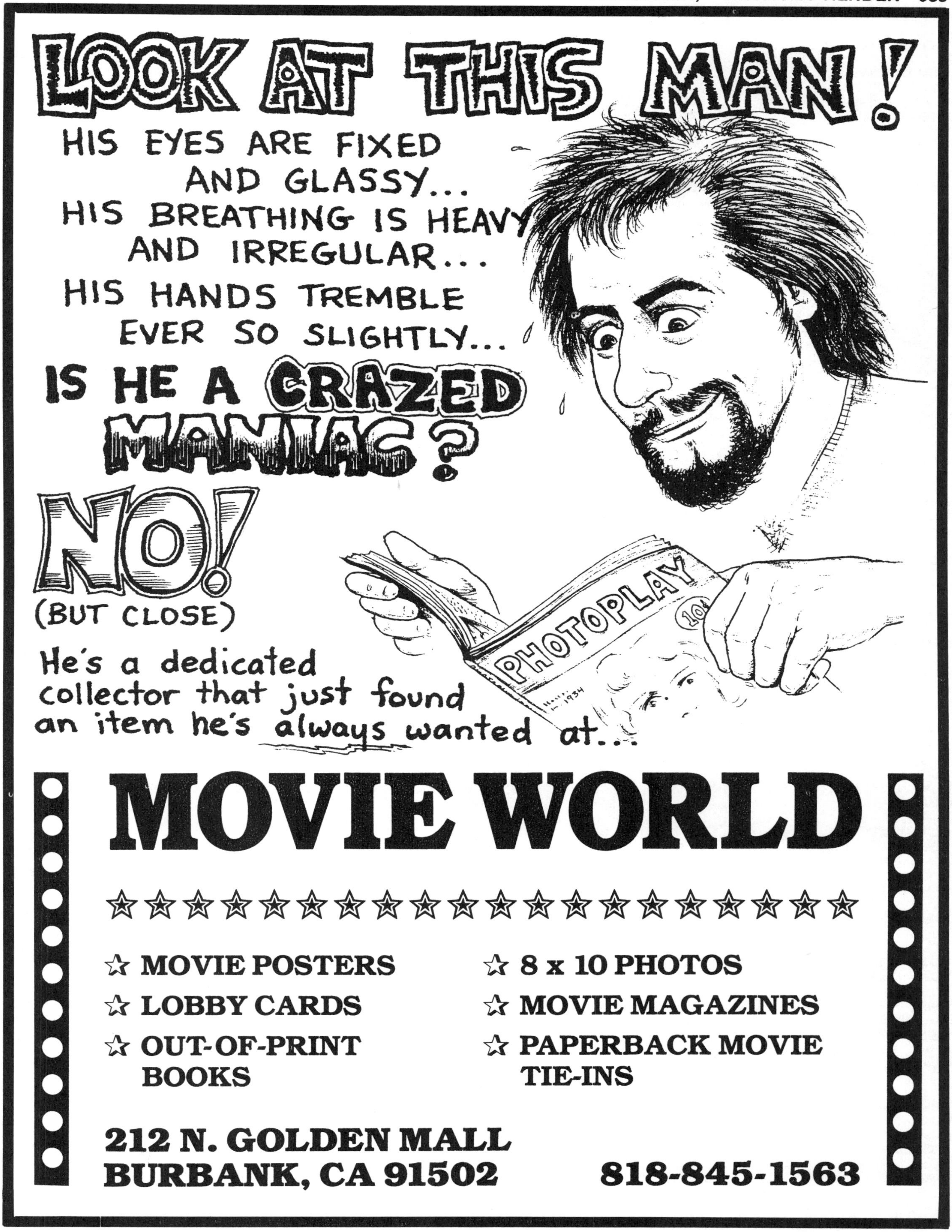

Name	Occupation	Address	City	Zip
YERVANIAN, ANI	MEZZO-SOPRANO	61 W 62ND ST #6-F	NEW YORK, NY	10023
YES	ROCK & ROLL GROUP	SUN ARTISTS, 9 HILLGATE ST	LONDON W8 7SP	ENGLAND
YETNIKOFF, WALTER	RECORD EXECUTIVE	CBS RECORDS COMPANY		
		1801 CENTURY PARK W	LOS ANGELES, CA	90067
YINGLING, JOHN	DIRECTOR	975 WINSTON AVE	SAN MARINO, CA	91108
YIP, DAVID	ACTOR	50-C GODOLPHIN RD	LONDON W12	ENGLAND
YIRCOV, CRUSHER	WRESTLER	SEE - BIGELOW, BAM BAM		
YNIGUEZ, RICHARD	ACTOR	5945 GRACIOSA DR	LOS ANGELES, CA	90068
YO	ROCK & ROLL GROUP	POST OFFICE BOX 2428	EL SEGUNDO, CA	90245
YO LA TENGO	ROCK & ROLL GROUP	POST OFFICE BOX 112		
		UPTOWN STATION	HOBOKEN, NJ	07030
YOAKAM, DWIGHT	SINGER-GUITARIST	POST OFFICE BOX 4003	BEVERLY HILLS, CA	90213
YODER, EDWIN M, JR	COLUMNIST	THE WASHINGTON POST		
		WRITERS GROUP		
		1150 15TH ST, NW	WASHINGTON, DC	20071
YODER, ERIC T	NEWS CORRESPONDENT	1210 N KENSINGTON ST #1	ARLINGTON, VA	22205
YOES, JANICE	SOPRANO	JCB, 155 W 68TH ST	NEW YORK, NY	10023
YOHE, JEFFREY E	MUSIC ARRANGER	371 WALLACE RD #H-55	NASHVILLE, TN	37211
YOHE, THOMAS G	DIRECTOR	WILD GOOSE LN	NORWALK, CT	06851
YOHN, ERICA	ACTRESS	10630 CHIQUITA ST	NORTH HOLLYWOOD, CA	91602
YOKLAVICH, JOSEPH	DIRECTOR	23451 SCHOOLCRAFT ST	CANOGA PARK, CA	91307
YOKOTA, VICTORIA SHERRAN	PHOTOGRAPHER	516 S 25TH ST	ARLINGTON, VA	22202
YOLL, YAEL R	DIRECTOR	PEA POND RD	BEDFORD VILLAGE, NY	10506
YOLLAND, PETER	TV DIRECTOR-PRODUCER	1 LAMBOURN RD	LONDON SW4 OLX	ENGLAND
YORK, BETH	SINGER	POST OFFICE BOX 3142	DURHAM, NC	27705
YORK, FRANCINE	ACTRESS	15010 VENTURA BLVD #234	SHERMAN OAKS, CA	91403
YORK, GERALD	ACTOR	8350 SANTA MONICA BLVD #102	LOS ANGELES, CA	90069
YORK, JAY S	ACTOR	AIMEE, 13743 VICTORY BLVD	VAN NUYS, CA	91401
YORK, KATHLEEN	ACTRESS	ICM, 8899 BEVERLY BLVD	LOS ANGELES, CA	90048
YORK, MARK	ACTOR	29633 STRAWBERRY HILL DR	AGOURA HILLS, CA	91301
YORK, MICHAEL	ACTOR	9100 CORDELL DR	LOS ANGELES, CA	90069
YORK, MICHAEL M	NEWS CORRESPONDENT	5102 FULTON ST, NW	WASHINGTON, DC	20016
YORK, REBECCA	ACTRESS	6310 SAN VICENTE BLVD #407	LOS ANGELES, CA	90048
YORK, SUSANNAH	ACTRESS	ICM, 388-396 OXFORD ST	LONDON W1	ENGLAND
YORK QUINTET	MUSICAL DUO	POST OFFICE BOX 131	SPRINGFIELD, VA	22150
YORKIN, ALAN "BUD"	WRITER-PRODUCER	250 DELFERN DR	LOS ANGELES, CA	90077
YOSHIDA, TOSHITAKA	NEWS CORRESPONDENT	5809 PLAINVIEW RD	BETHESDA, MD	20817
YOSHIOKA, ADELE	ACTRESS-DANCER-MODEL	3754 ROSEWOOD AVE	LOS ANGELES, CA	90066
YOSHIOKA, EMMETT G	COMPOSER-CONDUCTOR	5223 APO DR	HONOLULU, HI	96821
YOST, PETE	NEWS CORRESPONDENT	12805 SCRANTON CT, NW	WASHINGTON, DC	20070
YOST, ROBERT A	COMPOSER	11478 E WINCHELL ST	WHITTIER, CA	90606
YOUMAN, ROGER	EDITOR-WRITER	TV GUIDE, 100 MATSONFORD RD	RADNOR, PA	19088
YOUNG, AIDA	FILM-TV PRODUCER	LONDON MANAGEMENT, LTD		
		235-241 REGENT ST	LONDON W1A 2JT	ENGLAND
YOUNG, ALAN	ACTOR	7500 DEVISTA DR	LOS ANGELES, CA	90046
YOUNG, ANGEL	SINGER	SOUNDS, 1210 PALM ST	ABILINE, TX	79602
YOUNG, BARBARA	ACTRESS	59 BELSIZE AVE #1	LONDON NW3 4BN	ENGLAND
YOUNG, BOB	TV WRITER	8955 BEVERLY BLVD	LOS ANGELES, CA	90048
YOUNG, BRUCE	TALENT AGENT	POST OFFICE BOX 22129	SAN FRANCISCO, CA	94122
YOUNG, BUCK	ACTOR	10850 RIVERSIDE DR #501	NORTH HOLLYWOOD, CA	91602
YOUNG, BURT	ACTOR-SCREENWRITER	708 N ROXBURY DR	BEVERLY HILLS, CA	90210
YOUNG, CAMERON	ACTOR	10845 LINDBROOK DR #3	LOS ANGELES, CA	90024
YOUNG, CHARLES	ACTOR	3575 W CAHUENGA BLVD #320	LOS ANGELES, CA	90068
YOUNG, CHIP	GUITARIST	3600 HILLSBORO RD #G-1	NASHVILLE, TN	37215
YOUNG, CLINT	ACTOR	10850 RIVERSIDE DR #501	NORTH HOLLYWOOD, CA	91602
YOUNG, COLIN	FILM DIRECTOR	BEACONSFIELD STUDIOS		
		STATION RD, BEACONSFIELD	BUCKS HP9 1LG	ENGLAND
YOUNG, CURTIS E	GUITARIST	840 CLEMATIS DR	NASHVILLE, TN	37205
YOUNG, DALENE A	TV WRITER	8955 BEVERLY BLVD	LOS ANGELES, CA	90048
YOUNG, DAVE	FIREARMS EXPERT	2801 MEADOW LARK DR	SAN DIEGO, CA	92123
YOUNG, DAVID	ACTOR	8721 SUNSET BLVD #202	LOS ANGELES, CA	90069
YOUNG, DEAN	CARTOONIST	KING FEATURES SYNDICATE		
		235 E 45TH ST	NEW YORK, NY	10017
YOUNG, DEY	ACTRESS	427 N CANON DR #205	BEVERLY HILLS, CA	90210
YOUNG, DIANE	CASTING DIRECTOR	WARNER BROS, 4000 WARNER BLVD		
		NORTH ADMINISTRATION #11	BURBANK, CA	91522
YOUNG, EDDIE "BAMA"	GUITARIST	2305 JOYCE DR #102	CORPUS CHRISTI, TX	78416
YOUNG, FARON	SINGER-SONGWRITER	TESSIER, 505 CANTON PASS	MADISON, TN	37115
YOUNG, FLOYD R	GUITARIST	16460 HAWTHORNE	FONTANA, CA	92335
YOUNG, FREDDIE	CINEMATOGRAPHER	3 ROEHAMPTON CLOSE	LONDON SW15	ENGLAND
YOUNG, FREDERICK KIRBY	DRUMMER	ROUTE #1, BOX 156	EDMONTON, KY	42129
YOUNG, G J	TV WRITER	8955 BEVERLY BLVD	LOS ANGELES, CA	90048
YOUNG, GARY	SINGER	LUTZ, 5625 "O" STREET BLDG	LINCOLN, NE	68510
YOUNG, GARY	WRESTLER	UNIVERSAL WRESTLING FEDERATION		
		MID SOUTH SPORTS, INC		
		5001 SPRING VALLEY RD	DALLAS, TX	75244
YOUNG, GARY A	DIRECTOR	35 E 20TH ST	NEW YORK, NY	10003
YOUNG, GEORGIANA	ACTRESS	MONTALBAN, 9256 ROBIN DR	LOS ANGELES, CA	90069
YOUNG, JAMES P	DIRECTOR	POST OFFICE BOX 781	COUPEVILLE, WA	98239
YOUNG, JEFF	TV WRITER	555 W 57TH ST #1230	NEW YORK, NY	10019
YOUNG, JEFFREY	FILM DIRECTOR	DGA, 7950 SUNSET BLVD	HOLLYWOOD, CA	90046
YOUNG, JESSE COLIN	SINGER-SONGWRITER	POST OFFICE BOX 569	FRANKLIN, PA	16323
YOUNG, JOHN	PIANIST	SPRINGER, 1001 ROLANDVUE RD	BALTIMORE, MD	21204
YOUNG, JOHN BELL	PIANIST	POST OFFICE BOX 20548	NEW YORK, NY	10025
YOUNG, JOHN SACRET	TV WRITER	3456 WONDER VIEW DR	LOS ANGELES, CA	90068

YES

Chris Squire • Trevor Rabin • Tony Kaye • Alan White • Jon Anderson

ZZ TOP

Billy Gibbons • Frank Beard • Dusty Hill

Name	Occupation	Address	City	Zip
YOUNG, JOSEPH	NEWS CORRESPONDENT	1703 DALEWOOD PL	MC LEAN, VA	22101
YOUNG, KAC S	TV DIRECTOR	3474 LA SOMBRA DR	HOLLYWOOD, CA	90068
YOUNG, KAG	TV PRODUCER	ABC-TV, "GENERAL HOSPITAL"		
		1438 N GOWER ST	LOS ANGELES, CA	90028
YOUNG, KAREN	SINGER	SUNSHINE, 800 S 4TH ST	PHILADELPHIA, PA	19147
YOUNG, KEONE	ACTOR	8235 SANTA MONICA BLVD #202	LOS ANGELES, CA	90046
YOUNG, KRIS T	TV WRITER	8955 BEVERLY BLVD	LOS ANGELES, CA	90048
YOUNG, L MARTINA	DANCER	AFFILIATE ARTISTS, INC		
		37 W 65TH ST, 6TH FLOOR	NEW YORK, NY	10023
YOUNG, LEAH R	NEWS CORRESPONDENT	16101 GOODMAN CT	LAUREL, MD	20707
YOUNG, LINDA	SINGER	TC TALENT, 3725 HILLTOP LN	NASHVILLE, TN	37216
		ROCKEFELLER CENTER	NEW YORK, NY	10020
YOUNG, LINDA	NEWS REPORTER	TIME/TIME & LIFE BLDG		
YOUNG, LORETTA	ACTRESS	LEWIS, 1705 AMBASSADOR AVE	BEVERLY HILLS, CA	90210
YOUNG, MARK D	WRITER-PRODUCER	11123 LANDALE ST	NORTH HOLLYWOOD, CA	91602
YOUNG, MARL	COMPOSER	3602 COUNTRY CLUB DR	LOS ANGELES, CA	90019
YOUNG, MELISSA A	PHOTOJOURNALIST	5130 CONNECTICUT AVE #509, NW	WASHINGTON, DC	20008
YOUNG, MICHAEL	ACTOR	ICM, 8899 BEVERLY BLVD	LOS ANGELES, CA	90048
YOUNG, MICHAEL L	DRUMMER	4181 APACHE TRAIL	ANTIOCH, TN	37013
YOUNG, MIGHTY JOE	SINGER-GUITARIST	CAMERON, 822 HILLGROVE AVE	WESTERN SPRINGS, IL	60558
YOUNG, MURIEL	TV PRODUCER	ROSE COTTAGE, FORTON		
		LONGPARISH	HANTS	ENGLAND
YOUNG, NEIL	SINGER-SONGWRITER	LOOKOUT, 9120 SUNSET BLVD	LOS ANGELES, CA	90069
YOUNG, NELSON & THE SANDY VALLE	C & W GROUP	POST OFFICE BOX 25371	CHARLOTTE, NC	28212
YOUNG, OTIS	ACTOR	6716 ZUMIREZ DR	MALIBU, CA	90265
YOUNG, PATRICK	NEWS CORRESPONDENT	16101 GOODMAN CT	LAUREL, MD	20707
YOUNG, PAUL	SINGER-SONGWRITER	POST OFFICE BOX 40	LONDON WC2	ENGLAND
YOUNG, RAY	ACTOR	8443 KIRKWOOD DR	LOS ANGELES, CA	90046
YOUNG, RAYMOND	ACTOR	69 KINGSWOOD RD	LONDON SW19 3ND	ENGLAND
YOUNG, REGGIE	GUITARIST	ROUTE #32, BOX 31, BUCKNER RD	THOMPSON STATION, TN	37179
YOUNG, RHONDA	CASTING DIRECTOR	PARAMOUNT PICTURES CORPORATION		
		DIRECTORS BUILDING #401		
		5555 MELROSE AVE	LOS ANGELES, CA	90038
YOUNG, RICHARD	ACTOR	9200 SUNSET BLVD #909	LOS ANGELES, CA	90069
YOUNG, RICHARD E	ACTOR	9165 SUNSET BLVD #202	LOS ANGELES, CA	90069
YOUNG, ROBERT	ACTOR	31589 SADDLETREE DR	WESTLAKE VILLAGE, CA	91361
YOUNG, ROBERT	FILM DIRECTOR	HEATH, PARAMOUNT HOUSE		
		162-170 WARDOUR ST	LONDON W1V 3AT	ENGLAND
YOUNG, ROBERT M	WRITER-PRODUCER	125 W 76TH ST	NEW YORK, NY	10023
YOUNG, ROBERT MALCOLM	TV WRITER	8955 BEVERLY BLVD	LOS ANGELES, CA	90048
YOUNG, ROBERT W	WRITER-PRODUCER	STUDIO LAMBERT, 9 CARLISLE ST	LONDON W1	ENGLAND
YOUNG, ROGER	GUITARIST	225 BRIDGEWAY CIR	NASHVILLE, TN	37211
YOUNG, ROGER E	TV DIRECTOR	8439 SUNSET BLVD #402	LOS ANGELES, CA	90069
YOUNG, RON	SINGER	POST OFFICE BOX 29543	ATLANTA, GA	30359
YOUNG, SALLEE	ACTRESS	8150 BEVERLY BLVD #303	LOS ANGELES, CA	90048
YOUNG, SEAN	ACTRESS	1888 CENTURY PARK E #1400	LOS ANGELES, CA	90067
YOUNG, STEPHEN	ACTOR	400 S BEVERLY DR #216	BEVERLY HILLS, CA	90212
YOUNG, STEPHEN T	GUITARIST	2712 WESTWOOD AVE	NASHVILLE, TN	37212
YOUNG, STEVE	SINGER	POST OFFICE BOX 121264	NASHVILLE, TN	37212
YOUNG, TERENCE	FILM WRITER-DIRECTOR	61 EATON SQ	LONDON SW1	ENGLAND
YOUNG, TONY	ACTOR	1221 N KINGS RD #PH-405	LOS ANGELES, CA	90069
YOUNG, VICTORIA	ACTRESS	9229 SUNSET BLVD #306	LOS ANGELES, CA	90069
YOUNG, WILLIAM A	DIRECTOR	4525 MORSE AVE	STUDIO CITY, CA	91604
YOUNG, WILLIAM ALLEN	ACTOR	10000 SANTA MONICA BLVD #305	LOS ANGELES, CA	90067
YOUNG, WILLIAM L, JR	DIRECTOR	4819 WILLOW CREST AVE	NORTH HOLLYWOOD, CA	91601
YOUNG, WYCLIFFE	ACTOR	11030 VENTURA BLVD #3	STUDIO CITY, CA	91604
YOUNG FRESH FELLOWS	ROCK & ROLL GROUP	POST OFFICE BOX 95364	SEATTLE, WA	98145
YOUNGBLOOD, CHIEF MARK	WRESTLER	WORLD CLASS WRESTLING		
		SOUTHWEST SPORTS, INC		
		DALLAS SPORTATORIUM		
		1000 S INDUSTRIAL BLVD	DALLAS, TX	75207
YOUNGER, JACK	ACTOR	8831 SUNSET BLVD #402	LOS ANGELES, CA	90069
YOUNGER, JAMES & MICHAEL	VOCAL DUO	POST OFFICE BOX 973	ALIEF, TX	77411
YOUNGER BROTHERS, THE	C & W GROUP	POST OFFICE BOX 973	ALIEF, TX	77411
YOUNGFELLOW, BARRIE	ACTRESS	10927 MISSOURI AVE	LOS ANGELES, CA	90025
YOUNGMAN, HENNY	COMEDIAN	77 W 55TH ST	NEW YORK, NY	10019
YOUNGS, GAIL	ACTRESS	211 S BEVERLY DR #201	BEVERLY HILLS, CA	90212
		44 N CENTRAL AVE	ELMSFORD, NY	10523
YOUNT, ROBIN	BASEBALL	8140 E SANDS DR, BOX 545	SCOTTSDALE, AZ	85255
YOUNTS, BOB	DRUMMER	ROUTE #1, BOX 378	PLEASANT VIEW, TN	37146
YOURGRAU, TUGGELIN B	TV WRITER	555 W 57TH ST #1230	NEW YORK, NY	10019
YOUSSEFIAN, APICK	ACTRESS	3330 BARHAM BLVD #103	LOS ANGELES, CA	90068
YOUTH IN ASIA	ROCK & ROLL GROUP	FRONT LINE MANAGEMENT		
		80 UNIVERSAL CITY PLAZA	UNIVERSAL CITY, CA	91608
YOYAH AND FRIPP	ROCK & ROCK DUO	JEM RECORDS, 3619 KENNEDY RD	SOUTH PLAINFIELD, NJ	07080
YRIGOYEN, JOSEPH	DIRECTOR	32171 SAILVIEW LN	WESTLAKE VILLAGE, CA	91361
YUDAIN, SIDNEY L	NEWS CORRESPONDENT	4901 POTOMAC AVE, NW	WASHINGTON, DC	20007
YUDKIN, JON	MUSICIAN	321 PINEWAY DR, LOWER LEVEL	NASHVILLE, TN	37217
YULIN, HARRIS	ACTOR	1630 CRESCENT PL	VENICE, CA	90291
YUNE, JOHNNY	ACTOR	11574 IOWA AVE #114	LOS ANGELES, CA	90025
YUNG, ROBERT	DIRECTOR	DGA, 110 W 57TH ST	NEW YORK, NY	10019
YUNUS, TARIQ	ACTOR	OCA, 34 GRAFTON TERR	LONDON NW5 4HY	ENGLAND
YUNWEN, ZHANG	NEWS CORRESPONDENT	3706 MASSACHUSETTS AVE, NW	WASHINGTON, DC	20016
YURGATIS, ROBERT S	WRITER	8135 REDBUSH LN	PANORAMA CITY, CA	91402
YURICK, PAUL	TV WRITER	8955 BEVERLY BLVD	LOS ANGELES, CA	90048

YURO, ROBERT	ACTOR	6430 SUNSET BLVD #1203	LOS ANGELES, CA	90028
YUS, FRANCISCA G	NEWS CORRESPONDENT	444 N CAPITOL ST, NW	WASHINGTON, DC	20001
YUST, LARRY	DIRECTOR	520 S ROSSMORE AVE	LOS ANGELES, CA	90020
YUSUF, JAVED	WRITER-PRODUCER	31 CREIGHTON AVE	LONDON N10 1NX	ENGLAND

ZABA, TIBOR	WRITER	1634 TOWER GROVE DR	BEVERLY HILLS, CA	90210
ZABALA, TERESA ANN	PHOTOGRAPHER	3735 BENTON ST, NW	WASHINGTON, DC	20007
ZABALETA, NICANOR	HARPIST	MARIEDL ANDERS ARTISTS MGMT		
		535 EL CAMINO DEL MAR ST	SAN FRANCISCO, CA	94121
ZABILSKI, DOUG	ACTOR	5922 OAKDALE AVE	WOODLAND HILLS, CA	91367
ZABKA, STANLEY	COMPOSER-DIRECTOR	5723 STAR LN	WOODLAND HILLS, CA	91367
ZABKA, WILLIAM	ACTOR-SINGER	20121 VENTURA BLVD #343	WOODLAND HILLS, CA	91364
ZABRISKE, GRACE	ACTRESS	9744 WILSHIRE BLVD #206	BEVERLY HILLS, CA	90212
ZABRISKIE, P JAY	DIRECTOR	2377 N DANVILLE ST	ARLINGTON, VA	22207
ZACCARO, JAMES	DIRECTOR	315 E 68TH ST	NEW YORK, NY	10021
ZACHA, WILLIAM T	ACTOR-WRITER	22954 COLLINS ST	WOODLAND HILLS, CA	91367
ZACHARIAS, CHRISTIAN	PIANIST	CAMI, 165 W 57TH ST	NEW YORK, NY	10019
ZACHARIAS, STEFFEN	ACTOR-WRITER	6234 BAKMAN AVE	NORTH HOLLYWOOD, CA	91606
ZACHARIAS, STEVE	SCREENWRITER	165 N ANITA AVE	LOS ANGELES, CA	90049
ZACHARY, DOLLY	ACTRESS	100 THE STRAND	HERMOSA BEACH, CA	90254
ZACHEM, MARY SUSAN	NEWS CORRESPONDENT	8801 GLENVILLE RD	SILVER SPRING, MD	20901
ZACK, DOTTY	SINGER	234 POTTERS AVE	WARWICK, RI	02886
ZACK, EDDIE	SINGER	234 POTTERS AVE	WARWICK, RI	02886
ZACK, RICHIE	SINGER	234 POTTERS AVE	WARWICK, RI	02886
ZACKER, DENIS	ACTOR	5000 LANKERSHIM BLVD #5	NORTH HOLLYWOOD, CA	91601
ZACKS, RICHARD	VIDEO COLUMNIST	N Y TIMES SYNDICATION		
		130 5TH AVE	NEW YORK, NY	10011
ZADAN, CRAIG	FILM PRODUCER	TRI-STAR PICTURES COMPANY		
		1875 CENTURY PARK E	LOS ANGELES, CA	90067
ZADORA, PIA	ACTRESS-SINGER	23720 MALIBU COLONY DR	MALIBU, CA	90265
ZAENTZ, SAUL	FILM-RECORD PRODUCER	FANTASY RECORDS COMPANY		
		10TH & PARKER STS	BERKELEY, CA	94710
ZAGER, LYNANNE	ACTRESS	7045 VAN NOORD AVE	NORTH HOLLYWOOD, CA	91605
ZAGON, MARTY	ACTOR	1122 CLYBOURN AVE	BURBANK, CA	91505
ZAGONE, ROBERT	DIRECTOR	2300 VINE ST	BERKELEY, CA	94708
ZAGOR, MICHAEL STEWART	TV WRITER	8955 BEVERLY BLVD	LOS ANGELES, CA	90048
ZAHL, EDA	ACTRESS	2124 N BEACHWOOD DR #16	LOS ANGELES, CA	90068
ZAHLER, ANDREAS	DIRECTOR	49 HORATIO ST	NEW YORK, NY	10014
ZAHRN, WILL	ACTOR	1509 N CRESCENT HGTS BLVD #7	LOS ANGELES, CA	90069
ZAILLIAN, STEVEN	SCREENWRITER	8955 BEVERLY BLVD	LOS ANGELES, CA	90048
ZAJIC, DOLORA	MEZZO-SOPRANO	CAMI, 165 W 57TH ST	NEW YORK, NY	10019
ZAK, JOHN C	ACTOR-DIRECTOR	4455 LOS FELIZ BLVD #401	HOLLYWOOD, CA	90027
ZAKAI, MIRA	CONTRALTO	ANGLO-SWISS ARTISTS MGMT		
		16 MUSWELL HILL RD, HIGHGATE	LONDON N6 5UG	ENGLAND
ZAKARIAN, SEDMARA	PIANIST	POST OFFICE BOX 27539	PHILADELPHIA, PA	19118
ZAKOTNIK, JOHN	NEWS CORRESPONDENT	5550 FRIENDSHIP BLVD	CHEVY CHASE, MD	20815
ZAL, ROXANNA	ACTRESS	151 S EL CAMINO DR	BEVERLY HILLS, CA	90212
ZALA, NANCY	ACTRESS-WRITER	11514 VENTURA BLVD #10	STUDIO CITY, CA	91604
ZAMBALIS, STELLA	MEZZO-SOPRANO	ICM, 40 W 57TH ST	NEW YORK, NY	10019
ZAMMIT, EDDIE	ACTOR	247 S BEVERLY DR #102	BEVERLY HILLS, CA	90210
ZAMORA, DEL	ACTOR	15010 VENTURA BLVD #219	SHERMAN OAKS, CA	91403
ZAMPESE, ALAN	ACTOR	484 W 43RD ST #16-Q	NEW YORK, NY	10036
ZAMPIERI, MARA	SOPRANO	CAMI, 165 W 57TH ST	NEW YORK, NY	10019
ZANCANARO, GIORGIO	BARITONE	CAMI, 165 W 57TH ST	NEW YORK, NY	10019
ZAND, MICHAEL	ACTOR	9300 WILSHIRE BLVD #410	BEVERLY HILLS, CA	90212
ZAND, SHAR MICHAEL	ACTOR	3460 CABRILLO BLVD	LOS ANGELES, CA	90066
ZANDBERG, JEFF	ACTOR	3400 BEN LOMOND PL #317	LOS ANGELES, CA	90027
ZANE, FRANK	BODYBUILDER	POST OFFICE BOX 366	SANTA MONICA, CA	90406
ZANENGO, ROZ	CARTOONIST	POST OFFICE BOX 4203	NEW YORK, NY	10017
ZANETOS, DEAN	TV DIRECTOR-PRODUCER	3170 HOLLYRIDGE DR	HOLLYWOOD, CA	90068
ZANNOTH, SHERRY	SOPRANO	61 W 62ND ST #6-F	NEW YORK, NY	10023
ZANUCK, RICHARD	FILM PRODUCER	546 PALISADES BEACH RD	SANTA MONICA, CA	90402
ZAP, SAM	ACTOR	1355 1/4 N HAVENHURST DR	LOS ANGELES, CA	90046
ZAPANTA, DIANE	ACTRESS	FELBER, 2126 N CAHUENGA BLVD	LOS ANGELES, CA	90068
ZAPATA, CARMEN	ACTRESS	6107 ETHEL AVE	VAN NUYS, CA	91401
ZAPP	RHYTHM & BLUES GROUP	GTI, 1700 BROADWAY, 10TH FLOOR	NEW YORK, NY	10019
ZAPPA, DWEEZIL	ACTOR-SINGER	7885 WOODROW WILSON DR	LOS ANGELES, CA	90046
ZAPPA, FRANK	SINGER-MUSICAN	7885 WOODROW WILSON DR	LOS ANGELES, CA	90046
ZAPPA, MOON UNIT	SINGER	7885 WOODROW WILSON DR	LOS ANGELES, CA	90046
ZAPPACOSTA	ROCK & ROLL GROUP	41 BRITAIN ST #200	TORONTO, ONT	CANADA
ZAPPLE, ROB	ACTOR	11315 BLUE SAGE DR	SYLMAR, CA	91342

ZAPPO THE CLOWN	CLOWN	HALL, 138 FROG HOLLOW RD	CHURCHVILLE, PA	18966
ZARCOFF, MORTON	WRITER	1616 WARNALL AVE	LOS ANGELES, CA	90024
ZARKONS, THE	ROCK & ROLL GROUP	6253 HOLLYWOOD BLVD #727	HOLLYWOOD, CA	90028
ZAROU, ELIAS	ACTOR	4721 LAUREL CANYON BLVD #211	NORTH HOLLYWOOD, CA	91607
ZARRAS, BILL	RECORD EXECUTIVE	WEA MUSIC, 1810 BIRCHMONT RD	SCARBOROUGH, ONT	CANADA
ZASLOW, MICHAEL	ACTOR	9200 SUNSET BLVD #1210	LOS ANGELES, CA	90069
ZASTUPNEVICH, PAUL	COSTUME DESIGNER	73640 JOSHUA TREE	PALM DESERT, CA	92260
ZATESLO, GEORGE T	TV WRITER	11755 NEBRASKA AVE #9	LOS ANGELES, CA	90025
ZAVADA, ERVIN	WRITER-PRODUCER	16763 LONDELIUS ST	SEPULVEDA, CA	91343
ZAVAYNA, KEN	ACTOR	8949 SUNSET BLVD #203	LOS ANGELES, CA	90069
ZAY, BOB L	ACTOR	1121 N OLIVE DR #303	LOS ANGELES, CA	90069
ZAZOFSKY, PETER	VIOLINIST	59 E 54TH ST #81	NEW YORK, NY	10022
ZAZVORKA, LISA	ACTRESS	12119 MORRISON ST	NORTH HOLLYWOOD, CA	91607
ZBRZEZNY, ANTHONY	BASSO-BARITONE	45 W 60TH ST #4-K	NEW YORK, NY	10023
ZBYSZKO, LARRY	WRESTLER	AMERICAN WRESTLING ASSOC		
		MINNEAPLOIS WRESTLING		
		10001 WAYZATA BLVD	MINNETONKA, MN	55345
ZEAROTT, MICHAEL F	COMPOSER-CONDUCTOR	701 OHIO AVE #3	LONG BEACH, CA	90804
ZECHAR, DAVID B	NEWS CORRESPONDENT	ABC-TV, NEWS DEPARTMENT		
		1717 DE SALES ST, NW	WASHINGTON, DC	20036
ZEDNIK, HEINZ	TENOR	59 E 54TH ST #81	NEW YORK, NY	10022
ZEE, ELEANOR	ACTRESS	1322 N HAVENHURST DR #26	LOS ANGELES, CA	90046
ZEE, JOHN A	ACTOR	3800 BARHAM BLVD #303	LOS ANGELES, CA	90068
ZEFFERELLI, FRANCO	FILM DIRECTOR	VIA APPIA PIGNATELLI 1448	ROME	ITALY
ZEGLER, PAUL	ACTOR	1942 RODNEY DR #10	LOS ANGELES, CA	90027
ZEH, JANUARY	ACTRESS	6430 SUNSET BLVD #1203	LOS ANGELES, CA	90028
ZEHMS, CRAIG	ACTOR	438 N SYCAMORE AVE #7	LOS ANGELES, CA	90036
ZEHR, TIMOTHY	GUITARIST	104 HULL LN	HENDERSONVILLE, TN	37075
ZEIDEN, JAY	ACTOR	4724 FARMDALE AVE	NORTH HOLLYWOOD, CA	91602
ZEIDENBERG, LEONARD	NEWS CORRESPONDENT	5617 NORTHFIELD RD	BETHESDA, MD	20034
ZEIGLER, HEIDI	ACTRESS	3575 W CAHUENGA BLVD #320	LOS ANGELES, CA	90068
ZEIGLER, TED	ACTOR-WRITER	4040 SHADYGLADE AVE	STUDIO CITY, CA	91604
ZEITLIN, ZVI	VIOLINIST	204 WARREN AVE	ROCHESTER, NY	14618
ZEITMAN, JERRY	TALENT AGENT	10351 SANTA MONICA BLVD #211	LOS ANGELES, CA	90025
ZELENKA, JERRY	ACTOR	4410 HENLEY CT	WESTLAKE, CA	91361
ZELIGSON, WENDY S	NEWS CORRESPONDENT	400 NATIONAL PRESS BLDG		
		529 14TH ST, NW	WASHINGTON, DC	20045
ZELLER, ART	BODYBUILDER	POST OFFICE BOX 254	SANTA MONICA, CA	90406
ZELLIN, ROBERT F	COMPOSER	6643 LOCHE ALENE	PICO RIVERA, CA	90660
ZELLMAN, SHELLEY	TV WRITER	9869 EASTON DR	BEVERLY HILLS, CA	90210
ZELTSER, MARK	PIANIST	111 W 57TH ST #1203	NEW YORK, NY	10019
ZEMAN, JACKLYN	ACTRESS	12024 SARAH ST	STUDIO CITY, CA	91607
ZEMANN, DON	RECORD EXECUTIVE	POST OFFICE BOX 3082	LONG ISLAND CITY, NY	11103
ZEMECKIS, ROBERT	WRITER-DIRECTOR	1880 CENTURY PARK E #900	LOS ANGELES, CA	90067
ZENDAR, FRED V	DIRECTOR	134 CHAUTAUQUA BLVD	SANTA MONICA, CA	90402
ZENK, COLLEEN	ACTRESS	CBS-TV, "AS THE WORLD TURNS"		
		51 W 52ND ST	NEW YORK, NY	10019
ZENK, TOM	WRESTLER	POST OFFICE BOX 3859	STAMFORD, CT	06905
ZENOR, SUZANNE	ACTRESS	3158 OAKSHIRE DR	LOS ANGELES, CA	90068
ZENOVICH, NINON	ACTRESS	120 W VICTORY BLVD #104	BURBANK, CA	91501
ZENTALL, KATE	ACTRESS	2922 2ND ST #B	SANTA MONICA, CA	90405
ZENTNER, SIMON	COMPOSER-CONDUCTOR	4825 FAIRFAX AVE	LAS VEGAS, NV	89120
ZERBE, ANTHONY	ACTOR	SF & A, 121 N SAN VICENTE BLVD	BEVERLY HILLS, CA	90211
ZERBINI, JAQLIN	AERIAL ACT	POST OFFICE BOX 87	WEST LEBANON, NY	12195
ZETTEL, PHILIP	ACTOR	7300 LANKERSHIM BLVD	NORTH HOLLYWOOD, CA	91605
ZETTERLING, MAI	ACT-WRI-DIR	DOUGLAS RAE MANAGEMENT		
		28 CHARING CROSS RD	LONDON WC2	ENGLAND
ZEVNIK, NEIL	ACTOR	ABC-TV NETWORK, "LOVING"		
		1330 AVE OF THE AMERICAS	NEW YORK, NY	10019
ZEVON, WARREN	SINGER-SONGWRITER	1880 CENTURY PARK E #900	LOS ANGELES, CA	90067
ZHUKOV, BORIS	WRESTLER	AMERICAN WRESTLING ASSOC		
		MINNEAPLOIS WRESTLING		
		10001 WAYZATA BLVD	MINNETONKA, MN	55345
ZIEFF, HOWARD	FILM DIRECTOR	1243 SUNSET PLAZA DR	LOS ANGELES, CA	90069
ZIEGLER, BILL	CARTOONIST	NEWS AMERICA SYNDICATE		
		1703 KAISER AVE	IRVINE, CA	92714
ZIEGLER, DELORES	MEZZO-SOPRANO	HILLYER, 250 W 57TH ST	NEW YORK, NY	10107
ZIEGLER, JACK	CARTOONIST	NEW YORK MAGAZINE		
		25 W 43RD ST	NEW YORK, NY	10036
ZIEGLER, JAMES E	TV DIRECTOR	1640 REDESDALE AVE	LOS ANGELES, CA	90026
ZIEGLER, JAN	NEWS CORRESPONDENT	3726 CONNECTICUT AVE #508, NW	WASHINGTON, DC	20008
ZIEGMAN, JERALD L	TV WRITER	8955 BEVERLY BLVD	LOS ANGELES, CA	90048
ZIELKE, W D "OZ"	DIRECTOR	11948 RANCHO BERNARDO RD #D	SAN DEIGO, CA	92128
ZIEN, CHIP	ACTOR	10 E 44TH ST #700	NEW YORK, NY	10017
ZIFFRIN, MARILYN	COMPOSER	FINELL, 155 W 68TH ST	NEW YORK, NY	10023
ZIGAS, DAVID	NEWS CORRESPONDENT	3000 SPOUT RUN PARKWAY	ARLINGTON, VA	22201
ZIGMAN, JOSEPH	DIRECTOR	473 S HOLT AVE	LOS ANGELES, CA	90048
ZIKER, RICHARD	FILM DIRECTOR	11268 SUNSHINE TRAIL	STUDIO CITY, CA	91604
ZILIO, ELENA	MEZZO-SOPRANO	61 W 62ND ST #6-F	NEW YORK, NY	10023
ZILSKE, BRUCE	WRITER	2050 RODNEY DR #9	LOS ANGELES, CA	90027
ZIMBALIST, EFREM, JR	ACTOR	4750 ENCINO AVE	ENCINO, CA	91316
ZIMBALIST, STEPHANIE	ACTRESS	2121 AVE OF THE STARS #410	LOS ANGELES, CA	90067
ZIMERMAN, STEVE	VIOLINIST	1120 DUNCANWOOD DR	NASHVILLE, TN	37204
ZIMMER, KIM	ACTRESS	CBS-TV, "THE GUIDING LIGHT"		
		51 W 52ND ST	NEW YORK, NY	10019

Name	Occupation	Address	City	Zip
ZIMMER, LEE	ACTOR	51 5TH AVE	NEW YORK, NY	10003
ZIMMER-SMITH, DEBRA	DIRECTOR	DGA, 7950 SUNSET BLVD	LOS ANGELES, CA	90046
ZIMMERMAN, AMANDA	NEWS CORRESPONDENT	825 DUKE ST	ALEXANDRIA, VA	22314
ZIMMERMAN, CATHERINE B	PHOTOGRAPHER	607 DALE DR	SILVER SPRING, MD	20910
ZIMMERMAN, DICK	PHOTOGRAPHER	201 N ROBERTSON BLVD #A	BEVERLY HILLS, CA	90211
ZIMMERMAN, DONALD PAUL	DIRECTOR	DGA, 7950 SUNSET BLVD	LOS ANGELES, CA	90046
ZIMMERMAN, GAIL ABBOTT	DIRECTOR	205 W END AVE #1-N	NEW YORK, NY	10023
ZIMMERMAN, GORDON	ACTOR	1766 WASHINGTON WY	VENICE, CA	90291
ZIMMERMAN, JONATHAN	ACTOR	6909 1/2 BONITA TERR	HOLLYWOOD, CA	90068
ZIMMERMAN, MARGARITA	SINGER	2171 CAMPO SAN ROLO	VINCENZIA	ITALY
ZIMMERMAN, PAUL	COMEDIAN	POST OFFICE BOX 1556	GAINESVILLE, FL	32602
ZIMMERMAN, PAUL	SPORTS WRITER-EDITOR	SPORTS ILLUSTRATED MAGAZINE		
		TIME & LIFE BUILDING		
		ROCKEFELLER CENTER	NEW YORK, NY	10020
ZIMMERMAN, RICHARD G	NEWS CORRESPONDENT	125 10TH ST, SE	WASHINGTON, DC	20003
ZIMMERMAN, TERESA M	NEWS CORRESPONDENT	2900 CONNECTICUT AVE #232, NW	WASHINGTON, DC	20008
ZIMMERMAN, TERRY DEE	SINGER-GUITARIST	1100 THOMPSON PL #C-29	NASHVILLE, TN	37217
ZIMMERMAN, VERNON	WRITER-DIRECTOR	POST OFFICE BOX 900	BEVERLY HILLS, CA	90213
ZIMMERMANN, FRANK PETER	VIOLINIST	CAMI, 165 W 57TH ST	NEW YORK, NY	10019
ZIMMERMANN, GERHARDT	MUSIC ARRANGER	500 5TH AVE #2050	NEW YORK, NY	10110
ZIMMERMANN, MARGARITA	MEZZO-SOPRANO	CAMI, 165 W 57TH ST	NEW YORK, NY	10019
ZINBERG, MICHAEL	WRITER-PRODUCER	1539 SAN YSIDRO DR	BEVERLY HILLS, CA	90210
ZINC, TONY	WRESTLER	POST OFFICE BOX 3859	STAMFORD, CT	06905
ZINDEL, PAUL	PLAYWRIGHT	HARPER & ROW, 10 E 53RD ST	NEW YORK, NY	10022
ZINER, PETER	FILM EDITOR	334 ARNO WY	PACIFIC PALISADES, CA	90272
ZINGALE, MICHAEL C	DIRECTOR	11750 CLONLEE AVE	GRANADA HILLS, CA	91344
ZINKAN, JOSEPH	GUITARIST	18 ORCHARD VALLEY RD	HENDERSONVILLE, TN	37075
ZINMAN, DAVID	MUSIC DIRECTOR	ICM, 40 W 57TH ST	NEW YORK, NY	10019
ZINN, REUEL H	NEWS CORRESPONDENT	229 BROADWAY	HANOVER, PA	17331
ZINNEMANN, FRED	FILM DIRECTOR	128 MOUNT ST	LONDON W1	ENGLAND
ZINTL, ROBERT T	WRITER-EDITOR	TIME/TIME & LIFE BLDG		
		ROCKEFELLER CENTER	NEW YORK, NY	10020
ZIPP, DEBBIE	ACTRESS	211 S BEVERLY DR #107	BEVERLY HILLS, CA	90212
ZIPPER	ROCK & ROLL GROUP	POST OFFICE BOX 448	RADFORD, VA	24141
ZIPPER, HERBERT	CONDUCTOR	1091 PALISAIR PL	PACIFIC PALISADES, CA	90272
ZIPPRODT, PATRICIA	COSTUME DESIGNER	39 KING ST	NEW YORK, NY	10014
ZIRATO, BRUNO, JR	DIRECTOR	6330 N 3RD ST	PHOENIX, AZ	85012
ZIRINSKY, SUSAN	WRITER-NEWS CORRES	CBS NEWS, 2020 "M" ST, NW	WASHINGTON, DC	20036
ZIRYAB, TALLER	MUSICIAN	KAY, 58 W 58TH ST	NEW YORK, NY	10019
ZISKIN, LAURA E	WRITER	6473 RODGERTON DR	LOS ANGELES, CA	90068
ZITELLA, JAMES	ACTOR	5922 TAMPA AVE	TARZANA, CA	91356
ZITO, STEPHEN	TV WRITER	8955 BEVERLY BLVD	LOS ANGELES, CA	90048
ZITO, WILLIAM	GUITARIST	KAY, 58 W 58TH ST	NEW YORK, NY	10019
ZITZERMAN, ZELMA	CARTOONIST	POST OFFICE BOX 345		
		STATION A	TORONTO, ONT M5W 1C2	CANADA
ZIVONI, YOSSI	VIOLINIST	POST OFFICE BOX U	REDDING, CT	06875
ZIZZO, ALICIA	PIANIST	GEWALD, 58 W 58TH ST	NEW YORK, NY	10019
ZLATOFF-MIRSKY, EVERETT IGOR	VIOLINIST	240 GREENBAY RD	GLENCOE, IL	60022
ZLOTKIN, FREDERICK	CELLIST	HILLYER, 250 W 57TH ST	NEW YORK, NY	10107
ZLOTNICK, VICKI LYN	WRITER	2323 S BEVERLY BLVD #6	LOS ANGELES, CA	90064
ZLOTOFF, LEE D	TV WRITER	458 19TH ST	SANTA MONICA, CA	90402
ZMED, ADRIAN	ACTOR	1135 S BEVERLY DR #2	LOS ANGELES, CA	90035
ZMUDA, BOB	TV WRITER	8955 BEVERLY BLVD	LOS ANGELES, CA	90048
ZNOWHITE	ROCK & ROLL GROUP	5342 N WINTHROP AVE #2-E	CHICAGO, IL	60640
ZOGHBY, LINDA	SOPRANO	CAMI, 165 W 57TH ST	NEW YORK, NY	10019
ZOGLIN, RICHARD	WRITER-EDITOR	TIME/TIME & LIFE BLDG		
		ROCKEFELLER CENTER	NEW YORK, NY	10020
ZOHAR, RITA	ACTRESS	211 S BEVERLY DR #201	BEVERLY HILLS, CA	90212
ZOLA, MARION	WRITER	999 DOHENY DR #604	LOS ANGELES, CA	90069
ZOLO, VICTOR	CONDUCTOR	7060 FRANKLIN AVE #4	LOS ANGELES, CA	90028
ZON, CALVIN	NEWS CORRESPONDENT	2205 42ND ST #105, NW	WASHINGTON, DC	20007
ZOREK, MICHAEL	ACTOR	11927 MAGNOLIA BLVD #9	NORTH HOLLYWOOD, CA	91607
ZORI, CARMIT	VIOLINIST	CAMI, 165 W 57TH ST	NEW YORK, NY	10019
ZORICH, LOUS	ACTOR	SUSAN SMITH, 850 7TH AVE	NEW YORK, NY	10019
ZORINA, VERA	ACTRESS	10 GRACIE SQ	NEW YORK, NY	10009
ZSCHAU, MARILYN	SOPRANO	CAMI, 165 W 57TH ST	NEW YORK, NY	10019
ZSIGMOND, VILMOS	CINEMATOGRAPHER	9229 SUNSET BLVD #700	LOS ANGELES, CA	90069
ZUCKER, CHARLES	ACTOR	141 S EL CAMINO DR #205	BEVERLY HILLS, CA	90212
ZUCKER, DAVID	WRITER-PRODUCER	1849 SAWTELLE BLVD #500	LOS ANGELES, CA	90025
ZUCKER, JERRY	FILM WRI-DIR-PROD	481 DENSLOW AVE	LOS ANGELES, CA	90049
ZUCKERMAN, EDWARD	NEWS CORRESPONDENT	2431 59TH PL	CHEVERLY, MD	20785
ZUCKERMAN, FAYE	COLUMNIST	N Y TIMES SYNDICATION		
		130 5TH AVE	NEW YORK, NY	10011
ZUCKERMAN, HOWARD	DIRECTOR	5361 BLANCO AVE	WOODLAND HILLS, CA	91367
ZUCKERMAN, MORTIMER B	PUBLISH EXECUTIVE	U S NEWS & WORLD REPORT		
		2400 "N" ST, NW	WASHINGTON, DC	20037
ZUCKERMAN, ROBERT	NEWS CORRESPONDENT	3320 CLARIDGE CT	WHEATON, MD	20902
ZUCKERMAN, STEVE	COMPOSER-CONDUCTOR	5311 HAZELTINE AVE	VAN NUYS, CA	91401
ZUCKERT, BILL	ACTOR	3397 FLOYD TERR	LOS ANGELES, CA	90068
ZUERCHER, RICK	NEWS CORRESPONDENT	1864 WYOMING AVE, NW	WASHINGTON, DC	20009
ZUGSMITH, ALBERT	WRITER-PRODUCER	1210 N WETHERLY DR	LOS ANGELES, CA	90069
ZUKERMAN, EUGENIA	FLUTIST	BROOKLYN COLLEGE		
		MUSIC DEPARTMENT		
		BEDFORD AVE & AVE "H"	BROOKLYN, NY	11210
ZUKERMAN, JAY	ACTOR	15942 TOBIN WY	SHERMAN OAKS, CA	91403

ZUKERMAN, PINCHAS	VIOLINIST	173 RIVERSIDE DR	NEW YORK, NY	10024
ZUKOFSKY, PAUL	VIOLINIST	HILLYER, 250 W 57TH ST	NEW YORK, NY	10107
ZUKOR, EUGENE	FILM EXECUTIVE	1161 SHADOW HILL WY	BEVERLY HILLS, CA	90210
ZUKOW, CHARLES	ACTOR	13004 VALLEYHEART DR #10	STUDIO CITY, CA	91604
ZUKOWSKI, HELEN	TV WRITER	8955 BEVERLY BLVD	LOS ANGELES, CA	90048
ZULUS	ROCK & ROLL GROUP	11 TREMLETT ST	DORCHESTER, MA	02124
ZUMMOS, THE	ROCK & ROCK DUO	POST OFFICE BOX 118	HOLLYWOOD, CA	90078
ZUNIGA, DAPHNE	ACTRESS	11726 SAN VICENTE BLVD #300	LOS ANGELES, CA	90049
ZUNIGA, FRANK	FILM DIRECTOR	12050 VALLEYHEART DR #102	STUDIO CITY, CA	91604
ZUPONCIC, VEDA	PIANIST	POST OFFICE BOX U	REDDING, CT	06875
ZURAWIEC, RICHARD W	TV DIRECTOR	418 MACKINAW AVE	CALUMET CITY, IL	60409
ZURLA, LESLIE	DIRECTOR-PRODUCER	5746 RADFORD AVE	NORTH HOLLYWOOD, CA	91607
ZUROCHOV, BORIS	WRESTLER	SEE - ZHUKOV, BORIS		
ZURU, KOMA	TOP SPINNER	HALL, 138 FROG HOLLOW RD	CHURCHVILLE, PA	18966
ZUVICH, DENNIS M	CONDUCTOR	3916 VINELAND AVE	STUDIO CITY, CA	91604
ZWADIUK, OLEH	NEWS CORRESPONDENT	1201 CONNECTICUT AVE, NW	WASHINGTON, DC	20036
ZWANG, LARRAINE	TV DIRECTOR	88 LEXINGTON AVE	NEW YORK, NY	10016
ZWEBEN, JERRY	DIRECTOR	38 TWIN RIVERS DR N	EAST WINDSOR, NJ	08520
ZWECK, BRAD	NEWS CORRESPONDENT	1021 ARLINGTON BLVD	ARLINGTON, VA	22209
ZWEIBACK, A MARTIN	WRITER-DIRECTOR	1117 S BEDFORD ST	LOS ANGELES, CA	90035
ZWEIBEL, ALAN	TV WRITER-PRODUCER	555 W 57TH ST #1230	NEW YORK, NY	10019
ZWEIG, FREDERIC	CONDUCTOR	637 N SWEETZER AVE	LOS ANGELES, CA	90048
ZWERIUN, CHARLOTTE M	DIRECTOR-PRODUCER	43 MORTON ST	NEW YORK, NY	10014
ZWICK, EDWARD M	TV WRITER-DIRECTOR	309 SUMAC LN	SANTA MONICA, CA	90402
ZWICK, JOEL	DIRECTOR	9300 WILSHIRE BLVD #410	BEVERLY HILLS, CA	90212
ZWIRN, ROBERT S	COMPOSER-CONDUCTOR	1028 HI POINT ST	LOS ANGELES, CA	90035
ZYLIS-GARA, TERESA	SOPRANO	CAMI, 165 W 57TH ST	NEW YORK, NY	10019
ZZ TOP	ROCK & ROLL TRIO	POST OFFICE BOX 19744	HOUSTON, TX	77024

MOVIE & TELEVISION STARS

Portraits (P) & Movie Stills (S)

$1.00 each

JULIE ADAMS

JIM ARNESS

JULIE ANDREWS

BEVERLY AADLAND - P
WILLIE AAMES - P/S
BURMA ACQUANETTA
BROOKE ADAMS - P/S
CATLIN ADAMS - P
DON ADAMS - P
EDIE ADAMS - P
JULIE ADAMS - P
MASON ADAMS - P
MAUD ADAMS - P
NEILE ADAMS - P
ISABELLE ADJANI - P
IRIS ADRIAN - P
JOHN AGAR - P
JENNY AGUTTER - P
ANOUK AIMEE - P
ANNA MARIA ALBERGHETTI
EDDIE ALBERT - P
EDWARD ALBERT - P
LOLA ALBRIGHT - P
ALAN ALDA - P/S
KAY ALDRIDGE - P
JANE ALEXANDER - P
KIM ALEXIS - P
DEBBIE ALLEN - P
NANCY ALLEN - P
STEVE ALLEN - P
REX ALLEN, SR - P
FERNANDO ALLENDE - P
KIRSTIE ALLEY -P
JUNE ALLYSON - P
KIRK ALYN - P
DON AMECHE - P
ED AMES - P
LEON AMES - P
BIBI ANDERSON - P
JUDITH ANDERSON - P
LONI ANDERSON - P
MELISSA SUE ANDERSON
MELODY ANDERSON - P
RICHARD ANDERSON - P
RICHARD DEAN ANDERSON
URSULA ANDRESS - P/S
DANA ANDREWS - P
JULIE ANDREWS - P/S
TIGE ANDREWS - P
HEATHER ANGEL - P
ANN-MARGRET - P/S
MICHAEL ANSARA - P
SUSAN ANSPACH - P
LYSETTE ANTHONY - P
LAURA ANTONELLI - P
SUSAN ANTON - P/S
ALAN ARBUS - P
ANNE ARCHER - P/S
EVE ARDEN - P
ALAN ARKIN - P
ALICE ARMAND - P
BESS ARMSTRONG - P
DESI ARNAZ, JR - P
LUCY ARNAZ - P
JAMES ARNESS - P
JAMES ARNESS (MATT DILLON)
ROSANNA ARQUETTE - P
BEA ARTHUR - P
JEAN ARTHUR - P
ELIZABETH ASHLEY - P/S
EDWARD ASNER - P
CHUCK ASPEGREN - P
ARMAND ASSANTE - P/S
JOHN ASTIN - P
MARY ASTOR - P
CHRISTOPHER ATKINS - P
RICHARD ATTENBOROUGH - P
CLAUDINE AUGER - P
JEAN-PIERRE AUMONT - P
GENE AUTRY - P
NINA AXELROD - P
DAN AYKROYD - P
LEW AYRES - P

LAUREEN BACALL - P
BARBARA BACH - P/S
CATHERINE BACH - P
JIM BACKUS - P
KEVIN BACON - P
BUDDY BAER - P
PEARL BAILEY - P/S
BARBARA BAIN - P
SCOTT BAIO - P/S
CARROLL BAKER - P
JOE DON BAKER - P/S
WILLIAM BAKEWELL - P
BELINDA BALASKI - P
LUCILLE BALL - P
MARTIN BALSAM - P/S
ANNE BANCROFT - P
VILMA BANKY - P

JIM BANNON - P
ADRIENNE BARBEAU -P/S
BRIGITTE BARDOT - P
LYNN BARI - P
BINNIE BARNES - P
PRISCILLA BARNES - P/S
SONNY BARNES - S
DOUG BARR - P
MARIE BARRAULT - S
RONA BARRETT - P
MONA BARRIE - P
CHUCK BARRIS - P
GENE BARRY - P
DREW BARRYMORE - P
FREDDIE BARTHOLOMEW - P
LINA BASQUETTE - P
KIM BASSINGER - P
ALAN BATES - P
JAIME LYN BAUER - P
STEVEN BAUER - P
FRANCES BAVIER - P
LINDSAY BAXTER - P/S
MEREDITH BAXTER - P
JENNIFER BEALS - P
ORSON BEAN - P
NED BEATTY - P/S
WARREN BEATTY - P/S
BONNIE BEDELIA - P
BARBARA BEL GEDDES - P
SHARI BELAFONTE - P
MADGE BELLAMY - P
RALPH BELLAMY - P
KATHLEEN BELLER - P/S
JEAN PAUL BELMONDO - P/S
DIRK BENEDICT - P
RICHARD BENJAMIN - P/S
JOAN BENNETT - P
ROBBIE BENSON - P/S
BARBIE BENTON - P
TOM BERENGER - P
MERISSA BERENSON - P
CANDICE BERGEN - P
POLLY BERGEN - P/S
HERBERT BERGHOF - P
SANDAHL BERGMAN (CONAN)
MILTON BERLE - P
WARREN BERLINGER - S
ELIZABETH BERRIDGE - S
NOAH BERRY, JR - P
VALERIE BERTINELLI - P
BIBI BESCH - S
JOE BESSER - P
LYLE BETTGER - P
JACK BEUTEL - P
TURHAN BEY - P
BING BINGHAM - S
DAVID BIRNEY - P/S
JACQUELINE BISSET - P
JACQUELINE BISSET (WET SHIRT)

BILL BIXBY - P
KAREN BLACK - P/S
HONOR BLACKMAN - P
VIVIAN BLAINE - P
JANET BLAIR - P
LINDA BLAIR - P/S
AMANDA BLAKE - P
ROBERT BLAKE - P
ROBERT BLAKE (HOFFA)
RONNEE BLAKELY - P
SUSAN BLAKELY - P
CLAIRE BLOOM - P
BLUES BROTHERS - S
ANN BLYTH - P
HART BOCHNER - P
DIRK BOGARDE - P/S
HEIDI BOHAY - P
PETER BONERZ - P
LISA BONET - P
FRANK BONNER - P
SHIRLEY BOOTH - P
VICTOR BORGE - P
ERNEST BORGNINE - P/S
JOE BOTTOMS - P
SAM BOTTOMS - P
TIMOTHY BOTTOMS - P/S
BARBARA BOUCHET - P
CAROLE BOUQUET - P
JUDI BOWKER - S
BRUCE BOXLEITNER - P
PETER BOYLE - P/S
EDDIE BRACKEN - P
SONIA BRAGGA - P
NEVILLE BRAND - P
JOCELYN BRANDO - P/S
MARLON BRANDO - P/S
MICHAEL BRANDON - S
TRACY BREGMAN - P
MICHAEL BREHN - P
EILEEN BRENNAN - P
DAVID BRENNER - P
BEAU BRIDGES - P/S
JEFF BRIDGES - P/S
LLOYD BRIDGES - P/S
CHRISTIE BRINKLEY - P
MAY BRITT - P
MORGAN BRITTANY - P
BARBARA BRITTON - P
MATTHEW BRODERICK - P
JAMES BROLIN - P
CHARLES BRONSON - P/S
FOSTER BROOKS - P
MEL BROOKS - P/S
RAND BROOKS - P
RANDI BROOKS - P
PIERCE BROSNAN - P
CANDI BROUGH - P
RANDI BROUGH - P
BLAIR BROWN - P
JAMES BROWN - S

VILMA BANKY

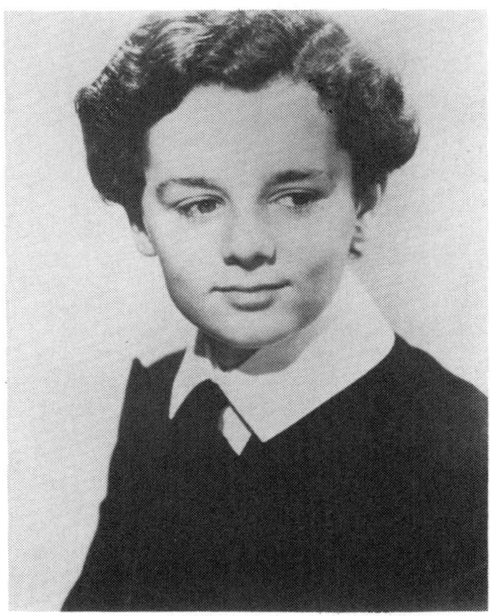

FREDDIE BARTHOLOMEW

PIERCE BROSNAN

IMOGENE COCA

CLAUDETTE COLBERT

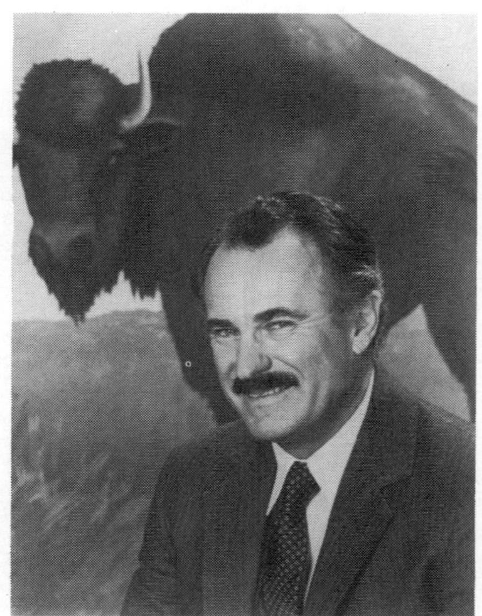
DABNEY COLEMAN

JIM BROWN - P/S
TOM BROWN - P
SUSAN BUCKNER - S
GENEVIEVE BUJOLD - P
BROOKE BUNDY - P
GARY BURGHOFF - P
TOM BURLINSON - P
CAROL BURNETT - P/S
GEORGE BURNS - P
RAYMOND BURR - P
ELLEN BURSTYN - P/S
LEVAR BURTON - P
GARY BUSEY - P/S
RED BUTTONS - P/S
PAT BUTTRAM - P
JEFFREY BYRON - P

MICHAEL CAINE - P/S
RORY CALHOUN - P/S
CORINNE CALVET - P
COLLEEN CAMP - P
JOSEPH CAMPANELLA - P
JOHN CANDY - P
DYAN CANNON - P/S
DIANA CANOVA - P
CANTINFLAS - P
KATE CAPSHAW - P
IRENE CARA - P
CLAUDIA CARDINALE - P
MC DONALD CAREY
MICHELLE CAREY - P
KITTY CARLISLE - P
MARY CARLISLE - P
ART CARNEY - P/S
LESLIE CARON - P/S
DAVID CARRADINE - P/S
JOHN CARRADINE - P/S
KEITH CARRADINE - P/S
ROBERT CARRADINE - P
SUNSET CARSON - P
LYNDA CARTER - P
LYNDA CARTER (WONDER WOMAN)
VERONICA CARTWRIGHT - P/S
PEGGY CASS - P
JOHN CASSAVETES - P/S
DAVID CASSIDY - P
JOANNA CASSIDY - P/S
JOANNA CASSIDY - P
SHAWN CASSIDY - P
NICK CASTLE - P
PHOEBE CATES - P/S
ANNE CAUDRY - S
JOAN CAULFIELD - P
CHRISTOPHER CAZENONE - P
GEORGE CHAKIRIS - P
MARILYN CHAMBERS - P
RICHARD CHAMBERLAIN - P
CAROL CHANNING - P
STOCKARD CHANNING - P/S
ROSALIND CHAO - S
GERALDINE CHAPLIN - P
JUDITH CHAPMAN - P
MARGUERITE CHAPMAN - P
CYD CHARISSE - P
CHEVY CHASE - P
CHEECH & CHONG - P/S
LOIS CHILES - P
LINDA CHRISTIAN - P
WILLIAM CHRISTOPHER (MASH)
CANDY CLARK - P
DANE CLARK - P
SUSAN CLARK - P
MAE CLARKE - P
MAE CLARKE (GRAPEFRUIT SCENE)
JILL CLAYBURGH - P/S
PAUL CLEMENS - S
DEBRA CLINGER - P
GLENN CLOSE - P
JAMES COBURN - P/S
IMOGENE COCA - P
CLAUDETTE COLBERT - P/S
DABNEY COLEMAN - P
GARY COLEMAN - P
JOHN COLICOS - P/S
GARY COLLINS - P
JACKIE COLLINS - P
JOAN COLLINS - P/S
ANJANETTE COMER - S
JENNIFER CONNELLY - P
SEAN CONNERY - P/S
CARROLL CONNORS - P
CHUCK CONNORS - P
MIKE CONNORS - P
ROBERT CONRAD - P
WILLIAM CONRAD - P
TIM CONWAY - P
JACKIE COOPER - P
JOAN COPELAND - P
TERI COPLEY - P
GRETCHEN CORBETT - S
ANN CORIO - P
LYDIA CORNELL - P
JOSEPH CORTESE - P
BILL COSBY - P/S
JOSEPH COTTEN - P/S
COURTNEY COX - P
RICHARD COX - P
RONNIE COX - P
YVONNE CRAIG - P
JEANNE CRAIN - P
NORMA CRANE - P

GEMMA CRAVEN - P
JOHNNY CRAWFORD - P
RICHARD CRENNA - P/S
LINDA CRISTAL - P/S
HUME CRONYN - P
CATHY LEE CROSBY - P
KATHRYN CROSBY - P
MARY CROSBY - P
LINDSAY CROUSE - P
TOM CRUISE - P
BILLY CRYSTAL - P/S
ROBERT CULP - S
PEGGY CUMMINS - P
ROBERT CUMMINGS - P
VALERIE CURTIN - P/S
BILLY CURTIS - S
JAMIE LEE CURTIS - P/S
KEN CURTIS - P
TONY CURTIS - P/S
PETER CUSHING - P/S

BEVERLY D'ANGELO - P/S
PATTI D'ARBANVILLE - P
DAGMAR - P
ARLENE DAHL - P/S
BILL DALY - P
TYNE DALY - P
BILL DANA - P
RODNEY DANGERFIELD - P
BLYTHE DANNER - P
SYBIL DANNING - P
ROYAL DANO - P
TED DANSON - P
TONY DANZA - P/S
KIM DARBY - P
SEVERIN DARDEN - P
JAMES DARREN - P/S
GAIL DAVIES - P
SAMMY DAVIS, JR - P
BETTE DAVIS - P
BRAD DAVIS - P
NANCY DAVIS - P
BRUCE DAVISON - P
PHYLLIS DAVIS - P
PAM DAWBER - P
DORIS DAY - P
LARRAINE DAY - P/S
ROSEMARY DE CAMP - P
YVONNE DE CARLO - P
DON DE FORE - P
GLORIA DE HAVEN - P
OLIVIA DE HAVILLAND - P/S
DOM DE LUISE - P/S
KATHARINE DE MILLE - P
REBECCA DE MORNAY - P

ROBERT DE NIRO - P/S
JOYCE DE WITT - P
PRISCILLA DEAN - P
FRANCIS DEE - P
RUBY DEE - P
SANDRA DEE - P/S
DON DEFOE - P
GABRIEL DELL - P
MYRNA DELL - P
GABRIEL DELL
ALAIN DELON - P/S
CAROL DEMPSTER - P
CATHERINE DENEUVE - P/S
RICHARD DENNING - P/S
SANDY DENNIS - P
BOB DENVER - P/S
BO DEREK - P/S
BO DEREK (SEMI NUDE)
JOHN DEREK - P
BRUCE DERN - P/S
WILLIAM DEVANE - P
COLLEEN DEWHURST - P
SUSAN DEY - P
ANGIE DICKINSON - P
MARLENE DIETRICH - P
URSULA "USCHI" DIGARD
PHYLLIS DILLER - P
BRADFORD DILLMAN - P
MATT DILLON - P
ANN DITCHBURN - P
DONNA DIXON - P
KEVIN DOBSON - P
FAITH DOMERGUE - P
ELEANOR DONAHUE - P
TROY DONAHUE - P
PETER DONAT - P
JAMES DOOHAN - P
ANN DORAN - P
DONNA DOUGLAS - P
KIRK DOUGLAS - P/S
MICHAEL DOUGLAS - P/S
SARAH DOUGLAS - P
BRAD DOURIF - S
BILLIE DOVE - P
TONY DOW - P
DORIS DOWLING - P
LESLIE-ANNE DOWN - P/S
BETSY DRAKE - P
ELLEN DREW - P/S
RICHARD DREYFUSS - P/S
JOANNE DRU - P
JAMES DRURY - P
FRED DRYER - P
HOWARD DUFF - P/S
PATRICK DUFFY - P
ANDREW DUGGAN - P
PATTY DUKE - P
KEIR DULLEA - P
FAYE DUNAWAY - P/S
SANDY DUNCAN - P/S
IRENE DUNNE - P
DEANNA DURBIN - P
CHARLES DURNING - P/S
ANN DUSENBERRY - P

BILLY CRYSTAL

KEN CURTIS

DANNY DE VITO

EMILO ESTEVEZ

DALE EVANS

ALICE FAYE

ROBERT DUVALL - P/S
SHELLY DUVALL - P/S

JEFF EAST - S
CLINT EASTWOOD - P/S
BUDDY EBSEN - P
BUDDY EBSEN
(JED CLAMPETT)
BARBARA EDEN - P
PENNY EDWARDS - P
VINCE EDWARDS - P
SAMANTHA EGGAR - P/S
LISA EICHORN - P/S
JILL EIKENBERRY - P/S
BRITT EKLAND - P
JACK ELAM - P
TAINA ELG - P
SAM ELLIOTT - P
STEPHEN ELLIOTT - P
MARIA ENGLISH - P
ERIK ESTRADA - P
DALE EVANS - P
LINDA EVANS - P
CHAD EVERETT - P/S
GREG EVIGAN - P
TOM EWELL - P

SHELLEY FABARES - P
NANETTE FABRAY - P
DOUGLAS FAIRBANKS, JR
MORGAN FAIRCHILD - P
MORGAN FAIRCHILD
(SEMI NUDE)
PETER FALK - P/S
JINX FALKENBERG - P
JAMES FARENTINO - P
ANTONIO FARGAS - P/S
RICHARD FARNSWORTH - P
FELICIA FARR - P
JAMIE FARR - P
CHARLES FARRELL - P
MIKE FARRELL - P
MIA FARROW - P/S
FARRAH FAWCETT - P/S
BARBARA FELDON - P
TOVAH FELDSHUH - P/S
NORMAN FELL - P
CRISTINA FERRARE - P
JOSE FERRER - P/S
LOU FERRIGNO - P
SALLY FIELD - P
SALLY FIELD (FLYING NUN)
KIM FIELDS - P
ALBERT FINNEY - P/S
CARRIE FISHER - P/S
GAIL FISHER - S
GERALDINE FITZGERALD - P
FANNIE FLAGG - P
ED FLANDERS - P
RHONDA FLEMING - P
LOUISE FLETCHER - P/S
WAYLAND FLOWERS & MADAME
NINA FOCH - P
JANE FONDA - P/S
PETER FONDA - P/S
JOAN FONTAINE - P
BRENDA FORBES - P
GLENN FORD - P/S
HARRISON FORD - P/S
FREDERIC FORREST - P
STEVE FORREST - P/S
JOHN FORSYTHE - P
JODI FOSTER (SEMI NUDE)
JODIE FOSTER - P/S
MEG FOSTER - P/S
SAMANTHA FOX - P
ROBERT FOXWORTH - P/S
REDD FOXX - P/S
ANN FRANCIS - P/S
ARLENE FRANCIS - P
GENIE FRANCIS - P
JAMES FRANCISCUS - P/S
TONY FRANCIOSA - P/S
GARY FRANK - P
BONNIE FRANKLIN - P
ARTHUR FRANZ - S
JANE FRAZEE - P
LYNN FREDERICK - P
MONA FREEMAN - P
ANNETTE FUNICELLO - P/S
ALLEN FUNT - P

EVA GABOR - P
ZSA ZSA GABOR - P
PETER GALLAGHER - P/S
RITA GAM - P
GRETA GARBO - P
VINCENT GARDENIA - P
AVA GARDNER - P
BEVERLY GARLAND - P
JAMES GARNER - P/S
TERI GARR - P
VITTORIO GASSMAN - P/S
JOHN GAVIN - P
BEN GAZZARA - P
MICHAEL GAZZO - S
TONY GEARY - P

LINDA DAY GEORGE - P
PHYLLIS GEORGE - P
GIL GERARD - P
RICHARD GERE - P
GIANCARLO GIANNINI - S
CINDY GIBB - P
MARLA GIBBS - P
HENRY GIBSON - P
MEL GIBSON - P/S
WYNN GIBSON - P
JOHN GIELGUD - P
MELISSA GILBERT - P
JACK GILFORD - S
HERMIONE GINGOLD - P
LILLIAN GISH - P
MICHAEL GLASER - P/S
SCOTT GLENN - P
SHARON GLESS - P
MARK GODDARD - P
PAULETTE GODDARD - P
WHOOPI GOLDBERG - P
GALE GORDON - P
FRANK GORSHIN - P
LOU GOSSETT - P
FARLEY GRANGER - P
STEWART GRANGER - P
LEE GRANT - P/S
BONITA GRANVILLE - P
PETER GRAVES - P
ERIN GRAY - P
LINDA GRAY - P
KATHRYN GRAYSON - P
LORNE GREENE - P
SHECKY GREENE - P
JANE GREER - P
ROSE GREGARIO - P
ANDRE GREGORY - P/S
JOEL GREY - P
PAM GRIER - P/S
ANDY GRIFFITH - P/S
TAMMY GRIMES - P
GEORGE GRIZZARD - P/S
CHARLES GRODIN - P
MICHAEL GROSS - P
HARRY GUARDINO - P
ROBERT GUILLAUME - P
ALEC GUINNESS - P
STEVE GUTTENBURG - P
FRED GWYNNE - P

SHELLY HACK - P
GENE HACKMAN - P/S
JULIE HAGERTY - P
DAN HAGGERTY - P
LARRY HAGMAN - P

BARBARA HALE - P
MONTE HALE - P
JACKIE EARL HALEY - P
HUNTZ HALL - P
LUKE HALPIN - P/S
VERONICA HAMEL - P
ANTHONY HAMILTON - P
GEORGE HAMILTON - P/S
LEIGH HAMILTON - P/S
HARRY HAMLIN - P/S
SUSAN HAMPSHIRE - P/S
DARRYL HANNAH - P
TESS HARPER - P
VALERIE HARPER - P
PAT HARRINGTON - P
BARBARA HARRIS - P
GREG HARRISON - P
JULIE HARRIS - P/S
PHIL HARRIS - P
REX HARRISON - P
REX HARRISON
(DR DOOLITTLE)
RICHARD HARRIS - P/S
KATHERINE HARROLD - P
JOHN HART - P
SUSAN HART - P
VERONICA HART - P
MARIETTE HARTLEY - P
DAVID HARTMAN - P
LISA HARTMAN - P
DAVID HASSELHOFF - P
MARILYN HASSETT - P/S
SIGNE HASSO - P
RICHARD HATCH - P
RUTGER HAUER - P
WINGS HAUSER - P
JUNE HAVER - P
JUNE HAVOC - P
GOLDIE HAWN - P/S
ALEXANDRA HAY - P
STERLING HAYDEN - P/S
HELEN HAYES - P
ROBERT HAYS - P
MARY HEALY - P
MYRON HEALY - P
JOHN HEARD - P/S
JOEY HEATHERTON - P
EILEEN HECKART - P
TIPPI HEDREN - P
SUSAN HELFOND - P/S
MARIEL HEMINGWAY - P/S
DAVID HEMMINGS - P
FLORENCE HENDERSON - P
GLORIA HENDRY - P
PAUL HENREID - P
BUCK HENRY - P
GREG HENRY - P/S
PAM HENSLEY - P
AUDREY HEPBURN - P/S
KATHARINE HEPBURN - P/S

GLENN FORD

LORNE GREENE

REX HARRISON

C. THOMAS HOWELL

DON JOHNSON

LYNN-HOLLY JOHNSON

EDWARD HERMANN - P
BARBARA HERSHEY - P/S
IRENE HERVEY - S
HOWARD HESSMAN - P
CHARLTON HESTON - P/S
CHARLTON HESTON (BEN HUR)
ANNE HEYWOOD - P/S
ARTHUR HILL - P
BENNIE HILL - P
DANA HILL - S
TERRENCE HILL - P/S
JOHN HILLERMAN - P
WENDY HILLER - P
PAT HINGLE - P
JUDD HIRSCH - P
EDDIE HODGES - P/S
DUSTIN HOFFMAN - P
DUSTIN HOFFMAN (TOOTSIE)
HAL HOLBROOK - P/S
HAL HOLBROOK (ABE LINCOLN)
SARAH HOLCOMB - P/S
REBECCA HOLDEN - P
JEFFREY HOLDER - P
EARL HOLLIMAN - P
STERLING HOLLOWAY - P
CELESTE HOLM - P
JENNIFER HOLT - P
BOB HOPE - P/S
ANTHONY HOPKINS - P
BO HOPKINS - P/S
DENNIS HOPPER - P/S
LEE HORSLEY - P
JOHN HOUSEMAN - P
KEN HOWARD - P
RON HOWARD - P
SUSAN HOWARD - P
TREVOR HOWARD - P
C THOMAS HOWELL - P
MARK HOWELL - P/S
SALLY ANN HOWES - P
SEASON HUBLEY - P
MARY BETH HUGHES - P
DIANE HULL - P
GAYLE HUNNICUT - P
MARSHA HUNT - P
KHAKI HUNTER - S
KIM HUNTER - P
TAB HUNTER - P
PAM HUNTINGTON - S
ISABELLE HUPPERT - P/S
MARY BETH HURT - P/S
OLIVIA HUSSEY - P
RUTH HUSSEY - P
JOHN HUSTON - P
BETTY HUTTON - P
LAUREN HUTTON - P
TIM HUTTON - P/S

MARTHA HYER - P

IMAN - P/S
JILL IRELAND - P/S
JOHN IRELAND - P
JEREMY IRONS - P/S
AMY IRVING - P/S

ANN JACKSON - P/S
GLENDA JACKSON - P/S
KATE JACKSON - P
SHERRY JACKSON - P/S
RICHARD JAECKEL - P
JOHN JAMES - P
CONRAD JANIS - P
GLORIA JEAN - P
ANN JEFFRIES - P
FRAN JEFFRIES - P
RITA JENRETTE - P
KAREN JENSEN - P
MAREN JENSEN - P/S
ADELE JERGENS - P
ANN JILLIAN - P
ZITA JOHANN - P
I S JOHAR - P
GLYNIS JOHNS - P
ARTE JOHNSON - P
BEN JOHNSON - P/S
DOROTHY JOHNSON - P
LYNN-HOLLY JOHNSON - P
MICHELLE JOHNSON - P
VAN JOHNSON - P/S
DEAN JONES - P/S
GRACE JONES - P
JAMES EARL JONES - P
JENNIFER JONES - P
L Q JONES - P
SAM J JONES - P
SHIRLEY JONES - P
TOMMY JONES - P
LOUIS JOURDAN - P
BRENDA JOYCE - P
CALVIN JUNG - P

MADELINE KAHN - P/S
STEVE KANALY - P
GABE KAPLAN - P/S

VALERIE KAPRISKY - P
ALEX KARRAS - P
ANNA KASHFI - P
WILLIAM KATT - P
CHRISTINE KAUFMAN - P/S
STACY KEACH - P/S
DIANE KEATON - P/S
RUBY KEELER - P
HARVEY KEITEL - P
BRIAN KEITH - P/S
DAVID KEITH - P
SALLY KELLERMAN - P/S
DE FORREST KELLY - P
GENE KELLY - P
GENE KELLY
(SINGING IN THE RAIN)
NANCY KELLY - P
PAULA KELLY - P
SUZY KENDALL - P
ARTHUR KENNEDY - P/S
GEORGE KENNEDY - P/S
ISAAC KENNEDY - P
JAYNE KENNEDY - P
DEBORAH KERR - P
LANCE KERWIN - P
EVELYN KEYES - P/S
PERSIS KHAMBATTA - P
MARGOT KIDDER - P
RICHARD KIEL - P/S
RICHARD KILEY - P
ALAN KING - P
ANDREA KING - P
JOHN KING - P
PERRY KING - P
BEN KINGSLEY - P
KLAUS KINSKI - P
NASTASSIA KINSKI - P
NASTASSIA KINSKI
(SEMI NUDE)
GEORGE KIRBY - P
PHYLLIS KIRK - P
EARTHA KITT - P
WERNER KLEMPERER - P
KEVIN KLINE - P
JACK KLUGMAN - P
HILDEGARDE KNEF - P
EVELYN KNIGHT - P
JUNE KNIGHT - P
SHIRLEY KNIGHT - P
DON KNOTTS - P
ELSIE KNOX - P
JON KORKES - P
HARVEY KORMAN - P
APOLLONIA KOTERO - P
YAPHET KOTTO - P/S
CONNIE KRESKI - P
ALICE KRIGE - P
SYLVIA KRISTEL - P
KRIS KRISTOFFERSON - P/S
SWOOZIE KURTZ - P
NANCY KWAN - P/S

LAURA LA PLANTE - P
LASH LA RUE - P
CHERYL LADD - P
HEDY LAMARR - P
HEDY LAMARR (NUDE)
DOROTHY LAMOUR - P
BURT LANCASTER - P/S
PAUL LAND - P/S
MARTIN LANDAU - P
AUDREY LANDERS - P
JUDY LANDERS - P/S
LORRAINE LANDON - P
MICHAEL LANDON - P
DIANE LANE - P
PRISCILLA LANE - P
ROCKY LANE - P
SUE ANN LANGDON - P
HOPE LANGE - P
JESSICA LANGE - P/S
KELLY LANGE - P
FRANK LANGELLA - P/S
ANGELA LANSBURY - P
ROBERT LANSING - P
LOUISE LASSER - P
TOM LAUGHLIN - P
PIPER LAURIE - P
DALIAH LAVI - P
LINDA LAVIN - P
VICKI LAWRENCE - P
GEORGE LAZENBY - P
KELLY LE BROCK - P
PAUL LE MAT - S
GLORIA LE ROY - P
HAL LE ROY - P
CLORIS LEACHMAN - P/S
AMANDA LEAR - NUDE
MICHAEL LEARNED - P
FRANCIS LEDERER - P
CHRISTOPHER LEE - P/S
MICHELLE LEE - P
PINKY LEE - P
JANET LEIGH - P
JACK LEMMON - P/S
KAY LENZ - P
JOAN LESLIE - P
JERRY LESTER - P
AL LEWIS - P
EMMANUEL LEWIS - P
JERRY LEWIS - P/S
RON LIEBMAN - P/S
HAL LINDEN - P
JENNIE LINDEN - S
VIVECA LINDFORS - P

STACY KEACH

CHERYL LADD

AUDREY LANDERS

ROB LOWE

SUSAN LUCCI

NANCY MC KEON

PAUL LINKE - P
LARRY LINVILLE - P
PEGGY LIPTON - P
VERNA LISI - P/S
JOHN LITHGOW - P
CLEAVON LITTLE - P
RICH LITTLE - P
BOB LIVINGSTON - P
CHRISTOPHER LLOYD - P
TONY LO BIANCO - P
SONDRA LOCKE - P
JUNE LOCKHART - P
HEATHER LOCKLEAR - P
JACQUELINE LOGAN - P
GINA LOLLOBRIGIDA - P/S
HERBERT LOM - P/S
JULIE LONDON - P/S
PAM LONG - P
SHELLY LONG - P/S
CLAUDINE LONGET - P
MICHEL LONSDALE - P/S
JACK LORD - P
SOPHIA LOREN - P/S
DOROTHY LOUDON - P
TINA LOUISE - P
LINDA LOVELACE - P
ROB LOWE - P
MYRNA LOY - P/S
SUSAN LUCCI - P
LORNA LUFT - P
KEYE LUKE - P
JOHN LUND - P
IDA LUPINO - P
JIMMY LYDON - P
CAROL LYNLEY - P
SUE LYON - P

JAMES MAC ARTHUR - P
ALI MAC GRAW - P/S
SHIRLEY MAC LAINE - P/S
PETER MAC LEAN - P/S
FRED MAC MURRAY - P/S
PATRICK MAC NEE - P
RALPH MACCHIO - P
GUY MADISON - P
GEORGE MAHARIS - P
JOCK MAHONEY - P/S
JOCK MAHONEY (TARZAN)
LEE MAJORS - P
KARL MALDEN - P/S
DOROTHY MALONE - P
ROBERT MANDAN - P
ROBERT MANDAN - P
SILVANO MANGANO - P
NANCY MARCHAND - P
JANET MARGOLIN - P
PHILIPPE MARLAND - P
JUNE MARLOWE - P
LUCY MARLOWE - P
MARION MARSH - P
E G MARSHALL - P/S
PENNY MARSHALL - P
ANNE MARIE MARTIN - P
DEAN MARTIN - P/S
ELSA MARTINELLI - P
MARY MARTIN - P
MARY MARTIN (PETER PAN)
LEE MARVIN - P/S
LEE MARVIN (CAT BALLOU)
MICHELLE MARVIN - P
MARSHA MASON - P/S
MARY ELIZABETH
MASTRANTOVIA - P
MARCELLO MASTROIANNI - P
JERRY MATHERS - P
TIM MATHESON - P
JOYCE MATHEWS - P
WALTER MATTHAU - P/S
VICTOR MATURE - P
JOHN MATUSZAK - P/S
ELAINE MAY - P
VIRGINIA MAYO - P
MIKE MAZURKI - P
PAUL MAZURSKY - P
ANDREA MC ARDLE - P
DIANE MC BAIN - P
DAVID MC CALLUM - P
IRISH MC CALLA - P
MERCEDES MC CAMBRIDGE - P
ANDREW MC CARTHY - P
KEVIN MC CARTHY - S
RUE MC CLANAHAN - P
RUE MC CLANAHAN - P
LEIGH MC CLOSKY - P
DOUG MC CLURE - P
MAUREEN MC CORMICK - P
PAT MC CORMICK - P
PATTY MC CORMICK - P
SIMON MC CORKINDALE - P
JOEL MC CREA - P/S
MALCOLM MC DONALD - P
RODDY MC DOWELL - P/S
SPANKY MC FARLAND - P
DARREN MC GAVIN - P
KELLY MC GILLIS - P
PATRICK MC GOOHAN - P
ELIZABETH MC GOVERN - P
MAUREEN MC GOVERN - P
DOROTHY MC GUIRE - P/S
JOHN MC INTYRE - P
GARDNER MC KAY - P
DOUG MC KEON - P
NANCY MC KEON - P
PHILIP MC KEON - P
LEO MC KERN - S
GAVIN MC LEOD - P

KEN MC MILLAN - P
STEPHEN MC NALLY - P/S
JIMMIE MC NICHOL - P
KRISTY MC NICHOL - P/S
BUTTERFLY MC QUEEN - P/S
AUDREY MEADOWS - P
JAYNE MEADOWS - P
ANN MEARA - P/S
RALPH MEEKER - P
MELINA MERCOURI - S
BURGESS MEREDITH - P/S
LEE MEREDITH - P
LEE MERIWETHER - P
UNA MERKEL - P
DINA MERRILL - P
ANN-LAURE MEURY - P
TOSHIRO MIFUNE - P
ALYSSA MILANO - P
JOANNA MILES - P
SARAH MILES - P/S
SYLVIA MILES - P
VERA MILES - P
PENELOPE MILFORD - S
TOMAS MILIAN - P
ANN MILLER - P
DENNIS MILLER (TARZAN)
PATSY RUTH MILLER - P
DONNA MILLS - P
HAYLEY MILLS - P
JOHN MILLS - P
YVETTE MIMIEUX - P
LIZA MINNELLI - P/S
CAMERON MITCHELL - P
JIM MITCHUM - P/S
ROBERT MITCHUM - P/S
RICARDO MONTALBAN - P/S
YVES MONTAND - P
ELIZABETH MONTGOMERY - P
GEORGE MONTGOMERY - P/S
CLEO MOORE - P
COLLEEN MOORE - P
CONSTANCE MOORE - P
DEMI MOORE - P
DUDLEY MOORE - P/S
MARY TYLER MOORE - P/S
ROGER MOORE - P/S
TERRY MOORE - P
ERIN MORAN - P
LOIS MORAN - P
RITA MORENO - P/S
HARRY MORGAN - P
CATHY MORIARTY - P
MICHAEL MORIARTY - P
LOUISA MORITZ - S
ROBERT MORLEY - P
GREG MORRIS - P
HOWARD MORRIS - P
PATRICIA MORRISON - P
ROBERT MORSE - P/S
DONNY MOST - P/S

MARY MURPHY - P
MICHAEL MURPHY - P
BILL MURRAY - P
DON MURRAY - P/S
JAN MURRAY - P/S
ORNELLA MUTI - P
JEAN MUIR - P
DIANA MULDAUR - P
KATE MULGREW - P
EDWARD MULHARE - P
MARTIN MULL - P/S
CAROLYN MUNRO - P

JIM NABORS - P
GEORGE NADER - P/S
ALAN NAPIER - P
KITTEN NATIVIDAD - P
JAMES NAUGHTON - P
PATRICIA NEAL - P
POLA NEGRI - P
NOEL NEILL- P
KATE NELLIGAN - P/S
BARRY NELSON - P
FRANCO NERO - P/S
LOIS NETTLETON - P
BOB NEWHART - P
ANTHONY NEWLEY - P
BARRY NEWMAN - P/S
LARRAINE NEWMAN - P
NANETTE NEWMAN - P
PAUL NEWMAN - P/S
JULIE NEWMAR - P/S
JACK NICHOLSON - P/S
KELLY NICHOLS - P
MICHELLE NICHOLS - P
BRIGETTE NIELSEN-STALLONE
LESLIE NIELSEN - P
LEONARD NIMOY - P/S
CHRIS NOEL - S
NICK NOLTE - P/S
CHRISTOPHER NORRIS - P
CHUCK NORRIS - P/S
JAY NORTH - P/S
SHEREE NORTH - P
RICHARD NORTON - S
KIM NOVAK - P/S
NURYEV - P/S
FRANCE NUYEN - P

HUGH O'BRIAN - P

EDDIE MURPHY

CHRISTOPHER NORRIS

SHEREE NORTH

CARROLL O'CONNOR

AL PACINO

SUSAN SARANDON

MARGARET O'BRIEN - S
CARROLL O'CONNOR - P
DONALD O'CONNOR - P/S
GLYNNIS O'CONNOR - P
NELL O'DAY - P
MARTHA O'DRISCOLL - P
JACK O'HALLORAN - P
MAUREEN O'HARA - P
CATLIN O'HEANNEY - S
MILES O'KEEFE - P
JENNIFER O'NEIL - P/S
PATRICK O'NEIL - P
RYAN O'NEIL - P/S
TATUM O'NEIL - P/S
MAUREEN O'SULLAVAN - P
RANDI OAKES - P
SUSAN OLIVER - P
SIR LAURENCE OLIVIER - P/S
NANCY OLSON - P
MICHAEL ONTKEAN - P/S
BILLY ORTEGA - S
CATHERINE OXENBERG - P

AL PACINO - P/S
ANITA PAGE - P
GENEVIEVE PAGE - P/S
GERALDINE PAGE - P
DEBRA PAGET - P/S
JANIS PAIGE - P
JACK PALANCE - P/S
BETSY PALMER - P
IRENE PAPPAS - P
ELEANOR PARKER - P
FESS PARKER - P
JAMESON PARKER - P/S
BARBARA PARKINS - P
MICHAEL PARKS - S
LESLIE PARRISH - P/S
ESTELLE PARSONS - P
NANCY PARSONS - P
MANDY PATINKIN - P
LORNA PATTERSON - P
JOHN PAYNE - P
GREGORY PECK - P/S
LISA PELIKAN - P
CHRISTOPHER PENN - P
SEAN PENN - P
GEORGE PEPPARD - P
ANTHONY PERKINS - P/S
GIGI PERREAU - P
VALERIE PERRINE - P
NEHEMIAH PERSOFF - P
DONNA PESCOW - P
JOE PESCOW - P/S
BERNADETTE PETERS - P
BROCK PETERS - P
JOANNA PETTIT - P
MICHELLE PFEIFFER - P
JOANNE PFLUG - P
MARY PHILBIN - P
MC KENZIE PHILLIPS - P
MICHELLE PHILLIPS - P
SIAN PHILLIPS - P
CINDY PICKETT - P/S
MOLLY PICON - S
MARIE FRANCE PISIER - P/S
MARY KAY PLACE - P
DONALD PLEASANCE - P
SUZANNE PLESHETTE - P
JOAN PLOWRIGHT - P
CHRISTOPHER PLUMMER - P/S
SIDNEY POITIER - P/S
MICHAEL J POLLARD - S
MARKIE POST - P
TOM POSTON - P
ANNIE POTTS - P
JANE POWELL - P
STEFANIE POWERS - P
PAULA PRENTISS - P/S
PRISCILLA PRESLEY - P
HARVE PRESNELL - P
VINCENT PRICE - P
VICTORIA PRINCIPAL - P
EILEEN PRINGLE - P
DOROTHY PROVINE - S
JULIETTE PROWSE - P
RICHARD PRYOR - P/S
LEE PURCELL - P
SARAH PURCELL - P
LINDA PURL - P/S

DENNIS QUAID - P/S
RANDY QUAID - P
ANTHONY QUALE - P/S
KATHLEEN QUINLAN - P
AILEEN QUINN - P
ANTHONY QUINN - P/S

GILDA RADNER - P
DEBORAH RAFFIN - P
STEVE RAILSBACK - P
LUISE RAINER - P
CHRISTINA RAINES - P
ELLA RAINES - P
JOHN RAITT - P
ESTHER RALSTON - P

VERA RALSTON - P
CHARLOTTE RAMPLING - P/S
TONY RANDALL - P/S
ALDO RAY - P/S
MARTHA RAYE - P
ROBERT REDFORD - P/S
LYNN REDGRAVE - P
VANESSA REDGRAVE - P
JERRY REED - P/S
OLIVER REED - P
PAMELA REED - P
CHRISTOPHER REEVE - P
STEVE REEVES - P
CARL REINER - P/S
ROB REINER - P
ROB REINER - P
ANN REINKING - P
LEE REMICK - P/S
KELLY RENO - P/S
TOMMY RETTIG - P
ANNE REVERE - P
DOROTHY REVERE - P
BURT REYNOLDS - P/S
DEBBIE REYNOLDS - P/S
MADELINE RHUE - P
DON RICKLES - P
COLLEEN RILEY - S
JEANNINE RILEY - P
JOHN RITTER - P/S
CHITA RIVERA - P
JOAN RIVERS - P
JASON ROBARDS - P/S
CLIFF ROBERTSON - P/S
DALE ROBERTSON - P
DORIS ROBERTS - P
ERIC ROBERTS - P
PERNELL ROBERTS - P
RACHEL ROBERTS - P
TANYA ROBERTS - P
ALEX ROCCO - P
EUGENE ROCHE - P
GINGER ROGERS - P
ROY ROGERS - P
WAYNE ROGERS - P
GILBERT ROLAND - P
RUTH ROMAN - P
CEASAR ROMERO - P
MICKEY ROONEY - P/S
ISABELLA ROSALINI - P
ROSE MARIE - P
KATHARINE ROSS - P/S
RICHARD ROUNDTREE - P
MISTY ROWE - P
GINA ROWLANDS - P
JANICE RULE - P
BARBARA RUSH - P
JANE RUSSELL - P/S
JOHN RUSSELL - P
KURT RUSSELL - P
MARK RUSSELL - P
ANN RUTHERFORD - P
PEGGY RYAN - P

EVA MARIE SAINT - P
SUSAN SAINT JAMES - P
SOUPY SALES - P/S
EMMA SAMMS - P
OLGA SAN JUAN - P
CHRIS SARANDON - S
SUSAN SARANDON - P
MICHAEL SARRAZIN - P
JOHN SAVAGE - P
TELLY SAVALES - P
JOHN SAXON - P
DIANE SCARWID - P
NATALIE SCHAFER - P
ROY SCHEIDER - P/S
MAXIMILIAN SCHELL - P
JOHN SCHNEIDER - P
MARIA SCHNEIDER - P/S
ROMY SCHNEIDER - P
BOB SCHOOT - S
MARIA SCHRIBER - P
RICKY SCHROEDER - P/S
ARNOLD SCHWARZENEGGER - P
ARNOLD SCHWARZENEGGER (CONAN)
PAUL SCOFIELD - P
TRACY SCOGGINS - P
ELIZABETH SCOTT - P
FRED SCOTT - P
GEORGE C SCOTT - P/S
MARTHA SCOTT - P
GEORGE SEGAL - P/S
SEKA - P
DAVID SELBY - P
CONNIE SELLECA - P
TOM SELLECK - P
MICHAEL SERRAULT - S
ANNE SEYMOUR - P
JANE SEYMOUR - P
OMAR SHARIF - P/S
RAY SHARKEY - P/S
CORNELIA SHARPE - P
KAREN SHARPE - P
WILLIAM SHATNER - P
WALLACE SHAWN - S
ALLEY SHEEDY - P
MARTIN SHEEN - P/S
CYBIL SHEPHERD - P
SAM SHEPHERD - P
BROOKE SHIELDS - P/S
JOANNE SHIMKUS - P
TALIA SHIRE - P/S

GEORGE C. SCOTT

JANE SEYMOUR

TALIA SHIRE

SYLVESTER STALLONE

JOHN STAMOS

MARY STEENBERGEN

ANNE SHIRLEY - P
SYLVIA SIDNEY - P
GREGORY SIERRA - P
JEAN SIMMONS - P/S
SIMONE SIMONE - P
O J SIMPSON - P
FRANK SINATRA - P/S
FRANK SINATRA (DIRTY DINGUS MAGEE)
LORI SINGER - P
MARC SINGER - P
PENNY SINGLETON - P
RED SKELTON - P/S
TOM SKERRITT - P
HELEN SLATER (SUPERGIRL)
HELEN SLATER - P
ALEXIS SMITH - P
BUBBA SMITH - P
BUFFALO BOB SMITH
JACQUELINE SMITH - P
MAGGIE SMITH - P/S
ROBERT SMITH - P
ROGER SMITH - P/S
SHELLY SMITH - P
CARRIE SNODGRASS - P
LEIGH SNOWDEN - P
ELKE SOMMER - P
JOANIE SOMMERS - P
SUZANNE SOMMERS - P
ANN SOTHERN - P
DAVID SOUL - P
CATHERINE SPAAK - P
SISSY SPACEK - P/S
CAMILLA SPARV - P
CLINTON SPILSBURY (LONE RANGER)
G D SPRADLIN - P
LILI ST CYR - P
RAYMOND ST JACQUES - P
JILL ST JOHN - P
ROBERT STACK - P
ROBERT STACK (ELLIOTT NESS)
SLYVESTER STALLONE - P/S
SYLVESTER STALLONE (RAMBO)
SYLVESTER STALLONE (ROCKY)
JOHN STAMOS - P
TERENCE STAMP - P
LIONEL STANDER - P
ARNOLD STANG - P
EILEEN STANLEY - P
HARRY DEAN STANTON - P
BARBARA STANWYCK - P/S
JEAN STAPLETON - P
MAUREEN STAPLETON - P
RINGO STARR - P/S
BOB STEELE - P
MARY STEENBERGEN - P/S
ROD STEIGER - P/S
DAVID STEINBERG - P
LINDA STERLING - P
ROBERT STERLING - P
TISHA STERLING - P
ANDREW STEVENS - P
CONNIE STEVENS - P
K T STEVENS - P
MC LEAN STEVENSON - P
PARKER STEVENSON - P
SHAWN STEVENS - S
STELLA STEVENS - P
JAMES STEWART - P
JAMES STEWART (GLENN MILLER)
PAULA STEWART - S
PEGGY STEWART - P
DAVID OGDEN STIERS - P
JERRY STILLER - P/S
DEAN STOCKWELL - P
GUY STOCKWELL - P/S
GAIL STORM - P
TEMPEST STORM - P
BEATRICE STRAIGHT - P
SUSAN STRASBERG - P
ROBIN STRASSER - P
PETER STRAUSS - P
MERYL STREEP - P
BARBRA STREISAND - P/S
WOODY STRODE - P
SALLY STRUTHERS - P
AMY STRYKER - S
BARRY SULLIVAN - P
DONALD SUTHERLAND - P/S
JANET SUZMAN - P
PAT SUZUKI - P
GABRIEL SWANN - P/S
PATRICK SWAYZE - P
INGA SWENSON - P
LORETTA SWIT - P
CYNTHIA SYKES - P
SYLVIA SYMS - S

MR T - P
GEORGE TAKEI - P
RUSS TAMBLYN - P
JESSICA TANDY - P
VIC TAYBACK - P
ELIZABETH TAYLOR - P/S
LEIGH TAYLOR-YOUNG - P
ROD TAYLOR - P
VERA TEASDALE - P
SHIRLEY TEMPLE - P

ALICE TERRY - P
TERRY-THOMAS - P/S
LAUREN TEWES - P
URSULA THIESS - P
ROY THINNES - P
DANNY THOMAS - P
MARLO THOMAS - P
PHILIP MICHAEL THOMAS - P
RICHARD THOMAS - P
TIM THOMERSON - S
JACK THOMPSON - P
LEA THOMPSON - P
GRETA THYSSEN - P
CHERYL TIEGS - P
GENE TIERNEY - P
MEG TILLY - P
CHARLENE TILTON - P
ANN TODD - P
UGO TOGNAZZI - P/S
LILY TOMLIN - P/S
LILY TOMLIN (ERNESTINE)
ANGEL TOMPKINS - P
REGIS TOOMEY - P
TOPOL - S
RIP TORN - P
RAQUEL TORRES - P
AUDREY TOTTER - P
CONSTANCE TOWERS - P
DANIEL TRAVANTI - P
JOHN TRAVOLTA - P/S
CLAIRE TREVOR - P
ANN TURKEL - P
KATHLEEN TURNER - P/S
LANA TURNER - P/S
RITA TUSHINGHAM - P
TWIGGY - P
CICELY TYSON - P
LIV ULLMAN - P
ROBERT URICH - P
PETER USTINOV - P/S

BRENDA VACCARO - P/S
KAREN VALENTINE - P
RAF VALLONE - P
JOAN VAN ARK - P
LEE VAN CLEEF - P/S
TRISH VAN DEVERE - P
MAMIE VAN DOREN - P
JOHM VAN DREELEN - P
DICK VAN DYKE - P/S
JO VAN FLEET - P
DICK VAN PATTEN - P
JIMMY VAN PATTEN - P
JOYCE VAN PATTEN - P
VINCE VAN PATTEN - S
DEBRA VAN VOLKENBURGH
DIANE VARSI - P
ROBERT VAUGHN - P
LENO VENTURA - P
GWEN VERDON - P
BEN VEREEN - P
MARTHA VICKERS - P
ROBERT VIHARO - P
HERVE VILLECHAIZE - P
JAN-MICHAEL VINCENT -
MITCH VOGEL - P
JON VOIGHT - P/S
MAX VON SYDOW - P/S

LYLE WAGGONER - P
LINDSAY WAGNER - P
ROBERT WAGNER - P
KEN WAHL - P
CHRISTOPHER WALKEN
CLINT WALKER - P
JIMMY WALKER - P
NANCY WALKER - P
DEE WALLACE - P/S
ELI WALLACH - P/S
JEAN WALLACE - P
RAY WALSTON - P
JESSICA WALTER - P
JULIE WALTERS - P
RACHEL WARD - P
JACK WARDEN - P/S
JENNIFER WARREN - P
LESLIE ANN WARREN - P/S
DIANE WARWICK - P
DENZEL WASHINGTON - P
SAM WATERSTON - P
DAVID WAYNE - P
PAT WAYNE - P/S
CARL WEATHERS - P/S
DENNIS WEAVER - P
SIGOURNEY WEAVER - P
PEGGY WEBBER - P
ROBERT WEBBER - P
RAQUEL WELCH - P/S
TAWNE WELCH - P
TUESDAY WELD - P
DAWN WELLS - P
ADAM WEST - P
ARLENE WHELAN - P
LISA WHELCHEL - P
STUART WHITMAN - P/S
JAMES WHITMORE - P
JAMES WHITMORE
(WILL ROGERS)
RICHARD WIDMARK - P/S
LARRY WILCOX - P
CORNEL WILDE - P

BARBARA STANWYCK

JAMES STEWART

HEATHER THOMAS

GUY WILLIAMS

FLIP WILSON

GENE WILDER - P/S
JUNE WILKINSON - P
ANDY WILLIAMS - P/S
BILLY DEE WILLIAMS - P/S
CINDY WILLIAMS - P
CLARENCE WILLIAMS, III - P
EDY WILLIAMS - P
EMLYN WILLIAMS - P
ESTHER WILLIAMS - P
FRED WILLIAMSON - P
GUY WILLIAMS (ZORRO)
HAL WILLIAMS - P
JO BETH WILLIAMS - P
NICOL WILLIAMSON - P
ROBIN WILLIAMS - P/S
TREAT WILLIAMS - P/S
BRUCE WILLIS - P
FLIP WILSON - P
LOIS WILSON - P
MARIE WINDSOR - P
PAUL WINFIELD - P
OPRAH WINFREY - P
DEBRA WINGER - P
HENRY WINKLER - P
JONATHAN WINTERS - P/S
ROLAND WINTERS - P
SHELLY WINTERS - P/S
JANE WITHERS - P
LANA WOOD - P/S
JAMES WOODS - P
JOANNE WOODWARD - P/S
JO ANN WORLEY - P
IRENE WORTH - P/S
FAY WRAY - P/S
TERESA WRIGHT - P
JANE WYATT - P
GRETCHEN WYLER - P
JANE WYMAN - P/S
PATRICE WYMORE - P
DANA WYNTER - P

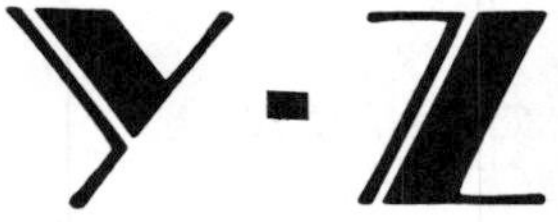

MICHAEL YORK - P/S
BURT YOUNG - P/S
LORETTA YOUNG - P
ROBERT YOUNG - P
PIA ZADORA - P
JACKLYN ZEMAN - P
ANTHONY ZERBE - P
EFREM ZIMBALIST - P
STEPHANIE ZIMBALIST - P
VERA ZORINA - P

SHELLY WINTERS

JOANNE WOODWARD

JANE WYMAN

MUSICAL PERFORMERS

All Portrait Photographs
$1.00 each

MARION ANDERSON
ANDREWS SISTERS
PAUL ANKA
ADAM ANT
TONI ARDEN
DESI ARNAZ, SR
FRANKIE AVALON
AVERAGE WHITE BAND

BURT BACHARACH
JOAN BAEZ
PEARL BAILEY
SHIRLEY BASSEY
BAY CITY ROLLERS
BEATLES
BEE GEES
HARRY BELAFONTE
PAT BENETAR
TONY BENNETT
IRVING BERLIN
LEONARD BERNSTEIN
TAKA BOOM
DEBBY BOONE
PAT BOONE
DAVID BOWIE
BOBBIE BREEN
TERESA BREWER
JACKSON BROWNE
ANITA BRYANT

KIM CANTRELL
LANA CANTRELL
CAPT & TENNILLE
IRENE CARA
VICKIE CARR
DIAHANN CARROLL
NELL CARTER
SHAWN CASSIDY
RAY CHARLES
CHARLIE
CHARO
CHUBBY CHECKER
CHER
JUNE CHRISTIE
DICK CLARK
PETULA CLARK
ROSEMARY CLOONEY
JOE COCKER
NATALIE COLE
BETTY COMDEN & ADOLPH GREEN
PERRY COMO
ALICE COOPER
ELVIS COSTELLO
CHRISTOPHER CROSS

ROGER DALTRY
VIC DAMONE
BILLY DANIELS
JAMES DARREN
JOHN DAVIDSON
MILES DAVIS
PATTI DAVIS
DENNIS DAY
DORIS DAY
JACKIE DE SHANNON
DEF LEPPARD
JOHN DENVER
JOHNNY DESMOND
NEIL DIAMOND
DION
FATS DOMINO
BOB DYLAN

SHEENA EASTON
BILLY ECKSTINE
JOE EGAN

FABIAN
LOLA FALANA
MARK FARNER
JOSE FELICIANO
EDDIE FISHER
ELLA FITZGERALD
PETER FRAMPTON

TONY BENNETT

PAT BOONE

NELL CARTER

GLADYS KNIGHT

LIBERACE

MADONNA

SERGIO FRANCHI
CONNIE FRANCIS
GARY FRANK
ARETHA FRANKLIN

ART GARFUNKEL
BOBBY GENTRY
BOY GEORGE
STAN GETZ
ANDY GIBB
GEORGIA GIBBS
BOBBY GOLDSBORO
ROBERT GOULET
GOGI GRANT
BUDDY GRECO

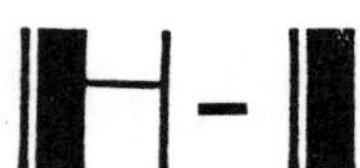

CONNIE HAINES
HALL & OATES
MARVIN HAMLISH
HERBIE HANCOCK
GEORGE HARRISON
DEBBIE HARRY
ISAAC HAYES
JERRY HERMAN
EDDIE HODGES
LENA HORNE
WHITNEY HOUSTON
ENGELBERT HUMPERDINCK
JULIO IGLESIAS

MICHAEL JACKSON
MICK JAGGER
JONI JAMES
HERB JEFFRIES
JOAN JETT
BILLY JOEL
ELTON JOHN
QUINCY JONES

KITTY KALLEN
LAINIE KAZAN
B B KING
PHYLLIS KIRK
KISS
EARTHA KITT
GLADYS KNIGHT

FRANKIE LAINE
ABBE LANE
FRANCIS LANGFORD
CYNDI LAUPER
CAROL LAWRENCE
STEVE LAWRENCE
PEGGY LEE
JULIAN LENNON
JEFF LEPPER
HUEY LEWIS
JERRY LEE LEWIS
LIBERACE
LITTLE RICHARD
KENNY LOGGINS
JULIE LONDON
TRINI LOPEZ

MADONNA
HENRY MANCINI
CHUCK MANGIONE
BARRY MANILOW
AL MARTINO
TONY MARTIN
JOHNNY MATHIS
PAUL MC CARTNEY
MARILYN MC COO
BARBARA MC NAIR
MEATLOAF
MENUDO
BETTE MIDLER
MITCH MILLER
STEVE MILLER
STEPHANIE MILLS
LIZA MINNELLI
JAYE P MORGAN
ELLA MAE MORSE
PATRICE MUNSEL

PETER NERO
ANTHONY NEWLEY
JUICE NEWTON
OLIVIA NEWTON-JOHN
WAYNE NEWTON
STEVIE NICKS
TED NUGENT

HELEN O'CONNELL
ORIGINAL WEAVERS
DONNY OSMOND
MARIE OSMOND

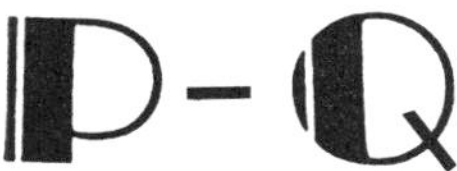

PATTI PAGE
ROY PARKER, JR
LUCIANO PAVORATTI
JOHNNY PAYCHECK
TEDDY PENDERGRASS
PETER, PAUL & MARY
ROBERT PLANT
ANDRE PREVIN
PRINCE
SUZI QUATRO

JOHN RAITT
LOU RAWLS
JOHNNY RAY
HELEN REDDY
LOU REED
DELLA REESE
LIONEL RICHIE
JEANNIE C RILEY
LINDA RONSTADT
DIANA ROSS
LEON RUSSELL
BOBBY RYDELL

SANDLER & YOUNG
TOMMY SANDS
BOZ SCAGGS
NEIL SEDAKA
BOBBY SHERMAN
ROBERTA SHERWOOD
DINAH SHORE
BEVERLY SILLS
PAUL SIMON
FRANK SINATRA
NANCY SINATRA
KEELY SMITH
SMOTHERS BROTHERS
JOANIE SOMMERS
DAVID SOUL
BRUCE SPRINGSTEEN
RICK SPRINGFIELD
JO STAFFORD
KAY STARR
RINGO STARR
TOMMY STEELE
CAT STEVENS
RAY STEVENS
ROD STEWART
DONNA SUMMER
SYLVIA

TONI TENNILLE
MERLE TRAVIS
TANYA TUCKER
TINA TURNER
BONNIE TYLER
LESLIE UGGAMS

JUNE VALI
EDDIE VAN HALEN
SYLVIE VARTON
SARAH VAUGHN
BENAY VENUTA
VILLAGE PEOPLE
BOBBY VINTON

PORTER WAGGONER
FRED WARING
FRAN WARREN
DIONNE WARWICK
ANDY WILLIAMS
PAUL WILLIAMS
NANCY WILSON
WOLFMAN JACK
FRANK ZAPPA

CHUCK MANGIONE

LUCIANO PAVAROTTI

PRINCE

JOHNNY CASH

EARL THOMAS CONLEY

AMY GRANT

COUNTRY & WESTERN STARS

All Portrait Photographs

$1.00 each

ALABAMA
BILL ANDERSON
JOHN ANDERSON
EDDY ARNOLD
CHET ATKINS
HOYT AXTON
ED BRUCE
GLEN CAMPBELL
CARLENE CARTER
JOHNNY CASH
ROY CLARK
JESSI COLTER
EARL THOMAS CONLEY
HELEN CORNELIUS
CHARLIE DANIELS
CHARLIE DANIELS BAND
MAC DAVIS
JIMMY DEAN
JOHN DENVER
JIMMIE DICKENS
EVERLY BROTHERS
FREDDIE FENDER
ERNIE FORD
JANE FRICKE
JERRY GARCIA
LARRY GATLIN
CRYSTAL GAYLE
VINCE GILL
GEORGE GOBEL
AMY GRANT
MERLE HAGGARD
TOM T HALL
GUS HARDIN
EMMY LOU HARRIS
HUDSON BROTHERS
BILL HUDSON
BRETT HUDSON
MARK HUDSON
BURL IVES
WAYLON JENNINGS
GEORGE JONES
THE JUDDS
PEE WEE KING
KRIS KRISTOFFERSON
BRENDA LEE
JERRY LEE LEWIS
LORETTA LYNN
BARBARA MANDRELL
LOUISE MANDRELL
KITTY MATTEA
ROGER MILLER
RONNIE MILSAP
GARY MORRIS
ANNE MURRAY
WILLIE NELSON
JIMMIE C NEWMAN
OAK RIDGE BOYS
ROY ORBISON
DOLLY PARTON
MINNIE PEARL
CARL PERKINS
WEBB PIERCE
RAY PRICE
CHARLIE PRIDE
EDDIE RABBIT
JERRY REED
CHARLIE RICH
RIDERS IN THE SKY
MARTY ROBBINS
JIMMIE RODGERS
KENNY ROGERS
JEAN SHEPARD
CARLY SIMON
RICKY SKAGGS
CARL SMITH
SYLVIA
THRASHER BROTHERS
MEL TILLIS
MERLE TRAVIS
ERNEST TUBB
CONWAY TWITTY
LEN WADE
KITTY WELLS
DOTTIE WEST
THE WHITES
KEITH WHITLEY
HANK WILLIAMS, JR
GARY WOLF
THE WRIGHT BROTHERS
TAMMY WYNETTE
GLEN YARBROUGH
FARON YOUNG

COWBOYS & COWGIRLS

All Portrait Photographs
$1.00 each

KAY ALDRIDGE
REX ALLEN
GENE AUTRY
SMITH BALLEW
JIM BANNON
DON "RED" BARRY
RICHARD BASEHART
REX BELL
TOM BERENGER
LYLE BETTGER
DAN BLOCKER
RICHARD BOONE
ADRIAN BOOTH
BILL BOYD
SCOTT BRADY
CHARLES BRONSON
RAND BROOKS
YUL BRYNNER
SMILEY BURNETTE
PAT BUTTRAM
JAMES CAAN
RORY CALHOUN
ROD CAMERON
YAKIMA CANNUTT
HARRY CAREY, JR
LEO CARRILLO
SUNSET CARSON
HOPALONG CASSIDY
CHUCK CONNORS
BUSTER CRABBE
KEN CURTIS
TONY CURTIS
JIM DAVIS - S
MYRNA DELL
RICHARD DENNING
JOHN DEREK
ANDY DEVINE
JAMES DRURY
CLINT EASTWOOD
JACK ELAM
DALE EVANS
RICHARD FARNSWORTH
GLENN FORD
TONY FRANCIOSA
ROBERT FULLER
JAMES GARNER
KIRBY GRANT
ANDY GRIFFITH
MONTE HALE
JACK HOLT
JENNIFER HOLT
BEN JOHNSON
BUCK JONES
VICTOR JORY
JOHN "DUSTY" KING
LASH LA RUE
ROCKY LANE
BOB LIVINGSTON
JOHNNY MAC BROWN
GUY MADISON
GEORGE MAHARIS
LEE MAJORS
DEAN MARTIN
LEE MARVIN
KEN MAYNARD
TIM MC COY
TOM MIX
GEORGE MONTGOMERY
CLAYTON MOORE
AUDIE MURPHY
DON MURRAY
NOEL NEILL
WILLIE NELSON
JACK PALANCE
GEORGE PEPPARD
JACK PERRIN
BROCK PETERS
SLIM PICKENS
DENVER PYLE
RONALD REAGAN
BURT REYNOLDS
TEX RITTER
CLIFF ROBERTSON
DALE ROBERTSON
ROY ROGERS
ROY ROGERS & DALE EVANS
JOHN RUSSELL
FRED SCOTT
RANDOLPH SCOTT
CAL SHRUM
DAVID SOUL
CLINTON SPILSBURY (LONE RANGER)
BARBARA STANWYCK
CHARLES STARRETT
LINDA STERLING
JIMMY STEWART
PEGGY STEWART
TOM TYLER
LEE VAN CLEEF
JIMMY WAKELY
CLINT WALKER
JOHN WAYNE
RAQUEL WELCH
WHIP WILSON

SMITH BALLEW

MYRNA DELL

ROGERS & EVANS

BERNARDO BERTOLUCCI

ALAN PAKULA

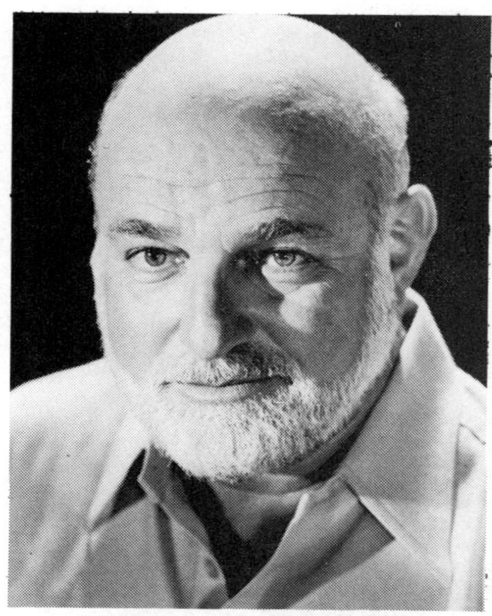

JOHN SCHLESSINGER

FILM & TV DIRECTORS

All Portrait Photographs
$1.00 each

LOU ADLER
JEAN-JACQUES ANNAUD
HAL ASHBY
JOHN G AVILSEN
JOHN BADHAM
RALPH BAKSHI
CARROLL BALLARD
INGMAR BERGMAN
BERNARDO BERTOLUCCI
TONY BILL
MEL BLANC
PETER BOGDANOVICH
JAMES CAAN
FRANK CAPRA
JOHN CARPENTER
ALLEN CARR
WILLIAM CASTLE
MICHAEL CIMENO
WALTER COBLENZ
FRANCIS COPPOLA
WILLIAM COWAN
DAN CURTIS
JOE DANTE
MARTIN DAVIDSON
DINO DE LAURENTIIS
BRIAN DE PALMA
JONATHAN DEMME
MICHAEL DEVILLE
CLIVE DONNER
RICHARD DONNER
RICHARD FLEISCHER
BRYAN FORBES
JOHN FOREMAN
GEORGE FORMAN
MILOS FORMAN
BOB FOSSE
JOHN FRANKENHEIMER
RICHARD FRANKLIN
COSTA GARVAS
LEWIS GILBERT
JEAN-LUC GODARD
ULA GROSBARD
GUY HAMILTON
RAY HARRYHAUSEN
JIM HENSEN
JOHN HUGHES
TIM HUNTER
JOHN IRVIN
JAMES JAMERSON
NORMAN JEWISON
LAMONT JOHNSON
JEREMY PAUL KAGAN
GARSON KANIN
STANLEY KUBRICK
DAVID LEAN
SERGIO LEONE
ART LINSON
SIDNEY LUMET
ROUBEN MAMOULIAN
ROBERT MARKOWITZ
LEO MC CAREY
VINCENT MINNELLI
RONALD NEAME
HAL NEEDHAM
MIKE NICHOLS
B W L NORTON
NOEL NOSSECK
ALAN PAKULA
ALAN PARKER
RICHARD PEARCE
LARRY PEERCE
ROMAN POLANSKI
SYDNEY POLLACK
OTTO PREMINGER
MICHAEL PRESSMAN
RICHARD QUINNE
KAREL RAISZ
ROB REINER
TONY RICHARDSON
MICHAEL RITCHIE
HAL ROACH
HERBERT ROSS
FRANKLIN J SCHAFFNER
JOHN SCHLESSINGER
PAUL SCHRADER
STEVE SHAGAN
JERRY SKOLIMOWSKI
STEVEN SPIELBERG
FRED C SULLIVAN
FRANCOIS TRUFFAUT
ROGER VADIM
KING VIDOR
JOSEPH WAMBAUGH
SOL ZAENTZ
FRANCO ZEFFIRELLI
HOWARD ZIFF
FRED ZINNEMAN

THE HONEYMOONERS

All Group Photographs

$1.00 each

ALL FOUR TAKING TRIP ON CRUISE SHIP
ALL FOUR DRINKING WINE AT KITCHEN TABLE
ALL FOUR IN KITCHEN
ALL FOUR ON BUS
ALL FOUR PERFORMING PLAY ON STAGE
ALL FOUR SINGING QUARTET
NORTON & KRAMDEN AT RESTAURANT COUNTER
NORTON TRYING TO PULL BOWLING BALL STUCK ON RALPH'S FINGER
NORTON EMERGING FROM SEWER
NORTON OPENING WALLET WITH TRIXIE LOOKING OVER SHOULDER
RALPH KRAMDEN PHOTO
RALPH & TRIXIE ARGUING OVER BOWLING BALL
RALPH GIVING TRIXIE BOUQUET OF FLOWERS
RALPH & NORTON LOOKING AT GIRLIE MAGAZINE
RALPH IN SPOLIGHT ALONE ON STAGE

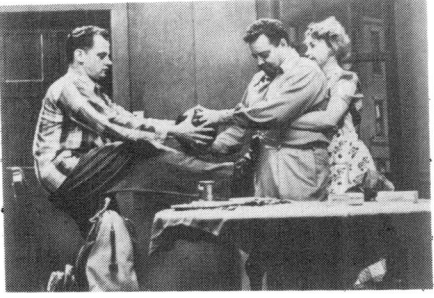

A-TEAM

ALICE

ALL IN THE FAMILY

TELEVISION & MOVIE CAST PHOTOS

$1.00 each

A-TEAM
ADAM 12
AFTER MASH
AIN'T MISBEHAVING
ALICE
ALL IN THE FAMILY
ALL'S FAIR
AVENGERS
BANACEK
BATMAN (BATMAN, ROBIN & VILLANS)
BEVERLY HILLBILLIES
BIG VALLEY
BONANZA
DANIEL BOONE
BRADY BUNCH
CAROL BURNETT SHOW
CAGNEY & LACEY
CHARLIE'S ANGELS (FARRAH FAWCETT)
CHARLIE'S ANGELS (TANYA ROBERTS)
CHARLIE'S ANGELS (CHERYL LADD)
CHEERS
THE COSBY SHOW
DALLAS
DONNY & MARIE SHOW
DUKES OF HAZZARD
DYNASTY
F B I
FACTS OF LIFE
FANTASY ISLAND
FATHER KNOWS BEST
FAMILY FEUD (RICHARD DAWSON)
FLAMINGO ROAD
FLYING NUN
GHOST & MRS MUIR
GOLDEN GIRLS
LOU GRANT
GREATEST AMERICAN HERO
GREEN ACRES
ANDY GRIFFITH SHOW
GUNSMOKE
HAPPY DAYS
HARDCASTLE & MC CORMICK
HART TO HART
HAWAIIAN EYE
HILL STREET BLUES
HONEYMOONERS (BUS SCENE)
HONEYMOONERS (KITCHEN SCENE)
BOB HOPE, GEORGE BURNS
& JOHNNY CARSON
HUNTER
I DREAM OF JEANNIE
I LOVE LUCY

THE AVENGERS

CHARLIE'S ANGELS

CHEERS

DUKES OF HAZZARD

DYNASTY

FACTS OF LIFE

FATHER KNOWS BEST

GUNSMOKE

HAPPY DAYS

BATMAN

BIG VALLEY

DALLAS

THE F.B.I.

MARY TYLER MOORE SHOW

HAWAIIAN EYE

THE HONEYMOONERS

I LOVE LUCY

POLICEWOMAN

SPACE 1999

SUPERMAN

TRAPPER JOHN, M.D.

77 SUNSET STRIP

STARSKY & HUTCH

TOO CLOSE FOR COMFORT

THE YELLOW ROSE

THE JEFFERSONS

JOANIE LOVES CHACHIE

BARNABY JONES

I SPY
JEFFERSONS
JOANIE LOVES CHACHIE
BARNABY JONES
KATE & ALLIE
KING KONG (ARMSTRONG & WRAY)
LAVERNE & SHIRLEY
LEAVE IT TO BEAVER
LOGANS RUN (TV SERIES)
LOVE AT FIRST BITE
LOVE BOAT
LOVE, SIDNEY
*M*A*S*H*
MAMA'S PLACE
MANNIX
MARY TYLER MOORE SHOW
BAT MASTERSON
MAUDE
MIAMI VICE
MISSION IMPOSSIBLE
MOD SQUAD
MORK & MINDY
MR ED (ALAN YOUNG)
MUNSTERS
NBC FOLLIES
ODD COUPLE
PARTNERS IN CRIME
POLICE WOMAN
MARY POPPINS
QUINCY
RAT PACK (SINATRA, DAVIS & MARTIN)
REMINGTON STEELE
RIPTIDE
ROCKFORD FILES
SCARECROW & MRS KING
77 SUNSET STRIP
SILVER SPOONS
SIMON & SIMON
SOAP
SPACE 1990
STAR TREK
STARSKY & HUTCH
TENSPEED & BROWNSHOE
THE BOLD ONES
THREE'S COMPANY
THREE'S COMPANY (W/ SOMERS)
TONIGHT SHOW
TOO CLOSE FOR COMFORT
TRAPPER JOHN, MD
TV BLOOPERS & PRACTICAL JOKES
UNTOUCHABLES
VALERIE
DICK VAN DYKE SHOW
WEBSTER
MARCUS WELBY, MD
WHAT'S HAPPENING!!
WONDERFUL WORLD OF ANIMALS
THE YELLOW ROSE

KATE & ALLIE

LEAVE IT TO BEAVER

LOVE BOAT

MIAMI VICE

PARTNERS IN CRIME

RIPTIDE

ROCKFORD FILES

MARCUS WELBY, M.D.

THE UNTOUCHABLES

BATMAN TV SERIES

All Character Photographs
$1.00 each

JOHN ASTIN (THE RIDDLER)
BATMAN & ROBIN (WITH 4 VILLANS)
ANNE BAXTER (ZELDA)
ART CARNEY (THE ARCHER)
YVONNE CRAIG (BATGIRL)
FRANK GORSHIN (THE RIDDLER)
VAN JOHNSON (THE MINSTREL)
BOB KANE (BATMAN ARTIST)
EARTHA KITT (CATWOMAN)
RODDY MC DOWALL (BOOKWORM)
BURGESS MEREDITH (THE PENGUIN)
LEE MERIWETHER (CATWOMAN)
ALAN NAPIER (THE BUTLER)
JULIE NEWMAR (CATWOMAN)
OTTO PREMINGER (MR FREEZE)
VINCENT PRICE (EGGHEAD)
CLIFF ROBERTSON (SHANE)
CESAR ROMERO (THE JOKER)
TISHA STERLING (LEGS)
ROBIN WARD (ROBIN)
DAVID WAYNE (MAD HATTER)
ADAM WEST & BURT WARD (BATMAN & ROBIN)
ADAM WEST (BATMAN)
SHELLY WINTERS (MA PARKER)

JOHN ASTIN

ART CARNEY

YVONNE CRAIG

FRANK GORSHIN

VAN JOHNSON

EARTHA KITT

RODDY MC DOWALL

BURGESS MEREDITH

LEE MERIWETHER

JULIE NEWMAR

CLIFF ROBERTSON

CESAR ROMERO

TISHA STERLING

WEST & WARD

ARNAZ & ROBERTS

BRONSON & IRELAND

CAINE & ROONEY

GROUP PHOTOGRAPHS

All Movie & Cast Scenes

$1.00 each

ISABELLE ADJANI & RYAN O'NEAL
EDWARD ALBERT & SUSAN GEORGE
EDWARD ALBERT, SUSAN ANSPACH & NOAH BEERY, JR
ALAN ALDA & LORETTA SWIT
ALAN ALDA & JANE FONDA
JULIE ANDREWS & JAMES GARNER
JULIE ANDREWS, DUDLEY MOORE & BO DEREK
SUSAN ANTON & JAMES COBURN
ALAN ARKIN & MARIETTE HARTLEY
BESS ARMSTRONG & DENNIS QUAID
LUCIE ARNAZ & TONY ROBERTS
FRED ASTAIRE & GINGER ROGERS
FRED ASTAIRE & CYD CHARISSE
CHRISTOPHER ATKINS & KRISTY MC NICHOL
LEW AYRES & LORRAINE DAY

BARBARA BACH & RINGO STARR
LUCILLE BALL & AVA GABOR
PRISCILLA BARNES & ROGER MOORE
ALAN BATES & BETTE MIDLER
NOAH BEERY & JAMES GARNER
ROBBY BENSON & KIM CATTRALL
ROBBY BENSON & LYNN-HOLLY JOHNSON
CANDICE BERGEN & JACQUELINE BISSET
DAVID BIRNEY & MEREDITH BAXTER
JACQUELINE BISSET & NICK NOLTE
BOB, CAROL, TED & ALICE
KAREN BLACK & ROBERT DUVALL
DEBBIE BOONE & PAT BOONE
PETER BOYLE & BILL MURRAY
BEAU BRIDGES & MARILYN HASSETT
BEAU BRIDGES & ANDY GRIFFITH
JEFF BRIDGES & SALLY FIELD
CHARLES BRONSON & RANDY QUAID
CHARLES BRONSON & JILL IRELAND
CHARLES BRONSON, JACQUELINE BISSET, MAXIMILLIAN SCHELL, ELLEN BURSTYN & TOM SKERRIT
LEVAR BURTON & CHUCK CONNORS

JAMES CAAN & JANE FONDA
MICHAEL CAINE & MAX VON SYDOW
MICHAEL CAINE & MICKEY ROONEY
DAVID CARRADINE & STOCKARD CHANNING
JOHNNY CASH & WAYLON JENNINGS
JOHN CASSAVETES, GENA ROWLANDS & MOLLY RINGWALD
PHOEBE CATES & WILLIE AAMES
KIM CATRALL, JACK LEMMON & ROBBY BENSON
CYD CHARISSE & GENE KELLY
CYD CHARISSE & FRED ASTAIRE
CHEECH & CHONG
LOIS CHILES & ROGER MOORE
JILL CLAYBURGH & ROBERT PRESTON

JOAN COLLINS & CHARLES GRODIN
CHUCK CONNORS & BEN VEREEN
TIM CONWAY, DON KNOTTS & HARVEY KORMAN
HUME CRONYN & JESSICA TANDY
JON CRYER & DEMI MOORE
JAMIE LEE CURTIS & STACY KEACH, JR
KEN CURTIS, SAM ELLIOTT & CYBILL SHEPHERD

MARGARET TRUMAN DANIEL & JAMES WHITMORE
DOM DE LUISE & PETER FALK
ROBERT DE NIRO & TONY CURTIS
ROBERT DE NIRO & BURGESS MEREDITH
CATHERINE DENEUVE & DAVID BOWIE
MATT DILLON & MEG TILLY
KEVIN DOBSON & DIANE LADD
TONY DOW & JERRY MATHERS
HUGH DOWNS & SENATOR EDWARD KENNEDY
ROBERT DUVALL & SISSY SPACEK

ROGER EBERT & GENE SISKEL
NELSON EDDY & JEANETTE MC DONALD
SAM ELLIOTT & KATHARINE ROSS

MIA FARROW & ROBERT REDFORD
MIA FARROW, BARBARA HERSHEY & DIANNE WEST
FARRAH FAWCETT & JEFF BRIDGES
SALLY FIELDS & HENRY WINKLER
ALBERT FINNEY & KAREN ALLEN
PETER FIRTH & NASTASSIA KINSKI
LOUISE FLETCHER & PETER FALK
JODY FOSTER & SALLY KELLERMAN

GREER GARSON & CESAR ROMERO
GIL GERARD & PAMELA HENSLEY
JACKIE GLEASON & TERI GARR
KATHERINE GRAYSON (DESERT SONG SCENE)
LORNE GREENE, MAREN JENSEN & RICHARD HATCH
JAMES GREGORY & ANGELA LANSBURY

GENE HACKMAN & BARBRA STREISAND
LARRY HAGMAN & BARBARA EDEN
H R HALDERMAN & MIKE WALLACE
GEORGE HAMILTON & SUZANNE PLESHETTE
SUSAN HAMILTON & SUSAN ST JAMES
HARRY HAMLEN & DEBORAH VAN VALKENBURGH
RICHARD HATCH & DIRK BENEDICT
HELEN HAYES & JODIE FOSTER
MARIEL HEMINGWAY & WOODY ALLEN
MARIEL HEMINGWAY & ERIC ROBERTS
PAM HENSLEY, DUKE BUTLER & HENRY SILVA
MARTIN HEWITT & BROOKE SHIELDS
ARTHUR HILL, MORGAN BRITTANY & DAVID BIRNEY
DUSTIN HOFFMAN & MERYL STREEP
DUSTIN HOFFMAN & KATHARINE ROSS
HAL HOLBROOK & MICHAEL DOUGLAS
RON HOWARD & HENRY WINKLER
GAYLE HUNNICUTT & MICHAEL SARAZIN
WILLIAM HURT & SIGORNEY WEAVER

CATRALL, LEMMON & BENSON

DOW & MATHERS

FLETCHER & FALK

IRELAND & MC CALLUM

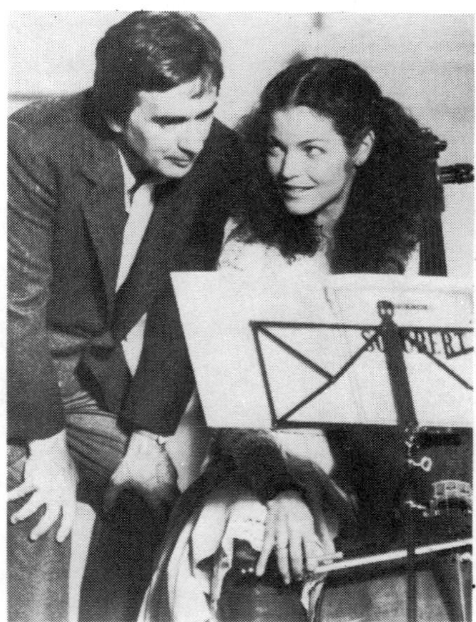

MOORE & IRVING

JONES & INGELS

JILL IRELAND & DAVID MC CALLUM
JEREMY IRONS & MERYL STREEP
AMY IRVING & DUDLEY MOORE
AMY IRVING, DUDLEY MOORE & ANN REINKING

BILLY JONES & ERNIE HARE
SHIRLEY JONES & MARTY INGLES
TOMMY JONES & SISSY SPACEK

ALEX KARRAS, HOWARD COSELL & FRANK GIFFORD
STACEY KEACH & JAMIE LEE CURTIS
HOWARD KEEL & DONNA REED
SALLY KELLERMAN & JODY FOSTER
GENE KELLY & FRED ASTAIRE
GENE KELLY & FRANK SINATRA
GENE KELLY & CYD CHARISSE
KIRK & MC COY (STAR TREK)
KEVIN KLINE & PETER MC NICHOL
KEVIN KLINE & MERYL STREEP
DON KNOTTS & TIM CONWAY
KRIS KRISTOFFERSON & TALIA SHIRE
KRIS KRISTOFFERSON & SARAH MILES

CHERYL LADD & KEN WAHL
STEVE LAWRENCE & EYDIE GORME
GEORGE LAZENBY & DIANA RIGG
VIVIAN LEIGH & BUTTERFLY MC QUEEN
JACK LEMMON & ROBBY BENSON
JACK LEMMON & SISSY SPACEK
RON LIEBMAN & DOLLY PARTON

SHIRLEY MAC LAINE & GENE KELLY
SHIRLEY MAC LAINE & ANNE BANCROFT
SHIRLEY MAC LAINE & TOM SKERRITT
RALPH MACCHIO & PAT MORITA
CHEECH MARIN & THOMAS CHONG
PENNY MARSHALL & CINDY WILLIAMS
DEAN MARTIN & JOE NAMATH
DEAN MARTIN & JERRY LEWIS
DEAN MARTIN & FRANK SINATRA
PAMELA MARTIN & PARKER STEVENSON
LEE MARVIN & BURT LANCASTER
MARSHA MASON & MATTHEW BRODERICK
MARSHA MASON & KRISTY MC NICHOL
MARSHA MASON & NEIL SIMON
MARY ELIZABETH MASTRONTONIO & STEVEN BAUER
TIM MATHESON & KATE CAPSHAW
WALTER MATTHAU & ROBIN WILLIAMS
MARILYN MC COO & BILLY DAVIS, JR
BURGESS MEREDITH & EILEEN HECKART
HAYLEY MILLS & JANE WYMAN
LIZA MINNELLI & MARISSA BERENSON
DUDLEY MOORE & MARY TYLER MOORE
ROGER MOORE & SUZANNA YORK
DEMI MOORE, AMY IRVING & ANN REINKING
RITA MORENO & CAROL BURNETT

JIM NABORS, DON KNOTTS & ANDY GRIFFITH

KARRAS, COSELL & GIFFORD

WAHL & LADD

MARTIN & LEWIS

MARTIN & STEVENSON

MACCHIO & MORITA

MARVIN & LANCASTER

DAVIS & MC COO

HECKERT & MEREDITH

PARTON & REYNOLDS

SHEEDY & PENN

SIEGFRIED & ROY

SONNY & CHER

WILLIE NELSON & ISELA VEGA
PAUL NEWMAN & ROBERT REDFORD
PAUL NEWMAN & SALLY FIELDS
PAUL NEWMAN & JOEL GREY
PAUL NEWMAN & GERALDINE CHAPLIN

MILES O'KEEFE & BO DEREK
RYAN O'NEAL & JACK WARDEN
RYAN O'NEAL & BRUCE DERN
PETER O'TOOLE & JOHN V LINDSAY
MICHAEL ONTKEAN & JO BETH WILLIAMS

ANTHONY PERKINS & YVONNE FURNEAUX
SUZANNE PLESHETTE, GIL GERARD & JAMIE FARR
VICTORIA PRINCIPAL & PATRICK DUFFY

TONY RANDALL & JACK KLUGMAN
BASIL RATHBONE & NIGEL BRUCE
ROBERT REDFORD & MIA FARROW
ROBERT REDFORD & LOIS CHILES
LYNN REDGRAVE & JANE FONDA
DONNA REED & HOWARD KEEL
BURT REYNOLDS & SALLY FIELD
BURT REYNOLDS & CANDICE BERGEN
BURT REYNOLDS & GENE HACKMAN
BURT REYNOLDS & DOLLY PARTON
TONY ROBERTS, JOSE FERRER, MIA FARROW & JULIE HAGGARTY
ROY ROGERS & DALE EVANS
DIANA ROSS & ANTHONY PERKINS
JOHN RUSSELL, ROY ROGERS, JOCK MAHONEY LEE MAJORS

MICHAEL SARRAZIN & CORNELIA SHARPE
MAXIMILLIAN SCHELL & ALI MAC GRAW
ARNOLD SCHWARZENEGGER & SALLY FIELD
ARNOLD SCHWARZENEGGER & SANDAHL BERGMAN
JANE SEYMOUR & CHRISTOPHER REEVE
WILLIAM SHATNER & LEE GRANT
ALLY SHEEDY & SEAN PENN
BROOKE SHIELDS & SHIRLEY KNIGHT
BROOKE SHIELDS & CHRISTOPHER ATKINS
SIEGFRIED & ROY
FRANK SINATRA & GENE KELLY
FRANK SINATRA, SOPHIA LOREN & CARY GRANT
FRANK SINATRA & SHIRLEY MAC LAINE
FRANK SINATRA & MARTHA HYER
FRANK SINATRA, DEAN MARTIN & SAMMY DAVIS, JR
TOM SKERRITT & SHIRLEY MAC LAINE
TOM SKERRITT & LYNN-HOLLY JOHNSON
SONNY & CHER
SONNY, CHER & CHASTITY
DAVID SOUL & FRIEND
SISSY SPACEK & ERIC ROBERTS
SISSY SPACEK, MINNIE PEARL & WAYLON JENNINGS
SPOCK & KIRK (STAR TREK)
STAR TREK CREW & PERSIS KHAMBATTA
SYLVESTER STALLONE & DOLLY PARTON

MARY STEENBURGEN & WOODY ALLEN
PARKER STEVENSON & SHAUN CASSIDY
MERYL STREEP & JEREMY IRONS
BARBRA STREISAND & ROBERT REDFORD
DONALD SUTHERLAND & BROOKE ADAMS
DONALD SUTHERLAND & SUZANNE SOMERS

GEORGE TAKAI & WALTER KOENIG
SHIRLEY TEMPLE & BUDDY EBSEN
MEG TILLY & MATT DILLON
LILY TOMLIN & JOHN TRAVOLTA

PETER USTINOV & MAGGIE SMITH

BEN VEREEN & MELBA MOORE
BEN VEREEN & JEFF GOLDBLUM

ROBERT WAGNER & STEFANIE POWERS
KEN WAHL & CHERYL LADD
JULIE WALTERS & MICHAEL CAINE
SIGOURNEY WEAVER & CHRISTOPHER PLUMMER
RICHARD WIDMARK & GENEVIEVE BUJOLD

BILLY DEE WILLIAMS & DIAHANN CARROLL
JO BETH WILLIAMS, KEVIN KLINE, WILLIAM HURT & GLENN CLOSE
ROBIN WILLIAMS & SHELLY DUVALL
FLIP WILSON & GLADYS KNIGHT

SMOTHERS BROTHERS

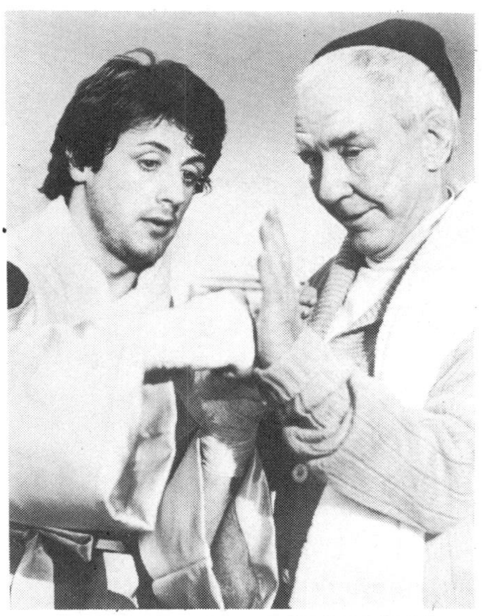

STALLONE & MEREDITH

WILLIAMS & DUVALL

WILSON & KNIGHT

REDFORD & STREISAND

MUHAMMAD ALI

PEGGY FLEMING

BRUCE JENNER

FAMOUS CELEBRITIES

All Portrait Photographs
$1.00 each

KAREEM ABDUL-JABBAR
PRINCESS YASMIN AGA KHAN
EDWARD ALBEE
MUHAMMAD ALI
JACK ANDERSON
YURI ANDROPOV
JACK ARMSTRONG
NEIL ARMSTRONG
ARTHUR ASHE

BURT BACHARACH
CHRISTIAN BARNARD
RONA BARRETT
CHARLES BECKWITH
MELVIN BELLI
IRVING BERLIN
LEONARD BERNSTEIN
BJORN BORG
JAMES BRADY
DR JOYCE BROTHERS
HELEN GURLEY BROWN
JACK BURNS

SAMMY CAHN
CAPUCINE
JOHNNY CARSON
JIMMY CARTER
ROSALYN CARTER
SUZY CHAFFEE
MARGE CHAMPION
CESAR CHAVEZ
LADY SARAH CHURCHILL
JACKIE COLLINS
BETTY COMDEN & ADOLPH GREEN
NADIA COMENICI
JIMMIE CONNORS
DOUGLAS CORRIGAN
HOWARD COSELL
JACQUES COUSTEAU
SCOTT CROSSFIELD

DR WILLIAM DE VRIES
JOE DI MAGGIO
PHIL DONAHUE

ABBA EBAN
RICHARD EBERHART
JULIUS ERVING
CHRIS EVERETT-LLOYD

PEGGY FLEMING
PEGGY FLEMING & BIG BIRD
BETTY FORD
JERRY FORD
DAVID FROST

JOHN KENNETH GAILBRAITH
GALLAGHER
GARBACHEV
JOHN GLENN
ALEXANDER GODUNOV
BILLY GRAHAM
MARTHA GRAHAM
ROCKY GRAZIANO
JOSE GRECO
DICK GREGORY
MERV GRIFFIN

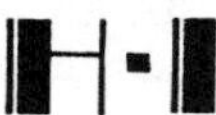

GENERAL ALEXANDER HAIG
ALEX HAILEY
ARTHUR HAILEY
DOROTHY HAMILL
DOUG HENNING
HULK HOGAN
LARRY HOLMES
VLADIMER HOROWITZ
ROBERT INDIANA

REV JESSE JACKSON
BIANCA JAGGER
DR ROBERT JARVICK
BRUCE JENNER
JASPER JOHN
ERICA JONG

YOUSIF KARASH
BOB KEESHAN
(CAPT KANGAROO)
EMMETT KELLY, JR
EDWARD KENNEDY
TED KEY
MICHAEL KIDD
JEANNE KILPATRICK
BILLIE JEAN KING
HENRY KISSINGER
EVIL KNIEVEL
WILLIAM C KNIGHT
MAYOR ED KOCH

JAKE LA MOTTA
MEADOWLARK LEMON
DAVID LETTERMAN
ART LINKLETTER
CLAIRE BOOTH LUCE

RAY "BOOM BOOM" MANCINI
WINNIE MANDELLA
MICKEY MANTLE
MARCEL MARCEAU
PETER MARTINS
MICHELLE MARVIN
WILLIE MAYS
JOHN MC ENROE
ROD MC KUEN
ED MC MAHON
DON MEREDITH
JAMES MICHNER
REV S M MOON
ARCHIE MOORE
GARY MOORE
MOTHER TERESA

JOE NAMATH
MARTINA NATRAVLOVA
LOUISE NEVELSON
RICHARD NIXON
KEN NORTON - S
TINA ONASSIS-NIARCHOS

BERT PARKS
JACK PARR
LINUS PAULING
PELE
ITZHAK PERLMAN
PALOMA PICASSO
JAMES PURDY

I I RABI
ELIZABETH RAY
MAUREEN REAGAN
NANCY REAGAN
RONALD REAGAN
RONALD REAGAN
(COWBOY)
RONALD REAGAN, JR
RONALD REAGAN & BONZO
CATHY RIGBY
HAROLD ROBBINS
ORAL ROBERTS
FRED ROGER (MR ROGERS)
MARK RUSSELL

DR CARL SAGAN
MORT SAHL
PAT SAJAK
MAX SCHMELLING
FRITZ SCHOLDER
ARIEL SHARON
A SHOSTEKOVICH
SIEGFRIED & ROY
RICHARD SIMMONS
ISAAC B SINGER
BOB SMITH &
HOWDY DOODY
STEVEN SONDHEIM
MICKEY SPILLANE
LEON SPINKS
MARK SPITZ

DR EDWARD TELLER
MOTHER TERESA
ALAN THICKE
ABIGAIL VAN BUREN
KURT VONNEGUT, JR

LECH WALESA
HERSCHEL WALKER
IRVING WALLACE
BARBARA WALTERS
ROBERT PENN WARREN
DR RUTH WESTHEIMIER
VANESSA WILLIAMS
PAUL WINCHELL &
JERRY MAHONEY
TOM WOLFE
ANDREW WYETH
WEIRD AL YANKOVIC
GENERAL CHUCK YEAGER
ANDREW YOUNG

MICKEY MANTLE

JOHN MC ENROE

GORE VIDAL

FRED ASTAIRE

LEX BARKER

DON "RED" BARRY

DECEASED TV & MOVIE STARS

All Portrait Photographs
$1.00 each

ABBOTT & COSTELLO
WALTER ABEL
DAWN ADDAMS
LUTHER ADLER
BRIAN AHERNE
JACK ALBERTSON
ROBERT ALDA
FRED ALLEN
GRACIE ALLEN
AMOS 'N" ANDY
EVELYN ANKERS
FATTY ARBUCKLE
RICHARD ARLEN
GEORGE ARLISS
LOUIS ARMSTRONG
DESI ARNAZ, SR
EDWARD ARNOLD
FRED ASTAIRE
FRED ASTAIRE (DANCING ON PIANO)
NILES ASTER
LIONEL ATWELL
MISHA AUER

FAY BAINTER
SMITH BALLEW
GEORGE BANCROFT
TALLULAH BANKHEAD
THEDA BARA
GEORGE BARBIER
LEX BARKER
DON "RED" BARRY
ETHEL BARRYMORE
JOHN BARRYMORE
LIONEL BARRYMORE
RICHARD BARTHELMESS
RICHARD BASEHART
ANNE BAXTER
WARNER BAXTER
JOHN BEAL
CECIL BEATON
NOAH BEERY, SR
WALLACE BEERY
REX BELL
JOHN BELUSHI
CONSTANCE BENNETT
JACK BENNY
EDGAR BERGEN & CHARLIE MC CARTHY
INGRID BERGMAN
WARREN BERLINGER
HERSCHEL BERNARDI
DAN BLOCKER
JOAN BLONDELL
ERIC BLORE
BEN BLUE
HUMPHREY BOGART
JOHN BOLES
RAY BOLGER (SCARECROW)
WARD BOND
BEAULAH BONDI
RICHARD BOONE
CLARA BOW
BILL BOYD
CHARLES BOYER
SCOTT BRADY
EL BRENDEL
GEORGE BRENT
FANNY BRICE
HELEN BRODERICK
BETTY BRONSON
JOE E BROWN
JOHNNY MACK BROWN
NIGEL BRUCE
VIRGINIA BRUCE
YUL BRYNNER
VICTOR BUONO - S
BILLIE BURKE
SMILEY BURNETTE
BOB BURNS
RICHARD BURTON
FRANCES X BUSHMAN

JAMES CAGNEY (GRAPEFRUIT SCENE)
ROD CAMERON
JUDY CANOVA
EDDIE CANTOR
YAKIMA CANUTT
HARRY CAREY
HOAGY CARMICHAEL
LEO CARRILLO

JOHN BARRYMORE

JOHN BELUSHI

INGRID BERGMAN

DAN BLOCKER

RAY BOLGER

BEAULAH BONDI

RICHARD BOONE

CHARLES BOYER

YUL BRYNNER

LEO G. CARROLL

NAT "KING" COLE

CHARLES CHAPLIN

JOHN CARROLL
LEO G CARROLL
JACK CARSON
PEGGY CASS
GOWER CHAMPION
JEFF CHANDLER
LON CHANEY, SR
LON CHANEY, JR
CHARLIE CHAPLIN
CHARLIE CHASE
ILKA CHASE
MAURICE CHEVALIER
MARGUERITE CHURCHILL
JIMMY CLANTON
BUDDY CLARK
MONTGOMERY CLIFT
ANDY CLYDE
LEE J COBB
CHARLES COBURN
JAMES COCO - P/S
NAT "KING" COLE
RONALD COLMAN
BETTY COMPSON
HANS CONREID
JACKIE COOGAN
GARY COOPER
GLADYS COOPER
MELVILLE COOPER
DOLORES COSTELLO
LOU COSTELLO
WALLY COX
BUSTER CRABBE
JAMES CRAIG
BOB CRANE
BRODERICK CRAWFORD
JOAN CRAWFORD
DONALD CRISP
BING CROSBY
SCATMAN CROTHERS
GEORGE CUKOR

FIFI D'ORSAY
BEBE DANIELS
ROYAL DANO
LINDA DARNELL
DANIELLE DARRIEUX
FRANKIE DARRO
JANE DARWELL
JIM DAVIS - S
MARION DAVIS
RUFE DAVIS
CECIL B DE MILLE
VITTORIO DE SICA
BILLY DE WOLFE
JAMES DEAN
DOLORES DEL RIO
WILLIAM DEMEREST
REGINALD DENNY
ANDY DEVINE
WALT DISNEY
BRIAN DONLEVY
DIANA DORS
JIMMY DORSEY
TOMMY DORSEY
MELVIN DOUGLAS
PAUL DOUGLAS
JESSICA DRAGONETTE
ANDREW DUGGAN
JAMES DUNN
JIMMY DURANTE
DAN DUREYA
ANN DVORAK

NELSON EDDY
SALLY EILERS
FAYE EMERSON
LEIF ERICKSON
LEON ERROL
STU ERWIN
MADGE EVANS

DOUGLAS FAIRBANKS, SR
FRANCES FARMER
MARTY FELDMAN
GRACIE FIELDS
KIM FIELDS
W C FIELDS
LARRY FINE
BARRY FITZGERALD
BESS FLOWERS
ERROLL FLYNN
HENRY FONDA
DICK FORAN
PRESTON FOSTER
EDDIE FOY, JR
EDDIE FOY, SR

CLARK GABLE
TONY GALENTE
JOHN GARFIELD
JUDY GARLAND

MONTGOMERY CLIFT

BUSTER CRABBE

BRODERICK CRAWFORD

JOAN CRAWFORD

SCATMAN CROTHERS

FRANCES FARMER

DICK FORAN

CLARK GABLE

JUDY GARLAND

ARTHUR GODFREY

BENNY GOODMAN

JETTA GOUDAL

PEGGY ANN GARNER
JANET GAYNOR
WILL GEER
CHIEF DAN GEORGE
ALICE GHOSTLEY
BILLY GILBERT
JAMES GLEASON
JACKIE GLEASON - P/S
JACKIE GLEASON (RALPH CRAMDEN)
ARTHUR GODFREY
SAMUEL GOLDWYN
BENNY GOODMAN
RUTH GORDON
JETTA GOUDAL
BETTY GRABLE
GLORIA GRAHAME - S
CARY GRANT
KIRBY GRANT
SYDNEY GREENSTREET
D W GRIFFITH
TEXAS GUINNAN
SIGRID GURIE

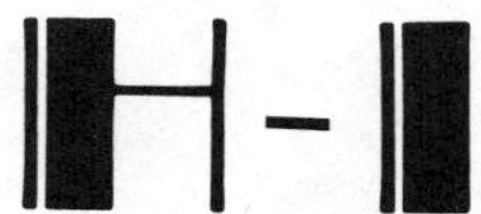

JOAN HACKETT
WILLIAM HAINES
BILL HALEY
JACK HALEY
MARGARET HAMILTON
NEIL HAMILTON
OLIVER HARDY
JEAN HARLOW
WILLIAM S HART
RAYMOND HATTON
SESSUE HAYAKAWA
GABBY HAYES
LOUIS HAYWARD
SUSAN HAYWARD
RITA HAYWORTH
EDITH HEAD
TED HEALY
JIMI HENDRIX
WANDA HENDRIX - P/S
SONJA HENIE
HUGH HERBERT
JEAN HERSHOLT
JON ERIK HEXUM
PAT HINGLE
ALFRED HITCHCOCK
JOHN HODIAK
WILLIAM HOLDEN
STERLING HOLLOWAY
JACK HOLT
LOU HOLTZ
MIRIAM HOPKINS
EDWARD EVERETT HORTON
LESLIE HOWARD
MOE HOWARD
WILLIE HOWARD
JACK HOXIE
ROCK HUDSON
HENRY HULL
WALTER HUSTON
JIM HUTTON

EMIL JANNINGS
CLAUDIA JENNINGS - S
GEORGE JESSEL
SONNY JOHNSON
AL JOLSON
BUCK JONES
CAROLYN JONES - P/S
SPIKE JONES
JANIS JOPLIN
VICTOR JORY
LEATRICE JOY
ARLENE JUDGE
CURT JURGENS - S
KURT JURGENS

BORIS KARLOFF
ROSCOE KARNS
JULIE KAVNER
JULIE KAVNER
SAMMY KAYE
DANNY KAYE - P/S
BUSTER KEATON
GRACE KELLY
DORIS KENYON
FUZZY KNIGHT
ERNIE KOVACS
OTTO KRUGER

JACK LA RUE
ALAN LADD
BERT LAHR (COWARDLY LION)
ARTHUR LAKE
VERONICA LAKE
FERNANDO LAMAS
ELSA LANCHESTER
ELISSA LANDI

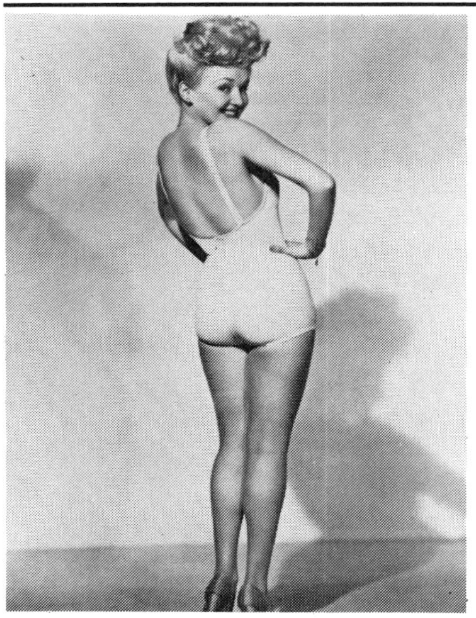
BETTY GRABLE

CARY GRANT

NEIL HAMILTON

JEAN HARLOW

SUSAN HAYWARD

ALFRED HITCHCOCK

JOHN HODIAK

DANNY KAYE

SAMMY KAYE

CAROLE LANDIS

CAROLE LOMBARD

BELA LUGOSI

CAROL LANDIS
ALLEN LANE
JOI LANSING
MARIO LANZA
JACK LARUE
CHARLES LAUGHTON
LAUREL & HARDY
PETER LAWFORD
GERTRUDE LAWRENCE
BRUCE LEE
ANDREA LEEDS
VIVIAN LEIGH
OSCAR LEVANT
MONICA LEWIS
TED LEWIS
HAROLD LLOYD
CAROLE LOMBARD
PETER LORRE
BESSIE LOVE
PAUL LUCAS
BELA LUGOSI
LUM & ABNER - P/S
JOHN LUND
WILLIAM LUNDIGAN
PAUL LYNDE -P/S
DIANA LYNN
BEN LYON
BERT LYTELL

MAE MAC AVOY
JAYNE MANSFIELD
HERBERT MARSHALL
DEAN PAUL MARTIN
STROTHER MARTIN
MARX BROTHERS
CHICO MARX
GROUCHO MARX
HARPO MARX
JAMES MASON
RAYMOND MASSEY
KEN MAYNARD
HATTIE MC DANIEL
JEANETTE MC DONALD
& NELSON EDDY
JEANETTE MC DONALD
FIBBER MC GEE & MOLLY
FRANK MC HUGH
VICTOR MC LAUGHLIN
STEVE MC QUEEN
KAY MEDFORD
DONALD MEEK
ADOLPH MENJOU
UNA MERKLE
ETHEL MERMAN
RAY MILLAND
GLENN MILLER
MARILYN MILLER
MILLS BROTHERS
MARY MILES MINTER
CARMEN MIRANDA
TOM MIX
MARILYN MONROE
DOUGLAS MONTGOMERY
ROBERT MONTGOMERY
GRACE MOORE
VICTOR MOORE
JEANNE MOREAU
DENNIS MORGAN
HELEN MORGAN
CHESTER MORRIS
WAYNE MORRIS
ALAN MOWBRAY
JEAN MUIR
AUDIE MURPHY - P/S
CLARENCE MUSE
CARMEL MYERS

J CARROL NASH
OLGA NAZIMOVA
ANNA NEAGLE
RICK NELSON
ANNA Q NIELSEN
DAVID NIVEN - P/S
MARION NIXON
LLOYD NOLAN
MABEL NORMAND
RAYMOND NOVARRO

EDMOND O'BRIEN
GEORGE O'BRIEN
PAT O'BRIEN
JACK OAKIE
SIMON OAKLAND
MERLE OBERON
WARNER OLAND
EDNA MAE OLIVER
OLSON & JOHNSON

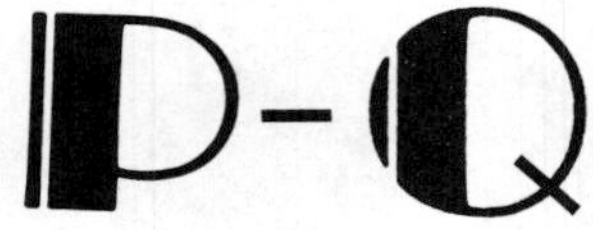

LILI PALMER
JEAN PARKER
LARRY PARKS

JEANETTE MAC DONALD

GROUCHO MARX

JAMES MASON

RAYMOND MASSEY

CARMEN MIRANDA

JACK OAKIE

EDMUND O'BRIEN

PAT O'BRIEN

LILI PALMER

TYRONE POWER

ELVIS PRESLEY

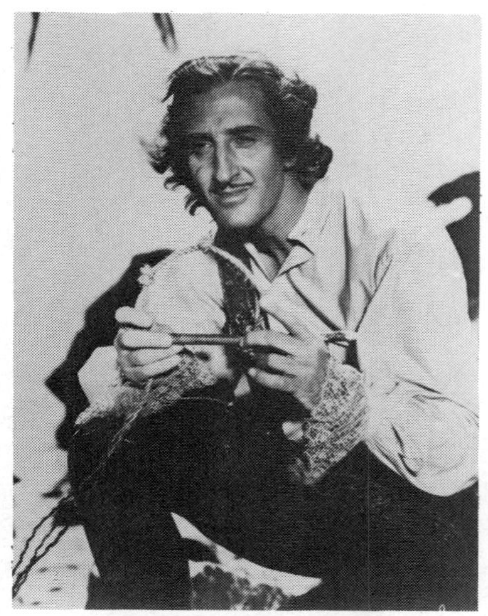
BASIL RATHBONE

SLIM PICKENS - P/S
WALTER PIDGEON
JAMES PIERCE
ENZIO PINZA
ZASU PITTS
SNUB POLLARD
LILY PONS
DICK POWELL
WILLIAM POWELL
TYRONE POWER
ELVIS PRESLEY
ROBERT PRESTON
EDMUND PURDOM

BASIL RATHBONE &
NIGEL BRUCE
BASIL RATHBONE (HOLMES)
GREGORY RATHOFF
MICHAEL REDGRAVE
DONNA REED
GEORGE REEVES
JIM REEVES
HARRY RICHMAN
TEX RITTER
PAUL ROBESON
BILL ROBINSON
EDWARD G ROBINSON
MAE ROBSON
WILL ROGERS, SR
LILLIAN ROTH
CHARLES RUGGLES
ROSALIND RUSSELL

SABU
CHICK SALE
WILL SAMPSON - P/S
JOSEPH SCHILDKRAUT
RANDOLPH SCOTT
ZACHARY SCOTT
JEAN SEBERG
PETER SELLERS - P/S
MACK SENNETT
ROBERT SHAW
DICK SHAWN - P/S
NORMA SHEARER
JACK SHELDON
ANN SHERIDAN
HERB SHRINER
MILTON SILLS
PHIL SILVERS - P/S
PHIL SILVERS - P/S
C AUBREY SMITH
GALE SONDERGAARD
NED SPARKS
AL (FUZZY) ST JOHN
CHARLES STARRETT
HENRY STEPHENSON
JAN STERLING
INGER STEVENS
LEWIS STONE
DOROTHY STRATTON
MARGARET SULLIVAN
GLORIA SWANSON
BLANCHE SWEET

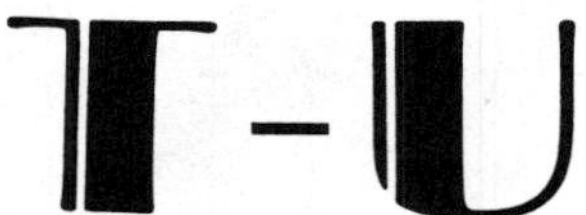

CONSTANCE TALMAGE
RICHARD TALMAGE
SHARON TATE
ROBERT TAYLOR - P/S
RUTH TAYLOR
CONWAY TEARLE
LAWRENCE TIBBETT
GEORGE TOBIAS
GENEVIEVE TOBIN
SIDNEY TOLER
FRANCHOT TONE
SPENCER TRACY
ARTHUR TREACHER
ERNEST TRUEX
FORREST TUCKER
SOPHIE TUCKER
SONNY TUFTS
TOM TULLY - S
BEN TURPIN
TOM TYLER

RUDOLPH VALENTINO
WALLY VERNON
MARTHA VICKERS
ERIC VON STROHEIM

JIMMY WAKELY
RAYMOND WALDBURN
H B WARNER
DINAH WASHINGTON
JOHN WAYNE
RICHARD WEBB
(CAPT MIDNIGHT)
CLIFTON WEBB - P/S
JOHNNY WEISSMULLER
ORSON WELLES - P/S
OSKAR WERNER
MAE WEST
MICHAEL WHALEN
BERT WHEELER
ALICE WHITE
RAY WHITLEY
PAUL WHITMAN
HENRY WILCOXON
MICHAEL WILDING
BIG BOY WILLIAMS
WARREN WILLIAMS
MARIE WILSON
WHIP WILSON
TOBY WING
ROLAND WINTERS
ANNA MAY WONG
NATALIE WOOD
GRETCHEN WYLER
KEENAN WYNN
ROLAND YOUNG
JOE YULE - S
E Z ZAKALL

GEORGE REEVES

EDWARD G. ROBINSON

PETER SELLERS

INGER STEVENS

TOM TYLER

JOHNNY WEISSMULLER

KEENAN WYNN

ROBERT BENCHLEY

FRANK BUCK

RICHARD E. BYRD

DECEASED CELEBRITIES

All Portrait Photographs
$1.00 each

ANSEL ADAMS
JANE ADAMS
LOUISA MAE ALCOTT
AMOS 'N' ANDY
SUSAN B ANTHONY
MAX BAER, SR
PHINNEAS T BARNUM
CLARA BARTON
COUNT BASIE
CLYDE BEATTY
ALEXANDER GRAHAM BELL
REX BELL
ROBERT BENCHLEY
FRANK BONNER
MAJOR EDWARD BOWES
WILLIAM JENNINGS BRYAN
FRANK BUCK
PEARL BUCK
LUTHER BURBANK
BURNS & ALLEN
EDGAR RICE BURROUGHS
RICHARD E BYRD
TRUMAN CAPOTE
HOAGY CARMICHAEL
ANDREW CARNEGIE
ENRICO CARUSO
CARRIE CHAPMAN COTT
BUDDY CLARK
SAMUEL CLEMENS
GEORGE M COHAN
NAT "KING" COLE
CALVIN COOLIDGE
CLARENCE DARROW
CHARLES DARWIN
JEFFERSON DAVIS
MOISHE DAYAN
DR LEE DE FORREST
JIMMY DORSEY
TOMMY DORSEY
JESSICA DRAGONETTE
W E B DU BOIS
AMELIA EARHART
GEORGE EASTMAN
THOMAS A EDISON
ALBERT EINSTEIN
RALPH WALDO EMERSON
DAVID FARRAGUT
WILLIAM FAULKNER
ENRICO FERMI
F SCOTT FITZGERALD
HENRY FORD, SR
STEPHEN FOSTER
SAMUEL GOLDWYN
SAMUEL GOMPERS
ULYSSES S GRANT
HORACE GREELEY
ZANE GREY
TITO GUIZAR
BILL HALEY
SIR ARTHUR HARRIS
NATHANIEL HAWTHORNE
TED HEALY
BEN HECHT
SONJA HEINIE
WILD BILL HITCHCOCK
SAM HOUSTON
ELIAS HOWE
WASHINGTON IRVING
GREGORY JARVIS
(CHALLENGER)
LYNDON B JOHNSON
BOBBY JONES
GEORGE S KAUFMAN
HELEN KELLER
EMMETT KELLY, SR
PRESIDENT J F KENNEDY
ROBERT F KENNEDY
DR MARTIN LUTHER KING
GERTRUDE LAWRENCE
SOL LESSER
CHARLES A LINDBERGH
SONNY LISTON
HENRY W LONGFELLOW
HORACE MANN
GUGLIELMO MARCONI
BAT MASTERSON
W SOMERSET MAUGHAN
SHARON CHRISTA
MC AULIFFE
(CHALLENGER)
CYRUS MC CORMICK
GEORGE B MC LELLAN
RONALD E MC NAIR
(CHALLENGER)
GEORGE MEADE
HERMAN MELVILLE
GLENN MILLER
GENERAL MONTGOMERY
(BRITISH)
GRACE MOORE
HENRY MOORE
LORD LOUIS MOUNTBATTEN

NAT "KING" COLE

GEORGE EASTMAN

THOMAS A. EDISON

F. SCOTT FITZGERALD

HENRY FORD, JR.

WILLIAM S. HART

GEORGE S. KAUFMAN

HELEN KELLER

EMMETT KELLY, SR.

MARTIN LUTHER KING, JR.

JOHN F. KENNEDY

GENERAL MONTGOMERY

HELEN MORGAN

ANNIE OAKLEY

PABLO PICASSO

CARRIE NATION
ANNIE OAKLEY
ELLISON S ONIZUKA
(CHALLENGER)
J ROBERT OPPENHEIMER
ROBERT E PERRY
PABLO PICASSO
EDGAR ALLEN POE
WILEY POST
ERNIE PYLE
SALLY RAND
WALTER REED
JUDITH RESNICK
(CHALLENGER)
NORMAN ROCKWELL
ELEANOR ROOSEVELT
FRANKLIN D ROOSEVELT
ARTUR RUBENSTEIN
BABE RUTH
ALBERT SCHWEITZER
DICK SCOBEE
(CHALLENGER)
ROD SERLING
WILLIAM H SEWARD
GEORGE BERNARD SHAW
WILLIAM T SHERMAN
MICHAEL J SMITH
(CHALLENGER)
JOHN PHILLIP SOUSA
ELIZABETH CODY
STANTON
CHARLES STEINMETZ
HARRIET BEECHER STOWE
ED SULLIVAN
PETER TCHAIKOWSY
HENRY THOREAU
LAURENCE TIBBETT
GENE TUNNEY
JACK WARNER
EARL WARREN
BOOKER T WASHINGTON
DINAH WASHINGTON
GEORGE WASHINGTON
CARVER
OLIVER WENDELL HOLMES
GEORGE WHITE
WALT WHITMAN
WALTER WINCHELL
ALEXANDER WOLCOTT
WILBUR & ORVILLE
WRIGHT
BRIGHAM YOUNG
DARRYL F ZANNUCK

WILEY POST

WALTER REID

BILL ROBINSON

WILL ROGERS

ALBERT SCHWEITZER

ROD SERLING

CHARLES STEINMETZ

WALTER WINCHELL

DARRYL F. ZANUCK

CAB CALLOWAY

FATS DOMINO

GENE KRUPA

ORCHESTRA LEADERS

All Portrait Photographs
$1.00 each

HERB ALPERT & TIJUANA BRASS
RAY ANTHONY
TEX BENEKE
CAB CALLOWAY
FATS DOMINO
MAYNARD FERGUSON
FERRANTE & TEICHER
PETE FOUNTAIN
DIZZY GILLESPIE
CONNIE HAINES
LIONEL HAMPTON
PHIL HARRIS
WOODY HERMAN
AL HIRT
GENE KRUPA
BUDDY RICH
ARTIE SHAW
GEORGE SHEARING

"THE WIZ" CHARACTERS

$1.00 each

LENA HORNE (GLINDA-GOOD WITCH)
MICHAEL JACKSON (STRAW MAN)
MABEL KING (WICKED WITCH)
DIANA ROSS (DOROTHY)
TED ROSS (COWARDLY LION)
NIPSEY RUSSELL (TIN MAN)

MISCELLANEOUS PHOTOS

$1.00 each

CHEWBACCA (STAR WARS)
KERMIT THE FROG
MISS PIGGY
R2D2

ORDER FORM

SY SUSSMAN PORTRAITS • 2962 S. MANN ST. • LAS VEGAS, NV 89102

COUPON

PHOTOS (   ) X $1.00 ...

POSTAGE & HANDLING 1.00

TOTAL ENCLOSED ....

SEND ORDER TO:

NAME

STREET

CITY

STATE ZIP

PHOTO CREDITS

A-TEAM	NBC-TV
ACE, JOHNNY	ABC/DUNHILL RECORDS
ADAMS, BROOKE	UNITED ARTISTS PICTURES
ADAMS, JULIE	UNIVERSAL PICTURES
AIR SUPPLY	JET MANAGEMENT
ALABAMA	RCA RECORDS
ALDA, ALAN	UNIVERSAL PICTURES
ALICE	CBS-TV
ALL IN THE FAMILY	CBS-TV
ALLEN, NANCY	FILMWAYS PICTURES
ALYN, KIRK	COLUMBIA PICTURES/D. C. COMICS
ANDERSON, RICHARD DEAN	LEONARDO'S CINEMA CLASSICS
ANKA, PAUL	RCA RECORDS
ANT, ADAM	EPIC RECORDS/ALLAN BALLARD
ARKIN, ALAN	20TH CENTURY-FOX PICTURES
ARNESS, JAMES	CBS-TV
ARNOLD, EDDY	RCA RECORDS
ASHFORD & SIMPSON	A & M RECORDS
ASIA	GEFFEN RECORDS
ASTIN, JOHN	ABC-TV
ATKINS, CHET	RCA RECORDS
AUSTIN, PATTI	QWEST RECORDS
AVENGERS, THE	ABC-TV
AXTON, HOYT	JEREMIAH RECORDS
B-52'S, THE	WARNER BROS RECORDS
BACH, BARBARA	UNITED ARTISTS PICTURES
BAILEY, PHILIP	COLUMBIA RECORDS/BOBBY HOLLAND
BAILEY, RAZZY	RCA RECORDS
BAKER, ANITA	ELEKTRA RECORDS/MARK WEISS
BANDY, MOE	COLUMBIA RECORDS
BANGLES, THE	COLUMBIA RECORDS/NEIL ZLOZOWER
BAR-KAYS, THE	MERCURY/POLYGRAM RECORDS
BARDOT, BRIGITTE	LEONARDO'S CINEMA CLASSICS
BARRYMORE, JOHN	MGM PICTURES
BARRYMORE, LIONEL	MGM PICTURES
BARYSHNIKOV, MIKHAIL	AMERICAN BALLET SOCIETY
BATMAN	ABC-TV
BEATLES, THE	UNITED ARTISTS PICTURES
BEGLEY, ED, SR.	PARAMOUNT PICTURES
BELLAMY BROTHERS, THE	CURB/WARNER BROS RECORDS
BELUSHI, JOHN	UNIVERSAL PICTURES
BENCHLEY, ROBERT	MGM PICTURES
BENEDICT, DIRK	LEONARDO'S CINEMA CLASSICS
BENSON, GEORGE	WARNER BROS RECORDS
BERGMAN, SANDAHL	20TH CENTURY-FOX PICTURES
BERTOLUCCI, BERNARDO	ITALIAN FILM DIRECTORS GUILD
BIG COUNTRY	MERCURY/POLYGRAM RECORDS
BIG VALLEY	ABC-TV
BLANC, MEL	HANNA-BARBERA PRODUCTIONS
BLASTERS, THE	SLASH/WARNER RECORDS/GARY LEONARD
BLOCKER, DAN	NBC-TV
BOLGER, RAY	MGM PICTURES
BON JOVI	POLYGRAM RECORDS
BOONE, PAT	BRUNO OF HOLLYWOOD
BOWIE, DAVID	RCA RECORDS
BOXLEITNER, BRUCE	LEONARDO'S CINEMA CLASSICS
BOYLE, PETER	UNIVERSAL PICTURES
BRANDAUER, KLAUS MARIA	20TH CENTURY-FOX PICTURES/KEN HOWARD
BRANDO, MARLON	COLUMBIA PICTURES
BRIDGES, BEAU	UNIVERSAL PICTURES
BRODERICK, MATTHEW	20TH CENTURY-FOX PICTURES/RALPH NELSON
BRODY, LANE	IN CONCERT INTERNATIONAL
BRONSON, CHARLES	PARAMOUNT PICTURES
BROSNAN, PIERCE	NBC-TV
BROWNE, JACKSON	ASYLUM RECORDS/RANDEE ST. NICHOLAS
BRUBECK, DAVE	TOMATO ARTISTS
BUCK, FRANK	COLUMBIA PICTURES
BUCKINGHAM, LINDSAY	ELEKTRA RECORDS/MATTHEW ROLSTON
BUFFETT, JIMMY	MCA RECORDS/TOM CORCORAN
BURTON, LEVAR	ABC-TV
CAMEO	POLYGRAM RECORDS
CARA, IRENA	NETWORK RECORDS/HARRY LANGDON
CARNEY, ART	ABC-TV
CARPENTERS, THE	A & M RECORDS
CARSON, JOHNNY	ABC-TV
CARTER FAMILY	BUDDY LEE ATTRACTIONS
CARTER, LYNDA	ABC-TV
CASH, JOHNNY	COLUMBIA RECORDS/SLICK LAWSON
CHAPIN, TOM	KRAGEN & COMPANY
CHARLES, RAY	ATLANTIC RECORDS
CHARLIE'S ANGELS	ABC-TV
CHEERS	NBC-TV
CLAPTON, ERIC	DUCK/WARNER BROS RECORDS
CLARK, ALAN	CLARK RECORDS
CLARK, DICK	ABC-TV
CLARK, ROY	MCA RECORDS
CLIFT & TAYLOR	LEONARDO'S CINEMA CLASSICS
COCHRAN, EDDIE	LIBERTY RECORDS
COE, DAVID ALLAN	RCA RECORDS
COLE, NAT "KING"	CAPITOL RECORDS
COLLINS, JOAN	LEONARDO'S CINEMA CLASSICS
COLLINS, PHIL	ATLANTIC RECORDS
COMMODORES, THE	MOTOWN RECORDS
CONLEE, JOHN	MCA RECORDS
CONLEY, EARL THOMAS	RCA RECORDS
COOKE, SAM	RCA RECORDS
COOPER, GARY	MGM RECORDS
CORY, HART	EMI AMERICA RECORDS
COSBY, BILL	WARNER BROS PICTURES
COSTELLO, ELVIS	UNITED ARTISTS PICTURES
CRAIG, YVONNE	ABC-TV
CROUCH, ANDRAE	WARNER BROS RECORDS
CRUISE, TOM	LEONARDO'S CINEMA CLASSICS
CRUSADERS, THE	MCA RECORDS
CRYSTALS, THE	JAMES J. KRIEGSMANN

DALLAS	CBS-TV/LORIMAR TELEPICTURES
DAVIS, MILES	WARNER BROS RECORDS/KEN FRANCKLING
DE LAURENTIIS, DINO	DE LAURENTIIS CORPORATION
DE NIRO, ROBERT	COLUMBIA PICTURES
DE YOUNG, DENNIS	A & M RECORDS
DEAN, G. R., JR.	CHOICE MAGAZINE
DELLS, THE	20TH CENTURY-FOX RECORDS
DENVER, JOHN	RCA RECORDS
DEPECHE MODE	SIRE RECORDS
DEREK, BO	20TH CENTURY-FOX PICTURES
DIETRICH, MARLENE	LEONARDO'S CINEMA CLASSICS
DILLARD, ALBERT N., JR.	CHOICE MAGAZINE
DILLON, MATT	LEONARDO'S CINEMA CLASSICS
DIRE STRAITS	WARNER/REPRISE RECORDS
DOUGLAS & TURNER	LEONARDO'S CINEMA CLASSICS
DUKES OF HAZZARD	CBS-TV
DYNASTY	CBS-TV
E, SHEILA	WARNER BROS RECORDS
EARTH, WIND & FIRE	COLUMBIA RECORDS
EASTWOOD, CLINT	WARNER BROS PICTURES
ECHO & THE BUNNYMEN	SIRE RECORDS/ANTON CORBIJN
EDEN, BARBARA	HARRY LANGDON
EDMUNDS, DAVE	SWAN SONG RECORDS
EDWARDS, VINCENT	ABC RECORDS
ESTEVEZ, EMILIO	20TH CENTURY-FOX PICTURES/HERB RITTS
EURYTHMICS, THE	RCA RECORDS
EVERY BROTHERS, THE	POLYGRAM RECORDS/ED CARAEFF
EXILE	WARNER/CURB RECORDS
F. B. I., THE	ABC-TV/QUINN MARTIN PRODUCTIONS
FACTS OF LIFE, THE	NBC-TV
FARGO, DONNA	WARNER BROS RECORDS
FATHER KNOWS BEST	CBS-TV, NBC-TV & ABC-TV
FENDER, FREDDY	MCA RECORDS
FERRELL, SHEA	LEONARDO'S CINEMA CLASSICS
FLYNN, ERROL	LEONARDO'S CINEMA CLASSICS
FOGARTY, JOHN	WARNER BROS RECORDS/CRAIG DIETZ
FORD, HARRISON	LEONARDO'S CINEMA CLASSICS
FOREIGNER	ATLANTIC RECORDS
FOUR TOPS, THE	MOTOWN RECORDS
FRAMPTON, PETER	A & M RECORDS
FRANCIS, CONNIE	JAMES J. KRIEGSMANN
FRICKE, JANIE	COLUMBIA PICTURES
FUNICELLO, ANNETTE	WALT DISNEY STUDIOS
GABLE, CLARK	MGM PICTURES
GABOR, ZSA ZSA	LEONARDO'S CINEMA CLASSICS
GABRIEL, PETER	GEFFEN RECORDS
GALLAGHER	UNITED ARTISTS RECORDS
GAYE, MARVIN	JAMES J. KRIEGMANN
GAYLE, CRYSTAL	COLUMBIA RECORDS/HAGIWARA/PARKER
GELDOF, BOB	ATLANTIC RECORDS
GEORGE, BOY	VIRGIN RECORDS/DAVID LEVINE
GIBSON, MEL	LEONARDO'S CINEMA CLASSICS
GILLEY, MICKEY	EPIC RECORDS
GLEASON, JACKIE	UNIVERSAL PICTURES
GOLD, ANDREW	ASYLUM RECORDS/JIM SHEA
GOLDBERG, WHOPPI	PARAMOUNT PICTURES
GOLDSBORO, BOBBY	CURB RECORDS/JIM MC GUIRE
GORDON, GALE	LEONARDO'S CINEMA CLASSICS
GORSHIN, FRANK	ABC-TV
GRANT, EDDY	PORTRAIT RECORDS
GREEN, KERRI	20TH CENTURY-FOX PICTURES
GUNSMOKE	CBS-TV
GUTHRIE, ARLO	WARNER BROS RECORDS
GWYNNE, FRED	CBS-TV
HAGGARD, MERLE	MCA RECORDS

HALL & OATES	RCA RECORDS
HAMILTON, GEORGE, IV	MCA RECORDS
HANKS, TOM	20TH CENTURY-FOX PICTURES/KARIN EPSTEIN
HAPPY DAYS	ABC-TV
HARMON, MARK	LEONARDO'S CINEMA CLASSICS
HARRIS, EMMYLOU	WARNER BROS RECORDS/ROBERT BLAKEMAN
HARRISON, REX	LEONARDO'S CINEMA CLASSICS
HARRY, DEBORAH	UNITED ARTISTS PICTURES
HAWAIIAN EYE	ABC-TV
HENDRIX, JIMI	WARNER BROS RECORDS
HENNER, MARILU	LEONARDO'S CINEMA CLASSICS
HONEYMOONERS, THE	CBS-TV
HOUSTON, THELMA	RCA RECORDS
HOWARD, JAN	SHORTY LAVENDER
HUBBARD, FREDDIE	COLUMBIA RECORDS/NTI
HUDSON, ROCK	ASSOCIATED FILM DISTRIBUTION
HYMAN, PHYLLIS	ARISTA RECORDS
I LOVE LUCY	CBS-TV
IDOL, BILLY	CHRYSALIS RECORDS
IGLESIAS, JULIO	COLUMBIA RECORDS/HARRY LANGDON
IMPRESSIONS, THE	20TH CENTURY-FOX RECORDS
JAMES, RICK	MOTOWN RECORDS
JARREAU, AL	WARNER BROS RECORDS
JEFFERSONS, THE	CBS-TV
JENNINGS, WAYLON	RCA RECORDS
JOANIE LOVES CHACHIE	ABC-TV
JOHN, LITTLE WILLIE	KING RECORDS
JOHNSON, DON	NBC-TV
JOHNSON, LYNN-HOLLY	UNITED ARTISTS PICTIRES/S. A. DANJAZ
JOHNSON, VAN	ABC-TV
JONES GIRLS, THE	RCA RECORDS
JONES, BARNABY	CBS-TV
JONES, GEORGE	EPIC RECORDS/ANTHONY DARIUS
JONES, GRACE	UNITED ARTISTS PICTURES
JONES, HOWARD	ELEKTRA RECORDS/SIMON FOWLER
JONES, RICKIE LEE	WARNER BROS RECORDS
JULIA, RAUL	LORIMAR MOTION PICTRURES
JUNIOR	MERCURY/POLYGRAM RECORDS
KARRAS, COSELL & GIFFORD	ABC-TV
KEACH, STACY, JR.	CBS-TV
KELLER, HELEN	INSTITUTE FOR THE BLIND
KENDALLS, THE	POLYGRAM RECORDS
KENNEDY, JOHN F.	FABIAN BACHRACH
KERSHAW, DOUG	ERIC PORTRAIT ASSOCIATED
KHAMBATTA, PERSIS	UNIVERSAL PICTURES/HARRY LANGDON
KHAN, CHAKA	WARNER BROS RECORDS/GORDON MUNRO
KING, B. B.	MCA RECORDS
KING, PERRY	LEONARDO'S CINEMA CLASSICS
KITT, EARTHA	ABC-TV
KLINE, KEVIN	UNIVERSAL PICTURES
KNIGHT, GLADYS	COLUMBIA RECORDS
KRIGE, ALICE	UNIVERSAL PICTURES
KRUPA, GENE	MAURICE SEYMOUR
LAKE, VERONICA	LEONARDO'S CINEMA CLASSICS
LAKESIDE	SOLAR RECORDS/RANDEE ST. NICHOLAS
LANCHESTER, ELSA	COLUMBIA PICTURES
LANDSBURY, ANGELA	LEONARDO'S CINEMA CLASSICS
LANGE, TED	LEONARDO'S CINEMA CLASSICS
LARSON, NICOLETTE	WARNER BROS PICTURES
LAUPIER, CYNDI	ERIC PORTRAIT ASSOCIATED/JOHN BELLISSIMO
LE BROCK, KELLY	LEONARDO'S CINEMA CLASSICS
LEAVE IT TO BEAVER	CBS-TV & ABC-TV
LEE, BRUCE	WARNER BROS PICTURES
LEMON, MEADOWLARK	SPOTLITE ENTERPRISES
LEWIS, HUEY & THE NEWS	CHRYSALIS RECORDS/DENNIS CALLAHN
LEWIS, JERRY	20TH CENTURY-FOX PICTURES

LEWIS, JERRY LEE	ELEKTRA RECORDS/JIM SHEA
LEWIS, RAMSEY	COLUMBIA RECORDS/SKREBNESKI
LIBERACE	JAMES J. KRIEGSMANN
LIGHTFOOT, GORDON	WARNER/REPRISE RECORDS
LITTLE, RICH	KRAGEN & COMPANY
LOCKE, SONDRA	WARNER BROS PICTURES
LOMBARD, CAROLE	PARAMOUNT PICTURES
LOREN, SOPHIA	MGM PICTURES
LOVE BOAT, THE	ABC-TV
MAC LEOD, GAVIN	ABC-TV
MACCHIO, RALPH	LEONARDO'S CINEMA CLASSICS
MADONNA	DAVID ELKOUBY
MANDEL, HOWIE	WARNER BROS RECORDS
MANDRELL, BARBARA	MCA RECORDS
MANILOW, BARRY	ARTISTA RECORDS/MARTHA SWOPE
MARIE, TEENA	EPIC RECORDS
MARY JANE GIRLS	MOTOWN RECORDS
MARY TYLER MOORE SHOW, THE	CBS-TV/MTM ENTERPRISES
MASON DIXON	DON SCHAFER PROMOTIONS
MATHERS & DOW	CBS-TV & ABC-TV
MATTEA, KATHY	MERCURY/POLYGRAM RECORDS
MATTHAU, WALTER	UNIVERSAL PICTURES
MATUSZAK, JOHN	UNITED ARTISTS PICTURES
MAYS, WILLIE	SAN FRANCISCO GIANTS
MAZE	CAPITOL RECORDS/CRAIG KOLB
MC CORKINDALE, SIMON	LEONARDO'S CINEMA CLASSICS
MC DOWALL, RODDY	ABC-TV
MC DOWELL, RONNIE	EPIC RECORDS/NORMAN SEEFF
MC GINLEY, TED	LEONARDO'S CINEMA CLASSICS
MC PHATTER, CLYDE	JAMES J. KRIEGSMANN
MELLENCAMP, JOHN COUGAR	RIVA/POLYGRAM RECORDS
MEN AT WORK	COLUMBIA RECORDS
MERIWETHER, LEE	ABC-TV
MESSINA, JIM	WARNER BROS RECORDS
MIAMI SOUND MACHINE	EPIC RECORDS
MILSAP, RONNIE	RCA RECORDS
MONEY, EDDIE	COLUMBIA RECORDS/RANDEE ST. NICHOLAS
MOODY BLUES, THE	POLYGRAM RECORDS
MOORE, DEMI	20TH CENTURY-FOX PICTURES/HERB RITTS
MOORE, ROGER	UNITED ARTISTS PICTURES/S. A. DANJAQ
MORENO, RITA	LEONARDO'S CINEMA CLASSICS
MORRIS, GARY	WARNER BROS RECORDS
MOTELS, THE	CAPITOL RECORDS
MURPHY, EDDIE	PARAMOUNT PICTURES
MURRAY, BILL	UNIVERSAL PICTURES
NAKED EYES	EMI AMERICA RECORDS
NAMATH, JOE	NEW YORK JETS
NEAL, PATRICIA	LEONARDO'S CINEMA CLASSICS
NELSON, WILLIE	COLUMBIA RECORDS/NORMAN SEEFF
NEWMAR, JULIE	ABC-TV
NITTY GRITTY DIRT BAND	WARNER BROS RECORDS/ALAN MESSER
O'CONNELL, HELEN	JAMES J. KRIEGSMANN
OAKLEY, ANNE	RICHARD K. FOX
OCEAN, BILLY	JIVE/ARISTA RECORDS
OHIO PLAYERS	JAMES J. KRIEGSMANN
OLIVIER, SIR LAURENCE	ASSOCIATED FILM DISTRIBUTION
OSBORNE, JEFFREY	A & M RECORDS
OSMOND, MARIE	OSMOND CORPORATION
OWENS, BUCK	WARNER BROS RECORDS
OXENBURG, CATHERINE	LEONARDO'S CINEMA CLASSICS
PACINO, AL	PARAMOUNT PICTURES
PARKER, RAY, JR	ARISTA RECORDS
PAUL, BILLY	PHILADELPHIA INT'L RECORDS
PAUL, LES & MARY FORD	CAPITOL RECORDS
PAYCHECK, JOHNNY	EPIC RECORDS/NORMAN SEEFF
PAYNE, FREDA	NTI
PERKINS, CARL	BRUNO OF HOLLYWOOD
PERRY, STEVE	COLUMBIA RECORDS
PERSUASIONS, THE	SUTTON ARTISTS
PETERS, BERNADETTE	MCA RECORDS/HARRY LANGDON
PHOTOGLO, JIM	20TH CENTURY-FOX RECORDS
PICKETT, WILSON	EMI RECORDS
PLANT, ROBERT	ESPARANZA/ATLANTIC RECORDS
POINTER SISTERS, THE	PLANET RECORDS
POLICEWOMAN	NBC-TV
PRESLEY, ELVIS	RCA RECORDS
PRETENDERS, THE	WARNER BROS RECORDS/EBET ROBERT
PRIDE, CHARLEY	RCA RECORDS
PRIME TIME	TOTAL EXPERIENCE RECORDS
PRINCE	WARNER BROS RECORDS
RABBITT, EDDIE	ELEKTRA RECORDS/LYNN GOLDSMITH
RAMONES, THE	SIRE RECORDS
RANDALL, BARTON	TRAVIS BICKEL
REYNOLDS, BURT	UNIVERSAL PICTURES
RICHIE, LIONEL	MOTOWN RECORDS
RIGG, DIANA	UNIVERSAL PICTURES
RIPTIDE	NBC-TV
ROBBINS, MARTY	COLUMBIA RECORDS
ROBERTSON, CLIFF	ABC-TV
ROBINSON, EDWARD G.	MGM PICTURES
ROCKFORD FILES, THE	NBC-TV
ROLLING STONES, THE	ROLLING STONES RECORDS
ROMERO, CESAR	ABC-TV
RONSTADT, LINDA	ASYLUM RECORDS
ROSS, DIANA	NANCY BARR
RUSH	MERCURY RECORDS
RUSHEN, PATRICE	ELEKTRA RECORDS
RUSSELL, JOHN	ABC-TV
S. O. S. BAND	TABU RECORDS/ERIC PORTRAIT ASSOCIATED
SAMMS, EMMA	LEONARDO'S CINEMA CLASSICS
SARDUCCI, FATHER GUIDO	WARNER BROS RECORDS/PATRICK JOHNSON
SAYER, LEO	WARNER BROS RECORDS
SCHEIDER, ROY	20TH CENTURY-FOX/COLUMBIA PICTURES
SCHNEIDER, JOHN	ERIC PORTRAIT ASSOCIATED
SEA LEVEL	ARISTA RECORDS
SEGER, BOB	CAPITOL RECORDS
SELLECK, TOM	CBS-TV
SELLERS, PETER	UNITED ARTISTS PICTURES
SEVENTY-SEVEN SUNSET STRIP	ABC-TV
SEVEREID, SUSANNE	DOUGLAS KIRKLAND
SHACKELFORD, TED	LEONARDO'S CINEMA CLASSICS
SHEAR, JULES	EMI AMERICA RECORDS/JUDY HERZI
SHEEN, CHARLIE	20TH CENTURY-FOX PICTURES
SHEPPARD, T. G.	CURB RECORDS
SHIELDS, BROOKE	NANCY BARR
SILVERS, PHIL	CBS-TV
SIMMONS, RICHARD	ELEKTRA RECRDS/BONNIE SCHIFFMAN
SIMON, PAUL	WARNER BROS RECORDS/MARIA RHODES
SISTER SLEDGE	COTILLION RECORDS
SLICK, GRACE	RCA RECORDS
SMOTHERS BROTHERS	NBC-TV
SNOW, HANK	RCA RECORDS
SONNY & CHER	ATCO RECORDS
SPACEK, SISSY	UNIVERSAL PICTURES
SPRINGSTEEN, BRUCE	NANCY BARR
STACK, ROBERT	ABC-TV
STALLONE & MEREDITH	UNITED ARTISTS PICTURES
STALLONE, FRANK	POLYDOR RECORDS
STALLONE, SYLVESTER	UNITED ARTISTS PICTURES
STARSKY & HUTCH	ABC-TV
STATLERS, THE	POLYGRAM RECORDS
STEENBURGEN, MARY	PARAMOUNT PICTURES
STERLING, TISHA	ABC-TV
STEVENS, CAT	A & M RECORDS
STEVENS, SHAKIN'	EPIC RECORDS
STEWART, AL	ARISTA RECORDS
STONE, SLY	WARNER BROS RECORDS
STREEP, MERYL	MGM/UA PICTURES
STREISAND & REDFORD	COLUMBIA PICTURES
SUN, JOE	ELEKTRA RECORDS
SUPERMAN	D. C. COMICS
SYLVESTER	FANTASY HONEY RECORDS

SYLVIA	RCA RECORDS
TALKING HEADS	SIRE RECORDS/DEBORAH FEINGOLD
TEARS FOR FEARS	MERCURY/POLYGRAM RECORDS
TEMPLE, SHIRLEY	20TH CENTURY-FOX PICTURES
TEMPTATIONS, THE	MOTOWN RECORDS
THOMAS, B. J.	MCA RECORDS
TILLIS, MEL	RCA RECORDS
TOO CLOSE FOR COMFORT ...	ABC-TV
TOTO	COLUMBIA RECORDS
TOWNSHEND, SIMON	POLYDOR RECORDS
TRAPPER JOHN, M.D.	CBS-TV
TRAVERS BAND, PAT	POLYDOR RECORDS/JIMM ROBERTS
TRAVIS, RANDY	WARNER BROS RECORDS/ JEFF KATZ
TRAVOLTA, JOHN	FILMWAYS PICTURES, INC.
TROWER, ROBIN	CHRYSALIS RECORDS
TUCKER, TANYA	MCA RECORDS
TURNER, KATHLEEN	20TH CENTURY-FOX PICTURES
TWITTY, CONWAY	MCA RECORDS
U-2	ANTON CORBIJN
UNTOUCHABLES, THE	ABC-TV
VANDROSS, LUTHER	EPIC RECORDS
VANELLI, GINO	ARISTA RECORDS
VANGELIS	POLYGRAM RECORDS
VANITY	MOTOWN RECORDS
VAUGHAN, STEVIE RAY & DOUBLE TROUBLE	EPIC RECORDS/BENNO FRIEDMAN
VEREEN, BEN	20TH CENTURY-FOX/COLUMBIA PICTURES
VINCENT, GENE	BRUNO OF HOLLYWOOD
WAITE, JOHN	EMI AMERICA RECORDS/GEOFFREY THOMAS
WALKER, JUNIOR	WHITFIELD RECORDS
WANG CHUNG	GEFFEN RECORDS
WARWICK, DIONNE	ARISTA RECORDS
WEAVER, DENNIS	CBS-TV
WEAVER, SIGOURNEY	20TH CENTURY-FOX PICTURES
WEISBERG, TIM	RCA RECORDS
WEISSMULLER, JOHNNY	MGM PICTURES
WELBY, MARCUS, MD.	ABC-TV
WELCH, RAQUEL	LEONARDO'S CINEMA CLASSICS
WEST, ADAM & BURT WARD ...	ABC-TV
WEST, DOTTIE	KRAGEN & COMPANY
WHISPERS, THE	SOLAR RECORDS
WHITE, TONY JOE	TONY RODRIQUEZ/LAUFER COMPANY
WHITES, THE	WARNER/CURB RECORDS
WHO, THE	WARNER BROS RECORDS
WILLIAMS & DUVALL	PARAMOUNT PICTURES
WILLIAMS, DEBBIE	SPOTLITE RECORDS
WILLIAMS, DENICE	COLUMBIA RECORDS/MARC RABOY
WILLIAMS, DON	MCA RECORDS
WILLIAMS, HANK, JR.	CURB RECORDS/JIM SHEA
WILLIAMS GUY	ABC-TV
WILLIS, BRUCE	ABC-TV
WILLS, DAVID	RCA RECORDS
WINTER, JOHNNY	BLUE SKY RECORDS
WINTERS, SHELLEY	LEONARDO'S CINEMA CLASSICS
WINWOOD, STEVE	ISLAND RECORDS/ARTHUR ELGORT
WONDER, STEVE	TAMALA RECORDS
WOODS, JAMES	20TH CENTURY FOX
WOODWARD, JOANNE	LEONARDO'S CINEMA CLASSICS
WRAY, FAY	RKO PICTURES CORP.
WRIGHT, GARY	WARNER BROS RECORDS
YANKOVIC, WEIRD AL	ROCK 'N' ROLL RECORDS
YELLOW ROSE, THE	NBC-TV
YES	ATCO RECORDS
YOUNG, FARON	MCA RECORDS
YOUNG, JESSE COLIN	ELEKTRA RECORDS/RANDEE ST. NICHOLAS
ZZ TOP	WARNER RECORDS